CONCISE ◆
MAJOR ◆
21ST- ◆
CENTURY ◆
WRITERS ◆

CONCISE MAJOR 21ST-CENTURY WRITERS

A Selection of Sketches from *Contemporary Authors*

Tracey L. Matthews, Project Editor

Volume 2: Co-Gr

THOMSON

GALE

Detroit • New York • San Francisco • New Haven, Conn. • Waterville, Maine • London • Munich

Concise Major 21st-Century Writers

Project Editor
Tracey L. Matthews

Editorial
Michelle Kazensky, Josh Kondek, Lisa Kumar,
Julie Mellors, Joyce Nakamura, Mary Ruby

Composition and Electronic Capture
Carolyn A. Roney

Manufacturing
Rita Wimberley

Library of Congress Control Number: 2006929297

ISBN 0-7876-7539-3 (hardcover : set), ISBN 0-7876-7540-7 (v. 1), ISBN 0-7876-7541-5 (v. 2),
ISBN 0-7876-7542-3 (v. 3), ISBN 0-7876-7543-1 (v. 4), ISBN 0-7876-7544-X (v. 5)

Printed in the United States of America
10 9 8 7 6 5 4 3 2 1

Contents

Introduction

Concise Major 21st-Century Writers (*CMTFCW*) is an abridgement of the 2004 eBook-only edition of Thomson Gale's *Major 21st-Century Writers* (*MTFCW*), a set based on Thomson Gale's award-winning *Contemporary Authors* series. *CMTFCW* provides students, educators, librarians, researchers, and general readers with a concise yet comprehensive source of biographical and bibliographical information on 700 of the most influential and studied authors at the turn of the twenty-first century as well as emerging authors whose literary significance is likely to increase in the coming decades.

CMTFCW includes sketches on approximately 700 authors who made writing literature their primary occupation and who have had at least part of their oeuvre published in English. Thus novelists, short story writers, nonfiction writers, poets, dramatists, genre writers, children's writers, and young adult writers of about sixty nationalities and ethnicities are represented. Selected sketches of authors that appeared in the 2004 edition of *MTFCW* are completely updated to include information on their lives and works through 2006. About thirty authors featured in *CMTFCW* are new to this set evidencing Thomson Gale's commitment to identifying emerging writers of recent eras and of many cultures.

How Authors Were Chosen for *CMTFCW*

The preliminary list of authors for *MTFCW* was sent to an advisory board of librarians, teaching professionals, and writers whose input resulted in informal inclusion criteria. In consultation with the editors, the list was narrowed to 700 authors for the concise edition plus criteria were established for adding authors. Criteria our editors used for adding authors not previously published in the last edition of *MTFCW* include:

- Authors who have won major awards

- Authors whose works are bestsellers

- Authors whose works are being incorporated into curricula and studied at the high school and/or college level

Broad Coverage in a Single Source

CMTFCW provides detailed biographical and bibliographical coverage of the most influential writers of our time, including:

- *Contemporary Literary Figures*: Mitch Albom, Sherman Alexie, Maya Angelou, Margaret Atwood, Dan Brown, Michael Chabon, J.M. Coetzee, Don DeLillo, Joan Didion, Dave Eggers, Gabriel Garcia Marquez, Nadine Gordimer, Khaled Hosseini, Toni Morrison, Joyce Carol Oates, Thomas Pynchon, J.K. Rowling, Salman Rushdie, Amy Tan, and John Updike, among many others.

- *Genre Writers*: Ray Bradbury, Tom Clancy, Philip K. Dick, Neil Gaiman, Sue Grafton, Dennis Lehane, Stephen King, Walter Mosley, Christopher Paolini, Anne Rice, Nora Roberts, Art Spiegelman, and Jane Yolen, among many others.

- *Novelists and Short Story Writers*: James Baldwin, Charles Baxter, Peter Carey, Carlos Fuentes, Graham Greene, Sebastian Junger, Sue Monk Kidd, John le Carré, Yann Martel, Rick Moody, Chuck Palahniuk, and Zadie Smith, among many others.

- *Dramatists*: Edward Albee, Samuel Beckett, Athol Fugard, Tony Kushner, David Mamet, Arthur Miller, Neil Simon, Tom Stoppard, Wendy Wasserstein, Alfred Uhry, Paula Vogel, and Tennessee Williams, among many others.

- *Poets*: Gwendolyn Brooks, Allen Ginsburg, Louise Glück, Jorie Graham, Seamus Heaney, Ted Kooser, Mary Oliver, Kenneth Rexroth, Adrienne Rich, Derek Walcott, and C.K. Williams, among many others.

How Entries Are Organized

Each *CMTFCW* biography begins with a series of rubrics that outlines the author's personal history, including information on the author's birth, death, family life, education, career, memberships, and awards. The *Writings* section lists a bibliography of the author's works along with the publisher and year published. The *Sidelights* section provides a biographical portrait of the author's development; information about the critical reception of the author's works; and revealing comments, often by the author, on personal interests, motivations, and thoughts on writing. The *Biographical/Critical Sources* section features a useful list of books, articles, and reviews about the author and his or her work. This section also includes citations for all material quoted in the *Sidelights* essay.

Other helpful sections include *Adaptations*, which lists the author's works that have been adapted by others into various media, including motion pictures, stage plays, and television or radio broadcasts, while the *Work in Progress* section lists titles or descriptions of works that are scheduled for publication by the author.

Using the Indexes

CMTFCW features a Nationality/Ethnicity index as well as a Subject/Genre index. More than sixty nations are represented in the Nationality/Ethnicity index, reflecting the international scope of this set and the multinational status of many authors. The Subject/Genre index covers over fifty genres and subject areas of fiction and nonfiction frequently referenced by educators and students, including social and political literature, environmental issues, and science fiction/science fantasy literature.

Citing *CMTFCW*

Students writing papers who wish to include references to information found in *CMTFCW* may cite sources in their bibliographies using the following format. Teachers adhering to other bibliographic formats may request that their students alter the citation below, which should only serve as a guide:

"Margaret Atwood." *Concise Major 21st-Century Writers*. Ed. Tracey L. Matthews. Detroit: Thomson Gale, 2006, pp. 214-223.

Comments Are Appreciated

CMTFCW is intended to serve as a useful reference tool for a wide audience, so your comments about this work are encouraged. Suggestions for authors to include in future editions of *CMTFCW* are also welcome. Send comments and suggestions to: *Concise Major 21st-Century Writers*, Thomson Gale, 27500 Drake Rd., Farmington Hills, MI 48331-3535; call at 1-248-699-4253; or fax at 1-248-699-8070.

Concise Major 21st-Century Writers
Advisory Board

In preparation for the first edition of *Major 20th-Century Writers* (*MTCW*), the editors of *Contemporary Authors* conducted a telephone survey of librarians and mailed a survey to more than 4,000 libraries to help determine the kind of reference resource the libraries wanted. Once it was clear that a comprehensive, yet affordable source of information on twentieth-century writers was needed to serve small and medium-sized libraries, a wide range of resources was consulted: national surveys of books taught in American high schools and universities; British secondary school syllabi; reference works such as the *New York Library Desk Reference, Reading Lists for College-Bound Students: The Books Most Recommended by America's Top Colleges, The List of Books, E.D. Hirsch's Cultural Legacy*, and volumes in Thomson Gale's Literacy Criticism and Dictionary of Literary Biography series. From these resources and with advice of an international advisory board, the author list for the first edition of *MTCW* was finalized, the sketches edited, and the volume published.

For the eBook edition of *Major 21st-Century Writers* (*MTFCW*), the editors compiled a preliminary author list based largely upon a list of authors included in the second print edition of *MTCW* with recommendations based on new inclusion criteria. This list was sent to an advisory board of librarians, authors, and teaching professionals in both the United States and Britain. In addition to vetting the submitted list, the advisors suggested other noteworthy writers. Recommendations made by the advisors ensure that authors from all nations and genres are represented.

Concise Major 21st-Century Writers (*CMTFCW*) is an abridgement of the eBook-only edition of *MTFCW*. The editors built upon the work of past advisors of the eBook edition to create a concise version and added authors who have earned increased recognition since the publication of *MTFCW*. The advisory board for *MTFCW* played a major role in shaping the author list for *CMTFCW*, and the editors wish to thank them for sharing their expertise. The twenty-seven member advisory board includes the following individuals:

- **Carl Antonucci,** Director of Library Services, Capital Community College, Hartford, Connecticut

- **Barbara Bibel,** Reference Librarian, Oakland Public Library, Oakland, California

- **Beverly A. Buciak,** Librarian, Brother Rice High School, Chicago, Illinois

- **Mary Ann Capan,** District Library Media Specialist, Sherrard Jr. Sr. High School, Sherrard, Illinois

- **Linda Carvell,** Head Librarian, Lancaster Country Day School, Lancaster, Pennsylvania

- **Anne Christensen,** Librarian II, Phoenix Public Library, Phoenix, Arizona

- **Peggy Curran,** Adult Services Librarian, Naperville Public Library, Naperville, Illinois

- **Eva M. Davis,** Youth Services Manager, Ann Arbor District Library, Ann Arbor, Michigan

- **Thomas Eertmoed,** Librarian, Illinois Central College, East Peoria, Illinois

- **Lucy K. Gardner,** Director, Howard Community College, Columbia, Maryland

- **Christine C. Godin,** Director of Learning Resources, Northwest Vista College, San Antonio, Texas

- **Francisca Goldsmith,** Senior Librarian, Berkeley Public Library, Berkeley, California

- **Nancy Guidry,** Reference Librarian, Bakersfield College, Bakersfield, California

- **Jack Hicks,** Administrative Librarian, Deerfield Public Library, Deerfield, Illinois

- **Charlie Jones,** School Library Media Specialist, Plymouth High School Library Media Center, Canton, Michigan

- **Carol M. Keeler,** Upper School Media Specialist, Detroit Country Day School, Beverly Hills, Michigan

- **Georgia Lomax,** Managing Librarian, King County Library System, Covington, Washington

- **Mary Jane Marden,** Librarian, M.M. Bennett Library, St. Petersburg College, Pinellas Park, Florida

- **Frances Moffett,** Materials Selector, Fairfax County Public Library, Chantilly, Virginia

- **Ruth Mormon,** Upper School Librarian, The Meadows School, Las Vegas, Nevada

- **Bonnie Morris,** Upper School Media Specialist, Minnehaha Academy, Minneapolis, Minneapolis

- **Nancy Pinkston,** English Teacher, Sherrard Jr. Sr. High School, Sherrard, Illinois

- **Robert Reginald,** Head of Technical Services and Collection Development, California State University, San Bernadino, California

- **Janet P. Sarratt,** Library Media Specialist, John E. Ewing Middle School, Gaffney, South Carolina

- **Brian Stableford,** 0.5 Lecturer in Creative Writing, University College, Winchester (formerly King Alfred's College), Reading, England

- **Stephen Weiner,** Director, Maynard Public Library, Maynard, Massachusetts

- **Hope Yelich,** Reference Librarian, College of William and Mary, Williamsburg, Virginia

Concise Major 21st-Century Writers

VOLUME 1: A-Cl

Abbey, Edward 1927-1989

Abe, Kobo 1924-1993

Achebe, Chinua 1930-

Ackroyd, Peter 1949-

Adams, Alice 1926-1999

Adams, Douglas 1952-2001

Affabee, Eric
  See Stine, R.L.

Aghill, Gordon
  See Silverberg, Robert

Albee, Edward 1928-

Albom, Mitch 1958-

Aldiss, Brian W. 1925-

Aldrich, Ann
  See Meaker, Marijane

Alegría, Claribel 1924-

Alexie, Sherman 1966-

Allan, John B.
  See Westlake, Donald E.

Allen, Paula Gunn 1939-

Allen, Roland
  See Ayckbourn, Alan

Allende, Isabel 1942-

Allison, Dorothy E. 1949-

Alvarez, A. 1929-

Alvarez, Julia 1950-

Amado, Jorge 1912-2001

Ambrose, Stephen E. 1936-2002

Amichai, Yehuda 1924-2000

Amis, Kingsley 1922-1995

Amis, Martin 1949-

Anand, Mulk Raj 1905-2004

Anaya, Rudolfo A. 1937-

Anderson, Laurie Halse 1961-

Anderson, Poul 1926-2001

Andrews, Elton V.
  See Pohl, Frederik

Angelou, Maya 1928-

Anouilh, Jean 1910-1987

Anthony, Peter
  See Shaffer, Peter

Anthony, Piers 1934-

Archer, Jeffrey 1940-

Archer, Lee
  See Ellison, Harlan

Ard, William
  See Jakes, John

Arenas, Reinaldo 1943-1990

Arias, Ron 1941-

Arnette, Robert
  See Silverberg, Robert

Aronson, Marc 1948-

Ashbery, John 1927-

Ashbless, William
  See Powers, Tim

Asimov, Isaac 1920-1992

Atwood, Margaret 1939-

Axton, David
  See Koontz, Dean R.

Ayckbourn, Alan 1939-

Bachman, Richard
  See King, Stephen

Bainbridge, Beryl 1934-

Baker, Nicholson 1957-

Baker, Russell 1925-

Baldacci, David 1960-

Baldwin, James 1924-1987

Ballard, J.G. 1930-

Bambara, Toni Cade 1939-1995

Banat, D.R.
  See Bradbury, Ray

Banks, Iain M. 1954-

Banks, Russell 1940-

Baraka, Amiri 1934-

Barclay, Bill
  See Moorcock, Michael

Barclay, William Ewert
  See Moorcock, Michael

Barker, Clive 1952-

Barnes, Julian 1946-

Baron, David
  See Pinter, Harold

Barrington, Michael
  See Moorcock, Michael

Barthelme, Donald 1931-1989

Bashevis, Isaac
  See Singer, Isaac Bashevis

Bass, Kingsley B., Jr.
  See Bullins, Ed

Baxter, Charles 1947-

Beagle, Peter S. 1939-

Beattie, Ann 1947-

Beauvoir, Simone de 1908-1986

Beckett, Samuel 1906-1989

Beldone, Phil "Cheech"
  See Ellison, Harlan

Bell, Madison Smartt 1957-

Bellow, Saul 1915-2005

Benchley, Peter 1940-2006

Benitez, Sandra 1941-

Berendt, John 1939-

Berger, Thomas 1924-

Berry, Jonas
    See Ashbery, John

Berry, Wendell 1934-

Bethlen, T.D.
    See Silverberg, Robert

Binchy, Maeve 1940-

Bird, Cordwainer
    See Ellison, Harlan

Birdwell, Cleo
    See DeLillo, Don

Blade, Alexander
    See Silverberg, Robert

Blais, Marie-Claire 1939-

Bliss, Frederick
    See Card, Orson Scott

Block, Francesca Lia 1962-

Bloom, Amy 1953-

Blount, Roy, Jr. 1941-

Blue, Zachary
    See Stine, R.L.

Blume, Judy 1938-

Bly, Robert 1926-

Boland, Eavan 1944-

Böll, Heinrich 1917-1985

Boot, William
    See Stoppard, Tom

Borges, Jorge Luis 1899-1986

Bowles, Paul 1910-1999

Box, Edgar
    See Vidal, Gore

Boyle, Mark
    See Kienzle, William X.

Boyle, T. Coraghessan 1948-

Brackett, Peter
    See Collins, Max Allan

Bradbury, Edward P.
    See Moorcock, Michael

Bradbury, Ray 1920-

Bradley, Marion Zimmer 1930-1999

Bragg, Rick 1959-

Brashares, Ann 1967-

Breslin, Jimmy 1930-

Brink, André 1935-

Brodsky, Iosif
Alexandrovich 1940-1996

Brodsky, Joseph
    See Brodsky, Iosif Alexandrovich

Brodsky, Yosif
    See Brodsky, Iosif Alexandrovich

Brookner, Anita 1928-

Brooks, Cleanth 1906-1994

Brooks, Gwendolyn 1917-2000

Brooks, Terry 1944-

Brown, Dan 1964-

Brown, Dee Alexander 1908-2002

Brown, Rita Mae 1944-

Brown, Sterling Allen 1901-1989

Brownmiller, Susan 1935-

Bruchac, Joseph, III 1942-

Bryan, Michael
    See Moore, Brian

Buckley, William F., Jr. 1925-

Buechner, Frederick 1926-

Bukowski, Charles 1920-1994

Bullins, Ed 1935-

Burke, Ralph
    See Silverberg, Robert

Burns, Tex
    See L'Amour, Louis

Busiek, Kurt

Bustos, F.
    See Borges, Jorge Luis

Butler, Octavia E. 1947-2006

Butler, Robert Olen 1945-

Byatt, A.S. 1936-

Cabrera Infante,
Guillermo 1929-2005

Cade, Toni
    See Bambara, Toni Cade

Cain, G.
    See Cabrera Infante, Guillermo

Caldwell, Erskine 1903-1987

Calisher, Hortense 1911-

Calvino, Italo 1923-1985

Camp, John 1944-

Campbell, Bebe Moore 1950-

Capote, Truman 1924-1984

Card, Orson Scott 1951-

Carey, Peter 1943-

Carroll, James P. 1943-

Carroll, Jonathan 1949-

Carruth, Hayden 1921-

Carter, Nick
    See Smith, Martin Cruz

Carver, Raymond 1938-1988

Cavallo, Evelyn
    See Spark, Muriel

Cela, Camilo José 1916-2002

Cela y Trulock, Camilo José
    See Cela, Camilo José

Cesaire, Aimé 1913-

Chabon, Michael 1963-

Chang, Iris 1968-2004

Chapman, Lee
    See Bradley, Marion Zimmer

Chapman, Walker
    See Silverberg, Robert

Charby, Jay
    See Ellison, Harlan

Chávez, Denise 1948-

Cheever, John 1912-1982

Chevalier, Tracy 1962-

Childress, Alice 1920-1994

Chomsky, Noam 1928-

Cisneros, Sandra 1954-

Cixous, Hélène 1937-

Clancy, Tom 1947-

Clark, Carol Higgins 1956-

Clark, Curt
    See Westlake, Donald E.

Clark, John Pepper
    See Clark Bekederemo, J.P.

Clark, Mary Higgins 1929-

Clark Bekederemo, J.P. 1935-

Clarke, Arthur C. 1917-

Clarke, Austin C. 1934-

Clavell, James 1925-1994

Cleary, Beverly 1916-

Clifton, Lucille 1936-

Clinton, Dirk
 See Silverberg, Robert

Clowes, Daniel 1961-

VOLUME 2: Co-Gr

Codrescu, Andrei 1946-

Coe, Tucker
 See Westlake, Donald E.

Coetzee, J.M. 1940-

Coffey, Brian
 See Koontz, Dean R.

Coleman, Emmett
 See Reed, Ishmael

Collins, Billy 1941-

Collins, Max Allan 1948-

Colvin, James
 See Moorcock, Michael

Condé, Maryse 1937-

Connell, Evan S., Jr. 1924-

Conroy, Pat 1945-

Cook, Roy
 See Silverberg, Robert

Cooper, J. California

Cooper, Susan 1935-

Coover, Robert 1932-

Cormier, Robert 1925-2000

Cornwell, Patricia 1956-

Corso, Gregory 1930-2001

Cortázar, Julio 1914-1984

Courtney, Robert
 See Ellison, Harlan

Cox, William Trevor
 See Trevor, William

Craig, A.A.
 See Anderson, Poul

Creeley, Robert 1926-2005

Crews, Harry 1935-

Crichton, Michael 1942-

Crowley, John 1942-

Crutcher, Chris 1946-

Cruz, Victor Hernández 1949-

Culver, Timothy J.
 See Westlake, Donald E.

Cunningham, E.V.
 See Fast, Howard

Cunningham, J. Morgan
 See Westlake, Donald E.

Cunningham, Michael 1952-

Curtis, Price
 See Ellison, Harlan

Cussler, Clive 1931-

Cutrate, Joe
 See Spiegelman, Art

Dahl, Roald 1916-1990

Dale, George E.
 See Asimov, Isaac

Danticat, Edwidge 1969-

Danziger, Paula 1944-2004

Davies, Robertson 1913-1995

Davis, B. Lynch
 See Borges, Jorge Luis

Deighton, Len 1929-

Delany, Samuel R. 1942-

DeLillo, Don 1936-

Demijohn, Thom
 See Disch, Thomas M.

Denis, Julio
 See Cortázar, Julio

Denmark, Harrison
 See Zelazny, Roger

dePaola, Tomie 1934-

Derrida, Jacques 1930-

Desai, Anita 1937-

DeWitt, Helen 1957-

Dexter, Colin 1930-

Dexter, John
 See Bradley, Marion Zimmer

Dexter, N.C.
 See Dexter, Colin

Dexter, Pete 1943-

Diamond, Jared 1937-

Dick, Philip K. 1928-1982

Didion, Joan 1934-

Dillard, Annie 1945-

Disch, Thomas M. 1940-

Disch, Tom
 See Disch, Thomas M.

Doctorow, E.L. 1931-

Domecq, H. Bustos
 See Borges, Jorge Luis

Domini, Rey
 See Lorde, Audre

Dorris, Michael 1945-1997

Douglas, Leonard
 See Bradbury, Ray

Douglas, Michael
 See Crichton, Michael

Dove, Rita 1952-

Doyle, John
 See Graves, Robert

Doyle, Roddy 1958-

Dr. A.
 See Asimov, Isaac

Dr. Seuss
 See Geisel, Theodor Seuss

Drabble, Margaret 1939-

Drummond, Walter
See Silverberg, Robert

Druse, Eleanor
See King, Stephen

Dubus, Andre, III 1959-

Due, Linnea A. 1948-

Due, Tananarive 1966-

Duke, Raoul
See Thompson, Hunter S.

Duncan, Lois 1934-

Duncan, Robert 1919-1988

Dunn, Katherine 1945-

Durang, Christopher 1949-

Dworkin, Andrea 1946-2005

Dwyer, Deanna
See Koontz, Dean R.

Dwyer, K.R.
See Koontz, Dean R.

Eco, Umberto 1932-

Edelman, Marian Wright 1939-

Edmondson, Wallace
See Ellison, Harlan

Eggers, Dave 1971-

Ehrenreich, Barbara 1941-

Eisner, Will 1917-2005

Eliot, Dan
See Silverberg, Robert

Elkin, Stanley L. 1930-1995

Elliott, Don
See Silverberg, Robert

Elliott, William
See Bradbury, Ray

Ellis, Alice Thomas 1932-

Ellis, Bret Easton 1964-

Ellis, Landon
See Ellison, Harlan

Ellison, Harlan 1934-

Ellison, Ralph 1914-1994

Ellroy, James 1948-

Emecheta, Buchi 1944-

Endo, Shusaku 1923-1996

Enger, L.L.
See Enger, Leif

Enger, Leif 1961-

Epernay, Mark
See Galbraith, John Kenneth

Erdrich, Louise 1954-

Erickson, Steve 1950-

Erickson, Walter
See Fast, Howard

Ericson, Walter
See Fast, Howard

Ernaux, Annie 1940-

Erwin, Will
See Eisner, Will

Esquivel, Laura 1951-

Estleman, Loren D. 1952-

Eugenides, Jeffrey 1960-

Everett, Percival L. 1956-

Fadiman, Anne 1953-

Faludi, Susan 1959-

Farmer, Philip José 1918-

Fast, Howard 1914-2003

Ferlinghetti, Lawrence 1919-

Ferré, Rosario 1938-

Fielding, Helen 1958-

Fitch, John, IV
See Cormier, Robert

Fitzgerald, Penelope 1916-2000

Fleur, Paul
See Pohl, Frederik

Flooglebuckle, Al
See Spiegelman, Art

Fo, Dario 1926-

Foer, Jonathan Safran 1977-

Foote, Horton 1916-

Foote, Shelby 1916-2005

Forché, Carolyn 1950-

Ford, Michael Thomas 1969-

Ford, Richard 1944-

Forsyth, Frederick 1938-

Fowler, Karen Joy 1950-

Fowles, John 1926-2005

Francis, Dick 1920-

Franzen, Jonathan 1959-

Fraser, Antonia 1932-

Frayn, Michael 1933-

Frazier, Charles 1950-

French, Marilyn 1929-

French, Paul
See Asimov, Isaac

Frey, James 1969-

Friedan, Betty 1921-2006

Friedman, Thomas L. 1953-

Frisch, Max 1911-1991

Fry, Christopher 1907-

Fuentes, Carlos 1928-

Fugard, Athol 1932-

Fundi
See Baraka, Amiri

Gaddis, William 1922-1998

Gaiman, Neil 1960-

Gaines, Ernest J. 1933-

Galbraith, John Kenneth 1908-

Gallant, Mavis 1922-

Garcia, Cristina 1958-

Garcia Marquez, Gabriel 1928-

Gardner, John 1933-1982

Gardner, Miriam
See Bradley, Marion Zimmer

Gardons, S.S.
See Snodgrass, W.D.

Garner, Alan 1934-

Gass, William H. 1924-

Gates, Henry Louis, Jr. 1950-

Gee, Maggie 1948-

Geisel, Theodor Seuss 1904-1991

Genet, Jean 1910-1986

Gibbons, Kaye 1960-

Gibson, William 1948-

Gibson, William2 1914-

Gilchrist, Ellen 1935-

Ginsberg, Allen 1926-1997

Ginzburg, Natalia 1916-1991

Giovanni, Nikki 1943-

Glück, Louise 1943-

Godwin, Gail 1937-

Golden, Arthur 1956-

Golding, William 1911-1993

Goodkind, Terry 1948-

Gordimer, Nadine 1923-

Goryan, Sirak
    See Saroyan, William

Gottesman, S.D.
    See Pohl, Frederik

Gould, Stephen Jay 1941-2002

Goytisolo, Juan 1931-

Grafton, Sue 1940-

Graham, Jorie 1950-

Grant, Skeeter
    See Spiegelman, Art

Grass, Günter 1927-

Graves, Robert 1895-1985

Graves, Valerie
    See Bradley, Marion Zimmer

Gray, Alasdair 1934-

Gray, Francine du Plessix 1930-

Gray, Spalding 1941-2004

Greeley, Andrew M. 1928-

Green, Brian
    See Card, Orson Scott

Greene, Graham 1904-1991

Greer, Richard
    See Silverberg, Robert

Gregor, Lee
    See Pohl, Frederik

Grisham, John 1955-

Grumbach, Doris 1918-

VOLUME 3: Gu-Ma

Guest, Judith 1936-

Gump, P.Q.
    See Card, Orson Scott

Guterson, David 1956-

Haddon, Mark 1962-

Hailey, Arthur 1920-2004

Halberstam, David 1934-

Hall, Donald 1928-

Hall, Radclyffe 1886-1943

Hamilton, Franklin
    See Silverberg, Robert

Hamilton, Jane 1957-

Hamilton, Mollie
    See Kaye, M.M.

Hamilton, Virginia 1936-2002

Handke, Peter 1942-

Hardwick, Elizabeth 1916-

Hargrave, Leonie
    See Disch, Thomas M.

Harjo, Joy 1951-

Harris, E. Lynn 1957-

Harris, Robert 1957-

Harris, Thomas 1940-

Harson, Sley
    See Ellison, Harlan

Hart, Ellis
    See Ellison, Harlan

Harvey, Jack
    See Rankin, Ian

Hass, Robert 1941-

Havel, Vaclav 1936-

Hawkes, John 1925-1998

Hawking, S.W.
    See Hawking, Stephen W.

Hawking, Stephen W. 1942-

Haycraft, Anna
    See Ellis, Alice Thomas

Hayes, Al
    See Grisham, John

Hazzard, Shirley 1931-

Head, Bessie 1937-1986

Heaney, Seamus 1939-

Hébert, Anne 1916-2000

Hegi, Ursula 1946-

Heinlein, Robert A. 1907-1988

Heller, Joseph 1923-1999

Hellman, Lillian 1906-1984

Helprin, Mark 1947-

Hempel, Amy 1951-

Henley, Beth 1952-

Herbert, Frank 1920-1986

Hersey, John 1914-1993

Hiaasen, Carl 1953-

Highsmith, Patricia 1921-1995

Hijuelos, Oscar 1951-

Hill, John
    See Koontz, Dean R.

Hillenbrand, Laura 1967-

Hillerman, Tony 1925-

Hinojosa, Rolando 1929-

Hinton, S.E. 1950-

Hoban, Russell 1925-

Hochhuth, Rolf 1931-

Høeg, Peter 1957-

Hoffman, Alice 1952-

Hollander, Paul
    See Silverberg, Robert

Homes, A.M. 1961-

hooks, bell 1952-

Hosseini, Khaled 1965-

Houellebecq, Michel 1958-

Houston, Jeanne Wakatsuki 1934-

Howard, Maureen 1930-

Howard, Warren F.
    See Pohl, Frederik

Hoyle, Fred 1915-2001

Hubbell, Sue 1935-

Hudson, Jeffrey
    See Crichton, Michael

Hughes, Ted 1930-1998

Humes, Edward

Hwang, David Henry 1957-

Ionesco, Eugene 1912-1994

Irving, John 1942-

Isaacs, Susan 1943-

Isherwood, Christopher 1904-1986

Ishiguro, Kazuo 1954-

Ives, Morgan
    See Bradley, Marion Zimmer

Jakes, John 1932-

James, Mary
    See Meaker, Marijane

James, P.D. 1920-

James, Philip
    See Moorcock, Michael

Janowitz, Tama 1957-

Jarvis, E.K.
    See Ellison, Harlan

Jarvis, E.K.2
    See Silverberg, Robert

Jenkins, Jerry B. 1949-

Jhabvala, Ruth Prawer 1927-

Jiang, Ji-li 1954-

Jimenez, Francisco 1943-

Jin, Ha 1956-

Johnson, Adam 1967-

Johnson, Angela 1961-

Johnson, Charles 1948-

Jones, Diana Wynne 1934-

Jones, Edward P. 1950-

Jones, Gayl 1949-

Jones, LeRoi
    See Baraka, Amiri

Jong, Erica 1942-

Jorgensen, Ivar
    See Ellison, Harlan

Jorgenson, Ivar2
    See Silverberg, Robert

Judd, Cyril
    See Pohl, Frederik

Junger, Sebastian 1962-

Karageorge, Michael A.
    See Anderson, Poul

Karr, Mary 1955-

Kastel, Warren
    See Silverberg, Robert

Kaufman, Moises 1963-

Kavanagh, Dan
    See Barnes, Julian

Kaye, M.M. 1908-2004

Kaye, Mollie
    See Kaye, M.M.

Keillor, Garrison 1942-

Kelly, Lauren
    See Oates, Joyce Carol

Keneally, Thomas 1935-

Kennedy, William 1928-

Kennilworthy Whisp
    See Rowling, J.K.

Kerr, M.E.
    See Meater, Marijane

Kerry, Lois
    See Duncan, Lois

Kesey, Ken 1935-2001

Keyes, Daniel 1927-

Kidd, Sue Monk

Kienzle, William X. 1928-2001

Kincaid, Jamaica 1949-

King, Stephen 1947-

King, Steve
    See King, Stephen

Kingsolver, Barbara 1955-

Kingston, Maxine Hong 1940-

Kinnell, Galway 1927-

Kinsella, Thomas 1928-

Kinsella, W.P. 1935-

Kizer, Carolyn 1925-

Knight, Etheridge 1931-1991

Knowles, John 1926-2001

Knox, Calvin M.
    See Silverberg, Robert

Knye, Cassandra
    See Disch, Thomas M.

Koch, Kenneth 1925-2002

Kogawa, Joy 1935-

Kolb, Edward W. 1951-

Kolb, Rocky
    See Kolb, Edward W.

Koontz, Dean R. 1945-

Kooser, Ted 1939-

Kosinski, Jerzy 1933-1991

Kozol, Jonathan 1936-

Krakauer, Jon 1954-

Kumin, Maxine 1925-

Kundera, Milan 1929-

Kunitz, Stanley 1905-

Kushner, Tony 1956-

L'Amour, Louis 1908-1988

L'Engle, Madeleine 1918-

La Guma, Alex 1925-1985

Lahiri, Jhumpa 1967-

Lamb, Wally 1950-

Lange, John
    See Crichton, Michael

Laredo, Betty
    See Codrescu, Andrei

Laurence, Margaret 1926-1987

Lavond, Paul Dennis
    See Pohl, Frederik

Leavitt, David 1961-

le Carré, John 1931-

Lee, Don L.
   See Madhubuti, Haki R.

Lee, Harper 1926-

Lee, Stan 1922-

Le Guin, Ursula K. 1929-

Lehane, Dennis 1965-

Leonard, Elmore 1925-

LeSieg, Theo.
   See Geisel, Theodor Seuss

Lessing, Doris 1919-

Lester, Julius 1939-

Lethem, Jonathan 1964-

Levi, Primo 1919-1987

Levin, Ira 1929-

Levon, O.U.
   See Kesey, Ken

Leyner, Mark 1956-

Lindbergh, Anne Morrow 1906-2001

Lively, Penelope 1933-

Lodge, David 1935-

Logan, Jake
   See Smith, Martin Cruz

Long, David 1948-

Loos, Anita 1893-1981

Lorde, Audre 1934-1992

Louise, Heidi
   See Erdrich, Louise

Lowry, Lois 1937-

Lucas, Craig 1951-

Ludlum, Robert 1927-2001

Lynch, B. Suarez
   See Borges, Jorge Luis

M.T.F.
   See Porter, Katherine Anne

Macdonald, Anson
   See Heinlein, Robert A.

MacDonald, John D. 1916-1986

Mackay, Shena 1944-

MacKinnon, Catharine A. 1946-

MacLeish, Archibald 1892-1982

MacLeod, Alistair 1936-

Maddern, Al
   See Ellison, Harlan

Madhubuti, Haki R.

Maguire, Gregory 1954-

Mahfouz, Naguib 1911-

Mailer, Norman 1923-

Makine, Andreï 1957-

Malabaila, Damiano
   See Levi, Primo

Malamud, Bernard 1914-1986

Malcolm, Dan
   See Silverberg, Robert

Malouf, David 1934-

Mamet, David 1947-

Mara, Bernard
   See Moore, Brian

Marchbanks, Samuel
   See Davies, Robertson

Marías, Javier 1951-

Mariner, Scott
   See Pohl, Frederik

Markandaya, Kamala 1924-2004

Markham, Robert
   See Amis, Kingsley

Marshall, Allen
   See Westlake, Donald E.

Marshall, Paule 1929-

Martel, Yann 1963-

Martin, Webber
   See Silverberg, Robert

Mason, Bobbie Ann 1940-

Mason, Ernst
   See Pohl, Frederik

Mass, William
   See Gibson, William2

Massie, Robert K. 1929-

Mathabane, Mark 1960-

Matthiessen, Peter 1927-

Maupin, Armistead 1944-

Mayo, Jim
   See L'Amour, Louis

VOLUME 4: Mc-Sa

McBride, James 1957-

McCaffrey, Anne 1926-

McCall Smith, Alexander 1948-

McCann, Edson
   See Pohl, Frederik

McCarthy, Cormac 1933-

McCourt, Frank 1930-

McCreigh, James
   See Pohl, Frederik

McCullough, Colleen 1937-

McCullough, David 1933-

McDermott, Alice 1953-

McEwan, Ian 1948-

McGuane, Thomas 1939-

McInerney, Jay 1955-

McKie, Robin

McKinley, Robin 1952-

McLandress, Herschel
   See Galbraith, John Kenneth

McMillan, Terry 1951-

McMurtry, Larry 1936-

McNally, Terrence 1939-

McPhee, John 1931-

McPherson, James Alan 1943-

Meaker, M.J.
    See Meaker, Marijane

Meaker, Marijane 1927-

Mehta, Ved 1934-

Members, Mark
    See Powell, Anthony

Méndez, Miguel 1930-

Merchant, Paul
    See Ellison, Harlan

Merrill, James 1926-1995

Merriman, Alex
    See Silverberg, Robert

Merwin, W.S. 1927-

Michener, James A. 1907-1997

Miéville, China 1973-

Miller, Arthur 1915-

Millett, Kate 1934-

Millhauser, Steven 1943-

Milosz, Czeslaw 1911-2004

Min, Anchee 1957-

Mitchell, Clyde
    See Ellison, Harlan

Mitchell, Clyde2
    See Silverberg, Robert

Momaday, N. Scott 1934-

Monroe, Lyle
    See Heinlein, Robert A.

Moody, Anne 1940-

Moody, Rick 1961-

Moorcock, Michael 1939-

Moore, Alan 1953-

Moore, Brian 1921-1999

Moore, Lorrie
    See Moore, Marie Lorena

Moore, Marie Lorena 1957-

Mora, Pat 1942-

Morgan, Claire
    See Highsmith, Patricia

Mori, Kyoko 1957-

Morris, Mary McGarry 1943-

Morrison, Chloe Anthony Wofford
    See Morrison, Toni

Morrison, Toni 1931-

Morrow, James 1947-

Mortimer, John 1923-

Mosley, Walter 1952-

Motion, Andrew 1952-

Mowat, Farley 1921-

Mukherjee, Bharati 1940-

Munro, Alice 1931-

Murdoch, Iris 1919-1999

Murray, Albert L. 1916-

Myers, Walter Dean 1937-

Myers, Walter M.
    See Myers, Walter Dean

Nafisi, Azar 1950-

Naipaul, Shiva 1945-1985

Naipaul, V.S. 1932-

Narayan, R.K. 1906-2001

Naylor, Gloria 1950-

Nemerov, Howard 1920-1991

Newt Scamander
    See Rowling, J.K.

Ngugi, James T.
    See Ngugi wa Thiong'o

Ngugi wa Thiong'o 1938-

Nichols, John 1940-

Nichols, Leigh
    See Koontz, Dean R.

North, Anthony
    See Koontz, Dean R.

North, Milou
    See Dorris, Michael

North, Milou2
    See Erdrich, Louise

Nosille, Nabrah
    See Ellison, Harlan

Novak, Joseph
    See Kosinski, Jerzy

Nye, Naomi Shihab 1952-

O'Brian, E.G.
    See Clarke, Arthur C.

O'Brian, Patrick 1914-2000

O'Brien, Edna 1932-

O'Brien, Tim 1946-

O'Casey, Brenda
    See Ellis, Alice Thomas

O'Faolain, Sean 1900-1991

O'Flaherty, Liam 1896-1984

Oates, Joyce Carol 1938-

Oates, Stephen B. 1936-

Oe, Kenzaburo 1935-

Okri, Ben 1959-

Olds, Sharon 1942-

Oliver, Mary 1935-

Olsen, Tillie 1912-

Ondaatje, Michael 1943-

Osborne, David
    See Silverberg, Robert

Osborne, George
    See Silverberg, Robert

Osborne, John 1929-1994

Oz, Amos 1939-

Ozick, Cynthia 1928-

Packer, Vin
    See Meaker, Marijane

Paglia, Camille 1947-

Paige, Richard
    See Koontz, Dean R.

Pakenham, Antonia
    See Fraser, Antonia

Palahniuk, Chuck 1962-

Paley, Grace 1922-

Paolini, Christopher 1983-

Parfenie, Marie
    See Codrescu, Andrei

Park, Jordan
    See Pohl, Frederik

Parker, Bert
    See Ellison, Harlan

Parker, Robert B. 1932-

Parks, Gordon 1912-2006

Pasternak, Boris 1890-1960

Patchett, Ann 1963-

Paton, Alan 1903-1988

Patterson, James 1947-

Payne, Alan
    See Jakes, John

Paz, Octavio 1914-1998

Peretti, Frank E. 1951-

Petroski, Henry 1942-

Phillips, Caryl 1958-

Phillips, Jayne Anne 1952-

Phillips, Richard
    See Dick, Philip K.

Picoult, Jodi 1966-

Piercy, Marge 1936-

Piers, Robert
    See Anthony, Piers

Pinsky, Robert 1940-

Pinta, Harold
    See Pinter, Harold

Pinter, Harold 1930-

Plimpton, George 1927-2003

Pohl, Frederik 1919-

Porter, Katherine Anne 1890-1980

Potok, Chaim 1929-2002

Powell, Anthony 1905-2000

Powers, Richard 1957-

Powers, Tim 1952-

Pratchett, Terry 1948-

Price, Reynolds 1933-

Prose, Francine 1947-

Proulx, E. Annie 1935-

Puig, Manuel 1932-1990

Pullman, Philip 1946-

Pygge, Edward
    See Barnes, Julian

Pynchon, Thomas, Jr. 1937-

Quindlen, Anna 1953-

Quinn, Simon
    See Smith, Martin Cruz

Rampling, Anne
    See Rice, Anne

Rand, Ayn 1905-1982

Randall, Robert
    See Silverberg, Robert

Rankin, Ian 1960-

Rao, Raja 1909-

Ravenna, Michael
    See Welty, Eudora

Reed, Ishmael 1938-

Reid, Desmond
    See Moorcock, Michael

Rendell, Ruth 1930-

Rensie, Willis
    See Eisner, Will

Rexroth, Kenneth 1905-1982

Rice, Anne 1941-

Rich, Adrienne 1929-

Rich, Barbara
    See Graves, Robert

Richler, Mordecai 1931-2001

Ríos, Alberto 1952-

Rivers, Elfrida
    See Bradley, Marion Zimmer

Riverside, John
    See Heinlein, Robert A.

Robb, J.D.
    See Roberts, Nora

Robbe-Grillet, Alain 1922-

Robbins, Tom 1936-

Roberts, Nora 1950-

Robertson, Ellis
    See Ellison, Harlan

Robertson, Ellis2
    See Silverberg, Robert

Robinson, Kim Stanley 1952-

Robinson, Lloyd
    See Silverberg, Robert

Robinson, Marilynne 1944-

Rodman, Eric
    See Silverberg, Robert

Rodríguez, Luis J. 1954-

Rodriguez, Richard 1944-

Roquelaure, A.N.
    See Rice, Anne

Roth, Henry 1906-1995

Roth, Philip 1933-

Rowling, J.K. 1965-

Roy, Arundhati 1960-

Rule, Ann 1935-

Rushdie, Salman 1947-

Russo, Richard 1949-

Rybczynski, Witold 1943-

Ryder, Jonathan
    See Ludlum, Robert

Sábato, Ernesto 1911-

Sacco, Joe 1960-

Sacks, Oliver 1933-

Sagan, Carl 1934-1996

Salinger, J.D. 1919-

Salzman, Mark 1959-

Sanchez, Sonia 1934-

Sanders, Noah
    See Blount, Roy, Jr.

Sanders, Winston P.
    See Anderson, Poul

Sandford, John
    See Camp, John

Saroyan, William 1908-1981

Sarton, May 1912-1995

Sartre, Jean-Paul 1905-1980

Satterfield, Charles
    See Pohl, Frederik

Saunders, Caleb
    See Heinlein, Robert A.

VOLUME 5: Sc-Z

Schaeffer, Susan Fromberg 1941-

Schulz, Charles M. 1922-2000

Schwartz, Lynne Sharon 1939-

Scotland, Jay
   See Jakes, John

Sebastian, Lee
   See Silverberg, Robert

Sebold, Alice 1963-

Sedaris, David 1957-

Sendak, Maurice 1928-

Seth, Vikram 1952-

Shaara, Jeff 1952-

Shaara, Michael 1929-1988

Shackleton, C.C.
   See Aldiss, Brian W.

Shaffer, Peter 1926-

Shange, Ntozake 1948-

Shapiro, Karl Jay 1913-2000

Shepard, Sam 1943-

Shepherd, Michael
   See Ludlum, Robert

Shields, Carol 1935-2003

Shreve, Anita 1946-

Siddons, Anne Rivers 1936-

Silko, Leslie 1948-

Sillitoe, Alan 1928-

Silverberg, Robert 1935-

Silverstein, Shel 1932-1999

Simic, Charles 1938-

Simon, David 1960-

Simon, Neil 1927-

Simpson, Louis 1923-

Singer, Isaac
   See Singer, Isaac Bashevis

Singer, Isaac Bashevis 1904-1991

Škvorecký, Josef 1924-

Smiley, Jane 1949-

Smith, Martin
   See Smith, Martin Cruz

Smith, Martin Cruz 1942-

Smith, Rosamond
   See Oates, Joyce Carol

Smith, Wilbur 1933-

Smith, Zadie 1976-

Snicket, Lemony 1970-

Snodgrass, W.D. 1926-

Snyder, Gary 1930-

Solo, Jay
   See Ellison, Harlan

Solwoska, Mara
   See French, Marilyn

Solzhenitsyn, Aleksandr I. 1918-

Somers, Jane
   See Lessing, Doris

Sontag, Susan 1933-2004

Soto, Gary 1952-

Soyinka, Wole 1934-

Spark, Muriel 1918-

Sparks, Nicholas 1965-

Spaulding, Douglas
   See Bradbury, Ray

Spaulding, Leonard
   See Bradbury, Ray

Spencer, Leonard G.
   See Silverberg, Robert

Spender, Stephen 1909-1995

Spiegelman, Art 1948-

Spillane, Mickey 1918-

Stack, Andy
   See Rule, Ann

Stacy, Donald
   See Pohl, Frederik

Stancykowna
   See Szymborska, Wislawa

Stark, Richard
   See Westlake, Donald E.

Steel, Danielle 1947-

Steig, William 1907-

Steinem, Gloria 1934-

Steiner, George 1929-

Steiner, K. Leslie
   See Delany, Samuel R.

Stephenson, Neal 1959-

Sterling, Brett
   See Bradbury, Ray

Sterling, Bruce 1954-

Stine, Jovial Bob
   See Stine, R.L.

Stine, R.L. 1943-

Stone, Robert 1937-

Stone, Rosetta
   See Geisel, Theodor Seuss

Stoppard, Tom 1937-

Straub, Peter 1943-

Styron, William 1925-

Swenson, May 1919-1989

Swift, Graham 1949-

Swithen, John
   See King, Stephen

Symmes, Robert
   See Duncan, Robert

Syruc, J.
   See Milosz, Czeslaw

Szymborska, Wislawa 1923-

Talent Family, The
   See Sedaris, David

Talese, Gay 1932-

Tan, Amy 1952-

Tanner, William
   See Amis, Kingsley

Tartt, Donna 1964-

Taylor, Mildred D. 1943-

Tenneshaw, S.M.
   See Silverberg, Robert

Terkel, Studs 1912-

Theroux, Paul 1941-

Thomas, D.M. 1935-

Thomas, Joyce Carol 1938-

Thompson, Hunter S. 1937-2005

Thornton, Hall
    See Silverberg, Robert

Tiger, Derry
    See Ellison, Harlan

Tornimparte, Alessandra
    See Ginzburg, Natalia

Tremblay, Michel 1942-

Trevor, William 1928-

Trillin, Calvin 1935-

Trout, Kilgore
    See Farmer, Philip José

Turow, Scott 1949-

Tyler, Anne 1941-

Tyree, Omar

Uchida, Yoshiko 1921-1992

Uhry, Alfred 1936-

Uncle Shelby
    See Silverstein, Shel

Updike, John 1932-

Urban Griot
    See Tyree, Omar

Uris, Leon 1924-2003

Urmuz
    See Codrescu, Andrei

Vance, Gerald
    See Silverberg, Robert

Van Duyn, Mona 1921-2004

Vargas Llosa, Mario 1936-

Verdu, Matilde
    See Cela, Camilo José

Vidal, Gore 1925-

Vile, Curt
    See Moore, Alan

Vine, Barbara
    See Rendell, Ruth

Vizenor, Gerald Robert 1934-

Vogel, Paula A. 1951-

Voigt, Cynthia 1942-

Vollmann, William T. 1959-

Vonnegut, Kurt, Jr. 1922-

Vosce, Trudie
    See Ozick, Cynthia

Wakoski, Diane 1937-

Walcott, Derek 1930-

Walker, Alice 1944-

Walker, Margaret 1915-1998

Wallace, David Foster 1962-

Walley, Byron
    See Card, Orson Scott

Ware, Chris 1967-

Warren, Robert Penn 1905-1989

Warshofsky, Isaac
    See Singer, Isaac Bashevis

Wasserstein, Wendy 1950-2006

Watson, James D. 1928-

Watson, John H.
    See Farmer, Philip José

Watson, Larry 1947-

Watson, Richard F.
    See Silverberg, Robert

Ways, C.R.
    See Blount, Roy, Jr.

Weldon, Fay 1931-

Wells, Rebecca

Welty, Eudora 1909-2001

West, Edwin
    See Westlake, Donald E.

West, Owen
    See Koontz, Dean R.

West, Paul 1930-

Westlake, Donald E. 1933-

White, Edmund 1940-

Wideman, John Edgar 1941-

Wiesel, Elie 1928-

Wilbur, Richard 1921-

Williams, C.K. 1936-

Williams, Juan 1954-

Williams, Tennessee 1911-1983

Willis, Charles G.
    See Clarke, Arthur C.

Wilson, August 1945-2005

Wilson, Dirk
    See Pohl, Frederik

Wilson, Edward O. 1929-

Winterson, Jeanette 1959-

Wolf, Naomi 1962-

Wolfe, Gene 1931-

Wolfe, Tom 1931-

Wolff, Tobias 1945-

Woodiwiss, Kathleen E. 1939-

Woodson, Jacqueline 1964-

Wouk, Herman 1915-

Wright, Charles 1935-

Wright, Judith 1915-2000

Xingjian, Gao 1940-

Yolen, Jane 1939-

York, Simon
    See Heinlein, Robert A.

Zelazny, Roger 1937-1995

Zindel, Paul 1936-2003

Co

CODRESCU, Andrei 1946-
(Betty Laredo, Marie Parfenie, Urmuz)

PERSONAL: Born December 20, 1946, in Sibiu, Romania; immigrated to the United States, 1966; naturalized U.S. citizen, 1981; son of Julius and Eva (Mantel) Codrescu; married Alice Henderson, 1968; children: Lucian, Tristan. *Education:* Attended University of Bucharest.

ADDRESSES: Agent—Jonathan Lazear, 930 First Ave. N., Suite 416, Minneapolis, MN 55401. *E-mail*—acodrescu@aol.com.

CAREER: Writer, journalist, editor, and translator. Johns Hopkins University, Baltimore, MD, visiting assistant professor, 1979-80; Naropa Institute, Boulder, CO, visiting professor; Louisiana State University, Baton Rouge, professor of English, beginning in 1984. Regular commentator on National Public Radio's *All Things Considered.* Appeared in the Peabody Award-winning documentary film *Road Scholar,* directed by Roger Weisberg, Metro-Goldwyn-Mayer, 1993.

MEMBER: American-Romanian Academy of Arts and Sciences, Modern Language Association of America, American Association of University Professors, Authors League of America, PEN American Chapter.

AWARDS, HONORS: Big Table Younger Poets Award, 1970, for *License to Carry a Gun*; National Endowment for the Arts fellowships, 1973, 1983; Pushcart Prize, 1980, for "Poet's Encyclopedia," and 1983, for novella *Samba de Los Agentes*; A.D. Emmart Humanities Award, 1982; National Public Radio fellowship, 1983; Towson University prize for literature, 1983, for *Selected Poems: 1970-1980*; National Endowment for the Arts grants, 1985, 1988; General Electric/CCLM Poetry Award, 1985, for "On Chicago Buildings"; American-Romanian Academy of Arts and Sciences Book Award, 1988; George Foster Peabody Award, Best Documentary Film, San Francisco Film Festival, Best Documentary Film, Seattle Film Festival, Cine Award, and Golden Eagle Award, all for *Road Scholar*; ACLU Civil Liberties Award, 1995; Romanian National Foundation Literature Award, 1996.

WRITINGS:

POETRY

License to Carry a Gun, Big Table/Follett (Chicago, IL), 1970.

A Serious Morning, Capra Press (Santa Barbara, CA), 1973.

The History of the Growth of Heaven, George Braziller (New York, NY), 1973, originally published in limited edition chapbook, Kingdom Kum Press (San Francisco, CA), 1973.

For the Love of a Coat, Four Zoas Press (Boston, MA), 1978.

The Lady Painter, Four Zoas Press (Boston, MA), 1979.

Necrocorrida, Panjandrum (Los Angeles, CA), 1982.

Selected Poems: 1970-1980, Sun Books (New York, NY), 1983.

Comrade Past and Mister Present, Coffee House Press (Minneapolis, MN), 1986, 2nd edition, 1991.

Belligerence, Coffee House Press (Minneapolis, MN), 1991.

Alien Candor: Selected Poems, 1970-1995, Black Sparrow Press (Santa Rosa, CA), 1996.

It Was Today: New Poems by Andrei Codrescu, Coffee House Press (Minneapolis, MN), 2003.

NOVELS

The Repentance of Lorraine, Pocket Books (New York, NY), 1976.

Monsieur Teste in America and Other Instances of Realism, Coffee House Press (Minneapolis, MN), 1987, Romanian edition translated by Traian Gardus and Lacrimioara Stoie, published as *Domnul Teste in America,* Editura Dacia (Cluj, Romania), 1993.

The Blood Countess, Simon & Schuster (New York, NY), 1995.

Messiah, Simon & Schuster (New York, NY), 1999.

Casanova in Bohemia, Free Press (New York, NY), 2002.

ESSAYS

A Craving for Swan, Ohio State University Press (Columbus, OH), 1986.

Raised by Puppets Only to Be Killed by Research, Addison-Wesley (Reading, MA), 1988.

The Disappearance of the Outside: A Manifesto for Escape, Addison-Wesley (Reading, MA), 1990, Romanian edition translated by Ruxandra Vasilescu, published as *Disparitia Lui Afara,* Editura Univers (Bucharest), 1995.

The Muse Is Always Half-Dressed in New Orleans and Other Essays, St. Martin's Press (New York, NY), 1993.

Zombification: Stories from NPR, St. Martin's Press (New York, NY), 1994.

The Dog with the Chip in His Neck: Essays from NPR and Elsewhere, St. Martin's Press (New York, NY), 1996.

Hail Babylon! In Search of the American City at the End of the Millennium, St. Martin's Press (New York, NY), 1998.

Ay, Cuba! A Socio-Erotic Journal, St. Martin's Press (New York, NY), 1999.

The Devil Never Sleeps and Other Essays, St. Martin's Press (New York, NY), 2000.

CHAPBOOKS; LIMITED EDITIONS

Why I Can't Talk on the Telephone (stories), Kingdom Kum Press (San Francisco, CA), 1972.

The Here What Where (poetry), Isthmus Press (San Francisco, CA), 1972.

Grammar and Money (poetry), Arif Press (Berkeley, CA), 1973.

A Mote Suite for Jan and Anselm (poetry), Stone Pose Art (San Francisco, CA), 1976.

Diapers on the Snow (poetry), Crowfoot Press (Ann Arbor, MI), 1981.

RADIO/AUDIO RECORDINGS

Traffic au bout du temps (poetry reading), Watershed Intermedia (Washington, DC), 1980.

American Life with Andrei Codrescu, National Public Radio (Washington, DC), 1984.

New Letters on the Air: Andrei Codrescu (poetry reading and interview), KSUR Radio (Kansas City, KS), 1987.

An Exile's Return, National Public Radio (Washington, DC), 1990.

Common Ground (radio series on world affairs), Stanley Foundation, 1991.

(With Spalding Grey, Linda Barry, Tom Bodett, and others) *First Words* (tape and compact disc; introductory recording to "Gang of Seven" spoken word series), BMG Distribution, 1992.

No Tacos for Saddam (tape and compact disc; "Gang of Seven" spoken word series), BMG Distribution, 1992.

Fax Your Prayers, Dove Audio (Los Angeles, CA), 1995.

Plato Sucks, Dove Audio (Los Angeles, CA), 1996.

Valley of Christmas, Gert Town, 1997.

OTHER

(Editor, with Pat Nolan) *The End over End,* privately printed, 1974.

(Translator) *For Max Jacob* (poetry), Tree Books (Berkeley, CA), 1974.

The Life and Times of an Involuntary Genius (autobiography), George Braziller, 1975.

In America's Shoes (autobiography), City Lights (San Francisco, CA), 1975.

(Editor and contributor) *American Poetry since 1970: Up Late* (anthology), Four Walls Eight Windows (New York, NY), 1987, 2nd edition, 1990.

(Editor) *The Stiffest of the Corpse: An Exquisite Corpse Reader,* City Lights (San Francisco, CA), 1988.

(Translator) Lucian Blaga, *At the Court of Yearning: Poems by Lucian Blaga,* Ohio State University Press (Columbus, OH), 1989.

The Hole in the Flag: A Romanian Exile's Story of Return and Revolution (reportage), Morrow (New York, NY), 1991.

Road Scholar (screenplay), directed by Roger Weisberg, Metro-Goldwyn-Mayer, 1993.

Road Scholar: Coast to Coast Late in the Century (reportage), with photographs by David Graham, Hyperion (New York, NY), 1993.

(Editor) *Reframing America: Alexander Alland, Otto Hagel & Hansel Mieth, John Gutmann, Lisette Model, Marion Palfi, Robert Frank,* University of New Mexico Press (Albuquerque, NM), 1995.

(Editor, with Laura Rosenthal) *American Poets Say Goodbye to the Twentieth Century,* Four Walls Eight Windows (New York, NY), 1996.

(Author of essay) *Walker Evans: Signs,* J. Paul Getty Museum (Los Angeles, CA), 1998.

A Bar in Brooklyn; Novellas & Stories 1970-1978, Black Sparrow Press (Santa Rosa, CA), 1999.

(Author of introduction) Kerri McCaffety, *Obituary Cocktail: The Great Saloons of New Orleans,* 2nd edition, Winter Books (New Orleans, LA), 1999.

(Author of commentary) *Land of the Free: What Makes Americans Different,* photographs by David Graham, Aperture (New York, NY), 1999.

(Editor, with Laura Rosenthal) *Thus Spake the Corpse: An Exquisite Corpse Reader, 1988-1998,* two volumes, Black Sparrow Press (Santa Rosa, CA), 2000.

An Involuntary Genius in America's Shoes and What Happened Afterwards, Black Sparrow Press (Santa Rosa, CA), 2001.

(Author of essay) Walker Evans, *Walker Evans, Cuba,* introduction by Judith Keller, J. Paul Getty Museum (Los Angeles, CA), 2001.

Also author, under pseudonym Betty Laredo, of *Meat from the Goldrush* and *36 Poems by Betty Laredo.* Author of novella *Samba de Los Agentes.* Contributor to anthologies, including *The World Anthology,* Bobbs-Merrill, 1969; *Another World,* Bobbs-Merrill, 1973; *The Fiction Collective Anthology,* Braziller, 1975; *Kaidmeon: An International Anthology,* Athens, 1976; *The Penguin Anthology of British and American Surrealism,* Penguin, 1978; *The Random House Anthology of British and American Surrealism,* Random House, 1979; *Longman Poetry Anthology,* Longman, 1985. Author of columns "La Vie Boheme," 1979-82, and "The Last Word," 1981-85, and a biweekly editorial column, "The Penny Post," all for the Baltimore *Sun*; author of monthly book column "The Last Word," for *Sunday Sun* and *Philadelphia Inquirer,* 1982—; author of weekly column "Caveman Cry," for *Soho Arts Weekly,* 1985-86; author of weekly book column "Melville &

Frisby," for the *City Paper* in Baltimore and Washington, DC; author of the column "Actual Size," for *Organica,* and of weekly book review for National Public Radio's *Performance Today.*

Contributor of poetry, sometimes under pseudonyms Urmuz and Marie Parfenie, to periodicals, including *Poetry, Poetry Review, Chicago Review, World, Antaeus, Sun, Confrontation, Isthmus,* and *Editions Change*; also contributor of short stories and book reviews to periodicals, including *Washington Post Book World, New York Times Book Review, American Book Review, Chicago Review, Playboy, Tri-Quarterly, Paris Review, World Press Review, Co-Evolution Quarterly,* and *New Directions Annual.* Poetry editor, *City Paper,* 1978-80, and Baltimore *Sun,* 1979-83; contributing editor, *San Francisco Review of Books,* 1978-83, and *American Book Review,* 1983—; editor, *Exquisite Corpse: A Journal of Books and Ideas,* 1983-1997; contributing editor, *Cover: The Arts,* 1986-88; editor, *American Poetry,* 1970—. Member of advisory board, *Performance Today* and *ARA: Journal of the American Romanian Academy of Arts and Sciences.*

Codrescu's writing has been translated into six languages. A collection of Codrescu's manuscripts is kept at the Hill Memorial Library, Louisiana State University.

ADAPTATIONS: The Blood Countess has been recorded by Simon & Schuster Audio, read by Codrescu and Suzanne Bartish, 1995.

SIDELIGHTS: A Romanian-born poet, fiction writer, editor, and journalist, Andrei Codrescu was expelled from the University of Bucharest for his criticism of the communist government and fled his homeland before he was conscripted into the army. Traveling to Rome, the young writer learned to speak fluent Italian; he then went to Paris and finally to the United States. Arriving in the United States in 1966 without any money or knowledge of English, Codrescu was nonetheless impressed with the social revolution that was occurring around the country. Within four years he had learned to speak colloquial English colorfully and fluently enough to write and publish his first poetry collection, *License to Carry a Gun.* The collection was hailed by many critics who recognized Codrescu to be a promising young poet.

Although Codrescu enjoys the artistic freedoms that exist in the United States, he is still as critical of bureaucracy in his adopted country as he was in his native

Romania—a skepticism that is made evident in his poetry and his autobiographies, *The Life and Times of an Involuntary Genius* and *In America's Shoes*. "In Mr. Codrescu's native Transylvania," Bruce Schlain observed in a *New York Times Book Review* article on the author's poetry collection *Comrade Past and Mister Present*, "poets are social spokesmen, and that perhaps explains his fearlessness of treading on the languages of philosophy, religion, politics, science or popular culture. His focus on a pet theme, oppression, is as much concerned with the private as with the public."

Just as *Comrade Past and Mister Present* compares East and West through poetry, in *The Disappearance of the Outside: A Manifesto for Escape* Codrescu discusses the matter in direct prose. He addresses here such subjects as the mind-numbing effects of television and mass marketing, the sexual and political implications that are a part of language, and the use of drugs and alcohol. "In line with his literary modernism," wrote Josephine Woll in the *Washington Post Book World*, "[Codrescu's] tastes run to the whimsical, the surreal (about which he writes with great understanding), even the perverse. He means to provoke, and he does. His ideas are worth thinking about." Codrescu's skill as an observant commentator about life in the United States has been praised by critics.

Codrescu returned to Romania after twenty-five years to observe firsthand the 1989 revolution that shook dictator Nicolai Ceausescu from power. The range of emotions Codrescu experienced during this time, from exhilaration to cynicism, are described in the volume *The Hole in the Flag: A Romanian Exile's Story of Return and Revolution*. Initially enthusiastic over the prospects of a new political system to replace Ceausescu's repressive police state, Codrescu became disheartened as neo-communists, led by Ion Iliescu, co-opted the revolution. Iliescu himself exhorted gangs of miners to beat student activists "who represented to Codrescu the most authentic part of the revolution in Bucharest," according to Alfred Stepan in the *Times Literary Supplement*. "It seemed to him the whole revolution had been a fake, a film scripted by the Romanian communists."

In preparation for the 1993 book and documentary film *Road Scholar: Coast to Coast Late in the Century*, Codrescu drove across the United States in a red Cadillac accompanied by photographer David Graham and a video crew. Encountering various aspects of the American persona in such cities as Detroit and Las Vegas, Codrescu filters his experiences through a distinctively wry point of view. "Codrescu is the sort of writer who

feels obliged to satirize and interplay with reality and not just catalogue impressions," observed Francis X. Clines in the *New York Times Book Review*, who compared Codrescu's journey to the inspired traveling of "road novelist" Jack Kerouac and poet Walt Whitman.

The title of Codrescu's 1995 novel *The Blood Countess* refers to Elizabeth Bathory, a sixteenth-century Hungarian noblewoman notorious for bathing in the blood of hundreds of murdered girls. "While during the day she functions as administrator for her and her husband's estates . . . at night, in her private quarters, she rages at, tortures, and frequently kills the endless supply of peasant maidens. . . . Convinced that blood restores the youth of her skin, she installs a cage over her bath, in which young girls are pierced to death," noted Robert L. McLaughlin in the *American Book Review*.

Codrescu tells Bathory's gruesome story in tandem with a contemporary narrative about the countess's descendant, Drake Bathory-Kereshtur, a U.S. reporter working in Budapest. Of royal lineage, Drake is called upon by Hungarian monarchists to become the next king (although the true goal of this group, which Drake soon suspects, is to install a fascist government). During the course of Drake's travels in Hungary, he meets up with various manifestations of Elizabeth and eventually is seduced by her spirit to commit murder. "Pleating the sixteenth century with the twentieth, Codrescu is nervously alert for recurrent patterns of evil and its handmaiden, absolute authority," pointed out *Time* contributor R.Z. Sheppard. "Both Elizabeth's and Drake's Hungarys are emerging from long periods of totalitarian culture," commented McLaughlin in the *American Book Review*. The critic further stated, "These monolithic systems, by tolerating no heresy, were able to establish virtually unquestioned order and stability for a period of time. But when these periods end, the societies are thrown into chaos." During the era of communist repression in Hungary, the violence inextricably linked to the land was dormant. But in the words of Nina Auerbach in the *New York Times Book Review*, "ancient agents of savagery" are roused from sleep in *The Blood Countess* after the fall of communism and during the resultant political upheaval—these evil forces "overwhelm modernity and its representative, the bemused Drake."

While some reviewers commented on the horrific aspects of *The Blood Countess*, Bettina Drew pointed out in the *Washington Post Book World* that "Codrescu has done more than tap into a Western fascination, whipped up by Hollywood Draculas and vampires. . . . He has written a vivid narrative of the sixteenth century . . . [and] has made the history of Hungary and its shifting contemporary situation entertaining and compelling." Although McLaughlin observed in the *American Book Review* that *The Blood Countess*'s "historical foundation is interesting; the incidents of its parallel plots keep one turning the pages; it has much to say about our world." Sheppard observed in *Time* that "*The Blood Countess* offers stylish entertainment," while *Entertainment Weekly* contributor Margot Mifflin found the book "beautifully written and meticulously researched."

Like *Zombification,* the volume of essays that follows it, *The Dog with the Chip in His Neck: Essays from NPR and Elsewhere* collects Codrescu's commentaries for National Public Radio's "All Things Considered" along with other essays and addresses that Codrescu has published or presented, as the title suggests, elsewhere. In an interview with *New Orleans Magazine,* Codrescu commented on the experience of writing poetry and fiction and of writing prose: "I write poetry and fiction for pleasure, and nonfiction for money. [Nonfiction] is plenty of fun; it's just slowed-down poetry." In this collection, Codrescu attempts to slow down the motion of mass culture in America. Joanne Wilkinson, writing for *Booklist,* noted that "Codrescu is a very distinctive writer, displaying a formidable command of the language, heady opinions, and a mordant sense of humor. This potent combination makes him perfectly suited to address America's strange brew of high culture and low."

In *Ay, Cuba! A Socio-Erotic Journey,* Codrescu addresses another strange brew, this time the mix of exotic sensuality and heavy-handed dogma in Castro's Cuba. Growing out of Codrescu's visit in late 1997 "to see for myself a decomposing ideology," the book "takes the form of an ironic travelogue-cum-report from the front," according to a *Publishers Weekly* contributor. What Codrescu found was an island surviving on a black market catering to Western tourists, including a number of Americans defying the U.S. travel ban, presided over by an aging revolutionary who keeps the faith while turning a blind eye to the hustlers, prostitutes, and illegal entrepreneurs who actually keep the economy from collapsing. But this is not a political exposé. Instead, it is a series of revealing encounters with a wide variety of Cubans, from street people to doctors, bureaucrats, and Santeria practitioners. "The result is a lively, tragicomic look at Cuba, enriched by insights gleaned from Codrescu's own experience with communism," noted *Library Journal* reviewer Boyd Childress. "In the end, it is refreshing to read a Cuban account where the human takes such firm precedence over the

political," concluded Henry Shukman in the *New York Times Book Review.*

Codrescu returned to the novel with *Casanova in Bohemia,* again fictionalizing a real historical figure and providing an odd connection to modern times. This time his subject is the legendary Giacomo Casanova, but at a time when old age has generally reduced his sexual adventures to voyeurism and storytelling. The stories are told largely to Laura Brock, a maidservant at the castle where Casanova works as librarian to Count Waldstein and completes his fascinating memoirs. "There is no plot to this novel. Rather it follows the ramblings of a nostalgic and learned man as he looks back in delight and forward with dread," noted reviewer Brigitte Weeks in the *Washington Post.* Along with the seductions that have made his very name part of the language, Casanova recounts his travels throughout Europe and his encounters with Benjamin Franklin, Mozart, Marie Antoinette, and other notables from his long and illustrious life. He also muses on a vast range of subjects, reminding the reader that he has authored books on physics, mathematics, and even the history of cheese. "Taking full advantage of the factual eccentricities of his subject, Codrescu succeeds in probing the depths and details of his fictional subject. The reader feels as if he or she has had a close, almost intimate relationship with the elderly roué. Codrescu's imagination is astounding," wrote Weeks.

But of course the sexual escapades, both real and imagined, play a central role throughout the novel, and "Codrescu fans will enjoy this tongue-in-cheek patchwork of bawdy escapades," noted Chicago *Tribune Books* reviewer Brian Bouldrey. "This is ultimately a fun and sexy romp through a libertine's freely fictionalized life," observed a *Kirkus Reviews* contributor. The main character is every bit the rake that has been imagined, but with one major difference: he is not the cold-blooded seducer some have portrayed, eagerly corrupting virgins before moving on to his next victim. "As Codrescu points out, Casanova's image has been reimagined and degraded 'by the likes of Federico Fellini and other unfair or rancorous assassins of his character.' . . . Codrescu's novel is a valuable corrective and a useful piece of pop history. It's also a blast," concluded *Times-Picayune* reviewer Phil Nugent. In the novel, Casanova gets to see that degradation up close, living well past his "official" death in 1798 to see his name dragged down and his works either banned or hopelessly sanitized, until 1960 when a proper French edition of his memoirs is finally published.

Codrescu returns to poetry in *It Was Today,* once again displaying his wide range. In one poem, he imagines a dialogue between two lovers in fourteenth-century China. The collection itself moves between lighter, everyday poems and more serious pieces, harking back to a grim youth in communist Romania and the struggles of a refugee in a foreign land. "No matter which poet is speaking, the effect is arresting," observed *Library Journal* reviewer Rochelle Ratner. For a *Publishers Weekly* contributor, these poems express the wisdom of a radical "whose pop and zing has been mellowed not with age so much as the bodily memory . . . of having seen more than most."

BIOGRAPHICAL AND CRITICAL SOURCES:

PERIODICALS

American Book Review, September-October, 1995, Robert L. McLaughlin, review of *The Blood Countess,* pp. 16, 23.

Booklist, July, 1996, Joanne Wilkinson, review of *The Dog with the Chip in His Neck: Essays from NPR and Elsewhere,* p. 1796.

Entertainment Weekly, September 8, 1995, Margot Mifflin, review of *The Blood Countess,* p. 76.

Kirkus Reviews, January 1, 2002, review of *Casanova in Bohemia,* p. 7.

Library Journal, March 1, 1999, Boyd Childress, review of *Ay Cuba! A Socio-Erotic Journal,* p. 102; August, 2003, Rochelle Ratner, review of *It Was Today,* p. 88.

New Orleans Magazine, October, 1996 (interview), p. 13.

New York Times Book Review, January 25, 1987, Bruce Schlain, review of *Comrade Past and Mister Present,* p. 15; May 9, 1993, Francis X. Clines, review of *Road Scholar: Coast to Coast Late in the Century,* pp. 1, 22-23; July 30, 1995, Nina Auerbach, review of *The Blood Countess,* p. 7; March 28, 1999, Henry Shukman, review of *Ay, Cuba!,* p. 19.

Publishers Weekly, January 18, 1999, review of *Ay Cuba!,* p. 19; July 21, 2003, review of *It Was Today,* p. 188.

Time, August 14, 1995, R.Z. Sheppard, "Gothic Whoopee," p. 70.

Times Literary Supplement, October 9, 1992, Alfred Stepan, review of *The Hole in the Flag: A Romanian Exile's Story of Return and Revolution,* p. 26.

Times-Picayune (New Orleans), February 24, 2002, Phil Nugent, "Lover, Come Back," p. D8.

Tribune Books (Chicago), April 14, 2002, Brian Bouldrey, review of *Casanova in Bohemia,* p. 14.

Washington Post Book World, July 29, 1990, Josephine Woll, "Persistence of Memory," p. WBK8; August 6, 1995, Bettina Drew, review of *The Blood Countess,* pp. 3, 10; July 7, 2002, Brigitte Weeks, "Lothario in Winter," p. 13.

* * *

COE, Tucker
   See WESTLAKE, Donald E.

* * *

COETZEE, J.M. 1940-
   (John Maxwell Coetzee)

PERSONAL: Born February 9, 1940, in Cape Town, South Africa; son of an attorney (father) and a schoolteacher (mother); married, 1963 (divorced, 1980); children: Nicholas, Gisela. *Education:* University of Cape Town, B.A., 1960, M.A., 1963; University of Texas, Austin, Ph.D., 1969.

ADDRESSES: Home—P.O. Box 92, Rondebosch, Cape Province 7700, South Africa. *Agent*—c/o Viking Publicity, 375 Hudson St., New York, NY 10014.

CAREER: International Business Machines (IBM), London, England, applications programmer, 1962-63; International Computers, Bracknell, Berkshire, England, systems programmer, 1964-65; State University of New York at Buffalo, NY, assistant professor, 1968-71, Butler Professor of English, 1984, 1986; University of Cape Town, Cape Town, South Africa, lecturer in English, 1972-82, professor of general literature, 1983—. Johns Hopkins University, Hinkley Professor of English, 1986, 1989; Harvard University, visiting professor of English, 1991.

MEMBER: International Comparative Literature Association, Modern Language Association of America.

AWARDS, HONORS: CNA Literary Award, 1977, for *In the Heart of the Country;* CNA Literary Award, James Tait Black Memorial Prize, and Geoffrey Faber Award, all 1980, all for *Waiting for the Barbarians;* CNA Literary Award, Booker-McConnell Prize, and Prix Femina Etranger, all 1984, all for *The Life and Times of Michael K;* D. Litt., University of Strathclyde, Glasgow, 1985; Jerusalem Prize for the Freedom of the Individual in Society, 1987; Sunday Express Book of the Year Prize, 1990, for *Age of Iron;* Premio Modello, 1994, and *Irish Times* International Fiction Prize, 1995, for *The Master of Petersburg;* Booker Prize, National Book League and Commonwealth Writer's Prize: Best Novel, for *Disgrace;* Life Fellow, University of Cape Town; Nobel Prize in Literature, 2003; longlisted for Booker Prize, 2003, for *Elizabeth Costello.*

WRITINGS:

NOVELS

Dusklands (contains two novellas, *The Vietnam Project* and *The Narrative of Jacobus Coetzee*), Ravan Press (Johannesburg, South Africa), 1974, Penguin Books (New York, NY), 1985.

From the Heart of the Country, Harper (New York, NY), 1977, published as *In the Heart of the Country,* Secker & Warburg (London, England), 1977.

Waiting for the Barbarians, Secker & Warburg (London, England), 1980, Penguin Books (New York, NY), 1982.

The Life and Times of Michael K., Secker & Warburg (London, England), 1983, Viking (New York, NY), 1984.

Foe, Viking (New York, NY), 1987.

Age of Iron, Random House (New York, NY), 1990.

The Master of Petersburg, Viking (New York, NY), 1994.

(With others) *The Lives of Animals,* edited with an introduction by Amy Gutmann, Princeton University Press (Princeton, NJ), 1999.

Disgrace, Viking (New York, NY), 1999.

Elizabeth Costello, Viking (New York, NY), 2003.

Slow Man, Viking (New York, NY), 2005.

OTHER

(Translator) Marcellus Emants, *A Posthumous Confession,* Twayne (Boston, MA), 1976.

(Translator) Wilma Stockenstroem, *The Expedition to the Baobab Tree,* Faber (London, England), 1983.

(Editor, with Andre Brink) *A Land Apart: A Contemporary South African Reader,* Viking (New York, NY), 1987.

White Writing: On the Culture of Letters in South Africa (essays), Yale University Press (New Haven, CT), 1988.

Doubling the Point: Essays and Interviews, edited by David Attwell, Harvard University Press (Cambridge, MA), 1992.

(With Graham Swift, John Lanchester, and Ian Jack) *Food: The Vital Stuff,* Penguin (New York, NY), 1995.

Giving Offense: Essays on Censorship, University of Chicago Press (Chicago, IL), 1996.

Boyhood: Scenes from Provincial Life, Viking (New York, NY), 1997.

(With Bill Reichblum) *What Is Realism?,* Bennington College (Bennington, VT), 1997.

(With Dan Cameron and Carolyn Christov-Bakargiev) *William Kentridge,* Phaidon (London, England), 1999.

Stranger Shores: Literary Essays, 1986-1999, Viking (New York, NY), 2001.

The Humanities in Africa/Die Geisteswissenschaften in Afrika, Carl Friedrich von Siemens Stiftung (Munich, Germany), 2001.

Youth: Scenes from Provincial Life II, Viking (New York, NY), 2002.

(Editor) *Landscape with Rowers: Poetry from the Netherlands,* Princeton University Press (Princeton, NJ), 2003.

Contributor of introduction, *The Confusions of Young Törless,* by Robert Musil, Penguin (New York, NY), 2001. Contributor of reviews to periodicals, including *New York Review of Books.*

ADAPTATIONS: An adaptation of *In the Heart of the Country* was filmed as *Dust,* by ICA (England), 1986.

SIDELIGHTS: J.M. Coetzee, recipient of the 2003 Nobel Prize in Literature, explores the implications of oppressive societies on the lives of their inhabitants, often using his native South Africa as a backdrop. As a South African, however, Coetzee is "too intelligent a novelist to cater for moralistic voyeurs," Peter Lewis declared in *Times Literary Supplement.* "This does not mean that he avoids the social and political crises edging his country towards catastrophe. But he chooses not to handle such themes in the direct, realistic way that writers of older generations, such as Alan Paton, preferred to employ. Instead, Coetzee has developed a symbolic and even allegorical mode of fiction—not to escape the living nightmare of South Africa but to define the psychopathological underlying the sociological, and in doing so to locate the archetypal in the particular."

Though many of his stories are set in South Africa, Coetzee's lessons are relevant to all countries, as *Books Abroad*'s Ursula A. Barnett wrote of *Dusklands,* which contains the novellas *The Vietnam Project* and *The Narrative of Jacobus Coetzee.* "By publishing the two stories side by side," Barnett remarked, "Coetzee has deliberately given a wider horizon to his South African subject. Left on its own, *The Narrative of Jacobus Coetzee* would immediately have suggested yet another tale of African black-white confrontation to the reader." Although each is a complete story, "their nature and design are such that the book can and should be read as a single work," Roger Owen commented in *Times Literary Supplement. Dusklands* "is a kind of diptych, carefully hinged and aligned, and of a texture so glassy and mirror-like that each story throws light on the other." Together the tales present two very different outcomes in confrontations between the individual and society.

The Vietnam Project introduces Eugene Dawn, employed to help the Americans win the Vietnam War through psychological warfare. The assignment eventually costs Dawn his sanity. The title character of *The Narrative of Jacobus Coetzee,* a fictionalized ancestor of the author, is an explorer and conqueror in the 1760s who destroys an entire South African tribe over his perception that the people have humiliated him through their indifference and lack of fear. H. M. Tiffin, writing in *Contemporary Novelists,* found that the novellas in *Dusklands* are "juxtaposed to offer a scarifying account of the fear and paranoia of imperialists and aggressors and the horrifying ways in which dominant regimes, 'empires,' commit violence against 'the other' through repression, torture, and genocide."

Coetzee's second novel, *In the Heart of the Country,* also explores racial conflict and mental deterioration. A spinster daughter, Magda, tells the story in diary form, recalling the consequences of her father's seduction of his African workman's wife. Both jealous of and repulsed by the relationship, Magda murders her father, then begins her own affair with the workman. The integrity of Magda's story eventually proves questionable. "The reader soon realizes that these are the untrustworthy ravings of a hysterical, demented individual consumed by loneliness and her love/hate relationship with her patriarchal father," Barend J. Toerien reported in *World Literature Today.* Magda's "thoughts range widely, merging reality with fantasy, composing and recomposing domestic dramas for herself to act in and, eventually introducing voices . . . to speak to her from the skies," Sheila Roberts noted in *World Literature Written in English.* "She imagines that the voices accuse her, among other things, of transforming her uneventful life into a fiction." *World Literature Today*'s Charles R. Larson found *In the Heart of the Country* "a perplexing novel, to be sure, but also a fascinating nov-

elistic exercise in the use of cinematic techniques in prose fiction," describing the book as reminiscent of an overlapping "series of stills extracted from a motion picture."

Coetzee followed *In the Heart of the Country* with *Waiting for the Barbarians,* in which he, "with laconic brilliance, articulates one of the basic problems of our time—how to *understand* . . . [the] mentality behind the brutality and injustice," Anthony Burgess wrote in *New York.* In the novel, a magistrate attempting to protect the peaceful nomadic people of his district is imprisoned and tortured by the army that arrives at the frontier town to destroy the "barbarians" on behalf of the Empire. The horror of what he has seen and experienced affects the magistrate in inalterable ways, bringing changes in his personality that he cannot understand. Doris Grumbach, writing in the *Los Angeles Times Book Review,* found *Waiting for the Barbarians* a book with "universal reference," an allegory which can be applied to innumerable historical and contemporary situations. "Very soon it is apparent that the story, terrifying and unforgettable, is about injustice and barbarism inflicted everywhere by 'civilized' people upon those it invades, occupies, governs." "The intelligence Coetzee brings us in *Waiting for the Barbarians* comes straight from Scripture and Dostoevsky," Webster Schott asserted in the *Washington Post Book World.* "We possess the devil. We are all barbarians."

Foe, a retelling of Daniel Defoe's *Robinson Crusoe,* marked a transitional stage for Coetzee, according to Maureen Nicholson in *West Coast Review.* Nicholson found many areas in which *Foe* differs from Coetzee's previous work. "Coetzee initially appeared to me to have all but abandoned his usual concerns and literary techniques" in *Foe,* Nicholson commented. "I was mistaken. More importantly, though, I was worried about why he has chosen *now* to write this kind of book; I found his shift of focus and technique ominous. Could he no longer sustain the courage he had demonstrated [in *Waiting for the Barbarians* and *The Life and Times of Michael K.*], turning instead to a radically interiorized narrative?" Nicholson concluded, "Perhaps *Foe* is best viewed as a pause for recapitulation and evaluation, transitional in Coetzee's development as a writer." Ashton Nichols, however, writing in *Southern Humanities Review,* found that Coetzee had not strayed far from his usual topics. "Like all of Coetzee's earlier works, *Foe* retains a strong sense of its specifically South African origins, a sociopolitical subtext that runs along just below the surface of the narrative," Nichols remarked. The reviewer emphasized Coetzee's role as "an archeologist of the imagination, an excavator of language who testifies to the powers and weaknesses of the words he discovers," a role Coetzee has performed in each of his novels, including *Foe*. Central to this idea are the mute Friday, whose tongue was cut out by slavers, and Susan Barton, the castaway who struggles to communicate with him. Daniel Foe, the author who endeavors to tell Barton's story, is also affected by Friday's speechlessness. Both Barton and Foe recognize their duty to provide a means by which Friday can relate the story of his escape from the fate of his fellow slaves who drowned, still shackled, when their ship sank; but both also question their right to speak for him. "The author, whether Foe or Coetzee, . . . wonders if he has any right to speak for the one person whose story most needs to be told," Nichols noted. "Friday is . . . the tongueless voice of millions."

In *Age of Iron* Coetzee addresses the crisis of South Africa in direct, rather than allegorical, form. The story of Mrs. Curren, a retired professor dying of cancer and attempting to deal with the realities of apartheid in Cape Town, *Age of Iron* is "an unrelenting yet gorgeously written parable of modern South Africa, . . . a story filled with foreboding and violence about a land where even the ability of children to love is too great a luxury," Michael Dorris wrote in Chicago *Tribune Books*. As her disease and the chaos of her homeland progress, Mrs. Curren feels the effects her society has had on its black members; her realization that "now my eyes are open and I can never close them again" forms the basis for her growing rage against the system. After her housekeeper's son and his friend are murdered in her home, Mrs. Curren runs away and hides beneath an overpass, leaving her vulnerable to attack by a gang. She is rescued by Vercueil, a street person she has gradually allowed into her house and her life, who returns her to her home and tends to her needs as the cancer continues its destruction. The book takes the form of a letter from Mrs. Curren to her daughter, living in the United States because she cannot tolerate apartheid. "Dying is traditionally a process of withdrawal from the world," Sean French commented in *New Statesman and Society*. "Coetzee tellingly reverses this and it is in her last weeks that [Mrs. Curren] first truly goes out in the baffling society she has lived in." As her life ends, Mrs. Curren's urgency to correct the wrongs she never before questioned intensifies. "In this chronicle of an aged white woman coming to understand, and of the unavoidable claims of her country's black youth, Mr. Coetzee has created a superbly realized novel whose truths cut to the bone," Lawrence Thornton wrote in the *New York Times Book Review*.

In Coetzee's next novel, *The Master of Petersburg*, the central character is the Russian novelist Fyodor Dosto-

evsky, but the plot is only loosely based on his real life. In Coetzee's story, the novelist goes to St. Petersburg upon the death of his stepson, Pavel. He is devastated by grief for the young man, and begins an inquiry into his death. He discovers that Pavel was involved with a group of nihilists and was probably murdered either by their leader or by the police. During the course of his anguished investigation, Dostoevsky's creative processes are exposed; Coetzee shows him beginning work on his novel *The Possessed*.

In real life, Dostoevsky did have a stepson named Pavel; but he was a foppish idler, a constant source of annoyance and embarrassment to the writer. The younger man outlived his stepfather by some twenty years, and as Dostoevsky died, he would not allow Pavel near his deathbed. Some reviewers were untroubled by Coetzee's manipulation of the facts. "This is not, after all, a book about the real Dostoevsky; his name, and some facts connected to it, form a mask behind which Coetzee enacts a drama of parenthood, politics and authorship," Harriett Gilbert explained in *New Statesman and Society*. She went on to praise Coetzee's depiction of "the barbed-wire coils of grief and anger, of guilt, of sexual rivalry and envy, that Fyodor Mikhailovich negotiates as he enters Pavel's hidden life. From the moment he presses his face to the lad's white suit to inhale his smell, to when he sits down, picks up his pen and commits a paternal novelist's betrayal, his pain is depicted with such harsh clarity that pity is burnt away. If the novel begins uncertainly, it ends with scorching self-confidence."

Coetzee's nonfiction works include *White Writing: On the Culture of Letters in South Africa, Doubling the Point: Essays and Interviews,* and *Giving Offense: Essays on Censorship*. In *White Writing,* the author "collects his critical reflections on the mixed fortunes of 'white writing' in South Africa, 'a body of writing [not] different in nature from black writing,' but 'generated by the concerns of people no longer European, yet not African,'" Shaun Irlam observed in *MLN*. The seven essays included in the book discuss writings from the late seventeenth century to the present, through which Coetzee examines the foundations of modern South African writers' attitudes. Irlam described the strength of *White Writing* as its ability "to interrogate succinctly and lucidly the presuppositions inhabiting the language with which 'white writers' have addressed and presumed to ventriloquize Africa." In *Doubling the Point: Essays and Interviews,* a collection of critical essays on Samuel Beckett, Franz Kafka, D. H. Lawrence, Nadine Gordimer, and others, Coetzee presents a "literary autobiography," according to Ann Irvine in a *Library Jour-*

nal review. Discussions of issues including censorship and popular culture and interviews with the author preceding each section round out the collection.

Giving Offense: Essays on Censorship was Coetzee's first collection of essays in nearly ten years, since *White Writing* appeared. The essays collected in *Giving Offense* were written over a period of about six years. Here Coetzee—a writer quite familiar with the varying forms of censorship and the writer's response to them—attempts to complicate what he calls "the two tired images of the writer under censorship: the moral giant under attack from hordes of moral pygmies and the helpless innocent persecuted by a mighty state apparatus." Coetzee discusses three tyrannical regimes: Nazism, Communism, and apartheid; and, drawing upon his training as an academic scholar as well as his experiences as a fiction writer, argues that the censor and the writer have often been "brother-enemies, mirror images one of the other" in their struggle to claim the truth of their position.

In *Boyhood: Scenes from Provincial Life,* Coetzee experiments with autobiography, a surprising turn for a writer, as Caryl Phillips noted in the *New Republic,* "whose literary output has successfully resisted an autobiographical reading." *Boyhood,* written in the third person, "reads more like a novella than a true autobiography. Coetzee develops his character, a young boy on the verge of adolescence, through a richly detailed interior monolog," wrote Denise S. Sticha in *Library Journal.* He recounts his life growing up in Worcester, South Africa, where he moved with his family from Cape Town after his father's latest business failure. There, he observes the contradictions of apartheid and the subtle distinctions of class and ethnicity with a precociously writerly eye. Rand Richards Cooper, writing for the *New York Times Book Review,* stated that "Coetzee's themes lie where the political, the spiritual, the psychological and the physical converge: the nightmare of bureaucratic violence; or forlorn estrangement from the land; a Shakespearean anxiety about nature put out of its order; and the insistent neediness of the body." Coetzee, an Afrikaner whose parents chose to speak English, finds himself between worlds, neither properly Afrikaner nor English. Throughout his boyhood, he encounters the stupid brutalities inflicted by arbitrary divisions between white and black, Native and Coloured, Afrikaner and English. Phillips speculated that "as a boy Coetzee feels compelled to learn how to negotiate the falsehoods that white South Africa offers up to those who wish to belong. In short, he develops the mentality of the writer. He fills his world with doubt, he rejects authority in all its forms—political, social, personal—

and he cultivates the ability to resign himself to the overwhelming insecurity of the heart."

Youth: Scenes from Provincial Life II begins six years after *Boyhood* ends. According to *New Yorker* critic John Updike, the sequel "lacks the bucolic bright spots and familial furies of *Boyhood* but has an overriding, suspenseful issue: when and how will our hero find his vocation, evident to us readers if not yet to him, as a world-class novelist?" Coetzee's narrator leaves South Africa to pursue his education in London, where, despite his desire to write poetry, he finds work as a computer programmer and drifts through a series of affairs. As Hazel Rochman noted in *Booklist,* "this wry, honest, edgy memoir is the portrait of the young artist as a failure." "Coetzee's delicate self-mockery threatens to become condescending," Updike remarked, "and *Youth*'s repeated rhetorical questions verge on burlesque." But Updike also observed that "the suspense attached to this stalled life is real, at least for any reader who has himself sought to find his or her voice and material amid the crosscurrents of late modernism. Coetzee, with his unusual intelligence and deliberation, confronted problems many a writer, more ebulliently full of himself, rushes past without seeing." As Penelope Mesic noted in *Book,* the narrator's growing awareness of the world's complexity is at the heart of the work: "He stands like a man on the edge of a great abyss, amid obscurity, fear, self-doubt and confusion. To discard what he has been told and act in accordance with his own true emotional responses to the world—to women, to cricket, to books, to political injustice—is something he is just learning to do. In that growing sense of authenticity lies the power that will carry him forward, to the passionately honest novels, including *The Life and Times of Michael K.* and *Disgrace,* that he will eventually write."

The Lives of Animals is a unique effort by Coetzee, incorporating his own lectures on animal rights with the fictional story of Elizabeth Costello, a novelist obsessed by the horrors of human cruelty to animals. In this "wonderfully inventive and inconclusive book," as Stephen H. Webb described it in *Christian Century,* Coetzee poses questions about the morality of vegetarianism and the guilt of those who use animal products. But his arguments are not simplistic: he wonders, for example, if vegetarians are really trying to save animals, or only trying to put themselves in a morally superior position to other humans. The character of Elizabeth Costello is revealed as deeply flawed, and the author's ambiguity about her "forces us to think," added Webb. Are her lectures "academic hyperbole and prophetic provocation? Are we meant to feel sorry for her or, angered by her poor reception, to stand up and defend her and her cause?" Following the novella, there are responses to Costello's arguments from four real-life scholars who have written about animals: Barbara Smuts, Peter Singer, Marjorie Garber, and Wendy Doniger. The sum of the book, wrote Marlene Chamberlain in *Booklist,* is valuable "for Coetzee fans and others interested in the links between philosophy, reason, and the rights of nonhumans."

Disgrace, Coetzee's next novel, is a strong statement on the political climate in post-apartheid South Africa. The main character, David Lurie, is an English professor at University of Cape Town. He sees himself as an aging, but still handsome, Lothario. He has seduced many young women in his day, but an affair with one of his students finally proves his undoing. Charged with sexual harassment, he leaves his post in disgrace, seeking refuge at the small farm owned by his daughter, Lucy. Lucy and David are anything but alike. While his world is refined and highly intellectualized, Lucy works at hard physical labor in simple surroundings. David has allowed his sexual desires to lead him, while Lucy is living a life of voluntary celibacy. While David was in an elitist position, Lucy works alongside her black neighbors. David's notions of orderliness are overturned when three men come to the farm, set him afire, and rape Lucy. Father and daughter survive the ordeal, only to learn that Lucy has become pregnant. Eventually, in order to protect herself and her simple way of life, she consents to become the third wife in her neighbor's polygamous family, even though he may have arranged the attack on her in order to gain control of her property.

The complex story of *Disgrace* drew praise from critics. "The novel's many literary allusions are remarkably cohesive on the subject of spiritual alienation: Lucifer, Cain, the tragedy of birth in Wordsworth—there is a full and even fulsome repertoire of soullessness," remarked Sarah Ruden in *Christian Century.* "The same theme can be found in many modernist and postmodernist writers, but Coetzee cancels the usual pretentious and self-pitying overtones." *Antioch Review* contributor John Kennedy noted, "In its honest and relentless probing of character and motive . . . this novel secures Coetzee's place among today's major novelists . . . . The impulses and crimes of passion, the inadequacies of justice, and the rare possibilities for redemption are played out on many levels in this brilliantly crafted book." The author's deft handling of the ambiguities of his story was also praised by Rebecca Saunders, who in *Review of Contemporary Fiction* warned that *Disgrace* is "not for the ethically faint of heart." Saunders felt

Coetzee has "strewn nettles in the bed of the comfortable social conscience," and his book is written in the style "we have come to expect" from him, "at once taciturn and blurting out the unspeakable."

Insight into the workings of Coetzee's mind is afforded through *Stranger Shores: Literary Essays, 1986-1999,* which collects twenty-six essays of literary criticism by the author, focusing on authors such as Franz Kafka, Salman Rushdie, Nadine Gordimer, and Jorge Luis Borges. "These are not puff pieces," warned James Shapiro in *New York Times Book Review.* In his criticism, "Coetzee wields a sharp scalpel, carefully exposing the stylistic flaws, theoretical shortcuts and, on occasion, bad faith of writers he otherwise admires." An *Economist* contributor found the tone of the book "dry tending to arid," and Alberto Manguel in *Spectator* suggested that the collection lacked a needed "touch of passion." Yet Shapiro thought that *Stranger Shores* is a fine model of "blunt, elegant and unflinching criticism at a time when novelists tend to go rather easy when reviewing their colleagues." Finally, Shapiro concluded, *Stranger Shores* is valuable for the "light it casts on a stage in the intellectual journey of one of the most cerebral and consequential writers of our day."

The 2003 work *Elizabeth Costello* "blurs the bounds of fiction and nonfiction while furthering the author's exploration of urgent moral and aesthetic questions," according to a critic in *Publishers Weekly.* In *Elizabeth Costello,* the title character, an aging Australian writer best known for a feminist novel she wrote in the 1960s, delivers a series of formal talks addressing issues such as animal rights and the nature of evil. A contributor in *Kirkus Reviews* noted that "Coetzee has here reimagined in semifictional form several of his recent nonfiction essays and lectures" and called the work "a disappointing hybrid that cannot, except by the loosest possible definition, be called fiction." *New Statesman* contributor Roy Robins believed that the work "has neither the gravity and compulsion of Coetzee's best fiction, nor the precision and intensity of his finest critical writing," Keir Graff offered a different opinion in *Booklist,* stating, "Coetzee may be exploding the genre, but *Elizabeth Costello* has real novelistic force."

In 2003 Coetzee was awarded the Nobel Prize in Literature. In announcing its selection, the Swedish Academy stated in *Africa News Service,* "J. M. Coetzee's novels are characterised by their well-crafted composition, pregnant dialogue, and analytical brilliance. But at the same time he is a scrupulous doubter, ruthless in his criticism of the cruel rationalism and cosmetic morality of western civilisation." Per Wästberg, a member of the Swedish Academy, observed, "Coetzee sees through the obscene poses and false pomp of history, lending voice to the silenced and the despised. Restrained but stubborn, he defends the ethical value of poetry, literature and imagination."

In 2005 Coetzee published *Slow Man.* In the story, a bicycle accident causes Paul Rayment to lose part of his leg. As an amputee, he isolates himself from everyone except his married nurse Marijana, with whom he begins to fall in love. The story becomes complicated with the unexplained appearance of novelist Elizabeth Costello, the protaganist from Coetzee's last novel. Costello's interruption is "either post-modern or pre-modern: it is in either case uncomfortable. What had seemed simple is not back in the realm of artifice," according to Anita Brookner in *Spectator.* Lee Henderson, writing in *Globe & Mail,* noted that the novel "can take place entirely in Rayment's apartment because physicality of any kind is strangely irrelevant to this kind of novel. The disfigured man is a study of consciousness; we read as Rayment's is pried open." Brookner concluded that "it is no small achievement to have created such a miasma of feeling, to leave us convinced and unsettled, and above all face to face with imponderables to which there is no solution." Vince Passaro, a reviewer for *Oprah* magazine, commented that in writing *Slow Man* Coetzee "unafraid, walks a high wire above philosophical uncertainty, love, loss, and death," in what Passaro called "an intense, astonishing work of art."

In addition to his writing, Coetzee has produced translations of works in Dutch, German, French, and Afrikaans, served as editor for others' work, and taught at the University of Cape Town. "He's a rare phenomenon, a writer-scholar," Ian Glenn, a colleague of Coetzee's, told the *Washington Post*'s Allister Sparks. "Even if he hadn't had a career as a novelist he would have had a very considerable one as an academic." Coetzee told Sparks that he finds writing burdensome. "I don't like writing so I have to push myself," he said. "It's bad if I write but it's worse if I don't." Coetzee hesitates to discuss his works in progress, and views his opinion of his published works as no more important than that of anyone else. "The writer is simply another reader when it is a matter of discussing the books he has already written," he told Sparks. "They don't belong to him anymore and he has nothing privileged to say about them—while the book he is engaged in writing is far too private and important a matter to be talked about."

BIOGRAPHICAL AND CRITICAL SOURCES:

BOOKS

Attwell, David, *J.M. Coetzee: South Africa and the Politics of Writing,* University of California Press (Berkeley, CA), 1993.

Coetzee, J.M., *Giving Offense: Essays on Censorship,* University of Chicago Press (Chicago, IL), 1996.

Contemporary Literary Criticism, Gale (Detroit, MI), Volume 66, 1991, Volume 117, 1997.

Contemporary Novelists, 7th edition, St. James Press (Detroit, MI), 2001.

Dictionary of Literary Biography, Volume 225: *South African Writers,* Gale (Detroit, MI), 2000.

Durrant, Sam, *Postcolonial Narrative and the Work of Mourning: J.M. Coetzee, Wilson Harris, and Toni Morrison,* State University of New York Press (Albany, NY), 2004.

Encyclopedia of World Biography, 2nd edition, Gale (Detroit, MI), 1998.

Gallagher, Susan V., *A Story of South Africa: J.M. Coetzee's Fiction in Context,* Harvard University Press (Cambridge, MA), 1991.

Goddard, Kevin, *J.M. Coetzee: A Bibliography,* National English Literary Museum (Grahamstown, South Africa), 1990.

Head, Dominic, *J.M. Coetzee,* Cambridge University Press (New York, NY), 1998.

Huggan, Graham, and Stephen Watson, editors, *Critical Perspectives on J.M. Coetzee,* introduction by Nadine Gordimer, St. Martin's Press (New York, NY), 1996.

Jolly, Rosemary Jane, *Colonization, Violence, and Narration in White South African Writing: Andre Brink, Breyten Breytenbach, and J.M. Coetzee,* Ohio University Press (Athens, OH), 1996.

Kossew, Sue, *Pen and Power: A Post-Colonial Reading of J.M. Coetzee and Andre Brink,* Rodopi (Atlanta, GA), 1996.

Kossew, Sue, editor, *Critical Essays on J.M. Coetzee,* G.K. Hall (Boston, MA), 1998.

Moses, Michael Valdez, editor, *The Writings of J.M. Coetzee,* Duke University Press (Durham, NC), 1994.

Penner, Dick, *Countries of the Mind: The Fiction of J.M. Coetzee,* Greenwood Press (New York, NY), 1989.

PERIODICALS

African Business, November, 1999, Stephen Williams, review of *Disgrace,* p. 42.

Africa News Service, October 3, 2003, "Coetzee Celebrates Nobel, in Private"; October 6, 2003, "Coetzee Swells South Africa's Nobel Haul"; December 22, 2003, "The Nobel Prize in Literature 2003—Presentation to J.M. Coetzee."

Africa Today, number 3, 1980.

America, September 25, 1982.

Antioch Review, summer, 2000, John Kennedy, review of *Disgrace,* p. 375.

Ariel, April, 1985, pp. 47-56; July, 1986, pp. 3-21; October, 1988, pp. 55-72.

Atlantic, March, 2000, Phoebe-Lou Adams, review of *Disgrace,* p. 116.

Book, July-August, 2002, "Confessions of a Computer Programmer," pp. 70- 71.

Booklist, November 1, 1994, p. 477; April 1, 1996, p. 1328; August, 1997, p. 1869; March 15, 1999, Marlene Chamberlain, review of *The Lives of Animals,* p. 1262; November 15, 1999, Hazel Rochman, review of *Disgrace,* p. 579; March 15, 2001, review of *Disgrace,* p. 1362; August, 2001, Donna Seaman, review of *Stranger Shores: Literary Essays, 1986-1999,* p. 2075; June 1, 2002, Hazel Rochman, review of *Youth: Scenes from a Provincial Life II,* p. 1666; September 15, 2003, Keir Graff, review of *Elizabeth Costello,* p. 180; February 1, 2004, Ray Olson, review of *Landscape with Rowers: Poetry from the Netherlands,* p. 943.

Books Abroad, spring, 1976.

Books and Culture, March, 1997, p. 30.

Books in Canada, August/September, 1982.

Boston Globe, November 20, 1994, p. B16.

British Book News, April, 1981.

Charlotte Observer, December 29, 1999, Lawrence Toppman, review of *Disgrace.*

Chicago Tribune Book World, April 25, 1982; January 22, 1984, section 14, p. 27; November 27, 1994, p. 3.

Choice, November, 1999, S.H. Webb, review of *The Lives of Animals,* p. 552.

Christian Century, May 19, 1999, Stephen H. Webb, review of *The Lives of Animals,* p. 569; August 16, 2000, Sarah Ruden, review of *Disgrace,* p. 840.

Christian Science Monitor, December 12, 1983; May 18, 1988, pp. 503-505; November 10, 1999, Ron Charles, "A Morality Tale with No Easy Answers," p. 20; November 18, 1999, review of *Disgrace,* p. 12.

Commentary, March, 2000, Carol Iannone, review of *Disgrace,* p. 62.

Contemporary Literature, summer, 1988, pp. 277-285; fall, 1992, pp. 419- 431.

Contrast, September, 1982, Peter Knox-Shaw, "Dusklands: A Metaphysics of Violence."

Critical Survey, May, 1999, Sue Kossew, "Resistance, Complicity, and Post-Colonial Politics," pp. 18-30, Myrtle Hooper, "'Sweets for My Daughter,'" pp. 31-44, and Derek Attridge, "J.M. Coetzee's *Boyhood,* Confession, and Truth," pp. 77- 93.

Critique: Studies in Modern Fiction, winter, 1986, pp. 67-77; spring, 1989, pp. 143-154; spring, 2001, review of *Foe,* p. 309.

Economist, June 18, 1988, "Oh, but Our Land Is Beautiful," p. 96; December 4, 1999, review of *Disgrace,* p. S4; September 15, 2001, review of *Stranger Shores,* p. 93; March 16, 2002, review of *Youth.*

Encounter, October, 1977; January, 1984.

English Journal, March, 1994, p. 97.

Entertainment Weekly, October 17, 2003, Rebecca Ascher-Walsh, review of *Elizabeth Costello,* p. 85.

Globe & Mail (Toronto, Ontario, Canada), August 30, 1986; October 2, 1999, review of *Disgrace,* p. D18; November 27, 1999, review of *Disgrace,* p. D49; October 22, 2005, Lee Henderson, "Go Disfigure," p. D17.

Harper's, June, 1999, review of *The Master of Petersburg,* p. 76.

Hudson Review, summer, 2000, Thomas Filbin, review of *Disgrace,* p. 333; Harold Fromm, review of *The Lives of Animals,* p. 336.

Journal of Commonwealth Literature, spring, 1996, Mike Marais, "Places of Pigs," p. 83.

Journal of Southern African Studies, October, 1982, Paul Rich, "Tradition and Revolt in South African Fiction."

Kirkus Reviews, February 15, 1999, review of *The Lives of Animals,* p. 264; May 1, 2002, review of *Youth,* p. 631; September 1, 2003, review of *Elizabeth Costello,* pp. 1087-1088.

Library Journal, June 1, 1992, p. 124; September 1, 1994, p. 213; March 15, 1996, p. 70; September 1, 1997, p. 181; December, 1999, Marc A. Kloszewski, review of *Disgrace,* p. 182; July, 2001, Gene Shaw, review of *Stranger Shores,* p. 89; May 15, 2002, Henry L. Carrigan, Jr., review of *Youth: Scenes from a Provincial Life II,* p. 97; October 1, 2003, Barbara Love, review of *Elizabeth Costello,* p. 114; October 15, 2003, Louis McKee, review of *Landscape with Rowers,* pp. 72-73.

Listener, August 18, 1977.

London Review of Books, September 13, 1990, pp. 17-18; October 14, 1999, reviews of *The Lives of Animals* and *Disgrace,* p. 12.

Los Angeles Times, October 3, 2003, Ann M. Simmons, "South African Wins Nobel Prize in Literature."

Los Angeles Times Book Review, May 23, 1982, p. 4; January 15, 1984; February 22, 1987; November 20, 1994, p. 3; December 12, 1999, review of *Disgrace,* p. 2.

Maclean's, January 30, 1984, p. 49.

MLN, December, 1988, pp. 1147-1150; December 17, 1990, pp. 777-780.

Nation, March 28, 1987, pp. 402-405; March 6, 2000, Joseph McElroy, review of *Disgrace,* p. 30.

Natural History, June, 1999, Steven N. Austad, review of *The Lives of Animals,* p. 18.

New Leader, December 13, 1999, Brooke Allen, review of *Disgrace,* p. 27; November-December, 2003, Rosellen Brown, "Countering the Obscene," pp. 35-37.

New Republic, December 19, 1983; February 6, 1995, pp. 170-172; October 16, 1995, p. 53; November 18, 1996, p. 30; February 9, 1998, p. 37; December 20, 1999, review of *Disgrace,* p. 42.

New Statesman, October 18, 1999, Douglas McCabe, review of *Disgrace,* p. 57; October 25, 1999, Jason Cowley, "The Ideal Chronicler of the New South Africa, He Deserves to Make Literary History as a Double Booker Winner," p. 18; November 29, 1999, review of *Disgrace,* pp. 79-80; April 22, 2002, Pankaj Mishra, "The Enigma of Arrival," pp. 50-51; September 15, 2003, Roy Robins, "Alter Ego," pp. 50-51; October 13, 2003, Jason Cowley, "Despite a Booker Nomination and a Nobel Prize, These Writers, Unheard in Their Own Land, Feel Oppressed by Emptiness," pp. 22- 24.

New Statesman and Society, September 21, 1990, p. 40; February 25, 1994, p. 41; November 21, 1997, p. 50.

Newsweek, May 31, 1982; January 2, 1984; February 23, 1987; November 15, 1999, review of *Disgrace,* p. 90.

Newsweek International, November 8, 1999, "South Africa's Prize Winner," p. 72.

New York, April 26, 1982, pp. 88, 90.

New Yorker, July 12, 1982; July 5, 1999, review of *The Lives of Animals,* p. 80; November 15, 1999, review of *Disgrace,* p. 110; July 15, 2002, John Updike, "The Story of Himself."

New York Review of Books, December 2, 1982; February 2, 1984; November 8, 1990, pp. 8- 10; November 17, 1994, p. 35; June 29, 2000, Ian Hacking, review of *The Lives of Animals,* p. 20; January 20, 2000, John Banville, review of *Disgrace,* p. 23; December 5, 2002, Ian Buruma, "Portraits of the Artists," pp. 52- 53.

New York Times, December 6, 1983, p. C22; February 11, 1987; April 11, 1987; November 18, 1994, p. C35; October 7, 1997, p. B7; October 26, 1999, Sarah Lyall, "South African Writer Wins Top British Prize for Second Time," p. A4; November 11, 1999, Christopher Lehmann-Haupt, "Caught in Shifting Values (and Plot)," p. B10; November 14, 1999, Rachel L. Swarns, "After Apartheid, White Anxiety," p. WK1; October 3, 2003, Alan Riding, Coetzee, "Writer of Apartheid, as Bleak Mirror, wins Nobel," p. A1, and Michiko Kakutani, "Chronicling Life Perched on a Volcano's Edge as Change Erupts," p. A6; October 21, 2003, Janet Maslin, "The Mockery Can Still Sting with a Target in the Mirror," p. E7.

New York Times Book Review, April 18, 1982; December 11, 1983, pp. 1, 26; February 22, 1987; September 23, 1990, p. 7; November 20, 1994, p. 9; September 22, 1996, p. 33; November 2, 1997, p. 7; November 28, 1999, review of *Disgrace,* p. 7; December 5, 1999, review of *Disgrace,* p. 8; September 16, 2001, James Shapiro, review of *Stranger Shores,* p. 29; July 7, 2002, William Deresiewicz, "Third-Person Singular," p. 6; July 14, 2002, "Youth (and Bear in Mind)," p. 22.

Novel, fall, 2000, Derek Attridge, review of *Disgrace,* p. 98.

Observer (London, England), July 18, 1999, review of *Disgrace,* p. 13.

Oprah, October, 2005, Vince Passaro, "Crash and Yearn: J.M. Coetzee's Twisty New Novel Explores Imagination and Desperate Love," p. 238.

Publishers Weekly, September 5, 1994, p. 88; January 22, 1996, p. 52; July 28, 1997, p. 59; February 8, 1999, review of *The Lives of Animals,* p. 193; November 1, 1999, Jean Richardson, "Coetzee Wins the Booker Again," p. 15; November 22, 1999, review of *Disgrace,* p. 42; September 22, 2003, review of *Elizabeth Costello,* pp. 80-81.

Quadrant, December, 1999, Paul Monk, review of *Disgrace,* p. 80.

Quarterly Review of Biology, June, 2001, David Fraser, review of *The Lives of Animals,* p. 215; May 6, 2002, review of *Youth,* p. 44.

Research in African Literatures, fall, 1984, Paul Rich, "Apartheid and the Decline of the Civilization Idea"; fall, 1986, pp. 370-392; winter, 1994, Chiara Briganti, "A Bored Spinster with a Locked Diary," pp. 33-49; summer, 2003, Sue Kossew, "The Politics of Shame and Redemption in J.M. Coetzee's *Disgrace,*" pp. 155- 162.

Review of Contemporary Fiction, summer, 2000, Rebecca Saunders, review of *Disgrace,* p. 167; spring, 2002, E. Kim Stone, review of *Stranger Shores,* p. 151.

Salmagundi, spring- summer, 1997, Joanna Scott, "Voice and Trajectory," pp. 82-102, and Regina Janes, "'Writing without Authority,'" pp. 103- 121.

Sewanee Review, winter, 1990, pp. 152-159; April, 1995, p. R48; fall, 2000, Merritt Moseley, review of *Disgrace,* p. 648; summer, 2001, John Reese Moore, review of *The Lives of Animals,* p. 462.

South Atlantic Quarterly, winter, 1994, pp. 1-9, 33-58, 83-110.

Southern Humanities Review, fall, 1987, pp. 384-386.

Speak, May-June, 1978, Stephen Watson, "Speaking: J.M. Coetzee."

Spectator, December 13, 1980; September 20, 1986; April 3, 1999, Antony Rouse, review of *The Lives of Animals,* p. 41; July 10, 1999, Katie Grant, review of *Disgrace,* p. 34; November 20, 1999, review of *Disgrace,* p. 47; September 22, 2001, Alberto Manguel, review of *Stranger Shores: Essays 1986- 1999,* p. 46; April 20, 2002, Hilary Mantel, "Craving Fire and Ardour," p. 39; September 13, 2003, Anita Brookner, *A Brave Stance to Take,* p. 63; September 10, 2005, Anita Brookner, "Take-Over Bid by a Stranger," p. 45.

Sun-Sentinel, December 22, 1999, Chauncey Mabe, review of *Disgrace.*

Time, March 23, 1987; November 28, 1994, pp. 89-90; November 29, 1999, review of *Disgrace,* p. 82; October 13, 2003, Rian Malan, "Only the Big Questions," p. 80.

Time International, November 15, 1999, Elizabeth Gleick, review of *Disgrace,* p. 96; September 15, 2003, Michael Fitzgerald, "Talking about Writing," p. 65.

Times (London, England), September 29, 1983; September 11, 1986; May 28, 1988.

Times Literary Supplement, July 22, 1977; November 7, 1980, p. 1270; January 14, 1983; September 30, 1983; September 23, 1988, p. 1043; September 28, 1990, p. 1037; March 4, 1994, p. 19; April 16, 1999, Maren Meinhardt, review of *The Lives of Animals,* p. 25; June 25, 1999, Ranti Williams, review of *Disgrace,* p. 23; May 19, 2000, Peter D. McDonald, "Not Undesirable," p. 14; October 5, 2001, Michael Gorra, review of *Stranger Shores,* p. 23; April 26, 2002, Peter Porter, "Bedsit Blues," p. 22; September 5, 2003, Oliver Herford, "Tears for Dead Fish," pp. 5- 6.

Tribune Books (Chicago, IL), February 15, 1987, pp. 3, 11; September 16, 1990, p. 3.

Tri-Quarterly, spring- summer, 1987, pp. 454-464.

U.S News and World Report, October 13, 2003, Lisa Stein, "A Novel Nobel," p. 13.

Village Voice, March 20, 1984.

Voice Literary Supplement, April, 1982.

Wall Street Journal, November 3, 1994, p. A16; October 26, 1999, Paul Levy, "Eyes on the Booker Prize," p. A24; November 26, 1999, Philip Connors, review of *Disgrace,* p. W8; July 5, 2002, Merle Rubin, review of *Youth,* p. W7.

Washington Post, October 29, 1983.

Washington Post Book World, May 2, 1982, pp. 1-2, 12; December 11, 1983; March 8, 1987; September 23, 1990, pp. 1, 10; November 27, 1994, p. 6.

West Coast Review, spring, 1987, pp. 52-58.

Whole Earth Review, summer, 1999, review of *The Lives of Animals,* p. 13.

World Literature Today, spring, 1978, pp. 245-247; summer, 1978, p. 510; autumn, 1981; autumn, 1988, pp. 718-719; winter, 1990, pp. 54-57; winter, 1995, p. 207; winter, 1996, "An Interview with J.M. Coetzee," pp. 107-110; autumn, 1996, p. 1038; winter, 2000, review of *Disgrace,* p. 228; spring, 2002, J. Roger Kurtz, review of *Stranger Shores,* p. 249; January-April, 2004, Kristjana Gunnars, "A Writer's Writer," pp. 11-13, Tony Morphet, "Reading Coetzee in South Africa," pp. 14-16, Richard A. Barney, "Between Swift and Kafka," pp. 17-23, Michael Fitzgerald, "Serendipity," pp. 24-25, and Charles Sarvan, "Disgrace?: A Path to Grace," pp. 26-29.

World Literature Written in English, spring, 1980, pp. 19-36; spring, 1986, pp. 34-45; autumn, 1987, pp. 153-161, 174-184, 207-215.

World Press Review, July, 1985, Bernard Genies,*Lifting Coetzee's Veil,* pp. 59-60.

ONLINE

David Higham Associates, http://www.davidhigham.co. uk/ (April 10, 2004), "J.M. Coetzee."

J.M. Coetzee Web site, http://www.tiac.net/users/jgm/ (April 8, 2002).

Nobel e-Museum, http://www.nobel.se/ (April 10, 2004), "John Maxwell Coetzee."

University of Chicago Chronicle, http://chronicle. uchicago.edu/ (April 8, 2002), Arthur Fournier, "J.M. Coetzee Honored with Booker Prize, Top British Fiction Award."

*   *   *

COETZEE, John Maxwell
See COETZEE, J.M.

*   *   *

COFFEY, Brian
See KOONTZ, Dean R.

*   *   *

COLEMAN, Emmett
See REED, Ishmael

COLLINS, Billy 1941-

PERSONAL: Born March 22, 1941, in New York, NY; son of William S. (an electrician) and Katherine M. (a nurse) Collins; married Diane (an architect), January 21, 1979. *Education:* College of the Holy Cross, B.A., 1963; University of California—Riverside, Ph.D. (romantic poetry), 1971. *Hobbies and other interests:* Jazz music.

ADDRESSES: Home—Somers, NY. *Agent*—Chris Calhoun, Sterling Lord Literistic, 65 Bleeker St., New York, NY 10012.

CAREER: Lehman College, City University of New York, Bronx, professor, then distinguished professor of English, 1971—. Writer-in-residence at Sarah Lawrence College. Performs poetry readings. Appears in video *On the Road with the Poet Laureate,* 2004.

AWARDS, HONORS: Poetry fellow, New York Foundation for the Arts, National Endowment for the Arts, and Guggenheim Foundation; *Poetry* magazine's Bess Hokin Award, Oscar Blumenthal Award, and Levinson Prize, all for poetry; appointed Literary Lion by New York Public Library; National Poetry Series competition winner, 1990, for "Questions about Angels"; U.S. poet laureate, 2001-03.

WRITINGS:

POETRY

Pokerface, limited edition, Kenmore, 1977.
Video Poems, Applezaba (Long Beach, CA), 1980.
The Apple That Astonished Paris, University of Arkansas Press (Fayetteville, AR), 1988.
Questions about Angels, Morrow (New York, NY), 1991.
The Art of Drowning, University of Pittsburgh Press (Pittsburgh, PA), 1995.
Picnic, Lightning, University of Pittsburgh Press (Pittsburgh, PA), 1998.
Taking off Emily Dickinson's Clothes, Picador (London, England), 2000.
The Eye of the Poet: Six Views of the Art and Craft of Poetry, edited by David Citino, Oxford University Press (New York, NY), 2001.
Sailing Alone around the Room: New and Selected Poems, Random House (New York, NY), 2001.

Nine Horses, Random House (New York, NY), 2002.
(Editor and author of introduction) *Poetry 180: A Turning Back to Poetry,* [New York, NY], 2003.

Contributor of poetry to university publications and journals, including *Flying Faucet Review* and *Oink.*

SIDELIGHTS: Billy Collins is an American poet who has earned the respect of high school students and such poets such as Edward Hirsch and Richard Howard. With fans such as John Updike and a legion of National Public Radio listeners, Collins has demonstrated a skill for "building a rare bridge of admiration for his work between serious literary fold and poetry novitiates," observed Bruce Weber in the *New York Times.* Collins gives commanding poetry readings, according to Weber, who complimented the poet's ability to hold the interest of a high school crowd. The poet "read[s] in a voice that leavens gravitas with a hint of mischief," described Weber, who declared: "It can be argued that with his books selling briskly and his readings packing them in, Mr. Collins is the most popular poet in America."

The poetry in *Questions about Angels* won Collins the 1990 National Poetry Series competition. Following this honor, the work—not his first—was published by mainstream publisher Morrow. In a review of the volume, a *Publishers Weekly* contributor applauded the poet's "strange and wonderful [images]" but believed that his poems—which are often "constricted by the novelty of a unifying metaphor"—"rarely induce an emotional reaction." In contrast, reviews of Collins' subsequent work have praised his ability to connect with readers. Assessing *Picnic, Lightning, Booklist* contributor Donna Seaman commented that "the warmth of his voice emanates from his instinct for pleasure and his propensity toward humor." John Taylor, writing in *Poetry,* lauded the poet's skill and style, noting that "Collins helps us feel the mystery of being alive." The poet has "a charming mixture of irony, wit, musing, and tenderness for the everyday," according to Taylor, who believed that "a funny-sad ambience characterizes his best work." Taylor also noted, "Rarely has anyone written poems that appear so transparent on the surface yet become so ambiguous, thought-provoking, or simply wise once the reader has peered into the depths."

Collins, who, as a poet, received a nearly unprecedented six-figure deal from Random House for his next three books, experienced a roadblock in the delivery of *Sailing around the Room: New and Selected Poems.* In a roundabout way, his popularity actually impeded the release of the 2000 publication. Due to the continued economic profitability of the poetry collections Collins published through the University of Pittsburgh Press—titles that include *The Art of Drowning* and *Picnic, Lightning*—the college press was extremely resistant to grant Random House the rights to the "selected poems" the New York-based publishing house was requesting for inclusion in *Sailing around the Room.* The battle between Random House and the University of Pittsburgh Press was cited in the *New York Times* by Weber, who expressed amazement that a university press would "unduly stand in the way of an author's success—and wishes."

Weber's article quoted poetry editor/poet Richard Howard, who said of Collins: "He has a remarkably American voice . . . that one recognizes immediately as being of the moment and yet has real validity besides, reaching very far into what verse can do." Collins described himself to Weber as "reader conscious." He also noted, "I have one reader in mind, someone who is in the room with me, and who I'm talking to, and I want to make sure I don't talk too fast, or too glibly. Usually I try to create a hospitable tone at the beginning of a poem. Stepping from the title to the first lines is like stepping into a canoe. A lot of things can go wrong." Collins further related to Weber: "I think my work has to do with a sense that we are attempting, all the time, to create a logical, rational path through the day. To the left and right there are an amazing set of distractions that we usually can't afford to follow. But the poet is willing to stop anywhere."

In 2002, Collins's fans who were anxiously awaiting his next collection of poems were finally satisfied when *Nine Horses: Poems* found its way to book stores. Prior to the volume's publication, Collins was named the U.S. Poet Laureate for 2001-2003 and, according to William Pratt writing in *World Literature Today,* "with this slim, impressive ninth volume of poetry, he shows that he deserves the honor." Pratt went on to note of Collins that "His poems contain lines that are worthy of quotation, as is true of few collections of poems these days, and he invents fresh metaphors, which Aristotle long ago established as the measure of poetry, all drawn from everyday experience rather than from fantasies or dreams." Focusing on ordinary activities, these poems include ruminations on such topics as traveling by train, listening to jazz on the radio, and lying on the beach. Collins also tackles more unusual circumstances, such as dying and discovering that when you get to heaven you have to write a poem about what you've found there.

Although immensely popular and well received by many critics, not everyone was overjoyed with *Nine Horses.* In a review for *New Criterion,* William Logan called Collins "a poet who doesn't respect his art enough to take it seriously." *Booklist* contributor Donna Seaman, however, praised the volume of poems, noting that "Collins is a connoisseur of muted moments and a coiner of whimsical yet philosophical revelations."

Collins's popularity has also led to the 2004 video, *On the Road with the Poet Laureate,* in which, as described by Cliff Glaviano in *Library Journal,* he "reads from his poetry, talks about poetry in his home office, and drives on the interstate highway." Glaviano added, "In this most fascinating film, Collins's readings bring alive the magic of poetry." In another poetry-related project, Collins has attempted to foster a wider appreciation of poetry through an online venture he started in 2002 called *Poetry 180.* Designed to encourage high school students to further appreciate and enjoy poetry, the *Poetry 180 Web site* contains 180 poems selected by Collins for each day of the school year, the focus on contemporary American poets whose work students would find accessible. Commenting in *Reading Today,* Collins noted, "Hearing a poem every day, especially well-written, contemporary poems that students do not have to analyze, might convince students that poetry can be an understandable, painless, and even eye-opening part of their everyday experience." Collins has supplemented his Internet venture by editing a collection of poems titled *Poetry 180: A Turning Back to Poetry.*

BIOGRAPHICAL AND CRITICAL SOURCES:

PERIODICALS

Booklist, March 1, 1998, Donna Seaman, review of *Picnic, Lightning,* p. 1086; November 1, 1998, p. 483; December 1, 2002, Donna Seaman, review of *Nine Horses,* p. 642.

Commonweal, January 11, 2002, Richard Alleva, "A Major Minor Poet: Billy Collins Isn't Just Funny," p. 21.

Library Journal, June 15, 1991, Ellen Kaufman, review of *Questions about Angels,* p. 81; February 15, 2004, Cliff Glaviano, review of *On the Road with the Poet Laureate,* p. 177.

Mother Jones, March-April, 2002, Laura Secor, "Billy Collins: Mischievous Laureate," p. 84.

New Criterion, December, 2003, William Logan, review of *Nine Horses,* p. 85.

New York Times, December 19, 1999, Bruce Weber, "On Literary Bridge, Poet Hits Roadblock," p. 1.

North American Review, November-December, 2003, Vincente F. Gotera, review of *Poetry 180: A Turning Back to Poetry,* p. 58.

Poetry, January, 1989, p. 232; February, 1992, p. 282; February, 2000, John Taylor, review of *Picnic, Lightning* and *The Art of Drowning,* p. 273.

Publishers Weekly, May 17, 1991, review of *Questions about Angels,* p. 59.

Reading Today, February-March, 2002, "U.S. Poet Laureate Launches New Project," p. 16.

U.S. News & World Report, October 28, 2002, Marc Silver, "Even He Wrote Teen-Angst Poems" (interview), p. 7.

World Literature Today, April-June, 2003, William Pratt, review of *Nine Horses,* p. 104.

ONLINE

CNN.com, http://www.cnn.com/ (June 22, 2001), "Billy Collins."

Poetry 180 Web site, http://www.loc.gov/poetry/180/ (August 10, 2004).

*   *   *

COLLINS, Max
See COLLINS, Max Allan

*   *   *

COLLINS, Max Allan 1948-
(Peter Brackett, Max Collins, Max Allan Collins, Jr.)

PERSONAL: Born March 3, 1948, in Muscatine, IA; son of Max Allan, Sr. (an executive) and Patricia Ann Collins; married Barbara Jane Mull (a writer), June 1, 1968; children: Nathan Allan. *Education:* Mescaline Community College, A.A., 1968; University of Iowa, B.A., 1970, M.F.A., 1972. *Politics:* Independent.

ADDRESSES: Home and office—301 Fairview Ave., Mescaline, IA 52761. *Agent*—Dominick Abel Literary Agency, Inc., 146 West 82nd St., 1B, New York, NY 10024.

CAREER: Professional musician, 1966-72, 1976-79, 1986—; songwriter for Tree International, Nashville, TN, 1967-71; reporter for *Muscatine Journal,* 1968-70; writer, 1972—; Muscatine Community College, Musca-tine, IA, instructor in English, journalism, and creative writing, 1971-77; instructor at Mississippi Valley Writers Conference 1973—; film producer/director/screenwriter, 1994—.

MEMBER: Mystery Writers of America (board of directors, 1980—), Private Eye Writers of America (board of directors, 1991—), Horror Writers of America (board of directors, 1997—), Iowa Motion Picture Association (board of directors, 1994—; president, 1998-2000), Iowa Screenwriters Alliance (board of directors, 1997—).

AWARDS, HONORS: Inkpot Award for outstanding achievement in comic arts, San Diego Comic Convention, 1982; Shamus Award for best hardcover novel, Private Eye Writers of America (PEWA), 1983, for *True Detective,* and 1991, for *Stolen Away: A Novel of the Lindbergh Kidnapping;* Edgar Allan Poe Special Award for critical/biographical work, Mystery Writers of America, 1984, for *One Lonely Knight: Mickey Spillane's Mike Hammer;* distinguished alumnus award, Muscatine Community College, 1985; Susan Glaspell Award for fiction, *Quad-City Times,* Davenport, IA, 1990; Best Screenplay, Iowa Motion Picture Awards, 1996, for *Mommy's Day;* Best Unproduced Screenplay, Iowa Motion Picture Awards, 1996, for *Blue Christmas;* Best Unproduced Screenplay, Iowa Motion Picture Awards, 1997, for *Spree;* Best Entertainment Program, Iowa Motion Picture Awards, 1999, for *Mike Hammer's Mickey Spillane;* Agatha Award nomination for nonfiction, 2002, for *The History of Mystery;* Shamus Award nomination for best hardcover novel, PEWA, 2002, for *Angel in Black.*

WRITINGS:

"NOLAN" SUSPENSE NOVEL SERIES

(Under name Max Collins) *Bait Money,* Curtis Books (New York, NY), 1973, revised edition, Pinnacle Books (New York, NY), 1981.

(Under name Max Collins) *Blood Money,* Curtis Books (New York, NY), 1973, revised edition, Pinnacle Books (New York, NY), 1981.

(Under name Max Collins) *Fly Paper,* Pinnacle Books (New York, NY), 1981.

(Under name Max Collins) *Hush Money,* Pinnacle Books (New York, NY), 1981.

(Under name Max Collins) *Hard Cash,* Pinnacle Books (New York, NY), 1982.

(Under name Max Collins) *Scratch Fever,* Pinnacle Books (New York, NY), 1982.

Spree, Tor Books (New York, NY), 1987.

Mourn the Living, Five Star (Unity, ME), 1999.

"QUARRY" SERIES

(Originally published under name Max Collins) *The Broker,* Berkley Publishing (New York, NY), 1976, published as *Quarry,* Foul Play, 1985.

(Originally published under name Max Collins) *The Broker's Wife,* Berkley Publishing, 1976, published as as *Quarry's List,* Foul Play, 1985.

(Originally published under name Max Collins) *The Dealer,* Berkley Publishing, 1976, published as *Quarry's Deal,* Foul Play, 1986.

(Originally published under name Max Collins) *The Slasher,* Berkley Publishing, 1977, published as *Quarry's Cut,* Foul Play, 1986.

Primary Target, Foul Play, 1987.

Quarry's Greatest Hits, Five Star (Waterville, ME), 2003.

"MALLORY" SERIES

(Under name Max Collins) *The Baby Blue Rip-Off,* Walker & Co. (New York, NY), 1983.

No Cure for Death, Walker & Co. (New York, NY), 1983.

Kill Your Darlings, Walker & Co. (New York, NY), 1984.

A Shroud for Aquarius, Walker & Co. (New York, NY), 1985.

Nice Weekend for a Murder, Walker & Co. (New York, NY), 1986.

"MEMOIRS OF NATHAN HELLER" HISTORICAL PRIVATE EYE SERIES

True Detective, St. Martin's Press (New York, NY), 1983.

True Crime, St. Martin's Press (New York, NY), 1984.

The Million-Dollar Wound, St. Martin's Press (New York, NY), 1986.

Neon Mirage, St. Martin's Press (New York, NY), 1988.

Stolen Away: A Novel of the Lindbergh Kidnapping, Bantam (New York, NY), 1991.

Dying in the Postwar World (short stories), Countryman Press, 1991.

Carnal Hours, Dutton (New York, NY), 1994.

Blood and Thunder, Dutton (New York, NY), 1995.

Damned in Paradise, Dutton (New York, NY), 1996.

Flying Blind, Signet (New York, NY), 1999.

Majic Man, Dutton, 1999.

Kisses of Death, Crippen & Landru, 2001.

Angel in Black, New American Library (New York, NY), 2001.

Chicago Confidential, New American Library (New York, NY), 2002.

"ELIOT NESS" HISTORICAL NOVEL SERIES

The Dark City, Bantam (New York, NY), 1987.

Butcher's Dozen, Bantam (New York, NY), 1988.

Bullet Proof, Bantam (New York, NY), 1989.

Murder by the Numbers, St. Martin's Press (New York, NY), 1993.

NONFICTION

(With Ed Gorman) *Jim Thompson: The Killers inside Him,* Fedora Press (Cedar Rapids, IA), 1983.

(With James L. Traylor) *One Lonely Knight: Mickey Spillane's Mike Hammer,* Popular Press (Bowling Green, OH), 1984.

(With John Javna) *The Best of Crime and Detective TV: Perry Mason to Hill Street Blues, The Rockford Files to Murder She Wrote,* Harmony (New York, NY), 1988.

COMIC-STRIP COLLECTIONS

(Under name Max Collins) *Dick Tracy Meets Angeltop,* Ace Books (New York, NY), 1980.

(Under name Max Collins) *Dick Tracy Meets the Punks,* Ace Books (New York, NY), 1980.

(Under name Max Collins) *The Mike Mist Minute Mysteries,* Eclipse Enterprises, 1981.

(With Terry Beatty) *The Files of Ms. Tree,* Volume 1, Aardvark-Vanaheim (Kitchener, Ontario, Canada), 1984, Volume 2: *The Cold Dish,* Renegade Press, 1985.

(With Dick Locher) *Dick Tracy: Tracy's Wartime Memories,* Ken Pierce, 1986.

(With Terry Beatty) *Ms. Tree,* Paper Jacks, 1988.

(Editor, with Dick Locher) *The Dick Tracy Casebook: Favorite Adventures, 1931-1990,* St. Martin's Press (New York, NY), 1990.

(Editor, with Dick Locher) *Dick Tracy: The Secret Files,* St. Martin's Press (New York, NY), 1990.

(With Dick Locher) *Dick Tracy's Fiendish Foes: A Sixtieth Anniversary Celebration,* St. Martin's Press (New York, NY), 1991.

SCREENPLAYS

The Expert, HBO, 1995.

Also author and director of *Mommy,* 1995, *Mommy's Day,* 1997, *Mike Hammer's Mickey Spillane* 1999, and *Real Time: Siege at Lucas Street Market,* 2000.

OTHER

(Coeditor) Mickey Spillane, *Mike Hammer: The Comic Strip,* Ken Pierce (Park Forest, IL), Volume 1, 1982, Volume 2, 1985.

(Editor) Mickey Spillane, *Tomorrow I Die,* Mysterious Press (New York, NY), 1984.

Midnight Haul, Foul Play (Woodstock, VT), 1986.

Dick Tracy (novelization of film), Bantam (New York, NY), 1990.

Dick Tracy Goes to War, Bantam (New York, NY), 1991.

Dick Tracy Meets His Match, Bantam (New York, NY), 1992.

In the Line of Fire (novelization of film), Jove (New York, NY), 1993.

Maverick (novelization of film), Signet (New York, NY), 1994.

(Under pseudonym Peter Brackett) *I Love Trouble* (novelization of film), Signet (New York, NY), 1994.

(Editor, with Mickey Spillane) *Murder Is My Business,* Dutton (New York, NY), 1994.

Waterworld (novelization of film), Boulevard (New York, NY), 1995.

NYPD Blue: Blue Beginning, Signet (New York, NY), 1995.

Daylight (novelization of film), Boulevard (New York, NY), 1996.

The Mystery Scene Movie Guide: A Personal Filmography of Modern Crime Pictures, Brownstone Books (San Bernardino, CA), 1996.

Earl MacPherson: The Sketchbook Pin-Ups, Collectors Press (Portland, OR), 1997.

NYPD Blue: Blue Blood, Signet (New York, NY), 1997.

Mommy, Leisure Books (New York, NY), 1997.

Air Force One (novelization of film), Ballantine (New York, NY), 1997.

Gil Elvgren: The Wartime Pin-Ups, Volume 1, Collectors Press (Portland, OR), 1997.

Pin-Up Poster Book: The Billy DeVorss Collection, Collectors Press (Portland, OR), 1997.

Road to Perdition (graphic novel), illustrated by Richard Piers Rayner, Paradox Press (New York, NY), 1998.

U.S. Marshals (novelization of film), Boulevard (New York, NY), 1998.

Mommy's Day, Leisure Books (New York, NY), 1998.

(With Drake Elvgren) *Elvgren: His Life and Art,* Collectors Press (Portland, OR), 1998.

Saving Private Ryan (novelization of film), Signet (New York, NY), 1998.

Swimsuit Sweeties, Collectors Press (Portland, OR), 1999.

Varga Girls I, Collectors Press (Portland, OR), 1999.

Varga Girls II, Collectors Press (Portland, OR), 1999.

Elvgren Girls I, Collectors Press (Portland, OR), 1999.

Elvgren Girls II, Collectors Press (Portland, OR), 1999.

Exotic Ladies, Collectors Press (Portland, OR), 1999.

The Mummy (novelization of film), Boulevard (New York, NY), 1999.

The Titanic Murders, Berkley (New York, NY), 1999.

(With Barbara Collins) *Regeneration,* Leisure Books (New York, NY), 1999.

For the Boys!: The Racy Pin-Ups of WWII, Collectors Press (Portland, OR), 2000.

(Editor and author of introduction) Barbara Collins, *Too Many Tomcats and Other Feline Tales of Suspense,* Five Star (Waterville, ME), 2000.

U-571 (novelization of film), Avon (New York, NY), 2000.

(Editor, with Jeff Gelb) *Flesh and Blood: Erotic Tales of Crime and Passion,* Mysterious Press (New York, NY), 2001.

Indian Maidens, Collectors Press (Portland, OR), 2001.

Pirate & Gypsy Girls, Collectors Press (Portland, OR), 2001.

Pin-Up Nudes, Collectors Press (Portland, OR), 2001.

Seaside Sweethearts, Collectors Press (Portland, OR), 2001.

Blue Christmas and Other Holiday Homicides, Five Star (Waterville, ME), 2001.

(With Barbara Collins) *Murder—His and Hers* (short stories), Five Star (Waterville, ME), 2001.

The History of Mystery, Collectors Press (Portland, OR), 2001.

The Pearl Harbor Murders, Berkley Prime Crime (New York, NY), 2001.

The Mummy Returns (novelization of film), Berkley Boulevard Books (New York, NY), 2001.

(Editor and author of introduction) Mickey Spillane *Together We Kill: The Uncollected Stories of Mickey Spillane,* Five Star (Waterville, ME), 2001.

The Lusitania Murders, Berkley Prime Crime (New York, NY), 2001.

(Editor, with Mickey Spillane) *A Century of Noir: Thirty-two Classic Crime Stories,* New American Library (New York, NY), 2002.

The Scorpion King (novelization of film), Berkley Boulevard Books (New York, NY), 2002.

Before the Dawn (based on television series), Ballantine Books (New York, NY), 2002.

I Spy (novelization of screenplay), HarperEntertainment (New York, NY), 2002.

Patriotic Pin-Ups, Collectors Press (Portland, OR), 2002.

Pin-Up Nudes II, Collectors Press (Portland, OR), 2002.

Cowgirl Pin-Ups, Collectors Press (Portland, OR), 2002.

Playful Pin-Ups, Collectors Press (Portland, OR), 2002.

Sin City, Pocket Star Books (New York, NY), 2002.

Calendar Girl: Sweet & Sexy Pin-Ups of the Postwar Era, Collectors Press (Portland, OR), 2003.

(Editor, with Jeff Gelb) *Flesh and Blood: Guilty as sin: Erotic Tales of Crime and Passion,* Mysterious Press (New York, NY), 2003.

CSI: Crime Scene Investigation, IDW Publications (San Diego, CA), 2003.

CSI: Crime Scene Investigation: Body of Evidence, Pocket Star Books (New York, NY), 2003.

CSI: Crime Scene Investigation: Cold Burn, Pocket Star Books (New York, NY), 2003.

Skin Game, Ballantine Books (New York, NY), 2003.

Batman: Child of Dreams (English adaptation), DC Comics, 2003.

On the Road to Perdition: Oasis, Paradox Press (New York, NY), 2003.

On the Road to Perdition: Sanctuary, Paradox Press (New York, NY), 2003.

Florida Getaway, Pocket Star Books (New York, NY), 2003.

(With wife, Barbara Collins) *Bombshell,* Five Star (Waterville, ME), 2004.

The London Blitz Murders, Berkley Prime Crime (New York, NY), 2004.

Road to Purgatory, William Morrow (New York, NY), 2004.

(With Kathy Reichs) *Bones: Buried Deep,* Pocket Star Books (New York, NY) 2006.

Author, under name Max Collins, of comic strip "Dick Tracy," distributed by Chicago Tribune/New York News Syndicate, 1977-93; writer of "The Comics Page," 1979-80, and of monthly *Ms. Tree* comic book. Contributor of scripts to *Batman* and *DC* comic books; cocreator, with Beatty, of *Wild Dog* comic-book feature; cocreator and writer of *Mickey Spillane's Mike Danger* comic book. Movie columnist for *Mystery Scene.* Contributor of short stories to numerous anthologies. Contributor of articles to magazines, including *Armchair Detective, Comics Feature,* and *Mystery Scene.*

Collins's manuscripts are collected at Bowling Green State University, Ohio.

ADAPTATIONS: Road to Perdition was directed by Sam Mendes, starred Tom Hanks, Jude Law, and Paul Newman, and was released by Twentieth-Century Fox and Dreamworks, 2002.

SIDELIGHTS: Max Allan Collins is a prolific novelist and freelance writer who has won widespread praise for his original detective fiction, yet among his best-known work is undoubtedly the "Dick Tracy" comic strip, which he wrote from 1977 to 1993. Also, Collins is the author for the "Nathan Heller" history-based mystery novels and has also penned a number of television and movie novelizations, among them book versions of popular films such as *U-571, The Scorpion King, Saving Private Ryan,* and *The Mummy Returns.*

"Dick Tracy," created by Chester Gould in 1931, was the first comic intended not to be humorous. The title character, a hard-boiled, two-fisted detective, quickly became a nationwide favorite. Collins and artist Richard Fletcher took over the series after Gould's retirement in 1977; when Fletcher died in 1983, Collins continued with artist Dick Locher. The two have edited several collections of the "Dick Tracy" strip, and Collins has also written three novels featuring the detective—one a novelization of the film *Dick Tracy,* and two sequels to it. Many reviewers agree that although the "Dick Tracy" novels are minor compared to Collins's other work, they are still worthwhile reading. "I consider my work in comics to play a supporting role in my career; . . . still, it often tends to take center-stage, since *Dick Tracy* is obviously more famous than anyone who merely writes it," Jon L. Breen quoted Collins as saying in *St. James Guide to Crime and Mystery Writers.*

"For many years now I've been in love with the private-eye novel: the lean prose, the sharp dialogue, the understated poetry at least as found in the works of those three proponents of the form, Dashiell Hammett, Raymond Chandler, and Mickey Spillane," Breen further quoted Collins. "But when I began writing my own suspense novels in the early 1970s I found myself uncomfortable with the private eye: my heroes tended to be antiheroes, perhaps reflecting the troubled times around me as I worked." Collins's first protagonist was Nolan, an aging thief who frequently becomes involved in detective work. His next creation was Quarry, a Vietnam veteran who now works as a hired killer. Breen named Quarry as "possibly the first detective in fiction to commit the murder before trying to solve it. He is among the least admirable characters (I think intentionally so) to be the protagonist of a series of crime novels. That he is acceptable in that role . . . is a tribute to Collins's talent." *Quarry's Greatest Hits* is an anthology of three "Quarry" short stories and one novel. Wes Lukowsky wrote in a *Booklist* review of the 2003 work that "The three stories included here reflect Collins' sardonic humor and his extraordinary ability to take his plots on an unexpected detour or two."

In the "Mallory" series, Collins introduced a young, small-town mystery writer who delivers meals to shut-ins and also solves mysterious crimes. Unlike Quarry and Nolan, Mallory is firmly on the right side of the law. Breen noted that "the 'Mallory' novels are softer edged, appropriate to a more conservative hardcover market, but in certain stretches the author's hard-boiled roots are apparent. Most notable about the Mallory books is their understanding depiction of the Vietnam generation and their sense of nostalgia for the recent past." Breen singled out *A Shroud for Aquarius* as the best of the Mallory novels, one that provides "a poignant look back at the 1960s."

One of Collins's historical series relates the fictional adventures of real-life gangbuster Eliot Ness during his days as a public safety officer in Cleveland. His most highly praised series, however, is probably the one featuring Nate Heller, described by Peter Robertson in *Booklist* as a 1930s "smart-mouthed, semihonest, gam-chasing" Chicago cop turned private investigator. In Breen's estimation, the "Nate Heller" series represents Collins's "major contribution to date." Over the course of several books, Heller becomes involved with notable, real-life historical figures including Al Capone, Eliot Ness, and Charles Lindbergh. "It's easier to bring a wholly fictitious creation to life in a novel than to animate real-life guest stars, but Collins does the job amazingly well," affirmed Breen. Collins has also been praised for the careful research that goes into his historical fiction. In Breen's opinion, "Collins achieves something else that many bestselling blockbuster writers do not: getting full measure from his thorough research without ever sounding like a history term paper."

The Heller novels often propose alternative solutions to mysterious crimes of the past. In *Stolen Away: A Novel of the Lindbergh Kidnapping,* Heller discovers the Lindbergh baby living in the Midwest, years after the world-famous early-twentieth-century abduction of the child of Charles and Anne Morrow Lindberg. A *Publishers Weekly* writer enthused: "Collins's . . . reconstruction of the Lindbergh case is so believable, one forgets that this is fiction," and a *Kirkus Reviews* contributor thought that *Stolen Away* is "a meaty, satisfying rehash of the crime of the century—required reading for people who still wonder." A collection of short stories about Heller, *Dying in the Postwar World,* was dismissed as "drab" by a *Publishers Weekly* contributor, and a contributor to *Kirkus Reviews* rated the collection "uneven." A *Booklist* writer judged the book very differently, however, saying that at least five of the stories are "gems: period yarns set in the postwar thirties and crisp with melodramatic cop slang and hard-nosed Chinatown urban detailing."

In *Blood and Thunder,* Heller is hired as a bodyguard to protect high-profile Louisiana senator Huey Long. "Collins's sense of place and time is unerringly acute, and he happily indulges in re-creating Long's fiery stump style," noted a *Publishers Weekly* reviewer. Wes Lukowsky rated *Blood and Thunder* a "highly recommended" title in *Booklist,* and a *Kirkus Reviews* speaker declared that publication of *Blood and Thunder* could be Collins's "finest hour."

Majic Man revolves around the alleged UFO crash in Roswell, New Mexico. The novel was lauded by critics. Wes Lukowsky in *Booklist* called the book a "typically intelligent, witty, and exciting examination of a real-life mystery." A *Publishers Weekly* critic concluded: "There's magic of a literary kind here: full-bore suspense coupled with an ingenious take on an overworked pop-historical touchstone."

In *Chicago Confidential,* set in the 1950s, Heller returns to the streets of Chicago, trying to dodge federal investigators examining the city's underworld—until a friend is killed. *Library Journal*'s Michael Rogers noted of the novel: "When it comes to noirish, hard-boiled PI thrillers, few writers can compete with Collins: the sex is hot and the killings cold. What else could you ask for?"

In the late 1990s, Collectors Press, a specialized publisher showcasing commercial art, issued a number of Collins' books on pin-up artists, including Billy DeVorss, Earl MacPherson, Gil Elvgren, and Alberto Vargas. "Elvgren, MacPherson, and Vargas are hardcore pinup artists, although pinup hard-core is perky, pert, clean as a whistle—in short, wholesomely sexy," commented Ray Olson in *Booklist.* Olson called Collins' text "apt and informative," and praised the quality reproductions. Mike Tribby lauded *Elvgren: His Life and Art* in a *Booklist* review: "This glowing volume offers an authoritative biography of Elvgren, analysis of his career, and lush reproduction of his work."

Breen concluded his assessment of Collins, calling the author "solidly entrenched in the hard and tough school of crime fiction. His protagonists have often been professional criminals. But his sense of humor and underlying humanity, coupled with a gift for intricate plotting and cinematically effective action scenes, make his novels palatable even to readers who normally would eschew the very hard-boiled."

BIOGRAPHICAL AND CRITICAL SOURCES:

BOOKS

St. James Guide to Crime and Mystery Writers, 4th edition, St. James Press (Detroit, MI), 1996.

PERIODICALS

Armchair Detective, July, 1978, pp. 300-304; winter, 1996, p. 109.
Booklist, July, 1990, p. 2075; March 15, 1991, p. 1435; October 15, 1991, p. 412; March 1, 1994, p. 1183; August, 1995, p. 1931; September 15, 1996; January 1, 1998, p. 761; August, 1998, p. 1974; September 15, 1998, p. 183; September 1, 1999, p. 71; May 1, 2003, p. 1538; October 15, 2003, Wes Lukowsky, review of *Quarry's Greatest Hits,* p. 393; May 1, 2004, review of *Bombshell,* p. 1503.
Chicago Tribune, November 2, 1990, section 3, p. 2; June 10, 1991, section 5, p. 3; December 13, 1991, section 5, p. 3.
Kirkus Reviews, March 15, 1991, p. 343; September 1, 1991, p. 1118; February 1, 1994, p. 97; July 1, 1995, p. 898; February 15, 2003, review of *Flesh and Blood: Guilty as Sin: Erotic Tales of Crime and Passion,* p. 272.
Library Journal, April 1, 1994, p. 137; April 1, 1997, p. 144; September 1, 1999, p. 237; April 1, 2004, review of *Bombshell,* p. 128.
New York Times Book Review, April 17, 1994, p. 19.
Publishers Weekly, April 5, 1991, p. 139; September 13, 1991, p. 66; February 14, 1994, p. 81; June 26, 1995, p. 93; August 23, 1999, p. 51; April 1, 2002, review of *Flesh and Blood: Dark Desires,* p. 56;

March 17, 2003, review of *Flesh and Blood: Guilty as Sin,* p. 58; September 22, 2003, review of *C.S.I.: Crime Scene Investigation: Serial,* p. 86; February 16, 2004, review of *On the Road to Perdition: Sanctuary,* p. 154.
Voice of Youth Advocates, October, 1990, p. 215; October, 1991, p. 223.

*   *   *

COLLINS, Max Allan, Jr.
    See COLLINS, Max Allan

*   *   *

COLVIN, James
    See MOORCOCK, Michael

*   *   *

CONDÉ, Maryse 1937-
    (Maryse Boucolon)

PERSONAL: Born February 11, 1937, Guadeloupe, West Indies; daughter of Auguste and Jeanne (Quidal) Boucolon; married Mamadou Condé, 1958 (divorced, 1981); married Richard Philcox (a translator), 1982; children: Denis; (first marriage) Sylvie, Aicha, Leila. *Education:* Sorbonne, University of Paris, Ph.D., 1976.

ADDRESSES: Home—Montebello, 97170 Petit Bourg, Guadeloupe, French West Indies. *Office*—Department of French and Romance Philology, 502 Philosophy Hall, Columbia University, New York, NY 10027.

CAREER: Ecole Normale Superieure, Conakry, Guinea, instructor, 1960-64; Ghana Institute of Languages, Accra, Ghana, 1964-66; Lycee Charles de Gaulle, Saint Louis, Senegal, instructor, 1966-68; University of Paris, Paris, France, assistant at Jussieu, 1970-72, lecturer at Nanterre, 1973-80, charge de cours at Sorbonne, 1980-85; University of California, Berkeley, professor of French, 1989-92; University of Maryland, College Park, professor of French, 1992-1995; Columbia University, New York, NY, professor of French, 1995—, chairperson of the French and Francophone Institute, 1997—. French Services of the British Broadcasting Corporation, London, England, program producer, 1968-70; Radio France Internationale, France Culture, program producer, 1980-85. Bellagio Writer-in-Residence, Rockefeller Foundation, 1986; visiting professor, California Institute of Technology, 1989, University of Virginia, 1993-95, and Harvard University, 1995; lecturer in United States, Africa, and the West Indies. Presenter of a literary program for Africa on Radio-France.

AWARDS, HONORS: Fulbright Scholar, 1985-86; Prix litteraire de la Femme, Prix Alain Boucheron, 1986, for *Moi, Tituba, Sorciere Noire de Salem;* Guggenheim fellow, 1987-88; Puterbaugh fellow, University of Oklahoma—Norman, 1993; Prix Carbet de la Caraibe, 1997, for *Desirada;* honorary member, Academie des Lettres du Quebec, 1998; Marguerite Yourcenar Prize, 1999, for *Tales from the Heart;* Lifetime Achievement Award, New York University Africana Studies Program and Institute of African-American Affairs, 1999; commandeur, l'Ordre des Arts et des Lettres (France), 2001. Honorary degrees from Occidental College, 1986, and Lehman College of the City University of New York, 1994.

WRITINGS:

(Editor) *Anthologie de la litterature africaine d'expression française,* Ghana Institute of Languages, 1966.

Dieu nous l'a donne (four-act play; title means "God Given"; first produced in Martinique, West Indies, at Fort de France, 1973), Oswald, 1972.

Mort d'Oluwemi d'Ajumako (four-act play; title means "Death of a King"; first produced in Haiti at Theatre d'Alliance Française, 1975), Oswald, 1973.

Le Morne de Massabielle, first produced in Puteaux, France, at Theatre des Hauts de Seine, 1974, translation by husband, Richard Philcox, produced in New York, NY, as *The Hills of Massabielle,* 1991.

(Translator into French with Richard Philcox) Eric Williams, *From Columbus to Castro: The History of the Caribbean,* Presence Africaine, 1977.

(Editor) *La Poesie antillaise* (also see below), Nathan (Paris, France), 1977.

(Editor) *Le Roman antillais* (also see below), Nathan, 1977.

La Civilisation du bossale (criticism), Harmattan (Paris, France), 1978.

Le profil d'une oeuvre: Cahier d'un retour au pays natal (criticism), Hatier (Paris, France), 1978.

La Parole des femmes: Essai sur des romancieres des Antilles de langue française (criticism), Harmattan, 1979.

Haiti Cherie (for children), Bayard Presse, 1987.

Pension les Alizes (play), Mercure de France, 1988, translated by Barbara Brewster Lewis and Catherine Temerson as *The Tropical Breeze Hotel,* produced in New York, NY, at Ubu Repertory Theater, 1994.

(Author of text) *Guadeloupe,* photographs by Jean de Boisberranger, Hoa-Qui (Paris, France), 1988.

An tan revolisyon: Elle court, elle court la liberte; piece de theatre, Conseil regional de la Guadeloupe, 1989.

Victor et les barricades (for children), Bayard Presse, 1989.

(Editor and contributor) *Bouquet de voix pour Guy Tirolien,* Editions Jasor, 1990.

Hugo le terrible, Sepia (Saint Maur), 1991.

Cellule familiale et developpement, U.P.L.G., 1992.

(Editor, with others) *L'heritage de Caliban,* Editions Jasor, 1992.

Comedie d'amour (play), first produced in Paris, France, at Theatre Fontaine, 1993, produced in New York, NY, 1993.

(With Madeleine Cottenet-Hage) *Penser la creolite,* Karthala (Paris, France), 1995.

(With Françoise Pfaff) *Entretiens avec Maryse Condé: Suivi d'une bibliographie compete,* translation published as *Conversations with Maryse Condé,* University of Nebraska Press (Lincoln, NE), 1996.

(Editor, with Lise Gauvin, and contributor) *Nouvelles d'Amerique* (short stories), L'Hexagone (Montreal, Quebec, Canada), 1998.

Le Coeur à Rire et à Pleurer (childhood memoir), Robert Laffont, 1999, translation by Richard Philcox published as *Tales from the Heart: True Tales from My Childhood,* Soho Press (New York, NY), 2001.

French Guadeloupe Writer Maryse Condé Reading from Her Work (sound recording), Archive of Hispanic Literature on Tape, Library of Congress (Washington, DC), 1999.

FICTION

Heremakhonon (novel), Union Generale d'Editions, 1976, translation by Richard Philcox, Three Continents Press (Washington, DC), 1982.

Une Saison a Rihata (novel), Robert Laffont (Paris, France), 1981, translation by Richard Philcox published as *A Season in Rihata,* Heinemann (London, England), 1988.

Segou: Les murailles de terre (novel), Robert Laffont, 1984, translation by Barbara Bray published as *Segu,* Viking (New York, NY), 1987.

Segou II: La terre en miettes (novel), Robert Laffont, 1985, translation by Linda Coverdale published as *The Children of Segu,* Viking (New York, NY), 1989.

Pays Mele; suivi de, Nanna-ya (short stories), Hatier, 1985, translation by Nicole Ball published as *Land of Many Colors, and Nanna-ya,* University of Nebraska Press (Lincoln, NE), 1999.

Moi, Tituba, sorciere noire de Salem (novel), Mercure de France (Paris, France), 1986, translation by Richard Philcox published as *I, Tituba, Black Witch of Salem,* University Press of Virginia (Charottesville, VA), 1992.

La Vie scelerate (novel), Seghers (Paris, France), 1987, translation by Victoria Reiter published as *Tree of Life: A Novel of the Caribbean,* Ballantine (New York, NY), 1992.

Traversee de la mangrove (novel), Mercure de France (Paris, France), 1990, translation by Richard Philcox published as *Crossing the Mangrove,* Doubleday (New York, NY), 1995.

Les derniers rois mages (novel), Mercure de France (Paris, France), 1992, translation by Richard Philcox published as *The Last of the African Kings,* University of Nebraska Press (Lincoln, NE), 1997.

La colonie du nouveau monde (novel), Robert Laffont (Paris, France), 1993.

La migration des coeurs (novel), Robert Laffont (Paris, France), 1995, translation by Richard Philcox published as *Windward Heights,* Faber (London, England), 1998, Soho Press (New York, NY), 1999.

Desirada (novel), Robert Laffont (Paris, France), 1997, translated by Richard Philcox, Soho Press (New York, NY), 2000.

Célanire cou-coupé: Roman fantastique, Robert Laffont (Paris, France), 2000, translation by Richard Philcox published as *Who Slashed Celanire's Throat? A Fantastical Tale,* Atria (New York, NY), 2004.

La belle Creole (novel), Mercure de France (Paris, France), 2001.

Histoire de la femme cannibale (novel), Mercure de France (Paris, France), 2003.

Also author of recordings for Record CLEF and Radio France Internationale. Contributor to anthologies, including *Othello: New Essays by Black Writers,* Howard University Press, 1997; *Caribbean Creolization,* University Press of Florida, 1998; and *Winds of Change: The Transforming Voices of Caribbean Women Writers and Scholars,* Peter Lang, 1998. Contributor to journals, including *Presence Africaine* and *Recherche Pedagogique.*

SIDELIGHTS: West Indian author Maryse Condé is a prolific novelist, playwright, and critic whose books explore the clash of cultures and races, particularly in Caribbean settings. In the *New York Times Book Review,* Anderson Tepper declared that Condé "has created an impressive body of work . . . that gives voice to the dispersed and historically silenced peoples of Africa and the Caribbean." Condé's work "deals with characters in domestic situations and employs fictitious narratives as a means of elaborating large-scale activities," asserted *World Literature Today* writers Charlotte and David Bruner. Drawing on her experiences in Paris, West Africa, and her native Guadeloupe, Condé has created several novels that "attempt to make credible on an increasingly larger scale the personal human complexities involved in holy wars, national rivalries, and migrations of peoples," the Bruners stated. A professor of French at Columbia University, Condé writes in French, but many of her novels have been translated into English. According to Erik Burns in the *New York Times Book Review,* she delivers "a vision of the black diaspora that challenges stereotypes by celebrating individual differences."

Condé's first novel, *Heremakhonon,* relates the journey of Veronica, an Antillean student searching for her roots in a newly liberated West African country. During her stay, Veronica becomes involved with both a powerful government official and a young school director opposed to the new regime; "to her dismay," David Bruner summarized, "she is unable to stay out of the political struggle, and yet she is aware that she does not know enough to understand what is happening." The result of Veronica's exploration, which is told with an "insinuating prose [that] has a surreal, airless quality," as Carole Bovoso related in the *Voice Literary Supplement,* is that "there were times I longed to rush in and break the spell, to shout at this black woman and shake her." The critic continued, "But no one can rescue Veronica, least of all herself; Condé conveys the seriousness of her plight by means of a tone of relentless irony and reproach." The Bruners noted, "Justly or not, one gains a comprehension of what a revolution is like, what new African nations are like, yet one is aware that this comprehension is nothing more than a feeling. The wise reader will go home as Veronica does," the critics concluded, "to continue more calmly, to reflect, and to observe."

Condé expands her scope in *Segu,* "a wondrous novel about a period of African history few other writers have addressed," noted *New York Times Book Review* contributor Charles R. Larson. In tracing three generations of a West African family during the early and mid-1800s, "Condé has chosen for her subject . . . [a] chaotic stage, when the animism (which she calls fetishism) native to the region began to yield to Islam," the critic described. "The result is the most significant historical novel about black Africa published in many a year." Beginning with Dousika, a Bambara nobleman caught up in court intrigue, *Segu* trails the exploits of his family, from one son's conversion to Islam to another's enslavement to a third's successful career in commerce, connected with stories of their wives, concubines, and servants. In addition, Condé's "knowledge of African history is prodigious, and she is equally versed in the continent's folklore," remarked Larson. "The unseen world haunts her characters and vibrates with the spirits of the dead."

Some critics, however, faulted the author for an excess of detail in *Segu. Washington Post* contributor Harold Courlander, for example, commented that "the plethora of happenings in the book does not always make for easy reading." The critic explained that "the reader is sometimes uncertain whether history and culture are being used to illuminate the fiction or the novel exists to tell us about the culture and its history." While Howard Kaplan reached a similar assessment, he added in the *Los Angeles Times Book Review* that *Segu* "glitters with nuggets of cultural fascination. . . . For those willing to make their way through this dense saga, genuine rewards will be reaped." The Bruners noted, "With such an overwhelming mass of data and with so extensive a literary objective, the risks of . . . producing a heavy, didactic treatise are, of course, great." They continued, "The main reason that Condé has done neither is, perhaps, because she has written here essentially as she did in her two earlier novels: she has followed the lives of the fictional characters as individuals dominated by interests and concerns which are very personal and often selfish and petty, even when those characters are perceived by other characters as powerful leaders in significant national or religious movements." Because of this, the Bruners concluded, *Segu* is "a truly remarkable book. . . . To know [the subjects of her work] better, as well as to know Maryse Condé even better, would be a good thing."

Subsequent Condé novels have varied in scope and setting from more sweeping historicals such as *Children of Segu* and *The Last of the African Kings,* to character-driven narratives such as *Crossing the Mangrove* and *I, Tituba, Black Witch of Salem.* In the *New York Times Book Review,* Howard Frank Mosher observed that one thread uniting all of Condé's work is the creation of "characters [who] not only survive the worst that life can throw at them but also often prevail, on their own terms, against overwhelming odds." Tituba is one such character. Little is known about the historical Tituba—a black female slave who was accused of witchcraft in Salem, Massachusetts—but Condé weaves a fully fleshed fictitious tale about the remarkable woman and her triumph over a wealth of adversity. Mosher called *I, Tituba, Black Witch of Salem* "an affirmation of a courageous and resourceful woman's capacity for survival."

The vagaries of survival are also at issue in *Crossing the Mangrove.* The fictitious villagers of Riviere au Sel in Guadeloupe gather at the wake of a mysterious visitor who had predicted his own death. The visitor, Francis Sancher, is drawn in detail through their orations and interior thoughts about him. "Together, the villagers and the intruder inhabit a world of unstable facts," declared Lawrence Thornton in the *New York Times Book Review.* "The multiple interpretations offered by the living reveal Riviere au Sel as a protean community, changed and changing still because of one man's brief sojourn there." In *Booklist,* George Needham concluded of *Crossing the Mangrove:* "This atmospheric novel is quite powerful."

In *Windward Heights,* Condé retells the classic *Wuthering Heights* story by Emily Brontë. Set at the beginning of the nineteenth century in Cuba and Guadeloupe, the novel explores the corrosive, obsessive love between dark-skinned Rayze, a foundling, and the mulatto Cathy Gagneur, who shuns Rayze for a lighter-skinned Creole husband. As with the novel upon which it is based, *Windward Heights* plays itself out over a series of generations, as Rayze's fury shapes his children and their choices into adulthood. *Library Journal* correspondent Janet Ingraham Dwyer called *Windward Heights* "a mesmerizing, vivid tale" and "a deft reinterpretation of a classic." Noting that Condé describes "a social and political moment far more complex than Brontë's," a *Publishers Weekly* reviewer commended *Windward Heights* as "a large and beautiful tapestry."

Desirada looks at the problems facing West Indians, but from the perspective of those engaged directly with ideas of European, rather than African, culture. Marie-Noelle, born on Guadeloupe to a fifteen-year-old mother in mysterious circumstances, begins a voyage of self-discovery that takes her first to France and then to the United States. "As she probes the mystery surrounding her birth," wrote *World Literature Today* contributor Mildred Mortimer, "Marie-Noelle embarks upon the healing process that allows her to come to terms with the troubled relationship with her mother and put the pain of rejection behind her." Yet Marie-Noelle is never able to resolve the central question surrounding her birth. Condé explained in a *World Literature Today* interview with Robert R. McCormick, Jr. "Marie-Noelle, who only wants to know the answer to some simple questions—Who is my father? Who am I? What happened?—won't ever find out. Because everyone lies. Not in a conscious and malicious way. Because, ultimately, to tell a story is to embellish it, to fabricate it according to one's tastes and desires, to create fiction." In *Desirada,* concluded a *Publishers Weekly* reviewer,

"Condé once again proves her ability to gracefully capture the voice of the Caribbean diaspora."

Histoire de la femme cannibale, a novel set primarily in post-apartheid South Africa, is, according to Edward Ousselin, writing in *World Literature Today,* "one of Condé's most personal and successful novels." The main character, Roselie Thibaudin, resembles the author is several ways. She is a successful black artist from Guadeloupe who is married to a white man. Although apartheid has officially ended, Roselie continues to feel estranged from her husband's white friends. To make matters even more difficult, many blacks feel her marriage represents a betrayal of her own race. The "cannibal" of the title, Fiela, is alleged to have killed, and partially eaten, her husband. Roselie follows Fiela's trial closely and, in the process, takes a big step toward realizing her own independence. Ousselin wrote that "the author paints a depressing picture of a violence-ridden South African society that has yet to shed most of the social consequences of decades of institutionalized racism."

Tales from the Heart: True Stories from My Childhood is a memoir of the author's childhood in Guadeloupe. Though black themselves, her parents tried to shield their daughter from the popular black culture on the island. Summer vacations were spent in Paris, where Condé was allowed much more freedom to play with friends and explore than she was back home. Having to attend school in Paris as a teenager only made her more curious about her own heritage. In a review for *Booklist,* GraceAnne A. DeCandido noted that "Conde conjures heat, and scent, and the childhood bitterness of loss and desire unfulfilled." The book won the 1999 Prix Yourcenar.

The literary culture of the Caribbean from which Condé writes is rooted both in the oral traditions of the West African *griot* and in the scripted literature of Europe. Critics of *Desirada* and Condé's other works have honored the author's use of French as a medium for relating the West Indian experience. Mortimer, for instance, praised Condé's "remarkable ability to use the French language as a vehicle for communicating Creole orality." "I write for my community (i.e., Guadeloupe) but they don't read," Condé stated in an online interview with Keidra Morris and Sydney Reece for the *Diaspora Web site.* "I write for them, but my largest readership comes from Europe." Condé also "celebrates the extent to which Jean Bernabe, Patrick Chamoiseau, Raphael Confiant, and others have 'allowed all West Indian writers to re-evaluate their relationship to the French language,'" explained *African American Review* contributor Kevin Meehan in a critique of *Conversations with Maryse Condé.* As Mosher concluded, "It is impossible to read her novels and not come away from them with both a sadder and more exhilarating understanding of the human heart, in all its secret intricacies, its contradictions and marvels."

BIOGRAPHICAL AND CRITICAL SOURCES:

BOOKS

Contemporary Literary Criticism, Thomson Gale (Detroit, MI), Volume 52, 1989, pp. 78-85, Volume 92, 1998, pp. 98-135.

PERIODICALS

African American Review, winter, 1996, Cilas Kemedijo, "The Curse of Writing: Genealogical Strata of a Disillusion; Orality, Islam-Writing, and Identities in the State of Becoming in Maryse Condé's *Segou,*" p. 124; spring, 1997, Arlene R. Keizer, review of *Crossing the Mangrove,* p. 175; fall, 2000, Kevin Meehan, review of *Conversations with Maryse Condé,* p. 548.
Booklist, February 15, 1995, George Needham, review of *Crossing the Mangrove,* p. 1057; April 15, 1999, Bonnie Johnston, review of *Land of Many Colors and Nanna-Ya,* p. 1513; August, 1999, Grace Fill, review of *Windward Heights,* p. 2023; September 15, 2001, GraceAnne A. DeCandido, review of *Tales from the Heart: True Stories from My Childhood,* p. 179.
Essence, November, 2000, review of *Desirada,* p. 80.
Library Journal, March 15, 1995, p. 96; June 1, 1999, Vicki J. Cecil, review of *Land of Many Colors and Nanna-Ya,* p. 180; August, 1999, Janet Ingraham Dwyer, review of *Windward Heights,* p. 136.
Los Angeles Times Book Review, March 8, 1987.
New York Times, February 22, 1995, p. C15.
New York Times Book Review, May 31, 1987, Charles R. Lawson, "Converts and Concubines," p. 47; October 25, 1992, Howard Frank Mosher, "Staying Alive," p. 11; July 16, 1995, Lawrence Thornton, "The Healer"; February 8, 1998, Erik Burns, review of *The Last of the African Kings;* September 5, 1999, Anderson Tepper, review of *Windward Heights.*
Publishers Weekly, June 29, 1992, review of *Tree of Life,* p. 50; January 23, 1995, review of *Crossing the Mangrove,* p. 65; July 12, 1999, review of *Windward Heights,* p. 76; October 9, 2000, review of *Desirada,* p. 73.

Research in African Literatures, winter, 1997, Ruth-marie H. Mitsch, "Maryse Condé's Mangroves," p. 54.

Washington Post, March 3, 1987.

World Literature Today, winter, 1982; winter, 1985, pp. 9-13; spring, 1985; summer, 1986; spring, 1987; summer, 1988; autumn, 1993, pp. 695-768; spring, 1998, Mildred Mortimer, review of *Desirada,* p. 437, Charlotte H. Bruner, review of *Pays mele,* p. 438; spring, 1999, Edward Ousselin, review of *Guadeloupe;* summer, 2000, Robert H. McCormick, Jr., "Desirada—A New Conception of Identity," p. 519; winter, 2000, review of *Windward Heights,* p. 222; October-December, 2003, Edward Ousselin, review of *Histoire de la femme cannibale,* p. 82.

ONLINE

Diaspora Web site, http://www.diaspora.sscnet.ucla.edu/ (March 6, 2001), Keidra Morris and Sydney Reece, interview with Condé.

*   *   *

CONNELL, Evan Shelby, Jr.
   See CONNELL, Evan S., Jr.

*   *   *

CONNELL, Evan S., Jr. 1924-
   (Evan Shelby Connell, Jr.)

PERSONAL: Born August 17, 1924, in Kansas City, MO; son of Evan Shelby (a surgeon) and Elton (Williamson) Connell. *Education:* Attended Dartmouth College, 1941-43; University of Kansas, A.B., 1947; graduate study at Stanford University, 1947-48, Columbia University, 1948-49, and San Francisco State College (now University).

ADDRESSES: Home—Fort Marcy 13, 320 Artist Rd., Santa Fe, NM 87501. *Agent*—Don Congdon, 156 5th Ave., Ste. 625, New York, NY 10010-7002.

CAREER: Poet, editor, novelist, and short story writer. *Military service:* U.S. Navy, pilot and flight instructor, 1943-45.

AWARDS, HONORS: Eugene F. Saxton fellow, 1953; Guggenheim fellow, 1963; Rockefeller Foundation grant, 1967; California Literature silver medal, 1974,

for *The Connoisseur;* National Book Critics Circle Award nomination, general nonfiction category, 1984, and *Los Angeles Times* Book Award, 1985, both for *Son of the Morning Star: Custer and the Little Bighorn;* American Academy and Institute of Arts and Letters award, 1987; Lifetime Achievement Award, Lannan Foundation, 2000.

WRITINGS:

FICTION

The Anatomy Lesson, and Other Stories, Viking (New York, NY), 1957.

Mrs. Bridge, Viking (New York, NY), 1959.

The Patriot, Viking (New York, NY), 1960.

At the Crossroads: Stories, Simon & Schuster (New York, NY), 1965.

The Diary of a Rapist, Simon & Schuster (New York, NY), 1966.

Mr. Bridge, Knopf (New York, NY), 1969.

The Connoisseur, Knopf (New York, NY), 1974.

Double Honeymoon, Putnam (New York, NY), 1976.

St. Augustine's Pigeon (short stories), North Point Press (Berkeley, CA), 1980.

The Alchymist's Journal, North Point Press (Berkeley, CA), 1991.

The Collected Stories of Evan S. Connell, Counterpoint (New York, NY), 1995.

Deus Lo Volt! Chronicle of the Crusades, Counterpoint (New York, NY), 2000.

OTHER

(Editor) Jerry Stoll, *I Am a Lover,* Angel Island Publications (Sausalito, CA), 1961.

Notes from a Bottle Found on the Beach at Carmel (epic poem), Viking (New York, NY), 1963.

(Editor) *Woman by Three,* Pacific Coast Publishers (Menlo Park, CA), 1969.

Points for a Compass Rose (epic poem), Knopf (New York, NY), 1973.

A Long Desire (nonfiction), Holt (New York, NY), 1979.

The White Lantern (nonfiction), Holt (New York, NY), 1980.

Son of the Morning Star: Custer and the Little Bighorn (nonfiction), North Point Press (Berkeley, CA), 1984.

Mesa Verde (nonfiction), Whitney Museum (New York, NY), 1992.

The Aztec Treasure House: New and Selected Essays (includes essays from *A Long Desire* and *The White Lantern*), Counterpoint (New York, NY), 2001.
Francisco Goya: A Life Counterpoint (New York, NY), 2004.

Contributor of short stories and reviews to periodicals, including *New York Times, Washington Post, Chicago Sun-Times, New York, San Francisco Chronicle, Carolina Quarterly, Paris Review,* and *Esquire.* Editor of *Contact* (literary magazine), 1959-65.

ADAPTATIONS: The novels *Mrs. Bridge* and *Mr. Bridge* were adapted as the film *Mr. and Mrs. Bridge* by Merchant-Ivory Productions in 1990, starring Paul Newman and Joanne Woodward. *Son of the Morning Star: Custer and the Little Bighorn* was adapted for television by Republic Pictures in 1991.

SIDELIGHTS: The works of Evan S. Connell, Jr., range widely in scope and theme, from domestic dramas of the modern middle class to fictitious historical treatises on the Crusades and alchemy. While his fiction has been widely reviewed, and adapted to film, it was his nonfiction work, *Son of the Morning Star: Custer and the Little Bighorn,* that placed him on the bestseller lists. According to William H. Nolte in the *Dictionary of Literary Biography,* Connell "would probably rank today as the most important American novelist if critical reception were the sole criterion for determining the reputation of a writer." Brooks Landon, in the *Dictionary of Literary Biography Yearbook 1981,* explained that "Connell's works have been successful with critics and have enjoyed respectable sales, but his impressive writing still remains one of America's best-kept literary secrets." A *Publishers Weekly* contributor noted that, while Connell "never developed a clear literary profile," he is nonetheless "a consummate craftsman who has enjoyed some remarkable successes."

The critical acclaim for Connell's work began with his first collection, *The Anatomy Lesson, and Other Stories.* At the time of the book's publication in 1957, Anne Chamberlain of the *New York Herald Tribune* wrote: "With a virtuoso's dexterity [Connell] explores theme and treatment, subject matter and attack, darting from the precious and the esoteric to almost legendary folk tales, laid in his native Midwest and in distant corners of America. This is a many-faceted writer." *New York Times* reviewer Siegfried Mandel called him "a craftsman who can evoke, sustain and dignify the 'small' tragedy that is often hidden from view." And William

Hogan, writing for the *San Francisco Chronicle,* said that the stories in *The Anatomy Lesson* are "well-observed, well-worked slices of life that exhibit craftsmanship, discipline and maturity. Connell is obviously a serious writer of promise and I look forward with great expectations to the publication of his first novel."

That first novel, *Mrs. Bridge,* is probably Connell's best-known work, as well as the one to which his subsequent books are most often compared. In it the author tells the story of India Bridge, an upper-class Midwestern woman, wife of a lawyer, mother of three children, who comes to personify Connell's concept of the idle rich. She is easily confused; she is bored with her leisure-class existence; and she is dominated by materialism and the need to be "socially correct." India Bridge, according to some critics, may be the most fully developed character in any post-World War II American novel. In her *New York Herald Tribune* review, Chamberlain said that Connell had achieved "a triumph of ironic characterization. In his heroine, who appears at first meeting the acme of mediocrity, he manages to create an interesting, a pathetically comic, a tragically lonely figure. . . . It is sad, somewhat terrifying to reflect upon the numberless Mrs. Bridges trotting befuddledly through this urgent age."

In the decade following the publication of *Mrs. Bridge,* Connell published two more novels, *The Patriot* and *The Diary of a Rapist,* one book-length poem, *Notes from a Bottle Found on the Beach at Carmel,* and a collection of short stories, *At the Crossroads: Stories.* Most of these were accepted by reviewers. He then returned to the Bridge family for his fourth novel, *Mr. Bridge,* which tells the Bridges' story from the husband's point of view. A *Playboy* critic called the book "a brilliant dissection of the quintessential small-town WASP—performed under the light of high art, with irony, insight, and a bleak pity." Webster Schott wrote in the *Washington Post Book World:* "Had Sinclair Lewis possessed compassion equal to his anger, discipline to complement his energy, he might have written *Mr. Bridge.* Evan Connell looks at his world straight. No artifice. But with full awareness of the quiet comedy, tenderness and tight-lipped waste. This job need not be done again. *Mr. Bridge* is a tour de force of contemporary American realism, a beautiful work of fiction." Some reviewers felt that the novel fell short of Connell's work in *Mrs. Bridge,* commenting that the characterization is somewhat weaker in the newer book. However, as John Gross of the *New York Review of Books* explained: "If *Mr. Bridge* is a less engaging work than its predecessor, it is chiefly because Walter Bridge himself has little of his wife's pathos. Where she was vulnerable in her innocence, funny and touching in her hapless cultural aspirations, he is rigid, efficient, proud of knowing his own mind. Not an especially likable man; but then Mr. Connell's purpose in writing about him is not to draw up a brief for the defense, but simply to restore a cliché-figure to humanity."

Connell's novel *The Alchymist's Journal* is a demanding work that features the journal entries of seven sixteenth-century men, all of them attempting alchemy: the transformation of basic metals into gold. Only one of the men is named—Paracelsus, who is based on the actual physician who experimented with new methods of treatment in the 1500s. The other men reflect readily identifiable types, such as a skeptic, a revolutionary, and a philosopher. As with many other Connell works, reviewers of this novel expressed admiration for the author's obvious painstaking research, experimental form, and intellectual daring. Bettina L. Knapp, writing in *World Literature Today,* praised the "highly cerebral and wisdom-filled work" as a "tour de force." *Hudson Review* critic William H. Pritchard, while calling the novel "erudite," admitted that "most of the entries were impenetrable to this uninformed sensibility." *New York Times Book Review* correspondent Sven Birkerts likewise commented that Connell "has here dared the unfashionable—a work that concedes nothing to the reader's appetite for dramatic structure or vivid historical tableaux."

In an interview with Melody Sumner for the *San Francisco Review of Books,* Connell brushed aside questions about the inaccessibility of *The Alchymist's Journal.* "I don't write to an audience," he said. "I wanted all seven of the journals to create a unity, but I was trying to avoid repetition. I went over it several times, just to make sure I wasn't using the same words again and again." In this task he succeeded. Birkerts concluded of the novel: "If we are willing to read with sustained attentiveness, facing the otherness and letting the indecipherable elements burn against our demand for clarity, we may at times feel as though we have stepped into a new place. We may get an inkling of what the world felt like some centuries before it assumed its modern contours." Sybil Steinberg, writing in *Publishers Weekly,* likewise felt that the book "commands thoughtful attention, its surface resplendent with forgotten lore of alchemy, science and love."

In 1995, many of Connell's short stories were collected and published as *The Collected Stories of Evan S. Connell.* Many of the collection's fifty-six stories were written in the 1950s and 1960s, while most of the remain-

der were products of the 1990s. All of the stories feature Connell's trademark minimalist prose; many offer wry commentaries on contemporary American life. The character of Koerner, a writer who in some ways resembles Connell, reappears in several of the stories, works that, to quote a *Kirkus Reviews* contributor, "[sparkle] with Connell's learnedness, sharp wit, and spare, concise prose."

If *The Alchymist's Journal* deals with the Middle Ages in an interior and cerebral manner, *Deus Lo Volt! A Chronicle of the Crusades* embraces the panoramic view of the age. A fictitious first-hand account of the European conquest of the Holy Land from 1095 through 1290, the book not only gives a history of the Crusades but also imparts that history from the perspective of a participant—with the enormous differences between the modern and the Medieval mind everywhere incorporated. Calling the novel "a massive, determinedly archaic history of the crusades from the point of view of a French knight," a *Publishers Weekly* reviewer recommended it as "a great feat of historic empathy." In *Booklist,* Michael Spinella observed that Connell "researches with the eye of an expert historical scholar and writes with the hand of an expert novelist."

Aside from his works of fiction, Connell's most notable work is *Son of the Morning Star,* his account of the Battle of the Little Bighorn, where Sioux Indian warriors, led by Sitting Bull, overwhelmed and slaughtered General George Armstrong Custer's band of American troops. A classic story of American history, "Custer's Last Stand" has been the subject of numerous books and articles since the 1880s. But despite the story's familiarity, Connell's account of the battle became a bestseller as well as a critical success. Besides winning a National Book Critics Circle Award nomination and the *Los Angeles Times* Book Award in history, *Son of the Morning Star* sold over 80,000 copies in hardcover, and paperback rights were sold for over $200,000. The book's success did not surprise Connell.

Research and writing for the book took Connell four years and involved reading dozens of books on the battle, the diaries of soldiers who participated in the campaign, and accounts by the Indians themselves. He visited the battle site in Montana on four occasions. The resulting manuscript was difficult to sell. Holt, publisher of some of his earlier fiction, declined *Son of the Morning Star.* They wanted Connell to rewrite the book as a straight biography of Custer or as an overview of the Indian Wars. Connell refused. Eventually North Point Press, a relatively small publisher in California, accepted the book as it was written.

Critical reception to *Son of the Morning Star* was enthusiastic. Ralph E. Sipper of the *Los Angeles Times* called it "a monumental study of the philosophical and cultural differences between red and white men that instigated so much mutual animosity and destruction. . . . In a masterly display of literary structure, Connell has drawn from hundreds of pertinent historical accounts and created the modern equivalent of a biblical work of witness." Writing in the *New York Times Book Review,* Page Stegner stated that "Connell's narrative of the life and times of General Custer becomes a narrative of the conflict between two cultures, and the battle Custer fought at the Little Bighorn [becomes] a metaphor for all the self-righteous hypocrisy that characterizes Indian-white negotiations to this day." Kenneth Turan, in *Time,* concluded that *Son of the Morning Star* is "a new American classic."

Connell became one of several biographers of the Spanish artist Francisco Goya (1746-1828) when he published *Francisco Goya: A Life.* What set his work apart and seemed to puzzle some of his critics was that, as Donna Seaman observed in her *Booklist* review, Connell seems to be "far more attuned to politics, lust, and eccentricity than he is to art." The biography does relate, however, how Goya's controversial paintings eventually led to his exile in France, and a *Kirkus Reviews* contributor described Connell's biography of him as "an idiosyncratic consideration" of "the contradictions and dangers inherent in being a member of the establishment during periods of serial oppression and liberation."

Critics were more enthusiastic in their appreciation of Connell's essay collection *The Aztec Treasure House: New and Selected Essays.* Though most of the essays had been published earlier in *The White Lantern* and *A Long Desire,* this edition represents a wide range of subject matter—science, religion, history, exploration, and astronomy, among other topics—that make it "a book to lay up for gloomy afternoons or rainy evenings," as a reviewer commented in the *Atlantic Monthly.* The collection reflects, as a *Publishers Weekly* contributor noted, the author's propensity for the "unexpected turns of fate and . . . strangely compelling details that historians often miss." From the mysteries of the lost city of Atlantis to the discoveries of the astronomer Galileo, and much more, Connell offers his readers a tantalizing panorama of "the human circus," concluded the *Atlantic Monthly* reviewer. The *Publishers Weekly* critic predicted that *The Aztec Treasure House* "will please any history, science or adventure buff."

BIOGRAPHICAL AND CRITICAL SOURCES:

BOOKS

Contemporary Authors Autobiography Series, Volume 2, Thomson Gale (Detroit, MI), 1985.
Contemporary Literary Criticism, Thomson Gale (Detroit, MI), Volume 4, 1975, Volume 6, 1976, Volume 45, 1987.
Dictionary of Literary Biography, Volume 2: *American Novelists since World War II,* Thomson Gale (Detroit, MI), 1978.
Dictionary of Literary Biography Yearbook: 1981, Thomson Gale (Detroit, MI), 1982.

PERIODICALS

Atlantic Monthly, February, 2002, review of *The Aztec Treasure House: New and Selected Essays,* pp. 102-103.
Booklist, January 1, 2000, Michael Spinella, review of *Deus Lo Volt! Chronicle of the Crusades,* p. 833; February 1, 2004, Donna Seaman, review of *Francisco Goya: A Life,* p. 941.
Hudson Review, autumn, 1991, William H. Pritchard, review of *The Alchymist's Journal,* p. 507.
Kirkus Reviews, August 15, 1995, review of *The Collected Stories of Evan S. Connell,* p. 1126; December 1, 2003, review of *Francisco Goya,* p. 1388.
Library Journal, March 1, 2000, David Keymer, review of *Deus Lo Volt!,* p. 123.
Los Angeles Times, October 3, 1984, Ralph E. Sipper, review of *Son of the Morning Star: Custer and the Little Bighorn,*
New York Herald Tribune Book Review, May 26, 1957, Anne Chamberlain, review of *The Anatomy Lesson and Other Stories;* January 18, 1959, Anne Chamberlain, review of *Mrs. Bridge.*
New York Review of Books, June 23, 1966; May 17, 1973, John Gross, review of *Mr. Bridge.*
New York Times, May 19, 1957, Siegfried Mandel, review of *The Anatomy Lesson and Other Stories.*
New York Times Book Review, January 20, 1985, Page Stegner, review of *Son of the Morning Star;* April 30, 1989; May 12, 1991, Sven Birkerts, "A World Ripe with Magic."
Playboy, June, 1969, review of *Mr. Bridge.*
Publishers Weekly, November 20, 1981, Patricia Holt, interview with Evan S. Connell, p. 12; February 22, 1991, Sybil Steinberg, review of *The Alchymist's Journal,* p. 208; August 21, 1995, review of *The Collected Stories of Evan S. Connell,* p. 47; Febru-

ary 21, 2000, review of *Deus Lo Volt!,* p. 61; October 2, 2000, "Nine Writers Win Lannan Awards," p. 12; July 2, 2001, review of *The Aztec Treasure House,* p. 59.

San Francisco Chronicle, May 28, 1957, William Hogan, review of *The Anatomy Lesson and Other Stories;* January 19, 1959; September 19, 1960.

San Francisco Review of Books, February, 1991, Melody Sumner, interview with Evan S. Connell, p. 26.

Time, November 5, 1984, Kenneth Turan, review of *Son of the Morning Star.*

Times Literary Supplement, July 29, 1983; August 18, 2000, Emily Wilson, review of *Deus lo Volt!,* p. 24.

Washington Post Book World, April 20, 1969, Webster Schott, review of *Mr. Bridge.*

World Literature Today, summer, 1992, Bettina L. Knapp, review of *The Alchymist's Journal,* p. 526.

*   *   *

CONROY, Donald Patrick
See CONROY, Pat

*   *   *

CONROY, Pat 1945-
(Donald Patrick Conroy)

PERSONAL: Born October 26, 1945, in Atlanta, GA; son of Donald (a military officer) and Frances Dorothy (Peek) Conroy; married Barbara Bolling, 1969 (divorced, 1977); married Lenore Gurewitz, March 21, 1981; children: (first marriage) Megan; Jessica, Melissa (stepdaughters); (second marriage) Susannah; Gregory, Emily (stepchildren). *Education:* The Citadel, B.A., 1967. *Politics:* Democrat

ADDRESSES: Office—Old New York Book Shop, 1069 Juniper St. N.E., Atlanta, GA 30309. *Agent*—IGM Literary, 825 Seventh Ave., Eighth Floor, New York, NY 10019.

CAREER: Novelist. Worked as an elementary school-teacher in Daufuskie, SC, 1969, and as a high school teacher in Beaufort, SC, 1967-69.

MEMBER: Authors Guild, Authors League of America, Writers Guild, PEN.

AWARDS, HONORS: Leadership Development grant, Ford Foundation, 1971; Anisfield-Wolf Award, Cleveland Foundation, 1972, for *The Water Is Wide;* National Endowment for the Arts award, 1974, for achievement in education; Georgia Governor's Award for Arts, 1978; Lillian Smith Award for fiction, Southern Regional Council, 1981; Robert Kennedy Book Award nomination, Robert F. Kennedy Memorial, 1981, for *The Lords of Discipline;* inducted into South Carolina Hall of Fame Academy of Authors, 1988; Academy Award nomination for best screenplay (with Becky Johnson), 1987, for *The Prince of Tides;* Thomas Cooper Society Literary Award, University of South Carolina, 1995; South Carolina Governor's Award in the Humanities for Distinguished Achievement, 1996; Georgia Commission on the Holocaust Humanitarian Award, 1996; Lotos Medal of Merit, 1996, for outstanding literary achievement.

WRITINGS:

The Boo, McClure Press (Verona, VA), 1970.
The Water Is Wide, Houghton (Boston, MA), 1972.
The Great Santini, Houghton (Boston, MA), 1976.
The Lords of Discipline, Houghton (Boston, MA), 1980.
The Prince of Tides, Houghton (Boston, MA), 1986.
Beach Music, Nan A. Talese/Doubleday (New York, NY), 1995.
My Losing Season, Nan A. Talese/Doubleday (New York, NY), 2002.
(Adaptor with Becky Johnson) *The Prince of Tides* (screenplay; based on Conroy's novel), Paramount, 1991.

Author of screenplays, including television movie *Invictus,* 1988, and (with Doug Marlett) film *Ex.*

ADAPTATIONS: The film *Conrack,* based on *The Water Is Wide,* was produced by Twentieth Century-Fox, 1974, and was adapted as a musical by Granville Burgess and produced off-off Broadway, 1987; *The Great Santini* was adapted as a film by Warner Brothers, 1979; *The Lords of Discipline* was adapted as a film by Paramount, 1983; Warner Bros. purchased film rights to *My Losing Season.* Several of Conroy's works have been recorded as audiobooks.

SIDELIGHTS: Best-selling novelist Pat Conroy has worked some of his most bitter experiences into stories that present ironic, often jarring, yet humorous views of life and relationships in the contemporary South. Garry Abrams in the *Los Angeles Times* reported that "misfortune has been good to novelist Pat Conroy. It gave him a family of disciplinarians, misfits, eccentrics, liars and loudmouths. It gave him a Southern childhood in which the bizarre competed with the merely strange. It gave him a military school education apparently imported from Sparta by way of Prussia. It gave him a divorce and a breakdown followed by intensive therapy. It gave him everything he needed to write best sellers, make millions and live in Rome." Brigitte Weeks touched on Conroy's appeal in the *Washington Post:* "With his feet set firmly on his native earth, Conroy is, above all, a storyteller. His tales are full of the exaggeration and wild humor of stories told around a camp fire." A critic for *Publishers Weekly* explained that "Conroy is beloved for big, passionate, compulsively readable novels propelled by the emotional jet fuel of an abusive childhood." According to an essayist for *Contemporary Novelists,* "If a reader has experienced a Conroy novel before, he knows the book will be flawed, he knows the book is 500-plus pages, and he knows the characters are, in many ways, the same ones he knew in the last Conroy novel. But in ways, it's like returning to old friends and familiar places, and the lyricism of the prose is more than most readers can resist."

Critics frequently consider Conroy's novels to be autobiographical. Conroy's father was a Marine Corps pilot from Chicago who believed in strong discipline; his mother was an outwardly yielding Southerner who actually ran the household. "When he [Conroy's father] returned home from work my sister would yell, 'Godzilla's home' and the seven children would melt into whatever house we happened to be living in at the time. He was no match for my mother's byzantine and remarkable powers of intrigue. Neither were her children. It took me 30 years to realize that I had grown up in my mother's house and not my father's," Conroy commented in the *Book-of-the-Month Club News.* Still, critics frequently mention the ambivalent father-son relationships that appear in his novels. Gail Godwin in the *New York Times Book Review* described Conroy's work as having "twin obsessions—oppressive fathers or father figures, and the South. Against both they fight furiously for selfhood and independence, yet they never manage to secede from their seductive entrappers. Some fatal combination of nostalgia and loyalty holds them back; they remain ambivalent sons of their families and their region, alternately railing against, then shamelessly romanticizing, the myths and strictures that imprison them."

Conroy's first work to receive national attention was openly autobiographical. After college graduation he taught English in public high schools, but unsatisfied, he looked for a new challenge. When a desired position in the Peace Corps did not surface, he took a job teaching semi-illiterate black children on Daufuskie Island, a small, isolated area off the South Carolina coast. But he was not prepared for his new students. They did not know the name of their country, that they lived on the Atlantic Ocean, or that the world was round. On the other hand, Conroy found that his pupils expected him to know how to set a trap, skin a muskrat, and plant okra. He came to enjoy his unusual class, but eventually his unorthodox teaching methods—such as his unwillingness to allow corporal punishment of his students and disregard for the school's administration—cost him his job. As a way of coping with his fury at the dismissal, Conroy wrote *The Water Is Wide,* an account of his experiences. As he told Ted Mahar for the *Oregonian,* "When you get fired like that, you have to do something. I couldn't get a job with the charges the school board leveled against me." The process of writing did more than cool him down however; he also gained a new perspective on his reasons for choosing Daufuskie—Yamacraw Island in the book—and on his own responses to racism. Anatole Broyard described Conroy in the *New York Times Book Review* as "a former redneck and self-proclaimed racist, [who] brought to Yamacraw the supererogatory fervor of the recently converted." In *The Water Is Wide,* Conroy agreed: "At this time of my life a black man could probably have handed me a bucket of cow p——, commanded me to drink it in order that I might rid my soul of the stench of racism, and I would only have asked for a straw. . . . It dawned on me that I came to Yamacraw for a fallacious reason: I needed to be cleansed, born again, resurrected by good works and suffering, purified of the dark cankers that grew like toadstools in my past."

After the successful publication of *The Water Is Wide,* Conroy began writing full-time. Although his next book, *The Great Santini,* is a novel, many critics interpreted it as representing the author's adolescence. A writer in the *Virginia Quarterly Review* stated that "the dialogue, anecdotes, and family atmosphere are pure Marine and probably autobiographical." Conroy does draw heavily on his family background in his story of tough Marine Bull Meecham, Bull's long-suffering wife Lillian, and his eldest son Ben, who is striving for independence outside his father's control. Robert E. Burkholder wrote in *Critique* that *The Great Santini* "is a curious blend of lurid reality and fantastic comedy. . . . It is primarily a novel of initiation, but central to the concept of Ben's initiation into manhood and to the meaning of the whole novel is the idea that individual myths must be stripped away from Ben and the other major characters before Ben can approach reality with objectivity and maturity."

Part of Ben's growing up involves rejecting the image of his father's infallibility. In one scene, Ben finally beats his father at a game of basketball. As the game ends, he tells him: "Do you know, Dad, that not one of us here has ever beaten you in a single game? Not checkers, not dominoes, not softball, nothing."

According to Robert M. Willingham in the *Dictionary of Literary Biography,* after his defeat, "Bull does not outwardly change. He still blusters, curses, flashes toughness and resoluteness, but his family has become more to him than before. When Colonel Meecham's plane crashes and he is killed, one learns that the crash was unavoidable, but Bull's death was not: 'Am commencing starboard turn to avoid populated area. Will attempt to punch out when wings are level. . . .' The priority was to avoid populated areas, 'where people lived and slept, where families slept. Families like my family, wives like my wife, sons like my sons, daughters like my daughters.' He never punched out."

Bull Meecham is modeled on Conroy's father, Colonel Donald Conroy, who "would make John Wayne look like a pansy," as Conroy told Bill McDonald for the South Carolina *State.* Conroy reported that his father initially disliked *The Great Santini,* telling *Chicago Tribune* contributor Peer Gorner: "Dad could only read the book halfway through before throwing it across the room. Then people started telling him he actually was lovable. Now, he signs Christmas cards *The Great Santini,* and goes around talking about childrearing and how we need to have more discipline in the home—a sort of Nazi Dr. Spock." The movie based on the novel helped to change the colonel's attitude. *The Great Santini* starred Robert Duvall, and the Colonel liked the way "his" character came across. In a *Washington Post* interview, Conroy related an incident of one-upmanship that seems borrowed from the book. "He (the Colonel) came to the opening of 'The Great Santini' movie here in Washington. I introduced the film to the audience, and in the course of my remarks I pointed out why he had chosen the military as a career. It was, of course, something that occurred to him on the day when he discovered that his body temperature and his IQ were the same number. Then, when it was his turn to talk, all he said was, 'I want to say that my body temperature has always been 160 degrees.' People laughed harder. So you see, I still can't beat him."

Another period of Conroy's life appeared in his next book, *The Lords of Discipline.* According to his father's wishes, Conroy attended the Citadel, South Carolina's venerable military academy. "Quirky, eccentric, and un-

forgettable" is how Conroy described the academy in the preface to *The Boo,* his first book, which takes a nostalgic look at the Citadel and its commander of cadets during the 1960s. Willingham described the Citadel in another way: "It is also an anachronism of the 1960s with a general disregard for the existence of the outside world." *The Lords of Discipline* paints an even bleaker picture of the institution through the fictionalized Carolina Military Institute. This school, stated Frank Rose in the *Washington Post Book World,* "combines some of the more quaint and murderous aspects of the Citadel, West Point, and Virginia Military Institute."

The Lords of Discipline concerns Will, the narrator, and his three roommates. Will is a senior cadet assigned to watch over the Institute's first black student. The novel's tension lies in the conflict between group loyalty and personal responsibility. Will eventually discovers the Ten, "a secret mafia whose existence has long been rumored but never proven, a silent and malevolent force dedicated . . . to maintain the purity of the Institute— racial purity included," commented Rose. He continued, "What Conroy has achieved is twofold; his book is at once a suspense-ridden duel between conflicting ideals of manhood and a paean to brother love that ends in betrayal and death. Out of the shards of broken friendship a blunted triumph emerges, and it is here, when the duel is won, that the reader finally comprehends the terrible price that any form of manhood can exact."

According to its author, *The Lords of Discipline* describes the love between men. "I wrote it because I wanted to tell about how little women understand about men," he explained in a *Washington Post* article. "The one cultural fact of life about military schools is that they are men living with men. And they love each other. The love between these men is shown only in obscure ways, which have to be learned by them. The four roommates who go through this book are very different from each other, but they have a powerful code. They have ways to prove their love to each other, and they're part of the rites of passage." And contradicting an old myth, Conroy added, "There is no homosexuality under these conditions. If you smile, they'll kill you. You can imagine what would happen to a homosexual."

While *The Lords of Discipline* portrays deep friendships, it also contains a theme common to many of Conroy's books: the coexistence of love and brutality. "This book . . . makes *The Lord of the Flies* sound like *The Sound of Music,*" wrote Christian Williams in the *Washington Post.* A *Chicago Tribune Book World* reviewer warned, "Conroy's chilling depictions of hazing are for strong stomachs only." And George Cohen in a later Chicago *Tribune Books* article described the novel's pull for readers: "It is our attraction to violence—observed from the safest of places—together with our admiration for the rebel who beats the system, and Conroy's imposing ability as a storyteller that make the novel engrossing."

Conroy's *The Prince of Tides* follows Tom Wingo, an unemployed high school English teacher and football coach, on a journey from coastal South Carolina to New York City to help his twin sister Savannah. Savannah, a well-known poet, is recovering from a nervous breakdown and suicide attempt. In an attempt to help Savannah's psychiatrist understand her patient, Tom relates the Wingo family's bizarre history. Despite the horrors the Wingos have suffered, including several rapes and the death of their brother, a sense of optimism prevails. Judy Bass stated in Chicago's *Tribune Books,* "Conroy has fashioned a brilliant novel that ultimately affirms life, hope and the belief that one's future need not be contaminated by a monstrous past. In addition, Conroy . . . deals with the most prostrating crises in human experience—death of a loved one, parental brutality, injustice, insanity—without lapsing into pedantry or oppressive gloom."

The Prince of Tides attracted critical attention due to its style alone. Some critics felt the novel is overblown: Richard Eder in the *Los Angeles Times Book Review* claimed that "inflation is the order of the day. The characters do too much, feel too much, suffer too much, eat too much, signify too much, and above all, talk too much. And, as with the classical American tomato, quantity is at the expense of quality." Godwin found that while "the ambition, invention and sheer irony in this book are admirable . . . , many readers will be put off by the turgid, high-flown rhetoric that the author must have decided would best match his grandiose designs. And as the bizarre, hyperbolic episodes of Wingo family life mount up, other readers are likely to feel they are being bombarded by whoppers told by an overwrought boy eager to impress or shock." But more critics appreciated what *Detroit News* contributor Ruth Pollack Coughlin called "spectacular, lyrical prose with a bitter sense of humor." The novel is long, admitted Weeks, "monstrously long, yet a pleasure to read, flawed yet stuffed to the endpapers with lyricism, melodrama, anguish and plain old suspense. Given all that, one can brush aside its lapses like troublesome flies."

In his long-awaited *Beach Music,* Conroy continues to mine his personal and family experiences. He weaves into this novel the difficulties of family relationships,

the pain of a mother's death, changing friendships, and the personal impact of global events such as the Holocaust, Vietnam, and present-day terrorism. What Conroy creates is a story of family, betrayal, and place. As Don Paul wrote in the *San Francisco Review of Books,* "In *Beach Music* Pat Conroy takes the theme of betrayal and fashions from it a story rambling and uneven and, like the family it portrays, erratic and flawed and magnificent. South Carolina overflows from his pages, sentimental and unforgiving, soft as sleepy pears and hard as turtle shells."

Beach Music is the story of Jack McCall. After his wife commits suicide, McCall leaves South Carolina and takes his young daughter to Italy to escape his memories and his strained relationships with his own and his wife's family. He returns home when his mother becomes ill with leukemia and finds himself caught up in the lives and intrigues of family and close friends. McCall and his friends are forced by current events to revisit the Vietnam era in their small South Carolina community. Some joined the military, some joined the antiwar movement, and some struggled with both. As Paul explained, "Central to the plot is the betrayal of the anti-war movement by a friend who turns out to be an FBI informer." The effect of this act continue to ripple into the novel's present.

The many characters, events, and themes make, in the opinion of *Detroit Free Press* contributor Barbara Holliday, for a long, convoluted book: "Conroy sets out to do too much and loses his focus in this novel. . . . But despite some fine passages, *Beach Music* finally becomes tiring, and that's too bad for one of the country's finer writers." A reviewer offered a more positive evaluation in *Publishers Weekly:* "Conroy has not lost his touch. His storytelling powers have not failed; neither has his fluid, poetic skill with words, nor his vivid imagination. His long-awaited sixth book sings with the familiar Southern cadences, his prose is sweepingly lyrical." And John Berendt, in a *Vanity Fair* profile of Conroy, called *Beach Music* "a novel rich in haunting imagery and seductive, suspenseful storytelling, a worthy successor to *The Prince of Tides.*" Berendt added, "In *Beach Music* . . . Conroy proves once again that he is the master of place, that he can take possession of any local—Rome, Venice, South Carolina—merely by wrapping his sumptuous prose around it."

Conroy turned to his stint as point guard for the Citadel's basketball team in his memoir *My Losing Season.* The 1966-67 season was a bad one for the team, with an 8-17 record, but Conroy's memory of the time paints it "as an odyssey of hardwood heroics, Olympian forti- tude and larger-than-life adversaries, with the occa- sional temptations of a coed siren," according to Don McLeese in *Book.* Conroy, in fact, argues that losing teaches you more than does winning. "This whole book is a love letter to losing and the lessons it teaches about friendship, courage, honesty and self-appraisal," ex- plained Malcolm Jones in *Newsweek.* A critic for *Kirkus Reviews* admitted that "Conroy can be entertaining and endearingly self-effacing," while Wes Lukowsky in *Booklist* found that "this is a coming-of-age memoir, re- ally, and it is in that context that Conroy's fans will most enjoy it."

Because of the autobiographical nature of Conroy's work, his family often judges his novels more harshly than do reviewers. Although Conroy's mother is the in- spiration for shrimper's wife Lila Wingo in *The Prince of Tides,* she died before he finished the novel and never read it. Conroy's sister, who did see the book, was of- fended. As Conroy told Rick Groen for the Toronto *Globe and Mail,* "Yes, my sister is also a poet in New York who has also had serious breakdowns. We were very close, but she has not spoken to me . . . since the book. I'm saddened, but when you write autobiog- raphy, this is one of the consequences. They're allowed to be mad at you. They have the right." This, however, was not the first time a family member reacted nega- tively to one of Conroy's books. *The Great Santini* in- furiated his Chicago relatives: "My grandmother and grandfather told me they never wanted to see me or my children again," Conroy told Sam Staggs for *Publishers Weekly.* Conroy's Southern relatives have also re- sponded to the sex scenes and "immodest" language in his books. Staggs related, "After *The Lords of Disci- pline* was published, Conroy's Aunt Helen telephoned him and said, 'Pat, I hope someday you'll write a book a Christian can read.' 'How far did you get?' her nephew asked. 'Page four, and I declare, I've never been so embarrassed.'"

Perhaps the most sobering moment for Conroy's auto- biographical impulse was when a tragic event from his writing came true. In early manuscripts of *Beach Music* Conroy included a scene where one of the characters, based on his younger brother Tom, commits suicide. Tom Conroy, a paranoid schizophrenic, did commit sui- cide in August of 1994. Devastated, Conroy removed the scene from *Beach Music.*

Hollywood has given Conroy's novels a warm recep- tion. In addition to the film adaptation of *The Great Santini, The Water Is Wide* was made into *Conrack,*

starring Jon Voight, and later became a musical. *The Lords of Discipline* kept the same title as a film featur- ing David Keith. Conroy himself cowrote the screen- play for *The Prince of Tides,* learning a lesson about Hollywood in the process.

Conroy explained his method of writing to Gorner: "When I'm writing, I have no idea where I'm going. People get married, and I didn't realize they were en- gaged. People die in these novels and I'm surprised. They take on this little subterranean life of their own. They reveal secrets to me even as I'm doing it. Maybe this is a dangerous way to work, but for me it becomes the pleasure of writing. . . . Critics call me a popular novelist, but writing popular novels isn't what urges me on. If I could write like Faulkner or Thomas Wolfe, I surely would. I'd much rather write like them than like me. Each book has been more ambitious. I'm trying to be more courageous."

An essayist for *Contemporary Southern Writers* con- cluded: "Conroy's work is distinguished by its focus on characters coping with and attempting to rise above of- ten bitter conflicts within families and relationships and by his loving recreation of Southern settings and culture. . . . Whether the conflicts are more overt and active, as in *The Great Santini,* or slowly revealed and psychological, as in *The Prince of Tides,* Conroy's work is repeatedly peopled with stern and demanding, some- times abusive father figures and characters attempting to transcend such harshness to establish a more life- embracing identity."

BIOGRAPHICAL AND CRITICAL SOURCES:

BOOKS

Contemporary Novelists, 7th edition, St. James Press (Detroit, MI), 2001.
Contemporary Popular Writers, St. James Press (De- troit, MI), 1997.
Contemporary Southern Writers, St. James Press (De- troit, MI), 1999.
Dictionary of Literary Biography, Volume 6: *American Novelists since World War II, Second Series,* Thom- son Gale (Detroit, MI), 1980.

PERIODICALS

Atlanta Journal-Constitution, March 27, 1988, p. J1.
Book, November-December, 2002, Don McLeese, re- view of *My Losing Season,* p. 82.

Booklist, August, 2002, Wes Lukowsky, review of *My Losing Season,* p. 1882.

Book-of-the-Month Club News, December, 1986.

Chicago Tribune, November 25, 1986.

Chicago Tribune Book World, October 19, 1980.

Cincinnati Enquirer, March 25, 1974.

Critique, Volume 21, number 1, 1979.

Detroit Free Press, July 9, 1995, p. 7G.

Detroit News, October 12, 1986; December 20, 1987.

Globe and Mail (Toronto, Ontario, Canada), February 28, 1987; November 28, 1987.

Kirkus Reviews, August 1, 2002, review of *My Losing Season,* p. 1089.

Library Journal, September 1, 2002, James Thorsen, review of *My Losing Season,* p. 184.

Los Angeles Times, February 19, 1983; October 12, 1986; October 19, 1986; December 12, 1986.

Los Angeles Times Book Review, October 19, 1986, p. 3.

Newsweek, October 14, 2002, Malcolm Jones, "Conroy's Literary Slam-Dunk: A Writer Revisits Life as a Jock, and as a Tortured Son," p. 63.

New York Times, January 10, 1987.

New York Times Book Review, July 13, 1972; September 24, 1972; December 7, 1980; October 12, 1986, p. 14.

Oregonian, April 28, 1974.

People, February 2, 1981, p. 67.

Publishers Weekly, May 15, 1972; September 5, 1986; May 8, 1995, p. 286: July 10, 1995, p. 16, July 31, 1995, p. 17; September 30, 2002, Tracy Cochran, "A Winning Career: Pat Conroy Proves That Writing Well Is the Best Revenge," p. 41, and review of *My Losing Season,* p. 60; October 28, 2002, Daisy Maryles, "Conroy's Winning Book," p. 20.

San Francisco Review of Books, July-August, 1995, p. 24.

State (Columbia, South Carolina), March 31, 1974.

Time, October 13, 1986, p. 97; June 26, 1995, p. 77.

Tribune Books (Chicago, IL), September 14, 1986, p. 23; October 19, 1986, p. 3; January 3, 1988, p. 3.

Vanity Fair, July, 1995, p. 108.

Virginia Quarterly Review, autumn, 1976.

Washington Post, October 23, 1980; March 9, 1992, p. B3.

Washington Post Book World, October 19, 1980; October 12, 1986.

ONLINE

Pat Conroy Web site, http://www.patconroy.com/ (November 6, 2003).

COOK, Roy
See SILVERBERG, Robert

*   *   *

COOPER, J. California
(Joan California Cooper)

PERSONAL: Born in Berkeley, CA; daughter of Joseph C. and Maxine Rosemary Cooper; children: Paris A. Williams. *Ethnicity:* Black *Education:* Attended technical high school and various colleges. *Religion:* Christian. *Hobbies and other interests:* Reading, nature, travel, painting, music, tap dancing.

CAREER: Writer.

AWARDS, HONORS: Black Playwright of the Year, 1978, for *Strangers;* Literary Lion Award and James Baldwin Award, both from the American Library Association, 1988; American Book Award, 1989, for *Homemade Love;* named Woman of the Year by the University of Massachusetts; named Best Female Writer in Texas.

WRITINGS:

NOVELS

Family: A Novel, Doubleday (New York, NY), 1991.

In Search of Satisfaction, Doubleday (New York, NY), 1994.

The Wake of the Wind, Doubleday (New York, NY), 1998.

Some People, Some Other Place, Doubleday (New York, NY), 2004.

SHORT STORY COLLECTIONS

A Piece of Mine (includes "$100 and Nothing!," "Loved to Death," "Sins Leave Scars," "The Free and the Caged," and "Color Me Real"), foreword by Alice Walker, Wild Trees Press (Navarro, CA), 1984.

Homemade Love (includes "The Magic Strength of Need," "Without Love," "Happiness Does Not Come in Colors," "Spooks," "Living," and "The Watcher"), St. Martin's (New York, NY), 1986.

Some Soul to Keep (includes "Sisters of the Rain," "Feeling for Life," "About Love and Money," "The Life You Live (May Not Be Your Own)," and "Red-Winged Blackbirds"), St. Martin's (New York, NY), 1987.

The Matter Is Life, Doubleday (New York, NY), 1991.

Some Love, Some Pain, Sometime, Doubleday (New York, NY), 1995.

The Future has a Past, Doubleday (New York, NY), 2000.

Wild Stars Seeking Midnight Suns: Stories, Doubleday (New York, NY), 2006.

OTHER

Author of seventeen plays, including *Strangers,* first produced in 1978, and *Loners;* also author of short story "Such Good Friends," 1990; contributor to *Center Stage: An Anthology of Twenty-One Contemporary Black-American Plays,* edited by Eileen Joyce Ostrow, University of Illinois Press (Champaign, IL), 1991.

SIDELIGHTS: J. California Cooper writes in a vernacular style that makes extensive use of African-American dialect. Usually set in small rural communities, her works focus on the lives of poor to middle-class black women who are searching for affection and respect from indifferent lovers or husbands. Her protagonists suffer many disappointments but manage to sustain optimism, courage, and a sense of humor as they discover ways to improve their lives, which often include finding a loving man, sometimes after leaving an abusive one. Her stories are generally told by a first-person narrator who is acquainted with the protagonist and relates the story's details in an intimate, almost gossipy style. Rooted in Christian ethics and morality, Cooper's works teach lessons and deliver an undeniable moral message. While some critics have faulted Cooper's subject matter as limited and have argued that her occasional didacticism curtails her writing's dramatic urgency, others have praised her attention to detail and creation of believable and compelling characters. In her foreword to Cooper's *A Piece of Mine,* Alice Walker remarked that "in its strong folk flavor, Cooper's work reminds us of Langston Hughes and Zora Neale Hurston. Like theirs, her style is deceptively simple and direct, and the vale of tears in which some of her characters reside is never so deep that a rich chuckle at a foolish person's foolishness can not be heard."

The twelve stories collected in *A Piece of Mine* deal largely with male-female relationships; in most of them, the women grow in strength and pride, while they gain revenge on men who have mistreated them. In "$100 or Nothing!," a businesswoman, whose husband resents and trivializes her accomplishments, decides to leave him only 100 dollars when she learns she is dying. In "Color Me Real," a mixed-race woman is able to leave behind the prejudices of both blacks and whites after she finds a supportive man who loves her, while the protagonist in "Sins Leave Scars" learns to accept herself despite the abuse she suffered as a girl.

A Piece of Mine earned Cooper critical praise for its relaxed, personal style and exploration of ordinary people's lives. "J. California Cooper possesses the ability to win the reader's trust and establish a rare intimacy as soon as she begins a story," wrote Diana Hinds in *Books and Bookmen.* "She writes often as the best friend, sometimes the sister, of the woman whose story she tells; and we believe her." Jeanette Winterson commented in the *Times Literary Supplement* that "Cooper . . . restores dignity and importance to the everyday." Winterson also praised the fact that "while the characters are all different, the narrative voice running through the book is the same; a continuity that improves each story and gives the whole the depth of the novel." Not all reviewers liked this quality, however; a *Kirkus Reviews* contributor criticized the collection's lack of variety.

Homemade Love, which received an American Book Award, consists of thirteen stories, again focusing on the lives and loves of everyday people. In many of these stories, characters searching for happiness find that what they wanted was within their grasp all along. The protagonist of "The Magic Strength of Need," for instance, becomes a successful entrepreneur, rejects a loving but less-prosperous suitor, but then goes back to him after a disastrous encounter with a wealthy man. "Living" concerns a man who leaves his wife and small-town life for what he thinks will be a more glamorous existence in a large city; he returns after only three days. In "Happiness Does Not Come in Colors," three women put aside their prejudices to find happiness with men they had not taken seriously as potential marriage partners.

As with her previous collection, reviewers of *Homemade Love* lauded Cooper's engaging characters. "The thirteen stories read as if they had been spoken for the benefit of a tape recorder hidden on the front porch of any home in any small Southern town," Michael Schumacher commented in *Writer's Digest.* "These are contemporary folk tales, laced with down-home flavor and Southern dialect." The stories, he continued, "pack a tremendous power that belies the simplicity in which they are told." Others, however, faulted the stories as monotonous and argued that Cooper had a tendency to moralize. Janet Boyarin Blundell, writing in *School Library Journal,* noted that "the stories are saved from preachiness by [Cooper's] wry and somewhat ingenuous tone."

The five stories collected in *Some Soul to Keep* are longer than those from Cooper's previous collections but cover familiar ground. "Sisters of the Rain" tells the tale of a long-suffering, hard-working woman who ends up happier than her wild-living friend. In "The Life You Live (May Not Be Your Own)" two women, kept apart by a lie spread by one's husband, eventually determine the truth and become friends. "Red-Winged Blackbirds" concerns the struggle for survival of a woman who narrowly escapes rape by a white supremacist, witnesses the murder of her parents by a racist mob, and keeps her virginity even while living with women who work as prostitutes.

Terry McMillan, writing in the *New York Times Book Review,* praised the intimacy of Cooper's style, remarking that "the stories enchant you because they are not stories; they are the truth reconstructed." However, McMillan found the stories "somewhat didactic" and noted that "the voice doesn't alter from one story to the next." A critic for *Publishers Weekly* expressed similar reservations: "Ultimately, no matter how admirable and lively these stories are individually, the sameness of their tone and structure . . . defuses the impact of the volume as a whole."

The characters and themes in *Family,* Cooper's first novel, recall those of her shorter fiction. The novel centers on a black family and traces its development over several generations, focusing primarily on slavery and its consequences before, during, and immediately after the Civil War. The narrator, Clora, is driven to suicide by plantation life, but her spirit keeps an eye on her descendants. While it details the tragedy of slavery, the novel is ultimately a tale of triumph over adversity, for it expresses optimism that racial distinctions will become irrelevant and that all people will consider themselves part of the same family. *Tribune Books* reviewer Melissa Walker argued that what "most distinguishes *Family* from . . . other narratives of slavery by black women writers is its persistent affirmation of the power of the human spirit to do battle with evil-and to win, even if only for a while."

Several reviewers praised the originality of the novel's narrative voice, which Sharon Dirlam, writing for the *Los Angeles Times Book Review* described as "both first-person and omniscient." A few, however, thought that Clora occasionally sounded anachronistic or implausibly scholarly. The novel also won compliments for its emotional power and ultimately hopeful outlook. Dirlam called the novel "original, stirring, vividly personal and painfully intense." Walker found *Family* less aesthetically rich than the works of Margaret Walker and Toni Morrison but praised its "compelling voice that speaks of the past in the present with a concern for those human traits that might make possible some kind of future." Roy Hoffman, writing in the *New York Times Book Review,* observed that "the lone woman talking to us . . . is as resilient at the end of her story as she was when it began." Hoffman added, "[But] she draws some homespun, though hard-won, conclusions, seeing us all enmeshed in a net of family ties that grows larger every day."

The Matter Is Life contains a novella, "The Doras," and seven short stories. "The Doras" centers on a woman named Dora and her four daughters, of whom the most unselfish, Splendora, is portrayed as the one most likely to find happiness. The short stories likewise contrast the emptiness of wealth and selfish pleasures with the rewards of a good life. As reviewer Carol Anshaw commented in *Tribune Books,* "If good and wise, [Cooper's characters] triumph in the end. If wicked and vain, they will surely receive their just desserts." *Booklist* contributor Donna Seaman, who, while calling Cooper's tales "moralistic," also termed them "gritty and authentic."

Cooper's second novel, *In Search of Satisfaction,* is a family chronicle of the post-slavery era, covering the 1880s through the first few decades of the twentieth century. Its primary characters are two half-sisters—both daughters of a former slave named Josephus—and the scandal-ridden members of the preeminent white family in their small town. Certain characters are obviously good, others overwhelmingly evil, while a half-black, half-white woman named Yinyang embodies both. These symbolic characters move through an allegorical story designed to transcend its historical period and comment on the desire for happiness common to all people.

Erin J. Aubry, reviewing the novel for the *Los Angeles Times,* called it "a mostly absorbing work, off-putting only when the author's trademark folksiness gets a bit cloying." The book's virtue, Aubry argued, is "Cooper's facile storytelling, as straight-ahead as a freight train but marvelously textured and layered with voices." Moments of whimsy and humor, Aubry said, balance

Cooper's tendency to moralize. Similarly, Carolyn Alessio observed in Chicago *Tribune Books:* "The moral commentary is insistent throughout *In Search of Satisfaction,* but Cooper expertly avoids pure invective by endowing her speakers with quirky voices." Valerie Smith, however, wrote in the *Washington Post Book World* that Cooper's narration often "slips into an uninspired flatness" and that her informal tone sometimes trivializes the tragic events of the book.

Cooper returned to short fiction with *Some Love, Some Pain, Sometime,* a collection of ten stories. As in her previous collections, Cooper's stories focus on black women seeking to improve their lot in life. Again, several critics objected to the stories' monotonous tone, while commending their realistic and down-to-earth manner and vernacular speech. A reviewer for *Publishers Weekly* stated that "Cooper's spirited use of the first person makes every tale [in *Some Love, Some Pain, Sometime*] engaging." The reviewer went on to note, "With thematic concerns tending to take precedence over technique, the author unabashedly indulges our romantic sensibilities."

After the release of *Some Love, Some Pain, Sometime,* Cooper took a three-year break from writing short stories in order to work on her novel, which was published as *The Wake of the Wind.* Afterwards, Cooper returned to her more prolific medium, and the result, *The Future has a Past,* is a collection of stories that was hailed as "deceptively simple" and simultaneously "rich," by *Booklist* critic Vanessa Bush. The stories are predominantly about women and their search for love and they are also about women's relationships with one another as mother, sister, and daughter. Many critics praised the collection and concluded that it had been worth the long wait. Indeed, Alicia Singleton, writing in *Black Issues Book Review,* noted that Cooper "delves into an emotional menagerie of human triumph and suffering." According to Singleton, "Once entangled in Cooper's gilded universe, you'll be able to think of no place else you'd rather be."

Cooper's novel *Some People, Some Other Place* is narrated by the unborn child of the protagonist and recounts the history of five generations of an African-American family. The novel is populated by somewhat allegorical settings, such as Dream Street and a town named Place. The protagonist, Eula Too, is named after her grandmother Eula, the family matriarch. Eula Too is raped, beaten, and left to die when she is on her way to Chicago during the Depression. Afterwards, she is befriended by the madam of a brothel. Although Eula Too

lives with the madam, she does not become a prostitute. While a *Publishers Weekly* contributor stated that the novel "aims to unveil the vastness of human experience," a *Kirkus Reviews* critic called the story "a very odd family saga." The *Publishers Weekly* contributor noted this 'oddness' by observing that the book is "a novel scattered in narrative." The contributor went on to note, however, that it is nonetheless "united in its humanity."

In *Wild Stars Seeking Midnight Suns: Stories,* Cooper focuses on love, success, and failure in nine stories about black women. One story is about Lily Bea, an unattractive woman who is married to a much older, and disagreeable, man. Lily escapes from her life by reading. Another story is about Willa Ways, who earns a Ph.D and finds success although she does not find satisfaction. Many of the stories feature dissatisfied characters who, ultimately, are the cause of their own unhappiness. Calling the book "warm-hearted, earthy and sly," a *Kirkus Reviews* contributor also noted: "What unifies and deepens these stories is the impish, ever-forgiving but gently judgmental narrator." A contributor to *TheBlackLibrary.com* Web site concluded that the collection is "a marvelous and satisfying suite of stories."

BIOGRAPHICAL AND CRITICAL SOURCES:

BOOKS

Cooper, J. California, *A Piece of Mine,* foreword by Alice Walker, Wild Trees Press (Navarro, CA), 1984.

PERIODICALS

Black Issues Book Review, January, 2001, Alicia Singleton, review of *The Future has a Past,* p. 17.
Books and Bookmen, February, 1986, Diana Hinds, review of *A Piece of Mine,* p. 18.
Booklist, October 15, 1998, Lillian Lewis, review of *The Wake of the Wind,* p. 399; October 15, 2000, Vanessa Bush, review of *The Future has a Past,* p. 417.
Kirkus Reviews, November 15, 1984, review of *A Piece of Mine,* p. 1056; January 1, 2006, review of *Wild Stars Seeking Midnight Suns: Stories,* p. 5; September 1, 2004, review of *Some People, Some Other Place,* p. 822.
Library Journal, October 15, 1998, Janis Williams, review of *The Wake of the Wind,* p. 96.

Los Angeles Times, August 5, 1991, Sharon Dirlam, review of *Family,* p. E2; October 14, 1994, Erin J. Aubry, review of *In Search of Satisfaction,* p. E5.

New York Times Book Review, November 8, 1987, Terry McMillan, review of *Some Soul to Keep,* p. 23; December 30, 1990, Roy Hoffman, review of *Familiy,* p. 12; January 26, 1992, p. 24.

Publishers Weekly, September 11, 1987, Sybil Steinberg, review of *Some Soul to Keep,* p. 79; July 31, 1995, review of *Some Love, Some Pain, Sometime,* pp. 66-7; September 2, 1996, review of *Some Love, Some Pain, Sometime,* p. 122; September 13, 2004, review of *Some People, Some Other Place,* p. 57.

School Library Journal, August, 1986, Janet Boyarin Blundell, review of *Homemade Love,* p. 168.

Times Literary Supplement, August 22, 1986, Jeanette Winterson, review of *A Piece of Mine,* p. 921.

Tribune Books (Chicago), February 24, 1991, Melissa Walker, review of *Family,* pp. 6-7; July 28, 1991, Carol Anshaw, review of *The Matter Is Life,* pp. 6-7; January 26, 1992, p. 8; November 6, 1994, Carolyn Alessio, review of *In Search of Satisfaction,* p. 5.

Washington Post Book World, October 11, 1994, Valerie Smith, review of *In Search of Satisfaction,* p. E3.

Writer's Digest, February, 1987, Michael Schumacher, review of *Homemade Love,* p. 21.

ONLINE

TheBlackLibrary.com, http://www.theblacklibrary.com/ (March 2, 2006), review of *Wild Stars Seeking Midnight Suns.*

*   *   *

COOPER, Joan California
See COOPER, J. California

*   *   *

COOPER, Susan 1935-
(Susan Mary Cooper)

PERSONAL: Born May 23, 1935, in Burnham, Buckinghamshire, England; immigrated to the United States, 1963; daughter of John Richard (an employee of the Great Western Railway) and Ethel May (a teacher; maiden name, Field) Cooper; married Nicholas J. Grant (a scientist and college professor), August 3, 1963 (divorced, 1983); married Hume Cronyn (an actor and playwright), 1996; children: (first marriage) Jonathan, Katharine; Anne, Bill, Peter (stepchildren); (second marriage) Tandy (stepchild). *Education:* Somerville College, Oxford, M.A., 1956. *Hobbies and other interests:* Music, islands.

ADDRESSES: Home—CT and New York, NY. *Agent*—c/o Author Mail, Margaret K. McElderry, Simon & Schuster, 1230 Ave. of the Americas, New York, NY 10020.

CAREER: Author, playwright, screenwriter, and journalist. *Sunday Times,* London, England, reporter and feature writer, 1956-63. Narrator, with others, of *George Balanchine's Nutcracker,* Warner Bros., 1993.

MEMBER: Society of Authors (United Kingdom), Authors League of America, Authors Guild, Writers Guild of America.

AWARDS, HONORS: Horn Book Honor List citation for *Over Sea, under Stone; Horn Book* Honor List and American Library Association (ALA) Notable Book citations, both 1970, both for *Dawn of Fear; Boston Globe-Horn Book* Award, Carnegie Medal runner-up, and ALA Notable Book citation, all 1973, and Newbery Award Honor Book, 1974, all for *The Dark Is Rising;* ALA Notable Book citation, for *Greenwitch;* Newbery Medal, Tir na N'og Award (Wales), Carnegie Medal commendation, *Horn Book* Honor List, and ALA Notable Book citation, all 1976, all for *The Grey King;* Tir na N'og Award, 1978, for *Silver on the Tree;* Parents' Choice Award, 1983, for *The Silver Cow;* Janusz Korczak Award, B'nai B'rith, and Universe Award runner-up, both 1984, both for *Seaward;* (with Hume Cronyn) Christopher Award, Humanitas Prize, Writers Guild of America Award, and Emmy Award nomination from Academy of Television Arts and Sciences, all 1984, all for *The Dollmaker;* Emmy Award nomination, 1987, and Writers Guild of America Award, 1988, for teleplay *Foxfire; Horn Book* Honor List citation, 1987, for *The Selkie Girl.*

WRITINGS:

FOR CHILDREN; FICTION

Dawn of Fear (historical fiction), illustrated by Margery Gill, Harcourt (New York, NY), 1970.

Jethro and the Jumbie (fantasy), illustrated by Ashley Bryan, Atheneum (New York, NY), 1979.

Seaward (fantasy), Atheneum (New York, NY), 1983.

(Reteller) *The Silver Cow: A Welsh Tale,* illustrated by Warwick Hutton, Atheneum (New York, NY), 1983.

(Reteller) *The Selkie Girl,* illustrated by Warwick Hutton, Margaret K. McElderry (New York, NY), 1986.

(Reteller) *Tam Lin,* illustrated by Warwick Hutton, Margaret K. McElderry (New York, NY), 1991.

Matthew's Dragon, illustrated by Joseph A. Smith, Margaret K. McElderry (New York, NY), 1991.

The Boggart (fantasy), Margaret K. McElderry (New York, NY), 1992.

Danny and the Kings, illustrated by Joseph A. Smith, Margaret K. McElderry (New York, NY), 1993.

The Boggart and the Monster (fantasy), Margaret K. McElderry (New York, NY), 1997.

(With Margaret Mahy, Uri Orlev, and Tjomg Khing) *Don't Read This! and Other Tales of the Unnatural* (short stories), Front Street, 1998.

King of Shadows (historical fiction), Margaret K. McElderry (New York, NY), 1999.

Frog, illustrated by Jane Browne, Margaret K. McElderry (New York, NY), 2002.

Green Boy, Margaret K. McElderry (New York, NY), 2002.

The Magician's Boy, Margaret K. McElderry Books (New York, NY), 2005.

Contributor to books, including *When I Was Your Age,* edited by Amy Ehrlich, Candlewick Press (New York, NY), 1996.

"DARK IS RISING" SERIES; FANTASY

Over Sea, under Stone, illustrated by Margery Gill, J. Cape (London, England), 1965, Harcourt (New York, NY), 1966.

The Dark Is Rising, illustrated by Alan E. Cober, Atheneum (New York, NY), 1973, illustrated by Lianne Payne, Puffin (London, England), 1994.

Greenwitch, Atheneum (New York, NY), 1974.

The Grey King, illustrated by Michael Heslop, Atheneum (New York, NY), 1975.

Silver on the Tree, Atheneum (New York, NY), 1977.

FOR ADULTS; NONFICTION, EXCEPT AS NOTED

Mandrake (science fiction), J. Cape (London, England), 1964.

Behind the Golden Curtain: A View of the U.S.A., Hodder & Stoughton (London, England), 1965, Scribner (New York, NY), 1966.

(Editor and author of preface) J.B. Priestley, *Essays of Five Decades,* Little, Brown (Boston, MA), 1968.

J.B. Priestley: Portrait of an Author, Heinemann (London, England), 1970, Harper (New York, NY), 1971.

Dreams and Wishes: Essays on Writing for Children, Margaret K. McElderry (New York, NY), 1996.

Contributor to books, including Michael Sissons and Philip French, editors, *The Age of Austerity: 1945-51,* Hodder & Stoughton (London, England), 1963, Scribner (New York, NY), 1966. Author of introductions to *The Christmas Revels Songbook: In Celebration of the Winter Solstice,* edited by John and Nancy Langstaff, David R. Godine, 1985, published as *The Christmas Revels Songbook: Carols, Processions, Rounds, Ritual, and Children's Songs in Celebration of the Winter Solstice,* 1995, and *A Revels Garland of Song: In Celebration of Spring, Summer, and Autumn,* edited by John Langstaff, Revels, Inc., 1996. Contributor of essays to *The Phoenix and the Carpet* by E. Nesbit, Dell, 1987, and to anthologies of children's literature criticism. Contributor to periodicals, including *Horn Book, New York Times Book Review, Magpies,* and *Welsh Review.*

PLAYS

(With Hume Cronyn) *Foxfire* (first produced in Stratford, Ontario, 1980; produced on Broadway at Ethel Barrymore Theatre, 1982; teleplay adaptation produced by Columbia Broadcasting System, Inc. [CBS], 1987), S. French (New York, NY), 1983.

(With Hume Cronyn) *The Dollmaker* (teleplay; adapted from the novel by Harriette Arnow), American Broadcasting Companies, Inc. (ABC), 1984.

To Dance with the White Dog (teleplay), CBS, 1993.

Also author of the teleplay *Dark Encounter,* 1976.

Cooper's papers are housed in the Lillian H. Smith collection, Toronto Public Library, Toronto, Ontario, Canada.

ADAPTATIONS: Cooper's Newbery Medal acceptance speech for *The Grey King* was released as a sound recording, Weston Woods, 1976; *The Dark Is Rising* was released on audio cassette, Miller-Brody, 1979; *The Silver Cow* was released as a filmstrip in 1985 and as a sound recording in 1986, both Weston Woods; *The Selkie Girl* was released as a filmstrip and on audio cassette, Weston Woods, 1988; *The Boggart* was released on audio cassette, Listening Library, 1994; *The Boggart and the Monster* was released on audio cassette, Listening Library, 1997.

SIDELIGHTS: Called "one of the most versatile, popular, and critically acclaimed children's writers of the twentieth century" by Joel D. Chaston in the *Dictionary of Literary Biography,* Susan Cooper is considered an exceptional author for the young whose works—fantasy novels and realistic fiction for young adults and stories and picture books for children—reflect her keen insight into human nature, her knowledge of folklore, history, and archaeology, and her ability to evoke place with authenticity. Credited with a rich, poetic literary style, Cooper is also well regarded as a writer of fiction, nonfiction, and plays for adult readers.

Characteristically, Cooper draws on the myths and legends of the British Isles as the basis for her works, and she is often praised for her ability to mesh the real and the fantastic, the ancient and the contemporary. She is best known as the creator of "The Dark Is Rising" series, a quintet of epic fantasies for young adults that depicts how a group of modern-day English children become involved in a cosmic battle between good and evil, which Cooper calls the Light and the Dark. As in several of her other books, volumes in the series feature magical experiences designed to prepare Cooper's young protagonists for conflicts which will occur throughout their lives. Favorably compared to the fantasies of J.R.R. Tolkien, C.S. Lewis, Ursula K. Le Guin, and Alan Garner, these works are rooted in the mythology of Britain and feature characters from and inspired by Arthurian legend, such as Merlin the great magician and Bran, the son of King Arthur and Guinevere. Cooper is often acknowledged for weaving social concerns within the supernatural events she depicts. In addition to her pervasive theme of the struggle between good and evil—a theme the author uses to explore the human potential for both qualities—Cooper addresses such issues as displacement, responsibility and choice, self-awareness, and the coexistence of magic and technology. Although her books include danger, violence, death, and a variety of manifestations of evil, Cooper is credited with presenting her readers with a positive view of human nature as well as with conclusions that demonstrate the ultimate triumph of good.

Critics have lauded Cooper as a gifted storyteller and superior craftsman whose works succeed in bringing together the ordinary and the extraordinary while capturing the thoughts and emotions of the young. Writing in *Children's Books and Their Creators,* Anne E. Deifendeifer noted that the "power of her fantasy for children places Cooper firmly among the best of children's authors. . . . The tremendous scope and intensity of Cooper's work marks her as a modern master of the high-fantasy genre." Commenting on what she called Cooper's "extraordinary prowess as an author of fantasy," *Twentieth Century Young-Adult Writers* contributor Karen Patricia Smith claimed that throughout her books "major themes resurface, allowing the reader to experience and internalize the depth of her commitment to her social ideals as well as to her art."

While often praised, Cooper has also been criticized by some reviewers for predictability and use of cliché in some of her books and for unevenness in "The Dark Is Rising" series; writing in *School Librarian,* David Rees claimed: "The whole quintet is shallow, relying on a box of magic tricks to disguise the poverty of the author's thinking and imagination." However, most observers view Cooper as the creator of rewarding, fascinating works with great relevance to their audience. Margaret K. McElderry wrote in *Horn Book* that Cooper is "one of the small and very select company of writers who—somehow, somewhere—have been touched by magic; the gift of creation is theirs, the power to bring to life, for ordinary mortals, 'the very best of symbolic high fantasy.' . . . Music and song, old tales and legends, prose and poetry, theater and reality, imagination and intellect, power and control, a strong sense of place and people both past and present— all are part of the magic that has touched Susan Cooper. . . . Her journeys add great luster to the world of literature."

When Cooper was four years old, World War II broke out in Great Britain, and would last until she was ten. By the time she was ten, Cooper had written original plays for a friend's puppet theater, a small illustrated book, and a weekly newspaper. She enjoyed reading, especially the books of Edith Nesbit, Arthur Ransome, Rudyard Kipling, John Masefield, and Jack London, and was entranced by poetry and by the rich tradition of mythology of Great Britain. In addition, she listened faithfully to the British Broadcasting Corporation (BBC) radio program *The Children's Hour,* which dramatized some of her favorite stories. Like her grandfather, Cooper was also enthralled by the theater, recalling, for example, the awe she felt when she saw her first pantomime at the age of three. At Slough High School, a school for girls, she was encouraged to develop her writing talent.

When she graduated, Cooper won a scholarship to Oxford, where she studied English literature and enjoyed what she later described as "a calm stretch of such good fortune that I can hardly describe it." While at Oxford, Cooper discovered and devoured the works of Shakespeare, Milton, and the English Metaphysical poets, heard lectures by J.R.R. Tolkien and C.S. Lewis, and worked for the university newspaper, becoming its first female editor. She also published her first short story and, on her last day at Oxford, submitted a long essay describing her feelings about the end of university life to the editors of the London *Times,* who published it in its entirety.

After her graduation, Cooper worked as a temporary reporter at the London *Sunday Express* before being hired by the *Sunday Times,* where she worked as a news reporter and feature writer for seven years, one of which she spent working for Ian Fleming, the author of the "James Bond" novels. Cooper wrote articles for the *Sunday Times* column "Mainly for Children"; later, she would use some of her subjects—King Arthur, medieval castles, Roman Britain, and brass rubbings—in her books for young people. While at the *Sunday Times,* Cooper began writing novels for adults. Her second attempt, the science-fiction novel *Mandrake,* was published in 1964. A dystopian novel in the manner of *Brave New World* and *1984,* the book addresses the concept of evil residing in ordinary people, a theme the author would later explore in her books for the young.

After completing *Mandrake,* Cooper began writing a children's story for a contest offered by publisher, Ernest Benn. The contest offered a prize in Victorian children's author Edith Nesbit's name for a family adventure story in the tradition of Nesbit's works. This project, Cooper once wrote, "offered the irresistible combination of a challenge, a deadline, and money, and I dived at it in delight." Cooper's story began, she noted, with the invention of "three rather Nesbitish children named Simon, Jane, and Barney Drew, and I sent them on a train journey from London to Cornwall." However, with the introduction of the children's great-uncle Merriman Lyon—actually Merlin the magician—the book transformed into something quite different than its author originally intended. "Merry took over," Cooper once wrote. "He led the book out of realism, to myth-haunted layers of story that took me way past a 'family adventure' and way past my deadline. Now I was no longer writing for a deadline or for money. I was writing for me, or perhaps for the child I once was and in part still am." When the book was finished, Cooper cut the first chapter about the railway journey; the result was *Over Sea, under Stone,* the first volume of "The Dark Is Rising."

Rejected by more than twenty publishers before its acceptance by Jonathan Cape, *Over Sea, under Stone* describes how the Drew children, who have traveled to Trewissick, Cornwall, for a holiday with their scholarly, white-haired great-uncle, use an ancient map they find in an attic to recover the Holy Grail. Plunged into the battle between good and evil, the children become misled by members of the Dark posing as the local vicar and a pair of tourists and encounter dangerous situations such as the kidnapping of Barney Drew. However, the powers of Great-Uncle Merry and the initiative of the children win a victory for the Light. At the end of the story, the Grail is placed in the British Museum and an ancient magical manuscript—which interprets the writing on the Grail, gives the outcome of the battle between the Light and the Dark, and promises that King Arthur will come again—is sent to the bottom of the sea. Writing in *Growing Point,* Margery Fisher commented that "perhaps this is a book with a theme too big for itself, but it is a fascinating book to read and it has considerable literary quality." *School Librarian* contributor C.E.J. Smith added: "The children are credible and their adventures shift so cunningly from the plausible to the legendary as to be totally absorbing. . . . The final scene on the jagged rocks amid an incoming tide is a feast for any imaginative twelve-or thirteen-year-old."

The London *Sunday Times* hired Cooper to cover U.S.-based stories, including the trial of Jack Ruby in Dallas. She also began to contribute a weekly column to the *Western Mail,* the national morning newspaper of Wales. Her column led to a nonfiction book for adults, *Behind the Golden Curtain: A View of the U.S.A.,* in which she explains the differences between the cultures of the United States and England. She also edited a collection of essays by friend J.B. Priestley, a notable English novelist, dramatist, and essayist, and later published a biography of Priestley. She also penned an autobiographical novel for adults about her childhood that was published in 1970 as *Dawn of Fear.*

Describing how a young boy is made aware of the horrors of World War II, *Dawn of Fear* outlines how Derek Brand—a middle grader who lives in a housing estate in the Thames Valley—learns the meaning of sadness, suffering, and fear when his best friend Peter and his family are killed by German bombs. Drawing parallels between Derek's private war—a rivalry between two gangs of local boys—and the larger one, Cooper is credited with evoking the pain of war while movingly describing the death of a child. A reviewer in *Publishers Weekly* commented that Cooper "has brought her insight and writing skills to creating another remarkable story." The critic concluded by calling *Dawn of Fear* a "moving chronicle of despair and of courage." Ethel L.

Heins in *Horn Book* praised *Dawn of Fear* as "an uncommon kind of war story," and a reviewer in *Junior Bookshelf* claimed, "To date I have not come across a book which makes anything like the same impression."

In *The Dark Is Rising* Cooper continues the story she began in *Over Sea, under Stone*. In this work, Will Stanton, the seventh son of a seventh son, learns on his eleventh birthday that he is the last of the Old Ones, immortal beings who serve the Light and who are committed to keeping the world safe from the Dark. Will undertakes a journey to find and join together the Six Signs of the Light—wood, bronze, iron, fire, water, and stone—to be used in a final battle against the Dark. In his quest, in which he is guided by the first of the Old Ones, Merriman Lyon, Will encounters evil forces who appear in different forms as he moves back and forth in time. Finally, the Dark rises during a winter filled with violent blizzards and floods, but Will, using both his intuition and the knowledge given him by Merry, successfully joins the Signs of the Light. A reviewer in the *Times Literary Supplement* noted, "With a cosmic struggle between good and evil as her subject, Susan Cooper invites comparison with Tolkien, and survives the comparison remarkably well." Writing in the *Washington Post Book World*, Virginia Haviland noted that the book "is exceptional by any standard," while S. William Alderson of the *Children's Book Review* commented that *The Dark Is Rising* "captures and holds one's imagination, almost as if the magic forces within the story were themselves reaching out to spellbind the reader." Ethel L. Heins in *Horn Book* noted the strength of Cooper's writing, which she described as "as rich and as eloquent as a Beethoven symphony," while Sally Emerson of *Books and Bookmen* concluded that anyone "who fears that they or their children are becoming rigidly sensible should buy this book to enrich imagination and recover wonderment."

The sequel to *The Dark Is Rising, Greenwitch,* again features the three Drew children, the protagonists of *Over Sea, under Stone*. The siblings work with their great-uncle Merry and Will Stanton, the main character from *The Dark Is Rising,* to recover the Holy Grail—which has been stolen from the British Museum by a painter who is an emissary of the Dark—as well as the ancient manuscript that accompanies it. As the children engage in their pursuit, the forces of Wild Magic embodied by the Greenwitch, a tree woman woven by Cornish villagers that is given life by an ocean goddess, come to their defense through the sympathies of middle child Jane Drew. Through her compassion, Jane obtains the manuscript from the Greenwitch, thus allowing the Old Ones to learn about the next part of their quest.

Writing in *Growing Point,* Margery Fisher claimed, "Fantasies like this depend most of all on the sheer power of the writing, on the literary synthesis between the sunlit world of here and now and the dark, misty otherwhere from which evil comes. The synthesis is less strong in this new book and the effect less consistent than in the other two books. . . . Nonetheless, it is a compelling story." A reviewer in the *Times Literary Supplement* predicted, "When Miss Cooper manages to knit her material into a single organic whole her achievement will be great."

The Grey King is often considered the most successful of the "Dark Is Rising" novels. In this book, Will Stanton has become ill with hepatitis and is sent to the seaside town of Tywyn, Wales, to recuperate. While in Wales, Will learns that he must undertake two quests: the recovery of a golden harp hidden in the nearby hills and the awakening of six ancient sleepers who are to be roused by the sound of the harp for the final battle between the Light and the Dark. Will is joined by Bran Davies, an albino boy who is revealed as the son of King Arthur, and Bran's white sheepdog Cafall. Bound by a preordained fate, the three retrieve the harp, but Will is thrust into a confrontation with the Grey King, an evil Lord of the High Magic who uses ghostly gray foxes and a crazed Welshman named Caradog Pritchard to carry out his wishes, which include the killing of Cafall. At the conclusion of the novel, the sleepers are raised and preparations begin for the final showdown between the opposing forces. Writing in *Horn Book,* Mary M. Burns called *The Grey King* a "spellbinding tour de force," while Zena Sutherland described it in her *Bulletin of the Center for Children's Books* review as a "compelling fantasy that is traditional in theme and components yet original in conception."

Two major fantasists, Natalie Babbitt and Jill Paton Walsh, also commented on *The Grey King*. Writing in the *New York Times Book Review,* Babbitt noted, "It is useless to try to recreate the subtleties of Susan Cooper's plotting and language. Enough to say that this volume, like those preceding it, is brimful of mythic elements and is beautifully told." Paton Walsh, reviewing *The Grey King* in the *Times Literary Supplement,* noted the book's "authentic evocative power" and the fact that Cooper "commands, to a rare degree, the power to thrill the reader, to produce a particular tremor of excitement and fear, in response not only to Arthurian magic . . . but rather to haunted places, to landscape deeply embedded in ancient fable, to a sense of secret forces breaking through." In 1976 *The Grey King* was awarded the Newbery Medal and the Tir na N'og Award; it also received a commendation for the Carnegie Medal.

The final volume of the "Dark Is Rising" sequence, *Silver on the Tree,* brings together the protagonists from the preceding books. In this story, which is again set in Wales, Will Stanton summons the Old Ones for a final battle with the forces of the Dark. Will, Bran, Merriman, and the Drew children travel through time to acquire the weapons needed for combat. At the end of their adventures, which range from incredibly dangerous to extremely beautiful, the children and the Old Ones find the legendary Midsummer Tree, the silver fruit of which determines the victor of the battle. At the end of the novel, the Six Sleepers finally defeat the Lords of the Dark, Will completes his tasks as the last of the Old Ones, and Bran, who is offered immortality, bids a final farewell to his father King Arthur by choosing to remain human. Writing in *Horn Book,* Ann A. Flowers called *Silver on the Tree* a "triumphant conclusion," while a reviewer for *Junior Bookshelf* commented that here, "crafted by the hand of a master, is a story of the ageless battle of good and evil, a book in one of the great traditions of children's literature and destined, perhaps, to become one of the high peaks of that tradition." Writing in *Growing Point,* Margery Fisher commented that the series "has given readers many moments of startled awareness and now that it is complete it deserves more deliberate consideration as a whole." Shirley Wilton of *School Library Journal* noted that Cooper "maintains a masterly control over the complex strands of her story sweeping readers along on a fantastic journey. It is an experience not to be missed and, for Cooper fans, a fitting wrap-up to the unfolding saga."

Following the completion of her fantasy quintet, Cooper began writing stories and picture books for younger children, an audience to whom most of her subsequent books have been directed. She returned to the genre of young-adult fantasy with her novel *Seaward.* Written during a particularly difficult period in her life—the author was dealing with a divorce from Nicholas Grant and the death of both her parents—*Seaward* describes how two teenagers, the girl Cally and the boy West, cross the borders of time as they try to reach the sea. Each involved with personal quests prompted by the deaths of their respective parents, Cally and West enter the world of Lady Taramis, who is actually Death, and her twin brother Lugan—Life—and encounter many dangers before they reach their destination. At the sea, the teens, who have fallen in love, learn the identity of Taramis and Lugan as well as the fact that Cally is the descendant of a selkie, a seal who can turn into a human. At the end of the novel Cally decides not to become a selkie and West decides to return to his own world; as a result, the friends are promised that, although they live in different countries, they will meet again and will spend their lives together. Writing in *Horn Book,* Paul Heins called *Seaward* an "uncanny, unconventional fantasy" and concluded that, like Scottish novelist and poet George MacDonald, Cooper "has endowed the concept of human responsibility—of human choice—with the face of fantasy." M. Hobbs noted in *Junior Bookshelf* that it "is a rare treat to have another novel from Susan Cooper" and concluded that *Seaward* is a "deeply moving, splendid novel, of unearthly beauty, and worthy of its predecessors."

The myths and legends of the British Isles have always been an important part of Cooper's novels. In 1983 she published *The Silver Cow: A Welsh Tale,* the first of several volumes of retellings illustrated by English artist Warwick Hutton. Another of Cooper's retellings, *The Selkie Girl,* is a story taken from the folk tales of Ireland and the Scottish Isles that, like *Seaward,* draws on the legends of seal maidens. The tale outlines how the lonely fisherman Donallan catches a beautiful selkie with whom he has fallen in love by stealing her seal skin so that she cannot go back to the sea. The couple has five children; when the youngest child finds the seal skin and tells his mother where it is hidden, she returns to her home in the water, where she also has five seal children. Before she goes, the selkie promises to meet with her land family once a year and blesses them with fine catches from their fishing. Writing in the *Junior Bookshelf,* Marcus Crouch noted that "Here, even in this small exercise, a master story-teller is at work, covering the bare bones of the story with living flesh." Ethel R. Twitchell concurred in her review for *Horn Book,* adding that Cooper "remains faithful to the spirit and magic of the story but gives it a fullness and inevitability that only a true storyteller can evoke."

Based on a Scottish ballad, *Tam Lin* is the third collaboration between Cooper and illustrator Hutton. The story outlines how Margaret, the spirited daughter of a king, runs away to a forbidden wood where she meets an enchanted knight, Tam Lin. Learning that Tam Lin is under a spell that can only be broken by the love of a mortal, Margaret holds on to Tam Lin on Midsummer's Eve as the fairy queen who cast the spell on him transforms him into a wolf, a snake, a deer, and a red-hot bar of iron; through Margaret's love, the enchantment of Tam Lin is broken. Writing in *Horn Book,* Heins called *Tam Lin* "a beautifully paced literary fairy tale, told and pictured with precision and restraint." Helen Gregory of *School Library Journal* noted that Cooper's version of the tale "is alive with dialogue." Critics also acknowledged the feminist slant brought by Cooper to her retelling.

With *The Boggart,* a humorous fantasy for middle graders, Cooper created one of her most popular books. The title character, a Scottish trickster spirit, has lived in Castle Keep as a companion of the MacDevon clan, who are the recipients of its lighthearted practical jokes. When the last MacDevon passes away, the Boggart is griefstricken until the Volnik family of Toronto—distant relatives of the MacDevons—come to the castle they have inherited. After arrangements are made for the castle's sale, the boggart is accidentally shipped back to Canada in an old desk. Emily Volnik and her younger brother Jessup, a computer whiz, recognize the spirit's presence when it starts playing practical jokes on the family, tricks that become dangerous when they begin to involve electricity. Although the children have become fond of the mischievous sprite, they realize it needs to return home to Scotland, so, in conjunction with their Scottish friend Tommy, they ship the spirit back to its castle on diskette via a computer game created by Jessup. Writing in the *New York Times Book Review*, Rafael Yglesias commented that while the "plot of a mysterious and possibly ancient being befriending modern kids and making trouble in their world will be familiar to any reader" familiar with modern movies, "that doesn't make its working out in *The Boggart* any less suspenseful or . . . surprising and moving." "The inevitable failure of a spirit to coexist with our dreary practical world isn't a new theme," Yglesias added, "although in *The Boggart* it seems fresher than ever." Calling the title creature "fascinating . . . , sly, ingenious, and endearing—as long as he belongs to someone else," Ann A. Flowers of *Horn Book* added that what "is most admirable is Susan Cooper's seamless fusion of the newest technology and one of the oldest forms of wild magic." Writing in *Five Owls*, Gary D. Schmidt noted that Cooper makes "rich distinctions between the bustle of Toronto and the quiet of Scotland, between the new technology and the Old Magic, between imagination and pseudo-scientific pretension." Schmidt concluded, "The result is a delightful and quick read, with a conclusion perhaps not as high and noble and cosmic as that of *Silver on the Tree* but in its own way just as satisfying and just as complete."

In addition to penning novels and picture books, Cooper has often written about her craft in books and magazines and has spoken to groups about both the genre of fantasy and her own literary career. In 1996 she published *Dreams and Wishes: Essays on Writing for Children*, a collection of fourteen essays drawn from various speeches in which she explores the craft of writing, outlines the nature of fantasy, and recalls her experiences as an author and reporter. Writing in *Voice of Youth Advocates*, Mary Ann Capan commented that, "Through these major speeches, the reader gains insight into the author's personal life as well as her creative

process." A critic in *Publishers Weekly* called *Dreams and Wishes* "essential reading not just for fans of Cooper or of fantasy novels, but for devotees of children's literature." Citing one of Cooper's anecdotes, the reviewer wrote that when a hurricane destroyed the author's family vacation home, her college-age son Jonathan nervously asked his mother if his favorite books from childhood, stories by the English writer Richmal Crompton, were unharmed. "I suspect," the critic concluded, "that under similar circumstances many other children might inquire worriedly about the safety of their Susan Cooper titles."

BIOGRAPHICAL AND CRITICAL SOURCES:

BOOKS

Celebrating Children's Books: Essays on Children's Literature in Honor of Zena Sutherland, edited by Betsy Hearne and Marilyn Kaye, Lothrop (New York, NY), 1981.

Children's Books and Their Creators, edited by Anita Silvey, Houghton Mifflin (Boston, MA), 1995.

Children's Literature Review, Volume 4, Thomson Gale (Detroit, MI), 1982.

Dictionary of Literary Biography, Volume 161: *British Children's Writers since 1960,* Thomson Gale (Detroit, MI), 1996.

Something about the Author Autobiography Series, Volume 6, Thomson Gale (Detroit, MI), 1989.

Speaking for Ourselves: Autobiographical Sketches by Notable Authors of Books for Young Adults, Volume 1, edited by Donald Gallo, National Council of Teachers of English, 1990.

Twentieth-Century Young-Adult Writers, St. James Press (Detroit, MI), 1994.

PERIODICALS

Booklist, October 15, 1993, Deborah Abbott, review of *Danny and the Kings,* p. 451; March 1, 1997, Stephanie Zvirin, review of *The Boggart and the Monster,* p. 1162; September 15, 1997, p. 226; October 15, 1999, Carolyn Phelan, review of *King of Shadows,* p. 442.

Books and Bookmen, October, 1973, Sally Emerson, review of *The Dark Is Rising,* pp. 130-131.

Bulletin of the Center for Children's Books, November, 1975, Zena Sutherland, review of *The Grey King,* p. 41; January, 1980, Zena Sutherland, review of *Jethro and the Jumbie,* p. 91; March, 1983, Zena

Sutherland, review of *The Silver Cow,* p. 124; February, 1994, Betsy Hearne, review of *Danny and the Kings,* p. 184; December, 1999, Janice M. Del Negro, review of *King of Shadows,* p. 126.

Children's Book Review, September, 1973, S. William Alderson, review of *The Dark Is Rising,* p. 112.

Five Owls, May-June, 1993, Gary D. Schmidt, review of *The Boggart,* p. 117.

Growing Point, September, 1965, Margery Fisher, "Arthurian Echoes," pp. 545-555; January, 1975, Margery Fisher, review of *Greenwitch,* pp. 2555-2556; March, 1978, Margery Fisher, "Dual Worlds," p. 3277.

Horn Book, October, 1970, Ethel L. Heins, review of *Dawn of Fear,* p. 477; June, 1973, Ethel L. Heins, review of *The Dark Is Rising,* p. 286; October, 1975, Mary M. Burns, review of *The Grey King,* p. 461; August, 1976, Margaret K. McElderry, "Susan Cooper," pp. 367-372; December, 1977, Ann A. Flower, review of *Silver on the Tree,* pp. 660-661; June, 1983, Mary M. Burns, review of *The Silver Cow,* pp. 287-288; February, 1984, Paul Heins, review of *Seaward,* pp. 59-60; November-December, 1986, Ethel R. Twitchell, review of *The Selkie Girl,* pp. 731-732; May-June, 1991, Ethel L. Heins, review of *Tam Lin,* pp. 340-341; May-June, 199 3, Ann A. Flowers, review of *The Boggart,* p. 330; JanuaryFebruary, 1997, p. 83; November-December, 1999, Jennifer M. Brabander, review of *King of Shadows,* p. 735.

Journal of Youth Services, spring, 1997, p. 305.

Junior Bookshelf, August, 1972, review of *Dawn of Fear,* p. 241; April, 1978, review of *Silver on the Tree,* pp. 99-100; April, 1984, M. Hobbs, review of *Seaward,* p. 80; April, 1988, Marcus Crouch, review of *The Selkie Girl,* pp. 77-78.

Kirkus Reviews, February 1, 1980, review of *Jethro and the Jumbie,* p. 120.

New York Times Book Review, November 28, 1975, Natalie Babbitt, review of *The Grey King,* pp. 10, 12; May 18, 1997, Jim Gladstone, "Magical Mysteries," p. 29; November 10, 1991, Susan Fromberg Schaeffer, "There's No Escaping Them," p. 53; May 16, 1993, Rafael Yglesias, "The Gremlin on the Floppy Disk," p. 23; January 16, 2000, David Paterson, review of *King of Shadows,* p. 27.

Publishers Weekly, August 31, 1970, Review of *Dawn of Fear,* p. 279; July 12, 1991, review of *Matthew's Dragon,* p. 65; May 27, 1996, review of *Dreams and Wishes,* p. 81.

School Librarian, December, 1965, C.E.J. Smith, review of *Over Sea, under Stone,* p. 358; September, 1984, David Rees, "Susan Cooper," pp. 197-205.

School Library Journal, December, 1977, Shirley Wilton, review of *Silver on the Tree,* p. 48; May, 1991,

Helen Gregory, review of *Tam Lin,* p. 88; May June, 1997, p. 315; November, 1999, Sally Margolis, review of *King of Shadows,* p. 156.

Times Educational Supplement, June 20, 1980, Virginia Makins, "Blithe Spirits," p. 44.

Times Literary Supplement, July 5, 1974, review of *Greenwitch,* p. 721; June 15, 1975, review of *The Grey King,* p. 685; December 5, 1975, Jill Paton Walsh, "Evoking Dark Powers," p. 1457.

Voice of Youth Advocates, August, 1996, Mary Ann Capan, review of *Dreams and Wishes,* p. 187.

Washington Post Book World, July 8, 1973, Virginia Haviland, "A Child's Garden of Ghosts, Poltergeists, and Werewolves," p. 13; July 7, 1996, p. 15.

*　　*　　*

COOPER, Susan Mary
See COOPER, Susan

*　　*　　*

COOVER, Robert 1932-
(Robert Lowell Coover)

PERSONAL: Born February 4, 1932, in Charles City, IA; son of Grant Marion and Maxine (Sweet) Coover; married Maria del Pilar Sans-Mallafré, June 3, 1959; children: Diana Nin, Sara Chapin, Roderick Luis. *Education:* Attended Southern Illinois University at Carbondale, 1949-51; Indiana University at Bloom ington, B.A., 1953; University of Chicago, M.A., 1965.

ADDRESSES: Home—Providence, RI. *Agent*—Georges Borchardt, Inc., 136 East 57th St., New York, NY 10022.

CAREER: Writer of fiction, plays, essays, and poetry. Instructor, Bard College, Annandale-on-Hudson, NY, 1966-67, University of Iowa, Iowa City, 1967-69, Princeton University, Princeton, NJ, 1972-73, Columbia University, New York, NY, 1972, Virginia Military Institute, Lexington, 1976, and Brandeis University, Waltham, MA, 1981; Brown University, Providence, RI, began as writer-in-residence, then distinguished professor, beginning 1981. Producer and director of film *On a Confrontation in Iowa City,* 1969. Organized conference on literature, "Unspeakable Practices: A Three-Day Celebration of Iconoclastic American Fiction," Brown University, 1988. *Military service:* U.S. Naval Reserve, 1953-57; became lieutenant.

MEMBER: American Academy of Arts and Letters.

AWARDS, HONORS: William Faulkner Award for best first novel, 1966, for *The Origin of the Brunists;* Rockefeller Foundation grant, 1969; Guggenheim fellowships, 1971, 1974; citation in fiction from Brandeis University, 1971; Academy of Arts and Letters award, 1975; National Book Award nomination, 1977, for *The Public Burning;* National Endowment for the Humanities award, 1985; Rea Award, Dungannan Foundation, 1987, for *A Night at the Movies;* DAAD fellowship, 1991.

WRITINGS:

NOVELS

The Origin of the Brunists, Putnam (New York, NY), 1966, reprinted, Grove Press (New York, NY), 2000.

The Universal Baseball Association, Inc., J. Henry Waugh, Prop., Random House (New York, NY), 1968.

The Public Burning, Viking (New York, NY), 1977.

Spanking the Maid, Bruccoli-Clark (Bloomfield Hills, MI), 1981.

Gerald's Party, Simon & Schuster (New York, NY), 1986.

Whatever Happened to Gloomy Gus of the Chicago Bears?, Simon & Schuster (New York, NY), 1987.

Pinocchio in Venice, Simon & Schuster (New York, NY), 1991.

John's Wife, Simon & Schuster (New York, NY), 1996.

Ghost Town, Holt (New York, NY), 1998.

The Adventures of Lucky Pierre: Directors' Cut, Grove Press (New York, NY), 2002.

The Grand Hotels (of Joseph Cornell) Burning Deck (New York, NY), 2002.

SHORT FICTION

Pricksongs & Descants, Dutton (New York, NY), 1969, reprinted, Grove Press (New York, NY), 2002.

The Water Pourer, Bruccoli-Clark (Bloomfield Hills, MI), 1972.

The Hair o' the Chine, Bruccoli-Clark (Bloomfield Hills, MI), 1979.

A Political Fable, Viking (New York, NY), 1980.

Charlie in the House of Rue, Penmaen Press (Great Barrington, MA), 1980.

The Convention, Lord John (Northridge, CA), 1981.

In Bed One Night and Other Brief Encounters, Burning Deck (Providence, RI), 1983.

Aesop's Forest (bound with *The Plot of the Mice and Other Stories* by Brian Swann), Capra Press (Santa Barbara, CA), 1986.

A Night at the Movies; or, You Must Remember This, Simon & Schuster (New York, NY), 1987.

Briar Rose, Grove Press (New York, NY), 1996.

PLAYS

The Kid (also see below), first produced in New York, NY, at American Place Theater, November 17, 1972, produced in London, England, 1974.

A Theological Position (contains *A Theological Position, Rip Awake, The Kid,* and *Love Scene;* also see below), Dutton (New York, NY), 1972.

Scène d'amour, first produced in Paris, France, at Troglodyte Theater, 1973, produced as *Love Scene* in New York, NY, March 20, 1974.

Rip Awake, first produced in Los Angeles, CA, 1975.

A Theological Position, first produced in Los Angeles, CA, 1977, produced in New York, NY, 1979.

Bridge Hand, first produced in Providence, RI, 1981.

Spanking the Maid, first produced, 1987.

A Pedestrian Accident, first produced, 1998.

Charlie in the House of Rue, first produced, 1999.

OTHER

(And director) *On a Confrontation in Iowa City* (screenplay), University of Iowa, 1969.

(Editor, with Kent Dixon) *The Stone Wall Book of Short Fiction,* Stone Wall Press (Washington, DC), 1973.

(Editor, with Elliott Anderson) *Minute Stories,* Braziller (New York, NY), 1976.

(Author of introduction) *Statements Two,* edited by Jonathan Baumbach, Fiction Collective Two (New York, NY), 1977.

After Lazarus: A Filmscript, Bruccoli-Clark (Bloomfield Hills, MI), 1980.

(Author of introduction) Wilfrido D. Nolledo, *But for the Lovers,* by Dalkey Archive Press, 1994.

Stepmother (fairy tale), illustrated by Michael Kupperman, McSweeney's, 2004.

Work represented in anthologies, including *New American Review 4,* New American Library (New York, NY), 1968, *New American Review 14,* Simon & Schuster (New York, NY), 1972, and *American Review,* Bantam (New York, NY), 1974. Contributor of short stories, poems, essays, reviews, and translations to numerous periodicals, including *Noble Savage, Quarterly Review, Argosy, Evergreen Review, Iowa Review, Antaeus, Saturday Review, New York Times Book Review, Granta, Fiction International,* and *Fiddlehead.* Fiction editor, *Iowa Review,* 1975-77.

ADAPTATIONS: The Baby Sitter has been adapted for the stage; "Pedestrian Accident" has been made into an opera; "The Leper's Helix" was performed as a chamber work.

SIDELIGHTS: Since beginning his career in the 1960s, Robert Coover has emerged as one of the leading American postmodern writers. As is true of his peers—John Barth, Donald Barthelme, William Gass, and Thomas Pynchon—Coover experiments with traditional fictional forms and familiar stories, twisting them in ways that challenge society's assumptions. He of ten mixes reality with illusion, creating alternative worlds. Critics have used such terms as "amazing," "fantastic," and "magic" to describe the effect of his fiction. *Time* contributor Paul Gray, for one, noted that Coover has won a "reputation as an avant-gardist who can do with reality what a magician does with a pack of cards: Shuffle the familiar into unexpected patterns." Coover usually begins his novels with ordinary subjects and events, then introduces elements of fantasy and fear that, when left unhindered, grow to equal, if not surpass, what is real within the situation. Michael Mason said in *Times Literary Supplement* that he believed Coover structures his novels around the idea of "an American superstition giving rise to its appropriate imaginary apocalypse."

The Origin of the Brunists, Coover's first and most conventional novel, chronicles the rise and fall of a fictitious religious cult. This cult arises when the sole survivor of a mining disaster, Giovanni Bruno, claims to have been visited by the Virgin Mary and rescued via divine intervention. As the cult gains followers and generates hysteria, the furor is fueled by a local newspaper editor until the situation reaches what Philip Callow of *Books & Bookmen* termed "apocalyptic proportions." Although some critics, including Callow, found the novel's conclusion disappointing and anticlimactic, others, such as *New Statesman* contributor Miles Burrows, described the book as being "a major work in the sense that it is long, dense, and alive to a degree that makes life outside the covers almost pallid."

In a *New Republic* review of Coover's second novel, *The Universal Baseball Association, Inc., J. Henry Waugh, Prop.,* Richard Gilman wrote, "What this novel

summons to action is our sense . . . of the possible substitution of one world for another, of the way reality implies alternatives." The book's protagonist, Henry Waugh, is bored with his job and his life. To alleviate his boredom, he creates, within his imagination, an entire baseball league, complete with statistics and team and player names and histories. Plays, players, and fates are determined by dice, and Waugh, according to Gilman, presides "over this world of chance with a creator's calm dignity." When the dice rule that a favored player must die during a game, both Waugh's imaginary and real worlds fall apart. Waugh could, of course, choose to ignore the dice's decision, but to do so would be in violation of "the necessary laws that hold the cosmos together," a *Time* reviewer explained. At the novel's end, Waugh disappears from the story, leaving his players to fashion their own existence, myths, and rituals.

National Observer critic Clifford A. Ridley commented that *The Universal Baseball Association, Inc.* "is a novel about continuity, about order, about reason, about God, and about the relationships between them. Which is to say that it is a parable of human existence, but do not feel put off by that; for it is a parable couched in such head-long, original prose and set down in a microcosmos of such consistent fascination that it is far too busy entertaining to stop and instruct." Red Smith, however, writing in the *Washington Post Book World,* disagreed, remarking that "A little fantasy goes a long way . . . and after an imaginary beanball kills an imaginary play er the author never finds the strike zone again. It all becomes a smothering bore." *New York Review* critic Ronald Sukenick shared Smith's assessment of the novel's second half: "Baseball has already been made to carry a heavy cargo in this book," he wrote, "but now it gets heavier. With the plausibility of the actual game lost, th e philosophical freight begins to take over."

Pricksongs & Descants, Coover's collection of short fiction pieces, has been widely praised. The author's experimental forms and techniques produce "extreme verbal magic," according to Christopher Lehmann-Haupt in *New York Times.* "Nothing in Mr. Coover's writing is quite what it seems to be," the critic continued. "In the pattern of the leaves there is always the smile of the Cheshire Cat." And Marni Jackson explained in *Critique* that "an innocent situation develops a dozen sinister possibilities, sprouting in the reader's imagination while they are suspended, open-ended, on the page. . . . Every disturbing twist the story might take is explored; all of them could have happened, or none. . . . Like a good conjurer, even when you recognize his gimmicks, the illusion continues to work."

With *The Public Burning* Coover returns to longer fiction and pushes his exploration of alternative realities to new levels, further blurring the distinction between fact and fiction. The book can be called a "factional" account of the 1953 conviction and execution of alleged spies Julius and Ethel Rosenberg. A satire on the mood and mentality of the nation at the time of the Rosenbergs' execution, the novel loosely combines events from both history and its author's imagination. Coover sets the site of the electrocutions in New York City's Times Square, adds surrealistic parodies of various personalities and events of the era, and provides then-Vice President Richard M. Nixon as the narrator-commentator. Reaction to the book has included admiration for Coover's creative efforts as well as criticism that those efforts go too far. Piers Brendon described the novel in *Books & Bookmen* as a "literary photo-montage" and "a paean of American self-hatred, a torrid indictment of the morally bankrupt society w here for so long Nixon was the one." Lehmann-Haupt stated in a *New York Times* review that he was "shocked and amazed" by the book; "*The Public Burning*," he explained, "is an astonishing spectacle. It does not invite us to participate. . . . It merely allows us to watch, somewhat warily, as its author performs."

In *New York Times Book Review* Thomas R. Edwards noted that "horror and anger are the governing feelings" in Coover's 1977 novel. "As a work of literary art," he commented, "*The Public Burning* suffers from excess. . . . But all vigorous satire is simplistic and excessive, and this book is an extraordinary act of moral p assion." Brendon was similarly impressed by the novel's scope and also aware of its ultimate shortcomings: "*The Public Burning* is an ambitious failure. It is a huge, sprawling, brilliant, original exercise in literary photo-montage. It combines fact and fiction, comedy and terror, surrealism and satire, travesty and tragedy. [But it] is too overblown, too undisciplined, too crude, too lurid."

The novel *Whatever Happened to Gloomy Gus of the Chicago Bears?* is another alternative reality story with Richard Nixon as a character. This time, a young Nixon follows his success on the football fields of Whittier, California, not with a career in politics but with a career in professional football. His rise and fall comes not in Washi ngton, but in Chicago. In the late 1930s, Nixon—known here as Gloomy Gus—falls in with several Chicago labor activists, including the book's narrator, Meyer, a sculptor. On Memorial Day of 1937, in a crowd of demonstrators picketing Republic Steel, Gus catches a police bullet and dies. Meyer looks back to tell this story—a story that challenges the reader by

warping historical events—and as Christopher Walker commented in *New Statesman,* "At [Nixon's] expense Coover reveals 'the inherent contradictions in the American dream' in a book which is both touching and hilariously funny."

While Coover often manipulates historical events for his artistic purposes, he does so with a solid knowledge of the facts. As Sara Paretsky noted in Chicago's *Tribune Books,* "Coover obviously knows Richard Nixon's life well. He displays the same careful research into events of the '30s on the streets of Chicago and the battlefields of Spain." And *New York Times Book Review* contributor Richard Kelly felt that Coover's fictionalized Nixon captures the essence of the man Americans came to know through his political ups and downs. "Gloomy Gus is Richard Nixon," Kelly said, "in all his awkward triumphs, in all the plodding determination every act takes, in the hars h light of the will that makes every act equal to every other." Still, Kelly believed that "Coover's Richard Nixon is a nobler, stupider character than history's." Through this character, he concluded, "Coover shows us the madness of the will as it operates without intelligence, and makes us think about that most secret of all our transg ressions, the deep sin of being innocent."

Kelly was impressed with Coover's artistry; he maintained that *Whatever Happened to Gloomy Gus of the Chicago Bears?* "has all Mr. Coover's delight in technique, his inventive brio, his earthy humor, along with the passion for justice that marks all his writings." He added that in this work in particular the author "takes hold of t he ordinary novel and, with apparent modesty, briskly renovates its traditional features." But *Los Angeles Times Book Review* contributor John Schulian dismissed the work as "an inflated short story." Schulian added that "Coover has undercut the very lesson his book was supposed to teach. He has paid attention to history, but he ha s repeated it—and himself—anyway." In Kelly's view, however, *Gloomy Gus* represents its author well. "Coover is one of our masters now," the critic wrote. "The tumultuous, Babylonian exuberance of his mind is fueled and directed by his equally passionate craftsmanship. He seems to be able to do anything, and this funny, bitter, h uman book is fair proof of it."

In *Pinocchio in Venice* Coover updates the story originated by the Italian writer Carlo Collodi in 1883 about the puppet who became a boy. "Coover's adult fable . . . comes closer to the stern morality of the early Italian story than Disney's saccharine film ever did," observed Constance Markey in Chicago's *Tribune Books*. *Times Literary Supplement* reviewer Lorna Sage characterized Coover's update as "a hilariously phallic riposte, a carnivalesque reprise all about the agonies and delights of turning back to wood. His Pinocchio, after a century of humanity, opts for the dry rot and the unstrung joints, follows his nose and looks to his roots." Coover's Pinocchio has grown up and grown old, one hundred years old. After a long career as a renowned professor and philosopher in U.S. universities, he decides to return to his native Italy. In Venice he encounters all the characters from his past—the fox, the cat, the puppets in the traveling show, and the blue fairy— all in new guises. "One ecstatic disaster follows on another," noted Sage, who went on to observe that Coover's fun "is perfectly nightmarish—murderous in its intensity, chilling in the thoroughness with which it scatters and splinters the remnants of 'character.'" In the end, according to Markey, Pinocchio's updated story "requires that the reader take a new hard look at his own wooden-headed ways, mulish choices and false blue fantasies."

As with his previous novels, Coover stretches the boundaries of content and form in his version of Pinocchio. By playing with reality, the author creates a type of magical realism, according to critic Anthony Burgess. However, as Burgess explained in the *New York Times Book Review*, "The Coover version is not magical realism of the Latin American and Salman Rushdie type but Rabelaisian fantasy, with no child readers allowed." As for the author's experimentation with form, Burgess commented that "Coover is one of America's quirkiest writers, if by 'quirky' we mean an unwillingness to abide by ordinary fictional rules and a conviction that a novel is primarily a verbal artifact unconvertible to other media." This manipulation of words pervades *Pinocchio in Venice,* and, according to a reviewer for the *Atlantic,* his language is more style than substance, his substance being "yet another lament for the human condition—the game that we all lose in the end." However, in the view of *Los Angeles Times Book Review* critic Richard Eder, "When you get through the bramble hedges of his wordplay and reality-play, you find a winning sympathy for his stick-figure pedant, along with a meditation on humanity vs. art." "In short, *Pinocchio in Venice* is one very funny, solid book; moving, too, with not a wooden line or ill-mortised joint to be found," concluded Brooke Horvath in *Review of Contemporary Fiction.*

John's Wife is a complex, convoluted novel that, according to Michael Harris in the *Los Angeles Times,* offers its reader many layers of meaning. The critic suggested that the novel is "on one level a bawdy and deadly satire of good-ol'-boy mores; on another level a complex portrait of the townspeople . . . on still another, a philosophical inquiry into the relationship between life and art." John is a builder whose money, ambition, and works are the heart of a small Midwestern town. He is an object of both love and hatred for his fellow townspeople, but his wife is an object of obsession. Each of the townspeople has his or her own image of John's wife; she stands at the center of each character's imagination while, in reality, she remains elusive. The result, as Jennifer Howard observed in *Washington Post Book World,* is that "the town . . . lives in a frenzy of desire, much of it unwholesome."

Brad Leithauser, writing in the *New York Times Book Review,* considered *John's Wife* to be "a rambling, reiterated and squalid affair" and dubbed Coover's writing "overworked: too much fuss, not enough fineness." Yet a reviewer for *Publishers Weekly* wrote that the novelist's "prose is, as always, biting and suggestive, a spicy blend of erudition and scatology, epic and farce." And, in Howard's opinion, "Coover knows how to put a sentence together, often brilliantly." She also commented that Coover's method for unraveling his plot has merits: "He employs a kind of circular storytelling technique that's intriguing if sometimes confusing." *New York Times* critic Lehmann-Haupt was intrigued by this storytelling technique as well. "At first, the proliferation of townspeople in 'John's Wife' is mind numbing," he noted. "But then gradually, almost eerily, as the narrative keeps circling back and digging deeper, you begin to remember their stories as vividly as your own past." Considering the author's crafting of the form and content of this novel, Harris conceded that "Coover's skills are formidable, and this story of the power of flux to disrupt memory, community and desire . . . has to be one of the year's most ambitious novels, and one of its funniest."

In a retelling of the Sleeping Beauty tale, Coover's *Briar Rose* reinterprets the conventions of a fairy tale. Infusing his version with more sexuality than the traditional version of the story, the author spins a tale about storytelling itself, in the opinion of *New York Times Book Review* contributor Michael Gorra. Using humor to energize the traditional tale, the author structures it so that, in Gorra's words, "this short and almost perfect book seems—paradoxically, blissfully—to go on forever." Michael Upchurch, writing in Chicago's *Tribune Books,* speculated that whereas other novelists work with the thought of film options foremost in their minds, *Briar Rose* "seems custom-designed to make a nifty computer game" since it "consists of almost nothing but false starts, wrong turns, spiral staircases, a 'door that is not a door' and other endlessly mutable narrative pathways that frustrate its beleaguered heroes." Thus Rose, the Sleeping Beauty figure held captive in a tower by a n old crone, is plagued by a series of nightmares that create an environment that, Upchurch suggested, should be "familiar to anyone who has . . . tried to track down reliable reference material on the Internet." These nightmares, induced by the crone's dark magical powers, create the impression of what Upchurch described as "false starts" and "wrong turns": in one, the handsome prince who will rescue Rose turns out to already have a wife; in another, not a prince but a toad wakes her, and—in a reversal of another fairy tale theme—his kiss turns her into a toad as well. "Coover's prose," warned Upchurch, "with its manneristic flourishes and acrobatic syntax, won't b e to everyone's liking"; nonetheless, he suggested that great rewards await those who give the book their full attention.

More recently, Coover published his version of a western novel with *Ghost Town*. Here, the author uses stereotyped characters and disconnected situations that skip around with no attention to plot development. As Allen Barra pointed out in a *Salon.com* review, the novel "isn't so much a western as a novel about westerns." The m ain character is a loner and drifter who finds himself in a stereotypical town complete with the usual ranchers, saloon keepers, outlaws, and saloon girls. However, in this town, people are constantly changing their roles, as does the loner himself, who shifts from outlaw to sheriff and back to outlaw. Even the buildings shift and rearrange themse lves from scene to scene. There is also a combination of humorous dialogue mixed with shoot-em-up violence in the book, though characters who are killed fail to stay dead; instead, they reappear later in other roles as if the reader were watching several different western movies starring the same actors. Adding to the confusion is the drifter's un reliable memory about things that have happened to him in the past. "Coover's concern is with the mythology of the western," said Barra, "but your reaction to *Ghost Town* is less likely to hinge on your feelings about westerns that about metafiction in general."

Review of Contemporary Fiction critic Robert L. McLaughlin felt that the overall effect of the book can cause readers to reconsider some American myths. "In subverting the narrative conventions of Westerns," McLaughlin wrote, "*Ghost Town* reveals a version of the American and a vision of America they usually keep masked. Coo ver has aimed at the dangerous absurdities of our national myth, as embodied in our stories of the frontier, and has hit his target with brilliant force."

Other critics, however, felt the book leaves something to be desired. For example, *World Literature Today* reviewer Robert Murray Davis found the story "dull and confusing," and Edward B. St. John, writing in *Library Journal,* remarked that although he admired the author's technical prowess, *Ghost Town* is still "a book easier to admire than to love."

In his ambitious novel *The Adventures of Lucky Pierre: Director's Cut,* Coover tackles the genre of pornography in order to "confront readers with assumptions about reality and how the mind works," according to Richard Bernstein in the *New York Times.* The story is about veteran porn actor Lucky Pierre, who despite abundant ple asure, doesn't feel so lucky. Lucky Pierre strides through Cinecity, a metropolis where porn movies are the stuff of life, thinking himself trapped "inside a box of artificial light even as it pulled him in all directions at once and has given him no life, no center of his own." With no name to hold on—he has different names in all his roles—and serving as a sex slave to women who are his directors and co-stars, Lucky Pierre cannot tell what around him is real and what is illusory.

Critics were divided about Coover's novel, *Los Angeles Times* contributor Susan Salter Reynolds expressing impatience with the novel's plot, which she found "so tenuous that its comprehension depends more on readers' imagination than is the case in more conventional fiction." *Entertainment Weekly* reviewer Troy Patterson stated that, given the novel's "cornucopia of cartoon depravities and the self-analytical orchestrations of its 'plot,' this pomo porno is begging to be called masturbatory." On the other hand, Bernstein among others applauded Coover's risk-taking, saying that in *The Adventures of Lucky Pierre* he "writes about sex as it's never bee n written about before, with a sly, detached precision that captures the unillusioned and undeterred Freudian id. Mr. Coover can be seen as the inverse of another writer about sex, the Marquis de Sade."

Because of his interest in experimenting with form, Coover has explored not only the novel and short story, but also poetry, plays, and filmscripts. His "interest in film has been evident in his fiction, which often relies blatantly on cinematic techniques," noted Larry McCaffery and Sinda J. Gregory in the *Dictionary of Literary Biography Yearbook: 1981.* "He finds interesting the notion of cinematic montage or juxtaposition, the ability of cinema to manipulate time, its great sense of immediacy, its mixture of what he calls 'magic and documentary power'—all of which have potential applications in fiction." He has also been intrigued by the possibilities of hype rtext—the branching, multiplex, interactive writing made possible by computers and the Internet. In a *New York Times Book Review* article on the growing presence of hypertext literature, Coover admitted he was not "likely to engage in any major hypertext fictions of my own. But, interested as ever in the subversion of the traditional bour geois novel and in fictions that challenge linearity, I felt that something was happening out (or in) there and that I ought to know what it was." To this end, Coover began reading and reviewing hypertext writing, launched a university course to introduce students to its possibilities, and has publicized both hypertext fictions and the software that makes them possible.

Coover is often cited as a major voice in the experimental branch of literature labeled "postmodern" fiction. As Joyce Carol Oates commented in *Southern Review:* the writer "exists blatantly and brilliantly in his fiction as an authorial consciousness. . . . He will remind readers of William Gass, of John Barth, of Samuel Beckett. He is as surprising as any of these writers, and as funny as Donald Barthelme; both crude and intellectual, predictable and alarming, he gives the impression of thoroughly enjoying his craft." Still, as Lois G. Gordon wrote in *Robert Coover: The Universal Fictionmaking Process,* the novelist "has developed a style unique among his conte mporaries, mixing so-called fact and fiction with realism and surrealism, merging narrative line with adjacent and 'descanting' poetic or fragmentary evocations of moral, mythic, historical, philosophical, and psychological dimensions." In his review of *Pricksongs & Descants* for the *New York Times,* Lehmann-Haupt dubbed Coover simply "among the best we now have writing."

BIOGRAPHICAL AND CRITICAL SOURCES:

BOOKS

Anderson, Richard, *Robert Coover,* Twayne (Boston, MA), 1981.

Contemporary Literary Criticism, Thomson Gale (Detroit, MI), Volume 3, 1975, Volume 7, 1977, Volume 15, 1980, Volume 32, 1985, Volume 46, 1988, Volume 87, 1995.

Cope, Jackson I., *Robert Coover's Fictions,* Johns Hopkins University Press (Baltimore, MD), 1986.

Dictionary of Literary Biography, Thomson Gale (Detroit, MI), Volume 2: *American Novelists since World War II,* 1978, Volume 227: *American Novelists since World War II, Sixth Series,* 2000.

Dictionary of Literary Biography Yearbook: 1981, Thomson Gale (Detroit, MI), 1982.

Gado, Frank, *First Person: Conversations on Writers and Writing,* Union College Press (Schenectady, NY), 1973.

Gass, William, *Fiction and the Figures of Life,* Knopf (New York, NY), 1971.

Gordon, Lois G., *Robert Coover: The Universal Fictionmaking Process,* Southern Illinois University Press (Carbondale, IL), 1983.

Kennedy, Thomas E., *Robert Coover: A Study of the Short Fiction,* Twayne (New York, NY), 1992.

LeClair, Thomas, and Larry McCaffery, *Interviews with Contemporary American Novelists,* University of Illinois Press (Urbana, IL), 1982.

Maltby, Paul, *Dissident Postmodernists: Barthelme, Coover, Pynchon,* University of Pennsylvania Press (Philadelphia, PA), 1991.

McCaffery, Larry, *The Metafictional Muse: The Works of Robert Coover, Donald Barthelme, and William Gass,* University of Pittsburgh Press (Pittsburgh, PA), 1982.

McKeon, Z. Karl, *Novels and Arguments,* University of Chicago Press (Chicago, IL), 1982.

Modern American Literature, fifth edition, St. James Press (Detroit, MI), 1999.

Pearce, Richard D., *The Novel in Motion: An Approach to Modern Fiction,* Ohio State University Press (Columbus, OH), 1983.

Pughe, Thomas, *Comic Sense: Reading Robert Coover, Stanley Elkin, Philip Roth,* Birkhauser Verlag (Basel, Switzerland), 1994.

Reference Guide to American Literature, fourth edition, St. James Press (Detroit, MI), 2000.

Schulz, Max, *Black Humor Fiction of the 1960s,* Ohio University Press (Athens, OH), 1973.

Semrau, Janusz, *American Self-Conscious Fiction of the 1960s and 1970s: Donald Barthelme, Robert Coover, Ronald Sukenick,* Poznan, 1986.

Sorkin, Adam J., editor, *Politics and the Muse: Studies in the Politics of Recent American Literature,* Bowling Green State University Popular Press (Bowling Green, OH), 1989.

PERIODICALS

Antioch Review, fall, 2003, Daniel Green, "Postmodern American Fiction," p. 729.

Atlanta Journal & Constitution, March 1, 1987.

Atlantic, November, 1977; February, 1991, p. 92.

Biblio, September, 1998, Nicholas A. Basbanes, "The Traditionalist and the Revolutionary," p. 10.

Booklist, October 1, 1992; August, 1998, Frank Casa, review of *Ghost Town,* p. 1960; September 1, 1998, Bill Ott, review of *The Universal Baseball Association, J. Henry Waugh, Prop.,* p. 168.

Books & Bookmen, May, 1967, Philip Callow, review of *The Origin of the Brunists;* August, 1978, Piers Brendon, review of *The Public Burning.*

Choice, September, 2003, B.H. Leeds, "Understanding Robert Coover," p. 147.

Critique, Volume 11, number 3, 1969, pp. 11-29; Volume 17, number 1, p. 78; Volume 31, number 2, 1990, p. 85; Volume 33, number 3, p. 29; Volume 34, number 4, 1993, p. 220; Volume 35, number 2, 1994, p. 67; fall, 2000 (special Coover issue), Larry McCaffery, "As Guilty as the Rest of Them: An Interview with Robert Coover," p. 115; s pring, 2004, Barbara Bond, "Postmodern Mannerism: An Examination of Robert Coover's Pinocchio in Venice," p. 273.

Cue, November 25, 1972.

Economist, November 14, 1998, review of *Ghost Town,* p. S6.

Entertainment Weekly, December 6, 2002, Troy Patterson, review of *Lucky Pierre,* p. 103.

Esquire, December, 1970.

Essays in Literature, fall, 1981, pp. 203-217.

Film Comment, May-June, 1987.

Harper's, June, 1999, Jonathan Dee, review of *The Public Burning,* p. 76.

Harvard Advocate, Volume 230, number 4, 1996.

Hollins Critic, April, 1970.

Library Journal, February 15, 1987; October 1, 1987; January 1991; March 1, 1996, p. 104; January, 1997, Barbara Hoffert, review of *Briar Rose,* p. 144; July, 1998, Edward B. St. John, review of *Ghost Town,* p. 134.

London Review of Books, April 17, 1986, p. 18; September 17, 1987, p. 19.

Los Angeles Times, February 6, 1987; April 22, 1996, p. E3.

Los Angeles Times Book Review, February 2, 1986, p. 2; October 25, 1987, p. 9; May 29, 1988, p. 14; January 27, 1991, p. 3; November 17, 2002, review of *Lucky Pierre,* p. 15.

Maclean's, April 13, 1987.

Modern Language Review, October 2003, Kathryn Hume, "Robert Coover: The Metaphysics of Bondage," p. 827.

Modern Fiction Studies, spring, 1987, p. 161.

Nation, December 8, 1969; June 24, 1996, pp. 32-33; February 10, 1997, Jennifer Starrels, review of *Briar Rose,* p. 35.

National Observer, July 29, 1968, Clifford A. Ridley, review of *The Universal Baseball Association, Inc., J. Henry Waugh, Prop.*

New Republic, August, 17, 1967; March 24, 1986, p. 28.

New Statesman, April 13, 1967, Miles Burrows, review of *The Origin of the Brunists;* June 16, 1978; May 16, 1986, p. 28; February 13, 1987; November 27, 1987, p. 33; July 1, 1988, p. 44.

Newsweek, December 1, 1969; January 5, 1987, p. 58.

New Yorker, December 23, 2002, review of *Lucky Pierre,* p. 155.

New York Review, March 13, 1969, Ronald Sukenick, review of *The Universal Baseball Association, Inc., J. Henry Waugh, Prop.*

New York Review of Books, April 24, 1986, p. 38; October 17, 1996, p. 48.

New York Times, June 13, 1968; October 22, 1969; November 18, 1972; September 7, 1977; December 19, 1985; January 7, 1987; August 22, 1987; January 15, 1991; April 1, 1996, p. B2; October 21, 1998, Richard Bernstein, review of *Ghost Town,* p. E9; November 13, 2002, Richard Bernstein, review of *The Adventures of Lucky Pierre,* p. E8.

New York Times Book Review, July 7, 1968; August 14, 1977, p. 9; June 27, 1982; December 29, 1985, p. 1; February 1, 1987, p. 15; September 27, 1987, p. 9; July 30, 1989, p. 28; January 27, 1991, pp. 3, 31; June 21, 1992, p. 1; January 3, 1993, p. 20; August 29, 1993, p. 1; April 7, 1996, p. 7; February 16, 1997, pp. 10-11; September 27, 1998, Sven Birkerts, "Horseman, Pass By!"

Notes on Contemporary Literature, November, 1995, p. 5.

Novel: A Forum on Fiction, spring, 1974, pp. 210-19; winter, 1979, pp. 127-148; fall, 1993, pp. 85-101.

Observer (London, England), April 13, 1986, p. 25; August 16, 1987, p. 23; June 25, 1989, p. 45; April 28, 1991, p. 59.

Partisan Review, fall, 1997, pp. 609-610.

Publishers Weekly, December 26, 1986; July 10, 1987; July 1, 1988; February 5, 1996, p. 75; November 25, 1996, p. 58; June 22, 1998, review of *Ghost Town,* p. 81; May 27, 2002, "The Grand Hotels (of Joseph Cornell)," p. 53.

Quill and Quire, May 1986, p. 29.

Review of Contemporary Fiction, fall, 1986, p. 143; fall, 1991, p. 267; fall, 1994, p. 9; summer, 1997, p. 272; fall, 1996, pp. 183-184; spring, 1999, Robert L. McLaughlin, review of *Ghost Town,* p. 174; summer 2003, Robert L. McLaughlin, review of *The Adventures of Lucky Pierre,* p. 137.

Saturday Review, August 31, 1968.

Short Story, fall, 1993, p. 89.

Southern Review, winter, 1971.

Studies in Short Fiction, spring, 199 4, p. 217.

Studies in the Novel, fall, 1993, p. 332.

Time, June 28, 1968; August 8, 1977.

Times (London, England), February 5, 1987; May 2, 1991.

Times Literary Supplement, June 16, 1978; May 2, 1986, p. 478; February 13, 1987; August 14, 1987, p. 873; July 1, 1988, p. 730; May 31, 1991, p. 19; February 12, 1999, Paul Quinn, review of *Ghost Town* and *The Pub lic Burning,* pp. 5, 21.

Tribune Books (Chicago, IL), January 18, 1987, p. 3; August 16, 1987, p. 3; January 6, 1991, p. 1; January 27, 1991, p. 1; February 9, 1997, p. 5.

Village Voice, July 30, 1970.

Voice Literary Supplement, April, 1986, p. 7.

Wall Street Journal, April 5, 1996, p. A6.

Washington Post, November 8, 1998, Marie Arana-Ward, review of *Ghost Town,* p. 5.

Washington Post Book World, July 7, 1968; November 2, 1969; May 11, 1982; January 18, 1986, p.5; March 1, 1987, p. 9; May 21, 1989, p. 12; January 6, 1991, p. 1; March 31, 1996, p. 6; November 8, 1998, Marie Arana-Ward, review of *Ghost Town,* p. 5.

World Literature Today, spring, 1997, Daniel R. Bronson, review of *John 's Wife,* p. 385; spring, 1999, Robert Murray Davis, review of *Ghost Town,* p. 333.

Yearbook of Comparative and General Literature, 1992, pp. 40, 83-8 9.

ONLINE

Metroactive Books Web site, http://www.metroactive.com/ (July 17, 2002), Allen Barra, "Robert Coover 's 'Ghost Town' Rides the Frontier of Our Cowboy Memories."

Salon.com, http://www.salon.com/ (July 17, 2002), Allen Barra, review of *Ghost Town.*

*　　*　　*

COOVER, Robert Lowell
See COOVER, Robert

*　　*　　*

CORMIER, Robert 1925-2000
(Robert Edmund Cormier, John Fitch, IV)

PERSONAL: Born January 17, 1925, in Leominster, MA; died of complications from a blood clot November 2, 2000, in Boston, MA; son of Lucien Joseph (a factory worker) and Irma Margaret (Collins) Cormier; married Constance B. Senay, November 6, 1948; children: Roberta Susan, P eter Jude, Christine Judith, Renee Elizabeth. *Education:* Attended Fitchburg State College, 1944. *Religion:* Roman Catholic

CAREER: Radio WTAG, Worcester, MA, writer, 1946-48; *Telegram and Gazette,* Worcester, reporter, 1948-55, writing consultant 1980-83; *Fitchburg Sentinel* (became *Fitchburg-Leominster Sentinel and Enterprise*), Fitchburg, MA, reporter, 1955-59, wire editor, 1959-66, associate editor, 1966-78; freelance writer, 1978-2000. Member of board of trustees of Leominster (MA) Public Library, 1978-93.

MEMBER: L'Union St. Jean Baptiste d'Amerique, PEN.

AWARDS, HONORS: Best human interest story of the year award, Associated Press in New England, 1959 and 1973; Bread Loaf Writers' Conference fellow, 1968; best newspaper column award, K.R. Thomson Newspapers, Inc., 1974; outstanding book of the year awards, *New York Times,* 1974, for *The Chocolate War,* 1977, for *I Am the Cheese,* and 1 979, for *After the First Death;* "Best Book for Young Adults" citations, American Library Association, 1974, for *The Chocolate War,* 1977, for *I Am the Cheese,* 1979, for *After the First Death,* and 1983, for *The Bumblebee Flies Anyway;* Maxi Award, *Media and Methods,* 1976; Doctor of Letters, Fitchburg Sta te College, 1977; Woodward School Annual Book Award, 1978, for *I Am the Cheese;* Lewis Carroll Shelf Award, 1979, for *The Chocolate War;* "Notable Children's Trade Book in the Field of Social Studies" citation, National Council for Social Studies and Children's Book Council, 1980, for *Eight Plus One;* Assembly on Literature for Adolescents (ALAN) Award, National Council of Teachers of English, 1982; "Best of the Best Books, 1970-1983" citations, American Library Association, for *The Chocolate War, I Am the Cheese,* and *After the First Death;* "Best Books of 1983" citation, *School Library Journal,* for *The Bumblebee Flies Anyway;* Car negie Medal nomination, 1983, for *The Bumblebee Flies Anyway;* Reader's Choice Award, 1983, for the *Eight Plus One* short story "President Cleveland, Where Are You?"; named Massachusetts Author of the Year, Massachusetts Library Association, 1985; "Honor List" citation from *Horn Book,* 1986, for *Beyond the Chocolate War;* Young Adult Services Division "Best Book for Young Adults" citation, American Library Association, 1988, for *Fade;* World Fantasy Award nomination, 1989, for *Fade;* Margaret A. Edwards Award, American Library Association, 1991, for *The Chocolate War, I Am the*

Cheese, and *After the First Death;* Best Books of the Year, *Publishers Weekly,* 1991, finalist for Best Young Adult award, Mystery Writers of America, 1992, California Reader Medal, 1993-94, and named to Best of the Best Books, American Library Association, 1994, all for *We All Fall Down;* Georgia Children's Book Award nomination, 1992-93, for *Other Bells for Us to Ring;* finali st for Best Young Adult award, Mystery Writers of America, 1996, for *In the Middle of the Night;* German Catholic Book of the Year, Bishops of Germany, 1997, for *Tunes for Bears to Dance To.*

WRITINGS:

YOUNG ADULT NOVELS, EXCEPT AS NOTED

The Chocolate War, Pantheon (New York, NY), 1974.
I Am the Cheese, Pantheon (New York, NY), 1977.
After the First Death, Pantheon (New York, NY), 1979.
Eight Plus One (short stories), Pantheon (New York, NY), 1980.
The Bumblebee Flies Anyway, Pantheon (New York, NY), 1983.
Beyond the Chocolate War, Knopf (New York, NY), 1985.
Other Bells for Us to Ring, Delacorte (New York, NY), 1990.
We All Fall Down, Delacorte (New York, NY), 1991.
Tunes for Bears to Dance To, Delacorte (New York, NY), 1992.
In the Middle of the Night, Delacorte (New York, NY), 1995.
Tenderness, Delacorte (New York, NY), 1997.
Heroes, Delacorte (New York, NY), 1998.
Frenchtown Summer (poetry), Delacorte (New York, NY), 1999.
The Rag and Bone Shop, Delacorte (New York, NY), 2001.

Also author of *The Rumple Country* and *In the Midst of Winter,* both unpublished novels.

ADULT NOVELS

Now and at the Hour, Coward (New York, NY), 1960.
A Little Raw on Monday Mornings, Sheed (New York, NY), 1963.
Take Me Where the Good Times Are, Macmillan (New York, NY), 1965.
Fade, Delacorte (New York, NY), 1988.

AUTOBIOGRAPHY/ESSAYS

I Have Words to Spend: Reflections of a Small-Town Editor, Delacorte (New York, NY), 1991.

CONTRIBUTOR

Betsy Hearne and Marilyn Kay, editors, *Celebrating Children's Books: Essays in Honor of Zena Sutherland,* Lothrop (New York, NY), 1981.
Sixteen: Short Stories by Outstanding Writers for Young Adults, Delacorte (New York, NY), 1984.
Mark I. West, editor, *Trust Your Children: Voices against Censorship in Children's Literature,* Neal-Schuman (New York, NY), 1987.

Fitchburg Sentinel, author of book review column "The Sentinel Bookman," 1964-78, and of human interest column under pseudonym John Fitch IV, 1969-78; also author of monthly human interest column "1177 Main Street," for *St. Anthony Messenger,* 1972-82. Contributor of articles and short stories to periodicals, most under t he pseudonym John Fitch IV, including *Catholic Library World, McCall's, Redbook, Saturday Evening Post, Sign,* and *Woman's Day.*

Several of Cormier's novels have been translated into French, Spanish, Italian, Swedish, Japanese, Danish, Hungarian, German, and other languages.

ADAPTATIONS: I Am the Cheese, a motion picture adapted from Cormier's novel of the same name, was released in 1983 by the Almi Group, starring Robert Wagner, Hope Lange, Robert Macnaughton, and featuring Cormier in the role of Mr. Hertz; *The Chocolate War* was released as a movie of the same title by Management Company Entertainment Group in 1989, directed by Keith Gordon and starring John Glover, Ilan Mitchell-Smith, and Wally Ward. *The Chocolate War, I Am the Cheese,* and *Tunes for Bears to Dance To* were all adapted as audio books, 1993, *Beyond the Chocolate War,* 1994; and *The Rag and Bone Shop,* 2002, all by Recorded Books, Inc.

SIDELIGHTS: Robert Cormier was widely acclaimed for his powerful and disturbing novels for young adult readers, though his realistic subject matter—including murder, sex, and terminal illness—at times made his work controversial. His novels, which include *The Chocolate War* and *I Am the Cheese,* often involve teenage protagonists faced with difficult, uncompromising situations. "A lot of people underestimate that intelligent teenager out there," Cormier noted in an interview for *Authors and Artists for Young Adults.* "These kids today, I'm talking about the sensitive, intelligent kid, are really far ahead of a lot of adults. They have been exposed to so much. Anybody who writes down to these people is making a mistake."

Cormier wrote and published three adult novels before writing *The Chocolate War* in 1974. Young adult readers received *The Chocolate War* with great enthusiasm, as they have all Cormier's young adult offerings. "Cormier seems to believe that teenagers are more idealistic today than in years past," Joe Stines observed in *Dict ionary of Literary Biography,* "and he affords them respect and responsibility in his writing while simultaneously awakening them to the harsh realities of life in contemporary America." Cormier did this only incidentally, though, his first and foremost intent was to tell a gripping story based on emotions, character, and plot. Cormier wro te *The Chocolate War* because of a true-life experience in which his son was the only person in his class to refuse to sell chocolates for a high school fund raiser, leading Cormier to ponder issues such as peer and faculty pressure and explore themes such as manipulation and what happens when an individual balks societal norms.

His other books have also been written to find answers to "what if?" questions. *I Am the Cheese,* for example, was written after Cormier read about the U.S. Witness Relocation Program. It tells the story of a boy whose father testified against organized crime figures, but even new identities do not protect the family from harm. News of terrorist hijackings drove Cormier to write *After the First Death.* So important was his need to be interested that if Cormier did not become emotionally engaged by the subject, he found himself unable to continue writing about it.

In *We All Fall Down,* Cormier tackles teenage violence firsthand with the story of a group of boys who vandalize a suburban home and attack a young girl. As is typical of a Cormier novel, he went on to further explore good and evil when one of the attackers falls in love with the girl's older sister. Clouding the arena further is the exis tence of a voyeur, known only as The Avenger. Nancy Vsilakis, writing for *Horn Book,* called the novel "a gripping page-turner," noting "The black hole down which the novelist draws the reader is both repellant and enthralling." "Most of us forget the aching awfulness of adolescence when we become adults. It's Cormi-

er's special b urden to remember," wrote Michael Cart in the *Los Angeles Times Book Review.* It was also Cormier's gift, Cart continued, "to be able to translate that memory into novels of intensity, immediacy and empathy." Citing Cormier's manipulation of the reader through "artificial" techniques, Mike Hayhoe of *School Librarian* admitt ed, "As an admirer of Cormier, I had an uneasy feeling that this [manipulation] sometimes moved towards the artifice of Stephen King; but I am confident that many readers will disagree strongly with me on that point!"

Cormier's 1995 novel, *In the Middle of the Night,* is based on a true event in which five hundred people died in a fire in an overcrowded nightclub. A busboy was initially blamed for lighting a match but was eventually exonerated. Cormier's story twists the nightclub into a cinema and the victims to children. He then picked up twenty-five years later with the usher receiving midnight phone calls from parents of the children while his sixteen-year-old son listens. "Unnerving and piercingly honest," noted Lois Metzger in the *New York Times Book Review.* While Elizabeth Hand in her review for *Washington Post Book World* called the plot "brazenly manipulative, the c haracterization unpleasant and dank," Patty Campbell, critic for *Horn Book,* called the tale "pure Cormier, a tight and spare construction of amazing complexity worthy of a place among his best works."

Cormier also wrote several books for a younger audience than the intended readers of *The Chocolate War.* Set during World War II, *Other Bells for Us to Ring* tells the story of eleven-year-old Darcy, who has just moved to Frenchtown, Massachusetts. In an article for *Horn Book,* Mary M. Burns, comparing the book to Cormier's pr evious books for older children, called it "no less thought-provoking, no less intense in its emotional impact, no less remarkable for carefully honed phrases and an unfailing sense of the right detail to convey an idea." Burns concluded her praise by calling *Other Bells for Us to Ring* "one of those rare and brilliant gems for all se asons and for all those who would be possessed by its honest poignancy and superb craftsmanship." Janice M. Del Negro, reviewer for *School Library Journal,* was less impressed. While Del Negro praised Cormier's "effective evoking" of a bygone time and place but called the characters "flat and two-dimensional."

Tunes for Bears to Dance To, published in 1992, was also aimed at younger children, although it retained Cormier's "enormous capacity for evoking the positive force of evil," as a reviewer for the *Junior Bookshelf* noted. Eleven-year-old Henry is the surviving child in a house where his older brother's death has traumatized hi s parents. After his family moves to a different home to banish these memories, Henry befriends a concentration camp survivor who spends his hours recreating the village he lived in before it was devastated by Nazis. In the *Washington Post Book World*, Anne Scott wrote that in the novel Cormier "stacks the deck of trouble and darkness more absolutely and less effectively than he has in his previous work." A *Kirkus Reviews* critic felt that the tale was "ultimately less grim" than Cormier's previous work and called it a "thought-provoking story."

Tenderness, the story of a cat-and-mouse game between a clean-cut, handsome eighteen-year-old serial killer and a veteran cop, involving a sexually precocious fifteen-year-old female runaway, is one of Cormier's darkest novels. According to a *Booklist* contributor "the sexual component here is far stronger than in Cormier's earli er books." Lori, a victim of sexual harassment and abuse, uses her sexuality to get what she wants; and, like Eric, the serial killer, she searches for genuine tenderness. "It is the idea of Eric's humanity that is the most disquieting aspect of the novel," maintained the critic for *Booklist*, adding that the killer's humanity was als o what "makes the book so seductive." A reviewer writing in *Kirkus Reviews* praised the "devastatingly ironic climax." A *Horn Book* contributor praised the style as "vintage Cormier: short pithy sentences and bends in the text that take the reader along startling paths." The reviewer also called Cormier a "master of ir ony" but lamented that "the basic premise—that there will be a serious exploration of tenderness—is unfulfilled."

Frenchtown Summer, published in 2000, is the story of a boy named Eugene, his observations on post World War II life, and his desire to connect with his father. A critic for *Publishers Weekly* wrote, "Eugene is a ghostly presence here, taking readers back in time and slowly mesmerizing them with his memories of coming of age." Written in verse through a series of vignettes, Cormier engaged his readers with a new writing style. Another reviewer for *Publishers Weekly* noted that the "novel-in-verse slowly mesmerizes." Patty Campbell for *Horn Book* wrote: "What an astonishment that the grandmaster of the YA novel has turned to poetry at this point in hi s career. . . . A treat for Cormier fans, and a revelation for others." "Cormier continues to demonstrate his unrivaled power to dazzle and delight his readers" commented Michael Cart for *Booklist*.

Cormier always maintained that he did not include explicit scenes or controversial subject matter for their market value. "All that controversial stuff, all that stuff that upsets people, is almost secondary in my mind as I write it," Cormier told to Roger Sutton in *School Library Journal*. "And yet there's always the qualifier the re, you know the readers are out there." Cornier went on to note that he often modified his scenes to make sure "[I] wasn't being titillating or exploitive, that I didn't make the acts sound attractive. I wanted to make them sound sordid, and I tried to make them brief. So there is that consciousness there as you're writing all the time. But again it's all bent on the altar of storytelling."

Whatever objections people have to Cormier's books, his works are commercially successful; avid fans in many countries have purchased millions of copies. "Cormier has acquired these fans," wrote Sylvia Patterson Iskander in *Concise Dictionary of American Literary Biography*, "because of his sensitive awareness about what actually o ccurs in the lives of teenagers today and his abundant talent for conveying that awareness through fiction. He has brought controversy and, simultaneously, a new dimension to the field of young-adult literature. He has earned the respect of his readers, regardless of their age, because of his refusal to compromise the truth as he sees it. His supe rb craftsmanship, his ability to create suspense and to shock the reader repeatedly, and his forcing the reader to think are all qualities which make Cormier's works entertaining, unique, and, indeed, unforgettable."

In 2001, Cormier's final novel *The Rag and Bone Shop* was published posthumously. The story focuses on twelve-year-old Jason who is being questioned by a detective named Trent who suspects him of murdering a young girl. As the last person to see her alive, Jason is the prime suspect. However, Trent, an expert interrogator, is more intent on w ringing out a confession from the young boy than on finding the truth. With his vast experience, Trent is able to make Jason doubt his memory and even his sense of reality. Roger Sutton, writing in *Horn Book*, felt that "the story elides reality too consistently and thoroughly to give its conclusion the impact it very much wants to h ave." Lori Atkins Goodson gave the book a favorable review in *Journal of Adolescent & Adult Literacy*, noting, "There are no winners in this book, except for the readers, who are treated to an intense voyage with the master of young adult novels at the helm." A *Publishers Weekly* contributor called the book "characteristi cally dark and though-provoking" and noted that the interrogation reflected "a taut, sinister mind game." The reviewer concluded, "The chilling results of the questioning will leave an indelible mark on readers and prompt heated discussions regarding the definition of guilt and the fine line between truth and deception."

In a *World and I* article reviewing Cormier's life and works, J.B. Cheaney noted that Cormier's YA novels are much more than novels "full of gratuitous violence, vulgar language and sex." Cheaney went on to note, "Cormier's concerns are much larger. Too many YA authors make innocent victims of their protagonists, or reduce their ch aracters' choices to whether or not to have sex or run away from home. Cormier alerts his readers that their problems may not be entirely 'out there'; some of the darkness is within."

BIOGRAPHICAL AND CRITICAL SOURCES:

BOOKS

Authors and Artists for Young Adults, Volume 3, Thomson Gale (Detroit, MI), 1990, pp. 65-76, interview with author.
Campbell, Patricia J., *Presenting Robert Cormier,* Twayne (Boston, MA), 1985.
Children's Literature Review, Volume 12, Thomson Gale (Detroit, MI), 1987.
Concise Dictionary of American Literary Biography: Broadening Views, 1968-1988, Thomson Gale (Detroit, MI), 1989, pp. 34-51.
Contemporary Literary Criticism, Volume 17, 1980; Volume 30, 1984.
Dictionary of Literary Biography, Volume 52: *American Writers for Children since 1960,* Thomson Gale (Detroit, MI), 1986, pp. 107-14.
Inglis, Fred, *The Promise of Happiness: Value and Meaning in Children's Fiction,* Cambridge University Press (New York, NY), 1981.
Rees, David, *The Marble in the Water: Essays on Contemporary Writers of Fiction for Children and Young Adults,* Horn Books (Boston, MA), 1980.
Twentieth-Century Children's Writers, 3rd edition, St. James Press (Chicago, IL), 1989.

PERIODICALS

Booklist, September 15, 1999, Michael Cart, review of *Frenchtown Summer,* p. 259.
Christian Science Monitor, February 10, 2000, review of *Frenchtown Summer,* p. 21.
English Journal, November, 1989; January, 1990; April, 1992; November, 1992.

Horn Book, March-April, 1985; May-June, 1985, pp. 289-96; March-April, 1989; November-December, 1990; November-December, 1991, p. 742; May-June, 1995, Patty Campbell, review of *In the Middle of the Night,* p. 365; February, 1997; September, 1999, Patty Campbell, review of *Frenchtown Summer,* p. 608; November-December, 2001, R oger Sutton, review of *The Rag and Bone Shop,* p. 742.
Journal of Adolescent & Adult Literacy, September, 2002, Lori Atkins Goodson, review of *The Rag and Bone Shop,* p. 87.
Junior Bookshelf, August, 1992, review of *Tunes for Bears to Dance To,* p. 161.
Kirkus Reviews, October 1, 1992, p. 1252; January 1, 1997.
Lion and the Unicorn: A Critical Journal of Children's Literature, June 12, 1988, pp. 12-18.
Los Angeles Times Book Review, October 27, 1991, Michael Cart, review of *We All Fall Down,,* p. 7.
New Statesman, April 17, 1987.
New York Times Book Review, February 12, 1989; July 16, 1995, Lois Metzger, review of *In the Middle of the Night,* p. 27.
Publishers Weekly, July 29, 1988; November 16, 1990, p. 57; October 25, 1991, p. 69; September 7, 1992, p. 97; July 19, 1999, review of *Frenchtown Summer,* p. 195; November 1, 1999, review of *Frenchtown Summer,* p. 57; October 15, 2001, review of *The Rag and Bone Shop,* p. 72.
School Librarian, August, 1992, Mike Hayhoe, review of *We All Fall Down,* p. 112.
School Library Journal, November, 1990; June, 1991, pp. 28-33; September, 1991, p. 277; September, 1992, p. 97; September, 1999, Edward Sullivan, review of *Frenchtown Summer,* p. 22.
Tribune Books (Chicago, IL), January 12, 1992, p. 6.
Voice of Youth Advocates, August, 1988, pp. 122-24.
Washington Post Book World, December 6, 1992, Anne Scott, review of *Tunes for Bears to Dance To,* p. 20; May 7, 1995.
World and I, December, 2001, J.B. Cheaney, "Teen Wars: The Young Adult Fiction of Robert Cormier," p. 256.

OBITUARIES:

PERIODICALS

Boston Globe, November 3, 2000.
New York Times, November 5, 2000.

CORMIER, Robert Edmund
See CORMIER, Robert

* * *

CORNWELL, David John Moore
See le CARRé, John

* * *

CORNWELL, Patricia 1956-
(Patricia Daniels Cornwell)

PERSONAL: Born June 9, 1956, in Miami, FL; daughter of Sam (an attorney) and Marilyn (a secretary; maiden name, Zenner) Daniels; married Charles Cornwell (a college professor), June 14, 1980 (divorced, 1990). *Education:* Davidson College, North Carolina, B.A., 1979. *Religion:* Presbyterian. *Hobbies and other interests:* Tennis.

ADDRESSES: Home—Greenwich, CT. *Office*—Cornwell Enterprises, P.O. Box 35686, Richmond, VA 23235. *Agent*—International Creative Management, 40 West 57th St., New York, NY 10019.

CAREER: Novelist. *Charlotte Observer,* Charlotte, NC, police reporter, 1979-81; Office of the Chief Medical Examiner, Richmond, VA, computer analyst and technical writer, 1985-91. President of Bell Vision Productions (film production company); worked as a volunteer police officer.

MEMBER: International Crime Writers Association, International Association of Chiefs of Police, International Association of Identification, National Association of Medical Examiners, Authors Guild, Authors League, Mystery Writers of America, Virginia Writers Club.

AWARDS, HONORS: Investigative reporting award, North Carolina Press Association, 1980, for a series on prostitution; Gold Medallion Book Award for biography, Evangelical Christian Publishers Association, 1985, for *A Time for Remembering: The Story of Ruth Bell Graham;* John Creasey Award, British Crime Writers Association, Edgar Award, Mystery Writers of America, Anthony Award, Boucheron/World Mystery Convention, and Macavity Award, Mystery Readers International, all for best first crime novel, all 1990, and French Prix du Roman d'Aventure, 1991, all for *Postmortem;* Gold Dagger award, for *Cruel and Unusual,* 1993.

WRITINGS:

NOVELS

Postmortem, Scribner (New York, NY), 1990.
Body of Evidence, Scribner (New York, NY), 1991.
All That Remains, Scribner (New York, NY), 1992.
Cruel and Unusual, Scribner (New York, NY), 1993.
The Body Farm, Scribner (New York, NY), 1994.
From Potter's Field, Scribner (New York, NY), 1995.
Cause of Death, Putnam (New York, NY), 1996.
Hornet's Nest, Putnam (New York, NY), 1997.
Unnatural Exposure, Putnam (New York, NY), 1997.
Three Complete Novels: Postmortem, Body of Evidence, All That Remains, Smithmark Publishers (New York, NY), 1997.
Point of Origin, Putnam (New York, NY), 1998.
Southern Cross, Putnam (New York, NY), 1998.
Black Notice, Putnam (New York, NY), 1999.
The Last Precinct Putnam (New York, NY), 2000.
Isle of Dogs, Little, Brown (Boston, MA), 2001.
Blow Fly, Putnam (New York, NY), 2003.
Trace, Putnam (New York, NY), 2004.
Predator, Putnam (New York, NY), 2005.
At Risk, Putnam (New York, NY), 2006.

OTHER

A Time for Remembering: The Story of Ruth Bell Graham (biography), Harper & Row (San Francisco, CA), 1983.
Scarpetta's Winter Table, Wyrick (Charleston, SC), 1998.
Life's Little Fable (children's book), illustrated by Barbara Leonard Gibson, Putnam (New York, NY), 1999.
(With Marlene Brown) *Food to Die For: Secrets from Kay Scarpetta's Kitchen,* Putnam (New York, NY), 2001.
Portrait of a Killer: Jack the Ripper—Case Closed, Putnam (New York, NY), 2002.

ADAPTATIONS: Brilliance Corp. released a sound recording of *Body of Evidence* in 1992; sound recordings are also available for *Postmortem, All That Remains, Cruel and Unusual, The Body Farm,* and *From Potter's*

Field; negotiations are in progress for the film rights to *From Potter's Field;* Columbia Pictures is planning a film treatment of *Cruel and Unusual* and *Unnatural Exposure.*

SIDELIGHTS: Since 1990 Patricia Cornwell's novels have followed Dr. Kay Scarpetta, a medical examiner called upon to solve murders with forensic sleuthing. The "Scarpetta" novels are praised for their accurate detail based upon research Cornwell did in the Virginia medical examiner's office, witnessing scores of autopsies. In addition to this, Cornwell also went out on police homicide runs. "I'm not sure I could have read my last book if I hadn't written it," Cornwell told Sandra McElwaine in *Harper's Bazaar.* "The violence is so real, I think it would have scared me to death."

Cornwell began her book-writing career in 1983 with a biography of Ruth Graham, wife of evangelist Billy Graham. It was Graham who encouraged her to pursue writing. "I felt she had real ability," Graham told Joe Treen in *People.* "I've kept every note I ever got from her." With Graham's encouragement, Cornwell went back to school at Davidson College in North Carolina, majoring in English. Right after graduation she married Charles Cornwell, one of her former professors, and began working as a crime reporter for the *Charlotte Observer.*

"I had a compulsion to get close to every story. I really wanted to solve crimes," Cornwell told McElwaine. In 1980, Cornwell received an investigative reporting award from the North Carolina Press Association for a series she did on prostitution. Unfortunately, just when she felt her career was getting underway, her husband decided that he wanted to become a minister, and the couple moved to Richmond, Virginia, where he attended Union Theological Seminary. "I did not want to give up the *Observer,*" she told Treen. "It was a very bad time for me."

Cornwell began working on a biography of her good friend Graham, which kept her busy for a few years until it was published in 1983. She had always pictured herself as a novelist, so she decided to try writing crime novels with the information she had gathered as a reporter. She realized that she would need to do more in-depth research to make her murder plots seem more believable. A friend recommended that she might try talking to the deputy medical examiner at the Virginia Morgue. Cornwell took the advice.

At her first appointment with Dr. Marcella Fierro, Cornwell was introduced to a whole world of high-tech forensic procedures that she knew nothing about. "I was

shocked by two things," Cornwell told Joanne Tangorra in *Publishers Weekly.* "One, by how fascinating it was, and two, by how absolutely little I knew about it. I realized I had no idea what a medical examiner would do—Did they put on gloves, wear lab coats and surgical greens? They do none of the above." After a short time, Cornwell began doing technical writing for the medical examiner's office.

Cornwell soon became a regular visitor at the forensic center and also took on technical writing projects for the morgue to absorb more of the forensic knowledge she craved. Working at the morgue led Cornwell to write her first novel, *Postmortem,* featuring the fictional investigative forensic pathologist, Dr. Kay Scarpetta.

Postmortem focuses on the rape and murder of several Richmond women by a serial killer. The book charts the work of Scarpetta, the chief medical examiner of Virginia, as she attempts to uncover the killer's identity. Frequently faced with sexism regarding her ability to handle a "man's job," Scarpetta aptly displays her knowledge of the innovative technologies of today's forensic medicine to crack the case. "Dr. Scarpetta has a terrible time with the chauvinists around her, one of whom in particular is malevolently eager for her to fail," wrote Charles Champlin in the *Los Angeles Times Book Review.* "These passages have the ring of truth as experienced, and so does the portrait of an investigative reporter who abets the solving."

Postmortem "won just about every mystery fiction award," declared *New York Times Book Review* contributor Bill Kent. "The follow-up novel, *Body of Evidence,* proved that Ms. Cornwell's success wasn't mere beginner's luck." *Body of Evidence* centers on Beryl Madison, a young woman who is writing a controversial book for which she has received death threats. Shortly after she reports these events she is murdered—apparently after allowing the killer to enter her home. Scarpetta must once again use tiny bits of evidence to track down the murderer.

In *Cruel and Unusual,* Cornwell introduces Temple Gault, a serial killer with intelligence to match Scarpetta's. Gault, who specializes in the murder of children, only narrowly escapes being captured by Scarpetta herself. "With his pale blue eyes and his ability to anticipate the best minds of law enforcement," wrote Elise O'Shaughnessy in the *New York Times Book Review,* "Gault is a 'malignant genius' in the tradition of Hannibal Lecter," the cannibalistic character in Thomas Harris's *The Silence of the Lambs.* "Like Lecter's bond with Clarice Starling," O'Shaughnessy concluded, "Gault's relationship with Scarpetta is *personal.*"

Gault appears again in the 1995 novel *From Potter's Field,* when he murders a young girl on Christmas Eve in Central Park. Scarpetta is called in to investigate the murder and ends up in a face- to-face confrontation with Gault. Critics again noted the research involved in the novel, as Mary B. W. Tabor commented in the *New York Times:* "There is something especially savory about novels set in real places, with real street names, real shops, real sights and smells that ring true for those who know the territory." *Booklist* reviewer Emily Melton compared reading *From Potter's Field* to "riding one of those amusement-park roller coasters . . . [that leave] the rider gasping and breathless." Melton lauded Cornwell's "magnificent plotting, masterful writing, and marvelous suspense," rating her among the top crime fiction writers.

Cornwell continued the Scarpetta series with *Cause of Death, Unnatural Exposure,* and *Point of Origin.* In the 1999 novel *Black Notice,* Scarpetta falls into an international mystery involving "the Werewolf," a killer named Jean-Baptiste Chandonne. *Library Journal* reviewer Leslie Madden observed, "This novel focuses on the features that made Cornwell's earliest novels so interesting—the slow unraveling of a mystery using Scarpetta's skill and intelligence." A reviewer for *Publishers Weekly* declared, "The forensic sequences boom with authority; the brief action sequences explode on the page." Cornwell continues the *Black Notice* storyline in *The Last Precinct* and *Blow Fly.* "Cornwell writes, as usual, with unwavering intensity in this grisly, fast-paced thriller. The effect: utterly chilling," concluded *Entertainment Weekly* reviewer, Jennifer Reese about *Blow Fly.*

In a column for *Mystery Scene* magazine, Cornwell shed some light on the nature of her heroine, Dr. Scarpetta. "Violence is filtered through her intellectual sophistication and inbred civility, meaning that the senseless cruelty of what she sees is all the more horrific," the author explained. She added that Dr. Scarpetta "approaches the cases with the sensitivity of a physician, the rational thinking of a scientist, and the outrage of a humane woman who values, above all else, the sanctity of life. Through Dr. Scarpetta's character I began to struggle with an irony that had eluded me before: the more expert one gets in dismantling death, the less he understands it."

Cornwell has written several other novels in addition to the Scarpetta series. *Hornet's Nest, Southern Cross,* and *Isle of Dogs* feature Judy Hammer and Andy Brazil as Virginia police officers. These books do not have the technical forensic writing of Cornwell's Scarpetta novels. In addition to her novels, Cornwell has coauthored a book of recipes titled *Food to Die For: Secrets from Kay Scarpetta's Kitchen,* and a similar novella called *Scarpetta's Winter Table,* which breaks down the ingredients for some of Scarpetta's favorite dishes, but lacks detailed recipes. She also wrote a children's book called *Life's Little Fable,* about a boy named Jarrod who lives in a land filled with sunlight, but whose curious nature leads him to explore a mysterious pond.

In 2002 Cornwell released the nonfiction book *Portrait of a Killer: Jack the Ripper—Case Closed.* The book is based on the infamous killer known as Jack the Ripper, who murdered prostitutes and terrorized London in the late 1880s. The book discusses Cornwell's forensic research and findings. Cornwell paints vivid pictures of Victorian London, specifically the crime scenes left behind by Jack the Ripper. In the book, Cornwell fingers artist Walter Sickert as the notorious killer. Though Cornwell has been criticized for basing her conclusion largely on circumstantial evidence, a *Publishers Weekly* reviewer described the book as "compassionate, intense, superbly argued, fluidly written and impossible to put down."

In *Trace,* the thirteenth Kay Scarpetta novel, Cornwell weaves a story about a human-ashes-obsessed psychopath named Edgar Allan Pogue, a dead teenager, and Scarpetta's angsty past. Called back to Virginia from Florida, where she has been working with her niece Lucy, Scarpetta is puzzled by the unexplained correlation between the deaths of the teenager and construction worker at a demolition site. She's less than pleased to deal with Dr. Marcus, who usurped her position as the state's medical examiner and ran her out of town five years ago. Numerous subplots weave danger and deceit from all directions as Scarpetta and sidekick Pete Marino try to sidestep the mayhem during their investigation. Critics agreed that the book would please Cornwell's fans. Though Leslie Madden of *Library Journal* said the book "[Lacks] the intensity of Cornwell's earlier works," Sean Daly of *People Weekly* called the climax "slick [and] unsettling" and complimented Cornwell on her ability to "generate willies with subtle poetic turns." A writer for *Kirkus Reviews* said the author "hits all her high notes," and Marilyn Stasio of the *New York Times Book Review* proclaimed *Trace* a welcome return to the series' former glory. Scarpetta's "recovery of her sharp tongue and imperious manner, as much as the state-of-the-art facilities of her beloved lab, fires her up to perform some of her best and most professionally rewarding work in years," Stasio wrote. "Although Cornwell's over- the-top series will probably never return to its realistic beginnings," she concluded, "it's a relief to find Scarpetta back in the lab where she belongs, up to her elbows in guts and gore."

In *Predator,* another Kay Scarpetta novel, Scarpetta takes the case of a psychopath who captures and tortures his victims in a house. Margaret Cannon, writing for the *Globe & Mail,* pointed out the novel's "solid plotline" but also commented that "this isn't [Cornwell's] worst novel . . . but it's far from her best." Stasio noted that "the contrived plot . . . plays out in too fragmented a form to sustain much suspense." However, she complimented Cornwell's ability to bring the killers "to full, frightening life."

BIOGRAPHICAL AND CRITICAL SOURCES:

BOOKS

American Women Writers: A Critical Reference Guide: From Colonial Time to the Present, St. James Press (Detroit, MI), 2000.

Beahm, George W., *The Unofficial Patricia Cornwell Companion,* St. Martin's Press (New York, NY), 2002.

Contemporary Southern Writers, St. James Press (Detroit, MI), 1999.

Mystery and Suspense Writers: The Literature of Crime, Detection, and Espionage, Scribner (New York, NY), 1998.

Newsmakers, Issue 1, Gale (Detroit, MI), 2003.

PERIODICALS

Armchair Detective, winter, 1991, p. 32.

Book, September, 1999, review of *Black Notice,* p. 70.

Booklist, May 1, 1995; December 15, 1999, Karen Harris, audio book review of *Southern Cross,* p. 798; May 1, 2000, Karen Harris, audio book review of *Black Notice,* p. 1626; September 1, 2000, Stephanie Zvirin, review of *The Last Precinct,* p. 6; October 15, 2001, Mark Knoblauch, review of *Food to Die For: Secrets from Kay Scarpetta's Kitchen,* p. 370; April 15, 2002, audio book review of *Isle of Dogs,* p. 1423; December 1, 2002, Brad Hooper, review of *Portrait of a Killer: Jack the Ripper—Case Closed,* p. 626.

Books, autumn, 1999, review of *Black Notice,* p. 18; Christmas 2001, review of *Isle of Dogs,* p. 18.

Bookseller, November 8, 2002, "Retailers Tied by Cornwell Embargo," p. 7.

Book World, October 17, 1999, review of *Black Notice,* p. 13.

Children's Book Review Service, August, 1999, review of *Life's Little Fable,* p. 157.

Children's Bookwatch, August, 1999, review of *Life's Little Fable,* p. 3.

Detroit Free Press, October 14, 2001, review of *Isle of Dogs,* p. 4E; April 14, 2002, review of *From Potter's Field,* p. 5E.

Economist (U.K.), June 19, 1999, review of *Black Notice,* p. S4.

Entertainment Weekly, June 26, 1992, p. 73; January 25, 2002, Matthew Flamm, "Between the Lines: The Inside Scoop on the Book World," p. 97; October 17, 2003, Jennifer Reese, review of *Blow Fly,* p. 86.

Europe Intelligence Wire, November 11, 2002, "Patricia Cornwell Fingers Painter As Jack the Ripper."

Globe & Mail (Toronto, Ontario, Canada), February 13, 1999, review of *Southern Cross,* p. D13; August 28, 1999, review of *Black Notice,* p. D17; October 20, 2001, review of *Isle of Dogs,* p. D22; November 24, 2001, audio book review of *Isle of Dogs,* p. D27; November 26, 2005, Margaret Cannon, "Have a Killer Christmas: Gifts. Family. Murder. Margaret Cannon Offers a Cozy Mix of Holiday Mayhem," p. D34.

Guardian, December 8, 2001, Fiachra Gibbons, "Does This Painting by Walter Sickert Reveal the Identity of Jack the Ripper?," p. 3; December 8, 2001, Mark Lawson, "A Novelist at the Scene of the Crime," p. 20.

Harper's Bazaar, August, 1992, pp. 46, 148.

Independent, November 17, 2001, Dina Rabinovitch, "Anatomy of a Gentle Ghoul," p. WR10.

Kirkus Reviews, June 1, 1995; January 1, 1999, review of *Southern Cross,* p. 30; July 1, 1999, review of *Black Notice,* p. 837; August 1, 2004, a review of *Trace,* p. 715.

Kliatt Young Adult Paperback Book Guide, November, 1999, audio book review of *Black Notice,* p. 48; March, 2001, audio book review of *The Last Precinct,* p. 52; March, 2002, audio book review of *Isle of Dogs,* p. 49.

Knight Ridder/Tribune News Service, August 4, 1999, Linda B. Blackford, review of *Black Notice,* p. K6581; October 18, 2000, Connie Ogle, review of *The Last Precinct,* p. K4862; November 1, 2000, Jeff Guinn, "Dissecting Patricia Cornwell," p. K1359; November 1, 200, Jeff Guinn, review of *The Last Precinct,* p. K2261; December 11, 2002, Oline H. Cogdill, audio book review of *Portrait of a Killer,* p. K4617.

Library Journal, September 1, 1994, p. 213; February 15, 1999, audio book review of *Point of Origin,* p. 126; April 15, 1999, Leslie Madden, review of *Point of Origin,* p. 142; July 1999, Leslie Madden, review of *Black Notice,* p. 129; September 1, 1999, Joyce Kessel, audio book review of *Southern Cross,* p. 252; November 15, 1999, Jennifer Belford, audio book review of *Black Notice,* p. 116; October 15, 2000, Leslie Madden, review of *The Last Precinct,* p. 101; February 15, 2001, audio book review of *Isle of Dogs,* p. 194; March 1, 2001, audio book review of *The Last Precinct,* p. 152; April 1, 2003, Joyce Kessel, audio book review of *Portrait of a Killer,* p. 147; September 15, 2004, Leslie Madden, a review of *Trace,* p. 48.

Los Angeles Times, March 28, 1991, p. F12; February 2, 2003, Eugen Weber, review of *Portrait of a Killer,* p. R11.

Los Angeles Times Book Review, February 11, 1990, p. 5; February 10, 1991, p. 9; September 20, 1992, p. 8; February 1, 1999, review of *Southern Cross,* p. 9.

M2 Best Books, April 18, 2002, Darren Ingram, review of *Food to Die For.*

Mystery Scene, January, 1990, pp. 56-57.

National Post, January 18, 2003, Lynn Crosbie, "Relentless Pursuit of the Elusive Ripper," review of *Portrait of a Killer,* p. SP4.

New Straits Times, February 6, 2001, Martin Spice, "In Better (If Not Best) Form," review of *The Last Precinct;* August 6, 2001, Manveet Kaur, review of *The Last Precinct.*

Newsweek, August 3, 1992; July 5, 1993.

New York Times Book Review, January 7, 1990; February 24, 1991; August 23, 1992; April 4, 1993, p. 19; July 4, 1993; September 16, 1994, pp. 38-39; January 10, 1999, Marilyn Stasio, review of *Southern Cross,* p. 18; August 8, 1999, Marilyn Stasio, review of *Black Notice,* p. 21; November 5, 2000, Marilyn Stasio, review of *The Last Precinct,* p. 32; December 15, 2002, Caleb Carr, review of *Portrait of a Killer,* p. 15; September 19, 2004, Marilyn Stasio, a review of *Trace,* p. 15; December 11, 2005, Marilyn Stasio, "Sex and Violet," p. 33.

Observer (London, England), February 28, 1999, review of *Southern Cross,* p. 12.

People, August 24, 1992, pp. 71- 72; October 3, 1994, pp. 37-38; November 5, 2001, review of *Isle of Dogs,* p. 51; December 9, 2002, Galina Espinoza, "Killer Instinct: Author Patricia Cornwell Thinks She Has Unmasked a Notorious Serial Killer. Critics Say She Doesn't Know Jack," p. 101; October 27, 2003, Edward Karam, review of *Blow Fly,* p. 50; September 13, 2004, Sean Daly, a review of *Trace,* p. 56.

Publishers Weekly, December 7, 1990, p. 76; February 15, 1991, pp. 71-72; June 15, 1992, p. 89; September 12, 1994; January 4, 1999, review of *Southern Cross,* p. 76; June 14, 1999, review of *Black Notice,* p. 52; September 25, 2000, review of *The Last Precinct,* p. 90; January 1, 2001, audio book review of *The Last Precinct,* p. 42; January 8, 2001, review of *The Last Precinct,* p. 35; October 15, 2001, review of *Food to Die For,* p. 65; November 11, 2002, review of *Portrait of a Killer,* p. 52; November 11, 2002, Jeff Zaleski, "On the Trail of Jack the Ripper," p. 53; January 6, 2003, audio book review of *Portrait of a Killer,* p. 20.

School Library Journal, December, 1992, pp. 146-147; July, 1999, review of *Life's Little Fable,* p. 68.

Scientist, February 10, 2003, Terry Melton, review of *Portrait of a Killer,* p. 16.

Skeptical Inquirer, March-April, 2003, Joe Nickell, review of *Portrait of a Killer,* p. 27.

Spectator, November 9, 2002, Richard Sloane, review of *Portrait of a Killer,* p. 84.

Sunday Times (London, England), August 13, 2000, John Harlow, "Thriller Queen Is World's Top Woman Writer," p. 20; November 18, 2001, Joan Smith, review of *Isle of Dogs,* p. C48.

Time, September 14, 1992; October 3, 1994.

Times (London, England), November 27, 2001, Penny Wark, "I'm Over Sex and Fame," p. S4.

Times Educational Supplement (London, England), December 17, 1999, review of *Black Notice,* p. 19.

Times Literary Supplement (London, England), July 16, 1993, p. 22; January 22, 1999, review of *Southern Cross,* p. 21; October 1, 1999, Lucy Atkins, review of *Black Notice,* p. 21; October 27, 2000, Heather O'Donoghue, review of *The Last Precinct,* p. 23.

Times of India, December 10, 2001, "Ripper: Mystery Unfolds Yet Again."

Wall Street Journal, August 27, 1999, Bob Hughes, review of *Black Notice,* p. W7.

Washington Post Book World, January 21, 1990, p. 6.

Wilson Library Bulletin, December, 1993.

Women's Quarterly, summer, 2001, Charlotte Hays and Ivy McClure Stewart, "Politically Correct Private Eyes," p. 18.

ONLINE

ABC News Web site, http://www.abcnews.com/ (October 29, 2003), "Stalking Jack the Ripper: A Crime Novelist Is Obsessed with a 113-Year-Old Case."

BookReporter.com, http://www.bookreporter.com/ (April 24, 2003).

Patricia Cornwell Web site, http://www.patricia cornwell.com/ (October 28, 2003).

Richmond Review Online, http://www.richmondreview. co.uk/ (April 24, 2003), Chris Wood, review of *Black Notice.*

Tangled Web UK Web site, http://www.twbooks.co.uk/ (October 29, 2003).

USA Weekend Online, http://www.usaweekend.com/ (October 29, 2003), Jeffrey Zaslow, "Straight Talk."

*   *   *

CORNWELL, Patricia Daniels
See CORNWELL, Patricia

*   *   *

CORSO, Gregory 1930-2001
(Nunzio Gregory Corso)

PERSONAL: Born March 26, 1930, in New York, NY; died from prostate cancer January 17, 2001, in Minneapolis, MN; son of Fortunato Samuel and Michelina (Colonni) Corso; married Sally November (a teacher), May 7, 1963 (divorced); married Belle Carpenter, 1968 (marriage ended); married Jocelyn Stern; children: (first marriage) Mirandia; (second marriage) Cybelle Nuncia, Max-Orphe. *Education:* Attended grammar school. *Politics:* "Individualism and freedom." *Religion:* "God."

CAREER: Writer. Manual laborer in New York, NY, 1950-51; employee of *Los Angeles Examiner,* Los Angeles, CA, 1951-52; merchant seaman on Norwegian vessels, 1952-53. English department, State University of New York at Buffalo, 1965-70. Appeared in Peter Whitehead's film, *Wholly Communion,* and in Andy Warhol's *Couch.*

AWARDS, HONORS: Longview Award for poem "Marriage"; Poetry Foundation award; Jean Stein Award for Poetry, American Academy and Institute of Arts and Letters, 1986.

WRITINGS:

The Vestal Lady on Brattle, and Other Poems, R. Brukenfeld (Cambridge, MA), 1955.

In This Hung-up Age (play) produced in Cambridge, MA, 1955.

Bomb (poem; broadside), [San Francisco, CA], 1958.

Gasoline (poems), introduction by Allen Ginsberg, City Lights (San Francisco, CA), 1958, new edition, 1992.

(With Henk Marsman) *A Pulp Magazine for the Dead Generation: Poems,* Dead Language, 1959.

(With William S. Burroughs, Brion Gysin, and Sinclair Beiles) *Minutes to Go,* Two Cities Editions (Paris, France), 1960.

Happy Birthday of Death (poems), New Directions (New York, NY), 1960.

(Editor with Walter Hollerer) *Junge Amerikanische Lyrik* (anthology), Carl Hansen Verlag, 1961.

The American Express (novel), Olympia Press, 1961.

(With Anselm Hollo and Tom Raworth) *The Minicab War,* Matrix Press, 1961.

Find It So Hard to Write the How Why & What . . . , Paterson Society, 1961.

Long Live Man (poems), New Directions (New York, NY), 1962.

Selected Poems, Eyre & Spottiswoode (London, England), 1962.

(With Lawrence Ferlinghetti and Allen Ginsberg) *Penguin Modern Poets 5,* Penguin (Harmondsworth, England), 1963.

The Mutation of the Spirit: A Shuffle Poem, Death Press, 1964.

There Is Yet Time to Run Back through Life and Expiate All That's Been Sadly Done (poems), New Directions (New York, NY), 1965.

The Geometric Poem: A Long Experimental Poem, Composite of Many Lines and Angles Selective, [Milan, Italy], 1966.

Ten Times a Poem: Collected at Random From Two Suitcases Filled with Poems—The Gathering of Five Years, Poets Press, 1967.

Elegiac Feelings American, New Directions (New York, NY), 1970.

Gregory Corso, Phoenix Book Shop, 1971.

Egyptian Cross, Phoenix Book Shop, 1971.

The Night Last Night Was at Its Nightest . . . , Phoenix Book Shop, 1972.

Earth Egg, Unmuzzled Ox, 1974.

Way Out: A Poem in Discord (play), Bardo Matrix (Kathmandu, Nepal), 1974.

The Japanese Notebook Ox, Unmuzzled Ox, 1974.

poesie, translated by Gianni Menarini, Guande, 1976.

Collected Plays, City Lights (San Francisco, CA), 1980.

Writings from Ox, edited by Michael Andre, Unmuzzled Ox, 1981.

Herald of the Autochthonic Spirit, New Directions (New York, NY), 1981.

Mindfield: New and Selected Poems, Thunder's Mouth Press (New York, NY), 1989.

An Accidental Autobiography: The Selected Letters of Gregory Corso, foreword by Patti Smith, New Directions (New York, NY), 2003.

Coauthor of screenplay *Happy Death,* 1965. Contributor to books, including Paris Leary and Robert Kelly, editors, *A Controversy of Poets,* Doubleday Anchor, 1965, and Bob Booker and George Foster, editors, *Pardon Me, Sir, But Is My Eye Hurting Your Elbow?* (screenplays), Bernard Geis, 1967; contributor to periodicals, including *Evergreen Review* and *Litterair Paspoort.*

SIDELIGHTS: Gregory Corso was a key member of the Beat movement, a group of convention-breaking writers who were credited with sparking much of the social and political change that transformed the United States in the 1960s. Corso's spontaneous, insightful, and inspirational verse once prompted fellow Beat poet Allen Ginsberg to describe him as an "awakener of youth." Although Corso enjoyed his greatest level of popularity during the 1960s and 1970s, he continued to influence contemporary readers and critics late into the twentieth century. Writing in the *American Book Review,* Dennis Barone remarked that Corso's 1989 volume of new and selected poems was a sign that "despite doubt, uncertainty, the American way, death all around, Gregory Corso will continue, and I am glad he will."

Born in 1930 to teenaged parents who separated a year after his birth, Corso spent his early childhood in foster homes and orphanages. At the age of eleven, he went to live with his natural father, who had remarried. A troubled youth, Corso repeatedly ran away and was eventually sent to a boys' home. One year later he was caught selling a stolen radio and was forced to testify in court against the dealer who purchased the illegal merchandise. While he was held as a material witness in the trial, the twelve-year-old boy spent several months in prison where he was abused. He later spent three months under observation at Bellevue Hospital.

When Corso was sixteen, he returned to jail to serve a three-year sentence for theft. There he read widely in the classics, including Fyodor Dostoevsky, Stendahl, Percy Bysshe Shelley, Thomas Chatterton, and Christopher Marlowe. After his release in 1950, he worked as a laborer in New York City, a newspaper reporter in Los Angeles, and a sailor on a boat to Africa and South America. It was in New York City that he first met Ginsberg, the Beat poet with whom he was most closely associated. The pair met in a Greenwich Village bar in 1950 while Corso was working on his first poems. Until then he had read only traditional poetry, and Ginsberg introduced him to contemporary, experimental work. Within a few years Corso was writing in long, Whitmanesque lines similar to those Ginsberg had developed in his own work. The surreal word combinations that began to appear in Ginsberg's work about the same time may in turn suggest Corso's reciprocal influence.

In 1954 Corso moved to Boston where several important poets, including Edward Marshall and John Wieners, were experimenting with the poetics of voice. The center for Corso's life there was not "the School of Boston," as these poets were called, but the Harvard University library, where he spent his days reading the great works of poetry. His first published poems appeared in the *Harvard Advocate* in 1954, and his play *In This Hung-up Age*—concerning a group of Americans who, after their bus breaks down midway across the continent, are trampled by buffalo—was performed by students at the university the following year.

Harvard and Radcliffe students underwrote the expenses of Corso's first book, *The Vestal Lady on Brattle, and Other Poems.* The poems featured in the volume are usually considered apprentice works heavily indebted to Corso's reading. They are, however, unique in their innovative use of jazz rhythms—most notably in "Requiem for 'Bird' Parker, Musician," which many call the strongest poem in the book—cadences of spoken English, and hipster jargon. Corso once explained his use of rhythm and meter in an interview with Gavin Selerie for *Riverside Interviews:* "My music is built in—it's already natural. I don't play with the meter." In other words, Corso believes the meter must arise naturally from the poet's voice; it is never consciously chosen.

In a review of *The Vestal Lady on Brattle* for *Poetry,* Reuel Denney asked whether "a small group jargon" such as bop language would "sound interesting" to those who were not part of that culture. Corso, he concluded, "cannot balance the richness of the bebop group jargon . . . with the clarity he needs to make his work meaningful to a wider-than-clique audience." Ironically, within a few years, that "small group jargon" became a national idiom.

Despite Corso's reliance on traditional forms and archaic diction, he remained a street-wise poet, described by Bruce Cook in *The Beat Generation* as "an urchin

Shelley." But the poems at their best are controlled by an authentic, distinctive, and enormously effective voice that can range from sentimental affection and pathos to exuberance and dadaist irreverence toward almost anything except poetry itself.

When Corso moved to San Francisco in 1956 he was too late to participate in the famous reading at the Six Gallery, at which Ginsberg read "Howl" and which, since it was widely noted in newspapers and popular magazines, is conventionally cited as the first major public event in the rise of the Beat movement. However, Corso was soon identified as one of the major figures of the movement and that notoriety undoubtedly contributed much to the fame of his poetry in the late 1950s and early 1960s. With Ginsberg, he also coauthored "The Literary Revolution in America," an article in which they declared that America now had poets who "have taken it upon themselves, with angelic clarions in hand, to announce their discontent, their demands, their hope, their final wondrous unimaginable dream."

From 1957 to 1958 Corso lived in Paris where, he once told Michael Andre in an *Unmuzzled Ox* interview, "things burst and opened, and I said, 'I will just let the lines go. . . .'" The poems that resulted from this effort were published in *Gasoline,* his first major book. *Gasoline* also contains poems written while Corso was traveling with Ginsberg in Mexico, and Ginsberg's influence is evident in much of the work. Here Whitman's long poetic line is adopted by Corso, much as it had been adopted by Ginsberg, and the diction is occasionally reminiscent of Ginsberg as well. "Ode to Coit Tower," for example, echoes "In the Baggage Room at Greyhound," on which Ginsberg was then working, and "Sun" utilizes structural devices and incantatory effects used in "Howl." However influential Ginsberg may have been, Corso always maintained his own distinctive voice. In an essay collected in *The Beats: Essays in Criticism,* Geoffrey Thurley summarized some of the principal characteristics that differentiated Corso from Ginsberg: "Where Ginsberg is all expression and voice, Corso is calm and quick, whimsical often, witty rather than humourous, semantically swift rather than prophetically incantatory."

The influence of bop is far more evident in *Gasoline* than in *The Vestal Lady on Brattle.* In his introduction, Ginsberg quotes Corso as saying that his poems were written the way Charlie Parker and Miles Davis played music. He would start with standard diction and rhythm but then be "intentionally distracted diversed sic into

my own sound." The result is an intricate linguistic pattern involving extremely subtle modulations of sound and rhythm. "For Corso," Neeli Cherkovski wrote in *Whitman's Wild Children: Profiles of Ten Contemporary American Poets,* "poetry is at its best when it can create a totally unexpected expression," and many of these linguistic fusions suggest the pleasure in invention for its own sake.

Corso shaped his poems from 1970 to 1974 into a book he planned to call *Who Am I—Who I Am,* but the manuscript was stolen, and there were no other copies. Aside from chapbooks and a few miscellaneous publications, he did not issue other work until 1981 when *Herald of the Autochthonic Spirit* appeared. Shorter than any of his major books since *Gasoline,* it contains several critically acclaimed poems, many of them written in clipped, almost prosaic lines more reminiscent of William Carlos Williams than of Whitman. "Return" deals with barren times in which there had been no poems but also asserts that the poet can now write again and that "the past is my future." The new poems, however, are generally more subdued than the earlier ones, though there are surreal flights, as in "The Whole Mess . . . Almost," in which the poet cleans his apartment of Truth, God, Beauty, Death, and essentially everything but Humor.

By the early 1980s, when Corso's *Herald of the Autochthonic Spirit* was published, language-centered writing, in which the conventions of language themselves become the subjects of poems, had long since surpassed the poetics of voice as the center of attention for many younger poets working outside academic traditions. Thus Corso's book was not widely reviewed, even though it contains some of the poet's best work. If the voice that shaped these poems was quieter than it had been a generation before, it nonetheless continued to affirm Kenneth Rexroth's characterization of Corso as "a real wildman." "At his worst," Rexroth added, "he is an amusing literary curiosity; at his best, his poems are metaphysical hotfoots and poetic cannon crackers."

In 1991 Corso published *Mindfield: New and Selected Poems.* The book consists of selections from five previously published books and close to sixty pages of previously unpublished poems, including one almost thirty pages long. Barone declared that the volume "provides for new readers the opportunity to be awakened and for those familiar with Corso's work a chance to be reawakened."

Although Corso greatly reduced his output in the years leading up to his death in 2001, he continued to believe in the power of poetry to bring about change. He once explained his Utopian vision: "I feel that in the future many many poets will blossom forth—the poetic spirit will spread and reach toward all; it will show itself not in words—the written poem—but rather in man's being and in the deeds he enacts. . . . A handful of poets in every country in the world can and have always been able to live in the world as well as in their own world; . . . and when such humankind becomes manifold, when all are embraced by the poetic spirit, by a world of poets, not by the written word but by deed and thought and beauty, then society will have no recourse but to become suitable for them and for itself. I feel man is headed in such a direction; he is fated and due to become aware of and knowledgeable about his time; his good intelligence and compassion will enable him to cope with almost all the bothersome, distracting difficulties that may arise—and when he becomes so, 'poet' will not be his name, but it will be his victory."

BIOGRAPHICAL AND CRITICAL SOURCES:

BOOKS

Bartlett, Lee, *The Beats: Essays in Criticism,* McFarland, 1981.

Chassman, Neil A., editor, *Poets of the Cities: New York and San Francisco, 1950-1965,* Dutton (New York, NY), 1974.

Cherkovski, Neeli, *Whitman's Wild Children: Profiles of Ten Contemporary American Poets,* Lapis Press, 1988.

Contemporary Literary Criticism, Thomson Gale (Detroit, MI), Volume 1, 1973, Volume 11, 1979.

Cook, Bruce, *The Beat Generation,* Scribner (New York, NY), 1971.

Dictionary of Literary Biography, Thomson Gale (Detroit, MI), Volume 5: *American Poets since World War II,* 1980, Volume 16: *The Beats: Literary Bohemianism in Postwar America,* 1983.

Gifford, Barry, and Lawrence Lee, *Jack's Book: An Oral Biography of Jack Kerouac,* St. Martin's Press (New York, NY), 1978.

Knight, Arthur, and Kit Knight, editors, *The Beat Vision: A Primary Sourcebook,* Paragon House, 1987.

Leary, Paris, and Robert Kelly, editors, *A Controversy of Poets,* Doubleday (New York, NY), 1965.

Nemerov, Howard, editor, *Poets on Poetry,* Basic Books (New York, NY), 1966.

Parkinson, Thomas, editor, *A Casebook on the Beat,* Crowell (New York, NY), 1961.

Rexroth, Kenneth, *Assays,* New Directions (New York, NY), 1961.

Selerie, Gavin, *Riverside Interviews 3: Gregory Corso,* Binnacle Press, 1982.

Tytell, John, *Naked Angels: The Lives and Literature of the Beat Generation,* McGraw, 1976.

Wilson, Robert A., *A Bibliography of Works by Gregory Corso, 1954-1965,* Phoenix Book Shop, 1966.

PERIODICALS

American Book Review, September, 1990, p. 17.
Hudson Review, spring, 1963.
Kenyon Review, spring, 1963.
Los Angeles Times, January 19, 2001.
New York Times, April 13, 1997.
North Dakota Quarterly, spring, 1982.
Partisan Review, fall, 1960.
Poetry, October, 1956.
Thoth, winter, 1971.
Unmuzzled Ox, winter, 1981.

OBITUARIES:

PERIODICALS

Chicago Tribune, January 17, 2001, sec. 1, p. 21.
Los Angeles Times, January 17, 2001, p. B7.
New York Times, January 17, 2001, p. C13.
Times (London, England), January 18, 2001.
Washington Post, January 17, 2001, p. B7.

*   *   *

CORSO, Nunzio Gregory
See CORSO, Gregory

*   *   *

CORTÁZAR, Julio 1914-1984
(Julio Denis)

PERSONAL: Born August 26, 1914, in Brussels, Belgium; held dual citizenship in Argentina and (beginning 1981) France; died of a heart attack February 12, 1984, in Paris, France; son of Julio Jose and Maria Herminia (Descotte) Cortázar; married former spouse A urora Bernardez, August 23, 1953. *Education:* Received degrees in teaching and public translating; attended Buenos Aires University. *Hobbies and other interests:* Jazz, movies.

CAREER: Writer. High school teacher in Bolivar and Chivilcoy, both in Argentina, 1937-44; teacher of French literature, University of Cuyo, Mendoza, Argentina, 1944-45; manager, Argentine Publishing Association (Camara Argentina del Libro), Buenos Aires, Argentina, 1946-48; public translator in Argentina, 1948-51; freelance translator for UNESCO, Paris, 1952-84. Member of jury, Casa de las Americas Award.

AWARDS, HONORS: Prix Medicis, 1974, for *Libro de Manuel;* Ruben Dario Order of Cultural Independence awarded by Government of Nicaragua, 1983.

WRITINGS:

FICTION

Bestiario (short stories; also see below), Sudamericana (Buenos Aires, Argentina), 1951, reprinted, 1983.

Final del juego (short stories; also see below), Los Presentes (Mexico City, Mexico), 1956, expanded edition, Sudamericana (Buenos Aires, Argentina), 1964, reprinted, 1983.

Las armas secretas (short stories; title means "The Secret Weapons"; also see below), Sudamericana (Buenos Aires, Argentina), 1959, reprinted, Catedra (Madrid, Spain), 1983.

Los premios (novel), Sudamericana (Buenos Aires, Argentina), 1960, reprinted, Ediciones B, 1987, translation by Elaine Kerrigan published as *The Winners,* Pantheon (New York, NY), 1965, reprinted, 1984.

Historias de cronopios y de famas (novel), Minotauro (Buenos Aires, Argentina), 1962, reprinted, Alfaguara (Madrid, Spain), 1984, translation by Paul Blackburn published as *Cronopios and Famas,* Pantheon (New York, NY), 1969.

Rayuela (novel), Sudamericana (Buenos Aires, Argentina), 1963, reprinted, 1984, translation by Gregory Rabassa published as *Hopscotch,* Pantheon (New York, NY), 1966, reprinted, 1987.

Cuentos (collection), Casa de las Americas (Havana, Cuba), 1964.

Todos los fuegos el fuego (short stories), Sudamericana (Buenos Aires, Argentina), 1966, reprinted, 1981, translation by Suzanne Jill Levine published as *All Fires the Fire, and Other Stories,* Pantheon (New York, NY), 1973, reprinted, 1988.

La vuelta al dia en ochenta mundos (essays, poetry, and short stories), Siglo Veintiuno (Mexico City, Mexico), 1967, reprinted, 1984, translation by Thomas Christensen published as *Around the Day in Eighty Worlds,* North Point Press (San Francisco, CA), 1986.

El perseguidor y otros cuentos (short stories), Centro Editor para America Latina (Buenos Aires, Argentina), 1967, reprinted, Bruguera (Barcelona, Spain), 1983.

End of the Game, and Other Stories, translated by Paul Blackburn (includes stories from *Final del juego, Bestiario,* and *Las armas secretas*), Pantheon (New York, NY), 1967, published as *Blow-Up, and Other Stories,* Collier (New York, NY), 1968, reprinted, Pantheon (New York, NY), 1985.

Ceremonias (collection), Seix Barral (Barcelona, Spain), 1968, reprinted, 1983.

62: Modelo para armar (novel), Sudamericana (Buenos Aires, Argentina), 1968, translation by Gregory Rabassa published as *62: A Model Kit,* Pantheon (New York, NY), 1972, New Directions (New York, NY), 2000.

Ultimo round (essays, poetry, and stories; title means "Last Round"), Siglo Veintiuno (Mexico City, Mexico), 1969, reprinted, 1984.

Relatos (collection), Sudamericana (Buenos Aires, Argentina), 1970.

La isla a mediodia y otros relatos (contains twelve previously published stories), Salvat (Estella, Spain), 1971.

Libro de Manuel (novel), Sudamericana (Buenos Aires, Argentina), 1973, translation by Gregory Rabassa published as *A Manual for Manuel,* Pantheon (New York, NY), 1978.

Octaedro (stories; title means "Octahedron"; also see below), Sudamericana (Buenos Aires, Argentina), 1974.

Antologí (collection), La Libreria (Buenos Aires, Argentina), 1975.

Fantomas contra los vampiros multinacionales (title means "Fantomas Takes on the Multinational Vampires"), Excelsior (Mexico City, Mexico), 1975.

Los relatos (collection), four volumes, Alianza (Madrid, Spain), 1976–1985.

Al guien que anda por ahí y otros relatos (short stories), Alfaguara (Madrid, Spain), 1977, translati on by Gregory Rabassa published as *A Change of Light, and Other Stories* (includes *Octae dro;* also see below), Knopf (New York, NY), 1980.

Te rritorios, Siglo Veintiuno (Mexico City, Mexico), 1978.

Un tal Lucas, Alfaguara (Madrid, Spain), 1979, translati on by Gregory Rabassa published as *A Certain Lucas,* Knopf (New York, NY), 1984.

Qu eremos tanto a Glenda, Alfaguara (Madrid, Spain), 1980, translati on by Gregory Rabassa published as *We Love Glenda So Much, and Other Tales,* Knopf (New York, NY), 1983.

Deshoras (short stories), Alfaguara (Madrid, Spain), 1982, translation by Alberto Manguel published as

Unreasonable Hours, Coach House Press (Toronto, Ontario, Canada), 1995.

Salvo el Crepusculo, translated by Stephen Kessler, published as *Save Twilight,* City Lights Books (San Francisco, CA), 1997.

Julio Cortázar: New Readings, edited by Carlos J. Alonso, Cambridge University Press (New York, NY), 1998.

Final Exam, translated by Alfred MacAdam, New Directions (New York, NY), 2000.

TRANSLATOR

Alfred Stern, *Filosofia de la risa y del llanto,* Iman (Buenos Aires, Argentina), 1950.

Lord Houghton, *Vida y cartas de John Keats,* Iman (Buenos Aires, Argentina), 1955.

Marguerite Yourcenar, *Memorias de Adriano,* Sudamericana (Buenos Aires, Argentina), 1955.

Edgar Allan Poe, *Obras en prosa,* two volumes, Revista de Occidente (Madrid, Spain), 1956.

Edgar Allan Poe, *Cuentos,* Editorial Nacional de Cuba (Havana, Cuba), 1963.

Edgar Allan Poe, *Aventuras de Arthur Gordon Pym,* Instituto del Libro (Havana, Cuba), 1968.

Poe, *Eureka,* Alianza (Madrid, Spain), 1972.

Daniel Defoe, *Robinson Crusoe,* Bruguera (Barcelona, Spain), 1981.

Also translator of works by G.K. Chesterton, Andre Gide, and Jean Giono, published in Argentina between 1948 and 1951.

OTHER

(Under pseudonym Julio Denis) *Presencia* (poems; title means "Presence"), El Bibliófilo (Buenos Aires, Argentina), 1938.

Los reyes (play; title means "The Monarchs"), Gulab y Aldabahor (Buenos Aires, Argentina), 1949, reprinted, Alfaguara (Madrid, Spain), 1982.

(Contributor) *Buenos Aires de la fundacion a la angustia,* Ediciones de la Flor (Buenos Aires, Argentina), 1967.

(With others) *Cuba por argentinos,* Merlin (Buenos Aires, Argentina), 1968.

Buenos Aires, Buenos Aires (includes French and English translations), Sudamericana (Buenos Aires, Argentina), 1968.

Viaje alrededor de una mesa (title means "Trip around a Table"), Cuadernos de Rayuela (Buenos Aires, Argentina), 1970.

(With Oscar Collazos and Mario Vargas Llosa) *Literatura en la revolucion y revolucion en la literatura,* Siglo Veintiuno (Mexico City, Mexico), 1970.

(Contributor) *Literatura y arte nuevo en Cuba,* Estela (Barcelona, Spain), 1971.

Pameos y meopas (poetry), Editorial Libre de Sivera (Barcelona, Spain), 1971.

Prosa del observatorio, Lumen (Barcelona, Spain), 1972.

La casilla de los Morelli (essays), edited by Jose Julio Ortega, Tusquets (Barcelona, Spain), 1973.

Convergencias, divergencias, incidencias, edited by Jose Julio Ortega, Tusquets (Barcelona, Spain), 1973.

(Author of text) *Humanario,* La Azotea (Buenos Aires, Argentina), 1976.

(Author of text) *Paris: Ritmos de una ciudad,* Edhasa (Barcelona, Spain), 1981.

Paris: The Essence of an Image, Norton (New York, NY), 1981.

(With Carol Dunlop) *Los autonautas de la cosmopista,* Muchnik (Barcelona, Spain), 1983.

Nicaragua tan violentamente dulce (essays), Nueva Nicaragua (Managua, Nicaragua), 1983.

Argentina: Anos de almabradas culturales (essays), edited by Saul Yurkievich, Muchnik (Barcelona, Spain), 1984.

Nada a pehuajo: Un acto; Adios, Robinson (plays), Katun, 1984.

Salvo el crepusculo (poems), Nueva Imagen (Mexico City, Mexico), 1984.

Textos politicos, Plaza y Janes (Barcelona, Spain), 1985.

Divertimento, Sudamericana/Planeta (Buenos Aires, Argentina), 1986.

El examen, Sudamericana/Planeta (Buenos Aires, Argentina), 1986.

Contributor to numerous periodicals, including *Revista Iberoamericana, Cuadernos Hispanoamericanos, Books Abroad,* and *Casa de las Americas.*

ADAPTATIONS: The story *Las babas del diablo,* from the collection *Las armas secretas* was the basis for Michaelangelo Antonioni's 1966 film *Blow Up.*

SIDELIGHTS: Argentine author Julio Cortázar was "one of the world's greatest writers," according to novelist Stephen Dobyns. "His range of styles," Dobyns wrote in the *Washington Post Book World,* "his ability to paint a scene, his humor, his endlessly peculiar mind makes many of his stories wonderful. His novel *Hopscotch* is considered one of the best novels written by a South American." A popular as well as a critical success, *Hopscotch* not only established Cortázar's reputation as a novelist of international merit but also, according to David W. Foster in *Currents in the Contemporary Argentine Novel,* prompted wider acceptance in the United S tates of novels written by other Latin Americans. For this reason many critics, such as Jaime Alazraki in *The Final Island,* viewed the book as "a turning point for Latin American literature." A *Times Literary Supplement* reviewer, for example, called *Hopscotch* "the first great novel of Spanish America."

Still other critics, including novelists Jose Donoso and C.D.B. Bryan, saw the novel in the context of world literature. Donoso, in his *The Boom in Spanish American Literature: A Personal History,* claimed that *Hopscotch* "humanized the novel." Cortázar was a writer, Donoso continued, "who [dared] to be dis cursive and whose pages [were] sprinkled with names of musicians, painters, art galleries, . . . movie directors, [and] all this had an undisguised place within his novel, something which I would never have dared to presume to be right for the Latin American novel, since it was fine for [German novelist] Thomas Mann b ut not for us." In the *New York Times Book Review,* Bryan stated: "I think *Hopscotch* is the most magnificent book I have ever read. No novel has so satisfactorily and completely and beautifully explored man's compulsion to explore life, to search for its meaning, to challenge its mysteries. Nor has any novel in recent memory lavi shed such love and attention upon the full spectrum of the writer's craft."

Cortázar attempted to perfect his craft by constant experimentation. In his longer fiction he pursued, as Leo Bersani observed in the *New York Times Book Review,* both "subversion and renewal of novelistic form." This subversion and renewal was of such importance to Cortázar that often the form of his novels overshadowe d the action that they described. Through the form of his fiction Cortázar invited the reader to participate in the writer's craft and to share in the creation of the novel. *Hopscotch* is one such novel. In *Into the Mainstream: Conversations with Latin-America Writers,* Luis Harss and Barbara Dohmann wrote that *Hopscotch* "is the first Latin American novel which takes itself as its own central topic or, in other words, is essentially about the writing of itself. It lives in constant metamorphoses, as an unfinished process that invents itself as it goes, involving the reader in such a way to make him part of the creative impulse."

Thus, *Hopscotch* begins with a "Table of Instructions" that tells the reader that there are at least two ways to read the novel. The first is reading chapters one to fifty-six in numerical order. When the reader finishes chapter fifty-six he can, according to the instructions, stop reading and "ignore what follows [nearly one hundred more short chapters] with a clean conscience." The other way of reading suggested by the instructions is to start with chapter seventy-two and then skip from chapter to chapter (hence, the title of the book), following the sequence indicated at the end of each chapter by a number which tells the reader which chapter is next. Read t he second way, the reader finds that chapter 131 refers him to chapter fifty-eight, and chapter fifty-eight to chapter 131, so that he is confronted with a novel that has no end. With his "Table of Instructions" Cortázar forces the reader to write the novel while he is reading it.

Cortázar's other experimental works include *62: A Model Kit* (considered a sequel to *Hopscotch*), *A Manual for Manuel, Ultimo round* ("Last Round"), and *Fantomas contra los vampiros multinacionales* ("Fantomas Takes on the Multinational Vampires"). *62: A Model Kit* is based on chapter sixty-two of *Hopscotch* in which a character, Morelli, expresses his desire to write a new type of novel. "If I were to write this book," Morelli states, "standard behavior would be inexplicable by means of current instrumental psychology. Everything would be a kind of disquiet, a continuous uprooting, a territory where psychological causality wou ld yield disconcertedly." In *62: A Model Kit* Cortázar attempted to put these ideas into action. Time and space have no meaning in the novel: although it takes place in Paris, London, and Vienna, the characters move and interact as if they are in one single space. The characters themselves are sketchily presented in fragments that must be assembled by the readers; chapters are replaced by short scenes separated by blank spaces on the pages of the novel. Cortázar noted in the book's introduction that once again the reader must help create the novel: "The reader's option, his personal montage of the elements in the tale, will in each case be the book he has chosen to read."

A Manual for Manuel continues in the experimental vein. Megan Marshall described the book in *New Republic* as "a novel that merges story and history, a supposed scrapbook of news clippings, journal entries, diagrams, transcripts of conversations, and much more." The book, about the kidnapping of a Latin American diplomat by a group of guerillas in Paris, is told from the double perspective of an unnamed member of the group, who takes notes on the plans for the kidnapping, and a nonmember of the group, Andres, who reads the notes. Periodically, these two narrations are interrupted by the inclusion of English-, French-, and Spanish-language texts reproduced in the pages of the novel. These texts, actual articles collected by Cortázar from various sources, form part of a scrapbook being assembled for Manuel, the child of two of the members of the group. On one page, for example, Cortázar reprinted a statistical table originally published in 1969 by the U.S. Department of Defense that shows how many Latin Americans have received military training in the United States. The reader reads about the compilation of the scrapbook for Manuel, while at the same time reading the scrapbook and reacting to the historical truth it contains.

Other such experimentation is found in *Ultimo round,* a collection of essays, stories, and poetry. William L. Siemens noted in the *International Fiction Review* that this book, like *Hopscotch* and *62: A Model Kit,* "is a good example of audience-participation art." In *Ultimo round,* he declared, "it is impos sible for the reader to proceed in a conventional manner. Upon opening the book the reader notes that there are two sets of pages within the binding, and he must immediately decide which of them to read first, and even whether he will go through by reading the top and then the bottom of page one, and so on."

Cortázar's brief narrative *Fantomas contra los vampiros multinacionales* is yet another experiment with new forms of fiction. It presents, in comic book form, the story of a "superhero," Fantomas, who gathers together "the greatest contemporary writers" to fight the destructive powers of the multinational corporations. Ch ilean Octavio Paz, Italian Alberto Moravia, and American Susan Sontag, along with Cortázar himself, appear as characters in the comic book. Although short, the work embodies several constants in Cortázar's fiction: the comic (the comic book form itself), the interplay of fantasy and reality (the appearance of historical figures in a fictional work), and a commitment to social activism (the portrayal of the writer as a politically involved individual). These three elements, together with Cortázar's experiments with the novelistic form, are the basic components of his fiction.

Cortázar explained how these elements function together in his essay "Algunos aspectos del cuento" ("Some Aspects of the Story"), which Alazraki quoted in *The Final Island.* His work, Cortázar claimed, was "an alternative to that false realism which assumed that everything can be neatly described as was upheld by the philosophic and scientific optimism of the eigh-

teenth century, that is, within a world ruled more or less harmoniously by a system of laws, of principles, of causal relations, of well defined psychologies, of well mapped geographies. . . . In my case, the suspicion of another order, more secret and less communicable [was one of the princ iples guiding] my personal search for a literature beyond overly naive forms of realism." Whatever the method, whether new narrative forms, unexpected humor, incursions into fantasy, or pleas for a more humane society, Cortázar strove to shake the reader out of traditional ways of thinking and seeing the world and to replace them wi th new and more viable models. Dobyn explained in the *Washington Post Book World,* "Cortázar wants to jolt people out of their self-complacency, to make them doubt their own definition of the world."

Cortázar's last full-length work of fiction, *A Certain Lucas,* for example, "is a kind of sampler of narrative ideas, a playful anthology of form, including everything from parables to parodies, folk tales to metafictions," as Robert Coover describes it in the *New York Times Book Review.* Including chapters with such tit les as "Lucas, His Shopping," "Lucas, His Battles with the Hydra," and "Lucas, His Pianists," the book "builds a portrait, montage-like, through a succession of short sketches (humorous set-pieces, really) full of outrageous inventions, leaping and dream-like associations and funny turns of phrase," states *Los Angeles Times Book Review* critic Charles Champlin. "Lucas is not Cortázar," Dobyns suggests in the *Washington Post Book World,* "but occasionally he seems to stand for him and so the book takes on an autobiographical quality as we read about Lucas' friends, his struggles with himself, his dreams, his tastes, his view of writing." The result, writes Champlin, might appear to be "no more than a series of extravagant jokes, [and] it would be an exceptional passing entertainment but no more than that. Yet under the cover of raillery, self-indicting foolishness and extremely tall tales," the critic continues, "Cortázar is discovered to be a thoughtful, deep-feeling man, impassioned, sentimental, angry, complicated, a philosopher exploring appearances vs. realities is the way of philosophers ever." "What we see in Lucas and in much of Cortázar's work is a fierce love of this earth, despite the awfulness, and a fierce respect for life's ridiculousness," concludes Dobyns. "And in the mi dst of this ridiculousness, Cortázar dances . . . and that dance comforts and eases our own course through the world."

This ridiculousness, or humor, in Cortázar's work often derived from what a *Time* reviewer referred to as the author's "ability to present common objects from strange perspectives as if he had just invented them."

Cortázar, declared Tom Bishop in *Saturday Review*, was "an intellectual humorist. . . . [He ha d] a rare gift for isolating the absurd in everyday life [and] for depicting the foibles in human behavior with an unerring thrust that [was] satiric yet compassionate." *Hopscotch* is filled with humorous elements, some of which Saul Yurkievich listed in *The Final Island*. He included "references to the ri diculous, . . . recourse to the outlandish, . . . absurd associations, . . . juxtaposition of the majestic with the popular or vulgar," as well as "puns . . . [and] polyglot insults." *New York Times* writer John Leonard called absurdity "obligatory" in a work by Cortázar and gave examples of the absurd found in *A Manual for Manuel*, such as "a turquoise penguin [is] flown by jet to Argentina; the stealing of 9,000 wigs . . . and obsessive puns."

In an interview with Evelyn Picon Garfield, quoted in *Books Abroad*, Cortázar called *Cronopios and Famas* his "most playful book." It is, he continued, "really a game, a very fascinating game, lots of fun, almost like a tennis match." This book of short, story-like narratives deals with two groups of creatures descr ibed by Arthur Curley in *Library Journal* as the "warm lifeloving cronopios and practical, conventional famas . . . imaginary but typical personages between whom communication is usually impossible and always ridiculous." One portion of the book, called "The Instruction Manual," contains detailed explanations of various everyday a ctivities, including how to climb stairs, how to wind a clock, and how to cry. In order to cry correctly, the author suggested thinking of a duck covered with ants. With these satiric instructions Cortázar, according to Paul West in *Book World*, "cleanses the doors of perception and mounts a subtle, bland assault on the mental rigid ities we hold most dear." By forcing us to think about everyday occurrences in a new way, Cortázar, Malva E. Filer noted in *Books Abroad*, "expresses his rebellion against objects and persons that make up our everyday life and the mechanical ways by which we relate to them." Filer continued: "In Cortázar's fictional w orld [a] routine life is the great scandal against which every individual must rebel with all his strength. And if he is not willing to do so, extraordinary elements are usually summoned to force him out of this despicable and abject comfort." These "extraordinary elements" enter into the lives of Cortázar's characters in the form of fantastic episodes which interrupt their otherwise normal existences.

Alexander Coleman observed in *Cinco maestros: Cuentos modernos de Hispanoamerica* (*Five Masters: Modern Spanish-American Stories*): "Cortázar's stories start in a disarmingly conversational way, with plenty of lo-

cal touches. But something always seems to go awry just when we least expect it." "Axolotl," a short story described by novelist Joyce Carol Oates in the *New York Times Book Review* as her favorite Cortázar tale, begins innocently: a man describes his trips to the Parisian botanical gardens to watch a certain type of salamander called an axolotl. But the serenity ends when the narrator admits, "Now I am an axolotl." In another story, a woman has a dream about a beggar who lives in Budapest (a city the woman has never visited). The woman ends up actually going to Budapest where she finds herself walking across a bridge as the beggar woman from her dream approaches from the opposite side. The two women embrace in the middle of the bridge and the first woman is transformed into the beggar woman—she can feel the snow seeping through the holes in her shoes—while she sees her former self walk away. In yet another story, a motorcyclist is involved in a minor traffic accident and suddenly finds himself thrown back in time where he becomes the victim of Aztec ritual sacrifice. Daniel Stern noted in *Nation* that with t hese stories and others like them "it is as if Cortázar is showing us that it is essential for us to reimagine the reality in which we live and which we can no longer take for granted."

Although during the last years of his life Cortázar was so involved with political activism that Jason Weiss described him in the *Los Angeles Times* as a writer with hardly any time to write, the Argentine had early in his career been criticized "for his apparent indifference to the brutish situation" of his fellow Latin Ameri cans, according to Leonard. Evidence of his growing political preoccupation is found in his later stories and novels. Leonard observed, for instance, that *A Manual for Manuel* "is a primer on the necessity of revolutionary action," and William Kennedy in the *Washington Post Book World* noted that the newspaper clippings included i n the novel "touch[ed] the open nerve of political oppression in Latin America." Many of the narratives in *A Change of Light, and Other Stories* are also politically oriented. Oates described the impact of one story in the *New York Times Book Review*. In "Apocalypse at Solentiname," a photographer develops his vacat ion photographs of happy, smiling people only to discover pictures of people being tortured. Oates commented, "The narrator . . . contemplates in despair the impotence of art to deal with in any significant way, the 'life of permanent uncertainty . . . [in] almost all of Latin America, a life surrounded by fear and death.'" Cortázar's fictional world, according to Alazraki in *The Final Island*, "represents a challenge to culture." This challenge is embedded in the author's belief in a reality that reaches beyond our everyday existence. Alazraki noted that Cortázar once declared, "Our daily reality masks a second reality which is neither mysterious nor theological, but profoundly human. Yet, due to a long series of mistakes, it has remained concealed under a reality prefabricated by many centuries of culture, a culture in which there are great achievements but also profound aberrations, profound distortions." Bryan further explained these ideas in the *New York Times Book Review:* Cortázar's "surrealistic treatment of the most pedestrian acts suggest[ed] that one way to combat alienation is to return to the original receptiveness of childhood, to recapture this original innocence, by returning to the concept of life as a game."

Cortázar confronted his reader with unexpected forms, with humor, fantasy, and unseemly reality in order to challenge him to live a more meaningful life. He summarized his theory of fiction (and of life) in an essay, "The Present State of Fiction in Latin America," which appeared in *Books Abroad.* The Argentine concluded: "T he fantastic is something that one must never say good-bye to lightly. The man of the future . . . will have to find the bases of a reality which is truly his and, at the same time, maintain the capacity of dreaming and playing which I have tried to show you . . . , since it is through those doors that the Other, the fantastic dimension, and the u nexpected will always slip, as will all that will save us from that obedient robot into which so many technocrats would like to convert us and which we will not accept—ever."

BIOGRAPHICAL AND CRITICAL SOURCES:

BOOKS

Alazraki, Jaime and Ivar Ivask, editors, *The Final Island: The Fiction of Julio Cortázar,* University of Oklahoma Press (Norman, OK), 1978.

Boldy, Steven, *The Novels of Cortázar,* Cambridge University Press (New York, NY), 1980.

Colas, Santiago, *Postmodernity in Latin America: The Argentine Paradigm,* Duke University Press (Durham, NC), 1994.

Coleman, Alexander, editor, *Cinco maestros: Cuentos modernos de Hispanoamerica,* Harcourt, Brace & World (New York, NY), 1969.

Contemporary Literary Criticism, Thomson Gale (Detroit, MI), Volume 2, 1974, Volume 3, 1975, Volume 5, 1976, Volume 10, 1979, Volume 13, 1980, Volume 15, 1980, Volume 33, 1985, Volume 34, 1985.

Dictionary of Literary Biography, Volume 113: *Modern Latin-American Fiction Writers, First Series,* Thomson Gale (Detroit, MI), 1992.

Donoso, Jose, *Historia personal del "boom,"* Anagrama (Barcelona, Spain), 1972, translation by Gregory Kolovakos published as *The Boom in Spanish American Literature: A Personal History,* Columbia University Press (New York, NY), 1977.

Foster, David W., *Currents in the Contemporary Argentine Novel,* University of Missouri Press (Columbia, MO), 1975.

Garfield, Evelyn Picon, *Cortázar por Cortázar* (interviews), Universidad Veracruzana (Veracruz, Mexico), 1981.

Garfield, Evelyn Picon, *Julio Cortázar,* Ungar (New York, NY), 1975.

Giacoman, Helmy F., editor, *Homenaje a Julio Cortázar,* Anaya (New York, NY), 1972.

Goloboff, Gerardo Mario, *Julio Cortázar: la biografia,* Seix Barral (Buenos Aires, Argentina), 1998.

Harss, Luis and Barbara Dohmann, *Into the Mainstream: Conversations with Latin-American Writers,* Harper (New York, NY), 1967.

Legaz, Maria Elena, and others, *Un Tal Julio: Cortázar, otras lecturas,* Alcion (Cordoba, Argentina), 1998.

Prego, Omar, *La fascinacion de las palabras* (interviews), Muchnik (Barcelona, Spain), 1985.

Ramirez, Sergio, *Hatful of Tigers: Reflections on Art, Culture, and Politics,* Curbstone Press (Willimantic, CT), 1995.

Standish, Peter, *Understanding Julio Cortázar,* University of South Carolina Press (Columbia, SC), 2001.

Stavans, Ilan, *Julio Cortázar: A Study of the Short Fiction,* Twayne (New York, NY), 1996.

Vasquez Amaral, Jose, *The Contemporary Latin American Narrative,* Las Americas (New York, NY), 1970.

PERIODICALS

America, April 17, 1965; July 9, 1966; December 22, 1973.

Atlantic, June, 1969; October, 1973.

Books Abroad, fall, 1965; winter, 1968; summer, 1969; winter, 1970; summer, 1976.

Book World, August 17, 1969.

Casa de las Americas, numbers 15-16, 1962.

Chicago Tribune, September 24, 1978; February 14, 1984.

Chicago Tribune Book World, November 16, 1980; May 8, 1983.

Christian Science Monitor, August 15, 1967; July 3, 1969; December 4, 1978; July 17, 1984, p. 24.

Commentary, October, 1966.

El Pais, April 19, 1981.

Globe and Mail (Toronto), February 18, 1984.

Hispania, December, 1973.

Hispanic Journal, spring, 1984, pp. 172-73.

Hudson Review, spring, 1974; autumn, 1983, pp. 549-62.

International Fiction Review, January, 1974; January, 1975.

Library Journal, July, 1967; September, 1969; September 15, 1980.

Listener, December 20, 1979.

Los Angeles Times, August 28, 1983; February 14, 1984.

Los Angeles Times Book Review, December 28, 1980; June 12, 1983; May 27, 1984; June 24, 1984, pp. 4, 14.

Nation, September 18, 1967.

National Review, July 25, 1967.

New Republic, April 23, 1966; July 15, 1967; October 21, 1978; October 25, 1980.

Newsweek, September 17, 1984, p. 82.

New Yorker, May 18, 1965; February 25, 1974.

New York Review of Books, March 25, 1965; April 28, 1966; April 19, 1973; October 12, 1978.

New York Times, November 13, 1978; March 24, 1983; February 13, 1984.

New York Times Book Review, March 21, 1965; April 10, 1966; June 15, 1969; November 26, 1972; September 9, 1973; November 19, 1978; November 9, 1980; March 27, 1983, pp. 1, 37-38; March 4, 1984; May 20, 1984.

Novel: A Forum on Fiction, fall, 1967.

Review of Contemporary Fiction (special Cortázar issue), fall, 1983.

Revista Iberoamericana, July-December, 1973.

Saturday Review, March 27, 1965; April 9, 1966.

Symposium, spring, 1983, pp. 17-47.

Time, April 29, 1966; June 13, 1969; October 1, 1973.

Times (London, England), February 14, 1984.

Times Literary Supplement, October 12, 1973; December 7, 1979.

Virginia Quarterly Review, spring, 1973.

Voice Literary Supplement, March, 1984.

Washington Post, February 13, 1984.

Washington Post Book World, November 18, 1973; November 5, 1978; November 23, 1980; May 1, 1983; June 24, 1984.

World Literature Today, winter, 1977; winter, 1980.

*   *   *

COURTNEY, Robert
See ELLISON, Harlan

COX, William Trevor
See TREVOR, William

*   *   *

CRAIG, A.A.
See ANDERSON, Poul

*   *   *

CREELEY, Robert 1926-2005
(Robert White Creeley)

PERSONAL: Born May 21, 1926, in Arlington, MA; died, March 30, 2005, in Odessa, TX; son of Oscar Slade (a physician) and Genevieve (Jules) Creeley; married Ann MacKinnon, 1946 (divorced, c. 1955); married Bobbie Louise Hall, January 27, 1957 (divorced, 1976); married Penelope Highton, 1977; children: (first marriage) David, Thomas, Charlotte; (second marriage) Kirsten (stepdaughter), Leslie (stepdaughter; deceased), Sarah, Katherine; (third marriage) William, Hannah. *Education:* Attended Harvard University, 1943-44 and 1945-46; Black Mountain College, B.A., c. 1955; University of New Mexico, M.A., 1960.

CAREER: Poet, novelist, short story writer, essayist, and editor. Divers Press, Palma, Mallorca, Spain, founder and publisher, 1950-54; Black Mountain College, Black Mountain, NC, instructor in English, 1954-55; instructor at school for young boys, Albuquerque, NM, beginning 1956; University of New Mexico, Albuquerque, instructor in English, 1961-62, lecturer, 1963-66, visiting professor, 1968-69 and 1978-80; University of British Columbia, Vancouver, instructor in English, 1962-63; University of New Mexico, visiting lecturer, 1961-62, lecturer in English, 1963-66, visiting professor, 1968-69, 1979, 1980-81; State University of New York at Buffalo, visiting professor, 1966-67, professor of English, 1967-78, David Gray Professor of Poetry and Letters, 1978-89, University of New York at Buffalo, Samuel P. Capen Professor of Poetry and Humanities, 1989-2003, director of poetics program, 1991-92; distinguished professor of English for the Graduate Program in Creative Writing at Brown University, 2003—. San Francisco State College, visiting lecturer in creative writing, 1970-71; State University of New York at Binghamton, visiting professor, 1985 and 1986. Bicentennial chair of American studies at University of Helsinki, Finland, 1988. New York State Poet, 1989. Participated in numerous poetry readings and writers' conferences. *Wartime service:* American Field Service, India and Burma, 1944-45.

MEMBER: American Academy of Arts and Letters.

AWARDS, HONORS: Levinson Prize, 1960, for group of ten poems published in *Poetry* magazine; D.H. Lawrence fellowship (for summer writing), University of New Mexico, 1960; National Book Award nomination, 1962, for *For Love;* Leviton-Blumenthal Prize, 1964, for group of thirteen poems published in *Poetry;* Guggenheim fellowship in poetry, 1964-65 and 1971; Rockefeller Foundation grant, 1966; Union League Civic and Arts Foundation Prize, 1967; Shelley Award, 1981, and Frost Medal, 1987, both from Poetry Society of America; National Endowment for the Arts grant, 1982; Deutsche Austauschdienst Programme residency in Berlin, 1983 and 1987; Leone d'Oro Premio Speziale, Venice, 1984; Frost Medal, Poetry Society of America, 1987; Fulbright Award, 1988, 1995; Walt Whitman citation of merit, 1989; named New York State Poet, 1989-91; named distinguished professor, State University of New York at Buffalo, 1989; D.Litt., University of New Mexico, 1993; Horst Bienek Lyrikpreis, Bavarian Academy of Fine Arts, Munich, 1993; America Award for Poetry, 1995; Lila Wallace/*Reader's Digest* Writers Award, 1996; Bollingen Prize, 1999; Chancellor Norton Medal, 1999; Before Columbus Lifetime Achievement Award, 1999; Lannan Lifetime Achievement Award (with Edward Said), Lannan Literary Foundation, 2001.

WRITINGS:

POETRY

Le Fou, Golden Goose Press, 1952.

The Kind of Act Of, Divers Press (Mallorca, Spain), 1953.

The Immoral Proposition, Jonathan Williams, 1953.

A Snarling Garland of Xmas Verse (published anonymously), Divers Press (Mallorca, Spain), 1954.

All That Is Lovely in Men, Jonathan Williams (Asheville, NC), 1955.

(With others) *Ferrin and Others,* Gerhardt (Germany), 1955.

If You, Porpoise Bookshop (San Francisco, CA), 1956.

The Whip, Migrant Books, 1957.

A Form of Women, Jargon Books (New York, NY), 1959.

For Love: Poems, 1950-1960, Scribner (New York, NY), 1962.

Distance, Terrence Williams, 1964.

Mister Blue, Insel-Verlag, 1964.

Two Poems, Oyez, 1964.

Hi There!, Finial Press, 1965.

Words (eight poems), Perishable Press, 1965.

Poems, 1950-1965, Calder & Boyars (London, England), 1966.

About Women, Gemini, 1966.

For Joel, Perishable Press, 1966.

A Sight, Cape Coliard Press, 1967.

Words (eighty-four poems), Scribner (New York, NY), 1967.

Robert Creeley Reads (with recording), Turret Books, 1967.

The Finger, Black Sparrow Press (Santa Rosa, CA), 1968, enlarged edition published as *The Finger Poems, 1966-1969,* Calder & Boyars (London, England), 1970.

5 Numbers (five poems), Poets Press (New York, NY), 1968, published as *Numbers* (text in English and German), translation by Klaus Reichert, Galerie Schmela (Dusseldorf, Germany), 1968.

The Charm: Early and Collected Poems, Perishable Press, 1968, expanded edition published as *The Charm,* Four Seasons Foundation (San Francisco, CA), 1969.

Divisions and Other Early Poems, Perishable Press, 1968.

Pieces (fourteen poems), Black Sparrow Press (Santa Rosa, CA), 1968.

The Boy (poem poster), Gallery Upstairs Press, 1968.

Mazatlan: Sea, Poets Press (New York, NY), 1969.

Pieces (seventy-two poems), Scribner (New York, NY), 1969.

Hero, Indianakatz (New York, NY), 1969.

A Wall, Bouwerie Editions (New York, NY), 1969.

For Betsy and Tom, Alternative Press, 1970.

For Benny and Sabrina, Samuel Charters, 1970.

America, Press of the Black Flag, 1970.

In London, Angel Hair Books, 1970.

Christmas: May 10, 1970, Lockwood Memorial Library, State University of New York at Buffalo (Buffalo, NY), 1970.

St. Martin's, Black Sparrow Press (Santa Rosa, CA), 1971.

1-2-3-4-5-6-7-8-9-0, drawings by Arthur Okamura, Shambhala (New York, NY), 1971.

Sea, Cranium Press, 1971.

For the Graduation, Cranium Press, 1971.

Change, Hermes Free Press, 1972.

One Day after Another, Alternative Press, 1972.

For My Mother: Genevieve Jules Creeley, 8 April 1887-7 October 1972 (limited edition), Sceptre Press (London, England), 1973.

His Idea, Coach House Press (Toronto, Ontario, Canada), 1973.

The Class of '47, Bouwerie Editions (New York, NY), 1973.

Kitchen, Wine Press, 1973.

Sitting Here, University of Connecticut Library, 1974.

Thirty Things, Black Sparrow Press (Santa Rosa, CA), 1974.

Backwards, Sceptre Press (London, England), 1975.

Hello, Hawk Press (Christchurch, New Zealand), 1976, expanded edition published as *Hello: A Journal, February 29-May 3, 1976,* New Directions (New York, NY), 1978.

Away, Black Sparrow Press (Santa Rosa, CA), 1976.

Presences (also see below), Scribner (New York, NY), 1976.

Selected Poems, Scribner (New York, NY), 1976, revised edition, University of California Press (Berkeley, CA), 1991.

Myself, Sceptre Press (London, England), 1977.

Later, Toothpaste (West Branch, IA), 1978, expanded edition, New Directions (New York, NY), 1979.

Desultory Days, Sceptre Press (London, England), 1979.

Corn Close, Sceptre Press (London, England), 1980.

Mother As Voice, Am Here Books/Immediate Editions, 1981.

The Collected Poems of Robert Creeley, 1945-1975, University of California Press (Berkeley, CA), 1982.

Echoes, Toothpaste (West Branch, IA), 1982, New Directions (New York, NY), 1994.

Going On: Selected Poems, 1958-1980, Dutton (New York, NY), 1983.

Mirrors, New Directions (New York, NY), 1983.

A Calendar: Twelve Poems, Coffee House Press (West Branch, IA), 1984.

The Collected Prose of Robert Creeley, Scribner (New York, NY), 1984.

Memories, Pig Press, 1984.

Memory Gardens, New Directions (New York, NY), 1986.

The Company, Burning Deck, 1988.

Window, edited by Richard Blevins, State University of New York at Buffalo (Buffalo, NY), 1988.

(With Libby Larsen) *A Creeley Collection: For Mixed Voices, Solo Tenor, Flute, Percussion, and Piano,* E.C. Schirmer, 1989.

(With Francesco Clemente) *64 Pastels,* Bruno Bischofberger, 1989.

Places, Shuffaloff Press, 1990.

Windows, New Directions (New York, NY), 1990.

Have a Heart, Limberlost Press, 1990.

Selected Poems, University of California Press (Berkeley, CA), 1991.

The Old Days, Ambrosia Press, 1991.

Gnomic Verses, Zasterle Press, 1991.

A Poetry Anthology, Edmundson Art Foundation, 1992.

Life and Death, Grenfell Press, 1993, New Directions (New York, NY), 1998.

Loops: Ten Poems, Nadja, 1995.

Ligeia: A Libretto, Granary Books, 1996.

So There: Poems 1976-83, New Directions (New York, NY), 1998.

(With Max Gimblett and Alan Loney) *The Dogs of Auckland,* Holloway Press, 1998.

(With John Millei) *Personal: Poems,* Peter Koch, 1998.

En Famille: A Poem by Robert Creeley, Granary Books, 1999.

(With Alex Katz) *Edges,* Peter Blum, 1999.

(With Daisy DeCapite) *Cambridge, Mass 1944,* Boog Literature, 2000.

Thinking, Z Press, 2000.

Clemente's Images, Backwoods Broadsides, 2000.

For Friends, Drive He Sd Books, 2000.

(With Archie Rand, illustrations) *Drawn and Quartered,* Distributed Art Publishers, 2001.

Just In Time: Poems, 1984-1994, New Directions (New York, NY), 2001.

If I Were Writing This, New Directions (New York, NY), 2003.

EDITOR

Charles Olson, *Mayan Letters,* Divers Press (Mallorca, Spain), 1953.

(With Donald M. Allen, and contributor) *New American Story,* Grove (New York, NY), 1965.

(And author of introduction) Charles Olson, *Selected Writings,* New Directions (New York, NY), 1966.

(With Donald Allen, and contributor) *The New Writing in the U.S.A.,* Penguin (New York, NY), 1967.

Whitman: Selected Poems, Penguin (New York, NY), 1973.

(And contributor) *The Essential Burns,* Ecco Press (New York, NY), 1989.

Tim Prythero, Peters Corporation, 1990.

Olson, Selected Poems, University of California Press (Berkeley, CA), 1993.

(With David Lehman) *The Best American Poetry 2002,* Scribner (New York, NY), 2002.

PROSE

The Gold Diggers (short stories), Divers Press (Mallorca, Spain), 1954, expanded edition published as *The Gold Diggers and Other Stories,* J. Calder, 1965.

The Island (novel), Scribner (New York, NY), 1963.

A Day Book (poems and prose), Scribner (New York, NY), 1972.

Mabel: A Story, and Other Prose (includes *A Day Book* and *Presences*), Calder & Boyars (London, England), 1976.

Collected Prose, Marion Boyars (New York, NY), 1984, corrected edition, University of California Press (Berkeley, CA), 1988, Dalkey Archive Press (Chicago, IL), 2001.

NONFICTION

An American Sense (essay), Sigma Press, 1965.

A Quick Graph: Collected Notes and Essays, edited by Donald M. Allen, Four Seasons Foundation (San Francisco, CA), 1970.

Notebook, Bouwerie Editions (New York, NY), 1972.

A Sense of Measure (essays), Calder & Boyars (London, England), 1972.

Inside Out (lecture), Black Sparrow Press (Santa Rosa, CA), 1973.

The Creative (lecture), Black Sparrow Press (Santa Rosa, CA), 1973.

Was That a Real Poem and Other Essays, Four Seasons Foundation (San Francisco, CA), 1979.

Collected Essays, University of California Press (Berkeley, CA), 1989.

Autobiography, Hanuman Books, 1990.

Day Book of a Virtual Poet (essays), Spuyten Duyvil (New York, NY), 1998.

OTHER

Listen (play; produced in London, 1972), Black Sparrow Press (Santa Rosa, CA), 1972.

Contexts of Poetry: Interviews, 1961-1971, Four Seasons Foundation (San Francisco, CA), 1973.

Charles Olson and Robert Creeley: The Complete Correspondence, ten volumes, edited by George F. Butterick, Black Sparrow Press (Santa Rosa, CA), 1980–96.

Jane Hammond, Exit Art, 1989.

Irving Layton and Robert Creeley: The Complete Correspondence, edited by Ekbert Faas and Sabrina Reed, University of Toronto Press (Toronto, Ontario, Canada), 1990.

Tales out of School: Selected Interviews, University of Michigan Press (Ann Arbor, MI), 1993.

Robert Creeley, reading with jazz musicians David Cast, Chris Massey, Steve Swallow, and David Torn accompanying, Cuneiform Records, 1998.

(Author of foreword) *The Turning,* Hilda Morley, Asphodel Press, 1998.

(With Elizabeth Licata and Amy Cappellazzo) *In Company: Robert Creeley's Collaborations* (from a traveling art show), University of North Carolina Press (Chapel Hill, NC), 1999.

(Contributor; with others) *Susan Rothenberg: Paintings from the Nineties,* Rizzoli International (New York, NY), 2000.

Work represented in numerous anthologies, including *The New American Poetry: 1945-1960,* edited by Donald Allen, Grove (New York, NY), 1960; *A Controversy of Poets,* edited by Paris Leary and Robert Kelly, Doubleday (New York, NY), 1965; *Norton Anthology of Modern Poetry,* edited by Richard Ellmann and Robert O'Clair, Norton (New York, NY), 1973; *The New Oxford Book of American Verse,* edited by Richard Ellmann, Oxford University Press (New York, NY), 1976; and *Poets' Encyclopedia,* edited by Michael Andre, Unmuzzled Ox Press, 1980. Contributor to literary periodicals, including *Paris Review, Nation, Black Mountain Review, Origin, Yugen,* and *Big Table.* Founder and editor, *Black Mountain Review,* 1954-57; advisory editor, *Sagetrieb,* 1983—; advisory editor, *American Book Review,* 1983—; contributing editor, *Formations,* 1984—; and advisory editor, *New York Quarterly,* 1984—.

The major collection of Creeley's manuscripts and correspondence is housed in Special Collections, Stanford University, Stanford, CA. Other collections include the Beinecke Rare Book and Manuscript Library of the Yale University Library, New Haven, CT (correspondence with William Carlos Williams), Humanities Research Center, University of Texas Libraries, Austin (correspondence with Ezra Pound), John M. Olin Library, Washington University, St. Louis, MO (manuscripts and correspondence predating 1965), Lilly Library, Indiana University, Bloomington (manuscripts and correspondence with Cid Corman), Simon Fraser University Library, Burnaby, British Columbia, Canada (correspondence with Richard Emerson), and University of Connecticut Library, Storrs (correspondence with Charles Olson).

SIDELIGHTS: Once known primarily for his association with the group called the "Black Mountain Poets," Robert Creeley has become an important and influential literary figure in his own right. His poetry is noted as much for its concision as its emotional power. Albert Mobilio, writing in the *Voice Literary Supplement,* observed: "Creeley has shaped his own audience. The much imitated, often diluted minimalism, the compression of emotion into verse in which scarcely a syllable is wasted, has decisively marked a generation of poets."

Creeley first began to develop his writing talents while attending Holderness School in Plymouth, New Hampshire, on a scholarship. His articles and stories appeared regularly in the school's literary magazine, and in his senior year he became its editor in chief. Creeley was admitted to Harvard in 1943, but his academic life was disrupted while he served as an ambulance driver for the American Field Service in 1944 and 1945.

Creeley returned to Harvard after the war and became associated with such writers as John Hawkes, Mitchell Goodman, and Kenneth Koch. He began corresponding with Cid Corman and Charles Olson, two poets who were to have a substantial influence on the direction of his future work. Excited especially by Olson's ideas about literature, Creeley began to develop a distinctive and unique poetic style.

Throughout the 1950s, Creeley was associated with the "Black Mountain Poets," a group of writers including Denise Levertov, Ed Dorn, Fielding Dawson, and others who had some connection with Black Mountain College, an experimental, communal college in North Carolina that was a haven for many innovative writers and artists of the period. Creeley edited the *Black Mountain Review* and developed a close and lasting relationship with Olson, who was the rector of the college. The two engaged in a lengthy, intensive correspondence about literary matters that has been collected and published as *Charles Olson and Robert Creeley: The Complete Correspondence.* Olson and Creeley together developed the concept of "projective verse," a kind of poetry that abandoned traditional forms in favor of a freely constructed verse that took shape as the process of composing it was underway. Olson called this process "composition by field," and his famous essay on the subject, "Projective Verse," was as important for the poets of the emerging generation as T.S. Eliot's "Tradition and the Individual Talent" was to the poets of the previous generation. Olson credited Creeley with formulating one of the basic principles of this new poetry: the idea that "form is never more than an extension of content."

Creeley was a leader in the generational shift that veered away from history and tradition as primary poetic sources and gave new prominence to the ongoing experiences of an individual's life. Because of this emphasis, the major events of his life loom large in his literary work. Creeley's marriage to Ann MacKinnon ended in divorce in 1955. The breakup of that relationship is chronicled in fictional form in his only novel, *The Island,* which drew upon his experiences on the island of Mallorca, off the coast of Spain, where he lived with MacKinnon and their three children in 1953 and 1954. After the divorce Creeley returned to Black Mountain College for a brief time before moving west to make a new life. He was in San Francisco during the flowering of the "San Francisco Poetry Renaissance" and became associated for a time with the writers of the Beat Generation: Allen Ginsberg, Jack Kerouac, Michael McClure, and others. His work appeared in the influential "beat" anthology *The New American Poetry: 1945-1960,* edited by Donald Allen.

In 1956 Creeley accepted a teaching position at a boys' school in Albuquerque, New Mexico, where he met his second wife, Bobbie Louise Hall. Though Creeley published poetry and fiction throughout the 1950s and 1960s and had even established his own imprint, the Divers Press, in 1952, his work did not receive important national recognition until Scribner published his first major collection, *For Love: Poems 1950-1960,* in 1962. This book collected work that he had been issuing in small editions and magazines during the previous decade. When *For Love* debuted, Mobilio wrote, "it was recognized at once as a pivotal contribution to the alternative poetics reshaping the American tradition. . . . The muted, delicately contrived lyrics . . . were personal and self-contained; while they drew their life from the everyday, their techniques of dislocation sprang from the mind's naturally stumbled syntax."

The very first poem in *For Love,* "Hart Crane," with its unorthodox, Williams-like line breaks, its nearly hidden internal rhymes, and its subtle assonance and sibilance, announces the Creeley style—a style defined by an intense concentration on the sounds and rhythms of language as well as the placement of the words on the page. This intensity produces a kind of minimal poetry, which seeks to extract the bare linguistic bones from ongoing life experiences. In his introduction to *The New Writing in the U.S.A.,* Creeley cites approvingly Herman Melville's definition of "visible truth"—"the apprehension of the absolute condition of present things"—and supplements it with William Burroughs's famous statement from *Naked Lunch* about the writer's task: "There is only one thing a writer can write about: what is in front of his senses at the moment of writing. . . . I am a recording instrument . . . I do not presume to impose 'story' 'plot' 'continuity.'"

In *Pieces, A Day Book, Thirty Things,* and *Hello: A Journal, February 29-May 3, 1976,* all published between 1968 and 1978, Creeley attempts to break down the concept of a "single poem" by offering his readers sequential, associated fragments of poems with indeterminate beginnings and endings. All of these works are energized by the same heightened attention to the present that characterizes Creeley's earlier work, but in *Hello,* a book written as journal entries over a five-week period while Creeley traveled in the Orient and South Pacific, he speculates on the possibility of using memory rather than the present as a poetic source. The poetry remains stubbornly rooted in the present despite the insistent intrusion of memories, both recent and long past.

Many of the poems in *Hello* refer to the last days of Creeley's relationship with his second wife, Bobbie. That marriage ended in divorce in 1976, the same year he met Penelope Highton, his third wife, while traveling in New Zealand. In this sense, the book may be described in much the same terms as Sherman Paul, in his book *The Lost America of Love,* describes *For Love,* "Poems of two marriages, the breakup of one, the beginning of another." For all of Creeley's experimentation, he has always been in some ways an exceedingly domestic poet; his mother, children, wives, and close friends are the subjects of his best work. Because Creeley's second marriage lasted nearly twenty years, the sense of a major chunk of his life drifting away from him is very strong in *Hello.* Creeley here conveys the traumatic emotional state that almost always accompanies the breakup of long-term relationships. En route to Perth, he writes: "Sitting here in limbo, there are / people walking through my head." In Singapore he remarks on his tenuous hold on things: "Getting fainter, in the world, / fearing something's fading. . . ." Although *Hello* is superficially a record of Creeley's travels, the poems are not really about the countries he has visited, but rather about the landscape of mind he has brought with him.

It was not until Creeley's next major collection, 1979's *Later,* that the poetry seemed to shift into a new phase characterized by a greater emphasis on memory, a new sense of life's discrete phases, and an intense preoccupation with aging. In "Myself," the first poem in *Later,* he writes: "I want, if older, / still to know / why, human, men / and women are / so torn, so lost / why hopes cannot / find a better world / than this." This futile but deeply human quest captures the spirit of Creeley's later work. It embodies a commonly shared realization: one becomes older but still knows very little about essential aspects of life, particularly the mysteries of human relationships. And as Alan Williamson observed in his *New York Times Book Review* assessment of *Later,* "In general, the stronger the note of elegiac bafflement and rage (the past utterly gone, the compensating wisdom not forthcoming), the better the writing."

The ten-part title poem, "Later," was written over a period of ten days in September of 1977. The poem presents a kaleidoscopic view of various times and events important to Creeley's life, beginning with an evocation of lost youth. Youth, in later life, can only become a palpable part of the present through the evocative power of memory. Another section of the poem comments on how certain empirical sensations are repositories of memory. A taste, a smell, a touch, can evoke a lost world. "Later" continues to present a flood of childhood memories: a lost childhood dog that Creeley fantasizes running into again after all these years; memories of his mother and friends and neighbors; sights and sounds of his early days all evoked and made a part of the poetry he is composing in an attic room in Buffalo, September, 1977.

In the work produced after the material included in *The Collected Poems of Robert Creeley, 1945-1975* there is an increasing tendency to derive poetry from what the English Romantic poet William Wordsworth called "emotion recollected in tranquility." It is a poetry that remembers and reflects and seems much less tied to the exigencies of the present than the earlier work.

Mirrors reveals how much a part of our characters memories become with each passing year, so that as we age we accumulate the mannerisms of our parents and reexperience past situations. This theme of the present incorporating the past is most literal in "Prospect," one of the most memorable poems in *Mirrors.* It is an atypical Creeley poem because it utilizes conventional elements of poetry—symbolism, metaphor, and imagery—in a surprisingly traditional manner. In fact, the poem has a remarkably unique resonance because Creeley's physical description of nature conveys both present and past psychological states. It takes no deep looking into the poem to see the landscape as emblematic of the state of Creeley's later life, invigorated by a new marriage and the birth of a new child, his son William. The poem concludes with the reflections awakened by a contemplation of the landscape, which is described as peaceful and beautiful, yet in the end "faintly painful." The final phrase surprises, coming at the end of an otherwise tranquil and nearly celebratory poem. It reminds the reader that although embarking on a new life can create the illusion that it is possible to exist in an Edenic landscape apart from time, in reality the past remains an integral part of the present. "Faintly painful," with its echoing first syllable rhyme, is exactly right to convey the contrary feelings of both relief and regret that the poem ultimately leaves the reader with— relief that the thoughtfulness the landscape provokes is not more painful, regret that there is any pain at all.

Another of Creeley's collections, *Life and Death,* examines the poet's increasing age and mortality. A *Publishers Weekly* reviewer wrote: "For all of his complexity, [Creeley's] responses to his own sense of aging are surprisingly witty, lyrical, and grounded." Speaking of two specific poems in the collection, *Yale Review* contributor Stephen Burt offered the following praise for Creeley's work: "The best poems in *Life and Death* do touch on subjects other than isolation and dying—subjects that triangulate, that help Creeley place his obsessions. One such poem is 'Old Poems'; another is 'Given,' whose unfinished sentences, loping through their subdued quatrains, depict childhood as old age remembers it. It seems to me an extraordinary success, in part a triumph of prosody, and in part a triumph of a few details—never has one doughnut done more verbal work."

But pain has been one of the most constant elements in Creeley's work, and his later poetry continues to search for words to express it with sensitivity and exactness and without the sometimes maudlin excesses of "confessional" verse. Though these poems are more rooted in memory than the earlier work, Creeley remains committed to the poetic task of getting things exactly right. This has been the task of his writing throughout his career, and as readers look into the "mirror" of Creeley's work, they can see not only his aging, but their own.

After *Life and Death,* other volumes of poetry followed in regular succession. Some of them are *Loops: Ten Poems,* in 1995; *Ligeia: A Libretto,* in 1996; *So There: Poems 1976-83,* in 1998; *En Famille: A Poem by Robert Creeley,* in 1999; *Cambridge, Mass 1944,* with Daisy DeCapite in 2000; *Thinking,* in 2000; *For Friends,* in 2000; *Drawn and Quartered,* with Archie Rand's illustrations in 2001; *Just In Time: Poems, 1984-1994,* in 2001; and *If I Were Writing This,* in 2003. R.D. Pohl in the *Buffalo News,* praised *If I Were Writing This* highly, declaring that it "contains some of the starkest and most memorable poems Creeley has written." For instance, "'Conversion to Her' is a dense and emotionally charged meditation on sexual identity that appears to suggest that the male ego succumbs to the feminine order of the universe only in death." Pohl and a *Publishers Weekly* reviewer both saw *If I Were Writing This* as a companion volume to *Life and Death,* each of them "composed primarily of poems dedicated to family and friends (dead and living), collaborative verses, and such poems as 'For You' in which intimacy of tone coincides with cryptic, lyrical abstraction." Pohl noted that *If I Were Writing This* is the first major volume to appear since Creeley joined the ranks of such poetic giants as Ezra Pound, William Carlos Williams, Wallace Stevens and

John Ashbery by winning the prestigious Yale University Bollingen Prize in 1999 and regretted that the publisher placed the fifty-four quatrains from Creeley's collaboration with artist Archie Rand early in the book without any explanation. "A casual or browsing reader might easily come to the mistaken conclusion that Creeley in his dotage had now turned to writing light verse," Pohl complained. However, Pohl delighted in the rest of the volume, in which, he said, Creeley "has no intention of presiding over his own canonization." He continued: "The fragility of our common experience in language and the world resonates through every line of Creeley's recent work" as in, "Somewhere in all the time that's passed / was a thing in mind became the evidence, / the pleasure even in fact of being lost / so quickly, simply that what it was could never last." To a question from J.M. Spalding of the 2003 *Cortland Review*—"What has changed in your work between *Echoes* and *Life and Death?*"—Creeley answered "Not a great deal. Perhaps a continuing relaxation, call it, an increased belief that says only being in the world matters at all and that it means, literally, finding one's way to others. I realized that just as childhood is lonely without other children to be with, old age is awful in isolation. One doesn't want to be stacked like planes waiting to take off, only with one's 'peer' group."

Creeley has also written a considerable amount of prose and been editor of a number of volumes, including *Best American Poetry 2002,* of which a *Publishers Weekly* writer remarked that it "is refreshing for what it isn't: a compendium of September 11 poems." Creeley, he said, has made a choice of poems that is "balanced and satisfying, providing space for contemplation, while opening a rare window on dissent." Among the poets included are John Ashbery, Frank Bidart, Anne Carson, W.S. Merwin, Sharon Olds, Carl Phillips, Charles Wright, Amiri Baraka, Alice Notley, Benjamin Friedlander, Steve Malmude, and Mong-Lan. The *Seattle Times*'s Richard Wakefield, however, asserted, "Most of the poems selected by Robert Creeley for inclusion in *The Best American Poetry 2002* are so awful that the reader is hard put to explain how five or ten good ones sneaked in." He found poems by W.S. Merwin, Donald Hall, and T. Alan Broughton among the few he would recommend. Amy Bracken Sparks in the *Plain Dealer,* on the other hand, enjoyed the "sea change" in poetry she recognized as "the avant-garde, going on fifty or so funneled from the margins by longtime progressive poet Robert Creeley." "It's thick," she wrote, "with lists, prose poems, fragments, foreign tongues and chunks of text dueling on the page." Even though she acknowledged that for "the legion of those who love Poet Laureate Billy Collins' poems," the poetry in this volume is not "accessible to all; they are innovative in both concept and structure, and therefore risk losing the reader," she added, "They are refreshingly unapologetic about being book-smart in an era when poetry has been dumbed-down at the microphone across America. Some have footnotes; one poem is entirely composed of them. Others juxtapose words in tight formation, or swing them across free-ranging lines that look like paint flung onto a canvas. Yes, it's a bit of work when not everything is explained. Pretension lurks about, but there's always Diane Di Prima keeping everything earthbound and Sharon Olds writing yet again about her father." As Eric McHenry of the Westchester *Journal News,* pointed out, "In the words of series editor David Lehman, *The Best American Poetry* is more properly viewed as a chronicle of 'the taste of our leading poets.' The best predictor of whether or not you'll like the poems in a given volume is whether or not you like the poetry of the person who chose them."

Creeley's prose includes a novel, essays, and short stories, as well as a play, collected letters, and an autobiography, published in 1990. But primarily a poet, he rejoices, as he says, in words, their immediacy, their availability to everyone, their insistence, in poems, that we just be with them. Don Byrd quoted him in *Contemporary Poets:* "I write to realize the world as one has come to live in it, thus to give testament. I write to move in *words,* a human delight. I write when no other act is possible." Asked by Spalding about "good" poems, Creeley, who had written in the introduction to *Best American Poetry 2002,* the poem is "that place we are finally safe in" where "understanding is not a requirement. You don't have to know why. Being there is the one requirement," responded, "If one only wrote 'good' poems, what a dreary world it would be. 'Writing writing' is the point. It's a process, like they say, not a production line. I love the story of Neal Cassidy writing on the bus with Ken Kesey, simply tossing the pages out the window as he finished each one. 'I wonder if it was any good,' I can hear someone saying. Did you ever go swimming without a place you were necessarily swimming to—the dock, say, or the lighthouse, the moored boat, the drowning woman? Did you always swim well, enter the water cleanly, proceed with efficient strokes and a steady flutter kick? I wonder if this 'good' poem business is finally some echo of trying to get mother to pay attention." Poets, he says, do not need encouragement. They live to write.

BIOGRAPHICAL AND CRITICAL SOURCES:

BOOKS

Allen, Donald M., editor, *Robert Creeley, Contexts of Poetry: Interviews, 1961-1971,* Four Seasons Foundation (San Francisco, CA), 1973.

Altieri, Charles, *Self and Sensibility in Contemporary American Poetry,* Cambridge University Press (New York, NY), 1984.

Butterick, George F., editor, *Charles Olson and Robert Creeley: The Complete Correspondence,* Black Sparrow Press (Santa Rosa, CA), 1980.

Clark, Tom, *Robert Creeley and the Genius of the American Common Place: Together with the Poet's Own Autobiography,* New Directions (New York, NY), 1993.

Conniff, Brian, *The Lyric and Modern Poetry: Olson, Creeley, Bunting,* Peter Lang (New York, NY), 1988.

Contemporary Authors Autobiography Series, Volume 10, Thomson Gale (Detroit, MI), 1989.

Contemporary Literary Criticism, Thomson Gale (Detroit, MI), Volume 1, 1973, Volume 2, 1974, Volume 4, 1975, Volume 8, 1978, Volume 11, 1979, Volume 15, 1980, Volume 36, 1986.

Contemporary Poets, 5th edition, edited by Tracy Chevalier, St. James Press (Detroit, MI), 1991.

Corman, Cid, editor, *The Gist of Origin,* Viking (New York, NY), 1975.

Creeley, Robert, *Hello,* Hawk Press (Christchurch, New Zealand), 1978.

Creeley, Robert, *Later,* Toothpaste (West Branch, IA), 1978.

Creeley, Robert, *If I Were Writing This,* New Directions (New York, NY), 2003.

Edelberg, Cynthia Dubin, *Robert Creeley's Poetry: A Critical Introduction,* University of New Mexico Press (Albuquerque, NM), 1978.

Faas, Ekbert, and Sabrina Reed, editors, *Irving Layton and Robert Creeley: The Complete Correspondence, 1953-1978,* McGill-Queen's University Press (Toronto, Ontario, Canada), 1990.

Faas, Ekbert, and Maria Trombaco, *Robert Creeley: A Biography,* University Press of New England (Hanover, NH), 2001.

Ford, Arthur L., *Robert Creeley,* Twayne (Boston, MA), 1978.

Foster, Edward Halsey, *Understanding the Black Mountain Poets,* University of South Carolina Press (Columbia, SC), 1995.

Fox, Willard, *Robert Creeley, Edward Dorn, and Robert Duncan: A Reference Guide.* G.K. Hall (Boston, MA), 1989.

Fredman, Stephen, *Poet's Prose: The Crisis in American Verse,* Cambridge University Press (New York, NY), 1983.

Giger, Esther, and Agnieszka Salska, editors, *Freedom and Form: Essays in Contemporary American Poetry.* Wydawnictwo Uniwersytetu Lódzkiego (Lódz, Poland), 1998.

Gwynn, R. S., editor, *New Expansive Poetry: Theory, Criticism, History,* Story Line (Ashland, OR), 1999.

Novik, Mary, *Robert Creeley: An Inventory, 1945-1970,* Kent State University Press (Kent, OH), 1973.

Oberg, Arthur, *Modern American Lyric: Lowell, Berryman, Creeley, and Plath,* Rutgers University Press (New Brunswick, NJ), 1977.

Paul, Sherman, *The Lost America of Love: Rereading Robert Creeley, Edward Dorn, and Robert Duncan,* Louisiana State University Press (Baton Rouge, LA), 1981.

Rifkin, Libbie, *Career Moves: Olson, Creeley, Zukofsky, Berrigan, and the American Avant-Garde,* University of Wisconsin Press (Madison, WI), 2000.

Roberts, Neil, editor, *A Companion to Twentieth-Century Poetry,* Blackwell (Oxford, England), 2001.

Sheffler, Ronald Anthony, *The Development of Robert Creeley's Poetry,* University of Massachusetts (Amherst, MA), 1971.

Tallman, Allen and Warren, editors, *The Poetics of the New American Poetry,* Grove (New York, NY), 1973.

Tallman, Warren, *Three Essays on Creeley,* Coach House Press (Toronto, Ontario, Canada), 1973.

Terrell, Carroll F., *Robert Creeley: The Poet's Workshop,* University of Maine Press (Orono, ME), 1984.

Von Hallberg, Robert, *American Poetry and Culture, 1945-80,* Harvard University Press (Cambridge, MA), 1985.

Wilson, John, editor, *Robert Creeley's Life and Work: A Sense of Increment,* University of Michigan Press (Ann Arbor, MI), 1987.

PERIODICALS

American Book Review, May-June, 1984.

American Poetry Review, November-December, 1976; May-June, 1997, p. 9; September-October, 1999, p. 17.

Atlantic Monthly, November, 1962; February, 1968; October, 1977.

Books Abroad, autumn, 1967.

Boundary 2, spring, 1975; spring and fall (special two-volume issue on Creeley), 1978.

Buffalo News, February 25, 1996, p. E1; February 7, 1999, p. E6; March 24, 2000, p. G18; September 7, 2003, p. G5.

Cambridge Quarterly, 1998, p. 87.

Christian Science Monitor, October 9, 1969.

Chronicle of Higher Education, November 1, 1996, p. B10.

Contemporary Literature, spring, 1972; fall, 1995, p. 79.

Cortland Review, April, 1998.

Critique, spring, 1964.

Denver Quarterly, winter 1997, p. 82.

ebr: The Alt-X Web Review, spring, 1999.

Encounter, February, 1969.

English: The Journal of the English Association, summer, 2001, p. 127.

Gentleman's Quarterly, June, 1996, p. 74.

Harper's, August, 1967; September, 1983.

Hudson Review, summer, 1963; summer, 1967; spring, 1970; summer, 1977.

Iowa Review, spring, 1982.

Journal News (Westchester, NY), August 31, 2003, p. 4E.

Journal of American Studies, August 1998, p. 263.

Kenyon Review, spring, 1970.

Library Journal, September 1, 1979; April 15, 1994, p. 81; April 1, 1997, p. 94; April 1, 1999, p, 95.

Listener, March 23, 1967.

London Magazine, June-July, 1973.

Los Angeles Times Book Review, April 17, 1983; October 30, 1983; March 4, 1984; June 24, 1984; June 23, 1991, p. 8.

Modern Language Quarterly, December, 1982, p. 369.

Modern Poetry Studies, winter, 1977.

Nation, August 25, 1962.

National Observer, October 30, 1967.

National Review, November 19, 1960.

New Leader, October 27, 1969.

New Orleans Review, spring, 1992, p. 14.

New Republic, October 11, 1969; December 18, 1976.

New Statesman, August 6, 1965; March 10, 1987.

New York Review of Books, January 20, 1966; August 1, 1968.

New York Times, June 27, 1967.

New York Times Book Review, November 4, 1962; September 22, 1963; November 19, 1967; October 27, 1968; January 7, 1973; May 1, 1977; March 9, 1980; August 7, 1983; June 24, 1984; September 23, 1984; November 3, 1991, p. 14.

North Dakota Quarterly, fall, 1987, p. 89.

Northwest Review, 2000, p. 102.

Observer (London, England), September 6, 1970.

Paris Review, fall, 1968.

Parnassus, fall-winter, 1984.

Partisan Review, summer, 1968.

Plain Dealer, September 29, 2002, p. J9.

Poetry, March, 1954; May, 1958; September, 1958; March, 1963; April, 1964; August, 1966; January, 1968; March, 1968; August, 1968; May, 1970; December, 1970; September, 1984.

Publishers Weekly, March 18, 1968; March 28, 1994; March 30, 1998, p. 77; September 24, 2001, p. 91; July 22, 2002, p. 170; September 1, 2003.

Review of Contemporary Fiction, fall, 1995, pp. 79, 82, 97, 107, 110, 116, 120, 127, 137, 141.

Sagetrieb: A Journal Devoted to Poets in the Imagist/ Objectivist Tradition, winter, 1982 (special issue); fall, 1988, p. 53; spring-fall, 1991, p. 209 (bibliog.); spring, 1999, pp. 131, 149.

San Francisco Chronicle, April 12, 1998, p. 12.

Saturday Review, August 4, 1962; December 11, 1965; June 3, 1967.

Seattle Times, October 6, 2002, p. L9.

Sewanee Review, winter, 1961.

Southwest Review, winter, 1964.

Talisman: A Journal of Contemporary Poetry and Poetics, 2001-2002, p. 49.

Time, July 12, 1971.

Times Literary Supplement, March 16, 1967; August 7, 1970; November 12, 1970; December 11, 1970; May 20, 1977; May 30, 1980; February 20, 1981; November 4, 1983; May 10, 1991, p. 22.

Village Voice, October 22, 1958; December 10, 1979; November 25, 1981.

Virginia Quarterly Review, summer, 1968; winter, 1972; spring, 1973.

Voice Literary Supplement, September, 1991, p. 14.

Washington Post Book World, August 11, 1991, p. 13.

Western Humanities Review, spring, 1970.

Winstom-Salem Journal, March 5, 2000, p. E1.

World Literature Today, autumn, 1984; summer, 1992; spring, 1995.

Yale Review, October, 1962; December, 1969; spring, 1970; April, 1999, p. 175.

ONLINE

Academy of American Poets: Poetry Exhibit, http:// www.poets.org/ (March 8, 2004).

Cortland Review, http://www.cortlandreview.com/ (April, 1998), interview with Creeley.

Levity, http://www.levity.com/ (March 8, 2004).

Providence Phoenix Book Reviews, http://www. providencephoenix.com/ (March 26-April 2, 1998), interview with Creeley.

Robert Creeley Home Page, http://wings.buffalo.edu/ epc/authors/creeley/ (April 26, 2000).

University of Illinois, Department of English, http:// www.english.uiuc.edu/ (March 8, 2004).

OBITUARIES:

BOOKS

Creeley, Robert, *Autobiography,* Hanuman Books, 1990.

PERIODICALS

Los Angeles Times, April 1, 2005, p. B9.
New York Times, April 1, 2005, p. C13.
Times (London, England), April 1, 2005, p. 62.
Washington Post, April 1, 2005, p. B6.

*   *   *

CREELEY, Robert White
See CREELEY, Robert

*   *   *

CREWS, Harry 1935-
(Harry Eugene Crews)

PERSONAL: Born June 6, 1935, in Alma, GA; son of Rey (a farmer) and Myrtice (Haselden) Crews; married Sally Thornton Ellis, January 24, 1960 (divorced); children: Patrick Scott (deceased), Byron Jason. *Education:* University of Florida, B.A., 1960, M.S.Ed., 1962.

ADDRESSES: Agent—c/o Author Mail, Simon & Schuster, 1230 Avenue of the Americas, New York, NY 10020.

CAREER: Writer. Broward Junior College, Ft. Lauderdale, FL, teacher of English, 1962-68; University of Florida, Gainesville, associate professor, 1968-74, professor of English, 1974-88. *Military service:* U.S. Marine Corps, 1953-56; became sergeant.

AWARDS, HONORS: Award from American Academy of Arts and Sciences, 1972.

WRITINGS:

NOVELS

The Gospel Singer, Morrow (New York, NY), 1968, reprinted, Perennial Library (New York, NY), 1988.

Naked in Garden Hills, Morrow (New York, NY), 1969.

This Thing Don't Lead to Heaven, Morrow (New York, NY), 1970.

Karate Is a Thing of the Spirit, Morrow (New York, NY), 1971.

Car, Morrow (New York, NY), 1972.

The Hawk Is Dying, Alfred A. Knopf (New York, NY), 1973.

The Gypsy's Curse, Alfred A. Knopf (New York, NY), 1974.

A Feast of Snakes, Atheneum (New York, NY), 1976.

All We Need of Hell, Harper & Row (New York, NY), 1987.

The Knockout Artist, Harper & Row (New York, NY), 1988.

Body, Poseidon Press (New York, NY), 1990.

Scar Lover, Poseidon Press (New York, NY), 1992.

The Mulching of America, Simon & Schuster (New York, NY), 1995.

Celebration, Simon & Schuster (New York, NY), 1998.

SHORT STORIES

The Enthusiast, Palaemon Press, 1981.

Two, Lord John (Northridge, CA), 1984.

Contributor of stories to *Florida Quarterly* and *Craft and Vision.*

OTHER

A Childhood: The Biography of a Place (autobiography), Harper & Row (New York, NY), 1978, reprinted, University of Georgia Press (Athens, GA), 1995.

Blood and Grits (nonfiction), Harper & Row (New York, NY), 1979.

Florida Frenzy (essays and stories), University Presses of Florida (Gainesville, FL), 1982.

Blood Issue (play), produced in Louisville, KY, 1989.

Madonna at Ringside, Lord John (Northridge, CA), 1991.

Classic Crews: A Harry Crews Reader, Poseidon Press (New York, NY), 1993.

Getting Naked with Harry Crews: Interviews, edited by Erik Bledsoe, University Press of Florida (Gainesville, FL), 1999.

Author of column "Grits" for *Esquire.* Contributor to *Sewanee Review, Georgia Review,* and *Playboy.*

SIDELIGHTS: Reading novelist Harry Crews, Allen Shepherd maintained in the *Dictionary of Literary Biography,* "is not something one wants to do too much of at a single sitting; the intensity of his vision is unsettling." This vision is both comic and tragic, nostalgic and grotesque, and is focused on the American South where Crews was raised and still lives. His characters, often physically deformed or strangely obsessed, are grotesques in the Southern gothic tradition, and his stories are violent and extreme. Michael Mewshaw, writing in the *Nation,* explained that Crews "has taken a cast of the misfit and malformed—freaks, side-show performers, psychopaths, cripples, midgets and catatonics—and yoked it to plots which are even more improbable than his characters." Frank W. Shelton of the *Southern Literary Journal* defined the world of Crews's fiction as "mysterious, violent and dangerous" and called his vision "a lonely and extremely sad one." But Mewshaw did not find Crews's vision essentially sad. He found that Crews is "beset by existential nausea but, like any normal American, is not blind to the humor of it all. Bleak, mordant, appalling, Harry Crews can also be hilarious." Vivian Mercier of the *World* echoed this idea, remarking that "reading Crews is a bit like undergoing major surgery with laughing gas."

Crews first began to create stories as a boy in rural Georgia during the Depression. Living in an area where, he claims in his *A Childhood: The Biography of a Place,* "there wasn't enough cash money . . . to close up a dead man's eyes," Crews and his friends found a wonderland in the Sears, Roebuck mail order catalog. The boys called the catalog their dream book because the models seemed unnaturally perfect to them, and the merchandise was far beyond their reach. While poring over the catalog pictures, Crews entertained his friends by spinning stories about the models and products. "I had decided that all the people in the catalog were related," he explains in *A Childhood,* "not necessarily blood kin but knew one another. . . . And it was out of this knowledge that I first began to make up stories."

After serving four years in the U.S. Marines, which he joined at the age of seventeen, Crews went to the University of Florida where he was inspired by writer-in-residence Andrew Lyle to begin writing seriously. In his first published novel, *The Gospel Singer,* Crews writes of his native Georgia. A popular traveling evangelist, the Gospel Singer appears in his hometown of Enigma during a concert tour. His local sweetheart has recently been murdered and, it is suspected, raped by a black man. The Singer is trailed into town by the Freak Fair, a sideshow of human oddities—including the show's owner, a man with an oversized foot—working the crowds attracted by the Singer's revival meetings. When the accused murderer is threatened with lynching, the Gospel Singer tries to save him by revealing that the murdered woman was not in fact a violated virgin but "the biggest whore who ever walked in Enigma," as Shepherd wrote. The result is chaos.

Response to *The Gospel Singer* was generally favorable. Though Walter Sullivan in *Sewanee Review* found the book has "all the hallmarks of a first novel: it is energetic but uneven, competent but clumsy, not finally satisfactory but memorable nonetheless," and believed that "Crews has a good eye, an excellent ear for voices, and a fine dramatic sense." Martin Levin, writing in the *New York Times Book Review,* commented that *The Gospel Singer* "has a nice wild flavor and a dash of Grand Guignol strong enough to meet the severe standards of Southern decadence." And Guy Davenport in *National Review* called the novel "a frenetic sideshow of Georgia poor white trash and their *Hochkultur.*"

Crews followed *The Gospel Singer* with *Naked in Garden Hills,* a book Jean Stafford of the *New York Times Book Review* believed "lives up to and beyond the shining promise of . . . *The Gospel Singer.* The novel is southern Gothic at its best, a Hieronymus Bosch landscape in Dixie inhabited by monstrous, darling pets." *Naked in Garden Hills* revolves around the almost helpless Mayhugh Aaron, known as the Fat Man because of his six-hundred-pound frame, and his valet John Henry Williams, a tiny black man who takes care of him. Fat Man owns most of Garden Hills, a town where the local phosphate mine is the only source of employment. When the mine is exhausted and closed, the town faces financial collapse. To avoid ruin, Dolly Ferguson opens a nightclub with go-go dancers and a sideshow to attract the tourist trade. She wants Fat Man as her star sideshow exhibit, but he refuses. As his employees, including Williams the valet, are one by one hired away by Dolly, and as his financial situation deteriorates, the Fat Man is reduced to a humiliated and helpless figure. He is finally forced to join the sideshow. "Bleeding, beaten by the mob of tourists, naked, and drooling, he crawls to his waiting cage and is lifted high in the light," Shepherd recounted.

Writing in the *New York Times Book Review,* Jonathan Yardley found *Naked in Garden Hills* "a convincing grotesque of a rotting American landscape and its decadent inhabitants," and Shelton wrote that the novel "treats religion in an almost allegorical way." He cited the book's title as a reference to the Garden of Eden, saw Jack O'Boylan, the out-of-state mine owner, as a God figure, and pictured Dolly Ferguson as a kind of savior meant to restore the town. But the novel's ending shows that "man's desire to find meaning in his life leads to degradation, exploitation and the denial of love," Shelton wrote.

A religious dimension can be found in *Karate Is a Thing of the Spirit,* in which Crews writes of an outlaw karate class that meets on a Florida beach and is barred from tournament competition because of its deadly reputation. John Kaimon wanders into this circle and becomes a member, undergoing the rigorous training under the hot sun. The star member of the class, brown belt Gaye Nell Odell, becomes pregnant, possibly by Kaimon. Shelton found both Kaimon and Odell searching for something—something they both find in the discipline of karate. The training, Shelton argued, "is an almost religious ritual through which people attempt to link and fulfill body and spirit." John Deck observed in the *New York Times Book Review* that, after a slow start, *Karate Is a Thing of the Spirit* "takes off, in the manner of a fire storm, rushing at amazing speed, eating up the oxygen, scorching everything it touches."

In *Car,* Crews examines another physical discipline, this one far less common than karate. Herman Mack, whose family is in the automobile junkyard business, decides it is his destiny to eat an automobile, four ounces at a time each day. His daily ingestion of the cut-up auto is broadcast on national television as a sports event. At first pleased with his instant notoriety, Herman falls in love with a prostitute and ends by abandoning his spectacle before it is finished. Yardley found Crews' ending to be "mere sentimentality" and a "flabby resolution," but nonetheless called the novel "a marvelous idea" and "exceedingly funny, indeed painfully so." A reviewer for the *Times Literary Supplement* viewed the novel as "a satire on two alleged vices of the American people: an extravagant fondness for motor-cars, and a taste for ghoulish spectacle." Christopher Lehmann-Haupt in the *New York Times* also saw larger implications in the story, concluding that *Car* "may very well be the best metaphor yet made up about America's passionate love affair with the automobile."

Another strange case of personal destiny dominates *The Hawk Is Dying.* George Gattling becomes obsessed with training a wild hawk, an obsession that estranges him from his family and friends. His efforts eventually reach fruition when "the hawk has finally been 'manned,' and flies free to kill and return again to Gattling's hand," resulting in "one moment of absolute value—and hence absolute beauty," as a critic for the *Times Literary Supplement* explained, adding that the story is told in "comic-horrific scenes." Mercier also found this odd mix in the novel, writing that "beauty and pity and terror coexist with satire and grotesque humor." Similarly, Phoebe Adams in an *Atlantic* review called *The Hawk Is Dying* "a bizarre mixture of tragedy and farce." But she went on to say that, though "the events of this novel are hardly realistic, . . . the book becomes immensely convincing because the underlying pattern of desperation over wasted time and neglected abilities is real and recognizable."

Crews examines a town's obsession with rattlesnakes in *A Feast of Snakes.* He fictionalizes a unique yearly custom in Mystic, Georgia, where the townspeople hold a Rattlesnake Roundup at which they crown a rattlesnake queen, hold a snake fight, and even dine on rattlesnake. The novel follows local resident Joe Lon Mackey, who is unhappily married, illiterate, and bitter about his life. Crews shows the pressures that drive Mackey to go on a murderous rampage at the snake roundup. The gruesome events leading up to this final outburst of violence are seen by many critics to be expertly handled. "Crews," Paul D. Zimmerman wrote in *Newsweek,* "has an ugly knack for making the most sordid sequences amusing, for evoking an absolutely venomous atmosphere, unredeemed by charity or hope. Few writers could pull off the sort of finale that has mad-eyed rednecks rushing in sudden bursts across a snake-scattered, bonfire-bright field, their loins enflamed by the local beauty contestants, their blood racing with whisky, their hearts ready for violence. Crews does." A critic for the *New Yorker* called Crews "a writer of extraordinary power. Joe Lon is a monster, but we are forced to accept him as human, and even as sympathetic. Mr. Crews' story makes us gag, but he holds us, in awe and admiration, to the sickening end."

Crews's nonfiction book *A Childhood* sheds some insight onto the sources of his fiction in its description of the first six years of the author's life. Childhood was a period, Crews claims, when "what has been most significant in my life had all taken place." His father died when he was two years old. His mother then married his uncle, a man she later left because of his violent rages. Crews had a bout with polio, which paralyzed his legs for a time and forced him to hobble. A fall into a tub of scalding water, used for removing the skin off slaughtered hogs, removed the first layer of skin on most of Crews's body. "The skin on the top of the wrist and the back of my hand, along with the fingernails," he remembers in the book, "all just turned loose and slid on down to the ground." Despite the hardships of his childhood, Crews presents the people of his home county in a warm, honest, and unapologetic manner. As the writer recounts, "It was a world in which survival depended on raw courage, a courage born out of desperation and sustained by a lack of alternatives." Robert Sherrill of the *New York Times Book Review* admitted: "It's easy to despise poor folks. *A Childhood* makes it more difficult. It raises almost to a level of heroism these people who seem of a different century."

Critical reaction to *A Childhood* was generally positive, with several critics citing Crews's restraint in recounting his life. Mewshaw, for example, found that throughout the book, Crews "maintains a precarious balance between sentiment and sensation, memory and madness, and manages to convince the reader of two mutually exclusive imperatives which have shaped his life—the desire to escape Bacon County and the constant ineluctable need to go back, if only in memory." A *New Yorker* critic wrote that Crews remembers his childhood with "a sense of grateful escape and shattering loss which have the confusing certainty of truth."

The author resumed writing longer works of fiction in late 1980s, producing the novels *All We Need of Hell* and *The Knockout Artist.* Like his books from previous decades, the works have been acclaimed for their gritty Southern flavor and offbeat characters. *All We Need of Hell* concerns Duffy Deeter, a driven attorney who constantly seeks to prove his manliness. When his wife throws him out of the house, Duffy commences a spree of exercise and drinking, a session that ends when a former enemy teaches Duffy the virtues of love, friendship, and forgiveness.

"If *All We Need of Hell* ran according to Harry Crews's earlier fictional form," remarked Lehmann-Haupt in the *New York Times,* "Duffy's misadventures would lead him to some bizarre or even ghoulish fate." Noting, though, that "something new has been added" to Crews's fiction, Lehmann-Haupt lamented that "there is something decidedly forced and even sentimental about [the story's positive] turn of events. . . . We come away from the novel regarding it as a distinctly lesser effort." Beaufort Cranford, writing in the *Detroit News* was similarly disappointed, commenting that "we readers of Crews suddenly find ourselves on alarmingly cheerful ground. . . . [The ending to] *All We Need of Hell* is a . . . shock, much like a sudden infusion of sugar." Despite complaints that Crews had softened his fiction, Lehmann-Haupt concluded that "we can't help forgiving him for it. There's still such a vividness to his characters. There's still such ease to his prose. . . . [And] he still has the power to make us smile and even laugh out loud."

Body centers around a backwoods Georgia girl named Dorothy Turnipseed who takes to working out in a gym and eventually goes on to compete, under the name Shereel Dupont, in the Ms. Cosmos competition. "In the world of the Ms. Cosmos competition, sex is for losing weight, food is for fuel, other people for rivalry, love for exploitation, family for leaving," novelist Fay

Weldon noted in her *New York Times Book Review* assessment of the book. Nevertheless, Dorothy/Shereel's family accompanies her all the way to the contest where they are conspicuous among the bodybuilders because of their immense bulk. Merle Rubin was unforgiving in her criticism of the book in the *Wall Street Journal,* labeling it a "violent comic-strip of a novel" that "mixes clenched, muscle-bound humor with lashings of fairly standard-style pornography." Weldon, however, was extremely enthusiastic, describing it as "electric . . . a hard, fast and brilliant book." She had special praise for Crews's ability to create convincing women: "Not for a moment, such is this male writer's skill, the throttled-back energy of his writing, do I doubt Mr. Crews's right to be as intimate as he is with his female characters. . . . Shereel's struggle between love and honor provides the book's tender, perfect fleshing out; the will-she-win, won't-she-win tension, mounting page by page, gives muscle, nerve and fervor to the whole." She added, however, that "it's Harry Crews's ability to describe physical existence, bodily sensation, that most impresses."

In *Scar Lover,* Crews featured a typical cast of outcasts and misfits, including a pair of scarred Rastafarian lovers and a woman who sings lullabies to her husband's skull. The protagonist is Peter Butcher, a man tormented by guilt because of an accident in which he left his younger brother permanently brain-damaged. Filled with self-loathing and reviled by the rest of his family, Peter eventually drifts into true love, fighting it all the way. "It may surprise the followers of Harry Crews to hear that his twelfth novel is a love story that is both life-affirming and tender," noted Robert Phillips in the *Hudson Review.* It is "a comic morality play which is less fierce and more tender than any of his previous works." In the reviewer's estimation, however, the positive messages in *Scar Lover* in no way blunt the power of the author's work. *Chicago Tribune* writer Gary Dretzka felt that the novel "is successful in promoting the healing powers of love and forgiveness" and that "Crews' familiar tenderness toward his outcast characters is here in spades, driven by typically muscular writing and energetic pacing."

A darker tone permeated *The Mulching of America,* a book described by a *Washington Post Book World* reviewer as "a satire of corporate America and the credo of success at any cost." The reviewer went on to say that "Crews's wicked satire sends up corporate culture's celebration of conformity and boundless personal sacrifice." The central characters are Hickum Looney, a door-to-door salesman for a soap company; Gaye Nell Odell, a homeless prostitute (seen previously in *Karate Is a*

Thing of the Spirit); and the Boss—the harelipped, hard-driving chief of the Soap for Life Company. Valerie Sayers, a contributor to the *New York Times Book Review,* found the characters predictable enough "for reader discomfort to set in." Still, she added that especially in the case of Hickum and Gaye Nell, "that their love story is sweetly compelling is the measure of Mr. Crews's ability to have his cartoon characters remind us, vaguely and laughably, of our own most compelling fears and humiliations." Sayers further credited the author with creating a successful portrayal of "Americans terrified of taking a step or making a moral choice," and concluded that "Crews is a storyteller who bears down on American enterprise with fierce eyes and a cackle. By the end of the story, he's not laughing and we are all ready to look away."

Some observers have judged Crews's stories to be excessive; "His harshest critics claim that Crews always pushes things too far—to the point where his characters turn into caricatures and his plots become cartoons," Mewshaw commented. One such critic was Sarah Blackburn, who in the *New York Times Book Review* described *The Hawk Is Dying* as "a festival of mangled animals, tortured sexuality and innocence betrayed." James Atlas in *Time* called Crews "a Southern gothic novelist who often makes William Faulkner look pastoral by comparison"; Crews's novel *A Feast of Snakes* was even banned in South Africa. However, Admirers of the writer continue to cite his ability to transform unusual or extreme subjects into credible, moving stories. Doris Grumbach, writing in the *Saturday Review,* admitted that Crews's novels possess a "bizarre, mad, violent, and tragic quality," but maintained that the writer "has a sympathy for maimed and deformed characters, a love of strange situations, and the talent to make it all, somehow, entirely believable." Shepherd, writing of *Car, The Hawk Is Dying,* and *A Feast of Snakes* in *Critique,* added that Crews displays "in these strangely powerful, outlandish, excessive, grotesquely alive novels a gift at once formidable and frightening."

BIOGRAPHICAL AND CRITICAL SOURCES:

BOOKS

Contemporary Literary Criticism, Thomson Gale (Detroit, MI), Volume 6, 1976, Volume 23, 1983, Volume 49, 1988.

Dictionary of Literary Biography, Thomson Gale (Detroit, MI), Volume 6: *American Novelists since World War II, Second Series,* 1980, Volume 143; *Third Series,* 1994.

Jeffrey, David K., editor, *A Grit's Triumph: Essays on the Works of Harry Crews*, Associated Faculty Press (Port Washington, NY), 1983.

PERIODICALS

Arkansas Review, spring, 1995, pp. 1, 82-94.

Atlanta Journal-Constitution, January 18, 1987, p. J8; June 26, 1988, p. J8; April 9, 1989, pp. N1, N2; September 2, 1990, p. N14; January 26, 1992, p. N8; March 8, 1992, p. N1; November 28, 1993, p. K8.

Atlantic, April, 1973, Phoebe Adams, review of *The Hawk Is Dying*.

Booklist, February 15, 1992, Eloise Kinney, review of *Scar Lover*, p. 1086; October 1, 1993, Martha Schoolman, review of *Classic Crews: A Harry Crews Reader*, p. 244; January 1, 1998, Donna Seaman, review of *Celebration*, p. 774.

Boston Globe, January 13, 1987, p. 59; May 3, 1988, p. 73; October 1, 1990, p. 32; February 21, 1992, p. 40; November 23, 1995, p. A26.

Chicago Tribune, February 1, 1987, sec. 14, p. 3; April 10, 1988, sec. 14, p. 6; August 27, 1990, sec. 5, p. 3; February 23, 1992, p. 6.

Chicago Tribune Book World, October 29, 1978; March 11, 1979; July 18, 1982; July 31, 1983; February 23, 1992, sec. 14, p. 6.

Critique, September, 1978; fall, 1986, pp. 45-53.

Detroit News, February 1, 1987, Beaufort Cranford, review of *All We Need of Hell*, p. H2.

Entertainment Weekly, February 28, 1992, Margot Mifflin, review of *Scar Lover*, p. 50; March 27, 1992, review of *Body*, p. 69; November 17, 1995, Michael Glitz, review of *The Mulching of America*, p. 75.

Georgia Review, fall 1987, pp. 627-631; fall 1994, pp. 537-553.

Harper's, August, 1986, p. 35.

Hudson Review, autumn, 1993, Robert Phillips, review of *Scar Lover*, pp. 492-493.

Journal of American Culture, fall, 1988, pp. 47-54.

Kirkus Reviews, December 1, 1997.

Library Journal, August, 1990, Robert H. Donahugh, review of *Body*, p. 139; February 1, 1992, Brack Stoval, review of *Scar Lover*, p. 121; November 15, 1995, Henry J. Carrigan, Jr., review of *The Mulching of America*, p. 98; December 1997, Wilda Williams, review of *Celebration*, p. 148.

Los Angeles Times, May 3, 1987, p. B8; May 22, 1988, p. B6; January 31, 1992, p. E2.

Los Angeles Times Book Review, May 3, 1987; May 22, 1988, p. 6; September 23, 1990, p. 3; October 21, 1990, p. 3; January 14, 1996, p. 2.

Maclean's, March 26, 1979.

Mississippi Quarterly, winter, 1987-88, pp. 1, 69-88.

Nation, February 3, 1979.

National Review, April 21, 1970, Guy Davenport, review of *The Gospel Singer*.

New Boston Review, February-March, 1979.

New Republic, March 31, 1973; May 8, 1989, Robert Brustein, theater review of *Blood Issue*, p. 28.

Newsweek, August 2, Paul D. Zimmerman, review of *A Feast of Snakes*, 1976.

New Yorker, July 15, 1974; July 26, 1976; November 6, 1978.

New York Times, March 2, 1972; March 21, 1973; April 30, 1974; July 12, 1976; December 11, 1978; February 6, 1979; January 12, 1987, Christopher Lehmann-Haupt, review of *All We Need of Hell*, p. C19; February 1, 1987, p. 9; February 19, 1987, Herbert Mitgang, "The 'Screwy' World of a Southern Writer,"; April 18, 1988, Christopher Lehmann-Haupt, review of *The Knockout Artist*, p. C21; May 1, 1988, p. 21; April 5, 1989, Mel Gussow, "Actors Theater," p. C19; November 20, 1995, Christopher Lehmann-Haupt, review of *The Mulching of America*, p. C16; January 8, 1998, Christopher Lehmann-Haupt, review of *Celebration*, p. B12.

New York Times Book Review, February 18, 1968; April 13, 1969; April 26, 1970; April 25, 1971; February 27, 1972; March 25, 1973; March 10, 1974; June 2, 1974; June 23, 1974; September 12, 1976; December 24, 1978; March 25, 1979; February 1, 1987, Russell Banks, review of *All We Need of Hell*, pp. 9, 11; May 1, 1988, Charles Nicol, review of *The Knockout Artist*, p. 21; September 9, 1990, Fay Weldon, review of *Body*, p. 14; March 15, 1992, p. 13; November 5, 1995, Valerie Sayers, review of *The Mulching of America*, p. 18.

Observer (London, England), October 30, 1994, p. 4.

People, June 8, 1987, Michelle Green, "Life-scarred and Weary of Battle, a Literary Guerrilla Calls Truce," p. 75; October 1, 1990, Lorenzo Carcaterra, review of *Body*, p. 41.

Playboy, August, 1990, p. 64.

Prairie Schooner, spring, 1974.

Publishers Weekly, April 15, 1988, Bob Summer, interview with Crews, p. 64; June 29, 1990, Sybil Steinberg, review of *Body*, p. 86; December 13, 1991, review of *Scar Lover*, p. 44; September 11, 1995, review of *The Mulching of America*, p. 76; November 17, 1997, review of *Celebration*, p. 54.

Saturday Review, November 11, 1978.

Sewanee Review, winter, 1969, Walter Sullivan, review of *The Gospel Singer*.

Shenandoah, summer, 1974.

Southern Literary Journal, spring, 1980; spring, 1984, pp. 132-135; spring, 1992, pp. 2, 3-10.

Spectator, January 22, 1977.

Studies in the Literary Imagination, fall, 1994, Robert C. Covel, "The Violent Bear It as Best They Can: Cultural Conflict in the Novels of Harry Crews," pp. 2, 75-86.

Texas Review, spring-summer, 1988, pp. 1-2, 96-109.

Time, September 13, 1976; October 23, 1978; March 5, 1979; April 17, 1989, review of *Blood Issue,* p. 70; March 2, 1992, Adam Begley, review of *Scar Lover,* p. 66.

Times Literary Supplement, February 2, 1973; January 11, 1974; January 24, 1975; January 21, 1977; December 7, 1979; December 30, 1994, p. 19.

Village Voice, October 30, 1978.

Virginia Quarterly Review, autumn, 1980, pp. 612-626.

Wall Street Journal, August 31, 1990, Merle Rubin, review of *Body,* p. A9.

Washington Post, March 29, 1979.

Washington Post Book World, April 15, 1973; July 24, 1983; May 1, 1988; August 19, 1990, p. 3; February 16, 1992, p. 4; October 17, 1993, p. 3; February 4, 1996, p. 8.

World, April 24, 1973.

Writers Digest, June, 1982, Jerry C. Hunter, interview with Crews, p. 30.

ONLINE

Harry Crews Web site, http://www.harrycrews.com/ (July 26, 2004).

*   *   *

CREWS, Harry Eugene
See CREWS, Harry

*   *   *

CRICHTON, John Michael
See CRICHTON, Michael

*   *   *

CRICHTON, Michael 1942-
(John Michael Crichton, Michael Douglas, a joint pseudonym, Jeffrey Hudson, John Lange)

PERSONAL: Surname is pronounced "*cry*-ton"; born October 23, 1942, in Chicago, IL; son of John Henderson (a corporate president) and Zula (Miller) Crichton; married Joan Radam, January 1, 1965 (divorced, 1970); married Kathleen St. Johns, 1978 (divorced, 1980); married Suzanne Childs (marriage ended); married Anne-Marie Martin, 1987 (divorced); children: (fourth marriage) Taylor (daughter). *Education:* Harvard University, A.B. (summa cum laude), 1964, M.D., 1969.

ADDRESSES: Office—(West Coast) Jenkins Financial Services, 433 North Camden Dr., Ste. 500, Beverly Hills, CA 90210-4443; (East Coast) Constant C Productions, 282 Katonah Ave., No. 246, Katonah, NY 10536-2110. *Agent*—International Creative Management, 40 West 57th Street, New York, NY, 10019.

CAREER: Author and physician, 1969—. Salk Institute for Biological Studies, La Jolla, CA, postdoctoral fellow, 1969-70; visiting writer, Massachusetts Institute of Technology, Cambridge, 1988.

Director of films and teleplays, including *Pursuit* (based on his novel *Binary*), American Broadcasting Companies, Inc., 1972, *Westworld,* Metro-Goldwyn- Mayer, 1973, *Coma,* United Artists (UA), 1978, *The Great Train Robbery,* UA, 1979, *Looker,* Warner Bros., 1981, *Runaway,* Tri-Star Pictures, 1984, *Physical Evidence,* Columbia, 1989, and *The Thirteenth Warrior* (also known as *Eaters of the Dead),* Buena Vista, 1999. Executive producer of film *Disclosure,* Warner Bros., 1994; producer of films, including *Twister,* Warner Bros., 1996, *Jurassic Park III,* 1997; *Sphere,* Warner Bros., 1998, and *The Thirteenth Warrior,* Buena Vista, 1999. Creator and executive producer, *ER* (television series), National Broadcast Company, Inc., 1994—.

MEMBER: Academy of Motion Picture Arts and Sciences, Aesculaepian Society, Authors Guild, Authors League of America, Directors Guild of America, Mystery Writers Guild of America (West), PEN, Phi Beta Kappa.

AWARDS, HONORS: Edgar Award, Mystery Writers of America, 1968, for *A Case of Need,* and 1979, for *The Great Train Robbery;* writer of the year award, Association of American Medical Writers, 1970, for *Five Patients: The Hospital Explained;* George Foster Peabody Award, 1995, and Emmy Award for Best Dramatic Series, 1996, both for *ER;* Modern Library Association Best Fiction List, 2001, for *Timeline.*

WRITINGS:

NOVELS

The Andromeda Strain, Knopf (New York, NY), 1969.

(With brother, Douglas Crichton, under joint pseudonym Michael Douglas) *Dealing; or, The Berkeley-to- Boston Forty-Brick Lost-Bag Blues,* Knopf (New York, NY), 1971.

The Terminal Man, Knopf (New York, NY), 1972.

Westworld, Bantam (New York, NY), 1974.

The Great Train Robbery, Knopf (New York, NY), 1975.

Eaters of the Dead: The Manuscript of Ibn Fadlan, Relating His Experiences with the Northmen in A.D. 922, Knopf (New York, NY), 1976.

Congo, Knopf (New York, NY), 1980.

Sphere, Knopf (New York, NY), 1987.

Jurassic Park, Knopf, 1990, published as *Michael Crichton's Jurassic World,* Knopf (New York, NY), 1997.

Rising Sun, Knopf (New York, NY), 1992.

Disclosure, Knopf (New York, NY), 1994.

The Lost World, Knopf (New York, NY), 1995.

Airframe, Knopf (New York, NY), 1996.

The Lost World, Jurassic Park: The Movie Storybook, (based on the motion picture and the novel), Grosset & Dunlap (New York, NY), 1997.

Timeline, Knopf (New York, NY), 1999.

Prey, HarperCollins (New York, NY), 2002.

State of Fear, HarperCollins (New York, NY), 2004.

NONFICTION

Five Patients: The Hospital Explained, Knopf (New York, NY), 1970.

Jasper Johns, Abrams (New York, NY), 1977, revised and expanded edition, 1994.

Electronic Life: How to Think about Computers, Knopf (New York, NY), 1983.

Travels (autobiography), Knopf (New York, NY), 1988.

SCREENPLAYS

Extreme Close- up, National General, 1973.

Westworld (based on novel of same title), Metro-Goldwyn-Mayer, 1973.

Coma (based on novel of same title by Robin Cook), United Artists, 1977.

The Great Train Robbery (based on novel of same title), United Artists, 1978.

Looker, Warner Bros., 1981.

Runaway, Tri-Star Pictures, 1984.

(With John Koepp) *Jurassic Park,* 1993.

(With Philip Kaufman and Michael Backes) *Rising Sun,* 1993.

Twister, Warner Bros., 1996.

UNDER PSEUDONYM JOHN LANGE

Odds On, New American Library (New York, NY), 1966.

Scratch One, New American Library (New York, NY), 1967.

Easy Go, New American Library (New York, NY), 1968, published as *The Last Tomb,* Bantam (New York, NY), 1974.

Zero Cool, New American Library (New York, NY), 1969.

The Venom Business, New American Library (New York, NY), 1969.

Drug of Choice, New American Library (New York, NY), 1970.

Grave Descend, New American Library (New York, NY), 1970.

Binary, Knopf (New York, NY), 1971.

UNDER PSEUDONYM JEFFREY HUDSON

A Case of Need, New American Library (New York, NY), 1968.

Contributor to periodicals, including *Wired,* and *Washington Monthly.*

ADAPTATIONS: The Andromeda Strain was filmed by Universal, 1971; *A Case of Need* was adapted as the film *The Carey Treatment* (also known as *Emergency Ward*) and filmed by Metro-Goldwyn-Mayer, 1972; *Binary* was filmed as *Pursuit,* ABC-TV, 1972; *The Terminal Man* was filmed by Warner Brothers, 1974; *Jurassic Park* was filmed by Steven Spielberg and released in 1994; *Congo* was filmed by Frank Marshall and released by Paramount, 1995; *Disclosure* was filmed and released in 1995; *The Lost World: Jurassic Park* was released by Universal, 1997; *Sphere* was adapted for the screen and released by Warner Brothers, 1998; *The Thirteenth Warrior* was released by Buena Vista, 1999; *Timeline* was filmed by Paramount Pictures, 2003. *Timeline* was also adapted as a computer game.

WORK IN PROGRESS: Developing a video game with Sega.

SIDELIGHTS: Michael Crichton has had a number of successful careers—physician, teacher, film director, screenwriter—but he is perhaps best known for pioneering the "techno-thriller" with novels such as *Jurassic*

Park, Andromeda Strain, and *Congo* and for creating and producing the hit television series, *ER.* Whether writing about a deadly microorganism, brain surgery gone awry, or adventures in the Congo, Crichton has the ability to blend the tight plot and suspense of the thriller with the technicalities of science fiction, making him a favorite with readers of all ages. Summing up Crichton's appeal in the *Dictionary of Literary Biography Yearbook,* Robert L. Sims wrote, "His importance lies in his capacity to tell stories related to that frontier where science and fiction meet . . . . Crichton's best novels demonstrate that, for the immediate future at least, technological innovations offer the same possibilities and limitations as their human creators."

Crichton's first brush with literary success occurred during medical school. To help pay for tuition and living expenses, he wrote paperback thrillers on the weekends and during vacations. One of these books, *A Case of Need,* became an unexpected hit. Written under a pseudonym, the novel revolves around a Chinese-American obstetrician who is unjustly accused of performing an illegal abortion on the daughter of a prominent Boston surgeon. Critical reaction to the book was very positive. "Read *A Case of Need* now," urged Fred Rotondaro in *Best Sellers,* "it will entertain you; get you angry—it will make you think." Allen J. Hubin, writing in the *New York Times Book Review,* similarly noted that the "breezy, fast-paced, up-to-date first novel . . . demonstrates again the ability of detective fiction to treat contemporary social problems in a meaningful fashion."

Also published while the author was still in medical school, *The Andromeda Strain* made Crichton a minor celebrity on campus (especially when the film rights were sold to Universal Studios). Part historical journal, the novel uses data such as computer printouts, bibliographic references, and fictional government documents to lend credence to the story of a deadly microorganism that arrives on Earth aboard a NASA space probe. The virus quickly kills most of the residents of Piedmont, Arizona. Two survivors, an old man and a baby, are taken to a secret government compound for study by Project Wildfire. The Wildfire team—Stone, a bacteriologist, Leavitt, a clinical microbiologist, Burton, a pathologist, and Hall, a practicing surgeon—must race against the clock to isolate the organism and find a cure before it spreads into the general population.

The mix of science and suspense in *The Andromeda Strain* brought varied reactions from reviewers. While admitting that he stayed up all night to finish the book,

Christopher Lehmann-Haupt, writing in the *New York Times,* observed that he felt cheated by the conclusion. Richard Schickel, writing in *Harper's,* was more concerned with a shortage of character development: "The lack of interest in this matter is . . . amazing. Perhaps so much creative energy went into his basic situation that none was left for people." Not all critics were as harsh in their evaluation of the novel, however. "The pace is fast and absorbing," claimed Alexander Cook in *Commonweal.* He went on to say, "The writing is spare and its quality is generally high; and the characters, if not memorable, are at any rate sufficiently sketched in and have been given little personal touches of their own."

Crichton also used the world of science and medicine as a backdrop for *The Terminal Man.* The title refers to computer scientist Harry Benson who, as the result of an automobile accident, suffers severe epileptic seizures. As the seizures grow in intensity, Benson has blackouts during which he commits violent acts. At the urging of his doctors, Benson undergoes a radical procedure in which an electrode is inserted into his brain. Hooked up to a packet in the patient's shoulder, the electrode is wired to locate the source of the seizures and delivers a shock to the brain every time an episode is about to occur. Something goes wrong, and Benson's brain is overloaded. As the shocks increase, Benson becomes more irrational, dangerous, and eventually, murderous.

John R. Coyne in the *National Review* found *The Terminal Man* "one of the season's best." He added, "Crichton proves himself capable of making the most esoteric material completely comprehensible to the layman . . . . Even more important, he can create and sustain that sort of suspense that forces us to suspend disbelief." And, in an *Atlantic* review of the novel, Edward Weeks opined that Crichton has "now written a novel quite terrifying in its suspense and implication."

In *The Great Train Robbery,* Crichton moved out of the realm of science and into the world of Victorian England. Loosely based on an actual event, the book explores master criminal Edward Pierce's attempt to steal a trainload of army payroll on its way to the Crimea. " *The Great Train Robbery* combines the pleasures, guilt, and delight of a novel of gripping entertainment with healthy slices of instruction and information interlarded," observed Doris Grumbach in the *New Republic.* Lehmann-Haupt enthused that he found himself "not only captivated because it is Mr. Crichton's best thriller to date . . . . but also charmed most of all by the story's Victorian style and content." And Weeks, writing in the *Atlantic Monthly*, called the novel "an exciting and very clever piece of fiction."

Congo marked Crichton's return to the field of science and technology. In the novel, three adventurers travel through the dense rain forests of the Congo in search of a cache of diamonds with the power to revolutionize computer technology. The trio is accompanied by an intelligent, linguistically-trained gorilla named Amy, the designated intermediary between the scientists and a band of killer apes who guard the gems. The small band's search is hampered by cannibals, volcanoes, and mutant primates; it is also marked by a sense of desperation, as the team fights to beat a Euro-Japanese rival company to the prize. In a review of *Congo* for *Best Sellers*, Justin Blewitt termed the novel "an exciting, fast-paced adventure. It rang very true and at the same time was a terrific page-turner. That's a rare combination . . . . [*Congo* is] really a lot of fun."

A scientific—and monetary—search is also the emphasis of *Sphere*. An American ship laying cable in the Pacific hits a snag; the snag turns out to be a huge spaceship, estimated to be at least three centuries old. An undersea research team investigates the strange craft from the relative safety of an underwater habitat. Among the civilian and military crew is psychologist Norman Johnson, whose apprehension about the entire project is validated by a number of increasingly bizarre and deadly events: a bad storm cuts the habitat off from the surface, strange messages appear on computer screens, and an unseen—but apparently huge—squid attacks the crew's quarters.

"Crichton's new novel . . . kept me happy for two hours sitting in a grounded plane," wrote Robin McKinley in the *New York Times Book Review*, adding that "no one can ask for more of a thriller. . . . Take this one along with you on your next plane ride." While noting that he had some problems with *Sphere*—including stilted dialogue and broad characterizations—James M. Kahn mused that Crichton "keeps us guessing at every turn . . . . [He is] a storyteller and a damned good one." And Michael Collins, writing in the *Washington Post Book World*, noted that "the pages turn quickly." He urged readers to "suspend your disbelief and put yourself 1,000 feet down."

Crichton also authored the blockbuster *Jurassic Park*, in which he brings the dinosaurs back from extinction. *Jurassic Park* chronicles the attempts of self-made bil-

lionaire John Hammond to build an amusement park on a remote island off the coast of Costa Rica. Instead of roller coasters and sideshows, the park features actual life-sized dinosaurs bred through the wonders of biotechnology and recombinant DNA. There are some problems before the park opens, however: workmen begin to die in mysterious accidents and local children are attacked by strange lizards. Fearful that the project's opening is in jeopardy, Hammond calls together a team of scientists and technicians to look things over. Led by a paleontologist named Grant, the group is initially amazed by Hammond's creation. Their amazement quickly turns to horror when the park's electronic security system is put out of commission and the dinosaurs are freed to roam at will. What ensues is a deadly battle between the vastly under-armed human contingent and a group of smarter-than-anticipated tyrannosaurs, pterodactyls, stegosaurs, and velociraptors.

Time correspondent John Skow considered *Jurassic Park* the author's "best [techno-thriller] by far since *The Andromeda Strain*." Skow added that Crichton's "sci-fi is convincingly detailed." In a piece for the *Los Angeles Times Book Review*, Andrew Ferguson remarked that, "having read Crichton's fat new novel . . . I have a word of advice for anyone owning real estate within ten miles of the La Brea tar pits: Sell." Ferguson criticized the novel, saying its "only real virtue" lies in "its genuinely interesting discussion of dinosaurs, DNA research, paleontology, and chaos theory." Gary Jennings of the *New York Times Book Review* was more appreciative, arguing that the book has "some good bits . . . . All in all, *Jurassic Park* is a great place to visit."

Crichton left the world of science in *Rising Sun*, a political thriller revolving around the murder of a young American woman during a party for a huge Japanese corporation. The case is given to detective Peter J. Smith, who finds himself up against an Oriental syndicate with great political and economic power. As Smith gets closer to the truth, the Japanese corporation uses all its influence to thwart his investigation—influence that includes corruption and violence. John Schwartz in *Newsweek* recognized that Crichton had "done his homework," but the critic still felt that *Rising Sun* is too full of "randy propaganda instead of a more balanced view" to be effective.

If *Rising Sun* was criticized as having a xenophobic view of the Far East, *Disclosure*, Crichton's 1994 bestseller, opened a whole new vista for debate and discussion. A techno-thriller with a twist, *Disclosure* opens as a computer company executive named Tom Sanders discovers that he has been passed over for a promotion in favor of a woman executive with whom he had once been romantically involved. When he arrives at his new boss's office, she makes a pass at him. Now happily married, Sanders dodges the boss's advances, only to find within days that he has been named as the aggressor in a sexual harassment suit. How Sanders digs his way from beneath the spurious charges—while simultaneously unearthing wider corruption in the computer company—forms the core of the novel.

While critics duly observed the theme of sexual harassment in *Disclosure,* they tended to dwell more upon the thriller aspect of the novel. In *New Statesman and Society,* Douglas Kennedy commended *Disclosure* as an "acidic glimpse into the nasty gamesmanship of U.S. corporate life," adding, "Sexual harassment becomes a minor consideration in a narrative more preoccupied by the wonders of virtual reality and the vicious corporate battlefield." *People* magazine reviewer Susan Toepfer found that by casting the woman as the wrongdoer, "Crichton offers a fresh and provocative story," but contended he did not sufficiently explore the situation's possibilities. *National Review* contributor Michael Coren likewise noted of the novel, "This is provocative stuff, for to question the racial or gender exclusivity of self-awarded victim status is to kick at the very foundations of modern liberalism."

Both *Disclosure* and *Jurassic Park* were produced as feature films, the latter proving to be one of the top-grossing movies of all time. Perhaps the vast success of *Jurassic Park* as a book and a film inspired Crichton to revisit his scheming raptors and vicious tyrannosaurs in *The Lost World.* Also set on an island off the coast of Costa Rica, *The Lost World* follows the adventures of another team of scientists—with a return appearance by mathematical theorist Ian Malcolm—as they try to escape the clutches of the dinosaurs *and* thwart the ambitions of some egg-stealing opportunists. Noted Susan Toepfer in *People,* "Characteristically clever, fast-paced and engaging, Michael Crichton's . . . work accomplishes what he set out to do: offer the still-harrowing thrills of a by-now-familiar ride."

In *Prey,* Crichton exposes the sinister in nanotechnology—tiny machines less than half the thickness of a human hair with the ability to reproduce, learn, and evolve. The story centers on Jack, a Mr. Mom-parent of three children and his workaholic wife's top-secret career which turns out to be developing dangerous nanotechnology for the military. In true Crichton form the

book is a page-turning adventure, extrapolating pages of both current and speculative science and technology into a best-selling novel. Critics had mixed reviews for the book, especially in comparison to Crichton's earlier successes. A *Kirkus Reviews* contributor described *Prey* as "nanotechnology [gone] homicidal" and considered the book a "disappointing effort from an author who simply refuses to change an old, tired template." Michael Hilzik of the *Los Angeles Times* agreed, calling *Prey* lean of drama, tension, and peril and "decidedly lesser Crichton." A *USA Today* reviewer considered the book "overly technical," while a *New York Times* reviewer described it as "irresistibly suspenseful" and said he "turned the pages feverishly."

In 2004 Crichton published *State of Fear,* a controversial work in which the validity of global warming is questioned and ecoterrorism exists. Critics felt strongly about Crichton's "work of thinly disguised political commentary," as Chris Mooney described the book in *Skeptical Inquirer.* Mooney called the main character "a vessel into which Crichton can pour his agenda-driven reading of the scientific evidence" and concluded that "such writing is pure porn for deniers of global warming." Bruce Barcott, writing for "New York Times Book Review," commented that "State of Fear is so over-the-top . . . that it wouldn't take much to turn it into a satiric parable of a liberal coming to his conservative senses." Andrew Stuttaford, reviewing the book for *National Review,* felt differently. He pointed out that the book is "packed with graphs, scientific discussion, footnotes, a manifesto, and an extensive bibliography," all elements which make for "a good, solid, exciting read."

Crichton's ability to mesh science, technology, and suspense is not limited to novels. Many of the films that the author has directed, such as *Westworld* and *Runaway,* feature a struggle between humans and technology. Despite the often grim outlook of both his films and novels, Crichton revealed in an interview with Ned Smith of *American Way* that his primary goal in making movies and writing books is to "entertain people." He continued, "It's fun to manipulate people's feelings and to be manipulated. To take a movie, or get a book and get very involved in it—don't look at my watch, forget about other things," he said. As for critical reaction to his work, Crichton told Smith: "Every critic assumes he's a code-breaker; the writer makes a code and the critic breaks it. And it doesn't work that way at all. As a mode of working, you need to become very uncritical."

BIOGRAPHICAL AND CRITICAL SOURCES:

BOOKS

Authors and Artists for Young Adults, Volume 10, Gale (Detroit, MI), 1993, pp. 63- 70.

Contemporary Literary Criticism, Gale (Detroit, MI), Volume 2, 1974, Volume 6, 1976, Volume 54, 1989.

Contemporary Novelists, 7th edition, St. James Press (Detroit, MI), 2001.

Dictionary of Literary Biography Yearbook: 1981, Gale (Detroit, MI), 1982.

St. James Encyclopedia of Popular Culture, St. James Press (Detroit, MI), 2000.

Shay, Don, and Jody Shay, *The Making of Jurassic Park,* Ballantine (New York, NY), 1993.

Trembley, Elizabeth A., *Michael Crichton: A Critical Companion,* Greenwood Press (Westport, CT), 1996.

PERIODICALS

American Spectator, May, 1992, John Podhhoretz, review of *Rising Sun,* p. 71.

Atlanta Journal- Constitution, September 30, 1999, Don O'Briant, "Medical Thrillers Pay Off for Former Doctor," p. C2.

Atlantic, May, 1972, pp. 108-110.

Best Sellers, August 15, 1968, pp. 207-208; February, 1981, p. 388.

Book, November, 1999, review of *Timeline,* p. 69.

Booklist, November 15, 1996, Ray Olson, review of *Airframe,* p. 548; January 1, 1997, review of *Timeline,* p. 763; January 1, 2000, review of *Timeline,* p. 819; February 15, 2001, Mary McCay, review of *Timeline,* p. 1166; May 1, 2001, Karen Harris, audio book review of *The Great Train Robbery,* p. 1616; December 1, 2002, Kristine Huntley, review of *Prey,* p. 628.

Boston Herald, November 28, 1999, review of *Timeline,* p. 59.

Business Week, December 6, 1999, review of *Timeline,* p. 12E10; December 2, 2002, review of *Prey,* p. 103.

Commonweal, August 9, 1969, pp. 493-494.

Daily Telegraph (London, England), December 14, 2002, Toby Clements, review of *Prey.*

Entertainment Weekly, December 3, 1990, p. 80; December 16, 1994, Cindy Pearlman, "Michael Crichton Gets Criticism from Doctors for His Television Show *ER,*" p. 16; December 30, 1994, Albert Kim, "The Entertainers"; 1994: Michael Crichton, p. 30; January 13, 1995, Lisa Schwarzbaum, review of *Disclosure,* pp. 52-53; September 22, 1995, Tom De Haven, review of *The Lost World,* pp. 72-73; November 26, 1999, "Joust for Kicks, review of *Timeline,*" p. 84; November 29, 2002, Benjamin Svetkey, "Michael Crichton Gets Small" (interview), p. 628.

Forbes, June 21, 1993, Steve Forbes, review of *Jurassic Park,* p. 24; September 13, 1993, Steve Forbes, review of *Congo,* p. 26; September 13, 1993, Steve Forbes, review of *Sphere,* p. 26; February 14, 1994, review of *Disclosure,* p. 26; February 21, 1994, p. 108.

Globe and Mail (Toronto, Ontario, Canada), December 4, 1999, review of *Timeline,* p. D16.

Guardian (London, England), December 4, 1999, Mark Lawson, "We Have Been Here Before: Mark Lawson Sees Michael Crichton Collide with the Talent of H.G. Wells," p. 10; March 9, 2002, Nicholas Lezard, "Pick of the Week: Nicholas Lezard Learns How to Review Books," p. 11; December 14, 2002, review of *Prey,* p. 29.

Harper's, August, 1969, p. 97.

Journal of the American Medical Association, September 8, 1993, Andrew A. Skolnick, review of *Jurassic Park,* p. 1252.

Kirkus Reviews, November 1, 1999, review of *Timeline,* p. 1673; November 15, 2002, review of *Prey,* p. 1639.

Kliatt Young Adult Paperback Book Guide, September, 1999, audio book review of *The Lost World,* p. 56.

Knight Ridder/Tribune News Service, November 27, 2002, Chris Cobbs, review of *Prey,* p. 56.

Library Journal, January, 1997, Mark Annichiarico, audio book review of *Airframe,* p. 172; October 15, 1999, Stephen L. Hupp, audio book review of *The Lost World,* p. 122; December, 1999, Jeff Ayers, review of *Timeline,* p. 184; April 1, 2000, Cliff Glaviano, audio book review of *Timeline,* p. 152.

Los Angeles Times, November 29, 2002, Bettijane Levine, "Tall Tech Tales; Michael Crichton's Macabre Vision Finds Another Perch in *Prey,*" p. E37; December 22, 2002, Michael Hiltzik, "It's a Small World after All," p. R10.

Los Angeles Times Book Review, July 12, 1987, pp. 1, 13; November 11, 1990, p. 4; October 29, 1995, p. 2; December 15, 1996, p. 3; November 14, 1999, review of *Timeline,* p. 3; December 22, 2002, "It's a Small World after All," p. R10.

Nation, May 11, 1992, Karl Taro Greenfeld, "The Outnation: A Search for the Soul of Japan," p. 637.

National Review, June 23, 1972, pp. 700-701; August 17, 1992, Anthony Lejeune, review of *Rising Sun,* p. 40; February 21, 1994, Michael Coren, review of *Disclosure,* p. 63; December 6, 1999, review of *Timeline,* p. 68; February 28, 2005, Andrew Stuttaford, "Global Warning," p. 52.

New Republic, June 7, 1975, pp. 30-1.

New Statesman, February 4, 1994, Douglas Kennedy, review of *Disclosure,* p. 49; December 20, 1997, p. 121.

New Statesman and Society, March 1, 1991, Elizabeth J. Young, review of *Jurassic Park,* p. 34.

Newsweek, November 19, 1990, Peter S. Prescott, review of *Jurassic Park,* p. 69; February 17, 1992, John Schwartz, review of *Rising Sun,* p. 64; January 17, 1994, David Gates, review of *Disclosure,* p. 52; December 9, 1996, Jeff Giles and Ray Sawhill, "Hollywood's Dying for Novel Ideas," p. 80; November 22, 1999, "Moving across Mediums: Why It's Hard to Get a Handle on Michael Crichton" (interview), p. 94.

New Yorker, February 7, 1994, review of *Disclosure,* p. 99; June 27, 1994, Anthony Lane, review of *Disclosure,* p. 81; December 16, 1996, John Lanchester, review of *Airframe,* p. 103.

New York Review of Books, April 23, 1992, Ian Buruma, review of *Rising Sun,* p. 3; August 12, 1993, Stephen Jay Gould, review of *Jurassic Park,* p. 51; February 29, 1996, pp. 20- 24; January 9, 1997, Louis Menand, review of *Airframe,* p. 16.

New York Times, May 30, 1969, p. 25; June 10, 1975; December 5, 1996, p. 35; October 15, 1999, Stephen L. Hupp, audio book review of *The Lost World,* p. 122; November 18, 1999, Christopher Lehmann-Haupt, review of *Timeline,* p. E9; November 24, 2002, Jim Holt, "It's the Little Things."

New York Times Book Review, August 18, 1968, p. 20; July 12, 1987, Robin McKinley, review of *Sphere,* p. 18; June 26, 1988, Patricia Bosworth, review of *Travels,* p. 30; November 1, 1990, pp. 14-15; November 11, 1990, Gary Jennings, review of *Jurassic Park,* p. 14; February 9, 1992, Robert Nathan, review of *Rising Sun,* p. 1; January 23, 1994, Maureen Dowd, review of *Disclosure,* p. 7; October 1, 1995, Mim Udovitch, review of *The Lost World,* pp. 9-10; December 15, 1996, Tom Shone, review of *Airframe,* p. 12; November 21, 1999, Daniel Mendelsohn, "Knights-errant: Michael Crichton's New Novel Employs Quantum Theory to Transport Some Twenty-first- Century Yalies into Fourteenth-Century France," p. 6; January 30, 2005, Bruce Barcott, "Not So Hot," p. 12.

Observer (London, England), December 5, 1999, review of *Timeline,* p. 11.

PC Magazine, May 27, 1997, Sebastian Rupley and Bill Howard, "Can the Web Hurt Schools? Author Michael Crichton and FCC Chief Reed Hundt Spar at PC Forum," p. 30; June 5, 2001, Les Freed, "Computer Game Review of *Timeline,*" p. 210.

People, January 17, 1994, Susan Toepfer, "Talking with . . . Michael Crichton: America's Tallest, Richest Writer?" (interview), p. 24; September 18, 1995, Susan Toepfer, review of *The Lost World,* p. 37.

Publishers Weekly, September 28, 1990, Sybil Steinberg, review of *Jurassic Park,* p. 84; January 27, 1992, review of *Rising Sun,* p. 91; July 22, 1996, p. 142; November 11, 1996, review of *Airframe,* p. 58; December 2, 1996, audio book review of *Airframe,* p. 30; December 16, 1996, Daisy Maryles, "Behind the Bestsellers," p. 20; November 1, 1999, "The High Concept of Michael Crichton" (interview), p. S3; November 8, 1999, review of *Timeline,* p. 51; October 28, 2002, review of *Prey,* p. 49; December 9, 2002, Daisy Maryles, review of *Prey,* p. 15.

St. Louis Post-Dispatch, November 21, 1999, "Crichton's Latest Thriller Takes Readers to Fourteenth-Century France," p. F13.

School Library Journal, April, 2000, Molly Conally, review of *Timeline,* p. 158.

Science Fiction Chronicle, April, 2001, review of *Timeline,* p. 38.

Skeptical Inquirer, May/June 2005, Chris Mooney, "Bad Science, Bad Fiction, and an Agenda," p. 53.

Time, November 12, 1990, John Skow, review of *Jurassic Park,* p. CB6; February 24, 1992, John Skow, review of *Rising Sun,* p. 63; January 10, 1994, Gregory Jaynes, "Pop Fiction's Prime Provocateur: Michael Crichton" (interview), p. 52; September 25, 1995, Gregory Jaynes, "Meet Mr. Wizard: Author Michael Crichton," p. 60; September 25, 1995, Michael D. Lemonick, "How Good Is His Science?," p. 65; December 9, 1996, p. 90; November 22, 1999, James Poniewozik, review of *Timeline,* p. 107; December 2, 2002, Lev Grossman, "Death Swarmed Over: Crichton's Latest Is a Soulless, By-the-Numbers Techno-Thriller—And You Won't Be Able to Put It Down" p. 96.

U.S. News and World Report, March 9, 1992, p. 50.

Vanity Fair, January, 1994, Zoe Heller, "The Admirable Crichton," p. 32- 49.

Wall Street Journal, December 9, 1996, Tom Nolan, review of *Airframe,* p. A12; December 11, 1996, p. B12; November 19, 1999, Thomas Bass, "Click Here for the Middle Ages, Review of *Timeline,* " p. W6.

Washington Post Book World, June 14, 1987, pp. 1, 14; September 5, 1999, review of *Timeline,* p. 3.

ONLINE

Official Michael Crichton Web site, http://www. crichton-official.com/ (November 9, 2003).

Random House Web site, http://www.randomhouse.com/ (November 9, 2003), "Michael Crichton."

CROWLEY, John 1942-

PERSONAL: Born December 1, 1942, in Presque Isle, ME; son of Joseph B. (a doctor) and Patience (Lyon) Crowley; married Laurie Block, 1984; children: two daughters. *Education:* Indiana University, B.A., 1964.

ADDRESSES: Home—Box 395, Conway, MA 01341.

CAREER: Photographer and commercial artist, 1964-66; fiction writer and freelance writer for films and television, 1966—. Yale University, visiting professor of creative writing.

AWARDS, HONORS: American Book Award nomination, 1980, for *Engine Summer;* Hugo Award nomination, Nebula Award nomination, and World Fantasy Award, all 1982, all for *Little, Big;* American Film Festival Award, 1982, for *America Lost and Found;* World Fantasy Award, 1990, for *Great Work of Time;* American Academy of Arts and Letters Award for literature; *Locus* award, for short story "Gone"; Academy Award nomination, 1991, for *The Restless Conscience: Resistance to Hitler within Germany 1933-1945,* and 1992, for *The Liberators: Fighting on Two Fronts in World War II.*

WRITINGS:

NOVELS

The Deep (also see below), Doubleday (New York, NY), 1975.
Beasts (also see below), Doubleday (New York, NY), 1976.
Engine Summer (also see below), Doubleday (New York, NY), 1979.
Little, Big, Bantam (New York, NY), 1981.
Ægypt (first novel in tetralogy), Bantam (New York, NY), 1987.
Great Work of Time (novella), Bantam (New York, NY), 1991.
Love and Sleep (second novel in tetralogy), Bantam (New York, NY), 1994.
Three Novels, Bantam (New York, NY), 1994.
Dæmonomania (third novel in tetralogy), Bantam (New York, NY), 2000.
The Translator, Morrow (New York, NY), 2002.

Otherwise: Three Novels (contains *The Deep, Beasts,* and *Engine Summer*), Perennial (New York, NY), 2002.
Lord Byron's Novel: The Evening Land, Morrow (New York, NY), 2005.

OTHER

(Editor, with Howard Kerr and Charles L. Crow) *The Haunted Dusk: American Supernatural Fiction, 1820-1920,* University of Georgia Press (Athens, GA), 1983.
Novelty (short stories), Bantam (New York, NY), 1989.
Antiquities: Seven Stories, Incunabula (Seattle, WA), 1993.
Novelties and Souvenirs: Collected Short Fiction, Perennial (New York, NY), 2004.

Author of screenplays for documentaries, including *America Lost and Found,* 1979, *No Place to Hide,* 1982, *America and Lewis Hine,* 1985, *The World of Tomorrow,* 1985, *Are We Winning Mommy? America and the Cold War,* 1986, *The World of Tomorrow,* 1989, *Fit: Episodes in the History of the Body,* 1990, *The Restless Conscience: Resistance to Hitler within Germany 1933-1945,* 1991, *Pearl Harbor: Surprise and Remembrance,* 1991, *The Liberators: Fighting on Two Fronts in World War II,* 1992, *The Gate of Heavenly Peace,* 1995, and *A Morning Sun,* 2003.

Work represented in anthologies, including *Shadows,* Doubleday (New York, NY), 1977; and *Elsewhere,* Ace Books (New York, NY), 1981. Author of television scripts for *America Lost and Found* and *No Place to Hide,* Public Broadcasting System (PBS). Contributor to periodicals, including *Omni.*

SIDELIGHTS: Author John Crowley has been praised by critics for his thoughtful, finely wrought works of science fiction and fantasy, which include the novels *The Deep, Ægypt, Love and Sleep,* and *Dæmonomania.* A successful television writer who has never pandered to popular tastes, Crowley infuses his genre writings with literary quality and "mind-catching philosophical musings," according to a *Publishers Weekly* reviewer of *Dæmonomania.* Suzanne Keen reported in *Commonweal* that his characters "are psychologically convincing, an accomplishment that makes the historical and fantastic elements of his [novel *Love and Sleep*] all the more thrilling." Whether his work visits far planets or local neighborhoods, some critics have suggested,

Crowley always challenges the accepted perceptions of things and offers multi-layered mysteries for his characters—and his readers—to explore. As a *Kirkus Reviews* contributor explained it in a review of *Dæmonomania*, "Crowley's work is a taste well worth acquiring, but you have to work at it."

In a *New York Times Book Review* piece on Crowley's first novel, *The Deep*, Gerald Jonas declared that "paraphrase is useless to convey the intensity of Crowley's prose; anyone interested in the risk-taking side of modern science fiction will want to experience it firsthand." Jonathan Dee noted, also in the *New York Times Book Review*, that Crowley "is an abundantly gifted writer, a scholar whose passion for history is matched by his ability to write a graceful sentence." Some reviewers observed that with his third novel, *Engine Summer*, Crowley developed more complex plots and characters, and his themes began reflecting the influence of the fantasy genre. Charles Nicol wrote in *Saturday Review:* "A lyric adventure as concerned with the meaning of actions as with the actions themselves, [*Engine Summer*] presents a meditative world that should appeal to lovers of the great fantasies. Crowley has published some science fiction previously; here he has gone beyond his genre into that hilly country on the borderlands of literature." Similarly, Crowley's Nebula and Hugo Award nominee *Little, Big* was described by John Clute in the *Washington Post Book World* as a "dense, marvelous, magic-realist family chronicle about the end of time and the new world to come."

Novelist Carolyn See, in a review for the *Los Angeles Times,* commented that Crowley's fifth novel, *Ægypt,* contains "some extraordinary storytelling." Incorporating fantasy, satire, and philosophical romance, the novel centers on Pierce Moffett, a professor of Renaissance history whose desire to write a book about finding the meaning in life leads him to a mythical area and a mysterious woman. *Washington Post Book World* contributor Michael Dirda remarked that *Ægypt* "is clearly a novel where thought speaks louder than action, where people, places and events are at once actual and allegorical. . . . Crowley wants readers to appreciate his foreshadowings, echoes, bits of odd lore, multiple voices—in the evolution of complex pattern is his art." Dirda also noted, however, that Crowley's narrative is so complex that it can occasionally be confusing. Commenting on this complexity, John Clute, in a review for the *New York Times Book Review,* suggested that *Ægypt* provides "a dizzying experience." *Ægypt* is the first novel in an ambitious tetralogy centering upon the intellectual and personal journey of Moffett.

In *Love and Sleep,* Crowley continues the tale begun in *Ægypt.* While *Ægypt* tells of Moffett's life during the 1960s and 1970s, *Love and Sleep* frames that period, returning to the 1950s and allowing readers a glimpse of Moffett's Kentucky childhood, a time full of "minor incidents and wonders," according to *Washington Post Book Review* critic Lawrence Norfolk, before leaping ahead of *Ægypt* in true sequel fashion. In the novel, Norfolk explained, Crowley hangs his plot upon the speculation that "between the old world of things as they used to be, and the new world of things as they would be instead, there has always fallen a sort of passage time, a chaos of unformed possibilities in which all sorts of manifestations could be witnessed." It has "an interim feel, a sense of its author treading water while the players are maneuvered into position" for the proposed third and fourth segments of the series, Norfolk continued. "As it stands, *Love and Sleep* is a collection of strange episodes, of hints and premonitions. The ultimate worth of this strange, teasing book hangs on the two yet to be written." Jonathan Dee offered a similar assessment of the work for the *New York Times Book Review:* while the first section of *Love and Sleep* "generates a true, expansive sense of human mystery . . . the novel's own vision, so crystal clear in that opening section, grows woollier and more diffuse" as Moffett's saga continues. Chicago *Tribune Books* contributor Robert Chatain maintained that the author's mixture of realism and fantasy "is not for every reader," yet the critic added: "to dislike fantasy is not to dismiss Crowley; he's one of the few writers who successfully crosses the razor-thin but definite line between genre fiction and literary fiction." Citing the author's "metaphysical conceits," Chatain concluded of Crowley, "there is no temptation to confuse [his novels] with other fictions; there's really nothing like them."

Dæmonomania continues the Pierce Moffett saga, as magic seeps further into the lives of Moffett and his acquaintances in Faraway Hills, New York. The title refers to a possible case of demonic possession, but the book portends even more massive shifts in what appears to be reality. For his part, Moffett comes to understand that magic once worked, that science has only temporarily halted the potency of magic, and that a "secret history," shared by a select few, actually directs the course of human actions. A *Kirkus Reviews* critic, while noting that the book will mean more to those who have read its two predecessors, called it "[d]eeply atmospheric, impressively learned, endlessly suggestive."

In 2002 Crowley went in a new direction with his writing, publishing *The Translator,* a work that "demonstrates to the reader . . . the escape that poetry and literature can provide in times of trouble," observed *Booklist* critic Ted Leventhal. Set in 1962, *The Transla-*

tor examines the relationship between Innokenti Falin, an exiled Russian poet, and Kit Malone, an American coed with a troubled past. The pair develop a close friendship, and Malone becomes Falin's translator. When the Cuban Missile Crisis erupts, their relationship is threatened by government officials who have been watching Falin. "Crowley's lovely, effortless writing and his accurate, earnest portraits of Russians make this a sad love story with an important piece of rhetoric at its heart," wrote a contributor in *Kirkus Reviews.* James Schiff, reviewing *The Translator* in *Book,* noted that "this simple and sincere novel, which masterfully renders a moment in history, possesses a certain beauty."

Novelties and Souvenirs: Collected Short Fiction, a 2004 work, contains fifteen tales of the fantastic. In an interview on *HarperCollins.com,* Crowley remarked that the stories "reflect matters . . . that have always been of deep interest to me. Among those is the malleability of reality, and what it would be like if it could be altered by human wishes; what goes on in the mind and heart of someone who makes such wishes . . . ; and the open-ended nature of the course of time, that produces unintended consequences, not always good or bad." A *Kirkus Reviews* contributor deemed *Novelties and Souvenirs* a "pleasing introduction to a very interesting writer's several 'worlds.'"

Crowley's works are noted for their lyrical, lucid style and diverse, provocative characters. In an interview with Gavin J. Grant on *Booksense.com,* the author was asked why he writes from such varied points of view. "I'm drawn to characters who seem to perceive the secret history of the world, or see a world-story proceeding, and don't trust themselves—and don't believe that they could know such a thing—but are drawn to it anyway," Crowley responded. "That's been a consistent direction all my writing has taken. I can think of people whose minds are active in that way in almost all the books I've written."

BIOGRAPHICAL AND CRITICAL SOURCES:

BOOKS

Contemporary Literary Criticism, Volume 57, Thomson Gale (Detroit, MI), 1990.

Dictionary of Literary Biography Yearbook 1982, Thomson Gale (Detroit, MI), 1983.

St. James Guide to Science Fiction Writers, 4th edition, St. James Press (Detroit, MI), 1996.

Turner, Alice K., and Michael Andre-Driussi, editors, *Snake's-Hands: The Fiction of John Crowley,* Cosmos Books (Canton, OH), 2003.

PERIODICALS

Analog: Science Fiction/Science Fact, June, 1977; August, 1987; December, 1989.

Atlantic, September, 1994, review of *Love and Sleep,* p. 112.

Berkshire Sampler, September 13, 1981.

Book, March-April, 2002, James Schiff, review of *The Translator,* p. 79.

Booklist, February 15, 2002, Ted Leventhal, review of *The Translator,* pp. 990-991.

Commonweal, December 2, 1994, Suzanne Keen, review of *Love and Sleep,* p. 26.

Extrapolation, spring, 1990.

Kirkus Reviews, June 15, 1994, review of *Love and Sleep;* June 15, 2000, review of *Dæmonomania,* p. 815; February 1, 2002, review of *The Translator,* p. 121; March 1, 2004, review of *Novelties and Souvenirs: Collected Short Fiction,* p. 194.

Library Journal, August, 2000, Rachel Singer Gordon, review of *Dæmonomania,* p. 168.

Locus, August, 1991; September, 1991; May, 2001, pp. 4-5, 66-67; February, 2002, Faren Miller, review of *The Translator.*

Los Angeles Times, May 4, 1987, Carolyn See, review of *Ægypt.*

Magazine of Fantasy and Science Fiction, April, 1980; December, 1987; January, 1992; June, 2002, Elizabeth Hand, review of *The Translator.*

New Statesman, November 20, 1987.

New York Review of Science Fiction, July, 1998, Jennifer Stevenson, "Memory and the World of John Crowley," pp. 1, 8-11; August, 1999, Alice K. Turner, "Deep Thoughts: John Crowley's Fifteenth-Century Game of Kings," pp. 1, 4-5, and Michael Andre-Driussi, "John Crowley's Great Blond Beasts," pp. 1, 6-12, and Alice K. Turner, "One Writer's Beginnings: John Crowley's *Engine Summer* as the Portrait of the Artist," pp. 17-18; October, 1999, Michael Andre-Driussi, "John Crowley," pp. 1, 4-7; January, 2000, Alice K. Turner, "Daily Alice's Childhood; *Little, Big* for Little Folk," pp. 9-10; October, 2000, Michael Andre-Driussi, "Off the Deep End," pp. 18-19; January, 2002, Sondra Ford Swift, "Pierce Moffett the Ass: Apuleian and Brunonian Theses in John Crowley's *Dæmonomania,*" pp. 1, 6-8; March, 2002, Bill Sheehan, "Life after *Ægypt,*" pp. 12-15.

New York Times Book Review, November 21, 1976, Gerald Jonas, review of *The Deep;* March 27, 1977; May 20, 1979; March 2, 1986; October 12, 1986; May 3, 1987, pp. 9, 11, John Clute, review of *Ægypt;* August 14, 1988; May 21, 1989; July 5, 1992; February 6, 1994, review of *Antiquities,* p. 22; September 4, 1994, Jonathan Dee, review of *Love and Sleep,* p. 9; September 17, 2000, Jeff Waggoner, review of *Dæmonomania,* p. 25; June 2, 2002, review of *The Translator,* p. 24.

Publishers Weekly, February 20, 1987; April 14, 1989; August 29, 1994, Robert K.J. Killheffer, "John Crowley: 'I Still Owe a Debt of Gratitude,'" p. 53; July 3, 2000, review of *Dæmonomania,* p. 53; January 14, 2002, review of *The Translator,* p. 38; May 24, 2004, p. 50.

Saturday Review, April 14, 1979.

Science Fiction and Fantasy Book Review, January-February, 1982.

Times Literary Supplement, May 28, 1982; November 20-26, 1987, p. 1274.

Tribune Books (Chicago, IL), October 18, 1981; June 18, 1989, p. 6; September 11, 1994, Robert Chatain, review of *Love and Sleep,* pp. 1, 13.

Village Voice, April 5, 2002, Elizabeth Hand, "Angels in America."

Voice Literary Supplement, September, 1994, p. 31.

Washington Post Book World, March 23, 1980; July 26, 1981; October 4, 1981; April 19, 1987, pp. 1, 7, Michael Dirda, review of *Ægypt;* March 19, 1989; December 6, 1992, review of *Little, Big,* p. 4; November 28, 1993, review of *Antiquities,* p. 8; July 10, 1994; August 14, 1994, Lawrence Norfolk, review of *Love and Sleep,* p. 5; March 24, 2002, Howard Norman, review of *The Translator.*

ONLINE

Booksense.com, http://www.booksense.com/ (August 17, 2004), Gavin J. Grant, "The Secret History of John Crowley."

HarperCollins Web site, http://www.harpercollins.com/ (August 20, 2004) "An Interview with John Crowley."

January Magazine Online, http://www.january magazine.com/ (April, 2002), David Dalgleish, "False Modesty."

Ransom Center Web site, http://www.hrc.utexas.edu/ (August 20, 2004), "John Crowley Papers."

Salon.com, http://www.salon.com/ (March 21, 2002), Laura Miller, review of *The Translator.*

CRUTCHER, Chris 1946-
(Christopher C. Crutcher)

PERSONAL: Born July 17, 1946, in Cascade, ID; son of John William (a county clerk) and Jewell (Morris) Crutcher. *Education:* Eastern Washington State College (now University), B.A., 1968. *Politics:* Independent

ADDRESSES: Home—East 3405 Marion St., Spokane, WA 99223. *Office*—Community Mental Health, South 107 Division, Spokane, WA 99202. *Agent*—Liz Darhansoff, 1220 Park Ave., New York, NY 10028.

CAREER: Kennewick Dropout School, Kennewick, WA, teacher of high school dropouts, 1970-73; Lakeside School, Oakland, CA, teacher, 1973-76, director of school, 1976-80; Community Mental Health, Spokane, WA, child protection team specialist, 1980-82, child and family therapist, 1982—.

AWARDS, HONORS: American Library Association's list of best books for young adults, 1983, for *Running Loose,* 1986, for *Stotan!,* 1989, for *Chinese Handcuffs,* 1991, for *Athletic Shorts,* 1993, for *Staying Fat for Sarah Byrnes,* and 1995, for *Ironman; School Library Journal's* best books for young adults list, and American Library Association's list of best books for young adults for *The Crazy Horse Electric Game,* both 1988; Michigan Library Association Best Young Adult Book of 1992, for *Athletic Shorts;* ALAN award for Significant Contribution to Adolescent Literature; National Intellectual Freedom Award, National Council of Teachers of English, 1998; ALA Margaret A. Edwards Award for lifetime achievement in writing for teenagers, 2000; Pacific Northwest Booksellers Association and Washington State Book awards for *Whale Talk,* 2002; "Writers Who Make a Difference" Award, *Writer,* 2004.

WRITINGS:

BOOKS FOR YOUNG ADULTS

Running Loose, Greenwillow (New York, NY), 1983, HarperTempest (New York, NY), 2003.
Stotan!, Greenwillow (New York, NY), 1986.
The Crazy Horse Electric Game, Greenwillow (New York, NY), 1987.
Chinese Handcuffs, Greenwillow (New York, NY), 1989.

Athletic Shorts: Six Short Stories, Greenwillow (New York, NY), 1991, HarperTempest (New York, NY), 2002.

Staying Fat for Sarah Byrnes, Greenwillow (New York, NY), 1993, HarperCollins (New York, NY), 2003.

Ironman, Greenwillow (New York, NY), 1995.

(Contributor) Lisa Rowe Fraustino, editor, *Dirty Laundry, Stories about Family Secrets*, Viking (New York, NY), 1998.

Whale Talk, Greenwillow (New York, NY), 2001.

OTHER

The Deep End, Morrow (New York, NY), 1991.

King of the Mild Frontier: An Ill-Advised Autobiography, Greenwillow Books/ HarperCollins (New York, NY), 2003.

Contributor to *Spokane* magazine.

ADAPTATIONS: Audio versions have been made of *Athletic Shorts, Ironman, Whale Talk,* and *Staying Fat for Sarah Byrnes*; screenplay for *Staying Fat for Sarah Byrnes* in production.

SIDELIGHTS: Chris Crutcher grew up in a town so small that a local athletic competition would bring business to a standstill. Crutcher played many sports in high school, did well in college swimming, and began participating in triathlons after college. It comes as no surprise then that competitive sports figure heavily in his writing. Throughout his schooling, as he describes in his autobiography, Crutcher was a self-professed academic underachiever, his family life was challenging, and he grew up with a violent temper. Yet he eventually earned a B.A. with a major in psychology and a minor in sociology, and became a high school social studies teacher, a school administrator, and a therapist at a mental health facility. After completing his education, Crutcher taught in tough, inner-city schools and ran an alternative school for inner-city kids in Oakland, California, before becoming a child and family therapist, all of which helped prepare him to write about a wide variety of serious problems with which adolescents are confronted daily in modern day American culture.

"Writing with a vitality and authority that stems from personal experiences in *Running Loose, Stotan!,* and *The Crazy Horse Electric Game,* Chris Crutcher gives readers the inside story on young men, sports, and growing up," wrote Christine McDonnell in *Horn Book.* "His

heroes—sensitive, reflective young men, far from stereotypic jocks—use sports as an arena to test personal limits; to prove stamina, integrity, and identity; and to experience loyalty and cooperation as well as competition." In *Staying Fat for Sarah Byrnes,* Crutcher teams a girl whose face is disfigured by a burn and her longtime overweight friend, "Moby" Calhoun, both of whom have the "terminal uglies," in the eyes of their schoolmates. The friends ultimately discover the shameful truth of how Sarah got her burn. In a New York Public Library "Author Chat," Crutcher told a caller: "The 'event' came from a real event in which a man burned his child in a drunken rage, and then handed her back to her mother and said, 'There's your pretty little girl for you.' The real people were very different from those in the story, and I did the 'what if' game to create characters who would help me tell the story the way I wanted to tell it." Crutcher does much to expose the real ugliness of what many children suffer, along with a message of courage and possibilities for healing.

In *Ironman* a high school senior, Bo Brewster, is locked "in a perpetual struggle with an authoritarian father and a battle with a tyrannical teacher," according to *New York Times* reviewer James Gorman. It is the story, Gorman wrote, of "Bo's search for self-understanding, self-possession and self-respect." Gorman noted that even if the book sounds like the plot of a television movie, "[Crutcher's] tale is a lot stronger than the flash that overlays it. He's a terrific storyteller with a wonderful handle on what it's like to be an adolescent." After a gap of six years, Crutcher produced *Whale Talk,* another story set in a small northwest town, where Tao (T.J.) Jones, a mixed-race high school athlete—"witty, self-assured, fearless, intelligent, and wise beyond his years" according to Todd Morning in the *School Library Journal,*—"has refused to play on the school teams and thus condone the Cutter High School cult of athletic privilege. He agrees to lead a startup swim team only to buck the system by signing up every needy misfit he can find—from a special ed. student to a 'one-legged psychopath'—and ensuring that each will win a Cutter High letterman's jacket. In quintessential Crutcher form, the unlikely athletes build up not only physical strength but emotional support as the team bus becomes a mobile group-therapy session," as a *Horn Book* reviewer described. *Booklist*'s Kelly Miller Halls quoted Crutcher on two swim team members: "I actually don't look at either of them as being disabled. I see them as warriors—guys who have really been through it and are struggling to stand up for what they have." T.J. fights elitism among school jocks, extreme racism in the stepfather of a friend, and an arrogant coach to bring his team through.

In 2003, Crutcher broke form by writing *King of the Mild Frontier: An Ill-Advised Autobiography.* A *Horn Book* reviewer praised the new venture: "Crutcher, best known for his novels and short stories, has discovered his most effective voice in this collection of episodic, autobiographical essays." In a *Journal of Adolescent and Adult Literature* interview, James Blasingame asked Crutcher about the ways he deals with death in his essays. The author responded, "The common issue is loss, and death is the trump card of loss. In the preface to one of the short stories in *Athletic Shorts . . .* I said there is a case to be made that from the time of birth, when we lose a warm, enclosed, safe place to be, our lives are made up of a series of losses and our grace can be measured by how we face those losses, and how we replace what is lost. What I'm talking about there is the process of grief, which is one of the most important things we do as humans—taking the risk of losing one thing so we can go on to the next. I believe our culture doesn't understand that very well, and it often tries to force us to hold on to old perceptions and beliefs that have little or no further use and that keep us stuck and afraid. If we do learn to face death, accommodate and accept it, there are few lesser changes that can tip us over, though there are certainly 'fates worse than death.' So, yeah, I think it's common for kids, at their developmental level, and it is common for us at ours." Crutcher, whose work has at times been censored by over-zealous librarians, parents, and teachers for his real-to-life dealing with the complexities—humorous and tragic—of teenage life, addresses these issues and shares stories from his growing up, which Joel Shoemaker in the *School Library Journal* described as "tough and tender reminiscences [which] focus primarily on family, social, and school conflicts, but lessons derived from his career as a teacher, therapist, and writer are also described. Hyperbole lightens the mood as the author portrays himself as a young crybaby, academic misfit, and athletic klutz, utterly without self-aggrandizement." It is his humility, wrote a *Publishers Weekly* reviewer, "that allows readers to laugh with young Chris, rather than at him" when he constantly gets into trouble under his older brother's tutelage, gets hit in the mouth with a softball bat showing off for the girls' team, and trembles as "a terrified 123-pound freshman ('with all the muscle definition of a chalk outline')."

Crutcher shared the following thoughts on writing: "It is a joy to write a tale that is believable, that is real. Writing is also a way to express humor and to present different human perspectives. I like to explore the different ways in which people make sense of what goes on around them—ways in which they respond to the wide range of random things that happen, and to the situations they create.

"Working in the mental health field provides me with some unique perspectives on the human drama—how people get stuck and how they grow. Every client—man, woman, or child, no matter how damaged—has shown me at least a small glimpse of how we're all connected."

BIOGRAPHICAL AND CRITICAL SOURCES:

BOOKS

Children's Literature Review, Volume 28, Thomson Gale (Detroit, MI), 1992.
Davis, Terry, *Presenting Chris Crutcher,* Twayne (Boston, MA), 1997.
Twentieth-Century Young Adult Writers, 1st edition, St. James Press (Detroit, MI), 1994.

PERIODICALS

ALAN Review, fall, 1994, "Chris Crutcher—Hero or Villain?"
Booklist, March 1, 1995, p. 1240; April 1, 2001, pp. 1462, 1463; April 15, 2003, p. 1469.
Buffalo News, July 12, 1998, p. F7.
Denver Post, April 15, 2001, p. F-01.
Detroit News, October 3, 2003, p. 05.
Emergency Librarian, January-February, 1991, pp. 67-71; May-June 1996, interview with Crutcher, p. 61.
English Journal, November, 1989, pp. 44-46; March 1996, 36.
Horn Book, May-June, 1988, p. 332; September-October, 1995, p. 606; May, 2001, p. 320; May-June, 2003, p. 368.
Journal of Adolescent and Adult Literacy, May, 2003, James Blasingame, interview with Crutcher, p. 696.
Kirkus Reviews, April 1, 2003, p. 532.
Knight Ridder/Tribune News Service, June 11, 2003, p. K1815.
Lion and the Unicorn: A Critical Journal of Children's Literature, June, 1992, p. 66.
Los Angeles Times Book Review, June 20, 1993, p. 3.
New York Times, May 18, 2003, p. 24.
New York Times Book Review, September 5, 1993, p. 17; July 2, 1995, p. 13.
Publishers Weekly, March 12, 2001, interview with Crutcher, p. 91; February 20, 1995, interview with Crutcher, p. 183; March 3, 2003, p. 77.
School Library Journal, February, 1996, p. 70; October, 1996, p. 78; January, 1997, p. 36; June 2000, interview with Crutcher, p. 42; May, 2001, p. 148;

April, 2003, p. 176; October, 2003, reviews of
Ironman, p. 99, and *Staying Fat for Sarah Byrnes*
(audiobook review), p. S68; November, 2003, Car-
ole Fazioli, review of *King of the Mild Frontier: An
Ill-Advised Autobiography,* p. 82.
Teacher Librarian, October, 2003, p. 36.
Tribune Books (Chicago, IL), August 11, 1991, p. 6.
VOYA: Voice of Youth Advocates, April, 1983, p. 36;
June 2002, p. 94.

ONLINE

Chris Crutcher Home Page, http://www.aboutcrutcher.
com/ (March 8, 2004).
New York Public Library,, http://summerreading.nypl.
org/ (July, 2002), interview with Crutcher.
Teenreads.com, http://www.teenreads.com/ (April 2,
2001), interview with Crutcher.

*　　*　　*

CRUTCHER, Christopher C.
See CRUTCHER, Chris

*　　*　　*

CRUZ, Victor Hernández 1949-

PERSONAL: Born February 6, 1949, in Aguas Buenas,
Puerto Rico; immigrated to the United States, 1954; son
of Severo and Rosa (Hernández) Cruz; divorced; children: Vitin Ajani, Rosa Luz. *Education:* Attended high
school in New York, NY.

ADDRESSES: Office—P.O. Box 40148, San Francisco,
CA 94140; P.O. Box 1047, Aguas Buenas, PR 00607.

CAREER: Poet. East Harlem Gut Theatre, New York,
NY, co-founder, 1968; University of California, Berkeley, guest lecturer, 1970-1971; San Francisco State University, 1973, Mission Neighborhood Center, San Francisco, Research/Writer. Visiting professor at University
of California, San Diego, 1993, 1995; and University of
Michigan, Ann Arbor, 1994. Also associated with San
Francisco Art Commission; co-founder, Before Columbus Foundation.

AWARDS, HONORS: Creative Artists in Public Service
award, 1974, for *Tropicalization;* National Endowment
for the Arts fellow, 1980; New York Poetry Foundation

award, 1989; Guggenheim Foundation, Latin America
and the Caribbean Fellow, 1991; finalist for Lenore
Marshall Poetry Prize, 2002, shortlist for Griffin Poetry
Prize, both for *Maraca.*

WRITINGS:

Papo Got His Gun! and Other Poems, Calle Once Pub-
lications, 1966.
Doing Poetry, Other Ways, 1968.
Snaps (poems), Random House (New York, NY), 1969.
(Editor with Herbert Kohl) *Stuff: A Collection of Po-
ems, Visions, and Imaginative Happenings from
Young Writers in Schools—Open and Closed,* Col-
lins & World, 1970.
Mainland (poems), Random House (New York, NY),
1973.
Tropicalization (poems and prose), Reed, Canon, 1976.
The Low Writings, Lee/Lucas Press, 1980.
By Lingual Wholes, Momo's Press, 1982.
Rhythm, Content and Flavor: New and Selected Poems,
Arte Publico Press (Tucson, AZ), 1989.
Red Beans, Coffee House Press (Minneapolis, MN),
1991.
(Editor with Leroy V. Quintana and Virgil Suarez) *Pa-
per Dance: Fifty-four Latino Poets,* Persea Books,
1994.
Paper Dance: 55 Latino Poets, Persea Books, 1995.
Panaramas, Coffee House Press (Minneapolis, MN),
1997.
Maracas: New and Selected Poems, 1966-2000, Coffee
House Press (Minneapolis, MN), 2001.

Poetry has appeared in anthologies, including *An Anthology of Afro-American Writing,* Morrow, 1968; *Giant
Talk: An Anthology of Third-World Writings,* Random
House, 1975; *Without Discovery: A Native Response to
Columbus* edited by Ray González, Broken Moon Press,
1992; *The Language of Life: A Festival of Poets,*
Doubleday, 1995; *Boricuas: Influential Puerto Rican
Writings,* edited by Roberto Santiago, One World, 1995;
and *The Latino Reader: An American Literary Tradition
from 1542 to the Present,* edited and with an introduc-
tion by Harold Augenbraum and Margarite Fernández
Olmos, Houghton Mifflin, 1997. Contributor to *Ever-
green Review, New York Review of Books, New York
Times Sunday Magazine, Village Voice, Ramparts, Down
Here,* and *Revista del Instituto de Estudios Puertor-
riquenos.* Editor, *Umbra* magazine, 1967-69.

SIDELIGHTS: In a *New York Times Book Review* of
Victor Hernández Cruz's 1982 book *By Lingual
Wholes,* Richard Elman remarked that the author

"writes poems about his native Puerto Rico and elsewhere which often speak to us with a forked tongue, sometimes in a highly literate Spanglish. . . . He's a funny, hard-edged poet, declining always into mother wit and pathos: 'So you see, all life is a holy hole. Bet hard on that.'" And Nancy Sullivan reflected in *Poetry* magazine: "Cruz allows the staccato crackle of English half-learned, so characteristic of his people, to enrich the poems through its touching dictional inadequacy. If poetry is arching toward the condition of silence as John Cage and Susan Sontag suggest, perhaps this mode of inarticulateness is a bend on the curve. . . . I think that Cruz is writing necessary poems in a period when many poems seem unnecessary."

Cruz's 1991 work *Red Beans*—the title of which is a play on the words "red beings," referring to Puerto Ricans—has also received critical attention. Reviewers have characterized the volume as a highly imaginative exploration of Puerto Rican history as well as the Puerto Rican's history in America. In a review for the *San Francisco Review of Books,* José Amaya commented that "Cruz experiments with the vast linguistic and cultural possibilities of 'indo-afro-hispano' poetry and comes up with a strong vision of American unity." Commenting on the development of Cruz's style, Amaya noted that the poet "is at his best in *Red Beans* when he portrays . . . the distinct sounds and voices of Caribbean life which crash into his poetic consciousness like a wild ocean surf." Calling Cruz a "vigorous bilingual Latino troubadour," Frank Allen in *Library Journal* declared *Red Beans* to be "a dance on the edges."

Cruz's previously published works have continued to be made available to new readers in anthologies such as *Maracas: New and Selected Poems,* which includes the poems collectively called "Seeds." W. Nick Hill, writing in *World Literature Today,* reported that "Seeds" are "recent poems in homage to a very personal group of people who all have functioned as 'seeds' in the sprouting of this powerful, meteoric poetry: Cantinflas, Nabokov, Marti, among others." A contributor for *Publishers Weekly* wrote that "Cruz's idioms hit highs and lows effortlessly, singularly and with political bite: 'Percolating out of edam cheese/ Curacao coconut bridge/ Colonialism is always/ Take and get/ Energy colonizes the cream.'"

As Cruz once wrote: "My family life was full of music, guitars and conga drums, maracas and songs. My mother sang songs. Even when it was five below zero in New York she sang warm tropical ballads." He continued: "My work is on the border of a new language, because I create out of a consciousness steeped in two of the important world languages, Spanish and English. A piece written totally in English could have a Spanish spirit. Another strong concern in my work is the difference between a tropical village, such as Aguas Buenas, Puerto Rico, where I was born, and an immensity such as New York City, where I was raised. I compare smells and sounds, I explore the differences, I write from the center of a culture which is not on its native soil, a culture in flight, living half the time on memories, becoming something totally new and unique, while at the same time it helps to shape and inform the new environment. I write about the city with an agonizing memory of a lush tropical silence. This contrast between landscape and language creates an intensity in my work."

BIOGRAPHICAL AND CRITICAL SOURCES:

BOOKS

Hernández, Carmen Dolores, *Puerto Rican Voices in English: Interviews with Writers,* Praeger (New York, NY), 1997.

PERIODICALS

Bilingual Review, Volume 1, 1974, pp. 312-319.
Library Journal, October 1, 1997.
MELUS, spring, 1989-90, pp. 43-58.
New York Times Book Review, September 18, 1983.
Poetry, May, 1970.
Publishers Weekly, September 22, 1997; September 3, 2001, review of *Maracas: New and Selected Poems.*
World Literature Today, summer-autumn, 2002, W. Nick Hill, review of *Maracas: New and Selected Poems,* p. 96.

ONLINE

Academy of American Poets Web site, http://www.poets.org/ (July 20, 2004), "Victor Hernández Cruz."

OTHER

Victor Hernandez Cruz (film), Lannan Foundation/ Metropolitan Pictures/EZTV, 1989.

Where Poems Come From (film), Metropolitan Pictures/ EZTV, 1989.

Palabra: A Sampling of Contemporary Latino Writers, Poetry Center/San Francisco State University, 1993.

*   *   *

CULVER, Timothy J.
     See WESTLAKE, Donald E.

*   *   *

CUNNINGHAM, E.V.
     See FAST, Howard

*   *   *

CUNNINGHAM, J. Morgan
     See WESTLAKE, Donald E.

*   *   *

CUNNINGHAM, Michael 1952-

PERSONAL: Born November 6, 1952, in Cincinnati, OH; son of Don (in advertising) and Dorothy (a real estate agent) Cunningham; companion of Ken Corbett since 1988. *Education:* Stanford University, B.A., 1975; University of Iowa, M.F.A., 1980.

ADDRESSES: Home—New York, NY, and Provincetown, MA. *Agent*—c/o Farrar, Straus, & Giroux, 19 Union Square W., New York, NY 10003.

CAREER: Writer. Worked for Carnegie Corp., New York, NY, beginning in 1986.

MEMBER: ACT-UP.

AWARDS, HONORS: Irish Times-Aer Lingus International Fiction Prize nomination, 1991; Guggenheim fellowship, 1993; *Lambda* Literary Award for gay men's fiction, 1995 and 1996, for *Flesh and Blood;* PEN/ Faulkner Award for fiction, and Pulitzer Prize for fiction, both 1999, both for *The Hours.*

WRITINGS:

NOVELS

Golden States, Crown (New York, NY), 1984.

A Home at the End of the World, Farrar, Straus (New York, NY), 1990.

Flesh and Blood, Farrar, Straus (New York, NY), 1995.

The Hours, Farrar, Straus (New York, NY), 1998.

Specimen Days, Farrar, Straus (New York, NY), 2005.

OTHER

Land's End: A Walk through Provincetown, Crown/ Journeys (New York, NY), 2002.

Contributor of fiction and nonfiction to periodicals, including *New Yorker, Atlantic, Los Angeles Times, Mother Jones,* and *Paris Review.*

ADAPTATIONS: Flesh and Blood was adapted for a play, 2001, for Portland Stage Company; *The Hours* was adapted for a film by the same title, directed by Stephen Daldry and starring Nicole Kidman, Julianne Moore, and Meryl Streep, was released by Miramax, 2002; *A Home at the End of the World* was adapted for a film by the same title by Warner Independent Pictures, starring Colin Farrell, 2004.

SIDELIGHTS: Winner of the Pulitzer Prize for Fiction as well as a PEN/Faulkner Award for his 1998 novel, *The Hours,* Michael Cunningham has earned not only critical acclaim, but also commercial success for his novels and for the adaptation of his works for the cinema. His works frequently feature homosexual characters and themes, but they do not lose sight of the world beyond the gay community. "Homosexuality is a lens through which the world is viewed, not a world unto itself," stated Joseph M. Eagan in *Gay and Lesbian Literature.* In novels that explore themes of family, friendship, identity, and commitment, he "places his gay and bisexual characters in the mainstream of American life, [viewing] their homosexuality as only one aspect of their identity," according to Eagan. The critic further noted that Cunningham has "been widely praised for his prose, sense of place, use of imagery, and psychological insight into his characters."

In 1984 Cunningham published his first novel, *Golden States,* which concerns an adolescent boy coming of age in southern California. The boy, twelve-year-old David Stark, is initially portrayed as a victim of his own preoccupations and manias. Living with his mother, older stepsister, and tirelessly obnoxious younger sister, David seems obsessed with safeguarding his home and family. At one point, he even sojourns, with an unloaded pistol, to San Francisco in a harebrained scheme to "save" his stepsister from her presumably dangerous fiancé. Eventually, David begins to understand and control his fears and anxieties even though his life becomes one of increasing isolation and domestic instability. Though abandoned by his father and rejected by his best friend, David develops a sense of security and self-understanding. Ever the protector, however, he continues to guard his suburban neighborhood home from prowling coyotes.

Golden States was generally perceived as a successful first venture into novel writing. Elizabeth Royte, writing in the *Village Voice,* deemed Cunningham's debut "a sweetly appealing book," while Anne F. Wittels declared in the *Los Angeles Times Book Review* that the work was "exceedingly well-written." Wittels objected only to the end, which she claimed "left a bad taste," but conceded that the book's "first seven-eighths was terrific." Ruth Doan MacDougall was more enthusiastic in her *Christian Science Monitor* appraisal. "However much one might object to the theme of the protection of women, one cannot help savoring every moment of this novel," she wrote. "Funny, tender, [*Golden States*] is a joy to read."

Despite the favorable reviews, *Golden States* only "sold seven or eight copies," the author joked to *Publishers Weekly* interviewer Michael Coffey. His real breakthrough came with his second novel, *A Home at the End of the World,* a story about sexual liberation in the age of acquired immune deficiency syndrome (AIDS). The novel provides perspectives on four characters—Jonathan, Bobby, Clare, and Alice—in detailing the complexities of a childhood friendship that develops into romantic love. Jonathan and Bobby meet as young boys in Cleveland, and in the ensuing years they become close friends. When Jonathan leaves for college in New York City, Bobby, whose own family life is empty, becomes a mainstay in his friend's family home. There, Bobby grows particularly close to Jonathan's mother, Alice, whose marriage is collapsing. Eventually, Bobby and Jonathan are reunited in New York City, where they begin living together. They are eventually joined in their quarters by Clare, a young divorced woman who is still rebelling against her wealthy family. Clare hopes to bear Jonathan's child. Instead, she bears Bobby's, a daughter. Jonathan becomes jealous of Bobby and Clare's relationship, but soon all three adults, plus child, begin living together in upstate New York. This idyll is undone, however, when one of Jonathan's former lovers arrives stricken with AIDS.

A Home at the End of the World has earned praise as a compelling portrait of modern times. In the *New York Times Book Review* Joyce Reiser likened Cunningham to authors Charles Dickens and E.M. Forster, and she hailed Cunningham's work as one of power and depth. She found *A Home at the End of the World* "memorable and accomplished." Another enthusiast, Richard Eder, was particularly impressed with Cunningham's craft, affirming in the *Los Angeles Times Book Review* that the novelist "writes with power and delicacy" and adding that the entire book "is beautifully written." And Patrick Gale, in his review for the *Washington Post Book World,* noted both the profundity of Cunningham's work and the subtlety with which he wrote it. Observing that the theme of the novel is nothing less than "the family and its alternatives in the overlapping aftermaths of sexual liberation and AIDS," Gale continued by commending Cunningham for his work's "careful structure." Especially successful to Gale is the use of memory, which enables *A Home at the End of the World* to provide readers with "a pleasing sense . . . of resolution, even if the characters are no less happy at the close than they were before."

Flesh and Blood, published in 1995, demonstrates Cunningham's continuing concerns for honoring all kinds of unconventional family units. This long, multigenerational saga centers on a Greek immigrant and his family. On the surface, Constantine and his wife, Mary, seem to have achieved the American dream: a nice house in the suburbs and three children. But Mary cannot curb her compulsion to shoplift, nor can Constantine resist the beauty of his eldest daughter. A cross-dressing son and a drug-using daughter who raises her illegitimate child with a transvestite partner fill out the picture. All the characters and their troubles "ring true, heartbreakingly true. And beautiful in a way no camera could capture," praised Kelli Pryor in *Entertainment Weekly.* A *Publishers Weekly* reviewer affirmed that, as in *A Home at the End of the World,* Cunningham's prose "is again rich, graceful and luminous, and he exhibits a remarkable maturity of vision and understanding of the human condition." The book was also praised by *Booklist* reviewer Donna Seaman, who called it "empathic and searing," and concluded: "Cunningham, in a remarkable performance, inhabits the psyche of each of his striking characters."

Cunningham received even higher praise for his 1998 publication, *The Hours.* This book is a complex tribute to early twentieth-century British author Virginia Woolf and her classic novel *Mrs. Dalloway,* and takes its title from Woolf's working title for her novel. Woolf is also a character in the book, which is strongly influenced by her unique style. A day in Woolf's life is skillfully meshed with brief episodes from two other lives: a lonely homemaker who escapes her family for a day to read *Mrs. Dalloway,* and a Greenwich Village lesbian who is called "Mrs. Dalloway" by her dying lover, a victim of AIDS. *Advocate* contributor Robert Plunket confided, "I have a very low tolerance for arty writers who publish stories in the *New Yorker* and then write novels that turn out to be homages to Virginia Woolf, which makes my reaction to Michael Cunningham's new novel . . . all the more remarkable. . . . Reading this book, I was overwhelmed by the possibilities of art."

Such high praise was heaped on Cunningham's novel by other reviewers, as well. A *Publishers Weekly* contributor declared that *The Hours* "makes a reader believe in the possibility and depth of a communality based on great literature, literature that has shown people how to live and what to ask of life." Similarly, a critic for *Kirkus Reviews* praised the "gorgeous, Woolfian, shimmering, perfectly-observed prose." The same contributor concluded, "Hardly a false note in an extraordinary carrying on of a true greatness that doubted itself." Brooke Allen, writing in the *New Criterion,* commented that Cunningham's story—about "a bunch of gay people in Greenwich Village unconsciously re-enacting Virginia Woolf's Dalloway"—sounded like "one of the worst ideas of all time." However, Allen found that Cunningham "succeeds brilliantly," and "proves once again that when a novelist has the right stuff, he can endow literally any subject with truth, poetry, and intelligence." Seaman writing in *Booklist,* felt that it "takes courage to emulate a revered and brilliant writer, not to mention transforming her into a character." Seaman noted further that, in fact, Cunningham "has done this and more in his third novel, a graceful and passionate homage to Virginia Woolf." While Jameson Currier, reviewing the book in the *Washington Post Book World,* found that Cunningham "enters his characters' minds and reconstitutes their days impressively," he also noted that *The Hours* "is not without its problems." According to Currier, these "problems" included a "few throwaway scenes . . . , some unrealized and stereotypical characters . . . , and some awkward and unnecessary shifts in point of view." However, the same critic went on to call *The Hours* Cunningham's "most mature and masterful work." And Richard Eder, writing in the *Los Angeles Times Book Review,* commended Cunningham's novel as a "fictional instrument of intricacy and remarkable beauty."

With both a Pen/Faulkner Award and Pulitzer Prize earned from *The Hours,* as well as a high-profile movie released, Cunningham was faced with a difficult follow-up act. While working on his next work of book-length fiction—a series of three linking novellas—he tackled a guidebook series entry on his part-time hometown, Provincetown, Massachusetts. With *Land's End: A Walk through Provincetown,* Cunningham "takes the reader on a leisurely, idiosyncratic tour of the fabled town at the tip of Cape Cod," according to a *Publishers Weekly* reviewer. A critic for *Kirkus Reviews* noted that Cunningham "takes his tour guide's responsibility seriously and eagerly, wanting readers to get both the grand and intimate view." For the same reviewer, Cunningham "intriguingly rendered" the world of Provincetown. *Booklist*'s Seaman had similar praise, finding that Cunningham's prose "has never been more gorgeously poetic" than in this work, and that the author demonstrates a "fascination with the peculiarities of our species and inspires tender and funny riffs on Provincetown's thriving gay and lesbian communities."

BIOGRAPHICAL AND CRITICAL SOURCES:

BOOKS

Contemporary Literary Criticism, Volume 34, Thomson Gale (Detroit, MI), 1985, pp. 40-42.
Gay and Lesbian Literature, Volume 2, St. James (Detroit, NY), 1998.

PERIODICALS

Advocate, June 13, 1995, p. 62; September 15, 1998, p. 63; December 8, 1998, Robert Plunket, "Imagining Woolf," p. 87.
American Theatre, October, 2001, "Novel to Stage: A Family's 2nd Act," p. 50.
Best Sellers, June, 1984, p. 87.
Booklist, March 15, 1984, p. 1027; January 15, 1995, Donna Seaman, review of *Flesh and Blood,* p. 868; September 15, 1998, Donna Seaman, review of *The Hours,* p. 173; July, 2002, Donna Seaman, review of *Land's End,* p. 1818.
Chicago, July, 1984, p. 156.
Christian Science Monitor, Ruth Doan MacDougall, review of *Golden States,* May 4, 1984, p. 20.
Christopher Street, Volume 13, number 9, 1990, pp. 4-5; January, 1991, p. 4; July 7, 1992, p. 3.
Daily Variety, December 17, 2002, Lily Oei, "Literati, Glitterati," p. 20.
Entertainment Weekly, May 8, 1992, p. 52; April 14, 1995, Kelli Pryor, review of *Flesh and Blood,* p. 59; May 10, 1996, p. 69.

Gay and Lesbian Review Worldwide, March-April, 2003, Tony Peregrin, "Michael Cunningham after Hours," pp. 30-31.

Glamour, November, 1990, p. 174; April, 1995, p. 198.

Kirkus Reviews, September 1, 1998, review of *The Hours;* May 1, 2002, review of *Land's End,* p. 632.

Lambda Book Report, May / June, 1995, p. 14.

Library Journal, April 1, 1984, p. 732; October 15, 1990, p. 102; March 15, 1994, p. 116; April 15, 1995, p. 112; October 1, 1998, Marc A. Kloszewski, p. 131.

London Review of Books, February 22, 1996, pp. 27-31.

Los Angeles Times Book Review, Alice F. Wittels, review of *Golden States,* April 22, 1984, p. 6; November 18, 1990, Richard Eder, review of *A Home at the End of the World,* pp. 3, 12; April 9, 1995, pp. 3, 7; November 15, 1998, Richard Eder, review of *The Hours,* p. 2.

Nation, July 1, 1991, pp. 21-25.

New Criterion, June, 1999, Brooke Allen, review of *The Hours,* p. 81.

New York, November 12, 1990, p. 30; April 10, 1995, pp. 72-73.

New Yorker, April 30, 1984, p. 118; October 5, 1998, p. 107.

New York Times Book Review, November 11, 1990, Joyce Reiser Kornblatt, review of *A Home at the End of the World,* pp. 12-13; April 16, 1995, p. 13; November 22, 1998, p. 6.

People, May 7, 1984, p. 19; February 10, 2003, Allison Adato, "Man of the Hours," p. 105.

Publishers Weekly, February 3, 1984, p. 393; August 17, 1990, p. 52; January 23, 1995, review of *Flesh and Blood,* p. 60; August 31, 1998, review of *The Hours,* p. 46; November 2, 1998, interview with Michael Coffey, "Michael Cunningham: New Family Outings," p. 53; May 20, 2002, review of *Land's End,* p. 55; July 15, 2002, John F. Baker, "Bookseller and Critical Favorite Michael Cunningham," p. 12.

Times Literary Supplement, August 11, 1995, p. 20.

Tribune Books (Chicago, IL), November 4, 1990, p. 6.

Vanity Fair, May, 1995, p. 96.

Village Voice, September 4, 1984, Elizabeth Royte, review of *Golden States,* p. 52.

Vogue, January, 1989, p. 62; November, 1998, p. 247.

Voice of Youth Advocates, October, 1984, p. 196.

Washington Post, April 8, 1999, David Streitfeld, "Cunningham Wins PEN Award," p. C1.

Washington Post Book World, December 9, 1990, Patrick Thomson Gale, review of *A Home at the End of the World,* p. 7; April 2, 1995, pp. 72-73; November 22, 1998, Jameson Currier, review of *The Hours,* p. 4.

ONLINE

Michael Cunningham Home Page, http://literati.net/Cunningham/ (July 24, 2004).

Steven Barclay Agency Web site, http://www.barclayagency.com/ (July 23, 2004), "Michael Cunningham."

*   *   *

CURTIS, Price
See ELLISON, Harlan

*   *   *

CUSSLER, Clive 1931-
(Clive Eric Cussler)

PERSONAL: Born July 15, 1931, in Aurora, IL; son of Eric E. and Amy (Hunnewell) Cussler; married Barbara Knight, August 28, 1955; children: Teri, Dirk, Dayna. *Education:* Attended Pasadena City College, 1949-50, and Orange Coast College. *Politics:* "Non-partisan." *Hobbies and other interests:* Collecting automobiles, searching for historic shipwrecks.

ADDRESSES: Home—Telluride, CO, and Paradise Valley, AZ. *Office*—National Underwater and Marine Agency, P.O. Box 5059, Scottsdale, AZ 85258. *Agent*—c/o Pitch Productions, 859 Hollywood Way, Ste. 212, Burbank, CA 91505.

CAREER: Bestgen and Cussler Advertising, Newport Beach, CA, owner, 1961-65; Darcy Advertising, Hollywood, CA, creative director, 1965-68; Mefford, Wolff and Weir Advertising, Denver, CO, vice president and creative director of broadcast, 1970-75; Aquatic Marine Dive Equipment, Newport Beach, CA, member of sales staff; National Underwater and Marine Agency (NUMA), founder and chair. Discoverer of more than sixty shipwrecks. Worked for a supermarket and a gas station. *Military service:* U.S. Air Force, 1950-54; served as aircraft mechanic, became sergeant.

MEMBER: National Society of Oceanographers (fellow), American Society of Oceanographers, Classic Car Club of America, Royal Geographic Society (London, England; fellow), Explorers Club of New York (fellow).

AWARDS, HONORS: Ford Foundation Consumer Award, 1965-66, for best promotional campaign; first prize, Chicago Film Festival, 1966, for best thirty-second live action commercial; International Broadcasting Awards, 1964, 1965, 1966, 1972, 1973, for year's best radio and TV commercials; first place award, Venice Film Festival, 1972, for sixty-second live commercial; Clio Awards, 1972, 1973, 1974, for TV and radio commercials; Lowell Thomas Award, Explorers Club of New York, for underwater exploration; numerous honors for work in shipwreck discoveries and marine archaeology, including NUMA's receiving a Lightspan Academic Excellence Award for outstanding contribution to education in the field of marine archaeology and historic preservation.

WRITINGS:

"DIRK PITT" ADVENTURE NOVELS

The Mediterranean Caper, Pyramid (New York, NY), 1973, also published as *May Day.*
Iceberg, Dodd, Mead (New York, NY), 1975.
Raise the Titanic, Viking (New York, NY), 1976.
Vixen 03, Viking (New York, NY), 1978.
Night Probe, illustrations by Errol Beauchamp, Bantam (New York, NY), 1981.
Pacific Vortex!, Bantam (New York, NY), 1983.
Deep Six, Simon & Schuster (New York, NY), 1984, premium edition, Pocket Star Books (New York, NY), 2006.
Cyclops, Simon & Schuster (New York, NY), 1986.
Treasure, Simon & Schuster (New York, NY), 1988.
Dragon, Simon & Schuster (New York, NY), 1990.
Sahara, Simon & Schuster (New York, NY), 1992.
Inca Gold, Simon & Schuster (New York, NY), 1994.
Shock Wave, Simon & Schuster (New York, NY), 1996.
Flood Tide, Simon & Schuster (New York, NY), 1997.
Atlantis Found, Putnam (New York, NY), 1999.
Valhalla Rising, Putnam (New York, NY), 2001.
Two Complete Novels (contains *Cyclops* and *Flood Tide*), Wings Books (New York, NY), 2001.
Trojan Odyssey, Putnam (New York, NY), 2003.
(With son, Dirk Cussler)*Black Wind,* Putnam (New York, NY), 2004.

"KURT AUSTIN" SERIES; WITH PAUL KEMPRECOS

Serpent: A Novel from the NUMA Files, Pocket (New York, NY), 1999.
Blue Gold: A Novel from the NUMA Files, Pocket (New York, NY), 2000.
Fire Ice, Putnam (New York, NY), 2002.
White Death, Putnam (New York, NY), 2003.

Lost City, Putnam (New York, NY), 2004.
Polar Shift, Putnam (New York, NY), 2005.

"OREGON FILES" SERIES

(With Craig Dirgo) *Golden Buddha,* Putnam (New York, NY), 2003.
(With Craig Dirgo) *Sacred Stone,* Putnam (New York, NY), 2004.
(With Jack DuBrul) *Dark Watch,* Putnam (New York, NY), 2004.

OTHER

(With Craig Dirgo) *The Sea Hunters: True Adventures with Famous Shipwrecks,* Simon & Schuster (New York, NY), 1996.
(With Craig Dirgo) *Clive Cussler and Dirk Pitt Revealed,* Pocket (New York, NY), 1998.
(With Craig Dirgo) *The Sea Hunters II: Diving the World's Seas for Famous Shipwrecks,* Putnam (New York, NY), 2002.
The Adventures of Vin Fiz (children's book), illustrated by William Farnsworth, Philomel Books (New York, NY), 2006.

Some novels adapted for young adult audiences beginning 1999.

ADAPTATIONS: Raise the Titanic, based on Cussler's novel and starring Jason Robards and Richard Jordan as Dirk Pitt, was released by Associated Film Distribution in 1980; Eco-Nova (Halifax, Canada) and *National Geographic* documentary series, "Clive Cussler's 'The Sea Hunters'"; Cussler's novel *Sahara* was adapted for film by screenwriter Thomas Dean Donnelly and director Breck Eisner. The film starred Matthew McConaughey and Penelope Cruz, and was released by Paramount Pictures in 2005. Cussler's books are available on audiotape.

SIDELIGHTS: Clive Cussler began writing novels to while away the time when his wife took a night-time job, but earned his living writing award-winning advertising copy until the success of his underwater adventure novels featuring his hero, Dirk Pitt, enabled him to leave the business world and pursue his writing interests full time. Since then, his adventure tales have sold over seventy million copies in more than forty languages and a hundred countries. Some sources cite the best-selling author as having more than ninety million fans, a number of which eagerly attend his book-signings and ask for his "famous" "personalized inscription[s]," wrote Daisy Maryles in a 1999 *Publishers Weekly* article recognizing the remarkable initial demand for Cussler's fifteenth Dirk Pitt novel, *Atlantis Found.* In a *People* review of that book, J.D. Reed described Cussler's writing—that it has two-dimensional characters, predictable story-lines, and "dialogue as sticky as Mississippi mud." "Still," qualified Reed, "we can't put down a Cussler Opus." Noting that Cussler "typically [exerts a] make-no-apologies enthusiasm," a *Publishers Weekly* critic declared: "For muscle-flexing, flag-waving, belief-suspending fare, [Cussler] has no equal." The *Publishers Weekly* critic's review specifically referred to *Atlantis Found* as "another wickedly engrossing yet predictably scripted tale of bravery against all odds."

"There are many things I'd rather be doing than writing a book," Cussler once said, according to Rebecca Ascher-Walsh in a 1997 *Entertainment Weekly* article. Acquiring cars and discovering shipwrecks are among his passions. Cussler has built a premier collection of over eighty-five classic and vintage automobiles. From European classic body styles to American town cars to 1950s convertibles, they are all carefully restored by Cussler and his crew of experts to concours d'elegance condition.

Cussler lives almost the same sort of adventurous life as his best-selling protagonist, Dirk Pitt: tramping the Southwest deserts and mountains in search of lost gold mines and ghost towns, as well as funding and leading more than thirty expeditions in search of lost ships and aircraft. He and his team of NUMA scientists and engineers (his fictional National Underwater and Marine Agency became a reality) have discovered and surveyed nearly seventy historically significant shipwrecks around the world, including the long-lost Confederate submarine *Hunley,* the German submarine *U-20* which sank the *Lusitania,* the famous Confederate raider *Florida,* the Navy dirigible *Akron* which crashed at sea during a storm in 1933, the troop transport *Leopoldville* which was torpedoed on Christmas Eve of 1944 off the coast of Cherbourg, France, killing over eight hundred American soldiers, and the *Carpathia,* which braved icebergs to rescue passengers of the *Titanic.* Cussler has donated all of his recovered artifacts from the archaeological sites to museums and universities.

Cussler's chosen genre, his avocations, and even his entry into publishing reveal his willingness to take risks. Almost thirty years ago, after his first manuscript re-

ceived numerous rejections, the author created a clever ploy to promote his second work: he printed up stationery with the name of a fabricated West Coast literary agent and used it to send recommendations for his books to major New York agencies. Within a month he had a contract, and has remained with the same (real) agent, Peter Lampack, ever since. After *Flood Tide,* his fourteenth Dirk Pitt adventure, however, he split with his longtime publisher Simon & Schuster. The Phoenix, Arizona, *Business Journal* reported that he left his former publisher in hopes of getting more respect through his new contract with G.P. Putnam and Sons: "Cussler would joke that Simon & Schuster executives lavished their attention on Mary Higgins Clark . . . . Cussler said. 'I get less respect than Rodney Dangerfield.'"

Cussler's widely read "Dirk Pitt" novels relate the adventures of a handsome, witty, courageous, devil-may-care character who, like his creator, collects classic cars and searches for lost ships. *Armchair Detective* reviewer Ronald C. Miller offered this description: "Dirk Pitt has the archeological background of Indiana Jones and the boldness of James Bond. He is as skilled and comfortable underwater as Jacques Cousteau, and, like Chuck Yeager, he can fly anything with wings." Yet Pitt is far from superhuman, Chicago's *Tribune Books* contributor David E. Jones observed: "Cussler has created a caring, cared-about, flesh and blood human being" who takes wrong turns and suffers from lapses in judgment, but who "also thinks faster on his feet than most and has an uncanny ability to turn negative situations into positive ones." This combination has proved to be tremendously appealing to readers, even though reviewers have often faulted Cussler's writing style and his improbable story lines. *New York Times Book Review* critic Newgate Callendar cited Cussler as "the cliche expert nonpareil" in a review of *Raise the Titanic* and asserted that "Cussler has revived the cliche and batters his reader with choice specimens: 'the cold touch of fear'; 'a set look of determination in the deep green eyes'; 'before death swept over him'; 'narrow brush with death.'" *Best Sellers* contributor Ralph A. Sperry dismissed the author's prose in *Cyclops* as "the prosaic in the service of the implausible."

Cussler shrugs off negative responses to his work. "Because I was locked in for eighteen years writing the short, snappy ad copy, I could never sit down and write a Fitzgerald-Hemingway-Bellow-type Great American Novel," he once told *CA.* "But [that experience] did prepare me to write easy, understandable prose, and also to look at writing and publishing from a marketing angle."

Cussler once recalled to *CA* that at the beginning of his writing career, "blood and guts adventure" was not universally accepted in the publishing field. Initially he was told that his adventures would never sell and that critical opinion was against him, but these views have softened with the growth of the author's popular appeal. When Cussler complained to his agent, Peter Lampack, about negative reviews, Lampack, Cussler said, "came back with a classic statement: 'Listen, when we start getting good literary reviews, we're in big trouble.'"

While early reviews of Cussler may have been dismissive, reviews of his later works have recognized his stories as full of action, fun to read—and extremely popular, while nonetheless pointing out the incredibility of his plots. Discussing *Dragon,* the author's 1990 release, *Publishers Weekly* critic Sybil Steinberg admitted that although the story line was "improbable," Cussler had still come up with "a page-turning romp that achieves a level of fast-paced action and derring-do that . . . practitioners of modern pulp fiction might well envy." Peter L. Robertson, in his *Tribune Books* review of *Treasure,* placed Cussler's stories "in the tradition of Ian Fleming's James Bond," and added, "Cussler has developed and patented a vibrant, rollicking narrative style that seldom shows signs of relenting." *Inca Gold,* which finds Pitt in the Amazonian jungles on a quest to thwart a group of smugglers, is "pure escapist adventure, with a wry touch of humor and a certain self-referential glee (Cussler himself makes a cameo appearance)," a *Publishers Weekly* reviewer noted, "but the entertainment value meets the gold standard." *Booklist* reviewer Joe Collins noted that the author's fans "are already familiar with his gift for hyperbole," and recommended that new readers take Cussler's "breathless approach with a grain of salt and just relax and enjoy the adventures of Pitt and company" in *Inca Gold.*

In 1997's *Flood Tide* Pitt's vacation plans go by the wayside as he uncovers a Chinese immigrant smuggling ring in waters near Seattle—an operation that is linked, through its leader, Qin Shang, to an attempt to cause "ecological and economic destruction from New Orleans to eastern Texas," related a *Publishers Weekly* reviewer, who also noted Cussler was tapping into "right-wing fears of a flood tide of nonwhite immigrants." The *Publishers Weekly* reviewer, as well as many other critics, determined that *Flood Tide* will please Cussler's fans. As Gilbert Taylor concluded in *Booklist,* "This bombastically scripted tale will satisfy Cussler faithfuls." The story is "packed with meticulous research and wonderfully quirky characters," remarked *People* contributor Cynthia Sanz, judging *Flood Tide* to be "as

fun as it is formulaic." "*Cussler's* story is entertaining, but suspending disbelief may be a problem," asserted Ray Vignovich in a *Library Journal* assessment of an audiobook edition of the novel.

In an interview with Connie Lauerman in the *Chicago Tribune,* Cussler reflected on his work. "I look upon myself more as an entertainer than merely a writer. It's my job to entertain the reader in such a manner that he or she feels that they received their money's worth when they reach *the end* of the book." Cussler also considers the impact of his books on young adults. "I have quite a large following of young people," he once told *CA.* "That's why I don't believe in using four-letter words, and any sex is simply alluded to, never detailed. I've had letters from kids as young as eight who enjoy Pitt and his adventures. And because I try to write my stories in a simple, forward manner, I'm especially pleased by letters from mothers and school teachers, who tell me their children and students had refused to read before they were given one of my books. Now they read everything in sight and are hooked on reading."

Cussler found that his readers enjoy the pictures of Pitt's cars included on the backs of his book jackets. *Clive Cussler and Dirk Pitt Revealed* provides a guide to the world of Pitt, including summaries of each novel of the Dirk Pitt series as well as details on weapons, vehicles, and locations from the writings. Cussler also once told *CA* that he has great fun with his cameo appearances. He and Pitt always meet up, with Cussler often supplying his hero with vital information before sending him on his way to subdue the villains. While his stories may seem tailor-made for Hollywood, Cussler emphasized that he refuses to sell them for adaptation until he can be assured of a quality production.

Asked how he comes up with his intricate plots, the author once told *CA:* "First comes the overall concept. This is, of course, the old cut-and-dried, time-tested *What-if.* What if, for example, they raise the *Titanic?* In *Night Probe,* what if Canada and the United States became one country? I also use a prologue that describes something in the past that sets up the plots in the present. Then I end with an epilogue that sews all the corners together. My plots are pretty convoluted; I usually juggle one main plot and as many as four subplots. Then the trick is to thread the needle in the end and give the readers a satisfying conclusion." Cussler has continually succeeded in giving readers a plot to escape in—even with his fifteenth "Dirk Pitt" adventure, published in 1999, twenty- three years after the series debut. Of *Atlantis Found,* Ronnie H. Terpening proclaimed in *Library Journal:* "Brilliantly conceived and boldly plotted . . . . his most imaginative yet . . . . A fascinating story . . . backed by meticulous research."

In 2005 Cussler penned another "Dirk Pitt" novel, this time in partnership with his son Dirk Cussler. In the story, two Japanese submarines carrying the deadly chimera virus intended for biological warfare are sunk off the coast of the United States. Decades later, the virus falls into the dangerous hands of Korean sleeper agent and industrialist Kang. Dirk Pitt and his children, Dirk Pitt, Jr. and Summer, are called on to prevent Kang from unleashing the virus. Pam Johnson, writing for *School Library Journal,* commented, "featuring plenty of intense action, the plot fairly runs across the pages, with even the quieter moments full of intrigue." She also pointed out that the science and history integrated into the novel give it "a sense of realism." "There are the usual harrowing encounters, close calls" and "daring exploits," noted George Cohen in *Booklist.*

Cussler continues to write novels in the Dirk Pitt series but, as Mark Graham in the *Rocky Mountain News* noted, he decided to add a couple of younger figures in a spinoff series planned by Cussler, written by Paul Kemprecos, and revised by Cussler, the "Kurt Austin" series which began publication in 1999: "Clive Cussler's James Bondesque undersea hero Dirk Pitt has starred in sixteen novels over the last four decades. And although Pitt is still capable of amazing feats, his bones are starting to creak, and he isn't quite as quick as he once was. If Pitt's National Underwater Marine Agency is going to keep up with the times, it obviously needs new blood. Recognizing this, the prolific Colorado author has not only taken on a partner (Paul Kemprecos, a Shamus Award-winning author of undersea thrillers in his own right), but created a new protagonist. Kurt Austin takes over as the 21st century Dirk Pitt clone." Graham found himself disappointed that "the only differences between Dirk Pitt and Kurt Austin are their names and ages" but acknowledged that "the key word here is fun. Like most of Dirk Pitt novels, what happens in *Fire Ice* is almost ludicrous in its improbability. Yet watching Cussler and Kemprecos maneuver around possible pitfalls (pun intended) in plot, action and setting makes for enjoyable light reading."

Serpent: A Novel from the NUMA Files, another book in the "Kurt Austin" series, tells of the adventures of Kurt Austin and his NUMA colleague Joe Zavala. A *Publishers Weekly* reviewer described the duo as "two young bucks without the seasoning and panache of Pitt but worthy successors, nonetheless." The coauthors used "the 1956 sinking of the Andrea Doria as the springboard for [this] thriller," stated Roland Green in *Booklist.* In *Serpent,* Austin and Zavala "are trying to find out why top archeologists are being killed, some of them butchered, at dig sites," recounted the writer for *Publishers Weekly* who judged the novel to be "great fun, if not a little top-heavy at times from flabby subplots and excessive detail." In the fourth adventure, *White Death,* as a *Publishers Weekly* reviewer stated, "All the villains have satanic smiles and pitiless eyes, and snarl their dialogue. If it all sounds highly preposterous, it is, but Cussler manages with his usual aplomb, impressively juggling his plots and bringing everyone home in an action-fueled, rip-roaring finale in which evil doers are soundly defeated and swashbuckling heroes reign supreme."

Rave reviews by avid readers are balanced by others who take a more jaundiced view of Cussler's productions. A *Publishers Weekly* reviewer of *White Death,* noted the way in which some of the villains are described, such as "swarthy, black-clad, facially tattooed Eskimos of the evil Kiolya tribe who guard the company's many operations." A.D. Sullivan in *Scrap Paper Review,* remarked of *Flood Tide,* that "Cussler waves the American flag so often one questions whether this is a novel or a bullfight. His facts—inserted to raise the peril of Japanese sovereignty over America—are often wrong or distorted, and his villains simplistic and cruel without attempt at understanding the complexity of America's addiction to foreign money." Cussler does, however, also slate a megalomaniac U.S. oil baron among his villains, as in *Valhalla Rising.*

In *Lost City,* the fifth novel about Kurt Austin's National Underwater Marine Agency, co-written with Paul Kemprecos, an enzyme that can prolong human life is discovered in the Lost City, a half- mile beneath the North Atlantic Ocean. Austin battles numerous forces bent on destruction, murder, and world domination in order to save the day. The plot ranges from a mountainous glacier, where the body of a frozen pilot is found, to an island populated by cannibals, and involves the fetching archaeologist Skye Labelle and the murderous mother-son team of Racine and Emil Fauchard, who put up quite a fight on their quest to take over the world. Along the way, Austin battles environmental disaster caused by monstrous seaweed and lumbering submarine that is up to no good. It's all good fun, according to a writer in *Publishers Weekly,* who called the novel "vintage Cussler," and Cohen, again writing for *Booklist,* deemed it "a page-turning adventure."

In 2005 Cussler and Kemprecos published the next novel featuring Kurt Austin and NUMA, *Polar Shift.* In the book, an anti-globalization group plans to set off an artificial polar shift, which will result in massive geological destruction. A *Kirkus Reviews* critic stated, "what matters most to Cussler/Kemprecos is the big bang, the monstrous cause-and-effect." Cohen concluded that "the plot is inconceivable, but Cussler's loyal fans won't care."

Finding—with four novels in the series at the top of charts immediately on publication—that this formula for success worked well, in 2003, Cussler added another series, the "Oregon Files." The first two books in the series, *Golden Buddha* and *Sacred Stone,* were written with the man who coauthored the two volumes of *The Sea Hunters* with him, Craig Dirgo. The series features "cool, brainy Chairman" of "the Corporation," Juan Cabrillo, according to Graham. A *Publishers Weekly* review of *Golden Buddha* quotes from the book's hero, Juan Cabrillo: "We [the Corporation] were formed to make a profit, that's for sure, but as much as we like the money, we are also cognizant of the chances that arise for us to somehow right the wrongs of others." The reviewer added, "They've been secretly hired by the U.S. government to find and acquire an ancient statue known as the Golden Buddha, stolen from the Dalai Lama upon his ouster from Tibet by the Chinese in 1959. An intricate plan is then set in motion culminating in the defeat of the Chinese in Tibet and the ascension of the Dalai Lama to his rightful place as the leader of the country. The list of characters, both good and evil, is long and sometimes confusing, but a useful directory is supplied. Cabrillo and crew are adept at high finance and diplomacy, playing the Russians off against the Chinese and winning over the United Nations." The "good guys" are certainly most often Americans and the "bad guys" as often not.

Cussler continued the "Oregon Files," series with 2004's *Sacred Stone* and 2005's *Dark Watch.* Of *Sacred Stone,* Cohen wrote "as always, the plot covers many locales around the world, and the dialogue contains lots of military jargon." Steve Dobosz, a reviewer for *Kliatt,* noted that in the novel "the graphic nature of the violence is held to a minimum, and in solving the dilemmas the authors display the morality and humanity of the Corporation." *Dark Watch,* coauthored with Jack DuBrul, contains "a few trite lines," according to Cohen, and the end "doesn't come as a surprise, but Cussler's countless fans won't care."

Cussler took his writing to another level in 2006 when he penned his first children's book, *The Adventures of Vin Fiz.* The story is about Casey and Lacey Nicefolk, twins who are given a device from a stranger that allows them to make their toys life-sized. They create a replica of a Wright brothers' plane and name it Vin Fiz. The siblings have many adventures flying across the country and aiding those in danger. "Unfortunately, the book suffers from a lack of characterization as well as problems with gender stereotypes," wrote Tasha Saecker in *School Library Journal.* However, a *Publishers Weekly* reviewer pointed out that "Cussler sprinkles his folksy narrative with instructional notes . . . and facts . . . and characters' names emphasize the text's tall-tale quality."

Cussler has held off on selling movie rights to Hollywood after, as he described it to *BookReporter.com*'s interviewer Ann Bruns, "They made such a botch of [*Raise the Titanic*]." He sold the movie rights to the Dirk Pitt novels in 2001 after, as he says, Hollywood "finally . . . gave me script and casting approval. So that's why I'm reading the script the screenwriter came up with. If it fails this time, it's my fault." The first movie to be produced will be *Sahara.*

BIOGRAPHICAL AND CRITICAL SOURCES:

BOOKS

Valero, Wayne, *The Collector's Guide to Clive Cussler,* 2000.

PERIODICALS

Americana, September- October, 1987, p. 10.
Armchair Detective, fall, 1994, p. 496.
Best Sellers, August, 1981; May, 1986.
Booklist, April 1, 1992, p. 1411; April 1, 1994, p. 1404; December 15, 1995, p. 667; August, 1997, p. 1846; June 1, 1999, p. 1741; November 15, 1999, p. 579; June 1, 2001, p. 1796; April 1, 2002, p. 1282; June 1, 2003, p. 1710; September 1, 2003, George Cohen, review of *Golden Buddha,* p. 53; November 1, 2003, David Pitt, review of *Trojan Odyssey,* p. 458; September 1, 2004, George Cohen, a review of *Lost City,* p. 60; October 15, 2004, George Cohen, review of *Sacred Stone,* p. 392; November 15, 2004, George Cohen, review of *Black Wind,* p. 564; September 1, 2005, George Cohen, review of *Polar Shift,* p. 62; October 15, 2005, George Cohen, review of *Dark Watch,* p. 29.
Books and Bookmen, May, 1984.
Buffalo News, April 23, 2000, p. F6.
Business Journal (Phoenix, AZ), December, 1999, p. 8.
Chicago Tribune, February 10, 1980; August 13, 1984.

Christian Science Monitor, October 10, 1996, p. 10.

Courier-Mail (Brisbane, Australia), February 1, 2003, p. M07.

Critic, summer, 1977.

Defense Week, August 14, 2000, p. 4.

Denver Business Journal, May 27, 1994, p.14A.

Entertainment Weekly, October 17, 1997, p. 66; September 7, 2001, p. 158; November 28, 2003, Jennifer Reese, review of *Trojan Odyssey,* p. 128.

Far Eastern Economic Review, December 18, 1997, p. 47.

Globe and Mail (Toronto, Ontario, Canada), August 10, 1985.

Grand Rapids Press, September 22, 2002, p. J5.

Inside Books, November, 1988, pp. 31-34.

Kirkus, October 15, 2003, review of *Trojan Odyssey,* p. 1239; August 1, 2005, review of *Polar Shift,* p. 804.

Kliatt, January, 2005, review of *Sacred Stone,* p. 12.

Library Journal, July, 1981, p. 1442; June 1, 1984, p. 1144; October 15, 1990, p. 116; November 1, 1990, p. 139; April 15, 1994, p. 111; April 1, 1995, p. 142; February 1, 1996, p. 97; September 1, 1996, p. 229; November 1, 1997, p. 130; November 15, 1999, p. 97; July 2001, p. 121; May 1, 2002, p. 132; September 15, 2003, Jeff Ayers, review of *Golden Buddha,* p. 90.

Los Angeles Magazine, September, 1990, p. 183; September, 1981, p. 259.

Los Angeles Times, June 21, 1979; September 25, 1981; March 21, 1986.

Los Angeles Times Book Review, August 5, 1984; March 20, 1988.

New Choices for the Best Years, March, 1991, p. 58.

New Yorker, June 27, 1994, p. 87.

New York Times Book Review, December 19, 1976; September 25, 1977; October 18, 1981, p. 46; February 16, 1986, p. 16; May 29, 1988, p. 14; June 17, 1990, p. 19; May 22, 1994, p. 39; January 21, 1996, p. 21.

Observer (London, England), July 20, 2003, p. 17.

People, July 2, 1984, p. 61; July 27, 1992, p. 25; September 21, 1992, p. 93; December 16, 1996, p. 36; November 10, 1997, p. 41; March 20, 2000, p. 47.

Playboy, April, 1986, p. 32.

PR Newswire, November 27, 2000, p. 4806; May 10, 2002.

Publishers Weekly, August 23, 1976; June 12, 1981, p. 46; February 26, 1982, p. 146; November 12, 1982, p. 64; April 13, 1984, p. 50; August 31, 1984, p. 312; January 3, 1986, p. 41; January 15, 1988, p. 69; March 18, 1988, p. 71; September 2, 1988, p. 71; May 4, 1990, p. 51; July 6, 1990, p. 46; April 13, 1992, p. 40; August 3, 1992, p. 26; March 28, 1994, p. 80; July 11, 1994, p. 58; September 19, 1994, p. 11; October 9, 1995, p. 18; December 18, 1995, p. 42; May 20, 1996, p. 37; August 26, 1996, p. 87; August 25, 1997, p. 46; March 16, 1998, p. 10; September 28, 1998, p. 20; March 1, 1999, p. 14; May 31, 1999, p. 65; November 22, 1999, p. 44; December 20, 1999, p. 17; July 30, 2001, p. 61; August 21, 2000, p. 24; August 27, 2001, p. 17; May 13, 2002, p. 50; June 17, 2002, p. 18; May 12, 2003, p. 40; June 30, 2003, p. 15; August 25, 2003, p. 37; October 27, 2003, review of *Trojan Odyssey,* p. 44; July 19, 2004, a review of *Lost City,* p. 145; December 19, 2005, review of *The Adventures of Vin Fiz,* p. 64.

Rocky Mountain News (Denver, CO), August 17, 2001, p. 25D; July 12, 2002, p. 30D.

School Library Journal, October, 1981, p. 160; October, 1990, p. 150; March, 1997, p. 217; December, 1997, p. 150; April, 1999, p. 130; May, 2000, p. 192; May, 2005, Pam Johnson, review of *Black Wind,* p. 168; February, 2006, Tasha Saecker, review of *The Adventures of Vin Fiz,* p. 94.

Skin Diver, November, 1984, p. 20; May, 1987, p. 151.

Star Tribune (Minneapolis, MN), February 2, 2003, p. 18F.

Tribune Books (Chicago, IL), March 20, 1988; June 21, 1992, p. 6; May 22, 1994, p. 6.

U.S. News and World Report, August 27, 1984, p. 45.

Washington Post, October 24, 1978; August 10, 1981; June 22, 1984; April 11, 1988.

Washington Post Book World, March 2, 1986; June 7, 1992, p. 8.

Writer, September, 1996, p. 15.

Writer's Digest, April, 1988, p. 31.

ONLINE

BookReporter.com, http://www.bookreporter.com/ (September 11, 2001), interview with Cussler.

Clive Cussler Collector's Society, http://www.cusslersociety.com/ (February 28, 2006), information about Cussler's collections.

National Underwater and Marine Agency, http://www.numa.net/ (February 28, 2006).

Scrap Paper Review, http://www.hourwolf.com/ (February 28, 2006), "Clive Cussler's Japan."

*   *   *

CUSSLER, Clive Eric
    See CUSSLER, Clive

*   *   *

CUTRATE, Joe
    See SPIEGELMAN, Art

D

DAHL, Roald 1916-1990

PERSONAL: Given name is pronounced "Roo-aal"; born September 13, 1916, in Llandaff, South Wales; died November 23, 1990, in Oxford, England; son of Harald (a shipbroker, painter, and horticulturist) and Sofie (Hesselberg) Dahl; married Patricia Neal (an actress), July 2, 1953 (divorced, 1983); married Felicity Ann Crosland, 1983; children: (first marriage) Olivia (deceased), Tessa, Theo, Ophelia, Lucy. *Education:* Graduate of British public schools, 1932.

CAREER: Shell Oil Co., London, England, member of eastern staff, 1933-37, member of staff in Dar-es-Salaam, Tanzania, 1937-39; writer. Host of a series of half-hour television dramas, *Way Out,* during early 1960s. *Military service:* Royal Air Force, fighter pilot, 1939-45; became wing commander.

AWARDS, HONORS: Edgar Award, Mystery Writers of America, 1954, 1959, and 1980; New England Round Table of Children's Librarians award, 1972, and Surrey School award, 1973, both for *Charlie and the Chocolate Factory;* Surrey School award, 1975, and Nene award, 1978, both for *Charlie and the Great Glass Elevator;* Surrey School award, 1978, and California Young Reader Medal, 1979, both for *Danny: The Champion of the World;* Federation of Children's Book Groups award, 1982, for *The BFG;* Massachusetts Children's award, 1982, for *James and the Giant Peach; New York Times* Outstanding Books award, 1983, Whitbread Award, 1983, and West Australian award, 1986, all for *The Witches;* World Fantasy Convention Lifetime Achievement Award, and Federation of Children's Book Groups award, both 1983; Maschler award runner-up, 1985, for *The Giraffe and Pelly and Me; Boston Globe/Horn Book* nonfiction honor citation, 1985, for *Boy: Tales of Childhood;* International Board on Books for Young People awards for Norwegian and German translations of *The BFG,* both 1986; Smarties Award, 1990, for *Esio Trot; The BFG, The Twits, Matilda,* and *Charlie and the Chocolate Factory* were all voted "one of the nation's 100 best-loved novels" by the British public as part of the BBC's The Big Read, 2003.

WRITINGS:

FOR ADULTS

Sometime Never: A Fable for Supermen (novel), Scribner, 1948.
My Uncle Oswald (novel), M. Joseph, 1979, Knopf, 1980.
Going Solo (autobiography), Farrar, Straus, 1986.

FOR CHILDREN

The Gremlins, illustrations by Walt Disney Productions, Random House, 1943.
James and the Giant Peach: A Children's Story (also see below), illustrations by Nancy Ekholm Burkert, Knopf, 1961, illustrations by Michel Simeon, Allen & Unwin, 1967.
Charlie and the Chocolate Factory (also see below), illustrations by Joseph Schindelman, Knopf, 1964, revised edition, 1973, illustrations by Faith Jaques, Allen & Unwin, 1967.
The Magic Finger (also see below), illustrations by William Pene du Bois, Harper, 1966, illustrations by Pat Marriott, Puffin, 1974.

Fantastic Mr. Fox (also see below), illustrations by Donald Chaffin, Knopf, 1970.

Charlie and the Great Glass Elevator: The Further Adventures of Charlie Bucket and Willy Wonka, Chocolate-Maker Extraordinary (also see below), illustrations by J. Schindelman, Knopf, 1972, illustrations by F. Jaques, Allen & Unwin, 1973.

Danny: The Champion of the World, illustrations by Jill Bennett, Knopf, 1975 (collected with *James and the Giant Peach* and *Fantastic Mr. Fox,* Bantam, 1983).

The Enormous Crocodile (also see below), illustrations by Quentin Blake, Knopf, 1978.

The Complete Adventures of Charlie and Mr. Willy Wonka (contains *Charlie and the Chocolate Factory* and *Charlie and the Great Glass Elevator*), illustrations by F. Jaques, Allen & Unwin, 1978.

The Twits, illustrations by Q. Blake, J. Cape, 1980, Knopf, 1981.

George's Marvelous Medicine, illustrations by Q. Blake, J. Cape, 1981, Knopf, 1982.

Roald Dahl's Revolting Rhymes, illustrations by Q. Blake, J. Cape, 1982, Knopf, 1983.

The BFG (also see below), illustrations by Q. Blake, Farrar, Straus, 1982.

Dirty Beasts (verse), illustrations by Rosemary Fawcett, Farrar, Straus, 1983, reprinted with illustrations by Q. Blake, Puffin (New York, NY), 2002.

The Witches (also see below), illustrations by Q. Blake, Farrar, Straus, 1983.

Boy: Tales of Childhood, Farrar, Straus, 1984.

The Giraffe and Pelly and Me, illustrations by Q. Blake, Farrar, Straus, 1985.

Matilda, illustrations by Q. Blake, Viking Kestrel, 1988.

Roald Dahl: Charlie and the Chocolate Factory, Charlie and the Great Glass Elevator, The BFG (boxed set), Viking, 1989.

Rhyme Stew (comic verse), illustrations by Q. Blake, J. Cape, 1989, Viking, 1990.

Esio Trot, illustrations by Q. Blake, Viking, 1990.

The Dahl Diary, 1992, illustrations by Q. Blake, Puffin Books, 1991.

The Minpins, Viking, 1991.

Three More from Roald Dahl (includes *The Witches, James and the Giant Peach,* and *Danny: The Champion of the World*), Puffin, 1991.

The Vicar of Nibbleswicke, illustrations by Q. Blake, Viking, 1992.

My Year, illustrations by Q. Blake, Viking Children's, 1994.

Roald Dahl's Revolting Recipes, illustrations by Quentin Blake, Viking (New York, NY), 1994.

The Mildenhall Treasure, pictures by Ralph Steadman, Knopf (New York, NY), 2000.

Some of Dahl's works have been translated into French and Spanish.

SHORT FICTION

Over to You: Ten Stories of Flyers and Flying (also see below), Reynal, 1946.

Someone Like You (also see below), Knopf, 1953.

Kiss, Kiss (also see below), Knopf, 1959.

Selected Stories of Roald Dahl, Modern Library, 1968.

Twenty-nine Kisses from Roald Dahl (contains *Someone Like You* and *Kiss, Kiss*), M. Joseph, 1969.

Switch Bitch (also see below), Knopf, 1974.

The Wonderful World of Henry Sugar and Six More, Knopf, 1977 (published in England as *The Wonderful Story of Henry Sugar and Six More,* Cape, 1977).

The Best of Roald Dahl (selections from *Over to You, Someone Like You, Kiss Kiss,* and *Switch Bitch*), introduction by James Cameron, Vintage, 1978.

Roald Dahl's Tales of the Unexpected, Vintage, 1979.

Taste and Other Tales, Longman, 1979.

A Roald Dahl Selection: Nine Short Stories, edited and introduced by Roy Blatchford, photographs by Catherine Shakespeare Lane, Longman, 1980.

More Tales of the Unexpected, Penguin, 1980 (published in England as *More Roald Dahl's Tales of the Unexpected,* Joseph, 1980, and as *Further Tales of the Unexpected,* Chivers, 1981).

(Editor) *Roald Dahl's Book of Ghost Stories,* Farrar, Straus, 1983.

Two Fables (contains "Princess and the Poacher" and "Princess Mammalia"), illustrations by Graham Dean, Viking, 1986.

The Roald Dahl Omnibus, Hippocrene Books, 1987.

A Second Roald Dahl Selection: Eight Short Stories, edited by Helene Fawcett, Longman, 1987.

Ah, Sweet Mystery of Life, illustrations by John Lawrence, J. Cape, 1988, Knopf, 1989.

The Collected Short Stories, Michael Joseph, 1991.

The Umbrella Man and Other Stories, Viking (New York, NY), 1998.

Contributor of short fiction to *Penguin Modern Stories 12,* 1972.

SCREENPLAYS

Lamb to the Slaughter (teleplay), *Alfred Hitchcock Presents,* Columbia Broadcasting System (CBS-TV), 1958.

(With Jack Bloom) *You Only Live Twice,* United Artists, 1967.

(With Ken Hughes) *Chitty Chitty Bang Bang,* United Artists, 1968.

The Night-Digger (based on *Nest in a Falling Tree,* by Joy Crowley), Metro-Goldwyn-Mayer, 1970.

Willie Wonka and the Chocolate Factory (motion picture; adaptation of *Charlie and the Chocolate Factory*), Paramount, 1971.

Also author of screenplays *Oh Death, Where Is Thy Sting-a-Ling-a-Ling?,* United Artists, *The Lightning Bug,* 1971, and *The Road Builder.*

OTHER

The Honeys (play), produced in New York City, 1955.

(With Felicity Dahl) *Memories with Food at Gipsy House,* Viking, 1991.

(With Felicity Dahl) *Roald Dahl's Cookbook,* Penguin Group, 1996.

The Roald Dahl Treasury, Viking (New York, NY), 1997.

Skin and Other Stories, Viking (New York, NY), 2000.

Dahl recorded *Charlie and the Chocolate Factory,* Caedmon, 1975, *James and the Giant Peach,* Caedmon, 1977, *Fantastic Mr. Fox,* Caedmon, 1978, and *Roald Dahl Reads His "The Enormous Crocodile" and "The Magic Finger,"* Caedmon, 1980, as well as an interview, *Bedtime Stories to Children's Books,* Center for Cassette Studies, 1973. Contributor to anthologies and periodicals, including *Harper's, New Yorker, Playboy, Collier's, Town and Country, Atlantic, Esquire,* and *Saturday Evening Post.*

ADAPTATIONS: 36 Hours (motion picture; adaptation of Dahl's short story "Beware of the Dog"), Metro-Goldwyn-Mayer, 1964; *Delicious Inventions* (motion picture; excerpted from film *Willie Wonka and the Chocolate Factory,* Paramount, 1971), Films, Inc., 1976: *Willie Wonka and the Chocolate Factory Storytime* (filmstrip; excerpted from the 1971 Paramount motion picture of the same name), Films, Inc., 1976: *Willie Wonka and the Chocolate Factory Learning Kit* (filmstrip; excerpted from the 1971 Paramount motion picture of the same name), Films, Inc., 1976; *The Witches,* screenplay by Allan Scott, Lorimar, 1990; *James and the Giant Peach* (animated motion picture; adapted from Dahl's novel of the same name), screenplay by Karey Kirkpatrick, Jonathan Roberts, and Steve Bloom,

Walt Disney, 1996; *Matilda* (based on Dahl's novel of the same name), screenplay by Robin Swicord and Nicholas Kazan, directed by Danny DeVito, 1996; *Tales of the Unexpected,* WNEW-TV, 1979; *Roald Dahl's Charlie and the Chocolate Factory: A Play,* by Richard George, introduction by Dahl, Knopf, 1976; *Roald Dahl's James and the Giant Peach: A Play,* by George, introduction by Dahl, Penguin, 1982. *The Great Switcheroo,* (recording) read by Patricia Neal, Caedmon, 1977; *Charlie and the Chocolate Factory* was adapted as a stage musical by Leslie Bricusse and Anthony Newley titled *Roald Dahl's Willy Wonka,* 2004 and the book is also scheduled to be adapted for film a second time. The forthcoming film will be directed by Tim Burton.

SIDELIGHTS: Roald Dahl, best known as the author of children's books *Charlie and the Chocolate Factory* and *James and the Giant Peach,* was also noted for his short stories for adults, and his enchanting autobiographical descriptions of growing up in England and flying in World War II. His children's fiction is known for its sudden turns into the fantastic, its wheeling, fast-moving prose, and its decidedly harsh treatment of any adults foolish enough to cause trouble for the young heroes and heroines. Similarly, his adult fiction often relies on a sudden twist that throws light on what has been happening in the story, a trait most evident in *Tales of the Unexpected,* which was made into a television series.

Dahl was born on September 13, 1916, the son of an adventurous shipbroker. He was an energetic and mischievous child and from an early age proved adept at finding trouble. His very earliest memory was of pedaling to school at breakneck speed on his tricycle, his two sisters struggling to keep up as he whizzed around curves on two wheels. In *Boy: Tales of Childhood,* Dahl recounted many of these happy memories from his childhood, remembering most fondly the trips that the entire family took to Norway, which he always considered home. Each summer the family would tramp aboard a steamer for the two-day trip to Oslo, where they were treated to a Norwegian feast with his grandparents, and the next day board a smaller ship for a trip north to what they called "Magic Island." On the island the family whiled away the long summer days swimming and boating.

Though Dahl's father died when the author was four, his mother abided by her husband's wish to have the children attend English schools, which he considered the best in the world. At Llandaff Cathedral School the young Dahl began his career of mischievous adventures and met up with the first of many oppressive, even cruel, adults. One exploit in particular foretold both the author's career in school and the major themes of his adult work. Each day on the way to and from school the seven-year-old Dahl and his friends passed a sweet-shop. Unable to resist the lure of "Bootlace Liquorice" and "Gobstoppers"—familiar candy to *Charlie and the Chocolate Factory* fans—the children would pile into the store and buy as much candy as they could with their limited allowances. Day after day the grubby, grouchy storekeeper, Mrs. Pratchett, scolded the children as she dug her dirty hands into the jars of candy; one day the kids had had enough of her abuse, and Dahl hatched the perfect plan to get back at her. The very next day, when she reached into the jar of Gobstoppers she clamped her hand around a very stiff, dead mouse and flung the jar to the ground, scattering Gobstoppers and glass all over the store floor. Mrs. Pratchett knew whom to blame, and when the boys went to school the next day she was waiting, along with a very angry Headmaster Coombes. Not only did Coombes give each of the boys a severe beating, but Mrs. Pratchett was there to witness it. "She was bounding up and down with excitement," Dahl remembered in *Boy*, "'Lay it into 'im!' she was shrieking. 'Let 'im 'ave it! Teach 'im a lesson!'"

Dahl's mother complained about the beating the boys were given, but was told that if she didn't like it she could find another school. She did, sending Roald to St. Peters Boarding School the next year, and later to Repton, a renowned private school. Of his time at St. Peters, Dahl said: "Those were days of horrors, of fierce discipline, of not talking in the dormitories, no running in the corridors, no untidiness of any sort, no this or that or the other, just rules, rules and still more rules that had to be obeyed. And the fear of the dreaded cane hung over us like the fear of death all the time."

Dahl received undistinguished marks while attending Repton, and showed little sign of his future prowess as a writer. His end-of-term report from Easter term, 1931, which he saved, declared him "a persistent muddler. Vocabulary negligible, sentences mal-constructed. He reminds me of a camel." Nevertheless, his mother offered him the option of attending Oxford or Cambridge when he finished school. His reply, recorded in *Boy*, was, "No, thank you. I want to go straight from school to work for a company that will send me to wonderful faraway places life Africa or China." He got his wish, for he was soon hired by the Shell Oil Company, and later shipped off to Tanganyika (now Tanzania), where he enjoyed "the roasting heat and the crocodiles and the

snakes and the log safaris up-country, selling Shell oil to the men who ran the diamond mines and the sisal plantations. . . . Above all, I learned how to look after myself in a way that no young person can ever do by staying in civilization."

In 1939, Dahl's adventures took on a more dangerous cast as he joined the Royal Air Force training squadron in Nairobi, Kenya. World War II was just beginning, and Dahl would soon make his mark as a fighter pilot combating the Germans all around the Mediterranean Sea. While strafing a convoy of trucks near Alexandria, Egypt, his plane was hit by machine-gun fire. The plane crashed to the ground and Dahl crawled from the wreckage as the gas tanks exploded. The crash left his skull fractured, his nose crumpled, and his eyes temporarily stuck shut. After six months of recovery he returned to his squadron in Greece and shot down four enemy planes, but frequent blackouts as a result of his earlier injuries eventually rendered him unable to fly.

Dahl was soon transferred to Washington, DC, to serve as an assistant air attache. One day C.S. Forester interviewed Dahl over lunch for an article he was writing for the *Saturday Evening Post,* but was too engrossed in eating to take notes himself. The notes that Dahl took for him turned out to be a story, which Forester sent to the magazine under Dahl's name. The magazine paid Dahl one thousand dollars for the story, which was titled "Piece of Cake" and later published in *Over to You: Ten Stories of Fliers and Flying.* Soon his stories appeared in *Collier's, Harper's, Ladies' Home Journal, Tomorrow* and *Town and Country.* Dahl indicated in a *New York Times Book Review* profile by Willa Petschek that "as I went on, the stories became less and less realistic and more fantastic. But becoming a writer was pure fluke. Without being asked to, I doubt if I'd ever have thought of it."

Dahl went on to publish numerous short story collections during the next several decades, some of which—notably 1953's *Someone Like You* and 1959's *Kiss, Kiss*—sold widely in the United States and earned Dahl a measure of fame. After 1960 Dahl's primary focus became children's fiction, although he did produce a short story collection, *Switch Bitch,* in 1974 as well as a novel, *My Uncle Oswald,* in 1979. Both of the latter works are marked by themes of sexual sadism and obsession; both were controversial and received criticism from reviewers for the sexual violence they portrayed. *Dictionary of Literary Biography* contributor John L. Grigsby summarized Dahl's achievements as a short fiction writer: "In his best stories Dahl presents skillfully composed plots that convey powerful insights into the frequently negative depths of the human psyche. . . . In his less effective works, however, Dahl's outsider status results in a kind of cynical condescension toward and manipulation of the reader in surprise-of-plot stories that stereotype characters outside his self-focused realm of psychological experience."

In 1943, Dahl wrote his first children's story, and coined a term, with *The Gremlins.* Gremlins were tiny saboteurs who lived on fighter planes and bombers and were responsible for all crashes. Mrs. Roosevelt, the president's wife, read the book to her children and liked it so much that she invited Dahl to dinner, and he and the president soon became friends. Through the 1940s and into the 1950s Dahl continued as a short story writer for adults, establishing his reputation as a writer of macabre tales with an unexpected twist. A *Books and Bookmen* reviewer called Dahl "a master of horror—an intellectual Hitchcock of the writing world." J.D. O'Hara, writing in *New Republic,* labeled him "our Supreme Master of Wickedness," and his stories earned him three Edgar Allan Poe Awards from the Mystery Writers of America.

In 1953 he married Hollywood actress Patricia Neal, star of such movies as *The Fountainhead* and, later, *Hud,* for which she won an Academy Award. Dahl recalled in *Pat and Roald* that "she wasn't at all movie-starish; no great closets filled with clothes or anything like that. She had a drive to be a great actress, but it was never as strong as it is with some of these nuts. You could turn it aside." Although the marriage did not survive, it produced five children. As soon as the children were old enough, he began making up stories for them each night before they went to bed. These stories became the basis for his career as a children's writer, which began in earnest with the publication of *James and the Giant Peach* in 1961. Dahl insisted that having to invent stories night after night was perfect practice for his trade, telling the *New York Times Book Review:* "Children are a great discipline because they are highly critical. And they lose interest so quickly. You have to keep things ticking along. And if you think a child is getting bored, you must think up something that jolts it back. Something that tickles. You have to know what children like." Sales of Dahl's books certainly attest to his skill: *Charlie and the Chocolate Factory* and *Charlie and the Great Glass Elevator* have sold over one million hardcover copies in America, and *James and the Giant Peach* more than 350,000.

James and the Giant Peach recounts the fantastic tale of a young boy who travels thousands of miles in a house-sized peach with as bizarre an assemblage of companions as can be found in a children's book. After the giant peach crushes his aunts, James crawls into the peach through a worm hole, making friends with a centipede, a silkworm, a spider, a ladybug, and a flock of seagulls that lifts the peach into the air and carries it across the ocean to Central Park. Gerald Haigh, writing in *Times Literary Supplement,* said that Dahl had the ability to "home unerringly in on the very nub of childish delight, with brazen and glorious disregard for what is likely to furrow the adult brow."

One way that Dahl delighted his readers was to exact often vicious revenge on cruel adults who harmed children. In *Matilda,* the Amazonian headmistress Miss Turnbull, who deals with unruly children by grabbing them by the hair and tossing them out windows, is finally banished by the brilliant, triumphant Matilda. *The Witches,* released as a movie in 1990, finds the heroic young character, who has been turned into a mouse, thwarting the hideous and diabolical witches who are planning to kill all the children of England. But even innocent adults receive rough treatment: parents are killed in car crashes in *The Witches,* and eaten by a rhinoceros in *James and the Giant Peach;* aunts are flattened by a giant peach in *James and the Giant Peach;* and pleasant fathers are murdered in *Matilda.* Many critics have objected to the rough treatment of adults. Eleanor Cameron, for example, in *Children's Literature in Education,* found that "Dahl caters to the streak of sadism in children which they don't even realize is there because they are not fully self-aware and are not experienced enough to understand what sadism is." And in *Now Upon a Time: A Contemporary View of Children's Literature,* Myra Pollack Sadker and David Miller Sadker criticized *Charlie and the Chocolate Factory* for its "ageism": "The message with which we close the book is that the needs and desires and opinions of old people are totally irrelevant and inconsequential."

However, Dahl explained in the *New York Times Book Review* that the children who wrote to him "invariably pick out the most gruesome events as the favorite parts of the books. . . . They don't relate it to life. They enjoy the fantasy. And my nastiness is never gratuitous. It's retribution. Beastly people must be punished." Alasdair Campbell, writing in *School Librarian,* argued that "normal children are bound to take some interest in the darker side of human nature, and books for them should be judged not by picking out separate elements but rather on the basis of their overall balance and effect." He found books such as *James and the Giant Peach, Charlie and the Chocolate Factory,* and *The Magic Finger* "ultimately satisfying, with the principles of justice clearly vindicated."

In *Trust Your Children: Voices Against Censorship in Children's Literature,* Dahl contended that adults may be disturbed by his books "because they are not quite as aware as I am that children are different from adults. Children are much more vulgar than grownups. They have a coarser sense of humor. They are basically more cruel." Dahl often commented that the key to his success with children was that he conspired with them against adults. Vicki Weissman, in her review of *Matilda* in the *New York Times Book Review,* agreed that Dahl's books are aimed to please children rather than adults in a number of ways. She thought that "the truths of death and torture are as distant as when the magician saws the lady in half," and delighted that "anarchic and patently impossible plots romp along with no regard at all for the even faintly likely." Just as children are more vulgar than adults, so too do they have more tolerance for undeveloped characters, loose linking of events, ludicrous word play, and mind-boggling plot twists. Eric Hadley, in his sketch of Dahl in *Twentieth Century Children's Writers,* suggested that the "sense of sharing, of joining with Dahl in a game or plot, is crucial: you admire him and his cleverness, *not* his characters." The result, according to Hadley, is that the audience has the "pleasure of feeling that they are in on a tremendous joke."

"The writer for children must be a jokey sort of a fellow. . . ," Dahl once told *Writer.* "He must like simple tricks and jokes and riddles and other childish things. He must be unconventional and inventive. He must have a really first-class plot." As a writer, Dahl encountered difficulty in developing plots. He filled an old school exercise book with ideas that he had jotted down in pencil, crayon, or whatever was handy, and insisted in *The Wonderful World of Henry Sugar and Six More* that every story he had ever written, for adults or for children, "started out as a three-or four-line note in this little, much-worn, red-covered volume." And each book was written in a tiny brick hut in the apple orchard about two hundred yards away from his home in Buckinghamshire, England. The little hut was rarely cleaned, and the walls were lined with "ill-fitting sheets of polystyrene, yellow with age and tobacco smoke, and spiders . . . [making] pretty webs in the upper corners," Dahl once declared. "The room itself is of no consequence. It is out of focus, a place for dreaming and floating and whistling in the wind, as soft and silent and murky as a womb."

Looking back on his years as a writer in *Boy,* Dahl contended that "the life of a writer is absolute hell compared with the life of a businessman. The writer has to force himself to go to work. . . . Two hours of writing fiction leaves this particular writer absolutely drained. For those two hours he has been miles away, he has been somewhere else, in a different place with totally different people, and the effort of swimming back into normal surroundings is very great. It is almost a shock. The writer walks out of his workroom in a daze. He wants a drink. He needs it. It happens to be a fact that nearly every writer of fiction in the world drinks more whisky than is good for him. He does it to give himself faith, hope, and courage. A person is a fool to become a writer. His only compensation is absolute freedom. He has no master except his own soul, and that, I am sure, is why he does it."

The Roald Dahl Museum and Story Centre opened in Great Missenden, England, on June 12, 2005.

BIOGRAPHICAL AND CRITICAL SOURCES:

BOOKS

Children's Literature Review, Thomson Gale, Volume 1, 1976, Volume 7, 1984.

Contemporary Literary Criticism, Thomson Gale, Volume 1, 1973, Volume 6, 1976, Volume 18, 1981, Volume 79, 1993.

Dahl, Lucy, *James and the Giant Peach: The Book and Movie Scrapbook,* Disney Press (New York, NY), 1996.

Dahl, Roald, *The Wonderful World of Henry Sugar and Six More,* Knopf, 1977.

Dahl, Roald, *Boy: Tales of Childhood,* Farrar, Straus, 1984.

Dahl, Roald, *Going Solo,* Farrar, Straus, 1986.

Dictionary of Literary Biography, Volume 139: *British Short-Fiction Writers, 1945-1980,* Thomson Gale, 1994.

Farrell, Barry, *Pat and Roald,* Random House, 1969.

McCann, Donnarae, and Gloria Woodard, editors, *The Black American in Books for Children: Readings in Racism,* Scarecrow, 1972.

Middleton, Haydn, *Roald Dahl,* Heinemann Library, 1998.

Powling, Chris, *Roald Dahl,* Hamish Hamilton, 1983.

Sadker, Myra Pollack, and David Miller Sadker, *Now Upon a Time: A Contemporary View of Children's Literature,* Harper, 1977.

Shavick, Andrea, *Roald Dahl: The Champion Storyteller,* Oxford University Press, 1998.

Treglown, Jeremy, *Roald Dahl: A Biography,* Farrar, Straus (New York City), 1994.

Twentieth-Century Children's Writers, 3rd edition, St. James Press, 1989, pp. 255-256.

Warren, Alan with Dale Salwak and Daryl F. Mallett, *Roald Dahl: From the Gremlins to the Chocolate Factory,* second edition, Borgo Press (San Bernadino, CA), 1994.

West, Mark I., interview with Roald Dahl in *Trust Your Children: Voices against Censorship in Children's Literature,* Neal-Schuman, 1988, pp. 71-76.

Wintle, Justin, and Emma Fisher, *Pied Pipers: Interviews with the Influential Creators of Children's Literature,* Paddington Press, 1975.

PERIODICALS

Atlantic, December, 1964.

Best Sellers, January, 1978.

Books and Bookmen, January, 1969; May, 1970.

Chicago Sunday Tribune, February 15, 1960; November 12, 1961.

Chicago Tribune, October 21, 1986.

Chicago Tribune Book World, August 10, 1980; May 17, 1981.

Children's Book News, March-April, 1968.

Children's Literature in Education, spring, 1975; summer, 1976, pp. 59-63.

Christian Century, August 31, 1960.

Christian Science Monitor, November 16, 1961.

Commonweal, November 15, 1961.

Entertainment Weekly, January 24, 1994, p. 57.

Horn Book, October, 1972; December, 1972; February, 1973; April, 1973; June, 1973; January/ February, 1989, p. 68; January/February, 1992, p. 64.

Kenyon Review, Volume 31, number 2, 1969.

Library Journal, November 15, 1961.

Life, August 18, 1972.

New Republic, October 19, 1974, p. 23; April 19, 1980.

New Statesman, October 29, 1960; March 5, 1971; November 4, 1977.

New Statesman & Society, November 24, 1989, p. 34.

New York, December 12, 1988.

New Yorker, December 12, 1988, p. 157; November 25, 1991, p. 146.

New York Herald Tribune Book Review, November 8, 1953; February 7, 1960.

New York Review of Books, December 17, 1970; December 14, 1972.

New York Times, November 8, 1953; April 29, 1980.

New York Times Book Review, February 7, 1960; November 12, 1961; October 25, 1964; November 8, 1970; September 17, 1972; October 27, 1974; October 26, 1975; December 25, 1977, pp. 6, 15; September 30, 1979; April 20, 1980; March 29, 1981;

January 9, 1983; January 20, 1985; October 12, 1986; January 15, 1989, p. 31; October 27, 1991, p. 27; May 1, 1994, p. 28.

Observer, September 8, 1991.

People, November 3, 1986; May 9, 1988.

Publishers Weekly, June 6, 1980; December 20, 1991, p. 82; January 24, 1994, p. 57; October 10, 1994, p. 69.

Punch, November 29, 1967; December 6, 1978.

Quill & Quire, November, 1991, p. 25.

San Francisco Chronicle, February 15, 1960; December 10, 1961.

Saturday Review, December 26, 1953; February 20, 1960; February 17, 1962; November 7, 1964; March 10, 1973.

School Librarian, June, 1981, pp. 108-114.

School Library Journal, November, 1991, p. 92; May, 1992, p. 112; March, 1993, p. 155; April, 1994, p. 136; March, 1995, p. 210.

Sewanee Review, winter, 1975.

Spectator, December, 1977; December 11, 1993, p. 45.

Springfield Republican, March 13, 1960.

Times (London, England), December 22, 1983; April 21, 1990.

Times Educational Supplement, November 19, 1982, p. 35.

Times Literary Supplement, October 28, 1960; December 14, 1967; June 15, 1973; November 15, 1974; November 23, 1979; November 21, 1980; July 24, 1981; July 23, 1982; November 30, 1984; September 12, 1986; May 6, 1988; July 12, 1991, p. 21; October 4, 1991, p. 28; November 22, 1991, p. 23.

Vanity Fair, January, 1994, p. 26.

Washington Post, October 8, 1986.

Washington Post Book World, November 13, 1977; April 20, 1980; May 8, 1983; January 13, 1985.

Wilson Library Bulletin, February, 1962; February, 1989; June, 1995, p. 125.

Writer, August, 1976, pp. 18-19.

Young Reader's Review, November, 1966.

OBITUARIES:

PERIODICALS

Los Angeles Times, November 24, 1990.

New York Times, November 24, 1990.

School Library Journal, January, 1991.

Times (London, England), November 24, 1990; December 19, 1990.

Washington Post, November 24, 1990.

DALE, George E.
    See ASIMOV, Isaac

*   *   *

DANTICAT, Edwidge 1969-

PERSONAL: Name is pronounced "Ed-*weedj* Dan-ti-*kah;*" born January 19, 1969, in Port-au-Prince, Haiti; immigrated to the United States, 1981; daughter of André Miracin (a cab driver) and Rose Souvenance (a textile worker) Danticat. *Ethnicity:* "Black." *Education:* Barnard College, B.A. 1990; Brown University, M.F.A., 1993.

ADDRESSES: Agent—c/o Author Mail, Scholastic Inc., 557 Broadway, New York, NY 10012.

CAREER: Writer. Clinica Estetico (filmmakers), New York, NY, production and research assistant, 1993-94; writer, educator, and lecturer, 1994—. New York University, professor, 1996-97; University of Miami, Coral Gables, FL, visiting professor of creative writing, spring, 2000.

MEMBER: Phi Beta Kappa, Alpha Kappa Alpha.

AWARDS, HONORS: National Book Award nomination, 1995, for *Krik? Krak!;* Lannan Foundation Fellowship, 2004; National Book Critics Circle Award nomination, 2004, and PEN/Faulkner Award nomination, 2005, both for *The Dew Breaker;* Pushcart Prize for short fiction; American Book Award, Before Columbus Foundation, for *The Farming of Bones;* fiction awards from periodicals, including *Caribbean Writer, Seventeen,* and *Essence.*

WRITINGS:

The Creation of Adam (play), produced in Providence, RI, 1992.
Dreams like Me (play), produced in Providence, RI, at Brown University New Plays Festival, 1993.
Breath, Eyes, Memory (novel), Soho Press (New York, NY), 1994.
Krik? Krak! (short stories), Soho Press (New York, NY), 1995.
Children of the Sea (play), produced in Roxbury Crossing, MA, at Roxbury Community College, 1997.

The Farming of Bones (novel), Soho Press (New York, NY), 1998.
(With Jonathan Demme) *Odillon Pierre, Artist of Haiti,* Kaliko Press (Nyack, NY), 1999.
(Editor) *The Beacon Best of 2000: Great Writing by Women and Men of All Colors and Cultures,* Beacon Press (Boston, MA), 2000.
(Editor) *The Butterfly's Way: Voices from the Haitian Dyaspora in the United States,* Soho Press (New York, NY), 2001.
(Translator and author of afterword, with Carrol F. Coates) Jackes Stephen Alexis, *In the Flicker of an Eyelid* (novel), University of Virginia Press (Charlottesville, VA), 2002.
After the Dance: A Walk through Carnival in Haiti, Crown Publishers (New York, NY), 2002.
Behind the Mountains (novel), Orchard Books (New York, NY), 2002.
The Dew Breaker (novel), Knopf (New York, NY), 2004.
Anacaona, Golden Flower: Haiti, 1490 (juvenile novel), Scholastic (New York, NY), 2005.

SIDELIGHTS: Fiction writer Edwidge Danticat conjures the history of her native Haiti in award-winning short stories and novels. She is equally at home describing the immigrant experience—what she calls "dyaspora"—and the reality of life in Haiti today. Danticat's fiction "has been devoted to an unflinching examination of her native culture, both on its own terms and in terms of its intersections with American culture," wrote an essayist in *Contemporary Novelists.* "Danticat's work emphasizes in particular the heroism and endurance of Haitian women as they cope with a patriarchal culture that, in its unswerving devotion to tradition and family, both oppresses and enriches them." Readers will find "massacres, rapes, [and] horrible nightmares in Danticat's fiction," wrote an essayist in the *St. James Guide to Young Adult Writers,* "but above all these are the strength, hope, and joy of her poetic vision."

Danticat's first novel, the loosely autobiographical *Breath, Eyes, Memory,* was a 1998 selection of the Oprah Winfrey Book Club, thus assuring its best-seller status. Other Danticat works have won warm praise as well, with some critics expressing surprise that such assured prose has come from an author so young. *Antioch Review* correspondent Grace A. Epstein praised Danticat for "the real courage . . . in excavating the romance of nationalism, identity, and home." *Time* reporter Christopher John Farley likewise concluded that Danticat's fiction "never turns purple, never spins wildly into the fantastic, always remains focused, with precise disciplined language, and in doing so, it uncovers moments of raw humanness."

Danticat was born in Haiti and lived there the first twelve years of her life. She came to the United States in 1981, joining her parents who had already begun to build a life for themselves in New York City. When she started attending junior high classes in Brooklyn, she had difficulty fitting in with her classmates because of her Haitian accent, clothing, and hairstyle. Danticat recalled for Garry Pierre-Pierre in the *New York Times* that she took refuge from the isolation she felt in writing about her native land. As an adolescent she began work on what would evolve into her first novel, the acclaimed *Breath, Eyes, Memory.* Danticat followed her debut with a collection of short stories, *Krik? Krak!*—a volume which became a finalist for that year's National Book Award. According to Pierre-Pierre, the young author has been heralded as "'the voice' of Haitian-Americans," but Danticat told him, "I think I have been assigned that role, but I don't really see myself as the voice for the Haitian-American experience. There are many. I'm just one."

Danticat's parents wanted her to pursue a career in medicine, and with the goal of becoming a nurse, she attended a specialized high school in New York City. But she abandoned this aim to devote herself to her writing. An earlier version of *Breath, Eyes, Memory* served as her master of fine arts thesis at Brown University, and the finished version was published shortly thereafter. Like Danticat herself, Sophie Caco—the novel's protagonist—spent her first twelve years in Haiti, several in the care of an aunt, before coming wide-eyed to the United States. But there the similarities end. Sophie is the child of a single mother, conceived by rape. Though she rejoins her mother in the United States, it is too late to save the still-traumatized older woman from self-destruction. Yet women's ties to women are celebrated in the novel, and Sophie draws strength from her mother, her aunt, and herself in order to escape her mother's fate.

Breath, Eyes, Memory caused some controversy in the Haitian-American community. Some of Danticat's fellow Haitians did not approve of her writing of the practice of "testing" in the novel. In the story, female virginity is highly prized by Sophie's family, and Sophie's aunt "tests" to see whether Sophie's hymen is intact by inserting her fingers into the girl's vagina. Haitian-American women, some of whom have never heard of or participated in this practice, felt that Danticat's inclusion of it portrayed them as primitive and abusive. American critics, however, appreciated *Breath, Eyes, Memory.* Joan Philpott in *Ms.* described the book as "intensely lyrical." Pierre-Pierre reported that reviewers "have praised Ms. Danticat's vivid sense of place and

her images of fear and pain." Jim Gladstone concluded in the *New York Times Book Review* that the novel "achieves an emotional complexity that lifts it out of the realm of the potboiler and into that of poetry." And Bob Shacochis, in his *Washington Post Book World* review, called the work "a novel that rewards a reader again and again with small but exquisite and unforgettable epiphanies." Shacochis added, "You can actually see Danticat grow and mature, come into her own strength as a writer, throughout the course of this quiet, soul-penetrating story about four generations of women trying to hold on to one another in the Haitian diaspora."

Krik? Krak! takes its title from the practice of Haitian storytellers. Danticat told Deborah Gregory of *Essence* that storytelling is a favorite entertainment in Haiti, and a storyteller inquires of his or her audience, "Krik?" to ask if they are ready to listen. The group then replies with an enthusiastic, "Krak!" The tales in this collection include one about a man attempting to flee Haiti in a leaky boat, another about a prostitute who tells her son that the reason she dresses up every night is that she is expecting an angel to descend upon their house, and yet another explores the feelings of a childless housekeeper in a loveless marriage who finds an abandoned baby in the streets. The *New York Times Book Review* reviewer, Robert Houston, citing the fact that some of the stories in *Krik? Krak!* were written while Danticat was still an undergraduate at Barnard College, felt that these pieces were "out of place in a collection presumed to represent polished, mature work." But *Ms.* contributor Jordana Hart felt that the tales in *Krik? Krak!* "are textured and deeply personal, as if the twenty-six-year-old Haitian-American author had spilled her own tears over each." Even Houston conceded that readers "weary of stories that deal only with the minutiae of 'relationships' will rejoice that they have found work that is about something, and something that matters."

Danticat's novel *The Farming of Bones* concerns a historical tragedy, the 1937 massacre of Haitian farm workers by soldiers of the Dominican Republic. In the course of less than a week, an estimated 12,000-15,000 Haitian workers in the Dominican Republic were slaughtered by the Dominican government or by private citizens in a classic case of "ethnic cleansing." *The Farming of Bones* is narrated by a young Haitian woman, Amabelle Desir, who has grown up in the Dominican Republic after being orphaned. As the nightmare unfolds around her, Amabelle must flee for her life, separated from her lover, Sebastien. In the ensuing decades as she nurses her physical and psychological wounds, Amabelle serves as witness to the suffering of her countrymen and the guilt of her former Dominican employers. The massacre, Danticat told Mallay Charters in *Publishers Weekly,* is "a part of our history, as Haitians, but it's also a part of the history of the world. Writing about it is an act of remembrance."

Dean Peerman wrote in *Christian Century* that "*Breath, Eyes, Memory* was an impressive debut, but *The Farming of Bones* is a richer work, haunting and heart-wrenching." In *Nation,* Zia Jaffrey praised Danticat for "blending history and fiction, imparting information, in the manner of nineteenth-century novelists, without seeming to." Jaffrey added: "Danticat's brilliance as a novelist is that she is able to put this event into a credible, human context." Farley also felt that the author was able to endow a horrific episode with a breath of humanity. "Every chapter cuts deep, and you feel it," he stated, continuing on to say that Amabelle's "journey from servitude to slaughter is heartbreaking." In *Americas,* Barbara Mujica concluded that Danticat has written "a gripping novel that exposes an aspect of Dominican-Haitian history rarely represented in Latin American fiction. In spite of the desolation and wretchedness of the people Danticat depicts, *The Farming of Bones* is an inspiring book. It is a hymn to human resilience, faith, and hope in the face of overwhelming adversity." Jaffrey ended her review by concluding that the novel is "a beautifully conceived work, with monumental themes."

Behind the Mountains takes the form of a diary of teenage Haitian Celiane Esperance. Celiane is happy in her home in the mountains of Haiti, but she hasn't seen her father since he left for the United States years before. She had intended to join him in New York, along with her mother and older brother, but visa applications are inexorably slow. After eight years, the visas are granted, and the family reunites in Brooklyn. After an initially joyful reunion, however, the family begins to slowly unravel. A child when her father left Haiti, Celiane is now a young woman with her own mind and will. Her brother, Moy, a nineteen-year-old artist, does not quietly slip back into the role of obedient child. Even more universal concerns, such as the freezing New York winters, difficulties at school, and the need to make a living, chip away at the family's unity. Good intentions go awry in a book showcasing "friction among family members" exacerbated by "the separation and adjustment to a new country," but especially by the inevitable maturation of younger family members and the unwillingness of parents to acknowledge it, wrote Diane S. Morton in *School Library Journal.* Hazel Rochman, writing in *Booklist,* praised the "simple, lyrical writing" Danticat demonstrates in the novel. "Danticat brings her formidable skill as a writer and her own firsthand knowledge of Haiti and immigrating to America to this heartfelt story told in the intimate diary format," wrote Claire Rosser in *Kliatt.*

In addition to her own works, Danticat has also edited the fiction of others, including *The Butterfly's Way: From the Haitian Dyaspora in the United States.* This work is a collection of stories, poems, and essays from Haitian writers living in America and Europe, many of whom are concerned with the feeling of displacement that is perhaps an inevitable consequence of emigration. Denolyn Carroll suggested in *Black Issues Book Review* that the pieces in *The Butterfly's Way* "help paint a vivid picture of what it is like to live in two worlds." Carroll also felt that the work adds "new dimensions of understanding of Haitian emigrant's realities. This compilation is a source of enlightenment for us all." *Booklist* contributor Donna Seaman found the book "a potent and piercing collection" that will help all Americans understand "the frustrations . . . of Haitians who are now outsiders both in Haiti and in their places of refuge."

After the Dance: A Walk through Carnival in Haiti is Danticat's nonfiction account of her first encounter with Carnival, the boisterous, sometimes debauched, sometimes dangerous celebrations that rock Haiti every year. As a child, she did not have the opportunity to attend Carnival. Her family inevitably packed up and left for a remote area in the Haitian mountains each year to escape the celebrations, perpetuating an almost superstitious distrust of the event. At times, though, staying clear has been a good idea. During the regime of Haitian dictator François "Papa Doc" Duvalier, carnival-goers were "subject to beatings and arrest by Duvalier's infamously unregulated militamen," wrote Judith Wynn in the *Boston Herald.* Danticat therefore approaches her first experience of Carnival uneasily. Her trip, however, beginning a week before the actual event, immerses her in the rich culture and history of Haiti, the cultural importance behind Carnival, and the background of the celebration itself. Danticat's "lively narrative" describes a country with a deep history, "influenced by Christianity, voodoo, Europeans, pirates, dictators, past slavery, and an uncertain economy," wrote Linda M. Kaufmann in *Library Journal.* Donna Seaman, writing in *Booklist,* observed that "as in her fiction, Danticat writes about her odyssey with an admirable delicacy and meticulousness," while a *Publishers Weekly* critic noted that the author "offers an enlightening look at the country—and Carnival—through the eyes of one of its finest writers."

The Dew Breaker is a work of mystery and violence. It is a collection of short stories (many previously unpublished) connected by the character of the Dew Breaker, a torturer whose nickname is based on the fact that he attacks in the dawn before the dew has disappeared in the light of day. The Dew Breaker ultimately moves from Haiti to Brooklyn, becomes a barber, and raises a loving family. In Danticat's stories, the Dew Breaker reveals his secrets out of guilt, and his victims reveal their secrets, too, to ease the pain of their memories. Danticat's "spare, lyrical prose is ever present," wrote Marjorie Valbrun in the *Black Issues Book Review*, "in the gentle telling of stories that are soft to the ear even when pain and violence seem to scream from the pages." "The text presents two levels of truth," commented Robert McCormick in *World Literature Today*. In the course of reading, one comes to understand much, he hinted, but "what we don't know . . . is just as important."

Anacaona, Golden Flower: Haiti, 1490 is a novel for the upper elementary and middle school grades, written in the form of a diary. Anacaona is a young princess of the Taíno people who comes of age in the time of Christopher Columbus. She weds a royal chieftain who lives nearby and undergoes military training to defend her island home. *Booklist* reviewer Gillian Engberg predicted that "readers will connect with Danticat's immediate, poetic language, Anacaona's finely drawn growing pains, and the powerful, graphic story."

"In order to create full-fledged, three-dimensional characters, writers often draw on their encounters, observations, collages of images from the everyday world, both theirs and others," Danticat remarked in a biographical essay in *Contemporary Novelists*. "We are like actors, filtering through our emotions what life must be like, or must have been like, for those we write about. Truly we imagine these lives, aggrandize, reduce, or embellish, however we often begin our journey with an emotion close to our gut, whether it be anger, curiosity, joy, or fear."

BIOGRAPHICAL AND CRITICAL SOURCES:

BOOKS

Contemporary Literary Criticism, Volume 94, Thomson Gale (Detroit, MI), 1996.
Contemporary Novelists, 7th edition, St. James Press (Detroit, MI), 2001.
St. James Guide to Young Adult Writers, Thomson Gale (Detroit, MI), 1999.
Short Stories for Students, Volume 1, Thomson Gale (Detroit, MI), 1997.

PERIODICALS

America, November 6, 1999, review of *The Farming of Bones*, p. 10.
Américas, January, 2000, Barbara Mujica, review of *The Farming of Bones*, p. 62; May, 2000, Michele Wucker, profile of Danticat, p. 40.
Antioch Review, winter, 1999, Grace A. Epstein, review of *The Farming of Bones*, p. 106.
Atlanta Journal-Constitution, October 29, 2000, Valerie Boyd, review of *The Beacon Best of 2000: Great Writing by Women and Men of All Colors and Cultures*, p. D3.
Belles Lettres, fall, 1994, Mary Mackay, "Living, Seeing, Remembering," pp. 36, 38; summer, 1995, pp. 12-15.
Black Issues Book Review, January, 1999, review of *The Farming of Bones*, p. 20; May, 2001, Denolyn Carroll, review of *The Butterfly's Way: Voices from the Haitian Dyaspora in the United States*, p. 60; July-August, 2004, Marjorie Valbrun, review of *The Dew Breaker*, p. 43.
Bloomsbury Review, September-October, 1994, p. 12.
Booklist, January 1, 1999, review of *The Farming of Bones*, p. 778; March 15, 1999, review of *The Farming of Bones*, p. 1295; June 1, 1999, review of *Breath, Eyes, Memory*, p. 1796; February 15, 2000, Deborah Taylor, review of *Breath, Eyes, Memory*, p. 1096; October 15, 2000, review of *The Beacon Best of 2000*, p. 416; February 15, 2001, Donna Seaman, review of *The Butterfly's Way*, p. 1096; January 1, 2002, review of *The Butterfly's Way*, p. 763; August, 2002, Donna Seaman, review of *After the Dance: A Walk through Carnival in Haiti*, pp. 1895-1896; October 1, 2002, Hazel Rochman, review of *Behind the Mountains*, p. 312; May 15, 2005, Gillian Engberg, review of *Anacaona, Golden Flower: Haiti, 1490*, p. 1674.
Boston Globe, Jordana Hart, "Danticat's Stories Pulse with Haitian Heartbeat," p. 70.
Boston Herald, November 17, 2000, Rosemary Herbert, "Writing in the Margins: Author-Editor Edwidge Danticat Celebrates Rich Pageant of Multicultural Stories," p. 43; September 1, 2002, Judith Wynn, review of *After the Dance*, p. 61.
Callaloo, spring, 1996, Renee H. Shea, interview with Danticat, pp. 382-389.
Christian Century, September 22, 1999, Dean Peerman, review of *The Farming of Bones*, p. 885.
Emerge, April, 1995, p. 58.
Entertainment Weekly, September 3, 1999, review of *The Farming of Bones*, p. 63.
Essence, November, 1993, Edwidge Danticat, "My Father Once Chased Rainbows," p. 48; April, 1995,

Deborah Gregory, "Edwidge Danticat: Dreaming of Haiti" (interview), p. 56; May, 1996.

Globe and Mail (Toronto, Ontario, Canada), June 12, 1999, review of *Breath, Eyes, Memory,* p. D4.

Kirkus Reviews, June 1, 2002, review of *After the Dance,* p. 782; September 15, 2002, review of *Behind the Mountains,* p. 1387.

Kliatt, November, 1999, review of *The Farming of Bones,* p. 16; November, 2002, Claire Rosser, review of *Behind the Mountains,* p. 8.

Library Journal, November 1, 2000, Barbara O'Hara, review of *The Butterfly's Way,* p. 80, Ann Burns and Emily Joy, review of *The Butterfly's Way,* p. 103; June 15, 2002, Linda M. Kaufmann, review of *After the Dance,* p. 83.

Ms., March-April, 1994, Joan Philpott, "Two Tales of Haiti," review of *Breath, Eyes, Memory,* pp. 77-78; March-April, 1995, Jordana Hart, review of *Krik? Krak!,* p. 75.

Nation, November 16, 1998, Zia Jaffrey, review of *The Farming of Bones,* p. 62.

Newsday, May 21, 1995, p. A52; March 30, 1995, Richard Eder, "A Haitian Fantasy and Exile," pp. B2, B25.

New York, November 20, 1995, Rebecca Mead, review of *Krik? Krak!,* p. 50.

New York Times, January 26, 1995, Garry Pierre-Pierre, "Haitian Tales, Flatbush Scenes," pp. C1, C8; October 23, 1995, p. B3.

New York Times Book Review, July 10, 1994, Jim Gladstone, review of *Breath, Eyes, Memory,* p. 24; April 23, 1995, Robert Houston, *Krik? Krak!,* p. 22; September 27, 1998, Michael Upchurch, review of *The Farming of Bones,* p. 18; December 5, 1999, review of *The Farming of Bones,* p. 104; December 10, 1999, review of *The Farming of Bones,* p. 36.

New York Times Magazine, June 21, 1998.

O, February, 2002, profile of Danticat, pp. 141-145.

Off Our Backs, March, 1999, review of *Krik? Krak!, The Farming of Bones,* and *Breath, Eyes, Memory,* p. 13.

People, September 28, 1998, review of *The Farming of Bones,* p. 51.

Poets and Writers, January, 1997.

Progressive, January, 1997, p. 39; December, 1998, Matthew Rothschild, review of *The Farming of Bones,* p. 44.

Publishers Weekly, January 24, 1994, pp. 39-40; May 25, 1998; August 17, 1998, Mallay Charters, review of *The Farming of Bones,* p. 42; November 2, 1998, review of *The Farming of Bones,* p. 40; September 11, 2000, review of *The Beacon Best of 2000,* p. 69; December 18, 2000, review of *The Butterfly's Way,* p. 65; May 13, 2002, review of *After the Dance,* pp. 58-59; October 28, 2002, review of *Behind the Mountains,* p. 72.

Quarterly Black Review, June, 1995, Kimberly Hebert, review of *Krik? Krak!,* p. 6.

Reference and User Services Quarterly, spring, 1999, review of *The Farming of Bones,* p. 253.

St. Louis Post-Dispatch, September 21, 1999, Shauna Scott Rhone, review of *The Farming of Bones,* p. D3.

School Library Journal, May, 1995, p. 135; October, 2002, Diane S. Marton, review of *Behind the Mountains,* p. 160.

Time, September 7, 1998, Christopher John Farley, review of *The Farming of Bones,* p. 78.

Times Literary Supplement, April 28, 2000, Helen Hayward, review of *The Farming of Bones,* p. 23.

Times (London, England), March 20, 1999, Rachel Campbell-Johnston, review of *The Farming of Bones,* p. 19.

Village Voice Literary Supplement, July, 1995, p. 11.

Voice of Youth Advocates, December, 1995, p. 299.

Washington Post Book World, April 3, 1994, Bob Shacochis, "Island in the Dark," p. 6; May 14, 1995, Joanne Omang, review of *Krik? Krak!,* p. 4.

World and I, February, 1999, review of *The Farming of Bones,* p. 290.

World Literature Today, spring, 1999, Jacqueline Brice-Finch, "Haiti," p. 373; January-April, 2005, Robert McCormick, review of *The Dew Breaker,* p. 83.

ONLINE

Free Williamsburg, http://www.freewilliamsburg.com/ (February 11, 2003), Alexander Laurence, interview with Danticat.

Voices from the Gaps, http://voices.cla.umn.edu/ (February 11, 2003), "Edwidge Danticat."

*   *   *

DANZIGER, Paula 1944-2004

PERSONAL: Born August 18, 1944, in Washington, DC; died July 8, 2004, in New York, NY, of complications from a heart attack; daughter of Samuel (worked in garment district) and Carolyn (a nurse) Danziger. *Education:* Montclair State College, B.A., 1967, M.A.

CAREER: Substitute teacher, Edison, NJ, 1967; Title I teacher, Highland Park, NJ, 1967-68; junior-high school English teacher, Edison, NJ, 1968-70; English teacher,

Lincoln Junior High School, West Orange, NJ, 1977-78; full-time writer, 1978–2004. Worked for the Educational Opportunity Program, Montclair State College, until 1977. Regular appearances on BBC-TV magazine shows, *Going Live!* and *Live and Kicking*.

AWARDS, HONORS: New Jersey Institute of Technology Award, and California Young Reader Medal nomination, California Reading Association (CRA), both 1976, Massachusetts Children's Book Award, first runner-up, 1977, winner, 1979, and Nene Award, Hawaii Association of School Librarians/Hawaii Library Association (HASL/HLA), 1980, all for *The Cat Ate My Gymsuit;* Children's Books of the Year citation, Child Study Association of America (CSAA), 1978, Massachusetts Children's Book Award, Education Department of Salem State College, 1979, Nene Award, HASL/HLA, 1980, California Young Reader Medal nomination, CRA, 1981, and Arizona Young Reader Award, 1983, all for *The Pistachio Prescription;* Children's Choice Award, International Reading Association and the Children's Book Council, 1979, for *The Pistachio Prescription*, 1980, for *The Cat Ate My Gymsuit* and *Can You Sue Your Parents for Malpractice?*, 1981, for *There's a Bat in Bunk Five,* and 1983, for *The Divorce Express*.New Jersey Institute of Technology Award, and Books for the Teen Age citation, New York Public Library, both 1980, and Land of Enchantment Book Award, New Mexico Library Association, 1982, all for *Can You Sue Your Parents for Malpractice?;* Read-a-Thon Author of the Year Award, Multiple Sclerosis Society, and Parents' Choice Award for Literature, Parents' Choice Foundation (PCF), both 1982, and South Carolina Young Adult Book Award, South Carolina Association of School Librarians, 1985, all for *The Divorce Express;* CRABbery Award, Prince George's County Memorial Library System (MD), 1982, and Young Readers Medal, 1984, both for *There's a Bat in Bunk Five;* Parents' Choice Award for Literature, PCF, Bologna International Children's Book Fair exhibitor, and Children's Books of the Year citation, CSAA, all 1985, all for *It's an Aardvark-Eat-Turtle World;* New Jersey Garden State Children's Book Award nomination, 1997, for *Amber Brown Is Not a Crayon.*

WRITINGS:

FOR CHILDREN

The Cat Ate My Gymsuit, Delacorte (New York, NY), 1974, Putnam (New York, NY), 2004.
The Pistachio Prescription, Delacorte (New York, NY), 1978.

Can You Sue Your Parents for Malpractice?, Delacorte (New York, NY), 1979.
There's a Bat in Bunk Five, Delacorte (New York, NY), 1980.
The Divorce Express, Delacorte (New York, NY), 1982.
It's an Aardvark-Eat-Turtle World, Delacorte, 1985, Puffin (New York, NY), 2000.
This Place Has No Atmosphere, Delacorte (New York, NY), 1986.
Remember Me to Harold Square, Delacorte (New York, NY), 1987.
Everyone Else's Parents Said Yes, Delacorte (New York, NY), 1989.
Make Like a Tree and Leave, Delacorte (New York, NY), 1990.
Earth to Matthew, Delacorte (New York, NY), 1991.
Not for a Billion, Gazillion Dollars, Delacorte (New York, NY), 1992.
Thames Doesn't Rhyme with James, Putnam (New York, NY), 1994.
(With Ann M. Martin) *P.S. Longer Letter Later,* Scholastic (New York, NY), 1998.
(With Ann M. Martin) *Snail Mail No More,* Scholastic Press (New York, NY), 2000.
United Tates of America, Scholastic (New York, NY), 2002.
Barfburger Baby, I Was Here First!, illustrated by G. Brian Karas, Putnam (New York, NY), 2004.

"AMBER BROWN" SERIES

Amber Brown Is Not a Crayon, illustrated by Tony Ross, Putnam (New York, NY), 1994.
You Can't Eat Your Chicken Pox, Amber Brown, illustrated by Tony Ross, Putnam (New York, NY), 1995.
Amber Brown Goes Fourth, illustrated by Tony Ross, Putnam (New York, NY), 1995.
Amber Brown Wants Extra Credit, illustrated by Tony Ross, Putnam (New York, NY), 1996.
Forever Amber Brown, illustrated by Tony Ross, Putnam (New York, NY), 1996.
Amber Brown Sees Red, illustrated by Tony Ross, Putnam (New York, NY), 1997.
Amber Brown Is Feeling Blue, illustrated by Tony Ross, Putnam (New York, NY), 1998.
I, Amber Brown, Putnam (New York, NY), 1999.
Amber Brown Is Green with Envy, illustrated by Tony Ross, Putnam (New York, NY), 2003.

"A IS FOR AMBER BROWN" SERIES

It's Justin Time, Amber Brown, illustrated by Tony Ross, Putnam (New York, NY), 2001.

What a Trip, Amber Brown, illustrated by Tony Ross, Putnam (New York, NY), 2001.

Get Ready for Second Grade, Amber Brown, illustrated by Tony Ross, Putnam (New York, NY), 2002.

It's a Fair Day, Amber Brown, illustrated by Tony Ross, Putnam (New York, NY), 2002.

Second Grade Rules, Amber Brown, illustrated by Tony Ross, Putnam (New York, NY), 2004.

Orange You Glad It's Halloween, Amber Brown?, illustrated by Tony Ross, Putnam (New York, NY), in press.

ADAPTATIONS: The Cat Ate My Gymsuit was adapted as a filmstrip and cassette by Cheshire, 1985.

SIDELIGHTS: Following the 1974 publication of her first novel, *The Cat Ate My Gymsuit,* Paula Danziger became one of America's most popular authors for young adults. Most of her books "center around young teenage girls faced with the problems of establishing a grownup identity," Alleen Pace Nilsen observed in *Twentieth-Century Children's Writers.* But while Danziger's characters frequently deal with personal and family problems, they do so with humor, wit, and spirit. As a result, Nilsen wrote, "teenagers begin to smile at themselves and come away from [Danziger's] books a little more confident that they too will make it."

"My life as an author began as a small child when I realized that was what I wanted to do and started mentally recording a lot of information and observations," Danziger told Marguerite Feitlowitz in an interview for *Authors and Artists for Young Adults (AAYA).* "That's also when I started to develop the sense of humor and the sense of perspective that allows me to write the way I do." While in high school, Danziger spent much of her time reading and also wrote for school and town newspapers. Nevertheless, she recalled, "I'd been raised to believe that I was not particularly bright, not college material. . . . Family dynamics were such that I fell into fulfilling their low expectations."

Despite her lackluster performance in school, Danziger was admitted to Montclair State College, where she studied to be a teacher. While in college, she was introduced to John Ciardi, a noted poet and author for children. She secured a semi-regular babysitting job with his family, including several summers when she accompanied the Ciardis to writers' conferences. The poet encouraged Danziger in her studies and frequently shared his literary knowledge and insight with her. The author related in her *AAYA* interview: "John Ciardi taught me more than anyone else about poetry and writing. Their house was full of books, and I borrowed liberally from the shelves. . . . It was the best lesson I've ever had in my life. He read the poems and explained them, giving me a sense of language structure."

After her graduation from college in 1967, Danziger began working as a substitute teacher—"an occupation that could have been a punishment in Dante's *Inferno,*" the author commented in *English Journal.* That job led to full-time positions as a junior high school English teacher. However, Danziger wanted to further her education, so she returned to school after three years to pursue a master's degree. Her studies were interrupted when she was involved in a bizarre series of car accidents. The first mishap was relatively minor, but it left her with a painful case of whiplash. Then, when she sought treatment several days later, the car she was traveling in was hit head-on by a drunken driver. Danziger hit the windshield of the car and suffered temporary brain damage that left her unable to read and haunted by nightmares.

To combat her fear and feelings of powerlessness, Danziger began writing a novel about a teenager beset by self-doubt and family troubles. "I felt very out of control," she once explained, and "the last time I felt that way was when I was a kid. When you're a kid, everyone seems to be in charge, to have the right to tell you what to do, how to feel. In hospitals and schools it seemed to be the same way. So I wanted to confront all that." In addition, the author continued, "I really missed teaching my eighth graders. . . . [so] I decided to write a book to talk to them about survival—learning to like oneself, dealing with school systems, and being able to celebrate one's own uniqueness. The result was *The Cat Ate My Gymsuit.*"

"The cat ate my gymsuit" is one of the excuses junior high school student Marcy Lewis gives her physical education teacher to avoid dressing for gym class. Uncomfortable with her looks, unhappy with her insensitive and uncommunicative parents, and unsatisfied with a school that stifles individuality, Marcy becomes involved in a student protest over a teacher's firing and learns to have faith in herself and her abilities. The result is "a thoroughly enjoyable, tightly written, funny/sad tale of an unglamorous but plucky girl who is imaginative, believable, and worthy of emulation," a reviewer commented in the *Journal of Reading.*

With its "fresh and funny" approach, *The Cat Ate My Gymsuit* "grabbed teenagers' attention because it was so different from the serious realistic novels that adult critics were raving over," Nilsen noted in *Twentieth-Century Children's Writers.* Despite the book's popularity, Danziger returned to teaching after recovering from her accident. Meanwhile, she continued working on a second book, *The Pistachio Prescription.* Eventually "the realization came that it was incredibly hard to be a good creative writer and a good creative teacher" at the same time, Danziger commented in *English Journal.* "Each was a full-time job. My choice was to write full time. I was never good at taking attendance, doing lesson plans, or getting papers back on time. I sold two ideas to Dell, took the advance money, and hoped for decent royalties."

The success of Danziger's next books allowed her the freedom to remain a full-time writer. *The Pistachio Prescription,* which details how an insecure teenager overcomes health problems and conflicts with her feuding parents, was considered "unusually well done" by *Bulletin of the Center for Children's Books* contributor Zena Sutherland. Sutherland added, "the characterization and dialogue are strong, the relationships depicted with perception, and the writing style vigorous." Sutherland likewise found that *Can You Sue Your Parents for Malpractice?* "has enough humor and breezy dialogue to make it fun to read, and enough solidity in the characters and relationships to make it thought-provoking." A story of a ninth grader confused by relationships with stubborn parents and unpredictable boyfriends, the novel has a "skillful balance between humor and pathos" which makes it "yet another to add to [Danziger's] growing list of successful efforts in literature that's particularly appropriate for junior high students," Michele Simpson commented in the *Journal of Reading.*

While Danziger's readers enjoy the humor and pacing of her books, some critics have faulted them as superficial, containing generic characters and situations. According to Perry Nodelman of *Children's Literature in Education,* for instance, the "typicality" of books such as *The Cat Ate My Gymsuit* means that "we cannot possibly understand the story unless we fill in its exceedingly vague outlines with knowledge from our own experience. . . . The book demands, not distance, but involvement." Sutherland, on the other hand, argued that *There's a Bat in Bunk Five,* which recounts Marcy Lewis's summer as a camp counselor, "has depth in the relationships and characterizations; and it's written with vigor and humor." While the novel contains elements of familiar camping stories, the critic explained, it "doesn't, however, follow a formula plot."

Responding to such criticism, Danziger told *AAYA*'s Feitlowitz: "For anyone who has ever felt alone—and

who hasn't, in truth—a book can make a very good friend. Like a good friend, a book can help you see things a little more clearly, help you blow off steam, get you laughing, let you cry." The author continued: "I think there is so much in life that is hard and sad and difficult and that there is so much in life that is . . . joyous and funny. There's also a lot of in between those two extremes. As a writer, I try to take all of those things and put them together. That way people can say 'I know that feeling' and identify with it."

This sense of identification helps to make Danziger's books so popular with her readers; as Nilsen and Kenneth L. Donelson stated in *Literature for Today's Young Adults,* Danziger's books "remain favorites . . . because they do not talk down to their readers, because they present real issues and real problems facing their readers, and because they do not pretend that there are easy answers to any problems." Danziger's sometimes negative portrayals of adults and quick one-liners "may annoy adults," the critics conclude, "but her humor is exactly what her readers want."

Though Danziger's later novels continue in her well-known humorous vein, they also include a science-fiction spoof, a book with a biracial protagonist, and series books for preteen readers. *This Place Has No Atmosphere* is set in the year 2057 and follows a teenager whose family moves to a colony on the moon. *The Divorce Express* presents Phoebe, who shuttles between her long-divorced parents. "Mercifully avoiding the . . . gloom and wearisome heart-searching of so many novels on this highly topical subject," Margery Fisher commented in *Growing Point,* "The Divorce Express makes its point in an agreeably relaxed and shrewd manner." The book also introduces Rosie, the biracial daughter of a mixed marriage; in *It's an Aardvark-Eat-Turtle World,* Rosie must cope with a new "family" when her mother combines households with her boyfriend. And the novels *Everyone Else's Parents Said Yes* and *Make Like a Tree and Leave,* which follow the adventures of sixth-grader Matthew Martin, continue "to reflect Danziger's awareness of what students of a certain age are like and what appeals to them," remarked Dona Weisman in a *School Library Journal* review of *Everyone Else's Parents Said Yes.* Matthew's adventures are continued in *Earth to Matthew* and *Not for a Billion, Gazillion Dollars.*

Aimed at even younger readers is the series that features Amber Brown. Reviewing *Amber Brown Is Not a Crayon,* Roger Sutton observed in the *Bulletin of the Center for Children's Books* that "Danziger's brisk and empathetic writing brings her the same kind of intuitive connection with kids she's made in books for older readers." These books deal not only with usual school traumas, but also with issues of divorce and blending families. The series has won praise for its ability to entice new readers and to make even kids who hate books find that reading can be fun.

The cast of the "Amber Brown" books continues in a second series about the spirited youngster, "A Is for Amber Brown." Aimed at a younger audience, this second series features the protagonist back in early elementary school, several years before the original "Amber Brown" series. In a *Publishers Weekly* review of the first two books, *It's Justin Time, Amber Brown,* and *What a Trip, Amber Brown,* a critic noted that "the emotions are real and recognizable." Discussing both *Get Ready for Second Grade, Amber Brown* and *It's a Fair Day, Amber Brown, School Library Journal* contributor Mary Elam thought that "the characters in these prequels for beginning readers lose nothing from their original portrayals in the longer books for older children."

Danziger joined forces with Ann M. Martin, author of the "Baby Sitters Club" series, in an epistolary novel titled *P.S. Longer Letter Later* and its sequel *Snail Mail No More.* The first book tells of two junior-high best friends, suddenly separated by hundreds of miles, who write to each other. Elizabeth's affluent parents suffer a reversal of fortune when her father's company is downsized. TaraStarr (as she signs herself) must cope with her young parents planning for their first "wanted" child. Ron Koertge, writing for the *New York Times Book Review,* described *P.S. Longer Letter Later* as a "spirited and readable book with none of the anemia or tendentiousness" associated with much YA writing. In the sequel, *Snail Mail No More,* pen pals Elizabeth and Tara are now in the twenty-first century and correspond via e-mail. Calling the book "alternately funny and poignant," a reviewer in *Publishers Weekly* noted that "the two characters approach life differently enough that there will likely be a response or suggestion that resonates with every reader, and both heroines share one important trait: they are all heart."

"As always, Danziger's characters are likable, and the dialogue and situations ring true" in the novel *United Tates of America,* Ronni Krasnow wrote in *School Library Journal.* Protagonist Sarah Kate "Skate" Tate narrates this story of adapting to middle school and coming to terms with the sudden death of her Great Uncle Mort, affectionately referred to as "GUM." "The fami-

ly's reactions to his death—a mix of sadness, happy memories, even anger and guilt—are poignantly portrayed in some of the novel's strongest scenes," thought *Horn Book*'s Peter D. Sieruta. Prior to his passing, GUM had enjoyed traveling the world, and in his will, he leaves the Tates a good deal of money with which to travel and expand their own horizons. The highlight of the book is a thirty-two page, full-color insert of the scrapbook Skate creates that year, which includes several photographs of the trip that the family took to Plymouth, Massachusetts, with part of their inheritance. "Young scrapbook artists, in particular, will take delight in this book's unique artwork," commented a *Publishers Weekly* contributor.

"So here I am a full-time writer, a 'grown-up' who chooses to write about kids," Danziger once commented. "I've made this choice because I think that kids and adults share a lot of the same feelings and thoughts, that we have to go through a lot of similar situations." As she explained in her *AAYA* interview, "All writers write from deep experience. For me, that is childhood. From it flow feelings of vulnerability, compassion, and strength. Perhaps it would be better to say that I write 'of' young people rather than 'for' or 'to' them. Writers tell the best stories we possibly can, hopefully in ways that others will like."

BIOGRAPHICAL AND CRITICAL SOURCES:

BOOKS

Authors and Artists for Young Adults, Volume 4, Thomson Gale (Detroit, MI), 1990, interview with author.
Beacham's Guide to Literature for Young Adults, Volumes 6 and 7, Beacham Publishing (Osprey, FL), 1990.
Children's Literature Review, Volume 20, Thomson Gale (Detroit, MI), 1990.
Contemporary Literary Criticism, Volume 21, Thomson Gale (Detroit, MI), 1982.
Drew, Bernard A., *The One Hundred Most Popular Young Adult Authors,* Libraries Unlimited (Englewood, CO), 1996.
Krull, Kathleen, *Presenting Paula Danziger,* Twayne Publishing (New York, NY), 1995.
Nilsen, Alleen Pace, and Kenneth L. Donelson, *Literature for Today's Young Adults,* 2nd edition, Scott, Foresman (Glenview, IL), 1985, pp. 335-369.
St. James Guide to Young Adult Writers, 2nd edition, St. James Press (Detroit, MI), 1999.
Twentieth-Century Children's Writers, 3rd edition, St. James Press (Detroit, MI), 1989.

PERIODICALS

Booklist, December 15, 2001, Ilene Cooper, review of *The Pistachio Prescription,* p. 729; April 15, 2002, Shelle Rosenfeld, review of *United Tates of America,* p. 1400; January 1, 2003, Jean Hatfield, review of *United Tates of America,* p. 924; September 1, 2003, Carolyn Phelan, review of *Amber Brown Is Green with Envy,* p. 119.

Books for Keeps, July, 1995, Chris Powling, "Autograph No. 93," pp. 14-15.

Bulletin of the Center for Children's Books, May, 1978, Zena Sutherland, review of *The Pistachio Prescription,* p. 140; June, 1979, Zena Sutherland, review of *Can You Sue Your Parents for Malpractice?,* pp. 172-173; December, 1980, Zena Sutherland, review of *There's a Bat in Bunk Five,* p. 68; June, 1994, Roger Sutton, review of *Amber Brown Is Not a Crayon,* pp. 316-317.

Children's Literature in Education, winter, 1981, Perry Nodelman, "How Typical Children Read Typical Books," pp. 177-185.

English Journal, November, 1984, Paula Danziger and others, "Facets: Successful Authors Talk about Connections between Teaching and Writing," pp. 24-27.

Growing Point, September, 1986, Margery Fisher, review of *The Divorce Express,* pp. 4673-4674.

Horn Book, March-April, 2002, Peter D. Sieruta, review of *United Tates of America,* pp. 210-211.

Journal of Reading, January, 1976, review of *The Cat Ate My Gymsuit,* pp. 333-335; February, 1980, Michele Simpson, review of *Can You Sue Your Parents for Malpractice?,* p. 473.

Kirkus Reviews, February 15, 2002, review of *United Tates of America,* p. 253; June 1, 2002, review of *It's a Fair Day, Amber Brown,* p. 803.

Kliatt, spring, 1979, Cyrisse Jaffe, review of *The Pistachio Prescription,* p. 6.

New York Times Book Review, January 5, 1975; March 18, 1979, Selma G. Lanes, review of *The Pistachio Prescription,* p. 26; June 17, 1979, Jane Langton, review of *Can You Sue Your Parents for Malpractice?,* p. 25; November 23, 1980; February 13, 1983; May 17, 1998, Ron Koertge, "Please Mr. Postman," review of *P.S. Longer Letter Later,* p. 27.

PEN Newsletter, September, 1988, Paula Danziger and others, "Writing for Children: Where Does It Come from and How Is It Different from Writing for Adults?," pp. 16-26.

Publishers Weekly, September 8, 1989, review of *Everyone Else's Parents Said Yes,* p. 70; September 12, 1994, review of *Thames Doesn't Rhyme with James,* p. 92; February 20, 1995, review of *You Can't Eat Your Chicken Pox, Amber Brown,* p. 201; June 7, 1999, review of *P.S. Longer Letter Later,* p. 53; September 20, 1999, review of *Amber Brown Is Feeling Blue,* p. 90; January 10, 2000, review of *Snail Mail No More,* p. 68; March 12, 2001, review of *It's Justin Time, Amber Brown* and *What a Trip, Amber Brown,* p. 91; February 4, 2002, review of *United Tates of America,* p. 77; July 21, 2003, review of *Amber Brown Is Green with Envy,* pp. 197-198.

School Library Journal, September, 1989, Dona Weisman, review of *Everyone Else's Parents Said Yes,* p. 249; October, 1990; July, 1997, Jackie Hechtkopf, review of *Amber Brown Sees Red,* p. 61; March, 2001, Genevieve Ceraldi, review of *It's Justin Time, Amber Brown,* p. 205; April, 2001, Holly Belli, review of *What a Trip, Amber Brown,* p. 105; June, 2002, Ronni Krasnow, review of *United Tates of America,* p. 136; July, 2002, Mary Elam, review of *Get Ready for Second Grade, Amber Brown* and *It's a Fair Day, Amber Brown,* pp. 87-88; November, 2002, Jane P. Fenn, review of *United Tates of America,* pp. 86-87; September, 2003, Maura Martin Smith, review of *Get Ready for Second Grade, Amber Brown,* pp. 73-74, Susan Mingee, review of *It's a Fair Day, Amber Brown,* p. 74, and Michele Shaw, review of *Amber Brown Is Green with Envy,* p. 176.

Storyworks, April, 2001, Alyssa Egts, review of *Remember Me to Harold Square,* p. 7.

Time for Kids, September 26, 2003, "Amber Brown Is Back," p. 3.

Voice of Youth Advocates, December, 1987, Nancy Headley Jones, review of *Remember Me to Harold Square,* p. 46.

ONLINE

Scholastic Books Web site, http://www.scholastic.com/ (February 13, 2004), "Meet Paula Danziger."

OBITUARIES:

PERIODICALS

Los Angeles Times, July 10, 2004, p. B19.
New York Times, July 10, 2004, p. B18.
Washington Post, July 13, 2004, p. B7.

DAVIES, Robertson 1913-1995
[A pseudonym]
(William Robertson Davies, Samuel Marchbanks)

PERSONAL: Born August 28, 1913, in Thamesville, Ontario, Canada; died of a stroke December 2, 1995, in Toronto, Ontario, Canada; son of William Rupert (a publisher) and Florence Sheppard (McKay) Davies; married Brenda Matthews (a stage manager and editor), February 2, 1940; children: Miranda, Jennifer (Mrs. C.T. Surridge), Rosamund (Mrs. John Cunnington). *Education:* Attended Upper Canada College, Toronto, and Queen's University at Kingston; Balliol College, Oxford, B.Litt., 1938.

CAREER: Old Vic Company, London, England, teacher and actor, 1938-40, appeared in *Traitor's Gate,* 1938, *She Stoops to Conquer,* 1939, *Saint Joan,* 1939, and *The Taming of the Shrew,* 1939; *Saturday Night,* Toronto, Ontario, Canada, literary editor, 1940-42; *Examiner,* Peterborough, Ontario, Canada, editor and publisher, 1942-62; University of Toronto, Toronto, Ontario, Canada, professor of English, 1960-81, master of Massey College, 1962-81, emeritus professor and master, 1981-95. Also worked as a newspaperman for *Whig Standard,* Kingston, Ontario, Canada. Senator, Stratford Shakespeare Festival, Stratford, Ontario, Canada.

MEMBER: Royal Society of Canada (fellow), Playwrights Union of Canada, Royal Society of Literature (fellow), American Academy and Institute of Arts and Letters (honorary member), Authors Guild, Authors League of America, Dramatists Guild, Writers' Union (Canada), PEN International.

AWARDS, HONORS: Louis Jouvet Prize for directing, Dominion Drama Festival, 1949; Stephen Leacock Medal for Humour, 1954, for *Leaven of Malice;* Lorne Pierce Medal, Royal Society of Canada, 1961; Companion of the Order of Canada, 1972; Governor General's Award for fiction, 1972, for *The Manticore;* LL.D., University of Alberta, 1957, Queen's University, 1962, University of Manitoba, 1972, University of Calgary, 1975, and University of Toronto, 1981; D.Litt., McMaster University, 1959, University of Windsor, 1971, York University, 1973, Mount Allison University, 1973, Memorial University of Newfoundland, 1974, University of Western Ontario, 1974, McGill University, 1974, Trent University, 1974, University of Lethbridge, 1981, University of Waterloo, 1981, University of British Columbia, 1983, University of Santa Clara, 1985, Trinity College, Dublin, 1990, University of Oxford, 1991, and University of Wales, 1995; LH.D., University of Rochester, 1983, Dowling College, NY, 1992, and Loyola University, Chicago, 1994; D.C.L., Bishop's University, 1967; D.Hum. Litt., University of Rochester, 1983; honorary fellow of Balliol College, Oxford, 1986, and Trinity College, University of Toronto, 1987; World Fantasy Convention Award for *High Spirits;* City of Toronto Book Award, Canadian Authors Association Literary Award for Fiction, and Booker Prize shortlist, all 1986, all for *What's Bred in the Bone;* Banff Centre School of Fine Arts National Award, 1986 and Lifetime Achievement Award from Toronto Arts Awards, both 1986; Gold Medal of Honor for Literature from National Arts Club (New York City), 1987; Order of Ontario, Diplome d'honneur, Canada Confederation of the Arts, Molson Prize in Arts, Canadian Council, and Neil Gunn International Fellow, Scottish Arts Council, all 1988; honorary fellowship, Royal Conservatory of Music, Toronto.

WRITINGS:

NONFICTION

Shakespeare's Boy Actors, Dent (London, England), 1939, Russell (New York, NY), 1964.

Shakespeare for Young Players: A Junior Course, Clarke, Irwin (Toronto, Ontario, Canada), 1942.

The Diary of Samuel Marchbanks (collection of newspaper pieces originally published under pseudonym Samuel Marchbanks; also see below), Clarke, Irwin (Toronto, Ontario, Canada), 1947.

The Table Talk of Samuel Marchbanks (collection of newspaper pieces originally published under pseudonym Samuel Marchbanks; also see below), Clarke, Irwin (Toronto, Ontario, Canada), 1949.

(With Tyrone Guthrie and Grant Macdonald) *Renown at Stratford: A Record of the Shakespearean Festival in Canada,* Clarke, Irwin (Toronto, Ontario, Canada), 1953, reprinted, 1971.

(With Tyrone Guthrie and Grant Macdonald) *Twice Have the Trumpets Sounded: A Record of the Stratford Shakespearean Festival in Canada,* Clarke, Irwin (Toronto, Ontario, Canada), 1954.

(With Tyrone Guthrie, Boyd Neal, and Tanya Moiseiwitsch) *Thrice the Brinded Cat Hath Mew'd: A Record of the Stratford Shakespearean Festival in Canada,* Clarke, Irwin (Toronto, Ontario, Canada), 1955.

A Voice from the Attic, Knopf (New York, NY), 1960, published as *The Personal Art: Reading to Good Purpose,* Secker & Warburg (London, England), 1961, reprinted, Darby Books, 1983.

Le Jeu de centenaire, Comission du Centenaire, c. 1967.

Samuel Marchbanks' Almanack (collection of newspaper pieces originally published under pseudonym Samuel Marchbanks; also see below), McClelland & Stewart (Toronto, Ontario, Canada), 1967.

The Heart of a Merry Christmas, Macmillan (Toronto, Ontario, Canada), 1970.

Stephen Leacock, McClelland & Stewart (Toronto, Ontario, Canada), 1970.

(Editor and author of introduction) *Feast of Stephen: An Anthology of Some of the Less Familiar Writings of Stephen Leacock,* McClelland & Stewart (Toronto, Ontario, Canada), 1970.

(With Michael R. Booth, Richard Southern, Frederick Marker, and Lise-Lone Marker) *The Revels History of Drama in English, Volume VI: 1750-1880,* Methuen (London, England), 1975.

One Half of Robertson Davies: Provocative Pronouncements on a Wide Range of Topics, Macmillan (Toronto, Ontario, Canada), 1977, published as *One Half of Robertson Davies,* Viking (New York, NY), 1978.

The Enthusiasms of Robertson Davies, edited by Judith Skelton Grant, McClelland & Stewart (Toronto, Ontario, Canada), 1979.

The Well-Tempered Critic: One Man's View of Theatre and Letters in Canada, edited by Judith Skelton Grant, McClelland & Stewart (Toronto, Ontario, Canada), 1981.

The Mirror of Nature (lectures), University of Toronto Press (Toronto, Ontario, Canada), 1983.

The Papers of Samuel Marchbanks (contains portions of *The Diary of Samuel Marchbanks, The Table Talk of Samuel Marchbanks,* and *Samuel Marchbanks' Almanack*), Irwin Publishing, 1985, Viking (New York, NY), 1986.

Conversations with Robertson Davies, edited by J. Madison Davis, University Press of Mississippi (Jackson, MS), 1989.

Reading and Writing (lectures), University of Utah Press (Salt Lake City, UT), 1994.

The Merry Heart: Reflections on Reading, Writing, and the World of Books, Viking (New York, NY), 1997.

Happy Alchemy: On the Pleasures of Music and the Theatre, Viking (New York, NY), 1998.

For Your Eye Alone: The Letters of Robertson Davies, edited by Judith Skelton Grant, Viking (New York, NY), 2001.

Contributor to books, including *Studies in Robertson Davies' Deptford Trilogy,* edited by Robert G. Lawrence and Samuel L. Macey, English Literary Studies, University of Victoria (Victoria, British Columbia, Canada), 1980. Columnist under pseudonym Samuel Marchbanks.

Davies's unpublished papers are collected in the National Archives of Canada.

PLAYS

Overlaid (also see below), produced in Peterborough, Ontario, Canada, 1947.

Eros at Breakfast (also see below), produced in Montreal, Quebec, Canada, 1948.

The Voice of the People (also see below), produced in Montreal, Quebec, Canada, 1948.

At the Gates of the Righteous (also see below), produced in Peterborough, Ontario, Canada, 1948.

Hope Deferred (also see below), produced in Montreal, Quebec, Canada, 1948.

Fortune, My Foe (first produced in Kingston, Ontario, Canada, 1948), Clarke, Irwin (Toronto, Ontario, Canada), 1949.

Eros at Breakfast and Other Plays (contains *Eros at Breakfast, Overlaid, The Voice of the People, At the Gates of the Righteous,* and *Hope Deferred*), with introduction by Tyrone Guthrie, Clarke, Irwin (Toronto, Ontario, Canada), 1949, revised edition published as *Four Favorite Plays,* 1968.

King Phoenix (also see below), produced in Peterborough, Ontario, Canada, 1950.

At My Heart's Core (first produced in Peterborough, Ontario, Canada, 1950), Clarke, Irwin (Toronto, Ontario, Canada), 1952.

A Masque of Aesop (first produced in Toronto, Ontario, Canada, May, 1952), Clarke, Irwin (Toronto, Ontario, Canada), 1952.

Hunting Stuart (also see below), produced in Toronto, Ontario, Canada, 1955.

A Jig for the Gypsy (first produced in Toronto, Ontario, Canada, 1954), Clarke, Irwin (Toronto, Ontario, Canada), 1955.

Love and Libel (based on Davies' novel *Leaven of Malice;* see below; first produced in Toronto, Ontario, Canada, November, 1960; first produced on Broadway at Martin Beck Theatre, December, 1960), Studio Duplicating Service, 1960.

A Masque of Mr. Punch (first produced in Toronto, Ontario, Canada, 1962), Oxford University Press (Oxford, England), 1963.

The Voice of the People, Book Society of Canada, 1968.

Hunting Stuart and Other Plays (contains *Hunting Stuart, King Phoenix,* and *General Confession*), New Press, 1972.

Brothers in the Black Art, first produced on Canadian Broadcasting Corporation, 1974.

Question Time (first produced in Toronto, Ontario, Canada, 1975), Macmillan (New York, NY), 1975.

Pontiac and the Green Man, first produced in Toronto, Ontario, Canada, 1977.

"Hunting Stuart" and "The Voice of the People": Two Plays, Simon & Pierre (Niagara Falls, NY), 1994.

(Author of libretto) *The Golden Ass* (opera), music by Randolph Peters, first produced in Toronto, Ontario, Canada, 1999.

FICTION

High Spirits (stories), Viking (New York, NY), 1983, reprinted, Penguin (New York, NY), 2002.

Murther and Walking Spirits (novel), Viking (New York, NY), 1991.

The Cunning Man (novel), McClelland & Stewart (Toronto, Ontario, Canada), 1994, Viking (New York, NY), 1995.

"SALTERTON TRILOGY"; NOVELS

Tempest-Tost, Clarke, Irwin (Toronto, Ontario, Canada), 1951, Rinehart (New York, NY), 1952, reprinted, Penguin (New York, NY), 1980.

Leaven of Malice, Clarke, Irwin (Toronto, Ontario, Canada), 1954, Scribners (New York, NY), 1955, reprinted, Penguin (New York, NY), 1980.

A Mixture of Frailties, Scribners (New York, NY), 1958, reprinted, Penguin (New York, NY), 1980.

The Salterton Trilogy (contains *Tempest-Tost, Leaven of Malice,* and *A Mixture of Frailties*), Penguin (New York, NY), 1986.

"DEPTFORD TRILOGY"; NOVELS

Fifth Business, Viking (New York, NY), 1970, reprinted, Penguin (New York, NY), 2001.

The Manticore, Viking (New York, NY), 1972.

World of Wonders, Macmillan (Toronto, Ontario, Canada), 1975, Viking (New York, NY), 1976.

The Deptford Trilogy (contains *Fifth Business, The Manticore,* and *World of Wonders*), Penguin (New York, NY), 1985.

"CORNISH TRILOGY"; NOVELS

The Rebel Angels, Viking (New York, NY), 1982.

What's Bred in the Bone, Viking (New York, NY), 1985.

The Lyre of Orpheus, Viking (New York, NY), 1988.

SIDELIGHTS: Robertson Davies was considered one of Canada's premier men of letters by virtue of his fiction, journalism, and essays on topics relating to literature and the theater. Davies trained for a career on the stage with London's prestigious Old Vic Company, but during World War II he returned to his native Canada and became internationally known for his novels of Canadian manners. *America* contributor Russell M. Brown wrote, "Learning how to move from constructing a character on the stage to creating one with words on the page, [Davies] exhibited the sharp eye for foible and pretension that later distinguished his fiction." In a *Maclean's* obituary for the author, Peter C. Newman concluded, "Robertson Davies was, if not a saint, certainly a genius, and most assuredly a sage and a visionary. It was to his credit and to our gain that he was also such a magnificent storyteller."

Davies was already well established on the Canadian literary scene when his *Deptford Trilogy,* consisting of the novels *Fifth Business, The Manticore,* and *World of Wonders,* brought him international attention. "These novels," Claude Bissell stated in *Canadian Literature,* "comprise the major piece of prose fiction in Canadian literature—in scope, in the constant interplay of wit and intelligence, in the persistent attempt to find a pattern in this [as Davies states in the trilogy] 'life of marvels, cruel circumstances, obscenities, and commonplaces.'" The trilogy traces the lives of three Canadian men from the small town of Deptford, Ontario, who are bound together by a single tragic event from their childhood. At the age of ten, Dunstan Ramsay and Percy "Boy" Staunton are throwing snowballs at one another. Staunton throws a snowball at Ramsay which contains a rock. Ramsay ducks. The snowball strikes Mrs. Mary Dempster in the head, causing her to give birth prematurely to a son, Paul Dempster, and to have a mental breakdown that ends in her permanent hospitalization. Each novel of the trilogy revolves around this tragedy and each deals primarily with one of the three men involved: *Fifth Business* with Dunstan Ramsay, who becomes a teacher; *The Manticore* with Boy Staunton, a politician; and *World of Wonders* with Paul Dempster, a stage magician. *Fifth Business* "provides the brickwork," John Alwyne observed in the *New Statesman,* "the two later volumes, the lath and plaster. But what a magnificent building is the result. [The trilogy] bears comparison with any fiction of the last decade."

Davies did not intend to write a trilogy when he first began *Fifth Business.* His initial story idea prompted him to write the novel, he once told an interviewer for Canada's *Time* magazine, "but he found almost as soon as he had finished that it wasn't all he wanted to say."

So Davies wrote *The Manticore* to tell more of his story. Reviewers then asked "to hear about the magician who appeared in the other two novels," Davies explained, "and I thought 'Well, I know a lot about magicians' and I wrote the third book.'"

Despite the unplanned development of the trilogy, it garnered extensive critical praise and each volume became an international bestseller. The first volume, *Fifth Business,* is, Sam Solecki maintained in *Canadian Forum,* "Davies' masterpiece and . . . among the handful of Canadian novels that count." In the form of an autobiographical letter written by Dunstan Ramsay upon his retirement, the novel delineates the course of Ramsay's life and how it was shaped by the pivotal snowball incident. Because he avoided being hit and thereby caused Mrs. Dempster's injury, Ramsay has lived his life suffering under a tremendous guilt. This guilt inspired an interest in hagiology, the study of saints, and Ramsay becomes in later years the foremost Protestant authority on the lives of the saints. "All the lore on saints and myth," Judith Skelton Grant stated in *Book Forum,* "is firmly connected to the central character, reflecting his interests, showing how he thinks, influencing his life, and playing a part in his interpretation of events." It is in terms of hagiology that Ramsay eventually comes to a realization about himself. His autobiographical letter finally "leads Ramsay to comprehension of his own nature—which is not saintly," John Skow reported in *Time.*

Much of this same story is reexamined in *The Manticore,* the second novel of the trilogy, which takes place after the mysterious death of prominent Canadian politician Boy Staunton. Staunton has been found drowned in his car at the bottom of Lake Ontario, a rock in his mouth. Investigation proves the rock to be the same one Staunton threw at Mrs. Dempster some sixty years before. Ramsay, obsessed with the incident, had saved it. But how Staunton died, and why he had the rock in his mouth, is unknown. During a performance by the magician Magnus Eisengrim—Paul Dempster's stage name—a floating brass head is featured that answers questions from the audience. Staunton's son David asks the head an explosive question, "Who killed Boy Staunton?" In the tumult caused by his outburst, David runs from the theater. His breakdown and subsequent Jungian psychoanalysis in Switzerland make up the rest of the novel. During his analysis, David comes to terms with his late father's career. "The blend of masterly characterization, cunning plot, shifting point of view, and uncommon detail, all fixed in the clearest, most literate prose, is superbly achieved," wrote Pat Barclay in *Canadian Literature.*

The life story of Paul Dempster is told in *World of Wonders,* the final volume of the trilogy. As a young boy, Dempster is kidnaped by a homosexual stage magician while visiting a traveling carnival. He stays with the carnival as it makes its way across Canada, intent on becoming a magician himself by learning the secrets of the man who abducted him. While learning the trade, Dempster works inside a mechanical fortune-telling gypsy, operating the gears that make it seem lifelike. When the carnival breaks up, he heads for Europe, where he finds work as a double for a popular stage actor. With his knowledge of magic and the stage manner he has acquired while working at the carnival, Dempster strikes out on his own as a magician, becoming one of the most successful acts on the continent. *World of Wonders,* Michael Mewshaw stated in the *New York Times Book Review,* is "a novel of stunning verbal energy and intelligence." L.J. Davis of *New Republic* believed the novel's "situation is shamelessly contrived, and the language fairly reeks of the footlights (to say nothing of, yes, brimstone)." Furthermore, Davis contended that *World of Wonders* "isn't so much a novel as it is a brilliant act whose strength lies in the complexity of its symbolism and the perfection of its artifice." It is, Davis judged, "a splendid conclusion" to the trilogy.

In each of these novels the lead character undergoes a psychological transformation. Dunstan Ramsay finds the key to himself in the study of saints and myth, using these archetypes for greater self-understanding. David Staunton relies on Jungian psychoanalysis to help him in discovering his true nature and in coming to terms with his father's disreputable life and mysterious death. Paul Dempster learns about reality and illusion from his work as a magician and his life in the theater, gaining insight into his own personality. The three novels are, Bissell explained, "essentially parts of a whole: three parallel pilgrimages." Grant, too, saw the essential search in which the three characters are engaged. She believed they explore different aspects of nature, however. "Dunstan moves toward God and Boy toward the Devil," Grant wrote, while Dempster "experiences both." The experience of both good and evil, Grant believed, allows those dark aspects of the mind to be exposed and confronted. "Not everything that has been labeled Evil proves to be so," Grant stated, "nor all that has been repressed ought to remain so. And the genuinely evil and justifiably banished are weaker if faced and understood." Grant felt that "together with the vigorous, lively and eccentric narrators of the [Deptford] trilogy, these moral . . . mythic and psychological ideas have given these books a place among the dozen significant works of fiction published in Canada during the seventies." Peter S. Prescott, writing in *News-*

week, saw the revelations of the three characters in similar terms. Davies, he contended, "means to recharge the world with a wonder it has lost, to re-create through the intervention of saints and miracles, psychoanalysts and sleight-of-hand a proper sense of awe at life's mystery and a recognition of the price that must be paid for initiation into that mystery."

Davies followed the *Deptford Trilogy* with another triptych, the *Cornish Trilogy.* "By the *Cornish Trilogy,* the Jungian matter has been absorbed into the novel's strategies allowing some experimentation with realism," observed a contributor to *Contemporary Novelists.* "*What's Bred in the Bone,* a revelation of the enigma of Francis Cornish, is narrated by Francis's psychic figures, his 'daimons.' *The Lyre of Orpheus* contains a commentary by the long-dead E.T.A. Hoffman, while the narrator of *Murther & Walking Spirits* is killed in the opening sentence to describe the novel from a vivid afterlife." The critic concluded: "These playful gestures of experimentation are part of the witty pleasures of Davies's novels but are harnessed to conservative ends." Russell M. Brown wrote: "For many, [the] 1970's novels remain the most appealing of all of Davies's fiction. But the Cornish trilogy of the 80's demonstrated the full range of Davies's wit and erudition and showed him attaining a new maturity. By marrying his previous concerns with myth and manners to large considerations of literary tradition, cultural conditions, art history, and opera, these later novels—*The Rebel Angels, What's Bred in the Bone,* and *The Lyre of Orpheus*—form a broad inquiry into the artist's relationship to the past."

Davies's 1994 novel, *The Cunning Man,* "is as substantial and as entertaining as any he has written," claimed Isabel Colegate in the *New York Times Book Review.* According to Paul Gray in *Time,* Davies "entertains with an old-fashioned fictional mixture that he seems to have invented anew: keen social observations delivered with wit, intelligence and free-floating philosophical curiosity." John Bemrose contended in *Maclean's* that "*The Cunning Man* takes the form of a memoir, but it reads more like an extended monologue by its narrator, Dr. Jonathan Hullah, a Toronto doctor nearing the end of his career." An aging physician who has assented to a series of interviews with a reporter writing a number of articles about "old Toronto," Hullah employs a notebook to separate his public reminiscences from his private reflections—those snippets of information and fact which he agrees to reveal in print, and those personal incidents in his own past which he prefers to keep to himself. As the notebook containing his personal thoughts and musings grows, he realizes he is actually recording and defining his own character analysis, cre-

ating a true lifetime retrospective. Although as a physician Hullah relies on scientific observation and qualitative inquiry, he combines his diagnostic approach with consideration of other factors, including psychological and spiritual elements. In an interview with Mel Gussow in the *New York Times Book Review,* the reviewer noted, "Davies has said he is 'a moralist possessed by humor,' a description that would serve equally for Dr. Hullah, who, he says, 'is a moralist not because he dictates morals but because he observes what's wrong with his patients.' For both the author and the character, physical and emotional causes of disease are inseparable." As Stephen Smith described it in *Quill and Quire,* Hullah "makes his narration a guide through a landscape full of recognizable Davies landmarks. There is a suspicious death on a church altar, a miracle, a murder, a disappointment in love, and sundry asides into . . . the past of that most 'flat-footed, hard-breathing' of Canadian cities, Toronto, as seen from its upper crust." Colegate further commented that the novel "enlarges joyously on many of [the author's] familiar themes; the one that underlies all the others is his belief that religion and science, poetry and medicine, theater and psychoanalysis have a kind of meeting place where no one is quite sufficient without the others."

The recurring theme of self-discovery follows the pattern established by psychologist Carl Jung, although Davies did not adhere strictly to Jungian psychology. He explored a number of models for "complete human identity," Patricia Monk claimed in her *The Smaller Infinity: The Jungian Self in the Novels of Robertson Davies.* Monk felt that though he had a "deep and long-lasting affinity with Jung . . . Davies eventually moves beyond his affinity . . . to a more impartial assessment of Jungianism as simply one way of looking at the universe, one myth among a number of others." Still, Roger Sale suggested in the *New York Review of Books* that, in common with the Jungian belief in archetypal influence on the human mind, Davies presents in his fiction characters who "discover the meaning of their lives, by discovering the ways those lives conform to ancient patterns." Peter Baltensperger, writing in *Canadian Literature,* saw this as a consistent theme in all of Davies's fiction. This theme Baltensperger defined as "the conquest of one's Self in the inner struggle and the knowledge of oneself as fully human."

Davies clarified the primary concern in all of his work in a short piece he wrote for *Contemporary Novelists.* "The theme which lies at the root of all my novels is the isolation of the human spirit," he explained. "I have not attempted to deal with it in a gloomy fashion but rather to demonstrate that what my characters do that might be called really significant is done on their own volition and usually contrary to what is expected of them. This theme is worked out in terms of characters who are trying to escape from early influences and find their own place in the world but who are reluctant to do so in a way that will bring pain and disappointment to others."

Many critics have labeled Davies a traditionalist who was a bit old-fashioned in his approach to writing. I.M. Owen, writing in *Saturday Night,* for example, placed Davies "curiously apart from the main stream of contemporary fiction." A critic for the *Washington Post Book World* characterized Davies as "a true novelist writing imagined stories, wonderful stories full of magic and incandescence, thought and literary art," something the critic did not find in other contemporary fiction. Davies was known as a moralist who believed in a tangible good and evil, a fine storyteller who consciously used theatrical melodrama to enliven his plots, and a master of a wide variety of genres and styles. In the *New York Times Book Review,* Peter Marks characterized the author as "a keen observer, defender and interpreter of all things Canadian, and to say that his status in that vast, sparsely populated nation was a kind of free-thinking Shavian figure is to reflect on both the breadth and vitality of his intellect and, perhaps, the all-too-limited boundaries of his influence, at least insofar as affairs of the day were concerned."

Calling Davies "a compellingly inventive storyteller" who garnered an "affectionate following," James Idema noted in the *Chicago Tribune Book World* that the continued appeal of Davies's fiction lies in "his way of placing ordinary humans in the midst of extraordinary events, of bringing innocent, resolutely straight characters into contact with bonafide exotics." Collections of Davies's essays have continued to appear posthumously, many of them edited by his wife and daughter. *The Merry Heart: Reflections on Reading and Writing and the World of Books* contains literary pieces, and *Happy Alchemy: On the Pleasures of Music and Theatre* presents his views on various theatrical productions and important figures in the English-speaking theater. A *Publishers Weekly* reviewer found *The Merry Heart* "remarkable for its continued freshness and invention," concluding that the work "has real wisdom from a witty, deeply humane man." Peter Marks declared that *Happy Alchemy* "in thoroughly entertaining fashion acquaints us with Davies's expansive erudition and gift for rendering literary and historical complexities in simple, human terms." In the *New York Times Book Review,* Diane Cole praised *Happy Alchemy* for "the ease with which Davies routinely transformed his sometimes erudite passions into delightful entertainments."

Davies was not always a politically correct writer, as he himself acknowledged, but "In his probing for the spiritual and his desire to be a decent man," noted Michael Peterman in his *Robertson Davies,* "he insisted on finding new means of expression appropriate to his growth, experience, and maturity." Critics in his homeland and abroad view Davies's work as a major addition to the Canadian literary canon seems assured. The author once commented on his particular affinity for Canada in a piece for *Maclean's.* "A lot of people complain that my novels aren't about Canada," he said. "I think they are, because I see Canada as a country torn between a very northern, rather extraordinary, mystical spirit which it fears, and its desire to present itself to the world as a Scotch banker. This makes for tension, and tension is the very stuff of art, plays, novels, the whole lot."

BIOGRAPHICAL AND CRITICAL SOURCES:

BOOKS

Anthony, Geraldine, editor, *Stage Voices: Twelve Canadian Playwrights Talk about Their Lives and Work,* Doubleday (Garden City, NY), 1978.
Bestsellers '89, issue 2, Thomson Gale (Detroit, MI), 1989.
Buitenhuis, Elspeth, *Robertson Davies,* Forum House Publishing (Toronto, Ontario, Canada), 1972.
Cameron, Donald, *Conversations with Canadian Novelists, Part 1,* Macmillan (Toronto, Ontario, Canada), 1973.
Contemporary Dramatists, 4th edition, St. James (Chicago, IL), 1988.
Contemporary Literary Criticism, Thomson Gale (Detroit, MI), Volume 2, 1974, Volume 7, 1977, Volume 13, 1980, Volume 25, 1983, Volume 42, 1987, Volume 75, 1993.
Contemporary Novelists, 5th edition, St. James (Detroit, MI), 1991.
Davis, J. Madison, editor, *Conversations with Robertson Davies,* University Press of Mississippi (Jackson, MS), 1989.
Diamond-Nigh, Lynne, *Robertson Davies: Life, Work, and Criticism,* York Press, 1997.
Dictionary of Literary Biography, Volume 68: *Canadian Writers, 1920-1959, First Series,* Thomson Gale (Detroit, MI), 1988.
Dooley, D. J., *Moral Vision in the Canadian Novel,* Irwin, 1978.
Grant, Judith Skelton, *Robertson Davies,* McClelland & Stewart (Toronto, Ontario, Canada), 1978.

Grant, Judith Skelton, *Robertson Davies: Man of Myth,* Penguin (Toronto, Ontario, Canada), 1994.

Heath, Jeffrey M., editor, *Profiles in Canadian Literature No. 2,* Dundum Press, 1980.

Jones, Joseph, and Johanna Jones, *Canadian Fiction,* Twayne (Boston, MA), 1981.

King, Bruce, *The New English Literatures: Cultural Nationalism in a Changing World,* St. Martin's Press (New York, NY), 1980.

Kirkwood, Hilda, *Between the Lines,* Oberon Press (Ottawa, Ontario, Canada), 1994.

Klinck, Carl F., editor, *Literary History of Canada,* University of Toronto Press (Toronto, Ontario, Canada), 2nd edition, 1976.

Lawrence, Robert G., and Samuel L. Macey, editors, *Studies in Robertson Davies' Deptford Trilogy,* English Literary Studies, University of Victoria (Victoria, British Columbia, Canada), 1980.

Lecker, David, and Ellen Luigley, editors, *Canadian Writers and Their Works,* Volume 6, ECW Press (Toronto, Ontario, Canada), 1985.

Lecker, Robert, and Jack David, editors, *The Annotated Bibliography of Canada's Major Authors,* Volume 3, ECW Press (Toronto, Ontario, Canada), 1982.

Little, Dave, *Catching the Wind in a Net: The Religious Vision of Robertson Davies,* ECW)Press (Toronto, Ontario, Canada), 1996.

Monk, Patricia, *The Smaller Infinity: The Jungian Self in the Novels of Robertson Davies,* University of Toronto Press (Toronto, Ontario, Canada), 1982.

Moore, Mavor, *Four Canadian Playwrights,* Holt (New York, NY), 1973.

Morley, Patricia, *Robertson Davies,* Gage Educational Publishing (Agincourt, Ontario, Canada), 1977.

Moss, John, *Sex and Violence in the Canadian Novel: The Ancestral Present,* McClelland & Stewart (Toronto, Ontario, Canada), 1977.

Moss, John, editor, *Heart and Now 1,* NC Press (Toronto, Ontario, Canada), 1979.

New, William H., editor, *Dramatists in Canada: Selected Essays,* University of British Columbia Press, 1972.

Peterman, Michael, *Robertson Davies,* Twayne (Boston, MA), 1986.

Stone-Blackburn, Susan, *Robertson Davies: Playwright,* University of British Columbia Press, 1985.

Stouck, David, *Major Canadian Authors: A Critical Introduction,* University of Nebraska Press (Omaha, NE), 1984.

Sutherland, Ronald, *The New Hero: Essays in Comparative Quebec/Canadian Literature,* Macmillan (Toronto, Ontario, Canada), 1977.

Twigg, Alan, *For Openers: Conversations with Twenty-four Canadian Writers,* Harbour Publishing (Madiera Park, British Columbia, Canada), 1981.

Wyatt, David, *Prodigal Sons: A Study in Authorship and Authority,* Johns Hopkins University Press (Baltimore, MD), 1980.

PERIODICALS

Acta Victoriana, Volume 97, number 2, 1973.

America, December 16, 1972.

American Spectator, May, 1989.

Ariel, July, 1979.

Atlantic, June, 1993.

Bloomsbury Review, May-June, 1996.

Book Forum, Volume 4, number 1, 1978.

Booklist, July, 1997, Donna Seaman, review of *The Merry Heart,* p. 1791; July, 1998, Jack Helbig, review of *Happy Alchemy,* p. 1849; January 1, 2000, Gilbert Taylor, review of *For Your Eye Alone: The Letters of Robertson Davies,* p. 900.

Books in Canada, November, 1985; August, 1988; February, 1996, p. 2.

Book World, December 13, 1970.

Canadian Drama, Volume 7, number 2, 1981 (special Davies issue).

Canadian Forum, June, 1950; December, 1975; October, 1977; December-January, 1981-82; February-March, 1989; November, 1991.

Canadian Literature, spring, 1960; winter, 1961; winter, 1967; spring, 1973; winter, 1974; winter, 1976; spring, 1982; winter, 1986.

Canadian Review, fall, 1976.

Chicago Tribune, July 26, 1986.

Chicago Tribune Book World, January 31, 1982.

Christian Century, February 1, 1989; January 29, 1992.

Christian Science Monitor, July 14, 1986.

Commonweal, December 20, 1985.

Dalhousie Review, autumn, 1981; fall, 1986.

Design for Arts in Education, May-June, 1989.

Detroit Free Press, January 22, 1989; February 6, 1989.

Economist, June 30, 1990.

English Studies in Canada, March, 1986; March, 1990.

Essays on Canadian Writing, spring, 1977; winter 1977-1978; winter, 1984-1985; spring, 1987; fall, 1989.

Financial Post, January 19, 1963.

Globe & Mail (Toronto), March 5, 1977; January 7, 1984; September 10, 1988; September 17, 1988.

Insight on the News, September 17, 1990.

Interview, March, 1989.

Journal of Canadian Fiction, winter, 1972; Volume 3, number 3, 1974; winter, 1982.

Journal of Canadian Studies, November, 1974; February, 1977 (special Davies issue).

Journal of Commonwealth Literature, Volume 22, number 1, 1987.

Library Journal, January, 1989; January, 1990; October 1, 1991; April 1, 1992; June 15, 1997, Caroline A. Mitchell, review of *The Merry Heart: Reflections on Reading and Writing and the World of Books,* p. 68; July, 1998, Eric Bryant, review of *Happy Alchemy,* p. 92; January 1, 2001, Morris Hounion, review of *For Your Eye Alone,* p. 106.

Library Quarterly, April, 1969.

Listener, April 15, 1971.

London Review of Books, November 10. 1988.

Los Angeles Times, January 29, 1982.

Los Angeles Times Book Review, December 1, 1985; January 29, 1989; January 30, 1989.

Maclean's, March 15, 1952; September, 1972; November 18, 1985; October 19, 1987; September 12, 1988; December 26, 1988; September 23, 1991; October 24, 1994, p. 54; April 26, 1999, John Bemrose, "Famous Last Words: Robertson Davies' Final Work Is a Triumph," p. 60.

Nation, April 24, 1982; October 24, 1994, p. 54.

New Republic, March 13, 1976; April 15, 1978; March 10, 1982; December 30, 1985; April, 24 1989.

New Statesman, April 20, 1973; April 4, 1980; October 14, 1988; November 22, 1991.

Newsweek, January 18, 1971; March 22, 1976; February 8, 1982.

New Yorker, January 27, 1986; February 10, 1992.

New York Review of Books, February 8, 1973; February 27, 1986; April 13, 1989.

New York Times, February 8, 1982; November 6, 1985; December 28, 1988; December 29, 1988; August 7, 1998, Peter Marks, "At the Theater with a Compulsive Companion," p. E40.

New York Times Book Review, December 20, 1970; November 19, 1972; April 25, 1976; February 14, 1982; December 15, 1985; October 30, 1988; January 8, 1989; November 17, 1991; December 1, 1991; February 5, 1995, Isabel Colgate, "Mind, Body and Dr. Hullah," pp. 1, 23, 24; July 26, 1998, Diane Cole, review of *Happy Alchemy: On the Pleasures of Music and Theatre;* March 4, 2001, Diane Cole, review of *For Your Eye Alone.*

Observer (London, England), May 31, 1987; October 2, 1988.

Performing Arts & Entertainment, summer, 1992.

Publishers Weekly, October 14, 1988; February 2, 1990; September 6, 1991; January 25, 1993; May 19, 1997, review of *The Merry Heart: Reflections on Reading and Writing and the World of Books,* p. 56.

Queen's Quarterly, spring, 1986.

Quill & Quire, August, 1988; September, 1994, pp. 1, 59, 62, 64.

Rolling Stone, December 1, 1977.

San Francisco Review of Books, spring, 1987.

Saturday Night, April 26, 1947; December 13, 1947; February 14, 1953; November, 1967; October, 1985; December, 1987; August, 1988; October, 1988; November, 1990; October, 1991; October, 1994, p. 58.

Saturday Review, December 26, 1970; April 3, 1976.

Spectator, August 21, 1982; October 8, 1988.

Studies in Canadian Literature, winter, 1978; Volume 7, number 2, 1982; Volume 12, number 1, 1987.

Sunday Times, September 1991.

Tamarack Review, autumn, 1958.

Time, January 11, 1971; May 17, 1976; December 26, 1988; March 13, 1995, pp. 100-101.

Time (Canada), November 3, 1975.

Times Literary Supplement, March 26, 1982; February 28, 1986; October 16, 1987; September 23, 1988.

Tribune Books (Chicago, IL), December 25, 1988.

University of Toronto Quarterly, number 21, 1952.

U.S. News & World Report, January 16, 1989.

Wall Street Journal, July 15, 1986.

Washington Post, January 11, 1989.

Washington Post Book World, May 30, 1976; February 7, 1982; October 30, 1983; November 17, 1985; July 20, 1986; June 5, 1988; December 18, 1988.

World Literature Today, autumn, 1995, Robert Ross, review of *The Cunning Man,* p. 793.

World Press Review, November, 1988.

OBITUARIES:

PERIODICALS

America, February 3, 1996, Russell M. Brown, "Robertson Davies (1913-95): In Memoriam," p. 19.

Maclean's, December 18, 1995, Peter C. Newman, "A Fond Farewell to 'Rob' Davies," p. 40.

New York Times, December 4, 1995.

Time, December 18, 1995, p. 25.

Washington Post, December 5, 1995, Charles Trueheart, "A Passion That Melted Snow: Canadian Writer Robertson Davies," p. D1.

*   *   *

DAVIES, William Robertson
See DAVIES, Robertson

*   *   *

DAVIS, B. Lynch
See BORGES, Jorge Luis

DEPAOLA, Thomas Anthony
   See DEPAOLA, Tomie

* * *

DE BEAUVOIR, Simone (Lucie Ernestine Marie Bertrand)
   See BEAUVOIR, Simone de

* * *

DEIGHTON, Len 1929-
   (Leonard Cyril Deighton)

PERSONAL: Born February 18, 1929, in Marylebone, London, England; married Shirley Thompson (an illustrator), 1960. *Education:* Attended St. Martin's School of Art, London, three years; Royal College of Art, graduate.

ADDRESSES: Office—25 Newman St., London W.1, England.

CAREER: Author. Worked as a railway lengthman, an assistant pastry cook at the Royal Festival Hall, 1951, a manager of a gown factory in Aldgate, England, a waiter in Piccadilly, an advertising man in London and New York City, a teacher in Brittany, a co-proprietor of a glossy magazine, and as a magazine artist and news photographer; steward, British Overseas Airways Corporation (BOAC), 1956-57; producer of films, including *Only When I Larf,* based on his novel of the same title, 1969.

WRITINGS:

Only When I Larf (novel), M. Joseph (London, England), 1968, published as *Only When I Laugh,* Mysterious Press (New York, NY), 1987.
Oh, What a Lovely War! (screenplay), Paramount, 1969.
Bomber: Events Relating to the Last Flight of an R.A.F. Bomber Over Germany on the Night of June 31, 1943 (novel), Harper (New York, NY), 1970.
Declarations of War (story collection), J. Cape (London, England), 1971, published as *Eleven Declarations of War,* Harcourt (New York, NY), 1975, reprinted, Thorndike Press (Thorndike, ME), 1992.
Close-Up (novel), Atheneum (New York, NY), 1972.
SS-GB: Nazi-Occupied Britain, 1941 (novel), J. Cape (London, England), 1978, Knopf (New York, NY), 1979.

Goodbye, Mickey Mouse (novel; Book-of-the-Month Club selection), Knopf (New York, NY), 1982.
Winter: A Novel of a Berlin Family (Book-of-the-Month Club alternate selection), Knopf (New York, NY), 1988.

Also author of television scripts *Long Past Glory,* 1963, and *It Must Have Been Two Other Fellows,* 1977. Also author of weekly comic strip on cooking, *Observer,* 1962—.

ESPIONAGE NOVELS

The Ipcress File, Fawcett (New York, NY), 1962, reprinted, Ballantine (New York, NY), 1982.
Horse Under Water (Literary Guild selection), J. Cape (London, England), 1963, Putnam (New York, NY), 1967.
Funeral in Berlin, J. Cape (London, England), 1964, Putnam (New York, NY), 1965.
The Billion Dollar Brain, Putnam (New York, NY), 1966.
An Expensive Place to Die, Putnam (New York, NY), 1967.
Spy Story, Harcourt (New York, NY), 1974.
Yesterday's Spy, Harcourt (New York, NY), 1975.
Twinkle, Twinkle, Little Spy, J. Cape (London, England), 1976, published as *Catch a Falling Spy,* Harcourt (New York, NY), 1976, reprinted, Compass Press, 2002.
XPD, Knopf (New York, NY), 1981.
Berlin Game, Knopf (New York, NY), 1983.
Mexico Set, Knopf (New York, NY), 1985.
London Match, Knopf (New York, NY), 1985.
Spy Hook, Knopf (New York, NY), 1988.
Spy Line, Knopf (New York, NY), 1989.
Spy Sinker, HarperCollins (New York, NY), 1990.
MAMista, HarperCollins (New York, NY), 1991.
City of Gold, HarperCollins (New York, NY), 1992.
Violent Ward, HarperCollins (New York, NY), 1993.
Faith, HarperCollins (New York, NY), 1995.
Hope, HarperCollins (New York, NY), 1995.
Charity, HarperCollins (New York, NY), 1996.

NONFICTION

(Editor) *Drinks-man-ship: Town's Album of Fine Wines and High Spirits,* Haymarket Press, 1964.
Ou est le garlic; or, Len Deighton's French Cookbook, Penguin, 1965, revised edition published as *Basic French Cooking,* J. Cape (London, England), 1979.

Action Cookbook: Len Deighton's Guide to Eating, J. Cape (London, England), 1965.

Len Deighton's Cookstrip Cook Book, Bernard Geis Associates, 1966.

(Editor with Michael Rand and Howard Loxton) *The Assassination of President Kennedy,* J. Cape (London, England), 1967.

(Editor and contributor) *Len Deighton's London Dossier,* J. Cape (London, England), 1967.

Len Deighton's Continental Dossier: A Collection of Cultural, Culinary, Historical, Spooky, Grim and Preposterous Fact, compiled by Victor and Margaret Pettitt, M. Joseph (London, England), 1968.

Fighter: The True Story of the Battle of Britain, J. Cape (London, England), 1977, Knopf (New York, NY), 1978.

(With Peter Mayle) *How to Be a Pregnant Father,* Lyle Stuart, 1977.

(With Arnold Schwartzman) *Airshipwreck,* J. Cape (London, England), 1978, Holt (New York, NY), 1979.

(With Simon Goodenough) *Tactical Genius in Battle,* Phaidon Press, 1979.

Blitzkrieg: From the Rise of Hitler to the Fall of Dunkirk, Coward (New York, NY), 1980.

Battle of Britain, Coward (New York, NY), 1980.

ABC of French Food, Bantam (New York, NY), 1990.

Blood, Tears, and Folly: An Objective Look at World War II, HarperCollins (New York, NY), 1993.

ADAPTATIONS: The Ipcress File was filmed by Universal in 1965, *Funeral in Berlin* by Paramount in 1966, *The Billion Dollar Brain* by United Artists in 1967, and *Only When I Larf* by Paramount in 1969; *Spy Story* was filmed in 1976; film rights to *An Expensive Place to Die* have been sold. Deighton's nameless British spy hero was given the name Harry Palmer in the film adaptations of his adventures. Several of the author's books have been adapted as audio recordings, including *The Ipcress File, Yesterday's Spy,* and *The True Story of the Battle of Britain.*

SIDELIGHTS: With his early novels, especially *The Ipcress File* and *Funeral in Berlin,* Len Deighton established himself as one of the mainstays of modern espionage fiction. He is often ranked—along with Graham Greene, John le Carre, and Ian Fleming—among the foremost writers in the field. Deighton shows a painstaking attention to accuracy in depicting espionage activities, and in his early novels this realism was combined with a light ironic touch that set his work apart. Deighton, David Quammen remarked in the *New York Times Book Review,* is "a talented, droll and original spy novelist."

Deighton's early novels are written in an elliptical style that emphasizes the mysterious nature of the espionage activities portrayed. They feature a nameless British intelligence officer who is quite different from the usual fictional spy. This officer is a reluctant spy, cynical, and full of wisecracks. Unlike many other British agents, he is also, Julian Symons stated in *Mortal Consequences: A History—From the Detective Story to the Crime Novel,* "a working-class boy from Brunley, opposed to all authority, who dislikes or distrusts anybody outside his own class. He is set down in a world of terrifying complexity, in which nobody is ever what he seems." T.J. Binyon wrote in the *Times Literary Supplement,* "The creation of this slightly anarchic, wise-cracking, working-class hero was Deighton's most original contribution to the spy thriller. And this, taken together with his characteristic highly elliptical expositional manner, with his fascination with the technical nuts and bolts of espionage, and with a gift for vivid, startling description, make the first seven [of Deighton's spy] stories classics of the genre." Peter S. Prescott of *Newsweek,* speaking of the early novels featuring Deighton's nameless hero, found that the style, marked by "oblique narration, nervous laughter and ironic detachment, . . . effectively transformed [Deighton's] spy stories into comedies of manners."

Deighton's elliptical style in these early books is clipped and episodic, deliberately omitting vital explanations of what his characters are discussing or thinking. This style, Robin W. Winks wrote in the *New Republic,* makes Deighton's "plots seem more complex than they are. . . . Because very little is stated explicitly, sequences appear to begin in mid-passage, and only through observation of the action does one come to understand either the motives of the villains, or the thought processes of the heroes." In these novels, Winks concludes, "Deighton had patented a style in which every third paragraph appeared to have been left out." Although this style confuses some readers—Prescott claims that Deighton's "specialty has always been a nearly incoherent plot." Writing in *New Leader,* Pearl K. Bell stated that Deighton's "obsessive reliance on the blurred and intangible, on loaded pauses and mysteriously disjointed dialogue, did convey the shadowy meanness of the spy's world, with its elusive loyalties, camouflaged identities and weary brutality."

Deighton was an immediate success with his first novel, *The Ipcress File,* a book that the late Anthony Boucher of the *New York Times Book Review* admitted "caused quite a stir among both critics and customers in England." Introducing Deighton's nameless protagonist in an adventure that takes him to a nuclear testing site on a Pacific atoll, to the Middle East, and behind the Iron Curtain, the book continues to be popular for its combination of a serious espionage plot with a parody of the genre. As Richard Locke observed in the *New York Times Book Review, The Ipcress File* possesses "a Kennedy-cool amorality . . . a cross of Hammett and cold war lingo."

Critics praised the book's gritty evocation of intelligence work, ironic narrative, and comic touches. Boucher called it "a sharply written, ironic and realistic tale of modern spy activities." Deighton's humor attracts the most attention from John B. Cullen of *Best Sellers,* who claimed that in *The Ipcress File* "Deighton writes with a tongue-in-cheek attitude. . . . No one is spared the needle of subtle ridicule, but the author still tells a plausible story which holds your attention throughout." However, for Robert Donald Spectar of the *New York Herald Tribune Book Review* Deighton's humor ruins the espionage story. "Deighton," Spectar wrote, "has combined picaresque satire, parody, and suspense and produced a hybrid more humorous than thrilling." But G.W. Stonier in the *New Statesman* compared Deighton with James Bond creator Ian Fleming. Stonier found Deighton to be "a good deal more expert and twice the writer" and believes "there has been no brighter arrival on the shady scene since Graham Greene." Even in 1979, some seventeen years after the book's initial publication, Julian Symons of the *New York Times Book Review* was moved to call *The Ipcress File* "a dazzling performance. The verve and energy, the rattle of wit in the dialogue, the side-of-the-mouth comments, the evident pleasure taken in cocking a snook at the British spy story's upper-middle-class tradition—all these, together with the teasing convolutions of the plot, made it clear that a writer of remarkable talent in this field had appeared."

Deighton's reputation as an espionage writer was enhanced by *Funeral in Berlin,* a story revolving around an attempt to smuggle a defecting East German biologist out of Berlin. With the assistance of a high-ranking Russian agent, former Nazi intelligence officers, and a freelance operator of doubtful allegiance, Deighton's unnamed hero arranges the details of the defection. The many plot twists, and Deighton's enigmatic presentation of his story, prompted Stephen Hugh-Jones of *New Statesman* to admit, "I spent most of the book wondering what the devil was going on." Boucher found the mysterious goings-on to be handled well. "The double and triple crosses involved," Boucher wrote, "are beautifully worked out." Published at the same time as John le Carré's classic espionage tale *The Spy Who Came in From the Cold,* a novel also set in Germany's divided

city, *Funeral in Berlin* compares favorably with its competitor. Boucher called its plot "very nearly as complex and nicely calculated," while Charles Poore of the *New York Times* maintained it is "even better" than le Carré's book. It is, Poore concluded, "a ferociously cool fable of the current struggle between East and West." Andy East of *Armchair Detective* claimed that *Funeral in Berlin* "has endured as Deighton's most celebrated novel."

Since these early novels, Deighton's style has evolved, becoming more expansive and less oblique. His "approach has grown more sophisticated," Mark Schorr related in the *Los Angeles Times Book Review.* "His more recent writings offer a deft balance of fact, scene-setting and the who-can-we-trust paranoia that makes spy novels engrossing." Peter Elstob of *Books and Bookmen* noted that Deighton "develops with each new book."

Of Deighton's later espionage novels, perhaps his most important work has been the trilogy comprised of *Berlin Game, Mexico Set,* and *London Match.* Here, Deighton spins a long story of moles (agents working within an enemy intelligence organization), defection, and betrayal that also comments on his own writing career, the espionage genre, and the cold war between East and West that has inspired such fiction. Derrick Murdoch of the Toronto *Globe and Mail* called the trilogy "Deighton's most ambitious project; the conventional spy-story turned inside-out."

The first novel of the trilogy, *Berlin Game,* opens with two agents waiting near the Berlin Wall for a defector to cross over from East Berlin. "How long have we been sitting here?" asks Bernie Samson, British agent and the protagonist of the trilogy. "Nearly a quarter of a century," his companion replies. With that exchange Deighton underlines the familiarity of this scene in espionage fiction, in his own early work and in the work of others, while commenting on the continuing relevance of the Berlin Wall as a symbol of East-West conflict, noted Anthony Olcott in the *Washington Post Book World.* Deighton, Olcott argued, "is not only aware of this familiarity, it is his subject. . . . Berlin and the Wall remain as much the embodiment of East-West rivalry as ever. . . . To read *Berlin Game* is to shrug off 25 years of acclimatization to the Cold War, and to recall what espionage fiction is about in the first place."

In *Berlin Game,* Samson works to uncover a Soviet agent secretly working at the highest levels of British intelligence. This, too, is a standard plot in spy fiction, inspired by the real-life case of Soviet spy Kim Philby. But, as the *New Yorker* critic pointed out, "Deighton, as always, makes the familiar twists and turns of spy errantry new again, partly by his grip of narrative, partly by his grasp of character, and partly by his easy, sardonic tone." Prescott claimed that the novel does not display the wit of Deighton's earlier works, but the book overcomes its faults because of Deighton's overall skill as a storyteller. "Each scene in this story," Prescott wrote, "is so adroitly realized that it creates its own suspense. Samson, the people who work for him, his wife, even the twits who have some reason to be working for Moscow, are interesting characters; what they say to each other is convincing. Besides, the book is full of Berlin lore: we can easily believe that Samson did grow up there and thinks of it as home."

Mexico Set continues the story begun in *Berlin Game.* In the first book, Samson uncovers the spy in British intelligence—his own wife—and she defects to East Germany. To redeem himself in the eyes of his superiors, who now harbor understandable doubts about his own loyalty, Samson works in *Mexico Set* to convince a Russian KGB agent to defect. But the agent may only be a plant meant to further discredit Samson and destroy his credibility. If Samson cannot convince him to defect, his superiors may assume that he is secretly working for the Russians himself. But the Russian may defect only to provide British intelligence with "proof" of Samson's treason. As in *Berlin Game,* Deighton relates this novel back to the origins of the cold war and, "just when you've forgotten what the Cold War was all about, Len Deighton takes you right back to the [Berlin] Wall and rubs your nose on it," Chuck Moss wrote in the *Detroit News.*

Samson's efforts to persuade the Russian agent to defect take him from London to Mexico, Paris, and Berlin. "Every mile along the way," Noel Behn wrote in the *Chicago Tribune,* "objectives seem to alter, friends and enemies become indistinguishable, perils increase, people disappear, people die." Behn found that it is Deighton's characters that make the story believable: "They strut forward one after the other—amusing, beguiling, arousing, deceiving, threatening—making us look in the wrong direction when it most behooves the prestidigitator's purpose." Writing in the *Washington Post Book World,* Ross Thomas reported that Deighton "serves up fascinating glimpses of such types as the nearly senile head of British intelligence; a KGB major with a passion for Sherlock Holmes; and Samson's boyhood friend and Jewish orphan, Werner Volkmann," all of whom Thomas found to be "convincing characters." Thomas concluded that *Mexico Set* is "one of [Deighton's] better efforts."

In the final novel of the trilogy, *London Match,* the Russian agent has defected to the British. But Samson must now decide whether the defector is telling the truth when he insists that a high-ranking member of British intelligence is a Russian mole. The situation grows more complicated when the suspected mole, one of Samson's superiors, comes to Samson for help in clearing his name. *London Match* "is the most complex novel of the trilogy," Julius Lester wrote in the *New York Times Book Review.* But Lester found *London Match*'s complexity to be a liability. He thought "the feeling it conveys of being trapped in a maze of distorting mirrors is almost a cliche in spy novels now." Similarly, Gene Lyons of *Newsweek* called *London Match* "not the most original spy story ever told." In his review of the book for the *Washington Post Book World,* J.I.M. Stewart criticized Deighton's characterization. He stated that "the characters, although liable to bore a little during their frequently over-extended verbal fencings, are tenaciously true to themselves even if not quite to human nature." But even critics with reservations about some of the novel's qualities find aspects of the book to praise. Stewart lauded Deighton's ability to recreate the settings of his story. "The places, whether urban or rural, can be described only as triumphs alike of painstaking observation and striking descriptive power," Stewart wrote. Lester found this strength, too, calling "the best character" in the book "the city of Berlin. It is a living presence, and in some of the descriptions one can almost hear the stones breathing."

Deighton continues Samson's adventures in the 1988 *Spy Hook,* the first story in a second trilogy about the British intelligence agent. In this thriller, Samson is charged with accounting for the disappearance of millions in Secret Service funds. At first, he suspects his ex-wife—who defected in the earlier *Berlin Game*—as the thief, but later Samson learns that his superiors have begun to suspect him for the crime. *Spy Hook* was chosen as a Book-of-the-Month Club selection and became a best seller. Critical reception of the work was generally favorable, with reviewers praising the book's carefully developed and intricate plot, detailed settings, and suspenseful atmosphere. A number of reviewers, however, reacted negatively to the book's ending, which they felt was too ambiguous. "Deighton's craftsmanship—his taut action and his insightful study of complex characters under pressure—is very much in place here, but many. . . unanswered questions raised in *Spy Hook* remain just that at the novel's conclusion," stated Don G. Campbell, for example, in the *Los Angeles Times Book Review.* Several critics, though, shared Margaret Cannon's Toronto *Globe and Mail* assessment of *Spy Hook* as matching Deighton's previous achievements in the espionage genre. The novel, she wrote, "promises to be even better than its terrific predecessors and proves that Deighton, the old spymaster, is still in top form."

Deighton followed *Spy Hook* with the trilogy's second installment, *Spy Line,* in 1989 and the concluding book, *Spy Sinker,* in 1990. *Spy Sinker* focuses on the clandestine efforts of Samson's wife to effect the fall of the Berlin Wall from inside East Germany. As it turns out, Samson's wife was working as a double agent all along. Her earlier defection and callous abandonment of her husband was ordered by British Intelligence as part of a long-term strategic plan to subvert East German internal order. "Here *Spy Sinker* shows Deighton at the top of his form, in his concentration upon the one player in this series whose story is not yet told," wrote Anthony Olcott in *Washington Post Book World.* Olcott added, "Deighton is able now to close in *Spy Sinker* by exploring what betrayal costs the betrayer, a woman who for higher loyalties leaves husband, home, and country, to incur even more betrayals in a cycle which may, in the end, destroy her."

According to Albert Hunt in *New Statesmen & Society,* "Everything slots together beautifully—Len Deighton has done as professional a job as Bernard Samson ever did." A *Time* reviewer similarly praised *Spy Sinker,* noting that Deighton accomplishes the near impossible— "winding up a closely plotted six-volume thriller . . . and still writing a credible novel. He makes a good job of it with a clever change of focus." However, *New York Times Book Review* contributor Morton Kondracke noted, "As a stand-alone spy novel, this book is implausible, often incomprehensible and, altogether, downright dull."

Deighton initiated another Samson trilogy with *Faith* and *Hope* in 1995. Set in Berlin in 1987, *Faith* involves Samson's participation in the defection of a Communist spy and relates complicated domestic circumstances surrounding the return of his wife after their long separation. "What raises Deighton's genre to art," according to Andy Solomon in *Washington Post Book World,* "is not only his absorbing characters but his metaphoric grace . . . droll wit . . . command of technical detail. . . and sure sense of place." Despite such praise, *New York Times Book Review* contributor Newgate Callendar described *Faith* as "dull and turgid." Likewise *Kirkus Reviews* criticized Deighton's "vapid characters, murky plot, and infelicitous descriptions." While noting slow passages concerning Samson's marital difficulties and Intelligence agency politics, *Times*

Literary Supplement reviewer John-Paul Flintoff wrote, "Deighton throws in plenty of plausible details—tricks of the trade, gun specifications, a picture of Berlin as a local would see it."

Deighton followed with *Hope,* in which Samson pursues his Polish brother-in-law despite official evidence of his death at the hands of Russian army deserters. Commenting on the strained relationship depicted between Samson and his wife, a *Times Literary Supplement* reviewer describes *Hope* as "an unexpectedly ambiguous novel, complicated by repressed emotions and jealousies as well as by double crosses and false identities." Scott Veale complained in the *New York Times Book Review,* "there's more secrecy than action in this novel, and too often it's easy to get lost in the plot's numerous byways." However, Chris Petrakos praised *Hope* in Chicago *Tribune Books,* noting that "as usual" Deighton puts forth "a taut, enigmatic effort." *Publishers Weekly* also commended *Hope* and hailed Deighton as "the only author other than le Carre who deserves to be known as 'spymaster.'"

In the final book of the trilogy, *Charity,* Samson's wife has returned home after finishing her duties as a double agent while Samson becomes more disillusioned with both his job and his growing estrangement from his wife. At the same time, he is looking into what he considers the very suspicious death of his sister-in-law Tessa. Writing in *Booklist,* Emily Melton noted that "this story also shows a darker, more despairing Bernard, who is as much a victim of his own doubts and insecurities as he is of the system he serves. A brilliant new entry in Deighton's superb repertoire." A *Publishers Weekly* contributor called the story "well crafted and reliably satisfying."

Although Deighton is best known for his espionage fiction, he has also written best-selling novels outside the espionage field, as well as books of military history. These other novels and books are usually concerned with the events and figures of World War II. Among the most successful of his novels have been *SS-GB: Nazi-Occupied Britain, 1941,* and *Goodbye, Mickey Mouse,* which have earned Deighton praise as a writer of military history. Deighton's writing in other fields has shown him, Symons wrote, to be "determined not to stay within the conventional pattern of the spy story or thriller."

SS-GB takes place in an alternative history of World War II, a history in which England lost the crucial Battle of Britain and Nazi Germany conquered the country.

The story takes place after the conquest when Scotland Yard superintendent Douglas Archer investigates a murder and finds that the trail leads to the upper echelons of the Nazi party. An underground plot to rescue the king of England, who is being held prisoner in the Tower of London, and the ongoing efforts of the Nazis to develop the atom bomb also complicate Archer's problems. "As is usual with Mr. Deighton," John Leonard wrote in *Books of the Times,* "there are as many twists as there are betrayals."

Deighton's ability to fully render what a Nazi-occupied Britain would be like is the most widely noted strength of the book. "The atmosphere of occupied England," Michael Demarest wrote in his review of *SS-GB* for *Newsweek,* "is limned in eerie detail. . . . In fact, Deighton's ungreened isle frequently seems even more realistic than the authentic backgrounds of his previous novels." "What especially distinguishes 'SS-GB,'" Leonard believed, "is its gritty atmosphere, the shadows of defeat on every page. Yes, we think, this is what martial law would feel like; this is the way the Germans would have behaved; this is how rationing and the black market and curfews and detention camps would work; this is the contempt for ourselves that we would experience." Paul Ableman of the *Spectator* criticized the plot and noted, "From about Page 100, the subversive thought kept surfacing: what is the point of this kind of historical 'might have been'?. . . I fear [the novel] ultimately lost its hold on me. We could have been given the same yarn set in occupied France." But Symons judged *SS-GB* a successful and imaginative novel and called it "a triumphant success. It is Mr. Deighton's best book, one that blends his expertise in the spy field with his interest in military and political history to produce an absorbingly exciting spy story that is also a fascinating exercise in might-have-been speculation."

Goodbye, Mickey Mouse, another Deighton novel about World War II, concerns a group of American pilots in England who run fighter protection for the bombers making daylight runs over Germany. It is described by Thomas Gifford of the *Washington Post Book World* as "satisfying on every imaginable level, but truly astonishing in its recreation of a time and place through minute detail." Equally high praise came from Peter Andrews, who wrote in his review for the *New York Times Book Review:* "Deighton's latest World War II adventure novel is such a plain, old-fashioned, good book about combat pilots who make war and fall in love that it defies a complicated examination. . . . 'Goodbye, Mickey Mouse' is high adventure of the best sort but always solidly true to life."

Not all reviewers were so enthusiastic, but even those with reservations about the novel's ultimate quality were impressed with the way Deighton presented the scenes of aerial combat. "As long as he keeps his propellers turning," Prescott allowed in his *Newsweek* review, "Deighton's book lives. He understands the camaraderie of pilots and to a lesser degree the politics of combat. . . . It's a pity that his people, like his prose, are built from plywood." Gifford of the *Washington Post Book World* interpreted the novel on a more serious level. Speaking of the generation who fought in the Second World War, many of whom are "approaching the time when they will one by one pass into our history," Gifford found Deighton's novel a tribute to that generation and its monumental fight. "Some of them," Gifford wrote, "are fittingly memorialized in Deighton's hugely assured novel."

The crucial Battle of Britain, which figures prominently in *SS-GB,* and the air battles of that period, which appear in *Goodbye, Mickey Mouse,* are further explored in the nonfiction *Fighter,* a history of the Royal Air Force defense of England during the Battle of Britain. A highly acclaimed popular account of what Noble Frankland of the *Times Literary Supplement* called "among the handful of decisive battles in British history," *Fighter* "is the best, most dispassionate story of the battle I have read," Drew Middleton stated in the *New York Times Book Review,* "and I say that even though the book destroyed many of my illusions and, indeed, attacks the validity of some of what I wrote as an eyewitness of the air battle 38 years ago."

The Battle of Britain took place over several months of 1940. After overrunning France, the Nazi leadership focused their attention on softening up England for a land invasion. They launched extensive bombing raids against the British Isles, attacking the city of London, air bases, factories, and seaports. The Royal Air Force, vastly outnumbered by their opponents, bravely fought the Germans to a standstill, which resulted in the proposed invasion being delayed and ultimately canceled. Or so most historians relate the story.

Deighton dispels some of the myths about the Battle of Britain still widely believed by most historians. He shows, for example, that a major reason for the failure of the German offensive was the decision to shift the main attack from British airfields to the city of London. The Nazis hoped that bombing the civilian population would cause Britain to sue for peace. But leaving the airfields alone only allowed the Royal Air Force to launch their fighter planes against the German bombers. And when bomber losses rose too high, the Nazi invasion plans were called off.

Other insights into the Battle of Britain include the facts "that British anti-aircraft fire was ineffective, that some R.A.F. ground personnel fled under fire, that the Admiralty provoked costly skirmishes. . . . The book resounds with exploded myths," Leonard Bushkoff wrote in the *Washington Post Book World.* Deighton also shows that British estimates of German losses were far higher than they actually were, while British losses were reported to be less serious than was actually the case. But Bushkoff sees the importance of these revelations to be inconsequential. "Is debunking sufficient to carry a book that essentially is a rehash of earlier works?" he asked. In his article for the *Saturday Review,* George H. Reeves reports that "there is a profusion of detail in *Fighter . . .* that will delight the military history specialist, and Deighton's well-paced narrative and techniques of deft characterization will also hold the attention of the general reader." He believed that Deighton "has turned his hand with commendable results to the writing of military history."

In all of his writing, whether fiction or nonfiction, Deighton shows a concern for an accurate and detailed presentation of the facts. He has included appendices in several novels to explain to his readers such espionage esoterica as the structure of foreign intelligence organizations and the effects of various poisons. Part of Deighton's research involves extensive travel throughout the world; he is reported to have contacts in cities as far-flung as Anchorage and Casablanca. These research trips have sometimes proven dangerous. For example, Russian soldiers once took him into custody in East Berlin. For *Bomber: Events Relating to the Last Flight of an R.A.F. Bomber Over Germany on the Night of June 31, 1943,* Deighton made three trips to Germany and spent several years in research, gathering some half million words in notes. Research for the books *Fighter* and *Blitzkrieg: From the Rise of Hitler to the Fall of Dunkirk* took nearly nine years.

Deighton turns to historical fiction in his 1987 book *Winter: A Novel of a Berlin Family.* The story of a well-to-do German family led by a banker and war financier, *Winter* depicts how cultural and historical factors influence the attitudes of his two sons, one of whom joins the murderous Nazi party, while the other moves to the United States and marries a Jewish woman. The mixed criticism for *Winter* revolved around Deighton's sympathetic portrayals of his Nazi characters and around the novel's wide historical scope, which some reviewers felt is inadequately represented, mainly through dialogue rather than plot.

"Unlike much of Deighton's work," wrote Gary Dretzka in Chicago *Tribune Books,* "'Winter' isn't much concerned with military strategy, suspense and spies as with people and relationships." According to Elizabeth Ward in *Washington Post Book World,* "*Winter* is neither fiction nor history but docudrama, running like a film script in a series of dutifully dated vignettes from New Year's Eve 1899 . . . to 1945." Favorably describing *Winter* as a fictional counterpart to William L. Shirer's acclaimed historical work *The Rise and Fall of the Third Reich,* Ward maintained that "*Winter* is an altogether silkier, less demanding and more entertaining read," adding, "Len Deighton certainly knows how to move a narrative along, build suspense and weave mysteries, even if history did write the larger plot for him." While praising Deighton's "scholarship and attention to detail," Dretzka noted, "In the end, it's almost as if the enormity of World War II devours the context of the novel, leaving little for the reader to feel except pity—which is fine for TV, but not enough for a serious, well-written piece of fiction about such a shocking period in history."

Deighton also produced *City of Gold* in 1992, another volume of historical fiction based on events during World War II. This novel is set in Cairo at the height of Nazi domination of North Africa under the command of General Erwin Rommel. The protagonist is Corporal Jim Ross, a British soldier who escapes court-martial by assuming the identity of Major Bert Cutler, a British Intelligence agent who dies of a heart attack on a train. With his new identity and security clearance, Ross (as Cutler) is assigned to uncover the source of Rommel's detailed information about Allied forces and their movements. Though critical of Deighton's unusually large cast of stereotyped characters, Michael Kernan wrote in *Washington Post Book World,* "The action scenes in the desert are as good as anything he has written." A *Kirkus Reviews* contributor praised Deighton's "terrific return" to the Second World War and the "rich drama of heroes and villains" in *City of Gold.* "In the finest Deighton form," wrote Dick Roraback in the *Los Angeles Times Book Review,* "the master sets up his row of people then surrounds them with the authentic sights, sounds, smells, the moods and mores of their locale."

Deighton's position as one of the most prominent of contemporary espionage writers is secure. Cannon, writing in the Toronto *Globe and Mail* described him as "one of the finest living writers of espionage novels." Writing in *Whodunit?: A Guide to Crime, Suspense and Spy Fiction* about his life as a writer, Deighton revealed: "I have no formal training and have evolved a muddled sort of system by trial and error. . . . My own writing is characterized by an agonizing reappraisal of everything I write so that I have to work seven days a week."

Summing up his feelings about being a best-selling author, Deighton concludes, "It's not such a bad job after all; except for sitting here at this damned typewriter."

BIOGRAPHICAL AND CRITICAL SOURCES:

BOOKS

Bestsellers 89, Issue 2, Thomson Gale (Detroit, MI), 1989.

Concise Dictionary of British Literary Biography: Contemporary Writers, 1960 to Present, Thomson Gale (Detroit, MI), 1992.

Contemporary Literary Criticism, Thomson Gale (Detroit, MI), Volume 4, 1975, Volume 7, 1977, Volume 22, 1982, Volume 46, 1988.

Dictionary of Literary Biography, Volume 87: *British Mystery and Thriller Writers since 1940,* First Series, Thomson Gale (Detroit, MI), 1989.

Keating, H.R. F., editor, *Whodunit?: A Guide to Crime, Suspense and Spy Fiction,* Van Nostrand (New York, NY), 1982.

Symons, Julian, *Mortal Consequences: A History—From the Detective Story to the Crime Novel,* Harper (New York, NY), 1972.

PERIODICALS

Armchair Detective, winter, 1986.

Best Sellers, November 15, 1963; January 1, 1968.

Booklist, June 1-15, 1993; October 15, 1996, Emily Melton, review of *Charity,* p. 379.

Books and Bookmen, September, 1967; December, 1971.

Books of the Times, February, 1979; August, 1981.

British Book News, December, 1980.

Chicago Tribune Book World, March 18, 1979; January 19, 1986.

Detroit News, February 3, 1985; February 9, 1986.

Globe and Mail (Toronto, Ontario, Canada), December 1, 1984; December 14, 1985.

Harper's, November, 1982.

Kirkus Reviews, May 1, 1992, p. 555; October 15, 1994, p. 1364.

Life, March 25, 1966.

London Review of Books, March 19-April 1, 1981.

Los Angeles Times, November 26, 1982; March 23, 1987.

Los Angeles Times Book Review, March 17, 1985; February 16, 1986; November 22, 1987; August 19, 1990, p. 8; July 26, 1992, p. 9.

New Leader, January 19, 1976.

New Republic, December 13, 1975.

New Statesman, December 7, 1962; September 8, 1964; May 12, 1967; June 18, 1976; August 25, 1978.

New Statesman and Society, September 14, 1990; September 6, 1991.

Newsweek, January 18, 1965; January 31, 1966; June 26, 1972; October 14, 1974; February 19, 1979; December 27, 1982; December 19, 1983; February 11, 1985; January 13, 1986.

New Yorker, February 3, 1968; May 7, 1979; February 6, 1984.

New York Herald Tribune Book Review, November 17, 1963, Robert Donald Spectar, review of *The Ipcress File.*

New York Times, January 12, 1965; October 17, 1970; October 16, 1976; September 20, 1977; May 13, 1981; June 21, 1981; December 7, 1982; December 12, 1983; December 21, 1987.

New York Times Book Review, November 10, 1963; January 17, 1965; May 21, 1967; January 14, 1968; October 4, 1970; April 13, 1975; July 9, 1978; February 25, 1979; May 3, 1981; November 14, 1982; January 8, 1984; March 10, 1985; December 1, 1985; January 10, 1988; December 25, 1988; September 2, 1990, p. 6; June 28, 1992; August 15, 1993; January 29, 1995, p. 21; February 25, 1996, p. 21.

Playboy, May, 1966.

Publishers Weekly, November 27, 1995, p. 53; November 4, 1996, review of *Charity,* p. 64.

Saturday Review, January 30, 1965; June 10, 1978.

Spectator, September 24, 1977; September 2, 1978; April 18, 1981.

Time, March 12, 1979; April 27, 1981; January 13, 1986; December 28, 1987; December 5, 1988; September 17, 1990, p. 79.

Times Literary Supplement, February 8, 1963; June 1, 1967; June 22, 1967; September 25, 1970; June 16, 1972; May 3, 1974; October 28, 1977; September 15, 1978; March 13, 1981; October 21, 1983; October 21, 1994; October 6, 1995.

Tribune Books (Chicago, IL), February 24, 1985; December 27, 1987; January 1, 1989; January 8, 1989; January 21, 1996, p. 6.

Village Voice, February 19, 1979.

Wall Street Journal, May 21, 1980.

Washington Post, October 9, 1970; December 20, 1987; December 13, 1988; December 12, 1989; July 12, 1992.

Washington Post Book World, September 29, 1974; June 4, 1978; March 20, 1979; April 14, 1981; November 7, 1982; January 8, 1984; January 27, 1985; December 15, 1985; December 20, 1987; September 23, 1990; February 12, 1995.

DeIGHTON, Leonard Cyril
   See DeIGHTON, Len

*   *   *

DELANY, Samuel R. 1942-
   (Richmond Arrley, Samuel Ray Delany, Jr., K. Leslie Steiner)

PERSONAL: Born April 1, 1942, in New York, NY; son of Samuel R. (a funeral director) and Margaret Carey (a library clerk; maiden name, Boyd) Delany; married Marilyn Hacker (a poet), August 24, 1961 (divorced, 1980); partner of Dennis Rickett; children: Iva Alyxander. *Education:* Attended City College (now City University of New York), 1960, 1962-63.

ADDRESSES: Office—English Department, Temple University, Anderson Hall, 10th Fl. (022-29), 1114 W. Berks St., Philadelphia, PA 19122-6090. *Agent*—Henry Morrison, Inc., Box 235, Bedford Hills, NY 10507. *E-mail*—sdelany@temple.edu.

CAREER: Writer and educator. Folk singer and guitarist in Greenwich Village, NY, 1960's; actor, teacher, and freelance writer, 1960-64; shrimp boat worker, 1965; musician with Heavenly Breakfast rock band, 1967; filmmaker and editor, 1970-71; State University of New York at Buffalo, Butler Professor of English, 1975; University of Wisconsin—Milwaukee, senior fellow at the Center for Twentieth-Century Studies, 1977; Cornell University, Ithaca, NY, senior fellow at the Society for the Humanities, 1987; University of Massachusetts—Amherst, professor of comparative literature, c. 1988-99; University of Michigan, Ann Arbor, fellow at Institute for the Humanities, 1993; State University of New York at Buffalo, NY, English professor, c. 1999-2001; Temple University, Philadelphia, PA, professor of English and creative writing, 2001—.

AWARDS, HONORS: Fellowship, Breadloaf Writers Conference, 1960; Nebula Awards, Science Fiction Writers of America, 1966, for best novel *Babel-17,* 1967, for best novel *The Einstein Intersection,* and for best short story "Aye and Gomorrah," and 1969, for best novelette "Time Considered as a Helix of Semi-Precious Stones"; Hugo Award for best short story, World Science Fiction Convention, 1970, for "Time Considered as a Helix of Semi-Precious Stones"; American Book Award nomination, 1980, for *Tales of Nèveryon;* Pilgrim Award for Excellence, Science Fic-

tion Research Association, 1985; Hugo Award for Best Nonfiction, World Science Fiction Society, 1989, for *The Motion of Light in Water: Sex and Science Fiction Writing in the East Village, 1957-1965;* William Whitehead Memorial Award for Lifetime Achievement for Gay and Lesbian Literature, 1993.

WRITINGS:

SCIENCE FICTION AND FANTASY

The Jewels of Aptor (abridged edition; bound with *Second Ending* by James White), Ace Books (New York, NY), 1962, new edition published with an introduction by Don Hausdorff, Gregg Press (Boston, MA), 1976.

Captives of the Flame (first novel in a trilogy; bound with *The Psionic Menace* by Keith Woodcott), Ace Books (New York, NY), 1963, revised edition published under author's original title *Out of the Dead City* (also see below), Sphere Books (London, England), 1968.

The Towers of Toron (second novel in a trilogy; also see below; bound with *The Lunar Eye* by Robert Moore Williams), Ace Books (New York, NY), 1964.

City of a Thousand Suns (third novel in a trilogy; also see below), Ace Books (New York, NY), 1965.

The Ballad of Beta- 2 (also see below; bound with *Alpha Yes, Terra No!* by Emil Petaja), Ace Books (New York, NY), 1965, hardcover edition published with an introduction by David G. Hartwell, Gregg Press (Boston, MA), 1977.

Empire Star (also see below; bound with *The Three Lords of Imeten* by Tom Purdom), Ace Books (New York, NY), 1966, hardcover edition published with an introduction by David G. Hartwell, Gregg Press (Boston, MA), 1977.

Babel-17, Ace Books (New York, NY), 1966, reprinted, Vintage Books (New York, NY), 2001.

The Einstein Intersection, slightly abridged edition, Ace Books (New York, NY), 1967, hardcover edition, Gollancz (London, England), 1968, complete edition, Ace Books (New York, NY), 1972.

Nova, Doubleday (New York, NY), 1968, reprinted, Vintage Books (New York, NY), 2002.

The Fall of the Towers (trilogy; contains *Out of the Dead City, The Towers of Toron,* and *City of a Thousand Suns*), Ace Books (New York, NY), 1970, hardcover edition published with introduction by Joseph Milicia, Gregg Press (Boston, MA), 1977, paperback edition reprinted, Vintage Books (New York, NY), 2004.

Driftglass: Ten Tales of Speculative Fiction, Doubleday (New York, NY), 1971.

The Tides of Lust, Lancer Books (New York, NY), 1973.

Dhalgren, Bantam (New York, NY), 1975, hardcover edition published with introduction by Jean Mark Gawron, Gregg Press (Boston, MA), 1978, published with foreword by William Gibson, Vintage Books (New York, NY), 2001.

The Ballad of Beta- 2 [and] *Empire Star,* Ace Books (New York, NY), 1975.

Triton, Bantam (New York, NY), 1976, published as *Trouble on Triton: An Ambiguous Heterotopia,* University Press of New England (Hanover, NH), 1996.

Empire: A Visual Novel, illustrations by Howard V. Chaykin, Berkley Books (New York, NY), 1978.

Distant Stars, Bantam (New York, NY), 1981.

Stars in My Pocket like Grains of Sand, Bantam (New York, NY), 1984 reprinted with foreword by Carl Freedman, Wesleyan University Press(Middletown, CT), 2004.

The Complete Nebula Award- winning Fiction, Bantam (New York, NY), 1986.

The Star Pits (bound with *Tango Charlie and Foxtrot Romeo*by John Varley), Tor Books (New York, NY), 1989.

They Fly at Ciron, Incunabula (Seattle, WA), 1992.

Equinox, Masquerade (New York, NY), 1994.

*Aye, and Gomorrah: Stories,*Vintage Books (New York, NY), 2003.

Phallos, Bamberger Books (Flint, MI), 2004.

"RETURN TO NÈVERŸON" SERIES; FANTASY NOVELS

Tales of Nèverÿon, Bantam (New York, NY), 1979.

Nèverÿona; or, The Tale of Signs and Cities, Bantam (New York, NY), 1983, published as *Nèverÿona; or, The Tale of Signs and Cities, Some Informal Remarks towards the Modular Calculus, Part Four,* University Press of New England (Hanover, NH), 1993.

Flight from Nèverÿon, Bantam (New York, NY), 1985.

The Bridge of Lost Desire, Arbor House (New York, NY), 1987, published as *Return to Nèverÿon,* University Press of New England (Hanover, NH), 1994.

OTHER

*The Jewel-Hinged Jaw: Notes on the Language of Science Fiction,*Dragon Press (Ithaca, NY), 1977, revised edition, Berkley Publishing (New York, NY), 1978.

The American Shore: Meditations on a Tale of Science Fiction by Thomas M. Disch— "Angouleme" (criticism), Dragon Press (Ithaca, NY), 1978.

Heavenly Breakfast: An Essay on the Winter of Love (memoir), Bantam (New York, NY), 1979.

(Editor) *Nebula Awards Thirteen,* 1980.

*Starboard Wine: More Notes on the Language of Science Fiction,*Dragon Press (Ithaca, NY), 1984.

The Motion of Light in Water: Sex and Science-Fiction Writing in the East Village, 1957- 1965, University of Minnesota Press(Minneapolis, MN), 1988.

Wagner/Artaud: A Play of Nineteenth- and Twentieth-Century Critical Fictions, Ansatz Press (New York, NY), 1988.

Straits of Messina (essays; originally published in magazines under pseudonym K. Leslie Steiner), Serconia Press (Seattle, WA), 1989.

Silent Interviews: On Language, Race, Sex, Science Fiction, and Some Comics: A Collection of Written Interviews, Wesleyan University Press (Middletown, CT), 1994.

The Mad Man (novel), Masquerade (New York, NY), 1994.

Atlantis: Three Tales, Wesleyan University (Middletown, CT), 1995.

Longer Views: Extended Essays, University Press of New England (Hanover, NH), 1996.

Bread and Wine: An Erotic Tale of New York City; An Autobiographical Account, Juno Books (New York, NY), 1998.

Hogg (novel), FC2 (Normal, IL), 1998.

Shorter Views: Queer Thoughts and the Politics of the Paraliterary, University Press of New England (Hanover, NH), 1999.

Times Square Red, Times Square Blue, New York University Press (New York, NY), 1999.

1984: Selected Letters, Voyant (Rutherford, NJ), 2000.

About Writing: Seven Essays, Four Letters, and Five Interviews, Wesleyan University Press (Middletown, CT), 2005.

Also author of scripts and director and editor for two short films, *Tiresias,* 1970, and *The Orchid,* 1971; author of two scripts for the "Wonder Woman" comic series, 1972, and of the radio play *The Star Pit,* based on his short story of the same title. Editor, *Quark,*1970-71; member of editorial board, *The Little Magazine,* 1981-86l; contributor to periodicals, including *New York Review of Science Fiction.*

SIDELIGHTS: "Samuel R. Delany is one of today's most innovative and imaginative writers of science-fiction," commented Jane Branham Weedman in her study of the author, *Samuel R. Delany*. Delany first appeared on the science-fiction horizon in the early 1960s, and in the decade that followed he established himself as one of the stars of the genre. Like many of his contemporaries who entered science fiction in the 1960s, he is less concerned with the conventions of the genre and more interested in science fiction as literature, literature that offers a wide range of artistic opportunities. As a result, maintained Weedman: "Delany's works are excellent examples of modern science-fiction as it has developed from the earlier and more limited science-fiction tradition, especially because of his manipulation of cultural theories, his detailed futuristic or alternate settings, and his stylistic innovations."

"One is drawn into Delany's stories because they have a complexity," observed Sandra Y. Govan in *Black American Literature Forum*, "an acute consciousness of language, structure, and form; a dexterous ability to weave together mythology and anthropology, linguistic theory and cultural history, gestalt psychology and sociology as well as philosophy, structuralism, and the adventure story." At the center of the complex web of personal, cultural, artistic, and intellectual concerns that provides the framework for all of his work is Delany's examination of how language and myth influence reality. "According to [the author]," wrote Govan in *Dictionary of Literary Biography*, "language identifies or negates the self. It is self-reflective; it shapes perceptions." By shaping perceptions, language in turn has the capacity to shape reality. Myths can exercise much the same power. In his science fiction, Delany "creates new myths, or inversions of old ones, by which his protagonists measure themselves and their societies against the traditional myths that Delany includes," Weedman observed. In this way, as Peter S. Alterman commented in *Dictionary of Literary Biography*, the author confronts "the question of the extent to which myths and archetypes create reality."

In societies in which language and myth are recognized as determinants of reality, the artist—one who works in language and myth—plays a crucial part. For this reason, the protagonist of a Delany novel is often an artist of some sort. "The role which Delany defines for the artist is to observe, record, transmit, and question paradigms in society," explained Weedman. Delany's artists, however, do more than chronicle and critique the societies of which they are a part. His artists are always on the margins of society; they are outcasts and often criminals. "The criminal and the artist both operate outside the normal standards of society," observed Alterman, "according to their own self-centered value systems." The artist/criminal goes beyond observation and

commentary. His actions at the margin push society's values to their limits and beyond, providing the experimentation necessary to prepare for eventual change.

Delany began his literary career in 1962 with the publication of his novel *The Jewels of Aptor*. Over the next six years, he published eight more novels, including *Babel-17, The Einstein Intersection*, and *Nova*, his first printed originally in hardcover. Douglas Barbour, writing in *Science Fiction Writers: Critical Studies of the Major Authors from the Early Nineteenth Century to the Present Day*, described these early novels as "colorful, exciting, entertaining, and intellectually provocative to a degree not found in most genre science fiction." Barbour added that although they do adhere to science fiction conventions, they "begin the exploration of those literary obsessions that define [Delany's] oeuvre: problems of communication and community; new kinds of sexual/love/family relationships; the artist as social outsider . . . cultural interactions and the exploration of human social possibilities these allow; archetypal and mythic structures in the imagination."

With the publication of *Babel-17* in 1966, Delany began to gain recognition in the science-fiction world. The novel, which earned its author his first Nebula Award, is a story of galactic warfare between the forces of the Alliance, which includes the Earth, and the forces of the Invaders. The poet Rydra Wong is enlisted by Alliance intelligence to decipher communications intercepted from its enemy. When she discovers that these dispatches contain not a code but rather an unknown language, she embarks on a quest to learn this mysterious tongue labeled *Babel-17*. While leading an interstellar mission in search of clues, Rydra gains insights into the nature of language and, in the process, discovers the unique character of the enigmatic new language of the Invaders.

Babel-17 itself becomes an exploration of language and its ability to structure experience. A central image in the novel, as George Edgar Slusser pointed out in his study *The Delany Intersection: Samuel R. Delany Considered as a Writer of Semi-Precious Words*, is that of "the web and its weaver or breaker." The web, continued Slusser, "stands, simultaneously, for unity and isolation, interconnectedness and entanglement." Weedman elaborated in her essay on the novel: "The language one learns necessarily constrains and structures what it is that one says." In its ability to connect and constrain is the power of the language/web. "Language . . . has a direct effect on how one thinks," explained Weedman, "since the structure of the language influences the processes by which one formulates ideas." At the center of the language as web "is one who joins and cuts—the artist-hero,"commented Slusser. And, in *Babel-17,* the poet Rydra Wong demonstrates that only she is able to master this new language weapon and turn it against its creators.

Delany followed *Babel-17* with another Nebula winner, *The Einstein Intersection.* This novel represents a "move from a consideration of the relationship among language, thought, action and time to an analytic and imaginative investigation of the patterns of myths and archetypes and their interaction with the conscious mind," wrote Alterman. Slusser saw this development in themes as part of a logical progression: "[Myths] too are seen essentially as language constructs: verbal scenarios for human action sanctioned by tradition or authority." Comparing this novel to *Babel-17,* he added: "Delany's sense of the language act, in this novel, has a broader social valence."

The Einstein Intersection relates the story of a strange race of beings that occupies a post-apocalyptic Earth. This race assumes the traditions—economic, political, and religious—of the extinct humans in an attempt to make sense of the remnant world in which they find themselves. "While they try to live by the myths of man," wrote Barbour in *Foundation,* "they cannot create a viable culture of their own. . . . Their more profound hope is to recognize that they do not have to live out the old myths at all, that the 'difference' they seek to hide or dissemble is the key to their cultural and racial salvation."

"Difference is a key word in this novel," Weedman explained, "for it designates the importance of the individual and his ability to make choices, on the basis of being different from others, which affect his life, thus enabling him to question the paradigms of his society." The artist is the embodiment of this difference; in *The Einstein Intersection* the artist is Lobey, a musician. The power of Lobey's music is its ability to create order, to destroy the old myths and usher in the new. At its core, then, "*The Einstein Intersection* is . . . a novel about experiments in culture," Weedman commented.

Delany's next novel, *Nova,* "stands as the summation of [his] career up to that time," wrote Barbour in *Science-Fiction Writers.* "Packing his story full of color and incident, violent action and tender introspective moments, he has created one of the grandest space operas ever

written." In this novel, Delany presents a galaxy divided into three camps, all embroiled in a bitter conflict caused by a shortage of the fuel illyrion on which they all depend. In chronicling one group's quest for a new source of the fuel, the author examines, according to Weedman, "how technology changes the world and philosophies for world survival. Delany also explores conflicts between and within societies, as well as the problems created by people's different perceptions and different reality models."

"In developing this tale," noted Slusser, "Delany has inverted the traditional epic relationship, in which the human subject (the quest) dominates the 'form.' Here instead is a 'subjunctive epic.' Men do not struggle against an inhuman system so much as inside an unhuman one." The system inside which these societies struggle is economic; the goal of the quester, who is driven by selfishness, is a commodity.

After the publication of *Nova,* Delany turned his creative urges to forms other than the novel, writing a number of short stories, editing four quarterlies of speculative fiction, and dabbling in such diverse media as film and comic books. Also at this time, he engaged himself in conceiving, writing, and polishing what would become his longest, most complex, and most controversial novel, *Dhalgren* —a work that earned him national recognition. On its shifting surface, this novel represents the experience of a nameless amnesiac, an artist/criminal, during the period of time he spends in a temporally and spatially isolated city scarred by destruction and decay. As Alterman related in the *Dictionary of Literary Biography,* "it begins with the genesis of a protagonist, one so unformed that he has no name, no identity, the quest for which is the novel's central theme." The critic went on to explain that "at the end Kid has a name and a life, both of which are the novel itself; he is a persona whose experience in *Dhalgren* defines him."

Dhalgren's length and complexity provide a significant challenge to readers, but as Gerald Jonas observed in the *New York Times Book Review,* "the most important fact about Delany's novel . . . is that nothing in it is clear. Nothing is meant to be clear." He added, "An event may be described two or three times, and each recounting is slightly disconcertingly different from the one before." What is more, continued the reviewer, "the nameless narrator experiences time discontinuously; whole days seem to be excised from his memory." According to Weedman: "Delany creates disorientation in *Dhalgren* to explore the problems which occur when reality models differ from reality." In Jonas's estimation, "If the book can be said to be *about* anything, it is about nothing less than the nature of reality."

Commenting that "*Dhalgren* has drawn more widely divergent critical response than any other Delany novel," *Dictionary of Literary Biography* contributor Govan wrote: "Some reviewers deny that it is science fiction, while others praise it for its daring and experimental form." For instance, *Magazine of Fantasy and Science Fiction* book reviewer Algis Budrys contended that "this book is not science fiction, or science fantasy, but allegorical quasi-fantasy on the [James Gould]Cozzens model. Thus, although it demonstrates the breadth of Delany's education, and many of its passages are excellent prose, it presents no new literary inventions." In his *Science-Fiction Writers* essay, Barbour described the same novel as "the very stuff of science fiction but lacking the usual structural emblems of the genre." "One thing is certain,"offered Jonas, "*Dhalgren* is not a conventional novel, whether considered in terms of S.F. or the mainstream."

Following the exhaustive involvement with Kid necessary to complete *Dhalgren*, Delany chose to write a novel in which he distanced himself from his protagonist, giving him a chance to look at the relationship between an individual and his society in a new light. "I wanted to do a psychological analysis of someone with whom you're just not in sympathy, someone whom you watch making all the wrong choices, even though his plight itself is sympathetic," Delany explained in an interview with Larry McCaffery and Sinda Gregory published in their book *Alive and Writing: Interviews with American Authors of the 1980s*. The novel is *Triton;* its main character is Bron. " *Triton* is set in a sort of sexual utopia, where every form of sexual behavior is accepted, and sex-change operations (not to mention 'refixations,' to alter sexual preference) are common,"observed Michael Goodwin in *Mother Jones*. In this world of freedom lives Bron, whom Govan described in *Black American Literature Forum* as "a narrow-minded, isolated man, so self-serving that he is incapable of reaching outside himself to love another or even understand another despite his best intentions." In an attempt to solve his problems, he undergoes a sex-change operation, but finds no happiness. "Bron is finally trapped in total social and psychological stasis, lost in isolation beyond any help her society can offer its citizens," commented Barbour in *Science-Fiction Writers*. In *Triton* he casts a critical eye, as Weedman pointed out, on "sexual persecution against women, ambisexuals, and homosexuals." Weedman concluded that the work is "on the necessity of knowing one's self despite sexual identification, knowing one's sexual identity is not one's total identity."

In the 1980s Delany continued to experiment in his fiction writing. In his "Nèverÿon" series, which includes *Tales of Nèverÿon, Nèverÿona; or, The Tale of Signs and Cities, Flight from Nèverÿon,* and *The Bridge of Lost Desire,* he chooses a different setting. "Instead of being set in some imagined future, [they] are set in some magical, distant past, just as civilization is being created," observed McCaffery in an interview with Delany. The books' focus, suggested Gregory in the same interview, is "power—all kinds of power: sexual, economic, even racial power via the issue of slavery."

Throughout these tales of a world of dragons, treasures, and fabulous cities Delany weaves the story of Gorgik, a slave who rises to power and abolishes slavery. In one story, the novel-length "Tale of Plagues and Carnivals," Delany shifts in time from his primitive world to present-day New York City and back to examine the devastating effects of a disease such as acquired immune deficiency syndrome (AIDS). And, in the appendices that accompany each of these books, he reflects on the creative process itself. Of the four, it is *Nèverÿona,* the story of Pryn—a girl who flees her mountain home on a journey of discovery—that has received the most attention from reviewers. *Science Fiction and Fantasy Book Review* contributor Michael R. Collings called it "a stirring fable of adventure and education, of heroic action and even more heroic normality in a world where survival itself is constantly threatened." Faren C. Miller found the book groundbreaking, writing in *Locus* that by "combining differing perspectives with extraordinary talent for the *details* of a world—its smells, its shadows, workaday furnishings, and playful frills—Delany has produced a sourcebook for a new generation of fantasy writers." The book also "presents a new manifestation of Delany's continuing concern for language and the magic of fiction, whereby words become symbols for other, larger things," Collings observed.

In *Stars in My Pocket like Grains of Sand* Delany returns to the future. The book is "a densely textured, intricately worked out novelistic structure which delights and astonishes even as it forces a confrontation with a wide range of thought-provoking issues," wrote McCaffery in *Fantasy Review*. Included are "an examination of interstellar politics among thousands of far flung worlds, a love story, a meandering essay on the variety of human relationships and the inexplicability of sexual attractiveness, and a hypnotic crash-course on a fascinating body of literature which does not yet exist," noted H.J. Kirchhoff in the Toronto *Globe & Mail*.

Beneath the surface features, as Jonas suggested in *New York Times Book Review,* the reader can discover the fullness of this Delany novel. "To unpack the layers of meaning in seemingly offhand remarks or exchanges of social pleasantries," noted Jonas, "the reader must be alert to small shifts in emphasis, repeated phrases or gestures that assume new significance in new contexts, patterns of behavior that only become apparent when the author supplies a crucial piece of information at just the proper moment." Here in the words and gestures of the characters and the subtle way in which the author fashions his work is the fundamental concern of the novel. "I take the most basic subject here to be the nature of information itself," McCaffery explained, "the way it is processed, stored and decoded symbolically, the way it is distorted by the present and the past, the way it has become a commodity . . . the way that the play of textualities defines our perception of the universe."

"This is an astonishing new Delany," according to Somtow Sucharitkul in the *Washington Post Book World,* "more richly textured, smoother, more colorful than ever before." Commending the novel because for the interaction it encourages with the reader, Jonas observed that, "Sentence by sentence, phrase by phrase, it invites the reader to collaborate in the process of creation, in a way that few novels do." He went on to note that "The reader who accepts this invitation has an extraordinarily satisfying experience in store for him/her." McCaffery concluded that " *Stars in My Pocket like Grains of Sand* . . . confirms that [Delany] is American SF's most consistently brilliant and inventive writer."

The novel *They Fly at Ciron* grew out of a short story that Delany wrote in thirty years before, in 1962. Although a version of the story, produced in collaboration with James Sallis, was published in 1971, Delany was not satisfied with it and subsequently reworked it into a novel. The action takes place in a nameless world that consists of small, independent village-states living in isolated harmony. This harmony, however, is shattered when a fierce, technologically advanced people known as the Myetrans begin pillaging the land, overpowering and slaughtering the inhabitants of every village they encounter. It is left to a pair of men—Kire, a former member of the Myetrans, and Rahm to thwart the warring Myetrans. The two men eventually overcome their nemesis by joining forces with the Winged Ones, a species of intelligent, flying beings. *New York Times Book Review* critic Gerald Jonas called the novel "a biting parable about the bloody roots of civilization" and praised the "spare beauty" of Delany's prose.

Critics often comment on how Delany, who is both gay and African American, uses fiction as a forum to call for greater acceptance of women's rights and gay rights;

yet, as Govan maintained in her *Dictionary of Literary Biography* contribution, "a recurring motif frequently overlooked in Delany's fiction is his subtle emphasis on race. Black and mixed-blood characters cross the spectrum of his speculative futures, both as a testimony to a future Delany believes will change to reflect human diversity honestly and as a commentary on the racial politics of the present."

In novels such as *Babel-17,* Delany demonstrates how language can be used to rob the black man of his identity. "White culture exerts a great influence because it can force stereotypic definitions on the black person," wrote Weedman. She added that "if the black person capitulates to the definition imposed on him by a force outside of his culture, then he is in danger of losing his identity." In his other novels, Govan pointed out, "Delany utilizes existing negative racial mythologies about blacks, but, in all his works, he twists the commonplace images and stereotypes to his own ends." In using his fiction to promote awareness of the race issue, he and black writers like him "have mastered the dominant culture's language and turned it against its formulators in protest," noted Weedman.

As Delany's fiction began to go out of print in the 1980s and 1990s, he focused more and more on writing criticism and essays, as well as teaching; he is currently a professor of comparative literature at the University of Massachusetts—Amherst. Although he had been writing criticism for decades, Delany has been receiving even more recognition lately as a perspicuous analyst of literature. "Delany is not only a gifted writer," claimed Barbour in his *Foundation* article, "he is one of the most articulate theorists of sf to have emerged from the ranks of its writers." In such critical works as *The Jewel-hinged Jaw: Notes on the Language of Science Fiction, The American Shore: Meditations on a Tale of Science Fiction by Thomas M. Disch—"Angouleme",* and *Starboard Wine: More Notes on the Language of Science Fiction,* "he has done much to open up critical discussion of sf as a genre, forcefully arguing its great potential as art," Barbour added. In his nonfiction, Delany offers a functional description of science fiction and contrasts it with other genres such as naturalistic fiction and fantasy. He also attempts to expand "the domain of his chosen genre by claiming it the modern mode of fiction *par excellence,*" commented Slusser, "the one most suited to deal with the complexities of paradox and probability, chaos, irrationality, and the need for logic and order."

Delany's books *Longer Views: Extended Essays* and *Shorter Views: Queer Thoughts and the Politics of the Paraliterary* have marked him not only as an astute critic of books but also of society. *Longer Views* is a collection that discusses such topics as Donna Haraway's "Manifesto for Cyborgs," gay identity (Delany notes that Hart Crane was gay and ponders how different criticism of Crane would have been had this been acknowledged), and Wagnerian opera. *Shorter Views* contains essays on critical theory and genres Delany labels "paraliterary," including comic books, graphic novels, and pornography. Reviewers have appreciated the fact that, as a self-educated intellectual, Delany can offer a fresh perspective on literature and other subjects outside of the academic world of which he is now a part. "One of the things I find most valuable about Delany," wrote *African American Review* contributor Robert Elliot Fox, "apart from his incredibly wide-ranging mind, his thoroughgoing grasp of so many different subjects, is his independence of thought, his terribly honest self-scrutiny." And although Charles Crawford cautioned in *Library Journal* that the author's erudition might be daunting for some readers, he added that *Shorter Views* "will strongly appeal to a select group of brave readers who have the patience to follow a daringly original mind at work." In a review of *Longer Views* for *African American Review,* Fox asserted that "increasingly . . . Delany is garnering serious attention as an original critical mind."

With the publication of *The Motion of Light in Water* Delany turned to writing about himself. This memoir of his early days as a writer in New York's East Village is "an extraordinary account of life experienced by a precocious black artist of the 1960s," as E. Guereschi described it in *Choice.* The book reveals much of Delany's sexual adventures with partners of both sexes at the time, his nervous breakdown, and the general sense of living on the edge during an exciting and innovative period. Moreover, the book tells of Delany's realization and eventual acceptance of his homosexuality. Thomas M. Disch, writing in *American Book Review,* found that Delany "can't help creating legends and elaborating myths. Indeed, it is his forté, the open secret of his success as an SF writer. [Delany's] SF heroes are variations of an archetype he calls The Kid." Disch continued, "In his memoir, the author himself [is] finally assuming the role in which his fictive alter-egos have enjoyed their success. That is the book's strength even more than its weakness." Guereschi believed that the memoir "defines an arduous search for identity," while Disch concluded that *The Motion of Light in Water* "has the potential of being as popular, as representative of its era, as *On the Road.*"

The inner workings of Delany's mind are also revealed in such works as *Silent Interviews: On Language, Race, Sex, Science Fiction, and Some Comics: A Collection of Written Interviews* and *1984: Selected Letters.* The former contains ten written interviews with Delany as well as one interview by him (of composer Anthony Davis) and features Delany discussing topics such as the state of science fiction, race, sexuality, language, and literary criticism. Paul Miller, reviewing the work in *Village Voice,* remarked that "the most interesting parts of *Silent Interviews* are not when [Delany] talks about the obvious aspects of sexuality and race, but when he discusses the ways they are encoded into our lives." In what a *Publishers Weekly* contributor called "a wonderful complement to his autobiographical writings," *1984* includes letters in which Delany talks about his attempts to curb his sexual behavior as he learns about the spread of the disease AIDS. Ultimately, his efforts are as unsuccessful as most dieters' attempts to cut back on food. The letter collection, however, is about more than this; there are many more intellectual passages. Delany, noted Thom Nickels in *Lambda Book Report,* "never stays put on any one subject too long. The good thing about these letters is the author's ability to balance."

In addition to his fiction and criticism, Delany is also becoming known for writing what many would label pornography, or, at least, gay erotica. This has been especially true with the novels *The Mad Man* and *Hogg,* which contain extreme scenes of sex and violence, including passages involving unsavory practices such as coprophilia, bestiality, and urolagnia. *The Mad Man* is about an African-American academic named John Marr who is studying the work of philosopher Timothy Hasler. Discovering that Hasler has been murdered, Marr becomes an amateur sleuth and begins to investigate his death. Fortunately for Marr, both he and Hasler are into unconventional sexual practices, and in the course of the many interludes in the story involving Marr's sexual dalliances with men, he uncovers clues that could lead to Hasler's murderer. "Although there are some themes and ideas in this book which relate to other work by Delany," noted Stan Leventhal in *Lambda Book Report,* "this new novel is quite a departure. All of the previous fiction which he has published has been firmly rooted in the science fiction and fantasy genres, and although his work has gotten more sexual in recent years, there is nothing else of his that can be classified as pornographic." Leventhal added, "Moreover, this text seems to embody a new genre that could be called anti-porn . . . : sexually explicit material that is so intense and over the top it fails to seduce the reader."

Delany's *Hogg* contains such explicit sexual content that for nearly thirty years the author was unable to get it published. Finally released in 1998, *Hogg* is told from the point of view of an eleven-year-old boy who is the sexual slave of the title character, a man who makes a living by being paid to rape women. He is a thoroughly disgusting character who does not even bother to find a rest room to go to the bathroom and enjoys urinating on people. "Even though Hogg's brutality had to be constructed in the context of abject poverty among hillbillies and 'nigger' fishermen," commented Bruce Benderson in *Lambda Book Report,* "the novel is neither a sociological study of the disadvantaged nor a psychological portrait of a degenerate. Instead, Hogg is a truly experimental novel, shining like a rare pearl in the tepid muck of today's postmodernism. Hogg is a minimalist testing of a single hypothesis. It wants to know to what limits appetite can suffuse consciousness before that consciousness stops being considered human." In a less laudatory review of the book, a *Publishers Weekly* critic complained that "in other works, Delany has examined the role of the criminal within society; with Hogg, he apparently was content merely to inhabit the criminal mind without exploring it."

In the nonfiction work *Times Square Red, Times Square Blue,* Delany writes lovingly of the porno scene in his native New York City, which in the 1990s was the target of a clean up effort by the city's government in an effort to make areas that were once filled with porno theaters more attractive to tourists. Delany complains that the triple-X theater district was actually safer in many ways than other parts of New York City because they were so crowded that one was actually reasonably safe walking down its streets. Although a great deal of illicit sex occurred there, he also laments the departure of the social scene, which has now been replaced by sterile office buildings that look like any other part of the business district. As Delany put it in his book, "because there's not enough intertwined commercial and residential variety to create a vital and lively street life, the neighborhood becomes a glass and aluminum graveyard." However, Delany later said in an interview with Tasha Robinson in the online *Onion A.V. Club* that although the area is much more "homogenized" now, "it does draw people, and I think that's good. I wish there was a little more variety in what was offered, but that may change."

Sexuality and urban life are also major themes of Delany's work. "New York," explained *Publishers Weekly* contributor Michael Bronski, "shines through all of Delany's writing . . . even in such early intergalactic tales as the Nèverÿon novels and *Dhalgren,* which are infused with the intensity and momentum of New York, and reflections on AIDS and gay life." Delany's auto-

biographical graphic novel *Bread and Wine: An Erotic Tale of New York,* wrote Bronski, "uses illustrations by Mia Wolff to recount how he and [his partner] Dennis [Ricketts], a New Yorker from a working-class Irish background, met seven years ago, when the latter was homeless and selling old books from a shopping cart on 72nd Street and Broadway."

Beginning in the late 1990s, Delany's work saw a resurgence in popularity as many of his books that had gone out of print were reissued. Although Delany feels that the reissuing of his books is more a matter of publishers believing there is profit to be made rather than a renewed public awareness of his work, he is encouraged that there has been more acceptance in recent years of gay, women's, and African-American literature among both academics and the general reading public. "While publishers are convinced fiction readers are only interested in reading about what they've read about before," Delany told Jayme Lynn Blaschke on the online *SF Site,* "the reality is, I suspect, more sanguine: People want new stories and new materials to explore and interrogate and have adventures in. The world—particularly the academic world—has been changing with a rapidity that, while astonishing, is still just slow enough to escape the eye of, say, the university student who has only been in school for four years, or even the graduate student who stays for eight or ten."

Delany's popularity is evidenced not only by the fact that his older science fiction books continue to be reprinted, but by the fact he continues to write and publish new works as well. Indeed, Delany has been writing and publishing books for nearly forty years. *Aye, and Gomorrah: Stories* features fifteen stories comprising most of the author's short fiction. Included in the volume are stories previously published in *Driftglass: Ten Tales of Speculative Fiction* and *Distant Stars.* Critics praised the collection and noted that Delany's famous traits were evident throughout. Writing in the *Library Journal,* Jackie Cassada noted that the book "encompasses both controversy and compassion." In addition, *Booklist* contributor Ray Olson wrote that Delany is considered a "titan" of the science-fiction genre and added that the volume's "ethically intriguing stories demonstrate why he has that reputation."

In *About Writing: Seven Essays, Four Letters, and Five Interviews,* the author discusses the art of fiction writing via 'seven essays, four letters, and five interviews.' The letters are addressed to fellow authors and explain the various factors that make for exceptional writing. Carl Hays, writing in *Booklist,* felt that this was an effective approach; he noted that the book "deserves a reading by aspiring wordsmiths in every genre." Noting that *About Writing,* is "not another how-to book," *Library Journal* contributor Nedra Crowe-Evers commented that the volume is also a "demonstration of how fiction fits into today's world."

In his long and varied career, Delany has branched far beyond the realms of science fiction in many of his writings, including his 2004 novella *Phallos.* "The story's fundamental conceit . . . is that a full-length anonymous gay porn novel called Phallos was published back in 1969," Delany told Stefen Styrsky in the *Lambda Book Report.* The author also told Styrsky: "A simple driver behind Phallos is the impulse to examine how pleasure integrates into one's ordinary life." Brandon Stosuy, writing in the *Village Voice* called the novel "a lapidary, digital-age *Pale Fire.*" Stosuy went on to state that the book is "emblematic of Delany's recent concerns, [and] the wee text offers a crib sheet for the writer's interests in the history of the novel and textual criticism."

Indeed, Delany is not an easily pigeonholed writer—a black man in a white society, a writer who suffers from dyslexia, an artist who is also a critic. His race, lifestyle, chosen profession, and chosen genre keep him far from the mainstream. "His own term 'multiplex' probably best describes his work (attitudes, ideas, themes, craftsmanship, all their inter-relations, as well as his relation as artist, to them all)," Barbour suggested, adding, "His great perseverance in continually developing his craft and never resting on his past achievements is revealed in the steady growth in [his] artistry." In Weedman's estimation, "Few writers approach the lyricism, the command of language, the powerful combination of style and content that distinguishes Delany's works. More importantly," she concluded, "few writers, whether in science fiction or mundane fiction, so successfully create works which make us question ourselves, our actions, our beliefs, and our society as Delany has helped us do."

BIOGRAPHICAL AND CRITICAL SOURCES:

BOOKS

Bleiler, E.F., editor, *Science- Fiction Writers: Critical Studies of the Major Authors from the Early Nineteenth Century to the Present Day,* Scribner (New York, NY), 1982.

Contemporary Black Biography, Volume 9, Gale (Detroit, MI), 1995.

Contemporary Literary Criticism, Gale (Detroit, MI), Volume 8, 1978, Volume 14, 1980, Volume 38, 1986.

Dictionary of Literary Biography, Gale (Detroit, MI), Volume 8: *Twentieth- Century American Science Fiction Writers,* 1981, Volume 33: *Afro-American Fiction Writers after 1955,* 1984.

Kostelanetz, Richard, editor, *American Writing Today,* Whitston, 1991.

Gay and Lesbian Literature, Volume 2, St. James Press (Detroit, MI), 1998.

McCaffery, Larry, and Sinda Gregory, editors, *Alive and Writing: Interviews with American Authors of the 1980s,* University of Illinois Press, 1987.

McEvoy, Seth, *Samuel R. Delany,* Ungar, 1984.

Modern Black Writers, 2nd edition, St. James Press (Detroit, MI), 2000.

Peplow, Michael W., and Robert S. Bravard, *Samuel R. Delany: A Primary and Secondary Bibliography, 1962- 1979,* G.K. Hall, 1980.

Platt, Charles, editor, *Dream Makers: The Uncommon People Who Write Science Fiction,* Berkley Books, 1980.

Reference Guide to American Literature, 4th edition, St. James Press (Detroit, MI), 2000.

St. James Guide to Science Fiction Writers, 4th edition, St. James Press (Detroit, MI), 1996.

Sallis, James, *Ash of Stars: On the Writing of Samuel R. Delany,* University Press of Mississippi (Jackson, MI), 1996.

Slusser, George Edgar, *The Delany Intersection: Samuel R. Delany Considered as a Writer of Semi- Precious Words,* Borgo, 1977.

Smith, Nicholas D., editor, *Philosophers Look at Science Fiction,* Nelson-Hall, 1982.

Weedman, Jane Branham, *Samuel R. Delany,* Starmont House (Mercer Island, WA), 1982.

PERIODICALS

African American Review, fall, 1994, Robert F. Reid-Pharr, "Disseminating Heterotopia," p. 347; spring, 1997, Sandra Y. Govan, review of *Silent Interviews: On Language, Race, Sex, Science Fiction, and Some Comics,* p. 164; spring, 1999, review of *Longer Views: Extended Essays,* p. 173; fall, 2001, Robert Elliot Fox, review of *Shorter Views: Queer Thoughts and the Politics of the Paraliterary,* p. 491.

American Book Review, January, 1989, Thomas M. Disch, review of *The Motion of Light in Water.*

Analog Science Fiction/Science Fact, April, 1985, Tom Easton, review of *Stars in My Pocket Like Grains of Sand,* p. 77; June, 1995, review of *They Fly at Ciron,* p. 168.

Black American Literature Forum, summer, 1984, Sandra Y. Govan, "The Insistent Presence of Black Folk in the Novels of Samuel R. Delany," pp. 43-48.

Booklist, December 15, 1994, Carl Hays, review of *They Fly at Ciron,* p. 740; May 1, 1995, Carl Hays, review of *Atlantis: Three Tales,* p. 1551; May 1, 1996, Carl Hays, review of *Longer Views,* p. 1484; February 15, 2003, Ray Olson, review of *Aye, and Gomorrah: Stories,* p. 1043; December 15, 2005, Carl Hays, review of *About Writing: Seven Essays, Four Letters and Five Interviews,* p. 13.

Choice, February, 1989, E. Guereschi, review of *The Motion of Light in Water.*

Chronicle, March, 2005, Don D'Ammassa, review of *Stars in My Pocket Like Grains of Sand,* p. 20.

Entertainment Weekly, June 8, 2001, Karen Valby, "Writer Redux: With the Reissue of Such Sci-Fi Classics as *Dhalgren* and *Babel-17,* Samuel Delany Is Back on the Shelf," p. 24.

Extrapolation, summer, 1995, Heather MacLean, review of *Silent Interviews,* p. 163.

Fantasy Review, December, 1984, Larry McCaffery, review of *Stars in My Pocket like Grains of Sand.*

Foundation, March, 1975, Douglas Barbour, review of *The Einstein Intersection.*

Gay and Lesbian Review, January, 2001, Michael Bronski, "Correspondence of a Compulsive Chronicler," p. 33.

Georgia Review, fall, 2000, Joe Bonomo, review of *Times Square Red, Times Square Blue,* p. 573.

Globe & Mail (Toronto, Ontario, Canada), February 9, 1985, H.J. Kirchhoff, review of *Stars in My Pocket like Grains of Sand.*

GLQ, March, 2001, Eric Rofes, review of *Times Square Red, Times Square Blue,* p. 101.

Lambda Book Report, July-August, 1994, Stan Leventhal, review of *The Mad Man,* p. 35; September-October, 1995, Bruce Benderson, reviews of *Hogg* and *Atlantis: Three Tales,* p. 20; September, 1997, Mike Varady, review of *Longer Views,* p. 17; October, 2000, Thom Nickels, "The Lost Art of Letters," p. 40; August-September, 2004, Stefen Styrsky, "Order out of Chaos: Samuel R. Delany on Codes, Science Fiction and Philosophy," p. 6.

Library BookWatch, April, 2005, review of *Stars in My Pocket Like Grains of Sand.*

Library Journal, January, 1994, Michael Rogers, review of *Nèverÿona; or, The Tale of Signs and Cities, Tales of Nèverÿon,* and *The Motion of Light in Water,* p. 172; May 1, 1995, Albert E. Wilheim, review

of *Atlantis,* p. 134; June 15, 1996, Charles C. Nash, review of *Longer Views,* p. 65; December, 1998, Michael Rogers, review of *The Einstein Intersection,* p. 163; July, 1999, Carol J. Binkowski, review of *Times Square Red, Times Square Blue,* p. 118; January, 2000, Charles Crawford, review of *Shorter Views,* p. 104; July, 2000, Robert L. Kelly, review of *1984: Selected Letters,* p. 122; March 15, 2003, Jackie Cassada, review of *Aye, and Gomorrah,* p. 121; December 1, 2005, Nedra Crowe-Evers, review of *About Writing,* p. 129.

Locus, summer, 1983, Faren C. Miller, review of *Nèverÿona; or, The Tale of Signs and Cities;* October, 1989; January, 1995, p. 54.

Magazine of Fantasy and Science Fiction, November, 1975, Algis Budrys, review of *Dhalgren;* June, 1980; May, 1989; February, 2001, Elizabeth Hand, review of *1984: Selected Letters,* p. 36; February, 2002, Elizabeth Hand, review of *Dhalgren,* p. 40.

Mother Jones, August, 1976, Michael Goodwin, review of *Triton.*

Nation, October 28, 1996, Scott McLemee, review of *Longer Views: Extended Essays,* p. 60.

New York Times Book Review, February 16, 1975, Gerald Jonas, review of *Dhalgren,* p. 27; February 10, 1985, Gerald Jonas, review of *Stars in My Pocket Like Grains of Sand,* p. 15; January 1, 1995, Gerald Jonas, review of< *They Fly at Ciron,* p. 22; October 29, 1995, Rose Kernochan, review of *Atlantis: Three Tales,* p. 42; December 29, 1996, Gerald Jonas, review of *Longer Views,* p. 15.

Parnassus, spring, 2000, Thomas M. Disch, review of *Times Square Red, Times Square Blue,* p. 324.

Publishers Weekly, January 29, 1988, Genevieve Stuttaford, review of *The Motion of Light in Water,* p. 424; October 19, 1992, review of *The Fly at Ciron,* p. 62; April 18, 1994, review of *The Mad Man,* p. 48; February 27, 1995, review of *Hogg,* p. 89; April 3, 1995, review of *Atlantis,* p. 47; May 6, 1996, p. 74; May 31, 1999, review of *Times Square Red, Times Square Blue,* p. 73; June 14, 1999, review of *Bread and Wine: An Erotic Tale of New York,* p. 62; July 12, 1999, Michael Bronski, "Samuel Delany: Ghosts of Times Square," p. 68; p. 68; November 1, 1999, review of *Times Square Red, Times Square Blue,* p. 49; November 15, 1999, review of *Shorter Views,* p. 46; May 22, 2000, review of *1984: Selected Letters,* p. 87.

Reason, December, 2005, Bidisha Banerjee, "Dhalgren in New Orleans: a Classic Science Fiction Novel Comes to life in the Big Easy," p. 68.

Review of Contemporary Fiction, spring, 1995, Steven Moore, review of *Atlantis,* p. 175; spring, 1996, Steven Moore, review of *The Mad Man,* p. 162; fall, 1996, K. Leslie Steiner, "An Interview with

Samuel R. Delany," p. 97; fall, 1996, Russell Blackford, "Jewels in Junk City: To Read 'Triton,'" p. 142; spring, 1997, David Ian Paddy, review of *Dhalgren*, p. 181; fall, 1997, James Sallis, review of *Longer Views*, p. 223.

Science Fiction and Fantasy Book Review, July/August, 1983, Michael R. Collings, review of *Nèverÿona*.

Science-Fiction Studies, November, 1990, Robert M. Philmus, Renee Lallier, and Robert Copp, "On 'Triton' and other Matters: an Interview with Samuel R. Delan," p. 295; November, 1990, Martha A. Bartter, " The (Science-Fiction) Reader and the Quantum Paradigm: Problems in Delany's *Stars in My Pocket Like Grains of Sand*," p. 325; July, 1995, David N. Samuelson, "Talking," p. 265; March, 1997, R.D. Mullen, review of *Longer Views*, p. 60; July, 2000, Carl Freedman, "Of Cities and Bodies," p. 356; November, 2000, Carl Freedman, review of *1984*, p. 523.

Symploke, winter- spring, 2000, Elizabeth Renn Crowley, review of *Times Square Red, Times Square Blue*, p. 223.

Village Voice, January 24, 1995, Paul Miller, review of *Silent Interviews*, p. 78; November 9, 2004, Brandon Stosuy, review of *Phallos.*.

Washington Post Book World, January 27, 1985, Somtow Sucharitkul, review of *Stars in My Pocket like Grains of Sand*.

Wilson Library Bulletin, April, 1995, Fred Lernier, review of *They Fly at Ciron*, p. 94.

ONLINE

Onion A.V. Club, http://www.theavclub.com/ (March 3, 2006), Tasha Robinson, interview with Samuel R. Delany.

SF Site, http://www.sfsite.com/ (March 3, 2006), Jayme Lynn Blaschke, "A Conversation with Samuel R. Delany."

Temple University Web site, http://www.temple.edu/ (March 3, 2006), faculty profile of author.

*   *   *

DELANY, Samuel Ray, Jr.
See DELANY, Samuel R.

*   *   *

DeLILLO, Don 1936-
(Cleo Birdwell)

PERSONAL: Born November 20, 1936, in New York, NY; married. *Education:* Fordham University, graduated, 1958.

ADDRESSES: Agent—c/o Scribner Publicity Department, Simon & Schuster, Inc., 1230 Avenue of the Americas, New York, NY 10020.

CAREER: Writer. Worked as an advertising copywriter in early 1960s.

MEMBER: American Academy of Arts and Letters, PEN.

AWARDS, HONORS: Guggenheim fellowship, 1979; American Academy of Arts and Letters Award in Literature, 1984; National Book Award in fiction, and National Book Critics Circle Award nomination, both 1985, both for *White Noise; Irish Times* International Fiction Prize, National Book Award nomination, and National Book Critics Circle Award nomination, all 1989, all for *Libra;* PEN/Faulkner Award, 1992, and Pulitzer Prize nomination, both for *Mao II;* National Book Award nomination, and National Book Critics Circle Award nomination, both 1997, Pulitzer Prize nomination, and William Dean Howells Medal, American Academy of Arts and Letters, 2000, all for *Underworld;* Jerusalem Prize, 2000.

WRITINGS:

NOVELS

Americana, Houghton (Boston, MA), 1971.
End Zone, Houghton (Boston, MA), 1972.
Great Jones Street, Houghton (Boston, MA), 1973.
Ratner's Star, Knopf (New York, NY), 1976.
Players, Knopf (New York, NY), 1977.
Running Dog, Knopf (New York, NY), 1978.
(Under pseudonym Cleo Birdwell)*Amazons: An Intimate Memoir by the First Woman Ever to Play in the National Hockey League*, Holt, Rinehart, and Winston (New York, NY), 1980.
The Names, Knopf (New York, NY), 1982.
White Noise, Viking (New York, NY), 1985.
Libra, Viking (New York, NY), 1988.
Mao II, Viking (New York, NY), 1991.
Underworld, Scribner (New York, NY), 1997, prologue published separately as *Pafko at the Wall*, 2001.
The Body Artist, Scribner (New York, NY), 2001.
Cosmopolis, Scribner (New York, NY), 2003.

OTHER

The Day Room (play; produced at American Repertory Theatre, Cambridge, MA, 1986), Knopf (New York, NY), 1987.

Valparaiso (play; produced at American Repertory Theatre, Cambridge, MA, 1999), Scribner (New York, NY), 1999.

Love-Lies-Bleeding (play), Scribner (New York, NY), 2005.

Also author of play *The Engineer of Moonlight,* published in *Cornell Review,* winter, 1979; author of one-minute plays *The Rapture of the Athlete Assumed into Heaven,* published in *Quarterly,* 1990, and *The Mystery at the Middle of Ordinary Life,* published in *Zoetrope,* winter, 2000. Work included in anthologies *Stories from Epoch,* edited by Baxter Hathaway, Cornell University Press, 1966; *The Secret Life of Our Times,* edited by Gordon Lish, Doubleday, 1973; *Cutting Edges,* edited by Jack Hicks, Holt, 1973; *On the Job,* edited by William O'Rourke, Random House, 1977; and *Great Esquire Fiction,* edited by L. Rust Hills, Viking, 1983. Contributor of essay to *Novel History: Historians and Novelists Confront America's Past (and Each Other),* edited by Mark C. Carnes, Simon & Schuster, 2001; contributor of essays and short stories to periodicals, including *Dimensions, New Yorker, New York Times Magazine, Conjunctions, Harper's, Grand Street, Paris Review, Esquire, Granta, Sports Illustrated, Kenyon Review,* and *Rolling Stone.*

ADAPTATIONS: DeLillo's novels have been adapted as audiobooks.

SIDELIGHTS: With each of his novels Don DeLillo has enhanced his literary reputation and gained a wider audience for his carefully crafted prose. He first attracted critical attention in the early 1970s when he published two ambitious and elusive novels about games: *End Zone,* an existential comedy that parlays football into a metaphor for thermonuclear war, and *Ratner's Star,* a surrealistic science fiction that is structurally akin to the mathematical formulas it employs. The verbal precision, dazzling intelligence, and sharp wit of these books made DeLillo a critical favorite, "but without bestseller sales figures or a dependable cult following, he has become something of a reviewer's writer," according to R.Z. Sheppard in *Time.*

DeLillo's 1985 novel *White Noise* received front-page *New York Times Book Review* coverage and garnered the National Book Award in fiction that year. His name became even more widely known after *Underworld* achieved bestsellerdom in several countries, including the United States. "In fact," wrote Chicago *Tribune Books* contributor John W. Aldridge, on the heels of

White Noise, "DeLillo has won the right not only to be ranked with [Thomas] Pynchon and [William] Gaddis but recognized as having surpassed them in brilliance, versatility, and breadth of imagination. DeLillo shares with them, but in a degree greater than theirs, that rarest of creative gifts, the ability to identify and describe, as if from the perspective of another galaxy, the exact look and feel of contemporary reality." DeLillo's novel *Libra,* is an account of the life of Lee Harvey Oswald, John F. Kennedy's assassin. A stunning success— *Libra* was nominated for the National Book Award and won the newly inaugurated International Fiction Prize from the *Irish Times*—Walter Clemons in *Newsweek* dubbed the work "overwhelming."

DeLillo's obsession with language links him to other members of literature's school. "Like his contemporaries, William Gass, Robert Coover, and John Barth, he may be termed a 'metafictionist,'" wrote Michael Oriard in *Critique.* "Like these writers, he is strongly aware of the nature of language and makes language itself, and the process of using language, his themes." In his *Contemporary Literature* interview with Thomas LeClair, DeLillo suggested that after writing *End Zone,* he realized "that language was a subject as well as an instrument in my work." Later, he elaborated: "What writing means to me is trying to make interesting, clear, beautiful language. Working at sentences and rhythms is probably the most satisfying thing I do as a writer. I think after a while a writer can begin to know himself through his language. He sees someone or something reflected back at him from these constructions. Over the years it's possible for a writer to shape himself as a human being through the language he uses. I think written language, fiction, goes that deep."

While DeLillo's sentiments may have intimidated some readers, they have attracted enthusiastic critics. Rising to his challenge of commitment, reviewers have offered thoughtful interpretations of his complex work, recognizing recurring themes which darken and turn more ominous as the work evolves. "From *Americana* to *End Zone* to *Great Jones Street* to *Ratner's Star* DeLillo traces a single search for the source of life's meaning," explained Oriard. "By the end of *Ratner's Star,* the quest has been literally turned inside out, the path from chaos to knowledge becomes a Moebius strip that brings the seeker back to chaos."

The quest in DeLillo's first novel, *Americana,* involves a disillusioned television executive's search for a national identity. Abandoning his job, producer David Bell embarks on a cross-country odyssey to "nail down the gas-driven, motel-housed American soul," *Village Voice* contributor Albert Mobilio explained. Even in this early work, DeLillo's obsession with language dominates the narrative: his first-person narrator describes his quest as a "literary venture," using images that compare the western landscape to linguistic patterns on a page. "For years I had been held fast by the great unwinding mystery of this deep sink of land, the thick paragraphs and imposing photos, the gallop of panting adjectives, prairie truth and the clean kills of eagles," says Bell. *Americana,* like most first novels, was not widely reviewed, but it did attract favorable notice from some established New York critics, who expressed enthusiasm for DeLillo's remarkable verbal gifts. "It is a familiar story by now, flawed in the telling," noted *New York Times* contributor Christopher Lehmann-Haupt in a representative review. "But the language soars and dips, and it imparts a great deal." *New York Times Book Review* contributor Thomas R. Edwards deemed it "a savagely funny portrait of middle-class anomie in a bad time," but also noted that the book is "too long and visibly ambitious, and too much like too many other recent novels, to seem as good as it should have."

Edwards found DeLillo's second novel—in which the quest for meaning is transferred from the American roadside to the sports arena—a more successful venture. "In *End Zone*," wrote Edwards, "DeLillo finds in college football a more original and efficient vehicle for his sense of things now." This episodic, largely plotless novel focuses on the final attempt college athlete Gary Harkness makes to prove himself as a football player in a small west Texas school. Gary, who spends his free time playing war games, is attracted to carefully structured systems of ordered violence that afford opportunities for complete control. Edwards speculates that "Gary's involvement with [football] is a version of his horrified fascination with the vocabulary, theory and technology of modern war." Out on the playing field, Gary wins all but one of his football games, but "it's a season of losses all the same," Edwards concludes, for not only do minor characters suffer setbacks and tragedies but Gary "ends up in the infirmary with a mysterious brain-fever being fed through plastic tubes."

Gary's hunger strike has been interpreted as a final existential attempt to exert control. "He's paring things down. He is struggling, trying to face something he felt had to be faced," DeLillo told LeClair. Thus the "end zone" of this novel becomes a symbolic setting that represents "not only the goal of the running back in a football game, but the human condition at the outer extremity of existence, a place where the world is on the verge of disintegration, and the characters teeter be-

tween genius and madness," Oriard believes. "In this region of end zones that DeLillo describes, characters struggle for order and meaning as their world moves inexorably towards chaos. DeLillo's men and women fight the natural law of entropy, while human violence hastens its inevitable consequences."

The next American milieu DeLillo tackles is the world of rock stars and the drug culture in the novel *Great Jones Street*. Walter Clemons's assessment of the novel as an "in-between book" is representative of critical opinion, and while critics realized DeLillo was extending himself as a writer, they were not completely satisfied with the result. "The rock stars, drug dealers and hangers-on that populate *Great Jones Street* are so totally freaked out, so slickly devoted to destruction and evil, so obsessed with manipulating and acquiring that they're beyond redemption," wrote *New York Times Book Review* contributor Sara Blackburn, who deemed the work "more of a sour, admirably written lecture than a novel, a book that is always puffing to keep up with the power and intensity of its subject."

DeLillo turned to the genre of science fiction for his fourth book, *Ratner's Star,* a pivotal work about a fourteen-year-old mathematical genius and Nobel laureate, Billy Twillig. "There is no easy way to describe *Ratner's Star,* a cheerfully apocalyptic novel," wrote Amanda Heller in the *Atlantic.* "Imagine *Alice in Wonderland* set at the Princeton Institute for Advanced Studies." A reviewer for the *New Yorker* found it "a whimsical, surrealistic excursion into the modern scientific mind." *New York Times Book Review* contributor George Stade described it as "not only interesting, but funny (in a nervous kind of way). From it comes an unambiguous signal that DeLillo has arrived, bearing many gifts. He is smart, observant, fluent, a brilliant mimic and an ingenious architect."

Modeled after Lewis Carroll's *Alice in Wonderland, Ratner's Star* is comprised of two sections, "Adventures" and "Reflections," that mimic the structural divisions of Carroll's book. "The comic, episodic discontinuous style of the book's first half is reflected in reverse in its symmetrically opposite second part," explained G.M. Knoll in *America.* He continued, "All that has been asserted or hypothesized about the signals from Ratner's Star is here denied. Billy's assignment is now to assist in the development of a language to answer the star's message rather than decipher the meaning of the signals." DeLillo's goal in this venture, according to *Time* reviewer Paul Gray, "is to show how the codification of phenomena as practiced by scientists leads to absurdity and madness." In his interview with LeClair, however, DeLillo says that his primary intention was "to produce a book that would be naked structure. The structure would be the book."

Ratner's Star marked a turning point in DeLillo's fiction, according to critics who noted a shift in the pacing and tone of the novelist's subsequent books. "Since *Ratner's Star,* the apogee or nadir of his mirrorgame experiments, DeLillo has opened his fiction to the possibilities of more extroverted action," observed *New Republic* contributor Robert Towers. "The speeded-up pace in both *Players* and *Running Dog* seems to me all to the good." Accompanying this accelerated narrative, however, is a noticeable change in the kinds of people DeLillo is writing about. Hardened by exposure to modern society, cynical in their views of life, these characters "are not sustained by the illusion that answers to cosmic questions can be found," Oriard believed. Nor are their self-serving quests particularly admirable, according to *Dictionary of Literary Biography* contributor Frank Day, who maintained that readers may have a hard time sympathizing with protagonists whose lives are "parables of betrayal and degeneration. The frail, confused youths of the early novels are here displaced by characters influenced by popular espionage fiction."

In *Players* DeLillo employs a prologue—a sophisticated bit of pure fiction in which the characters are temporarily suspended outside the apparatus of the story—to introduce his themes. Before the narrative starts, DeLillo collects his as-yet-unnamed protagonists on an empty airplane, seating them in the lounge to watch a grisly film. "The Movie," as this prelude is called, depicts an unsuspecting band of Sunday golfers being attacked and murdered by marauding hippies who splatter the scenic green landscape with blood. Without earphones the passengers can not hear the dialogue, so the pianist improvises silent-movie music to accompany the scene. "The passengers laugh, cheer, clap," noted *New York Times Book Review* contributor Diane Johnson. "It is the terrorists whom they applaud." When the movie ends, the lights come up and the passengers, now identified as protagonists Lyle and Pammy Wynant and friends, step off the plane and into the story—a tale of terrorists, murder, and wasted lives.

A hip New York couple, Pammy and Lyle are bored to distraction by each other and their jobs. Pammy works as a promotional writer at the Grief Management Council, an organization that "served the community in its efforts to understand and assimilate grief," while Lyle is a stockbroker on Wall Street who spends his free time

parked in front of the TV set, flipping channels, not in hopes of finding a good program, but because "he simply enjoyed jerking the dial into fresh image burns."

Pammy moves out, heading off to Maine with a pair of homosexual lovers, one of whom will become her lover and commit suicide, but she will ultimately return home. Lyle takes up with a mindless secretary who is linked to a terrorist group responsible for murdering a man on the stock exchange floor. Intrigued by the glamour of revolutionary violence, Lyle joins forces with the terrorists, but also covers himself by informing on their activities to law enforcement agencies. "The end," noted John Updike in the *New Yorker,* "finds him in a motel in Canada, having double-crossed everybody but on excellent terms, it seems, with himself." Both he and Pammy have become players in the game.

Noting that DeLillo is that rare kind of novelist who looks "grandly at the whole state of things," Johnson postulated that, "since Freud, we've been used to the way novelists normally present a character: looks normal, is secretly strange and individual. In the first of many inversions of appearance and reality that structure the book, Pammy and Lyle look interesting and seem to do interesting things, but do not interest themselves. The richness is only superficial . . . . Pammy and Lyle have no history; they are without pasts, were never children, come from nowhere. They worry that they have become too complex to experience things directly and acutely, but the opposite is true. They are being reduced by contemporary reality to numb simplicity, lassitude."

DeLillo followed *Players* with two psychological thrillers, *Running Dog* and *The Names,* the latter of which was praised for its improved characterization. But it was with *White Noise* that DeLillo most impressed critics with his rendition of fully realized characters in a minimalist prose style. Noting that with each book DeLillo has become increasingly elliptical, *Village Voice* contributor Albert Mobilio observed that "the distillation is matched by a more subtle and convincing treatment of his characters' inner lives. This broadened emotional vocabulary charges *White Noise* with a resonance and credibility that makes it difficult to ignore. Critics who have argued that his work is too clever and overly intellectual should take notice: DeLillo's dark vision is now hard-earned. It strikes at both heart and head."

A novel about technology and death, *White Noise* unfolds as the first-person narrative of Jack Gladney, chair of the department of Hitler studies at a small liberal arts school, College-on-the-Hill. Gladney lives with his fourth wife Babette—an ample, disheveled woman who teaches an adult education class in posture and reads to the blind—and their four children from previous marriages: Wilder, Steffie, Denise, and Heinrich. Life seems full for the Gladneys, but early on Jack confesses that he and Babette are obsessed with a troubling question: "Who will die first?" Even as they debate it, small signs of trouble begin to surface: the children are evacuated from grade school because of an unidentified toxin in the atmosphere, and Babette's memory is impaired, a side effect of a prescribed medication. One winter day a major chemical spill jeopardizes the whole city. Everyone is forced to evacuate and, on his way to the shelter Jack stops to get gas, inadvertently exposing himself to the "airborne toxic event." Informed that "anything that puts you in contact with actual emissions means we have a situation," Jack becomes convinced he is dying. (As proof, his computerized health profile spews out "bracketed numbers with pulsing stars.") When Jack discovers Babette's medication—which she has committed adultery to obtain—is an experimental substance said to combat fear of death, he vows to find more of the substance for himself. His quest to obtain the illicit drug at any cost forms the closing chapters of the novel.

Newsweek contributor Walter Clemons wrote that *White Noise* should win DeLillo "wide recognition, till now only flickeringly granted as one of the best American novelists. Comic and touching, ingenious and weird, *White Noise* looks, at first, reassuringly like an example of a familiar genre, the campus novel." But, Clemons went on to say, the novel "tunes us in on frequencies we haven't heard in other accounts of how we live now. Occult supermarket tabloids are joined with TV disaster footage as household staples providing nourishment and febrile attractions. Fleeting appearances or phone calls from the Gladneys' previous spouses give us the start of surprise we experience when we learn that couples we know have a previous family we haven't heard about." Also commenting on DeLillo's depiction of domestic scenes, Jay McInerney wrote in the *New Republic* that the novelist's "portrait of this postnuclear family is one of the simpler pleasures of this novel." Bert Testa hypothesized in the Toronto *Globe and Mail* that " *White Noise* plays off the familiar and the disturbing without ever tipping into the merely grotesque. When DeLillo constantly returns to Jack's quotidian family life, he means his readers to enter a firmly drawn circle that not even a little toxic apocalypse can break."

"The world of *Libra* is not the modern or technological world that characters in my other novels try to confront," DeLillo explained to *New York Times* reviewer

Herbert Mitgang of his 1988 novel. In *Libra* the author mixes fact with fiction in a discussion of the events that led to the assassination of President John F. Kennedy on November 22, 1963, in Dallas, Texas. He dispels the accepted truth that Kennedy was shot by a lone gunman, Lee Harvey Oswald, by uncovering information supporting a conspiracy theory acknowledged by some historians. DeLillo spent three years researching and writing about Oswald's life, tracing the assassin's career as a Marxist in the U.S. military and his consequent defection to the USSR and return to the United States. DeLillo surmises that a coterie of underworld and U.S. government figures—enemies of Kennedy—recruited Oswald as a scapegoat for an assassination attempt that should have been botched.

"At what point exactly does fact drift over into fiction?" Anne Tyler asked in her *New York Times Book Review* critique of *Libra*. "The book is so seamlessly written that perhaps not even those people who own . . . copies of the Warren report could say for certain." Richard Eder in the *Los Angeles Times Book Review* agreed, noting that in the novel "DeLillo disassembles his plots with the finest of jigsaw cuts, scrambles their order and has us reassemble them. As the assorted characters go about their missions, we discern them more by intuition than by perception. The chronology goes back and forth, disorienting us. We do not so much follow what is going on as infiltrate it." Robert Dunn observed in *Mother Jones* that in his study of the president's assassin DeLillo "has found a story beyond imagination, one whose significance is indisputable and ongoing . . . and he carefully hews to known facts and approaches all events with respect, even awe. By giving Oswald and the forces he represents full body, DeLillo has written his best novel."

Mao II, further solidified DeLillo's place in the leading ranks of contemporary American novelists. The winner of the 1992 PEN/Faulkner Award for fiction, the novel revolves around a reclusive novelist, Bill Gray, whose first two works made him famous but who has labored for more than twenty years to produce his third novel. Completely hidden from public view on his rural New York estate, Gray has human contact only with his secretary and helper, Scott, and a young woman, Karen, who is coping with the dissolution of her marriage. In typical DeLillo fashion, Karen's was not a standard marriage: the novel's opening scene shows her wedding her husband along with six thousand other couples in a ceremony staged by the Reverend Sun Myung Moon at Yankee Stadium. Convinced that Gray's long-awaited novel will be a failure, Scott urges him not to publish it, arguing that his cult-like celebrity will increase if the novel never appears in print. Gray, however, tiring of his isolation, does something more momentous than publishing his novel: he allows himself to be photographed by Brita, a Swedish photographer.

In *Underworld* DeLillo paints an encyclopedic portrait of late-twentieth-century American life through the story of accused murderer Nick Shay, as Shay's path collides with great moments of history, including the 1951 ball game in which the Giants won the pennant. Michiko Kakutani reviewed *Underworld* admiringly in the *New York Times,* calling it a "remarkable" tale of "the effluvia of modern life, all the detritus of our daily and political lives" that has been "turned into a dazzling, phosphorescent work of art." Like most of DeLillo's novels, time is not a straight trajectory in *Underworld,* and a current of conspiracy, paranoia, and terrorism weaves through the story. This technique brings the alienated protagonist in close contact with events that define his century, including the political suspense of the cold war. In a review for the *New York Times,* Martin Amis claimed that *Underworld* "may or may not be a great novel," but added: "there is no doubt that . . . DeLillo is a great novelist." Noting that nuclear war is the central theme of the book, Amis added that *Underworld*'s "main actors are psychological 'downwinders,' victims of the fallout from all the blasts—blasts actual and imagined."

Coming on the heels of the impressive *Underworld, The Body Artist* reinforced the belief held by many critics that DeLillo is not a writer to traverse the same path more than once. *The Body Artists* opens to the breakfast-table rambling of married couple Lauren and Rey; only later in the book do readers learn that Rey has committed suicide that same day. The rest of the novel focuses on Lauren, a performance artist who creates different characters by transforming her physical self. Grieving over Rey, she withdraws and becomes housebound, then begins to hear noises. Finally she discovers a strange, diminutive man, Mr. Tucker, who has the strange ability to repeat back to her the last rambling conversations between Lauren and her husband. Who Mr. Tucker is—a real, perhaps mentally disturbed person or a figment of Lauren's overwrought imaginings—is purposefully never made clear, DeLillo's central purpose to cause readers to reflect on "the fragility of identity, the nature of time, the way the words we employ in the face of death have become . . . worn to the point of transparency," according to *Newsweek* contributor Malcolm Jones. "Like all DeLillo's fiction," added a *Publishers Weekly* contributor, *The Body Artist* "offers a vision of contemporary life that expresses itself most clearly in how the story is told." While an *Economist* critic found

the novel as "slight as a blade of grass," Donna Seaman praised the challenging work in *Booklist,* noting that "Each sentence is like a formula that must be solved, and each paragraph adds up to unexpected disclosures regarding our sense of time, existence, identity, and connection."

More compressed in time than *The Body Artist, Cosmopolis* takes place for the most part inside a stretch limousine belonging to wealthy, twenty-something, and less-than-likeable financier Eric Packer. Packer's trip across town to the barber is thwarted by traffic snarls into an all-day excursion, forcing the mildly paranoid Packer to turn to his in-car computer to track his financial wheelings and dealings, teleconference with clients and lackeys, and make brief excursions from the limo to eat, shop, take in the sights of midtown Manhattan, and even commit murder. While the movement of Packer's limo is "glacial," according to an *Economist* reviewer, *Cosmopolis,* "with Mr. DeLillo at the wheel, zooms along, blowing up great billowing clouds of rhetorical dust . . . . full of wordy ruminations on the relationship between technology and capitalism."

Critics responded with characteristic vigor to *Cosmopolis,* although the novel, DeLillo's thirteenth, was not treated with overwhelming kindness. "There is no real plot," bemoaned *Spectator* contributor Peter Dempsey, "there are no fully rounded characters nor any character development, and though the novel ends dramatically, there is no sense of a conventionally satisfying conclusion." Noting that such expectations on the part of many critics are intentionally unmet by DeLillo, Dempsey described *Cosmopolis* as "a meditation on various kinds of speculation, most importantly financial and philosophical," that, as a work of fiction, "is redeemed by its beguiling structure and the cool intensity of its compelling descriptions of New York City." "Where did DeLillo lose me exactly?," Richard Lacayo queried in *Time.* "It may have been the scene in which Packer gets a digital rectal exam in his parked limousine while he chats with . . . his chief of finance. I like surrealism too, but sometimes I wish they would keep it in France." In contrast, *Review of Contemporary Fiction* critic Robert L. McLaughlin stayed the course, writing that the author "has captured the essence of a particular American moment," and ranked the novel as "a beautiful and brilliant book." "One senses that DeLillo continues to challenge himself," added Kyle Minor in *Antioch Review,* "and the result is a mature work of fiction, greatly satisfying."

In 2005 DeLillo published his third play, *Love-Lies-Bleeding.* In the play, an artist named Alex persists in a vegetative state after his second stroke. His son and ex-wife travel to his home in the desert to convince his current wife to let him die. John Leonard, reviewing the book in *Harper's,* called the play "a philosophical romance rooted in the tactile, textured and landscaped from shoe trees, shopping carts, and painted caves to larkspur, mariposa, and Apache plume." M.C. Duhing, writing in *Library Journal,* noted, "DeLillo has become increasingly confident as a dramatist, and we can only hope that he continues his endeavors in this genre."

BIOGRAPHICAL AND CRITICAL SOURCES:

BOOKS

Civello, Paul, *American Literary Naturalism and Its Twentieth-Century Transformations: Frank Norris, Ernest Hemingway, Don DeLillo,* University of Georgia Press (Athens, GA), 1994.

Contemporary Literary Criticism, Gale (Detroit, MI), Volume 8, 1978, Volume 10, 1979, Volume 13, 1980, Volume 27, 1984, Volume 39, 1986, Volume 54, 1989, Volume 76, 1993.

DeLillo, Don, *Americana,* Houghton (Boston, MA), 1971.

Dictionary of Literary Biography, Volume 6: *American Novelists since World War II, Second Series,* Gale (Detroit, MI), 1980.

Hantke, Steffen, *Conspiracy and Paranoia in Contemporary American Fiction: The Works of Don DeLillo and Joseph McElroy,* P. Lang (New York, NY), 1994.

Jackson, Thomas DePietro, editor, *Conversations with Don DeLillo,* University of Mississippi, 2005.

LeClair, Tom, *In the Loop: Don DeLillo and the Systems Novel,* University of Illinois Press, 1988.

Lentricchia, Frank, *Introducing Don DeLillo,* Duke University Press, 1991.

Lentricchia, Frank, editor, *New Essays on White Noise,* Cambridge University Press (New York, NY), 1991.

Osteen, Mark, *American Magic and Dread: Don DeLillo's Dialogue with Culture,* University of Pennsylvania Press, 2000.

Ruppersburg, Hugh M., and Tim Engles, editors,*Critical Essays on Don DeLillo,* G.K. Hall (New York, NY), 2000.

PERIODICALS

America, August 7, 1976; July 6-13, 1985.

Antioch Review, spring, 1972; winter, 1983; summer, 2003, Kyle Minor, review of *Cosmopolis,* p. 581.

Atlantic, August, 1976; February, 1985.

Booklist, November 1, 1993, p. 499; October 1, 2000, Donna Seaman, review of *The Body Artist,* p. 292; December 1, 2002, Donna Seaman, review of *Cosmopolis,* p. 628.

Choice, April, 1988, p. 1242.

Christian Century, May 2, 2001, Gordon Houser, review of *The Body Artist,* p. 27.

Commonweal, August 9, 1991, pp. 490-491.

Contemporary Literature, winter, 1982, Tom LeClair, "An Interview with Don DeLillo," pp. 19-31

Critique, Volume XX, number 1, 1978.

Detroit News, February 24, 1985.

Economist (U.S.), February 17, 2001, review of *The Body Artist,* p. 8; April 19, 2003, review of *Cosmopolis.*

Entertainment Weekly, April 11, 2003, Chris Nashawaty, "Prophet Statement" (interview), p. 48; April 18, 2003, Ken Tucker, review of *Cosmopolis,* p. 72.

Esquire, February, 2000, Sven Birkerts, review of *The Body Artist,* p. 38.

Financial Post, November 1, 1997, Allan Hepburn, review of *Underworld,* p. 28.

Globe and Mail (Toronto, Ontario, Canada), March 9, 1985; August 27, 1988.

Harper's, September, 1977; December, 1982; June, 1999, Jonathan Dee, review of *Libra,* p. 76; January, 2006, John Leonard, review of *Love-Lies-Bleeding,* p. 81.

Hudson Review, summer, 1999, Richard Hornby, review of *Valparaiso,* p. 287.

Journal of Men's Studies, fall, 1999, p. 73.

Journal of Modern Literature, spring, 1996, p. 453.

Kirkus Reviews, January 1, 2003, review of *Cosmopolis,* p. 8.

Library Journal, January, 1988, p. 96; January 1, 2001, Mirela Roncevic, review of *The Body Artist,* p. 152l; December, 2002, Edward B. St. John, review of *Cosmopolis,* p. 176; November 15, 2005, M.C. Duhig, review of *Love-Lies-Bleeding,* p. 67.

Los Angeles Times, July 29, 1984; August 12, 1988; October 8, 1997, David L. Ulin, "Merging Myth and Mystery," p. E1; December 14, 1997, Richard Eder, review of *Underworld,* p. 11.

Los Angeles Times Book Review, November 7, 1982; January 13, 1985; July 31, 1988; June 9, 1991, p. 3.

Maclean's, November 13, 1978, pp. 62, 64; August 29, 1988.

Modern Fiction Studies, summer, 1994, p. 229.

Mother Jones, September, 1988.

Nation, September 17, 1977; October 18, 1980; December 11, 1982; February 2, 1985; September 19, 1988.

National Review, October 28, 1977.

New Republic, October 7, 1978; November 22, 1982; February 4, 1985.

New Statesman, February 2, 1979, p. 158.

Newsweek, June 7, 1976; August 29, 1977; October 25, 1982; January 21, 1985; August 15, 1988; January 15, 2001, Malcolm Jones, review of *The Body Artist,* p. 61.

New Yorker, July 12, 1976; March 27, 1978; September 18, 1978; April 4, 1983; September 15, 1997, David Remnick, "Exile on Main Street," pp. 42-48.

New York Review of Books, June 29, 1972; December 16, 1982; March 14, 1985; June 9, 1991, pp. 7, 49; June 27, 1991, pp. 17-18; February 22, 2001, John Leonard, review of *The Body Artist,* p. 14.

New York Times, May 6, 1971; March 22, 1972; April 16, 1973; May 27, 1976; August 11, 1977; September 16, 1980; October 12, 1982; January 7, 1985; December 20, 1987; December 21, 1987; July 19, 1988; May 18, 1989; September 24, 1989; September 16, 1997, Michiko Kakutani, review of *Underworld,* p. E1; October 5, 1997, p. E2; September 10, 1998, David Firestone, "Reticent Novelist Talks Baseball, Not Books," p. B2; February 24, 1999, Peter Marks, "Ticket Mix-up Brings Fifteen Minutes of Fame," p. E1.

New York Times Book Review, May 30, 1971; April 9, 1972; April 22, 1973; June 20, 1976; September 4, 1977; November 12, 1978; October 10, 1982, Robert R. Harris, "A Talk with Don DeLillo," p. 23; January 13, 1985, Caryn James, "I Never Set out to Write an Apocalyptic Novel," p. 31; May 28, 1991, p. C15; October 5, 1997, Martin Amis, review of *Underworld,* p. 12; December 7, 1997, review of *Underworld,* p. 95; July 24, 1998, Kim Heron, "Haunted by His Book," p. 23.

New York Times Magazine, May 19, 1991, Vince Passaro, "Dangerous Don DeLillo," pp. 36-38, 76-77.

Partisan Review, number 3, 1979.

Publishers Weekly, August 19, 1988; November 20, 2000, review of *The Body Artist,* p. 43; December 9, 2002, review of *Cosmopolis,* p. 58.

Review of Contemporary Fiction, spring, 2001, David Seed, review of *The Body Artist,* p. 189; summer, 2003, Robert L. McLaughlin, review of *Cosmopolis,* p. 120.

Saturday Review, September 3, 1977; September 16, 1978.

Spectator, September 7, 1991, pp. 34-35; June 7, 2003, Peter Dempsey, review of *Cosmopolis,* p. 38.

Time, June 7, 1976; November 8, 1982; January 21, 1985; August 1, 1988; June 10, 1991, p. 68; April 21, 2003, Richard Lacayo, review of *Cosmopolis,* p. 74.

Times (London, England), January 23, 1986.

Times Literary Supplement, September 14, 1973; December 9, 1983; January 17, 1986.

Tribune Books (Chicago, IL), November 7, 1982; January 13, 1985; July 31, 1988; June 23, 1991, pp. 1, 4.

USA Today, January 11, 1985.

Vanity Fair, September, 1997, David Kamp, "DeLillo's Home Run," pp. 202-204.

Variety, March 1, 1999, Markland Taylor, review of *Valparaiso,* p. 93.

Village Voice, April 30, 1985; June 18, 1991, p. 65.

Voice Literary Supplement, December, 1981; November, 1982; October, 1988.

Wall Street Journal, June 13, 1991, review of *Mao II,* p. A14; September 26, 1997, James Bowman, review of *Underworld,* p. A20.

Washington Post, August 24, 1988; May 11, 1989; May 14, 1992, "Don DeLillo's Gloomy Muse," p. C1; November 11, 1997, David Streitfeild, "Don DeLillo's Hidden Truths," p. D1.

Washington Post Book World, April 16, 1972; April 15, 1973; June 13, 1976; August 21, 1977; October 15, 1978; October 10, 1982; January 13, 1985; July 31, 1988; May 26, 1991, pp. 1-2.

World and I, October, 2001, Linda Simon, "Voice from a Silent Landscape," p. 253.

World Literature Today, winter, 1992.

Yale Review, April, 1995, p. 107.

*   *   *

DEMIJOHN, Thom
  See DISCH, Thomas M.

*   *   *

DENIS, Julio
  See CORTÁZAR, Julio

*   *   *

DENMARK, Harrison
  See ZELAZNY, Roger

*   *   *

dePAOLA, Tomie 1934-
(Thomas Anthony dePaola)

PERSONAL: Some sources cite surname as de Paola; name pronounced "Tommy de-*pow*la"; born September 15, 1934, in Meriden, CT; son of Joseph N. (a union official) and Florence (Downey) dePaola; married in the 1950s (marriage dissolved). *Education:* Pratt Institute, B.F.A., 1956; California College of Arts and Crafts, M.F.A., 1969; Lone Mountain College, doctoral equivalency, 1970. *Religion:* Roman Catholic

ADDRESSES: Home—New London, NH. *Agent*—c/o Author Mail, Penguin Putnam, Putnam Juvenile Publicity, 345 Hudson St., New York, NY 10014.

CAREER: Professional artist and designer, and teacher of art, 1956—; writer and illustrator of children's books; creative director of Whitebird Books, imprint at G.P. Putnam's Sons. Newton College of the Sacred Heart, Newton, MA, instructor, 1962-63, assistant professor of art, 1963-66; San Francisco College for Women (now Lone Mountain College), San Francisco, CA, assistant professor of art, 1967-70; Chamberlayne Junior College, Boston, MA, instructor in art, 1972-73; Colby-Sawyer College, New London, NH, associate professor, designer, and technical director in speech and theater department, writer and set and costume designer for Children's Theatre Project, 1973-76; New England College, Henniker, NH, associate professor of art, 1976-78, artist-in-residence, 1978-79. Painter and muralist; graphic designer and illustrator; designer of theatrical sets. Member of board of directors of Society of Children's Book Writers of Los Angeles. *Exhibitions:* Individual shows at Botolph Group, Boston, MA, 1961, 1964, 1967; Putnam Art Center, Newton College of the Sacred Heart, 1971-72, 1975, 1978; Alliance Corporation, Boston, 1972; Library Arts Center, Newport, NH, 1975, 1982, 1984; Rizzoli Gallery, New York, NY, 1977; Clark County Library, Las Vegas, NV, 1979; Englewood (NJ) Library, 1980; Louisiana Arts and Science Center, Baton Rouge, LA, 1981; University of Minnesota, Minneapolis, 1981; Children's Theatre, Minneapolis, 1981; Yuma City-County (AZ) Library, 1981; Charles Fenton Gallery, Woodstock, VT, 1984; Arts and Science Center, Nashua, NH, 1985, 1986; Bush Galleries, Norwich, VT, 1987; and Women's Club, Minneapolis, 1988. Work exhibited in group shows at South Vermont Art Center, Manchester, 1958; Grail Festival of the Arts, Brooklyn, 1959; Botolph Group, 1962, 1964, 1969; San Francisco College for Women, 1969; Immaculate Heart College, Los Angeles, 1969; Library Arts Center, Newport, NH, 1975; Everson Museum, Syracuse, NY, 1977; Japan, 1977, 1979, 1981; Children's Book Fair, Bologna, Italy, 1978; Museum of Fine Arts, Houston, 1978; Dayton Art Institute, 1978; Brattleboro Museum and Art Center, 1980; Harley School, Rochester, NY, 1980-88; Port Washington, NY, Public Library, 1981; University of Connecticut Library, Storrs, 1982; Society of Illustrators, New York,

1982, 1983, 1984, 1985; Metropolitan Museum of Art, 1982, 1983; Museum of Fine Art, Houston, 1982; Dog Museum of America, New York, NY, 1983; Boulder Center for Visual Arts, 1983; University of New Hampshire, Durham, 1983; Simmons College, Boston, 1984; Bush Galleries, Norwich, VT, 1985; Congress Square Gallery, Portland, ME, 1985; Denver Public Library, 1986; Colorado Academy, 1986; New London, NH, Historical Society, 1985, 1986, 1988; Aetna Institute Gallery, Hartford, CT, 1986; Miami Youth Museum, 1986; and New Hampshire Historical Society, Concord, 1988. Works are also included in many private collections. Mural installations in Catholic churches and monasteries in New England. Member, National Advisory Council of the Children's Theater Company of Minneapolis; Ballet of the Dolls Dance Company, Minneapolis, member of board of directors.

MEMBER: Society of Children's Book Writers (member of board of directors), Authors Guild.

AWARDS, HONORS: Boston Art Directors' Club awards for typography and illustration, 1968; Child Study Association children's book of the year citations, 1968, for *Poetry for Chuckles and Grins,* 1971, for *John Fisher's Magic Book,* 1974, for *David's Window* and *Charlie Needs a Cloak,* 1975, for *Strega Nona* and *Good Morning to You, Valentine,* 1986, for *Strega Nona's Magic Lessons, Tattie's River Journey, Tomie dePaola's Mother Goose,* and *The Quilt Story,* 1987, for *Teeny Tiny* and *Tomie dePaola's Favorite Nursery Tales;* Franklin Typographers Silver Award for poster design, 1969; three books included in American Institute of Graphic Arts exhibit of outstanding children's books, *The Journey of the Kiss,* 1970, *Who Needs Holes?,* 1973, and *Helga's Dowry,* 1979; two books included on *School Library Journal*'s list of best picture books, *Andy, That's My Name,* 1973, and *Charlie Needs a Cloak,* 1974; Friends of American Writers Award as best illustrator of a children's book, 1973, for *Authorized Autumn Charts of the Upper Red Canoe River Country;* two books chosen as Children's Book Showcase titles, *Authorized Autumn Charts of the Upper Red Canoe River Country,* 1973, and *Charlie Needs a Cloak,* 1975; Brooklyn Art Books for Children Award, Brooklyn Museum and Brooklyn Public Library, 1975, for *Charlie Needs a Cloak,* and 1977, 1978, and 1979, for *Strega Nona,* which also received the Caldecott Honor Book Award, 1976, and the Nakamore Prize (Japan), 1978; *The Quicksand Book* and *Simple Pictures Are Best* were both chosen one of *School Library Journal*'s Best Books for Spring, 1977; Chicago Book Clinic Award, 1979, for *The Christmas Pageant; Helga's Dowry* was chosen a Children's Choice by the

International Reading Association and the Children's Book Council, 1978, *The Popcorn Book, Pancakes for Breakfast, The Clown of God, Four Scary Stories, Jamie's Tiger,* and *Bill and Pete,* all 1979, *Big Anthony and the Magic Ring* and *Oliver Button Is a Sissy,* both 1980, *The Comic Adventures of Old Mother Hubbard and Her Dog,* 1982, *Strega Nona's Magic Lessons,* 1983, *The Carsick Zebra and other Animal Riddles,* 1984, and *The Mysterious Giant of Barletta,* 1985; Garden State Children's Book Award for Younger Nonfiction, New Jersey Library Association, 1980, for *The Quicksand Book;* Kerlan Award, University of Minnesota, 1981, for "singular attainment in children's literature"; Golden Kite Award for Illustration, Society of Children's Book Writers, 1982, for *Giorgio's Village,* and 1983, for *Marianna May and Nursey; Boston Globe-Horn Book* Award Honor Book for Illustration, 1982, and Critici in Erba commendation from Bologna Biennale, 1983, both for *The Friendly Beasts;* Regina Medal, Catholic Library Association, 1983, for "continued distinguished contribution to children's literature"; *Sing, Pierrot, Sing* was chosen one of *School Library Journal*'s Best Books, 1983; *Mary Had a Little Lamb* was chosen as a Notable Book by the Association of Library Service to Children (ALA), 1984; *Clown of God* was selected a Notable Children's Film, 1984; *Sing, Pierrot, Sing* was selected a Notable Children's Trade Book in the Field of Social Studies by the National Council of Social Studies and the Children's Book Council, 1984, and *The Mysterious Giant of Barletta,* 1985; Award from the Bookbuilders West Book Show, 1985, for *Miracle on 34th Street;* Redbook Children's Picturebook Award Honorable Mention, 1986, for *Tomie dePaola's Favorite Nursery Tales; Horn Book* Honor List citation, 1986, for *Tomie dePaola's Mother Goose;* Golden Kite Honor Book for Illustration, 1987, for *What the Mailman Brought; The Art Lesson* was named one of the *New York Times*' best picture books of the year, 1989; American nominee in illustration for the Hans Christian Andersen Award, 1990; Smithsonian Medal, 1990; Helen Keating Ott Award, 1993; University of Southern Mississippi Medallion, 1995; Keene State College Children's Literature Festival Award, 1998; Newbery Award Honor Book, 2000, for *26 Fairmount Avenue.*

WRITINGS:

Criss-Cross, Applesauce, illustrations by B.A. King and his children, Addison House (Danbury, NH), 1979.
Strega Nona Takes a Vacation, Putnam (New York, NY), 2000.
Jamie O'Rourke and the Pooka, Putnam (New York, NY), 2000.

Also author of *The Legend of the Persian Carpet,* illustrated by Claire Ewart.

AND ILLUSTRATOR

The Wonderful Dragon of Timlin, Bobbs-Merrill (Indianapolis, IN), 1966.
Fight the Night, Lippincott (Philadelphia, PA), 1968.
Joe and the Snow, Hawthorn (New York, NY), 1968.
Parker Pig, Esquire, Hawthorn (New York, NY), 1969.
The Journey of the Kiss, Hawthorn (New York, NY), 1970.
The Monsters' Ball, Hawthorn (New York, NY), 1970.
(Reteller) *The Wind and the Sun,* Ginn (Lexington, MA), 1972.
Andy, That's My Name, Prentice-Hall (New York, NY), 1973.
Charlie Needs a Cloak, Prentice-Hall (New York, NY), 1973.
Nana Upstairs and Nana Downstairs, Putnam (New York, NY), 1973, reissued, 1997.
The Unicorn and the Moon, Ginn (Lexington, MA), 1973.
Watch Out for the Chicken Feet in Your Soup, Prentice-Hall (New York, NY), 1974.
The Cloud Book: Word and Pictures, Holiday House (New York, NY), 1975, translation by Teresa Mlawer, published as *El Libro de las Arenas Movedizas,* Holiday House, 1993.
Michael Bird-Boy, Prentice-Hall (New York, NY), 1975.
(Reteller) *Strega Nona: An Old Tale,* Prentice-Hall (New York, NY), 1975, published as *The Magic Pasta Pot,* Hutchinson (London, England), 1979.
Things to Make and Do for Valentine's Day, F. Watts (New York, NY), 1976.
When Everyone Was Fast Asleep, Holiday House (New York, NY), 1976.
Four Stories for Four Seasons, Prentice-Hall (New York, NY), 1977.
Helga's Dowry: A Troll Love Story, Harcourt (New York, NY), 1977.
The Quicksand Book, Holiday House (New York, NY), 1977, translation by Mlawer, published as *El libro de las nubes,* Holiday House, 1993.
Bill and Pete, Putnam (New York, NY), 1978.
The Christmas Pageant, Winston (Minneapolis, MN), 1978, published as *The Christmas Pageant Cutout Book,* 1980.
(Adapter) *The Clown of God: An Old Story,* Harcourt (New York, NY), 1978.
Pancakes for Breakfast, Harcourt (New York, NY), 1978.

The Popcorn Book, Holiday House (New York, NY), 1978.

Big Anthony and the Magic Ring, Harcourt (New York, NY), 1979.

Flicks, Harcourt (New York, NY), 1979.

The Kids' Cat Book, Holiday House (New York, NY), 1979.

Oliver Button Is a Sissy, Harcourt (New York, NY), 1979.

Songs of the Fog Maiden, Holiday House (New York, NY), 1979.

The Family Christmas Tree Book, Holiday House (New York, NY), 1980.

The Knight and the Dragon, Putnam (New York, NY), 1980.

The Lady of Guadalupe, Holiday House (New York, NY), 1980.

The Legend of the Old Befana: An Italian Christmas Story, Harcourt (New York, NY), 1980.

(Reteller) *The Prince of the Dolomites: An Old Italian Tale,* Harcourt (New York, NY), 1980.

The Comic Adventures of Old Mother Hubbard and Her Dog, Harcourt (New York, NY), 1981.

(Reteller) *Fin M'Coul, the Giant of Knockmany Hill,* Holiday House (New York, NY), 1981.

The Friendly Beasts: An Old English Christmas Carol, Putnam (New York, NY), 1981.

The Hunter and the Animals: A Wordless Picture Book, Holiday House (New York, NY), 1981.

Now One Foot, Now the Other, Putnam (New York, NY), 1981.

Strega Nona's Magic Lessons, Harcourt (New York, NY), 1982.

Francis, the Poor Man of Assisi, Holiday House (New York, NY), 1982.

Giorgio's Village, Putnam (New York, NY), 1982.

(Adapter) *The Legend of the Bluebonnet: An Old Tale of Texas,* Putnam (New York, NY), 1983.

Marianna May and Nursey, Holiday House (New York, NY), 1983.

Noah and the Ark, Winston (Minneapolis, MN), 1983.

Sing, Pierrot, Sing: A Picture Book in Mime, Harcourt (New York, NY), 1983.

(Adapter) *The Story of the Three Wise Kings,* Putnam (New York, NY), 1983.

(Adapter) *David and Goliath,* Winston (Minneapolis, MN), 1984.

Esther Saves Her People, Winston (Minneapolis, MN), 1984.

The First Christmas: A Festive Pop-up Book, Putnam (New York, NY), 1984.

(Adapter) *The Mysterious Giant of Barletta: An Italian Folktale,* Harcourt (New York, NY), 1984.

Tomie dePaola's Country Farm, Putnam (New York, NY), 1984.

Tomie dePaola's Mother Goose Story Streamers, Putnam (New York, NY), 1984.

Tomie dePaola's Mother Goose, Putnam (New York, NY), 1985.

Pajamas for Kit, Simon & Schuster (New York, NY), 1986.

Katie and Kit at the Beach, Simon & Schuster (New York, NY), 1986.

Katie's Good Idea, Simon & Schuster (New York, NY), 1986.

Katie, Kit and Cousin Tom, Simon & Schuster (New York, NY), 1986.

Merry Christmas, Strega Nona, Harcourt (New York, NY), 1986.

(With others) *Once upon a Time: Celebrating the Magic of Children's Books in Honor of the Twentieth Anniversary of Reading Is Fundamental,* Putnam (New York, NY), 1986.

(Adapter) *Queen Esther,* Winston (Minneapolis, MN), 1986, revised edition, Harper (New York, NY), 1987.

Tomie dePaola's Favorite Nursery Tales, Putnam (New York, NY), 1986.

Bill and Pete Go down the Nile, Putnam (New York, NY), 1987.

An Early American Christmas, Holiday House (New York, NY), 1987.

The Legend of the Indian Paintbrush, Putnam (New York, NY), 1987.

The Miracles of Jesus, Holiday House (New York, NY), 1987.

The Parables of Jesus, Holiday House (New York, NY), 1987.

Tomie dePaola's Book of Christmas Carols, Putnam (New York, NY), 1987.

Tomie dePaola's Diddle, Diddle, Dumpling and other Poems and Stories from Mother Goose (selections from *Tomie dePaola's Mother Goose*), Methuen (London, England), 1987.

Tomie dePaola's Three Little Kittens and other Poems and Songs from Mother Goose (selections from *Tomie dePaola's Mother Goose*), Methuen (London, England), 1987.

Baby's First Christmas, Putnam (New York, NY), 1988.

(Reteller) *Hey Diddle Diddle: And other Mother Goose Rhymes* (selections from *Tomie dePaola's Mother Goose*), Putnam (New York, NY), 1988.

Tomie dePaola's Book of Poems, Putnam (New York, NY), 1988.

(With others) *The G.O.S.H. ABC Book,* Aurum Books for Children (London, England), 1988.

The Art Lesson, Putnam (New York, NY), 1989.

Haircuts for the Woolseys, Putnam (New York, NY), 1989.

My First Chanukah, Putnam (New York, NY), 1989.

Tony's Bread: An Italian Folktale, Putnam (New York, NY), 1989.

Too Many Hopkins, Putnam (New York, NY), 1989.

Little Grunt and the Big Egg, Holiday House (New York, NY), 1990.

Tomie dePaola's Book of Bible Stories, Putnam/Zondervan (New York, NY), 1990.

Bonjour, Mr. Satie, Putnam (New York, NY), 1991.

My First Easter, Putnam (New York, NY), 1991.

My First Passover, Putnam (New York, NY), 1991.

My First Halloween, Putnam (New York, NY), 1991.

My First Thanksgiving, Putnam (New York, NY), 1992.

Country Angel Christmas, Putnam (New York, NY), 1995.

Days of the Blackbird: A Tale of Northern Italy, Putnam (New York, NY), 1997.

Tomie's Little Mother Goose, Putnam (New York, NY), 1997.

Big Anthony: His Story, Putnam (New York, NY), 1998.

The Night of Las Posadas, Putnam (New York, NY), 1999.

26 Fairmount Avenue (first book in the "26 Fairmount Avenue" series), Putnam (New York, NY), 1999.

Tomie dePaola's Rhyme Time, Grosset & Dunlap (New York, NY), 2000.

Here We All Are (second book in the "26 Fairmount Avenue" series) Putnam (New York, NY), 2000.

Meet the Barkers: Morgan and Moffat Go to School (first book in the "Barkers" series), Putnam (New York, NY), 2001.

Hide-and-Seek All Week (second book in the "Barkers" series), Grosset & Dunlap (New York, NY), 2001.

On My Way (third book in the "26 Fairmount Avenue" series), Putnam (New York, NY), 2001.

Adelita: A Mexican Cinderella Story, Putnam (New York, NY), 2002.

Four Friends at Christmas, Simon & Schuster (New York, NY), 2002.

Boss for a Day (third book in the "Barkers" series), Grosset & Dunlap (New York, NY), 2002.

A New Barker in the House (fourth book in the "Barkers" series), Putnam (New York, NY), 2002.

T-Rex Is Missing! (fifth book in the "Barkers" series), Grosset & Dunlap (New York, NY), 2002.

What a Year, Putnam (New York, NY), 2002.

Four Friends in Summer, Simon & Schuster (New York, NY), 2003.

Frida Kahlo: The Artist Who Painted Herself, Grosset & Dunlap (New York, NY), 2003.

Marcos Colors: Red, Yellow, Blue, Putnam (New York, NY), 2003.

Marcos Counts: One, Two, Three, Putnam (New York, NY), 2003.

Things Will Never Be the Same, Putnam (New York, NY), 2003.

Trouble in the Barkers' Class (sixth book in the "Barkers" series), Putnam (New York, NY), 2003.

Four Friends in Autumn, Simon & Schuster (New York, NY), 2004.

Pascual and the Kitchen Angels, Putnam (New York, NY), 2004.

Also author and illustrator of *Jingle, the Christmas Clown,* 1992, *Jamie O'Rourke and the Big Potato,* 1992, *Patrick: Patron Saint of Ireland,* 1992, *Tom,* 1993, *Kit and Kat,* 1994, *Christopher: The Holy Giant,* 1994, *The Legend of the Poinsettia,* 1994, *Strega Nona Meets Her Match,* 1995, *Country Angel Christmas,* 1995, *The Baby Sister,* 1996, *Strega Nona: Her Story,* 1996, *Mary: The Mother of Jesus,* 1997, and *Tomie's Little Mother Goose,* 1997.

ILLUSTRATOR:

Lisa Miller (pseudonym of Bernice Kohn Hunt) *Sound,* Coward (New York, NY), 1965.

Pura Belpre, *The Tiger and the Rabbit and other Tales,* Lippincott (Philadelphia, PA), 1965.

Lisa Miller, *Wheels,* Coward (New York, NY), 1965.

Jeanne B. Hardendorff, editor, *Tricky Peik and Other Picture Tales,* Lippincott (Philadelphia, PA), 1967.

Joan M. Lexau, *Finders Keepers, Losers Weepers,* Lippincott (Philadelphia, PA), 1967.

Melvin L. Alexenberg, *Sound Science,* Prentice-Hall (New York, NY), 1968.

James A. Eichner, *The Cabinet of the President of the United States,* F. Watts (New York, NY), 1968.

Leland Blair Jacobs, compiler, *Poetry for Chuckles and Grins,* Garrard (Champaign, IL), 1968.

Melvin L. Alexenberg, *Light and Sight,* Prentice-Hall (New York, NY), 1969.

Robert Bly, *The Morning Glory,* Kayak (San Francisco, CA), 1969.

Sam and Beryl Epstein, *Take This Hammer,* Hawthorn (New York, NY), 1969.

Mary C. Jane, *The Rocking-Chair Ghost,* Lippincott (Philadelphia, PA), 1969.

Nina Schneider, *Hercules, the Gentle Giant,* Hawthorn (New York, NY), 1969.

Eleanor Boylan, *How to Be a Puppeteer,* McCall (New York, NY), 1970.

Duncan Emrich, editor, *The Folklore of Love and Courtship,* American Heritage Press (New York, NY), 1970.

Duncan Emrich, editor, *The Folklore of Weddings and Marriage,* American Heritage Press (New York, NY), 1970.

Sam and Beryl Epstein, *Who Needs Holes?,* Hawthorn (New York, NY), 1970.

Barbara Rinkoff, *Rutherford T. Finds 21B,* Putnam (New York, NY), 1970.

Philip Balestrino, *Hot As an Ice Cube,* Crowell (New York, NY), 1971.

Sam and Beryl Epstein, *Pick It Up,* Holiday House (New York, NY), 1971.

John Fisher, *John Fisher's Magic Book,* Prentice-Hall (New York, NY), 1971.

William Wise, *Monsters of the Middle Ages,* Putnam (New York, NY), 1971.

Peter Zachary Cohen, *Authorized Autumn Charts of the Upper Red Canoe River Country,* Atheneum (New York, NY), 1972.

Sibyl Hancock, *Mario's Mystery Machine,* Putnam (New York, NY), 1972.

Jean Rosenbaum and Lutie McAuliff, *What Is Fear?,* Prentice-Hall (New York, NY), 1972.

Rubie Saunders, *The Franklin Watts Concise Guide to Babysitting,* F. Watts, 1972, published as *Baby-Sitting: For Fun and Profit,* Archway, 1979.

Sam and Beryl Epstein, *Hold Everything,* Holiday House (New York, NY), 1973.

Sam and Beryl Epstein, *Look in the Mirror,* Holiday House (New York, NY), 1973.

Kathryn F. Ernst, *Danny and His Thumb,* Prentice-Hall (New York, NY), 1973.

Valerie Pitt, *Let's Find Out about Communications,* F. Watts (New York, NY), 1973.

Charles Keller and Richard Baker, compilers, *The Star-Spangled Banana and other Revolutionary Riddles,* Prentice-Hall (New York, NY), 1974.

Alice Low, *David's Window,* Putnam (New York, NY), 1974.

Mary Calhoun, *Old Man Whickutt's Donkey,* Parents' Magazine Press, 1975.

Norma Farber, *This Is the Ambulance Leaving the Zoo,* Dutton (New York, NY), 1975.

Lee Bennett Hopkins, compiler, *Good Morning to You, Valentine* (poems), Harcourt (New York, NY), 1975.

Martha and Charles Shapp, *Let's Find Out about Houses,* F. Watts (New York, NY), 1975.

Eleanor Coerr, *The Mixed-up Mystery Smell,* Putnam (New York, NY), 1976.

John Graham, *I Love You, Mouse,* Harcourt (New York, NY), 1976.

Bernice Kohn Hunt, *The Whatchamacallit Book,* Putnam (New York, NY), 1976.

Steven Kroll, *The Tyrannosaurus Game,* Holiday House (New York, NY), 1976.

Martha and Charles Shapp, *Let's Find Out about Summer,* F. Watts (New York, NY), 1976.

Barbara Williams, *If He's My Brother,* Harvey House, 1976.

Lee Bennett Hopkins, compiler, *Beat the Drum: Independence Day Has Come* (poems), Harcourt (New York, NY), 1977.

Daniel O'Connor, *Images of Jesus,* Winston (Minneapolis, MN), 1977.

Belong, Winston (Minneapolis, MN), 1977.

Journey, Winston (Minneapolis, MN), 1977.

(With others) Norma Farber, *Six Impossible Things before Breakfast,* Addison-Wesley (Reading, MA), 1977.

Jean Fritz, *Can't You Make Them Behave, King George?,* Coward (New York, NY), 1977.

Patricia Lee Gauch, *Once upon a Dinkelsbühl,* Putnam (New York, NY), 1977.

Tony Johnston, *Odd Jobs,* Putnam (New York, NY), 1977, published as *The Dog Wash,* Scholastic (New York, NY), 1977.

Steven Kroll, *Santa's Crash-Bang Christmas,* Holiday House (New York, NY), 1977.

Stephen Mooser, *The Ghost with the Halloween Hiccups,* F. Watts (New York, NY), 1977.

Annabelle Prager, *The Surprise Party,* Pantheon (New York, NY), 1977.

Malcolm E. Weiss, *Solomon Grundy, Born on Oneday: A Finite Arithmetic Puzzle,* Crowell (New York, NY), 1977.

Nancy Willard, *Simple Pictures Are Best* (Junior Literary Guild selection), Harcourt (New York, NY), 1977.

Jane Yolen, *The Giants' Farm,* Seabury (New York, NY), 1977.

Sue Alexander, *Marc, the Magnificent,* Pantheon (New York, NY), 1978.

William Cole, compiler, *Oh, Such Foolishness!* (poems), Lippincott (Philadelphia, PA), 1978.

Tony Johnston, *Four Scary Stories,* Putnam (New York, NY), 1978.

Steven Kroll, *Fat Magic,* Holiday House (New York, NY), 1978.

Naomi Panush Salus, *My Daddy's Moustache,* Doubleday (New York, NY), 1978.

Jan Wahl, *Jamie's Tiger,* Harcourt (New York, NY), 1978.

The Cat on the Dovrefell: A Christmas Tale, translation from the Norse by George Webbe Dasent, Putnam (New York, NY), 1979.

Lee Bennett Hopkins, compiler, *Easter Buds Are Springing: Poems for Easter* (poems), Harcourt (New York, NY), 1979.

Anne Rose, *The Triumphs of Fuzzy Fogtop,* Dial (New York, NY), 1979.

Daisy Wallace, compiler, *Ghost Poems,* Holiday House (New York, NY), 1979.

Jane Yolen, *The Giants Go Camping,* Seabury (New York, NY), 1979.

Patricia L. Gauch, *The Little Friar Who Flew,* Putnam (New York, NY), 1980.

Patricia MacLachlan, *Moon, Stars, Frogs, and Friends,* Pantheon (New York, NY), 1980.

Clement Moore, *The Night before Christmas,* Holiday House (New York, NY), 1980.

Daniel M. Pinkwater, *The Wuggie Norple Story,* Four Winds (New York, NY), 1980.

Pauline Watson, *The Walking Coat,* Walker (New York, NY), 1980.

Malcolm Hall, *Edward, Benjamin and Butter,* Coward (New York, NY), 1981.

Michael Jennings, *Robin Goodfellow and the Giant Dwarf,* McGraw-Hill (New York, NY), 1981.

Stephen Mooser, *Funnyman's First Case,* F. Watts (New York, NY), 1981.

Annabelle Prager, *The Spooky Halloween Party,* Pantheon (New York, NY), 1981.

Jeanne Fritz, adapter, *The Good Giants and the Bad Pukwudgies,* Putnam (New York, NY), 1982.

Tony Johnston, *Odd Jobs and Friends,* Putnam (New York, NY), 1982.

Ann McGovern, *Nicholas Bentley Stoningpot III,* Holiday House (New York, NY), 1982.

David A. Adler, *The Carsick Zebra and other Animal Riddles,* Holiday House (New York, NY), 1983.

Tony Johnston, *The Vanishing Pumpkin,* Putnam (New York, NY), 1983.

Shirley Rousseau Murphy, *Tattie's River Journey,* Dial (New York, NY), 1983.

Valentine Davies, *Miracle on 34th Street,* Harcourt (New York, NY), 1984.

Sarah Josepha Hale, *Mary Had a Little Lamb,* Holiday House (New York, NY), 1984.

Stephen Mooser, *Funnyman and the Penny Dodo,* F. Watts (New York, NY), 1984.

Tony Johnston, *The Quilt Story,* Putnam (New York, NY), 1985.

(With others) Hans Christian Andersen, *The Flying Trunk and other Stories by Andersen,* new English version by Naomi Lewis, Andersen Press (Atlanta, GA), 1986.

Jill Bennett, reteller, *Teeny Tiny,* Putnam (New York, NY), 1986.

Tom Yeomans, *For Every Child a Star: A Christmas Story,* Holiday House (New York, NY), 1986.

Sanna Anderson Baker, *Who's a Friend of the Water-Spurting Whale?,* Chariot (Elgin, IL), 1987.

Carolyn Craven, *What the Mailman Brought* (Junior Literary Guild selection), Putnam (New York, NY), 1987.

Jeanne Fritz, *Shh! We're Writing the Constitution,* Putnam (New York, NY), 1987.

Nancy Willard, *The Mountains of Quilt,* Harcourt (New York, NY), 1987.

Elizabeth Winthrop, *Maggie and the Monster,* Holiday House (New York, NY), 1987.

Caryll Houselander, *Petook: An Easter Story,* Holiday House (New York, NY), 1988.

Tony Johnston, *Pages of Music,* Putnam (New York, NY), 1988.

Cindy Ward, *Cookie's Week,* Putnam (New York, NY), 1988.

Tony Johnston, adapter, *The Badger and the Magic Fan: A Japanese Folktale,* Putnam (New York, NY), 1990.

Jane Yolen, *Hark! A Christmas Sampler,* Putnam (New York, NY), 1991.

Mice Squeak, We Speak, Putnam (New York, NY), 1997.

Benny's Big Bubble, Grosset & Dunlap (New York, NY), 1997.

Erandi's Braids, Putnam (New York, NY), 1999.

The Holy Twins: Benedict and Scholastica, Putnam (New York, NY), 2001.

Annabelle Prager, *The Surprise Party,* Random House (New York, NY), 2003.

Also illustrator of *I Love You Sun, I Love You Moon,* 1994, *The Tale of Rabbit & Coyote,* 1994, *The Bubble Factory,* 1996, and *Get Dressed Santa,* 1996.

DePaola's books have been published in many countries, including Denmark, Germany, Netherlands, Sweden, Norway, Japan, Italy, France and South Africa. His work is represented at the Kerlan Collection at the University of Minnesota and at the Osborne Collection, Toronto, Ontario, Canada.

ADAPTATIONS: Wind and the Sun (sound filmstrip), Xerox Films/Lumin Films, 1973; *Andy* (sound filmstrip), Random House, 1977; *Charlie Needs a Cloak* (filmstrip with cassette), Weston Woods, 1977; *Strega Nona* (filmstrip with cassette), Weston Woods, 1978, (musical, adapted by Dennis Rosa, based on *Strega Nona, Big Anthony and the Magic Ring,* and *Strega Nona's Magic Lessons*), first produced in Minneapolis, MN, by the Children's Theatre Company, 1987, (videocassette), CC Studios, 1985; *Clown of God* (play; adapted by Thomas Olson), first produced in Minneapolis by the Children's Theatre Company, 1981, (16mm film; videocassette), Weston Woods, 1984; *Strega Nona's Magic Lessons and other Stories* (record and cassette; includes *Strega Nona's Magic Lessons, Strega Nona, Big Anthony and the Magic Ring, Helga's Dowry, Oliver Button Is a Sissy, Now One Foot, Now the Other, Nana Upstairs and Nana Downstairs*), read by Tammy Grimes, Caedmon, 1984; *Big Anthony and Helga's Dowry,* Children's Radio Theatre, 1984; *The Night before Christmas* (cassette), Live Oak Media, 1984; *The Vanishing Pumpkin* (filmstrip with cassette), Random House; *The Legend of the Bluebonnet: An Old Tale of Texas* (filmstrip with cassette), Random House, 1985; *The Mysterious Giant of Barletta* (cassette), Random House, 1985; *Mary Had a Little Lamb* (filmstrip with cassette), Weston Woods, 1985; *The Legend of the Indian Paintbrush* (filmstrip with cassette), Listening Library, 1988; *Tomie dePaola's Christmas Carols* (cassette), Listening Library, 1988; *Merry Christmas, Strega Nona* (cassette), Listening Library, (play; adapted by Thomas Olson), first produced in Minneapolis by the Children's Theatre Company, 1988; *Tomie dePaola's Mother Goose* (play; adapted by Constance Congdon), first produced in Minneapolis by the Children's Theatre Company, 1990. *Charlie Needs a Cloak* has been adapted into Braille and *Strega Nona* has been produced as a talking book. Filmstrips of *Let's Find Out about Houses, Let's Find Out about Summer, The Surprise Party, Pancakes for Breakfast, Sing, Pierrot, Sing,* and *Tattie's River Journey* have been produced.

SIDELIGHTS: "Tomie dePaola is one of the most popular creators of picture books for children in America today," state Richard F. Abrahamson and Marilyn Colvin in the *Reading Teacher.* Calling dePaola "an artist and writer of seemingly boundless energy," Anne Sherrill noted in an essay for the *Dictionary of Literary Biography* that he "has worked in several areas of children's literature." In addition to the scores of books he has written himself, dePaola's gently drawn, brightly colored illustrations fill the pages of many books written by other authors. Several critics, such as Abrahamson and Colvin, observed that dePaola is at his best, though, "when he both illustrates and writes a picture book," and considered his retold folk tales to "represent some of the most beautiful picture storybooks available today."

DePaola was born in 1934, near the end of the Great Depression, to Irish and Italian parents in Meriden, Connecticut. This talented and prolific author and illustrator grew up during World War II, before television deposed radio in American homes, in a family that appreciated books and creativity. He has frequently said

that he decided to become an artist when he was only four. "I must have been a stubborn child," he once commented, "because I never swayed from that decision." By the time he was a sophomore in high school, dePaola knew that he wanted to attend Pratt Institute in New York and wrote to them to find out what classes he should be taking to prepare for his studies there. In 1952 he entered Pratt, earning a degree in 1956.

After graduation from Pratt, dePaola entered a Benedictine Monastery in Vermont where he stayed for six months. He has stated that he used the time there to solidify some deep spiritual values. Because the Benedictines are involved in the arts, he also learned the value of culture. DePaola maintained his association with the monastery when he returned to the secular life. In addition to crafting liturgical art, he designed fabric for their weaving studio and designed Christmas cards. Living in the monastery influenced the subject matter of his writing as well. Several of his children's books draw upon religious stories or themes, often from the perspective of legend. *The Clown of God: An Old Story,* for example, is a retelling of the story about the rise and fall of a juggler and the miracle that occurs at his final astonishing performance before a statue of the Virgin Mary and Christ Child. Sherrill remarked that dePaola's tale "was inspired by Anatole France's version of the legend about a juggler who offers his talent as a gift to the Christ Child. DePaola retells it with an Italian Renaissance setting."

Beginning his career as a teacher of art at Newton College of the Sacred Heart in Massachusetts in 1962, dePaola first illustrated Lisa Miller's science book, *Sound,* in 1965. The following year, he illustrated the first of his own books, *The Wonderful Dragon of Timlin.* In 1967, he traveled west to teach at San Francisco College for Women, which became Lone Mountain College. While in California, he earned a master of fine arts degree from the California College of Arts and Crafts in 1969, and a doctoral equivalency a year later at Lone Mountain College. "The time I spent in San Francisco also helped raise my consciousness—about women's issues especially—and to realign my thinking about antiwar and peace organizations," dePaola told Lisa Lane in a *Chicago Tribune* interview. Following his graduate work, he returned to New England where he continued to teach art, adding theatrical writing, technical direction, and set design to his professorial tasks. DePaola has also exhibited his work extensively in numerous one-man and group shows, both nationally and internationally. He is the recipient of numerous awards and honors as well as high praise from reviewers for his appealing retellings of religious and ethnic folktales, realistic fiction with elements of fantasy, and concept books that combine fiction with educational topics. But as Abrahamson and Colvin remarked, "Can there be a higher honor for a creator of children's books than to be selected by children as a favorite? In 1978, children across the United States chose four of Tomie dePaola's works among their favorites. No other creator of children's books during that year was given such an honor."

DePaola's family was a closely connected one and some of his stories for children focus upon relationships among family members. One of dePaola's first books, *Nana Upstairs and Nana Downstairs,* is "based upon the death of his grandmother," noted Lane, adding that he admitted that "it was a highly personal and challenging book to write." It is the story of Tommy, whose grandmother and great-grandmother both live in the same house with him. When he is very young, his great-grandmother dies; several years later, his grandmother passes away also. Remarking that "years later when the grandmother dies, he thinks of them both as Nana Upstairs," Sherrill added that "though the book deals with the death of loved ones, the focus is on affection and fond memories."

A companion piece to *Nana Upstairs and Nana Downstairs* is *Now One Foot, Now the Other,* which involves young Bobby and his grandfather, Bob, who enjoy doing many things together. When the grandfather suffers a stroke, though, Bobby helps him to learn to walk again. Indicating that the "explanations are forthright and appropriate to readers' level of understanding," Karen Harris added in *School Library Journal,* "The tone is gentle and low-key and the illustrations are, as usual, first-rate." Natalie Babbitt remarked in the *New York Times Book Review* that although "this is a big and difficult story compressed into a small and simple story," dePaola omits nothing and is able to "present a warm and positive picture of the power of love." She also found that "the illustrations are exactly right. In calm browns and blues, with figures that are just realistic enough, they reinforce the straightforward tone of the prose."

Strega Nona: An Old Tale, which was named a Caldecott Honor Book and received the Nakamore Prize in Japan, is a traditional tale about a magic pot that, upon the recitation of a verse, produces food and ceases only with the recitation of another verse. In *Strega Nona* ("Grandmother Witch") has hired a helper, Anthony, who secretly observes her and believes that he too can make the pot perform magically. What Anthony has

missed is that Strega Nona also blows three kisses to the pot to get it to stop. Chaos ensues, threatening the entire town. Strega Nona sets things right and chooses to punish Anthony not by hanging him, as the townspeople suggest, but by forcing him to eat all the pasta he has created—"an ending children will probably enjoy tremendously," remarked Zena Sutherland in *Bulletin of the Center for Children's Books.*

In *Helga's Dowry: A Troll Love Story,* the story of a beautiful but poor troll who accumulates a dowry and attracts the handsome king of the trolls as her suitor but discards him for another of her own choice, dePaola invents his own tale in the folktale tradition. According to Jennifer Dunning in the *New York Times Book Review,* dePaola's inspiration often comes from faculty-meeting doodles. "A troll appeared on the doodle pad," Mr. dePaola recalled. "I thought, 'Gee, must be a troll story inside me.' So I did a lot of research on trolls and found the women are condemned to wander the face of the earth if they have no dowry." DePaola's troll acquires her dowry from doing enormous tasks for others—cows for laundry, land for clearing trees; and, according to Sutherland in *Bulletin of the Center for Children's Books,* "Most of the fun is in Helga's magical despatch of loot-producing tasks." DePaola also has some very definite ideas about the presence of sexual stereotyping in children's books. According to Sherrill, dePaola has frequently said that he "consciously tries to avoid presenting sexual stereotypes, and certainly the independent Helga underscores that."

In *Fin M'Coul: The Giant of Knockmany Hill,* Celtic motifs frame the half-page illustrations and text involving the legendary Irish hero Cu Chulainn. M'Coul is huge and powerful good giant who is afraid of being beaten by Cucullin, who is larger than he is. M'Coul's clever wife comes to his rescue, and he appears dressed as a baby stuffed into a real cradle. Cucullin retreats fearing that if the giant M'Coul could produce a child the size of the baby before him, what must the father be like? "Fin M'Coul comes alive through Tomie dePaola's comic illustrating and retelling of this tale," wrote Fellis L. Jordan in *Children's Book Review Service.* "You can almost hear Fin's Irish brogue as you read the story." "Much as we may admire the sheer cleverness of the book it is the humour that lives longest in the mind," stated a reviewer in the *Junior Bookshelf.* "This is the perfect version of the immemorial theme of the triumph of cunning over force, and Mr. dePaola tells it for all it is worth."

Critics have repeatedly praised dePaola's illustrations, noting that he has an almost primitive style reminiscent of folk art. "Although colored inks and watercolors on handmade watercolor paper are used most frequently as a base for dePaola's books, he also uses pencil drawings, etchings, charcoal drawings, and other techniques," wrote Sherrill, adding that his "characters in the stories are made distinctive through dePaola's treatment of eyes, facial expressions, noses, hair, and mouths. Tousle-haired children have become an identifying characteristic of his work." Considering his use of color "distinctive," dePaola added, "I think my style of illustration has been refined over the years. Style has to do with the kinds of things you are drawn to personally, and I'm drawn to Romanesque and folk art. I think that my style is very close to those—very simple and direct. I simplify."

"The child dePaola once was shines through all his works, captivating readers and enriching the field of children's books," remarked Barbara Elleman in *Twentieth-Century Children's Writers*. This is especially true in dePaola's autobiographical series of chapter books. In the Newbery Honor winner *26 Fairmount Avenue,* the first in the series, five-year-old Tomie tells about moving from an apartment to his family's new and only house. Tomie also details his first day of kindergarten and "an unfortunate but funny episode with a laxative," noted *Booklist*'s Linda Perkins. "DePaola successfully evokes the voice of a precocious, inquisitive five-year-old everyone would want to befriend," concluded a *Publishers Weekly* contributor. Perkins also praised dePaola's writing, noting "the colloquial narrative gently meanders, introducing family, friends, and neighbors, noting holidays, and anticipating moving day."

Young Tomie continues his tales in *Here We All Are,* and *On My Way,* both of which are sequels to *26 Fairmount Avenue.* In *Here We All Are* the family is settled in their new house and Tomie continues kindergarten. Tomi begins tap-dancing lessons and takes a stand against his tough Italian grandmother. *On My Own* focuses on change as Tomie graduates kindergarten and enters first grade. The narrator also vividly describes his fears as his sister battles pneumonia. Noted a *Horn Book* reviewer about *On My Own:* "DePaola's writing and recollective skills are so fresh that kids will feel like he's sitting right next to them, telling his tales in and out of school with disarming charisma and not a hint of nostalgia."

In *Meet the Barkers: Morgan and Moffat Go to School,* dePaola introduces readers to two dogs dressed as elementary students, who are starting school. In *School Library Journal,* reviewer Wanda Meyers-Hines ob-

served, "Moffie is smart, outspoken, and always has to be first." Moffie is proud of her elementary school accomplishments, especially her gold stars and ability to count to ten. Morgie, on the other hand, is most proud of his new friendship with a classmate who also likes dinosaurs. After the teacher talks to Moffie about always having to answer first in class, Moffie realizes that she has no friends, a situation that is quickly resolved. "Although never stated, the concept of complementary talents is very clear, and children will get the point," contended Perkins. A *Publishers Weekly* reviewer praised that "many of the situations here will strike a cord with young children and their parents, and dePaola's sunny, gently humorous acrylic paintings are as winning as ever."

DePaola continued the "Barkers" series with *Hide-and-Seek All Week, Boss for a Day, A New Barker in the House, T-Rex Is Missing,* and *Trouble in the Barkers' Class.* Of these, *A New Barker in the House* received the most critical attention because of the international adoption featured in the book. Moffie and Morgie learn that their parents are adopting Marcos, a Spanish-speaking three-year-old. When Marcos arrives, they teach him English and he, in turn, teaches them Spanish. "With Spanish words woven into the narrative, the bicultural intent of the story is obvious, but never didactic," noted Perkins. She added that the book is "brimming with dePaola's characterization, charm, and clarity." A contributor to *Kirkus Reviews* explained, "While the children's adjustment to the adoption may be a bit unrealistically smooth, their feelings of excitement will be familiar and contagious to readers."

"Of all the zillions of things that could be said about Tomie dePaola," observed Robert D. Hale in *Horn Book,* "the one that comes most strongly to mind is his exuberance. He is joyful, ebullient. His exhilaration fills all the spaces around him, wrapping everyone present in rare high spirits. The books he creates radiate this quality of good cheer, even when they have serious messages to impart. . . . Everything Tomie does is done with gusto and zest—which is why his work appeals to all generations. Tomie's softly colorful illustrations invite tots, while at the other end of the cycle adults appreciate his sharing of feelings." "For me," dePaola once remarked, "my expression is always the sum total of my personal experience with people. Not that it shows consciously or conspicuously, but it is the inner support that makes the terrifying experience of starting a new project less frightening."

BIOGRAPHICAL AND CRITICAL SOURCES:

BOOKS

Dictionary of Literary Biography, Volume 61, *American Writers for Children since 1960: Poets, Illustrators, and Nonfiction Authors,* Thomson Gale (Detroit, MI), 1987, pp. 15-26.

Kingman, Lee, and others, compilers, *Illustrators of Children's Books: 1957-1966,* Horn Book (Boston, MA), 1968.

Marquardt, Dorothy A., and Martha E. Ward, *Illustrators of Books for Young People,* Scarecrow Press (Metuchen, NJ), 1975.

Roginski, Jim, compiler, *Newbery and Caldecott Medalists and Honor Book Winners,* Libraries Unlimited (Littleton, CO), 1982.

Twentieth-Century Children's Writers, 3rd edition, St. James Press (Detroit, MI), 1989, pp. 279-281.

PERIODICALS

Booklist, February 15, 1992, Carolyn Phelan, review of *Jamie O'Rourke and the Big Potato: An Irish Folktale,* p. 1108; March 15, 1992, Hazel Rochman, review of *Patrick: Patron Saint of Ireland,* p. 1382; October 1, 1992, Ilene Cooper, review of *Jingle, the Christmas Clown,* p. 328; November 1, 1993, Carolyn Phelan, review of *Strega Nona Meets Her Match,* p. 730; May 1, 1994, Ilene Cooper, review of *Christopher: The Holy Giant,* p. 1603; May 15, 1994, Karen Harvey, review of *The Tale of Rabbit and Coyote,* p. 1678; August, 1994, Ilene Cooper, review of *The Legend of Poinsettia,* p. 2050; January 1, 1995, Carolyn Phelan, review of *The Unicorn and the Moon,* pp. 824-826, Ilene Cooper, review of *Kit and Kat,* p. 827; March 15, 1995, Ilene Cooper, review of *Alice Nizzy Nazzy: The Witch of Sante Fe,* p. 1334; September 1, 1995, Carolyn Phelan, review of *Mary: The Mother of Jesus,* p. 56; September 15, 1995, Carolyn Phelan, review of *Country Angel Christmas,* p. 169; March 15, 1996, Hazel Rochman, review of *The Baby Sister,* p. 1268; October 1, 1996, Ilene Cooper, review of *Mary,* p. 338; March 15, 1997, Susan Dove Lempke, review of *Days of the Blackbird: A Tale of Northern Italy,* p. 1247; July, 1997, Annie Ayres, review of *The Eagle and the Rainbow: Timeless Tales from Mexico,* pp. 1815-1817; September 15, 1997, Hazel Rochman, review of *Mice Squeak, We Speak,* p. 231; February 15, 1998, Michael Cart, review of *Nana Upstairs and Nana Downstairs,* p. 1020; May 15, 1998, Carolyn Phelan, review of *Bill and Pete to the Rescue,* p. 1629; November 15, 1998, Michael Cart, review of *Big Anthony: His Story,* p. 595, Isabel Schon, review of *La Leyenda de la flor de Nochebuena (The Legend of Poinsettia),* p. 599; January 1, 1999, Hazel Rochman, review of *Erandi's Braids,* p. 861; September 1,

1999, Ilene Cooper, review of *The Night of Las Posadas,* p. 147; August 9, 1999, review of *Andy: That's My Name,* p. 355; August, 1999, Linda Perkins, review of *26 Fairmount Avenue,* p. 2048; June, 2001, Linda Perkins, review of *Meet the Barkers: Morgan and Moffat Go to School,* p. 1890; February 1, 2002, Carolyn Phelan, review of *Boss for a Day,* p. 949, review of *Hide-and-Seek All Week,* p. 949; July, 2002, Linda Perkins, review of *A New Barker in the House,* pp. 1856-1858; August, 2002, Ilene Cooper, review of *Adelita: A Mexican Cinderella Story,* pp. 1967-1969; March, 2003, John Peters, review of *Things Will Never Be the Same,* pp. 1193-1195; April 1, 2003, Ilene Cooper, review of *Marcos Colors: Red, Yellow, Blue,* p. 1401, and review of *Adelita: A Mexican Cinderella Story,* pp. 1967-1969; John Peters, review of *Things Will Never Be the Same,* pp. 1193-1195.

Books for Your Children, summer, 1980, pp. 2-3.

Bulletin of the Center for Children's Books, October, 1973, pp. 24-25; November, 1975, p. 42; October, 1995, review of *Country Angel Christmas,* p. 14.

Chicago Tribune, February 13, 1989.

Children's Book Review Service, May, 1981, p. 81.

Children's Playmate, December, 1996, Samantha Hill, review of *Country Angel Christmas,* p. 13.

Entertainment Weekly, December 11, 1992, Michele Landsberg, review of *Jingle at Christmas,* p. 82; April 30, 1993, Leonard S. Marcus, review of *Tom,* p. 70.

Family Life, May 1, 2001, Sara Nelson, "Books," p. 89.

Hartford Courant (Hartford, CT), September 13, 1985.

Horn Book, April, 1974; August, 1975; October, 1975; November-December, 1985, pp. 770-772; January 15, 1993, Deborah Abbott, review of *Tom,* p. 898; July-August, 1993, Hanna B. Zeiger, review of *Tom,* p. 441; November-December, 1993, Hanna B. Zeiger, review of *Strega Nona Meets Her Match,* p. 730; May-June, 1994, Margaret M. Burns, review of *Christopher,* pp. 333-335, May-June, 1994, Elizabeth S. Watson, review of *The Tale of Rabbit and Coyote,* pp. 340-342; November-December, 1994, Hanna B. Zeiger, review of *The Legend of Poinsettia,* pp. 710-712; September 15, 1996, Carolyn Phelan, review of *Strega Nona: Her Story,* p. 246; January-February, Mary M. Burns, review of *Mary,* p. 89; November-December, 1996, Maria B. Salvadore, *Strega Nona: Her Story,* p. 722; March-April, 1997, Margaret A. Bush, review of *Days of the Blackbird,* p. 205; May, 1999, review of *26 Fairmount Avenue,* p. 351; March, 2001, review of *On My Way,* p. 228; March-April, 2002, Roger Sutton, review of *What a Year,* p. 228.

Instructor, April, 2003, Judy Freeman, review of *Adelita,* p. 55.

Junior Bookshelf, August, 1981, p. 144.

Kirkus Reviews, January 1, 2002, review of *What a Year,* p. 43; September 1, 2002, review of *Adelita,* pp. 1307-1309; November 1, 2002, review of *Four Friends at Christmas,* p. 1617; January 15, 2003, review of *Things Will Never Be the Same,* p. 141.

Language Arts, March, 1979.

New York Times Book Review, November 13, 1977, pp. 42, 45; September 20, 1981, p. 30.

Publishers Weekly, July 19, 1976; July 23, 1982; September 7, 1992, Elizabeth Devereaux, review of *My First Thanksgiving,* p. 62, and *Jingle, the Christmas Clown,* p. 67; January 25, 1993, review of *Tom,* p. 86; July 19, 1993, review of *Strega Nona Meets Her Match,* p. 251; November 1, 1993, review of *The Legend of the Persian Carpet,* p. 78; April 18, 1994, review of *The Tale of Rabbit and Coyote,* p. 60; February 27, 1995, review of *Alice Nizzy Nazzy,* p. 103; September 18, 1995, review of *Country Angel Christmas,* p. 100; February 19, 1996, review of *The Baby Sister,* p. 214; July 26, 1996, review of *Strega Nona: Her Story,* p. 241; December 16, 1996, review of *Days of the Blackbird,* p. 59; April 18, 1997, review of *Mice Sqeak, We Speak,* p. 91; April 20, 1998, review of *Bill and Pete to the Rescue,* pp. 65-67; September 7, 1998, review of *Big Anthony,* p. 94; March 29, 1999, review of *26 Fairmount Avenue,* p. 105; April 12, 1999, review of *The Next Best Thing,* p. 29; September, 1999, review of *The Night of Las Posadas,* p. 60; April 16, 2001, review of *Bill and Pete to the Rescue,* p. 67; July 2, 2001, review of *Meet the Barkers,* p. 75; July 11, 2001, review of *Big Anthony,* p. 87; July 16, 2001, p. 150; August 27, 2001, review of *The Holy Twins: Benedict and Scholastica,* p. 82; February 4, 2002, p. 78; March 25, 2002, "Beginning Reader Buddies," p. 66; June 3, 2002, review of *On My Way,* p. 91; July 1, 2002, review of *Adelita,* p. 79.

Reading Teacher, December, 1979, pp. 264-269; November, 1995, review of *The Legend of the Poinsettia,* p. 253.

School Library Journal, September, 1973, p. 56; November, 1974, pp. 46-47; September, 1981, pp. 105-106; February, 1992, Jacqueline Elsner, review of *My First Halloween,* p. 72, and Jean H. Zimmerman, review of *The Great Adventure of Christopher Columbus,* p. 81; April, 1992, Lisa Dennis, review of *Jamie O'Rourke and the Big Potato,* p. 104; May, 1992, Lisa S. Murphy, review of *Patrick,* pp. 98-100; April, 1993, Karen James, review of *Tom,* p. 95; November, 1993, Rose Zertuch Trevino, review of *El Libro de las Arenas Movedizas,* p. 138, review of *El Libro de las nubes,* p. 138D; March, 1994, Joy Fleishhacker, review of *Christopher,*

p. 60; October, 1994, Jane Marino, review of *The Legend of Poinsettia,* p. 30; May, 1996, Susan Hepler, review of *The Baby Sitter,* p. 91; March, 1997, Heide Piehler, review of *Days of the Blackbird,* p. 150; May, 1997, Teresa Bateman, "A Visit with Tomie dePaola," p. 81; October, 1997, Susan Garland, review of *Mice Squeak, We Speak,* p. 110; November 1, 1998, Sue Sherif, review of *Big Anthony,* p. 83; January, 1995, Emily Kutler, review of *I Love You, Sun; I Love You Moon,* p. 91; December, 1995, Patricia Pearl Dole, review of *Mary,* p. 96; October, 1995, review of *Country Angel Christmas,* p. 36; December, 1995, review of *Mary,* p. 96; October, 1996, Jane Marino, review of *Get Dressed, Santa,* p. 34; October, 1996, Karen MacDonald, review of *Strega Nona: Her Story,* p. 91; May, 1998, Heide Piehler, review of *Bill and Pete to the Rescue,* p. 113; February, 1999, Ann Welton, review of *Erandi's Braids,* p. 87; June, 1999, Heide Piehler, review of *26 Fairmount Avenue,* p. 112; August, 2001, Coop Renner, review of *The Baby Sister,* p. S60, Wanda Meyers-Hines, review of *Meet the Barkers,* p. 146; September, 2001, Coop Renner, review of *The Baby Sister,* p. S60, Patricia Pearl Dole, review of *The Holy Twins: Benedict and Scholastica,* p. 220; February, 2002, Debbie Stewart, review of *Boss for a Day,* p. 98; March, 2002, Alice Casey Smith, review of *What a Year,* p. 209; April 8, 2002, "Ongoing Series," pp. 229-231; June, 2002, Shara Alpern, review of *A New Barker in the House,* p. 92; September, 2002, Ann Welton, review of *Adelita,* pp. 210-212; February, 2003, Patricia Manning, review of *T-Rex Is Missing,* p. 104.

Top of the News, April, 1976.

Wilson Library Bulletin, October, 1977; February, 1992, Donnarae McCann and Olga Richard, review of *The Great Adventure of Christopher Columbus: A Pop-Up Book,* p. 82; January, 1995, Donnarae McCann and Olga Richard, review of *I Love You, Sun; I Love You, Moon,* p. 120.

World of Children's Books, spring, 1978, pp. 38-39.

*   *   *

DERRIDA, Jacques 1930-

PERSONAL: Born July 15, 1930, in El Biar, Algeria; son of Aime and Georgette (Safar) Derrida. *Education:* Attended École Normale Superieure, 1952-56; University of Paris, Sorbonne, Licence es Lettres, 1953, Licence de Philosophie, 1953, Diplome d'Etudes Superieures, 1954; received Certificat d'Ethnologie, 1954,

Agregation de Philosophie, 1956, Doctorat en Philosophie, 1967, Doctorat d'Etat es Lettres, 1980; graduate study at Harvard University, 1956-57.

ADDRESSES: Home—Paris, France. *Office*—École des Hautes Etudes en Sciences Sociales, 54 bis Raspail, 75006 Paris, France. *Agent*—c/o Author Mail, University of Chicago Press, 5801 South Ellis Ave., Chicago, IL 60637.

CAREER: Philosopher and educator. Lycée du Mans, professor, 1959-60; University of Paris, Sorbonne, Paris, France, professor of philosophy, 1960-64; École Normale Superieure, Paris, professor of philosophy, 1964-84; École des Hautes Etudes en Sciences Sociales, Paris, director, 1984—. College International de Philosophie, member of planning board, 1982-83, director, 1983-84, member of administrative council, 1986. Visiting professor and lecturer at numerous universities in Europe and the United States, including Johns Hopkins University, Yale University, University of California—Irvine, Cornell University, and City University of New York.

MEMBER: Institut des Textes et Manuscrits Modernes (member of steering committee, 1983-86), Groupe de Recherches sur l'Enseignement Philosophique (president), Association Jan Hus (vice president), Fondation Culturelle Contre l'Apartheid, American Academy of Arts and Sciences (foreign honorary member), Modern Language Association of America (honorary member), Academy for the Humanities and Sciences (honorary member).

AWARDS, HONORS: Prix Cavailles, Societe des Amis de Jean Cavailles, 1964, for translation into French of Edmund Husserl's *Origin of Geometry;* named to Liste d'Aptitude a l'Enseignement Superieur, 1968; named chevalier, 1968, officier, 1980, of Palmes Academiques; named Commandeur des Arts et des Lettres, 1983; Prix Nietzsche, Association Internationale de Philosophie, 1988; named Chevalier, Legion d'Honneur (France), 1995. Honorary doctorates from Columbia University, 1980, University of Louvain, 1983, and University of Essex, 1987.

WRITINGS:

(Translator and author of introduction) Edmund Husserl, *L'origine de la geometrie,* Presses Universitaires de France (Paris, France), 1962, translation by John P. Leavy published as *Edmund Husserl's "Origin of Geometry": An Introduction,* Nicolas-Hays (York Beach, ME), 1977.

La voix et le phenomene: introduction au probleme du signe dans la phenomenologie de Husserl, Presses Universitaires de France (Paris, France), 1967, translation by David B. Allison published as *Speech and Phenomena and Other Essays on Husserl's Theory of Signs,* Northwestern University Press (Evanston, IL), 1973.

L'ecriture et la difference, Seuil (Paris, France), 1967, translation by Alan Bass published as *Writing and Difference,* University of Chicago Press (Chicago, IL), 1978.

De la grammatologie, Minuit (Paris, France), 1967, translation by Gayatri Chakravorty Spivak published as *Of Grammatology,* Johns Hopkins University Press (Baltimore, MD), 1976.

La dissemination, Seuil (Paris, France), 1972, translation by Barbara Johnson published as *Dissemination,* University of Chicago Press (Chicago, IL), 1981.

Marges de la philosophie, Minuit (Paris, France), 1972, translation by Alan Bass published as *Margins of Philosophy,* University of Chicago Press (Chicago, IL), 1982.

Positions: entretiens avec Henri Ronse, Julia Kristeva, Jean-Louis Houdebine, Guy Scarpetta (interviews), Minuit (Paris, France), 1972, translation by Alan Bass published as *Positions,* University of Chicago Press (Chicago, IL), 1981.

L'archeologie du frivole (first published as introduction to Etienne de Condillac, *L'essai sur l'origine des connaissances humaines,* Galilée, 1973), Denoël (Paris, France), 1976, translation by John P. Leavey, Jr., published as *The Archaeology of the Frivolous: Reading Condillac,* Duquesne University Press (Atlantic Highlands, NJ), 1980.

Glas, Galilée (Paris, France), 1974, translation by John P. Leavey, Jr., and Richard Rand published as *Glas,* University of Nebraska Press (Lincoln, NE), 1986.

Eperons: les styles de Nietzsche, Flammarion (Paris, France), 1976, translation by Barbara Harlow published as *Spurs: Nietzsche's Styles,* University of Chicago Press (Chicago, IL), 1979.

Limited Inc: abc, Johns Hopkins University Press (Baltimore, MD), 1977.

La vérité en peinture (title means "Truth in Painting"), Flammarion (Paris, France), 1978.

La carte postale: de Socrate a Freud et au-dela, Flammarion (Paris, France), 1980, translation by Alan Bass published as *The Post Card: From Socrates to Freud and Beyond,* University of Chicago Press (Chicago, IL), 1987.

L'oreille de l'autre: otobiographies, transferts, traductions; textes et debats, VLB (Montreal, Quebec, Canada), 1982, translation by Peggy Kamuf published as *The Ear of the Other: Otobiography, Transference, Translation,* Schocken (New York, NY), 1985.

D'un ton apocalyptique adopte naguere en philosophie, Galilée (Paris, France), 1983.

Feu la cendre/Cio'che resta del fuoco, Sansoni (Florence, Italy), 1984, published as *Feu la cendre,* Des Femmes, 1987.

Signeponge/Signsponge (French and English text; English translation by Richard Rand), Columbia University Press (New York, NY), 1984, revised, Seuil (Paris, France), 1988.

Otobiographies: l'enseignement de Nietzsche et la politique du nom propre, Galilée (Paris, France), 1984.

Droit de regards, Minuit (Paris, France), 1985.

La faculté de juger, Minuit (Paris, France), 1985.

Parages, Galilée (Paris, France), 1986.

De l'esprit: Heidegger et la question, Galilée (Paris, France), 1987, translation by Geoffrey Bennington and Rachel Bowlby published as *Of Spirit: Heidegger and the Question,* University of Chicago Press (Chicago, IL), 1989.

Psyche: inventions de l'autre, Galilée (Paris, France), 1987.

Memoires: pour Paul de Man, Galilée (Paris, France), 1988, translation by Cecile Lindsay, Jonathan Culler, and Eduardo Cadava published as *Memoires: Lectures for Paul de Man,* Columbia University Press (New York, NY), 1989.

Le probleme de la genese dans la philosophie de Husserl, Presses Universitaires de France (Paris, France), 1990.

De droit a la philosophie, Galilée (Paris, France), 1990.

Memoires de'aveugle, l'autoportrait et autres ruins, Reunion des musees nationaux, 1990, translation by Pascale Ann Brault and Michael Nass published as *Memoirs of the Blind, the Self-Portrait and Other Ruins,* University of Chicago Press (Chicago, IL), 1993.

Donner le temps, 1, Fausse monnai, Galilée (Paris, France), 1991, translation by Peggy Kamuf published as *Given Time, 1: Counterfeit Money,* University of Chicago Press (Chicago, IL), 1992.

L'autre cap; suivre de la democratie ajournaee, Minuit (Paris, France), 1991, translation by Pascale-Anne Brault and Michael Naas published as *The Other Heading: Reflections of Today's Europe,* Indiana University Press (Bloomington, IN), 1992.

A Derrida Reader: Between the Blinds, edited by Peggy Kamuf, Columbia University Press (New York, NY), 1991.

Cinders, translation by Ned Lukacher, University of Nebraska Press (Lincoln, NE), 1991.

(With Geoffrey Derrida) *Jacques Derrida,* Seuil (Paris, France), 1991.

Prejuges, Passagen, 1992.

Acts of Literature, edited by Derek Attridge, Routledge (London, England), 1992.

Donner la mort, Seuil (Paris, France), 1992, translation by David Wells published as *The Gift of Death,* University of Chicago Press (Chicago, IL), 1995.

Passions, Galilée (Paris, France), 1993.

Khora, Galilée (Paris, France), 1993.

Apories: mourir-s'attendre aux "limites de la vérite," Galilée (Paris, France), 1993, translation by Thomas Dutoit published as *Aporias: Dying-Awaiting (One Another at) the "Limits of Truth,"* Stanford University Press (Stanford, CA), 1993.

Spectres de Marx: l'état de la dette, le travail du deuil et la nouvelle internationale, Galilée (Paris, France), 1993, translation by Peggy Kamuf published as *Spectres of Marx, State of the Debt, the Work of Mourning, and the New International,* Routledge (London, England), 1994.

Force de loi; le "fondement mystique de l'autorité," Galilée (Paris, France), 1994.

Politiques de l'amitié, Galilée (Paris, France), 1994, translation by George Collins published as *The Politics of Friendship,* Verso (London, England), 1997.

On the Name, edited by Thomas Dutoit, translated by David Wood and others, Stanford University Press (Stanford, CA), 1995.

Mal d'archive, une impression freudienne, Galilée (Paris, France), 1995, translation by Eric Predowitz published as *Archive Fever: A Freudian Impression,* University of Chicago Press (Chicago, IL), 1996.

Deconstruction and Philosophy: The Texts of Jacques Derrida, translation by David Wells, University of Chicago Press (Chicago, IL), 1995.

(With others) *Deconstruction and Pragmatism,* Routledge (London, England), 1996.

Résistances, de la psychanalyse, Galilée (Paris, France), 1996, published as *Resistances of Psychoanalysis,* Stanford University Press (Stanford, CA), 1998.

La monolinguisme de l'autre, ou La prothèse d'origine, Galilée (Paris, France), 1996, translation by Patrick Mensa published as *Monolingualism of the Other; or, The Prosthesis of Origin,* Stanford University Press (Stanford, CA), 1998.

Passions de la littaerature: avec Jacques Derrida, Galilée (Paris, France), 1996.

(With Bernard Stiegler) *Echographies de la télévision,* Galilée (Paris, France), 1996.

(With Peter Eisenman) *Chora L Works,* Monacelli Press, 1997.

Deconstruction in a Nutshell: A Conversation with Jacques Derrida, edited by John D. Caputo, Fordham University Press (Bronx, NY), 1997.

(With Paule Thevenin) *Secret Art of Antonin Artaud,* translation by Mary Ann Caws, MIT Press (Cambridge, MA), 1997.

Cosmopolites de tous les pays, encore un effort, Galilée (Paris, France), 1997, translated as *On Cosmopolitanism and Forgiveness,* Routledge (New York, NY), 2001.

Adieu à Emmanuel Lévines, Galilée (Paris, France), 1997, translation by Pascale-Anne Brault and Michael Naas published as *Adieu to Emmanuel Levinas,* Stanford University Press (Stanford, CA), 1999.

De l'hospitalité/Anne Duformantelle invite Jacques Derrida à répondre, Calmann Levy (Paris, France), 1997, translation by Rachel Bowlby published as *Of Hospitality: Anne Dufourmantelle Invites Jacques Derrida to Respond,* Stanford University Press (Stanford, CA), 2000.

Sur parole: instantanés philosophiques, Aube (Tour d'Aigues, France), 1999.

Le toucher, Jean-Luc Nancy/Jacques Derrida: accompagné de travaux de lecture de Simon Hantai, Galilée (Paris, France), 1999.

(With Catherine Malabou) *Jacques Derrida: La contre-allée,* Quinzaine litteraire-Louis Vuitton (Paris, France), 1999.

Du droit à la philosophie, Galilée (Paris, France), 2000, portions translated by Jan Plug as *Who's Afraid of Philosophy? Right to Philosophy,* Volume 1, Stanford University Press (Stanford, CA), 2003.

Demeure: Fiction and Testimony (published with *The Instant of My Death* by Maurice Blanchot), translated by Elizabeth Rottenberg, Stanford University Press (Stanford, CA), 2000.

(With Safaa Fathy) *Tourner les mots: Au bord d'un film,* Galilée (Paris, France), 2000.

Etats d'âme de la psychanalyse: l'impossible au-delà d'une souveraine cruauté, Galilée (Paris, France), 2000.

The Work of Mourning, edited by Pascale-Anne Brault and Michael Naas, University of Chicago Press (Chicago, IL), 2001.

L'univerité sans condition, Galilée (Paris, France), 2001.

Papier machine: le ruban de machine à écrire et autres résponses, Galilée (Paris, France), 2001.

(With Elisabeth Roudinesco) *De qui demain—dialogue,* Galilée (Paris, France), 2001, translation by Jeff Fort published as *For What Tomorrow: A Dialogue,* Stanford University Press (Stanford, CA), 2004.

Derrida Downunder, edited by Laurence Simmons and Heather Worth, Dunmore Press (Palmerston North, New Zealand), 2001.

Negotiations: Interventions and Interviews, 1971-2001, edited and translated by Elizabeth Rottenberg, Stanford University Press (Stanford, CA), 2002.

Fichus: discours de Francfort, Galilée (Paris, France), 2002.

Des humanités et de la discipline philosophique, [Paris, France], translated and edited by Peter Pericles Trifonas as *Ethics, Institutions, and the Right to Philosophy,* Rowman & Littlefield (Lanham, MD), 2002.

Artaud le Moma: interjections d'appel, Galilée (Paris, France), 2002.

Acts of Religion, edited by Gil Anidjar, Routledge (New York, NY), 2002.

Without Alibi (collected essays), translated and edited by Peggy Kamuf, Stanford University Press (Stanford, CA), 2002.

(With Giovanna Borradori and Jürgen Habermas) *Philosophy in a Time of Terror: Dialogues with Jürgen Habermas and Jacques Derrida,* University of Chicago Press (Chicago, IL), 2003.

Voyous: deux essais sur la raison, Galilée (Paris, France), 2003.

The Problem of Genesis in Husserl's Philosophy, translated by Marian Hobson, University of Chicago Press (Chicago, IL), 2003.

Also author of *Moscou aller-retour,* Aube.

Contributor to books, including *Tableau de la litterature francaise,* Gallimard (Paris, France), 1974; *Mimesis,* Flammarion (Paris, France), 1976; *Politiques de la philosophie,* Grasset (Paris, France), 1976; *Qui a peur de la philosophie?,* Flammarion (Paris, France), 1977; *Les États Generaux de la philosophie,* Flammarion (Paris, France), 1979; *Deconstruction and Criticism,* Seabury Press (New York, NY), 1979; *Philosophy in France Today,* Cambridge University Press (Cambridge, England), 1983; Joseph H. Smith and William Kerrigan, editors, *Taking Chances: Derrida, Psychoanalysis, and Literature,* Johns Hopkins University Press (Baltimore, MD), 1984; *Text und Interpretation,* Fink, 1984; *Poststructuralist Joyce,* Cambridge University Press (Cambridge, England), 1984; *La faculté de juger,* Minuit (Paris, France), 1985; *Qu'est-ce que Dieu?,* [Brussels], 1985; *Difference in Translation,* Cornell University Press (Ithaca, NY), 1985; *Genese de Babel, Joyce et la creation,* Editions du CNRS (Paris, France), 1985; *Paul Celan,* Galilée (Paris, France), 1986; *La grève des philosophes: école et philosophie,* Osiris, 1986, published as *Raising the Tone of Philosophy,* edited by Peter Fenves, Johns Hopkins University Press (Baltimore, MD), 1993; *La case vide,* Achitectural Association (London, England), 1986; *Pour Nelson Mandela,* Gallimard (Paris, France), 1986; *Romeo et Juliette,* Papiers, 1986; and *Questioning Judaism* (interviews), Stanford University Press (Stanford, CA), 2004.

Codirector of collection *Philosophie en effet.* Member of editorial boards of *Critique, Structuralist Review, Contemporary Studies in Philosophy and the Human Sciences,* and *Revue senegalaise de philosophie.* Associated with *Tel Quel* during 1960s and 1970s.

SIDELIGHTS: Algerian-born French philosopher Jacques Derrida is the leading light of the post-structuralist intellectual movement that significantly influenced philosophy, the social sciences, and literary criticism during the late twentieth century. By means of a "strategy of deconstruction," Derrida and other post-structuralists have sought to reveal the play of multiple meanings in cultural products and expose the tacit metaphysical assumptions they believe exist beneath much of contemporary social thought. The deconstructionist project ignited intense controversy among intellectuals in Europe and the United States, with detractors dismissing it as a particularly insidious form of nihilism, while its advocates argued that deconstructive practice allows the possibility of creating new values amid what they view as cynicism and spiritual emptiness of postmodern society.

Derrida first outlined his seminal ideas in a lengthy introduction to his 1962 French translation of German philosopher Edmund Husserl's *Origin of Geometry.* The strategy of deconstruction is rigorously delineated in Derrida's difficult masterwork, *Of Grammatology,* but the philosopher explained some of his basic concepts in more accessible terms in a 1972 collection of interviews titled *Positions.* Derrida's thought builds on a variety of so-called subversive literature, including the writings of German philosophers Friedrich Nietzsche and Martin Heidegger, who both sought to overturn established values and depart from the traditional approach to the study of metaphysics; the political, social, and cultural insights of political economist Karl Marx and psychoanalyst Sigmund Freud, who postulated underlying contradictory phenomena beneath the surface of everyday social life; and the linguistic analysis of the Swiss linguist Ferdinand de Saussure, who posited that language functions in a self-referential manner and has no "natural" relation to external reality. Many of Derrida's texts are subtle analyses of the writings of these

thinkers and the literature of the modern structuralist movement, another strong influence on the philosopher. While accepting the structuralist notion, derived from Saussure, that cultural phenomena are best understood as self-referential systems of signs, Derrida denies the existence of a common intellectual structure capable of unifying the diverse cultural structures.

In the *New York Times Magazine,* Colin Campbell explained "Post-structuralism" as "a term that lumps together various French and other thinkers who write as though they want to overthrow oppressive philosophic structures by subverting language. Deconstruction was invented by Jacques Derrida . . . and Derrida is still the movement's leading theoretician." Campbell added: "In 1966, Derrida delivered his first lectures in the United States. The movement has been upsetting people and texts since."

Derrida's insistence on the inadequacy of language to render a complete and unambiguous representation of reality forms the basis for his deconstructivist strategy of reading texts. As Campbell stated: "To 'deconstruct' a text is pretty much what it sounds like—to pick the thing carefully apart, exposing what deconstructors see as the central fact and tragic little secret of Western philosophy—namely, the circular tendency of language to refer to itself. Because the 'language' of a text refers mainly to other 'languages' and texts—and not to some hard, extratexual reality—the text tends to have several possible meanings, which usually undermine one another. In fact, the 'meaning' of a piece of writing—it doesn't matter whether it's a poem or a novel or a philosophic treatise—is indeterminate."

In reading, Derrida studies texts for the multiple meanings that underlie and subvert the surface meaning of every piece of writing. To do this, he scrutinizes seemingly marginal textual elements such as idiosyncrasies of vocabulary and style, and subverts what appear to be simple words and phrases with a battery of puns, allusions, and neologisms. He illuminates in particular the continual play of differences in language, a phenomenon he calls "differance." As he wrote in *Positions,* differance prevents any simple element of language from being "*present* in and of itself, referring only to itself." Rather, every element contains differences and spaces within itself and *traces* of other elements that interweave to transform one text into another. There is, in Derrida's famous phrase, "nothing outside the text," that is, no clear and simple meaning represented by words, but only the play of differance and the multiplication of meanings in the deconstructive project. Although a deconstructive reading is never definitive, it is also not arbitrary, and the textual transformations can be followed systematically and even subjected to a structural analysis. Derrida's own deconstructive analyses of philosophical and literary texts include *Margins of Philosophy, Dissemination,* and *Spurs: Nietzsche's Styles.* "Derrida, in a typically bold and outrageous way, has gone so far as to say that writing is more basic than speaking, that speaking is only a form of writing," Campbell related. "But there's more. Because all writing is said to be metaphorical, working by tropes and figures, it follows that trained deconstructors should be able to interpret texts of all sorts, not just 'literature.'"

Given his devotion to textual analysis, Derrida has strongly influenced literary criticism, particularly in France and in the United States. J. Hillis Miller and the late Paul de Man of Yale University are among the best-known American deconstructivists, but younger scholars have also adopted the method. Derrida himself, meanwhile, has attempted to deconstruct the distinction between criticism and creative writing in books such as *Glas* and *The Post Card. Glas* is considered one of the most unusual books ever printed; its pages are divided into two columns, one being a philosophical, psychological, and biographical portrait of the German philosopher G.W.F. Hegel, and the other a critical analysis of the writings of French playwright Jean Genet. The columns are, in turn, fractured within themselves into sub-columns and boxes. Both texts begin and end in mid-sentence and appear at first to be completely independent from each other—indeed, they can be read that way. The reader can also create his or her own text by uncovering the textual traces that link the two columns and illuminate their differences. In fact, there is a virtually infinite number of ways to read and interpret *Glas,* which stoutly resists any total understanding.

"The disorderly philosophical conduct of this work is so magnificent that it defies linear exposition," Geoffrey H. Hartman remarked of *Glas* in his *Saving the Text: Literature/Derrida/Philosophy.* "Not since *Finnegans Wake* has there been such a deliberate and curious work: less original . . . and mosaic than the *Wake,* even flushed and overreaching, but as intriguingly, wearyingly allusive." *New York Times Book Review* contributor John Sturrock noted that *Glas* "is so made as to impose a certain vagrancy on the eyes and attention of whoever reads it and to break us of our nasty linear habits."

Derrida's strategy of deconstruction had implications far beyond literary criticism in the postmodern age, in the opinion of some moral philosophers. At a time when both religion and secular humanist ideologies had failed for many people, the post-structuralist celebration of difference offered an escape from alienated individualism. The metaphysical search is nostalgic and totalizing—seeking origin and end—while the deconstructive project recognizes no permanence and subverts all hierarchies. Dismissed by some readers and critics as nihilistic, this radical insistence on difference, incompleteness, and ephemerality impressed others as a positive grounding for social tolerance, mutual respect, and open discourse as the world entered the twenty-first century.

Within the fields of philosophy, political philosophy, and literary criticism, Derrida's impact has been felt most strongly. "Derrida is a philosopher from whom many of us have learned what we judge to be important and seductive truths about the nature of language," Sturrock declared, "and it would be good to go on learning from him." Also in the *New York Times Book Review,* Perry Meisel observed: "In fact, literary study in America has never been in better shape. Enriched by a variety of European methodologies since the early 1970s, it has grown into a vast, synthetic enterprise characterized by powerful continuities rather than by disjunctions. Feminism, deconstruction, 'reader-response,' 'New Historicism,' 'postcolonialism'—all share similar ends and similar ways of getting there in a momentous collaboration."

BIOGRAPHICAL AND CRITICAL SOURCES:

BOOKS

Behler, Ernst, *Confrontations: Derrida/Heidegger/Nietzsche,* Stanford University Press (Stanford, CA), 1991.

Caputo, John D., *The Prayers and Tears of Jacques Derrida: Religion without Religion,* Indiana University Press (Bloomington, IN), 1997.

Collins, Jeff, *Introducing Derrida,* Totem Books, 1997.

Contemporary Literary Criticism, Volume 24, Thomson Gale (Detroit, MI), 1983.

Derrida, Jacques, *Positions: entretiens avec Henri Ronse, Julia Kristeva, Jean-Louis Houdebine, Guy Scarpetta* (interviews), Minuit (Paris, France), 1972, translation by Alan Bass published as *Positions,* University of Chicago Press (Chicago, IL), 1981.

Garver, Newton, *Derrida and Wittgenstein,* Temple University Press (Philadelphia, PA), 1994.

Gasche, Rodolphe, *The Train of the Mirror: Derrida and the Philosophy of Difference,* Harvard University Press (Cambridge, MA), 1986.

Hartman, Geoffrey H., *Saving the Text: Literature/Derrida/Philosophy,* Johns Hopkins University Press (Baltimore, MD), 1981.

Harvey, Irene E., *Derrida and the Economy of Difference,* Indiana University Press (Bloomington, IN), 1986.

Llewelyn, John, *Derrida on the Threshold of Sense,* Macmillan (New York, NY), 1986.

Lucy, Niall, *Debating Derrida,* Melbourne University Press, 1995.

Magliola, Robert R., *Derrida on the Mend,* Purdue University Press (West Lafayette, IN), 1984.

Megill, Allan, *Prophets of Extremity,* University of California Press (Berkeley, CA), 1985.

Norris, Christopher, *Derrida,* Harvard University Press (Cambridge, MA), 1987.

Staten, Henry, *Wittgenstein and Derrida,* University of Nebraska Press (Lincoln, NE), 1984.

Sturrock, John, editor, *Structuralism and Since: From Levi-Strauss to Derrida,* Oxford University Press (Oxford, England), 1979.

PERIODICALS

Australian Journal of Political Science, July, 2002, Paul Patton, review of *On Cosmopolitanism and Forgiveness,* p. 383.

Choice, June, 2002, S. Barnett, review of *A Taste for the Secret,* p. 1782; September, 2002, R. Puligandia, review of *Acts of Religion,* p. 118.

Contemporary Literature, spring, 1979.

Contemporary Review, June, 2002, review of *On Cosmopolitanism and Forgiveness,* p. 381.

Critical Inquiry, summer, 1978.

Criticism, summer, 1979; winter, 1993.

Ethics, July, 2003, Samir J. Daddad, review of *Who's Afraid of Philosophy?,* p. 923.

International Philosophical Quarterly, September, 2003, David Michael Levin, "Cinders, Traces, Shadows on the Page: The Holocaust in Derrida's Writing," p. 269.

Journal of Ethnic and Migration Studies, March, 2003, Alastair Bonnett, review of *On Cosmopolitanism and Forgiveness,* p. 399.

Journal of the American Academy of Religion, September, 2002, Elliot R. Wolfson, "Assaulting the Border: Kabbalistic Traces in the Margins of Derrida," p. 475.

Modern Theology, April, 2002, James K.A. Smith, "A Principle of Incarnation in Derrida's 'Jungenschriften'," p. 217.

New Literary History, autumn, 1978.

New Republic, April 16, 1977.

New York Review of Books, March 3, 1977; January 14, 1993; June 25, 1998, Mark Lilla, "The Politics of Jacques Derrida," pp. 36-41.

New York Times Book Review, February 1, 1987; September 13, 1987, John Sturrock, "The Book Is Dead, Long Live the Book!" p. 3; May 28, 2000, Perry Meisel, "Let a Hundred Isms Blossom."

New York Times Magazine, February 9, 1986, Colin Campbell, "The Tyranny of the Yale Critics," p. 20.

Partisan Review, number 2, 1976; number 2, 1981.

Research in African Literatures, winter, 2002, p. 124.

Theological Studies, December, 2002, Silvia Benso, review of *A Taste for the Secret,* p. 894.

Time, November 25, 2002, Joel Stein, "Life with the Father of Deconstructionism" (interview), p. 104.

Times Literary Supplement, February 15, 1968; September 30, 1983; December 5, 1986.

Virginia Quarterly Review, winter, 1992.

OTHER

Dick, Kirby, and Amy Ziering Kofman, *Derrida* (documentary film), 2002.

*   *   *

DESAI, Anita 1937-

PERSONAL: Born June 24, 1937, in Mussoorie, India; daughter of D.N. (an engineer) and Toni Mazumdar; married Ashvin Desai (an executive), December 13, 1958; came to United States, 1987; children: Rahul, Tani, Arjun, Kiran. *Education:* Delhi University, B.A. (with honors), 1957.

ADDRESSES: Home—Cambridge, MA. *Office*—The Program in Writing and Humanistic Studies, Massachusetts Institute of Technology, Cambridge, MA 02139.

CAREER: Writer and educator. Smith College, Northampton, MA, Elizabeth Drew Professor of English, 1987-88; Mount Holyoke College, South Hadley, MA, Purington Professor of English, 1988-93; Massachusetts Institute of Technology, Cambridge, MA, professor of writing, 1993—. Girton College, Cambridge, Helen Cam visiting fellow, 1986-87, honorary fellow, 1988; Clare Hall, Cambridge, Ashby fellow, 1989, honorary fellow, 1991.

MEMBER: Royal Society of Literature (fellow), American Academy of Arts and Letters (honorary fellow).

AWARDS, HONORS: Winifred Holtby Prize, Royal Society of Literature, 1978, for *Fire on the Mountain;* Sahitya Academy award, 1979; Booker Prize shortlist, 1980, for *Clear Light of Day,* 1984, for *In Custody,* and 1999, for *Feasting, Fasting; Guardian* Prize for Children's Fiction, 1983, for *The Village by the Sea; Hadassah* Prize, 1989, for *Baumgartner's Bombay;* Padma Sri, 1990; Literary Lion Award, New York Public Library, 1993; Neil Gunn fellowship, Scottish Arts Council, 1994; Moravia Award (Rome, Italy), 1999; Benson Medal, Royal Society of Literature, 2003.

WRITINGS:

NOVELS

Cry, the Peacock, P. Owen (London, England), 1963.
Voices in the City, P. Owen (London, England), 1965.
Bye-Bye, Blackbird, Hind Pocket Books (Delhi, India), 1968.
Where Shall We Go This Summer?, Vikas Publishing House (New Dehli, India), 1975.
Fire on the Mountain, Harper & Row (New York, NY), 1977.
Clear Light of Day, Harper & Row (New York, NY), 1980.
In Custody, Heinemann (London, England), 1984, Harper & Row (New York, NY), 1985.
Baumgartner's Bombay, Alfred A. Knopf (New York, NY), 1989.
Journey to Ithaca, Alfred A. Knopf (New York, NY), 1995.
Fasting, Feasting, Chatto & Windus (London, England), 1999, Houghton Mifflin (Boston, MA), 2000.
The Zigzag Way, Houghton Mifflin (Boston, MA), 2004.

JUVENILE

The Peacock Garden, India Book House (Jaipur, India), 1974.
Cat on a Houseboat, Orient Longmans (Calcutta, India), 1976.
The Village by the Sea, Heinemann (London, England), 1982.

OTHER

Games at Twilight and Other Stories, Heinemann (London, England), 1978, Harper & Row (New York, NY), 1980.

(Author of introduction) Lady Mary Wortley Montagu, *Turkish Embassy Letters,* edited by Malcolm Jack, University of Georgia Press (Athens, GA), 1993.
Diamond Dust and Other Stories, Houghton Mifflin (Boston, MA), 2000.
(Author of introduction) E.M. Forster, *Arctic Summer,* Hesperus Press (London, England), 2003.
(Author of introduction) D.H. Lawrence, *Daughters of the Vicar,* Hesperus Press (London, England), 2004.

Contributor of short stories to periodicals, including *Thought, Envoy, Writers Workshop, Quest, Indian Literature, Illustrated Weekly of India, Femina, Harper's Bazaar,* and *Granta.*

ADAPTATIONS: The Village by the Sea was filmed by the British Broadcasting Corporation (BBC), 1992; *In Custody* was filmed by Merchant Ivory Productions, 1993.

SIDELIGHTS: Anita Desai focuses her novels upon the personal struggles of her Indian characters to cope with the problems of contemporary life. In this way, she manages to portray the cultural and social changes that her native country has undergone since the departure of the British. One of Desai's major themes is the relationships between family members, especially the emotional tribulations of women whose independence is suppressed by Indian society. Her first novel, *Cry, the Peacock,* concerns a woman who finds it impossible to assert her individuality; the theme of the despairing woman is also explored in Desai's *Where Shall We Go This Summer?* Other novels explore life in urban India (*Voices in the City*), the clash between Eastern and Western cultures (*Bye-Bye, Blackbird*), and the differences between the generations (*Fire on the Mountain*). Desai was shortlisted for Britain's prestigious Booker Prize three times: in 1980, for *Clear Light of Day;* in 1984, for *In Custody;* and in 1999, for *Fasting, Feasting.*

Exile—physical as well as psychological—is also a prominent theme in Desai's writings. In *Baumgartner's Bombay,* Desai (whose father was Indian and mother was German) details the life of Hugo Baumgartner, a German Jew who flees Nazi Germany for India, where he "gradually drifts down through Indian society to settle, like sediment, somewhere near the bottom," wrote Rosemary Dinnage in the *New York Review of Books.* She added: "Baumgartner is a more thoroughly displaced person than Anglicized Indians, and more solitary, for Desai's Indian characters are still tied to family and community, however irksomely. She has drawn on her dual nationality to write on a subject new, I think, to English fiction—the experience of Jewish refugees in India." Pearl K. Bell made a similar statement. "Baumgartner is the loneliest, saddest, most severely dislocated of Desai's fictional creatures," Bell noted in the *New Republic*. However, he "is also a representative man, the German Jew to whom things happen, powerless to resist the evil wind that swept him like a vagrant weed from Berlin to India." Jean Sudrann, writing in the *Yale Review,* praised Desai's narrative skill "in making us feel the cumulative force of Hugo's alienation." At a reading at Northeastern University transcribed on *Northeastern University Brudnick Center on Violence and Conflict* Web site, the novelist said of her protagonist: "You remarked about his being so passive a character. Yes, I did mean him to be an entirely passive character. For the whole idea was to show how history sweeps people up and, like a juggernaut, often crushes them under its wheels. I wanted to write about such a person."

Desai's descriptive powers have been acclaimed by several critics. In the *New Leader,* Betty Falkenberg called *Baumgartner's Bombay* "a mathematical problem set and solved in exquisite prose." Bell observed that "there is a Dickensian rush and tumble to her portrayals of the bazaars, the crowded streets, the packed houses of an Indian metropolis." In general, Desai's "novels are quite short, but they convey a sharply detailed sense of the tangled complexities of Indian society, and an intimate view of the tug and pull of Indian family life."

While noting Desai's mixed German-Indian ancestry, *Spectator* contributor Caroline Moore commended the author for the authentic Indian flavor of her works. "Westerners visiting India find themselves reeling under the outsider's sense of 'culture shock,' which is compounded more of shock than culture," the critic wrote. "To Anita Desai, of course, the culture is second nature. Yet that intimacy never becomes mere familiarity: her achievement is to keep the shock of genuine freshness, the eyes of the perpetual outsider." This particular engagement with India is evident in many of Desai's novels, as A.G. Mojtabai noted in the *New York Times Book Review*. "Desai is a writer of Bengali-German descent, who stands in a complicated but advantageous relation to India," said the reviewer. "Insiders rarely notice this much; outsiders cannot have this ease of reference." Mojtabai found that Desai is able to delineate characters, settings, and feelings intricately, yet economically, without extraneous detail or excessively populated scenes: "This author has no need of crowds. Properly observed, a roomful of people is crowd enough, and in

the right hands—as Anita Desai so amply illustrates—*world* enough."

The complexities of outsiders facing Indian culture form the basis of Desai's 1995 novel *Journey to Ithaca*. The story revolves around an ex-hippie European couple who travel to India for quite different reasons—the husband to find enlightenment, the wife to enjoy a foreign experience. As the husband, Matteo, becomes involved with a spiritual guru known as the Mother, wife Sophie goes on a quest of her own: to find the guru's roots in an effort either to debunk or to understand her. Calling the work "a kind of love triangle set against the madness of extreme spiritual searching," *New York Times* reviewer Richard Bernstein said of *Journey to Ithaca* that "Desai writes with intelligence and power. She has a remarkable eye for substance, the things that give life its texture. Nothing escapes her power of observation, not the thickness of the drapes that blot out the light in a bourgeois Parisian home, or the enamel bowl in the office of an Indian doctor." Moore, in the *Spectator,* though commenting that the main characters are drawn rather sketchily, commended the book as "superbly powerful . . . emotionally and intellectually haunting, teasing and tugging our minds even through its imperfections."

Gabriele Annan, writing in the *Times Literary Supplement,* found other flaws in *Journey to Ithaca*. "This is a curiously inept book for a novelist of Desai's experience," Annan wrote. "The narrative is full of gaps and improbabilities, as well as clichés," and "the dialogue is stagey and unconvincing." *Wall Street Journal* contributor Brooke Allen, while admiring Desai's style of writing, also found much of the story unbelievable. Spiritually inclined readers may find the action plausible, but "others will remain incredulous," Allen asserted.

Fasting, Feasting, Desai's third novel to be shortlisted for the Booker Prize, "tells the apparently spare story of one Indian family and the varying fates of its two daughters and single son; it is only on the novel's final, quiet page that Desai's intricate structure becomes clear and the complexity of her emotional insight makes itself felt," explained Sylvia Brownrigg in *Salon.com.* Uma, the oldest daughter, is charged with the care of her demanding parents, while her sister, Aruna, is unhappily married but has escaped the responsibilities that hinder her older sister. Arun, the brother, is the focus of the second half of the novel. He is smothered by his parents' expectations of his life, and he eventually finds his way to Boston where he attends school, staying with an American family, the Pattons, during a break between semesters. "Arriving in the United States, Arun had exulted in his newfound anonymity: 'no past, no family . . . no country.' But he has not escaped family after all, just stumbled into a plastic representation of it," commented J.M. Coetzee in the *New York Review of Books*. The Pattons, with their excesses, counter the values of the Indian household. "Arun himself, as he picks his way through a minefield of puzzling American customs, becomes a more sympathetic character, and his final act in the novel suggests both how far he has come and how much he has lost," explained a critic for *Publishers Weekly*.

Critics were overwhelmingly positive in their assessment of the novel. "*Fasting, Feasting* is a novel not of plot but of comparison," wrote Brownrigg. "In beautifully detailed prose Desai draws the foods and textures of an Indian small town and of an American suburb. In both, she suggests, family life is a complex mixture of generosity and meanness, license and restriction." Donna Seaman, writing in *Booklist,* commented: "Desai has been compared to Jane Austen, and, indeed, she is a deceptively gracious storyteller, writing like an embroiderer concealing a sword as she creates family microcosms that embody all the delusions and cruelties of society-at-large." Though Coetzee faulted Desai's America as feeling "as if it comes out of books," he lauded her writing, particularly her portraits of India. "Desai's strength as a writer has always been her eye for detail and her ear for the exact word . . . her gift for telling metaphor, and above all her feel for sun and sky, heat and dust, for the elemental reality of central India."

Desai is frequently praised by critics for her ability to capture the local color of her country and the ways in which Eastern and Western cultures have blended together there, and for developing this skill further with each successive novel. A large part of this skill is due to her use of imagery, one of the most important devices in her novels. Because of this emphasis on imagery, she is referred to by reviewers such as *World Literature Today* contributor Madhusudan Prasad as an "imagist-novelist" whose use of imagery is "a remarkable quality of her craft that she has carefully maintained" in her mature novels. Employing this imagery to suggest rather than overtly explain her themes, Desai's stories sometimes appear deceptively simple; but, as Anthony Thwaite pointed out in the *New Republic*, "she is such a consummate artist that she [is able to suggest], beyond the confines of the plot and the machinations of her characters, the immensities that lie beyond them—the immensities of India." In the London *Observer*, Salman Rushdie described Desai's fiction as being "illuminated by the author's perceptiveness, delicacy of language and sharp wit."

BIOGRAPHICAL AND CRITICAL SOURCES:

BOOKS

Afzal-Khan, Fawzia, *Cultural Imperialism and the Indo-English Novel: Genre and Ideology in R.K. Narayan, Anita Desai, Kamala Markandaya, and Salman Rushdie,* Pennsylvania State University Press (University Park, PA), 1993.

Bellioppa, Meena, *The Fiction of Anita Desai,* Writers Workshop, 1971.

Choudhury, Bidulata, *Women and Society in the Novels of Anita Desai,* Creative Books (New Delhi, India), 1995.

Contemporary Literary Criticism, Thomson Gale (Detroit, MI), Volume 19, 1981, Volume 37, 1986.

Contemporary Novelists, 6th edition, St. James Press (Detroit, MI), 1996.

Feminist Writers, St. James Press (Detroit, MI), 1996.

Khanna, Shashi, *Human Relationships in Anita Desai's Novels,* Sarup & Sons (New Delhi, India), 1995.

Parker, Michael, and Roger Starkey, editors, *Postcolonial Literature: Achebe, Ngugi, Desai, Walcott,* St. Martin's Press (New York, NY), 1995.

Pathania, Usha, *Human Bonds and Bondages: The Fiction of Anita Desai and Kamala Markandaya,* Kanishka Publishers (New Delhi, India), 1992.

St. James Guide to Children's Writers, 5th edition, St. James Press (Detroit, MI), 1999.

Sharma, Kajali, *Symbolism in Anita Desai's Novels,* Abhinav Publications (New Delhi, India), 1991.

Singh, Sunaina, *The Novels of Margaret Atwood and Anita Desai: A Comparative Study in Feminist Perspectives,* Creative Books, 1994.

Sivanna, Indira, *Anita Desai as an Artist: A Study in Image and Symbol,* Creative Books, 1994.

Solanki, Mrinalini, *Anita Desai's Fiction: Patterns of Survival Strategies,* Kanishka Publishers (New Delhi, India), 1992.

PERIODICALS

Belles Lettres, summer, 1989, p. 4.

Booklist, December 15, 1999, Donna Seaman, review of *Fasting, Feasting,* p. 739.

Boston Globe, August 15, 1995, p. 26.

Chicago Tribune, September 1, 1985.

Globe and Mail (Toronto, Ontario, Canada), August 20, 1988.

Kirkus Reviews, June 15, 1995, p. 799.

Lancet, January 12, 2002, Robin Gerster, "Geographies of the Imagination (Diamond Dust and Other Stories)," p. 178.

Library Journal, February 1, 2000, Dianna Moeller, review of *Fasting, Feasting,* p. 115; June 1, 2000, Faye A. Chadwell, review of *Diamond Dust,* p. 206.

Los Angeles Times, July 31, 1980.

Los Angeles Times Book Review, March 3, 1985; April 9, 1989.

New Leader, May 1, 1989, Betty Falkenberg, review of *Baumgartner's Bombay.*

New Republic, March 18, 1985; April 3, 1989; April 6, 1992, p. 36; August 15, 1994, p. 43.

New York Review of Books, June 1, 1989; December 6, 1990, p. 53; January 16, 1992, p. 42; March 3, 1994, p. 41; May 23, 1996, p. 6; May 25, 2000, J.M. Coetzee, review of *Fasting, Feasting,* pp. 33-35.

New York Times, November 24, 1980; February 22, 1985; March 14, 1989; August 30, 1995, p. B2.

New York Times Book Review, November 20, 1977; June 22, 1980; November 23, 1980; March 3, 1985, p. 7; April 9, 1989, p. 3; January 27, 1991, p. 23; September 17, 1995, p. 12.

Observer (London, England), October 7, 1984, p. 22.

Publishers Weekly, December 6, 1999, review of *Fasting, Feasting,* p. 55.

Spectator, June 3, 1995, pp. 41-42.

Time, July 1, 1985; August 21, 1995, p. 67.

Times (London, England), September 4, 1980.

Times Higher Education Supplement, April 7, 1995, pp. 16-17.

Times Literary Supplement, September 5, 1980; September 7, 1984; October 19, 1984; July 15-21, 1988, p. 787; June 2, 1995, p. 501.

Tribune Books (Chicago, IL), August 23, 1981; March 5, 1989.

Wall Street Journal, August 24, 1995, p. A14.

Washington Post Book World, January 11, 1981, p. 3; October 7, 1984; March 31, 1985; February 26, 1989.

World Literature Today, summer, 1984, pp. 363-369; winter, 1997, p. 221.

Yale Review, spring, 1990, p. 414.

ONLINE

Northeastern University Brudnick Center on Violence and Conflict Web Site, http://www.violence.neu.edu/ (April 18-20, 2001) "Third World Views of the Holocaust."

Salon.com, http://www.salon.com/ (February 17, 2000), Sylvia Brownrigg, review of *Fasting, Feasting.*

DeWITT, Helen 1957-

PERSONAL: Born 1957, in Takoma Park, MD. *Education:* Attended Smith College, 1975; attended Somerville College, Oxford, c. 1988-89.

ADDRESSES: Home—Chesterfield, Derbyshire, England. *Office*—c/o Author Mail, Hyperion, 77 West 66th St., 11th Floor, New York, NY 10023.

CAREER: Author.

AWARDS, HONORS: International IMPAC DUBLIN Literary Award nomination, 2002, for *The Last Samurai.*

WRITINGS:

The Last Samurai, Hyperion (New York, NY), 2000.

SIDELIGHTS: Helen DeWitt's novel *The Last Samurai* is the story of Ludo, a child prodigy who loves to learn, can read at age two, and has learned several languages by the time he is four years old. Ludo is raised by his single mother, Sibylla, who is struggling to make ends meet while working as a typist in England during the 1980s. Both Sibylla and Ludo are fans of Akira Kurosawa's film *The Seven Samurai,* and watch it many times a week. Sibylla believes that *The Seven Samurai* will serve her son as a guide or moral development. As Ludo gets older he becomes curious about his father, about whom his mother will tell him nothing, and at age eleven he seeks out seven men he sees as potential father figures, among them a travel writer, a painter, and a Nobel Prize-winning astronomer. Ludo's search for answers about his father ultimately leads him to a better understanding of his mother and of himself.

The Last Samurai drew critical praise from many quarters, as much for its compelling plot as its learnedness, a reflection of DeWitt's grounding in philosophy, literature, and the classics. Calling the novel "unlike anything you've ever read," *Atlanta Journal-Constitution* reviewer Greg Changnon praised it as a work of prose "as comfortable dipping into Japanese and Arabic as it is quoting the screenplay of Akira Kurosawa's 'The Seven Samurai.'" While praising the book as "witty and learned," *Observer* contributor David Mattin was quick to bolster the courage of potential readers, noting that *The Last Samurai* "does not bash the reader over the head with writerly prose"; instead, he explained, DeWitt spins a plot "that unashamedly attempts to charm." Calling DeWitt's fiction debut "ambitious," a *Publishers Weekly* contributor praised *The Last Samurai* as "energetic and relentlessly unpredictable," strengthened by the relationship between Sibylla and her son. In an enthusiastic review for the *Washington Post Book World* in which he dubbed the novelist "this year's It Girl of postmodernism," Steven Moore noted that DeWitt "is formidably intelligent but engagingly witty. . . . [with her] wide-ranging interests and en extraordinarily original mind; she is a joy to read." *Booklist* contributor Grace Fill called *The Last Samurai* "a touching story of a child's maturing love [that] . . . illuminates the ways in which a parent's issues can overtly or covertly affect the life of a child."

BIOGRAPHICAL AND CRITICAL SOURCES:

PERIODICALS

Atlanta Journal-Constitution (Atlanta, GA), February 25, 2001, Greg Changnon, review of *The Last Samurai.*

Booklist, July, 2000, Grace Fill, review of *The Last Samurai,* p. 1974.

Boston Globe, September 24, 2000, review of *The Last Samurai.*

Kirkus Reviews, July 1, 2000, review of *The Last Samurai,* p. 903.

Observer (London, England), October 28, 2001, David Mattin, review of *The Last Samurai.*

Publishers Weekly, August 7, 2000, review of *The Last Samurai,* p. 75.

Washington Post Book World, September 17, 2000, Steven Moore, review of *The Last Samurai.*

*   *   *

DEXTER, Colin 1930-
(N.C. Dexter, Norman Colin Dexter)

PERSONAL: Born September 29, 1930, in Stamford, England; son of Alfred (a taxi driver) and Dorothy (Towns) Dexter; married Dorothy Cooper (a physiotherapist), March 31, 1956; children: Sally, Jeremy. *Education:* Christ's College, Cambridge, B.A., 1953, M.A., 1958.

ADDRESSES: Home—56 Banbury Rd., Oxford OX2 7RG, England.

CAREER: Wyggeston School, Leicester, England, assistant classics master, 1954-57; Loughborough Grammar School, Loughborough, England, sixth form classics master, 1957-59; Corby Grammar School, Corby, England, senior classics master, 1959-66; Oxford Local Examination Board, Oxford, England, assistant secretary, 1966-76, senior assistant secretary, 1976-87. *Military service:* Royal Corps of Signals, 1949-50.

MEMBER: Crime Writers Association, Detection Club.

AWARDS, HONORS: Honorary M.A., Oxford University, 1966; Silver Dagger Award, Crime Writers Association, 1979, for *Service of All the Dead,* and 1981, for *The Dead of Jericho;* Gold Dagger Award, Crime Writers Association, 1989, for *The Wench Is Dead,* and 1992, for *The Way through the Woods;* honorary M.A., Leicester University, 1996; Medal of Merit, Lotus Club, 1996; Cartier Diamond Dagger, Crime Writers Association, 1997, for outstanding services to crime literature.

WRITINGS:

"INSPECTOR MORSE" MYSTERIES

Last Bus to Woodstock, St. Martin's Press (New York, NY), 1975.

Last Seen Wearing (also see below), St. Martin's Press (New York, NY), 1976.

The Silent World of Nicholas Quinn, St. Martin's Press (New York, NY), 1977.

Service of All the Dead, Macmillan (London, England), 1979, St. Martin's Press (New York, NY), 1980.

The Dead of Jericho, St. Martin's Press (New York, NY), 1981.

The Riddle of the Third Mile (also see below), Macmillan (New York, NY), 1983.

The Secret of Annexe 3 (also see below), Macmillan (London, England), 1986, St. Martin's Press (New York, NY), 1987.

The Wench Is Dead, Macmillan (London, England), 1989, St. Martin's Press (New York, NY), 1990.

The Jewel That Was Ours, Macmillan (London, England), 1991, Crown (New York, NY), 1992.

The Way through the Woods, Macmillan (London, England), 1992, Crown (New York, NY), 1993.

Morse's Greatest Mystery and Other Stories (contains "As Good as Gold," "Morse's Greatest Mystery," "Evans Tries an O-Level," "Dead as a Dodo," "At the Lulu-Bar Motel," "Neighbourhood Watch," "A

Case of Mis-Identity," "The Inside Story," "Monty's Revolver," "The Carpet-Bagger," and "Last Call"), Macmillan (London, England), 1993.

The Daughters of Cain, Macmillan (London, England), 1994, Crown (New York, NY), 1995.

Death Is Now My Neighbour, Macmillan (London, England), 1996, Crown (New York, NY), 1997.

The Remorseful Day: The Final Inspector Morse Novel, Crown (New York, NY), 1999.

OTHER

(Under name N.C. Dexter, with E.G. Rayner) *Liberal Studies: An Outline Course,* 2 volumes, Macmillan(London, England), 1964, revised edition, 1966.

(Under name N.C. Dexter, with E.G. Rayner) *Guide to Contemporary Politics,* Pergamon (London, England), 1966.

Work represented in several anthologies, including *Murder Ink,* edited by Dilys Winn, Workman Pub. (New York, NY), 1977; *Winter's Crimes 9,* edited by George Hardinge, St. Martin's Press (New York, NY), 1978; *Winter's Crimes 13,* edited by Hardinge, St. Martin's Press, 1982; and *Winter's Crimes 21,* edited by Hilary Hale, Macmillan(London, England), 1989.

ADAPTATIONS: Stories based on Dexter's Inspector Morse character were adapted for television and aired on the PBS program *Mystery!; Inspector Morse: Driven to Distraction* by Anthony Minghella is a screenplay based on characters created by Dexter and published by University of Cambridge Press, 1994. Several of Dexter's novels have also been recorded and released as audio books.

SIDELIGHTS: "To most readers of Colin Dexter's books," wrote *Dictionary of Literary Biography* contributor Bernard Benstock, "his major accomplishment is the creation of his particular detective hero, Detective Chief Inspector Morse of the Thames Valley Constabulary of Kidlington, Oxon." Inspector Morse is an irascible figure, fond of beer and tobacco, but nonetheless held in awe by his associate, Detective Sergeant Lewis. "At times," Benstock revealed, "his seediness is similar to the seediness of a Graham Greene character, his bluster and swagger similar to John Mortimer's Rumpole of the Bailey, but always there is an element of the pathetic to counterbalance the braggadocio. Morse's vulnerable and remarkable character unfolds serially from book to book, so that eventually there are no mysteries about him—except for his given name."

Dexter introduced Inspector Morse in 1975 in *Last Bus to Woodstock,* which established many of the central characteristics of Dexter's work. "*Last Bus to Woodstock* concerns the brutal murder (and possible sex-murder) of a scantily clad female hitchhiker, whose companion at the bus stop fails to identify herself," wrote Benstock. "Several young women are likely possibilities for the companion, but Morse is frustrated by their refusal to be honest with him." Morse finds himself sidetracked after having identified the wrong person as the murderer. "The grisly deaths of a husband and wife, each of whom had confessed to the murder," Benstock continued, "bring matters to a head, and Morse apprehends the woman murderer—an attractive young woman he had admired, who confesses that she has fallen in love with him—as she is taken away to stand trial." Dexter treats each of the Morse mysteries as a puzzle, complete with misleading clues, red herrings, and false trails. "Once you choose the wrong word," explained a *Virginia Quarterly Review* contributor, "the whole puzzle can be filled incorrectly."

Morse's irritability is balanced by his companion in mystery-solving, Detective Sergeant Lewis. Cushing Strout, writing in *Armchair Detective,* compared the relationship between Lewis and Morse to that of Arthur Conan Doyle's Sherlock Holmes and John Watson, calling Dexter's work "the best contemporary English example of adapting and updating Doyle's technique." Like Holmes, Strout continued, "Morse is a bachelor," but, "in spite of his generally cynical expectations about human nature and the world, unlike Holmes he is always romantically vulnerable (in spite of disappointing experience) to being smitten by love at first sight for some attractive and intelligent, but quite inappropriate woman." In contrast to Morse, Strout continued, Sergeant Lewis "is working class, a family man, and a competent policeman in a routine way. He has a refreshing common sense that Morse often sorely lacks, and the two men (like Holmes and Watson in this respect) know how to tease each other."

Dexter, Strout explained, "has collated his novels under the heading of 'what may be termed (though it sounds a bit posh) the exploitation of reader-mystification.'" This is a traditional attribute of English detective fiction: the ability to mislead the reader, who is trying to identify the culprit. The classic mystery novel, as set forth by one of the earliest practitioners of the genre, G.K. Chesterton, should present the reader with all the clues available to the detective, but in such a way that the reader fails to make the connection with the criminal until after the detective uncovers the guilty party. "Inferior writers," Strout continued, "tend to cast suspicion on so many characters that it is . . . like hiding one card amid the rest of the deck, rather than performing the much more difficult classic trick, wherein the 'money card' is one of only three cards." "Dexter," the critic concluded, "keeps shifting the pieces, like a conjuror misdirecting the audience by giving a specious explanation of his trick, until they finally make a coherent and credible picture with the lagniappe of a last surprise." In a review of *The Daughters of Cain* for the *New York Times Book Review,* Marilyn Stasio advised readers "to get out their pencils, timetables and aspirin."

As the series progresses, Dexter also begins to play highly literate games with his readers, ranging from apparently gratis references to literature, such as James Joyce's *Ulysses* in *The Riddle of the Third Mile* and Sophocles' Oedipus trilogy of plays in *The Dead of Jericho.* He also uses inscriptions and epigraphs at the beginning of each chapter like a chorus in a Greek play to comment on the story's action and the state of Morse's mind. "The basic norm in the Dexter novels," Benstock declared, "is best characterized by the epigraph to chapter 14 of *The Riddle of the Third Mile:* 'Preliminary investigations are now in full swing, and Morse appears unconcerned about the contradictory evidence that emerges.'"

Morse demonstrates many of his best points in the Gold Dagger award-winning novel, *The Wench Is Dead.* Critics have compared the book to Josephine Tey's classic detective novel *The Daughter of Time,* in which her detective, Alan Grant, immobilized in hospital with a fractured spine, tries to solve a historical mystery—the disappearance of young Edward V and his brother Richard of York in the Tower of London during the reign of Richard III. Morse is hospitalized with a bleeding ulcer, and to ease his boredom he reopens a Victorian murder case that took place in Oxford: the death by drowning of a female passenger on a canal boat in the mid-nineteenth century. Morse's wits and temper, wrote Stasio in the *New York Times Book Review,* "tug the reader into the detective's hospital bed to share his single-minded pursuit of the truth."

Dexter ended the "Inspector Morse" series in 1999 with his final case, *The Remorseful Day: The Final Inspector Morse Novel.* Morse is called in to re-investigate the two-year-old murder of a local nurse, a woman with whom he was once romantically involved. In the course of the investigation, Morse's long-time health problems come to the fore, leading to a final ending not only to the story but to the Morse series. "This finale to a grand series," noted the critic for *Publishers Weekly,* "presents a moving elegy to one of mystery fiction's most celebrated and popular characters." Reviewing the novel for *Booklist,* Bill Ott described it as "an audaciously clever and surprisingly moving finale."

Dexter's "Inspector Morse" novels have established him as a pivotal figure in modern English detective fiction. Throughout the series, Benstock stated, "the comic vies with the grotesque, pathos with the tragic, within an effective evocation of the mundane. The surface realities of ordinary life consistently color the criminal situations without impinging on the careful artifice of the usual murders and the bumbling but brilliant methods of investigation undertaken almost in spite of himself by Chief Inspector E. Morse." According to the essayist for the *St. James Guide to Crime and Mystery Writers,* with his series Dexter "has established himself in the forefront of British writers with some of the cleverest and most complicated plots, delighting a vast and ever growing band of devoted readers." Michael Leapman, writing in the *New Statesman,* called Morse "one of the great detectives of English fiction."

BIOGRAPHICAL AND CRITICAL SOURCES:

BOOKS

Contemporary Popular Writers, St. James Press (Detroit, MI), 1997.
Dictionary of Literary Biography, Volume 87: *British Mystery and Thriller Writers since 1940, First Series,* Thomson Gale (Detroit, MI), 1989.
St. James Guide to Crime and Mystery Writers, 4th edition, St. James Press (Detroit, MI), 1996.

PERIODICALS

Armchair Detective, winter, 1989, pp. 76-77; fall, 1990, p. 497; summer, 1993, review of *The Jewel That Was Ours,* p. 45; summer, 1994, p. 272; summer, 1995, review of *The Daughters of Cain,* p. 342; fall, 1995, pp. 434-437.
Booklist, March 1, 1995, Emily Melton, review of *The Daughters of Cain,* p. 1139; October 1, 1995, Emily Melton, review of *Morse's Greatest Mystery,* p. 212; December 1, 1996, Bill Ott, review of *Death Is Now My Neighbor,* p. 619; December 1, 1999, Bill Ott, review of *The Remorseful Day,* p. 660.
Books, November, 1994, review of *The Daughters of Cain,* p. 16.

Entertainment Weekly, April 23, 1993, Gene Lyons, review of *The Way through the Woods,* p. 50; April 4, 1997, Nikki Amdur, review of *Death Is Now My Neighbor,* p. 79; December 12, 1997, Tom De Haven, review of *The Way through the Wood,* p. 78.

Insight on the News, May 22, 1995, Elizabeth M. Cosin, review of *Daughters of Cain,* p. 25.

Kirkus Reviews, March 1, 1995, review of *The Daughters of Cain,* p. 270.

Library Journal, February 1, 2000, Fred M. Gervat, review of *The Remorseful Day,* p. 121.

Listener, July 8, 1976; June 30, 1977.

Los Angeles Times Book Review, April 9, 1995, review of *The Daughters of Cain,* p. 12.

New Republic, March 4, 1978.

New Statesman, September 20, 1996, Boyd Tonkin, "Watching the Detectives," p. 45; October 25, 1999, Michael Leapman, review of *The Remorseful Day,* p. 54; November 20, 2000, Andrew Billen, "Requiem for a Cop," p. 47.

New York Times Book Review, May 20, 1990, p. 53; April 4, 1993; April 16, 1995, review of *The Daughters of Cain,* p. 29; March 2, 1997, review of *Death Is Now My Neighbor,* p. 20.

People, May 8, 1995, Cynthia Sanz, review of *The Daughters of Cain,* p. 46.

Publishers Weekly, March 8, 1993, review of *The Way through the Woods,* p. 71; March 13, 1995, review of *The Daughters of Cain,* p. 63; October 9, 1995, review of *Morse's Greatest Mystery,* p. 79; December 30, 1996, review of *Death Is Now My Neighbor,* p. 57; January 24, 2000, review of *The Remorseful Day,* p. 296.

Time, April 26, 1993, p. 65, William A. Henry III, review of *The Way through the Woods,* p. 65.

Times Literary Supplement, September 26, 1975; April 23, 1976; August 26, 1977; June 5, 1981; October 25, 1991, p. 21; October 23, 1992, p. 22; December 23, 1994, review of *The Daughters of Cain,* p. 21.

Virginia Quarterly Review, autumn, 1992, p. 131.

Wall Street Journal, April 27, 1995, review of *The Daughters of Cain,* p. A12; March 28, 1997, review of *Death Is Now My Neighbor,* p. A14.

Washington Post Book World, December 20, 1987, p. 8.

*   *   *

DEXTER, John
   See BRADLEY, Marion Zimmer

*   *   *

DEXTER, N.C.
   See DEXTER, Colin

DEXTER, Norman Colin
   See DEXTER, Colin

*   *   *

DEXTER, Pete 1943-

PERSONAL: Born 1943, in Pontiac, MI; married (divorced); married second wife, Dian; children: (second marriage) Casey. *Education:* Received degree from University of South Dakota, 1970. *Hobbies and other interests:* Boxing.

ADDRESSES: Home—1170 Markham Way, Sacramento, CA 95818. *Office*—Sacramento Bee, 21st and Q Streets, Box 15779, Sacramento, CA 95852. *Agent*—Esther Newberg, International Creative Management, 40 West 57th St., New York, NY 10019.

CAREER: Novelist, journalist, and columnist. *West Palm Beach Post,* Palm Beach, FL, reporter, 1971-72; *Philadelphia Daily News,* Philadelphia, PA, columnist, 1972-84; *Sacramento Bee,* Sacramento, CA, columnist, 1985—; has also worked as a truck driver, gas station attendant, mail sorter, construction laborer, and salesperson.

AWARDS, HONORS: National Endowment for the Arts grant to write poetry; National Book Award, and National Book Critics Circle Award nomination, both 1988, both for *Paris Trout.*

WRITINGS:

NOVELS

God's Pocket, Random House (New York, NY), 1984.
Deadwood, Random House (New York, NY), 1986.
Paris Trout, Random House (New York, NY), 1988.
Brotherly Love, Random House (New York, NY), 1993.
The Paperboy, Random House (New York, NY), 1995.

SCREENPLAYS

Rush, Metro-Goldwyn-Mayer, 1991.
(With others) *Michael,* New Line Cinema, 1996.

Also author of screenplay *Mulholland Falls.* Contributor to periodicals, including *Esquire, Sports Illustrated,* and *Playboy.*

ADAPTATIONS: Dexter's work has been adapted for audiocassette.

WORK IN PROGRESS: Screenplays for *Deadwood* and *Paris Trout;* a novel.

SIDELIGHTS: National Book Award-winning author Pete Dexter is noted for his novels that mix violence with humor, display a sharp ear for dialogue and an eye for local color, and contain well-rounded and often eccentric characters. An outspoken journalist with the *Philadelphia Daily News* for twelve years and with the *Sacramento Bee* since 1985, Dexter turned to writing fiction after nearly being beaten to death by readers who were infuriated by one of his *Daily News* columns. Thus no stranger to brutality, he focuses in his novels on how communities react to violence and murder. Dexter's first book, *God's Pocket,* turns on the death of an abrasive white construction worker in Philadelphia; *Deadwood* relates the assassination of legendary outlaw "Wild Bill" Hickok in a western gold-rush town; *Paris Trout* explores the aftermath of the shooting of an innocent black girl in Georgia; and *The Paperboy* recounts the upcoming execution of an innocent man.

Born in Michigan and raised in Georgia and South Dakota, Dexter graduated from the University of South Dakota in 1970 after attending for eight years (he would quit when the weather got cold). He secured a job as a reporter with the *West Palm Beach Post* but left after two years ("I wasn't the best writer there," he explained in the *New York Times Book Review*). He then worked at a gas station with another former *Post* reporter but quit ("I wasn't even the best writer in the gas station") to join the *Philadelphia Daily News* in 1972. A decade later he was badly beaten in a barroom brawl by baseball-bat and tire-iron-wielding denizens of a Philadelphia neighborhood who were angered by a column he had written about a drug-related murder that happened there. Dexter survived with a broken back and hip and an altered sense of taste from the blows to his head. Forced to give up his favorite pastime, drinking (beer, according to Dexter, now tastes like battery acid), he devoted his spare time to writing. The result was three critically acclaimed novels.

Dexter's first work, *God's Pocket,* begins with what Julius Lester in *New York Times Book Review* called an "auspicious comic opening": "Leon Hubbard died ten minutes into lunch break on the first Monday in May, on the construction site of the new one-story trauma wing at Holy Redeemer Hospital in South Philadelphia. One way or the other, he was going to lose the job." Drug-addict bricklayer Leon prompted his own demise when he threatened a black coworker named Lucien with a straight razor; Lucien consequently bashed Leon in the back of the head with a lead pipe. Glad to be rid of the troublemaker, the other workers and the foreman told the police it was an accidental death. This "random incident," according to Paul Gray in *Time,* turns "into a picaresque romp" when Leon's devoted mother, Jeanie, and her second husband, Mickey, who is constantly trying to prove his devotion to her, believe otherwise. At the grieving mother's request, Mickey must tap his underground connections to find out who killed Leon.

Reviewers of *God's Pocket* commended Dexter for his masterful control of comic situations, fluent prose, and idiomatic dialogue. Gray also appreciated the novel's "impressive ballast of local color," noting that the rough working-class Philadelphia neighborhood called God's Pocket "seems all too real: narrow houses, streets, lives; a place where the Hollywood Bar, the social hub of the area, does 'half its business before noon.'" Some critics, however, criticized *God's Pocket* for being too ambitious. Gray, for instance, complained that Dexter "piles on more complications and coincidences than his novel ought to carry" and added that there are too many characters and subplots. Mickey, for example, in addition to having to please Jeanie by identifying Leon's murderer, must raise six thousand dollars to bury him in a mahogany casket. But because he cannot pay the undertaker for the funeral due to his losing efforts at the racetrack, Mickey is forced to drive Leon's embalmed corpse around in his refrigerated meat truck, which he uses to sell stolen meat for his two-bit mobster boss. For another subplot Dexter created Richard Shellburn, an alcoholic Philadelphia newspaper columnist who is also suspicious of Leon's mysterious demise. Shellburn is later beaten to death by the threatened residents of God's Pocket.

Dexter's second novel, *Deadwood,* focuses on the death of American folk hero James Butler "Wild Bill" Hickok. In the novel, Hickok, his longtime partner "Colorado" Charley Utter, and follower Malcolm Nash escort a wagon train of prostitutes to the Dakota gold rush town of Deadwood in 1876. Hickok, once renowned as the best pistol shot in the West, is now an aging Wild West-show performer who drinks to overcome the pain of syphilis. About a third of the way into *Deadwood* he is shot to death by a hired killer while playing poker in a saloon. "The rest of this hilarious and rousing novel," according to Dennis Drabelle in Chicago's *Tribune Books,* concerns itself with how "the other characters cope with [Hickok's] transformation from living to dead legend."

New York Times Book Review contributor Ron Hansen remarked that after his hero's death Dexter fills the pages of the novel with "some intriguingly extravagant minor characters." Populating Dexter's town of Deadwood are China Doll, a prostitute seeking revenge on Utter for burning the corpse of her brother; her pimp, Al Swearingen, who brutally rapes Nash; "Calamity" Jane Cannery, who claims that she is the widow of Hickok; and trapeze artist Agnes Lake, Hickok's true widow, who befriends Cannery. "All of them become threads in the tapestry of Deadwood," Drabelle noted, "and the town itself becomes the protagonist."

Critics praised *Deadwood* for its local color, shrewd characterization, and deftly handled bawdy situations. "*Deadwood* is unpredictable, hyperbolic and, page after page, uproarious," Hansen attested. It is "a joshing book written in high spirits and a raw appreciation for the past." "The writing is engagingly colloquial without being silly, and well suited to the multiple character points of view," *Village Voice* contributor M. George Stevenson assessed. "And the book *is* very funny and filled with wry observations about the surfaces of frontier life." "With its stylish humor and convincing demonstration of how the fables of the Wild West originated," Drabelle concluded, "*Deadwood* may well be the best Western ever written."

Dexter received the National Book Award and was shortlisted for the National Book Critics Circle Award for his third book, *Paris Trout.* Set in the 1950s in the town of Cotton Point, Georgia, the novel concerns the amoral Paris Trout, a white hardware-store owner and loan shark to the black community who is nonetheless locally respected. When a young black man, Henry Ray Boxer, refuses to make payments on a car he bought from Trout after it was hit by a truck, Trout and a crony barge into the man's home to collect on the loan. Not finding him there, Trout shoots Boxer's mother in the back and kills a fourteen-year old girl who lives with the family.

Reluctantly, the authorities arrest, try, and sentence Trout to three years' hard labor. Convinced of his right to collect on a debt and determined not to do time for what he does not consider a crime, Trout bribes his way out of going to prison. In the aftermath he grows in-creasingly demented and becomes, in the words of *Los Angeles Times Book Review* contributor Richard Eder, "a primal evil, all will and no humanity." "Before it is over," *Book World* contributor Judith Paterson noted, "[Trout's] unyielding conviction that everything he does is right has thrown the whole town off its moral center and exposed the link between Trout's depravity and the town's silent endorsement of all kinds of inhumanities—including racism, sexism and economic exploitation."

"If *Paris Trout* is about a community hamstrung by its accommodations," Eder continued, "it is also, at every moment, about the individuals caught in the accommodation. Dexter portrays them with marvelous sharpness." An increasingly paranoid Trout sleeps with a sheet of lead under his bed to shield himself from assassination and is convinced that his wife, Hanna, is trying to poison him. Hanna, a stoical schoolteacher who married Trout late in life to escape spinsterhood, is psychologically and sexually brutalized by him throughout their marriage. She consequently has an affair with Trout's gentleman defense lawyer, Harry Seagraves, who represented Trout out of social obligation but abandoned him after the trial. Hanna also hires local attorney Carl Bonner to represent her in divorce proceedings against her husband. "Perfectly offsetting graphic horror and comedy," Dean Faulkner Wells assessed in Chicago's *Tribune Books,* "Dexter brings all these characters together in an explosive conclusion."

"With a touch of the mastery that graces the best fiction about the South," Pete Axthelm observed in his *Newsweek* review of *Paris Trout,* "Dexter has conjured up characters stroked broadly, voices that ring true—and vignettes crafted in miniature in a way that haunts." Numerous critics mentioned similarities between Dexter and various Southern writers, claiming that his dark humor is reminiscent of the works of Flannery O'Connor and that his use of violence is Faulknerian. Dexter is quick to mention, though, that he is not a "Southern" writer (*Paris Trout* is his only book set in the South), but he is grateful for the praise. George Melly in *New Statesman and Society,* in fact, found differences between William Faulkner and Dexter. He noted that although *Paris Trout* is set in Faulkner's South, "it is free of Faulkner's convoluted style. The prose is taut, the feeling for time and place exact."

Dexter also denied the claim of some reviewers that *Paris Trout* symbolizes "racism, class war and inhumanity in the pre-civil-rights-era South," according to Glenn Collins of the *New York Times.* The author told the journalist that the events of *Paris Trout* "could have happened anywhere. The South has no lock on violence. In fact, South Philadelphia is more violent than the South." Deborah Mason in the *New York Times Book Review* commended Dexter for this insight, noting that "at a time when virulent racial incidents can no longer be conveniently fenced off in small Southern towns, Mr. Dexter's great accomplishment is to remind us, with lucidity and stinging frankness, the lengths to which we will go to deny our own racism and to reassure ourselves that we are innocent." Eder agreed. "The monstrousness, even of the decent people, hangs over the entire book," he confessed. "It is one of the elements that make *Paris Trout* a masterpiece, complex and breathtaking."

Dexter's novel *Brotherly Love* begins in an unlikely place—with the death of the two main characters, as reported in a newspaper article. Within the novel's remaining pages, Dexter details how the two men, Peter Flood and his cousin, Michael, grow up in Philadelphia, mature, and end up as targets of separate mob hits. Haunted by the death of his baby sister, which he was unable to prevent, Peter takes morbid thrills in jumping off buildings. He finds some release from the pain of his memories and the pressures of his life in boxing lessons. He becomes a labor racketeer for little other reason than that's what his father did. Peter has little interest in it, except that it's the "family business." Michael becomes a union leader in South Philly. Peter finds himself acting as little more than hired hand for the increasingly vicious Michael. Tired, afraid, and alarmed by Michael's cruelty, Peter finally severs the "now-destructive symbiotic relationship in a deed that caps the series of violent deaths that have gone before," wrote a *Publishers Weekly* reviewer. John Shaw, writing in *Time,* compared *Brotherly Love* with one of Dexter's previous novels, noting that "Though *Brotherly Love* is intentionally a narrower, less spacious novel than *Paris Trout,* its quality is just as high." A *Publishers Weekly* critic commented that the book is "a taut, gripping narrative that memorably examines the dark wellsprings of human behavior." Leah Rozen, writing in *People,* concluded, "All in all, it's an exhilarating novel."

In *The Paperboy,* Dexter draws on his experiences in journalism to tell the story of a pair of reporters exploring what looks like an unjust conviction—and looming execution—in Florida. The sheriff of Moat Country, Florida, Thurmond Call, is an unrepentant racist who "even by Moat county standards, had killed an inappropriate number of Negroes in the line of duty," according to narrator Jack James, recently kicked out of college and a delivery truck driver for his father's newspaper, the *Miami Times.* Spiraling further and further out of control, Sheriff Call stomps to death the drunk and handcuffed Jerome Van Wetter, a member of a poor, inbred family of white swamp-dwelling locals who hunt alligators and shun most contact with anyone outside their clan. Shortly after Jerome's death, Sheriff Call is found in the road near his police cruiser, gutted and dead. Another Van Wetter, Hillary, is arrested, tried, and convicted for the sheriff's murder and is sent to await his own demise on Death Row.

Four years later, investigative reporters Ward James (Jack's brother) and Yardely Acherman discover the case when Charlotte Bess, an aging beauty with a tendency to romance and become engaged to convicted men, comes to them with considerable evidence of Hillary's innocence. The two reporters sense a gross miscarriage of justice. They are sent to investigate by their employer, the *Miami Times.* Ward hires Jack to serve as his and Acherman's chauffeur and assistant—Jack, awed by the famed reporters, gladly agrees, since both journalists lost their driver's licenses over DWI offenses. When the trio arrives in Moat County, however, they discover a town unwilling to talk; even the Van Wetter family, mysterious and more than slightly dangerous, won't help save their kin. With persistence, and Ward's continual confrontations with belligerent sources such as the police, the locals, and the Van Wetters themselves, evidence does emerge, but it is not solid. The stylish Acherman, however, is willing to cut corners and go with what they have—and when Ward is hospitalized after a beating, Acherman simply makes up what's needed to finish the story. Hillary Van Wetter is freed, Ward and Acherman win a Pulitzer for their efforts, but the fabrications of the story are eventually discovered. Paul Gray, writing in *Time,* called *The Paperboy* "hip, hard-boiled, and filled with memorable eccentrics. The reporters' encounters with members of the Van Wetter clan comically—and ominously—juxtapose modern types with people ancient in their cunning and evil." Gilbert Taylor, writing in *Booklist,* observed that Dexter leaves "too many loose ends," but concluded that he "has created vibrant characters who fit snugly in their hot, languid setting." A critic from the *Mystery Guide* Web site remarked that *The Paperboy* is a "wonderful novel, which works in many ways at once: as a study of a family, as a chronicle of a town, and a psychological thriller." The novel has "a special quality seldom seen in fiction—a mesmerizing power of finality," observed Jon Saari in the *Antioch Review.* To reviewer Gene Lyons, writing in *Entertainment Weekly,* "*The Paperboy* is anything but a perfect novel," but he concluded, "It's a wise and fascinating tale well told."

BIOGRAPHICAL AND CRITICAL SOURCES:

BOOKS

Contemporary Literary Criticism, Thomson Gale (Detroit, MI), Volume 34, 1985, Volume 55, 1989.

Contemporary Popular Writers, St. James Press (Detroit, MI), 1997.

Modern American Literature, 5th edition, St. James Press (Detroit, MI), 1999.

PERIODICALS

American Journalism Review, April, 1995, review of *The Paperboy,* p. 56.

Antioch Review, summer, 1995, Jon Saari, review of *The Paperboy,* pp. 375-376.

Bestsellers 89, 1989, Issue 2.

Booklist, September 1, 1991, review of *Brotherly Love,* p. 4; September 15, 1991, review of *Brotherly Love,* p. 182; April 15, 1992, Jeanette Larson, review of *Brotherly Love,* p. 1547; November 15, 1994, Gilbert Taylor, review of *The Paperboy,* pp. 555-556; January 1, 1996, review of *Paris Trout,* p. 788; March 15, 1996, review of *The Paperboy,* p. 1272.

Books, March, 1992, review of *Brotherly Love,* p. 21; summer, 1995, review of *The Paperboy,* p. 27.

Bookwatch, December, 1995, review of *The Paperboy* (audio version), p. 3.

Christian Science Monitor, October 28, 1991, Jim Bencivenga, review of *Brotherly Love,* p. 13; February 16, 1995, Catherine Foster, review of *The Paperboy,* p. 12.

Entertainment Weekly, January 27, 1995, Gene Lyons, review of *The Paperboy,* pp. 42-43; January 26, 1996, review of *The Paperboy,* p. 53; May 3, 1996, Ken Tucker, review of *Mulholland Falls,* p. 62.

Gentlemen's Quarterly, February, 1995, Thomas Mallon, review of *The Paperboy,* p. 87.

Guardian, June 20, 1993, review of *Brotherly Love,* p. 28.

Hudson Review, summer, 1992, Dean Flower, review of *Brotherly Love,* pp. 331-332.

Independent, March 27, 1993, Anthony Quinn, "Hellraiser Who Never Met an Adjective He Liked," interview with Pete Dexter, p. 31.

Kirkus Reviews, August 1, 1991, review of *Brotherly Love,* p. 949; November 1, 1994, review of *The Paperboy,* p. 1430.

Kliatt Young Adult Paperback Book Guide, January, 1993, review of *Brotherly Love,* p. 6; March, 1996, review of *The Paperboy,* p. 8.

Law Institute Journal, December, 1996, Christ Hurley, review of *The Paper Boy,* pp. 60-61.

Legal Times, February 20, 1995, Joel Chineson, review of *The Paperboy,* p. 62.

Library Journal, October 1, 1991, Albert E. Wilhelm, review of *Brotherly Love,* pp. 139-140; October 1, 1991, Randy Pitman, review of *Paris Trout,* p. 155; February 15, 1992, Roxanna Herrick, review of *Brotherly Love,* p. 216; January, 1995, David Dodd, review of *The Paperboy,* p. 136.

London Review of Books, October 5, 1995, review of *The Paperboy,* p. 23.

Los Angeles Times, December 1, 1988.

Los Angeles Times Book Review, July 24, 1988; October 6, 1991; January 1, 1995, review of *The Paperboy,* p. 3.

Nation, March 10, 1984.

New Republic, May 27, 1996, Stanley Kauffmann, review of *Mulholland Falls,* pp. 28-29; March 3, 1997, review of *Michael.*

New Statesman, June 30, 1995, Nick Kimberley, review of *The Paperboy,* pp. 38-39; September 6, 1996, Boyd Tonkin, review of *Mulholland Falls,* p. 43.

New Statesman and Society, October 7, 1988, George Melly, review of *Paris Trout,* pp. 38-39.

Newsweek, September 26, 1988, Pete Axthelm, review of *Paris Trout,* p. 74.

New York, September 30, 1991, Rhoda Koenig, review of *Brotherly Love,* p. 75; May 13, 1996, David Denby, review of *Mulholland Falls,* pp. 58-59; September 30, 1991, p. 75.

New York Law Journal, June 8, 1995, Carole Shapiro, review of *The Paperboy,* p. 2.

New York Review of Books, February 16, 1989, Robert Towers, review of *Paris Trout,* pp. 18-19.

New York Times, December 5, 1988; October 4, 1991, Michiko Kakutani, review of *Brotherly Love,* p. C29; January 12, 1995, Christopher Lehmann-Haupt, review of *The Paperboy,* p. C24.

New York Times Book Review, February 19, 1984; April 20, 1986; July 24, 1988, Deborah Mason, review of *Paris Trout,* pp. 7-8; October 13, 1991, Robert Stone, review of *Brotherly Love,* p. 3; April 19, 1992; September 6, 1992, review of *Brotherly Love,* p. 24; April 4, 1993; January 22, 1995, Brent Staples, review of *The Paperboy,* p. 7; January 22, 1995, Barth Healey, "Interview with Pete Dexter," p. 7; June 11, 1995, review of *The Paperboy,* p. 38; December 3, 1995, review of *The Paperboy,* p. 76; January 14, 1996, review of *The Paperboy,* p. 28.

Observer (London, England), June 11, 1995, review of *The Paperboy,* p. 14.

People, October 21, 1991, Leah Rozen, review of *Brotherly Love,* pp. 31-32; January 30, 1995, Dani Shapiro, review of *The Paperboy,* p. 27; May 6, 1996, Ralph Novak, review of *Mulholland Falls,* pp. 18-19.

Publishers Weekly, May 13, 1988, p. 262; August 2, 1991, review of *Brotherly Love,* p. 63; October 4, 1991, Wendy Smith, "Pete Dexter: After His Roistering Lifestyle, His Career As a Novelist Is a Different Kind of Adventure," pp. 70-71; July 13, 1992, review of *Brotherly Love,* p. 52; November 7, 1994, review of *The Paperboy,* p. 62; February 13, 1995, p. 17.

Quill & Quire, July, 1995, audio review of *The Paperboy,* p. 7.

Rapport, January 1, 1992, review of *Brotherly Love,* p. 20; April, 1992, review of *Brotherly Love,* p. 30; May, 1995, review of *The Paperboy,* p. 22.

Southern Living, March, 1995, review of *The Paperboy,* p. 142.

Spectator, November 18, 1995, review of *The Paperboy,* p. 49.

Sports Illustrated, February 23, 1987.

Time, April 2, 1984; November 4, 1991, John Shaw, review of *Brotherly Love,* p. A4; January 23, 1995, Paul Gray, review of *The Paperboy,* p. 58.

Times Educational Supplement, March 6, 1992, review of *Brotherly Love,* p. 35.

Times Literary Supplement, November 25, 1988, Andrew Rosenheim, review of *Paris Trout,* p. 1306; February 21, 1992, John Sutherland, review of *Brotherly Love,* p. 32; May 19, 1995, Gordon Burn, review of *The Paperboy,* p. 19; December 1, 1995, review of *The Paperboy,* p. 10.

Tribune Books (Chicago, IL), April 6, 1986; August 7, 1988; Dean Faulkner Wells, review of *Paris Trout,* pp. 3, 9; September 6, 1992, review of *Brotherly Love,* p. 2; January 29, 1995, review of *The Paperboy,* p. 6.

Village Voice, June 17, 1986.

Virginia Quarterly Review, summer, 1995, review of *The Paperboy,* p. 95.

Vogue, October, 1991, Mark Marvel, review of *Brotherly Love,* p. 192.

Wall Street Journal, October 7, 1991, Julie Salamon, review of *Brotherly Love,* p. A12.

Washington Post, November 28, 1988.

Washington Post Book World, June 1, 1986; July 10, 1988, Judith Paterson, review of *Paris Trout,* p. 8; November 30, 1988; September 13, 1992, review of *Brotherly Love,* p. 12.

Western American Literature, winter, 1987, Margaret A. Lukens, p. 360.

World & I, March, 1995, review of *The Paperboy,* p. 322.

ONLINE

Mostly Fiction, http://www.mostlyfiction.com/ (December 17, 2002), review of *The Paperboy.*

Mystery Guide, http://www.mysteryguide.com/ (December 17, 2002).

*   *   *

DIAMOND, Jared 1937-
(Jared Mason Diamond)

PERSONAL: Born September 10, 1937, in Boston, MA; son of Louis K. and Flora K. Diamond; married Marie M. Cohen, 1982; children: two (twins). *Education:* Harvard University, B.A., 1958; Cambridge University, Ph. D., 1961.

ADDRESSES: Office—Department of Physiology, School of Medicine, 1251A Bunche Hall, University of California, Los Angeles, CA 90024. *E-mail*—jdiamond@geog.ucla.edu.

CAREER: Physiologist, ecologist, and author, specializing in evolutionary biology, ecology, bird faunas of New Guinea and other South West Pacific islands, and biological membranes. Harvard Medical School, Cambridge, MA, associate in biophysics, 1965-66; University of California Medical School, Los Angeles, associate professor of physiology, 1966-68, professor, 1968—. American Museum of Natural History, Department of Ornithology, research associate, 1973—; Los Angeles County Museum of Natural History, research associate, 1985—. National Science Foundation, fellow, 1958-61, 1961-62; Trinity College, Cambridge, fellow in physiology, 1961-65; Harvard University Society of Fellows, junior fellow, 1962-65.

MEMBER: National Science Academy, American Academy of Arts and Sciences (fellow), American Ornithologists Union (fellow), American Physiological Society, Biophysics Society, American Society of Naturalists, American Philosophical Society.

AWARDS, HONORS: Bowditch Prize, American Physiological Society, 1976; Kroc Foundation lecturer, Western Association of Physicians, 1978; Burr Award, National Geographic Society, 1979; MacArthur Foundation fellowship, 1985; *Los Angeles Times* Book Prize, 1992, and Science Book Prize, *New Scientist*

(London, England), 1992, both for *The Third Chimpanzee: The Evolution and Future of the Human Animal;* Pulitzer Prize in nonfiction, and Japan's Cosmos Prize, both 1998, both for *Guns, Germs, and Steel: The Fates of Human Societies.*

WRITINGS:

Avifauna of the Eastern Highlands of New Guinea, Nuttall Ornithological Club (Cambridge, MA), 1972.
(Editor, with Martin L. Cody) *Ecology and Evolution of Communities,* Belknap Press of Harvard University Press (Cambridge, MA), 1975.
(With Mary Lecroy) *Birds of Karkar and Bagabag Islands, New Guinea,* American Museum of Natural History (New York, NY), 1979.
(Editor, with Ted J. Case) *Community Ecology,* Harper & Row (New York, NY), 1986.
The Third Chimpanzee: The Evolution and Future of the Human Animal, HarperCollins (New York, NY), 1992, published as *The Rise and Fall of the Third Chimpanzee,* Hutchinson Radius (London, England), 1992.
Why Is Sex Fun? The Evolution of Human Sexuality, HarperCollins (New York, NY), 1997.
Guns, Germs, and Steel: The Fates of Human Societies, W.W. Norton (New York, NY), 1997.
(With Ernst Mayr) *The Birds of Northern Melanesia: Speciation, Dispersal, and Ecology,* Oxford University Press (New York, NY), 2001.
Why Did Human History Unfold Differently on Different Continents for the Last 13,000 Years?, RAND Corp. (Santa Monica, CA), 2001.
Collapse: How Societies Choose to Fail or Succeed, Viking Press (New York, NY), 2004.

Contributor to books, including D. Noble and C.A.R. Boyd's *Evolutionary Physiology,* Oxford University Press (New York, NY), 1993; contributor to periodicals, including *Discover, Natural History,* and *Nature.* Author of more than three hundred research papers on physiology, ecology, and ornithology.

SIDELIGHTS: Physiologist, ecologist, and author Jared Diamond "is a polymath," declared anthropologist Mark Ridley in the *Times Literary Supplement.* Diamond has established himself as an expert in both bird ecology and membrane physiology, two technical specialties that are not related, according to Ridley, and has established a reputation for turning out top-quality research papers at such a rate that "some suspect he is really a committee." On the *Edge* Web site, Diamond

commented: "I've set myself the modest task of trying to explain the broad pattern of human history, on all the continents, for the last 13,000 years. Why did history take such different evolutionary courses for peoples of different continents? This problem has fascinated me for a long time, but it's now ripe for a new synthesis because of recent advances in many fields seemingly remote from history, including molecular biology, plant and animal genetics and biogeography, archaeology, and linguistics."

Diamond assembled and extensively revised many of his short pieces to produce *The Third Chimpanzee: The Evolution and Future of the Human Animal.* The book consists of five sections, the first dealing with human prehistory, the second with the biology of human nature—including human sexuality, which Diamond compares and contrasts with that of other primates, a section on such uniquely human traits as art, language, and addiction, a section on human destructiveness, and a finale in which contemporary human society is placed in the context of the past. Human beings, explains Diamond, share ninety-eight percent of their genetic endowment with chimpanzees; indeed to the uninformed observer, such as an extraterrestrial scientist, prehistoric human beings would have looked merely like a third species of chimpanzee. Diamond sets forth to show the ways in which the remaining two percent of a human's genetic endowment impelled the vast cultural difference between humanity and its ape relatives.

According to Phoebe-Lou Adams in the *Atlantic,* Diamond is not entirely successful in tracing human distinctiveness to that genetic two percent, but nevertheless "succeeds well in his intention to arouse intelligent concern for social and environmental reform." Among the book's other reviewers were several well-known writers on science—for example, Elizabeth Marshall Thomas who in the *Los Angeles Times Book Review* termed *The Third Chimpanzee* "wonderful," and praised Diamond especially for his efforts to lead readers toward conservation of the environment. Thomas found "intriguing" Diamond's discussion of human beings' unusual proclivity for having sex in private. Lionel Tiger, also writing in the *Atlantic,* called Diamond "particularly enlightening on the subject of the biology of race." Race, Diamond asserts, evolved not for reasons of natural selection but for ones of sexual selection: within local populations, the traits that are now associated with the different races were chosen for their beauty. "Diamond has a clear sense of how to advance his evolutionary arguments through lively examples," explained Tiger. This reviewer, however, also expressed a few qualms: notably, that Diamond overemphasizes the novelty of some of his material and gives short shrift to the similar ideas of his predecessors. Tiger also thought that Diamond's view of human beings is less complex and "risk-taking" than a truly demanding reader would have hoped for. Nevertheless, concluded Tiger, Diamond's book "makes us take a searching look in the mirror that will be as unsettling to some as it will be enlightening to many."

Ridley, in the *Times Literary Supplement,* praised Diamond in particular for his ability to synthesize and digest a great deal of diverse material; he enjoyed the anecdotes of Diamond's New Guinea experiences, as did primatologist Frans B.M. de Waal in the *New York Times Book Review,* and lauded Diamond's topic selection, expressing gratitude for discussions of the origins of Indo-European language, of agriculture, and of genocide. "Every page is thick with examples, usually unfamiliar ones," commented Ridley. De Waal, for his part, applauded Diamond's treatment of linguistic diversity, though he also found some "rather implausible scenarios" in Diamond's evaluation of the relationship between Cro-Magnons and Neanderthals. Even these "farfetched theses" according to de Waal, have positive value, however, for they force the reader to think imaginatively about human evolution and human destiny.

Roger Lewin of the *Washington Post Book World,* singled out Diamond's discussion of language in *The Third Chimpanzee.* Lewin termed the chapter "Bridges to Human Language" "glorious" for its material on Creole, pidgin, and nonhuman communication systems. Lewin praised Diamond, in addition, for two theoretical views that counterbalance each other nicely: Diamond refuses to see the development of agriculture and industrialism as a march of progress, but he also refuses to see the prehistoric hunter-gatherer way of life as a golden age. Likewise, Michael Kenward in the *New Scientist*—the same journal which awarded *The Third Chimpanzee* its Science Book Prize—enjoyed Diamond's vision of hunter-gatherer societies; "I like books that bash perceived wisdom," Kenward wrote. Kenward was among the critics disapproving of Diamond's literary style; he compared it to that of a scientific paper, with the exception that "big words" had been excised. Several commentators had a far different view, including Lewin, who concluded: "No one writes about these things better than Diamond." And Steve Jones, in the *London Review of Books,* called *The Third Chimpanzee* "literate, informative and impassioned." Jones especially approved of Diamond's writings on human sexuality and found that Diamond's view of the evolutionary basis of human behavior is "less startling than the author makes out." Lewin declared that *The Third Chim-*

panzee is "composed with erudition and elegance" and that it offers "some of the best popular writing on human biology and prehistory."

In *Guns, Germs, and Steel: The Fates of Human Societies* Diamond's ambitions take him even further into the realm of the social sciences. In this book, which won the 1998 Pulitzer Prize in nonfiction, Diamond seeks to explain how the peoples of Europe and Asia were able to conquer those of the Americas, Africa, and Australia. His thesis is not that Europeans and Asians are inherently superior, but that an accident of geography made it possible for them to develop advanced weaponry, immunity to disease, and social structures that enabled them to gain control over other continents. The Eurasian land mass, he points out, was the source of many more domesticable plants than the rest of the world, and Eurasia's east-west orientation made it easy for these plants to spread to areas with similar climates. This gave rise to agriculture, which in turn gave rise to dense and settled populations. Technology and, in time, armaments production, flourished in these societies, as did centralized government. Eurasia also had a larger number of domesticable animals; living in proximity to animals and to each other allowed Eurasians to be exposed to and eventually to become immune to numerous diseases. These diseases were unknown in many parts of the world until European explorers arrived, and so a combination of microbes and military might helped the Europeans subdue native populations in the Americas and elsewhere. As *New Statesman* contributor Roz Kaveney put it: "Cortes and Pizarro thought of themselves as all-conquering heroes, but mostly they were just carriers of smallpox, measles and whooping cough."

Newsweek reviewer Sharon Begley, noting that the arguments in *Guns, Germs, and Steel* are based on a long-neglected concept known as geographic determinism, declared that "Diamond's attempt to explain the past is one of the boldest in generations. If he's right, then pride in the power and the glories of European civilization should be tempered with a little humility: were it not for cowpox, history might have been very different." Begley found Diamond's explanations inadequate in some areas; for instance, she pointed out, "geographic predestination does not explain why Europe subjugated China for years, even though China was the most advanced nation in the world by 1400."

Other commentators raised other questions; for example, in the *New Leader* Thomas M. Disch wrote that while he was sympathetic to Diamond's ideas, he was not completely convinced by Diamond's reasoning. To account for his uncertainty, Disch cited new archeological evidence that the Americas may have been inhabited 1,000 years earlier than Diamond and other scientists believe. "This impacts his argument concerning the extinction of larger mammals by the first Asians to colonize the Americas, and their consequent unavailability for domestication," Disch observed. "Such new findings raise doubts about Diamond's conclusions." M.E. Sharpe, writing in *Challenge,* questioned the importance placed by Diamond on Eurasia's east-west orientation and other continents' north-south orientation; there are many more important factors that determine how differences in civilization evolve, Sharpe contended. That reviewer also took Diamond to task for paying scant attention to the role of capitalism in global development: "Columbus, after all, came to the Americas looking for a route to the West Indies. His voyage was not taken on a whim or because of an axis but because European merchants were engaged in an increasingly profitable trade with eastern and southern Asia and were feverishly looking for an easier and cheaper way to get there." *National Review* critic Steven Sailer took issue with Diamond's dismissal of the possibility that genetic differences among ethnic groups might explain much about world history. "Diamond appears to confuse the concepts of genetic superiorities (plural) and genetic supremacy (singular)," Sailer asserted. "The former are circumstance-specific. . . . In contrast, genetic supremacy is the dangerous fantasy that one group is everything."

Still, several reviewers, even some who voiced reservations, found much to admire in *Guns, Germs, and Steel.* In the *New York Times Book Review,* James Shreeve commented that Diamond's "multilayered analysis . . . should be consumed with a grain of salt. Its sheer depth compels him to wear the hats of anthropologist, archeologist, plant geneticist, epidemiologist, and social, military and technological historian. . . . Each of these disciplines into which he delves to further his argument is rife with uncertainties, differing interpretations and opposing viewpoints. A closer examination of them would have only strengthened an already formidable work." Kaveney noted that other scholars have put forth theories similar to Diamond's, and that Diamond has had to simplify complicated arguments. However, she added: "What Diamond offers is a look behind the glamour of history . . . behind the empires and the gold are the peasants, and behind the peasants are the ox, the chicken and the wheat stalk. This has the strength of all the best books, it makes us see things afresh." And Disch concluded that *Guns, Germs, and Steel* "is one long crescendo of inductive logic, and deserves the attention of anyone concerned with the his-

tory of mankind at its most fundamental level. It is an epochal work."

In his introduction to a talk given by Diamond and subsequently published as *Why Did Human History Unfold Differently on Different Continents for the Last 13,000 Years?,* John Brockman commented that one of the biggest questions Diamond deals with is "how to turn the study of history into a science." Brockman noted that in his theories concerning human development and the rise of civilization, Diamond combines history and biology and, in the process, questions long-held race-based theories surrounding human development—theories in which one group of people believes certain other groups of people are not capable of being educated and are thus different and less than human. "Most people are explicitly racists," Brockman quoted Diamond as saying. "In parts of the world—so called educated, so-called western society—we've learned that it is not polite to be racist, and so often we don't express racist views, but nevertheless I've given lectures on this subject, and members of the National Academy of Sciences come up to me afterwards and say, but native Australians, they're so primitive. Racism is one of the big issues in the world today." Brockman commented that Diamond believes the primary reason so many people resort to racist explanations of the rise of global civilization is because they have no other explanation and that, until a convincing answer is provided to the question of why history took the course it did, people will continue to see racism as the answer.

Diamond continues his examination of societies from around the globe in *Collapse: How Societies Choose to Fail or Succeed.* In contrast with *Guns, Germs, and Steel,* which explains how access to weapons, an immunity to diseases, and advances in technology allowed the people of the Eurasian continent to achieve success throughout the world over the course of thousands of years, *Collapse* examines the reasons behind the failure of certain societies throughout history. Diamond asserts that many times the failure of a society is directly related to a mismanagement of environmental resources. Among the examples Diamond cites in his book are the Mayan empire, the Easter Islanders, the Anasazi, and the Vikings of Greenland. As Kathy Tewell explained in *School Library Journal,* "the author shows how a combination of environmental factors such as habitat destruction, the loss of biodiversity, and degradation of the soil caused complex, flourishing societies to suddenly disintegrate."

"Diamond cites a string of examples of societies that failed for a variety of reasons, some because of outside forces, but many simply from poor use of their once abundant natural resources," wrote Paul Wilkes in *America.* Diamond also points to the environmental problems in modern societies, such as Rwanda and Haiti, that have already begun to collapse, and others, such as China, Australia, and even the state of Montana, that could face major problems in the near future. Diamond argues, according to Kevin Shapiro of *Commentary,* that the collapse of societies "is a consequence of 'ecocide'—environmental damage caused by deforestation, intensive agriculture, and the destruction of local flora and fauna." Not everyone agreed with the argument put forth by Diamond in *Collapse,* however. Writing for *National Review,* Victor Davis Hanson pointed out that "most of Diamond's examples are slanted: They involve fragile, mostly isolated or island landscapes that witnessed colonists, renegades, or adventurers who sought in their greed or ignorance to put too many people in the wrong place." Hanson continued, "The main problem . . . is that Diamond's well-meaning, environmentally correct storytelling cannot impart any coherent lesson of why in fact societies fail. Environmental degradation, climate change, hostilities, political and cultural failures, and trade are cited as the roots of collapse, but are used so interchangeably that we never learn to what degree mismanagement of nature or of people brings on doom." In a critique for *History Today,* Jeremy Black noted that he was "uneasy about the sweep of *Collapse,* and the extent to which, at times, it appears all-explaining." Despite these shortcomings, Black commented, "Throughout the book, there is evidence of a thoughtful and wide-ranging mind, and the attempt to relate environmental management to social issues and political polices . . . is particularly successful."

In an interview with Will Boisvert of *Publishers Weekly,* Diamond revealed that the mystery behind the collapse of certain societies intrigued him. He remarked that "many of these mystery collapses involved a component of environmental damage. It was the most exciting thing in large-scale comparative history that I could think of." As for his hopes for *Collapse,* Diamond said, "I hope people will come away from this book feeling that there are environmental problems, but we can solve them."

BIOGRAPHICAL AND CRITICAL SOURCES:

BOOKS

Diamond, Jared, *Why Did Human History Unfold Differently on Different Continents for the Last 13,000 Years?,* RAND Corp. (Santa Monica, CA), 2001.

PERIODICALS

America, May 16, 2005, Paul Wilkes, review of *Collapse: How Societies Choose to Fail or Succeed,* p. 16.

Atlantic, May, 1992, Phoebe-Lou Adams, review of *The Third Chimpanzee: The Evolution and Future of the Human Animal,* p. 128.

Challenge, March-April, 1998, M.E. Sharpe, review of *Guns, Germs, and Steel: The Fates of Human Societies,* p. 118.

Commentary, April, 2005, Kevin Shapiro, review of *Collapse,* p. 85.

Economist (U.S.), July 19, 1997, review of *Guns, Germs, and Steel,* p. 84.

History Today, April, 2005, Jeremy Black, review of *Collapse,* p. 55.

Library Journal, February 15, 2005, Gloria Maxwell, review of *Collapse,* p. 154.

London Review of Books, September 10, 1992, Steve Jones, review of *The Third Chimpanzee,* p. 17.

Los Angeles Times Book Review, March 22, 1992, p. 4; November 8, 1992, p. 9.

National Review, May 19, 1997, Steven Sailer, review of *Guns, Germs, and Steel,* p. 51; April 11, 2005, Victor Davis Hanson, "Decline and Fall," review of *Collapse,* p. 43.

New Leader, March 10, 1997, Thomas M. Disch, review of *Guns, Germs, and Steel,* p. 18.

New Scientist, May 23, 1992, Michael Kenward, review of *The Third Chimpanzee,* pp. 39-40.

New Statesman, August 22, 1997, Roz Kaveney, review of *Guns, Germs, and Steel,* p. 48.

Newsweek, June 16, 1997, Sharon Begley, review of *Guns, Germs, and Steel,* p. 47.

New York Times Book Review, March 15, 1992, Frans B.M. de Waal, review of *The Third Chimpanzee,* p. 10; June 15, 1997, James Shreeve, review of *Guns, Germs, and Steel.*

Population and Development Review, December, 1997, Garret Hardin, review of *Guns, Germs, and Steel,* p. 889.

Publishers Weekly, January 13, 1997, review of *Guns, Germs, and Steel,* p. 60; November 15, 2004, Will Boisvert, "Apocalypse Then," interview with Jared Diamond, p. 48; February 7, 2005, review of *Collapse,* p. 35.

School Library Journal, June, 2005, Kathy Tewell, review of *Collapse,* p. 190.

Science News, January 29, 2005, review of *Collapse,* p. 79.

Times Literary Supplement, August 2, 1991, Mark Ridley, review of *The Third Chimpanzee,* pp. 3-4.

Washington Post Book World, April 19, 1992, Roger Lewin, review of *The Third Chimpanzee,* pp. 3-4.

ONLINE

Edge, http://www.edge.org/3rd_culture/ (July 26, 2004). "Jared Diamond."

*   *   *

DIAMOND, Jared Mason
   See DIAMOND, Jared

*   *   *

DICK, Philip K. 1928-1982
(Philip Kindred Dick, Richard Phillips)

PERSONAL: Born December 16, 1928, in Chicago, IL; died of heart failure following a stroke, March 2, 1982, in Santa Ana, CA; son of Joseph Edgar (a government employee) and Dorothy (Kindred) Dick; married, 1949; wife's name Jeannette (divorced); married, 1951; wife's name Kleo (divorced); married, 1958; wife's name Ann (divorced); married April 18, 1967; wife's name Nancy (divorced); married Tessa Busby, April 18, 1973 (divorced); children: (third marriage) Laura; (fourth marriage) Isolde; (fifth marriage) Christopher. *Education:* Attended University of California—Berkeley, 1950. *Politics:* "Anti-war, pro-life." *Religion:* Episcopalian.

CAREER: Writer. Hosted classical music program on KSMO Radio, 1947; worked in a record store, 1948-52; occasional lecturer at California State University—Fullerton; active in drug rehabilitation and anti-abortion work.

MEMBER: Science Fiction Writers of America, Animal Protection Institute.

AWARDS, HONORS: Hugo Award, World Science Fiction Convention, 1962, for *The Man in the High Castle;* John W. Campbell Memorial Award, 1974, for *Flow My Tears, the Policeman Said;* guest of honor, Science Fiction Festival, Metz, France, 1978; Philip K. Dick Memorial Award was created by Norwescon, an annual science-fiction convention in Seattle, WA; inducted into the Science Fiction Hall of Fame in Seattle, Washington, 2005).

WRITINGS:

SCIENCE-FICTION NOVELS

Solar Lottery (bound with *The Big Jump* by Leigh Brackett), Ace Books (New York, NY), 1955, published separately, Gregg, 1976, published as *World of Chance,* Rich & Cowan (London, England), 1956, reprinted under original title, Vintage (New York, NY), 2003.

The World Jones Made (bound with *Agent of the Unknown* by Margaret St. Clair), Ace Books (New York, NY), 1956.

The Man Who Japed (bound with *The Space-Born* by E.C. Tubb), Ace Books (New York, NY), 1956, published separately, Vintage (New York, NY), 2002.

Eye in the Sky, Ace Books (New York, NY), 1957, reprinted, Vintage (New York, NY), 2003.

The Cosmic Puppets (bound with *Sargasso of Space* by Andrew North), Ace Books (New York, NY), 1957, published separately, Berkley Publishing (New York, NY), 1983, reprinted, Vintage (New York, NY), 2004.

Time out of Joint, Lippincott (Philadelphia, PA), 1959, reprinted, Vintage (New York, NY), 2002.

Dr. Futurity (also see below; bound with *Slavers of Space* by John Brunner), Ace Books (New York, NY), 1960, published with *The Unteleported Man* by Dick, 1972, published separately, Berkley Publishing (New York, NY), 1984.

Vulcan's Hammer (bound with *The Skynappers* by John Brunner), Ace Books (New York, NY), 1960, reprinted, Vintage (New York, NY), 2004.

The Man in the High Castle, Putnam (New York, NY), 1962.

The Game-Players of Titan, Ace Books (New York, NY), 1963.

Martian Time-Slip, Ballantine (New York, NY), 1964.

The Penultimate Truth, Belmont-Tower, 1964, reprinted, Vintage (New York, NY), 2004.

The Simulacra, Ace Books (New York, NY), 1964, reprinted, Vintage (New York, NY), 2002.

Clans of the Alphane Moon, Ace Books (New York, NY), 1964, reprinted, Vintage (New York, NY), 2002.

Dr. Bloodmoney; or, How We Got Along after the Bomb, Ace Books (New York, NY), 1965, reprinted, Vintage (New York, NY), 2002.

The Three Stigmata of Palmer Eldritch, Doubleday (New York, NY), 1965.

Now Wait for Last Year, Doubleday (New York, NY), 1966.

The Crack in Space (also see below), Ace Books (New York, NY), 1966.

The Unteleported Man (also see below; bound with *The Mind Monsters* by Howard L. Cory), Ace Books (New York, NY), 1966, reprinted (bound with *Dr. Futurity* by Dick), 1972, reprinted separately, Berkley Publishing (New York, NY), 1983.

(With Ray Nelson) *The Ganymede Takeover,* Ace Books (New York, NY), 1967.

Counter-Clock World, Berkley Publishing (New York, NY), 1967, reprinted, Vintage (New York, NY), 2002.

The Zap Gun, Pyramid Publications, 1967, reprinted, Vintage (New York, NY), 2002.

Do Androids Dream of Electric Sheep?, Doubleday, (New York, NY) 1968, published as *Blade Runner,* Ballantine (New York, NY), 1982.

Ubik (also see below), Doubleday (New York, NY), 1969.

Galactic Pot-Healer, Doubleday (New York, NY), 1969.

A Philip K. Dick Omnibus (contains *The Crack in Space, The Unteleported Man,* and *Dr. Futurity*), Sidgwick & Jackson (London, England), 1970.

A Maze of Death, Doubleday (New York, NY), 1970.

Our Friends from Frolix 8, Ace Books (New York, NY), 1970, reprinted, Vintage (New York, NY), 2003.

We Can Build You, DAW Books (New York, NY), 1972.

Flow My Tears, the Policeman Said, Doubleday (New York, NY), 1974.

(With Roger Zelazny) *Deus Irae,* Doubleday (New York, NY), 1976, reprinted, Vintage (New York, NY), 2003.

A Scanner Darkly, Doubleday (New York, NY), 1977.

VALIS, Bantam (New York, NY), 1981.

The Divine Invasion, Pocket Books (New York, NY), 1981.

The Transmigration of Timothy Archer, Pocket Books (New York, NY), 1982.

The Man Whose Teeth Were All Exactly Alike, Zeising, 1984.

Radio Free Albemuth, Arbor House, 1987.

Nick and the Glimmung, Gollancz (London, England), 1988.

The Little Black Box, Gollancz (London, England), 1990.

The Minority Report, Pantheon (New York, NY), 2002.

SHORT FICTION

A Handful of Darkness, Rich & Cowan (London, England), 1955.

The Variable Man and Other Stories, Ace Books (New York, NY), 1957.

The Preserving Machine and Other Stories, Ace Books (New York, NY), 1969.

The Book of Philip K. Dick, DAW Books (New York, NY), 1973, published as *The Turning Wheel and Other Stories,* Coronet (London, England), 1977.

The Best of Philip K. Dick, Ballantine (New York, NY), 1977.

The Golden Man, Berkley Publishing (New York, NY), 1980.

Robots, Androids, and Mechanical Oddities: The Science Fiction of Philip K. Dick, edited by Patricia Warrick and Martin H. Greenberg, Southern Illinois University Press, 1984.

Lies, Inc., Gollancz (London, England), 1984, revised edition, Vintage (New York, NY), 2004.

I Hope I Shall Arrive Soon, Doubleday (New York, NY), 1985.

The Short Happy Life of the Brown Oxford, and Other Classic Stories, introduction by Roger Zelazny, Citadel Press (New York, NY), 1987.

The Collected Stories, five volumes, Underwood Miller, 1987.

Selected Stories of Philip K. Dick, introduction by Jonatham Lethem, Pantheon (New York, NY), 2002.

Paycheck, and Twenty-four Other Classic Stories, Kensington (New York, NY), 2003.

Contributor to anthologies, including *Time to Come,* edited by August Derleth, Farrar, Straus (New York, NY), 1954; *Star Science Fiction Stories #3,* edited by Frederik Pohl, Ballantine (New York, NY), 1955; *A Treasury of Great Science Fiction,* Volume I, edited by Anthony Boucher, Doubleday (New York, NY), 1959; *Dangerous Visions: Thirty-three Original Stories,* edited by Harlan Ellison, Doubleday, 1967; *Final Stage,* edited by Edward L. Ferman and Barry N. Malzberg, Charterhouse, 1974; *Science Fiction: The Academic Awakening,* edited by Willis E. McNelly, College English Association, 1974; and *Science Fiction at Large,* edited by Peter Nicholls, Gollancz (London, England), 1976, Harper (New York, NY), 1977.

OTHER

Confessions of a Crap Artist, Jack Isidore (of Seville, Calif.): A Chronicle of Verified Scientific Fact, 1945-1959 (novel), Entwhistle Books, 1975.

A Letter from Philip K. Dick (pamphlet), Philip K. Dick Society, 1983.

In Milton Lumky Territory (novel), Ultramarine, 1984.

Ubik: The Screenplay (based on novel of same title), Corroboree, 1985.

Puttering About in a Small Land (novel), Academy (New York, NY), 1985.

Mary and the Giant (novel), Arbor House, 1987.

The Broken Bubble (novel), Arbor House, 1988.

The Selected Letters of Philip K. Dick, 1974, edited by Paul Williams, Underwood-Miller (Novato, CA), 1991.

Gather Yourselves Together (novel), WCS Books (Herndon, VA), 1994.

The Shifting Realities of Philip K. Dick: Selected Literary and Philosophical Writings, edited by Lawrence Sutin, Pantheon (New York, NY), 1995.

The Philip K. Dick Reader, Carol Publishing Group (Secaucus, NJ), 1997.

The Selected Letters of Philip K. Dick, 1938-1971, Underwood Books, 1997.

What If Our World Is Their Heaven?: The Final Conversations of Philip K. Dick, Overlook Press (Woodstock, NY), 2000.

Also author of unpublished novels *A Time for George Stavros, Nicholas and the Higs,* and *Voices from the Street.* Author of radio scripts for Mutual Broadcasting System. Contributor of over 100 stories, some under pseudonym Richard Phillips, to *Magazine of Fantasy and Science Fiction, Galaxy, Amazing Science Fiction Stories,* and other magazines.

ADAPTATIONS: Do Androids Dream of Electric Sheep? was filmed as *Blade Runner* by Warner Bros., 1982. "We Can Remember It for You Wholesale" was filmed as *Total Recall,* 1990. *Imposter,* directed by Gary Felder, was based on a story by Dick. *The Minority Report* was adapted for a film of the same name, directed by Steven Spielberg, Twentieth Century-Fox, 2002. *Paycheck,* based on *Paycheck and Other Short Stories,* was released by Paramount Pictures, 2003.

SIDELIGHTS: The central problem when reading Philip K. Dick's science fiction is how to distinguish the real from the unreal. Dick once told an interviewer: "My major preoccupation is the question, 'What is reality?'" In novel after novel, Dick's characters find that their familiar world is in fact an illusion, either self-created or imposed on them by others. Dick "liked to begin a novel," Patricia Warrick wrote in *Science-Fiction Studies,* "with a commonplace world and then have his characters fall through the floor of this normal world into a strange new reality." Drug-induced hallucinations, robots and androids, mystical visions, paranoic delusions, and alternate or artificial worlds are the stuff of which Dick's flexible universe is made. "All of his work," Charles Platt wrote in *Dream Makers: The Uncommon People Who Write Science Fiction,* "starts with the basic assumption that there cannot be one, single, objective reality. Everything is a matter of perception. The ground is liable to shift under your feet. A protago-

nist may find himself living out another person's dream, or he may enter a drug-induced state that actually makes better sense than the real world, or he may cross into a different universe completely."

Despite the mutable and often dangerous nature of Dick's fictional worlds, his characters retain at least a faint hope for the future and manage to survive and comfort one another. Dick's characters are usually ordinary people—repairmen, housewives, students, salesmen—caught up in overwhelming situations that call into question their basic beliefs about themselves and their world. In *The Three Stigmata of Palmer Eldritch* powerful drugs create such believable hallucinations that users find it difficult to know when the hallucination has ended and the real world has returned. A character in *Time out of Joint* discovers that he does not really live in a mid-twentieth-century American town as he had believed. He lives in an artificial replica of an American town built by a government of the future for its own purposes. In *Eye in the Sky* eight people at a research facility are pushed by a freak accident into a state of consciousness where each one's subjective reality becomes real for the entire group for a time. They experience worlds where the ideas of a religious cult member, a communist, a puritan, and a paranoid are literally true. The ability of Dick's characters to survive these situations, preserving their sanity and humanity in the process, is what Dick celebrated. His novels presented a "world where ordinary people do the best they can against death-driven, malevolent forces," Tom Whalen wrote in the *American Book Review.*

In many of his works, Dick stresses the importance of emotion, "which in his view made men human," Steven Kosek wrote in the *Chicago Tribune Book World.* In *Now Wait for Last Year* it is the ability to feel for others that distinguishes the aliens from the Earthlings, while in *Do Androids Dream of Electric Sheep?* a similar ability separates the androids from human beings. This emphasis on human emotions is usually contrasted with the technological environment in which Dick's characters find themselves. The typical Dick novel is set in a technologically advanced, near-future America which is falling apart in some way. Caught in the accelerating chaos, his characters need all of their humanity to survive. "There are no heroics in Dick's books," Ursula K. LeGuin explained in the *New Republic,* "but there are heroes. One is reminded of [Charles] Dickens: what counts is the honesty, constancy, kindness and patience of ordinary people."

Dick had, John Clute maintained in the *Washington Post Book World,* a "self-lacerating, feverish, deeply argued refusal to believe that the diseased prison of a

world we all live in could possibly be the 'real' world."
As Dick himself explained it in his introduction to the
story collection *The Golden Man:* "I want to write about
people I love, and put them into a fictional world spun
out of my own mind, not the world we actually have,
because the world we actually have does not meet my
standards." In the afterword to that same collection,
Dick explained why he chose to write science fiction:
"SF is a field of rebellion: against accepted ideas, institutions, against all that is. In my writing I even question
the universe; I wonder out loud if it is real, and I wonder out loud if all of us are real."

This questioning of reality was often accomplished
through the use of "two basic narrative situations,"
Patrick G. Hogan, Jr. wrote in the *Dictionary of Literary Biography,* adding that Dick's "favorite plot device
is that of alternate universes or parallel worlds." Dick,
Hogan added, "is also fascinated by what he characteristically calls simulacra, devices ranging from merely
complex mechanical and electronic constructs to androids, and by the paradoxes created by their relationships to organic life, especially that of human beings."
Many critics considered the best of Dick's novels about
alternate universes to be *The Man in the High Castle,
The Three Stigmata of Palmer Eldritch,* and *Flow My
Tears, the Policeman Said. Do Androids Dream of Electric Sheep?* is probably his best-known novel about
simulacra.

The Man in the High Castle, winner of the Hugo Award
and generally considered Dick's best novel, is set in a
world in which America, which lost World War II, has
been divided in two and is occupied by the Germans
and Japanese. Most of the novel takes place on the
Japanese-occupied West Coast and revolves around a
group of Americans who are trying to cope with their
status as subject people. Concerned primarily with creating a believable alternate society, the novel reveals in
the process "how easily this nation would have surrendered its own culture under a Japanese occupation and
how compatible American fears, prejudices, and desires
were with Nazism," as Hogan remarked. The novel's
"man in the high castle" is the author of an underground
best-seller about an alternate world where America won
the war. "I did seven years of research for *The Man in
the High Castle,*" Dick once explained in an interview
for the *Missouri Review.* "I had prime-source material
at the Berkeley-Cal library right from the gestapo's
mouth—stuff that had been seized after World War
II. . . . That's . . . why I've never written a sequel to
it: it's too horrible, too awful. I started several times to
write a sequel, but I [would have] had to go back and
read about Nazis again, so I couldn't do it." Dick used

the I Ching, an ancient Chinese divining system, to plot
The Man in the High Castle. At each critical juncture in
the narrative, Dick consulted the I Ching to determine
the proper course of the plot.

The alternate universes in *The Three Stigmata of Palmer
Eldritch* are created by powerful hallucinogenic drugs.
The novel is set in the near-future when the increasing
heat of the sun is making life on Earth impossible. The
United Nations begins forcing people to immigrate to
Mars, an inhospitable desert waste where colonists must
live in underground hovels. Because of the boredom of
colony life, a drug-induced fantasy world has been devised that uses small dolls and miniature settings. When
a colonist takes the drug Can-D, he becomes one of the
dolls and lives for a brief time in an Earth-like setting.
The manufacturer of the dolls and settings—a company
named Perky Pat Layouts, after the female doll—also
sells Can-D. When Palmer Eldritch returns from a deep-
space exploration, he brings with him a supply of the
new and more powerful drug Chew-Z. Eldritch has also
acquired three "stigmata"—an artificial metallic arm,
enormous steel teeth, and artificial eyes. His Chew-Z is
cheaper and longer-lasting than Can-D, and he soon is
selling it to the Martian colonists. But Chew-Z does not
seem to wear off; the user is moved into a world that
seems like his own but with the important difference
that Palmer Eldritch has god-like powers. Bruce
Gillespie, writing in *Philip K. Dick: Electric Shepherd,*
called *Palmer Eldritch* "one of the few masterpieces of
recent science fiction."

Dick received the John W. Campbell Memorial Award
for *Flow My Tears, the Policeman Said,* a near-future
novel in which popular television talk show host Jason
Taverner wakes up one morning in a world where he is
unknown. No record even exists of his having been
born, an awkward situation in the records-conscious police state that Taverner's California has become. The
explanation for this impossibility is that Taverner is living within the drug hallucination of Alys Buckner, and
in that hallucination there is no place for him. The powerful drug, able to impose Alys's hallucination on reality itself, eventually kills her, and Taverner is set free.
"Dick skillfully explores the psychological ramifications of this nightmare," Gerald Jonas commented in
the *New York Times Book Review,* "but he is even more
interested in the reaction of a ruthlessly efficient computerized police state to the existence of a man, who,
according to the computers, should not exist."

Do Androids Dream of Electric Sheep? is Dick's most
celebrated novel about simulacra, mechanical objects
which simulate life. In this novel Dick posits a world in

which androids are so highly developed that it is only by the most rigid testing that one can distinguish them from human beings. The key difference is the quality of empathy which humans have for other living things. When some androids escape from a work colony and make their way to Earth, bounty hunter Rick Deckard must find them. But Deckard gradually comes to feel compassion for the androids, realizing that the tests he gives measure only a subtle difference between androids and humans. In contrast to this officially sanctioned tracking and killing of androids, this near-future society accepts artificial animals of all kinds—everything from sheep to spiders. With most real animals extinct, replicas are fashionable to own. One of the rarest animals is the toad, and when Deckard discovers one in the desert, he believes he has made an important find. But even in the desert there are no real animals. Deckard notices a small control panel in the toad's abdomen. Nonetheless, he takes the toad home and cares for him. His wife, touched by his concern for the "creature," buys some electric flies for the toad to eat. "Against this bizarre background of pervasive fakery," Philip Strick wrote in *Sight and Sound,* "the erosion of authentic humanity by undetectable android imitations has all the plausibility of a new and lethal plague whereby evolution would become substitution and nobody would notice the difference." Writing in *Philip K. Dick,* Patricia S. Warrick called *Do Androids Dream of Electric Sheep?* "one of Dick's finest novels," citing its "complexity of structure and idea." The novel was loosely adapted as the film *Blade Runner* in 1982.

Several critics have commented on the structure of Dick's fiction, pointing out that many novels end inconclusively and are often filled with deliberate paradoxes and inconsistencies. Angus Taylor, writing in his *Philip K. Dick and the Umbrella of Light,* explained that Dick "undermines the plot in its superficial aspect by throwing roadblocks in the way of the smooth succession of events, and asks us to divert our attention, to search out and accept the poetic core of the work; he tries to focus our attention on the plot as a 'net' for catching something strange and otherworldly." In similar terms, Roger Zelazny noted in *Philip K. Dick* that "the subjective response, . . . when a Philip Dick book has been finished and put aside is that, upon reflection, it does not seem so much that one holds the memory of a story; rather, it is the after effects of a poem rich in metaphor that seem to remain." Writing in *Extrapolation,* Mary Kay Bray saw Dick's novels as using a "mandalic" structure. "The key to mandalic structure," Bray wrote, "is that it radiates from a center and must suggest that center in all its patterns and images. In point of view and details of landscape and character, Dick's novels

manage just that." Also writing in *Extrapolation,* Warrick argued that in Dick's novels, he creates a "bi-polar construction" of reality. This construction presents both sides of a question simultaneously, expecting a synthesis from the reader. This synthesis results in the reader seeing "from opposite directions simultaneously. He is rewarded with a fleeting epiphany—Dick's vision of 'process reality,'" Warrick wrote. "Ultimately, however, one intuits, not analyzes, Dick's meaning."

In several of his novels, Dick drew upon his own life experiences. *A Scanner Darkly,* for example, is dedicated to a list of Dick's friends who died or suffered permanent health damage because of drugs. The novel concerns undercover narcotics agent Bob Arctor, who is assigned to investigate himself. His superiors are unaware of his undercover identity and Arctor cannot afford to reveal it. He investigates himself to avoid suspicion. While conducting the investigation, however, Arctor is taking the drug Substance D. The drug splits his personality until he no longer recognizes himself in surveillance videotapes. Arctor's condition worsens until he is finally put into a drug rehabilitation program. "The novel," Patrick Parrinder wrote in the *Times Literary Supplement,* "is a frightening allegory of the process of drug abuse, in which some of the alternative realities experienced are revealed as the hallucinations of terminal addicts." "Drug misuse is not a disease," Dick wrote in an author's note to the novel, "it is a decision, like the decision to step out in front of a moving car." Dick himself suffered pancreatic damage from his involvement with drugs. His use of amphetamines resulted in the high blood pressure which eventually ended in his fatal stroke. Dick once admitted to Platt that he had "regarded drugs as dangerous and potentially lethal, but I had a cat's curiosity. It was my interest in the human mind that made me curious. . . . These were essentially religious strivings that were appearing in me."

Dick's interest in religion crystallized in 1974 in a mystical experience that changed the course of his career. "I experienced an invasion of my mind," Dick explained to Platt, "by a transcendentally rational mind, as if I had been insane all my life and suddenly I had become sane." For several months, this presence took over Dick's mind and directed his actions. He claimed that it straightened out his health and finances and put his business affairs in order. Despite numerous efforts to rationalize the experience, Dick was unable to come to any conclusions about it. In *VALIS, The Divine Invasion,* and *The Transmigration of Timothy Archer,* Dick wrote of theological paradoxes and seekers after truth, exploring various religious concepts for possible answers. Dick realized the disturbing appearance of his claims, and in *VALIS* questioned his own sanity through two characters who are aspects of himself. Horselover Fat is a half-mad mystic who hears God's voice in his head. The other character, Phil Dick, is a writer who tries to understand Horselover, although he regards him in a bemused manner. It is revealed in the course of the novel that Horselover is actually a psychological projection of Phil. He has been created as a way to deal with the death of Phil's loved ones, to act as a shield against accepting those deaths. With this revelation, Clute observed, "we begin to see the artfulness in the way Dick has chosen to handle . . . material too nutty to accept, too admonitory to forget, too haunting to abandon." After asking the question "Was Phil Dick sane?," Peter Nicholls wrote in *Science Fiction Review* that "the question has no absolute answer. . . . Phil thought that God had reached into his mind. To this day I am not sure whether he meant this literally or metaphorically."

Prior to his success as a science-fiction writer, Dick attempted to find a niche as a mainstream author in the 1950s and 1960s. Two of the books he produced during this period were posthumously published as *Mary and the Giant* and *The Broken Bubble,* and both revolve around 1950s suburban California. The protagonist of *Mary and the Giant* is an undereducated twenty-year-old woman who whirls in the vacuum of her life options. These include marriage or love with several different lovers, including an elderly record-store owner, an African-American lounge singer, and an underachieving pianist. A *Publishers Weekly* critic called Dick "one of the most compelling chroniclers of life and love in 1950s California that we have had." Colin Greenland of the *Times Literary Supplement* stated that "this neglected early novel reveals Philip K. Dick's remarkable insight into a society on the eve of change and a young woman on the edge of panic." "The narrative voice is ever clear and sensitive, forcing sympathies in unlikely places," noted Nancy Forbes in her *New York Times Book Review* appraisal of *Mary and the Giant,* adding, "In this *film noir* world, people may be good, but they are never nice." Greenland concluded that Dick's "bald, assertive style prefigures the work of contemporary writers like Frederick Barthelme, Tobias Wolff, and Ellen Gilchrist, who attempt to articulate, in their own terms, the dramas of individuals whose moral perceptions are smothered by a culture of compliance and consumption."

The Broken Bubble centers on narrator Jim Briskin, a radio announcer who is still in love with his ex-wife, Pat. The story unfolds as Jim introduces Pat to two of his fans, teenage couple Art and Rachel, thereby unwittingly setting into motion a complex relationship between the four. In the *New York Times Book Review,* George Blooston said of the characters: "Their willfulness is riveting. But by the time the dust clears and the morally strong have saved the weak, the rewards of the novel seem meager. Without the humor or wisdom of Dick's science fiction, this portrait of 1950's anomie is dominated by its bleak naturalism and soap-operate earnestness." Clute of the *Times Literary Supplement* commented, "It is a slippery plot to hold, but although Dick sometimes loses control . . . the mature, deft, probing tenderness with which he presents his four protagonists exhibits a rather more than scattershot talent."

At his best, Dick is generally regarded as one of the finest science-fiction writers of his time, and many of his books have remained in print more than three decades after their initial publication. Nicholls believed him to be "one of the greatest science fiction writers in history, and one of [the twentieth] century's most important writers in any field." Dick was, Whalen maintained, "one of America's best writers. . . . He was a great science fiction writer, so much so, that one is reluctant to apply the SF label, with its undeserved stigma, to his writing." Similarly, Clute held that Dick was the "greatest of science fiction writers—though he's by no means the best writer of science fiction" to clarify that what Dick wrote was concerned with the human condition, not with the technological progress of the future. In her evaluation of Dick's work, LeGuin stressed that it is easy to misinterpret him. A reader "may put the book down believing that he's read a clever sci-fi thriller and nothing more," LeGuin wrote. "The fact that what Dick is entertaining us about is reality and madness, time and death, sin and salvation—this has escaped most readers and critics. Nobody notices; nobody notices that we have our own homegrown [Jorge Luis] Borges, and have had him for thirty years." According to Kosek, Dick held a "very intense and morally significant vision of life," and this vision imbues his "long string of compelling, idiosyncratic novels. . . , most of which embodied a single urgent message: Things are not what they seem to be."

BIOGRAPHICAL AND CRITICAL SOURCES:

BOOKS

Aldiss, Brian W., *The Shape of Future Things,* Faber (London, England), 1970.
Aldiss, Brian W., *The Billion Year Spree,* Doubleday (New York, NY), 1973.

Contemporary Literary Criticism, Thomson Gale (Detroit, MI), Volume 10, 1979, Volume 30, 1984, Volume 72, 1992.

Dick, Anne R., *Search for Philip K. Dick, 1928-1982: A Memoir and Biography of the Science Fiction Writer,* Edwin Mellen Press (Lewiston, NY), 1996.

Dictionary of Literary Biography, Volume 8: *Twentieth-Century American Science-Fiction Writers,* two volumes, Thomson Gale (Detroit, MI), 1981.

Gillespie, Bruce, editor, *Philip K. Dick: Electric Shepherd,* Norstrilia Press (Melbourne, Australia), 1975.

Greenberg, Martin Harry, and Joseph D. Olander, editors, *Philip K. Dick,* Taplinger (New York, NY), 1983.

Ketterer, David, *New Worlds for Old: The Apocalyptic Imagination, Science Fiction, and American Literature,* Indiana University Press, 1974.

Knight, Damon, *In Search of Wonder,* 2nd edition, Advent Publishers, 1967.

Levack, Daniel J.H. and Steven Owen Godersky, *PKD: A Philip K. Dick Bibliography,* Underwood/ Miller, 1981.

Moskowitz, Sam, *Seekers of Tomorrow,* Ballantine (New York, NY), 1967.

Mullen, R. D., and Darko Suvin, editors, *Science-Fiction Studies: Selected Articles on Science Fiction, 1973-1975,* Gregg, 1976.

Nicholls, Peter, editor, *Science Fiction at Large,* Harper (New York, NY), 1976.

Parrinder, Peter, *Science Fiction: A Critical Guide,* Longman (London, England), 1979.

Platt, Charles, *Dream Makers: The Uncommon People Who Write Science Fiction,* Berkley Publishing (New York, NY), 1980.

Rickman, Gregg, *Philip K. Dick: In His Own Words,* Fragments, 1984.

Scholes, Robert, and Eric S. Rabkin, *Science Fiction: History, Science, Vision,* Oxford University Press (New York, NY), 1977.

Spinrad, Norman, *Modern Science Fiction,* Doubleday (New York, NY), 1974.

Taylor, Angus, *Philip K. Dick and the Umbrella of Light,* T-K Graphics, 1975.

Tolley, Michael, and Kirpal Singh, editors, *The Stellar Gauge,* [Carlton, Australia], 1981.

Wolfe, Gary K., editor, *Science Fiction Dialogues,* Academy Chicago (Chicago, IL), 1982.

PERIODICALS

American Book Review, January, 1984.

Best Sellers, November, 1976; May, 1977.

Booklist, November 1, 2002, Roland Green, review of *Selected Stories of Philip K. Dick,* p. 480.

Books in Canada, Parkrick Burger, "Homeostatic Kipple: Meditations on Philip K. Dick," pp. 46-47.

Chicago Tribune Book World, July 4, 1982.

Extrapolation, summer, 1979; summer, 1980; summer, 1983; winter, 2000, Darko Suvin, "Goodbye and Hello: Differentiating within the Later P.K. Dick," p. 368.

Fantasy Newsletter, April-May, 1982.

Fantasy Review, October, 1984.

Library Journal, December, 2002, p. 186; May 15, 2003, Michael Rogers, review of *Our Friends from Frolix 8;* August, 2003, Michael Rogers, review of *Eye in the Sky,* p. 143.

Listener, May 29, 1975.

Los Angeles Times Book Review, September 6, 1981; February 9, 1986, p. 4.

Magazine of Fantasy and Science Fiction, June, 1963; August, 1968; January, 1975; August, 1978; July, 1980.

Missouri Review, Volume VII, number 2, 1984.

New Republic, October 30, 1976; November 26, 1977; December 6, 1993, p. 34.

New Statesman, December 17, 1976; December 16, 1977; October 9, 1987, p. 29.

New Worlds, March, 1966; May, 1969.

New York Times Book Review, July 20, 1975; December 1, 1985, p. 24; January 12, 1986, p. 22; April 26, 1987, p. 24; October 16, 1988, p. 36; January 26, 1992, p. 24.

Observer (London, England), December 8, 1974.

Philip K. Dick Society Newsletter, 1983—.

Publishers Weekly, March 20, 1987, p. 68; May 27, 1988, p. 50.

San Francisco Review of Books, Volume 6, number 13, 1991.

Science Fiction Chronicle, October, 1985, p. 42; May, 1986, p. 37; May, 1988, p. 42.

Science Fiction Review, Volume V, number 2, 1976; Volume V, number 4, 1976; February, 1977; summer, 1983; November, 1983.

Science-Fiction Studies, March, 1975; July, 1980; July, 1982; July, 1983; March, 1984; March, 1992, p. 105.

Sight and Sound, summer, 1982.

Spectator, November 19, 1977.

Times Literary Supplement, June 12, 1969; July 8, 1977; January 27, 1978; February 7, 1986, p. 150; February 19, 1988, p. 186; December 8, 1989, p. 1368.

Vertex, February, 1974.

Voice Literary Supplement, August, 1982.

Washington Post, March 4, 1982.

Washington Post Book World, February 22, 1981; May 23, 1982; June 30, 1985; May 25, 1986; August 2, 1987.

OBITUARIES:

PERIODICALS

Chicago Tribune, March 4, 1982.
Los Angeles Times, March 8, 1982.
Newsweek, March 15, 1982.
New York Times, March 3, 1982.
Publishers Weekly, March 19, 1982.
Time, March 15, 1982.
Times (London, England), March 15, 1982.

*   *   *

DICK, Philip Kindred
   See DICK, Philip K.

*   *   *

DIDION, Joan 1934-

PERSONAL: Born December 5, 1934, in Sacramento, CA; daughter of Frank Reese and Eduene (Jerrett) Didion; married John Gregory Dunne (a writer), January 30, 1964 (deceased, 2003); children: Quintana Roo (daughter; deceased, 2005). *Education:* University of California, Berkeley, B.A., 1956.

ADDRESSES: Agent—Lynn Nesbit, Janklow & Nesbit, 445 Park Ave., 13th Fl., New York, NY 10022.

CAREER: Writer. *Vogue,* New York, NY, 1956-63, began as promotional copywriter, became associate feature editor. Visiting regents lecturer in English, University of California—Berkeley, 1976.

AWARDS, HONORS: First prize, *Vogue*'s Prix de Paris, 1956; Bread Loaf fellowship in fiction, 1963; National Book Award nomination in fiction, 1971, for *Play It As It Lays*; Morton Dauwen Zabel Award, National Institute of Arts and Letters, 1978; National Book Critics Circle Prize nomination in nonfiction, 1980, and American Book Award nomination in nonfiction, 1981, both for *The White Album*; *Los Angeles Times* Book Prize nomination in fiction, 1984, for *Democracy*; Edward MacDowell Medal, 1996; Gold Medal for Belles Lettres, American Academy of Arts and Letters, in honor of distinguished writing career; National Book Award for nonfiction, National Book Foundation, 2005, for *The Year of Magical Thinking.*

WRITINGS:

NOVELS

Run River, Obolensky (New York, NY), 1963.
Play It As It Lays (also see below), Farrar, Straus (New York, NY), 1970, revised edition with introduction by David Thomson, Farrar, Straus (New York, NY), 2005.
A Book of Common Prayer, Simon & Schuster (New York, NY), 1977.
Democracy, Simon & Schuster (New York, NY), 1984.
The Last Thing He Wanted, Knopf (New York, NY), 1996.

SCREENPLAYS; WITH HUSBAND, JOHN GREGORY DUNNE

Panic in Needle Park (based on James Mills's book of the same title), Twentieth Century-Fox, 1971.
Play It As It Lays (based on Didion's book of the same title), Universal, 1972.
(With others) *A Star Is Born,* Warner Bros., 1976.
True Confessions (based on John Gregory Dunne's novel of the same title), United Artists, 1981.
Hills Like White Elephants (based on Ernest Hemingway's short story), HBO, 1990.
Broken Trust (based on the novel *Court of Honor* by William Wood), TNT, 1995.
Up Close and Personal, Touchstone, 1996.

NONFICTION

Slouching toward Bethlehem, Farrar, Straus (New York, NY), 1968.
The White Album, Simon & Schuster (New York, NY), 1979.
Salvador, Simon & Schuster (New York, NY), 1983.
Joan Didion: Essays & Conversations, Ontario Review Press (Princeton, NJ), 1984.
Miami, Simon & Schuster (New York, NY), 1987.
Robert Graham: The Duke Ellington Memorial in Progress, Los Angeles County Museum of Art (Los Angeles, CA), 1988.
After Henry, Simon & Schuster (New York, NY), 1992, published in England as *Sentimental Journeys,* HarperCollins (London, England), 1993.
Political Fictions, Knopf (New York, NY), 2001.
Where I Was From, Knopf (New York, NY), 2003.
Fixed Ideas: America since 9.11, New York Review of Books (New York, NY), 2003.

Vintage Didion, Vintage Books (New York, NY), 2004.
The Year of Magical Thinking, Knopf (New York, NY),
2005.

Author of introduction, Robert Mapplethorpe, *Some
Women,* Bulfinch Press (Boston, MA), 1992. Author of
column, with John Gregory Dunne, "Points West," *Saturday Evening Post,* 1967-69, and "The Coast," *Esquire,* 1976-77; former columnist, *Life.* Contributor of
short stories, articles, and reviews to periodicals, including *Vogue, Saturday Evening Post, Holiday,Harp-
er's Bazaar,* and *New York Times Book Review, New
Yorker,* and *New York Review of Books.* Former contributing editor, *National Review.*

SIDELIGHTS: Throughout her long literary career, Joan
Didion has distinguished herself with her highly polished style, her keen intelligence, and her provocative
social commentary. Although her work frequently criti-
cizes trends in the contemporary world, which she sees
as increasingly chaotic, "her moral courage and tenacious search for truth deeply honor American values.
No literary journalist currently writing is better able to
shape the shards of American disorder into a living history of this time," commended Paul Ashdown in *Dictionary of Literary Biography.* The author of novels, essays, and screenplays, Didion has always identified
herself as being more interested in images than in ideas,
and she is noted for her use of telling details. In addition to being "a gifted reporter," according to *New York
Times Magazine* contributor Michiko Kakutani, Didion
"is also a prescient witness, finding in her own experiences parallels of the times. The voice is always precise, the tone unsentimental, the view unabashedly
subjective. She takes things personally." Didion has
written a great deal about her native state, California, a
place which seemed to supply her with ample evidence
of the disorder in society. Her theme has remained essentially unchanged, but as the years have passed she
has found new ways to express it, writing about
troubles of Latin America, Southeast Asia, and the
American political scene.

After graduating from the University of California at
Berkeley in 1956, Didion took a job at *Vogue* magazine's New York office, where she remained for eight
years, rising from promotional copywriter to associate
feature editor. During this period, she met John Gregory
Dunne and, after several years of friendship, they married, becoming not just matrimonial partners but writing
collaborators as well. While still at *Vogue,* Didion began her first novel, *Run River,* which was published in
1963. The story concerns two families prominent in the

Sacramento Valley, the Knights and the McClellans.
Everett and Lily are children of these two prosperous
families who elope. Before long they have two children, but their marriage slides into danger when Everett
must leave home to serve in the armed forces during
World War II. In his absence, Lily has an affair, which
leads to her pregnancy. Everett returns and convinces
Lily to abort the child, but their marriage can never recover; they live out their lives engaged in mutual recrimination, eventually ending in violence. "The novel
depicts the social fragmentation of California that results from the dashed dreams of people drawn to the
state by its promise of prosperity," mused Mark Royden
in another *Dictonary of Literary Biography* essay.
"What is finally ennobling about Lily's western experience, Didion seems to be saying, is not the dream that
gave it birth, but the life force that enables her to survive the failure of that dream."

In 1964, Didion and Dunne moved back to the West
Coast, where she was determined to earn a living as a
freelance reporter. Working on a series of magazine columns about California for the *Saturday Evening Post,*
the couple earned a meager $7,000 in their first year.
But their writing did attract widespread attention, and
when Didion's columns were collected and published in
1968 as *Slouching toward Bethlehem,* her reputation as
an essayist soared. The collection takes its theme from
William Butler Yeats's poem "The Second Coming,"
which reads: "Things fall apart; the center cannot hold;
/ Mere anarchy is loosed upon the world." For Didion
those words sum up the chaos of the 1960s, a chaos so
far-reaching that it affected her ability to perform. Convinced "that writing was an irrelevant act, that the world
as I had understood it no longer existed," Didion, as
she states in the book's preface, realized, "If I was to
work again at all, it would be necessary for me to come
to terms with disorder." She went to Haight-Ashbury to
explore the hippie movement and out of that experience
came the title essay. Most critics reserved high praise
for *Slouching toward Bethlehem.* Writing in the *Christian Science Monitor,* Melvin Maddocks suggested that
Didion's "melancholy voice is that of a last survivor
dictating a superbly written wreckage report onto a tape
she doubts will ever be played." And while *Best Sellers*
reviewer T. O'Hara argued that "the devotion she gives
to America-the-uprooted-the-lunatic-and-the- alienated
is sullied by an inability to modulate, to achieve a respectable distance," most critics applauded her subjectivity. "Nobody captured the slack-jawed Haight-
Ashbury hippies any better," acknowledged *Saturday
Review* contributor Martin Kasindorf.

In 1970 Didion published *Play It As It Lays,* a best-
selling novel that received a National Book Award

nomination and, at the same time, created enormous controversy with its apparently nihilistic theme. The portrait of a woman on what *New York Times Book Review* contributor Lore Segal called a "downward path to wisdom," *Play It As It Lays* tells the story of Maria Wyeth's struggle to find meaning in a meaningless world. "The setting is the desert; the cast, the careless hedonists of Hollywood; the emotional climate, bleak as the surroundings," Kakutani reported in the *New York Times Magazine*. Composed of eighty-four brief chapters, some less than a page in length, the book possesses a cinematic quality and such technical precision that Richard Shickel remarked in *Harper's* that it is "a rather cold and calculated fiction—more a problem in human geometry . . . than a novel that truly lives."

A Book of Common Prayer continues the author's theme of social disintegration with the story of Charlotte Douglas, a Californian "immaculate of history, innocent of politics." Until her daughter Marin abandoned home and family to join a group of terrorists, Charlotte was one who "understood that something was always going on in the world but believed that it would turn out all right." When things fall apart, Charlotte takes refuge in Boca Grande, a fictitious Central American country embroiled in its own domestic conflicts. There she idles away her days at the airport coffee shop, futilely waiting for her daughter to surface and eventually losing her life in a military coup.

Because Charlotte's story is narrated by Grace, an American expatriate and long-time Boca Grande resident, the book presented several technical problems. "The narrator was not present during most of the events she's telling you about. And her only source is a woman incapable of seeing the truth," Didion explained to Diehl. In her *New York Times Book Review* article, Joyce Carol Oates speculated that Didion employs this technique because Grace permits Didion "a free play of her own speculative intelligence that would have been impossible had the story been told by Charlotte. The device of an uninvolved narrator is a tricky one, since a number of private details must be presented as if they were within the range of the narrator's experience. But it is a measure of Didion's skill as a novelist that one never questions [Grace's] near omniscience in recalling Charlotte's story." Christopher Lehmann-Haupt, on the other hand, maintained in the *New York Times* that Didion "simply asks too much of Charlotte, and overburdened as she is by the pitiless cruelty of the narrator's vision, she collapses under the strain."

After *A Book of Common Prayer*, Didion published *The White Album*, a second collection of magazine essays similar in tone to *Slouching towards Bethlehem*. "I don't

have as many answers as I did when I wrote *Slouching*," Didion explained to Kakutani. She called the book *The White Album* in consideration of a famous Beatles album that captured for her the disturbing ambiance of the sixties. "I am talking here about a time when I began to doubt the premises of all the stories I had ever told myself," Didion writes in the title essay. "This period began around 1966 and continued until 1971." During this time, says Didion, "all I knew was what I saw: flash pictures in variable sequence, images with no 'meaning' beyond their temporary arrangement, not a movie but a cuttingroom experience."

Salvador stands as one of Didion's most successful reportorial works. Originally published as two articles in the *New York Review of Books*, it was also nominated for a Pulitzer Prize. The piece was based on a two-week visit Didion and Dunne made to the embattled Republic of El Salvador in June, 1982. A repressive military regime had taken hold there and horrific violence was a daily occurrence. Like Joseph Conrad's *Heart of Darkness, Salvador* "contemplates the meaning of existence when one confronts absolute evil," stated Ashman. "Taken only as a short, impressionistic report on the war, *Salvador* would be a slight work. Something much more is intended, however, than telling the facts about El Salvador. Like Conrad's tale, *Salvador* is a journey into the interior of the human soul." Although highly acclaimed for its literary merits, *Salvador* did generate criticism as well as praise. *Newsweek* reviewer Gene Lyon, for example, allowed that "Didion gets exactly right both the ghastliness and the pointlessness of the current killing frenzy in El Salvador," but then suggested that "ghastliness and pointlessness are Didion's invariable themes wherever she goes. Most readers will not get very far in this very short book without wondering whether she visited that sad and tortured place less to report than to validate the Didion world view."

A year after *Salvador* was published, Didion produced *Democracy*. The book was to have been the story of a family of American colonialists whose interests were firmly entrenched in the Pacific at a time when Hawaii was still a territory, but Didion abandoned this idea. The resulting novel features Inez Christian and her family. In the spring of 1975—at the time the United States completed its evacuation of Vietnam and Cambodia—Inez's father is arrested for a double murder with political and racial overtones. "The Christians and their in-laws are the emblems of a misplaced confidence," according to John Lownsbrough in Toronto's *Globe and Mail*, "the flotsam and jetsam of a Manifest Destiny no longer so manifest. Their disintegration as a family in the spring of 1975 . . . is paralleled by the fall of Saigon a bit later that year and the effective disintegration of the American expansionist dream in all its ethnocentric optimism." Somehow, her family's tragedy enables Inez to break free of her marriage to a self-serving politician and escape to Malaysia with Jack Lovett, a freelance CIA agent and the man she has always loved. Though he dies abruptly, Inez holds on to her freedom, choosing to remain in Kuala Lumpur where she works among the Vietnamese refugees.

New York Review of Books critic Thomas R. Edwards believed *Democracy* "finally earns its complexity of form. It is indeed 'a hard story to tell' and the presence in it of 'Joan Didion' trying to tell it is an essential part of its subject. Throughout one senses the author struggling with the moral difficulty that makes the story hard to tell—how to stop claiming what Inez finally relinquishes, 'the American exemption' from having to recognize that history records not the victory of personal wills over reality . . . but the 'undertow of having and not having, the convulsions of a world largely unaffected by the individual efforts of anyone in it.'"

Miami once again finds Didion on the literary high wire, in a work of nonfiction that focuses on the cultural, social, and political impact the influx of Cuban exiles has had upon the city of Miami and, indeed, upon the entire United States. Culminating in an indictment of American foreign policy from the presidential administrations of John F. Kennedy through Ronald Reagan, *Miami* "is a thoroughly researched and brilliantly written meditation on the consequences of power, especially on power's self- addictive delusions," according to *Voice Literary Supplement* reviewer Stacey D'Erasmo. The book explores the thirty- year history of the community of Cuban immigrants which now comprises over half the population of that city. Didion paints these émigrés as existing within a country that threatens their political agenda, and a city full of enemies. "The shadowy missions, the secret fundings, the conspiracies beneath conspiracies, the deniable support by parts of the U.S. government and active discouragement by other parts," Richard Eder wrote in the *Los Angeles Times Book Review,* paraphrasing Didion's argument, "all these things have fostered a tensely paranoid style in parts of our own political life . . . . Miami is us." While noting that Didion's intricate—if journalistic—style almost overwhelms her argument, Eder compared *Miami* to a luxury hunting expedition: "You may look out the window and see some casually outfitted huntsman trudging along. You may wonder whether his experience is more authentic than yours. Didion's tour is overarranged, but that is a genuine lion's carcass strapped to our fender."

After Henry, published in the United Kingdom as *Sentimental Journeys,* is a collection of twelve essays organized loosely around three geographical areas that Didion has focused on throughout her writing career: Washington, D.C., California, and New York City. "For her they are our Chapels Perilous," declared Robert Dana in the *Georgia Review,* "where power and dreams fuse or collide." The title essay is a tribute to Didion's friend and mentor Henry Robbins, who served as her editor prior to his death in 1979.

Politics are discussed in the section titled "Washington." The essay "In the Realm of the Fisher King" is an analysis of the years of the Reagan presidency. "Her difficulty with politics is that she really doesn't know it as well as she imagines," stated Jonathan Yardley in the *Washington Post Book World,* "and brings to it no especially useful insights." However, reviewer Hendrik Hertzberg lauded "Inside Baseball," Didion's essay on the 1988 presidential campaign, in the *New York Times Book Review:* "Her cool eye sees sharply when it surveys the rich texture of American public folly . . . . What she has to say about the manipulation of images and the creation of pseudo-events makes familiar territory new again." But, Hertzberg added, Didion's "focus on the swirl of 'narratives' is useful as a way of exploring political image- mongering, but surprisingly limited as a way of describing the brute political and social realities against which candidates and ideas must in the end be measured."

Included among the remaining works in *After Henry* is "Sentimental Journeys," a three-part "attack on New York City and the sentimentality that distorts and obscures much of what is said and done there, and which has brought the city to the edge of bankruptcy and collapse," according to Dana. One section explores the way in which the highly publicized 1990 rape of a white investment banker jogging in New York City's Central Park—and the trial that followed—was transformed by the media into what Didion terms a "false narrative." Combined with her illuminating discussion of the many rapes occurring in the city that are not given such intensive press coverage and the decreasing competitive edge possessed by the city when viewed in real terms, "Didion's portrait is one of a city drugged nearly to death on the crack of its own myths," according to Dana, "its own 'sentimental stories told in defense of its own lazy criminality.'"

After a twelve-year hiatus, Didion returned to fiction with *The Last Thing He Wanted.* Set in 1984, the year *Democracy* was published, it contains some of the same elements, but this time in a different outpost of American foreign- policy gamesmanship, Central America. Told from the viewpoint of a "not quite omniscient" narrator, it is the story of Elena McMahon, a writer who walks away from a job covering the presidential campaign and returns to Florida and her widowed father. A shady wheeler-dealer fading into senility, her father sees a chance to turn a huge profit by supplying arms to Nicaragua's anticommunist *contras,* and Elena flies to Costa Rica to close the deal. Before long, she is caught in a web of gunrunners, CIA operatives, and a conspiracy that stretches from the JFK assassination to the Iran-Contra scandal. Some reviewers criticized the narrator, and by extension the novel, as too vague and unreal. "The problem of *The Last Thing He Wanted,* " according to *New Republic* critic James Wood, "is not that our author is 'not quite omniscient.' It is that our narrator is not quite a person." Michiko Kakutani, writing in the *New York Times,* found the novel equally unconvincing: "Despite Ms. Didion's nimble orchestration of emotional and physical details, despite her insider's ear for lingo, her conspiratorial view of history never feels terribly persuasive . . . . In the end, what's meant to be existential angst feels more like self-delusion; what's meant to be disturbing feels more like paranoia." Other critics, however, found this "unreality" oddly appropriate. For example, John Weir wrote in the *New Yorker:* "A dream is disorienting but it adheres to its own particular logic. By contrast, the real life events on which novels are traditionally based have lately taken on a quality that almost defies their being retold. 'This is something different,' Didion's narrator writes about the story she's driven to tell. The result is entrancing—a dream without the logic of a dream, the way we live now."

Didion published another collection of her essays in 2001. *Political Fictions* is made up of pieces previously printed in the *New York Review of Books.* Her central theme is that political life in the United States has become increasingly inauthentic, designed for and shaped by the media, and controlled by a small elite class that shows complete disregard for the majority of the electorate. She is acerbic in her criticism of the media's part in this state of affairs, claiming that they are willing accomplices with the political powers that be. Her time frame begins with the rivalry between Michael Dukakis and George Bush, Sr., continues through the years of the Clinton administration and on to the bitter battle of the presidential campaign in 2000. Again and again she reaches the conclusion that democracy in modern America is "not a system of majority rule or an expression of voter choice; it is a cheap spectacle acted out by the craven officials and smug journalists of Wash-

ington's 'political class,'" explained Sean McCann in *Book.* McCann found some of the author's conclusions "questionable," but added that the "anger and beauty of Didion's work" is so great that "while one reads, it is hard not to nod one's head in assent." A *Publishers Weekly* writer stated that "at her best, Didion is provocative, persuasive and highly entertaining." Noting that Democrats, Republicans, and political reporters all come under fire from Didion, the writer added: "Didion's willingness to skewer nearly everyone is one of the pleasures of the book."

Didion published two books in 2003: *Where I Was From* and *Fixed Ideas: America since 9.11.* The first returned to one of her favorite subjects, the state of California. She had actually started the book in the 1970s, but found it so difficult to write that she set it aside for many years. The death of her mother finally provided the impetus for her to finish it. Her aim was to explore the vast gap between the reality of California and the popular image of the state. Coming from a long line of Californians, Didion explored many family stories in the course of her narrative. The picture she paints of modern-day California is not flattering; she sees "greed, acquisitiveness and wasteful extravagance lurking beneath the state's eternal sunshine," wrote a *Publishers Weekly* reviewer. Even in its earlier days, now greatly romanticized, California was in fact a place where bigotry and other forms of inhumanity flourished. While many people might find her opinions debatable, "the book is a remarkable document precisely because of its power to trigger a national debate that can heighten awareness and improve conditions on the West Coast and throughout the country," concluded the reviewer. Terren Ilana Wein, a writer for *Library Journal,* defined *Where I Was From* as "a complex and challenging memoir, difficult to enter into but just as difficult to put down . . . . Those who have long admired the clarity and precision of her prose will not be disappointed with this partly autobiographical, partly historical, but fully engrossing account."

Didion critiqued the political aftermath of the September 11, 2001, destruction of the World Trade Center towers in her book *Fixed Ideas: America since 9.11.* "In times of national crisis, the public turns to such proven, clear- eyed observers of American society to place events within a historical and political context," stated Donna Seaman in *Booklist.* She noted, however, that meaningful discussion as to the roots of the tragedy was difficult because those who tried to initiate it were "instantly branded as traitors" by the Bush administration. Didion dissects the administration's tactics and strategies for managing the public perception of the terrorist attacks and the war on Iraq that followed. Her analysis proves her to be a "shrewd, seasoned, and superbly articulate interpreter of the machinations of American politics, particularly the art of spin." The author was quoted by Chauncey Mabe, a contributor to the *South Florida Sun-Sentinel,* as saying: "My immediate thought after 9/11 was that it would alter everything . . . . But whatever did change doesn't seem to include the political process. I knew this as soon as President Bush made his first speech to the nation, and all the commentators were analyzing how it played, how it was an 'up thing' that took attention off the economy. That was pretty discouraging." Discouraged or not, Didion stands as a significant witness to the modern world. "Her prose is a literary seismograph," claimed Dana, "on which are clearly registered the tremors and temblors that increasingly shake the bedrock of the American social dream."

In 2005 Didion published *The Year of Magical Thinking,* a memoir of the year of her life following the death of her husband, writer John Gregory Dunne. The couple had returned home from visiting their only daughter, Quintana Roo, who was admitted to a hospital when a progressive flu developed into pneumonia and then sepsis, a severe bloodstream infection. That evening, Dunne died suddenly of a massive heart attack. "She gave away her husband's clothes but not his shoes; he would need them if he somehow returned to her. This, she says, was the beginning of her year of magical thinking," commented Linda Hall in *American Prospect.* Robert Pinsky, writing in *New York Times Book Review,* called the book an "exact, candid and penetrating account of personal terror and bereavement." Pinsky further noted, "Didion's book is thrilling and engaging—sometimes quite funny—because it ventures to tell the truth . . . . grief makes us crazy." Pinsky also commented on Didion's writing style, stating that her use of "repeated, vague, nearly meaningless phrases . . . dramatize both the inner numbness of shock and the outer reality of the emergency, a terminal reality that is uniquely complicated and simple." Sadly, after the book was published, Quintana Roo died in August of 2005, although the end of the memoir suggested she may recover. Didion did not feel it was necessary to change the book to reflect the passing of her daughter. The same year, Didion was awarded the National Book Award for nonfiction for her moving story of personal loss.

BIOGRAPHICAL AND CRITICAL SOURCES:

BOOKS

Concise Dictionary of American Literary Biography: Broadening Views, 1968-1988, Gale (Detroit, MI), 1989.

Contemporary Literary Criticism, Gale (Detroit, MI), Volume 1, 1973, Volume 3, 1975, Volume 8, 1978, Volume 14, 1980.

Contemporary Novelists, St. James Press (Detroit, MI), 2001.

Dictionary of Literary Biography, Gale (Detroit, MI), Volume 2: *American Novelists since World War II,* 1978; Volume 173: *American Novelists since World War II,* fifth series, 1996; Volume 185: *American Literary Journalists, 1945-1995,* first series, 1997.

Dictionary of Literary Biography Yearbook, Gale (Detroit, MI), 1981, 1986.

Friedman, Ellen G., editor, *Joan Didion: Essays and Conversations,* Ontario Review Press (Princeton, NJ), 1984.

Henderson, Katherine, *Joan Didion,* Ungar (New York, NY), 1981.

Loris, Michelle, *Innocence, Loss, and Recovery in the Art of Joan Didion,* Peter Lang (New York, NY), 1989.

St. James Encyclopedia of Popular Culture, St. James Press (Detroit, MI), 2000.

Winchell, Mark, *Joan Didion,* Twayne (Boston, MA), 1980.

PERIODICALS

America, April 5, 1997, Lewis A. Turlish, review of *The Last Thing He Wanted,* p. 28.

American Prospect, February 25, 2002, Ronald Brownstein, review of *Political Fictions,* p. 33; November, 2005, Linda Hall, "The Last Thing She Wanted," p. 39.

American Scholar, winter, 1970- 71.

American Spectator, September, 1992.

Atlantic Monthly, April, 1977.

Belles Lettres, fall, 1992, p. 14.

Book, September, 2001, Sean McCann, review of *Political Fictions,* p. 75.

Booklist, March 1, 1992; July, 1996, Donna Seaman, review of *The Last Thing He Wanted,* p. 1779; October 15, 1998, Mary Carroll, review of *The Last Thing He Wanted,* p. 397; August, 2001, Donna Seaman, review of *Political Fictions,* p. 2075; May 15, 2003, Donna Seaman, review of *Fixed Ideas: America since 9.11,* p. 1621.

Boston Globe, May 17, 1992, p. 105.

Boston Magazine, September, 1996, Sven Birkerts, review of *The Last Thing He Wanted,* p. 124.

Chicago Tribune, June 12, 1979.

Chicago Tribune Book World, July 1, 1979; April 3, 1983; April 15, 1984.

Chicago Tribune Magazine, May 2, 1982.

Christian Science Monitor, May 16, 1968; September 24, 1970; July 9, 1979; June 1, 1992, p. 13.

Commentary, June, 1984, pp. 62- 67; October, 1996, Elizabeth Powers, review of *The Last Thing He Wanted,* p. 70.

Commonweal, November 29, 1968; October 23, 1992.

Critique, spring, 1984, pp. 160- 170.

Detroit News, August 12, 1979.

Dissent, summer, 1983.

Economist, August 22, 1992.

Entertainment Weekly, September 20, 1996, Vanessa V. Friedman, review of *The Last Thing He Wanted,* p. 75.

Esquire, March, 1996, p. 36.

Georgia Review, winter, 1992, pp. 799-802.

Globe and Mail (Toronto, Ontario, Canada), April 28, 1984.

Harper's, August, 1970; December, 1971; November, 2005, Jennifer Szalai, "The Still Point of the Turning World: Joan Didion and the Opposite of Meaning," p. 97.

Harper's Bazaar, September, 1996, Philip Weiss, review of *The Last Thing He Wanted,* p. 124.

Harvard Advocate, winter, 1973.

Interview, September, 1996, Mark Marvel, interview with Joan Didion, p. 84; November, 2001, Amy Spindler, interview with Joan Didion, p. 80.

Library Journal, July, 1996, Barbara Hoffert, review of *The Last Thing He Wanted,* p. 156; October 1, 2001, Cynthia Harrison, review of *Political Fictions,* p. 124; June 15, 2003, Terren Ilana Wein, review of *Where I Was From,* p. 72.

London Review of Books, December 10, 1987, pp. 3, 5-6; October 21, 1993, pp. 12- 13.

Los Angeles, September, 2001, Tom Carson, review of *Political Fictions,* p. 137; March, 1996, Peter Rainer, review of *Up Close and Personal,* p. 145.

Los Angeles Times, May 9, 1971; July 4, 1976.

Los Angeles Times Book Review, March 20, 1983; September 27, 1987, pp. 3, 6.

Maclean's, March 4, 1996, Brian D. Johnson, review of *Up Close and Personal,* p. 79.

Miami Herald, December 2, 1973.

Ms., February, 1977.

Nation, September 26, 1979; September 30, 1996, John Leonard, review of *The Last Thing He Wanted,* p. 23.

National Review, June 4, 1968; August 25, 1970; October 12, 1979; November 23, 1987; June 22, 1992, pp. 53- 54.

New Republic, June 6, 1983; April 9, 1984; November 23, 1987; October 14, 1996.

Newsweek, August 3, 1970; December 21, 1970; March 21, 1977; June 25, 1979; March 28, 1983; April 16, 1984; March 4, 1996, David Ansen, review of *Up Close and Personal,* p. 70; September 9, 1996, Laura Shapiro, review of *The Last Thing He Wanted,* p. 68.

New York, February 15, 1971; June 13, 1979; March 4, 1996, David Denby, review of *Up Close and Personal,* p. 66; September 2, 1996, Linda Hall, interview with Joan Didion, p. 28.

New Yorker, June 20, 1977; April 18, 1983; January 25, 1988, p. 112; March 11, 1996, James Wolcott, review of *Up Close and Personal,* p. 107; September 16, 1996.

New York Observer, September 17, 2001, Susan Faludi, review of *Political Fictions,* p. 14.

New York Review of Books, October 22, 1970; May 10, 1984; December 20, 2001, Joseph Lelvveld, review of *Political Fictions,* p. 8.

New York Times, July 21, 1970; October 30, 1972; March 21, 1977; June 10, 1979; June 5, 1979; March 11, 1983; April 6, 1984; September 14, 1984; February 8, 1987; September 3, 1996; September 30, 2001, review of *Political Fictions,* p. 22.

New York Times Book Review, July 21, 1968; August 9, 1970; April 3, 1977; June 17, 1979; March 13, 1983; April 22, 1984; October 25, 1987, p. 3; May 17, 1992, pp. 3, 39; September 8, 1996, Michael Wood, review of *The Last Thing He Wanted,* p. 10; September 20, 2001, review of *Political Fictions,* p. 22; October 7, 2001, review of *Political Fictions,* p. 26; October 6, 2002, Scott Veale, review of *Political Fictions,* p. 36; October 9, 2005, Robert Pinsky, "Goodbye to All That," p. 1L.

Observer (London, England), March 27, 1988, p. 43; January 24, 1993, p. 53; January 12, 2003, Jemima Hunt, "The Didion Bible," p. 3.

People, October 28, 1996, Paula Chin, review of *The Last Thing He Wanted,* p. 40.

Plain Dealer (Cleveland, OH), September 30, 2001, John Freeman, review of *Political Fictions,* p. J9.

Publishers Weekly, June 24, 1996, review of *The Last Thing He Wanted,* p. 43; August 6, 2001, review of *Political Fictions,* p. 72; October 15, 2001, Natasha Wimmer, interview with Joan Didion, p. 41; June 30, 2003, Joel Hirschhorn, review of *Where I Was From,* p. 68.

Quill and Quire, December, 1987, p. 30.

St. Louis Post- Dispatch, September 25, 2002, Jane Henderson, "Fans May Be Stuck in the '60s, but . . . Didion Has Moved on," p. D1.

San Francisco Chronicle, September 25, 2001, John M. Hubbell, "A Sharp Eye on Politics," p. B1.

San Francisco Review of Books, May, 1977.

Saturday Review, August 15, 1970; March 5, 1977; September 15, 1979; April 1982.

Sewanee Review, fall, 1977.

South Florida Sun-Sentinel, November 20, 2002, Chauncey Mabe, review of *Political Fictions.*

Star-Ledger (Newark, NJ), September 30, 2001, Jonathan Schell, review of *Political Fictions,* p. 5; October 14, 2001, Deborah Jerome-Cohen, review of *Political Fictions,* p. 5.

Time, August 10, 1970; March 28, 1977; August 20, 1979; April 4, 1983; May 7, 1984; June 29, 1992; March 4, 1996, Richard Corliss, review of *Up Close and Personal,* p. 63; September 9, 1996, Paul Gray, review of *The Last Thing He Wanted,* p. 69.

Times Literary Supplement, February 12, 1970; March 12, 1971; July 8, 1977; November 30, 1979; June 24, 1983; January 29, 1993, p. 10; November 5, 1993, p. 28.

Tribune Books (Chicago, IL), May 10, 1992, pp. 3, 7.

Variety, March 4, 1996, Leonard Klady, review of *Up Close and Personal,* p. 72.

Village Voice, February 28, 1977; June 25, 1979; May 26, 1992, pp. 74-76.

Vogue, April, 2002, Susan Orlean, interview with Joan Didion, p. 281.

Voice Literary Supplement, October 1987, pp. 21-22.

W, October, 2001, James Reginato, "Joan of Arch," p. 110.

Washington Post, April 8, 1983.

Washington Post Book World, June 17, 1979; March 13, 1983; April 15, 1984; May 10, 1992, p. 3.

Writer, March, 1999, Lewis Burke Frumkes, interview with Joan Didion, p. 14.

ONLINE

Metroactive, http://www.metroactive.com/ (July 10, 2003), "Why Ask Why?"

Salon.com, http://www.salon.com/ (July 10, 2003), interview with Joan Didion.

*   *   *

DILLARD, Annie 1945-

PERSONAL: Born April 30, 1945, in Pittsburgh, PA; daughter of Frank and Pam (Lambert) Doak; married Richard Dillard (a professor and writer), June 5, 1964 (divorced); married Gary Clevidence (a writer), April 12, 1980 (divorced); married Robert D. Richardson, Jr. (a professor and writer), 1988; children: (second marriage) Cody Rose; Carin, Shelly (stepchildren). *Education:* Hollins College, B.A., 1967, M.A., 1968. *Religion:* Roman Catholic

ADDRESSES: Agent—Timothy Seldes, Russell and Volkening, 50 West 29th St., New York, NY 10001.

CAREER: Writer and educator. *Harper's Magazine,* editor, 1973-85; Western Washington University, Bellingham, scholar-in-residence, 1975-79; Wesleyan University, Middletown, CT, distinguished visiting professor, 1979-81, full adjunct professor, 1983-98, writer-in-residence, 1987-98; professor emeritus, 1999—. Member of U.S. cultural delegation to China, 1982. Board member for various organizations, including Western States Arts Foundation, Milton Center, and Key West Literary Seminar; Wesleyan Writers' Conference, board member and chair, 1991—. Member, New York Public Library national literacy committee, National Committee for U.S.-China relations, and Catholic Commission on Intellectual and Cultural Affairs. Member of usage panel, *American Heritage Dictionary*; member of McNair Mentors Program; has served as a juror for various writing prizes, including Yale University Bollingen Prize, Pulitzer Prize in general nofiction, and PEN Martha Albrand Award in nonfiction.

MEMBER: International PEN, Poetry Society of America, Society of American Historians, National Association for the Advancement of Colored People, National Citizens for Public Libraries, Phi Beta Kappa.

AWARDS, HONORS: Pulitzer Prize in general nonfiction, 1975, for *Pilgrim at Tinker Creek;* New York Press Club Award for Excellence, 1975, for "Innocence in the Galapagos"; Washington State Governor's Award for Literature, 1977; grants from National Endowment for the Arts, 1982-83, and Guggenheim Foundation, 1985-86; *Los Angeles Times* Book Prize nomination, 1982, for *Living by Fiction;* honorary degrees from Boston College, 1986, and Connecticut College, and University of Hartford, both 1993; National Book Critics Circle Award nomination, 1987, for *An American Childhood*; Appalachian Gold Medallion, University of Charleston, 1989; St. Botolph's Club Foundation Award, 1989; English-Speaking Union Ambassador Book Award, 1989, for *The Writing Life;* Best Book of the 1980s, *Boston Globe,* for *Teaching a Stone to Talk;* Best Foreign Book Award (France), 1990, for *Pilgrim at Tinker Creek,* and 2002, for *For the Time Being*; History Maker Award, Historical Society of Western Pennsylvania, 1993; Connecticut Governor's Arts Award, 1993; Campion Medal, *America* magazine, 1994; Milton Prize, 1994; inducted into Connecticut Women's Hall of Fame, 1997; Academy Award in Literature, American Academy of Arts and Letters, 1998; fellow, American Academy of Arts and Letters, 1999.

WRITINGS:

Tickets for a Prayer Wheel (poems), University of Missouri Press (Columbia, MO), 1974.

Pilgrim at Tinker Creek (also see below), Harper's Magazine Press (New York, NY), 1974.

Holy the Firm (also see below), Harper (New York, NY), 1977.

The Weasel, Rara Avis Press (Claremont, CA), 1981.

Living by Fiction (also see below), Harper (New York, NY), 1982.

Teaching a Stone to Talk: Expeditions and Encounters (also see below), Harper (New York, NY), 1982.

Encounters with Chinese Writers, Wesleyan University Press (Middletown, CT), 1984.

An American Childhood (also see below), Harper (New York, NY), 1987.

(Editor, with Robert Atwan) *The Best American Essays, 1988,* Houghton Mifflin (Boston, MA), 1988.

The Annie Dillard Library (contains *Living by Fiction, An American Childhood, Holy the Firm, Pilgrim at Tinker Creek,* and *Teaching a Stone to Talk*), Harper (New York, NY), 1989.

The Writing Life (also see below), Harper (New York, NY), 1989.

Three by Annie Dillard (contains *Pilgrim at Tinker Creek, An American Childhood,* and *The Writing Life*), Harper (New York, NY), 1990.

The Living (novel), HarperCollins (New York, NY), 1992.

The Annie Dillard Reader, HarperCollins (New York, NY), 1994.

(Editor, with Cort Conley) *Modern American Memoirs,* HarperCollins (New York, NY), 1995.

Mornings Like This: Found Poems, HarperCollins (New York, NY), 1995.

For the Time Being, Knopf (New York, NY), 1999.

Also author of "Innocence in the Galapagos." Columnist, *Living Wilderness,* 1973-75. Contributing editor, *Harper's,* 1974-81, and 1983-85. Contributor to *Inventing the Truth: The Art and Craft of Memoir,* edited by William Zinsser, Houghton (Boston, MA), 1987. Contributor of fiction, essays, and poetry to numerous periodicals and anthologies, including *Atlantic Monthly, American Scholar, Poetry, Mill Mountain Review, Black Warrior Review, Esquire, Ploughshares, Yale Review, American Heritage, Antioch Review, Carolina Quarterly, TriQuarterly, North American Review, New York Times Magazine, New York Times Book Review, Chicago Review, The Lure of Tahiti, The Norton Reader,* and *Incarnation*

ADAPTATIONS: Several of Dillard's writings have been adapted as plays or as readings to accompany music and art.

SIDELIGHTS: Annie Dillard has carved a unique niche for herself in the world of American letters. Over the course of her career, Dillard has written essays, a memoir, poetry, literary criticism—even a Western novel. In whatever genre she works, Dillard distinguishes herself with her carefully wrought language, keen observations, and original, metaphysical insights. Her first significant publication, 1974's *Pilgrim at Tinker Creek,* drew numerous comparisons to Henry David Thoreau's *Walden;* in the years since, Dillard's name has come to stand for excellence in writing.

Tickets for a Prayer Wheel was Dillard's first publication. This slim volume of poetry—which expresses the author's yearning for a hidden God—was praised by reviewers. Within months of its appearance, however, Dillard's debut work was completely overshadowed by the release of her second, *Pilgrim at Tinker Creek.*

Dillard lived quietly on Tinker Creek in Virginia's Roanoke Valley, observing the natural world, taking notes, and reading voluminously in a wide variety of disciplines, including theology, philosophy, natural science, and physics. Following the progression of seasons, in *Pilgrim at Tinker Creek* she probes the cosmic significance of the beauty and violence coexisting in the natural world.

"One of the most pleasing traits of the book is the graceful harmony between scrutiny of real phenomena and the reflections to which that gives rise," noted a *Commentary* reviewer of *Pilgrim at Tinker Creek.* "Anecdotes of animal behavior become so effortlessly enlarged into symbols by the deepened insight of meditation. Like a true transcendentalist, Miss Dillard understands her task to be that of full alertness." Other critics found fault with Dillard's work, however, calling it self-absorbed or overwritten. Charles Deemer of the *New Leader,* for example, claimed that "if Annie Dillard had not spelled out what she was up to in this book, I don't think I would have guessed. . . . Her observations are typically described in overstatement reaching toward hysteria." A more charitable assessment came from Muriel Haynes of *Ms.* While finding Dillard to be "susceptible to fits of rapture," Haynes asserted that the author's "imaginative flights have the special beauty of surprise."

Dillard's next book delves into the metaphysical aspects of pain. *Holy the Firm* was inspired by the plight of one of her neighbors, a seven-year-old child who was badly burned in a plane crash. As Dillard reflects on the maimed child and on a moth consumed by flame, she struggles with the problem of reconciling faith in a loving God with the reality of a violent world. Only seventy-six pages long, *Holy the Firm* overflows with "great richness, beauty and power," according to Frederick Buechner in the *New York Times Book Review,* while *Atlantic* reviewer C. Michael Curtis found that "Dillard writes about the ferocity and beauty of natural order with . . . grace."

Elegant writing also distinguishes *Living by Fiction,* Dillard's fourth book, in which the author analyzes the differences between modernist and traditional fiction. "Everyone who timidly, bombastically, reverently, scholastically—even fraudulently—essays to live 'the life of the mind' should read this book," advised Carolyn See in the *Los Angeles Times.* See went on to describe *Living by Fiction* as "somewhere between scholarship, metaphysics, an acid trip and a wonderful conversation with a most smart person." "Whether the field of investigation is nature or fiction, Annie Dillard digs for ultimate meanings as instinctively and as determinedly as hogs for truffles," remarked *Washington Post Book World* contributor John Breslin. "The resulting upheaval can be disconcerting . . . still, uncovered morsels are rich and tasty."

Dillard returns again to reflecting on nature and religion in *Teaching a Stone to Talk: Expeditions and Encounters.* In minutely detailed descriptions of a solar eclipse, visits to South America and the Galapagos Islands, and other, more commonplace events and locations, she continues "the pilgrimage begun at Tinker Creek with an acuity of eye and ear that is matched by an ability to communicate a sense of wonder," according to Beaufort Cranford in the *Detroit News. Washington Post Book World* contributor Douglas Bauer was similarly pleased with the collection, judging Dillard's essays to be "almost uniformly splendid." In his estimation, Dillard's "art . . . is to move with the scrutinous eye through events and receptions that are random on their surfaces and to find, with grace and always-redeeming wit, the connections."

Dillard looked deeply into her past to produce another best-seller, *An American Childhood.* On one level, *An American Childhood* details the author's upbringing in an idiosyncratic, wealthy family; in another sense, the memoir tells the story of a young person's awakening to consciousness. In the words of *Washington Post* writer Charles Trueheart, Dillard's "memories of childhood are like her observations of nature: they feed her acrobatic thinking, and drive the free verse of her prose." Critics also applauded Dillard's keen insight into the unique perceptions of youth, as well as her exuberant spirit. "Loving and lyrical, nostalgic without being wistful, this is a book about the capacity for joy," stated *Los Angeles Times Book Review* contributor Cyra McFadden, while Noel Perrin of the *New York Times Book Review* observed that "Dillard has written an autobiography in semimystical prose about the growth of her own mind, and it's an exceptionally interesting account."

The activity that has occupied most of Dillard's adulthood serves as the subject of *The Writing Life.* With regard to content, *The Writing Life* is not a manual on craft nor a guide to getting published; rather, it is a study of a writer at work and the processes involved in that work. Among critics, the book drew mixed reaction. "Dillard is one of my favorite contemporary authors," Sara Maitland acknowledged in the *New York Times Book Review.* "Dillard is a wonderful writer and *The Writing Life* is full of joys. These are clearest to me when she comes at her subject tangentially, talking not of herself at her desk but of other parallel cases—the last chapter, a story about a stunt pilot who was an artist of air, is, quite simply, breathtaking. There are so many bits like this. . . . Unfortunately, the bits do not add up to a book." *Washington Post Book World* contributor Wendy Law-Yone voiced similar sentiments, finding the book "intriguing but not entirely satisfying" and "a sketch rather than a finished portrait." Nevertheless, the critic wondered, "Can anyone who has ever read Annie Dillard resist hearing what she has to say about writing? Her authority has been clear since *Pilgrim at Tinker Creek*—a mystic's wonder at the physical world expressed in beautiful, near-biblical prose."

Dillard ventured into new territory with her 1992 publication, *The Living,* a sprawling historical novel set in the Pacific Northwest. Reviewers hailed the author's first novel as masterful. "Her triumph is that this panoramic evocation of a very specific landscape and people might as well have been settled upon any other time and place—for this is, above all, a novel about the reiterant, precarious, wondrous, solitary, terrifying, utterly common condition of human life," exclaimed Molly Gloss in a review for the *Washington Post Book World.* Dillard's celebrated skill with words is also much in evidence here, according to Gloss, who noted that the author "uses language gracefully, releasing at times a vivid, startling imagery." Carol Anshaw concurred in the *Los Angeles Times Book Review:* "The many readers who have been drawn in the past to Dillard's work for its elegant and muscular language won't be disappointed in these pages."

Following the 1994 publication of *The Annie Dillard Reader,* a collection of poems, stories, and essays that prompted a *Publishers Weekly* reviewer to term Dillard "a writer of acute and singular observation," Dillard produced two works during 1995. *Modern American Memoirs,* which she edited with Cort Conley, is a collection of thirty-five pieces excerpted from various writers' memoirs. Authors whose work appears here include Ralph Ellison, Margaret Mead, Reynolds Price, Kate Simon, and Russell Baker. "Many of these memoirs are striking and memorable despite their brevity," commented Madeline Marget in a *Commonweal* review of the collection.

Mornings Like This: Found Poems, Dillard's other 1995 publication, is an experimental volume of verse. To create these poems, Dillard culled lines from other writers' prose works—Vincent Van Gogh's letters and a Boy Scout Handbook, for example—and "arranged" the lines "in such a way as to simulate a poem originating with a single author," explained John Haines in the *Hudson Review.* While commenting that Dillard's technique works better with humorous and joyful pieces than with serious ones, a *Publishers Weekly* critic added that "these co-op verses are never less than intriguing." Haines expressed concern over the implications of Dillard's experiment: "What does work like this say about the legitimacy of authorship?" He concluded, however, that "on the whole the collection has in places considerable interest."

In 1999 Dillard produced another book of theological musings that has been praised as a worthy successor to her earlier works in the genre. *For the Time Being* specifically addresses the questions of cruelty and suffering. In this volume, Dillard displays a fascination with statistics, quoting facts about the number of dead people in the earth versus the number of living; how many suicides take place each day; what percentage of the population is mentally retarded; and how many people die each day. She describes in clinical detail various birth defects, the wholesale slaughter of enemies practiced by rulers throughout history, and the ritual burial of thousands of living soldiers and concubines with deceased Chinese rulers. As Jean Bethke Elshtain put it in the *Journal of Religion,* the author "does this through a variety of genres that are not often on display in a single text. Weaving together poetry, vignette, ethnography, autobiography, history, theology, Dillard provides multiple entry points into the mysteries of time, history, natural calamity, and the possibility of grace." *For the Time Being* "is, among other things, an impressionist picture of [a] tempest-tossed world," remarked Michael J. Farrell in *National Catholic Reporter.* "The book is a

gradual unveiling of the world as Dillard is obsessed by it, which also, of course, is a gradual unveiling of the author." Maggie Mortimer noted in the *National Post* that *For the Time Being* "embodies the cryptic and the insightful," and that "*For the Time Being* sometimes reaches heights that can only be deemed inspirational."

"Few writers depict what's wrong with the world as vividly as Dillard," concluded Farrell. "At the end of the most brutal century in human history, we, weary, search desperately for the happy ending, the escape, while Dillard urges us not to turn away, coaxes us instead to look Life in the eye. . . . Relentlessly. Her books are one tour de force after another." Andre La-Sana, critiquing *For the Time Being* in *First Things,* described Dillard's work as "a valuable attempt to cut us loose from a complacent acceptance of life's enigmas."

BIOGRAPHICAL AND CRITICAL SOURCES:

BOOKS

Anderson, Chris, *Literary Nonfiction: Theory, Criticism, Pedagogy,* Southern Illinois University Press (Carbondale, IL), 1989.

Carnes, Mark C., *Novel History: Historians and Novelists Confront America's Past (and Each Other),* Simon & Schuster (New York, NY), pp. 109-118.

Contemporary Literary Criticism, Thomson Gale (Detroit, MI), Volume 9, 1978, Volume 60, 1990.

Detweiler, Robert, *Breaking the Fall: Religious Readings of Contemporary Fiction,* Harper (New York, NY), 1989.

Dictionary of Literary Biography Yearbook: 1980, Thomson Gale (Detroit, MI), 1981.

Elder, John, *Imagining the Earth: Poetry and the Vision of Nature,* University of Illinois Press (Chicago, IL), 1985.

Fritzell, Peter A., *Nature Writing and America: Essays on a Cultural Type,* Iowa State University Press (Ames, IA), 1990.

Hassen, Ihab, *Selves at Risk: Patterns of Quest in Contemporary American Letters,* University of Wisconsin Press (Madison, WI), 1991.

Johnson, Sandra Humble, *The Space Between: Literary Epiphany in the Works of Annie Dillard,* Kent State University Press (Kent, OH), 1992.

Lohafer, Susan, and Jo Ellyn Clarey, editors, *Short Story Theory at a Crossroads,* Louisiana State University Press (Baton Rouge, LA), 1989.

Parrish, Nancy C., *Lee Smith, Annie Dillard, and the Hollins Group: A Genesis of Writers,* Louisiana State University Press (Baton Rouge, LA), 1998.

Rainwater, Catherine, and William J. Scheick, editors, *Contemporary American Women Writers: Narrative Strategies,* University Press of Kentucky (Lexington, KY), 1985.

Slovac, Scott, *Seeking Awareness in American Nature Writing: Henry Thoreau, Annie Dillard, Edward Abbey, Wendell Berry, Barry Lopez,* University of Utah Press (Salt Lake City, UT), 1992.

Smith, Linda, *Annie Dillard,* Twayne (Boston, MA), 1991.

PERIODICALS

America, April 20, 1974; February 11, 1978, pp. 363-364; May 6, 1978, pp. 363-364; April 16, 1988, p. 411; November 25, 1989, p. 1; November 19, 1994, p. 2.

American Heritage, December, 1993, p. 104.

American Literature, March, 1987.

American Scholar, summer, 1990, p. 445.

Atlantic, December, 1977; October, 1984, p. 126.

Best Sellers, December, 1977.

Booklist, February 15, 1992, p. 1066; August, 1993, p. 2081; November 1, 1994, p. 530; November 15, 1994, p. 572; February 15, 1995, p. 1104; June 1, 1995, p. 1721; October 1, 1995, p. 245; February 1, 1999, p. 939.

Chicago Tribune, October 1, 1987.

Christian Century, November 14, 1984, p. 1062; June 7, 1989, p. 592; November 15, 1989, p. 1063; October 7, 1992, p. 871; June 4, 1997, p. 569.

Christianity Today, May 5, 1978, pp. 14-19, 30-31; January 5, 1983, p. 23; May 18, 1983, p. 483; July 15, 1983, p. 50; December 11, 1987, p. 58; April 8, 1988, p. 30; September 14, 1992, p. 46.

Commentary, October, 1974.

Commonweal, October 24, 1975, pp. 495-496; February 3, 1978; December 3, 1982, p. 668; November 6, 1987, p. 636; March 9, 1990, p. 151; April 5, 1996, p. 32.

Cross Currents, fall, 2000, Peggy Rosenthal, "Joking with Jesus in the Poetry of Kathleen Norris and Annie Dillard," p. 383.

Denver Quarterly, fall, 1985, Mary Davidson McConahay, "Into the Bladelike Arms of God: The Quest for Meaning through Symbolic Language in Thoreau and Annie Dillard," pp. 103-116.

Detroit News, October 31, 1982, p. 2H.

English Journal, April, 1989, p. 90; May 1, 1989, p. 69; December, 1989, Joan Bischoff, "Fellow Rebels: Annie Dillard and Maxine Hong Kingston," pp. 62-67.

Entertainment Weekly, August 7, 1992, p. 54.

Esquire, August, 1985, p. 123.

Fifty Plus, December, 1982, p. 56.

First Things, April, 2000, Andre LaSana, review of *For the Time Being,* p. 74.

Globe and Mail (Toronto, Ontario, Canada), November 28, 1987.

Hudson Review, winter, 1996, p. 666.

Journal of Religion, Jean Bethke Elshtain, review of *For the Time Being,* p. 541.

Library Journal, March 15, 1982, p. 638; September 1, 1982, p. 1660; November 15, 1984, p. 2150; September 1, 1987, p. 177; May 1, 1989, p. 69; March 1, 1992, p. 136; March 15, 1992, p. 124; July, 1992, p. 146; March 1, 1994, p. 138; April 1, 1994, p. 150; December, 1994, p. 155; May 15, 1995, p. 76; October 1, 1995, p. 83; April 1, 1999, p. 103.

Los Angeles Times, April 27, 1982; November 19, 1982.

Los Angeles Times Book Review, October 31, 1982, p. 2; November 18, 1984, p. 11; July 6, 1986, p. 10; September 20, 1987, pp. 1, 14; May 31, 1992, pp. 1, 7.

Mosaic, spring, 1989, Susan M. Felch, "Annie Dillard: Modern Physics in a Contemporary Mystic," pp. 1-14.

Ms., August, 1974; June, 1985, p. 62; December, 1985, p. 80; October, 1987, p. 78.

Nation, November 20, 1982, pp. 535-536; October 16, 1989, pp. 435-436; May 25, 1992, p. 692.

National Catholic Reporter, November 3, 1989, p. 14; May 11, 1990, p. 28; May 7, 1999, p. 29.

National Post, May 20, 2000, Maggie Mortimer, "Imparting New Meaning to the Personal Narrative," p. B8.

New Leader, June 24, 1974; November 2, 1987, p. 17; August 10, 1992, p. 17.

New Republic, April 6, 1974.

New Statesman, June 10, 1988, p. 42; December 23, 1988, p. 30; November 9, 1990, p. 34.

Newsweek, June 8, 1992, p. 57.

New Yorker, May 17, 1982, p. 140; February 14, 1983, p. 118; December 25, 1989, p. 106; July 6, 1992, p. 80.

New York Times, September 21, 1977; March 12, 1982, p. C18; November 25, 1982, p. C18.

New York Times Book Review, March 24, 1974, pp. 4-5; September 25, 1977, pp. 12, 40; July 1, 1979, p. 21; May 9, 1982, pp. 10, 22-23; July 4, 1982, p. 38; November 28, 1982, pp. 13, 19; December 5, 1982, p. 34; January 1, 1984, p. 32; September 23, 1984, p. 29; September 27, 1987, p. 7; September 17, 1989, p. 15; April 26, 1992, p. 34; May 3, 1992, p. 9; March 28, 1999, p. 9.

New York Times Magazine, April 26, 1992, p. 34.

Old Northwest, winter, 1989-90, Eugene H. Pattison, "The Great Lakes Childhood: The Experience of William Dean Howells and Annie Dillard," pp. 311-329.

People, October 19, 1987, p. 99; July 20, 1992, p. 27.

Progressive, June, 1982, p. 61; December, 1987, p. 31.

Publishers Weekly, January 29, 1982, p. 60; July 20, 1984, p. 73; July 24, 1987, p. 180; September 23, 1988, p. 70; July 14, 1989, p. 62; September 1, 1989, pp. 67-68; February 24, 1992, p. 41; July 6, 1992, p. 22; April 4, 1994, p. 15; October 31, 1994, p. 45; April 24, 1995, p. 65.

Reason, April, 1990, p. 56.

Religion and Literature, summer, 1985, David Lavery, review of *Living by Fiction, Teaching a Stone to Talk,* and *Encounters with Chinese Writers,* pp. 61-68.

Saturday Review, March, 1982, p. 64; April, 1986, p. 64; May-June, 1986, p. 23.

School Library Journal, April, 1988, p. 122.

Smithsonian, November, 1982, p. 219.

South Atlantic Quarterly, spring, 1986, pp. 111-122.

Studia Mystica, fall, 1983, Joseph Keller, "The Function of Paradox in Mystical Discourse."

Theology Today, July, 1986, Eugene H. Peterson, "Annie Dillard: With Her Eyes Open," pp. 178-191.

Threepenny Review, summer, 1988.

Time, March 18, 1974; October 10, 1977.

Tribune Books (Chicago, IL), September 12, 1982, p. 7; November 21, 1982, p. 5; September 13, 1987, pp. 1, 12; December 18, 1988, p. 3; August 27, 1989, p. 6.

U.S. Catholic, September, 1992, p. 48.

Village Voice, July 13, 1982, pp. 40-41.

Virginia Quarterly Review, autumn, 1974, pp. 637-640; spring, 1996, p. 57.

Washington Post, October 28, 1987.

Washington Post Book World, October 16, 1977, p. E6; April 4, 1982, p. 4; January 2, 1983, p. 6; September 9, 1984, p. 6; July 6, 1986, p. 13; September 6, 1987, p. 11; August 14, 1988, p. 12; August 27, 1989, p. 6; September 24, 1989, p. 4, May 3, 1992, pp. 1-2.

Writer's Digest, April, 1989, p. 53.

Yale Review, October, 1992, p. 102.

*   *   *

DISCH, Thomas M. 1940-
  (Thom Demijohn, a joint pseudonym, Thomas Michael Disch, Tom Disch, Leonie Hargrave, Cassandra Knye, a joint pseudonym)

PERSONAL: Born February 2, 1940, in Des Moines, IA; son of Felix Henry and Helen (Gilbertson) Disch.

Education: Attended Cooper Union and New York University, 1959-62.

ADDRESSES: Agent—Karpfinger Agency, 500 Fifth Ave., Ste. 2800, New York, NY 10110.

CAREER: Writer, 1964—. Majestic Theatre, New York City, part-time checkroom attendant, 1957-62; Doyle Dane Bernbach, New York City, copywriter, 1963-64; theater critic for *Nation,* 1987-91; theater critic for the *New York Daily News,* 1993—. Artist-in-residence, College of William and Mary, 1996—. Lecturer at universities.

MEMBER: P.E.N, National Book Critics Circle (board member, 1988-91, secretary, 1989-91), Writers Guild East.

AWARDS, HONORS: O. Henry Prize, 1975, for story "Getting into Death," and 1979, for story "Xmas"; John W. Campbell Memorial Award, and American Book Award nomination, both 1980, both for *On Wings of Song;* Hugo Award and Nebula Award nominations, 1980, and British Science Fiction Award, 1981, all for novella *The Brave Little Toaster.*

WRITINGS:

NOVELS

The Genocides, Berkley Publishing (New York City), 1965, Vintage Books (New York, NY), 2000.

Mankind under the Leash (expanded version of his short story, *"White Fang Goes Dingo"* [also see below]), Ace Books (New York City), 1966, published in England as *The Puppies of Terra,* Panther Books, 1978.

(With John Sladek under joint pseudonym Cassandra Knye) *The House That Fear Built,* Paperback Library, 1966.

Echo Round His Bones, Berkley Publishing, 1967.

(With Sladek under joint pseudonym Thom Demijohn) *Black Alice,* Doubleday (New York City), 1968.

Camp Concentration, Hart-Davis, 1968, Doubleday, 1969.

The Prisoner, Ace Books, 1969.

334, MacGibbon & Kee, Avon (New York City), 1974, Vintage Books (New York, NY), 1999.

(Under pseudonym Leonie Hargrave) *Clara Reeve,* Knopf (New York City), 1975.

On Wings of Song, St. Martin's (New York City), 1979, Vintage Books (New York, NY), 2002.

Triplicity (omnibus volume), Doubleday, 1980.

(With Charles Naylor) *Neighboring Lives,* Scribner, 1981.

The Businessman: A Tale of Terror, Harper, 1984.

Amnesia (computer-interactive novel), Electronic Arts, 1985.

The Silver Pillow: A Tale of Witchcraft, M.V. Ziesing (Willimantic, CT), 1987.

The M.D.: A Horror Story, Knopf, 1991.

The Priest: A Gothic Romance, Knopf, 1995.

The Sub: A Study in Witchcraft, Knopf, 1999.

STORY COLLECTIONS

One Hundred and Two H-Bombs and Other Science Fiction Stories (also see below), Compact Books (Hollywood, FL), 1966, revised edition published as *One Hundred and Two H-Bombs,* Berkeley Publishing, 1969, published in England as *White Fang Goes Dingo and Other Funny S.F. Stories,* Arrow Books, 1971.

Under Compulsion, Hart-Davis, 1968, also published as *Fun with Your New Head,* Doubleday, 1969.

Getting into Death: The Best Short Stories of Thomas M. Disch, Hart-Davis, 1973, revised edition, Knopf, 1976.

The Early Science Fiction Stories of Thomas M. Disch (includes *Mankind under the Leash* and *One Hundred and Two H-Bombs*), Gregg (Boston, MA), 1977.

Fundamental Disch, Bantam, 1980.

The Man Who Had No Idea, Bantam, 1982.

POETRY

(With Marilyn Hacker and Charles Platt) *Highway Sandwiches,* privately printed, 1970.

The Right Way to Figure Plumbing, Basilisk Press, 1972.

ABCDEFG HIJKLM NOPQRST UVWXYZ, Anvil Press Poetry (Millville, MN), 1981.

Orders of the Retina, Toothpaste Press (West Branch, IA), 1982.

Burn This, Hutchinson, 1982.

Here I Am, There You Are, Where Were We?, Hutchinson, 1984.

Yes, Let's: New and Selected Poetry, Johns Hopkins University Press (Baltimore, MD), 1989.

Dark Verses and Light, Johns Hopkins University Press, 1991.

(Under name Tom Disch) *A Child's Garden of Grammar,* University Press of New England (Hanover, NH), 1997.

JUVENILE

The Tale of Dan de Lion: A Fable, Coffee House Press, 1986.

The Brave Little Toaster: A Bedtime Story for Small Appliances, Doubleday, 1986.

The Brave Little Toaster Goes to Mars, Doubleday, 1988.

EDITOR

(Ghost editor with Robert Arthur) *Alfred Hitchcock Presents: Stories that Scared Even Me,* Random House, 1967.

The Ruins of the Earth: An Anthology of Stories of the Immediate Future, Putnam, 1971.

Bad Moon Rising: An Anthology of Political Foreboding, Harper, 1975.

(With Naylor) *New Constellations: An Anthology of Tomorrow's Mythologies,* Harper, 1976.

(With Naylor) *Strangeness: A Collection of Curious Tales,* Scribner, 1977.

Ringtime (short story), Toothpaste Press, 1983.

(Author of introduction) Michael Bishop, *One Winter in Eden,* Arkham House (Sauk City, WI), 1984.

Torturing Mr. Amberwell (short story), Cheap Street (New Castle, VA), 1985.

(Author of preface) Pamela Zoline, *The Heat Death of the Universe and Other Stories,* McPherson & Company (New Paltz, NY), 1988.

(Author of introduction) Philip K. Dick, *The Penultimate Truth,* Carroll & Graf, 1989.

The Castle of Indolence: On Poetry, Poets, and Poetasters, Picador (New York City), 1995.

Also editor of *The New Improved Sun: An Anthology of Utopian Science Fiction,* 1975.

OTHER

(Adaptor) *Ben Hur* (play), first produced in New York City, 1989.

The Cardinal Detoxes (verse play), first produced in New York City by RAPP Theater Company, 1990.

The Dreams Our Stuff Is Made Of: How Science Fiction Conquered the World, Simon & Schuster, 1998.

The Castle of Perseverance: Job Opportunities in Contemporary Poetry, University of Michigan Press (Ann Arbor, MI), 2002.

On SF, University of Michigan Press (Ann Arbor, MI), 2005.

Also librettist of *The Fall of the House of Usher* (opera), produced in New York City, 1979, and of *Frankenstein* (opera), produced in Greenvale, NY, 1982.

Contributor to *Science Fiction at Large,* edited by Peter Nicholls, Harper, 1976. Also contributor to numerous anthologies. Also contributor to periodicals, including *Playboy, Poetry,* and *Harper's.* Regular reviewer for *Times Literary Supplement* and *Washington Post Book World.*

ADAPTATIONS: The Brave Little Toaster was produced as an animated film by Hyperion-Kushner-Lockec, 1987.

SIDELIGHTS: An author of science fiction, poetry, historical novels, opera librettos, and computer-interactive fiction, [Thomas M.] Disch has been cited as "one of the most remarkably talented writers around" by a reviewer for the *Washington Post Book World.* Disch began his career writing science fiction stories that featured dark themes and disturbing plots. Many of Disch's early themes reappear in his short stories and poetry; the result, according to Blake Morrison in the *Times Literary Supplement,* is "never less than enjoyable and accomplished." While many of his best-known works are aimed at an adult audience, Disch is also the author of well-received children's fiction, including two fantasies, *The Brave Little Toaster* and *The Brave Little Toaster Goes to Mars.*

Disch grew up in Minnesota and graduated from high school in St. Paul. As a youngster he devoured horror comic books and science fiction magazines, including the influential *Astounding Science Fiction.* He learned his craft by reading and re-reading the work of authors such as Robert A. Heinlein and Isaac Asimov—found in the pages of *Astounding Science Fiction.* After a series of low-paying jobs in Minnesota (which included employment as night watchman in a funeral parlor), Disch moved to New York City. While living there, he worked as a checkroom attendant and advertising copywriter. His first fiction appeared in a magazine called

Fantastic Stories in 1962. Between that periodical and another one called *Amazing Stories* he would publish nine more stories that year and the next. Although Disch has admitted to not thinking that highly of his first publishing success, he found his second effort at writing a full-length story more satisfactory. This story, titled "White Fang Goes Dingo," was first published in its short form, then in an expanded version as the author's second novel, *Mankind under the Leash* (later published under the title Disch prefers, *The Puppies of Terra*).

In 1964, having secured an advance from Berkley Books, Disch left advertising to become a full-time writer. He published his first novel the following year, a science fiction tale titled *The Genocides.* In large part the story of an alien invasion of Earth, *The Genocides* describes the last grim days of human existence, an existence where people are reduced to little more than insects in the aliens' global garden. Critics found the book frightening. "The novel . . . is powerful in the way that it forces the reader to alter his perspective, to reexamine what it means to be human," wrote Erich S. Rupprecht in the *Dictionary of Literary Biography.* Disch followed *The Genocides* with a series of thought-provoking science fiction tales, such as *Camp Concentration* and *334,* as well as horror novels such as *The Businessman* and *The M.D.*

Camp Concentration, 334, and *On Wings of Song* are widely considered Disch's best works. All three appeared in a mid-1980s survey by David Pringle titled *Science Fiction: The 100 Best Novels. Camp Concentration* is set at a secret prison camp run by the U.S. Army where selected prisoners are being treated with a new drug that increases their intelligence. Unfortunately, this drug also causes the prisoners' early deaths. The novel is in the form of a diary kept by one of the prisoners. The diary's style grows more complex as the narrative develops, reflecting the prisoner's increasing intelligence. Rupprecht drew a parallel between *Camp Concentration* and *The Genocides.* In both novels, he argues, the characters must survive inescapable situations. Disch's continuing theme, Rupprecht summarizes, is "charting his characters' attempts to keep themselves intact in a world which grows increasingly hostile, irrational, inhuman."

This theme is also found in *334,* a novel set in a New York City housing project of the future. Divided into six loosely related sections, the novel presents the daily lives of residents of the building, which is located at 334 East Eleventh Street. The characters live in boredom and poverty; their city is rundown and dirty. In his analysis of the book Rupprecht noted the similarity between the novel's setting and the world of the present. He found *334* to be "a slightly distorted mirror image of contemporary life." Although the *Washington Post Book World* reviewer judged the setting to be "an interesting, plausible and unpleasant near-future world where urban life is even more constricted than now," he nonetheless believed that "survival and aspiration remain possible." Rupprecht praises *334* as Disch's "most brilliant and disturbing work. . . . One can think of few writers—of science fiction or other genres—who could convey a similar sense of emptiness, of yearning, of ruin with this power and grace. . . . Like all great writers, Disch forces his readers to see the reality of their lives in a way that is fresh, startling, disturbing, and moving."

Like *334, On Wings of Song* deals with a future time that resembles our own. Describing the general atmosphere of the novel in the *New York Times Book Review,* Gerald Jonas noted: "Politically and economically, things seem to be going downhill, but in between crises, people can still assure themselves that they are living in 'normal' times." In the *Village Voice,* John Calvin Batchelor called *On Wings of Song* Disch's "grandest work." The critic maintains that the novel links Disch with other great social critics of the past, including H.G. Wells and George Orwell. "Disch," he wrote, "is an unapologetic political writer, a high-minded liberal democrat, who sees doom in Western Civilization and says so, often with bizarre, bleak scenarios."

Continuing to explore many literary avenues, in the 1980s and 1990s Disch published novels, stories, poetry, a libretto and an interactive computer novel. Three novels published during this period, the first of the "Supernatural Minnesota" series, further the social criticism seen in earlier works. In *The Businessman: A Tale of Terror, The M.D.: A Horror Story,* and *The Priest: A Gothic Romance,* Disch combines classic thriller techniques with a critical look at the corruption he sees in the three professions mentioned in the titles. The plots are replete with the type of strange occurrences Disch's readers have grown to expect, and the works show Disch's usual blend of styles. Writing about *The M.D.* in *Kliatt,* Larry W. Prater noted: "The novel combines elements of the macabre, of fantasy and of SF." Evidently, in life as well as literature, categories aren't important to Disch. In a *Publishers Weekly* interview with David Finkle, Disch refuses to see *The M.D.* as just a horror novel and with equal fervor defends his right to remain unburdened by a convenient label. "Every book has its own slightly different ground rules from the others," he maintained. "As long as the book plays by its own rules and those are clear, I don't think genre borderlines are especially helpful. I don't spend my life trying to determine what category I'm in." Disch told Platt: "Part of my notion of a proper ambition is that one should excel at a wide range of tasks."

Disch's 1999 novel *The Sub: A Study in Witchcraft* continues his "Supernatural Minnesota" series. The story revolves around Diana Turney, a substitute teacher who has recovered memories of being molested as a child at the hands of her father. Diana soon realizes that she is in control of a potent witchcraft—she is able to turn men into their totem animals, i.e., the animal they most resemble in personality. Critical reaction to the novel was largely positive. Alicia Graybill in *Library Journal* recommended the book, citing its "memorable characters and . . . darkly humorous plot." Though *New York Times Book Review* critic Scott Sutherland faulted the work for being too laden with allusions, a *Publishers Weekly* reviewer claimed the work "builds on the achievement of its predecessors and secures [Disch's] tenure as the [Jonathan] Swift of supernatural satire."

The variety found in Disch's novels and stories also extends to his poetry and work for children. Disch's work as a children's author includes titles such as *The Brave Little Toaster* and *The Tale of Dan de Lion.* In these works, Disch fully embraces the fantastic. *The Brave Little Toaster* tells the story of a group of small appliances—(including the toaster, a clock radio, and an electric blanket)—who come to life in order to search for their missing master. *The Tale of Dan de Lion,* presented in a series of couplets, concerns the adventures of a dandelion, his weedy family, and the rose breeder who wants to destroy them. Critics praised Disch's children's works both for the author's use of language and sense of whimsy. *The Brave Little Toaster* gained further recognition when it was produced as a popular animated film in 1987.

BIOGRAPHICAL AND CRITICAL SOURCES:

BOOKS

Aldiss, Brian W., *Trillion Year Spree: The History of Science Fiction,* Atheneum, 1986.

Bleiler, E. F., editor, *Science Fiction Writers: Critical Studies of the Major Authors from the Early Nineteenth Century to the Present Day,* Scribner, 1982, pp. 351-56.

Children's Literature Review, Volume 18, Thomson Gale (Detroit), 1989.

Contemporary Literary Criticism, Thomson Gale, Volume 7, 1977, pp. 86-87; Volume 36, 1986, pp. 123-28.

Contemporary Poets, St. James Press (Chicago), 5th edition, 1991.

Delany, Samuel R., *The American Shore: Meditations on a Tale of Science Fiction by Thomas M. Disch,* Dragon (Elizabethtown, NY), 1978.

Dictionary of Literary Biography, Volume 8: *Twentieth-Century Science Fiction Writers,* Thomson Gale, 1981, pp. 148-54.

Something about the Author Autobiography Series, Volume 15, Thomson Gale, 1993, pp. 107-23.

Stephens, Christopher P.,*A Checklist of Thomas M. Disch,* Ultramarine (Hastings-on-Hudson, NY), 1991.

PERIODICALS

Atlantic Monthly, June, 1998, p. 114.

Booklist, April, 1998, p. 1293; April 15, 1999, p. 1451.

Kliatt, September, 1992, p. 20.

Library Journal, April 15, 1998, p. 78; June 1, 1999, p. 172.

Los Angeles Times, February 3, 1981; November 21, 1982, p. 13; August 13, 1989, p. 3.

Nation, June 15, 1998.

New Statesman, July 13, 1984, p. 28.

Newsweek, March 9, 1981; July 2, 1984; July 11, 1988, pp. 66-67.

New York Times Book Review, March 21, 1976, p. 6; October 28, 1979, p. 15, 18; August 26, 1984, p. 31; April 20, 1986, p. 29; August 9, 1998; August 1, 1999.

Publishers Weekly, January 7, 1974, p. 56; January 5, 1976, p. 59; August 29, 1980, p. 363; April 19, 1991, pp. 48-49; April 20, 1998, p. 54; May 31, 1999, p. 63.

Reason, August-September, 1998.

Science Fiction Chronicle, February, 1993, p. 35.

Spectator, May 1, 1982, p. 23.

Time, July 28, 1975; February 9, 1976, pp. 83-84; July 9, 1984, pp. 85-86.

Times Literary Supplement, February 15, 1974, p. 163; June 12, 1981, p. 659; August 27, 1982, p. 919; May 25, 1984, p. 573; November 28, 1986, p. 343; September 15-21, 1989, p. 1000; November 11, 1994, p. 19.

Tribune Books, (Chicago) March 22, 1982.

Village Voice, August 27-September 2, 1980, pp. 35-36.

Voice of Youth Advocates, April, 1981, p. 39.

Washington Post, September 23, 1979, p. 7.

Washington Post Book World, July 26, 1981, pp. 6-7; August 6, 1989, p. 5.

*   *   *

DISCH, Thomas Michael
See DISCH, Thomas M.

*   *   *

DISCH, Tom
See DISCH, Thomas M.

*   *   *

DOCTOROW, Edgar Laurence
See DOCTOROW, E.L.

*   *   *

DOCTOROW, E.L. 1931-
(Edgar Laurence Doctorow)

PERSONAL: Born January 6, 1931, in New York, NY; son of David R. (a music store proprietor) and Rose (a pianist; maiden name, Levine) Doctorow; married Helen Esther Setzer (a writer), August 20, 1954; children: Jenny, Caroline, Richard. *Education:* Kenyon College, A.B. (with honors), 1952; Columbia University, graduate study, 1952- 53.

ADDRESSES: Home—New Rochelle, NY. *Office*—Department of English, New York University, 19 University Pl., New York, NY, 10003. *Agent*—Amanda Urban, I.C.M., 40 West 57th St., New York, NY 10019. *E-mail*—eld1@nyu.edu.

CAREER: New American Library, New York, NY, senior editor, 1959-64; Dial Press, New York, NY, editor-in-chief, 1964-69, vice president and publisher, 1968-69; University of California—Irvine, writer-in-residence, 1969-70; Sarah Lawrence College, Bronxville, NY, member of faculty, 1971-78; New York University, New York, NY, Glucksman Professor of English and American Letters, 1982—. Script reader, Columbia Pictures Industries, Inc., 1956-58; creative writing fellow, Yale School of Drama, 1974-75; visiting professor, University of Utah, 1975; visiting senior fellow, Princeton University, 1980-81. *Military service:* U.S. Army, Signal Corps, 1953- 55.

MEMBER: American Academy and Institute of Arts and Letters, Authors Guild, PEN, Writers Guild of America, Century Association.

AWARDS, HONORS: Guggenheim fellowship, 1973; Creative Artists Service fellow, 1973-74; National Book Critics Circle Award and American Academy of Arts and Letters award, 1976, both for *Ragtime;* L.H.D., Kenyon College, 1976; Litt.D., Hobart and William Smith Colleges, 1979; National Book Critics Circle Award, 1982, for *Loon Lake,* and 1989, for *Billy Bathgate;* National Book Award, 1986, for *World's Fair;* L.H.D., Brandeis University, 1989; Edith Wharton Citation of Merit for Fiction, and New York State Author, both 1989-91; PEN/Faulkner Award, and William Dean Howells Medal, American Academy of Arts and Letters, both 1990, both for *Billy Bathgate;* National Humanities Medal, 1998; PEN/Faulkner Award, and National Book Critics Circle prize for fiction, both 2006, both for *The March.*

WRITINGS:

NOVELS

Welcome to Hard Times, Simon & Schuster (New York, NY), 1960, published as *Bad Man from Bodie,* Deutsch (London, England), 1961.

Big as Life, Simon & Schuster (New York, NY), 1966.

The Book of Daniel, Random House (New York, NY), 1971, new edition, Modern Library (New York, NY), 2005.

Ragtime, Random House (New York, NY), 1975.

Loon Lake, Random House (New York, NY), 1980.

World's Fair, Random House (New York, NY), 1985.

Billy Bathgate, Random House (New York, NY), 1989.

Three Complete Novels, Wings (New York, NY), 1994.

The Waterworks, Random House (New York, NY), 1994.

City of God, Random House (New York, NY), 2000.

The March, Random House (New York, NY), 2005.

OTHER

Drinks before Dinner (play; first produced off-Broadway at Public Theater, 1978), Random House (New York, NY), 1979.

(Author of text) *American Anthem,* photographs by Jean-Claude Suares, Stewart, Tabori & Chang (New York, NY), 1982.

Daniel (screenplay; based on author's *The Book of Daniel;* also see below), Paramount, 1983.

Lives of the Poets: Six Stories and a Novella, Random House (New York, NY), 1984.

(Author of text) Eric Fischl, *Scenes and Sequences: Fifty-eight Monotypes* (limited edition), Peter Blum (New York, NY), 1989.

Reading and Interview (sound recording), American Audio Prose Library (Columbia, MO), 1991.

The People's Text: A Citizen Reads the Constitution (limited edition), with wood engravings by Barry Moser, Nouveau Press (Jackson, MS), 1992.

Jack London, Hemingway, and the Constitution: Selected Essays, 1977-1992, Random House (New York, NY), 1993.

(Editor, with Katrina Kenison) *The Best American Short Stories 2000,* Houghton Mifflin (Boston, MA), 2000.

(Author of text) *Lamentation 9/11,* photographs by David Finn, Ruder-Finn Press (New York, NY), 2002.

Reporting the Universe (essays), Harvard University Press (Cambridge, MA), 2003.

Three Screenplays (includes *Daniel, Ragtime,* and *Loon Lake*), introduction, commentaries, and interviews by Paul Levine, Johns Hopkins University Press (Baltimore, MD), 2003.

Sweet Land Stories (short stories), Random House (New York, NY), 2004.

ADAPTATIONS: In 1967 Metro-Goldwyn-Mayer produced a movie version of *Welcome to Hard Times,* written and directed by Burt Kennedy and starring Henry Fonda. Doctorow was involved, for a time, with the film version of *Ragtime,* released in 1981 and directed by Milos Forman from a screenplay by Michael Weller; it starred James Cagney in his last screen performance. *Ragtime* was adapted as a musical, with book by Terrence McNally and music and lyrics by Stephen Flahery and Lynn Ahrens, and produced on Broadway in 1998. A film of *Billy Bathgate,* written by Tom Stoppard, directed by Robert Benton, and starring Dustin Hoffman, Nicole Kidman, and Bruce Willis, was released by Touchstone in 1991.

SIDELIGHTS: E.L. Doctorow is a highly regarded novelist and playwright known for his serious philosophical probings, the subtlety and variety of his prose style, and his unusual use of historical figures in fictional works, among them Julius and Ethel Rosenberg in *The Book of Daniel,* Emma Goldman, Harry Houdini, J.P. Morgan, and others in *Ragtime,* and Dutch Schultz in *Billy Bathgate.* Novelist Anne Tyler called Doctorow "a sort of human time machine" in an assessment of the latter novel for the *New York Times Book Review. Times Literary Supplement* critic Stephen Fender, meanwhile, observed that "The project of Doctorow's fiction has been to deconstruct crucial episodes in American political history and to rebuild them out of . . . his own speculative imagination," and *Listener* commentator Andrew Clifford remarked that "Doctorow's trademark of using historical fact to brew up brilliantly imaginative fiction has helped him stake a claim to be the present-day Great American Novelist." His work as a teacher and editor and his nonfiction essays on social and political issues have further contributed to Doctorow's reputation as one of the most important literary figures of the late twentieth century.

Doctorow's father, a lover of literature, named his son after Edgar Allan Poe. Young Edgar quickly developed a passion for words as well; he was in third grade when he decided to make writing his career, he once told an interviewer. He wrote plays while serving in the U.S. Army, and when he left the service he got a job as a script reader for Columbia Pictures, an assignment that led to his first novel, *Welcome to Hard Times.* In an interview for the *Miami Herald,* he told Jonathan Yardley that he "was accursed to read things that were submitted to this company and write synopses of them . . . . I had to suffer one lousy Western after another, and it occurred to me that I could lie about the West in a much more interesting way than any of these people were lying. I wrote a short story, and it subsequently became the first chapter of that novel."

The resulting book, unlike many Westerns, is concerned with serious issues. As Wirt Williams noted in the *New York Times Book Review,* the novel addresses "one of the favorite problems of philosophers: the relationship of man and evil . . . . Perhaps the primary theme of the novel is that evil can only be resisted psychically: when the rational controls that order man's existence slacken, destruction comes. [Joseph] Conrad said it best in *Heart of Darkness,* but Mr. Doctorow has said it impressively. His book is taut and dramatic, exciting and successfully symbolic." Similarly, Kevin Stan, writing in the *New Republic,* remarked that *Welcome to Hard Times* "is a superb piece of fiction: lean and mean, and thematically significant . . . . [Doctorow] takes the thin, somewhat sordid and incipiently depressing materials of the Great Plains experience and fashions them into a myth of good and evil . . . . He does it marvelously, with economy and with great narrative power."

After writing a Western of sorts, Doctorow turned to another form not usually heralded by critics: science fiction. In *Big as Life* two naked human giants material-

ize in New York harbor. The novel examines the ways in which its characters deal with a seemingly impending catastrophe. Like *Welcome to Hard Times, Big as Life* won substantial critical approval. A *Choice* reviewer, for example, commented that "Doctorow's deadpan manner . . . turns from satire to tenderness and human concern. A performance closer to James Purdy than to [George] Orwell or [Aldous] Huxley, but in a minor key." In spite of praise from critics, however, *Big as Life,* like *Welcome to Hard Times,* was not a significant commercial success.

The Book of Daniel, Doctorow's third book, uses yet another traditional form: the historical novel. It is a fictional account based on the relationship between Julius and Ethel Rosenberg and their children. The Rosenbergs were Communists who were convicted of and executed for conspiracy to commit treason. Many feel that they were victims of the sometimes hysterical anticommunist fever of the 1950s. As with *Welcome to Hard Times* and *Big as Life,* Doctorow modified the traditional form to suit his purposes. The work is not an examination of the guilt or innocence of the Rosenbergs but, as David Emblidge observed in *Southwest Review,* a look at the central character Daniel's psychology, his attempts to deal with the trauma he suffered from his parents' death. Thus many critics considered the book, unlike typical historical novels, to be largely independent of historical fact. In *Partisan Review,* Jane Richmond wrote that "if Julius and Ethel Rosenberg had never existed, the book would be just as good as it is." In like manner, Stanley Kauffmann, in the *New Republic,* remarked, "I haven't looked up the facts of the Rosenberg case; it would be offensive to the quality of this novel to check it against those facts."

Kauffmann joined several other critics in deeming *The Book of Daniel* a novel of high quality indeed. Kauffmann termed it "the political novel of our age, the best American work of its kind that I know since Lionel Trilling's *The Middle of the Journey.*" P. S. Prescott in *Newsweek* added that *The Book of Daniel* is "a purgative book, angry and more deeply felt than all but a few contemporary American novels, a novel about defeat, impotent rage, the passing of the burden of suffering through generations . . . . There is no question here of our suspending disbelief, but rather how when we have finished, we may regain stability." And Richmond called it "a brilliant achievement and the best contemporary novel I've read since reading Frederick Exley's *A Fan's Notes. . . .* It is a book of infinite detail and tender attention to the edges of life as well as to its dead center."

In *Ragtime* Doctorow delves further into historical territory. The novel interweaves the lives of an upper-middle-class white family, a poor European immigrant family, and the family of a black ragtime musician together with historical figures such as Morgan, Houdini, Goldman, Henry Ford, and Evelyn Nesbit. Doctorow shows famous people involved in unusual, sometimes ludicrous, situations. In the *Washington Post Book World*, Raymond Sokolov noted that "Doctorow turns history into myth and myth into History . . . . [He] continually teases our suspicion of literary artifice with apparently true historical description . . . . On the one hand, the 'fact' tugs one toward taking the episode as history. On the other, the doubt that lingers makes one want to take the narrative as an invention." Sokolov argued that Doctorow "teases" the reader in order to make him try "to sort out what the author is doing. That is, we find ourselves paying Doctorow the most important tribute. We watch to see what he is doing."

Newsweek's Walter Clemons also found himself teased by *Ragtime*'s historical episodes: "The very fact that the book stirs one to parlor-game research is amusing evidence that Doctorow has already won the game: I found myself looking up details because I wanted them to be true." George Stade, in the *New York Times Book Review*, expressed an opinion similar to Sokolov's. "In this excellent novel," Stade wrote, "silhouettes and rags not only make fiction out of history but also reveal the fictions out of which history is made. It incorporates the fictions and realities of the era of ragtime while it rags our fictions about it. It is an anti-nostalgic novel that incorporates our nostalgia about its subject."

Ragtime also is a deeply political story, and some reviewers, especially those writing for conservative publications, looked less than favorably on its political viewpoint, considering it far-left and simplistic. Hilton Kramer of *Commentary*, for instance, thought that "the villains in *Ragtime*, drawn with all the subtlety of a William Gropper cartoon, are all representatives of money, the middle class, and white ethnic prejudice . . . . *Ragtime* is a political romance . . . . The major fictional characters . . . are all ideological inventions, designed to serve the purposes of a political fable." Similarly, Jeffrey Hart, writing in the *National Review*, made the case that Doctorow judges his revolutionary and minority characters much less harshly than the middle-and upper-class figures, which results in "what can be called left-wing pastoral," a form of sentimentality.

In *Loon Lake* Doctorow continues to experiment with prose style and to evoke yet another period in American history: the Great Depression. The novel's plot revolves

around the various relationships between an industrial tycoon, his famous aviatrix wife, gangsters and their entourage, an alcoholic poet, and Joe, a young drifter who stumbles onto the tycoon's opulent residence in the Adirondack Mountains of New York State. The novel works on several levels with "concentrically expanding ripples of implication," according to Robert Towers in the *New York Times Book Review*. For the most part, however, it is Doctorow's portrait of the American dream versus the American reality that forms the novel's core. As Christopher Lehmann-Haupt of the *New York Times* explained, *Loon Lake* "is a complex and haunting meditation on modern American history."

Time contributor Paul Gray believed that "Doctorow is . . . playing a variation on an old theme: The American dream, set to the music of an American nightmare, the Depression." Lehmann-Haupt saw a similar correlation and elaborated, "This novel could easily have been subtitled *An American Tragedy Revisited*. . . . *Loon Lake* contains [several] parallels to, as well as ironic comments on, the themes of [Theodore] Dreiser's story . . . . Had Dreiser lived to witness the disruptions of post-World War II American society—and had he possessed Mr. Doctorow's narrative dexterity—he might have written something like *Loon Lake*."

Doctorow's narrative style generated much critical comment. "The written surface of *Loon Lake* is ruffled and choppy," Gray remarked. "Swatches of poetry are jumbled together with passages of computerese and snippets of mysteriously disembodied conversation. Narration switches suddenly from first to third person, or vice versa, and it is not always clear just who is telling what." A reviewer for the *Chicago Tribune* found such "stylistic tricks" annoyingly distracting. "We balk at the frequent overwriting, and the clumsy run-on sentences," he observed. "We can see that Doctorow is trying to convey rootlessness and social unrest through an insouciant free play of language and syntax . . . the problem is that these eccentricities draw disproportionate attention to themselves, away from the characters and their concerns."

Doctorow's play *Drinks before Dinner* seems to have been created through an analogous act of exploration. In the *Nation*, Doctorow stated that the play "originated not in an idea or a character or a story but in a sense of heightened language, a way of talking. It was not until I had the sound of it in my ear that I thought about saying something. The language preceded the intention . . . . The process of making something up is best experienced as fortuitous, unplanned, exploratory. You write to find out what it is you're writing." In composing *Drinks before Dinner,* Doctorow worked from sound to words to characters. Does this "flawed" method of composition show a "defective understanding of what theater is supposed to do?" he wondered. His answer: "I suspect so. Especially if we are talking of the American theater, in which the presentation of the psychologized ego is so central as to be an article of faith. And that is the point. The idea of character as we normally celebrate it on the American stage is what this play seems to question."

When the play was produced, *Village Voice* critic Michael Feingold observed that in *Drinks before Dinner,* Doctorow "has tried to do something incomparably more ambitious than any new American play has done in years—he has tried to put the whole case against civilization in a nutshell." Feingold, however, found the ambition thwarted by a "schizoid" plot and "flat, prosy, and empty" writing. "I salute his desire to say something gigantic," Feingold concluded, "how I wish he had found a way to say it fully, genuinely, and dramatically." Richard Eder, writing in the *New York Times,* responded more positively: "Doctorow's turns of thought can be odd, witty and occasionally quite remarkable. His theme—that the world is blindly destroying itself and not worrying about it—is hardly original, but certainly worth saying. And he finds thoughtful and striking ways of saying it." Eder added, "and Mr. Doctorow's [ideas] are sharp enough to supplement intellectual suspense when the dramatic suspense bogs down."

Doctorow's novels *World's Fair* and *Billy Bathgate* are set in 1930s New York, and both received much critical acclaim. *World's Fair* relates a boy's experiences in New York City, growing up in a loving, if somewhat financially stressed, Jewish family during the Great Depression, and ends with his visit to the 1939 World's Fair. Numerous reviewers considered it autobiographical—the young protagonist and narrator has Doctorow's first name, Edgar; his parents, like Doctorow's, are named Rose and David; David runs a music store, as Doctorow's father did. Doctorow confirmed that the novel had autobiographical origins. *World's Fair* "is really a story about memory," he told Herbert Mitgang in an interview for the *New York Times.* "I started writing it before I knew what I was doing. The title came to me one-third of the way through the book."

"'World's Fair' is Doctorow's portrait of the artist as a young child," commented Richard Eder in the *Los Angeles Times Book Review.* "The author's alter-ego, Edgar Altschuler, grows into an awareness that the world stretches far beyond the protective confines of a Bronx Jewish household." While "the subject of growing up is not so much a literary theme as a literary subspecies," Eder continued, Doctorow's "implacable intelligence" makes this novel stand out among the ranks of coming-of-age stories, "not necessarily in front, but unmistakably by itself." Doctorow, he remarked, "has renewed an old theme in his quite individual way." Edmund White, reviewing for the *Nation,* also found *World's Fair* distinctive. "In so many autobiographical novels the writer is tempted to gift himself with nearly perfect recall and to turn his early experiences into signs of his own later genius," White observed. "Doctorow avoids these temptations and sticks close to memory, its gaps and haziness as well as its pockets of poetic lucidity. He never divines in his Jewish middle-class Bronx childhood of the 1930s the extraordinary eloquence and wisdom he was later to win for himself." The novel, White added, "never becomes just an excursion down memory lane," with Edgar's recollections instead "constructing the anthropology of twentieth-century America." The critic concluded, "Doctorow finds feelings that are deep in the settings of a more innocent past. His past purrs and hisses and is capable of scratching deep enough to draw blood."

Billy Bathgate has the same setting as *World's Fair,* but where that book, as Anne Tyler put it in the *New York Times Book Review,* was a "lingering, affectionate, deeply textured evocation of the Bronx in the 30s . . . with a memoir's loose, easygoing story line, this new book has a plot as tightly constructed as that of 'Huckleberry Finn.' It is Mr. Doctorow's shapeliest piece of work: a richly detailed report of a fifteen-year-old boy's journey from childhood to adulthood, with plenty of cliff-hanging adventure along the way." Indeed, although *World's Fair* received the American Book Award, some critics laud *Billy Bathgate* as an even greater achievement. The story of teenager Billy Behan's initiation into the world of organized crime under the mentorship of Dutch Schultz is a "grand entertainment that is also a triumphant work of art," according to Pete Hamill, writing in the *Washington Post Book World.* Certain reviewers especially appreciated Doctorow's ability to avoid cliched characters. "Even the various gangsters are multidimensional," Tyler remarked. The completion of *Billy Bathgate* was also a milestone for its author. While discussing the novel in the *Washington Post,* Doctorow revealed that he felt he had been "liberated by it to a certain extent . . . . Certain themes and preoccupations, that leitmotif that I've been working with for several years. I think now I can write anything. The possibilities are limitless. I've somehow been set free by this book."

In *The Waterworks,* Doctorow imaginatively revisits old New York of the 1870s, an era of widespread corruption in a city which enjoyed great prosperity because of profiteering during the U.S. Civil War. In this novel, Doctorow's protagonist is a journalist named McIlvaine, who investigates reports that a wealthy man, believed deceased, has been spotted in public on at least two occasions in the city. To his horror, McIlvaine discovers several such specimens of the living dead as well as their reanimator—a rogue scientist named Wrede Sartorius who is either a madman or a genius ahead of his time. Sartorius is capable of bringing to life the recently deceased, using "fluids" obtained from anonymous street urchins held captive in his lair. Major scenes are set at the municipal waterworks, the holding reservoir into which flows Manhattan's water supply from upstate. In this novel, explained Luc Sante in the *New York Review of Books,* the waterworks facility "is identified with the machinery of civilization, a matter of considerable ambiguity. It is both the locus of possibly nefarious deeds and a marvel of engineering no less impressive today than it was then. Within its precincts Sartorius carries out his experiments, which are futuristic and quaint, morally questionable and straightforwardly inquisitive." Paul Gray, reviewing for *Time,* found *The Waterworks* "an entertaining and sometimes truly haunting story," while *Spectator* critic John Whitworth called it "a marvelous book," a novel "of the prelapsarian state, a late nineteenth-century novel, something out of Conrad and James, out of Stevenson and Wells and Conan Doyle."

The story of Doctorow's *City of God* "is at first difficult to discern," noted a *Publishers Weekly* reviewer, "because the abruptly changing voices are not identified. But the episodic selections prove to be passages in a notebook" kept by Doctorow's protagonist, a writer named Everett. *Time* reviewer Gray commented that after thirty pages, the reader "will get the hang of things." In the story, Everett is looking for something to write about and finds an idea that interests him: an incident involving a brass cross that was stolen from an Episcopal church tended by a faith-doubting Thomas Pemberton. The cross turns up on the roof of the Synagogue for Evolutionary Judaism. Pemberton is murdered after a trip to eastern Europe, and Everett eventually becomes attracted to Pemberton's widow. The plot does not come across so straightforwardly, however. *City of God,* explained *New York Times Book Review* critic A.O. Scott, "features shifting narrative points of view and loose ends scattered like snippets of telephone wire, as well as extended passages of philosophical speculation, theological rumination and blankish verse." Among the topics Doctorow explores, observed Mark Harris in *Entertainment Weekly,* are "the origins of the known universe and of life on earth, the fathomless horror of the Holocaust, the place of Jewish and Christian worship and of religious faith in general at the dawn of a new millennium, jazz, desire, movies, war, writing . . . in other words, one of our senior literary lions has decided to grapple with cosmic questions."

"Through all its convolutions," noted John Bemrose in *Maclean's,* "*City of God* creates a gripping sense of the moral and spiritual dilemmas faced by humans at the turn of the millennium." *Nation* contributor Melvin Bukiet called the novel Doctorow's "most vital—and most difficult—work yet . . . . Without linear plot or unified voice, *City of God* is tessellated, a mosaic touching on love and loneliness, faith and physics. It glints and glimmers, reflecting off rather than building upon itself, and adding up to a sum greater than its multifarious parts." Francine Prose, reviewing for *People,* wrote that "*City of God* puts great faith in the intelligence and patience of its readers." Prose felt that readers who "rise to the challenge" will find the novel rewarding. Writing in *Library Journal,* Mirela Roncevic termed the novel "courageous" and, praising Doctorow for sensitivity and perceptiveness, described the work as "essential reading." Gray concluded in *Time* that "the true miracle of *City of God* is the way its disparate parts fuse into a consistently enthralling and suspenseful whole. In such novels as *Ragtime* (1975) and *Billy Bathgate* (1989), Doctorow mixed historical and fictional figures in ways that magically challenged ordinary notions of what is real. His new novel repeats this process, with even more intriguing and unsettling consequences."

Doctorow's subsequent publications include collections of screenplays, essays, and short stories. *Three Screenplays* features the screenplay for *Daniel*—for which Doctorow did see his script used—as well as his unproduced adaptations of *Ragtime* and *Loon Lake.* When *Ragtime* was being prepared for film by director Robert Altman, Doctorow worked for a time on the screenplay, but he left the project after Milos Forman replaced Altman, as Forman and Doctorow disagreed on several aspects of the production. In the preface to *Three Screenplays,* Doctorow reveals that he dislikes writing film scripts: the screenplays, he says, "were motivated only by my desire to protect my work from oversimplification, bowdlerization, and general mauling by other hands."

The essay compilation *Reporting the Universe* and the short-fiction collection *Sweet Land Stories* find Doctorow in literary forms he apparently enjoys more than screenwriting. The pieces in *Reporting the Universe*, originally a series of lectures delivered by Doctorow at Harvard University, deal with some of the subjects that have informed his fiction: his boyhood, American social and political culture, spirituality, freedom of expression. Doctorow's arguments "are brilliantly reasoned and beautifully expressed," related Amanda Heller in the *Boston Globe*. Both this collection and *Sweet Land Stories* show the author "burrowing hard toward the Big Questions," commented Art Winslow in Chicago's *Tribune Books*, adding: "When he examines the role of the writer in society in 'Reporting the Universe,' one can turn to 'Sweet Land Stories' and see how those ideas play out in his fiction." Doctorow's characters in the short stories include murderers, a self-anointed prophet, an abandoned child, and people who abandon or abduct children. "One of Doctorow's great strengths," Winslow remarked, "is in presenting the aberrant mind and antisocial act as relatively rational, under the circumstances . . . . The characters speak to us engagingly from the Dark Fields of Doctorow's Republic." In *Sweet Land Stories*, Doctorow is "boring like a laser into the failures of the American dream," a *Publishers Weekly* reviewer observed, while *Library Journal* contributor Barbara Hoffert reported that "Doctorow takes a simple story and creates a universe," and the collection as a whole "reminds one of the distinction between merely good and truly great authors."

In 2005 Doctorow turned his attention once again to novels. He penned the historical fiction work *The March*, which documents General William Tecumseh's notorious march through the southern states during the Civil War. The march was first popularized by Margaret Mitchell's *Gone with the Wind*, but Doctorow "makes it more frightening, more destructive, more triumphant, more liberating and far more historically accurate," according to Deirdre Donahue in *USA Today*. Donahue also commented on how the author "masterfully weaves together historical figures with imagined ones." Walter Kirn, reviewing the book for *New York Times Book Review*, wrote about the author's "peristaltic storytelling: that process by which a writer captures his audience . . . by swallowing the reader whole and then conveying him—firmly, steadily, irresistibly—toward a fated outcome." Other critics similarly praised the work; Donna Seaman, writing in *Booklist*, pointed out, "never before has [Doctorow] so fully occupied the past, or so gorgeously evoked its generation of the forces that seeded our times." Doctorow was awarded his second PEN/Faulkner Award and his first National Book Critics Circle prize for fiction for *The March* in 2006.

BIOGRAPHICAL AND CRITICAL SOURCES:

BOOKS

Bloom, Harold, editor, *E.L. Doctorow*, Chelsea House Publishers (Philadelphia, PA), 2002.

Concise Dictionary of American Literary Biography: Broadening Views, 1968-1988, Gale (Detroit, MI), 1989.

Contemporary Literary Criticism, Gale (Detroit, MI), Volume 6, 1976, Volume 11, 1979, Volume 15, 1980, Volume 18, 1981, Volume 37, 1986, Volume 44, 1987, Volume 65, 1991.

Contemporary Novelists, 7th edition, St. James Press (Detroit, MI), 2001.

Dictionary of Literary Biography, Gale (Detroit, MI), Volume 2: *American Novelists since World War II*, 1978, Volume 28: *Twentieth-Century American-Jewish Fiction Writers*, 1984.

Dictionary of Literary Biography Yearbook: 1980, Gale (Detroit, MI), 1981.

Doctorow, E.L., *Three Screenplays*, Johns Hopkins University Press (Baltimore, MD), 2003.

Encyclopedia of World Literature in the Twentieth Century, St. James Press (Detroit, MI), 1999.

Johnson, Diane, *Terrorists and Novelists*, Knopf (New York, NY), 1982.

Levine, Paul, *E.L. Doctorow*, Methuen (New York, NY), 1985.

Morris, Christopher, *Models of Misrepresentation: On the Fiction of E.L. Doctorow*, University Press of Mississippi (Jackson, MS), 1991.

Morris, Christopher, *Conversations with E.L. Doctorow*, University Press of Mississippi (Jackson, MS), 1999.

Parks, John, *E.L. Doctorow*, Continuum (New York, NY), 1991.

Tokarczyk, Michelle, and E.L. Doctorow, *E.L. Doctorow: An Annotated Bibliography*, Garland (New York, NY), 1988.

Trenner, Richard, editor, *E.L. Doctorow: Essays and Conversations*, Ontario Review Press (Princeton, NJ), 1983.

Williams, John, *Fiction as False Document: The Reception of E.L. Doctorow in the Postmodern Age*, Camden House (Columbia, SC), 1996.

PERIODICALS

American Literary History, summer, 1992.
American Studies, spring, 1992.
Atlanta Journal and Constitution, February 8, 1998.

Atlantic, September, 1980.

Booklist, October 1, 1994, p. 238; January 1, 2000, Bonnie Smothers, review of *City of God,* p. 833; August, 2005, Donna Seaman, review of *The March,* p. 1952.

Boston Globe, June 22, 2003, Amanda Heller, review of *Reporting the Universe,* p. D7.

Chicago Tribune, September 28, 1980.

Chronicle of Higher Education, May 30, 2003, Jennifer Ruark, "Professor Seeks to Make Film about Lawyer Who Defended Racist Murderers; Scholarly Press Publishes Screenplays of Three Novels by Doctorow," p. 16.

Commentary, October, 1975; March, 1986.

Detroit Free Press, February 19, 1989.

Detroit News, November 10, 1985.

Drama, January, 1980.

Entertainment Weekly, June 17, 1994, p. 46; February 25, 2000, Mark Harris, review of *City of God,* p. 73.

Globe and Mail (Toronto, Ontario, Canada), March 11, 1989.

Hudson Review, summer, 1986.

Library Journal, March 1, 2000, Mirela Roncevic, review of *City of God,* p. 123; March 1, 2004, Barbara Hoffert, review of *Sweet Land Stories,* p. 110.

Listener, September 14, 1989, Andrew Clifford, "True-ish Crime Stories," p. 29.

London Magazine, February, 1986.

Los Angeles Times Book Review, November 24, 1985, Richard Eder, review of *World's Fair,* p. 3; March 5, 1989, Richard Eder, "Siege Perilous in the Court of Dutch Schultz," p. 3.

Maclean's, July 25, 1994, p. 54; April 17, 2000, John Bemrose, review of *City of God,* p. 56.

Manchester Guardian, February 23, 1986.

Miami Herald, December 21, 1975, Jonathan Yardley, "E.L. Doctorow: Mr. 'Ragtime,'" pp. 88-89.

Midwest Quarterly, autumn, 1983.

Nation, June 2, 1979; September 27, 1980; November 17, 1984; November 30, 1985, Edmund White, review of *World's Fair;* April 3, 1989; June 6, 1994; March 13, 2000, Melvin Bukiet, review of *City of God,* p. 23.

National Review, August 15, 1975; March 14, 1986.

New Leader, December 16-30, 1985.

New Republic, June 5, 1971; July 5, 1975; September 6, 1975; September 20, 1980; December 3, 1984; July 18, 1994, p. 44; March 6, 2000, Robert Alter, review of *City of God,* p. 27.

New Statesman, June 17, 1994, p. 40.

Newsweek, June 7, 1971; July 14, 1975; November 4, 1985; February 21, 2000, Peter Plagens, review of *City of God,* p. 58.

New York, September 29, 1980; November 25, 1985.

New Yorker, December 9, 1985; June 27, 1994, p. 41.

New York Herald Tribune, January 22, 1961.

New York Review of Books, August 7, 1975; December 19, 1985; June 23, 1994, p. 12.

New York Times, August 4, 1978; November 24, 1978; September 12, 1980; March 1, 1981, Tom Buckley, "The Forman Formula," section 6, p. 28; November 6, 1984; October 31, 1985; November 11, 1985, Herbert Mitgang, "Doctorow Revisits the 'World's Fair' of His Novel," p. C13; February 9, 1989; July 8, 1994.

New York Times Book Review, September 25, 1960; July 4, 1971; July 6, 1975; September 28, 1980; December 6, 1984; November 10, 1985; February 26, 1989, Anne Tyler, "An American Boy in Gangland," p. 1; June 19, 1994, p. 1; March 5, 2000, A. O. Scott, review of *City of God,* p. 7; September 25, 2005, Walter Kirn, "Making War Hell," p. 1L.

Partisan Review, fall, 1972.

People, March 20, 1989; July 4, 1994, p. 28; March 13, 2000, Francine Prose, review of *City of God,* p. 55.

Progressive, March, 1986.

Publishers Weekly, June 30, 1975; June 27, 1994, p. 51; January 24, 2000, review of *City of God,* p. 292; August 28, 2000, review of *The Best American Short Stories 2000,* p. 53; March 22, 2004, review of *Sweet Land Stories,* p. 59.

Saturday Review, July 17, 1971; July 26, 1975; September, 1980.

South Atlantic Quarterly, winter, 1982.

Southwest Review, autumn, 1977.

Spectator, May 28, 1994, p. 33.

Time, July 14, 1975; September 22, 1980; December 18, 1985; June 20, 1994, p. 66; February 14, 2000, Paul Gray, review of *City of God,* p. 82.

Times Literary Supplement, February 14, 1986; May 27, 1994, Stephen Fender, "The Novelist as Liar," p. 20.

Tribune Books (Chicago, IL), April 25, 2004, Art Winslow, "Illuminating Stories," p. 2.

USA Today, September 20, 2005, Deirdre Donahue, "*The March* Strides into History," p. 4D.

Village Voice, July 7, 1975; August 4, 1975; December 4, 1978; November 26, 1985.

Wall Street Journal, February 7, 1986.

Washington Post, March 9, 1998.

Washington Post Book World, July 13, 1975; September 28, 1980; November 11, 1984; November 17, 1985; February 19, 1989.

*   *   *

DOMECQ, H. Bustos
See BORGES, Jorge Luis

DOMINI, Rey
    See LORDE, Audre

* * *

DORRIS, Michael 1945-1997
    (Michael Anthony Dorris, Milou North, a joint pseudonym)

PERSONAL: Born January 30, 1945, in Louisville, KY (some sources say Dayton, WA); committed suicide April 11, 1997, in Concord, NH; son of Jim and Mary Besy (Burkhardt) Dorris; married Louise Erdrich (a writer), 1981; children: Reynold Abel, Jeffrey Sava, Madele Hannah, Persia Andromeda, Pallas Antigone, Aza Marion. *Education:* Georgetown University, B.A. (cum laude), 1967; Yale University, M.Phil., 1970.

CAREER: University of Redlands, Johnston College, Redlands, CA, assistant professor, 1970; Franconia College, Franconia, NH, assistant professor, 1971-72; Dartmouth College, Hanover, NH, instructor, 1972-76, assistant professor, 1976-79, associate professor, 1979, professor of anthropology, 1979-88, chair of Native American studies department, 1979-85, chair of Master of Arts in Liberal Studies program, 1982-85, adjunct professor, 1989-97. University of New Hampshire, visiting senior lecturer, 1980. Director of urban bus program, summers, 1967, 1968, and 1969. Society for Applied Anthropology, fellow, 1977-97; Save the Children Foundation, board member, 1991-92, advisory board member, 1992-97; U.S. Advisory Committee on Infant Mortality, member, 1992-97. Consultant to National Endowment for the Humanities, 1976-97, and to television stations, including Los Angeles Educational Television, 1976, and Toledo Public Broadcast Center, 1978. Appeared on numerous radio and television programs.

MEMBER: PEN, Author's Guild, Writer's Guild, Modern Language Association of America (delegate assembly and member of minority commission, 1974-77), American Anthropological Association, American Association for the Advancement of Science (opportunities in science commission, 1974-77), National Indian Education Association, National Congress of American Indians, National Support Committee (Native American Rights Fund), Save the Children (board of directors, 1993-94), Research Society on Alcoholism, National Organization for Fetal Alcohol Syndrome, Phi Beta Kappa, Alpha Sigma Nu.

AWARDS, HONORS: Woodrow Wilson fellow, 1967 and 1980; fellowships from National Institute of Mental Health, 1970 and 1971, John Simon Guggenheim Memorial Foundation, 1978, Rockefeller Foundation, 1985, National Endowment for the Arts, 1989, and Dartmouth College, 1992; Indian Achievement Award, 1985; best book citation, American Library Association, 1988, for *A Yellow Raft in Blue Water;* PEN Syndicated Fiction Award, 1988, for "Name Games"; honorary degree, Georgetown University, 1989; National Book Critics Circle Award for general nonfiction, 1989, and Christopher Award, Heartland Prize, and Outstanding Academic Book, *Choice,* all 1990, all for *The Broken Cord: A Family's Ongoing Struggle with Fetal Alcohol Syndrome;* Medal of Outstanding Leadership and Achievement, Dartmouth College, 1991; Sarah Josepha Hale Literary Award, 1991; Scott Newman Award, 1992, and Gabriel Award for National Entertainment Program, ARC Media Award, Christopher Award, Writers Guild of America award, and Media Award, American Psychology Association, all for television film of *The Broken Cord: A Family's Ongoing Struggle with Fetal Alcohol Syndrome;* Montgomery fellow, Dartmouth College, 1992; International Pathfinder Award, World Conference on the Family, 1992; Award for Excellence, Center for Anthropology and Journalism, 1992, for essays on Zimbabwe; Scott O'Dell Award for Historical Fiction, American Library Association, 1992, for *Morning Girl.*

WRITINGS:

Native Americans: Five Hundred Years After (nonfiction), photographs by Joseph C. Farber, Crowell (New York, NY), 1977.

(As Michael A. Dorris, with Arlene B. Hirschfelder and Mary Gloyne Byler) *A Guide to Research on North American Indians* (nonfiction), American Library Association (Chicago, IL), 1983.

A Yellow Raft in Blue Water (novel), Holt (New York, NY), 1987.

The Broken Cord: A Family's Ongoing Struggle with Fetal Alcohol Syndrome (nonfiction), foreword by wife, Louise Erdrich, Harper (New York, NY), 1989, published as *The Broken Cord: A Father's Story,* Collins (New York, NY), 1990.

(With Louise Erdrich) *The Crown of Columbus* (novel), HarperCollins (New York, NY), 1991.

(With Louise Erdrich) *Route Two and Back,* Lord John, 1991.

Morning Girl (young adult novel), Hyperion (New York, NY), 1992.

Rooms in the House of Stone (nonfiction), Milkweed Editions (Minneapolis, MN), 1993.

Working Men (stories), Holt (New York, NY), 1993.

Paper Trail (essays), HarperCollins (New York, NY), 1994.

Guests (young adult novel), Hyperion (New York, NY), 1995.

Sees behind Trees, Hyperion (New York, NY), 1996.

Cloud Chamber (novel), Scribners (New York, NY), 1997.

The Window (young adult novel), Hyperion (New York, NY), 1997.

(Editor) *The Most Wonderful Books: Writers on Discovering the Pleasures of Reading,* Milkweed Editions, 1997.

Also author of article "House of Stone" and short story "Name Games." Contributor to books, including *Racism in the Textbook,* Council on Interracial Books for Children, 1976; *Separatist Movements,* edited by Ray Hall, Pergamon, 1979; and *Heaven Is under Our Feet,* edited by Don Henley and Dave Marsh, Longmeadow Press, 1991. Contributor of articles, poems, short stories, and reviews to periodicals, including *Chicago Tribune, Life, Los Angeles Times, Mother Jones, New York Times Book Review, Parents* magazine, *Vogue,* and *Woman* (with Louise Erdrich, under the joint pseudonym Milou North). *Viewpoint,* editor, 1967; *American Indian Culture and Research Journal,* member of editorial board, 1974-97; *MELUS,* member of editorial board, 1977-79. Author of screen treatment to *Sleeping Lady,* Mirage Films/Sydney Pollack, 1991; author of songs with Judy Rodman, Warner-Chappell Music, 1993.

ADAPTATIONS: The Broken Cord: A Family's Ongoing Struggle with Fetal Alcohol Syndrome was produced for television by Universal Television/ABC-TV, 1992. *A Yellow Raft in Blue Water* and *The Broken Cord: A Family's Ongoing Struggle with Fetal Alcohol Syndrome* were released on audiocassette by HarperAudio, 1990; *The Crown of Columbus* was released on audiocassette by HarperAudio, 1991. Film rights to *The Crown of Columbus* were sold to Cinecom.

SIDELIGHTS: Deemed by many reviewers as one of the most renowned Native American writers of his generation, Michael Dorris helped to promote the study of Native American culture through his works of nonfiction and fiction. Part Modoc on his father's side, Dorris coauthored a North American Indian research guide, founded the Native American Studies Department at Dartmouth College, created juvenile stories about Native American life, and researched Fetal Alcohol Syndrome (FAS)—the abnormalities occurring in a child when alcohol consumption during pregnancy destroys the brain cells of the fetus. FAS is a particular concern of some Native Americans since the rate of alcohol abuse is higher than the national average on reservations.

Dorris first became aware of FAS when, as a single parent, he adopted a three-year-old Sioux boy who had been taken from his neglectful, alcoholic mother. Dorris, unaware of the physical and mental impact of FAS, initially believed that with love and security his adopted son would outgrow many of his health and behavior problems. Over time, however, developmental impairments in the child became more obvious and limitations more pronounced. In addition to seizures and physical dysfunctions, his son experienced poor vision, near deafness, and slow growth, and was unable to relate cause and effect. After consulting with numerous professionals, Dorris regretfully learned that his son was not getting better. In 1982 Dorris discovered that his son's problems stemmed from FAS; the boy's biological mother, who died of alcohol poisoning, drank heavily during her pregnancy. The discovery inspired Dorris to confront the topic of alcoholism among Native Americans. His extensive research and personal story led to the publication of *The Broken Cord: A Family's Ongoing Struggle with Fetal Alcohol Syndrome*—also published as *The Broken Cord: A Father's Story*—a semi-autobiographical account of the events leading up to and succeeding the adoption of his son (called Adam in the book) along with the information Dorris unearthed on FAS.

Granted the National Book Critics Circle Award for general nonfiction, *The Broken Cord* received widespread praise for Dorris's sharing of his personal story as well as the statistical information he gathered. "*The Broken Cord,* beautifully written, angry, dispassionate, painfully honest, is the deeply moving and fierce story of Michael Dorris's search for answers," noted *Detroit News* contributor Stephen Salisbury. "Part memoir, part mystery, part love story, polemic, and social and public-health study, this is that rare book that focuses attention like a magnifying glass on a hot, sunny day. It burns." Carl A. Hammerschlag wrote in the *Los Angeles Times Book Review* that "it is not enough to say that *The Broken Cord . . .* is good. Written like a prayer from the heart of someone strong enough to share his pain, it tells a tale of crimes against Native American children that approach the dimensions of genocide. . . . Whatever the theories of causation, alcohol is threatening to destroy 1.5 million contemporary Indian people. The annihilation is almost unimaginable. Dorris gives all this a name, a face and a personal history that make it impossible for the reader to remain detached." According to Phyllis Theroux of the *Washington Post*, "Dorris gradually uncovers the ghastly dimensions of [FAS], clearly intending *The Broken Cord* to be an [alarm] that neither lay nor professional readers can ignore. He succeeds brilliantly."

In addition to nonfiction topics, Dorris wrote fictional accounts about such notable events as the arrival of Columbus in America. In 1992, the five-hundredth anniversary of Christopher Columbus's discovery of the Americas, Dorris published his first book for young adults, *Morning Girl,* a story of Bahamian youths living in 1492. Morning Girl, who loves the day, and Star Boy, who prefers the night, are siblings who are like two sides of the same coin and often display their conflicting feelings about one another. As their identities develop and emerge, however, the children discover similarities in their caring for their family. The daily adventures of the young narrators are the focus of the novel, and Dorris interweaves the backdrop of nature and the prominent role of the natural world in the children's native culture. The book comes to a close when Columbus's crew from the *Nina* lands on the island. "This sad, lovely and timely tale gives us an alternative view of America's 'discovery,'" related Suzanne Curley in the *Los Angeles Times Book Review.*

Dorris's second book for young adults, *Guests,* was published in 1995. The novel tells the story of Moss, a young Native-American boy growing up several centuries ago; the guests of the title are Europeans invited by Moss's father to a celebratory dinner in honor of the harvest. "As in *Morning Girl,* . . . Dorris writes lyrically of nature. The descriptions fill the senses," praised Linda Perkins in the *New York Times Book Review.* Nancy Vasilakis, writing in *Horn Book,* stated, "The narrative voice in this book is natural and believable, though this book, like [*Morning Girl,*] is very much an introspective novel." A reviewer for the Chicago *Tribune Books* concluded that in *Guests* "Dorris brings readers close to his characters at the same time he evokes how far away they were."

Dorris also wrote collaboratively with his wife, author Louise Erdrich, and among their works is *The Crown of Columbus,* an adult novel about explorer Christopher Columbus. Columbus's story is framed by a love story about two Dartmouth professors, Vivian Twostar and Roger Williams, with little in common but a physical attraction. Both are involved in the research of Christopher Columbus; Vivian, a Native-American single parent, has been assigned the task of writing an academic piece on Columbus from the Native American view-

point, while Roger, an English professor and poet, is writing an epic poem about Columbus for *People* magazine. The research leads them on an adventure and eventually forces them to question the impact of Columbus's journey for the contemporary world, especially Native Americans.

The Crown of Columbus received mixed reactions. Some reviewers believed that the work was below the standards of both Dorris's and Erdrich's previous books and claimed it was manufactured to become a bestseller rather than a literary effort. Other reviewers found Vivian and Roger's adventures amusing, vibrant, and charming. "Erdrich and Dorris, who write so convincingly elsewhere from their own experience, seem here to have been a little hasty in trying to exploit Columbus's," claimed Kirkpatrick Sale in the *Nation.* Sale also found *The Crown of Columbus* "difficult to read without remembering that the Dorris-Erdrich team got some $1.5 million to turn out a book from their Indian perspective for the Quincentenary." More enthusiastic about the couple's effort, *Library Journal*'s Ann Fisher declared the book "a sure-fire winner on all levels" and praised the authors' depiction of the relationship of the two main characters as "funny, vivid, and life-affirming." *New York Times Book Review* contributor Robert Houston complimented the "moments of genuine humor and compassion, of real insight and sound satire," but also commented that, "in the end, *The Crown of Columbus* never really finds itself."

Cloud Chamber, published just prior to Dorris's death in 1997, refers readers back to his novel *A Yellow Raft in Blue Water,* a 1987 work that introduces fifteen-year-old Rayona Taylor, part African American, part Native American. While *Yellow Raft* describes Rayona's adventures as a feisty tomboy, including entering a bronco-riding contest, *Cloud Chamber* traces the teen's lineage back to her great-great-grandmother from Ireland. In doing so, it relates the complex love relationships that have patterned the family over the years. John Skow of *Time* called the novel "intricate and brooding."

Dorris also published a book of short stories titled *Working Men.* A number of the stories included were previously published in other publications such as *Mother Jones, Ploughshares,* and *Northwest Review.* Despite its title, the collection examines the lives of men and women, straight and gay, young and old in a variety of settings. Noted Phillip Graham in the Chicago *Tribune Books,* "No two of these stories are the same, though each rests on the solid authority of a distinctive human voice and a slyly elastic definition of work."

Working Men received praise from a number of reviewers. "All [of the stories] are strikingly different and are told with flair and efficiency and honed craftsmanship," praised Ron Hansen in the *Los Angeles Times Book Review.* "*Working Men* is admirable not just for its mastery and variety, but for Michael Dorris's faith in the heroism and importance of ordinary American life." Mentioning the stories "The Vase" and "Jeopardy" specifically, Charles R. Larson wrote in the *Washington Post Book World* that *Working Men* "contains two stories as good as we are likely to find by anyone writing today, and that is all the measure needed for any artist worthy of serious attention."

While *The Crown of Columbus* was the first novel to result from the Dorris-Erdrich collaboration, the couple worked closely together on all of their books. As Dorris once explained to Dulcy Brainard in a *Publishers Weekly* interview: "The person whose name is on the book is the one who's done most of the primary writing. The other helps plan, reads it as it goes along, suggests changes in direction, in character and then acts as editor." Considering their popular following, the system seemed to work well for Dorris and Erdrich. *New York Times Magazine*'s Vince Passaro pointed out that "one senses the act of collaboration serves a vital, extra-literary function, perhaps as a fortification against an insinuating and inevitable competition. If every work that leaves their hands is in some sense a joint work, they can escape the awful consequences of one talent overshadowing another."

Despite seemingly successful careers intertwined with a solid marriage, Erdrich and Dorris quietly separated in 1996 and were undergoing divorce proceedings when Dorris ended his life in April of 1997. Following his death, it became public that Dorris was under investigation for child abuse and that he had previously attempted suicide two weeks prior to his death. However, in an interview with the *New York Times,* Erdrich said that her husband's depression had existed throughout their marriage: "Suicide. It's a very tangled road, a tangle of paths and dead ends and clear places and it's gone. He descended inch by inch, fighting all the way."

BIOGRAPHICAL AND CRITICAL SOURCES:

BOOKS

Erdrich, Louise, and Michael Dorris, *Conversations with Louise Erdrich and Michael Dorris,* University Press of Mississippi (Jackson, MS), 1994.

Native North American Literature, Thomson Gale (Detroit, MI), 1994.

Weil, Ann, *Michael Dorris,* Raintree Steck-Vaughn (Austin, TX), 1997.

PERIODICALS

America, May 10, 1997, p. 7.
Bloomsbury Review, May-June, 1995, p. 19.
Christian Science Monitor, March 2, 1989, pp. 16-17.
Georgia Review, summer, 1995, p. 523.
Horn Book, January-February, 1995, p. 58.
Library Journal, March 15, 1991, p. 114.
Los Angeles Times, September 18, 1988, sec. 6, pp. 8-9.
Los Angeles Times Book Review, June 21, 1987, p. 2; September 27, 1992, p. 12; August 3, 1993, p. 11; November 7, 1993, p. 2; October 30, 1994, p. 8.
Missouri Review, 1988, pp. 79-99.
New Statesman and Society, September 7, 1990, p. 44.
Newsweek, June 16, 1997, p. 54.
New York, June 16, 1997, p. 30.
New York Times, April 19, 1991, p. C5; February 2, 1992, sec. L, pp. 29, 38.
New York Times Book Review, June 7, 1987, p. 7; July 30, 1989, pp. 1, 20; April 28, 1991, p. 10; August 1, 1993, p. 18; May 18, 1994, p. 18; January 1, 1995, p. 20; January 29, 1995, p. 20.
New York Times Magazine, April 21, 1991, pp. 35-40, 76.
North Dakota Quarterly, winter, 1987, pp. 196-218.
Publishers Weekly, August 4, 1989, pp. 73-74; August 10, 1992, p. 71.
Time, February 17, 1997; April 28, 1997, p. 68.
Times Literary Supplement, August 24, 1990, p. 893; July 19, 1991, p. 21; December 2, 1994.
Tribune Books (Chicago, IL), May 10, 1987, pp. 6-7; July 23, 1989, pp. 1, 11; April 28, 1991, p. 5; October 24, 1993, pp. 6-7; August 14, 1994, p. 7.
U.S. Catholic, May, 1997, p. 46.
Washington Post Book World, October 17, 1993, p. 6.
Western American Literature, February, 1992, pp. 369-371.
Women's Review of Books, October, 1991, pp. 17-18.

OBITUARIES:

PERIODICALS

Entertainment Weekly, April 25, 1997, p. 14.
Guardian (Manchester, England), April 22, 1997, p. T6.

Newsweek, April 28, 1997, p. 82.
People, April 28, 1997, p. 61.

*   *   *

DORRIS, Michael Anthony
    See DORRIS, Michael

*   *   *

DOUGLAS, Leonard
    See BRADBURY, Ray

*   *   *

DOUGLAS, Michael
    See CRICHTON, Michael

*   *   *

DOVE, Rita 1952-
    (Rita Frances Dove)

PERSONAL: Born August 28, 1952, in Akron, OH; daughter of Ray A. (a chemist) and Elvira E. (Hord) Dove; married Fred Viebahn (a writer), March 23, 1979; children: Aviva Chantal Tamu Dove-Viebahn. *Education:* Miami University, B.A. (summa cum laude), 1973; attended Universität Tübingen (West Germany), 1974-75; University of Iowa, M.F.A., 1977.

ADDRESSES: Home—Charlottsville, VA. *Office*—Department of English, 219 Bryan Hall, University of Virginia, Charlottesville, VA 22903; fax: 434-924-1478. *E-mail*—rita_dove@Virginia.edu.

CAREER: Arizona State University, Tempe, assistant professor, 1981-84, associate professor, 1984-87, professor of English, 1987-89; University of Virginia, Charlottesville, professor of English, 1989-93, Commonwealth Professor of English, 1993—. Writer-in-residence at Tuskegee Institute, 1982. National Endowment for the Arts, member of literature panel, 1984-86, chair of poetry grants panel, 1985. Commissioner, Schomburg Center for the Preservation of Black Culture, New York Public Library, 1987—; judge, Walt Whitman Award, Academy of American Poets, 1990, Pulitzer Prize in poetry, 1991 and 1997, Ruth Lilly Prize, 1991, National Book Award (poetry), 1991 and 1998, Anisfield-Wolf Book Awards, 1992—; jury mem-

ber, Amy Lowell fellowship, 1997, and Shelley Memorial Award, 1997. Library of Congress consultant in poetry, 1993-95, special consultant in poetry, 1999-2000, member of board of student achievement services, 2002—. Member, Afro-American studies visiting committee, Harvard University, and Council of Scholars, Library of Congress, 2002—. Has made numerous appearances on radio and television, including *Today Show, Charlie Rose Show, Bill Moyers' Journal, A Prairie Home Companion, All Things Considered,* and National Public Radio's *Morning Edition.*

MEMBER: PEN, Associated Writing Programs (member of board of directors, 1985-88; president, 1986-87), Poetry Society of America, American Society of Composers, Authors, and Publishers, American Philosophical Society, Poets and Writers, Phi Beta Kappa (senator, 1994-2000), Phi Kappa Phi.

AWARDS, HONORS: Fulbright fellow, 1974-75; grants from National Endowment for the Arts, 1978, and Ohio Arts Council, 1979; International Working Period for Authors fellow for West Germany, 1980; John Simon Guggenheim fellow, 1983; Peter I.B. Lavan Younger Poets Award, Academy of American Poets, 1986; Pulitzer Prize in poetry, 1987, for *Thomas and Beulah;* General Electric Foundation Award for Younger Writers, 1987; Bellagio (Italy) residency, Rockefeller Foundation, 1988; Ohio Governor's Award, 1988; Mellon fellow, National Humanities Center, 1988-89; Ohioana Award, 1991, for *Grace Notes;* Literary Lion Medal, New York Public Library, 1991; inducted into Ohio Women's Hall of Fame, 1991; appointed Poet Laureate of the United States, 1993-94 and 1994-95; Women of the Year Award, *Glamour* magazine, 1993; Great American Artist Award, National Association for the Advancement of Colored People, 1993; Harvard University Phi Beta Kappa Lecturer, 1993; Distinguished Achievement medal, Miami University Alumni Association, 1994; Golden Plate Award, American Academy of Achievement, 1994; Renaissance Forum Award for leadership in the literary arts, Folger Shakespeare Library, 1994; Carl Sandburg Award, International Platform Association, 1994; Fund for New American Plays grant, 1995; Heinz Award in arts and humanities, 1996; Charles Frankel Prize/National Humanities Medal, 1996; Sara Lee Frontrunner Award, 1997; Barnes & Noble Writers for Writers Award, 1997; Levinson Prize, *Poetry* magazine, 1998; Frederick Nims Translation Award (with Fred Viebahn), *Poetry,* 1999; Library Lion Medal, New York Public Library, 2000; Twenty-five Books to Remember list, New York Public Library, and National Book Critics Circle Award nomination, both 2000, both for *On the Bus with Rosa Parks;* Margaret

Raynal Virginia Writer of Distinction, Randolph-Macon Woman's College, 2001; Duke Ellington Lifetime Achievement Award, 2001; Emily Couric Leadership Award, 2003. Awarded honorary doctorates from Miami University, 1988, Knox College, 1989, Tuskegee University, 1994, University of Miami, 1994, Washington University—St. Louis, 1994, Case Western Reserve University, 1994, University of Akron, 1994, Arizona State University, 1995, Boston College, 1995, Dartmouth College, 1995, Spelman College, 1996, University of Pennsylvania, 1996, Notre Dame, 1997, Northeastern University, 1997, University of North Carolina—Chapel Hill, 1997, Columbia University, 1998, State University of New York—Brockport, 1999, Washington and Lee University, 1999, Howard University, 2001, Pratt Institute, 2001, and Skidmore College, 2004.

WRITINGS:

Ten Poems (chapbook), Penumbra Press (Lisbon, IA), 1977.

The Only Dark Spot in the Sky (poetry chapbook), Porch Publications (Phoenix, AZ), 1980.

The Yellow House on the Corner (poems; also see below), Carnegie Mellon University Press (Pittsburgh, PA), 1980.

Mandolin (poetry chapbook), Ohio Review (Athens, OH), 1982.

Museum (poems; also see below), Carnegie-Mellon University Press (Pittsburgh, PA), 1983.

Fifth Sunday (short stories), University of Kentucky Press (Lexington, KY), 1985, 2nd edition, University Press of Virginia (Charlottesville, VA), 1990.

Thomas and Beulah (poems; also see below), Carnegie-Mellon University Press (Pittsburgh, PA), 1986.

The Other Side of the House (poems), photographs by Tamarra Kaida, Pyracantha Press (Tempe, AZ), 1988.

Grace Notes (poems), Norton (New York, NY), 1989.

Through the Ivory Gate (novel), Pantheon (New York, NY), 1992.

Selected Poems (contains *The Yellow House on the Corner, Museum,* and *Thomas and Beulah*), Pantheon (New York, NY), 1993.

Lady Freedom among Us, Janus Press (Burke, VT), 1993.

The Darker Face of the Earth: A Play (first produced at Oregon Shakespeare Festival, 1996; produced at Kennedy Center, 1997; produced in London, England, 1999), Story Line Press (Brownsville, OR), 1994, 3rd revised edition, 2000.

Mother Love: Poems, Norton (New York, NY), 1995.

(Author of foreword) *Multicultural Voices: Literature from the United States,* Scott Foresman (Glenview, IL), 1995.

The Poet's World, Library of Congress (Washington, DC), 1995.

Evening Primrose (poetry chapbook), Tunheim-Santrizos (Minneapolis, MN), 1998.

On the Bus with Rosa Parks: Poems, Norton (New York, NY), 1999.

(Editor) *The Best American Poetry 2000,* Scribner (New York, NY), 2000.

(Selector and author of introduction) Natasha Trethewey, *Domestic Work: Poems,* Graywolf Press (Saint Paul, MN), 2000.

Conversations with Rita Dove, edited by Earl G. Ingersoll, University Press of Mississippi (Jackson, MS), 2003.

American Smooth, (poems), Norton (New York, NY), 2004.

Work represented in anthologies. Author of weekly column "Poet's Choice," in *Washington Post Book World,* 2000-02. Contributor of poems, stories, and essays to magazines, including *Agni Review, Antaeus, Georgia Review, Nation, New Yorker,* and *Poetry.* Member of editorial board, *National Forum,* 1984-89, *Isis,* and *Ploughshares;* associate editor, *Callaloo,* 1986-98; advisory editor, *Gettysburg Review, TriQuarterly, Callaloo, Georgia Review, Bellingham Review, International Quarterly,* and *Mid-American Review.*

AUTHOR OF LYRICS

The House Slave, music by Alvin Singleton, first presented at Spelman College, 1990.

(With Linda Pastan) *Under the Resurrection Palm,* music by David Liptak, first presented by Eastman American Music series, 1993.

Umoja: Each One of Us Counts, music by Alvin Singleton, first presented in Atlanta, GA, 1996.

Singin' Sepia, music by Tania Leon (first presented in New York, NY), Continuum International Publishing (New York, NY), 1996.

Grace Notes, music by Bruce Adolphe, first presented in New York, NY, 1997.

The Pleasure's in Walking Through, music by Walter Ross, first presented in Charlottesville, VA, 1998.

Seven for Luck, music by John Williams, first presented in Tanglewood, MA, 1998.

Song for the Twentieth Century, music by John Williams, first presented in Washington, DC, as part of Stephen Spielberg's film *The Unfinished Journey,* 1999.

Thonas and Beulah, music by Amnon Wolman, first presented in Chicago, IL, 2001.

SOUND RECORDINGS

Rita Dove and Edward Hirsch Reading Their Poems, Library of Congress (Washington, DC), 1986.

Poets in Person: Rita Dove with Helen Vendler, Modern Poetry Association (Chicago, IL), 1991.

Grace Cavalieri Interviews United States Poet Laureate Rita Dove, Library of Congress (Washington, DC), 1993.

Rita Dove Reading from Her Poetry, Library of Congress (Washington, DC), 1993.

A Handful of Inwardness: The World in the Poet, Library of Congress (Washington, DC), 1994.

Stepping Out: The Poet in the World, Library of Congress (Washington, DC), 1994.

Rita Dove Reading Her Poems in the Montpelier Room, May 4, 1995, Library of Congress (Washington, DC), 1995.

Oil on the Waters: The Black Diaspora: Panel Discussions and Readings Exploring the African Diaspora through the Eyes of Its Artists, Library of Congress (Washington, DC), 1995.

Former Poet Laureate Rita Dove Discusses the Thomas Jefferson Rough Draft of the Declaration of Independence, Library of Congress (Washington, DC), 1997.

(With others) *Sharing the Gifts: Readings by 1997-2000 Poet Laureate Consultant in Poetry Robert Pinsky, 1999-2000 Special Poetry Consultants Rita Dove, Louise Glück, W.S. Merwin, 1999 Witter Bynner fellows David Gewanter, Campbell McGrath, Heather McHugh,* Library of Congress (Washington, DC), 1999.

The Poet and the Poem from the Library of Congress— Favorite Poets, Library of Congress (Washington, DC), 1999.

(With others) *Poetry and the American People,* Library of Congress (Washington, DC), 2000.

SIDELIGHTS: Rita Dove, who served as poet laureate of the United States from 1993 until 1995, has been described as a quiet leader and as an artist who weaves African-American experience into the broader perspective of international culture. Dove's lyrical and accessible poetry reflects the author's interest in music and drama, as well as her commitment to social justice and her sensitivity to women's issues. As Dove explained in the *Washington Post:* "Obviously, as a black woman, I am concerned with race. . . . But certainly not every poem of mine mentions the fact of being black. They are poems about humanity, and sometimes humanity happens to be black. I cannot run from, I won't run from any kind of truth." According to Renee H. Shea in

Women in the Arts, "Reflections on the spaces where public and private histories intersect are familiar terrain" in Dove's work. Shea added that in the poems, "every line, every image, is a testament to her gift for language, her wide-ranging and curious intellect, and her continuous research on life."

When she was appointed poet laureate in 1993, Dove was forty years old—the youngest poet ever to be elected to that honorary position. She was also the first poet laureate to see the appointment as a mandate to generate public interest in the literary arts. She traveled widely during her term, giving readings in a variety of venues from schools to hospitals. As the first African-American poet laureate, Dove noted in the *Washington Post* that her appointment was "significant in terms of the message it sends about the diversity of our culture and our literature."

Born in Akron, Ohio, in 1952, Dove is the daughter of a research chemist who broke the color barrier in the tire industry. She grew up in a home full of books and was an avid reader who also enjoyed writing and staging plays. In 1970, she was named a presidential scholar, one of the top one hundred high school graduates in the country that year. She earned a national merit scholarship to Miami University in Ohio, graduating Phi Beta Kappa in 1973. After that, she received a Fulbright fellowship to attend the University of Tübingen in West Germany, and then completed a master of fine arts at the prestigious Iowa Writers' Workshop. Although Dove published two chapbooks of poetry in 1977 and 1980, she made her formal literary debut in 1980 with the poetry collection *The Yellow House on the Corner,* which received praise for its sense of history combined with individual detail.

Dove's next volume, *Museum,* also received praise for its lyricism, its finely crafted use of language, and its detailed depiction of images drawn from her travels in Europe. Alvin Aubert of *American Book Review,* however, faulted the volume for an avoidance of personal issues and experiences, such as that of ethnicity. "I would like to know more about Rita Dove as a woman, including her ethnicity, and on her home ground," he asserted. Calvin Hernton of *Parnassus,* in contrast, praised the "universal" sensibility of the poems in *Museum,* which, he noted, "lack anything suggesting that they were written by a person of African, or African-American, artistic or cultural heritage."

Dove turned to prose fiction with the publication of *Fifth Sunday,* a short-story collection. Reviewers emphasized Dove's minimalist style and her interest in what a critic for *Southern Humanities Review* called "the fable-like aspects of middle class life." While considered promising, the volume generally received mixed reviews, with some critics finding the quality and detail of the writing uneven.

Dove is best known for her book of poems *Thomas and Beulah,* which garnered her the 1987 Pulitzer Prize in poetry. The poems in this collection are loosely based on the lives of Dove's maternal grandparents and are arranged in two sequences: one devoted to Thomas, born in 1900 in Wartrace, Tennessee, and the other to Beulah, born in 1904 in Rockmart, Georgia. *Thomas and Beulah* is viewed as a departure from Dove's earlier works in both its accessibility and its chronological sequence that has, to use Dove's words, "the kind of sweep of a novel." On the book's cover is a snapshot of a black couple in Akron, Ohio, in the 1940s (actually depicting not the author's grandparents, but an aunt and uncle). *New York Review of Books* contributor Helen Vendler observed that "though the photograph, and the chronology of the lives of Thomas and Beulah appended to the sequence, might lead one to suspect that Dove is a poet of simple realism, this is far from the case. Dove has learned . . . how to make a biographical fact the buried base of an imagined edifice."

The poems in *Grace Notes* are largely autobiographical. Alfred Corn remarked in *Poetry* that "glimpses offered in this collection of middle-class Black life have spark and freshness to them inasmuch as this social category hasn't had poetic coverage up to now." In *Parnassus,* Helen Vendler described Dove's poems as "rarely without drama," adding, "I admire Dove's persistent probes into ordinary language of the black proletariat." Jan Clausen noted in the *Women's Review of Books* that Dove's "images are elegant mechanisms for capturing moods and moments which defy analysis or translation." In the *Washington Post Book World,* A.L. Nielsen felt that the poems "abound in the unforgettable details of family character." Nielsen added that Dove "is one of those rare poets who approach common experience with the same sincerity with which the objectivist poets of an earlier generation approached the things of our world."

A more recent work, the novel *Through the Ivory Gate,* tells the story of Virginia King, a gifted young black woman who takes a position as artist-in-residence at an elementary school in her hometown of Akron, Ohio. The story alternates between past and present as Virginia's return stirs up strong, sometimes painful memories of her childhood. Barbara Hoffert observed in the *Li-brary Journal* that the "images are indelible, the emotions always heartfelt and fresh." In the *New York Times Book Review,* Geoff Ryman noted that *Through the Ivory Gate* "is mature in its telling of little stories—Virginia's recollections of life with a troupe of puppeteers, of visiting the rubber factory where her father worked, of neighborhood boys daubing a house so that it looked as if it had measles." He concluded, "The book aims to present the richness of a life and its connections to family and friends, culture, place, seasons, and self. In this it succeeds."

In 1993 Dove published *Selected Poems,* which contains three of her previously published volumes: *The Yellow House on the Corner, Museum,* and *Thomas and Beulah.* Assessing the collection for *Women's Review of Books,* Akasha (Gloria) Hull remarked that "In the guise of poet," Dove is transformed into "many types of women and men, and takes us readers into their consciousness, helping us to feel whatever it is we all share that makes those journeys possible."

Dove explores yet another genre with her first full-length play, *The Darker Face of the Earth.* "There's no reason to subscribe authors to particular genres," she commented in *Black American Literature Forum,* "I'm a writer, and I write in the form that most suits what I want to say." Depicting the events that ensue when a wealthy white woman named Amalia gives birth to a slave's child, *The Darker Face of the Earth* imbues the theme of slavery with high drama as well as the murderous elements reminiscent of the classical Greek drama *Oedipus Rex.* Hull, again writing for *Women's Review of Books,* commented that *The Darker Face of the Earth* "transfers the oedipal myth of patricide and maternal incest to antebellum South Carolina, and though we can guess the end from the very beginning, we read with continuing interest, sustained by Dove's poetic dialogue." *The Darker Face of the Earth* was produced at the Kennedy Center for the Performing Arts in Washington, DC. In *African American Review,* Theodora Carlisle suggested that the work "draws on a transcendent power, a dynamic that is at once erotic, compassionate, and creative. . . . This reading is endowed with both compassion and clearheaded responsibility to face and recognize the horrors as well as the richness implicit in the past."

While Dove's forays into fiction and drama have been well received, many observers would agree with Vendler, who commented in the *New Yorker* that Dove is "primarily a poet" because her greatest concern is language itself. Dove returned to writing poetry with her volumes *Mother Love* and *On the Bus with Rosa Parks*, two works that "deepen a dialogue over what might be described as public history versus private," to quote Matthew Flamm in the *New York Times Book Review*. Dedicated to Dove's daughter, Aviva, *Mother Love* takes its unifying structure from the Greek mother-daughter myth of Demeter and Persephone. Vendler praised Dove's unsentimental portrayal of motherhood, emphasizing her often wry and sometimes startling tone. "Dove brings into close focus the pained relation between mothers and daughters," noted Vendler. *Times Literary Supplement* correspondent Sarah Maguire likewise affirmed, "Dove's handling of the variety of voices and styles woven through the book shows a wonderful control of register and music."

On the Bus with Rosa Parks is also partly inspired by Dove's daughter, for on one occasion the poet and her daughter actually found themselves on a bus trip with the celebrated civil rights heroine. To quote Brenda Shaughnessy in *Publishers Weekly*, "Dove's tenacious belief in personal responsibility for public affairs is echoed throughout her new book, most notably in the sections about Rosa Parks, wherein the poet examines the critical moment when the woman whose name is now synonymous with the civil rights movement stepped into history by sitting down." Shaughnessy added, "Dove is a master at transforming a public or historic element—re-envisioning a spectacle and unearthing the heartfelt, wildly original private thoughts such historic moments always contain." *Library Journal* correspondent Ellen Kaufman felt that Dove's audience "will relish the delicious combination of a young girl, a dry wit, and a mature soul" in *On the Bus with Rosa Parks*. In an *American Visions* review of the collection, Denolyn Carroll concluded, "Their lyrical quality raises [Dove's] poems to the level of masterpieces."

Dove told a *Women in the Arts* interviewer: "I've always been obsessed by the voices that are not normally heard. I think it comes from the women I knew as a child, the women in the kitchen who told the best stories. They knew how the world worked, about human nature, and they were wise, are wise. When you are marginalized in any way—race, gender, age, class—you must learn to listen and pay attention very carefully if you are going to survive, and—women have known this since time immemorial—you have to anticipate what is expected of you, what you can get away with, how far you can push yourself. That makes you an extremely sensitive human being. It's the lemonade you get out of the lemons."

BIOGRAPHICAL AND CRITICAL SOURCES:

BOOKS

Contemporary Women Poets, St. James Press (Detroit, MI), 1998.
Keller, Lynn, *Forms of Expansion*, University of Chicago Press (Chicago, IL), 1997.
Novy, Marianne, editor, *Transforming Shakespeare*, St. Martin's Press (New York, NY), 1999.
Pereira, Malin, *Rita Dove's Cosmopolitanism*, University of Illinois Press, 2003.
Steffen, Therese, *Crossing Color: Transcultural Space and Place in Rita Dove's Poetry, Fiction, and Drama*, Oxford University Press (New York, NY), 2001.
Vendler, Helen Hennessy, *The Given and the Made: Strategies of Poetic Redefinition*, Harvard University Press (Cambridge, MA), 1995.

PERIODICALS

African American Review, spring, 2000, Theodora Carlisle, "Reading the Scars: Rita Dove's *The Darker Face of the Earth*," p. 135; summer, 2002, Malin Pereira, "'When the Pear Blossoms/ Cast Their Pale Faces on/ the Darker Face of the Earth': Miscegenation, the Primal Scene, and the Incest Motif in Rita Dove's Work," pp. 195-212.
American Book Review, July, 1985.
American Poetry Review, January, 1982, 36.
American Visions, April-May, 1994, p. 33; October, 1999, Denolyn Carroll, review of *On the Bus with Rosa Parks*, p. 34.
Belles Lettres, winter, 1993-94, pp. 38-41.
Black American Literature Forum, fall, 1986, pp. 227-240.
Booklist, February 1, 1981, p. 743; August, 1983; March 15, 1986, p. 1057; February 15, 1997.
Callaloo, winter, 1986; spring, 1991; winter, 1996.
Detroit Free Press, July 24, 1993, pp. 5A, 7A.
Georgia Review, summer, 1984; winter, 1986.
Kliatt, March, 1994, p. 25.
Library Journal, August, 1992; November 15, 1993, p. 81; March 1, 1994, p. 88; April 1, 1997; May 15, 1999, Ellen Kaufman, review of *On the Bus with Rosa Parks*, p. 99.
Michigan Quarterly Review, spring, 1987, pp. 428-438.
New Yorker, May 15, 1995.
New York Review of Books, October 23, 1986.

New York Times Book Review, October 11, 1992; April 11, 1999, Matthew Flamm, review of *On the Bus with Rosa Parks,* p. 24.

North American Review, March, 1986.

Parnassus, spring-summer-fall-winter, 1985; Volume 16, number 2, 1991.

Poetry, October, 1984; October, 1990, pp. 37-39; March, 1996, Ben Howard, review of *Mother Love,* p. 349.

Publishers Weekly, August 3, 1992; January 31, 1994, p. 83; April 12, 1999, Brenda Shaughnessy, "Rita Dove: Taking the Heat," p. 48; July 31, 2000, review of *Best American Poetry 2000,* p. 90.

Southern Humanities Review, winter, 1988, p. 87.

Times Literary Supplement, February 18, 1994; November 17, 1995, p. 29.

USA Weekend, March 25-27, 1994, p. 22.

Virginia Quarterly Review, spring, 1988, pp. 262-276.

Washington Post, April 17, 1987; May 19, 1993; November 7, 1997.

Washington Post Book World, April 8, 1990, p. 4; July 30, 1995, p. 8.

Women in the Arts, spring, 1999, Renee H. Shea, "Irresistible Beauty: The Poetry and Person of Rita Dove," pp. 6-9.

Women's Review of Books, July, 1990, pp. 12-13; May, 1994, p. 6; May, 1996.

ONLINE

Rita Dove Home Page, http://www.people.virginia.edu/~rfd4b/ (June 28, 2003).

*   *   *

DOVE, Rita Frances
  See DOVE, Rita

*   *   *

DOYLE, John
  See GRAVES, Robert

*   *   *

DOYLE, Roddy 1958-

PERSONAL: Born May 8, 1958 in Dublin, Ireland; son of Rory (a printer) and Ida (a secretary; maiden name, Bolger) Doyle; married; wife's name Belinda; children: two sons. *Education:* Attended University College (Dublin, Ireland).

ADDRESSES: Agent—Patti Kelly, Viking Books, 375 Hudson St., New York, NY 10014.

CAREER: Playwright, screenwriter, educator, and novelist. Greendale Community School, Kilbarrack, Dublin, Ireland, English and geography teacher, 1980—.

AWARDS, HONORS: The Van was shortlisted for the Booker Prize, British Book Trust, 1991; Booker Prize, 1993, for *Paddy Clarke Ha Ha Ha;* W.H. Smith Children's Book of the Year Award shortlist, 2001, for *The Giggler Treatment.*

WRITINGS:

NOVELS

The Commitments, Heinemann (London, England), 1988, Random House (New York, NY), 1989.

The Snapper, Secker & Warburg (London, England), 1990, Penguin (New York, NY), 1992.

The Van, Viking (New York, NY), 1991.

The Barrytown Trilogy, Secker & Warburg, (London, England), 1992.

Paddy Clarke Ha Ha Ha, Secker & Warburg, (London, England), 1993.

The Woman Who Walked into Doors, Viking (New York, NY) 1996.

A Star Called Henry, Viking (New York, NY), 1999.

SCREENPLAYS

(With Dick Clement and Ian La Frenais) *The Commitments* (based on the novel by Doyle), Twentieth Century-Fox, 1991.

The Snapper (based on the novel by Doyle), Miramax Films, 1993.

The Van (based on the novel by Doyle), British Broadcasting Corp. (BBC), 1996.

Famine, Crom Films, 1998.

OTHER

Brownbread (play; produced in Dublin, Ireland; also see below), Secker & Warburg (London, England), 1987.

War (play; produced in Dublin, Ireland; also see below), Passion Machine (Dublin, Ireland), 1989.

Brownbread and War (plays), Minerva (London, England), 1993, Penguin Books (New York, NY), 1994.

Family (television script), BBC, 1994.

The Giggler Treatment (for children), drawings by Brian Ajhar, Arthur A. Levine Books (New York, NY), 2000.

Rover Saves Christmas (for children), drawings by Brian Ajhar, Arthur A. Levine Books (New York, NY), 2001.

Rory and Ita (memoir), Viking (New York, NY), 2002.

Also author of screenplay *When Brendan Met Trudy*, 2001. Contributor to anthologies, including *My Favorite Year*, Witherby (London, England), 1993, and *Yeats Is Dead!: A Mystery by Fifteen Irish Writers*, edited by Joseph O'Connor, Knopf (New York, NY), 2001.

SIDELIGHTS: Roddy Doyle's trilogy of novels about the Irish Rabbitte family, known informally as the "Barrytown trilogy," has been internationally acclaimed for wit, originality, and powerful dialogue. Each of the three books—*The Commitments, The Snapper,* and *The Van*—focuses on a single character of the large Rabbitte family who live in Barrytown, Dublin. They are "a like-able, rough, sharp-witted clan," observed Lawrence Dugan in the *Chicago Tribune.* Typical working-class citizens, the Rabbittes are a vivacious and resilient household, lustily displaying an often ribald sense of humor. "These books are funny all the way down to their syntax," claimed Guy Mannes-Abbott in the *New Statesman & Society,* "enabling Doyle to sustain my laughter over two or three pages."

The Commitments is, perhaps, Doyle's most well-recognized work. The successful novel was adapted in 1991 into a very popular screenplay by Doyle, Dick Clement, and Ian La Frenais, and directed by award-winning filmmaker Alan Parker. In both the novel and the film, Doyle's wit and originality are evident. The main character, Jimmy Rabbitte, inspired by the rhythm and blues music of James Brown, B.B. King, and Marvin Gaye, resolves to form an Irish soul band in Dublin. He places a musicians-wanted ad in the paper: "Have you got Soul? If yes, . . . contact J. Rabbitte." And so is born the "Commitments," with Jimmy as the manager of a group which includes Imelda, a singer, and Joey "The Lips" Fagan, a musician who claims to have "jammed with the man" James Brown. "The rehearsals, as Mr. Doyle chronicles them," wrote Kinky Friedman in the *New York Times,* "are authentic, joyous, excruciating and funny as hell." Dugan, in the *Chicago Tribune,* described *The Commitments* as "a beautifully told

story about the culture that absorbed the Vikings, Normans, Scots, and British now trying its luck with black America." The film version stars an all-Irish cast, including Robert Arkins, Andrew Strong, and singer Maria Doyle performing such 1960s hits as "Mustang Sally" and "In the Midnight Hour." A *People* critic reviewed the film and concluded, "The cathartic power of music has never been more graphically demonstrated."

Doyle's second novel, *The Snapper,* focuses on Sharon Rabbitte, Jimmy's older sister, who is young, unmarried, and pregnant. As Sharon refuses to reveal the identity of the father of her "snapper," her predicament has the Rabbitte household in a tizzy, and she becomes the target of humorous speculations by the Barrytown citizens. As a result of Sharon's pregnancy, relationships within the family undergo various transformations ranging from the compassionate (dad Jimmy, Sr.) to the murderous (mom Veronica), while Sharon herself tries to understand the changes within her own body. A *Los Angeles Times Book Review* critic noted that "few novels depict parent-child relationships—healthy relationships, no less—better than this one, and few men could write more sensitively about pregnancy."

Like *The Commitments, The Snapper* is written in the Irish vernacular, with little descriptive intrusion and with an enormous sense of humor. John Nicholson in the London *Times* pointed out Doyle's "astonishing talent for turning the humdrum into high comedy" in the novel. He also singled out the characters' vernacular banter for critical praise—"the dialogue of *The Snapper* crackles with wit and authenticity." This is a "very funny" novel, admitted Tania Glyde in the London *Times,* yet she further pointed out that "it is also sad . . . Sharon's life . . . would be tragic without the support of her large and singular family." *Times Literary Supplement* critic Stephen Leslie asserted, "*The Snapper* is a worthy successor to *The Commitments.*"

Shortlisted for Britain's prestigious Booker Prize, Roddy Doyle's third Rabbitte novel, *The Van,* changes the focus to Jimmy, Sr., the Rabbitte family's ribald, fun-loving father, who has been recently laid off work. Jimmy and his best friend, Bimbo, open a portable fast-food restaurant—Bimbo's Burgers—housed in a greasy van that is a health inspector's nightmare. The antics of the two friends running the business provide much of the hilarity of the book; for example, they mistakenly deep-fry a diaper, serve it up to a customer like cod, and then flee—restaurant and all—from his wrath, hurling frozen fish at their victim from the back of the van. Jimmy and his friends are Irish laborers "whose idea of wit and repartee is putting on fake Mexican accents and 'burstin' their shite' at jokes about farting," wrote Anne-Marie Conway in the *Times Literary Supplement.* "*The Van* is not just a very funny book," insisted Mannes-Abbott, "it is also faultless comic writing."

Critical response toward *The Van* was enthusiastic, with many reviewers finding a special appeal in what a *Publishers Weekly* commentator called Doyle's "brash originality and humor that are both uniquely Irish and shrewdly universal." Reviewer Tim Appelo, in the *Los Angeles Times Book Review,* maintained that "Doyle has perfect pitch from the get-go. He can write pages of lifelike, impeccably profane dialogue without a false note or a dull fill, economically evoking every lark and emotional plunge in the life of an entire Irish family."

Doyle's next book, *Paddy Clarke Ha Ha Ha,* was awarded the prestigious Booker Prize in 1993. The novel is written from the point of view of Paddy Clarke, a ten-year-old Irish boy, whose often humorous escapades become gradually more violent and disturbing as the story progresses. John Gallagher in the *Detroit News and Free Press* commented on Doyle's effective use of a stream-of-consciousness narrative, and noted a "theme of undeserved suffering. . . . *Paddy Clarke Ha Ha Ha* matures into an unforgettable portrait of troubled youth."

In the *New York Times,* Mary Gordon established her admiration for Doyle by stating that "perhaps no one has done so much to create a new set of images for the Ireland of the late twentieth century as Roddy Doyle." Doyle's book *The Woman Who Walked into Doors* is about an abused, beaten wife who continually goes to the hospital emergency room and is never questioned by the staff, who merely "chalk [her repeat visits] up to her drinking or clumsiness or bad luck." Paula came from a family with loving, affectionate parents and three sisters, and her marriage started out with a "blissful honeymoon at the seaside." Gordon ruminates about Doyle's description of "what it's like to be beaten by your lover, the father of your children," and feels that it "is a masterpiece of virtuoso moves. Nothing is blinked; nothing is simplified." Paula finally comes to her senses when she sees her husband "looking at their daughter, not with desire . . . but with hate and a wish to annihilate. She stops being a battered wife when she becomes a protective mother."

In *A Star Called Henry,* Doyle delves into Irish history and nationalism as experienced by the book's title character, Henry Smart. "Henry is the dark horse of Irish history, Forrest Gump with a brain, and an attitude—the man cropped out of the official photographs, the boy soldier not credited for even his dirtiest work," wrote Robert Cremins in the *Houston Chronicle.* Born into poverty in the early 1900s, Henry is streetwise by the age of three, wandering the lanes and alleys with his year-old brother Victor, stealing what the pair needs to survive. His mother is weary with a bleak outlook, and his father is a one-legged bouncer at a brothel, a sometime murderer, and drop-of-the-hat brawler. Henry's single day of formal education ends with him being ousted by the head nun, but he cements a relationship with his teacher, Miss O'Shea, that will be taken up again in earnest later in life. Victor dies, his father abandons them, and he loses contact with his mother. Despite his disadvantages, Henry is clever and cunning, strikingly handsome, and able to use the brains that nature gave him. He inherits his father's wooden leg, and uses it both as a weapon and as a talisman to remind him where he came from and where he wants to go.

While still a teen, Henry joins the Irish Republican Army (IRA), doing so "because of his resentment of the squalor he grew up in, rather than any passion for nationhood," wrote Anthony Wilson-Smith in *Maclean's.* In his first combat against the British, Henry is more interested in shooting out store windows—symbols of the wealth and life he never had—than at British soldiers.

At age fourteen, Henry finds himself fighting along legendary Irish revolutionaries Michael Collins, James Connolly, and Padraig Pearce in the Easter Uprising of 1916 and the occupation of the General Post Office. "The account of the 1916 Easter Uprising, the occupation of the GPO, and the bloodshed that follows must be one of the boldest and vivid descriptions of civil strife in a familiar city ever penned," observed a *Publishers Weekly* reviewer. Henry meets up again with Miss O'Shea, and the two consummate their relationship on stacks of unused stamps in the basement of the post office. They are separated after the fierce battle of Easter, 1916—Henry barely escapes with his life, and continues to rise in the ranks of the IRA. Henry and Miss O'Shea meet again—and marry—three years later, with Henry deliberately avoiding knowledge of her given name ("We became man and wife without me hearing her first name," Henry says. "She was and stayed my Miss O'Shea. I never knew her name.").

Henry emerges from the story as larger-than-life, a prodigy, and a kind of home-grown superhero of the stature of Finn McCool. "Fact and fiction aside, historians and non-historians alike will find little not to like about Henry Smart—his confidence, his humor, his pride," wrote Clare Bose in *Europe.* "He is a myth and not a legend, more Butch and Sundance than Bonnie and Clyde, but a very well-created myth at that." David Kirby, writing in *Atlanta Journal-Constitution,* also found Henry to be an engaging character, writing, "He's an impetuous, lucky fellow who always manages to find a way out of the fire and back into the frying pan, saved again and again either by some gooey-eyed damsel or his pop's prosthesis, surely the oddest good luck charm in all literature."

James Hopkin, writing in the *New Statesman,* observed, "There are enough fine moments in *A Star Called Henry* to remind us that Doyle is an accomplished writer; his dialogue is earthy and effective, he can render a scene as well as anyone, and a simple poetry plays around the edges of his prose." Still, for Hopkin, "stylistic flaws and heavy doses of sentiment" mar the story. Other critics, including Grace Fill in *Booklist,* remarked that "Doyle expertly weaves his well-known wit into even the most violent and most tender passages of the tale." Colleen Kelly-Warren, writing in the *St. Louis Post-Dispatch,* commented that "Doyle's writing combines rhythmic, cadenced prose, rich description, and dialogue that's real enough to feel overheard." Critic William Hutchings, in a *World Literature Today* review, remarked that the novel's "psychological insights into an adolescent gunman are remarkable, and its portrait of childhood homelessness in the streets and slums of turn-of-the-century Dublin, where rat-catching for profit provides a means of subsistence, is unforgettable, heartrending, and harrowingly real."

Doyle has also turned his keen observations and wit to good use in a pair of children's books. In *The Giggler Treatment,* adults who are mean to children are given the signature treatment of the Gigglers: a smear of dog excrement on their shoes. The furry little Gigglers have placed their smelly payload directly in the path of Mister Mack, a cookie taster who is thought to have transgressed against his children. The action and suspense of the book—whether Mister Mack will step in the dog poo or not—takes less than a minute, but throughout Doyle digresses and diverges into such material as a history of gigglers, secrets about dogs, and a dictionary of Irish terms. However, it emerges that Mister Mack is innocent of any wrongdoing, and his entire family, including a Giggler and dog Rover, rush to ensure his shoes remain clean. A *Publishers Weekly* reviewer called the book a "bracingly rude dose of fun," while Steven Engelfried, writing in *School Library Journal,* observed that "the imaginative narrative and clever plotting make this more than just another silly read."

Rover Saves Christmas finds the usually steadfast and resolute Rudolph suffering from a cold and a possible mid-life crisis. Santa asks talking-dog Rover to take over for the incapacitated reindeer. The Mack children (from *The Giggler Treatment*), their friend Victoria, and lizards Hans and Heidi join Santa and Rover on the worldwide journey on Christmas Eve. The non-linear text constantly veers from the main story to other features, including glossaries of Irish words, warnings to children, funny commercials, descriptions, and even the rebellion of the surly chapter six. "Such digressions have a joyous, vigorous lunacy, absolutely in tune with a child's way of thinking," commented Sarah Crompton in the *Daily Telegraph.* A *Publishers Weekly* critic called the book "enormously entertaining," and Regan McMahon, writing in *San Francisco Chronicle,* remarked that *Rover Saves Christmas* "may not be the first story of how Christmas gets saved just in the nick of time, but it may be the funniest."

Doyle's *Rory & Ita,* is the nonfiction biography of his parents. "It's Roddy's job to take his parents' oral history of their times and relationship and transform it into something interesting," wrote Steven E. Alford in the *Houston Chronicle.* "And in *Rory & Ita,* his first nonfiction work, he largely succeeds." Ita was born in 1925, and "so surrounded was she by poverty that she didn't recognize deprivation and hardship for what it was," Alford wrote. After a dubious first meeting at a local dance—Rory was inebriated and unappealing—their courtship thrived, and they were married in 1951. "Doyle's art consists in taking these disjointed memories and, through discreet stitching, turning them into a smooth narrative fabric," Alford observed.

"This is a charming story of two ordinary people whose lives were beset by routine struggles, most of them occasioned by the lack of money," Alford remarked. "Now and then, the account offers insight into the lifestyle changes over a single generation," wrote a *Publishers Weekly* reviewer. Some poignant moments, such as the death of the Doyles' third baby, are recounted. Rory's past as a member of the IRA is hinted at. But mostly, the book emerges as "a study in ordinariness," wrote Charlotte Moore in the *Spectator.* "Either you like this kind of thing or you don't," Moore observed. "I love it. I relished every word of *Rory & Ita.*" Some critics remarked that because of their ordinary lives, the Doyles may not merit a full-blown biography. However, "all personal testimony is of historical interest," Moore declared. "This book is Doyle's very personal endeavor at capturing his family's history, and his parents come across as lovely, genuine people," wrote Elsa Gaztambide in *Booklist.* "It's a pity we can't all have our memories handled with such dignity and care," Moore concluded.

BIOGRAPHICAL AND CRITICAL SOURCES:

BOOKS

Contemporary Literary Criticism, Volume 81, Thomson Gale (Detroit), 1994.

Dictionary of Literary Biography, Volume 194: *British Novelists since 1960, Second Series,* Thomson Gale (Detroit, MI), 1998.

Doyle, Roddy, *The Commitments,* Heinemann (London, England), 1988, Random House (New York, NY), 1989.

Doyle, Roddy, *A Star Called Henry,* Viking (New York, NY), 1999.

Drabble, Margaret, editor, *Oxford Companion to English Literature,* 6th edition, Oxford University Press (New York, NY), 2000.

Modern British Literature, 2nd edition, St. James Press (Detroit, MI), 2000.

Stade, George, and Sarah Hanna Goldstein, editors, *British Writers,* Scribner (New York, NY), 1999.

PERIODICALS

America, February 19, 2000, James Martin, James S. Torrens, and John Breslin, review of *A Star Called Henry,* p. 25.

Atlanta Journal-Constitution, October 10, 1999, David Kirby, "Doyle's *Star* Casts a Pall of Darkness on Irish Life," review of *A Star Called Henry,* p. L10.

Book, September, 1999, review of *A Star Called Henry,* p. 69.

Booklist, June 1, 1999, Grace Fill, review of *A Star Called Henry,* p. 1741; June 1, 1999, review of *The Woman Who Walked into Doors,* p. 1797; March 15, 2000, review of *A Star Called Henry,* p. 1337; February 1, 2002, Joanne Wilkinson, review of *A Star Called Henry,* p. 925; November 15, 2002, Elsa Gaztambide, review of *Rory & Ita,* p. 562.

Book World, September 5, 1999, review of *A Star Called Henry,* p. 3; October 31, 1999, review of *A Star Called Henry,* p. 4.

Boston Globe, December 19, 1993.

Chicago Tribune, August 9, 1992, p. 5.

Christian Science Monitor, September 16, 1999, review of *A Star Called Henry,* p. 16; November 18, 1999, review of *A Star Called Henry,* p. 12.

Commonweal, November 19, 1999, review of *A Star Called Henry,* p. 56.

Daily Telegraph (London, England), December 1, 2002, Sarah Crompton, review of *Rover Saves Christmas.*

Detroit News and Free Press, December 12, 1993,

Entertainment Weekly, September 17, 1999, review of *A Star Called Henry,* p. 74; December 24, 1999, review of *A Star Called Henry,* p. 144.

Europe, March, 2000, Claire Bose, review of *A Star Called Henry,* p. 34.

Globe and Mail (Toronto, Ontario, Canada), September 11, 1999, review of *A Star Called Henry,* p. D18; November 27, 1999, review of *A Star Called Henry,* p. D50; December 1, 2001, review of *Rover Saves Christmas,* p. D16.

Guardian (London, England), September 2, 2000, review of *A Star Called Henry,* p. 11.

Horn Book Guide, spring, 2001, review of *The Giggler Treatment,* p. 60.

Houston Chronicle, October 10, 1999, Robert Cremins, review of *A Star Called Henry,* p. 15; December 15, 2002, Steven E. Alford, review of *Rory & Ita,* p. 23.

Independent (London, England), April 14, 1996, p. 32.

Kirkus Reviews, June 15, 1999, review of *A Star Called Henry,* p. 901; November 1, 2001, review of *Rover Saves Christmas,* p. 1548; September 15, 2002, review of *Rory & Ita,* p. 1363.

Knight Ridder/Tribune News Service, Dave Ferman, review of *Rita and Ita,* p. K6369.

Library Journal, August, 1999, Heather McCormack, review of *A Star Called Henry,* p. 137.

Literary Review, summer, 1999, Karen Sbrockey, "Something of a Hero: An Interview with Roddy Doyle," p. 537.

Los Angeles Times Book Review, July 19, 1992, p. 6; September 20, 1992, p. 3; October 3, 1999, review of *A Star Called Henry,* p. 2.

Maclean's August 30, 1993, p. 50; October 25, 1999, Anthony Wilson-Smith, review of *A Star Called Henry,* p. 93.

Nation, April 16, 2001, Tim Appelo, review of *When Brendan Met Trudy,* p. 35.

New Republic, September 16, 1991, p. 30.

New Statesman, September 6, 1999, James Hopkin, review of *A Star Called Henry,* p. 54.

New Statesman & Society, August 23, 1991, pp. 35-36; June 18, 1993, p. 39.

New Straits Times, August 7, 1996.

Newsweek, December 27, 1993, p. 48.

Newsweek International, September 20, 1999, Carla Power, "The Myths of Rebellion: A New Novel Takes on Freedom Fighters," review of *A Star Called Henry,* p. 35.

New Yorker, January 24, 1994, p. 91; February 5, 1996, p. 56; October 4, 1999, Daphne Merkin, review of *A Star Called Henry,* pp. 110-117.

New York Review of Books, February 3, 1994, p. 3.

New York Times, July 23, 1989, p. 11; December 13, 1993, p. B2; May 16, 1997, p. B12; September 10, 1999, Richard Bernstein and Eric Asimov, review of *A Star Called Henry,* p. B42; September 10, 1999, review of *A Star Called Henry,* p. E44.

New York Times Book Review, October 11, 1992, p. 15; October 8, 1993; January 2, 1994, pp. 1, 21; April 28, 1996, p. 7; May 2, 1999, Katharine Weber, "Finbar's Hotel," p. 19; September 12, 1999, Richard Eder, review of *A Star Called Henry,* p. 7; December 5, 1999, p. 6; December 5, 1999, review of *A Star Called Henry,* p. 106; September 17, 2000, "So Watch Your Step," p. 33; December 16, 2001, review of *Rover Saves Christmas,* p. 20.

Observer (London, England), October 31, 1993, p. 18; August 29, 1999, review of *A Star Called Henry,* p. 11; September 12, 1999, review of *A Star Called Henry,* p. 7; October 28, 2001, review of *Rover Saves Christmas,* p. 16.

People, August 26, 1991, pp. 13-14.

Philadelphia Inquirer, January 20, 1994, pp. E1, E7.

Publishers Weekly, May 25, 1992, p. 36; March 25, 1996, pp. 55-56; July 12, 1999, review of *A Star Called Henry,* p. 70; October 4, 1999, review of *A Star Called Henry,* p. 36; November 1, 1999, review of *A Star Called Henry,* p. 45; July 24, 2000, review of *The Giggler Treatment,* p. 94; September 24, 2001, review of *Rover Saves Christmas,* p. 54; September 24, 2001, review of *The Giggler Treatment,* p. 95; September 23, 2002, review of *Rory & Ita,* p. 59.

Reading Teacher, May, 2001, review of *The Giggler Treatment,* p. 827.

Rolling Stone, September 21, 1989, p. 27.

St. Louis Post-Dispatch, September 19, 1999, Colleen Kelly Warren, "Doyle's Exuberant, Bleak Story Introduces Henry Smart, an IRA Assassin Born to the Job," review of *A Star Called Henry,* p. F10.

San Francisco Chronicle, October 2, 1999, Sam Whiting, "A Star Called Roddy Doyle: Irish Novelist's Latest Best-seller Delves into History, Both Personal and National," profile of Roddy Doyle, p. B1; December 16, 2001, Regan McMahon, review of *Rover Saves Christmas,* p. 4.

School Library Journal, November, 2000, Steven Engelfried, review of *The Giggler Treatment,* p. 119; October, 2001, review of *Rover Saves Christmas,* p. 64.

Sewanee Review, fall, 1999, Floyd Skloot, review of *A Star Called Henry,* p. C3.

Spectator, September 4, 1999, Kevin Myers, review of *A Star Called Henry,* pp. 32-33; November 30, 2002, Charlotte Moore, "In Their Own Words," review of *Rory & Ita,* p. 54.

Star-Telegram (Fort Worth, TX), February 5, 2003, Dave Ferman, review of *Rory & Ita.*

Time, December 6, 1993, p. 82; September 6, 1999, review of *A Star Called Henry,* p. 76; October 4, 1999, Walter Kirn, "The Best of the Boyos: Roddy Doyle Vividly Portrays the Wild Passions of an Irish Everyman in *A Star Called Henry,*" p. 102.

Times (London, England), August 16, 1990; October 5, 1991, p. 51.

Times Educational Supplement, July 2, 1993, p. 18.

Times Literary Supplement, December 21-27, 1990, p. 1381; August 16, 1991, p. 22; June 11, 1993, p. 21; November 5, 1993, p. 14; September 3, 1999, review of *A Star Called Henry,* p. 8.

Wall Street Journal, September 10, 1999, Allen Barra, review of *A Star Called Henry,* p. W7; March 9, 2001, Joe Morgenstern, review of *When Brendan Met Trudy,* p. W4.

Washington Post, February 4, 1995.

Washington Post Book World, August 10, 1992, p. B2.

World Literature Today, summer, 2000, William Hutchings, review of *A Star Called Henry,* p. 594.

World of Hibernia, winter, 1999, John Boland, review of *A Star Called Henry,* p. 155.

ONLINE

Guardian Online, http://guardian.co.uk/ (January 14, 2003), "Roddy Doyle."

Salon.com, http://www.salon.com/ (October 28, 1999), Charles Taylor, interview with Doyle.

*   *   *

DR. A
   See ASIMOV, Isaac

*   *   *

DRABBLE, Margaret 1939-

PERSONAL: Born June 5, 1939, in Sheffield, England; daughter of John Frederick (a judge) and Kathleen Marie (Bloor) Drabble; married Clive Walter Swift (an actor with the Royal Shakespeare Company), June, 1960 (divorced, 1975); married Michael Holroyd (an author), 1982; children: (first marriage) Adam Richard George, Rebecca Margaret, Joseph. *Education:* Newnham College, Cambridge, B.A. (first class honors), 1960. *Hobbies and other interests:* Walking, dreaming.

ADDRESSES: Agent—Peters, Fraser, and Dunlop, 5th Floor, The Chambers, Chelsea Harbour, Lots Road, London SW10 0XF, England.

CAREER: Novelist, biographer, critic, editor, and short-story writer. Member of Royal Shakespeare Company for one year.

MEMBER: National Book League (deputy chair, 1978-80; chair, 1980-82).

AWARDS, HONORS: John Llewelyn Rhys Memorial Award, 1966, for *The Millstone;* James Tait Black Memorial Book Prize, 1968, for *Jerusalem the Golden;* Book of the Year Award, *Yorkshire Post,* 1972, for *The Needle's Eye;* E.M. Forster Award, National Institute and American Academy of Arts and Letters, 1973; *The Middle Ground* named a notable book of 1980 by the American Library Association, 1981; honorary fellow of Sheffield City Polytechnic, 1989. D.Litt., University of Sheffield, 1976, University of Manchester, 1987, University of Keele, 1988, University of Bradford, 1988, University of Hull, 1992, University of East Anglia, 1994, and University of York, 1995.

WRITINGS:

NOVELS

A Summer Bird-Cage, Weidenfeld & Nicolson (London, England), 1963, Morrow (New York, NY), 1964.

The Garrick Year, Weidenfeld & Nicolson (London, England), 1964, Morrow (New York, NY), 1965.

The Millstone, Weidenfeld & Nicolson (London, England), 1965, Morrow (New York, NY), 1966, published with new introduction by Drabble, Longman (London, England), 1970, published as *Thank You All Very Much,* New American Library (New York, NY), 1973.

Jerusalem the Golden, Morrow (New York, NY), 1967.

The Waterfall, Knopf (New York, NY), 1969.

The Needle's Eye, Knopf (New York, NY), 1972.

The Realms of Gold, Knopf (New York, NY), 1975.

The Ice Age, Knopf (New York, NY), 1977.

The Middle Ground, Knopf (New York, NY), 1980.

The Radiant Way (first novel in a trilogy), Knopf (New York, NY), 1987.

A Natural Curiosity (second novel in a trilogy), Viking (New York, NY), 1989.

The Gates of Ivory (third novel in a trilogy), Viking (New York, NY), 1991.

Margaret Drabble in Tokyo, edited by Fumi Takano, Kenkyusha (Tokyo, Japan), 1991.

The Witch of Exmoor, Viking (New York, NY), 1996.

The Peppered Moth, Harcourt (New York, NY), 2001.

The Seven Sisters, Harcourt (New York, NY), 2002.

OTHER

Laura (television play), Granada Television, 1964.

Wadsworth (criticism), Evans Brothers (London, England), 1966, Arco, 1969.

(Author of dialogue) *Isadora* (screenplay), Universal, 1968.

Thank You All Very Much (screenplay; based on Drabble's novel, *The Millstone*), Columbia, 1969, released as *A Touch of Love,* Palomar Pictures, 1969.

Bird of Paradise (play), first produced in London, England, 1969.

(Editor, with B.S. Johnson) *London Consequences* (group novel), Greater London Arts Association, 1972.

Virginia Woolf: A Personal Debt, Aloe Editions (New York, NY), 1973.

Arnold Bennett (biography), Knopf (New York, NY), 1974.

(Editor) *Jane Austen, Lady Susan, the Watsons and Sanditon,* Penguin (New York, NY), 1975.

(Editor, with Charles Osborne) *New Stories 1,* Arts Council of Great Britain (London, England), 1976.

(Editor) *The Genius of Thomas Hardy,* Knopf (New York, NY), 1976.

For Queen and Country: Britain in the Victorian Age, Deutsch (London, England), 1978, published as *For Queen and Country: Victorian England,* Houghton (New York, NY), 1979.

A Writer's Britain: Landscape and Literature, photographs by Jorge Lewinski, Knopf (New York, NY), 1979.

(Editor) *The Oxford Companion to English Literature,* 5th edition, Oxford University Press (Oxford, England), 1985, sixth edition, 2000.

(Editor, with Jenny Stringer) *The Concise Oxford Companion to English Literature,* Oxford University Press (New York, NY), 1987, second edition, 2004.

Stratford Revisited, Celandine Press (Shipston-on-Stour, Warwickshire, England), 1989.

Safe as Houses, Chatto & Windus (London, England), 1990.

(Editor) Emily Brontë, *Wuthering Heights, and Poems,* Charles E. Tuttle Co., 1993.

Angus Wilson: A Biography, St. Martin's Press (New York, NY), 1996.

(Author of introduction) Thomas Hardy, *The Woodlanders,* Knopf (New York, NY), 1997.

Contributor to *Contemporary Fiction,* selected by Lorna Sage, Book Trust, 1988. Author of story for "A Roman Marriage," Winkast Productions. Contributor to numerous anthologies.

SIDELIGHTS: On the strength of her first three novels, *A Summer Bird-Cage, The Garrick Year,* and *The Millstone,* Margaret Drabble made her reputation in the early 1960s as the preeminent novelist of the modern woman, and she has gone on in subsequent novels to reaffirm her standing. Sister of fellow novelist A.S. Byatt, Drabble focuses her fiction on women attempting to make something of themselves in modern England, moving, as in novels ranging from the early *A Summer Bird-Cage* to the later *A Peppered Moth* and *The Seven Sisters,* the concerns of her protagonist to align with her own. As Stephanie Foote noted in a review of the 2002 novel *The Seven Sisters* for *Book:* "A master of quirky, richly drawn characters, Drabble is attuned to people on the brink of unexpected change." In addition to her fiction, Drabble has also made her mark as a biographer and has served as editor for several highly respected literary reference works.

Drabble's characters Sarah Bennett of *A Summer Bird-Cage* and Rosamund Stacey of *The Millstone,* are, like the author herself, Oxbridge graduates. Sarah has given up the notion of going on to get a higher degree because "you can't be a sexy don," and she has spent a year rather aimlessly looking for something to do that is worthy of her talents and education. In the course of the novel, she considers her options, partly represented by her beautiful sister Louise, who has sacrificed any ambition she had to marry a rich, fussy, rather sexless man, and partly by her Oxford friends, most of whom are working at dull jobs in London and falling short of their ambitions almost as badly as Louise is. In the end, Sarah is preparing to marry her long-time Oxford boyfriend, though she insists that she will "marry a don" as opposed to becoming "a don's wife." Rosamund, a Cambridge graduate, is more determined and less conventional. Not only does she earn her doctorate in English literature during the course of the novel, but she also becomes pregnant, has the baby on her own, and experiences mother-love at the same time.

At age twenty-six, somewhat older than the other two characters and the mother of two small children, Emma Evans of *The Garrick Year* experiences other problems. Having just been offered a chance to escape from the domestic routine for part of the day by reading the news on television, she finds that she must move her family from London to Hereford, where her actor husband has a year's engagement with a provincial theatre company. There she tries to escape the even more intense boredom by having an affair with her husband's director. Like Rosamund, Emma finds that motherhood is the dominant factor in her life and that both she and her husband are bound to their marriage by that most important factor, the children.

Drabble's approach is realistic in her early novels as she explores the extreme ambivalence her characters feel toward motherhood and the enforced domesticity accompanying it. As Valerie Grosvenor Myer put it in *Margaret Drabble: Puritanism and Permissiveness,* "The woman undergraduate's interest is divided between her academic work and her feminine destiny, which at the university stage appears as though it will take the conventional social forms. The conflict is between the duty of the self-imposed task and instinct." The early Drabble heroine is constantly fighting the opposing forces of ambition—the need to do something in the world, "the greater gifts, greater duty to society line," as she described it in *A Summer Bird-Cage*—and the social and biological urge to get married and/or have babies.

The two novels that followed these early treatments of women, *Jerusalem the Golden* and *The Waterfall,* represent a considerable development for Drabble as a novelist. Ellen Cronan Rose contended in *Critical Essays on Margaret Drabble* that *Jerusalem the Golden* is Drabble's "first wholly realized novel, economical in its construction, finely precise in its characterization of the heroine. In later novels she will be more profound; never will she be more completely in control of her material than in this relatively early work."

The Waterfall returns to the solipsistic protagonist but treats her in a much more self-conscious way. The most experimental of Drabble's novels, *The Waterfall* has as its primary stylistic characteristic a divided narrative point of view. The first half of the book is written in the third person, narrated from the point of view of protagonist Jane Grey, a young woman on the verge of agoraphobia. She is the mother of a small child, and her husband has left her during the sixth month of her second pregnancy. The novel opens with the birth of Jane's second child and her falling in love with her cousin's husband and continues with Jane's experience of the ensuing affair, which is presented as the highest and most consuming of passions. In the middle of the novel, however, Jane breaks out in the first person, exclaiming, "Lies, lies, it's all lies. A pack of lies. . . . What have I tried to describe? A passion, a love, an unreal life, a life in limbo, without anxiety, guilt, corpses." The two voices then alternate, the third-person narrator creating an intense and unreal story of passionate love and the first-person narrator training an objective, almost cynical eye on the novel's events and characters. In one sense, this split expresses a division that runs throughout Drabble's fiction, between a romantic yearning for coherence through love and a realistic skepticism prompted by the awareness of conflict and incoherence.

Critics have been divided both on the nature of the split in point of view and on its success. Writing in *Journal of Narrative Technique,* Caryn Fuoroli maintained that it results from Drabble's "inability to control narration" and that the novel fails because the technique keeps her from realizing "the full potential of her material." Rose believed that the novel works because its point of view is a dramatization of the conflict of the woman artist: "She has divided herself into Jane, the woman (whose experience is liquid), and Jane Grey, the artist (who gives form, order, and shapeliness to that experience)." Rose contends in *Contemporary Literature* that this is the fundamental truth the novel succeeds in expressing: "In order to be whole (and wholly a woman), Drabble suggests, a woman must reconcile these divisions. And if a woman writer is to articulate this experience of what it is to be a woman, she must devise a form, as Drabble has done in *The Waterfall,* which amalgamates feminine fluidity and masculine shapeliness."

Jerusalem the Golden's broader canvas and *The Waterfall*'s self-conscious narration were perhaps necessary first steps toward Drabble's full development in the mid-1970s. Her two biggest novels, *The Needle's Eye* and *The Realms of Gold,* were written during this period, and together they represent her fullest exploration of substantial themes: *The Needle's Eye* of personal morality and *The Realms of Gold* of the possibilities for individual achievement despite limitations beyond the individual's physical, social, familiar, psychological, and spiritual control.

The Needle's Eye reflects both Drabble's deep interest in ethics and morality and her lack of orthodoxy. Like her, the novel's heroine, Rose Vassiliou, is unsure of her theology but possessed of a conviction that she must do right. As a young heiress she achieved a certain amount of notoriety by giving up her inheritance to marry Christopher Vassiliou, an unsavory and radical young immigrant. After their marriage, she infuriates Christopher by giving away a thirty-thousand-pound legacy to a rather dubious African charity and refusing

to move out of their working class house into a more fashionable middle-class neighborhood when he begins to make his own fortune. At the time of the novel, Rose is living in her house with her children and has divorced the violent Christopher, who is trying to get her back or to get custody of the children.

Marion Vlastos Libby wrote in *Contemporary Literature* that *The Needle's Eye* is a "complex and passionate evocation of a fatalism deriving from the human condition and the nature of the world" and that its greatness "lies in portraying the tension, real and agonizing, between the hounds of circumstance and the force of the individual will." The best Drabble can say for Rose is that she has been "weathered into identity" by the hostile forces she confronts. In other words, she has developed a soul and found a way to grace, and in that sense she has won her battle. But she has "ruined her own nature against her own judgment, for Christopher's sake, for the children's sake. She had sold them for her own soul . . . the price she had to pay was the price of her own living death, her own conscious lying, her own lapsing, slowly, from grace."

If *The Needle's Eye* represents the human will at its weakest and circumstance at its strongest, Drabble moves to the opposite extreme in *The Realms of Gold.* The protagonist in this novel, Frances Wingate, is the apotheosis of the high-powered heroine. A celebrated archaeologist in her mid-thirties, Frances has divorced the wealthy man she married at an early age and is raising their four children on her own. She has a satisfying love affair with Karel Schmidt, an historian and survivor of the Holocaust, whom she eventually marries. She is rich, accomplished, and a little smug, recognizing in herself "amazing powers of survival and adaptation," and openly admits to herself that she is a "vain, self-satisfied woman."

Frances has her frailties but is not affected by her limitations in any fundamental way, because she does not allow them to affect her. She is Drabble's quintessential personification of will: "I must be mad, she thought to herself. I imagine a city, and it exists. If I hadn't imagined it, it wouldn't have existed." She is an obvious extreme, and Drabble sets her in opposition to the other extremes in the novel. While she makes her mark on her family, her profession, her society, even—in discovering a lost city in the desert—upon nature, she is surrounded by people who are destroyed by circumstances: environment, heredity, psychology, and fate. As Mary Hurley Moran noted in *Margaret Drabble: Existing within Structures,* "Drabble's fiction portrays a bleak, often menacing universe, ruled over by a harsh deity who allows human beings very little free will." Drabble's emphatic statement in *The Realms of Gold,* however, is that the will does count for something, that what hope there is for survival lies precisely in the individual's exercise of will in the face of what may seem overwhelming external forces.

The Ice Age and *The Middle Ground* present what has become the typical struggle of the individual in Drabble's work to survive and to maintain an identity in the face of a disintegrating social order. Drabble remarked that *The Ice Age* is in one sense a novel about money. Its protagonist, Anthony Keating, is a thoughtful man who made a fortune in real estate development during the boom times of the 1960s and lost it during the recession of the early 1970s. At the beginning of the novel he is recuperating from a heart attack and trying to come to terms with his new position in life. Meanwhile, the spoiled teenaged daughter of his fiancée Alison Murray has gotten herself into trouble in an eastern European country, and his former partner, Len, has landed himself in prison through his shady dealings. The novel is about money in many senses: about the failing British economy, about the effects that making a lot of money has on people, about the interaction of old money and new money, and about the class structures that underlie everyone's thinking about money. However, it is also about the forces that individuals in contemporary Britain are up against, from the natural fact of Alison's retarded younger daughter to the threat that an alien totalitarian government poses to her older one.

The interesting artistic fact about *The Ice Age* is that its narrative is not centered in one character, but is divided among Anthony, Alison, Len, and Len's girlfriend, Maureen. This is in part a reflection of the general disintegration going on in the world Drabble is presenting, in part a somewhat ironic move toward community. Not one of these characters has the force of will that makes Frances Wingate the central presence she is. Each of them is severely handicapped in some way, but they do manage to function in concert. There is some power in community.

The Middle Ground returns to a central character who is very much like Frances Wingate. Kate Armstrong is a successful writer with teenaged children who lives a very comfortable expense-account life. Because she resides in the world of *The Ice Age,* however, Kate is less confident than Frances of her future. In one sense *The Middle Ground* is about middle age. After the ending of a ten-year love affair and the abortion of a fetus with

spina bifida, Kate at age forty-one is asking what is left for her to do with the rest of her life: "Work? Living for others? Just carrying on, from day to day, enjoying as much of it as one could? Responding to demands as they came, for come they would?" Faced with the decay of urban London, the realities of the Third World visited upon her in the shape of a house-guest called Mujid, the apparent failure of the women's movement, and the turning off of the youth in her world, Kate is not sure what course she should take.

In addition to stand-alone novels, Drabble has authored a trilogy that follows the lives of three women whose friendship began while they were students at Cambridge in the 1950s. In the first book, *The Radiant Way,* Drabble introduces Liz, a successful psychotherapist; Alix, an idealist whose socialistic principles have led her to work at low-paying, altruistic jobs; and Esther, a scholar whose main interest lies with minor artists of the Italian Renaissance. By following these three characters through the years in *The Radiant Way* and into their middle age in *A Natural Curiosity,* the author "also attempts to show us how a generation managed (or mismanaged) its hopes and dreams," commented Michiko Kakutani in the *New York Times.* Kakutani found this approach similar to that of Mary McCarthy's *The Group,* a novel about former Vassar students, and criticized the tendency in both books "to substitute exposition for storytelling, sociological observation for the development of character and drama." But in a *Newsweek* review by Laura Shapiro, the critic approved of Drabble's willingness to explore all the facets of her characters' lives "at a time when skimpy prose, skeletal characterizations, frail plots and a sense of human history that stops sometime around last summer have become the new standards for fiction." Shapiro concluded: "Drabble reminds us here as in all her books exactly why we still love to read."

The Gates of Ivory, which completes the trilogy, differs from *The Radiant Way* and *A Natural Curiosity* in several significant ways. For example, "in *The Gates of Ivory,*" declared *Concise Dictionary of British Literary Biography* contributor Barbara C. Millard, "Drabble eschews a conventional plot in favor of a compelling scrutiny of her ongoing characters." Also, while the first two books centered on crime—the murder of one of Alix's students in *The Radiant Way* and Alix's attempts to understand the murderer's motivation in *A Natural Curiosity*—*The Gates of Ivory* follows Liz's actions on behalf of her friend, journalist Stephen Cox, in his attempt to interview Khmer Rouge leader Pol Pot. Cox disappears while traveling through rural Cambodia, and Liz becomes involved in the situation first in London, when she tries to trace his route, and then in Cambodia itself, when she travels there to look for him. In the process, Drabble combines elements of the traditional domestic novel, for which she is celebrated, with journalism and literary criticism, and examines such diverse topics as the Vietnam War, the novels of Joseph Conrad, and the restoration of the ancient temple complex at Angkor Wat. "The novel," stated Mary Kaiser in *World Literature Today,* "is multilayered, breathtaking in its ability to connect the First and Third Worlds." Disappointed with the novel's unrealized potential, the reviewer concluded: "Although Drabble has flirted with the explosive possibilities of leaving the domestic novel and inventing a new form, her allegiance to traditional realism prevents her from breaking the form in order to engage fully the undomesticated facts of our complex and violent times."

In *The Peppered Moth* Drabble tells the fictionalized story of her mother, Bessie Bawtry Baron, who was born and raised in a coal-mining town in South Yorkshire. Despite her working-class background and the prejudices against women at the time, she attends Cambridge University on a scholarship, becomes a teacher, and eventually marries her long-time boyfriend. In the book's afterword, Drabble comments, "I wrote this book to try and understand my mother better." Except for Bessie, none of the other characters in the novel are based on real people, and the subplots of the book are also invented. In the *Houston Chronicle,* Shelby Hearon commented that the subplots, one of which involves the tracing of 8,000-year-old DNA, "seem forced," and "come alive only as they relate to the central story." Charles Matthews wrote in a *Knight-Ridder/Tribune News Service* review that Drabble's use of a "neo-Victorian omniscient narrator," who often intrudes on the reader, can be "irritating and coy" and noted that "there are evasions and compromises in Drabble's storytelling." Overall, however, he found "much that is sharp and insightful in the novel." A *Booklist* reviewer praised the novel, noting, "Drabble glories in the musicality and pliancy of language in this exuberant, intelligent, and thoroughly entertaining saga." In the *New York Times,* Daphne Merkin called *The Peppered Moth* "one of the more absorbing novels I have read in a long time, both for its sheer storytelling ability and for its powers of imaginative conjecture."

Drabble's models have been the great British novelists of the eighteenth and nineteenth century—George Eliot, Anthony Trollope, the Brontës, Arnold Bennett, and, to a lesser extent, Jane Austen and Virginia Woolf—as well as Henry James. Elaine Showalter quoted her in *A Literature of Their Own* as saying, "I don't want to write an experimental novel to be read by people in fifty years, who will say, oh, well, yes, she foresaw what was coming. I'm just not interested." It is this kind of thinking that has led Drabble to be seen, as Michael F. Harper noted in *Contemporary Literature,* "as a late twentieth-century novelist who writes what many reviewers have taken to be good, solid nineteenth-century novels."

While some reviewers have criticized her approach as anachronistic, Harper maintained that Drabble's style "is not the result of unthinking acceptance of Victorian conventions, or of nostalgia for 'the riches of the past.' It is rather a working back to a reconstituted realism, in which Drabble begins with modernism and subjects it to a critique that is profound and contemporary." Drabble's realistic world, he said, "is something painfully and with difficulty constructed by the author and her characters, something not assumed but affirmed in an act of faith, achieved at the end of an odyssey of doubt and questioning of both the world and the self."

Drabble's realism may very well be her personal mediation between two extreme visions that permeate her world: the vestigial yearning for a transformation of the ordinary into an ideal unity and the post-modernist view that contemporary society has disintegrated beyond the possibility of unity or coherence, beyond the possibility of even a coherent description of its disintegration. She continues to insist both on the reality of the writer and on the reality of the world she describes. And while she sees very clearly the extreme tensions in society—from the contrary pulls on a talented woman who wants both to be a mother and to make her mark on the world to the economic and political forces that threaten the precarious stability of social institutions—she continues to believe in the human striving for something transcendent, something spiritual or ideal.

In addition to her novels, Drabble has also written well-regarded works of criticism and biography and has edited several influential volumes, including two editions of the esteemed *Oxford Companion to English Literature.* Her biographies include 1974's *Arnold Bennett* and 1996's *Angus Wilson: A Biography.* In the latter work, Drabble chronicles the life of Angus Wilson, a well-known British writer who became a friend of Drabble's during the 1960s. While some reviewers felt that Drabble fails to offer a fully realized portrait of Wilson's inner life, others remarked that her own training as a novelist assisted her in analyzing Wilson's character and his writing. Commenting in the *London Review of Books,* Frank Kermode stated, "Altogether, with the assistance and consent of [Wilson's longtime companion] Tony Garrett, . . . she has given a minute, intimate and candid account . . . of Wilson's hectic life."

BIOGRAPHICAL AND CRITICAL SOURCES:

BOOKS

Allan, Tuzyline Jita, *Womanist and Feminist Aesthetics: A Comparative Review,* Ohio University Press (Athens, OH), 1995.

Blain, Virginia, Patricia Clements, and Isobel Grundy, *The Feminist Companion to Literature in English,* Yale University Press (New Haven, CT), 1990.

Bokat, Nicole Suzanne, *The Novels of Margaret Drabble: This Freudian Family Nexus,* Peter Lang (New York, NY), 1998.

Concise Dictionary of British Literary Biography: Contemporary Writers, 1960 to the Present, Thomson Gale (Detroit, MI), 1992.

Contemporary Literary Criticism, Thomson Gale (Detroit, MI), Volume 2, 1974, Volume 3, 1975, Volume 5, 1976, Volume 8, 1978, Volume 10, 1979, Volume 22, 1982, Volume 53, 1989.

Creighton, Joanne V., *Margaret Drabble,* Methuen (London, England), 1985.

Dictionary of Literary Biography, Thomson Gale (Detroit, MI), Volume 14: *British Novelists since 1960,* 1983, Volume 155: *Twentieth-Century British Literary Biographers,* 1995.

Drabble, Margaret, *A Summer Bird-Cage,* Weidenfeld & Nicolson (London, England), 1963, Morrow (New York, NY), 1964.

Drabble, Margaret, *The Middle Ground,* Knopf (New York, NY), 1980.

Drabble, Margaret, *The Needle's Eye,* Knopf (New York, NY), 1972.

Drabble, Margaret, *The Realms of Gold,* Knopf (New York, NY), 1975.

Drabble, Margaret, *The Waterfall,* Knopf (New York, NY), 1969.

Moran, Mary Hurley, *Margaret Drabble: Existing within Structures,* Southern Illinois University Press (Carbondale, IL), 1983.

Myer, Valerie Grosvenor, *Margaret Drabble: Puritanism and Permissiveness,* Vision Press (London, England), 1974.

Packer, Joan Garrett, *Margaret Drabble: An Annotated Bibliography,* Garland (New York, NY), 1988.

Quiello, Rose, *Breakdowns and Breakthoughts: The Figure of the Hysteric in Contemporary Novels by Women,* Peter Lang (New York, NY), 1996.

Rose, Ellen Cronan, *The Novels of Margaret Drabble: Equivocal Figures,* Barnes & Noble (New York, NY), 1980.

Rose, Ellen Cronan, editor, *Critical Essays on Margaret Drabble,* Hall, 1985.

Roxman, Susanna, *Guilt and Glory: Studies in Margaret Drabble's Novels 1963-1980,* Almquist and Wiksell (Stockholm, Sweden), 1984.

Sadler, Lynn Veach, *Margaret Drabble,* Twayne (New York, NY), 1986.

Schmidt, Dory, and Jan Seale, editors, *Margaret Drabble: Golden Realms,* Pan American University (Edinberg, TX), 1982.

Showalter, Elaine, *A Literature of Their Own,* Princeton University Press (Princeton, NJ), 1977.

Soule, George, *Four British Women Novelists: Anita Brookner, Margaret Drabble, Iris Murdoch, Barbara Pym; An Annotated and Critical Secondary Bibliography,* Salem Press (Pasadena, CA), 1998.

Staley, Thomas F., editor, *Twentieth-Century Women Novelists,* Barnes & Noble (New York, NY), 1982.

Stovel, Nora Foster, *Margaret Drabble: Symbolic Moralist,* Borgo Press (San Bernardino, CA), 1989.

Todd, Janet, *Gender and Literary Voice,* Holmes & Meier (New York, NY), 1980.

Wojcik-Andrews, Ian, *Margaret Drabble's Female Bildungsroman: Theory, Genre, and Gender,* Peter Lang (New York, NY), 1995.

Wynne-Davies, Marion, editor, *The Bloomsbury Guide to English Literature,* Prentice Hall General Reference (Paramus, NJ), 1990.

PERIODICALS

American Scholar, winter, 1973.

Atlantic, January, 1976; December, 1977; November, 1980; April, 2001, p. 106; November, 2002, review of *The Seven Sisters,* pp. 125-126.

Book, November-December, 2002, Stephanie Foote, review of *The Seven Sisters,* p. 85.

Booklist, February 15, 2001, Donna Seaman, review of *The Peppered Moth,* p. 1084.

Books and Bookmen, September, 1969.

Bookview, January, 1978.

Canadian Forum, November, 1977.

Chicago Tribune Book World, August 31, 1980.

CLA Journal, September, 1984.

College Literature, fall, 1982.

Commentary, December, 1977.

Commonweal, June 18, 1976; February 13, 1981.

Comparative Literature Studies, February, 1998, p. 116.

Contemporary Literature, Volume 14, 1973; Volume 16, 1975; Volume 21, 1980; Volume 23, 1982.

Contemporary Review, April, 1972; January, 1976; January, 1978.

Critic, August, 1979.

Critique, number 15, 1973; number 21, 1980.

Daily Telegraph (London, England), February 12, 2000, p. 6.

Detroit News, October 19, 1980.

Economist, July 13, 1974; February 14, 1976.

English Review, November, 2001, p. 35.

English Studies, number 59, 1978.

Frontiers, number 3, 1978.

Globe and Mail (Toronto, Ontario, Canada), April 11, 1987; October 7, 1989.

Guardian, May 29, 1969; January 15, 1972; April 8, 1972; May 13, 1972; July 20, 1974; October 4, 1975; November 11, 1979; July 13, 1980; June 26, 1999, p. S6; October 14, 2000, p. 9; December 16, 2000, p. S38; December 8, 2001, p. 3.

Harper's, November, 1969; October, 1977; October, 1980.

History Today, March, 1980.

Houston Chronicle, May 13, 2001, Shelby Hearon, "Margaret Drabble's Mother: Paradise Gained and Lost," p. 13.

Hudson Review, winter, 1970; winter, 1973; winter, 1975; summer, 1975; spring, 1978; spring, 1981.

Journal of Narrative Technique, spring, 1981.

Knight-Ridder/Tribune News Service, May 2, 2001, Charles Matthews, review of *The Peppered Moth,* p. K4997.

Library Journal, June 1, 1998, p. 187; February 1, 2001, p. 125; November 1, 2002, Starr E. Smith, review of *The Seven Sisters,* p. 128; March 1, 2004, Marilyn Lary, review of *The Concise Oxford Companion to Literature,* p. 64.

London Review of Books, June 8, 1995, p. 3.

Los Angeles Times, December 28, 1980; November 25, 1982; June 21, 1987; October 23, 1989; April 9, 2001, p. E3.

Los Angeles Times Book Review, October 18, 1987; September 24, 1989; June 9, 1996, p. 3.

Maclean's, September 29, 1980.

Midwest Quarterly, Volume 16, 1975.

Modern Fiction Studies, Volume 25, 1979-80.

Modern Language Review, April, 1971.

Ms., August, 1974; July, 1978; November, 1980.

Nation, October 23, 1972; April 5, 1975.

National Review, December 23, 1977; March 20, 1981.

New Leader, July 24, 1972; April 26, 1976; January 30, 1978; September 22, 1980.

New Republic, July 8, 1972; September 21, 1974; October 22, 1977.

New Statesman, May 23, 1969; March 31, 1972; July 12, 1974; September 26, 1975; March 19, 1976; September 9, 1977; December 7, 1979; July 11, 1980; May 26, 1995, p. 24.

Newsweek, September 9, 1974; October 17, 1977; October 6, 1980; November 2, 1987.

New Yorker, October 4, 1969; December 16, 1972; December 23, 1974; January 12, 1976; December 26, 1977; July 11, 1980.

New York Review of Books, October 5, 1972; October 31, 1974; November 27, 1975; November 10, 1977; July 19, 1979; November 20, 1980; July 5, 2001, p. 33.

New York Times, October 31, 1975; October 4, 1977; July 4, 1985; October 21, 1987; August 22, 1989; May 6, 2001, Daphne Merkin, "Unnatural Selection."

New York Times Book Review, November 23, 1969; June 11, 1972; December 3, 1972; September 1, 1974; December 1, 1974; December 7, 1975; April 18, 1976; June 26, 1977; August 21, 1977; October 9, 1977; November 20, 1977; December 23, 1977; September 7, 1980; February 14, 1982; November 7, 1982; July 14, 1985; November 1, 1987; September 3, 1989; May 30, 1993; May 28, 2001, p. E1; June 3, 2001, p. 26.

New York Times Magazine, September 11, 1988.

Novel, Volume 11, 1978.

Observer, April 2, 1972; September 23, 1973; July 14, 1974; September 28, 1975; December 14, 1975; March 21, 1976; April 17, 1977; September 4, 1977; December 18, 1977; June 29, 1980; July 13, 1980.

Partisan Review, number 46, 1979.

People, October 13, 1980.

Prairie Schooner, spring-summer, 1981.

Progressive, January, 1981.

Publishers Weekly, May 31, 1985; February 26, 2001, p. 55.

Regionalism and the Female Imagination, number 4, 1978.

Saturday Review, November 15, 1975; January 10, 1976; February 21, 1976; August 20, 1977; January 7, 1978.

Sewanee Review, January, 1977; April, 1978; January, 1982.

Spectator, April 1, 1972; July 20, 1974; September 27, 1975; February 7, 1976; February 14, 1976; July 5, 1980; May 27, 1995, p. 38; January 6, 2001, p. 29.

Studies in the Literary Imagination, Volume 11, 1978.

Time, September 9, 1974; November 3, 1975; June 26, 1976; October 17, 1977; September 15, 1980; November 16, 1987.

Times (London, England), June 30, 1980; April 25, 1985; April 27, 1987; April 30, 1987; July 8, 1987.

Times Literary Supplement, July 12, 1974; September 26, 1975; September 2, 1977; July 11, 1980; April

26, 1985; July 12, 1985; May 1, 1987; September 29, 1989; June 9, 1995, p. 24; January 12, 2001, p. 22.

Tribune Books (Chicago, IL), November 8, 1987; August 20, 1989.

Victorian Studies, spring, 1978.

Village Voice, November 24, 1975; October 24, 1977.

Virginia Quarterly Review, spring, 1976; summer, 1976; summer, 1978.

Voice Literary Supplement, May, 1982.

Washington Post, January 1, 1980.

Washington Post Book World, September 14, 1980; June 2, 1985; September 21, 1986; October 25, 1987; August 27, 1989.

Women's Studies, Volume 6, 1979.

World Literature Today, spring, 1993.

Yale Review, March, 1970; June, 1978.

* * *

DR. SEUSS
See GEISEL, Theodor Seuss

* * *

DRUMMOND, Walter
See SILVERBERG, Robert

* * *

DRUSE, Eleanor
See KING, Stephen

* * *

DUBUS, Andre, III 1959-

PERSONAL: Born September 11, 1959, in Oceanside, CA; son of Andre II (a fiction writer and educator) and Patricia (a social worker; maiden name, Lowe) Dubus; married Fontaine Dollas (a dancer), June 25, 1989. *Education:* Bradford College, A.A., 1979; University of Texas at Austin, B.A. (sociology), 1981; attended Vermont College. *Politics:* Liberal Democrat *Religion:* Roman Catholic.

ADDRESSES: Home—Newburyport, MA. *Agent*—Philip G. Spitzer Literary Agency, 788 Ninth Ave., New York, NY 10019.

CAREER: Fiction writer. Boulder Community Treatment Center, Boulder, CO, counselor, 1982-83; worked variously as a bartender, bounty hunter, prison counselor, and actor, c. 1980s; carpenter, 1988—. Part-time writing instructor at Emerson College, Boston, MA.

MEMBER: International Sociology Honor Society, Authors Guild, Authors League, Alpha Kappa Delta.

AWARDS, HONORS: National Magazine Award for Fiction, 1985; American Library Association Notable Book selection, and finalist for National Book Award, *Los Angeles Times* book award, L.L. Winship/PEN New England Award, and Booksense Book of the Year award, all 2000, all for *House of Sand and Fog.*

WRITINGS:

The Cage Keeper and Other Stories, Dutton (New York, NY), 1989.

House of Sand and Fog, Norton (New York, NY), 1999.

Bluesman, Norton (New York, NY), 2001.

Contributor of stories and reviews to periodicals, including *Playboy, Crazyhorse Quarterly,* and *Crescent Review.*

House of Sand and Fog has been translated into over twenty-two languages.

ADAPTATIONS: House of Sand and Fog was adapted as a motion picture directed by Vadim Perelman, Dreamworks, 2003. The novel was also adapted as an audiobook read by Dubus and his wife, Fontaine Dubus, HarperAudio, 2001.

SIDELIGHTS: Andre Dubus III is the son of the late famed short-fiction writer of the same name. Dubus III has also had success with the short-story form, but he is perhaps best known for his acclaimed 2000 novel, *House of Sand and Fog. House of Sand and Fog*—which took Dubus four years to write and which was turned down by over twenty publishers before being accepted by Norton—follows the collision course of an ex-Iranian colonel named Behrani and Kathy Nicolo, a young former drug addict whose modest bungalow Behrani purchases during a bank foreclosure auction. Complicating the plot is one of the officers who evicts Kathy, who then starts dating her and helping her fight to get her house back. Although the novel did well after publication, moving to the top of the *New York Times* bestseller list, it became a publishing phenomenon after being chosen by talk show personality Oprah Winfrey as an *Oprah* Book Club selection.

Reviewers of *House of Sand and Fog* had unqualified praise for Dubus's debut novel. Donna Seaman, writing in *Booklist,* noted that the book's characters "are headed for a resolution of stunningly tragic dimensions." Liz Keuffer, discussing *House of Sand and Fog* for *BookReporter,* praised the novel as well, concluding that Dubus "chronicles the clash of cultures between the Americans and the Iranians while keeping the humanity of everyone involved at the forefront." Reflecting also on the culture clash that is at the core of Dubus's novel, Joanna Burkhardt commented in *Library Journal* that "the frustration and anger are visceral, the tension intense." *House of Sand and Fog* "captures the hope, confusion, resolve, and uncertainty" of a cast of compelling characters.

Dubus told *CA:* "Every one of us needs to express himself in some way. I feel very fortunate that creative writing has tapped me on the shoulder."

BIOGRAPHICAL AND CRITICAL SOURCES:

PERIODICALS

Booklist, February 1, 1999, Donna Seaman, review of *House of Sand and Fog,* p. 961.

Library Journal, January, 1989, Starr E. Smith, review of *The Cage Keeper and Other Stories,* p. 101; May 15, 1993, Charles Michaud, review of *Bluesman,* p. 96; March 1, 1999, Reba Leiding, review of *House of Sand and Fog,* p. 108; May 1, 2001, Joanna Burkhardt, review of *House of Sand and Fog,* p. 145.

Macclean's, May 14, 2001, "House That Oprah Built," p. 53.

New York Times Book Review, February 5, 1989, Deborah Solomon, review of *The Cage Keeper and Other Stories,* p. 24; April 25, 1999, Bill Sharp, review of *House of Sand and Fog,* p. 104.

People, March 12, 2001, "Blood Knot: Bestselling Novelist Andre Dubus III Knew One Thing Growing Up—He Wouldn't Be a Writer Like His Father," p. 75.

Publishers Weekly, October 21, 1988, review of *The Cage Keeper and Other Stories,* p. 48; November 1, 1999, review of *House of Sand and Fog,* p. 45.

Times Literary Supplement, April 7, 2000, Henry Hitchings, review of *House of Sand and Fog,* p. 28.

ONLINE

BookReporter, http://www.bookreporter.com/ (May 1, 2003).

House of Sand and Fog Official site, http://www.dreamworks.com/houseofsandandfog/ (January 14, 2004).

*   *   *

DUE, Linnea A. 1948-

PERSONAL: Born April 3, 1948, in Berkeley, CA; daughter of Floyd O. (a psychoanalyst) and Ellen (a nurse; maiden name, Anderson) Due. *Education:* Sarah Lawrence College, B.A., 1970; University of California—Berkeley, M.A., 1971.

ADDRESSES: Home and office—5846 Vallejo St., Oakland, CA 94608.

CAREER: Educational Development Corp., Menlo Park, CA, writer, 1973-74; Classified Flea Market, Oakland, CA, graphic designer, 1974-78; Diana Press, Oakland, in advertising, 1978; Oakland Graphics, Oakland, typesetter, 1978—. Editor for Straight Arrow Press, 1973-75.

AWARDS, HONORS: High and Outside was listed among best books for young adults by American Library Association, 1980.

WRITINGS:

High and Outside (young adult novel), Harper (New York, NY), 1980.

Give Me Time, Morrow (New York, NY), 1985.

Life Savings, Spinsters, 1992.

(Editor, with Lily Burana and Roxxie) *Dagger: On Butch Women,* Cleis Press, 1994.

Joining the Tribe: Growing Up Gay and Lesbian in the 1990s, Anchor (New York, NY), 1995.

(Editor) *Hot Ticket: Tales of Lesbians, Sex, and Travel,* Alyson Books (Los Angeles, CA), 1997.

(Editor) *Uniform Sex: Erotic Stories of Women in Service,* Alyson (Los Angeles, CA), 2000.

SIDELIGHTS: Linnea A. Due broke new ground with her YA novel about teenage alcoholism in 1980. As she once explained: "I began *High and Outside* when I returned from a trip—I had a week off work, and no one knew I was in town—so I locked myself in my study and started writing. I became so involved with my characters I wouldn't have been surprised in the least if they'd rung my doorbell one morning. This is the joy of writing for me—when the characters assume their own identities and run away with the story, leaving my idea of the book behind. Listening to the characters is much more interesting than writing about them, and eventually, I suspect, results in a better book."

Due followed the success of *High and Outside* with her 1992 novel *Life Savings,* about which a *Publishers Weekly* contributor commented: "This novel raises important questions about money, power and social responsibility. Mostly, however, it entertains. Each character is carefully drawn, with her own quirks, flaws and personal history."

In 1995, Due published *Joining the Tribe: Growing Up Gay and Lesbian in the 1990s,* a collection of interviews with gay and lesbian youth that a *Publishers Weekly* critic called "moving and vital." The teens Due interviewed "vividly recount the assaults they suffer in their families and schools and in the broader society," the reviewer added, noting that "name-calling, beatings and death threats" were not uncommon. The *Publishers Weekly* critic also thought that the book reflects the voice of these young Americans through Due's commentary and "sensitive editing." Due has edited three more collections, including lesbian fiction, interviews, and travel tales.

BIOGRAPHICAL AND CRITICAL SOURCES:

PERIODICALS

Best Sellers, September, 1980.
Lambda Book Report, July-August, 1994, Victoria A. Brownworth, review of *Dagger: On Butch Women,* p. 19; July, 1998, Susan Branch Smith, review of *Hot Ticket: Tales of Lesbians, Sex, and Travel,* p. 35.
Library Journal, June 15, 1980.
Publishers Weekly, August 31, 1992, review of *Life Savings,* p. 69; August 21, 1995, review of *Joining the Tribe: Growing Up Gay and Lesbian in the 1990s,* p. 59.
Women's Review of Books, March, 1996, review of *Joining the Tribe,* p. 16.

DUE, Tananarive 1966-

PERSONAL: Name is pronounced "tah-nah-nah-*reeve* doo"; born 1966; daughter of John Dorsey (an attorney) and Patricia (a civil rights activist; maiden name, Stephens) Due; married Steven Barnes (a science fiction novelist and screenwriter); children: Lauren Nicole Barnes (stepdaughter). *Education:* Northwestern University, B.S., 1987; University of Leeds (England), M.A., 1988. *Religion:* African Methodist Episcopal. *Hobbies and other interests:* playing piano and keyboard, rollerblading.

ADDRESSES: Home—1105 15th Ave. #D-227, Longview, WA 98632. *Agent*—c/o John Hawkins & Associates, 71 West 23rd St., Ste. 1600, New York, NY 10010. *E-mail*—tdue@tananarivedue.com.

CAREER: Journalist and novelist. Columnist for *Miami Herald;* former intern at *New York Times* and *Wall Street Journal.* Has performed with Rockbottom Remainders (rock band that includes authors Stephen King, Dave Barry, and Amy Tan) as keyboardist/vocalist/dancer.

AWARDS, HONORS: Finalist, Bram Stoker Award for Outstanding Achievement in a First Novel, Horror Writers Association, 1995, for *The Between; Publishers Weekly* Best Book citation, 1997, for *My Soul to Keep,* and 2001, for *The Living Blood;* National Association for the Advancement of Colored People Image Award nomination for *The Black Rose;* American Book Award, 2002, for *The Living Blood.*

WRITINGS:

The Between (novel), HarperCollins (New York, NY), 1995.
My Soul to Keep (novel), HarperCollins (New York, NY), 1997.
The Black Rose: The Magnificent Story of Madam C.J. Walker, America's First Black Female Millionaire, Ballantine (New York, NY), 2000.
The Living Blood (novel), Pocket Books (New York, NY), 2001.
(With mother, Patricia Stephens Due) *Freedom in the Family: A Mother-Daughter Memoir of the Fight for Civil Rights,* One World (New York, NY), 2003.
The Good House (novel), Atria (New York, NY), 2003.

Contributor to *Naked Came the Manatee,* Putnam (New York, NY), a comic thriller written by thirteen southern writers, each contributing a chapter.

ADAPTATIONS: Film rights to *My Soul to Keep* were obtained by Fox Searchlight.

SIDELIGHTS: Miami-based journalist and novelist Tananarive Due set her sights on a writing career at an early age. As a sixth-grader watching the landmark television miniseries *Roots,* Due—the daughter of an attorney and a civil-rights activist—traced her own family's history, calling her work *My Own Roots.* As a young woman, Due attended a summer program for young writers at Northwestern University and won numerous awards for both writing and oratory. After earning her bachelor's degree in journalism, she completed a Rotary Foundation scholarship in Leeds, England. There she completed her master's degree, concentrating her studies on Nigerian literature. Due began her professional career at the *Miami Herald* as a columnist; at the same time she began sending her short stories to publishers, although none responded in the affirmative. "No one likes rejection," Due told Alison Hibbert of the *Miami Times,* "but as long as I got rejection slips, I knew I had to keep going. I had my mind set on being a serious writer."

An interview with Anne Rice, author of such gothics as *The Vampire Lestat,* inspired Due to try her hand at horror. She drafted her first novel, *The Between,* in her spare time before and after work. This time Due caught the attention of a publisher, and *The Between* was released in 1995. That novel and subsequent work helped set the author apart in the genre of mystery/horror: her books feature African-American characters.

The Between is "a skillful blend of horror and the supernatural," according to a reviewer for *Publishers Weekly.* The story centers on a forty-year-old social worker in Miami's inner city who is plagued by nightmares that seem to indicate either his insanity or his status as a person "in between" life and death. As a child, Hilton James barely escaped death by drowning in the same accident that killed his grandmother; now, as the husband of the only African-American woman judge in Miami, he seems to be receiving messages through his subconscious that indicate his survival all those years ago was a mistake that must be rectified. Due's portrait of Hilton's crumbling personality is "sympathetic and credible," according to a *Publishers Weekly* critic, who nevertheless felt that the rest of the

cast fails to achieve the same verisimilitude. M.J. Simmons, who reviewed *The Between* for *Library Journal,* noted that, rather than a tale of supernatural horror, Due's first novel is "a chilling and sympathetic portrait of a man whose madness needs explanation in the psychic realm." Although Simmons found Due's ending a disappointment, Lillian Lewis, who reviewed the book for *Booklist,* praised the book's "intriguing and suspenseful plot," concluding that "Due may very well develop a loyal following with her first novel."

Due followed *The Between* with *My Soul to Keep,* another tale of supernatural horror in which reporter Jessica discovers that her otherwise-perfect husband David is actually a five-hundred-year-old member of an Ethiopian band of immortals willing to kill to keep its members' existence a secret. David reveals his secret to Jessica, endangering himself and the family he has come to love when the brotherhood sends another member of the band to make sure their secret does not get out. *Booklist* critic Lewis found Due's second novel "more compelling than her first" and compared *My Soul to Keep* with Octavia Butler's *Kindred* for its grounding in "African and African-American heritage and culture." Critics lauded Due's realistic details and strong sense of family life, which provide a convincing foundation for a somewhat melodramatic plot. *My Soul to Keep* is "a novel populated with vivid, emotional characters that is also a chilling journey to another world," concluded a reviewer for *Publishers Weekly.*

Returning to gothic fiction, in 2001 Due published *The Living Blood,* a sequel to *My Soul to Keep.* The story rejoins Jessica and David as Jessica joins her husband among the immortals after a ceremonial infusion of magical blood. Now a part of the ancient Life Brothers society, Jessica finds herself alone and pregnant after David, accused of murder, disappears. She raises her daughter, Fana, to age two and discovers the child possesses the Life Brothers' psychic powers. She embarks on a desperate mission to find David in Africa. Larger in scope than *My Soul to Keep, The Living Blood* drew mixed reaction from some reviewers. Patricia Altner commented in *Library Journal* that the sequel suffers from a "poorly executed" plot and "flaccid" writing. On the other hand, *Booklist*'s Lewis welcomed the novel, saying that even newcomers to the Jessica-and-David saga will likely enjoy the story. While noting that the author "does not fully develop the fascinating theological implications of her story," *Black Issues Book Review* contributor Paulette Richards still praised *The Living Blood* as "an engrossing, well-paced narrative." The book won an American Book Award in 2002.

Also in the supernatural vein is Due's 2003 novel *The Good House.* Divorcee Angela Toussaint moves with her teenaged son Corey to Washington, where the family has a summer home built in 1907 and once occupied by Angela's Creole "mambo" grandmother Marie, a suspected witch. When an ancient evil is brought back to life, voodoo, family ties, murder, and suicide all figure in a story in which "Due keeps richly packed and layered description alive with suspense," maintained a *Kirkus* reviewer, concluding that in *The Good House* Due "weaves a stronger net than ever." Praising the novel's "themes of family ties, racial identity and moral responsibility," a *Publishers Weekly* reviewer noted that Due traverses the intricate plot deftly, "interjecting powerfully orchestrated moments of supernatural horror that sustain the tale's momentum." Although of the opinion that the novel would have been better served by a stronger ending, Jennifer Baker praised *The Good House* in *Library Journal* as "a cleverly plotted tale of possession and magic gone awry."

By the late 1990s Due had gained enough of a reputation as a novelist and journalist for the estate of the late author Alex Haley to assign her the project of finishing a biographical novel begun by Haley and based on the life of pioneering African-American executive Madam C.J. Walker. In the early twentieth century Walker—born Sarah Breedlove and the daughter of former slaves—rose from laundress to millionaire on the strength of her business savvy and her line of hair-care products. At the time of his death in 1992, Haley left behind an outline for the Walker novel, along with reams of archival clippings, letters, and photographs. "I had heard she was the first self-made Black female millionaire," Due remarked to an *Indianapolis Recorder* interviewer, "but I knew nothing about her struggle."

The resulting book, 2002's *The Black Rose: The Magnificent Story of Madam C.J. Walker, America's First Black Female Millionaire,* traces Walker from childhood to her death at age fifty-two. Combining fiction and fact, *The Black Rose* uses Walker's point of view to explore the challenges of life in the segregated South of the early twentieth century. Recognizing a need for beauty products aimed at underserved black women, Walker not only created her own products, but recruited as many as 20,000 women to sell them door to door—"empowering them, in many cases, to transform themselves from cooks or maids to entrepreneurs," according to Valerie Boyd in an *Atlanta Journal-Constitution* piece. Boyd labeled Due's account "compelling," adding: "with the patience of a born storyteller, [the author] slowly allows Walker's stirring story to unfold." The reviewer also cited Due for presenting a well-rounded, flaws-and-all picture of her subject.

In 2003 Due once again turned to nonfiction with *Freedom in the Family: A Mother-Daughter Memoir of the Fight for Civil Rights.* Written with her mother, Patricia Stephens Due, the volume relates a personal history of the struggle for equality, from the lunch-counter sit-ins of the 1950s to a racially motivated police raid on the Due family's Miami home decades later. The book, noted a *Publishers Weekly* contributor, is "cathartic in its recounting of past obstacles, and optimistic of its hopes for the future."

Talking to *Publishers Weekly* contributor Stefan Dziemianowicz about her supernatural novels, Due remarked that she "really never set out to write a trilogy or create a franchise." But she didn't rule out the idea of a third book in the gothic series about Jessica and David, saying that with the completion *Freedom in the Family,* "it may be time to revisit the immortals."

Due told *CA:* "I've wanted to write since I was four years old, when I wrote a picture book called 'Baby Bobby.' It seems to me that I came into this world wanting to tell stories and write. Hopefully, I have absorbed some of the lessons of the great writers I have read over the years—Toni Morrison, Stephen King, Jane Austen, Octavia E. Butler, Franz Kafka, Gloria Naylor, Richard Wright—although my own voice is unique. I'm happiest when I can write a story the way I did when I was a kid: finding the place the story naturally begins and having great fun in the telling. I have found myself preoccupied with issues of illness, death and loss, and writing helps me work through my own fears.

"What continues to surprise me is that writing doesn't get easier—in fact, if anything, sometimes I think it gets more difficult with each book. My standards are continually changing and growing, and I'm always trying to stretch myself. *My Soul to Keep* has been a reader favorite, but my new favorite novel is *The Good House* because I was challenging myself. I am also very grateful I was able to coauthor *Freedom in the Family: A Mother-Daughter Memoir of the Fight for Civil Rights* with my mother. A project like that is priceless to a family."

BIOGRAPHICAL AND CRITICAL SOURCES:

BOOKS

Contemporary Black Biography, Thomson Gale (Detroit, MI), 2001.

PERIODICALS

Atlanta Journal-Constitution, July 16, 2000, Valerie Boyd, "Black Female Entrepreneur Finally Gets Her Due," p. L8.

Black Issues Book Review, July, 2000, Natasha Tarpley, review of *The Black Rose: The Magnificent Story of Madam C.J. Walker, America's First Black Female Millionaire,* p. 19; May, 2001, Paulette Richards, review of *The Living Blood,* p. 18.

Booklist, May 15, 1995, Lillian Lewis, review of *The Between,* p. 1631; July 19, 1997, Lillian Lewis, review of *My Soul to Keep;* April 15, 2000, Brad Hooper, review of *The Black Rose,* p. 1500; April 1, 2001, Lillian Lewis, review of *The Living Blood,* p. 1447.

Ebony, July, 2000, review of *The Black Rose,* p. 14; June, 2001, review of *The Living Blood,* p. 23.

Houston Chronicle, August 13, 1997; May 27, 2001, Mark Johnson, review of *The Living Blood,* p. 21.

Kirkus Reviews, May 15, 1997, p. 738; November 1, 2002, review of *Freedom in the Family: A Mother-Daughter Memoir of the Fight for Civil Rights,* p. 1585; August 15, 2003, review of *The Good House,* p. 1033.

Library Journal, June 1, 1995, M.J. Simmons, review of *The Between,* p. 158; February 15, 2001, Patricia Altner, review of *The Living Blood,* p. 200; November 1, 2002, Ann Burns, review of *Freedom in the Family,* p. 115; August, 2003, Jennifer Baker, review of *The Good House,* p. 129.

Miami Times, May 18, 1995, p. 18; April 30, 1998, p. 10.

Publishers Weekly, April 24, 1995, review of *The Between,* p. 60; June 2, 1997, review of *My Soul to Keep,* p. 55; November 8, 1999, John Baker, "First Black Millionaire," p. 14; March 15, 2000, review of *The Black Rose,* p. 87; March 19, 2001, Stefan Dziemianowicz, "PW Talks to Tananarive Due" and review of *The Living Blood,* p. 81; December 23, 2002, review of *Freedom in the Family,* p. 56; July 14, 2003, review of *The Good House,* p. 61.

St. Louis Post-Dispatch, July 16, 2000, Naima Wartts, "Novel Tells Fact-Based Story of First Black Female Millionaire," p. F10.

School Library Journal, December, 2000, review of *The Black Rose,* p. 168.

Science Fiction Chronicle, August, 2001, review of *The Living Blood,* p. 34.

Washington Post Book World, November 23, 1997; February 4, 2001, review of *The Black Rose,* p. 10; May 6, 2001, review of *The Living Blood,* p. 8.

ONLINE

Tananarive Due Web site, http://www.tananrivedue. com/ (September 24, 2002).

DUKE, Raoul
See THOMPSON, Hunter S.

*   *   *

DUNCAN, Lois 1934-
(Lois Kerry)

PERSONAL: Born Lois Duncan Steinmetz, April 28, 1934, in Philadelphia, PA; daughter of Joseph Janney (a magazine photographer) and Lois (a magazine photographer; maiden name, Foley) Steinmetz; married an attorney, 1953 (marriage ended, c. 1962); married Donald Wayne Arquette (an electrical engineer), July 15, 1965; children: (first marriage) Robin, Kerry, Brett; (second marriage) Donald Jr., Kaitlyn (deceased). *Education:* Attended Duke University, 1952-53; University of New Mexico, B.A. (cum laude), 1977.

ADDRESSES: Agent—c/o Penguin Putnam Inc., 375 Hudson St., New York, NY 10014. *E-mail*—lois duncan@arquettes.com.

CAREER: Writer; magazine photographer; instructor in department of journalism, University of New Mexico, 1971-82. Lecturer at writers' conferences.

MEMBER: National League of American PEN Women, Society of Children's Book Writers, New Mexico Press Women, Phi Beta Kappa.

AWARDS, HONORS: Three-time winner during high school years of *Seventeen* magazine's annual short story contest; Seventeenth Summer Literary Award, Dodd, Mead & Co., 1957, for *Debutante Hill;* Best Novel Award, National Press Women, 1966, for *Point of Violence;* Edgar Allan Poe Award runner-ups, Mystery Writers of America, 1967, for *Ransom,* 1969, for *They Never Came Home,* 1985, for *The Third Eye,* 1986, for *Locked in Time,* and 1989, for *The Twisted Window;* Zia Award, New Mexico Press Women, 1969, for *Major André: Brave Enemy;* grand prize winner, *Writer's Digest* Creative Writing Contest, 1970, for short story; Theta Sigma Phi Headliner Award, 1971; Best Books for Young Adults citations, American Library Association (ALA), 1976, for *Summer of Fear,* 1978, for *Killing Mr. Griffin,* 1981, for *Stranger with My Face,* 1982, for *Chapters: My Growth as a Writer,* and 1990, for *Don't Look behind You;* Best Books for Children citations, *New York Times,* 1981, for *Stranger with My Face,* and 1988, for *Killing Mr. Griffin;* Ethical Culture

School Book Award, Library of Congress' Best Books citation, and *English Teacher's Journal*and University of Iowa's Best Books of the Year for Young Adults citation, all 1981, and Best Novel Award, National League of American Pen Women, 1982, all for *Stranger with My Face;* Notable Children's Trade Book in the Field of Social Studies, National Council for Social Studies/ Children's Book Council, 1982, for *Chapters: My Growth as a Writer;* Children's Books of the Year citation, Child Study Association of America, 1986, for *Locked in Time* and *The Third Eye;* Children's Book Award, National League of American Pen Women, 1987, for *Horses of Dreamland;* Margaret A. Edwards Award, 1991, *School Library Journal*/Young Adult Library Services Association, for body of work; ALA Best Adult Book for Young Adults, *School Library Journal* Best Book of the Year, and Pacific Northwest Young Readers Award for *Who Killed My Daughter?: The True Story of a Mother's Search for Her Daughter's Murderer;* Junior Literary Guild award winner for *The Twisted Window, Locked in Time, The Third Eye, Summer of Fear,* and *They Never Came Home.* Duncan has also received numerous librarians', parents', children's choice, and readers awards from the states of Alabama, Arizona, California, Colorado, Florida, Indiana, Iowa, Massachusetts, Nevada, New Mexico, Oklahoma, Tennessee, Texas, South Carolina, and Vermont, as well as from groups in England and Australia.

WRITINGS:

YOUNG ADULT NOVELS

Debutante Hill, Dodd (New York, NY), 1958.

(Under pseudonym Lois Kerry) *Love Song for Joyce,* Funk (New York NY), 1958.

(Under pseudonym Lois Kerry) *A Promise for Joyce,* Funk (New York NY), 1959.

The Middle Sister, Dodd (New York, NY), 1961.

Game of Danger, Dodd (New York, NY), 1962.

Season of the Two-Heart, Dodd (New York, NY), 1964.

Ransom, Doubleday (Garden City, NY), 1966, published as *Five Were Missing,* New American Library (New York, NY), 1972.

They Never Came Home, Doubleday (Garden City, NY), 1969.

I Know What You Did Last Summer, Little, Brown (Boston, MA), 1973.

Down a Dark Hall, Little, Brown (Boston, MA), 1974.

Summer of Fear, Little, Brown (Boston, MA), 1976.

Killing Mr. Griffin, Little, Brown (Boston, MA), 1978.

Daughters of Eve, Little, Brown (Boston, MA), 1979.

Stranger with My Face, Little, Brown (Boston, MA), 1981.

The Third Eye, Little, Brown (Boston, MA), 1984, published as *The Eyes of Karen Connors,* Hamish Hamilton (London, England), 1985.

Locked in Time, Little, Brown (Boston, MA), 1985.

The Twisted Window, Delacorte (New York, NY), 1987.

Don't Look behind You, Delacorte (New York, NY), 1989.

Gallows Hill, Delacorte (New York, NY), 1997.

FOR CHILDREN

The Littlest One in the Family, illustrated by Suzanne K. Larsen, Dodd (New York, NY), 1960.

Silly Mother, illustrated by Suzanne K. Larsen, Dial (New York, NY), 1962.

Giving Away Suzanne, illustrated by Leonard Weisgard, Dodd (New York, NY), 1963.

Hotel for Dogs, illustrated by Leonard Shortall, Houghton Mifflin (Boston, MA), 1971.

A Gift of Magic, illustrated by Arvis Stewart, Little, Brown (Boston, MA), 1971.

From Spring to Spring: Poems and Photographs, photographs by the author, Westminster, 1982.

The Terrible Tales of Happy Days School (poetry), illustrated by Friso Henstra, Little, Brown (Boston, MA), 1983.

Horses of Dreamland, illustrated by Donna Diamond, Little, Brown (Boston, MA), 1985.

Wonder Kid Meets the Evil Lunch Snatcher, illustrated by Margaret Sanfilippo, Little, Brown (Boston, MA), 1988.

The Birthday Moon (poetry), illustrated by Susan Davis, Viking (New York, NY), 1989.

Songs from Dreamland (poetry), illustrated by Kay Chorao, Alfred A. Knopf (New York, NY), 1989.

The Circus Comes Home: When the Greatest Show on Earth Rode the Rails, photographs by Joseph Janney Steinmetz, Delacorte (New York, NY), 1993.

The Magic of Spider Woman, illustrated by Shonto Begay, Scholastic (New York, NY), 1996.

The Longest Hair in the World, illustrated by Jon McIntosh, Bantam (New York, NY), 1999.

I Walk at Night, illustrated by Steve Johnson and Lou Fancher, Viking Penguin (New York, NY), 2000.

Song of the Circus, illustrated by Meg Cundiff, Philomel (New York, NY), 2001.

OTHER

Point of Violence (adult), Doubleday (New York, NY), 1966.

Major André: Brave Enemy (young adult nonfiction), illustrated by Tran Mawicke, Putnam (New York, NY), 1969.

Peggy (young adult nonfiction), Little, Brown (Boston, MA), 1970.

When the Bough Breaks (adult), Doubleday (New York, NY), 1974.

How to Write and Sell Your Personal Experiences (nonfiction), Writers Digest, 1979.

Chapters: My Growth as a Writer (autobiography), Little, Brown (Boston, MA), 1982.

A Visit with Lois Duncan (videotape), RDA Enterprises, 1985.

Dream Songs from Yesterday (cassette), RDA Enterprises, 1987.

Our Beautiful Day (cassette), RDA Enterprises, 1988.

The Story of Christmas (cassette), RDA Enterprises, 1989.

Who Killed My Daughter?: The True Story of a Mother's Search for Her Daughter's Murderer, Delacorte (New York, NY), 1992.

Psychics in Action (audio cassette series), Silver Moon Productions, 1993.

(With William Roll) *Psychic Connections: A Journey into the Mysterious World of Psi,* Delacorte (New York, NY), 1995.

(Editor) *Night Terrors: Stories of Shadow and Substance,* Simon & Schuster (New York, NY), 1996.

(Editor) *Trapped! Cages of Mind and Body,* Simon & Schuster (New York, NY), 1998.

(Editor) *On the Edge: Stories at the Brink,* Simon & Schuster (New York, NY), 2000.

Contributor of over five hundred articles and stories to periodicals, including *Good Housekeeping, Redbook, McCall's, Woman's Day, Writer, Reader's Digest, Ladies' Home Journal, Saturday Evening Post,* and *Writer's Digest.* Contributing editor, *Woman's Day.*

ADAPTATIONS: Summer of Fear was adapted as the television movie *Strangers in Our House,* NBC-TV, 1978; *Killing Mr. Griffin* was adapted as a television movie, NBC-TV, 1997; *I Know What You Did Last Summer* was adapted as a feature film, Mandalay, 1997; *Gallows Hill* was adapted as a television movie, NBC-TV, 1998; and *Ransom* was adapted as a television movie. Listening Library made cassettes of *Down a Dark Hall,* 1985, *Killing Mr. Griffin,* 1986, *Summer of Fear,* 1986, and *Stranger with My Face,* 1986; *Don't Look Behind You,* adapted as a "made-for-TV movie" by Fox Family Channel. RDA Enterprises made cassettes of *Selling Personal Experiences to Magazines,* 1987, and *Songs from Dreamland,* 1987. *Stranger With My Face* was adapted as a screen play in 2004.

WORK IN PROGRESS: A sequel to *Who Killed My Daughter?,* with working title *The Tally Keeper.*

SIDELIGHTS: Award-winning writer Lois Duncan's young adult novels of suspense and the supernatural have made her a favorite of adult critics and young readers alike. According to *Times Literary Supplement* reviewer Jennifer Moody, Duncan is "popular . . . not only with the soft underbelly of the literary world, the children's book reviewers, but with its most hardened carapace, the teenage library book borrower." Equally enthusiastic was critic Sarah Hayes, who observed in *Times Literary Supplement* that "Duncan understands the teenage world and its passionate concerns with matters as diverse as dress, death, romance, school, self-image, sex and problem parents." But Hayes added that while other writers for young adults show life in a humorous, optimistic light, "Duncan suggests that life is neither as prosaic nor as straightforward as it seems at first."

In most of Duncan's books, her protagonists are high school students—usually young women—who find themselves suddenly confronted with a sinister threat to their "normal" existence. "It is a mark of Duncan's ability as a writer that the evils she describes are perfectly plausible and believable," noted an essayist in *St. James Guide to Young Adult Writers.* "As in her use of the occult, her use of warped human nature as a tool to move the plot along briskly never seems contrived or used solely for shock effect; it is integral to the story."

Born in Philadelphia, Pennsylvania, and raised in Sarasota, Florida, Duncan grew up in a creative household where her early efforts at writing were encouraged by her parents, internationally renowned photographers Joseph and Lois Steinmetz. She started writing stories for magazines as a pre-teen and progressed to book-length manuscripts as she matured. She enrolled in Duke University in 1952 but found it a difficult adjustment after the relaxed, creative environment in which she had been raised. She also grew frustrated with the lack of privacy in dormitory life, and decided to leave after one year to get married.

One of her first serious efforts at publication was a love story for teens, *Debutante Hill,* which she wrote in between magazine articles as a way of passing the lonely hours as a young homemaker and mother while her first husband served first in the U.S. Air Force and then enrolled in law school. She entered the book in Dodd, Mead and Company's Seventeenth Summer Literary

Contest. The manuscript "was returned for revisions because in it a young man of twenty drank a beer," Duncan once observed. "I changed the beer to a Coke and resubmitted the manuscript. It won the contest, and the book was published." While Duncan considered the story "sweet and sticky . . . pap," a reviewer for the *Christian Science Monitor* maintained that Duncan "writes exceptionally well, and has the happy ability to make a reader care what happens to her characters." Still, the prize—one thousand dollars and a book contract—did much to encourage the budding novelist, who, in 1958, suddenly found herself a published novelist at the age of twenty-four.

When her first marriage ended in divorce, Duncan returned to magazine writing to support her family. In 1962, she relocated to Albuquerque, New Mexico, got a teaching job at the University of New Mexico's department of journalism, and eventually earned her master's degree. In 1965, she married engineer Don Arquette, and since "the financial pressure was off, I also felt free to turn back to my non-lucrative, but immeasurably enjoyable, hobby of writing teenage novels," she once recalled. Over the years, young adult novels had changed, however, and Duncan found she was no longer constricted by many of the taboos of the 1950s. The result of this newfound freedom was *Ransom,* an adventure story of five teenagers kidnapped by a school-bus driver. When Duncan's publisher refused to handle the book because it deviated from her former style, Doubleday took it on, and *Ransom* became a runner-up for the prestigious Edgar Allan Poe Award. It also received a healthy dose of critical praise, with reviewer Dorothy M. Broderick commenting in the *New York Times Book Review* that the character of Glenn Kirtland, whose consistently selfish behavior endangers the whole group, "sets the book apart and makes it something more than another good mystery." *Ransom* established Duncan in a genre she would master to great success.

While teaching, studying, and raising her five children, Duncan continued to publish young adult suspense novels, such as *I Know What You Did Last Summer, Down the Hall,* and *Summer of Fear.* Duncan's style remained consistent in its simplicity; as a writer for *Twentieth-Century Children's Writers* observed, Duncan "places an individual or a group of normal, believable young people in what appears to be a prosaic setting such as a suburban neighborhood or an American high school; on the surface everything is as it should be, until Duncan introduces an element of surprise that gives the story an entirely new twist." These elements are often supernatural; *Summer of Fear* features a young witch who charms herself into an unsuspecting family, while *Down*

a *Dark Hall* involves a girls' boarding school whose students are endangered by the malevolent ghosts of dead artists and writers.

In a similar fashion, *Stranger with My Face* details a young girl's struggle to avoid being possessed by her twin sister, who uses astral projection to take over others' bodies. While the novel's premise might be difficult to accept, "Duncan makes it possible and palatable by a deft twining of fantasy and reality, by giving depth to characters and relationships, and by writing with perception and vitality," stated Zena Sutherland of the *Bulletin of the Center for Children's Books.* This depth is typical of all of Duncan's mystic novels; as the writer for *Twentieth-Century Children's Writers* commented, "an element of the occult is an integral part of [Duncan's] fast-moving plot, but it is always believable because Duncan never carries her depiction of the supernatural into the sometimes goofy realms that a writer such as Stephen King does. Character and plot are always predominant; the books are first and foremost good mysteries made even more interesting for young readers by some aspect of the unusual."

Duncan doesn't rely solely on supernatural events to provide suspense, however. In *Killing Mr. Griffin,* a teenage boy guides a group of friends into kidnapping their strict high school teacher and intimidating him into giving less homework. The teacher dies when he misses his heart medication, and the students try to cover up their involvement. "Duncan breaks some new ground in a novel without sex, drugs or black leather jackets," commented Richard Peck in *New York Times Book Review.* "But the taboo she tampers with is far more potent and pervasive: the unleashed fury of the permissively reared against any assault on their egos and authority. . . . The value of the book lies in the twisted logic of the teenagers and how easily they can justify anything."

While Peck liked the beginning of *Killing Mr. Griffin,* he criticized the ending for descending "into unadulterated melodrama. . . . The book becomes an 'easy read' when it shouldn't." For her part, Duncan pointed to her readers to explain the style of her writing, noting that, to be read, her books have to be tailored to a generation of teens more familiar with television than novels. "Television has had an enormous effect upon youth books," she once stated. "Few of today's readers are patient enough to wade through slow paced, introductory chapters as I did at their ages to see if a book is eventually going to get interesting." Television "has conditioned its viewers to expect instant entertainment," the author continued, and because of this, "writers have been forced into utilizing all sorts of TV techniques to hold their readers' attention."

Perhaps one of Duncan's most well-known novels, *Daughters of Eve*, features a dangerous leader: a faculty adviser who leads a high school girls' club into increasingly more violent acts in the name of feminism. The book's portrayal of a negative feminist element drew some strong remarks from critics. "It has an embittered tone of hatred that colors the characterization," suggested Zena Sutherland in her *Bulletin of the Center for Children's Books* review. Jan M. Goodman presented a similar assessment in *Interracial Books for Children Bulletin*: Duncan "clearly places a harsh value judgment on violent solutions, and . . . she leaves the impression that fighting for women's rights leads to uncontrollable anger and senseless destruction. . . . The book's deceptive interpretation of feminism plus its dangerous stereotypes make it a harmful distortion of reality." But Natalie Babbitt found the work "refreshing" and liked the fact that "there are no lessons." In *New York Times Book Review*, Babbitt compared the novel to William Golding's *Lord of the Flies* and concluded that *Daughters of Eve* "is strongly evenhanded, for it lets us see that women can be as bloodthirsty as men ever were."

Even though she features extraordinary events in her books, "the things I have written about as fiction in suspense novels are no part of our everyday lives," Duncan once commented. This reassuring fact, however, was shattered in 1989 when her youngest daughter, Katilyn, was murdered in an incident that paralleled the plot of *Don't Look behind You,* a novel Duncan had published just a month before the crime took place. In the novel, the character April—who was based on Kaitlyn—is run down and killed by a hit man in a Camaro. "In July 1989," Duncan recalled, "Kait was chased down and shot to death by a hit man in a Camaro." This brutal crime would involve Duncan and her family in a police investigation similar to that described in *Killing Mr. Griffin,* and dealings with a psychic like the one described in Duncan's novel *The Third Eye.* While three men were arrested, none were charged with the murder.

Duncan shared her tragic experience with readers in *Who Killed My Daughter?: The True Story of a Mother's Search for Her Daughter's Murderer,* which was published in 1992 in the hope that it might be read by someone with information on her daughter's murder. Through private investigators hired by the family, she learned that her daughter's boyfriend had been involved in an insurance fraud scam, and she suspects that Kaitlyn learned of the scam and was planning to break up with him. As the facts became known, Duncan realized that other circumstances surrounding her daughter's murder paralleled the novel she had just published. "It was as if these things I'd written about as fiction became hideous reality," Duncan explained to interviewer Roger Sutton in *School Library Journal.*

Who Killed My Daughter?, Duncan's first work of nonfiction, was praised by numerous reviewers and was nominated for teen reading awards in nine states. According to *Kliatt* contributor Claire Rosser, readers "will find this tragedy all the more poignant simply because it is horrifyingly true." While Mary Jane Santos noted in her appraisal for *Voice of Youth Advocates* that readers might "get lost in the myriad of minutia" Duncan marshals in her effort to solve the crime—numerous transcripts and other factual evidence is presented in the book—the critic went on to add that "the strength and tenacity of Duncan is admirable."

Several years after the murder, Duncan and her husband moved to the West Coast to attempt to rebuild their lives. Meanwhile, the coincidences between her daughter's murder and her own YA novel had led Duncan to contact Dr. William Roll, a director at the Psychical Research Foundation and an expert in extrasensory perception (ESP), who explained to Duncan that, as she told Sutton, "precognition is very much a proven reality, that it's also been proven that people who are creative individuals have much more psychical ability than others."

For several years, Duncan focused on editing collections of suspenseful short fiction and penning books for younger readers, such as *The Circus Comes Home: When the Greatest Show on Earth Rode the Rails,* about the Ringling Brothers-Barnum & Bailey circus that wintered near Duncan's childhood home in Florida, and *The Magic of Spider Woman,* a retelling of a Navajo myth that a *Publishers Weekly* contributor praised for its "thoughtful message, grounded in well-chosen details and adeptly relayed through [Duncan's] personable storytelling." However, with *Gallows Hill,* Duncan returned to her characteristic suspense format, as protagonist Sarah, the new girl in town, attempts to gain popularity by starting a fortune-telling business. When her fortunes prove accurate and she becomes haunted by dreams of the Salem Witch Trials of the seventeenth century, Sarah's plan backfires, and soon she is looked on with suspicion by what a *Publishers Weekly* contributor described as "adults [who] are unsympathetic and clueless, allowing their teens to run rampant into the alluring arms" of an evil Sarah's supernatural ability seems to have unleashed. In *Voice of Youth Advocates,* critic Delia A. Culberson praised Duncan's ability to meld historical fact with compelling fiction, dubbing *Gallows Hill* "an unusual and intriguing tale peopled with believable characters. . . . [that] illustrates how ignorance and bigotry can prevail against fairness and common sense."

In 1995, Duncan teamed with Roll to write *Psychic Connections: A Journey into the Mysterious World of Psi,* which provides teens with explanations of various types of psychic phenomenon—ghosts, telepathy, ESP, psychic healing—from a balanced perspective. Duncan shows how data and facts can be misconstrued, and she also explores how the psychic interviewing process works, relating such things to her own inconclusive experiences with the paranormal in the case of her daughter. The book received a somewhat ambivalent reaction from *Bulletin for the Center of Children's Books* critic Deborah Stevenson, who viewed *Psychic Connections* as "successful neither as a collection of true mysterious tales nor as a science-based defense of a controversial subject." However, *School Library Journal* contributor Cathy Chauvette found the book "compelling," while Nancy Glass Wright praised the work in *Voice of Youth Advocates* as "a comprehensive overview" that is "sometimes riveting."

Several of Duncan's books have found their way onto television, and one even appeared on movie screens in 1997. Pleased with television adaptations of *Summer of Fear* and *Killing Mr. Griffin,* Duncan was understandably excited when movie rights to *I Know What You Did Last Summer* were sold and production on the 1997 motion picture release began. However, she was dismayed by the film version starring actress Jennifer Love Hewitt. "They made it into a slasher film," Duncan told Susan Schindehette in *People.* "And I don't think murder is funny."

BIOGRAPHICAL AND CRITICAL SOURCES:

BOOKS

Contemporary Literary Criticism, Volume 26, Thomson Gale (Detroit, MI), 1983.

Duncan, Lois, *Chapters: My Growth as a Writer,* Little, Brown (Boston, MA), 1982.

St. James Guide to Young Adult Writers, 2nd edition, St. James Press (Detroit, MI), 1999.

Something about the Author Autobiography Series, Volume 2, Thomson Gale (Detroit, MI), 1986.

*Twentieth-Century Children's Writers,*3rd edition, edited by Tracy Chevalier, St. James Press (Detroit, MI), 1989.

PERIODICALS

Best Sellers, August 1978, Hildagarde Gray, review of *Killing Mr. Griffin,* pp. 154-155.

Booklist, April 15, 1992, Ilene Cooper, review of *Who Killed My Daughter?: The True Story of a Mother's Search for Her Daughter's Murderer,* p. 1482; February 15, 1994, Ilene Cooper, review of *The Circus Comes Home,* p. 1078; June 1, 1995, Ilene Cooper, review of *Psychic Connections,* p. 1743; May 15, 1996, Stephanie Zvirin, review of *Night Terrors,* p. 1581; April 15, 1997, Ilene Cooper, review of *Gallows Hill,* p. 1420; July, 1998, Roger Leslie, review of *Trapped!,* p. 1873; February 15, 1999, Karen Harris, review of *Don't Look behind You,* p. 1984; February 1, 2000, Gillian Engberg, review of *I Walk at Night,* p. 1028; June 1, 2000, G. Engberg, review of *On the Edge,* p. 1882.

Bulletin of the Center for Children's Books, February 1974; January 1980, Zena Sutherland, review of *Daughter of Eve,* pp. 92-93; April 1982, Zena Sutherland, review of *Stranger with My Face,* p. 146; July-August 1987; September 1995, Deborah Stevenson, review of *Psychic Connections,* pp. 12-13; July-August, 1998, p. 393.

Children's Book Review Service, spring 1982, Leigh Dean, review of *Chapters: My Growth as a Writer,* p. 116.

Christian Science Monitor, February 5, 1959, "Widening Horizons: Debutante Hill," p. 11.

Horn Book, February 1965, Ruth Hill Viguers, review of *Season of the Two-Heart,* p. 59; April 1977, Ethel L. Heins, review of *Summer of Fear,* p. 167; February 1982; November-December 1993, Margaret A. Bush, review of *The Circus Comes Home,* p. 754; July-August 1996, Elizabeth S. Watson, review of *The Magic of Spider Woman,* p. 470.

Interracial Books for Children Bulletin, Volume 11, number 6, 1980, Jan M. Goodman, review of *Daughters of Eve,* pp. 17-18.

Kirkus Reviews, September 1, 1973, review of *I Know What You Did Last Summer,* p. 972; January 1, 1982, review of *Stranger with My Face,* p. 11.

Kliatt, May 1994, Claire Rosser, review of *Who Killed My Daughter?,* p. 26.

New York Times Book Review, June 5, 1966, Dorothy M. Broderick, review of *Ransom,* p. 42; June 8, 1969, Richard F. Shepard, review of *They Never Came Home,* p. 42; November 10, 1974, Gloria Levitas, "Haunts and Hunts," pp. 8, 10; March 6, 1977, Julia Whedon, "Witches and Werewolves," p. 29; April 30, 1978, Richard Peck, "Teaching Teacher a Lesson," p. 54; January 27, 1980, Natalie Babbitt, review of *Daughters of Eve,* p. 24; August 16, 1998, p. 14.

People, November 24, 1997, Susan Schindehette, "Who Killed My Daughter? An Eight-Year-Old Unsolved Slaying Still Plagues Writer Lois Duncan," p. 103.

Publishers Weekly, April 20, 1992, Maria Simpson, "'Who Killed My Daughter?' Lois Duncan (and Delacorte) Search for an Answer," p. 19; March 11, 1996, review of *The Magic of Spider Woman,* p. 64; March 17, 1997, review of *Gallows Hill,* p. 84; June 1, 1998, review of *Trapped!,* p. 48; January 10, 2000, review of *I Walk at Night,* p. 67; June 26, 2000, review of *On the Edge,* p. 76; September 18, 2000, review of *The Magic of Spider Woman,* p. 113; February 12, 2001, review of *The Longest Hair in the World,* p. 214.

School Library Journal, November 1971, Peggy Sullivan, review of *A Gift of Magic,* p. 122; April 1974, Linda Silver, review of *I Know What You Did Last Summer,* p. 64; September 1979, Cyrisse Jaffee, review of *Daughters of Eve,* p. 155; November 1981; July 1989; June 1992, Roger Sutton, interview with Lois Duncan, pp. 20-24; August 1992 Barbara Lynn, review of *Who Killed My Daughter?,* p. 190; May, 1995, Cathy Chauvette, review of *Psychic Connections,* p. 125; May 1997, Bruce Anne Shook, review of *Gallows Hill,* p. 132; March 2000, review of *I Walk at Night,* p. 194.

Times Literary Supplement, March 26, 1982, Jennifer Moody, "The Onset of Maturity," p. 343; February 22, 1985, Anthony Horowitz, "Parent Problems," p. 214; January 29-February 4, 1988, Sarah Hayes, "Fatal Flaws," p. 119.

Voice of Youth Advocates, December 1992, Mary Jane Santos, review of *Who Killed My Daughter?,* p. 304; August 1995, Nancy Glass Wright, review of *Psychic Connections,* p. 181; April 1997, Delia A. Culberson, review of *Gallows Hill,* p. 28.

ONLINE

Lois Duncan Web site, http://loisduncan.arquettes.com/ (July 26, 2004).

DUNCAN, Robert 1919-1988
(Robert Edward Duncan, Robert Symmes)

PERSONAL: Born Edward Howard Duncan, January 7, 1919, in Oakland, CA; died of a heart attack February 3, 1988, in San Francisco, CA; son of Edward Howard (a day laborer) and Marguerite (Wesley) Duncan; adopted by Edwin Joseph (an architect) and Minnehaha (Harris) Symmes; adopted name, Robert Edward Symmes; in 1941 he took the name Robert Duncan; companion of Jess Collins (a painter). *Education:* Attended University of California, Berkeley, 1936-38, 1948-50.

CAREER: Poet. Worked at various times as a dishwasher and typist. Organizer of poetry readings and workshops in San Francisco Bay area; *Experimental Review,* co-editor with Sanders Russell, publishing works of Henry Miller, Anaís Nin, Lawrence Durrell, Kenneth Patchen, William Everson, Aurora Bligh (Mary Fabilli), Thomas Merton, Robert Horan, and Jack Johnson, 1940-41; *Berkeley Miscellany,* editor, 1948-49; lived in Banyalbufar, Majorca, 1955-56; taught at Black Mountain College, Black Mountain, NC, spring and summer, 1956; assistant director of Poetry Center, San Francisco State College, under a Ford grant, 1956-57; associated with the Creative Writing Workshop, University of British Columbia, 1963; lecturer in Advanced Poetry Workshop, San Francisco State College, spring, 1965. *Military service:* U.S. Army, 1941; discharged on psychological grounds.

AWARDS, HONORS: Ford Foundation grant, 1956-57; Union League Civic and Arts Foundation Prize, *Poetry* magazine, 1957; Harriet Monroe Prize, *Poetry,* 1961; Guggenheim fellowship, 1963-64; Levinson Prize, *Poetry,* 1964; Miles Poetry Prize, 1964; National Endowment for the Arts grants, 1965, 1966-67; Eunice Tietjens Memorial Prize, *Poetry,* 1967; nomination for National Book Critics Circle Award, 1984, for *Ground Work: Before the War;* first recipient of National Poetry Award, 1985, in recognition of lifetime contribution to the art of poetry; Before Columbus Foundation American Book Award, 1986, for *Ground Work: Before the War;* Fred Cody Award for Lifetime Literary Excellence from Bay Area Book Reviewers Association, 1986.

WRITINGS:

Heavenly City, Earthly City (poems), drawings by Mary Fabilli, Bern Porter, 1947.

Medieval Scenes (poems), Centaur Press (San Francisco), 1950, with preface by Duncan and afterword by Robert Bertholf, Kent State University Libraries, 1978.

Poems, 1948-49, Berkeley Miscellany, 1950.

The Song of the Border-Guard (poem), Black Mountain Graphics Workshop, 1951.

The Artist's View, [San Francisco], 1952.

Fragments of a Disordered Devotion, privately printed, 1952, reprinted, Gnomon Press, 1966.

Caesar's Gate: Poems, 1949-55, Divers Press (Majorca, Spain), 1956, 2nd edition, Sand Dollar, 1972.

Letters (poems), drawings by Duncan, J. Williams (Highlands, NC), 1958.

Faust Foutu: Act One of Four Acts, A Comic Mask, 1952-1954 (first produced in San Francisco, CA, 1955; produced in New York, 1959-60), decorations by Duncan, Part I, White Rabbit Press (San Francisco, CA), 1958, reprinted, Station Hill Press, 1985, entire play published as *Faust Foutu,* Enkidu sur Rogate (Stinson Beach, CA), 1959.

Selected Poems, City Lights Books (San Francisco, CA), 1959.

The Opening of the Field (poems), Grove (New York, NY), 1960, revised edition, New Directions (New York, NY), 1973.

(Author of preface) Jess [Collins], *O!,* Hawk's Well Press (New York, NY), 1960.

(Author of preface) Jonathan Williams, *Elegies and Celebrations,* Jargon, 1962.

On Poetry (radio interview), Yale University (New Haven, CT), 1964.

Roots and Branches (poems), Scribner (New York, NY), 1964.

Writing Writing: A Composition Book of Madison 1953, Stein Imitations, Sumbooks, 1964.

As Testimony: The Poem and the Scene (essay), White Rabbit Press (San Francisco, CA), 1964.

Wine, Auerhahn Press/Oyez (Berkeley, CA), 1964.

Uprising (poems), Oyez (Berkeley, CA), 1965.

The Sweetness and Greatness of Dante's "Divine Comedy," 1263-1965 (lecture), Open Space (San Francisco, CA), 1965.

Medea at Kolchis; [or] The Maiden Head (play; first produced at Black Mountain College, 1956), Oyez (Berkeley, CA), 1965.

Adam's Way: A Play on Theosophical Themes, [San Francisco, CA], 1966.

Of the War: Passages 22-27, Oyez (Berkeley, CA), 1966.

A Book of Resemblances: Poems, 1950-53, drawings by Jess Collins, Henry Wenning, 1966.

Six Prose Pieces, Perishable Press (Rochester, MI), 1966.

The Years as Catches: First Poems, 1939-46, Oyez (Berkeley, CA), 1966.

Boob (poem), privately printed, 1966.

Audit/Robert Duncan (also published as special issue of *Audit/Poetry,* Volume 4, number 3), Audit/Poetry, 1967.

Christmas Present, Christmas Presence! (poem), Black Sparrow Press, 1967.

The Cat and the Blackbird (children's storybook), illustrations by Jess Collins, White Rabbit Press (San Francisco, CA), 1967.

Epilogos, Black Sparrow Press (San Francisco, CA), 1967.

My Mother Would Be a Falconress (poem), Oyez (Berkeley, CA), 1968.

Names of People (poems), illustrations by Jess Collins, Black Sparrow Press (San Francisco, CA), 1968.

The Truth and Life of Myth: An Essay in Essential Autobiography, House of Books (New York, NY), 1968.

Bending the Bow (poems), New Directions (New York, NY), 1968.

The First Decade: Selected Poems, 1940-50, Fulcrum Press (London, England), 1968.

Derivations: Selected Poems, 1950-1956, Fulcrum Press (London, England), 1968.

Achilles Song, Phoenix (London, England), 1969.

Playtime, Pseudo Stein; 1942, A Story [and] A Fairy Play: From the Laboratory Records Notebook of 1953, A Tribute to Mother Carey's Chickens, Poet's Press, c.1969.

Notes on Grossinger's "Solar Journal: Oecological Sections," Black Sparrow Press (San Francisco, CA), 1970.

A Selection of Sixty-five Drawings from One Drawing Book, 1952-1956, Black Sparrow Press (San Francisco, CA), 1970.

Tribunals: Passages 31-35, Black Sparrow Press (San Francisco, CA), 1970.

Poetic Disturbances, Maya (San Francisco, CA), 1970.

Bring It up from the Dark, Cody's Books, 1970.

A Prospectus for the Prepublication of Ground Work to Certain Friends of the Poet, privately printed, 1971.

An Interview with George Bowering and Robert Hogg, April 19, 1969, Coach House Press, 1971.

Structure of Rime XXVIII; In Memoriam Wallace Stevens, University of Connecticut (Storrs, CT), 1972.

Poems from the Margins of Thom Gunn's Moly, privately printed, 1972.

A Seventeenth-Century Suite, privately printed, 1973.

Dante, Institute of Further Studies (New York, NY), 1974.

(With Jack Spicer) *An Ode and Arcadia,* Ark Press, 1974.

The Venice Poem, Poet's Mimeo (Burlington, VT), 1978.

Veil, Turbine, Cord & Bird: Sets of Syllables, Sets of Words, Sets of Lines, Sets of Poems, Addressing . . . , J. Davies, c. 1979.

Fictive Certainties: Five Essays in Essential Autobiography, New Directions (New York, NY), 1979.

The Five Songs, Friends of the University of California, San Diego Library, 1981.

Towards an Open Universe, Aquila Publishing, 1982.

Ground Work: Before the War, New Directions (New York, NY), 1984.

A Paris Visit, Grenfell Press, 1985.

The Regulators, Station Hill Press, 1985.

Ground Work II: In the Dark, New Directions (New York, NY), 1987.

Selected Poems, edited by Robert J. Bertholf, New Directions (New York, NY), 1993.

Selected Prose, New Directions (New York, NY), 1995.

Faust Foutu: A Comic Masque, Barrytown (Barrytown, NY), 2001.

The Letters of Robert Duncan and Denise Levertov, Stanford University Press (Stanford, CA), 2004.

Contributor to books, including Howard Nemerov, editor, *Poets on Poetry,* Basic Books, 1966; Edwin Haviland Miller, editor, *The Artistic Legacy of Walt Whitman: A Tribute to Gay Wilson Allen,* New York University Press, 1970; Ian Young, editor, *The Male Muse: Gay Poetry Anthology,* Crossing Press, 1973. Also author of *The H.D. Book,* a long work in several parts, published in literary journals. Represented in anthologies, including *Faber Book of Modern American Verse,* edited by W.H. Auden, 1956, *The New American Poetry: 1945-1960,* edited by Donald M. Allen, 1960, and many others. Contributor of poems, under name Robert Symmes, to *Phoenix* and *Ritual.* Contributor to *Atlantic, Poetry, Nation, Quarterly Review of Literature,* and other periodicals.

SIDELIGHTS: Though the name of American poet Robert Duncan is not well known outside the literary world, within that world Duncan has become associated with a number of superlatives. Kenneth Rexroth, writing in *Assays,* named Duncan "one of the most accomplished, one of the most influential" of U.S. postwar poets. An important participant in the Black Mountain school of poetry led by Charles Olson, Duncan became "probably the figure with the richest natural genius" from among that group, suggested M.L. Rosenthal in *The New Poets: American and British Poetry since*

World War II. Duncan was also, in Rosenthal's opinion, perhaps "the most intellectual of our poets from the point of view of the effect upon him of a wide, critically intelligent reading." In addition, "few poets have written more articulately and self-consciously about their own intentions and understanding of poetry," reported *Dictionary of Literary Biography* contributor George F. Butterick. The homosexual companion of San Francisco painter Jess Collins, Duncan was also one of the first poets to call for a new social consciousness that would accept homosexuality. Largely responsible for the establishment of San Francisco as the spiritual hub of contemporary American poetry, Duncan left, at his death, a significant contribution to American literature through the body of his writings and through the many poets who felt the influence of the theory behind his poetics.

Duncan's poetics were formed by the events of his early life. His mother died while giving him birth, leaving his father, a day laborer, to care for him. Six months later, he was adopted by a couple who selected him on the basis of his astrological configuration. Their reverence for the occult in general, and especially their belief in reincarnation and other concepts from Hinduism, was a lasting and important influence on Duncan's poetic vision. Encouraged by a high school English teacher who saw poetry as an essential means of sustaining spiritual vigor, Duncan chose his vocation while still in his teens. Though his parents wanted him to have a European education in medieval history, he remained in San Francisco, living as a recluse so as not to embarrass the academic figure who was his lover. He continued reading and writing, eventually became the student of Middle Ages historian Ernst Kantorowicz, and throughout his life "maintained a profound interest in occult matters as parallel to and informing his own theories of poetry," Michael Davidson reported in another *Dictionary of Literary Biography* essay.

Minnesota Review contributor Victor Contoski suggested that Duncan's essays in *The Truth and Life of Myth* comprise "the best single introduction to his poetry," which, for Duncan, was closely related to mysticism. Duncan, noted a London *Times* reporter, was primarily "concerned with poetry as what he called 'manipulative magic' and a 'magic ritual', and with the nature of what he thought of (in a markedly Freudian manner) as 'human bisexuality.'" Reported James Dickey in *Babel to Byzantium,* "Duncan has the old or pagan sense of the poem as a divine form of speech which works intimately with the animism of nature, of the renewals that believed-in ceremonials can be, and of the sacramental in experience; for these reasons and others that neither he nor I could give, there is at least part of a very good poet in him." While this emphasis on myth was an obstacle to some reviewers, critic Laurence Liebermann, writing in a *Poetry* review, said of Duncan's *The Opening of the Field* that it "announced the birth of a surpassingly individual talent: a poet of mysticism, visionary terror, and high romance."

Duncan wrote some of the poems in *The Opening of the Field* in 1956, while he taught at Olson's Black Mountain College. Olson promoted projective verse, a poetry shaped by the rhythms of the poet's breath, which he defined as an extension of nature. These poems found their own "open" forms unlike the prescribed measures and line lengths that ruled traditional poetry. "Following Olson's death, Duncan became the leading spokesman for the poetry of open form in America," noted Butterick. Furthermore, explained some critics, Duncan fulfilled Olson's dictum more fully than Olson had done; whereas Olson projected the poem into a space bounded by the poet's natural breath, Duncan carried this process farther, defining the poem as an open field without boundaries of any kind.

Duncan was a syncretist possessing "a bridge-building, time-binding, and space-binding imagination" in which "the Many are One, where all faces have their Original Being, and where Eternal Love encompasses all reality, both Good and Evil," wrote Stephen Stepanchev in *American Poetry since 1945*. A Duncan poem, accordingly, is like a collage, "a compositional field where anything might enter: a prose quotation, a catalogue, a recipe, a dramatic monologue, a diatribe," Davidson explained. The poems draw together into one dense fabric materials from sources as diverse as works on ancient magic, Christian mysticism, and the *Oxford English Dictionary*. Writing in the *New York Times Book Review*, Jim Harrison called the structure of a typical Duncan poem multi-layered and four-dimensional—"moving through time with the poet"—and compared it to "a block of weaving. . . . *Bending the Bow* is for the strenuous, the hyperactive reader of poetry; to read Duncan with any immediate grace would require Norman O. Brown's knowledge of the arcane mixed with Ezra Pound's grasp of poetics. . . . [Duncan] is personal rather than confessional and writes within a continuity of tradition. It simply helps to be familiar with Dante, [William] Blake, mythography, medieval history, H.D., William Carlos Williams, Pound, [Gertrude] Stein, [Louis] Zukofsky, Olson, [Robert] Creeley and [Denise] Levertov."

Process, not conclusion, drew Duncan's focus. In some pages from a notebook published in Donald Allen's *The New American Poetry: 1945-1960*, Duncan stated: "A longing grows to return to the open composition in which the accidents and imperfections of speech might awake intimations of human being. . . . There is a natural mystery in poetry. We do not understand all that we render up to understanding. . . . I study what I write as I study out any mystery. A poem, mine or another's, is an occult document, a body awaiting vivisection, analysis, X-rays." The poet, he explained, is an explorer more than a creator. "I work at language as a spring of water works at the rock, to find a course, and so, blindly. In this I am not a maker of things, but, if maker, a maker of a way. For the way is itself." As in the art of marquetry—the making of patterns by enhancing natural wood grains—the poet is aware of the possible meanings of words and merely brings them out. "I'm not *putting* a grain into the wood," he once told Jack R. Cohn and Thomas J. O'Donnell in a *Contemporary Literature* interview. Later, he added, "I acquire language lore. What I am supplying is something like . . . grammar of design, or of the possibilities of design." The goal of composition, Duncan also wrote in a *Caterpillar* essay, was "not to reach conclusion but to keep our exposure to what we do not know."

Each Duncan poem builds itself by a series of organic digressions, in the manner of outward-reaching roots or branches. The order in his poems is not an imposed order, but a reflection of correspondences already present in nature or language. At times, the correspondences inherent in language become insistent so that the poet following an organic method of writing is in danger of merely recording what the language itself dictates as possible. Duncan was highly susceptible to impressions from other literature—perhaps too susceptible, he once noted in a *Boundary 2* interview. In several interviews, for example, Duncan referred to specific early poems as "received" from outside agents, "poems in which angels were present." After reading Rainer Marie Rilke's *Duino Elegies,* he came to dread what he called "any angelic invasion"—an insistent voice other than his own. One poem that expresses this preference is "Often I Am Permitted to Return to a Meadow," the first poem in *The Opening of the Field*. As Duncan once explained to Cohn and O'Donnell, "When I wrote that opening line . . . I recognized that this was my permission, and that this meadow, which I had not yet identified, would be the thematic center of the book. In other words, what's back of that opening proposition I understood immediately: twice *you* wanted to compel me to have a book that would have angels at the center, but *now* I am permitted, often you have permitted me, to return to a mere meadow." His originality consisted of his demand that the inner life of the poem be his own, not received from another spiritual or literary source. "Whether he is working from Dante's prose Renaissance meditative poems, or Thom Gunn's *Moly* sequence, he works *from* them and *to* what they leave open or unexamined," explained Thomas Parkinson in *Poets, Poems, Movements.*

At the same time, Duncan recognized his works as derivative literature for several reasons. "I am a traditionalist, a seeker after origins, not an original," he was noted as saying by Herbert Mitgang in the *New York Times.* Often Duncan claimed Walt Whitman as his literary father, seeking in poetry to celebrate the experiences common to all men and women of all times, trying to manifest in words the underlying unity of all things that was essential to his beliefs. Complete originality is not possible in such a cosmos. In fact, the use of language—an inherited system of given sounds and symbols—is itself an imitative activity that limits originality. Even so, the poet, he believed, must be as free as possible "from preconceived ideas, whether structural or thematic, and must allow the internal forces of the composition at hand to determine the final form," Robert C. Weber observed in *Concerning Poetry.* This position, Duncan recognized, was bequeathed to him by Whitman and Pound, who viewed a poet's life work as one continuous "unfinished book," Parkinson noted.

Duncan's works express social and political ideals conversant with his poetics. The ideal environment for the poet, Duncan believed, would be a society without boundaries. In poetry he found a vocation where there was no prohibition against homosexuality, James F. Mersmann observed in *Out of the Viet Nam Vortex: A Study of Poets and Poetry against the War.* Duncan's theory, Mersmann added, "not only claims that the poem unfolds according to its own law, but envisions a compatible cosmology in which it may do so. It is not the poem alone that must grow as freely as the plant: the life of the person, the state, the species, and indeed the cosmos itself follows a parallel law. All must follow their own imperatives and volition; all activity must be free of external coercion."

Political commitment is the subject of *Bending the Bow.* Duncan was "one of the most astute observers of the malpractices of Western governments, power blocs, etc., who [was] always on the human side, the *right* side of such issues as war, poverty, civil rights, etc., and who therefore [did] not take an easy way out," though his general avoidance of closure sometimes weakened his case, Harriet Zinnes remarked in a *Prairie Schooner* review. Highly critical of the Vietnam War, pollution, nuclear armament, and the exploitation of native peoples and natural resources, the poems in *Bending the Bow*

include "Up-Rising," "one of the major political poems of our time," according to Davidson. For Duncan, the essayist continued, "the American attempt to secure *one* meaning of democracy by eliminating all others represents a massive violation of that vision of polis desired by John Adams and Thomas Jefferson and projected through Walt Whitman." Though such poems voice an "essentially negative vision," noted Weber, "it is a critical part of Duncan's search for the nature of man since he cannot ignore what man has become. . . . These themes emerge from within the body of the tradition of the poetry he seeks to find; politics are a part of the broad field of the poet's life, and social considerations emerge from his concern with the nature of man."

The difference between organic and imposed order, for Duncan, explained Mersmann, "is the difference between life and death. The dead matter of the universe science dissects into tidy stacktables; the living significance of creation, the angel with which the poet wrestles, is a volatile whirlwind of sharp knees and elbows thrashing with a grace beyond our knowledge of grace." The only law in a dancing universe, the critic added, is its inherent "love of the dance itself." Anything opposed to this dance of freedom is seen as evil. Both Duncan's poetics and his lifestyle stemmed from "a truly different kind of consciousness, either a very old or a very new spirituality," Mersmann concluded.

Duncan's method of composition based on this spirituality results in several difficulties for even the sympathetic reader. His "drifting conglomerations" are an exercise of poetic freedom that sometimes inspires, "but more often I feel suicidal about it," Dickey commented. Davidson noted that Duncan "never courted a readership but rather a special kind of reader, who grants the poet a wide latitude in developing his art, even in its most extreme moments. . . . The number of such readers is necessarily limited, but fierce in devotion." A large number of Duncan's poems are most accessible to an inner circle familiar with the personal and literary contexts of his writings, observed a *Times Literary Supplement* reviewer, who pointed out that "not everyone can live in California."

Duncan's method of composition has presented some difficulties for critics, as well. The eclectic nature of *Bending the Bow,* for example, remarked Hayden Carruth in the *Hudson Review,* excludes it from "questions of quality. I cannot imagine my friends, the poets who gather to dismember each other, asking of this book, as they would of the others in this review, those narrower in scope, smaller in style, 'Is it good or is it bad?' The question doesn't arise; not because Duncan is a good poet, though he is superb, but because the comprehensiveness of his imagination is too great for us."

After the publication of *Bending the Bow* in 1968, Duncan announced he would not publish a major collection for another fifteen years. During this hiatus he hoped to produce process-oriented poems instead of the "overcomposed" poems he wrote when he thought in terms of writing a book. In effect, this silence kept him from receiving the widespread critical attention or recognition he might otherwise have enjoyed. However, Duncan had a small but highly appreciative audience among writers who shared his concerns. Distraught when *Ground Work: Before the War,* the evidence of nearly twenty years of significant work, did not win the attention they thought it deserved from the publishing establishment, these poets founded the National Poetry Award and honored Duncan by making him the first recipient of the award in 1985. The award, described in a *Sagetrieb* article, was "a positive action affirming the admiration of the poetic community for the dedication and accomplishment of a grand poet."

Duncan concluded the project he began with *Ground Work: Before the War* with *Ground Work II: In the Dark,* which was published shortly before his death. Leonard Schwartz noted in the *American Book Review* that while not as groundbreaking in technique as the first, the poems in *In the Dark* are "much more surer and more complete than those in *I . . .* [which] is *. . .* an exploration of words to find their fullest senses." Schwartz concluded, "*II* is the fruit of that exploration, finished works brought back and thereby bringing to term a specific condition of consciousness." Thom Gunn, writing in the *Times Literary Supplement,* found that Duncan "trusts his spontaneity so completely that he encourages it to *trip up* his conscious intentions." Gunn noted that "It is this current that accounts for the most exciting, and the most exasperating of Duncan's writing."

Selected Poems, published posthumously in 1993, gathers together Duncan's writings from throughout his career, resulting in a comprehensive review of the poet's innovative technical and spiritual poetics. In comparing Duncan to other Black Mountain poets, Mark Ford in the *London Review of Books* remarked that "Duncan's work . . . exhibits a far more nuanced awareness of its own relationship to the traditions of poetry that it aims to modify." A *Publishers Weekly* reviewer stated that even readers familiar with the author's poetry will "become more sensitized to his . . . imagery and consistency" after reviewing this collection. Dachine

Ranier, contributor to *Agenda,* called the collection "a lovely offering of the work of an American poet, unjustly neglected for decades."

BIOGRAPHICAL AND CRITICAL SOURCES:

BOOKS

Allen, Donald M., *The New American Poetry, 1945-1960,* Grove (New York, NY), 1960.

Allen, Donald M., *The Poetics of the New American Poetry,* Grove (New York, NY), 1973.

Bertholf, Robert J., and Ian W. Reid, editors, *Robert Duncan: Scales of the Marvelous,* New Directions (New York, NY), 1979.

Charters, Samuel, *Some Poems/Poets: Studies in American Underground Poetry since 1945,* Oyez (Berkeley, CA), 1971.

Contemporary Literary Criticism, Thomson Gale (Detroit, MI), Volume 1, 1973, Volume 2, 1974, Volume 4, 1975, Volume 7, 1977, Volume 15, 1980, Volume 41, 1987, Volume 55, 1989.

Dickey, James, *Babel to Byzantium,* Farrar, Straus (New York, NY), 1968.

Dictionary of Literary Biography, Thomson Gale (Detroit, MI), Volume 5: *American Poets since World War II,* 1980, Volume 16: *The Beats: Literary Bohemians in Postwar America,* 1983.

Faas, Ekbert, editor, *Towards a New American Poetics: Essays and Interviews,* Black Sparrow Press (San Francisco, CA), 1978.

Fass, Ekbert, *Young Robert Duncan: Portrait of the Homosexual in Society,* Black Sparrow Press (San Francisco, CA), 1983.

Fauchereau, Serge, *Lecture de la poesie americaine,* Editions de Minuit (Paris, France), 1969.

Foster, Edward Halsey, *Understanding the Black Mountain Poets,* University of South Carolina Press (Columbia, SC), 1995.

Mersmann, James F., *Out of the Viet Nam Vortex: A Study of Poets and Poetry against the War,* University Press of Kansas, 1974.

Parkinson, Thomas, *Poets, Poems, Movements,* University of Michigan Research Press (Ann Arbor, MI), 1987.

Pearce, Roy Harvey, *Historicism once More: Problems and Occasions for the American Scholar,* Princeton University Press (Princeton, NJ), 1969.

Rexroth, Kenneth, *Assays,* New Directions (New York, NY), 1961.

Rexroth, Kenneth, *American Poetry in the Twentieth Century,* Herder and Herder, 1971.

Rosenthal, M. L., *The New Poets: American and British Poetry since World War II,* Oxford University Press (New York, NY), 1967.

Stepanchev, Stephen, *American Poetry since 1945,* Harper (New York, NY), 1965.

Tallman, Warren, *Godawful Streets of Man,* Coach House Press, 1976.

Weatherhead, Kingsley, *Edge of the Image: Marianne Moore, William Carlos Williams, and Some Other Poets,* University of Washington Press (Seattle, WA), 1967.

PERIODICALS

Agenda, autumn-winter, 1970; autumn, 1994, p. 308.
American Book Review, May, 1989, p. 12.
Audit/Poetry (special Duncan issue), number 3, 1967.
Boundary 2, winter, 1980.
Caterpillar, numbers 8-9, 1969.
Centennial Review, fall, 1975; fall, 1985.
Concerning Poetry, spring, 1978.
Contemporary Literature, spring, 1975.
History Today, January, 1994, p. 56.
Hudson Review, summer, 1968.
Library Journal, March 1, 1993, p. 81; August, 1994, p. 132; September 15, 2003, Scott Hightower, review of *The Letters of Robert Duncan and Denise Levertov,* p. 58.
London Review of Books, March 10, 1994, p. 20.
Maps (special Duncan issue), 1974.
Minnesota Review, fall, 1972.
New York Review of Books, June 3, 1965; May 7, 1970.
New York Times Book Review, December 20, 1964; September 29, 1968; August 4, 1985.
Poetry, March, 1968; April, 1969; May, 1970.
Publishers Weekly, February 15, 1993, p. 232; May 16, 1994, p. 63.
Sagetrieb, winter, 1983; (special Duncan issue) fall-winter, 1985.
Saturday Review, February 13, 1965; August 24, 1968.
School Library Journal, August, 1994, p. 132.
Southern Review, spring, 1969; winter, 1985.
Sulfur 12, Volume 4, number 2, 1985.
Times Literary Supplement, May 1, 1969; July 23, 1971; November 25, 1988, p. 1294.
Unmuzzled Ox, February, 1977.
Voice Literary Supplement, November, 1984.
World Literature Today, autumn, 1988, p. 659; spring, 1994, p. 373.

OBITUARIES:

PERIODICALS

Los Angeles Times, February 4, 1988.

New York Times, February 2, 1988.
Times (London, England), February 11, 1988.

*   *   *

DUNCAN, Robert Edward
See DUNCAN, Robert

*   *   *

DUNN, Katherine 1945-
(Katherine Karen Dunn)

PERSONAL: Born October 24, 1945, in Garden City, KS; daughter of Jack (a linotype operator) and Velma (Golly) Dunn; children: Eli Malachy Dunn Dapolonia. *Education:* Attended Portland State College (now University) and Reed College.

AWARDS, HONORS: Music Corporation of America writing grant; Rockefeller writing grant.

WRITINGS:

NOVELS

Attic, Harper (New York City), 1970, reprinted, Warner Books, 1990.
Truck, Harper, 1971, reprinted, Warner Books, 1990.
Geek Love, Knopf (New York City), 1989, reprinted, Warner Books, 1990.

OTHER

Why Do Men Have Nipples? And Other Low-Life Answers to Real-Life Questions, Warner Books, 1992.
(Introduction) *Death Scenes: A Homicide Detective's Scrapbook,* by Jack Huddleston, Feral House, 1996.

Also author of film script of *Truck.*

SIDELIGHTS: Katherine Dunn's novel *Geek Love* is, according to Jeff VanderMeer in the *St. James Guide to Horror, Ghost and Gothic Writers,* "a modern Gothic classic." VanderMeer explains that "the book's artistic success depends upon its risky structure: two strands (past and present) that alternate chapters, each strand offering insight into the other. Much like the novel's Siamese twins, the two stories intertwine to form one cohesive narrative. This double story-line forces the reader to continually re-evaluate the characters and to reassess Dunn's slant on morality."

Both story strands are narrated by the same character, Olympia Binewski, "an albino hunchback dwarf," as VanderMeer describes her. In the present-day narrative, Olympia tells of her attempts to keep her daughter out of the clutches of a wealthy, sadistic woman. The past narrative describes Olympia's childhood among carnival performers, one of whom has created a cult in which people without deformities purposely mutilate themselves to become "freaks." *Geek Love*, VanderMeer notes, contains "commentaries on society [which] run like a hidden vein of satire throughout the book. Dunn's explorations of the utter mercilessness of science when applied by human beings provides a needed counterpoint to her sometimes repetitive lesson that the true monsters are often hidden behind handsome faces with charming smiles."

Dunn once told *CA:* "I have been a believer in the magic of language since, at a very early age, I discovered that some words got me into trouble and others got me out. The revelations since then have been practically continuous.

"There are other inclinations that have shaped the form and direction of my work: rampant curiosity, a cynical inability to accept face-values balanced by lunatic optimism, and the preoccupation with the effervescing qualities of truth that is probably common to those afflicted by absent-mindedness, prevarication, and general unease in the presence of facts. But the miraculous nature of words themselves contains the discipline.

"Writing is, increasingly, a moral issue for me. The evasion of inexpensive facility, the rejection of the flying bridges built so seductively into the language, require a constant effort of will. The determination required for honest exploration and analysis of the human terrain is often greater than I command. But the fruits of that determination seem worthy of all my efforts."

BIOGRAPHICAL AND CRITICAL SOURCES:

BOOKS

St. James Guide to Horror, Ghost and Gothic Writers, St. James Press (Detroit), 1998.

PERIODICALS

Life, October 24, 1969.
Nation, August 3, 1970.
New York Times, July 1, 1970.
New York Times Book Review, June 21, 1970.

*   *   *

DUNN, Katherine Karen
    See DUNN, Katherine

*   *   *

DURANG, Christopher 1949-
    (Christopher Ferdinand Durang)

PERSONAL: Born January 2, 1949, in Montclair, NJ; son of Francis Ferdinand and Patricia Elizabeth Durang. *Education:* Harvard University, B.A., 1971; Yale University, M.F.A., 1974. *Religion:* "Raised Roman Catholic."

ADDRESSES: Office—Creative Artists Agency, 9830 Wilshire Blvd., Beverly Hills, CA 90212-1804. *Agent*—Helen Merrill, Helen Merrill Agency, 337 W. 22nd St., New York, NY 10011-2607.

CAREER: Yale Repertory Theatre, New Haven, CT, actor, 1974; Southern Connecticut College, New Haven, teacher of drama, 1975; Yale University, New Haven, teacher of playwriting, 1975-76; playwright, 1976-. Actor in plays, including *The Idiots Karamazov* and *Das Lusitania Songspiel;* actor in film and television, including *The Secret of My Success, Joe's Apartment, Mr. North, Housesitter, The Butcher's Wife, The Cowboy Way, Penn and Teller Get Killed,* and *Fraiser;* director of plays. Currently cochair of the playwriting program at Juilliard. Starred in a revival of *Laughing Wild,* produced by the Huntington Theater Company in Boston on June 16, 2005.

MEMBER: Dramatists Guild, Writers Guild, Actors Equity Association, American Society of Composers, Authors, and Publishers.

AWARDS, HONORS: Fellow of Columbia Broadcasting System (CBS), 1975-76; Rockefeller Foundation grant, 1976-77; Guggenheim fellow, 1978-79; Antoinette

Perry Award (Tony) nomination for best book of a musical, League of New York Theatres and Producers, 1978, for *A History of the American Film*; grant from Lecomte du Nouy Foundation, 1980-81; off-Broadway Award (Obie), *Village Voice*, 1980, for *Sister Mary Ignatius Explains It All for You,* and 1999, for *Betty's Summer Vacation*; Kenyon Festival Playwriting award, 1983; Hull-Warriner Award, Dramatists Guild, 1985; Lila Wallace-*Reader's Digest* Fund Writer's Award, 1994-96.

WRITINGS:

PLAYS

The Nature and Purpose of the Universe (first produced in Northampton, MA, 1971; produced in New York, NY, 1975), Dramatists Play Service (New York, NY), 1979.

Robert, first produced in Cambridge, MA, 1971; produced as *'dentity Crisis* in New Haven, CT, 1975.

Better Dead Than Sorry, first produced in New Haven, CT, 1972; produced in New York, NY, 1973.

(With Albert Innaurato) *I Don't Generally Like Poetry, But Have You Read "Trees"?,* first produced in New Haven, CT, 1972; produced in New York, NY, 1973.

(With Albert Innaurato) *The Life Story of Mitzi Gaynor; or, Gyp,* first produced in New Haven, CT, 1973.

The Marriage of Betty and Boo (first produced in New Haven, CT, 1973; revised version produced in New York, NY, 1979), Dramatists Play Service, 1985.

(With Albert Innaurato) *The Idiots Karamazov* (first produced in New Haven at Yale Repertory Theatre, October 10, 1974), Dramatists Play Service (New York, NY), 1980.

Titanic (first produced in New Haven, CT, 1974; produced off-Broadway at Van Dam Theatre, May 10, 1976), Dramatists Play Service (New York, NY), 1983.

Death Comes to Us All, Mary Agnes, first produced in New Haven, CT, 1975.

(With Wendy Wasserstein) *When Dinah Shore Ruled the Earth,* first produced in New Haven, CT, 1975.

(With Sigourney Weaver) *Das Lusitania Songspiel,* first produced off-Broadway at Van Dam Theatre, May 10, 1976.

A History of the American Film (first produced in Hartford, CT, at Eugene O'Neill Playwrights Conference, summer, 1976; produced on Broadway at American National Theatre, March 30, 1978), Avon (New York, NY), 1978.

The Vietnamization of New Jersey (first produced in New Haven, CT, at Yale Repertory Theatre, October 1, 1976), Dramatists Play Service (New York, NY), 1978.

Sister Mary Ignatius Explains It All for You (first produced in New York City at Ensemble Studio Theatre, December, 1979), Dramatists Play Service (New York, NY), 1980; adapted for film as *Sister Mary Explains It All,* Showtime, 2001.

The Nature and Purpose of the Universe, Death Comes to Us All, Mary Agnes, 'dentity Crisis: Three Short Plays, Dramatists Play Service (New York, NY), 1979.

Beyond Therapy (first produced off-Broadway at Phoenix Theatre, January 5, 1981), Samuel French (New York, NY), 1983.

The Actor's Nightmare (first produced in New York at Playwrights Horizons, October 21, 1981), Dramatists Play Service (New York, NY), 1982.

Christopher Durang Explains It All for You (contains *The Nature and Purpose of the Universe, 'dentity Crisis, Titanic, The Actor's Nightmare, Sister Mary Ignatius Explains It All for You,* and *Beyond Therapy,*) Avon (New York, NY), 1982.

Baby with the Bathwater (first produced in Cambridge, MA, 1983; produced in New York, NY, 1983), Dramatists Play Service (New York, NY), 1984.

Sloth, first produced in Princeton, NJ, 1985.

Laughing Wild (first produced in New York, NY, 1987; revival produced in Boston, June 16, 2005), Dramatists Play Service (New York, NY), 1996.

Cardinal O'Connor [and] *Woman Stand-Up,* first produced as part of musical revue *Urban Blight,* New York, NY, 1988.

Chris Durang and Dawne (cabaret), first produced in New York, NY, 1990.

Naomi in the Living Room, first produced in New York, NY, 1991.

Media Amok, first produced in Boston, MA, 1992.

Putting It Together, first produced in New York, NY, 1993.

Shaken, Not Stirred, first produced at Fountainhead Theater in Los Angeles, CA, 1993.

For Whom the Southern Belle Tolls, first produced in New York, NY, 1994.

Durang Durang (six short plays, including *For Whom the Southern Belle Tolls* and *A Stye in the Eye*), first produced in New York, NY, 1994.

Twenty-seven Short Plays, Smith & Kraus (Lyme, NH), 1995.

Collected Works, Smith & Kraus (Lyme, NH), 1995.

Sister Mary Ignatius Explains It All for You; and The Actor's Nightmare: Two Plays, Dramatists Play Service (New York, NY), 1995.

Complete Full-Length Plays, Smith & Kraus (Lyme, NH), 1996.

Sex and Longing, first produced at Cort Theater, 1996.

Betty's Summer Vacation, Grove Press (New York, NY), 1999.

Wanda's Visit, first produced at Blue Heron Arts Center, New York, NY, 2001.

Monologues, edited by Erick Kraus, Smith & Kraus (Hanover, NH), 2002.

Also author, with Robert Altman, of screenplay *Beyond Therapy,* 1987. Writer for television series *Comedy Zone* and for the *Carol Burnett Special.* Lyricist of songs for plays.

SIDELIGHTS: Early in Christopher Durang's career, a *New York Times* reviewer included him in the constellation of "new American playwrights," dramatists such as Michael Cristofer, Albert Innaurato, David Mamet, and Sam Shepard who follow in the footsteps of Tennessee Williams, Arthur Miller, and Edward Albee. Writers like Durang, the reviewer explained, "are not one-play writers—a home run and back to the dugout—but artists with staying power and growing bodies of work."

Stylistically, Durang specializes in collegiate humor. He deals in cartoons and stereotypes, employing mechanical dialogue and brand names to exploit clichés. In his works for the stage, Durang has parodied drama, literature, movies, families, the Catholic church, show business, and society. But his lampoons are not vicious or hostile; they are controlled comedies. He "is a parodist without venom," wrote *Horizon* magazine contributor Antonio Chemasi. "At the moment he fixes his pen on a target, he also falls in love with it. His work brims with an unlikely mix of acerbity and affection and at its best spills into a compassionate criticism of life."

Durang's first target as a professional playwright was literature. In 1974 the Yale Repertory Theatre produced *The Idiots Karamazov,* a satire of Dostoyevsky's *The Brothers Karamazov.* The play, featuring Durang in a leading role, was praised by critics for its "moments of comic inspiration." "I was . . . impressed—with their [Durang's and coauthor Albert Innaurato's] wit as well as their scholarship," Mel Gussow stated in the *New York Times.* The playwright followed *The Idiots Karamazov* by collaborating with well-known actress Sigourney Weaver on *Das Lusitania Songspiel,* a musical travesty that met with critical and popular success.

Durang's major success of the 1970s was *A History of the American Film,* for which he was nominated for a Tony Award in 1978. A tribute to movie mania, the play illustrates America's perceptions of Hollywood from 1930 to the present. *A History of the American Film* parodies some two hundred motion pictures and chronicles the evolution of movie stereotypes in American culture. There are five characters: a tough gangster typified by James Cagney, an innocent Loretta Young type, a sincere guy, a temptress, and a girl who never gets the man of her dreams. The production parodies movies such as *The Grapes of Wrath, Citizen Kane,* and *Casablanca.* Show girls dressed up like vegetables satirize the razzmatazz of big Hollywood productions by singing "We're in a Salad." And the character portraying Paul Henreid's role in *Now, Voyager* is forced to smoke two cigarettes when Bette Davis's character refuses one because she does not smoke. "In Durang's hands," wrote *Time* critic Gerald Clarke, "the familiar images always take an unexpected turn, however, and he proves that there is nothing so funny as a cliché of a different color."

After the success of *A History of the American Film,* Durang wrote two satires of suburban families: *The Vietnamization of New Jersey* and *The Nature and Purpose of the Universe,* as well as a parody of the Catholic church, *Sister Mary Ignatius Explains It All for You.* Called a "savage cartoon" by Mel Gussow, *Sister Mary Ignatius Explains It All for You* uses the character of an elderly nun to expose the hypocrisies of Catholicism. The nun, Gussow observed, is "a self-mocking sister [who] flips pictures of hell, purgatory and heaven as if they are stops on a religious package tour." Her list of the damned includes David Bowie, Betty Comden, and Adolph Green, and she lists hijacking planes alongside murder as a mortal sin. "Anyone can write an angry play—all it takes is an active spleen," observed Rich. "But only a writer of real talent can write an angry play that remains funny and controlled even in its most savage moments. *Sister Mary Ignatius Explains It All for You* confirms that Christopher Durang is just such a writer." The play was also adapted as a film for Showtime Television.

In October, 1981, the Obie-winning *Sister Mary Ignatius* was presented on the same playbill as *The Actor's Nightmare,* a satire of show business and the theater. Using the play-within-a-play technique for *The Actor's Nightmare,* Durang illustrates the comedy that ensues when an actor is forced to appear in a production he has never rehearsed. Earlier in 1981 the Phoenix Theatre produced Durang's *Beyond Therapy,* a parody in which a traditional woman, Prudence, and a bisexual man, Bruce, meet through a personal ad, only to have their relationship confounded by their psychiatrists. Hers is a lecherous, he-man Freudian; his is an absent-minded comforter. "Some of Durang's satire . . . is sidesplitting," commented a *New York* reviewer, "and there are many magisterial digs at our general mores, amores, and immores."

A writer heaped with honors early in his career may begin to feel the weight of the mantle later on. *Daily News* reviewer Douglas Watt wrote of Durang's 1983 drama, *Baby with the Bathwater,* Durang "continues to write like a fiendishly clever undergrad with some fresh slants but an inability to make them coalesce into a fully sustained evening of theater." Frank Rich, writing in the *New York Times,* commented: "We can't ignore that Act I of *Baby with the Bathwater* is a strained variation on past Durang riffs. We're so inured by now to this writer's angry view of parental authority figures that at intermission we feel like shaking him and shouting: 'Enough already! Move on!'" *New York Magazine* contributor John Simon sounded a similar theme: "Christopher Durang is such a funny fellow that his plays cannot help being funny; now, if they could only help being so undisciplined. . . . Free-floating satire and rampant absurdism are all very well, but even the wildest play must let its characters grow in wildness and match up mouth with jokes." But *Nation* reviewer Eliot Sirkin stated that Durang "is, at heart, a writer who divides humanity into the humiliators and the humiliated." Sirkin compared Durang's methods to those of Tennessee Williams: "When Williams created an overwhelming woman, he didn't create a psychopathic fiend—at least not always. . . . Durang's witches are *just* witches."

Durang's next play, *The Marriage of Bette and Boo,* draws from the playwright's own childhood. *New York Post* reviewer Clive Barnes summarized the characters: "The father was a drunk, the mother rendered an emotional cripple largely by her tragic succession of stillborn children, the grandparents were certifiably nutty, the family background stained with the oppression of the Roman Catholic Church, and the son himself is primarily absorbed in a scholarly enquiry into the novels of Thomas Hardy. Just plain folks!" *New York Times* critic Frank Rich explained, "*Bette and Boo* is sporadically funny and has been conceived with a structural inventiveness new to the writer's work. . . . But at the same time, Mr. Durang's jokemaking is becoming more mannered and repetitive. . . . *Bette and Boo* has a strangely airless atmosphere." *New York Magazine* critic John Simon wrote, "Christopher Durang's latest, *The Marriage of Bette and Boo,* is more recycling than writing. Here again, the quasi-autobiographical boy-hero growing up absurd." A *Contemporary Dramatists* writer was more complimentary about this play, calling *The*

Marriage of Bette and Boo "a trenchantly amusing dissection of the contemporary Catholic family. . . . The playwright gives an outrageously satiric view of society that characterizes his best work."

In a 1990 *Chicago Tribune* interview with Richard Christiansen, Durang revealed that he felt "burned out on New York, and that includes its theater." For a time Durang left the theater to tour with a one-hour cabaret act, *Chris Durang and Dawne.* Durang explained his "premise" to Christiansen: "I was fed up with being a playwright and had decided to form my own lounge act with two back-up singers and go on a tour of Ramada Inns across the country."

In 1992 Durang returned to the theater with *Media Amok,* a lampoon of the characters and obsessions of television talk shows. Noting its content, Durang told *Boston Globe* critic Kevin Kelly that he had become "more political." The play features an elderly couple watching television talk shows which assault them constantly with the same three topics: abortion, gay rights, and racial tension. All of the topics are handled in a flippant and inflammatory fashion.

In 1994 *Durang Durang,* a series of six sketches taking swipes at fellow playwrights Tennessee Williams, Sam Shepard and David Mamet, debuted in New York City. One section, the one-act play titled *For Whom the Southern Belle Tolls,* is a parody of *The Glass Menagerie,* while *A Stye in the Eye* focuses on Shepard's typical cowboy characters. In a *New Yorker* review, Nancy Franklin called the play "Beckett with a joy buzzer. . . . Sitting through *Durang Durang* is a little like going on the bumper cars at an amusement park: you're so caught up in the exhilarating hysteria that it doesn't matter to you that you're not actually going anywhere except—momentarily, blissfully—outside yourself." In a *New York Times* review, Ben Brantley described *Durang Durang* as "endearing and exasperating . . . juvenile and predictable."

Lulu, a nymphomaniac, and Justin, a nearly as insatiable homosexual, share an apartment in the play *Sex and Longing.* A philandering and drunkard senator and his puritanical wife, as well as a reverend from the political right, also figure into the plot. *Newsweek* critic Marc Peyser remarked: "This intersection of sex, religion, hypocrisy and spiritual emptiness was bracing two decades ago . . . now it's trite and labored and, worst of all, almost devoid of humor." *New York* critic John Simon, who thought the play's humorlessness stems from its silliness bordering on the ridiculous, wrote that the play "is strictly anti-realistic absurdist farce, but even as such it ought to know where it is going. . . . It is all rather like automatic writing with a glitch in the automation." *Variety* contributor Greg Evans noted that Durang "can mine any laughs at all from such perversity," noting that the "characters [are] so broadly drawn that to call them stereotypes would be an understatement." Still, Evans observed, "Despite his misstep here, the playwright retains a distinctive voice—one that finds its way even through the indulgences of this play."

Durang's 1999 effort, *Betty's Summer Vacation,* is "a summer sandstorm of horrifying fun," according to Everett Evans in the *Houston Chronicle.* The critic explained, "Sensible, normal Betty has come to a seaside 'summer share' with a simple wish for rest and quiet. As soon as we meet the fellow tenants to which fate has subjected her, we realize this is to be a comedy of excruciating frustration." These characters include a very talkative victim of childhood incest, a serial killer, and a flasher. Steven Winn, reviewing a local production of the play for the *San Francisco Chronicle,* mentioned the chorus of voices that Durang included in the script. "These offstage voices are the American public," wrote Winn, and "the whole thing's a kind of tabloid catharsis, like waking up from a bad dream and finding yourself in the studio audience of *The Jerry Springer Show.*" As Holly Hildebrand explained in *Back Stage West,* "Who better to take a poke—not to mention quite a number of stabs—at this bizarre entertainment business than Durang, who's never shrunk from satirizing American society and culture." Durang premiered a briefer effort, *Wanda's Visit,* in 2001. Laura Weinert, also reviewing for *Back Stage West,* summed it up as "the lighter side of Durang, an uproarious glimpse at what happens when the world of tired, static marrieds Marsha and Jim is upset by a surprise knock on the door by Jim's high school sweetheart Wanda."

BIOGRAPHICAL AND CRITICAL SOURCES:

BOOKS

American Theatre Annual, 1979-1980, Thomson Gale (Detroit, MI), 1981.
Contemporary Dramatists, 6th edition, St. James Press (Detroit, MI), 1999.
Contemporary Literary Criticism, Thomson Gale (Detroit, MI), Volume 27, 1984, Volume 38, 1986.

PERIODICALS

Advocate, April 27, 1999, Don Shewey, review of *Betty's Summer Vacation,* p. 79.

American Theatre, December, 1999, Christopher Durang, "An Interview with the Playwright by Himself," review of *Betty's Summer Vacation,* p. 37.
Atlanta Constitution, March 18, 1994, p. P17.
Back Stage West, April 7, 2000, Karl Levett, "Durang, Durang and More Durang," p. 42; July 27, 2000, Brad Schreiber, review of *The Marriage of Bette and Boo,* p. 18; February 15, 2001, Madeleine Shaner, review of *Baby with the Bathwater,* p. 13; May 24, 2001, Holly Hildebrand, "Durang Delivers," p. 11; August 15, 2002, Kristina Mannion, "*Sister Mary Ignatius Explains It All for You* and *The Nature and Purpose of the Universe* at the Empire Theater," p. 23; September 19, 2002, Laura Weinert, "Durang, Make It a Double! at the Complex," p. 13, and Gi-Gi Downs, "*Beyond Therapy* at the Cassius Carter Centre Stage," p. 13.
Boston Globe, March 22, 1992, p. B25.
Chicago Tribune, January 21, 1990.
Daily News (New York, NY), March 31, 1978; November 9, 1983.
Entertainment Weekly, April 16, 1993, p. 31.
Horizon, March, 1978.
Houston Chronicle, May 7, 2001, Everett Evans, "Pack Your Bags for Comic *Betty's Summer Vacation,*" p. 5.
Library Journal, August, 1997, Howard E. Miller, "Complete Full-Length Plays," p. 86.
Los Angeles Times, August 11, 1989, p. 8; November 25, 1994, p. 1.
Nation, April 15, 1978; February 18, 1984, pp. 202-204.
New Leader, October 7, 1996, Stefan Kanfer, review of *Sex and Longing,* p. 23.
New Republic, April 22, 1978.
Newsweek, April 10, 1978; October 21, 1996, Marc Peyser, review of *Sex and Longing,* p. 89.
New York, April 17, 1978; January 19, 1981; October 23, 1989, p. 166; November 28, 1994, p. 76; October 21, 1996, pp. 76-77; March 29, 1999, John Simon, review of *Betty's Summer Vacation,* p. 46.
New Yorker, May 24, 1976; April 10, 1978; January 19, 1981; November 28, 1994, pp. 153-55.
New York Magazine, November 21, 1983, pp. 65-68; June 3, 1985, pp. 83-84.
New York Post, March 31, 1978; November 9, 1983; December 12, 1983, p. 80; May 17, 1985, pp. 268-269.
New York Times, November 11, 1974; February 13, 1977; March 17, 1977; May 11, 1977; August 21, 1977; June 23, 1978; December 27, 1978; February 24, 1979; December 21, 1979; February 8, 1980; August 6, 1980; January 6, 1981; October 22, 1981; November 9, 1983, p. C21; May 17, 1985,

p. 3; June 27, 1994, p. C13; November 14, 1994, p. 11; March 14, 1999, Bob Morris, review of *Betty's Summer Vacation,* p. AR7; March 15, 1999, Ben Brantley, review of *Betty's Summer Vacation,* p. E1; January 15, 2001, Sarah Boxer, review of *The Idiots Karamazov,* p. B9; May 25, 2001, Caryn James, review of *Sister Mary Ignatius Explains It All for You,* p. E23.

San Francisco Chronicle, May 22, 2001, Steven Winn, "*Vacation* Feeds on Craving for Sex and Gore; Actors Theatre Takes on Durang's Biting Satire," p. B5.

Saturday Review, May 27, 1978.

Time, May 23, 1977.

USA Today, May 17, 1985.

Variety, November 14, 1994, p. 54; October 14-20, 1996, p. 72; March 22, 1999, Charles Isherwood, review of *Betty's Summer Vacation,* p. 46; May 28, 2001, Steven Oxman, review of *Sister Mary Ignatius Explains It All for You,* p. 29.

Washington Post, December 11, 1994, p. 4.

Women's Wear Daily, May 20, 1985.

World Literature Today, summer, 1991, p. 487.

ONLINE

Moonstruck Web site, http://www.imagi-nation.com/moonstruck/ (May 1, 2003), author profile.

*   *   *

DURANG, Christopher Ferdinand
See DURANG, Christopher

*   *   *

DWORKIN, Andrea 1946-2005

PERSONAL: Born September 26, 1946, in Camden, NJ; died April 9, 2005, in Washington, DC; daughter of Harry (a retired guidance counselor) and Sylvia (a secretary; maiden name, Spiegel) Dworkin; married (divorced, 1972). *Education:* Bennington College, B.A., 1968. *Politics:* "Radical feminist."

CAREER: Writer and lecturer. University of Minnesota, visiting professor, 1983. Lectured at universities in the United States, England, Ireland, Scotland, Canada, and Sweden, and at "Take Back the Night" rallies across the United States and Canada. A ppeared on television

shows, including *Donahue, 60 Minutes, Nightwatch, CBS Evening News, MacNeil-Lehrer Report, 48 Hours,* and the hour long documentary "Against Pornography: The Feminism of Andrea Dworkin" in the British Broadcasting Corporation (BBC) series *Omnibus.* Worked variously as a waitress, receptionist, secretary, typist, salesperson, factory worker, Head Start teacher, paid political organizer, and teacher. Previously member of usage panel for American Heritage Dictionary.

MEMBER: Amnesty International, PEN, Women's Institute for Freedom of the Press (fellow), Authors Guild, Authors League of America, Planned Parenthood, National Organization for Women, National Council on Women and Family Law (former adviser), National Abortion Rights Action League, National Women's Political Caucus, the Abortion Fund (founding sponsor), Coalition against Trafficking in Women, Southern Poverty Law Center.

WRITINGS:

NONFICTION

Woman Hating, Dutton (New York, NY), 1974.

Our Blood: Prophecies and Discourses on Sexual Politics (essays), Harper (New York, NY), 1976.

Pornography: Men Possessing Women, Putnam (New York), 1981, published with a new introduction by the author, 1989.

Right-Wing Women: The Politics of Domesticated Females, Putnam, 1983.

Intercourse, Free Press (New York, NY), 1987, tenth anniversary edition, Free Press, 1997.

(With Catharine A. MacKinnon) *Pornography and Civil Rights: A New Day for Women's Equality,* Organizing against Pornography, 1988.

Letters from a War Zone: Writings, 1976-1989 (essays), Dutton, 1989.

Life and Death: Unapologetic Writings on the Continuing War against Women, Free Press, 1997.

(Editor, with Catherine A. MacKinnon) *In Harm's Way: The Pornography Civil Rights Hearings,* Harvard University Press (Cambridge, MA), 1998.

Scapegoat: The Jews, Israel, and Women's Liberation, Free Press, 2000.

Heartbreak: The Political Memoir of a Feminist Militant, Basoc Books, 2002.

Also author of *Marx and Gandhi Were Liberals: Feminism and the "Radical" Left,* 1977, and *Why So-called Radical Men Love and Need Pornography,* 1978. Contributor to anthologies, including *Take Back the Night: Women on Pornography,* Morrow, 1980, *Transforming a Rape Culture,* edited by Emilie Buchwald, Milkweed, 1993; *Making Violence Sexy: Feminist Views on Pornography,* edited by Diana E.H. Russell, Teachers College Press, 1993; and *The Price We Pay: The Case Against Racist Speech, Hate Propaganda, and Pornography,* edited by Laura Lederer and Richard Delgado, Hill & Wang, 1995. Author of introduction, *Sexual Harassment: Women Speak Out,* Crossing, 1993. Contributor to periodicals, including *America Report, Christopher Street,Times Higher Education Supplement, Gay Community News, Ms., Social Policy,* and *Village Voice.* Works translated into several languages, including French, German, Dutch, Russian, Norwegian, Swedish, Spanish, Russian, Hebrew, Japanese, Korean, Chinese, and Lithuanian.

FICTION

The New Woman's Broken Heart (short stories), Frog in the Well (East Palo Alto, CA), 1980.
Ice and Fire, Secker & Warburg (London), 1986.
Mercy, Secker & Warburg, 1990, Four Walls Eight Windows (New York, NY), 1991.

Also author of the novel *Ruins.*

SIDELIGHTS: Called "one of the most compelling voices" in the women's movement by *Ms.* critic Carole Rosenthal, Andrea Dworkin, self-proclaimed radical feminist, author, and lecturer, "is still out there fighting . . . against the way American culture treats women," observes Lore Dickstein in the *New York Times Book Review.* Author of fiction about victimized women, Dworkin is perhaps best known for the forceful expression of her politics in controversial nonfiction about sexual roles in contemporary society.

"The role polarity of sex in our culture, which stresses the differences of man and woman, creates problems of power and violence that a culture which stresses the similarities between the sexes can peacefully avoid," explained Jeanne Kinney in a *Best Sellers* review of Dworkin's 1974 book, *Woman Hating.* And although Dworkin's graphic examples of sexual abuses of women repelled her, Kinney stated that "it also awakened me to Woman as Victim in ways I never knew existed." In *Our Blood: Prophecies and Discourses on Sexual Politics,* according to Rosenthal, Dworkin "scrutinizes historical and psychological issues, including female mas-

ochism, rape, the slavery of women in 'Amerika,' and the burning of nine million witches during the Middle Ages. Then she calls for—insists upon, really—a complete cultural transformation, the rooting out of sex roles from our society."

In *Right-Wing Women,* which appeared almost ten years after the publication of her first book, Dworkin theorizes that fear of male violence has forced many women to seek protection by accepting the rigid, predetermined social order of conservatism, which promises "form, shelter, safety, rules, and love," in exchange for female subservence. She cautions that the price for this protection is high, suggesting that with the possibility of laboratory reproduction comes the only role sanctioned by men for women—the prostitute. Consequently, she envisions a "gynocide," or female holocaust, with survivors reduced to the status of worker ants in a brothel-ghetto. The problem with the book, suggested Anne Tyler in *New Republic,* is that Dworkin "avoids the particular and makes generalizations so sweeping that the reader blinks and draws back."

Intercourse "consists of accounts of the attitudes and behavior of men in sexual relations with women," wrote Naomi Black in the Toronto *Globe and Mail.* "Some of them documentary, most of them literary, these accounts are harrowing." Although she declared that "Dworkin uses texts selectively to support her argument," Black concluded that "it is surely crucial to accept women's own accounts of their experience, which distinguish by implication between more and less harmful versions of male sexuality." In Dworkin's opinion, wrote Black, "heterosexuality is necessarily exploitative" because of the typically dominant role of the male, and such exploitation extends throughout heterosexual society. When accused of being a man-hater, Dworkin's response, reported Catherine Bennett in a London *Times* review of *Intercourse,* is: "Women are supposed to be loyal and devoted to men. And if you don't have loyalty and devotion you are called a man hater. I am not loyal and devoted but I am deeply responsive to men of integrity, who care about women's rights."

Although critics have faulted Dworkin on stylistic grounds, especially her use of language, her strong convictions and passionate language usually impress even those reviewers who do not agree with her politics. Bennett pointed to "the unvarying, obstreperous crudity of her language," and the "relentless battering" of her prose style. However, in a *Punch* review of *Pornography: Men Possessing Women,* Stanley Reynolds proclaimed that "Dworkin writes like a Leon Trotsky of the sex war. Short, sharp sentences, full of repetitions but never boring. She is full of power and energy. She writes—dare I say it?—with an aggressive manner, like a man. Except that no men write with such utter conviction these days." Similarly, Rosenthal stated that although Dworkin's revolutionary demands are sometimes unrealistic, her "relentless courage" in calling for drastic social reform is admirable. "If she overstates her case, it is because she is a true revolutionary," noted Reynolds.

Dworkin believes that pornography is one of the primary weapons used by men to control women. It is not about sex, she says, but about male power. *Pornography: Men Possessing Women,* stated Reynolds, analyzes numerous pornographic stories to illustrate that they "all—even those dealing with homosexuals—demonstrate the male lust for violence and power." By portraying women as masochistic, submissive playthings for men, "it creates hostility and aggression toward women, causing both bigotry and sexual abuse," she told *Contemporary Authors.* Dworkin discusses the subtle effects of pornography upon both the sexes and believes, as Sally O'Driscoll pointed out in the *Village Voice,* that "men make pornography to justify their treatment of women in real life, but at the same time men treat real women that way because pornography proves that's how they are. It's a vicious cycle."

Dworkin has not limited her crusade against pornography to her writings; she and lawyer Catharine A. MacKinnon, with whom she wrote *Pornography and Civil Rights: A New Day for Women's Equality,* are responsible for a controversial anti-pornography ordinance that was passed in Indianapolis, twice passed and twice vetoed in Minneapolis, and is being considered in other cities. The ordinance defines pornography as a form of sex discrimination and allows any person who feels harassed by pornography to sue its maker or seller. Opponents of the legislation have said that it violates the First Amendment and restricts basic personal freedoms. Dworkin disagrees in *Ms.:* "The law really doesn't have anything to say about what people do in their private lives, unless they're forcing pornography on somebody or coercing somebody or assaulting somebody. If personal, private sexual practice involves the use of pornography that someone else has to produce, the question then is, do they have a right to that product no matter what it costs the people who have to produce it?"

In her fiction, which she has had difficulty publishing in the United States, Dworkin attempts to convey to the reader the emotional impact of her nonfictional topics.

Her first novel, *Ice and Fire,* begins with recollections of childhood by a disillusioned young woman. Increasingly contemptuous of men and the violence she sees at their core, the narrator descends into a squalid life of drugs, prostitution, and panhandling in New York City, and is eventually rescued by the act of writing. "Dworkin creates an atmosphere that evokes the suffocating intensity and impotent panic of a nightmare," wrote Sherie Posesorski in the Toronto *Globe and Mail.* "The scenes flash like strobe lights. Her short, punchy paragraphs and assertive syntax establish a rhythm of explosive anger." Jean Hanff Korelitz contended in the *Times Literary Supplement* that "Dworkin completely fails to flesh out any of the points made in her non-fiction works," but Posesorski maintained that the novel "invades the consciousness like a migraine headache; its provocative aura and disturbing vision vibrate with unforgettable urgency."

A more recent novel, *Mercy,* is about "a young woman whose journey through the misogynist world . . . constitutes an almost encyclopaedic survey of male sexual violence," wrote Zoe Heller in a *Times Literary Supplement* review. The main character, named Andrea, has her first sexual encounter at the age of nine, when she is molested in a movie theater. As a teenager, she frequents Greenwich Village where she lives on the street, penniless. She marries a European revolutionary, only to be beaten and otherwise abused by him. Unable to verbalize her anger, she expresses it by beating up male tramps at night. As her life and her identity disintegrate, she continues to repeat three facts: her name, her place of birth, and the address of Walt Whitman's home in Camden, New Jersey. A reviewer for *Publishers Weekly* commented that "Andrea's high-pitched voice is at first hard to take," yet concluded that "its vehemence and candor build to a convincing indictment of a society that tolerates violence against women." A *Time Out* contributor similarly observed that the novel "offers a strangely moving account of the girl's recognition of the major and minor, deliberate and casual denigration of women." Heller found that "Dworkin has written a mad, bad novel; and one doesn't have to be a man, a rapist, or a self-hating woman to admit as much." And Brian Morton called Dworkin a "considerably underrated novelist," adding in his *Bookseller* review that "for all the skeltering violence and fury of her fiction, there is a unity of voice and a dim hope of transcendence in the telling that keeps one (this one; personally) to the page." In the *Glasgow Herald,* Morton suggested, "There is hope, too, in Dworkin's writing. The fact that she *is* writing is a gesture of hope in itself."

Life and Death: Unapologetic Writings on the Continuing War against Women is a collection of essays and speeches by this "eloquent, impassioned, but often stunningly illogical feminist," as Dworkin is described by a *Kirkus Reviews* writer. Her subjects include the O.J. Simpson murder trial and the years of abuse his slain ex-wife, Nicole Brown Simpson, endured at Simpson's hands; the systematic rape of Croatian and Muslim women in Serbian death camps; pornography; and her own experiences as a battered wife. The *Kirkus Reviews* contributor found Dworkin's arguments unbalanced, stating that she is "melodramatic" about attacks on her work and inaccurate in her claims of being censored. The reviewer concluded, "Those already converted to Dworkin's strain of feminism will find much to admire here; those who disagree with her will likely remain unconvinced. But political specifics aside, her critique of our culture's vicious and persistent woman-hating is powerful and painful." A writer for *Publishers Weekly* singled out Dworkin's report on a visit to Israel as a unique condemnation of the Jewish state as theocratic, racist, and founded on dispossession and theft. That reviewer further commented on a particular strength of Dworkin's: the ability to "forcefully link the personal to the political." *Library Journal* reviewer Barbara Hutcheson summarized: "Her language is powerful but controlled; the images . . . often brutal; her logic is inescapable."

Dworkin expanded on her thoughts about Israel in *Scapegoat: The Jews, Israel, and Women's Liberation.* In this book, she illustrates ways in which the modern world has been shaped by institutionalized male violence against women, children, and Jews. Equating these victims with the "scapegoat"—an animal sacrificed for the sins of a group—she then takes a look at the principle of the scapegoat in Nazi Germany and contemporary Israel. The use of these two settings to illustrate her point is only one of many startling aspects of *Scapegoat.* Her book serves as a "towering indictment and call to action," declared a *Booklist* reviewer, who also stated that the author's prose "has never been sharper, or her feminist vision more arresting." Identifying herself as a "lapsed pacifist," Dworkin exhorts women to start accepting responsibility for putting an end to violent crimes against humanity committed by men. Her book is an "onslaught of information, statistics and analysis," reported a *Publishers Weekly* writer. Cautioning that she "frequently overstates her case," the reviewer credited Dworkin with making "potent points" and concluded: "This weighty treatise unfailingly engages and provokes."

BIOGRAPHICAL AND CRITICAL SOURCES:

BOOKS

Contemporary Authors Autobiography Series, Volume 21, Thomson Gale (Detroit), 1995.

Contemporary Literary Criticism, Volume 43, Thomson Gale, 1987.

Dworkin, Andrea, *Right-Wing Women,* Putnam, 1983.

Jenefsky, Cindy, and Ann Russo, *Without Apology: Andrea Dworkin's Art and Politics,* Westview (Boulder, CO), 1997.

PERIODICALS

American Book Review, October, 1994, review of *Letters from a War Zone,* p. 9.

Belles Lettres, spring, 1994, review of *Letters from a War Zone,* p. 74.

Best Sellers, July 1, 1974.

Booklist, February 15, 1997, Donna Seaman, review of *Life and Death,* p. 978; July, 2000, review of *Scapegoat,* p. 1994.

Bookseller, September 21, 1990, p. 837.

Choice, October, 1974.

Glasgow Herald, October 4, 1990.

Globe and Mail (Toronto), August 2, 1986; July 11, 1987.

Kirkus Reviews, January 1, 1997, review of *Life and Death,* p. 32.

Lambda Book Report, January, 1993, review of *Mercy,* p. 43; September, 1993, review of *Letters from a War Zone,* p. 47.

Library Journal, June 1, 1974; January, 1997, Barbara Hutcheson, review of *Life and Death,* p. 127.

Listener, December 3, 1981.

Los Angeles Times, August 10, 1983.

Los Angeles Times Book Review, May 3, 1987; March 16, 1997, review of *Life and Death,* p. 9.

Ms., February, 1977; June, 1980; March, 1981; June, 1983; April, 1985; January-February, 1994, p. 32; March, 1997, review of *Life and Death,* p. 82.

New Pages, spring, 1982.

New Republic, February 21, 1983; June 25, 1984; August 11-18, 1997, review of *Life and Death,* p. 36.

New Statesman, November 6, 1981; July 29, 1983; June 5, 2000, Andrea Dworkin, "The Day I Was Drugged and Raped," p. 13.

Newsweek, March 18, 1985.

New Yorker, March 28, 1977.

New York Times Book Review, July 12, 1981; May 3, 1987; October 29, 1989.

Observer, May 16, 1982; September 28, 1997, review of *Life and Death,* p. 18; October 26, 1997, review of *Life and Death,* p. 18.

OnIssues, summer, 1994, review of *Pornography,* p. 47.

Playboy, October, 1992, p. 36.

Progressive, November, 1993, L.A. Winokur, review of *Sexual Harassment,* p. 38.

Psychology Today, July, 1987, Beryl Lieff Benderly, review of *Intercourse,* p. 69.

Publishers Weekly, February 25, 1974; July 25, 1991, review of *Mercy,* p. 36; September 27, 1993, review of *Letters from a War Zone,* p. 61; September 9, 1996, Judy Quinn, "Dworkin Returns to the Free Press," p. 30; December 30, 1996, review of *Life and Death,* p. 46; April 24, 2000, *Scapegoat,* p. 69.

Punch, February 10, 1982.

Spectator, August 5, 2000, Michael Moorcook, review of *Scapegoat,* pp. 31-32.

Time Out, September 26, 1990, p. 1049.

Times (London), June 4, 1987; May 18, 1988.

Times Literary Supplement, January 1, 1982; June 6, 1986, p. 622; October 16, 1987; June 3-9, 1988; October 5-11, 1988; October 5, 1990, p. 1072; September 4, 1998, review of *Life and Death,* p. 28; September 1, 2000, David Vital, review of *Scapegoat,* p. 24.

Tribune Books, November 1, 1992, review of *Mercy,* p. 8.

Village Voice, July 15-21, 1981.

Washington Post Book World, June 21, 1981.

West Coast Review of Books, March-April, 1983.

Woman's Journal, January, 1998, review of *Life and Death,* p. 11.

ONLINE

No Status Quo, http://www.nostatusquo.com/ (August 23, 2000) Graham Broad, "Andrea Dworkin and the New Evangelists".

*   *   *

DWYER, Deanna
See KOONTZ, Dean R.

*   *   *

DWYER, K.R.
See KOONTZ, Dean R.

E

ECO, Umberto 1932-

PERSONAL: Born January 5, 1932, in Alessandria, Italy; son of Giulio and Giovanna (Bisio) Eco; married Renate Ramge (a teacher) September 24, 1962; children: Stefano, Carlotta. *Education:* University of Turin, Ph.D., 1954.

ADDRESSES: Office—Universita di Bologna, Via Toffano 2, Bologna, Italy.

CAREER: Italian Radio-Television (RAI), Milan, Italy, editor for cultural programs, 1954-59; University of Turin, Turin, Italy, assistant lecturer, 1956-63, lecturer in aesthetics, 1963-64; Casa Editore Bompiani (publisher), Milan, Italy, nonfiction senior editor, 1959-75; University of Milan, lecturer in architecture, 1964-65; University of Florence, Florence, Italy, professor of visual communications, 1966-69; Milan Polytechnic, professor of semiotics, 1969-71; University of Bologna, Bologna, Italy, associate professor, 1971-75, professor of semiotics, 1975—, director of doctorate program in semiotics, 1986—, chair of Corso di Laurea in Scienze della comunicazione, 1993—, founder of publishing-studies program, 2003. Visiting professor, New York University, 1969, 1976, Northwestern University, 1972, University of California, San Diego, 1975, Yale University, 1977, 1980, 1981, and Columbia University, 1978; visiting fellow at Italian Academy and Columbia University. Lecturer on semiotics at various institutions throughout the world, including Tanner Lecturer, Cambridge University, 1990, Norton Lecturer, Harvard University, 1992-93, University of Antwerp, École Pratique des Hautes Etudes, University of London, Nobel Foundation, University of Warsaw, University of Budapest, University of Toronto, Murdoch University/Perth, and Amherst College. Member of the Council for the United States and Italy. *Military service:* Italian Army, 1958-59.

MEMBER: International Association for Semiotic Studies (secretary-general, 1972-79; vice president, 1979—), James Joyce Foundation (honorary trustee).

AWARDS, HONORS: Premio Strega and Premio Anghiari, both 1981, both for *Il Nome della rosa;* named honorary citizen of Monte Cerignone, Italy, 1982; Prix Medicis for best foreign novel, 1982, for French version of *Il Nome della rosa; Los Angeles Times* fiction prize nomination, 1983, and best fiction book award from Association of Logos Bookstores, both for *The Name of the Rose;* Marshall McLuhan Teleglobe Canada Award from UNESCO's Canadian Commission, 1985, for achievement in communications; Commandeur de l'Ordre des Arts et des Lettres (France), 1985; Chevalier de la Legion d'Honneur (France), 1993; Golden Cross of the Dodecannese, Patmos (Greece), 1995; Cavaliere di Gran Croce al Merito della Repubblica Italiana, 1996; honorary degrees from Catholic University, Leuven, 1985, Odense University, 1986, Loyola University, Chicago, 1987, State University of New York at Stony Brook, 1987, Royal College of Arts, London, 1987, Brown University, 1988, University of Paris, Sorbonne Nouvelle, 1989, University of Glasgow, 1990, University of Tel Aviv and University of Buenos Aires, both 1994, and University of Athens, Laurentian University at Sudbury, Ontario, and Academy of Fine Arts, Warsaw, all 1996.

WRITINGS:

IN ITALIAN

Filosofi in liberta, Taylor (Turin, Italy), 1958, 2nd edition, 1959.

Apocalittici e integrati: Comunicazioni di massa e teoria della cultura di massa, Bompiani (Milan, Italy), 1964, revised edition, 1977.

Le Poetiche di Joyce, Bompiani (Milan, Italy), 1965, 2nd edition published as *Le Poetiche di Joyce dalla "Summa" al "Finnegan's Wake,"* 1966.

Appunti per una semiologia delle comunicazioni visive (also see below), Bompiani (Milan, Italy), 1967.

(Author of introduction) Mimmo Castellano, *Noi vivi,* Dedalo Libri, 1967.

(Coeditor) *Storia figurata delle invenzioni. Dalla selce scheggiata al volo spaziale,* Bompiani (Milan, Italy), 1968.

La Struttura assente (includes *Appunti per una semiologia delle comunicazioni visive*), Bompiani (Milan, Italy), 1968, revised edition, 1983.

La Definizione dell'arte (title means "The Definition of Art"), U. Mursia, 1968, reprinted, Garzanti, 1978.

(Editor) *L'Uomo e l'arte,* Volume 1: *L'Arte come mestiere,* Bompiani (Milan, Italy), 1969.

(Editor, with Remo Faccani) *I Sistemi di segni e lo strutturalismo sovietico,* Bompiani (Milan, Italy), 1969, 2nd edition published as *Semiotica della letteratura in URSS,* 1974.

(Editor) *L'Industria della cultura,* Bompiani (Milan, Italy), 1969.

(Editor) *Dove e quando? Indagine sperimentale su due diverse edizioni di un servizio di "Almanacco,"* RAI, 1969.

(Editor) *Socialismo y consolacion: Reflexiones en torno a "Los Misterios de Paris" de Eugene Sue,* Tusquets, 1970, 2nd edition, 1974.

Le Forme del contenuto, Bompiani (Milan, Italy), 1971.

(Editor, with Cesare Sughi) *Cent'anni dopo: Il ritorno dell'intreccio,* Bompiani (Milan, Italy), 1971.

Il Segno, Isedi, 1971, 2nd edition, Mondadori (Milan, Italy).

(Editor, with M. Bonazzi) *I Pampini bugiardi,* Guaraldi, 1972.

(Editor) *Estetica e teoria dell'informazione,* Bompiani (Milan, Italy), 1972.

(Editor) *Eugenio Carmi: Una Pittura de paesaggio?,* G. Prearo, 1973.

Il Costume di casa: Evidenze e misteri dell'ideologia italiano, Bompiani (Milan, Italy), 1973.

Beato di Liebana: Miniature del Beato de Fernando I y Sancha, F.M. Ricci, 1973.

Cristianesimo e politica: Esame della presente situazione culturale, G.B. Vico, 1976.

(Coeditor) *Storia di una rivoluzione mai esistita l'esperimento Vaduz,* Servizio Opinioni, RAI, 1976.

Dalla periferia dell'impero, Bompiani (Milan, Italy), 1976.

Il Superuomo di massa: Studi sul romanzo popolare, Cooperativa Scrittori, 1976, revised edition, Bompiani (Milan, Italy), 1978.

Come si fa una tesi di laurea, Bompiani (Milan, Italy), 1977.

(Coeditor) *Le Donne al muro: L'Immagine femminile nel manifesto politico italiano, 1945-1977,* Savelli, 1977.

(Coauthor) *Informazione: Consenso e dissenso,* Saggiatore, 1979.

(Coauthor) *Strutture ed eventi dell'economia alessandrina: Cassa di risparmio di Alessandria: Umberto Eco, Carlo Beltrame, Francesco Forte,* La Pietra, 1981.

Testa a testa, Images 70, 1981.

Sette anni di desiderio, Bompiani (Milan, Italy), 1983.

Conceito de texto, Queiroz, 1984.

(Coeditor) *Cremonini: Opere dal 1960 al 1984,* Grafis, 1984.

(Coauthor) *Carnival!,* Mouton Publishers (Hague, Netherlands), 1984.

L'Espresso, 1955/85, Editoriale L'Espresso, 1985.

La Rosa dipinta: Trentuno illustratori per "Il Nome della rosa," Azzurra, 1985.

Sugli specchi e altri saggi, Bompiani (Milan, Italy), 1985.

De bibliotheca, Echoppe, 1986.

Faith in Fakes: Essays, Secker & Warburg (London, England), 1986.

(Coauthor) *Le Ragioni della retorica: Atti del Convegno "Retorica, verita, opinione, persuasione": Cattolica, 22 febbrario-20 aprile 1985,* Mucchi, 1986.

(Coauthor) *Le Isole del tesoro: Proposte per la riscoperta e la gestione delle risorse culturali,* Electa, 1988.

(Author of introduction) Maria Pia Pozzato and others, *L'Idea deforme: Interpretazioni esoteriche di Dante,* Bompiani (Milan, Italy), 1989.

Lo Strano caso della Hanau 1609, Bompiani (Milan, Italy), 1989.

(Coauthor) *Leggere i promessi sposi: Analisi semiotiche,* Bompiani (Milan, Italy), 1989.

I Limiti dell'interpretazione, Bompiani (Milan, Italy), 1990.

Stelle e stellette, Melangolo, 1991.

Vocali, Guida, 1991.

(Coauthor) *Enrico Baj: Il Giardino delle delizie,* Fabbri, 1991.

Semiotica: Storia, teoria, interpretazione: Saggi intorno a Umberto Eco, Bompiani (Milan, Italy), 1992.

(With Eugenio Carmi) *Gli gnomi di gnu,* Bompiani (Milan, Italy), 1992.

(Coeditor) Flaminio Gualdoni, *La Ceramica di Arman,* Edizioni Maggiore, 1994.

(Editor) *Povero Pinocchio,* Comix, 1995.

(Coauthor) *Carmi,* Edizioni L'Agrifoglio, 1996.

Incontro, Guernica Editions, 1997.

La Bustina di Minerva, Bompiani (Milan, Italy), 1999.

Contributor to books, including *Momenti e problema di storia dell'estetica,* Marzorati, 1959; *Documenti su il nuovo medioevo,* Bompiani (Milan, Italy), 1973; *Convegno su realta e ideologie dell'informazione,* 1978, Il Saggiatore, 1979; *Carolina Invernizio, Matilde Serao, Liala,* La Nuova Italia, 1979; and *Perche continuiamo a fare e a insegnare arte?,* Cappelli, 1979.

Eco's works have been translated into several languages, including Spanish and French.

IN ENGLISH TRANSLATION

Il Problema estetico in San Tommaso, Edizioni di Filosofia, 1956, 2nd edition published as *Il Problema estetico in Tommaso d'Aquino,* Bompiani (Milan, Italy), 1970, translation by Hugh Bredin published as *The Aesthetics of Thomas Aquinas,* Harvard University Press (Cambridge, MA), 1988.

(Editor, with G. Zorzoli) *Storia figurata delle invenzioni: Dalla selce scheggiata al volo spaziali,* Bompiani (Milan, Italy), 1961, 2nd edition, 1968, translation by Anthony Lawrence published as *The Picture History of Inventions from Plough to Polaris,* Macmillan (New York, NY), 1963.

Opera aperta: Forma e indeterminazione nelle poetiche contemporanee (includes *Le poetiche di Joyce;* also see below), Bompiani (Milan, Italy), 1962, revised edition, 1972, translation by Anna Cancogni published as *The Open Work,* Harvard University Press (Cambridge, MA), 1989.

Diario minimo, Mondadori (Milan, Italy), 1963, 2nd revised edition, 1976, translation by William Weaver published as *Misreadings,* Harcourt (San Diego, CA), 1993.

(Editor, with Oreste del Buono) *Il Caso Bond,* Bompiani (Milan, Italy), 1965, translation by R. Downie published as *The Bond Affair,* Macdonald (London, England), 1966.

I Tre cosmonauti (juvenile), illustrated by Eugenio Carmi, Bompiani (Milan, Italy), 1966, revised edition, 1988, translation published as *The Three Astronauts,* Harcourt (New York, NY), 1989.

La Bomba e il generale (juvenile), illustrated by Eugenio Carmi, Bompiani (Milan, Italy), 1966, revised edition, 1988, translation by William Weaver published as *The Bomb and the General,* Harcourt (New York, NY), 1989.

(Editor, with Jean Chesneaux and Gino Nebiolo) *I Fumetti di Mao,* Laterza, 1971, translation by Frances Frenaye published as *The People's Comic Book: Red Women's Detachment, Hot on the Trail, and Other Chinese Comics,* Anchor Press (New York, NY), 1973.

Trattato di semiotica generale, Bompiani (Milan, Italy), 1975, translation published as *A Theory of Semiotics,* Indiana University Press (Bloomington, IN), 1976.

Lector in fabula: La Cooperazione interpretative nei testi narrativa, Bompiani (Milan, Italy), 1979, translation published as *The Role of the Reader: Explorations in the Semiotics of Texts,* Indiana University Press (Bloomington, IN), 1979.

Il Nome della rosa (novel), Bompiani (Milan, Italy), 1980, translation by William Weaver published as *The Name of the Rose,* Harcourt (New York, NY), 1983.

Semiotica e filosofia del linguaggio, G. Einaudi, 1984, translation published as *Semiotics and the Philosophy of Language,* Indiana University Press (Bloomington, IN), 1984.

Postscript to "The Name of the Rose" (originally published in Italian), translation by William Weaver, Harcourt (New York, NY), 1984.

Art and Beauty in the Middle Ages (originally published in Italian), translation by Hugh Bredin, Yale University Press (New Haven, CT), 1986.

Travels in Hyper Reality (originally published in Italian), edited by Helen Wolff and Kurt Wolff, translation by William Weaver, Harcourt (New York, NY), 1986.

Il Pendolo di Foucault (novel), Bompiani (Milan, Italy), 1988, translation by William Weaver published as *Foucault's Pendulum,* Harcourt (New York, NY), 1989.

The Aesthetics of Chaosmos: The Middle Ages of James Joyce (originally published in Italian), translation by Ellen Esrock, Harvard University Press (Cambridge, MA), 1989.

La Quete d'une langue parfaite dans l'histoire de la culture europeenne: Lecon inaugurale, faite le vendredi 2 octobre 1992, College de France, 1992, published in Italian as *La Ricerca della lingua perfetta nella cultura europea,* Laterza (Bari, Italy), 1993, translation by James Fentress published as *The Search for the Perfect Language,* Blackwell (Oxford, England), 1994.

How to Travel with a Salmon and Other Essays (originally published in Italian as *Il Secondo diario minimo*), translation by William Weaver, Harcourt (New York, NY), 1994.

L'Isola del giorno prima (novel), Bompiani (Milan, Italy), 1994, translation by William Weaver published as *The Island of the Day Before,* Harcourt (New York, NY), 1995.

Kant e l'ornitorinco, Bompiani (Milan, Italy), 1997, translation by Alastair McEwen published as *Kant and the Platypus: Essays on Language and Cognition,* Harcourt Brace (New York, NY), 2000.

Cinque scritti morali, Bompiani (Milan, Italy), 1997, translation by Alastair McEwen published as *Five Moral Pieces,* Harcourt (New York, NY), 2001.

Serendipities: Language and Lunacy, translation by William Weaver, Columbia University Press (New York, NY), 1998.

Baudolino, Bompiani (Milan, Italy), 2000, translation by William Weaver, Harvard University Press (Cambridge, MA), 2002.

Experiences in Translation, translation by Alastair McEwen, University of Toronto Press (Toronto, Canada), 2001.

On Literature, translation by Martin McLaughlin, Harcourt (Orlando, FL), 2004.

The Mysterious Flame of Queen Loana: An Illustrated Novel, translated by Geoffrey Brock, Harcourt (Orlando, FL), 2005.

IN ENGLISH

(Coauthor) *Environmental Information: A Methodological Proposal,* UNESCO, 1981.

(Editor, with Thomas A. Sebeok) *Sign of the Three: Dupin, Holmes, Peirce,* Indiana University Press (Bloomington, IN), 1984.

(Editor, with others) *Meaning and Mental Representations,* Indiana University Press (Bloomington, IN), 1988.

(Editor, with Costantino Marmo) *On the Medieval Theory of Signs,* John Benjamins, 1989.

The Limits of Interpretation, Indiana University Press (Bloomington, IN), 1990.

(With Richard Rorty, Jonathan Culler, and Christine Brooke-Rose) *Interpretation and Overinterpretation,* Cambridge University Press (Cambridge, England), 1992.

Misreadings, Harcourt (New York, NY), 1993.

Apocalypse Postponed: Essays, Indiana University Press (Bloomington, IN), 1994.

Six Walks in the Fictional Woods, Harvard University Press (Cambridge, MA), 1994.

(Author of text) *Leonardo Cremonini: Paintings and Watercolors, 1976-1986,* Claude Bernard Gallery, 1987.

The Cult of Vespa, Gingko Press, 1997.

(Coauthor) *Conversations about the End of Time: Umberto Eco . . . [and others],* produced and edited by Catherine David, Frederic Lenoir, and Jean-Philippe de Tonnac, Fromm International (New York, NY), 2000.

(With Carlo Maria Martini) *Belief or Nonbelief?: A Confrontation,* translation by Minna Proctor, Arcade (New York, NY), 2000.

Contributor to numerous encyclopedias, including *Enciclopedia filosofica* and *Encyclopedic Dictionary of Semiotics.* Also contributor to proceedings of First Congress of the International Association for Semiotic Studies. Columnist for *Il Giorno, La Stampa, Corriere della sera,* and other newspapers and magazines. Contributor of essays and reviews to numerous periodicals, including *Espresso, Corriere della sera, Times Literary Supplement, Revue internationale de sciences sociales,* and *Nouvelle revue française.* Member of editorial board, *Semiotica, Poetics Today, Degres, Structuralist Review, Text, Communication, Problemi dell'informazione,* and *Alfabeta;* editor, *VS-Semiotic Studies.*

ADAPTATIONS: Jean-Jacques Annaud directed a 1986 film adaptation of Eco's novel *The Name of the Rose,* starring Sean Connery as William of Baskerville.

SIDELIGHTS: No one expected *The Name of the Rose* to become an internationally acclaimed best-seller, least of all its author, Umberto Eco. A respected Italian scholar, Eco has built his literary reputation on specialized academic writing about semiotics: the study of how cultures communicate through signs. Not only was *The Name of the Rose* Eco's first novel, it was also a complex creation, long on philosophy and short on sex—definitely not blockbuster material, especially not in Italy where the market for books is small.

Some experts attribute the novel's success to the rising interest in fantasy literature. "For all its historical accuracy, *The Name of the Rose* has the charm of an invented world," Drenka Willen, Eco's editor at Harcourt, told *Newsweek.* Others chalk it up to snob appeal. "Every year there is one great *unread* best-seller. A lot of people who will buy the book will never read it," Howard Kaminsky, president of Warner Books, suggested in that same *Newsweek* article.

But perhaps the most plausible explanation is the one offered by Franco Ferrucci in the *New York Times Book Review:* "The answer may lie in the fact that Mr. Eco is the unacknowledged leader of contemporary Italian culture, a man whose academic and ideological prestige has grown steadily through years of dazzling and solid work."

On one level *The Name of the Rose* is a murder mystery in which a number of Catholic monks are inexplicably killed. The setting is an ancient monastery in northern Italy, the year is 1327, and the air is rife with evil. Dissension among rival factions of the Franciscan order threatens to tear the church apart, and each side is preparing for a fight. On one side stand the Spiritualists and the emperor Louis IV who endorse evangelical poverty; on the other stand the corrupt Pope John XXII and the monks who believe that the vow of poverty will rob the church of earthly wealth and power. In an effort to avoid a confrontation, both sides agree to meet at the monastery—a Benedictine abbey that is considered neutral ground. To this meeting come William of Baskerville, an English Franciscan empowered to represent the emperor, and Adso, William's disciple and scribe. Before the council can convene, however, the body of a young monk is discovered at the bottom of a cliff, and William, a master logician in the tradition of Sherlock Holmes, is recruited to solve the crime, assisted by Adso, in Watson's role.

Nowhere is the importance of decoding symbols more apparent than in the library—an intricate labyrinth that houses all types of books, including volumes on pagan rituals and black magic. The secret of the maze is known to only a few, among them the master librarian whose job it is to safeguard the collection and supervise the circulation of appropriate volumes. William suspects that the murder relates to a forbidden book—a rare work with "the power of a thousand scorpions"—that some of the more curious monks have been trying to obtain. "What the temptation of adultery is for laymen and the yearning for riches is for secular ecclesiastics, the seduction of knowledge is for monks," William explains to Adso. "Why should they not have risked death to satisfy a curiosity of their minds, or have killed to prevent someone from appropriating a jealously guarded secret of their own?"

If William speaks for reason, Adso—the young novice who, in his old age, will relate the story—represents the voice of faith. Ferrucci believed that Adso reflects the author's second side: "The Eco who writes *The Name of the Rose* is Adso: a voice young and old at the same time, speaking from nostalgia for love and passion. William shapes the story with his insight; Adso gives it his own pathos. He will never think, as William does, that 'books are not made to be believed but to be subjected to inquiry'; Adso writes to be believed."

Another way *The Name of the Rose* can be interpreted is as a parable of modern life. The vehement struggle between church and state mirrors much of recent Italian history with its "debates over the role of the left and the accompanying explosion of terrorist violence," wrote Sari Gilbert in the *Washington Post*. Eco acknowledges the influence that former Italian premier Aldo Moro's 1978 kidnapping and death had on his story, telling Gilbert that it "gave us all a sense of impotence," but he also warned that the book was not simply a *roman à clef*. "Instead," he told Herbert Mitgang in a *New York Times Book Review* article, "I hope readers see the roots, that everything that existed then—from banks and the inflationary spiral to the burning of libraries—exists today. We are always approaching the time of the antiChrist. In the nuclear age, we are never far from the Dark Ages."

As with his first novel, Eco's second novel was an international best-seller. Published in 1989 in English as *Foucault's Pendulum,* the book is similar to *The Name of the Rose* in that it is a semiotic murder mystery wrapped in several layers of meaning. The plot revolves around Casaubon, the narrator, and two Milan editors who break up the monotony of reviewing manuscripts on the occult by combining information from all of them into one computer program called the Plan. Initially conceived as a joke, the Plan connects the Knights Templar—a medieval papal order that fought in the Crusades—with other occult groups throughout history. The program produces a map indicating the geographical point at which the powers of the earth can be controlled. That point is in Paris, France, at Foucault's Pendulum. When occult groups, including Satanists, get wind of the Plan, they go so far as to kill one of the editors in their quest to gain control of the earth. Beyond the basic plot, readers will also encounter William Shakespeare, Rene Descartes, Tom and Jerry, Karl Marx, Rhett Butler and Scarlett O'Hara, Sam Spade, and Frederick the Great of Prussia, as well as assorted Nazis, Rosicrucians, and Jesuits. Eco orchestrates all of these and other diverse characters and groups into his multilayered semiotic story.

Some of the interpretations of *Foucault's Pendulum* critics have suggested include reading it as nothing more than an elaborate joke, as an exploration of the ambiguity between text as reality and reality as text, and as a warning that harm comes to those who seek knowledge through bad logic and faulty reasoning. Given this range of interpretation and Eco's interest in semiotics, *Foucault's Pendulum* is probably best described as a book about many things, including the act of interpretation itself.

Foucault's Pendulum generated a broad range of commentary. Some critics faulted it for digressing too often into scholarly minutia, and others felt Eco had only mixed success in relating the different levels of his tale. Several reviewers, however, praised *Foucault's Pendulum*. Comparing the work to his first novel, Herbert Mitgang, for example, said in the *New York Times* that the book "is a quest novel that is deeper and richer than *The Name of the Rose*. It's a brilliant piece of research and writing—experimental and funny, literary and philosophical—that bravely ignores the conventional expectations of the reader." Eco offered his own opinion of his novel in *Time:* "This was a book conceived to irritate the reader. I knew it would provoke ambiguous, nonhomogeneous responses because it was a book conceived to point up some contradictions."

Eco's third novel, *The Island of the Day Before,* like *The Search for the Perfect Language,* explained Toronto *Globe and Mail* contributor Patrick Rengger, "is also, and in more ways than one, attempting to excavate truths by sifting language and meaning." The book takes place during the early seventeenth century and tells the story of an Italian castaway, Roberto della Griva, who is marooned on an otherwise deserted ship in the South Pacific. "While exploring the ship," stated Mel Gussow in the *New York Times,* "the protagonist drifts back into his past and recalls old battles as well as old figments of his imagination." *The Island of the Day Before* "is dazzling in its range," *Los Angeles Times Book Review* contributor Marina Warner declared, "its linguistic fireworks ('Babelizing' as Eco calls it) and sheer learning."

In *Baudolino* Eco draws readers back into the early thirteenth century to tell the life story of a man involved in most major events of the period, including the search for the Holy Grail and the fourth Crusade. An admitted liar, Baudolino tells his story to Byzantine scribe Niketas Choniates, a member of the court of Frederick Barbarossa, while all around the two men the city of Constantinople is undergoing destruction. "The implicit contrast between the refined civilization of Byzantium and the barbarity of the Crusaders who willfully put it to the torch is as forceful now as ever," noted Ingrid D. Rowland in a review for the *New Republic;* "the destruction of Constantinople in *Baudolino,* like the destruction of the library in *The Name of the Rose,* threatens to slay civility itself." Noting that the novel leaves the reader puzzling over what is fact and what is fiction—Niketas Choniates was an actual person, whereas Baudolino is not—*Seattle Times* contributor Terry Tazioli wrote that the novel "becomes so fun, so fanciful and so intricate that Eco must be chuckling all the way to the corner trattoria, simply anticipating his readers' befuddlement and fun." Calling *Baudolino* both "beguiling and exasperating," *Time* reviewer Richard Lacayo maintained that through his novel Eco once

again illustrates that "the thing we call knowledge—of ourselves, one another, the world at large—. . . [is] mostly a matter of which illusions we choose to believe."

Apart from his novels, Eco has been a prolific contributor to Italian letters, and many of his works have been translated into English. *The Search for the Perfect Language* is a history of the attempts to reconstruct a "natural" original language. *London Review of Books* contributor John Sturrock called it "a brisk, chronological account of the many thinkers about language, from antiquity onwards, who have conceived programmes for undoing the effects of time and either recovering the ur-language that they believed must once have existed only later to be lost, or else inventing a replacement for it." Eco pursues this search as a semiotician, because he believes language is the most common human symbol. However, as *The Search for the Perfect Language* reveals, more often than not the thinkers only reveal their own linguistic prejudices in their conclusions. This search for the primal tongue is, Sturrock continued, a "history of a doomed but often laudably ingenious movement to go against the linguistic grain and rediscover a truly natural language: a language of Nature or of God as it were, the appropriateness of whose signs there could be no denying."

Eco's *Apocalypse Postponed* is a collection of essays on culture written between the 1960s and the 1980s. The book discusses a variety of topics, including cartoons, literacy, Federico Fellini, and the counterculture movement, and reflects the alarm of many intellectuals at the proliferation of pop culture during the period. Divided into four parts, which reflect the topics of mass culture, mass media, countercultures, and Italian intellectualism, the book was summarized by a *Kirkus* reviewer as "substantial, lucid, humane, and a great deal of fun." *Serendipities: Language and Lunacy* is, as Tom Holland reported in the *New Statesman,* "really nothing more than a collection of footnotes to an earlier and much more detailed work," *The Search for the Perfect Language.* In *Booklist,* Michael Spinella wrote, "This slim but pithy volume offers an approachable introduction to the intellectual history of language and the foundation of linguistic study."

In *Kant and the Platypus* Eco considers questions of meaning: how do we identify and classify something that is totally new to us? The book revisits and revises ideas of semiotics that Eco previously discussed in *A Theory of Semiotics* and *Semiotics and the Philosophy of Language.* According to Simon Blackburn in the

New Republic, Eco said, "This is a hard-core book. It's not a page-turner. You have to stay on every page for two weeks with your pencil. In other words, don't buy it if you are not Einstein." However, in *World Literature Today,* Rocco Capozzi commented that the author has "an outstanding talent for teaching and entertaining at the same time, even as he examines complicated theoretical, philosophical, linguistic, and cultural issues." And in *Publishers Weekly,* a reviewer called *Kant and the Platypus* "valuable and pleasurable for anyone seeking a gallant introduction to the philosophy of language." In *Five Moral Pieces,* Eco presents five essays on ethical principles in postmodern culture. The essays originated as lectures and were each prompted by a social crisis—such as the Gulf War, the trial of a Nazi criminal, or the rise of extreme conservatives in Europe—or by an invitation for Eco to contribute his thoughts on a topic. In *Library Journal,* Ulrich Baer wrote that the collection "cogently argues and periodically sparkles with . . . wit and insight."

Eco, who directs programs for communication sciences and publishing at the University of Bologna, frequently travels to the United States and elsewhere to speak and teach. He continues to produce scholarly treatises, contributes to several Italian and foreign newspapers, and edits a weekly column for the magazine *L'Espresso.*

BIOGRAPHICAL AND CRITICAL SOURCES:

BOOKS

Bondanella, Peter E., *Umberto Eco and the Open Text: Semiotics, Fiction, Popular Culture,* Cambridge University Press (New York, NY), 1997.

Capozzi, Rocco, editor, *Reading Eco: An Anthology,* Indiana University Press (Bloomington, IN), 1997.

Contemporary Literary Criticism, Thomson Gale (Detroit, MI), Volume 28, 1984, Volume 60, 1991.

Inge, Thomas M., editor, *Naming the Rose: Essays on Eco's "The Name of the Rose,"* University Press of Mississippi (Jackson, MS), 1988.

Santoro-Brienza, Liberato, editor, *Talking of Joyce: Umberto Eco, Liberato Santoro-Brienza,* University College Dublin Press (Dublin, Ireland), 1998.

Tanner, William E., Anne Gervasi, and Kay Mizell, editors, *Out of Chaos: Semiotics; A Festschrift in Honor of Umberto Eco,* Liberal Arts Press (Arlington, TX), 1991.

PERIODICALS

America, August 3, 1983.
American Historical Review, June, 1997, p. 776.

American Scholar, autumn, 1987.
Antioch Review, winter, 1993, p. 149.
Atlantic, November, 1989; November, 1998, p. 138.
Bloomsbury Review, September, 1992.
Booklist, April 15, 1998, p. 1369; February 15, 1997, p. 1038; October 15, 1998, p. 377; April 1, 2000, p. 1414; April 15, 2000, p. 1502; September 1, 2001, p. 43; March 15, 2003, Ted Hipple, review of *Baudolino,* p. 1338.
Books, autumn, 1999, p. 18.
Books in Canada, December, 2002, David Solway, review of *Baudolino,* p. 10.
Boston Book Review, July, 1999, p. 32; December, 1999, p. 33.
Boston Globe, March 30, 1994, p. 75.
Choice, December, 2000, p. 720; September, 2001, p. 108.
Corriere della sera, June 1, 1981.
Critique, spring, 2001, p. 271; summer, 2003, Thomas J. Rice, "Mapping Complexity in the Fiction of Umberto Eco," pp. 349-369.
Daily Telegraph (London, England), December 18, 1999, p. 3.
Drama Review, summer, 1993.
Economist, October 28, 1989.
Emergency Librarian, May, 1997, p. 9.
Esquire, August, 1994, p. 99.
Globe and Mail, (Toronto, Ontario, Canada), January 6, 1996, p. C7.
Guardian, March 24, 1998; December 18, 1999, p. 1.
Harper's, August, 1983; May, 1993, p. 24; January, 1995, p. 33.
International Philosophical Quarterly, June, 1980.
Interview, November, 1989.
Journal of Communication, autumn, 1976.
Kirkus Reviews, March 15, 1994; September 1, 1998, p. 1253; November 1, 1999, p. 1705; August 1, 2001, p. 1085.
Language, Volume 53, number 3, 1977.
Language in Society, April, 1977.
Library Journal, October 15, 1998, p. 70; November 1, 1999, p. 86; December, 1999, p. 158; April 15, 2000, p. 96; August, 2001, p. 107.
London Review of Books, October 5, 1995, p. 8; November 16, 1995; December 9, 1999, p. 9.
Los Angeles Times, November 9, 1989; June 1, 1993, p. E4; March 18, 2000, p. B2; December 3, 2001, p. E3.
Los Angeles Times Book Review, June 4, 1989; April 13, 1994; November 13, 1994, p. 6; December 17, 1995.
Maclean's, July 18, 1983.
Medieval Review, July 3, 1998.
Nation, January 6, 1997, p. 35.

National Review, January 22, 1990.

New Republic, September 5, 1983; November 27, 1989; February 7, 2000, p. 34; November 18, 2002, Ingrid D. Rowland, review of *Baudolino,* p. 33.

New Scientist, April 3, 1999, p. 50.

New Statesman, December 15, 1989; April 22, 1994; February 26, 1999, p. 54.

Newsweek, July 4, 1983; September 26, 1983; September 29, 1986; November 13, 1989.

New Yorker, May 24, 1993, p. 30; August 21-28, 1995, p. 122.

New York Review of Books, July 21, 1983; February 2, 1995; June 9, 1994, p. 24; June 22, 1995, p. 12; April 10, 1997, p. 4; June 15, 2000, p. 62.

New York Times, June 4, 1983; December 13, 1988; October 11, 1989; January 9, 1991, p. C15; November 28, 1995, pp. B1-B2.

New York Times Book Review, June 5, 1983; July 17, 1983; October 15, 1989; July 25, 1993, p. 17; October 22, 1995; March 14, 1993, p. 31; November 3, 2002, Peter Green, review of *Baudolino,* p. 14.

Observer (London, England), February 7, 1999, p. 13.

People, August 29, 1983.

Publishers Weekly, February 24, 1989, p. 232; September 28, 1998, p. 83; October 25, 1999, p. 61; March 27, 2000, p. 59; September 10, 2001, p. 69; November 4, 2002, Daisy Maryles, review of *Baudolino,* p. 18.

Quadrant, January, 1997, p. 113.

Reference and Research Book News, February, 1999, p. 153.

Review of Contemporary Fiction, spring, 1999, p. 180.

San Francisco Chronicle, December 12, 1999, p. 11.

San Francisco Review of Books, spring, 1991, pp. 18-19.

Seattle Times, November 13, 2002, Terry Tazioli, review of *Baudolino.*

Sight and Sound, November, 1994, p. 37.

Spectator, June 12, 1993, pp. 49-50; November 19, 1994, p. 48; March 27, 1999, p. 41; January 15, 2000, p. 35.

Time, June 13, 1983; March 6, 1989; November 6, 1989; November 4, 2002, Richard Lacayo, review of *Baudolino,* p. 86.

Times (London, England), September 29, 1983; November 3, 1983.

Times Higher Education Supplement, January 23, 1998, p. 18; January 22, 1999, p. 33.

Times Literary Supplement, July 8, 1977; March 3, 1989; April 7-13, 1989, p. 380; February 1, 1991, p. 9; December 6, 1991, p. 12; July 30, 1993, p. 8; June 11, 1999, p. 26; February 25, 2000, p. 7; September 21, 2001, p. 31; May 2, 2003, Peter

Hainsworth, "Dialects and Ecos: Italian Fiction Is in Good Shape," p. 14-15.

UNESCO Courier, June, 1993.

U.S. News and World Report, November 20, 1989.

Voice Literary Supplement, October, 1983; November, 1989.

Wall Street Journal, June 20, 1983; November 14, 1989.

Washington Post, October 9, 1983; November 26, 1989.

Washington Post Book World, June 19, 1983; October 29, 1989.

Washington Times, November 11, 2001, p. 6.

World Literature Today, spring, 1999, p. 313; autumn, 2000, p. 877.

ONLINE

The Modern Word, http://www.themodernword.com/ (January 18, 2002), "Umberto Eco."

*   *   *

EDELMAN, Marian Wright 1939-

PERSONAL: Born June 6, 1939, in Bennettsville, SC; daughter of Arthur J. and Maggie (Bowen) Wright; married Peter Benjamin Edelman, July 14, 1968; children: Joshua Robert, Jonah Martin, Ezra Benjamin. *Education:* Attended University of Paris and University of Geneva, 1958-59; Spelman College, B.A., 1960; Yale University, LL.B., 1963.

ADDRESSES: Office—Children's Defense Fund, 122 C St. N.W., Washington, DC 20001.

CAREER: National Association for the Advancement of Colored People (NAACP), Legal Defense and Education Fund, Inc., New York, NY, staff attorney, 1963-64, director of office in Jackson, MS, 1964-68; partner of Washington Research Project of Southern Center for Public Policy, 1968-73; Children's Defense Fund, Washington, DC, founder and president, 1973—. W.E.B. Du Bois Lecturer at Harvard University, 1986. Member of Lisle Fellowship's U.S.-USSR Student Exchange, 1959; member of executive committee of Student Non-Violent Coordinating Committee (SNCC), 1961-63; member of Operation Crossroads Africa Project in Ivory Coast, 1962; congressional and federal agency liaison for Poor People's Campaign, summer, 1968; director of Harvard University's Center for Law and Education, 1971-73. Member of Presidential Commission on Americans Missing and Unaccounted for in Southeast Asia (Woodcock Commission), 1977, United States-South Africa leadership Exchange Program, 1977, National Commission on the International Year of the Child, 1979, and President's Commission for a National Agenda for the Eighties, 1979; member of board of directors of Carnegie Council on Children, 1972-77, Aetna Life and Casualty Foundation, Citizens for Constitutional Concerns, U.S. Committee for UNICEF, and Legal Defense and Education Fund of the NAACP; member of board of trustees of Martin Luther King, Jr., Memorial Center, and Joint Center for Political Studies.

MEMBER: Council on Foreign Relations, Delta Sigma Theta (honorary member).

AWARDS, HONORS: Merrill scholar in Paris and Geneva, 1958-59; honorary fellow of Law School at University of Pennsylvania, 1969; Louise Waterman Wise Award, 1970; Presidential Citation, American Public Health Association, 1979; Outstanding Leadership Award, National Alliance of Black School Educators, 1979; Distinguished Service Award, National Association of Black Women Attorneys, 1979; National Award of Merit, National Council on Crime and Delinquency, 1979; named Washingtonian of the Year, 1979; Whitney M. Young Memorial Award, Washington Urban League, 1980; Professional Achievement Award, Black Enterprise magazine, 1980; Outstanding Leadership Achievement Award, National Women's Political Caucus and Black Caucus, 1980; Outstanding Community Service Award, National Hookup of Black Women, 1980; Woman of the Year Award, Big Sisters of America, 1980; Award of Recognition, American Academy of Pedodontics, 1981; Rockefeller Public Service Award, 1981; Gertrude Zimand Award, National Child Labor Committee, 1982; Florina Lasker Award, New York Civil Liberties Union, 1982; Anne Roe Award, Graduate School of Education at Harvard University, 1984; Roy Wilkins Civil Rights Award, National Association for the Advancement of Colored People (NAACP), 1984; award from Women's Legal Defense Fund, 1985; Hubert H. Humphrey Award, Leadership Conference on Civil Rights, 1985; fellow of MacArthur Foundation, 1985; Grenville Clark Prize from Dartmouth College, 1986; Compostela Award of St. James Cathedral, 1987; Gandhi Peace Award, 1989; Fordham Stein Prize, 1989; Murray-Green-Meany Award, AFL-CIO, 1989; Frontrunner Award, Sara Lee Corporation, 1990; Jefferson Award, American Institute for Public Service, 1991; recipient of more than thirty honorary degrees.

WRITINGS:

Families in Peril: An Agenda for Social Change, Harvard University Press (Cambridge, MA), 1987.

The Measure of Our Success: A Letter to My Children and Yours, Beacon Press (Boston, MA), 1992, with a new preface, 1994.
Guide My Feet: Prayers and Meditations on Loving and Working for Children, Beacon Press (Boston, MA), 1995.
Stand for Children, Hyperion Books for Children (New York, NY), 1998.
Lanterns: A Memoir of Mentors, HarperPerennial (New York, NY)), 1999.
I'm Your Child, God: Prayers for Children and Teenagers, Hyperion Books for Children (New York, NY), 2002.

Also author of *School Suspensions: Are They Helping Children?,* 1975, and *Portrait of Inequality: Black and White Children in America,* 1980. Contributor to books, including *Raising Children in Modern America: Problems and Prospective Solutions,* edited by Nathan B. Talbot, Little, Brown, 1975; and *Toward New Human Rights: The Social Policies of the Kennedy and Johnson Administrations,* edited by David C. Warner, Lyndon B. Johnson School of Public Affairs, University of Texas at Austin, 1977.

SIDELIGHTS: Dubbed "the 101st Senator on children's issues" by U.S. Senator Edward Kennedy, Marian Wright Edelman left her law practice in 1968, just after the assassination of civil rights leader Martin Luther King, Jr., to work toward a better future for American children. She was the first black woman to join the Mississippi Bar and had been a civil rights lawyer with the National Association for the Advancement of Colored People (NAACP). "Convinced she could achieve more as an advocate than as a litigant for the poor," wrote Nancy Traver in *Time,* Edelman moved to Washington, DC, and began to apply her researching and rhetorical skills in Congress. She promotes her cause with facts about teen pregnancies, poverty, and infant mortality and—with her Children's Defense Fund—has managed to obtain budget increases for family and child health care and education programs. In *Ms.* magazine Katherine Bouton described Edelman as "the nation's most effective lobbyist on behalf of children . . . an unparalleled strategist and pragmatist."

Edelman's book *Families in Peril: An Agenda for Social Change* was judged "a powerful and necessary document" of the circumstances of children by *Washington Post* reviewer Jonathan Yardley, and it urges support for poor mothers and children of all races. The book is based on the 1986 W.E.B. Du Bois Lectures that Edelman gave at Harvard University. In making her case for increased support for America's children, Edelman offers numerous statistics that paint a grim portrait of life for the country's poor. Don Wycliff, reviewing the book for the *New York Times Book Review,* questioned Edelman's solutions as overly dependent on government support and neglectful of parental responsibility for children: "Governmental exertions . . . are indispensable. But . . . Edelman doesn't satisfactorily address how [parents] can be induced to behave wisely and responsibly *for their child's benefit.*" A *Kirkus Review* contributor, however, termed the book "graphic and eloquent."

In *Measure of Our Success: A Letter to My Children and Yours,* Edelman again deals with the problems and possible solutions of poverty and the neglect of children, in part by discussing her own experience as a parent. The book is divided into five sections: "A Family Legacy"; "Passing on the Legacy of Service"; "A Letter to My Sons"; "Twenty-five Lessons for Life"; and "Is the Child Safe?" Writing in the *New York Times Book Review* about the chapter "Twenty-five Lessons for Life," Clifton L. Taulbert commented, "In the twenty-five lessons for life that she presents here, she issues a call for parental involvement, a commitment of personal time on behalf of others, the primacy of service over self, and the assumption of individual responsibility for our nation's character."

Edelman's *I'm Your Child, God: Prayers for Our Children* follows in the footsteps of her previous collections of prayers, *Guide My Feet: Prayers and Meditations on Loving and Working for Children.* Divided into specific segments for younger children, young adults, and special occasions, the work features language that *Booklist* contributor Gillian Engberg described as at times "clunky and even banal." Nonetheless, the critic added, among the works Edelman assembles are some deeply "heartfelt selections." "She offers kids support, peace and empowerment in prayers," added a *Publishers Weekly* reviewer, the critic going on to state that *I'm Your Child, God* is "a book many will welcome."

Edelman once commented: "I have been an advocate for disadvantaged Americans throughout my professional career. The Children's Defense Fund, which I have been privileged to direct, has become one of the nation's most active organizations concerned with a wide range of children's and family issues, especially those which most affect America's children: our poorest Americans.

"Founded in 1968 as the Washington Research Project, the Children's Defense Fund monitors and proposes improvements in federal, state, and local budgets, legisla-

tive and administrative policies in the areas of child and maternal health, education, child care, child welfare, adolescent pregnancy prevention, youth employment, and family support systems. In 1983 the Children's Defense Fund initiated a major long-term national campaign to prevent teenage pregnancy and provide positive life options for youth. Since then, we have launched a multimedia campaign that includes transit advertisements, posters, and television and radio public service announcements, a national prenatal care campaign, and Child Watch coalitions in more than seventy local communities in thirty states to combat teen pregnancy.

"The Children's Defense Fund also has been a leading advocate in Congress, state legislatures, and courts for children's rights. For example, our legal actions blocked out-of-state placement of hundreds of Louisiana children in Texas institutions, guaranteed access to special education programs for tens of thousands of Mississippi's children, and represented the interests of children and their families before numerous federal administrative agencies."

BIOGRAPHICAL AND CRITICAL SOURCES:

PERIODICALS

Black Issues Book Review, January-February 2003, review of *I'm Your Child, God: Prayers for Our Children,* p. 71.

Booklist, October 1, 2002, Gillian Engberg, review of *I'm Your Child, God,* p. 340.

Ebony, July, 1987.

Harper's, February, 1993, p. 154.

Kirkus Reviews, February 1, 1987, p. 189; October 1, 2002, review of *I'm Your Child, God,* p. 1467.

Library Journal, March 1, 1987, p. 66.

Ms., July-August, 1987.

New Republic, March 4, 1996, p. 33.

Newsweek, June 10, 1996, p. 32.

New York Times Book Review, June 7, 1987, p. 12; August 23, 1992, p. 13.

Psychology Today, July-August, 1993, p. 26.

Publishers Weekly, October 28, 2002, review of *I'm Your Child, God,* p. 69.

School Library Journal, September, 1992, p. 290; December, 1992, p. 29; December 2002, Marge Louch-Wouters, review of *I'm Your Child, God,* p. 158.

Time, March 23, 1987.

Washington Post, March 4, 1987.

Washington Post Book World, April 19, 1992, p. 13.

EDMONDSON, Wallace
   See ELLISON, Harlan

*   *   *

EGGERS, Dave 1971(?)-

PERSONAL: Born c. 1971; married Vendela Vida (an author and magazine editor), 2003.

ADDRESSES: Office—c/o McSweeney's, 826NYC, 372 Fifth Ave. Brooklyn, NY 11215; 826 Valencia St., San Francisco, CA 94110.

CAREER: Writer. *Might* magazine, founder and editor, beginning 1997. Also editor at *Esquire* and *Timothy McSweeney's Quarterly Concern.* Consultant for ESPN. Has appeared on various radio and television shows, including *This American Life,* for National Public Radio (NPR), and *The Real World,* for Music Television (MTV).

WRITINGS:

(And editor, with others) *For the Love of Cheese: The Editors of Might Magazine,* Boulevard Books (New York, NY), 1996.

A Heartbreaking Work of Staggering Genius (memoir), Simon & Schuster (New York, NY), 2000.

You Shall Know Our Velocity (novel), self-published, 2002.

(Editor, with Michael Cart) *The Best American Nonrequired Reading 2002,* Mariner Books, 2002.

(Editor, with Zadie Smith) *The Best American Nonrequired Reading 2003,* Houghton Mifflin, 2003.

(Editor) *The Best American Nonrequired Reading 2004,* Mariner Books, 2004.

(Editor, with others) *Created in Darkness by Troubled Americans: The Best of McSweeney's Humor Category,* Knopf, 2004.

Sacrament! (play; adapted from *You Shall Know Our Velocity,*) produced at the Campo Santo Company, San Francisco, CA, 2004.

How We Are Hungry (short stories), McSweeney's, 2004.

Contributor to numerous periodicals.

ADAPTATIONS: A Heartbreaking Work of Staggering Genius is being adapted as a screenplay by Nick Hornby and D.V. DeVincentis.

SIDELIGHTS: Founder in 1994 and former editor of *Might* magazine, writer Dave Eggers edits *Timothy McSweeney's Quarterly Concern,* a quarterly journal and Web site in existence since 1998. Jeff Daniel of the St. Louis *Post-Dispatch* likened Eggers to avant-garde pop musicians Radiohead and the movie-making Coen brothers, placing him among the "rare breed that has managed to marry commercial and critical success." Daniel called Eggers a "self-starter and self-promoter," praising him for his work ethic and writing talent. Daniel, too, noted that *McSweeney's* continues to be commended for promoting clever writing. Christopher Lydon, interviewer for *WBUR Boston,* commented that *McSweeney's* is a "quirky" Monty Python-style publication as well as a "postmodern examination of everything." Only a few years prior to the development and launch of *Might,* Eggers and his three siblings faced the grim reality of having seen both their parents die within weeks of each other. After two of Eggers' siblings moved to California, he decided to take on the task of raising his eight-year-old brother, Christopher, or Toph, on his own. That experience, as well as many others, prompted Eggers to write *A Heartbreaking Work of Staggering Genius.*

Daniel Handler, in *Voice Literary Supplement,* stated that "whether [Eggers is] discussing early *Might* meetings or parent-teacher conferences, he invariably finds a perfect tone and zeroes in on the triple paradox of . . . slacker days: you want to do something, preferably the right thing, but are paralyzed by self-awareness; despite self-awareness you do something anyway." Handler commented that Eggers "may end up becoming something he richly deserves and probably does not aspire to be: the voice of a generation." Mark Horowitz, reviewing *A Heartbreaking Work of Staggering Genius* for *New York,* praised Eggers' honest voice, noting that he "lays everything out in exquisite, excruciating detail." Horowitz called the book "a heart-wrenching yet often very funny memoir."

Sara Mosle, in the *New York Times Book Review,* commented on the humor in *A Heartbreaking Work of Staggering Genius,* calling the work "a book of finite jest, which is why it succeeds so brilliantly." Mosle commented that the book "goes a surprisingly long way toward delivering on its self-satirizing, hyperbolic title," and that it "is a profoundly moving, occasionally angry and often hilarious account of those odd and silly things, usually done in the name of Toph." Elise Harris described in *Nation* how "conviction and doubt, depth and humor, are placed side by side," and that "each is a style, and each is true and false at once." According to Harris, Eggers "won't let the reader make a choice between them—we don't know where he really falls. The result is exhausting and frustrating, but trustworthy." James Poniewozik, in *Time,* stated that in *A Heartbreaking Work of Staggering Genius* "literary gamesmanship and self-consciousness are trained on life's most unendurable experience, used to examine memory too scorching to stare at, as one views an eclipse by projecting sunlight onto paper through a pinhole." Grace Fill, a reviewer in *Booklist,* was another reviewer who commented on Eggers' use of humor, stating that his "piercingly observant style allows hilarity to lead the way in a very personal and revealing recounting of the loss of his parents." A reviewer in *Publishers Weekly* said that "literary self-consciousness and technical invention mix unexpectedly in this engaging memoir." Eric Bryant, a reviewer in *Library Journal,* "highly recommended" the book, calling the work "a surprisingly moving tale of family bonding and resilience."

Eggers' first novel, *You Shall Know Our Velocity,* concerns two young men on a week-long trip around the world with the goal of giving away an unexpected windfall of cash one of them received. Kyle Minor of the *Antioch Review* pointed out the plot is simply a way for Eggers to conduct a philosophical character analysis of the duo as they deal with feelings of guilt and attempt to come to grips with a friend's death. Minor felt the Eggers produced a "convincing booklength dialogue between them that works on multiple levels," remarking that, it is a "minor work, but it is a satisfying and meritorious effort." Benjamin Markovitz noted in the *New Statesman* that Eggers draws the title for his novel from "a lengthy anecdote about a harmless, foolish, and ambitious South American tribe who believed they could jump their way to heaven. Its relation to the story is clear, and explains why their failure and nobility appealed to Eggers." Markovits also commented that Eggers' writing is more "grown up in style" and the plot tighter than in his memoir, yet he still exhibits some of the irreverence shown in his first book. "He deserves his success," commented Markovitz. "He writes well and he practises what he preaches: he teaches literacy at his own foundation in San Francisco, while *McSweeney's,* the independent literary magazine and press that he founded, is now the place publishers look for new talent."

BIOGRAPHICAL AND CRITICAL SOURCES:

PERIODICALS

Antioch Review, spring, 2003, Kyle Minor, review of *You Shall Know Our Velocity,* p. 373.

Booklist, January 1, 2000, Grace Fill, review of *A Heartbreaking Work of Staggering Genius,* p. 860.

Entertainment Weekly, March 3, 2000, Clarissa Cruz, "His So-Called Life: Author du jour Dave Eggers' Crazy Existence Gets Even Crazier," p. 67.

Library Journal, November 15, 1999, Eric Bryant, review of *A Heartbreaking Work of Staggering Genius,* p. 77.

Nation, March 20, 2000, Elise Harris, "Infinite Jest," p. 45.

New Statesman, February 24, 2003, Benjamin Markovitz, review of *You Shall Know Your Velocity,* p. 53.

New York, January 31, 2000, Mark Horowitz, "Laughing through His Tearjerker," pp. 30-33.

New York Times Book Review, February 20, 2000, Sara Mosle, "My Brother's Keeper," p. 6.

Publishers Weekly, December 13, 1999, review of *A Heartbreaking Work of Staggering Genius,* p. 72.

St. Louis Post-Dispatch, July 17, 2003, Jeff Daniel, "Quirky Dave Eggers Comes to Town to Promote His New Book," p. 5.

Time, February 7, 2000, James Poniewozik, "Dave Eggers' Mystery Box: With a Curious Journal and an Ambitious New Memoir of Orphanhood, This Young Editor and Writer Opens a Package of Literary Surprises," p. 72.

U.S. News & World Report, February 7, 2000, Linda Kulman, "He's Ingenious and He Knows It," p. 62.

Voice Literary Supplement, February-March, 2000, Daniel Handler, "Reality Writes," p. 107.

ONLINE

Timothy McSweeney's Internet Tendency, http://www.mcsweeneys.net/ (August 14, 2004).

WBUR Boston Web site, http://www.wbur.org/ (February 22, 2000), Christopher Lydon, "Dave Eggers, Novelist and Editor of *McSweeney's.*"

*   *   *

EHRENREICH, Barbara 1941-

PERSONAL: Born August 26, 1941, in Butte, MT; daughter of Ben Howes and Isabelle Oxley (Isely) Alexander; married John Ehrenreich, August 6, 1966 (marriage ended); married Gary Stevenson, December 10, 1983; children: (first marriage) Rosa, Benjamin. *Education:* Reed College, B.A., 1963; Rockefeller University, Ph.D., 1968. *Politics:* "Socialist and feminist."

ADDRESSES: Agent—c/o Author Mail, Henry Holt & Co., Inc., 115 West 18th St., New York, NY 10011.

CAREER: Health Policy Advisory Center, New York, NY, staff member, 1969-71; State University of New York College at Old Westbury, assistant professor of health sciences, 1971-74; writer, 1974—; *Seven Days* magazine, editor, 1974—; *Mother Jones* magazine, columnist, 1986-89; *Time* magazine, essayist, 1990; *Guardian,* London, England, columnist, 1992—. New York Institute for the Humanities, associate fellow, 1980—; Institute for Policy Studies, fellow, 1982—. Co-chair, Democratic Socialists of America, 1983—.

AWARDS, HONORS: National Magazine award, 1980; Ford Foundation award for Humanistic Perspectives on Contemporary Issues, 1981; Guggenheim fellowship, 1987; Christopher Award and *Los Angeles Times* Book Award in current-interest category, both 2002, both for *Nickel and Dimed: On (Not) Getting by in America.*

WRITINGS:

(With husband, John Ehrenreich) *Long March, Short Spring: The Student Uprising at Home and Abroad,* Monthly Review Press (New York, NY), 1969.

(With John Ehrenreich) *The American Health Empire: Power, Profits, and Politics: A Report from the Health Policy Advisory Center,* Random House (New York, NY), 1970.

(With Deirdre English) *Witches, Midwives, and Nurses: A History of Women Healers,* Feminist Press (Old Westbury, NY), 1972.

(With Deirdre English) *Complaints and Disorders: The Sexual Politics of Sickness,* Feminist Press, 1973.

(With Deirdre English) *For Her Own Good: One Hundred-fifty Years of the Experts' Advice to Women,* Doubleday (New York, NY), 1978.

The Hearts of Men: American Dreams and the Flight from Commitment, Doubleday (New York, NY), 1983.

(With Annette Fuentes) *Women in the Global Factory* (pamphlet), South End Press (Boston, MA), 1983.

(Coauthor) *Poverty in the American Dream: Women and Children First,* Institute for New Communications, South End Press (Boston, MA), 1983.

(With Elizabeth Hess and Gloria Jacobs) *Re-making Love: The Feminization of Sex,* Anchor Press/Doubleday (New York, NY), 1986.

(With Fred Block, Richard Cloward, and Frances Fox Piven) *The Mean Season: An Attack on the Welfare State,* Pantheon (New York, NY), 1987.

Fear of Falling: The Inner Life of the Middle Class, Pantheon (New York, NY), 1989.

The Worst Years of Our Lives: Irreverent Notes from a Decade of Greed, Pantheon, 1990.

Kipper's Game, Farrar, Straus (New York, NY), 1993.

The Snarling Citizen: Essays, Farrar, Straus (New York, NY), 1995.

Blood Rites: Origins and History of the Passions of War, Metropolitan Books (New York, NY), 1997.

Nickel and Dimed: On (Not) Getting by in America, Holt (New York, NY), 2001.

(Editor with Arlie Russell Hochschild) *Global Woman: Nannies, Maids, and Sex Workers in the New Economy,* Metropolitan Books (New York, NY), 2003.

Contributor to magazines, including *Radical America, Nation, Esquire, Vogue, New Republic,* and *New York Times Magazine.* Contributing editor, *Ms.,* 1981—, and *Mother Jones,* 1988—. Guest columnist, *New York Times.*

ADAPTATIONS: "Wage Slaves: Not Getting by in America," a segment of the A&E series *Investigative Reports,* was based in part on *Nickel and Dimed: On (Not) Getting by in America* and aired August 26, 2002.

SIDELIGHTS: The images circulating in 2004, during the War on Terror, of Iraqi prisoner abuse by U.S. soldiers dashed some of Barbara Ehrenreich's hope that women "would eventually change the military, making it more respectful of other people and cultures, more capable of genuine peace keeping." Ehrenreich's remarks were made during her commencement address to the 2004 graduates of Barbard College in New York City. "What we need is a tough new kind of feminism with no illusions. . . . We need a kind of woman who doesn't want to be one of the boys when the boys are acting like sadists or fools." An outspoken feminist and socialist party leader, Ehrenreich crusades for social justice in her books. Although many of her early works were shaped by her formal scientific training—she earned a Ph.D. in biology—her more recent works have moved beyond health care concerns to the plight of women and the poor. In addition to her numerous nonfiction books, Ehrenreich is widely known for her weekly columns published in *Time* and the *Guardian.*

Early in her career, while working for the Health Policy Advisory Center, Ehrenreich published a scathing critique of the American health "empire," exposing its inefficiency, inhumanity, and self-serving policies. Then, turning from the population in general to women in particular, Ehrenreich and her coauthor Deirdre English unveiled the male domination of the female health care system in *Complaints and Disorders: The Sexual Politics of Sickness* and *For Her Own Good: One Hundred Fifty Years of the Experts' Advice to Women.* In a controversial work, *The Hearts of Men: American Dreams and the Flight from Commitment,* Ehrenreich takes on the whole male establishment, challenging the assumption that feminism is at the root of America's domestic upheaval.

Describing *The Hearts of Men* as a study of "the ideology that shaped the breadwinner ethic," Ehrenreich surveys the three decades between the 1950s and the 1980s, showing how male commitment to home and family collapsed during this time. "The result," according to *New York Times* contributor Eva Hoffman, "is an original work of cultural iconography that supplements—and often stands on its head—much of the analysis of the relations between the sexes that has become the accepted wisdom of recent years." Ehrenreich's interpretation of the evidence led her to the surprising conclusion that anti-feminism evolved in response not to feminism, but to men's abdication of their breadwinner role.

The seeds of male revolt were planted as far back as the 1950s, according to Ehrenreich, when what she calls "the gray flannel dissidents" began to balk at their myriad responsibilities. "The gray flannel nightmare of the commuter train and the constant pressure to support a houseful of consumers caused many men to want to run away from it all," Carol Cleaver wrote in the *New Leader.* What held these men in check, says Ehrenreich, was the fear that, as bachelors, they would be associated with homosexuality. Hugh Hefner banished that stigma with the publication of *Playboy,* a magazine whose name alone "defied the convention of hard-won maturity," Ehrenreich maintains in her book. "The magazine's real message was not eroticism, but escape . . . from the bondage of breadwinning."

In the decades that followed, men's increasing "flight from commitment" was sanctioned by pop psychologists and other affiliates of the human potential movement, who banished guilt and encouraged people to "do their own thing." Unfortunately for women, Ehrenreich concludes that men abandoned the breadwinner role "without overcoming the sexist attitudes that role has perpetuated: on the one hand, the expectation of female nurturance and submissive service as a matter of right; on the other hand a misogynist contempt for women as 'parasites' and entrappers of men." In response to male abdication, women increasingly adopted one of two

philosophies: they became feminists, committed to achieving economic and social parity with men, or they became anti-feminists, who tried to keep men at home by binding themselves ever more tightly to them. Despite such efforts, Ehrenreich concludes that women have not fared well, but instead have found themselves increasingly on their own "in a society that never intended to admit us as independent persons, much less as breadwinners for others."

Widely reviewed in both magazines and newspapers, *The Hearts of Men* was hailed for its provocative insights, even as individual sections of the study were soundly criticized. In her *Village Voice* review, for instance, Judith Levine was both appreciative of the work and skeptical of its conclusions: "Ehrenreich—one of the finest feminist-socialist writers around—has written a witty, intelligent book based on intriguing source material. *The Hearts of Men* says something that needs saying: men have not simply reacted to feminism— skulking away from women and children, hurt, humiliated, feeling cheated of their legal and emotional rights. Men, as Ehrenreich observes, have, as always, done what they want to do. . . . I applaud her on-the-mark readings of *Playboy,* medical dogma, and men's liberation; her insistence that the wage system punishes women and children when families disintegrate; her mordant yet uncynical voice." At the same time, Levine judged the central thesis of the book as "wrong": "When she claims that the glue of families is male volition and the breadwinner ideology—and that a change in that ideology caused the breakup of the family—I am doubtful," commented the critic. "The ideology supporting men's abdication of family commitment is not new. It has coexisted belligerently with the breadwinner ethic throughout American history."

In 1986's *Re-making Love: The Feminization of Sex,* coauthored with Elizabeth Hess and Gloria Jacobs, Ehrenreich reports and applauds the freer attitudes toward sex that women adopted in the 1970s and 1980s. The authors assert that women have gained the ability to enjoy sex just for the sake of pleasure, separating it from idealistic notions of love and romance. In her review of *Re-making Love* for the *Chicago Tribune,* Joan Beck noted that the book "is an important summing up of what has happened to women and sex in the last two decades and [that it] shows why the sex revolution requires re-evaluation." Beck, however, argued that the authors ignore the "millions of walking wounded"— those affected by sexually transmitted diseases, unwanted pregnancy, or lack of lasting relationships. *Washington Post Book World* contributor Anthony Astrachan also expressed a wish for a deeper analysis, but nevertheless found *Re-making Love* "full of sharp and sometimes surprising insights that come from looking mass culture full in the face."

Ehrenreich's next work to attract critical notice, *Fear of Falling: The Inner Life of the Middle Class,* examines the American middle class and its attitudes toward people of the working and poorer classes. Jonathan Yardley stated in the *Washington Post* that what Ehrenreich actually focuses on is a class "composed of articulate, influential people. . . . in fact what most of us think of as the upper-middle class." According to Ehrenreich this group perceives itself as threatened, is most concerned with self-preservation, and has isolated itself, feeling little obligation to work for the betterment of society. This attitude, Ehrenreich maintains, is occurring at a time when the disparity in income between classes has reached the greatest point since World War II and has become "almost as perilously skewed as that of India," as Joseph Coates quoted from *Fear of Falling* in Chicago's *Tribune Books.*

Globe and Mail contributor Maggie Helwig, while praising *Fear of Falling* as "witty, clever, [and] perceptive," described as unrealistic Ehrenreich's hope for a future when everyone could belong to the professional middle class and hold fulfilling jobs. Similarly, David Rieff remarked in the *Los Angeles Times Book Review* that Ehrenreich's proposed solutions to class polarization are overly optimistic and tend to romanticize the nature of work. "Nonetheless," Rieff concluded, "*Fear of Falling* is a major accomplishment, a breath of fresh thinking about a subject that very few writers have known how to think about at all." The book elicited even higher praise from Coates, who deemed it "a brilliant social analysis and intellectual history, quite possibly the best on this subject since Tocqueville's."

In *The Worst Years of Our Lives: Irreverent Notes from a Decade of Greed* Ehrenreich discusses in a series of reprinted articles what some consider to be one of the most self-involved and consumeristic decades in American history: the 1980s. Most of these articles first appeared in *Mother Jones,* but some come from such periodicals as *Nation, Atlantic Monthly,* the *New York Times,* and the *New Republic.* Together, they summarize "what Ms. Ehrenreich sees as the decade's salient features: blathering ignorance, smug hypocrisy, institutionalized fraud and vengeful polarization—all too dangerous to be merely absurd," according to H. Jack Geiger in the *New York Times Book Review.* "One of Mrs. Ehrenreich's main themes," observed *New York Times* reviewer Herbert Mitgang, "is that the Reagan Administration,

which dominated the . . . [1980s], cosmeticized the country and painted over its true condition. The author writes that the poor and middle class are now suffering the results of deliberate neglect."

The Snarling Citizen: Essays collects fifty-seven previously published essays, most of which Ehrenreich contributed to *Time* and the London *Guardian.* The essays once again reveal the author's passion for social justice and feminism. Although some reviewers have taken exception to Ehrenreich's opinions in these pieces, nearly all have lavished praise on her well-honed writing style. Writing in the Chicago *Tribune Books,* for example, Penelope Mesic remarked that the pieces in *The Snarling Citizen* "startle and invigorate because those who espouse liberal causes—feminism, day care and a strong labor movement—all too often write a granola of prose: a mild, beige substance that is, in a dull way, good for us. Ehrenreich is peppery and salacious, bitter with scorn, hotly lucid." *Women's Review of Books* contributor Nan Levinson commended the author for her "writing, a hymn to pithiness and wit, and her ear, attuned to the ways in which language redefined becomes thought reconstructed and politics realigned." Andrew Ferguson, however, writing in the *American Spectator,* took issue with what he called the author's habit of building entire essays around "casual misstatements" of fact. In addition, while conceding that Ehrenreich "knows that caricature can be a verbal art," Ferguson maintains that "too often her fondness for exaggeration and hyperbole drags her into mere buffoonery." While noting that the collection's pieces are all so similar in "size, . . . voice and essentially . . . subject" that they "resemble a box of Fig Newtons," Levinson declared: "Ehrenreich is a rare thing in American public life today—a freelance thinker."

In June 1998 Ehrenreich embarked on what was to become perhaps her best-known project. "I leave behind everything that normally soothes the ego and sustains the body—home, career, companion, reputation, ATM card—," as she explained in a *Harper's* article, "and plunge into the low-wage workforce." Following up on such previous studies as *Fear of Falling,* Ehrenreich spent two years living the life of the American working class, and what she discovered turned into the bestselling 2001 exposé *Nickel and Dimed: On (Not) Getting by in America.*

A successful, affluent, Ph.D. candidate, the author created a new persona—Barbara Ehrenreich, divorced homemaker with some housekeeping experience—and set off on a tour of the country attempting to sustain herself at what are commonly called "entry-level" jobs. In Ehrenreich's case, that meant waiting tables and cleaning hotel rooms in Key West, Florida; working at a nursing home in Portland, Maine; and becoming a Wal-Mart "associate" in Minneapolis. As she points out, Ehrenreich herself is not too far removed from the working class: her father was a copper miner, her husband a warehouse worker, and her sister an employee in the kind of low-wage jobs the author now was sampling. Nor did she harbor any illusions about her temporary status among the working class: "My aim is nothing so mistily subjective as to 'experience poverty' or find out how it 'really feels' to be a long-term low-wage worker," she asserted in *Harper's*. "And with all my real-life assets—bank account, IRA, health insurance, multiroom home—waiting indulgently in the background, I am, of course, thoroughly insulated from the terrors that afflict the genuinely poor."

As the author related in the *Harper's* piece that was expanded into *Nickel and Dimed*, "My first task is to find a place to live. I figure that if I can earn $7 an hour—which, from the want ads, seems doable—I can afford to spend $500 [per month] on rent." In affluent Key West, that amount might finance "flophouses and trailer homes," the latter featuring "no air-conditioning, no screens, no fans, no television and, by way of diversion, only the challenge of evading the landlord's Doberman pinscher." But even that rent was $675 per month—out of Ehrenreich's reach. "It is a shock to realize that 'trailer trash' has become, for me, a demographic category to aspire to."

Though she equipped herself with three essentials for her study—a car, a laptop computer, and $1,300 startup funds—Ehrenreich quickly learned that earning money for the basics of life came much harder in the service sector. She discovered a booming trade in Key West's "hospitality industry" and noted that her demographic—white, female, English-speaking—gave her an advantage at hiring time. She initially dismissed such options as desk-clerking—too much standing—waitressing—too much walking—and telemarketing—wrong personality type. That left Ehrenreich to fill out applications at hotels, supermarkets, inns, and guest-houses. But her phone seldom rang. To the author's surprise, she learned that the larger chains often run continual help-wanted ads, even when no jobs are open, to build a candidate safety net against the constant turnover in the service field. Ehrenreich finally landed a job at a small chain-hotel's restaurant, as a server. She doled out drinks, made salads and desserts, and tended to "side work," which she defines as "sweeping, scrubbing, slicing, refilling, and restocking." The break room, servers were

informed by management, was not a right, but a privilege. Her wage came to $5.15 per hour, not including tips that dried up with the summer heat. Ehrenreich realized she could not afford her $500 efficiency apartment and must find a second job. She took a job at "Jerry's," her alias for a large, well-known family restaurant chain. If anything, the conditions were even worse: "The break room typifies the whole situation: there is none, because there are no breaks at Jerry's. For six to eight hours in a row, you never sit except to pee." She later landed what she considered a dream job of housekeeping in a hotel: stripping beds, scrubbing bathrooms, and handling giant vacuum cleaners on four-hour, no-break shifts. A month working in Key West netted Ehrenreich approximately $1,040; after expenses she was left with $22, and had no health insurance.

"How former welfare recipients and single mothers will (and do) survive in the low-wage workforce, I cannot imagine," Ehrenreich wrote. This comment is a running theme of *Nickel and Dimed*, as the jobs the author described are typical of those taken by the some twelve-million women who are the objects of welfare reform, "workfare," or other such governmental policies. To *Salon* reviewer Laura Miller, "one of the sly pleasures of 'Nickel and Dimed' is the way it dances on the line between straightforward social protest and an edgier acknowledgment of inconvenient truths."

Other critical reaction to Ehrenreich's book ranged from skeptical to admiring. In the former camp was Julia Klein, whose question in *American Prospect* was, "In the end, what has [Ehrenreich] accomplished? It's no shock that the dollars don't add up; that affordable housing is hard, if not impossible, to find; and that taking a second job is a virtual necessity for many of the working poor." After labeling the author "a prickly, self-confident woman and the possessor of a righteous, ideologically informed outrage at America's class system that can turn patronizing at times," Klein went on to acknowledge that *Nickel and Dimed* is still "a compelling and timely book whose insights sometimes do transcend the obvious." Similarly, *Humanist* contributor Joni Scott mentioned an early reluctance to read the memoirs of an affluent person living temporarily as poor, but found that Ehrenreich's work is "an important literary contribution and a call to action that I hope is answered. I believe this book should be required reading for corporate executives and politicians." "This book opens one's eyes very wide indeed," declared a reviewer for *M2 Best Books*. And in the view of Bob Hulteen of *Sojourners*, "Definitional books come around about once a decade. Such books so describe the reality of the age in simple terms that the impact is felt from after-dinner conversations to federal policy discussions." *Nickel and Dimed,* he added, "will likely join this pantheon."

BIOGRAPHICAL AND CRITICAL SOURCES:

BOOKS

Ehrenreich, Barbara, and Arlie Russell Hochschild, editors, *Global Woman: Nannies, Maids, and Sex Workers in the New Economy,* Metropolitan Books (New York, NY), 2003.

PERIODICALS

American Prospect, July 30, 2001, Julia Klein, review of *Nickel and Dimed: On (Not) Getting by in America,* p. 43.
American Spectator, August, 1995, Andrew Ferguson, review of *The Snarling Citizen: Essays,* p. 66.
Armed Forces & Society, fall, 1999, Daniel Moran, review of *Blood Rites: Origins and History of the Passions of War,* p. 111.
Barron's, August 6, 2001, review of *Nickel and Dimed,* p. 37.
Booklist, March 15, 1998, review of *Blood Rites,* p. 1209; April 1, 2001, George Cohen, review of *Nickel and Dimed,* p. 43.
Business Week, May 28, 2001, review of *Nickel and Dimed,* p. 24; December 10, 2001, review of *Nickel and Dimed,* p. 22.
Chicago Tribune, September 25, 1986, Joan Beck, review of *Re-making Love; The Feminization of Sex.*
Christian Century, August 1, 2001, Lillian Daniel, review of *Nickel and Dimed,* p. 30.
Christian Science Monitor, July 12, 2001, review of *Nickel and Dimed,* p. 17; November 15, 2001, review of *Nickel and Dimed,* p. 14.
Dissent, fall, 2001, review of *Nickel and Dimed,* p. 131.
Entertainment Weekly, May 29, 1998, review of *Blood Rites,* p. 69; December 21, 2001, review of *Nickel and Dimed,* p. 132.
European Intelligence Wire, May 21, 2004, "Commencement: Author Barbara Ehrenreich Calls for New Kind of Feminism to Counter Images of Prison Abuse."
Foreign Affairs, March, 1998, review of *Blood Rites,* p. 146.
Globe and Mail (Toronto, Ontario, Canada), August 26, 1989, Maggie Helwig, review of *Fear of Falling: The Inner Life of the Middle Class.*

Harper's, January, 1999, Barbara Ehrenreich, "Nickel and Dimed," p. 107.
Harvard Business Review, January, 2002, review of *Nickel and Dimed,* p. 107.
Humanist, January-February, 1992, p. 11; November, 1998, Edd Doerr, review of *Blood Rites,* p. 47; September, 2001, Joni Scott, review of *Nickel and Dimed,* p. 40.
International Journal on World Peace, December, 1998, Gordon Anderson, review of *Blood Rites,* p. 111.
Journal of Affordable Housing & Community Development Law, winter, 2002, Lynn Cunningham, review of *Nickel and Dimed,* pp. 159-161.
Journal of Peace Research, September, 1999, review of *Blood Rites,* p. 611.
Kirkus Reviews, April 1, 2001, review of *Nickel and Dimed,* p. 475.
Kliatt, July, 2003, Julia Klein, review of *Nickel and Dimed,* p. 5.
Library Journal, May 1, 2001, review of *Nickel and Dimed,* p. 115.
Long Island Business News, July 19, 2002, review of *Nickel and Dimed,* p. A25.
Los Angeles Times, July 24, 1983; June 15, 2001, David Ulin, "Life at the Bottom of the Food Chain," p. E1.
Los Angeles Times Book Review, August 20, 1989, David Rieff, review of *Fear of Falling;* May 27, 2001, review of *Nickel and Dimed,* p. 4; December 2, 2001, review of *Nickel and Dimed,* p. 24.
M2 Best Books, May 2, 2002, review of *Nickel and Dimed;* October 22, 2003.
Marine Corps Gazette, August, 1998, review of *Blood Rites,* p. 73.
Ms., May-June, 1995, p. 75; April-May, 2001, Vivien Labaton, review of *Nickel and Dimed,* p. 88.
Nation, December 24, 1983.
Naval War College Review, autumn, 1998, review of *Blood Rites,* p. 157.
New Leader, July 11, 1983, Carol Cleaver, review of *The Hearts of Men.*
New Republic, July 11, 1983.
New Statesman & Society, May 17, 1991, p. 37, May 20, 1994, Vicky Hutchings, review of *Kipper's Game,* p. 37.
Newsweek, June 4, 2001, review of *Nickel and Dimed,* p. 57.
New York Review of Books, July 1, 1971.
New York Times, January 20, 1971; August 16, 1983, Eva Hoffman, review of *The Hearts of Men;* May 16, 1990, Herbert Mitgang, review of *The Worst Years of Our Lives: Irreverent Notes from a Decade of Greed;* July 13, 1993, p. C18; July 30, 2001, Bob Herbert, "Unmasking the Poor," p. A21.

New York Times Book Review, March 7, 1971; June 5, 1983; August 6, 1989; May 20, 1990, H. Jack Geiger, review of *The Worst Years of Our Lives;* August 8, 1993, p. 18; May 28, 1996, p. 12; June 14, 1998, review of *Blood Rites,* p. 32; May 13, 2001, Dorothy Gallagher, "Making Ends Meet," p. 10; May 20, 2001, review of *Nickel and Dimed,* p. 67; June 3, 2001, review of *Nickel and Dimed,* p. 30.

New York Times Magazine, June 26, 1996, p. 28.

Observer (London, England), October 11, 1998, review of *Blood Rites,* p. 16.

Progressive, January, 1995, p. 47; February, 1995, p. 34; January, 2002, review of *Nickel and Dimed,* p. 42.

Public Interest, winter, 2002, review of *Nickel and Dimed,* p. 141.

Publishers Weekly, July 26, 1993, p. 46; May 14, 2001, review of *Nickel and Dimed,* p. 67.

Readings, September, 2001, review of *Nickel and Dimed,* p. 33.

Reference & User Services Quarterly, spring, 1998, review of *Blood Rites,* p. 274.

School Library Journal, December, 2001, Barbara Genco, review of *Nickel and Dimed,* p. 57.

Social Service Review, March, 2002, review of *Nickel and Dimed,* p. 196.

Sojourners, January-February, 2002, Bob Hulteen, review of *Nickel and Dimed,* p. 56.

Time, May 7, 1990.

Times Literary Supplement, July 22, 1977; April 10, 1998, review of *Blood Rites,* p. 3.

Tribune Books (Chicago, IL), November 8, 1987; September 24, 1989, Joseph Coates, review of *Fear of Falling;* May 13, 1990; May 28, 1995, Penelope Mesic, review of *The Snarling Citizen,* p. 3.

Utne Reader, May-June, 1995, p. 70.

Village Voice, February 5, 1979; August 23, 1983, Judith Levine, review of *The Hearts of Men.*

Wall Street Journal, May 18, 2001, review of *Nickel and Dimed,* p. W10.

Washington Post, August 23, 1989, Jonathan Yardley, review of *Fear of Falling;* June 10, 2001, Katherine Newman, "Desperate Hours," p. T03.

Washington Post Book World, August 19, 1979; July 24, 1983; November 9, 1986, Anthony Astrachan, review of *Re-making Love; The Feminization of Sex;* February 25, 2001, review of *Nickel and Dimed,* p. 6; June 10, 2001, review of *Nickel and Dimed,* p. 3.

Whole Earth Review, winter, 1995, p. 86.

Women's Review of Books, October, 1995, Nan Levinson, review of *The Snarling Citizen,* p. 25; July, 2001, Jacqueline Jones, review of *Nickel and Dimed,* p. 5, author interview, p. 6; January, 2004, Martha Nicols, "Global Woman," p. 12.

World & I, December, 2001, review of *Nickel and Dimed,* p. 250.

ONLINE

Alter Net, http://www.alternet.org/ (May 15, 2001), Tamara Straus, review of *Nickel and Dimed.*

Onion A.V. Club, http://wwwtheonion.com/ (September 19, 2001), Noel Murray, author interview.

Salon.com, http://www.salon.com/ (May 9, 2001), Laura Miller, review of *Nickel and Dimed.*

*   *   *

EISNER, Will 1917-2005
(William Erwin Eisner, Will Erwin, Willis Rensie)

PERSONAL: Born March 6, 1917, in New York, NY; died January 3, 2005, in Fort Lauderdale, FL; son of Samuel (a furrier) and Fannie (maiden name, Ingber) Eisner; married Ann Louise Weingarten (a director of volunteer hospital services), June 15, 1950; children: John David, Alice Carol (deceased). *Education:* Attended Art Students League, New York, NY, 1935.

CAREER: Author, cartoonist, publisher. *New York American,* New York, NY, staff artist, 1936; Eisner & Iger, New York, NY, founder, partner, 1937-40; Eisner-Arnold Comic Group, New York, NY, founder, publisher, 1940-46; author and cartoonist of syndicated newspaper feature, "The Spirit," 1940-52; founder and president of American Visuals Corp., beginning in 1949; president of Bell McClure North American Newspaper Alliance, 1962-64; executive vice-president of Koster-Dana Corp., 1962-64; president of Educational Supplements Corp., 1965-72; chair of the board of Croft Educational Services Corp., 1972-73; member of faculty of School of Visual Arts, New York, NY, beginning 1973. President of IPD Publishing Co., Inc. Member of board of directors of Westchester Philharmonic. *Military service:* U.S. Army, Ordnance, 1942-45.

MEMBER: Princeton Club (New York, NY).

AWARDS, HONORS: Comic book artist of the year, National Cartoonists Society, 1967; best artist, National Cartoonists Society, 1968-69; award for quality of art in comic books, Society of Comic Art Research, 1968; International Cartoonist Award, 1974; named to Hall of Fame of the Comic Book Academy; Eisner Award for Best Archival Collection, 2001, for *The Spirit Archives.*

WRITINGS:

A Pictorial Arsenal of America's Combat Weapons, Sterling (New York, NY), 1960.

America's Space Vehicles: A Pictorial Review, edited by Charles Kramer, Sterling (New York, NY), 1962.

A Contract with God, and Other Tenement Stories, Baronet (New York, NY), 1978.

(With P.R. Garriock and others) *Masters of Comic Book Art,* Images Graphiques (New York, NY), 1978.

Odd Facts, Ace Books (New York, NY), 1978.

Dating and Hanging Out (for young adults), Baronet (New York, NY), 1979.

Funny Jokes and Foxy Riddles, Baronet (New York, NY), 1979.

Ghostly Jokes and Ghastly Riddles, Baronet (New York, NY), 1979.

One Hundred and One Half Wild and Crazy Jokes, Baronet (New York, NY), 1979.

Spaced-Out Jokes, Baronet (New York, NY), 1979.

The City (narrative portfolio), Hollygraphic, 1981.

Life on Another Planet (graphic novel), Kitchen Sink (Princeton, WI), 1981.

Will Eisner Color Treasury, text by Catherine Yronwode, Kitchen Sink (Princeton, WI), 1981.

Spirit: Color Album, Kitchen Sink (Princeton, WI), 1981–1983.

Illustrated Roberts Rules of Order, Bantam (New York, NY), 1983.

(Catherine Yronwode, with Denis Kitchen) *The Art of Will Eisner,* introduction by Jules Feiffer, Kitchen Sink (Princeton, WI), 1982.

(Coauthor, with Jules Feiffer and Wallace Wood) *Outer Space Spirit, 1952,* edited by Denis Kitchen, Kitchen Sink (Princeton, WI), 1983.

Signal from Space, Kitchen Sink (Princeton, WI), 1983.

Will Eisner's Quarterly, Kitchen Sink (Princeton, WI), 1983–86.

Will Eisner's 3-D Classics Featuring. . . , Kitchen Sink (Princeton, WI), 1985.

Comics and Sequential Art, Poorhouse (Tamarac, FL), 1985.

Will Eisner's Hawks of the Seas, 1936-1938, edited by Dave Schreiner, Kitchen Sink (Princeton, WI), 1986.

Will Eisner's New York, the Big City, Kitchen Sink (Princeton, WI), 1986.

Will Eisner's The Dreamer, Kitchen Sink (Princeton, WI), 1986.

The Building, Kitchen Sink (Princeton, WI), 1987.

A Life Force, Kitchen Sink (Princeton, WI), 1988.

City People Notebook, Kitchen Sink (Princeton, WI), 1989.

Will Eisner's Spirit Casebook, Kitchen Sink (Princeton, WI), 1990–98.

Will Eisner Reader: Seven Graphic Stories by a Comics Master, Kitchen Sink (Princeton, WI), 1991.

To the Heart of the Storm, Kitchen Sink (Princeton, WI), 1991.

The White Whale: An Introduction to "Moby Dick," Story Shop (Tamarac, FL), 1991.

The Spirit: The Origin Years, Kitchen Sink (Princeton, WI), 1992.

Invisible People, Kitchen Sink (Northampton, MA), 1993.

The Christmas Spirit, Kitchen Sink (Northampton, MA), 1994.

Sketchbook, Kitchen Sink (Northampton, MA), 1995.

Dropsie Avenue: The Neighborhood, Kitchen Sink (Northampton, MA), 1995.

Graphic Storytelling, Poorhouse (Tamarac, FL), 1996.

(Adapter) *Moby Dick by Herman Melville,* NBM (New York, NY), 1998.

A Family Matter, Kitchen Sink (Northampton, MA), 1998.

(Reteller) *The Princess and the Frog by the Grimm Brothers,* NBM (New York, NY), 1999.

Minor Miracles: Long Ago and Once upon a Time, Back when Uncles Were Heroic, Cousins Were Clever, and Miracles Happened on Every Block, DC Comics (New York, NY), 2000.

The Last Knight: An Introduction to "Don Quixote" by Miguel de Cervantes, NBM (New York, NY), 2000.

Last Day in Vietnam: A Memory, Dark Horse (Milwaukie, OR), 2000.

Will Eisner's The Spirit Archives, DC Comics (New York, NY), 2000.

The Name of the Game, DC Comics (New York, NY), 2001.

Will Eisner's Shop Talk, Dark Horse (Milwaukie, OR), 2001.

(With Dick French, Bill Woolfolk, and others) *The Blackhawk Archives,* DC Comics (New York, NY), 2001.

Fagin the Jew, Doubleday (New York, NY), 2003.

(Adapter) *Sundiata: A Legend of Africa,* NMB (New York, NY), 2003.

For U.S. Department of Defense, creator of comic strip instructional aid, *P.S. Magazine,* 1950, and for U.S. Department of Labor, creator of career guidance series of comic booklets, *Job Scene,* 1967. Also creator of comic strips, sometimes under pseudonyms Will Erwin and Willis Rensie, including "Uncle Sam," "Muss 'em Up Donovan," "Sheena," "The Three Brothers," "Blackhawk," "K-51," and "Hawk of the Seas." Author of newspaper feature, "Odd Facts." Also contributor to *Artwork for "9-11 Emergency Relief,"* issued by Alternative Comics, 2001.

SIDELIGHTS: Cartoonist Will Eisner, the creator of many popular comic strips, was also well known as a pioneer in the educational applications of this medium. Throughout his fifty-plus-year career, he created a host of comic-book characters to guide young people in their choice of a career, to instruct military personnel, and simply to entertain children of all ages. Eisner has also produced a series of comic-book training manuals for developing nations, which teach modern farming techniques and the maintenance of military equipment. These booklets are used by the Agency for International Development, the United Nations, and the U.S. Department of Defense.

Eisner's career began in the mid-1930s, when he sold his first comic feature, "Scott Dalton," to *Wow!* magazine. He went on to create more comic strips, including "Sheena, Queen of the Jungle" and his best-known work, "The Spirit," a weekly adventure series published as an insert in Sunday papers from 1940 to 1951. This strip featured protagonist Denny Colt, a private investigator who is seriously injured, and presumed dead, after an explosion in the laboratory of evil scientist Dr. Cobra. Once Colt recovers, he vows to exploit his new anonymity to enhance his ability to bring hardened criminals to justice. The strip, renowned for its social satire, also featured the first African-American character to make ongoing appearances in an American comic feature.

In 1942, Eisner was drafted into the U.S. Army, where he was put to work designing safety posters. He also used cartoon-strip techniques to simplify the military's training manual for equipment maintenance, *Army Motors.* After his discharge in 1946, Eisner continued to write and illustrate "The Spirit," but decided to discontinue the strip in 1951. He then founded the American Visuals Corporation, a company that produced comic books for schools and businesses. In 1967, the U.S. Department of Labor asked Eisner to create a comic book that would appeal to potential school dropouts. The result was *Job Scene,* a series of booklets designed to introduce career choices to young people in the hope that they would see the need for further education. *Job Scene* proved so successful that several national publishers have issued similar series.

Eisner also developed *P.S. Magazine,* an instructional manual for the U.S. Department of Defense designed to replace the verbose, unwieldy technical manuals formerly used by military trainers. Eisner wrote in a 1974 article for *Library Journal:* "The significance of comics as a training device is perhaps not so much the use of time-honored sequential art as the language accompanying the pictures. For example, *P.S. Magazine* . . . em-

ployed the soldier's argot, rendering militarese into common language. The magazine said 'Clean away the crud from the flywheel' instead of 'All foreign matter should be removed from the surface of the flywheel and the rubber belt which it supports.'" Eisner's version reduced the original one-hundred-word section describing that procedure to a sequence of three panels which quickly and simply presented the necessary instruction.

The immediate visual impact and simple language used in *P.S. Magazine* are assets which Eisner believes make comics desirable in more traditional classroom situations. Critics, however, complain that while teachers are trying to instill a healthy respect for proper language, comic books and strips violate every rule of grammar. In his *Publishers Weekly* article, Eisner responded: "This is an understandable criticism, but it is based on the assumption that cartoons are designed primarily to teach language. *Comics are a message in themselves!* . . . To readers living in the ghetto and playing in the street and school yard, comic books, with their inventive language, argot, and slang, serve as no other literature does."

Eisner believes it is remarkable that many reading teachers are still reluctant to adapt this "inviting material." He praises those educators who have recognized the merit in his art form. Eisner concluded his *Publishers Weekly* article with a commentary on the improving status of comics in the schools: "In schools, comic strip reprints are reaching reluctant readers who are either unresponsive or hostile to traditional books. . . . Certain qualities distinctive to comic books support their educational importance. Perhaps their most singular characteristic is *timeliness.* Comics appeal to readers when they deal with 'now' situations, or treat them in a 'now' manner. Working in a high-speed transmission, the author faces instant acceptance or rejection. He or she is writing for a transient audience who are in a hurry to savor vicarious experiences. Loyalties are to the characters themselves, so the need for imaginative storytelling is great. Equally vital is the choice of terms. The reader's instant recognition of symbols and concepts challenges the ingenuity and empathy of comic-book creators."

Satisfying as his educational-and-vocational-based work had been, Eisner was drawn back to narrative forms again in the mid-1970s, after he attended a comic-book convention and was inspired by the innovative work he saw there, in particular that of underground cartoonist R. Crumb. In 1975 he began work on what he called a "graphic novel," published three years later as *A Con-*

tract with God and Other Tenement Stories. Unlike his earlier adventure comics, this work is a serious treatment of such serious themes as religious faith, sexual betrayal, and prejudice. Other graphic novels, which depicted the lives of Jewish immigrants in America, followed, including *Life on Another Planet, Big City, A Life Force,* and *Minor Miracles.* Eisner's 2001 graphic novel, *The Name of the Game,* is a multigenerational family saga about the Arnheim family, who expand their businesses from corset manufacturing to stock brokering. Though *Booklist* reviewer Gordon Flagg found the book melodramatic and predictable, the critic appreciated Eisner's "expressive" artwork and noted that the book reflects "a sensibility somehow appropriate to the period and subject."

Eisner has also used the comic-strip medium to adapt literary classics, including *Don Quixote* and *Moby Dick* as well as fairy tales by the Brothers Grimm. These projects have received mixed reviews. Susan Weitz of *School Library Journal* found Eisner's version of *Moby Dick* "simplistic" and disappointing; *Booklist* contributor Francisca Goldsmith, however, considered it highly successful in conveying the original work's plot, characterizations, and mood. Similar differences marked critical reception to *The Last Knight: An Introduction to "Don Quixote" by Miguel de Cervantes.* Marian Drabkin commented in *School Library Journal* that, in Eisner's hands, Don Quixote becomes merely a "clownish madman whose escapades are slapstick and pointless," while Cervantes depicted him as a much more complex character. *Booklist* critic Roger Leslie, on the other hand, felt that Eisner's book is "faithful to the spirit of the original" and an excellent introduction to the great classic.

In *Comics and Sequential Art,* Eisner explains the unique aspects of sequential art: imagery, frames, timing, and the relationship between written word and visual design. Ken Marantz, reviewing the book's twenty-first printing for *School Arts,* praised its clarity, creativity, and detailed descriptions, and concluded that the book is a valuable introduction to an innovative medium for creative expression.

Despite being an octogenarian, Eisner has continued to work vigorously. In *Fagin the Jew,* published in 2003, Eisner takes the famous character from Charles Dickens's *Oliver Twist* and tells his personal story, one in which Fagin comes out in a much better light. As told by Eisner, Fagin was virtually forced into crime as a youth because of circumstances, not the least of which was the general prejudice against his family as Ash-

kenazi Jews. "As written by Eisner, Fagin gains depth and humanity, and he could have found success on the right side of the law had not persecution, poverty, and bad luck hindered him," wrote Steve Raiteri in *Library Journal.* The graphic novel includes a foreword explaining the probable historical antecedents of the tale and how they related to Dickens's portrayal of Jews. While noting that Eisner's depiction of nineteenth-century London is "wholly convincing," a *Publishers Weekly* reviewer felt that "the story errs on the side of extreme coincidence and melodrama." *Library Journal* contributor Steve Weiner commented that "Eisner masterfully weaves a Dickensian story of his own focusing on racism and stereotypes." Francisca Goldsmith, writing in *School Library Journal* noted that the book would appeal to readers looking for another view of the Dickens classic but was "also for those concerned with media influence on stereotypes and the history of immigration issues."

In another 2003 publication, Eisner adapted an African story set in the thirteenth century for the graphic novel, *Sundiata: A Legend of Africa.* The story revolves around the death of the Mali peoples' leader and their subsequent conquest by a tyrant, who can control the elements. Sundiata, son of the former Mali leader, eventually leads his people in victory against their oppressor. *Booklist* contributor Carlos Orellana felt that the ending was unsatisfying but noted that "the plot flows smoothly; the telling never feels rushed; and the sequential art, which is full of movement and expression, gives the familiar good-versus-evil theme extra depth." Steve Raiteri, writing in *Library Journal,* commented that the book would interest not only children but that teens and adults as well would "appreciate Eisner's concise and clear storytelling and his dramatic artwork, distinctively colored in grays and earth tones."

BIOGRAPHICAL AND CRITICAL SOURCES:

PERIODICALS

Booklist, August, 1998, Gordon Flagg, review of *A Family Matter,* p. 1948; December 15, 1999, Stephanie Zvirin, review of *The Princess and the Frog by the Grimm Brothers,* p. 780; June 1, 2000, Roger Leslie, review of *The Last Knight: An Introduction to "Don Quixote" by Miguel de Cervantes,* p. 1884; August, 2000, Gordon Flagg, review of *The Spirit Archives,* p. 2094; September 15, 2000, Gordon Flagg, review of *Minor Miracles,* p. 200; November 15, 2001, Francisca Goldsmith, review of *Moby Dick by Herman Melville,* p. 568, and "Sequential Art Meets the White Whale," p. 569; February 1, 2002, Gordon Flagg, review of *The Name of the Game,* p. 914; February 1, 2003, Carlos Orellana, review of *Sundiata: A Legend of Africa,* p. 984; September 1, 2003, Gordon Flagg, review of *Fagin the Jew,* p. 76.

College English, February, 1995, George Dardess, review of *Comics and Sequential Art,* p. 213.

Library Journal, October 15, 1974, Will Eisner, "Comic Books in the Library"; June 1, 1991, Keith R.A. DeCandido, review of *To the Heart of the Storm,* p. 134; October 15, 1974; September 15, 2000, Stephen Weiner, review of *Minor Miracles,* p. 66; March 1, 2003, Steve Raiteri, review of *Sundiata: A Legend of Africa,* p. 74; November 1, 2003, Steve Raiteri, review of *Fagin the Jew,* p. 60.

New York Review of Books, June 21, 2001, David Hajdu, "The Spirit of the Spirit," p. 48.

Philadelphia Magazine, August, 1984, Jack Curtin, "Signals from Space," p. 70.

Publishers Weekly, October 4, 1985, review of *Comics and Sequential Art,* p. 75; March 25, 1988, review of *A Life Force,* p. 61; March 22, 1991, review of *To the Heart of the Storm,* p. 76; June 21, 1991, review of *Will Eisner Reader: Seven Graphic Stories by a Comics Master,* p. 58; May 8, 1995, review of *Dropsie Avenue: The Neighborhood,* p. 293; January 3, 2000, review of *The Princess and the Frog,* p. 78; November 17, 2003, review of *Fagin the Jew,* p. 46.

School Arts, April, 2002, Ken Marantz, review of *Comics and Sequential Art,* p. 58.

School Library Journal, July, 2000, Marian Drabkin, review of *The Last Knight,* p. 115; January, 2002, Susan Weitz, review of *Moby Dick by Herman Melville,* p. 138; February, 2003, John Peters, review of *Sundiata,* p. 129; January, 2004, Francisca Goldsmith, review of *Fagin the Jew,* p. 166.

Variety, September 28, 1988, "Comic Book Confidential," p. 30.

Whole Earth, spring, 1998, review of *The Spirit,* p. 25.

ONLINE

Will Eisner Web site, http://willeisner.tripod.com/ (July 22, 2002).

OBITUARIES:

PERIODICALS

Economist, January 13, 2005.
New York Times, January 5, 2005.

EISNER, William Erwin
See EISNER, Will

*   *   *

ELIOT, Dan
See SILVERBERG, Robert

*   *   *

ELKIN, Stanley L. 1930-1995
(Stanley Lawrence Elkin)

PERSONAL: Born May 11, 1930, in New York, NY; died May 31, 1995, of heart failure in St. Louis, MO; son of Phil (a salesman) and Zelda (Feldman) Elkin; married Joan Marion Jacobson, February 1, 1953; children: Philip Aaron, Bernard Edward, Molly Ann. *Education:* University of Illinois, A.B., 1952, M.A., 1953, Ph.D., 1961. *Religion:* Jewish.

CAREER: Washington University, St. Louis, Mo., instructor, 1960-62, assistant professor, 1962-66, associate professor, 1966-69, professor of English, 1969-95. Visiting professor at Smith College, 1964-65, University of California, Santa Barbara, 1967, University of Wisconsin—Milwaukee, 1969, University of Iowa, 1974, Yale University, 1975, and Boston University, 1976. *Military service:* U.S. Army, 1955-57.

MEMBER: Modern Language Association of America, American Academy and Institute of Arts and Letters.

AWARDS, HONORS: Longview Foundation award, 1962; *Paris Review* humor prize, 1965; Guggenheim fellow, 1966-67; Rockefeller Foundation grant, 1968-69; National Endowment for the Arts and Humanities grant, 1972; American Academy of Arts and Letters award, 1974; Richard and Hinda Rosenthal Award, 1980; *Sewanee Review* prize, 1981, for *Stanley Elkin's Greatest Hits;* National Book Critics Circle Award, 1982, for *George Mills;* Brandeis University, creative arts award, 1986; New York University, Elmer Holmes Bobst award, 1991; National Book Critics Circle Award for Fiction, 1995, for *Mrs. Ted Bliss;* honorary degrees: L.H.D., University of Illinois, 1986, D.Litt., Bowling Green State University, 1992.

WRITINGS:

Boswell: A Modern Comedy (novel), Random House (New York, NY), 1964, reprinted, Dalkey Archive Press (Normal, IL), 1999.

Criers and Kibitzers, Kibitzers and Criers (stories), Random House (New York, NY), 1966, reprinted, Dalkey Archive Press (Normal, IL), 2000.

A Bad Man (novel), Random House (New York, NY), 1967, reprinted, with an introduction by David C. Dougherty, Dalkey Archive Press (Normal, IL), 2003.

The Dick Gibson Show (novel), Random House (New York, NY), 1971, reprinted, Dalkey Archive Press (Normal, IL), 1998.

The Making of Ashenden (novella; also see below), Covent Garden Press (London, England), 1972.

Searches and Seizures (contains *The Bailbondsman, The Making of Ashenden,* and *The Condominium*), Random House (New York, NY), 1973 (published in England as *Eligible Men: Three Short Novels,* Gollancz, 1974), published as *Alex and the Gypsy: Three Short Novels,* Penguin (New York, NY), 1977.

The Franchiser (novel), Farrar, Straus (New York, NY), 1976, reprinted, with a foreword by William H. Gass, Dalkey Archive Press (Normal, IL), 2001.

The Living End (contains three contiguous novellas, *The Conventional Wisdom, The Bottom Line,* and *The State of the Art,* which first appeared, in slightly different form, respectively in *American Review, Antaeus,* and *TriQuarterly*), Dutton (New York, NY), 1979, reprinted, with an afterword by Curtis White, Dalkey Archive Press (Normal, IL), 2004.

Stanley Elkin's Greatest Hits, foreword by Robert Coover, Dutton (New York, NY), 1980.

(Editor with Shannon Ravenel and author of introduction) *The Best American Short Stories, 1980,* Houghton (Boston, MA), 1980.

The First George Mills (novel), Pressworks (Dallas, TX), 1981, reprinted, with an introduction by Chris Lehmann, Dalkey Archive Press (Normal, IL), 2003.

George Mills, Dutton (New York, NY), 1982.

The Magic Kingdom, Dutton (New York, NY), 1985, reprinted, with an introduction by Rick Moody, Dalkey Archive Press (Normal, IL), 2000.

Early Elkin, Bamberger Books (Flint, MI), 1985.

The Rabbi of Lud, Scribner (New York, NY), 1987.

The Six-Year Old Man, Bamberger Books (Flint, MI), 1987.

The Coffee Room (radio play), KWMU-FM in St. Louis, 1988.

The MacGuffin: A Novel, Viking Penguin (New York, NY), 1991.

Pieces of Soap, Simon and Schuster (New York, NY), 1992.

Van Gogh's Room at Arles: Three Novellas, Viking Penguin (New York, NY), 1992.

Mrs. Ted Bliss, Hyperion (New York, NY), 1995.

Also author of film scenario "The Six-Year-Old Man," published in *Esquire,* December, 1968. Stories appeared in *The Best American Short Stories,* Houghton, 1962, 1963, 1965, and 1978. Contributor to *Epoch, Views, Accent, Esquire, American Review, Antaeus, TriQuarterly, Perspective, Chicago Review, Journal of English and Germanic Philology, Southwest Review, Paris Review, Harper's, Oui,* and *Saturday Evening Post.*

ADAPTATIONS: "The Bailbondsman" was filmed as "Alex and the Gypsy." The film rights to *Boswell* and *A Bad Man* have been purchased.

SIDELIGHTS: "'What happens next?' is a question one doesn't usually ask in Stanley L. Elkin's [works]," wrote Christopher Lehmann-Haupt of the *New York Times.* "Plot is not really Mr. Elkin's game. His fiction runs on language, on parody, on comic fantasies and routines. Give him conventional wisdom and he will twist it into tomfoolery. . . . Give [him] cliché and jargon and he will fashion of it a kind of poetry." Long recognized and praised for his extraordinary linguistic vitality and comic inventiveness, Elkin, though he dislikes these terms, has been described as a "stand-up literary comedian" and a "black humorist" who invites us to laugh at the painful absurdities, frustrations, and disappointments of life. His books "aren't precisely satires," according to Bruce Allen in the *Chicago Tribune Book World,* but rather are "unillusioned yet affectionate commemorations of rascally energy and ingenuity." Ironically, in the view of some critics, Elkin's strength has often been his weakness as well, for he is sometimes criticized for carrying his high-energy rhetoric and comic monologues to extremes. Nonetheless, Josh Greenfeld, who considered Elkin "at once a bright satirist, a bleak absurdist, and a deadly moralist," declared in the *New York Times Book Review,* "I know of no serious funny writer in this country who can match him."

Searches and Seizures, a collection of three novellas, "should provide the uninitiated with an ideal introduction to [Elkin's] art even as it confirms addicts like me in our belief that no American novelist tells us more about where we are and what we're doing to ourselves," claimed Thomas R. Edwards in the *New York Times Book Review.* "This is an art that takes time—his scenes are comic turns that build cunningly toward climax in deflative bathos, and in the novels there's an inclination toward the episodic, the compulsive storyteller's looseness about connections and logic. [The first novella,] 'The Bailbondsman,' . . . is just about perfectly scaled to Elkin's imagination; we have a tight focus, one day in the life of an aging Cincinnati bondsman of Phoenician descent, which nevertheless accommodates an astonishing thickness of texture, a weaving of events and psychic motifs that is as disturbing as it is funny."

The other two stories in *Searches and Seizures* are *"The Making of Ashenden"* and *"The Condominium."* The former is, in the words of Clancy Sigal in the *New Republic,* "a fantasy satirizing Brewster Ashenden, an idle wastrel in love with Jane Loes Lipton, a kind of Baby Jane Holzer with a Schweitzerian yen to do good. The 'shocking' climax, within the dream landscape of a rich Englishman's private zoo, has Brewster interminably screwing a bear." The man-bear sex scene "is vigorous, raunchy, painful, smelly—and downright *touching,*" exclaimed Bruce Allen in the *Hudson Review,* and it forces Brewster, humbly and hilariously, to admit his animal nature.

"The Condominium" is a tale about a graduate student who inherits his father's Chicago condominium and "then gets fatally drawn into the numbing quality of its community life," noted Christopher Lehmann-Haupt in the *New York Times.* Though the pieces of these stories seem to be always "flying apart," Lehmann-Haupt concluded: "In some subtle way that defies all equations—metaphorical, symbolical, allegorical, or otherwise—everything connects with everything else. And tells us in a way that lies just beyond explanation, in crazy poetic searches and seizures, much about loneliness, sex, and mortality."

According to Michael Wood in the *New York Review of Books,* "the real subject of the three short novels contained in *Searches and Seizures* is a complicated invention of character by means of snowballing language. The writer invents characters who invent themselves as they talk and thereby invent him, the writer." The protagonist of *"The Bailbondsman,"* for example, introduces himself as "Alexander Main the Bailbondsman. I go surety. . . . My conditions classic and my terms terminal. Listen, I haven't much law—though what I have is on my side, binding as clay, advantage to the house—but am as at home in replevin, debenture, and gage as someone on his own toilet seat with the door closed and the house empty." "The motive force of Elkin's writing," said William Plummer in the *New Republic,* "is 'the conventional wisdom' itself. His aggressive, high energy rhetoric comes into being under the pressure of cliche, which is not to suggest that his *métier* is either satire or camp. Rather, he seems to share with Emerson the vaguely platonic idea that the hackneyed is 'fossile poetry'—the Truth in tatters, in its fallen condition."

Thomas R. Edwards in *New York Times Book Review* claimed the first story "shows that an art founded on aggression, on assaults against the reader's habits of association and sense of good manners, can be both wrenchingly funny and oddly moving." Plummer called *"The Bailbondsman"* "one of the great works in the language—right up there, perhaps, with [Faulkner's] 'The Bear' and [Melville's] 'Bartleby.'" He added, however, one qualification: "But you must grant Elkin his premises. He has no interest in 'the arduous, numbing connections' in plot or even structure. He's not anti-story, . . . but rather has an insatiable 'sweet tooth' for instance," which he treats with "gags, interpolated tales, catalogues and assorted pieces. Like *Tristram Shandy,* he believes in progress by digression."

But Clancy Sigal, also writing in the *New Republic,* did not grant Elkin's premises, noting, "Elkin's monologues, at which he excels, are the alienated patter of a brilliant, but turned off, stand-up literary comic. I'm very suspicious of it in large doses." Moreover, L.J. Davis charged in the *Washington Post Book World* that Elkin's focus on language weakens the characterization. "Elkin's characters," declared Davis, "are artifacts, superbly sculptured statuary adorned with rich garlands of prose. Sedentary, separate from us, their gestures frozen, they are meant to be observed but not experienced, admired but not touched. The strength of the writing imbues them with a kind of static life, but it does not bestow upon them either an autonomous vitality or a poignant humanity. They exist to prove a point." Davis concluded, "In a way, the prose itself becomes a hero."

Far from seeing Elkin's characters as passive instruments, however, Jonathan Raban argued in *Encounter* that the heroes in *Searches and Seizures* are tragic, in the classical sense: "They build up glittering verbal palaces around themselves, in cascading rhetorical monologues, in dreams, in deep wordy caverns of introspection. Their worlds are perfected right down to the final bauble on the last minaret. Then the crunch comes. They discover that no one else is living there but them. The brilliant talker is the proprietor and sole inhabitant of his universe, and he might as well be adrift in outer space. His fatal proficiency in language has taken him clean out of the world of other people. This is the central theme."

The Dick Gibson Show, Elkin's third novel, "contains enough comic material for a dozen nightclub acts," noted R.Z. Sheppard in *Time,* "yet it is considerably more than an entertainment." Joseph McElroy claimed in the *New York Times Book Review* that this "absolutely American compendium . . . may turn out to be our classic about radio." The hero of the book is a disc jockey who has worked for dozens of small-town radio stations across the country. "As the perpetual apprentice, whetting his skills and adopting names and accents to suit geography," said Sheppard, "he evolves into part of American folklore. As Dick Gibson, the paradox of his truest identity is that he is from Nowhere, U.S.A."

A radio talk-show host, Gibson is the principal listener for a bizarre cast of callers: Norman, the "caveman from Africa," whose linguistic equivalent for "chief" is "Aluminum Siding Salesman"; a rich orphaned boy—his skydiving parents accidentally parachuted into a zoo's tiger den—who has fears of being adopted for his money; a woman who wants to trade a bow and arrow, and in exchange will accept nothing but used puppets. Sheppard surmised that Gibson is "a McLuhan obfuscation made flesh—a benevolent witch doctor in an electronic village of the lonely, the sick, and the screwed up." In the *New York Times Book Review* McElroy argued that Elkin "unites manic narrative and satiric wit to ensure that we know Dick Gibson [as] . . . receiver of an America whose invisibility speaks live into the great gap of doubt inside him, itinerant listener in this big-hearted country where it's so hard to get anyone to listen."

Christopher Lehmann-Haupt of the *New York Times,* however, believed that while it could be argued that Dick Gibson is "the sound of American silence, . . . this is forcing things somewhat. . . . The bitter-sweet and seriocomic truth is that Stanley Elkin is [merely] stringing routines together. . . . Which is not to say that I didn't love . . . passages like 'the wide laps beneath her nurse's white uniform with its bas-relief of girdle and garter like landmarks under a light snow.' Or that I didn't sink to my knees from laughing time and again. It's just that after a while one gets tired, can predict the patterns, begins to look for more than gags, and can't really find much."

Geoffrey Wolf of *Newsweek* found that the novel's loose structure is patterned after that of radio itself. Acknowledging that the book "flies straight in the teeth of fiction's decorums," Wolff concludes that Elkin "insists on his freedom, radio's freedom to wander, and seems to accept radio's risk, the risk that the audience's attention will wander." McElroy, also noted that Elkin's digressions enhance the thematic concerns of the novel and commented, "Far from seeming prolix, Mr. Elkin's expansiveness—notably in the lunatic monologues of one horrendous talk-show night fourteen years after [World War II]—proves a rich and anxious means of further surrounding his theme."

John Leonard, writing in *Saturday Review,* considered *The Franchiser* to be the closest of Elkin's novels to *The Dick Gibson Show;* he also deemed it Elkin's best. "It is a brilliant conceit—the franchising of America on the prime interest rate; manifest destiny on credit," stated Leonard. "It is also considerably more than a conceit. It is a frenzied parable, rather as though the Wandering Jew and Willy Loman had gotten together on a vaudeville act. Who, after all, is displaced by the franchise? Ben Flesh, [the protagonist,] knows: 'Kiss off the neighborhood grocers and corner druggists and little shoemakers.' Kiss off, in other words, ethnicity, roots. Assimilate. Homogenize."

Some critics, however, fault the book for its digressiveness—a common flaw in Elkin's novels according to Robert Towers and John Irving. Towers said in the *New York Times Book Review:* "While he can invent wonderful scenes full of madness and power, Elkin seems unable to create a sustaining comic action or plot that could energize the book as a whole and carry the reader past those sections where invention flags or becomes strained. Without the onward momentum of plot . . . we are left with bits, pieces and even large chunks that tend to cancel each other out and turn the book into a kind of morass." Towers went on to note, "The need is especially felt in a book as long as *The Franchiser.*" Novelist John Irving, also writing in the *New York Times Book Review,* declared that the "rap against Elkin is that he's too funny, and too fancy with his prose, for his own good. . . . It is brilliant comedy, but occasionally stagnant: the narrative flow is interrupted by Elkin's forays into some of the best prose-writing in English today; it is extraordinary writing, but it smacks at times of showing off—and it is digressive. Despite the shimmering language, the effect is one of density; I know too many readers who say they admire Stanley Elkin as a writer, but they haven't finished a single Elkin novel." Other reviewers praised Elkin's stylistic pyrotechnics in *The Dick Gibson Show.* Michael Wood of the *New York Review of Books,* for example, wrote that jokes and "gags for Elkin seem to represent some sort of hold on randomness, serve both to clarify and to stave off the dizzying sense that nothing has to happen the way it does, and they afford Elkin and his heroes a recurring, cheerfully defeated stance."

The Living End is, in the opinion of many critics, Elkin's best work. John Irving in the *New York Times Book Review,* for example, called it a "narrative marvel [with] a plot and such a fast pace that a veteran Elkin reader may wonder about the places where he lost interest, or lost his way, in reading Elkin before." The book consists of three contiguous novellas, *"The Conven-*

tional Wisdom," "The Bottom Line," and "The State of the Art," which provide the kind of conventional, "beginning-middle-end," structure often lacking in Elkin's other novels. The titles of the novellas also reflect Elkin's characteristic attention to cliche, according to Harold Robbins in the *Washington Post Book World*. Robbins pointed out that Elkin "knows that clichés are the substance of our lives, the coinage of human intercourse, the ways and means that hold our messy selves and sprawling nation intact. To exploit their vigor and set them forth with unexpected force has been the basis of his success as a novelist; no writer has maneuvered life's shoddy stock-in-trade into more brilliantly funny forms."

In addition to the strenuous language and the book's structural balance, "in *The Living End* Elkin has finally found a subject worthy of him," wrote Geoffrey Stokes in the *Village Voice.* "No more does he diddle with the surrogates, no more leave us wiping the laughter from our eyes and wondering if we really care quite all that much about One-Hour Martinizing. This time, Elkin goes directly for the big one: God, He Who, etc." Writing in *Time,* R.Z. Sheppard commented that with *The Living End* "Elkin must finally be recognized as the grownup's Kurt Vonnegut, the Woody Allen for those who prefer their love, death, and cosmic quarrels with true bite and sting."

With a vision that is sometimes blasphemous, the book begins with Ellerbee, a Minneapolis liquor-store owner and "the nicest of guys," noted Sheppard, who goes to Heaven after being gunned down behind the counter during a robbery. His surprise at Heaven's unsurprising sights, sounds, and smells—pearly gates, angels with harps, ambrosia, manna, and a choir that sings "Oh dem golden slippers"—however, turns to shock when St. Peter tells him, "beatifically," to go to Hell. The "ultimate ghetto," Hell also gives Ellerbee a sense of *deja vu,* with the devils' horns and pitchforks, and the sinners raping and mugging each other endlessly and pointlessly; moreover, there is cancer, angina, indigestion, headache, toothache, earache, and a painful, third-degree burning itch everywhere. "What Ellerbee discovers," declared Irving, "is that everything [about the afterlife] is true. . . . It's like life itself, of course, but so keenly exaggerated that Elkin manages to make the pain more painful, and the comedy more comic."

After several years God visits Hell, and Ellerbee asks why he, a good man, has been condemned. A mean-spirited and petty God charges him with selling the demon rum, keeping his store open on the Sabbath, utter-

ing an occasional oath, having impure thoughts, and failing to honor his parents, even though he was orphaned as an infant. Sheppard noted that Ellerbee "ignored what Elkin labels 'the conventional wisdom.' The corollary: in a cosmos ruled by an unforgiving stickler, 'one can never have too much virtue.'"

Jeffrey Burke pointed out in *Harper's* that Elkin "founds his irreverence on the truths of contemporary religion, that is, on the myriad inconsistencies, cliches, superstitions, and insanities derived from centuries of creative theology," but claimed that Elkin's purpose lies beyond satire. Harold Robbins explained: "Unlike others of his generation . . . Elkin does not identify with the laughter of the gods, he does not dissociate himself from the human spectacle by taking out a franchise on the cosmic joke. Hard and unyielding as his comic vision becomes, Elkin's laughter is remission and reprieve, a gesture of willingness to join the human mess, to side with the damned, to laugh in momentary grace at whatever makes life Hell."

The remainder of the story leads up to the Day of Judgment, when God appears before the Heavenly Host to reveal that the purpose of creation was theatrical, though He never found His audience: "'Goodness? Is that what you think? . . . Were you born yesterday? You've been in the world. Is that how you explain trial and error, history by increment, God's long Slap and Tickle, His Indian-gift wrath? *Goodness?* No. It was Art! It was always Art. I work by the contrasts and metrics, by beats and the silences. It was all Art. *Because it makes a better story is why.*'" "Precisely because it's God talking," surmised Geoffrey Stokes, "the question of why He does what He does is genuinely important—especially when it turns out that Elkin is ultimately addressing the obligations of all creators. And suddenly—when the eternally-disfigured Christ learns that his suffering occurred solely because God thought it would make a better story—the laughter stops, and the very funny, very serious Elkin goes deeper than he's ever gone before. *The Living End* makes it at once possible to forgive God, and unnecessary to forgive Stanley Elkin."

In his novel *The MacGuffin,* Elkin recounts the story of Bobbo Druff, a small-time city commissioner with failing health, a wife who is going deaf, and a grown-up son who still lives at home. Seeing his life slipping away from him, Druff creates a paranoid conspiracy theory that involves his ultimate demise and may include everyone he knows. The title of the novel comes from the term movie director Alfred Hitchcock used to denote anything that, as Paul Gray noted in *Time*, "gives spurious meaning to a plot." As explained by Thomas R. Edwards in the *New Republic*, the title reflects Druff's tendency to impute "some sinister coherence to the contingencies of ordinary experience." Edwards called the novel "splendid" and commented that the "conflict between randomness and purpose has always been a large theme in Elkin's fiction." Edwards also noted that "the climax of *The MacGuffin* is one of the most knowing and affecting treatments of the parent-child relationship that I can recall."

Van Gogh's Room at Arles: Three Novellas was published in 1992 and tells the story of "three more victims in a difficult world," as noted by Marvin J. LaHood in *World Literature Today*. In the first novella, "Her Sense of Timing," a university professor who is an invalid is abandoned by his wife and must turn for help to a corporation that cares for the elderly and disabled. In "Tom Crier Exclusive, Confessions of a Princess Manqua," the narrator recounts her missed chance to become the Queen of England. The final novella, "Van Gogh's Room at Arles," focuses on another college professor who wins a grant to go to Arles to study how prestigious academics from colleges view community colleges. LaHood noted that this novella was the best of the three in its portrayal of how a "mean-spirited" man is transformed. LaHood went on to note, "Stanley Elkin has portrayed an epiphany as moving as any in literature." Louisa Ermelino, writing in *People*, praised the novellas, commenting, "The three novellas of his 16th book treat us again to his cornucopian delight in language." Ermelino also noted, "In these tales everyone is caught on the flypaper of situations that are tragic, absurd and hilarious."

Elkins's final novel, 1995's *Mrs. Ted Bliss*, won the National Book Critics Circle Award for Fiction. It tells the tale of an elderly Russian-born Jewish widow who lives in a condominium overlooking Biscayne Bay. Although not self-reflective and easily pleased by the mundane things of life, the disinterested Mrs. Bliss finds herself encountering a number of intrigues involving profiteers, drug dealers, and a general unraveling of her and her condo neighbors' secure lives. James P. Degnan, writing in *America*, found the novel disappointing and "vitiated by authorial intrusion." A *Publishers Weekly* contributor commented that "it is the trenchant quips about the way of all flesh, and memory, that will give Dorothy Bliss a life after death." Arthur M. Saltzman, writing in the *Review of Contemporary Fiction* noted that *Mrs. Ted Bliss* is "a quieter volume" than many of the author's other works. Saltzman concluded that the novel "is a fitting conclusion to Elkin's career of refuting human foibles and the failings of the flesh with the most vital, surprising, passionate style around."

BIOGRAPHICAL AND CRITICAL SOURCES:

BOOKS

Bailey, Peter Joseph, *Reading Stanley Elkin*, University of Illinois Press (Urbana, IL) 1985.

Bargen, Doris G. *The Fiction of Stanley Elkin*, Lang (Cirencester, United Kingdom), 1980.

Charney, Maurice, *Jewish Wry: Essays on Jewish Humor*, Indiana University Press (Bloomington, IN), 1987.

Contemporary Literary Criticism, Thomson Gale (Detroit, MI), Volume 4, 1975, Volume 6, 1976, Volume 9, 1978, Volume 14, 1980, Volume 27, 1984, Volume 51, 1989.

Dictionary of Literary Biography, Thomson Gale (Detroit, MI), Volume II: *American Novelists since World War II*, 1978; *Yearbook: 1980*, 1981.

Dougherty, David C., *Stanley Elkin*, Twayne (Boston, MA), 1990.

Elkin, Stanley, *Searches and Seizures* (contains *The Bailbondsman, The Making of Ashenden*, and *The Condominium*), Random House (New York, NY), 1973.

Elkin, Stanley, *The Living End* (contains *The Conventional Wisdom, The Bottom Line*, and *The State of the Art*), Dutton (New York, NY), 1979.

Elkin, Stanley, *The Dick Gibson Show* (novel), Random House (New York, NY), 1971.

Guttman, Allan, *The Jewish Writer in America: Assimilation and the Crisis of Identity*, Oxford University Press (New York, NY), 1971, pp. 79-86.

Lebowitz, Naomi, *Humanism and the Absurd in the Modern Novel*, Northwestern University Press (Evanston, IL), 1971, pp. 126-29.

Olderman, Raymond M., *Beyond the Waste Land: A Study of the American Novel in the 1960s*, Yale University Press (New Haven, CT), 1972, pp. 53-73, 175-81.

Pughe, Thomas, *Comic Sense: Reading Robert Coover, Stanley Elkin, and Philip Roth*, Birkhauser Verlag (Boston, MA), 1994.

Short Story Criticism, Thomson Gale (Detroit, MI), Volume 12, 1993.

Tanner, Tony, *City of Words*, J. Cape, 1971.

PERIODICALS

America, December 12, 1992; April 27, 1996, James P. Degnan, *Mrs. Ted Bliss*, p. 27.

Booklist, December 15, 1992; February 1, 1992.

Books and Bookmen, May, 1968.

Book Week, June 21, 1964.

Chicago, June, 1987; January, 1988; March, 1991; February, 1992.

Chicago Tribune Book World, July 8, 1979.

Choice, October, 1966.

Christian Science Monitor, May 12, 1966.

Commonweal, December 8, 1967.

Contemporary Literature, Spring, 1975, pp. 131-62.

Critique, Volume XXI, Number 2, 1979.

Delta, February, 1985.

Encounter, February, 1975.

Esquire, November, 1980.

Fiction International Spring/Fall, 1974, pp. 140-44.

Harper's, July, 1979; November, 1982; May, 1988; January, 1993.

Hollins Critic, June, 1982.

Hudson Review, Spring, 1974.

Iowa Review, Winter, 1976, pp. 127-39.

Library Journal, January 15, 1966; October 15, 1987; February 1, 1991; January, 1993.

Life, October 27, 1967.

Listener, March 28, 1968.

Los Angeles Times Book Review, July 15, 1979.

Massachusetts Review, Summer, 1966, pp. 597-600.

Nation, November 27, 1967; August 28, 1976; June 1, 1985.

New Leader, December 4, 1967.

New Republic, November 24, 1973; March 23, 1974; June 12, 1976; June 23, 1979; June, 1980; May 20, 1991, Thomas R. Edwards, review of *The MacGuffin,* p. 44.

Newsweek, April 19, 1971; June 18, 1979.

New York, June 18, 1979; October 12, 1987; February 25, 1991; March 8, 1993.

New Yorker, February 24, 1968; April 19, 1993.

New York Review of Books, February 3, 1966; January 18, 1967; March 21, 1974; August 5, 1976; August 16, 1979.

New York Times, February 17, 1971; October 9, 1973; May 21, 1976; May 25, 1979.

New York Times Book Review, July 12, 1964; January 23, 1966; October 15, 1967, p. 40; February 21, 1971; October 21, 1973; June 13, 1976; June 10, 1979; March 24, 1985; November 8, 1987; March 10, 1991; March 21, 1993; September 17, 1995, p. 7.

New York Times Magazine, March 3, 1991.

Paris Review, Summer, 1976.

People, March 29, 1993, Louisa Ermelino, review of *Van Gogh's Room at Arles,* p. 26.

Present Tense, January-February, 1989.

Publishers Weekly, October 22, 1973; September 11, 1987; January 18, 1991, Sybil Steinberg, *The MacGuffin,* p. 46; December 13, 1991; December 14, 1992; May 29, 1995, review of *Mrs. Ted Bliss,* p. 64.

Punch, March 27, 1968; January 1, 1969.

Review of Contemporary Fiction, spring, 1996, Arthur M. Saltzman, *Mrs. Ted Bliss,* p. 145.

Rocky Mountain Review of Language and Literature, Volume 32, 1978.

Saturday Review, August 15, 1964; January 15, 1966; November 18, 1967; May 29, 1976.

Studies in American Jewish Literature, Volume 2, 1982, pp. 132-43.

Studies in Short Fiction, Fall, 1974.

Time, October 27, 1967; March 1, 1971; October 29, 1973; May 24, 1976; June 4, 1979; November 10, 1980; March 25, 1991, Paul Gray, *The MacGuffin,* p. 70.

Times Literary Supplement, October 22, 1964; August 27, 1971; January 18, 1980.

TriQuarterly, Spring, 1975.

Village Voice, August 20, 1979.

Washington Post Book World, October 22, 1967; October 29, 1967; March 7, 1971; October 28, 1973; June 13, 1976; January 7, 1979; July 1, 1979.

World Literature Today, autumn, 1994, Marvin J. La-Hood, review of *Van Gogh's Room at Arles,* p. 811.

Yale Review, July, 1993.

OBITUARIES:

PERIODICALS

Chicago Tribune, June 1, 1995, section 2, p. 6.

Time, June 12, 1995, p. 21.

*   *   *

ELKIN, Stanley Lawrence
   See ELKIN, Stanley L.

*   *   *

ELLIOTT, Don
   See SILVERBERG, Robert

*   *   *

ELLIOTT, William
   See BRADBURY, Ray

ELLIS, Alice Thomas 1932-
[A pseudonym]
(Anna Haycraft, Anna Margaret Haycraft, Brenda O'Casey)

PERSONAL: Born Anna Margaret Lindholm, September 9, 1932, in Liverpool, England; married Colin Haycraft (a publisher), 1956 (died, 1994); children: five sons, two daughters (one son and one daughter deceased). *Religion:* Roman Catholic.

ADDRESSES: Home—Wales. *Office*—c/o Author Mail, Duckworth & Co. Ltd., The Old Piano Factory, 43 Gloucester Crescent, London NW1 7DY, England.

CAREER: Writer. Duckworth & Co. (publishers), London, England, fiction editor.

MEMBER: Royal Society of Literature (fellow, 1989.

AWARDS, HONORS: Arts Council of Wales Literature Award, 1977 for *The Sin Eater;* Booker-McConnell Prize shortlist, 1982, for *The Twenty-seventh Kingdom,* and 1986, for *Unexplained Laughter;* Writers' Guild Award for best fiction, 1990, for *The Inn at the Edge of the World.*

WRITINGS:

(Under pseudonym Brenda O' Casey) *Natural Baby Food: A Cookery Book,* Duckworth (London, England), 1977, published under name Anna Haycraft, Fontana (London, England), 1985.
(With Caroline Blackwood) *Darling, You Shouldn't Have Gone to So Much Trouble* (cookbook), J. Cape (London, England), 1980.
(Editor) Mary Keene, *Mrs. Donald/Mary Keene,* Hogarth Press (Oxford, England), 1983.
Home Life (essays), Duckworth (London, England), 1986.
(With Tom Pitt-Aikens) *Secrets of Strangers* (nonfiction), Duckworth (London, England), 1986.
More Home Life, Duckworth (London, England), 1987.
Home Life Three, illustrations by Ze, Duckworth (London, England), 1988.
(With Tom Pitt-Aikens) *Loss of the Good Authority: The Cause of Delinquency,* Viking (London, England), 1989.
Home Life Four, Duckworth (London, England), 1989.

(Editor) *Wales: An Anthology,* illustrations by Kyffin Williams, Collins (London, England), 1989.
A Welsh Childhood, photographs by Patrick Sutherland, M. Joseph (London, England), 1990.
Cat among the Pigeons: A Catholic Miscellany, Flamingo (London, England), 1994.
The Evening of Adam, Viking (Harmondsworth, Middlesex, England), 1994.
Serpent on the Rock: A Personal View of Christianity, Hodder & Stoughton (London, England), 1994.
(Editor) *Valentine's Day,* Duck Editions (London, England), 2000.

NOVELS

The Sin Eater, Duckworth (London, England), 1977.
The Birds of the Air, Duckworth (London, England), 1980, Viking (New York, NY), 1981.
The Twenty-seventh Kingdom, Duckworth (London, England), 1982, Moyer Bell (Wakefield, RI), 1999.
The Other Side of the Fire, Duckworth (London, England), 1983, Viking (New York, NY), 1984.
Unexplained Laughter, Duckworth (London, England), 1985.
The Clothes in the Wardrobe (also see below), Duckworth (London, England), 1987.
The Skeleton in the Cupboard (also see below), Duckworth (London, England), 1988.
The Fly in the Ointment (also see below), Duckworth (London, England), 1989.
The Inn at the Edge of the World, Viking (London, England), 1990, Trafalgar Square (New York, NY), 2001.
Pillars of Gold, Viking (London, England), 1992.
The Summer House: A Trilogy (contains *The Clothes in the Wardrobe, The Skeleton in the Cupboard,* and *The Fly in the Ointment*), Penguin Books (London, England), 1994.
Fairy Tale, Viking (London, England), 1996, Moyer Bell (Wakefield, RI), 1998.
A Gallimaufry of Books and Cooks, Duckworth (London, England), 2004.

OTHER

Columnist for *Spectator, Universe,* 1989-91, *Catholic Herald,* 1990-96, and *Oldie,* 1996—.

ADAPTATIONS: The Clothes in the Wardrobe was filmed as *The Summer House,* 1992.

SIDELIGHTS: "Literary history is full of cliques, those intense and gossip-riven clubs of like-minded souls whose personal interrelations reflected the solidarity of their works," observed John Walsh in *Books and Bookmen.* According to Walsh, Alice Thomas Ellis, fiction editor for Britain's Duckworth publishing house, was at the center of just such a group in the 1980s. Dubbed the Duckworth Gang, and comprised of Ellis and novelists Beryl Bainbridge, Caroline Blackwood, and Patrice Chaplin, the group evolved a distinctive, immediately recognizable style, reported Walsh, which reviewers refer to as "the Duckworth style." Works in the Duckworth mode—usually novels of about 150 pages—are generally written by women and feature women; they are set in the United Kingdom during modern times, with plots focusing on the domestic and marital strife of a main character, sometimes leading to physical violence; and style is important, while traditional expository techniques are de-emphasized. The books also, in Walsh's words, "guarantee devilish entertainment."

Ellis has written what Walsh considers classics in the genre. Her novels have earned the author acclaim as "brilliant" and "clever," with praise for her books extending from appreciation of her elegant prose style to admiration for her ability to create eccentric characters. In the estimation of Harriet Waugh, reviewing for *Spectator,* Ellis writes "short, edgy comedies of human failure in the face of some ultimate good. . . . [She] maneuvers to pit the world against the spirit and then stands back to see which will win. Her stories are domestic in nature, her protagonists often women taking an understandable interest in the oddities they inadvertently manage to collect around themselves. She writes intelligent novels . . . and she writes with clarity and wit."

The Sin Eater, Ellis's first novel, is set in Wales and concerns the interaction within a family—also surnamed Ellis—as the impending death of the father draws family members home. More important than plot in this work is the atmosphere, the sense of impending doom evoked through Ellis's interweaving of a biting wit with vivid imagery and Welsh mythology. Indeed, the distinguishing quality of the book, Peter Ackroyd commented in *Spectator,* is "its wit: the relentlessness of domestic life, the knives only just sheathed in time, the tart little phrases bouncing around like Molotov cocktails." And Jeremy Treglown, reviewing for the *New Statesman,* offered a similar assessment, observing that *The Sin Eaters* "has some of the satirical malice, the implacable cruelty of plotting and the snobbish humour of early [Evelyn] Waugh, and a lot of Virginia Woolf's narrative

method. . . . It is a fiction . . . satirising both the pretensions of the rulers and the inadequacies of the ruled."

Following *The Sin Eater* is *The Birds of the Air,* both "an anatomy of various kinds of grief" and a "savage attack on English Christmases," appraised Anatole Broyard in a *New York Times* review. This second novel centers on the Marsh family: Mrs. Marsh, a widow who feels no one appreciates her; her daughters Mary, who grieves for her deceased, illegitimate son Robin, and Barbara, who is obsessed with her husband's infidelity; Sebastian, Barbara's husband, described by Ellis as a professor whose "insistence on ordinary language and absolute clarity of expression rendered his discourse unintelligible to the ordinary person"; and Sam, Barbara's son, whose rebellious nature and dislike of hypocrisy prompt him to dye his hair green for Christmas.

Ellis's "characterizations are deft and devastating," wrote Linda Barrett Osborne in the *Washington Post Book World,* showing "with stunning accuracy how people can live together day after day without knowing each other at all." Mary, the main character, resides in an inner world of grief, providing a sharp contrast to the Christmas season with its expectations of peace and joy. She and Sam together, explained Jennifer Uglow in a *Times Literary Supplement* critique of *The Birds of the Air,* "belong to a more elemental world" than do their relatives. Although misunderstood by their family as uncaring, the two are "passionate beings." As in *The Sin Eater,* continued Uglow, in this more recent novel Ellis "presents the submerged world of irrationality and disorder which they inhabit as more powerful than the civilized surface . . . this short novel is densely packed, strengthened by a network of imagery, almost overburdened by urgent blasts against modern society."

Ellis's 1982 novel, *The Twenty-seventh Kingdom,* was shortlisted for Britain's most prestigious literary honor, the Booker-McConnell Prize, and despite its popularity did not reach American readers until 1999. It is "a brittle, anarchic theological fantasy set in the Chelsea of the 1950s," remarked A.N. Wilson in the *Spectator,* while Linda Taylor, critiquing for the *Times Literary Supplement,* reflected that the novel is a book wherein "eccentricity rules." Aunt Irene, whose looks had "disappeared under waves of creamy, curdling flesh," is the main character and, reported Taylor, all who approach her residence, Dancing Master House, become to some extent subject to its bizarre rules. It is "clever and funny," observed Taylor, adding that Ellis "beguiles the reader with the oddity of coincidence, an air of mystery. . . . Like Aunt Irene, she's a master of the deceptive appearance." Describing the novel as "witty," a *Publishers Weekly* contributor added praise for Ellis's "whiplash humor" and noted that readers will "marvel . . . at the ease with which she depicts eccentric but fully recognizable members of society."

The Twenty-seventh Kingdom is also, according to Wilson, "a tale of sacred love, and the miraculous." In contrast, *The Other Side of the Fire,* in Wilson's opinion, "is a merciless little story of profane love unrequited." Claudia, the protagonist, has been married to staid, boring Charles for fifteen years when she falls in love with her stepson, Philip, whom everyone but Claudia recognizes as a homosexual. In an effort to thwart her passion, Claudia introduces her stepson to Evvie, daughter of her bohemian friend Sylvie. Evvie, however, thinks love is ridiculous. Sylvie herself no longer cares about love, and Charles, suspecting that something is amiss with Claudia, turns to Sylvie for advice.

Although reviewer John Nicholson suggested in the London *Times* that *The Other Side of the Fire* provides another example of "Ellis's chillingly effective dissections of the damage people do to each other when they stretch out the hand of friendship or, worse still, love," he cautioned that the author's seriousness should not obscure her reputation as "one of the wittiest writers currently at work." Indeed Claudia is ludicrous in her infatuation, with Ellis continually poking fun at the lunacy of love. In the London *Times* Pat Raine, for example, noted that "some splendid passages from a low-brow love story are merrily inserted into [the book's] elegant narrative," while in the *New Statesman* Harriet Gilbert lauded the work as "a fast and funny novel, its cynicism warmed by compassion."

Ellis's *Unexplained Laughter* "is an elusive novel teetering on the edge of comedy but remaining faintly and unexpectedly sombre," opined reviewer Harriet Waugh. The protagonist is Lydia, a London journalist taking sanctuary in Wales following the end of a love affair. Betty, kind-hearted and frumpy, is Lydia's foil, and together the two explore the local community and meet its inhabitants. In the process, reported Julia O'Faolain in the *Times Literary Supplement,* there is much taboo-breaking "as the unsayable keeps getting said. . . . Lydia's sharp tongue links her to the eighteenth century. Hers is a classic wit. Lucid and rational, it encapsulates and sums up with utter clarity." Confident though she is, Lydia finds herself shaken upon hearing the mysterious laughter that emanates from a Welsh valley. There is no clear explanation for the laughter, which not ev-

eryone is able to hear. "One is not," as Isabel Raphael pointed out in her critique for the London *Times,* "allowed to sit comfortably in Alice Thomas Ellis's world. She enjoys teasing, too . . . and every gust of laughter is counterbalanced by a shiver in recognition of the human condition." And O'Faolain concluded that "in the end the novel cannot be summarized and this is proof of its excellence. The author's quicksilver perceptions can be conveyed adequately in no words but her own."

Ellis's "Summerhouse Trilogy," consisting of *The Clothes in the Wardrobe, The Skeleton in the Cupboard,* and *The Fly in the Ointment,* tells the same story from three different points of view. Set in a London suburb, the events concern the impending marriage of a young woman, Margaret, to forty-year-old Syl. Margaret has no desire to marry Syl; the marriage has been arranged by Syl's and Margaret's mother, who control much of their middle-aged children's lives. Margaret, as narrator of *The Clothes in the Wardrobe,* recalls her life prior to her engagement: her education in Egypt, a disastrous first love affair there, and her witnessing of a murder committed by her lover. Though she had wanted to become a nun, she feels unworthy of the vocation after helping to dispose of the body and sinks into a silent, colorless way of life. She is saved from marriage to the worthless Syl when Lili, an exotic friend from Egypt, seduces the betrothed man and contrives to have the wedding guests witness the act, thereby giving Margaret a way out of the doomed union. Margaret is then able to pursue life in a convent. *The Skeleton in the Cupboard,* narrated by Syl's mother, reveals that Margaret was sexually abused by her father.

The Fly in the Ointment is told from Lili's viewpoint, and shows that her promiscuity is part of her struggle to keep from falling into a deep depression. "Her narrative style is sometimes conversational, sometimes dramatic with breathless ellipses," noted *Dictionary of Literary Biography* contributor Catherine Burgass. "She also has a tendency, shared with Margaret, toward archaic biblical-sounding forms of expression." Burgass noted that, "while the comic or farcical aspects of her public seduction of Syl . . . are presented in the first two novels, in Lili's account the scene has elements of tragedy. Reviewers have described the novel as elegant, malicious, and darkly comic." The three books, taken together, present the idea that memory is highly fallible, for although the same events are described in each novel, the different narrators tell vastly different stories.

Ellis puts a group of strangers disappointed and hoping to avoid the forced festivities of the Christmas holidays together in her award-winning 1990 novel *The Inn at the Edge of the World.* Each person in the group has been lured to an island off the coast of Scotland in the hope of avoiding holiday events at home. Ronald is a distressed psychoanalyst whose wife and cleaning lady have abandoned him simultaneously; Jessica is an actress who is paid huge amounts of money to pitch bath soap and tea bags; and Anita is an out-of-sorts retail store manager. Noting that, despite its premise, the novel remains upbeat, *Atlantic* contributor Martha Spaulding added that "Ellis's ironic sense of humor pokes up everywhere like crocuses in March."

Ellis's 1996 novel, *Fairy Tale,* is an offbeat story set in a Welsh village full of eccentric characters. Clare and Miriam are two London women who visit the village, where Clare's daughter, Eloise, lives. Eloise longs for a child, but her husband does not. One day she comes home with a strange, silver-haired, green-eyed baby. It turns out to be a changeling and is eventually taken into the care of three fairies who, throughout the story, have appeared in various human guises. *Booklist* reviewer Whitney Scott found the book "charming in moments," but cautioned readers that "its sometimes downright slow pacing, may delight one reader while working like Sominex on another." A *Publishers Weekly* reviewer noted as well that "even if the novel's plot and pacing are not always consistently on cue, the ironic charm and whimsical humor are consistently sharp."

In addition to her novels, Ellis, who converted to Roman Catholicism during her late teens and studied briefly as a postulate in a nunnery, has written numerous books and essays on religion and the Catholic Church. In 1996 she was dismissed as a columnist for the *Catholic Herald* after writing some scathing pieces about "what she sees as the general degeneration of Catholic practices," reported Burgass. Ellis's views are clearly expressed in her book *Serpent on the Rock: A Personal View of Christianity. Commonweal* reviewer Paul Baumann dubbed Ellis a "ferocious" writer, adding: "Make no mistake about it, Ellis believes in Hell as well as in the devil and especially in clerical garb and the Latin Mass. When at her best, she can make you believe too. . . . Her description of the ineradicable nature of grief and loss is utterly persuasive, as is her matter-of-fact acceptance of the self-sacrifice motherhood demands. . . . Her wry views about sex as the world's most overrated pleasure are very amusing, and not unconnected to her dismissal of men as a species of dithering idiots." Baumann concluded that Ellis's work has its flaws, but she is, nevertheless, "a writer of . . . moral imagination and sure dramatic instinct." In *Contemporary Review* Richard Mullen also had praise for Ellis's work, noting that Ellis, among the "finest and most perceptive novelists" of her generation, "has a genius for seeing how small details reveal so much about peoples' lives." Despite her concerns over the state of the Catholic Church following Vatican II, Ellis "has that rare gift of being able to denounce without rancour" and throughout *Serpent on the Rock* she threads "a radiance of how a strong, deep and highly emotional fiath can guide someone through the troubles of our time."

BIOGRAPHICAL AND CRITICAL SOURCES:

BOOKS

Contemporary Literary Criticism, Volume 40, Thomson Gale (Detroit, MI), 1986.
Contemporary Novelists, St. James Press (Detroit, MI), 1996.
Dictionary of Literary Biography, Volume 194: *British Novelists since 1960, Second Series,* Thomson Gale (Detroit, MI), 1998.
Ellis, Alice Thomas, *The Birds of the Air,* Duckworth (London, England), 1980.
Ellis, Alice Thomas, *The Twenty-seventh Kingdom,* Duckworth (London, England), 1982, Moyer Bell (Wakefield, RI), 1999.
Ellis, Alice Thomas, *A Welsh Childhood,* photographs by Patrick Sutherland, M. Joseph (London, England), 1990.

PERIODICALS

Atlantic, April, 2001, Martha Spaulding, review of *The Inn at the Edge of the World,* p. 104.
Booklist, March 15, 1998, p. 1200; December 15, 2000, Whitney Scott, review of *Valentine's Day: Women against Men,* p. 788.
Books and Bookmen, February, 1983; January, 1984, p. 20.
Commonweal, December 4, 1981; August 16, 1996, Paul Baumann, review of *Serpent on the Rock,* p. 26.
Contemporary Review, January, 1995, Richard Mullen, review of *Serpent on the Rock,* p. 52.
Globe and Mail (Toronto, Ontario, Canada), March 28, 1987.
Guardian, April 1, 1996, p. 4.
Library Journal, July, 1981, p. 1442; September 15, 1984, p. 1771; June 1, 1987, p. 128; March 1, 1992, p. 133; October 1, 1995, p. 86; January, 1997, p. 110; March 1, 1998, p. 126.
Listener, July 22, 1982, p. 24.

Los Angeles Times, October 19, 1984.

New Statesman, December 16, 1977, p. 855; October 24, 1980, p. 26; August 13, 1982, p. 22; November 11, 1983, p. 30; August 23, 1985, p. 28; July 28, 1989, p. 31; December 1, 1989, p. 36; September 21, 1990, p. 45; April 17, 1992, p. 47; September 2, 1994, p. 39.

New York, September 7, 1981, p. 64; October 15, 1984, p. 92.

New Yorker, January 14, 1985; July 18, 1994, p. 81.

New York Review of Books, June 23, 1994, p. 46.

New York Times, August 5, 1981, p. C22.

New York Times Book Review, October 18, 1987, p. 22; April 24, 1994, p. 13; April 20, 1997, p. 21; April 26, 1998, p. 26; December 20, 1998, p. 13.

Observer (London, England), July 4, 1982, p. 28.

People, August 24, 1981, p. 11.

Publishers Weekly, June 5, 1981, p. 79; July 20, 1984, p. 70; June 5, 1987, p. 70; January 20, 1997, p. 382; March 2, 1998, p. 60; August 24, 1998, review of *The Sin Eater,* p. 46; July 26, 1999, review of *The Twenty-seventh Kingdom,* p. 62.

Saturday Review, August, 1981, p. 1442.

Spectator, December 24, 1977, pp. 29-30; December 31, 1983; August 31, 1985, pp. 24-25.

Sunday Times (London, England), August 17, 1980, p. 33; June 27, 1982, p. 40.

Times (London, England), September 4, 1980; December 1, 1983; August 22, 1985, p. 9; November 12, 1986; November 29, 1986.

Times Literary Supplement, November 25, 1977; August 15, 1980; July 2, 1982; November 18, 1983; September 6, 1985; December 19, 1986.

Village Voice, November 27, 1984, p. 56.

Washington Post Book World, August 30, 1981.

OBITUARIES:

BOOKS

Ellis, Alice Thomas, *A Welsh Childhood,* M. Joseph (London, England), 1990.

PERIODICALS

Independent (London, England), March 10, 2005, p. 35.

Los Angeles Times, March 15, 2005, p. B9.

New York Times, March 12, 2005, p. A27.

Times (London, England), March 10, 2005, p. 67.

Washington Post, March 12, 2005, p. B7.

ELLIS, Bret Easton 1964-

PERSONAL: Born March 7, 1964, in Los Angeles, CA; son of Robert Martin (a real estate investment analyst) and Dale (a homemaker; maiden name, Dennis) Ellis. *Education:* Bennington College, B.A., 1986. *Hobbies and other interests:* Piano, playing keyboards in bands, reading.

ADDRESSES: Agent—c/o Knopf Publicity, 1745 Broadway, New York, NY 10019.

CAREER: Writer; appeared in the documentary film *This Is Not an Exit: The Fictional World of Bret Easton Ellis,* First Run Features, 2000.

MEMBER: Authors Guild, PEN, Writers Guild (West).

WRITINGS:

Less Than Zero (novel), Simon & Schuster (New York, NY), 1985.

The Rules of Attraction (novel), Simon & Schuster (New York, NY), 1987, Vintage (New York, NY), 1998.

American Psycho (novel), Vintage (New York, NY), 1991.

Informers (short stories), Knopf (New York, NY), 1994.

Glamorama (novel), Knopf (New York, NY), 1999.

Lunar Park (novel), Knopf (New York, NY), 2005.

Contributor of articles to periodicals, including *Rolling Stone, Vanity Fair, Wall Street Journal,* and *Interview.*

ADAPTATIONS: Less Than Zero was adapted as a film, produced by Twentieth Century Fox, 1987. *American Psycho* was adapted as a film, released by Lions Gate Films, 2000. *The Rules of Attraction* was adapted as a film, released by Lions Gate Films, 2002.

SIDELIGHTS: In 1985, twenty-one-year-old Bret Easton Ellis jolted the literary world with his first novel, *Less Than Zero.* Many reviewers' reactions to the book echoed that of *Interview* magazine's David Masello, who called it "startling and hypnotic." Eliot Fremont-Smith of the *Voice Literary Supplement* pronounced the book "a killer"—and, like other critics, was impressed not only with the novel itself but also with its author's youth. "As a first novel, [*Less Than Zero*] is exceptional," John Rechy declared in the *Los Angeles Times Book Review*; it is "extraordinarily accomplished," a *New Yorker* critic concurred. *Less Than Zero,* wrote Larry McCarthy in *Saturday Review,* "is a book you simply don't forget." A college undergraduate at the time of the novel's publication, Ellis has been hailed by more than one critic as the voice of his generation. Upon the publication of his third novel, *American Psycho,* Ellis again attracted attention, this time for writing a story so disturbing and violent that Matthew Tyrnauer of *Vanity Fair* called Ellis "the most reviled writer in America, the Salman Rushdie of too much, too fast."

The somewhat-autobiographical *Less Than Zero* grew out of a writing project Ellis began at Bennington College under his professor, writer Joe McGinniss. Comprised of vignettes, the book centers on Clay, an eighteen-year-old freshman at an eastern college who returns to Los Angeles for Christmas vacation. Drugs, sex, expensive possessions, and an obsession with videotapes, video games, and music videos fill the lives of Clay and his jaded peers. Events others might find horrifying—hardcore pornography, a corpse in an alley, and a girl who is kidnapped, drugged, and raped—become passive forms of entertainment for this group.

The novel's grim subject matter is related in a detached, documentary-style prose, leading *New York Times* reviewer Michiko Kakutani to state that *Less Than Zero* was "one of the most disturbing novels [she had] read in a long time." *Time* magazine's Paul Gray asserted that "Ellis conveys the hellishness of aimless lives with economy and skill," while Alan Jenkins of the *Times Literary Supplement* found that "at times [the novel] reproduces with numbing accuracy the intermittent catatonic lows of a psycho-physical system artificially stimulated beyond normal human endurance."

Some critics drew comparisons between *Less Than Zero* and J.D. Salinger's *Catcher in the Rye,* the 1950s classic of disaffected youth. But Anne Janette Johnson, writing in the *Detroit Free Press,* explained that such comparisons could not extend "beyond the fact that both [novels] concern teenagers coming of age in America. Salinger's [Holden Caulfield] had feelings—anger, self-pity, desire. The youths in [*Less Than Zero*] are merely consuming automatons, never energetic enough to be angry or despairing." For some critics, the novel brought to mind Jack Kerouac and similar "beat generation" writers of the 1950s. And Kakutani found echoes of Raymond Chandler, Joan Didion, and Nathanael West in Ellis's evocation of Los Angeles. Ellis himself has admitted to the influence that Didion has

had on his work. He told an interviewer for the Random House Web site that "Didion's essays and fiction appealed to the Southern Californian side of me and I think as a prose writer she's a genius. And I completely ripped her off when I wrote *Less Than Zero,* and I'm proud of it."

Ellis's second novel, *The Rules of Attraction,* continued in the vein of *Less Than Zero*; as R.Z. Sheppard, writing in *Time* magazine, noted: "The village of the damned goes East." *Rules* is set at Camden College, a fictional East Coast school which bears a striking similarity to Bennington College in Vermont, where Ellis earned his degree. Despite the academic setting, many reviewers noted the absence of the usual rigors of higher education. Richard Eder announced in the *Los Angeles Times Book Review* that "we actually catch a glimpse of one professor . . . and he is asleep on his office couch and reeks of pot." What is present, however, are "drunken parties, drugs, sex, shoplifting, [and] pop music," according to Campbell Geeslin in *People.* The three main characters, Paul, Sean, and Lauren, are involved in a frustrating love triangle: Paul, a homosexual, desires the bisexual Sean; Sean meanwhile longs to deepen his involvement with Lauren, who is pining after someone else. *New York Times Book Review* contributor Scott Spencer stated that these characters "live in a world of conspicuous and compulsive consumption—consuming first one another, and then drugs, and then anything else they can lay their hands on."

Spencer praised Ellis for "portraying the shallowness of [his characters'] desires," but objected to what he deemed the author's gratuitous use of brand names which he felt served no function in the narrative. Spencer also surmised that Ellis is a potentially adept satirist, but that in *The Rules of Attraction* "his method of aping the attitudes of the burnt-out works against him . . . . One closes the book feeling that this time out the author has stumbled over the line separating cool from cold. Where we ought to be saying, 'Oh my God, no,' we are, instead, saying, 'Who cares?'" *Newsweek* reviewer David Lehman also found Ellis's authorial skill to be somewhat deficient, and he concluded that "like *Less Than Zero, The Rules of Attraction* is more effective as a sociological exhibit than as a work of literary art." One unlikely proponent of the book was Gore Vidal, whom Tyrnauer quoted as remarking, "I thought it was really rather inspired . . . . These nutty characters, each on his own track—and the tracks keep crossing. It was a wonderfully comic novel." When Roger Avary directed the film version of *The Rules of Attraction,* which appeared on theater screens in 2002, he updated the tale to contemporary times rather than the 1980s.

A minor character from *The Rules of Attraction* —Sean's older brother, Patrick—became the central figure in Ellis's third novel, *American Psycho.* Like Ellis's other protagonists, Patrick Bateman is young, greedy, wealthy, and devoid of morals. A Wall Street executive who shops at the most expensive stores and dines at the trendiest restaurants, Patrick also enjoys torturing, mutilating, and murdering people at random, mostly from New York City's underclass. His crimes are described in the same emotionless detail that he devotes to his observations on food, clothing, and stereo equipment. Though he drops many hints of his covert activities to friends and authorities, he is never caught, and none of the victims seems to be missed.

Ellis has stated that he intended *American Psycho* to be a satirical black comedy about the lack of morality in modern America, and some critics believe that he achieved this aim. Other commentators, however, accused him of pandering to readers' most base desires by producing a novel with all the artistic worth of a low-budget horror movie. Man, woman, child, and animal all meet grisly ends at the hands of Bateman, and the book's violence toward women in particular prompted one chapter of the National Organization for Women to organize to boycott not only the book itself, but all books by its publisher, Vintage, and its parent company, Random House. The novel generated controversy from the very beginning, however. Ellis's first publisher, Simon & Schuster, refused to carry through on their agreement to publish it, even though they had already given the author a $300,000 advance.

Some critics saw little literary merit in the book. In a *Washington Post* review, Jonathan Yardley called *American Psycho* "a contemptible piece of pornography, the literary equivalent of a snuff flick" and urged readers to forego the experience. Andrew Motion echoed Yardley's sentiments in the London *Observer,* calling the book "deeply and extremely disgusting . . . . Sensationalist, pointless except as a way of earning its author some money and notoriety." Similarly, Albert Manguel of *Saturday Night* also reported that his reaction to the book was not as the author intended: "not intellectual terror, which compels you to question the universe, but physical horror—a revulsion not of the senses but of the gut, like that produced by shoving a finger down one's throat." John Leonard of the *Nation,* however, argued that "There is no reason this couldn't have been funny: if not Swiftian, at least a sort of *Bonfire of the Vanities* meets *The Texas Chainsaw Massacre* . . . . Ellis has an ear for the homophobic and misogynistic fatuities of his social set . . . . When Patrick tells people that he's 'into murders and executions,' what they hear him say is 'mergers and acquisitions.'"

Director David Cronenberg considered making a film version, and author Michael Tolkin argued, as Tyrnauer reported: "There was a massive denial about the strengths of the book . . . . People scapegoated the violence, but that wasn't his sin. He made a connection between the language of fashion writing and serial murder." The film was eventually made in 2000, however, and after actor Leonardo DiCaprio first agreed and then declined to take on the role of Patrick Bateman, it went to Christian Bale. Several critics lauded the work of director Mary Harron, including Gavin Smith in *Film Comment,* who noted that "she and screenplay collaborator-actress Guinevere Turner . . . have done an exemplary job of adaptation—distilling, sharpening, and fleshing out the malignant essence of the novel," and that "the result is a mordantly funny and agreeably blatant satire with genuinely subversive bite." Similarly, Richard Corliss in *Time* felt that "Harron and . . . Turner do understand the book, and they want their film to be understood as a period comedy of manners."

The debate over Ellis's style continued with his 1994 publication, *The Informers.* A book of short stories constructed from loosely related short pieces which take place once again in Los Angeles and concern rich and beautiful college students, the book displays the deadpan prose and scenes of horror on which Ellis's reputation has been built. The book contains graphic depictions of vampirism and murder on a par with those in *American Psycho,* but violence is not the book's focus. A multitude of friends and acquaintances, mostly tan, blonde, and sleeping with each other, find their lives uprooted by several random murders and mutilations of their relatives and peers. As it turns out, two of these young trendy types, Dirk and Jamie, are vampires. But once again Ellis focuses on the emptiness of the 1980s and on characters consumed with style and materialism who have contempt for any real analysis of their lives. "The *Informers* is full of scintillating chitchat," wrote Leonard in the *Nation.* "What Ellis has digitized, instead of a novel, is a video. He channel-surfs—from bloody bathroom to bloodier bedroom; from herpes to anorexia," he continued. For Neal Karlen, reviewer for the *Los Angeles Times Book Review, The Informers* represented "a further slide down for an author who long ago had it." Karlen dismissed the book as full of "a rancid phoniness" and characterized all of Ellis's later work as being "opaque and bitter, devoid of both humanity and meaning" because "Ellis apparently has not learned the lesson of empathy, either on the page or in life." Conversely, for *New York Times Book Review* contributor George Stade, *The Informers* was "spare, austere, elegantly designed, telling in detail, coolly ferocious, sardonic in its humor." Stade concluded that

Ellis himself was "a covert moralist and closet sentimentalist, the best kind, the kind who leaves you space in which to respond as your predispositions nudge you, whether as a commissar or hand-wringer or, like me, as an admirer of his intelligence and craft."

Ellis published his fourth novel, *Glamorama,* in 1999. As he explained on the Random House Web site, *Glamorama* differs from his previous work because, "to put it bluntly, it has a plot, or at least an identifiable narrative that my other novels really don't have." In it, protagonist and senator's son Victor Ward is a male model who leaves his shallow milieu to become unwittingly involved in a European terrorist ring. Ellis further observed, "I think the connection I'm making has to do with the tyranny of beauty in our culture and the tyranny of terrorism. Of course that's a metaphor and the idea of models actually blowing up hotels and airlines is farfetched." After quoting a particularly gruesome passage of *Glamorama* in a critique for the *National Review,* however, James Panero asked, "Now did the tyranny of beauty ever make you feel that uneasy?" Panero also presented another question about Ellis in discussing *Glamorama*: "The plot is nihilistic; the characters, depraved. And page after page is filled with horrible, graphic violence. So why do I get the feeling Ellis is a closet conservative?" A reviewer from *Esquire* was less impressed, stating that while Ellis "may even be said to succeed at rendering a certain world whole, in its squirming, teeming entirety," the author "neglects to . . . make the world of his choosing interesting." Likewise, an *Entertainment Weekly* critic felt that the novel's "overly complicated plot drags on and on." Robert Plunket in the *Advocate,* however, praised *Glamorama* as "sick, twisted, and possibly brilliant," commenting further that the book "secures [Ellis's] reputation as the Jeffrey Dahmer of novelists—dangerous and deranged . . . . Clearly, here is a man who is doing what he is born to do."

In 2005 Ellis penned the novel *Lunar Park,* a faux memoir turned horror story about a novelist named Bret Easton Ellis who marries, moves to the suburbs, and is ultimately haunted by demons that torment his life. Rene Rodriguez, reviewing the book for *Miami Herald,* noted that "at times" the book contains "genuinely frightening and violent passages. But other elements . . . come off as hokey." Rodriguez added, "*Lunar Park* is a story about the momentous pain parents inflict on their children, and Ellis' appropriation of his own life, which initially seems like a vainglorious stunt, ends up adding an extra layer of poignancy to this most personal of novels." A reviewer for *Publishers Weekly* called the novel "a fascinating look at a once controversial celebrity as a middle-aged man."

In Tyrnauer's interview with Ellis, he noted that "a certain slangy level of ironic detachment informs even his most serious statements—and not everybody gets it. 'I am an incredibly moralistic person . . . . A lot of people totally mistake the books in some cases as advocating a certain behavior or as glorifying a certain form of behavior.'" Commenting on his role as a spokesperson for his generation, Ellis told *CA* that "I . . . don't believe that there's one or two spokespeople for a generation, one collective voice who's going to speak for the whole lot . . . . What you have to do . . . is just feel safe enough about your own opinion and go ahead and state it."

BIOGRAPHICAL AND CRITICAL SOURCES:

BOOKS

Authors and Artists for Young Adults, Volume 43, Gale (Detroit, MI), 2002.
Contemporary Literary Criticism, Gale (Detroit, MI), Volume 39, 1986, Volume 71, 1992.
Contemporary Novelists, 7th edition, St. James Press (Detroit, MI), 2001.
St. James Encyclopedia of Popular Culture, St. James Press (Detroit, MI), 2000.

PERIODICALS

Advocate, February 2, 1999, Robert Plunket, review of *Glamorama,* p. 65.
Chicago Tribune, September 13, 1987.
Current Biography, November, 1994, p. 23.
Detroit Free Press, August 18, 1985.
Detroit News, August 11, 1985.
Entertainment Weekly, August 19, 1994; January 22, 1999, "Glitter Haughty," p. 95.
Esquire, October, 1994, p. 158; February, 1999, "Bret Easton Ellis Plays Tom Wolfe," p. 26.
Film Comment, December, 1985; March, 2000, Gavin Smith, review of *American Psycho,* p. 72.
Guardian, January 9, 1999, "Leader of the Bret Pack."
Hollywood Reporter, October 7, 2002, Frank Scheck, review of *The Rules of Attraction,* pp. 10-11.
Interview, June, 1985; January, 1991, p. 54.
Library Journal, January, 1991; July, 1994.
Los Angeles Times Book Review, May 26, 1985; September 13, 1987.
Mademoiselle, June, 1986.

Miami Herald, August 17, 2005, Rene Rodriguez, "*Lunar Park:* A Fortysomething Writer Tries to Straighten Out His Life in This Could-Be Autobiography Sprinkled with Horror."

Nation, April 1, 1991, p. 426; September 5, 1994, p. 238.

National Review, February 14, 1986; June 24, 1991; September 12, 1994, p. 86; June 17, 1996, p. 56; March 8, 1999, James Panero, "Ellis's Island," p. 53.

New Republic, June 10, 1985; September 5, 1994, p. 46.

New Statesman, November 11, 1994, p. 40; January 15, 1999, Scott Reyburn, review of *Glamorama,* p. 49.

Newsweek, July 8, 1985; September 7, 1987; March 4, 1991, p. 58.

New Yorker, July 29, 1985; October 26, 1987, p. 142.

New York Review of Books, May 29, 1986.

New York Times, June 8, 1985; January 5, 1999, Michiko Kakutani, "Fashion Victims Take Terrorist Chic Seriously," p. E8.

New York Times Book Review, June 16, 1985; June 22, 1986; September 13, 1987, p. 14; December 16, 1990, p. 3; September 18, 1994, p. 14; January 24, 1999, Daniel Mendelsohn, "Lesser Than Zero," p. 8.

Observer, April 21, 1991, p. 61; January 3, 1999, Andrew Motion, "What Do You Give a Man with Two Girlfriends? A Really Hard Time."

People Weekly, July 29 1985; September 28, 1987.

Playboy, July, 1991, p. 26.

Publishers Weekly, June 13, 1994; June 27, 2005, review of *Lunar Park,* p. 38.

Rolling Stone, September 26, 1985.

Saturday Night, July-August, 1991, pp. 46-47, 49.

Saturday Review, July-August, 1985.

Time, June 10, 1985; October 19, 1987; March 18, 1991, p. 14; April 17, 2000, Richard Corliss, "A Yuppie's Killer Instinct," p. 78.

Times Literary Supplement, February 28, 1986.

USA Today Magazine, July, 2000, Christopher Sharrett, "American Psychosis," p. 67.

Vanity Fair, April, 1994, p. 108; August, 1994, p. 94.

Voice Literary Supplement, May, 1985.

Washington Post, February 27, 1991, pp. B1, B3; April 28, 1991, pp. C1, C4.

Writer's Digest, December, 1986.

ONLINE

Good Reports, http://www.goodreports.net/glaell.htm/ (March 6, 1999), review of *Glamorama.*

Random House, http://www.randomhouse.com/ (May 2, 2003), "An Interview with Bret Easton Ellis."

OTHER

This Is Not an Exit: The Fictional World of Bret Easton Ellis (film), First Run Features, 2000.

*   *   *

ELLIS, Landon
   See ELLISON, Harlan

*   *   *

ELLISON, Harlan 1934-
(Lee Archer, a house pseudonym, Phil "Cheech" Beldone, a house pseudonym, Cordwainer Bird, Jay Charby, Robert Courtney, a house pseudonym, Price Curtis, a house pseudonym, Wallace Edmondson, a house pseudonym, Landon Ellis, a house pseudonym, Harlan Jay Ellison, Sley Harson, a house pseudonym, Ellis Hart, E.K. Jarvis, a house pseudonym, Ivar Jorgensen, a house pseudonym, Alan Maddern, a house pseudonym, Paul Merchant, Clyde Mitchell, a joint pseudonym, Nabrah Nosille, a house pseudonym, Bert Parker, a house pseudonym, Ellis Robertson, a joint pseudonym, Jay Solo, Derry Tiger, a house pseudonym)

PERSONAL: Born May 27, 1934, in Cleveland, OH; son of Louis Laverne (a dentist and jeweler) and Serita (Rosenthal) Ellison; married Charlotte B. Stein, February 19, 1956 (divorced, 1959); married Billie Joyce Sanders, November 13, 1961 (divorced, 1962); married Lory Patrick, January 30, 1965 (divorced, 1965); married Lori Horwitz, June 5, 1976 (divorced, 1977); married Susan Toth, 1986. *Education:* Attended Ohio State University, 1953-54.

ADDRESSES: Home—P.O. Box 55548, Sherman Oaks, CA 91413-0548. *Agent*—Richard Curtis Associates, Inc., 171 East 74th St., New York, NY 10021.

CAREER: Freelance writer, 1954—. Part-time actor at Cleveland Playhouse, Cleveland, OH, 1944-49; editor, *Rogue* (magazine), 1959-60; founder and editor, Regency Books, 1961-62. Editorial commentator, Canadian Broadcasting Co. (CBC), 1972-78; president of Kilimanjaro Corp., Sherman Oaks, CA, 1979—. Creator of weekly television series (sometimes under pseudonym Cordwainer Bird), including *The Starlost,* syndicated, 1973, *Brillo* (with Ben Bova), American Broadcasting Companies, Inc. (ABC), 1974, and *The Dark Forces* (with Larry Brody), National Broadcasting Corporation, Inc. (NBC), 1986; creative consultant and director of television series (sometimes under pseudonym Cordwainer Bird), including *The Twilight Zone,* Columbia Broadcasting Systems, Inc. (CBS), 1984-85, and *Cutter's World,* 1987-88; conceptual consultant, *Babylon 5,* syndicated, beginning 1993. Host of cable magazine show, *Sci-Fi Buzz,* the Sci-Fi Channel, 1993; host of radio series *Beyond 2000,* National Public Radio (NPR), 2000; actor and voice-over talent. Has lectured at various universities, including Yale Political Union, Harvard University, Massachusetts Institute of Technology, London School of Economics, Michigan State University, University of California—Los Angeles, Duke University, Ohio State University, and New York University. West Coast spokesman, Chevrolet GEO Imports, 1988-89. Member of board of advisors, Great Expectations (video dating service). *Military service:* U.S. Army, 1957-59.

MEMBER: Science Fiction Writers of America (co-founder; vice president, 1965-66), Writers Guild of America (former member of board of directors for West chapter), Screen Actors Guild.

AWARDS, HONORS: Writers Guild of America Award, 1965, for *Outer Limits* television series episode "Demon with a Glass Hand," 1967, for original teleplay of *Star Trek* television series episode "The City on the Edge of Forever," 1973, for original teleplay of *Starlost* television pilot episode "Phoenix without Ashes," and 1986, for *Twilight Zone* television series episode "Paladin of the Lost Hour"; Nebula Awards, Science Fiction Writers of America, best short story, 1965, for "'Repent, Harlequin!' Said the Ticktockman," and 1977, for "Jeffty Is Five," best novella, 1969, for *A Boy and His Dog*; Hugo Awards, World Science Fiction Convention, best short fiction, 1965, for "'Repent, Harlequin!' Said the Ticktockman," best short story, 1967, for "I Have No Mouth, and I Must Scream," 1968, for "The Beast That Shouted Love at the Heart of the World," 1977, for "Jeffty Is Five," and 1986, for "Paladin of the Lost Hour," best dramatic presentation, 1967, for *Star Trek* television series episode "The City on the Edge of Forever," and 1976, for film *A Boy and His Dog,* best novelette, 1973, for "The Deathbird," 1974, for "Adrift, Just Off the Islets of Langerhans. . . "; special plaques from the World Science Fiction Convention, 1968, for *Dangerous Visions: Thirty-three Original Stories,* and 1972, for *Again, Dangerous Visions: Forty-six Original Stories;* Nova Award, 1968, for most outstanding contribution to the field of science fiction; Locus Awards,

Locus (magazine), best short fiction, 1970, for "The Region Between," 1972, for "Basilisk," 1973, for "The Deathbird," 1975, for "Croatoan," 1977, for "Jeffty Is Five," 1978, for "Count the Clock That Tells the Time," 1985, for "With Virgil Oddum at the East Pole," and 1988, for "Eiddons," best original anthology, 1972, for *Again, Dangerous Visions,* and 1986, for *Medea: Harlan's World,* best novelette, 1974, for "Adrift, Just Off the Islets of Langerhans. . . ," 1982, for "Djinn, No Chaser," 1985, for "Paladin of the Lost Hour," and 1988, for "The Function of Dream Sleep," best nonfiction, 1984, for *Sleepless Nights in the Procrustean Bed,* best short story collection, 1988, for *Angry Candy;* Jupiter Awards, Instructors of Science Fiction in Higher Education, best novelette, 1973, for "The Deathbird," and best short story, 1977, for "Jeffty Is Five"; Bram Stoker Awards, Horror Writers of America, 1988, for *The Essential Ellison: A Thirty-five Year Retrospective,* and 1990, for *Harlan Ellison's Watching;* Edgar Allan Poe Awards, Mystery Writers of America, 1974, for "The Whimper of Whipped Dogs," and 1988, for "Soft Monkey"; PEN International Silver Pen award for journalism, 1988, for column "An Edge in My Voice"; *Angry Candy* was named one of the major works of American literature by *Encyclopedia Americana Annual,* 1988; World Fantasy Awards, best short story collection, 1989, for *Angry Candy,* and 1993, for lifetime achievement; honored by PEN for continuing commitment to artistic freedom and battle against censorship, 1990; inducted into Swedish National Encyclopedia, 1992; selection of short story "The Man Who Rowed Christopher Columbus to Freedom" for inclusion in *The Best American Short Stories,* 1993; nominated for Nebula Award, 1993, for "The Man Who Rowed Christopher Columbus to Freedom," and 1994 for novella *Mefisto in Onyx;* recipient of Milford Award for lifetime achievement in editing; Bradbury Award, Science Fiction and Fantasy Writers of America, 2000.

WRITINGS:

SHORT STORY COLLECTIONS

The Deadly Streets, Ace Books (New York, NY), 1958.
(Under pseudonym Paul Merchant) *Sex Gang,* Nightstand (San Diego, CA), 1959.
A Touch of Infinity, Ace Books (New York, NY), 1960.
Children of the Streets, Ace Books (New York, NY), 1961, also published as *The Juvies.*
Gentleman Junkie, and Other Stories of the Hung-Up Generation, Regency Books (Evanston, IL), 1961.
Ellison Wonderland, Paperback Library (New York, NY), 1962.

Paingod, and Other Delusions (includes "'Repent, Harlequin!' Said the Ticktockman"), Pyramid Books (New York, NY), 1965.

I Have No Mouth and I Must Scream (also see below), Pyramid Books (New York, NY), 1967.

From the Land of Fear, Belmont (New York, NY), 1967.

Love Ain't Nothing But Sex Misspelled, Trident (New York, NY), 1968.

The Beast That Shouted Love at the Heart of the World (includes novella *A Boy and His Dog*), Avon (New York, NY), 1969.

Over the Edge: Stories from Somewhere Else, Belmont (New York, NY), 1970.

Alone against Tomorrow: Stories of Alienation in Speculative Fiction, Macmillan (New York, NY), 1971, abridged editions published as *All the Sounds of Fear,* Panther (London, England), 1973, and *The Time of the Eye,* Panther (London, England), 1974.

(With others) *Partners in Wonder: SF Collaborations with Fourteen Other Wild Talents,* Walker & Co. (New York, NY), 1971.

Approaching Oblivion: Road Signs on the Treadmill toward Tomorrow, Walker & Co. (New York, NY), 1974.

Deathbird Stories: A Pantheon of Modern Gods (includes "The Whimper of Whipped Dogs"; also see below), Harper (New York, NY), 1975.

No Doors, No Windows, Pyramid Books (New York, NY), 1975.

Harlan! Harlan Ellison Reads Harlan Ellison (sound recording), Alternate World Recordings, 1976.

Approaching Oblivion: Road Signs on the Treadmill toward Tomorrow: Eleven Uncollected Stories, Millington (London, England), 1976.

Blood!: The Life and Future Times of Jack the Ripper (sound recording), Alternate World Recordings, 1977.

Strange Wine: Fifteen New Stories from the Nightside of the World, Harper (New York, NY), 1978.

The Illustrated Harlan Ellison, edited by Byron Preiss, Baronet (New York, NY), 1978.

The Fantasies of Harlan Ellison, Gregg (Boston, MA), 1979.

Shatterday (also see below), Houghton (New York, NY), 1980.

Stalking the Nightmare, Phantasia Press (Huntington Woods, MI), 1982.

Harlan Ellison Reads Jeffty Is Five (sound recording), Harlan Ellison Record Collection, 1982.

Prince Myshkin, and Hold the Relish (sound recording), Harlan Ellison Record Collection, 1982.

Loving Reminiscences of the Dying Gasp of the Pulp Era (sound recording), Harlan Ellison Record Collection, 1982.

I'm Looking for Kadak (sound recording), Harlan Ellison Record Collection, 1982.

On the Road with Ellison (sound recording), Harlan Ellison Record Collection, 1983.

The Prowler in the City at the Edge of the World (sound recording), Harlan Ellison Record Collection, 1983.

The Beast That Shouted Love at the Heart of the World, Bluejay Books (New York, NY), 1984.

On the Downhill Side (sound recording), H. Ellison, 1984.

Ellison Wonderland, Bluejay Books (New York, NY), 1984.

The Essential Ellison: A Thirty-five Year Retrospective, edited by Terry Dowling, with Richard Delap and Gil Lamont, with an introduction by Dowling, Nemo Press (Omaha, NE), 1986.

The Harlan Ellison Roast (sound recording), Kilimanjaro Corp. (London, England), 1986.

Angry Candy, Houghton (New York, NY), 1988.

Dreams with Sharp Teeth (includes revised editions of *I Have No Mouth and I Must Scream, Deathbird Stories,* and *Shatterday*), Book-of-the-Month-Club (New York, NY), 1991.

Spider Kiss, Armchair Detective Library (New York, NY), 1991.

Mind Fields: The Art of Jacek Yerka, the Fiction of Harlan Ellison, Morpheus International (Beverly Hills, CA), 1994.

Slippage: Precariously Poised, Previously Uncollected Stories, Houghton (Boston, MA), 1994.

Mind Fields: Thirty Short Stories Inspired by the Art of Jacek Yerka, illustrated by Jacek Yerka, Morpheus (Beverly Hills, CA), 1994.

Chanuka Lights 1995 (sound recording), NPR, 1995.

Edgeworks, four volumes, White Wolf Pub. (Clarkston, GA), 1996–97.

Repent, Harlequin! Said the Ticktockman: The Classic Story, illustrated by Rick Berry, Underwood Books (Novato, CA), 1997.

(Author of introduction) *The Outer Limits: Armageddon Dreams,* Quadrillion Media (Scottsdale, AZ), 2000.

Contributor to *The HR Giger Screen Saver* (computer file), by H.R. Giger, Cyberdreams, 1995. Contributor of short story to *I Have No Mouth, and I Must Scream: The Official Strategy Guide,* by Mel Odom, Prima (Rocklin, CA), 1995. Also contributor of over eleven hundred short stories, some under pseudonyms, to numerous publications, including *Magazine of Fantasy and Science Fiction, Ariel, Twilight Zone, Cosmopolitan, Datamation, Omni, Ellery Queen's Mystery Magazine, Analog, Heavy Metal,* and *Galaxy.*

NOVELS

Rumble, Pyramid Books (New York, NY), 1958, published as *Web of the City,* 1975.

The Man with Nine Lives (also see below) [and] *A Touch of Infinity* (stories), Ace Books (New York, NY), 1960.

The Sound of a Scythe (originally published as *The Man with Nine Lives*), Ace Books (New York, NY), 1960.

Spider Kiss, Fawcett (New York, NY), 1961, also published as *Rockabilly.*

Doomsman (bound with *Telepower* by Lee Hoffman), Belmont (New York, NY), 1967, reprinted (bound with *The Thief of Thoth* by Lin Carter), 1972.

(With Edward Bryant) *The Starlost #1: Phoenix without Ashes,* Fawcett (New York, NY), 1975.

All the Lies That Are My Life, Underwood-Miller (Novato, CA), 1980.

Footsteps, illustrated by Ken Snyder, Footsteps Press (Round Top, NY), 1989.

Run for the Stars (bound with *Echoes of Thunder* by Jack Dann and Jack C. Haldeman II), Tor Books (New York, NY), 1991.

Mefisto in Onyx (novella), Mark V. Ziesing Books (Shingletown, CA), 1993.

ESSAYS

Memos from Purgatory: Two Journeys of Our Times, Regency Books (Evanston, IL), 1961.

The Glass Teat: Essays of Opinion on the Subject of Television, Ace Books (New York, NY), 1970.

The Other Glass Teat: Further Essays of Opinion on Television, Pyramid Books (New York, NY), 1975.

The Book of Ellison, edited by Andrew Porter, Algol Press (Brooklyn, NY), 1978.

Sleepless Nights in the Procrustean Bed, edited by Marty Clark, Borgo (San Bernardino, CA), 1984.

An Edge in My Voice, Donning (Norfolk, VA), 1985.

Harlan Ellison's Watching, Underwood-Miller (Novato, CA), 1989.

The Harlan Ellison Hornbook (autobiographical), Penzler (New York, NY), 1990.

EDITOR

Dangerous Visions: Thirty-three Original Stories, Doubleday (New York, NY), 1967.

Nightshade and Damnations: The Finest Stories of Gerald Kersh, Fawcett (New York, NY), 1968.

Again, Dangerous Visions: Forty-six Original Stories, Doubleday (New York, NY), 1972.

(With others, and contributor) *Medea: Harlan's World* (includes "With Virgil Oddum at the East Pole"), Bantam (New York, NY), 1985.

EDITOR; "DISCOVERY" SERIES OF FIRST NOVELS

James Sutherland, *Stormtrack,* Pyramid Books (New York, NY), 1974.

Marta Randall, *Islands,* Pyramid Books (New York, NY), 1976.

Terry Carr, *The Light at the End of the Universe,* Pyramid Books (New York, NY), 1976.

Arthur Byron Cones, *Autumn Angels,* Pyramid Books (New York, NY), 1976.

Bruce Sterling, *Involution Ocean,* Pyramid Books (New York, NY), 1977.

SCREENPLAYS

(With Russell Rouse and Clarence Greene) *The Oscar* (based on the novel by Richard Sale), Embassy, 1966.

Harlan Ellison's Movie: An Original Screenplay, Twentieth Century-Fox, Mirage Press (Baltimore, MD), 1990.

(With Isaac Asimov) *I, Robot: The Illustrated Screenplay* (see also below), Warner (New York, NY), 1994.

Also author of screenplays *Would You Do It for a Penny?,* Playboy Productions, *Stranglehold,* Twentieth Century-Fox, *Seven Worlds, Seven Warriors,* De Laurentiis, *I, Robot,* Warner Bros., *Swing Low, Sweet Harriet,* Metro-Goldwyn-Mayer, *The Dream Merchants,* Paramount, *Rumble,* American International, *Khadim,* Paramount, *Bug Jack Barron,* Universal, *None of the Above, Blind Voices, The Whimper of Whipped Dogs, Nick the Greek,* and *Best by Far.*

TELEPLAYS

The Starlost (series), syndicated, 1973.

Brillo (series), ABC, 1974.

The Tigers Are Loose (special), NBC, 1974.

The Dark Forces (series), NBC, 1986.

The Twilight Zone (series), CBS, 1986.

(And author of introduction) *The City on the Edge of Forever,* Borderlands (Brooklandville, MD), 1994.

Also author of telefilms and pilots *A Boy and His Dog, The Spirit, Dark Destroyer, Man without Time, The Other Place, The Tigers Are Loose, Cutter's World, Our Man Flint, Heavy Metal, Tired Old Man, Mystery Show, Astral Man, Astra/Ella, Project 120, Bring 'Em Back Alive, Postmark: Jim Adam, The Contender,* and *The Sniper.*

Author of teleplays for series, including *Star Trek, Outer Limits, Voyage to the Bottom of the Sea, Dark Room, Circle of Fear, Rat Patrol, Amos Burke—Secret Agent, The Great Adventure, Empire, Batman, Ripcord, The Man from UNCLE, Cimarron Strip, Burke's Law, The Young Lawyers, The Name of the Game, Manhunter, The Flying Nun, Route 66, The Alfred Hitchcock Hour, Logan's Run, Twilight Zone,* and *Babylon 5.*

OTHER

The City on the Edge of Forever (play; based on the teleplay by Ellison), published in *Six Science Fiction Plays,* edited by Roger Elwood, Pocket Books (New York, NY), 1976.
Demon with a Glass Hand (graphic novel; illustrated by Marshall Rogers), D.C. Comics (New York, NY), 1986.
Night and the Enemy (graphic novel; illustrated by Ken Steacy), Comico (Norristown, PA), 1987.
Vic and Blood: The Chronicles of a Boy and His Dog (graphic novel; based on Ellison's novella *A Boy and His Dog*), edited by Jan Strand, illustrated by Richard Corben, St. Martin's (New York, NY), 1989.
I Have No Mouth and I Must Scream (computer game), Cyberdreams, 1995.
(Author of preface) Mel Odom, *I Have No Mouth and I Must Scream: The Official Strategy Guide,* Prima Pub., 1995.

Also author of four books on juvenile delinquency. Contributor to *Faster than Light,* edited by Jack Dann and George Zebrowski, Harper (New York, NY), 1976. Columnist, "The Glass Teat" and "Harlan Ellison Hornbook," *Los Angeles Free Press,* 1972-73, and of "An Edge in My Voice," *Future Life,* 1980-81, and *L.A. Weekly,* 1982-83; author of syndicated film review column "Watching"; publisher of *Dimensions* magazine (originally *Science Fantasy Bulletin*).

ADAPTATIONS: A Boy and His Dog was filmed by LQJaf in 1975; much of Ellison's work has been cited as the inspiration for the motion picture *The Terminator,*

Orion, 1984; several of Ellison's short stories have been adapted for television. The film rights to *Mefisto in Onyx* have been optioned by Metro-Goldwyn-Mayer.

SIDELIGHTS: Described by fellow author J.G. Ballard as "an aggressive and restless extrovert who conducts his life at a shout and his fiction at a scream," Harlan Ellison is a writer who actively resists being labeled. Though he has written or edited more than seventy books and has authored more than twelve hundred short stories, he dislikes being called prolific; though his works of fiction and nonfiction are often considered iconoclastic, opinionated, and confrontational, he bristles at the label irrepressible; and, though he has garnered numerous major awards from science fiction organizations, including several Hugo and Nebula awards, he adamantly refuses to be categorized as a science fiction writer, preferring the term magic realism to define his writing.

Ellison began his writing career in the mid-1950s after being dismissed from college over a disagreement with a writing teacher who told Ellison that he had no talent. Ellison moved to New York City to become a freelance writer and in his first two years there sold some 150 short stories to magazines in every genre from crime fact to science fiction. It was the science fiction genre, however, that most appreciated Ellison's talent—both to Ellison's benefit and chagrin. Reviewers quickly associated him with the New Wave of science fiction writers—a group that included such authors as Brian W. Aldiss, J.G. Ballard, and Robert Silverberg. James Blish, writing under the pseudonym William Atheling, Jr., proclaimed in *More Issues at Hand* that "Harlan Ellison is not only the most audible but possibly the most gifted of the American members of the New Wave." Donald A. Wolheim similarly said in *The Universe Makers,* "Harlan Ellison is one of those one-man phenomena who pop up in a field, follow their own rules, and have such a terrific charisma and personal drive that they get away with it. They break all the rules and make the rest like it."

In response to such reviews, Ellison not only denied his role in the New Wave of science fiction but rejected the notion of a New Wave entirely. "For the record, and for those who need to be told bluntly, I do not believe there is such a thing as 'New Wave' in speculative fiction," he announced in the introduction to *The Beast That Shouted Love at the Heart of the World.* "It is a convenient journalese expression for inept critics and voyeur-observers of the passing scene, because they have neither the wit nor the depth to understand that this richness of new voices is *many* waves: each composed of one writer." Still, Wolheim maintained, the nature of Ellison's fiction places him firmly among the New Wave school of writing: "In the sense that [his] short stories have most certainly charted new paths in writing, in that he has indeed found new ultramodern ways of narration which yet manage to keep comprehension, . . . in that he takes the downbeat view of the far future and therefore, by implication, seems to accept the view that there is no real hope for humanity. . . . In that sense Harlan Ellison is New Wave [and] is the best of them all."

In the more than forty years since the publication of his first book, Ellison has written essays, reviews, screenplays, teleplays, and drama; yet he is still plagued with the science fiction label. "In the earliest days when I began writing I was a science fiction fan," he once explained, "so I gravitated toward the genre, naturally; but I wrote far more mystery fiction, far more mainstream fiction than ever I wrote science fiction." Ellison also told a *Publishers Weekly* contributor: "I've long ago ceased to write anything even remotely resembling science fiction, if indeed I ever really did write it." His chief reason for not wanting to be lumped among other science fiction writers, Ellison once commented is that "I conceive of the mass of science fiction writers as very bad writers indeed." According to *Times Literary Supplement* writer Eric Korn, however, this observation serves only to place Ellison more firmly within the science fiction genre, for he believed Ellison's writing "exhibits all that is hateful about SF: the biographical and autobiographical logorrhea, the cute titles, the steamy, cosy, encounter-group confessional tone, the intrusively private acknowledgments, the blurbs and afterwords." Some critics, such as Joseph McLellan of *Washington Post,* have suggested that to call Ellison a science fiction writer is too limiting. McLellan maintained that "the categories are too small to describe Harlan Ellison. Lyric poet, satirist, explorer of odd psychological corners, moralist, one-line comedian, purveyor of pure horror and of black comedy; he is all these and more."

Ellison employs the term "magic realism" to describe his writing, a term that he says can be applied to the work of many other writers, including Kurt Vonnegut, John Barth, Jorge Luis Borges, and Luisa Valenzuela. In 1967, after reading a short story by Thomas Pynchon, Ellison was inspired to edit a collection of "magic realism" stories as a means of better defining the term and distinguishing it from science fiction. The result was *Dangerous Visions: Thirty-three Original Stories.* Specifically designed to include those stories too controversial, too experimental, or too well written to ap-

pear in popular magazines, *Dangerous Visions* broke new ground in both theme and style. "[*Dangerous Visions*] was intended to shake things up," Ellison wrote in his introduction to the book. "It was conceived out of a need for new horizons, new forms, new styles, new challenges in the literature of our times."

Critical reaction to the book was largely favorable. For example, Damon Knight, writing in *Saturday Review,* called it "a gigantic, shapeless, exuberant, and startling collection [of] vital, meaningful stories." Of the thirty-three stories in *Dangerous Visions,* seven became winners of either the Hugo or Nebula Award while another thirteen stories were nominees. The collection received a special plaque from the World Science Fiction Convention. *Again, Dangerous Visions: Forty-six Original Stories,* Ellison's sequel to *Dangerous Visions,* met with the same success as its predecessor: J.B. Post predicted in *Library Journal* that *Again, Dangerous Visions* "will become a historically important book," and W.E. Mc-Nelly of *America* claimed that the collection was "so experimental in design, concept, and execution that this one volume may well place science fiction in the very heart of mainstream literature."

Both *Dangerous Visions* and *Again, Dangerous Visions* employ a unique format. Each story is preceded by a short introduction by Ellison, who speaks about the author and why the story was chosen for the collection. The story is then followed by an afterword from the author, who describes how the story came to be written. The format serves to personalize each story and to highlight its place in the collection. Theodore Sturgeon, writing in *National Review,* described Ellison's introductions to *Dangerous Visions* as a "one-man isometrics course [that] will stretch your laugh-muscles, your retch-muscles, your indignation-, wonder-, delight-, mad-, appall-, admiration-, and disbelief-muscles, and strongly affect your blood-pressure thing. You may have perceived that I have not used the word 'dull.' [Ellison] might numb you, but you will not be bored."

Through his fiction and, in particular, his essays, Ellison has earned a reputation as a polemic. Michael Schrage, writing in *Washington Post,* identified Ellison as "brash, arrogant, funny and provocative to the point of insulting." Though he noted that the essays in Ellison's collection *An Edge in My Voice* "may reek of ego and self-indulgence . . . they are very, very funny and very, very entertaining." Wolheim called Ellison "a unique sort of genius who can lead where others can never successfully follow, who can hold an audience enthralled yet never gain a convert, [and] who can insult and have only the stupid offended." Schrage warned, however, that "people who don't like smart-mouthed writers with a flair for caustic repartee are advised to steer clear" of Ellison.

However provocative it may be, Ellison's fiction has been ranked among America's best. Blish noted in *More Issues at Hand* that Ellison is "a born writer, almost entirely without taste or control but with so much fire, originality and drive, as well as compassion, that he makes the conventional virtues of the artist seem almost irrelevant." In his book-length study *Harlan Ellison: Unrepentant Harlequin,* George Edgar Slusser called Ellison "a tireless experimenter with forms and techniques" and concluded that he "has produced some of the finest, most provocative fantasy in America today."

Of all his short stories, one that is frequently singled out by critics and fans alike as Ellison's best is "'Repent, Harlequin!' Said the Ticktockman." It describes a future civilization in which citizens are held responsible for every second of their day; value is determined by productivity, and tardiness is loathed above all things; in fact, if one is late for an appointment, that time is subtracted from his or her life. Promptness is enforced by the tyrannical Master Timekeeper, known colloquially as the Ticktockman. The protagonist is Everett Marm, the Harlequin, who dresses in motley, is always late, and plays pranks on his coworkers simply to make them laugh. Though in the end the Harlequin is brainwashed and subsumed by the system, his actions create ripples in the pond, planting within his coworkers the seeds of civil disobedience. The moral of "'Repent, Harlequin!'" is, according to Slusser, that "the 'real' men in society are not those who abdicate all freedom of judgment to serve the machine, but those who resist dehumanization through acts of conscience, no matter how small. . . . If such a sacrifice brings even the slightest change, it is worth it." "'Repent, Harlequin!' Said the Ticktockman" is one of the ten most reprinted stories in the English language.

"Many of Ellison's stories turn on the problems created by [the] conception of identity," noted Thomas F. Dillingham in *Dictionary of Literary Biography.* "In some cases, an unself-conscious, weak individual becomes aware of his situation and fights to throw off the false or stereotypic characteristics imposed by genes, environment, or a malevolent external force. In others, a strong character encounters an attack on his autonomy and fights to protect it. The outcomes of these conflicts are not necessarily simple or consistent solutions to these identity crises. In some cases character is destiny, but in others—where certain of the variables of character are not readily visible—it is the vehicle of a trenchant irony."

Another classic Ellison story on this theme is "I Have No Mouth and I Must Scream." In this tale, the world superpowers have constructed three subterranean supercomputers to oversee and run their war campaigns, but when these intelligent computers decide to unite, they form one supercomputer with a massive intellect that calls itself AM. AM, seeing the human race as flawed and impure, decides to destroy everyone on the planet. However, AM preserves five human beings whom it brings underground with the devilish purpose of making them immortal and then tormenting them for all eternity. In a final effort to retain some human dignity, one of the humans, Ted, kills the other four people so that they, at least, can escape AM's sadism. Noted Dillingham: "Ted's own fate, however, is a grisly mirror image of the harlequins: where Everett Marm is 'regularized' by the machine and returned to 'normal' existence, Ted is reduced to a subhuman physical existence, but his mind remains intact. He is a prisoner inside an inexpressive body, incapable of uttering his humanity, but doomed to witness it to himself for an indefinite period of 'life.'" Ellison later adapted "I Have No Mouth and I Must Scream" into a computer game for Cyberdreams.

Another popular work of Ellison's that warns against humanity's relentless pursuit of technology is the 1968 novella *A Boy and His Dog,* which was made into a movie in 1975. In the year 2024, shortly after the devastating climax of World War IV, Vic and his dog, Blood, wander the wastes of the American southwest. The relationship between boy and dog is unusual for two reasons: first, Blood is telepathic, allowing him to communicate with Vic; second, the roles of human and animal have been reversed—Vic is little more than a scavenger, while Blood is literate and cultured. Blood teaches his "master" reading, speech, arithmetic, and history; however, he has forgotten his animal instincts, and must rely upon Vic to hunt game and find shelter. John Crow and Richard Erlich, reviewing *A Boy and His Dog* for *Extrapolation,* described the novella as "a cautionary fable" that "demands consideration of just how consciously our own society is proceeding into its technological future."

But war and intelligent computers are not the only possible dangers that Ellison has raged against in his writings. He also sees television as something that is sapping people of intelligence, culture, and a sense of history. The essay collections *The Glass Teat: Essays of Opinion of the Subject of Television* and *The Other Glass Teat: Further Essays of Opinion on Television* fully explore these views. As he told John Krewson online in *Onion A.V. Club,* he warns people in these books, "'Hey, folks! This sucker [television] is gonna steal your souls and you're gonna turn into morons! Well, it's come to pass.'" Nevertheless, Ellison has written extensively for television because he recognizes it as an unavoidable medium for writers. "If I had my druthers," he told Krewson, "I would not work in television at all; but again, it's a cultural medium from which most people derive their knowledge and education. For a writer today to stay in business, just to stay a writer, means that you have to have some kind of public profile." Ellison has written for numerous television series, including *The Twilight Zone, The Outer Limits,* and *Babylon 5.* He has also been a consultant for these series and even helped create *Babylon 5,* in which he also had an acting role.

Possibly the most famous contribution Ellison has made to television, however, is the episode he wrote for the original *Star Trek* series, "The City on the Edge of Forever." In this episode, Captain Kirk of the starship *Enterprise* and his first officer, Spock, must go back into the past to prevent Dr. McCoy from accidentally changing the course of events back in Depression-era America. McCoy has saved the life of a woman named Edith whose strong message of peace delays the Allies from taking action against Germany, which results in the Nazis winning World War II. To put history back on the correct course, Kirk, who has fallen in love with Edith, must allow her to die in an auto accident. *Star Trek* creator Gene Roddenberry made extensive changes to Ellison's story, which made the author furious, but he was later vindicated when his original script ended up winning Hugo and Writers Guild of America awards. In 1994, Ellison had his screenplay published in a book that was highly praised by reviewers. Ray Olson, for one, lauded the story in a *Booklist* review, adding that he particularly enjoyed the author's "sputtering, raging, fuming introduction in which he sets the record straight." This experience understandably turned Ellison off of writing television; however, his name today affords him such great respect that he has gained complete authority over the scripts he now writes, such as in his work for the revised *Outer Limits* series. "Nobody touches the script but me," he told Krewson. "If they don't like it, I give 'em their money back and I take my script back."

Ellison's stories in the 1980s and 1990s have been concerned more and more with thoughts of death and mortality, especially after the author's brush with death af-

ter a 1996 heart attack. These concerns are evident in such collections as *Slippage: Precariously Poised, Previously Uncollected Stories, Angry Candy,* and the four-volume *Edgeworks.* In the short stories in these collections, individuals again often struggle to assert their identity and humanity. One of Ellison's themes here is most pointedly revealed in his story "The Man Who Rowed Christopher Columbus Ashore," which is about an immortal trickster figure who manipulates people and events according to his own peculiar whims. Told in segments that vacillate "wildly between moments of humor, suffering, pathos, tragedy, absurdity, and extreme violence," as a contributor to *Contemporary Popular Writers* observed, "the cumulative effect of these aphoristic narrative fragments is to disrupt ideas of fate, causality, or structure in human existence, and to highlight the randomness of life's events. In the end, all that is left is the responsibility of the individual."

One of the stories collected in *Edgeworks,* "Mefisto in Onyx," was later published as a separate novella. The protagonist is Rudy Pairis, a gifted black man with the ability to read minds. He is employed by Deputy District Attorney Allison Roche to exonerate a convicted serial killer who awaits an impending death sentence. Though Roche prosecuted the convicted murderer herself, days before his execution she doubts his guilt and persuades Pairis to probe his mind for evidence of his innocence. David Gianatasio praised the Pairis character in an *Armchair Detective* review. "Like most Ellison anti-heroes, Pairis's inability to fully accept his heightened mental powers—and in a larger sense, to accept himself—makes him an outcast in his own world." Gianatasio added, "Pairis's ability to accept who and what he is . . . is the key to his final transcendence." Tom Auer concluded in *Bloomsbury Review,* "This story is a page-turner, quick, lively, and entertaining, and very funny in parts, but colored throughout with a deep sense of humankind's insufferable inhumanity."

Ellison continued to defy the marketing concerns of movie producers when he published *I, Robot: The Illustrated Screenplay,* which he wrote with Isaac Asimov, after a protracted and ultimately failed attempt to produce a film version of the story. Based on Asimov's *I, Robot* series and elements of Orson Welles' *Citizen Cane,* Ellison grafts various Asimov subplots and his own material into a story about a journalist's persistent effort to interview Susan Calvin, a reclusive octogenarian, upon the death of her reputed lover, Stephen Byerly. Though commending Ellison's achievement, *Locus* reviewer Gary K. Wolfe wrote that "*I, Robot* was probably never a very good idea for a movie" because "most of the stories were intellectual puzzles based on permutations of the laws of robotics." However, Wolfe added, "As a potential moviegoer, there's nothing here to convince me that this relatively simple story about a lonely woman in a lost future is impossible to film." An *Analog* reviewer similarly concluded, "Ellison did indeed make a compelling story of Asimov's material, and the script would indeed make a grand movie."

Commenting on Ellison's style and central themes, Auer said, "Ellison's prose is powerful and ingenious, but often angry, sometimes sinister, occasionally gloomy, and often with an edge that can cut quickly to and through the heart of his subject, or that of his reader for that matter." He also observed, "The bloody truth of our violent times, a subject he writes about with regularity and ease, practically drips from some of his finely crafted pages. He also has a sense of humor, but we don't see it often, and it is frequently black as midnight when we do."

Ellison once commented: "Everything I write is concerned with the world of today. . . . I explain the world through which we move by reflecting it through the lens of fantasy turned slightly askew, so that you can see it from a new angle. I talk about the things people have always talked about in stories: pain, hate, truth, courage, destiny, friendship, responsibility, growing old, growing up, falling in love, all of these things. I don't write about far-flung galactic civilizations; I don't write about crazed robots; I don't write gimmick stories. What I try to write about are the darkest things in the soul, the mortal dreads. . . . The closer I get to the burning core of my being, the things which are most painful to me, the better is my work."

"It is a love/hate relationship that I have with the human race," Ellison continued. "I am an elitist, and I feel that my responsibility is to drag the human race along with me—that I will never pander to, or speak down to, or play the safe game. Because my immortal soul will be lost."

"I write because I cannot *not* write," he once explained in *Bloomsbury Review.* "That's what I *do.* . . . It amazes me when I get an interview with someone who says, 'You're so prolific, you've done forty-two books and thousands of short stories.' And I say, 'If I were a plumber, and I had fixed a thousand toilets, you wouldn't say that, you wouldn't say what a prolific plumber I am.' That's what I *do.*'"

BIOGRAPHICAL AND CRITICAL SOURCES:

BOOKS

Atheling, William Jr., *More Issues at Hand,* Advent, 1970.

Contemporary Literary Criticism, Thomson Gale (Detroit, MI), Volume 1, 1973; Volume 13, 1980; Volume 42, 1987.

Contemporary Popular Writers, St. James Press (Detroit, MI), 1997.

Dictionary of Literary Biography, Volume 8: *Twentieth-Century American Science Fiction Writers,* Thomson Gale (Detroit, MI), 1981, pp. 161-169.

Ellison, Harlan, editor, *Dangerous Visions: Thirty-three Original Stories,* Doubleday (New York, NY), 1967.

Ellison, Harlan, *The Beast That Shouted Love at the Heart of the World,* Avon (New York, NY), 1969.

Platt, Charles, *The Dream Makers: The Uncommon People Who Write Science Fiction,* Berkley, 1980.

Porter, Andrew, editor, *The Book of Ellison,* Algol Press, 1978.

St. James Guide to Science Fiction Writers, fourth edition, St. James Press (Detroit, MI), 1996.

Slusser, George Edgar, *Harlan Ellison: Unrepentant Harlequin,* Borgo, 1977.

Swigart, Leslie Kay, *Harlan Ellison: A Bibliographical Checklist,* Williams Publishing (Dallas, TX), 1973.

Walker, Paul, *Speaking of Science Fiction: The Paul Walker Interviews,* Luna, 1978.

Wolheim, Donald A., *The Universe Makers,* Harper (New York, NY), 1971.

PERIODICALS

America, June 10, 1972, W.E. McNelly, review of *Again, Dangerous Visions: Forty-six Original Stories.*

Analog, September, 1960; December, 1962; May, 1968; June, 1968; August, 1970; April, 1973; September, 1995, review of *I, Robot: The Illustrated Series,* p. 185.

Armchair Detective, spring, 1994, David Gianatasio, review of "Mefisto in Onyx," p. 245.

Bloomsbury Review, January, 1985; February, 1985; May-June, 1994, Tom Auer, review of "Mefisto in Onyx," p. 1.

Booklist, December 1, 1995, Ray Olson, review of *The City on the Edge of Forever,* p. 606.

Chicago Tribune, September 24, 1961; June 2, 1985; January 17, 1989.

Esquire, January, 1962.

Extrapolation, May, 1977; winter, 1979, John Crow and Richard Erlich, review of *A Boy and His Dog.*

Fantasy Newsletter, April, 1981.

Galaxy, April, 1968; May, 1972.

Guardian (Manchester, England), July 4, 1963.

Library Journal, April 15, 1972, J.B. Post, review of *Again, Dangerous Visions: Forty-six Original Stories;* February 1, 1995, p. 75; July, 1996, Michael Rogers, review of *Edgeworks,* Volume 1, p. 172; August, 1997, Michael Rogers, review of *Edgeworks,* Volume 3, p. 142; October 15, 1997, Susan Hamburger, review of *Slippage: Previously Uncollected, Precariously Poised Stories,* p. 97; February 1, 1998, Michael Rogers, review of *Edgeworks,* Volume 4, p. 118.

Locus, November, 1994, Gary K. Wolfe, review of *I, Robot: The Illustrated Screenplay,* p. 61.

Los Angeles Times, September 20, 1988.

Los Angeles Times Book Review, October 24, 1982, p. 14; June 30, 1985, p. 7; January 1, 1989, p. 9.

Luna Monthly, May, 1970; July, 1970; May-June, 1971; June, 1972; September, 1972.

Magazine of Fantasy and Science Fiction, January, 1968; November, 1971; September, 1972; October, 1975; July, 1977; June, 1998, Robert K.J. Killheffer, review of *Slippage,* p. 39; April, 2002, Charles De Lint, review of *The Essential Ellison,* p. 34.

National Review, July 12, 1966; May 7, 1968, Theodore Sturgeon, review of *Dangerous Visions: Thirty-three Original Stories.*

New Statesman, March 25, 1977.

New York Times, September 21, 1997, Eric P. Nash, review of *Slippage.*

New York Times Book Review, October 26, 1958; June 30, 1960; August 20, 1961; June 30, 1968; September 3, 1972; March 23, 1975; April 1, 1979; January 8, 1989, p. 31; September 17, 1989, p. 12; March 18, 1990, p. 32.

Publishers Weekly, February 10, 1975; July 28, 1997, review of *Slippage,* p. 55; February 1, 1999, review of *Goodbye, Columbus and Five Short Stories* (sound recording), p. 35.

Renaissance, summer, 1972.

Review of Contemporary Literature, fall, 1994, p. 229.

Saturday Review, December 30, 1967, Damon Knight, review of *Dangerous Visions: Thirty-three Original Stories.*

Science Fiction Review, January, 1971; September-October, 1978.

Spectator, January, 1971.

Times Literary Supplement, April 16, 1971; January 14, 1977; July 9, 1982, p. 739.

Tribune Books (Chicago, IL), June 2, 1985, p. 35.

Variety, July 8, 1970; March 17, 1971.

Washington Post, August 3, 1978; July 30, 1985.

Washington Post Book World, January 25, 1981; December 26, 1982; June 30, 1985; September 25, 1988, p. 8; October 28, 1990, p. 10; February 2, 1992, p. 12.

Worlds of If, July, 1960; September-October, 1971.

ONLINE

Onion A.V. Club, http://theavclub.com/ (September 17, 1998), John Krewson, "The World Is Turning into a Cesspool of Imbeciles."

*   *   *

ELLISON, Harlan Jay
   See ELLISON, Harlan

*   *   *

ELLISON, Ralph 1914-1994
   (Ralph Waldo Ellison)

PERSONAL: Born March 1, 1914, in Oklahoma City, OK; died of cancer April 16, 1994, in New York, NY; son of Lewis Alfred (a construction worker and tradesman) and Ida (Millsap) Ellison; married Fanny McConnell, July, 1946. *Education:* Attended Tuskegee Institute, 1933-36. *Hobbies and other interests:* Jazz and classical music, photography, electronics, furniture-making, bird-watching, gardening.

CAREER: Writer, 1937-94. Researcher and writer for Federal Writers' Project, New York, NY, 1938-42; *Negro Quarterly,* editor, 1942; U.S. Information Agency, tour of Italian cities, 1956; Bard College, Annandale-on-Hudson, NY, instructor in Russian and American literature, 1958-61; New York University, New York, NY, Albert Schweitzer Professor in Humanities, 1970-79, professor emeritus, 1979-94. Alexander White Visiting Professor, University of Chicago, 1961; visiting professor of writing, Rutgers University, 1962-64; visiting fellow in American studies, Yale University, 1966. Lecturer at Salzburg Seminar, Austria, 1954; Gertrude Whittall Lecturer, Library of Congress, 1964; Ewing Lecturer, University of California—Los Angeles, 1964; lecturer at colleges and universities throughout the United States, including Columbia University, Fisk University, Princeton University, Antioch University, and Bennington College. Member of Carnegie Commission on Educational Television, 1966-67; honorary consultant in American letters, Library of Congress, 1966-72. Trustee, Colonial Williamsburg Foundation, John F. Kennedy Center for the Performing Arts, 1967-77, Educational Broadcasting Corp., 1968-69, New School for Social Research (now New School University), 1969-83, Bennington College, 1970-75, and Museum of the City of New York, 1970-86. Charter member of National Council of the Arts, 1965-67, and National Advisory Council, Hampshire College. *Military service:* U.S. Merchant Marine, World War II.

MEMBER: PEN (vice president, 1964), Authors Guild, Authors League of America, American Academy and Institute of Arts and Letters, Institute of Jazz Studies (member of board of advisors), Century Association (resident member).

AWARDS, HONORS: Rosenwald grant, 1945; National Book Award and National Newspaper Publishers' Russwurm Award, both 1953, both for *Invisible Man;* Certificate of Award, *Chicago Defender,* 1953; Rockefeller Foundation award, 1954; Prix de Rome fellowships, American Academy of Arts and Letters, 1955 and 1956; *Invisible Man* selected as the most distinguished postwar American novel and Ellison as the sixth most influential novelist by *New York Herald Tribune Book Week* poll, 1965; award honoring Oklahomans in the arts from governor of Oklahoma, 1966; Medal of Freedom, 1969; made Chevalier de l'Ordre des Arts et Lettres (France), 1970; Ralph Ellison Public Library, Oklahoma City, OK, named in his honor, 1975; National Medal of Arts, 1985, for *Invisible Man* and teaching at numerous universities. Honorary doctorates from Tuskegee Institute, 1963, Rutgers University, 1966, Grinnell College, 1967, University of Michigan, 1967, Williams College, 1970, Long Island University, 1971, Adelphi University, 1971, College of William and Mary, 1972, Harvard University, 1974, Wake Forest College, 1974, University of Maryland, 1974, Bard College, 1978, Wesleyan University, 1980, and Brown University, 1980.

WRITINGS:

Invisible Man (novel), Random House (New York, NY), 1952, with illustrations by Steven H. Stroud, Franklin Library, 1980, thirtieth-anniversary edition with new introduction by author, Random House, 1982, edited and with an introduction by Harold Bloom, Chelsea House (New York, NY), 1996.

(Author of introduction) Stephen Crane, *The Red Badge of Courage and Four Great Stories,* Dell (New York, NY), 1960.

Shadow and Act (essays), Random House (New York, NY), 1964.

(With Karl Shapiro) *The Writer's Experience* (lectures; includes "Hidden Names and Complex Fate: A Writer's Experience in the U.S.," by Ellison, and "American Poet?," by Shapiro), Gertrude Clarke Whittall Poetry and Literature Fund for Library of Congress (Washington, DC), 1964.

(With Whitney M. Young and Herbert Gans) *The City in Crisis,* introduction by Bayard Rustin, A. Philip Randolph Education Fund (Washington, DC), 1968.

(Author of introduction) Romare Bearden, *Paintings and Projections* (catalogue of exhibition), State University of New York at Albany (Albany, NY), 1968.

(Author of foreword) Leon Forrest, *There Is a Tree More Ancient than Eden,* Random House (New York, NY), 1973.

Going to the Territory (essays), Random House (New York, NY), 1986.

The Collected Essays of Ralph Ellison, Modern Library (New York, NY), 1995.

Flying Home and Other Stories, edited by John F. Callahan, preface by Saul Bellow, Random House (New York, NY), 1996.

Juneteenth (novel), edited by John F. Callahan, Random House (New York, NY), 1999.

Living with Music: Ralph Ellison's Jazz Writings, edited by Robert G. O'Meally, Modern Library (New York, NY), 2001.

OTHER

Ralph Ellison: An Interview with the Author of Invisible Man (sound recording), Center for Cassette Studies (Hollywood, CA), 1974.

(With William Styron and James Baldwin) *Is the Novel Dead?: Ellison, Styron, and Baldwin on Contemporary Fiction* (sound recording), Center for Cassette Studies (Hollywood, CA), 1974.

Ralph Ellison Reading from a Novel in Progress, Gertrude Clarke Whittall Poetry and Literature Fund for Library of Congress (Washington, DC), 1983.

Conversations with Ralph Ellison, edited by Maryemma Graham and Amritjit Singh, University Press of Mississippi (Jackson, MS), 1995.

Trading Twelves: The Selected Letters of Ralph Ellison and Albert Murray, edited by Albert Murray and John F. Callahan, Modern Library (New York, NY), 2000.

Contributor to books, including *The Living Novel: A Symposium,* edited by Granville Hicks, Macmillan (New York, NY), 1957; *Education of the Deprived and Segregated* (report), Bank Street College of Education (New York, NY), 1965; *Who Speaks for the Negro?,* by Robert Penn Warren, Random House (New York, NY), 1965; *To Heal and to Build: The Programs of Lyndon B. Johnson,* edited by James MacGregor Burns, prologue by Howard K. Smith, epilogue by Eric Hoffer,

McGraw Hill (New York, NY), 1968; and *American Law: The Third Century, the Law Bicentennial Volume,* edited by Bernard Schwartz, New York University School of Law (New York, NY), 1976. Work represented in numerous anthologies, including *American Writing,* edited by Hans Otto Storm and others, J.A. Decker (Prairie City, IL), 1940; *Best Short Stories of World War II,* edited by Charles A. Fenton, Viking Press (New York, NY), 1957; *The Angry Black,* edited by John Alfred Williams, Lancer Books (New York, NY), 1962, 2nd edition published as *Beyond the Angry Black,* Cooper Square (Totowa, NJ), 1966; *Soon, One Morning: New Writing by American Negroes, 1940-1962* (includes previously unpublished section from original manuscript of *Invisible Man*), edited by Herbert Hill, Alfred A. Knopf (New York, NY), 1963, published as *Black Voices,* Elek Books (London, England), 1964; *Experience and Expression: Reading and Responding to Short Fiction,* edited by John L. Kimmey, Scott, Foresman (Glenview, IL), 1976; and *The Treasury of American Short Stories,* compiled by Nancy Sullivan, Doubleday (New York, NY), 1981.

ADAPTATIONS: Avon Kirkland directed the documentary *Ralph Ellison: An American Journey,* 2002. *Living with Music, Invisible Man,* and *Juneteenth* were adapted as audiobooks.

SIDELIGHTS: Growing up in Oklahoma, a "frontier" state that "had no tradition of slavery" and where "relationships between the races were more fluid and thus more human than in the old slave states," American author and educator Ralph Ellison became conscious of his obligation "to explore the full range of American Negro humanity and to affirm those qualities which are of value beyond any question of segregation, economics or previous condition of servitude." This sense of obligation, articulated in his 1964 collection of critical and biographical essays, *Shadow and Act,* led to Ellison's staunch refusal to limit his artistic vision to the "uneasy sanctuary of race" and commit instead to a literature that explores and affirms the complex, often contradictory frontier of an identity at once black and American and universally human. For Ellison, whom John F. Callahan in a *Chant of Saints: A Gathering of Afro-American Literature, Art, and Scholarship* essay called a "moral historian," the act of writing was fraught with both great possibility and grave responsibility. As Ellison once asserted, writing "offers me the possibility of contributing not only to the growth of the literature but to the shaping of the culture as I should like it to be. The American novel is in this sense a conquest of the frontier; as it describes our experience, it creates it."

For Ellison, then, the task of the novelist was a moral and political one. In his preface to the thirtieth anniversary edition of his best-known work, *Invisible Man,* Ellison argued that the serious novel, like the best politics, "is a thrust toward a human ideal." Even when the ideal is not realized in the actual, he declared, "there is still available that fictional *vision* of an ideal democracy in which the actual combines with the ideal and gives us representations of a state of things in which the highly placed and the lowly, the black and the white, the Northerner and the Southerner, the native-born and the immigrant are combined to tell us of transcendent truths and possibilities such as those discovered when Mark Twain set Huck and Jim afloat on the raft." Ellison saw the novel as a "raft of hope" that may help readers stay above water as they try "to negotiate the snags and whirlpools that mark our nation's vacillating course toward and away from the democratic ideal."

Early in his career, Ellison conceived of his vocation as a composer of symphonies. When he entered Alabama's Tuskegee Institute in 1933 he enrolled as a music major; he wonders in *Shadow and Act* if he did so because, given his background, it was the only art "that seemed to offer some possibility for self-definition." The act of writing soon presented itself as an art through which the young student could link the disparate worlds he cherished, could verbally record and create the "affirmation of Negro life" he knew was so intrinsic a part of the universally human. To move beyond the old definitions that separated jazz from classical music, vernacular from literary language, the folk from the mythic, he would have to discover a prose style that could equal the integrative imagination of the "Renaissance Man."

Because Ellison did not get a job that paid him enough to save money for tuition, he stayed in New York, working and studying composition until his mother died. After his return to the family home in Dayton, Ohio, Ellison and his brother supported themselves by hunting. Though Ellison had hunted for years, he did not know how to wing-shoot; it was from Hemingway's fiction that he learned this process. Ellison also studied Hemingway to learn writing techniques; from the older writer he also learned a lesson in descriptive accuracy and power, in the close relationship between fiction and reality. Like his narrator in *Invisible Man,* Ellison did not return to college; instead he began his long apprenticeship as a writer, his long and often difficult journey toward self-definition.

Ellison's early days in New York, before his return to Dayton, provided him with experiences that would later translate themselves into his theory of fiction. Two days after his arrival in "deceptively 'free' Harlem," he met black poet Langston Hughes who introduced him to the works of Andre Malraux, a French writer defined as Marxist. Though attracted to Marxism, Ellison sensed in Malraux something beyond a simplistic political sense of the human condition. Ellison began to form his definition of the artist as a revolutionary concerned less with local injustice than with the timelessly tragic.

Ellison's view of art was furthered after he met black novelist Richard Wright. Wright urged him to read Joseph Conrad, Henry James, James Joyce, and Feodor Dostoevsky and invited Ellison to contribute a review essay and then a short story to the magazine he was editing. Wright was then in the process of writing *Native Son,* much of which Ellison read, he declared in *Shadow and Act,* "as it came out of the typewriter." Though awed by the process of writing and aware of the achievement of the novel, Ellison, who had just read works by Malraux, began to form his objections to the "sociological," deterministic ideology which informed the portrait of the work's protagonist, Bigger Thomas. In *Shadow and Act,* which Arthur P. Davis in *From the Dark Tower: Afro-American Writers, 1900 to 1960* described as partly an *apologia provita sua* (a defense of his life), Ellison articulated the basis of his objection: "I . . . found it disturbing that Bigger Thomas had none of the finer qualities of Richard Wright, none of the imagination, none of the sense of poetry, none of the gaiety." Ellison thus refuted the depiction of the black individual as an inarticulate victim whose life is one only of despair, anger, and pain. He insisted that art must capture instead the complex reality, the pain and the pleasure of black existence, thereby challenging the definition of the black person as something less than fully human.

From 1938 to 1944 Ellison published a number of short stories and contributed essays to journals such as *New Masses.* As with other examples of Ellison's work, these stories have provoked disparate readings. In an essay in *Black World,* Ernest Kaiser called the earliest stories and the essays in *New Masses* "the healthiest" of Ellison's career. The critic praised the economic theories that inform the early fiction, and he found Ellison's language pure, emotional, and effective. Lamenting a change he attributed to Ellison's concern with literary technique, Kaiser charged the later stories, essays, and novels with being no longer concerned with people's problems and with being "unemotional." Other critics, like Marcus Klein in *After Alienation: American Novels in Mid-Century,* saw the early work as a progressive preparation for Ellison's mature fiction and theory. In the earliest of these stories, "Slick Gonna Learn," Ellison draws a character shaped largely by an ideological,

naturalistic conception of existence, the very type of character he later repudiated. From this imitation of proletarian fiction, Ellison's work moved towards psychological and finally metaphysical explorations of the human condition. His characters thus were freed from restrictive definitions as Ellison developed a voice that was his own, Klein maintained.

In the two latest stories of the 1938-1944 period, "Flying Home" and "King of the Bingo Game," Ellison creates characters congruent with his sense of pluralism and possibility and does so in a narrative style that begins to approach the complexity of *Invisible Man.* As Arthur P. Davis noted, in "Flying Home" Ellison combines realism, folk story, symbolism, and a touch of surrealism to present his protagonist, Todd. In a fictional world composed of myriad levels of the mythic and the folk, the classical and the modern, Todd fights to free himself of imposed definitions. In "King of the Bingo Game," Ellison experiments with integrating sources and techniques. As in all of Ellison's early stories, the protagonist is a young black man fighting for his freedom against forces and people that attempt to deny it. In "King of the Bingo Game," Robert G. O'Meally argued in *The Craft of Ralph Ellison,* "the struggle is seen in its most abstracted form." This abstraction results from the "dreamlike shifts of time and levels of consciousness" that dominate the surrealistic story and also from the fact that "the King is Ellison's first character to sense the frightening absurdity of everyday American life." In an epiphany that frees him from illusion and which places him, even if for only a moment, in control, the King realizes "that his battle for freedom and identity must be waged not against individuals or even groups, but against no less than history and fate," O'Meally declared. Ellison saw his black hero as one who wages the oldest battle in human history: the fight for freedom to be timelessly human, to engage in the "tragic struggle of humanity," as the writer asserted in *Shadow and Act.*

Whereas the King achieves awareness for a moment, the Invisible Man not only becomes aware but is able to articulate fully the struggle. As Ellison noted in his preface to the anniversary edition of the novel, too often characters have been "figures caught up in the most intense forms of social struggle, subject to the most extreme forms of the human predicament but yet seldom able to articulate the issues which tortured them." The Invisible Man is endowed with eloquence; he is Ellison's radical experiment with a fiction that insists upon the full range and humanity of the black character.

Ellison began *Invisible Man* in 1945. Although he was at work on a never-completed war novel at the time, he recalled in his 1982 preface that he could not ignore the "taunting, disembodied voice" he heard beckoning him to write *Invisible Man*. Published in 1952 after a seven-year creative struggle on the part of its author, and awarded the National Book Award in 1953, *Invisible Man* received critical acclaim. Although some early re-viewers were puzzled or disappointed by the experi-mental narrative techniques, many now agree that these techniques give the work its lasting force and account for Ellison's influence on modern fiction. The novel is a fugue of cultural fragments—echoes of Homer, Joyce, Eliot, and Hemingway join forces with the sounds of spirituals, blues, jazz, and nursery rhymes. The Invis-ible Man is as haunted by Louis Armstrong's "What did I do/ To be so black/ And blue?" as he is by Heming-way's bullfight scenes and his matadors' grace under pressure. The linking together of these disparate cul-tural elements allows the Invisible Man to draw the portrait of his inner face that is the way out of his waste-land.

In the novel, Ellison clearly employed the traditional motif of the bildungsroman, or novel of education: the Invisible Man moves from innocence to experience, darkness to light, from blindness to sight. Complicating this linear journey, however, is the narrative frame pro-vided by the prologue and epilogue which the narrator composes after the completion of his above-ground educational journey. Yet readers begin with the pro-logue, written in his underground chamber on the "bor-der area" of Harlem where he is waging a guerrilla war against the Monopolated Light & Power Company by invisibly draining their power. At first denied the story of his discovery, readers must be initiated through the act of re-experiencing the events that led them and the narrator to this hole. Armed with some suggestive hints and symbols, readers then start the journey toward a re-visioning of the Invisible Man, America, and them-selves.

The act of writing, of ordering and defining the self, is what gives the Invisible Man freedom and what allows him to manage the absurdity and chaos of everyday life. Writing frees the self from imposed definitions, from the straitjacket of all that would limit the produc-tive possibilities of the self. Echoing the pluralism of the novel's form, the Invisible Man insists on the free-dom to be ambivalent, to love and to hate, to denounce and to defend the America he inherits. Ellison himself was well acquainted with the ambivalence of his Ameri-can heritage; nowhere is it more evident than in his name. Named after the nineteenth-century essayist and poet Ralph Waldo Emerson, whom Ellison's father ad-mired, the name created for Ellison embarrassment,

confusion, and a desire to be the American writer his namesake called for. And Ellison placed such emphasis on his unnamed yet self-named narrator's breaking the shackles of restrictive definitions, of what others call reality or right, he also freed himself, as Robert B. Stepto argued in *From behind the Veil: A Study of Afro-American Narrative,* from the strictures of the tradi-tional slave narratives of Frederick Douglass and W.E.B. Du Bois. By consciously invoking this form but then not bringing the motif of "ascent and immersion" to its traditional completion, Ellison revoiced the form, made it his own, and stepped outside it.

In a *PMLA* essay, Susan Blake argued that Ellison's in-sistence that black experience be ritualized as part of the larger human experience results in a denial of the unique social reality of black life. Because Ellison so thoroughly adapted black folklore into the Western tra-dition, Blake found that the definition of black life be-comes "not black but white"; it "exchanges the self-definition of the folk for the definition of the masters." Thorpe Butler, in a *College Language Association Jour-nal* essay, defended Ellison against Blake's criticism. He declared that Ellison's depiction of specific black experience as part of the universal does not "diminish the unique richness and anguish" of that experience and does not "diminish the force of Ellison's protest against the blind, cruel dehumanization of black Americans by white society." This debate extends arguments that have appeared since the publication of the novel. Underlying these controversies is the old, uneasy argument about the relationship of art and politics, of literary practice and social commitment.

Although the search for identity is the major theme of *Invisible Man,* other aspects of the novel have also re-ceived critical attention. Among them, as Joanne Giza noted in *Black American Writers: Bibliographical Es-says,* are literary debts and analogies, comic elements, the metaphor of vision, use of the blues, and folkloric elements. Although all of these concerns are part of the larger issue of identity, Ellison's use of blues and folk-lore has been singled out as a major contribution to contemporary literature and culture. Since the publica-tion of *Invisible Man,* scores of articles have appeared on these two topics, a fact which in turn has led to a re-discovery and revisioning of the importance of blues and folklore to American literature and culture in gen-eral.

Much of Ellison's groundbreaking work is presented in *Shadow and Act.* Published in 1964, this collection of essays, said Ellison, is "concerned with three general themes: with literature and folklore, with Negro musical expression—especially jazz and the blues—and with the complex relationship between the Negro American subculture and North American culture as a whole." This volume has been hailed as one of the more prominent examples of cultural criticism to appear in the twentieth century. Writing in *Commentary*, Robert Penn Warren praised the astuteness of Ellison's perceptions; in *New Leader*, Stanley Edgar Hyman proclaimed Ellison "the profoundest cultural critic we have." In the *New York Review of Books*, R.W.B. Lewis explored Ellison's study of black music as a form of power and found that "Ellison is not only a self-identifier but the source of self-definition in others."

Published in 1986, *Going to the Territory* is a second collection of essays reprising many of the subjects and concerns treated in *Shadow and Act*: literature, art, music, the relationships of black and white cultures, fragments of autobiography, tributes to such noted black Americans as Richard Wright, Duke Ellington, and painter Romare Beardon. With the exception of "An Extravagance of Laughter," a lengthy examination of Ellison's response to Jack Kirkland's dramatization of Erskine Caldwell's novel *Tobacco Road*, the essays in *Going to the Territory* are reprints of previously published articles or speeches, most of them dating from the 1960s.

Ellison's influence as both novelist and critic, as artist and cultural historian, has been enormous. In special issues of *Black World* and *College Language Association Journal* devoted to Ellison, strident attacks appear alongside equally spirited accolades. Perhaps another measure of Ellison's stature and achievement was his readers' vigil for his long-awaited second novel. Although Ellison often refused to answer questions about the work-in-progress, there was enough evidence during the author's lifetime to suggest that the manuscript was very large, that all or part of it had been destroyed in a fire and was being rewritten, and that its creation was a long and painful task. Most readers waited expectantly, believing that Ellison, who writes in *Shadow and Act* that he "failed of eloquence" in *Invisible Man*, intended to wait until his second novel equaled his imaginative vision of the American novel as conqueror of the frontier, equaled the Emersonian call for a literature to release all people from the bonds of oppression.

Eight excerpts from this novel-in-progress were originally published in journals such as *Quarterly Review of Literature, Massachusetts Review*, and *Noble Savage*. Set in the South in the years spanning the Jazz Age and the civil rights movement, these fragments seem an attempt to recreate modern American history and identity. The major characters are the Reverend Hickman, a one-time jazz musician, and Bliss, the light-skinned boy whom Hickman adopts and who later passes into white society and becomes Senator Sunraider, an advocate of white supremacy. As O'Meally noted in *The Craft of Ralph Ellison*, the major difference between Bliss and Ellison's earlier young protagonists is that despite some harsh collisions with reality, Bliss refuses to divest himself of his illusions and accept his personal history. Said O'Meally: "Moreover, it is a renunciation of the blackness of American experience and culture, a refusal to accept the American past in all its complexity."

After Ellison's death on April 16, 1994, speculation about the existence of the second novel reignited, and it was eventually announced that Ellison had left a manuscript of over 1,000 pages. In 1999, five years after the writer's death, rumors surrounding this second novel were finally answered—at least in part—with the publication of *Juneteenth*. The novel was culled from Ellison's voluminous manuscript by John F. Callahan, who became Ellison's literary executor. According to Callahan, the published form of *Juneteenth* consists of several distinct elements: a 1959 published story titled "And Hickman Arrives"; one of three long narratives—referred to as "Book Two" in Ellison's notes—in the novel that Ellison had been working on for years before he died; a thirty-eight page draft titled "Bliss's Birth"; and a single paragraph from a short fictional piece titled "Cadillac Flambe." The chief characters remain the same as those from the earlier published excerpts: the white, race-baiting Senator Sunraider (also called "Bliss") and the black minister Alonzo Hickman, who raised Bliss as a child.

The action of *Juneteenth* is set in motion via a visit by Hickman to the Senate chambers to hear Bliss speak. During the speech, Bliss is mortally wounded by a gunman, and the remainder of the novel features a dying Bliss and a watchful Hickman—the only person Bliss allows to see him—reminiscing about their earlier relationship. Much like *Invisible Man*, the novel addresses such themes as the black-white divide in America, the nature of identity, and the interaction between politics and religion. The novel's title, in fact, comes from a combined religious/political holiday celebrated by African Americans to commemorate a day in June 1865, when black slaves in Texas finally discovered that they were free—more than two years after Abraham Lincoln issued the Emancipation Proclamation.

Given the unusual circumstances of the book's publication, reviewers perhaps inevitably focused as much on these circumstances as on the merits of the work itself. Specifically, critics focused on Callahan's role in shaping a single narrative out of Ellison's sprawling manuscript despite the lack of any instructions from the author himself about what he intended the novel to be. Lamenting that Callahan had excised two of the three narratives that made up Ellison's manuscript, *New York Times Book Review* contributor Louis Menand noted, "It seems unfair to Ellison to review a novel he did not write. . . . A three-part work implies counterpoint: whatever appears in a Book 2 must be designed to derive its novelistic significance from whatever would have appeared in a Book One and a Book Three." According to Gerald Early in Chicago's *Tribune Books*, the new work "reads very much like the pastiche it is, with uneven characterization, clashing styles of writing and shifting points of view, and a jumbled narrative. The reader should be warned that this is a very unfinished product." Some reviewers reserved praise for certain prose sections that reflect Ellison's dazzling technical ability; Early, for instance, remarked on the "passages of affecting, sometimes tour-de-force writing and some deft wordplay," while a *Publishers Weekly* reviewer commented that the book's "flashbacks showcase Ellison's stylized set pieces, among the best scenes he has written." In the end, though, critics expressed reservations that the book should ever have been released. Menand concluded forcefully, "This is not Ralph Ellison's second novel," while Early stated that "I wonder if the world and Ralph Ellison have been best served by the publication of this work."

Despite concerns over *Juneteenth*, critics noted that Ellison's literary reputation—relying heavily on the landmark *Invisible Man*—remains secure. In 2003, a fifteen-foot-high bronze tribute honoring Ellison and *Invisible Man* was unveiled in New York's Riverside Park in West Harlem, facing the apartment building in which Ellison lived for more than thirty years.

BIOGRAPHICAL AND CRITICAL SOURCES:

BOOKS

Benstion, Kimberly W., editor, *Speaking for You: The Vision of Ralph Ellison*, Howard University Press (Washington, DC), 1987.

Bishop, Jack, *Ralph Ellison*, Chelsea House (New York, NY), 1988.

Bloom, Harold, editor, *Ralph Ellison: Modern Critical Views*, Chelsea House (New York, NY), 1986.

Busby, Mark, *Ralph Ellison*, Twayne (Boston, MA), 1991.

Callahan, John F., *In the African-American Grain: The Pursuit of Voice in Twentieth-Century Black Fiction*, University of Illinois Press (Urbana, IL), 1988.

Concise Dictionary of American Literary Biography: The New Consciousness, 1941-1948, Thomson Gale (Detroit, MI), 1987.

Contemporary Literary Criticism, Thomson Gale (Detroit, MI), Volume 1, 1973, Volume 3, 1975, Volume 11, 1979, Volume 54, 1989.

Cooke, Michael, *Afro-American Literature in the Twentieth Century: The Achievement of Intimacy*, Yale University Press (New Haven, CT), 1984.

Davis, Arthur P., *From the Dark Tower: Afro-American Writers, 1900 to 1960*, Howard University Press (Washington, DC), 1974.

Dictionary of Literary Biography, Thomson Gale (Detroit, MI), Volume 2: *American Novelists since World War II*, 1978, Volume 76: *Afro-American Writers, 1940-1955*, 1988.

Ellison, Ralph, *Invisible Man* (thirtieth-anniversary edition with new introduction by author), Random House, 1982.

Ellison, Ralph, *Shadow and Act* (essays), Random House (New York, NY), 1964.

Graham, Maryemma, and Amritjit Singh, editors, *Conversations with Ralph Ellison*, University Press of Mississippi (Jackson, MS), 1995.

Harper, Michael S., and Robert B. Stepto, *Chant of Saints: A Gathering of Afro-American Literature, Art, and Scholarship*, University of Illinois Press (Urbana, IL), 1979.

Inge, M. Thomas, editor, *Black American Writers: Bibliographic Essays, Volume 2: Richard Wright, Ralph Ellison, James Baldwin, and Amiri Baraka*, St. Martin's Press (New York, NY), 1978.

Jothiprakash, R., *Commitment as a Theme in African American Literature: A Study of James Baldwin and Ralph Ellison*, Wyndham Hall Press (Bristol, IN), 1994.

Klein, Marcus, *After Alienation: American Novels in Mid-Century*, World Publishing (Cleveland, OH), 1964.

Lynch, Michael F., *Creative Revolt: A Study of Wright, Ellison, and Dostoevsky*, P. Lang (New York, NY), 1990.

McSweeney, Kerry, *Invisible Man: Race and Identity*, Twayne (Boston, MA), 1988.

Nadel, Alan, *Invisible Criticism: Ralph Ellison and the American Canon*, University of Iowa Press (Iowa City, IA), 1988.

O'Meally, Robert G., *The Craft of Ralph Ellison*, Harvard University Press (Cambridge, MA, 1980.

O'Meally, Robert G., *New Essays on Invisible Man*, Cambridge University Press (Cambridge, England), 1988.

Parr, Susan Resneck, and Pancho Savery, editors, *Approaches to Teaching Ellison's "Invisible Man,"* Modern Language Associates of America (New York, NY), 1989.

Stepto, Robert B., *From behind the Veil: A Study of Afro-American Narrative*, University of Illinois Press (Champaign, IL), 1979.

Sundquist, Eric J., editor, *Cultural Contexts for Ralph Ellison's Invisible Man*, Bedford Books (Boston, MA), 1995.

Watts, Jerry Gafio, *Heroism and the Black Intellectual: Ralph Ellison, Politics, and Afro-American Intellectual Life*, University of North Carolina Press (Chapel Hill, NC), 1994.

PERIODICALS

African American Review, summer, 2002, Christopher A. Shinn, "Masquerade, Magic, and Carnival in Ralph Ellison's Invisible Man," pp. 243-263.

America, August 27, 1994, p. 26.

Atlantic, July, 1952; December, 1970; August, 1986.

Black American Literature Forum, summer, 1978.

Black World, December, 1970 (special Ellison issue).

Carleton Miscellany, winter, 1980 (special Ellison issue).

Chicago Review, Volume 19, number 2, 1967.

Chicago Tribune, June 18, 1992, p. 1.

Chicago Tribune Book World, August 10, 1986.

College Language Association Journal, December, 1963; June, 1967; March, 1970 (special Ellison issue); September, 1971; December, 1971; December, 1972; June, 1973; March, 1974; September, 1976; September, 1977; number 25, 1982; number 27, 1984.

Commentary, November, 1953; number 39, 1965.

English Journal, September, 1969; May, 1973; November, 1984.

Harper's, October, 1959; March, 1967; July, 1967.

Jet, May 19, 2003, "Memorial to Famed Author Ralph Ellison Is Unveiled in New York," pp. 12-14.

Los Angeles Times, August 8, 1986.

Massachusetts Review, autumn, 1967; autumn, 1977.

Modern Fiction Studies, winter, 1969-70.

Nation, May 10, 1952; September 9, 1964; November 9, 1964; September 20, 1965.

Negro American Literature Forum, July, 1970; summer, 1973; Number 9, 1975; spring, 1977.

Negro Digest, May, 1964; August, 1967.

Negro History Bulletin, May, 1953; October, 1953.

New Criterion, September, 1983.

New Leader, October 26, 1964.

New Republic, November 14, 1964; August 4, 1986.

Newsweek, August 12, 1963; October 26, 1964; May 2, 1994, p. 58.

New Yorker, May 31, 1952; November 22, 1976; March 14, 1994, p. 34.

New York Herald Tribune Book Review, April 13, 1952.

New York Review of Books, January 28, 1964; January 28, 1965.

New York Times, April 13, 1952; April 24, 1985; April 17, 1994, p. A38; April 20, 1994, p. C13; April 18, 1996, pp. B1, B2.

New York Times Book Review, April 13, 1952; May 4, 1952; October 25, 1964; January 24, 1982; August 3, 1986; June 20, 1999, p. 4.

New York Times Magazine, November 20, 1966; January 1, 1995, p. 22.

PMLA, January, 1979.

Publishers Weekly, March 22, 1999, p. 68.

Renascence, spring, 1974; winter, 1978.

Saturday Review, April 12, 1952; March 14, 1953; December 11, 1954; January 1, 1955; April 26, 1958; May 17, 1958; July 12, 1958; September 27, 1958; July 28, 1962; October 24, 1964.

Southern Humanities Review, winter, 1970.

Southern Literary Journal, spring, 1969.

Southern Review, fall, 1974; summer, 1985.

Studies in American Fiction, spring, 1973.

Studies in Black Literature, autumn, 1971; autumn, 1972; spring, 1973; spring, 1975; spring, 1976; winter, 1976.

Time, April 14, 1952; February 9, 1959; February 1, 1963; April 6, 1970.

Times Literary Supplement, January 18, 1968.

Tribune Books (Chicago, IL), April 24, 1994, p. 3; June 13, 1999, p. 1.

Village Voice, November 19, 1964.

Washington Post, August 19-21, 1973; April 21, 1982; February 9, 1983; March 30, 1983; July 23, 1986; April 18, 1994, p. C1; April 25, 1994, p. C2.

Washington Post Book World, May 17, 1987.

Washington Times, February 16, 2002, Marlene L. Johnson, "Well-rounded Look at Ellison; Documentary Sees Many Sides of 'Invisible Man' Author," p. D04.

ONLINE

Center X (University of California—Los Angeles) Web Site, http://centerx.gseis.ucla.edu/ (April 6, 2004).

OBITUARIES:

PERIODICALS

Time, April 25, 1994.

*   *   *

ELLISON, Ralph Waldo
   See ELLISON, Ralph

*   *   *

ELLROY, James 1948-

PERSONAL: Born March 4, 1948, Los Angeles, CA; son of Geneva (a nurse; maiden name, Hilliker) Ellroy; married Mary Doherty, 1988 (marriage ended); married Helen Knode (a journalist and author).

ADDRESSES: Home—New Canaan, CT. *Agent*—Nat Sobel, Sobel, Weber Associates, Inc., 146 East 19th St., New York, NY 10003.

CAREER: Writer. Worked at a variety of jobs, including as a golf caddy in California and New York, 1977-84. *Military service:* U.S. Army, 1965.

AWARDS, HONORS: Edgar Award nomination, Mystery Writers of America, 1982, for *Clandestine;* Prix Mystere Award, 1990, for *The Big Nowhere.*

WRITINGS:

"L.A. QUARTET" CRIME NOVELS

The Black Dahlia, Mysterious Press (New York, NY), 1987.
The Big Nowhere, Mysterious Press (New York, NY), 1988.
L.A. Confidential, Mysterious Press (New York, NY), 1990.
White Jazz, Knopf (New York, NY), 1992.

NOVELS

Brown's Requiem, Avon (New York, NY), 1981.
Clandestine, Avon (New York, NY), 1982.

Blood on the Moon (also see below), Mysterious Press (New York, NY), 1984.
Because the Night (also see below), Mysterious Press (New York, NY), 1984.
Killer on the Road, Avon (New York, NY), 1986.
Suicide Hill (also see below), Mysterious Press (New York, NY), 1986.
Silent Terror, introduction by Jonathan Kellerman, Avon (New York, NY), 1986.
Hollywood Nocturnes, Otto Penzler Books (New York, NY), 1994.
American Tabloid, Knopf (New York, NY), 1995.
L.A. Noir, (contains *Blood on the Moon, Because the Night,* and *Suicide Hill*), Mysterious Press (New York, NY), 1998.
The Cold Six Thousand, Knopf (New York, NY), 2001.
Destination: Morgue!: L.A. Tales, Knopf (New York, NY), 2004.

OTHER

(Author of introduction) Jim Thompson, *Heed the Thunder,* Armchair Detective Library (New York, NY), 1991.
My Dark Places: An L.A. Crime Memoir, Knopf (New York, NY), 1996.
Crimewave: Reportage and Fiction from the Underside of L.A., Random House (New York, NY), 1999.
(Author of afterword) Bill O'Reilly, *The No-Spin Zone: Confrontations with the Powerful and Famous in America,* Broadway Books (New York, NY), 2001.
(Editor, with Otto Penzler) *The Best American Mystery Stories, 2002,* American Library Association (New York, NY), 2002.

Author of the story "Dark Blue." Author's personal archives, including handwritten manuscripts and correspondence with editors, are housed at the University of South Carolina's Thomas Cooper Library.

ADAPTATIONS: Blood on the Moon was filmed as *Cop,* Atlantic, 1988. *L.A. Confidential* was filmed in 1997 by New Regency, directed by Curtis Hanson and starring Kevin Spacey, Russell Crowe, Danny DeVito, and Kim Basinger. *L.A. Noir* is available as an audiobook, Books on Tape, 1998. Robert Greenwald directed *James Ellroy's Los Angeles* as a mini-series containing characters from Ellroy's novels, as well as a film version of *My Dark Places;* the 2003 United Artists film *Dark Blue* was adapted from Ellroy's story by David Ayer, directed by Ron Shelton; *The Black Dahlia* was adapted for a film directed by Brian DePalma; a film version of *White Jazz* was in production.

WORK IN PROGRESS: A script for a film about Hollywood lawyer Sidney Korshak titled *The Man Who Kept Secrets.*

SIDELIGHTS: James Ellroy is a prominent crime novelist who has won acclaim for his vivid portraits of Los Angeles, California's seamier aspects. Ellroy himself spent many years on the Los Angeles streets. After an arduous childhood—his parents divorced when he was four, his mother was murdered six years later, and his father died seven years after that—Ellroy took to the streets. Having already been expelled from both high school for excessive truancy and the military for faking a nervous breakdown, he turned to crime, committing petty burglaries to fund his increasing alcohol dependency. From 1965 to 1977 Ellroy was arrested for such crimes as drunkenness, shoplifting, and trespassing on approximately thirty occasions. Twelve times he was convicted and was imprisoned for eight months.

In 1977 Ellroy's life changed radically after he was hospitalized with double pneumonia. Profoundly shaken by his brush with death, he entered an Alcoholics Anonymous program and then managed, through a friend, to obtain employment as a caddy at posh Hollywood golf courses. By this time Ellroy was already determined to pursue a literary career. Before he had been hospitalized, he had spent many hours in public libraries, where he drank discreetly while poring through twentieth-century American literature. He also read the more than two hundred crime novels he had stolen from various markets and bookstores, and it was the crime genre that eventually enticed him into commencing his own literary career.

In 1979, while continuing with his job as a caddy, Ellroy began writing his first book. The result, after more than ten months of steady writing in longhand, was *Brown's Requiem,* the story of a private investigator who uncovers a deadly band of extortionists roaming the streets of Los Angeles.

Brown's Requiem won Ellroy immediate acceptance from an agent who in turn quickly managed to place the manuscript with a publisher. Ellroy's actual earnings from the novel, though, were not enough to support him, and so he remained a golf caddy while he produced a second novel, *Clandestine.* This novel, in which a former police officer tracks down his ex-lover's killer, received a nomination for the crime genre's prestigious Edgar Award from the Mystery Writers of America.

Ellroy followed *Clandestine* with *Blood on the Moon,* the story of two brilliant men—a somewhat unstable police detective, Lloyd Hopkins, and a psychopathic murderer—who clash in Los Angeles. In 1984, the year that this novel appeared in print, Ellroy finally managed to leave his caddying job and devote himself fully to writing. Among the next few novels he published were *Because the Night, Killer on the Road,* and *Suicide Hill,* the last in which Lloyd Hopkins, the temperamental protagonist of the earlier *Blood on the Moon,* opposes a vicious bank robber.

In 1987 Ellroy produced *The Black Dahlia,* the first volume in his "L.A. Quartet" series. *The Black Dahlia* is based on the actual 1947 unsolved murder of prostitute Elizabeth Short, whose severed body was found on a Los Angeles street. The murder bears similarities to that of Ellroy's own mother. Like the Black Dahlia case, the murder of Ellroy's mother was never solved, but in Ellroy's novel he proposes a possible solution to the Black Dahlia mystery. "Ellroy's novel is true to the facts as they are known," wrote David Haldane in the *Los Angeles Times.* "But it provides a fictional solution to the crime consistent with those facts." Haldane added that in tracing the Black Dahlia case Ellroy "conducts an uncompromising tour of the obscene, violent, gritty, obsessive, darkly sexual world" that existed within Los Angeles during the 1940s, "complete with names and places."

Ellroy continued to chart the Los Angeles underworld in *The Big Nowhere,* in which two criminal investigations converge with shocking results. The novel takes place during the McCarthy era of the 1950s, when fear of the communist threat in the United States was widespread. In one investigation, a deputy sheriff probes a rash of killings in the homosexual community. The other case involves a city investigator's efforts to further his career by exposing a band of alleged communists circulating within the film industry. The two cases become one when the ambitious investigator employs the deputy as a decoy to lure an influential leftist known as the Red Queen. This collaborative operation leads to unexpected discoveries.

The Big Nowhere won Ellroy substantial recognition as a proficient writer. According to London *Times* writer Peter Guttridge, it established its author as one "among that handful of crime writers whose work is regarded as literature." Among the novel's enthusiasts was Bruce Cook, who proclaimed in the *Washington Post Book World* that Ellroy has produced "a first-rate crime novel, a violent picture in blood-red and grays, set against a fascinating period background."

Ellroy realized further acclaim with *L.A. Confidential,* in which three police officers cross paths while conducting their affairs in 1950s Los Angeles. The protagonists here are wildly different: Bud White is a brutish, excessively violent law enforcer; Trashcan Vincennes is a corrupt narcotics investigator; and Ed Exley is a rigid, politically ambitious sergeant. The three men come together while probing a bizarre incident in which several coffee shop patrons were gunned down. The ensuing plot, reported Kevin Moore in Chicago's *Tribune Books,* "plays itself out with all the impact—and excess—of a shotgun blast." *People* reviewer Lorenzo Carcaterra judged that *L.A. Confidential* is "violently unsettling" and "ugly yet engrossing." *White Jazz,* the concluding volume in the "L.A. Quartet," appeared in 1992.

After completing his four-book series, Ellroy decided upon a change in course. "I think," he told Guttridge in the London *Times,* "it's time I moved beyond Los Angeles." Ellroy added, however, that he planned to continue to pursue what he called his "one goal—to be the greatest crime writer of all time."

Move beyond Los Angeles he did in his next novel, *American Tabloid,* an ambitious, tightly plotted narrative of national and international conspiracy and crime in the 1960s that culminates with the great "unsolved" American crime: the Kennedy assassination. Two FBI agents and a CIA operative make up the three central characters through which Ellroy spins this complex, disturbing, and visceral tale of American history "from the bottom up," in the words of a *Booklist* critic. *American Tabloid,* rife with Ellroy's signature staccato language and over-the-top violence, sold well and invited positive reviews and colorful critical descriptions. A contributor to *Booklist* characterized the novel as being about the "most potent drug of all"—power. "It's as if Ellroy injects us with a mainline pop of the undiluted power that surges through the veins of his obsessed characters," the critic added. In *Time,* Paul Gray called *American Tabloid* "American history as well as Hellzapoppin, a long slapstick routine careening around a manic premise: What if the fabled American innocence is all shuck and jive?" Gray went on to praise the novel as "a big, boisterous, rude and shameless reminder of why reading can be so engrossing and so much fun."

With his next project, 1996's "crime memoir" *My Dark Places,* Ellroy returns not only to Los Angeles, but also to his own unresolved past. With his early novel *The Black Dahlia,* Ellroy had attempted to put to rest questions about his mother's death, but here he sets out to solve his mother's murder himself. He enlists the help of a retired Los Angeles police officer and starts retracing the evidence of the almost thirty-year-old crime. Ellroy reports the facts of the investigation in great de-

tail, using a style similar to that of his crime novels, a decision critics found only partially successful. A writer for *Kirkus Reviews* described the language as "a punchy but monotonous rhythm that's as relentless as a jackhammer," while Bruce Jay Friedman in the *New York Times Review* compared it to something that "might've been fired out of a riveting gun." Ellroy never finds the murderer, but he does speculate on the impact of his mother's death on his character and career and learns more about her life. Although a *Kirkus Reviews* critic warned that "Those expecting an autobiographical exposé of the writer's psychological clockwork will feel stonewalled by macho reserve," Friedman found the psychological dimension satisfying. "All in all, a rough and strenuously involving book," he commented in his review of *My Dark Places.* "Early on, Mr. Ellroy makes a promise to his dead mother that seems maudlin at first: 'I want to give you breath.' But he's done just that and—on occasion—taken ours away."

After *My Dark Places,* Elroy publically stated that he was no longer interested in the genre. "I'm not writing crime fiction anymore," he told Jeff Guinn for the *Knight Ridder/Tribune News Service.* "I've moved on with what I wanted to do. I wanted to write fiction about history, to have rewritten history to my own specifications." Despite disappointing crime fans, he kept true to his word; his 2001 novel, *The Cold Six Thousand,* is a follow-up to *American Tabloid* and the second in the projected "Underworld U.S.A." trilogy about politics and racism in America during the 1960s and 1970s. *The Cold Six Thousand* covers the years 1963 through 1968 and includes such historical figures as Howard Hughes, J. Edgar Hoover, Martin Luther King, Jr., and Robert Kennedy. Probing the dark side of America, Ellroy tells of Hoover's hatred of King, a Central Intelligence Agency that smuggles dope, and the mess of the Vietnam War. The story focuses primarily on a Las Vegas police officer named Wayne Tedrow, Jr., who inadvertently becomes involved in the cover up of President John F. Kennedy's assassination. Through the course of the novel Tedrow becomes involved in various unsavory organizations, including the Mafia and the Ku Klux Klan, as Ellroy offers his vision of an America that is anything but innocent. Although Tedrow is the novel's "hero," by the end he has become a corrupted, ruthless, and vengeful killer who plays a role in the assassination of King. Commenting on the book during an interview with Dorman T. Shindler for *Writer,* Ellroy noted: "The *Cold Six Thousand* is a story about violent men in a violent time doing terrible, violent things. This is the epic of bad white men doing bad things in the name of authority. This is the humanity of bad white men."

Reviewing *The Cold Six Thousand* for the *Knight Ridder/Tribune News Service,* Fred Grimm wondered if perhaps "Ellroy was outdone this time by wider ambition." The novel's look at the assassinations of John and Bobby Kennedy and of King "offers only another variation of theories explored by 10,000 wild-eyed paranoids," the critic added. A *Publishers Weekly* contributor, however, praised the novel as "a career performance," and went on to note that, "With Ellroy's ice-pick declarative prose . . . plus his heart-trembling, brain-searing subject matter, readers will feel kneed, stomped upon and then kicked-right up into the maw of hard truth." Thomas Auger, writing in the *Library Journal,* called the book "readable yet complex in its character development and critical examination of U.S. public policy." Paul Gray wrote in *Time* that *The Cold Six Thousand* is an "exceedingly nasty piece of work," and went on to note: "Yet it is often funny . . . and traces an unexpectedly moral arc through all its mayhem. Pick it up if you dare; put it down if you can."

BIOGRAPHICAL AND CRITICAL SOURCES:

BOOKS

Twentieth-Century Crime and Mystery Writers, 3rd edition, St. James Press (Detroit, MI), 1991, pp. 347-348.

PERIODICALS

Armchair Detective, spring, 1987, p. 206; winter, 1991, p. 31.
Booklist, January 15, 1995.
Christian Science Monitor, October 2, 1987, p. B5.
Interview, December, 1996, p. 70.
Kirkus Reviews, September 15, 1996.
Knight Ridder/Tribune News Service, May 30, 2001, Fred Grimm, review of *The Cold Six Thousand,* p. K7849; June 13, 2001, Jeff Guinn, "Political History, as Told by James Ellroy," p. K5306.
Library Journal, April 15, 2001, Thomas Auger, review of *The Cold Six Thousand,* p. 131.
Los Angeles Times, October 4, 1987; May 27, 1990.
Los Angeles Times Book Review, June 3, 1984, p. 18; September 13, 1987, p. 16; October 9, 1988, p. 12; July 8, 1990, p. 8.
Nation, December 2, 1996, p. 25.
New Statesman, June 19, 1987, p. 31; January 22, 1988, p. 33.
New York Times, November 3, 2003, Virginia Heffernan, "A Writer, Hard-boiled and Shaped by Murder," p. E8.
New York Times Book Review, July 22, 1984, p. 32; July 6, 1986, p. 21; November 8, 1987, p. 62; October 9, 1988, p. 41; September 3, 1989, p. 20; July 15, 1990, p. 26; June 30, 1991, p. 32; November 24, 1996.
Observer, May 13, 1984, p. 23.
People, December 14, 1987; July 2, 1990; November 25, 1996, p. 93.
Publishers Weekly, June 15, 1990, pp. 53-54; May 21, 2001, review of *The Cold Six Thousand,* p. 83.
Spectator, July 21, 1984, p. 29.
Time, April 10, 1995, p. 74; November 25, 1996, p. 115; May 21, 2003, Paul Gray, review of *The Cold Six Thousand,* p. 90.
Times (London, England), November 10, 1990.
Tribune Books (Chicago, IL), September 3, 1989, p. 5; June 10, 1990, p. 1.
Washington Post Book World, October 23, 1988, p. 10.
West Coast Review of Books, January, 1983, p. 43; September, 1983, p. 20; September, 1986, p. 27.
Writer, September, 2001, Dorman T. Shindler, "Fierce Ambition," interview with Ellroy, p. 28.

ONLINE

Salon.com, http://www.salon.com/ (December 9, 1996), interview with Ellroy.

*   *   *

EMECHETA, Buchi 1944-
(Florence Onye Buchi Emecheta)

PERSONAL: Born July 21, 1944, in Yaba, Lagos, Nigeria; daughter of Jeremy Nwabudike (a railway worker and molder) and Alice Ogbanje (Okwuekwu) Emecheta; married Sylvester Onwordi, 1960 (separated, 1966); children: Florence, Sylvester, Jake, Christy, Alice. *Education:* University of London, B.Sc. (with honors), 1972, Ph.D., 1991. *Religion:* Anglican *Hobbies and other interests:* Gardening, attending the theatre, listening to music, reading.

ADDRESSES: Home—7 Briston Grove, Crouch End, London N8 9EX, England.

CAREER: British Museum, London, England, library officer, 1965-69; Inner London Education Authority, London, youth worker and sociologist, 1969-76; community worker, Camden, NJ, 1976-78. Writer and lecturer, 1972—. Visiting professor at several universities throughout the United States, including Pennsylvania State University, University of California—Los Angeles, and University of Illinois—Urbana-Champaign, 1979; senior resident fellow and visiting professor of English, University of Calabar, Nigeria, 1980-81; lecturer, Yale University, 1982, London University, 1982—; fellow, London University, 1986. Proprietor, Ogwugwu Afor Publishing Company, 1982-83. Member of Home Secretary's Advisory Council on Race, 1979—, and of Arts Council of Great Britain, 1982-83.

AWARDS, HONORS: Jock Campbell Award, *New Statesman,* 1978, for literature by new or unregarded talent from Africa or the Caribbean; selected as the Best Black British Writer, 1978, and one of the Best British Young Writers, 1983.

WRITINGS:

In the Ditch, Barrie & Jenkins (London, England), 1972.
Second-Class Citizen (novel), Allison & Busby (London, England), 1974, Braziller (New York, NY), 1975.
The Bride Price: A Novel, Braziller (New York, NY), 1976, also published as *The Bride Price: Young Ibo Girl's Love; Conflict of Family and Tradition.*
The Slave Girl: A Novel, Braziller (New York, NY), 1977.
The Joys of Motherhood: A Novel, Braziller (New York, NY), 1979.
Destination Biafra: A Novel, Schocken (New York, NY), 1982.
Naira Power (novelette), Macmillan (London, England), 1982.
Double Yoke (novel), Schocken (New York, NY), 1982.
The Rape of Shavi (novel), Ogwugwu Afor (Ibuza, Nigeria), 1983, Braziller (New York, NY), 1985.
Adah's Story: A Novel, Allison & Busby (London, England), 1983.
Head above Water (autobiography), Ogwugwu Afor (Ibuza, Nigeria), 1984, Collins (London, England), 1986.
The Family (novel), Braziller (New York, NY), 1990.
Gwendolen (novel), Collins (London, England), 1990.
Kehinde, Heinemann (Portsmouth, NH), 1994.
The New Tribe, Heinemann (Portsmouth, NH), 2000.

FOR CHILDREN

Titch the Cat (based on story by daughter Alice Emecheta), Allison & Busby (London, England), 1979.

Nowhere to Play (based on story by daughter Christy Emecheta), Schocken (New York, NY), 1980.
The Moonlight Bride, Oxford University Press (Oxford, England), 1981.
The Wrestling Match, Oxford University Press (Oxford, England), 1981, Braziller (New York, NY), 1983.
Family Bargain (publication for schools), British Broadcasting Corp. (London, England), 1987.

OTHER

(Author of introduction and commentary) Maggie Murray, *Our Own Freedom* (book of photographs), Sheba Feminist (London, England), 1981.
A Kind of Marriage (teleplay; produced by BBC-TV), Macmillan (London, England), 1987.

Also author of teleplays *Tanya, a Black Woman,* produced by BBC-TV, and *The Juju Landlord.* Contributor to journals, including *New Statesman, Times Literary Supplement,* and *Guardian.*

SIDELIGHTS: Although Buchi Emecheta has resided in London since 1962, she is "Nigeria's best-known female writer," commented John Updike in the *New Yorker.* "Indeed, few writers of her sex . . . have arisen in any part of tropical Africa." Emecheta enjoys great popularity in Great Britain, and she has gathered an appreciative audience on this side of the Atlantic as well. Although Emecheta has written children's books and teleplays, she is best known for her historical novels set in Nigeria, both before and after independence. Concerned with the clash of cultures and the impact of Western values upon agrarian traditions and customs, Emecheta's work is strongly autobiographical, and, as Updike observed, much of it is especially concerned with "the situation of women in a society where their role, though crucial, was firmly subordinate and where the forces of potential liberation have arrived with bewildering speed."

Born to Ibo parents in Yaba, a small village near Lagos, Nigeria, Emecheta indicates that the Ibos "don't want you to lose contact with your culture," wrote Rosemary Bray in the *Voice Literary Supplement.* Bray explained that the oldest woman in the house plays an important role in that she is the "big mother" to the entire clan. Said Bray: "'She was very old and almost blind,'" Buchi recalls, "'And she would gather the young children around her after dinner and tell stories to us.'" The stories the children heard were about their origins and ancestors; and, according to Bray, Emecheta recalls: "I thought to myself 'No life could be more important than this.' So when people asked me what I wanted to do when I grew up I told them I wanted to be a storyteller—which is what I'm doing now."

In the Ditch, her first book, originally appeared as a series of columns in the *New Statesman.* Written in the form of a diary, it "is based on her own failed marriage and her experiences on the dole in London trying to rear alone her many children," stated Charlotte and David Bruner in *World Literature Today.* Called a "sad, sonorous, occasionally hilarious . . . extraordinary first novel," by Adrianne Blue of the *Washington Post Book World,* it details her impoverished existence in a foreign land, as well as her experience with racism, and "illuminates the similarities and differences between cultures and attitudes," remarked a *Times Literary Supplement* contributor, who thought *In the Ditch* merits "special attention."

Similarly autobiographical, Emecheta's second novel, *Second-Class Citizen,* "recounts her early marriage years, when she was trying to support her student-husband—a man indifferent to his own studies and later indifferent to her job searches, her childbearing, and her resistance to poverty," observed the Bruners. The novel is about a young, resolute, and resourceful Nigerian girl who, despite traditional tribal domination of females, manages to continue her own education; she marries a student and follows him to London, where he becomes abusive toward her. "Emecheta said people find it hard to believe that she has not exaggerated the truth in this autobiographical novel," reported Nancy Topping Bazin in *Black Scholar.* "The grimness of what is described does indeed make it painful to read." Called a "brave and angry book" by Marigold Johnson in the *Times Literary Supplement,* Emecheta's story, however, "is not accompanied by a misanthropic whine," noted Martin Levin in the *New York Times Book Review.* Alice Walker, who found it "one of the most informative books about contemporary African life" that she has read, observed in *Ms.* that "it raises fundamental questions about how creative and prosaic life is to be lived and to what purpose."

"Emecheta's women do not simply lie down and die," observed Bray. "Always there is resistance, a challenge to fate, a need to renegotiate the terms of the uneasy peace that exists between them and accepted traditions." Bray added that "Emecheta's women know, too, that between the rock of African traditions and the hard place of encroaching Western values, it is the women who will be caught."

Concerned with the clash of cultures, in *The Bride Price: A Novel,* Emecheta tells the story of a young Nigerian girl "whose life is complicated by traditional attitudes toward women," wrote Richard Cima in *Library Journal.* The young girl's father dies when she is thirteen; and, with her brother and mother, she becomes the property of her father's ambitious brother. She is permitted to remain in school only because it will increase her value as a potential wife. However, she falls in love with her teacher, a descendant of slaves; and because of familial objections, they elope, thereby depriving her uncle of the "bride price." When she dies in childbirth, she fulfills the superstition that a woman would not survive the birth of her first child if her bride price had not been paid. Susannah Clapp maintained in the *Times Literary Supplement,* that the quality of the novel "depends less on plot or characterization than on the information conveyed about a set of customs and the ideas which underlay them." Calling it "a captivating Nigerian novel lovingly but unsentimentally written, about the survival of ancient marriage customs in modern Nigeria," Valerie Cunningham added in *New Statesman* that this book "proves Buchi Emecheta to be a considerable writer."

Emecheta's *Slave Girl: A Novel* is about "a poor, gently raised Ibo girl who is sold into slavery to a rich African marketwoman by a feckless brother at the turn of the century," wrote a *New Yorker* contributor. Educated by missionaries, she joins the new church where she meets the man she eventually marries. In *Library Journal,* Cima thought that the book provides an "interesting picture of Christianity's impact on traditional Ibo society." Perceiving parallels between marriage and slavery, Emecheta explores the issue of "freedom within marriage in a society where slavery is supposed to have been abolished," wrote Cunningham in the *New Statesman,* adding that the book indicts both "pagan and Christian inhumanity to women." And although a contributor to *World Literature Today* suggested that the "historical and anthropological background" in the novel tends to destroy its "emotional complex," another contributor to the same journal believed that the sociological detail has been "unobtrusively woven into" it and that *The Slave Girl* represents Emecheta's "most accomplished work so far. It is coherent, compact and convincing."

"Emecheta's voice has been welcomed by many as helping to redress the somewhat one-sided picture of African women that has been delineated by male writers," according to a contributor to *A New Reader's Guide to African Literature.* Writing in *African Literature Today,* Eustace Palmer indicated that "the African novel has until recently been remarkable for the absense of what might be called the feminine point of view." Because of the relatively few female African novelists, "the presentation of women in the African novel has been left almost entirely to male voices . . . and their interest in African womanhood . . . has had to take second place to numerous other concerns," continued Palmer. "These male novelists, who have presented the African woman largely within the traditional milieu, have generally communicated a picture of a male-dominated and male-oriented society, and the satisfaction of the women with this state of things has been . . . completely taken for granted." Palmer added that the emergence of Emecheta and other "accomplished female African novelists . . . seriously challenges all these cozy assumptions. The picture of the cheerful contented female complacently accepting her lot is replaced by that of a woman who is powerfully aware of the unfairness of the system and who longs to be else's appendage." For instance, Palmer noted that *The Joys of Motherhood: A Novel* "presents essentially the same picture of traditional society . . . but the difference lies in the prominence in Emecheta's novel of the female point of view registering its disgust at male chauvinism and its dissatisfaction with what it considers an unfair and oppressive system."

The Joys of Motherhood is about a woman "who marries but is sent home in disgrace because she fails to bear a child quickly enough," wrote Bazin. "She then is sent to the city by her father to marry a man she has never seen. She is horrified when she meets this second husband because she finds him ugly, but she sees no alternative to staying with him. Poverty and repeated pregnancies wear her down; the pressure to bear male children forces her to bear child after child since the girls she has do not count." Palmer observed that "clearly, the man is the standard and the point of reference in this society. It is significant that the chorus of countrymen say, not that a woman without a child is a failed woman, but that a woman without a child *for her husband* is a failed woman." Bazin observed that in Emecheta's novels, "a woman must accept the double standard of sexual freedom: it permits polygamy and infidelity for both Christian and non-Christian men but only monogamy for women. These books reveal the extent to which the African woman's oppression is engrained in the African mores."

Acknowledging that "the issue of polygamy in Africa remains a controversial one," Palmer stated that what Emecheta stresses in *The Joys of Motherhood* is "the resulting dominance, especially sexual, of the male, and the relegation of the female into subservience, domesticity and motherhood." Nonetheless, despite Emeche-

ta's "angry glare," said Palmer, one can "glean from the novel the economic and social reasons that must have given rise to polygamy. . . . But the author concentrates on the misery and deprivation polygamy can bring." Palmer praised Emecheta's insightful psychological probing of her characters' thoughts: "Scarcely any other African novelist has succeeded in probing the female mind and displaying the female personality with such precision." Blue likewise suggested that Emecheta "tells this story in a plain style, denuding it of exoticism, displaying an impressive, embracing compassion." Calling it a "graceful, touching, ironically titled tale that bears a plain feminist message," Updike added that "in this compassionate but slightly distanced and stylized story of a life that comes to seem wasted, [Emecheta] sings a dirge for more than African pieties. The lives within *The Joys of Motherhood* might be, transposed into a different cultural key, those of our own rural ancestors."

Emecheta's "works reveal a great deal about the lives of African women and about the development of feminist perspectives," observed Bazin, explaining that one moves beyond an initial perspective of "personal experience," to perceive "social or communal" oppression. This second perspective "demands an analysis of the causes of oppression within the social mores and the patriarchal power structure," added Bazin. Finding both perspectives in Emecheta's work, Bazin thought that her descriptions reveal "what it is like to be for" millions of black African women. Although her feminist perspective is anchored in her own personal life, said Bazin, Emecheta "grew to understand how soon preference, bride price, polygamy, menstrual taboos, . . . wife beating, early marriages, early and unlimited pregnancies, arranged marriages, and male dominance in the home functioned to keep women powerless." The Bruners wrote that "obviously Emecheta is concerned about the plight of women, today and yesterday, in both technological and traditional societies, though she rejects a feminist label." Emecheta told the Bruners: "The main themes of my novels are African society and family; the historical, social, and political life in Africa as seen by a woman through events. I always try to show that the African male is oppressed and he too oppresses the African women. . . . I have not committed myself to the cause of African women only. I write about Africa as a whole."

Emecheta's *Destination Biafra: A Novel* is a story of the "history of Nigeria from the eve of independence to the collapse of the Biafran secessionist movement," wrote Robert L. Berner in *World Literature Today*. The novel has generated a mixed critical response, though.

In the *Times Literary Supplement,* Chinweizu felt that it "does not convey the feel of the experience that was Biafra. All it does is leave one wondering why it falls so devastatingly below the quality of Buchi Emecheta's previous works." Noting, however, that Emecheta's publisher reduced the manuscript by half, Berner suggested that "this may account for what often seems a rather elliptical narrative and for the frequently clumsy prose which too often blunts the novel's satiric edge." Finding the novel "different from any of her others . . . larger and more substantive," the Bruners stated: "Here she presents neither the life story of a single character nor the delineation of one facet of a culture but the whole perplexing canvas of people from diverse ethnic groups, belief systems, levels of society all caught in a disastrous civil war." Moreover, the Bruners felt that the "very objectivity of her reporting and her impartiality in recounting atrocities committed by all sides, military and civilian, have even greater impact because her motivation is not sadistic."

At about the same time that Emecheta published *Destination Biafra,* her novel *Double Yoke* also saw print. *Double Yoke* details the difficulties facing African women in the academic world; though at first, the heroine Nko's boyfriend seems progressive, he later repudiates her for allowing him to have sex with her before marriage. Nko must also deal with a professor who extorts sexual favors from her under the threat of preventing her from receiving her degree. According to Jewelle Gomez in *Black Scholar,* "Here, as in Emecheta's other novels, she speaks with an undeniably Nigerian voice; makes clear the Nigerian woman's circumscribed position in society and her skillful adaptation to it."

The Rape of Shavi represents somewhat of a departure in that "Emecheta attempts one of the most difficult of tasks: that of integrating the requirements of contemporary, realistic fiction with the narrative traditions of myth and folklore," wrote Somtow Sucharitkul in the *Washington Post Book World.* Roy Kerridge described the novel's plot in the *Times Literary Supplement:* "A plane crashes among strange tribespeople, white aviators are made welcome by the local king, they find precious stones, repair their plane and escape just as they are going to be forcibly married to native girls. The king's son and heir stows away and has adventures of his own in England." Called a "wise and haunting tale" by a *New Yorker* contributor, *The Rape of Shavi* "recounts the ruination of this small African society by voracious white interlopers," said Richard Eder in the *Los Angeles Times.* A few critics suggested that in *The Rape of Shavi,* Emecheta's masterful portrayal of her Shavian community is not matched by her depiction of the foreigners. Eder, for instance, called it a "lopsided fable," and declared: "It is not that the Shavians are noble and the whites monstrous; that is what fables are for. It is that the Shavians are finely drawn and the Westerners very clumsily. It is a duet between a flute and a kitchen drain." However, Sucharitkul thought that portraying the Shavians as "complex individuals" and the Westerners as "two dimensional, mythic types" presents a refreshing, seldom expressed, and "particularly welcome" point of view.

Although in the *New York Times* Michiko Kakutani called *The Rape of Shavi* "an allegorical tale, filled with ponderous morals about the evils of imperialism and tired aphorisms about nature and civilization," Sucharitkul believed that "the central thesis of [the novel] is brilliantly, relentlessly argued, and Emecheta's characters and societies are depicted with a bittersweet, sometimes painful honesty." The critic also praised Emecheta's "persuasive" prose: "It is prose that appears unusually simple at first, for it is full of the kind of rhythms and sentence structures more often found in folk tales than in contemporary novels. Indeed, in electing to tell her multilayered and often very contemporary story within a highly mythic narrative framework, the author walks a fine line between the pitfalls of preciosity and pretentiousness. By and large, the tightrope act is a success."

Following *The Rape of Shavi,* Emecheta seemed to be more concerned with discussing the lives of African immigrants to England and other western countries. The title character of *Gwendolen* is a young Jamaican girl whose parents move to England in search of a better life, leaving her in the care of her grandmother. Her grandmother's boyfriend molests her, and when she eventually rejoins her parents in England, her own father rapes her. Despite these troubles, and her father's suicide, she eventually finds happiness. "This modern ending," in the words of Kirsten Holst Peterson in the *Concise Dictionary of World Literary Biography,* "rests on a new set of relationships formed on the basis of personal choice rather than on blind acceptance of the established pattern of race and family relationships." Peterson concluded that "there seems to be an implicit suggestion that this alternative mode of social organization might avoid a repeat of the experiences of the main character."

In 1994's *Kehinde,* the heroine is Kehinde Okolo, described by a *Contemporary Black Biography* essayist as "a thirty-five-year-old Londoner of Nigerian descent with a management position in international banking."

She is happy and successful in England, but when her husband wishes to return home to his village in Nigeria, where his social status is greatly increased, she follows him. She stays in London to sell their home, however, and by the time she arrives in Nigeria, he has taken another wife who has provided him with children, and her own social status is greatly lowered.

Emecheta takes the stand that even African men are better off in Western countries in her 2000 novel, *The New Tribe.* Chester, a boy of Nigerian descent, is adopted by a white British family, but as an adult travels to Nigeria to get in touch with his ethnic origins. There, he is "tricked out of his passport and his money," as Bruce King reported in *World Literature Today,* and becomes "disillusioned by the corruption, violence, filth, and unhealthy environment," which causes him to contract malaria. His black English girlfriend comes to rescue him and take him back to England, which he now "accepts . . . as home," in King's words.

"Emecheta has reaffirmed her dedication to be a full-time writer," said the Bruners. Her fiction is intensely autobiographical, drawing on the difficulties she has both witnessed and experienced as a woman, and most especially as a Nigerian woman. Indicating that in Nigeria, however, "Emecheta is a prophet without honor," Bray added that "she is frustrated at not being able to reach women—the audience she desires most. She feels a sense of isolation as she attempts to stake out the middle ground between the old and the new." Remarking that "in her art as well as in her life, Buchi Emecheta offers another alternative," Bray quoted the author: "What I am trying to do is get our profession back. Women are born storytellers. We keep the history. We are the true conservatives—we conserve things and we never forget. What I do is not clever or unusual. It is what my aunt and my grandmother did, and their mothers before them."

BIOGRAPHICAL AND CRITICAL SOURCES:

BOOKS

Allan, Tuzyline Jita, *Womanist and Feminist Aesthetics: A Comparative Review,* Ohio University Press (Athens, OH), 1995.

Concise Dictionary of World Literary Biography, Volume 3, Thomson Gale (Detroit, MI), 1999.

Contemporary Black Biography, Thomson Gale (Detroit, MI), 2001.

Contemporary Literary Criticism, Thomson Gale (Detroit, MI), Volume 14, 1980, Volume 28, 1984.

Contemporary Novelists, 7th edition, St. James Press (Detroit, MI), 2001.

Umeh, Marie, *Emerging Perspectives on Buchi Emecheta,* Africa World Press (Trenton, NJ), 1995.

Zell, Hans M., and others, *A New Reader's Guide to African Literature,* 2nd revised and expanded edition, Holmes & Meier, 1983.

PERIODICALS

African Literature Today, number 3, 1983.

Atlantic, May, 1976.

Black Scholar, November-December, 1985, Jewelle Gomez, review of *Double Yoke,* p. 51; March-April, 1986.

International Fiction Review, January, 2002, Teresa Derrickson, "Class, Culture, and the Colonial Context: The Status of Women in Buchi Emecheta's *The Joys of Motherhood,*" pp. 40-52.

Library Journal, September 1, 1975; April 1, 1976; January 15, 1978; May 1, 1979; May 15, 1994, p. 98.

Listener, July 19, 1979.

Los Angeles Times, October 16, 1983; March 6, 1985; January 16, 1990.

Ms., January, 1976; July, 1984; March, 1985.

New Statesman, June 25, 1976; October 14, 1977; June 2, 1978; April 27, 1979.

New Yorker, May 17, 1976; January 9, 1978; July 2, 1979; April 23, 1984; April 22, 1985.

New York Times, February 23, 1985; June 2, 1990.

New York Times Book Review, September 14, 1975; November 11, 1979; January 27, 1980; February 27, 1983; May 5, 1985; April 29, 1990.

School Library Journal, September, 1994, p. 255.

Times Literary Supplement, August 11, 1972; January 31, 1975; June 11, 1976; February 26, 1982; February 3, 1984; February 27, 1987; April 20, 1990.

Voice Literary Supplement, June, 1982.

Washington Post Book World, May 13, 1979; April 12, 1981; September 5, 1982; September 25, 1983; March 30, 1985.

World Literature Today, spring, 1977; summer, 1977; spring, 1978; winter, 1979; spring, 1980; winter, 1983; autumn, 1984; spring, 2001, Bruce King, review of *The New Tribe,* p. 310.

*   *   *

EMECHETA, Florence Onye Buchi
See EMECHETA, Buchi

ENDO, Shusaku 1923-1996

PERSONAL: Born March 27, 1923, in Tokyo, Japan; died September 29, 1996; son of Tsuneshia and Iku (Takei) Endo; married Junko Okado, September 3, 1955; children: Ryunosuke (son). *Education:* Keio University, Tokyo, B.A., 1949; Lyon University (Lyon, France), student in French literature, 1950-53.

CAREER: Writer.

MEMBER: International PEN (president of Japanese Centre, 1969), Association of Japanese Writers (member of executive committee, 1966).

AWARDS, HONORS: Akutagawa prize (Japan), 1955, for *Shiroihito;* Tanizaki prize (Japan), 1967, and Gru de Oficial da Ordem do Infante dom Henrique (Portugal), 1968, both for *Chinmoku;* Sanct Silvestri, awarded by Pope Paul VI, 1970; Noma prize, 1980.

WRITINGS:

IN ENGLISH TRANSLATION

Umi to Dokuyaku (novel), Bungeishunju, 1958, translation by Michael Gallagher published as *The Sea and Poison,* P. Owen (London, England), 1971, Taplinger, 1980.

Kazan (novel), [Japan], 1959, translation by Richard A. Schuchert published as *Volcano,* P. Owen (London, England), 1978, Taplinger, 1980.

Obaka-san, [Japan], 1959, translation by Francis Mathy published as *Wonderful Fool,* Harper (New York, NY), 1983, reprinted, Dufour Editions (Chester Springs, PA), 2000.

Chinmoku (novel), Shinchosha (Tokyo, Japan), 1966, translation by William Johnston published as *Silence,* P. Owen (London, England), 1969, Taplinger, 1979.

Ougon no Ku (play), Shinchosha (Tokyo, Japan), 1969, translation by Francis Mathy published as *The Golden Country,* Tuttle (Tokyo, Japan), 1970.

Iseu no shogai, [Japan], 1973, translation by Richard A. Schuchert published as *A Life of Jesus,* Paulist Press, 1978.

Kuchibue o fuku toki (novel), [Japan], 1974, translation by Van C. Gessel published as *When I Whistle,* Taplinger, 1979.

Juichi no iro-garasu (short stories), [Japan], 1979, translation published as *Stained Glass Elegies,* Dodd (New York, NY), 1985.

Samurai (novel), [Japan], 1980, translation by Van C. Gessel published as *The Samurai,* Harper (New York, NY), 1982.

Scandal, translated by Van C. Gessel, Dodd (New York, NY), 1988.

Foreign Studies, translated by Mark Williams, P. Owen (London, England), 1989.

The Final Martyrs, translated by Van C. Gessel, New Directions (New York, NY), 1994.

Deep River, translated by Van C. Gessel, New Directions (New York, NY), 1994.

Watashi ga suteta onna (see also below), translation by Mark Williams published as *The Girl I Left Behind,* New Directions (New York, NY), 1995.

Five by Endo: Stories, translated by Van C. Gessel, New Directions (New York, NY), 2000.

Song of Sadness (originally published as *Kanashimi no uta*), translated by Teruyo Shimizu, University of Michigan Center for Japanese Studies (Ann Arbor, MI), 2003.

IN JAPANESE

Shiroihito (novel), Kodansha (Tokyo, Japan), 1955.

Seisho no Naka no Joseitachi (essays; title means "Women in the Bible"), Shinchosha (Tokyo, Japan), 1968.

Bara no Yakat (play), Shinchosha (Tokyo, Japan), 1969.

Yumoa shosetsu shu (short stories), Kodansha (Tokyo, Japan), 1974.

France no daigakusei (essays on travel in France), Kadokawashoten, 1974.

Kitsunegata tanukigata (short stories), Kodansha (Tokyo, Japan), 1976.

Watashi ga suteta onna, Kodansha (Tokyo, Japan), 1976.

Yukiaru kotoba (essays), Shinchosha (Tokyo, Japan), 1976.

Nihonjin wa Kirisuto kyo o shinjirareru ka, Shogakukan, 1977.

Kare no ikikata, Shinchosha (Tokyo, Japan), 1978.

Kirisuto no tanjo, Shinchosha (Tokyo, Japan), 1978.

Ningen no naka no X (essays), Shuokoronsha, 1978.

Rakuten taisho, Kodansha (Tokyo, Japan), 1978.

Ju to jujika (biography of Pedro Cassini), Shuokoronsha, 1979.

Marie Antoinette (fiction), Asahi Shinbunsha, 1979.

Chichioya, Shinchosha (Tokyo, Japan), 1980.

Kekkonron, Shufunotomosha, 1980.

Sakka no nikki (diary excerpts), Toju-sha, 1980.

Endo Shusaku ni yoru Endo Shusaku, Seidosha, 1980.
Meiga Iesu junrei, Bungei Shunju, 1981.
Onna no issho (fiction), Asahi Shinbunsha, 1982.
Endo Shusaku to Knagaeru, PHP Kekyujo, 1982.
Fuyu no yasashisa, Bunka Shuppakyoku, 1982.
Enishi no ito: bunshu, Sekai Bunkasha (Tokyo, Japan), 1998.

Also author of *Watakusi no Iesu,* 1976, *Usaba kagero nikki,* 1978, *Shinran,* 1979, *Tenshi,* 1980, *Ai to jinsei o meguru danso,* 1981, and *Okuku e no michi,* 1981.

SIDELIGHTS: Of all leading twentieth-century Japanese novelists, Shusaku Endo is considered by many critics as the most accessible to Western readers. Endo's Roman Catholic upbringing is often cited as the key to his accessibility, for it gave him a philosophical background shaped by Western traditions rather than those of the East. Christianity is a rarity in Japan, where two sects of Buddhism predominate. As Garry Wills explained in the *New York Review of Books,* "Christ is not only challenging but embarrassing [to the Japanese] because he has absolutely no 'face'. . . . He will let anyone spit on him. How can the Japanese ever honor such a disreputable figure?" While strongly committed to his adopted religion, Endo often described the sense of alienation felt by a Christian in Japan. Most of his novels translated into English address the clash of Eastern and Western morals and philosophy, as well as illustrate the difficulty and unlikelihood of Christianity's establishment in Japan.

John Updike wrote in the *New Yorker* that Endo's first novel in English translation, *Silence,* is "a remarkable work, a somber, delicate, and startlingly empathetic study of a young Portuguese missionary during the relentless persecution of the Japanese Christians in the early seventeenth century." The young missionary, Rodrigues, travels to Japan to investigate rumors that his former teacher, Ferreira, has not only converted to Buddhism but is even participating in the persecution of Christians. As Updike noted, "One can only marvel at the unobtrusive, persuasive effort of imagination that enables a modern Japanese to take up a viewpoint from which Japan is at the outer limit of the world."

Rodrigues is captured soon after his clandestine entry into Japan and is handed over to the same jailer who effected Ferreira's conversion. Rodrigues is never physically harmed but is forced to watch the sufferings of native converts while repeatedly being told that his public denouncement of Christ is the only thing that will save them. At first he resists, anticipating a glorious martyrdom for himself, but eventually a vision of Christ convinces him of the selfishness of this goal. He apostatizes, hoping to save at least a few of the Japanese converts by his example. This "beautifully simple plot," wrote Updike, "harrowingly dramatizes immense theological issues."

Endo sought to illustrate Japan's hostility toward a Christ figure in another of his translated novels, *Wonderful Fool.* Set in modern times, this story centers on a Frenchman, Gaston Bonaparte. Gaston is a priest who longs to work with missionaries in Japan; after being defrocked, he travels there alone to act as a lay missionary. Completely trusting, pure-hearted, and incapable of harming anyone, Gaston is seen only as a bumbling fool by the Japanese. At their hands he is "scorned, deceived, threatened, beaten and finally drowned in a swamp," reported *Books Abroad* contributor Kinya Tsuruta. "In the end, however, his total faith transforms all the Japanese, not excluding even a hardened criminal. Thus, the simple Frenchman has successfully sowed a seed of good will in the corrupting mud swamp, Endo's favorite metaphor for non-Christian Japan."

Wonderful Fool was seen by some reviewers as Endo's condemnation of his country's values. "What shocks him. . . ," noted a *Times Literary Supplement* contributor, "is the spiritual emptiness of what he calls 'mud-swamp Japan,' an emptiness heightened by the absence of any appropriate sense of sin. . . . [But] is it not, perhaps, too self-righteous to ask whether Japan needs the sense of sin which the author would have it assume?" Addressing this issue in a *New Republic* review, Mary Jo Salter believed that "ultimately it is the novelist's humor—slapstick, corny, irreverent—that permits him to moralize so openly."

Louis Allen suggested in the *Listener* that Endo "is one of Japan's major comic writers." Praising the author's versatility, Allen went on to write: "In *When I Whistle,* he explores yet another vein, a plain realism behind which lingers a discreet but clear symbolism." *When I Whistle* tells two parallel stories, that of Ozu and his son, Eiichi. Ozu is an unsuccessful businessman who thinks nostalgically of his childhood in pre-war Japan and his youthful romance with the lovely Aiko. Eiichi is a coldly ambitious surgeon who "despises his father—and his father's generation—as sentimentally humanist," explained Allen. The parallel stories merge when Eiichi, in the hopes of furthering his career, decides to use experimental drugs on a terminal cancer patient—Ozu's former sweetheart, Aiko.

Like *Wonderful Fool, When I Whistle* presents "an unflattering version of postwar Japan," noted Allen, adding that while *Wonderful Fool* is marked by its humor, "Sadness is the keynote [of *When I Whistle*], and its symbol the changed Aiko: a delicate beauty, unhoused and brought to penury by war, and ultimately devoured by a disease which is merely a pretext for experiment by the new, predatory generation of young Japan." *When I Whistle* differs from many of Endo's novels in its lack of an overtly Christian theme, but here as in all his fiction, maintained *New York Times Book Review* contributor Anthony Thwaite, "what interests Mr. Endo—to the point of obsession—are the concerns of both the sacred and secular realms: moral choice, moral responsibility. . . . 'When I Whistle' is a seductively readable—and painful—account of these issues."

Endo returned to the historical setting of *Silence*—the seventeenth century—with *The Samurai.* This novel—his most popular work among Japanese readers—is, like *Silence,* based on historical fact. Whereas *Silence* gave readers a Portuguese missionary traveling to Japan, *The Samurai* tells of a Japanese warrior journeying to Mexico, Spain, and finally the Vatican. The samurai, Hasekura, is an unwitting pawn in his shogun's complex scheme to open trade routes to the West. Instructed to feign conversion to Christianity if it will help his cause, Hasekura does so out of loyalty to the shogun, although he actually finds Christ a repulsive figure. Unfortunately, by the time he returns to Japan five years later, political policy has been reversed, and he is treated as a state enemy for his "conversion." Finally, through his own suffering, Hasekura comes to identify with Jesus and becomes a true Christian.

Geoffry O'Brien judged *The Samurai* to be Endo's most successful novel, giving particular praise to its engrossing storyline and to the novelist's "tremendously lyrical sensory imagination" in a *Village Voice* review. *Washington Post Book World* contributor Noel Perrin claimed that *The Samurai* functions well as an adventure story but maintained that "Endo has done far more than write a historical novel about an early and odd encounter between East and West. Taking the history of Hasekuru's embassy as a mere base, he has written a really quite profound religious novel. . . . It is calm and understated and brilliantly told. Simple on the surface, complex underneath. Something like a fable from an old tapestry. . . . If you're interested in how East and West really met, forget Kipling. Read Endo."

In *Scandal,* Endo relates the self-referential story of Suguro, an aging Japanese-Catholic novelist who, upon receiving crowning accolades in a public ceremony, is accused of leading a double life in the brothels of Tokyo. Haunted by his striking semblance in a portrait displayed in a sordid hotel, and hounded by Kobari, a muckraking journalist, Suguro immerses himself in the Tokyo underworld to pursue his doppelganger. Here Suguro is introduced to Mrs. Naruse, a sadomasochist nurse who engages the author's lurid yearnings and arranges for him to view his double as he engages in sex with Mitsu, a young girl. The distinction between reality and illusion becomes ambiguous as Suguro discovers his shocking other self and struggles to reconcile the moral dichotomy. According to Charles Newman in the *New York Times Book Review,* "Suguro is left with a knowledge more complex than that of a moral hypocrite and more human than that of a writer who had commonly confused the esthetic dualism with the spiritual," reflecting instead "the irreducible evil at the core of his own character." In the end, as Louis Allen observed in the *Times Literary Supplement,* "The sure grip Suguro thought he had on his world is gradually pried loose. His relationship to his wife is falsified, and his art is seen to be built on self-deception. He realizes that 'sin' and the salvation which can arise from it are somehow shallow and superficial things." Nicci Gerrard praised *Scandal* in the London *Observer,* writing that Endo "is fastidious and yet implacable in exposing the dark side of human nature and is painstakingly lucid about unresolvable mysteries."

Foreign Studies, originally published in Japan in 1965, is a collection of three tragic stories that portray the reception of Japanese students in Europe, reflecting Endo's own education in France. The first, "A Summer in Rouen," describes a Japanese student's stay with a Catholic family in post-war France. Kudo, the student, is viewed as a reincarnation of the hostess's dead son and is even called by his name. Unable to express himself because of his poor French and taciturn nature, Kudo retreats into quiet misery among his European sponsors. The brief second piece, "Araki Thomas," anticipates the themes of *Silence* and *The Samurai* in the story of a seventeenth-century Japanese student who travels to Rome to study theology. Upon his return to Japan, however, a changed political climate and torture induce Araki Thomas to apostatize his new religion. As a result he suffers from his dual betrayal of self and his fellow Christians who continue to receive punishment.

The third and longest story in *Foreign Studies,* "And You, Too," is generally regarded as the most significant. "And You, Too" conveys the acute psychological pain caused by acculturation. Tanaka, a Japanese student, visits Paris in the mid-1960s to study literature, in particular the writings of the Marquis de Sade. His preference for European writers is the source of scorn among the other Japanese expatriates, except for a failed architecture student whom he befriends until tuberculosis forces the friend's premature departure. Isolated and disconsolate in Paris, Tanaka ventures to Sade's castle near Avignon where, in a highly symbolic denouement, he wanders about the ruins and coughs blood onto the snow as he leaves, signifying his final inability to reconcile the cultures of East and West and his imminent return to Japan. As John B. Breslin noted in a *Washington Post Book World* review, Endo's prefatory comments for the English translation indicated his belief that "East and West could never really understand one another on the deep level of 'culture,' only on the relatively superficial level of 'civilization.'" Marleigh Grayer Ryan praised the collection in *World Literature Today,* writing that "the three pieces taken together constitute a strong statement of the abyss that separates the Japanese mind and the sensibility from the West."

The Final Martyr is a collection of eleven short stories produced by Endo between 1959 and 1985. However, as Karl Schoenberger qualifies in the *Los Angeles Times Book Review,* "these are not short stories at all, but rather character sketches and rambling essays in the confessional *zuihitsu* style," some with extensive footnotes that display Endo's incorporation of historical detail. As several reviewers observe, the collection reveals Endo's frequent use of the short story to develop themes and characters for later novels. Joseph R. Graber writes in the *San Francisco Review of Books* that "*The Final Martyrs* is a fascinating study of how the writer's mind works." The title story, originally published in 1959, describes the persecution of nineteenth-century Catholic villagers in southern Japan and foreshadows the novel *Silence.* Here the central figure is a weak-minded villager who renounces Christianity under torture and experiences acute guilt as he betrays both state and God. Endo also offers unabashed autobiographic examination in "A Sixty-Year-Old Man," written upon the author's sixtieth birthday, which describes an aging Catholic writer's lust for a young girl he encounters at the park. In the final story, "The Box," Endo contemplates whether talking to plants encourages their growth as he recounts wartime events revealed in an old box of postcards and photographs. Paul Binding concludes in a *New Statesman and Society* review, "It is Endo's triumph that his sense of the totalitarian power of suffering does not diminish his insights into quotidian, late twentieth century urban life—and vice versa."

In *Deep River,* set in India along the Ganges, Endo describes the spiritual quest of Otsu, a rejected Catholic priest who carries corpses to the funeral pyres, and a Japanese tourist group, including a recently widowed businessman who pursues the reincarnation of his wife, a former soldier who survived the Burmese Highway of Death during World War II, a nature writer, and Mitsuko, a cynical, divorced woman who once seduced and spurned Otsu. Through their experiences Endo explores the transcendent wisdom and salvation of Hinduism, Buddhism, and Catholicism, symbolically reflected in Mitsuko's characterization of God as an onion. Robert Coles commented in the *New York Times Book Review* that "Endo is a master of the interior monologue, and he builds 'case' by 'case,' chapter by chapter, a devastating critique of a world that has 'everything' but lacks moral substance and seems headed nowhere." Praising the novel as among Endo's most effective, Andrew Greeley wrote in the *Washington Post Book World* that "this moving story about a pilgrimage of grace, must be rated as one of the best of them all."

The Girl I Left Behind, written some thirty-five years earlier but not published until a year before its author's death in 1996, recounts lifelong encounters between Yoshioka Tsutomu, a Japanese salesman, and Mitsu, a simple country girl whom he seduced as a college student. Though Endo himself acknowledges the immaturity of this early work in an afterword, the sentimental story adumbrates the author's skill for characterization and powerful Christian allusions, here represented by Mitsu's Christ-like goodness and charity. Confined to a leprosarium managed by Catholic nuns until informed of her misdiagnosis, Mitsu learns to live among the lepers and devotes her life to their care. Despite its noted awkwardness and technical shortcomings, P.J. Kavanagh regarded the novel as "remarkably convincing" in a review for the *Spectator* and a *Publishers Weekly* reviewer concluded that Endo's writing is redeemed by "moments of sparkling intelligence and clarity."

BIOGRAPHICAL AND CRITICAL SOURCES:

BOOKS

Contemporary Literary Criticism, Thomson Gale (Detroit, MI), Volume 7, 1977, Volume 14, 1980, Volume 19, 1981, Volume 54, 1989.

Dictionary of Literary Biography, Volume 182: *Japanese Fiction Writers since World War II,* Thomson Gale (Detroit, MI), 1997.

Endo, Shusaku, *Foreign Studies,* translated by Mark Williams, P. Owen (London, England), 1989.

Rimer, J. Thomas, *Modern Japanese Fiction and Its Traditions: An Introduction,* Princeton University Press (Princeton, NJ), 1978.

PERIODICALS

America, June 21, 1980; February 2, 1985; October 13, 1990; August 1, 1992; November 19, 1994, pp. 18, 28.

Antioch Review, winter, 1983.

Best Sellers, November, 1980.

Books Abroad, spring, 1975.

Chicago Tribune Book World, October 7, 1979.

Christian Century, September 21, 1966.

Christianity Today, March 17, 1989.

Commonweal, November 4, 1966; September 22, 1989; May 19, 1995.

Contemporary Review, April, 1978.

Critic, July 15, 1979.

Kirkus Reviews, October 1, 1995.

Listener, May 20, 1976; April 12, 1979.

London Magazine, April-May, 1974.

London Review of Books, May 19, 1988.

Los Angeles Times, November 13, 1980; December 1, 1983.

Los Angeles Times Book Review, December 5, 1982; September 18, 1994.

New Republic, December 26, 1983.

New Statesman, May 7, 1976; April 13, 1979; April 30, 1993.

Newsweek, December 19, 1983.

New Yorker, January 14, 1980.

New York Review of Books, February 19, 1981; November 4, 1982.

New York Times Book Review, January 13, 1980; June 1, 1980; December 26, 1982; November 13, 1983; July 21, 1985; August 28, 1988; May 6, 1990; May 28, 1995.

Observer (London, England), April 24, 1988.

Publishers Weekly, July 4, 1994, p. 25; September 11, 1995, p. 72.

San Francisco Review of Books, October-November, 1994.

Saturday Review, July 21, 1979.

Spectator, May 1, 1976; April 14, 1979; May 15, 1982; November 19, 1994.

Times (London, England), April 18, 1985.

Times Literary Supplement, July 14, 1972; January 25, 1974; May 5, 1978; May 21, 1982; October 26, 1984; April 29, 1988; October 28, 1994.

Vanity Fair, February, 1991.

Village Voice, November 16, 1982.

Washington Post Book World, September 2, 1979; October 12, 1980; October 24, 1982; June 23, 1985; May 6, 1990; June 25, 1995.

World Literature Today, summer, 1979; winter, 1984; winter, 1990; winter, 1996.

ENGER, Leif 1961-
(L.L. Enger, a joint pseudonym)

PERSONAL: Born 1961, in Osakis, MN; married; wife's name Robin; children: two sons. *Education:* Minnesota State University, Moorhead, B.A., 1983.

ADDRESSES: Home—Brainerd Lakes area of Minnesota. *Agent*—Paul Cirone, Aaron Priest Agency, 703 Third Ave., 23rd Fl., New York, NY 10017.

CAREER: Novelist. Minnesota Public Radio, reporter and producer, 1984-2000.

AWARDS, HONORS: Best Book of the Year, *Amazon.com,* 2001, for *Peace like a River. Peace like a River* was also chosen for the "One Book, One Denver" reading program in 2004.

WRITINGS:

(With brother, Lin Enger, under joint pseudonym L.L. Enger) *Sacrifice* (novel) Pocket Books (New York, NY), 1993.

(With brother, Lin Enger, under joint pseudonym L.L. Enger) *The Sinners' League: A Gun Pedersen Mystery* (novel), O. Penzler Books (New York, NY), 1994.

Peace like a River (novel), Atlantic Monthly Press (New York, NY), 2001.

Also author, with brother Lin Enger, under joint pseudonym L.L. Enger, of the mystery novels *Swing, Comeback,* and *Strike,* all published by Pocket Books (New York, NY).

SIDELIGHTS: Leif Enger is a writer who has won acclaim for his first solo novel, *Peace like a River.* Enger's literary debut, which begins in rural Minnesota during the early 1960s, tells the story of Reuben Land, an adolescent beset with a chronic respiratory disorder and a wayward brother, Davy. When Davy guns down two home invaders and leaves town, Reuben joins his father, a poetry aficionado working as a school janitor, and his little sister, a tomboy obsessed with reading cowboy novels and preparing her own verse about a gunslinger, in searching for the runaway brother. The family's ensuing travels lead them into strange and miraculous experiences, including an encounter with a seemingly bottomless soup pot at a roadside eatery. "By the end," reported Susan Salter Reynolds in the *Los Angeles Times,* "life itself seems miraculous and strange: from the fact of breath to the possibility of justice."

Upon publication in 2001, *Peace like a River* received recognition as a uniquely entertaining novel. "The miracle of *Peace like a River* is the irresistibility of a well-told tale," wrote C.K. Hubbuch in *Ruminator Review.* Hubbuch noted, "Enger writes on the precarious edge of traditionalism. He veers toward sentimentality, but the strength of his story and characters keeps his novel real." Another reviewer, Rob Thomas, described Enger's novel, in a *Capital Times* assessment, as "an odd little novel that mixes a wintry Minnesota setting with flashes of magical realism." But Greg Changnon, writing in the *Atlanta Journal-Constitution,* praised *Peace like a River* as "a book full of wisdom and grace, a literary potboiler that celebrates the glory of faith." Michael Pearson, in another *Atlanta Journal-Constitution* review, expressed similar praise, stating that Enger's novel "has the power to convince that, despite sorrow, human experience is a miracle of ordinary truth and extraordinary love." Katherine Dieckmann was less impressed, commenting in the *New York Times Book Review* that "Enger's world . . . seems unlikely to have ever existed," though she thought, "he manages to infuse sections of this novel with some surprisingly lively writing and deftly turned sentences." Brad Hooper concluded in another *Booklist* appraisal, "Enger's profound understanding of human nature stands behind his compelling prose."

Enger—in collaboration with his brother Lin Enger—has also published several mystery novels centering on the exploits of a former baseball player. "It was one of those mercenary adventures that comes up empty-handed," Enger told *BookPage* interviewer Alden Mudge. "Nobody really read them and they didn't get much attention and we didn't get paid very much for them." He added, "We had a lot of fun doing it, and it was a fabulous apprenticeship for me."

BIOGRAPHICAL AND CRITICAL SOURCES:

PERIODICALS

Atlanta Journal-Constitution, October 14, 2001, Michael Pearson, "A Miraculously Good Tale with a Western Twang," p. B5; November 25, 2001, Greg Changnon, review of *Peace like a River,* p. C5.

Booklist, May 15, 2001, Brad Hooper, review of *Peace like a River,* p. 1707; June 1, 2001, Joanne Wilkinson, review of *Peace like a River,* p. 1838.
Economist (London, England), September 8, 2001, "Big, Bold, Bare, and Spare," p. 112.
Entertainment Weekly, September 28, 2001, Karen Valby, review of *Peace like a River,* p. 68.
Los Angeles Times Book Review, September 2, 2001, Susan Salter Reynolds, review of *Peace like a River,* p. 11.
New York Times Book Review, September 9, 2001, Katherine Dieckmann, "Miracle Worker," p. 19.
People, October 8, 2001, Bella Stander, review of *Peace like a River,* p. 59.
Publishers Weekly, July 16, 2001, review of *Peace like a River,* p. 166; September 3, 2001, Daisy Maryles, "An Indie Favorite," p. 20.
Ruminator Review, fall, 2001, C.K. Hubbuch, "Magical Mystery Tour," p. 48.

ONLINE

Amazon.com, http://amazon.com/ (April 22, 2002), "Claire Dederer, *Amazon.com's* Best of 2001."
BookPage, http://www.bookpage.com/ (December 2, 2001), Alden Mudge, "Riding the Wave of Leif Enger's Dazzling Debut."
Capital Times, http://captimes.com/ (September 14, 2001), Rob Thomas, "*Peace like a River* Just Too Unreal."

*   *   *

ENGER, L.L.
    See ENGER, Leif

*   *   *

EPERNAY, Mark
    See GALBRAITH, John Kenneth

*   *   *

ERDRICH, Karen Louise
    See ERDRICH, Louise

*   *   *

ERDRICH, Louise 1954-
    (Karen Louise Erdrich, Heidi Louise, a joint pseudonym, Milou North, a joint pseudonym)

PERSONAL: Born June 7 (one source says July 6), 1954, in Little Falls, MN; daughter of Ralph Louis (a teacher with the Bureau of Indian Affairs) and Rita Joanne (affiliated with the Bureau of Indian Affairs; maiden name, Gourneau) Erdrich; married Michael Anthony Dorris (a writer and professor of Native-American studies), October 10, 1981 (died, April 11, 1997); children: Reynold Abel (died, 1991), Jeffrey Sava, Madeline Hannah, Persia Andromeda, Pallas Antigone, Aza Marion. *Education:* Dartmouth College, B.A., 1976; Johns Hopkins University, M.A., 1979. *Politics:* Democrat. *Religion:* "Anti-religion." *Hobbies and other interests:* Quilting, running, drawing, "playing chess with daughters and losing, playing piano badly, speaking terrible French."

ADDRESSES: Agent—Andrew Wylie Agency, 250 W. 57th St., Ste. 2114, New York, NY 10107-2199.

CAREER: Writer. North Dakota State Arts Council, visiting poet and teacher, 1977-78; Johns Hopkins University, Baltimore, MD, writing instructor, 1978-79; Boston Indian Council, Boston, MA, communications director and editor of the *Circle,* 1979-80; Charles Merrill Co., textbook writer, 1980. Previously employed as a beet weeder in Wahpeton, ND; waitress in Wahpeton, Boston, MA, and Syracuse, NY; psychiatric aide in a Vermont hospital; poetry teacher at prisons; lifeguard; and construction flag signaler. Has judged writing contests.

MEMBER: International Writers, PEN (member of executive board, 1985-88), Authors Guild, Authors League of America.

AWARDS, HONORS: Johns Hopkins University teaching fellow, 1978; MacDowell Colony fellow, 1980; Yaddo Colony fellow, 1981; Dartmouth College visiting fellow, 1981; First Prize, Nelson Algren fiction competition, 1982, for "The World's Greatest Fisherman"; National Endowment for the Arts fellowship, 1982; Pushcart Prize, 1983; National Magazine Fiction awards, 1983 and 1987; Virginia McCormack Scully Prize for best book of the year dealing with Indians or Chicanos, National Book Critics Circle Award for best work of fiction, and *Los Angeles Times* Award for best novel, all 1984, and Sue Kaufman Prize for Best First Novel, American Academy and Institute of Arts and Letters, American Book Award, Before Columbus Foundation, and named among best eleven books of 1985 by the *New York Times Book Review,* all for *Love Medicine;* Guggenheim fellow, 1985-86; *The Beet Queen* named one of *Publishers Weekly*'s best books, 1986; First Prize, O. Henry awards, 1987; National Book Critics

Circle Award nomination; World Fantasy Award for Best Novel, World Fantasy Convention, 1999, for *The Antelope Wife;* National Book Award for fiction finalist, 2001, for *The Last Report on the Miracles at Little No Horse,* and 2003, for *The Master Butchers Singing Club;* Scott O'Dell Award for historical fiction, 2006, for *The Game of Silence.*

WRITINGS:

NOVELS

Love Medicine, Holt (New York, NY), 1984, expanded edition, 1993.
The Beet Queen, Holt (New York, NY), 1986.
Tracks, Harper (New York, NY), 1988.
(With husband, Michael Dorris) *The Crown of Columbus,* HarperCollins (New York, NY), 1991.
The Bingo Palace, HarperCollins (New York, NY), 1994.
Tales of Burning Love, HarperCollins (New York, NY), 1996.
The Antelope Wife, HarperFlamingo (New York, NY), 1998.
The Last Report on the Miracles at Little No Horse, HarperCollins (New York, NY), 2001.
The Master Butchers Singing Club, HarperCollins (New York, NY), 2003.
Four Souls, HarperCollins (New York, NY), 2004.

POETRY

Jacklight, Holt (New York, NY), 1984.
Baptism of Desire, Harper (New York, NY), 1989.
Original Fire: New and Selected Poems, HarperCollins (New York, NY), 2003.

FOR CHILDREN

Grandmother's Pigeon, illustrated by Jim LaMarche, Hyperion (New York, NY), 1996.
(And illustrator) *The Birchbark House,* Hyperion Books for Children (New York, NY), 1999.
The Game of Silence, HarperCollins (New York, NY), 2004.

OTHER

Imagination (textbook), C.E. Merrill (New York, NY), 1980.

Louise Erdrich and Michael Dorris Interview with Kay Bonetti, (sound recording), American Audio Prose Library, 1986.

(Author of preface) Michael Dorris, *The Broken Cord: A Family's Ongoing Struggle with Fetal Alcohol Syndrome,* Harper (New York, NY), 1989.

(Author of preface) Desmond Hogan, *A Link with the River,* Farrar, Straus (New York, NY), 1989.

(With Allan Richard Chavkin and Nancy Feyl Chavkin) *Conversations with Louise Erdrich and Michael Dorris,* University Press of Mississippi (Jackson, MS), 1994.

The Falcon: A Narrative of the Captivity and Adventures of John Tanner, Penguin (New York, NY), 1994.

The Blue Jay's Dance: A Birth Year, (memoir), Harper-Collins (New York, NY), 1995.

Books and Islands in Ojibwe Country, National Geographic (Washington, DC), 2003.

Author of short story, "The World's Greatest Fisherman"; contributor to anthologies, including *Norton Anthology of Poetry; Best American Short Stories of 1981-83, 1983, and 1988;* and *Prize Stories: The O. Henry Awards,* 1985 and 1987. Contributor of stories, poems, essays, and book reviews to periodicals, including *New Yorker, New England Review, Chicago, American Indian Quarterly, Frontiers, Atlantic, Kenyon Review, North American Review, New York Times Book Review, Ms., Redbook* (with her sister Heidi, under the joint pseudonym Heidi Louise), and *Woman* (with Dorris, under the joint pseudonym Milou North).

ADAPTATIONS: The Crown of Columbus has been optioned for film production.

SIDELIGHTS: The daughter of a Chippewa Indian mother and a German-American father, Louise Erdrich explores Native-American themes in her works, with major characters representing both sides of her heritage. In an award-winning series of related novels and short stories, Erdrich has visited and re-visited the North Dakota lands where her ancestors met and mingled, creating "a Chippewa experience in the context of the European American novelistic tradition," to quote P. Jane Hafen in the *Dictionary of Literary Biography.* Many critics claim Erdrich has remained true to her Native ancestors' mythic and artistic visions while writing fiction that candidly explores the cultural issues facing modern-day Native Americans and mixed heritage Americans. As an essayist for *Contemporary Novelists* observed: "Erdrich's accomplishment is that she is weaving a body of work that goes beyond portraying contemporary Native American life as descendants of a politically dominated people to explore the great universal questions—questions of identity, pattern versus randomness, and the meaning of life itself." In fact, as Hafen put it, Erdrich's "diverse imageries, subjects, and textual strategies reaffirm imperatives of American Indian survival."

A contributor to *Contemporary Popular Writers* credited Erdrich with a body of work that is "more interested in love and survival than in recrimination." The critic added: "Past wrongs and present hardships do figure in her work but chiefly as the backdrop against which the task of 'protecting and celebrating' takes on added force and urgency. . . . Erdrich's sense of loss never gives way to a sense of grievance; her characteristic tone is hopeful, not mournful, and springs from her belief in the persistence and viability of certain Native American values and the vision to which they give rise." The author's creative impulse has led to a significant accomplishment. Elizabeth Blair declared in *World and I:* "In an astonishing, virtuoso performance sustained over more than two decades, Erdrich has produced . . . interlinked novels that braid the lives of a series of fallible, lovable, and unpredictable characters of German, Cree, métis, and Ojibwe heritage." Blair concluded: "The painful history of Indian-white relations resonates throughout her work. In her hands we laugh and cry while listening to and absorbing home truths that, taken to heart, have the power to change our world. We listen because these truths come sinew-stitched into the very fabric of the tapestry she weaves so artfully."

Erdrich's first year at Dartmouth College, 1972, was the year the college began admitting women, as well as the year the Native-American studies department was established. The author's future husband and collaborator, anthropologist Michael Dorris, was hired to chair the department. In his class, Erdrich began the exploration of her own ancestry that would eventually inspire her novels. Intent on balancing her academic training with a broad range of practical knowledge, Erdrich told Miriam Berkley in an interview with *Publishers Weekly,* "I ended up taking some really crazy jobs, and I'm glad I did. They turned out to have been very useful experiences, although I never would have believed it at the time." In addition to working as a lifeguard, waitress, poetry teacher at prisons, and construction flag signaler, Erdrich became an editor for the *Circle,* a Boston Indian Council newspaper. She told *Writers Digest* interviewer Michael Schumacher: "Settling into that job and becoming comfortable with an urban community—which is very different from the reservation community—gave me another reference point. There were lots of people with mixed blood, lots of people who had their own confusions. I realized that this was part of my life—it wasn't something that I was making up—and that it was something I *wanted* to write about." In 1978, the author enrolled in an M.A. program at Johns Hopkins University, where she wrote poems and stories incorporating her heritage, many of which would later become part of her books. She also began sending her work to publishers, most of whom sent back rejection slips.

After receiving her master's degree, Erdrich returned to Dartmouth as a writer-in-residence. Dorris—with whom she had remained in touch—attended a reading of Erdrich's poetry there and was impressed. A writer himself—Dorris would later publish the best-selling novel *A Yellow Raft in Blue Water* and receive the 1989 National Book Critics Circle Award for his nonfiction work *The Broken Cord: A Family's Ongoing Struggle with Fetal Alcohol Syndrome*—he decided then that he was interested in working with Erdrich and getting to know her better. When he left for New Zealand to do field research and Erdrich went to Boston to work on a textbook, the two began sending their poetry and fiction back and forth with their letters, laying a groundwork for a literary relationship. Dorris returned to New Hampshire in 1980, and Erdrich moved back there as well. The two began collaborating on short stories, including one titled "The World's Greatest Fisherman." When this story won five thousand dollars in the Nelson Algren fiction competition, Erdrich and Dorris decided to expand it into a novel—*Love Medicine*. At the same time, their literary relationship led to a romantic one and in 1981 they were married.

The titles Erdrich and Dorris chose for their novels—such as *Love Medicine* and *A Yellow Raft in Blue Water*—tend to be rich poetic or visual images, and was often the initial inspiration from which their novels were drawn. Erdrich told Schumacher, "I think a title is like a magnet: It begins to draw these scraps of experience or conversation or memory to it. Eventually, it collects a book." Erdrich and Dorris's collaborative process began with a first draft, usually written by whomever had the original idea for the book, the one who would ultimately be considered the official author. After the draft was written, the other person edited it, and then another draft was written; often five or six drafts would be written in all. Finally, the two read the work aloud until they agreed on each word. Although the author had the original voice and the final say, ultimately, both collaborators were responsible for what the work became. This "unique collaborative relationship," according to Alice Joyce in *Booklist,* is covered in *Con-*

versations with Louise Erdrich and Michael Dorris, a collection of twenty-five interviews with the couple. By 1997, when Dorris committed suicide, the pair had separated and were no longer actively collaborating. Erdrich alone is responsible for much of her work in the 1990s and all of her publications since the turn of the twenty-first century.

Erdrich's novels *Love Medicine, The Beet Queen, Tracks, The Bingo Palace,* and *Tales of Burning Love* encompass the stories of three interrelated families living in and around a reservation in the fictional town of Argus, North Dakota, from 1912 through the 1980s. The novels have been compared to those of William Faulkner, mainly due to the multi-voice narration and non-chronological storytelling which he employed in works such as *As I Lay Dying.* Erdrich's works, linked by recurring characters who are victims of fate and the patterns set by their elders, are structured like intricate puzzles in which bits of information about individuals and their relations to one another are slowly released in a seemingly random order, until three-dimensional characters—with a future and a past—are revealed. Through her characters' antics, Erdrich explores universal family life cycles while also communicating a sense of the changes and loss involved in the twentieth-century Native-American experience.

Poet Robert Bly, describing Erdrich's nonlinear storytelling approach in the *New York Times Book Review,* emphasized her tendency to "choose a few minutes or a day in 1932, let one character talk, let another talk, and a third, then leap to 1941 and then to 1950 or 1964." The novels' circular format is a reflection of the way in which the works are constructed. Although Erdrich is dealing with a specific and extensive time period, "The writing doesn't start out and proceed chronologically. It never seems to start in the beginning. Rather, it's as though we're building something around a center, but that center can be anywhere."

Erdrich published her first novel, *Love Medicine,* in 1984. "With this impressive debut," stated *New York Times Book Review* contributor Marco Portales, "Louise Erdrich enters the company of America's better novelists." *Love Medicine* was named for the belief in love potions which is a part of Chippewa folklore. The novel explores the bonds of family and faith which preserve both the Chippewa tribal community and the individuals that comprise it.

The story begins at a family gathering following the death of June Kashpaw, a prostitute. The characters introduce one another, sharing stories about June which reveal their family history and their cultural beliefs. Albertine Johnson, June's niece, introduces her grandmother, Marie, her grandfather, Nector, and Nector's twin brother, Eli. Eli represents the old way—the Native American who never integrated into the white culture. He also plays a major role in *Tracks,* in which he appears as a young man. The story of Marie and Nector brings together many of the important images in the novel, including the notion of "love medicine." As a teenager in a convent, Marie is nearly burned to death by a nun who, in an attempt to exorcise the devil from within her, pours boiling water on Marie. Immediately following this incident, Marie is sexually assaulted by Nector. Marie and Nector are later married, but in middle age, Nector begins an affair with Lulu Lamartine, a married woman. In an attempt to rekindle Nector and Marie's passion, their grandson Lipsha prepares "love medicine" for Nector. But Lipsha has difficulty obtaining a wild goose heart for the potion. He substitutes a frozen turkey heart, which causes Nector to choke to death.

Reviewers responded positively to Erdrich's debut novel, citing its lyrical qualities as well as the rich characters who inhabit it. *New York Times* contributor D.J.R. Bruckner was impressed with Erdrich's "mastery of words," as well as the "vividly drawn" characters who "will not leave the mind once they are let in." Portales, who called *Love Medicine* "an engrossing book," applauded the unique narration technique which produces what he termed "a wondrous prose song." The novel won numerous awards, including the National Book Critics Circle Award for best work of fiction in 1984.

After the publication of *Love Medicine,* Erdrich told reviewers that her next novel would focus less exclusively on her mother's side, embracing the author's mixed heritage and the mixed community in which she grew up. Her 1986 novel, *The Beet Queen,* deals with whites and half-breeds, as well as American Indians, and explores the interactions between these worlds. The story begins in 1932, during the Depression. Mary and Karl Adare's recently-widowed mother flies off with a carnival pilot, abandoning the two children and their newborn brother. The baby is taken by a young couple who have just lost their child. Karl and eleven-year-old Mary ride a freight train to Argus, seeking refuge with their aunt and uncle. When they arrive in the town, however, Karl, frightened by a dog, runs back onto the train and winds up at an orphanage. Mary grows up with her aunt and uncle, and the novel follows her life—as well as those of her jealous, self-centered cousin Sita and their part-Chippewa friend Celestine James—for the next forty years, tracing the themes of

separation and loss that began with Mary's father's death and her mother's grand departure.

The Beet Queen was well received by critics, some of whom found it even more impressive than *Love Medicine.* Many commented favorably on the novel's poetic language and symbolism; Bly noted that Erdrich's "genius is in metaphor," and that the characters "show a convincing ability to feel an image with their whole bodies." Josh Rubins, writing in *New York Review of Books,* called *The Beet Queen* "a rare second novel, one that makes it seem as if the first, impressive as it was, promised too little, not too much." Other reviewers had problems with *The Beet Queen,* but they tended to dismiss the novel's flaws in light of its positive qualities. *New Republic* contributor Dorothy Wickenden considered the characters unrealistic and the ending contrived, but she lauded *The Beet Queen*'s "ringing clarity and lyricism," as well as the "assured, polished quality" which she felt was missing in *Love Medicine.* Although Michiko Kakutani found the ending artificial, the *New York Times* reviewer called Erdrich "an immensely gifted young writer." "Even with its weaknesses," proclaimed Linda Simon in *Commonweal,* "*The Beet Queen* stands as a product of enormous talent."

After Erdrich completed *The Beet Queen,* she was uncertain as to what her next project should be. The four-hundred-page manuscript that would eventually become *Tracks* had remained untouched for ten years; the author referred to it as her "burden." She and Dorris took a fresh look at it, and decided that they could relate it to *Love Medicine* and *The Beet Queen.* While more political than her previous novels, *Tracks* also deals with spiritual themes, exploring the tension between the Native Americans' ancient beliefs and the Christian notions of the Europeans. *Tracks* takes place between 1912 and 1924, before the settings of Erdrich's other novels, and reveals the roots of *Love Medicine*'s characters and their hardships. One of the narrators, Nanapush, is the leader of a tribe that is suffering on account of the white government's exploitation. He feels pressured to give up tribal land in order to avoid starvation. While Nanapush represents the old way, Pauline, the other narrator, represents change. The future mother of *Love Medicine*'s Marie Lazarre, Pauline is a young half-breed from a mixed-blood tribe "for which the name was lost." She feels torn between her Indian faith and the white people's religion, and is considering leaving the reservation. But at the center of *Tracks* is Fleur, a character whom *Los Angeles Times Book Review* contributor Terry Tempest Williams called "one of the most haunting presences in contemporary American literature." Nanapush discovers this young woman—the last survivor of a family killed by consumption—in a cabin in the woods, starving and mad. Nanapush adopts Fleur and nurses her back to health.

Reviewers found *Tracks* distinctly different from Erdrich's earlier novels, and some felt that her third novel lacked the characteristics that made *Love Medicine* and *The Beet Queen* so outstanding. *Washington Post Book World* critic Jonathan Yardley stated that, on account of its more political focus, the work has a "labored quality." Robert Towers, in the *New York Review of Books,* found the characters too melodramatic and the tone too intense. Katherine Dieckmann, writing in the *Village Voice Literary Supplement,* affirmed that she "missed [Erdrich's] skilled multiplications of voice," and called the relationship between Pauline and Nanapush "symptomatic of the overall lack of grand orchestration and perspectival interplay that made Erdrich's first two novels polyphonic masterpieces." According to *Commonweal* contributor Christopher Vecsey, however, although "a reviewer might find some of the prose overwrought, and the two narrative voices indistinguishable . . . readers will appreciate and applaud the vigor and inventiveness of the author."

Other reviewers enjoyed *Tracks* even more than the earlier novels. Williams stated that Erdrich's writing "has never appeared more polished and grounded," and added, "*Tracks* may be the story of our time." Thomas M. Disch lauded the novel's plot, with its surprising twists and turns, in the *Chicago Tribune.* The critic added: "Erdrich is like one of those rumored drugs that are instantly and forever addictive. Fortunately in her case you can *just say yes.*"

Erdrich and Dorris's jointly authored novel *The Crown of Columbus* explores Native-American issues from the standpoint of the authors' current experience, rather than the world of their ancestors. Marking the quincentennial anniversary of Spanish explorer Christopher Columbus's voyage in a not-so-celebratory fashion, Erdrich and Dorris raise important questions about the meaning of that voyage for both Europeans and Native Americans today. The story is narrated by the two central characters, both Dartmouth professors involved in projects concerning Columbus. Vivian Twostar is a Native-American single mother with eclectic tastes and a teenage son, Nash. Vivian is asked to write an academic article on Columbus from a Native-American perspective and is researching Columbus's diaries. Roger Williams, a stuffy New England Protestant poet, is writing an epic work about the explorer's voyage. Vivian and Roger become lovers—parenting a girl

named Violet—but have little in common. Ultimately acknowledging the destructive impact of Columbus's voyage on the Native-American people, Vivian and Roger vow to redress the political wrongs symbolically by changing the power structure in their relationship. In the end, as Vivian and Roger rediscover themselves, they rediscover America.

Some reviewers found *The Crown of Columbus* unbelievable and inconsistent, and considered it less praiseworthy than the individual authors' earlier works. However, *New York Times Book Review* contributor Robert Houston appreciated the work's timely political relevance. He also stated: "There are moments of genuine humor and compassion, of real insight and sound satire." Other critics also considered Vivian and Roger's adventures amusing, vibrant, and charming.

Erdrich returned to the descendants of Nanapush with her 1994 novel, *The Bingo Palace.* The fourth novel in the series that began with *Love Medicine, The Bingo Palace* weaves together a story of spiritual pursuit with elements of modern reservation life. Erdrich also provided continuity to the series by having the novel primarily narrated by Lipsha Morrissey, the illegitimate son of June Kapshaw and Gerry Nanapush from *Love Medicine.* After working at a Fargo sugar beet factory, Lipsha has returned home to the reservation in search of his life's meaning. He finds work at his uncle Lyman Lamartine's bingo parlor and love with his uncle's girlfriend, Shawnee Ray Toose. Thanks to the magic bingo tickets provided to him by the spirit of his dead mother, June, he also finds modest wealth. The character of Fleur Pillager returns from *Tracks* as Lipsha's great-grandmother. After visiting her, Lipsha embarks on a spiritual quest in order to impress Shawnee and learn more about his own tribal religious rites. Family members past and present are brought together in his pursuit, which comprises the final pages of the novel.

Reviewers' comments on *The Bingo Palace* were generally positive. While Lawrence Thornton, in the *New York Times Book Review,* found "some of the novel's later ventures into magic realism . . . contrived," his overall impression was more positive: "Erdrich's sympathy for her characters shines as luminously as Shawnee Ray's jingle dress." Pam Houston, writing for the *Los Angeles Times Book Review,* was especially taken by the character of Lipsha Morrissey, finding in him "what makes this her most exciting and satisfying book to date."

The Bingo Palace was also reviewed in the context of the series as a whole. *Chicago Tribune* contributor Michael Upchurch concluded, *The Bingo Palace* "falls somewhere between *Tracks* and *The Beet Queen* in its accomplishment." He added, "The best chapters in *The Bingo Palace* rival, as *Love Medicine* did, the work of Welty, Cheever, and Flannery O'Connor."

Erdrich turned to her own experience as mother of six for her next work, *The Blue Jay's Dance*. Her first book of nonfiction, *The Blue Jay's Dance* chronicles Erdrich's pregnancy and the birth year of her child. The title refers to a blue jay's habit of defiantly "dancing" towards an attacking hawk, Erdrich's metaphor for "the sort of controlled recklessness that having children always is," noted Jane Aspinall in *Quill & Quire*. Erdrich has been somewhat protective of her family's privacy and has stated the narrative actually describes a combination of her experience with several of her children. Sue Halpern, in the *New York Times Book Review*, remarked on this difficult balancing act between public and private lives but found "Erdrich's ambivalence inspires trust . . . and suggests that she is the kind of mother whose story should be told."

Some reviewers noted that Erdrich's description of the maternal relationship was a powerful one: "the bond between mother and infant has rarely been captured so well," commented a *Kirkus Reviews* contributor. While the subject of pregnancy and motherhood is not a new one, Halpern noted that the book provided new insight into the topic: "What makes *The Blue Jay's Dance* worth reading is that it quietly places a mother's love and nurturance amid her love for the natural world and suggests . . . how right that placement is." Although the *Kirkus Reviews* contributor found *The Blue Jay's Dance* to be "occasionally too self-conscious about the importance of Erdrich's role as Writer," others commented positively on the book's examination of the balance between the work of parenting and one's vocation. A *Los Angeles Times Book Review* reviewer remarked: "this book is really about working and having children, staying alert and . . . focused through the first year of a child's life."

Erdrich retained her focus on children with her first children's book, *Grandmother's Pigeon*. Published in 1996, it is a fanciful tale of an adventurous grandmother who heads to Greenland on the back of a porpoise, leaving behind grandchildren and three bird's eggs in her cluttered bedroom. The eggs hatch into passenger pigeons, thought to be extinct, through which the children are able to send messages to their missing grandmother. A *Publishers Weekly* reviewer commented, "As in her fiction for adults . . . , Erdrich makes every word count in her bewitching debut children's story."

Within the same year, Erdrich returned to the character of June Kashpaw of *Love Medicine* in her sixth novel, *Tales of Burning Love*. More accurately, it is the story of June's husband, Jack Mauser, and his five—including June—ex-wives. To begin the tale, Jack meets June while they are both inebriated and marries her that night. In reaction to his inability to consummate their marriage, she walks off into a blizzard and is found dead the next day. His four subsequent marriages share the same elements of tragedy and comedy, culminating in Jack's death in a fire in the house he built. The story of each marriage is told by the four ex-wives as they are stranded together in Jack's car during a blizzard after his funeral. Again, Erdrich references her previous work in the characters of Gerry and Dot Nanapush, Dot as one of Jack's ex-wives and Gerry as Dot's imprisoned husband.

Reviewers continued to note Erdrich's masterful descriptions and fine dialogue in this work. According to Penelope Mesic in the *Chicago Tribune*, "Erdrich's strength is that she gives emotional states—as shifting and intangible, as indefinable as wind—a visible form in metaphor." A *Times Literary Supplement* contributor compared her to Tobias Wolff—"[like him], she is . . . particularly good at evoking American small-town life and the space that engulfs it"—as well as Raymond Carver, noting her dialogues to be "small exchanges that . . . map out the barely navigable distance between what's heard, what's meant, and what's said."

Tales of Burning Love also focuses Erdrich's abilities (and perhaps Dorris's collaborative talents) on the relationship between men and women. As the *Times Literary Supplement* reviewer continued, "Erdrich also shares Carver's clear and sophisticated view of the more fundamental distance between men and women, and how that, too, is negotiated." However, Mark Childress in the *New York Times Book Review* commented that while "Jack's wives are vivid and fully realized . . . whenever [Jack's] out of sight, he doesn't seem as interesting as the women who loved him."

While Erdrich covers familiar territory in *Tales of Burning Love,* she seems, claim several critics, to be expanding her focus slightly. Roxana Robinson, in *Washington Post Book World*, remarked, "The landscape, instead of being somber and overcast . . . is vividly illuminated by bolts of freewheeling lunacy: This is a mad Gothic comedy." Or as Verlyn Klinkenborg noted in the *Los Angeles Times Book Review,* "this book marks a shift in [Erdrich's] career, a shift that is suggested rather than fulfilled . . . there is new country coming into [her] sight, and this novel is her first welcoming account of it."

The Antelope Wife was the first book Erdrich released following Dorris's suicide, and although the author disavowed any relationship between herself and her characters, the story does include a self-destructive husband who inadvertently kills his child in a botched suicide attempt. The episodic plot revolves around the history of Rozin, married to the suicidal Richard and in love with another man, and Richard's friends Klaus Shawano and Sweetheart Calico—the latter the "Antelope Wife" of the title. Intercut with the modern tale of these four are the stories of their ancestors, Native and European, who live out their lives and passions on the plains. Erdrich reveals how the Antelope Wife received her mystical powers and how a dog named Almost Soup cheats mortality. *People* reviewer V.R. Peterson called the novel "a captivating jigsaw puzzle of longing and loss."

New York Times Book Review correspondent Diana Postlethwaite suggested that the Native-American craft of beadwork serves as a metaphor for the linked narratives in *The Antelope Wife*. As Postlethwaite wrote: "Family—both immediate and ancestral—is a tensile bond that links the novel's characters, as much a hangman's noose as a lifeline." The critic concluded that reading *The Antelope Wife* "offers a . . . rich taste of the bitter and the sweet." In a *New York Times* review Michiko Kakutani described *The Antelope Wife* as "one of [Erdrich's] most powerful and fully imagined novels yet." Kakutani added: "Erdrich has returned to doing what she does best: using multiple viewpoints and strange, surreal tales within tales to conjure up a family's legacy of love, duty and guilt, and to show us how that family's fortunes have both shifted—and endured—as its members have abandoned ancient Indian traditions for a modern fast-food existence. . . . As for Ms. Erdrich's own storytelling powers, they are on virtuosic display in this novel. She has given us a fiercely imagined tale of love and loss, a story that manages to transform tragedy into comic redemption, sorrow into heroic survival. She has given us a wonderfully sad, funny and affecting novel."

Erdrich has also embarked upon a series of novels for children based on lives of Native-American young people at the time of white encroachment. *The Birchbark House,* published in 1999, tells the story of seven-year-old Omakayas, who lives with her extended family on an island in Lake Superior. In rich detail, Erdrich describes Omakayas's hardships and triumphs as she learns the lessons of her heritage and completes the routines of daily living. Heartache comes too, as Omakayas fails to nurse her beloved baby brother back to health when he contracts smallpox. *Booklist* con-tributor Hazel Rochman found the characters in *The Birchbark House* "wonderfully individualized, humane and funny," adding that readers of the "Little House" series by Laura Ingalls Wilder "will discover a new world, a different version of a story they thought they knew."

A peripheral character from Erdrich's previous novels, Father Damien, takes center stage in *The Last Report on the Miracles at Little No Horse.* Having served the parishioners of a North Dakota Indian reservation for eight decades, Father Damien is finally dying—and is revealed to be a woman named Agnes DeWitt who was once ousted from a convent for playing Chopin piano pieces in the nude. Agnes's passion finds an outlet amongst the families of the reservation, whose names and deeds are already familiar from other Erdrich novels. What this story provides is a stage upon which the author can address the collaboration between Native beliefs and Catholicism. "This is the miracle of Erdrich's writing," stated Ann-Janine Morey in the *Christian Century.* "She conveys the fluidity of meanings across religious systems and across time through her full, rich characters." Elizabeth Blair likewise noted: "In this tale of passion and compassion, a priest meets an elder possessing love medicine and under his tutelage constructs a hybrid religious life that abounds with mysteries and miracles."

Again the reviewers found much to praise in *The Last Report on the Miracles at Little No Horse.* Kakutani found the portrait of Father Damien "so moving, so precisely observed." The critic further commented: "By turns comical and elegiac, farcical and tragic, the stories span the history of this Ojibwe tribe and its members' wrestlings with time and change and loss. . . . Erdrich has woven an imperfect but deeply affecting narrative and in doing so filled out the history of that postage-stamp-size world in Ojibwe country that she has delineated with such fervor and fidelity in half a dozen novels." *New York Times Book Review* contributor Verlyn Klinkenborg maintained that in *The Last Report on the Miracles at Little No Horse* Erdrich "takes us farther back in time than she ever has, so far back that she comes, in a sense, to the edge of the reservation that has been her fictional world. What makes it possible is the Ojibwa language, which is both as fresh and as ancient as rain. It is the leading edge of a discovery that will, one hopes, take Erdrich even farther." In the *New Leader* Lynne Sharon Schwartz declared: "*The Last Report* . . . comes from the 'dictates of a great love,' the author's for her land and her people. Love alone never produced a fine novel, but Erdrich's gifts are abundant enough to subsume melodrama and quash disbelief. She has made this improbable saga moving and luminous."

Although Erdrich continues to dedicate herself to her saga involving Native-American characters, she steps away from that world to touch on her German-American heritage with *The Master Butchers Singing Club,* the 2003 novel that made her a National Book Award finalist for the second time. The title is indicative of the inventive plot that does indeed include singing and intertwines the lives of a German World War I veteran and his wife with those of circus performers and other small-town residents. Erdrich's fans will find themselves in familiar territory, as this story is set in North Dakota like previous Erdrich novels; however this time there are few Native-American characters. The book was highly praised, a *Booklist* contributor commenting that, "Combining a cast of remarkable characters, a compelling plot, and an unforgiving North Dakota setting, Erdrich tells the story of indefatigable Fidelis Waldgovel, a butcher with a talent for singing."

With *Four Souls,* released in 2004, Erdrich picks up the thread of previous tales by returning to the story of Fleur Pillager from *The Last Report on the Miracles at Little No Horse.* Fleur wants revenge and her target is the man who swindled her out of her land, but this revenge not only takes its toll on the intended, but on Fleur as well. Critical reaction to *Four Souls* was mixed; the common complaint was Erdrich's lyrical style. The verdict from a *People* contributor was that while, "On occasion Erdrich's lyrical descriptions of Ojibwe beliefs run on and overwhelm the story," the author nonetheless "sustains a literary voice like no other." Noting the author's growing body of long fiction, in the *Dictionary of Literary Biography,* Peter G. Beidler ranked Erdrich among "the most important contemporary Native American writers," and maintained that "her novels, particularly, deserve to be read, discussed, and appreciated."

BIOGRAPHICAL AND CRITICAL SOURCES:

BOOKS

American Women Writers: A Critical Reference Guide from Colonial Times to the Present, 2nd edition, St. James Press (Detroit, MI), 2000.

Chavkin, Allan, and Nancy Feyl Chavkin, editors, *Conversations with Louise Erdrich and Michael Dorris,* University Press of Mississippi (Jackson, MS), 1994.

Chavkin, Allan, editor, *The Chippewa Landscape of Louise Erdrich,* University of Alabama Press (Tuscaloosa, AL), 1999.

Concise Dictionary of American Literary Biography: Modern Writers, 1900-1998, Thomson Gale (Detroit, MI), 1998, pp. 44-55.

Contemporary Literary Criticism, Thomson Gale (Detroit, MI), Volume 39, 1986, Volume 54, 1989, Volume 120, 1999.

Contemporary Novelists, 7th edition, St. James Press (Detroit, MI), 2001.

Contemporary Poets, 6th edition, St. James Press (Detroit, MI), 1996.

Contemporary Popular Writers, St. James Press (Detroit, MI), 1997.

Contemporary Women Poets, St. James Press (Detroit, MI), 1998.

Cooperman, Jeannette Batz, *The Broom Closet: Secret Meanings of Domesticity in Postfeminist Novels,* Peter Lang (New York, NY), 1999.

Dictionary of Literary Biography, Thomson Gale (Detroit, MI), Volume 152: *American Novelists since World War II, Fourth Series,* 1995, Volume 175: *Native American Writers of the United States,* 1997, pp. 84-100, Volume 206: *Twentieth-Century American Western Writers, First Series,* 1999, pp. 85-96.

Erdrich, Louise, *Tracks,* Harper (New York, NY), 1988.

Erdrich, Louise, *Baptism of Desire,* Harper (New York, NY), 1989.

Jacobs, Connie A., *The Novels of Louise Erdrich: Stories of Her People,* Peter Lang (New York, NY), 2001.

Lyons, Rosemary, *A Comparison of the Works of Antonine Maillet of the Acadian Tradition of New Brunswick, Canada, and Louise Erdrich of the Ojibwe of North America with the Poems of Longfellow,* Edwin Mellen Press (Lewiston, NY), 2002.

Pearlman, Mickey, *American Women Writing Fiction: Memory, Identity, Family, Space,* University Press of Kentucky (Lexington, KY), 1989, pp. 95-112.

Peterson, Nacy J., *Against Amnesia: Contemporary Women Writers and the Crises of Historical Memory,* University of Pennsylvania Press (Philadephia, PA), 2001.

Scott, Steven D., *The Gamefulness of American Postmodernism: John Barth and Louise Erdrich,* Peter Lang (New York, NY), 2000.

PERIODICALS

America, May 14, 1994, p. 7.

American Indian Culture and Research Journal, 1987, pp. 51-73; winter, 1999, Peter G. Beidler, review of

The Antelope Wife, p. 219; spring, 2001, Peter G. Beidler, review of *The Last Report on the Miracles at Little No Horse,* p. 179.

American Literature, September, 1990, pp. 405-422.

Atlantic, March, 2003, p. 108; July-August, 2004, p. 164.

Belles Lettres, summer, 1990, pp. 30-31.

Book, January-February, 2003, p. 67.

Booklist, January 15, 1995, p. 893; April 1, 1999, Hazel Rochman, review of *The Birchbark House,* p. 1427; February 15, 2001, Bill Ott, review of *The Last Report on the Miracles at Little No Horse,* p. 1085; January 1, 2002, p. 767; October 1, 2002, pp. 334-335; December 1, 2002, p. 629; May 1, 2003, p. 1568; September 15, 2003, p. 195; April 15, 2004, p. 1405.

Chicago Tribune, September 4, 1988, pp. 1, 6; January 1, 1994, pp. 1, 9; April 21, 1996, pp. 1, 9.

Christian Century, September 26, 2001, Ann-Janine Morey, review of *The Last Report on the Miracles at Little No Horse,* p. 36.

College Literature, October, 1991, pp. 80-95.

Commonweal, October 24, 1986, pp. 565, 567; November 4, 1988, p. 596.

Economist, May 15, 2001, p. 8.

Entertainment Weekly, June 25, 2004, p. 169.

Explicator, summer, 2002, pp. 241-243; summer, 2003, pp. 248-250; winter, 2003, pp. 119-121.

Horn Book, May, 1999, review of *The Birchbark House,* p. 329.

Kirkus Reviews, February 15, 1996, p. 244; April 15, 1996, p. 600; August 15, 2002, p. 1222; November 15, 2002, p. 1640; April 15, 2004, p. 347.

Library Journal, January, 2002, p. 49; December, 2002, p. 177; August, 2003, pp. 88-89; May 15, 2004, p. 114.

Los Angeles Times Book Review, October 5, 1986, pp. 3, 10; September 11, 1988, p. 2; May 12, 1991, pp. 3, 13; February 6, 1994, p. 1, 13; May 28, 1995, p. 8; June 16, 1996, p. 3.

MELUS, fall, 2002, pp. 113-132, 147-159.

Midwest Quarterly, summer, 2004, pp. 427-428.

Mothering, summer, 1997, Lisa Solbert-Sheldon, review of *The Blue Jay's Dance: A Birth Year,* p. 50.

Mother Jones, May, 2001, Josie Rawson, "Louise Erdrich: Cross-Dressing the Divine," p. 102.

Nation, October 21, 1991, pp. 465, 486-490.

New Leader, May, 2001, Lynne Sharon Schwartz, "Corporate Sinners and Crossover Saints," p. 35.

New Republic, October 6, 1986, pp. 46-48; January 6-13, 1992, pp. 30-40.

Newsday, November 30, 1986.

Newsweek, February 17, 2003, p. 66.

New York Review of Books, January 15, 1987, pp. 14-15; November 19, 1988, pp. 40-41; May 12, 1996, p. 10.

New York Times, December 20, 1984, p. C21; August 20, 1986, p. C21; August 24, 1988, p. 41; April 19, 1991, p. C25; March 24, 1998, Michiko Kakutani, "Myths of Redemption Amid a Legacy of Loss"; April 6, 2001, Michiko Kakutani, "Saintliness, Too, May Be in the Eye of the Beholder."

New York Times Book Review, August 31, 1982, p. 2; December 23, 1984, p. 6; October 2, 1988, pp. 1, 41-42; April 28, 1991, p. 10; July 20, 1993, p. 20; January 16, 1994, p. 7; April 16, 1995, p. 14; April 12, 1998, Diana Postlethwaite, "A Web of Beadwork"; April 8, 2001, Verlyn Klinkenborg, "Woman of the Cloth."

People, June 10, 1991, pp. 26-27; April 13, 1998, V.R. Peterson, review of *The Antelope Wife,* p. 31; July 19, 2004, p. 45.

Playboy, March, 1994, p. 30.

Progressive, April, 2002, pp. 36-40.

Publishers Weekly, August 15, 1986, pp. 58-59; April 22, 1996, p. 71; January 29, 2001, review of *The Last Report on the Miracles at Little No Horse,* p. 63, "PW Talks with Louise Erdrich," p. 64; July 2, 2001, review of *The Last Report on the Miracles at Little No Horse,* p. 31; September 9, 2002, p. 67; December 23, 2002, pp. 43-44; October 6, 2003, pp. 80-81; May 10, 2004, p. 33.

Quill & Quire, August, 1995, p. 30.

Time, February 7, 1994, p. 71; April 28, 1997, Elizabeth Gleick, "An Imperfect Union," p. 68.

Times Literary Supplement, February 14, 1997, p. 21.

Village Voice Literary Supplement, October, 1988, p. 37.

Washington Post Book World, August 31, 1986, pp. 1, 6; September 18, 1988, p. 3; February 6, 1994, p. 5; April 21, 1996, p. 3.

Western American Literature, February, 1991, pp. 363-364.

World and I, September, 2001, Elizabeth Blair, review of *The Last Report on the Miracles at Little No Horse,* p. 214.

World Literature Today, winter, 2000, Howard Meredith, review of "The Antelope Wife," p. 214.

Writer's Digest, June, 1991, Michael Schumacher, interview with Erdrich, pp. 28-31.

ONLINE

Bedford/St. Martin's Web site, http://www.bedford stmartins.com/ (August 23, 2004), "Louise Erdrich."

Carol Hurst's Children's Literature Site, http://www.
carolhurst.com/ (December 2, 2001), review of *The
Birchbark House.*

Salon.com, http://www.salon.com/ (August 23, 2004),
interview with Erdrich.

* * *

ERICKSON, Steve 1950-

PERSONAL: Born Stephen Michael Erickson, April 20,
1950, in Santa Monica, CA; son of Milton Ivan (a
printer and photographer) and Joanna (a theater director; maiden name, DeGraff) Erickson. *Education:* University of California—Los Angeles, B.A., 1972, M.A.,
1973.

ADDRESSES: Home—Topanga, CA. *Office*—c/o Black
Clock, CalArts, 24700 McBean Parkway, Valencia, CA
91355.

CAREER: Freelance editor and writer in London, England, Paris, France, Rome and Venice, Italy, Amsterdam, the Netherlands, and Los Angeles, CA, 1973-86;
arts and film editor, *Los Angeles Weekly,* 1989-93; film
critic, *Los Angeles Magazine;* editor, *Book Forum;*
California Institute for the Arts, MFA writing faculty
member, Valencia, CA; editor, *Black Clock,* California
Institute of the Arts, 2004—.

AWARDS, HONORS: Samuel Goldwyn Award for fiction, University of California—Los Angeles, 1972; fellowship from National Endowment for the Arts, 1987;
MacDowell Colony Fellow, 2002-2003.

WRITINGS:

Days between Stations, Poseidon (New York, NY),
1985.
Rubicon Beach, Poseidon (New York, NY), 1986.
Tours of the Black Clock, Poseidon (New York, NY),
1989.
Leap Year (nonfiction), Poseidon (New York, NY),
1989.
Arc d'X, Poseidon (New York, NY), 1993.
Amnesiascope, Holt (New York, NY), 1996.
American Nomad (nonfiction), Holt (New York, NY),
1997.
The Sea Came in at Midnight, Bard (New York, NY),
1999.
Our Ecstatic Days, Simon & Schuster (New York, NY),
2005.

Author of column "Guerrilla Pop" and contributing editor for *Los Angeles Reader,* 1982-85; film columnist for
California Magazine. Contributor to *Esquire, Los Angeles Magazine, Los Angeles Times, Los Angeles Herald
Examiner, Chicago Reader, Free Paper* (Washington,
DC), *East Bay Express* (Berkeley, CA), *L.A. Weekly,
PSA Magazine, New York Times Sunday Magazine, Rolling Stone,* and *Village Voice;* film columnist, *Los Angeles Magazine.* Contributor of essays to Web sites, including *Book Forum, Conjunctions, Salon, and Salon
(Media Circus).* Contributor of entry "L.A.'s Top 100"
to *Best Music Writing 2002,* edited by R.J. Smith, Da
Capo Press (Cambridge, MA), 2001.

SIDELIGHTS: Readers of Steve Erickson's novels frequently find themselves lost in time. Like a disjointed
dream sequence, historical characters appear in the
present as prisoners of an enduring fate while those
born in the here and now can find themselves just as
suddenly displaced to a past they never knew they had.
Erickson's work stretches the limit of the novel form in
its attempt to incorporate the qualities of other media,
such as film and art.

According to *Complete Review,* Steve Erickson "writes
on the edge of science fiction: his novels tend to feature
slightly altered (un)realities, dystopias that are closer to
us than we care to imagine. . . . He sets his scenes
fairly well, using his post-apocalyptic visions effectively while rarely losing himself in the details of his
imagined worlds. And he has some decent stories to
tell." In an interview with Rob Trucks for *Blue Moon
Review,* Erickson stated of his work, "It's not fantasy,
it's not surrealism, it's not magical realism, it's not
mainstream, it's not avant-garde, it's not conventional
and it's not necessarily hip. It just doesn't lend itself to
a niche."

Many of Erickson's novels take place in Los Angeles,
which, according to *Complete Review,* the author has
"gotten bogged down in . . . destroy[ing] and recreat-
[ing] it in almost every book." Erickson said of this
city, in his interview with Trucks, "My relationship
with Los Angeles is touch and go. I didn't set out to
write about it so much. It just naturally lent itself to
what I was doing."

In the author's first novel, *Days between Stations,* futuristic lovers Lauren and Michel travel the post-
apocalyptic world in search of the latter's pre-amnesic

identity. A reel of silent film recorded by his Parisian grandfather is the only clue Michel possesses of his past; his bleak European journey, in which he finds Paris plunged into primeval darkness, reveals little about his past or his current situation. Writing in the *New York Times Book Review,* Frederika Randall observed, "There is a healthy dose of cinematic surrealism in . . . Erickson's moody first novel," its narrative unfolding "with the magical ease of a movie that floats back and forth in space and time." *Los Angles Times* critic Carolyn See also noted that *Days between Stations* "demands concentration and a very close reading [as] characters change names at the drop of a hat . . . incidents repeat themselves, [and] . . . diction shifts."

See further stated that Erickson's interest in "the essential duality of things, image versus reality, past versus present, dreams versus wakening," is plotted logically, but that the book defies a "symbolic exegesis or a plot summary." Deeming the book a serious, risk-taking endeavor, See predicted a distinguished future for the author.

Discussing Erickson's second novel, *Rubicon Beach,* in the *New York Times Book Review,* Paul Auster observed that the author has again "shunned the strictures of realistic fiction." Describing the work as "part science fiction, part surrealist love story, [and] part political fable," Auster noted that its three distinct parts often intersect and ultimately converge. "Characters vanish from one world and reappear in another . . . names and identities slide" and "imagery is far more important . . . than plot." Noting the "Jungian tonality" of the book's events, Auster suggested that *Rubicon Beach* "is in some sense intended as a warning to those who lack the courage to cross the Rubicon of their imaginations." While the reviewer acknowledged "moments when [Erickson's] energies outstrip his ideas," Auster nonetheless judged the work a success. "One does not think twice about following him down the labyrinthine paths of his bizarre and striking tale." The critic praised the author's prose as well, concluding that Erickson "is a young writer to be watched."

Tours of the Black Clock, Erickson's third novel, blends future with past and history with fantasy. The plot concerns Banning Jainlight, who becomes Adolf Hitler's pornographer. Erickson "effectively creates a brooding, self-enclosed world of driven sensuality," remarked Tom Clark in the *Los Angeles Times Book Review,* adding that the novelist's "effort to engage history on a cosmic scale . . . is affected negatively by a serious case of overreaching." Kathy Acker, however, praised

Erickson in her *New York Times Book Review* article, saying that the novel "is more than a story: it becomes a meditation on evil, on 'the most evil man in the world.' Since the narrator of this meditation is himself a murderer, hardly free of the taint of evil, the *absolute* quality of evil is being questioned." Acker pronounced the novel "a gorgeous argument against a culture of absolutes and for a way of life based on questioning."

In *Arc d'X,* Erickson expounds on a favorite theme: the lost ideals and dreams of America. The book takes place during Thomas Jefferson's diplomatic sojourn in Paris, though it is Jefferson's slave and reputed lover, Sally Hemings, who is the focus of attention. In Paris, Sally is a free woman, but love proves more important to her than freedom, and she accompanies Jefferson back to America and remains his slave.

The plot shifts from eighteenth-century France to an apocalyptic city ravaged by religious extremists, then again to Berlin in 1999 where Jefferson reappears to kill the novelist, who is a character in his own work of fiction. "Characters, objects, and events jump across time and space," commented Walt Bode of the *Voice Literary Supplement.* While Bode found some of Erickson's writing confusing, he added that "there is luminous and sensual prose about bodies, the weather and revolution; there are breathtaking leaps of the imagination, but too often obliqueness seems to be the goal." For Michiko Kakutani of the *New York Times, Arc d'X* has "moments of genuine brilliance," including "haunting descriptions of pre-Revolutionary Paris and post-unification Berlin and imaginative depictions of a futuristic city-state perched precariously between ruin and redemption."

In his interview with Erickson for *HotWired,* John Alderman called the author's sixth novel, *Amnesiascope,* "bleakly funny," particularly in its "nightmarish" depiction of a futuristic Los Angeles. *Amnesiascope* "seems to describe not just an architecture of the imagination but an urban sprawl of the imagination," Alderman commented. While the book is clearly a work of science fiction, it is also a semi-autobiographical account that contains scenes that Alderman noted "are embarrassing to read" because they are so intensely personal.

The protagonist of *Amnesiascope* is, as Erickson once was, a film critic for an alternative local newspaper, a position that leaves the former novelist artistically and financially dissatisfied. S, as the character is called, roams a divided Los Angeles, encircled by rings of fire to separate it from the rest of the country, to visit the city's underside of prostitution, drugs, and strip joints. Alvin Lu of the *San Francisco Bay Guardian* found the book "dazzling" and "mind-blowing," but mentioned what he considers a recurrent fault of the author's work: "at times his articulation is impatient, unwilling to work out the details; ultimately the brilliance becomes blinding." In his interview with Trucks, Erickson, himself, noted this shortcoming in his work. "My greatest flaw [as a novelist]," Erickson remarked, "is I'm really not as careful an observer as I should be and my books wind up being a little too imagined when they ought to be better observed. I expect that's because I've spent a whole lifetime living inside my own head and I'm more comfortable there. I'm more fascinated with what's in my own head than I am with the world around me. There are a lot of bad things that journalism does to one's writing but one of the good things it does is force you out of your own head and to record the world around you in ways that I wish I was better at than I am."

Kakutani of the *New York Times* complained that *Amnesiascope's* series of "peculiar events" never become a coherent story. These events are S and his girlfriend's plans to kidnap a stripper, a review of an imagined movie that somehow everyone in Los Angeles thinks is real, and S's efforts to track down the woman of his dreams after spotting her on a billboard. Kakutani wrote that these events "feel like the sort of drug-induced riffs college students like to spin out for one another late at night." Despite this criticism, Kakutani observed that *Amnesiascope* reveals "passages far more emotionally intimate—and in some cases, far more engaging—than anything he has written before."

In the category of nonfiction, Erickson has produced two books recounting his experiences covering two presidential elections. But, as G. Michael O'Toole warned in his *West Coast Review of Books* article, no one should expect from Erickson "your standard 'Making-of-the-President'-type fare." The first of these works, *Leap Year,* finds the author on the road with the 1988 campaign. "He was in Atlanta for the Democratic convention, but mainly bagged the event by television in his hotel room," noted *Los Angeles Times Book Review* writer Charles Bowden. "He was in New Orleans for the Republican Convention, but split before it began in order to take in the music and bars of Austin, TX. . . . He was periodically hounded by Sen. Albert Gore and his wife Tipper—they kept showing up either wasted or demented as Erickson hallucinated his way across the landscape of the United States."

The author, Bowden continued, uses the election and the candidates "as props in his discussion of what's

gone wrong with this country. And his novelist's feel for the language is a relief from either the dead newspaper prose or poli-sci jargon that lurks in election books." In devoting an entire article to Erickson's works, *Village Voice* writer Greg Tate singled out *Leap Year* as the author's "most melancholic work, a *Mr. Smith Goes to Washington* for the '90s."

An unexpected character in *Leap Year* materializes in the ghost of Sally Hemings—the same historical figure who also appeared in the novel *Arc d'X.* Hemings' voice, according to Tate, "is symbolic of all those locked out of Jefferson's vision of democracy by his ofay will to power." Hemings is portrayed searching for Jefferson and locating him during the election year 1988, living in a Hopi Reservation.

Journalist and critic David Yepsen, for one, found elements of *Leap Year* rough going; as he told *Washington Post Book World,* what with the ghost of Hemings and the author's side trips "the book gets so confused . . . [that] the political junkie looking for some counterculture insights will find [*Leap Year*] to be too much work." Still, Yepsen acknowledged, Erickson "makes some worthwhile points about all the rot of the 1988 campaign that aren't often made by those of us who covered it."

With *American Nomad,* Erickson covered the 1996 Oval Office race; this time he was on assignment for *Rolling Stone* magazine. "For a while [Erickson carried] off the pretense of being a more or less normal campaign correspondent," remarked *New York Times Book Review* contributor Barbara Ehrenbach. But he was subsequently fired by publisher Jann Wenner for what was perceived as increasingly bizarre dispatches.

No matter, as Ehrenbach continued in her *New York Times Book Review* piece. In *American Nomad* the author retains "his eagle eye for the ambient madness, rage and yearning of the Presidential election season. He understands the cheap redemption white America sought in Colin Powell and how, when another high-profile African-American was acquitted of murder, white America decided to blow off redemption and stick with resentment and guilt."

At his best, the critic added, Erickson "functions like some high-tech psycho-medical sensing devise inserted into the ravaged soul of American politics." Less impressed was *Washington Post Book World*'s Jonathan Yardley, who deemed *American Nomad* a book "overloaded with sweeping, cosmic generalizations almost none of which is capable of holding more than a couple ounces of water." While he cited the author for areas of "clear, straight thinking," Yardley also pointed to passages like "America had [become] a country of nomads, who wandered the hallways of the American soul not sure if they were in a funhouse or a cancer ward" as evidence that Erickson "simply cannot resist the formulation of glib oversimplifications that quickly reach the level of *reductio ad absurdum.*"

To a *Kirkus Review* critic, on the other hand, *American Nomad* "operates brilliantly as both a political chronicle and a zany memoir." And in Ehrenbach's view, Erickson "establishes one thing in this beautiful, crazed and weirdly patriotic book: [in firing Erickson] Jann Wenner made a big mistake."

Publishing much in print and electronically, Erickson has written numerous essays on politics, as well as culture and film, for such periodicals as *New York Times Sunday Magazine, Village Voice, Esquire, Los Angeles Magazine, Los Angeles Times, Los Angeles Herald Examiner,* and *Chicago Reader,* and the Web sites *Book Forum, Conjunctions, Salon,* and *Salon (Media Circus).* He also contributed to a music review, "L.A.'s Top 100," for *Best Music Writing 2002.* In a review for *Rock Critics,* by Scott Woods, Erickson classified his work as "one hundred soundtracks for a city that has always liked to think of itself as utopia or one hundred utopias." Woods categorized the work as a "great reference piece."

In addition to teaching writing at the California Institute for the Arts, Erickson also edits their semi-annual literary magazine, *Black Clock.* The first issue of the journal featured the works of such notable writers as David Foster Wallace, Bruce Bauman, Nicholas Royle, Heidi Julavits, and Rick Mood, or "enough heavyweights to collapse newsstand shelves," according to Matthew C. Duersten, in a review for *Los Angeles Weekly.* Duersten classified Erickson as "arguably one of the most definitive L.A. writers of the last twenty years." David Kipen, in the *San Francisco Chronicle,* provided additional accolades for Erickson's literary journal. "*Black Clock* vaults into the upper echelon of literary magazines," Kipen stated. "[It] contains what may be the single greatest author interview I've ever read . . . a sit-down between the unclassifiable author of the novel *Dhalgren,* Samuel R. Delany, and *Black Clock* editor Steve Erickson. . . . Somehow they manage to say something new about science fiction, Hemingway and God knows what all else, and nothing old or predictable about anything."

BIOGRAPHICAL AND CRITICAL SOURCES:

BOOKS

Contemporary Literary Criticism, Volume 64, Thomson Gale (Detroit, MI), 1991.

PERIODICALS

Atlanta Journal and Constitution, March 5, 1989.
Boston Globe, December 30, 1988.
HotWired, April 18-20, 1997.
Kirkus Reviews, March 15, 1997, p. 434.
Los Angeles Herald Examiner, August 20, 1985.
Los Angeles Times, May 20, 1985; September 8, 1986.
Los Angeles Times Book Review, January 29, 1989; October 15, 1989, pp. 3-7.
Los Angeles Weekly, May 17, 1985; August 29, 1986; January 13, 1989, December 26, 2003-January 1, 2004; February 13-19, 2004.
New Statesman & Society, April 8, 1994, p. 40.
New York Times, January 7, 1989; April 6, 1993, p. C17; June 11, 1996, p. B2.
New York Times Book Review, May 12, 1985; September 21, 1986; March 5, 1989; May 2, 1993, p. 9; June 6, 1993, p. 37; June 8, 1997, p. 6.
New York Times Sunday Magazine, July 30, 2000; March 30, 2003.
Philadelphia Inquirer, August 8, 1985; October 26, 1986.
Publishers Weekly, March 22, 1993, p. 59; March 25, 1996, p. 60.
San Francisco Bay Guardian, May 29, 1996.
San Francisco Chronicle, March 19, 1989.
Village Voice, October 7, 1986; April 3, 1990, p. 75.
Voice Literary Supplement, May, 1993, p. 5.
Wall Street Journal, March 13, 1989.
Washington Post Book World, October 8, 1989; May 9, 1993, p. 4; May 4, 1997.
West Coast Review of Books, November-December, 1989, p. 41.

ONLINE

Austin Chronicle Online, http://www.austinchronicle.com/ (July 26, 2004), Michael Ventura, "Letters at 3AM."
Blue Moon Web site, http://www.thebluemoon.com/ (1998), Rob Trucks, "A Conversation with Steve Erickson."

BookForum.com, http://www.bookforum.com/ (July 26, 2004), Steve Erickson, "California Scheming: The Noir Novels of James M. Cain."

Complete Review, http://www.complete-review.com/ (July 26, 2004).

Los Angeles Weekly Online, http://www.laweekly.com/ (March 19-25, 2004), Matthew C. Duersten, "Tour de Force of the *Black Clock.*"

Rock Critics, http://www.rockcritics.com/ (July 26, 2004), Scott Woods, review of "We Are Worthy."

Salon.com, http://www.salon.com/ (July 26, 2004).

San Francisco Chronicle Online, http://www.sfgate.com/cgi-bin/ (May 16, 2004), David Kipen, review of *Black Clock.*

Village Voice Online, http://www.villagevoice.com/ (January 15-11, 2000), Steve Erickson, "World's Fare: Distributing the Wealth."

*   *   *

ERICKSON, Walter
See FAST, Howard

*   *   *

ERICSON, Walter
See FAST, Howard

*   *   *

ERNAUX, Annie 1940-

PERSONAL: Born September 1, 1940, in Lillebonne, France; daughter of Alphonse (a grocer) and Blanche (a grocer; maiden name, Dumenil) Duchesne; married Philippe Ernaux, 1964 (divorced, 1985); children: Eric, David. *Education:* Rouen University, Agregation of (French) Modern Literature, 1971.

ADDRESSES: Home—La Favola, 23 Allee des Lozeres, 95000 Cergy, France. *Agent*—c/o Author Mail, Seven Stories Press, 140 Watts St., New York, NY 10013.

CAREER: Novelist and memoirist. Has worked as a secondary school teacher of French in Haute-Savoie and the Paris region, 1966-77; Centre National d'Enseignement par Correspondance, professor, 1977-2000.

AWARDS, HONORS: Renaudot prize, 1984, for *La place.*

WRITINGS:

Les armoires vides, Gallimard (Paris, France), 1974, translation by Carol Sanders published as *Cleaned Out,* Dalkey Archive Press (Normal, IL), 1990.

Ce qu'ils disent ou rien, Gallimard (Paris, France), 1977.

La femme gelée, Gallimard (Paris, France), 1981, translation by Linda Coverdale published as *A Frozen Woman,* Four Walls Eight Windows (New York, NY), 1995.

La place, Gallimard (Paris, France), 1984, translation by Tanya Leslie published as *A Man's Place,* Four Walls Eight Windows (New York, NY), 1992.

Une femme, Gallimard (Paris, France), 1987, translation by Tanya Leslie published as *A Woman's Story,* Four Walls Eight Windows (New York, NY), 1991.

Passion simple, Gallimard (Paris, France), 1991, translation by Tanya Leslie published as *Simple Passion,* Four Walls Eight Windows (New York, NY), 1993.

Journal du dehors, Gallimard (Paris, France), 1993, translation by Tanya Leslie published as *Exteriors,* Seven Stories Press (New York, NY), 1996.

La Honte, Gallimard (Paris, France), 1997, translation by Tanya Leslie published as *Shame,* Seven Stories Press (New York, NY), 1998.

Je ne suis pas sortie de ma nuit, Gallimard (Paris, France), 1997, translation by Tanya Leslie published as *I Remain in Darkness,* Seven Stories Press (New York, NY), 1999.

L'evenement, Gallimard (Paris, France), 2000, translation by Tanya Leslie published as *Happening,,* Seven Stories Press (New York, NY), 2001.

La vie exterieure: 1993-1999, Gallimard (Paris, France), 2000.

Se perdre (title means "Losing Oneself"), Gallimard (Paris, France), 2001.

L'occupation, Gallimard (Paris, France), 2002.

(With Frédéric Yves Jeannet) *L'écriture comme un couteau,* Stock (Paris, France), 2003.

SIDELIGHTS: French writer Annie Ernaux creates work that "is remarkably of a piece," according to James Sallis, writing in the *Review of Contemporary Fiction,* "each book circling back to paraphrase, correct, emendate, and reinvest earlier ones." Sallis went on to note that Ernaux's work, "with its blurring of fictional, autobiographical, and confessional elements, of the discursive and the representational, leads us virtually with each sentence to question supposed borders between finding and making, re-creation and reinvention; to question the notion of literature itself."

Ernaux is the author of a number of short autobiographical novels that have been praised for their compellingly honest exploration of human emotions as well as their spare, well-wrought prose style. As Sonja Bolle commented in the *Los Angeles Times Book Review,* "When Annie Ernaux sits down to write, it is as if she has carefully washed her hands, switched on a brilliant desk lamp, and is examining a rare artifact under a magnifying glass." And Maria Simson observed in *Publishers Weekly,* "All writers draw on their own lives in their work, but few subject their past to the kind of unflinching examination that Annie Ernaux does." Kathryn Harrison, meanwhile, writing in the *New York Times Book Review,* called Ernaux "the sort of writer who practices vivisection. With words, she lays open a life . . . she has dismantled and coolly examined her early youth and her strivings to escape the humiliations of her parents' blue-collar world for the seemingly rarified realm of academia, dissecting the consolations and disappointments of transcending her parents' social class as well as the agonies of self-loathing that ensued." Simson quoted Ernaux as describing her approach to writing in this fashion: "I'm not trying to write a real autobiography. I don't believe that feelings, experiences, encounters that happen to me are interesting because they happen to me. Rather they are things that happen to a person, who happens to be me."

In Ernaux's first novel, *Les armoires vides,* translated as *Cleaned Out,* a young female college student recovering from an illegal abortion recalls the pain of her childhood, seeking to understand how she has come to be in such a state of desperation and lamenting the fact that circumstances have resulted in her alienation from her working-class parents, who sacrificed themselves for her well-being. "*Cleaned Out . . .* describes a childhood and youth in Normandy that paralleled Ernaux's," Simson related. "The novel is a raw, often angry depiction of a young girl's burgeoning sexuality; of her distance from, and her disdain for, her uncouth parents."

With the appearance of *Une femme* (*A Woman's Story*), the second of Ernaux's books to be translated into English, the author began to be compared to Simone de Beauvoir for her insights into women's lives, and to Albert Camus for her spare prose and harsh, simply-told truths. *A Woman's Story,* based on Ernaux's relationship with her mother, portrays the death of a rural, working-class woman through the eyes of her estranged, university-educated daughter. Through the elder woman's life story—in which she and her husband save enough money to buy a small grocery-café that enables them to send their daughter to university, where she becomes alienated from them—Ernaux examines class, age, and gender issues. Lillian S. Robinson wrote in the *Nation* that "Ernaux does not attempt to put words into her mother's mouth and tell her full story but rather to use the medium of literary language to show why her mother could never tell her own story." Despite the peculiarly French nature of some of the mother-daughter conflicts depicted in *A Woman's Story,* several American critics found a universal message in the book. Ginger Danto commented in the *New York Times Book Review* that *A Woman's Story* "is every woman's story, the story of every daughter who loses a mother, every matriarch whose power ebbs with time and every widow who surreptitiously loosens her fierce grip on life." Miranda Seymour, also writing in the *New York Times Book Review,* judged *A Woman's Story* "extraordinarily evocative literature."

A Man's Place, the translation of Ernaux's memoir of her father, *La place,* was equally enthusiastically reviewed. Like *A Woman's Story, A Man's Place* begins with the death of the parent as the catalyst for the reminiscences that follow: the peasant upbringing, the myriad ways in which his humble origins set the limits for his adult life, and the inevitable gulf that separates him from his daughter as she becomes more educated. This book marked the appearance of a "more streamlined" style in Ernaux's work, noted Simson in *Publishers Weekly;* the work is "not so much a narrative as an accretion of descriptive scenes." Simson quoted Ernaux as saying, "I had started to write about my father in the same style in which I'd written my first two novels, and I started to see this as a form of betrayal. If I wanted to be true to my father's life, to a life that was dictated by indignities, a life that did not lend itself to novelistic transformation, then the narrative had to be spare and factual." Several critics perceived this quality in the work; Ann Fortune, writing in the *Times Literary Supplement,* commented on the "ferocious economy" of the narrative, while Charles Solomon, writing in the *Los Angeles Times Book Review,* commended the author's "unsparing honesty." Seymour, in her *New York Times Book Review* assessment of *A Man's Place,* concluded: "The victim, as in *A Woman's Story,* turns out to be the author herself, viewed with a hard, unsparing eye as she fails to bridge the gap between the two worlds. It is this bleak honesty, this refusal to let herself off the hook of guilt, that gives Ms. Ernaux's two books their uncommon strength."

Passion simple, which appeared in English as *Simple Passion,* is a record of a woman's obsessive two-year affair with a married man. Caryn James commented in the *New York Times Book Review* that the novel "embraces the crazed adolescent behavior that can crop up at any age, yet is intelligent enough to wrap those details in a taut literary shape and defiantly unemotional language." Other critics emphasized Ernaux's characteristic attention to the minutiae of her subject's emotional life, and the unabashed, not always flattering, manner in which she exposes her subject's sexual behavior and desires. "This memoir falls into the reader's lap like a steaming lump of truth, smelling of sexual hunger, indifferent to the shamelessness or the pathos of its cause," remarked Daphne Merkin in the *New Yorker*.

Ernaux continued her blend of memoir and novel in two further books during the 1990s: *Exteriors* and *Shame*. The former title is a "slim, deceptively slight paste-up of daily encounters," according to *Nation's* Joe Knowles. Reviewing that same novel, a contributor for *Publishers Weekly* acknowledged that "Ernaux's best subject is Ernaux." The same reviewer concluded that this "loose and largely unremarkable series of vignettes . . . [is] not yet literature," unlike earlier novels from Ernaux that "succeeded brilliantly." In *Shame* Ernaux reconstructs the day in 1952 when she watched her father try to kill her mother. For *Booklist's* Donna Seaman, this "beautifully crafted and unsettling narrative offers a telling glimpse," while a contributor for *Publishers Weekly* concluded that "Ernaux strips herself and her memories of any comforting myth and in the process, she forces us to face the jarring facts of being human."

I Remain in Darkness, published in French as *Je ne suis pas sortie de ma nuit,* is a journal that details the final years of Ernaux's mother's life, during which the older woman's mind and body deteriorated from Alzheimer's disease. Ernaux opened her home to her mother for a time, then had to place her in a nursing home, where the elderly woman died in 1986. Ernaux describes vividly the sights and smells of her mother's sickroom and offers observations of the other patients in the nursing home. She also examines the still-tortured mother-daughter relationship; she feels both love and hatred emanating from her mother and is aware of a "sadistic streak" in herself. This book "is a sequel in a way to *A Woman's Story,*" related Richard Bernstein in the *New York Times*. As Harrison explained in the *New York Times Book Review,* "there is little inconsistency between the two works. Details and even scenes are repeated, sometimes almost word for word . . . but the sympathy between novel and memoir is not a matter of mere repetition. While *I Remain in Darkness* will not give readers new information, it serves as a more intimate revelation of the slow death that prompted her to bear witness of the life that was ebbing." Bernstein commented that the book has "flashes of genius" and

that fans of Ernaux's work will desire it, "even though it is a less gripping work than her earlier works." This book "is so thin and undeveloped as to lack the quiet impact of her others," he remarked. Harrison, however, praised the book with less reservation, asserting that "as revealed by Ernaux, the details of a loved one's deterioration have such emblematic force and terror that the particular becomes universal. . . . Ernaux renders the plight of the dying with a seemingly effortless economy."

Ernaux returns again to personal stories in *Happening,* and to the illegal abortion she had as a young woman in the 1960s that she first fictionalized in *Cleaned Out.* Writing in the *Review of Contemporary Fiction,* Gregory Howard felt that in *Happening* Ernaux "succeeds in rendering the numbing grind of diurnal unhappiness, fearful accounts of her trips to the abortionist, and harrowing . . . [details of having] the miscarriage in her dorm room with beauty and riveting detail." Similarly, Mary Paumier Jones, writing in *Library Journal,* found *Happening* "deeply affecting." More praise came from *Booklist's* Donna Seaman who called the book an "important, moving testimony in the history of women's rights." In *Publishers Weekly* a contributor described *Happening* as an "important, resonant work."

In *Se perdre* Ernaux recounts an affair she had with a married Russian diplomat in the 1980s. A reviewer for the *Economist* found that Ernaux's "matter-of-fact account manages to avoid the pitfalls of exhibitionism, while forcefully demonstrating how self-awareness can be achieved through alienation." Julia Abramson, writing in *World Literature Today,* concluded that "the yearning for perfection, a recurring motif in *Se perdre,* thus characterizes both Ernaux's experience of the love affair and her esthetic in writing." And in the 2003 *L'occupation,* a novel of jealousy and remorse, Ernaux "continues her exploration of the psychic interior and the relation between emotional states and literature," according to Michele Levy in *World Literature Today.* Levy further praised all of Ernaux's books as "slim texts" that "blur the boundaries between autobiography and fiction," and commended *L'occupation* in particular, for enabling readers to "comprehend, confront, and thus resist our own 'occupations.'"

A contributor for the *Complete Review Web site* described Ernaux's novels as "powerful little reads. They are short fictions, based in her life, most only a hundred pages or so in length. Similar territory is revisited and reexamined from book to book as she tries to come to terms with her childhood, her parents, her love affairs, and still she manages to create something new each time." For her own part, Ernaux once explained that "The recurring motif in my books is the social and cultural divide that I myself have experienced. Born of small shopkeepers, I went to university and was taken away from my original background: I gradually changed in my tastes, my habits, and ultimately, in my whole outlook on the world. My literary goal, as I expressed it in *A Woman's Story,* is 'something between history, sociology, and literature.'"

BIOGRAPHICAL AND CRITICAL SOURCES:

PERIODICALS

Atlantic, October 1, 1998, Phoebe-Lou Adams, review of *Shame,* p. 116.

Booklist, May 1, 1995, Donna Seaman, review of *A Frozen Woman,* p. 1551; July, 1998, Donna Seaman, review of *Shame,* p. 1850; November 1, 1999, Ray Olson, review of *I Remain in Darkness,* p. 503; September 15, 2001, Donna Seaman, review of *Happening,* p. 179.

Economist, July 14, 2001, review of *Se perdre,* p. 5.

French Forum, spring, 2002, p. 131; fall, 2002, p. 99.

Journal of European Studies, September, 1998, M.A. Hutton, "Challenging Autobiography," p. 231.

Library Journal, November 15, 1999, Wilda Williams, review of *I Remain in Darkness,* p. 90; November 1, 2001, Mary Paumier Jones, review of *Happening,* p. 90.

Los Angeles Times Book Review, August 29, 1993, p. 6; September 26, 1993, p. 8.

Nation, August 26, 1991, Lillian S. Robinson, review of *A Woman's Story,* pp. 234-236; December 16, 1996, Joe Knowles, review of *Exteriors,* p. 31.

New Yorker, December 27, 1993, Daphne Merkin, review of *Simple Passion,* pp. 154-159.

New York Times, November 22, 1999, Richard Bernstein, "When a Parent Becomes the Child."

New York Times Book Review, May 19, 1991, Ginger Danto, review of *A Woman's Story,* p. 13; May 10, 1992, Miranda Seymour, review of *A Man's Place,* pp. 5-6; October 24, 1993, Caryn James, review of *Simple Passion;* May 21, 1995, p. 13; November 28, 1999, Kathryn Harrison, "As She Lay Dying."

North American Review, May-June, 1993, Margaret Peller Feeley, review of *A Woman's Story,* p. 46.

Observer Review, December 30, 1984, p. 19.

Publishers Weekly, September 14, 1990, Sybil Steinberg, review of *Cleaned Out,* p. 112; March 8, 1991, Sybil Steinberg, review of *A Woman's Story,* p. 67; September 6, 1991; March 9, 1992, review of *A Man's Place,* p. 48; July 19, 1993, review of *Simple Passion,* p. 236; March 20, 1995, review of *A Frozen Woman,* p. 41; September 16, 1996, review of *Exteriors,* p. 69; December 9, 1996, Maria Simson, "Annie Ernaux: Diaries of Provincial Life," p. 49; June 15, 1998, review of *Shame,* p. 50; October 11, 1999, review of *I Remain in Darkness,* p. 54; August 20, 2001, review of *Happening,* p. 68.

Review of Contemporary Fiction, spring, 1994, James DeRossitt, review of *Simple Passion,* p. 230; spring, 1997, review of *Exteriors,* p. 182; spring, 1999, Robert Buckeye, review of *Shame,* p. 175; spring, 2000, James Sallis, review of *I Remain in Darkness,* p. 193; summer, 2002, Gregory Howard, review of *Happening,* p. 246.

Times Literary Supplement, April 26, 1991, Ann Fortune, review of *A Man's Place,* p. 23.

World Literature Today, winter, 2002, Julia Abramson, review of *Se perdre,* p. 171, E. Nicole Meyer, review of *La vie exterieurre: 1993-1999,* p. 179; October-December, 2003, Michele Levy, review of *L'occupation,* p. 108.

ONLINE

Complete Review Web site, http://www.complete-review.com/ (August 10, 2004), "Annie Ernaux at the Complete Review."

*   *   *

ERWIN, Will
   See EISNER, Will

*   *   *

ESQUIVEL, Laura 1951(?)-

PERSONAL: Born c. 1951, in Mexico; daughter of Julio Caesar Esquivel (a telegraph operator) and Josephina Esquivel; married Alfonso Arau (a film director); children: Sandra. *Education:* Attended Escuela Normal de Maestros, Mexico. *Hobbies and other interests:* Cooking.

ADDRESSES: Home—Mexico City, Mexico. *Agent*—Doubleday, 666 5th Avenue, New York, NY 10103.

CAREER: Novelist and screenwriter; writer and director for children's theater. Worked as a teacher for eight years.

AWARDS, HONORS: Ariel Award nomination for best screenplay, Mexican Academy of Motion Pictures, Arts and Sciences, for *Chido One.*

WRITINGS:

Chido One (screenplay), 1985.
Como agua para chocolate: novela de entregas mensuales con recetas, amores, y remedios caseros (novel), Editorial Planeta Mexicana, 1989, translation by Carol Christensen and Thomas Christensen published as *Like Water for Chocolate: A Novel in Monthly Installments, with Recipes, Romances, and Home Remedies,* Doubleday (New York, NY), 1991.
Like Water for Chocolate (screenplay, based on her novel of the same title), Miramax, c. 1993.
Little Ocean Star (screenplay for children), 1994.
Ley del amor (novel), translation by Margaret Sayers Peden published as *The Law of Love,* Crown Publishers (New York, NY), 1996.
Intimas suculencias: Tratado filosofico de cocina (novel), Ollero & Ramos (Madrid, Spain), 1998.
Between Two Fires: Intimate Writings on Life, Love, Food, and Flavor (novel), translation by Stephen Lytle, Crown Publishers (New York, NY), 2000.
Tan velos como el deseo (novel), Plaza y Janes Editores (Barcelona, Spain), 2001, translation by Stephen Lytle published as *Swift as Desire,* Crown Publishers (New York, NY), 2001.
Malinche (Spanish language novel), Atria, 2006.

Like Water for Chocolate was also published in serial format in its entirety in the *New York Times'* Metro Section, 2004.

SIDELIGHTS: Mexican author Laura Esquivel, who gained international recognition with her first novel, *Como agua para chocolate* (*Like Water for Chocolate*), began writing when she worked in a theater workshop for children and found that there was little material available for them to perform. She then moved into writing for children's public television, and then into screenwriting.

Working in partnership with her husband, Mexican director Alfonso Arau, Esquivel wrote the screenplay for the 1985 Mexican release *Chido One,* which Arau directed. The film's success prompted the couple to continue their collaboration, and Arau became the director when Esquivel adapted *Like Water for Chocolate* for

the screen. Both the novel and movie were enormously popular. A number-one best-seller in Mexico in 1990, the book has been translated into numerous languages, including an English version, which enjoyed a longstanding run on the *New York Times Book Review* bestseller list in 1993. The movie, according to *Publishers Weekly,* became one of the highest-grossing foreign films of the decade. Employing in this work the brand of magic realism that Gabriel García Márquez popularized, Esquivel blends culinary knowledge, sensuality, and alchemy with fables and cultural lore to capture what *Washington Post* reviewer Mary Batts Estrada called "the secrets of love and life as revealed by the kitchen."

Like Water for Chocolate is the story of Tita, the youngest of three daughters born to Mama Elena, the tyrannical owner of the De la Garza ranch. Tita is a victim of tradition: as the youngest daughter in a Mexican family she is obliged to remain unmarried and to care for her mother. Experiencing pain and frustration as she watches Pedro, the man she loves, marry her older sister Rosaura, Tita faces the added burden of having to bake the wedding cake. But because she was born in the kitchen and knows a great deal about food and its powers, Tita is able to bake her profound sense of sorrow into the cake and make the wedding guests ill. "From this point," as James Polk remarked in the *Tribune Books,* "food, sex and magic are wondrously interwoven." For the remainder of the novel, Tita uses her special culinary talents to provoke strange reactions in Mama Elena, Rosaura, Tita's other sister, Gertrudis, and many others.

Food has played a significant role in Esquivel's life since she was a child. Remembering her early cooking experiences and the aromas of foods cooked in her grandmother's house, she told Molly O'Neill of the *New York Times* that "I watch cooking change the cook, just as it transforms the food. . . . Food can change anything." For Esquivel, cooking is a reminder of the alchemy between concrete and abstract forces. Writing in the *Los Angeles Times Book Review,* Karen Stabiner remarked that Esquivel's novel "is a wondrous, romantic tale, fueled by mystery and superstition, as well as by the recipes that introduce each chapter." James Polk, in the *Chicago Tribune,* wrote that " *Like Water for Chocolate* (a Mexican colloquialism meaning, roughly, agitated or excited) is an inventive and mischievous romp—part cookbook, part novel."

Esquivel followed with *The Law of Love,* a highly imaginative novel that features reincarnation and cosmic retribution and attests to the primacy of love. The story opens with the sixteenth-century Spanish conquest of Tenochtitlan, the future site of Mexico City, and the rape of an Aztec princess atop a temple. Many centuries later the principal actors of this earlier drama reappear as astro-analyst Azucena, her missing soul mate Rodrigo, and planetary presidential candidate Isabel in a confrontation that finally breaks the cycle of vengeance and hatred with love and forgiveness. The text is accompanied by a compact disc with music and cartoon illustrations. This "multimedia event," as described by Lilian Pizzichini in the *Times Literary Supplement,* incorporates elements of magic realism, science fiction, and New Age philosophy. "The result," wrote *Library Journal* reviewer Barbara Hoffert, "is at once wildly inventive and slightly silly, energetic and clichéd." Pizzichini concluded, "Esquivel dresses her ancient story in a collision of literary styles that confirm her wit and ingenuity. She sets herself a mission to explore the redemptive powers of love and art and displays boundless enthusiasm for parody."

In *Swift as Desire,* Esquivel explores communication between people, telling the story of Jubilo, a former telegraph operator who now has Parkinson's disease and is mostly blind and mute. His daughter Lluvia, hoping to help him to communicate and also hoping to bring him back together with her mother Lucha, from whom he is estranged, installs telegraph equipment in his bedroom so that he can tap out messages in Morse code; a computer translates them into written words. Jubilo's life story is told in flashbacks, revealing how he learned of the power of communication and words when he became a telegraph operator and sent messages of love and fate over the wires. Jubilo has certain gifts: his hearing is so sensitive that he can hear the movements of a fetus in his wife's womb; he can hear people's true thoughts, which are often different from the telegraph messages they send. In the *New York Times,* William Ferguson wrote that although Esquivel's prose is occasionally "cloying," the book "has many charms." In a *Knight-Ridder/Tribune News Service* review, Katrinka Blickle noted that the storyline is sometimes interrupted by digressions on sunspots or World War II history. However, she wrote, "Jubilo is a fascinating character." In another *Knight-Ridder/Tribune News Service* review, Marta Barber wrote, "the love story of Jubilo and Lucha warms the heart even when it doesn't jolt the mind." In *School Library Journal,* Adriana Lopez praised the book as "a smooth, simple read for devotees of a quality romance." A *Publishers Weekly* reviewer commented, "Esquivel's storytelling abilities are in top form here, and despite its unoriginality, the novel succeeds in conveying a touching message of the power of familial and romantic love."

BIOGRAPHICAL AND CRITICAL SOURCES:

BOOKS

Authors and Artists for Young Adults, Volume 29, Thomson Gale (Detroit, MI), 1999.

PERIODICALS

Americas, September, 1999, Cecilia Novella, review of *Intimas suculencias: Tratago filosofico de cocina,* p. 60.
Antioch Review, winter, 1998, p. 113.
Booklist, July, 1999, p. 1965; June 1, 2001, Kathleen Hughes, review of *Swift as Desire,* p. 1798.
Entertainment Weekly, April 23, 1993, p. 52; December 31, 1993, pp. 203-204; January 7, 1994, p. 47.
Hispanic Times, December/January 1996, p. 42.
Kirkus Reviews, July 1, 1996, p. 917.
Knight-Ridder/Tribune News Service, September 26, 2001, Marta Baber, review of *Swift as Desire,* p. K7344; October 10, 2001, Katrinka Blicke, review of *Swift as Desire,* p. K5186.
Library Journal, January, 1996, p. 81; July, 1996, p. 156; December, 2000, Wendy Miller, review of *Between Two Fires: Intimate Writings on Life, Love, Food, and Flavor,* p. 131; July, 2001, Mary Margaret Brown, review of *Swift as Desire,* p. 122; August, 2001, p. S33.
Los Angeles Times Book Review, November 1, 1992, p. 6.
Ms., November/ December, 1993, p. 75.
Nation, June 14, 1993, p. 846.
New Republic, March 1, 1993, pp. 24-25.
New Statesman, August 27, 2001, Rachel Cooke, "Pleasure Zone," p. 39.
New Yorker, June 27, 1994, p. 80.
New York Times, March 31, 1993, pp. C1, C8; October 7, 2001, William Ferguson, review of *Swift as Desire,* p. 22.
New York Times Book Review, November 17, 1996, p. 11.
Publishers Weekly, May 17, 1993, p. 17; August 15, 1994, p. 13; October 3, 1994, p. 40; February 5, 1996, p. 24; July 3, 2000, John F. Baker, "Esquival Back to Family for Crown," p. 12; December 4, 2000, review of *Between Two Fires,* p. 70; July 16, 2001, review of *Swift as Desire,* p. 165.
School Library Journal, September, 2001, Adriana Lopez, review of *Swift as Desire,* p. S33; November, 2001, Molly Connally, review of *Swift as Desire,* p. 191.

Time, April 5, 1993, pp. 62-63.
Times Literary Supplement, October 18, 1996, p. 23; October 5, 2001, Claudia Pugh-Thomas, review of *Swift as Desire,* p. 26.
Tribune Books (Chicago), October 18, 1992, p. 8.
Washington Post, September 25, 1992, p. B2.
World Press Review, February, 1996, p. 43.

*   *   *

ESTLEMAN, Loren D. 1952-

PERSONAL: Born September 15, 1952, in Ann Arbor, MI; son of Leauvett Charles (a truck driver) and Louise (a postal clerk; maiden name, Milankovich) Estleman; married Carole Ann Ashley (a marketing and public relations specialist), September 5, 1987. *Education:* Eastern Michigan University, B.A., 1974.

ADDRESSES: Home—Whitmore Lake, MI. *Agent*—c/o Morgan and Associates, P.O. Box 2976, Ann Arbor, MI 48106.

CAREER: Writer. *Michigan Fed,* Ann Arbor, MI, cartoonist, 1967-70; *Ypsilanti Press,* Ypsilanti, MI, reporter, 1973; *Community Foto-News,* Pinckney, MI, editor in chief, 1975-76; *Ann Arbor News,* Ann Arbor, special writer, 1976-77; *Dexter Leader,* Dexter, MI, staff writer, 1977-80. Has been an instructor for Friends of the Dexter Library, and a guest lecturer at colleges.

MEMBER: Mystery Writers of America, Author's Guild, Western Writers of America (vice president and president-elect, 1998), Private Eye Writers of America, Napoleonic Association of America.

AWARDS, HONORS: American Book Award nomination, 1980, for *The High Rocks; New York Times Book Review* notable book citations, 1980, for *Motor City Blue,* and 1982, for *The Midnight Man;* Golden Spur Award for best Western historical novel, Western Writers of America, 1982, for *Aces & Eights;* Shamus Award nomination for best private eye novel, Private Eye Writers of America, 1984, for *The Glass Highway;* Pulitzer Prize in letters nomination, 1984, for *This Old Bill;* Shamus Awards, 1985, for novel *Sugartown,* and for short story "Eight Mile and Dequindre"; Golden Spur Award for best Western short story, 1986, for "The Bandit"; Michigan Arts Foundation Award for Literature, 1986; Michigan Library Association Author of the Year Award, 1997; Shamus Award for best short story, 2004, for "Lady on Ice."

WRITINGS:

The Oklahoma Punk (crime novel), Major Books (Canoga Park, CA), 1976.
Sherlock Holmes vs. Dracula; or, The Adventure of the Sanguinary Count (mystery-horror novel), Doubleday (New York, NY), 1978.
Dr. Jekyll and Mr. Holmes (mystery-horror novel), Doubleday (New York, NY), 1979.
The Wister Trace: Classic Novels of the American Frontier (criticism), Jameson Books, 1987.
Red Highway (novel), PaperJacks, 1988.
Peeper (mystery novel), Bantam (New York, NY), 1989.
The Best Western Stories of Loren D. Estleman, edited by Bill Pronzini and Martin H. Greenberg, Ohio University Press (Athens, OH), 1989.
Sweet Women Lie, Thorndike Press, 1990.
Whiskey River, Bantam (New York, NY), 1990.
Motown, Bantam (New York, NY), 1992.
Sudden Country, Bantam (New York, NY), 1992.
Crooked Way, Eclipse (New York, NY), 1993.
King of the Corner, Bantam (New York, NY), 1993.
City of Widows, Tor Books (New York, NY), 1994.
The Judge, Forge (New York, NY), 1994.
Edsel, Mysterious Press (New York, NY), 1995.
Stress, Mysterious Press (New York, NY), 1996.
Jitterbug: A Novel of Detroit, Forge (New York, NY), 1998.
The Rocky Mountain Moving Picture Association, Forge (New York, NY), 1999.
Thunder City: A Novel of Detroit, Forge (New York, NY), 1999.
The Hours of the Virgin, Mysterious Press (New York, NY), 1999.
White Desert, Forge (New York, NY), 2000.
A Smile on the Face of the Tiger, Mysterious Press (New York, NY), 2000.
Writing the Popular Novel: A Comprehensive Guide to Crafting Fiction That Sells, Writer's Digest Books (Cincinnati, OH), 2004.
The Undertaker's Wife, Forge (New York, NY), 2005.

"AMOS WALKER" MYSTERY SERIES

Motor City Blue, Houghton (Boston, MA), 1980.
Angel Eyes, Houghton (Boston, MA), 1981.
The Midnight Man, Houghton (Boston, MA), 1982.
The Glass Highway, Houghton (Boston, MA), 1983.
Sugartown, Houghton (Boston, MA), 1984.
Every Brilliant Eye, Houghton (Boston, MA), 1986.
Lady Yesterday, Houghton (Boston, MA), 1987.

Downriver, Houghton (Boston, MA), 1988.

General Murders (short story collection), Houghton (Boston, MA), 1988.

Silent Thunder, Houghton (Boston, MA), 1989.

Never Street, Mysterious Press (New York, NY), 1997.

The Witchfinder, Mysterious Press (New York, NY), 1998.

Sinister Heights, Mysterious Press (New York, NY), 2002.

Poison Blonde, Mysterious Press (New York, NY), 2003.

Retro, Forge (New York, NY), 2004.

"PETER MACKLIN" MYSTERY SERIES

Kill Zone, Mysterious Press (New York, NY), 1984.

Roses Are Dead, Mysterious Press (New York, NY), 1985.

Any Man's Death, Mysterious Press (New York, NY), 1986.

Something Borrowed, Something Black, Forge (New York, NY), 2002.

WESTERN NOVELS

The Hider, Doubleday (New York, NY), 1978.

Aces & Eights (first book in historical Western trilogy), Doubleday (New York, NY), 1981.

The Wolfer, Pocket Books (New York, NY), 1981.

Mister St. John, Doubleday (New York, NY), 1983.

This Old Bill (second book in historical Western trilogy), Doubleday (New York, NY), 1984.

Gun Man, Doubleday (New York, NY), 1985.

Bloody Season, Bantam (New York, NY), 1988.

Western Story, Doubleday (New York, NY), 1989.

Billy Gashade, Forge (New York, NY), 1997.

Journey of the Dead, Forge (New York, NY), 1998.

The Master Executioner, Tom Doherty Associates (New York, NY), 2001.

(Editor) *American West: Twenty New Stories*, Forge (New York, NY), 2001.

Black Powder, White Smoke, Tom Doherty Associates (New York, NY), 2002.

"PAGE MURDOCK" WESTERN SERIES

The High Rocks, Doubleday (New York, NY), 1979.

Stamping Ground, Doubleday (New York, NY), 1980.

Murdock's Law, Doubleday (New York, NY), 1982.

The Stranglers, Doubleday (New York, NY), 1984.

Port Hazard, Forge (New York, NY), 2004.

OTHER

(Editor, with Martin H. Greenberg) *P.I. Files*, Ivy Books, 1990.

Contributor to books, including Robert J. Randisi, editor, *The Eyes Have It: The First Private Eye Writers of America Anthology*, Mysterious Press, 1984; and Edward D. Hoch, editor, *The Year's Best Mystery and Suspense Stories, 1986*, Walker & Co., 1986. Contributor to periodicals, including *Alfred Hitchcock's Mystery Magazine, Baker Street Journal, Fiction Writers Magazine, A Matter of Crime, Mystery, New Black Mask, Pulpsmith, Roundup, Saint Magazine, TV Guide, Writer,* and *Writer's Digest.*

ADAPTATIONS: The "Amos Walker" mysteries *Motor City Blue, Angel Eyes, The Midnight Man, Sugartown, The Glass Highway,* and *Every Brilliant Eye,* were adapted as audiobooks, read by David Regal, for Brilliance Corp. (Grand Haven, MI), 1988. *Sherlock Holmes vs. Dracula* was broadcast by the British Broadcasting Corporation. One of Estleman's Western novels has been optioned by a California film company.

SIDELIGHTS: Loren D. Estleman, the prolific author of what James Kindall described in *Detroit* as "hard-bitten mysteries, a herd of reality-edged westerns and an occasional fantasy or two," is perhaps best known for his series of hard-boiled mysteries that unravel in an authentically evoked Detroit. "A country boy who has always lived outside of Detroit, he writes with convincing realism about inner city environments," stated Kindall, adding that "probably no other area pensmith can lay as convincing a claim to the title of Detroit's private eye writer as Estleman." Had it not been for the success of fellow Detroiter and mystery writer Elmore Leonard, pronounced William A. Henry in *Time,* "Estleman would doubtless be known as the poet of Motor City."

Estleman has crafted an increasingly popular series of mysteries around the character of Amos Walker, a witty and rugged Detroit private investigator who recalls Raymond Chandler's Philip Marlowe and Dashiell Hammett's Sam Spade. Considered "one of the best the hard-boiled field has to offer" by Kathleen Maio in *Wilson Library Bulletin,* "Walker is the very model of a

Hammett-Chandler descendant," observed *New York Times Book Review* contributor Newgate Callendar. "He is a big man, very macho, who talks tough and is tough. He hates hypocrisy, phonies and crooks. He pretends to cynicism but is a teddy bear underneath it all. He is lonely, though women swarm all over him." Conceding to Ross that the character represents his "alter ego," Estleman once refused a six-figure offer from a major film company for exclusive rights to Walker, explaining to Kindall: "Twenty years from now, the money would be spent and I'd be watching the umpteenth movie with Chevy Chase or Kurt Russell playing Amos with the setting in Vegas or L.A. and blow my brains out."

Walker "deals with sleaze from top to bottom—Motor City dregs, cop killers and drug dealers," remarked Andrew Postman in *Publishers Weekly,* and reviewers admire the storytelling skills of his creator. Walker made his debut searching the pornographic underworld of Detroit for the female ward of an aging ex-gangster in *Motor City Blue,* a novel Kristiana Gregory appraised in the *Los Angeles Times Book Review* as "a dark gem of a mystery." About *Angel Eyes,* in which a dancer who anticipates her own disappearance hires Walker to search for her, the *New Republic*'s Robin W. Winks believed "Estleman handles the English language with real imagination . . . so that one keeps reading for the sheer joy of seeing the phrases fall into place." In *The Midnight Man,* which Callendar described as "tough, side-of-the-mouth stuff, well written, positively guaranteed to keep you awake," Walker encounters a contemporary bounty hunter in his pursuit of three cop killers; and writing about *The Glass Highway,* in which Walker is hired to locate the missing son of a television anchor and must contend with a rampaging professional killer, Callendar believed Estleman "remains among the top echelon of American private-eye specialists."

Walker disappeared for most of the 1990s as Estleman worked on other projects, then made a comeback in *Never Street* after a eight-year hiatus. *Never Street* spins an intriguing and self-reflexive tale by setting up a mystery based on one character's obsession with the classic film noir *Pitfall,* which leaves Walker "wandering the '90s in search of 1952," in the words of a writer for *Booklist.* Estleman refers to plot devices and conventions of the film noir genre as well as scenes from the actual movie as the mystery unwinds, "producing a novel that is part parody, part tribute," according to the *Booklist* reviewer. *New York Times Book Review* contributor Marilyn Stasio applauded Walker's return, saying that he has come back "just in time to slap some sense into a genre that's getting dumber and dumber by the minute."

General Murders contains a collection of ten previously published short stories and novelettes featuring Walker. "Dating from 1982 to 1987, these samplings are good indicators of the pleasures in Estleman's longer works," remarked a reviewer for *Publishers Weekly,* while a *Booklist* contributor noted that, "Like the best short story writers, Estleman creates characters with a phrase and sets scenes with a sentence." Yet *New York Times Book Review* contributor Edna Stumpf concluded that, "In general, however, the short story form reveals the intense stylization of Loren Estleman's fiction in an unkind way."

In another series of mysteries, Estleman slants the perspective to that of a criminal, Peter Macklin, who also freelances out of Detroit. "Macklin is the result of my wanting to do an in-depth study of a professional killer," Estleman told Bob McKelvey in the *Detroit Free Press.* "It presents a challenge to keep a character sympathetic who never has anything we would call morals." Kindall suggested that, "although a killer, he always seems to end up facing opponents even lower on the evolutionary scale, which shades him into the quasi-hero side." However, in a review of *Kill Zone,* the first novel in the "Macklin" series, Callendar felt that "not even Mr. Estleman's considerable skill can hide the falsity of his thesis" that even hired killers can be admirable characters. The plot of the novel concerns the seizure of a Detroit river boat by terrorists who hold hundreds of passengers hostage, attracting other professional killers from organized crime and a governmental agency as well. This all makes for a plot that a *Publishers Weekly* contributor found "confusing and glutted with a plethora of minor characters who detract from the story's credibility." Although Peter L. Robertson detected an implausibility of plot in the second of the "Macklin" series' novels, *Roses Are Dead,* in which Macklin tries to determine who and why someone has contracted to kill him, the critic noted in *Booklist* that the novel is "a guaranteed page-turner that features an intoxicating rush of brutal events and a fascinating anti-hero."

Describing the action of *Any Man's Death,* in which Macklin is hired to guard the life of a television evangelist and is caught in the struggle between rival mob families for control of a proposed casino gambling industry in Detroit, Wes Lukowsky suggested in *Booklist* that Estleman "has created a surprisingly credible and evolving protagonist." And as a *Time* contributor remarked: "For urban edge and macho color . . . nobody tops Loren D. Estleman."

The Hider, a novel about the last buffalo hunt in America, was Estleman's first Western novel and was purchased immediately—a rarity in the genre. He has since written several other successful Western novels plus a critical analysis of Western fiction itself, *The Wister Trace: Classic Novels of the American Frontier;* and several of his books about the American West have earned critical distinction. *The High Rocks,* for instance, which is set in the mountains of Montana and relates the story of a man's battle with the Indians who murdered his parents, was nominated for an American Book Award. And the first two books of his proposed historical Western trilogy have also earned honors: *Aces & Eights,* about the murder of Wild Bill Hickok, was awarded the Golden Spur, and *This Old Bill,* a fable based on the life of William Frederick "Buffalo Bill" Cody, was nominated for a Pulitzer Prize.

In the *Los Angeles Times Book Review,* David Dary discussed Estleman's *Bloody Season,* an extensively researched historical novel about the gunfight at the O.K. Corral: "The author's search for objectivity and truth, combined with his skill as a fine writer, have created a new vision of what happened in Tombstone . . . , and he avoids the hackneyed style that clutters the pages of too many Westerns." Dary concluded that although it is a fictional account, the novel "probably comes closer to the truth" than anything else published on the subject. In *Twentieth-Century Western Writers,* Bill Crider observed: "All of Estleman's books appear solidly researched, and each ends in a way which ties all the story threads together in an effective pseudo-historical manner, giving each an air of reality and credibility."

Estleman again displays his ability to balance parody and tribute in the 1997 Western *Billy Gashade,* the story of a young man from a wealthy family who flees his New York home after the 1863 draft riots and lights out for the territories, encountering on his journey such figures as Jesse James, Calamity Jane, Billy the Kid, and Crazy Horse. The narrative, told from the vantage point of the eighty-eight-year-old protagonist living in Depression-era Hollywood, tells of Billy's wanderings as an itinerant piano player. A contributor to *Publishers Weekly* called the novel "a song, lyrical and alive with biting wit, drama, and grace," praising Estleman's ability to take "potshots at our conventional understanding of western heroes and their legends." A critic for *Booklist* was impressed that the novel "somehow manages to avoid collapsing under the weight of its epic scope," while a writer for *Kirkus Reviews* assessed *Billy Gashade* as "a fine, picaresque tale that brings to vivid, mock-heroic life many of American history's western icons."

Estleman followed the upbeat *Billy Gashade* with a Western of a much darker tone. *Journey of the Dead* picks up the thread of another figure whose life has been touched by the legendary Billy the Kid: his killer, Sheriff Pat Garrett. Garrett's life, described by a *Kirkus Reviews* contributor as "sunbaked torture," was irreparably shaken by his intervention in history. A writer for *Publishers Weekly* described Garrett as "a convincingly tragic western figure who never quite understands the praise and blame attached to him for an act he can never live down." The novel tells not only of the violent events themselves, but also of Garrett's lingering nightmares, taking place on a bleak strip of landscape called La Journada del Muerto, from which the novel takes its title. *Journey of the Dead* "deserves blue ribbons and rosettes," according to the *Kirkus Reviews* critic. "As he shows once more, [Estleman] has no rival—not even Louis L'Amour—in invoking the American Southwest."

The city of Detroit is the central character of Estleman's crime series originally projected to be a trilogy but now encompassing additional volumes. The first installment, *Whiskey River,* covers the wars between rival gangs during the Prohibition years and is narrated by newspaper columnist Connie Minor. "Estleman's novel is a wizard piece of historical reconstruction, exciting as a gangster film but with a texturing of the characters and the times that rises well above genre," hailed Charles Champlin in the *Los Angeles Times Book Review.* "Occasionally the details fail," remarked Walter Walker in the *New York Times Book Review.* "But [Estleman] does a marvelous job of setting clues, bringing seemingly loose ends together and surprising his readers, leaving them nearly incapable of stopping at the end of any given chapter."

Motown is set in the turbulent year of 1966, when big cars, mobs, labor unions, racial tension, and power politicians dominated Detroit. Intertwining real and fictional events, Estleman weaves plots concerning race wars between the black and Italian mobs, racketeering, and the safety records of the cars produced by the Big Three automakers. Connie Minor appears again, this time as an investigative reporter who finds an incriminating photograph of a labor leader. Thomas Morawetz declared in the *Washington Post Book World* that "this wonderful cornucopia of a novel [has] quicksilver dialogue, incisive characterizations and canny interweaving of observations and events."

The series' third novel, *King of the Corner,* continues the themes of racial tension, dirty politics, and organized crime. The central character is "Doc" Miller, an overweight ex-Tigers baseball pitcher just out of prison for the death of a girl in his hotel room. Though he intends to do honest work, Miller soon finds himself involved with Detroit's black drug dealers and political corruption. "Neither as colorful nor as vigorous as the earlier volumes—but, still, a pleasing if rather rambling mystery-thriller," commented a *Kirkus Reviews* contributor.

The additional novels in the series focus on other decades in the Motor City. In *Edsel*, Connie Minor has become a copywriter for the Ford Motor Company touting its new dream car of the 1950s, the Edsel. Because of his questioning of guys on the line, Minor comes under suspicion of spying on the rank-and-file and gets caught up in intrigue by the unions. "The conspiracy he ultimately discovers and untangles may be fairly anticlimactic, but Minor's observation and irreverence combine to keep the reader comfortably—even avidly—in the passenger's seat," declared Jean Hanff Korelitz in a review for the *Washington Post Book World*. Noted Marilyn Stasio in the *New York Times Book Review*, "Estleman is a pithy, punchy writer who can also deliver the action by spitting images out of the side of his mouth." *Stress* takes place in the 1970s as Detroit is recovering from the sixties race riots, and focuses on Charlie Battle, a young black cop confronting a racist department and violent black militant groups. In *Booklist*, Wes Lukowsky called the novel "a fine installment in an innovative series," while a *Publishers Weekly* reviewer stated: "It's difficult to believe that Detroit will ever find a more eloquent poet than Estleman, who here . . . celebrates the gristle and sinew of the city as well as its aching heart."

Poison Blond, Estelman's fiftieth published book, was described by *Library Journal* reviewer Rex Klett as the author's "latest spell-binding adventure." Another installment in the "Amos Walker" series, the plot focuses on Walker's latest client, a Latino singer who performs under a borrowed name to hide from death squads from her home country. A reviewer in *Publishers Weekly* praised Estleman as a "wordsmith par excellence" who "has Amos deliver passionate laments for his city that add a melancholy counterpoint like background music." In reviewing the audiobook version of the novel, *Library Journal* critic Barbara Perkins called *Poison Blond* "another crackling good book. . . . This is Estleman at his very best."

A *Publishers Weekly* critic declared Estleman "at the top of his game," in a review of *Port Hazard*, in which U.S. Marshal Page Murdock takes on a conspiracy plot to renew the Civil War by murdering prominent lawmen and public officials. Murdock dives into the cor-

ruption of San Francisco's Barbary Coast, mixing it up with gamblers, vigilantes, whores, Chinese gangs, and crooked politicians. The "snappy dialogue, fast-paced action, colorful characters and plenty of bullets, booze and blood make this western crime drama a wicked romp," continued the *Publishers Weekly* critic. A contributor to *Kirkus Reviews* dubbed the novel "a historical western in mirror-smooth mahogany prose," and *Booklist* reviewer Brad Hooper praised *Port Hazard* as a "wildly entertaining romp with great period atmosphere."

BIOGRAPHICAL AND CRITICAL SOURCES:

BOOKS

Contemporary Literary Criticism, Volume 48, Thomson Gale (Detroit, MI), 1988, pp. 102-107.

Twentieth-Century Crime and Mystery Writers, 2nd edition, St. Martin's Press (New York, NY), 1985.

Twentieth-Century Western Writers, Thomson Gale (Detroit, MI), 1982.

PERIODICALS

Ann Arbor News, September 24, 1978.

Ann Arbor Observer, July, 1978.

Armchair Detective, summer, 1987, p. 311; spring, 1988, p. 218; summer, 1989, p. 329; fall, 1989, p. 434; summer, 1990, p. 250; spring, 1991, p. 250; winter, 1991, pp. 5-11, p. 28; summer, 1995, p. 285.

Booklist, November 15, 1984; September 1, 1985; October 15, 1986; September 15, 1988, p. 123; April 1, 1990, p. 1530; June 15, 1991, pp. 1932, 1948; March 15, 1994, p. 1327; March 15, 1996, p. 1242; November 15, 2002; April 1, 2003; November 15, 2003; May 1, 2004; May 15, 2004.

Chicago Tribune Book World, January 18, 1981; August 10, 1986.

Detroit, March 8, 1987.

Detroit Free Press, September 26, 1984.

Detroit News, May 18, 1979; August 21, 1983.

Kirkus Reviews, August 1, 1988, p. 1100; August 1, 1989, p. 1116; June 15, 1991, p. 746; April 1, 1992, p. 412; February 15, 1994, p. 160; February 1, 1995, p. 90; December 1, 1997; September 1, 2002; March 1, 2003; November 15, 2003; May 1, 2004.

Library Journal, September 1, 1989, p. 219; March 15, 1994, p. 100; March 1, 1996, p. 109; October 15, 2002; October 15, 2003.

Los Angeles Times Book Review, August 21, 1983, p. 7; January 19, 1986, p. 9; January 24, 1988, p. 12; September 9, 1990, p. 10; April 11, 1991, p. 5; August 11, 1991, p. 5; May 10, 1992, p. 17.

New Republic, November 25, 1981.

New York Times Book Review, November 11, 1979, p. 24; October 26, 1980, p. 20; November 1, 1981, p. 41; August 22, 1982, p. 26; August 14, 1983, p. 27; October 23, 1983, p. 38; December 2, 1984; December 23, 1984, p. 24; March 24, 1985, p. 29; November 24, 1985, p. 43; April 20, 1986, p. 32; October 26, 1986, p. 47; March 6, 1988, p. 22; January 29, 1989, p. 34; April 9, 1989, p. 42; April 16, 1989, p. 31; October 15, 1989, p. 45, p. 56; May 20, 1990, p. 53; July 8, 1990, p. 28; October 14, 1990, p. 50; September 15, 1991, p. 34; February 9, 1992, p. 28; July 5, 1992, p. 17; May 8, 1994, p. 18; March 19, 1995, p. 29; February 22, 1998.

Observer (London, England), September 16, 1990, p. 55

Publishers Weekly, August 23, 1985; January 22, 1988; August 12, 1988, p. 442; May 3, 1991, p. 64; March 14, 1994, p. 64; January 29, 1996, p. 84; September 16, 2002; April 21, 2003; December 8, 2003.

Time, July 31, 1978, p. 83; December 22, 1986, p. 75; August 17, 1987, p. 63; February 1, 1988, p. 66; March 16, 1998, p. 80.

Times (London, England), November 20, 1986; November 29, 1986; December 31, 1987.

Times Literary Supplement, March 14, 1986; April 10, 1987; August 12, 1988, p. 893; September 8, 1989, p. 969; August 10, 1990, p. 855; September 13, 1991, p. 22.

Tribune Books (Chicago, IL), February 24, 1987, p. 41; March 1, 1987, p. 8; January 31, 1988, p. 6; March 26, 1989, p. 6; November 5, 1989, p. 6; July 21, 1991, p. 3; May 3, 1992, p. 6.

Village Voice, February 24, 1987.

Washington Post Book World, September 21, 1980, p. 14; October 18, 1981, p. 6; May 17, 1987, p. 6; October 21, 1990, p. 10; August 18, 1991, p. 10; July 26, 1992, p. 1; August 16, 1992, p. 6; March 26, 1995, p. 2.

Wilson Library Bulletin, March, 1985, p. 487.

*   *   *

EUGENIDES, Jeffrey 1960(?)-

PERSONAL: Born c. 1960, in Grosse Pointe Park, MI; son of Constantine (a mortgage banker) and Wanda Eugenides; married, wife's name Karen (an artist); children: a daughter. *Education:* Brown University, B.A. (magna cum laude), 1983; Stanford University, M.A., 1986. *Religion:* Greek Orthodox

ADDRESSES: Agent—Lynn Nesbit, Janklow & Nesbit Associates, 445 Park Ave., New York, NY 10022.

CAREER: Writer. *Yachtsman* magazine, photographer and staff writer; American Academy of Poets, New York, NY; various positions including newsletter editor, beginning in 1988. Has worked as a cab driver, busboy, and a volunteer with Mother Teresa in India.

AWARDS, HONORS: Aga Khan Prize for fiction, *Paris Review,* 1991, for an excerpt from the *The Virgin Suicides;* Writers Award, Whiting Foundation, 1993; Henry D. Vursell Memorial Award, American Academy of Arts and Letters; Pulitzer Prize in fiction, 2003, for *Middlesex;* recipient of fellowships from Guggenheim Foundation, National Endowment for the Arts, and Academy of Motion Picture Arts and Sciences; Berlin Prize fellowship, American Academy in Berlin, 2000-2001; fellow of the Berliner Kuenstlerprogramm of the DAAD.

WRITINGS:

The Virgin Suicides, Farrar, Straus & Giroux (New York, NY), 1993.

Middlesex, Farrar, Straus & Giroux (New York, NY), 2002.

Contributor to periodicals, including *Paris Review.*

ADAPTATIONS: The Virgin Suicides, a film adaptation written and directed by Sofia Coppola, was released by Paramount Pictures, 2000.

SIDELIGHTS: Novelist Jeffrey Eugenides received critical acclaim for his first novel, *The Virgin Suicides,* a tale of five teenaged sisters who one by one kill themselves. His sequel, *Middlesex,* published nine years later, won a Pulitzer Prize for fiction.

The Michigan-born writer had worked in various fields before graduating from Brown University, including driving a cab in downtown Detroit and working alongside Mother Teresa in Calcutta, India. He later wrote for the American Academy of Poets in New York, and pushed to complete his opus when he learned the organization would soon terminate his position. Eugenides also wrote part of his first novel, *The Virgin Suicides,* while traveling down the Nile through Egypt. An excerpt from the book was published in the *Paris Review* in 1991 and won the literary journal's Aga Khan Prize for fiction that year.

The author got the idea for *The Virgin Suicides* while visiting his brother's house in Michigan and chatting with the babysitter. The young woman said that she and her sisters had all attempted suicide at one point. When Eugenides asked why, she replied simply, "pressure." The theme of inexplicable adolescent trauma amid a placid suburban landscape gave birth to the plot of the novel. *The Virgin Suicides* is set in an unnamed affluent suburb remarkably similar to Eugenides's hometown of Grosse Pointe Park, Michigan, and is told in the collective narrative voice of a group of men who were obsessed with the girls as teenagers. Now nearing middle age, they are still trying to fathom the mysterious suicides of twenty years before, haunted by their memories of the sisters.

The Virgin Suicides juxtaposes the innocence and eroticism of early-1970s suburbia against the unaccountable force that drove the young women to their deaths. The Lisbon family consists of the five lovely daughters, an overprotective and devoutly Catholic mother, and a rather invisible father. The girls are garbed in shapeless, oversized clothes and forbidden to date. The neighborhood boys, entranced by their remoteness, spy on them and rummage through the family's garbage for such collectibles as discarded cosmetics and homework papers. The reader learns how the suicides began as the voice recounts when one of them sneaked into the Lisbon house through a sewer tunnel and peeped in on the youngest, thirteen-year-old Cecilia, as she bathed. To his horror she had also slit her wrists, and her intruder turns out to be a temporary rescuer when he notifies the police. Yet a short time later, during an unlikely party at the somber Lisbon house, Cecilia jumps to her death from a window, impaling herself on a fencepost. The death of a peer fascinates the neighborhood boys: "We had stood in line with her for smallpox vaccinations," the narrator recalls of Cecilia, "had held polio sugar cubes under our tongues with her, had taught her to jump rope, to light snakes, had stopped her from picking her scabs on numerous occasions, and had cautioned her against touching her mouth to the drinking fountain at Three Mile Park."

Soon the girls are grounded permanently and disappear even from the normalcy of a school routine, further piquing the boys' obsession. They watch as one of the sisters, the sexually precocious Lux, fornicates on the roof of the house with mysterious men at night, while neighbors begin to complain about the family's unkempt lawn and the strange odors emanating from the Lisbon house. The boys maintain a distant relationship with the girls, calling them on the phone and signaling to them from neighboring houses. Finally they hatch a plan to rescue the girls in which they will all escape to Florida in a stolen car. In the end, however, the remaining girls commit suicide, leaving the boys to their lifelong preoccupation with the unexplained deaths.

Many reviewers praised the author's use of the wry, anonymous narrative. Tom Prince, in *New York* magazine, described the work as "a highly polished novel about the coarseness of adolescence, relentlessly mournful but also gruesomely funny." *New York Review of Books* critic Alice Truax remarked that "if anything is offensive about *The Virgin Suicides,* perhaps it's that reading it is such a pleasurable, melancholy experience—in spite of its ostensible subject matter." Commenting on Eugenides's style, Truax said "On his first page, he makes it clear that his title means what it says, and that he plans to spin a dreamy, elegiac tale from its terrible promise."

"Eugenides never loses his sense of humor," Kristin McCloy wrote in the *Los Angeles Times Book Review.* "Mordant to be sure, and always understated, Eugenides's sense of the absurd is relentless." Michiko Kakutani of the *New York Times* warned that unexplained elements in the novel might "grate on the reader's nerves, momentarily breaking the spell of [Eugenides's] tale." Kakutani, however, described the book's end result as "by turns lyrical and portentous, ferocious and elegiac," and noted that *The Virgin Suicides* insinuates itself into our minds as a small but powerful opera in the unexpected form of a novel." And *People*'s Joseph Olshan added that "the novel manages to maintain a high level of suspense in what is clearly an impressive debut."

Nine years passed between *The Virgin Suicides* and the publication of *Middlesex.* The author returned to Grosse Pointe to tell about a multigenerational Greek-American family through the eyes of its most unusual member: the hermaphroditic Cal (Calliope) Stephanides. Using a male/female narrator posed a challenge: "I wanted the book to be first-person," Eugenides told Dave Welch of *Powells.* "In many ways, the point of the book is that we're all an *I* before we're a he or a she, so I needed that *I.*" For practical reasons, the author added, "I wanted the *I* because I didn't want that terrible situation where the character is she, then you turn the page and she becomes he—or even the more dreaded s/he."

In *Middlesex*, Cal's gender is the product of speculation even before conception. Parents Milton and Tessie long for a girl, and heed an uncle's advice to engage in sex twenty-four hours before ovulation; that way "the swift male sperm would rush in and die off. The female sperm, sluggish but more reliable, would arrive just as the egg dropped." After Tessie becomes pregnant, rancor builds among the relatives when grandma Desdemona, dangling a silver spoon over Tessie's abdomen, declares the child inside a boy. However, the baby born shortly after is deemed female. Calliope spends her childhood and early adolescence as what Laura Miller of the *New York Times* called a "relatively unremarkable daughter." All that changes at puberty when "she" begins sprouting facial hair and speaking in a deepening voice. It is discovered during a doctor's examination that Calliope is a hermaphrodite, possessing equally the physical and sexual characteristics of male and female. "To the extent that fetal hormones affect brain chemistry and histology," the narrator declares, "I've got a male brain."

The girl's horrified parents take her to sexologist Dr. Luce, who proposes a radical "final solution" to Cal's predicament: surgery to remove all outward traces of maleness, and hormonal therapy to reinforce the female characteristics. But for Calliope, that is not the answer. Instead, the character embraces his male identity, and grows to adulthood as an academic in Berlin (where the author lives). Meanwhile, he recounts a twentieth-century family saga that illustrates how Calliope/Cal came to be. He reveals, for example, that grandparents Desdemona and Lefty were brother and sister; and that Cal's own parents married as first cousins.

"Though its premise makes the novel sound as if it's either sensational or clinical—or both," Charles Matthews in a *Knight Ridder/Tribune News Service* review, "it isn't. That's because [*Middlesex*] is as much about the Stephanides family as it is about Cal/Calliope." Matthews added that "even with the element of incest, the story of the Stephanides family doesn't become weirdly titillating or turn into a sentimental problem drama about what's now known as intersexuality. Instead, it's a story based on the familiar dynamics of belonging and displacement." Lisa Schwarzbaum, in *Entertainment Weekly*, said the writing itself "is also about mixing things up, grafting flights of descriptive fancy with hunks of conventional dialogue, pausing briefly to sketch passing characters or explain a bit of a bygone world."

"Because it's long and wide and full of stuff," wrote Miller, the novel "will be associated by some readers with books by David Foster Wallace and Jonathan Franzen, brilliant members of Eugenides's cohort." But unlike those hard-line satirists, the critic added, Eugenides "is sunnier; the book's length feels like its author's arms stretching farther and farther to encompass more people, more life."

But Keith Gessen of *Nation* acknowledged that this "politically effective" novel displays "too much energy . . . expended" on "the assurance of the author's good intentions. The result is often a measured, highly adequate bloodlessness." Yet to *New Republic* contributor James Wood, the author showcases just the right intentions. "Eugenides's charm, his life-jammed comedy, rescues the novel from its occasional didacticism," he wrote. "One can put it this way: a novel narrated by a hermaphrodite comes to seem largely routine, as if Calliope were simply fat or tall. A fact that might scream its oddity, and that might have been used again and again heavily to explore fashionable questions of identity and gender, is here blissfully domesticated."

Comparing the two Eugenides novels, Mark Lawson of *Europe Intelligence Wire* found that while *The Virgin Suicides* "reflected on connections between sex and death, its successor considers the links between sex, life and inheritance." Lawson also found it strange that "in a novel with such a long gestation, occasional phrases seem hasty." In ten years the novelist had produced only two books, though both well-received; Rachel Collins, in *Library Journal,* said "it is Eugenides's dedication to his stories, his characters, and, yes, even his readers, that compels him to spend years on a manuscript." As for his 2003 Pulitzer Prize-winner, Eugenides told Collins that *Middlesex* "really is Cal's" book, "and I think there is nothing ugly about his life. In fact, it's as close to a triumphant story as I'm ever likely to write."

BIOGRAPHICAL AND CRITICAL SOURCES:

BOOKS

Eugenides, Jeffrey, *The Virgin Suicides,* Farrar, Straus & Giroux (New York, NY), 1993.

PERIODICALS

Atlantic Monthly, September, 2002, Stewart O'Nan, review of *Middlesex,* p. 157.

Book, September-October, 2002, Penelope Mesic, "Identity Crisis," p. 70.

Booklist, June 1, 2002, Joanne Wilkinson, review of *Middlesex,* p. 1644.

Bookseller, July 5, 2002, "A Family Story with a Difference," p. 35.

British Medical Journal, October 26, 2002, John Quin, review of *Middlesex,* p. 975.

Detroit News, April 3, 1993, review of *The Virgin Suicides,* pp. 1C, 3C.

Economist, October 5, 2002, review of *Middlesex.*

Entertainment Weekly, September 13, 2002, Lisa Schwarzbaum, "Work of Genes," p. 146.

Europe Intelligence Wire, October 5, 2002, Mark Lawson, "Gender Blender"; October 6, 2002, Geraldine Bedell, "He's Not Like Other Girls."

Kirkus Reviews, July 15, 2002, review of *Middlesex,* p. 977.

Knight Ridder/Tribune News Service, September 11, 2002, Margaria Fichtner, review of *Middlesex,* p. K7215; September 18, 2002, Charles Matthews, review of *Middlesex,* p. K2795; October 2, 2002, Carlin Romano, review of *Middlesex,* p. K4158; October 30, 2002, Marta Salij, "Pointe of View," p. K4969.

Library Journal, July, 2002, Rachel Collins, review of *Middlesex,* p. 116, author interview, p. 121.

Los Angeles Times Book Review, June 20, 1993, Kristin McCloy, review of *The Virgin Suicides,* pp. 2, 5.

Nation, October 14, 2002, Keith Gessen, "Sense and Sexibility," p. 25.

New Republic, October 7, 2002, James Wood, "Unions," p. 31.

Newsweek, September 23, 2002, David Gates, "The Gender Blender," p. 71.

New York, April 26, 1993, Tom Prince, review of *The Virgin Suicides,* pp. 54-58; September 9, 2002, John Homans, "Helen of Boy," p. 131.

New York Review of Books, June 10, 1993, Alice Truax, review of *The Virgin Suicides,* pp. 45-46; November 7, 2002, Daniel Mendelsohn, "Mighty Hermaphrodite," p. 17.

New York Times, March 19, 1993, Michiko Kakutani, review of *The Virgin Suicides,* p. C23; September 15, 2002, Laura Miller, "My Big Fat Greek Gender Identity Crisis."

People, April 19, 1993, Joseph Olshan, review of *The Virgin Suicides,* p. 27.

Spectator, October 5, 2002, Sebastian Stone, "Putting It All In," p. 43.

Time, September 23, 2002, Richard Lacayo, review of *Middlesex,* p. 78.

Times Literary Supplement, October 4, 2002, Paul Quinn, "In the Centre of the Labyrinth," p. 24.

ONLINE

Bomb, http://www.bombsite.com/ (April 9, 2003), Jonathan Safran Foer, author interview.

Powells, http://www.powells.com/ (April 9, 2003), Dave Welch, "Jeffrey Eugenides Has It Both Ways."

Read, http://www.randomhouse.ca/ (April 9, 2003), author interview.

Salon, http://www.salon.com/ (October 15, 2002), Laura Miller, "Interview with Jeffrey Eugenides."

*   *   *

EVERETT, Percival L. 1956-

PERSONAL: Born December 22, 1956, in Ft. Gordon, GA; son of Percival Leonard (a dentist) and Dorothy (Stinson) Everett. *Education:* University of Miami, A.B., 1977; attended University of Oregon, 1978-80; Brown University, A.M., 1982.

ADDRESSES: Office—c/o University Park Campus, English Department, University of Southern California, Los Angeles, CA 90089. *E-mail*—peverett\@usc.edu.

CAREER: Worked as jazz musician, ranch worker, and high school teacher; University of Kentucky, Lexington, associate professor of English, 1985-89, director of graduate creative writing program, 1985-89; University of Notre Dame, Notre Dame, IN, professor of English, 1989-92; University of California at Riverside, professor of creative writing and chairman of program, 1992-99; University of Southern California, Los Angeles, professor of creative writing, American studies, and critical theory, 1999—; writer.

MEMBER: Writers Guild of America (West), Modern Language Association.

AWARDS, HONORS: D.H. Lawrence fellowship, University of New Mexico, 1984; Lila Wallace-*Reader's Digest* fellowship; New American Writing Award, for *Zulus;* PEN/Oakland Josephine Miles Award, for *Big Picture;* Academy Award for Literature, American Academy of Arts and Letters, 2003; Hurston/Wright Legacy Award; Hillsdale Award.

WRITINGS:

Suder (novel), Viking (New York, NY), 1983.
Walk Me to the Distance (novel), Ticknor & Fields (Boston, MA), 1985.

Cutting Lisa (novel), Ticknor & Fields (Boston, MA), 1986.

The Weather and Women Treat Me Fair (short stories), August House (Little Rock, AK), 1989.

Zulus (novel), Permanent Press (Sag Harbor, NY), 1989.

For Her Dark Skin (novel), Owl Creek Press (Seattle, WA), 1989.

The One That Got Away (children's book), illustrations by Dirk Zimmer, Clarion Books (New York, NY), 1992.

God's Country (novel), Faber (Boston, MA), 1994.

The Body of Martin Aguilera, Owl Creek Press (Seattle, WA), 1994.

Big Picture (short stories), Graywolf Press (St. Paul, MN), 1996.

Watershed (novel), Graywolf Press (St. Paul, MN), 1996.

Frenzy (novel), Graywolf Press (St. Paul, MN), 1996.

Glyph (novel), Graywolf Press (St. Paul, MN), 1999.

Grand Canyon, Inc. (novel), Versus Press, 2001.

Erasure (novel), Hyperion (New York, NY), 2002.

(Author of foreword) *Making Callaloo: Twenty-five Years of Black Literature, 1976-2000,* edited by Charles Henry Rowell, afterword by Carl Phillips, St. Martin's Press (New York, NY), 2002.

American Desert (novel), 2004.

Damned If I Do (short fiction), 2004.

(With James Kincaid) *A History of the African-American People (Proposed) by Strom Thurmond, As Told to Percival Everett and James Kincaid* (novel), Akashic Books, 2004.

Work represented in anthologies, including *From Timberline to Tidepool: Contemporary Fiction from the Northwest,* edited by Rich Ives, Owl Creek Press, 1989. Contributor of stories to periodicals, including *Montana Review, Callaloo, Aspen Journal of the Arts, Modern Short Stories,* and *Black American Literature Forum.*

SIDELIGHTS: Percival L. Everett is an educator and writer who has won acclaim with his comic fiction. Everett gained acclaim in 1983 with his first novel, *Suder,* which tells the story of a baseball player who reacts to a slump and family problems by suddenly embarking on a trip across the American northwest. Carolyn See, writing in the *Los Angeles Times,* described *Suder* as a "mad work of comic genius," and Alice Hoffman affirmed in the *New York Times Book Review* that the novel "gives us a story of a life filled with chance events, some laughable, others tragic." *Walk Me to the Distance,* Everett's second novel, concerns a Vietnam veteran who finds seclusion at a Wyoming ranch house he shares with an aging widow and her mentally impaired son. The hero finds a measure of contentment with the widow, with whom he eventually adopts a Vietnamese girl. But when the widow's son, scorned by his mother, violates the girl, the hero is drawn to vigilante justice. Reviewing *Walk Me to the Distance* in the *Los Angeles Times,* Don Strachan said that the novel "forces us to examine our moral positions," and he added that Everett demonstrates an ability "to plumb a deep emotional well with a detail."

In 1986 Everett produced his third novel, *Cutting Lisa,* and he followed that volume in 1989 with his first short-story collection, *The Weather and Women Treat Me Fair.* In 1989 he also published *Zulus,* a fantasy about the last fertile woman on a post-thermonuclear Earth. The heroine is an obese woman who avoids forced sterilization and subsequently becomes pregnant after being raped. With her potential for childbearing, the heroine proves valuable to rebels interested in rejuvenating the human race. Reviewing *Zulus* in the *Washington Post,* Clarence Major drew comparisons to Aldous Huxley's classic, *Brave New World,* and stated that Everett's novel "is a curious, troublesome and, at times, delightful addition to the literature of the antiheroic and the futuristic." In addition, Major hailed Everett as "one of America's most promising young novelists" and noted that his "gifts as a lyrical writer are vividly on display."

Everett followed *Zulus* with another novel, *For Her Dark Skin.* He then published *The One That Got Away,* a children's book about the high jinks that ensue when a band of cowboys capture the numeral "one." A *Kirkus Reviews* critic conceded that *The One That Got Away* is "sort of a one-joke story" but nonetheless summarized it as a "novel idea, developed with high style and wit."

In 1994 Everett published *God's Country,* a novel about a cowardly racist who requires a black tracker's services after his wife is kidnapped by white men posing as Indians. *Booklist* reviewer Brian McCombie deemed *God's Country* "laugh-out-loud funny, thoughtful, and shocking," and a *Publishers Weekly* critic found it "corrosively funny and disquieting." A *Kirkus Reviews* critic, meanwhile, contended that "as a spoof, this tale hits the mark," and David Bowman, writing in the *New York Times Book Review,* declared that *God's Country* "starts sour, then abruptly turns into Cowpoke Absurdism, ending with an acute hallucination of blood, hate and magic." He added, "The novel sears."

Everett's *Big Picture,* which appeared two years later, contains short stories exemplifying what a *Kirkus Reviews* critic acknowledged as Everett's "usual subtlety and eccentric comic flourishes." Among the tales in *Big Picture* are "Cerulean," where an artist indulges his long-held desire to consume paint; "Dicotyles Tajacu," in which a forlorn painter bonds with a stuffed, one-eyed pig; and "Squeeze," wherein a cowhand falls victim to a prankster sporting a friend's dentures. A *Publishers Weekly* critic, while contending that *Cerulean* "caves in on itself," concluded that other tales in the collection "steer clear of abstract self-preoccupation and make for good reading." A *Kirkus Reviews* critic similarly summarized the stories in *Big Picture* as "eminently readable," while Maggie Garb, writing in the *New York Times Book Review,* affirmed that Everett sometimes manages to enrich his characters with "a strangely appealing complexity."

In 1996, the same year he issued *Big Picture,* Everett also produced two novels: *Watershed* and *Frenzy. Watershed* depicts a black hydrologist contending with both a faltering romance and a federal investigation for murder. The novel begins with the hero surrounded by police in the mountains of Colorado. It then retraces events—including the hero's involvement in a dispute between Indians and the U.S. government—culminating in the standoff. A *Kirkus Reviews* critic claimed that *Watershed* provides "few breathtaking vistas" but conceded that it includes "nice touches of humor and essential humanity." A *Publishers Weekly* critic was likewise ambivalent, noting the novel's "rueful irony and political bite" but adding that the various relationships "lack the nuance of the cultural background [Everett] gives them." James Polk, though, declared in the *New York Times Book Review* that *Watershed* "tells an important story."

Frenzy, meanwhile, is set in the world of Greek mythology. The novel tells of Vlepo, assistant to the half-man, half-God Dionysus. Vlepo, who possesses the ability to read minds, travels back in time in an attempt to help Dionysus grasp his own fate. A *Publishers Weekly* critic deemed *Frenzy* "playful," and *Library Journal* reviewer Robert E. Brown proclaimed it "interesting." A *Kirkus Reviews* critic, however, concluded that some readers might find *Frenzy* "a strained, rather precious exercise."

The novel *Glyph* concerns an infant genius—his studies include philosophy and physics—who blackmails his father before being kidnapped by, successively, a deranged psychologist and conspiratorial government agents. A *Kirkus Reviews* critic described the novel's conclusion as "a final free-for-all that involves [the hero's] previous captors, the Catholic Church, and [former Filipino dictator] Ferdinand Marcos." *Kirkus Reviews*

deemed *Glyph* "a smart, rollicking sendup," and a *Publishers Weekly* reviewer described the novel as an "off-kilter academic spoof." Barbara Hoffert, writing in *Library Journal,* was less impressed, claiming that Everett's protagonist is "insufferable enough to leave a sour taste." But *Booklist* critic George Needham called *Glyph* a novel "that can be enjoyed by almost anyone."

Everett continued his prolific production of fiction with the 2001 novella *Grand Canyon, Inc.,* which was followed the next year by the novel *Erasure.* Described by a *Publishers Weekly* critic as an "an over-the-top masterpiece," *Erasure* features as its protagonist one Thelonius "Monk" Ellison, an African-American writer who has built a limited readership for his intellectual essays and experimental novels. Having observed the success of other black writers who have opted to "write black," Monk decides to try his hand at "ghetto prose." His proposal for a novel titled *My Pafology,* written under the pseudonym of Stagg R. Leigh, quickly produces a huge advance from a major publisher and an even larger offer for movie rights to the story. The resulting novel becomes a best-seller and is nominated for an important book award. In the *Review of Contemporary Fiction,* Trey Strecker wrote, "*Erasure*'s acerbic satire on race and publishing is balanced by Monk's heartfelt attempt to reconcile himself to tumultuous—and typically late-twentieth-century—changes in his family life: his sister's murder, his mother's Alzheimer's disease, his brother's coming out, and his father's suicide." In *Publishers Weekly* a reviewer concluded, "Percival's talent is multifaceted, sparked by a satiric brilliance that could place him alongside Wright and Ellison as he skewers the conventions of racial and political correctness."

Everett's *American Desert* projects an even stranger tale. Ted Street, a disgruntled college professor, is en route to commit suicide when he is killed in a car crash. At his funeral he comes back to life, and then embarks on a bizarre journey of soul searching. Reviewing the novel for *Booklist,* Vanessa Bush called *American Desert* a "biting and satirical" story "about the meaning of life and death and one man's search for redemption."

BIOGRAPHICAL AND CRITICAL SOURCES:

PERIODICALS

Booklist, May 15, 1994, Brian McCombie, review of *God's Country;* April 1, 1996, Brad Hooper, review of *Watershed,* p. 1342; January 1, 1997, Brian Mc-

Combie, review of *Frenzy,* p. 818; October 15, 1999, George Needham, review of *Glyph;* April 1, 2004, Vanessa Bush, review of *American Desert,* p. 1346.

Kirkus Reviews, March 1, 1992, review of *The One That Got Away;* March 15, 1994, review of *God's Country;* February 15, 1996, reviews of *Watershed* and *Big Picture;* November 1, 1996, review of *Glyph.*

Library Journal, January, 1997, Robert E. Brown, review of *Frenzy;* November 1, 1999, Barbara Hoffert, review of *Glyph.*

Los Angles Times, July 31, 1983, pp. 1, 8.

New York Times Book Review, October 2, 1983, pp. 9, 26; March 24, 1985, p. 24; June 5, 1994, David Bowman, "Cowpoke Absurdism"; September 15, 1996, Maggie Garb, review of *Big Picture;* December 1, 1996, James Polk, review of *Watershed.*

Publishers Weekly, April 18, 1994, review of *God's Country,* p. 46; March 4, 1996, reviews of *Watershed,* p. 53, and *Big Picture,* p. 61; November 18, 1996, review of *Frenzy,* p. 67; November 8, 1999, review of *Glyph;* August 13, 2001, review of *Erasure,* p. 283.

Review of Contemporary Fiction, summer, 2002, Trey Strecker, review of *Erasure,* p. 228.

Washington Post, May 20, 1990, p. 4.

ONLINE

University of Southern California Web site, http://www.usc.edu/ (September 27, 2003).

F

FADIMAN, Anne 1953-

PERSONAL: Born August 7, 1953, in New York, NY; daughter of Clifton (a writer and editor) and Annalee Whitmore Jacoby (a writer) Fadiman; married George Howe Colt (a writer), March 4, 1989; children: two. *Education:* Harvard University, B.A., 1975.

ADDRESSES: Agent—c/o Farrar, Straus & Giroux, 19 Union Sq. W., New York, NY 10003.

CAREER: Literary journalist and editor. *American Scholar,* editor, 1998-2004; worked nine years as an editor and staff writer for *Life* magazine; worked for three years as editor-at-large and columnist for *Civilization.*

AWARDS, HONORS: National Book Critics Circle Award for Nonfiction, *Los Angeles Times* Book Award for Current Interest, both 1997, and Boston Book Review Rea Nonfiction Prize, 1998, all for *The Spirit Catches You and You Fall Down: A Hmong Child, Her American Doctors, and the Collision of Two Cultures;* National Magazine Award.

WRITINGS:

The Spirit Catches You and You Fall Down: A Hmong Child, Her American Doctors, and the Collision of Two Cultures, Farrar, Straus (New York, NY), 1997.
Ex Libris: Confessions of a Common Reader, Farrar, Straus (New York, NY), 1998.
(Editor, with Robert Atwan) *Best American Essays, 2003,* Houghton Mifflin (Boston, MA), 2003.

Contributor of articles to periodicals.

SIDELIGHTS: Spending nine years as an editor and staff writer for *Life* magazine served author Anne Fadiman well in the writing of her debut book *The Spirit Catches You and You Fall Down: A Hmong Child, Her American Doctors, and the Collision of Two Cultures.* The three years she spent as a columnist for *Civilization,* the magazine of the Library of Congress, led to her second volume, *Ex Libris: Confessions of a Common Reader.* Fadiman comes from a family laden with literary talent: her father is the writer and editor Clifton Fadiman and her mother is the journalist Annalee Whitmore Jacoby Fadiman.

The Spirit Catches You and You Fall Down is a case study of a young refugee girl living in California who was severely stricken with epilepsy. Because her family had their own cultural beliefs about her condition and how to treat it, the child's encounter with California doctors and Western medicine became a trying ordeal for all involved. The book details the life of this child, Lia Lee.

Lia and her parents, Foua Yang and Nao Kao Lee, are Hmong, a people from the mountains of Laos. Since that country fell to the communists in 1975, the Hmong were seen as enemies of the new People's Democratic Republic of Laos, largely because they had supported the previous government that was toppled by the communist troops. As a result, the Hmong became the target of wholesale extermination and were forced to flee. Many of these 150,000 refugees came to the United States, settling primarily in California and Minnesota. Although the United States had received a multitude of immigrants for centuries, the social customs and behavior of the Hmong are unique. In 1980 Nao Kao Lee and his wife Foua Yang, were two of those who arrived in the United States.

In 1982, when the Lees were living in Merced, California, Foua gave birth to Lia. When she was three months old, Lia was diagnosed as having epilepsy. However, the Lees believed the girl was suffering from what they referred to as *qaug dab peg* ("the spirit catches you and you fall down"), despite American doctors' efforts to explain the realities of the malady. Physicians prescribed drugs such as Depakene and Valium; the Lees attempted to "fix her spirit" by employing a shaman, sacrificing chickens and pigs in their living-room, and rubbing coins on Lia's body. It was a case of Western and Eastern medicinal practices clashing. With the Laotian forests a world away, the Lees were unable to attain the traditional roots and herbs they and their people had always used to treat such afflictions. As a result, they had to turn to the Merced County medical system. Unfortunately, the doctors and physicians within that system believed that the Lees' holistic approach was plagued by ignorance and superstition. Lia's medical chart soon expanded to five volumes, weighing nearly fourteen pounds. Finally, her condition became so serious that Merced officials deemed it necessary to use legal means to take custody of the child, a fact that devastated her family. As the dispute continued between the two parties, Lia suffered a massive seizure and was declared brain dead.

Fadiman first met the Lees in 1988, intending simply to write a magazine article about them. She became fascinated with their case, eventually devoting thousands of hours of her time to the family in interviews and support. She also spent a great deal of time with the doctors and officials who treated Lia. Because of this diligence, her book is a well-documented portrayal of Lia's case. She also plainly lays out the differences between Eastern and Western thinking in medical matters. "The Hmong view of health care seemed to me to be precisely the opposite of the prevailing American one, in which the practice of medicine has fissioned into smaller and smaller subspecialties, with less and less truck between bailiwicks. The Hmong carried holism to its ultima Thule," Fadiman remarks.

In *The Spirit Catches You and You Fall Down* Fadiman attempts to make American readers understand the motivations behind the Lees' actions and beliefs. "The history of the Hmong yields several lessons that anyone who deals with them might do well to remember," she wrote. "Among the most obvious of these are that the Hmong do not like to take orders; that they do not like

to lose; that they would rather flee, fight, or die than surrender; that they are not intimidated by being outnumbered; that they are rarely persuaded that the customs of other cultures, even those more powerful than their own, are superior; and that they are capable of getting very angry."

The Spirit Catches You and You Fall Down was praised by numerous critics who described it as a powerful tale of culture clash. "The mysteries of Hmong language and ritual are balanced throughout the book with passages that portray Western medicine as having its own impenetrable language and ritual," Jennifer Ruark wrote in the *Chronicle of Higher Education.* Rebecca Cress-Ingebo, reviewing the book for *Library Journal,* proclaimed it to be a "riveting, cross-cultural medicine classic," and declared the story a "haunting lesson for every healthcare provider." Calling Fadiman's work a "profoundly memorable book," Sherwin B. Nuland, in the *New Republic,* applauded the effort. Nuland wrote that Fadiman has "expertly woven together all the fascinating narrative threads in the story." "This is a book that should be deeply disturbing to anyone who has given so much as a moment's thought to the state of American medicine," Nuland concluded.

Fadiman's parents, husband, and other family members are featured in the essays collected and published as *Ex Libris: Confessions of a Common Reader.* Here Fadiman chronicles her lifelong love of books and the written word. A contributor for *Publishers Weekly* found the collection to be "fussy" at times, and recommended that "these essays are best when just nibbled one or two at a time." Writing for *Booklist,* Donna Seaman had more praise for the book, writing that, "As delectable and witty as these divulgences are, it is Fadiman's profound appreciation and knowledge of books and all that they convey that hit home."

BIOGRAPHICAL AND CRITICAL SOURCES:

BOOKS

Fadiman, Anne, *The Spirit Catches You and You Fall Down: A Hmong Child, Her American Doctors, and the Collision of Two Cultures,* Farrar, Straus (New York, NY), 1997.

PERIODICALS

Booklist, September 15, 1997, William Beatty, review of *The Spirit Catches You and You Fall Down: A Hmong Child, Her American Doctors, and the Col-*

lision of Two Cultures, pp. 184-185; October 1, 1998, Donna Seaman, review of *Ex Libris: Confessions of a Common Reader,* p. 303.

Chronicle of Higher Education, November 28, 1997, pp. A15-16.

Commonweal, January 16, 1998, Robert Coles, review of *The Spirit Catches You and You Fall Down,* p. 18.

Discover, May, 1998, Tony Dajer, review of *The Spirit Catches You and You Fall Down,* pp. 97-98.

Entertainment Weekly, October 23, 1998, review of *Ex Libris: Confessions of a Common Reader,* p. 74.

Journal of American Ethnic History, summer, 1999, Jo Ann Koltyk, review of *The Spirit Catches You and You Fall Down,* pp. 193-194.

Lancet, January 24, 1998, Charles Gropper, review of *The Spirit Catches You and You Fall Down,* p. 301; February 6, 1999, Faith McLellan, "A Most Uncommon Reader," p. 508.

Library Journal, September 1, 1997, Rebecca Cress-Ingebo, review of *The Spirit Catches You and You Fall Down,* pp. 208-209; September 15, 1998, Wilda Williams, review of *Ex Libris,* p. 78.

National Catholic Reporter, June 15, 2001, Stephen Schloesser, review of *The Spirit Catches You and You Fall Down,* p. 17.

New Republic, October 13, 1997, Sherwin B. Nuland, review of *The Spirit Catches You and You Fall Down,* pp. 31-39.

Pediatric Nursing, March-April, 1998, Antia J. Catlin, review of *The Spirit Catches You and You Fall Down,* pp. 170-171; March-April, 1998, June L. Harney Boffman, review of *The Spirit Catches You and You Fall Down,* pp. 172-173.

Progressive, December, 1998, Ruth Conniff, review of *The Spirit Catches You and You Fall Down,* p. 39.

Publishers Weekly, August 11, 1997, review of *The Spirit Catches You and You Fall Down,* p. 393; August 24, 1998, *Ex Libris,* p. 34.

ONLINE

Atlantic Unbound, http://www.theatlantic.com/ (October 28, 1998), Katie Bolick, "Coming to Life: An Interview with Anne Fadiman."

Salon.com, http://www.salon.com/ (October 7, 1998), Dan Cryer, review of *Ex Libris: Confessions of a Common Reader.*

*   *   *

FALUDI, Susan 1959-

PERSONAL: Born April 18, 1959, in New York, NY; daughter of Steven (a photographer) and Marilyn Lanning (an editor) Faludi. *Education:* Harvard University, B.A. (summa cum laude), 1981.

ADDRESSES: Home—San Francisco, CA. *Agent*—Sandra Dijkstra, Sandra Dijkstra Literary Agency, 1155 Camino del Mar, Ste. 515, Del Mar, CA 92014.

CAREER: Journalist. *New York Times,* New York, NY, copy clerk, 1981-82; *Miami Herald,* Miami, FL, reporter, 1983; *Atlanta Constitution,* Atlanta, GA, reporter, 1984-85; *West* magazine, San Jose, CA, staff writer, 1985-89; *Mercury News,* San Jose, reporter, 1986-88; Institute for Research on Women and Gender, Stanford University, staff member, 1989-91; *Wall Street Journal,* San Francisco bureau, staff writer, 1990-92; contributing editor to *Newsweek.*

AWARDS, HONORS: Robert F. Kennedy Memorial Journalism Award citation, 1989; John Hancock Award, 1991; Pulitzer Prize, Columbia University Graduate School of Journalism, 1991, for *Wall Street Journal* article on the leveraged buyout of Safeway supermarkets; National Book Critics Circle Award nomination, 1992, for *Backlash: The Undeclared War against American Women.*

WRITINGS:

Backlash: The Undeclared War against American Women, Crown (New York, NY), 1991.
Stiffed: The Betrayal of the American Man, Morrow (New York, NY), 1999.

Contributor of articles to periodicals, including *Mother Jones, California Business,* and *Ms.*

ADAPTATIONS: Backlash was adapted as an audio cassette read by the author, Publishing Mills, 1992.

WORK IN PROGRESS: A book about the goals of contemporary American women, for Holt.

SIDELIGHTS: Pulitzer Prize-winning journalist Susan Faludi gained nationwide attention with her first book, *Backlash: The Undeclared War against American Women,* in which the author investigates the attacks she observed on feminism and women's social, economic, and political progress during the 1980s. From advertisements for plastic surgery that term small breasts a "disease" to blue-collar men who harass their few female coworkers, and from right-wing preachers who denounce feminists as "witches" and "whores" to Hollywood films that depict single career women as desperate and crazed, Faludi found a "backlash" against women virtually everywhere. The culmination of four years of research, *Backlash* drew praise and stirred controversy, with some critics maintaining that Faludi essentially claims society conspires to keep women oppressed. "So much of the criticism [of *Backlash*] seems to be about a book I didn't write," Faludi told a *Time* magazine contributor. "I'm charged with saying there's a male conspiracy out there to put women down. Anyone who says that can't possibly have read the book. . . . This is not a book about hating men." Indeed, Faludi tried to show that her arguments apply just as much to men as they do to women when she released her second book, *Stiffed: The Betrayal of the American Man.*

Faludi, who served as an editor of both her high school and college newspapers, is no stranger to controversy. In high school she wrote about school meetings of born-again Christian students and teachers, gatherings that, by virtue of being held on public-school grounds, did not maintain the separation of church and state and were therefore unconstitutional. As an undergraduate at Harvard University, she penned a story about ongoing sexual harassment on campus. Though a guilty professor and the dean tried to convince her not to print it, the story appeared in the paper and the university subsequently asked the professor to take a leave of absence.

After graduating from college, Faludi worked as a copy clerk for the *New York Times,* and while there and at her succeeding positions she gained a reputation as "a superb crusading journalist, attacking injustice with a rare passion," according to Carol Pogash in *Working Woman.* She wrote about how former president Ronald Reagan's budget cuts affected poor children, how companies in California's Silicon Valley were replacing older employees with younger, more cost-effective workers, and about the human impact of Safeway Stores' leveraged buyout. Faludi received a Pulitzer Prize for the last story, which appeared in the *Wall Street Journal.* "Then as now," Pogash observed, "her stories were laden with research and punch-in-the-gut images—the writer, part academian, part assassin."

Faludi was inspired to write *Backlash* by a 1986 marriage study that made national headlines. The study, which was then being conducted by researchers at Harvard and Yale universities, stated that college-educated, thirty-year-old women had only a twenty-percent chance of ever getting married, and by age thirty-five the odds dropped to five percent. After one of the researchers talked to a reporter about the unpublished study's find-

ings, newspapers, popular magazines, and talk shows began running stories about the "marriage crunch" and "man shortage" in America. Women who postponed marriage in favor of educations and careers, the researchers reasoned, would have difficulty finding a husband. "I hadn't been worrying about marriage," Faludi recalled to Kim Hubbard in *People* magazine, "but suddenly I felt morose and grouchy."

Skeptical of the researchers' statistics, Faludi contacted the U.S. Census Bureau and other sources and learned that the methodology used to generate the marriage study was flawed and that the report's conclusions were suspect. She and other journalists wrote articles about this discovery, but their input was virtually ignored by the national media. "What was remarkable to me," Faludi told Hubbard, "was that there was so little interest in finding out whether the study was true or false. The story simply fit the notion of where women were at that point in history."

Faludi points out in *Backlash* that many accepted ideas about women's status in the 1980s were also myths. In addition to the nationally trumpeted marriage study, the author discredits other media-trend stories in her book, including accounts of professional women abandoning the work force in large numbers to care for their homes and children, and reports of single and career women suffering from depression, nervous breakdowns, and burnout in epidemic proportions. Upon examining these claims, Faludi discovered that they had no empirical basis. A number of studies comparing working and non-working women, for example, concluded that women who work are actually mentally and physically healthier than their non-working counterparts. According to Faludi, myths about single and working women are "the chisels of a society-wide backlash. They are part of a relentless whittling-down process—much of it amounting to outright propaganda—that has served to stir women's private anxieties and break their political wills."

Though conventional wisdom suggests that the women's movement had achieved its aims by the late twentieth century, Faludi notes in *Backlash* that women still receive mixed messages about equality. She explains that the media and politicians often present women's liberation as the source of women's problems. Feminists, for instance, are often portrayed as women who are unable to attract men, working women are depicted as poor mothers, and independent single women are shown to be desperate to marry and bear children. The moral of these stories, Faludi maintains, is that "it must be all that equality that's causing all that pain. Women are unhappy precisely *because* they are free."

Faludi challenges this conclusion in her book by detailing how the backlash against women's rights continued to be perpetuated by newspapers, magazines, television programs, movies, the fashion and beauty industry, popular psychology, anti-abortion activists, and national politics. She also cites an array of statistics that give a different and, she argues, more accurate picture of women's progress. According to Faludi, women still struggle for equality in politics, the workplace, and at school and home, and this is truly the cause of the unhappiness they express. The author observes in *Backlash,* for instance, that by 1990 the average female college graduate earned less than the average man with a high school diploma, and that American women "face the worst gender-based pay gap in the developed world." The lack of child care and family leave policies, Faludi asserts, also undermines women's equality in the workplace. At home, women "still shoulder seventy percent of the household duties. . . . Furthermore, in thirty states, it is still generally legal for husbands to rape their wives; and only ten states have laws mandating arrest for domestic violence—even though battering was the leading cause of injury of women in the late '80s."

In what some critics consider *Backlash*'s most effective section, Faludi profiles a number of notable antifeminists, including George Gilder, a speechwriter for former President Ronald Reagan and author of *Wealth and Poverty;* Allen Bloom, author of *The Closing of the American Mind,* a book that decries feminism's influence in higher education; Robert Bly, a founder of the men's movement and author of *Iron John;* and Sylvia Ann Hewlett, author of *A Lesser Life: The Myth of Women's Liberation in America.* She also interviews philosophy professor Michael Levin, who wrote *Feminism and Freedom,* a book denouncing feminism as an "antidemocratic, if not totalitarian, ideology," Faludi notes. Levin also claims that men are naturally better at math and that women prefer to take on household duties such as cooking. During her interview with Levin, Faludi learned that Levin's wife, Margarita, is a professor of the philosophy of mathematics, that the Levins split child care and household tasks equally, and that cooking is the favorite activity of one of their young sons. Gayle Greene remarked in a *Nation* review that "Faludi must be a crackerjack interviewer, letting subjects babble on until they blurt out marvelously self-incriminating revelations, offering up the real reasons they hate and fear feminists—motives that are self-serving, silly, often sinister—which Faludi simply, deadpan, recounts."

Published in 1991, *Backlash* quickly became a bestseller. Though the response from critics was generally favorable, some reviewers found the book to be over-

long or disagreed that a backlash against women's progress existed. *Business Week* writer Walecia Konrad commented that, "even for committed feminists, Faludi's analysis is an eye-opener. But her relentless presentation of facts, figures, anecdotes, polls, and interviews is so dense that at times the book is hard to read." In *Commentary* Charlotte Allen opined that *Backlash* has "none of the sustained theorizing or distanced observation that we might expect from a work of cultural criticism." In contrast, however, *Newsweek* contributor Laura Shapiro compared Faludi's book to Simone de Beauvoir's *The Second Sex* and Betty Friedan's *The Feminine Mystique* and described *Backlash* as "less visionary than theirs but just as gripping. She's not a theorist, she's simply a reporter."

Backlash was described by other admirers, Hubbard reported, as "feminism's new manifesto." Greene noted that the "book offers a rich compendium of fascinating information and an indictment of a system losing its grip and reeling from changes it does not begin to understand." Konrad called *Backlash* "a thinking person's book. Instead of spoon-feeding answers, Faludi offers compelling and disturbing evidence that some of the toughest battles for women are still to come." And Shapiro reported that "once you've read this hair-raising but meticulously documented analysis, you may never read a magazine or see a movie or walk through a department store the same way again."

Backlash's success soon made Faludi a sought-after guest on talk shows and the subject of a *Time* magazine cover story with noted feminist Gloria Steinem. But despite the attention she received, she remained reluctant to promote herself as feminism's new spokeswoman. "It's strange, since in my book I'm fairly critical of instant experts," Faludi told Hubbard. "I don't want to set myself up as a sort of seer." The author remarked to Pogash in *Working Woman:* "To the extent that *Backlash* arms women with information and a good dose of cynicism, I think it will have served its purpose." She added, "It's also very large, so it can be thrown at misogynists."

After completing *Backlash,* Faludi felt that her first work did not answer the question of why men were resisting the feminist movement in the first place. She therefore spent six years interviewing men in all sorts of occupations to get at the heart of the matter. But while the original question for her was why men seemed to be so disturbed by the prospects of female empowerment, her research led her to an entirely different question: Why are men allowing themselves to be subjugated by a shallow, materialistic, appearance-obsessed society, and why are they not doing anything to fight against it? The result of her studies became the book *Stiffed: The Betrayal of the American Man.* Here she examines the lives of men living a wide variety of lifestyles, including cadets at the Citadel, laid-off blue-collar workers, Christian Promise Keepers, astronauts, porn stars, and street gang members, rounding out her survey with a thirty-page examination of actor Sylvester Stallone, who serves as a model of ideal manhood. She found that the men of the 1990s, especially those of the Baby Boomer generation, felt disconnected and disempowered because they grew up with emotionally distant fathers and because they found themselves locked in an "ornamentalist" culture that demands good looks over substance, for men just as much as for women.

Faludi blames rampant capitalism, which has laid off so many working-class people in favor of beefing up stock prices, for leaving many men feeling emasculated because they cannot earn enough to support their families or fulfill a sense of purpose in their lives. "Interestingly," observed Cathy Young in *Reason,* "unlike many feminists, Faludi does not equate traditional masculinity with abusive, egotistical dominance. Rather, she notes that cultural concepts of manhood have always been based on care-taking, social responsibility, and productivity." The author further discovered that the ability of men to be productive was not necessarily tied to a strong economy. "I found that as the economy improved," she told Sue Halpern in *Mother Jones,* "the men I was talking to were still stricken with a sense that they had been betrayed, and that the betrayal went much deeper than a paycheck. It had to do with loyalty and a social pact that they had been led to believe was bedrock and part of being a man."

The solution to modern American men's dilemma, however, remains elusive, according to Faludi. As *New Republic* contributor James Wolcott explained in his review of *Stiffed,* all the author can offer is "the prospect of men joining like-minded women to create 'a new paradigm of human progress.'" As she commented in a *Newsweek* interview, however, Faludi is somewhat optimistic that the post-Baby Boom generation will fare better than their fathers: "The one bright light in this otherwise pretty bleak story is that the younger generation are more open, caring fathers. That's largely the result of the women's movement—that men need to have a full life by having a meaningful domestic life."

A number of reviewers of Faludi's *Stiffed* argued with her portrayal of men facing a "bleak" world. For one thing, several critics pointed out that the author's sampling of men avoids including those who are content and successful in their lives. "The polls tell us that there are many men in America who are generally satisfied with their lot," commented Midge Decter in the *National Review.* Writing in *Progressive,* Laura Flanders also noted that Faludi's sampling of men is misleading as supporting evidence for her conclusions. "Faludi's study of gender gets mixed up with class because she focuses almost exclusively on men who fit the stereotypical image of masculinity—brawny laborers and evangelical/militaristic macho types (and Sylvester Stallone). . . . If she'd interviewed some affluent traders making pots of money in the market or business executives or Silicon Valley nerds, she could have filled a crucial gap. And plenty of men are doing just fine, thank you, with the traditional model."

Adding that "the author's failure to choose a representative sample of men is not her book's most serious shortcoming," Decter said that in trying to find out what is troubling men Faludi "has finally achieved little more than to raise the volume on that most tiresome and least enlightening form of human expression. I am referring to the Whine." The critic went on to write that "what men need above all is the simple recognition of their full and necessary value in the lives of women. Such a recognition would go a very long way toward the healing understanding that this book and its author claim to seek"; yet in failing to address this, Faludi's "researches will have virtually nothing to teach us." Rebecca Abrams, writing in the *New Statesman,* similarly felt that Faludi is not exactly saying anything new in *Stiffed.* "The disappointing aspect of this book," according to Abrams, "is that although Faludi appears to be breaking new ground, in a sense all she actually does is graft accepted feminist 'truths' on to male experience. After all, feminism pioneered mother-blame decades ago. Compared to the battle that daughters were waging—consciously or unconsciously—on the dire influence of their mothers, patriarchy was always something of a picnic."

Despite these criticisms, however, a number of reviewers found *Stiffed* to be, as Abrams put it, "a rewarding read. Faludi is a meticulous and sensitive interviewer, and her compendium of American men . . . grows into a gallery of compelling and detailed portraits." Other critics also found that Faludi's reporting, compared to her concluding arguments, is the strong point of the book. "Her reporting is stellar," asserted Flanders, "as it was in *Backlash.*" An *Economist* writer found the author's retelling of men's personal accounts of their disappointments in life to be "often fascinating. *Stiffed* displays Ms. Faludi's formidable research skills and her keen journalistic nose"; and the reviewer added that "in her explorations of different male subcultures, Ms. Faludi is always alert and almost never dull." Although *Library Journal* contributor Rebecca Miller felt that Faludi's conclusions "won't surprise anyone," the critic concluded that "this important book is sure to spark dialog."

In the end, as Faludi told Halpern, her point is that men and women should overcome the dictates of American culture and work together so as not to "be judged according to superficial and ephemeral and impossible-to-attain objectives." Although she feels the solution to creating this kind of change is "not obvious . . . we need to start at square one and figure out what the forces are and respond to them."

BIOGRAPHICAL AND CRITICAL SOURCES:

BOOKS

Faludi, Susan, *Backlash: The Undeclared War against American Women,* Crown (New York, NY), 1991.

PERIODICALS

American Enterprise, June, 2000, Evan Gahr, review of *Stiffed: The Betrayal of the American Man,* p. 59.

Atlantic, December, 1991, pp. 123-126.

Business Week, November 4, 1991, Walecia Konrad, review of *Backlash,* pp. 12, 17.

Christian Century, December 1, 1999, Mary Stewart Van Leeuwen, review of *Stiffed,* p. 1166.

Commentary, February, 1992, Charlotte Allen, review of *Backlash,* pp. 62-64.

Economist, November 13, 1999, "American Men: What Do They Really Want?," p. 5.

Entertainment Weekly, October 15, 1999, Lisa Schwarzbaum, "Men Overboard: In Her Provocative New Book, *Stiffed,* Susan Faludi Makes a Strong Case That Macho America Ain't What It Used to Be," p. 72.

Forbes, March 16, 1992, Gretchen Morgenson, "A Whiner's Bible," p. 152; November 29, 1999, Virginia Postrel, "Who's in Charge? You Are," p. 112.

Fortune, November 22, 1999, Albert Mobilio, "Angry White Knuckleheads," p. 86.

Insight on the News, June 5, 1995, Suzanne Fields, "Invasion of the Neoclassical Feminist Body-Snatchers," p. 40; November 15, 1999, Suzanne Fields, "Betrayal of the American Woman," p. 48.

Library Journal, October 15, 1999, Rebecca Miller, review of *Stiffed,* p. 90.

Maclean's, November 1, 1999, Anthony Wilson-Smith, "Gender Armistice: A Leading Feminist Argues That Men Are Victims, Too," p. 70.

Mother Jones, September-October, 1999, Sue Halpern, "Susan Faludi: The Mother Jones Interview."

Nation, February 10, 1992, Gayle Greene, review of *Backlash,* pp. 166-170.

National Review, March 30, 1992, Maggie Gallagher, review of *Backlash,* p. 41; October 25, 1999, Midge Decter, "Guy Talk," p. 58.

New Republic, March 16, 1992, pp. 30-34; November 15, 1999, James Wolcott, "The Male Eunuch," p. 36.

New Statesman, November 1, 1999, Rebecca Abrams, "Pity the Boys," p. 56.

New Statesman and Society, April 3, 1992, pp. 44-45.

Newsweek, October 21, 1991, Laura Shapiro, review of *Backlash,* pp. 41-44; September 13, 1999, "This Time, a Backlash for Guys: What's a Nice Feminist Like Susan Faludi Doing Writing a Book about Men?," p. 59.

New Yorker, December 23, 1991, p. 108.

New York Times Book Review, October 27, 1991, pp. 1, 36.

People, November 11, 1991, pp. 138-140; October 25, 1999, "Male-ady: Feminist Author Susan Faludi Says American Men Must Be Liberated from Superficial Values That Have Long Bedeviled Women," p. 143.

Progressive, June, 1993, Ruth Conniff, "Susan Faludi," p. 35; November, 1999, Laura Flanders, review of *Stiffed,* p. 41.

Publishers Weekly, May 25, 1992, Gayle Feldman, "Faludi's New Book on Men Goes to Morrow/Avon," p. 18; July 6, 1992, review of *Backlash* (sound recording), p. 23; September 13, 1999, review of *Stiffed,* p. 69.

Reason, December, 1999, Virginia Postrel, "Reactionary Running Mates," p. 4; March, 2000, Cathy Young, "The Man Question," p. 64.

Tikkun, March, 2000, Janna Malamud Smith, "Where Have All the Fathers Gone?," p. 73.

Time, March 9, 1992, pp. 56-57; October 4, 1999, Elizabeth Gleick, "Men on the Edge: Feminist Susan Faludi Comes to the Defense of the American Male," p. 100; October 25, 1999, Joel Stein, "The Emasculation Proclamation," p. 46.

Times (London, England), March 26, 1992.
Working Woman, April, 1992, pp. 64-67, 104.

*   *   *

FARMER, Philip José 1918-
(Kilgore Trout, John H. Watson)

PERSONAL: Born January 26, 1918, in North Terre Haute, IN; son of George (a civil and electrical engineer) and Lucile Theodora (Jackson) Farmer; married Elizabeth Virginia Andre, May 10, 1941; children: Philip Laird, Kristen. *Education:* Attended University of Missouri, 1936-37, 1942; Bradley University, B.A., 1950; Arizona State University, graduate study, 1961-62.

ADDRESSES: Home—5911 North Isabell Ave., Peoria, IL 61614. *Agent*—Ted Chichak of Scovil, Chichak, Galen, 381 Park Avenue South, Suite 1020, New York, NY, 10016.

CAREER: Worked at various jobs, 1936-56, with some periods as full-time writer; General Electric, Syracuse, NY, technical writer, 1956-58; Motorola, Scottsdale, AZ, technical writer, 1959-62; Bendix, Ann Arbor, MI, 1962; Motorola, Phoenix, AZ, 1962-65; McDonnell-Douglas, Santa Monica, CA, technical writer, 1965-69; freelance writer, 1965-67, 1969—. *Military service:* U.S. Army Air Forces, 1942-43, aviation cadet.

MEMBER: Authors Guild, Authors League of America, Society of Technical Writers and Editors, Burroughs Bibliophiles, American Association for the Advancement of Science.

AWARDS, HONORS: Hugo Award, World Science Fiction Convention, 1952, for best new writer in the science fiction field, 1967, for best novella, "Riders of the Purple Wage," and 1971, for best novel, *To Your Scattered Bodies Go;* guest of honor at 26th World Science Fiction Convention, 1968, and at other science fiction conventions; Nebula Award Grand Master, Science Fiction and Fantasy Writers of America, 2000; World Fantasy Award for Lifetime Achievement, 2001; First Fandom Hall of Fame award, World Science Fiction Convention, 2003.

WRITINGS:

The Green Odyssey, Ballantine (New York, NY), 1957, reprinted, Gregg (New York, NY), 1978.

Flesh (also see below), Beacon Books (New York, NY), 1960.
Strange Relations, Ballantine (New York, NY), 1960, reprinted, Avon (New York, NY), 1978.
A Woman a Day, Beacon Books (New York, NY), 1960, published as *The Day of Timestop,* Lancer Books (New York, NY), 1968, published as *Timestop!,* Quartet (London, England), 1973.
The Lovers, Ballantine (New York, NY), 1961.
The Alley God, Ballantine (New York, NY), 1962.
Fire and the Night, Regency (London, England), 1962.
Tongues of the Moon, Pyramid Press (New York, NY), 1964.
Inside Outside, Ballantine (New York, NY), 1964, reprinted, Gregg (New York, NY), 1980.
Cache from Outer Space, also published as *The Celestial Blueprint, and Other Stories,* Ace Books (New York, NY), 1965, revised edition published as *The Cache,* Tor Books (New York, NY), 1981.
Dare, Ballantine (New York, NY), 1965, reprinted, Gregg (New York, NY), 1980.
The Gates of Creation, Ace Books (New York, NY), 1966, special revised edition, Phantasia Press (Huntington Woods, MI), 1981.
The Gate of Time, Belmont Books (New York, NY), 1966, expanded edition published as *Two Hawks from Earth,* Ace Books (New York, NY), 1979.
Night of Light, Berkley Publishing (New York, NY), 1966.
The Image of the Beast: An Exorcism, Ritual One (also see below), Essex House (London, England), 1968.
Blown; or, Sketches among the Ruins of My Mind: An Exorcism, Ritual Two (sequel to *The Image of the Beast;* also see below), Essex House (London, England), 1969.
A Feast Unknown: Volume IX of the Memoirs of Lord Grandrith, Essex House (London, England), 1969.
Keepers of the Secrets, Sphere Books (London, England), 1970, reprinted, Severn House (London, England), 1985.
Lord of the Trees: Volume X of the Memoirs of Lord Grandrith (also see below), Ace Books (New York, NY), 1970.
The Mad Goblin (bound with *Lord of the Trees;* also see below), Ace Books (New York, NY), 1970.
Lord Tyger (also see below), Doubleday (New York, NY), 1970.
Love Song: A Gothic Romance, Brandon House (North Hollywood, CA), 1970, limited edition, D. McMillan (Missoula, MT), 1983.
The Stone God Awakens, Ace Books (New York, NY), 1970.
Down in the Black Gang, and Other Stories, Doubleday (New York, NY), 1971.

The Wind Whales of Ishmael, Ace Books (New York, NY), 1971.

Tarzan Alive: A Definitive Biography of Lord Greystoke, Doubleday (New York, NY), 1972.

Time's Last Gift, Ballantine (New York, NY), 1972.

The Book of Philip José Farmer; or, The Wares of Simple Simon's Custard Pie and Space Man, Daw Books (New York, NY), 1973, revised edition, Berkley Books (New York, NY), 1982.

Doc Savage: His Apocalyptic Life, Doubleday (New York, NY), 1973.

The Other Log of Phileas Fogg, Daw Books (New York, NY), 1973, reprinted, Tor Books (New York, NY), 1988.

Traitor to the Living, Ballantine (New York, NY), 1973.

Hadon of Ancient Opar, illustrations by Roy Krenkel, Daw Books (New York, NY), 1974.

(Under pseudonym Kilgore Trout) *Venus on the Half-Shell,* Dell (New York, NY), 1975.

Flight to Opar, Daw Books (New York, NY), 1976.

(With J.H. Rosny) *Ironcastle,* Daw Books (New York, NY), 1978.

Dark Is the Sun, Ballantine (New York, NY), 1979.

Riverworld and Other Stories, Berkley Publishing (New York, NY), 1979.

Image of the Beast (contains *Image of the Beast* and *Blown*), Berkley Publishing (New York, NY), 1979.

Jesus on Mars (also see below), Pinnacle Books (New York, NY), 1979.

Lord of the Trees [and] *The Mad Goblin,* Ace Books (New York, NY), 1980.

Riverworld War: The Suppressed Fiction of Philip José Farmer (contains *Jesus on Mars*), Ellis Press (Peoria, IL), 1980.

The Unreasoning Mask, Putnam (New York, NY), 1981.

Flesh [and] *Lord Tyger,* New American Library (New York, NY), 1981.

A Barnstormer in Oz; or, A Rationalization and Extrapolation of the Split-level Continuum, Phantasia Press (Huntington Woods, MI), 1982.

River of Eternity, Phantasia Press (Huntington Woods, MI), 1983.

The Grand Adventure, Berkley Publishing (New York, NY), 1984.

The Classic Philip José Farmer, 1952-1964, edited by Martin H. Greenberg, Crown (New York, NY), 1984.

Father to the Stars, Pinnacle Books (New York, NY), 1981.

Stations of the Nightmare, Tor Books (New York, NY), 1982.

Red Orc's Rage, Tor Books (New York, NY), 1991.

Escape from Loka, Bantam (New York, NY), 1991.

(With Piers Anthony) *The Caterpillar's Question,* Ace Books (New York, NY), 1992.

(With Jack London) *Fantastic Tales,* edited by Dale L. Walker, Bison Books Corporation (London, England), 1998.

Nothing Burns in Hell, Forge (New York, NY), 1998.

"WORLD OF TIERS" SERIES

The Maker of Universes: The Enigma of the Many-leveled Cosmos, Ace Books (New York, NY), 1965, revised edition, Phantasia Press (Huntinton Woods, MI), 1980.

The Gates of Creation, Ace Books (New York, NY), 1966.

A Private Cosmos, Ace Books (New York, NY), 1968, special revised edition, Phantasia Press (Huntington Woods, MI), 1981.

Behind the Walls of Terra, Ace Books (New York, NY), 1970.

The Lavalite World, Ace Books (New York, NY), 1977.

The World of Tiers, two volumes (Volume 1 contains *The Maker of Universes* and *The Gates of Creation;* Volume 2 contains *A Private Cosmos, Behind the Walls of Terra,* and *The Lavalite World*), Thomas Nelson-Doubleday (New York, NY), 1980.

Greatheart Silver, illustrations by Nick Cuti, Tor Books (New York, NY), 1982.

The Purple Book, Tor Books (New York, NY), 1982.

More than Fire, Tor Books (New York, NY), 1993.

"RIVERWORLD" SERIES

To Your Scattered Bodies Go, Putnam (New York, NY), 1971, reprinted, Ballantine (New York, NY), 1998.

The Fabulous Riverboat, Putnam (New York, NY), 1971.

The Dark Design, Berkley Publishing (New York, NY), 1977.

The Magic Labyrinth, Berkley Publishing (New York, NY), 1981.

The Complete Riverworld Novels, five volumes, Berkley Publishing (New York, NY), 1982.

Gods of Riverworld, Phantasia Press (Huntington Woods, MI), 1983.

Quest to Riverworld, Warner Books (New York, NY), 1993.

Gods of Riverworld, Del Rey (New York, NY), 1998.

The Dark Heart of Time, Del Rey (New York, NY), 1999.

"DAYWORLD" SERIES

Dayworld, Putnam (New York, NY), 1985.
Dayworld Rebel, Putnam (New York, NY), 1987.
Dayworld Breakup, Tor Books (New York, NY), 1989.

OTHER

(Compiler) *Mother Was a Lovely Beast: A Feral Man Anthology—Fiction and Fact about Humans Raised by Animals,* Chilton (Philadelphia, PA), 1974.
(Author under pseudonym John H. Watson; editor under name Philip José Farmer) *The Adventure of the Peerless Peer,* Aspen Press (Boulder, CO), 1974.
(Editor) *Naked Came the Farmer,* Mayfly Productions, 1998.

Work appears in anthologies. Contributor to *Visual Encyclopedia of Science Fiction.* Contributor of short stories to *Adventure, Magazine of Fantasy and Science Fiction, Startling Stories,* and other magazines.

Farmer's work has been translated into twenty-one languages and published in over forty countries.

ADAPTATIONS: The film rights to the "Riverworld" series, including *To Your Scattered Bodies Go, The Fabulous Riverboat, The Dark Design, The Magic Labyrinth,* and *Gods of Riverworld,* were sold to Walt Disney Productions, 1990.

SIDELIGHTS: Philip José Farmer is a prolific science-fiction writer whose success is based on his deft mixture of three primary components, "religion, sex, and violence," in each of his many works, according to Franz Rottensteiner in *Science-Fiction Studies.* In addition, he is often credited with introducing the first mature depiction of human-alien sexual encounters into the genre with his 1961 book, *The Lovers.* Both Farmer's inclusion of the sex act itself within his fiction and the fact that it involved an alien being triggered off a controversy within science-fiction circles. Despite the initial reaction, *The Lovers* stands as an historically important work in the field.

Although Farmer is sometimes dismissed as a writer of formula fiction whose least-successful works are written "hastily, sometimes downright sloppily," as reviewer Leslie A. Fiedler charged in the *Los Angeles Times,* admirers find his exploration of timeless themes within an action-oriented adventure plot a winning combination. Furthermore, "the number, richness, and complexity of Farmer's series," according to Thomas L. Wymer in the *Dictionary of Literary Biography,* "can lay claim to uniqueness." In *The Universe Makers,* Donald A. Wollheim called Farmer's work "veritable fireworks of new concepts in biology and fantasy lands." In *Science Fiction Chronicle* Paul Levinson was quoted as noting: since *The Lovers* appeared in 1952, Farmer has "pioneered the exploration of critical human relations and dimensions in science fiction and inspired a generation of writers, from Samuel R. Delany to Jonathan Lethem."

Farmer's talent for new concepts is given full rein in his "Riverworld" series, which Roland Green of *Booklist* called "one of the largest, most ambitious, and least conventional works of modern science fiction." The series concerns the planet Riverworld, a single, million-mile river valley into which the entire human race is reincarnated at the same time. A few of the reborn humans, including such diverse characters as Mark Twain, Cyrano de Bergerac, and Hermann Göring, search for the headwaters of the River in the hope that it may hold the answer to their reincarnation.

Farmer began the "Riverworld" series in 1952 when he entered a writing contest sponsored by two publishing companies. He won the contest with his first "Riverworld" novel but, before he collected his $4,000 prize, one of the publishers went bankrupt, taking his prize money with it. Worse, Farmer lost the rights to his book for many years. It wasn't until the late 1960s that he revived the "Riverworld" idea. He wrote a series of novelettes for magazine publication that contained "very little of the original novel, aside from the basic concept," as Farmer stated in *Dream Makers: The Uncommon People Who Write Science Fiction.* When these novelettes were published together as a novel, the result was the Hugo Award-winning *To Your Scattered Bodies Go,* and the "Riverworld" series was on its way.

As Peter Stoler wrote in *Time,* "the auspicious opening" of Farmer's "Riverworld" series "was a difficult act to follow, and many Farmerites wondered whether the Riverworld was wide enough to sustain a projected tetralogy. The author's next works allayed all fears." In subsequent novels Farmer's characters build a paddle wheel boat, several blimps, and even an air force of small planes in their quest for the headwaters of the River. Besides fighting among themselves and against hostile peoples they must voyage past during their journey, the explorers must be on guard against agents of the Ethicals, the mysterious creators of Riverworld, who are secretly in their midst. In the course of this adventure, many theological, political, and cultural questions are raised and discussed by historical figures from widely different times and cultures. Farmer's juxtaposition of historical figures from widely divergent periods "insinuates strands of history and myth, philosophy and ribaldry" into the multi-volume adventure story, according to Stoler.

Further examples of Farmer's innovative concepts are found in the "World of Tiers" series, which concerns a highly advanced race of humans who, through the use of technology, create entire self-contained universes governed by arbitrary natural laws. Although other writers have examined man's evolution and technological development, in Wollheim's view Farmer implies "that God Himself might be just another mortal playing at scientific games."

Though the "World of Tiers" series was scheduled to end with the fourth installment, *The Magic Labyrinth,* which followed *The Dark Design* in 1980, Farmer returned in 1983 with *Gods of Riverworld,* encouraging a reviewer for *Publishers Weekly* to remark: "The Riverworld seems to pull Farmer as the Mississippi did Twain." In *Gods of Riverworld* the humans who discovered the secret of the Ethicals' power take control of Riverworld and contend with the consequences of their newfound authority. Although critics found the work flawed, it was noted that this novel, like its precursors, contains "enough action, intrigue, and Farmer's habitual game-playing with historical characters" to satisfy fans of the series, according to *Booklist* critic Roland Green.

Like the "Riverworld" series, the "World of Tiers" series relies heavily on action-packed plots. Novels in this series "are marked by an intense sense of pulp action-adventure, with fast-paced and very physical action, battles and contests, intrigues, disguises, and surprises," remarked Wymer. "But Farmer combines this action with a fascinating sense of psychological exploration." In the first installment, *The Maker of Universes,* Robert Wolff enters the World of Tiers and leads a revolt against its lords, an evil remnant of a technologically advanced race that rule these pocket universes for their own pleasure. Although other writers have examined man's evolution and technological development, Farmer makes "the implication that God Himself might be just another mortal playing at scientific games," Wollheim added.

Gates of Creation, the second work in the series, finds Wolff's own father leading an invasion of the world over which Wolff now reigns. In the next three novels

in the series—*A Private Cosmos, Behind the Walls of Terra,* and *The Lavalite World*—the focus shifts to Kickaha, a secondary figure in the first two books and, according to Wymer, an exemplum of Farmer's "ideal non-neurotic man, afraid only of real threats and ready to risk his life without hesitation." The series ends with *Red Orc's Rage* and *More than Fire,* books that stage a lingering battle between good and evil, represented by Kickaha and Lord Red Orc, leader of the creators of the pocket universes.

Farmer turns to the Earth of the future in the "Dayworld" series, in which overpopulation—caused by the conquering of poverty, hunger, and pollution—is resolved by dividing humanity into seven categories, each allowed one day of consciousness per week then consigned to suspended animation the other six. Jeff Caird is a Daybreaker, a rebel against the system who assumes seven different personalities in his quest to remain conscious seven days a week. *Dayworld,* the first book in the series, recounts Caird's struggles to integrate his personalities and escape the grip of the Earth's corrupt leaders. This book "provides further evidence of the author's vivid imagination and ingenious storytelling skills," enthused Peter L. Robertson in *Booklist.* The first sequel, *Dayworld Rebel,* finds Farmer's protagonist—now known as Duncan—imprisoned by the authorities, escaping, and leading a band of rebels to Los Angeles. Still running in *Dayworld Breakup,* Duncan enlists the aid of a female cop in leading a revolution to end the Dayworld system. Although some critics found that the final two novels failed to live up to the promise of the first, reviewers tended to recommend that libraries purchase the books anyway, considering Farmer's popularity. "A definite acquisition, given Farmer's vast audience," concluded Roland Green in his review of *Dayworld Breakup.*

In other books, such as *The Adventure of the Peerless Peer* and *Tarzan Alive,* Farmer plays tongue-in-cheek games using famous literary characters. In *The Peerless Peer,* he writes a new Sherlock Holmes adventure under the pseudonym of Holmes's assistant, John H. Watson. *Tarzan Alive* is a thorough biography of the "real" Tarzan that answers questions, a reviewer for the *New York Times* held, that "have been plaguing practically nobody at all for many years now. . . . Rarely has so much been written so obscurely about so little." He concluded that Farmer is "some kind of a genius of Dada."

Under the pseudonym Kilgore Trout, Farmer wrote *Venus on the Half-Shell,* a parody of a work by novelist Kurt Vonnegut. Trout, a character in several of Vonnegut's novels, is a science-fiction writer who has authored hundreds of books, all of them unfortunately published by pornography houses that marketed them under rather non-SF titles. "I thought people would flip their minds," Farmer explained in *Dream Makers,* "if they saw a book by Trout, a supposedly fictional character, on the stands. Also, I did it as a tribute, the highest, to an author whom I loved and admired at that time. And I identify with Trout." Farmer's parody was so well done that several critics assumed Vonnegut had written the book. "Who is Kilgore Trout?" Walton R. Collins of the *National Observer* asked. "The odds are good that he is Vonnegut. . . . You can't read a dozen pages anywhere in *Venus* without becoming morally certain you're reading Vonnegut. The style is unmistakable."

Farmer has published several collections of his shorter pieces, including the short stories and novellas that made his early reputation. In a review of *The Classic Philip José Farmer,* a critic for *Kirkus Reviews* remarked, that the author "was instrumental in kicking science fiction out of its late-1940s puritanical rut—and these six iconoclastic, imaginative yarns aptly show how and why." *Library Journal* contributor Susan L. Nickerson recommended that readers "who know Farmer only for his more recent tepid efforts" seek out this resource for examples of his early work. *Voice of Youth Advocates* contributor Susan B. Madden found Farmer's *Purple Book,* containing "Riders of the Purple Wage," "Spiders of the Purple Mage," and others, "punny, irreverent, raunchy and bizarre." *The Grand Adventure,* which includes early pieces presaging the "Riverworld" series among other works, was also highly recommended by critics, who compared these pieces favorably to more recent efforts by the popular author. "The stories are 'classic' Farmer, well constructed, readable, and more satisfying than most of his contemporary esoteric pieces," wrote Jerry L. Parsons in *Fantasy Review.*

The influence of Farmer's immense body of work stretches across boundaries. Not only have his books been translated into over twenty languages, they also have been published in more than forty countries, establishing him as one of the preeminent voices in modern science fiction and fantasy literature. In 2001 Farmer was honored with the World Fantasy Award for Lifetime Achievement, just one of many accolades he has received. Writing in the *St. James Guide to Science Fiction Writers,* critic Mary Turzillo Brizzi commented on the traits that have made Farmer a unique voice in the literary world. "Farmer attacks convention. He startles readers with scenes of alien and human sex and repro-

duction. He speculates on metaphysical verities, the nature of the soul and the uncertainty of human knowledge. He refutes conventional theology," Brizzi wrote. "Immortality, the conflict between individual and society, religious conversion, impossible physical perfection, the drive for power and knowledge—such are his themes."

With his publishing career spanning nearly five decades, Farmer has few regrets about what he has written. He prefers to concentrate his energies on future writings. Speaking of his many novels, Farmer stated in *Dream Makers:*"I can see where I could have done better. I can see innumerable cases. But it's no good to go back and rewrite them, because if you did you'd lose a certain primitive vigor that they have. The thing to do is to go on and write new stuff." The Philip José Farmer Society, an organization for enthusiasts and collectors of Farmer's work, was founded in 1978.

BIOGRAPHICAL AND CRITICAL SOURCES:

BOOKS

Authors and Artists for Young Adults, Volume 28, Thomson Gale (Detroit, MI), 1999.

Beacham's Encyclopedia of Popular Fiction, Beacham (Osprey, FL), 1996.

Brizzi, Mary, *The Reader's Guide to Philip José Farmer,* Starmont, 1980.

Clareson, Thomas D., editor, *Voices for the Future,* Volume 2, Bowling Green University Popular Press, 1979.

Contemporary Literary Criticism, Thomson Gale (Detroit, MI), Volume 1, 1973, Volume 19, 1981.

Dictionary of Literary Biography, Volume 8: *Twentieth-Century American Science-Fiction Writers,* Thomson Gale (Detroit, MI), 1981.

Farmer, Philip José, *The Book of Philip José Farmer,* DAW (New York, NY), 1973.

Knapp, Lawrence J., *The First Editions of Philip José Farmer, Science Fiction Bibliographies 2,* David G. Turner, 1976.

Moskowitz, Sam, *Seekers of Tomorrow: Masters of Modern Science Fiction,* Hyperion (New York, NY), 1974.

Platt, Charles, *Dream Makers: The Uncommon People Who Write Science Fiction,* Berkley Publishing (New York, NY), 1980.

Walker, Paul, *Speaking of Science Fiction: The Paul Walker Interviews,* Luna, 1978.

Wollheim, Donald A., *The Universe Makers,* Harper (New York, NY), 1971.

PERIODICALS

Amazing Science Fiction, October, 1961.

Analog Science Fiction and Fact, December, 1977; July, 1978; December, 1980; February, 1992, Tom Easton, review of *Red Orc's Rage,* p. 155; May, 1992, Tom Easton, review of *Escape from Loki,* p. 164; January, 1994, Tom Easton, review of *More than Fire,* p. 306.

Booklist, October 1, 1977; July 15, 1980; September 1, 1992, Roland Green, review of *The Caterpillar's Question,* p. 37; September 15, 1993, Roland Green, review of *More than Fire,* p. 132; April 15, 1998, David Pitt, review of *Nothing Burns in Hell,* p. 1381.

Books and Bookmen, December, 1966.

Bulletin. Science Fiction and Fantasy Writers of America, summer, 2001, Darrell Schweitzer, interview with Farmer, p. 35.

Extrapolation, May, 1976; December, 1976; May, 1977; winter, 1994, review of *Night of Light,* p. 342.

Galaxy, January, 1958.

Kirkus Reviews, August 15, 1993, review of *More than Fire,* p. 1036; April 1, 1998, review of *Nothing Burns in Hell,* p. 448.

Library Journal, August, 1980, Rosemary Herbert, review of *The Magic Labyrinth* and *Riverworld War,* p. 1665; September 15, 1981, Susan L. Nickerson, review of *The Unreasoning Mask,* p. 1756; February 15, 1985, review of *Dayworld,* p. 181; June 15, 1987, Jackie Cassada, review of *Dayworld Rebel,* p. 88; June 15, 1990, Jackie Cassada, review of *Dayworld Breakup,* p. 139; September 15, 1992, Jackie Cassada, review of *The Caterpillar's Question,* p. 97; May 1, 1998, Rex E. Klett, review of *Nothing Burns in Hell,* p. 142.

Locus, September, 1992, review of *Tales of Riverworld,* p. 25; January, 1993, review of *Red Orc's Rage,* p. 45; May, 1993, review of *The Other Log of Phileas Fogg,* p. 48; September, 1993, review of *Quest to Riverworld,* p. 64; October, 1993, review of *More than Fire,* p. 21; July, 1994, review of *The Image of the Beast,* p. 56.

Los Angeles Times, April 23, 1972.

Louisville Eccentric Observer, August 21, 2002, p. 16.

Magazine of Fantasy and Science Fiction, October, 1953; July, 1962; September, 1965; May, 1967; February, 1978; July, 1980.

National Observer, May 17, 1975.

National Review, April 14, 1972.

New York Times, April 22, 1972.

New York Times Book Review, April 28, 1985.

Observer, December 21, 1969, August 8, 1976.

Psychiatric Times, July 2001, p. 7.

Publishers Weekly, March 20, 1981, Sally A. Lodge, review of *The Magic Labyrinth,* p. 60; August 7, 1981, Barbara A. Bannon, review of *The Unreasoning Mask,* p. 68; February 5, 1982, review of *Behind the Walls of Terra,* p. 384; July 30, 1982, review of *A Barnstormer in Oz,* p. 77; February 4, 1983, Barbara A. Bannon, review of *The Lavalite World,* p. 364; January 4, 1985, review of *Dayworld,* p. 62; May 15, 1987, Sybil Steinberg, review of *Dayworld Rebel,* p. 270; May 11, 1990, Sybil Steinberg, review of *Dayworld Breakup,* p. 252; September 21, 1992, review of *The Caterpillar's Question,* p. 81; October 4, 1993, review of *More than Fire,* p. 68; March 30, 1998, review of *Nothing Burns in Hell,* p. 73.

Rapport, April, 1992, review of *Red Orc's Rage,* p. 31; June, 1994, review of *More than Fire,* p. 25.

School Library Journal, October, 1981, John Adams, review of *The Unreasoning Mask,* p. 160; April, 1993, Linda Vretos, review of *The Caterpillar's Question,* p. 149.

Science Fiction Chronicle, June, 1992, reviews of *Riders of the Purple Wage,* p. 33; August, 1992, review of *Tales of Riverworld,* p. 49; February, 1994, review of *More than Fire,* p. 5; July, 1998, review of *Nothing Burns in Hell,* p. 45; April, 2001, p. 5; July, 2001, pp. 2, 5.

Science Fiction Collector, September, 1977.

Science Fiction Review, August, 1975; November, 1977; February, 1978.

Science Fiction Studies, Volume 1, 1973; Volume 4, 1977.

Spectator, August 4, 1973.

Time, July 28, 1980, Peter Stoler, "'Riverworld' Revisited," pp. 68-69.

Times Literary Supplement, January 8, 1970; April 12, 1974.

Village Voice, June 13, 1974.

Voices of Youth Advocates, June, 1992, review of *Escape from Loki,* p. 93; April, 1994, review of *More than Fire,* p. 36.

Washington Post Book World, November 27, 1983; June 28, 1987; August 26, 1990.

Xenophile, September-October, 1977; September-October, 1979.

ONLINE

Official Philip José Farmer Home Page, http://www.pj farmer.com/ (August 18, 2004).

FAST, Howard 1914-2003

(E.V. Cunningham, Walter Erickson, Walter Ericson, Howard Melvin Fast)

PERSONAL: Born November 11, 1914, in New York, NY; died March 12, 2003, in Old Greenwich, CT; son of Barney (an ironworker, cable car gripper, tin factory worker, and dress factory cutter) and Ida (a homemaker; maiden name, Miller) Fast; married Bette Cohen (a painter and sculptor), June 6, 1937 (died November, 1994); married Mimi O'Connor, June 17, 1999; children: (first marriage) Rachel, Jonathan; stepchildren: three. *Education:* Attended National Academy of Design. *Religion:* Jewish. *Hobbies and other interests:* "Home, my family, the theater, the film, and the proper study of ancient history. And the follies of mankind."

CAREER: Worked at several odd jobs and as a page in the New York Public Library prior to 1932; writer, beginning 1932. Foreign correspondent for *Esquire* and *Coronet,* 1945. Taught at Indiana University, 1947; member of World Peace Council, 1950-55; American Labor Party candidate for U.S. Congress, 23rd New York District, 1952; owner, Blue Heron Press, New York, 1952-57; film writer, 1958-67; chief news writer, Voice of America, 1982-84. Gave numerous lectures and made numerous appearances on radio and television programs. *Military service:* Affiliated with U.S. Office of War Information, 1942-44; correspondent with special Signal Corps unit and war correspondent in China-India-Burma theater, 1945.

MEMBER: Century Club, Fellowship of Reconciliation.

AWARDS, HONORS: Bread Loaf Literary Award, 1937; Schomberg Award for Race Relations, 1944, for *Freedom Road;* Newspaper Guild award, 1947; National Jewish Book Award, Jewish Book Council, 1949, for *My Glorious Brothers;* International Peace Prize from the Soviet Union, 1954; Screenwriters annual award, 1960; annual book award, National Association of Independent Schools, 1962; American Library Association notable book citation, 1972, for *The Hessian;* Emmy Award for outstanding writing in a drama series, American Academy of Television Arts and Sciences, 1975, for episode "The Ambassador," *Benjamin Franklin;* Literary Lions Award, New York Public Library, 1985; Prix de la Policia (France), for books under name E.V. Cunningham.

WRITINGS:

Two Valleys, Dial (New York, NY), 1933.
Strange Yesterday, Dodd (New York, NY), 1934.

Place in the City, Harcourt (New York, NY), 1937.
Conceived in Liberty: A Novel of Valley Forge, Simon & Schuster (New York, NY), 1939.
The Last Frontier, Duell, Sloan & Pearce (New York, NY), 1941, reprinted, North Castle Books (Armonk, NY), 1997.
The Romance of a People, Hebrew Publishing (New York, NY), 1941.
Lord Baden-Powell of the Boy Scouts, Messner (New York, NY), 1941.
Haym Salomon, Son of Liberty, Messner (New York, NY), 1941.
The Unvanquished, Duell, Sloan & Pearce (New York, NY), 1942, reprinted, M.E. Sharpe (Armonk, NY), 1997.
The Tall Hunter, Harper (New York, NY), 1942.
(With wife, Bette Fast) *The Picture-Book History of the Jews,* Hebrew Publishing (New York, NY), 1942.
Goethals and the Panama Canal, Messner (New York, NY), 1942.
Citizen Tom Paine, Duell, Sloan & Pearce (New York, NY), 1943.
The Incredible Tito, Magazine House (New York, NY), 1944.
Tito and His People, Contemporary Publishers (Winnipeg, Manitoba, Canada), 1944.
Freedom Road, Duell, Sloan & Pearce (New York, NY), 1944, new edition with foreword by W.E.B. DuBois, introduction by Eric Foner, M.E. Sharpe (Armonk, NY), 1995.
Patrick Henry and the Frigate's Keel, and Other Stories of a Young Nation, Duell, Sloan & Pearce (New York, NY), 1945.
The American: A Middle Western Legend, Duell, Sloan & Pearce (New York, NY), 1946.
(With William Gropper) *Never Forget: The Story of the Warsaw Ghetto,* Book League of the Jewish Fraternal Order, 1946.
(Editor) Thomas Paine, *Selected Works,* Modern Library (New York, NY), 1946.
The Children, Duell, Sloan & Pearce (New York, NY), 1947.
(Editor) Theodore Dreiser, *Best Short Stories,* World Publishing (New York, NY), 1947.
Clarkton, Duell, Sloan & Pearce (New York, NY), 1947.
My Glorious Brothers, Little, Brown (Boston, MA), 1948, new edition, Hebrew Publications (New York, NY), 1977.
Departure and Other Stories, Little, Brown (Boston, MA), 1949.
Intellectuals in the Fight for Peace, Masses & Mainstream (New York, NY), 1949.

The Proud and the Free, Little, Brown (Boston, MA), 1950.

Literature and Reality, International Publishers (New York, NY), 1950.

Spartacus, Blue Heron (New York, NY), 1951, reprinted with new introduction, North Castle Books (Armonk, NY), 1996.

Peekskill, U.S.A.: A Personal Experience, Civil Rights Congress (New York, NY), 1951.

(Under pseudonym Walter Erickson) *Fallen Angel,* Little, Brown (Boston, MA), 1951.

Tony and the Wonderful Door, Blue Heron (New York, NY), 1952.

Spain and Peace, Joint Anti-Fascist Refugee Committee, 1952.

The Passion of Sacco and Vanzetti: A New England Legend, Blue Heron (New York, NY), 1953.

Silas Timberman, Blue Heron (New York, NY), 1954.

The Last Supper, and Other Stories, Blue Heron (New York, NY), 1955.

The Story of Lola Gregg, Blue Heron (New York, NY), 1956.

The Naked God: The Writer and the Communist Party (memoir), Praeger (New York, NY), 1957.

Moses, Prince of Egypt, Crown (New York, NY), 1958, with new introduction by the author, Pocket Books (New York, NY), 2000.

The Winston Affair, Crown (New York, NY), 1959.

The Howard Fast Reader, Crown (New York, NY), 1960.

April Morning, Crown (New York, NY), 1961.

The Edge of Tomorrow (stories), Bantam (New York, NY), 1961.

Power, Doubleday (New York, NY), 1962.

Agrippa's Daughter, Doubleday (New York, NY), 1964.

The Hill, Doubleday (New York, NY), 1964.

Torquemada, Doubleday (New York, NY), 1966.

The Hunter and the Trap, Dial (New York, NY), 1967.

The Jews: Story of a People, Dial (New York, NY), 1968, Cassell (London, England), 1960.

The General Zapped an Angel, Morrow (New York, NY), 1970.

The Crossing (based on his play of the same title), Morrow (New York, NY), 1971, New Jersey Historical Society, 1985.

The Hessian, Morrow (New York, NY), 1972, reprinted with new foreword, M.E. Sharpe (Armonk, NY), 1996.

A Touch of Infinity: Thirteen Stories of Fantasy and Science Fiction, Morrow (New York, NY), 1973.

Mohawk (screenplay; short film), Paulist Productions, 1974.

Time and the Riddle: Thirty-one Zen Stories, Ward Richie Press (Pasadena, CA), 1975.

The Immigrants, Houghton Mifflin (Boston, MA), 1977.

The Art of Zen Meditation, Peace Press (Culver City, CA), 1977.

The Second Generation, Houghton Mifflin (Boston, MA), 1978.

The Establishment, Houghton Mifflin (Boston, MA), 1979.

The Legacy, Houghton Mifflin (Boston, MA), 1980.

The Magic Door (juvenile), Avon (New York, NY), 1980.

Max, Houghton Mifflin (Boston, MA), 1982.

The Outsider, Houghton Mifflin (Boston, MA), 1984.

The Immigrant's Daughter, Houghton Mifflin (Boston, MA), 1985.

The Dinner Party, Houghton Mifflin (Boston, MA), 1987.

The Call of Fife and Drum: Three Novels of the Revolution (contains *The Unvanquished, Conceived in Liberty,* and *The Proud and the Free*), Citadel, 1987.

The Pledge, Houghton Mifflin (Boston, MA), 1988.

The Confession of Joe Cullen, Houghton Mifflin (Boston, MA), 1989.

Being Red: A Memoir, Houghton Mifflin (Boston, MA), 1990.

The Trial of Abigail Goodman: A Novel, Crown (New York, NY), 1993.

War and Peace: Observations on Our Times, M.E. Sharpe (Armonk, NY), 1993.

Seven Days in June: A Novel of the American Revolution, Carol (Secaucus, NJ), 1994.

The Bridge Builder's Story, M.E. Sharpe (Armonk, NY), 1995.

An Independent Woman, Harcourt (New York, NY), 1997.

Redemption, Harcourt (New York, NY), 1999.

Greenwich, Harcourt (New York, NY), 2000.

Masuto Investigates (contains *Samantha* and *The Case of the One-Penny Orange;* also see below), ibooks (New York, NY), 2000.

Author of weekly column, *New York Observer,* 1989-92; also columnist for *Greenwich Time* and *Stamford Advocate.*

PLAYS

The Hammer, produced in New York, NY, 1950.

Thirty Pieces of Silver (produced in Melbourne, 1951), Blue Heron (New York, NY), 1954.

George Washington and the Water Witch, Bodley Head (London, England), 1956.

The Crossing, produced in Dallas, TX, 1962.

The Hill (screenplay; produced for television by A&E, 1999), Doubleday (New York, NY), 1964.

The Hessian, 1971.

David and Paula, produced in New York at American Jewish Theater, November 20, 1982.

Citizen Tom Paine: A Play in Two Acts (produced in Williamstown, MA, then in Washington, DC, at the John F. Kennedy Center for the Performing Arts, 1987), Houghton Mifflin (Boston, MA), 1986.

The Novelist (produced in Williamstown, MA, then Mamaroneck, NY, 1991), published as *The Novelist: A Romantic Portrait of Jane Austen,* Samuel French (New York, NY), 1992.

Also wrote for television series *Benjamin Franklin,* Columbia Broadcasting System (CBS), 1974 and *How the West Was Won,* American Broadcasting Companies (ABC), 1978-79.

NOVELS; UNDER PSEUDONYM E.V. CUNNINGHAM

Sylvia, Doubleday (New York, NY), 1960, published under name Howard Fast, Carol, 1992.

Phyllis, Doubleday (New York, NY), 1962.

Alice, Doubleday (New York, NY), 1963.

Shirley, Doubleday (New York, NY), 1963.

Lydia, Doubleday (New York, NY), 1964.

Penelope, Doubleday (New York, NY), 1965.

Helen, Doubleday (New York, NY), 1966.

Margie, Morrow (New York, NY), 1966.

Sally, Morrow (New York, NY), 1967, published under name Howard Fast, Chivers, 1994.

Samantha, Morrow (New York, NY), 1967.

Cynthia, Morrow (New York, NY), 1968.

The Assassin Who Gave Up His Gun, Morrow (New York, NY), 1969.

Millie, Morrow (New York, NY), 1973.

The Case of the One-Penny Orange, Holt (New York, NY), 1977.

The Case of the Russian Diplomat, Holt (New York, NY), 1978.

The Case of the Poisoned Eclairs, Holt (New York, NY), 1979.

The Case of the Sliding Pool, Delacorte (New York, NY), 1981.

The Case of the Kidnapped Angel, Delacorte (New York, NY), 1982.

The Case of the Angry Actress, Delacorte (New York, NY), 1984.

The Case of the Murdered Mackenzie, Delacorte (New York, NY), 1984.

The Wabash Factor, Doubleday (New York, NY), 1986.

Author of introduction for *Saving the Fragments: From Auschwitz to New York,* by Isabella Leitner and Irving A. Leitner, New American Library (New York, NY), 1985; *Red Scare in Court: New York versus the International Workers Order,* by Arthur J. Sabin, University of Pennsylvania Press (Philadelphia, PA), 1993; and *The Sculpture of Bette Fast,* M.E. Sharpe (Armonk, NY), 1995.

ADAPTATIONS: The film *Rachel and the Stranger,* RKO Radio Pictures, 1948, was based on the novels *Rachel* and *Neighbor Sam; Spartacus* was filmed in 1960 by Universal Pictures, directed by Stanley Kubrick and Anthony Mann, and starred Kirk Douglas, Laurence Olivier, Tony Curtis, Jean Simmons, Charles Laughton, and Peter Ustinov. Other works by Fast have been adapted to film, including *Man in the Middle,* Twentieth Century-Fox, 1964, based on his novel *The Winston Affair; Mirage,* based on a story he wrote under the pseudonym Walter Ericson, Universal, 1965; *Fallen Angel,* based on his novel of the same title; *Sylvia,* Paramount, 1965, based on the novel of the same title; *Penelope,* Metro-Goldwyn-Mayer (MGM), 1966, based on the novel of the same title written under the pseudonym E.V. Cunningham; and *Jigsaw,* Universal, 1968, based on the screenplay for *Mirage* which was based on Fast's novel *Fallen Angel.* Writings by Fast have also been adapted for television, including *The Face of Fear,* CBS, 1971, based on the novel *Sally,* written under the pseudonym E.V. Cunningham; *What's a Nice Girl Like You. . . ?,* ABC, 1971, based on his novel *Shirley; 21 Hours at Munich,* ABC, 1976, based on a story by Fast; *The Immigrants,* syndicated, 1978, based on his novel of the same title; *Freedom Road,* National Broadcasting Corporation (NBC), 1979, based on the novel of the same title; *April Morning,* broadcast as a *Hallmark Hall of Fame* movie, CBS, 1988, based on the novel of the same title; and *The Crossing,* Arts and Entertainment (A&E), 2000, based on the novel of the same name. *The Crossing* was recorded on cassette, narrated by Norman Dietz, Recorded Books, 1988; *The Immigrant's Daughter* was recorded on cassette, narrated by Sandra Burr, Brilliance Corporation, 1991; *Spartacus* was adapted for a miniseries, USA cable network, 2002.

SIDELIGHTS: A prolific writer, Howard Fast published novels, plays, screenplays, stories, historical fiction, and biographies in a career that dated from the early days of the Great Depression until his death in 2003. Fast's works have been translated into eighty-two languages and have sold millions of copies worldwide. Some observers have ranked him as the most widely read writer of the twentieth century. *Los Angeles Times* contributor

Elaine Kendall wrote: "For half a century, Fast's novels, histories, and biographies have appeared at frequent intervals, a moveable feast with a distinct political flavor." *Washington Post* correspondent Joseph McLellan found Fast's work "easy to read and relatively nourishing," adding that the author "demands little of the reader, beyond a willingness to keep turning the pages, and he supplies enough activity and suspense to make this exercise worthwhile."

The grandson of Ukrainian immigrants and son of a British mother, Fast was raised in New York City. His family struggled to make ends meet, so Fast went to work as a teen and found time to indulge his passion—writing—in his spare moments. His first published novel, *Two Valleys,* was released in 1933 when he was only eighteen. Thereafter Fast began writing full time, and within a decade he had earned a considerable reputation as an historical novelist with his realistic tales of American frontier life. *Dictionary of Literary Biography* contributor Anthony Manousos commented, "As a storyteller, Fast has his greatest appeal: his knack for sketching lifelike characters and creating brisk, action-packed narratives has always insured him a wide readership, despite occasionally slipshod writing."

Fast found himself drawn to the downtrodden peoples in America's history—the Cheyenne Indians and their tragic attempt to regain their homeland (*The Last Frontier*), the starving soldiers at Valley Forge (*Conceived in Liberty: A Novel of Valley Forge*), and African Americans trying to survive the Reconstruction era in the South (*Freedom Road*). In *Publishers Weekly,* John F. Baker called these works "books on which a whole generation of radicals was brought up." A *Christian Science Monitor* contributor likewise noted: "Human nature rather than history is Howard Fast's field. In presenting these harassed human beings without any heroics he makes us all the more respectful of the price paid for American liberty." *Freedom Road* in particular was praised by the nation's black leaders for its depiction of one race's struggle for liberation; the book became a best-seller and won the Schomberg Award for Race Relations in 1944.

During the World War II, Fast worked as a correspondent for several periodicals and for the Office of War Information. After the conflict ended he found himself at odds with the Cold War mentality developing in the United States. At the time Fast was a member of the Communist Party and a contributor of time and money to a number of antifascist causes. His writing during the period addressed such issues as the abuse of power, the suppression of labor unions, and communism as the basis for a utopian future. Works such as *Clarkton, My Glorious Brothers,* and *The Proud and the Free* were widely translated behind the Iron Curtain and earned Fast the International Peace Prize in 1954.

Baker noted that Fast's political views "made him for a time in the 1950s a pariah of the publishing world." The author was jailed for three months on a contempt of Congress charge for refusing to testify before the House Committee on Un-American Activities about his political views. Worse, he found himself blacklisted to such an extent that no publishing house would accept his manuscripts. Fast's persecution seemed ironic to some observers, because in the historical and biographical novels he had already published—like *Conceived in Liberty: A Novel of Valley Forge* and *The Unvanquished*—as well as in his work for the Office of War Information, Fast emphasized the importance of freedom and illuminated the heroic acts that had built American society. As a correspondent for the radio program that would become the Voice of America, he was entrusted with the job of assuring millions of foreigners of the country's greatness and benevolence during World War II.

Fast makes the relatively unknown or forgotten history of the United States accessible to millions of Americans in books like *The Last Frontier,* in which he writes a fictional account of the real-life 1878 rebellion by a tribe of northern Cheyenne Indians. According to *Twentieth-Century Western Writers* contributor David Marion Holman, "Starved and denuded of pride, the small group of 300 men, women, and children illegally leave the reservation to return to their ancestral homeland. After eluding the U.S. cavalry for weeks . . . part of the tribe is eventually captured. As a result of their unwavering determination not to return to the Oklahoma reservation, the imprisoned Indians suffer from starvation and exposure, and are eventually massacred when they attempt a desperate escape." Because of this tragedy, the Secretary of the Interior eventually grants the rest of the tribe its freedom. Holman concluded, "Throughout the novel, Fast impresses upon the reader the inherent racism of American settlers' treatment of the Indian and points out the irony of double standards of freedom in a democracy."

Fast subsequently learned of Stalin's atrocities and broke his ties with the Communist Party in 1956; but he did not regret the decision he had made in 1944. His experience as the target of political persecution evoked some of his best and most popular works. It also led

Fast to establish his own publishing house, the Blue Heron Press. In a discussion of Fast's fiction from 1944 through 1959, *Nation* correspondent Stanley Meisler contended that the "older writings must not be ignored. They document a unique political record, a depressing American waste. They describe a man who distorted his vision of America to fit a vision of communism, and then lost both." Fast published *Spartacus* under the Blue Heron imprint in 1951. A fictional account of a slave revolt in ancient Rome, *Spartacus* became a bestseller after it was made into a feature film in 1960.

Fast went on to publish five books chronicling the fictional Lavette family, beginning with *The Immigrants* in 1977. *The Immigrants* and its sequels represent some of his most popular work. The first book of the series is set mostly in San Francisco, where Dan Lavette, the son of an Italian fisherman, lives through the great earthquake in that city and goes on to build a fortune in the shipping business. The fates of an Irish family and a Chinese family are also entwined with those of the Lavettes. *The Immigrant's Daughter* relates the story of Barbara Lavette—Dan Lavette's daughter—and her political aspirations. Denise Gess in the *New York Times Book Review* called *The Immigrant's Daughter* "satisfying, old-fashioned storytelling" despite finding the novel occasionally "soap-operatic and uneven." Barbara Conaty, reviewing the novel in *Library Journal,* called Fast a "smooth and assured writer." A reviewer for *Publishers Weekly* commented that, "smoothly written, fast-paced, alive with plots and subplots, the story reads easily." With the publication of *The Immigrant's Daughter,* the series appeared to reach its conclusion, but in 1997, Fast surprised readers with a sixth installment in the saga, *An Independent Woman.* This book relates the final years of Barbara Lavette's life. Barbara has some things in common with her creator: like him, she is a reporter, a victim of McCarthyism, and a worker for civil rights. The twilight years of her life continue to be dynamic. She battles injustice and cancer, finds romance, and astonishes her family by marrying again. A *Kirkus Reviews* writer called *An Independent Woman* "a muted, somewhat puzzling, addenda to a lively (and successful) series."

Fast published another politically charged novel in 1989, with *The Confession of Joe Cullen.* Focusing on U.S. military involvement in Central America, *The Confession of Joe Cullen* is the story of a C.I.A. pilot who confesses to New York City police that, among other things, he murdered a priest in Honduras, and has been smuggling cocaine into the United States. Arguing that the conspiracy theory that implicates the federal government in drug trafficking and gun running has never

been proved, Morton Kondracke in the *New York Times Book Review* had reservations about the "political propaganda" involved in *The Confession of Joe Cullen.* Robert H. Donahugh, however, highly recommended the novel in *Library Journal,* calling it "unexpected and welcome," and lauding both the "fast-moving" storyline and the philosophical probing into Catholicism. Denise Perry Donavin, in *Booklist,* found the politics suiting the characters "without lessening the pace of a powerful tale."

Fast focuses on another controversial subject, the issue of abortion, in his 1993 novel, *The Trial of Abigail Goodman.* As a *Publishers Weekly* critic noted, Fast views America's attitude toward abortion as "parochial," and is sympathetic to his protagonist, a college professor who has an abortion during the third trimester in a southern state with a retroactive law forbidding such acts. Critical reaction to the novel was mixed. Ray Olson in *Booklist* argued that "every anti-abortion character" is stereotyped, and that Fast "undermines . . . any pretensions to evenhandedness," and called the novel "an execrable work." A *Publishers Weekly* critic, on the other hand, found *The Trial of Abigail Goodman* "electrifying" and considered Fast "a master of courtroom pyrotechnics." Many critics, including Susan Dooley in the *Washington Post,* viewed the novel as too polemical, failing to flesh out the characters and the story. Dooley argued that Fast "has not really written a novel; his book is a tract for a cause, and like other similar endeavors, it concentrates more on making converts than creating characters." A reviewer for *Armchair Detective* concluded that the novel would have been much stronger if "there were some real sincerity and some well-expressed arguments from the antagonists." A *Rapport* reviewer commented, "Fast is more than capable of compelling character studies. There's a kernel of a powerful trial novel here, but this prestigious writer chooses not to flesh it out."

Fast returns to the topic of the American Revolution in *Seven Days in June: A Novel of the American Revolution.* A *Publishers Weekly* critic summarized: "Fictionalizing the experiences of British commanders, loyalists to the crown and a motley collection of American revolutionaries, Fast . . . fashions this dramatic look at a week of profound tension that will erupt [into] the battle of Bunker Hill." Some critics saw *Seven Days in June* as inferior to Fast's *April Morning,* also a novel about the American Revolution, which was considered by some to be a minor masterpiece. Charles Michaud in *Library Journal* found that *Seven Days* "is very readable pop history, but as a novel it is not as involving as . . . *April Morning.*" A *Kirkus Reviews* critic faulted the novel for repetitiveness and a disproportionate amount of focus on the sexual exploits of the British commanders, concluding that *Seven Days* "has a slipshod, slapdash feel, cluttered with hurried, lazy characterizations." The critic for *Publishers Weekly,* however, argued that the novel "ekes genuine suspense" and lauded Fast's "accomplished storytelling."

The Bridge Builder's Story tells of Scott Waring and his young bride, Martha, who honeymoon in Europe during the Nazi era and find themselves persecuted by Hitler's thuggish minions. After Martha is killed by the Gestapo, Scott makes his way to New York, where his ensuing sessions with a psychiatrist provide much of the narrative. Albert Wilheim, writing in *Library Journal,* thought that the novel tested "the limits of credibility," but praised Fast's "skillful narration." And Alice Joyce, in *Booklist,* opined that in *The Bridge Builder's Story* "Fast's remarkable prowess for storytelling" results in a "riveting tale, sure to satisfy readers."

Fast's time as a communist in Cold War America provided him with an extraordinary story to share in his autobiographical works, which included *Being Red: A Memoir.* Charles C. Nash of *Library Journal* called *Being Red* "indispensable to the . . . literature on America's terrifying postwar Red Scare." Fast once told *CA:* "There is no way to imagine war or to imagine jail or to imagine being a father or a mother. These things can only be understood if you live through them. Maybe that's a price that a writer should pay." Fast told Ken Gross in *People* that he wrote the book at the request of his son Jonathan, who wanted to share the story with his own children. Rhoda Koenig of *New York* magazine remarked that Fast's story is "a lively and gripping one," and that he "brings alive the days of parochial-school children carrying signs that read 'KILL A COMMIE FOR CHRIST.'"

With a critical eye, Ronald Radosh claimed in *Commentary* that *Being Red* contains information and perspectives that contradict portions of Fast's 1957 memoir, *The Naked God: The Writer and the Communist Party.* In Radosh's opinion, *Being Red* was the author's attempt to "rehabilitate" the Communist Party he had admonished in *The Naked God.* "Now, nearly thirty-five years later, it almost sounds as though Fast wants to end his days winning back the admiration of those unreconstructed Communists," Radosh asserted, even calling them "some of the noblest human beings I have ever known."

In 1999 Fast published *Redemption,* a suspense novel featuring Ike Goldman, a character who seems to be the author's alter ego. Goldman is a retired professor, highly intelligent, and the veteran of numerous political and social struggles. Driving through New York City one night, he sees a woman, Elizabeth, about to jump from a bridge. He talks Elizabeth out of her desperate act and, in the weeks that follow, finds himself falling in love with her. The two are planning to wed, when Elizabeth's ex-husband is found dead in suspicious circumstances, making her a suspect. Goldman does all he can to aid in her defense, but as the evidence against her mounts, his own doubts about her innocence increase. "The story moves along sedately in Fast's most relaxed style ever, with the author . . . plainly enjoying and indulging himself in this smoked salmon of romantic fantasy, adding plot dollops to keep the reader alert. . . . Fast's followers won't be disappointed," advised a contributor to *Kirkus Reviews.* The following year, Fast published *Greenwich,* a tale of eight people invited to a high-society dinner party in Greenwich, Connecticut. The comfortable life they enjoy masks an evil undercurrent; Fast suggests that guilt is widespread, and redemption is vital. Although faulting the book as stylistically "bland," a *Kirkus Reviews* writer nevertheless added: "It doesn't have to be a classic if it comes from the heart."

Fast also published a number of detective novels under the pseudonym E.V. Cunningham, for which he was awarded with a Prix de la Policia. Many of these novels feature a fictional Japanese-American detective named Masao Masuto, who works with the Beverly Hills Police Department. Fast told *Publishers Weekly,* "Critics can't stand my mainline books, maybe because they sell so well, [but] they love Cunningham. Even the *New Yorker* has reviewed him, and they've never reviewed me." In the *New York Times Book Review,* Newgate Callendar called detective Masuto "a well-conceived character whose further exploits should gain him a wide audience." *Toronto Globe and Mail* contributor Derrick Murdoch also found Masuto "a welcome addition to the lighter side of crime fiction." "Functional and efficient, Fast's prose is a machine in which plot and ideals mesh, turn and clash," *Los Angeles Times* contributor Elaine Kendall concluded, adding, "The reader is constantly being instructed, but the manner is so disarming and the hectic activity so absorbing that the didacticism seldom intrudes upon the entertainment."

Fast's voice interpreted America's past and present and helped shape its reputation at home and abroad. One of his own favorites among his novels, *April Morning,* has been standard reading in public schools for generations. The film *Spartacus* has become a popular classic, and *Being Red* offers an account of American history that Americans may never want to forget, whether or not they agree with Fast's perspectives. As Victor Howes commented in *Christian Science Monitor,* if Howard Fast "is a chronicler of some of mankind's most glorious moments, he is also a register of some of our more senseless deeds."

Upon Fast's death in 2003, Holly J. Morris wrote an obituary in the *U.S. News & World Report* recounting a story demonstrating that readers did not have to agree with Fast's politics. At a 1987 party, Pat Buckley, wife of William Buckley, told Fast she read all of his books. Fast was doubtful, noting that his beliefs were diametrically opposite to the staunch conservative couple. According to Morris, Buckley replied, "'Oh, I don't care about that—I love your books.'" In a *Knight-Ridder/ Tribune News Service* obituary appearing in the *Chicago Tribune,* Ron Grossman noted that Fast never enjoyed the same popularity he did as a young writer, but his books will survive. Grossman opined, "Years from now, some young person, trapped in the poverty Fast knew, will find his books, preserved in those heavy library bindings, on a shelf somewhere. He or she will realize that others have made life's difficulty journey before them, while reading that remarkable passage in *Freedom Road* where those anxious women, who had so recently been slaves, see a distant sign of a better world to come." Brad Hooper perhaps summed up Fast's popularity best in *Booklist,* commenting, "The bottom line is that when it comes to reading Howard Fast, we continue to understand and appreciate that, simply, he could tell a darn good story."

BIOGRAPHICAL AND CRITICAL SOURCES:

BOOKS

Authors and Artists for Young Adults, Volume 16, Thomson Gale (Detroit, MI), 1995.

Contemporary Authors Autobiography Series, Volume 18, Thomson Gale (Detroit, MI), 1994.

Contemporary Literary Criticism, Thomson Gale (Detroit, MI), Volume 23, 1983, Volume 131, 2000.

Contemporary Novelists, 6th edition, St. James Press (Detroit, MI), 1996.

Contemporary Popular Writers, St. James Press (Detroit, MI), 1997.

Dictionary of Literary Biography, Volume 9: *American Novelists, 1910-1945,* Thomson Gale (Detroit, MI), 1981.

MacDonald, Andrew, *Howard Fast: A Critical Companion,* Greenwood (Westport, CT), 1996.

Meyer, Hershel, D., *History and Conscience: The Case of Howard Fast,* Anvil-Atlas (New York, NY), 1958.

St. James Guide to Crime and Mystery Writers, 4th edition, St. James Press (Detroit, MI), 1996.

St. James Guide to Young Adult Writers, 2nd edition, St. James Press (Detroit, MI), 1999.

Twentieth-Century Romance and Historical Writers, 3rd edition, St. James Press (Detroit, MI), 1994.

Twentieth-Century Western Writers, St. James Press (Detroit, MI), 1991.

PERIODICALS

Antioch Review, winter, 1993, review of *Sylvia,* p. 156.

Armchair Detective, spring, 1994, review of *The Trial of Abigail Goodman,* p. 218.

Atlantic Monthly, September, 1944; June, 1970.

Best Sellers, February 1, 1971; September 1, 1973; January, 1979; November, 1979.

Booklist, June 15, 1989, p. 1739; July, 1993, review of *The Trial of Abigail Goodman,* p. 1916; October 1, 1995, review of *The Bridge Builder's Story,* p. 252; May 1, 1997, review of *An Independent Woman,* p. 1460; February 15, 1999, review of *Redemption,* p. 1003; February 1, 2000, review of *Greenwich,* p. 996.

Book Week, May 9, 1943.

Chicago Tribune, April 21, 1987; January 20, 1991, section 14, p. 7.

Christian Science Monitor, July 8, 1939; August 23, 1972, p. 11; November 7, 1977, p. 18; November 1, 1991, p. 12; August 12, 1999, review of *Redemption,* p. 20.

Commentary, March, 1991, pp. 62-64.

Detroit News, October 31, 1982.

Entertainment Weekly, August 1, 1997, review of *An Independent Woman,* p. 69; July 30, 1999, review of *Redemption,* p. 66.

Globe and Mail (Toronto, Ontario, Canada), September 15, 1984; March 1, 1986; July 17, 1999, review of *Redemption,* p. D14.

Kirkus Reviews, June 15, 1993, review of *The Trial of Abigail Goodman,* p. 739; June 15, 1994, review of *Seven Days in June,* p. 793; July 15, 1995, review of *The Bridge Builder's Story,* p. 968; June 15, 1997, review of *An Independent Woman,* p. 909; May 1, 1999, review of *Redemption,* p. 650.

Library Journal, November 15, 1978; September 15, 1985, p. 92; May 15, 1989, p. 88; October 1, 1990, p. 96; August, 1991, p. 162; July, 1994, review of *Seven Days in June,* p. 126; September 1, 1995, review of *The Bridge Builder's Story,* p. 206; February 1, 1997, p. 112; June 15, 1997, review of *An Independent Woman,* p. 96; May 15, 1999, review of *Redemption,* p. 125.

Los Angeles Times, November 11, 1982; November 11, 1985; November 21, 1988.

Los Angeles Times Book Review, December 9, 1990.

Nation, April 5, 1952; May 30, 1959.

New Republic, August 17, 1942, p. 203; August 14, 1944; November 4, 1978; May 27, 1992.

New Statesman, August 8, 1959.

New York, November 5, 1990, pp. 124-125.

New Yorker, July 1, 1939; May 1, 1943.

New York Herald Tribune Book Review, July 21, 1963.

New York Herald Tribune Books, July 27, 1941, p. 3.

New York Times, October 15, 1933; June 25, 1939; April 25, 1943; February 3, 1952; September 24, 1984; February 9, 1987, p. C16; March 10, 1987; April 21, 1991, pp. 20-21; October 23, 1991, p. C19; November 19, 1993, p. A2.

New York Times Book Review, October 13, 1933; April 25, 1943; February 3, 1952; March 4, 1962; July 14, 1963; February 6, 1966; October 2, 1977, p. 24; October 30, 1977; May 14, 1978; June 10, 1979; September 15, 1985, p. 24; March 29, 1987, p. 22; August 20, 1989, p. 23; February 28, 1993, review of *The Jews: Story of a People,* p. 32; October 22, 1995, review of *The Bridge Builder's Story,* p. 37.

People, January 28, 1991, pp. 75-79.

Publishers Weekly, August 6, 1979; April 1, 1983; July 19, 1985, p. 48; November 28, 1986, p. 66; July 22, 1988, p. 41; June 30, 1989, p. 84; June 21, 1993, review of *The Trial of Abigail Goodman,* p. 83; July 11, 1994, review of *Seven Days in June,* p. 66; September 4, 1995, review of *The Bridge Builder's Story,* p. 49; May 26, 1997, review of *An Independent Woman,* p. 64; May 17, 1999, review of *Redemption,* p. 54.

Rapport, number 1, 1994, review of *The Trial of Abigail Goodman,* p. 38.

Reference and Research Book News, November, 1995, review of *Freedom Road,* p. 69; February, 1998, review of *The Unvanquished,* p. 150.

Saturday Review, March 8, 1952; January 22, 1966; September 17, 1977.

Saturday Review of Literature, July 1, 1939; July 26, 1941, p. 5; May 1, 1943; December 24, 1949.

Science and Society, spring, 1993, review of *Being Red,* p. 86.

Time, November 6, 1977.

Times Literary Supplement, November 11, 1939.

Tribune Books (Chicago, IL), February 8, 1987, pp. 6-7.

Washington Post, October 4, 1979; September 26, 1981; September 25, 1982; September 3, 1985; February 9, 1987; March 3, 1987; September 6, 1993, p. C2.

Washington Post Book World, October 23, 1988; November 25, 1990; November 17, 1996, p. 12; August 8, 1999, review of *Redemption,* p. 4.

ONLINE

New York Times Online, http://www.nytimes.com/ (March 13, 2003).

OBITUARIES:

PERIODICALS

Booklist, May 15, 2003, Brad Hooper, "A Tribute to Howard Fast," p. 1639.

Chicago Tribune (Knight-Ridder/Tribune News Service), March 18, 2003, Ron Grossman, "Howard Fast, The Last of the Proletarian Writers."

Los Angeles Times, March 14, 2003, p. B13.

New York Times, March 13, 2003, p. C12.

Times (London, England), March 20, 2003.

U.S. News & World Report, March 24, 2003, Holly J. Morris, "The Steadfast Howard Fast," p. 8.

*   *   *

FAST, Howard Melvin
    See FAST, Howard

*   *   *

FERLING, Lawrence
    See FERLINGHETTI, Lawrence

*   *   *

FERLINGHETTI, Lawrence 1919-

    (Lawrence Ferling, Lawrence Monsanto Ferlinghetti)

PERSONAL: Born Lawrence Ferling, March 24, 1919, in Yonkers, NY; original family name of Ferlinghetti restored, 1954; son of Charles S. (an auctioneer) and Clemence (Mendes Monsanto) Ferling; married Selden Kirby-Smith, April, 1951 (divorced, 1976); children: Julie, Lorenzo. *Education:* University of North Carolina, A.B., 1941; Columbia University, M.A., 1947;

Sorbonne, University of Paris, doctorat (with honors), 1949. *Politics:* "Now an enemy of the State." *Religion:* "Catholique manque."

ADDRESSES: Home—San Francisco, CA. *Office*—City Lights Books, 261 Columbus Ave., San Francisco, CA 94133.

CAREER: Poet, playwright, editor, and painter; worked for *Time*, New York, NY, post-World War II; taught French in an adult education program, San Francisco, CA, 1951-52; City Lights Pocket Bookshop (now City Lights Books), San Francisco, co-owner, 1953—, founder, publisher, and editor of City Lights Books, 1955—. Participant in literary conferences, art exhibitions, and poetry readings. *Military service:* U.S. Naval Reserve, 1941-45; became lieutenant commander; was commanding officer during Normandy invasion.

AWARDS, HONORS: National Book Award nomination, 1970, for *The Secret Meaning of Things;* Notable Book of 1979 citation, *Library Journal*, 1980, for *Landscapes of Living and Dying;* Silver Medal for poetry, Commonwealth Club of California, 1986, for *Over All the Obscene Boundaries;* poetry prize, City of Rome, 1993; San Francisco street named in his honor, 1994; named first poet laureate of San Francisco, 1998; *Los Angeles Times* Robert Kirsch Award, 2001, for body of work; PEN Center West Literary Award, 2002, for lifetime achievement; award for creative publishing, Association of American Publishers, 2005.

WRITINGS:

(Translator) Jacques Prevert, *Selections from "Paroles,"* City Lights (San Francisco, CA), 1958.
Her (novel), New Directions (New York, NY), 1960.
Howl of the Censor (trial proceedings), edited by J.W. Ehrlich, Nourse Publishing, 1961.
(With Jack Spicer) *Dear Ferlinghetti*, White Rabbit Press, 1962.
The Mexican Night: Travel Journal, New Directions (New York, NY), 1970.
A World Awash with Fascism and Fear, Cranium Press, 1971.
A Political Pamphlet, Anarchist Resistance Press, 1976.
Northwest Ecolog, City Lights (San Francisco, CA), 1978.
(With Nancy J. Peters) *Literary San Francisco: A Pictorial History from the Beginning to the Present*, Harper (New York, NY), 1980.

The Populist Manifestos (includes "First Populist Manifesto"), Grey Fox Press, 1983.
Seven Days in Nicaragua Libre (journal), City Lights (San Francisco, CA), 1985.
Leaves of Life: Fifty Drawings from the Model, City Lights (San Francisco, CA), 1985.
(Translator with others) Nicanor Parra, *Antipoems: New and Selected*, New Directions (New York, NY), 1985.
(Translator, with Francesca Valente) Pier Paolo Pasolini, *Roman Poems*, City Lights (San Francisco, CA), 1986.
Love in the Days of Rage (novel), Dutton (New York, NY), 1988.
(With Alexis Lykiard) *The Cool Eye: Lawrence Ferlinghetti Talks to Alexis Lykiard*, Stride, 1993.
(With Christopher Felver) *Ferlinghetti: Portrait*, Gibbs Smith, 1998.
What Is Poetry?, Creative Arts (Berkeley, CA), 2000.
(Translator, with others) Homero Aridjis, *Eyes to See Otherwise*, New Directions (New York, NY), 2002.
Life Studies, Life Stories: Drawings, City Lights (San Francisco, CA), 2003.

POETRY

Pictures of the Gone World, City Lights (San Francisco, CA), 1955, enlarged edition, 1995.
Tentative Description of a Dinner Given to Promote the Impeachment of President Eisenhower, Golden Mountain Press, 1958.
A Coney Island of the Mind, New Directions (New York, NY), 1958.
Berlin, Golden Mountain Press, 1961.
One Thousand Fearful Words for Fidel Castro, City Lights (San Francisco), 1961.
Starting from San Francisco (with recording), New Directions (New York, NY), 1961, revised edition (without recording), 1967.
(With Gregory Corso and Allen Ginsberg) *Penguin Modern Poets 5*, Penguin (New York, NY), 1963.
Thoughts of a Concerto of Telemann, Four Seasons Foundation, 1963.
Where Is Vietnam?, City Lights (San Francisco), 1965.
To F—-Is to Love Again, Kyrie Eleison Kerista; or, The Situation in the West, Followed by a Holy Proposal, F—-You Press, 1965.
Christ Climbed Down, Syracuse University (Syracuse, NY), 1965.
An Eye on the World: Selected Poems, MacGibbon & Kee, 1967.
Moscow in the Wilderness, Segovia in the Snow, Beach Books, 1967.

After the Cries of the Birds, Dave Haselwood Books, 1967.

Fuclock, Fire Publications, 1968.

Reverie Smoking Grass, East 128, 1968.

The Secret Meaning of Things, New Directions (New York, NY), 1969.

Tyrannus Nix?, New Directions (New York, NY), 1969.

Back Roads to Far Places, New Directions (New York, NY), 1971.

Love Is No Stone on the Moon, ARIF Press, 1971.

The Illustrated Wilfred Funk, City Lights (San Francisco, CA), 1971.

Open Eye, Open Heart, New Directions (New York, NY), 1973.

Director of Alienation: A Poem, Main Street, 1976.

Who Are We Now? (also see below), City Lights (San Francisco, CA), 1976.

Landscapes of Living and Dying (also see below), New Directions (New York, NY), 1979.

Mule Mountain Dreams, Bisbee Press Collective, 1980.

A Trip to Italy and France, New Directions (New York, NY), 1980.

Endless Life: Selected Poems (includes "Endless Life"), New Directions (New York, NY), 1984.

Over All the Obscene Boundaries: European Poems and Transitions, New Directions (New York, NY), 1985.

Inside the Trojan Horse, Lexikos, 1987.

Wild Dreams of a New Beginning: Including "Landscapes of Living and Dying" and "Who Are We Now?," New Directions (New York, NY), 1988.

When I Look at Pictures, Peregrine Smith Books, 1990.

These Are My Rivers: New and Selected Poems, 1955-1993, New Directions (New York, NY), 1993.

A Far Rockaway of the Heart, New Directions (New York, NY), 1997.

San Francisco Poems, City Lights (San Francisco, CA), 2001.

How to Paint Sunlight: Lyric Poems and Others, 1997-2000, New Directions (New York, NY), 2001.

PLAYS

Unfair Arguments with Existence: Seven Plays for a New Theatre (contains *The Soldiers of No Country* [produced in London, England, 1969], *Three Thousand Red Ants* [produced in New York, NY, 1970; also see below], *The Alligation* [produced in San Francisco, 1962; also see below], *The Victims of Amnesia* [produced in New York, NY, 1970; also see below], *Motherlode, The Customs Collector in*

Baggy Pants [produced in New York, NY, 1964], and *The Nose of Sisyphus*), New Directions (New York, NY), 1963.

Routines (includes *The Jig Is Up, His Head, Ha-Ha,* and *Non-Objection*), New Directions (New York, NY), 1964.

Three by Ferlinghetti: Three Thousand Red Ants, The Alligation, [and] *The Victims of Amnesia,* produced in New York, NY, 1970.

EDITOR

Beatitude Anthology, City Lights (San Francisco, CA), 1960.

Pablo Picasso, *Hunk of Skin,* City Lights (San Francisco, CA), 1969.

Charles Upton, *Panic Grass,* City Lights (San Francisco, CA), 1969.

City Lights Anthology, City Lights (San Francisco, CA), 1974, reprinted, 1995.

City Lights Pocket Poets Anthology, City Lights (San Francisco, CA), 1995.

RECORDINGS

(With Kenneth Rexroth) *Poetry Readings in "The Cellar,"* Fantasy, 1958.

Tentative Description of a Dinner to Impeach President Eisenhower, and Other Poems, Fantasy, 1959.

Tyrannus Nix? and Assassination Raga, Fantasy, 1971.

(With Gregory Corso and Allen Ginsberg) *The World's Greatest Poets 1,* CMS, 1971.

OTHER

Author of narration, *Have You Sold Your Dozen Roses?* (film), California School of Fine Arts Film Workshop, 1957. Contributor to numerous periodicals, including *San Francisco Chronicle, Nation, Evergreen Review, Liberation, Chicago Review, Transatlantic Review,* and *New Statesman.* Editor, *Journal for the Protection of All Beings, Interim Pad,* and *City Lights Journal.*

Ferlinghetti's manuscripts are collected at Columbia University, New York, NY.

ADAPTATIONS: Ferlinghetti's poem "Autobiography" was choreographed by Sophie Maslow, 1964. *A Coney Island of the Mind* was adapted for the stage by Steven Kyle Kent, Charles R. Blaker, and Carol Brown and produced at the Edinburgh Festival, Scotland, 1966; poem was adapted for television by Ted Post on *Second Experiment in Television,* 1967.

SIDELIGHTS: As poet, playwright, publisher, and spokesman, Lawrence Ferlinghetti helped to spark the San Francisco literary renaissance of the 1950s and the subsequent "Beat" movement. Ferlinghetti was one of a group of writers—labeled the "Beat Generation"—who felt strongly that art should be accessible to all people, not just a handful of highly educated intellectuals. His career has been marked by a constant challenge to the status quo in art; his poetry engages readers, defies popular political movements, and reflects the influence of American idiom and modern jazz. In *Lawrence Ferlinghetti: Poet-at-Large,* Larry Smith noted that the author "writes truly memorable poetry, poems that lodge themselves in the consciousness of the reader and generate awareness and change. And his writing sings, with the sad and comic music of the streets."

Ferlinghetti performed numerous functions essential to the establishment of the Beat movement while also creating his own substantial body of work. His City Lights bookstore provided a gathering place for the fertile talents of the San Francisco literary renaissance, and the bookstore's publishing arm offered a forum for publication of Beat writings. He also became "America's best-selling poet of the twentieth century," according to Paul Varner in *Western American Literature.* As Smith noted in the *Dictionary of Literary Biography,* "What emerges from the historical panorama of Ferlinghetti's involvement is a pattern of social engagement and literary experimentation as he sought to expand the goals of the Beat movement." Smith added, however, that Ferlinghetti's contribution far surpasses his tasks as a publisher and organizer. "Besides molding an image of the poet in the world," the critic continued, "he created a poetic form that is at once rhetorically functional and socially vital." *Dictionary of Literary Biography* essayist Thomas McClanahan likewise contended that Ferlinghetti "became the most important force in developing and publicizing antiestablishment poetics."

Ferlinghetti was born Lawrence Monsanto Ferling, the youngest of five sons of Charles and Clemence Ferling. His father, an Italian immigrant, had shortened the family name upon arrival in America. Only years later, when he was a grown man, did Ferlinghetti discover the lengthier name and restore it as his own.

A series of disasters struck Ferlinghetti as a youngster. Before he was born, his father died suddenly. When he was only two, his mother suffered a nervous breakdown that required lengthy hospitalization. Separated from his brothers, Lawrence went to live with his maternal uncle, Ludovic Monsanto, a language instructor, and Ludovic's French-speaking wife, Emily. The marriage disintegrated, and Emily Monsanto returned to France, taking Lawrence with her. During the following four years, the youngster lived in Strasbourg and spoke only French.

Ferlinghetti's return to America began with a stay in a state orphanage in New York; he was placed there by his aunt while she sought work in Manhattan. The pair were reunited when the aunt found a position as governess to the wealthy Bisland family in Bronxville. Young Ferlinghetti endeared himself to the Bislands to such an extent that when his aunt disappeared suddenly, he was allowed to stay. Surrounded by fine books and educated people, he was encouraged to read and learn fine passages of literature by heart. His formal education proceeded first in the elite Riverdale Country Day School and later in Bronxville public schools. As a teenager he was sent to Mount Hermon, a preparatory academy in Massachusetts.

Ferlinghetti enrolled at the University of North Carolina in 1937. There he majored in journalism and worked with the student staff of the *Daily Tarheel.* He earned his bachelor's degree in the spring of 1941 and joined the U.S. Navy that fall. His wartime service included patrolling the Atlantic coast on submarine watch and commanding a ship during the invasion of Normandy. After his discharge Ferlinghetti took advantage of the G.I. Bill to continue his education. He did graduate study at Columbia University, receiving his master's degree in 1948, and he completed his doctoral degree at the University of Paris in 1951.

Ferlinghetti left Paris in 1951 and moved to San Francisco. For a short time he supported himself by teaching languages at an adult education school and by doing freelance writing for art journals and for the *San Francisco Chronicle.* In 1953 he joined with Peter D. Martin to publish a magazine, *City Lights,* named after a silent film starring actor Charlie Chaplin. In order to subsidize the magazine, Martin and Ferlinghetti opened the City Lights Pocket Book Shop in a neighborhood on the edge of Chinatown.

Before long the City Lights Book Shop was a popular gathering place for San Francisco's avant-garde writers, poets, and painters. "We were filling a big need," Ferlinghetti told the *New York Times Book Review.* "City Lights became about the only place around where you could go in, sit down, and read books without being pestered to buy something. That's one of the things it was supposed to be. Also, I had this idea that a bookstore should be a center of intellectual activity; and I knew it was a natural for a publishing company too."

In addition to his new career as an entrepreneur, Ferlinghetti was busy creating his own poetry, and in 1955 he launched the City Lights Pocket Poets publishing venture. First in the "Pocket Poets" series was a slim volume of his own, *Pictures of the Gone World.* In *Lawrence Ferlinghetti,* Smith observed that, from his earliest poems onwards, the author writes as "the contemporary man of the streets speaking out the truths of common experience, often to the reflective beat of the jazz musician. As much as any poet today he . . . sought to make poetry an engaging oral art." McClanahan wrote: "The underlying theme of Ferlinghetti's first book is the poet's desire to subvert and destroy the capitalist economic system. Yet this rather straightforward political aim is accompanied by a romantic vision of Eden, a mirror reflecting the Whitmanesque attempts to be free from social and political restraints."

These sentiments found an appreciative audience among young people of the mid-twentieth century, who were agonizing over the nuclear arms race and cold war politics. By 1955 Ferlinghetti counted among his friends such poets as Kenneth Rexroth, Allen Ginsberg, and Philip Whalen, as well as the novelist Jack Kerouac. Ferlinghetti was in the audience at the watershed 1955 poetry reading "Six Poets at the Six Gallery," at which Ginsberg unveiled his poem *Howl.* Ferlinghetti immediately recognized *Howl* as a classic work of art and offered to publish it in the "Pocket Poets" series. The first edition of *Howl and Other Poems* appeared in 1956 and sold out quickly. A second shipment was ordered from the publisher's British printer, but U.S. customs authorities seized it on the grounds of alleged obscenity. When federal authorities declined to pursue the case and released the books, the San Francisco Police Department arrested Ferlinghetti on charges of printing and selling lewd and indecent material.

Ferlinghetti engaged the American Civil Liberties Union for his defense and welcomed his court case as a test of the limits to freedom of speech. Not only did he win the suit on October 3, 1957, he also benefitted from the publicity generated by the case. In the *Dictionary of Literary Biography,* Smith wrote: "The importance of this court case to the life and career of Ferlinghetti as well as to the whole blossoming of the San Francisco renaissance in poetry and the West Coast Beat move-

ment is difficult to overestimate. Ferlinghetti and Ginsberg became national as well as international public figures leading a revolution in thinking as well as writing. The case solidified the writing into a movement with definite principles yet an openness of form."

For Ferlinghetti, these "principles" included redeeming poetry from the ivory towers of academia and offering it as a shared experience with ordinary people. He began reading his verses to the accompaniment of experimental jazz and reveled in an almost forgotten oral tradition in poetry. In 1958 New York's New Directions press published Ferlinghetti's *A Coney Island of the Mind,* a work that has since sold well over one million copies in America and abroad. In his *Dictionary of Literary Biography* piece, Smith called *A Coney Island of the Mind* "one of the key works of the Beat period and one of the most popular books of contemporary poetry. . . . It launched Ferlinghetti as a poet of humor and satire, who achieves an open-form expressionism and a personal lyricism." Walter Sutton offered a similar assessment in *American Free Verse: The Modern Revolution in Poetry.* Sutton felt that the general effect of the book "is of a kaleidoscopic view of the world and of life as an absurd carnival of discontinuous sensory impressions and conscious reflections, each with a ragged shape of its own but without any underlying thematic unity or interrelationship." Sutton added, "To this extent the collection suggests a Surrealistic vision. But it differs in that meanings and easily definable themes can be found in most of the individual poems, even when the idea of meaninglessness is the central concern."

In *Lawrence Ferlinghetti,* Smith suggested that the poems in *A Coney Island of the Mind* demonstrate the direction Ferlinghetti intended to go with his art. The poet "enlarged his stance and developed major themes of anarchy, mass corruption, engagement, and a belief in the surreality and wonder of life," to quote Smith. "It was a revolutionary art of dissent and contemporary application which jointly drew a lyric poetry into new realms of social—and self-expression. It sparkles, sings, goes flat, and generates anger or love out of that flatness as it follows a basic motive of getting down to reality and making of it what we can." Smith concluded: "Loosely, the book forms a type of 'Portrait of the Artist as a Young Poet of Dissent.' There are some classic contemporary statements in this, Ferlinghetti's—and possibly America's—most popular book of modern poetry. The work is remarkable for its skill, depth, and daring."

If certain academics grumbled about Ferlinghetti's work, others found it refreshing for its engagement in current social and political issues and its indebtedness to a bardic tradition. "Ferlinghetti has cultivated a style of writing visibly his own," claimed Linda Hamalian in the *American Book Review*. "He often writes his line so that it approximates the rhythm and meaning of the line. He also has William Carlos Williams' gift of turning unlikely subjects into witty poems. . . . He introduces the unexpected, catching his readers open for his frequently sarcastic yet humorous observations." *Poetry* contributor Alan Dugan maintained that the poet "has the usual American obsession, asking, 'What is going on in America and how does one survive it?' His answer might be: By being half a committed outsider and half an innocent Fool. He makes jokes and chants seriously with equal gusto and surreal inventiveness, using spoken American in a romantic, flamboyant manner."

Two collections of Ferlinghetti's poetry provide insight into the development of the writer's overarching style and thematic approach: *Endless Life: Selected Poems* and *These Are My Rivers: New and Selected Poems, 1955-1993.* Ferlinghetti chose selections from among his eight books of poetry and his work in progress, written over twenty-six years, for inclusion in *Endless Life.* The poems reflect the influences of e. e. cummings, Kenneth Rexroth, and Kenneth Patchen and are concerned with contemporary themes, such as the antiwar and antinuclear movements. Some critics have dismissed Ferlinghetti "as either sentimental or the literary entrepreneur of the Beat generation," noted John Trimbur in *Western American Literature,* the critic adding that he feels such labels are unjustified. Ferlinghetti writes a "public poetry to challenge the guardians of the political and social status quo for the souls of his fellow citizens," Trimbur maintained, noting that the poet does so while "risking absurdity." In *World Literature Today,* J. Martone acknowledged that while Ferlinghetti has produced heralded poetry, some of that poetry is stagnant. "Ferlinghetti never moves beyond—or outgrows—the techniques of [his] early poems," maintained Martone, adding that "his repertoire of devices (deliberately casual literary allusion, self-mockery, hyperbole) becomes a bit tedious with repetition." However, Joel Oppenheimer praised the poet in the *New York Times Book Review,* contending that Ferlinghetti "learned to write poems, in ways that those who see poetry as the province of the few and the educated had never imagined."

Ferlinghetti focuses on current political and sexual matters in *These Are My Rivers.* As Rochelle Ratner noted in *Library Journal,* the poems are experimental in technique, often lacking common poetic devices such as stanza breaks, and they appear in unusual ways on the page, "with short lines at the left margin or moving across the page as hand follows eye." Yet, despite its visual effect, Ashley Brown commented in *World Literature Today,* "Ferlinghetti writes in a very accessible idiom; he draws on pop culture and sports as much as the modern poets whom he celebrates." Ratner averred that "Ferlinghetti is the foremost chronicler of our times." Indeed, the collection shows "Ferlinghetti still speaking out against academic poetry just as he did when the Beat Movement began," remarked Varner in *Western American Literature.* "Ferlinghetti, always the poet of the topical now, still sees clearly the 1990s," the critic added.

Drama has also proved a fertile ground for Ferlinghetti. He carried his political philosophies and social criticisms into experimental plays, many of them short and surrealistic. In *Lawrence Ferlinghetti,* Smith contended that the writer's stint as an experimental dramatist "reflects his stronger attention to irrational and intuitive analogy as a means of suggesting the 'secret meaning' behind life's surface. Though the works are provocative, public, and oral, they are also more cosmic in reference, revealing a stronger influence from Buddhist philosophy." In *Dialogue in American Drama,* Ruby Cohn characterized the poet's plays as "brief sardonic comments on our contemporary life-style. . . . The themes may perhaps be resolved into a single theme—the unfairness of industrial, consumer-oriented, establishment-dominated existence—and the plays are arguments against submission to such existence."

In 1960 Ferlinghetti's first novel, *Her,* was published. An autobiographical, experimental work that focuses on the narrator's pursuit of a woman, the novel received very little critical comment when it was published. According to Smith in the *Dictionary of Literary Biography, Her* "is an avant-garde work that pits character and author in a battle with the subjective relativity of experience in a quest for ideals; a surrealistic encounter with the subconscious—filled with phallic symbols and prophetic visions of desire. At once existential, absurd, symbolic, expressionistic, cinematic and surrealistic in vision and form, *Her* is controlled, as all of Ferlinghetti's work is, by a drive toward expanded consciousness." Smith concluded, "The book is truly a spirited, though somewhat self-mocking, projection of the optimistic goals the Beat and San Francisco poetry movements placed on a grand imaginative scale."

Ferlinghetti published another novel in 1988, *Love in the Days of Rage.* This chronicles a love affair between an expatriate American painter named Annie, and a Parisian banker of Portuguese extraction named Julian.

Their relationship takes place against the backdrop of 1968 Paris, during the student revolution that took place during that year. Though at first Annie thinks Julian is conservative, because of his clothing style and occupation, he eventually reveals his involvement in a subversive plot—which she supports him in. Alex Raksin, discussing *Love in the Days of Rage* in the *Los Angeles Times Book Review,* praised the work as an "original, intense novel" in which Ferlinghetti's "sensitivity as a painter . . . is most apparent." Patrick Burson, critiquing for the *San Francisco Review of Books,* explained that "*Love in the Days of Rage* challenges the reader on several stylistic levels as it attemps to mirror the anarchistic uprising of '68 which briefly united intellectuals, artists, and proletariats in common cause." Burson went on to conclude that the book is "an uneven ride, at times maddeningly confused, but noble in intent and final effect."

Ferlinghetti, who continues to operate the City Lights bookstore, travels frequently to give poetry readings. His paintings and drawings have been exhibited in San Francisco galleries; his plays have been performed in experimental theaters. He also continues to publish new poetry, including the 1997 collection *A Far Rockaway of the Heart,* which is to some degree a follow-up to *A Coney Island of the Mind.* In 2001 readers saw the arrival of two books by Ferlinghetti: *How to Paint Sunlight: Lyric Poems and Others, 1997-2000* and *San Francisco Poems.* As Smith observed in the *Dictionary of Literary Biography,* Ferlinghetti's life and writing "stand as models of the existentially authentic and engaged. . . . His work exists as a vital challenge and a living presence to the contemporary artist, as an embodiment of the strong, anticool, compassionate commitment to life in an absurd time." *New York Times Book Review* correspondent Joel Oppenheimer cited Ferlinghetti's work for "a legitimate revisionism which is perhaps our best heritage from those raucous [Beat] days—the poet daring to see a different vision from that which the guardians of culture had allowed us." As *New Pages* contributor John Gill concluded, reading a work by Ferlinghetti "will make you feel good about poetry and about the world—no matter how mucked-up the world may be."

BIOGRAPHICAL AND CRITICAL SOURCES:

BOOKS

Cherkovski, Neeli, *Ferlinghetti: A Biography,* Doubleday (New York, NY), 1979.
Cohn, Ruby, *Dialogue in American Drama,* Indiana University Press, 1971.

Contemporary Literary Criticism, Thomson Gale (Detroit, MI), Volume 2, 1974, Volume 6, 1976, Volume 10, 1979, Volume 27, 1984, Volume 111, 1998.
Contemporary Poets, 7th edition, St. James Press (Detroit, MI), 2001.
Dictionary of Literary Biography, Volume 16: *The Beats: Literary Bohemians in Post-War America,* Thomson Gale (Detroit, MI), 1983.
Parkinson, Thomas, *Poets, Poems, Movements,* UMI Research Press, 1987.
Poetry Criticism, Volume 1, Thomson Gale (Detroit, MI), 1991.
Rexroth, Kenneth, *American Poetry in the Twentieth Century,* Herder & Herder, 1971.
Rexroth, Kenneth, *Assays,* New Directions (New York, NY), 1961.
Silesky, Barry, *Ferlinghetti: The Artist in His Time,* Warner Books (New York, NY), 1990.
Smith, Larry, *Lawrence Ferlinghetti: Poet-at-Large,* Southern Illinois University Press (Carbondale, IL), 1983.
Sutton, Walter, *American Free Verse: The Modern Revolution in Poetry,* New Directions (New York, NY), 1973.

PERIODICALS

American Book Review, March-April, 1984.
American Poetry Review, September-October, 1977.
Arizona Quarterly, autumn, 1982.
Booklist, November 15, 1995, p. 532; May 15, 1997, p. 1557.
Chicago Tribune, May 19, 1986; September 13, 1988.
Chicago Tribune Book World, February 28, 1982.
Critique, Volume 19, number 3, 1978.
Explicator, winter, 2001, Marilyn Ann Fontane, "Ferlinghetti's 'Constantly Risking Absurdity,'" p. 106.
Georgia Review, winter, 1989.
Guardian, April 16, 1998, p. T20.
Library Journal, November 15, 1960; October 1, 1993, p. 98; March 15, 1998, p. 107.
Life, September 9, 1957.
Listener, February 1, 1968.
Los Angeles Times, July 20, 1969; March 18, 1980; September 27, 1985.
Los Angeles Times Book Review, August 24, 1980; October 19, 1980; March 24, 1985; September 4, 1988, Alex Raksin, review of *Love in the Days of Rage,* p. 4.
Midwest Quarterly, autumn, 1974.
Minnesota Review, July, 1961.
Nation, October 11, 1958.
New Pages, spring-summer, 1985.

New York Times, April 14, 1960; April 15, 1960; April 16, 1960; April 17, 1960; February 6, 1967; February 27, 1967; September 13, 1970.

New York Times Book Review, September 2, 1956; September 7, 1958; April 29, 1962; July 21, 1968; September 8, 1968; September 21, 1980; November 1, 1981; November 6, 1988; November 6, 1994.

Observer (London, England), November 1, 1959; April 9, 1967.

Parnassus, spring-summer, 1974.

Poetry, November, 1958; July, 1964; May, 1966.

Prairie Schooner, fall, 1974; summer, 1978.

Publishers Weekly, September 26, 1994, p. 59; November 27, 1995, p. 67; March 31, 1997, p. 69; September 28, 1998, p. 24.

Punch, April 19, 1967.

San Francisco Chronicle, March 5, 1961.

San Francisco Review of Books, September, 1977; fall, 1988, Patrick Burnson, "Passionate Spring," p. 44.

Saturday Review, October 5, 1957; September 4, 1965.

Sewanee Review, fall, 1974.

Sunday Times (London, England), June 20, 1965.

Times (London, England), October 27, 1968.

Times Literary Supplement, April 27, 1967; November 25, 1988.

Virginia Quarterly Review, autumn, 1969; spring, 1974.

Washington Post Book World, August 2, 1981.

West Coast Review, winter, 1981.

Western American Literature, spring, 1982, p. 79; winter, 1995, p. 372.

Whole Earth, summer, 1999, Lawrence Ferlinghetti, "A Far Rockaway of the Heart," p. 38.

World Literature Today, summer, 1977; spring, 1982, p. 348; autumn, 1994, p. 815; winter, 1998, p. 138.

ONLINE

City Lights Web site, http://www.citylights.com/ (May 3, 2003), "Lawrence Ferlinghetti."

*   *   *

FERLINGHETTI, Lawrence Monsanto
See FERLINGHETTI, Lawrence

*   *   *

FERRÉ, Rosario 1938-

PERSONAL: Born September 28, 1938, in Ponce, Puerto Rico; daughter of Luis A. (an engineer and former governor of Puerto Rico) and Lorenza Ramirez de Arellano de Ferré; married Benigno Trigo (a businessman), 1960 (divorced); married Jorge Aguilar Mora (a writer; marriage ended); married Agustin Costa (an architect); children: Rosario Trigo Costanzo, Benigno Trigo Ferré, Luis Trigo Ferré. *Education:* University of Puerto Rico, M.A.; University of Maryland, Ph.D., 1986. *Religion:* Roman Catholic

ADDRESSES: Agent—Susan Bergholz, 17 West 10th St., New York, NY 10011.

CAREER: Writer. Advisory board member, Americas Literary Initiative series, University of Wisconsin Press, 2003.

AWARDS, HONORS: Critics Choice Award, 1995, and National Book Award nomination, 1996, both for *The House on the Lagoon.*

WRITINGS:

Papeles de Pandora (title means "Pandora's Roles"; stories), Joaquin Mortiz (Mexico City, Mexico), 1976, Vintage (New York, NY), 2000, translation by the author published as *The Youngest Doll,* University of Nebraska Press (Lincoln, NE), 1991.

El Medio pollito: Siete cuentos infantiles (title means "The Half Chicken"; children's stories), Ediciones Huracan (Rio Piedras, Puerto Rico), 1976.

La Muñeca menor/ The Youngest Doll (bilingual edition), illustrations by Antonio Martorell, Ediciones Huracan (Rio Piedras, Puerto Rico) 1980.

Sitio a Eros: Trece ensayos literarios, Joaquin Mortiz (Mexico City, Mexico), 1980, 2nd edition published as *Sitio a Eros: Quince ensayos literarios,* 1986.

Los Cuentos de Juan Bobo (title means "The Tales of Juan Bobo"; children's stories), Ediciones Huracan (Rio Piedras, Puerto Rico) 1981.

La Mona que le pisaron la cola (title means "The Monkey Whose Tail Got Stepped On"; children's stories), Ediciones Huracan (Rio Piedras, Puerto Rico) 1981.

Fábulas de la garza desangrada, Joaquin Mortiz (Mexico City, Mexico), 1982.

Puerto Rican Writer Rosario Ferré Reading from Her Prose and Poetry (sound recording), recorded for the Archive of Hispanic Literature on Tape in the Library of Congress Recording Laboratory, 1982.

La C Lisa Rowe Fraustino, ed., aja de cristal, La Maquina de Escribir (Mexico), 1982.

Maldito amor (title means "Cursed Love"), Joaquin Mortiz (Mexico City, Mexico), 1986, revised and translated by Ferré and published as *Sweet Diamond Dust* (see also below), Ballantine (New York, NY), 1988.

El Acomodor: Una lectura fantástica de Felisberto Hernández, Fondo de Cultura Economica (Mexico), 1986.

Sonatinas, Ediciones Huracan (Rio Piedras, Puerto Rico) 1989.

El Árbol y sus sombras, Fondo de Cultura Economica (Mexico), 1989.

El Coloquio de las perras, Cultural (San Juan, Puerto Rico), 1990, selections translated by the author and published as "On Destiny, Language, and Translation; or, Ophelia Adrift in the C & O Canal," in *The Youngest Doll,* 1991.

El Cucarachita Martina, Ediciones Huracan (Rio Piedras, Puerto Rico), 1990.

Cortázar, Literal (Washington, DC), 1991.

Las Dos Venecias (title means "The Two Venices"), Joaquin Mortiz (Mexico City, Mexico), 1992.

Memorias de Ponce: Autobiografia de Luis A. Ferré, Editorial Norma (Barcelona, Spain), 1992.

La Batalla de las vírgenes, Editorial de la Universidad de Puerto Rico, (San Juan, Puerto Rico), 1993.

Antología personal: 1992-1976, Editorial Cultural, 1994.

The House on the Lagoon, Farrar, Straus (New York, NY), 1995, translated by the author as *La Casa de la laguna,* Vintage (New York, NY), 1997.

Sweet Diamond Dust and Other Stories, Plume (New York, NY), 1996.

El Sombrero magico (title means "The Magical Hat"), Santillana Publishing, 1997.

La Sapita sabia y otros cuentos (title means "The Smart Frog and Other Stories"), Santillana Publishing, 1997.

Pico Rico Mandorico y otros cuentos (title means "Pico Rico Manorico and Other Stories"), Santillana Publishing, 1997.

Eccentric Neighborhoods, Farrar, Straus (New York, NY), 1998, translated by the author as *Vecindarios eccentricos,* Vintage (New York, NY), 1999.

La Extrana muerte del Capitancito Candelario, Plaza & Janes Editores, 1999.

A la sombra de tu nombre (essays), Alfaguara (Mexico), 2001.

Flight of the Swan, Farrar, Straus (New York, NY), 2001, translated by the author as *Vuelo del cisne,* Vintage (New York, NY), 2002.

Contributor to books, including *Contextos: Literarios hispanoamericanos,* edited by Teresa Mindez-Faith, Holt (New York, NY), 1985; *Anthology of Contemporary Latin American Literature, 1960-1984,* Fairleigh Dickinson University Press, 1986; *Reclaiming Medusa: Short Stories by Contemporary Puerto Rican Women,* Spinsters Aunt Lute (San Francisco, CA), 1988; and In-terviews with Latin American Writers, edited by Marie-Lisa Gazarian Gautier, Dalkey Archive Press, 1989. Some of Ferré's writings have also been anthologized in *Ritos de iniciacion: Tres novelas cortas de Hispanoamerica,* a textbook for intermediate and advanced students of college Spanish, by Grinor Rojo, and *Anthology of Women Poets.*

SIDELIGHTS: "Rosario Ferré," wrote *Dictionary of Literary Biography* contributor Carmen S. Rivera, "has become the 'translator' of the reality of Puerto Rican women, opening the doors for the feminist movement on the island. By combining classical mythology with indigenous folktales that usurp the traditional actions of female characters, Ferré has interpreted, translated, and rewritten a more active and satisfying myth of Puerto Rican women." Ferré—the daughter of a former governor of Puerto Rico—writes about politics (she favors Puerto Rican independence), about literature, and about the status of women in modern Puerto Rican society. A former student of Angel Rama and Mario Vargas Llosa, she often utilizes magic realist techniques to communicate her points. "Many critics believe that with the publication of her first book," Rivera continued, "Ferré began the feminist movement in Puerto Rico and became, if not its only voice, one of its most resonant and forceful spokespersons."

Chronologically, Ferré's first work was the short-story collection *Papeles de Pandora.* Its original Spanish-language version was published in Mexico in 1976, but it was not until 1991 that an English-language translation by the author became available. "Defiant magic feminism challenges all our conventional notions of time, place, matter and identity in Rosario Ferré's spectacular new book, *The Youngest Doll,* " declared Patricia Hart in the *Nation. New York Times Book Review* contributor Cathy A. Colman stated that "Ferré . . . writes with an irony that cloaks anger about the oppression and danger inherent in being either a protected upper-class woman or a marginalized working-class woman caught in Puerto Rico's patriarchal society." In the story "Sleeping Beauty," for example, a young woman's desire to become a dancer is railroaded by her family, who wants her to marry an aristocratic young man. The protagonist of "The Poisoned Story" starts out as a Cinderella figure (she marries a sugarcane planter) but ends up playing the role of a wicked stepmother to his daughter. "From beginning to end . . . whether she is conceiving stories, translating them or providing commentary," Hart concluded, "Rosario Ferré shines, and it is high time for English-speaking readers to bask in her light."

Ferré's first work to be translated into English was *Sweet Diamond Dust,* a short novel telling the stories of influential Puerto Rican women in different time periods. "Ferré parodies novels about the land, a popular genre during the first half of the [twentieth] century, as she sets out to rewrite Puerto Rican history from a woman's perspective," Rivera declared. "She describes how the island (*isla* is a female noun in Spanish) is oppressed by the government and American businesses—both of which are rendered as masculine in Spanish—while drawing parallels to the situation of women." Reviewer Alan Cheuse, writing in the *Chicago Tribune,* called Ferré "one of the most engaging young Latin American fiction writers at work today," and added, "Ferré shows off her linguistic talent as well as her inventiveness by giving us her own English version of the book."

The House on the Lagoon, Ferré's first work composed in English, was nominated for the National Book Award in 1996. "Most of this novel," declared a *Publishers Weekly* reviewer, "is comprised of . . . semi-fictionalized family history." The book tells of a Puerto Rican couple, Quintin Mendizabal and Isabel Monfort, who come into conflict over politics—she favors independence for the island, he favors close ties with the United States—their attitudes—he believes in traditional women's roles, she favors feminism—and the history she is writing, which includes stories about her husband's family. The family's black servant Petra Aviles also plays a role in the family dynamic. "The novel's conclusion affirms in the strongest terms the necessity of interracial alliances, both sexual and familial, to the future of a Puerto Rican community," wrote Judith Grossman in the *Women's Review of Books.* "Ferré dramatizes the issue of who gets to write history," stated a *Publishers Weekly* contributor, "gracefully incorporating it into a compelling panorama of Puerto Rican experience that is rich in history, drama and memorable characters." "*The House on the Lagoon,*" Grossman concluded, "gives us a performance of great accomplishment and wit, and the sense of a world held in measured but deeply affectionate memory."

In *Flight of the Swan,* a novel that melds history and fiction, Ferré tells the story of her version of ballet legend Anna Pavlova, who due to historical upheavals in Russia, finds herself stranded with her dance troupe in Puerto Rico in 1917. She explores the themes of love and betrayal, politics, sex and art, through the voyeuristic narrator Masha, a member of Madame Pavlova's corps de ballet and her slavishly devoted servant. In the end Masha comes to see that, in spite of her mistress's foibles, Pavlova is ready to sacrifice everything for her art, which in turn forces Masha to question her own choices. Praising the novel as "fascinating," *Americas* contributor Barbara Mujica added that *Flight of the*

Swan is "an entertaining and thought-provoking book that raises serious questions about class, race, sex, art, and politics. Both Madame and Masha are freely drawn characters whose conflicting perspectives shed light on both Puerto Rican politics during the early decades of the twentieth century and on the hierarchical world of Russian ballet."

Diana Postlethwaite wrote in the *New York Times* that while "the premise of Masha as earthy observer describing the misadventures of an ethereal drama queen is a promising one," "her voice is never consistently sustained." In addition, Postlethwaite noted, Ferré, whose command of English often forces her to rely on prefabricated prose, further complicates her story by telling it in a Russian voice. *Publishers Weekly* contributor Jeff Zaleski concurred that Ferré's writing in her second language "may account for the pedestrian quality of this novel," and that "the imaginatively conceived but strangely lackluster story" is overwhelmed by "an excess of historical details and long monologues." On the other hand, *Washington Post* contributor Laura Jacobs maintained that "Ferré writes beautifully when she is direct . . . but strains language in heated moments." She argued that "there is a shorter, stronger book inside *Flight of the Swan,* if only Ferré had put the manuscript through a final, fat-burning fast."

BIOGRAPHICAL AND CRITICAL SOURCES:

BOOKS

Dictionary of Literary Biography, Volume 145: *Modern Latin-American Fiction Writers,* Thomson Gale (Detroit, MI), 1994.
Latina Self-Portraits: Interviews with Contemporary Women Writers, University of New Mexico Press (Albuquerque, NM), 2000.
Sobre castas y puentes: Conversaciones con Elena Poniatowska, Rosario Ferré y Diamela Eltit, Editorial Cuarto Propio (Santiago, Chile), 2000.

PERIODICALS

Americas, January-February, 2002, Barbara Mujica, review of *Flight of the Swan,* p. 60.
Book, July, 2001, Susan Tekulve, review of *Flight of the Swan,* p. 76.
Chicago Tribune, January 13, 1989.

Critique, summer, 2000, Ronald D. Morrison, "Remembering and Recovering Goblin Market in Rosario Ferré's 'Pico Rico, Mandorico,'" p. 365.

Library Journal, August, 1995, p. 115; June 1, 2001, Ed Morales, review of *A la sombra de tu nombre,* p. 37.

Nation, May 6, 1991, pp. 597-598.

New York Times Book Review, March 24, 1991, p. 24; July 29, 2001, Diana Postlethwaite, review of *Flight of the Swan,* p. 21.

Progressive, August, 1998, Lisa Chipongian, review of *Eccentric Neighborhoods,* p. 43.

Publishers Weekly, July 3, 1995, review of *The House on the Lagoon,* p. 47; November 24, 1997, review of *Eccentric Neighborhoods,* p. 51; May 7, 2001, Jeff Zaleski, review of *Flight of the Swan,* p. 219.

Review of Contemporary Fiction, spring, 1996, p. 168.

Studies in Short Fiction, spring, 1995, Augustus Puelo, "The Intersection of Race, Sex, Gender, and Class in a Short Story of Rosario Ferré," p. 227.

Washington Post, July 1, 2001, Laura Jacobs, review of *Flight of the Swan,* p. T09.

Woman's Review of Books, February, 1996, Judith Grossman, review of *The House on the Lagoon,* p. 5.

World Literature Today, summer, 1996, Ilan Stavans, review of *The House on the Lagoon,* p. 690; spring, 2002, Catherine E. Wall, review of *Flight of the Swan,* p. 151.

*   *   *

FIELDING, Helen 1958-

PERSONAL: Born February 19, 1958, in England; daughter of a mill manager and a homemaker; companion of Kevin Curran (a television writer and producer); children: one son. *Education:* Oxford University, 1979.

ADDRESSES: Agent—c/o Author Mail, Penguin Putnam, 375 Hudson St., New York, NY 10014.

CAREER: BBC-TV, England, producer, 1979-89; freelance writer, c. 1989—; columnist for the London *Independent,* 1995–97, 2005—.

AWARDS, HONORS: British Book Award, 1997, for *Bridget Jones's Diary.*

WRITINGS:

(With Simon Bell and Richard Curtis) *Who's Had Who, in Association with Berk's Rogerage: An Historical Rogister Containing Official Lay Lines of History from the Beginning of Time to the Present Day,* Faber & Faber (Boston, MA), 1987, reissued as *Who's Had Who: An Historical Rogister Containing Official Lay Lines of History from the Beginning of Time to the Present Day,* Warner Books (New York, NY), 1990.

Cause Celeb (novel), Picador (London, England), 1994, Viking (New York, NY), 2001.

Bridget Jones's Diary (novel), Picador (London, England), 1996, Viking (New York, NY), 1998.

Bridget Jones: The Edge of Reason, Viking (New York, NY), 2000.

Bridget Jones's Guide to Life, Penguin (New York, NY), 2001.

Olivia Joules and the Overactive Imagination, Picador (London, England), 2003, Viking (New York, NY), 2004.

Contributor to the *Independent* (London, England) and *Newsweek.* Coauthor of screenplays for *Bridget Jones's Diary* and *Bridget Jones: The Edge of Reason.*

ADAPTATIONS: A film version of *Bridget Jones's Diary* was released in 2001 by Miramax. *Bridget Jones: The Edge of Reason* was released in 2004 by Universal Pictures and Mirimax.

SIDELIGHTS: Helen Fielding achieved international fame with her humorous novel *Bridget Jones's Diary,* which sold more than four million copies worldwide, and was published in thirty countries. Fielding had already established herself as a producer for the British Broadcasting Corporation; in 1994, she had published her first novel, *Cause Celeb.* Its success led to an offer from the London *Independent* for Fielding to do a column in the persona of a character. The author responded by creating the beloved Bridget Jones, who discussed the often humorous trials of a single British woman over thirty in the column. Bridget and the column proved so popular that Fielding turned her adventures into a novel, *Bridget Jones's Diary,* which became a best-seller in 1996 in the author's native country, and then, two years later, in the United States. *Bridget Jones's Diary* also garnered Fielding the prestigious British Book Award, was made into a highly successful motion picture, and generated two sequels, *Bridget Jones: The Edge of Reason* and *Bridget Jones's Guide to Life.*

Even before *Cause Celeb,* Fielding collaborated with Simon Bell and Richard Curtis on the 1987 volume, *Who's Had Who, in Association with Berk's Rogerage:*

An Historical Rogister Containing Official Lay Lines of History from the Beginning of Time to the Present Day. A spoof on the famous volume that outlines the ancestry of all of Great Britain's nobility, the "rogerage" and "rogister" of the subtitles play on the British slang verb "to roger," which means to have sex. One of Fielding's partners in this literary effort, Richard Curtis, was a classmate of hers at Oxford University, and went on to write the screenplay for the popular British film *Four Weddings and a Funeral*.

Cause Celeb features the adventures of Rosie Richardson, an administrator with an international food charity who attempts to escape the consequences of a bad love affair by traveling to Africa to aid famine relief. The book uses flashbacks to show readers Rosie's difficulties with television presenter Oliver Marchant, but in the novel's present timelines, she finds herself attracted to a young doctor also employed by her relief agency. The pair investigate the rumored possibility of a locust plague that threatens to send the region they explore into starvation; when their agency ignores the evidence, they return to England to enlist the aid of various celebrities, including Marchant, to publicize the coming disaster.

Reviewers of *Cause Celeb* frequently commented on Fielding's mingling humor with the serious subject of African famine relief. Nicola Walker in the *Times Literary Supplement* maintained that the novel was not completely successful. "*Cause Celeb* is neatly plotted and its attack on the iniquities of the Western media machine is topical and legitimate," Walker conceded. "However, Fielding is not a subtle or imaginative satirist, and the result is an uneasy combination of celebrity-bashing and African misery." In contrast, Kate Kellaway noted in the *Observer* that "*Cause Celeb* is amazingly poised. The plot is about as challenging as walking to Africa in stilettos but is managed without a wobble. What makes it such a pleasure to read," Kellaway continued, "is its variety of tone: flip, flirtatious, serious, mocking and moving." Another *Observer* reviewer praised the "bitter-sweet power" of Fielding's "comedy of manners."

It was Fielding's second novel that made her a literary celebrity. For *Bridget Jones's Diary*, the author knew that she could not just take the columns and put them into book form. According to Sarah Van Boven in *Newsweek*, Fielding based "the story on *Pride and Prejudice*" by Jane Austen. She quipped to Van Boven: "There's several hundred years of market testing on that plot." Hence the last name of the man that Bridget fi-

nally ends up with is Darcy. Bridget takes note of the irony before taking a liking to him: "It struck me as pretty ridiculous to be called Mr. Darcy and to stand on your own looking snooty at a party. It's like being called Heathcliff and insisting on spending the entire evening in the garden, shouting 'Cathy!' and banging your head against a tree." Before Bridget and Darcy come together, however, many pages are filled with Bridget's laments about bad dates, inappropriate relationships in the workplace, her parents' pressure on her to find a husband, and family friends who make ticking noises at her to suggest the running out of her biological clock. Bridget also struggles with her weight, or her perceptions of it; Fielding confided to Alexandra Jacobs in *Entertainment Weekly* that "Bridget's height is kept deliberately vague, like her age, so people can fill in the rest as they choose to imagine and identify with their chosen level of paranoia." The heroine fights daily to quit drinking and smoking, and records the amount of alcohol consumed and the number of cigarettes she smoked in each day's diary entry along with her caloric intake.

Bridget Jones's Diary was met with predominantly favorable response, though some feminist critics lambasted the novel. Alex Kuczynski in the *New York Times* explained that she knew that "*Bridget Jones* is satire, a sassy spoof of urban manners. But Bridget is such a sorry spectacle, wallowing in her man-crazed helplessness, that her foolishness cannot be excused." Van Boven, however, asserted that "Bridget's post-feminist sorrows could be tedious in the hands of a less charming writer—they include such trivialities as the inability to find a pair of tights in her bureau without holes or bits of tissue stuck all over them." But, the critic countered, "Fielding has managed to create an unforgettably droll character." Similarly, Shane Watson hailed Bridget in *Harper's Bazaar* as "a wonderfully quirky comic creation," and elaborated: "To come up with a character who is loveable, ingenuous and a crack social commentator called for a mixture of kooky wit and razor-sharp professionalism." Schulman, in another review for the *Times Literary Supplement,* declared: "Quotation fails this novel. Its humour is not remotely aphoristic; and no quotation can convey the quality that constitutes Bridget's claim to be as durable a comic figure as Nigel Molesworth or the Provincial Lady." She went on to conclude that: "*Bridget Jones's Diary* rings with the unmistakable tone of something that is true to the marrow; it defines what it describes. I know for certain that if I were a young, single, urban woman, I would finish this book crying, 'Bridget Jones, c'est moi.'"

The success of *Bridget Jones's Diary* led to a sequel: *Bridget Jones: The Edge of Reason*. The fast-paced plot includes Bridget's disastrous interview with actor Colin Firth, her apparent happiness with Mr. Darcy, notes on her mother's trip to Africa, and even her imprisonment in a jail in Thailand. "Fans will adore this," advised Francine Fialkoff in *Library Journal,* who remarked that *The Edge of Reason* "actually has more of a plot than the original." Fialkoff found that "sidesplitting humor is still present" in Fielding's writing, and noted that if Jones seems "dumber and ditzier" here than in the original book, "it's not necessarily a drawback," as these qualities are part of Bridget's charm. Other reviewers found that another volume of Bridget was too much, especially since the character seemed to have learned nothing from any of her experiences. For example, Elizabeth Gleick wrote in *Time,* "Hapless can be endearing. But hapless with no sign of a learning curve, in a sequel that has none of the novelty of the original yet is much longer now that will try the patience of even a Bridget fan." The reviewer observed that Bridget seemed "unable to learn from her mistakes, move forward or pull herself together the tiniest bit," and concluded: "The fact that the reader is so much smarter and more observant than Bridget is, this time round, irritating rather than suspenseful." A reviewer for *Publishers Weekly* allowed that after a time, "Bridget's propensity to misunderstand and bungle everything becomes predictable," but still had praise for the book. The heroine's ups and downs with her Mr. Darcy, her attempts to deal with the impossible assignments handed out by her boss, and her trials in dealing with a carpenter who ruins her apartment are humorous, and Bridget's disastrous vacation in Thailand is "a genuinely suspenseful and hilarious episode." Fielding further capitalized on the popularity of her heroine by publishing a short parody of a self-help book, titled *Bridget Jones's Guide to Life.*

In her next book, Fielding created a heroine who is superficially worlds away from Bridget Jones. *Olivia Joules and the Overactive Imagination* is a fast-paced thriller featuring a young, female spy who must confront terrorists, bombs, and assorted other life-threatening scenarios. Reviewing the book for *Asia Africa Intelligence Wire,* Julian Satterthwaite called it "shamelessly of-the-minute," adding: "The novel aims to satisfy the airport blockbuster crowd with a litany of brand names and far-flung locations." While the title character may seem a far cry from Bridget Jones, however, Satterthwaite notes that like Fielding's earlier creation, Joules also struggles with male-female relationships and phones her girlfriends when things go wrong. The novel is really "firmly in Fielding territory," according to Satterthwaite; "indeed, it reads like the fantasies Bridget Jones might have had while not occupied

pursuing Mr. Darcy. Get the guy and save the world, all while wearing the right accessories: This is Bridget Jones empowered." Amy Jenkins, reviewing the book for the London *Observer,* also noted that while Olivia is trim, effective, and superficially confident, "Bridget keeps bubbling back up to the surface, primarily because Fielding cannot resist those klutzy BJ moments." Jenkins wrote, however, that "What was lovable in Bridget is mildly irritating in Olivia." Yet the reviewer concluded that "there is plenty of lively action and amusement to sweep you along, to say nothing of a marvellously cosy tone that is very addictive, even if it doesn't supply much dramatic tension."

Discussing her work with John Walsh in an interview for the London *Independent,* Fielding commented: "I'm interested in trying different kinds of writing. But I prefer being funny as a way of looking at things, because it's more enjoyable to read. I don't like books that are trying to impress rather than entertain. I like books that make you want to turn the page and see what happens."

BIOGRAPHICAL AND CRITICAL SOURCES:

BOOKS

Dictionary of Literary Biography, Volume 231: *British Novelists since 1960, Fourth Series,* Thomson Gale (Detroit, MI), 2000.
Newsmakers 2000, Issue 4, Thomson Gale (Detroit, MI), 2000.

PERIODICALS

Asia Africa Intelligence Wire, November 22, 2003, Boniface Linley, "From the Diary to the Dire"; December 14, 2003, Julian Satterthwaite, review of *Olivia Joules and the Overactive Imagination.*
Book, January, 2001, Mimi O'Connor, review of *Cause Celeb,* p. 70.
Booklist, December 1, 2000, Kristine Huntley, review of *Cause Celeb,* p. 675; July, 2000, Mary McCay, review of *Bridget Jones: The Edge of Reason,* p. 2054.
Daily Telegraph, June 6, 1998; April 13, 2000.
Dallas Morning News, April 16, 2000, p. 9J.
Entertainment Weekly, June 19, 1998, p. 68; July 31, 1998, p. 14; March 3, 2000, Lisa Schwarzbaum, review of *Bridget Jones: The Edge of Reason,* p. 65.
Harper's Bazaar, July, 1998, p. 62.

Independent (London, England), November 10, 2003, John Walsh, "From Singletons to Spies," p. 2.

Library Journal, December, 1999, Catherine Swenson, review of *Bridget Jones's Diary,* p. 205; February 1, 2000, Francine Fialkoff, review of *Bridget Jones: The Edge of Reason,* p. 116; June 15, 2000, Catherine Swenson, review of *Bridget Jones: The Edge of Reason* (audio version), p. 136; December, 2000, Francine Fialkoff, review of *Cause Celeb,* p. 187; September 15, 2001, Catherine Swenson, review of *Cause Celeb,* p. 127.

New Republic, September 7, 1998, p. 36.

New Statesman, July 26, 1999, review of *Bridget Jones's Diary,* p. 51; November 24, 2003, Zoe Williams, "Killer Joules," p. 54.

Newsweek, May 4, 1998, p. 82; June 29, 1998, pp. 64, 66; March 6, 2000, p. 69.

Newsweek International, November 29, 1999, p. 101.

New York, April 23, 2001, Peter Rainer, review of *Bridget Jones's Diary* (motion picture), p. 138.

New Yorker, April 16, 2001, Anthony Lane, review of *Bridget Jones's Diary* (motion picture), p. 90.

New York Times, June 14, 1998, section 9, p. 1; February 27, 2000.

New York Times Book Review, February 27, 2000, Anita Gates, review of *Bridget Jones: The Edge of Reason,* p. 12; February 25, 2001, Maggie Galehouse, review of *Cause Celeb,* p. 20.

New York Times Magazine, February 20, 2000, Susan Dominus, interview with Helen Fielding, p. 18.

Observer, July 17, 1994, p. 17; July 24, 1994, p. 14; November 9, 2003, Amy Jenkins, review of *Olivia Joules and the Overactive Imagination,* p. 15.

People, June 22, 1998, p. 199.

Publishers Weekly, January 24, 2000, review of *Bridget Jones: The Edge of Reason,* p. 293; April 3, 2000, review of *Bridget Jones: The Edge of Reason,* p. 36; December 11, 2000, review of *Cause Celeb,* p. 61; May 13, 2000, p. 22.

Rocky Mountain News, July 12, 1998, p. 1E.

Rolling Stone, April 26, 2001, Peter Travers, review of *Bridget Jones's Diary* (motion picture), p. 66.

Time, March 13, 2000, Elizabeth Gleick, review of *Bridget Jones: The Edge of Reason,* p. 88.

Time Canada, March 27, 2000, review of *Bridget Jones: The Edge of Reason,* p. 52A.

Time International, April 16, 2001, Richard Corliss, review of *Bridget Jones's Diary* (motion picture), p. 68.

Times Literary Supplement, August 19, 1994, p. 20; November 1, 1996, p. 26.

USA Today, May 28, 1998, p. 5D.

Vogue, February, 2001, Hilton Als, review of *Cause Celeb,* p. 196.

ONLINE

Internet Movie Database, http://www.imdb.com/ (November 7, 2003).

*   *   *

FITCH, John, IV
   See CORMIER, Robert

*   *   *

FITZGERALD, Penelope 1916-2000

PERSONAL: Born December 17, 1916, in Lincoln, England; died of complications from a stroke, April 28, 2000, in Highgate, London, England; daughter of Edmund Valpy (editor of *Punch*), and Christina (Hicks) Knox; married Desmond Fitzgerald, August 15, 1953 (died, 1976); children: Edmund Valpy, Maria. *Education:* Somerville College, Oxford (first-class honors), 1939. *Religion:* Christian.

CAREER: Writer. Broadcasting House (British Broadcasting Corporation), London, England, recorded program assistant, 1939-53; also worked in a bookstore and as a teacher affiliated with Westminster Tutors, London.

AWARDS, HONORS: Booker Prize shortlist for fiction, 1978, for *The Bookshop;* Booker Prize for fiction, 1979, for *Offshore;* Heywood Hill Literary Prize for lifetime achievement in literature, 1996; National Book Critics Circle Prize, 1998, for *Blue Flower.*

WRITINGS:

NOVELS

The Golden Child, Scribner (New York, NY), 1977.

The Bookshop, Duckworth (London, England), 1978, Houghton Mifflin (Boston, MA), 1997.

Offshore, Collins (London, England), 1979, Holt (New York, NY), 1987.

Human Voices, Collins (London, England), 1980, Houghton Mifflin (Boston, MA), 1999.

At Freddie's, Collins (London, England), 1982, Godine (Boston, MA), 1985.

Innocence, Holt (New York, NY), 1986, Houghton Mifflin (Boston, MA), 1998.

The Beginning of Spring, Collins (London, England), 1988, Holt (New York, NY), 1989.

The Gate of Angels, Collins (London, England), 1990, Doubleday (Garden City, NY), 1992.

The Blue Flower, Flamingo (London, England), 1996, Houghton Mifflin (Boston, MA), 1997.

BIOGRAPHIES

Edward Burne-Jones, M. Joseph (London, England), 1975, Sutton (Stroud, Gloucestershire, England), 1998.

The Knox Brothers, Macmillan (London, England), 1977, published as *The Knox Brothers: Edmund (Evoe), 1881-1971, Dillwyn, 1883-1943, Wilfred, 1886-1950, Ronald, 1888-1957,* Coward, McCann & Geoghegan (New York, NY), 1977.

Charlotte Mew and Her Friends, Collins (London, England), 1984, published as *Charlotte Mew and Her Friends: With a Selection of Her Poems,* Addison-Wesley (Reading, MA), 1988.

OTHER

Means of Escape (short stories), Houghton Mifflin (Boston, MA), 2000.

The Afterlife, edited by Terrence Dooley, Christopher Carduff, and Mandy Kirkby, Houghton Mifflin (Boston, MA), 2000.

Contributor to *Modern Women's Short Stories,* Penguin (New York, NY), 1998. A collection of Penelope Fitzgerald's papers are held at the Harry Ransom Humanities Research Center at the University of Texas at Austin.

ADAPTATIONS: The Gate of Angels has been adapted as an audiobook.

SIDELIGHTS: Penelope Fitzgerald published her first novel when she was fifty-nine years old. Some two decades and a Booker Prize later, she had established a reputation as an ironic, spare, and richly comic author. Even when the settings for her novels range as far afield as Florence, pre-revolutionary Moscow, and Germany in the 1790s, she is praised for her sense of detail and her clear observations of human nature. In the *Spectator,* Anita Brookner characterized Fitzgerald as

"one of the mildest and most English of writers," adding: "Mild, yes, but there is authority behind those neat, discursive and unresolved stories of hers. . . . She is so unostentatious a writer that she needs to be read several times. What is impressive is the calm confidence behind the apparent simplicity of utterance." *Los Angeles Times Book Review* contributor Richard Eder noted that Fitzgerald's writing is "so precise and lilting that it can make you shiver . . . an elegy that nods at what passes without lamentation or indifference."

Some of Fitzgerald's early novels are loosely based upon her own work experiences. Born of a "writing family," she was educated at Oxford and was employed by the British Broadcasting Corporation during World War II. After her marriage in 1953, she worked as a clerk in a bookstore in rural East Suffolk; later she and her family lived on a barge on the Thames. These episodes in her life helped Fitzgerald to present, in her fiction, "a small, specialist world which she opens for the reader's inspection," to quote *Dictionary of Literary Biography* contributor Catherine Wells Cole. In *The Bookshop,* for instance, a courageous entrepreneur named Florence Green defies the stuffy prejudices of her town, Hardborough, by stocking Vladimir Nabokov's novel *Lolita. The Bookshop* was described by Valentine Cunningham in the *Times Literary Supplement* as "on any reckoning a marvelously piercing fiction. . . . There are the small circumstances that give rise naturally to a Hardy-like gothic, complete with a rapping poltergeist, and to a fiction where character inevitably comes to 'characters.' And Penelope Fitzgerald's resources of odd people are impressively rich."

Offshore, published in 1979 in England, presents a community of eccentric characters living in barges (much as the author did at one time) on Battersea Reach on the Thames River. As the tide ebbs and flows, so do the lives in the unconventional community, in both comic and tragic ways. *Offshore* won the Booker Prize in 1979 for Fitzgerald, who, at sixty-three, was still something of a novice writer. In *Books and Bookmen,* reviewer Mollie Hardwick described the work as "a delicate water-colour of a novel . . . a small, charming, Whistler etching." Similar praises greeted *Human Voices,* Fitzgerald's novelistic take on wartime work at Broadcasting House in London. There, one character wishes for a quick peace because he might be called upon to provide more typewriters than he has available; another one muses about the challenge of recording the sounds of tanks rolling across a beach. In *Encounter,* correspondent Penelope Lively found the novel "a clever fictional rendering of the way in which a random selection of people, flung together for impersonal reasons, will set up a pattern of relationships and reactions . . . told in a voice that is both idiosyncratic and memorable."

Beginning in 1986 with the publication of *Innocence,* Fitzgerald began to range farther afield for her stories. Set in Florence, Italy, during the postwar era, *Innocence* follows the fortunes of a patrician family in decline. In a *Times Literary Supplement* review of the work, Anne Duchene wrote of Fitzgerald: "Her writing, as ever, has a natural authority, is very funny, warm, and gently ironic, and full of tenderness towards human beings and their bravery in living." *The Beginning of Spring* presents an off-beat comedy of manners set in the household of a British expatriate in 1913 Moscow. As the thoughtful and upright Frank Reid faces the sudden departure of his wife—leaving him with three young children—he receives dubious assistance from some of his friends, both English and Russian. To quote *New York Times Book Review* correspondent Robert Plunket, with *The Beginning of Spring* Fitzgerald has become "that refreshing rarity, a writer who is very modern but not the least bit hip. Ms. Fitzgerald looks into the past, both human and literary, and finds all sorts of things that are surprisingly up to date. Yet as *The Beginning of Spring* reaches its triumphant conclusion, you realize that its greatest virtue is perhaps the most old-fashioned of all. It is a lovely novel."

Fitzgerald produced the well-received novels *The Gate of Angels* and *The Blue Flower* (for which she was the surprise recipient of the U.S. National Book Critics Circle Prize) in the 1990s. *The Gate of Angels,* published in the United States in 1992, concerns a fictitious Cambridge college for physicists in Edwardian England, and describes how the cloistered academy changes after one of its junior fellows, Fred Fairly, suffers a bicycle accident. "This funny, touching, wise novel manages, despite its brevity, to seem leisurely," remarked Nina King in the *New York Times Book Review.* "It is vibrant with wonderful minor characters, ablaze with ideas." *Listener* reviewer Kate Kellaway noted that, in *The Gate of Angels,* Fitzgerald "unostentatiously fills her story with quietly original observations so that you are constantly recognising and discovering through her eyes." John Bayley in the *New York Review of Books* observed that "Penelope Fitzgerald is not only an artist of a high order but one of immense originality, wholly her own woman. She composes with an innocent certainty which avoids any suggestion that she might have a feminist moral in mind, or a dig against science, or a Christian apologetic. The translucent little tale keeps quite clear of such matters, and yet it is certainly about goodness, and . . . successful at giving us the experience and conviction of it."

In *The Blue Flower,* according to Adam Begley of *People:* "Penelope Fitzgerald squeezes tragedy, history and philosophy into a short, beautifully written, desperately sad novel." Set in the eighteenth century, the novel is based on a true story: the spontaneous and overwhelming infatuation of twenty-two-year-old poet prodigy Friedrich von Hardenberg (later to become renowned under the pen name Novalis) with a young girl named Sophie whom he sees standing by a window. Novalis is a penniless aristocrat who nevertheless has attended the best universities. "Sophie," as described by Begley, "is an empty-headed twelve-year-old whose best feature is a guileless laugh." Fitzgerald chronicles their tragic three-year courtship, contrasting Novalis's aristocratic background with Sophie's thoroughly middle-class one. At the same time she brings to life the era in which they lived. A *Publishers Weekly* reviewer commented: "There's scads of research here, into daily life in Enlightenment-era Saxony, German reactions to the French Revolution and Napoleon, early-nineteenth-century German philosophy. . . . But history aside, this is a smart novel. Fitzgerald . . . witty and poignant . . . has created an alternately biting and touching exploration of the nature of Romanticism—capital 'R' and small."

The Means of Escape, published just after Fitzgerald's death in 2000, is a collection of eight short-short stories set in many places and times—Tasmania, England, France, Turkey and from the present back to the seventeenth century. In the *Spectator,* Philip Hennsher argued of Fitzgerald's writing in general and the title story in particular, "The interest in farce is constant; one of her best short stories, 'The Means of Escape,' is revealed, only at the very end, to be a farce, as well as, as the reader had always suspected, a crime story, a miniature psychological thriller." He added that she draws the farce into reality by describing her characters with minute realism. Additionally, *World and I* commentator Maude McDaniel noted that Fitzgerald "refuses to take sides herself" with her characters in *The Means of Escape.* "In these stories, she seems curiously detached from her own creatures, leaving readers to make of things what they will—a surrender of authority that has always annoyed me with other writers. Somehow it seems right with these offerings, which are less inclined to heavy preaching than individual nuancing," and, as McDaniel continued, often turning the reader's expectations on their head. "The reader cannot be sure of anything in ['The Red-Haired Girl']—except that in some way, lives have been touched and consequences changed." McDaniel quoted Fitzgerald in an interview: "I have remained true to my deepest convictions. I mean the courage of those who are born to be defeated, the weaknesses of the strong, and the tragedy of misunderstandings and lost opportunities, which I have done my best to treat as comedy—for otherwise how can we manage to bear it?"

In addition to her many novels, Fitzgerald published several biographies, including one of Pre-Raphaelite painter Edward Coley Burne-Jones, and one titled *The Knox Brothers,* which recounts the lives of her father and his brothers, each of whom contributed to British society in a special—and individual—way. Her 1984 biography *Charlotte Mew and Her Friends* examines the life and work of a British poet that Fitzgerald feels contemporary critics have for the most part overlooked. Once praised by novelist Thomas Hardy as "far and away the best living woman poet," Charlotte Mew (1869-1928) did not lead a happy life. Throughout her childhood her family's fortunes descended increasingly into poverty. She saw three of her brothers die before the age of five, and another brother and sister institutionalized for schizophrenia. Only her younger sister Anne, a painter of decorative screens, accompanied her into adulthood. In addition, Mew was a lesbian with the unfortunate habit of forming attachments to women who were not, attachments that invariably remained unfulfilled. Mew began writing short stories at an early age and soon became a regular contributor to *Yellow Book,* one of the popular periodicals of the day. Her fiction is consciously imitative of other writers of the era, such as Henry James, and has been dismissed by most critics as inferior work. In her poetry, however, Mew found her own voice, a distinct and original one of considerable power. April Bernard of the *New Republic* stated, "The poems are masterpieces of the lyric macabre, throat-catching, heart-stopping effulgences of rage and despair and love. . . . Mew's work is really only like itself, busting drunkenly out of whatever scheme it seems the poem has set, into long flailing lines and unsuspected rhymes." In her forties, Mew saw her work recognized and praised by writers who congregated around London's influential Poetry Bookshop. Her readings at the Poetry Bookshop were considered mesmerizing and the shop's owners published her first collection in 1916. The poverty Mew had experienced throughout her life was relieved when she received both a government artist's pension and a small inheritance from an uncle. However, after the death of her mother and sister, both of whom she'd lived with all her life, Mew's grief led to her confinement in a nursing home where she committed suicide. Phoebe-Lou Adams, reviewing *Charlotte Mew and Her Friends* for the *Atlantic,* felt that "Ms. Fitzgerald reconstructs her Mew's sad story with grace and intelligence, while the selection of poems the American edition appended to the biography

makes it clear that Mew at her best was, if not a great poet, decidedly a good one." Bernard noted, "It is greatly to Penelope Fitzgerald's credit that she has not turned this biography into one of those ghoulish mystery stories reserved for suicides, wherein the entire life is cast retrospectively in the shadow of the subject's death."

In an essay for the *Contemporary Authors Autobiography Series,* Fitzgerald wrote of herself: "Biographies and novels are the forms which I feel I can just about manage. They are the outcome of intense curiosity about other people and about oneself." That "intense curiosity" has produced a body of work that casts an eye on such intangibles as personal relationships, social institutions, history, and the interactions between them. "On a superficial reading Fitzgerald's novels may appear slight," concluded Catherine Wells Cole, "but their real strength lies in what they omit, in what has been pared away. Their skill and grace is not simply displayed technical achievement, but derives instead from Fitzgerald's absolute concern, often conveyed through humor and comedy, for the moral values of the tradition she follows so precisely."

Fitzgerald once told *CA:* "I've begun to write at rather a late stage in life because I love books and everything to do with them. I believe that people should write biographies only about people they love, or understand, or both. Novels, on the other hand, are often better if they're about people the writer doesn't like very much."

BIOGRAPHICAL AND CRITICAL SOURCES:

BOOKS

Contemporary Authors Autobiography Series, Volume 10, Thomson Gale (Detroit, MI), 1989, pp. 101-109.

Contemporary Literary Criticism, Thomson Gale (Detroit, MI), Volume 19, 1981, pp. 172-175; Volume 51, 1989, pp. 123-127; Volume 61, 1989, pp. 114-124.

Dictionary of Literary Biography, Volume 14: *British Novelists since 1960,* Thomson Gale (Detroit, MI), 1983, pp. 302-308.

PERIODICALS

America, November 11, 2000, p. 22.
Atlanta Journal-Constitution, March 26, 1998, p. E2.

Atlantic, August, 1988, p. 80.

Austin American-Statesman, June 1, 1997, p. D6; November 12, 2000, p. L6.

Australian (Sydney, New South Wales, Australia), September 13, 2000, p. B20.

Birmingham Post (Birmingham, England), October 10, 1998, p. 37.

Booklist, September 1, 1997, p. 57; October 1, 2000, p. 321; November 15, 2003, Donna Seaman, review of *The Afterlife,* p. 563.

Books and Bookmen, December 1979, pp. 16-17.

Christian Science Monitor, June 26, 1997, p. B1; May 6, 1999, p. 20.

Commonweal, June 19, 1998, p. 27; September 10, 1999, p. 32; June 16, 2000, p. 20; November 3, 2000, p. 32.

Courier-Mail (Brisbane, Australia), February 24, 1996, p. 007.

Dickens Studies Annual: Essays on Victorian Fiction, 1982, p. 143.

Encounter, January 1981, pp. 53-59.

Essays in Arts and Sciences, October 1997, p. 1.

Explicator, summer, 2001, p. 204.

Financial Times, October 7, 2000, p. 4.

Guardian (London, England), March 27, 1998, p. 21; December 16, 2000, p. 10; December 21, 2002, p. 31.

Harper's, June 1999, p. 76.

Herald (Glasgow, Scotland), November 4, 2000, p. 20.

Independent (London, England), January 26, 2002.

Independent on Sunday (London, England), September 1, 1996, p. 37; October 1, 2000, p. 73; January 26, 2002, p. 11.

International Herald Tribune, March 26, 1998, p. 20.

Journal of the William Morris Society, autumn, 1998, p. 25.

Kirkus Reviews, October 1, 2003, Donna Seaman, review of *The Afterlife,* p. 1218.

Knight Ridder/Tribune News Service, November 29, 2000, p. K5334; January 3, 2001, p. K3072.

Library Journal, September 1, 1997, p. 217; May 1, 1998, p. 144; May 1, 1999, p. 109; October 15, 2000, p. 107.

Listener, August 23, 1990, p. 24.

London Review of Books, October 13, 1988, pp. 20-21; October 5, 1995, p. 7; May 23, 2002, p. 17.

Los Angeles Times Book Review, April 23, 1989, p. 3; January 12, 1992, pp. 3, 7; April 13, 1997, p. 5; December 24, 1997, p. 11; October 15, 2000, p. 11.

New Criterion, March 1992, p. 33.

New Republic, August 22, 1988, p. 36; August 2, 1999, p. 39.

New Statesman, October 3, 1980, p. 24; November 6, 2000, p. 52.

New Statesman and Society, October 6, 1995, p. 38; January 28, 2002, p. 54.

New Yorker, February 7, 2000, p. 80.

New York Review of Books, April 9, 1992, p. 13; October 5, 1995, p. 7; July 17, 1997, p. 4; June 10, 1999, p. 28.

New York Times, September 8, 1985, p. 24; April 28, 1987, p. C17; March 26, 1998, p. B11; May 5, 1999, p. E9; August 31, 2000, p. E8.

New York Times Book Review, April 1, 1979, p. 21; June 29, 1980, p. 3; September 8, 1985, p. 24; May 10, 1987, p. 20; September 13, 1987, p. 51; August 7, 1988, p. 15; May 7, 1989, p. 15; March 1, 1992, pp. 7, 9; April 13, 1997, p. 9; September 7, 1997, p. 11; December 7, 1997, p. 12; May 9, 1999, p. 22; November 26, 2000, p. 8; September 16, 2001, p. 32.

New York Times Magazine, August 15, 1999, p. 30.

Observer (London, England), September 17, 1995, p. 15; September 8, 1996, p. 18; October 29, 2000, p. 11; December 24, 2000, p. 19.

People, April 14, 1997, p. 29.

Publishers Weekly, March 10, 1997, p. 51; July 21, 1997, p. 183; April 5, 1999, p. 219; May 17, 1999, p. 51; September 4, 2000, p. 28; September 25, 2000, p. 88.

St. Louis Dispatch, October 5, 1997, p. 05C.

San Francisco Chronicle, March 30, 1997, p. 5; April 6, 1997, p. 11; August 24, 1997, p. 5; March 3, 1998, p. B3; March 25, 1998, p. E2; May 30, 1999, p. 11.

Scotsman (Edinburgh, Scotland), February 28, 1998, p. 3; November 4, 2000, p. 4.

Seattle Post-Intelligencer, March 25, 1998, p. E5.

Seattle Times, April 20, 1997, p. M3; March 25, 1998, p. E6; September 6, 1998, p. M9; June 6, 1999, p. M11; September 26, 1999, p. M9.

Spectator, October 1, 1988, pp. 29-30; September 23, 1995, p. 38; April 11, 1998, p. 33; October 21, 2000, p. 44.

Star Ledger (Newark, NJ), July 12, 1997, p. 006; July 4, 1999, p. 004.

Sunday Herald (Glasgow, Scotland), October 15, 2000, p. 6.

Sunday Times (London, England), May 7, 2000, p. 18; October 15, 2000, p. 50.

Time, May 15, 2000, p. 35.

Time International, April 6, 1998, p. 13.

Times (London, England), April 13, 1998, p. 10, interview with Fitzgerald; August 8, 1998, p. 20; October 11, 2000, pp. 17; December 29, 2000, p. 27.

Times Literary Supplement, November 17, 1978, p. 1333; September 12, 1986, p. 995.

Wall Street Journal, April 8, 1997, p. A20; May 28, 1999, p. W6; September 26, 2000, p. A24.
Washington Post, October 1, 2000, p. X15.
Washington Post Book World, February 23, 1992, pp. 1, 8; June 1997, pp. 3, 13.
Women's Review of Books, October, 1997, p. 6.
World and I, January, 2001, p. 254.
World Literature Today, spring, 1998, p. 371.

ONLINE

Second Circle, http://www.thesecondcircle.com/ (March 9, 2004), review of *The Blue Flower.*

OBITUARIES:

PERIODICALS

Guardian (London, England), May 3, 2000, p. 22; May 24, 2000, p. 24.
Herald Sun (Melbourne, Australia), May 15, 2000, p. 109.
Independent (London, England), May 3, 2000, p. 5; May 9, 2000, p. 6.
Los Angeles Times, May 4, 2000, p. A8.
Milwaukee Journal-Sentinel, May 5, 2000, p. 04.
New York Times, May 3, 2000, p. A29.
Seattle Times, May 3, 2000, p. A19.
Times (London, England), May 6, 2000, p. 24; October 11, 2000, p. 22.

*   *   *

FLEUR, Paul
    See POHL, Frederik

*   *   *

FLOOGLEBUCKLE, Al
    See SPIEGELMAN, Art

*   *   *

FO, Dario 1926-

PERSONAL: Born March 24, 1926, in San Giano, Lombardy, Italy; son of Felice (a railroad stationmaster) and Pina (Rota) Fo; married Franca Rame (a playwright and actress), June, 1954; children: three. *Education:* Attended Accademia di Belle Arti, Milan, Italy.

ADDRESSES: Home—Milan, Italy. *Office*—Michael Imison Playwrights Ltd, 28 Almeida St., London, NI 1 1TD, England; also, CTFR, Corso di Porta Romania 132, 201228 Milan, Italy. *Agent*—Maria Nadotti, 349 East 51st St., New York, NY 10022.

CAREER: Playwright, director, actor, and theatrical company leader. Has written more than forty plays, many of which have been translated and performed in more than thirty countries, 1953—; performs plays in Italy, Europe, and the United States, and runs classes and workshops for actors, 1970s—. Worked as a member of small theatrical group, headed by Franco Parenti, performing semi-improvised sketches for radio before local audiences, 1950; wrote and performed comic monologues for his own radio program, *Poer nana* ("Poor Dwarf"), broadcast by the Italian national radio network RAI, 1951; formed revue company, *I Dritti* ("The Stand-Ups"), with Giustino Durano and Parenti, 1953; screenwriter in Rome, 1956-58; formed improvisational troupe *Compagnia Fo-Rame,* with wife, Franca Rame, 1958; named artistic director of Italian state television network's weekly musical revue, *Chi l'ha visto?* ("Who's Seen It?"), and writer and performer of sketches for variety show *Canzonissima* ("Really Big Song"), 1959; formed theater cooperative *Nuova Scena,* with Rame, 1968, and *La Comune,* 1970.

AWARDS, HONORS: Sonning Award, Denmark, 1981; Off Broadway Award, *Village Voice,* 1987; Nobel Prize in Literature, 1997; Lusanto Jullare Francesco, 1999.

WRITINGS:

PLAYS

Teatro comico, Garzanti (Italy), 1962.
Le Commedie, Einaudi (Turin, Italy), 1966, enlarged edition published as *Le Commedie di Dario Fo,* six volumes, Einaudi (Turin, Italy), 1974, reprinted, 1984.
Vorrei morire anche stasera se dovessi pensare che no e servito a niente, E.D.B., 1970.
Morte e resurrezione di un pupazzo, Sapere Edizioni, 1971.
Teatro comico, Garzanti (Italy), 1971.
Ordine!, Bertani (Verona, Italy), 1972.
Ordine! Per Dio, Bertani (Verona, Italy), 1972.
Pum, pum! Chi e? La polizia! (title means "Knock, Knock! Who's There? Police!"), Bertani (Verona, Italy), 1972.

Tutti uniti! Tutti insieme! Ma scusa quello non e il padrone? (title means "United We Stand! All Together Now! Oops, Isn't That the Boss?"), Bertani (Verona, Italy), 1972.

Guerra di popolo in Cile (title means "The People's War in Chile"), Bertani (Verona, Italy), 1973.

Mistero buffo: Giullarata popolare, Bertani (Verona, Italy), 1974, reprinted, Einaudi (Torino, Italy), 2003.

Mistero buffo (title means "The Comic Mystery"; first produced in Milan, Italy, 1969; produced on Broadway at the Joyce Theater, May 27, 1986), Bertani (Verona, Italy), 1973, revised, 1974.

Ballate e canzoni (title means "Ballads and Songs"), introduction by Lanfranco Binni, Bertani (Verona, Italy), 1974, reprinted, Newton Compton (Rome, Italy), 1976.

Non si paga, non si paga (first produced in Milan, 1974), La Comune (Milan, Italy), 1974; adapted by Bill Colvill and Robert Walker, Pluto Press (London, England), 1978; translation by Lino Pertite reprinted as *Can't Pay? Won't Pay!,* Pluto Press (London, England), 1982, North American version by R.G. Davis published as *We Won't Pay! We Won't Pay!,* Samuel French (New York, NY), 1984.

Morte accidentale di un anarchico (first produced in Milan, December, 1970; produced on Broadway at Belasco Theater, November 15, 1984), Einaudi (Turin, Italy), 1974, translation by Gavin Richards published as *Accidental Death of an Anarchist,* Pluto Press (London, England), 1980, published as *Morte accidentale di un anarchio [Accidental Death of an Anarchist],* Manchester University Press (New York, NY), 1998.

La Guillarata, Bertani (Verona, Italy), 1975.

Il Fanfani rapito, Bertani (Verona, Italy), 1975.

La Marjuana della mamma e la piu bella, Bertani (Verona, Italy), 1976.

La Signora e da buttare (title means "The Old Girl's for the Scrapheap"), Einuadi (Turin, Italy), 1976.

Il Teatro politico, G. Mazzotta (Milan, Italy), 1977.

Dario Fo parla di Dario Fo, Lerici (Cosenza, Italy), 1977.

(With wife, Franca Rame) *Tutta casa, letto e chiesa* (title means "All House, Bed, and Church"), Bertani (Verona, Italy), 1978, translation published as *Orgasmo Adulto Escapes from the Zoo,* Bertani (Verona, Italy), 1978, translation by Estelle Parsons, Broadway Play Publishing (New York, NY), 1985.

La Storia di un soldato, photographs by Silvia Lelli Masotti, commentary by Ugo Volli, Electa (Milan, Italy), 1979.

Storia della tigre ed altre storie, La Comune (Milan, Italy), 1980.

Storia vera di Piero d'Angera: Che alla crociata non c'era, La Comune (Milan, Italy), 1981.

Fabulazzo osceno, F.R. La Comune (Milan, Italy), 1982.

L'Opera dello sghignazzo: dalla "Beggar's opera di John Gay" e da alcune idee di mio figlio Jacopo, F.R. La Comune (Milan, Italy), 2nd edition, 1982.

Dario Fo and Franca Rame: Theatre Workshops at Riverside Studios, London, April 28th, May 5th, 12th, 13th & 19th, 1983, Red Notes (London, England), 1983.

Coppia aperta, Tip.-Lit. "La Musica moderna," 1984.

Il Ratto della Francesca: Commedia in due tempi, La Comune (Milan, Italy), 1986.

About Face: A Political Farce, translated by Ron Jenkins, S. French (New York, NY), 1989.

Archangels Don't Play Pinball [Arcangeli non giocano a flipper], translated by Ron Jenkins, S. French (New York, NY), 1989.

Dario Fo, dialogo provocatorio sul comico, il tragico, la follia e la ragione con Luigi Allegri, Laterza (Rome, Italy), 1990.

Johan Padan a la descoverta de le Americhe, Giunti (Firenze, Italy), 1992.

(Coauthor) *Parliamo di donne: Il Teatro,* Kaos (Milan, Italy), 1992.

Abducting Diana: Il Ratto della Francesca, adapted by Stephen Stenning, Oberon Books (London, England), 1994.

Toto: Manuale dell'attor comico, Vallecchi (Firenze, Italy), 1995.

(Illustrator) *Una Strega, una pizza e un orco con la stizza,* by Bianca Fo Garambois, FATATRAC (Rome, Italy), 1995.

Il Diavolo con le Zinne, G. Einaudi (Turin, Italy), 1998.

Federico Fellini & Dario Fo: Disegni geniali, Mazzotta (Milan, Italy), 1999.

La Vera storia di Ravenna, F.C. Panini (Modena, Italy), 1999.

OTHER PLAYS; IN ENGLISH TRANSLATION

(With Franca Rame) *Female Parts: One Woman Plays,* translated by Margaret Kunzle and Stuart Hood, adapted by Olwen Wymark, Pluto Press (London, England), 1981.

Car Horns, Trumpets and Raspberries (first produced in Milan, January, 1981; produced in the United States at the Yale Repertory Theater as *About Face,* 1981), translated by R.C. McAvoy and A.H. Giugni, Pluto Press (London, England), 1981, reprinted, 1984.

(With Franca Rame) *The Open Couple—Wide Open Even,* Theatretexts (London, England), 1984.

The Tale of a Tiger: A Comic Monologue [Storia della tigre], Theatretexts (London, England), 1984.

One Was Nude and One Wore Tails: A One-Act Farce [Uomo nudo e l'uomo in frak], Theatretexts (London, England), 1985.

Elizabeth, Almost by Chance a Woman [Quasi per caso una donna, Elisabetta], translated by Ron Jenkins, S. French (New York, NY), 1989.

The Open Couple and an Ordinary Day, Heinemann (London, England), 1990.

The Pope and the Witch, Heinemann (London, England), 1993, translated by Joan Holden, S. French (New York, NY), 1997.

(With Franca Rame) *Plays, Two* (contains *Can't Pay? Won't Pay!, The Open Couple,* and *An Ordinary Day*), Methuen (London, England)), 1994.

Plays, Methuen Drama (London, England), 1997.

Johan Padan and the Discovery of the Americas, Grove Press (New York, NY), 2001.

We Won't Pay! We Won't Pay! and Other Plays: The Collected Plays of Dario Fo, edited by Franca Rame, translated by Ron Jenkins, Theatre Communications Group (New York, NY), 2001.

Also author of *The Devil with Boobs.*

OTHER PLAYS; PRODUCED ONLY

Il Dito nell'occhio (title means "A Finger in the Eye"), first produced in Milan at Piccolo Teatro, June, 1953.

I Sani da legare (title means "A Madhouse for the Sane"), first produced in Milan at Piccolo Teatro, 1954.

Ladri, manachini e donne nude (title means "Thieves, Dummies, and Naked Women"), first produced in Milan at Piccolo Teatro, 1958.

Gli arcangeli non giocano a flipper (title means "Archangels Don't Play Pinball,") first produced in Milan at Teatro Odeon, September, 1959.

Isabella, tre caravelle, e un cacciaballe (title means "Isabella, Three Ships, and a Con Man"), first produced in Milan at Teatro Odeon, 1963.

L'Anomal bicefalo (title means "Two-Headed Anomaly"), frist produced in Milan at Piccolo Teatro, 2003.

Also author of numerous other plays produced in Italy, including *Aveva due pistole con gli occhi bianchi e neri* (title means "He Had Two Pistols with White and Black Eyes"), 1960; *Grande pantomima con bandiere e pupazzi piccoli e medi* (title means "Grand Pantomime with Flags and Small and Medium-Sized Puppets"), October, 1968; *Fedayn,* 1971; *Il Fabulazzo osceno* (title means "The Obscene Fable"), 1982; and *Hellequin, Arlekin, Arlechino,* 1986. Other stage credits include an adaptation of Bertolt Brecht's *Threepenny Opera,* for Teatro Stabile di Torino and Teatro Il Fabbricone of Prato, and *Patapumfete,* for the clown duo I Colombaioni.

OTHER

Manuale minimo dell'attore (title means "Basic Handbook for the Actor"), Einuadi (Turin, Italy), 1987, reprinted, 1997.

The Tricks of the Trade, translation by Joe Farrell, Routledge (New York, NY), 1991.

Marino libero! Marino e innocente!, Einaudi (Turin, Italy), 1998.

Teatro, G. Einaudi (Turin, Italy)), 2000.

L'Ascensione di Alessandro Magno portato in cielo da due grifoni: Dal romanzo greco dello pseudo-Callistene vissuto ad Alessandria d'Egitto nel IV secolo d.c., illustrated by Rachele Lo Piano, Sinnos (Rome, Italy), 2001.

Cinquant'anni di storia italiana attraverso il teatro: Dario Fo e Franca Rame: Tournee 2001-2002, M. Baroni (Lucca, Italy)), 2002.

(With Franca Rame) *Il Paese dei Mezaràt: I Miei primi sette anni* (e qualcuno in più), Feltrinelli (Milano, Italy), 2002.

The Peasants Bible and The Story of the Tiger, translated by Ron Jenkins, Grove Press (New York, NY), 2004.

SIDELIGHTS: Noted Italian playwright and Nobel laureate Dario Fo began refining his animated method of storytelling as a child, listening to the tales told by the locals in San Giano, the small fishing village in northern Italy where he was born. After leaving Milan's Academy of Fine Arts without earning a degree, Fo wrote and performed with several improvisational theatrical groups. He first earned acclaim as a playwright in 1953 with *Il Dito nell'occhio,* a socially satiric production that presented Marxist ideas against a circus-like background. His 1954 attack on the Italian government in *I Sani da legare,* in which Fo labeled several government officials fascist sympathizers, resulted in the cutting of some material from the original script and the mandated presence of state inspectors at each performance of the play to insure that the country's strict libel laws were not violated.

Following a brief stint as a screenwriter in Rome, Fo, together with his wife, actress Franca Rame, returned to the theater and produced a more generalized, less explicitly political brand of social satire. Widely regarded as his best work during this phase of his career, *Gli arcangeli non giocano a flipper* was the first of Fo's plays to be staged outside of Italy. As quoted by Irving Wardle in the London *Times,* the heroic clown in *Archangels* voices the playwright's basic contention, stating, "My quarrel is with those who organize our dreams."

In 1968 Fo and Rame rejected the legitimate theater as an arm of the bourgeoisie and, backed by the Italian Communist party, they formed Nuova Scena, a noncommercial theater group designed to entertain and inform the working class. The plays produced by this company centered on political issues and grew increasingly radical in tone. The communist government withdrew its support from Nuova Scena after the staging of *Grande pantomima con bandiere e pupazzi piccoli e medi,* a satire of Italy's political history in the wake of World War II. The highly symbolic play depicts the birth of capitalism (portrayed by a beautiful woman) from fascism (a huge monster puppet) and the subsequent seduction of communism by capitalism. Through the play Fo demonstrated his disenchantment with the authoritative, antirevolutionary policies of the Italian Communist party, allowing communism to succumb to capitalism's enticement.

Steeped in an atmosphere of political and social unrest, the 1960s proved to be a decade of increased popularity for Fo, providing him with new material and a receptive audience. *Mistero buffo,* generally considered his greatest and most controversial play was first performed in 1969. An improvised production based on a constantly changing script, the play is a decidedly irreverent retelling of the gospels that indicts landowners, government, and, in particular, the Catholic Church as public oppressors. Fo based the show's format on that of the medieval mystery plays originally parodied by *giullari,* strolling minstrel street performers of the Middle Ages. *Mistero buffo* was written in Italian as a series of sketches for a single actor—Fo—to perform on an empty stage. The playwright introduces each segment of the work with an informal prologue to establish a rapport with his audience. He links together the satiric religious narratives, portraying up to a dozen characters at a time by himself. The sketches include a reenactment of Lazarus's resurrection, complete with opportunists who pick the pockets of the awestruck witnesses; the tale of a contented cripple's efforts to avoid being cured by Jesus; an account of the wedding feast at Cana as told by a drunkard; and an especially dark portrait of the corrupt Pope Boniface VIII.

Writing in *American Theatre,* Ron Jenkins considered Fo's black humor and "sense of moral indignation" most effectively illuminated in a fable from *Mistero buffo* titled "The Birth of the Giullare," which explains how the minstrel received his narrative gift. A former peasant, the *giullare* had been humiliated and victimized by corrupt politicians, priests, and landowners. In his despair, he decides to kill himself but is interrupted by a man asking for water. The man is Jesus Christ, who, in kissing the peasant's lips gives him the facility to mesmerize an audience—and deflate the very authorities that had oppressed him—with his words. Jenkins remarked, "Fo performs the moment of the miracle with an exhilarating sense of musicality. . . . The triumph of freedom over tyranny is palpable in [his] every sound and movement."

According to Charles C. Mann in the *Atlantic Monthly,* Fo took pleasure in the Vatican's description of the play, which was taped and broadcast on television in 1977, as "the most blasphemous" program ever televised. *Mistero buffo* was nevertheless a critical and popular success throughout Europe. The staging of the play in London in 1983 single-handedly saved from bankruptcy the financially ailing theater in which it was performed. Despite the reception of his masterpiece abroad, Fo was unable to perform the play in the United States until 1986 when he and Rame were finally granted permission to enter the country. The couple had been denied visas in 1980 and 1984 because of their alleged involvement in fund-raising activities for an Italian terrorist organization. Fo and his wife dismissed the accusation and maintained their innocence. Through the efforts of civil libertarian and cultural groups in Europe and the United States, Fo and Rame ultimately received visas, and *Mistero buffo* opened in New York in the spring of 1986. Jenkins termed the play "a brilliant one-man version of biblical legends and church history" whose comedy "echo[es] the rhythms of revolt."

Fo's penchant for justice prompted him to compose the absurdist play *Morte accidentale di un anarchico,* produced in English as *Accidental Death of an Anarchist,* in response to the untimely death of anarchist railway man Giuseppe Pinelli in late 1969. Pinelli's death was apparently connected to efforts by right-wing extremists in Italy's military and secret service agencies to discredit the Italian Communist party by staging a series of seemingly leftist-engineered bombings. The railway worker was implicated in the worst of these bombings, the 1969 massacre at Milan's Agricultural Bank. While being held for interrogation, Pinelli fell—it was later shown that he was pushed—from the fourth-floor window of Milan's police headquarters.

In *Accidental Death,* Fo introduces a stock medieval character, the maniac, into the investigation of the bombing to illuminate the truth. Fo commented in *American Theatre,* "When I injected absurdity into the situation, the lies became apparent. The maniac plays the role of the judge, taking the logic of the authorities to their absurd extremes," thus demonstrating that Pinelli's death could not have occurred in the way the police had described. John Lahr reported in the *Los Angeles Times* that because of their part in the exposure of the police cover-up, Fo was assaulted and jailed and Rame kidnapped and beaten in the first few years that the play was staged.

Accidental Death of an Anarchist was a smash hit in Italy, playing to huge crowds for more than four years. When officials pressured a theater in Bologna to halt plans for production, the play was alternatively staged in a sports stadium for an audience of more than six thousand people. After receiving rave reviews throughout Europe—Lahr, writing in *New Society,* called the show "loud, vulgar, kinetic, scurrilous, smart, [and] sensational. . . . Everything theatre should be"—and enjoying a thirty-month run in London, *Accidental Death* opened in the United States in 1984, only to close a short time later.

Because Fo's plays are often either loosely translated or performed in Italian and center on historical, political, and social events that bear more significance for audiences in Italy than in the States, American versions of the playwright's works are frequently considered less dazzling than their Italian counterparts. In an article for the *New York Times,* Mel Gussow pointed out that "dealing with topical Italian materials in colloquial Italian language . . . presents problems for adapters and directors." For instance, a few critics found the presence of a translator on stage during *Mistero buffo* mildly distracting. And many reviewers agreed that the English translation of *Accidental Death* lacked the power of the Italian production. Frank Rich insisted in the *New York Times* that adapter Richard Nelson's introduction of timely American puns into the *Accidental Death* script "wreck[ed] the play's farcical structure and jolt[ed] both audience and cast out of its intended grip."

Fo's 1978 collaboration with Rame, *Tutta casa, letto e chiesa,* produced in the United States as *Orgasmo Adulto Escapes from the Zoo,* also "may have lost some of its punch crossing the Atlantic," asserted David Richards in the *Washington Post.* A cycle of short sketches written for a single female player, *Orgasmo* focuses on women's status in a patriarchal society. Richards felt

that, to an American audience in the mid-1980s when the play was produced in the United States, "the women in *Orgasmo* seem to be fighting battles that have long been conceded on these shores." Still, if not timely, the performances were judged favorably for their zest and honesty in portraying Italian sexism.

The Tricks of the Trade, published in 1991, is a collection of notes, talks, and workshop transcripts by Fo that deal with numerous aspects of the theater and their historical origins and modern roles: mimes and clowns, masks, and puppets and marionettes. Fo also discusses his own plays and his distinctive approach to playwriting and performing. "*The Tricks of the Trade* offers inspiration for theatre practitioners of all sorts, while celebrating a revival of the power and predominance of the politically inspired clown," remarked James Fisher in *Drama Review.* Writing in *World Literature Today,* Giovanni d'Angelo commented that the book "is technically robust and exhaustive" and termed Fo's style "fluent and graceful."

In the *New York Times* Gussow noted, "For Mr. Fo, there are no sacred cows, least of all himself or his native country," and concluded that Fo's social commentary is more "relevant" than "subversive." Commenting on the underlying philosophy that shapes and informs his works, Fo asserted in *American Theatre,* "My plays are provocations, like catalysts in a chemical solution. . . . I just put some drops of absurdity in this calm and tranquil liquid, which is society, and the reactions reveal things that were hidden before the absurdity brought them out into the open."

Fo's winning of the Nobel Prize for Literature in 1997 caused quite a stir. Italian literature enjoys a long, distinguished history, going back to the fourteenth century to the work of Petrarch and Boccaccio. When Fo won the coveted prize many people were surprised. They thought him "a mere writer and clownish performer of rather buffoonish comedies," wrote Jack Helbig for *Booklist.* However, audiences who have witnessed his works, continued Helbig, "have seen his anarchistic farces descry serious intent just below their mad comic surfaces." In a statement expressing the reasons for giving the prize to Fo, the academy stated that it was awarded for Fo's commitment to uphold the dignity of the downtrodden in modern society. Upon winning the prize, Fo reportedly telephoned his wife, Rame, referring to her as Mrs. Nobel, acknowledging her lifelong commitment to their shared work.

Fo's *Mistero Buffo* was the first of his plays to be staged in New York in the spring of 1986. The following year, he and his wife won an Obie Award under the category of special citations. More recently, a revival of Fo's *Johan Padan and the Discovery of the Americas,* was presented at the American Repertory Theatre in Cambridge, MA, in 2001. In a review for *American Theatre,* Jenkins noted that despite the fact that Fo adapted his play from sixteenth-century explorers' diaries, "its sly satirical examination of racism, religious warfare, ethnic cleansing and the mass migration of homeless refugees resonates with today's headlines." In this play, Johan Padan is a stowaway on one of Christopher Columbus's ships. However, when Padan arrives in the New World, he sides with the Native Americans in their fight against Columbus and his men. As *Variety's* Markland Taylor put it, Johan does so, having learned that "the so-called savages of the Americas are a good deal less savage than the Europeans." *Boston Herald* theatre critic Terry Byrne found that this particular play "blends Fo's best skills as a traditional storyteller and political satirist." The play was staged in several U.S. cities, including New York, as a fiftieth anniversary celebration of Fo's career on stage with Rame.

The 2001 publication of *We Won't Pay! We Won't Pay! and Other Plays: The Collected Plays of Dario Fo* once again brought Fo's name to the forefront of discussions about drama in the States. *Library Journal* reviewer Thomas E. Luddy described Fo and Rame as "modern commedia dell'arte entertainers," and claimed that this new study of their collaborative work was "a much-needed critical review." The title of this book comes from one of Fo's most often performed plays. In an article about the titled play, after it was staged back in 1998, *Los Angeles Times'* Laurie Winer, referred to *We Won't Pay! We Won't Pay!* as a classical example of how Fo earned his Nobel Prize, with the play's main theme of upholding the rights of those less fortunate. Winer wrote that the play "blends wacky kitchen-sink comedy with diatribes on how the workers need to grab power from capitalist crooks."

Fo, in his seventies, continues to work. As Maureen Paton wrote in an interview with Fo for the London *Times:* he "still has plenty to rebel against." Despite the fact that he has spent time in jail in Italy for his writing and performance, that his wife has suffered abuse from people who disagreed with the couple's creative material, that his theatre was burnt, and an attempt was made to set his house on fire, Fo has never lacked the courage to express exactly what is on his mind.

Fo was called "a Left-leaning anti-cleric," by Bruce Johnston in London's *Daily Telegraph;* and "a clown with a tongue that slashed the establishment, including the Vatican," by the *Boston Herald's* Iris Fanger. No matter what he is called, Fo continues to speak in what Winer described as his "anarchic voice," the same one that was heard by the Nobel committee when they awarded him the prize in Stockholm.

If his critics and opponents thought their verbal or physical attacks would intimidate Fo, his scathing 2003 play *Two-Headed Anomaly,* which was performed at Milan's Piccolo Teatro, proved them wrong. This time, Fo turns his attention to Italy's notorious prime minister, Silvio Berlusconi. In the satire, Fo attacks the prime minister for a variety of abuses of power, including passing laws for his own benefit, creating a media monopoly, and censoring journalistic criticism of the government. At one stage in the play, the prime minister, played by Fo, has Russian leader Vladimir Putin's brain transplanted into his head, making him a drunken, confused, Russian speaking, two-and-a-half foot dwarf. Much of the play focuses on the prime minister with his wife, played by Fo's wife, Rame. "These scenes give the play its greatest force. Berlusconi is depicted as a petulant adolescent who is constantly in need of approval while Lario is like a stern mother figure humoring her unruly, mischievous child with patronizing words," wrote Antonion D'Ambroso in the *Progressive.* D'Ambroso went on to note that the play "represents Fo at his best, placing him in the tradition of Moliere and Ruzzante Beolco, the father of the commedia dell'-arte." The play has so outraged some of those in power that Italian senator Marcello Dell'Utri, an associate of the prime minister, brought suit against Fo, asking for $1.25 million in damages. Nick Vivarelli, writing in *Variety,* quoted Fo as responding, "It's just caricature. Any elements from reality have been widely reported and even written in books. The truth is, this is an attempt to shut us up. But we aren't going to stop." Fo is also author of *The Peasants Bible and The Story of the Tiger,* in which Fo takes five monologues from various Italian folklore stories and reworks them for his own satirical purposes.

BIOGRAPHICAL AND CRITICAL SOURCES:

BOOKS

Artese, Erminia, *Dario Fo parla di Dario Fo,* Lerici (Cosenza, Italy), 1977.

Behan, Tom, *Dario Fo: Revolutionary Theatre,* Pluto Press (London, England), 2000.

Contemporary Literary Criticism, Thomson Gale (Detroit, MI), Volume 32, 1985, Volume 109, 1998.

Farrell, Joseph, and Antonio Scuderi, editors, *Dario Fo: Stage, Text, and Tradition,* Southern Illinois University Press (Carbondale, IL), 2000.

Fellini, Federico, *Federico Fellini & Dario Fo: Disegni Geniali,*Mazzotta (Milan, Italy), 1999.

Hirst, David L., *Dario Fo and Franca Rame,* Macmillan (London, England), 1989.

McAvoy, R. C., editor, *Dario Fo and Franca Rame: The Theatre Workshops at Riverside Studios,* Red Notes (London, England), 1983.

Mitchell, Tony, *Dario Fo: People's Court Jester,* Methuen (London, England), 1984.

Pertile, Lino, "Dario Fo," in *Writers & Society in Contemporary Italy,* St. Martin's Press (New York, NY), 1984, pp. 167-90.

Trussler, Simon, editor, *File on Fo,* Methuen (London, England), 1989.

PERIODICALS

American Theatre, June, 1986; February 1998, Ron Jenkins, "The Nobel Jester," pp. 22-24; October, 2001, Ron Jenkins, review of *Johan Padan and the Discovery of the Americas,* p. 12.

Aperture, summer, 1993; Ron Jenkins, "Drawing from the Imagination: The Comic Art of Dario Fo," pp. 12-19.

Atlantic Monthly, September, 1985.

Booklist, February 1, 2002, Jack Helbig, review of *We Won't Pay! We Won't Pay! and Other Plays: The Collected Plays of Dario Fo,*p. 917.

Boston Herald, April 19, 1999, Iris Fanger, review of *We Won't Pay! We Won't Pay!,* p. O39; September 10, 2001, Terry Byrne, review of *Johan Padan and the Discovery of the Americas,* p. O36.

Choice, March, 1992, p. 1090.

Daily Telegraph (London, England), November 17, 2000, Bruce Johnston, "Dario Fo Is Tipped As Milan Mayor."

Drama, summer, 1979; third quarter, 1985, Phoebe Tait, "Political Clown," pp. 28-29.

Drama Review, September, 1972, A. Richard Sogliuzzo, "Dario Fo: Puppets for Proletarian Revolution," pp. 71-77; June 1975, Suzanne Cowan, "The Throw-Away Theatre of Dario Fo," pp. 102-13; winter, 1992, James Fisher, review of *Tricks of the Trade,* p. 171.

Library Journal, February 15, 2002, Thomas E. Luddy, review of *We Won't Pay! We Won't Pay! and Other Plays: The Collected Plays of Dario Fo,* p. 143.

Los Angeles Times, January 16, 1983; January 21, 1983; September 3, 1998, Laurie Winer, "Nobel Prize Winner's Anarchic, Loony Tone Comes through in *We Won't Pay!,*" pp. 6, 29.

Modern Drama, June, 1985, Martin W. Walsh, "The Proletarian Carnival of Fo's *Non si paga! Non si paga!,*" pp. 211-222; December, 1989, Mimi D'Aponte, "From Italian Roots to American Relevance: The Remarkable Theatre of Dario Fo," pp. 532-544; March, 1990, Joylynn Wing, "The Performances of Power and the Power of Performance: Rewriting the Police State in Dario Fo's *Accidental Death of an Anarchist,*" pp. 139-149; spring, 1998, Joseph Farrell, "Variations on a Theme: Respecting Dario Fo," pp. 19-29.

National Catholic Reporter, November 13, 1992.

New Republic, December 17, 1984.

New Society, March 13, 1980.

New Statesman, August 7, 1981.

New Yorker, February 23, 1981.

New York Times, December 18, 1980; April 17, 1983; August 5, 1983; August 14, 1983; August 27, 1983; February 15, 1984; October 31, 1984; November 16, 1984; May 29, 1986; May 30, 1986; May 9, 1987; November 27, 1987.

New York Times Book Review, February 2, 1998, p. 31.

Opera News, October, 1993.

Partisan Review, 1984, Joel Schechter, "The Un-American Satire of Dario Fo," pp. 112-119.

Progressive, April, 2004, Antonion D'Ambroso, "The Playwright vs. the Prime Minister," review of *Two-Headed Anomaly,* p. 32.

Theatre, spring, 1979, Suzanne Cowan, "Dario Fo, Politics, and Satire: An Introduction to *Accidental Death of an Anarchist,*" pp. 7-11.

Theatre Journal, October 1993, J.L. Wing, "The Iconicity of Absence: Dario Fo and the Radical Invisible," pp. 303-315.

Times (London, England), November 17, 1984; September 22, 1986; September 25, 1986; May 15, 2002, Maureen Paton, "Still a Worthy Fo: Interview," p. 4.

Times Literary Supplement, December 18, 1987.

Variety, August 4, 1982; May 11, 1992; September 17, 2001, Markland Taylor, review of *Johan Padan and the Discovery of the Americas,* p. 28; January 19-January 25, Nick Vivarelli, "Beauty of a 'Beast' Dispute: Berlusconi Play Adds Court Date to Its Run," p. 5.

Washington Post, August 27, 1983; November 17, 1984; January 17, 1985; June 12, 1986.

World Literature Today, autumn, 1992, Giovanni d'Angelo, review of *Tricks of the Trade,* p. 707.

ONLINE

Nobel Prize Internet Archive, http://almaz.com/nobel/ (July 18, 2002).

FOER, Jonathan Safran 1977-

PERSONAL: Born 1977, in Washington, DC. *Education:* Attended Princeton University. *Religion:* Jewish.

ADDRESSES: Home—Brooklyn, NY. *Agent*—c/o Houghton Mifflin Company, Trade Division, Adult Editorial, 8th Fl., 222 Berkeley St. Boston, MA 02116-3764.

CAREER: Writer. Worked as receptionist at public relations firm, morgue assistant, jewelry seller, farm sitter, and ghostwriter.

AWARDS, HONORS: Zoetrope fiction prize, 2000; Guardian Prize for a First Book and National Jewish Book Award, both 2002, both for *Everything is Illuminated;* New York Public Library's Young Lion Award, 2003, for *Everything Is Illuminated.*

WRITINGS:

(Editor) *A Convergence of Birds: Original Fiction and Poetry Inspired by the Work of Joseph Cornell,* Distributed Art Publishers (New York, NY), 2001.
Everything Is Illuminated (novel), Houghton Mifflin (Boston, MA), 2002.
Extremely Loud and Incredibly Close (novel), Houghton Mifflin (Boston, MA), 2005.

Contributor to magazines, including *Paris Review* and *Conjunctions.*

ADAPTATIONS: Everything Is Illuminated was made into a film starring Elijah Wood, directed by Liev Schreiber, and released by Warner Independent Pictures in 2005; *Extremely Loud and Incredibly Close* has been optioned for film by Scott Rudin Productions in conjunction with Warner Brothers and Paramount Pictures.

WORK IN PROGRESS: A novel tentatively titled *The Zelnik Museum.*

SIDELIGHTS: Jonathan Safran Foer's first novel, *Everything Is Illuminated,* was the subject of eager anticipation after an excerpt was published in the *New Yorker* in 2001. The novel grew out of a trip he made to the Ukraine in 1997 in an effort to increase his knowledge of his family history, especially of his late maternal grandfather. The grandfather had escaped the Holocaust with the help of a woman in his Ukrainian hometown, the small Jewish village, or shtetl, of Trachimbrod, but the family knew nothing beyond that. Foer's visit illuminated him no further—for one thing, the only trace of Trachimbrod was a memorial plaque—so he began writing a fictional version of his search, interwoven with an imagined history of the town from its founding in 1791 to its destruction in World War II.

In the novel, the protagonist bears the author's name and is the same age, twenty, that Foer was when he went to the Ukraine. The fictional Jonathan Safran Foer joins forces with an entrepreneurial young Ukrainian translator, Alex Perchov, a gentile whose family travel business caters to Jews seeking their roots. Accompanying them in their week-long search are Alex's curmudgeonly grandfather and the grandfather's none-too-bright seeing-eye dog, which, although female, is named after Sammy Davis, Jr., with an extra "Jr." The novel takes the form of correspondence between Alex and Jonathan after Jonathan returns to the United States. Alex sends letters filled with reflections on Jonathan's visit, written in "thesaurus-bludgeoned English," as *Los Angeles Times* reporter Lynell George put it. In reply, Jonathan sends excerpts from his novel in progress, a fictionalized chronicle of his ancestral village, which *Time* reviewer Lev Grossman called "a lyrical, fairy-tale creation, a Yiddish idyll of the *Fiddler on the Roof* variety, inhabited by randy, gossipy villagers," including Jonathan's grandfather, a man of remarkable sexual prowess.

"The two voices come at the plot from both ends at once," Grossman explained, later adding, "The two stories collide when the searchers stumble on Trachimbrod's last surviving inhabitant, who tells the horrifying secret of how the dreamy little village met its end in the nightmare of World War II." The novel's mix of comedy and tragedy drew comment from several reviewers. "The author offers sympathy and irony without shrinking from their contrasts," observed Molly McQuade in Chicago *Tribune Books.* "Although the novel seeks to resurrect the memory of a community of Jews massacred by the Germans, Foer doesn't shy away from applying warm mockery to the wiles of their forebears, so spiritually fractious that they had to split into two righteous bodies, the Upright Synagogue and the Slouching Synagogue."

Alex's mangling of the English language provides much humor as well. "Alex's vocabulary mistakes, turned by Mr. Foer into a source of great delight, are easily understood," reported Janet Maslin in the *New York Times*. "When he picks the wrong synonym for 'hard,' he winds up with phrases like 'amid a rock and a rigid place' and 'an American in Ukraine is so flaccid to recognize.'" Alex's distinctive voice, however, is more than comic relief, according to some critics. McQuade remarked, "Alex's words embody, syllable by syllable and clause by clause, the character's struggle to learn his place in the future and Jonathan's place in the past. They graze the reader with a furious, greedy, uncompromising impurity that is sheer inspiration."

Maslin concluded that *Everything Is Illuminated* "is a complex, ambitious undertaking, especially as its characters and events begin to run together in keeping with the author's ultimate plan. Mr. Foer works hard on these effects, and sometimes you will, too. But the payoff is extraordinary: a fearless, acrobatic, ultimately haunting effort to combine inspired mischief with a grasp of the unthinkable." *Washington Post Book World* critic Marie Arana thought Foer had lived up to the high expectations created by the *New Yorker* excerpt. "Rarely does a writer as young as Jonathan Foer display such virtuosity and wisdom," she commented. "His prose is clever, challenging, willfully constructed to make you read it again and again. His novel is madly complex, at times confusing, overlapping, unforgiving. But read it, and you'll feel altered, chastened—seared in the fire of something new."

Foer followed the success of his first novel with *Extremely Loud and Incredibly Close*. In the story, Oskar Schell's father has just been killed in the September 11, 2001 attack on the World Trade Center. Oskar's journey begins when he finds a key labeled "Black" in his father's things. As he sets off to find all New Yorkers bearing that last name, he "meets a range of eccentric characters whose peculiarities mirror and even equal his own," according to Francine Prose in *People*. Matthew L. Moffett, writing in *School Library Journal*, commented that the novel's "humor works as a deceptive, glitzy cover for a fairly serious tale about loss and recovery," and Foer leads the story to "a powerful conclusion that will make even the most jaded hearts fall."

BIOGRAPHICAL AND CRITICAL SOURCES:

PERIODICALS

Book, January- February, 2002, Elaine Szewczyk, "Jonathan Safran Foer," p. 37.
Independent (London, England), April 21, 2002, Sarah Bernard, "The Natural Surrealist," pp. 12, 14.

Kirkus Reviews, January 1, 2002, review of *Everything Is Illuminated,* p. 10.
Los Angeles Times, May 30, 2002, Lynell George, "A Light Is Shined on the Edges of Truth," p. 1.
Los Angeles Times Book Review, April 28, 2002, Mark Rozzo, review of *Everything Is Illuminated,* p. 14.
New York Times, April 22, 2002, Janet Maslin, "Searching for Grandfather and a Mysterious Shtetl," p. E6; April 24, 2002, Joyce Wadler, "Seeking Grandfather's Savior, and Life's Purpose," p. B2.
Observer (London, England), June 2, 2002, Clark Collis, "Foer Play," p. 28.
People April 11, 2005, Francine Prose, review of *Extremely Loud and Incredibly Close,* p. 51.
Publishers Weekly, February 4, 2002, review of *Everything Is Illuminated,* p. 48.
Review of Contemporary Fiction, summer, 2001, Peter Donahue, review of *A Convergence of Birds: Original Fiction and Poetry Inspired by the Work of Joseph Cornell,* p. 167.
School Library Journal, July, 2005, Matthew L. Moffett, review of *Extremely Loud and Incredibly Close,* p. 131.
Time, April 29, 2002, Lev Grossman, "Laughter in the Dark," p. 73.
Tribune Books (Chicago, IL), May 19, 2002, Molly McQuade, "Novel's Joint Narrative Creates an Enchanting World," p. 4.
Washington Post Book World, April 21, 2002, Marie Arana, "Dream Time," p. 5.

ONLINE

Jewish Week, http://www.thejewishweek.com/ (December 20, 2001), Susan Josephs, "The New New Thing."
Jonathan Safran Foer Official Site, http://www.jonathan safranfoerbooks.com/ (March 2, 2006).
New York Magazine, http://www.nymag.com/ (April 15, 2002), Sarah Bernard, "A Fan's Notes."
The Project Museum, http://www.jonathansafranfoer. com/ (March 2, 2006).

*   *   *

FOOTE, Horton 1916-

PERSONAL: Born Albert Horton Foote, Jr., March 14, 1916, in Wharton, TX; son of Albert (a merchant and cotton farmer) and Hallie (Brooks) Foote; married Lillian Vallish, June 4, 1945; children: Barbarie Hallie, Albert Horton, Walter Vallish, Daisy Brooks. *Education:* Studied at Pasadena Playhouse School of Theatre, 1933-35, and Tamara Darkarhovna School of Theatre, 1937-39.

ADDRESSES: Home—505 North Houston St., Wharton, TX 77488. *Office*—c/o Luckyroll, 390 West End Ave., New York, NY 10024.

CAREER: Writer for stage, screen, and television. Actor in Broadway plays, 1932-42, including *The Eternal Road, The Fifth Column, The Coggerers,* and *Texas Town;* manager and instructor in playwriting and acting for Productions, Inc. (a semi-professional theatre), Washington, DC, 1945-49. Writer of dramatic teleplays for Columbia Broadcasting Company (CBS), National Broadcasting Company (NBC), American Broadcasting Company (ABC), and British Broadcasting Corp. (BBC); contributor of scripts to dramatic television series, including *Kraft Playhouse, DuPont Show of the Week,* and *Playhouse 90.*

MEMBER: Writers Guild of America, Authors Guild, Dramatists Guild, Texas Institute of Letters, Fellowship of Southern Writers.

AWARDS, HONORS: Academy Award for best screenplay, Academy of Motion Picture Arts and Sciences, and Writers Guild of America Screen Award, both 1962, both for *To Kill a Mockingbird;* Academy Award for best screenplay, 1983, and Christopher Award, both for *Tender Mercies;* Academy Award nomination for best screenplay, 1985, and Writers Guild Award nomination, both for *The Trip to Bountiful;* Capostelo Award, 1987; elected to Fellowship of Southern Writers, 1988; Evelyn Burkey Award, Writers Guild, 1989; William Inge Lifetime Achievement Award, 1989; Dickinson College Arts Award, 1989; Alley Theatre Award, Houston, TX, 1991; Headliners' Club Award, 1991; Torch of Hope Award, Barbara Barondess Theatre Lab Alliance, 1992; Laurel Award, Writers Guild of America, West, 1993; Lontinkle Award, Texas Institute of Letters, 1994; Lifetime Achievement Award, Heartland Film Festival, 1995; Outer Critics Circle Special Achievement Award, 1995; Academy Award in Literature, American Academy of Arts and Letters, Lucille Lortel Award, and Pulitzer Prize for drama, all 1995, all for *The Young Man from Atlanta;* inducted into Theatre Hall of Fame, 1996; Emmy Award, 1997, for teleplay, *Old Man;* American Academy of Arts and Letters Gold Medal for Drama, 1998, for lifetime achievement; elected to American Academy of Arts and Letters Department of Literature,

1998; RCA Crystal Heart, Career Achievement Award, Heartland Film Festival, 1998; Ian McKellan Hunter Memorial Award for Lifetime Achievement, Writer's Guild of America, East, 1999; Annual Bookend Award, Texas Book Festival, 1999; Pen/Laura Pels Foundation Award for Drama to a master American dramatist, 2000; Last Frontier Playwright Award, Edward Albee Theatre Conference, 2000; New York State Governor's Arts Award, New York State Council on the Arts, 2000; National Medal of Arts, 2000; Texas Medal of Arts Award in Literary Arts, Texas Cultural Trust Council, 2001; honorary degrees received from Drew University, Austin College, and American Film Institute, Spalding University, University of the South, and University of Hartford.

WRITINGS:

PLAYS

Only the Heart (three-act; produced in New York, NY at Bijou Theatre, 1944; broadcast by NBC, 1947), Dramatists Play Service (New York, NY), 1944.
The Chase (also see below; three-act; produced on Broadway, 1952), Dramatists Play Service (New York, NY), 1952.
The Trip to Bountiful (also see below; three-act; broadcast by NBC, 1953; produced on Broadway, 1953), Dramatists Play Service (New York, NY), 1954.
A Young Lady of Property (also see below; contains *The Dancers* [broadcast by NBC, 1954, produced in Los Angeles at Fiesta Hall, 1963], *A Young Lady of Property, The Old Beginning, John Turner Davis* [broadcast by NBC, 1953, produced in New York, NY, 1958], *Death of the Old Man,* and *The Oil Well*), Dramatists Play Service (New York, NY), 1954.
The Traveling Lady (also see below; three-act; produced on Broadway, 1954; broadcast by CBS, 1957), Dramatists Play Service (New York, NY), 1955.
The Midnight Caller (one-act; broadcast by NBC, 1953; produced in New York, NY, 1958), Dramatists Play Service (New York, NY), 1959.
Harrison, Texas: Eight Television Plays, Harcourt (New York, NY), 1959.
Three Plays (also see below; contains *Roots in a Parched Ground* and two plays based on stories by Faulkner, *Old Man* and *Tomorrow*), Harcourt (New York, NY), 1962.
Tomorrow (also see below; based on a story by William Faulkner, broadcast by CBS, 1960; produced Off-Broadway, 1985), Dramatists Play Service (New York, NY), 1963, revised edition, 1996.

The Roads to Home (broadcast by ABC, 1955; produced in New York, NY at Manhattan Punch Line Theatre, 1982), Dramatists Play Service (New York, NY), 1982.

Blind Date (one-act; part of "Marathon '86;" produced in New York, NY at Ensemble Studio Theatre, 1986), Dramatists Play Service (New York, NY), 1986.

Selected One-Act Plays of Horton Foote, edited by Gerald C. Wood, SMU Press (Dallas, TX), 1988.

Habitation of Dragons (produced at Pittsburgh Playhouse, 1988), Dramatists Play Service (New York, NY), 1993.

The Man Who Climbed the Pecan Trees, Dramatists Play Service (New York, NY), 1989.

Horton Foote: Four New Plays, Smith & Kraus, 1993.

The Tears of My Sister, The Prisoner's Song, The One-Armed Man, The Land of the Astronauts, Dramatists Play Service (New York, NY), 1993.

The Young Man from Atlanta, Dramatists Play Service (New York, NY), 1995.

Laura Dennis, Dramatists Play Service (New York, NY), 1996.

Taking Pictures, Dramatists Play Service (New York, NY), 1996.

Night Seasons, Dramatists Play Service (New York, NY), 1996.

Getting Frankie Married—and Afterwards and Other Plays, Smith & Kraus, 1999.

The Last of the Thorntons (produced in New York, NY by Signature Theater, 2000), Overlook Press (Woodstock, NY), 2000.

The Carpetbagger's Children; The Actor, Two Plays Overlook Press (Woodstock, NY), 2003,

UNPUBLISHED PLAYS

Texas Town, produced in New York, NY at Weidman Studio, 1941, produced Off-Broadway, 1942.

Out of My House, produced in New York, NY, 1942.

Celebration (one-act), produced in New York, NY at Maxine Elliott Theatre, 1948.

(Author of book) *Gone with the Wind* (musical version of Margaret Mitchell's novel), produced in London's West End, 1972, produced in Los Angeles at Dorothy Chandler Pavilion, 1973.

The Road to the Graveyard (one-act; part of "Marathon '85"), produced in New York, NY at Ensemble Studio Theatre, 1985.

Dividing the Estate, produced in Princeton, NJ, at McArthur Theatre, 1989.

Talking Pictures, produced in Sarasota, FL, at Asolo Theater, 1990.

Vernon Early, produced in Montgomery, AL at Carolyn Blount Theater, 1998.

The Prisoner's Song, produced in New York, NY, 2002.

Also author of plays produced Off-Broadway, including *The Night Seasons, In a Coffin in Egypt, The Old Friends,* and *Arrival and Departure.* Author of play *Wharton Dance,* produced by American Actors Company.

"ORPHANS' HOME" CYCLE

Roots in a Parched Ground (also see below; broadcast by CBS under title *The Night of the Storm,* 1960), Dramatists Play Service (New York, NY), 1962.

Convicts, produced in New York, NY at Ensemble Studio Theatre, 1983.

Courtship (also see below; produced in Louisville, KY, by Actors' Theatre, 1984), Dramatists Play Service (New York, NY), 1984.

Lily Dale (also see below), produced Off-Broadway, 1986.

The Widow Claire (also see below), produced Off-Broadway, 1986.

"Courtship," "Valentine's Day," and "1918": Three Plays from "The Orphans' Home" Cycle (broadcast by PBS as *The Story of a Marriage,* 1987), Grove Press (New York, NY), 1987.

On Valentine's Day (also see below; produced Off-Broadway, 1980), Dramatists Play Service (New York, NY), 1987.

1918 (also see below; produced Off-Broadway, 1982), Dramatists Play Service (New York, NY), 1987.

"Roots in a Parched Ground," "Convicts," "Lily Dale," and "The Widow Claire" (also see below), Grove Press (New York, NY), 1988.

The Death of Papa (also see below), Dramatists Play Service (New York, NY), 1989.

"Cousins" and "The Death of Papa": Two Plays from "The Orphans' Home" Cycle (also see below), Grove Press (New York, NY), 1989.

Cousins (produced in Los Angeles at The Loft, 1984), Dramatists Play Service (New York, NY), 1990.

SCREENPLAYS

Storm Fear (based on novel by Clinton Seeley), United Artists, 1956.

To Kill a Mockingbird (based on the novel by Harper Lee), Universal, 1962, published as *The Screenplay of "To Kill a Mockingbird,"* Harcourt (New York, NY), 1964.

Baby, the Rain Must Fall (based on Foote's play, *The Traveling Lady*), Columbia, 1965.

(With Thomas Ryan) *Hurry Sundown* (based on the novel by K.B. Glidden), Paramount, 1966.

Tomorrow (based on the story by William Faulkner), Filmgroup, 1971.

Tender Mercies, Universal, 1983.

1918, Cinecom International, 1984.

On Valentine's Day, Angelika Films, 1985.

The Trip to Bountiful, Island Pictures, 1985.

"To Kill a Mockingbird," "Tender Mercies," and "The Trip to Bountiful": Three Screenplays, Grove Press (New York, NY), 1989.

Convicts, M.C.E.G., 1991.

Of Mice and Men (adapted from the novel by John Steinbeck), 1991.

Lily Dale, Showtime, 1996.

Also author of screenplay, *Spring Moon* (based on the novel by Bette Bao Lord), 1987.

TELEVISION PLAYS

Ludie Brooks, CBS, 1951.

The Travelers, NBC, 1952.

The Old Beginning, NBC, 1953.

The Trip to Bountiful, 1953.

The Oil Well, NBC, 1953.

The Rocking Chair, NBC, 1953.

Expectant Relations, NBC, 1953.

John Turner Davis, 1953.

The Midnight Caller, 1953.

Tears of My Sister, NBC, 1953.

Young Lady of Property, NBC, 1953.

Death of the Old Man, NBC, 1953.

Shadow of Willie Greer, NBC, 1954.

The Dancers, 1954.

The Roads to Home, 1955.

Flight, NBC, 1956.

Drugstore: Sunday Noon, ABC, 1956.

Member of the Family, CBS, 1957.

Old Man (based on the novel by William Faulkner), CBS, 1959, revised version, Hallmark Hall of Fame, 1997.

The Shape of the River, CBS, 1960.

The Night of the Storm, 1960.

The Gambling Heart, NBC, 1964.

The Displaced Person (based on a story by Flannery O'Connor), PBS, 1977.

Barn Burning (based on a story by William Faulkner), PBS, 1980.

Keeping On, PBS, 1983.

Habitation of Dragons, 1991.

Lily Dale, 1996.

Alone, 1997.

Horton Foote's The Shape of the River: The Lost Teleplay about Mark Twain, with History and Analysis, by Mark Dawidziak, Applause Theatre & Cinema Books, 2003.

OTHER

The Chase (novel), based on Foote's play, Rinehart (New York, NY), 1956.

Farewell: A Memoir of a Texas Childhood, Scribner (New York, NY), 1999.

Beginnings: A Memoir, Scribner (New York, NY), 2001.

Genesis of an American Playwright, edited and with an introduction by Marion Castleberry, Baylor University Press, 2004.

ADAPTATIONS: The Chase was adapted to film by Lillian Hellman for Columbia Pictures, 1965.

SIDELIGHTS: Horton Foote is a prolific writer for stage and screen whose dramas of rural Texas reveal the fundamentals and universals of the human condition. Awarded a National Medal of Arts by U.S. President Bill Clinton in 2000, Foote is perhaps best known for his films, including *To Kill a Mockingbird* and *Tender Mercies.* It is on the stage, however, where the author's artistry most manifests itself. "Much of Foote's drama treats the common man and woman realistically in disturbing but strangely comforting stories," observed an essayist for *Contemporary Dramatists.* "The pathos that ordinary people undergo, the nobility of the neglected and the forgotten, the profound humor in unsuspected houses and families, the suffering around every corner, the substantiality of what is taken for granted, the high stakes wagered in backstairs games—these constitute his subject." In a career spanning more than sixty years of writing about small-town life, Foote has become affectionately known for works that pierce to the core of human relationships from the cradle to the nursing home.

"From the beginning," Foote once wrote, "most of my plays have taken place in the imaginary town of Harrison, Texas, and it seems to me a more unlikely subject could not be found in these days of Broadway and world theatre, than this attempt of mine to recreate a small Southern town and its people. But I did not choose this task, this place, or these people to write about so much as they chose me, and I try to write of them with honesty." At a time when the sensational and carnal preside over a great portion of the popular dramatic arts, Foote continues to stress the subtle and the intimate with lean dialogue and understated action. "What seems remarkable about Foote's career," wrote Charles Champlin in the *Los Angeles Times,* "is that across all the media and amid all the conflicts of art versus commerce, in which art is always the long-odds underdog, he has produced a coherent body of work. . . . It is most often an intimate, loving, perceptive exploration of ordinary people and their often extraordinary resilience, courage, persistence and wisdom in the face of trials, disappointments and dreams that have had to be deferred or abandoned."

Foote was born in Wharton, Texas, and was raised in a well-to-do family. He showed precocious reading habits from early youth, enrolling in the Book-of-the-Month club when he was twelve. After high school he left Texas to enroll in the Pasadena Playhouse School of Theatre, and at the height of the Great Depression he arrived in New York, NY in search of an acting job. He was cast in several Off-Broadway plays during the late 1930s, and it was while performing with the American Actors Company between 1939 and 1942 that Foote realized his talent as a dramatist. In 1942 his play *Texas Town* was produced in New York City. For the next three years Foote operated a production company in Washington, DC, and managed to get two more works produced in New York, 1942's *Out of My House* and 1944's *Only the Heart.* "It is impossible not to believe absolutely in the reality of his characters," wrote Brooks Atkinson in his review of *Texas Town* for the *New York Times.* Of *Out of My House,* Atkinson commented: "Foote pulls himself together in a vibrant and glowing last act that is compact and bitterly realistic."

Foote's early plays—emotionally restrained dramas emphasizing character development and set within the social context of the rural South—established a recognizable pattern from which he has rarely wavered. The *Contemporary Dramatists* contributor wrote: "The rhetoric of Foote's work suggests that the language we regularly use be taken as fully adequate to our condition and that our condition consists precisely of the people we know, the work we do, and the era in which we live. . . . Nothing and no one is unrelated, even by choice." As James M. Wall put it in the *Christian Century,* Foote's "writing is deceptively simple, filled with quiet exchanges between people who desperately want to understand what is happening to them but are constantly confronted by loss and suffering over which they have no final control." A contributor to *Contempo-*

rary Southern Writers similarly noted: "In [Foote's] plays and screenplays life, even common, middle-class life, is full of quiet terror and mystery. . . . But in Foote's world things never are quite hopelessness, for balancing out the world's unpleasant surprises is always the possibility of love, a kind of countervailing, benevolent mystery."

In the late 1940s, while still writing for the stage, Foote also began working in television. He adapted many of his own dramas for such showcases as *Playhouse 90* and *Kraft Playhouse,* and occasionally adapted the work of other Southern writers to television, including William Faulkner's *Old Man* and *Tomorrow.* In all, Foote adapted more than thirty dramas for television. His book *Harrison, Texas,* a collection of eight television plays written and produced between January, 1953, and March, 1954, elicited reviewer praise. "Television is in redemptive hands as long as it can work with art like this," wrote a *Saturday Review* critic.

In Foote's acclaimed 1953 teleplay, *The Trip to Bountiful,* an elderly widow longs to escape the cramped Houston, Texas apartment she shares with her unsupportive son and his lazy wife. The widow eventually journeys to her small-town birthplace, only to find desolation instead of a sentimental homecoming. Prompted by *Bountiful*'s television success, Foote adapted it for the theater, and it ran on Broadway that same year. Later, a film version earned Foote an Oscar nomination for best screenplay.

In 1956, Foote's play *The Chase* was published as a novel and received critical acclaim for its dramatic power and strong characterizations. Anthony Boucher made these comments: "Sharply effective as a melodrama of violence, it is also powerful as a novel of character, probing deeply into many lives . . . and studying the inherent moral and psychological problems of violence." While *Commonweal*'s W.J. Smith found the book's lengthy epilogue to be ineffective, he was enthusiastic about the story itself: "The characterizations are excellent, the action is fast and suspenseful and the ramifications of the plot neatly interlocked. The novel attains a level beyond that of the mere thriller—psychological melodrama, perhaps, describes it better."

With the demise of live television in the late 1950s, Foote moved his dramatic efforts to the movie screen. His adaptation of Harper Lee's novel *To Kill a Mockingbird* won the 1962 Academy Award for best screenplay, and Gregory Peck received the award for best actor for his portrayal of Atticus Finch, the father. Concentrating on the lives of two children in depression-era, rural Alabama, the film reveals the prevailing bigotry of a small town as the children watch their father defend in court a black man falsely accused of rape. The film culminates in a guilty verdict, but not before the children witness the harmful consequences of prejudice and learn through their father's noble efforts the value of integrity. Bosley Crowther lauded the film's "feeling for children." In the *New York Times* Crowther wrote: "There is . . . so much delightful observation of their spirit, energy, and charm. . . . Especially in their relations with their father."

Following the success of *To Kill a Mockingbird,* Foote wrote such screenplays as *Baby, the Rain Must Fall, Hurry Sundown,* and an adaptation of Faulkner's *Tomorrow.* But he withdrew into semi-retirement during the 1970s to live on a farm in New Hampshire with his family. There he concentrated upon playwriting, producing his acclaimed "Orphans' Home" cycle, based upon his father's childhood and coming of age. Foote's reemergence in Hollywood came at the suggestion of a friend, actor Robert Duvall, who requested a screenplay from the writer. The result was *Tender Mercies,* the 1983 movie that won Foote a second Academy Award for best screenplay and Duvall an Oscar for best actor.

The film portrays a famous country singer who succumbs to alcoholism and loses his career and marriage. Eventually he finds solace with a young widow and her son in a Texas roadside motel. True to Foote's enduring, subtle style, "the excitement of *Tender Mercies* lies below the surface," wrote David Sterritt in the *Saturday Evening Post.* "It's not the quick change of fast action, the flashy performances or the eye-zapping cuts. Rather, it's something much more rare—the thrill of watching characters grow, personalities deepen, relationships ripen and mature. It's the pleasure of rediscovering the dramatic richness of decency, honesty, compassion and a few other qualities that have become rare visitors to the silver screen." Vincent Canby wrote in the *New York Times* that Foote's screenplay "doesn't overexplain or overanalyze. It has a rare appreciation for understatement, which is the style of its characters if not of the actual narrative." Canby called *Tender Mercies* "the best thing [Foote's] ever done for films."

Even before his successful return to the screen, Foote had begun work on a nine-part dramatic cycle called "Orphans' Home." The cycle follows several generations of the Robedaux family and depicts their hardships amid the decline of the plantation aristocracy in

southern Texas during the early part of the twentieth century. The character who unites the cycle is Horace Robedaux, a boy abandoned by his mother after the death of his father. How Horace persists in the face of tragedy forms the crux of each play. In *1918,* for example, Horace and his fellow small-town Texans follow the news of World War I even as a deadly influenza outbreak brings mounting casualties to their own world. *Lily Dale* explores Horace's attempt to connect with the mother and sister who left him behind for a better life in Houston. The concluding play in the cycle, *The Death of Papa,* reveals a family's disintegration after Horace's grandfather dies. Foote is quoted in the *Southern Literary Journal* as having written of the cycle: "These plays, I feel, are about change, unexpected, unasked for, unwanted, but to be faced and dealt with or else we sink into despair or a hopeless longing for a life that is gone."

Critical response to the series, which included the televised productions *1918, On Valentine's Day,* and *Convicts,* has been divided between opponents and proponents of Foote's typically subdued style. Writing in the *National Review,* Chilton Williamson, Jr. thought Foote "trivializes life into a banal serenity," while Canby argued that Foote's characters, "being so resolutely ordinary, become particular." Canby called *1918* a "writer's movie. . . . One that, for better or worse, pays no attention to the demands for pacing and narrative emphasis that any commercially oriented Hollywood producer would have insisted on. The very flatness of its dramatic line is its dramatic point." Author Reynolds Price is quoted in *Christian Century* as saying that the "Orphans' Home" cycle "will take its rightful place near the center of our largest American dramatic achievements."

Foote continued to write through his eighties, producing new plays and directing plays by his daughter, Daisy. In 1995 he earned a Pulitzer Prize for his play *The Young Man from Atlanta.* Set in the 1950s, *The Young Man from Atlanta* follows the struggles of Will and Lily Dale Kidder as they seek to reconcile themselves to their son's death, a possible suicide. A young man claiming to have been the son's roommate accepts huge sums of money from Lily Dale in exchange for information, but Will staunchly refuses to see him. Although the son's homosexuality is implied—and his roommate's integrity is challenged by a third party—neither question is fully resolved during the drama. In a review for *Advocate,* Dick Scanlan declared: "At 81, Foote's artistic heart remains in good shape, his instinct for truth intact. *Young Man* addresses the futile pursuit of the American dream a la *Death of a Salesman* while adding heterosexuality as a component of that dream." *Variety* correspondent Greg Evans felt that the play's "affecting portrait of shattered illusions . . . won't soon be forgotten."

The Last of the Thorntons, produced in New York in 2000, is set in a nursing home. There the elderly residents and their visitors, all of whom hail from the same small Texas town, review their lives both past and present with varying degrees of resignation. "As befits an 84-year-old playwright, this small but haunting work is about final endings and the ghosts of the past," maintained Karl Levett in *Back Stage.* "It is presented in a straightforward, slice-of-life fashion, but with echoing reverberations way beyond the here and now. With complete mastery over his material, Foote achieves his effects with never a false note, making it all seem deceptively simple." In *Variety,* Charles Isherwood described the play as "a piece of chamber music more than a drama. It makes the kind of quiet inroads into our hearts that music does. By the end you're surprised at how deeply—and almost imperceptibly—you've been affected, how impatience has quietly turned into empathy."

Foote has also authored two autobiographies, *Farewell: A Memoir of a Texas Childhood* and *Beginnings.* Together the two books take Foote from birth to his years as an actor and budding playwright. Andrew O'Hehir noted in the *New York Times Book Review* that, at first, *Farewell* seems like "nostalgic musings for a bygone era of small-town America." The critic added, however, that the work "provides a key to the birth of [Foote's] distinctive sensibility." *Wilson Quarterly* reviewer Larry L. King commended Foote for writing *Farewell* "deliberately, in detail, and unhurriedly." King added: "In time, one realizes that his wanderings are not without purpose, and that he has achieved a surprising economy of words." A *Publishers Weekly* contributor wrote of *Beginnings:* "Foote's chronicle is still as charming as his plays and will be welcomed by his fans."

Marion Castleberry, in conjunction with Foote, has edited *Genesis of an American Playwright,* which collects previously published essays and includes a chronology of Foote's life as well as an appendix listing cast and details of all plays, screenplays, and teleplays. *Genesis* "reveals both the private man and the prolific artist," Joanne Brannon Aldridge writing for the *Charlotte Observer* reported and "Foote's comments are rich and generous." Castleberry has been instrumental in creating the Horton Foote American Playwrights Festival and the Horton Foote Society at Baylor University.

Some years ago, Foote moved back to his hometown to reside in the family homestead, although he also kept an apartment in Greenwich Village. In the *New York Times Magazine,* Samuel G. Freedman reflected on the Texan's distinctive style: "The key to Foote's writing, the signature of his style, is the ability to convey both melodramatic events and loquacious language in a spare, reductive manner. While his plots suggest Faulkner, his style shares more with Katharine Anne Porter, and he is influenced primarily by poetry, the most skeletal of forms."

BIOGRAPHICAL AND CRITICAL SOURCES:

BOOKS

Briley, Rebecca Luttrell, *You Can Go Home Again: The Focus on Family in the Works of Horton Foote,* Peter Lang (New York, NY), 1993.
Contemporary Dramatists, 6th edition, St. James Press (Detroit, MI), 1999.
Contemporary Literary Criticism, Volume 51, Thomson Gale (Detroit, MI), 1989.
Contemporary Southern Writers, St. James Press (Detroit, MI), 1999.
Contemporary Theatre, Film, and Television, Volume 15 Thomson Gale (Detroit, MI), 1996.
Dictionary of Literary Biography, Volume 26: *American Screenwriters,* Thomson Gale (Detroit, MI), 1984.
Foote, Horton, *Beginnings: A Memoir,* Scribner (New York, NY), 2001.
Foote, Horton, *Farewell: A Memoir of a Texas Childhood,* Scribner (New York, NY), 1999.
Porter, Laurin, *Orphans' Home: The Voice and Vision of Horton Foote,* Louisiana State University Press (Baton Rouge, LA), 2003.
Prunty, Wyatt, editor, *Sewanee Writers on Writing,* Louisiana State University Press (Baton Rouge, LA), 2000.
Watson, Charles S., *Horton Foote: A Literary Biography,* University of Texas Press (Austin, TX), 2003.
Wood, Gerald C., *Horton Foote and the Theater of Intimacy,* Louisiana State University Press (Baton Rouge, LA), 1999.

PERIODICALS

Advocate, April 29, 1997, Dick Scanlan, review of *The Young Man from Atlanta,* p. 61.
America, May 10, 1986.
Atlanta Journal-Constitution, April 25, 1999, Dan Hulbert, review of *Farewell: A Memoir of a Texas Childhood,* p. S10.

Back Stage, December 8, 2000, Karl Levett, review of *The Last of the Thorntons,* p. 56.

Booklist, February 15, 1999, Jack Helbig, review of *Getting Frankie Married—and Afterwards and Other Plays,* p. 1027; May 1, 1999, Jack Helbig, review of *Farewell,* p. 1572.

Charlotte Observer, Joanne Brannon Aldridge, review of *Genesis*Fri, Jul. 23, 2004.

Chicago Tribune, May 14, 1985; February 7, 1986; January 8, 1987.

Christian Century, February 19, 1997, James M. Wall, "Home, Family, Religion," p. 179.

Commonweal, March 16, 1956; February 26, 1988, p. 110.

Explicator, winter, 1998, Ron Evans, "Faulkner's 'Tomorrow,'" p. 95.

Houston Chronicle, February 18, 1996, Everett Evans, "A Stage of Life," p. 8.

Library Journal, April 1, 1989, p. 89; May 1, 1999, Barry X. Miller, review of *Farewell,* p. 80.

Los Angeles Times, March 4, 1983; April 3, 1983; April 3, 1984; April 17, 1984; June 12, 1985; December 23, 1985; March 15, 1986; December 13, 1987; June 8, 1996, Robert Koehler, "'Lily Dale' Withers in Face of Conflict," p. 6.

Modern Maturity, December, 1996, Sheila Benson, interview with Foote.

National Review, June 14, 1985; June 6, 1986.

New Leader, March 24, 1997, Stefan Kanfer, review of *The Young Man from Atlanta,* p. 22.

New Republic, March 31, 1986.

Newsday, November 21, 1986.

New York, May 26, 1986; January 5, 1987; April 6, 1987.

New Yorker, December 29, 1986; April 14, 1997, John Lahr, review of *The Young Man from Atlanta,* p. 86; September 10, 2001, John Lahr, "Texas Bittersweet," p. 102.

New York Herald Tribune Book Review, February 6, 1956.

New York Magazine, April 6, 1992, p. 87.

New York Times, April 30, 1941; January 8, 1942; December 7, 1942; April 5, 1944; April 16, 1952; November 4, 1953; October 28, 1954; February 19, 1956; April 12, 1982; February 8, 1983; March 4, 1983; March 13, 1983; April 21, 1985; April 26, 1985; April 28, 1985; May 27, 1985; December 20, 1985; April 11, 1986; April 13, 1986; May 4, 1986; May 13, 1986; August 15, 1986; October 8, 1986; October 17, 1986; November 21, 1986; December 18, 1986; April 5, 1987; December 2, 1989; December 3, 1989; December 4, 2000, Ben Brantley, "Wry Smiles Temper the Anguish of Old Age," p. B1; December 10, 2001, Mel Gussow, "The Creativity Born of a Town in Texas," p. E4.

New York Times Book Review, August 15, 1999, Andrew O'Hehir, review of *Farewell,* p. 18; December 30, 2001, N. Graham Nesmith, review of *Beginnings,* p. 17.

New York Times Magazine, February 9, 1986.

North American Review, March-April, 1996, Robert L. King, review of *The Young Man from Atlanta,* p. 44.

Publishers Weekly, December 13, 1993, p. 67; May 10, 1999, review of *Farewell,* p. 50; September 10, 2001, review of *Beginnings,* p. 71.

San Francisco Chronicle, February 26, 1956.

Saturday Evening Post, October, 1983.

Saturday Review, February 18, 1956.

Southern Literary Journal, fall, 1999, Michael Gallagher, "Horton Foote: Defying Heraclitus in Texas," p. 77.

Texas Monthly, July 1991, p. 110.

Time, April 14, 1986.

TV Guide, April 4, 1987.

Variety, March 31, 1997, Greg Evans, review of *The Young Man from Atlanta,* p. 98; June 29, 1998, Chris Jones, review of *Vernon Early,* p. 49; June 7, 1999, Markland Taylor, review of *The Death of Papa,* p. 47; December 11, 2000, Charles Isherwood, review of *The Last of the Thorntons,* p. 29; August 20, 2001, Peter Ritter, review of *The Carpetbagger's Children,* p. 31.

Washington Post, February 8, 1983; April 29, 1983; January 31, 1985; April 25, 1986; June 9, 1996, Linton Weeks, "A Pale 'Lily Dale,'" p. G5.

Wilson Quarterly, autumn, 1999, Larry L. King, review of *Farewell,* p. 116.

ONLINE

Horton Foote Society Web site, http://www3.baylor.edu/Horton_Foote_Society/ (August 3, 2004).

*   *   *

FOOTE, Shelby 1916-2005

PERSONAL: Born November 17, 1916, in Greenville, MS; died June 27, 2005, in Memphis TN; son of Shelby Dade (a business executive) and Lillian (Rosenstock) Foote; married Gwyn Rainer, September 6, 1956; children: Margaret Shelby, Huger Lee. *Education:* Attended University of North Carolina, 1935-37.

CAREER: Novelist, historian, and playwright. Novelist-in-residence, University of Virginia, Charlottesville, 1963; playwright-in-residence, Arena Stage, Washington, DC, 1963-64; writer-in-residence, Hollins College, Roanoke, VA, 1968. Judge, National Book Award in history, 1979. *Military service:* U.S. Army, artillery, 1940-44; became captain. U.S. Marine Corps, 1944-45.

MEMBER: American Academy of Arts and Letters, Society of American Historians, Fellowship of Southern Writers.

AWARDS, HONORS: Guggenheim fellowships, 1955, 1956, and 1957; Ford Foundation grant, 1963; Fletcher Pratt Award, 1964, for *The Civil War: A Narrative;* named distinguished alumnus, University of North Carolina, 1974; Dos Passos Prize for Literature, 1988; Charles Frankel Award, 1992; St. Louis Literary Award, 1992; Nevins-Freeman Award, 1992; honorary D.Litt. degrees from University of the South, 1981, Southwestern University, 1982, University of South Carolina, 1991, University of North Carolina, 1992, Millsaps University, 1992, Notre Dame University, 1994, Loyola University, 1999, and College of William and Mary, 1999.

WRITINGS:

NOVELS

Tournament, Dial (New York, NY), 1949.
Follow Me Down (also see below), Dial (New York, NY), 1950.
Love in a Dry Season (also see below), Dial (New York, NY), 1951.
Shiloh, Dial (New York, NY), 1952.
Jordan County: A Landscape in Narrative (also see below), Dial (New York, NY), 1954.
Three Novels (contains *Follow Me Down, Love in a Dry Season,* and *Jordan County: A Landscape in Narrative*), Dial (New York, NY), 1964.
September September, Random House (New York, NY), 1979.
Child by Fever, Random House (New York, NY), 1995.
Ride Out, Modern Library (New York, NY), 1996.

OTHER

The Civil War: A Narrative, Random House (New York, NY), Volume 1: *Fort Sumter to Perryville,* 1958, Volume 2: *Fredericksburg to Meridian,* 1963, Volume 3: *Red River to Appomattox,* 1974, fortieth anniversary edition, Time-Life Books, 1998.

Jordan County: A Landscape in the Round (play), produced in Washington, DC, 1964.
A Novelist's View of History (nonfiction), 1981.
(Editor) *Chickamauga, and Other Civil War Stories* (short stories), Dell (New York, NY), 1993.
Stars in Their Courses: The Gettysburg Campaign (history), Random House (New York, NY), 1994.
The Beleaguered City: The Vicksburg Campaign, December 1862-July 1863 (originally published in Volume 2 of *The Civil War: A Narrative*), Modern Library (New York, NY), 1995.
The Correspondence of Shelby Foote and Walker Percy, edited by Jay Tolson, Center for Documentary Studies (New York, NY), 1997.
(Author of introduction) Anton Chekhov, *Early Short Stories, 1883-1888,* Modern Library (New York, NY), 1999.
(Author of introduction) Anton Chekhov, *Later Short Stories, 1888-1903,* Modern Library (New York, NY), 1999.
(Editor and author of introduction) Anton Chekhov, *Longer Stories from the Last Decade,* Modern Library (New York, NY), 1999.

ADAPTATIONS: Many of Foote's nonfiction writings, including *The Civil War: A Narrative, Stars in Their Courses,* and *The Beleaguered City,* have been adapted as audiobooks.

SIDELIGHTS: Although his novels have been favorably received, Shelby Foote is best known for his three-volume narrative history of the U.S. Civil War. Originally envisioned as a one-volume work, Foote's *The Civil War: A Narrative* grew into what critics have praised as a monumental project that took some twenty years to complete. In the *New York Times Book Review,* Nash K. Burger explained that after writing the Civil War novel *Shiloh,* "Mississippi-born Shelby Foote was asked by a New York publisher to write a short, one-volume history of that conflict. Foote agreed. It seemed a nice change of pace before his next novel. Now, twenty years later, the project is completed."

In Foote's work, the three volumes are divided up between the stages of the war, and appropriately titled *Fort Sumter to Perryville, Fredericksburg to Meridian,* and *Red River to Appomattox,* Noting the scope of Foote's almost three-thousand-word narrative, Burger praised *The Civil War* as "a remarkable achievement, prodigiously researched, vigorous, detailed, absorbing."

Other reviewers have voiced similar praise. In *Newsweek* Peter S. Prescott stated that "the result [of Foote's labor] is not only monumental in size, but a truly impressive achievement." Prescott added that "Foote the novelist cares less for generalizations about dialectics, men and motives than for creating 'the illusion that the observer is not so much reading a book as sharing an experience.'" According to M.E. Bradford in the *National Review,* in this endeavor Foote succeeds admirably. "There is, of course, a majesty inherent in the subject," noted Bradford of the U.S. Civil War, going on to note that "the credit for recovering such majesty to the attention of our skeptical and unheroic age will hereafter belong . . . to Mr. Foote."

Foote's account of the war is strictly a military one, detailing the battles, men, and leaders on both sides of the conflict. "The War itself . . . is indeed Foote's subject," Bradford remarked. "The *war,* the *fighting*—and not its economic, intellectual, or political causes." Lance Morrow echoed this summation in a *Time* review, noting that Foote's "attention is focused on the fighting itself—fortification, tactics, the strange chemistries of leadership, the workings in the generals' minds. Foote moves armies and great quantities of military information with a lively efficiency."

Critics have noted that although military histories concerning the U.S. Civil War abound, Foote's is among the most comprehensive, covering as it does the Union and Confederate Armies in both the eastern and western theaters of the war. Moreover, many reviewers have expressed admiration for the author's balanced and objective view of the still-somewhat divisive conflict. C. Vann Woodward commented in the *New York Review of Books* that "in spite of his Mississippi origins, Foote . . . attempts to keep an even hand in giving North and South their due measure of praise and blame." Burger agreed, adding that although Foote's chronicle begins and ends with reports on the activities of Confederate President Jefferson Davis, this introduction "is not indicative of any bias in favor of the South or its leader. . . . The complete work," Burger continued, "is a monumental, even-handed account of this country's tragic, fratricidal conflict."

In discussing Foote's concentration on the war itself and "therefore the persons who made, died in, or survived that conflict," Bradford asserted that it is not "an exaggeration to speak of the total effect produced by this emphasis as epic." Prescott concluded: "To read Foote's chronicle is an awesome and moving experience. History and literature are rarely so thoroughly combined as here; one finishes [the last] volume convinced that no one need undertake this particular enterprise again."

Foote became something of a national celebrity during the early 1990s for his on-camera commentary as part of documentary filmmaker Ken Burns's epic Public Television documentary *The Civil War,* which became something of a national event when it first aired in 1990. Sparked by his appearance on the cover of *Newsweek* magazine in the fall of that year, interest in Foote's work as an historian increased markedly, and his *The Civil War: A Narrative* received renewed interest among critics and general readers alike when it was made available as an audiobook. In addition to continuing to pen novels, in the mid-1990s Foote also collected short fiction of the Civil War period as *Chickamauga, and Other Civil War Stories,* and produced an in-depth history of one of the most dramatic battles of the war in *Stars in Their Courses: The Gettysburg Campaign.*

BIOGRAPHICAL AND CRITICAL SOURCES:

BOOKS

Carter, William C., editor, *Conversations with Shelby Foote,* University Press of Mississippi, 1995.

Phillips, Robert L., Jr., *Shelby Foote: Novelist and Historian,* University Press of Mississippi, 1992.

Tolson, Jay, *The Correspondence of Shelby Foote and Walker Percy,* Center for Documentary Studies, 1997.

White, Helen, and Redding S. Sugg, Jr., *Shelby Foote,* Twayne Publishers, 1982.

PERIODICALS

American Heritage, July-August, 1991.

Atlantic, May, 1952; December, 1963.

Book Week, December 15, 1963.

Chicago Sunday Tribune, November 16, 1958.

Christian Science Monitor, December 4, 1963.

Commonweal, January 9, 1959.

English Journal, September, 1992, Penny Turk, review of *Shiloh,* p. 98.

Library Journal, September 1, 1992, Michael Rogers, review of *Jordan County,* p. 220; March 1, 1995, Michael T. Fein, review of *Stars in Their Courses: The Gettysburg Campaign,* p. 119; March 15, 1996, Barbara Mann, review of *The Beleaguered City: The Vicksburg Campaign,* p. 113.

Military Law Review, fall, 1994, pp. 275-279.

National Review, February 14, 1975.

Newsweek, December 2, 1974; January 30, 1978; October 8, 1990, Harry F. Waters, "Prime Time's New Star," p. 60.

New York Herald Tribune Book Review, July 16, 1950; October 21, 1951; April 6, 1952; May 2, 1954; November 23, 1958.

New York Review of Books, March 6, 1975.

New York Times, September 25, 1949; September 23, 1951; April 6, 1952; April 25, 1954; November 16, 1958; December 1, 1996.

New York Times Book Review, December 1, 1963; December 15, 1974; March 5, 1978.

Paris Review, summer, 1999, Donald Faulkner, interview with Foote, p. 48.

People, October 15, 1990, Michelle Greene, "The Civil War Finds a Homer in Writer Shelby Foote," p. 60.

San Francisco Chronicle, November 28, 1958.

Saturday Review, November 19, 1949; June 5, 1954; December 13, 1958.

Southern Literary Journal, fall, 2003, p. 21.

Time, July 3, 1950; January 27, 1975.

OBITUARIES:

PERIODICALS

New York Times, June 29, 2005.

ONLINE

CNN.com, http://www.cnn.com/ (June 28, 2005).

*   *   *

FORCHÉ, Carolyn 1950-
(Carolyn Louise Forché)

PERSONAL: Surname is pronounced "for-*shay*"; born April 28, 1950, in Detroit, MI; daughter of Michael Joseph (a tool and die maker) and Louise Nada (a journalist; maiden name, Blackford) Sidlosky; married Henry E. Mattison (a news photographer), December 27, 1984; children: Sean-Christophe. *Education:* Michigan State University, B.A., 1972; Bowling Green State University, M.F.A., 1975.

ADDRESSES: Home—Maryland. *Office*—George Mason University, 4400 University Dr., Fairfax, VA, 22030-4444. *Agent*—Virginia Barber, 353 West 21st St., New York, NY 10011. *E-mail*—cforchem@osf1.gmu.edu.

CAREER: Justin Morrill College, Michigan State University, East Lansing, visiting lecturer in poetry, 1974; San Diego State University, San Diego, CA, visiting lecturer, 1975, assistant professor, 1976-78; journalist and human rights activist in El Salvador, 1978-80; University of Virginia, Charlottesville, visiting lecturer, 1979, visiting associate professor, 1982-83; University of Arkansas, Fayetteville, assistant professor, 1980, associate professor, 1981; New York University, New York, NY, visiting writer, 1983, 1985; correspondent for National Public Radio's *All Things Considered* in Beirut, 1983; Vassar College, Poughkeepsie, NY, visiting writer, 1984; Writer's Community, New York, NY, visiting poet, 1984; State University of New York—Albany, Writer's Institute, writer-in-residence, 1985; Columbia University, adjunct associate professor, 1984-85; University of Minnesota, visiting associate professor, summer, 1985; George Mason University, Fairfax, VA, associate professor, 1994—. Consultant on Central America and member of Commission on U.S.-Central American Relations.

MEMBER: Amnesty International, PEN American Center (member of Freedom to Write and Silenced Voices committees), Poetry Society of America, Academy of American Poets, Associated Writing Programs (president, beginning 1994), Institute for Global Education, Coalition for a New Foreign Policy, Theta Sigma Phi.

AWARDS, HONORS: Devine Memorial fellowship in poetry, 1975; First Award in Poetry, *Chicago Review,* 1975; Yale Series of Younger Poets Award, 1975, for *Gathering the Tribes;* Tennessee Williams fellowship in poetry, Bread Loaf Writers Conference, 1976; National Endowment for the Arts fellowships, 1977 and 1984; John Simon Guggenheim Memorial fellowship, 1978; Emily Clark Balch Prize, *Virginia Quarterly Review,* 1979; Alice Fay di Castagnola Award, Poetry Society of America, 1981; Lamont Poetry Selection Award, Academy of American Poets, 1981, for *The Country between Us;* H.D.L., Russell Sage College, 1985; Lannan Foundation Literary fellowship, 1992; *Los Angeles Times* Book Award for Poetry, 1994, for *The Angel of History;* Edita and Ira Morris Hiroshima Foundation Award (Japan) for her use of poetry as a "means to attain understanding, reconciliation, and peace within communities and between communities," 1997; National Book Critics Circle Award, 2003, for poem "Blue Hour."

WRITINGS:

(With Martha Jane Soltow) *Women in the Labor Movement, 1835-1925: An Annotated Bibliography,* Michigan State University Press (East Lansing, MI), 1972.

Gathering the Tribes (poetry), Yale University Press (New Haven, CT), 1976.

The Colonel, Bieler Press (St. Paul, MN), 1978.

(Editor) *Women and War in El Salvador,* Women's International Resource Exchange (New York, NY), 1980.

(Coauthor) *History and Motivations of U.S. Involvement in the Control of the Peasant Movement in El Salvador: The Role of AIFLD in the Agrarian Reform Process,* EPICA (Washington, DC), 1980.

The Country between Us (poetry), Copper Canyon Press (Port Townsend, WA), 1981.

(Translator) Claribel Alegría, *Flowers from the Volcano,* University of Pittsburgh Press (Pittsburgh, PA), 1982.

Carolyn Forché and George Starbuck Reading Their Poems, Library of Congress (Washington, DC), 1982.

(Author of text) *El Salvador: The Work of Thirty Photographers,* edited by Harry Mattison, Susan Meiselas, and Fae Rubenstein, Writers and Readers Publishing Cooperative (New York, NY), 1983.

"The Poet and the Poem" at the Library of Congress, (sound recording), Library of Congress (Washington, DC), 1990.

(Translator, with William Kulik) *The Selected Poems of Robert Desnos,* Ecco Press (New York, NY), 1991.

(Editor and author of introduction) *Against Forgetting: Twentieth-Century Poetry of Witness* (anthology of poetry), Norton (New York, NY), 1993.

The Angel of History (poetry), HarperCollins (New York, NY), 1994.

Colors Come from God—Just like Me! Abingdon Press (New York, NY), 1995.

(Author of introduction) Natalie Kenvin, *Bruise Theory: Poems,* Boa Editions (Brockport, NY), 1995.

The Angel of History, HarperPerennial (New York, NY), 1995.

(With others) *Lani Maestro/Cradle Cradle Ugoy* (exhibition catalog), Art in General (New York, NY), 1996.

(Author of introduction) George Trakl, *Autumn Sonata,* translated by Daniel Simko, Moyer Bell (Kingston, RI), 1998.

(With others) *Seven Washington Poets Reading Their Poems in the Coolidge Auditorium,* Library of Congress (sound recording), Library of Congress (Washington, DC), 1998.

(Translator) Claribel Alegría, *Saudade=Sorrow,* Curbstone Press (Willimantic, CT), 1999.

(Editor, with Philip Gerard) *Writing Creative Nonfiction: Instruction and Insights from Teachers of the Associated Writing Programs,* Story Press (Cincinnati, OH), 2001.

(Translator and editor, with Munir Akash, Sinan Antoon, and Amira El-Zein) Mahmoud Darwish, *Unfortunately, It Was Paradise: Selected Poems,* University of California Press (Berkeley, CA), 2003.

Blue Hour (poetry), HarperCollins (New York, NY), 2003.

Contributor to books, including *Martyrs: Contemporary Writers on Modern Lives of Faith,* edited by Susan Bergman, HarperSanFrancisco, 1996. Contributing editor, *The Pushcart Prize: Best of the Small Presses,* Volume 3; poetry coeditor of *The Pushcart Prize: Best of the Small Presses,* Volume 8. Work represented in anthologies, including *The Pushcart Prize: Best of the Small Presses,* Volume 6 and Volume 8; *The American Poetry Anthology;* and *Anthology of Magazine Verse: Yearbook of American Poetry.* Contributor of poetry, articles, and reviews to periodicals, including *Parnassus, New York Times Book Review, Washington Post Book World, Ms., Antaeus, Atlantic,* and *American Poetry Review.* Poetry editor of *New Virginia Review,* 1981; contributing editor of *Tendril.*

SIDELIGHTS: "Perhaps no one better exemplifies the power and excellence of contemporary poetry than Carolyn Forché, who is not only one of the most affecting . . . poets in America, but also one of the best poets writing anywhere in the world today," Jonathan Cott wrote in the introduction to his interview with Forché for *Rolling Stone.* Such praise was not new to Forché. Her first book of poetry, *Gathering the Tribes,* recounts experiences of the author's adolescence and young-adult life and won the 1975 Yale Series of Younger Poets Award; her second, *The Country between Us,* was named the 1981 Lamont Poetry Selection and became that most-rare publication: a poetry bestseller. In a critique for the *Los Angeles Times Book Review,* Art Seidenbaum maintained that the poems of the second volume "chronicle the awakening of a political consciousness and are themselves acts of commitment: to concepts and persons, to responsibility, to action." According to Joyce Carol Oates in the *New York Times Book Review,* Forché's ability to wed the "political" with the "personal" places her in the company of such poets as Pablo Neruda, Philip Levine, and Denise Levertov.

By the time she was twenty-four years old, Forché had completed *Gathering the Tribes,* described by Stanley Kunitz in the book's foreword as a work centering on kinship. In these poems, Forché "remembers her childhood in rural Michigan, evokes her Slovak ancestors, immerses herself in the American Indian culture of the

Southwest, explores the mysteries of flesh, tries to understand the bonds of family, race, and sex," related Kunitz. "Burning the Tomato Worms," for example, deals with a young woman's sexual coming of age. But this poetic tale of "first sexual experience," Mark Harris stated in a *Dictionary of Literary Biography* essay, "is told against the larger backdrop of her grandmother's life and death and their meaning to a woman just grown."

If *Gathering the Tribes* "introduced a poet of uncommon vigor and assurance," as Oates wrote, then *The Country between Us* served as "a distinct step forward." A *Ms.* reviewer called the second collection "a poetry of dissent from a poet outraged." Forché herself told Cott: "The voice in my first book doesn't know what it thinks, it doesn't make any judgments. All it can do is perceive and describe and use language to make some sort of re-creation of moments in time. But I noticed that the person in the second book makes an utterance."

Forché's first two volumes of poetry were separated by a period of five years, during the course of which she was involved with Amnesty International and with translating the work of Salvadoran poets. In those years, she also had the opportunity to go to Central America as a journalist and human rights advocate where she learned firsthand of violations against life and liberty. While there, she viewed inadequate health facilities that had never received the foreign aid designated for them and discovered that sixty-three out of every thousand children died from gastrointestinal infections before age one; she saw for herself the young girls who had been sexually mutilated; she learned of torture victims who had been beaten, starved, and otherwise abused; and she experienced something of what it was like to survive in a country where baby food jars are sometimes used as bombs.

Her experiences found expression in *The Country between Us.* As reviewer Katha Pollitt observed in the *Nation,* Forché "insists more than once on the transforming power of what she has seen, on the gulf it has created between herself and those who have seen less and dared less." The poet herself admitted to the compelling nature of her Central American experience. "I tried not to write about El Salvador in poetry, because I thought it might be better to do so in journalistic articles," she told Cott. "But I couldn't—the poems just came." El Salvador became the primary subject of *The Country between Us.* In these poems Forché "addresses herself unflinchingly to the exterior, historical world," Oates explained. She did so at a time when most of her

contemporaries were writing poetry in which there is no room for politics—poetry, Pollitt stated, "of wistful longings, of failed connections, of inevitable personal loss, expressed in a set of poetic strategies that suit such themes."

Forché is considered particularly adept at depicting cruelty and the helplessness of victims, and in so doing, Paul Gray wrote in *Time,* she "makes pain palpable." More than one critic singled out her poem "The Colonel," centering on her now-famous encounter with a Salvadoran colonel who, as he made light of human rights, emptied a bag of human ears before Forché. The poem concludes: "Something for your poetry, no? he said. Some of the ears on the floor caught this scrap of his voice. Some of the ears on the floor were pressed to the ground." Pollitt remarked that "at their best, Forché's poems have the immediacy of war correspondence, postcards from the volcano of twentieth-century barbarism."

A dozen years passed between the publication of *The Country between Us* and Forché's editing of *Against Forgetting: Twentieth-Century Poetry of Witness,* an anthology collecting the works of poets addressing human-rights violations on a global level. The poems in this anthology present what Matthew Rothschild in the *Progressive* called "some of the most dramatic antiwar and anti-torture poetry written in this benighted century." The poems provide, Gail Wronsky pointed out in the *Antioch Review,* "irrefutable and copious evidence of the human ability to record, to write, to speak in the face of those atrocities." Building on the tradition of social protest and the antiwar poems of the late 1960s, Forché presents a range of approaches: "Many of the poems here are eyes-open, horrifyingly graphic portrayals of human brutality," observed Rothschild. "But others are of defiance, demonstrating resolve and extracting hope even in the most extreme circumstances."

Against Forgetting begins with poets who witnessed the Ottoman Turk genocide of one-and-a-half million Armenians between 1909 and 1918. In this section, the executed Armenian poet Siamento seems to speak for all the other poets in the collection: "Don't be afraid. I must tell you what I say / so people will understand / the crimes men do to men." Another section includes poems by Americans, Germans, and Japanese about the effects of World War II upon those who witnessed and recorded the events. There are also sections on the Holocaust, the Spanish Civil War, the Soviet Union, Central and Eastern Europe, the Mediterranean, the Middle East, Latin America, South Africa, and China.

Critics were divided upon both the selections in and the importance of *Against Forgetting*. Wronsky, for example, questioned why "women of all races and ethnicities are underrepresented here (124 male poets to 20 female)," while Phoebe Pettingell in the *New Leader* argued that the work's flaws are "outweighed by the anthology's breadth and scope, and by the excellence of most of its entries. *Against Forgetting*," Pettingell continued, "preaches the hope that humanity, after a century of unparalleled brutality met largely by helplessness, can finally learn to mend its ways." John Bayley, writing in the *New York Review of Books,* called the collection "a remarkable book. Not only in itself and for the poems it contains, but for the ideas that lie behind their selection as an anthology."

In an article in the *Mason Gazette,* Forché commented that "The poetry of witness reclaims the social from the political and in so doing defends the individual against illegitimate forms of coercion." The year following the publication of *Against Forgetting* saw Forché bring out her own book of witness, *The Angel of History,* which won the 1994 *Los Angeles Times* Book Award for poetry. The book is divided into five sections dealing with the atrocities of war in France, Japan, and Germany and with references to the poet's own experiences in Beirut and El Salvador. The title figure, the Angel of History—a figure imagined by German philosopher and critic Walter Benjamin—can record the miseries of humanity yet is unable either to prevent these miseries from happening or from suffering from the pain associated with them. Kevin Walker, in the *Detroit Free Press,* called the book "a meditation on destruction, survival and memory." Don Bogen, in the *Nation,* saw this as a logical development, since Forché's work with *Against Forgetting* was "instrumental in moving her poetry beyond the politics of personal encounter. *The Angel of History* is rather an extended poetic mediation on the broader contexts—historical, aesthetic, philosophical—which include [the twentieth] . . . century's atrocities," wrote Bogen.

Critical response to *The Angel of History* was generally supportive. Calvin Bedient in the *Threepenny Review* claimed that *The Angel of History* is "instantly recognizable as a great book, the most humanitarian and aesthetically 'inevitable' response to a half-century of atrocities that has yet been written in English." Steven Ratiner, reviewing the work for the *Christian Science Monitor,* called it one that "addresses the terror and inhumanity that have become standard elements in the twentieth-century political landscape—and yet affirms as well the even greater reservoir of the human spirit."

While Forché is a poet of social and political conscience in an era when poetry is often criticized for being self-centered and self-absorbed, her verse does not always succeed, according to some critics. Pollitt noted an "incongruity between Forché's themes and her poetic strategies," and also commenting on a certain lack of "verbal energy" in her work. William Logan, critiquing for the *Times Literary Supplement,* explained that "in her attempt to offer a personal response to the horrors she has witnessed, Forché too often emphasizes herself at their expense. . . . Forché's work relies on sensibility, but she has not found a language for deeper feeling." Nevertheless, recognizing Forché's achievement, Pollitt commended the poet for "her brave and impassioned attempt to make a place in her poems for starving children and bullet factories, for torturers and victims." While some critics emphasize that she might not be a reassuring poet, in the words of Gray, "she is something better, an arresting and often unforgettable voice."

In 1997, Forché was presented with the Edita and Ira Morris Hiroshima Foundation Award for using her poetry as a "means to attain understanding, reconciliation, and peace within communities and between communities." Hope J. Smith commented in the *Madison Gazette* that while it was "surprising for a poet to receive recognition for her work outside of the usual genre prizes, . . . Forché's work is unusual in that it straddles the realms of the political and the poetic, addressing political and social issues in poetry when many poets have abandoned these subjects altogether. In recognizing the link Forché has made between these worlds, the Hiroshima Foundation recognizes her human rights work as much as it does her writing."

BIOGRAPHICAL AND CRITICAL SOURCES:

BOOKS

Contemporary Literary Criticism, Thomson Gale (Detroit, MI), Volume 25, 1983, Volume 83, 1994, Volume 86, 1995.
Contemporary Poets, 5th edition, St. James Press (Detroit, MI), 1991.
Dictionary of Literary Biography, Volume 5: *American Poets since World War II,* Thomson Gale (Detroit, MI), 1980.
Forché, Carolyn, *Gathering the Tribes,* Yale University Press (New Haven, CT), 1976.
Poetry Criticism, Volume 10, Thomson Gale (Detroit, MI), 1994.

PERIODICALS

American Poetry, spring, 1986, pp. 51-69.

American Poetry Review, November-December, 1976, p. 45; July-August, 1981, pp. 3-8; January-February, 1983, pp. 35-39; November-December, 1988, pp. 35-40.

Antioch Review, summer, 1994, Gail Wronsky, review of *Against Forgetting: Twentieth-Century Poetry of Witness,* p. 536.

Bloomsbury Review, September-October, 1994, p. 19.

Book Forum, annual, 1976, pp. 369-399.

Boston Globe, July 24, 1994, p. 42.

Centennial Review, spring, 1986, pp. 160-180.

Chicago Tribune, December 13, 1982, pp. 1-3.

Christian Science Monitor, April 20, 1994, Steven Ratiner, review of *The Angel of History,* p. 20.

Commonweal, November 25, 1977.

Detroit Free Press, May 27, 1982; May 22, 1994, Kevin Walker, review of *The Angel of History,* p. 8.

Detroit News, June 8, 1982.

Georgia Review, winter, 1982, pp. 911-922; summer, 1994, pp. 361-366.

Library Journal, May 1, 1993, p. 88.

Los Angeles Times, August 24, 1982; October 17, 1982; February 22, 1984.

Los Angeles Times Book Review, May 23, 1982; October 17, 1982.

Ms., January, 1980; September, 1982, review of *The Country between Us.*

Nation, May 8, 1982; October 16, 1982; December 27, 1993, pp. 809, 814; October 24, 1994, Don Bogen, review of *The Angel of History,* p. 464.

New England Review, spring, 1994, pp. 144-154.

New Leader, May 17, 1993, Phoebe Pettingell, review of *Against Forgetting,* pp. 23-24.

New York Review of Books, June 24, 1993, John Bayley, review of *Against Forgetting,* pp. 20-22.

New York Times Book Review, August 8, 1976; April 4, 1982; April 19, 1982; December 4, 1983.

Parnassus, spring-summer, 1982, pp. 9-21.

Progressive, October, 1993, Matthew Rothschild, review of *Against Forgetting,* pp. 45-46.

Publishers Weekly, February 1, 1993, review of *Against Forgetting,* p. 78; January 31, 1994, review of *The Angel of History,* p. 7.

Rolling Stone, April 14, 1983, Jonathan Cott, interview with Forché, pp. 81, 83-87, 110-111.

Text and Performance Quarterly, January, 1990, pp. 61-70.

Threepenny Review, summer, 1994, Calvin Bedient, review of *The Angel of History,* pp. 19-20.

Time, March 15, 1982.

Times Literary Supplement, June 10, 1983.

Triquarterly, winter, 1986, pp. 30, 32-38.

Village Voice, March 29, 1976.

Virginia Quarterly Review, autumn, 1994, p. 136.

Washington Post Book World, May 30, 1982.

Whole Earth Review, spring, 1996, p. 70.

Women's Review of Books, July, 1995, p. 3.

ONLINE

Daily Mason Gazette Online, http://gazette.gmu.edu/ (April 26, 2005).

George Mason University Web site, http://mason.gmu. edu/ (July 27, 2004), "Carolyn Forché."

*   *   *

FORCHÉ, Carolyn Louise
    See FORCHÉ, Carolyn

*   *   *

FORD, Michael Thomas 1969(?)-

PERSONAL: Born c. 1969. *Hobbies and other interests:* SCUBA diving.

ADDRESSES: Home—San Francisco, CA. *Agent*—c/o Mitchell Waters, Curtis Brown Ltd., 10 Astor Place, New York, NY 10003. *E-mail*—writemtf@ michaelthomasford.com.

CAREER: Novelist, columnist, author of nonfiction, and radio commentator.

AWARDS, HONORS: American Library Association (ALA) best book for young adults, 1992, for *One Hundred Questions and Answers about AIDS;* ALA best book for young adults, *Booklist* editor's choice, and National Science Teachers Association/Children's Book Council (CBC) outstanding science trade book designation, all 1995, all for *The Voices of AIDS;* National Council of Social Studies/CBC Notable Children's Book, 1998, for *Outspoken;* Lambda Literary Award for best humor book, 1999, for *Alec Baldwin Doesn't Love Me, and Other Trials of My Queer Life,* 2000, for *That's Mr. Faggot to You: Further Trials from My Queer Life,* 2001, for *It's Not Mean If It's True,* and 2002, for *The Little Book of Neuroses;* New York Public Library best book for the teen age designation, 2000, for *Paths of Faith: Conversation about Religion and Spirituality;* Lambda Literary Award for best romance novel, 2004, for *Last Summer.*

WRITINGS:

NONFICTION

One Hundred Questions and Answers about AIDS: A Guide for Young People, New Discovery Books (New York, NY), 1992, published as *One Hundred Questions and Answers about AIDS: What You Need to Know Now,* Beech Tree Books (New York, NY), 1993.

The Voices of AIDS: Twelve Unforgettable People Talk about How AIDS Has Changed Their Lives, Morrow Junior Books (New York, NY), 1995.

The World out There: Becoming Part of the Lesbian and Gay Community, New Press (New York, NY), 1996.

Alec Baldwin Doesn't Love Me, and Other Trials of My Queer Life, Alyson Books (Los Angeles, CA), 1998.

Outspoken: Role Models from the Lesbian and Gay Community, Morrow Junior Books (New York, NY), 1998.

That's Mr. Faggot to You: Further Trials from My Queer Life, Alyson Books (Los Angeles, CA), 1999.

It's Not Mean if It's True: More Trials from My Queer Life, Alyson Books (Los Angeles, CA), 2000.

Paths of Faith: Conversation about Religion and Spirituality, Simon & Schuster Books for Young Readers (New York, NY), 2000.

The Little Book of Neuroses: Ongoing Trials from My Queer Life, Alyson Books (Los Angeles, CA), 2001.

My Big Fat Queer Life: The Best of Michael Thomas Ford, Alyson Books (Los Angeles, CA), 2003.

Ultimate Gay Sex, DK Publishers (New York, NY), 2004.

Author of "My Queer Life" (syndicated newspaper column), beginning 1996; contributor to *Instinct* magazine and to Web sites.

FICTION

(With others) *Masters of Midnight,* Kensington Books (New York, NY), 2003.

Last Summer, Kensington Books (New York, NY), 2003.

Looking for It, Kensington Books (New York, NY), 2004.

(With others) *Midnight Thirsts,* Kensington Books (New York, NY), 2004.

Author of young adult fiction under various pseudonyms. Also author of musical *Alec Baldwin Doesn't Love Me.*

ADAPTATIONS: Selections from Ford's columns have been recorded as *My Queer Life,* Fluid Word, 2000.

WORK IN PROGRESS: Television-script projects and screenplays.

SIDELIGHTS: As the author of "My Queer Life," a syndicated column that touches on everything from Life after Viagra to the legal troubles of oft-reviled and equally admired business tycoon Martha Stewart, Michael Thomas Ford has been compared to writers such as James Thurber, and been called everything from the "gay Erma Bombeck" to the "gay Everyman." Ford has been widely applauded throughout the gay community for his dry humor, which is reflected in the titles of several anthologies of his columns: *Alec Baldwin Doesn't Love Me, and Other Trials of My Queer Life; That's Mr. Faggot to You: Further Trials from My Queer Life,* and *The Little Book of Neuroses: Ongoing Trials from My Queer Life.* The last book, in particular, showcases what a *Publishers Weekly* reviewer dubbed Ford's "delightfully inventive wit" in its tackling of such compelling subjects as "how *Tiger Beat* magazine made him gay" as well as providing "relationship tips for the neurotically inclined and mus[ing] . . . on how eBay allows us to relive our childhood by buying back our past." However, he also has a more serious side that has also been expressed in his award-winning books for young adults, such as *One Hundred Questions and Answers about AIDS: A Guide for Young People* and *Outspoken: Role Models from the Lesbian and Gay Community.*

Interviews are an important component of all of Ford's books for teen readers; they have been particularly important in making his nonfiction books on coming-of-age issues popular among a readership for whom peer identification is important. In *One Hundred Questions and Answers about AIDS* he talks to four teens who are HIV positive, supplementing those discussions with what a *Publishers Weekly* contributor noted are "concise, very candid explanations" of the symptoms and effects of the disease. Ford's 1995 book *The Voices of AIDS* continues to address the concerns of teens, particularly those in the gay community, by introducing a range of men and women who either have the disease, are involved with an infected lover or family member, or are educators or AIDS activists. "Ford's careful, pointed questions bring out issues related to self-esteem, stereotyping, and discrimination that make the people he's talking to seem very real," noted Stephanie Zvirin in *Booklist,* reflecting the view of other appreciative critics.

From books addressing the most important issue facing young gay Americans—AIDS—Ford has also addressed the social issues that, to many adolescents dealing with their own homosexuality, can often feel as devastating. *Outspoken: Role Models from the Lesbian and Gay Community* does more than just present interviews with eleven gay and lesbian Americans: it allows readers the opportunity to meet eleven men and women who have allowed their differences to make them stronger individuals. Praising Ford's skill in posing "good, interesting questions" to his subjects—which include boxer Mark Leduc, actor Dan Butler, Rabbi Lisa Edwards, and artist Alison Bechdel—Christine Heppermann added in a *Horn Book* review that *Outspoken* "illustrates that there are as many different ways of coming to and participating in the gay community as there are people in it." In *Booklist,* Zvirin praised the book as "Accessible, informative, and sensitive" to its intended audience.

Continuing his focus on teens, Ford has also gone beyond issues of sexuality to address another aspect of personal identity in *Paths of Faith: Conversations about Religion and Spirituality.* Again centering his book on interviews, he talks with Wiccan writer Starhawk, Catholic Archbishop John Cardinal O'Connor, and representatives of Shaker, Islamic, Episcopal, Quaker, Hindu, Jewish Reform, and Buddhist spiritual communities. "Just as good biography can bring to life an historical era, these individuals' stories provide intriguing introductions to a variety of religious faiths," noted a *Horn Book* contributor, while a *School Library Journal* reviewer dubbed *Paths of Faith* "a thoughtful look at contemporary religious practice in the United States." Although some critics noted that the individuals interviewed reflect predominately liberal religious views, as a *Publishers Weekly* contributor maintained, "for does an expert job of balancing discussions about the particulars of a religion with the overarching concerns common to most faiths."

From his stance as a commentator on gay culture, Ford continues to strike a balance between entertainment and education in his writing. While continuing his column, he has also branched out into fiction, and his novels of gay life and love have been praised for their likeable characters and insights into romantic relationships even

as they have gained a following for due to their sexual content. Ford also remains outspoken on serious issues within the gay community at large, particularly racial issues, drug and alcohol abuse, and depression. As he commented during an interview with Paul J. Willis for *Lambda Book Report,* "What we call the queer 'community' is really an extremely diverse group of people united by one commonality—our sexuality. . . . Because of that one commonality, we've been brought together as a family that has to learn how to support one another and look out for one another. Until we do that, then gay rights laws and marriage initiatives and all of those things will mean very little. If the individual members of a community are not working together, then there is no community."

BIOGRAPHICAL AND CRITICAL SOURCES:

PERIODICALS

Advocate, September 26, 2000, Edward Guthmann, "Seriously Funny," p. 73.

Booklist, August, 1995, Stephanie Zvirin, review of *The Voices of Aids,* p. 1948; July, 1996, Ray Olson, review of *The World out There: Becoming Part of the Lesbian and Gay Community,* p. 1783; May 1, 1998, Stephanie Zvirin, review of *Outspoken: Role Models from the Lesbian and Gay Community,* p. 1516; October 1, 20000, Ilene Cooper, review of *Paths of Faith: Conversations about Religion and Spirituality,* p. 353; November 1, 2001, Michael Spinella, review of *The Little Book of Neuroses: Ongoing Trials from My Queer Life,* p. 456; August, 2003, review of *Last Summer,* p. 1952; August, 2004, Whitney Scott, review of *Looking for It,* p. 1908.

Entertainment Weekly, September 23, 2003, review of *Last Summer,* p. 158.

Horn Book, May-June, 1998, Christine Heppermann, review of *Outspoken,* p. 358; January, 2001, review of *Paths of Faith,* p. 108.

Lambda Book Report, July-August, 1999, Louis Bayard, review of *That's Mr. Faggot to You,* p. 24; September, 2000, Paul J. Willis, "Michael Thomas Ford Tells the Awful Truth" (interview), p. 8; April, 2001, Nancy Garden, review of *Paths of Faith,* p. 24; May, 2004, Jonathan Harper, review of *Ultimate Gay Sex,* p. 29.

Publishers Weekly, October 12, 1992, review of *One Hundred Questions and Answers about AIDS,* p. 81; November 13, 1995, review of *The Voices of AIDS,* p. 63; April 5, 1999, review of *That's Mr.*

Faggot to You, p. 226; August 14, 2000, review of *It's Not Mean if It's True,* p. 339; January 29, 2001, review of *Paths of Faith,* p. 87; October 8, 2001, review of *The Little Book of Neuroses,* p. 58; August 4, 2993, review of *Last Summer,* p. 56; April 5, 2004, review of *Ultimate Gay Sex,* p. 58; July 19, 2004, review of *Looking for It,* p. 145.

School Library Journal, January, 2001, Elaine Fort Weischedel, review of *Paths of Faith,* p. 144.

ONLINE

Michael Thomas Ford Web site, http://www.michael thomasford.com/ (August 24, 2004).

*   *   *

FORD, Richard 1944-

PERSONAL: Born February 16, 1944, in Jackson, MS; son of Parker Carrol (in sales) and Edna (Akin) Ford; married Kristina Hensley (a research professor), 1968. *Education:* Michigan State University, B.A., 1966; attended Washington University Law School, 1967-68; University of California—Irvine, M.F.A., 1970.

ADDRESSES: Agent—Amanda Urban, International Creative Management, 40 West 57th St., New York, NY 10019.

CAREER: Writer, 1976—. University of Michigan, Ann Arbor, lecturer, 1974-76; Williams College, Williamstown, MA, assistant professor of English, 1978-79; Princeton University, Princeton, NJ, lecturer, 1979-80; Harvard University, Cambridge, MA, instructor, 1994.

MEMBER: Writers Guild (East), PEN.

AWARDS, HONORS: University of Michigan Society of Fellows, 1971-74; Guggenheim fellow, 1977-78; National Endowment for the Arts fellow, 1979-80, 1985-86; *The Sportswriter* was chosen one of the five best books of 1986, *Time* magazine; PEN/Faulkner citation for fiction, 1987, for *The Sportswriter;* literature award, Mississippi Academy of Arts and Letters, 1987; literature award, American Academy and Institute of Arts and Letters, 1989; Literary Lion Award, New York Public Library, 1989; Echoing Green Foundation award, 1991; Rea Award for the Short Story, 1995; PEN/

Faulkner Award for fiction, Folger Shakespeare Library, and Pulitzer Prize for fiction, Columbia University, both 1996, both for *Independence Day.*

WRITINGS:

FICTION

A Piece of My Heart (novel), Harper (New York, NY), 1976.
The Ultimate Good Luck (novel), Houghton Mifflin (Boston, MA), 1981.
The Sportswriter (novel), Vintage (New York, NY), 1986.
Rock Springs: Stories (includes "Children" and "Great Falls"), Atlantic Monthly Press (New York, NY), 1987.
Wildlife (novel), Atlantic Monthly Press (New York, NY), 1990.
Independence Day (novel), Knopf (New York, NY), 1995.
Women with Men: Three Stories, Knopf (New York, NY), 1997.
A Multitude of Sins: Stories, Harvill (London, England), 2001, Knopf (New York, NY), 2002.
Vintage Ford (collected stories), Vintage (New York, NY), 2003.

EDITOR

(With Shannon Ravenel) *The Best American Short Stories 1990,* Houghton Mifflin (Boston, MA), 1990.
The Granta Book of the American Short Story, Viking (New York, NY), 1992.
A.J. Liebling, *The Fights,* photographs by Charles Hoff, Chronicle Books (San Francisco, CA), 1996.
(With Michael Kreyling) Eudora Welty, *Complete Novels*, Library of America (New York, NY), 1998.
(With Michael Kreyling), Eudora Welty, *Stories, Essays, and Memoir,* Library of America (New York, NY), 1998.
The Essential Tales of Chekhov, Norton (New York, NY), 1998.
The Best American Sports Writing, Houghton Mifflin (Boston, MA), 1999.

OTHER

American Tropical (play), produced in Louisville, KY, 1983.

(Author of introduction) *Juke Joint: Photographs by Birney Imes,* University Press of Mississippi (Jackson, MS), 1990.

Bright Angel (screenplay; based on Ford's short stories "Children" and "Great Falls"), Hemdale, 1991.

(Author of introduction) Richard Bausch, *Aren't You Happy for Me? and Other Stories*, Macmillan (London, England), 1995.

(Author of text) Jane Kent, *Privacy* (etchings), 2000.

(Author of foreword) William Albert Allard, *Portraits of America,* National Geographic Society (Washington, DC), 2001.

(Translator, with David Satcher) Alejandrina Drew, *Abra Cadabra, Patas de Cabra: A Spanish/English Story for Young Readers,* Eakin, 2001.

(Author of introduction) Richard Yates, *Revolutionary Road,* Methuen (London, England), 2001.

Contributor to books, including *Fifty Great Years of Esquire Fiction,* edited by L. Rust Hills, Viking (New York, NY), 1983; *The Great Life: A Man's Guide to Sports, Skills, Fitness, and Serious Fun,* Penguin (New York, NY), 2000; and *Maine: The Seasons,* Knopf, 2001. Contributor of stories and essays to periodicals.

Ford's papers are housed at Michigan State University Libraries, East Lansing, MI.

ADAPTATIONS: Ford's story "Communist" was adapted for the stage and produced in San Francisco, CA, 1999.

SIDELIGHTS: "Writing is the only thing I've done with persistence, except for being married," claimed novelist and short fiction author Richard Ford in an interview with *Publishers Weekly,* "and yet it's such an inessential thing. Nobody cares if you do it, and nobody cares if you don't." The Pulitzer Prize-winning author of the novel *Independence Day,* Ford undoubtedly believed that statement, yet numerous reviewers have demonstrated how much they do care about Ford's work by lavishing it with praise. He is "a formidably talented novelist" and "one of the best writers of his generation," according to Walter Clemons of *Newsweek.* He is "the leading short story writer in the United States today," in the opinion of Toronto *Globe and Mail* contributor Alberto Manguel.

Ford, who was raised in Mississippi and Arkansas and had to overcome dyslexia as a child, turned to fiction-writing after a brief, unsatisfying stint as a law student. He enrolled in the M.F.A. program at the University of California—Irvine, where he studied with such writers as E.L. Doctorow and Oakley Hall. Following his graduation, Ford worked on short stories and his first novel, the latter which was published in 1976 under the title *A Piece of My Heart.* The book is the tale of an Arkansas drifter and a Chicago law student whose paths cross on an uncharted island deep in the Mississippi delta.

A Piece of My Heart received mixed reviews, although many critics praised Ford for his skillful evocation of the South and its people. "Faulknerian in setting and atmosphere, the novel reveals a writer with his own cadence and tone," observed Nolan Miller in the *Antioch Review.* Writing in the *New York Times Book Review,* Larry McMurtry also raised a comparison between Ford and Faulkner, although with a less-laudatory result. "If the vices this novel shares with its many little Southern cousins could be squeezed into one word, the word would be neo-Faulknerism. . . . Pronouns drifting toward a shore only dimly seen, a constant backward tilt toward a past that hasn't the remotest causal influence on what is actually happening, plus a more or less constant tendency to equate eloquence with significance: these are the familiar qualities in which Mr. Ford's narrative abounds." Still, McMurtry acknowledged that he saw promise in Ford's first novel and concluded that Ford's "minor characters are vividly drawn, and his ear is first-rate. If he can weed his garden of some of the weeds and cockleburrs of his tradition, it might prove very fertile."

Ford himself has expressed frustration with attempts to qualify fiction as "Southern" or any other label. He declared in *Harper's:* "Categorization (women's writing, gay writing, Illinois writing) inflicts upon art exactly what art strives at its best never to inflict on itself: arbitrary and irrelevant limits, shelter from the widest consideration and judgment, exclusion from general excellence. When writing achieves the level of great literature, of great art (even good art), categories go out the window. William Faulkner, after all, was not a great Southern writer: he was a great writer who wrote about the South."

Ford's second novel, *The Ultimate Good Luck,* recounts the tale of a Vietnam veteran who, in an attempt to reclaim the affections of his ex-girlfriend, journeys to Mexico to rescue her brother from prison, where he is being held for his part in a drug deal. Gilberto Perez panned the book in the *Hudson Review,* writing that it "calls to mind a cheap action picture in which hastily collaborating hacks didn't quite manage to put a story together." *Newsweek* reviewer Walter Clemons had a different assessment, calling *The Ultimate Good Luck* "a tighter, more efficient book" than *A Piece of My Heart,* "and a good one." While Clemons did feel Ford has "jimmied himself into the confines of the existentialist thriller with a conspicuous sacrifice of his robust gift for comedy," he wrote that the author has "larger capabilities" than those manifested in this novel and declared that, "sentence by sentence, *The Ultimate Good Luck* is the work of a formidably talented novelist." Toronto *Globe and Mail* reviewer Douglas Hill was even more enthusiastic, crediting Ford with creating "a thriller that is also a love story, and at its core a meditation upon the precariousness and impotence of post-Vietnam U.S. values."

Ford's reputation and popularity soared with the publication of his third book, *The Sportswriter,* which sold more than 60,000 copies. Writing in the London *Times,* James Wood described it as "a desperately moving and important book, at once tremulous and tough." *The Sportswriter* is narrated by its protagonist, Frank Bascombe. Bascombe is "deceptively amiable, easygoing and sweet natured," reported *Newsweek* reviewer Clemons. "As he tells his story in a chipper, uncomplaining tone, we gradually learn that he's a damaged man who's retreated into cushioned, dreamy detachment to evade grief and disappointment." Once a promising novelist and short-story writer, Bascombe has abandoned the difficulties of creating fiction for the simpler, more immediate gratifications of sports reporting and suburban life in New Jersey. The death of his son brings on a spiritual crisis he tries to avoid, and he distracts himself with extramarital affairs which eventually leads his wife to divorce him.

Although he continually asserts his happiness, Bascombe "asserts so hard that we are made to feel the hollowness," explained *Los Angeles Times* book critic Richard Eder. "Negation by assertion is the narrative's central device, in fact, giving it a flatness and a dead tone." Eder explained that "the point of *The Sportswriter* is not the plot, but the quality of thought and feeling with which the narrator assays his life." The reviewer found it to be "a dull point" because, in his opinion, "Bascombe is not very nice and not very interesting." Clemons also thought that Bascombe's behavior is often "less than admirable," but in his view this increases Ford's literary achievement, for "only a scrupulously honest novelist could make us sympathetic to such an unheroic nature. Ford makes us feel we're more like Bascombe than we often care to admit." *New York Times* reviewer Michiko Kakutani called the novel "powerful," noting that while Bascombe's monologue is

occasionally "long winded and overly meditative . . . his voice . . . is so pliant and persuasive that we are insistently drawn into his story. . . . We come to see Frank not only as he sees himself (hurt, alienated, resigned to a future of diminishing returns) but also as he must appear to others—essentially kind and decent, but also wary, passive and unwilling to embrace the real possibilities for happiness that exist around him."

"*The Sportswriter* . . . established a glittering reputation" for Ford, asserted a *Time* contributor, adding: "The stories in *Rock Springs* confirm it." Set mostly in Montana, the stories in *Rock Springs* portray characters in transit, moving from one town or one way of life to another. "If the term 'perfect' still means 'thoroughly accomplished,' then *Rock Springs* is a perfect book," said Manguel in his *Globe and Mail* review. *New York Times* contributor Kakutani also found the collection to be an impressive work. "Ford has managed to find a wholly distinctive narrative voice . . . a voice that can move effortlessly between neat, staccato descriptions and rich, lyrical passages," Kakutani wrote, adding: His "stories stand as superb examples of the storyteller's craft, providing us with both the pleasures of narrative and the sad wisdom of art." Kakutani pronounced enthusiastically: "This volume should confirm his emergence as one of the most compelling and eloquent storytellers of his generation."

Ford returned to the novel form with 1990's *Wildlife.* Describing the inner workings of the Brinson family, the novel uses the central metaphor of a raging forest fire to symbolize the uncontrolled forces sweeping through the family. Reviewers were again divided in their assessment of this work. Jonathan Yardley, reviewing *Wildlife* for the *Washington Post,* was not pleased with the way the characters smooth "each other's passage through life with pearls of pop-psychological wisdom," or with the abundance of metaphors in the narrative. "Like a puppy with a slipper, Ford sinks his teeth into those metaphors, shakes them all over the place and refuses to let them go," quipped Yardley. Victoria Glendinning commented of Ford in the London *Times* that "there is something obsessional and over-tidy in the jigsaw neatness of his writing, his interlocking themes and images, his modest conclusions," but she allowed that *Wildlife* is "beautifully made" and noted: Ford "has far more to teach Europeans about ordinary American life and the American psyche than have the flashier East Coast novelists."

The mixed critical responses to Ford's work stand as proof of its worth, maintained Toronto *Globe and Mail* contributor Trevor Ferguson, who rated *Wildlife* "a superb novel." Ferguson added that the novel "is also, like its characters and like its vision of America, strangely contradictory—at once affirmative and self-limiting. Applaud or berate him as he assumes a position in the front rank of American letters, Ford and his stylistic decisions deserve heated debate."

Independence Day, Ford's sequel to *The Sportswriter,* finds protagonist Frank Bascombe "sunk deep into a morass of spiritual lethargy," observed Michiko Kakutani in the *New York Times.* Much has changed in the years between the two stories. First, Frank is no longer a sportswriter; he is a real estate agent in his hometown in New Jersey. His ex-wife has taken their two living children to her new home and husband in Connecticut. "Frank wryly yet seriously portrays his current life in sharply-observed detail," Merle Rubin wrote in the *Christian Science Monitor,* adding that "it is Richard Ford's great gift as a novelist that he makes the details matter." Bascombe's experiences reflect those of American society during the late 1980s. As Kakutani wrote, "Not only does Mr. Ford do a finely nuanced job of delineating Frank's state of mind . . . , but he also moves beyond Frank, to provide a portrait of a time and a place, of a middle-class community caught on the margins of change and reeling, like Frank, from the wages of loss and disappointment and fear."

Independence Day follows Bascombe during the long Fourth of July weekend of 1988. Frank hopes to reconnect with his troubled fifteen-year-old son through a father-son trip that includes the Basketball Hall of Fame in Massachusetts and the Baseball Hall of Fame in New York. "Displaying again his astonishing mastery of New Jersey, Connecticut, Massachusetts, and New York roadmaps—their physical as well as moral landscapes—Ford sweeps us in a four-day whirl through an election-year America which de Toccqueville foretold—filled with ambitious men but empty of lofty ambitions," Raymond A. Schroth commented in *Commonweal.* The lasting merit of *Independence Day,* according to *Times Literary Supplement* contributor Gordon Burn, comes in Ford's uncommon ability to bring together all of these elements: the man, the family, the society, and the landscape. In Burn's words, "Ford's achievement in *Independence Day . . .* is to reclaim the strangeness of a country which he knows is at least as beguiling as it is wretched, and to rescue it from its worst own image. Amazingly, this late in the American century, he gives every impression of cruising through a territory nobody has laid claim to, nailing it with such a devouring—such an undeceived—eye that it begins to seem new again and in need of a writer of Ford's marvelous talents to explain and translate it." Concluded Kakutani,

"With *Independence Day,* Mr. Ford has written a worthy sequel to *The Sportswriter* and galvanized his reputation as one of his generation's most eloquent voices."

Women with Men is a collection of three short stories—"The Womanizer," "Jealous," and "Occidentals"—that each feature "men pondering their complicated relationships with women," Michael Pearson explained in the *Atlanta Journal-Constitution.* Two of the stories take place in Paris and are told from the perspective of mature men, while the third focuses on a seventeen-year-old living in Montana. Still, they all share a certain quality, "a kind of moody but sweet ennui . . . ," in the words of *Boston Globe* contributor Gail Caldwell, "like being suddenly enveloped in a warm fog on what you believed was a sunny beach. Maybe it will pass in twenty minutes; maybe you won't get out alive." Because of this overall quality, as Pearson noted, "Each of the three principal characters in this new collection is a lost soul."

While conceding Ford's skills as a storyteller, some reviewers concluded that *Women with Men* does not represent the author's best effort. Christopher Lehmann-Haupt in the *New York Times* called Ford's characters "not complex enough to hold one's interest," while James Marcus commented in the *Village Voice* that "Ford never makes [his male protagonists] . . . into mere whipping boys for an assortment of masculine sins: he has a sneaking sympathy for their foolishness, and for the women they tend to inflict it on." Moreover, in the opinion of Peter S. Prescott of the *Wall Street Journal,* Ford takes readers "inside the thoughts of two entirely unremarkable men, men who can be defined by their limitations, and made the exercise interesting." David Nicholson, in his review for the *Washington Post,* faulted the stories in *Women with Men* for being "slight," although Caldwell offered a different take. Ford "doesn't insist on something happening, even in a short story, since he seems to grasp that most of life is lived in between occurrences," Caldwell noted in the *Boston Globe.* Pearson found in *Women with Men* a kinship to *Men without Women,* a collection of stories by Ernest Hemingway that Ford's fiction invoked for the critic. "Similar to Hemingway's stories," Pearson noted, "Ford's are like the tips of icebergs, only a small portion of the emotion showing and always something chilling beneath the surface."

The 2001 story collection *A Multitude of Sins* was described by Ford in the *Austin American-Statesman* as "a group of stories about how people fail each other" and themselves. Of the ten stories—one of which is a novella—William H. Pritchard noted in *Commonweal* that Ford "defuses the word sin into 'sin,' and since adultery is the condition of or fact behind most of these stories, its sinful nature—or lack of such—is explored rather than assumed." In *Maclean's,* John Bemrose expanded on Pritchard's observation: "To say that Ford's subject is duplicity is to miss his full achievement. Many of his characters manifest their own kind of integrity and courage in painful situations, such as the narrator in the splendid 'Calling,' who recalls his youth as the son of a selfish, abandoning father." Jenny Shank in the *Rocky Mountain News,* commented on the same story, "The son narrates all this from many years hence, after his mother and father have died. Reflecting on his father, he makes an observation that encapsulates all the stories in this collection: 'My father did only what pleased him, and believed that doing so permitted others the equal freedom to do what they wanted. Only that isn't how the world works, as my mother's life and mine were living proof. Other people affect you. It's really no more complicated than that.'"

Bemrose suggested that the subtle themes in *A Multitude of Sins* offer "some deeper insights into the workings of the American mind. . . . The adventures of the mad Captain Ahab—the protagonist of . . . *Moby Dick,* which chronicles the pursuit of a great white whale—may well have more to say about where the U.S. [middle class] is headed in the long run than the latest bulletin from CNN." Julie Myerson wrote in the London *Guardian:* "Ford's sheer mastery of the short-story form is jaw-dropping. . . . Each of these tales boasts the satisfying density of a novel, yet reaches its pay-off in a matter of minutes. Almost every one of his characters is rounded enough to carry 300 pages, yet we usually say goodbye to them after a brisk and dazzling thirty."

Characteristic of critical reaction to Ford's work, some critics were less than enthusiastic in their response to *A Multitude of Sins.* John de Falbe, writing in the *Spectator,* questioned: "These stories are not rib-ticklers then, but are they good? . . . If care were enough to guarantee excellence, then Ford could not be faulted, but it is his extreme care that betrays him. Nobody could accuse him of not thinking through his characters' feelings—he has done so exhaustively, so that one sometimes longs for a clear image in place of half a page of analysis. Yet to criticise him for failing to use images is not quite just because he often uses them well. Too often they seem ponderous or tired, however." *New Statesman* contributor John Dugdale compared the collection with *The Sportswriter* and *Independence Day,* which thrive on "the juggling of passion and profession." In *A Multitude of Sins,* Dugdale wrote, "this balance has gone askew. Ford sketches what his cheating and cheated figures do from nine to five with tantalising skill, but never shows them doing it. . . . Ford's couples never discuss politics, current affairs, religion, high and popular culture, celebrities, sport or even sex, focusing myopically on their relationship. No wonder they're fed up with one another. But why isn't Ford bored of writing about them?" Interviewer John Marshall countered in the *Seattle Post-Intelligencer* that "Ford is a fearless explorer of American spaces. . . . Ambiguity, unease, excess, failings." "Ford enters these shadowy areas in his prize-winning fiction," Marshall added, "then reports back from places where many people would rather not admit they have tread."

Ford commented to Marshall, "Unlike novels, short stories seem perfectible, but getting them perfected is very frustrating. Novels are comfortable, large, forgiving—novels can have all sorts of structural inadequacies, but still be great books. A story with that will be seen as some failed thing. . . . There is such an economy of gesture in short stories that everything takes on added weight. I constantly find I am asking myself, 'Gee, how do you do this?'"

Returning to the novel form following *A Multitude of Sins,* Ford featured Frank Bascombe in a third novel, titled *The Lay of the Land.* Meanwhile, his most popular short fiction was collected and published in 2003 as *Vintage Ford.*

BIOGRAPHICAL AND CRITICAL SOURCES:

BOOKS

Contemporary Literary Criticism, Volume 46, Thomson Gale (Detroit, MI), 1988.

Contemporary Novelists, 6th edition, St. James Press (Detroit, MI), 1996.

Folks, Jeffrey J., and James A. Perkins, editors, *Southern Writers at Century's End,* University Press of Kentucky (Lexington, KY), 1997.

Folks, Jeffrey J., and Nancy Summers Folks, editors, *The World Is Our Culture: Society and Culture in Contemporary Southern Writing,* University Press of Kentucky (Lexington, KY), 2000.

Guagliardo, Huey, editor, *Perspectives on Richard Ford,* University Press of Mississippi (Jackson, MS), 2000.

Guagliardo, Huey, editor, *Conversations with Richard Ford,* University Press of Mississippi (New York, NY), 2001.

Hobson, Fred, *The Southern Writer in the Postmodern World,* University of Georgia Press, 1991.

Iftekharuddin, Farhat, Mary Rohrberger, and Maurice Lee, editors, *Speaking of the Short Story: Interviews with Contemporary Writers,* University Press of Mississippi (Jackson, MS), 1997.

Lyons, Bonnie, and Bill Oliver, editors, *Passion and Craft: Conversations with Notable Writers,* University of Illinois Press (Urbana, IL), 1998.

Walker, Elinor Ann, *Richard Ford,* Twayne (New York, NY), 2000.

PERIODICALS

America, December 9, 1995, p. 26.

Antioch Review, winter, 1977, p. 124.

Atlanta Journal-Constitution, July 2, 1995, p. L9; September 24, 1995, p. M3; June 19, 1997, p. E5.

Atlantic, March, 2002, p. 116.

Austin American-Statesman, March 3, 2003, p. E1.

Black Issues Book Review, March-April 2003, p. 14.

Bloomsbury Review, July-August, 1996, p. 22.

Book Collector, spring, 1995, p. 67.

Booklist, May 15, 1997, p. 1540; August 1999, p. 2024; September 1, 1999, p. 60; April 1, 2001, p. 1444; December 15, 2001, p. 683.

Boston Globe, October 19, 1987; June 18, 1995, p. B45; August 22, 1996, p. E1; June 22, 1997, p. N15.

Boston Herald, December 26, 1999, p. 47.

Canadian Literature, autumn, 1995, p. 51.

Chicago Tribune, June 22, 1995, section 5, p. 9.

Chicago Tribune Book World, April 19, 1981.

Christian Science Monitor, July 3, 1995, p. 13.

Commentary, November, 1995, p. 130.

Commonweal, October 6, 1995, p. 27; June 19, 1998, p. 28; April 5, 2002, p. 30.

Daily Telegraph (London, England), November 6, 2001, p. 6.

Economist, August 12, 1995, p. 73; October 27, 2001, p. 126.

Entertainment Weekly, June 23, 1995, p. 47; July 28, 1995, p. 55; May 31, 1996, p. 55; Feb 15, 2002, p. 62.

Globe and Mail (Toronto, Ontario, Canada), July 18, 1987; October 3, 1987; July 7, 1990.

Guardian (London, England), February 28, 2003, p. 20.

Harper's, August, 1986, pp. 35, 42-43.

Hudson Review, winter, 1981-82, pp. 606-620.

Independent (London, England), November 17, 2001, p. 13; October 18, 2002, p. 12.

Kenyon Review, summer-fall, 2001, p. 123; fall, 2002, p. 123.

Library Journal, June 1, 1995, p. 160; October 15, 1997, p. 55; December, 1998, p. 159; May 5, 1999, p. 146; October 1, 1999, p. 103; February 1, 2002, p. 134.

London Review of Books, August 24, 1995, p. 23.

Los Angeles Times, March 12, 1986; June 28, 1996, p. E1.

Los Angeles Times Book Review, October 30, 1988, p. 10; June 30, 1991, p. 14; July 2, 1995, p. 1; July 13, 1997, p. 2; February 10, 2002, p. 3.

Louisiana English Journal, New Series, 1999, p. 81.

Maclean's, July 10, 1995, p. 42; July 14, 1997, p. 61; October 29, 2001, p. 60.

Mississippi Quarterly, winter, 1998-1999, p. 73; summer, 2000, p. 459.

Missouri Review, 1987, p. 71.

National Review, November 12, 1976, pp. 1240-1241; September 25, 1995, p. 93.

New Leader, January-February 2002, p. 29.

New Republic, September 18, 1995, p. 48.

New Statesman, July 14, 1995, p. 39; October 29, 2001, p. 57; October 17, 1997, p. 55.

Newsweek, May 11, 1981, pp. 89-90; April 7, 1986, p. 82; June 12, 1995, p. 64; February 18, 2002, p. 69.

New York, July 7, 1997, p. 55.

New York Review of Books, April 24, 1986, pp. 38-39; August 10, 1995, p. 11; July 18, 2002, p. 53.

New York Times, February 26, 1986, p. C21; September 20, 1987; April 10, 1988; June 1, 1990; June 13, 1995, p. C17; August 22, 1995, p. C13; November 5, 1995, section 9, p. 7; April 18, 1996, p. C17; June 16, 1997, p. C16; February 4, 2002, p. E7; December 7, 2002, p. B7; February 2, 2003, p. 24.

New York Times Book Review, October 24, 1976, p. 16; May 31, 1981, pp. 13, 51; March 23, 1986, p. 14; September 16, 1990, pp. 1, 32; June 18, 1995, p. 1; July 13, 1997, p. 5; March 3, 2002, p. 8; March 10, 2002, p. 22; March 17, 2002, p. 22; March 24, 2002, p. 18; June 2, 2002, p. 23; February 2, 2003, p. 24.

New York Times Magazine, September 20, 1998, p. 63.

Observer (London, England), October 13, 2001, p. 9; November 18, 2001, p. 16.

People, July 17, 1995, p. 30; September 8, 1997, p. 35.

Ploughshares, fall, 1996, p. 226.

Publishers Weekly, May 18, 1990, pp. 66-67; April 24, 1995, p. 59; May 12, 1997, p. 57; September 6, 1999, p. 92; October 2, 2000, p. 79; December 17, 2001, p. 62.

Reason, December, 1996, p. 53.

Rocky Mountain News, February 1, 2002, p. D24.

San Francisco Chronicle, June 15, 1997, p. 3; February 3, 2002, p. 1; February 10, 2002, p. 2; March 18, 2002, p. D1.

San Francisco Review of Books, November-December, 1995, p. 32.

School Library Journal, July, 2001, p. 74.

Seattle Post-Intelligencer, March 29, 2002, p. 21.

Seattle Times, February 24, 2002, p. J12.

South Carolina Review, fall, 2002, p. 209.

Southern Literary Journal, fall, 1990, p. 93.

Southern Quarterly, winter, 1999, p. 16.

Southern Review, summer, 1998, p. 609.

Spectator, November 3, 2001, p. 57.

Sunday Telegraph (London, England), September 8, 2002, p. 3.

Tikkun, March-April, 1996, p. 74.

Time, November 16, 1987, p. 89; June 19, 1995, p. 60; July 7, 1997, p. 111.

Times (London, England), August 28, 1986; June 11, 1987; June 20, 1987; July 11, 1987; May 5, 1988; August 9, 1990.

Times Literary Supplement, July 14, 1995, p. 21.

Tribune Books (Chicago, IL), June 25, 1995, p. 3; September 7, 1997, p. 3.

Village Voice, June 24, 1997, p. 53.

Wall Street Journal, June 27, 1997, p. A13.

Washington Post, June 20, 1990; April 17, 1996, p. C1; July 8, 1997, p. E2.

Washington Post Book World, February 20, 1977, p. N3; March 30, 1986, p. 3; July 2, 1995, p. 4.

Writer, December, 1996, p. 9.

ONLINE

BookPage, http://www.bookpage.com/ (February, 2002).

Off Course, http://www.albany.edu/offcourse/ (November, 1998).

Salon.com, http://www.salon.com/ (July 8, 1996), interview with Ford.

*   *   *

FORSYTH, Frederick 1938-

PERSONAL: Born in 1938, in Ashford, Kent, England; son of a furrier, shopkeeper, and rubber tree planter; married Carole Cunningham (a model), September, 1973 (marriage ended); married Sandy Molloy, 1994; children: (first marriage) Frederick Stuart, Shane Richard. *Education:* Attended University of Granada. *Hobbies and other interests:* Sea fishing, snooker.

ADDRESSES: Home—St. John's Wood, London, England. *Agent*—c/o Author Mail, Bantam Books, 62/63 Uxbridge Rd., London W5 5SA, England.

CAREER: Author. *Eastern Daily Press,* Norwich, England, and King's Lynn, Norfolk, reporter, 1958-61; Reuters News Agency, reporter in London, England, and Paris, France, 1961-63, bureau chief in East Berlin, East Germany, 1963-64; British Broadcasting Corporation (BBC), London, reporter, 1965-66, assistant diplomatic correspondent, 1967-68; freelance journalist in Nigeria, 1968-69. *Military service:* Royal Air Force, 1956-58; pilot.

AWARDS, HONORS: Edgar Allan Poe Award, Mystery Writers of America, 1971, for *The Day of the Jackal.*

WRITINGS:

NOVELS

The Day of the Jackal, Viking (New York, NY), 1971.

The Odessa File, Viking (New York, NY), 1972.

The Dogs of War, Viking (New York, NY), 1974.

The Shepherd, Hutchinson (London, England), 1975, Viking (New York, NY), 1976.

The Novels of Frederick Forsyth (contains *The Day of the Jackal, The Odessa File,* and *The Dogs of War*), Hutchinson (London, England), 1978, published as *Forsyth's Three,* Viking (New York, NY), 1980, published as *Three Complete Novels,* Avenel Books (New York, NY), 1980.

The Devil's Alternative, Hutchinson (London, England), 1979, Viking (New York, NY), 1980.

The Four Novels (contains *The Day of the Jackal, The Odessa File, The Dogs of War,* and *The Devil's Alternative*), Hutchinson (London, England), 1982.

The Fourth Protocol, Viking (New York, NY), 1984.

The Negotiator, Bantam (New York, NY), 1989.

The Deceiver, Bantam (New York, NY), 1991.

The Shepherd, Bantam (New York, NY), 1992.

The Fist of God, Bantam (New York, NY), 1994.

Icon, Bantam (New York, NY), 1996.

The Phantom of Manhattan, St. Martin's Press (New York, NY), 1999.

Avenger, St. Martin's Press (New York, NY), 2003.

OTHER

The Biafra Story (nonfiction), Penguin (London, England), 1969, revised edition published as *The Making of an African Legend: The Biafra Story,* 1977.

Emeka (biography), Spectrum Books (Ibadan, Nigeria), 1982, 2nd edition, 1993.

No Comebacks: Collected Short Stories, Viking (New York, NY), 1982.

(And executive producer) *The Fourth Protocol* (screenplay; based on his novel of the same title), Lorimar, 1987.

Chacal, French and European Publications, 1990.

(Editor) *Great Flying Stories,* Norton (New York, NY), 1991.

I Remember: Reflections on Fishing in Childhood, Summersdale (London, England), 1995.

The Veteran and Other Stories, Bantam (London, England), 2001.

Also author of *The Soldiers,* a documentary for BBC. Contributor to *Visitor's Book: Short Stories of Their New Homeland by Famous Authors Now Living in Ireland,* Arrow Books, 1982. Contributor of articles to newspapers and magazines, including *Playboy.*

ADAPTATIONS: The Day of the Jackal was filmed by Universal in 1973; *The Odessa File* was filmed by Columbia in 1974; *The Dogs of War* was filmed by United Artists in 1981. The Mobil Showcase Network filmed two of Forsyth's short stories ("A Careful Man" and "Privilege") under the title *Two by Forsyth* in 1984; *The Fourth Protocol* was filmed by Lorimar in 1987; "A Careful Man" was also videotaped and broadcast on Irish television.

SIDELIGHTS: British writer Frederick Forsyth "helped define the international conspiracy thriller," according to *Booklist*'s Connie Fletcher. Further, he established, as a critic for *Publishers Weekly* noted, the "traditional formula of thrillers that educate as well as entertain." Realism is the key word behind Forsyth's novels, which originated a new genre, the "documentary thriller." Forsyth found sudden fame with the publication of his smash best-seller, *The Day of the Jackal,* a book that combines the suspense of an espionage novel with the detailed realism of the documentary novel, first made popular by Truman Capote's *In Cold Blood.* The detail in Forsyth's novels depends not only on the months of research he spends on each book, but also on his own varied personal experiences, which lend even greater authenticity to his writing. As *Dictionary of Literary Biography* contributor Andrew F. Macdonald explained, "The sense of immediacy, of an insider's view of world affairs, of all-too-human world figures," as well as quick-paced plots, are the keys to the author's popularity.

Critics, however, have sometimes faulted the novelist for shallow characterization and a simplistic writing style. Forsyth does not deny his emphasis on plotting over other considerations. In a *Los Angeles Times* interview he remarked, "My books are eighty percent plot and structure. The remaining twenty percent is for characters and descriptions. I try to keep emotions out. Occasionally a personal opinion will appear in the mouth of one of my characters, but only occasionally. The plot's the thing. This is how it works best for me." These plots find their resolution in Forsyth's painstaking attention to detail. "Forsyth's forte, with the added bonus of precise technical description worthy of a science writer," Macdonald explained, is "how things work, ranging from the construction of a special rifle (*The Day of the Jackal*) and improvised car bombs (*The Odessa File*), to gunrunning (*The Dogs of War*) and the innards of oil tankers (*The Devil's Alternative*), to the assembly of miniature nuclear bombs (*The Fourth Protocol*)."

For Forsyth the road to becoming a best-selling novelist was a long, circuitous route filled with adventurous detours that would later work their way into his writing. Early in his life, Forsyth became interested in becoming a foreign correspondent when his father introduced him to the world news as reported in the London *Daily Express.* In a London *Times* interview with John Mortimer, Forsyth related how his father "would get out the atlas and show me where the trouble spots were. And, of course, father had been to the Orient, he told me about tiger shoots and the headhunters in Borneo." Impatient to experience life for himself, Forsyth left school at the age of seventeen and went to Spain, where he briefly attended the University of Granada while toying with the idea of becoming a matador. However, having previously trained as a Tiger Moth biplane pilot, Forsyth decided to join the Royal Air Force in 1956. He learned to fly a Vampire jet airplane, and—at the age of nineteen—he was the youngest man in England at the time to earn his wings.

But Forsyth still dreamed of becoming a foreign correspondent, and toward that end he left the service to join the staff of the *Eastern Daily Press.* His talent for languages (Forsyth is fluent in French, German, Spanish, and Russian) later landed him his dream job as a correspondent for the Reuters News Agency and then for the British Broadcasting Corporation (BBC). It was during an assignment for the BBC that Forsyth's career took a sudden turn. Assigned to cover an uprising in the Nigerian region of Biafra, Forsyth began his mission believing he was going to meet an upstart rebellious colonel who was misleading his followers. He soon realized, though, that this leader, Colonel Ojukwu, was actually an intelligent man committed to saving his people from an English-supported government whose corrupt leaders were allowing millions to die of starvation in order to obtain their oil-rich lands. When Forsyth reported his findings, he was accused of being unprofessional, and his superiors reassigned him to covering politics at home. Outraged, Forsyth resigned, and he told Henry Allen in a *Washington Post* article that this experience destroyed his belief "that the people who ran the world were men of good will." This disillusionment is reflected in his writing. Forsyth revealed to Mortimer that he prefers "to write about immoral people doing immoral things. I want to show that the establishment's as immoral as the criminals."

Going back to Africa, Forsyth did freelance reporting in Biafra and wrote an account of the war, *The Biafra Story,* which *Spectator* critic Auberon Waugh asserted "is by far the most complete account, from the Biafran side [of the conflict], that I have yet read." In 1970, when the rebels were finally defeated and Ojukwu went into exile, Forsyth returned to England to find that his position on the war had effectively eliminated any chances he had of resuming a reporting career. He decided, however, that he could still put his journalism experience to use by writing fiction. Recalling his days in Paris during the early 1960s, when rumors were spreading that the Secret Organization Army had hired an assassin to shoot President Charles de Gaulle, Forsyth sat down and in just over a month wrote *The Day of the Jackal* based on this premise.

Forsyth had problems selling the manuscript at first because publishers could not understand how there could be any suspense in a plot about a presidential assassination that had obviously never come to pass. As the author explained to Allen, however, "The point was not whodunit, but how, and how close would he get?" The fascinating part of *The Day of the Jackal* lies in Forsyth's portrayal of the amoral, ultra-professional killer known only by his code name, "Jackal," and detective Claude Lebel's efforts to stop him. Despite what *New York Times Book Review* critic Stanley Elkin called Forsyth's "graceless prose style," and characterization that, according to J.R. Frakes in a *Book World* review, uses "every stereotype in the filing system," the author's portrayal of his nemesis weaving through a non-stop narrative has garnered acclaim from many critics and millions of readers. By boldly switching his emphasis from the side of the law to the side of the assassin, Forsyth adds a unique twist that gives his novel its appeal. "So plausible has Mr. Forsyth made his implausible villain . . . and so exciting does he lead him on his mur-

derous mission against impossible odds," said Elkin, "that even saintly readers will be hard put not to cheer this particular villain along his devious way." The author, however, noted that he considered the positive response to his villain a distinctly American response. "There is this American trait of admiring efficiency," he explained to a *Washington Post* interviewer, "and the Jackal is efficient in his job."

"*The Day of the Jackal* established a highly successful formula," wrote Macdonald, "one repeated by Forsyth and a host of other writers." Using a tight, journalistic style, Forsyth creates an illusion of reality in his writing by intermixing real-life people and historical events with his fictional characters and plots; "the ultimate effect is less that of fiction than of a fictional projection into the lives of the real makers of history," Macdonald attested. The author also fills his pages with factual information about anything from how to assemble a small nuclear device to shipping schedules and restaurant menus. But the main theme behind the author's novels is the power of the individual to make a difference in the world, and even change the course of history. Macdonald described the Forsyth protagonist as "a maverick who succeeds by cutting through standard procedure and who as a result often has difficulty in fitting in, [yet he] lives up to his own high professional standards. Forsyth suggests that it is the lone professionals, whether opposed to the organization or part of it, who truly create history, but a history represented only palely on the front pages of newspapers."

Since Forsyth had a three-book contract with Viking, he quickly researched and wrote his next two novels, *The Odessa File,* about a German reporter's hunt for a Nazi war criminal, and *The Dogs of War,* which concerns a mercenary who orchestrates a military coup in West Africa. Forsyth drew on his experience as a reporter in East Berlin for *The Odessa File,* as well as interviewing experts such as Nazi hunter Simon Wiesenthal, to give the novel authenticity. Background to *The Dogs of War* also came from the author's personal experiences—in this case, his time spent in Biafra. When it comes to details about criminal doings, however, Forsyth goes right to the source. In a Toronto *Globe and Mail* interview with Rick Groen, Forsyth said, "There are only two kinds of people who really know the ins and outs of illegal activities: those who practice them and those who seek to prevent them from being practiced. So you talk to cops or criminals. Not academics or criminologists or any of those sorts." This tactic has gotten Forsyth into some dangerous situations. In a *Chicago Tribune* interview the author regaled Michael Kilian with one instance when he was researching *The Dogs of War.*

Trying to learn more about gun trafficking in the black market, Forsyth posed as a South African interested in buying arms. The ploy worked until one day when the men he was dealing with noticed a copy of *The Day of the Jackal* in a bookstore window. It was "probably the nearest I got to being put in a box," said the author.

The Dogs of War became a highly controversial book when a London *Times* writer accused Forsyth of paying $200,000 to mercenaries attempting a coup against the President of Equatorial Guinea, Francisco Marcias Nguema. At first, the novelist denied any involvement. Later, however, David Butler and Anthony Collins reported in *Newsweek* that Forsyth admitted to having "organized a coup attempt for research purposes, but that he had never intended to go through with it." The controversy did not hurt book sales, though, and *The Dogs of War* became Forsyth's third best-seller in a row.

After *The Dogs of War* Forsyth did not attempt another thriller for several years. He credits exhaustion to this lengthy hiatus. "Those first three novels had involved a lot of research, a lot of traveling, a half-million words of writing, a lot of promotion," the novelist told *New York Times Book Review* contributor Tony Chiu. "I was fed up with the razzmatazz. I said I would write no more." To avoid heavy English taxes, Forsyth moved to Ireland, where tax laws are lenient on writers. One explanation as to why he returned to writing has been offered by *New York Times Book Review* critic Peter Maas, who recorded that when a tax man came to Forsyth's door one day and explained that only actively writing authors were eligible for tax breaks, Forsyth quickly told him that he was working on a novel at that moment. "I hasten to say," Maas wrote, "that all this may be apocryphal, but in the interests of providing us a greater truth, I like to think it happened. It's a wonderful thought, the idea of a tax person forcing a writer into more millions."

Forsyth made his comeback with *The Devil's Alternative,* an intricately plotted, ambitious novel about an American president who must choose between giving in to the demands of a group of terrorists and possibly causing a nuclear war in the process, or refusing their demands and allowing them to release the biggest oil spill in history from the tanker they have hijacked. "The vision is somewhat darker than in Forsyth's earlier works, in which a moral choice was possible," noted Macdonald. "Here . . . somebody must get hurt, no matter which alternative is chosen." The usual complaints against Forsyth's writing have been trained against *The Devil's Alternative.* Peter Gorner, for one, argued in the *Chicago Tribune Book World* that "his characters are paper-thin, the pages are studded with cliches, and the plot is greased by coincidence." But Gorner added that "things move along so briskly you haven't much time to notice." *Los Angeles Times* critic Robert Kirsch similarly noted that "Forsyth's banal writing, his endless thesaurus of cliches, his Hollywood characters do not interfere with page turning." Nevertheless, *New York Times Book Review* contributor Irma Pascal Heldman expressed admiration for Forsyth's ability to accurately predict some of the political crises that came to pass not long after the book was published. She also praised the "double-whammy ending that will take even the most wary reader by surprise. *The Devil's Alternative* is a many-layered thriller."

As with *The Devil's Alternative,* Forsyth's *The Fourth Protocol* and *The Negotiator* offer intrigue on a superpower scale. *The Fourth Protocol* is the story of a Soviet plot to detonate a small atomic device in a U.S. airbase in England. The explosion is meant to be seen as an American error and help put the leftist, antinuclear Labour Party into power. Reviews on the novel were mixed. *Time* magazine reviewer John Skow faulted the author for being too didactic: "[Forsyth's] first intention is not to write an entertainment but to preach a political sermon. Its burden is that leftists and peaceniks really are fools whose habitual prating endangers civilization." Michiko Kakutani of the *New York Times* also felt that, compared to Forsyth's other novels, *The Fourth Protocol* "becomes predictable, and so lacking in suspense." But other critics, including *Washington Post Book World* reviewer Roderick MacLeish, maintained a contrary view. MacLeish asserted that it is Forsyth's "best book so far" because the author's characters are so much better developed. "Four books and a few million pounds after *Jackal* Frederick Forsyth has become a well-rounded novelist."

Of *The Negotiator,* Forsyth's tale of the kidnapping of an American president's son, *Globe and Mail* critic Margaret Cannon declared that "while nowhere nearly as good as *The Day of the Jackal* or *The Odessa File,* it's [Forsyth's] best work in recent years." Harry Anderson, writing in *Newsweek,* also called the novel "a comparative rarity; a completely satisfying thriller." Critics such as *Washington Post* reviewer John Katzenbach have resurrected the old complaints that Forsyth "relies on shallow characters and stilted dialogue," and that while "the dimensions of his knowledge are impressive, rarely does the information imparted serve any greater purpose." Acknowledging that *The Negotiator* has "too many characters and a plot with enough twists to fill a pretzel factory," Cannon nevertheless added that "the endless and irrelevant descriptive passages are gone and someone has averted Forsyth's tendency to go off on tiresome tangents."

"Perhaps recognizing the need for sharply defined heroes and villains," stated Andrew Macdonald in the *St. James Guide to Crime and Mystery Writers*, "Forsyth's next book, *The Deceiver*, is a nostalgic look back to the good old days (at least for field agents and writers) of the Cold War, when political positions seemed eternally frozen and villainy could be motivated simply by nationality." For British agent Sam McCready, those days were a series of successes. With the collapse of the Soviet Union, however, the government is poised to eliminate his position. As part of his protest against the retirement forced on him, McCready recounts four of his most successful exploits. McCready loses the protest and is sent into retirement. Forsyth nonetheless ends the novel on an uncertain note, with Saddam Hussein's invasion of Kuwait. "The notion that international crises are over, that a new and peaceful world order will prevail, is immediately proved wrong," Macdonald noted. "All that has changed is the names, cultures, and ideologies of the players, and there will always be a need for new versions of Sam McCready, Forsyth suggests."

The author revisits this changing world order in *The Fist of God*, which tells of a secret mission to Iraq in an attempt to prevent the use of a catastrophic doomsday weapon. The intelligence situation in Iraq's closed society has become critical, and the western allies recruit a young version of Sam McCready—Major Mike Martin—to obtain the information they need. Martin's mission is to contact an Israeli "mole," a secret agent planted in Iraq by the Mossad, Israel's secret service, years before. In the process he also encounters rumors of Saddam's ultimate weapon—a weapon he must destroy in order to ensure a western victory. "As with his best works," wrote Macdonald in the *St. James Guide to Crime and Mystery Writers*, "Forsyth gives a sense of peering behind the curtains created by governments and media, allowing a vision of how the real battles, mostly invisible, were carried out."

In *Icon*, Forsyth turns to contemporary Russian politics for a thriller about a presidential candidate with ties to the Russian mafia and plans for wholesale ethnic cleansing at home and renewed Russian aggression abroad. Jason Monk, ex-CIA agent, is hired by an unlikely group of Russian and American global players to get rid of candidate Igor Komarov before the election. "As usual," wrote a reviewer for *Publishers Weekly*, "For-

syth interweaves speculation with historical fact, stitching his plot pieces with a cogent analysis of both Russian politics and the world of espionage." Although Anthony Lejeune, writing in the *National Review*, believed that "the scale is too large, the mood too chilly, for much personal involvement" with the novel's characters, J.D. Reed claimed in *People* that "*Icon* finds the master in world-class form."

Forsyth experimented with untypical projects in 1999 with his sequel to *Phantom of the Opera*, and in 2000 with a group of five short stories and a novella originally published online and then in book form. With *The Phantom of Manhattan*, Forsyth posits a new life for the Phantom, Erik Muhlheim, subject of the gothic classic and the fabulously popular musical. In Forsyth's take, Muhlheim makes it to New York where he makes millions on Wall Street, opens his own opera house, and hires his long-desired love interest, Christine de Chagney, to sing for him. A critic for *Publishers Weekly* found that Forsyth "brings the Phantom to life in a new way, in an invigorating parable about loneliness, greed, and love." With *The Veteran and Other Stories*, Forsyth presents a mixture of tales, from a police procedural, to a high-class art scam to Custer's Last Stand. Ronnie H. Terpening, writing in *Library Journal*, felt that the usual Forsyth trademarks, or "revenge, mystery, murder, [and] deception," are all present in these stories "that showcase the author's ability to capture character and generate suspense in remarkably few words." D.J. Taylor, reviewing the collection in the *Spectator*, also had praise for these five "'tall stories': brisk little conceits or incidents that in lesser hands would dry up in a dozen pages or so but which Forsyth's narrative guile has no trouble in fleshing out to, in some cases, novella length." However, for Taylor the downside to Forsyth's usual compilation of detail is that "it is clearly now an authorial fixation, a pageant of rococo embellishments that frequently elbows aside the narrative it adorns."

Forsyth has more scope for such accumulation of detail in his 2003 thriller *Avenger*, a "story of revenge and loyalty," according to Nola Theiss writing in *Kliatt*. This "taut suspense thriller . . . brings current world events and personal relationships into play," Theiss further commented. Calvin Dexter was a special operations man in Vietnam who worked in the tunnels stalking his Vietcong victims. Now a lawyer by day, he is the Avenger at other times, tracking down and bringing to justice those who try to escape the law. Hired by a mining tycoon to find the Serbian killer of his grandson in Bosnia, Dexter takes on the mission of his life, tracking the killer to South America and battling both the Serbian killer's impeccable security apparatus as well as an FBI man trying to use the killer as bait to capture the terrorist Usama bin Laden.

Critics spoke of this novel being on a par with the author's first three books. For example, a critic for *Publishers Weekly* felt that this "strong and memorable novel is [Forsyth's] best in decades," and that the machinations of the Avenger in getting his man are "pure gold." *Booklist*'s Connie Fletcher commended Forsyth's "crisp narration" as well as his "extraordinary care with detail, his solid voice, and his exquisite pacing." All these factors combined to make *Avenger* a "totally engrossing thriller," according to Fletcher. Similarly, *Library Journal*'s Robert Conroy dubbed the novel "gripping, complex, and exciting." Conroy concluded that this "well-written tale of evil and retribution" compares "favorably" to Forsyth's classic *The Day of the Jackal.*

It has always been the plots and technical details in his novels that have most fascinated Forsyth. "Invention of the story is the most fun," the author told Peter Gorner in the *Chicago Tribune.* "It's satisfying, like doing a jigsaw or a crossword." He admitted to Groen that he loves the research: "I quite enjoy going after the facts. I put into my books a pretty heavy diet of factuality." Recognizing that Forsyth is aiming to entertain his audience with these techniques, Macdonald wrote that a "common element in all the criticism [against the author] is a refusal to accept Forsyth's docudrama formula for what it is, but rather to assume it should be more conventionally 'fictional.'" Forsyth has sold over thirty million books to readers who know, as *Detroit News* contributor Jay Carr put it, that the thrill of the author's books lies not in finding out how "Forsyth is going to defuse the bomb whose wick he ignites, but rather to see how he works out the details."

BIOGRAPHICAL AND CRITICAL SOURCES:

BOOKS

Bestsellers 89, Issue 4, Thomson Gale (Detroit, MI), 1990.
Contemporary Literary Criticism, Volume 36, Thomson Gale (Detroit, MI), 1986.
Contemporary Novelists, 7th edition, St. James Press (Detroit, MI), 2001.
Critical Survey of Mystery and Detective Fiction, Salem Press (Pasadena, CA), 1988.
Dictionary of Literary Biography, Volume 87: *British Mystery and Thriller Writers since 1940, First Series,* Thomson Gale (Detroit, MI), 1989.
St. James Guide to Crime and Mystery Writers, 4th edition, St. James (Detroit, MI), 1996.

PERIODICALS

American Theatre, April, 2000, Celia Wren, "Money Sings," p. 49.
Armchair Detective, May, 1974; winter, 1985.
Atlantic, December, 1972; August, 1974.
Book, November-December, 2001, Helen M. Jerome, "Return to Formula: Frederick Forsyth Is Back in Business," p. 24.
Book and Magazine Collector, June, 1989.
Booklist, March 1, 1994, p. 1139; October 15, 1999, Ray Olson, review of *The Phantom of Manhattan,* p. 417; August, 2001, David Pitt, review of *The Veteran and Other Stories,* p. 2096; July, 2003, Connie Fletcher, review of *Avenger,* p. 1845.
Book World, September 5, 1971, J.R. Frakes, review of *The Day of the Jackal.*
Boston Herald, November 22, 1999, Terry Byrne Mug, "Frederick Forsyth's Uninspired Sequel Skimps on Story: *Phantom* Sequel Is Unmasked," p. 37.
Chicago Tribune, October 16, 1984; April 16, 1989; June 14, 1989.
Chicago Tribune Book World, March 2, 1980, Peter Gorner, review of *The Devil's Alternative.*
Christian Science Monitor, September 7, 1984.
Daily News, September 30, 1984.
Daily Telegraph, December 18, 1999, Hugh Massingberd, "After the Phantom Vanished into Thin Air Hugh Massingberd Is Hooked by the Sequel to a Tale of Obsessive and Unrequited Passion"; October 6, 2001, Will Cohu, "Let's Twist Again."
Detroit News, February 10, 1980; August 15, 1982; April 30, 1989.
Economist, December 7, 1996, p. S3; October 18, 2003, review of *Avenger,* p. 84.
Entertainment Weekly, May 20, 1994, p. 55; October 3, 2003, Marc Bernardin, review of *Avenger,* p. 78.
Globe and Mail (Toronto, Ontario, Canada), September 8, 1984; August 29, 1987; April 29, 1989, Margaret Cannon, review of *The Negotiator;* November 27, 1999, p. D38.
Guardian (London, England), August 16, 1994, p. 3.
Independent (London, England), December 12, 2001, p. S8.
Insight on the News, July 11, 1994, p. 28.
Kirkus Reviews, October 1, 1999, p. 1517.
Kliatt, March, 1998, p. 48; March 2001, p. 18; January, 2004, Nola Theiss, review of *Avenger* (audiobook), 40-41.
Library Journal, September 1, 2001, Ronnie H. Terpening, review of *The Veteran and Other Stories,* p. 237.
Life, October 22, 1971.

Listener, June 17, 1971; September 28, 1972; January 10, 1980.

Los Angeles Times, March 19, 1980; March 28, 1980; May 7, 1982; August 28, 1987; January 27, 2002, Eugene Weber, review of *The Veteran and Other Stories,* p. R8.

Los Angeles Times Book Review, April 16, 1989.

National Observer, October 30, 1971.

National Review, August 2, 1974; December 23, 1996, Anthony Lejeune, review of *Icon,* p. 56.

New Leader, April 7, 1980.

New Statesman, September 20, 1974; January 15, 1988.

New Statesman & Society, September 6, 1991, pp. 35-36.

Newsweek, July 22, 1974, Anthony Collins, review of *The Dogs of War;* May 1, 1978; April 24, 1989, Harry Anderson, review of *The Negotiator.*

New York Post, September 21, 1974.

New York Times, October 24, 1972; April 18, 1978; January 17, 1980; August 30, 1984, Michiko Kakutani, review of *The Fourth Protocol;* August 28, 1987; November 16, 1999, Alan Cowell, "Jackal's Day Has Passed: Forsyth Tails the Phantom," p. E1.

New York Times Book Review, August 15, 1971; December 5, 1971; November 5, 1972; July 14, 1974; October 16, 1977; February 24, 1980; March 2, 1980; May 9, 1982; September 2, 1984; April 16, 1989.

Observer (London, England), June 13, 1971; September 24, 1972; September 22, 1974.

People, October 22, 1984; July 18, 1994, p. 24; October 21, 1996, J.D. Reed, review of *Icon,* p. 40.

Playboy, July, 1989, p. 26; November, 1991, p. 34.

Publishers Weekly, August 9, 1971; September 30, 1974 March 17, 1989; August 9, 1991, p. 43; March 7, 1994, p. 51; August 12, 1996, review of *Icon,* p. 61; May 18, 1998, Jean Richardson, "Forsyth's *Phantom* Sequel," p. 22; September 6, 1999, review of *The Phantom of Manhattan,* p. 77; November 20, 2000, review of *The Veteran and Other Stories,* p. 37; July 28, 2003, review of *Avenger,* p. 77.

Saturday Review, September 4, 1971; September 9, 1972.

Spectator, August 2, 1969, Auberon Waugh, review of *The Biafra Story;* December 11, 1999, p. 62; September 8, 2001, D.J. Taylor, review of *The Veteran and Other Stories,* p. 41.

Time, September 3, 1984, John Skow, review of *The Fourth Protocol.*

Times (London, England), August 22, 1982; March 17, 1987; May 13, 1989; November 17, 2001, p. W1.

Times Educational Supplement, December 17, 1999, p. 19.

Times Literary Supplement, July 2, 1971; October 25, 1974; December 19, 1975; November 19, 1999, p. 24.

Wall Street Journal, April 12, 1989; April 18, 1989.

Washington Post, August 19, 1971; September 26, 1971; December 12, 1978; February 13, 1981; March 28, 1984; August 29, 1987; April 21, 1989, John Katzenbach, review of *The Negotiator.*

Washington Post Book World, February 3, 1980; August 26, 1984, Roderick MacLeish, review of *The Fourth Protocol.*

World Press Review, March, 1980; May, 1987.

ONLINE

Unofficial Frederick Forsyth Homepage, http://www. whirlnet.co.uk/forsyth/ (July 25, 2004).

*   *   *

FOWLER, Karen Joy 1950-

PERSONAL: Born February 7, 1950, in Bloomington, IN; daughter of Cletus (an animal psychologist) and Joy Arthur (a schoolteacher; maiden name, Fossum) Burke; married Hugh Fowler, 1972; children: Ryan, Shannon. *Education:* Attended University of California, Berkeley, 1968-70, B.A., 1972; attended State University of New York, 1970-71; University of California, Davis, M.A., 1974.

ADDRESSES: Agent—Wendy Weil, Wendy Weil Agency, 747 Third Ave., New York, NY 10017. *E-mail*—webspinner@sfwa.org.

CAREER: Novelist, short story writer, and educator. Cleveland State University, Cleveland, OH, writer-in-residence.

AWARDS, HONORS: John W. Campbell Memorial Award (Hugo Award) for best new writer, World Science Fiction Society, 1987; grant from the National Endowment for the Arts, 1988; Commonwealth Club Medal, 1991, for *Sarah Canary;* World Fantasy Award for best collection, World Fantasy Convention, 1999, for *Black Glass: Short Fictions;* finalist for PEN/ Faulkner Award, 2002, for *Sister Noon;* Nebula Award for best short story, 2004, for "What I Didn't See."

WRITINGS:

Artificial Things (story collection), Bantam (New York, NY), 1986.

Peripheral Vision (story collection), Pulphouse (Eugene, OR), 1990.

Sarah Canary (novel), Holt (New York, NY), 1991.

(Contributor) Kim Stanley Robinson, editor, *"Pulphouse" Science-Fiction Short Stories,* Pulphouse (Eugene, OR), 1991.

The Sweetheart Season: A Novel, Holt (New York, NY), 1996.

Black Glass: Short Fictions, Holt (New York, NY), 1998.

Sister Noon, Putnam (New York, NY), 2001.

The Jane Austen Book Club, Putman (New York, NY), 2004.

Work represented in periodicals, including *Pulphouse* and *Science Fiction.*

ADAPTATIONS: The Jane Austen Book Club has been optioned for film by Sony Pictures Entertainment and was adapted for audio by Listen & Live, 2004.

SIDELIGHTS: Winner of the 1987 Hugo Award for best new writer, Karen Joy Fowler is the author of short story collections and novels that use fantastical characters and situations to bring to light various aspects of human nature. Her work has been well received by critics.

In her first story collection, *Artificial Things,* Fowler compiled thirteen short stories, many of which had appeared previously in periodicals. Applauding the stories as worthy "examples of both literary form and style," *Voice of Youth Advocates*'s Allison Rogers Hutchison especially recommended the work to writing students. The critic also praised Fowler's skillful use of fantastic plotlines and characters to show the human world in a different light. Fowler accomplishes this by presenting humans through the eyes of her alien characters. For instance, in one story, insectile aliens probe the mind of a poet, while in another, humans in the far future study replicants who reenact historical events. Karen S. Ellis noted in *Kliatt* that although many of the stories in *Artificial Things* were abstract, the "study of human nature" was an important theme in Fowler's work.

In 1990 Fowler issued her second collection of short stories. Titled *Peripheral Vision,* the volume garnered further praise for Fowler as an emerging writer. Reviewing the work in the *Washington Post Book World,* Gregory Feeley lauded Fowler as a "writer of clarity and humor." In particular, the reviewer cited "The Faithful Companion at Forty" and "Contention" as examples

of the author's interest in writing modern stories which, he felt, retained the element of fantasy "without shifting their centers of gravity."

This sense of fantasy also pervades Fowler's novel *Sarah Canary.* Set in the late nineteenth-century, it recounts the adventures of a mysterious woman called Sarah Canary and a Chinese immigrant laborer named Chin. The book begins when Sarah—who has been described variously by critics as a mysterious wild creature and an enigmatic woman who speaks in grunts and strange sounds—is entrusted to Chin's care after she wanders into his labor camp. Chin is asked to take Sarah to an asylum, but before he can accomplish this task, he is jailed. Separated from Sarah, the imprisoned Chin vows to free her, marking the beginning of their adventures together. Accompanying them on their journey are B.J., an escapee from a mental institution, and Adelaide Dixon, a free-thinking lecturer. The narrative follows the characters through a bizarre series of events until they reach San Francisco, where Chin escapes to China and eventually becomes a government bureaucrat. Sarah, on the other hand, vanishes without a trace or explanation.

The plot of *Sarah Canary* is loosely structured and has lent itself to numerous interpretations. Barbara Quick, writing in the *New York Times Book Review,* said that the story presents a "dreamscape" through which Fowler reveals a "tableau of the Pacific Northwest in the 1870s." *Los Angeles Times Book Review* contributor Richard Eder described *Sarah Canary* as "part ghost story, part picaresque adventure," an unusual narrative style that has allowed Fowler to present an ironic and painful vision of late nineteenth-century America. Explaining that the main characters of the book are representative of the victims of that age, Eder drew parallels between events in history and the action of the story. For example, he believed the character of Chin evokes the large number of Chinese immigrants who worked on building American railroads, while the female characters reveal the plight of women at the time. Another reviewer, Michael Dorris, wrote in the Chicago *Tribune Books* that *Sarah Canary* is a "full-tilt allegory, an uncompromising work of imagination that asks its readers to not merely suspend disbelief but to surrender it." Describing the landscape of the book as mythic, Dorris called Sarah "a cipher, an embodiment of each individual's deeply buried need for mystery in life." Quick noted in her final assessment that *Sarah Canary* "is an extraordinarily strong first novel" that "whets the appetite for what . . . [Fowler] will serve up next."

Fowler next served up an optimistic novel about a mill town that makes breakfast cereal. *The Sweetheart Sea-*

son: A Novel takes place in 1947, and the mill owner decides to form an all-girl traveling baseball team. He hopes this will promote his business and lift the girls' spirits, as they are bemoaning the fact that the war is over, but none of the boys wants to come back to his hometown. By going on the road, he reasons, they have a better chance of meeting nice, young bachelors. A *Kirkus Reviews* contributor called the story "a sluggish though skillful second novel, . . . alternately a romp and a slog." Deirdre McNamer, however, wrote in the *New York Times Book Review*: "Ms. Fowler's willingness to take detours, her unapologetic delight in the odd historical fact, her shadowy humor and the elegant unruliness of her language, all elevate her story from the picaresque to the grand."

In *Black Glass: Short Fictions*, the author presents fifteen varied short stories, ranging in scope from a Drug Enforcement Agency (DEA) agent who encounters the spirit of Carry A. Nation to aliens taking lessons on love Earth style. Christine DeZelar-Tiedman, writing in the *Library Journal*, called the collection "stunning" and noted that despite the extraordinary conceits of the stories the author makes "what should seem incredible . . . fully believable." A *Publishers Weekly* contributor commented that the author "delights in the arcane," adding that the stories "are occasionally puzzling but never dull." Elizabeth Hand, writing in the *Magazine of Fantasy and Science Fiction,* noted: "This is a superior collection, gracefully written but also utterly absorbing. I only wish it had been twice as long."

Set in 1890s San Francisco, Fowler's 2001 novel *Sister Noon* tells the story of Lizzie Hayes, a single woman in her forties who volunteers to work at the Ladies' Relief and Protection Society Home. Known for her reliability, Hayes nevertheless involves herself in adventure and intrigue when the notorious Mrs. Mary Ellen Pleasant arrives at the home with a young orphan girl named Jenny Ijub in tow. The parents of Jenny are unknown but rumors abound, including one that Jenny's father is wealthy, leading Lizzie to think of a possible donation to the home. Meanwhile, Mrs. Pleasant may be much more than she seems, perhaps even a voodoo priestess. "The story is a blend of history, suspense, and commentary on societal norms and social pretensions that both guide and confine," wrote Eileen Hardy in *Booklist*. Starr E. Smith, writing in the *Library Journal*, called the effort "a deft blend of historical fact, urban myth, social satire, and romance." A *Publishers Weekly* contributor wrote that the author "moves her principals through time and space seamlessly and gracefully, and exquisitely renders San Francisco."

Perhaps Fowler's most successful novel in terms of widespread recognition is *The Jane Austen Book Club.*

Optioned for film shortly after its spring 2004 release, the story offers an exploration of Austen's novels as it follows the activities of six book club members. The members are diverse in age and life experience: only one is a man, and he becomes an object of constant speculation by the others. However, the characters all have one common thread besides their love of reading—each exhibits strong character traits shared by some of Austen's characters or the author herself. "Fowler shares Austen's fascination with the power of stories, and explores the same timeless aspects of human behavior that Austen so masterfully dramatizes," wrote Donna Seaman in *Booklist*. Calling the novel "ingenious," John Freeman, writing in *People*, added that "the real pleasure comes from watching Fowler pay homage to Austen's gift." A *Publishers Weekly* contributor commented that "the novelty of Fowler's package should attract significant numbers of book club members, not to mention the legions of Janeites craving good company and happy endings."

BIOGRAPHICAL AND CRITICAL SOURCES:

BOOKS

Twentieth-Century Science-Fiction Writers, 3rd edition, St. James Press (Detroit, MI), 1991.

PERIODICALS

Booklist, May 15, 2001, Eileen Hardy, review of *Sister Noon*, p. 1731; March 15, 2004, Donna Seaman, review of *The Jane Austen Book Club*, p. 1265.

Kirkus Reviews, August 1, 1996, review of *The Sweetheart Season: A Novel*, p. 1074.

Kliatt, April, 1987, Karen S. Ellis, review of *Artificial Things,* pp. 29-30.

Library Journal, February 1, 1998, Christine DeZelar-Tiedman, review of *Black Glass: Short Fictions,* p. 114; May 1, 2001, Starr E. Smith, review of *Sister Noon*, p. 126.

Los Angeles Times Book Review, October 20, 1991, Richard Eder, review of *Sarah Canary*, pp. 3, 7; September 29, 1996, review of *The Sweetheart Season: A Novel*, p. 2.

Magazine of Fantasy & Science Fiction, May, 1992, Orson Scott Card, review of *Sarah Canary*, p. 50; August, 1998, Elizabeth Hand, review of *Black Glass*, p. 30.

New York Times Book Review, November 10, 1991, Barbara Quick, review of *Sarah Canary*, p. 18; October 13, 1996, Deirdre McNamer, review of *The Sweetheart Season*, p. 27.

People, May 24, 2004, John Freeman, review of *The Jane Austen Book Club*, p. 47.

Publishers Weekly, January 5, 1998, review of *Black Glass*, p. 59; April 9, 2001, review of *Sister Noon*, p. 48; March 22, 2004, review of *The Jane Austen Book Club*, p. 59; August 23, 2004, John F. Bank, "The Jane Austen Book Club by Karen Joy Fowler, a Bestseller for Marian Wood's Imprint at Putnam, Has Been Optioned as a Movie by Sony Pictures Entertainment, with John Calley as Producer," p. 12.

Tribune Books (Chicago, IL), December 15, 1991, Michael Dorris, review of *Sarah Canary*, section 14, pp. 1, 9.

Voice of Youth Advocates, June, 1987, Allison Rogers Hutchison, review of *Artificial Things*, pp. 89-90.

Washington Post Book World, April 29, 1990, Gregory Feeley, review of *Peripheral Vision*, p. 8.

ONLINE

Science Fiction and Fantasy Writers of America, Inc., Web site, http://www.sfwa.org/ (November 17, 2005), KJF Web page includes biography of and news on Karen Joy Fowler.

*   *   *

FOWLES, John 1926-2005
(John Robert Fowles)

PERSONAL: Born March 31, 1926, in Leigh-on-Sea, Essex, England; died November 5, 2005, in Lyme Regis, Dorset, England; son of Robert John and Gladys May (Richards) Fowles; married Elizabeth Whitton, April 2, 1954 (died, 1990); married Sarah Smith, 1998. *Education:* Attended University of Edinburgh; New College, Oxford, B.A. (honors), 1950.

CAREER: Writer and educator. University of Poitiers, Poitiers, France, lecturer in English, 1950-51; Anargyrios and Korgialenios School of Spetses, Spetsai, Greece, teacher, 1951-52; Ashridge College, teacher, 1953-54; St. Godric's College, London, England, teacher, 1954-63. *Military service:* Royal Marines; became lieutenant.

AWARDS, HONORS: Silver Pen Award, English Centre of International PEN, W.H. Smith Literary Award, both 1970, for *The French Lieutenant's Woman;* honorary curator of Lyme Regis Museum, 1979-88; Christopher Award, 1982, for *The Tree; The Magus* was voted 'one of the nation's 100 best-loved novels' by the British public as part of the British Broadcasting Corporation's project *The Big Read,* 2003; honorary fellowships from Modern Language Association and New College, Oxford; Litt.D., University of East Anglia and Chapman University.

WRITINGS:

NOVELS

The Collector (also see below), Little, Brown (Boston, MA), 1963.

The Magus (also see below), Little, Brown (Boston, MA), 1966, revised edition, 1977.

The French Lieutenant's Woman (also see below), Little, Brown (Boston, MA), 1969.

Daniel Martin, Little, Brown (Boston, MA), 1977.

Mantissa, Little, Brown (Boston, MA), 1982.

A Maggot, Little, Brown (Boston, MA), 1985.

OTHER

The Aristos: A Self-Portrait in Ideas, Little, Brown (Boston, MA) 1964, 2nd revised edition published as *The Aristos,* Jonathan Cape (London, England), 1980.

(With Stanley Mann and John Kohn) *The Collector* (screenplay; based on Fowles's novel of the same title), Columbia Pictures, 1965.

The Magus (screenplay; based on Fowles's novel of the same title), Twentieth Century-Fox, 1969.

Poems, Ecco Press (New York, NY), 1973.

The Ebony Tower (short stories), Little, Brown (Boston, MA), 1974.

(Adaptor and translator) Charles Perrault, *Cinderella,* Jonathan Cape (London, England), 1974, Little, Brown (Boston, MA), 1976.

(Translator) Clairie de Dufort, *Ourika* (novel), W. Thomas Taylor (Austin, TX), 1977.

(Author of text) *Islands* (photograph collection), photographs by Fay Godwin, Little, Brown (Boston, MA), 1978.

(Author of text) *The Tree* (photograph collection), photographs by Frank Horvat, Little, Brown (Boston, MA), 1980.

The Enigma of Stonehenge, photographs by Barry Brukoff, Summit Books (New York, NY), 1980.

(Literary editor) John Aubrey, *Monumenta Brittanica* (nonfiction), Little, Brown (Boston, MA), Parts 1 and 2, 1980, Part 3 and Index, 1982.

A Short History of Lyme Regis, Little, Brown (Boston, MA), 1983.

(Editor and author of introduction) *Thomas Hardy's England,* Little, Brown (Boston, MA), 1985.

(Editor) *Land* (photograph collection), photographs by Fay Godwin, Little, Brown (Boston, MA), 1985.

Lyme Regis Camera, Little, Brown (Boston, MA), 1990.

(Translator, with Robert D. MacDonald and Christopher Hampton) Corneille, *Landmarks of French Classical Drama,* Heinemann (London, England), 1991.

Wormholes: Essays and Occasional Writings, Holt (New York, NY), 1998.

The Journals: Volume 1: 1949-1965, edited and with an introduction by Charles Drazin, Jonathan Cape (London, England), 2003, Alfred A. Knopf (New York, NY), 2005, *Volume II,* edited by Drazin, Jonathan Cape (London, England), 2005.

Shorter works include text for the photograph collection *"Shipwreck,"* photographs by the Gibsons of Scilly, Jonathan Cape (London, England), 1974". Author of introduction, glossary, and appendix, *Mehalah: A Story of the Salt Marshes,* by Sabine Baring-Gould, Chatto & Windus (London, England), 1969; and *The French Lieutenant's Woman: A Screenplay,* by Harold Pinter (based on Fowles's novel of the same title), Little, Brown (Boston, MA), 1981; author of afterword, *The Man Who Died: A Story,* by David H. Lawrence, Ecco Press (New York, NY), 1994; contributor to several other books and anthologies, including *Afterwords: Novelists on Their Novels,* 1969, *New Visions of Franz Kafka,* 1974, and *Britain: A World by Itself: Reflections on the Landscape by Eminent British Writers,* 1984.

ADAPTATIONS: The Collector was made into a film in 1965, and adapted for the stage and produced in London at the King's Head Theatre in 1971; *The French Lieutenant's Woman* was made into a film in 1981; a version of Fowles's novella *The Ebony Tower* was broadcast on television in 1984.

SIDELIGHTS: John Fowles "is an enigma in broad daylight," commented critic Lance St. John Butler in *The British and Irish Novel since 1960.* "He is exceptionally open about his feelings and opinions, yet it is hard to be absolutely certain that one has understood his work or his position in post-1960s fiction." Fowles was a novelist first and foremost, but he also wrote short fiction, essays, poetry, commentaries on the world

of letters, and translations. His novels earned for him a great deal of popularity among the reading public, especially outside his native England in America and France. As Ellen Pifer explained in the *Dictionary of Literary Biography,* "Fowles's success in the marketplace derives from his great skill as a storyteller. His fiction is rich in narrative suspense, romantic conflict, and erotic drama." Yet, as Pifer added, this popularity comes despite the fact that Fowles took an approach to his writing that was most often appreciated in literary circles. "Remarkably," she wrote, "he manages to sustain such effects at the same time that, as an experimental writer testing conventional assumptions about reality, he examines and parodies the traditional devices of storytelling."

Fowles's interest in exploring and challenging the traditional devices of storytelling goes hand in hand with his primary thematic concern: freedom. The concept of freedom played a significant role throughout much of Fowles's writing career. Not only did Fowles refuse to be put into a "cage labeled 'novelist,'" as he stated in *The Aristos: A Self-Portrait in Ideas,* but he also rejected any label limiting him to a particular kind of writing. Known primarily as a novelist, Fowles seemed to write every possible kind of novel, as well as works of poetry and short fiction. An overview of Fowles's diverse writings helps to explain this characteristic and why it leaves some readers and reviewers perplexed. Many who enjoyed *The Collector,* a thriller and Fowles's first published novel, were subsequently puzzled when *The Magus* departed from its pattern. Unlike the tight and compact form of the thriller, *The Magus* spreads to the length of an "apprentice novel," a form which, like Charles Dickens's *Great Expectations,* usually follows the chronology of a youth's development. *The French Lieutenant's Woman,* a historical novel set in the 1860s, overtly guides readers into Fowles's method of transforming and recreating established forms for a new era. *The Ebony Tower* is unique, for it contains short works that are connected thematically to each other and to several of Fowles's earlier books. *Mantissa* represents a parody of the literary theories of the post-structuralists. And *A Maggot* is another historical novel, but it is also a sort of detective story that raises questions about our ability to discern the truth of events by reconstructing them from human accounts.

Despite the variety of forms that he employed, Fowles remained true to his concern with freedom. He pursued the question of whether a human being can act independently from the psychological and social pressures of his/her environment. While this is not his only theme, he wrote in his nonfiction manifesto, *The Aristos,* that the very "terms of existence encourage us to change, to evolve" if we are to be free; and thus the theme provides a unifying thread throughout much of his work.

Fowles's first published work, *The Collector,* deals with freedom on a variety of levels. Fred Clegg, a lower-class clerk who has won a fortune in a football pool, buys an isolated house and rigs up a basement room as a secret cell for Miranda, a twenty-year-old, upper-middle-class scholarship art student, whom he has kidnapped. The situation allows Fowles to examine how two types of people and their views of freedom and authority play out in contemporary society. As Susana Onega explained in *Form and Meaning in the Novels of John Fowles,* "The collector is the least imaginative of men, for in order to exist he must tangibly possess the objects that obsess him, while the creator rejects this material reality and uses his imagination to create his own subjective alternatives to it." Fowles allows each of these points of view to give an account of the kidnapping by dividing the book into two halves. Onega reported, "In *The Collector,* John Fowles offers us two complementary versions of the events—Frederick Clegg's 'objective' first-person account counterbalanced and undermined by Miranda's much more literary version recorded in her diary."

The action of the novel consists of the working out of two lines of freedom, both based on Miranda's response to Clegg's imposition of his illegitimate authority over her, which she terms "the hateful tyranny of weak people." One line of freedom is Miranda's tentative, temporary, or pretended acceptance of the imposed authority that wins her small degrees of freedom within the limited boundaries that Clegg will permit. The second line consists of Miranda's successive attempts to escape Clegg's control altogether, a struggle that takes on societal and universal human dimensions as the novel progresses. In this struggle, Miranda's diary takes on special significance, one that alludes to Fowles's view of the artist's work. "In *The Collector,* Miranda intuits that it is possible to destroy her awful reality by striving to create a fictional alternative to it with her diary," suggested Onega. In the end, however, Miranda dies. She catches pneumonia because of the poor conditions in her basement prison, and Clegg refuses to take action.

While the imprisonment of a young woman in a locked room dramatizes lost freedom in *The Collector,* Fowles deals with the issue more subtly and ironically in *The Magus.* Nicholas, a young, well-educated Englishman, is an English teacher at a private boys' school on the Greek island of Phraxos. He makes the acquaintance of Conchis, a local wealthy villa owner who has set out to create his own world. This creation includes a "god-game," a series of dramas in which Nicholas and others in Conchis's circle serve as living actors. Fowles and Conchis contrive for Nicolas a trial to learn that freedom in a world of psychological and societal influences requires self-knowledge. Although Nicholas has embraced the concepts of existentialism precisely because of their emphasis on the possibility of knowing one's self and acting authentically upon such knowledge, Fowles demonstrates how the character, in fact, uses them as an almost ironclad defense against self-knowledge.

The French Lieutenant's Woman again addresses the issues of freedom starkly dramatized in *The Collector* and more developed in *The Magus.* While Fowles again depicts characters struggling for physical and psychic liberation, he places them in the restrictive atmosphere of Victorian England. Here Charles Smithson, engaged to Ernestina Freeman, becomes entranced by another woman, Sarah Woodruff, the object of rumors of a failed affair with a French lieutenant. In playing out the story of Charles's growing obsession, Fowles desires to see his characters freed, not only from society but also from his own control of them as author; thus the composing process becomes part of the novel's subject. And finally, Fowles liberates even himself from the limitations of the novel form; he devises separate endings for the novel, making the reader his implied consultant on the creation of the book. In this way, as Pifer pointed out in the *Dictionary of Literary Biography,* Fowles creates in *The French Lieutenant's Woman* "a remarkable evocation of the historical and social matrix of the Victorian age . . . [that] is also a parody of the conventions, and underlying assumptions, that operate within the Victorian novel."

By giving characters their freedom, Fowles also liberates himself from the tyranny of the rigid plan; but there remains a more basic limitation of fiction, and from this Fowles frees himself by means of his double ending. "The novelist is still a god," Fowles wrote in *The French Lieutenant's Woman,* "since he creates (and not even the most aleatory avant-garde modern novel has managed to extirpate its author completely); what has changed is that we are no longer the gods of the Victorian image, omniscient and decreeing; but in the new theological image, with freedom our first principle, not authority." Thus, although the novel seems in many ways a Victorian novel, the author reminds the reader that it is not; it is actually a novel of our time, with "this self-consciousness about the processes of art [that] is a hallmark of much twentieth-century fiction."

Fowles said in a personal note set in the middle of *The Ebony Tower* that he "meant to suggest variations on both certain themes in previous books of mine and in methods of narrative presentation." Themes and narrative methods combine to weave an intricate pattern of connection, not only with earlier works but among the novella, the three short stories, and the translation of a Celtic medieval romance that make up this collection. This translation, of Marie de France's *Eliduc,* is crucial to the connectedness of these short works. "By including his prose translation of this romance among the original stories collected in this volume," observed Pifer, "Fowles encourages his readers to look for thematic correspondences and common motifs. He thus continues to provoke the reader's interest in the literary process as well as in the product."

In the title work, a novella, Fowles follows the character of David Williams, a minor British abstract painter and art critic. For a contribution to an upcoming art book, David is assigned an interview with one of the leading British painters of an earlier generation. Henry Breasley, now in his seventies, has long lived in Brittany, France, in self-imposed exile. As the story unfolds, the elder artist challenges the younger, accusing him and his contemporaries of isolating themselves in an ebony tower. "A modern variant of the traditional 'ivory tower' idealism," Pifer explained, "the ebony tower signifies the contemporary artist's retreat from reality. Obscurity and cool detachment mask his fear of self-exposure and his failure to engage with life's vital mysteries." David is offered the opportunity to make changes, but he fails to do so. As Carol M. Barnum noted in *The Fiction of John Fowles: A Myth for Our Time,* "David has spent his life avoiding the challenge, living comfortably but superficially. When he finds himself faced with the dark tower of his existence, he cannot rise to meet it."

Returning to the novel format, Fowles published *Daniel Martin.* "This novel is patterned on the quest motif, the main character's search for an authentic self," Pifer wrote. Specifically, the title character is a relatively successful screenwriter who is not satisfied with the life that he has made. As a result, he contemplates writing a novel about his own life, and in the writing, recreating himself. "Unlike Fowles's previous novels," suggested Pifer, "this one does not proceed with rapid forward momentum, catching the reader up in its ingenious twists and turns." Even so, assured the critic, "*Daniel Martin* is not simply nor unartfully constructed; its design is extremely complex." As Jacqueline Costello explained in *University of Hartford Studies in Literature,* in this novel, "Fowles analyzes the ways in which fic-

tion can restrict or expand our ideas, our relationships, and our beings as he explores the extent to which one can write and revise one's life. His juxtaposition of the then and now, the real and reported, the narrator's first and third persons, discovers a realm in which fiction and reality, author and character, past, present, and future are no longer limited by clear distinctions."

In setting up these juxtapositions, Fowles offers Daniel Martin the opportunity to recognize his own as well as his generation's failings, mainly selfishness. In this recognition, "Fowles appears more concerned than ever before with the relationship of the individual to his society, and with the necessary balance between personal freedom and social restraint," Pifer pointed out. In the end, Costello found, "*Daniel Martin* assumes the moral shape of the epic romance as it replays the protagonist's return to domesticity, community, and culture after travel and trial, after quelling id and confronting neurosis." Thus, concluded Pifer, "At the end of *Daniel Martin,* the protagonist finds himself . . . poised on the brink of a possible new life, the "chance of a new existence.""

In *Mantissa,* Fowles draws the reader into a story about a writer who is suffering from amnesia, and his doctor, who offers her brand of sexual therapy as a cure. Yet, as is always the case with Fowles, there is more here than immediately meets the eye, issues of freedom and the writer's role. As Raymond J. Wilson III commented in *Twentieth-Century Literature,* this novel is a complex work that folds an allegory about writing into a parody of one particular philosophy of writing. Wilson suggested that Fowles has essentially called the bluff of post-structuralists such as Roland Barthes, Jacques Derrida, and Jacques Lacan. In other words, asked Wilson, "What would a novel look like if the post-structuralists are right? John Fowles's answer: If they are right, a novel will look like *Mantissa.*" Wilson continued, "Drawing primarily from Roland Barthes but also from Jacques Derrida and Jacques Lacan, Fowles ridicules the sexual theory of the text while simultaneously transforming it into an interesting and plausible allegorical expression of the creative process." Contrary to what the post-structuralists argue, that the author does not exist or is at best inconsequential, Fowles demonstrates through the union of the amnesic author and his muse doctor that this view is absurd and that he, John Fowles, does exist and does control the text. "When Fowles parodies our modern philosophers in *Mantissa,* he transcends parody by re-crafting the post-structuralist sexual theory of the text into his own demonstrated sexual allegory of the creative process," reiterated Wilson.

In *A Maggot* Fowles turns his attention to the eighteenth century in much the same way as he had explored the nineteenth century in *The French Lieutenant's Woman.* The two novels share a number of similarities. Frederick M. Holmes outlined the similarities in a *Contemporary Literature* review. "Both are unconventional historical novels which bring an explicitly modern authorial consciousness to bear on the past rather than pretending to be of the historical period during which the action takes place." Furthermore, Holmes observed, "*A Maggot* features both segments of narrative in the manner of a realistic novel . . . and the discursive reflections of a self-consciously literary narrator." However, Fowles employs several new devices to draw readers into the eighteenth-century world he is creating and to distract them from the fact that it is a creation. *A Maggot* "incorporates other kinds of documents, some of which Fowles has taken from authentic, eighteenth-century sources and some of which he has composed to masquerade as eighteenth-century texts," Holmes explained.

The novel is centered on the disappearance of Mr. Bartholomew and the efforts of the barrister Henry Ayscough to reconstruct the events of his disappearance. In the course of his investigation, the rational Ayscough must face the intuitive, artistic Rebecca, who may have witnessed the events in question. Because she has offered two different accounts of the trip to a cave in rural England from which Bartholomew never returned, and though both versions seem unreliable, Ayscough's efforts to recreate the past only muddle it more. "Like the majority of Fowles's fiction, [*A Maggot*] suggests that to impose finality on narratives is to falsify the existential uncertainty which is an inescapable part of being alive," wrote Holmes.

A Maggot was Fowles's last novel. As he confided to *Washington Post Book World* contributor David Streitfeld, "the idea of writing yet another story suddenly seems rather boring." Instead, Fowles became increasingly interested in poetry. "I hope to write a book-length attempt at various poems," he told Streitfeld. "I think when you get old, suddenly poetry becomes more real, more important."

The major philosophical and literary concerns of Fowles's career are presented in *Wormholes,* a miscellany of several decades' worth of essays and occasional writings. These are grouped as autobiographical writings, pieces on culture and society, essays on literature and criticism, reflections on nature, and "An Interview." Critics appreciated the book's liveliness and originality. In the *New York Times Book Review,* Roger Kimball hailed the volume as "various, quirkily learned, beguil-ing, opinionated and, in parts, as sumptuously written as Fowles's fiction." Christopher Lehmann-Haupt, in the *New York Times,* especially welcomed Fowles's comments on writing and literature, as well as his travel writing about France and Greece. Though the critic disliked the occasional bouts of over-seriousness in the book, he considered it, in general, to be "a useful and stimulating tour through nature, literature and the art of the novel."

Nearly twenty years after the publication of *A Maggot,* Fowles reappeared on the literary scene, through the editorial efforts of Charles Drazin, with the first of two volumes of the novelist's journals. *The Journals: Volume 1: 1949-1965,* describe Fowles's youthful adventures in France and Greece, his emergence from obscurity at nearly forty years of age with the publication of *The Collector,* and the ensuing fame that threatened to overwhelm him, ending with the author's retreat circa 1969 to the peace and quiet of Lyme Regis, where he remained until his death. Some critics expressed pleasant surprise at the news that Fowles had published a "remarkably detailed, analytical" documentation of a relatively private life, as Donna Seaman noted in her *Booklist* review. She recommended Fowles's journal as a "fascinating . . . story of his evolution as a writer." *Contemporary Review* contributor Geoffrey Heptonstall counted the journal among the best of Fowles's literary accomplishments. "Private thoughts made public," he observed, can surprise the unsuspecting reader, "but the intemperate frankness here revealed is a necessary prelude to the singularly enriching clarity of perception." A second volume of *The Journals* was published in 2005.

Fowles's refusal to limit himself opened his work to much of life. He sifted elements of culture, art, and historical experience into such familiar structures as the thriller, the adolescent-learning novel, the historical novel, the book of short fiction, and the mainstream modernist novel. He re-created and made these forms his own, mixing his insight about human beings and life into the transformed structures. Literature and myth enter through the many allusions that he made central to the movement of the novels. Finally, while many of Fowles's novels make significant social comments and provide insights into human character, his variety of forms open continual opportunities for new possibilities. Such diversity, although presenting the reader with difficulties of adjustment from novel to novel, supplies evidence that Fowles pushed ahead, activated by his own major theme: the drive for freedom. For this reason, Pifer concluded in the *Dictionary of Literary Biography,* "Fowles has indeed proved himself a dynamic rather than a static artist. Generations of readers will doubtless continue to be enlightened as well as entertained by his fiction."

Fowles died at his home in Lyme Regis, England on November 5, 2005, after a prolonged period of illness.

BIOGRAPHICAL AND CRITICAL SOURCES:

BOOKS

Acheson, James, editor, *The British and Irish Novel since 1960,* Macmillan Academic (London, England), 1991.

Acheson, James, *John Fowles,* St. Martin's Press (New York, NY), 1998.

Conradi, Peter, *John Fowles,* Methuen (London, England), 1982.

Contemporary Fiction in America and England, 1950-1970, Thomson Gale (Detroit, MI), 1976.

Contemporary Literary Criticism, Thomson Gale (Detroit, MI), Volume 1, 1973, Volume 2, 1974, Volume 3, 1975, Volume 4, 1975, Volume 6, 1976, Volume 9, 1978, Volume 10, 1979, Volume 15, 1980, Volume 33, 1985, Volume 87, 1995.

Contemporary Novelists, 6th edition, St. James Press (Detroit, MI), 1996.

Dictionary of Literary Biography, Thomson Gale (Detroit, MI), Volume 14: *British Novelists since 1960,* 1983, Volume 139: *British Short-Fiction Writers,* 1994.

Fawkner, H. W., *The Timescapes of John Fowles,* Fairleigh Dickinson University Press (East Brunswick, NJ), 1984.

The Fiction of John Fowles: A Myth for Our Time, Penkevill Publishing (Greenwood, FL), 1988.

Fowles, John, *The Aristos: A Self-Portrait in Ideas,* Little, Brown (Boston, MA) 1964, 2nd revised edition published as *Aristos,* J. Cape (London, England), 1980.

Fowles, John, *The French Lieutenant's Woman,* Little, Brown (Boston, MA), 1969.

Fowles, John, *The Ebony Tower,* Little, Brown (Boston, MA), 1974.

Fowles, John, *The Journals: Volume 1: 1949-1965,* Jonathan Cape (London, England), 2003.

Hayman, Ronald, *The Novel Today, 1967-75,* Longman (New York, NY), 1976.

Higdon, David L., *Time and English Fiction,* Macmillan (New York, NY), 1977.

Huffaker, Robert, *John Fowles,* Twayne (Boston, MA), 1980.

Loveday, Simon, *The Romances of John Fowles,* St. Martin's (New York, NY), 1985.

McSweeney, Kerry, *Four Contemporary Novelists,* McGill-Queen's University Press (Montreal, Quebec, Canada), 1983.

Newquist, Roy, *Counterpoint,* Simon & Schuster (New York, NY), 1964.

Olshen, Barry, *John Fowles,* Ungar (New York, NY), 1978.

Olshen, Barry, and Toni Olshen, *John Fowles: A Reference Guide,* G.K. Hall (Boston, MA), 1980.

Onega, Susan, *Form and Meaning in the Novels of John Fowles,* UMI Research Press (Ann Arbor, MI), 1989.

Palmer, William J., *The Fiction of John Fowles: Tradition, Art, and the Loneliness of Selfhood,* University of Missouri Press (Columbia, MO), 1974.

Runyon, Randolph, *Fowles/Irving/Barthes: Canonical Variations on an Apocryphal Theme,* Ohio State University Press (Columbus, OH), 1981.

Salami, Mahmoud, *John Fowles's Fiction and the Poetics of Postmodernism,* Associated University Presses (Cranbury, NJ), 1992.

Shaw, Philip, and Peter Stockwell, editors, *Subjectivity and Literature from the Romantics to the Present Day,* Pinter Publishers (London, England), 1991.

Tarbox, Katherine, *The Art of John Fowles,* University of Georgia Press (Athens, GA), 1998.

Vipond, Dianne L., editor, *Conversations with John Fowles,* University Press of Mississippi (Jackson, MS), 1999.

Warburton, Eileen, *John Fowles: A Life In Two Worlds,* Viking (New York, NY), 2004.

Weber, Brom, editor, *Sense and Sensibility in Twentieth-Century Writing,* Southern Illinois University Press (Carbondale, IL), 1970.

Wolfe, Peter, *John Fowles: Magus and Moralist,* Bucknell University Press (Cranbury, NJ), 1976, revised edition, 1979.

Woodcock, Bruce, *Male Mythologies: John Fowles and Masculinity,* Barnes & Noble (New York, NY), 1984.

PERIODICALS

Booklist, May 1, 2005, Donna Seaman, review of *The Journals,* p. 1560.

Contemporary Literature, summer, 1986, Frederick M. Holmes, review of *A Maggot,* p. 160.

Contemporary Review, May, 1996, p. 262; April, 2004, Geoffrey Heptonstall, review of *The Journals,* p. 246.

New York Times, May 11, 1998, Christopher Lehmann-Haupt, review of *Wormholes: Essays and Occasional Writings.*

New York Times Book Review, May 31, 1998, Roger Kimball, review of *Wormholes.*

Publishers Weekly, March 28, 2005, review of *The Journals,* p. 67.

Twentieth-Century Literature, Volume 28, 1982, Raymond J. Wilson III, review of *Mantissa.*

University of Hartford Studies in Literature, Volume 22, number 1, 1990, article by Jacqueline Costello, p. 31.

Washington Post Book World, May 31, 1998, David Streitfeld, interview, p. X15.

OBITUARIES:

PERIODICALS

New York Times, November 8, 2005.

*   *   *

FOWLES, John Robert
    See FOWLES, John

*   *   *

FRANCIS, Dick 1920-
    (Richard Stanley Francis)

PERSONAL: Born October 31, 1920, in Tenby, Pembrokeshire, Wales; son of George Vincent (a professional steeplechase rider and stable manager) and Molly (Thomas) Francis; married Mary Brenchley (a teacher and assistant stage manager), June 21, 1947 (died, September 30, 2000); children: Merrick, Felix. *Education:* Attended Maidenhead County School. *Religion:* Church of England. *Hobbies and other interests:* Boating, fox hunting, tennis.

ADDRESSES: Agent—c/o John Johnson Ltd., 45/46 Clerkenwell Green, London EC1R 0HT, England.

CAREER: Novelist. Amateur steeplechase rider, 1946-48; professional steeplechase jockey, 1948-57; *Sunday Express,* London, England, racing correspondent, 1957-73. *Military service:* Royal Air Force, 1940-46; became flying officer (pilot).

MEMBER: Crime Writers Association (chair, 1973-74), Mystery Writers of America, Writers of Canada, Detection Club, Racecourse Association, Garrick Club (London, England).

AWARDS, HONORS: Steeplechase jockey championship, 1954; Silver Dagger Award, Crime Writers Association, 1965, for *For Kicks;* Edgar Allan Poe Award, Mystery Writers of America, 1969, for *Forfeit,* 1980, for *Whip Hand,* and 1996, for *Come to Grief;* Gold Dagger Award, Crime Writers Association, 1980, for *Whip Hand;* named commander, Order of the British Empire, 1984; L.H.D., Tufts University, 1991; Grand Master Award and Best Novel award, Mystery Writers of America, both 1996, both for *Come to Grief;* elected fellow, Royal Society of Literature, 1997.

WRITINGS:

MYSTERY NOVELS

Dead Cert, Holt (New York, NY), 1962, reprinted, Armchair Detective Library (New York, NY), 1989.

Nerve, Harper (New York, NY), 1964, reprinted, Armchair Detective Library (New York, NY), 1990.

For Kicks, Harper (New York, NY), 1965, reprinted, Armchair Detective Library (New York, NY), 1990.

Odds Against, Michael Joseph (London, England), 1965, Harper (New York, NY), 1966, reprinted, Edito-Service S.A. (Geneva, Switzerland), 1982.

Flying Finish, Michael Joseph (London England), 1966, Harper (New York, NY), 1967.

Blood Sport, Harper (New York, NY), 1967.

Forfeit, Harper (New York, NY), 1968.

Enquiry, Harper (New York, NY), 1969.

Rat Race, Harper (New York, NY), 1970.

Bonecrack, Harper (New York, NY), 1971.

Smokescreen, Harper (New York, NY), 1972.

Slayride, Harper (New York, NY), 1973.

Knockdown, Harper (New York, NY), 1974.

High Stakes, Harper (New York, NY), 1975.

In the Frame, Harper (New York, NY), 1976.

Risk, Harper (New York, NY), 1977.

Trial Run, Harper (New York, NY), 1978.

Whip Hand, Harper (New York, NY), 1979, reprinted, ImPress (Pleasantville, NY), 2001.

Reflex, Michael Joseph (London, England), 1980, Putnam (New York, NY), 1981.

Twice Shy, Michael Joseph (London, England), 1981, Putnam (New York, NY), 1982.

Banker, Michael Joseph (London, England), 1982, Putnam (New York, NY), 1983.

The Danger, Michael Joseph (London, England), 1983, Putnam (New York, NY), 1984.

Proof, Michael Joseph (London, England), 1984, Putnam (New York, NY), 1985.

Break In, Michael Joseph (London, England), 1985, Putnam (New York, NY), 1986, reprinted, Jove Books (New York, NY), 2001.

Bolt, Michael Joseph (London, England), 1986, Putnam (New York, NY), 1987.

Hot Money, Michael Joseph (London, England), 1987, Putnam (New York, NY), 1988.

The Edge, Michael Joseph (London, England), 1988, Putnam (New York, NY), 1989.

Straight, Putnam (New York, NY), 1989.

Longshot, Putnam (New York, NY), 1990.

Comeback, Putnam (New York, NY), 1991.

Driving Force, Putnam (New York, NY), 1992.

Decider, Putnam (New York, NY), 1993.

Wild Horses, Putnam (New York, NY), 1994.

Come to Grief, Putnam (New York, NY), 1995.

To the Hilt, Putnam (New York, NY), 1996.

10 Lb. Penalty, Putnam (New York, NY), 1997.

Second Wind, Putnam (New York, NY), 1999.

Shattered, Putnam (New York, NY), 2000.

Win, Place, or Show (collection of "Sid Halley" stories), Berkely Prime Crime (New York, NY), 2004.

OTHER

The Sport of Queens (racing autobiography), Michael Joseph (London, England), 1957, Armchair Detective Library (New York, NY), 1993.

(Editor, with John Welcome) *Best Racing and Chasing Stories,* Faber (London, England), 1966.

(Editor, with John Welcome) *Best Racing and Chasing Stories II,* Faber (London, England), 1969.

The Racing Man's Bedside Book, Faber (London, England), 1969.

A Jockey's Life: The Biography of Lester Piggott, Putnam (New York, NY), 1986, published as *Lester, the Official Biography,* Michael Joseph (London, England), 1986.

(Editor, with John Welcome) *The Dick Francis Treasury of Great Racing Stories,* G.K. Hall (Boston, MA), 1990.

(Editor, with John Welcome) *Classic Lines: More Great Racing Stories,* Bellew Publications (London, England), 1991.

(Editor, with John Welcome) *The New Treasury of Great Racing Stories,* Norton (New York, NY), 1992.

Field of Thirteen (short-story collection), Putnam (New York, NY), 1998.

Work published in anthologies, including *Winter's Crimes 5,* edited by Virginia Whitaker, Macmillan, 1973; *Stories of Crime and Detection,* edited by Joan D. Berbrich, McGraw, 1974; *Ellery Queen's Crime Wave,* Putnam, 1976; and *Ellery Queen's Searches and Seizures,* Davis, 1977. Contributor to periodicals, including *Horseman's Year, Sports Illustrated, In Praise of Hunting,* and *Stud and Stable.*

Francis's works have been translated into Japanese, Norwegian, Czechoslovakian, and thirty-one other languages.

ADAPTATIONS: Dead Cert was filmed by United Artists in 1973; *Odds Against* was adapted for Yorkshire Television as *The Racing Game,* 1979, and also broadcast as part of the Public Broadcasting System television series *Mystery!,* 1980-81. Francis's works were adapted for television as *Dick Francis Mysteries,* 1989; *Blood Sport* was adapted for television as *Dick Francis: Blood Sport,* Comedia Entertainment, 1989. All of Francis's books have been recorded on audiocassette.

SIDELIGHTS: When steeplechase jockey Dick Francis retired from horse racing at age thirty-six, he recalls, he speculated that he would be remembered as "the man who didn't win the National," England's prestigious Grand National steeplechase. If Francis had not turned to fiction, his prediction might have been correct, but with the publication of his first novel, *Dead Cert,* in 1962, he launched a second career that has become even more successful than his first: he became a mystery writer and since that time has averaged a thriller a year, astounding critics with the fecundity of his imagination.

Francis has garnered important awards such as Britain's Silver Dagger—in 1965 for *For Kicks*—three "best mystery novel" Edgars—for *Forfeit* in 1969, *Whip Hand* in 1980, and *Come to Grief* in 1996—and the prestigious Grand Master citation from the Mystery Writers of America in 1996. In his autobiography, *Sport of Queens,* Francis reflects on his books and their success: "I still find the writing . . . grindingly hard, and I approach Chapter 1 each year with deeper foreboding." Gina MacDonald, writing in the *Dictionary of Literary Biography,* noted that Francis's method of writing his books is very precise. He usually thinks of a plot by midsummer, and spends the rest of the year researching the book. He finally starts writing the following year and finishes the book by spring. Most of his books concern horses, and racing still figures prominently in his life. This affinity for the racetrack enriches his prose, according to Julian Symons, who declared in the *New York Times Book Review* that "what comes most naturally to [Francis] is also what he does best—writing about the thrills, spills and chills of horse racing."

Before he began writing, Francis experienced one of racing's most publicized "spills" firsthand. In 1956, when he was already a veteran jockey, he had the privilege of riding Devon Loch—the Queen Mother's horse—in the annual Grand National. Fifty yards from the finish line, with the race virtually won, the horse inexplicably collapsed. Later examination revealed no physical injury and no clue was ever found. "I still don't have the answer," Francis told Peter Axthelm of *Newsweek.* "Maybe he was shocked by the noise of 250,000 people screaming because the royal family's horse was winning. But the fact is that with nothing wrong with him, ten strides from the winning post he fell. The other fact is," he added, "if that mystery hadn't happened, I might never have written all these other ones."

Though each of his novels deals with what many consider a specialized subject, Francis's books have broad appeal. As Judith Rascoe declared in the *Christian Science Monitor,* "You needn't know or care anything about racing to be his devoted reader." And, writing in the *New York Times,* reviewer John Leonard claimed: "Not to read Dick Francis because you don't like horses is like not reading Dostoyevsky because you don't like God. . . . Race tracks and God are subcultures. A writer has to have a subculture to stand upon."

Francis's ability to make this subculture come alive for his readers—to create what Rascoe termed "a background of almost Dickensian realism for his stories"—is what sets him apart from other mystery writers. "In particular," observed Charles Champlin in the *Los Angeles Times,* "his rider's view of the strains and spills, disappointments and exaltations of the steeplechase is breathtaking, a far cry from the languid armchair detecting of other crime solvers." Writing in the *London* magazine, John Welcome expressed similar admiration, especially praising Francis's ability to infuse his races with a significance that extends beyond the Jockey Club milieu: "One can hear the smash of birch, the creak of leather and the rattle of whips. The sweat, the strain, the tears, tragedies and occasional triumphs of the racing game are all there, as well as its seductive beauty. In this—as in much else—no other racing novelist can touch him. He has made racing into a microcosm of the contemporary world."

While critics initially speculated that Francis's specialized knowledge would provide only limited fictional opportunities, most have since changed their minds. "It is fascinating to see how many completely fresh and unexpected plots he can concoct about horses," marveled Anthony Boucher in the *New York Times Book Review.* Philip Pelham took this approbation one step further, writing in the *London* magazine that Francis "improves with every book as both a writer of brisk, lucid prose and as a concocter of ingenious and intricately worked-out plots." His racetrack thrillers deal with such varied story lines as stolen stallions—*Blood Sport*—crooks transporting horses by air—*Flying Finish*—and a jockey who has vanished in Norway—*Slayride.* To further preserve the freshness of his fiction, Francis creates a new protagonist for each novel and often develops subplots around fields unrelated to racing. "His books," noted Axthelm, "take him and his readers on global explorations as well as into crash courses in ventures like aviation, gold mining and, in *Reflex,* amateur photography."

Notwithstanding such variations in plot and theme, Francis is known as a formula writer whose novels, while well written, are ultimately predictable. In all the Francis novels, wrote Welcome, "the hard-done-by chap [is] blindly at grips with an unknown evil, the threads of which he gradually unravels. Frequently—perhaps too frequently—he is subjected to physical torture described in some detail. His heroes are hard men used to injury and pain and they learn to dish it out as once they had to learn to take it. Racing has made them stoics."

Barry Bauska, writing in the *Armchair Detective,* offered a more detailed version of the "typical" Francis thriller. "At the outset something has happened that looks wrong (a jockey is set down by a board of inquiry that seemed predetermined to find him guilty; a horse falls going over a final hurdle it had seemed to clear; horses perfectly ready to win consistently fail to do so). The narrator protagonist (usually not a detective, but always inherently curious) begins to poke around to try to discover what has occurred. In so doing he inevitably pokes too hard and strikes a hornets' nest. The rest of the novel then centers on a critical struggle between the searcher-after-truth and the mysterious agent of evil, whose villainy had upset things in the first place."

Despite the formulaic nature of his work, Francis deals with problems prevalent in modern society, according to Marty Knepper in *Twelve Englishmen of Mystery.*

Knepper felt that Francis's works deal with social and moral issues "seriously and in some depth . . . including some topics generally considered unpleasant." For example, in *Blood Sport* the hero is struggling with his own suicidal urges. In Knepper's words, "To read *Blood Sport* . . . is to learn what it feels like to be lonely, paranoid and suicidal."

Character development also plays an important part in Francis's novels. Knepper suggested that biographical similarities between Francis's heroes may blind the reader to the important differences among them. For example, Francis's heroes have a wide variety of professions. This gives the author a chance to examine professionalism and the responsibilities that accompany it, in fields other than racing and detection. Each of Francis's heroes, according to Knepper, is "a unique person, but each hero . . . changes as a result of his adventures."

While a number of Francis's books include a love story, a much more pressing theme, according to Axthelm, is that of pain. "Again and again," the critic wrote in *Newsweek,* the author's "villains probe the most terrifying physical or psychic weakness in his heroes. A lifetime's most treasured mementos are destroyed by mindless hired thugs; an already crippled hand is brutally smashed until it must be amputated. The deaths in Francis novels usually occur 'off-camera.' The tortures are more intimate affairs, with the reader forced to watch at shudderingly close range."

The prevalence of such violence, coupled with Francis's tendency to paint the relationship between hero and villain as a confrontation between good and evil, have made some reviewers uneasy. In his *Times Literary Supplement* review of *Risk,* for example, Alex de Jong commented that "characterization is sometimes thin and stylized, especially the villains, out to inflict pain upon the accountant who has uncovered their villainy, crooked businessmen and trainers, all a little too well dressed, florid and unexpectedly brutal bullies, created with a faint hint of paranoia." Francis, however, justifies the punishment he metes out to his characters as something his fans have come to expect. "Somehow the readers like to read about it," he told Judy Klemesrud in the *New York Times Book Review.* "But I don't subject them to anything I wouldn't put up with myself. This old body has been knocked around quite a bit."

While the violence of his early novels is largely external, Francis's later novels emphasize more internal stress, according to critics who believe that this shift has added a new dimension to the author's work. Welcome, for instance, observed that in *Reflex* Francis's lessened emphasis on brutality has enabled him to "flesh out his characters. The portrait of Philip Nore, the mediocre jockey nearing the end of his career, is created with real insight; as is the interpretation of his relations with the horses he rides." MacDonald commented that Francis's more recent books "concentrate more specifically on psychological stress." In her opinion, his writing has gone beyond the "dramatic presentation of heroic action" to a deeper level, where the hero "is less a man who can endure torture than one who has the strength to face self-doubt, fear, and human inadequacy and still endure and thrive." Bauska expressed a similar view when he said that Francis's more current works, although not that different in the plot, focus on the protagonist. According to Bauska, Francis is increasingly "considering what goes into the making not so much of a 'hero' as of a good man." The focus of Francis's work is no longer the war outside, though the books are still action-packed, but on the struggle within the protagonist's mind, and his attempts to conquer his own doubts and fears. Bauska attributed this shift in focus to Francis's own growing distance from his racing days. The result, he said, "is that Dick Francis is becoming less a writer of thrillers and more a creator of literature."

While not all reviewers have found Francis's work to be the stuff of literature, his ability to create nearly every year a fresh racing mystery that still retains a creative spark in its focus and technique has been continually remarked upon. Patricia Craig maintained in the *Times Literary Supplement:* "Unreality aside, the Dick Francis story line works through a combination of energy and amiability, the doggedness and right-thinking of the central character, and a certain expertise in the evocation of atmosphere." Citing Francis's *Driving Force* as an example, Craig continued: "Francis shows that he has such a hold on his readers that he can dwell on the properties of horseboxes without fear of being judged uncompelling." Even when Francis returns to the same protagonist, Sid Halley—known to readers of *Odds Against, Whip Hand,* and *Come to Grief*—he manages to shed new light on the character. Dick Adler, contributing to the *Chicago Tribune,* stated: "In spite of a certain predictability in the plot . . . *Come to Grief* is in fact one of [Francis's] most engrossing recent efforts."

Francis's continuing ability to engage both new readers and longtime fans in his stories is perhaps his greatest strength. Christopher Wordsworth, reviewing *Wild Horses* for the London *Observer,* dubbed the novelist "an institution." Indeed, as Elizabeth Tallent noted in the *New York Times Book Review,* while Francis's former position as jockey for the Queen Mother is often mentioned in reviews of the writer, "At this point in his illustrious writing career, the Queen Mother might wish to note in her *vita* that the writer Dick Francis once rode for her."

Francis made an important revelation about his work in the weeks following his wife's death in the autumn of 2000. It had long been understood that Francis himself was a high-school dropout and Mary Francis, who was college-educated, helped to research and edit his books. Only after her death did the author reveal that she indeed helped him to write them as well. "She was more than my right arm, she was both arms, really," he told the *Knight-Ridder/Tribune News Service.* He added: "Mary never allowed her name to be on the books, but it was a double act really." Francis also intimated that he might not try writing any more novels without her, leading to the possibility that his 2000 title, the aptly named *Shattered,* might be his final work. Whether or not that proves to be the case, Francis can certainly lay claim to a long and distinguished career. As Emily Melton put it in *Booklist,* his "ingenious plotting, pared-down writing style, wry humor, and skillful characterizations" make Francis "a sheer delight to read."

BIOGRAPHICAL AND CRITICAL SOURCES:

BOOKS

Bargainnier, Earl F., editor, *Twelve Englishmen of Mystery,* Bowling Green University Popular Press (Bowling Green, OH), 1984.

Barnes, Melvyn, *Dick Francis,* Ungar (New York, NY), 1986.

Bestsellers 89, Issue 3, Thomson Gale (Detroit, MI), 1989.

Contemporary Literary Criticism, Thomson Gale (Detroit, MI), Volume 2, 1974, Volume 22, 1982, Volume 42, 1987, Volume 102, 1998.

Davis, J. Madison, *Dick Francis,* Twayne (Boston, MA), 1989.

Dictionary of Literary Biography, Volume 87: *British Mystery and Thriller Writers since 1940, First Series,* Thomson Gale (Detroit, MI), 1989.

Francis, Dick, *The Sport of Queens,* Michael Joseph (London, England), 1957.

PERIODICALS

Architectural Digest, June, 1985.

Armchair Detective, July, 1978; spring, 1982; winter, 1986; summer, 1993; winter, 1996, p. 102.

Atlantic, March, 1969.

Booklist, January 15, 1986; September 15, 1998, Emily Melton, review of *Field of Thirteen,* p. 202; September 1, 1999, Emily Melton, review of *Second Wind,* p. 7; August, 2000, Connie Fletcher, review of *Shattered,* p. 2073.

British Book News, October, 1984.

Chicago Tribune, October 2, 1994, p. 9; September 3, 1995, p. 4.

Christian Science Monitor, July 17, 1969.

Clues, fall-winter, 2000, Rachel Schaffer, "Dick Francis's Six-Gun Mystique," p. 17.

Family Circle, July, 1970.

Forbes, November 21, 1994, p. 26.

Globe and Mail (Toronto, Ontario, Canada), November 16, 1985; August 12, 1989.

Kirkus Reviews, July 15, 1995, p. 986.

Knight-Ridder/Tribune News Service,.

Life, June 6, 1969.

London, February-March, 1975; March, 1980; February-March, 1981.

Los Angeles Times, March 27, 1981; April 9, 1982; September 12, 1984.

National Review, January 20, 1992.

Newsweek, April 6, 1981.

New Yorker, March 15, 1969; April 16, 1984; April 22, 1985.

New York Times, March 6, 1969; April 7, 1971; March 20, 1981; December 18, 1989; October 9, 2000, Doreen Carvajal, "Mary Francis, 76, Quiet Force behind Dick Francis's Novels," p. A19.

New York Times Book Review, March 21, 1965; March 10, 1968; March 16, 1969; June 8, 1969; July 26, 1970; May 21, 1972; July 27, 1975; September 28, 1975; June 13, 1976; July 10, 1977; May 20, 1979; June 1, 1980; March 29, 1981; April 25, 1982; February 12, 1989; March 27, 1983; March 18, 1984; March 24, 1985; March 16, 1986; October 18, 1992, p. 32; October 2, 1994, p. 26; September 10, 2000, Marilyn Stasio, review of *Shattered,* p. 38.

New York Times Magazine, March 25, 1984.

Observer (London, England), October 2, 1994, p. 18.

People, June 7, 1976; November 23, 1982; January 24, 1994, p. 32; November 22, 1999, "Who Done It? Millions of Books Later, a Mystery Gallops up on Dick Francis: Did His Wife Cowrite His Bestsellers?," p. 202.

Publishers Weekly, January 24, 1986; August 14, 2000, review of *Shattered,* p. 326.

School Library Journal, January, 1995, p. 145.

Sports Illustrated, November 15, 1993.

Time, March 11, 1974; July 14, 1975; May 31, 1976; July 7, 1978; May 11, 1981.

Times (London, England), December 18, 1986.

Times Literary Supplement, October 28, 1977; October 10, 1980; December 10, 1982; October 30, 1992, p. 21; October 7, 1994, p. 30; November 17, 1995, p. 28.

U.S. News and World Report, March 28, 1988.

Washington Post, October 3, 1986.

Washington Post Book World, April 30, 1972; February 18, 1973; April 19, 1980; April 18, 1982; March 27, 1983; March 17, 1985; February 21, 1988; February 5, 1989.

*   *   *

FRANCIS, Richard Stanley
See FRANCIS, Dick

*   *   *

FRANZEN, Jonathan 1959-

PERSONAL: Born August 17, 1959, in Western Springs, IL; son of Earl T. (a civil engineer) and Irene (a homemaker) Franzen; married Valerie Cornell (a writer), c. 1982 (divorced, 1994). *Education:* Swathmore College, B.A., 1981.

ADDRESSES: Home—140 E. 81st St. #10G, New York, NY 10028. *Agent*—Susan Golomb, 875 6th Ave., No. 2302, New York, NY 10001.

CAREER: Writer, 1981—.

AWARDS, HONORS: Fulbright fellow at Free University of Berlin, 1981-82; Massachusetts Artists fellow, 1986; Whiting Writers' Award, 1988, for *The Twenty-Seventh City;* Guggenheim fellow, 1996; National Book Award, 2001, Pulitzer Prize for fiction and PEN/Faulkner Award finalist, and James Tait Black Memorial Prize for fiction, all 2002, all for *The Corrections. The Corrections* was also a finalist for the National Book Critics Circle Award, Los Angeles Book Prize, and IMPAC/Dublin Award.

WRITINGS:

NOVELS

The Twenty-Seventh City, Farrar, Straus (New York, NY), 1988.

Strong Motion, Farrar, Straus (New York, NY), 1992.

The Corrections, Farrar, Straus (New York, NY), 2001.

OTHER

How to Be Alone: Essays, Farrar, Straus (New York, NY), 2002.

Contributor to *New Yorker.*

ADAPTATIONS: The Corrections was optioned for film.

SIDELIGHTS: Jonathan Franzen is a novelist and essayist whose writings reveal "one of the most nuanced minds at work in the dwindling republic of letters," according to Richard Lacayo in *Time* magazine. Franzen's first novel, *The Twenty-Seventh City,* created an evocative portrait of modern America as seen through the lens of St. Louis, Missouri; his second novel, *Strong Motion,* again offered social commentary, this time in a story set in Boston, Massachusetts. Several years passed before the author completed and published his third novel, *The Corrections,* a complex family saga that earned Franzen a National Book Award and a Pulitzer Prize nomination. *The Corrections* is, according to Donald Antrim in *Bomb,* "an absolutely thrilling work, brave and funny and beautiful and, above all, generous. There is something monumental about this novel. It is the product of a deep and prolonged struggle. Its intelligence is everywhere apparent. I could go on in search of words to praise this novel, words that might in some way be truly compatible with, might truly address, Jonathan's achievement. Reading *The Corrections,* I feel myself to be in the presence of a work of art."

Franzen's writing has drawn praise from the start of his career. His debut novel, *The Twenty-Seventh City,* was published just a few years after the author graduated from Swathmore College. Ostensibly set in St. Louis, Missouri, the narrative is laced with references to real-life streets and settings of the city, but readers are not "likely to confuse Franzen's fictional replica of America's twenty-seventh largest city with the real St. Louis," reflected John Blades in the Chicago *Tribune Books.* Rather, he explained, "Franzen has transformed St. Louis into a paranoid reflection of itself, comically and grotesquely distorted, cracked and splintered, a xenophobic fantasyland." St. Louis was, according to the author, once America's fourth largest city; by 1984, the year in which the book is set, its rank has dropped to twenty-seventh. In the book, the population of St. Louis is dominated by Asian Indians. The plot follows the political machinations and psychological warfare of the newly-appointed police chief, S. Jammu. Jammu, a former Bombay police chief who is a cousin of Indian prime minister Indira Gandhi, resorts to seductions, pet-killings, bombings, and kidnappings to convert opponents to her plan for revitalizing downtown business and residential districts. Her methods, however, suggest to some that she is actually seeking total control of the city.

Richard Eder analyzed Franzen's premise in the *Los Angeles Times Book Review:* "The United States is in a decline—in its economy, its health, its social vigor—and risks being superseded by non-Western societies of greater discipline and purpose." Some reviewers, including Eder, found the book's plot overly complex; yet Eder praised the young novelist's imagination and foresight, and added that Franzen's view of America is "startlingly exact." Calling *The Twenty-Seventh City* "unsettling and visionary," Michele Slung noted in the *Washington Post Book World* that it "is not a novel that can be quickly dismissed or easily forgotten: it has elements of both 'Great' and 'American.'" Desmond Christy, reviewing *The Twenty-Seventh City* for the Manchester *Guardian,* wrote: "Novelists are expected to understand their characters; few bring a city to life so vividly as Franzen."

Strong Motion, Franzen's next novel, was another densely-plotted story, one that describes how complacency in the city of Boston is literally shaken loose by a series of devastating earthquakes. The book's central characters are Louis Holland, who works at a failing radio station, and Renee Seitchek, a Harvard seismologist who is investigating a series of mysterious earthquakes. Also central to the plot of *Strong Motion* are Louis's father, a former hippie turned college professor; his socially ambitious mother; and his older sister Eileen, a would-be hipster who is beginning to embrace middle-class values. Louis's mother inherits a million dollars' worth of stock in a chemical company that coincidentally turns out to be responsible for the quakes. Renee then discovers that the company has been disposing of waste products by injecting them into abandoned wells beneath the city. A subplot of the novel involves women's reproductive rights and Renee's conflict with a Christian anti-abortion group.

Franzen told an interviewer for *Publishers Weekly* that in writing *Strong Motion,* he "specifically set out to write a second book that was different from *The Twenty-*

Seventh City: "I wanted it to be. . . a more personal book, I wanted it to be about the kind of people I know, as opposed to the kind of people I knew watching my parents' friends as I grew up in St. Louis." Reviewing *Strong Motion* for *Newsday,* Dan Cryer called it "equally ambitious and even better than his first—more emotionally gripping, more grounded in the everyday. With maximalist gusto, it summons up Boston cityscapes and some of the great social torments of our time, notably the controversies over abortion and environmental decay. With tender regard, it charts the uncertain course of romance between two love-shy protagonists. Blending John Updike's eye for social observation, John Irving's penchant for broad Dickensian plotting and Don DeLillo's gift for quirkily beautiful phrasing, Franzen emerges as a hugely talented original."

Franzen's third novel, *The Corrections,* was more than eight years in the making. It relates the story of a dysfunctional American family, headed by Enid and Alfred Lambert, a long-married couple entering their twilight years. Alfred was once the dominant force of the pair, but now suffers from Parkinson's disease; his affliction forces Enid to take charge of their lives. She decides to invite their three children home for one final Christmas before their father passes away. The eldest son, Gary, is married, with two children and a wife who disparages him. The second son, Chip, has lost his tenure as a college professor after seducing a student, and is trying to escape into an affair with a married woman. Denise, the youngest of the trio, has been fired from her job as a chef after sleeping with her boss's wife. Franzen reveals the lives of his subjects in great detail, shifting back and forth between children, parents, and a host of subsidiary characters. The family does eventually come together for the Christmas reunion, which is related in the final hundred pages of the book. The Lamberts' story illuminates the relationship between generations, as well as providing biting commentary on the state of modern life.

Reviewing *The Corrections* in *New York Review of Books,* John Leonard wrote: "Full of understatment and overreaction, irony and anger, anthropology and surrealism, glut and glee—the rising gorge, the falling tear, politics, parody, pratfall, and prophetic snit—*The Corrections* is the whole package, as if nobody ever told Franzen that the social novel is dead and straight white males vestigial. You will laugh, wince, groan, weep, leave the table and maybe the country, promise never to go home again, and be reminded of why you read serious fiction in the first place: to console and complicate the extreme self with the beauty and truth of sinewy sentences and the manners and mystery of characters from outer space, to see the shadow, and then the teeth, of social context and momentous history." Sven Birkerts, reviewing the book in *Esquire,* observed that while there are many books exploring the theme of life at the end of the twentieth century, "none moves so perfectly between black comedy and tragic pathos." Franzen stirred up considerable controversy after *The Corrections* was selected for the Oprah Book Club, hosted by television talk-show personality Oprah Winfrey. The author expressed some misgivings about having Winfrey's trademark logo appear on the cover of his book, which in turn led Winfrey to cease her discussion of the novel, although it did remain on her list of book club selections.

In 2002, Franzen published *How To Be Alone: Essays,* a collection of previously-published writings. All of the essays comment in some fashion on the modern world, and on the effects a media-saturated culture brings to bear on both writers and their readers. "In tones that are sober but never lugubrious, Franzen weighs the pressures upon the self in a culture that manages the neat trick of discouraging real solitude and genuine community, substituting for both the paradox of media-overloaded isolation," mused Lacayo. In "Why Bother?," a revised version of a piece he had published six years earlier, Franzen looks to serious fiction to bridge the gap of cultural alienation, and seeks to define his place as a writer in the modern world; according to Lacayo, this piece is the "keystone" of the collection. Kyle Minor, assessing *How To Be Alone* in *Antioch Review,* found that the essays in this book show the continued development of Franzen's writing and his thought. He is, according to Minor, "a master novelist emerging as a man of letters."

BIOGRAPHICAL AND CRITICAL SOURCES:

PERIODICALS

Antioch Review, spring, 2003, review of *How to Be Alone: Essays,* p. 370.

Bomb, fall, 2001, Donald Antrim, interview with Jonathan Franzen, pp. 72-78.

Book, July-August, 2003, Stephen King, review of *How To Be Alone,* p. 42.

Boston Globe, August 14, 1988; January 17, 1992, Matthew Gilbert, review of *Strong Motion.*

Chicago Tribune, January 12, 1992, review of *Strong Motion.*

Entertainment Weekly, February 14, 1992, L.S. Klepp, review of *Strong Motion,* p. 48; Benjamin Svetkey, "Domestic Drama: Jonathan Franzen's Carefully Crafted *The Corrections* Finds One Family on the Edge of a Nervous Breakdown," p. 85.

Esquire, October, 2001, Sven Birkerts, review of *The Corrections.*

Globe and Mail (Toronto, Ontario, Canada), December 24, 1988; August 28, 2001, Simon Houpt, interview with Jonathan Franzen, pp. R1, R9; October 27, 2001, Sandra Martin, "Judging Oprah by the Cover," p. R11.

Guardian (Manchester, England), January 29, 1998, Desmond Christy, review of *The Twenty-Seventh City,* p. 17.

Houston Post, March 1, 1992, Jonathan Yardley, review of *Strong Motion.*

Journal of European Studies, December, 2003, Catherine Toal, "Corrections: Contemporary American Melancholy," p. 305.

Library Journal, October 1, 2002, review of *How To Be Alone,* p. 94.

Los Angeles Times, February 2, 1992, Richard Eder, review of *Strong Motion*; November 1, 2001, David L. Ulin, "A Reluctant Member of the Club," p. E1.

Los Angeles Times Book Review, September 4, 1988.

Mirabella, January, 1992, Will Dana, review of *Strong Motion,* pp. 50-51.

New Republic, December 2, 2002, James Wolcott, review of *How To Be Alone,* p. 36.

Newsday, August, 1988, Dan Cryer, review of *The Twenty-Seventh City*; January 5, 1992, Dan Cryer, review of *Strong Motion.*

Newsweek, August 29, 1988; September 17, 2001, Malcolm Jones, "The Emperor's New Pravda?," p. 66.

New Yorker, December 19, 1988, Terrence Raffert, review of *The Twenty-Seventh City,* pp. 101-106.

New York Review of Books, September 20, 2001, John Leonard, review of *The Corrections,* pp. 33-35.

New York Times, August 17, 1988, Michiko Kakutani, review of *The Twenty-Seventh City,* p. C21; September 4, 2001, Michiko Kakutani, review of *The Corrections,* p. E1; October 21, 2001, Monica Corcoran, "On the Dust Jacket, to O or Not to O"; October 29, 2001, David D. Kirkpatrick, "'Oprah' Gaffe by Jonathan Franzen Draws Ire and Sales."

New York Times Book Review, October 9, 1988, Peter Andrews, review of *The Twenty-Seventh City,* p. 22; September 9, 2001, David Gates, review of *The Corrections,* p. 10.

People, October 17, 1988, review of *The Twenty-Seventh City,*; September 9, 2001, Maggie Haberman, review of *The Corrections,* p. 51.

Philadelphia Inquirer, January 19, 1992, Ephraim Paul, review of *Strong Motion,* p. L1; January 25, 1992, Carlin Romano, "A Writer Basking in the Raves."

Poets and Writers, September-October, 2001, Joanna Smith Rakoff, interview with Jonathan Franzen, pp. 27-33.

Publishers Weekly, October 4, 1991, review of *Strong Motion,* p. 79; December 6, 1991, Michael Coffey, "Jonathan Franzen: A Distinct Turn to More Personal Issues Marks His Second Novel," p. 53; September 2, 2002, review of *How To Be Alone,* p. 65.

San Francisco Chronicle, September 25, 1988.

Sydney Morning Herald, May 10-11, 2003, Malcolm Knox, interview with Jonathan Franzen, pp. 4-5.

Time, November 25, 2002, Richard Lacayo, review of *How To Be Alone,* p. 93.

Tribune Books, August 21, 1988, John Blades, review of *The Twenty-Seventh City,* p. 1.

Washington Post Book World, September 4, 1988, Michele Slung, review of *The Twenty-Seventh City,* p. 1.

Yale Review, April, 2002, T.M. McNally, review of *The Corrections,* p. 161-170.

ONLINE

American Prospect, http://www.prospect.org/ (April 20, 2005), Keith Gessen, review of *The Corrections.*

Now Culture, http://www.nowculture.com/ (February 17, 2002), review of *The Corrections.*

Oprah.com, http://www.oprah.com/ (October 15, 2001), review of *The Corrections.*

Slate, http://slate.msn.com/ (November 1, 2001), "Jonathan Franzen: A Defense."

*   *   *

FRASER, Antonia 1932-
(Antonia Pakenham)

PERSONAL: Born August 27, 1932, in London, England; daughter of Francis Aungier Pakenham, seventh Earl of Longford (a politician and writer) and Elizabeth Pakenham, Countess of Longford (a writer; maiden name, Harman); married Hugh Charles Patrick Joseph Fraser (member of parliament), September 25, 1956 (marriage ended, 1977); married Harold Pinter (a playwright), November 27, 1980; children: (first marriage) Rebecca, Flora, Benjamin, Natasha, Damian, Orlando. *Education:* Oxford University, B.A., 1953; received M.A. *Religion:* Roman Catholic *Hobbies and other interests:* Swimming, "life in the garden."

ADDRESSES: Home—London, England. *Agent*—Curtis Brown Ltd., 28-29 Haymarket, London SW1Y 4SP.

CAREER: Writer, 1954—. Also worked as broadcaster and lecturer; panelist on British Broadcasting Corporation's *My Word!* radio program. Member of Arts Council, 1970-71.

MEMBER: English PEN (president, 1988-1990; vice president, 1990—), Society of Authors (chairperson, 1974-75), Crimewriters Association (vice chairperson, 1984; chairperson, 1985-87), Detection, Vanderbilt, Writers in Prison Committee (chairman, 1985-88, 1990-).

AWARDS, HONORS: James Tait Black Memorial Prize for biography, 1969, for *Mary, Queen of Scots;* Woltson Prize for history, 1984, and Prix Caumont-La Force, 1985, both for *The Weaker Vessel;* D. Litt., Hull, 1986, Sussex, 1990, Nottingham, 1993, St. Andrew's College, 1994; Crime Writers' Association Non-Fiction Gold Dagger, 1996; St. Louis Literary Award, 1996; Commander of the British Empire, 1999; North Medicott Medal, Historical Association, 2000; Franco-British Society Literary Prize.

WRITINGS:

HISTORICAL NONFICTION

Mary, Queen of Scots (biography), Delacorte (New York, NY), 1969, new edition, Weidenfeld & Nicolson (London, England), 1994.

Cromwell, the Lord Protector (biography), Knopf (New York, NY), 1973, published in England as *Cromwell, Our Chief of Men,* Weidenfeld & Nicolson (London, England), 1973.

Mary, Queen of the Scots, and the Historians, Royal Stuart Society (Ilford, Essex, England), 1974.

King James VI of Scotland, I of England (biography), Weidenfeld & Nicolson (London, England), 1974, Knopf (New York, NY), 1975.

Royal Charles: Charles II and the Restoration, (biography), Knopf (New York, NY), 1979, published in England as *King Charles II,* Weidenfeld and Nicolson (London, England), 1979, revised edition published as *Charles II: His Life and Times,* Weidenfeld and Nicolson (London, England), 1993.

The Weaker Vessel: Woman's Lot in Seventeenth-Century England, Knopf (New York, NY), 1984.

The Warrior Queens, Knopf (New York, NY), 1988, published in England as *Boadicea's Chariot: The Warrior Queens,* Weidenfeld & Nicolson (London, England), 1988.

The Wives of Henry VIII, Knopf (New York, NY), 1992, published in England as *The Six Wives of Henry VIII,* Weidenfeld & Nicolson (London, England), 1992.

Faith and Treason: The Story of the Gunpowder Plot, Doubleday (New York, NY), 1996; published in England as *The Gunpowder Plot: Terror and Faith,* Weidenfeld & Nicolson (London, England), 1996.

Marie Antoinette: The Journey, Weidenfeld & Nicolson (London, England), 2001, Doubleday (New York, NY), 2001.

"JEMIMA SHORE" MYSTERY SERIES

Quiet As a Nun, Viking (New York, NY), 1977.

The Wild Island: A Mystery, Norton (New York, NY), 1978.

A Splash of Red, Norton (New York, NY), 1981.

Cool Repentance, Norton (New York, NY), 1982.

Oxford Blood, Norton (New York, NY), 1985.

Jemima Shore's First Case and Other Stories, Methuen (New York, NY), 1986.

Your Royal Hostage, Atheneum (New York, NY), 1988.

The Cavalier Case, Bantam (New York, NY), 1990.

Jemima Shore at the Sunny Grave and Other Stories, Bloomsbury (London, England), 1991, Bantam (New York, NY), 1993.

Political Death, Bantam (New York, NY), 1996.

EDITOR

The Lives of the Kings and Queens of England (also see below), Knopf (New York, NY), 1975, revised edition, University of California Press (New York, NY), 1998.

Scottish Love Poems: A Personal Anthology, Canongate (Edinburgh, Scotland), 1975, Viking (New York, NY), 1976, new expanded edition, illustrated by James Hutcheson, Canongate (Edinburgh, Scotland), 2002.

Love Letters: An Anthology, Weidenfeld & Nicolson (London, England), 1976, Knopf (New York, NY), 1977, reprinted as *Love Letters: An Illustrated Anthology,* Contemporary Books (Chicago, IL), 1989.

Heroes and Heroines, Weidenfeld & Nicolson (London, England), 1980.

Mary, Queen of Scots: An Anthology of Poetry, Eyre Methuen (London, England), 1981.

Oxford and Oxfordshire in Verse, illustrated by Rebecca Fraser, Secker & Warburg (London, England), 1982.

Love Letters: An Illustrated Anthology, Contemporary Books (New York, NY), 1989.

The Pleasure of Reading, Random House (New York, NY), 1992.

Maurice Ashley, *The Stuarts* (excerpted from *Lives of the Kings and Queens of England*), University of California Press (Berkeley, CA), 2000.

Anthony Cheetham, *The Wars of the Roses* (excerpted from *Lives of the Kings and Queens of England*), University of California Press (Berkeley, CA), 2000.

John Clarke, *The Houses of Hanover and Sax-Coburg-Gotha* (excerpted from *Lives of the Kings and Queens of England*), University of California Press (Berkeley, CA), 2000.

John Gillingham, *The Middle Ages* (excerpted from *Lives of the Kings and Queens of England*), University of California Press (Berkeley, CA), 2000.

Andrew Roberts, *The House of Windsor* (excerpted from *Lives of the Kings and Queens of England*), University of California Press (Berkeley, CA), 2000.

Neville Williams, *The Tudors* (excerpted from *Lives of the Kings and Queens of England*), University of California Press (Berkeley, CA), 2000.

OTHER

(Under name Antonia Pakenham) *King Arthur and the Knights of the Round Table* (juvenile), Weidenfeld & Nicolson (London, England), 1954, Knopf (New York, NY), 1970.

(Translator; under name Antonia Pakenham) Jean Monsterleet, *Martyrs in China,* Longman (London, England), 1956.

(Under name Antonia Pakenham) *Robin Hood* (juvenile), Weidenfeld & Nicolson (London, England), 1957, Knopf (New York, NY), 1971.

(Translator; under name Antonia Pakenham) *Dior by Dior: The Autobiography of Christian Dior,* Weidenfeld & Nicolson (London, England), 1957.

Dolls, Putnam (New York, NY), 1963.

A History of Toys, Delacorte (New York, NY), 1966, revised edition, Springer Books, 1972.

Mary, Queen of Scots (phonodisc), National Portrait Gallery, 1971.

(With Gordon Donaldson) *Sixteenth-Century Scotland* (phonotape), Holt Information Systems, 1972.

Contributor to anthologies, including *Winter's Crimes 15,* edited by George Hardinge, St. Martin's Press (New York, NY), 1983, and *John Creasey's Crime Collection*

1983, edited by Herbert Harris, Gollancz (London, England), 1983, and *More Women of Mystery,* Severn House, 1994. Also author of scripts for television series *Jemima Shore Investigates,* 1983. Also author of radio plays *On the Battlements,* 1975,*The Heroine,* 1976, and *Penelope,* 1976; author of television play *Charades,* 1977, "Mister Clay, Mister Clay" for the *Time for Murder* series, 1985, *Have a Nice Death,* 1985. General editor, "Kings and Queens of England" series, Weidenfeld & Nicolson, 1953-55.

ADAPTATIONS: The novel *A Splash of Red* was adapted for television as *Jemima Shore Investigates.*

SIDELIGHTS: Versatile writer Antonia Fraser "has won many accolades for her meticulous research and attention to detail," wrote Edie Gibson in the *Chicago Tribune,* "[and for] bringing a lively narrative style to historical writing, capturing readers who typically shun such scholarly endeavors." Fraser secured her position as a noteworthy biographer with *Mary, Queen of Scots,* and has subsequently chronicled the lives of other British figures such as Oliver Cromwell, James I, and Charles II. With her acclaimed biography *Marie Antoinette: The Journey,* Fraser showed that she could write as well about subjects who were not British. In addition to her biographies of individuals, she has also written histories that are wider in scope. In *The Weaker Vessel,* Fraser examines the place of women in seventeenth-century England, and *The Warrior Queens* illuminates the leadership roles women often assume in times of war. Fraser has also proven herself adept at writing fiction; in a popular series of mysteries, she details the adventures of Jemima Shore, a liberated investigative television reporter who has a knack for solving mysteries.

The eldest child of highly educated and politically active parents, Fraser was raised at Oxford where her father was a don, and academic pursuits were strongly encouraged by both parents. At thirteen, following the example set by her parents, she chose to convert to Catholicism and transferred to a Catholic school. She told Ray Connolly of the *London Times* of her initial attraction to the church: "I loved all the ritual, the white veils on Sunday and the black veils for going to mass every morning." She launched her writing career shortly after graduating from Oxford, but until her reputation as an author was solidified, Fraser was more known for being a prominent member of London society.

Mary, Queen of Scots, Fraser's first biography, established the standard for her historical writing: thorough research, vivid character portraits, and sound scholar-

ship presented in a manner that appealed to a wide audience. Jean Stafford of *Book World* noted that Fraser conveys "a vivid sense of the mores of the sixteenth century" in *Mary, Queen of Scots.* In addition, "she succeeds in almost completely clarifying the muddied maelstrom in which Europe and the British Isles were thrashing and trumpeting," Stafford continued, with "a narrative dexterity that makes her sad tale seem told for the first time." "Mary emerges neither as a Jezebel nor as a saint," declared a reviewer for *Time,* "but as a high-spirited woman who was brave, rather romantic, and not very bright." "Satisfying to scholars," commented a *Times Literary Supplement* critic, "the book is eminently one for the general reader, its style both spirited and graceful."

Fraser's early works, critics have noted, are strict biography in the sense that they examine the life of a single person, but they do not attempt to discuss the individual's actions in terms of the age in which he or she lived. In *Cromwell, the Lord Protector, King James VI of Scotland, I of England,* and *Royal Charles,* Fraser's portrayals of eminent historical figures are brought "so vividly to life that the history of the age in which they play so arresting a part tends to lose itself in the background," according to Peter Stansky of the *New York Times Book Review.* In reviewing *Royal Charles,* Stansky commented on the difference between pure biography and historical biography: "Unlike, for example, Barbara Tuchman, who sees biography as a 'Prism of History,' and admits to using it 'less for the sake of the individual subject than as a vehicle for exhibiting an age,' Lady Antonia is wholeheartedly committed to the life of the individual subject."

Fraser altered her strict biographical approach with her 1984 award-winning study *The Weaker Vessel: Woman's Lot in Seventeenth-Century England.* Rather than focusing on a single character as her earlier biographies had done, *The Weaker Vessel* looks at many roles of women in the 1600s, with special emphasis on "marriage, birth, widowhood, divorce, prostitution, the stage, business, and so forth," summarized Brigitte Weeks in the *Washington Post.* "Each chapter is a maze of interconnected life stories of women, almost always pregnant, ending all too often in sudden death, mostly in childbirth," Weeks continued. Fraser investigated women's varied responsibilities during the English Civil War: holding custody of castles, leading troops into battle, writing treatises, and presenting petitions to parliament. After the war, however, these newly won liberties were rescinded, leaving women in much the same position as they were before the conflict. "One of the lies about historical progress," declared Peter S. Prescott in a

Newsweek review of *The Weaker Vessel* "is that it hunches inexorably along its way. In fact, progress is cyclical; it jumps sporadically, only to be set back again." Fraser's analysis of the gamut of class roles, from dairymaid to actress to heiress, prompted Maureen Quilligan of the *Nation* to acknowledge that "it will be hard for anyone to paint a fuller, more vivid or more abundantly detailed portrait of women in seventeenth-century England."

The Warrior Queens, another survey of women's history, grew out of the research Fraser did for *The Weaker Vessel.* The work focuses on women who have led their countries into war, women such as the Egyptian queen Cleopatra, the British tribal leader Boadicea, and Zenobia, the third-century Queen of the desert city of Palmyra, all of whom led forces against the Roman Empire. Also included are modern-day leaders such as Israel's Golda Meir and Great Britain's Margaret Thatcher. "Seeking explanations for these women's rise to power and their enormous personal magnetism," wrote Barbara Benton in *MHQ: The Quarterly Journal of Military History,* "she attempts to isolate common themes in their stories."

In *The Warrior Queens,* Fraser categorizes the patterns of behavior that these women leaders have utilized in wielding their power. Victoria Glendenning enumerated these in the London *Times:* "The Appendance Syndrome, according to which the Warrior Queen justifies herself by stressing her connection with a famous father or husband, or fights allegedly on behalf of her son; the Shame Syndrome, otherwise the Better-man Syndrome, which means she shows up the chaps by being braver than they are; the Tomboy Syndrome, which implies that she never played with dolls when she was a little girl; and the Only-a-Weak-Woman Syndrome, when she puts on a sudden show of weakness or modesty for strategic purposes." In addition to these is the "voracity syndrome" in which powerful women are separated into models of virtue or monsters of lust. Fraser's conclusions, summarized Margaret Atwood in the *Los Angeles Times Book Review,* show that "public women are put through different tests of nerve, attract different kinds of criticism, and are subject to different sorts of mythologizing than are men, and *The Warrior Queens* indicates what kinds."

Continuing her interest in the lives of prominent women in history, Fraser wrote *The Wives of Henry VIII,* which provided new interpretations of the six women who, according to Fraser, are often "defined in a popular sense not so much by their lives as by the way these lives ended," quoted Angeline Goreau in the *New York Times Book Review.* During his reign from 1509-1547, Henry VIII's unsuccessful quest to produce a male heir to succeed him left four wives dead and two in the unceremonious state of being divorced. From Catherine of Aragon to Catherine Parr, Fraser explores the lives of those she proclaims were "intelligent and fascinating people who were variously misused, abandoned, and executed" by the king, according to Bonnie Angelo in *Time.* Fraser analyzes the effect of divorce on Catherine of Aragon and Anne of Cleves and illustrates its impact on the rest of their lives; an aspect that prompted Goreau to deem the book "a deeply engaging portrait of a marriage—in serial." About this notorious episode of history, Angelo concluded that "Fraser brings to it insights—and a keen feminist edge—based on meticulous research."

In *Faith and Treason: The Story of the Gunpowder Plot,* Fraser shed new light on the events that are now commemorated every year on Guy Fawkes' Day—a November 5 holiday that is celebrated with huge bonfires and the burning in effigy of the Pope. In 1605, Roman Catholics were subject to terrible persecution in England, despite the fact that King James I was the son of one Catholic and the husband of another. Dissidents hatched a plan to blow up the unsympathetic king and most of his nobles at the opening of Parliament that year. The plan failed miserably, and the unsuccessful rebels have been reviled throughout most of English history. "Antonia Fraser, with her usual combination of careful scholarship and a nose for a good subject, has now told the plotters' story," advised Michael Elliott in the *New York Times.* "It is such a good yarn that one wonders why nobody has tried to popularize it before."

"Fraser's searching look at the failed conspiracy of Robert Catesby (the actual planner) and Guy Fawkes could not be more timely," reported a *Publishers Weekly* writer. The author draws parallels between the Gunpowder Plot and modern terrorism, asking "the old but difficult questions: When does persecution excuse violence? How far should a cause of conscience be defended?" said Elliott. Another reviewer, *New Statesman* contributor Diarmaid MacCulloch, noted that there are many books on the Gunpowder Plot, but names Fraser's as "a good place to start for a serious, balanced treatment of the still-mysterious affair. She manages to combine scholarly breadth and historical sympathy with readability and wit. Writing with fellow-feeling for the Roman Catholic plotters and those they dragged down to disaster, she nevertheless avoids . . . partisanship."

In 2001, Fraser took a fresh look at one of history's most reviled women: Marie Antoinette, the last queen of France. Beheaded in 1793 along with her husband,

Louis XVI, she was slandered in her lifetime as a heartless spendthrift and a pervert. This reputation has stayed with her throughout the passing centuries. Yet Fraser's characteristically painstaking research shows that in the years before the French Revolution reached the boiling point, Marie Antoinette was reputed to be a kind-hearted queen, one whose virtue was far beyond that of most of her contemporaries. While some accounts of her life report that Marie Antoinette had many lovers of both sexes, Fraser concludes that there was probably only one, despite Louis XVI's apparent inability to consummate his marriage for many years. Fraser paints Marie as extravagant and somewhat desperate for happiness, but her portrait is sympathetic to the young woman who led a lonely, manipulated life. A *Kirkus Reviews* writer credited Fraser with skill in turning "this spoiled, not-too-bright princess into a likable character." The biography shows how Marie was groomed by her powerful mother, the Empress Maria Teresa, but barely educated enough to learn to write her name. This spirited girl was sent to the French court when she has just fourteen years old, where she was a captive in the opulent, decadent world of court life and court intrigue. Yet she showed her independence by asserting her own will in such matters as giving birth in private and wearing simple dresses and little makeup after the birth of her children. Her calmness and dignity on being led to the guillotine has been frequently remarked upon. The real villains in Marie Antoinette's story, according to a writer for the *Economist,* "were the journalists and cartoonists who pilloried the queen, creating a monster from one whose chief crime was to be careless about her public image." *Houston Chronicle* reviewer Fritz Lanham called *Marie Antoinette: The Journey* "the best sort of biography: vigorously argued, richly detailed, with a clear viewpoint on its subject. . . . Despite the melancholy subject matter, it's hard to put down."

"Despite the fact that she was able to bring a personal style to the writing of history," declared Rosemary Herbert in a *Publishers Weekly* interview with the author, "in the mid-'70s Fraser 'felt that there was something in myself that history didn't express.' She gave in to the impulse to write fiction and created the TV commentator/sleuth Jemima Shore, a stylish, liberated woman who shares some of the author's characteristics." Fraser further told Herbert that mystery writing fulfilled her need to "preserve a sort of order. I'm very interested in good and evil and the moral nature of my [characters]. People in my books tend to get their just desserts." P.D. James, herself a well-known mystery writer, greeted the investigator's debut in *Quiet As a Nun* with pleasure, noting that the story "is written with humour and sympathy and has a heroine of whom, happily, it is promised that we shall know more."

Though not as "lovably eccentric as Peter Wimsey, Jane Marple, Hercule Poirot, or the great Sherlock Holmes," wrote Anne Tolstoi Wallach in the *New York Times Book Review,* Jemima Shore is nevertheless "prettier, sexier, and far more in tune with today's London." Margaret Cannon, writing in the Toronto *Globe and Mail,* was fascinated by the details that Fraser provides about the upper class settings through which Shore moves—circles in which Fraser herself travels. In the seventh Jemima Shore mystery, *The Cavalier Case,* Shore ventures to a haunted estate to produce a television segment about the ghost of a seventeenth-century poet who has apparently caused several deaths. During her investigation, Shore becomes involved with the new viscount of the manor. Though crime is not in short supply in Fraser's Jemima Shore novels, the incidents tend to be relatively mild because, as Fraser stated in the *St. James Guide to Crime and Mystery Writers,* she has "a horror of blood dripping from the page," adding, "my books are therefore aimed at readers who feel likewise."

Jemima Shore at the Sunny Grave and Other Stories is a collection of nine mystery stories, most of which involve Fraser's well-known heroine and are set on remote islands. The title story involves the murder of an elderly heiress at her plantation mansion in the Caribbean, where Jemima Shore is preparing a television documentary. In another story, "The Moon Was to Blame," Fraser recounts an Englishman's Greek-island vacation with his wife punctuated by murder and eroticism. Brad Hooper noted in a *Booklist* review that Fraser displays "precision" and "characteristic èlan." The collection is described by *Kirkus Reviews* as "highly civilized, suavely written—and immensely readable."

In *Political Death* Jemima Shore resolves a longstanding British political scandal from the 1960s. During a heated political campaign, Lady Imogen Swain, the aged former mistress of a contemporary political candidate, reveals her intimate knowledge of the "Faber Mystery," involving the disappearance of a man accused of selling government secrets. After offering her story and incriminating diaries to Shore, Lady Imogen dies from a suspicious fall, prompting Shore to pursue a trail of evidence through the British theater and political scenes to solve the case.

Many critics agree that Fraser's detective stories are worthy additions to the illustrious heritage of British detective writing. Beverly Lyon Clark wrote in the *New York Times Book Review* that *Oxford Blood* is "in the tradition of the British whodunit, especially that of the

Tea Cake and Country House mystery—or, in this case, the Champagne and Maserati sort. . . . Antonia Fraser is not quite Dorothy Sayers, not quite P.D. James. But she does have a seductive style." Shore believed, according to Cannon, that "there's nothing in the detective code of ethics that says you have to dress badly, get married or pass up an interesting one-night stand. It's a long way from St. Mary Mead, but I somehow think that [Agatha Christie's detective] Miss Marple, shrewd student of human nature that she was, would approve."

Lyn Pykett, a contributor to *St. James Guide to Crime and Mystery Writers,* also declared Fraser's detective novels to be very much in the classic English tradition. Like so many of the fictional detectives before her, Jemima Shore is an upper-middle-class amateur in the sleuthing game. She is "a modern, 'liberated' version of the inquisitive spinster detective. Like her predecessors, Shore is propelled into her investigations by her 'Eve-like' curiosity . . . and like theirs her success in detection derives in large measure from her class and gender position," asserted Pykett. "She is usually a privileged insider in the social circles which form the locus of her investigations. She is often on the scene before the crime occurs and the police arrive, and her convent-educated, Cambridge-honed brain, and her social savoir-faire take her in directions where flat-footed policemen may not tread. Ultimately she is, perhaps, in the tradition of Dorothy L. Sayers's Harriet Vane, rather than Agatha Christie's Miss Marple. She is a thoroughly modern young woman, unconventional and with a natural love of mischief." Pykett also noted that the "cool journalistic professionalism" possessed by Fraser's heroine "is offset by her apparent attraction to dangerous situations, and the fact that she is prone to sudden extremes of sexual attraction, often to rather unsuitable men." The commentator concluded: "Oxford, literary London, and the glamorous world of the media are Fraser's stock-in-trade in the Jemima Shore novels. Famous names and designer labels abound. Fraser's novels are always bright and witty, and their denouements are usually surprising."

Fraser has entertained many readers with her intriguing tales of both fact and fiction. Her historical interpretation, wrote Lawrence Stone of the *New York Review of Books,* displays "good judgment and a subtle appreciation of human psychology" and is complimented by her mysteries which *Spectator* reviewer Harriet Waugh called "jokey, accomplished, and action-packed." Wallach summarized that Fraser "writes both history and mystery with zest and verve, and her primary interest is people—foolish queens, military commanders, former wives, rival siblings or stepdaughters desperate for attention."

BIOGRAPHICAL AND CRITICAL SOURCES:

BOOKS

Authors in the News, Volume 2, Thomson Gale (Detroit, MI), 1976.
St. James Guide to Crime and Mystery Writers, 4th edition, St. James Press (Detroit, MI), 1996.

PERIODICALS

Booklist, November 15, 1992, p. 563; March 15, 1996, p. 1242; August, 2001, Brad Hooper, review of *Marie Antoinette: The Journey,* p. 2046; January 1, 2002, review of *Marie Antoinette: The Journey,* p. 757; March 1, 2002, Donna Seaman, review of *Faith and Treason: The Story of the Gunpowder Plot,* p. 1085.
Book World, November 16, 1969.
Boston Herald, September 28, 2001, Rosemary Herbert, review of *Marie Antoinette: The Journey,* p. 48.
Chicago Tribune, March 16, 1988.
Chicago Tribune Book World, September 30, 1984.
Christian Science Monitor, December 7, 1979.
Daily Telegraph, June 16, 2001, Andy Martin, review of *Marie Antoinette: The Journey,* p. 5; January 19, 2002, Helen Brown, review of *Marie Antoinette: The Journey.*
Economist, July 14, 2001, review of *Marie Antoinette: The Journey,* pp. 6, 100.
Gay and Lesbian Review Worldwide, November-December, 2001, review of *Marie Antoinette: The Journey,* p. 35.
Globe and Mail (Toronto, Ontario, Canada), August 25, 1984.
Guardian (London, England), July 14, 2001, Hazel Mills, review of *Marie Antoinette: The Journey,* p. 8.
History Today, October, 2000, Daniel Snowman, "Antonia Fraser," p. 26; May, 2002, John Rogister, review of *Marie Antoinette: The Journey,* p. 75.
House and Garden, March, 1985, "Lady Antonia's Secret Garden."
Houston Chronicle, January 6, 2002, Fritz Lanham, review of *Marie Antoinette: The Journey,* p. 20.
Interview, September, 2001, review of *Marie Antoinette: The Journey,* p. 130.
Kirkus Reviews, November 1, 1992, p. 1336; January 15, 1996, p. 104; March 15, 2001, review of *Cromwell,* p. 366; August 1, 2001, review of *Marie Antoinette: The Journey,* p. 1087.

Kliatt Young Adult Paperback Book Guide, March, 1998, review of *Faith and Treason,* p. 32; September, 1998, review of *The Warrior Queens* (audio version), p. 69; September, 1999, review of *Lives of the Kings and Queens of England* (audio version), p. 64.

Library Journal, August, 2001, Bruce H. Webb, review of *Marie Antoinette: The Journey,* p. 122.

Los Angeles Times, September 25, 1980; October 21, 2001, Cara Mia Dimassa, review of *Marie Antoinette: The Journey,* p. 5.

Los Angeles Times Book Review, September 23, 1984; April 2, 1989.

Maclean's, December 31, 1979.

MHQ: The Quarterly Journal of Military History, autumn, 1989.

Nation, September 22, 1984, pp. 244-246.

New Republic, December 29, 1979.

New Statesman, August 30, 1996, p. 48; July 16, 2001, Michele Roberts, review of *Marie Antoinette: The Journey,* p. 54.

Newsweek, September 10, 1984.

New Yorker, September 24, 2001, review of *Marie Antoinette: The Journey,* p. 93.

New York Review of Books, April 11, 1985.

New York Times, November 13, 1979; November 14, 1984; October 13, 1985, p. 24; May 17, 1989, p. 15; April 9, 1989, p. 47; January 6, 1991; October 27, 1996; September 4, 2001, Mel Gussow, review of *Marie Antoinette: The Journey,* p. B1.

New York Times Book Review, November 18, 1984; April 2, 1989; January 6, 1991; December 20, 1992, p. 11; July 31, 1994, p. 28; February 8, 1998, review of *Faith and Treason,* p. 28; September 23, 2001, Francine du Plessix Gray, review of *Marie Antoinette: The Journey,* p. 11; September 30, 2001, review of *Marie Antoinette: The Journey,* p. 22.

New York Times Magazine, September 9, 1984, Mel Gussow, "Antonia Fraser: The Lady Is a Writer."

People, February 3, 1997, p. 35.

Publishers Weekly, June 19, 1987, pp. 104-105; February 5, 1996, p. 79; July 23, 2001, review of *Marie Antoinette: The Journey,* p. 64.

Spectator, September 26, 1987, pp. 34-35; June 23, 2001, Douglas Johnson, review of *Marie Antoinette: The Journey,* p. 37.

Time, October 17, 1969; September 17, 1984; December 21, 1992.

Times (London, England), May 3, 1984; October 7, 1988; October 15, 1988; March 3, 1990.

Times Literary Supplement, July 3, 1969; May 27, 1977; June 8, 1984; November 11-17, 1988; July 20, 2001, Robert Gildea, review of *Marie Antoinette: The Journey,* p. 31.

Tribune Books (Chicago, IL), April 2, 1989.

Virginia Quarterly Review, autumn, 2001, review of *A Royal History of England,* p. 121.

Vogue, January, 1993, p. 71; September, 2001, Amanda Foreman, review of *Marie Antoinette: The Journey,* p. 502.

Washington Post, October 7, 1984; October 7, 2001, review of *Marie Antoinette: The Journey,* p. T8; December 15, 2001, Alona Wartofsky, review of *Marie Antoinette: The Journey,* p. C1.

Washington Post Book World, March 12, 1989; April 21, 1996.

*   *   *

FRAYN, Michael 1933-

PERSONAL: Born September 8, 1933, in London, England; son of Thomas Allen (a manufacturer's representative) and Violet Alice (Lawson) Frayn; married Gillian Palmer (a psychotherapist), February 18, 1960 (divorced, 1989); married Claire Tomalin (an author), June 5, 1996; children: (first marriage) three daughters. *Education:* Emmanuel College, Cambridge, B.A., 1957.

ADDRESSES: Agent—Green & Heaton, 37a Goldhawk Rd., London W12 8QQ, England.

CAREER: Novelist and playwright. *Guardian,* Manchester, England, general-assignment reporter, 1957-59, "Miscellany" columnist, 1959-62; *Observer,* London, England, columnist, 1962-68. *Military service:* British Army, 1952-54.

MEMBER: Royal Society of Literature.

AWARDS, HONORS: Somerset Maugham Award, 1966, for *The Tin Men;* Hawthornden Prize, 1967, for *The Russian Interpreter;* National Press Club Award for distinguished reporting, International Publishing Corporation, 1970, for *Observer* articles on Cuba; Best Comedy of the Year awards, London *Evening Standard,* 1975, for *Alphabetical Order,* and 1982, for *Noises Off;* Society of West End Theatre Award for best comedy of the year, 1976, for *Donkeys' Years,* and 1982, for *Noises Off;* Best Play of the Year award, *Evening Standard,* Society of West End Theatre Award for best play of the year, and Laurence Olivier Award for best play, all 1984, and *Plays and Players* Award for best new play, and New York Drama Critics' Circle Award for best new foreign play, both 1986, all for *Benefactors;* Antoinette Perry ("Tony") Award nomination for best play, 1984, for *Noises Off;* International Emmy Award, 1989, for *First and Last;* Emmy Award, 1990; *Sunday Express* Book of the Year Award, 1991, for *A Landing on the Sun; Evening Standard* Award for best play, Critics Circle Award for best play, and South Bank Show Award, all 1998, Moliè Award (Paris, France), and Tony Award for best play, 2000, all for *Copenhagen;* Booker Prize shortlist, 1999, for *Headlong;* honorary doctorate, Cambridge University, 2001; Whitbread Novel of the Year Award, 2002, and Twenty-first Century Award for best foreign novel (China), both for *Spies; Evening Standard* Award for best play, Critic's Circle Award for best play, and South Bank Show Award, all 2003, all for *Democracy;* New York Public Library for the Performing Arts tribute, 2003; S.T. Dupont Award for Lifetime Achievement in Literature, PEN English Centre, 2003; Tony Award nomination, 2005, for *Democracy..*

WRITINGS:

The Day of the Dog (columns; originally published in *Guardian*), illustrations by Timothy Birdsall, Collins (London, England), 1962, Doubleday (New York, NY), 1963.

The Book of Fub (columns; originally published in *Guardian*), Collins (London, England), 1963, published as *Never Put off to Gomorrah,* Pantheon (New York, NY), 1964.

On the Outskirts, Collins (London, England), 1964.

At Bay in Gear Street (columns; originally published in *Observer*), Fontana (Huntington, NY), 1967.

Constructions (philosophy), Wildwood House (London, England), 1974.

The Original Michael Frayn, Salamander Press (Edinburgh, Scotland), 1983.

Speak after the Beep (ollected columns), Methuen (London, England), 1995.

The Additional Michael Frayn, Methuen (London, England), 2000.

NOVELS

The Tin Men, Collins (London, England), 1965, Little, Brown (Boston, MA), 1966.

The Russian Interpreter, Viking (New York, NY), 1966.

Towards the End of the Morning, Collins (London, England), 1967, reprinted, Harvill (London, England), 1987, published as *Against Entropy,* Viking (New York, NY), 1967.

A Very Private Life, Viking (New York, NY), 1968.

Sweet Dreams, Collins (London, England), 1973, Viking (New York, NY), 1974.

The Trick of It, Viking (London, England), 1989, Viking (New York, NY), 1990.

A Landing on the Sun, Viking (London, England), 1991, Viking (New York, NY), 1992.

Now You Know, Viking (London, England), 1992, Viking (New York, NY), 1993.

Headlong, Metropolitan Books (New York, NY), 1999.

(With David Burke) *Celia's Secret: An Investigation* (based on the play *Copenhagen*), Faber (London, England), 2000, published as *The Copenhagen Papers,* Metropolitan Books (New York, NY), 2001.

Spies, Metropolitan Books (New York, NY), 2002.

STAGE PLAYS

(With John Edwards) *Zounds!* (musical comedy), produced in Cambridge, England, 1957.

The Two of Us: Four One-Act Plays for Two Players (contains *Black and Silver, The New Quixote, Mr. Foot,* and *Chinamen;* first produced in London's West End, 1970), Fontana (London, England), 1970.

The Sandboy (first produced in London, England, 1971), Fontana (London, England), 1971.

Alphabetical Order (first produced in London's West End, 1975), published with *Donkeys' Years,* Methuen (London, England), 1977.

Donkeys' Years (first produced in London's West End, 1976; produced off-off Broadway, 1987; also see below), S. French (New York, NY), 1977.

Clouds (also see below; first produced in London, England, 1976), S. French (New York, NY), 1977.

Alphabetical Order [and] *Donkeys' Years,* Methuen (London, England), 1977.

Balmoral (also see below; first produced in Guildford, Surrey, England, 1978, revised version produced as *Liberty Hall* in London, England, 1980, produced under original title in London, 1987), Methuen (London, England), 1977, revised, 1987.

Make and Break (also see below; first produced in Hammersmith, England, then in London's West End, 1980; produced at John F. Kennedy Center for the Performing Arts, 1982), Methuen (London, England), 1980.

Noises Off (three-act; also see below; first produced in Hammersmith, England, then London's West End, 1982, produced in New York, NY, 1983; revival produced on London's West End, 2000, then Broadway, 2001), S. French (New York, NY), 1982, revised version, Doubleday (New York, NY), 2002.

Benefactors (also see below; two-act; first produced in London's West End, 1984; produced on Broadway, 1985), Methuen (London, England), 1984.

(Translator from the French) Jean Anouilh, *Number One* (first produced in London, England, 1984), S. French (New York, NY), 1985.

Plays: One (contains *Alphabetical Order, Donkeys' Years, Clouds, Make and Break,* and *Noises Off*), Methuen (London, England), 1985.

Look Look (first produced as *Spettattori* in Rome, Italy, 1989; produced as *Look Look* in London, England, 1990), Methuen (London, England), 1990, first act published as *Audience,* S. French (New York, NY), 1991.

Listen to This (short plays), Methuen (London, England), 1990.

Plays: Two (contains *Benefactors, Balmoral,* and *Wild Honey*), Methuen (London, England), 1992.

Here (first produced at Donmar Warehouse, 1993), Methuen (London, England), 1993.

(Translator from the French) Jacques Offenbach, *La belle Vivette* (opera), first produced at Rome Coliseum, 1995.

Now You Know (first produced in London, England, 1995), Methuen (London, England), 1995.

Alarms and Excursions, first produced in Guilford, England, 1998.

Copenhagen (first produced in Cottesloe, England, 1998, produced in London's West End, 1999; produced in New York, NY), Methuen Drama (London, England), 1998.

Plays: Three, Methuen Drama (London, England), 2000.

Democracy, first produced in London's West End, 2003; produced in New York, 2004.

TRANSLATOR FROM THE RUSSIAN; AND ADAPTER

(And author of introduction) Anton Chekhov, *The Cherry Orchard* (four-act; first produced in London's West End, 1978), Methuen (London, England), 1978.

(And author of introduction) Leo Tolstoy, *The Fruits of Enlightenment* (four-act; first produced in London's West End, 1979), Methuen (London, England), 1979.

Anton Chekhov, *Wild Honey: The Untitled Play* (also known as *Platonov;* also see above; produced in London's West End, 1984; produced in New York, NY, 1986), Methuen (London, England), 1984.

(And author of introduction) Anton Chekhov, *Three Sisters* (four-act; produced in Manchester, England, 1985), Methuen (London, England), 1983.

(And author of introduction) Anton Chekhov, *The Seagull* (produced in London's West End, 1986), Methuen (London, England), 1986.

Trifonov, *Exchange* (produced at Guildhall School of Drama, 1986, then on BBC Radio 3), Methuen (London, England), 1990.

Anton Chekhov, *Uncle Vanya* (produced in London, England, 1988), Methuen (London, England), 1987.

Anton Chekhov, *Chekhov: Plays* (includes *The Seagull, Uncle Vanya, Three Sisters,* and *The Cherry Orchard*), Methuen (London, England), 1988.

(And adaptor) Anton Chekhov, *The Sneeze* (short stories and sketches; produced in London's West End, 1988), Methuen (London, England), 1989.

TELEVISION WORK

1962–66 *What the Papers Say* (documentary series), Granada TV.

(With John Bird) *Second City Reports* (series), Granada TV, 1964.

Jamie, on a Flying Visit (teleplay; also see below), British Broadcasting Corp. (BBC-TV), 1968.

(And presenter) *One Pair of Eyes* (documentary film), BBC-TV, 1968.

Birthday (teleplay; also see below), BBC-TV, 1969.

(With John Bird and Eleanor Bron) *Beyond a Joke* (series), BBC-TV, 1972.

(And presenter) *Laurence Sterne Lived Here* (documentary film), BBC-TV, 1973.

Making Faces (six-part comedy miniseries), BBC-TV, 1975.

(And presenter) *Imagine a City Called Berlin* (documentary film), BBC-TV, 1975.

(And presenter) *Vienna: The Mask of Gold* (documentary film), BBC-TV, 1977.

Alphabetical Order (adapted from Frayn's stage play), Granada TV, 1978.

(And presenter) *Three Streets in the Country* (documentary film), BBC-TV, 1979.

Donkeys' Years (adapted from Frayn's stage play), ATV, 1980.

(And presenter) *The Long Straight,* BBC-TV, 1980.

(And presenter) *Jerusalem* (documentary film), BBC-TV, 1984.

Make and Break (adapted from Frayn's stage play), BBC-TV, 1987.

Benefactors (adapted from Frayn's stage play), BBC-TV, 1989.

First and Last (movie; broadcast on BBC-TV, 1989), Methuen, 1989.

Jamie, on a Flying Machine [and] *Birthday* (teleplays), Methuen (London, England), 1990.

(And presenter) *Magic Lantern: Prague* (documentary film), BBC-TV, 1993.

A Landing on the Sun (movie; adapted from Frayn's novel), BBC-TV, 1994.

(And presenter) *Budapest: Written in Water* (documentary film), BBC-TV, 1996.

Copenhagen (movie; adapted from Frayn's stage play), BBC-TV, 2002.

OTHER

(Editor) John Bingham Morton, *The Best of Beachcomber,* Heinemann (London, England), 1963.

(Editor, with Bamber Gascoigne) *Timothy: The Drawings and Cartoons of Timothy Birdsall,* M. Joseph (London, England), 1964.

(With others) *Great Railway Journeys of the World* (based on film broadcast by BBC-TV; contains Frayn's segment on Australia), BBC (London, England), 1981, Dutton (New York, NY), 1982.

Clockwise (screenplay; produced by Universal, 1986), Methuen (London, England), 1986.

Noises Off (screenplay; adapted from Frayn's stage play), Touchstone, 1992.

Remember Me? (screenplay), Channel Four Films, 1997.

Contributor to Michael Sissons and Philip French, *Age of Austerity,* Hodder & Stoughton (London, England), 1963.

SIDELIGHTS: Though best known in the United States as the author of the hit stage farce *Noises Off* and the multi-award-winning play *Copenhagen,* British playwright Michael Frayn has actually produced a wide variety of writings during his long career. Frayn's beginnings as a columnist and critic for two newspapers—the Manchester *Guardian* and the London *Observer*—led to a number of published collections, while his novels, including *Headlong, The Russian Interpreter,* and *Spies,* have garnered praise for both their humor and their insights into the complications of modern times. Among his plays, Frayn's translations of Anton Chekhov's classics draw particular attention. In 1986 the writer ventured into cinema with the produced screenplay *Clockwise,* and has also written for television.

A native Londoner, "Frayn believes his sense of humor began to develop during his years at Kingston Grammar School where, to the delight of his classmates, he practiced the 'techniques of mockery' on his teachers," re-

ported Mark Fritz in the *Dictionary of Literary Biography.* As an adult, he quickly established himself as a keen social satirist on two newspapers, the *Guardian* and *Observer.* For the former, as Frayn saw it, his task in his "Miscellany" column "was to write cool, witty interviews with significant film directors passing through, but there were never enough film directors so he started making up humorous paragraphs to fill," according to Terry Coleman in the *Guardian.* Malcolm Page explained in the *Dictionary of Literary Biography* that Frayn "invented for the column the Don't Know Party and such characters as the trendy Bishop of [Twicester] . . . ; Rollo Swavely, a public relations consultant; and the ambitious suburban couple" Christopher and Lavinia Crumble.

Comparing Frayn's "wit, sophistication, and imagination" to "that of American humorist S.J. Perelman," Fritz declared that Frayn's "satire is sharper." That sense of satire, along with an emerging seriousness, carried the author to his first novel, *The Tin Men.* The story, a satire about the suitability of computers to take over the burden of human dullness, won the Somerset Maugham Award for fiction in 1966.

After *The Tin Men* Frayn produced *The Russian Interpreter,* "a spy story which deals more with the deceit between individuals than between nations," according to Fritz. The action resolves around an English research student studying in Moscow who becomes embroiled in a series of swiftly paced intrigues involving a mysterious businessman, stolen books, and a Russian girl and eventually is incarcerated in a Russian prison. Page characterized the book, which was awarded the Hawthornden Prize, as one of Frayn's more conventional novels, as opposed to his fantasies and satires.

Frayn's novel *A Very Private Life,* written in the future tense, "explains how life has grown more private, first through physical privacy, then through the development of drugs to cope with anger and uncertainty," wrote Page. To *Spectator* reviewer Maurice Capitanchik, "Frayn, in his parable of the horrific future, does not escape the impress which [George] Orwell and [Aldous] Huxley have made upon the genre, nor does he really go beyond the area of authoritarian oppression so brilliantly illumined by [Franz] Kafka, but he does something else both valuable and unique: he shows that his 'Brave New World' is really our cowardly old world, if we did but, shudderingly, know it, in a prose which is often beautiful and, almost, poetry."

In the novel *Sweet Dreams* a young architect dies and goes to a distinctly familiar sort of English heaven, "a terribly decent place, really, where one's pleasantest dreams come true and one's most honest longings are fulfilled," as *Washington Post Book World* critic L.J. Davis described it. Caught in a permanent fantasy world, Howard, the architect, "immediately joins the small, intimate, and brilliantly unorthodox architectural firm he'd always yearned for," Davis continued. After redesigning the Matterhorn, engaging in a dramatic love affair, and realizing other superlative encounters, Frayn's protagonist "sells out to the movies, purges himself with a spell of rustic simplicity, rallies the best minds of his generation by means of letters to *The Times,* meets God . . . and eventually winds up, crinkle-eyed and aging, as prime minister. It is all rather poignant," noted Davis. Page found *Sweet Dreams* to be a "shrewd, sardonic and deceptively charming tale" that Frayn relates with "wit and flourish."

After *Sweet Dreams,* Frayn abandoned the novel form for a decade and a half in order to establish his reputation both as an original playwright and a translator of Chekhov's plays. He returned to the novel in 1989 with *The Trick of It,* in which a young lecturer in literature becomes personally involved with a slightly older, celebrated author on whom he is an expert. During his involvement with the woman, which includes marriage, the man hopes to unravel the secret to her creative success, attempts to influence her writing, and tries unsuccessfully to become a creative writer himself. Told entirely through letters, the novel was described by Page as "a highly original work . . . linked more closely with a real world than [Frayn's] fantasies." George Craig in the *Times Literary Supplement* called *The Trick of It* "an intensely discomfiting novel, precisely because the elements of farce, social comedy and adventure remain present throughout as potential directions, even as darker and more destructive elements proliferate."

Civil servants are leading characters in Frayn's novels *A Landing on the Sun* and *Now You Know.* In the former, civil servant Brian Jessel is assigned to investigate the supposedly accidental death of colleague Stephen Summerchild fifteen years earlier. Jessel uncovers that Summerchild was overseeing government research into happiness by Elizabeth Serafin, an Oxford philosophy don, and that the two had set up a hidden garret for meetings. "*A Landing on the Sun* tells the wacky and exhilarating story of how Summerchild and Serafin got up into the garret, what they did there and what became of them," explained Richard Eder in the *Los Angeles Times Book Review.* "On that level, it is loony comedy with a mournful ending. Intermittently, it is a lovely satirical speculation on the ways of bureaucracies and academics, on the uses of order and disorder, and the deepest opposite twists in men and women." Page found *A*

Landing on the Sun "less ingenious" than *Sweet Dreams,* "although it cleverly unfolds as narrative and explores significant ideas."

In *Now You Know,* a novel-related, play-like work, told through a series of dramatic monologues, Hilary Wood quits her job at the Home Office after meeting Terry Little, who heads OPEN, an organization demanding truth from the government. When she leaves, Hilary illegally takes a file about a police fatality case, the details of which OPEN wants made known. Yet, despite all the talk of openness, secrecy abounds. *Now You Know* is "ingenious, witty, thoughtful and smart. . . . It is also a provocative meditation on the pitfalls of letting it all—most particularly, the truth—hang out," Jonathan Yardley noted in the *Washington Post Book World.* Calling *Now You Know* a book about "truth and when lying may be justified," Yardley added that Frayn's more recent novels "have in common wit, elegance, page-turning storytelling, and a playful treatment of serious themes."

Short-listed for the Booker Prize, the novel *Headlong* is a fascinating mix of comedy, art history, and human desire. Art historian Martin Clay discovers a painting, a lost masterpiece, in a run-down country estate while on vacation in England for a week. Believing Flemish master Pieter Bruegel may have created the painting, Clay is determined to deceive the unsuspecting owner in an effort to claim the painting for himself and sell it for millions of dollars. Complications abound and the young art historian soon discovers that some things are not worth risking everything for. "Clay's five days that shook the world become, in the hands of Frayn, a small jewel of comic shine," according to Terri Natale of the *New Statesman.*

Set in World War II, Frayn's novel *Spies* chronicles the story of two British boys who suspect their neighbors of Nazi espionage and begin following them. The friends—Keith and Steven—live in a quiet little neighborhood until they convince themselves that it is really a network of underground passages and secret laboratories for German infiltrators. "Frayn perfectly captures the dynamics of childhood friendships," stated a *Booklist* critic, while a *Publishers Weekly* reviewer added that Frayn's "enigmatic melodrama will keep readers' attention firmly in hand." Interestingly, *Spies,* which won Frayn the 2002 Whitbread Award for best novel, found its author going head to head against his wife, biographer Claire Tomalin, whose Whitbread Award-winning biography *Samuel Pepys: The Unequalled Self* ultimately won out against *Spies* as the Whitbread Book of the Year.

From his beginnings as a journalist and novelist, Frayn's dramatic work started with television plays, and advanced to satiric and humorous work for the stage. *Contemporary Dramatists* essayist Christopher Innes viewed the playwright's work in terms of "a return to traditional comic values," in response to the didactic "political drama that was sweeping the English stage at the beginning of the 1970s." Discussing the thematic content of Frayn's plays as a whole, Innes stated: "Frayn deals with society in terms of organizations—the news media, a manufacturing industry, the commercial theatre—which intrinsically threaten the survival of humanity. Deadening order is always subverted, however unintentionally; and the life force triumphs, though at the expense of what the individuals concerned are striving for." Frayn, himself, described the overriding theme of his dramatic work as "the way in which we impose our ideas on the world around us."

Among Frayn's stage plays, *Alphabetical Order* and *Donkeys' Years* earned plaudits, profits, and some measure of reputation for their author. In *Alphabetical Order,* the happy disarray of a newspaper's research department—the "morgue"—is changed forever when a hyper-efficient young woman joins the staff. "By the second act she has transformed [the morgue] into a model of order and efficiency. But somehow the humanness is gone," noted Fritz. "The young woman then proceeds to reorganize the personal lives of the other characters as well. She is not a total villain, however. In a way, the newspaper staff needs her: without a strong-willed person to manipulate them, weak-willed people often stagnate. At the heart of the play is the question: which is better, order or chaos?" Innes pointed out that the play is satirizing "the illusory nature of what our news-fixated culture considers important."

The successful *Donkeys' Years* focuses upon a group of university graduates reunited twenty years later, only to revert to their adolescent roles and conflicts. Voted the best comedy of 1972 by London's Society of West End Theatre, the play was praised by Stephen Holden in the *New York Times* as a "well-made farce that roundly twits English propriety."

Frayn's early theatrical background included a sojourn with the Cambridge Footlights revue during his college days and a walk-on in a production of Nikolai Gogol's *The Inspector General,* the latter a disaster that prefigured the backstage slapstick of his most popular play, *Noises Off.* "I pulled instead of pushed at the door, it jammed in the frame, and there was no other way off," the writer told Benedict Nightingale for a *New York Times Magazine* profile. "So I waited for what seemed like many, many hours while stagehands fought with crowbars on the other side and the audience started to slow-handclap. I've never been on the stage since."

Although many renowned comedies and dramas have used the play-within-a-play format in the past—it is a device that predates Shakespeare—perhaps no self-referential play has been so widely received in this generation as *Noises Off,* a no-holds-barred slapstick farce. Using the kind of manic entrances and mistaken identities reminiscent of French master Georges Feydeau, *Noises Off* invites the audience to witness the turmoil behind a touring company of has-beens and never-weres as they attempt to perform a typically English sex farce called "Nothing On." Referring to the production as "a show that gave ineptitude a good name," *Insight* writer Sheryl Flatow indicated that *Noises Off* was criticized by some as nothing more than a relentless, if effective, laugh-getting machine. The charge of being too funny, however, is not the sort of criticism that repels audiences, and *Noises Off* enjoyed a long run on the West End and Broadway. Describing the play in *Plays: One,* Frayn stated: "The fear that haunts [the cast] is that the unlearned and unrehearsed—the great dark chaos behind the set, inside the heart and brain—will seep back on to the stage. . . . Their performance will break down, and they will be left in front of us naked and ashamed."

"The fun begins even before the curtain goes up," Frank Rich reported in his *New York Times* review of Frayn's comedy. "In the Playbill, we find a program-within-the-program. . . . Among other things, we learn that the author of 'Nothing On' is a former 'unsuccessful gents hosiery wholesaler' whose previous farce 'Socks before Marriage' ran for nine years." When the curtain does rise, Rich continued, "it reveals a hideous set . . . that could well serve all those sex farces . . . that do run for nine years." As the story opens, the "Nothing On" cast and crew are blundering through their final rehearsal; importantly, everyone establishes his onstage and offstage identities. Remarked Rich: "As the run-through is mostly devoted to setting up what follows, it's also the only sporadically mirthless stretch of Mr. Frayn's play: We're asked to study every ridiculous line and awful performance in 'Nothing On' to appreciate the varied replays yet to come. Still, the lags are justified by the payoff: Having painstakingly built his house of cards in Act I, the author brings it crashing down with exponentially accelerating hilarity in Acts II and III."

While the backstage romances simmer, the troupe systematically skewers whatever appeal the cheesy "Nothing On" should have provided. Even the props get involved: by Act II, a plate of sardines is as important an element to the play as any of the actors. By this time, "Frayn's true inspiration strikes," wrote *Washington Post* reviewer David Richards. "The company is a month into its tour and the set has been turned around, so that we are viewing 'Nothing On' from backstage. The innocent little romances in Act I have turned lethal and, while the actors are still vaguely mindful of their cues, they are more mindful of wreaking vengeance upon one another. . . . An ax is wielded murderously, a skirt is torn off, toes are stomped on, shoelaces are tied together, bone-crunching tumbles are taken, bouquets are shredded, a cactus is sat upon and, of course, the ingenue's damned [contact] lens pops out again!"

Noises Off established Frayn as a farceur on the order of Feydeau and Ben Travers. To that end, the author told *Los Angeles Times* reporter Barbara Isenberg that farce is serious business. Its most important element, he explained, is "the losing of power for coherent thought under the pressure of events. What characters in farce do traditionally is try to recover some disaster that occurred, by a course of behavior that is so ill-judged that it makes it worse. In traditional farce, people are caught in a compromising situation, try to explain it with a lie and, when they get caught, have then to explain both the original situation *and* the lie. And, when they're caught in that lie, they have to have another one." The play was revised for a revival debuting at London's National Theatre in the fall of 2000 and from there quickly moved across the Atlantic to Broadway.

Frayn's first produced screenplay, *Clockwise,* closely resembles *Noises Off* in its wild construction. Like the play, the film takes a simple premise and lets circumstances run amok. In *Clockwise* protagonist Brian Stimpson (played by Monty Python star John Cleese), a small-town headmaster who is obsessed with punctuality, wins Headmaster of the Year honors and must travel by train to a distant city to deliver his acceptance speech. Inevitably, Brian catches the wrong train, and the thought that he may arrive late drives him to desperate means. By the film's end, he has stolen a car, invaded a monastery, robbed a man of his suit, and set two squadrons of police on his trail. "It isn't the film's idea of taking a prim, controlled character and letting him become increasingly unhinged that makes *Clockwise* so enjoyable; it's the expertise with which Mr. Frayn's screenplay sets the wheels in motion and keeps them going," wrote Janet Maslin in the *New York Times.* Noting that *Clockwise* is "far from perfect—it has long sleepy stretches and some pretty obvious farce situations," *Washington Post* critic Paul Attanasio nonethe-

less added that, "at its best, here is a comedy unusual in its layered complexity, in the way Frayn has worked everything out. 'Gonna take a bit o' sortin' out, this one,' says one of the pursuing bobbies. The joke, of course, is in the understatement. And rarely has the 'sortin' out' been so much fun."

Departing from farce, Frayn also wrote the stage work *Benefactors,* an acerbic look at a 1960s couple wrestling with their ideals as they try to cope with their troubled neighbors, a couple caught in a failing marriage. Comparing *Benfactors* with *Noises Off,* Frank Rich wrote in the *New York Times:* "It's hard to fathom that these two works were written by the same man. Like *Noises Off, Benefactors* is ingeniously constructed and has been directed with split-second precision . . . but there all similarities end. Mr. Frayn's new play is a bleak, icy, microcosmic exploration of such serious matters as the nature of good and evil, the price of political and psychological change and the relationship of individuals to the social state. Though *Benefactors* evokes Chekhov, *Othello* and *The Master Builder* along its way, it is an original, not to mention demanding, achievement that is well beyond the ambitions of most contemporary dramatists." Likewise, Mel Gussow of the same newspaper found strong ties between Chekhov and Frayn: "Thematically . . . the work remains [close] to Chekhov; through a closely observed, often comic family situation we see the self-defeating aspects of misguided social action."

Also dark in focus, Frayn's *Democracy* features a fractured Cold-War Germany and West German Chancellor Willy Brandt's fall from power. While focusing on Brandt and Günter Guillaume, the communist who caused Brant's downfall, *Democracy* also has a subtext: "the complexity of human beings" and the idea that each individual "contains all the lives that he or she might once have been or could be again," in the words of *Hollywood Reporter*'s Ray Bennett.

Frayn's Tony Award-winning play *Copenhagen* focuses on a meeting during World War II between Nobel Prize-winning nuclear physicists Niels Bohr and Werner Heisenberg. Before the war, their work together had revolutionized atomic physics, and their meeting—which has been heavily debated over the years—has been the subject of much speculation. Both men gave opposing accounts of their meeting following the war, and the real purpose of the encounter remained a mystery. Frayn's play is inspired, in part, by the book *Heisenberg's War: The Secret History of the German Bomb,* which focuses on Heisenberg's efforts to discourage the Nazi atomic bomb program. Moral ambiguities are one of the primary themes Frayn addresses in his play, and as the playwright told a *Guardian* contributor: "whatever was said at the meeting, and whatever Heisenberg's intentions, there is something profoundly characteristic of the difficulties in human relationships, and profoundly painful, in that picture of the two ageing men."

While Frayn has gone on to produce such popular comic works as *Democracy,* his work during the twentieth century is viewed as particularly influential. "Although one cannot say that Michael Frayn's plays revolutionized the British stage during [the late twentieth century], they certainly helped to enliven it," concluded Fritz. Like many of his contemporaries, in his early work he "experimented with dramatic structures borrowed from film and television—perhaps an attempt to find new methods of expression," and went on to produce "a string of lively, witty comedies with some serious philosophical questions lurking beneath the surfaces." Discussing Frayn's overall impact on modern theatre, Innes grouped Frayn with playwrights Trevor Griffiths, Peter Barnes, and Tom Stoppard as creators "of the most inventive contemporary comedy" of their generation.

BIOGRAPHICAL AND CRITICAL SOURCES:

BOOKS

Contemporary Dramatists, 5th edition, St. James Press (Detroit, MI), 1993.

Contemporary Literary Criticism, Thomson Gale (Detroit, MI), Volume 3, 1975, Volume 7, 1977, Volume 31, 1985, Volume 47, 1988.

Contemporary Novelists, 6th edition, St. James Press (Detroit, MI), 1996.

Dictionary of Literary Biography, Thomson Gale (Detroit, MI), Volume 13: *British Dramatists since World War II,* 1982, Volume 14: *British Novelists since 1960,* 1983.

Page, Malcolm, *File on Frayn,* Methuen Drama (London, England), 1994.

PERIODICALS

American Theatre, October, 2001, Celia Wren, review of *The Copenhagen Papers,* p. 121.

Art in America, July, 2000, Paula Harper, review of *Headlong,* p. 35.

Atlanta Journal-Constitution, April 7, 2002, Steve Murray, review of *Spies,* p. H4.

Back Stage, April 21, 2000, David A. Rosenberg, review of *Copenhagen,* p. 64.

Back Stage West, January 17, 2002, Kristina Mannion, review of *Copenhagen,* p. 16.

Booklist, July, 1999, Brad Hooper, review of *Headlong,* p. 1893; March 15, 2001, Whitney Scott, review of *Headlong,* p. 1412; April 1, 2001, Jack Helbig, review of *The Copenhagen Papers,* p. 1442; February 15, 2002, Joanne Wilkinson, review of *Spies,* p. 991.

Boston Herald, April 19, 2002, Rosemary Herbert, review of *Spies,* p. 35.

Chicago Tribune, November, 1988.

Commonweal, June 16, 2000, Celia Wren, review of *Copenhagen,* p. 17.

Dallas Morning News, May 15, 2002, Jerome Weeks, "A Success on Stages and Pages" (interview with Frayn).

Drama, summer, 1975; July, 1980.

Entertainment Weekly, September 3, 1999, review of *Headlong,* p. 65; December 24, 1999, review of *Headlong,* p. 2145.

Fortune, April 16, 2001, review of *Copenhagen,* p. 460.

Globe and Mail (Toronto, Ontario, Canada), October 30, 1999, review of *Headlong,* p. D19.

Guardian (London, England), October 1, 1968; March 11, 1975; February 9, 2002, Peter Bradshaw, review of *Spies,* p. 10; March 23, 2002, review of *Copenhagen,* p. A1.

Hollywood Reporter, November 27, 2002, Jay Reiner, review of *Copenhagen,* p. 20; October 7, 2003, Ray Bennett, review of *Democracy,* p. 24.

Horizon, January-February, 1986.

Hudson Review, summer, 2000, Abraham Pais, review of *Copenhagen,* p. 182, and Thomas Filbin, review of *Headlong,* p. 330.

Insight, February 3, 1986.

Kirkus Reviews, November 15, 1991, p. 1421; July 15, 1999, review of *Headlong,* p. 1071; March 1, 2001, review of *The Copenhagen Papers,* p. 311; February 1, 2002, review of *Spies,* p. 122.

Library Journal, June 15, 1999, Edward B. St. John, review of *Headlong,* p. 106; April 1, 2001, Mingming Shen Kuo, review of *The Copenhagen Papers,* p. 101; August, 2002, Elizabeth Stifter, review of *Noises Off,* p. 94.

Listener, January 21, 1965; January 15, 1966; March 20, 1975.

London Review of Books, October 8, 1992, p. 13; October 14, 1999, review of *Headlong,* p. 22.

Los Angeles Times, October 30, 1984; February 3, 1985; February 12, 1985; October 10, 1986; July

20, 1987; January 7, 2002, Daryl H. Miller, review of *Copenhagen*, p. F10.

Los Angeles Times Book Review, February 16, 1992, p. 3; September 5, 1999, review of *Headlong*, p. 11.

Massachusetts Review, summer, 2001, Robert L. King, review of *Copenhagen*, p. 165.

New Statesman, October 4, 1968; November 1, 1974; January 26, 1996, p. 32; September 13, 1999, Terri Natale, review of *Headlong*, p. 55; November 29, 1999, review of *Headlong*, p. 82; February 4, 2002, Hugo Barnacle, review of *Spies*, p. 57; January 5, 2004, John Gordon Morrison, review of "The Last Laugh: Why the Art of Farce Is an Extremely Serious Business," p. 32.

Newsweek, February 18, 1974; January 20, 1986.

New Yorker, September 20, 1999, review of *Headlong*, p. 128; April 1, 2002, John Updike, review of *Spies*, p. 94.

New York Review of Books, May 14, 1992, p. 41; December 2, 1999, review of *Headlong*, p. 23.

New York Times, September 11, 1970; June 13, 1971; June 3, 1979; December 12, 1983; July 23, 1984; January 28, 1985; December 23, 1985; January 5, 1986; March 19, 1986; September 4, 1986; October 10, 1986; December 14, 1986; December 19, 1986; March 12, 1987; August 24, 1999, review of *Headlong*, p. E8; October 25, 1999, Sarah Lyall, "Enter Farce and Eruditon," p. B1; March 21, 2000, James Glanz, William J. Broad, review of *Copenhagen*, p. D1; April 12, 2000, Ben Brantley, review of *Copenhagen*, p. B1; May 14, 2000, Rick Marin, review of *Copenhagen*, p. WK2; June 13, 2001, Richard Bernstein, review of *Copenhagen*, p. B9; February 9, 2002, James Glanz, review of *Copenhagen*, p. A15; April 9, 2002, Michiko Kakutani, review of *Spies*, p. B7; April 14, 2002, Jennifer Schuessler, review of *Spies*, p. B7.

New York Times Book Review, September 15, 1968; March 18, 1990; February 16, 1992; January 17, 1993, p. 1; August 29, 1999, review of *Headlong*, p. 7; December 5, 1999, review of *Headlong*, p. 8; January 5, 2003, Scott Veale, review of *Spies*, p. 16.

New York Times Magazine, December 8, 1985.

Observer (London, England), June 11, 1967; July 18, 1976; April 27, 1980; April 4, 1984; August 22, 1999, review of *Headlong*, p. 11; October 3, 1999, review of *The Original Michael Frayn*, p. 16.

Opera News, August, 1996, p. 49.

Plays and Players, September, 1970; March, 1980; December, 1984.

Publishers Weekly, December 6, 1991; November 23, 1992; July 5, 1999, review of *Headlong*, p. 54; May 7, 2001, review of *The Copenhagen Papers*, p. 234; February 4, 2002, review of *Spies*, p. 48.

St. Louis Post-Dispatch, April 7, 2000, Calvin Wilson, review of *Copenhagen*, p. F3.

San Francisco Chronicle, January 14, 2001, David Perlman, review of *Copenhagen*, p. D1.

Saturday Review, January 15, 1966.

Science, April 14, 2000, David Voss, review of *Copenhagen*, p. 278.

Sewanee Review, fall, 2000, Merritt Moseley, review of *Headlong*, p. 648.

Spectator, November 23, 1962; October 4, 1968; August 29, 1992, p. 28; December 10, 1983; August 7, 1999, Anita Brookner, review of *Headlong*, p. 34; July 24, 2000, Robert Winder, review of *Celia's Secret: An Investigation*, p. 54; January 26, 2002, Jane Gardam, review of *Spies*, p. 53.

Sunday Times (London, England), January 27, 1980.

Time, September 27, 1968; July 12, 1982; January 5, 1987.

Times (London, England), February 25, 1982; February 15, 1983; April 6, 1984; March 14, 1986; November 10, 1986.

Times Literary Supplement, February 1, 1980; March 5, 1982; September 22-28, 1989; August 20, 1999, Hal Jensen, review of *Headlong*, p. 19; September 1, 2000, Maggie Gee, review of *Celia's Secret*, p. 34; February 1, 2002, Jonathan Keats, review of *Spies*, p. 22.

Wall Street Journal, April 12, 2000, Amy Gamerman, review of *Copenhagen*, p. A24.

Washington Post, October 16, 1983; October 27, 1983; December 24, 1985; October 25, 1986.

Washington Post Book World, January 10, 1974; January 31, 1993, p. 3; September 5, 1999, review of *Headlong*, p. 15.

ONLINE

Bomb Online, http://www.bombsite.com/ (May 28, 2002), Marcy Kahan, interview with Frayn.

London Review of Books Online, http://www.lrb.co.uk/ (May 28, 2002), Michael Wood, review of *Headlong*.

Washington Post Online, http://www.washingtonpost.com/ (May 28, 2002), Michael Dirda, review of *Headlong*.

World Socialist Web site, http://www.wsws.org/ (May 28, 2002), Trevor Johnson, review of *Copenhagen*.

* * *

FRAZIER, Charles 1950-

PERSONAL: Born November 4, 1950, in Asheville, NC; son of Charles O. (a high school principal) and Betty (a school librarian and administrator) Frazier; married, c. 1976; wife's name Katherine (an accounting professor); children: Annie. *Education:* University of North Carolina-Chapel Hill, B.A., 1973, University of South Carolina, Ph.D., 1976; graduate study at Appalachian State University.

ADDRESSES: Home—A farm near Raleigh, NC. *Agent*—Amanda Urban, International Creative Management, Inc., 40 West 57th St., New York, NY 10019.

CAREER: Writer, university professor, and horse breeder. University of Colorado, Boulder, instructor in early American literature; taught literature at a college in North Carolina, prior to 1990; freelance writer, 1990—. Raises horses on farm near Raleigh, North Carolina.

AWARDS, HONORS: National Book Award for fiction, from the National Book Foundation, 1997, for *Cold Mountain.*

WRITINGS:

(With Donald Secreast) *Adventuring in the Andes: The Sierra Club Travel Guide to Ecuador, Peru, Bolivia, the Amazon Basin, and the Galapagos Islands* (nonfiction), Sierra Club Books (San Francisco, CA), 1985.
Cold Mountain (novel), Atlantic Monthly Press (New York, NY), 1997.

Also author of the introduction to a paperback edition of *The Book of Job.*

ADAPTATIONS: Cold Mountain was adapted for film by MGM and Miramax in 2003, directed by Anthony Minghella and starring Jude Law, Nicole Kidman, and Renee Zellweger.

WORK IN PROGRESS: Another novel, about a one hundred-year-old white man who grew up with the Cherokees in North Carolina, and who was found in a North Carolina psychiatric hospital near the turn of the century.

SIDELIGHTS: Before publishing his award-winning first novel, *Cold Mountain,* in 1997, Charles Frazier taught early American literature, first at the University of Colorado and later in his native North Carolina. He also traveled extensively in South America, his experi-

ences becoming the basis for a book written in collaboration with Donald Secreast that appeared in 1985, *Adventuring in the Andes: The Sierra Club Travel Guide to Ecuador, Peru, Bolivia, the Amazon Basin, and the Galapagos Islands.* Around 1990, he left academic life to focus on the story that would become *Cold Mountain.* Frazier's first novel brought him considerable critical acclaim, winning a National Book Award and reaching the top of the *New York Times* bestseller list.

Adventuring in the Andes contains a variety of knowledge useful to anyone planning a vacation near the South American mountain range—from people who want strenuous hiking to those who merely want a comfortable hotel stay in an exotic location. The volume discusses one hundred hiking trails, including the Inca trail to Machu Picchu; it also describes the cuisine available in each region. In addition, Frazier and his coauthor warn readers of the various types of disease and other medical complications they might encounter during their travels in South America. John Brosnahan noted in *Booklist* that "The book supplies a generous amount of . . . information." A *Kliatt* reviewer called *Adventuring in the Andes* "excellent" and "invaluable," while Harold M. Otness in the *Library Journal* summed it up as "a fine choice for travel collections."

Frazier has also hiked extensively in the North Carolina mountains, not coincidentally the setting of *Cold Mountain.* He got the idea for the novel from the life of one of his ancestors, a great-great uncle named W.P. Inman who, after being wounded, deserted from the Confederate Army during the War between the States. Frazier tells the story of Inman's three-hundred-mile-long journey home to the woman and the mountain he loves, evading troops from the North as well as Southern Home Guard patrols bent on capturing and executing deserters as he winds his way through the mountains. Frazier alternates Inman's chapters with others written from the viewpoint of Inman's sweetheart Ada, a genteel Southern woman from Charleston whose life has been changed drastically by the war and by her father's death. Another interesting character featured in Ada's chapters is Ruby, a more practical woman who helps Ada homestead a farm. More importantly, perhaps, Ruby teaches Ada how to be self-sufficient, and steeps her in the old Appalachian folklore that guides her in her interactions with the natural world surrounding Cold Mountain.

Critics have been as quick to praise *Cold Mountain* as readers have been in sending it to the bestseller list. Mel Gussow in the *New York Times* asserted that the novel "is filled with flavorful details: language (tools like maul and froe, spurtle, fleam and snath), crops, food, books and Cherokee legends," and went on to note that "Mr. Frazier is a stickler for authenticity." The difference, Gussow noted, between this and other popular novels about the Civil War is that in this one, "the war is in the background." Frazier told Gussow that he was aiming at "an *Odyssey* rather than an *Iliad.*" Civil War historian Shelby Foote read the book and liked it, in part, according to Gussow, because Frazier "did not presume to step inside historical characters." A reviewer for *Publishers Weekly* lauded *Cold Mountain* as "rich in evocative physical detail and timeless human insight." Likewise, David A. Berona in the *Library Journal* proclaimed it both "a remarkable effort" and a "monumental novel." Malcolm Jones, Jr. in *Newsweek* cited Frazier's acknowledgment in which he apologizes for not being completely true to the facts of his ancestor's life and to "the geography surrounding Cold Mountain," and concluded: "One must assume that he is merely being polite. This writer owes apologies to no one." One of the few voices of dissent came from Greil Marcus, reviewing the novel in *Esquire.* "I was halfway through *Cold Mountain . . .* when I realized it was only going to get worse," the critic remarked. Marcus went on to maintain that "*Cold Mountain* is a ridiculous book. Not for its story, which is merely picaresque when it's Inman's and uplifting when it's Ada's, but for its language: denatured, tangled, squeamish."

Frazier discussed with Gussow his feelings about the ways *Cold Mountain* compares with other novels about the Civil War. "When you grow up in the South," he told the reporter, "you get this concept of the war as this noble, tragic thing, and when I think about my own family's experience, it doesn't seem so noble in any direction." He added, "These people were sort of duped by a kind of war-fever hysteria. To go off and fight for a cause they had not much relation to: that's the part I see as tragic." Speaking of Civil War novels such as Stephen Crane's *The Red Badge of Courage* and Michael Shaara's *The Killer Angels,* Frazier told Gussow: "I felt those battle books had been done and in many cases done well. What I was interested in was the old lost culture of the southern Appalachians." To Jones, Frazier asserted what is perhaps his answer to Marcus's criticism. "I want the diction of the book to make people understand this is a different world," he stated.

Frazier worked for approximately seven years on *Cold Mountain* before it was ready for publication, and has frequently acknowledged the roles that family members and friends played in its creation. His daughter read drafts of the novel aloud for him, and Frazier told

Michelle Green in *People* that "it really helped to hear it in somebody else's voice and to see if she was getting the rhythm of the sentences." The author also revealed his gratitude to his wife Katherine to Green, saying "I don't know many wives who would have said to a forty-year-old man, 'Sure, honey, quit your job. Write that novel.'" Also, one of the members of the Fraziers' parental car pool who took turns driving the neighborhood children to activities turned out to be novelist Kaye Gibbons. Frazier showed a draft of *Cold Mountain* to Gibbons, who in turn encouraged him to show it to agents and publishers.

Though Frazier's accomplishment of selling *Cold Mountain* to Atlantic Monthly Press for a six-figure advance on the basis of the first one hundred pages of his draft is impressive, he has since sold his follow-up book for over eight million dollars on the basis of a one-page outline. Several sources have reported that the subject of Frazier's next novel comes "from research he had come across while writing *Cold Mountain,*" as an article about the author in *Newsmakers* put it. "Around 1900," the piece continued, "a North Carolina state psychiatric hospital housed a 100-year-old man who sometimes refused to speak any language but Cherokee. He was not a Native American, but rather had grown up among the Cherokee in North Carolina, and represented them in Washington for a time." Frazier has already sold the film rights to the story. *Cold Mountain,* on the other hand, has been made into a film directed by Anthony Minghella and starring Jude Law, Nicole Kidman, and Renee Zellweger. Zellweger's performance earned her an Oscar in 2004 for best actress in a supporting role.

BIOGRAPHICAL AND CRITICAL SOURCES:

BOOKS

Authors and Artists for Young Adults, Volume 34, Thomson Gale (Detroit, MI), 2000.
Contemporary Southern Writers, St. James Press (Detroit, MI), 1999.
Newsmakers, Issue 2, Thomson Gale (Detroit, MI), 2003.

PERIODICALS

Atlanta Journal-Constitution, April 5, 1998, Bo Emerson, "Author Deals with a Mountain of Success," p. M1; September 27, 1998, Greg Changnon, "The Reading Room," p. L11.

Booklist, September 1, 1985, p. 23.

Entertainment Weekly, September 26, 1997, pp. 46-47.

Esquire, November, 1998, Greil Marcus, "The Maiden Takes Her Easement," pp. 70-72.

Guardian (London), April 9, 1998, Roger Clarke, "American Odyssey," p. 16.

Kliatt, fall, 1985, p. 57.

Library Journal, June 1, 1985, p. 127; May 15, 1997, p. 100.

Mississippi Quarterly, spring, 1999, Bill McCarron and Paul Knoke, "Images of War and Peace: Parallelism and Antithesis in the Beginning and Ending of *Cold Mountain,*" p. 273; winter, 2001, Terry Gifford, "Terrain, Character, and Text: Is *Cold Mountain* by Charles Frazier a Post-Pastoral Novel?," pp. 87-96.

New Statesman, April 29, 2002, Jason Cowley, "Books Diary," p. 53.

Newsweek, June 23, 1997, p. 73; July 28, 1997, Malcolm Jones, Jr., interview with Charles Frazier, pp. 64-65; April 15, 2002, Malcolm Jones, "Publishing: King of the Mountain," p. 54.

New York Times, August 27, 1997, pp. B1, B7.

People, February 23, 1998, Michelle Green, interview with Charles Frazier, p. 107.

Publishers Weekly, May 5, 1997, pp. 196-197.

San Francisco Chronicle, October 6, 1998, Jon Carrol, "Five Thoughts on *Cold Mountain,*" p. B10.

Variety, April 8, 2002, Jonathan Ding, "'Mountain' Man Books $11 Mil for Next Novel," pp. 1-2.

ONLINE

Cold Mountain Official Web site, http://www.miramax. com/cold_mountain/ (November 8, 2003).

*   *   *

FRENCH, Marilyn 1929-
(Mara Solwoska)

PERSONAL: Born November 21, 1929, in New York, NY; daughter of E. Charles and Isabel (Hazz) Edwards; married Robert M. French, Jr. (a lawyer), June 4, 1950 (divorced, 1967); children: Jamie, Robert M. III. *Education:* Hofstra College (now University), B.A., 1951, M.A., 1964; Harvard University, Ph.D., 1972. *Hobbies and other interests:* Amateur musician; parties, cooking, travel.

ADDRESSES: Home—New York, NY. *Agent*—Charlotte Sheedy Literary Agency, 145 West 86th St., New York, NY 10024.

CAREER: Writer and lecturer. Hofstra University, Hempstead, NY, instructor in English, 1964-68; College of the Holy Cross, Worcester, MA, assistant professor of English, 1972-76; Harvard University, Cambridge, MA, Mellon Fellow in English, 1976-77. Artist-in-residence at Aspen Institute for Humanistic Study, 1972.

MEMBER: Modern Language Association of America, Society for Values in Higher Education, Virginia Woolf Society, James Joyce Society, Phi Beta Kappa.

WRITINGS:

The Book As World: James Joyce's "Ulysses," Harvard University Press (Cambridge, MA), 1976, reprinted, Paragon House (New York, NY), 1993.

The Women's Room (novel), Summit Books (New York, NY), 1977, with an afterword by Susan Faludi, Ballantine Books (New York, NY), 1993.

The Bleeding Heart (novel), Summit Books (New York, NY), 1980.

Shakespeare's Division of Experience, Summit Books (New York, NY), 1981.

Beyond Power: On Women, Men, and Morals (essays), Summit Books (New York, NY), 1985.

Her Mother's Daughter (novel), Summit Books (New York, NY), 1987.

(Author of introduction) Edith Wharton, *Summer,* Macmillan (New York, NY), 1987.

(Author of afterword) Jane Wagner, *The Search for Signs of Intelligent Life in the Universe: Now a Major Motion Picture Starring Lily Tomlin,* HarperCollins (New York, NY), 1991.

The War against Women (nonfiction), Summit (New York, NY), 1992.

Our Father (novel), Little, Brown (Boston, MA), 1994.

My Summer with George, Knopf (New York, NY), 1996.

A Season in Hell: A Memoir, Knopf (New York, NY), 1998.

From Eve to Dawn: A History of Women, McArthur (Toronto, Ontario, Canada), 2002.

Also author of two unpublished novels. Contributor of articles and stories, sometimes under pseudonym Mara Solwoska, to journals, including *Soundings* and *Ohio Review.*

ADAPTATIONS: The Women's Room was produced a television movie, 1980.

SIDELIGHTS: Novelist, educator, and literary scholar Marilyn French is perhaps best known for her cogent synthesis of the late-twentieth-century feminist perspective. "My goal in life," she once asserted in an *Inside Books* interview with Ray Bennett, "is to change the entire social and economic structure of western civilization, to make it a feminist world." "Feminism isn't a question of what kind of genitals you possess," she explained, "it's a kind of moral view. It's what you think with your head and feel with your heart." French, whose own feminism was heightened by her life experiences, was married with children before she read Simone de Beauvoir's *The Second Sex,* a book thematically concerned with the importance of women not living through men. Considered by many to be the first text of the twentieth-century feminist movement, the book greatly impressed and influenced French, and soon thereafter she began to write short stories that expressed her own feelings and frustrations. Divorced in 1967, she earned a doctorate from Harvard through fellowships, and then launched an impressive academic career marked by the publication of her thesis, *The Book As World: James Joyce's "Ulysses."* In 1977, the success of French's explosive and provocative first novel *The Women's Room,* allowed her to pursue writing full-time. The work also became a major novel of the women's movement.

"I wanted to tell the story of what it is like to be a woman in our country in the middle of the twentieth century," French explained to a *New York Times* interviewer about *The Women's Room.* Calling it "a collective biography of a large group of American citizens," Anne Tyler described the novel's characters in the *New York Times Book Review:* "Expectant in the 40's, submissive in the 50's, enraged in the 60's, they . . . arrived in the 70's independent but somehow unstrung, not yet fully composed after all they've been through." The novel is about Mira, a submissive and repressed young woman whose conventional childhood prepares her for a traditional marriage that ends in divorce and leaves her liberated but alone. "The tone of the book is rather turgid, but exalted, almost religious," noted Anne Duchene in the *Times Literary Supplement,* "a huge jeremiad for a new kind of Fall, a whole new experience of pain and loss."

Writing about *The Women's Room* in the *Washington Post Book Review,* Brigitte Weeks contended that "the novel's basic thesis—that there is little or no foreseeable future for coexistence between men and women—is powerfully stated, but still invokes a lonely chaos repellent to most readers." Uncomfortable with what she perceives as the woman-as-victim perspective in *The Women's Room,* Sara Sanborn elaborated in *Ms.:* "My main objection is not that French writes about the sufferings of women; so have the best women writers. But the women of, say, George Eliot or Virginia Woolf, hampered as they are, live in the world of choice and consequence. They are implicated in their own fates, which gives them both interest and stature. The characters in this book glory in the condition which some men have ascribed to women: they are not responsible." In her interview with *People* magazine's Gail Jennes, French stated: "Books, movies, TV teach us false images of ourselves. We learn to expect fairy-tale lives. Ordinary women's daily lives—unlike men's—have not been the stuff of literature. I wanted to legitimate it and I purposely chose the most ordinary lives [for the characters in the novel]—not the worst cases. . . . I wanted to break the mold of conventional women's novels." However, in the *New York Times Book Review,* Rosellen Brown noted that *The Women's Room* "declared the independence of one victimized wife after another."

"French wonders not only if male-female love is *possible,* but whether it's *ethical* in the contemporary context," wrote Lindsey Van Gelder in a *Ms.* review of French's second novel, *The Bleeding Heart.* "How, in other words, does one reconcile one's hard-won feminist insights about the way the System works with one's longing to open one's heart completely to a man who, at the very least, benefits from an oppressive System buttressed, in part, by women's emotional vulnerability?" *The Bleeding Heart* centers on Dolores, a liberated professor of Renaissance literature, who is on leave and researching a new book at Oxford University when she meets Victor, an unhappily married father of four in England on business. Compromising her feminist principles by engaging in an impassioned but frustratingly combative affair with him, Dolores ultimately realizes that she cannot live with Victor without descending into predictably prescribed roles. Commenting in *Newsweek* that "French makes her point and touches lots of raw contemporary nerves," Jean Strouse queried, "What happens when nobody wants to be the wife?" According to Brown, *The Bleeding Heart* represents "an admirably honest admission of the human complications that arise after a few years of lonely integrity: What now? Must one wait for love until the world of power changes hands? Is there a difference between accommodation and compromise among lovers? Accommodation and surrender? How to spell out the terms of a partial affirmation?"

In the *Village Voice,* Laurie Stone observed the political thesis of *The Bleeding Heart:* "Although a feminist may love a man, she will ultimately have to reject him, since men axiomatically live by values inimical to women." Describing it as "a novel of love and despair in the seeming ruins of post-'60s angst and the ill-defined emotional territory of the '70s," Thomas Sanchez suggested in the *Los Angeles Times Book Review* that the work "is less a novel of people and their fierce concerns for survival than a melodrama of symbols clothed in philosophical and political garb." Furthermore, Sanchez called *The Bleeding Heart* "maddening" in the sense that "French has mistaken politics for prose." But according to R.Z. Sheppard in *Time,* French softened her militancy in the work: "Her soul on ice, Marilyn French sounded like a feminist Eldridge Cleaver [in *The Women's Room*]. *The Bleeding Heart* suggests a slight thaw. Its core is a seemingly endless and inconclusive dialogue—SALT talks in the gender wars." And *Nation* contributor Andrea Freud Loewenstein suggested that although *The Bleeding Heart* is "a depressed and depressing book," it is "not a destructive one." In the words of Alice Hoffman in the *New York Times Book Review,* "French continues to write about the inner lives of women with insight and intimacy. What she's given us this time is a page-turner with a heart."

French's novel *Our Father* depicts the troubled "family reunion" that occurs after a wealthy man, Stephen Upton, suffers a stroke, sparking a visit from his four estranged daughters—all of whom have different mothers. Each hoping to gain either money or acknowledgment from their father, the women initially compete and bicker. The daughters' discovery that they have all been the victims of incest during their childhood, however, becomes a source of bonding and mutual support. Reviews of the work have been mixed. Citing an element of flatness in French's characters and scenes, Georgia Jones-Davis in the *Los Angeles Times Book Review* commented: "French has written a polemic, not a novel. . . . [The work] is too preachy and badly written to count as literature and too static to be good mind candy." Maude McDaniel, reviewing the book for Chicago's *Tribune Books,* also found the author's prose style "pedestrian," but nevertheless argued that *Our Father* "should strike a chord with every woman who is willing to think honestly about the place of femaleness in the world." While noting that the novel lacks realism in terms of character and environmental detail, Meg Wolitzer of the *New York Times Book Review* also found the book fascinating: " *Our Father* is a big novel that is fueled by anger, revenge, and the possibilities of recovery," Wolitzer noted. "It is overly long and often wildly melodramatic, but somehow these failings also give it an odd power."

A criticism frequently leveled at French's fiction is that "her novels suffer from a knee-jerk feminist stereotype in which all men are at worst, brutal and, at best, insensitive," noted Susan Wood in the *Washington Post Book World.* Astonished at the bitterness and anger French expresses in *The Women's Room* and *The Bleeding Heart,* for instance, critics have cited the author's strident anti-male stance. For example, Libby Purves wrote in the London *Times* that *The Women's Room* is "a prolonged—largely autobiographical—yell of fury at the perversity of the male sex. . . . The men in the novel are drawn as malevolent stick figures, at best appallingly dull and at worst monsters." And referring in the *Chicago Tribune Book World* to a "persistently belligerent anti-male bias" in *The Bleeding Heart,* Alice Adams felt the novel's one-sided characterization only serves to disenfranchise many readers who might otherwise read and learn from French's literature. Richard Phillips commented in the *Chicago Tribune* that "to read one of her novels . . . means wincing through hundreds of pages of professed revulsion over the male species of human kind. Man means power, control, rage. Even the nice guys finish last. Men are bastards. Women suffer. It is a message written with all the subtlety of a sledgehammer, but one that, French argues, is only a mirror reflection of what men themselves are taught from birth: contempt for women." But, as French explained to Phillips, "Contempt for women is not an accident, it is not a by-product of our culture. It is the heart. The culture is founded on it. It is the essential central core; without it, the culture would fall apart."

"Just as feminists have identified and denounced misogyny in books written by men, it behooves us all to arraign those books which exude a destructive hatred of men," opined Suzanne Fields in the *Detroit News.* "Such feelings can infect and calcify in dangerous ways. To intersperse torrid sex scenes with tirades against men for the imagined crime of being men merely allows villains and victims to exchange places. The rules of the game, weighted as they are to create those villains and victims, go unchallenged." However, to those critics who have charged that French portrays male characters as "stick figures," "empty men," and "cardboard villains," French responded in the *New York Times:* "The men are there as the women see them and feel them—impediments in women's lives. That's the focus. . . . Aristotle managed to build a whole society without mentioning women once. Did anyone ever say: 'Are there women in (Joseph Conrad's) *Nigger of the Narcissus* ?'"

Praising French's skill in eliciting response from her readers, Weeks declared that "as a polemic [*The Women's Room*] is brilliant, forcing the reader to accept the reactions of the women as the only possible ones." Noting that "the reader, a willing victim, becomes enmeshed in mixed feelings," Weeks observed that the novel "forces confrontations on the reader mercilessly." Although Weeks acknowledged the novel's flaws, she concluded that the novel is "full of life and passions that ring true as crystal. Its fierceness, its relentless refusal to compromise are as stirring as a marching song." Yet, as Van Gelder pointed out in *Ms.,* despite the fact that it "is a book whose message is 'the lesson all women learn: men are the ultimate enemy,'" men do not seem to be "especially threatened by the book"; those who choose to read it probably have some degree of commitment to feminism in the first place. "The best compliment I can pay it is that I kept forgetting that it was fiction," remarked *New York Times* contributor Christopher Lehmann-Haupt. "It seized me by my preconceptions and I kept struggling and arguing with its premises. Men can't be that bad, I kept wanting to shout at the narrator. There must be room for accommodation between the sexes that you've somehow overlooked. And the damnable thing is, she's right."

In *Her Mother's Daughter,* a forgiving look at motherhood, French writes about the maternal legacy bequeathed to daughters by examining four generations of an immigrant family through the experiences of its women. Anastasia, the narrator, attempts to overcome several generations of wrongs by living like a man, sexually free and artistically and commercially successful. Her success, however, is juxtaposed with the hardships and sufferings endured by the women before her, and her emancipation, according to Anne Summers in the *Times Literary Supplement,* "is shown to be more illusory than real; despite every conceivable change in outward forms, it is the older women's experience which imprints itself on her inner life." Reviewing the novel in Chicago's *Tribune Books,* Beverly Fields indicated that *Her Mother's Daughter* focuses on "the ways in which female submission to male society, with its accompanying suppression of rage, is passed like contagion from mother to daughter." Marie Olesen Urbanski observed in the *Los Angeles Times Book Review* that "the more educated or liberated the mother is, the more pervasive is her sense of a guilt from which there is no absolution. . . . *Her Mother's Daughter* celebrates mothers. It depicts the high price mothers pay for children who say they do not want, but who must have their sacrifices. . . . Has Mother's Day come at last?"

In other nonfiction works French seeks the origins of male dominance in society. In *Shakespeare's Division of Experience,* for example, she posits that the female's capacity to bear children has historically aligned her with nature and, consequently, under man's compulsion to exercise power over it. In the *New York Times Book Review,* Geoffrey H. Hartman described the subject of the book as "the relationship between political power and the 'division' of experience according to gender principles. It is a division that has proved disastrous for both sexes, she writes: To the male is attributed the ability to kill; to the female the ability to give birth; and around these extremes there cluster 'masculine' and 'feminine' qualities, embodied in types or roles that reinforce a schizoid culture and produce all sorts of fatal contradictions." Calling *Shakespeare's Division of Experience* "the finest piece of feminist criticism we have yet had," Laurence Lerner noted in the *Times Literary Supplement* that the author's "concern is not merely with Shakespeare." Recognizing that French "believes the identification of moral qualities with genders impoverishes and endangers our society," Lerner added that she thinks "every human experience should be reintegrated." Lerner continued that "whereas for Shakespeare the greatest threat may have lain in nature, it now lies in control; she therefore confesses an animus against 'the almost total dedication to masculine values that characterizes our culture.'"

Remarking that "French is intelligent, nothing if not ingenious, and obviously sincere," Anne Barton suggested in the *New York Review of Books* regarding *Shakespeare's Division of Experience* that "there is something very limiting . . . about the assumption upon which all her arguments are based." For example, Barton continued, "Although she does grudgingly admit from time to time that rationality, self-control, individualism, and 'permanencies' may have some little value, she is distrustful of 'civilization,' and of the life of the mind. She also leaves a major contradiction in her position unexplored. On the one hand, she indignantly denies that women are any 'closer to nature' than men. . . . On the other hand, it is not clear that the qualities she values, and according to which she would like to see life lived by both sexes, are all—in her terms—feminine." According to S. Schoenbaum in the *Washington Post Book World,* French "accepts what is after all common knowledge: that the gender principles aren't gender-specific—biological males can accommodate feminine values, and females aren't exempt from masculine power struggles. And, along with overlap, there exists the possibility for synthesis."

Beyond Power: On Women, Men, and Morals, wrote Lawrence Stone in the *New York Times Book Review,* "is a passionate polemic about the way men have treated women over the past several millenniums." And according to Paul Robinson in the *Washington Post Book World,* "Nothing in her previous books . . . prepares one for the intellectual range and scholarly energy" of the work, "which is nothing less than a history of the world (from the cavewomen to the Sandinistas) seen through the critical prism of contemporary feminism." Mary Warnock explained in the *Times Literary Supplement* that French's "general thesis is that men, who have hitherto governed the world, have always sought power above all else, and, in the interests of power, have invented the system of patriarchy which dominates all Western art, philosophy, religion, and education. Above all it now dominates industry and politics."

Agreeing with French's thesis, Stone stated of *Beyond Power:* "The history of the treatment of women by men in the last 2,500 years of Western civilization is truly awful. One therefore has to sympathize with her passionate indignation and admire the single-minded zeal with which she has pursued her theory through the millenniums." Nevertheless, Stone found the book flawed. For instance, pointing to the "relentless cruelty and selfishness" anthropologists have discovered among some of the primitive societies French has perceived as utopian, Stone commented: "French's attempt to resuscitate the noble savage in feminist drag is not convincing. Moreover, worship of a female does not do much to affect the lot of women one way or the other." Observing that "she is a formidable woman to argue with," Purves wondered whether the patriarchal system, whether "strife, competition, rivalry, the concentration of power, and even war itself," is not responsible for even a few benefits to the world. French responded by explaining, "We are always told this. That commercial links and inventions and knowledge of other nations come from war, but who is to say that these things wouldn't have happened anyway? There is no way we can know how the world would have been without men's domination." Calling it "a brilliant study of power and control showing how those two related systems have affected the lives of men and women throughout human history," Richard Rhodes concluded in the *Chicago Tribune Book World* that "*Beyond Power* ranks high among the most important books of the decade."

French's *The War against Women* surveys the oppression of women on a global scale. Considering such activities as ritualized female genital mutilation in Africa and bride burning in India, along with economic disparities between women and men, French argues that women have become "increasingly disempowered, degraded, and subjugated" by patriarchal societies. Comparing the book with Susan Faludi's more popular feminist tract, *Backlash: The Undeclared War against Women,* Julie Wheelwright of the *New Statesman* found *The War against Women* simplistic in light of then-current developments in contemporary feminist thought. In particular, Wheelwright objected to French's insistence on the universal victimization and "moral superiority" of women. In contrast, Isabelle de Courtivron, writing in the *New York Times Book Review,* praised "French's chilling and well-documented research," noting the disturbing validity of many of her observations.

From Eve to Dawn traces the history of women in three volumes. As Marian Botsford Fraser explained in a review for the Toronto *Globe and Mail,* the book revisits *Beyond Power:* "Before there were patriarchal states, there were matrilineal societies; something equivalent to the Big Bang happened to the human race about 10,000 years ago; states and patriarchy resulted and changed profoundly the nature of all societies; understanding this history will enable the world to move beyond patriarchy, but not to matriarchy which would also be a bad thing. Matriarchy, in which women have power over men, has never existed, according to French." Fraser admired the author's "chutzpah" in writing the book, but found *From Eve to Dawn* "impossible to read except in short bursts, or by browsing." What it lacks, Fraser pointed out, is a "narrative, story-telling quality." "It is a fascinating cornucopia of historical tidbits and arcane detail," the critic concluded, citing "a half-page on the Tlingit of Alaska, a page on the !Kung of the Kalahari Desert, an 'overview' of ancient Mesopotamia," and short examinations of the world's three major religions among the book's focus. "If you are satisfied with just a superficial graze . . . or can use the book as introductory . . . it has served [its] purpose," Fraser concluded.

BIOGRAPHICAL AND CRITICAL SOURCES:

BOOKS

Contemporary Literary Criticism, Thomson Gale (Detroit, MI), Volume 10, 1979, Volume 18, 1981, Volume 60, 1990.

PERIODICALS

Booklist, March 15, 1992; October 15, 1993.
Chicago Tribune, May 4, 1980; February 7, 1988.
Chicago Tribune Book World, March 9, 1980; June 23, 1985.
Detroit News, April 20, 1980.
Economist, March 21, 1992.
Entertainment Weekly, April 24, 1992.

Globe and Mail (Toronto, Ontario, Canada), July 6, 2002, Marian Botsford Fraser, review of *From Eve to Dawn.*

Ladies' Home Journal, October, 1987.

Library Journal, November 15, 1977; October 15, 1987; May 1, 1992; November 15, 1993.

Los Angeles Times Book Review, May 4, 1980; April 19, 1981; August 25, 1985; October 18, 1987; February 27, 1994, p. 12.

Modern Language Review, January, 1979.

Ms., January, 1978; April, 1979; May, 1980; April, 1987; April, 1989; July-August, 1990; March-April, 1991.

Nation, January 30, 1988.

New Statesman, February 21, 1986; April 3, 1992, p. 44.

Newsweek, March 17, 1980; January 24, 1994, p. 66.

New York, October 12, 1987.

New York Review of Books, June 11, 1981.

New York Times, October 27, 1977; March 10, 1980; March 16, 1981.

New York Times Book Review, October 16, 1977; November 11, 1977; March 16, 1980; March 22, 1981; June 12, 1983; June 23, 1985; October 25, 1987; July 17, 1988; September 24, 1989; July 5, 1992, p. 8; January 16, 1994, p. 12.

Observer (London, England), January 26, 1986.

People, February 20, 1978; January 24, 1994.

Psychology Today, August, 1985.

Publishers Weekly, August 29, 1977; August 21, 1978; March 7, 1980; September 11, 1987; September 2, 1988; March 2, 1992; October 18, 1993.

Spectator, April 4, 1992, p. 39.

Time, March 17, 1980; July 29, 1985.

Times (London, England), March 18, 1982; January 22, 1986; October 15, 1987; October 19, 1987.

Times Literary Supplement, February 18, 1977; April 21, 1978; May 9, 1980; June 4, 1982; January 24, 1986; October 23, 1987; June 19, 1992, p. 3.

Tribune Books (Chicago, IL), October 11, 1987; January 2, 1994.

Village Voice, March 24, 1980.

Virginia Quarterly Review, Volume 54, number 2, 1978.

Washington Post, May 7, 1980.

Washington Post Book World, October 9, 1977; March 9, 1980; March 8, 1981; June 2, 1985; October 18, 1987.

Women's Review of Books, October, 1986; April, 1988.

*   *   *

FRENCH, Paul
See ASIMOV, Isaac

FREY, James 1969-

PERSONAL: Born 1969; married; wife's name, Maya (an advertising executive); children: one daughter. *Education:* Attended Denison University.

ADDRESSES: Home—New York, NY. *Agent*—c/o Author Mail, Penguin Group, c/o Riverhead Books Publicity, 375 Hudson St., New York, NY 10014.

CAREER: Writer, memoirist, and screenwriter. Has worked variously as a camp counselor, a bouncer, a film director, a skateboard salesman, a picture-framer, a film producer, a busboy, a hotel security guard, and as costumed characters such as Santa Claus and the Easter Bunny in department store promotions.

AWARDS, HONORS: Hermosa Beach Film Festival, best film (director), 1998, and No Dance Film Festival, best director, 1999, both for *Sugar: The Fall of the West.*

WRITINGS:

Kissing a Fool (screenplay), MCA/Universal Pictures, 1998.

Sugar: The Fall of the West (screenplay), Next Generation, 1998.

A Million Little Pieces (memoir), N.A. Talese/Doubleday (New York, NY), 2003.

My Friend Leonard (memoir), Riverhead Books (New York, NY), 2005.

SIDELIGHTS: Author and memoirist James Frey reveals the brutal, deeply harrowing side of both addiction and recovery in the detailed accounts of his struggles, *A Million Little Pieces* and *My Friend Leonard.*

At the beginning of *A Million Little Pieces,* the twenty-three-year-old Frey has been an alcoholic for ten years and a crack addict for three. He awakens on a plane, not knowing where he has come from or where he is going, covered in a mixture of leaked and expelled bodily fluids, missing four front teeth and bearing a broken nose and a nickel-sized hole through his cheek. He is completely bereft of hope, physically and mentally, worn to his lowest possible point by his multiple and converging addictions. He shortly finds out that his battered state was due to a face-first fall down a fire escape and that he is on a plane to meet with his parents in Chicago, who plan to send him to a rehab clinic in rural Minnesota since identified as Hazelden. The bulk of the book describes in raw detail the exhausting, soul-wrenching work of kicking a half-lifetime's worth of destructive habits and physical addictions. "Frey's lacerating, intimate debut chronicles his recovery from multiple addictions with adrenal rage and sprawling prose," commented a *Kirkus Reviews* critic.

Frey's approach to his recovery immediately puts him at odds with the staff of Hazelden. He refuses to commit to the required twelve-step program, declines to surrender an iota of his life to any higher power, and declares that he will beat his addictions on his own terms and in his own way. He takes full responsibility for the condition he is in and for the person who may emerge after treatment. He refuses to see his addiction as a disease. "What sets *Pieces* apart from other memoirs about 12-stepping is Frey's resistance to the concept of a higher power," commented a *Publishers Weekly* reviewer.

He also describes the many characters he meets during treatment, including Leonard, an affable mobster; Lily, a heroin-addicted ex-prostitute with whom he falls in love; and a variety of other lost and abandoned people who forge deep friendships in the crucible of treatment that will lead to lives changed by recovery or doomed by addictions that cannot be overcome. "Frey discovers that, aside from being some of the most tormented souls on the planet, these are the nicest people he's ever met; together, they shakily plumb the depths," observed *Spectator* contributor William Leith.

"Starkly honest and mincing no words, Frey bravely faces his struggles head on, and readers will be mesmerized by his account of his ceaseless battle against addiction," commented Kristine Huntley, writing in *Booklist*. "What really separates this title from other rehab memoirs, apart from the author's young age, is his literary prowess," observed *School Library Journal* reviewer Jamie Watson. *Library Journal* contributor Rachel Collins commented that "this raw and intense book reveals a rare author whose approach to memoir writing is as original as his method to getting straight." Jennifer Reese, writing in *Entertainment Weekly*, noted that "all the ferocious energy and will Frey once devoted to self-destruction he turned toward fixing himself. Frey's prose is muscular and tough, ideal for conveying extreme physical anguish and steely determination" to succeed. A *Publishers Weekly* reviewer called the book "a remarkable memoir of addic-

tion and recovery." Louis Bayard, writing on the *Salon.com* Web site, stated that "if this bullheaded, lionhearted book doesn't reach the level of masterpiece, it's not for lack of trying. Frey has devised a rolling, pulsing style that really *moves*—an acquired taste, perhaps, but undeniably striking."

In *My Friend Leonard,* Frey resumes his story after gaining his sobriety and leaving treatment. The book begins with him in jail, serving his time for offenses committed while he was in the grip of his multiple addictions. When he is released, he heads to Chicago to see Lily, but learns that she has committed suicide only hours before. Torn with grief, Frey once again finds himself teetering on the edge of the abyss. However, before he can descend, he renews his friendship with avuncular mobster Leonard, who offers him financial support and the occasional simple odd job, usually courier work, which is likely illegal. The memoir dwells on Frey's relationship with Leonard and the contradictory elements of the man's life of crime and stoic dedication to his friends. Leonard teaches Frey that addictive substances are not the answer to any problem, and that enjoying life and its simple pleasures are its own best reward. Though there are still tragedies to endure, with Leonard's support, financial assistance, and genuine affection, Frey manages to maintain the discipline of his recovery and avoid any relapses into addiction.

"Frey's extraordinary relationship with Leonard is alive, a flesh-and-blood bond forged in the agony of rehab and sustained through honesty and trust," commented a writer in *Publishers Weekly*. "As smart as it is heartfelt, this tribute to friendship is a far sunnier book than Frey's debut," remarked *Newsweek* reviewer Malcolm Jones. A *Kirkus Reviews* reviewer called the book "a fine, grim tale, full of smarting immediacy, with stylistic tics—repetitions, an aversion to commas, run-ons—that skip close to the irritating but lend a musicality and remind the reader to pay attention."

In 2006 a *Smoking Gun* article reported that parts of Frey's memoir *A Million Little Pieces* were fabricated. Frey did not confirm or deny the allegations, although the book's publisher, Doubleday, an imprint of Random House, offered refunds to its direct customers. In addition, talk-show host Oprah Winfrey, who had chosen *A Million Little Pieces* for her popular book club, defended the overall message of the memoir as valuable despite any suspected embellishments. Later, as more evidence indicated the extent of the fabrications, Doubleday reported that new copies of Frey's memoir would contain a note with an explanation of the controversy and an apology; the note was also posted on the Random House web site. Frey's literary manager Kassie Evashevski with Brillstein-Grey Entertainment, announced that she would no longer represent Frey. Ultimately, Winfrey apologized to her viewers for initially defending Frey's memoir and confronted him about the inaccuracies on her show. She also officially removed the author from her book club. Due to the scandal surrounding the book, Frey was dropped by his publisher.

BIOGRAPHICAL AND CRITICAL SOURCES:

BOOKS

Frey, James, *A Million Little Pieces,* N.A. Talese/ Doubleday (New York, NY), 2003.
Frey, James, *My Friend Leonard,* Riverhead Books (New York, NY), 2005.

PERIODICALS

Booklist, April 15, 2003, Kristine Huntley, review of *A Million Little Pieces,* p. 1432.
Entertainment Weekly, April 4, 2003, Karen Valby, "James Frey Does Not Care What You Think about Him (Please Love Him): The Author of the Memoir *A Million Little Pieces* Kicked Crack and Alcohol on His Own Terms. Now, He Wants to Kick the Literary World's Ass the Same Way," profile of James Frey, p. 60; April 25, 2003, Jennifer Reese, "Straight Story: With Unflinching Honesty, James Frey Describes the Filth and Fury of His Substance Abuse and Recovery," review of *A Million Little Pieces,* p. 152; June 17, 2005, Thom Geier, review of *My Friend Leonard,* p. 86.
Kirkus Reviews, February 1, 2003, review of *A Million Little Pieces,* p. 204; May 1, 2005, review of *My Friend Leonard,* p. 523.
Library Journal, March 1, 2003, Rachel Collins, review of *A Million Little Pieces,* p. 106; April 15, 2005, Dale Raben, review of *My Friend Leonard,* p. 99.
Miami Herald, June 29, 2005, Andy Diaz, "In His Latest Memoir, James Frey Can't Make the Reader Care Whether He's Drunk or Sober," review of *My Friend Leonard.*
New Statesman (1996), May 26, 2003, Julian Keeling, "The Yellow Gloom of Sleepless Nights," review of *A Million Little Pieces,* p. 52.
Newsweek, June 27, 2005, Malcolm Jones, "Friends in Low Places: The Author of *A Million Little Pieces* Gets Happy," review of *My Friend Leonard,* p. 65.

People, June 27, 2005, "Great Reads," review of *My Friend Leonard,* p. 47.
Publishers Weekly, February 24, 2003, Charlotte Abbott, "One in a Million: In His Debut, James Frey Rewrites the Recovery Memoir with Hubris to Spare," review of *A Million Little Pieces,* p. 17; March 10, 2003, review of *A Million Little Pieces,* p. 67; August 18, 2003, John F. Baker, "Riverhead Gets Frey Sequel," p. 14; March 28, 2005, review of *My Friend Leonard,* p. 64.
School Library Journal, August, 2003, Jamie Watson, review of *A Million Little Pieces,* p. 188.
Spectator, May 24, 2003, William Leith, "Plumbing the Lower Depths," review of *A Million Little Pieces,* p. 40.

ONLINE

CNN.com, http://www.cnn.com/ (January 12, 2006), "Some 'Pieces' Buyers Offered Refund"; "Winfrey Stands Behind 'Pieces' Author."
Salon.com, http://www.salon.com/ (April 19, 2003), Louis Bayard, "The Sound Bite and the Fury," profile of James Frey.

*   *   *

FRIEDAN, Betty 1921-2006
(Betty Naomi Friedan)

PERSONAL: Born February 4, 1921, in Peoria, IL; died February 4, 2006, in Washington, DC, of heart failure; daughter of Harry (a jeweler) and Miriam (Horowitz) Goldstein; married Carl Friedan (a theater producer), June, 1947 (divorced May, 1969); children: Daniel, Jonathan, Emily. *Education:* Smith College, A.B. (summa cum laude), 1942; further study at University of California, Berkeley, University of Iowa, and Esalen Institute. *Politics:* Democrat.

CAREER: Feminist organizer, writer, and lecturer at universities, institutes, and professional associations worldwide, including Harvard Law School, University of Chicago, Vassar College, Smithsonian Institution, New York Bar Association, U.S. Embassy in Bogota, Colombia, and in Sweden, the Netherlands, Brazil, Israel, and Italy, beginning in the 1960s; organizer and director, First Women's Bank &Trust Co., New York City, 1974-. Organizer, Women's Strike for Equality, 1970, International Feminist Congress, 1973, and Economic Think Tank for Women, 1974; consultant for

President's Commission on the Status of Women, 1964-65, and Rockefeller Foundation project on education of women, 1965. Delegate, White House Conference on Family, 1980, United Nations Decade for Women Conferences in Mexico City, Copenhagen, and Nairobi. Instructor in creative writing and women's studies, New York University, 1965-73; visiting professor, Yale University, 1974, and Queens College of the City University of New York, 1975; visiting scholar, University of Southern Florida, Sarasota, 1985; distinguished visiting professor, School of Journalism and Social Work, University of Southern California.

MEMBER: National Organization for Women (NOW; founding president, 1966-70; member of board of directors of legal defense and education fund), National Women's Political Caucus (founder; member of national policy council, 1971-73), National Association to Repeal Abortion Laws (vice-president, 1972-74), National Conference of Public Service Employment (member of board of directors), Girl Scouts of the U.S.A. (member of national board), Women's Forum, American Sociological Association, Association for Humanistic Psychology, Gerontological Society of America, PEN, American Federation of Television and Radio Artists (AFTRA), American Society of Journalists and Authors, Authors Guild, Authors League of America, Women's Ink, Women's Forum, Society of Magazine Writers, Phi Beta Kappa, Coffee House.

AWARDS, HONORS: New World Foundation-New York State Education Department grant, 1958-62; Wilhelmina Drucker Prize for contribution to emancipation of men and women, 1971; Humanist of the Year award, 1975; American Public Health Association citation, 1975; Mort Weisinger Award for outstanding magazine article, American Society of Journalists and Authors, 1979; Author of the Year, American Society of Journalists and Authors; L.H.D., Smith College, 1975, State University of New York at Stony Brook, 1985, and Cooper Union, 1987; Chubb fellow, Yale University, 1985; Andrus Center for Gerontology fellow, University of Southern California, 1986; Eleanor Roosevelt Leadership Award, 1989; Doctorate (honorary), Columbia University, 1994.

WRITINGS:

The Feminine Mystique, Norton (New York, NY), 1963, revised edition, 1974, twentieth-anniversary edition, 1983, rerprinted with a new introduction by the author, 1997, reprinted with an introduction by Anna Quindlen, 2001.

It Changed My Life: Writings on the Women's Movement, Random House, 1976, published with a new introduction by the author, Norton, 1985.

The Second Stage, Summit Books, 1981, revised edition with a new introduction and afterword by the author, 1986, reprinted with a new introduction by the author, Harvard University Press (Cambridge, MA), 1998.

The Fountain of Age, Simon &Schuster (New York City), 1993.

Beyond Gender: The New Politics of Work and Family, Woodrow Wilson Center Press (Washington, DC), 1997.

Life So Far, Simon &Schuster, 2000.

Contributor to books, including *Voices of the New Feminism,* edited by Mary Lou Thompson, Beacon Press, 1970, and to anthologies, including *Anatomy of Reading,* edited by L.L. Hackett and R. Williamson, McGraw, 1966; *Gentlemen, Scholars, and Scoundrels: Best of "Harper's" 1850 to the Present*; and *A College Treasury.* Contributor of articles to periodicals, including *Saturday Review, New York Times Magazine, Harper's, Redbook, Mademoiselle, Ladies' Home Journal, Newsday,* and *Working Woman*; contributing editor and columnist for *McCall's,* 1971-74; member of editorial board for *Present Tense.*

The Schlesinger Library of Radcliffe College maintains a collection of Friedan's personal papers.

SIDELIGHTS: When Betty Friedan's first book, *The Feminine Mystique,* was published in 1963 it helped launch the modern women's movement by debunking the myth of the post-war woman—a content homemaker who deferred her own ambitions and interests to take care of her family. Friedan was the first writer to analyze how the perpetration of this stereotype belied the complexity of most women's lives; she called this phenomenon "the feminine mystique." With the publication of the book, she immediately became one of the women's movement's most visible proponents, participating in the founding of the National Organization for Women (NOW) in 1966 and lobbying incessantly for such causes as the passage of the Equal Rights Amendment and legalization of abortion. By the 1990s her concerns had shifted to issues pertaining to aging. Her book *The Fountain of Age* was prompted by "feelings of *deja vu* [that washed] over me as I hear[d] geriatric experts talk about the aged with the same patronizing 'compassionate' denial of their personhood that I heard when experts talked about women 20 years ago," Friedan wrote in the *New York Times Magazine.*

Friedan's journey to political activism began in the early-1960s when she lost her job as a newspaper reporter after requesting her second maternity leave. Although she graduated from college with honors in psychology, she turned down a fellowship at University of California at Berkeley in order to devote herself to her growing family. In her spare time she began to write articles for women's magazines and soon discovered a pattern of bias on the part of the magazines' editors. "They claimed a woman painting a crib was interesting to their readers, but a woman painting a picture was not," summarized Marilyn French in *Esquire*. "The reality of women's lives . . . was censored; what appeared was a fantasy, a picture-book image of happy female domesticity," French continued. *The Feminine Mystique* addressed this generation of women whose lives were supposed to be made more convenient by the proliferation of time-saving appliances and the trappings of suburbia. Instead, many of these women turned to tranquilizers or lived with vague feelings of uneasiness and unfulfillment. A *Times Literary Supplement* reviewer defined the mystique as a "victorian homelife made roseate by the women's magazines and the ad-men, and made intellectually respectable by pseudo-Freud."

Criticism of the book was diverse. Sylvia Fleis Fava, writing in the *American Sociological Review,* noted that "Friedan tends to set up a counter-mystique; that all women must have creative interests outside the home to realize themselves. This can be just as confining and tension-producing as any other mold." Fava also explained that Friedan was not warmly received by all feminists in those early years-especially the movement's more radical elements who saw her views as somewhat reactionary and bourgeois. This discord resulted in the fracturing of the women's movement in the early 1970s in which other prominent feminists, most notably Gloria Steinem and Bella Abzug, gained control of the National Women's Political Caucus and NOW, two of the most powerful feminist organizations at the time.

Friedan's next two books, *It Changed My Life: Writings on the Women's Movement* and *The Second Stage,* document the women's movement as it pertains to her own experiences. *It Changed My Life* is a compilation of Friedan's writings from the 1960s and 1970s in which she sorts out the healthy, productive elements of the movement from the petty, divisive ones in an attempt to gain a new focus—"She wants us to *get together* in a cause that is right and good for all of us, women, men, children, grandparents, single people, everybody," wrote Eliot Fremont-Smith in the *Village Voice*. Accounts of the activities of the National Women's Political Caucus

detail the maneuvering that typified the movement at that point, as alliances shifted and allegations were made that resulted in a less-than-unified front. However, Stephanie Harrington of the *New York Times Book Review* questioned Friedan's "half-light between innuendo and substantiated accusation, juxtaposing names and her version of events and letting the implications fall where they may" approach. Friedan also received criticism for her assertion that lesbianism is a private matter and therefore should not be an issue for the women's movement—an opinion that infuriated many lesbians who considered themselves integral to the movement. Such fringe groups, Friedan argued, threatened basic gains for all women, especially passage of the Equal Rights Amendment. Many critics further faulted Friedan for her maternal attitude towards her accomplishments; Sara Sanborn in the *Saturday Review* described it as "a self-justifying, even self-regarding tone . . . as though Friedan were afraid that we might forget our debt to her."

The Second Stage explains how the backlash from the first wave of feminism caused a "feminist mystique" to emerge in the form of the "superwoman" stereotype—she who effortlessly combines family, career, and satisfying social life. This new prevailing wisdom enabled "the Moral Majority, Ronald Reagan, and various Neanderthal forces [to] bear down with a wrecker" and threaten the gains women have made, wrote Webster Schott of the *Washington Post Book World*. Friedan defines the "second stage" as "the restructuring of our institutions on the basis of real equality for women and men, so we can live a new 'yes' to life and love, and *choose* to have children." She urges those in the women's movement to make the family its central focus. Furthermore, she proposes revised standards of performance for women's roles, because expecting women to perform at their highest levels in both the workplace and the home is unrealistic; they no longer have the luxury of concentrating on a single role as previous generations of women did. The "feminist mystique," Friedan said in an interview with Paula Gribetz Gottlieb in *Working Woman*, refers to "an agenda so concentrated on that which had been denied . . . that it denies that there are other aspects to her life. . . . What is needed now is an integration of the two."

With the publication of *The Fountain of Age* in 1993, Friedan moved to the forefront of another emerging movement-one that seeks to improve the quality of life and amount of respect for older people. The goal of this movement, Friedan states, is for society to see aging not as a process whereby individuals become useless, but as a new phase of life that is none the less vital or interesting than youth. Enumerating statistics illustrating that people are living longer than ever, that women live longer than men, and that people over sixty-five are the fastest growing demographic in the country, Friedan sets out to overturn stereotypes that cast the elderly as nonparticipants in society. According to Friedan, the "age mystique" is the unacceptable view "that aging is acceptable only if it passes for youth," wrote Carol Kleiman in Chicago *Tribune Books*.

After three decades of promoting her own strain of feminism, Friedan finally admits in *The Fountain of Age* "with relief and excitement, my liberation from the power politics of the women's movement. I recognized my own compelling need now to transcend the war between the sexes, the no-win battles of women as a whole sex, oppressed victims, against men as a whole sex, the oppressors. . . . The unexpectedness of this new quest has been my adventure into age." However, Friedan does credit feminism for providing women with a greater ability to adapt to the challenges of aging. Though Friedan's ideas are not necessarily groundbreaking or revolutionary—"word has been out for years that old age need not be synonymous with deterioration," stated David Gates in *Newsweek*—they bring the issue into the mainstream with discussions and anecdotes about life after menopause, mountain-climbing expeditions, and maintaining healthy relationships.

Criticism of *The Fountain of Age* came from Nancy Mairs in the *New York Times Book Review,* who warned that the author "generalizes from the conditions and experiences of a predominately white middle-class population . . . for people from diverse ethnic and economic backgrounds aging may present altogether different challenges." Others have faulted Friedan's writing for what they see as a lack of organization and excessive length due to repetition; "a prose style that resembles nothing so much as a community bulletin board, full of flabby words," according to Christopher Lehman-Haupt in the *New York Times*. Kleiman was puzzled by Friedan's support for the lifestyle *Playboy* magnate Hugh Hefner has adopted in his later years while simultaneously dismissing Steinem, now in her fifties, who is still a high-profile feminist activist. Diane Middlebrook, writing in the *Los Angeles Times Book Review,* also commented on Friedan's interpretation of cultural attitudes toward aging by determining that "Friedan is better as a muckraker challenging the disease model by which the conditions of aging are approached by medical and social institutions." When it comes to research priorities and allocation of funds, for example, Friedan thinks the medical establishment focuses too heavily on sickness and disability while ig-

noring the healthy, active populace over sixty-five. Despite this, Kleiman wrote, "She shows no desire to evade issues, no matter how delicate and difficult." Middlebrook concluded that "readers not turned off by her occasional nervous preening will find much to enlighten and provoke as they join her in the contemplation of possibilities."

Friedan died on February 4, 2006, of congestive heart failure.

BIOGRAPHICAL AND CRITICAL SOURCES:

BOOKS

Contemporary Issues Criticism, Volume 2, Thomson Gale (Detroit), 1984.
Mitchell, Juliet, *Psychoanalysis and Feminism,* Random House, 1974.

PERIODICALS

American Sociological Review, December, 1963, pp. 1053-54.
Business Week, November 1, 1993, p. 18.
Chicago Tribune Book World, November 8, 1981.
Encounter, February, 1983.
Esquire, December, 1983.
Humanist, January/ February, 1991, pp. 26-27.
Insight on the News, October 25, 1993, p. 12; June 27, 1994, p. 40.
Life, fall, 1990, p. 107.
Los Angeles Times, December 27, 1981.
Los Angeles Times Book Review, September 19, 1993.
Nation, November 14, 1981; November 28, 1981.
National Review, February 5, 1982.
New Republic, April 27, 1974; January 20, 1982; July 1, 1983; October 11, 1993, p. 49.
Newsweek, October 4, 1993, p. 78.
New York Times, August 3, 1976; April 25, 1983; June 2, 1986; October 11, 1993.
New York Times Book Review, July 4, 1976, pp. 7-8; November 22, 1981; October 3, 1993, p. 1.
New York Times Magazine, July 5, 1981; February 27, 1983; November 3, 1985.
People Weekly, October 4, 1993, p. 26.
Psychology Today, November-December, 1993, p. 20.
Publishers Weekly, June 28, 1993, p. 61.
Saturday Review, July 24, 1976; October, 1981.
Tikkun, March-April, 1994, p. 79.

Times Literary Supplement, May 31, 1963; July 30, 1982.

Tribune Books (Chicago), September 12, 1993.

Village Voice, June 28, 1976, pp. 43-44.

Washington Post Book World, August 8, 1976, p. F7; November 1, 1981; October 19, 1983.

Working Woman, February, 1982.

OBITUARIES:

PERIODICALS

New York Times, February 5, 2006.

*   *   *

FRIEDAN, Betty Naomi
See FRIEDAN, Betty

*   *   *

FRIEDMAN, Thomas L. 1953-
(Thomas Loren Friedman)

PERSONAL: Born July 20, 1953, in Minneapolis, MN; son of Harold Abraham and Margaret (a retired real estate broker; maiden name, Philips) Friedman; married Ann Louise Bucksbaum (a copyeditor), November 23, 1978; children: two daughters. *Education:* Brandeis University, B.A. (summa cum laude), 1975; St. Antony's, Oxford, M.Phil., 1978. *Religion:* Jewish. *Hobbies and other interests:* Golf.

ADDRESSES: Home—Bethesda, MD. *Office*—New York Times, 1627 I St. NW, Washington, DC 20006.

CAREER: United Press International, correspondent in London, England, 1978-79, and Beirut, Lebanon, 1979-81; *New York Times,* New York, NY, business reporter, 1981-82, Beirut bureau chief, 1982-84, Jerusalem bureau chief, 1984-89, Washington, DC, bureau chief and diplomatic correspondent, 1989-95, foreign affairs columnist, 1995—. Former visiting professor, Harvard University. Has also hosted television documentaries for the Discovery Channel.

MEMBER: Phi Beta Kappa.

AWARDS, HONORS: Overseas Press Club award, 1980, for best business reporting from abroad; George Polk Award, 1982, and Pulitzer Prize and Livingston Award for Young Journalists, both 1983, all for coverage of war in Lebanon; Page One Award, New York Newspaper Guild, 1984; Colonel Robert D. Heinl, Jr., Memorial Award in Marine Corps History, Marine Corps Historical Foundation, 1985; Pulitzer Prize, 1988, for coverage of Israel; National Book Award, National Book Foundation, 1989, for *From Beirut to Jerusalem;* Overseas Press Club award, 2000, for *The Lexus and the Olive Tree;* Pulitzer Prize, 2002, for commentary; New Israel Fund Award for Outstanding Reporting from Israel. Recipient of several honorary degrees.

WRITINGS:

(Author of text) *War Torn* (photo collection), Pantheon (New York, NY), 1984.

From Beirut to Jerusalem, Farrar, Straus (New York, NY), 1989.

(With Richard Rhodes) *Writing in an Era of Conflict,* Library of Congress (Washington, DC), 1990.

Israel, a Photobiography: The First Fifty Years, Simon & Schuster (New York, NY), 1998.

The Lexus and the Olive Tree: Understanding Globalization, Thorndike Press (Thorndike, ME), 1999.

Longitudes and Attitudes: Exploring the World after September 11, Farrar, Strauss (New York, NY), 2002.

The World Is Flat: A Brief History of the Twenty-first Century, Farrar, Straus (New York, NY), 2005.

Contributor to *New York Times Magazine. From Beirut to Jerusalem* has been translated into more than two dozen languages.

SIDELIGHTS: Having survived five years of reporting from one of the most war-torn areas of the Middle East, Thomas L. Friedman decided he had had enough when he awoke one night in 1984 to find his Beirut neighborhood under mortar attack. The constant warfare had become so commonplace that it was no longer even considered news, so he decided to return home. From his assignment in Beirut, Friedman moved on to a posting in Jerusalem, where he remained until 1989. Two Pulitzer Prizes and innumerable war stories later, Friedman returned to the United States as chief diplomatic correspondent for the Washington, DC, bureau of the *New York Times.*

From Beirut to Jerusalem represents the culmination of Friedman's experiences covering the Middle East, with glimpses of his youth and background. As a Jewish

American, Friedman brings an enlightening perspective to discussions of Middle Eastern affairs, according to reviewers. For example, Barbara Newman observed in the *Los Angeles Times Book Review* that Friedman "has written an intimate portrait of his ten years of reporting in the Middle East, chronicling his change from awe-struck lover of Israel to outspoken critic." Friedman's infatuation with Israel began at the age of fifteen, when he visited the country with his parents. In the introductory chapter of *From Beirut to Jerusalem,* he relates an anecdote from his high school days: "I was insufferable. When the Syrians arrested thirteen Jews in Damascus, I wore a button that said, 'Free the Damascus 13,' which most of my classmates thought referred to an underground offshoot of the Chicago 7."

From Beirut to Jerusalem is divided into two sections consisting of discussions of Beirut and of Jerusalem, corresponding to Friedman's assignments first as Beirut bureau chief and later as Jerusalem bureau chief for the *New York Times.* "Mr. Friedman is different when writing of Beirut than he is when writing of Jerusalem," commented Roger Rosenblatt in the *New York Times Book Review.* "When he arrives in Jerusalem for the second stage of his assignment, and for the second half of the book, he becomes the political and historical analyst. Reporting from Beirut, he is, for the most part, Pandemonium's correspondent, detailing scenes of pathos and hysteria." Friedman concluded in *From Beirut to Jerusalem* that the situation in the Middle East is not hopeless, but will require the intervention of the United States for its resolution. "Only a real friend tells you the truth about yourself," he wrote. "An American friend has to help jar these people out of their fantasies by constantly holding up before their eyes the mirror of reality."

Rosenblatt praised Friedman's treatment of his subject. "For a writer to appear evenhanded discussing the Jews and Arabs in this situation takes little more than giving each equal space in print and ascribing as many errors and atrocities to one as to the other. Mr. Friedman, who leaves no question as to the ardor of his Jewishness, is more interestingly evenhanded in that he rarely makes judgments on specific actions. When he delivers opinions, the judgments are so cosmic and melancholy that the question of fairness does not arise. First and last he is a reporter." Conor Cruise O'Brien asserted in the *New York Times,* "I warmly recommend *From Beirut to Jerusalem.* But I do have some reservations. Mr. Friedman is splendid when he is interpreting events of which he has firsthand experience. His grasp on the previous history of the Arab-Israeli conflict is not so sure." O'Brien cited a section of the book that documents

Egyptian President Anwar el-Sadat's efforts to negotiate a peace treaty with Israel only after waging war in 1973. O'Brien contended that Sadat made an unreciprocated attempt for peace in 1971. "Most Israelis have forgotten that episode," O'Brien said. "It is odd that so staunch a critic of Israel as Mr. Friedman should share in that Israeli amnesia."

Over the years, Friedman has expanded his focus to encompass not only the Middle East, but also the entire world. The hotly debated subject of globalization formed the thesis for his book *The Lexus and the Olive Tree: Understanding Globalization.* In it, he writes that, because it is driven by technology, globalization is inevitable; and he discusses the changes, some of them painful, that technology brings as the world becomes smaller and more interconnected. "We all increasingly know how each other lives. And when we all increasingly know how each other lives, we all start to demand the same things. And when we don't get them, we get mad. . . . Oh, in globalization you get mad!" He further sees globalization and access to technology as empowering the individual.

Partly because of its timeliness and partly because of its controversial topic, *The Lexus and the Olive Tree* received massive critical attention from the business, political, and technology communities, as well as the literary community. *New York Times* critic Richard Eder called it "a spirited and imaginative exploration of our new order of economic globalization." Robert A. Simons went further in his *Appraisal* evaluation of the book, stating in a 2004 review: "The book was written before [the terrorist attacks of] 9/11, but the basic premise of the book is robust enough to withstand the shock of that terrorist calamity to the international capital markets. In some ways, Friedman foresaw and characterized the possibility of a major terrorist event (backlash) and its implications."

The Lexus and the Olive Tree earned Friedman another Overseas Press Club award in 2000, and in 2002 he won his third Pulitzer Prize. By this time, Friedman had gained the status of a guru on not only the Middle East but also international trends as a whole. He added to this reputation with his 2005 book, *The World Is Flat: A Brief History of the Twenty-first Century.* A kind of follow-up to his previous book in which he discussed globalization, in *The World Is Flat* he declares that the Internet is effectively creating a "flat" economy in which the location of workers is irrelevant so long as they have access to computers and the World Wide Web. An added caveat is that workers need to be technologically skilled, a need that is becoming a chronic problem in the United States. The exponential growth of this phenomenon since the 1990s has made such things possible as call centers located in India that serve customers in real time online in the United States. While such a dramatic change in the global economy will no doubt result in growing pains for America as some developing countries abroad take advantage of the technology, overall Friedman sees this as a positive development. "In the Friedman worldview," related Justin Fox in a *Fortune* article, "revolutions are mostly good things, so *The World Is Flat* is imbued with a winning optimism." "This is a very important and very readable book," concluded Monica Bay *Law Technology News,* "that brings to life how our world is changing dramatically through technology."

BIOGRAPHICAL AND CRITICAL SOURCES:

BOOKS

Friedman, Thomas L., *From Beirut to Jerusalem,* Farrar, Straus (New York, NY), 1989.
Friedman, Thomas L., *The Lexus and the Olive Tree: Understanding Globalization,* Thorndike Press (Thorndike, ME), 1999.

PERIODICALS

Appraisal, January, 2004, Robert A. Simons, review of *The Lexus and the Olive Tree: Understanding Globalization,* p. 80.
Fortune, September 19, 2005, Justin Fox, "Rockin' in the Flat World: He Dazzles Crowds. He Brews Conventional Wisdom. He Charms CEOs. And He Drives Some People Crazy. Meet Tom Friedman, the Oracle of the Global Century," p. 154.
Law Technology News, July, 2005, Monica Bay, "Technology & the Global Village."
New York Times, July 6, 1989, Conor Cruise O'Brien, review of *From Beirut to Jerusalem;* April 26, 1999, Richard Eder, "The Global Village Is Here. Resist at Your Peril," review of *The Lexus and the Olive Tree,* p. E8.
New York Times Book Review, July 9, 1989, Roger Rosenblatt, review of *From Beirut to Jerusalem,* pp. 1, 26.

ONLINE

Thomas L. Friedman Home Page, http://www.thomaslfriedman.com/ (January 10, 2006).

FRIEDMAN, Thomas Loren
See FRIEDMAN, Thomas L.

*   *   *

FRISCH, Max 1911-1991
(Max Rudolf Frisch)

PERSONAL: Born May 15, 1911, in Zurich-Hottgen, Switzerland; died of cancer, April 4, 1991, in Zurich, Switzerland; son of Franz Bruno (an architect) and Lina (Wildermuth) Frisch; married Gertrud Anna Constance von Meyenburg (an architecture student), July 30, 1942 (divorced, 1959); married Marianne Öllers, December, 1968 (divorced); children: (first marriage) Ursula, Hans Peter, Charlotte. *Education:* Attended University of Zurich, 1931-33; Federal Institute of Technology, Zurich, diploma in architecture, 1940.

CAREER: Freelance journalist for various Swiss and German newspapers, including *Neue Zürcher Zeitung* and *Frankfurter Zeitung,* beginning 1933; architect in Zurich, Switzerland, 1945-55; full-time writer, 1955-1991. *Military service:* Swiss Army, 1939-45, served as cannoneer and later as border guard on the Austrian and Italian frontiers.

MEMBER: Deutsche Akademie für Sprache und Dichtung, Akademie der Künste, PEN, American Academy and Institute of Arts and Letters (honorary member), American Academy of Arts and Sciences (honorary member), Comunita degli Scrittori.

AWARDS, HONORS: Conrad Ferdinand Meyer Prize, 1938; Rockefeller Foundation grant for drama, 1951; Georg Büchner Prize, German Academy of Language and Poetry, 1958; Literature Prize of the City of Zurich, 1958; Literature Prize of Northrhine-Westphalia, 1963; Prize of the City of Jerusalem, 1965; Grand Prize, Swiss Schiller Foundation, 1974; Peace Prize, German Book Trade, 1976; Commandeur de l'Ordre des Arts et des Lettres, 1985; Common Wealth Award, Modern Language Association of America, 1986; International Neustadt Prize for Literature, University of Oklahoma, 1987. Has received honorary doctorates from the City University of New York, 1982, Bard College, Philipps University (Marburg, Germany), and Technische Universität (Berlin).

WRITINGS:

NOVELS

Jürg Reinhart: Eine sommerliche Schicksalsfahrt, Deutsche Verlags-Anstalt (Stuttgart, Germany), 1934, revised edition published as *J'adore ce qui me brule; oder, Die Schwierigen,* Atlantis (Zurich, Switzerland), 1943, 2nd revised edition published as *Die Schwierigen; oder, J'adore ce qui me brule,* Atlantis (Zurich, Switzerland), 1957.

Antwort aus der Stille: Eine Erzählung aus den Bergen (title means "Answer Out of the Silence: A Tale from the Mountains"), Deutsche Verlags-Anstalt (Stuttgart, Germany), 1937.

Bin; oder, Die Reise nach Peking (title means "Am; or, the Trip to Peking"), Atlantis (Zurich, Switzerland), 1945.

Stiller, Suhrkamp (Frankfurt am Main, Germany), 1954, Reclam (Leipzig, Germany), 1986, translation by Michael Bullock published as *I'm Not Stiller,* Abelard (New York, NY), 1958, with a new foreword by Michael Bullock, Harcourt (San Diego, CA), 1994.

Homo Faber, Suhrkamp (Frankfurt am Main, Germany), 1957, translation by Michael Bullock published as *Homo Faber: A Report,* Abelard (New York, NY), 1959, Harcourt (San Diego, CA), 1994.

Meine Name sei Gantenbein, Suhrkamp (Frankfurt am Main, Germany), 1964, translation by Michael Bullock published as *A Wilderness of Mirrors,* Methuen (London, England), 1965, Random House (New York, NY), 1966, same translation published as *Gantenbein,* Harcourt (San Diego, CA), 1982.

Montauk, Suhrkamp (Frankfurt am Main, Germany), 1975, translation by Geoffrey Skelton published as *Montauk,* Harcourt (New York, NY), 1976.

Der Mensch erscheint im Holozän, Suhrkamp (Frankfurt am Main, Germany), 1979, translation by Geoffrey Skelton published as *Man in the Holocene: A Story,* Harcourt (New York, NY), 1980.

Blaubart, Suhrkamp (Frankfurt am Main, Germany), 1982, translation by Geoffrey Skelton published as *Bluebeard,* Harcourt (San Diego, CA), 1983.

PLAYS

Nun singen sie wieder: Versuch eines Requiems (two-act; title means "Now They Sing Again: An Attempt at a Requiem"; first produced at the Schauspielhaus, Zurich, March 29, 1945), Schwabe (Switzerland), 1946, translation by David Lommen published as *Now They Sing Again* in *Contemporary German Theatre,* edited by Michael Roloff, Avon (New York, NY), 1972.

Santa Cruz: Eine Romanz (five-act; first produced at the Schauspielhaus, Zurich, March 7, 1946), Suhrkamp (Frankfurt am Main, Germany), 1946.

Die chinesische Mauer: Eine Farce (also see below; first produced at the Schauspielhaus, Zurich, October 10, 1946), Schwabe (Switzerland), 1947, 2nd revised edition, 1972, translation by James L. Rosenberg published as *The Chinese Wall,* Hill & Wang (New York, NY), 1961.

Als der Kriege zu Ende war: Schauspiel (also see below; title means "When the War Was Over"; first produced at the Schauspielhaus, Zurich, January 8, 1948), Schwabe (Switzerland), 1949, edited by Stuart Friebert, Dodd (New York, NY), 1967.

Graf Öderland: Ein Spiel in Zehn Bildern (also see below; title means "Count Öderland: A Play in Ten Scenes"; first produced at the Schauspielhaus, Zurich, February 10, 1951; produced in Washington, D.C., at Arena Stage as *A Public Prosecutor Is Sick of It All,* 1973), Suhrkamp (Frankfurt am Main, Germany), 1951, revised edition published as *Graf Öderland: Eine Moritat in zwölf Bildern,* Suhrkamp (Frankfurt am Main, Germany), 1963, edited by George Salamon, Harcourt (New York, NY), 1966.

Don Juan; oder, die Liebe zur Geometrie: Eine Komödie in fünf Akten (also see below; title means "Don Juan; or, The Love of Geometry: A Comedy in Five Acts"; first produced at the Schauspielhaus, Zurich, May 5, 1953), Suhrkamp (Frankfurt am Main, Germany), 1953.

Herr Biedermann und die Brandstifter: Hörspiel (also see below; radio play; first produced in Germany, 1953; first stage adaptation produced as *Biedermann und die Brandstifter: Eine Lehrstück ohne Lehre, mit einem Nachspiel* at the Schauspielhaus, Zurich, March 29, 1958; produced in London as *The Fire Raisers,* 1961; produced at the Maidman Playhouse as *The Firebugs,* February, 1963), Suhrkamp (Frankfurt am Main, Germany), 1958, translation by Michael Bullock published as *The Fire Raisers: A Morality without Moral, with an Afterpiece,* Methuen (London, England), 1962, translation by Mordecai Gorelick published as *The Firebugs: A Learning Play without a Lesson,* Hill & Wang (New York, NY), 1963.

Die grosse Wut des Philipp Hotz (also see below; one-act; first produced at the Schauspielhaus, Zurich, March 29, 1958; produced at the Barbizon-Plaza Theatre as *The Great Fury of Philipp Hotz,* November, 1969), translation published as *Philipp Hotz's Fury* in *Esquire,* October, 1962.

Andorra: Stück in zwölf Bildern (also see below; one-act radio play; first broadcast in West Germany, 1959; stage adaptation first produced at the Schauspielhaus, November 2, 1961; produced on Broadway at the Biltmore Theatre, February 9, 1963), Suhrkamp (Frankfurt am Main, Germany), 1962, version edited by Peter Hutchinson published by Routledge (London, England), 1994, translation by Michael Bullock published as *Andorra: A Play in Twelve Scenes,* Hill & Wang (New York, NY), 1964; revived Off-Broadway, 2002.

Three Plays (contains *The Fire Raisers, Count Öderland,* and *Andorra*), translation by Michael Bullock, Methuen (London, England), 1962, with an introduction by Peter Löffler, Ronsdale Press (Vancouver, British Columbia, Canada), 2002.

Zurich-Transit: Skizze eines Films (television play; first produced on German television, January, 1966), Suhrkamp (Frankfurt am Main, Germany), 1966.

Three Plays (contains *Don Juan; or, the Love of Geometry: A Comedy in Five Acts, The Great Rage of Philipp Hotz,* and *When the War Was Over*), translation by J.L. Rosenberg, Hill & Wang (New York, NY), 1967.

Biografie: Ein Spiel (also see below; two-act; first produced at the Schauspielhaus, Zurich, February 1, 1968), Suhrkamp (Frankfurt am Main, Germany), 1967, revised edition, 1968, translation by Michael Bullock published as *Biography: A Game,* Hill & Wang (New York, NY), 1969.

Four Plays: The Great Wall of China, Don Juan; or, the Love of Geometry, Philipp Hotz's Fury, Biography: a Game, translation by Michael Bullock, Methuen (London, England), 1969.

Rip van Winkle: Hörspiel (radio play; first produced in Germany, 1953), Reclam (Stuttgart, Germany), 1969.

Triptychon: Drei szenische Bilder, Suhrkamp (Frankfurt am Main, Germany), 1978, translation by Geoffrey Skelton published as *Triptych: Three Scenic Panels,* Harcourt (New York, NY), 1981.

Also author of plays *Stahl* (title means "Steel"), 1927, and *Judith,* 1948, and *Herr Quixote,* a radio play, 1955.

OTHER

Geschrieben im Grenzdienst 1939, [Germany], 1940.

Blätter aus dem Brotsack (diary; title means "Pages from the Knapsack"), Atlantis (Zurich, Switzerland), 1940.

Marion und die Marionetten: Ein Fragment, Gryff-Presse (Basel, Switzerland), 1946.

Das Tagebuch mit Marion (title means "Diary with Marion"), Atlantis (Zurich, Switzerland), 1947, revised and expanded version published as *Tagebuch, 1946-1949,* Drömer Knaur (Munich, Germany), 1950, translation by Geoffrey Skelton published as *Sketchbook, 1946-49,* Harcourt (New York, NY), 1977.

(With Lucius Burckhardt and Markus Kutter) *Achtung, die Schweiz: Ein Gespräch über unsere Lage und ein Vorschlag zur Tat,* Handschin (Basel, Switzerland), 1956.

(With Lucius Burckhardt and Markus Kutter) *Die Neue Stadt: Beiträge zur Diskussion,* Handschin (Basel, Switzerland), 1956.

Ausgewählte Prosa, edited by Stanley Corngold, Suhrkamp (Frankfurt am Main, Germany), 1961, Harcourt (New York, NY), 1968.

Stücke, two volumes, Suhrkamp (Frankfurt am Main, Germany), 1962.

(Author of texts with Kurt Hirschfeld and Oskar Waelterlin) Teo Otto, *Skizzen eines Bühnenbildners: 33 Zeichnungen,* Tschudy (St. Gallen, Switzerland), 1964.

Öffentlichkeit als Partner (essays), Suhrkamp (Frankfurt am Main, Germany), 1967.

Erinnerungen an Brecht, Friedenauer (West Berlin, Germany), 1968.

Dramaturgisches: Ein Briefwechsel mit Walter Höllerer, Literarisches Colloquium (West Berlin, Germany), 1969.

(With Rudolf Immig) *Der Mensch zwischen Selbstentfremdung und Selbstverwirklichung,* Calwer (Stuttgart, Germany), 1970.

Glück: Eine Erzählung, Brunnenturm-Presse, 1971.

Wilhelm Tell für die Schule, Suhrkamp (Frankfurt am Main, Germany), 1971.

Tagebuch, 1966-71, Suhrkamp (Frankfurt am Main, Germany), 1972, translation by Geoffrey Skelton published as *Sketchbook, 1966-71,* Harcourt (New York, NY), 1974.

Dienstbuchlein, Suhrkamp (Frankfurt am Main, Germany), 1974.

Stich-Worte, Suhrkamp (Frankfurt am Main, Germany), 1975.

(With Hartmut von Hentig) *Zwei Reden zum Friedenspreis des Deutschen Buchhandels 1976,* Suhrkamp (Frankfurt am Main, Germany), 1976.

Gesammelte Werke in zeitlicher Folge, six volumes, Suhrkamp (Frankfurt am Main, Germany), 1976.

Frisch: Kritik, Thesen, Analysen, Francke (Bern, Switzerland), 1977.

Erzählende Prosa, 1939-1979, Volk und Welt (West Berlin, Germany), 1981.

Forderungen des Tages, Suhrkamp (Frankfurt am Main, Germany), 1983.

Novels, Plays, Essays, edited by Rolf Kieser, foreword by Peter Demetz, Continuum (New York, NY), 1989.

Schweize ohne Armee?: Ein Palavar (title means "Switzerland without an Army? A Palaver"), Limmat (Zurich, Switzerland), 1989.

Schweiz als Heimat?: Versuche über 50 Jahre, edited and with an afterword by Walter Obschlager, Suhrkamp (Frankfurt am Main, Germany), 1990.

"Ich stelle mir vor": ein Lesebuch, edited by Rof Niederhauser, Suhrkamp (Frankfurt am Main, Germany), 1995.

(With Friedrich Dürrenmatt) *Briefwechsel,* with an essay by Peter Rüedi, Diogenes (Zurich, Switzerland), 1998.

Jetzt ist Sehenzeit: Briefe, Notate, Dukumente 1943-1963, edited and with an afterword by Julian Schütt, Suhrkamp (Frankfurt am Main, Germany), 1998.

(With Uwe Johnson) *Der Briefwechsel: Max Frisch, Uwe Johnson, 1964-1983,* edited by Eberhard Fahlke, Suhrkamp (Frankfurt am Main, Germany), 1999.

Im übrigen bin ich immer völlig allein: Briefwechsel mit der Mutter 1933: Eishockeyweltmeisterschaft in Prag, edited by Walter Obschlager, Suhrkamp (Frankfurt am Main, Germany), 2000.

(With Carl Zuckmayer and Carl Jacob Burckhardt) *Die Briefwechsel mit Carl Jacob Burckhardt und Max Frisch: mit einer Dokumentation,* edited by Claudia Mertz-Rychner, Röhrig (St. Ingbert, Germany), 2000.

Jetzt—Max Frisch: mit zahlreichen Fotos, Dokumenten und Zeichnungen, edited by Luis Bolliger, Walter Obschlager, and Julian Schütt, Suhrkamp (Frankfurt am Main, Germany), 2001.

Author of annotations to *Sieben Lithographien,* by Robert S. Gessner, Hürlimann (Zurich, Switzerland), 1952; author of foreword to *Wir selber bauen unsere Stadt: Ein Hinweis auf die Möglichkeiten staatlicher Baupolitik,* by Markus Kutter and Lucius Burckhardt, Handschin (Basel, Switzerland), 1956; author of afterword to *Drei Gedichten,* by Bertold Brecht, [Zurich], 1959; contributor to *Gesammelte Werke,* Volume 1, Atlantis (Zurich, Switzerland), 1961, and *Siamo italiani/Die Italiener: Gespräche mit italienischen Arbeitern in der Schweiz,* EVZ Verlag (Zurich, Switzerland), 1965; author of preface to *Die grossen Städte: Was sie zerstört und was sie retten kann,* by Gody Suter, Lübbe (Bergisch Gladbach, Germany), 1966; author of postscript to *Wie ich mir die Zukunft vorstelle: Gedanken ueber Fortschritt, friedliche Koexistenz und geistige Freiheit,* by Andrei Sakharov, Diogenes (Zurich, Switzerland), 1969. Contributor to periodicals in West Germany and Switzerland, including *Neue Schweizer Rundschau, Der Spiegel,* and *Atlantis;* contributor to newspapers, including *Neue Zürcher Zeitung* and *Süddeutsche Zeitung.*

SIDELIGHTS: Along with fellow Swiss dramatist Friedrich Dürrenmatt, Max Frisch "has been a major force in German drama for the generation since 1945," Arrigo Subiotto declared in *The German Theatre: A Symposium.* Best known for such works as *I'm Not Stiller* and *The Firebugs,* Frisch is esteemed as both a novelist and playwright. Winning numerous literary awards, including the Georg Büchner Prize and Neustadt International Prize, he was also a perennial candidate for the Pulitzer Prize for several years. His writing, characterized by its surrealistic style, "is a sort of poetry," Joseph McLellan remarked in the *Washington Post Book World,* "but a poetry of the mind rather than the senses—sparse and austere, with every detail chosen for its resonances." Several critics have commented on not only the remarkable consistency of this style, which *Dictionary of Literary Biography* contributor Wulf Koepke thought was "discernable since the early 1940s," but also on Frisch's inventiveness in expressing "a single theme: the near impossibility of living truthfully," Sven Birkerts concluded in his *New Republic* article.

As a student of German literature at the University of Zurich, Frisch admired such writers as Albin Zollinger and Gottfried Keller. His father's death, however, made it necessary for him to leave school to support himself and his mother. Becoming a freelance journalist for various German and Swiss newspapers, he traveled widely in Europe throughout the 1930s. During this time, Frisch also wrote fiction; but, as Koepke notes, he "grew increasingly disenchanted with his writing, and in 1937 he burned all his manuscripts." Opting for a more utilitarian career, he temporarily abandoned his writing goals to attend architecture classes at the Federal Institute of Technology in Zurich, where he received his diploma in 1940. However, he was not able to refrain totally from writing, and, while serving as a border guard in the Swiss army, he wrote *Jürg Reinhart: Eine sommerliche Schicksalsfahrt, Antwort aus der Stille: Eine Erzählung aus den Bergen, Blätter aus dem Brotsack,* and *Bin; oder, die Reise nach Peking.*

These lesser-known works, considering they were written during the time of Hitler's Third Reich, "astound the reader by their absolutely apolitical character," observed Mona and Gerhard Knapp in *World Literature Today.* Frisch was by no means unconcerned with the war's effects, however. Characterized by *New York Times Book Review* contributor Richard Gilman as "politically liberal, a pacifist," the author "was very much aware of his own unique position regarding the war; as a Swiss, apparently unaffected by the conflict surrounding his own country, Frisch could only attempt to present the lessons of the war from a bipartisan point of view," Manfred Jurgensen observed in *Perspectives on Max Frisch.* This is precisely what the dramatist attempts to do in his first plays written after the war.

Invited in 1945 by the director of the Zurich Schauspielhaus, Kurt Hirschfeld, to write plays for his theater, the author's *Nun singen sie wieder: Versuch eines Requiems* ("Now They Sing Again: An Attempt at a Requiem") explores prejudice by placing characters from both the Axis and Allied countries into the world of the afterlife, where they become equals. In his next play about the war, *Als der Krieg zu Ende war* ("When the War Was Over"), Frisch writes of a German woman who falls in love with a Russian soldier, demonstrating, as Carol Petersen said in his book, *Max Frisch,* "that by true human feelings all kinds of prejudices can and must be overcome."

However, "Frisch has no real hope that [such social] evils can be remedied," remarked Koepke, and his plays and novels are therefore largely pessimistic. For example, in *The Theater of Protest and Paradox: Developments in the Avant-Garde Drama,* George Wellwarth noted that "Frisch's two best plays, [*The Chinese Wall*] and [*The Firebugs: A Learning Play without a Lesson*], are consciously foredoomed pleas for a better world. The irony implicit in them no longer sounds like the scornful laughter of the gods we hear in Dürrenmatt; it sounds like the self-reproaching wailing of the damned." Underlying this pessimism is, as Jurgensen remarked, Frisch's frustration with "man's incorrigible selfishness and his inability or unwillingness to learn, to change, to think dynamically." According to Petersen, the lesson of *The Chinese Wall* is therefore that "freedom is only in the realm of the spirit; for, in the real world, the possessors of power end up by doing the same things over and over again."

Approaching this theme from another angle in what *World Literature Today* contributor Adolf Muschg calls Frisch's "most successful play internationally," *The Firebugs* creates a character who, instead of trying to prevent disaster, actually fosters it. In this play, a weak-willed hair lotion manufacturer named Gottlieb Biedermann is unable to admit to himself the true intentions of two arsonists, and knowingly allows them to enter and destroy his home. Several interpretations of the political implications of this play have been proposed, as Subiotto explained: "[*The Firebugs*] can be seen as a metaphor of Hitler's legitimate 'seizure of power' or of the way in which the nations of the world are playing with nuclear bombs as deterrents. . . . It also offers a 'model' of liberal societies allowing freedom of action, in the name of liberty, to extremist elements in their midst (whether of right or left) whose avowed aim is to destroy those societies." According to Koepke, the author endorses the interpretation that *The Firebugs* is about "the weakness of capitalist society." *The Firebugs* is also significant for its development of Frisch's "theme of the true identity behind an artificial mask, the de-

struction of false conventions, and the feeling of the self from deeply ingrained prejudices," Alex Natan wrote in his introduction to *German Men of Letters: Twelve Literary Essays.*

According to the Knapps, *Andorra: A Play in Twelve Scenes,* along with *The Firebugs,* "catapulted [Frisch] to international theatrical prominence." *Andorra* revolves around the theme of anti-Semitism to illustrate the imposition of images. The story concerns the deception of a schoolteacher, living in fictional Andorra, who hides the identity of his illegitimate son Andri by telling his neighbors that Andri is a Jewish boy whom he has saved from the oppressive "Blacks." With the increasing strength of the Blacks, the Andorrans begin to impose more and more stereotypes on Andri until he eventually accepts himself as Jewish. Even when he learns the truth about who he really is, Andri is unable to shed this false identity; and, when the Blacks invade Andorra, he chooses to die under their persecution.

The struggle for self-truth in a world which prefers the stereotypes and simplicity of the image to an authentic existence is also evident in *Don Juan; or, the Love of Geometry.* Here, in what Petersen called "an uncommonly clever, wittily pointed play, which offers a broad view of the relativity of all human sentiment," Frisch twists the legend of Don Juan by describing Juan as a lover of geometry who is forced into the role of philanderer by the demands and expectations of society. He actually prefers the logic and precision of geometry to the capricious ways of the women who surround him. Compared to the traditional version of Don Juan, critics like Petersen believed that "the twentieth-century man, inclined to rationalism, can more readily recognize himself in Frisch's Don Juan."

The three novels that deal with the theme of identity on its most introspective, individual level are *I'm Not Stiller, Homo Faber: A Report,* and *A Wilderness of Mirrors.* Along with a number of other critics, Charles Hoffman, a contributor to *The Contemporary Novel in German: A Symposium,* felt that with these books, Frisch "has created three of the most important novels of [the mid-nineteenth century]. Taken together, these books are perhaps the most meaningful [in] recent German writing." The years in which they were written, from 1954 to 1964, were also "of singular importance in establishing Frisch's international reputation," added the Knapps.

Like *Don Juan, Homo Faber* appeals to the modern man, but on a much more serious note. Submerging himself in a love of technology over actual human emotions, Frisch's protagonist, engineer Walter Faber, unwittingly enters into a relationship with a woman whom he later discovers to be his illegitimate daughter. Because he cannot face the emotions that result from this discovery, Faber "is punished for his 'blindness' by her loss" when she dies of a snake bite, explained the Knapps. In this description of a man who becomes alienated from his own identity through his reverence for modern technology, "Frisch has captured that essential anguish of modern man which we find in the best of Camus," Richard Plant declared in *Spectator*. But *Homo Faber* is also one of Frisch's more optimistic works because, noted Koepke, in the "last period of his life, characterized by a growing awareness of human existence, [Faber] not only comes into contact with his own past failures and their long-term consequences but also begins to see the truth of nontechnological realities."

I'm Not Stiller "established [for Frisch] a claim to major status in the history of the novel in post-war Germany and Switzerland," Michael Butler claimed in his *The Novels of Max Frisch*. The book is Frisch's most critically acclaimed novel concerning the theme of escape from the self. Told mostly through the point-of-view of the sculptor Anatol Stiller, *I'm Not Stiller* is the story of a man who assumes the identity of an American named White in an effort to flee his feelings of failure as an artist, husband, and lover. Confronted with his true identity by the Swiss government, which has accused him of having worked with the Communists, Stiller is forced to face his true identity. The resulting personal struggle, which Frisch chronicles in Stiller's journal, "consumes not only all his own moral and artistic energy," said the Knapps, "but also that of his frail wife Julika, who soon dies." The last section of *I'm Not Stiller* is told by Stiller's prosecutor, who moralizes: "As long as a person does not accept himself, he will always have the fear of being misunderstood and misconstrued by his environment." Although some critics, such as Plant, felt that the novel's "provocative idea [has] been spoiled . . . by excessive detail and over-decoration," a number of others thought that *I'm Not Stiller* is one of Frisch's best works. Butler declared, for example, that in *I'm Not Stiller* "Frisch suddenly produced a narrative work of unsuspected depth and fascination."

After *Montauk* the author's books betray his awareness of his advancing years. Koepke explained: "While in *Montauk* numerous quotes from Frisch's earlier works indicate self-acceptance, the past has become threatening in the last works. Old age and death are dominant themes, but even more prevalent may be regret of the past-one's own and that of the human race." For example, Jurgensen noted that in *Triptychon* "Frisch shows . . . how all acts, thoughts, and misunderstandings are repeated in death; death becomes the stage for re-enacting our lives. The finality does not lie in death but in our unthinking life, in our inability to do anything other than repeat ourselves." "*Triptychon*'s real subject is a social death," Jurgensen concluded, "in fact: the death of society."

Jurgensen also noted that this pessimistic theme is similar to that of *The Firebugs;* and Frisch's next book, *Man in the Holocene*, also resembles *The Firebugs* in its "unsettling notion that some rational, well-meaning force is actually *willing* catastrophe," according to *Nation* reviewer Arthur Sainer. In what McLellan called "a small book but a major achievement," *Man in the Holocene* relates the last few days in the life of a ageing man named Geiser who becomes trapped in his alpine valley home by a landslide. Battling against his own encroaching senility and a dwindling food supply, Geiser ironically passes up the chance to escape his isolation, eventually suffering from a stroke before he finally dies. *Man in the Holocene*, like *Triptychon*, reiterates Frisch's suspicion of the transience of the human race. McLellan explained it this way: in *Man in the Holocene* "the old man's life itself is being eroded, as are all men's lives—as is, perhaps, the life of the entire species."

Frisch returns to his more familiar theme of identity in *Bluebeard*. But, Sven Birkerts said in a *New Republic* review, the author "is not so much returning to earlier themes as he is bringing the preoccupations of a lifetime under a more calculated and intense pressure." As in *I'm Not Stiller,* the story's events are related by the protagonist, Dr. Schaad, through his memories about his trial. This time, the main character is accused of being a wife murderer, like the infamous Bluebeard, and this role is forced upon him to the point where he eventually assimilates it. Marga I. Weigel noted the similarity between Dr. Schaad's identity crisis and that of another Frisch character. Writing in *World Literature Today*, Weigel observed: "[Dr. Schaad] works himself more and more into the role of the murderer. He is now convinced he is the person others consider him to be-an attitude identical to the reaction of Andri in *Andorra*."

After Frisch's death in 1991, much of his correspondence was collected, edited, and published in several volumes, including *Briefwechsel*, which contains the correspondence between Frisch and Dürrenmatt, and *Der Briefwechsel: Max Frisch, Uwe Johnson, 1964-*

1983, which includes not only letters to and from Frisch and his friend (and sometimes editor) Johnson, but also over 150 pages of Johnson's manuscript notes on the second volume of Frisch's *Tagebuch.* "As an access to the thought and works of two of the most prominent German-language authors of the twentieth century," commented a reviewer in *World Literature Today,* "the volume marks a valuable contribution to our understanding" of this great writer.

BIOGRAPHICAL AND CRITICAL SOURCES:

BOOKS

Butler, Michael, *The Novels of Max Frisch,* Oswald Wolff (London, England), 1976.

Contemporary Literary Criticism, Thomson Gale (Detroit, MI), Volume 3, 1975; Volume 9, 1978; Volume 14, 1980; Volume 18, 1981; Volume 32, 1985; Volume 44, 1987.

Daemmrich, Horst S., and Diether H. Haenicke, *The Challenge of German Literature,* Wayne State University Press (Detroit, MI), 1971.

Dictionary of Literary Biography, Thomson Gale (Detroit, MI), Volume 69: *Contemporary German Fiction Writers,* 1988; Volume 124: *Twentieth-Century German Dramatists,* 1992.

Esslin, Martin, *Reflections: Essays on Modern Theatre,* Doubleday (New York, NY), 1969.

Garten, Hugh Frederic, *Modern German Drama,* Methuen (London, England), 1959.

Hayman, Ronald, *The German Theatre: A Symposium,* Barnes & Noble (New York, NY), 1975.

Heitner, Robert R., editor, *The Contemporary Novel in German: A Symposium,* University of Texas Press (Austin, TX), 1967.

Lumley, Frederick, *New Trends in 20th Century Drama,* Oxford University Press (New York, NY), 1967.

Natan, Alex, editor, *German Men of Letters: Twelve Literary Essays,* Volume 3, Oswald Wolff (London, England), 1968.

Petersen, Carol, *Max Frisch,* translated by Charlotte La Rue, Ungar (New York, NY), 1972.

Probst, Gerhard F., and Jay F. Bodine, editors, *Perspectives on Max Frisch,* University Press of Kentucky (Lexington, KY), 1982.

Weber, Brom, editor, *Sense and Sensibility in Twentieth-Century Writing,* Southern Illinois University Press (Carbondale, IL), 1970.

Weisstein, Ulrich, *Max Frisch,* Twayne (New York, NY), 1967.

Wellwarth, George, *The Theater of Protest and Paradox: Developments in the Avant-Garde Drama,* New York University Press (New York, NY), 1964.

White, Alfred D., *Max Frisch, the Reluctant Modernist,* E. Mellen Press (Lewiston, NY), 1995.

PERIODICALS

Back Stage, September 18, 1992, Irene Backalenick, review of *Andorra,* p. 52; January 1, 1993, Sy Syna, review of *The Firebugs,* p. 27.

Biography News, June, 1974.

Books Abroad, winter, 1968.

Chicago Sun-Times, May 5, 1974.

Chicago Tribune Book World, September 28, 1980.

Christian Science Monitor, February 12, 1968.

Forum for Modern Language Studies, July, 1982.

Germanic Review, fall, 1995, Peter C. Thornton, "Man the Maker: Max Frisch's *Homo Faber* and the Daedalus Myth," pp. 153-143.

German Life and Letters, October, 1974.

Los Angeles Times Book Review, August 10, 1980.

Modern Drama, December, 1975.

Nation, July 3, 1976; September 20, 1980, Arthur Sanier, review of *Man in the Holocene,* pp. 259-260.

New Republic, July 11, 1983, Sven Birkerts, review of *Bluebeard,* pp. 32-35.

New Statesman, August 6, 1982, Marion Glastonbury, review of *I'm Not Stiller,* p. 23.

New Yorker, May 24, 1976; July 11, 1977.

New York Review of Books, September 24, 1981.

New York Times, July 2, 1968; November 27, 1969; May 17, 1970; May 22, 1980, John Leonard, review of *Man in the Holocene,* section C, p. 25.

New York Times Book Review, February 20, 1966; April 28, 1974; May 16, 1976; May 27, 1976; April 3, 1977; March 19, 1978; May 11, 1980, Herbert Mitgang, "The Frischest Frisch," p. 51; June 22, 1980, George Stade, review of *Man in the Holocene,* pp. 1-2; July 10, 1983, review of *Bluebird,* p. 9; September 29, 1983.

Observer, July 25, 1982; March 13, 1983.

Saturday Review, April 12, 1958; May 7, 1960; February 26, 1966.

Spectator, April 11, 1958; May 7, 1960, Richard Plant, review of *Homo Faber: A Report.*

Swiss News, April, 2001, Michael Maupin, "Remembering Max Frisch," p. 20.

Times (London, England), February 24, 1983.

Times Literary Supplement, November 11, 1965; January 25, 1968; September 29, 1972; September 12, 1980; June 4, 1982; July 30, 1982.

Tulane Drama Review, March, 1962.

Village Voice, July 11, 1968.

Washington Post Book World, July 18, 1976; July 27, 1980, Joseph McClellan, review of *Man in the Holocene;* July 17, 1983, Paul West, review of *Bluebeard,* p. 9.

World Literature Today, spring, 1977; spring, 1979; spring 1983; autumn, 1984; autumn, 1986; spring, 1996, Theodore Ziolkowski, review of *"Ich stelle mir vor": ein Lesebuch,* pp. 401-402; spring, 1999, Theodore Ziolkowski, review of *Briefwechsel,* p. 323; winter, 2000, review of *Der Briefwechsel: Max Frisch, Uwe Johnson, 1964-1983,* p. 152.

OBITUARIES:

PERIODICALS

Time, April 15, 1991, p. 52.

*   *   *

FRISCH, Max Rudolf
   See FRISCH, Max

*   *   *

FRY, Christopher 1907-

PERSONAL: Born Christopher Fry Harris, December 18, 1907, in Bristol, England; son of Charles John (an architect) and Emma Marguerite Fry (Hammond) Harris; married Phyllis Marjorie Hart, December 3, 1936 (died, 1987); children: one son. *Education:* Attended Bedford Modern School, Bedford, England, 1918-26. *Religion:* Church of England.

ADDRESSES: Home—The Toft, East Dean, near Chichester, West Sussex PO18 0JA, England. *Agent*—ACTAC Ltd., 16 Cadogan Ln., London SW1, England.

CAREER: Playwright, screenwriter, translator, critic. Bedford Froebel Kindergarten, teacher, 1926-27; Citizen House, Bath, England, actor and office worker, 1927; Hazelwood Preparatory School, Limpsfield, Surrey, England, schoolmaster, 1928-31; secretary to H. Rodney Bennett, 1931-32; Tunbridge Wells Repertory Players, founding director, 1932-35, 1940, 1944-46; Dr. Barnardo's Homes, lecturer and editor of school magazine, 1934-39; Oxford Playhouse, director, 1940; Arts Theatre Club, London, England, director, 1945, staff dramatist, 1947. Visiting director, Oxford Playhouse, 1945-46, Arts Theatre Club, 1947. *Military service:* Pioneer Corps, 1940-44.

MEMBER: Dramatists Guild, Garrick Club.

AWARDS, HONORS: Shaw Prize Fund award, 1948, for *The Lady's Not for Burning*; William Foyle Poetry Prize, 1951, for *Venus Observed*; New York Drama Critics Circle Award, 1951, for *The Lady's Not for Burning,* 1952, for *Venus Observed,* and 1956, for *Tiger at the Gates*; Queen's Gold Medal for Poetry, 1962; Heinemann Award, Royal Society of Literature, 1962, for *Curtmantle*; D.A., 1966, and Honorary Fellow, 1988, Manchester Polytechnic, 1966; Writers Guild Best British Television Dramatization award nomination, 1971, for "The Tenant of Wildfell Hall"; Doctor of Letters, Lambeth and Oxford University, 1987, De Monfort University and University of Sussex, both in 1994; Fellow and recipient of Benson Silver medal, Royal Society of Literature, 2000.

WRITINGS:

PLAYS

(With Monte Crick and F. Eyton) *She Shall Have Music,* first produced in London, England, 1934.

Open Door, first produced in London, England, 1936.

The Boy with a Cart: Cuthman, Saint of Sussex, (first produced in Coleman's Hatch, Sussex, England, 1938; produced in the West End at Lyric Theatre, January 16, 1950), Oxford University Press (Oxford, England), 1939, 2nd edition, Muller (London, England), 1956.

(Author of libretto) *Robert of Sicily: Opera for Children,* first produced in 1938.

The Tower (pageant), first produced at Tewkesbury Festival, Tewkesbury, England, July 18, 1939.

Thursday's Child: A Pageant (first produced in London, 1939), Girl's Friendly Press (London, England), 1939.

(Author of libretto) *Seven at a Stroke: A Play for Children,* first produced in 1939.

A Phoenix Too Frequent (first produced in London at Mercury Theatre, April 25, 1946; produced on Broadway, 1950), Hollis & Carter (London, England), 1946, Oxford University Press (Oxford, England), 1949.

The Firstborn (broadcast on radio, 1947; first produced at Gateway Theatre, Edinburgh, Scotland, September 6, 1948), Cambridge University Press (Cambridge, England), 1946, 3rd edition, Oxford University Press (Oxford, England), 1958.

The Lady's Not for Burning (first produced in London at Arts Theatre, March 10, 1948; produced in the West End, May 11, 1949, produced on Broadway at Royale Theatre, November 8, 1950), Oxford University Press (Oxford, England), 1949, revised edition, 1973.

Thor, with Angels (first produced at Chapter House, Canterbury, England, June, 1948; produced in the West End at Lyric Theatre, September 27, 1951), H.J. Goulden, 1948, Oxford University Press (Oxford, England), 1949.

Venus Observed (first produced in London at St. James Theatre, January 18, 1950; produced on Broadway at Century Theatre, February 13, 1952), Oxford University Press, 1950.

A Sleep of Prisoners (first produced in Oxford, England, at University Church, April 23, 1951; produced in London at St. Thomas's Church, May 15, 1951), Oxford University Press (Oxford, England), 1951, 2nd edition, 1965.

The Dark Is Light Enough: A Winter Comedy (first produced in the West End at Aldwych Theatre, April, 30, 1954; produced on Broadway at ANTA Theatre, February 23, 1955) Oxford University Press (Oxford, England), 1954.

Curtmantle (first produced in Dutch in Tilburg, Netherlands, at Stadsschouwburg, March 1, 1961, produced on the West End at Aldwych Theatre, October 6, 1962), Oxford University Press (Oxford, England), 1961.

A Yard of Sun: A Summer Comedy (first produced at Nottingham Playhouse, Nottingham, England, July 11, 1970; produced on the West End at Old Vic Theatre, August 10, 1970), Oxford University Press (Oxford, England), 1970.

One Thing More, or Caedmon Construed (first produced at Chelmsford Cathedral, England, 1986; broadcast on radio, 1986), Oxford University Press (Oxford, England), 1985, Dramatists Play Service (New York, NY), 1987.

A Ringing of Bells, (first produced in a staged reading at the National Theatre in London, 2001), Samuel French (New York, NY), 2001.

Also author of the play "Youth of the Peregrines," produced at Tunbridge Wells with premiere production of George Bernard Shaw's "Village Wooing." Author of radio plays for "Children's Hour" series, 1939-40, and of "Rhineland Journey," 1948.

SCREENPLAYS AND TELEPLAYS

The Canary, British Broadcasting Corp. (BBC-TV), 1950.

The Queen Is Crowned (documentary), Universal, 1953.

(With Denis Cannan) *The Beggar's Opera,* British Lion, 1953.

Ben Hur, Metro-Goldwyn-Mayer, 1959.

Barabbas, Columbia Broadcasting Systems, 1961.

(With Jonathan Griffin, Ivo Perilli, and Vittorio Bonicelli) *The Bible: In the Beginning,* Twentieth Century-Fox, 1966.

The Tenant of Wildfell Hall, BBC-TV, 1968.

The Brontes of Haworth (four teleplays), BBC-TV, 1973.

The Best of Enemies, BBC-TV, 1976.

Sister Dora, BBC-TV, 1977.

Star over Bethlehem, BBC-TV, 1981.

TRANSLATOR AND ADAPTER

Ring round the Moon: A Charade with Music (adapted from *L'Invitation au Chateau* by Jean Anouilh; first produced in the West End at Globe Theatre, January 26, 1950), Oxford University Press (Oxford, England), 1950.

Jean Giraudoux, *Tiger at the Gates* (first produced in the West End at Apollo Theatre, October 3, 1955), Methuen, 1955, 2nd edition, 1961, Oxford University Press (Oxford, England), 1956; (produced as *The Trojan War Will Not Take Place*), London, 1983, Methuen (London, England), 1983.

Jean Anouilh, *The Lark* (first produced in the West End at Lyric Theatre, May 11, 1955; produced on Broadway at Longacre Theatre, November 17, 1955), Methuen, 1955 (London, England), Oxford University Press (New York, NY), 1956.

Duel of Angels (adapted from *Pour Lucrece* by Jean Giraudoux; first produced in the West End at Apollo Theatre, April 22, 1958; produced on Broadway at Helen Hayes Theatre, April 19, 1960), Methuen (London, England), 1958, Oxford University Press (New York, NY), 1959.

Jean Giraudoux, *Judith* (first produced in the West End at Her Majesty's Theatre, June 20, 1962), Methuen (London, England), 1962.

Sidonie Gabrielle Colette, *The Boy and the Magic,* Dobson (London, England), 1964, Putnam (New York, NY), 1965.

Henrik Ibsen, *Peer Gynt* (first produced at Chichester Festival Theatre, Chichester, England, May 13, 1970), Oxford University Press (Oxford University Press), 1970, revised edition, 1989.

Edmond Rostand, *Cyrano de Bergerac* (first produced at Chichester Festival Theatre, May 14, 1975), Oxford University Press (Oxford, England), 1975, reprinted, with an introduction by Fry, 1996.

OMNIBUS VOLUMES

Three Plays: The Firstborn; Thor, with Angels; A Sleep of Prisoners, Oxford University Press (Oxford, England), 1960.

(Translator) Jean Giraudoux, *Plays* (contains *Judith, Tiger at the Gates,* and *Duel of Angels*), Methuen (London, England), 1963.

Plays (contains *Thor, with Angels* and *The Lady's Not for Burning*), Oxford University Press (Oxford, England), 1969.

Plays (contains *The Boy with a Cart: Cuthman, Saint of Sussex; The Firstborn;* and *Venus Observed*), Oxford University Press (Oxford, England), 1970.

Plays (contains *A Sleep of Prisoners, The Dark Is Light Enough,* and *Curtmantle*), Oxford University Press (Oxford, England), 1971.

Selected Plays (contains *The Boy with a Cart: Cuthman, Saint of Sussex; A Phoenix Too Frequent; The Lady's Not for Burning; A Sleep of Prisoners;* and *Curtmantle*), Oxford University Press (Oxford, England), 1985.

OTHER

(Contributor) *An Experience of Critics and the Approach to Dramatic Criticism,* edited by Kaye Webb, Perpetua, 1952, Oxford University Press (Oxford, England), 1953.

(Author of libretto) *Crown of the Year* (cantata), first produced in 1958.

(Contributor) *The Modern Theatre,* edited by Robert W. Corrigan, Macmillan (London, England), 1964.

The Boat That Mooed (juvenile fiction), Macmillan (London, England), 1965.

(Contributor) *The Drama Bedside Book,* edited by H.F. Rubinstein, Atheneum (New York, NY), 1966.

(With Jonathan Griffin) *The Bible: Original Screenplay,* Pocket Books (New York, NY), 1966.

The Brontes of Haworth, two volumes, Davis-Poynter (London, England), 1975.

Root and Sky: Poetry from the Plays of Christopher Fry, edited by Charles E. Wadsworth and Jean G. Wadsworth, Godine (Boston, MA), 1975.

Can You Find Me: A Family History, Oxford University Press (Oxford, England), 1978.

(Adaptor) *Paradise Lost* (first produced in Chicago, 1978), Schott (Mainz, German), 1978.

Death Is a Kind of Love (lecture; drawings by Charles E. Wadsworth), Tidal Press (Cranberry Isles, ME), 1979.

(Author of introduction) *Charlie Hammond's Sketch Book,* Oxford University Press (Oxford, England), 1980.

Genius, Talent, and Failure (lecture), King's College (Cambridge, England), 1987.

(Author of foreword) *A Sprinkle of Nutmeg: Letters to Christopher Fry, 1943-45,* by Phyl Fry, Enitharmon Press (London, England), 1992.

The Early Days (lecture), Society for Theatre Research (London, England), 1997.

SIDELIGHTS: British playwright, screenwriter, translator, and critic Christopher Fry is perhaps best known for his elegant verse plays, which emerged in the 1940s and 1950s as a sharp contrast to the naturalism and realism popular since the late nineteenth century. When Fry's blank-verse comedy *The Lady's Not for Burning* first appeared on stage in London during the 1950s, it became an immediate sensation. According to Harold Hobson in *Drama:* "It is difficult to exaggerate the sense of freshness and excitement that swept through the theatrical world when *The Lady's Not for Burning,* with the extraordinary brilliance of the fancies, the conceits, and the imagination of its dialogue, the originality of its verse-form, and the joyous medieval paradox of its story seemed to shatter the by then somnolent reign of naturalism on the British stage." Derek Stanford recalled in *Christopher Fry: An Appreciation:* "Without the creaking machinery of any cranked-up manifesto, the plays of Fry appeared on the stage, receiving a progressive succession of applause. For the first time for several centuries, we were made to realise that here was a poet addressing the audience from the boards with that immediacy of effect which had seemed to have deserted the muse as far as its dramatic office was concerned. . . . Like a man who is conscious of no impediment, and does not anticipate embarrassing rebuffs, Fry spoke out with a power natural to him. He was heard—with surprise, with pleasure, and relief."

Fry's style attracted as many detractors as devotees; some thought his rapidly moving, glittering language masked weak plots and shallow characterizations. In a *Times Literary Supplement* review of *The Lady's Not for Burning,* a critic found the play "without the comparatively pedestrian power of developing character and situation," and added: "It is surprising how rich a play may be in fine speeches and yet be a bad play because the speeches alter nothing." But Stanford determined that "so readily magniloquent and rich, in fact, is Fry that in an age of verbal paucity his own Elizabethan munificence of diction appears to our 'austerity' reviewers as suspect. None of these critics, it is true, has been able to deny the impact of his language, but have rather tended to minimise its import by treating it as the playwright's sole talent." A 2002 London production of *The Lady's Not for Burning* prompted *Guardian* reviewer Lyn Gardner to remark: "The real surprise is that the verse turns out to be such an affable and accessible form and that the language is so exciting. Relax into it," she continued, "and it is like having your mind stroked by a velvet glove."

The Lady's Not for Burning, directed by and starring John Gielgud, was the first installment of a series of four comedies, each corresponding to a different season. The series continued with *Venus Observed* (autumn), *The Dark Is Light Enough* (winter), and concluded, twenty-two years after its commencement, with *A Yard of Sun* (summer). While the other plays, especially *Venus Observed,* received critical acclaim, none surpassed *The Lady's Not for Burning* in popularity. *The Lady's Not for Burning* is set in a somewhat fantastic medieval world, and primarily concerns two characters: Thomas, an embittered ex-soldier who wishes to die, and Jennet, a wealthy young orphan who loves life, but has been sentenced to burn on a trumped-up witchcraft charge so that the town may inherit her property. The play intertwines irony and comedy, with a dense mayor, his practical wife, and their two quarrelling sons all playing clownish roles. *Dictionary of Literary Biography* contributor Audrey Williamson described the play as "a lyric of spring: it has an April shimmer, like the dust of pollination shot by sunlight." Williamson continued: "There is a kind of golden haze about it that is penetrated by the occasional bawdiness of the humor: for Fry has combined the robustness of the Elizabethans with touches of the cheerful blasphemy that mingled with piety in the medieval morality play. But the sense of the abundance, mystery, and poetry of life is unimpaired."

Venus Observed involves an emotionally remote and aging duke who intends to choose a wife from his many ex-lovers. But in the process he becomes infatuated with the young woman his son also loves. The role of the elderly man was played by Laurence Olivier in London and Rex Harrison in New York; *Theatre Arts* contributor L.N. Roditte wrote of the character: "The Duke is a hero of considerable magnitude; his story, though mild and witty, has an element of tragedy. . . . [Fry] has created an extraordinary part that other great actors

will want to play." Although *Venus Observed* was well received by the public and critics, Fry's style again received criticism. According to *Saturday Review* contributor John Mason Brown: "Mr. Fry is blessed with one of the most delightful talents now contributing to the theatre. He has a wit, nimble and original; an agile and unpredictable mind, as playful as it is probing; and a love of language which can only be described as a lust." But Brown continued by explaining that Fry "is an anachronism, if you will; a fellow who has wandered from one Elizabethan age into another," and concluded: "Mr. Fry concentrates on all the sensuous splendors of the flesh, ignoring the skeleton of sustained ideas or dramatic structure." *New Republic* contributor Harold Clurman, however, felt differently: "Let no one say that Fry's work consists of playful, euphonious words and no more. The meaning is clear to anyone who will pay attention. . . . And the meaning . . . is historically or (socially) revealing. Fry's plays are poems of resignation in which tragic substance is flattened into lovely ornament."

The Dark Is Light Enough delves into the past, this time using the background of revolutions on the Hungarian border in 1848. The heroine, Countess Rosmarin, is an elderly lady who attempts to rescue her ex-son-in-law, an army deserter, from execution. While the play ends with the Countess's death, "the viewer senses a summer radiance on which winter has set its feathered touch, light and cold as the snowflakes descending outside the window," explained Williamson. In *Ariel,* Stanley Wiersma also described the conclusion as a positive one: "The Countess . . . finds warmth enough in the winter of our discontent, goodness enough in a wicked world, life enough in death." *Chicago Sunday Tribune* contributor F.E. Faverty noted a conflict between the plot and dialogue, however. "In spite of the heavy themes, the dialogue is light and sparkling," he wrote. "There is a quotable epigram on every page. Nonetheless, one's final impression is that there is too much talk and too little action." But Williamson admired the interplay: "Fry adapts his verse to his theme, conveying wisdom and a new verbal austerity," she continued. "It makes for a play of dramatic tension and fascination."

Fry's abhorrence of violence is an important part of *The Dark Is Light Enough.* Wiersma identified the play's themes as "violence as self-assertion, violence as loyalty to the state, violence as loyalty to God, and, finally, violence to be endured but not to be inflicted," and explains that the playwright sees such violence as "an infection with its own irrational necessities. The violence in the situation and within the people is moving toward a duel; who fights it or against whom is beside the point." Fry's answer to violence is love: love that endures pain but refuses to inflict it. Emil Roy, in his monograph on Fry, found this treatment unique: "Unlike most of his contemporaries, Fry has not given man's meanness, animality, and evil a central position in his work. If men are selfish, egoistic, and blind to love, it belongs to his more enlightened, self-controlled, and discerning characters to bring their understanding and tolerance to bear upon the pain and anguish that results."

A Yard of Sun ends the quartet; it deals with the return of two absent members of an Italian family: the black sheep and a betrayed friend. A *Times Literary Supplement* reviewer called the characters and situation "stereotyped" and claimed they "receive a thick coating of Fry's Christmas-tree versification which serves to convert clichés into fanciful imagery and camouflage the fact that no issue is being squarely faced." But according to Williamson, the play contains "a concentrated glow of language, pared to a new, more austere structure. The Italianate characterization is vivid and varied, and the story line taut and gripping." And a *Newsweek* reviewer wrote that *A Yard of Sun* "shimmers with poetry and affirms Fry's belief in a basically mystical Christian benevolence."

Yet Fry did not begin his career with *The Lady's Not for Burning,* nor did he confine his art to this quartet of plays. He had a moderate success in 1946 with the one-act *A Phoenix Too Frequent,* which, as a writer for *Contemporary Dramatists* reported, "was taken from the ancient tale of the young Roman widow romantically committed to a fast to the death in her husband's tomb until she and an equally romantic young soldier agree to substitute the husband's body for the corpse the soldier was guarding with his life." The critic continued: "With the lightest of touches, the widow decides for life, and youth and love supplant social convention and death, a joyful illustration of the life force at work." The playwright followed *Phoenix* with *The Firstborn,* a drama about the life of Moses which poignantly depicted the emotional toll inflicted on the famed Biblical patriarch in having to call down plagues upon the Egyptian people who had raised him. Fry eventually took his flair for writing Biblical characters to Hollywood, working on the screenplays for such epics as *Ben Hur, Barabbas,* and *The Bible.* As *Manchester Guardian Weekly* critic W.J. Weatherby noted, however, "When all the film work was done, he did not allow himself to be sucked further into the Hollywood dream world, but broke away and came home to England to begin again on his play about Henry [II, *Curtmantle.*]" Fry has also translated the plays of several French playwrights, in-

cluding Jean Anouilh and Edmond Rostand, and written scripts for several BBC television dramas, including *The Tenant of Wildfell Hall* and *The Brontes of Haworth.*

Fry also received critical acclaim for his 1951 drama, *A Sleep of Prisoners.* This play uses the dreams of soldiers being held prisoner in a church to illustrate several Old Testament stories which are "chosen to illustrate facets of the idea of violence," according to *Contemporary Dramatists.* A writer for *Contemporary Poets* praised Fry's *A Sleep of Prisoners* as "perhaps his most entirely successful piece."

In 2001, at the age of ninety-three, Fry published a dramatic tribute to the preceding one hundred years entitled *A Ringing of Bells.* Discussing a staged reading of this piece in London's National Theatre, *Spectator* writer Morley noted that "it managed in forty minutes to cover with wondrous poetic lyricism everything crucial about the twentieth century, from the first world war to the Big Bang theory of Stephen Hawking."

Overall, Stanford viewed Fry as a joyous freethinker in a narrow world: "In a universe often viewed as mechanic, he has posited the principle of mystery; in an age of necessitarian ethics, he has stood unequivocally for ideas of free-will. In theatre technique, he has gaily ignored the sacrosanct conventions of naturalistic drama; and in terms of speech he has brought back poetry onto the stage with undoctored abandon." Roy explained: "Fry has occasionally seemed wordy, sentimental, and lacking in conventional kinds of conflict, but he has more than compensated with vital and compassionate characters, the courage to deal with contemporary human conflicts and issues, and some of the most vital language in the theater today." And Williamson wrote: "In Fry's hands the English theater turned, for an elegantly creative period, away from prosaic reality and explored both the poetry and the mystery of life."

BIOGRAPHICAL AND CRITICAL SOURCES:

BOOKS

Contemporary Authors Autobiography Series, Volume 23, Thomson Gale (Detroit, MI), 1996.
Contemporary Dramatists, 6th edition, St. James Press (Detroit, MI), 1999.
Contemporary Poets, 7th edition, St. James Press (Detroit, MI), 2001.

Dictionary of Literary Biography, Volume 13: *British Dramatists since World War II,* Thomson Gale (Detroit, MI), 1982.

Leeming, Glenda, *Poetic Drama,* Macmillan (New York, NY), 1989.

Leeming, Glenda, *Christopher Fry,* Twayne (Boston, MA), 1990.

Roy, Emil, *Christopher Fry,* Southern Illinois University Press (Carbondale, IL), 1968.

Sangal, Mahendra Pratap, *Christopher Fry and T.S. Eliot,* Brij Prakashan, 1968.

Stanford, Derek, *Christopher Fry: An Appreciation,* Peter Nevill (London, England), 1951.

Wiersma, Stanley, *More Than the Ear Discovers: God in the Plays of Christopher Fry,* Loyola University Press (Chicago, IL), 1983.

Wiersma, Stanley, *Christopher Fry: A Critical Essay,* Eerdmans (Grand Rapids, MI), 1970.

PERIODICALS

Ariel, October, 1975.

Back Stage West, February 14, 2002, T.H. McCulloh, review of *The Lady's Not for Burning,* p. 15.

Drama, spring, 1979.

Guardian (London, England), December 8, 1997, p. T12; May 30, 2002, Lyn Gardner, review of *The Lady's Not for Burning,* p. 20.

Literary Half-Yearly, July, 1971.

Los Angeles Times, July 19, 2001, Michael Phillips, review of *The Lady's Not for Burning,* p. F39; February 14, 2002, Philip Brandes, review of *The Lady's Not for Burning,* p. E47.

Manchester Guardian Weekly, November 10, 1959, article by W.J. Weatherby, p. 14.

New Republic, August 20, 1951; March 3, 1952; December 2, 1978.

Newsweek, July 27, 1970.

New York Times Book Review, January 21, 1979.

New York Times Magazine, March 12, 1950.

Parabola, fall, 1995, p. 61.

Plays and Players, December, 1987.

Poetry, August, 1995, p. 280.

Saturday Review, March 1, 1952; March 21, 1953.

Spectator, July 7, 2001, Sheridan Morley, review of *A Ringing of Bells,* p. 38.

Sunday Telegraph (London, England), June 2, 2002, John Gross, "Antidote to Depression: Theatre," p. 9.

Theatre Arts, September, 1950.

Times Literary Supplement, April 2, 1949; August 21, 1970; October 20, 1978.

Tulane Drama Review, March, 1960.

FUENTES, Carlos 1928-

PERSONAL: Born November 11, 1928, in Panama City, Panama; Mexican citizen; son of Rafael Fuentes Boettiger (a career diplomat) and Berta Macias Rivas; married Rita Macedo (a movie actress), 1959 (divorced, 1969); married Sylvia Lemus (a television journalist), 1973; children: (first marriage) Cecilia; (second marriage) Carlos Rafael, Natasha. *Education:* National University of Mexico, LL.B., 1948; graduate study, Institute des Hautes Etudes (Geneva, Switzerland). *Politics:* Independent leftist. *Hobbies and other interests:* Reading, travel, swimming, visiting art galleries, listening to classical and rock music, motion pictures, the theater.

ADDRESSES: Home—Mexico City, Mexico; and London, England. *Agent*—c/o Alfaguara, S.A.-Grupo Santillana, Torrelaguna, 60, 28043 Madrid, Spain.

CAREER: Writer. International Labor Organization, Geneva, Switzerland, began as member, became secretary of the Mexican delegation, 1950-52; Ministry of Foreign Affairs, Mexico City, Mexico, assistant chief of press section, 1954; National University of Mexico, Mexico City, Mexico, secretary and assistant director of cultural dissemination, 1955-56, head of department of cultural relations, 1957-59; Mexican ambassador to France, 1975-77; Cambridge University, Norman Maccoll Lecturer, 1977, Simon Bolivar Professor, 1986-87; Barnard College, New York, NY, Virginia Gildersleeve Professor, 1977; Columbia University, New York, NY, Henry L. Tinker Lecturer, 1978; University of Pennsylvania, professor of English, 1978-83; Harvard University, Cambridge, MA, Robert F. Kennedy Professor of Latin American studies, 1987. Fellow at Woodrow Wilson International Center for Scholars, 1974; lecturer or visiting professor at University of Mexico, University of California—San Diego, University of Oklahoma, University of Concepción in Chile, University of Paris, University of Pennsylvania, and George Mason University; Modern Humanities Research Association, president, 1989—; member of Mexican National Commission on Human Rights.

MEMBER: American Academy and Institute of Arts and Letters (honorary).

AWARDS, HONORS: Centro Mexicano de Escritores fellowship, 1956-57; Biblioteca Breve Prize, Seix Barral (publishing house, Barcelona, Spain), 1967, for *Cambio de piel;* Xavier Villaurrutia Prize (Mexico), 1975; Romulo Gallegos Prize (Venezuela), 1977, for

Terra Nostra; Alfonso Reyes Prize (Mexico), 1979, for body of work; National Award for Literature (Mexico), 1984, for "Orchids in the Moonlight"; nominated for *Los Angeles Times* Book Award in fiction, 1986, for *The Old Gringo;* Miguel de Cervantes Prize, Spanish Ministry of Culture, 1987; Ruben Dario Order of Cultural Independence (Nicaragua) and literary prize of Italo-Latino Americano Institute, both 1988, for *The Old Gringo;* Medal of Honor for Literature, National Arts Club (New York, NY), 1988; Rector's Medal, University of Chile, 1991; Casita Maria Medal, 1991; Order of Merit (Chile), 1992; French Legion of Honor, 1992; Menedez Pelayo International Award, University of Santander, 1992; named honorary citizen of Santiago de Chile, Buenos Aires, and Veracruz, 1993; Principe de Asturias Prize, 1994; Premio Grinzane-Cavour, 1994; candidate for Neustadt International Prize for Literature, 1996; Ruben Dario Prize, 1998; nominated for the 2002 Impac Dublin Literary Award for *The Years with Laura Díaz;* Common Wealth Award for Distinguished Service, 2002; Chubb Fellowship, Yale, 2004; honorary degrees from Bard College, Cambridge University, Columbia College, Chicago State University, Dartmouth College, Essex University, Georgetown University, Harvard University, and Washington University.

WRITINGS:

NOVELS

La región más transparente, Fondo de Cultura Economica (Mexico City, Mexico), 1958, translation by Sam Hileman published as *Where the Air Is Clear,* Ivan Obolensky, 1960.

Las buenas consciencias, Fondo de Cultura Economica (Mexico City, Mexico), 1959, translation published as *The Good Conscience,* Ivan Oblensky, 1961.

La muerte de Artemio Cruz, Fondo de Cultura Economica (Mexico City, Mexico), 1962, translation by Sam Hileman published as *The Death of Artemio Cruz,* Farrar, Straus (New York, NY), 1964.

Aura (also see below), Era, 1962, reprinted, 1982, translation by Lysander Kemp, Farrar, Straus (New York, NY), 1965.

Zona sagrada, Siglo XXI, 1967, translation by Suzanne Jill Levine published as *Holy Place* (also see below), Dutton (New York, NY), 1972.

Cambio de piel, Mortiz, 1967, translation by Sam Hileman published as *A Change of Skin,* Farrar, Straus (New York, NY), 1968.

Cumpleaños, Mortiz, 1969, translation published as *Birthday* (also see below).

Terra Nostra (also see below), Seix Barral (Barcelona, Spain), 1975, translation by Jill Levine, afterword by Milan Kundera, Farrar, Straus (New York, NY), 1976.

La cabeza de hidra, Mortiz, 1978, translation by Margaret Sayers Peden published as *Hydra Head,* Farrar, Straus (New York, NY), 1978.

Una familia lejana, Era, 1980, translation by Margaret Sayers Peden published as *Distant Relations,* Farrar, Straus (New York, NY), 1982.

El gringo viejo, Fondo de Cultura Economica (Mexico City, Mexico), 1985, translation with Margaret Sayers Peden published as *The Old Gringo,* Farrar, Straus (New York, NY), 1985.

Cristóbal Nonato, Fondo de Cultura Economica (Mexico City, Mexico), 1987, translated as *Christopher Unborn,* Farrar, Straus (New York, NY), 1989.

La frontera de cristal, Alfaguara (Mexico City, Mexico), 1995, translated as *The Crystal Frontier: A Novel in Nine Stories.*

Diana, the Goddess Who Hunts Alone, introduction by Alfred J. Mac Adam, Farrar, Straus (New York, NY), 1995.

Años con Laura Díaz, Alfaguara (Mexico City, Mexico), 1999, translation by Alfred Mac Adam published as *The Years with Laura Díaz,* Farrar, Straus (New York, NY), 2000.

Instinto de Inez, Alfaguara (Mexico City, Mexico), 2001, translation by Margaret Sayers Peden published as *Inez,* Farrar, Straus (New York, NY), 2002.

La silla del águila, Alfaguara (Mexico City, Mexico), 2003.

Also author of *Holy Place & Birthday: Two Novellas,* Farrar, Straus (New York, NY).

SHORT STORIES

Los días enmascarados (also see below), Los Presentes, 1954.

Cantar de ciegos (also see below), Mortiz, 1964.

Dos cuentos mexicanos (title means "Two Mexican Stories"; previously published in *Cantar de ciegos*), Instituto de Cultura Hispanica de Sao Paulo, Universidade de Sao Paulo, 1969.

Poemas de amor: Cuentos del alma, Imp. E. Cruces (Madrid, Spain), 1971.

Chac Mool y otros cuentos, Salvat, 1973.

Agua quemada (anthology), Fondo de Cultura Economica (Mexico City, Mexico), 1981, translation by Margaret Sayers Peden published as *Burnt Water,* Farrar, Straus (New York, NY), 1980.

Constancia y otras novelas para vírgenes, Mondadori (Madrid, Spain), 1989, translation by Thomas Christensen published as *Constancia and Other Stories for Virgins,* Farrar, Straus (New York, NY), 1989.

Inquieta compañía, (title means "Uneasy Company"), Alfaguara (Mexico City, Mexico), 2004.

PLAYS

Todos los gatos son pardos (also see below), Siglo XXI, 1970.

El tuerto es rey (also see below; produced in French in 1970), Mortiz, 1970.

Los reinos originarios (contains *Todos los gatos son pardos* and *El tuerto es rey*), Seix Barral (Barcelona, Spain), 1971.

Orquídeas a la luz de la luna (produced in English as *Orchids in the Moonlight* at American Repertory Theater in Cambridge, MA, 1982), Seix Barral (Barcelona, Spain), 1982.

NONFICTION

The Argument of Latin America: Words for North Americans, Radical Education Project, 1963.

(Contributor) *Whither Latin America?* (political articles), Monthly Review Press, 1963.

París: La revolución de mayo, Era, 1968.

La nueva novela hispanoamericana, Mortiz, 1969.

(Contributor) *El mundo de José Luis Cuevas,* Tudor (Mexico City, Mexico), 1969.

Casa con dos puertas (title means "House with Two Doors"), Mortiz, 1970.

Tiempo mexicano (title means "Mexican Time"), Mortiz, 1971.

Cervantes; o, La crítica de la lectura, Mortiz, 1976, translation published as *Don Quixote; or, The Critique of Reading,* Institute of Latin American Studies, University of Texas at Austin (Austin, TX), 1976.

On Human Rights: A Speech, Somesuch Press (Dallas, TX), 1984.

Latin America: At War with the Past, CBC Enterprises, 1985.

Myself with Others: Selected Essays, Farrar, Straus (New York, NY), 1988.

Buried Mirror: Reflections on Spain in the New World, Houghton Mifflin (Boston, MA), 1992.

A New Time for Mexico, Farrar, Straus (New York, NY), 1996.

El Espejo Enterrado, Alfaguara (Mexico City, Mexico), 2001.

En esto creo, Seix Barral (Barcelona, Spain), 2002.

Carlos Fuentes: viendo visions, Fondo de Cultura Económica (Mexico City, Mexico), 2003.

This I Believe: An A to Z of a Life, translated by Kristina Cordero, Random House (New York, New York), 2005.

OTHER

(Editor and author of prologue) Octavio Paz, *Los signos en rotacion, y otros ensayos,* Alianza, 1971.

Cuerpos y ofrendas (anthology; includes selections from *Los días enmascarados, Cantar de ciegos, Aura,* and *Terra Nostra,*) introduction by Octavio Paz, Alianza, 1972.

(Author of introduction) Milan Kundera, *La vida está en otra parte* (Spanish translation of *Life Is Elsewhere*), Seix Barral (Barcelona, Spain), 1977.

(Author of introduction) Omar Cabezas, *Fire from the Mountain,* Crown (New York, NY), 1988.

Valiente Mundo Nuevo, Fondo de Cultura Economica (Mexico City, Mexico), 1990.

The Campaign, Farrar, Straus (New York, NY), 1991.

Geografía de la novela, Fondo de Cultura Economica (Mexico City, Mexico), 1993.

El naranjo, o los circulos del tiempo, Alfaguara (Mexico City, Mexico), 1993.

The Orange Tree, introduction by Mac Adam, Farrar, Straus (New York, NY), 1994.

The Writings of Carlos Fuentes, edited by Raymond L. Williams, University of Texas Press (Austin, TX), 1996.

Los cinco soles de México: Memoria de un milenio, Seix Barral (Barcelona, Spain), 2000.

(Author of introduction) Michael L. Sand, editor, *Witnesses of Time,* photographs by Flor Garduno, Aperture Foundation (New York, NY), 2000.

Contributor to *Juan Rulfo: México,* Lunwerg Editores (Barcelona, Spain), 2001, translation by Margaret Sayers Peden published as *Juan Rulfo's Mexico,* Smithsonian Institution Press, 2002, and *Nudes/Desnudos: The photographs of Manuel Alvarez,* edited by Ariadne Kimberly Huque, Distributed Art Publishers (New York, NY), 2002. Collaborator on several film scripts, including *Pedro Paramo,* 1966, *Tiempo de morir,* 1966, and *Los caifanes,* 1967. Work represented in numerous anthologies, including *Antología de cuentos hispanoamericanos,* Nueva Decada (Costa Rica), 1985. Contributor to periodicals in the United States, Mexico, and France, including *New York Times, Washington Post,* and *Los Angeles Times.* Founding editor, *Revista Mexicana de Literatura,* 1954-58; coeditor, *El Espectador,* 1959-61, *Siempre,* 1960, and *Politica,* 1960.

ADAPTATIONS: Two short stories from *Cantar de ciegos* were made into films in the mid-1960s; *The Old Gringo* was adapted into a film of the same title by Fonda Films, 1989.

WORK IN PROGRESS: A novel about the assassination of Emiliano Zapata.

SIDELIGHTS: "Carlos Fuentes," stated Robert Maurer in *Saturday Review,* is "without doubt one of Mexico's two or three greatest novelists." He is part of a group of Latin American writers whose writings, according to Alistair Reid's *New Yorker* essay, "formed the background of the Boom," a literary phenomenon Reid described as a period in the 1960s when "a sudden surge of hitherto unheard-of writers from Latin America began to be felt among [U.S.] readers." Fuentes, however, is singled out from among the other writers of the Boom in José Donoso's autobiographical account, *The Boom in Spanish American Literature: A Personal History,* in which the Chilean novelist called Fuentes "the first active and conscious agent of the internationalization of the Spanish American novel." Since the 1960s, Fuentes has continued his international influence in the literary world; his 1985 novel, *The Old Gringo,* for example, was the first written by a Mexican to ever appear on the *New York Times* best-seller list.

Although, as Donoso observed, early worldwide acceptance of Fuentes's novels contributed to the internationalization of Latin American literature, his work is an exploration of the culture and history of one nation, his native Mexico. Critics note the thematic presence of Mexico in nearly all Fuentes's writing. Robert Coover commented in the *New York Times Book Review* that in *The Death of Artemio Cruz,* for instance, Fuentes delineated "in the retrospective details of one man's life the essence of the post-Revolutionary history of all Mexico." Mexico is also present in Fuentes's novel *Terra Nostra,* in which, according to *Washington Post Book World* contributor Larry Rohter, "Fuentes probes more deeply into the origins of Mexico—and what it means to be a Mexican—than ever before." *Old Gringo,* published more than twenty years after *The Death of Artemio Cruz,* returns to the same theme as it explores Mexico's relationship with its northern neighbor, the United States.

Fuentes explained his preoccupation with Mexico, and particularly with Mexican history, in a *Paris Review* interview. "Pablo Neruda used to say," he told Alfred MacAdam and Charles Ruas, "that every Latin American writer goes around dragging a heavy body, the body of his people, of his past, of his national history. We have to assimilate the enormous weight of our past so that we will not forget what gives us life. If you forget your past, you die." Fuentes also noted that the development of the same theme in his novels unifies them so that they may be considered part of the same work. The author observed in the same interview, "In a sense my novels are one book with many chapters: *Where the Air Is Clear* is the biography of Mexico City; *The Death of Artemio Cruz* deals with an individual in that city; [and] *A Change of Skin* is that city, that society, facing the world, coming to grips with the fact that it is part of civilization and that there is a world outside that intrudes into Mexico."

Along with thematic unity, another characteristic of Fuentes's work is his innovative narrative style. In a *New Yorker* review, Anthony West compared the novelist's technique to "a rapid cinematic movement that cuts nervously from one character to another." Evan Connell stated in the *New York Times Book Review* that Fuentes's "narrative style—with few exceptions—relies on the interruption and juxtaposition of different kinds of awareness." Reviewers Donald Yates and Karen Hardy also commented on Fuentes's experimental style. In the *Washington Post Book World,* Yates called Fuentes "a tireless experimenter with narrative techniques and points of view." In *Hispania,* Hardy noted that in Fuentes's work "the complexities of a human or national personality are evoked through . . . elaborate narrative devices."

The Death of Artemio Cruz and *Terra Nostra* are especially good examples of his experimental techniques. The first novel deals with a corrupt Mexican millionaire who, on his deathbed, relives his life in a series of flashbacks. In the novel Fuentes uses three separate narrations to tell the story, and for each of these he uses a different narrator. *New York Review of Books* contributor A. Alvarez explained the three-part narration of the novel: "Cruz's story is told in three persons. 'I' is the old man dying on his bed; 'you' is a slightly vatic, 'experimental' projection of his potentialities into an unspecified future. . . . 'he' is the real hero, the man whose history emerges bit by bit from incidents shuffled around from his seventy-one years." In John S. Brushwood's *Mexico in Its Novel: A Nation's Search for Identity,* the critic praised Fuentes's technique, commenting: "The changing narrative viewpoint is extremely effective, providing a clarity that could not have been accomplished any other way. I doubt that there is anywhere in fiction a character whose wholeness is more apparent than in the case of Artemio Cruz."

Coover observed that in *Terra Nostra,* Fuentes once again uses a variety of narrators to tell his story. Commenting favorably on Fuentes's use of the "you" narrative voice in the novel, Coover wrote: "Fuentes's second person [narration] is not one overheard on a stage: the book itself, rather than the author or a character, becomes the speaker, the reader or listener a character, or several characters in succession." Spanish novelist Juan Goytisolo similarly stated in *Review:* "One of the most striking and most successful devices [in *Terra Nostra*] is the abrupt shift in narrative point of view (at times without the unwary reader's even noticing), passing from first-person narration to second . . . and simultaneously rendering objective and subjective reality in one and the same passage with patent scorn for the rules of discourse that ordinarily govern expository prose." In the *Paris Review,* Fuentes commented on his use of the second person narrative, calling it "the voice poets have always used and that novelists also have a right to use."

Fuentes's use of the second person narrative and other experimental techniques makes his novels extremely complex. In a *New York Times Book Review* interview with Frank MacShane concerning the structure of *Terra Nostra,* Fuentes described the intricacy of the work: "My chief stylistic device in *Terra Nostra* is to follow every statement by a counter statement and every image by its opposite." This deliberate duplicity by the author, along with the extensive scope of the novel, caused some reviewers to criticize *Terra Nostra* for being inaccessible to the average reader. Maurer, for instance, called the novel "a huge, sprawling, exuberant, mysterious, almost unimaginably dense work of 800 pages, covering events on three continents from the creation of man in Genesis to the dawn of the twenty-first century," and added that "*Terra Nostra* presents a common reader with enormous problems simply of understanding what is going on." *Newsweek*'s Peter S. Prescott noted: "To talk about [*Terra Nostra*] at all we must return constantly to five words: excess, surreal, baroque, masterpiece, [and] unreadable."

Other critics, however, have written more positive reviews, seeing *Terra Nostra* and other Fuentes works as necessarily complex. *Village Voice* contributor Jonah Raskin found Fuentes is at his best when the novelist can "plunge readers into the hidden recesses of his char-

acters' minds and at the same time allow language to pile up around their heads in thick drifts, until they feel lost in a blizzard of words that enables them to see, to feel, in a revolutionary way." Fuentes also defended the difficulty of his works in a *Washington Post* interview with Charles Truehart. Recalling his conversation with Fuentes, Truehart quoted him as saying: "I believe in books that do not go to a ready-made public. . . . I'm looking for readers I would like to *make.* . . . To *win* them . . . to *create* readers rather than to give something that readers are expecting. That would bore me to death."

In 1992 Fuentes produced *The Buried Mirror: Reflections on Spain in the New World,* a historical work that discusses the formation and development of the Latin American world. The title refers to polished rocks found in the tombs of ancient Mediterranean and Amerindian peoples, presaging, in Fuentes's view, the convergence of these distant cultures. Fuentes wrote that his book is "dedicated to a search for the cultural continuity that can inform and transcend the economic and political destiny and fragmentation of the Hispanic world." Attempting to disentangle the complex legacy of Spanish settlement in the New World, Fuentes first addresses the mixed ethnicity of the Spanish conquerors, whose progeny include Celts, Phoenicians, Greeks, Romans, Arabs, and Jews, and the consequent diversity produced in Latin America through war, colonization, and miscegenation.

Praising Fuentes's intriguing though broad subject, Nicolas Shumway wrote in the *New York Times Book Review,* "The range of the book is both its principal defect and its chief virtue. Beginning with the prehistoric cave paintings at Altamira in Spain and ending with contemporary street art in East Los Angeles, Mr. Fuentes seeks to cover all of Spanish and Spanish-American history, with frequent digressions on a particular artist, political figure, novel or painting." *The Buried Mirror,* according to David Ewing Duncan in a *Washington Post Book World* review, is "invigorated by the novelist's sense of irony, paradox and sensuality. Here is a civilization, he says, that defies whatever stereotypes we may hold, a society at once erotic and puritanical, cruel and humane, legalistic and corrupt, energetic and sad." Guy Garcia noted in *Time* that the book "represents an intellectual homecoming for Fuentes, who conceived of the project as 'a fantastic opportunity to write my own cultural biography.'"

Four years later Fuentes followed with *A New Time for Mexico,* a collection of essays on the internal injustice and international indignity suffered by Mexico. Viewed as a sequel to his 1971 publication, *Tiempo mexicano* (translated as "Mexican Time"), Fuentes addresses current events in his native country, including political reform, the Chiapas rebellion, social inequities, and the significance of the North American Free Trade Agreement (NAFTA) for Mexico and its perception in the United States. Though noting the bias of Fuentes's strong nationalism, Roderic A. Camp maintained in *Library Journal* that his "brief cultural vignettes" are "appealing and insightful." A *Publishers Weekly* reviewer commended Fuentes's "lapidary, lyrical meditations on Mexico as a land of continual metamorphosis."

The Orange Tree offers five novellas whose subjects span several centuries, each connected by the image of the orange. For Fuentes the orange tree signifies the possibilities of beauty, sustenance, transplantation, and rejuvenation. Its seeds were introduced to Spain through Roman and Moorish invaders, reached the New World with the conquistadors, and have flourished since. Fuentes illustrates various manifestations of violence, deception, and suffering by recounting episodes from the conquest of Roman Iberia and Mexico, a contemporary corporate takeover, and the death wish of an American actor.

"In all this intercourse between Old World and New, Rome and Africa and Spain, past and present," Alan Cheuse wrote in Chicago's *Tribune Books,* "Fuentes makes the older material resonate with all of the exotic and yet familiar attraction of compelling human behavior." Michael Kerrigan praised the work in a *Times Literary Supplement* review, noting that "The challenge and opportunity *The Orange Tree* presents its reader are those of escaping from 'a more or less protected individuality' into a wider existence of multiple possibility and a cyclical history that holds past and present in simultaneity and in ceaseless renewal." Kerrigan concluded, "What strikes the reader first in Fuentes' work may be his erudition and intellectual rigour, but what remains in the mind is his sympathy, his concern to commemorate the countless lives sacrificed in pain and obscurity so that we might live."

In 1995 Fuentes published *Diana, the Goddess Who Hunts Alone,* a semi-autobiographical novel that follows a love affair between an unnamed, married Mexican novelist and an American film actress, Diana Soren. The fictional romance, however, contains obvious parallels to the author's real-life affair with film actress Jean Seberg. Mirroring actual events surrounding the liaison between Fuentes and Seberg, the writer meets Soren at a New Year's Eve party in 1969 and follows her to a Santiago film location where they enjoy a passionate, albeit brief, relationship. After several months of literary conversation and tenuous intimacy, the self-absorbed writer is abandoned by the unstable actress, who maintains a second relationship via telephone with a Black Panther, and keeps a photograph of her last lover, Clint Eastwood, by her bed.

Though the book received mixed reviews, Rosanne Daryl Thomas observed in Chicago's *Tribune Books* that the novel reveals "the tensions between imagination, language and reality, between generosity born of love and the profound selfishness often found in artists." Thomas concluded, "Carlos Fuentes takes off the mask of literary creation and reveals a man nakedly possessed by a desperate passion. Then he raises the mask to his face and tells a fascinating, frightening tale of heartbreak."

While Fuentes's innovative use of theme and structure has gained the author an international reputation as a novelist, he believes that only since *Terra Nostra* has he perfected his craft. "I feel I'm beginning to write the novels I've always wanted to write and didn't know how to write before," he explained to Philip Bennett in a *Boston Globe Magazine* interview. "There were the novels of youth based on energy, and conceptions derived from energy. Now I have the conceptions I had as a young man, but I can develop them and give them their full value."

Fuentes delivered a narrative history of twentieth-century Mexico and insightful commentary on his country's past in *The Years with Laura Díaz.* The novel turns on the life story of Laura Díaz, a woman whose passionate nature and dramatic love life place her close to many of the key people and events in recent Mexican history. The story is narrated by Laura's grandson, who has traveled to Detroit to photograph murals by Diego Rivera—paintings that feature Laura's image. As Laura's story unfolds for readers, her interactions provide a way for Fuentes to present discourses on political subjects such as the opposition between fascism and communism. "Fuentes's emotional commitment to his subject shows in the lucidity of the book's underlying intellectual dialogues," commented a *Publishers Weekly* reviewer, who added that the author animates his commentary "with a learned lyricism that should make this volume one of his most admired and memorable." Some reviewers voiced reservations about *The Years with Laura Díaz,* finding the book overburdened with social discourse and reflection. Richard Eder, writing in the *New York Times Book Review,* noted that the heroine was "not much more than an effigy." While acknowledging that the author "writes well of places, ideas, confrontations," Eder felt that "it is characters that defeat him." Emiliana Sandoval, a writer for *Knight-Ridder/ Tribune News Service,* described Laura as frequently "maddeningly opaque, just a pair of eyes through which we look at Mexico." But while warning that *The Years with Laura Díaz* is "not light reading," Sandoval ultimately recommended it as "evocative and absorbing." And *Library Journal* contributor Jack Shreve stated, "this fictionalized memoir brilliantly recaptures the turbulent and exciting history of twentieth-century Mexico. . . . This roman fleuve of a novel can hardly fail to entertain and enlighten."

Describing his writing method to Caleb Bach for *Americas,* Fuentes said, "I work from seven to noon, when I go out on my walk. By then I feel I've said what I want to say and am at peace with myself. I am a Calvinist! That's my rhythm, I go right on through the weekend. When I get tired after three or four weeks, I go off on vacation to the beach, read novels, walk, see other things." Bach commented, "Any reader who has entered the Fuentian realm never fails to be astounded by the spectacular somersaults he makes through time and space, audacious games he plays with fact and fiction, the precarious balancing act he performs."

Part of the genius of Fuentes is his involvement in different worlds and his ability to bring them together. He does not separate art from politics. Officially he was Mexico's ambassador to France in the seventies, but his works have always taken on the role of ambassador as well. Fuentes continued to meditate on Mexico in many of the essays found in *En esto creo,* published in 2002 and in 2003 with the novel *La silla del águila.* These books use different genres, but both discuss Mexico's growing pains and its place in the world. In an article for *Financial Times,* John Authers and Sara Silver characterized *La silla del águila* as a "devastatingly accurate futuristic novel of politics," adding that "Fuentes' idea was to use a thriller set in the future to warn about the present. But he worries that his fantasies could turn into prophesies." These worries are not without merit, since some of his visions from *Cristóbal Nonato,* published in 1989, were quite accurate.

BIOGRAPHICAL AND CRITICAL SOURCES:

BOOKS

Authors in the News, Volume 2, Thomson Gale (Detroit, MI), 1976.

Brushwood, John S., *Mexico in Its Novel: A Nation's Search for Identity,* University of Texas Press (Austin, TX), 1966.

Conde Ortega, José Francisco and Arturo Trejo, editors, *Carlos Fuentes: 40 años de escritor,* Universidad Autónoma Metropolitana (Mexico City, Mexico), 1993.

Contemporary Literary Criticism, Thomson Gale (Detroit, MI), Volume 3, 1975, Volume 8, 1978, Volume 10, 1979, Volume 13, 1980, Volume 22, 1982, Volume 41, 1987, Volume 60, 1991.

Dictionary of Hispanic Biography, Thomson Gale (Detroit, MI), 1996.

Dictionary of Literary Biography, Volume 113: *Modern Latin American Fiction Writers, First Series,* Thomson Gale (Detroit, MI), 1992.

Donoso, José, *The Boom in Spanish American Literature: A Personal History,* Columbia University Press (New York, NY), 1977.

Encyclopedia of World Biography, second edition, seventeen volumes, Thomson Gale (Detroit, MI), 1998.

Faris, Wendy B., *Carlos Fuentes,* Frederick Ungar (New York, NY), 1983.

Feijoo, Gladys, *Lo fantástico en los relatos de Carlos Fuentes: aproximación teórica,* Senda Nueva de Ediciones (New York, NY), 1985.

García-Gutiérrez, Georgina, editor, *Carlos Fuentes desde la crítica,* Universidad Nacional Autónoma de México (Mexico City, Mexico), 2001.

García Núñez, Fernando, *Fabulación de la fe: Carlos Fuentes,* Universidad Veracruzana (Xalapa, Mexico), 1989.

González, Alfonso, *Carlos Fuentes; Life, Work, and Criticism,* York Press (Fredericton, New Brunswick, Canada), 1987.

Helmuth, Chalene, *The Postmodern Fuentes,* Associated University Press (Cranbury, NJ), 1997.

Herández de López, Ana María, *La obra de Carlos Fuentes: una visión múltiple,* Pliegos (Madrid, Spain), 1988.

Hispanic Literature Criticism, Thomson Gale (Detroit, MI), 1994.

Ibsen, Kristine, *Author, Text, and Reader in the Novels of Carlos Fuentes,* P. Lang (New York, NY), 1993.

Lindstrom, Naomi, *Twentieth-Century Spanish American Fiction,* University of Texas Press (Austin, TX), 1994.

Ordiz, Francisco Javier, *El mito en la obra de Carlos Fuentes,* Universidad de León (León, Spain), 1987.

Plimpton, George, editor, *Writers at Work: The Paris Review Interviews, Sixth Series,* Penguin, 1984.

Short Story Criticism, Volume 24, Thomson Gale (Detroit, MI), 1997.

Van Delden, Maarten, *Carlos Fuentes, Mexico and Modernity,* Vanderbilt University Press (Nashville, TN), 1998.

Williams, Raymond Leslie, *The Writings of Carlos Fuentes,* University of Texas Press (Austin, TX), 1996.

World Literature Criticism, Thomson Gale (Detroit, MI), 1992.

PERIODICALS

Americas (English edition), April, 2000, Caleb Bach, "Time to Imagine," p. 22; January-February 2002, Barbara Mujica, review of *Instinto de Inez,* p. 62.

Antioch Review, winter, 1998, review of *A New Time for Mexico,* p. 114.

Book, May-June 2002, Beth Kephart, review of *Inez,* p. 77.

Booklist, September 1, 2000, Veronica Scrol, review of *The Years with Laura Díaz,* p. 6; November 1, 2000, Brad Hooper, review of *The Vintage Book of Latin American Short Stories,* p. 519; April 1, 2002, Donna Seaman, review of *Inez,* p. 1283.

Boston Globe Magazine, September 9, 1984.

Financial Times, July 1, 2004, John Authers and Sara Silver, "A visionary approach: Mexican writer and democrat Carlos Fuentes' cautionary writing has a knack of predicting his country's political future," p. 26.

Foreign Policy, March-April, 2004, Christopher Dominguez Michael, "Mexico's former future," pp. 84-85.

Hispania, May, 1978.

Hispanic, June, 1998, review of *The Crystal Frontier,* p. 70.

Journal of Latin American Studies, Amit Thakkar, review of *Juan Rulfo's Mexico,* pp. 393-394.

Kirkus Reviews, April 15, 1996, p. 575; September 1, 1997, review of *The Crystal Frontier,* p. 1328; April 1, 2002, review of *Inez,* p. 441.

Knight-Ridder/Tribune News Service, November 15, 2000, Emiliana Sandoval, review of *The Years with Laura Díaz,* p. K24.

Library Journal, January, 1994, p. 96; January, 1995, p. 77; January, 1996, p. 81; May 1, 1996, p. 112; August, 1997, review of *The Crystal Frontier,* p. 137; July, 1999, review of *Los Años con Laura Díaz,* p. 76; October 1, 2000, Jack Shreve, review of *The Years with Laura Díaz,* p. 147; August, 2001, David Garza, review of *Instinto de Inez,* p. S33, Isabel Cuadrado, review of *Los cinco soles de México: Memoria de un milenio,* p. S48; May 15, 2002, Barbara Hoffert, review of *Inez,* p. 124.

London Review of Books, May 10, 1990, p. 26.

Los Angeles Times Book Review, April 10, 1994, p. 6; October 26, 1997, review of *The Crystal Frontier,* p. 9; December 14, 1997, review of *The Crystal Frontier,* p. 4.

Nation, February 17, 1992, p. 205.

New Perspectives, spring, 1994, p. 54.

New Statesman, August 26, 1994, p. 37; September 29, 1995, p. 57; July 17, 1998, review of *The Crystal Frontier,* p. 46.

Newsweek, November 1, 1976.

Newsweek International, May 17, 2004, Scott Johnson "Carlos Fuentes: A Tropical Stalinism," p. 72.

New Yorker, March 4, 1961; January 26, 1981; February 24, 1986; November 3, 1997, review of *The Crystal Frontier,* p. 109.

New York Review of Books, June 11, 1964.

New York Times Book Review, November 7, 1976; October 19, 1980; October 27, 1985, Earl Shorris, review of *The Old Gringo,* p. 1; October 6, 1991, p. 3; April 26, 1992, p. 9; October 22, 1995, p. 12; October 26, 1997, review of *The Crystal Frontier,* p. 20; December 7, 1997, review of *The Crystal Frontier,* p. 60; December 20, 1998, review of *The Crystal Frontier,* p. 28; November 12, 2000, Richard Eder, review of *The Years with Laura Díaz,* p. 8.

Observer (London, England), April 1, 1990, p. 67; November 28, 1999, review of *The Picador Book of Latin American Stories,* p. 14.

Paris Review, winter, 1981.

Publishers Weekly, April 15, 1996, p. 55; August 11, 1997, review of *The Crystal Frontier,* p. 381; November 10, 1997, review of *A New Time for Mexico,* p. 71; September 18, 2000, review of *The Years with Laura Díaz,* p. 85; November 6, 2000, "December Publications," p. 72; May 6, 2002, review of *Inez,* p. 35.

Review, winter, 1976.

Review of Contemporary Fiction, spring, 2001, Steve Tomasula, review of *The Years with Laura Díaz,* p. 191; fall, 2002, Christopher Paddock, review of *Inez,* p. 165.

Saturday Review, October 30, 1976.

School Library Journal, September, 2001, David Garza, "Inez's Instinct," p. 533; June, 2003, Bruce Jensen, review of *The Seat of Power,* p. SS36.

Time, June 29, 1992, p. 78.

Time for Kids, September 20, 2001, Ronald Buchanan, "Telling Mexico's story: Author Carlos Fuentes shares his unique view of Mexico with the world through his books, plays, stories and essays," p. 6.

Times Literary Supplement, June 10, 1994, p. 23; September 29, 1995, p. 27; February 20, 1998, review of *A New Time for Mexico,* p. 27; June 5, 1998, review of *The Crystal Frontier,* p. 24.

Translation Review Supplement, July, 1997, review of *A New Time for Mexico,* p. 14, review of *Diana: The Goddess Who Hunts Alone,* p. 38.

Tribune Books (Chicago, IL), April 19, 1992; April 11, 1994, p. 6; December 17, 1995, p. 3.

Village Voice, January 28, 1981; April 1, 1986.

Washington Post, May 5, 1988.

Washington Post Book World, October 26, 1976; January 14, 1979; March 29, 1992; October 19, 1997, review of *The Crystal Frontier: A Novel in Nine Stories,* p. 1.

World Literature Today, autumn, 1994, p. 794; spring, 1997, review of *La Frontera de Cristal,* p. 354.

ONLINE

Center for Book Culture Web site, http://www.centerforbookculture.org/ (August 2, 2004), Debra A. Castillo, "Travailing Time: An Interview with Carlos Fuentes."

Librynth Web site, http://www.themodernworld.com/ (August 2, 2004), biography of Carlos Fuentes.

Mexico Connect Web site, http://www.mexconnect.com/ (1999), Jim Tuck, "Rebel, Internationalist, Establishmentarian: The Meadering Road of Carlos Fuentes."

Speakers Worldwide Web site, http://www.speakersworldwide.com (2000), biography of Carlos Fuentes.

*   *   *

FUGARD, Athol 1932-
(Harold Athol Fugard)

PERSONAL: Born June 11, 1932, in Middelburg, Cape Province, South Africa; son of Harold David (an owner of a general store) and Elizabeth Magdalena (a tea room manager; maiden name, Potgiefer) Fugard; married Sheila Meiring (a novelist, poet, and former actress), 1956; children: Lisa. *Education:* Attended Port Elizabeth Technical College, 1946-50, and University of Cape Town, 1950-53. *Hobbies and other interests:* Jogging, music, poetry.

ADDRESSES: Office—P.O. Box 5090, Walmer, Port Elizabeth 6065, Republic of South Africa. *Agent*—Esther Sherman, William Morris Agency, 1350 Avenue of the Americas, New York, NY 10019.

CAREER: Actor, director, and playwright. Crew member of tramp steamer bound from Port Sudan to the Far East, 1953-55; *Port Elizabeth Evening Post,* Port Elizabeth, South Africa, journalist, 1954; South African Broadcasting Corporation, Port Elizabeth and Cape Town, reporter, 1955-57; Fordsburg Native Commissioner's Court, Johannesburg, South Africa, clerk, 1958; African Theatre Workshop, Sophiatown, South Africa, cofounder, 1958-59; New Africa Group, Brussels, Belgium, cofounder, 1960; Serpent Players, Port Elizabeth, cofounder, director, and actor, 1963—; Ijinle Company, London, cofounder, 1966; The Space (experimental theatre), Cape Town, cofounder, 1972. Has worked as actor and director in various theatre productions in New York City, London, and South Africa. Actor in television film *The Blood Knot* for British Broadcasting Corp. (BBC-TV), 1968; actor in motion pictures, including *Boesman and Lena,* 1973, *Meetings with Remarkable Men,* 1979, *Marigolds in August,* 1980, *Gandhi,* 1982, *The Killing Fields,* 1984, and *The Road to Mecca,* 1992.

MEMBER: Royal Society of Literature (fellow), American Academy of Arts and Letters, Dramatists Guild, Mark Twain Society.

AWARDS, HONORS: Obie Award for distinguished foreign play from *Village Voice,* 1971, for *Boesman and Lena; Plays & Players* Award for best new play, 1973, for *Sizwe Banzi Is Dead;* London Theatre Critics Award, 1974; Ernest Artaria Award, Locarno Film Festival, 1977; Golden Bear, Berlin Film Festival, 1980; Yale University fellow, 1980; Antoinette Perry Award nominations for best play, 1975, for *Sizwe Banzi Is Dead and the Island,* 1981, for *A Lesson from Aloes,* 1982, for *"Master Harold" . . . and the Boys,* and 1986, for *Blood Knot;* New York Drama Critics Circle Award for best play, 1982, for *A Lesson from Aloes;* Drama Desk Award and New York Drama Critics Circle Award for best play, 1983, and *Evening Standard* Award, London, 1984, for *"Master Harold" . . . and the Boys;* Commonwealth Award, 1984, for contribution to the American theatre; Drama League Award, 1986; New York Drama Critics Circle Award, 1988; Helen Hayes Award, 1990, for direction; honorary degrees from Yale University, Georgetown University, Natal University, Rhodes University, Cape Town University, Emory University, and the University of Port Elizabeth, South Africa.

WRITINGS:

Tsotsi (novel), Collings, 1980, Random House (New York, NY), 1981.

Notebooks, 1960-1977, edited by Mary Benson, Faber (London, England), 1983, Knopf (New York, NY), 1984.

Writer and Region: Athol Fugard (essay), Anson Phelps Stokes Institute (New York, NY), 1987.

Cousins: A Memoir, Theatre Communications Group (New York, NY), 1997.

PLAYS

No-Good Friday (also see below), first produced in Cape Town, South Africa, 1956.

Nongogo (also see below), first produced in Cape Town, 1957; produced in New York City, 1978.

The Cell, produced in Cape Town, 1957.

Klaas and The Devil, produced in Cape Town, 1957.

The Blood Knot (first produced in Johannesburg, South Africa, and London, 1961; produced Off-Broadway, 1964; also see below), Simondium (Johannesburg, South Africa), 1963, Odyssey Press (New York, NY), 1964 (published with other plays as *Blood Knot and Other Plays,* Theatre Communications Group [New York, NY], 1991).

Hello and Goodbye (first produced in Johannesburg, 1965; produced Off-Broadway at Sheridan Square Playhouse, September 18, 1969; also see below), A.A. Balkema (Cape Town, South Africa), 1966, Samuel French (New York, NY), 1971.

The Coat, first produced in Port Elizabeth, South Africa, 1966 (bound with *The Third Degree,* by Don MacLennan, A.A. Balkema [Cape Town, South Africa], 1971).

The Occupation: A Script for Camera, published in *Ten One-Act Plays,* edited by Cosmos Pieterse, Heinemann (New York, NY), 1968.

Boesman and Lena (first produced in Grahamstown, South Africa, 1969; produced Off-Broadway at Circle in the Square, June 22, 1970; produced on the West End at Royal Court Theatre Upstairs, July 19, 1971; also see below), Buren, 1969, revised and rewritten edition, Samuel French (New York, NY), 1971 (published with *The Blood Knot, People Are Living There* [also see below], and *Hello and Goodbye* as *Boesman and Lena, and Other Plays,* Oxford University Press [Oxford, England], 1978).

People Are Living There (first produced in Cape Town at Hofmeyr Theatre, June 14, 1969; produced on Broadway at Forum Theatre, Lincoln Center, November 18, 1971), Oxford University Press (Oxford England), 1970, Samuel French (New York, NY), 1976.

The Last Bus, first produced in Port Elizabeth, South Africa, 1970.

Friday's Bread on Monday, first produced in Port Elizabeth, South Africa, 1970.

Orestes, produced in Cape Town, 1971 (published with other plays in *Theatre One: New South African Drama,* edited by Stephen Gray, Donker [Johannesburg, South Africa], 1978).

(With John Kani and Winston Ntshona) *Sizwe Banzi Is Dead* (also see below), first produced in Cape Town, 1972, produced in New York City, 1974.

Statements (contains *Sizwe Banzi Is Dead, The Island,* [also see below] and *Statements after an Arrest under the Immorality Act,* first produced in Cape Town, 1972; produced in London, 1974), Oxford University Press (Oxford, England), 1974.

(With John Kani and Winston Ntshona) *Die Hodoshe Span,* first produced in Cape Town at The Space Theatre, 1973; revised as *The Island* (also see below) first produced in South Africa, 1972; produced on the West End at Royal Court Theatre, December, 1973; produced in New York at Edison Theatre, November, 1974 (published with *Sizwe Banzi Is Dead* as *Sizwe Banzi Is Dead and The Island,* VIking Press [New York, NY], 1976).

Three Port Elizabeth Plays: The Blood Knot, Hello and Goodbye, Boesman and Lena, Viking (New York, NY), 1974.

Dimetos, first produced in Edinburgh, 1975, produced in London and New York City, 1976 (published with *No-Good Friday* and *Nongogo* as *Dimetos and Two Early Plays,* Oxford University Press [Oxford, England], 1977).

(With Ross Devenish) *The Guest: An Episode in the Life of Eugene Marais* (screenplay; also see below), Donker (Johannesburg, South Africa), 1977.

A Lesson from Aloes (first produced in Johannesburg, December, 1978; produced in New York, 1980), Oxford University Press (Oxford, England), 1981, Random House (New York, NY), 1981.

The Drummer, produced in Louisville, Kentucky, 1980.

(With Ross Devenish) *Marigolds in August* (screenplay), Donker (Johannesburg, South Africa), 1982 (published with *The Guest* as *Marigolds in August and The Guest: Two Screenplays,* Theatre Communications Group [New York, NY], 1992).

"Master Harold" . . . and the Boys (first produced in New Haven, Connecticut, March, 1982; produced on Broadway at Lyceum Theatre, May 5, 1982), Knopf (New York, NY), 1982, Oxford University Press (Oxford, England), 1983 (published with *The Blood Knot, Hello and Goodbye,* and *Boesman and Lena* as *Selected Plays,* Oxford University Press, 1987).

The Road to Mecca (first produced in New Haven, 1984; produced in London at Lyttelton Theatre,

March 1, 1985; produced in New York at Prom-
enade Theatre, April, 1988), Faber, (Boston, MA),
1985.

A Place with the Pigs: A Personal Parable, (produced
in New Haven, 1987; also see below), Faber (Boston, MA), 1988.

My Children! My Africa! (produced in Johannesburg
and New York City, 1989), Theatre Communications Group (New York, NY), 1990.

Playland, first produced in Cape Town, 1992 (published
with *A Place with the Pigs* as *Playland and A
Place with the Pigs,* Theatre Communications
Group [New York, NY], 1993).

The Township Plays (contains *No-Good Friday, Nongogo, The Coat, Sizwe Banzi Is Dead,* and *The Island*), Oxford University Press (Oxford, England),
1993.

My Life (also see below), first produced in Grahamstown, South Africa, National Festival of the Arts,
July 8, 1994.

Valley Song, (produced in Market Theater, Johannesburg, and McCarter Theater, Princeton, NJ, 1995),
Theatre Communications Group (New York, NY),
1996 (published with *My Life* as *My Life and Valley
Song,* Hodder and Stoughton, and Witwatersrand
University Press [Johannesburg, South Africa],
1996).

The Captain's Tiger: A Memoir for the Stage (produced
at City Center Stage, New York, 1999), Withwa-
tersrand University Press (Johannesburg, South Africa), 1997, Theatre Communications Group (New
York, NY), 1999.

Sorrows and Rejoicings (first produced at the Second
Stage Theater, New York, 2002), Theatre Communications Group (New York, NY), 2001.

Author of teleplays *Mille Miglia* and *The Guest at
Steenkampskraal.* Produced screenplays include *Boesman and Lena* (based on his play), 1972, *The Guest,*
1976, *Meetings with Remarkable Men,* 1979, *Marigolds
in August,* 1980, *Gandhi,* 1982, and *The Killing Fields,*
1984. Plays reprinted in various anthologies, including
Text & Teaching: The Search for Excellence, edited by
Michael Collins, Georgetown University Press, 1991.

WORK IN PROGRESS: A play about Hildegard of Bin-
gen, a twelfth-century German abbess.

SIDELIGHTS: As a white child growing up in segregated South Africa, Athol Fugard resisted the racist upbringing society offered him. Nevertheless, the boy who
would become, in the words of Gillian MacKay of *Maclean's,* "perhaps South Africa's most renowned literary

figure, and its most eloquent anti-apartheid crusader
abroad" did not completely escape apartheid's
influence—he insisted that the family's black servants
call him Master Harold, and he even spat at one of
them. Fugard told MacKay that the servant, an "extraordinary" man who had always treated him as a close
friend, "grieved for the state" of Fugard's soul and for-
gave him instead of beating him "to a pulp."

Fugard never forgot this incident, which he transformed
into a powerful scene in the play, *"Master Harold"
. . . and the Boys.* He told Lloyd Richards of *Paris
Review* that the event is like a deep stain which has
"soaked into the fabric" of his life. In Fugard's career
as a playwright, director, and actor, he has forced himself and his audiences to consider their own "stains."
As Frank Rich remarked in a 1985 *New York Times* review of *The Blood Knot,* "Mr. Fugard doesn't allow
anyone, least of all himself, to escape without examining the ugliest capabilities of the soul."

Despite Fugard's insistence that he is not a political
writer and that he speaks for no one but himself, his
controversial works featuring black and white characters have found favor with critics of apartheid. According to Brendan Gill of the *New Yorker, The Blood Knot,*
the play that made Fugard famous, "altered the history
of twentieth-century theatre throughout the world" as
well as the world's "political history." Not all critics of
apartheid, however, have appreciated Fugard's works.
Some "see a white man being a spokesman for what
has happened to black people and they are naturally in-
tolerant," Fugard explained to Paul Allen in *New Statesman and Society.*

Whether Fugard's theatrical explorations of passion,
violence, and guilt played a role in undermining apartheid or not, it is clear that he was involved in breaking
physical and symbolic barriers to integration. He defied
the apartheid system by founding the first enduring
black theater company in South Africa, by collaborating
with black writers, and by presenting black and white
actors on stage together for integrated audiences. He insisted upon performing plays for local audiences in
South Africa as well as for those in New York City and
London; his plays carried messages that people around
the world needed to hear. Even after the government
took Fugard's passport and banned his work, he refused
to consider himself an exile or to renounce his country.
Love, and not hate for South Africa, Fugard maintained,
would help it break the chains of apartheid. "Wouldn't
it be ironic if South Africa could teach the world something about harmony?," he asked MacKay.

Fugard is highly regarded by literary and theater critics. Stephen Gray of *New Theatre Quarterly* noted that the author has been called "the greatest active playwright in English." His works are renowned for their multifaceted, marginalized characters, realistic yet lyrical dialogue, and carefully crafted, symbolic plots. Critics have also praised Fugard's ability to write scenes which elicit emotion without declining into melodrama. Fugard has forged new paths in theater by directing and acting in many of his own plays and by writing and composing plays with the actors who perform in them.

Fugard credits his parents with shaping his insights about South African society. As a child, he developed close relationships with both his English-speaking South African father, Harold, and his mother, Elizabeth, the daughter of Dutch-speaking Afrikaners. Harold, a jazz musician and amputee who spent a great deal of time in bed, amused the boy with fantastic stories and confused him with his unabashed bigotry. Fugard's mother Elizabeth supported the family by efficiently managing their tea room. In an interview with Jamaica Kincaid for *Interview,* Fugard described his mother as "an extraordinary woman" who could "barely read and write." In Fugard's words, she was "a *monument* of decency and principle and just anger" who encouraged Fugard to view South African society with a thoughtful and critical eye.

If Fugard learned the power of words from his father, and if he discovered how to question society from his mother, he gained an understanding of the complexity of human nature from both parents. Like Fugard's characters, his parents were neither entirely good or evil. Nevertheless, as Fugard explained to Kincaid, "I think at a fairly early age I became suspicious of what the system was trying to do to me. . . . I became conscious of what attitudes it was trying to implant in me and what *prejudices* it was trying to pass on to me." Fugard fed his intellectual appetite with conversations with his mother and daily trips to the local library. By the time he began college, he knew he wanted to be a writer. He accepted a scholarship at the University of Cape Town and studied philosophy, but he left school before graduating to journey around the Far East on a steamer ship.

At this time in his life, Fugard entertained notions of writing a great South African novel. Yet his first attempt at writing a novel, as he saw it, was a failure, and he destroyed it. After Fugard met and married Sheila Meiring, an out-of-work South African actress, he developed an interest in writing plays. *The Cell* and *Klaas and the Devil* were the first results of this ambition.

Not until after Fugard began to keep company with a community of black writers and actors near Johannesburg did he experience a revelation in his work. During this time, he witnessed the frustration of the black writers and learned the intricacies of a system which shrewdly and cruelly thwarted their efforts to live and work freely. The plays he penned at this time, *No-Good Friday* and *Nongogo,* were performed by Fugard and his black actor friends for private audiences.

In 1959 Fugard moved to England to write. His work received little attention there, and Fugard began to realize that he needed to be in South Africa to follow his muse. Upon his return home in 1961, Fugard wrote a second novel. Although he tried to destroy this work, a pair of graduate students later found the only surviving copy, and it was published in 1981. Critics have noticed the presence of many of the elements which would re-emerge in Fugard's more famous plays in this novel, *Tsotsi.*

Tsotsi portrays the life of David, a young black man whose nickname, "Tsotsi," means "hoodlum." Tsotsi spends his time with his gang of thieving, murderous friends. He has no family and cannot remember his childhood. It is not until a woman he is about to attack gives him a box with a baby in it, and David gives the baby his name, that he begins to experience sympathy and compassion, and to recall his childhood. When David is about to kill a crippled old man he has been pursuing, he suddenly remembers how his mother was arrested and never came home, and how he began to rove with a pack of abandoned children. It is not long before he recalls the trauma that led to his violent life on the streets. Fugard does not allow David's character to revel in his newly discovered emotions or to continue his search for God: at the novel's end, David is crushed under a bulldozer in an attempt to save David, the baby.

Critics appreciate *Tsotsi* for the insight it provides into the lives of even minor characters. Fugard did not allow his readers to categorize characters as "good" or "bad"; instead, he forced readers to understand their complexity. In the *New York Times Book Review,* Ivan Gold called *Tsotsi* "a moving and untendentious book" which demonstrates Fugard's ability to "uncannily insinuate himself into the skins of the oppressed majority and articulate its rage and misery and hope." Although Barbara A. Bannon in *Publishers Weekly* commented that *Tsotsi* is "altogether different in tone" from some of his plays, she also observed that the "milieu is much the same as the one that has made Fugard . . . the literary conscience of South Africa."

While Fugard generally works on one project at a time (typically writing with pens instead of word processors), he wrote *Tsotsi* and *The Blood Knot* simultaneously. The inspiration for *The Blood Knot* came when the author walked into a room and saw his brother asleep in bed one night. His brother had lived a difficult life, and his pain was apparent in his face and body. Realizing that there was nothing he could do to save his brother from suffering, Fugard experienced guilt. By writing *The Blood Knot,* Fugard recalled to Richards in *Paris Review,* he "was trying to examine a guilt more profound than racial guilt—the existential guilt that I feel when another person suffers, is victimized, and I can do nothing about it. South Africa afforded me the most perfect device for examining this guilt."

The Blood Knot is the story of two brothers born to the same mother. Morris, who has light skin, can "pass" for white; he confronts the truth about his identity when he returns home to live with his dark-skinned brother, Zachariah. Although the opening scene of the play finds Morris preparing a bath for hard-working Zachariah's feet, it soon becomes clear that the brothers' relationship is a tenuous one. The tension between the brothers is heightened when Zach's white pen pal (a woman who thinks Zach is white) wants to meet him, and Morris must pretend to be the white man with whom she has been corresponding.

Morris's attempts to look and sound white are painful for both brothers: To convincingly portray a white man, Morris must treat his black brother with the cruelty of a racist. In his role as a white man, Morris sits in the park and calls insults at his brother, who chases black children from the presence of his "white" brother. By the last scene, the "game" is out of control, and Zach tries to kill Morris. According to Robert M. Post in *Ariel,* the brothers in *The Blood Knot* "are typical victims of the system of apartheid and bigotry" and "personify the racial conflict of South Africa."

Fugard had little support in producing the play; it was not until actor Zakes Mokae joined the project that the production emerged. As a result of this collaboration, the first production of *The Blood Knot* was controversial not only for its content, but also because it featured a black actor and a white actor on stage together. Fugard played the light-skinned brother who "passes" for a white man, while Mokae played the darker-skinned brother. *The Blood Knot* opened in front of a mixed-race, invitation-only audience in a run-down theatre. As Derek Cohen noted in *Canadian Drama,* this first production of *The Blood Knot* "sent shock waves" through South Africa. "Those who saw the initial performance knew instinctively that something of a revolution had taken place in the stodgily Angloid cultural world of South Africa," he wrote. "Whites, faced boldly with some inescapable truths about what their repressive culture and history had wrought, were compelled to take notice."

Responses to *The Blood Knot* varied. As Cohen notes, some Afrikaners believed that the play's message was that blacks and whites could not live together in peace, and some black critics called the work racist. Many now accept the interpretation of the play as a sad commentary on the way racism has twisted and tangled our understanding of brotherhood and humanity. More specifically, according to Cohen, *The Blood Knot* is "about the hatred which South African life feeds on."

According to Dennis Walder in his book *Athol Fugard,* many of Fugard's plays "approximate . . . the same basic model established by *The Blood Knot:* a small cast of 'marginal' characters is presented in a passionately close relationship embodying the tensions current in their society, the whole first performed by actors directly involved in its creation, in a makeshift, 'fringe' or 'unofficial' venue." Since the first production of *The Blood Knot,* the substance of Fugard's plays as well as the means of their production have reflected the historical circumstances in which they evolved. Fugard insists that individual performances of each of his plays represent the legitimate play; he personally selects the actors and also continues to direct and act in them himself.

Boesman and Lena, produced in 1969, was Fugard's next great success; Cohen called it "possibly the finest of Fugard's plays." This work develops around the image of an old, homeless woman Fugard once saw, presenting a homeless couple (both "colored") who wander without respite. According to Cohen, it is a "drama of unrelieved and immitigable suffering" which becomes "more intense as the characters, impotent against the civilization of which they are outcasts, turn their fury against each other."

Fugard suffered from writer's block after he wrote *Boesman and Lena,* but went on to work in collaboration with actors to create *Orestes* in 1971. *Orestes* developed as a collection of images which, Walder remarked, "defies translation into a script" and explores "the effect of violence upon those who carry it out."

Fugard's next project began after two amateur actors, John Kani and Winston Ntshona, asked Fugard to help them become professional actors. As Fugard explained to Richards in his *Paris Review* interview, "at that point in South Africa's theater history . . . the notion that a black man could earn a living being an actor in South Africa was just the height of conceit." Nevertheless, the trio decided to create their own play. Three plays eventually emerged from this plan in 1972—*The Island, Sizwe Banzi Is Dead,* and *Statements after an Arrest under the Immorality Act,* also known as *The Statements Trilogy* or *The Political Trilogy.*

In these plays, personal experiences, along with the direction of Fugard, combine to provoke audiences. Post commented that *The Island* and *Statements* share "the basic conflict of the individual versus the government." In *The Island,* prisoners (portrayed by John and Winston) in a South African jail stage Sophocles's *Antigone;* the play within the play suggests that, according to Post, the "conflict between individual conscience and individual rights . . . and governmental decrees . . . corresponds to the conflict between the individual conscience and the rights of black prisoners and white government." *Statements* follows the relationship between a white librarian and a black teacher who become lovers despite their fear of being caught and castigated; eventually, their "illegal" love is uncovered by the police.

The development of *Sizwe Banzi Is Dead* began with an image of a black man in a new suit, seated and smiling, that Fugard saw in a photographer's store. Speculation about why the man was smiling led to a story about the passbook that blacks had to carry around with them under the apartheid system. Before Sizwe Banzi can get his passbook in order, he must symbolically die by trading his identity for another. The play was performed "underground" until, as Fugard told Richards, it "had played in London and New York" and earned a reputation that "protected" its writers and cast. In 1974, Kani won a Tony Award for his New York performance in *Sizwe Banzi Is Dead.*

Fugard unveiled *A Lesson from Aloes* in 1978. Like his other works, this play demonstrates the extent to which apartheid effects everyone in South African society. Piet, a Dutch Afrikaner living in Port Elizabeth in 1963, tends his collection of hardy, bitter aloe plants and joins a group of political activists. When the group's bus boycott is disrupted by the police and Piet's only friend Steve is found to have mixed blood and sent away, Piet is blamed. Even Piet's wife, whose diaries have been read by the police, believes he betrayed Steve.

Instead of defending himself, Piet isolates himself in his quiet aloe garden, and even the audience is unsure of his innocence. At the same time, Gladys, his wife,

laments the violation of her diaries and goes insane. Fugard explained that he wanted to demonstrate the "complexity" of the Afrikaner in *A Lesson from Aloes.* He told Richards in his *Paris Review* interview, "[we will] never understand how we landed in the present situation or what's going to come out of it" if we "simply dispose of the Afrikaner as the villain in the South African situation."

"Master Harold" . . . and the Boys communicates similar notions. Hallie, whose childhood parallels Fugard's, is troubled by his father's thoughtless and unthinking attitude. Although he has a close relationship with his family's black servants, Sam and Willie, even he is not immune to the evil of apartheid; at one point in the play, the boy spits in Willie's face. Fugard tells Richards how the relationship shared by Hallie, Sam, and Willie is autobiographical, and how he really did spit in Willie's face. He felt that it was "necessary" to deal with what he'd done by writing *"Master Harold" . . . and the Boys.*

"Master Harold" . . . and the Boys was the second of Fugard's plays to open in the United States, where it earned critical acclaim. Despite this American success, the play provoked criticism from individuals and groups who, as Jeanne Colleran noted in *Modern Drama,* either asserted that characters like Sam exhibit "Uncle Tom-ism," or demanded that Fugard present his plays in South Africa instead of abroad, in "languages of the black majority." Colleran suggested that because of this criticism, "Fugard cannot write of Johannesburg or of township suffering without incurring the wrath of Black South Africans who regard him as a self-appointed and presumptuous spokesman; nor can he claim value for the position previously held by white liberals without being assailed by the more powerful and vociferous radical left. . . . Ironically . . . Fugard has been forced to practice a kind of self-censorship by those whose cause he shared."

"Master Harold" . . . and the Boys also received negative attention from the South African government, which claimed that it was subversive. The government proclaimed it illegal to import or distribute copies of the play. Fugard later managed to present *"Master Harold" . . . and the Boys* in Johannesburg, because the government did not forbid the play's performance.

The publication of *Notebooks, 1960-1977* reinforced Fugard's growing popularity in the United States. This book provides what Pico Iyer of *Time* calls "the random scraps out of which Fugard fashioned his plays" and "a trail of haunting questions." Richard Eder of the *Los Angeles Times Book Review* asserted that, in addition to providing "the most vivid possible picture of an artist striving to shape his material even as it was detonating all around him," the *Notebooks* are "an illuminating, painful and beguiling record of a life lived in one of those tortured societies where everything refers back, sooner or later, to the situation that torments it."

When *The Road to Mecca* opened in 1984 at the Yale Repertory Theatre, American audiences were captivated by Fugard's mastery once again. Nevertheless, this play reinforced Fugard's reputation as a regional writer by reconstructing the character and life of a woman who lived in Karoo, where Fugard kept his South African home. Unable to take comfort from the Karoo community, Helen Martins isolates herself at home; there, she produces sculpture after sculpture from cement and wire. Benedict Nightingale noted in *New Statesman* that while Helen Martins actually committed suicide by "burning out her stomach with caustic soda," Fugard recreates her as "a docile old widow" with a beautiful life; "that paranoia, that suicide are ignored" by the playwright. The central problem in the play consists of the local pastor's attempts to get Helen to enter a home for the elderly to hide his secret love for her. As Jack Kroll observed in *Newsweek,* although *The Road to Mecca* "doesn't seem to be a political play at all," it "concerns love and freedom, and for Fugard that is the germ cell of the South African problem."

With some exceptions, *The Road to Mecca* was lauded by critics. While Nightingale appreciates the presentation of the Afrikaner pastor "in the round, from his own point of view as much as that from the liberal outsider," he also finds the play to be "exasperatingly uneven, as unreal and real a play as Fugard has ever yet penned." According to Colleran, *The Road to Mecca* was "extraordinarily well received," playing at Britain's National Theatre and on Broadway. Graham Leach asserted in *Listener* that *The Road to Mecca* is "universal" and "a major piece of theatre. . . . Many people here believe it may well end up being judged Fugard's finest work."

A Place with the Pigs, as Colleran recounted in *Modern Drama,* is a personal parable "concerning the forty years spent in a pigsty" by a "Red Army deserter." It premiered at the Yale Repertory Theatre in 1987 with Fugard in the leading role. Unlike *The Road to Mecca,* *A Place with the Pigs* did not receive critical acclaim. Colleran suggested that the play may have failed to

gain positive attention because it "simply does not conform to the audience's expectations of what a work by Athol Fugard should be like." In her opinion, the "dismissal" of *A Place with the Pigs* is unfortunate, in part because this "parable of one segment of South African society—the white South African who is committed both to dismantling apartheid and to remaining in his homeland—it adds a new voice, an authentic one, to those clamoring to decide the future of South Africa."

My Children! My Africa! was the first of Fugard's plays to premiere in South Africa in years. According to Gray in *New Theatre Quarterly,* Fugard believed that "South African audiences should have this play first." Fugard ensured that many audiences were exposed to this work: After a long run at the Market Theatre in Johannesburg, *My Children! My Africa!* was performed for six weeks in a tour of black townships in South Africa in 1989 with Lisa Fugard, Fugard's daughter, and John Kani in starring roles.

Like *"Master Harold" . . . and the Boys, My Children! My Africa!* portrays the struggles of youths to live with or confront the division between races in South Africa. Yet, as Allen of *New Statesman and Society* observed, the play marks "the first time Fugard . . . put the struggle itself on stage." Fugard was inspired by the story of a black teacher who refused to participate in a school boycott and was later murdered in Port Elizabeth by a group that believed he was a police informer.

Playland was the first of Fugard's plays to appear after the fall of apartheid. It is set on New Year's Eve in a traveling amusement park in Karoo. Here, a black night watchman painting a bumper car and a white South African whose car has broken down meet, discuss their lives, and reveal their darkest secrets: the white man tells how he killed blacks in a border war, and the black man confesses that he killed a white man who tried to force his fiancée (who was working as the white man's servant) to have sexual intercourse with him. John Simon of *New York* criticized the play: "There is hardly a situation, a snatch of dialogue, an object that isn't, or doesn't become, a symbol." But, according to Edith Oliver in a *New Yorker* review of the play, the spell cast by the actors' performances "is rooted in Mr. Fugard's moral passion." She concluded: "I have rarely seen an audience so mesmerized, or been so mesmerized myself."

Set after Nelson Mandela's election as South Africa's new president, *Valley Song* portrays four "colored" characters as they prepare to face the challenges of the future. Fugard was happy to premiere *Valley Song* at the Market Theatre in Johannesburg. As Donald G. McNeil, Jr., of the *New York Times* reported, Fugard was also optimistic about the future of South Africa: "We're pulling off a political miracle here." In a *World Literature Today* article, Harold A. Waters stated: "*Valley Song* is a paean to post-apartheid."

Fugard published an autobiography in 1997, entitled *Cousins: A Memoir*. In it, the playwright describes his relationship to Johnnie, his cousin of Afrikaner descent, and Garth, his English cousin. Fugard considers that as different as the two men's characters may have been, each served as an important inspiration to him in his literary work. This memoir also includes some hints of autobiographical events that appear in his plays. "A readable gem of a memoir," wrote Katherine K. Koenig in *Library Journal*. In a *Booklist* review, Jack Helbig commented that *Cousins* is a "warmhearted memoir." A reviewer for *Publishers Weekly* called the book "an excellent complement to [Fugard's] plays."

Cousins was followed by a dramatic memoir, *The Captain's Tiger: A Memoir for the Stage*, which first appeared in Johannesburg and Pretoria. This play is concerned with the twenty-year-old writer as he travels from Africa to Japan on a steamer. During his sea journey, the young man makes an inner journey through his attempt to recount the story of his mother's life. "Athol Fugard has cooked up a rare feast for theatergoers," wrote David Sheward in *Back Stage*. In a *Variety* review, Charles Isherwood voiced conflicting sentiments about the play. "It's suffused with a tenderly evoked sympathy for [Fugard's] mother," said Isherwood, but, he continued, "it's a minor-key and ultimately rather uninvolving play." Later in the article, the critic stated: "The play feels like a piece of prose only half transformed into stage material." Robert L. Daniels called *The Captain's Tiger* "a sweetly autobiographical memory play" that demonstrates Fugard's "lyrical sense of storytelling." Daniels remarked in his article in *Variety*: "Fugard is delightfully feisty and impish" in his role as the ship's steward. The critic concluded that the co-directors (Fugard and Susan Hilferty) had directed *The Captain's Tiger* "with tasteful simplicity."

Sorrows and Rejoicings is yet another drama in Fugard's series of post-apartheid plays. It involves an Afrikaner poet, David Olivier, who goes into exile in England when his writings are banned in South Africa. He returns to his homeland, along with his wife, Allison, shortly before his death. As the play begins, David has already died, and his story is recounted by his wife, his "colored" mistress, and his illegitimate daughter. The ghost of David appears onstage to interact with the women in his life.

Critics greeted this play with mixed reviews. "Fugard's sparsely populated and sparely plotted tone poems are an advanced model of the most literary kind," said Sean Mitchell in a *Los Angeles Times* review. He also noted that the writer's words "fail to gather much steam as drama," despite the fact that they "offer enduring images of a beautiful, cruel land." Charles Isherwood called *Sorrows and Rejoicings* an "eloquent, moving and piercingly sad new play . . . which has been sensitively staged." "The play does not succeed so well as most of [Fugard's] earlier work," commented Robert L. King in *North American Review*. In a *Variety* article, Robert L. Daniels stated that *Sorrows and Rejoicings* is "a romantic memory play heightened by the playwright's poetic storytelling gifts." Ed Kaufman praised Fugard as "a writer-poet with power and passion." In his *Hollywood Reporter* review, the critic considered the play to be Fugard's "most personal statement about the political, social and moral dynamics within South Africa."

Twenty-eight years after its premiere, a revival of *The Island* appeared in London in 2002, featuring the original actors, Kani and Ntshona. Since the play was written and staged during the apartheid period, it might well have seemed outdated; the theater critics, however, did not find that to be the case. "The production makes the prisoners' experience seem vividly of-the-moment as well as universal in application," wrote Dominic Cavendish in *Daily Telegraph*. Michael Billington of the *Guardian* praised Fugard's "astonishing collaborative play" that is staged with "sheer theatrical intelligence."

In an interview with Simon Hattenstone, Athol Fugard considered his work in the light of post-apartheid. When apartheid first ended, Fugard thought he might become "South Africa's first literary redundancy." After further reflection, however, he considered "that the new complicated South Africa needs more vigilance than ever before." Although the country's politics have changed, Fugard finds himself faced with a challenge: "What do I do now? That is the question and I'm trying to answer that question . . . by way of the three post-apartheid plays I've written."

BIOGRAPHICAL AND CRITICAL SOURCES:

BOOKS

Benson, Mary, *Athol Fugard and Barney Simon: Bare Stage, a Few Props, Great Theatre*, Ravan Press (Randburg, South Africa), 1997.

Bigsby, Christopher, *Writers in Conversation,* Pen & Inc. (Norwich, England), 2001.

Forsyth, Alison, *Gadamer, History, and the Classics: Fugard, Marowitz, Berkoff, and Harrison Rewrite the Theatre,* Peter Lang (New York, NY), 2002.

Fugard, Athol, *Notebooks, 1960-1977,* Faber (London, England), 1983, Knopf (New York, NY), 1984.

Gray, Stephen, *Athol Fugard,* McGraw Hill (New York, NY), 1982.

Hauptfleisch, Temple, *Athol Fugard: A Source Guide,* Donker (Johannesburg, South Africa), 1982.

Vandenbroucke, Russell, *Truths the Hand Can Touch: The Theatre of Athol Fugard,* Theatre Communications Group (New York, NY), 1985.

Walder, Dennis, *Athol Fugard,* Macmillan (New York, NY), 1984.

Walton, J. Michael, and Marianne McDonald, editors, *Amid Our Troubles,* Methuen (London, England), 1984.

Wertheim, Albert, *The Dramatic Art of Athol Fugard: From South Africa to the World,* Indiana University Press (Bloomington, IN), 2000.

PERIODICALS

America, March 21, 1992, pp. 250-251.

Ariel, July, 1985, pp. 3-17.

Back Stage, January 29, 1999, David Sheward, review of *The Captain's Tiger,* p. 64; February 8, 2002, Julius Novick, review of *Sorrows and Rejoicings,* p. 56; February 22, 2002, Simi Horwitz, "In Search of the New Classics," p. 7-8.

Booklist, December 1, 1982, p. 478; Jack Helbig, review of *Cousins: A Memoir,* p. 301.

Canadian Drama, spring, 1980, pp. 151-61.

Chicago, March, 1989, p. 34.

Commonweal, June 3, 1988, pp. 342-343.

Guardian (London), January 24, 2002, Michael Billington, review of *The Island;* March 18, 2002, Simon Hattenstone, interview with Athol Fugard, p. 4; March 26, 2002, Michael Billington, review of *Sorrows and Rejoicings,* p. 16.

Hollywood Reporter, February 27, 2002, Frank Scheck, review of *Sorrows and Rejoicings,* p. 44-45; May 24, 2002, Ed Kaufman, review of *Sorrows and Rejoicings,* p. 34.

Interview, August, 1990, pp. 64-69.

Kirkus Reviews, December 1, 1980, p. 1530; September 1, 1997, review of *Cousins,* p. 87.

Library Journal, November 1, 1997, Katherine K. Koenig, review of *Cousins: A Memoir,* p. 74.

Listener, December 13, 1984, p. 20.

Los Angeles Times, March 13, 1982; July 17, 1983; April 8, 1984, pp. 3, 5; July 29, 1983; May 24, 2002, Sean Mitchell, review of *Sorrows and Rejoicings,* p. 30.

Maclean's, June 18, 1990, pp. 58-59.

Modern Drama, March, 1990, pp. 82-92.

New Republic, July 25, 1970; December 21, 1974.

New Statesman and Society, March 8, 1985, pp. 30-31; September 7, 1990, p. 38.

Newsweek, May 28, 1984, pp. 85-86; May 2, 1988, p. 73.

New Theatre Quarterly, February, 1990, pp. 25-30.

New York, June 6, 1970; December 2, 1974; February 20, 1978; May 17, 1982; January 6, 1986; June 21, 1993, pp. 71-72.

New Yorker, December 11, 1978; December 23, 1985, pp. 78, 80; June 28, 1993, p. 9; February 18, 2002, John Lahr, review of *Sorrows and Rejoicings,* p. 196-198.

New York Times, September 19, 1969; May 17, 1970; June 4, 1970; July 6, 1970; December 17, 1974; February 2, 1977; April 1, 1980; April 5, 1980; November 16, 1980; February 1, 1981, pp. 8, 27; June 6, 1981; March 21, 1982; May 5, 1982; November 12, 1982; December 5, 1982; May 15, 1984; December 11, 1985, p. C23; April 3, 1987; May 28, 1987; April 10, 1988; April 13, 1988; April 24, 1988; January 13, 1995, p. C2; January 18, 1998, Lisa Michaels, review of *Cousins,* p. 16; January 5, 1999, Mel Gussow, review of *The Captain's Tiger,* p. E1; January 20, 1999, Peter Marks, review of *The Captain's Tiger,* p. E1; September 3, 2002, Rachel L. Swarns, review of *Sorrows and Rejoicings,* p. E1.

North American Review, March-April, 2002, "New Plays and a Modern Master," Robert L. King, p. 45-46.

Paris Review, summer, 1989, pp. 128-151.

Publishers Weekly, December 19, 1980, p. 38; September 1, 1997, review of *Cousins,* p. 87.

Theater, fall-winter, 1984, pp. 40-42.

Theatre Journal, March, 1998, Mark Reynolds, "Valley Song," p. 103-105.

Time, April 30, 1984, pp. 76-77.

Times (London), March 23, 2002, Benedict Nightingale, review of *Sorrows and Rejoicings,* p. 23.

Times Literary Supplement, May 2, 1980; March 1, 1985.

Travel and Leisure, December, 1992, pp. 118-122.

Variety, May 18, 1998, Robert L. Daniels, review of *The Captain's Tiger,* p. 82-83; January 25, 1999, Charles Isherwood, review of *The Captain's Tiger* p. 84; May 14, 2001, Robert L. Daniels, review of *Sorrows and Rejoicings,* p. 33; March 15, 1993, p. 70; February 11, 2002, Charles Isherwood, review of *Sorrows and Rejoicings,* p. 49.

Village Voice, February 20, 1978.

Wall Street Journal, February 6, 2002, Barbara D. Phillips, review of *Sorrows and Rejoicings,* p. A16.

Washington Post, April 13, 1985; September 29, 1987; September 29, 1998, William Triplett, review of *The Captain's Tiger,* p. D10.

World Literature Today, summer, 1983, pp. 369-71; Spring, 1998, Harold A. Waters, "Valley Song," p. 444.

FUGARD, Harold Athol
	See FUGARD, Athol

*   *   *

FUNDI
	See BARAKA, Amiri

G

GADDIS, William 1922-1998

PERSONAL: Born 1922, in New York, NY; died of prostate cancer December 16, 1998, in East Hampton, NY; children: one son, one daughter. *Education:* Attended Harvard College, 1941-45.

CAREER: New Yorker, New York, NY, fact checker, 1946-47; lived in Latin America, Europe, and North Africa, 1947-52; freelance writer of film scripts, speeches, and corporate communications, 1956-70; novelist. Also taught at universities. Distinguished visiting professor at Bard College, 1977.

MEMBER: American Academy of Arts and Letters, American Academy of Arts and Sciences.

AWARDS, HONORS: National Institute of Arts and Letters grant, 1963; National Endowment for the Arts grants, 1967 and 1974; Rockefeller grant and National Book Award for fiction, both 1976, both for *J R;* Guggenheim fellowship, 1981; MacArthur Foundation fellowship, 1982; nomination for PEN/Faulkner Award, 1985, for *Carpenter's Gothic;* National Book Award, 1994, and National Book Critics' Circle Award, 1995, both for *A Frolic of His Own.*

WRITINGS:

NOVELS

The Recognitions, Harcourt (New York, NY), 1955, corrected edition, Penguin (New York, NY), 1993.
J R, Knopf (New York, NY), 1975, corrected edition, Penguin (New York, NY), 1993.

Carpenter's Gothic, Viking (New York, NY), 1985.
A Frolic of His Own, Simon & Schuster (New York, NY), 1994.
Agape, Agape, Viking (New York, NY), 2002.
The Rush for Second Place: Essays and Occasional Writings, Penguin (New York, NY), 2002.

OTHER

Contributor to periodicals, including *Atlantic, Antaeus, New Yorker, New York Times,* and *Harper's.*

SIDELIGHTS: William Gaddis was one of the most highly regarded yet least-read novelists in late twentieth-century America, and was described by *New York Times Book Review* contributor George Stade as "a presiding genius . . . of post-war American fiction." Although many readers remain unfamiliar with Gaddis's work, certain critics have made extravagant claims for it. Richard Toney, in the *San Francisco Review of Books,* described the novelist's first book, *The Recognitions,* as a work "of stunning power, 956 pages of linguistic pyrotechnics and multi-lingual erudition unmatched by any American writer in this century—perhaps in any century." L.J. Davis, in the *National Observer,* wrote that Gaddis's second novel, *J R,* "is the equal of—if not superior to—its predecessor"; but the work remains, as Frederick Karl asserted in *Conjunctions,* "perhaps the great unread novel of the postwar era." With the publication in 1994 of *A Frolic of His Own,* which won a National Book Award, Gaddis's work received wider recognition.

Gaddis drew heavily on his own background for the settings of his novels. Born in Manhattan in 1922, he was raised in Massapequa, Long Island, in the house that was the model for the Bast home in *J R*. Like the Basts, Gaddis's maternal relatives were Quakers, though he himself was raised in a Calvinist tradition, as is Wyatt Gwyon, protagonist in *The Recognitions*. Like Otto in the same novel and Jack Gibbs in *J R*, Gaddis grew up without a father. Haunting all four novels, in fact, is the spirit of a dead or absent father who leaves a ruinous state of affairs for his children, a situation that may be extrapolated to include Gaddis's literary vision of a world abandoned by God and plunged into disorder. The writer's fifth through thirteenth years were spent at a boarding school in Berlin, Connecticut, which not only furnished the fictional Jack Gibbs with the bleak memories recalled in *J R* but also provided the unnamed New England setting for the first chapter of *The Recognitions*. Returning to Long Island to attend Farmingdale High School, Gaddis contracted the illness that debilitates Wyatt in the first novel and that kept Gaddis out of World War II. Instead he attended Harvard University and edited the *Harvard Lampoon* until circumstances required him to leave college in 1945 without a degree.

Back in New York, Gaddis worked as a fact checker at the *New Yorker,* a job he later recalled as "terribly good training, a kind of post-graduate school for a writer, checking everything, whether they were stories or profiles or articles. . . . A lot of the complications of high finance and so forth in *J R*—I tried very hard to get them all right. And it was very much that two years at the *New Yorker,*" he once told Miriam Berkley in a *Publishers Weekly* interview. At this time he also mingled in the Greenwich Village milieu recreated in the middle section of *The Recognitions*. Here he became acquainted with future Beat writers William Burroughs, Allen Ginsberg, Alan Ansen, Chandler Brossard, and Jack Kerouac. (In fact, Kerouac converted Gaddis into a character named Harold Sand in his 1958 novel *The Subterraneans*.) In 1947 Gaddis set off on a five-year trip wandering through Mexico, Central America, Spain, France, and North Africa. In 1952 he returned to America to complete his first novel.

Published in 1955, *The Recognitions* is an account of personal integration amid collective disintegration, of an individual finding himself in a society losing itself. Protagonist Wyatt Gwyon, a failed seminarian, turns to forging the paintings of the Old Masters in an earnest but misguided attempt to return to an era when art was authentic and sanctioned by God. Gaddis sets Wyatt in stark contrast to most of the other artist figures in the novel: Otto, the playwright; Esme, the poet; Max, the painter; Sinisterra, the counterfeiter—all of whom plagiarize, falsify, or discredit the artistic process. These

personages, along with the rest of the novel's large cast of characters, are representative of a society crumbling in a shoddy world so encrusted with counterfeit that "recognitions" of authenticity are nearly impossible.

The action in *The Recognitions* runs on two narrative planes that occasionally intersect. On one plane lives Wyatt, whom Karl in *Conjunctions* calls "an avenging Messiah . . . because he perceives himself as bringing a purifying and cleansing quality, a 'recognition,' to a society that has doomed itself with corruptive sophistication." But Wyatt is hobbled in his pursuit of a "vision of order"—as it is later defined in *Carpenter's Gothic*—by a psychologically crippling boyhood that has instilled in him a mixture of guilt, secrecy, and alienation. The author exposes the compromised worlds of religion and art in the first two chapters, and Wyatt's brief fling with conventionality—complete with wife and nine-to-five job—fails by chapter three, leaving him open to the temptations of the novel's Mephistopheles, Recktall Brown, a corrupt art dealer. Selling his soul to the devil, Wyatt retreats offstage for the entrance of his parodic counterpart, Otto Pivner, whose comic misadventures in Central America and Greenwich Village constitute the second narrative plane of the novel.

Here the "corruptive sophistication" mentioned by *Conjunctions*'s Karl appear as endless discussions of art and religion are carried on through endless parties and bar conversations by those whom Gaddis lampoons as "the educated classes, an ill-dressed, underfed, overdrunken group of squatters with minds so highly developed that they were excused from good manners, tastes so refined in one direction that they were excused for having none in any other, emotions so cultivated that the only aberration was normality, all afloat here on sodden pools of depravity calculated only to manifest the pricelessness of what they were throwing away, the three sexes in two colors, a group of people all mentally and physically the wrong size."

With the realization that the major cause for the godless condition embodied by and surrounding modern humanity may be attributed to the absence of love, Wyatt abandons forgery, travels to Spain where his mother is entombed, and finds the love necessary to baptize his new life. Spurning love, the rest of the novel's characters are last seen rushing headlong into death, madness, or disintegration.

The Recognitions presents a multi-layered complexity necessary to dramatize the novel's themes of imitation versus reality. As Tony Tanner pointed out in the *New*

York Times Book Review, "If at times we feel lost, displaced, disoriented as we move through the complicated edifice of the book, we are only experiencing analogically a lostness that is felt in varying ways by all the characters in the book." Often eschewing traditional narrative exposition, Gaddis abandons the reader at the various scenes of action, forcing the reader instead to overhear the confused gropings, deliberate lies, and mistaken notions of the characters, to sort them out as best he can. In other words, the reader must participate in the novel and make the same "recognitions" demanded of its characters by the title. An immense network of allusions, references, motifs, and gestures are introduced and repeated in countless convoluted permutations, demanding much more than casual attention from the reader. The novel is also very erudite, but any negative effects of this characteristic have often been overemphasized; the sense, if not the literal meaning, of Gaddis's hundreds of references, allusions, and foreign language phrases is usually clear enough from the context.

The Recognitions had little immediate critical impact upon publication. Unfortunately, 1955 was "one of American criticism's weakest hours," as Maurice Dolbier noted in a *New York Herald Tribune* article seven years later, and most reviewers were put off by this gargantuan novel by an unknown writer. A few readers recognized its greatness immediately, but only in later years did a historical perspective allow critics to gauge its importance. In a *Saturday Review* assessment of Gaddis's second novel, John W. Aldridge adopted such a perspective: "As is usually the case with abrasively original work, there had to be a certain passage of time before an audience could begin to be educated to accept *The Recognitions,*" commented the critic, who added that "The most authoritative mode in the serious fiction of the Fifties was primarily realistic, and the novel of fabulation and Black Humor—of which *The Recognitions* was later to be identified as a distinguished pioneering example—had not yet come into vogue. In fact, the writers who became the leaders of the Black Humor movement had either not been heard from in 1955 or remained undiscovered. Their work over the past 20 years has created a context in which it is possible to recognize Gaddis's novel as having helped inaugurate a whole new movement in American fiction. Rereading it with the knowledge of all that this movement has taught us about modern experience and the opening of new possibilities for the novel, one can see that *The Recognitions* occupies a strikingly unique and primary place in contemporary literature."

Little was heard of Gaddis in the decade and a half after 1955. Denied the life of a "successful" novelist, he

began a long line of jobs in industry, working first in publicity for a pharmaceutical firm, then writing films for the U.S. Army, and later writing speeches for corporate executives. With the 1970 appearance in the *Dutton Review* of what would later become the opening pages of his second novel, Gaddis broke his fifteen-year silence. Two more fragments from *J R* appeared, in *Antaeus* and *Harper's,* before the novel was published in the fall of 1975 to much stronger reviews than those received by *The Recognitions. J R* won the National Book Award for the best fiction of the year and has since earned the praise of such writers as Saul Bellow, Mary McCarthy, William H. Gass, Stanley Elkin, Joseph McElroy, and Don DeLillo.

Although Gaddis's intricate, 726-page novel resists easy summary, it is essentially a satire of corporate America, a "country" so obsessed with money that failure is all but inevitable for anyone who does not sell his soul to Mammon. The first word of the novel is "money," a word that reappears throughout the novel as its debasing touch besmirches everything from education to science, from politics to marriage, from the arts to warfare. At the center of the novel is eleven-year-old J.R. Vansant, a slovenly but clever boy who transforms a small "portfolio" of mail order acquisitions and penny stocks into an unwieldy paper empire in an improbably short time. The most radical feature of the novel is its narrative mode: except for an occasional transitional passage, the novel is composed entirely of dialogue. While novels composed totally of dialogue had been written before, none followed Gaddis's extreme format. For his dialogue is not the literary dialogue of most novels, tidied up and helpfully sprinkled with conversational conventions and explanatory asides by the author helping to clarify what the characters actually mean. Instead, *J R* reads like a tape-recorded transcription of real voices: ungrammatical, often truncated, with constant interruptions by other characters (and by telephones, radios, and televisions), with rarely an identifying or interpretive remark by the author.

Such a literary mode makes unusual demands upon the reader; it requires that he read actively with involvement and concentration, rather than passively, awaiting entertainment. Jack Gibbs, a major character, pinpoints this problem during a drunken conversation with Edward Bast, a young composer: "Problem most God damned readers rather be at the movies. Pay attention here bring something to it take something away problem most God damned writing's written for readers perfectly happy who they are rather be at the movies, come in empty-handed go out the same God damned way I told him Bast. Ask them to bring one God damned bit of effort want everything done for them they get up and go to the movies." In his interview with *Publishers Weekly,* Gaddis reiterated the point: "For me it is very much a proposition between the reader and the page. That's what books are about. And he must bring something to it or he won't take anything away. . . . Television is hot, it provides everything. In the so-called situation comedies, you go with a completely blank mind, which is preoccupied for a half hour, and then you turn it off. You have brought nothing to it and you take nothing home. Much bad fiction is like this. Everything is provided for you, and you forget it a week later." What the attentive reader takes home from *J R* is a ringing in the ears from what Sarah E. Lauzen, in *Postmodern Fiction,* labeled "the constant cacophony of America selling America."

Just as everyone in the counterfeit cultural world of *The Recognitions* moves in relation to Wyatt, everyone in the phony paper world of *J R* moves in relation to the young title figure, who embodies what Gaddis called in his *Publishers Weekly* interview: "Simple naked cheerful greed, no meanness, no nastiness, and not a great deal of intelligence, as I say. Just doing what you're supposed to do." J.R. gleefully accepts the corrupt civilization handed down to him, wanting only to know how fast he can get his share. By following the letter of the law at the expense of its spirit, he is able to build his "family of companies" with the assistance of adults as amoral as he is.

The only adults who attempt to infuse a moral sense into J.R. are his teacher, Amy Joubert, and his reluctant business associate, Edward Bast, a struggling musician. But Amy is too preoccupied with her own problems to be of much help, and Bast causes more problems than he solves. Although one of the major conflicts in the novel is between such outwardly directed people as J.R. and such inwardly directed people as the book's artists, all of the latter figures have largely themselves to blame for their artistic failures rather than the crass business world to which they belong. Despite their failures, however, most are seen at work on new art projects at the novel's end, for as Johan Thielemans noted in an essay in *In Recognition of William Gaddis,* "Artistic perfection represents the only possible escape from entropic processes."

The term "entropy" is introduced in the novel almost as early as "money," and this concept—the tendency for any system to move from a state of order to one of disorder—operates throughout the novel. Nearly everyone in Gaddis's novel is caught up in a desperate at-

tempt to hold things together in the face of encroaching disorder and dissolution. But the attempts are largely futile: families break up, artists burn out and/or commit suicide, businesses close or are swallowed up by conglomerates, children are abandoned, coitus is interrupted, and communication breaks down. In *J R,* everyone's life is chaotic, and the exclusive use of dialogue creates what Thomas LeClair described in *Modern Fiction Studies* as "a massive consistency in which characters with different backgrounds, money-men and artists alike, come to have the same rushed habits of speech, the inability to complete a message or act." As *Saturday Review*'s Aldridge concluded about *J R:* "It is undoubtedly inevitable that the novel promises at almost every point to fall victim to the imitative fallacy, that it is frequently as turgid, monotonous, and confusing as the situation it describes. Yet Gaddis has a strength of mind and talent capable of surmounting this very large difficulty. He has managed to reflect chaos in a fiction that is not itself artistically chaotic because it is imbued with the conserving and correcting power of his imagination. His awareness of what is human and sensible is always present behind his depiction of how far we have fallen from humanity and sense."

Like its predecessor, *J R* is primarily a comic novel. As Alicia Metcalf Miller noted in the Cleveland *Plain Dealer,* "If Gaddis is a moralist, he is also a master of satire and humor. *J R* is a devastatingly funny book. Reading it, I laughed loudly and unashamedly in public places, and at home, more than once, I saw my small children gather in consternation as tears of laughter ran down my face." Such is the reader response for which *J R* aims.

Gaddis's underground reputation surfaced somewhat following the publication of *J R* in 1975. The National Book Award for fiction was followed by a steady stream of academic essays and dissertations, culminating in 1982 with the first book on Gaddis's work, a special issue of the *Review of Contemporary Fiction,* and his receipt of a MacArthur Foundation fellowship. Two years later, the second book on his work appeared, Gaddis was elected to the American Academy and Institute of Arts and Letters, and he finished his third novel.

For this novel—originally titled *That Time of Year: A Romance* but published in the summer of 1985 as *Carpenter's Gothic*—Gaddis turned away from the "meganovel" and set out to write a different as well as shorter—262 pages—book. As he once explained in a *Washington Post* interview with Lloyd Grove: "I wanted it to move very fast. Everything that happens on one page is preparing for the next page and the next chapter and the end of the book. When I started I thought, 'I want 240 pages'—that was what set I out for. It preserved the unity: one place, one very small amount of time, very small group of characters, and then, in effect, there's a nicer word than 'cliche,' what is it? Staples. That is, the staples of the marriage, which is on the rocks, the obligatory adultery, the locked room, the mysterious stranger, the older man and the younger woman, to try to take these and make them work."

Gaddis restores to worn-out literary clichés some of their original drama and intensity, particularly in *Carpenter's Gothic*. Like *The Recognitions*, his third novel is concerned with the ambiguous nature of reality; "there's a very fine line between the truth and what really happens" is an oft-repeated line in *Carpenter's Gothic*. The novel also attacks the perversions done in the name of religion. From *J R* it takes its narrative technique—an almost total dependence on dialogue—and its contempt for the motivating factor of capitalism. Sometimes seen by critics as a smaller, less-important reflection of the author's two preceding novels, this novel presents Gaddis's most characteristic themes and techniques with economy and flair.

Carpenter's Gothic is rooted in a specific time and place: the action takes place over a month's time—internal references date it between October and November of 1983—in a "carpenter gothic" style Victorian house in a small Hudson River Valley town. (Gaddis owned just such a house on Ritie Street in Piermont, New York.) Almost continuously on stage is Elizabeth Booth: "Bibbs" to her brother Billy, "Liz" to her husband Paul, and "Mrs. Booth" to McCandless, the house's owner and a failed novelist. These men subject Liz to the bullying, self-serving dialogue that makes up the bulk of the novel and that brings the outside world onto Gaddis's one-set stage. With newspapers and telephone calls filling the roles of messengers, a complicated plot quickly unfolds concerning Christian fundamentalism, political chicanery, African mineral rights, and a half-dozen family disputes. Long-suffering Liz endures it all, helpless to prevent her men from rushing headlong into—and even creating—the Armageddon that looms on the final pages of the novel.

In *Carpenter's Gothic,* as in all of Gaddis's novels, the males do most of the talking and create most of the problems. Like Esme in *The Recognitions* and Amy in *J R,* Liz is the still point in a frantic male world, "the only thing that holds things together," as her brother Billy admits. Though flawed, she is perhaps the most sympathetic figure in all three of Gaddis's novels. For that reason, her sudden death at the end gives *Carpenter's Gothic* its bleaker, more despairing tone.

Liz's husband Paul, a Vietnam veteran once attacked by his own men, is in one sense a grown-up J.R. Vansant—an identification Gaddis encourages when someone dismisses Paul for "know[ing] as much about finance as some snot nosed sixth grader." Like J. R., Paul simply does what people do to "make it" in America, never examining for an instant the ethics or morality of his questionable dealings. But the man who brings the greatest disorder into Liz's life is McCandless, the mysterious owner of the house, whom she transforms into a wearily romantic figure out of Charlotte Brontë's *Jane Eyre,* a movie version of which serves as a backdrop to Liz and Paul's joyless lovemaking. McCandless, no longer feeling any connection between his world and himself and outraged at the stupidity that has severed that connection, can only envision a bleak future.

This vision of deep disorder and empty outlook belongs to Gaddis as well, for *Carpenter's Gothic,* as Peter Prescott declared in *Newsweek,* "is surely Gaddis's most pessimistic, his most savage novel." No one in the novel demonstrates any possibility of sidestepping, much less overcoming, the novelist's vision of the world's crushing stupidity. An escape hatch through which characters such as Wyatt and Bast can save themselves is present in the first two novels, but no such option exists in *Carpenter's Gothic.* As Robert Kelly noted in *Conjunctions,* Gaddis does not seem to have "an optimistic bone in his body—at least not in his writing hand." This pessimism bothers many readers, but Kelly explained: "We are foolish if we expect the skilful anatomist who excoriates vicious folly to provide a cure for it too—and doubly foolish if we credit any panacea he does trick himself into prescribing."

In *Listener* Peter Kemp described the work as Gaddis's "grimmest book," observing, "A scathing, exacerbated *tour de force, Carpenter's Gothic* seems the last word on a society whose doomed babble it so vehemently transmits." In the *Nation,* Terrence Rafferty mentioned the novel's "sour, contemptuous tone and its formal bad faith," adding: "The real story of *Carpenter's Gothic* isn't the end of the world, it's the end of the imagination, the world gone dark in the writer's head." Carol Iannone remarked in *Commentary* that "Gaddis means to show us the consequences of stupidity. . . . *Carpenter's Gothic* shows that Gaddis is not so much an artist as an anti-artist, working with cartoon characters and disembodied ideas."

Even art, the panacea prescribed in the first two novels, is suspect in the third book. On one level, *Carpenter's Gothic* is a meditation on fiction, specifically on the dubious motives for writers' fiction-making impulses. For Liz—as perhaps for the younger Gaddis—fiction offers "some hope of order restored, even that of a past life in tatters, revised, amended, fabricated in fact from its very outset to reorder its unlikelihoods, what it all might have been." But McCandless insisted on the suspect, compromised nature of art in his commentary on the carpenter-gothic style of his house, a passage that doubles as a description of the novel itself: "All they had were the simple dependable old materials, the wood and their hammers and saws and their own clumsy ingenuity bringing those grandiose visions the masters had left behind down to a human scale with their own little inventions, . . . a patchwork of conceits, borrowings, deceptions, the inside's a hodgepodge of good intentions like one last ridiculous effort at something worth doing even on this small a scale." In this sense, any reader who flees the disorder of life for the order of art will find cold comfort in *Carpenter's Gothic*.

Throughout Gaddis's novels there is a sense of bitter disappointment at America for not fulfilling its potential, for events not working out as planned. In this regard Gaddis resembles his beloved Russian novelists of the nineteenth century; in the *New York Times Book Review* William H. Gass reported a talk of Gaddis's in Lithuania where he insisted "the comic and satiric side of his work was attempting to save his version of his country as the earlier Russian writers had endeavored to redeem theirs." In the third novel, however, America seems to have reached the bottom of the psychosocial abyss. *Carpenter's Gothic* implies that it is too late to reverse the tide, to restore the promise of the American dream, too late for anything more than "one last ridiculous effort at something worth doing."

Emphasizing litigiousness and greed as characteristics of contemporary American society, Gaddis's award-winning novel *A Frolic of His Own* focuses on Oscar Crease, his family, his friends, and the various lawsuits in which they are all enmeshed. Employing elements of humor and farce, Gaddis exhaustively details the absurdities of his characters' suits and subsequent countersuits. For example, Oscar is plaintiff in a plagiarism case he has brought against Constantine Kiester, a top Hollywood producer whose real name is Jonathan Livingston Siegal. Oscar is also, paradoxically, plaintiff and defendant in a suit concerning a hit-and-run accident in which he was hit by his own car—a Sosumi ("so sue me"). Taking its title from a British legal phrase used to describe an employee's actions which, though

they resulted in on-the-job injuries, do not entitle the employee to compensation, *A Frolic of His Own* is largely noted for its satire of justice and law in contemporary American society and for its unusual narrative structure.

Except for the inclusion of excerpts from Oscar's writings, legal documents, and court opinions, Gaddis relayed the novel's story line primarily through dialogue that is unattributed and only lightly punctuated. Critics have praised Gaddis's realistic depiction of everyday speech—complete with pauses, interruptions, and unfinished thoughts—and stressed the difficulty such a narrative technique, reminiscent of stream-of-consciousness writing, places on readers. As Steven Moore observed in the *Nation*, *A Frolic of His Own* "is both cutting-edge, state-of-the-art fiction and a throwback to the great moral novels of Tolstoy and Dickens. That it can be both is just one of the many balancing acts it performs: It is bleak and pessimistic while howlingly funny; it is a deeply serious exploration of such lofty themes as justice and morality but is paced like a screwball comedy; it is avant-garde in its fictional techniques but traditional in conception and in the reading pleasures it offers; it is a damning indictment of the United States, Christianity and the legal system, but also a playful frolic of Gaddis's own." Zachary Leader in the *Times Literary Supplement* called *A Frolic of His Own* a "bleak, brilliant, exhausting novel."

BIOGRAPHICAL AND CRITICAL SOURCES:

BOOKS

Aldridge, John W., *In Search of Heresy,* McGraw (New York, NY), 1956.

Comnes, Gregory, *The Ethics of Indeterminacy in the Novels of William Gaddis,* University Press of Florida (Gainesville, FL), 1994.

Contemporary Literary Criticism, Thomson Gale (Detroit, MI), Volume 1, 1973, Volume 3, 1975, Volume 6, 1976, Volume 8, 1978, Volume 10, 1979, Volume 19, 1981, Volume 43, 1987, Volume 86, 1995.

Dictionary of Literary Biography, Volume 2: *American Novelists since World War II,* Thomson Gale (Detroit, MI), 1978.

Gaddis, William, *Carpenter's Gothic,* Viking (New York, NY), 1985.

Gaddis, William, *J R,* Knopf (New York, NY), 1975, corrected edition, Penguin (New York, NY), 1985.

Gaddis, William, *The Recognitions,* Harcourt (New York, NY), 1955, corrected edition, Penguin (New York, NY), 1985.

Gardner, John, *On Moral Fiction,* Basic Books (New York, NY), 1978.

Knight, Christopher J., *Hints and Guesses: William Gaddis's Fiction of Longing,* University of Wisconsin Press, 1997.

Kuehl, John, and Steven Moore, editors, *In Recognition of William Gaddis,* Syracuse University Press (Syracuse, NY), 1984.

Madden, David, *Rediscoveries,* Crown (New York, NY), 1971.

Magill, Frank N., editor, *Literary Annual,* Salem Press, 1976.

Magill, Frank N., editor, *Survey of Contemporary Literature,* supplement, Salem Press, 1972.

McCaffery, Larry, editor, *Postmodern Fiction,* Greenwood Press (Westport, CT), 1986.

Moore, Steven, *A Reader's Guide to William Gaddis's "The Recognitions,"* University of Nebraska Press (Lincoln, NE), 1982.

Tanner, Tony, *City of Words,* Harper (New York, NY), 1971.

Wiener, Norbert, *The Human Use of Human Beings,* Houghton (Boston, MA), 1954.

Wolfe, Peter, *A Vision of His Own: The Mind and Art of William Gaddis,* Fairleigh Dickinson University Press (Rutherford, NJ), 1996.

PERIODICALS

Atlantic, April, 1985.

Berkeley Gazette, March 16, 1962.

Booklist, September 15, 2002, Donna Seaman, review of *Agape Agape,* p. 194.

Chicago Tribune Book World, July 14, 1985.

Christian Science Monitor, September 17, 1985, pp. 25-26.

Commentary, December, 1985, pp. 62-65.

Commonweal, April 15, 1955.

Conjunctions, number 7, 1985; number 8, 1985.

Contemporary Literature, winter, 1975.

Critique, winter, 1962-63; Volume 19, number 3, 1978; Volume 22, number 1, 1980.

Genre, number 13, 1980.

Hollins Critic, April, 1977.

Hungry Mind Review, spring, 1994, pp. 34, 42-43.

International Fiction Review, Volume 10, number 2, 1983.

Kirkus Reviews, August 15, 2002, review of *The Rush for Second Place: Essays and Occasional Writings,* p. 1193.

Library Journal, September 15, 2002, David W. Henderson, review of *Agape Agape,* p. 89.

Listener, March 13, 1986, pp. 28-29.

London Review of Books, May 12, 1994, pp. 20-21.

Los Angeles Times Book Review, July 14, 1985.

Modern Fiction Studies, number 27, 1981-82.

Nation, April 30, 1955; November 16, 1985, p. 496; April 25, 1994, pp. 569-71.

National Observer, October 11, 1975.

New Leader, January 17-31, 1994, pp. 18-19.

New Republic, September 2, 1985, pp. 30-32; February 7, 1994, pp. 27-30.

Newspaper, numbers 12-14, 1962.

Newsweek, March 14, 1955; November 10, 1975; July 15, 1985; January 17, 1994, p. 52.

New York, January 3, 1994, p. 34.

New Yorker, April 9, 1955.

New York Herald Tribune, April 14, 1962.

New York Herald Tribune Book Review, March 13, 1955.

New York Review of Books, February 17, 1994, pp. 3-4, 6.

New York Times, July 3, 1985, p. C22; November 15, 1987; January 4, 1994, p. C20.

New York Times Book Review, March 13, 1955; July 14, 1974; November 9, 1975; June 20, 1976; June 6, 1982; July 7, 1985; February 2, 1986; January 9, 1994, pp. 1, 22.

New York Times Magazine, November 15, 1987.

Observer Weekend Review, September 9, 1962.

People, May 9, 1994, p. 29.

Plain Dealer (Cleveland, OH), October, 1975.

Publishers Weekly, July 12, 1985; November 21, 1994, p. 26; September 23, 2002, review of *Agape Agape,* p. 48.

Pynchon Notes, number 11, 1983.

Queen's Quarterly, summer, 1962.

Review of Contemporary Fiction, Volume 2, number 2, 1982.

San Francisco Review of Books, February, 1976.

Saturday Review, March 12, 1955; October 4, 1975.

Scotsman, April 10, 1965.

Studies in American Humor, number 1, 1982.

Time, March 14, 1955; July 22, 1985; January 24, 1994, p. 67.

Times Literary Supplement, February 28, 1986; June 3, 1994, p. 22.

TREMA, number 2, 1977.

United States Quarterly Book Review, June, 1955.

Village Voice, November 1, 1962.

Village Voice Literary Supplement, April, 1991, p. 26.

Virginia Quarterly Review, summer, 1976.

Wall Street Journal, August 26, 1985, p. 14.

Washington Post, August 23, 1985.

Washington Post Book World, July 7, 1985, p. 1; January 23, 1994, pp. 1, 10.
Western Review, winter, 1956.
Wisconsin Studies in Contemporary Literature, summer, 1965.
Yale Review, September, 1951.

OBITUARIES:

PERIODICALS

Chicago Tribune, December 19, 1998, p. 23.
Los Angeles Times, December 18, 1998, p. B6.
New York Times, December 17, 1998, p. B15.
Times (London, England), January 14, 1999.
Washington Post, December 19, 1998, p. B6.

*   *   *

GAIMAN, Neil 1960-
(Neil Richard Gaiman)

PERSONAL: Born November 10, 1960, in Portchester, England; son of David Bernard (a company director) and Sheila (a pharmacist; maiden name, Goldman) Gaiman; married Mary Therese McGrath, March 14, 1985; children: Michael Richard, Holly Miranda, Madeleine Rose Elvira. *Politics:* "Wooly." *Religion:* Jewish. *Hobbies and other interests:* "Finding more bookshelf space."

ADDRESSES: Agent—Merilee Heifetz, Writer's House, 21 W. 26th St., New York, NY 10010.

CAREER: Freelance journalist, 1983-87; full-time writer, 1987—.

MEMBER: Comic Book Legal Defense Fund (board of directors), International Museum of Cartoon Art (advisory board), Science Fiction Foundation (committee member), Society of Strip Illustrators (chair, 1988-90), British Fantasy Society.

AWARDS, HONORS: Mekon Award, Society of Strip Illustrators, and Eagle Award for best graphic novel, both 1988, both for *Violent Cases;* Eagle Award for best writer of American comics, 1990; Harvey Award for best writer, 1990 and 1991; Will Eisner Comic Industry Award for best writer of the year and best graphic al-

bum (reprint), 1991; World Fantasy Award for best short story, 1991, for "A Midsummer Night's Dream"; Will Eisner Comic Industry Award for best writer of the year, 1992; Harvey Award for best continuing series, 1992; Will Eisner Comic Industry Award for best writer of the year and best graphic album (new), 1993; Gem Award, Diamond Distributors, for expanding the marketplace for comic books, 1993; Will Eisner Comic Industry Award for best writer of the year, 1994; Guild Award, International Horror Critics, and World Fantasy Award nomination, both 1994, both for *Angels and Visitations: A Miscellany* and short story "Troll Bridge;" GLAAD Award for best comic of the year, 1996, for *Death: The Time of Your Life;* Eagle Award for best comic, 1996; Lucca Best Writer Prize, 1997; *Newsweek* list of best children's books, 1997, for *The Day I Swapped My Dad for Two Goldfish;* Defender of Liberty Award, Comic Book Legal Defense Fund, 1997; MacMillan Silver Pen Award, 1999, for *Smoke and Mirrors: Short Fictions and Illusions;* Hugo Award nomination, 1999, for *Sandman: The Dream Hunters;* Mythopoeic Award for best novel for adults, 1999, for *Stardust: Being a Romance within the Realms of Faerie;* Nebula Award nomination, 1999, for screenplay for the film *Princess Mononoke;* Hugo Award for best science fiction/fantasy novel, Bram Stoker Award for best novel, Horror Writers Association, and British Science Fiction Association (BSFA) Award nomination, all 2002, all for *American Gods;* BSFA Award for best short fiction, Elizabeth Burr/Worzalla Award, Bram Stoker Award, Horror Writers Association, Hugo Award nomination, Nebula Award for best novella, and Prix Tam Tam Award, all 2003, all for *Coraline;* British Science Fiction Association Award for short fiction, Bram Stoker Award nomination, Locus Award nomination, International Horror Guild Nomination, all 2004, all for *The Wolves in the Walls;* Bram Stoker award for illustrated narrative, Locus Award, both 2004, both for *The Sandman: Endless Nights;* Hugo Award for short story, Locus Award for novelette, both 2004, both for "A Study in Emerald;" Locus Award for short story, 2004, for "Closing Time;" Quill Book Award for graphic novel, 2005, for *Marvel 1602, volume 1.* Gaiman has received international awards from Austria, Brazil, Canada, Finland, France, Germany, Italy, and Spain. His script *Signal to Noise* received a SONY Radio Award; Hugo Award for Best Short Story, 2004, for "A Study in Emerald".

WRITINGS:

GRAPHIC NOVELS AND COMIC BOOKS

Violent Cases, illustrated by Dave McKean, Titan (London, England), 1987, Tundra (Northampton, MA), 1991, Dark Horse Comics (Milwaukie, OR), 2003.

Black Orchid (originally published in magazine form in 1989), illustrated by Dave McKean, D.C. Comics (New York, NY), 1991.

Miracleman, Book 4: The Golden Age, illustrated by Mark Buckingham, Eclipse (Forestville, CA), 1992.

Signal to Noise, illustrated by Dave McKean, Dark Horse Comics (Milwaukie, OR), 1992.

The Books of Magic (originally published in magazine form, four volumes), illustrated by John Bolton and others, D.C. Comics (New York, NY), 1993.

The Tragical Comedy, or Comical Tragedy, of Mr. Punch, illustrated by Dave McKean, VG Graphics (London, England), 1994, Vertigo/ D.C. Comics (New York, NY), 1995, also published as *Mr. Punch.*

(Author of text, with Alice Cooper) *The Compleat Alice Cooper: Incorporating the Three Acts of Alice Cooper's The Last Temptation,* illustrated by Michael Zulli, Marvel Comics (New York, NY), 1995, published as *The Last Temptation,* Dark Horse Comics (Milwaukie, OR), 2000.

Angela, illustrated by Greg Capullo and Mark Pennington, Image (Anaheim, CA), 1995, published as *Spawn: Angela's Hunt,* Image (Anaheim, CA), 2000.

1997–98 *Stardust: Being a Romance within the Realms of Faerie,* illustrated by Charles Vess, D.C. Comics (New York, NY), text published as *Stardust,* Spike (New York, NY), 1999.

(Author of text, with Matt Wagner) *Neil Gaiman's Midnight Days,* D.C. Comics (New York, NY), 1999.

Green Lantern/Superman: Legend of the Green Flame, D.C. Comics (New York, NY), 2000.

Harlequin Valentine, illustrated by John Bolton, Dark Horse Comics (Milwaukie, OR), 2001.

Murder Mysteries (based on play of the same title, also see below), illustrated by P. Craig Russel, Dark Horse Comics (Milwaukie, OR), 2002.

Creatures of the Night, illustrated by Michael Zulli, Dark Horse Comics (Milwaukie, OR), 2004.

Marvel 1604, illustrated by Andy Kubert and Richard Isanove, Marvel Comics (New York, NY), 2004.

MirroMask, illustrated by Dave McKean, HarperCollins (New York, NY), 2005.

"SANDMAN" SERIES

Sandman: The Doll's House (originally published in magazine form), illustrated by Mike Dringenberg and Malcolm Jones III, D.C. Comics (New York, NY), 1990.

Sandman: Preludes and Nocturnes (originally published as *Sandman,* Volumes 1-8), illustrated by Sam Keith, Mike Dringenberg, and Malcolm Jones III, D.C. Comics (New York, NY), 1991.

Sandman: Dream Country (originally published as *Sandman,* Volumes 17-20; includes "A Midsummer's Night's Dream"), illustrated by Kelley Jones, Charles Vess, Colleen Doran, and Malcolm Jones III, D.C. Comics (New York, NY), 1991.

Sandman: Season of Mists (originally published as *Sandman,* Volumes 21-28), illustrated by Kelley Jones, Malcolm Jones III, Mike Dringenberg, and others, D.C. Comics (New York, NY), 1992.

Sandman: A Game of You (originally published as *Sandman,* Volumes 32-37), illustrated by Shawn McManus and others, D.C. Comics (New York, NY), 1993.

Sandman: Fables and Reflections (originally published as *Sandman,* Volumes 29-31, 38-40, 50), illustrated by Bryan Talbot, D.C. Comics (New York, NY), 1994.

Death: The High Cost of Living (originally published in magazine form, three volumes), illustrated by Dave McKean, Mark Buckingham, and others, D.C. Comics (New York, NY), 1994.

Sandman: Brief Lives (originally published as *Sandman,* Volumes 41-49), illustrated by Jill Thompson, Dick Giordano, and Vince Locke, D.C. Comics (New York, NY), 1994.

Sandman: World's End (originally published as *Sandman,* Volumes 51-56), illustrated by Dave McKean, Mark Buckingham, Dick Giordano, and others, D.C. Comics (New York, NY), 1994.

(Author of text, with Matt Wagner) *Sandman: Midnight Theatre,* illustrated by Teddy Kristiansen, D.C. Comics (New York, NY), 1995.

(Editor, with Edward E. Kramer) *The Sandman: Book of Dreams,* HarperPrism (New York, NY), 1996.

Sandman: The Kindly Ones (originally published as *Sandman,* Volumes 57-69), illustrated by Marc Hempel, Richard Case, and others, D.C. Comics (New York, NY), 1996.

Death: The Time of Your Life, illustrated by Mark Buckingham and others, D.C. Comics (New York, NY), 1997.

(Author of commentary and contributor) *Dustcovers: The Collected Sandman Covers, 1989-1997,* illustrated by Dave McKean, Vertigo/D.C. Comics (New York, NY), 1997, published as *The Collected Sandman Covers, 1989-1997,* Watson-Guptill (New York, NY), 1997.

Sandman: The Wake, illustrated by Michael Zulli, Charles Vess, and others, D.C. Comics (New York, NY), 1997.

(Reteller) *Sandman: The Dream Hunters,* illustrated by Yoshitaka Amano, D.C. Comics (New York, NY), 1999.

The Quotable Sandman: Memorable Lines from the Acclaimed Series, D.C. Comics (New York, NY), 2000.

The Sandman: Endless Nights, illustrated by P. Craig Russell, Milo Manara, and others, D.C. Comics (New York, NY), 2003.

OTHER FICTION

(With Terry Pratchett) *Good Omens: The Nice and Accurate Prophecies of Agnes Nutter, Witch* (novel), Gollancz (London, England), 1990, revised edition, William Morrow (New York, NY), 2006.

(With Mary Gentle) *Villains!* (short stories), edited by Mary Gentle and Roz Kaveney, ROC (London, England), 1992.

(With Mary Gentle and Roz Kaveney) *The Weerde: Book One* (short stories), ROC (London, England), 1992.

(With Mary Gentle and Roz Kaveney) *The Weerde: Book Two: The Book of the Ancients* (short stories), ROC (London, England), 1992.

Angels and Visitations: A Miscellany (short stories), illustrated by Steve Bissette and others, DreamHaven Books and Art (Minneapolis, MN), 1993.

Neverwhere (novel), BBC Books (London, England), 1996, Avon (New York, NY), 1997.

Smoke and Mirrors: Short Fictions and Illusions (short stories), Avon (New York, NY), 1998.

American Gods (novel), William Morrow (New York, NY), 2001.

(Reteller) *Snow Glass Apples,* illustrated by George Walker, Biting Dog Press (Duluth, GA), 2003.

SCREENPLAYS

(With Lenny Henry) *Neverwhere,* BBC2 (London, England), 1996.

Signal to Noise, BBC Radio 3 (London, England), 1996.

Day of the Dead: An Annotated Babylon 5 Script (originally aired as the episode "Day of the Dead" for the series *Babylon 5,* Turner Broadcasting System, 1998), DreamHaven (Minneapolis, MN), 1998.

Princess Mononoke (motion picture; English translation of the Japanese screenplay by Hayao Miyazak), Miramax (New York, NY), 1999.

MirrorMask (motion picture), Sony Pictures (Culver City, CA), 2005.

FOR CHILDREN

The Day I Swapped My Dad for Two Goldfish (picture book), illustrated by Dave McKean, Borealis/White Wolf (Clarkson, GA), 1997, HarperCollins (New York, NY), 2004.

Coraline (fantasy), illustrated by Dave McKean, Bloomsbury (London, England), HarperCollins (New York, NY), 2002.

The Wolves in the Walls (picture book), illustrated by Dave McKean, HarperCollins (New York, NY), 2003.

OTHER

Duran Duran: The First Four Years of the Fab Five (biography), Proteus (New York, NY), 1984.

Don't Panic: The Official Hitch-Hiker's Guide to the Galaxy Companion, Titan (London, England), Pocket Books (New York, NY), 1988, revised edition with additional material by David K. Dickson published as *Don't Panic: Douglas Adams and the Hitchhiker's Guide to the Galaxy,* Titan (London, England), 1993.

Warning: Contains Language (readings; compact disc), music by Dave McKean and the Flash Girls, DreamHaven (Minneapolis, MN), 1995.

(Co-illustrator) *The Dreaming: Beyond the Shores of Night,* D.C. Comics (New York, NY), 1997.

(Co-illustrator) *The Dreaming: Through the Gates of Horn and Ivory,* D.C. Comics (New York, NY), 1998.

Neil Gaiman: Live at the Aladdin (videotape), Comic Book Legal Defense Fund (Northampton, MA), 2001.

(With Gene Wolfe) *A Walking Tour of the Shambles* (nonfiction), American Fantasy Press (Woodstock, IL), 2001.

Murder Mysteries (play), illustrated by George Walker, Biting Dog Press (Duluth, GA), 2001.

Adventures in the Dream Trade (nonfiction and fiction), edited by Tony Lewis and Priscilla Olson, NESFA Press (Framingham, MA), 2002.

(With Dave McKean) *The Alchemy of MirrorMask,* Collins Design (New York, NY), 2005.

EDITOR

(With Kim Newman) *Ghastly beyond Belief,* Arrow (London, England), 1985.

(With Stephen Jones) *Now We Are Sick: A Sampler,* privately published, 1986, published as *Now We Are Sick: An Anthology of Nasty Verse,* DreamHaven (Minneapolis, MN), 1991.

(With Alex Stewart) *Temps,* ROC (London, England), 1991.

(With Alex Stewart) *Euro Temps,* ROC (London, England), 1992.

Also author of the comic book *Outrageous Tales from the Old Testament*. Creator of characters for comic books, including Lady Justice; Wheel of Worlds; Mr. Hero, Newmatic Man; Teknophage; and Lucifer. Coeditor of *The Utterly Comic Relief Comic,* a comic book that raised money for the UK Comic Relief Charity in 1991. Contributor to *The Sandman Companion,* D.C. Comics (New York, NY), 1999, and has contributed prefaces and introductions to several books. Gaiman's works, including the short story "Troll Bridge," have been represented in numerous anthologies. Contributor to newspapers and magazines, including *Knave, Punch, Observer, Sunday Times* (London, England) and *Time Out.* Gaiman's books have been translated into other languages, including Bulgarian, Danish, Dutch, Finnish, French, German, Greek, Hungarian, Italian, Japanese, Norwegian, Spanish, and Swedish. He has written scripts for the films *Avalon, Beowulf, The Confessions of William Henry Ireland, The Fermata, Modesty Blaise,* and others.

ADAPTATIONS: The Books of Magic was adapted into novel form by Carla Jablonski and others into several individual volumes, including *The Invitation, The Blindings,* and *The Children's Crusade,* issued by HarperCollins (New York, NY). *Neverwhere* was released on audio cassette by HighBridge (Minneapolis, MN), 1997; *American Gods* was released on cassette by Harper (New York, NY), 2001; *Coraline* was released as an audio book read by the author, Harper (New York, NY), 2002; *Two Plays for Voices* (*Snow Glass Apples* and *Murder Mysteries*) was released as an audio book and on audio CD, Harper (New York, NY), 2003. Several of Gaiman's works have been optioned for film, including *Sandman,* by Warner Bros.; *The Books of Magic,* by Warner Bros.; *Death: The High Cost of Living,* by Warner Bros.; *Good Omens,* by Renaissance Films; *Neverwhere,* by Jim Henson Productions; *Chivalry,* by Miramax; *Stardust,* by Miramax and Dimension Films; and *Coraline,* by Pandemonium Films. *Signal to Noise* was made into a stage play by NOWtheater (Chicago, IL).

WORK IN PROGRESS: A screen adaptation of the classic work *Beowulf,* for Sony Pictures, expected 2007.

SIDELIGHTS: An English author of comic books, graphic novels (text and pictures in a comic-book format published in book form), prose novels, children's books, short fiction, nonfiction, and screenplays, Neil Gaiman is a best-selling writer who is considered perhaps the most accomplished and influential figure in modern comics as well as one of the most gifted of contemporary fantasists. Characteristically drawing from mythology, history, literature, and popular culture to create his works, Gaiman blends the everyday, the fantastic, the frightening, and the humorous to present his stories, which reveal the mysteries that lie just outside of reality as well as the insights that come from experiencing these mysteries. He refers to the plots and characters of classical literature and myth—most notably fairy tales, horror stories, science fiction, and traditional romances—while adding fresh, modern dimensions. In fact, Gaiman is credited with developing a new mythology with his works, which address themes such as what it means to be human; the importance of the relationship between humanity and art; humanity's desire for dreams and for attaining what they show; and the passage from childish ways of thinking to more mature understanding. Although most of the author's works are not addressed to children, Gaiman often features child and young adult characters in his books, and young people are among Gaiman's greatest and most loyal fans. The author has become extremely popular, developing a huge cult-like following as well as a celebrity status. The author perhaps is best known as the creator of the comic-book and graphic-novel series about the Sandman. This character, which is based loosely on a crime-fighting superhero that first appeared in D.C. Comics in the 1930s and 40s, is the protagonist of an epic series of dark fantasies that spanned eight years and ran for seventy-five monthly issues. Gaiman introduces the Sandman as an immortal being who rules the Dreaming, a surreal world to which humans go when they fall asleep. As the series progresses, the Sandman discovers that he is involved with the fate of human beings on an intimate basis and that his life is tied intrinsically to this relationship. The "Sandman" series has sold millions of copies in both comic book and graphic novel formats and has inspired companion literature and a variety of related merchandise.

As a writer for children, Gaiman has been the subject of controversy for creating *Coraline,* a fantasy for middle-graders about a young girl who enters a bizarre alternate world that eerily mimics her own. Compared to Lewis Carroll's nineteenth-century fantasy *Alice's Adventures in Wonderland* for its imaginative depiction of a surreal adventure, *Coraline* has been questioned as an appropriate story for children because it may be too frightening for its intended audience. Gaiman also is the creator of two picture books for children, *The Day I Swapped My Dad for Two Goldfish,* a comic-book-style fantasy about a boy who trades his dad for two attractive goldfish, and *The Wolves in the Walls,* which features a brave girl who faces the wolves that have taken over her house. The author's adult novel *American*

Gods, the tale of a young drifter who becomes involved with what appears to be a magical war, was a critical and popular success that helped to bring Gaiman to a mainstream audience. Among his many works, Gaiman has written a biography of the English pop/rock group Duran Duran; a comic book with shock-rocker Alice Cooper that the latter turned into an album; a satiric fantasy about the end of the world with English novelist Terry Pratchett; comic books about Todd MacFarlane's popular character Spawn; and scripts for film, television, and radio, both original scripts and adaptations of his own works. Gaiman wrote the English-language script for the well-received Japanese anime film *Princess Mononoke;* the script of the episode "Day of the Dead" for the television series *Babylon 5;* and both a television script and a novel called *Neverwhere* that describes how an office worker rescues a young woman who is bleeding from a switchblade wound and is transported with her to London Below, a mysterious and dangerous world underneath the streets of England's largest city. Throughout his career, Gaiman has worked with a number of talented artists in the fields of comic books and fantasy, including John Bolton, Michael Zulli, Yoshitaka Amaro, Charles Vess, and longtime collaborator Dave McKean.

As a prose stylist, Gaiman is known for writing clearly and strongly, using memorable characters and striking images to build his dreamlike worlds. Although his books and screenplays can range from somber to creepy to horrifying, Gaiman is commended for underscoring them with optimism and sensitivity and for balancing their darkness with humor and wit. Reviewers have praised Gaiman for setting new standards for comic books as literature and for helping to bring increased popularity to both them and graphic novels. In addition, observers have claimed that several of the author's works transcend the genres in which they are written and explore deeper issues than those usually addressed in these works. Although Gaiman occasionally has been accused of being ponderous and self-indulgent, he generally is considered a phenomenon, a brilliant writer and storyteller whose works reflect his inventiveness, originality, and wisdom. Writing in *St. James Guide to Horror, Ghost, and Gothic Writers,* Peter Crowther noted that when Gaiman "is on form (which is most of the time), he is without peer . . . . His blending of poetic prose, marvelous inventions, and artistic vision has assured him of his place in the vanguard of modern-day dark fantasists." Keith R. A. DeCandido of *Library Journal* called Gaiman "arguably the most literate writer working in mainstream comics." Referring to Gaiman's graphic novels, Frank McConnell of *Commonweal* stated that the author "may just be the most gifted and

important storyteller in English" and called him "our best and most bound-to-be-remembered writer of fantasy."

Born in Portchester, England, Gaiman was brought up in an upper-middle-class home. His father, David, was the director of a company, while his mother, Sheila, worked as a pharmacist. As a boy, Gaiman was "a completely omnivorous and cheerfully undiscerning reader," as he told Pamela Shelton in an interview for *Authors and Artists for Young Adults (AAYA).* In an interview with *Booklist* writer Olson Gaiman recalled that he first read *Alice in Wonderland* "when I was five, maybe, and always kept it around as default reading between the ages of five and twelve, and occasionally picked up and reread since. There are things Lewis Carroll did in *Alice* that are etched onto my circuitry." Gaiman was a voracious reader of comic books until the age of sixteen, when he felt that he outgrew the genre as it existed at the time. At his grammar school, Ardingly College, Gaiman would get "very grumpy . . . when they'd tell us that we couldn't read comics, because 'if you read comics you will not read OTHER THINGS.'" He asked himself, "Why are comics going to stop me reading?" Gaiman proved that his teachers were misguided in their theory: he read the entire children's library in Portchester in two or three years and then started on the adult library. He told Shelton, "I don't think I ever got to 'Z' but I got up to about 'L'."

When he was about fourteen, Gaiman began his secondary education at Whitgift School. When he was fifteen, Gaiman and his fellow students took a series of vocational tests that were followed by interviews with career advisors. Gaiman told Shelton that these advisors "would look at our tests and say, 'Well, maybe you'd be interested in accountancy,' or whatever. When I went for my interview, the guy said, 'What do you want to do?' and I said, 'Well, I'd really like to write American comics.' And it was obvious that this was the first time he'd ever heard that. He just sort of stared at me for a bit and then said, 'Well, how do you go about doing that, then?' I said, 'I have no idea—you're the career advisor. Advise.' And he looked like I'd slapped him in the face with a wet herring; he sort of stared at me and there was this pause and I went on for a while and then he said, 'Have you ever thought about accountancy?'" Undeterred, Gaiman kept on writing. He also was interested in music. At sixteen, Gaiman played in a punk band that was about to be signed by a record company. Gaiman brought in an attorney who, after reading the contract being offered to the band, discovered that the deal would exploit them; consequently, Gaiman refused to sign the contract. By 1977, he felt that he was ready to become a professional writer. That same year, Gaiman left Whitgift School.

After receiving some rejections for short stories that he had written, Gaiman decided to become a freelance journalist so that he could learn about the world of publishing from the inside. He wrote informational articles for British men's magazines with titles like *Knave.* Gaiman told Shelton that being a journalist "was terrific in giving me an idea of how the world worked. I was the kind of journalist who would go out and do interviews with people and then write them up for magazines. I learned economy and I learned about dialogue." In 1983, he discovered the work of English comic-strip writer Alan Moore, whose *Swamp Thing* became a special favorite. Gaiman told Shelton, "Moore's work convinced me that you really could do work in comics that had the same amount of intelligence, the same amount of passion, the same amount of quality that you could put in any other medium." In 1984, Gaiman produced his first book, *Duran Duran: The First Four Years of the Fab Five.* Once he had established his credibility as a writer, Gaiman was able to sell the short stories that he had done earlier in his career. In 1985, Gaiman married Mary Therese McGrath, with whom he has three children: Michael, Holly, and Madeleine (Maddy). At around this time, Gaiman decided that he was ready to concentrate on fiction. In addition, the comics industry was experiencing a new influx of talent, which inspired Gaiman to consider becoming a contributor to that medium.

In 1986, Gaiman met art student Dave McKean, and the two decided to collaborate. Their first work together was the comic book *Violent Cases.* Serialized initially in *Escape,* a British comic that showcased new strips, *Violent Cases* was published in book form in 1987. The story recounts the memories of an adult narrator—pictured by McKean as a dark-haired young man who bears a striking resemblance to Gaiman—who recalls his memories of hearing about notorious Chicago gangland leader Al Capone from an elderly osteopath who was the mobster's chiropractor. As a boy of four, the narrator had his arm broken accidentally by his father. In the office of the osteopath, the boy was transfixed by lurid stories about Chicago of the 1920s but, in the evenings, he had nightmares in which his own world and that of Capone's would intersect. As the story begins, the adult narrator is trying to make sense of the experience. According to Joe Sanders of the *Dictionary of Literary Biography,* the narrator "discover[s] that grownups are as prone to uncertainty, emotional outbursts, and naïve rationalization as children. The boy is delighted, the grownup narrator perplexed, to see how

'facts' change to fit an interpreter's needs." Writing in London's *Sunday Times,* Nicolette Jones called *Violent Cases* "inspired and ingenious," while Cindy Lynn Speer, writing in an essay on the author's Web site, dubbed it "a brilliant tale of childhood and memory."

At around the same time that *Violent Cases* was published in book form, Gaiman produced the comic book *Outrageous Tales from the Old Testament,* which is credited with giving him almost instant notoriety in the comic-book community. Gaiman teamed with McKean again to do a limited-run comic series, *Black Orchid,* the first of the author's works to be released by D.C. Comics, the publisher of the original "Superman" and "Batman" series. A three-part comic book, "Black Orchid" features an essentially nonviolent female heroine who fights villains that she hardly can remember. Gaiman then was offered his choice of inactive D.C. characters to rework from the Golden Age of Comics (the 1930s and 1940s). He chose the Sandman. Originally, the character was millionaire Wesley Dodds who hunted criminals by night wearing a fedora, cape, and gas mask. Dodds would zap the crooks with his gas gun and leave them sleeping until the police got to them. When Gaiman began the series in 1988, he changed the whole scope of the character. The Sandman, who is also called Dream, Morpheus, Oneiros, Lord Shaper, Master of Story, and God of Sleep, became a thin, enigmatic figure with a pale face, dark eyes, and a shock of black hair. The Sandman is one of the Endless, immortals in charge of individual realms of the human psyche. The Sandman's brothers and sisters in the Endless are (in birth order) Destiny, Death, Destruction, the twins Desire and Despair, and Delirium (formerly Delight); Dream (the Sandman) falls between Death and Destruction.

In the "Sandman" book *Preludes and Nocturnes,* Gaiman introduces the title character, the ageless lord of dreams, who has just returned home after being captured by a coven of wizards and held in an asylum for the criminally insane for seventy-two years. Dream finds that his home is in ruins, that his powers are diminished, and that his three tools—a helmet, a pouch of sand, and a ruby stone—have been stolen. He finds his missing helpers and the young girl who has become addicted to the sand from his pouch; he also visits Hell to find the demon who stole his helmet and battles an evil doctor who has unleashed the power of dreams on the unsuspecting people of Earth. Dream comes to realize that his captivity has affected him: he has become humanized, and he understands that he eventually will have to die. In *The Doll's House,* Dream travels across the United States searching for the Arcana, the stray dreams and nightmares of the twentieth century that have taken on human form; the story is interwoven with a subplot about a young woman, Rose Walker, who has lost her little brother. In *Dream Country,* Gaiman features Calliope, a muse and the mother of Dream's son, Orpheus; the story also brings in a real character, actor/ playwright William Shakespeare. In *Season of Mists,* Dream meets Lucifer, who has left his position as ruler of Hell and has left the choice of his successor to Dream.

A Game of You features Barbara (nicknamed Barbie), a character who had appeared in *The Doll's House.* Barbie is drawn back into the dream realm that she ruled as a child in order to save it from the evil Cuckoo, who plans to destroy it. *Fables and Reflections* is a collection of stories featuring the characters from the series and includes Gaiman's retelling of the Greek myth of Orpheus. In *Brief Lives,* Dream and Delirium embark on a quest to find their little brother Destruction, who exiled himself to Earth three hundred years before. *World's End* includes a collection of tales told by a group of travelers who are waiting out a storm in an inn. *The Kindly Ones* brings the series to its conclusion as Hippolyta (Lyta) Hall takes revenge upon Dream for the disappearance of her son. Lyta, who has been driven mad by anger and grief, asks the help of the title characters, mythological beings also known as the Furies. The Kindly Ones take out Lyta's revenge on Dream, who succumbs to their attack. The tale comes full cycle, and Dream's destiny is joined with that of humans in death. In the final chapter of the series, *The Wake,* a funeral is held for Dream; however, as Gaiman notes thematically, dreams really never die, and Dream's role in the Endless is taken on in a new incarnation. The Sandman also appears in a more peripheral role in *The Dream Hunters,* a retelling of the Japanese folktale "The Fox, the Monk, and the Mikado of All Night's Dreaming."

Next to the Sandman, Death, Dream's older sister, is the most frequently featured and popular character in the series. Death is charged with shepherding humans who are about to die through their transitions. Once a century, she must come to Earth as a sixteen-year-old girl in order to remind herself what mortality feels like. In contrast to Dream, who characteristically is isolated, brooding, and serious, Death, who is depicted as a spike-haired young woman who dresses like a punk rocker or Goth girl, has a more open and kindly nature. Death is featured in two books of her own, *Death: The High Cost of Living* and *Death: The Time of Your Life.* In the first story, she helps Sexton, a teen who is contemplating suicide, rediscover the joys in being alive as

they journey through New York City and, in the second, she helps Foxglove, a newly successful musician, to reveal her true sexual orientation as her companion Hazel prepares to die. Death and the rest of the Endless are also featured in *The Sandman: Endless Nights,* in which Gaiman devotes an individual story to each of the seven siblings.

Writing in *Commonweal* about the "Sandman" series, Frank McConnell stated, " *Sandman* is not just one of the best pieces of fiction being done these days; . . . it emerges as *the* best piece of fiction being done these days." McConnell stated that what Gaiman has done with the series "is to establish the fact that a comic book can be a work of high and very serious art—a story that other storytellers, in whatever medium they work, will have to take into account as an exploration of what stories can do and what stories are for." The critic concluded, "I know of nothing quite like it, and I don't expect there will be anything like it for some time . . . . Read the damn thing; it's important." Peter Crowder of the *St. James Guide to Horror, Ghost, and Gothic Writers* noted that, with the "Sandman" series of comic books, Gaiman "has truly revolutionized the power of the medium." Crowder called the various volumes of collected stories "almost uniformly excellent, and any one of them would make a good starting point for those readers who, while well-versed in the field of Gothic prose literature, have yet to discover the rare but powerful joy inherent in a great comic book." In 1996, D.C. Comics surprised the fans of "Sandman" by announcing the cancellation of the series while it was still the company's best-seller; however, D.C. had made this arrangement with Gaiman at the beginning of the series. "Sandman" has sold more than seven million copies; individual copies of the stories also have sold in the millions or in the hundreds of thousands. "A Midsummer's Night's Dream," a story from *Dream Country,* won the World Fantasy Award for the best short story of 1991. This was the first time that a comic book had won an award that was not related to its own medium, and the event caused an uproar among some fantasy devotees. The "Sandman" stories have inspired related volumes, such as a book of quotations from the series, and merchandise such as action figures, stuffed toys, trading cards, jewelry, and watches.

In 1994, Gaiman told Ken Tucker of *Entertainment Weekly,* "Superhero comics are the most perfectly evolved art form for preadolescent male power fantasies, and I don't see that as a bad thing. I want to reach other sorts of people, too." In 1995, he told Shelton, "If you're too young for *Sandman,* you will be bored silly by it. It's filled with long bits with people having conversations." Speaking to Nick Hasted of the *Guardian* in 1999, Gaiman said, "Right now, as things stand, *Sandman* is my serious work . . . . It is one giant, overarching story, and I'm proud of it. Compared to *Sandman,* all the prose work so far is trivia." In 2003, Gaiman wrote an introduction to *The Sandman: King of Dreams,* a collection of text and art from the series with commentary by Alisa Kwitney. He commented, "If I have a concern over *The Sandman,* the 2,000-page story I was able to tell between 1988 and 1996, it is that the things that have come after it, the toys (whether plastic and articulated or soft and cuddly), the posters, the clothes, the calendars and candles, the companion volume, and even the slim book of quotations, along with the various spin-offs and such—will try people's patience and goodwill, and that a book like this will be perceived, not unreasonably, as something that's being used to flog the greasy patch in the driveway where once, long ago, a dead horse used to lie. The ten volumes of *The Sandman* are what they are, and that's the end of it."

Throughout his career, Gaiman has included young people as main characters in his works. For example, *The Books of Magic,* a collection of four comics published in 1993, predates J. K. Rowling's "Harry Potter" series by featuring a thirteen-year-old boy, Tim Hunter, who is told that he has the capabilities to be the greatest wizard in the world. Tim, a boy from urban London who wears oversized glasses, is taken by the Trenchcoat Brigade—sorcerers with names like The Mysterious Phantom Stranger, the Incorrigible Hellblazer, and the Enigmatic Dr. Occult—on a tour of the universe to learn its magical history. Tim travels to Hell, to the land of Faerie, and to America, among other places, each of them showing him a different aspect of the world of magic. He also searches for his girlfriend, Molly, who has been abducted into the fantasy realms; after he finds her, the two of them face a series of dangers as they struggle to return to their own world. At the end of the story, Tim must make a decision to embrace or reject his talents as a wizard. *The Books of Magic* also includes cameos by the Sandman and his sister Death. Writing in *Locus,* Carolyn Cushman said, "It's a fascinating look at magic, its benefits and burdens, all dramatically illustrated [by John Bolton, Scott Hampton, Charles Vess, and Paul Johnson], and with a healthy helping of humor." Speaking of the format of *The Books of Magic,* Michael Swanwick of *Book World* noted, "The graphic novel has come of age. This series is worth any number of movies."

In 1994, Gaiman produced *The Tragical Comedy, or Comical Tragedy, of Mr. Punch* (also published as *Mr. Punch*), a work that he considers one of his best. In this

graphic novel, which is illustrated by Dave McKean, a young boy is sent to stay with his grandparent by the seaside while his mother gives birth to his baby sister. While on his visit, the boy encounters a mysterious puppeteer and watches a Punch and Judy show, a sometimes violent form of puppet-theater entertainment. Through a series of strange experiences, he ends up rejecting Mr. Punch's promise that everyone in the world is free to do whatever they want. Sanders of the *Dictionary of Literary Biography* called *Mr. Punch* "perhaps Gaiman and McKean's most impressive collaboration," while Crowder called it "an impressive work, rich not only in freshness and originality but also in compassion, Gaiman's hallmark. . . . The collective impact is literally breathtaking." Writing in *Commonweal,* Frank McConnell noted, "This stunning comic book- graphic novel—whatever—is easily the most haunting, inescapable story I have read in years."

In 1996, Gaiman and McKean produced their first work for children, the picture book *The Day I Swapped My Dad for Two Goldfish.* In this tale, a little boy trades his father for two of his neighbor's goldfish while his little sister stares, horrified. When their mother finds out what has happened, she is furious. She makes the children go and get back their father who, unfortunately, has already been traded for an electric guitar. While on their quest to find him, the siblings decide that their father is a very good daddy after all. The children finally retrieve their father, who has been reading a newspaper all during his adventure. At home, their mother makes the children promise not to swap their dad any more. Writing in *Bloomsbury Review,* Anji Keating called *The Day I Swapped My Dad for Two Goldfish* "a fabulously funny tale" and dubbed the protagonists' journey to fetch their father "delightful." Malcolm Jones of *Newsweek* predicted that Gaiman and McKean "may shock a few grandparents . . . but in fact the most shocking thing they've done in this droll story is to take the illegible look of cutting-edge magazines like *Raygun* and somehow make it readable."

In 2003, Gaiman and McKean produced a second picture book, *The Wolves in the Walls.* In this work, young Lucy hears wolves living in the walls of the old house where she and her family live; of course, no one believes her. When the wolves emerge to take over the house, Lucy and her family flee. However, Lucy wants her house back, and she also wants the beloved pig-puppet that she left behind. She talks her family into going back into the house, where they move into the walls that had been vacated by the wolves. Lucy and her family frighten the usurpers, who are wearing their clothes and eating their food. The wolves scatter, and everything seems to go back to normal until Lucy hears another noise in the walls; this time, it sounds like elephants. In her *Booklist* review of *The Wolves in the Walls,* Francisca Goldsmith found the book "visually and emotionally sophisticated, accessible, and inspired by both literary and popular themes and imagery." Writing in *School Library Journal,* Marian Creamer commented that "Gaiman and McKean deftly pair text and illustration to convey a strange, vivid story," and predicted, "Children will delight in the 'scary, creepy tone.'"

Gaiman's first story for middle-graders, *Coraline,* outlines how the title character, a young girl who feels that she is being ignored by her preoccupied parents, enters a terrifying, malevolent alternate reality to save them after they are kidnapped. The story begins when Coraline and her parents move into their new house, which is divided into apartments. Left to her own devices, bored Coraline explores the house and finds a door in the empty flat next door that leads to a world that is a twisted version of her own. There, she meets two odd-looking individuals who call themselves her "other mother" and "other father." The Other Mother, a woman who looks like Coraline's except for her black-button eyes and stiletto fingernails, wants Coraline to stay with her and her husband. Tempted by good food and interesting toys, Coraline considers the offer. However, when the girl returns home, she finds that her parents have disappeared. Coraline discovers that they are trapped in the other world, and she sets out to save them. The Other Mother, who turns out to be a soul-sucking harpy, enters into a deadly game of hide-and-seek with Coraline, who discovers new qualities of bravery and resolve within herself. Before returning home, Coraline saves herself, her parents, and some ghost children who are trapped in the grotesque world.

After its publication, *Coraline* became a subject of dispute. Some adult observers saw it as a book that would give nightmares to children. However, other observers have noted that the children of their acquaintance who read the book consider it an exciting rather than overly frightening work. A reviewer in *Publishers Weekly* noted that Gaiman and illustrator McKean "spin an electrifyingly creepy tale likely to haunt young readers for many moons. . . . Gaiman twines his tale with a menacing tone and crisp prose fraught with memorable imagery . . . , yet keeps the narrative just this side of terrifying." Writing in *School Library Journal,* Bruce Anne Shook commented, "The story is odd, strange, even slightly bizarre, but kids will hang on every word . . . . This is just right for all those requests for a scary book." Stephanie Zvirin of *Booklist* added that Gaiman offers

"a chilling and empowering view of children, to be sure, but young readers are likely to miss such subtleties as the clever allusions to classic horror movies and the references to the original dark tales of the Brothers Grimm." A critic in *Kirkus Reviews* found *Coraline* "not for the faint-hearted—who are mostly adults anyway—but for stouthearted kids who love a brush with the sinister, *Coraline* is spot on." *Coraline* has won several major fantasy awards and has become an international best-seller.

In 2005, Gaiman released the adult novel *Anansi Boys,* which focuses on Charles "Fat Charlie" Nancy—son of an *American Gods* character, the trickster god Anansi. Fat Charlie calls his father to announce his engagement, only to find out that the man has passed away and the funeral is the next day. Charlie attends the funeral only to find out his father's status as a god and that he has a brother, Spider. Spider comes to visit Charlie, turning his life upside-down—he is fired, his fiancee sleeps with Spider thinking it is Charlie, and he is even arrested for a white-collar crime. Charlie enlists the help of other gods to get Spider back out of his life, and that is when things begin to get even stranger. *Anansi Boys* is a "quirky, inventive fantasy," according to *School Library Journal* contributor Matthew L. Moffett, who said of the work, "Darkly funny and heartwarming to the end, this book is an addictive read not easily forgotten." Charles De Lint agreed with this positive assessment in a *Magazine of Science Fiction and Fantasy* review, observing that Gaiman "has shown us how to find all the interesting bits in the world around us that otherwise we might simply continue to take for granted." Discussing *Anansi Boys* in comparison with Gaiman's other works, De Lint noted that "it might be the best one yet."

In his interview with Shelton, Gaiman said, "What I enjoy most is when people say to me, 'When I was sixteen I didn't know what I was going to do with my life and then I read *Sandman* and now I'm at university studying mythology' or whatever. I think it's wonderful when you've opened a door to people and showed them things that would never have *known* they would have been interested in." Gaiman finds it satisfying to introduce his readers to mythology. He told Shelton, "You gain a cultural understanding to the last 2,500 to 3,000 years, which, if you lack it, there's an awful lot of stuff that you will simply never quite understand." He noted that, in *Sandman,* even readers unfamiliar with the Norse god Loki or the three-headed spirit of Irish mythology "sort of half-know; there's a gentle and sort of delightful familiarity with these tales. It feels right. And I think that's probably the most important thing. Giving people this stuff, pointing out that it can be interesting, but also pointing out what mythologies do know. And how they affect us." In an interview with Nick Hasted in the *Guardian,* Gaiman stated, "What I'm fighting now is the tendency to put novelists in a box, to make them write the same book over and over again. I want to shed skins. I want to keep awake. I definitely have a feeling that if I'm not going forward, if I'm not learning something, then I'm dead."

BIOGRAPHICAL AND CRITICAL SOURCES:

BOOKS

Authors and Artists for Young Adults, Gale (Detroit, MI), Volume 19 (author interview with Pamela Shelton), 1996, Volume 42, 2002.
Dictionary of Literary Biography, Volume 261: *British Fantasy and Science Fiction Writers since 1960,* Gale (Detroit, MI), 2002.
Kwitney, Alisa, *The Sandman: King of Dreams,* introduction by Neil Gaiman, Chronicle Books (San Francisco, CA), 2003.
St. James Guide to Horror, Ghost, and Gothic Writers, St. James Press (Detroit, MI), 1998.

PERIODICALS

Bloomsbury Review, July-August, 1997, Anji Keating, review of *The Day I Swapped My Dad for Two Goldfish,* p. 21.
Booklist, August, 2002, Ray Olson, "The *Booklist* Interview: Neil Gaiman," p. 19, and Stephanie Zvirin, review of *Coraline,* p. 1948; August, 2003, Francisca Goldsmith, review of *The Wolves in the Walls,* p. 1989.
Book World, April 7, 2002, Michael Swanwick, "Reel Worlds," p. 3.
Commonweal, December 2, 1994, Frank McConnell, review of *Mister Punch,* p. 27; October 20, 1995, Frank McConnell, review of *Sandman,* p. 21; June 19, 1998, Frank McConnell, review of *Neverwhere,* p. 21
Entertainment Weekly, June 24, 1994, Ken Tucker, review of *Sandman,* pp. 228-229.
Guardian (London, England), July 14, 1999, Nick Hasted, "The Illustrated Man," p. 12.
Kirkus Reviews, June 15, 2002, review of *Coraline,* p. 88.
Library Journal, September 15, 1990, Keith R. A. DeCandido, review of *The Golden Age,* p. 104.

Locus, April, 1993, Carolyn Cushman, review of *The Books of Magic,* p. 29.
Magazine of Fantasy and Science Fiction, March, 2006, Charles DeLint, review of *Anansi Boys,* p. 33.
Newsweek, December 1, 1997, Malcolm Jones, review of *The Day I Swapped My Dad for Two Goldfish,* p. 77.
Publishers Weekly, June 24, 2002, review of *Coraline,* p. 57; September 5, 2005, review of *The Las Temptation,* p. 41.
School Library Journal, August, 2002, Bruce Anne Shook, review of *Coraline,* p. 184; September, 2003, Marian Creamer, review of *The Wolves in the Walls,* p. 178; January 2006, Matthew L. Moffett, review of *Anansi Boys,* p. 172.
Sunday Times (London, England), July 15, 1990, Nicolette Jones, review of *Violent Cases.*

ONLINE

Neil Gaiman Home Page, http://www.neilgaiman.com/ (May, 2002), Cindy Lynn Speer, "An Essay on Neil Gaiman and Comics."

* * *

GAIMAN, Neil Richard
See GAIMAN, Neil

* * *

GAINES, Ernest J. 1933-
(Ernest James Gaines)

PERSONAL: Born January 15, 1933, in Oscar, LA; son of Manuel (a laborer) and Adrienne J. (Colar) Gaines; married Dianne Saulney (an attorney), 1993. *Education:* Attended Vallejo Junior College; San Francisco State College (now University), B.A., 1957; graduate study at Stanford University, 1958-59. *Hobbies and other interests:* Listening to music ("Bach to Coltrane"), watching television, reading, spending time in the gym.

ADDRESSES: Office—128 Buena Vista Blvd., Lafayette, LA, 70503-2059; and Department of English, University of Southwestern Louisiana, P.O. Box 44691, Lafayette, LA 70504-0001. *Agent*—JCA Literary Agency, Inc., 242 West 27th St., New York, NY 10001.

CAREER: Novelist. Denison University, Granville, OH, writer-in-residence, 1971; Stanford University, Stanford, CA, writer-in-residence, 1981; University of Southwestern Louisiana, Lafayette, professor of English and writer-in-residence, beginning 1983. Whittier College, visiting professor, 1983, writer-in-residence, 1986. *Military service:* U.S. Army, 1953-55.

AWARDS, HONORS: Wallace Stegner fellow, Stanford University, 1957; Joseph Henry Jackson Award, San Francisco Foundation, 1959, for "Comeback" (short story); National Endowment for the Arts award, 1967; Rockefeller grant, 1970; Guggenheim fellow, 1971; Black Academy of Arts and Letters award, 1972; fiction gold medal, Commonwealth Club of California, 1972, for *The Autobiography of Miss Jane Pittman,* and 1984, for *A Gathering of Old Men;* Louisiana Library Association award, 1972; honorary doctorate of letters from Denison University, 1980, Brown University, 1985, Bard College, 1985, Whittier College, 1986, and Louisiana State University, 1987; award for excellence of achievement in literature, San Francisco Arts Commission, 1983; American Academy and Institute of Arts and Letters literary award, 1987; MacArthur Foundation fellowship, 1993; National Book Critics Circle Award for fiction, 1993, for *A Lesson before Dying;* made Commander of the Order of Arts and Letters (France), 1996; inducted into Literary Hall of Fame for Writers of African Descent, Chicago State University, 1998; Emmy Award for best television movie, 1999, for adaptation of *A Lesson before Dying;* National Humanities Medal, National Endowment for the Humanities, 2000.

WRITINGS:

FICTION

Catherine Carmier (novel), Atheneum (New York, NY), 1964.

Of Love and Dust (novel), Dial (New York, NY), 1967.

Bloodline (short stories; also see below), Dial (New York, NY), 1968, reprinted, Vintage Contemporaries (New York, NY), 1997.

A Long Day in November (originally published in *Bloodline*), Dial (New York, NY), 1971.

The Autobiography of Miss Jane Pittman (novel), Dial (New York, NY), 1971.

In My Father's House (novel), Knopf (New York, NY), 1978.

A Gathering of Old Men (novel), Knopf (New York, NY), 1983.

A Lesson before Dying (novel), Knopf (New York, NY), 1993.

OTHER

Conversations with Ernest Gaines, edited by John Lowe, University Press of Mississippi (Jackson, MS), 1995.

Gaines's works have been translated into other languages, including German and French.

ADAPTATIONS: The Autobiography of Miss Jane Pittman, adapted from Gaines's novel, aired on the Columbia Broadcasting System (CBS-TV), 1974, and won nine Emmy Awards. "The Sky Is Gray," a short story originally published in *Bloodline,* was adapted for public television in 1980. *A Gathering of Old Men,* adapted from Gaines's novel, aired on CBS-TV, 1987. *In My Father's House* was adapted for audiocassette. *A Lesson before Dying* was filmed for Home Box Office, 1999, and was adapted for the stage by Romulus Linney, 2001.

SIDELIGHTS: The fiction of Ernest J. Gaines, including his 1971 novel *The Autobiography of Miss Jane Pittman* and his 1993 novel *A Lesson before Dying,* is deeply rooted in the African-American culture and storytelling traditions of rural Louisiana where the author was born and raised. His stories have been noted for their convincing characters and powerful themes presented within authentic, often folk-like, narratives that tap into the complex world of the rural South. Gaines depicts the strength and dignity of his black characters in the face of numerous struggles: the dehumanizing and destructive effects of racism; the breakdown in personal relationships as a result of social pressures; and the choice between secured traditions and the sometimes radical measures necessary to bring about social change. Although the issues presented in Gaines's fiction are serious and often disturbing, "this is not hot-and-breathless, burn-baby-burn writing," Melvin Maddocks pointed out in *Time;* rather, it is the work of "a patient artist, a patient man." Expounding on Gaines's rural heritage, Maddocks continued: Gaines "sets down a story as if he were planting, spreading the roots deep, wide and firm. His stories grow organically, at their own rhythm. When they ripen at last, they do so inevitably, arriving at a climax with the absolute rightness of a folk tale."

Gaines's experiences growing up on a Louisiana plantation provide the foundation upon which much of his fiction is based. Particularly important, he told Paul

Desruisseaux in the *New York Times Book Review*, were "working in the fields, going fishing in the swamps with the older people, and, especially, listening to the people who came to my aunt's house, the aunt who raised me." Although Gaines moved to California at the age of fifteen and subsequently went to college there, his fiction has been based in an imaginary Louisiana plantation region called Bayonne, which a number of critics have compared to William Faulkner's fictional Yoknapatawpha County. Gaines has acknowledged looking to Faulkner, in addition to Ernest Hemingway, for language, and to such French writers as Gustave Flaubert and Guy de Maupassant for style. A perhaps greater influence, however, have been the writings of nineteenth-century Russian authors.

Gaines's first novel, *Catherine Carmier*, is "an apprentice work more interesting for what it anticipates than for its accomplishments," noted William E. Grant in the *Dictionary of Literary Biography*. The novel chronicles the story of a young black man, Jackson Bradley, who returns to Bayonne after completing his education in California. Jackson falls in love with Catherine, the daughter of a Creole sharecropper who refuses to let members of his family associate with anyone darker than he, believing Creoles to be racially and socially superior. The novel portrays numerous clashes of loyalty: Catherine is torn between her love for Jackson and for her father; Jackson is caught between a bond to the community he grew up in and the experience and knowledge he has gained in the outside world. "Both Catherine and Jackson are immobilized by the pressures of [the] rural community," noted Keith E. Byerman in the *Dictionary of Literary Biography*, which produces "twin themes of isolation and paralysis [that] give the novel an existential quality. Characters must face an unfriendly world without guidance and must make crucial choices about their lives." The characters in *Catherine Carmier*—as in much of Gaines's fiction—are faced with struggles that test the conviction of personal beliefs. Winifred L. Stoelting explained in the *CLA Journal* that Gaines is concerned more "with how [his characters] . . . handle their decisions than with the rightness of their decisions—more often than not predetermined by social changes over which the single individual has little control."

Gaines sets *Catherine Carmier* in the time of the U.S. civil rights movement, yet avoids making it a primary force in the novel. "In divorcing his tale from contemporary events," Grant commented, "Gaines declares his independence from the political and social purposes of much contemporary black writing. Instead, he elects to concentrate upon those fundamental human passions and conflicts which transcend the merely social level of human existence." Grant found Gaines "admirable" for doing this, yet also believed Jackson's credibility is marred because he remains aloof from contemporary events. For Grant, the novel "seems to float outside time and place rather than being solidly anchored in the real world of the modern South." Byerman held a similar view, stating that the novel "is not entirely successful in presenting its major characters and their motivations." Nonetheless, he pointed out that in *Catherine Carmier*, "Gaines does begin to create a sense of the black community and its perceptions of the world around it. Shared ways of speaking, thinking, and relating to the dominant white society are shown through a number of minor characters."

Gaines's next novel, *Of Love and Dust*, is also a story of forbidden romance, and, as in *Catherine Carmier*, a "new world of expanding human relationships erodes the old world of love for the land and the acceptance of social and economic stratification," wrote Stoelting. *Of Love and Dust* is the story of Marcus Payne, a young black man bonded out of prison by a white landowner and placed under the supervision of a Cajun overseer, Sidney Bonbon. Possessed of a rebellious and hostile nature, Marcus is a threat to Bonbon, who in turn does all that he can to break the young man's spirit. In an effort to strike back, Marcus pays special attention to the overseer's wife; the two fall in love and plot to run away. The novel ends with a violent confrontation between the two men in which Marcus is killed. After the killing, Bonbon claims that to spare Marcus would have meant his own death at the hands of other Cajuns. Grant noted a similarity between *Of Love and Dust* and *Catherine Carmier* in that the characters are "caught up in a decadent social and economic system that determines their every action and limits their possibilities." Similarly, the two novels are marked by a "social determinism [that] shapes the lives of all the characters, making them pawns in a mechanistic world order rather than free agents."

Of Love and Dust demonstrates Gaines's development as a novelist, offering a clearer view of the themes and characters that have come to dominate his work. Stoelting noted that "in a more contemporary setting, the novel . . . continues Gaines's search for human dignity, and when that is lacking, acknowledges the salvation of pride," adding that "the characters themselves grow into a deeper awareness than those of [his] first novel. More sharply drawn . . . [they] are more decisive in their actions." Byerman remarked that the novel "more clearly condemns the economic, social, and racial system of the South for the problems faced by its characters." Likewise, the first-person narrator in the novel—a coworker of Marcus—"both speaks in the idiom of the place and time and instinctively asserts the values of the black community."

Gaines turns to a first-person narrator again in his next novel, *The Autobiography of Miss Jane Pittman,* which many consider to be his masterwork. Miss Jane Pittman—well over one hundred years old—relates a personal history that spans the time from the U.S. Civil War and slavery up through the civil rights movement of the 1960s. "To travel with Miss Pittman from adolescence to old age is to embark upon a historic journey, one staked out in the format of the novel," wrote Addison Gayle, Jr. in *The Way of the World: The Black Novel in America.* "Never mind that Miss Jane Pittman is fictitious, and that her 'autobiography,' offered up in the form of taped reminiscences, is artifice," added Josh Greenfield in *Life,* "the effect is stunning." Gaines's gift for drawing convincing characters is clearly demonstrated in *The Autobiography of Miss Jane Pittman.* "His is not . . . an 'art' narrative, but an authentic narrative by an authentic ex-slave, authentic even though both are Gaines's inventions," Jerry H. Bryant commented in the *Iowa Review.* "So successful is he in *becoming* Miss Jane Pittman, that when we talk about her story, we do not think of Gaines as her creator, but as her recording editor."

The character of Jane Pittman could be called an embodiment of the black experience in America. "Though Jane is the dominant personality of the narrative—observer and commentator upon history, as well as participant—in her odyssey is symbolized the odyssey of a race of people; through her eyes is revealed the grandeur of a people's journey through history," maintained Gayle. "The central metaphor of the novel concerns this journey: Jane and her people, as they come together in the historic march toward dignity and freedom in Sampson, symbolize a people's march through history, breaking old patterns, though sometimes slowly, as they do." The important historical backdrop to Jane's narrative—slavery, Reconstruction, the civil rights era, segregation—does not compromise, however, the detailed account of an individual. "Jane captures the experiences of those millions of illiterate blacks who never had a chance to tell their own stories," Byerman explained. "By focusing on the particular yet typical events of a small part of Louisiana, those lives are given a concreteness and specificity not possible in more general histories."

In his fourth novel, *In My Father's House,* Gaines focuses on a theme that appears in varying degrees throughout his fiction: the alienation between fathers and sons. As the author told Desruisseaux, "In my books there always seems to be fathers and sons searching for each other. That's a theme I've worked with since I started writing. Even when the father was not in the story, I've dealt with his absence and its effects on his children. And that is the theme of this book." *In My Father's House* tells of prominent civil rights leader Reverend Phillip Martin, who, at the peak of his career, is confronted with a troubled young man named Robert X. Although Robert's identity is initially a mystery, eventually he is revealed to be one of three offspring from a love affair Martin had in an earlier, wilder life and then abandoned. Robert arrives to confront and kill the father whose neglect he sees as responsible for the family's disintegration: his sister has been raped, his brother imprisoned for the murder of her attacker, and his mother alone and reduced to poverty. Although the son's intent to kill his father is never carried out, Martin is forced "to undergo a long and painful odyssey through his own past and the labyrinthine streets of Baton Rouge to learn what really happened to his first family," wrote William Burke in the *Dictionary of Literary Biography Yearbook.* Larry McMurtry, in the *New York Times Book Review,* noted that as the book traces the lost family, "we have revealed to us an individual, a marriage, a community and a region, but with such an unobtrusive marshaling of detail that we never lose sight of the book's central thematic concern: the profoundly destructive consequences of the breakdown of parentage, of a father's abandonment of his children and the terrible and irrevocable consequences of such an abandonment."

A Gathering of Old Men, Gaines's fifth novel, presents a cast of aging Southern black men who, after a life of subordination and intimidation, make a defiant stand against injustice. Seventeen of them, together with the thirty-year-old white heiress of a deteriorating Louisiana plantation, plead guilty to murdering Beau Boutan, a member of a violent Cajun clan. While a confounded sheriff and vengeful family wait to lynch the black they have decided is guilty, the group members—toting recently fired shotguns—surround the dead man and "confess" their motives. "Each man tells of the accumulated frustrations of his life—raped daughters, jailed sons, public insults, economic exploitation—that serve as sufficient motive for murder," wrote Byerman. "Though Beau Boutan is seldom the immediate cause of their anger, he clearly represents the entire white world that has deprived them of their dignity and manhood. The confessions serve as ritual purgings of all the hostility and self-hatred built up over the years." Over a dozen characters—white, black, and Cajun—advance the story through individual narrations, creating "thereby a range of social values as well as different perspectives on the action," Byerman noted. *New York Times Book Review* contributor Reynolds Price noted that the black narrators "are nicely distinguished from one another in rhythm and idiom, in the nature of what they see and report, especially in their specific laments for past passivity in the face of suffering." The accumulated effect, observed Elaine Kendall in the *Los Angeles Times Book Review,* is that the "individual stories coalesce into a single powerful tale of subjugation, exploitation and humiliation at the hands of landowners."

Another theme of *A Gathering of Old Men,* according to *America*'s Ben Forkner, is "the simple, natural dispossession of old age, of the traditional and well-loved values of the past, the old trades and the old manners, forced to give way to modern times." Sam Cornish commented in the *Christian Science Monitor* that the novel's "characters—both black and white—understand that, before the close of the novel, the new South must confront the old, and all will be irrevocably changed. Gaines portrays a society that will be altered by the deaths of its 'old men,' and so presents an allegory about the passing of the old and birth of the new."

A Lesson before Dying, issued ten years after *A Gathering of Old Men,* continues the author's historical reflections on the South. The setting is a characteristic one: a plantation and jail in Bayonne during a six-month span in 1948. The unlikely hero is Jefferson, a scarcely literate, twenty-one-year-old man-child who works the cane fields of the Pichot plantation. Trouble finds the protagonist when he innocently hooks up with two men; they then rob a liquor store and are killed in the process along with the shop's proprietor, leaving Jefferson as an accomplice. The young man's naivete in the crime is never recognized as he is brought to trial before a jury of twelve white men and sentenced to death. Jefferson's defense attorney ineffectively attempts to save his client by presenting him as a dumb animal, as "a thing that acts on command. A thing to hold the handle of a plow, a thing to load your bales of cotton." When Jefferson's godmother learns of this analogy, she determines that her nephew will face his execution as a man, not as an animal. Thus, she enlists the help of young teacher Grant Wiggins, who is initially resistant but works to help Jefferson to resolutely shoulder his fate in his final days.

According to Sandra D. Davis in the *Detroit Free Press,* "*A Lesson before Dying* begins much like many other stories where racial tension brews in the background." Yet, as in Gaines's other works, the racial tension in this novel is more of a catalyst for his tribute to the perseverance of the victims of injustice. Unexpectedly, pride, honor, and manhood in a dehumanizing environment emerge as the themes of this novel. Through Wiggins, the young narrator and unwilling carrier of the "burden" of the community, and his interaction with the black community, as represented by Jefferson's godmother and the town's Reverend Ambrose, Gaines "creates a compelling, intense story about heroes and the human spirit," contended Davis. Ironically, Jefferson and Reverend Ambrose ultimately emerge as the real teachers, showing Wiggins that, as Davis asserted, "education encompasses more than the lessons taught in school." Wiggins is also forced to admit, according to Jonathan Yardley in the *Washington Post Book World,* "his own complicity in the system of which Jefferson is a victim." *Commonweal* critic Madeline Marget likened Jefferson's ordeal to the crucifixion of Jesus Christ: "*A Lesson before Dying* is Gaines's retelling of the Passion—a layered and sensual story of a suffering man and his life-changing struggle," one that Gaines explores "through a narrative of tremendous velocity."

Of that community which yields the lessons of Gaines's fiction and his relation to it, Alice Walker wrote in the *New York Times Book Review:* Gaines "claims and revels in the rich heritage of Southern Black people and their customs; the community he feels with them is unmistakable and goes deeper even than pride . . . Gaines is mellow with historical reflection, supple with wit, relaxed and expansive because he does not equate his people with failure." The novelist has been criticized by some, however, who feel his writing does not more directly focus on problems facing blacks. Gaines responded to Desruisseaux that he feels "too many blacks have been writing to tell whites all about 'the problems,' instead of writing something that all people, including their own, could find interesting, could enjoy." Gaines has also remarked that more can be achieved than strictly writing novels of protest. In an interview for *San Francisco,* the author stated: "So many of our writers have not read any farther back than [Richard Wright's] *Native Son.* So many of our novels deal only with the great city ghettos; that's all we write about, as if there's nothing else." Gaines continued: "We've only been living in these ghettos for seventy-five years or so, but the other three hundred years—I think this is worth writing about."

In *Conversations with Ernest Gaines,* the author reveals to editor John Lowe some of the factors behind his popularity and critical acclaim. "While a notable consistency in themes and setting is evident within the body of his writing," stated critic Valerie Babb, writing about *Conversations with Ernest Gaines* in the *African American Review,* "in novel ways this talented writer consistently re-envisions and reworks the material that inspires him. . . . The best commentary is Gaines's own . . . as he assesses his art." "Critiques of racial essentialism are many," Babb concluded, "and there is increased scholarly emphasis on finding voice and telling story, two elements that imbue Gaines's works with their own unique pyrotechnics. With greater appreciation of how small details make great fiction, it seems our critical age is indeed ready to appreciate the fiction of Ernest Gaines."

Gaines's output has been slow but steady, and his focus remains restricted to Louisiana's past. "I can write only about the past," he explained to Jerome Weeks of the *Knight Ridder/Tribune News Service.* "I let it sink into me for a long time, let it stay there. I can't write about something that happened last week." Although his works number less than a dozen, their influence has been widespread. His novels have become part of the mainstay of high school and college literature courses because his characters struggle to define themselves within themselves, their communities, society, and humanity. "We must all try to define ourselves. It's a human struggle," he told Weeks.

BIOGRAPHICAL AND CRITICAL SOURCES:

BOOKS

Babb, Valerie-Melissa, *Ernest Gaines,* Twayne (Boston, MA), 1991.

Beavers, Herman, *Wrestling Angels into Song: The Fictions of Ernest J. Gaines and James Alan McPherson,* University of Pennsylvania Press (Philadelphia, PA), 1995.

Bruck, Peter, editor, *The Black American Short Story in the Twentieth Century: A Collection of Critical Essays,* B.R. Gruner (Amsterdam, Netherlands), 1977.

Carmean, Karen, *Ernest J. Gaines: A Critical Companion,* Greenwood Press (Westport, CT), 1998.

Children's Literature Review, Thomson Gale (Detroit, MI), Volume 62, 2002.

Concise Dictionary of American Literary Biography: Broadening Views, 1968-1988, Thomson Gale (Detroit, MI), 1989.

Contemporary Literary Criticism, Thomson Gale (Detroit, MI), Volume 3, 1975, Volume 11, 1979, Volume 18, 1981.

Dictionary of Literary Biography, Thomson Gale (Detroit, MI), Volume 2: *American Novelists since World War II,* 1978, Volume 33: *Afro-American Fiction Writers after 1955,* 1984.

Dictionary of Literary Biography Yearbook: 1980, Thomson Gale (Detroit, MI), 1981.

Estes, David C., *Critical Reflections on the Fiction of Ernest J. Gaines,* University of Georgia Press (Athens, GA), 1994.

Gaudet, Marcia, and Carl Wooton, *Porch Talk with Ernest Gaines: Conversations on the Writer's Craft,* Louisiana State University Press (Lafayette, LA), 1990.

Gayle, Addison, Jr., *The Way of the New World: The Black Novel in America,* Doubleday (New York, NY), 1975.

Hicks, Jack, *In the Singer's Temple: Prose Fictions of Barthelme, Gaines, Brautigan, Piercy, Kesey, and Kosinski,* University of North Carolina Press (Chapel Hill, NC), 1981.

Hudson, Theodore R., *The History of Southern Literature,* Louisiana State University Press (Lafayette, LA), 1985.

Lowe, John, editor, *Conversations with Ernest Gaines,* University Press of Mississippi (Jackson, MS), 1995.

O'Brien, John, editor, *Interview with Black Writers,* Liveright (New York, NY), 1973.

PERIODICALS

African American Review, fall, 1994, p. 489; February, 1998, p. 350.

America, June 2, 1984.

Atlanta Journal-Constitution, October 26, 1997; July 28, 2002, Teresa K. Weaver, "National Black Arts Festival: The Importance of Reading Ernest (Gaines)," p. L1.

Black American Literature Forum, Volume 11, 1977; Volume 24, 1990.

Black Issues Book Review, May, 2002, review of *In My Father's House* (audio version), p. 26.

Booklist, June 1, 1999, review of *A Lesson before Dying,* p. 1796; November 15, 2001, review of *Catherine Carmier,* p. 555.

Callaloo, Volume 7, 1984; Volume 11, 1988; winter, 1999, Keith Clark, "Re-(w)righting Black Male Subjectivity: The Communal Poetics of Ernest Gaines's *A Gathering of Old Men,*" p. 195; winter, 2001, review of *A Lesson before Dying,* p. 346.

Chicago Tribune Book World, October 30, 1983.

Christian Science Monitor, December 2, 1983.

Chronicle of Higher Education, May 11, 1994, p. A23.

CLA Journal, March, 1971; December, 1975.

Commonweal, June 16, 2000, Madeline Marget, review of *A Lesson before Dying,* p. 23.

Detroit Free Press, June 6, 1993, p. 7J.

Essence, August, 1993, p. 52.

Globe and Mail (Toronto, Ontario, Canada), June 12, 1999, review of *A Lesson before Dying,* p. D4.

Guardian (London, England), March 18, 2000, Nick Hasted, "Nick Hasted Ghosthunts with Ernest Gaines in Altered Southern States," p. 11.

Iowa Review, winter, 1972, Jerry H. Bryant, "From Death to Life: The Fiction of Ernest J. Gaines," pp. 206-120.

Knight Ridder/Tribune News Service, February 28, 2001, Jerome Weeks, "Author Ernest J. Gaines Mines His Rich Southern Past," p. K882.

Library Journal, May 15, 2001, Nancy Pearl, review of *A Lesson before Dying,* p. 192.

Life, April 30, 1971.

Los Angeles Times, March 2, 1983.

Los Angeles Times Book Review, January 1, 1984.

MELUS, Volume 11, 1984; spring, 1999, Wolfgang Lepschy, "Ernest J. Gaines" (interview), p. 197.

Mississippi Quarterly, spring, 1999, Jeffrey J. Folks, "Communal Responsibility in Ernest J. Gaines's *A Lesson before Dying,*" p. 259.

Nation, February 5, 1968; April 5, 1971; January 14, 1984.

Negro Digest, November, 1967; January, 1968; January, 1969.

New Orleans Review, Volume 1, 1969; Volume 3, 1972; Volume 14, 1987.

New Republic, December 26, 1983.

New Statesman, September 2, 1973; February 10, 1984; May 29, 2000, Nicola Upson, review of *A Gathering of Old Men,* p. 57.

Newsweek, June 16, 1969; May 3, 1971.

New Yorker, October 24, 1983.

New York Times, July 20, 1978.

New York Times Book Review, November 19, 1967; May 23, 1971; June 11, 1978; October 30, 1983; May 22, 1999, Ron Wertheimer, review of *A Lesson before Dying,* p. B15; September 19, 2000, Bruce Weber, "Last-Minute Lessons for a Condemned Prisoner in the Jim Crow South," p. E1.

Observer (London, England), February 5, 1984.

Publishers Weekly, March 21, 1994, p. 8.

San Francisco, July, 1974.

Sojourners, September-October, 2002, Dale Brown, "A Lesson for Living," pp. 30-33.

Southern Review, Volume 10, 1974; Volume 21, 1985.

Studies in Short Fiction, summer, 1975.

Studies in the Humanities, June-December, 2001, Lorna Fitzsimmons, "*The Autobiography of Miss Jane Pittman:* Film, Intertext, and Ideology," pp. 94-109.

Time, May 10, 1971; December 27, 1971.

Times (London, England), March 18, 2000, Paul Connolly, review of *A Gathering of Old Men,* p. 21.

Times Literary Supplement, February 10, 1966; March 16, 1973; April 6, 1984.

Voice Literary Supplement, October, 1983.

Wall Street Journal, September 20, 2000, Amy Gamerman, review of *A Lesson before Dying,* p. A24.

Washington Post, January 13, 1976; May 22, 1999, Ken Ringle, review of *A Lesson before Dying,* p. C01.

Washington Post Book World, June 18, 1978; September 21, 1983; March 28, 1993, p. 3; May 23, 1993.

Writer, May, 1999, p. 4.

ONLINE

NewOrleans, http://www.neworleans.com/lalife/ (summer, 1997), Faith Dawson, "A Louisiana Life: Ernest J. Gaines."

OTHER

Louisiana Stories: Ernest Gaines (television film), WHMM-TV, 1993.

*   *   *

GAINES, Ernest James
See GAINES, Ernest J.

*   *   *

GALBRAITH, John Kenneth 1908-2006
(Mark Epernay, Herschel McLandress)

PERSONAL: Born October 15, 1908, in Iona Station, Ontario, Canada; naturalized United States citizen, 1937; died April 29, 2006, in Cambridge, MA; son of William Archibald (a politician and farmer) and Catherine (Kendall) Galbraith; married Catherine Atwater, September 17, 1937; children: John Alan, Peter, James, Douglas (deceased). *Education:* University of Toronto, B.S. (agriculture), 1931; University of California, Berkeley, M.S., 1933, Ph.D. (economics), 1934; attended Cambridge University, 1937-38. *Politics:* Democrat.

ADDRESSES: Home—30 Francis Ave., Cambridge, MA 02138; Newfane, VT (summer); Gstaad, Switzerland (winter). *Office*—207 Littauer Center, Harvard University, Cambridge, MA 02138.

CAREER: Harvard University, Cambridge, MA, instructor and tutor, 1934-39; Princeton University, Princeton, NJ, assistant professor of economics, 1939-42; U.S. Office of Price Administration, Washington, D.C., administrator in charge of price division, 1941-42, department administrator, 1942-43; *Fortune* magazine, member of board of editors, 1943-48; Harvard University, lecturer, 1948-49, professor, 1949-59, Paul M. Warburg Professor of Economics, 1959-75, Paul M. Warburg Professor emeritus, 1975—. Reith Lecturer, 1966; Trinity College, Cambridge, visiting fellow, 1970-71. Director of U.S. Strategic Bombing Survey, 1945, and Office of Economic Security Policy, U.S. Department of State, 1946; presidential adviser to John F. Kennedy and Lyndon B. Johnson; U.S. Ambassador to India, 1961-63. Affiliated with television series *The Age of Uncertainty*, on the British Broadcasting Corporation (BBC), 1977.

MEMBER: American Academy and Institute of Arts and Letters (president, 1984-87), American Academy of Arts and Sciences (fellow), American Economic Association (president, 1972), Americans for Democratic Action (chairman, 1967-69), American Agricultural Economics Association, Twentieth Century Fund (trustee), Century Club (New York, NY), Federal City Club (Washington, DC), Harvard Club (New York, NY), Saturday Club (Boston).

AWARDS, HONORS: Research fellowship, University of California, 1931-34; Social Science Research Council fellowship, 1937-38; Medal of Freedom, 1946; Sarah Josepha Hale Award, Friends of the Richards Free Library, 1967; President's Certificate of Merit; honorary degrees include LL.D., Bard College, 1958, Miami University (Ohio), 1959, University of Toronto, 1961, Brandeis University, 1963, University of Massachusetts, 1963, University of Guelph, 1965, University of Saskatchewan, 1965, Rhode Island College, 1966, Boston College, 1967, Hobart and William Smith Colleges, 1967, University of Paris, 1975, Harvard University, 1988, Moscow State University, 1988, Smith College, 1989, and Oxford University, 1990; Medal of Freedom Award, by the President of the United States, 2000; Padma Vibhushan Award (India's second highest civilian honor), by the Indian ambassador Lalit Mansingh, 2001.

WRITINGS:

(With Henry Sturgis Dennison) *Modern Competition and Business Policy,* Oxford University Press, 1938.

A Theory of Price Control, Harvard University Press, 1952, reprinted with new introduction by Galbraith, 1980.

American Capitalism: The Concept of Countervailing Power, Houghton, 1952, reprinted with new introduction by Galbraith, M.E. Sharpe, 1980, revised edition, Transaction Publishers, 1993.

Economics and the Art of Controversy, Rutgers University Press, 1955.

The Great Crash, 1929, Houghton, 1955, reprinted with new introduction by Galbraith, 1988, reprinted Houghton Mifflin, 1995.

(With Richard H. Holton and others) *Marketing Efficiency in Puerto Rico,* Harvard University Press, 1955.

Journey to Poland and Yugoslavia, Harvard University Press, 1958.

The Affluent Society, Houghton, 1958, 4th edition, 1984.

The Liberal Hour, Houghton, 1960.

Economic Development in Perspective, Harvard University Press, 1962, revised edition published as *Economic Development,* 1964.

(Under pseudonym Mark Epernay) *The McLandress Dimension* (satire), Houghton, 1963, revised edition, New American Library, 1968.

The Scotch (memoir), Houghton, 1964, 2nd edition, 1985 (published in England as *Made to Last,* Hamish Hamilton, 1964, and as *The Non-potable Scotch: A Memoir on the Clansmen in Canada,* Penguin, 1964).

The Underdeveloped Country (text of five radio broadcasts), Canadian Broadcasting Corp., 1965.

The New Industrial State, Houghton, 1967, 4th edition, 1985.

How to Get Out of Vietnam: A Workable Solution to the Worst Problem of Our Time, New American Library, 1967.

The Triumph: A Novel of Modern Diplomacy, Houghton, 1968.

(With Mohinder Singh Randhawa) *Indian Painting: The Scene, Themes and Legends,* Houghton, 1968.

How to Control the Military, Doubleday, 1969.

Ambassador's Journal: A Personal Account of the Kennedy Years, Houghton, 1969.

(Author of introduction) David Levine, *No Known Survivors: David Levine's Political Prank,* Gambit, 1970.

Who Needs the Democrats, and What It Takes to Be Needed, Doubleday, 1970.

A Contemporary Guide to Economics, Peace, and Laughter (essays), edited by Andrea D. Williams, Houghton, 1971.

Economics and the Public Purpose, Houghton, 1973.

A China Passage, Houghton, 1973.

(Author of introduction) Frank Moraes and Edward Howe, editors, *India,* McGraw-Hill, 1974.

Money: Whence It Came, Where It Went, Houghton, 1975, revised edition, 1995.

The Age of Uncertainty (based on the 1977 BBC television series), Houghton, 1977.

The Galbraith Reader: From the Works of John Kenneth Galbraith, selected and with commentary by the editors of *Gambit,* Gambit, 1977.

(With Nicole Salinger) *Almost Everyone's Guide to Economics,* Houghton, 1978.

Annals of an Abiding Liberal, edited by Williams, Houghton, 1979.

The Nature of Mass Poverty, Harvard University Press, 1979.

A Life in Our Times: Memoirs, Houghton, 1981.

The Anatomy of Power, Houghton, 1983.

The Voice of the Poor: Essays in Economic and Political Persuasion, Harvard University Press, 1983.

A View from the Stands: Of People, Politics, Military Power, and the Arts, edited by Williams, Houghton, 1986.

Economics in Perspective: A Critical History, Houghton, 1987, published as *A History of Economics,* 1987.

(With Stanislav Menshikov) *Capitalism, Communism and Coexistence: From the Bitter Past to a Better Present,* Houghton, 1988.

A Tenured Professor (novel), Houghton, 1990.

The Culture of Contentment, Houghton, 1992.

(Editor and author of introduction) Thomas H. Eliot, *Recollections of the New Deal: When the People Mattered,* Northeastern University Press, 1992.

A Short History of Financial Euphoria: A Hymn of Caution, Whittle Books/ Viking, 1993.

The Triumph: A Novel of Modern Diplomacy, Houghton, 1993.

A Journey through Economic Time: A Firsthand View, Houghton, 1994.

The World Economy since the Wars: An Eyewitness Account, Houghton, 1994.

The Good Society: The Humane Dimension, Houghton, 1996.

Letters to Kennedy (correspondence), edited by James Goodman, Harvard University Press, 1998.

The Socially Concerned Today, Victoria University and the University of Toronto Press, 1998.

Name-Dropping: From F.D.R. On, Houghton Mifflin, 1999.

The Unfinished Business of Our Century, American College, 1999.

Contributor to books, including *Can Europe Unite?,* Foreign Policy Association (New York, NY), 1950, and *The Past Speaks to the Present,* by Yigael Yadin, Granada TV Network Limited, 1962. Author of drafts of speeches for political leaders, including Franklin D. Roosevelt, Adlai Stevenson, John F. Kennedy, Lyndon B. Johnson, and Robert Kennedy. Editor of "Harvard Economic Studies" series, Harvard University Press. Contributor to scholarly journals. Reviewer, under pseudonym Herschel McLandress, of *Report from Iron Mountain.*

Galbraith's works have been translated into numerous languages.

SIDELIGHTS: John Kenneth Galbraith was considered one of the twentieth century's foremost writers on economics and among its most influential economists. A prolific and diverse writer, whose more than forty books range over a variety of topics, Galbraith was the author of such classic texts as *The Affluent Society* and *The New Industrial State.* In addition to his writings, he has also held positions as a government economist, presidential adviser, and foreign ambassador, and for more than fifteen years he was the Paul M. Warburg Professor of Economics at Harvard University. Galbraith's blend of skills make him a rarity among economists. "As a raconteur and a literary stylist, he stands with the best," stated James Fallows in the *New York Times Book Review,* while "as a thinker," noted Lowell Ponte in the *Los Angeles Times Book Review,* "Galbraith has made major contributions to the economic arguments of our time." In addition to originating several terms that are part of the vernacular of economists and laymen alike—such as "affluent society," "conventional wisdom," and "countervailing power"—Galbraith is famous as a witty guide to twentieth-century economics. A *New Yorker* reviewer called him "a wizard at packing immense amounts of information into a style so entertaining that the reader does not realize he is being taught." Eugene D. Genovese wrote in the *New York Times Book Review* that Galbraith "has admirably demonstrated that respect for the English language provides everything necessary to demystify economics and render its complexities intelligible."

Galbraith's writing abilities, including his accessibility to non-economist audiences, have at times overshadowed his achievements as an economist. "Galbraith's irreverent wit and lucid style lead many to underestimate his importance in the history of economic thought," Walter Russell Mead notes in the *Los Angeles Times Book Review.* "Like Adam Smith . . . Galbraith has spent a career attacking the entrenched errors of conventional wisdom." Galbraith is well known as a formidable critic of modern economic policies and economists. Richard Eder in the *Los Angeles Times* depicted him as "liberal, witty, polemical and a man who tends to charm his antagonists because the dunce caps he fits on them are so finely made that they almost flatter." As a critic, Galbraith has made significant contributions to economics by highlighting its shortcomings. According to Genovese, Galbraith's "services" include: "his early warnings that Keynesians were paying inadequate attention to the danger of inflation; his thoughtful if not always convincing discussions of the political and economic relationship of the free market sector to the managed sector; his bold exploration of the possibilities and actualities of socialism; and his humane concern for the problems of women, the poor, the blacks and others conveniently forgotten by most academic economists." Godfrey Hodgson, in the *Washington Post Book World,* compared Galbraith to eighteenth-century French satirist Voltaire, "a man whose sardonic wit and careful urbanity are worn like masks to hide both the anger he feels for sham and complacent greed, and the pity he feels for their victims."

The son of a Canadian politician and farmer, Galbraith became interested in the study of economics during the Depression. In the 1930s and early 1940s, he taught at both Harvard University and Princeton University and became influenced by economist John Maynard Keynes. In 1941, at the age of 33, he was appointed administrator of the price operations of the U.S. Office of Price Administration and was responsible for setting prices in the United States. His 1952 book *A Theory of Price Control* outlines many of Galbraith's fundamental economic principles, as does another early book, *American Capitalism: The Concept of Countervailing Power,* which explores postwar American economy and the role of labor as a countervailing force in a market economy. Samuel Lubell in the *New York Herald Tribune Book World* called *American Capitalism* "one of the most provocative economic essays since the writings of the late John Maynard Keynes," adding that "even where one disagrees, [Galbraith's] ideas stimulate a spring cleaning of old beliefs and outworn, if cherished, notions—which is perhaps all that can be asked of any new theory." Galbraith commented to Victor Navasky in the *New York Times Book Review* on his decision to write about economics: "I made up my mind I would never again place myself at the mercy of the technical economists who had the enormous power to ignore what I had written. I set out to involve a large community. I would involve economists by having the larger public say to them 'Where do you stand on Galbraith's idea of price control?' They would *have* to confront what I said."

Galbraith broadened his readership with his 1955 book *The Great Crash, 1929,* which recounts the harried days leading up to the stock market crash and Great Depression. Written at the suggestion of historian Arthur Schlesinger, Jr., who queried Galbraith as to why no one had ever written an economic account of the depression, *The Great Crash, 1929* was praised for being both illuminating and readable. "Economic writings are seldom notable for their entertainment value, but this book is," C.J. Rolo commented in *Atlantic Monthly,* adding, "Galbraith's prose has grace and wit, and he distills a good deal of sardonic fun from the whopping errors of the nation's oracles and the wondrous antics of the financial community." R.L. Heilbroner wrote in the *New York Herald Tribune Book Review:* "Galbraith has told the tale of the great bust with all the verve, pace, and suspense, of a detective story. . . . For any one who is interested in understanding the recent past or attempting to achieve a perspective on the future of American economic history, . . . this book will be of great interest."

Following these books, Galbraith wrote the bestseller *The Affluent Society.* A major assessment of the U.S. economy, *The Affluent Society* questions priorities of production and how wealth is to be divided. As Galbraith stated in the book: "The final problem of the productive society is what it produces. This manifests itself in an implacable tendency to provide an opulent supply of some things and a niggardly yield of others. This disparity carries to the point where it is a cause of social discomfort and social unhealth." According to Heilbroner, Galbraith raised three important issues: "One of these is the moral problem of how an Affluent Society may be prevented from becoming merely a Rich one. A second is the efficacy of Mr. Galbraith's reforms to offset the inertia and the vested interests of a powerful social structure. A third is what form of social cohesion can replace our troublesome but useful absorption in Production." Heilbroner called *The Affluent Society* "as disturbing as it is brilliant. . . . with which it is easy to cavil or to disagree, but which it is impossible to dismiss."

Galbraith's 1967 bestseller *The New Industrial State,* a sequel to *The Affluent Society,* examines the diminishing role of individual choice in the market enterprise. "I reached the conclusion that in 'The Affluent Society' I had only written half the book I should have," Galbraith commented to the *New York Times Book Review.* "'The Affluent Society' says the more you have the more you want. And for obvious reasons, as people become richer it is easier to persuade them as to their wants. But I hadn't really examined the role of the great corporations, the industrial system, in the persuasion process." Arthur Selwyn Miller commented in the

New Republic: "If Galbraith is correct—and I am inclined to agree in large part with him—then we . . . are ruled by nameless and faceless managers in the technostructures of the private governments of the supercorporations and their counterparts in the public bureaucracy. That's an event of considerable significance." Raymond J. Saulnier in the *New York Times Book Review* called *The New Industrial State* "a tightly organized, closely reasoned book, notable for what it says about the dynamics of institutional change and for certain qualities of its author: a sardonic wit, exercised liberally at the expense of conservatives, and unusual perception."

In his 1973 book *Economics and the Public Purpose* Galbraith, according to Leonard Silk in the *New York Times,* goes "beyond his earlier books to describe the whole modern capitalist economy, which he sees as split roughly in twain between 'the planning system' and what he calls 'the market system'—a collection of imperfect competitors and partial monopolists that includes such producers as farmers, television repairmen, retailers, small manufacturers, medical practitioners, photographers and pornographers." The *New Yorker's* Naomi Bliven commented that Galbraith "offers his account of the American economic system and his ideas of how to correct—a word he uses frequently—its irrationality." She added that although "his intensity sometimes makes his wit painfully abrasive. . . . because his work is intelligent, stimulating, and comprehensive—Galbraith knows (in fact, insists) that an economic theory implies an ethical system, a political purpose, and a psychological hypothesis—one forgives this unrelenting critic."

In addition to more than twenty-five other books on economics, the prolific Galbraith is also the author of novels and acclaimed volumes of memoirs. As in his other books, critics found that these writings display Galbraith's characteristic wit and insight. His 1968 novel *The Triumph,* set amidst a revolution in a fictional Latin American nation, depicts the bungled efforts of U.S. foreign policy officials to put an acceptable leader in power. Robert Brown in the *New Republic,* while expressing reservations about the novel's tone, which he described as "loftily condescending and relentlessly witty," called the book "quite devastating" and acknowledged Galbraith's "detailed knowledge of the scene." Galbraith's 1990 novel, *A Tenured Professor,* is the tale of a professor who, with his wife, develops a successful stock forecasting mechanism that makes them very wealthy. With their new money, the couple begins supporting various liberal causes, such as identifying companies that do not employ women in top

executive positions. "Lurking in the background of his story is enough economics to satisfy Wall Street game players and enough of a cheerful fairy tale for grown-ups to please the most liberal dreamers," notes Herbert Mitgang in the *New York Times.* "A whimsical fellow is John Kenneth Galbraith, who knows that money makes people and institutions jump through hoops and over their own cherished principles." He added: "Readers who know and admire the author as an acerbic political voice are not shortchanged in his biting new novel. . . . Satirical one-liners and paragraphs fall lightly from the pen of the author and from the lips of his characters all through the story."

Galbraith's memoirs give insights into his diverse career as economist, writer, and participant in the political scene. Regarding *A Life in Our Times,* Ward Just commented in the *Chicago Tribune Book World:* "[Galbraith] has rarely been at the center of events, though he has been on the fringes of most everything, so this is not a memoir of the and-then-I-told-the-President variety. . . . The charm and consequence of this book is not the career as such, but the manner in which the author has chosen to describe it, with singular range, style, and wit, and a sure grasp of absurdity and pomposity, particularly as they apply to government and politics." Regarding the essays in *A View from the Stands: Of People, Politics, Military Power, and the Arts,* Richard Eder wrote in the *Los Angeles Times* that Galbraith "has a priceless sense of the absurd. . . . [Yet,] for someone who makes an art out of polite irreverence, Galbraith manages to be equally artistic in his strong admirations. . . . His portraits of, among others, Ambassador Chester Bowles, President Lyndon B. Johnson and First Lady Eleanor Roosevelt are both warm and strikingly perceptive." *A View from the Stands* reveals a man, according to John Freeman in the *Times Literary Supplement,* who is "substantial, interesting, frequently perverse, occasionally silly, almost always stimulating—at least hardly ever a bore—opinionated, funny, fastidious, loyal, on the whole generous and magnificently infallible even when he is wrong."

In *The Culture of Contentment,* Galbraith "scathingly denounces a society in which the affluent have come to dominate the political arena, guaranteeing their continued comfort while refusing to address the needs of the less fortunate," claimed Victor Dwyer in *Maclean's.* Galbraith asserted that satisfied citizens—those whose earning are in the top twenty percent and who live a moneyed lifestyle—tend, by their very prosperity, to guarantee their eventual downfall by ignoring the fundamental requirements of the underclasses. Their blindness to social reform has historically led to inflation and the need for greater government intervention, the author maintained, thereby causing a resulting eventual decline in economic security even for the elite. Galbraith warned that the upper class ignores economic, political, and social necessities of the lower classes at its own peril. Galbraith told Dwyer that *The Culture of Contentment* exceeds the scope of his other books: "'What I am attempting is to formulate the political consequences of self-satisfied well-being,' said Galbraith. 'In the wake of Mr. Reagan and Mr. Bush,' he added, 'it seemed that the time was right.'" Robert N. Bellah observed in the *New York Times Book Review,* "'The Culture of Contentment' is certainly no savage jeremiad. It is a very amusing volume, but by the end one's laughter has turned hollow and one wants to weep. For all its gentle appearances, it is a bombshell of a book, and the story it tells is one of devastation." Aidan Rankin commented in the *Times Literary Supplement:* "The reassuring, old-fashioned elegance of John Kenneth Galbraith's prose is at once the most striking and the most disturbing feature of *The Culture of Contentment.* Striking, because it contrasts so markedly with the jargon and euphemism of modern economics, disturbing in the force and clarity of its critique of contemporary democracy."

About *A Short History of Financial Euphoria: A Hymn of Caution,* Robert Krulwich explained in the *New York Times Book Review* that it "is John Kenneth Galbraith's quick tour through four centuries of financial bubbles, panics and crashes, with an eye toward instructing today's investors on how to see cautionary signs before it is too late." The book describes, through myriad examples, a historic pattern of financial ebb and flow creating highs and lows in the economic climate. Galbraith denounces the oblivious attitude engendered by successful investments, blinding individuals to warning signs and potential disasters. As Krulwich put it, "How people become blockheads is the real subject of his treatise." He concluded that Galbraith reminds readers that "rich people aren't smart. They're just lucky."

A Journey through Economic Time: A Firsthand View traces economic development from the time of World War I (or the "Great War") through the highlights of the twentieth century, including other wars and military conflicts, the philosophies of influential pundits, and the practices and ideologies of various presidential administrations. "Somehow, with an astonishing and no doubt deceptive ease, Mr. Galbraith is able to compress eras, reducing their unwieldy bulk to graspable essence and extracting coherence from their thematic tangle," remarked Alan Abelson in the *New York Times Book Review.* Abelson admired the readability of the book, asserting, "He's opinionated, incorrigibly sardonic and

murder on fools. . . . In a profession in which statistical surfeit, abused syntax and impenetrable prose are prerequisites to standing, Mr. Galbraith's lucidity and grace of articulation are excommunicable offenses." Donald McCloskey hailed Galbraith's tome in the Chicago *Tribune Books,* summarizing, "What makes it good is the Old Economist showing you page after page how to think like one," ultimately urging readers to "buy it or borrow it. You'll be a better citizen and will not believe so easily the latest economic idiocy from Washington or the Sierra Club or the other fonts of conventional wisdom."

William Keegan noted in *New Statesman and Society* that *The World Economy since the Wars: An Eyewitness Account* "can be thoroughly recommended to those interested in the economic debate, but [who are] not quite sure where to start." Galbraith's efforts involve "sifting and reducing a lifetime's observations to an essential core," described Keegan. While the reviewer suggested that much of this volume had already appeared in other forms in earlier books, he nevertheless maintained, "This is a highly engaging memoir, which holds the attention even of people, such as myself, who are thoroughly familiar with most of Galbraith's work."

Two years after the Republican party won control of Congress in the 1994 elections, Galbraith produced *The Good Society: The Humane Dimension,* reiterating his economic and political vision for the creation of a just and equitable society. While suggesting that big government and the welfare state are the products of historical forces rather than liberal policies, Galbraith advocated reform on behalf of the poor and disenfranchised, including health care, unemployment compensation, government regulation of working conditions, education, environmental protection, and progressive taxation. As Paul Craig Roberts summarized in the *National Review,* Galbraith "defines 'the good society' as one that is politically organized to coerce 'the favored' for the poor. The instrument for this coercion 'must be the Democratic Party.'" According to Todd Gitlin in the *Nation,* "Galbraith has written perhaps the most chastened manifesto in American history. Deliberately so. His goal in this brief handbook is to sketch 'the achievable, not the perfect.'" *The Good Society,* as Matthew Miller observed in the *New York Times Book Review,* contains "Mr. Galbraith's vintage cultural complaints. He denounces the equation of wealth with intelligence, the role of advertising in ginning up consumer desire, the injustice of private affluence alongside public squalor . . . and, of course, the perils of bureaucracy."

For more than half a century, Galbraith has proven himself a brilliant writer, critical thinker, perspicacious social analyst, and astute economic observer/commentator. Rankin opined in the *Times Literary Supplement* that "Galbraith has contributed substantially to the liberal tradition in the United States and the social democratic tradition in Western Europe." About the author's multiple interests and abilities, McCloskey commented in the *Chicago Tribune Books,* "As much as he would rather be a writer, converting people to his government-loving faith, he [is] an economist down to his shoes." Dwyer described Galbraith in *Maclean's* as "America's foremost liberal thinker," adding that he "is most passionate about the state of American society." McCloskey concluded, "We need more of him because he's an economist who can speak to non-economists. . . . Galbraith is one of a handful of professors who can make the Dismal Science sing."

An interview with Galbraith appears in *Contemporary Authors, New Revision Series,* Volume 34.

BIOGRAPHICAL AND CRITICAL SOURCES:

BOOKS

Contemporary Issues Criticism, Volume 1, Thomson Gale (Detroit), 1982.
Galbraith, John Kenneth, *The Affluent Society,* Houghton, 1958.
Galbraith, John Kenneth, *The Scotch,* Houghton, 1964.
Galbraith, John Kenneth, *A Life in Our Times: Memoirs,* Houghton, 1981.
Galbraith, John Kenneth, *A View from the Stands: Of People, Politics, Military Power, and the Arts,* Houghton, 1986.
Galbraith, John Kenneth, *A Journey through Economic Time: A Firsthand View,* Houghton, 1994.
Galbraith, John Kenneth, *The World Economy since the Wars: An Eyewitness Account,* Houghton, 1994.
Reisman, D. A., *Galbraith and Market Capitalism,* New York University Press, 1980.
Reisman, D.A., *Tawney, Galbraith, and Adam Smith,* St. Martin's, 1982.
Stanfield, J. Ron, *John Kenneth Galbraith,* St. Martin's, 1996.
Parker, Richard, *John Kenneth Galbraith: His Life, His Politics, His Economics,* Farrar, Straus, 2005.

PERIODICALS

American Economic Review, December, 1952.
Atlantic Monthly, June, 1955; January, 1987.

Chicago Tribune, June 1, 1958.
Chicago Tribune Book World, April 19, 1981.
Fortune, June 13, 1994, p. 149.
Kirkus Reviews, February 15, 1996, p. 273.
Library Journal, May 15, 1993, pp. 78-79.
Look, March 27, 1970.
Los Angeles Times, December 3, 1986.
Los Angeles Times Book Review, May 24, 1981; November 11, 1987; March 4, 1990; June 19, 1994, pp. 4, 11.
Maclean's, May 25, 1992, pp. 61-62.
Nation, July 30, 1955; May 6, 1996, p. 28.
National Review, October 10, 1994, p. 75; June 17, 1996, p. 52.
New Republic, June 9, 1958; July 8, 1967; May 4, 1968.
New Statesman and Society, January 28, 1994, p. 14; February 18, 1994, p. 24; July 22, 1994, p. 47.
Newsweek, June 26, 1967; July 3, 1967.
New Yorker, January 6, 1968; December 31, 1973; May 2, 1977.
New York Herald Tribune Book Review, June 29, 1952; April 24, 1955; June 9, 1958.
New York Review of Books, May 26, 1994, p. 40.
New York Times, June 1, 1958; September 18, 1973; February 24, 1990.
New York Times Book Review, June 25, 1967; September 7, 1975; May 3, 1981; February 11, 1990; April 5, 1992, p. 10; July 18, 1993, p. 8; June 19, 1994, p. 9.
Playboy (interview), June, 1968.
Publishers Weekly, May 17, 1993, p. 58.
Spectator, November 10, 1967.
Time, February 16, 1968.
Times Literary Supplement, March 13, 1987; May 29, 1992, p. 26.
Tribune Books (Chicago), February 18, 1990; September 25, 1994, p. 4.
Washington Monthly, July-August, 1994, p. 20.
Washington Post Book World, October 21, 1979; February 11, 1990.

* * *

GALINDO, P.
   See HINOJOSA, Rolando

* * *

GALLANT, Mavis 1922-

PERSONAL: Born Mavis Young, August 11, 1922, in Montreal, Quebec, Canada. *Education:* Educated at schools in Montreal and New York, NY.

ADDRESSES: Home—37 West 12th St., New York, NY 10011-8502. *Agent*—Georges Borchardt, 136 East 57th St., New York, NY 10022.

CAREER: Worked at National Film Board of Canada, Montreal, early 1940s; *Standard*, Montreal, Quebec, feature writer and critic, 1944-50; freelance writer, 1950—. Writer-in-residence at University of Toronto, 1983-84.

MEMBER: PEN, Authors Guild, Authors League of America, American Academy and Institute of Arts and Letters (foreign honorary member), Royal Society of Literature (fellow).

AWARDS, HONORS: Canadian Fiction Prize, 1978; named Officer of the Order of Canada, 1981; Governor General's Award, 1981, for *Home Truths: Selected Canadian Stories;* honorary doctorates from University of St. Anne, Nova Scotia, and York University, Ontario, both 1984, University of Western Ontario, 1990, Queen's University, 1992, and University of Montreal and Birnap's University, both 1995; Canada-Australia Literary Prize, 1985; Canadian Council Molson Prize for the Arts, 1997.

WRITINGS:

FICTION

The Other Paris (short stories), Houghton (Boston, MA), 1956.

Green Water, Green Sky (novel), Houghton (Boston, MA), 1959.

My Heart Is Broken: Eight Stories and a Short Novel, Random House (New York, NY), 1964, published in England as *An Unmarried Man's Summer,* Heinemann (London, England), 1965.

A Fairly Good Time (novel), Random House (New York, NY), 1970.

The Pegnitz Junction: A Novella and Five Short Stories, Random House (New York, NY), 1973.

The End of the World and Other Stories, McClelland & Stewart (Toronto, Ontario, Canada), 1974.

From the Fifteenth District: A Novella and Eight Short Stories, Random House (New York, NY), 1979.

Home Truths: Selected Canadian Stories, Macmillan (Toronto, Ontario, Canada), 1981, Random House (New York, NY), 1985.

Overhead in a Balloon: Stories of Paris, Macmillan (Toronto, Ontario, Canada), 1985, Random House (New York, NY), 1987.

In Transit: Twenty Stories, Viking (Markam, Ontario, Canada), 1988, Random House (New York, NY), 1989.

Across the Bridge: Nine Short Stories, Random House (New York, NY), 1993.

The Moslem Wife and Other Stories, McClelland & Stewart (Toronto, Ontario, Canada), 1993.

The Collected Stories of Mavis Gallant, Random House (New York, NY), 1996.

(Author of introduction) *The Wandering Jews,* W.W. Norton (New York, NY), 2000.

Paris Stories, New York Review Books (New York, NY), 2002.

Varieties of Exile: Stories, New York Review Books (New York, NY), 2003.

OTHER

(Author of introduction) Gabrielle Russier, *The Affair of Gabrielle Russier,* Knopf (New York, NY), 1971.

(Author of introduction) J. Hibbert, *The War Brides,* PMA (Toronto, Ontario, Canada), 1978.

What Is to Be Done? (play; produced in Toronto, Ontario, Canada, 1982), Quadrant, 1983.

Paris Notebooks: Essays and Reviews, Macmillan (Toronto, Ontario, Canada), 1986.

Contributor of essays, short stories, and reviews to numerous periodicals, including the *New Yorker, New York Times Book Review, New Republic, New York Review of Books,* and *Times Literary Supplement.*

WORK IN PROGRESS: A novel.

SIDELIGHTS: Canadian-born Mavis Gallant is often described as one of the finest crafters of short stories in the English language. Her works, most of which appeared initially in the *New Yorker* magazine, are praised for sensitive evocation of setting and penetrating delineation of character. In the words of *Maclean's* contributor Mark Abley, Gallant "is virtually unrivaled at the art of short fiction"; an exacting artist, her pieces reveal "an ability to press a lifetime into a few resonant pages as well as a desire to show the dark side of comedy and the humor that lurks behind despair." *Time* contributor Timothy Foote called Gallant "one of the prose masters of the age," and added that no modern writer "casts a colder eye on life, on death and all the angst and eccentricity in between."

Since 1950 Gallant has lived primarily in Paris, but she has also spent extended periods of time in the United States, Canada, and other parts of Europe. Not surprisingly, her stories and novellas show a wide range of place and period; many feature refugees and expatriates forced into self-discernment by rootlessness. As Anne Tyler noted in the *New York Times Book Review,* each Gallant fiction "is densely—woven, . . . rich in people and plots—a miniature world, more satisfying than many full-scale novels. . . . There is a sense of limitlessness: each story is like a peephole opening out into a very wide landscape."

Dictionary of Literary Biography essayist Ronald B. Hatch observed that the subject of children, "alone, frightened, or unloved," recurs often in Gallant's work. This, he noted, reflects Gallant's own difficult youth. The author underwent a solitary and transient childhood, attending seventeen different schools in the United States and Canada. Her father died while she was in grade school, and her mother, soon remarried, moved to the United States, leaving the child with strangers. Reflecting upon how her formative years influenced her writing, Gallant told the *New York Times:* "I think it's true that in many, many of the things I write, someone has vanished. And it's often the father. And there is often a sense that nothing is very safe, and you're often walking on a very thin crust." One advantage of Gallant's far-flung education has endured, however. As a primary schooler in her native Montreal, she learned French, and she remained bilingual into adulthood.

Gallant matured into a resourceful young woman determined to be a writer. At the age of twenty-one she became a reporter with the *Montreal Standard,* a position that honed her writing talents while it widened her variety of experiences. Journalism, she told the *New York Times,* "turned out to be so valuable, because I saw the interiors of houses I wouldn't have seen otherwise. And a great many of the things, particularly in . . . [fiction] about Montreal, that I was able to describe later, it was because I had seen them, I had gone into them as a journalist." She added: "If I got on with the people, I had no hesitation about seeing them again. . . . I went right back and took them to lunch. I could see some of those rooms, and see the wallpaper, and what they ate, and what they wore, and how they spoke, . . . and the way they treated their children. I drew it all in like blotting paper." From these encounters Gallant began to write stories. In 1950 she decided to leave Montreal and begin a new life as a serious fiction writer in Paris. At the same time she began to send stories to the *New Yorker* for publication. Her second submission, a piece called "Madeline's Birthday," was accepted, beginning a four-decade relationship with the prestigious periodical. Gallant used the six-hundred-dollar check for her story to finance her move abroad. Paris has been her permanent home ever since.

Expatriation provided Gallant with new challenges and insights that have formed central themes in her fiction. In *The Other Paris* and subsequent story collections, her characters are "the refugee, the rootless, the emotionally disinherited," to quote a *Times Literary Supplement* reviewer, who added: "It is a world of displacement where journeys are allegorical and love is inadequate." Gallant portrays postwar people locked into archaic cultural presuppositions; often dispossessed of their homes by haphazard circumstances, they are bewildered and insecure, seeking refuge in etiquette and other shallow symbols of tradition. *Time* correspondent Patricia Blake maintained that Gallant's "natural subject is the varieties of spiritual exile. . . . All [her characters] are bearers of a metaphorical 'true passport' that transcends nationality and signifies internal freedom. For some this serves as a safe-conduct to independence. For others it is a guarantee of loneliness and despair." Gallant also presents the corollary theme of the past's inexorable grip on its survivors. In her stories, *New York Review of Books* essayist V.S. Pritchett contended, "we are among the victims of the wars in Europe which have left behind pockets of feckless exiles. . . . History has got its teeth into them and has regurgitated them and left them bizarre and perplexed." Whether immersed in the past or on the run from it, vainly trying to "turn over a new leaf," Gallant's characters "convey with remarkable success a sense of the amorphousness, the mess of life," to quote *Books & Bookmen* contributor James Brockway. Spiritually and physically marginal, they yearn paradoxically for safety, order, and freedom. "Hearts are not broken in Mavis Gallant's stories," concluded Eve Auchincloss in the *New York Review of Books.* "Roots are cut, and her subject is the nature of the life that is led when the roots are not fed."

Most critics applaud Gallant's ability to inhabit the minds of her characters without resorting to condescension or sentimentality. Abley claimed that the author "can write with curiosity and perceptiveness about the kind of people who would never read a word of her work—a rarer achievement than it might sound. She is famous for not forgiving and not forgetting; her unkindness is usually focused on women and men who have grown complacent, never reflecting on their experience, no longer caring about their world. With such people she is merciless, yet with others, especially children bruised by neglect, she is patient and even kind. In the end, perhaps, understanding can be a means of forgiveness. One hopes so, because Mavis Gallant understands us terribly well." In Chicago's *Tribune Books,* Civia Tamarkin suggested that Gallant's works "impose a haunting vision of man trapped in an existential world. Each of the stories is a sensitive, though admirably understated, treatment of isolation, loneliness, and despair. Together they build an accumulating sense of the frustrating indifference of the cosmos to human hopes."

While best known for her short stories and novellas, Gallant has also penned two novels, *Green Water, Green Sky* and *A Fairly Good Time.* Hatch contended that these works continue the author's "exploration of the interaction between an individual's thoughts and his external world." In *Green Water, Green Sky,* according to Constance Pendergast in the *Saturday Review,* Gallant "writes of the disaster that results from a relationship founded on the mutual need and antagonism of a woman and her daughter, where love turns inward and festers, bringing about inevitably the disintegration of both characters." Elmer Borklund, writing in *Contemporary Novelists,* found Gallant's first attempt at longer fiction to be less successful than her short stories: "*Green Water, Green Sky,* despite a vivid central section, suffers from an uncertainty of focus." Borklund also faulted Gallant's portrayal of the daughter's descent into madness, stating that "Florence remains an intriguing and pathetic puzzle; our questions are unanswered, our sympathies largely unresolved." In contrast, Borklund had high praise for Gallant's second novel, describing *A Fairly Good Time* as "splendidly complex. . . . a spectacular *tour de force:* the writing is disconcertingly vivid, full of the unmediated poetry of near-hallucination, yet nothing is irrelevant or misplaced." Lighter in tone than its predecessor, *A Fairly Good Time* follows the blundering adventures of a Canadian, Shirley Perrigny, her life in France, and the dissolution of her marriage to a Parisian journalist. Hatch noted that the novel "may well be the funniest of all [Gallant's] works. . . . As a satire on the self-satisfied habits of the French, *A Fairly Good Time* proves enormously high-spirited. Yet the novel offers more than satire. As the reader becomes intimately acquainted with Shirley, her attempts to defeat the rigidity of French logic by living in the moment come to seem zany but commendable."

Home Truths: Selected Canadian Stories, first published in 1981, has proven to be one of Gallant's most popular collections. In Abley's view, the volume "bears repeated witness to the efforts made by this solitary, distant writer to come to terms with her own past and her own country." The stories focus on footloose Canadians who are alienated from their families or cultures; the characters try "to puzzle out the ground rules of their situations, which are often senseless, joyless and contradictory," to quote *Nation* reviewer Barbara Fisher Williamson. *New York Times Book Review* contributor Maureen Howard observed that in *Home Truths,* Canada "is not a setting, a backdrop; it is an adversary, a constraint, a comfort, the home that is almost understandable, if not understanding. It is at once deadly real and haunting, phantasmagoric." Phyllis Grosskurth elaborated in *Saturday Night:* "Clearly [Gallant] is still fighting a battle with the Canada she left many years ago. Whether or not that country has long since vanished is irrelevant, for it has continued to furnish the world of her imagination. . . . She knows that whatever she writes will be in the language that shaped her sensibility, though the Canada of her youth imposed restraints from which she could free herself only by geographic separation. Wherever she is, she writes out of her roots. . . . Her Montreal is a state of mind, an emotion recalled, an apprenticeship for life." *Home Truths* won the 1981 Governor General's Award, Canada's highest literary honor. *Books in Canada* correspondent Wayne Grady concluded that it is not a vision of Gallant's native country that emerges in the book, but rather "a vision of the world, of life: it is in that nameless country of the mind inhabited by all real writers, regardless of nativity, that Mavis Gallant lives. We are here privileged intruders."

The *New Yorker* has been the initial forum for almost all of Gallant's short fiction—and much of her nonfiction, too—since 1950. Critics, among them *Los Angeles Times* reviewer Elaine Kendall, felt that Gallant's work meets the periodical's high literary standards; in Kendall's words, Gallant's stories "seem the epitome of the magazine's traditional style." Readers of the *New Yorker* expect to find challenging stories, and according to Hatch, Gallant offers such challenges. "The reader finds that he cannot comprehend the fictional world as something given, but must engage with the text to bring its meanings into being," Hatch wrote. "As in life, so in a Gallant story, no handy editor exists ready to point the moral." Foote expressed a similar opinion. "Gallant rarely leaves helpful signs and messages that readers tend to expect of 'literature': This way to the Meaning or This story is about the Folly of Love," the critic concluded. "In the end the stories are simply there—haunting, enigmatic, printed with images as sharp and durable as the edge of a new coin, relentlessly specific."

In Transit, published in 1988, consists of twenty stories that appeared in the *New Yorker* during the 1950s and 1960s. Most of the stories in this well-praised collection are set in Europe and portray the sense of dislocation experienced by various expatriates, refugees, tourists, and natives. In the title story, French newlyweds overhear the dispute of an older American couple while waiting in a Helsinki airport lounge, inducing private reflection on their own nuptial misgivings. Gerald Mangan wrote in the *Times Literary Supplement,* "Elegant wit and a pin-sharp intelligence give her prose a dazzling surface; but her characters live entirely by their own lights, by virtue of a compassionate imagination, and she is generous enough to leave all the judgments to the reader." According to Ronald Bryden in the *New York Times Book Review,* "Transit, noise, and the symbiosis between them, one might argue, are Mavis Gallant's major themes—noise, that is, in the philosopher's definition of data that carry no meaning to the senses they fall on." He added that Gallant "spends much of her work demonstrating quietly how much of language, culture, and their ideological designs on us is simply noise to most people, in this shifting world where fewer and fewer of us are at home, linguistically or otherwise."

Across the Bridge, a collection of short stories, appeared in 1993. In each of these pieces, most set in either Montreal or Paris, Gallant explores the familiar themes of dislocation and alienation as reflected in arranged marriage, language, national identity, and modern consumer society. John McGahern wrote in the *New York Times Book Review,* "French is the natural language of many of her characters, and it is a palpable presence in her lucid, elegant sentences." McGahern added, "The general climate of the bourgeois or petit-bourgeois world she describes is philistine, never more so than when airbrushed with culture: Proust or Chateaubriand is interchangeable with Gucci or Armani." Barbara Gabriel wrote in a *Canadian Forum* review, "As always in Gallant, the main protagonist in these stories is history itself. Readers who have followed her as one of the great chroniclers of the human fallout of World War II and its redrawn borders, will see the special ironies in the new twists and turns of fate inaugurated by the fall of the Berlin Wall." McGahern similarly commented on "Gallant's remarkable gift for introducing whole lives and future histories in a few swift, brief strokes." Rita Donovan observed in a *Books in Canada* review, "Gallant writes of her origins from 'away'; this is interesting, first, because her grasp of Montreal, and the Montreal of the past, is undiluted and, second, because it ties in nicely with many of her other stories that deal with the emigre experience."

The Collected Stories of Mavis Gallant appeared in 1996. This nine-hundred-page volume brings together over fifty stories, all selected by Gallant, covering the span of her career from the 1930s through the 1990s. *America* contributor Judith Farr noted: "Although each story is memorably distinct, the fictional world Gallant creates has recognizable characteristics that have remained the same throughout six decades. Her characters mostly inhabit European or Canadian cities, where they are for various reasons not quite at home and where perils, great and small, await them." Gallant has arranged the collection chronologically, with the addition of four sections devoted to recurring characters. The stories centering on the character Linnet Muir, who often describes her youth in Canada, are probably the most autobiographical of Gallant's creations. The lighter side of her work is most apparent in the final section of the book, devoted to the adventures of the French literary hack and charlatan Henri Grippes, who supports himself in style by means of one scam after another. Pearl K. Bell, writing in *New Republic,* stated that a "rich and tantalizing lode of absurdity runs through all of the Grippes stories," and felt they offer "splendid proof that Gallant in her seventies has not lost her touch." Farr felt that language—"its uses and disuse, how it is regarded, learned, avoided or even transcended"—is one of the central keys to understanding Gallant's fiction. She found *The Collected Stories* to be a book in which "there is a largesse of sympathy that recalls both fluent speech and compassionate silence." Bell stressed the fact that although the flavor and concerns of *New Yorker* fiction have changed radically over six decades, Gallant has remained a significant contributor to the magazine. She saw this as a testament to the "steadiness and subtlety" of Gallant's stories, concluding that "her sober commitment to reality has not wavered."

Gallant's collection *Paris Stories* appeared in 2002 and was edited by renowned author Michael Ondaatje. The book compiles the best of her many short stories set in Paris. Her usual cast of characters appears, including the expatriate, the disillusioned youth, and the exiled family member. Critics consider Gallant a master at reintroducing these characters in new and unusual ways.

Critical reception to Gallant's work has been almost universally positive. *Washington Post Book World* reviewer Elizabeth Spencer suggested that there is "no writer in English anywhere able to set Mavis Gallant in second place. Her style alone places her in the first rank. Gallant's firmly drafted prose neglects nothing, leaves no dangling ends for the reader to tack up. . . . She is hospitable to the metaphysics of experience as well as to the homeliest social detail." Grosskurth wrote: "Gallant's particular power as a writer is the sureness with which she catches the ephemeral; it is a wry vision, a blend of the sad and the tragi-comic. She is a born writer who happens to have been born in Canada, and her gift has been able to develop as it has only because she could look back in anger, love, and nostalgia." *New York Times Book Review* contributor Phyllis Rose praised Gallant for her "wicked humor that misses nothing, combined with sophistication so great it amounts to forgiveness." The critic concluded: "To take up residence in the mind of Mavis Gallant, as one does in reading her stories, is a privilege and delight."

Gallant told *Publishers Weekly* interviewer David Finkle: "It's fragile, fiction. It takes me a long time to write a story. . . . You have to be ruthless. When in doubt, cut it. . . . I write every day. I get up early in the morning and do it. People say it's discipline. It isn't."

BIOGRAPHICAL AND CRITICAL SOURCES:

BOOKS

Contemporary Literary Criticism, Thomson Gale (Detroit, MI), Volume 7, 1977, Volume 18, 1981, Volume 38, 1986.

Contemporary Novelists, 6th edition, St. James Press (Detroit, MI), 1996.

Dictionary of Literary Biography, Volume 53: *Canadian Writers since 1960, First Series,* Thomson Gale (Detroit, MI), 1986.

Encyclopedia of World Literature in the 20th Century, Volume 2: E-K, St. James Press (Detroit, MI), 1999.

Lecker, Robert and Jack David, editors, *The Annotated Bibliography of Canada's Major Authors,* Volume 5, ECW (Ontario, Canada), 1984.

Literature Lover's Companion, Prentice Hall (Englewood Cliffs, NJ).

Merler, Grazia, *Mavis Gallant: Narrative Patterns and Devices,* Tecumseh, 1978.

Moss, John, editor, *Present Tense,* NC Press (Toronto, Ontario, Canada), 1985.

Reference Guide to Short Fiction, St. James Press (Detroit, MI), 1993, 1999.

Short Story Criticism, Volume 5, Thomson Gale (Detroit, MI), 1990.

PERIODICALS

America, March 5, 1994, p. 28; February 8, 1997, p. 33.

Atlantis, autumn, 1978.

Books and Bookmen, July, 1974.

Books in Canada, October, 1979; October, 1981; April, 1984; October, 1985; October, 1993, p. 38.

Canadian Fiction, number 28, 1978; number 43, 1982.

Canadian Forum, February, 1982; November, 1985; March, 1994, p. 38.

Canadian Literature, spring, 1973; spring, 1985; winter, 1991, p. 235.

Christian Science Monitor, June 4, 1970.

Entertainment Weekly, October 11, 1996, p. 87.

Globe and Mail (Toronto, Ontario, Canada), October 11, 1986; October 15, 1988.

Los Angeles Times, April 15, 1985.

Los Angeles Times Book Review, November 4, 1979; May 24, 1987.

Maclean's, September 5, 1964; November 9, 1981; November 22, 1982.

Nation, June 15, 1985; October 18, 1993, p. 66.

New Republic, August 25, 1979; May 13, 1985; March 28, 1994, p. 43; November 25, 1996, p. 31.

New York Review of Books, June 25, 1964; January 24, 1980.

New York Times, June 5, 1970; October 2, 1979; April 20, 1985; July 9, 1985; March 4, 1987.

New York Times Book Review, February 26, 1956; September 16, 1979; May 5, 1985; March 15, 1987; May 28, 1989, p. 3; September 12, 1993, p. 7.

Observer, February 4, 1990, p. 60.

People, January 13, 1997, p. 29.

Publishers Weekly, August 5, 1996, p. 431; October 7, 1996, p. 46.

Quill & Quire, October, 1981; June, 1984.

Rubicon, winter, 1984-85.

Saturday Night, September, 1973; November, 1981; October, 1996, p. 109.

Saturday Review, October 17, 1959; August 25, 1979; October 13, 1979.

Spectator, August 29, 1987; February 20, 1988.

Time, November 26, 1979; May 27, 1985.

Times (London, England), February 28, 1980.

Times Literary Supplement, March 14, 1980; February 28, 1986; September 25-October 1, 1987; January 22-28, 1988; April 13, 1990, p. 403.

Tribune Books (Chicago, IL), November 11, 1979.

Virginia Quarterly Review, spring, 1980.

Washington Post Book World, April 14, 1985; March 29, 1987.

*   *   *

GAO XINGJIAN
See XINGJIAN, Gao

GARCIA, Cristina 1958-

PERSONAL: Born July 4, 1958, in Havana, Cuba; immigrated to the United States, c. 1960; daughter of Frank M. and Hope Lois Garcia; married Scott Brown, December 8, 1990; children: Pilar Akiko. *Education:* Barnard College, B.A., 1979; Johns Hopkins University, M.A., 1981. *Politics:* "Registered Democrat." *Hobbies and other interests:* Contemporary dance, music, travel, foreign languages.

ADDRESSES: Agent—Ellen Levine, 15 East 26th St., Suite 1801, New York, NY 10010.

CAREER: Journalist and author. *Time* (magazine), New York, NY, reporter and researcher, 1983-85, correspondent, 1985-90, bureau chief in Miami, FL, 1987-88.

MEMBER: Amnesty International, PEN American Center.

AWARDS, HONORS: National Book Award finalist, National Book Foundation, 1992, for *Dreaming in Cuban;* Hodder fellowship, Princeton University, 1992-93; Cintas fellowship, 1992-93; Whiting Writers Award, 1996.

WRITINGS:

Dreaming in Cuban (novel), Knopf (New York, NY), 1992.
Cars of Cuba (essay), created by D.D. Allen, photographs by Joshua Greene, Abrams (New York, NY), 1995.
The Aguero Sisters (novel), Knopf (New York, NY), 1997.
Monkey Hunting (novel), Knopf (New York, NY), 2003.
(Editor and author of introduction) *Cubanismo!: The Vintage Book of Contemporary Cuban Literature,* Vintage (New York, NY), 2003.

Dreaming in Cuban and *The Aguero Sisters* have been translated into Spanish.

WORK IN PROGRESS: Poems and novels.

SIDELIGHTS: A reporter and correspondent for *Time* magazine during the 1980s, Cristina Garcia published her first novel, *Dreaming in Cuban,* in 1992. Inspired by Garcia's Cuban heritage, the book was highly acclaimed and became a finalist for the National Book Award. Reviewer Michiko Kakutani remarked in the *New York Times:* "Fierce, visionary, and at the same time oddly beguiling and funny, *Dreaming in Cuban* is a completely original novel. It announces the debut of a writer, blessed with a poet's ear for language, a historian's fascination with the past and a musician's intuitive understanding of the ebb and flow of emotion."

Dreaming in Cuban chronicles three generations of a Cuban family. The matriarch, Celia, falls in love with a married Spaniard and writes him letters for twenty-five years. Despite this long-distance affair, Celia marries a man she does not love, and the couple has two daughters, Lourdes and Felicia, and a son, Javier. Celia also becomes enamored of the Cuban Revolution and its leader, Fidel Castro. Lourdes, however, is raped by a revolutionary, and carries her hatred of the revolution with her when she moves to New York with her husband and opens two successful bakeries. Felicia stays in Cuba with her mother, but she marries a sailor who gives her syphilis, and she eventually meets a tragic end. Javier becomes a scientist and immigrates to Czechoslovakia, only to return a bitter alcoholic. As for the next generation, Thulani Davis explained in *New York Times Book Review,* "Celia's grandchildren can only be described as lost and abandoned by the obsessions of the parents. Of these, Lourdes's daughter, Pilar Puente del Pino, a would-be painter and student in New York, becomes the secret sharer, a distant repository of the family's stories and some of its demons." Pilar is also the one who reunites the family, dragging her mother along with her on a trip to Cuba to see her grandmother.

In detailing this family history, Alan West observed in *Washington Post Book World,* "Garcia deftly shifts the narrative from third to first person, mixing in a series of Celia's letters to her long-lost Spanish lover, Gustavo. Likewise, she shifts from the past to the present, from Brooklyn to Havana, from character to character caught in the web that blood and history have set up for them, often with cruel irony." Richard Eder, writing in the *Los Angeles Times,* called *Dreaming in Cuban* "poignant and perceptive," noting that "the realism is exquisite." Davis concluded in *New York Times Book Review:* "I have no complaints to make. Cristina Garcia has written a jewel of a first novel."

Garcia's second novel, *The Aguero Sisters,* tells of two Cuban sisters, Constancia and Reina, who have been separated for thirty years. Constancia and her husband, who has recently retired from his cigar business, have moved from New York to Key Biscayne, Florida, and she has become a successful businesswoman and entrepreneur with her own line of homemade, natural body and face creams made from such ingredients as over-ripe peaches and avocado pits. Heberto, though, disappears from the main plot as he embarks on a new career as a counterrevolutionary, embroiled in a Bay of Pigs-like plot to overthrow the Cuban government.

Reina still lives in Cuba as a traveling electrician, and she has been nicknamed "Companera Amazonas" for her voluptuousness and free-spirited sexuality. While Constancia is somewhat prudish and has only had two lovers in her entire life—her two husbands—the uninhibited libertine Reina relishes the pleasure men provide her. As Garcia describes her, "Often, Reina selects the smallest, shiest electrician in a given town for her special favors, leaving him weak and inconsolable for months. After she departs, black owls are frequently sighted in the Ceiba trees." *Washington Post Book World* editor Nina King noted, "The sudden appearance of those ominous black owls is typical of Garcia's stylistic shifts from reality to myth to the heightened reality of 'magic realism.'"

According to *Time* reviewer Pico Iyer, "Both Aguero sisters share something deep as blood: a matter-of-fact commitment to the magic of their island of honey and rum. Constancia makes spells for women in the form of the 'luscious unguents' she markets; Reina casts spells over men." This is typical of a mystical parallelism that runs throughout the novel; for example, at approximately the same time Constancia elects cosmetic surgery that inadvertently leaves her with her mother's face, Reina is struck by lightning and must undergo experimental skin grafts—her skin becomes a patchwork contributed by friends and family.

As Kakutani commented in a *New York Times* review, "In Cristina Garcia's haunting new novel, *The Aguero Sisters,* a strange scar is handed down generation to generation. Blanca Aguero, the clan's ill-fated matriarch, receives the mysterious mark on her heel while swimming in Las Casas river during her honeymoon. Years later, while escaping from Cuba to the United States, Blanca's daughter Constancia leaves a similar mark on the foot of *her* daughter, Isabel, while trying to revive her from heatstroke. Isabel, in turn, eventually has a boy named Raku, who is born with a red birthmark on his foot in the same place as his mother's wound."

When the two sisters are reunited in Miami, they work to strip away the lies that constitute their lives. By the novel's denouement, their respective daughters, the artist, Isabel, and former volleyball coach-turned-prostitute, Dulce, are united, as well. The primary element that connects all four women, aside from their kinship per se, is the quest to learn the truth about the death of Constancia and Reina's mother, Blanca Mestre de Aguero. Blanca and her husband were both ornithologists, documenting the endangered wildlife of Cuba when her estranged husband, Ignacio, brutally murdered her. The reader is told, early on, the nature of her fate, but the protagonists must untwist truth from lies.

Ruth Behar noted in Chicago's *Tribune Books* that "Garcia offers an even more gorgeously written, even more flamboyant feminist vision of Cuban and American history, women's lives, memory and desire" than her previous novel, *Dreaming in Cuban*. The critic added, "Constancia and Reina, the feisty and rebellious Aguero sisters, are strong female protagonists whose meditations on men, sex, power and longing are among the great joys of Garcia's novel." Kakutani noted "the force of Ms. Garcia's powerfully imagined characters" and "the magic of her prose." In *Nation*, Ilan Stavans mentioned Garcia's "astonishing literary style and dazzling attention to telling detail," and deemed her "an immensely talented writer, whose work . . . is renewing American fiction." And, describing Garcia as "a wise and generous storyteller," Iyer praised the novelist. "Garcia has crafted a beautifully rounded work of art," the reviewer noted, "as warm and wry and sensuous as the island she clearly loves."

With 2003's *Monkey Hunting,* Garcia tackles another multigenerational saga with a twist: this time, the family she follows is of mixed Chinese and Cuban descent. The story begins with Chen Pan, who travels from his homeland in China to Cuba in the 1850s, where he is at first enslaved and forced to work in the sugarcane fields. However, Chen surmounts this challenge to become a successful Havana businessman who falls in love with a mulata named Lucrecia and finds happiness as a family man. The story then follows his descendants, whose experiences vary widely: their son Lorenzo becomes a physician; his daughter Chen Fang lives in China, where she becomes a teacher and counterrevolutionary; and, finally, her son Domingo Chen, ends up in New York City, where he encounters racism and ends up a soldier fighting in Vietnam. Critics delighted in Garcia's deft handling of shifts in time and point of view in a novel that is relatively short, given the expanse of years it covers. For example, Mary Margaret Benson, writing in *Library Journal,* called *Monkey Hunting* "a brilliantly conceived work—and it's also delightful reading." And although a *Publishers Weekly* reviewer wished that Garcia had taken more time in her story to develop the characters further, the critic praised the author's third novel as "a richly patterned mini-epic, a moving chorus of distinct voices." *New York Times* critic Michiko Kakutani, however, felt that *Monkey Hunting* "lacks the fierce magic and unexpected humor of Ms. Garcia's remarkable debut novel." Jennifer Schuessler, in *New York Times Book Review,* expressed a similar judgment, noting that, though the novel "leaps sure-footedly between the branches of a bushy and far-flung family tree," it does not convey the "spark of life that allows the Chen family to survive and transcend its forced march through endless war and revolution." Margot Livesey, on the other hand, observed in *Atlantic Monthly* that the novel combines "gorgeous writing" with extraordinary empathy and understanding.

BIOGRAPHICAL AND CRITICAL SOURCES:

BOOKS

Contemporary Literary Criticism, Volume 76, Thomson Gale (Detroit, MI), 1993.
Contemporary Novelists, 7th edition, St. James (Detroit, MI), 2001.
Notable Hispanic American Women, 2nd edition, Thomson Gale (Detroit, MI), 1998.

PERIODICALS

Atlantic Monthly, May, 2003, Margot Livesey, "Time Travel," p. 123.
Boston Globe, May 25, 1997, p. N15.
Entertainment Weekly, March 27, 1992, p. 68; March 26, 1993, p. 74.
Globe and Mail (Toronto, Ontario, Canada), March 21, 1992, p. C9.
Library Journal, March 15, 1997, Barbara Hoffert, review of *The Aguero Sisters,* p. 88; April 1, 2003, Mary Margaret Benson, review of *Monkey Hunting,* p. 128; June 15, 2003, Ron Ratliff, review of *Cubanismo!: The Vintage Book of Contemporary Cuban Literature,* p. 71.
Los Angeles Times, March 12, 1992, p. E10.
Los Angeles Times Book Review, November 19, 1995, p. 11; June 8, 1997, p. 8.
MELUS, fall, 2000, Katherine Payant, "From Alienation to Reconciliation in the Novels of Cristina Garcia," p. 163.
Nation, May 19, 1997, p. 32.
Newsweek, April 20, 1992, p. 78-79; April 28, 1997, p. 79.
New Yorker, June 1, 1992, p. 86.
New York Times, February 25, 1992, p. C17; May 27, 1997, p. C16; June 24, 2003, Michiko Kakutani, review of *Monkey Hunting,* p. E6.
New York Times Book Review, May 17, 1992, p. 14; June 15, 1997, p. 38; May 18, 2003, Jennifer Schuessler, "Fantasy Island," p. 11.
Observer, August 10, 1997, p. 15.
Publishers Weekly, January 13, 1992, review of *Dreaming in Cuban,* p. 46; March 10, 1997, review of *The Aguero Sisters,* p. 48; April 7, 2003, review of *Monkey Hunting,* p. 48.
Review of Contemporary Fiction, fall, 1997, Jane Juffer, review of *The Aguero Sisters,* p. 243.
Time, March 23, 1992, p. 67; May 12, 1997, Pico Ayer, review of *The Aguero Sisters,* p. 88.
Tribune Books (Chicago, IL), June 8, 1997, section 14, p. 1.
Washington Post Book World, March 1, 1992, p. 9; July 13, 1997, p. 1.
World Literature Today, winter, 1998, Ana Maria Hernandez, review of *The Aguero Sisters,* p. 134; winter, 2000, Rocio G. Davis, "Back to the Future: Mothers, Languages, and Homes in Cristina Garcia's *Dreaming in Cuban,*" p. 60.

*   *   *

GARCIA MARQUEZ, Gabriel 1928-
(Gabriel José Garcia Marquez)

PERSONAL: Born March 6, 1928, in Aracataca, Colombia; son of Gabriel Eligio Garcia (a telegraph operator) and Luisa Santiaga Marquez Iguaran; married Mercedes Barcha, March, 1958; children: Rodrigo, Gonzalo. *Ethnicity:* Hispanic *Education:* Attended Universidad Nacional de Colombia, 1947-48, and Universidad de Cartagena, 1948-49.

ADDRESSES: Home—P.O. Box 20736, Mexico City D.F., Mexico. *Agent*—c/o Knopf Publicity, 1745 Broadway, New York, NY 10019.

CAREER: Began career as a journalist, 1947; reporter for *Universal,* Cartegena, Colombia, late 1940s, *El heraldo,* Barranquilla, Colombia, 1950-52, and *El espectador,* Bogota, Colombia, until 1955; freelance journalist in Paris, London, and Caracas, Venezuela, 1956-58; worked for *Momento* magazine, Caracas, 1958-59; helped form Prensa Latina news agency, Bogota, 1959, and worked as its correspondent in Havana, Cuba, and New York City, 1961; writer, 1965—. Fundacion Habeas, founder, 1979, president, 1979—.

MEMBER: American Academy of Arts and Letters (honorary fellow).

AWARDS, HONORS: Colombian Association of Writers and Artists Award, 1954, for story "Un dia despues del sabado"; Premio Literario Esso (Colombia), 1961, for *La mala hora;* Chianciano Award (Italy), 1969, Prix de Meilleur Livre Etranger (France), 1969, and Romulo Gallegos prize (Venezuela), 1971, all for *Cien anos de soledad;* LL.D., Columbia University, 1971; Books Abroad/Neustadt International Prize for Literature, 1972; Nobel Prize for Literature, 1982; *Los Angeles Times* Book Prize nomination for fiction, 1983, for *Chronicle of a Death Foretold; Los Angeles Times* Book Prize for fiction, 1988, for *Love in the Time of Cholera;* Serfin Prize, 1989; Ariels (Mexican equivalent of Oscars) for scripwriting from La Academia Mexicana de Ciencias y Artes Cinematograficas; Reconocimiento a las Humanidades y Ciencias Sociales Tecnologico de Monterrey, Mexico, July 2003.

WRITINGS:

FICTION

La hojarasca (novella; title means "Leaf Storm"; also see below), Ediciones Sipa (Bogota, Colombia), 1955, reprinted, Bruguera (Barcelona, Spain), 1983.

El coronel no tiene quien le escriba (novella; title means "No One Writes to the Colonel"; also see below), Aguirre Editor (Medellin, Colombia), 1961, reprinted, Bruguera (Barcelona, Spain), 1983.

La mala hora (novel; also see below), Talleres de Graficas "Luis Perez" (Madrid, Spain), 1961, reprinted, Bruguera (Barcelona, Spain), 1982, English translation by Gregory Rabassa published as *In Evil Hour,* Harper (New York, NY), 1979.

Los funerales de la Mama Grande (short stories; title means "Big Mama's Funeral"; also see below), Editorial Universidad Veracruzana (Mexico), 1962, reprinted, Bruguera (Barcelona, Spain), 1983.

El Gallo de Oro, (with Carlos Fuentes) screenplay from novel by Juan Rulfo, made into a film, 1964.

Cien anos de soledad (novel), Editorial Sudamericana (Buenos Aires, Argentina), 1967, reprinted, Catedra, 1984, English translation by Gregory Rabassa published as *One Hundred Years of Solitude,* Harper (New York, NY), 1970, with a new foreword by Rabassa, Knopf (New York, NY), 1995.

Isabel viendo llover en Macondo (novella; title means "Isabel Watching It Rain in Macondo"; also see below), Editorial Estuario (Buenos Aires, Argentina), 1967.

No One Writes to the Colonel and Other Stories (includes "No One Writes to the Colonel," and stories from *Los Funerales de la Mama Grande*), translated by J.S. Bernstein, Harper (New York, NY), 1968, Perennial Classics (New York, NY), 2005.

La increible y triste historia de la candida Erendira y su abuela desalmada (short stories; also see below), Barral Editores, 1972.

El negro que hizo esperar a los angeles (short stories), Ediciones Alfil (Montevideo, Uraguay), 1972.

Ojos de perro azul (short stories; also see below), Equisditorial (Argentina), 1972.

Leaf Storm and Other Stories (includes "Leaf Storm," and "Isabel Watching It Rain in Macondo"), translated by Gregory Rabassa, Harper (New York, NY), 1972, 2005.

El otono del patriarca (novel), Plaza and Janes Editores (Barcelona, Spain), 1975, translation by Gregory Rabassa published as *The Autumn of the Patriarch,* Harper (New York, NY), 1976, 1999.

Todos los cuentos de Gabriel Garcia Marquez: 1947-1972 (title means "All the Stories of Gabriel Garcia Marquez: 1947- 1972"), Plaza y Janes Editores, 1975.

Innocent Erendira and Other Stories (includes "Innocent Erendira and Her Heartless Grandmother" and stories from *Ojos de perro azul*), translated by Gregory Rabassa, Harper (New York, NY), 1978, Perennial Classics (New York, NY), 2005.

Dos novelas de Macondo (contains *La hojarasca* and *La mala hora*), Casa de las Americas (Havana, Cuba), 1980.

Cronica de una muerte anunciada (novel), La Oveja Negra (Bogota, Colombia), 1981, translation by Gregory Rabassa published as *Chronicle of a Death Foretold,* J. Cape (London, England), 1982, Knopf (New York, NY), 1983.

Viva Sandino (play), Editorial Nueva Nicaragua, 1982, 2nd edition published as *El asalto: el operativo con que el FSLN se lanzo al mundo,* 1983.

El rastro de tu sangre en la nieve: El verano feliz de la senora Forbes, W. Dampier Editores (Bogota, Colombia), 1982.

El secuestro: Guion cinematografico (unfilmed screenplay), Oveja Negra (Bogota, Colombia), 1982.

Erendira (filmscript; adapted from his novella *La increible y triste historia de la candida Erendira y su abuela desalmada*), Les Films du Triangle, 1983.

Collected Stories, translated by Gregory Rabassa and Bernstein, Harper (New York, NY), 1984, reprinted, Penguin (New York, NY), 1996.

El amor en los tiempos del colera, Oveja Negra, 1985, English translation by Edith Grossman published as *Love in the Time of Cholera,* Knopf (New York, NY), 1988.

A Time to Die (filmscript), ICA Cinema, 1988.

Diatribe of Love against a Seated Man (play; first produced at Cervantes Theater, Buenos Aires, 1988), Arango Editores (Santafe de Bogota, Colombia), 1994.

El general en su labertino, Mondadori (Madrid, Spain), 1989, English translation by Edith Grossman published as *The General in His Labyrinth,* Knopf (New York, NY), 1990.

Collected Novellas, HarperCollins (New York, NY), 1990.

Doce cuentos peregrinos, Mondadori (Madrid, Spain), 1992, English translation by Edith Grossman published as *Strange Pilgrims: Twelve Stories,* Knopf (New York, NY), 1993.

The Handsomest Drowned Man in the World: A Tale for Children, translated by Gregory Rabazza, Creative Education (Mankato, MN), 1993.

Del amor y otros demonios, Mondadori (Barcelona, Spain), 1994, English translation by Edith Grossman published as *Of Love and Other Demons,* Knopf (New York, NY), 1995.

(Contributor) *The Picador Book of Latin American Stories,* Picador (New York, NY), 1998.

Individually bound series of single stories, including *El verano feliz de la senora Forbes*, illustrated by Carmen Sole Vendrell, Groupo Editorial Norma (Bogota, Colombia), 1999.

(Contributor) J.H. Blair, ed., *Caliente!: The Best Erotic Writing in Latin American Fiction.* Penguin/Putnam (New York, NY), June 2002.

Memoria de mis putas tristes (novel), Mondadori (Barcelona, Spain), 2004, English translation by Edith Grossman published as *Memories of My Melancholy Whores,* Knopf (New York, NY), 2005.

NONFICTION

(With Mario Vargas Llosa) *La novela en America Latina: Dialogo,* Carlos Milla Batres (Lima, Peru), 1968.

Relato de un naufrago (journalistic pieces), Tusquets Editor (Barcelona, Spain), 1970, English translation by Randolph Hogan published as *The Story of a Shipwrecked Sailor,* Knopf (New York, NY), 1986.

Cuando era feliz e indocumentado (journalistic pieces), Ediciones El Ojo de Camello (Caracas, Venezuela), 1973.

Operacion Carlota, (essays) 1977.

Cronicas y reportajes (journalistic pieces), Oveja Negra, 1978.

Periodismo militante (journalistic pieces), Son de Maquina (Bogota, Colombia), 1978.

De viaje por los paises socialistas: 90 dias en la "Cortina de hierro" (journalistic pieces), Ediciones Macondo (Colombia), 1978.

(Contributor) *Los sandanistas,* Oveja Negra, 1979.

(Contributor) Soledad Mendoza, editor, *Asi es Caracas,* Editorial Ateneo de Caracas (Caracas, Venezuela), 1980.

Obra periodistica (journalistic pieces), edited by Jacques Gilard, Bruguera, Volume 1: *Textos constenos,* 1981, Volumes 2- 3: *Entre cachacos,* 1982, Volume 4: *De Europa y America (1955-1960),* 1983.

El olor de la guayaba: Conversaciones con Plinio Apuleyo Mendoza (interviews), Oveja Negra, 1982, English translation by Ann Wright published as *The Fragrance of Guava,* Verso (London, England), 1983.

(With Guillermo Nolasco-Juarez) *Persecucion y muerte de minorias: dos perspectivas,* Juarez Editor (Buenos Aires, Argentina), 1984.

(Contributor) *La Democracia y la paz en America Latina,* Editorial El Buho (Bogota, Colombia), 1986.

La aventura de Miguel Littin, clandestino en Chile: Un reportaje, Editorial Sudamericana, 1986, English translation by Asa Zatz published as *Clandestine in Chile: The Adventures of Miguel Littin,* Holt (New York, NY), 1987.

Primeros reportajes, Consorcio de Ediciones Capriles (Caracas, Venezuela), 1990.

(Author of introduction) Mina, Gianni, *An Encounter with Fidel: An Interview,* translated by Mary Todd, Ocean Press (Melbourne, Australia), 1991.

Notas de prensa, 1980- 1984, Mondadori (Madrid, Spain), 1991.

Elogio de la utopia: Una entrevista de Nahuel Maciel, Cronista Ediciones (Buenos Aires, Argentina), 1992.

News of a Kidnapping, translated from the Spanish by Edith Grossman, Knopf (New York, NY), 1997.

(With Reynaldo Gonzales) *Cubano 100%,* with photographs by Gianfranco Gorgoni, Charta, 1998.

For the Sake of a Country Within Reach of the Children, Villegas Editores, 1998.

(Author of introduction), Castro, Fidel, *My Early Years,* LPC Group, 1998.

Vivir Para Contarla (title means "To Live to Tell It") (memoir), [Colombia], 2002, published as *Living to Tell the Tale,* Knopf (New York, NY), 2003.

Author of weekly syndicated column.

ADAPTATIONS: A play, *Blood and Champagne,* was based on Garcia Marquez's *One Hundred Years of Solitude; Maria de me Corazon* film 1983; *I'm the One You're Looking For, Letters from the Park* (extracted from *Love in the Time of Cholera*), *Miracle in Rome, The Summer of Miss Forbes,* films 1988; *Nobody Writes to the Colonel,* adapted for film, 1999; an adaptation of the story "A Very Old Man With Enormous Wings" was put on the stage for children in Minneapolis, MN, September 2002; the novella *Chronicle of a Death Foretold* produced by Repertorio Espanol in New York City 1999-2003, and by the The National Theatre of Colombia, January 2003, in Sydney; the novella *Erendira and her Heartless Grandmother* were adapted for the stage in New York, NY, in March 2003; film rights have been sold to producer Scot Steindorff at Stone Village Pictures for an adaptation of *Love in the Time of Cholera.*

SIDELIGHTS: Winner of the 1982 Nobel Prize for Literature for *One Hundred Years of Solitude,* Colombian writer Gabriel Garcia Marquez is widely considered one of the deans of Latin American writing. From his fabulous tales of rural Colombian life to his volumes of journalistic reportage, Garcia Marquez has emerged as "one of the small number of contemporary writers from Latin America who have given to its literature a maturity and dignity it never had before," to quote John Sturrock in the *New York Times Book Review.* "More than any other writer in the world," declared David Streitfeld in the *Washington Post,* "Gabriel Garcia Marquez combines both respect (bordering on adulation) and mass popularity (also bordering on adulation)." *Time* magazine correspondent R.Z. Sheppard simply deemed the author "one of the greatest living storytellers."

One Hundred Years of Solitude is perhaps Garcia Marquez's best-known contribution to the awakening of interest in Latin American literature. It has sold more than twenty million copies and has been translated into over thirty languages. According to an *Antioch Review* critic, the popularity and acclaim for *One Hundred Years of Solitude* signaled that "Latin American literature will change from being the exotic interest of a few to essential reading and that Latin America itself will be looked on less as a crazy subculture and more as a fruitful, alternative way of life." So great was the novel's initial popularity, noted Mario Vargas Llosa in *Garcia Marquez: Historia de un deicido,* that not only was the first Spanish printing of the book sold out within one week, but for months afterwards Latin American readers alone exhausted each successive printing. Translations of the novel similarly elicited enthusiastic responses from critics and readers around the world.

In this outpouring of critical opinion, which *Books Abroad* contributor Klaus Muller-Bergh called "an earthquake, a maelstrom," various reviewers termed *One Hundred Years of Solitude* a masterpiece of modern fiction. For example, Chilean poet Pablo Neruda, himself a Nobel laureate, was quoted in *Time* as calling the book "the greatest revelation in the Spanish language since the *Don Quixote* of Cervantes." Similarly enthusiastic was William Kennedy, who wrote in the *National Observer* that " *One Hundred Years of Solitude* is the first piece of literature since the Book of Genesis that should be required reading for the entire human race." And Regina Janes, in her study *Gabriel Garcia Marquez: Revolutions in Wonderland,* described the book as "a 'total novel' that [treats] Latin America socially, historically, politically, mythically, and epically," adding that *One Hundred Years of Solitude* is also "at once accessible and intricate, lifelike and self-consciously, self-referentially fictive."

The novel is set in the imaginary community of Macondo, a village on the Colombian coast, and follows the lives of several generations of the Buendia family. Chief among these characters are Colonel Aureliano Buendia, perpetrator of thirty-two rebellions and father of seventeen illegitimate sons, and Ursula Buendia, the clan's matriarch and witness to its eventual decline. Besides following the complicated relationships of the Buendia family, *One Hundred Years of Solitude* also reflects the political, social, and economic troubles of South America. Many critics have found the novel, with its complex family relationships and extraordinary events, to be a microcosm of Latin America itself.

The mixture of historical and fictitious elements that appears in *One Hundred Years of Solitude* places the novel within that genre of Latin American fiction that critics have termed "magical realism." Janes attributed the birth of this style of writing to Alejo Carpentier, a Cuban novelist and short story writer, and concluded that Garcia Marquez's fiction follows ideas originally formulated by the Cuban author. The critic noted that Carpentier "discovered the duplicities of history and elaborated the critical concept of 'lo maravilloso americano' the 'marvelous real,' arguing that geographically, historically, and essentially, Latin America was a space marvelous and fantastic . . . and to render that reality was to render marvels." Garcia Marquez presented a similar view of Latin America in his *Paris Review* interview with Peter H. Stone: "It always amuses me that the biggest praise for my work comes for the imagination while the truth is that there's not a single line in all my work that does not have a basis in reality." The author further explained in his *Playboy* interview with Claudia Dreifus: "Clearly, the Latin American environment is marvelous. Particularly the Caribbean . . . . The coastal people were descendants of pirates and smugglers, with a mixture of black slaves. To grow up in such an environment is to have fantastic resources for poetry. Also, in the Caribbean, we are capable of believing anything, because we have the influences of all those different cultures, mixed in with Catholicism and our own local beliefs. I think that gives us an open-mindedness to look beyond apparent reality."

But along with the fantastic episodes in Garcia Marquez's fiction appear the historical facts or places that inspired them. An episode involving a massacre of striking banana workers is based on a historical incident. In reality, Garcia Marquez told Dreifus, "there were very few deaths . . . [so] I made the death toll 3,000 because I was using certain proportions in my book." But while *One Hundred Years of Solitude* is the fictional account of the Buendia family, the novel is also, as John Leonard stated in the *New York Times*, "a recapitulation of our evolutionary and intellectual experience. Macondo is Latin America in microcosm." Robert G. Mead Jr. similarly observed in *Saturday Review* that "Macondo may be regarded as a microcosm of the development of much of the Latin American continent." Mead added: "Although [*One Hundred Years of Solitude*] is first and always a story, the novel also has value as a social and historical document." Garcia Marquez responded to these interpretations in his interview with Dreifus, commenting that his work "is not a history of Latin America, it is a *metaphor* for Latin America."

The "social and historical" elements of *One Hundred Years of Solitude* reflect the journalistic influences at work in Garcia Marquez's fiction. Although known as a novelist, the author began his writing career as a reporter and still considers himself to be one. In fact, in 1999, he used money from his Nobel prize to buy the then-failing *Cambio,* a weekly news magazine which employs some of Colombia's finest journalists, according to Frank Bajak in the Melbourne *Herald Sun*. As Garcia Marquez remarked to Stone, "I've always been

convinced that my true profession is that of a journalist." Janes asserted that the evolution of Garcia Marquez's individual style is based on his experience as a correspondent. In addition, this same experience has led Janes and other critics to compare the Colombian to Ernest Hemingway. "[The] stylistic transformation between *Leaf Storm* and *No One Writes to the Colonel* was not exclusively an act of will," Janes claimed. "Garcia Marquez had had six years of experience as a journalist between the two books, experience providing practice in the lessons of Hemingway, trained in the same school." And George R. McMurray, in his book *Gabriel Garcia Marquez,* maintained that Hemingway's themes and techniques have "left their mark" on the work of the Colombian writer.

Garcia Marquez has been compared to another American Nobel-winner, William Faulkner, who also elaborated on facts to create his fiction. Faulkner based his fictional territory Yoknapatawpha County on memories of the region in northern Mississippi where he spent most of his life. Garcia Marquez based Macondo, the town appearing throughout his fiction, on Aracataca, the coastal city of his birth. A *Time* reviewer called Macondo "a kind of tropical Yoknapatawpha County." *Review* contributor Mary E. Davis pointed out further resemblances between the two authors: "Garcia Marquez concentrates on the specific personality of place in the manner of the Mississippean, and he develops even the most reprehensible of his characters as idiosyncratic enigmas." She concluded: "Garcia Marquez is as fascinated by the capacity of things, events, and characters for sudden metamorphosis as was Faulkner." Nevertheless, *Newsweek* writer Peter S. Prescott maintained that it was only after Garcia Marquez shook off the influence of Faulkner that he was able to write *One Hundred Years of Solitude.* Prescott argued that in this novel Garcia Marquez's "imagination matured: no longer content to write dark and fatalistic stories about a Latin Yoknapatawpha County, he broke loose into exuberance, wit and laughter." Thor Vilhjalmsson similarly observed in *Books Abroad* that while "Garcia Marquez does not fail to deal with the dark forces, or give the impression that the life of human beings, one by one, should be ultimately tragic, . . . he also shows every moment pregnant with images and color and scent which ask to be arranged into patterns of meaning and significance while the moment lasts." While the Colombian has frequently referred to Faulkner as "my master," Luis Harss and Barbara Dohmann added in their *Into the Mainstream: Conversations with Latin-American Writers* that in his later stories, "the Faulknerian glare has been neutralized. It is not replaced by any other. From now on Garcia Marquez is his own master."

The phenomenal worldwide success of *One Hundred Years of Solitude* has proven to be both boon and bane for its author. In *Contemporary Popular Writers,* Jack Shreve observed that with *One Hundred Years of Solitude,* Garcia Marquez "emerged as the leading literary talent of the Spanish-speaking world . . . and many began to speak of him as the greatest author in the Spanish language since Cervantes." The critic added: "But like Cervantes after writing *Don Quixote,* Garcia Marquez has subsequently had to contend with critics who are disinclined to acknowledge that his masterpiece can ever be equaled or surpassed." Indeed, while all of Garcia Marquez's subsequent writings have been praised by critics and bought in quantity by readers, none has elicited the outpouring of praise that attended—and still attends— *One Hundred Years of Solitude.*

In *The Autumn of the Patriarch* Garcia Marquez uses a more openly political tone in relating the story of a dictator who has reigned for so long that no one can remember any other ruler. Elaborating on the kind of solitude experienced by Colonel Aureliano Buendia in *One Hundred Years of Solitude,* Garcia Marquez explores the isolation of a political tyrant. "In this fabulous, dream-like account of the reign of a nameless dictator of a fantastic Caribbean realm, solitude is linked with the possession of absolute power," described Ronald De Feo in the *National Review.* Rather than relating a straightforward account of the general's life, *The Autumn of the Patriarch* skips from one episode to another using detailed descriptions. *Times Literary Supplement* contributor John Sturrock found this approach appropriate to the author's subject, calling the work "the desperate, richly sustained hallucination of a man rightly bitter about the present state of so much of Latin America." Sturrock noted that "Garcia Marquez's novel is sophisticated and its language is luxuriant to a degree. Style and subject are at odds because Garcia Marquez is committed to showing that our first freedom—and one which all too many Latin American countries have lost—is of the full resources of our language." *Time* writer R. Z. Sheppard similarly commented on Garcia Marquez's elaborate style, observing that "the theme is artfully insinuated, an atmosphere instantly evoked like a puff of stage smoke, and all conveyed in language that generates a charge of expectancy." The critic concluded: "Garcia Marquez writes with what could be called a stream-of-consciousness technique, but the result is much more like a whirlpool."

Some critics, however, found both the theme and technique of *The Autumn of the Patriarch* lacking. J.D. O'Hara, for example, wrote in the *Washington Post*

Book World that for all his "magical realism," Garcia Marquez "can only remind us of real-life parallels; he cannot exaggerate them." For the same reason, the critic added, "although he can turn into grisly cartoons the squalor and paranoia of actual dictatorships, he can scarcely parody them; reality has anticipated him again." *Newsweek* columnist Walter Clemons found the novel somewhat disappointing: "After the narrative vivacity and intricate characterization of the earlier book [*The Autumn of the Patriarch*] seems both oversumptuous and underpopulated. It is—deadliest of compliments—an extended piece of magnificent writing." Other critics believed that the author's skillful style enhances the novel. Referring to the novel's disjointed narrative style, Wendy McElroy commented in *World Research INK* that "this is the first time I have seen it handled properly. Gabriel Garcia Marquez ignores many conventions of the English language which are meant to provide structure and coherence. But he is so skillful that his novel is not difficult to understand. It is bizarre; it is disorienting . . . but it is not difficult. Moreover, it is appropriate to the chaos and decay of the general's mind and of his world." Similarly, De Feo maintained that "no summary or description of this book can really do it justice, for it is not only the author's surrealistic flights of imagination that make it such an exceptional work, but also his brilliant use of language, his gift for phrasing and description." The critic concluded: "Throughout this unique, remarkable novel, the tall tale is transformed into a true work of art."

"With its run-on, seemingly free-associative sentences, its constant flow of images and color, Gabriel Garcia Marquez's last novel, *The Autumn of the Patriarch,* was such a dazzling technical achievement that it left the pleasurably exhausted reader wondering what the author would do next," commented De Feo in the *Nation.* The author's next work, *Chronicle of a Death Foretold* "is, in miniature, a virtuoso performance," stated Jonathan Yardley in the *Washington Post Book World.* In contrast with the author's "two masterworks, *One Hundred Years of Solitude* and *The Autumn of the Patriarch,*" continued the critic, "it is slight . . . its action is tightly concentrated on a single event. But in this small space Garcia Marquez works small miracles; *Chronicle of a Death Foretold* is ingeniously, impeccably constructed, and it provides a sobering, devastating perspective on the system of male 'honor'." In the novella, described Douglas Hill in the Toronto *Globe & Mail,* Garcia Marquez "has cut out an apparently uncomplicated, larger-than- life jigsaw puzzle of passion and crime, then demonstrated, with laconic diligence and a sort of concerned amusement, how extraordinarily difficult the task of assembling the pieces can be." The story is based on a historical incident in which a young woman is returned after her wedding night for not being a virgin and her brothers set out to avenge the stain on the family honor by murdering the man she names as her "perpetrator." The death is "foretold" in that the brothers announce their intentions to the entire town, but circumstances conspire to keep Santiago Nasar, the condemned man, from this knowledge, and he is brutally murdered.

"In telling this story, which is as much about the towns-people and their reactions as it is about the key players, Garcia Marquez might simply have remained omniscient," observed De Feo. But instead "he places himself in the action, assuming the role of a former citizen who returns home to reconstruct the events of the tragic day—a day he himself lived through." This narrative maneuvering, claimed the critic, "adds another layer to the book, for the narrator, who is visible one moment, invisible the next, could very well ask himself the same question he is intent on asking others, and his own role, his own failure to act in the affair contributes to the book's odd, haunting ambiguity." This recreation after the fact has an additional effect, as Gregory Rabassa noted in *World Literature Today:* "From the beginning we know that Santiago Nasar will be and has been killed, depending on the time of the narrative thread that we happen to be following, but Garcia Marquez does manage, in spite of the repeated foretelling of the event by the murderers and others, to maintain the suspense at a high level by never describing the actual murder until the very end." Rabassa explained: "Until then we have been following the chronicler as he puts the bits and pieces together ex post facto, but he has constructed things in such a way that we are still hoping for a reprieve even though we know better." "As more and more is revealed about the murder, less and less is known," wrote Leonard Michaels in the *New York Times Book Review,* "yet the style of the novel is always natural and unselfconscious, as if innocent of any paradoxical implication."

In approaching the story from this re-creative standpoint, Garcia Marquez once again utilizes journalistic techniques. As *Chicago Tribune Book World* editor John Blades maintained, "Garcia Marquez tells this grisly little fable in what often appears to be a straight-faced parody of conventional journalism, with its dependence on 'he-she-they told me' narrative techniques, its reliance on the distorted, contradictory and dreamlike memories of 'eyewitnesses'." Blades added, however, that "at the same time, this is precision-tooled fiction; the author subtly but skillfully manipulates his chronol-

ogy for dramatic impact." *New York Times* correspondent Christopher Lehmann-Haupt similarly noted a departure from the author's previous style: "I cannot be absolutely certain whether in *Chronicle* Gabriel Garcia Marquez has come closer to conventional storytelling than in his previous work, or whether I have simply grown accustomed to his imagination." The critic added that "whatever the case, I found *Chronicle of a Death Foretold* by far the author's most absorbing work to date. I read it through in a flash, and it made the back of my neck prickle." "It is interesting," remarked *Times Literary Supplement* contributor Bill Buford, that Garcia Marquez chose to handle "a fictional episode with the methods of a journalist. In doing so he has written an unusual and original work: a simple narrative so charged with irony that it has the authority of political fable." Buford concluded: "If it is not an example of the socialist realism [Garcia] Marquez may claim it to be elsewhere, *Chronicle of a Death Foretold* is in any case a mesmerizing work that clearly establishes [Garcia] Marquez as one of the most accomplished, and the most 'magical' of political novelists writing today." In *Review,* Edith Grossman concluded: "Once again Garcia Marquez is an ironic chronicler who dazzles the reader with uncommon blendings of fantasy, fable and fact."

Another blending of fable and fact, based in part on Garcia Marquez's recollections of his parents' marriage, *Love in the Time of Cholera* "is an amazing celebration of the many kinds of love between men and women," according to Elaine Feinstein of the London *Times.* "In part it is a brilliantly witty account of the tussles in a long marriage, whose details are curiously moving; elsewhere it is a fantastic tale of love finding erotic fulfillment in ageing bodies." The novel begins with the death of Dr. Juvenal Urbino, whose attempt to rescue a parrot from a tree leaves his wife of fifty years, Fermina Daza, a widow. Soon after Urbino's death, however, Florentino Ariza appears on Fermina Daza's doorstep. The rest of the novel recounts Florentino's determination to resume the passionate courtship of a woman who had given him up over half a century before. In relating both the story of Fermina Daza's marriage and her later courtship, *Love in the Time of Cholera* "is a novel about commitment and fidelity under circumstances which seem to render such virtues absurd," recounted *Times Literary Supplement* contributor S. M.J. Minta. "[It is] about a refusal to grow old gracefully and respectably, about the triumph sentiment can still win over reason, and above all, perhaps, about Latin America, about keeping faith with where, for better or worse, you started out from."

Although the basic plot of *Love in the Time of Cholera* is fairly simple, some critics have accused Garcia Marquez of over-embellishing his story. Calling the plot a "boy-meets-girl" story, Chicago *Tribune Books* contributor Michael Dorris remarked that "it takes a while to realize this core [plot], for every aspect of the book is attenuated, exaggerated, overstated." The critic also argued that "while a Harlequin Romance might balk at stretching this plot for more than a year or two of fictional time, Garcia Marquez nurses it over five decades," adding that the "prose [is] laden with hyperbolic excess." Some critics have claimed that instead of revealing the romantic side of love, *Love in the Time of Cholera* "seems to deal more with libido and self-deceit than with desire and mortality," as Angela Carter termed it in the *Washington Post Book World*. Dorris expressed a similar opinion, writing that while the novel's "first 50 pages are brilliant, provocative, . . . they are [an] overture to a discordant symphony" which portrays an "anachronistic" world of machismo and misogyny. In contrast, Toronto *Globe & Mail* contributor Ronald Wright believed that the novel works as a satire of this same kind of "hypocrisy, provincialism and irresponsibility of the main characters' social milieu." Wright concluded: " *Love in the Time of Cholera* is a complex and subtle book; its greatest achievement is not to tell a love story, but to meditate on the equivocal nature of romanticism and romantic love."

Other reviewers have agreed that although it contains elements of his other work, *Love in the Time of Cholera* is a development in a different direction for Garcia Marquez. Author Thomas Pynchon, writing in the *New York Times Book Review,* commented that "it would be presumptuous to speak of moving 'beyond' *One Hundred Years of Solitude* but clearly Garcia Marquez has moved somewhere else, not least into deeper awareness of the ways in which, as Florentino comes to learn, 'nobody teaches life anything'." Countering criticisms that the work is overemotional, Minta claimed that "the triumph of the novel is that it uncovers the massive, submerged strength of the popular, the cliched and the sentimental." While it "does not possess the fierce, visionary poetry of *One Hundred Years of Solitude* or the feverish phantasmagoria of *The Autumn of the Patriarch*," as *New York Times* critic Michiko Kakutani described it, *Love in the Time of Cholera* "has revealed how the extraordinary is contained in the ordinary, how a couple of forgotten, even commonplace lives can encompass the heights and depths of grand and eternal passion." "The result," concluded the critic, "is a rich commodious novel, a novel whose narrative power is matched only by its generosity of vision." "The Garcimarquesian voice we have come to recognize from the other fiction has matured, found and developed new resources," asserted Pynchon, "[and] been brought to a

level where it can at once be classical and familiar, opalescent and pure, able to praise and curse, laugh and cry, fabulate and sing and when called upon, take off and soar." Pynchon concluded: "There is nothing I have read quite like [the] astonishing final chapter, symphonic, sure in its dynamics and tempo . . . . At the very best [this remembrance] results in works that can even return our worn souls to us, among which most certainly belongs *Love in the Time of Cholera,* this shining and heartbreaking novel."

For his next novel, *The General in His Labyrinth,* Garcia Marquez chose another type of story. His protagonist, the General, is Simon Bolivar. Known as "the Liberator," Bolivar is remembered as a controversial and influential historical figure. His revolutionary activities during the early nineteenth century helped free South America from Spanish control. The labyrinth evoked in the title consists of what John Butt described in the *Times Literary Supplement* as "the web of slanders and intrigues that surrounded [Bolivar's] decline." The book focuses on Bolivar's last months, once the leader had renounced the Colombian presidency and embarked on a long journey that ended when he died near the Caribbean coast on December 17, 1830. Even as he neared death, Bolivar staged one final, failed attempt to reassert leadership in the face of anarchy. In the *New York Times Book Review* author Margaret Atwood declared: "Had Bolivar not existed, Mr. Garcia Marquez would have had to invent him." Atwood called the novel "a fascinating literary tour de force and a moving tribute to an extraordinary man," as well as "a sad commentary on the ruthlessness of the political process."

The political process is, indeed, an integral aspect of *The General in His Labyrinth.* "Latin American politicians and intellectuals have long relied on a more saintly image of Bolivar to make up for the region's often sordid history," Tim Padgett wrote in *Newsweek.* Although Garcia Marquez presents a pro-Bolivar viewpoint in his novel, the book was greeted with controversy. Butt observed that Garcia Marquez had "managed to offend all sides . . . . From the point of view of some pious Latin Americans he blasphemes a local deity by having him utter the occasional obscenity and by showing him as a relentless womanizer, which he was. Others have detected the author's alleged 'Caribbean' tropical and lowland dislike of *cachacos* or upland and *bogotano* Colombians." The harshest criticism, Butt asserted, emanated from some Colombian historians "who claim that the novel impugns the basis of their country's independence by siding too openly with the Liberator" to the detriment of some of Bolivar's political contemporaries. Garcia Marquez earned wide praise for the quality of documentary research that contributed to the novel, although Butt, for one, lamented that the book "leaves much unexplained about the mental processes of the Liberator." He elaborated: "We learn far more about Bolivar's appearance, sex-life, surroundings and public actions than about his thoughts and motives."

In the works, off and on, for nearly two decades, *Strange Pilgrims: Twelve Stories* marked Garcia Marquez's return to the short story collection. Garcia Marquez's pilgrims are Latin American characters placed in various European settings, many of them in southern Italy. "Thematically, these dozen stories explore familiar Marquesan territory: human solitude and quiet desperation, unexpected love (among older people, between generations), the bizarre turns of fate, the intertwining of passion and death," Michael Dirda asserted in the *Washington Post Book World.* At each story's core, however, "lies a variant of that great transatlantic theme—the failure of people of different cultures, ages or political convictions to communicate with each other." In *Strange Pilgrims,* Margaret Sayers Peden asserted in the *Chicago Tribune,* "Latins do not fare well in their separation from native soil." In "The Saint," for example, an old Colombian man has brought the intact corpse of his young daughter to Rome. For decades he journeys through the Vatican bureaucracy, trying to get his child canonized. "Absurd and oddly serene," Richard Eder wrote in the *Los Angeles Times Book Review,* "['The Saint'] says a great deal about Latin American boundlessness in a bounded Europe." In another story, "I Only Came to Use the Phone," a Mexican woman is mistakenly identified as a mental patient and is trapped in a Spanish insane asylum—no one heeds her cry that she only entered the building to place a telephone call.

"Rich with allusion and suggestion, colourful like a carnival," wrote Ian Thomson in *Spectator,* "these short stories nevertheless lack the graceful charm of *Love in the Time of Cholera,* say, or of other novels by [Garcia] Marquez. There's a deadpan acceptance of the fantastic, though, which allows for a degree of comedy." In a similar vein, Dirda asserted: "Many of the stories in *Strange Pilgrims* might be classified as fantastic . . . . Still, none of them quite possesses the soul-stirring magic of Garcia Marquez's earlier short fiction." He continued: "For all their smooth execution, [the stories] don't feel truly haunted, they seldom take us to fictive places we've never been before . . . . And yet. And yet. One could hardly wish for more readable entertainments, or more wonderful detailing." Edward Waters Hood, however, declared in *World Literature Today* that these "interesting and innovative stories . . . complement and add several new dimensions to Gabriel Garcia Marquez's fictional world."

Garcia Marquez returned to his Maconderos in his next novel, *Of Love and Other Demons.* The story stems from an event the author witnessed early in his journalistic career. As a reporter in Cartagena in 1949, he was assigned to watch while a convent's tomb was opened to transfer burial remains—the convent was being destroyed to clear space for a hotel. There soon emerged twenty-two meters of vibrant human hair, atttached to the skull of a young girl who had been buried for two centuries. Remembering his grandparents' stories about a twelve-year-old aristocrat who had died of rabies, Garcia Marquez began to reconstruct the life and death of a character named Sierva Maria. Jonathan Yardley remarked in the *Washington Post Book World* that the author's mood in this novel "is almost entirely melancholy and his manner is, by contrast with his characteristic ebullience, decidedly restrained." In the *Los Angeles Times Book Review,* Eder judged the novel to be "a good one though not quite among [Garcia Marquez's] best."

As the daughter of wealthy but uninterested parents, Sierva Maria grows up with the African slaves on her family's plantation. When she is bitten by a rabid dog, a local bishop determines that she requires exorcism. The girl is taken to the Convent of Santa Clara, where the bishop's pious delegate, Father Cayetano Delaura, is charged with her case. But Delaura himself is soon possessed by the demon of love, his forbidden love for the young woman. Yardley wrote: "Here most certainly we are in the world of Gabriel Garcia Marquez, where religious faith and human love collide in agony and passion." In *Time* magazine R. Z. Sheppard asserted that in telling "a story of forbidden love," Garcia Marquez "demonstrates once again the vigor of his own passion: the daring and irresistible coupling of history and imagination." Yardley warned, however, that "readers hoping to re-experience 'magical realism' at the level attained in the author's masterpieces will be disappointed." In the *Nation,* John Leonard stated: "My only complaint about this marvelous novella is its rush toward the end. Suddenly, [the author is] in a hurry . . . when we want to spend more time" with his characters.

The origins behind *Of Love and Other Demons* emphasize once again the dual forces of journalism and fiction in Garcia Marquez's oeuvre. The author elaborated in his interview with Dreifus: "I'm fascinated by the relationship between literature and *journalism.* I began my career as a journalist in Colombia, and a reporter is something I've never stopped being. When I'm not working on fiction, I'm running around the world, practicing my craft as a reporter." His work as a journalist has produced controversy, for in journalism Garcia Marquez not only sees a chance to develop his "craft," but also an opportunity to become involved in political issues. His self-imposed exile from Colombia was prompted by a series of articles he wrote in 1955 about the sole survivor of a Colombian shipwreck, claiming that the government ship had capsized due to an overload of contraband. In 1986, Garcia Marquez wrote *Clandestine in Chile: The Adventures of Miguel Littin,* a work about an exile's return to the repressive Chile of General Augusto Pinochet. The political revelations of the book led to the burning of almost 15,000 copies by the Chilean government. In addition, Garcia Marquez has maintained personal relationships with such political figures as Cuban President Fidel Castro, former French President Francois Mitterand, and the late Panamanian leader General Omar Torrijos.

Because of this history of political involvement, Garcia Marquez has often been accused of allowing his politics to overshadow his work, and has also encountered problems entering the United States. When asked by *New York Times Book Review* contributor Marlise Simons why he is so insistent on becoming involved in political issues, the author replied that "If I were not a Latin American, maybe I wouldn't [become involved]. But underdevelopment is total, integral, it affects every part of our lives. The problems of our societies are mainly political." The Colombian further explained that "the commitment of a writer is with the reality of all of society, not just with a small part of it. If not, he is as bad as the politicians who disregard a large part of our reality. That is why authors, painters, writers in Latin America get politically involved."

Perhaps not surprisingly, Garcia Marquez's political involvement has led him to examine the role that drug cartels have played in destabilizing Colombian society. *News of a Kidnapping,* a nonfiction account of several audacious kidnappings engineered by the Medellin drug cartel, is written in a consciously even-handed journalistic style but nevertheless reflects the author's dismay not only with the native drug dealers but with the American government that seeks to extradite and punish them. In the *New York Times,* Michiko Kakutani wrote: " *News of a Kidnapping* not only provides a fascinating anatomy of 'one episode in the biblical holocaust that has been consuming Colombia for more than 20 years,' but also offers the reader new insights into the surreal history of Mr. Garcia Marquez's native country. Indeed, the reader is reminded by this book that the magical realism employed by Mr. Garcia Marquez and other Latin American novelists is in part a narrative strategy for grappling with a social reality so hallucinatory, so irrational that it defies ordinary naturalistic description."

Centered on the abduction of three prominent Colombian women, *News of a Kidnapping* describes the women's suffering as hostages of the drug lords as well as the negotiations to free them. "By now the world is well acquainted with hostage holding as a grotesque basis for personal relationships," noted R.Z. Sheppard. "But here the unusual experience of living in close quarters with your potential killers is intensified in prose as precise and deadpan as a coroner's report. And as he does so often, Garcia Marquez makes the fantastic seem ordinary." In the *New York Times Book Review,* Robert Stone declared: "Mr. Garcia Marquez is a former journalist, and *News of a Kidnapping* resembles newspaper journalism of the better sort, with a quick eye for the illuminating detail and a capacity for assembling fact. It will interest those who follow the details of the drug problem more than it will appeal to the literary following of Mr. Garcia Marquez . . . . Still, the horrors and the absurdities, the touches of tender humanity and the stony cruelty that are part of this story—and of Colombia—all appear."

Despite the controversy that his politics and work have engendered, Garcia Marquez's *One Hundred Years of Solitude* is enough to ensure the author "a place in the ranks of twentieth century masters," claimed Curt Suplee in the *Washington Post.* The Nobel-winner's reputation, however, is grounded in more than this one masterpiece. The Swedish Academy's Nobel citation states, "Each new work of his is received by critics and readers as an event of world importance, is translated into many languages and published as quickly as possible in large editions." "At a time of dire predictions about the future of the novel," observed McMurray, Garcia Marquez's "prodigious imagination, remarkable compositional precision, and wide popularity provide evidence that the genre is still thriving." Janes, in the *Reference Guide to World Literature,* noted, "Often humorous, at times bitterly ironic or grotesque, occasionally tinged with pathos, Garcia Marquez's work possesses a rare power of invention. Deficient in the psychological and linguistic density characteristic of some modern writers, Garcia Marquez at his best achieves continuous surprise in the elaboration of a rococo, tessellated prose surface that makes the reader aware of the simultaneous insistence and insufficiency of interpretation." And as *Tribune Books* contributor Harry Mark Petrakis described him, Garcia Marquez "is a magician of vision and language who does astonishing things with time and reality. He blends legend and history in ways that make the legends seem truer than truth. His scenes and characters are humorous, tragic, mysterious and beset by ironies and fantasies. In his fictional world, anything is possible and everything is believable." Concluded the critic:

"Mystical and magical, fully aware of the transiency of life, his stories fashion realms inhabited by ghosts and restless souls who return to those left behind through fantasies and dreams. The stories explore, with a deceptive simplicity, the miracles and mysteries of life."

Garcia Marquez continues, too, to elude those who wish to pigeonhole him and to resist pressure to be "politically correct." He has continued to support the actions of Cuba's Fidel Castro against sometimes loud objections, while at the same time pointing out that he has helped many Cubans leave Cuba safely. He has returned to journalism in his later years, buying the failing newspaper *Cambio* in 1999 and writing regularly for it thereafter and increasing its sales five-fold. Of his (and other South American writers') early and continuing political involvement, Brooke Allen in the *New Leader* said, "There is hardly an ivory tower litterateur among the bunch. Their vital engagement seems to derive from the continual political chaos in South and Central America. 'In both America and Latin America,' commented Manuel Puig, 'the young writer usually doesn't like the system, with a capital "S," in his country. But in Latin America the possibility exists of actually shaking that system, because Latin American systems are shaky. Young writers who don't like the American way of life feel impotent, because it's really tough to shake Wall Street. You may not like Wall Street, but it works somehow . . . . Ironically, Latin American countries, in their instability, give writers and intellectuals the hope that they are needed. In Latin America there's the illusion that a writer can change something; of course, it's not that simple.' It is therefore not surprising that so many prominent Latin American writers have taken active political roles."

In 2002 Garcia Marquez published a memoir, volume one covering approximately the first thirty years of his life, *Vivir Para Contarla*. Two million copies were sold between late November and May 2003, not counting pirate copies that flooded the streets, prompting Knopf to publish the U.S. and Spanish versions a year ahead of their planned time. Elise Christensen of *Newsweek* recounted, "Photocopied versions have been peddled in Puerto Rico, and armed police guarded bookstores in Mexico in October after a delivery truck was reportedly hijacked in Colombia." And, according to Sandra Hernandez in a May, 2003 *Knight Ridder* report, "In an unprecedented move, major newspapers including the *Los Angeles Times* reviewed the Spanish language version rather than wait for the English edition due out in November together with the next volume in Spanish." Adriana Lopez, writing in the *New York Times,* reported that "for weeks, propelled by the buzz in the Latin

American news media, Latino readers have been flocking to Little Colombia, where copies have found their way to street vendors and independently owned Latino bookstores. On Roosevelt Avenue, under the shadow of the elevated No. 7 train, street vendors like Ms. Luna do a brisk business hawking copies of the memoir, which they get from her buyers in South America and Spain, for up to $40 apiece . . . . Some customers shy away from the street vendors in response to a Colombian news media campaign urging readers not to buy illegal copies of the book. Some pirated copies are said to be circulating clandestinely. But the majority of Little Colombia's street booksellers appear to be selling the real thing, a quality-bound edition whose cover bears a haunting sepia image of the author as a child. Mr. Ramirez's wife, Irma, recalls the day she realized how much the book was touching a nerve among her fellow Colombians. 'I saw a young man sitting in Flushing Meadows Park reading a copy,' she said. 'And the tears were just running down his face'." The English translation appeared in late 2003 as *Living to Tell the Tale.*

Caleb Bach, with his son Joel photographing, conducted an informal interview with Garcia Marquez for the May-June 2003 *Americas.* They found him working six hours a day on the next volume of the memoir because as Garcia Marquez told them, "If I don't write, I get bored," adding, "I keep writing so as not to die." He confided that he has a prodigious memory and uses no outside researchers: "I was a chain smoker for thirty years, but at age fifty abruptly I quit after a doctor in Barcelona told me my habit would cause memory loss." "If I can't remember something, it didn't happen," he said. Bach and his son found Garcia Marquez to be a "kind, thoughtful, dignified man who has enriched the lives of so many people the world over never forgets his own humble origins and struggle to give purpose to his life. It is his nature to help others, especially young people, as they set out on their own journey." This impression was confirmed by an *Economist (U.S.)* reviewer who remarked, "Interestingly, his memoir reveals its author to be a man of few deep convictions, for whom friendship is far more important than politics."

Nicaraguan poet Gioconda Belli relished the memoir, saying that she ultimately realized that, hoping to find the boundary between Garcia Marquez's fiction and reality, "This is a journey in which each family anecdote and tale brings us back to characters we've met in his books or reveals to us the promise of many stories yet to be written. Through it, we find the hidden genetic codes of the Buendias, of Remedios the Beauty and Petra Cotes, and we come to realize that we've penetrated the looking glass, thinking we would be able to separate fiction from reality only to discover that they're in-separable." She went on, *"Vivir para contarla* is, from the start, an empirical argument to demonstrate both the reality of magic and the magic of reality. Garcia Mar-quez brings up the idea more than once in that playful way of his, so far removed from academic parsimony. Referring to *The Arabian Nights,* for example, he says: [I even dared to think that the wonders Scheherazade told about had really happened in the daily life of her time and that they stopped happening because of the disbelief and cowardice of succeeding generations]." She concluded, "His talent to blend magic and reality relieves us from the rationalist Cartesian split—so un-healthy for the spirit—and presents an alternative, wholesome way to embrace both. This is precisely why his writings provoke such a sensual joy. They let our imagination roam free in our bodies and infuse us with the magical powers inherent in the human condition. His writing shows us, Latin Americans, a credible ver-sion of our own history: not the academic vision of the history books that in no way resembles our experience but the version we learned by living in forsaken towns and in cities where lunatics and crocodiles roamed the streets and where dictators kept prisoners in cages alongside their pet lions and jaguars. In a world in-creasingly suffering the unreal, Garcia Marquez has fooled reality once more, this time by remaining faith-ful to it." Belli also cited the memoir as explanation of the author's political development from the moment he was witness to the murder of presidential candidate, Jorge Eliecer Gaitan, a populist in whom many had hope for peace, in 1948.

Searching for those who did not relate positively to the memoir was a futile task, though the U.S. *Economist*'s writer did find, "This memoir may not win over those who have resisted being persuaded that Mr. Garcia Mar-quez is a great, rather than a very good, writer. His style is one of much poetry but sometimes less meaning than meets the eye: in a typical sentence, he says of his grandfather that 'I knew what he was thinking by the changes in his silence.' And fecund though it was, magi-cal realism has much to answer for: Mr. Garcia Mar-quez has rarely let historical fact get in the way of a good story, and Latin American journalism has suffered much from the blurring of its boundaries with fiction. But most readers will not mind. They will simply enjoy the anecdotes and the prose of a master of the narrative art and of the Spanish language." Given Latin Ameri-can commentary on the different view taken of the seam between "cold" reality and "magic" in less rationalistic South American countries (as evidenced in Belli's re-view), even this slight denigration can be seen as a cul-tural misprision. Hopefully, there is rather something to

be learned from the understanding that reality, imagina-tion, magic, history are bound together in such a way they cannot be so easily separated and reduced. The first volume of the memoir, presenting Garcia Marquez' early life, reveals in it the realities that appear as magic in the novels. As Lois Zamora commented in the *Hous-ton Chronicle,* "Garcia Marquez is often called a 'magi-cal realist,' but when you finish this autobiography you will be convinced of what he has long insisted in repu-diation of the term: that he is not a magical realist but a realist and has never written about anything that he hasn't seen himself or known someone who has."

After the success of his memoir, Garcia Marquez turned his attention back to fiction in 2004 by publishing the novel *Memoria de mis putas tristes,* translated as *Memo-ries of My Melancholy Whores.* In the story, a 90-year-old man gives himself the gift of a virgin adolescent prostitute for his birthday. After sleeping with more than 500 prostitutes in his lifetime, he is surprised to find himself falling in love with the young girl, with whom he never has sex but merely adores while sleep-ing. In reviewing the book for the *New York Times Book Review,* Terrence Rafferty noted that with "this sprightly, perverse little fable about looking forward" Garcia Mar-quez "is now old enough, at last, to feel that every new story arrives as a miracle, and to understand that as long as he writes he can keep being born again." Peter Oliva, writing in *Globe & Mail,* concluded, "the book is quick; it flies. It is a surefire antidote for melancholy. There are hallucinations, dreams, fortune telling and murder. There is old love and there is madness. And with all this crazed love there is spanking new self-awareness. The result is a delight, a clean gem from a master storyteller."

BIOGRAPHICAL AND CRITICAL SOURCES:

BOOKS

Balderston, Daniel, and Schwartz, Marcy, eds., *Voice-Overs: Translation and Latin American Literature.* State University of New York Press (Albany, NY), 2002.

Bell, Michael, *Gabriel Garcia Marquez: Solitude and Solidarity,* St. Martin's Press (New York, NY), 1993.

Bell-Villada, Gene H., *Garcia Marquez: The Man and His Work,* University of North Carolina Press (Chapel Hill, NC), 1990; editor, *Conversations with Gabriel Garcia Marquez,* University Press of Mis-sissippi (Jackson, MS), 2005.

Brotherson, Gordon, *The Emergence of the Latin American Novel,* Cambridge University Press (New York, NY), 1979.

Contemporary Literary Criticism, Gale (Detroit, MI), Volume 2, 1974, Volume 3, 1975, Volume 8, 1978, Volume 10, 1979, Volume 15, 1980, Volume 27, 1984, Volume 47, 1988, Volume 55, 1989.

Contemporary Popular Writers, St. James Press (Detroit, MI), 1997, pp. 159- 160.

Cruz Mendizábal, Juan, and Fernández Jiménez, Juan, eds., *Visión de la narrativa hispánica: Ensayos.* Department of Spanish and Classical Languages, Indiana University of Pennsylvania (Indiana, PA), 1999.

Dictionary of Literary Biography, Volume 113: *Modern Latin-American Fiction Writers,* Gale (Detroit, MI), 1992.

Dictionary of Literary Biography Yearbook: 1982, Gale (Detroit, MI), 1983.

Dolan, Sean, *Gabriel Garcia Marquez,* Chelsea House (New York, NY), 1994.

Fernandez-Braso, Miguel, *Gabriel Garcia Marquez,* Editorial Azur (Madrid, Spain), 1969.

Fiddian, Robin W., *Garcia Marquez,* Longman (New York, NY), 1995.

Fuentes, Carlos, *Gabriel Garcia Marquez and the Invention of America,* 1987.

Gabriel Garcia Marquez, nuestro premio Nobel, La Secretaria de Informacion y Prensa de la Presidencia de la Nacion (Bogota, Colombia), 1983.

Gallagher, David Patrick, *Modern Latin American Literature,* Oxford University Press (Oxford, England), 1973.

Garcia Marquez, Eligio, *Tras las claves de Melquiades: Historia de Cien anos de soledad,* 2001.

Guibert, Rita, *Seven Voices,* Knopf (New York, NY), 1973.

Harss, Luis, and Barbara Dohmann, *Into the Mainstream: Conversations with Latin-American Writers,* Harper (New York, NY), 1967.

Janes, Regina,*Gabriel Garcia Marquez: Revolutions in Wonderland,* University of Missouri Press (Columbia, MO), 1981.

Jaramillo, Maria Mercedes, Osorio, Betty, and Robledo, Angela I., eds., *Literatura y cultura: Narrativa colombiana del siglo XX, I: La nación moderna: Identidad; II: Diseminación, cambios, desplazamientos; III: Hibridez y alteridades.* Ministerio de Cultura (Bogota, Colombia), 2000.

Lopez Cruz, Humberto, ed., *Encuentro con la literatura panamena.* Circulo de Lectura de la Universidad Catolica Santa Maria La Antigua (Panama City, Panama), 2003.

Lopez Parada, Esperanza. *Una mirada al sesgo: Literatura hispanoamericana desde los margenes.* Iberoamericana-Vervuert (Madrid, Spain), 1999.

Mantilla, Alfonso Renteria, compiler, *Garcia Marquez habla de Garcia Marquez,* Renteria (Colombia), 1979.

McGuirk, Bernard, and Richard Cardwell, editors, *Gabriel Garcia Marquez: New Readings,* Cambridge University Press (New York, NY), 1988.

McMurray, George R., *Gabriel Garcia Marquez,* Ungar (New York, NY), 1977.

Moretti, Franco, *The Modern Epic: The World-System from Goethe to Garcia Marquez,* 1996.

Penuel, Arnold M., *Intertextuality in Garcia Marquez,* 1994.

Porrata, Francisco E., and Fausto Avedano, *Explicacion de Cien anos de soledad Garcia Marquez,* Editorial Texto (Costa Rica), 1976.

Pritchett, V.S., *The Myth Makers,* Random House (New York, NY), 1979.

Reference Guide to World Literature, 2nd edition, St. James Press (Detroit, MI), 1995, pp. 454-458.

Rincon, Carlos. *Garcia Marquez, Hawthorne, Shakespeare, De La Vega and Co. Unltd.* Instituto Caro y Cuervo (Bogota, Colombia), 1999.

Rodman, Selden, *Tongues of Fallen Angels,* New Direction (New York, NY), 1974.

Scarlett, Elizabeth, and Wescott, Howard B., eds., *Convergencias Hispanicas: Selected Proceedings and Other Essays on Spanish and Latin American Literature, Film, and Linguistics.* Cuesta (Newark, DE), 2001.

Simas, Rosa, *Circularity and Visions of the New World in William Faulkner, Gabriel Garcia Marquez, and Osman Lins,* 1993.

Sommer, Doris, ed., *The Places of History: Regionalism Revisited in Latin America.* Duke University Press (Durham, NC), 1999.

Vargas Llosa, Mario, *Garcia Marquez: Historia de un deicido,* Barral Editores, 1971.

Wood, Michael, *Gabriel Garcia Marquez: One Hundred Years of Solitude,* Cambridge University Press (New York, NY), 1990.

PERIODICALS

Acta Neophilologica, 2001, pp. 87, 124.

Afro-Hispanic Review, fall, 2000, p. 80.

Alba de America: Revista Literaria, March 1999, pp. 109, 277.

American Journalism Review, October, 1997, p. 60.

Americas (English edition), May-June, 2003, pp. 14, 60.

Antioch Review, winter, 1991, p. 154.

ARIEL, October, 1998, p. 53.

Boletin de la Academia Colombiana, January-June, 2000, p. 140.

Booklist, March 15, 1997; January 1, 2003, p. 809; October 15, 2003, review of *Living To Tell the Tale,* p. 354; January 1, 2004, review of *Living To Tell the Tale,* p. 773.

Books Abroad, winter, 1973; summer, 1973; spring, 1976.

Book World, February 22, 1970; February 20, 1972.

Business Wire, October 4, 2000, p. 2011.

Chicago Tribune, March 6, 1983; October 31, 1993.

Chicago Tribune Books, August 10, 1997, p. 3, 6.

Christian Science Monitor, April 16, 1970; October 15, 2002, p. 7.

Ciberletras, August, 1999.

Circulo: Revista de Cultura, 2001, p. 171.

CLCWeb: Comparative Literature and Culture: A WW-Web Journal, March 2001, p. 13, paragraphs.

CLIO, June 22, 1999, p. 375.

College Literature, spring, 1999, p. 59.

Commonweal, March 6, 1970; September 26, 1997, p. 20.

Comparatist: Journal of the Southern Comparative Literature Association, May, 2000, p. 146.

Cuento en Red: Estudios Sobre la Ficcion Breve, spring, 2002.

Daily Telegraph, (Surry Hills, Australia), January 20, 2003, p. 012.

Detroit News, October 27, 1982; December 16, 1984.

Economist, February 15, 2003.

El Norte (Mexico D.F., Mexico), August 18, 2003, p. 1; August 23, 2003, p. 6; September 8, 2003, p. 7.

El Pais, January 22, 1981.

Entertainment Weekly, November 29, 2002, p. 109; November 14, 2003, review of *Living To Tell the Tale,* p. 129.

Especulo: Revista de Estudios Literarios, July-October 2000; March-June 2003.

Estudios de Literatura Colombiana, January-June, 1999, p. 23.

Eureka Studies in Teaching Short Fiction, fall, 2001, p. 50.

Explicator, fall, 2000, p. 46.

Feminaria Literaria, July, 1999, p. 95.

Foreign Policy, March- April, 2003, p. 78.

Globe & Mail (Toronto, Ontario, Canada), April 7, 1984; September 19, 1987; May 21, 1988; October 29, 2005, Peter Oliva, "Master of Melancholy," p. D21.

Guardian (London, England), September 2, 2000, p. 1.

Hispania, September, 1976; September, 1993, pp. 439-445; March, 1994, pp. 80-81.

Hispanic, October, 1997, p. 92; April, 1999, p. 13; September, 2001, p. 16.

Hispanic Journal, fall, 2000, p. 395.

Hispanic Review, spring, 2001, p. 175.

Hispanofila, September, 2001, p. 95.

Horizontes: Revista de la Universidad Catolica de Puerto Rico, April 2001, p. 265.

Houston Chronicle, February 2, 2003, p. 17.

Irish Studies Review, April, 2002, p. 63.

Journal of Latin American Studies, May 1998, p. 395.

Journal of Modern Literature, fall, 2000, p. 173.

Kanina: Revista de Artes y Letras de la Universidad de Costa Rica, January-June 1999, pp. 19, 27.

Knight Ridder/Tribune Business News, October 20, 2002.

Knight Ridder/Tribune News Service, April 10, 1996, p. 410K6295; January 26, 1996, p. 126K3199; October 18, 2002, p. K6143; May 7, 2003, p. K5549.

Lamar Journal of the Humanities, spring, 2002, p. 5.

Lancet, October 18, 1997, p. 1169.

Library Journal, June 15, 1997, p. 85; July, 1997, p. 68; June 1, 2001, p. S26; June 1, 2002, p. 198; November 15, 2003, review of *Living To Tell the Tale,* p. 67.

Literature/Film Quarterly, 2003, p. 118.

London Magazine, April-May, 1973; November, 1979.

Lit: Literature Interpretation Theory, February, 2001, p. 403.

London Review of Books, October 30, 1997, p. 29.

Los Angeles Times, October 22, 1982; January 25, 1987; August 24, 1988; November 1, 2002, p. E-1; January 15, 2003, p. A-1; February 16, 2003, p. R5.

Los Angeles Times Book Review, April 10, 1983; November 13, 1983; December 16, 1984; April 27, 1986; June 7, 1987; April 17, 1988; October 24, 1993, pp. 3, 10; May 14, 1995, pp. 3, 5; June 1, 1997, pp. 10-11.

Maclean's, July 24, 1995, p. 50; September 1, 1997, p. 56.

Magazine Litteraire, October 1998, p. 127.

Manila Bulletin, May 2, 2003.

Melbourne Herald Sun, January 27, 1999, p. 027.

Mural (Mexico D.F., Mexico), August 22, 2003, p. 39; August 23, 2003, p. 9.

Nation, December 2, 1968; May 15, 1972; May 14, 1983; June 12, 1995, pp. 836-840; July 2, 2001, p. 36; January 26, 2004, review of *Living To Tell the Tale,* p. 23.

National Observer, April 20, 1970.

National Review, May 27, 1977; June 10, 1983; May 1, 2000.

Neophilologus, January 1999, p. 59.

New Leader, January- February 2003, p. 24.

New Republic, April 9, 1977; October 27, 1979; May 2, 1983; August 25, 1997, p. 30.

New Statesman, June 26, 1970; May 18, 1979; February 15, 1980; September 3, 1982; August 1, 1997, p. 46.

Newsweek, March 2, 1970; November 8, 1976; July 3, 1978; December 3, 1979; November 1, 1982; October 8, 1990, p. 70; December 16, 2002, p. 10; November 10, 2003, review of *Living To Tell the Tale,* p. 65.

New York Review of Books, March 26, 1970; January 24, 1980; April 14, 1983; January 11, 1996, p. 37; October 9, 1997, p. 19.

New York Times, July 11, 1978; November 6, 1979; October 22, 1982; March 25, 1983; December 7, 1985; April 26, 1986; June 4, 1986; April 6, 1988; June 19, 1997; March 3, 1999, p. A4; October 9, 2002, p. E1; November 17, 2002, p. 6; April 6, 2003, p. 3.

New York Times Book Review, September 29, 1968; March 8, 1970; February 20, 1972; October 31, 1976; July 16, 1978; September 16, 1978; November 11, 1979; November 16, 1980; December 5, 1982; March 27, 1983; April 7, 1985; April 27, 1986; August 9, 1987; April 10, 1988; September 16, 1990, pp. 1, 30; May 28, 1995, p. 8; June 15, 1997; November 6, 2005, Terrence Rafferty, "Client of the Year," p. 14.

New Yorker, September 27, 1999, pp. 56, 68.

Notes on Contemporary Literature, September, 1999, pp. 5, 10.

Observer (London, England), August 30, 1998, p. 16; January 21, 2001, p. 19; June 3, 2001, p. 5.

Opinion, March 1, 2003.

Palabra (Mexico D.F., Mexico), July 27, 2003, p. 20; August 23, 2003, p. 6; September 5, 2003, p. 8; September 6, 2003, p. 6.

People, July 24, 1995, p. 26; December 8, 2003, review of *Living To Tell the Tale,* p. 55.

Playboy, February, 1983.

Publishers Weekly, May 13, 1974; December 16, 1983; July 6, 1990, p. 58; March 27, 1995, pp. 72- 73; June 10, 1996, p. 45; November 25, 2002, p. 16; December 9, 2002, p. 78.

Razon y Fe: Revista Hispanoamericana de Cultura, July-August, 2000, p. 91.

Readerly/Writerly Texts: Essays on Literature, Literary/ Textual Criticism, and Pedagogy, spring- winter, 2001, p. 159.

Reforma (Mexico D.F., Mexico), August 28, 2003, p. 4.

Review, number 24, 1979; September-December, 1981.

Review: Latin American Literature and Arts, fall, 2002, p. 48.

Revista Canadiense de Estudios Hispanicos, winter, 2000, p. 397.

Revista de Critica Literaria Latinoamericana, 1999, p. 199; 2000, p. 269.

Revista de Estudios Colombianos, 1999, p. 37.

Revista de Filologia y Linguistica de la Universidad de Costa Rica, January-June, 2001, pp. 7, 53.

Revista de Literatura Hispanoamericana, July-December, 1999, p. 103; January-June, 2001, p. 19.

Revista Hispanica Moderna, June, 1999, p. 135.

Revista de Literaturas Modernas, 2000, p. 169.

Revista Universidad de Antioquia, April-June, 2000, p. 60.

Rivista di Studi Italiani, June, 2000, p. 127.

Romance Notes, spring, 1999, p. 345.

San Francisco Chronicle, January 26, 1999, p. B10.

Saturday Review, December 21, 1968; March 7, 1970.

School Library Journal, December, 2002, p. S42.

Scotsman (Edinburgh, Scotland), August 8, 2000, p. 9.

Seattle Times, January 26, 2003, p. L8.

Southwest Review, summer, 1973.

Spectator, October 16, 1993, pp. 40-41; June 28, 1997, p. 43; December 6, 2003, review of *Living To Tell the Tale,* p. 48.

Star Tribune (Minneapolis, MN), September 6, 2002, p. 01E; September 13, 2002, p. 03E.

Studies in the Linguistic Sciences, spring, 2001, p. 121.

Suplemento Cultura La Nacion (Buenos Aires, Argentina), July 29, 2001, p. 3.

Taller de Letras, November 1999, p. 191; November 2002, p. 7.

Tesserae: Journal of Iberian and Latin American Studies, June 2001, p. 55.

Time, March 16, 1970; November 1, 1976; July 10, 1978; November 1, 1982; March 7, 1983; December 31, 1984; April 14, 1986; May 22, 1995; June 2, 1997, p. 79; November 17, 2003, review of *Living To Tell the Tale,* p. 148.

Time International, May 24, 1999, p. 104.

Times (London, England), November 13, 1986; June 30, 1988; January 24, 2001, p. 12; November 13, 2002, p. 15.

Times Literary Supplement, April 15, 1977; February 1, 1980; September 10, 1982; July 1, 1988; July 14- 20, 1989, p. 781; July 7, 1995.

Torre: Revista de la Universidad de Puerto Rico, April-June, 1999, p. 433.

Translation Review, 2000, p. 32.

Tribune Books (Chicago, IL), November 11, 1979; November 7, 1982; April 3, 1983; November 18, 1984; April 27, 1986; June 28, 1987; April 17, 1988.

UNESCO Courier, February, 1996, p. 4.

Variety, March 25, 1996, p. 55.

Veltro: Rivista della Civilta Italiana, January-April, 2000, p. 227.

Wasafiri: Journal of Caribbean, African, Asian and Associated Literatures and Film, spring, 2001, p. 23.

Washington Post, October 22, 1982; April 10, 1994, p. F1; September 12, 1997, p. C1.

Washington Post Book World, November 14, 1976; November 25, 1979; November 7, 1982; March 27, 1983; November 18, 1984; July 19, 1987; April 24, 1988; October 31, 1993, p. 7; May 14, 1995, p. 3.

World Literature Today, winter, 1982; winter, 1991, p. 85; autumn, 1993, pp. 782- 783.

World Policy Journal, summer, 1996.

World Press Review, April, 1982.

World Research INK, September, 1977.

ONLINE

Books and Writers, http://www.kirjasto.sci.fi/marquez. htm/ (March 10, 2004).

Modern Word, http://www.themodernword.com/gabo/ (March 10, 2004), "Macondo," web resource on Garcia Marquez.

Paris Review, http://www.parisreview.com/ (March 2, 2006), Paternostro, Silvana, "Solitude and Company: An Oral Biography of Gabriel Garcia Marquez."

*   *   *

GARCIA MARQUEZ, Gabriel Jose
See GARCIA MARQUEZ, Gabriel

*   *   *

GARDNER, John 1933-1982
(John Champlin Gardner, Jr.)

PERSONAL: Born July 21, 1933, in Batavia, NY; died in a motorcycle accident, September 14, 1982, in Susquehanna, PA; son of John Champlin (a dairy farmer) and Priscilla (a high school literature teacher; maiden name, Jones) Gardner; married Joan Louise Patterson, June 6, 1953 (divorced, 1976); married Liz Rosenberg, 1980 (divorced); children: Joel, Lucy. *Education:* Attended De Paul University, 1951-53; Washington University (St. Louis, MO), A.B., 1955; State University of Iowa, M.A., 1956, Ph.D., 1958.

CAREER: Oberlin College, Oberlin, OH, instructor, 1958-59; Chico State College (now California State University), Chico, CA, instructor, 1959-62; San Francisco State College (now San Francisco State University), San Francisco, CA, assistant professor of English, 1962-65; Southern Illinois University—Carbondale, professor of English, 1965-74; Bennington College, Bennington, VT, instructor, 1974-76; Williams College, Williamstown, MA, and Skidmore College, Saratoga Springs, NY, instructor, 1976-77; author, 1976-82; George Mason University, Fairfax, VA, instructor, 1977-78; founder and director of writing program, State University of New York—Binghamton, 1978-82. Distinguished visiting professor, University of Detroit, 1970-71; visiting professor, Northwestern University, 1973.

MEMBER: Modern Language Association of America, American Association of University Professors.

AWARDS, HONORS: Woodrow Wilson fellowship, 1955-56; *Grendel* named one of 1971's best fiction books by *Time* and *Newsweek;* National Education Association award, 1972; Danforth fellowship, 1972-73; Guggenheim fellowship, 1973-74; *October Light* named one of the ten best books of 1976 by *Time* and *New York Times;* National Book Critics Circle Award for fiction, 1976, for *October Light;* Armstrong Prize, 1980, for *The Temptation Game.*

WRITINGS:

NOVELS

The Resurrection, New American Library (New York, NY), 1966.

The Wreckage of Agathon, Harper (New York, NY), 1970.

Grendel, Knopf (New York, NY), 1971.

The Sunlight Dialogues, Knopf (New York, NY), 1972.

Jason and Medeia (novel in verse), Knopf (New York, NY), 1973.

Nickel Mountain: A Pastoral Novel, Knopf (New York, NY), 1973.

October Light, Knopf (New York, NY), 1976.

Freddy's Book, Knopf (New York, NY), 1980.

Mickelsson's Ghosts, Knopf (New York, NY), 1982.

FOR CHILDREN

Dragon, Dragon, and Other Timeless Tales, Knopf (New York, NY), 1975.

Gudgekin the Thistle Girl, and Other Tales, Knopf (New York, NY), 1976.

In the Suicide Mountains, Knopf (New York, NY), 1977.

A Child's Bestiary (light verse), Knopf (New York, NY), 1977.

King of the Hummingbirds, and Other Tales, Knopf (New York, NY), 1977.

Vlemk, the Box Painter, Lord John Press, 1979.

CRITICISM

(Editor, with Lennis Dunlap) *The Forms of Fiction,* Random House (New York, NY), 1961.

(Editor and author of introduction) *The Complete Works of the Gawain-Poet in a Modern English Version with a Critical Introduction,* University of Chicago Press (Chicago, IL), 1965.

(Editor, with Nicholas Joost) *Papers on the Art and Age of Geoffrey Chaucer,* Southern Illinois University Press (Urbana, IL), 1967.

(Editor and author of notes) *The Gawain-Poet: Notes on Pearl and Sir Gawain and the Green Knight, with Brief Commentary on Purity and Patience,* Cliffs Notes, 1967.

Morte D'Arthur Notes, Cliffs Notes, 1967.

Sir Gawain and the Green Knight Notes, Cliffs Notes, 1967.

(Editor and author of notes) *The Alliterative Morte Arthure, The Owl and the Nightingale and Five Other Middle English Poems* (modern English version), Southern Illinois University Press (Urbana, IL), 1971.

The Construction of the Wakefield Cycle, Southern Illinois University Press (Urbana, IL), 1974.

The Construction of Christian Poetry in Old English, Southern Illinois University Press (Urbana, IL), 1975.

The Life and Times of Chaucer, Knopf (New York, NY), 1977.

The Poetry of Chaucer, Southern Illinois University Press (Urbana, IL), 1978.

On Moral Fiction, Basic Books (New York, NY), 1978.

On Becoming a Novelist, Harper (New York, NY), 1983.

The Art of Fiction: Notes on Craft for Young Writers, Knopf (New York, NY), 1984.

On Writers and Writing, foreword by Stewart O'Nan, Addison-Wesley (Reading, MA), 1994.

OTHER

The King's Indian and Other Fireside Tales (novellas), Knopf (New York, NY), 1974, published as *The King's Servant,* J. Cape (London, England), 1975.

(Contributor) Matthew Bruccoli and C.E. Frazer Clark, Jr., editors, *Pages,* Volume 1, Gale (Detroit, MI), 1976.

William Wilson (libretto; also see below), New London Press, 1978.

Poems, Lord John Press, 1978.

Three Libretti (includes *William Wilson, Frankenstein,* and *Rumpelstiltskin*), New London Press, 1979.

MSS: A Retrospective, New London Press, 1980.

The Art of Living and Other Stories, Knopf (New York, NY), 1981.

(Editor, with Shannon Ravenel) *The Best American Short Stories of 1982,* Houghton (Boston, MA), 1982.

(Translator, with Nobuko Tsukui) Kikuo Itaya, *Tengu Child,* Southern Illinois University Press (Urbana, IL), 1983.

(Translator, with John R. Maier) *Gilgamesh: A Translation,* Knopf (New York, NY), 1984.

Stillness and Shadows, edited by Nicholas Delbanco, Knopf (New York, NY), 1986.

Lies! Lies! Lies!: A College Journal of John Gardner, University of Rochester Libraries (Rochester, NY), 1999.

Also author of *The Temptation Game* (radio play), 1980. Contributor of short stories to *Southern Review, Quarterly Review of Literature,* and *Perspective;* of poetry to *Kenyon Review, Hudson Review,* and other literary quarterlies; and of articles to *Esquire, Saturday Evening Post,* and other magazines. Founder and editor, *MSS* (literary magazine).

ADAPTATIONS: An animated film version of *Grendel* called *Grendel, Grendel, Grendel* was produced by Victorian Film Corporation in Australia in 1981. *Nickel Mountain* was loosely adapted for film as *Heavy. In the Suicide Mountains* was adapted by Michael Keck as the musical stage play *A Village Fable,* Dramatic Publishing, 2001.

SIDELIGHTS: John Gardner was a philosophical novelist, a twentieth-century medievalist well versed in the classics, an educator, and an opinionated critic. Described by *Village Voice* contributor Elizabeth Stone as "Evel Knievel at the typewriter," Gardner was an advocate of conservation of values from the past, yet he also maintained a lifelong love-hate relationship with "the rules." Though he championed the moral function of literature, his long hair, leather jacket, and motorcycle classed him with the nonconformists of the baby boom generation. The typical conflict in Gardner's work pits individual freedom against institutions that dominate by means of cultural "myths." In Gardner's novels and stories, Paul Gray summarized in *Time,* "Gardner sets conflicting metaphysics whirling, then records the patterns thrown out by their lines of force. One situation consistently recurs, . . . an inherited past must defend itself against a plotless future."

Gardner's novels have provoked a wide range of critical responses, but, unlike many academic fictions, also gained him a large audience, three even going on to become bestsellers. "Very few writers, of any age, are alchemist enough to capture the respect of the intellectual community *and* the imagination of others who lately prefer [Jacqueline] Susann and [Judith] Krantz. Based on critical acclaim, and sales volume, it would seem that this man accomplished both," Craig Riley wrote in *Best Sellers.* As Carol A. MacCurdy reported in the *Dictionary of Literary Biography Yearbook, 1982,* "Many critics consider *Grendel* (1971) a modern classic, *The Sunlight Dialogues* an epic of the 1970s, and *October Light* a dazzling piece of Americana." *October Light* won the National Book Critics Circle Award for fiction in 1976.

Gardner's notes on *Morte D'Arthur, Sir Gawain and the Green Knight,* and the Gawain poet have helped younger readers appreciate these classics, while also drawing from the author's knowledge of medieval literature. Gardner's retellings of ancient stories for children are fairy tales retold with original twists, "hip" tales in which familiar characters speak in modern cliches or where unlikely contemporary characters are revived by the magic of the past. For example, in *Dragon, Dragon, and Other Timeless Tales* losers win and heroes lose. "Kings prove powerless, young girls mighty. The miller wins the princess, but she proves to be a witch. Tables are turned this way and that, with consequences that are hilarious and wonderful," Jonathan Yardley related in the *New York Times Book Review.* Like most of Gardner's fairy tales, *In the Suicide Mountains*—the story of three outcasts who find happiness after hearing some old folktales—is for adults as well.

Gardner, who always worked on several book projects at a time, did not publish his novels in the order that they were completed. His first published novel, *The Resurrection,* traces a philosophy professor's thoughts after he learns his life will be shortened by leukemia. As David Cowart observed in the *Dictionary of Literary Biography,* "The book asks the question Gardner would ask in every succeeding novel: how can existential man—under sentence of death—live in such a way

as to foster life-affirming values, regardless of how ultimately provisional they may prove?" *The Resurrection* introduces features that recur in other books by Gardner: an embedded second narrative, usually a "borrowed" text; a facility with fictional techniques; and an emotional impact Cowart described as "harrowing."

Gardner's second published novel, *The Wreckage of Agathon,* showcases his skill as an antiquarian, as a writer who can bring forward materials from ancient history and weave them into "a novel transcending history and effectively embracing all of it, a philosophical drama that accurately describes the wreckage of the twentieth century as well as of Agathon, and a highly original work of imagination," according to Christopher Lehmann-Haupt in the *New York Times.* Built of mostly dialogue, *The Wreckage of Agathon* reveals its author's "manic glee in disputation," or "delight in forensic and rhetorical flashiness for its own sake," as Cowart observed. The novel's themes include the relation between individuals and the social orders they encounter. *The Wreckage of Agathon* "delineates the mental motion of the individual as sacred, whether he's a seer or not . . . and it exuberantly calls into question society's categorical insistances—the things brought into being at our own expense to protect us against ourselves, other people, and, putatively, other societies," as Paul West wrote in the *New York Times Book Review.*

The Sunlight Dialogues also grapples with this theme. In a *Washington Post Book World* review, Geoffrey Wolff called this novel "an extended meditation on the trench warfare between freedom and order." The Sunlight Man—a policeman-turned-outlaw embittered by the loss of his family—and Police Chief Fred Clumly, who is obsessed with law and order, duel to the death in this novel. Emerging in the conflict between them is Gardner's examination of how these two forces impinge on art. Wolff commented, "While all men wish for both—freedom and order—the conflict between them is dramatized by every decision that an artist makes. The artist will do what he will. . . . No: the artist does what he must, recognizes the limits, agrees to our rules so that we can play too. No; . . . it's *his* cosmos. And so it goes."

Gardner's well-known *Grendel* retells the *Beowulf* tale from the monster's point of view. This new take on the sea of the familiar hero myth allows the author a canvas on which to fathom new insights into the conflict between order and chaos. In the *New York Times,* Richard Locke explained how the uncivil behavior of "civilized" man contributes to Grendel's murderous career:

"Though twice he attempts to shed his monsterhood, become human, join these other verbal creatures, . . . he's misunderstood on both occasions, and the rat-like humans attack him in fear. So, racked with resentment, pride and vengeful nihilism, outraged by mankind's perversity (for the noble values of the poet's songs are betrayed in a trice by the beery warlords), Grendel commences his cynical war." Though confirmed in cynicism, the monster remains haunted by the words of the Shaper, the poet who revives inspiration and hope in the hearts of his listeners. In this way, Gardner demonstrated the power of art and its role in Western culture.

Nickel Mountain: A Pastoral Novel explores again the complex relationship between order and chaos, particularly as they relate to human responsibility for events in a world that seems to give random accident free play. Narrator Henry Soames, proprietor of an all-night diner, has a ringside seat to the "horror of the random," to cite Cowart, in the lives of his patrons. Slow-moving and dominated by routine, the pastoral life around the diner is interrupted by a series of fatal accidents, including auto wrecks and house fires, as well as emotions sparked by Soames' love for a young woman. Touching Soames more closely is the man who fell to his death on the stairs while recoiling from the diner-owner's shout. Debates ensue about limits to the assignment of blame, and some of Gardner's characters express the belief that the assignment of guilt, though painful, is preferable to viewing themselves as victims of mere chance. "Here, as in his other fiction," wrote Michael Wood in the *New York Review of Books,* "Gardner shows a marvelous gift for making *stories* ask balanced, intricate questions, for getting his complex questions into tight stories."

Henry's bout with guilt in *Nickel Mountain* has its roots in a personal tragedy Gardner suffered early in his life. At age eleven the author was at the wheel of a tractor which ran over and killed his seven-year-old brother David. Though it was an accident, Gardner believed he could have prevented it. Daily flashbacks to the accident troubled him until he wrote "Redemption," a 1979 story based on his memory of the accident. Because writing this story demanded concentration on the scene in order to take narrative control of it, Gardner's terror was diffused. However, the question of human responsibility versus chance continued to surface in many of Gardner's novels and stories, suggesting that this question had become, for him, a habit of mind.

What functions as an internal conflict in *Nickel Mountain* is openly debated in Gardner's next bestseller. *October Light* pits American conservativism against liberalism via a seventy-year-old Vermont farmer and his eighty-year-old feminist sister. In a characteristic rage about declining morals, James Paige shoots Sally's television set and locks her into an upstairs room. While the pair shout their arguments through the closed door, Sally finds a store of apples in the attic and parts of a trashy book about marijuana smugglers, *The Smugglers of Lost Soul's Rock,* in which she find parallels in the plot to her conflict with James. More vulnerable to the old man's intimidating anger is James's son Richard, who commits suicide. Gardner exposes the regrettable stubbornness of both sides of their conflict and at the same time implies the paucity of absurdist literature in the "trashy" parody of postmodern literature Sally reads.

By the novel's end, James has revised his opinions to accommodate a wider range of sensibility. "In *October Light,* then," reasoned Cowart, "we have a rustic world where the same horrors obtain as in the black-comic, nihilistic, 'smart-mouth satirical' novels typified by *Smugglers,* but Gardner convinces us that James Page can, at the age of seventy-two, come to self-knowledge—and that the thawing of this man's frozen heart holds much promise for all people who, bound in spiritual winter, have ever despaired of the spring."

While writing *Mickelsson's Ghosts,* Gardner deliberately tried to make the novel radically different from his prior works. The result, by comparison, said Curt Suplee of the *Washington Post,* "is a highbrow potboiler. . . . And it takes a wide-bodied and fast-moving narrative to carry all Gardner's themes, aiming them at the totalitarian threats in modern culture (metaphorically embedded in the Mormons and tax men) and a grand theological synthesis." As Gardner once explained to Suplee, "The two sort of big ghosts in the thing are [Friedrich] Nietzsche and [Martin] Luther: Luther's saying none of your works mean anything; and Nietzsche's saying works are everything. And if you get those two things together, you have courtly love. The lover does the most that he can possibly do, and then the grace of the lady saves him."

The title character of *Mickelsson's Ghosts* is a philosophy professor who is troubled with a proliferation of "ghosts." The farm on which he has taken refuge from the world is haunted by apparitions of its previous owners, including Mormonism founder Joseph Smith and the still-living Hell's Angel gang member who sold the professor the farm. Harassed by the Internal Revenue Service and the Sons of Dan—a fictional group of fanatic assassins—Mickelsson is haunted by his own crimes. After a teen he sleeps with gets pregnant, he robs an elderly man, hoping to pay the girl not to have an abortion, but during the robbery his victim dies of a heart attack. Should Mickelsson think of himself as the murderer of the elderly miser? This and other questions of ethics—including how to assess the worth of individual human lives, are the center of what Jack Miles dubbed a "huge and ambitious book" in the *Los Angeles Times Book Review*.

In addition to novels, Gardner wrote a number of thought-provoking works on the purpose and craft of fiction, and his criticism was hailed—as were his novels—as "disturbing." *On Moral Fiction*, written in part before Gardner's own novels were published, contains many blunt and occasionally contradictory statements that negatively assess the works of other major novelists. Gardner's view is sometimes overstated, understated, or unclear, and some took his judgments as insults, causing certain critics to evaluate Gardner's own creative works from a fighting stance. Other critics have forgiven the book its faults because they find merit in Gardner's overall assessment about the essentially humane quality of great literature.

On Becoming a Novelist expresses Gardner's thoughts about his vocation and also outlines what it takes to be a professional novelist. Most important, he claims, are "drive"—an unyielding persistence to write and publish; and faith—confidence in one's own abilities and belief in one's eventual success. The book also restates its author's moral aesthetic. *Los Angeles Times Book Review* contributor Richard Rodriguez was struck by Gardner's passionate rejection of fictions that substitute "inconclusiveness," "pointlessly subtle games," or obsessive "puzzle-making" for essential storytelling. A similar work, Gardner's *The Art of Fiction: Notes on Craft for Young Writers* "originated as the so-called 'Black Book,' an underground text passed from hand to hand in university creative-writing departments," Stuart Schoffman explained in the *Los Angeles Times Book Review*. John L'Heureux remarked in the *New York Times Book Review* that "Gardner was famous for his generosity to young writers, and *The Art of Fiction* is his posthumous gift to them."

Twelve years after Gardner's death in a motorcycle accident, a volume of his literary reviews and essays was published as *On Writers and Writing*. The collection includes Gardner's critical response to the fiction of John Steinbeck, William Styron, John Cheever, Walker Percy, and Bernard Malamud, among others, as well as an autobiographical essay and a posthumously discovered plan for *The Sunlight Dialogues*. According to William

Hutchings in *World Literature Today*, "Gardner's essays are remarkable for his astringent intelligence, his pugnaciousness, his lucid style, and his relentless pontifications about The True Nature of Art and the 'great persons' who create it." Commenting on Gardner's extreme "seriousness" and daunting standards, *New York Times Book Review* contributor Brooke Allen concluded of the late author and scholar: "what Gardner always sought was great art, something to place alongside Melville and Tolstoy, the literary yardsticks against which he continually measured lesser writers. Needless to say, he was usually disappointed, therefore unnecessarily harsh in his judgements."

BIOGRAPHICAL AND CRITICAL SOURCES:

BOOKS

Bellamy, Joe David, editor, *The New Fiction: Interviews with Innovative American Writers*, University of Illinois Press, 1974, pp. 169-193.

Burns, Alan, and Charles Sugnet, *The Imagination on Trial: British and American Writers Discuss Their Working Methods*, Allison & Busby (London, England), 1981.

Chavkin, Allan, *Conversations with John Gardner*, University Press of Mississippi (Jacksonville, MS), 1990.

Contemporary Literary Criticism, Thomson Gale (Detroit, MI), Volume 2, 1974, Volume 3, 1975, Volume 5, 1976, Volume 7, 1977, Volume 8, 1978, Volume 10, 1979, Volume 18, 1981, Volume 28, 1984, Volume 34, 1985.

Cowart, David, *Arches and Light: The Fiction of John Gardner*, Southern Illinois University Press (Urbana, IL), 1983.

Dictionary of Literary Biography, Volume 2: *American Novelists since World War II*, Thomson Gale (Detroit, MI), 1978.

Dictionary of Literary Biography Yearbook, 1982, Thomson Gale (Detroit, MI), 1983.

Ekelund, Bo G., *In the Pathless Forest: John Gardner's Literary Project*, Coronet Books, 1994.

Henderson, Jeff, editor, *Thor's Hammer: Essays on John Gardner*, University of Central Arkansas Press, 1985.

Howell, John M., *John Gardner: A Bibliographical Profile*, Southern Illinois University Press (Urbana, IL), 1980.

Howell, John M., *Understanding John Gardner*, University of South Carolina Press, 1993.

Morace, Robert A., *John Gardner: An Annotated Secondary Bibliography,* Garland Publishing (New York, NY), 1984.

Morace, Robert A., and Kathryn Van Spanckeren, editors, *John Gardner: Critical Perspectives,* Southern Illinois University Press (Urbana, IL), 1982.

Nutter, Ronald Grant, *A Dream of Peace: Art and Death in the Fiction of John Gardner,* Peter Lang (New York, NY), 1997.

Plimpton, George, editor, *Writers at Work: The Paris Review Interviews,* Viking (New York, NY), 1981.

Short Story Criticism, Thomson Gale (Detroit, MI), Volume 7, 1991.

Winther, Per, *The Art of John Gardner: Instruction and Exploration,* State University of New York Press (Albany, NY), 1992.

PERIODICALS

Atlantic, May, 1977, pp. 43-47; January, 1984.
Best Sellers, April, 1984.
Chicago Review, spring, 1978, pp. 73-87.
Chicago Tribune, March 16, 1980; April 13, 1980.
Chicago Tribune Book World, May 24, 1981; June 13, 1982; April 1, 1984.
Choice, October, 1994, p. 280.
Contemporary Literature, autumn, 1979, pp. 509-512.
Critique, number 2, 1977, pp. 86-108.
Esquire, January, 1971; June, 1982.
Los Angeles Times Book Review, May 30, 1982; December 5, 1982; June 12, 1983; May 30, 1982; February 12, 1984.
Midwest Quarterly, summer, 1979, pp. 405-415.
Mosaic, fall, 1975, pp. 19-31.
National Review, November 23, 1973.
New Republic, February 5, 1977; March 10, 1979, pp. 25, 28-33.
Newsweek, December 24, 1973; April 11, 1977.
New York Review of Books, March 21, 1974; June 24, 1982.
New York Times, September 4, 1970; November 14, 1976; December 26, 1976; January 2, 1977.
New York Times Book Review, November 16, 1975; March 23, 1980; May 17, 1981; May 31, 1981; June 20, 1982; February 26, 1984; July 20, 1986; March 27, 1994, p. 26.
New York Times Magazine, July 8, 1979, pp. 13-15, 34, 36-39.
Paris Review, spring, 1979, pp. 36-74.
Prairie Schooner, winter, 1980-81, pp. 70-93.
Sewanee Review, summer, 1977, pp. 520-531.
Time, January 1, 1973; December 30, 1974; December 20, 1976.

Times Literary Supplement, October 23, 1981; October 22, 1982; July 29, 1983.
Village Voice, December 27, 1976.
Washington Post, July 25, 1982; March 1, 1983.
Washington Post Book World, December 24, 1972; March 23, 1980; May 3, 1981; May 14, 1982.
World Literature Today, autumn, 1994, p. 819.

*   *   *

GARDNER, John Champlin, Jr.
See GARDNER, John

*   *   *

GARDNER, Miriam
See BRADLEY, Marion Zimmer

*   *   *

GARDONS, S.S.
See SNODGRASS, W.D.

*   *   *

GARNER, Alan 1934-

PERSONAL: Born October 17, 1934, in Cheshire, England; son of Colin and Marjorie Garner; married Ann Cook, 1956 (marriage ended); married Griselda Greaves, 1972; children: (first marriage) Adam, Ellen, Katharine; (second marriage) Joseph, Elizabeth. *Education:* Attended Magdalen College, Oxford.

ADDRESSES: Home—Blackden, Holmes Chapel, Cheshire CW4 8BY, England.

CAREER: Author; writer and director of documentary films. *Military service:* British Army; became second lieutenant.

MEMBER: Portico Library Club (Manchester, England).

AWARDS, HONORS: Carnegie Medal, 1967, and Guardian Award, 1968, both for *The Owl Service;* Lewis Carroll Shelf Award, 1970, for *The Weirdstone of Brisingamen;* first prize, Chicago International Film

Festival, for *Images,* 1981; Mother Goose Award for *A Bag of Moonshine,*1987; Phoenix Award, Children's Book Association, 1996, for *The Stone Book.*

WRITINGS:

The Weirdstone of Brisingamen: A Tale of Alderley, Collins (London, England), 1960, published as *The Weirdstone: A Tale of Alderley,* F. Watts (New York, NY), 1961, revised edition, Walck (New York, NY), 1969, reprinted, Magic Carpet Books (San Diego, CA), 1998.

The Moon of Gomrath, Walck (New York, NY), 1963, published as *The Moon of Gomrath: A Tale of Alderley,* Magic Carpet Books, (San Diego, CA), 1998.

Elidor, Walck (New York, NY), 1965, reprinted, Magic Carpet Books (San Diego, CA), 1999.

Holly from the Bongs, Collins (London, England), 1966.

The Owl Service, Walck (New York, NY), 1967, reprinted, Magic Carpet Books (San Diego, CA), 1999.

The Old Man of Mow, illustrated by Roger Hill, Doubleday (New York, NY), 1967.

(Editor) *A Cavalcade of Goblins,* illustrated by Krystyna Turska, Walck (New York, NY), 1969, published as *The Hamish Hamilton Book of Goblins,* Hamish Hamilton (London, England), 1969.

Red Shift (also see below), Macmillan (New York, NY), 1973.

The Breadhorse, Collins (London, England), 1975.

The Guizer, Greenwillow Books (New York, NY), 1976.

The Stone Book, Collins (London, England), 1976.

Tom Fobble's Day, Collins (London, England), 1977.

Granny Reardun, Collins (London, England), 1977.

The Aimer Gate, Collins (London, England), 1978.

The Golden Brothers, Collins (London, England), 1979.

The Girl of the Golden Gate, Collins (London, England), 1979.

The Golden Heads of the Well, Collins (London, England), 1979.

The Princess and the Golden Mane, Collins (London, England), 1979.

Alan Garner's Fairytales of Gold, Philomel Books (New York, NY), 1980.

The Lad of the Gad, Collins (London, England), 1980, Philomel Books (New York, NY), 1981.

Alan Garner's Book of British Fairytales, Collins (London, England), 1984.

A Bag of Moonshine (folk stories), Delacorte (New York, NY), 1986.

The Stone Book Quartet, Dell (New York, NY), 1988.

(Reteller) *Jack and the Beanstalk,* illustrated by Julek Heller, Doubleday (New York, NY), 1992.

Once upon a Time, Though It Wasn't in Your Time, and It Wasn't in My Time, and It Wasn't in Anybody Else's Time. . . ., Dorling Kindersley (New York, NY), 1993.

The Alan Garner Omnibus (contains *Elidor, The Weirdstone of Brisingamen,* and *The Moon of Gomrath*), Lions, 1994.

(Reteller) *Little Red Hen,* illustrated by Norman Messenger, D.K. Publishers (New York, NY), 1996.

Strandloper, Harvill Press (London, England), 1996.

Lord Flame (play), Harvill Press (London, England), 1996.

Pentecost (play), Harvill Press (London, England), 1997.

The Voice That Thunders, Harvill Press (London, England), 1997.

(Reteller) *The Well of the Wind,* D.K. Publishers (New York, NY), 1998.

Thursbitch, Harvill (London, England), 2003.

Also author of play *Holly from the Bongs,* 1965, and of dance drama *The Green Mist,* 1970; author of libretti for *The Bellybag* (music by Richard Morris), 1971, and *Potter Thompson* (music by Gordon Crosse), 1972; author of plays *Lamaload,* 1978, *Lurga Lom,* 1980, *To Kill a King,* 1980, *Sally Water,* 1982, and *The Keeper,* 1983; author of screenplays for documentary films *Places and Things,* 1978, and *Images,* 1981, and for feature film *Strandloper,* 1992; author of film adaptation of *Red Shift,* 1978. Member of International Editorial Board, Detskaya Literatura Publishers (Moscow), 1991—.

SIDELIGHTS: Considered among the most important children's authors of the later twentieth century, British author Alan Garner is noted for his use of folk traditions and the multiple layers of meaning contained in his stories. His early books, including *The Weirdstone of Brisingamen: A Tale of Alderley, The Moon of Gomrath,* and *Elidor,* are reminiscent of the fantasy literature popularized by J.R.R. Tolkien. With more recent works as *The Owl Service* and *The Stone Book Quartet,* however, Garner's interest in fantasy has become more closely enmeshed with the realistic English landscape of his childhood, and his efforts to preserve the folk tales and cultural heritage of his native England have been cited as exemplary by several reviewers.

Born into a family of craftsmen who have lived for several generations near Alderley Edge in Cheshire, England, Garner proved unsuited for pursuing the way of life that had been in his family for many years. Following an education at Manchester Grammar School, Garner attended Magdalen College, Oxford, where he read classics. Returning to Cheshire without completing his degree, he began working on his first work of fiction, *The Weirdstone of Brisingamen.* His development as a writer was closely related to his embrace of his Cheshire homeland and dialect, reflecting what Roderick McGillis in the *Dictionary of Literary Biography* called his "romantic quest to rediscover the mother tongue."

Though Garner was once considered a "children's" author, the increasing complexity of his stories has led many reviewers to reevaluate their original assessment of his work. For many, the turning point in his status was the publication of *The Owl Service,* an eerie tale of supernatural forces that interweaves ancient symbolism from Welsh folklore with a modern plot and original details. A story "remarkable not only for its sustained and evocative atmosphere, but for its implications," *The Owl Service* is "a drama of young people confronted with the challenge of a moral choice; at the same time it reveals, like diminishing reflections in a mirror, the eternal recurrence of the dilemma with each generation," according to a writer in *Children's Book World.* A critic from the *Christian Science Monitor* described it as "a daring juxtaposition of legend from the *Mabinogion,* and the complex relationship of two lads and a girl [in which] old loves and hates are . . . reenacted. Mr. Garner sets his tale in a Welsh valley and touches with pity and terror the minds of the reader who will let himself feel its atmosphere. This is not a book 'for children'; its subtle truth is for anyone who will reach for it." A writer for the *Times Literary Supplement* echoed this sentiment, noting that with *The Owl Service* "Garner has moved away from the world of children's books and has emerged as a writer unconfined by reference to age-groups; a writer whose imaginative vein is rich enough to reward his readers on several different levels."

In an essay excerpted in the *Times Literary Supplement,* Garner himself alluded to the many levels of meaning in his work. Speaking of his readers, he explained: "The age of the individual does not necessarily relate to the maturity. Therefore, in order to connect, the book must be written for all levels of experience. This means that any given piece of text must work at simple plot level, so that the reader feels compelled to turn the page, if only to find out what happens next; and it must also work for me, and for every stage between. . . . I try to write onions."

One book by Garner that is so complex that some critics have viewed it as almost impenetrable is *Red Shift,* a novel comprised of three different stories with separate sets of characters who are linked only by a Bronze Age axe-head, which functions as a talisman, and a rural setting in Cheshire. Composed almost wholly of dialogue, *Red Shift* jump-cuts from the days of the Roman conquest to the seventeenth century to the present time. Writing in *Horn Book,* Aidan Chambers compared the book to "a decorated prism which turns to show—incident by incident—first one face, then another. In the last section, the prism spins so fast that the three faces merge into one color, one time, one place, one set of people, one meaning." Michael Benton believed that *Red Shift* "expresses the significance of place and the insignificance of time. . . . Certainly in style and structure the book is uncompromising: the familiar literary surface of the conventional novel is stripped away and one is constantly picking up hints, catching at clues, making associations and allowing the chiselled quality of the writing to suggest new mental landscapes."

Despite the fact that Garner's novels are difficult, especially for young American readers unfamiliar with the local British dialects he employs so freely, Garner "takes his craft very seriously, gives far more time to each book than the majority of present-day writers and has probably given more thought to the theory and practice of writing for children than anyone else," wrote Frank Eyre in *British Children's Books in the Twentieth Century.*

Derived from the folklore of the British Isles, Garner's *A Bag of Moonshine* presents twenty-two short stories that some have described as fables of human cunning and folly. Critics have praised Garner's use of the folk tradition, including what E.F. Bleiler in the *Washington Post Book World* termed "fascinating rustic and archaic turns of phrase." Neil Philip concurred in the *Times Educational Supplement,* observing that "Garner has taken a number of lesser-known English and Welsh stories and, as it were, set them to music, establishing in each text a tune or cadence based on local speech patterns." Also a unique retelling of folk tales for children, Garner's *Once upon a Time* presents "The Fox, the Hare, and the Cock," "The Girl and the Geese"—both Russian tales—and "Battibeth," which Joanne Schott of *Quill & Quire* described as "a surrealistic and dreamlike story of a girl's search for her mother's missing knife."

Alan Garner's Fairytales of Gold employs the author's successful technique of drawing upon the plots and themes of traditional stories and then embellishing this material with a highly original use of language and detail. The collection presents four English tales: "The Golden Brothers," "The Girl of the Golden Gate," "The Three Golden Heads of the Well," and "The Princess and the Golden Mane." Reviewers observed that Garner's retellings maintain the general moral perspective, along with many of the thematic tenets of the original stories: the magic power of words, the use of incantations, the motif of fantastic quests, and the morality of kindness rewarded and evil punished. "Garner's interest is in reanimating a tradition of British stories; he laments the passing of traditional fairy tales that were meant for the whole family, not just the children," commented Roderick McGillis in the *Dictionary of Literary Biography.* "The fairy tales he recreates are a link to the British past, and, as he writes, 'a healthy future grows from its past.'"

With *The Stone Book,* Garner presents a "quartet" of interrelated stories depicting four generations of a working-class family in Cheshire, England, spanning the mid-nineteenth-century through the World War II era. Set in Victorian England, the first volume of the series, *The Stone Book,* tells the story of a young girl who begins to learn the significance of history, cultural meaning, and time when her father takes her to a remote cave and tells her to "read" the ancient paintings on the wall. "The ultimate idea [of the book] shines through with an elemental wisdom," asserted Paul Heins in *Horn Book,* noting that the book reflects "the continuity of life, the perception of a collective past." *Granny Reardun,* the second volume of the series, treats the theme of family and history through another angle, depicting a boy who decides to abandon his grandfather's stone masonry trade in favor of apprenticeship to a blacksmith. The saga continues with the final stories of the quartet, *The Aimer Gate,* in which the destructive impact of World War I is addressed, followed by *Tom Fobble's Day,* a coming-of-age story in which a young boy acquires the courage and confidence to sled down one of the highest hills he can find. Although reviewers occasionally question the accessibility of Garner's historical setting and English idiom to contemporary American children, *The Stone Book* has consistently received high praise for the multilayered quality of its treatment of the theme of family history. Offering a laudatory assessment of the series in *Times Literary Supplement,* Margaret Meek commented: "In the Stone Book Quartet we have moved away from a kind of nineteenth-century writing which is still found in books for twentieth-century children. This is a book of our day, for all its Victorian and Edwardian settings."

Reviewing Garner's *The Well of the Wind,* a reviewer for *Publishers Weekly* called the piece "a thought-provoking fantasy full of enchantment," in which a

quest taken by abandoned siblings ends in the brother and sister finding their parents. In *Booklist* reviewer Stephanie Zvirin commented that *The Well of the Wind* "is pure fantasy, and the language, lyrical and quiet, is replete with imagery that blossoms outward" from the plot. *Thursbitch* unveils an eighteenth-century mystery surrounding the death of a packman in the snow. The body is found eerily surrounded by a woman's footprints. M. John Harrison, reviewing the novel for the London *Guardian,* commented that, as a demanding novel, *Thursbitch* "isn't a story that takes life lightly, nor does it expect to be taken lightly in turn."

Garner's 1997 essay collection *The Voice That Thunders* is a work that Shelley Cox described in a *Library Journal* review as "an informal autobiography," one that contains both talks and lectures. In *Commonweal* Daria Donnelly praised the collection, noting that while Garner consistently "extends the reach of children's literature," in his essays in particular "he argues that the rise of a separate sphere called children's literature has had spirit-wasting effects. It has put adults beyond the reach of myth and tales that they urgently need." In addition, Donnelly noted, according to Garner "it has left children vulnerable to the didactic and the reductive in both literature and the teaching of literature."

BIOGRAPHICAL AND CRITICAL SOURCES:

BOOKS

British Children's Books in the Twentieth Century, Dutton (New York, NY), 1971.
Contemporary Literary Criticism, Volume 17, Thomson Gale (Detroit, MI), 1981.
Dictionary of Literary Biography, Volume 161: *British Children's Writers since 1960, First Series,* Thomson Gale (Detroit, MI), 1996.

PERIODICALS

Booklist, March 1, 1981, p. 963; August 1998, p. 2006.
Books for Keeps, May, 1987, p. 15.
Children's Book World, November 3, 1968.
Children's Literature in Education, March, 1974.
Christian Science Monitor, November 2, 1967.
Commonweal, April 7, 2000, Daria Donnelly, review of *The Voice That Thunders,* p. 23; June 16, 2000, p. 26.
Globe and Mail (Toronto, Ontario, Canada), April 4, 1987.

Guardian, October 18, 2003, M. John Harrison, review of *Thursbitch.*

Horn Book, October, 1969, p. 531; February, 1970, p. 45; October, 1973; December, 1976, p. 636; April, 1979, p. 192; October, 1979, p. 533.

Kirkus Reviews, December 1, 1993, p. 1523.

Library Journal, December 15, 1970, p. 4349; October 15, 1998, p. 70.

New York Times Book Review, October 22, 1967, p. 62; October 28, 1973; July 22, 1979.

Observer (London, England), October 7, 1979, p. 39.

Publishers Weekly, September 14, 1998, p. 68.

Quill & Quire, January, 1994, p. 39.

School Library Journal, October, 1976, p. 116; March, 1981, p. 132; March, 1982, p. 157; April, 1987, p. 94; March, 1994, p. 215.

Spectator, April 12, 1975, p. 493.

Times Educational Supplement, December 5, 1986, p. 25.

Times Literary Supplement, May 25, 1967; November 30, 1967; September 28, 1973; March 25, 1977; December 2, 1977; September 29, 1978; November 30, 1984; November 28, 1986, p. 1346, December 5, 1995; May 24, 1996, p. 24.

Tribune Books (Chicago, IL), November 10, 1985.

Village Voice, December 25, 1978.

Washington Post Book World, July 8, 1979; November 10, 1985; November 9, 1986, p. 19; November 8, 1992, p. 11.

*   *   *

GASS, William H. 1924-
(William Howard Gass)

PERSONAL: Born July 30, 1924, in Fargo, ND; son of William Bernard and Claire (Sorensen) Gass; married Mary Patricia O'Kelly, June 17, 1952; married Mary Alice Henderson, September 13, 1969; children: (first marriage) Richard G., Robert W., Susan H.; (second marriage) Elizabeth, Catherine. *Education:* Kenyon College, A.B., 1947; Cornell University, Ph.D., 1954.

ADDRESSES: Home—6304 Westminster Pl., St. Louis, MO 63130. *Office*—International Writers Center, Washington University, Campus Box 1071, 1 Brookings Dr., St. Louis, MO 63130-4899. *Agent*—Lynn Nesbit, International Creative Management, 40 West 57th St., New York, NY 10019. *E-mail*—iwl@artsci.wustl.edu.

CAREER: College of Wooster, Wooster, OH, instructor in philosophy, 1950-54; Purdue University, Lafayette, IN, assistant professor, 1954-60, associate professor,

1960-66, professor of philosophy, 1966-69; Washington University, St. Louis, MO, professor of philosophy, 1969-79, David May Distinguished University Professor in the Humanities, beginning 1979, now emeritus, director of International Writers Center, 1990-2000. Visiting lecturer in English and philosophy, University of Illinois, 1958-59. Member of Rockefeller Commission on the Humanities, 1978-80; member of literature panel, National Endowment for the Arts, 1979-82. *Military service:* U.S. Navy, 1943-46; served in China and Japan; became ensign.

MEMBER: PEN, American Philosophical Association, American Academy and Institute of Arts and Letters (fellow, 1983—), American Academy of Arts and Sciences (fellow, 1982—).

AWARDS, HONORS: Longview Foundation Award in fiction, 1959, for "The Triumph of Israbestis Tott"; Rockefeller Foundation grant for fiction, 1965-66; Standard Oil Teaching Award, Purdue University, 1967; Sigma Delta Chi Best Teacher Award, Purdue University, 1967 and 1968; *Chicago Tribune* award for Big-Ten teachers, 1967; Indiana University Writers' Conference Award for Fiction, 1968; Guggenheim fellowship, 1969-70; Alumni Teaching Award, Washington University, 1974; National Institute for Arts and Letters prize for literature, 1975; Pushcart Prize, 1976, 1983, 1987, 1992; American Academy and Institute of Arts and Letters National Medal of Merit for fiction, 1979; National Book Critics Circle award for criticism, 1986, for *The Habitations of the Word: Essays;* Getty Scholar, 1993; PEN/Faulkner Award for Fiction and American Book Award, both 1996, for *The Tunnel;* National Book Critics Circle criticism award, 1997, for *Finding a Form;* Lifetime Achievement Award, The Lannan Foundation Literary Awards, 1997; National Book Critics Circle award for criticism, and PEN/Spielvogel Diamonstein Award for the art of the essay from the PEN American Center, both for *Tests of Time: Essays,* 2003. D.Litt., Kenyon College, 1974 and 1985; D.Litt., George Washington University, 1982; D.Litt., Purdue University, 1985.

WRITINGS:

FICTION

Omensetter's Luck (novel), New American Library (New York, NY), 1966, reprinted, Penguin Books (New York, NY), 1997.

In the Heart of the Heart of the Country (short stories), Harper (New York, NY), 1968, revised edition, David R. Godine (Boston, MA), 1981.

Willie Masters' Lonesome Wife (novella; first published in *TriQuarterly* magazine, 1968), Knopf (New York, NY), 1971, reprinted, Dalkey Archive Press (Normal, IL), 1998.

The First Winter of My Married Life (short stories), Lord John Press (Northridge, CA), 1979.

Culp (short stories), Grenfell Press (New York, NY), 1985.

The Tunnel (novel), Ticknor & Fields (New York, NY), 1994.

Cartesian Sonata and Other Novellas, Knopf (New York, NY), 1998.

NONFICTION

Fiction and the Figures of Life, Knopf (New York, NY), 1970.

(Author of introduction) *The Geographical History of America,* Random House (New York, NY), 1973.

On Being Blue: A Philosophical Inquiry, David R. Godine (Boston, MA), 1975.

The World within the Word (essays), Knopf (New York, NY), 1978, Basic Books, 2000.

(With Peter Eisenman) *The House VI Book,* David R. Godine (Boston, MA), 1980.

The Habitations of the Word: Essays, Simon & Schuster (New York, NY), 1984.

Words about the Nature of Things, Washington University (St. Louis, MO), 1985.

A Temple of Texts, Washington University (St. Louis, MO), 1990.

Fifty Literary Pillars: A Temple of Texts: An Exhibition to Inaugurate the International Writers Center, Special Collections, Olin Library, Washington University (St. Louis, MO), 1991.

Finding a Form: Essays, Knopf (New York, NY), 1996.

(Editor, with Lorin Cuoco) *The Writer in Politics,* Southern Illinois University Press (Carbondale, IL), 1996.

(Contributor) *Catherine Wagner: Art & Science, Investigating Matter,* Washington University Gallery of Art, 1996.

Art and Science: Investigating Matter, Nazraeli Press (St. Louis, MO), 1996.

(With Johanna Drucker) *The Dual Muse: The Writer as Artist, the Artist as Writer* (essays), John Benjamins (Philadelphia, PA), 1997.

(Contributor) *Sabina Ott: Everywhere There Is Somewhere,* Forum for Contemporary Art (St. Louis, MO), 1997.

Reading Rilke: Reflections on the Problems of Translation, Knopf (New York, NY), 1999.

(Editor, with Cuoco) *Literary St. Louis: A Guide,* Missouri Historical Society Press (St. Louis, MO), 2000.

(Editor, with Cuoco) *The Writer and Religion,* Southern Illinois University Press (Carbondale, IL), 2000.

(Contributor) *Three Essays,* Missouri Historical Society Press, 2000.

(Editor) Robert Burton and Holbrook Jackson, *The Anatomy of Melancholy,* New York Review of Books, Inc., 2001.

Tests of Time (essays), Alfred A. Knopf (New York, NY), 2002.

(Author of afterword) Desiderius Erasmus, *Praise of Folly,* translated by Clarence H. Miller, Yale University Press, 2003.

OTHER

Interview with William Gass (sound recording), American Audio Prose Library, 1981.

Old Folks: William Gass Reading "The Tunnel" (sound recording), American Audio Prose Library, 1981.

Gerald Early and William H. Gass Reading from Their Work (sound recording), 1993.

Conversations with William H. Gass, edited by Theodore G. Ammon, University Press of Mississippi (Jackson, MS), 2003.

Contributor to numerous periodicals, including *New York Review of Books, New York Times Book Review, New Republic, Nation, TriQuarterly, Salmagundi,* and to philosophical journals. William Gass's manuscripts have been collected in the Washington University Library.

SIDELIGHTS: "Both as an essayist and as a writer of fiction, William Gass has earned the reputation of being one of the most accomplished stylists of his generation," wrote Arthur M. Saltzman in *Contemporary Literature.* Gass, who is the director of the International Writers Center at Washington University, is a principal advocate of the primacy of language in literature and of the self-referential integrity of literary texts. *Times Literary Supplement* reviewer Robert Boyers contended that Gass's fictions—consisting of novels, novellas, and short stories—"give heart to the structuralist enterprise," while his essays "may be said to promote the attack on realist aesthetics." Viewed as a whole, Boyers concluded, Gass's work constitutes "the most vigorous anti-realist literary 'programme' we have had in our time."

A philosopher by training, Gass "maintains an art-for-art's-sake 'ethic' of infinite aesthetic value, in a structure of the sublime grotesque, as his principle of creativity," to quote *Criticism* contributor Reed B. Merrill. Merrill added: "His interest lies in the pleasures of the imagination, in model making, and in aesthetic projections composed in the face of an all-pervasive determinism." Whatever his views, Gass remains one of the most respected creative literary minds in modern American letters. In the *New York Times Book Review*, Robert Kiely noted that the author "has written some of the freshest and most finely disciplined fictional prose to have appeared in America since World War II . . . The unlikely combination of criticism, philosophy and metaphorical inventiveness has resulted in a kind of poetry." *New York Times* correspondent Christopher Lehmann-Haupt perhaps best summarized Gass's sensibility by declaring: "For three decades now, he has been saying that the words in a worthwhile work of fiction do not describe a world outside that fiction; instead those words embody the fiction and the fiction embodies the words."

Although born in Fargo, North Dakota, Gass grew up primarily in Warren, Ohio, the son of an alcoholic mother and a father who was crippled by arthritis. His schooling at Kenyon College was interrupted by his service as an ensign in the Navy in World War II. He returned to Kenyon to receive a bachelor's degree in philosophy in 1947. According to Larry McCaffery in the *Dictionary of Literary Biography,* "Gass was a voracious reader, his tastes focusing on such literary formalists as James, Faulkner, Joyce and—somewhat later—the three writers who would probably most directly influence his own writing career: [Rainer Maria] Rilke, Gertrude Stein, and [Paul] Valery." He also attended Cornell as a graduate student, later working with Max Black studying the philosophy of language and the theory of metaphor. He taught philosophy at the College of Wooster and eventually received his Ph.D. from Cornell in 1954. At that point, he began teaching at Purdue University, remaining there for fifteen years.

Gass's training in the philosophy of language under Black manifests itself in his later work, principally in a sense of the musical and intellectual nature of words, sentences, and paragraphs. *Los Angeles Times Book Review* correspondent Jonathan Kirsch observed that the author "does not merely celebrate language; quite the contrary, he is gifted with the nagging intellectual curiosity that prompts a precocious child to take apart a pocket watch to see what makes it tick." In the *Saturday Review,* Brom Weber commented on the fusion of fiction and philosophy in Gass's view. "Gass holds that philosophy and fiction are alike in that both are fictional constructions, systems based on concepts expressed linguistically, worlds created by minds whose choice of language specifies the entities and conditions comprising those worlds," Weber explained. "The reality of these fictional worlds does not depend upon correspondence with or reflection of other worlds, such as the socio-physical one customarily regarded as the 'real' world. Consequently, such concepts as cause and effect—designed to explain the 'real' world—are not necessarily relevant to a fictional world if its creator's language does not encompass causality." Kiely put it more succinctly when he suggested Gass holds that "philosophy and fiction are both 'divine games,' that they do not so much interpret reality as contribute to it."

To call Gass's opinion on fiction a "theory" is perhaps to overstep the bounds of his intentions. He told the *Southwest Review* that especially in his own fiction, he is "not interested in trying to write according to some doctrine." He continued: "When I'm writing fiction, it's very intuitive, so that what happens, or what I do, or how it gets organized, is pretty much a process of discovery, not a process of using some doctrine that you can somehow fit everything into." Gass merely feels that fictions should constitute their own worlds of words and not necessarily attempt to represent some external reality—a position consistent with postmodernism. Weber noted that the author "is dissatisfied with 'character,' 'plot,' 'realism,' and similar conceptual terms that relate fiction to more than itself, and dislikes explication and paraphrase as analytic methods that superimpose 'meaning' upon fiction." Boyers elaborated: "We all know what Gass is writing against, including the tiresome use of novels for purposes of unitary moral uplift and penetrating 'world-view.' What he detests is the goody sweepstakes, in which works of art are judged not by their formal complexity or nuances of verbal texture but by their ability to satisfy easy moral imperatives." The critic declared that, as essayist and fiction writer, Gass "has had some hand in discrediting the kind of righteous moralism that so corrupts ordinary apprehension of the literary arts."

"The esthetic aim of any fiction is the creation of a verbal world, or a significant part of such world, alive through every order of its Being," Gass declared in *Fiction and the Figures of Life.* "The artist's task is therefore twofold. He must show or exhibit his world, and to do this he must actually make something, not merely describe something that might be made." Gass is calling for a literature that makes demands on both its creator and its readers; reaching beyond reportage, it is its own reality unfolding on the page. In *Critique: Studies in Modern Fiction,* Richard J. Schneider claimed that Gass "suggests that any philosophic separation of spirit from body, reason from emotion, experience from innocence, and words from deeds is destructive of life. He reminds us (and we need reminding) that fiction, like poetry, should not merely mean but, above all, be." *New York Times Book Review* contributor Frederic Morton addressed the ways in which Gass's fictions reflect this concept. Gass, noted Morton, "chooses the small gray lulls in life: rural twilights, small-town still-lifes, shadowed backyards. From them he draws dolor and music and a resonance touching us all. Gass is, in fact, a virtuoso with homely textures. They are the perfect foils for the nightmare leaps of his language. . . . In brief, Gass engenders brand-new abrupt vulnerabilities. We read about the becalmed Midwest, about farmers mired in their dailiness, and realize too late that we've been exposed to a deadly poetry."

Omensetter's Luck, Gass's first novel, was "immediately recognized as a stunning achievement," according to Larry McCaffery in the *Dictionary of Literary Biography.* Published in 1966 after numerous rejections, the book established the unique verbal qualities that would come to be associated with all of Gass's work. The novel resists summarization; set in an Ohio river town, it explores the relationship between Brackett Omensetter, a happily unself-conscious "prelapsarian Adam," to quote McCaffery, and two self-conscious and thoughtful men, Henry Pimber and Jethro Furber. A *Newsweek* correspondent called the book "a masterpiece of definition, a complex and intricate creation of level within level, where the theme of Omensetter's luck becomes an intense debate on the nature of life, love, good and evil, and finally, of death. . . .[It] is a story of life and death in the little countries of men's hearts." Richard Gilman offered a different interpretation in *The Confusion of Realms.* The novel, wrote Gilman, "*is* Gass's prose, his style, which is not committed to something beyond itself, not an instrument of an idea. In language of amazing range and resiliency, full of the most exact wit, learning and contemporary emblems, yet also full of lyric urgency and sensuous body, making the most extraordinary juxtapositions, inventing, coining, relaxing at the right moments and charging again when they are over, never settling for the rounded achievement or the finished product, he fashions his tale of the mind, which is the tale of his writing a novel."

Given the difficulty Gass endured trying to find a publisher for *Omensetter's Luck,* he must have been immensely gratified by the critical reception the work received once it found its way into print. Gilman has called it "the most important work of fiction by an American in this literary generation . . . marvelously original, a whole Olympic broad jump beyond what almost any other American has been writing, the first full replenishment of language we have had for a very long time, the first convincing fusion of speculative thought and hard, accurate sensuality that we have had, it is tempting to say, since [Herman] Melville." *Nation* reviewer Shaun O'Connell described *Omensetter's Luck* as "a difficult, dazzling first novel, important in its stylistic achievement and haunting in its dramatic evocation of the most essential human questions." Not every assessment was entirely favorable, however. In his *Bright Book of Life: American Novelists and Storytellers from Hemingway to Mailer,* Alfred Kazin stated: "Everything was there in *Omensetter's Luck* to persuade the knowing reader of fiction that here was a great step forward: the verve, the bursting sense of possibility, the gravely significant atmosphere of contradiction, complexity of issue at every step. But it was all in the head, another hypothesis to dazzle the laity with. Gass had a way of dazzling himself under the storm of his style." Conversely, *Harper's* reviewer Earl Shorris praised Gass's stylistic achievement. *Omensetter's Luck,* Shorris concluded, is, "page after page, one of the most exciting, energetic, and beautiful novels we can ever hope to read. It is a rich fever, a parade of secrets, a novel as American as [Mark Twain's] *Huckleberry Finn* and as torturously comic as [James Joyce's] *Ulysses.*"

Gass followed *Omensetter's Luck* with *In the Heart of the Heart of the Country,* a short story collection "whose highly original form exactly suits its metafictional impulses," to quote McCaffery. McCaffery described the book as a development of the related themes of isolation and the difficulties of love, through the use of experimental literary forms. The characters "control their lives only to the extent that they can organize their thoughts and descriptions into meaningful patterns. Not surprisingly, then, we come to know them mainly as linguistic rather than psychological selves, with their actions usually less significant to our understanding of them than the way they project their inner selves through language." Critics once again praised the volume as a significant contribution to American letters. *Hudson Review* correspondent Robert Martin Adams noted that Gass's techniques, "which are various and imaginative, are always in the service of vision and feeling. Mr. Gass's stories are strict and beautiful pieces of writing without waste or falsity or indulgence." In the *New Republic,* Richard Howard wrote: "This is a volume of fictions which tell the truth, and speak even beyond the truth they tell; it is in that outspokenness, the risk of leaving something standing in his mind, that the authority of William Gass persists." *Nation* contributor Philip Stevick contended that *In the Heart of the Heart of the Country* "finally amounts to an eccentric and ingratiating book, like no other before it, full of grace and wit, displaying a mind in love with language, the human body, and the look of the world."

No Gass work reveals "a mind in love with language" more clearly than *Willie Masters' Lonesome Wife.* Merrill felt that the piece is "perhaps [Gass's] best work to date . . . Structurally, it is clear from the beginning that the subject of this book is the act of creation, and that [the narrator] Babs is William Gass's 'experimental structure' composed of language and imagination. The book *is* literally Babs. The book is a woman from beginning to end. The covers are the extrinsic flesh, the pages are the intrinsic contents of Babs's consciousness—her interior world. It would be difficult to find a better example of the use of structural principles than in Gass's stylistic combination of form and content in his book." In a *Critique* essay, McCaffery called the novella "a remarkably pure example of metafiction" and added: "As we watch 'imagination imagining itself imagine,' . . . we are witnessing a work self-consciously create itself out of the materials at hand—words. As the best metafiction does, *Willie Masters' Lonesome Wife* forces us to examine the nature of fiction-making from new perspectives. If Babs (and Gass) have succeeded, our attention has been focused on the act of reading words in a way we probably have not experienced before. The steady concern with the *stuff* of fiction, words, makes Gass's work unique among metafictions which have appeared thus far." *New York Review of Books* contributor Michael Wood observed that the work reveals "a real urgency, a powerful vision of the loneliness inherent in writing . . . and of writing as a useful and articulate image for loneliness of other kinds."

Gass's magnum opus, *The Tunnel,* took him nearly 30 years to write. He began the novel in 1966, publishing portions of it in a number of literary journals such as the *Review of Contemporary Fiction,* and as "fine press books," according to Steven Moore in the *Review of Contemporary Fiction.* It is the story of William Frederick Kohler, "fat and fifty-something . . . a bitter man, but a literate one," according to Moore. Kohler has almost completed *his* magnum opus, *Guilt and Innocence in Hitler's Germany.* All that remains is the introduction, but he is unable to write it. Instead, he begins to write his own life story, which is what readers of *The Tunnel* end up reading. At one point in the story, Kohler begins digging a tunnel (hence the title) in his basement. The act, though it seems to have no real purpose,

consumes the historian, taking him ever farther from any hope of finishing the introduction. In an interview with Tobin Harshaw of the *New York Times Book Review,* Gass said of his protagonist, "Better to have him on the page than inside of you." According to Harshaw, Gass "describes *The Tunnel* as an exploration of 'the inside of history'—the ambiguity and confusion hidden beneath any intellectual attempt at understanding the past."

Gass's standing as a writer and the impact that his long-awaited novel had in the literary community is evident in the depth and passion of the critical response to it. A number of reviewers lauded Gass's continuing gift for language and creating a world within the text. Noted Moore, "The sheer beauty and bravura of Gass's sentences are overwhelming, breathtaking; the novel is a pharaoh's tomb of linguistic treasures." *New Republic* reviewer Robert Alter observed: "The line between reality and textuality blurs, and everything turns into text. . . . [We are] constantly reminded by Gass of the textual artifice of the words that we are reading. Much of this is done typographically. There are sketches, cartoons, diagrams, printer's symbols, a dozen varieties of typefaces." As for the structure that emerges from Gass's craft, Alter commented, " *The Tunnel* is loose, unimpeded, free-associative flow. The principle of artful selection is renounced. The basic rhetorical form of the novel is the run-on catalog." For this reason, Moore warned that readers who "prefer their prose straight are advised to look elsewhere." Michael Dirda in *Washington Post Book World* offered a similar evaluation. Calling *The Tunnel* "an extraordinary achievement, a literary treat," he continued: "For 650 pages one of the consummate magicians of English prose pulls rabbits out of sentences and creates shimmering metaphors before your very eyes. He dazzles and amazes. But be warned: He does so on his own terms and some readers may be confused, bored or repulsed."

These "repulsive" aspects of *The Tunnel* and its loose structure are the focus of a number of reviews that seek to calculate the balance of the novel's merits and faults. Sven Birkerts found that the work "is a vast bog of uneven surface and unmeasured depth in which lie embedded, fully preserved, perceptions, memories, breathtaking cadenzas of longing, and stunning detailings that have been rendered with the precision of a Nabokov." Yet, he added in an *Atlantic Monthly* article, "*The Tunnel* is at the same time a dyspeptic slugfest, a den of vituperation, a vast catalogue of hatreds, a place where innocence is defeated and turned upon itself." And, finally, according to a *Publishers Weekly* reviewer, "In this endless ramble of a novel, Gass . . . though here, as always, possessed of a bewitching and spectacularly fluid and allusive style, fails to find a suitable home for his narrator's wickedly dyspeptic views of history, marriage and culture." Alter objected to what he believed to be Gass's attempts to examine Kohler's experience in light of the Holocaust. "Domestic rage, intimidation and resentment are terrible things," allowed the critic, "but they are not the moral or psychological equivalent of being herded into gas chambers and shoveled into furnaces. . . . The real obscenity of his novel is not its hideous language or its scatological imaginings, but its trivialization of the enormity of genocide by absorbing it into the nickel-and-dime nastiness that people perpetrate in everyday life."

Still, the outrage that it stirred up in the world it created with words seemed for other reviewers to be one of the essential features of *The Tunnel,* one which gives it its literary impact. Will Blythe explained in *Esquire,* "*The Tunnel* turns out to be the grand opus of entropy, the anti-epic, the super sulk, the anatomy of failure, the pseudonarrative that peters out in a snit." Blythe continued, "Line by line, paragraph by paragraph, Gass writes brilliantly: aphorisms, lists, curses, metaphors so baroque they have plots. . . . Out of these sentences emerges a ripe, overluscious, deliquescent world, rotten through and through, but so solid that you try to flick the flies off the page." For this reason, reviewers have compared Gass's work to that of a weighty group of literary giants, including Theodore Dreiser, Fyodor Dostoevsky, Thomas Pynchon, James Joyce, and Samuel Beckett. James McCourt in *The Yale Review* maintained, "Reading Gass is like reading Thomas Mann: *The Tunnel's* moral seriousness matches *The Magic Mountain's* and *Doctor Faustus's,* but I find Gass the better writer." As Birkerts put it, "Fashions come and go, and readerships wax and wane, but if a writer has been able to stir syllables to life, he or she has done something permanent, something that goes beyond our judging."

Something so permanent may require time in order to be adequately judged. Although *The Tunnel* was judged worthy of both the PEN/Faulkner Award for Fiction and the American Book Award in 1996, critics such as Moore noted that students will be reaping additional treasures from its pages for years to come. Concluded Moore, "It will take years of study to excavate fully the artistry of *The Tunnel.*"

Whatever the subject at hand, Gass's essays are invariably artistic creations. *Village Voice* reviewer Sam Tanenhaus noted that each piece "is a performance or foray: [Gass] announces a topic, then descants with im-

pressive erudition and unbuttoned ardor for the surprising phrase. The results often dazzle, and they're unfailingly original, in the root sense of the word—they work back toward some point of origin, generally a point where literature departs from the external world to invent a world of its own." Gass may serve as a spokesman for technical experimentation in fiction and for the value of innovative form, but his nonfiction also "asks us to yield ourselves in loving attentiveness to the being of language, poetic word, and concept, as it unfolds and speaks through us," according to Jeffrey Maitland in *Modern Fiction Studies.* V.S. Pritchett offered a similar view in the *New Yorker:* "Gass is a true essayist, who certainly prefers traveling to arriving, who treats wisdom as a game in which no one wins. . . . His personality, his wit and affectations are part of the game." Kiely, on the other hand, discovered a common core in Gass's meditations. The critic contended that "by means of startling metaphor and philosophical cajolery . . . [Gass] does the same thing in each essay: he calls our attention to art." The "art" to which attention is called is one that resists ease and proves imagination, beginning and ending with itself. "Gass is not 'ordering experience,' sending us on to higher morality," explained Shorris. "He is not documenting anything. The work is there, and the work is beautiful. The experience of it is a significant and exciting ordeal from which we cannot emerge unchanged."

The cumulative impression left by Gass's essays is, to quote Kiely, "that of a man thinking." Gass calls his whole imagination into play and then develops his obsessions stylistically with complicated flights of prose. *New Republic* essayist Robert Alter deemed Gass "clearly a writer willing to take chances" with a "freewheeling inventiveness." Alter suggested, however, that the "casting aside of inhibitions also means that unconscious materials are constantly popping through the surface of the writing, often in ways that subvert its effectiveness." *New York Times Book Review* correspondent Denis Donoghue also admitted a certain discomfort with some of Gass's assertions. Still, Donoghue claimed, "his sentences, true or false, are pleasures. Reading them, I find myself caring about their truth or error to begin with, but ending up not caring as much as I suppose I ought, and taking them like delicacies of the palate." Boyers remarked: "Gass's books are wonderful books because they raise all of the important aesthetic issues in the starkest and most inventive way. The writing is informed by a moral passion and a love of beautiful things that are never compromised by the author's compulsive addiction to aesthecizing formulations." Wood put it another way: "The writer speaks tenderly to his paper, and, by caring for his words, constructs a world for his readers."

Gass's collection of essays, *Finding a Form,* is loosely grouped around the subject of writing. Essays on the Pulitzer Prize, the present tense, Ezra Pound, and the state of nature emphasize Gass's "belief in the autonomy of language in fiction," according to Christopher Lehmann-Haupt in the *New York Times.* Lehmann-Haupt found this particular volume of essays a mixed bag, noting: "Many in this volume are incisively to the point," while in a few, "the author labors the obvious . . . and wanders aimlessly straining at gnats." Jim Lewis in *Artforum* conceded some faults but believed this collection of essays to be even better than those that have gone before. "Now the paragraphs are modulated with utter confidence, and if the argument sometimes wanders, we know nonetheless that Gass is leading us someplace. *Finding a Form* is a grand peroration, from a man who has thought and studied and written with extraordinary diligence and love of his chosen art." Lewis characterized *Finding a Form* as "a beautiful book, a dignified and deeply ambitious book, a dazzling book, and in many regards a troubling book." The National Book Critics Circle recognized the book's merits and gave it the group's criticism award in 1997. The award was well-earned, according to Lewis, for in his opinion, "As a promoter of difficult pleasures, more precious for being hard won, Gass has no contemporary equal."

In *Reading Rilke: Reflections on the Problems of Translation,* Gass addresses a number of issues pertinent to a deep understanding of the work of German poet Rainer Maria Rilke. The book is a study of Rilke's *Duino Elegies,* and it ranges widely through biography, linguistic and thematic criticism, and a comparison of English translations. Himself a Rilke translator, Gass also includes an essay on the challenges of rendering poetry from one language to another, and the book ends with Gass's own translations of the *Elegies.* In a *Boston Review* piece on *Reading Rilke,* Nicole Krauss addressed the complexity of the project: "Gass, himself an extraordinary writer, is not the sort who can easily hide himself behind the curtain of translation. His lyrical gift is irrepressible, impossible to restrain behind the dam of another's—even Rilke's—stanzas, and the resulting torrent of words makes for an unorthodox initiation into the most elusive of Rilke's poems."

"Few contemporary writers are as well suited to the task of unraveling Rilke and his work as Gass," declared Daniel Mendelsohn in the *New York Times Book Review.* For Mendelsohn, *Reading Rilke* succeeds on many levels, from the purely literary to the novelistic: "You've been given such profound access to the poet's life, and gained so many insights into his poetic language and mission, that the oscillations and conflicts that may once have made Rilke's work look too formidable seem to have resolved themselves into an organic harmony." The critic further praised the volume as "a work that does what the best poetry does: leaves you feeling more human."

As Candyce Dostert noted in the *Wilson Library Bulletin,* to read William Gass "is to accompany an extraordinary mind on a quest for perfection, an invigorating voyage for the strong of heart." Gass is acclaimed equally for his ground-breaking fiction and for the essays that defend the fiction's aesthetics. In the *Dictionary of Literary Biography,* McCaffery stated: "Certainly no other writer in America has been able to combine his critical intelligence with a background as a student of both the literary and philosophical aspects of language and to make this synthesis vital." Edmund White came to a similar conclusion in the *Washington Post Book World.* Gass's "discursive prose always reminds us that he is an imaginative writer of the highest order," White contended. "Indeed, among contemporary American writers of fiction, he is matched as a stylist only by a very select group." Another *Washington Post Book World* contributor, Paul West, observed that Gass's world "*is* words, *his* way of being . . . Gass sings the flux, under this or that commercial pretext, and in the end renders what he calls 'the interplay of genres . . . skids of tone and decorum' into cantatas of appreciative excess. A rare gift that yields startling art."

Gass has given numerous interviews on his art to scholarly periodicals. In one for the *Chicago Review,* he said of his fiction: "What you want to do is create a work that can be read non-referentially. There is nothing esoteric or mysterious about this. It simply means that you want the work to be self-contained. A reader can do with a work what he or she wants. You can't force interpretations and you can't prevent them." He added: "I'm interested in how the mind works—though not always well—by sliding off into sneakily connected pathways, parking the car at another level of discourse, arriving by parachute."

BIOGRAPHICAL AND CRITICAL SOURCES:

BOOKS

Bassoff, Bruce, *The Secret Sharers,* AMS Press (New York, NY), 1983.

Bellamy, Joe David, editor, *The New Fiction: Interviews with Innovative American Writers,* University of Illinois Press (Urbana, IL), 1974.

Bruss, Elizabeth W., *Beautiful Theories: The Spectacle of Discourse in Contemporary Criticism*, Johns Hopkins University Press (Baltimore, MD), 1982.

Contemporary Fiction in America and England, 1950-1970, Thomson Gale (Detroit, MI), 1976.

Contemporary Literary Criticism, Thomson Gale (Detroit, MI), Volume 1, 1973, Volume 2, 1974, Volume 8, 1978, Volume 11, 1979, Volume 15, 1980, Volume 39, 1986.

Contemporary Novelists, 6th edition, St. James Press (Detroit, MI), 1996.

Dictionary of Literary Biography, Volume 2: *American Novelists since World War II*, Thomson Gale (Detroit, MI), 1978.

Gass, William H., *Fiction and the Figures of Life*, Knopf (New York, NY), 1970.

Gilman, Richard, *The Confusion of Realms*, Random House (New York, NY), 1969.

Holloway, Watson L., *William Gass*, Twayne (Boston, MA), 1990.

Kaufmann, Michael, *Textual Bodies: Modernism, Postmodernism, and Print*, Bucknell University Press (Lewisburg, PA), 1994.

Kazin, Alfred, *Bright Book of Life: American Novelists and Storytellers from Hemingway to Mailer*, Little, Brown (Boston, MA), 1973.

McCaffery, Lawrence, *Metafictional Muse: The Works of Robert Coover, Donald Barthelme, and William H. Gass*, University of Pittsburgh Press (Pittsburgh, PA), 1982.

Quendler, Christian, *From Romantic Irony to Postmodernist Metafiction: A Contribution to the History of Literary Self-Reflexivity in Its Philosophical Context*, P. Lang (New York, NY), 2001.

Saltzman, Arthur M., *The Fiction of William Gass: The Consolation of Language*, Southern Illinois University Press (Carbondale, IL), 1986.

Scholes, Robert, *Fabulation and Metafiction*, University of Illinois Press (Champaign, IL), 1979.

Short Story Criticism, Volume 12, Thomson Gale (Detroit, MI), 1993.

Vidal, Gore, *Matters of Fact and of Fiction: Essays 1973-1976*, Random House (New York, NY), 1977.

Ziegler, Heide, editor, *Facing Texts: Encounters between Contemporary Writers and Critics*, Duke University Press (Durham, NC), 1988.

PERIODICALS

America, July 17, 1999, Richard Fusco, "All Too Human," p. 28.

American Scholar, winter, 2000, Susan Miron, review of *Reading Rilke: Reflections on the Problems of Translation*, p. 155.

Atlantic Monthly, June, 1995, p. 122.

Artforum, February, 1997, p. 19.

Book World, November 21, 1971.

Boston Review, summer, 2000, Nicole Krauss, review of *Reading Rilke: Reflections on the Problems of Translation*, p. 58.

Bulletin of Bibliography, July-September, 1974.

Chicago Daily News, February 1, 1969.

Chicago Review, autumn, 1978.

Commonweal, April 19, 1968, p. 154.

Contemporary Literature, summer, 1984.

Criticism, fall, 1976, p. 305.

Critique: Studies in Modern Fiction, December, 1972, p. 89; summer, 1976, p. 36; fall, 1988, p. 49.

Delaware Literary Review, Volume 1, 1972.

Esquire, March, 1995, p. 164.

Falcon, winter, 1972.

Harper's, May, 1972; October, 1978; February, 1990, p. 38.

Harvard Advocate, winter, 1973.

Hudson Review, spring, 1968.

Iowa Review, winter, 1976, p. 96.

Kirkus Reviews, June 15, 1996, p. 873.

Los Angeles Times Book Review, March 24, 1985; January 26, 1986.

Modern Fiction Studies, spring, 1973, p. 97; autumn, 1973; winter, 1977-78; winter, 1983.

Nation, May 9, 1966; April 29, 1968, p. 573; March 22, 1971; January 29, 1977; March 20, 1995, p. 388.

National Review, May 1, 1995, p. 82.

New Republic, May 7, 1966; May 18, 1968; March 20, 1971; October 9, 1976; May 20, 1978; March 11, 1985; March 27, 1995, p. 29; March 24, 1997, p. 25; May 8, 2000, Brian Phillips, "The Angel and the Egotist—The Human Cost of Rilke's Art," p. 38.

Newsweek, April 18, 1966; February 15, 1971; March 25, 1985.

New Yorker, January 10, 1977.

New York Review of Books, June 23, 1966; April 11, 1968; December 14, 1972, p. 12; July 15, 1974; April 17, 1975; May 1, 1975; May 15, 1975; August 5, 1976; October 14, 1976; July 13, 1995, p. 8; December 2, 1999, J.M. Coetzee, "Going All the Way," p. 37.

New York Times, October 4, 1976; February 14, 1985; February 23, 1995, p. C17; December 19, 1996, Christopher Lehmann-Haupt, "How Words Become the Real World," p. B2.

New York Times Book Review, April 17, 1966; April 21, 1968, p. 4; February 21, 1971; November 14, 1971; November 7, 1976, July 9, 1978; June 3, 1979; March 10, 1985; February 26, 1995, p. 1, 18;

March 9, 1997, Maureen Howard, "In the Heart of the Heart of the Text," p. 6; January 30, 2000, Daniel Mendelsohn, "A Line-by-Line Safari," p. 7.

Pacific Coast Philology, Volume 9, 1974.

Paris Review, 1977.

Partisan Review, summer, 1966.

Publishers Weekly, October 3, 1994, p. 13; January 2, 1995, p. 59; June 3, 1996, p. 66.

Record (Washington University in St. Louis), October 9, 2000, "Exhibit Honors Bill Gass on His Retirement."

Review of Contemporary Fiction, spring, 1989; fall, 1991, pp. 78, 88, 102, 124.

Salmagundi, fall, 1973.

Saturday Review, March 2, 1968; September 21, 1968, p. 29; May 29, 1971.

Shenandoah, winter, 1976.

Southern Review, spring, 1967.

Southwest Review, spring, 1979; autumn, 1985.

Studies in Short Fiction, summer, 1980, p. 348; fall, 1989, p. 497.

Sub-Stance, Volume 9, number 2, 1980, p. 56.

Time, November 15, 1976.

Times Literary Supplement, May 18, 1967; August 14, 1969; April 22, 1977; November 3, 1978.

Twentieth Century Literature, May, 1976.

Village Voice, June 4, 1985.

Washington Post Book World, November 21, 1971, p. 12; July 9, 1978; March 3, 1985; February 2, 1992, p. 12; March 12, 1995, p. 1.

Western Humanities Review, winter, 1978.

Wilson Library Bulletin, May, 1985.

World Literature Today, spring, 1979; winter, 1987.

Yale Review, July, 1995, p. 159.

ONLINE

Dalkey Archive Press, http://www.dalkeyarchive.com/ (November 6, 2000), Arthur M. Saltzman, interview with Gass.

*　　*　　*

GASS, William Howard
See GASS, William H.

*　　*　　*

GATES, Henry Louis, Jr. 1950-

PERSONAL: Born September 16, 1950, in Keyser, WV; son of Henry Louis and Pauline Augusta (Coleman) Gates; married Sharon Lynn Adams (a potter), September 1, 1979; children: Maude Augusta Adams, Elizabeth Helen-Claire. *Ethnicity:* "Black." *Education:* Yale University, B.A. (summa cum laude), 1973; Clare College, Cambridge, M.A., 1974, Ph.D., 1979. *Religion:* Episcopalian. *Hobbies and other interests:* Jazz, pocket billiards.

ADDRESSES: Office—Department of Afro-American Studies, Harvard University, 12 Quincy St., Cambridge, MA 02138. *Agent*—Carl Brandt, Brandt & Brandt Literary Agents, Inc., 1501 Broadway, New York, NY 10036.

CAREER: Anglican Mission Hospital, Kilimatinde, Tanzania, general anesthetist, 1970-71; John D. Rockefeller gubernatorial campaign, Charleston, WV, director of student affairs, 1971, director of research, 1972; *Time,* London Bureau, London, England, staff correspondent, 1973-75; Yale University, New Haven, CT, lecturer, 1976-79, assistant professor, 1979-84, associate professor of English and Afro-American Studies, 1984-85, director of undergraduate Afro-American studies, 1976-79; Cornell University, Ithaca, NY, professor of English, comparative literature, and African studies, 1985-88, W.E.B. DuBois Professor of Literature, 1988-90; Duke University, Durham, NC, John Spencer Bassett Professor of English and Literature, 1990—; Harvard University, Cambridge, MA, W.E.B. DuBois Professor of the Humanities, professor of English, chair of Afro-American studies, and director of W.E.B. DuBois Institute for Afro-American Research, 1991—. Virginia Commonwealth, visiting professor, 1987; visiting scholar, Princeton University, Institute for Advanced Study, 2003-2004. Created the Public Broadcasting Service (PBS) television series *The Image of the Black in the Western Imagination,* 1982, and *Wonders of the African World with Henry Louis Gates, Jr.,* 1999.

MEMBER: Council on Foreign Relations, American Antiquarian Society, Union of Writers of the African Peoples, Association for Documentary Editing, African Roundtable, African Literature Association, Afro-American Academy, American Studies Association, Trans-Africa Forum Scholars Council, Association for the Study of Afro-American Life and History (life member), Caribbean Studies Association, College Language Association (life member), Modern Language Association, Stone Trust, Zora Neale Hurston Society, Cambridge Scientific Club, American Civil Liberties Union National Advisory Council, German American Studies Association, National Coalition against Censorship, American Philosophical Society, Saturday Club, New England Historic Genealogical Society, Phi Beta Kappa.

AWARDS, HONORS: Carnegie Foundation Fellowship for Africa, 1970-71; Phelps Fellowship, Yale University, 1970-71; Mellon fellowships, Cambridge University, 1973-75, and National Humanities Center, 1989-90; grants from Ford Foundation, 1976-77 and 1984-85, and National Endowment for the Humanities, 1980-86; A. Whitney Griswold Fellowship, 1980; Rockefeller Foundation fellowships, 1981 and 1990; MacArthur Prize Fellowship, MacArthur Foundation, 1981-86; Yale Afro-American teaching prize, 1983; award from Whitney Humanities Center, 1983-85; Princeton University Council of the Humanities lectureship, 1985; Award for Creative Scholarship, Zora Neale Hurston Society, 1986; associate fellowship from W.E.B. DuBois Institute, Harvard University, 1987-88 and 1988-89; John Hope Franklin Prize honorable mention, American Studies Association, 1988; Woodrow Wilson National Fellow, 1988-89 and 1989-90; Candle Award, Morehouse College, 1989; American Book Award and Anisfield-Wolf Book Award for Race Relations, both 1989, both for *The Signifying Monkey: Towards a Theory of Afro-American Literary Criticism;* recipient of honorary degrees from many universities, including Dartmouth College, 1989, University of West Virginia, 1990, University of Rochester, 1990, Pratt Institute, 1990, University of Bridgeport, 1991 (declined), University of New Hampshire, 1991, Bryant College, 1992, Manhattan Community College, 1992, George Washington University, 1993, University of Massachusetts at Amherst, 1993, Williams College, 1993, Emory University, 1995, Colby College, 1995, Bard College, 1995, and Bates College, 1995; Richard Wright Lecturer, Center for the Study of Black Literature and Culture, University of Pennsylvania, 1990; Potomac State College Alumni Award, 1991; Bellagio Conference Center Fellowship, 1992; Clarendon Lecturer, Oxford University, 1992; Best New Journal of the Year award (in the humanities and the social sciences), Association of American Publishers, 1992; elected to the American Academy of Arts and Sciences, 1993; Golden Plate Achievement Award, 1993; African-American Students Faculty Award, 1993; George Polk Award for Social Commentary, 1993; Heartland Prize for Nonfiction, 1994, for *Colored People: A Memoir;* Lillian Smith Book Award, 1994; West Virginian of the Year, 1995; Humanities Award, West Virginia Humanities Council, 1995; Ethics Award, *Tikkun* (magazine), 1996; Distinguished Editorial Achievement, *Critical Inquiry,* 1996; voted one of the twenty-five most influential Americans, *Time* magazine, 1997; National Humanities Medal, 1998; elected to American Academy of Arts and Letters, 1999; named honorary citizen of Benin, 2001; W.D. Weatherford Award; elected chair of the Pulitzer Prize Board, April, 2005.

WRITINGS:

Figures in Black: Words, Signs, and the Racial Self, Oxford University Press (New York, NY), 1987.

The Signifying Monkey: Towards a Theory of Afro-American Literary Criticism, Oxford University Press (New York, NY), 1988.

Loose Canons: Notes on the Culture Wars (essays), Oxford University Press (New York, NY), 1992.

Colored People: A Memoir, Knopf (New York, NY), 1994.

Speaking of Race, Speaking of Sex: Hate Speech, Civil Rights, and Civil Liberties, New York University Press (New York, NY), 1995.

(With Cornel West) *The Future of the Race,* Knopf (New York, NY), 1996.

Thirteen Ways of Looking at a Black Man, Random House (New York, NY), 1997.

Wonders of the African World, Knopf (New York, NY), 1999.

(With Cornel West) *The African-American Century: How Black Americans Have Shaped Our Country,* Free Press (New York, NY), 2000.

(Author of text) *Come Sunday: Photographs by Thomas Roma,* Museum of Modern Art (New York, NY), 2002.

Back to Africa, Duke University Press (Durham, NC), 2002.

The Trials of Phillis Wheatley: America's First Black Poet and Her Encounters with the Founding Fathers, BasicCivitas Books (New York, NY), 2003.

America behind the Color Line: Dialogues with African Americans, Warner (New York, NY), 2004.

EDITOR

(And author of introduction) *Black Is the Color of the Cosmos: Charles T. Davis's Essays on Afro-American Literature and Culture, 1942-1981,* Garland Publishing (New York, NY), 1982.

(And author of introduction) Harriet E. Wilson, *Our Nig; or, Sketches from the Life of a Free Black,* Random House (New York, NY), 1983.

(And author of introduction) *Black Literature and Literary Theory,* Methuen (New York, NY), 1984.

(And author of introduction, with Charles T. Davis) *The Slave's Narrative: Texts and Contexts,* Oxford University Press (New York, NY), 1986.

(Editor, with James Gibbs and Ketu H. Katrak) *Wole Soyinka: A Bibliography of Primary and Secondary Sources,* Greenwood Press (Westport, CT), 1986.

(And author of introduction) *"Race," Writing, and Difference,* University of Chicago Press (Chicago, IL), 1986.

(And author of introduction) *The Classic Slave Narratives,* New American Library (New York, NY), 1987.

(And author of introduction) *In the House of Oshugbo: A Collection of Essays on Wole Soyinka,* Oxford University Press (New York, NY), 1988.

(Series editor) *The Oxford-Schomburg Library of Nineteenth-Century Black Women Writers,* thirty volumes, Oxford University Press (New York, NY), 1988.

W.E.B. DuBois, *The Souls of Black Folk,* Bantam Books (New York, NY), 1989.

James Weldon Johnson, *The Autobiography of an Ex-Coloured Man,* Vintage (New York, NY), 1989.

Three Classic African-American Novels, Vintage (New York, NY), 1990.

Zora Neale Hurston, *Their Eyes Were Watching God,* introduction by Mary Helen Washington, Harper (New York, NY), 1990.

Zora Neale Hurston, *Jonah's Gourd Vine,* introduction by Rita Dove, Harper (New York, NY), 1990.

Zora Neale Hurston, *Tell My Horse,* introduction by Ishmael Reed, Harper (New York, NY), 1990.

Zora Neale Hurston, *Mules and Men,* introduction by Arnold Rampersad, Harper (New York, NY), 1990.

Reading Black, Reading Feminist: A Critical Anthology, Meridian Book (New York, NY), 1990.

Voodoo Gods of Haiti, introduction by Ishmael Reed, Harper (New York, NY), 1991.

The Schomburg Library of Nineteenth-Century Black Women Writers, ten-volume supplement, Oxford University Press (New York, NY), 1991.

(With Randall K. Burkett and Nancy Hall Burkett) *Black Biography, 1790-1950: A Cumulative Index,* Chadwyck-Healey (Teaneck, NJ), 1991.

(With George Bass) Langston Hughes and Zora Neale Hurston, *Mulebone: A Comedy of Negro Life,* HarperPerennial (New York, NY), 1991.

Bearing Witness: Selections from African-American Autobiography in the Twentieth Century, Pantheon Books (New York, NY), 1991.

(With Anthony Appiah) *Gloria Naylor: Critical Perspectives Past and Present,* Amistad (New York, NY), 1993.

(With Anthony Appiah) *Alice Walker: Critical Perspectives Past and Present,* Amistad (New York, NY), 1993.

(With Anthony Appiah) *Langston Hughes: Critical Perspectives Past and Present,* Amistad (New York, NY), 1993.

(With Anthony Appiah) *Richard Wright: Critical Perspectives Past and Present,* Amistad (New York, NY), 1993.

(With Anthony Appiah) *Toni Morrison: Critical Perspectives Past and Present,* Amistad (New York, NY), 1993.

(With Anthony Appiah) *Zora Neale Hurston: Critical Perspectives Past and Present,* Amistad (New York, NY), 1993.

The Amistad Chronology of African-American History from 1445-1990, Amistad (New York, NY), 1993.

(And annotations) *Frederick Douglass: Autobiographies,* Library of America, 1994.

(With Anthony Appiah) *The Dictionary of Global Culture,* Knopf (New York, NY), 1995.

The Complete Stories of Zora Neale Hurston, HarperCollins (New York, NY), 1995.

(With Anthony Appiah) *Identities,* University of Chicago (Chicago, IL), 1996.

(With N.Y. McKay) *The Norton Anthology of African-American Literature,* Norton (New York, NY), 1996.

Ann Petry: Critical Perspectives Past and Present, Amistad (New York, NY), 1997.

Chinua Achebe: Critical Perspectives Past and Present, Amistad (New York, NY), 1997.

Harriet A. Jacobs: Critical Perspectives Past and Present, Amistad (New York, NY), 1997.

Ralph Ellison: Critical Perspectives Past and Present, Amistad (New York, NY), 1997.

Wole Soyinka: Critical Perspectives Past and Present, Amistad (New York, NY), 1997.

Frederick Douglass: Critical Perspectives Past and Present, Amistad (New York, NY), 1997.

The Essential Soyinka: A Reader, Pantheon (New York, NY), 1998.

(Coeditor) *Pioneers of the Black Atlantic: Five Slave Narratives from the Enlightenment, 1772-1815,* Civitas (Washington, DC), 1998.

(Coeditor) *Black Imagination and the Middle Passage,* Oxford University Press (New York, NY), 1999.

(Coeditor) *The Civitas Anthology of African-American Slave Narratives,* Civitas/ Counterpoint (Washington, DC), 1999.

Wonders of the African World, Random House (New York, NY), 1999.

Slave Narratives, Library of America (New York, NY), 2000.

Harvard Guide to African-American History, Harvard University Press (Cambridge, MA), 2001.

Schomburg Library of Nineteenth-Century Black Women Writers, Oxford University Press (New York, NY), 2002.

Hannah Crafts, *The Bondwoman's Narrative,* Warner (New York, NY), 2002.

(With Anthony Appiah) *Africana: The Encyclopedia of the African and African-American Experience,* Running Press (New York, NY), 2003.

*In the House of Oshugbo: Critical Essays on Wole Soy-
    inka,* Oxford University Press (New York, NY),
    2003.
(With Anthony Appiah) *Transition 96,* Soft Skull Press,
    2004.
(With Anthony Appiah) *Transition 97/98,* Soft Skull
    Press, 2004.
(With Evelyn Brooks Higginbotham) *African-American
    Lives,* Oxford University Press (New York, NY),
    2004.

Also editor, with Anthony Appiah, of "Amistad Critical
Studies in African-American Literature" series, 1993,
and editor of the Black Periodical Literature Project.
Advisory editor of "Contributions to African and Afro-
American Studies" series for Greenwood Press (West-
port, CT), "Critical Studies in Black Life and Culture"
series for Garland Press, and "Perspectives on the Black
World" series for G.K. Hall (Boston, MA). General edi-
tor of *A Dictionary of Cultural and Critical Theory;
Middle-Atlantic Writers Association Review.* Coeditor of
Transition. Associate editor of *Journal of American
Folklore.* Member of editorial boards including, *Critical
Inquiry, Studies in American Fiction, Black American
Literature Forum, PMLA, Stanford Humanities Review,*
and *Yale Journal of Law and Liberation.*

SIDELIGHTS: Henry Louis Gates, Jr. is one of the
best-known humanities professors in the United States,
and one of the most respected and controversial scholars in the field of African-American studies. Educated
at Yale and a professor at Harvard, he had a humble
start in Keyser, West Virginia, where the majority of the
population worked for a paper mill. The town was a
strictly segregated community in his youth, but Gates
remembered its strong sense of community in a mostly
positive light in his memoir *Colored People.* Gates's father worked as a loader at the mill, and also as a janitor
for the telephone company. Young Gates excelled in
school, where integration occurred relatively smoothly.
During the tumultuous 1960s, Gates was a young student who was gaining an awareness of Africa from
studying current events. In 1968, he graduated as the
class valedictorian, delivering a commencement address
with a militant tone. He moved on to Potomac State
College of West Virginia University the following autumn, with the thought of going on to medical school.
A professor named Duke Anthony Whitmore saw the
spark of genius in Gates, however, and encouraged him
to apply to top-tier schools. Gates was soon accepted at
Yale University, where he graduated summa cum laude
in 1973. He then traveled to Cambridge University to
earn a master of arts degree. He began his teaching ca-

reer at Yale, and distinguished himself early on by discovering and reissuing an 1859 novel written by a black
woman, titled *Our Nig; or, Sketches from the Life of a
Free Black.* Publication of this work sparked considerable interest in recovering other works by early black
women writers.

Gates moved on to take a post at Cornell University,
and during his tenure there he published the multi-
volume *Schomburg Library of Nineteenth-Century Black
Women Writers,* a landmark work that showed black
women had written their own stories more than had
ever been previously acknowledged. In 1988, he became the W.E.B. DuBois Professor of Literature at Cornell, becoming the first African-American man to hold
an endowed chair at that institution. His star continued
to rise as he moved on to a position at Duke and then
to Harvard University, where he was W.E.B. DuBois
Professor of the Humanities at Harvard and head of its
Afro-American Studies program. Gates breathed new
life and enthusiasm into the program, which at the time
of his arrival had very few students and only one full-
time professor. He hired high-profile lecturers such as
film director Spike Lee and authors Jamaica Kincaid
and Wole Soyinka. Under Gates's leadership, the number of students in the program tripled within a few
years.

Gates had detractors as well as admirers, however. Some
of his colleagues found him to be insufficiently Afro-
centric. He engaged in certain high-profile activities
that were regarded by some as inappropriate self-
promotion, for example, publicly testifying at the obscenity trial of rap group 2 Live Crew, stating that their
extreme lyrics were merely part of an African oral tradition. Still, even those who objected to Gates's flashy
public activities rarely argued with his credentials, or
denied his many important contributions to Afro-
American scholarship, as he has written and edited numerous books of literary and social criticism. According
to James Olney in the *Dictionary of Literary Biography,* Gates's mission is to reorder and reinterpret "the
literary and critical history of Afro-Americans in the
context of a tradition that is fully modern but also continuous with Yoruba modes of interpretation that are
firmly settled and at home in the world of black Americans."

In his approach to literary criticism, Gates is avowedly
eclectic and defines himself as a centrist who rejects extreme positions on either end of the spectrum. Neither
the white, Western tradition nor the African tradition is
superior; they should coexist and inform each other, in

Gates's view. Like the American novelist Ralph Ellison, Gates sees the fluid, indeed porous, relationship between black and white culture in the United States. Gates argues that our conception of the literary canon needs to be enlarged accordingly.

Black Literature and Literary Theory, which Gates edited, is considered by many reviewers to be an important contribution to the study of black literature. Calling it "an exciting, important volume," Reed Way Dasenbrock wrote in *World Literature Today:* "It is a collection of essays . . . that attempts to explore the relevance of contemporary literary theory, especially structuralism and poststructuralism, to African and Afro-American literature. . . . Anyone seriously interested in contemporary critical theory, in Afro-American and African literature, and in black and African studies generally will need to read and absorb this book." R.G. O'Meally wrote in *Choice* that in *Black Literature and Literary Theory* Gates "brings together thirteen superb essays in which the most modern literary theory is applied to black literature of Africa and the U.S. . . . For those interested in [the] crucial issues—and for those interested in fresh and challenging readings of key texts in black literature—this book is indispensable." Finally, Terry Eagleton remarked in the *New York Times Book Review* that "the most thought-provoking contributions to [this] collection are those that not only enrich our understanding of black literary works but in doing so implicitly question the authoritarianism of a literary 'canon.'"

One of Gates's best-known works is *Loose Canons: Notes on the Culture Wars,* in which he discusses gender, literature, and multiculturalism and argues for greater diversity in American arts and letters. Writing in the *Virginia Quarterly Review,* Sanford Pinsker noted that according to Gates "the cultural right . . . is guilty of 'intellectual protectionism,' of defending the best that has been thought and said within the Western Tradition because they are threatened by America's rapidly changing demographic profile; while the cultural left 'demands changes to accord with population shifts in gender and ethnicity.' *Loose Canons* makes it clear that Gates has problems with both positions." "The society we have made," Gates argues in *Loose Canons,* "simply won't survive without the values of tolerance. And cultural tolerance comes to nothing without cultural understanding. . . . If we relinquish the ideal of America as a plural nation, we've abandoned the very experiment that America represents." Writing in the *Los Angeles Times,* Jonathan Kirsch praised the humor and wit that infused Gates's arguments. *Loose Canons,* Kirsch concluded, is "the work of a man who has mastered

the arcane politics and encoded language of the canon makers; it's an arsenal of ideas in the cultural wars. But it is also the outpouring of a humane, witty and truly civilized mind."

Colored People: A Memoir played to a wider audience than did *Loose Canons.* In it, Gates recalls his youth in Piedmont, West Virginia, at a time when the town was becoming integrated. It "explores the tension between the racially segregated past and the integrated modernity that the author himself represents," commented David Lionel Smith in *America.* While affirming the progress brought by desegregation, Gates also laments the loss of the strong, united community feeling that segregation created among blacks—a feeling epitomized in the annual all-black picnic sponsored by the paper mill that provided jobs to most of Piedmont's citizens. Numerous reviewers pointed out the gentle, reminiscent tone of Gates's narrative, but some considered this a weakness in light of the momentous changes Gates lived through. Smith remarked: "From an author of Gates's sophistication, we expect more than unreflective nostalgia." Comparing it to other recent African-American memoirs and autobiographies, he concluded, "Some of them address social issues more cogently and others are more self-analytical, but none is more vivid and pleasant to read than *Colored People.*" *Los Angeles Times Book Review* contributor Richard Eder affirmed that *Colored People* was an "affecting, beautifully written and morally complex memoir," and Joyce Carol Oates, in her *London Review of Books* assessment, described it as an "eloquent document to set beside the grittier contemporary testimonies of black male urban memoirists; in essence a work of filial gratitude, paying homage to such virtues as courage, loyalty, integrity, kindness; a pleasure to read and, in the best sense, inspiring."

Gates wrote *The Future of the Race* with Cornel West, a professor of Afro-American studies at Harvard University. This work contains an essay by Gates, an essay by West, and two essays by black intellectual W.E.B. DuBois, the latter of which are preceded by a foreword by Gates. Writing in the *New York Times Book Review,* Gerald Early noted: "The question . . . that the authors wish to answer—what is their duty to the lower or less fortunate class of blacks?—indicates the black bourgeoisie's inability to understand precisely what their success means to themselves or blacks generally." Early also observed that while "the pieces seem hastily written," Gates's essay is "engagingly witty and journalistic" as well as "charming and coherent."

Gates offers insight into the position of the black male in American society in *Thirteen Ways of Looking at a Black Man.* Through a series of discussions recorded over several years and documented in various magazine articles, Gates brings a broad cross-section of African-American hopes and ideals to the reader's attention. Interviewees include such major black American figures as James Baldwin, Harry Belafonte, Colin Powell, and Bill T. Jones. Writing in *Library Journal,* Michael A. Lutes referred to *Thirteen Ways of Looking at a Black Man* as a "riveting commentary on race in America."

A belief that tolerance proceeds from education and familiarity led Gates to devote himself to working with a variety of media and corporate resources to enlighten the general public about African-American heritage and contributions to society. His efforts in this realm range from writing a set of booklets about black history, distributed at McDonald's restaurants, to creating multi-part television documentaries on black heritage for the Public Broadcasting System (PBS). He also worked with a team of other scholars to fulfil a dream of the late W.E.B. DuBois: to create an answer to the *Encyclopedia Britannica,* called *Encyclopedia Africana* that would take into consideration African influences and contributions to the world. Working with Microsoft, Gates helped to create the CD-ROM version of the *Encyclopedia Africana,* and he also launched *Africana.com,* a Web site that was later sold to AOL Time Warner.

Gates also brought his message to the masses with his PBS television series, *Wonders of the African World with Henry Louis Gates, Jr.* In this program, Gates took viewers on a journey through Africa that illustrated the remains of the great cultures that once flourished on that continent. Contemporary Africa was also explored, and Gates shared his personal experience of the journey. In making the series, Gates hoped to "debunk the myths of Africa being this benighted continent civilized only when white people arrived," as Lorraine Eaton of the *Virginia Pilot* quoted him as saying. He continued: "In fact, Africans had been creators of culture for thousands of years before. These were very intelligent, subtle and sophisticated people, with organized societies and great art."

Gates continued to bring forth newly discovered works by African Americans of early generations, such as *The Bondwoman's Narrative,* a melodramatic story of a slave's life written by Hannah Crafts. More significant than the literary content of the book are the facts and attitudes it reveals within the slaves' world, and the fact that its author was most likely an escaped slave herself. He looked into the life and work of Phillis Wheatley, the first published black poet in the United States, in *The Trials of Phillis Wheatley: America's First Black Poet and Her Encounters with the Founding Fathers.* Reviewing the volume for *Booklist,* Vanessa Bush commented, "Gates brings scholarly insight and a love of black literature to this examination of how Wheatley, the first published African-American poet, has survived the judgment of past and contemporary critics." When first published in 1773, Wheatley's poems stirred up questions of their authenticity among those who could not believe a black person could create poetry. When their authenticity was established, Wheatley's work was attacked on other grounds. "In this slim, lively volume, Gates extols Wheatley's enduring literary significance and Jefferson's contribution to spurring a tradition of black literature that was first aimed at proving equality and came to signify a black aesthetic," concluded Bush.

The stellar make-up of Harvard's African-American studies department was diminished when Anthony Appiah and Cornel West, two of the department's top scholars, announced they would be moving to other universities after disagreements with Harvard's leadership on the direction of the program. Gates chose to remain at Harvard to continue to try to keep the program vital and forward-looking. He was instrumental in restructuring the department, adding five new faculty members, including an African scholar, a linguist, and even an expert on hip-hop. Gates did, however, take a year's leave from Harvard to join the Institute for Advanced Study in Princeton, New Jersey—a so-called "think tank" most famous for its association with Albert Einstein.

BIOGRAPHICAL AND CRITICAL SOURCES:

BOOKS

Contemporary Black Biography, Thomson Gale (Detroit, MI), 2003.
Contemporary Southern Writers, St. James Press (Detroit, MI), 1999.
Dictionary of Literary Biography, Volume 67: *Modern American Critics since 1955,* Thomson Gale (Detroit, MI), 1988.
Notable Black American Men, Thomson Gale (Detroit, MI), 1998.

PERIODICALS

America, December 31, 1994, p. 24.
American Spectator, April-May, 1994, p. 69.

Atlanta Journal-Constitution, November 21, 1999, Michael Skube, "Harvard Don on a Mission to Show Africa in All Its Glory," p. K1; December 6, 2000, John Head, interview with Henry Louis Gates, Jr., p. D1.

Black Issues Book Review, November-December, 2003, Herb Boyd, review of *The Trials of Phillis Wheatley: America's First Black Poet and Her Encounters with the Founding Fathers,* p. 66.

Black Issues in Higher Education, January 17, 2002, "Rift between Harvard Scholars, President Makes National News," p. 14; February 28, 2002, "Gates Ponders Move to Princeton," p. 17; June 5, 2003, "Harvard's Gates to be Visiting Scholar at Princeton Think Tank," p. 14.

Booklist, September 1, 2000, Vanessa Bush, review of *The African-American Century: How Black Americans Have Shaped Our Country,* p. 3; February 15, 2001, Nora Harris, review of *The Norton Anthology of African-American Literature,* p. 1172; November 15, 2001, Candace Smith, review of *Wonders of the African World,* p. 588; June 1, 2003, Vanessa Bush, review of *The Trials of Phillis Wheatley,* p. 1728.

Boston Globe, October 20, 1990, p. 3; May 12, 1991, p. 12; April 23, 1992, p. 70; November 7, 1992, p. 15; December 1, 1992, p. 23; April 29, 1993, p. 53; May 29, 1994, p. A13; April, 2002, Greg Lalas, review of *The Bondwoman's Narrative,* p. 161.

Boston Herald, April 9, 2002, Dana Bisbee, review of *The Bondwoman's Narrative,* p. 45.

Callaloo, spring, 1991.

Chicago Tribune, February 18, 1993, section 5, p. 3; November 18, 1993, section 1, p. 32; July 17, 1994, section 14, p. 3; August 24, 1994, section 5, p. 1.

Choice, May, 1985; March, 1995, p. 1059.

Christian Century, January 19, 1994, pp. 53-54.

Christian Science Monitor, April 10, 1992, p. 11; June 7, 1994, p. 13.

Commonweal, December 18, 1992, pp. 22-23.

Criticism, winter, 1994, pp. 155-161.

Emerge, November, 1990, p. 76.

Guardian (London, England), July 6, 2002, Maya Jaggi, "Henry the First," p. 20.

Humanities Magazine, July-August, 1991, pp. 4-10; March-April, 2002, interview with Henry Louis Gates, Jr., p. 6.

International Herald Tribune, July 17, 2003, Sara Rimer, "Harvard Refocuses Afro-American Unit," p. 7.

Jet, August 27, 2001, *Henry Louis Gates, Jr. Named Honorary Citizen of Benin,* p. 31; January 21, 2002, "Harvard University President Meets with Black Scholars to Mend Rift There," p. 36.

Journal of American Ethnic History, fall, 2000, Donald R. Wright, review of *Black Imagination and the Middle Passage,* p. 78.

Kirkus Reviews, October 1, 2003, review of *America behind the Color Line: Dialogues with African Americans,* p. 1207.

Library Journal, February, 1997; November 1, 2000, review of *The African-American Century,* p. 102; November 15, 2000, Thomas J. Davis, review of *The African-American Century,* p. 80; June 1, 2002, Roger A. Berger, review of *The Bondwoman's Narrative,* p. 147.

London Review of Books, July 21, 1994, pp. 22-23; January 12, 1995, p. 14.

Los Angeles Times, October 29, 1990, p. A20; March 25, 1992, p. E2; June 3, 1994, p. E1; February 6, 2000, review of *Africana,* p. E1.

Los Angeles Times Book Review, May 8, 1994, pp. 3, 12.

New Leader, September 12, 1994, pp. 12-13.

New Literary History, autumn, 1991.

New Republic, July 4, 1994, p. 33; June 16, 1997.

New Statesman & Society, February 10, 1995, p. 43.

New York Review of Books, November 2, 2000, George M. Frederickson, review of *Slave Narratives,* p. 61.

New York Times, December 6, 1989, p. B14; April 1, 1990, section 6, p. 25; June 3, 1992, p. B7; May 16, 1994, p. C16; May 8, 2003, Karen W. Arenson, "Harvard Scholar to Visit Princeton Institute," p. A26; July 16, 2003, Sara Rimer, "Harvard Scholar Rebuilds African Studies Department," p. A16.

New York Times Book Review, December 9, 1984; August 9, 1992, p. 21; June 19, 1994, p. 10; April 21, 1996, p. 7; February 9, 1997; May 12, 2002, Mia Bay, review of *The Bondwoman's Narrative,* p. 30.

New York Times Magazine, April 1, 1990.

Plain Dealer (Cleveland, OH), July 28, 2002, Margaret Bernstein, review of *The Bondwoman's Narrative,* p. J11.

Publishers Weekly, October 16, 2000, review of *The African-American Century,* p. 57; April 1, 2002, review of *The Bondwoman's Narrative,* p. 53.

Rocky Mountain News, May 10, 2002, review of *The Bondwoman's Narrative,* p. 29D.

San Francisco Chronicle, May 20, 2002, Steven Winn, review of *The Bondwoman's Narrative,* p. D1.

Seattle Times, May 5, 2002, John Gamino, review of *The Bondwoman's Narrative,* p. K9.

Spectator, February 18, 1995, pp. 31-32.

Time, April 22, 1991, pp. 16, 18; May 23, 1994, p. 73.

Times Literary Supplement, May 17, 1985; February 24, 1995, p. 26.

Tribune Books (Chicago, IL), July 17, 1994, pp. 3, 5; October 9, 1994, p. 11.

U.S. News and World Report, March, 1992; September 18, 2000, Matthew Benjamin, "Africana Dot Sold," p. 64.

Village Voice, July 5, 1994, p. 82.

Virginian Pilot, January 23, 2000, "Gates Refuses to Yield to Popular Opinions," p. E2.

Virginia Quarterly Review, summer, 1993, pp. 562-568.

Voice Literary Supplement, June, 1985.

Washington Post, October 20, 1990, p. D1; August 11, 1992, p. A17.

Washington Post Book World, July 3, 1983; June 7, 1992, p. 6; May 15, 1994, p. 3.

Washington Times, January 2, 2002, Julia Duin, "Cultural Critic Gates named NEH Lecturer," p. 2.

World Literature Today, summer, 1985.

ONLINE

Salon.com, http://www.salon.com/ (June 16, 1999), Craig Offman, "The Making of Henry Louis Gates, CEO."

*   *   *

GEE, Maggie 1948-
(Maggie Mary Gee)

PERSONAL: Born November 2, 1948, in Poole, Dorset, England; daughter of Victor Valentine and Aileen Mary (Church) Gee; married Nicholas Winton Rankin, August 6, 1983; children: one daughter. *Education:* Somerville College, Oxford, M.A., 1970, M.Litt., 1973; Wolverhampton Polytechnic, Ph.D., 1980.

ADDRESSES: Home—London, England. *Agent*—c/o David Godwin Associates, 55 Monmouth St., London WC2H 9DG, England.

CAREER: Elsevier International Press, Oxford, England, editor, 1972-74; research assistant at Wolverhampton Polytechnic, 1975-79; Northern Arts writer in residence, 1996; Sussex University, visiting fellow, 1986—; writer.

MEMBER: Society of Authors, Campaign for Nuclear Disarmament.

AWARDS, HONORS: Eastern Arts Writing Fellow, University of East Anglia, 1982; named among best young British novelists, 1983; Royal Society of Literature fellow, 1994—; shortlist, Orange Prize for Fiction, 2002, for *The White Family.*

WRITINGS:

Dying, in Other Words (novel), Harvester (Brighton, England), 1981, Faber (Boston, MA), 1984.

(Editor) *Anthology of Writing against War: For Life on Earth,* University of East Anglia (Norwich, England), 1982.

The Burning Book (novel), St. Martin's (New York, NY), 1983.

Light Years (novel), St. Martin's (New York, NY), 1985.

Grace (novel), Heinemann (London, England), 1988, Weidenfeld & Nicolson (New York, NY), 1989.

Where Are the Snows (novel), Heinemann (London, England), 1991, published as *Christopher and Alexandra,* Ticknor & Fields (New York, NY), 1992.

Lost Children (novel), Flamingo (London, England), 1994.

How May I Speak in My Own Voice? Language and the Forbidden (text of lecture), Birkbeck College (London, England), 1996.

The Ice People (novel), Richard Cohen Books (London, England), 1998.

The White Family (novel), Saqi Books (London, England), 2002.

The Flood (novel), Saqi Books (London, England), 2004.

My Cleaner (novel), Saqi Books (London, England), 2005.

Also author of several short stories and a radio play, "Over and Out," 1984. Contributor to *Diaspora City: The London New Writing Anthology,* Arcadia Books, 2003. Contributor to periodicals, including *Daily Telegraph, Sunday Times* (London), and *Times Literary Supplement.*

SIDELIGHTS: Maggie Gee has a reputation as an original and versatile voice in British literature. Her writings have earned comparisons to those of such acclaimed authors as Virginia Woolf, Vladimir Nabokov, and Samuel Beckett, whom she considers her "chief twentieth-century models," she told *Contemporary Novelists.* Gee's work has not been confined to any single genre; she has used the conventions of crime novels and science fiction, for instance, and has established herself as a technically adept experimentalist whose works are introspective, dark, and wryly humorous.

"Gee's importance as a novelist rests on her stylistic innovations and choices of subject matter, which is often political: Gee is, for example, a fierce opponent of nuclear armament," reported Martha Genn in the *Dictionary of Literary Biography.* Gee is also concerned with the environment, race and gender relations, and distinctions between the rich and the poor. Genn noted that Gee is "inventive and artful in the construction of narrative" and that her novels "vary in genre and yet frequently share concerns, including most notably the lasting, profound, and unpredictable effects of the actions and events of individual lives on surrounding persons and sequences of events."

Gee's debut novel, *Dying, in Other Words,* is an unusual thriller populated by a vast array of eccentric characters, including a murderous milkman. Published in 1981, the book begins with a disclaimer by Gee in which she denies that the work is "a serious novel." *Dying, in Other Words* centers on the mysterious death of young writer Moira Penny. Moira's naked body is found outside the window of her Oxford flat—she has apparently committed suicide. As an inordinate number of the dead woman's acquaintances also die under strange circumstances, authorities begin to suspect foul play in Moira's case. An ensuing investigation reveals the true and unexpected nature of Moira's death.

"Penny's suicide is dropped, as it were, into the pool of lives around her and the ripples spread and impinge on the lives of others and, what makes the novel remarkable, on the continuum of the past and present of those lives," related a contributor to *Contemporary Novelists.* Commenting in the *Times Literary Supplement* on the frequent manipulation of narrative prose and monologue in *Dying, in Other Words,* Stoddard Martin remarked, "Some of the surrealistic scenery is vivid, but the thickets surrounding are impenetrable." While some other critics pointed to the novel's extreme self-consciousness and fragmentation as a source of obscurity, they also thought that Gee's first work had brought a provocative new twist to the thriller genre. In a review for the Toronto *Globe and Mail,* Douglas Hill wrote that *Dying, in Other Words* possesses "a cosmic implication, the death of a planet, the extinction of humanity as the reality of everyday imagination. Death and fiction, for Gee, are inseparable."

Gee continues her thematic exploration of death in her 1983 work, an apocalyptic novel titled *The Burning Book,* which uses the genre of the sprawling family saga. Tracing four generations of an English family through both world wars, *The Burning Book* focuses on ordinary people struggling to exist in a world that hovers on the threshold of nuclear destruction. Gee weaves evocations of Hiroshima and Nagasaki into her narrative, imbuing the world of the novel with a sense of bleakness and impending doom. The uninspired, unfulfilled characters—lacking a sense of political and social consciousness—become victims of their own self-absorption and are ultimately annihilated.

Although some reviewers found the text difficult, *The Burning Book* received praise as well. Linda Taylor, writing in the *Times Literary Supplement,* deemed it "an odd kind of novel but a marvelously cogent anti-war statement." The *Contemporary Novelists* essayist noted, "As a nuclear warning the book certainly succeeds; and it succeeds as a work of literature as well." Especially impressed by Gee's descriptive powers, attention to detail, and skillful infusion of the work with a haunting sense of urgency, *New York Times Book Review* contributor Ronald De Feo observed, "At its best, it is a wonderfully inventive saga of dreams and disillusionment." The reviewer added that *The Burning Book*'s "tragic ending is suggestively, almost poetically conveyed, and it is terribly affecting."

Gee's next novel, a touchingly humorous romance titled *Light Years,* chronicles a year in the lives of a middle-aged husband and wife following their breakup. The book's construction—fifty-five chapters divided into twelve sections—mirrors the year of their estrangement. During this time, each engages in a superficial affair, but the self-centered Harold and spoiled, rich Lottie are reunited by the novel's end. In a review for the *Spectator,* Christopher Hawtree theorized that "the effect of *Light Years* is to convey the gravitational forces which, however much they are impeded and however ill-matched the participants might appear, bring people together."

Some critics deemed the plot of *Light Years* overly contrived, but some praised the book as having vivid character portraits and effortless narrative technique. *Dictionary of Literary Biography*'s Henn remarked, "Though Harold and especially Lottie are problematic people, they are rounded and reasonably relatable. While the novel still possesses a complex structure, it is far easier to comprehend than the intricacies of her first novels." Roz Kaveney, writing in the *Times Literary Supplement,* concluded: "This is so fine a novel because so completely a planned and crafted one. . . . The book's posed philosophical view pile[s] up all of human possibility and perception as a barrier against the cold and the dark."

Grace is a thriller with an antinuclear theme; it was inspired by the murder in 1984 of antinuclear activist Hilda Murrell. Its primary characters are an unconventional eighty-five-year-old woman, Grace Stirling, who is a veteran supporter of liberal causes, and her niece Paula Timms, a writer who is involved in the antinuclear movement and is working on a book about Murrell. A British government agent is spying on them, even tailing them on trips. More than Murrell's murder, Henn noted, "the most significant crime in the context of the novel . . . is the global perpetuation of nuclear radiation through nuclear energy and armaments."

Henn thought the novel "occasionally stretches credibility" in pursuit of its political agenda. The *Contemporary Novelists* essayist, though, found *Grace* "an exciting and considerable advance in the art of Gee's novels," as "the threads of the story and the lives they describe gradually and skillfully converge and intermesh" while illuminating Gee's antinuclear theme, which is "fundamental to the story."

Where Are the Snows is about a wealthy, heedless, globe-trotting couple, Christopher and Alexandra Court (whose first names provide the title for the U.S. edition). They bring unhappiness to most of the people in their lives, including their son and daughter, who are teenagers when Christopher and Alexandra take off on an extended journey and grow to troubled adulthood in their parents' absence. The Courts also bring unhappiness to each other, with Alexandra having an extramarital affair and Christopher shooting her lover. And despite all their travels, they miss their chance to see snow, which is vanishing because of global warming.

"The slow but steady eradication from the earth of snowfall mirrors the slow corruption of earthly and personal purity," explained Henn. A *Publishers Weekly* reviewer commented that some readers may find it hard to care about the Courts, but Henn remarked, "It is a measure of Gee's talent that readers are consistently concerned about the fates of her major characters, despite the fact that they are almost always unlikable." The *Publishers Weekly* critic praised the novel overall, calling it "a memorable tale" written "in stylish prose."

In *Lost Children,* it is a child who leaves the parents behind to deal with the loss. Sixteen-year-old Zoe Bennett runs away from home, shocking her mother, Alma, who has always believed their relationship to be an uncommonly good one. The strain leads Alma to separate from her husband, Paul, and further distances her from

their law-student son, Adam, to whom she has never been close. Alma goes into therapy "to explore her childhood as a means of rediscovering the self she lost during marriage and motherhood," reported Mary Scott in *New Statesman and Society.* Therapy leads her to think she may have been sexually abused in girlhood, by her father, her stepfather, or perhaps a stranger; she believes her mother let her down in some way but fails to recognize her own imperfections as a mother to Adam and Zoe.

"The implication of the novel's title," noted Henn, "is that Adam and Zoe are not the novel's only lost children but that all of the characters could be considered as such." Isobel Armstrong, writing in the *Times Literary Supplement,* pointed out that the lost children include "the children our past selves were" and "the actual children, unparented, deprived, frequently abused, who inhabit the urban London of our present." Henn found it typical of Gee that her "focus on individuals takes place simultaneously with her investigation of some breakdown of the social order—primarily homelessness," as numerous homeless people are camped near the London real estate office where Alma works. Gee presents the plight of these people against the background of the self-centered and materialistic attitudes of Alma's coworkers, whom Armstrong described as "small-time yuppies." Armstrong praised Gee's "brilliantly evoked" character portraits and her "cool, lucid writing," concluding that *Lost Children* is a "searching and ambitious novel."

In *The Ice People,* Gee deals with social issues through the science fiction genre. The novel is set in England the middle of the twenty-first century, when a new ice age is on its way. Also in this period, the services once provided by the government have been privatized; disease has devastated the population; class distinctions are sharper than ever; most people are deeply apathetic about politics; and the sexes are largely segregated, voluntarily. For a time, the book's main character and narrator, Saul, is an exception to the latter trend, living with a woman named Sarah. But Saul and Sarah eventually break up, and she moves to a women's community, bringing along their son, Luke. Saul then kidnaps Luke and takes him on a journey with the intended destination of Africa, a location attractive to many so-called ice people from northern lands.

The title also refers, however, to "the present chilly state of love," commented Eric Korn in the *Times Literary Supplement.* Gee "distributes the blame equitably" to both sexes, Korn reported, showing both Saul's and

Sarah's flaws and frailties. He called the novel "stirring, witty, beautifully written" and "mordantly comic, unsparing, politically savvy, a beautifully clear and bracingly nasty vision," concluding, "Anyone who has ever been involved in human relations must take it personally."

Race relations are the concern of *The White Family,* set in a working-class London neighborhood, once exclusively white but now attracting numerous new black and Asian residents, many of them from England's former colonies. The whites—including the Whites, the novel's central family—have been "shocked to find that the Empire had landed on their doorstep," Heather Clark explained in the *Times Literary Supplement.* The neighborhood's changing complexion brings varying responses from the members of the White family—park groundskeeper Alfred; his homemaker wife, May; and their three adult children. Racism brews in some of them, acceptance in others, and emotional barriers go up between them.

Gee uses multiple narrators, a device that generally "enriches our understanding of the Whites' predicament," Clark observed, although she thought the shifts occasionally distracting. She also found "much to admire in the way the novel both implicates and absolves the Whites of their transgressions," as "Gee moves skillfully between compassion and disgust." In London's *Sunday Times,* Margaret Walters wrote that "although Gee's novel adds up to a telling indictment of blind prejudice, she is too fine a writer to lapse into simple pessimism," with some characters "allowed happy or, rather, hopeful, endings." Walters summed up the book as "somberly perceptive" and Gee as "one of our most ambitious and challenging novelists."

BIOGRAPHICAL AND CRITICAL SOURCES:

BOOKS

Contemporary Novelists, 7th edition, St. James Press (Detroit, MI), 2001.
Dictionary of Literary Biography, Volume 207: *British Novelists since 1960, Third Series,* Thomson Gale (Detroit, MI), 1999, pp. 123-130.

PERIODICALS

Globe and Mail (Toronto), February 16, 1985.
New Statesman and Society, April 22, 1994, Mary Scott, review of *Lost Children,* p. 48.

New York Times Book Review, October 14, 1984.
Publishers Weekly, December 13, 1991, review of *Christopher and Alexandra,* p. 46.
Spectator, September 24, 1983, October 5, 1985.
Sunday Times (London), May 12, 2002, Margaret Walters, "Dark Visions of a Black and White World," p. 48.
Times Literary Supplement, July 17, 1981; September 23, 1983; October 4, 1985; April 29, 1994, Isobel Armstrong, "Bloody Parents," p. 20; October 2, 1998, Eric Korn, "Cold Comforts," p. 25; May 3, 2002, Heather Clark, "Empire on the Doorstep," p. 23.
Washington Post, May 2, 1986.

*   *   *

GEE, Maggie Mary
   See GEE, Maggie

*   *   *

GEISEL, Theodor Seuss 1904-1991
   (Dr. Seuss, Theo. LeSieg, Rosetta Stone, a joint pseudonym)

PERSONAL: Surname is pronounced *Guy*-zel; born March 2, 1904, in Springfield, MA; died of cancer, September 24, 1991, in La Jolla, CA; son of Theodor Robert (a superintendent of a public park system) and Henrietta (Seuss) Geisel; married Helen Palmer (an author and vice president of Beginner Books), November 29, 1927 (died, October 23, 1967); married Audrey Stone Diamond, August 6, 1968. *Education:* Dartmouth College, A.B., 1925; graduate study at Lincoln College, Oxford, 1925-26, and Sorbonne, University of Paris.

CAREER: Author and illustrator. Freelance cartoonist, beginning 1927; advertising artist, Standard Oil Company of New Jersey, 1928-41; *PM* (magazine), New York, NY, editorial cartoonist, 1940-42; publicist, War Production Board of U.S. Treasury Department, 1940-42; Random House, Inc., New York, NY, founder and president of Beginner Books imprint, 1957-91. *Life* (magazine), correspondent in Japan, 1954. Trustee, La Jolla, CA, Town Council, beginning 1956. *Exhibitions:*One-man art exhibitions at San Diego Arts Museum, 1950, Dartmouth College, 1975, Toledo Museum of Art, 1975, La Jolla Museum of Contemporary Art, 1976, and Baltimore Museum of Art, 1987. *Military service:* U.S. Army Signal Corps, Information and Education Division, 1942-46; became lieutenant colonel; received Legion of Merit.

MEMBER: Authors League of America, American Society of Composers, Authors, and Publishers (ASCAP), Sigma Phi Epsilon.

AWARDS, HONORS: Academy Award, 1946, for *Hitler Lives,* 1947, for *Design for Death,* 1951, for *Gerald McBoing-Boing,* and 1977, for *Halloween Is Grinch Night;* Randolph Caldecott Honor Award, 1948, for *McElligot's Pool,* 1950, for *Bartholomew and the Oobleck,* and 1951, for *If I Ran the Zoo;* Young Reader's Choice Award, Pacific Northwest Library Association, 1950, for *McElligot's Pool;* Lewis Carroll Shelf Award, 1958, for *Horton Hatches the Egg,* and 1961, for *And to Think That I Saw It on Mulberry Street;* Boys' Club of America Junior Book Award, 1966, for *I Had Trouble in Getting to Solla Sollew;* Peabody Award, 1971, for animated cartoons *How the Grinch Stole Christmas* and *Horton Hears a Who;* Critics' Award, International Animated Cartoon Festival, and Silver Medal, International Film and Television Festival of New York, both 1972, both for *The Lorax;* Los Angeles County Library Association Award, 1974; Southern California Council on Literature for Children and Young People Award, 1974, for special contribution to children's literature; named Outstanding California Author, California Association of Teachers of English, 1976; Roger Revelle Award, University of California— San Diego, 1978; Children's Choice election, 1978; Laura Ingalls Wilder Award, American Library Association, 1980; Dr. Seuss Week proclaimed by state governors, March 2-7, 1981; Regina Medal, Catholic Library Association, 1982; National Association of Elementary School Principals special award, 1982, for distinguished service to children; Pulitzer Prize, 1984, for "special contribution over nearly half a century to the education and enjoyment of America's children and their parents"; PEN Los Angeles Center Award for children's literature, 1985, for *The Butter Battle Book.* Honorary degrees include L.H.D., Dartmouth College, 1956, American International College, 1968, Lake Forest College, 1977; D.Litt., Whittier College, 1980; D.F.A., Princeton University, 1985; D.H.L., University of Hartford, 1986; and L.H.D., Brown University, 1987.

WRITINGS:

UNDER PSEUDONYM DR. SEUSS; SELF-ILLUSTRATED, EXCEPT WHERE NOTED

And to Think That I Saw It on Mulberry Street, Vanguard (New York, NY), 1937.

The 500 Hats of Bartholomew Cubbins, Vanguard (New York, NY), 1938.

The Seven Lady Godivas, Random House (New York, NY), 1939, reprinted, 1987.

The King's Stilts, Random House (New York, NY), 1939.

Horton Hatches the Egg, Random House (New York, NY), 1940.

McElligot's Pool, Random House (New York, NY), 1947.

Thidwick, the Big-hearted Moose, Random House (New York, NY), 1948.

Bartholomew and the Oobleck, Random House (New York, NY), 1949.

If I Ran the Zoo, Random House (New York, NY), 1950.

Scrambled Eggs Super! (also see below), Random House (New York, NY), 1953.

The Sneetches and Other Stories, Random House (New York, NY), 1953.

Horton Hears a Who! (also see below), Random House (New York, NY), 1954.

On beyond Zebra, Random House (New York, NY), 1955.

If I Ran the Circus, Random House (New York, NY), 1956.

Signs of Civilization! (booklet), La Jolla Town Council (La Jolla, CA), 1956.

The Cat in the Hat (also see below), Random House (New York, NY), 1957.

How the Grinch Stole Christmas (also see below), Random House (New York, NY), 1957.

The Cat in the Hat Comes Back!, Beginner Books (New York, NY), 1958.

Yertle the Turtle and Other Stories, Random House (New York, NY), 1958.

Happy Birthday to You!, Random House (New York, NY), 1959, revised as *Happy Birthday to You!: A Pop-Up Book,* paper engineering by William Wolff, 2003.

One Fish, Two Fish, Red Fish, Blue Fish, Random House (New York, NY), 1960.

Green Eggs and Ham, Beginner Books (New York, NY), 1960, adapted by Aristides Ruiz as *Green Eggs and Ham: With Fabulous Flaps and Peel-off Stickers,* Random House (New York, NY), 2001.

Dr. Seuss' Sleep Book, Random House (New York, NY), 1962.

Hop on Pop, Beginner Books (New York, NY), 1963, revised as a board book, 2004.

Dr. Seuss' ABC, Beginner Books (New York, NY), 1963.

(With Philip D. Eastman) *The Cat in the Hat Dictionary, by the Cat Himself,* Beginner Books (New York, NY), 1964.

Fox in Socks, Beginner Books (New York, NY), 1965.

I Had Trouble in Getting to Solla Sollew, Random House (New York, NY), 1965.

Dr. Seuss' Lost World Revisited: A Forward-Looking Backward Glance (nonfiction), Award Books (New York, NY), 1967.

The Cat in the Hat Songbook, Random House (New York, NY), 1967.

The Foot Book, Random House (New York, NY), 1968, adapted as a lift-the-flap book, 2002.

I Can Lick Thirty Tigers Today! and Other Stories, Random House (New York, NY), 1969.

My Book about Me, by Me Myself, I Wrote It! I Drew It! With a Little Help from My Friends Dr. Seuss and Roy McKie, illustrated by Roy McKie, Beginner Books (New York, NY), 1969.

Mr. Brown Can Moo! Can You?, Random House (New York, NY), 1970.

I Can Draw It Myself, Random House (New York, NY), 1970.

The Lorax, Random House (New York, NY), 1971.

Marvin K. Mooney, Will You Please Go Now?, Random House (New York, NY), 1972.

Did I Ever Tell You How Lucky You Are?, Random House (New York, NY), 1973.

The Shape of Me and Other Stuff, Random House (New York, NY), 1973.

Great Day for Up!, illustrated by Quentin Blake, Beginner Books (New York, NY), 1974.

There's a Wocket in My Pocket!, Random House (New York, NY), 1974.

Dr. Seuss Storytime (includes *Horton Hears a Who*), Random House (New York, NY), 1974.

Oh, the Thinks You Can Think!, Random House (New York, NY), 1975.

The Cat's Quizzer, Random House (New York, NY), 1976.

I Can Read with My Eyes Shut, Random House (New York, NY), 1978.

Oh Say Can You Say?, Beginner Books (New York, NY), 1979.

The Dr. Seuss Storybook (includes *Scrambled Eggs Super!*), HarperCollins (New York, NY), 1979.

Hunches in Bunches, Random House (New York, NY), 1982.

The Butter Battle Book (also see below), Random House (New York, NY), 1984.

You're Only Old Once, Random House (New York, NY), 1986.

The Tough Coughs As He Ploughs the Dough: Early Writings and Cartoons by Dr. Seuss, edited by Richard Marschall, Morrow (New York, NY), 1986.

I Am Not Going to Get Up Today!, illustrated by James Stevenson, Beginner Books (New York, NY), 1987.

Oh, the Places You'll Go!, Random House (New York, NY), 1990, revised as *Oh, the Places You'll Pop-Up!,* paper engineering by William Wolff, 2002.

Six by Seuss (includes *And To Think I Saw It on Mulberry Street*), Random House (New York, NY), 1991.

Daisy-Head Mayzie, Random House (New York, NY), 1994.

My Many Colored Days, illustrated by Steve Johnson and Lou Fancher, Knopf (New York, NY), 1996.

What Was I Scared Of?, Random House (New York, NY), 1997.

A Hatful of Seuss (includes *The Sneetches and Other Stories*), Random House (New York, NY), 1997.

Seuss-isms: Wise and Witty Prescriptions for Living from the Good Doctor, Random House (New York, NY), 1997.

Can You Speak Gink?, illustrated by Josie Yee, Random House (New York, NY), 1997.

1 2 3, a Wubbulous Countdown, illustrated by Josie Yee, Random House (New York, NY), 1997.

The Birthday Moose, illustrated by the Thompson Bros., Random House (New York, NY), 1997.

The Big Brag, Random House (New York, NY), 1998.

(With Jack Prelutsky and Lane Smith) *Hooray for Diffendoofer Day!,* Knopf (New York, NY), 1998.

The Grinch Pops Up, Random House (New York, NY), 2002.

How Do You Do?: By Thing One and Thing Two (As Told to the Cat in the Hat), illustrated by Christopher Moroney, Random House (New York, NY), 2003.

Gerald McBoing-Boing Sound Book, Random House (New York, NY), 2003.

Your Favorite Seuss, compiled by Janet Schulman and Cathy Goldmsith, Random House (New York, NY), 2004.

UNDER PSEUDONYM THEO. LESIEG

Ten Apples up on Top!, illustrated by Roy McKie, Beginner Books (New York, NY), 1961.

I Wish That I Had Duck Feet, illustrated by B. Tokey, Beginner Books (New York, NY), 1965.

Come Over to My House, illustrated by Richard Erdoes, Beginner Books (New York, NY), 1966.

The Eye Book, illustrated by Roy McKie, Random House (New York, NY), 1968.

(Self-illustrated) *I Can Write—By Me, Myself,* Random House (New York, NY), 1971.

In a People House, illustrated by Roy McKie, Random House (New York, NY), 1972.

The Many Mice of Mr. Brice, illustrated by Roy McKie, Random House (New York, NY), 1973.

Wacky Wednesday, illustrated by George Booth, Beginner Books (New York, NY), 1974.

Would You Rather Be a Bullfrog?, illustrated by Roy McKie, Random House (New York, NY), 1975.

Hooper Humperdink . . . ? Not Him!, Random House (New York, NY), 1976.

Please Try to Remember the First of Octember!, illustrated by Arthur Cummings, Beginner Books (New York, NY), 1977.

Maybe You Should Fly a Jet! Maybe You Should Be a Vet, illustrated by Michael J. Smullin, Beginner Books (New York, NY), 1980.

The Tooth Book, Random House (New York, NY), 1981.

SCREENPLAYS

Your Job in Germany (documentary short subject), U.S. Army, 1946, released under title *Hitler Lives,* Warner Bros., 1946.

(With wife, Helen Palmer Geisel) *Design for Death* (documentary feature), RKO Pictures, 1947.

Gerald McBoing-Boing (animated cartoon), United Productions of America (UPA)/Columbia, 1951.

(With Allen Scott) *The 5,000 Fingers of Dr. T* (musical), Columbia, 1953.

Also author of screenplays for *Private Snafu* film series, for Warner Bros.

TELEVISION SCRIPTS

How the Grinch Stole Christmas, Columbia Broadcasting System (CBS-TV), first aired December 18, 1966.

Horton Hears a Who, CBS-TV, 1970.

The Cat in the Hat, CBS-TV, 1971.

Dr. Seuss on the Loose, CBS-TV, 1973.

Hoober-Bloob Highway, CBS-TV, 1975.

Halloween Is Grinch Night, American Broadcasting Companies (ABC-TV), 1977.

Pontoffel Pock, Where Are You?, ABC-TV, 1980.

The Grinch Grinches the Cat in the Hat, ABC-TV, 1982.

The Butter Battle Book, Turner Network Television (TNT-TV), 1989.

OTHER

(Illustrator) *Boners,* Viking (New York, NY), 1931.

(Illustrator) *More Boners,* Viking (New York, NY), 1931.

(With Michael Frith, under joint pseudonym Rosetta Stone) *Because a Little Bug Went Ka-Choo!,* illustrated by Frith, Beginner Books (New York, NY), 1975.

Dr. Seuss from Then to Now (museum catalog), Random House (New York, NY), 1987.

The Secret Art of Dr. Seuss, Random House (New York, NY), 1995.

(Illustrator) Alexander Abingdon, *Herrings Go About the Sea in Shawls—,* Viking (New York, NY), 1997.

Contributor of cartoons and prose to magazines, including *Judge, College Humor, Liberty, Vanity Fair,* and *Life.* Editor, *Jack-o'-Lantern* (Dartmouth College humor magazine), until 1925.

The manuscript *The 500 Hats of Bartholomew Cubbins* is housed in the collection of Dartmouth College, Hanover, NH. Other manuscripts are in the Special Collections Department of the University of California Library, Los Angeles.

The author's books have been translated into several languages, including French, Spanish, and Latin.

ADAPTATIONS: Geisel's animated cartoon character Gerald McBoing-Boing appeared in several UPA pictures, including *Gerald McBoing-Boing's Symphony,* 1953, *How Now McBoing-Boing,* 1954, and *Gerald McBoing-Boing on the Planet Moo,* 1956. From 1956-58 McBoing-Boing appeared in his own animated variety show, *The Gerald McBoing-Boing Show,* on CBS-TV. The musical *Seussical,* based on Geisel's works and written by Lynn Ahrens and Stephen Flaherty, was produced on Broadway, 2000. *How the Grinch Stole Christmas* was adapted as a screenplay for a film starring Jim Carrey, Universal, 2000. *The Cat in the Hat* was adapted for film, 2002. *Green Eggs and Ham* was adapted as a musical for children by Robert Kapilow titled *Green Eggs and Hamadeus,* 2003.

SIDELIGHTS: Theodor Seuss Geisel, better known under his pseudonym "Dr. Seuss," was "probably the best-loved and certainly the best-selling children's book writer of all time," wrote Robert Wilson of the *New York Times Book Review.* Geisel entertained several generations of young readers with his zany nonsense books. Speaking to Herbert Kupferberg of *Parade,* Geisel once claimed: "Old men on crutches tell me, 'I've been brought up on your books.'" His "rhythmic verse rivals Lewis Carroll's," stated Stefan Kanfer in *Time,* "and his freestyle drawing recalls the loony sketches of Edward Lear." Because of his work in publishing books for young readers and for the many innovative children's classics he wrote himself, during the second half of the twentieth century Geisel "had a tremendous impact on children's reading habits and the way reading is taught and approached in the school system," declared Miles Corwin of the *Los Angeles Times*.

Geisel had originally intended to become a professor of English, but soon "became frustrated when he was shunted into a particularly insignificant field of research," reported Myra Kibler in the *Dictionary of Literary Biography*. After leaving graduate school in 1926, Geisel worked for a number of years as a freelance magazine cartoonist, selling cartoons and humorous prose pieces to the major humor magazines of the 1920s and 1930s. Many of these works are collected in *The Tough Coughs As He Ploughs the Dough*. One of Geisel's cartoons—about "Flit," a spray-can pesticide—attracted the attention of the Standard Oil Company, manufacturers of the product. In 1928 they hired Geisel to draw their magazine advertising art and, for the next fifteen years, he created grotesque, enormous insects to illustrate the famous slogan "Quick, Henry! The Flit!" He also created monsters for the motor oil division of Standard Oil, including the Moto-Raspus, the Moto-Munchus, and the Karbo-Nockus, that, said Kibler, are precursors of his later fantastic creatures.

It was quite by chance that Geisel began writing for children. Returning from Europe by boat in 1936, he amused himself by putting together a nonsense poem to the rhythm of the ship's engine. Later he drew pictures to illustrate the rhyme and in 1937 published the result as *And to Think That I Saw It on Mulberry Street*, his first children's book. Set in Geisel's home town of Springfield, Massachusetts, *And to Think That I Saw It on Mulberry Street* is the story of a boy whose imagination transforms a simple horse-drawn wagon into a marvelous and exotic parade of strange creatures and vehicles. Many critics regard it as Geisel's best work.

And to Think That I Saw It on Mulberry Street, along with *The 500 Hats of Bartholomew Cubbins, Horton Hatches the Egg*, and *McElligot's Pool*, introduces many of the elements for which Geisel became famous. *Mulberry Street* features rollicking anapestic tetrameter verse that complements the author's boisterous illustrations. Jonathan Cott, writing in *Pipers at the Gates of Dawn: The Wisdom of Children's Literature*, declared that "the unflagging momentum, feeling of breathlessness, and swiftness of pace, all together [act] as the mo-

tor for Dr. Seuss's pullulating image machine." Whimsical fantasy characterizes *The 500 Hats of Bartholomew Cubbins*, while *Horton Hatches the Egg* introduces an element of morality and *McElligot's Pool* marks the first appearance of the fantasy animal characters for which Geisel became famous.

The outbreak of World War II forced Geisel to give up writing for children temporarily and to devote his talents to the war effort. Working with the Information and Education Division of the U.S. Army, he made documentary films for American soldiers. One of these army films—*Hitler Lives*—won an Academy Award, a feat Geisel repeated with his documentary about the Japanese war effort, *Design for Death*, and the UPA cartoon *Gerald McBoing-Boing*, about a little boy who can only speak in sound effects. The screenplay for the film *The 5,000 Fingers of Dr. T*, which Geisel wrote with Allen Scott, achieved cult status during the 1960s among music students on college campuses. Later, Geisel adapted several of his books into animated television specials, the most famous of which—*How the Grinch Stole Christmas*—has become a holiday favorite.

The success of his early books confirmed Geisel as an important new children's writer. However, it was *The Cat in the Hat* that solidified his reputation and revolutionized the world of children's book publishing. By using a limited number of different words, all simple enough for very young children to read, and through its wildly iconoclastic plot—when two children are alone at home on a rainy day, the Cat in the Hat arrives to entertain them, wrecking their house in the process—*The Cat in the Hat* provided an attractive alternative to the simplistic "Dick and Jane" primers then in use in American schools, and critics applauded its appearance. Helen Adams Masten in the *Saturday Review* marveled at the way Geisel, using "only 223 different words, . . . has created a story in rhyme which presents an impelling incentive to read." The enthusiastic reception of *The Cat in the Hat* led Geisel to found Beginner Books, a publishing company specializing in easy-to-read books for children. In 1960 Random House acquired the company and made Geisel president of the Beginner Books division.

Geisel and Beginner Books created many modern classics for children, from *Green Eggs and Ham*, about the need to try new experiences, and *Fox in Socks*, a series of increasingly boisterous tongue-twisters, to *The Lorax*, about environmental preservation, and *The Butter Battle Book*, a fable based on the nuclear arms race. In

1986, at the age of eighty-two, Geisel produced his most uncharacteristic book, *You're Only Old Once,* a work geared for the "obsolete children" of the world. The story follows an elderly gentleman's examination at "The Golden Age Clinic on Century Square," where he has gone for "Spleen Readjustment and Muffler Repair." The gentleman, who is never named, is subjected to a number of seemingly pointless tests by merciless physicians and grim nurses, ranging from a diet machine that rejects any appealing foods to an enormous eye chart that asks, "Have you any idea how much these tests are costing you?" Finally, the patient is dismissed, the doctors telling him: "You're in pretty good shape / For the shape that you're in!"

In its cheerful conclusion *You're Only Old Once* is typically Geisel. "The other ending is unacceptable," the author confided to *New York Times Book Review* contributor David W. Dunlap. In other ways, however, the book is very different in that it is much more autobiographical than any of his other stories. Robin Marantz Henig, writing in the *Washington Post Book World,* called *You're Only Old Once* "lighthearted, silly, but with an undertone of complaint. Being old is sometimes tough, isn't it . . . Seuss seems to be saying." *Los Angeles Times Book Review* contributor Jack Smith declared that in the book Geisel "reveals himself as human and old, and full of aches and pains and alarming symptoms, and frightened of the world of geriatric medicine, with its endless tests, overzealous doctors, intimidating nurses, Rube Goldberg machines and demoralizing paperwork." Nonetheless, Henig concluded, "We should all be lucky enough to get old the way this man, and Dr. Seuss himself, has gotten old."

In 2004, Random House began a yearlong celebration in honor of the one hundredth anniversary of Geisel's birth. Having sold more books for Random House than any other author, Geisel was also depicted on a stamp issued by the U.S. Postal Service. The celebration included one hundred days of events in memory of Geisel held in forty cities throughout the United States. Events included live theatrical performances, readings of his works, costume character appearances, and interactive workshops. "The celebration encompasses his life as a whole and not just him as a children's book illustrator," Random House executive Judith Haut told Joy Bean in *Publishers Weekly.* "He revolutionized how children learned to read, and so we knew the celebration had to equal the passion people have for his books."

BIOGRAPHICAL AND CRITICAL SOURCES:

BOOKS

Children's Literature Review, Thomson Gale (Detroit, MI), Volume 1, 1976, Volume 9, 1985.

Cott, Jonathan, *Pipers at the Gates of Dawn: The Wisdom of Children's Literature,* Random House (New York, NY), 1983.

Dictionary of Literary Biography, Volume 61: *American Writers for Children since 1960: Poets, Illustrators, and Nonfiction Authors,* Thomson Gale (Detroit, MI), 1987.

Fensch, Thomas, *Of Sneetches and Whos and the Good Dr. Seuss: Essays on the Writings and Life of Theodor Geisel,* McFarland (Jefferson, NC), 1997.

Greene, Carol, *Dr. Seuss: Writer and Artist for Children,* Children's Press (Chicago, IL), 1993.

Lanes, Selma G., *Down the Rabbit Hole: Adventures and Misadventures in the Realm of Children's Literature,* Atheneum (New York, NY), 1972.

Lathem, Edward Connery, editor, *Theodor Seuss Geisel, Reminiscences and Tributes,* Dartmouth College (Hanover, NH), 1996.

Morgan, Judith, and Neil Morgan, *Dr. Seuss and Mr. Geisel: A Biography,* Random House (New York, NY), 1995.

PERIODICALS

Chicago Tribune, May 12, 1957; April 15, 1982; April 17, 1984; June 29, 1986; January 14, 1987.

Education Digest, December, 1992.

English Journal, December, 1992.

Horn Book, September-October, 1992.

Interview, April, 1995.

Los Angeles Times, November 27, 1983; October 7, 1989.

Los Angeles Times Book Review, March 9, 1986.

New York Review of Books, December 20, 1990.

New York Times, May 21, 1986; December 26, 1987.

New York Times Book Review, November 11, 1952; May 11, 1958; March 20, 1960; November 11, 1962; November 16, 1975; April 29, 1979; February 26, 1984; March 23, 1986; February 26, 1995.

Parade, February 26, 1984.

Publishers Weekly, February 10, 1984; August 9, 1993; January 23, 1995; February 2, 2004, Joy Bean, "Celebrating Dr. Seuss: Random House Launches a Horton-Sized, Year-Long Tribute to Ted Geisel," p. 23.

Reader's Digest, April, 1992.
Saturday Review, May 11, 1957; November 16, 1957.
Time, May 7, 1979.
Washington Post, December 30, 1987.
Washington Post Book World, March 9, 1986.
Yankee, December, 1995.

OBITUARIES:

PERIODICALS

Chicago Tribune, September 26, 1991.
Detroit Free Press, September 26, 1991; September 27, 1991.
Detroit News, September 26, 1991.
Los Angeles Times, September 26, 1991.
School Library Journal, November, 1991.
Times (London, England), September 27, 1991.

* * *

GENET, Jean 1910-1986

PERSONAL: Born December 19, 1910, in Paris, France; died of throat cancer, April 15, 1986 in Paris, France; never knew his parents; was abandoned by his mother, Gabrielle Genet, to the *Assistance publique,* and was raised by a family of peasants.

CAREER: Novelist, dramatist, and poet.

AWARDS, HONORS: Village Voice Off-Broadway (Obie) Awards, 1960, for *The Balcony,* and 1961, for *The Blacks.* Literary Grand Prix (France), 1983.

WRITINGS:

Notre-Dame-des-Fleurs (novel), dated from Fresnes prison, 1942, limited edition, L'Arbalète, 1943, revised edition published by Gallimard (Paris, France), 1951, French & European Publications (New York, NY), 1966, translation by Bernard Frechtman published as *Our Lady of the Flowers,* Morihien (Paris, France), 1949, published with introduction by Jean-Paul Sartre, Grove (New York, NY), 1963, reprinted, 1991.
Miracle de la rose (prose-poem), dated from La Sante and Tourelles prisons, 1943, L'Arbalète, 1946, 2nd edition, L'Arbalète, 1956, translation by Frechtman published as *Miracle of the Rose,* Blond, 1965, Grove (New York, NY), 1966.

Chants secrets (poems), privately printed (Lyons), 1944.
Querelle de Brest, privately printed, 1947, translation by Gregory Streatham published as *Querelle of Brest,* Blond, 1966, translation by Anselm Hollo published as *Querelle,* Grove (New York, NY), 1974.
Pompes funebres, privately printed, c. 1947, revised edition, 1948, translation by Frechtman published as *Funeral Rites,* Grove (New York, NY), 1969.
Poemes, L'Arbalète, 1948, 2nd edition, 1962.
Journal du voleur, Gallimard (Paris, France), 1949, French & European Publications (New York, NY), 1966, translation by Frechtman published as *The Thief's Journal,* foreword by Sartre, Olympia Press, 1954, Grove (New York, NY), 1964, reprinted, 1987.
Haute surveillance (play; first performed at Theatre des Mathurins, February, 1949), Gallimard (Paris, France), 1949, French & European Publications (New York, NY), 1965, translation by Frechtman published as *Deathwatch: A Play* (also see below; produced as *Deathwatch,* Off-Broadway at Theatre East, October 9, 1958), Faber (Boston, MA), 1961.
L'Enfant criminel et 'Adame Miroir, Morihien, 1949.
Les beaux gars, [Paris], 1951.
Les Bonnes (play; first performed in Paris, April 17, 1947), Pauvert, 1954, French & European Publications (New York, NY), 1963, translation by Frechtman published as *The Maids* (also see below; produced in New York at Tempo Playhouse, May 6, 1955), introduction by Sartre, Grove (New York, NY), 1954, augmented French edition published as *Les Bonnes et comment jouer Les Bonnes,* M. Barbezat, 1963.
The Maids [and] *Deathwatch,* introduction by Sartre, Grove (New York, NY), 1954, revised edition, 1962.
Le Balcon (play; produced in Paris at Theatre du Gymnase, May 18, 1960), illustrated with lithographs by Alberto Giacometti, L'Arbalète, 1956, French & European Publications (New York, NY), 1962, translation by Frechtman published as *The Balcony,* (produced in London at London Arts Theatre Club, April 22, 1957; produced on Broadway at Circle in the Square, March 3, 1960), Faber (Boston, MA), 1957, Grove (New York, NY), 1958, revised edition, Grove (New York, NY), 1960, reprint of French edition edited by David Walker, published under original title, Century Texts, 1982.
Les Negres: Clownerie (play; first produced at Theatre de Lutece, October 28, 1959), M. Barbezat, 1958, 3rd edition, published with photographs, M. Barbezat, 1963, translation by Frechtman published as

The Blacks: A Clown Show (produced as *The Blacks* Off-Broadway at St. Mark's Playhouse, May 4, 1961, and revived as *The Blacks: A Clown Story* by the Classical Theater of Harlem, 2003), Grove (New York, NY), 1960.

Les Paravents (play; produced in Stockholm, Sweden at Alleteatern Theatre, 1964), M. Barbezat, 1961, French & European Publications (New York, NY), 1976, translation by Frechtman published as *The Screens* (produced in Brooklyn, NY, at Brooklyn Academy of Music, November, 1971), Grove (New York, NY), 1962.

Lettres a Roger Blin, Gallimard (Paris, France), 1966, translation by Richard Seaver published as *Letters to Roger Blin: Reflections on the Theater,* Grove (New York, NY), 1969 (same translation published in England as *Reflections on the Theatre, and Other Writings,* Faber (Boston, MA), 1972).

May Day Speech (delivered in 1970 at Yale University), with description by Allen Ginsberg, City Lights (San Francisco, CA), 1970.

The Complete Poems of Jean Genet, Man-Root, 1980.

Treasures of the Night: Collected Poems of Jean Genet, Gay Sunshine, 1981.

Un Captif Amoureux, Gallimard (Paris, France, 1986.

Rembrandt, translated by Randolph Hough, Hanuman Books (New York, NY), 1988.

Lettres à Olga et Marc Barbezat, L'Arbalète (Décines, France), 1988.

Elle, edited by Albert Dichy, L'Arbalète, (Décines, France), 1989, translation by Terri Gordon produced at Zipper Theater, New York, 2002.

Genet à Chatila, Solin, (Arles, France), 1992.

Splendid's: Pièce en 2 Actes, edited by Albert Dichy, L'Arbalète, (Décines, France), 1993, translation by Neil Bartlett published as *Splendid's,* introduction by Edmund White, Faber (Boston, MA), 1995.

The Selected Writings of Jean Genet, edited and with an introduction by Edmund White, Ecco Press (Hopewell, NJ), 1993.

Le Bagne, (theatrical scenario), L'Arbalète (Décines, France), 1994.

Le Condamné à mort et autres poèmes, suivi de funambule, Gallimard (Paris, France), 1999.

Lettres au Petit Franz (1943-1944), edited by Claire Degans and François Sentein, Gallimard (Paris, France), 2000.

Théâtre Complet, edited by Michel Corvin and Albert Dichy, Gallimard (Paris, France), 2002.

Prisoner of Love, translated by Barbara Bray; introduction by Ahdaf Soueif, New York Review Books (New York, NY), 2003.

Fragments of the Artwork, translated by Charlotte Mandell, Stanford University Press (Stanford, CA), 2003.

The Declared Enemy: Texts and Interviews, edited by Albert Dichy, translated by Jeff Fort, Stanford University Press (Stanford, CA), 2004.

OMNIBUS VOLUMES

Oeuvres completes, 6 volumes, Gallimard (Paris, France), 1951–79, portions published in six volumes, French & European Publications (New York, NY), 1951–53.

L'Atelier d'Alberto Giacometti; Les Bonnes, suivi d'une lettre; L'Enfant criminel [and] *Le Funambule,* L'Arbalète, 1958.

OTHER

Work represented in anthologies, including *Seven Plays of the Modern Theatre,* edited by Harold Clurman, Grove (New York, NY), 1962. Creator of the film, "A Song of Love," based on Genet's poem "Un Chant d'amour." Author of scenario, "Mademoiselle," Woodfall Films, 1966. Contributor to *Esquire.*

ADAPTATIONS: Le Balcon was filmed and released as *The Balcony* by Continental in 1963 and adapted as an opera by Peter Eotvos that premiered at the Aix Festival in Aix-en-Provence, 2002; *Querelle de Brest* was filmed as *Querelle of Brest* and *Haute surveillance* was filmed as *Deathwatch;* a filmed stage performance of *The Maids* was released in 1975. Selections from Genet's works have been recorded on Caedmon Records, including a reading by Genet, in French, from *Journal du voleur.*

SIDELIGHTS: Jean Genet's works rarely inspire indifference. For some readers, he was a creative genius; for others, he was a mere pornographer. Indeed, his works, his attitudes, his theories, and the criticism written about him seem founded on irreconcilable oppositions.

Although the facts of Genet's life are mixed with fiction, it is certain that he was born in 1910 in Paris. His father was unknown, and his mother, Gabrielle Genet, abandoned him at birth. As a ward of the *Assistance publique,* he spent his early childhood in an orphanage. As a young boy he was assigned to a peasant family in the Morvan region of France. The foster parents, who were paid by the state to raise him, accused him of theft; and some time between the age of ten and fifteen he was sent to the Mettray Reformatory, a penal colony for adolescents. After escaping from Mettray and joining and deserting the Foreign Legion, Genet spent the next twenty years wandering throughout Europe where he made his living as a thief and male prostitute.

According to the legend, he began writing his first novels in jail and quickly rose to literary prominence. Having been sentenced to life in prison for a crime he did not commit, he received a presidential pardon from Vincent Auriol in 1948, primarily because of a petition circulated by an elite group of Parisian writers and intellectuals. After 1948 Genet devoted himself to literature, the theatre, the arts, and various social causes—particularly those espoused by the Black Panthers.

Francois Mauriac, a fervent opponent of Genet's work, rebuked him in a 1949 article "The Case of Jean Genet" ("Le Cas Jean Genet") for what Mauriac saw as Genet's literary exploitation of vice and crime. Many critics conceded Genet's talent but deplored its use, which, ironically, helped confirm Genet's stature as a writer. At the opposite end of the critical pole were the Parisian intellectuals, led by Jean-Paul Sartre and Jean Cocteau, who quickly became ardent defenders of Genet and his work. Sartre's 1952 portrayal of the writer as existential hero in *Saint Genet: Actor and Martyr (Saint Genet, comedien et martyr)* elevated him to the status of cult hero and his work to a legitimate object of scholarly research.

Unfortunately, Sartre's seminal work fostered almost as many legends about Genet as Genet himself had created; Sartre accommodated Genet's life, theories, and early works to his own existential philosophy. To give but one example, Sartre maintained that Genet loathed "history and historicity," an idea that is easily refuted given the historical content of so much of his creative work. Sartre's use of Genet for his own purposes, however, in no way detracted from the value of *Saint Genet* as a source for valid interpretation of the writer. For, be it the thesis (Genet as existential saint), or the antithesis (Genet as Mauriacian Lucifer), modern criticism clearly agrees that Genet and his works are best represented by the concept, first identified by Sartre, of the "eternal couple of the criminal and the saint."

Recent analyses of Genet's works have become less occupied with their morality than with their complexities of style, thematic structures, aesthetic theories, and transformations of the life into the legend. In addition, scholarship has revised many of the early opinions of his works. It is now clear, for example, that Genet pur-

posely created myths about his life and art. The once widely accepted story of the uneducated convict creating works of genius in a jail cell was undoubtedly created to enhance his opportunities for financial and literary success. It is now certain that Genet had read Proust and that he was aware of his literary ancestors, such as de Sade, Rimbaud, Lautreamont, Celine, Jouhandeau, Pirandello, and the surrealists.

One useful aspect of the Genet myth is the idea that his development as a writer was from poetry to novels to plays. According to the legend, his initial creative effort was a poem written in prison, and, in fact, his first published work was his poem *"The Condemned Man"* (*"Le condamne a mort"*), of 1942. The period from 1942 to 1948 was dominated by four major novels and one fictionalized autobiography. He also wrote two plays, of which one, *The Maids (Les Bonnes)*, was produced by Louis Jouvet in 1947. Although Genet made two films between 1949 and 1956 (*Imagenetions* and *Song of Love*), he commented in a 1965 *Playboy* interview that "Sartre's book created a void which made for a kind of psychological deterioration . . . [and I] remained in that awful state for six years." His most successful theatrical period was from 1956 to 1962. During that time, he wrote and presented three plays—all successful major productions. Various ballets, mimes, films, aesthetic criticism and socio-political statements were interspersed throughout his years of productivity, from about 1937 to 1979. Weakened by ill health, Genet published little after 1979.

From his first poem *The Condemned Man*, to his last work, the play *The Screens (Les Paravents)*, Genet dealt with constant subjects: homosexuality, criminality (murder, theft, corruption), saintliness, reality and illusion, history, politics, racism, revolution, aesthetics, solitude. Many people have been shocked not only by his themes but also by his attitude toward himself, his life, and his material—and most of all by his stated intention to corrupt. He openly professed his homosexuality, his admiration for crime and criminals, his joy in theft, and his contempt for the society that rejected him. His vitriolic and scatological attacks on accepted social values made him the target of innumerable moralists.

Genet, whose work is often defended on the basis of its poetic style and inspiration, has been very little studied as a poet. In Richard C. Webb's *Jean Genet: An Annotated Bibliography, 1943-1980,* the section devoted to studies of the poetry consists of one page: two entries and ten cross-references. By comparison, entries for the plays require 295 pages. Clearly, the poetry has been seen as the least important part of Genet's work. Scholars point out that his poetic style and structure follow nineteenth-century models and that there are obvious borrowings from Valery, Verlaine, Hugo, and Baudelaire. Camille Naish in *A Genetic Approach to Structures in the Work of Jean Genet* established that the poems could be specifically linked in theme and structure with his subsequent works. However, Naish also quoted Genet as disparaging his own poems, "finding them 'too much influenced by Cocteau and neo-classicism.'"

Genet's early success as a novelist may certainly be attributed to various factors—to the support of Cocteau and Sartre, to the scandal arising from his subject matter, and to the notoriety of the thief as novelist. The critics long continued to accept the simplistic legend of the unlettered convict genius despite the classical references and other literary allusions, the sophisticated structures, and the sheer volume of work purportedly created between 1942 and 1948. The legend persisted until 1970 when Richard N. Coe published, in *The Theatre of Jean Genet: A Casebook,* an essay by Lily Pringsheim in which she reported that the Genet she had known in Germany in 1937 was of "a truly astonishing intelligence. . . . I could scarcely believe the extent of his knowledge of literature." She also revealed that Genet begged her "to store away a number of manuscripts . . . and that he shared [with her friend Leuschner] an uncontrollable thirst for knowledge, for Leuschner, like Genet, carried books about with him everywhere he went: Shakespeare, language textbooks, scientific treatises."

A simple count of the major works supposedly created by Genet between 1942 and 1948, when he was in and out of prison, should have led some critics to question the legend. The staggering production of this period allegedly included four novels, an autobiography, two plays, three poems, and a ballet. Pringsheim's testimony supports the idea that a major portion of the work was done at an earlier date and in libraries with reference sources. In his very first novel, *Our Lady of the Flowers* (*Notre-Dame-des-Fleurs*), supposedly written in Fresnes prison, Genet accurately quoted from *The Constitutional and Administrative History of France* by the nineteenth-century historian Jean-Baptiste-Honore-Raymond Capefigue. Furthermore, in a letter to the author of this essay, Genet confirmed that he had read *The Memoires on the Private Life of Marie Antoinette* by Madame Genet-Campan. The fact that Genet had read these rather unusual works, had quoted accurately from one of them (supposedly while in prison), and had used the other as a source for material in his play *The Maids,* leads one to several conclusions: major portions of *Our*

Lady were written outside prison, Genet was extremely well read and undoubtedly an habitue of libraries, and he probably received the basics of a traditional French education while incarcerated as a boy at the Mettray reformatory.

Of the five novels, counting the fictionalized autobiography, *The Thief's Journal* (*Journal du voleur*), critics consider *Our Lady of the Flowers* and *Miracle of the Rose* (*Miracle de la rose*) to be the best. Genet's first novel was brought to Jean Cocteau's attention by three young men who had become acquainted with Genet who was then selling books (some stolen) from a bookstall along the Seine. Cocteau recognized the literary merit of *Our Lady.* This novel's uniqueness stems from its basic philosophy, its sophisticated literary technique, and its composite central character Genet-Divine-Culafroy. Some critics think that Genet, the uneducated convict, should be considered a precursor of the "new novel"—that literary movement which came into being as a protest against the traditional novel. Genet's works, like those of the well-known "new novelists" Alain Robbe-Grillet and Michel Butor, may be considered untraditional in their disregard of conventional psychology, their lack of careful transitions, their confused chronologies, and their disdain for coherent plot structures.

To understand *Our Lady,* or any of Genet's works, one must turn to Sartre's *Saint Genet* for an explanation of the "sophistry of the Nay." In *Saint Genet: Actor and Martyr,* Sartre explained Genet's view of the world by relating it to the concept of the saint. According to Sartre, saintliness results from refusing something—honors, power, or money, for example—and the seekers after saintliness soon "convince themselves and others that they have refused everything." Sartre went on to comment, "With these men appeared the sophistry of the Nay . . . [and] in a destructive society which places the blossoming of being at the moment of its annihilation, the Saint, making use of divine meditation, claims that a Nay carried to the extreme is necessarily transformed into a Yea. Extreme poverty is wealth, refusal is acceptance, the absence of God is the dazzling manifestation of his presence, to live is to die, to die is to live, etc. One step further and we are back at the sophisms of Genet: sin is the yawning chasm of God." From this concept, Sartre postulated the concept of the "eternal couple of the criminal and the saint": hence, the legitimacy of the pursuit of saintliness by the homosexual thief Genet-Divine-Culafroy, the hero/heroine of *Our Lady.* The plot of this "epic of masturbation," as Sartre first labeled it, is difficult to follow because Genet wanders from past to present without transition in an episodic celebration of perversity. Louis Culafroy, a twenty-year-old peasant, arrives in Paris from the provinces. He assumes the name Divine and makes his living as a thief and male prostitute. Through the story of Our Lady's conviction for the murder of a helpless old pederast, it is the development of the Genet-Divine-Culafroy character which focuses the novel and provides its true literary merit.

Genet's seeking to canonize this homosexual thief and his use of metaphors combining the sacred and the obscene caused the moralists to rally to the defense of the traditional and the acceptable. Francis L. Kunkle in his *Passion and the Passion: Sex and Religion in Modern Literature* is representative of those critics who reject Genet's work; Kunkle found *Our Lady* to be "a kind of endless linguistic onanism which often collapses into obscene blasphemy." Most critics, however, consider *Our Lady* innovative in its treatment of time and its concept of gesture-as-act, sophisticated in its self-conscious aesthetic, and poetic in its use of incantatory language. In *Jean Genet: A Critical Appraisal*, Philip Thody defended the worth of the book: "There are a number of reasons for considering *Our Lady of the Flowers* as Genet's best novel, and the work in which his vision of reality is given its most effective expression. It has a unity which stems from its concentration upon a single character, and Genet's projection of his own problems on to Divine creates a detachment and irony that are not repeated in any other of his works."

In his next two "novels," Genet followed the successful formula used in *Our Lady*. *Miracle of the Rose* relates the story of Harcamone, "graduate" of the Mettray reformatory, who, betrayed by a fellow convict, murders a prison guard in order to die "gloriously" rather than serve a life sentence. The novel concludes with the mystical experience that Genet, the work's narrator, supposedly underwent the night prior to Harcamone's execution. Although this novel provides certain insights into Genet's life, the reader must be cautious about regarding the work as strictly autobiographical. The writer stipulated that his life must "be a legend, in other words, legible, and the reading of it must give birth to a certain new emotion that I call poetry." *Miracle,* which is easier to follow than *Our Lady,* may be marred by the excessive self-consciousness of its technique. Yet, as in *Our Lady,* Genet set forth in *Miracle* his inversion of good and evil, his longing for deification through degradation, and his homo-eroticism.

In *The Thief's Journal* Genet reveals much about his incredible odyssey through the criminal underworld and the sordid prisons of Europe in the 1930s and 1940s.

Even if only partially factual, the book remains a fascinating social document. But whether Genet's works are primarily social documents or private mythologies is a question that frequently occupies critics. For example, Lucian Goldmann, in *La Creation culturelle dans la societe moderne (Cultural Creation in Modern Society),* labeled Genet the "greatest advocate of social revolt in contemporary French literature." Yet, in *Narcissus Absconditus, the Problematic Art of Autobiography in Contemporary France,* Germaine Bree stressed the mythological aspect of his work saying that *Journal* "gyrates upon itself, proclaiming its symbol-laden ceremonies to be fiction."

Funeral Rites (Pompes funebres) and *Querelle of Brest (Querelle de Brest)* are Genet's least successful works. *Funeral* is Genet's lament for a lover killed during the liberation of Paris, and *Querelle* relates the depressing story of a sailor who is a murderer, thief, and opium smuggler. Both works concentrate on homosexuality, and *Querelle* is the only Genet novel that is not fictionalized autobiography. The critical judgments about his novels reflect the antitheses so often associated with the author and his works: the novels are considered poetic eroticism or pornographic trash, lyrical incantations or demented exhibitionism, sociological documents or masturbatory fantasies. They have been described—and this is only a partial catalogue of labels employed—as existentialist, solipsistic, ambiguous, mythological, homosexual, popular, Freudian, semi-mystical, humorous, basically romantic, adolescent, obscene, blasphemous, ahistorical, archetypal.

After the publication of *The Thief's Journal* Genet turned to the theatre for the presentation of his radical views of the world. Perhaps because of his obsession with religion, the theatre proved a better vehicle for his ideas and techniques than did the novel, since the theatrical experience is, by definition and tradition, a form of ceremony, a rite. However, Genet had some problems in adjusting to the new medium, in seeing his fantasies corrupted by realistic treatment; during Peter Zadek's 1957 London production of *The Balcony (Le Balcon),* for example, he was barred from the theatre for disrupting the production. Yet he soon learned to stage his fantasies within the context of theatrical reality. More importantly, he met and accepted Roger Blin as his future director and interpreter. Under Blin's guidance, his theatrical genius blossomed in the productions of *The Blacks* and *The Screens.*

Critical reactions to the plays are as divergent as they are to the novels. In *Theatre and Anti-Theatre: New Movements since Beckett,* Ronald Hayman labeled Genet's plays "anti-theatrical." Lucien Goldmann focused on the socio-political aspects of the plays, which he considered examples of revolutionary, social realism. Between those two extremes exists a wide range of terms often applied to Genet's drama, including ritualistic, absurd, metaphysical, neurotic, nonrealistic, and cruel.

Genet's works for the theatre may be divided into two periods—1947 to 1949 and 1956 to 1962. It is generally accepted that although *The Maids* was the first play produced, *Deathwatch* (*Haute Surveillance*) was written earlier. The several revisions that Genet made of *Deathwatch* suggest that he was little satisfied with the original version of the play so often compared to Sartre's *No Exit*. This first play by the "convict-genius" is tightly constructed, almost classical in conception and presentation. The unities of time, place, and action are strictly observed. However, the concept of decorum is violated by the on-stage murder of Maurice by Lefranc, and the language and premise of the author are definitely not classical. Once again, the spectators and the critic are confronted with the concept of the "criminal and the saint."

Genet established a criminal-religious hierarchy—that is, the more serious the crime the more "saintly" the criminal. Within this hierarchy Genet developed those subjects consistently found throughout his work: betrayal, murder, homosexuality, theft, and solitude. Although there is some dispute over who the "hero" really is in *Death Watch,* it seems obvious that Lefranc, not Green Eyes, is the preferred Genetian hero because he chooses his murder and opts for prison, whereas Green Eyes repudiates his murder. Furthermore, Lefranc admits that he is provoked to murder Maurice by an imaginary spray of lilacs, symbol of fate and death. Lefranc seeks to become the "Lilac Murderer" in imitation of other thugs who have acquired exotic nick-names appropriate to their crimes—the Avenger, the Panther, the Tornado, for example. *Deathwatch* thus serves as an excellent example of Genet's creative process. As the author of an essay in the *French Review* commented, "he began with a basic symbol, that is, it is unlucky to take lilacs into a house for they will cause a death, and then expanded this symbol to include the basic themes of the play—murder, betrayal, fate, sex, and the criminal-religious hierarchy. By bedecking his criminals with lilacs, Genet has created a gigantic and a new flower-symbol."

The Maids, based on an actual murder committed by the Papin sisters, is a one-act play that serves as a brilliant example of Genet's ability to create complex structures for what Sartre called his "whirligig of reality and illusion." Genet wanted very much to have the female roles performed by young men. He also wanted a sign posted to inform the audience of the deception. This would have added two more levels of illusion to the already complicated role-playing wherein one of the maids assumes the guise of their mistress and her sister plays the role of the sister playing the mistress. As the author of an essay in *Kentucky Romance Quarterly* noted, a remarkably complicated work results: "The complexity of Genet's genius is such that he can create a play such as *The Maids* based on 'historical materials' which is at the same time an illustration of the philosophical concept of the eternal couple of the criminal and the saint, a 'Fable' based on the history of Marie Antoinette and the French Revolution, and an example of a black mass."

The Balcony, unlike the first two plays in which there is a certain classical simplicity of form, is a long and complex series of scenes that take place primarily in Madame Irma's "House of Illusions," a brothel where various rooms are reserved for the ritualized performance of erotic fantasies based on such equations as sex/power, sex/religion, and sex/revolution. In the preface to the definitive edition of the play, Genet stressed that his play was not a satire but the "glorification of the Image and the Reflection. . . ." Richard N. Coe, in *The Vision of Jean Genet,* considered *The Balcony* an example of Genet's essential conception of drama: "The highest, most compelling form of experience—the experience which Genet describes as sacred and which forms the basis of all his mysticism—occurs when the human consciousness becomes simultaneously aware of the two co-existent dimensions of existence: the real and the transcendental. This, as Genet sees it, is the underlying miracle of the Christian Eucharist; and it is also the principle of all true theatre." Given Genet's obsession with religion and saintliness, it becomes more understandable why he objected so strenuously to Zadek's realistic London production of *The Balcony.* For, as Martin Esslin pointed out in *The Theatre of the Absurd,* Genet desired that "his fantasies of sex and power . . . be staged with the solemnity and the outward splendor of the liturgy in one of the world's great cathedrals."

In a real sense, the first and last scenes of this complex play are summations of Genet's theories and theatrical techniques. The first tableau opens with a character wearing bishop's vestments in a whore house (attack on conventional morality). The bishop is a fake who turns out to be a gas-meter reader (whirligig of illusion and reality). Like the other Western power figures (the judge, the general, the chief of police, and the revolutionary), the bishop's existence is predicated on its opposite. The cleric can exist only if sin exists, for his function, which is to forgive sinners, depends on the antithesis of holiness (antithetical power relationship of the sinner and the saint). Within this same antithetical concept, the bishop later seeks to betray the chief of police (betrayal as necessary adjunct to saintliness). Concomitantly, the bishop is "holy" because he plays the role of a clergyman in a whorehouse, but he is less "holy" than the prostitutes because they are not playing the roles of but are truly prostitutes. Thus in Genet's upside-down world they are saints (sophistry of the Nay).

After a series of tableaux illustrating various Genetian subjects—betrayal, murder, the nature of royalty, illusion and reality, sex and power, the futility of revolution, function versus appearance—Madame Irma, the sole character who is not a victim of the need to live an "illusion," turns to the audience and advises them to "go home, where everything—you may be quite sure—will be falser than here". By breaking the theatrical conventions in addressing the audience directly, by blurring the distinction between the illusion of the theatre and the "reality" outside the theatre, the conclusion thereby reflects Genet's desire that the play be the "glorification of the Image and the Reflection." Genet the thief has once again "robbed" the bourgeois audience. An experienced crook, he diverts their attention with shock tactics while he tries to strip them of their values. The irony is that he not only tries to undermine their moral certainties but that he is enriched by their willingness to pay to be insulted and deceived. There is, in his mind, very little difference between picking a victim's pocket and doing what he does in the theatre. As the play ends, the sounds of a new revolution are heard, by which Genet intended that smug, self-righteous men be reminded that thieves, murderers, and revolutionaries will constantly strive to wreck their complacency.

Genet's last two major artistic creations, *The Blacks* (*Les Negres*) and *The Screens* may well have provided him with his most satisfying moments in his war on society. Both plays, in which racism or colonialism are presented within the context of Genetian ritual and ceremony, are vitriolic attacks on bourgeois values. *The Blacks,* written in 1957 and performed in 1959, is a play within a play. The audience, which must always include a white person or an effigy of one, is entertained with a ritual re-enactment of the murder of a white woman by a black man. The murderer is convicted by a white court—blacks wearing white masks. However, the trial of the murderer is a diversion from the real crime—a black traitor's execution—that is sup-

posedly taking place off-stage. Presenting blacks acting out their hatred of whites and of white society, the play had its greatest success and most profound impact at the time of the race riots in America in the late 1960s. Although Bettina Knapp declared in *Jean Genet* that nothing real occurs on stage, that "The whole ritual on stage, then, is a big joke, a game, a 'clownerie' (the subtitle of the play)," it is more often believed that Genet's play was one of the first theatrical productions in which black actors confronted a primarily white audience with an expression of their suppressed hatreds and prejudices.

Criticism of *The Blacks* attested that, even in the black community, there was, as usual, a wide divergence of opinion. E. Bullins, the editor of *Black Theatre,* attacked the play and its author: "Jean Genet is a white, self-confessed homosexual with dead, white Western ideas—faggoty ideas about Black Art, Revolution, and people. His empty masochistic activities and platitudes on behalf of the Black Panthers should not con Black people. . . . Beware of whites who plead the Black cause." However, most critics, black or white, saw the play as an expression of black liberation, of black psychology, and of the bitterness in race relations. Very few critics accepted what director Roger Blin insisted was Genet's intention: to present a play that was an exercise in aesthetics, not in politics or psychology.

Genet's last work, *The Screens,* is an obvious attack on French colonialism and a virulent condemnation of the war in Algeria. As a result, it provoked hostile reactions from the right-wing element in France. Published in 1961, the play was not performed in its entirety until 1964 in Stockholm. Due to its explosive content, *The Screens* was banned in France until 1966, when it was presented for a total of forty performances at the behest of Andre Malraux, Minister of Culture. It must have delighted Genet's sense of irony to see his play produced at the Odeon, the theatre of France, for the play is an attack on the nation. Even more ironic was the need for police protection because of the violence directed at the actors and the author by "honest patriots." The outcast, the rejected orphan, the despised homosexual and thief, had had the last word.

It is a difficult if not impossible task to summarize *The Screens,* Genet's most complex play. Some ninety-six characters create "artistic" patterns on screens during the performance of a very complicated plot while dressed, for the most part, in fantastic costumes. The plot concerns Said, the poorest man in Algeria, who can afford to marry only the ugliest woman. An ascetic figure, Said wishes to become as abject as possible through self-degradation; Leila, Said's intended, supports his intentions and seeks to become even uglier in order to help him achieve his goal. Having stolen, not from the French but from his Arab neighbors, Said is cast out by his own kind and ultimately arrested. The "hero" of this play is not only poor and ugly, a thief and an outcast, he is loathsome—or worse—dull. Of all of Genet's plays and of all of his heroes, *The Screens* and Said are the most calculatedly vile. Genet's images of filth and excrement abound, and both the French and the Arabs are portrayed as vermin. As Richard N. Coe wrote in *The Vision of Jean Genet:* "One might almost suspect that Genet, in a last desperate attempt to reconcile his artist's aestheticism with politics, is trying to use the conventional concept of Beauty—which he himself now identifies unhesitatingly with the enemy society—as an argument in favour of the outcast. But, in spite of the ingenious twists of logic involved . . . the argument defeats itself. For if beauty is sufficient to invalidate the claim of Monsieur Blankensee to so many kilometers of Algerian countryside, unfortunately it invalidates the claims of the Arabs simultaneously. What remains is not Arab-owned economy, but simply a Void, a *zero.*"

Although Genet and Blin insisted that the play was nonpartisan, that it was a poetic and not a political statement, the hostilities began soon after the opening performance. The stage became a target for stink bombs and rotten eggs; numerous fights broke out between actors and spectators and between partisan spectators. In particular, a scene where French soldiers break wind in the face of a dead French officer caused howls of protest, mostly from cadets of Saint Cyr and from members of various veterans' organizations.

Although a definitive judgment of Genet and his works is difficult to make, a quantitative statement about the critical attention to him is revealing. Webb's *Jean Genet: An Annotated Bibliography, 1943-1980,* lists some 1,790 books, articles, theses, and other scholarly works; and this number does not count the many critical reviews of specific productions that Webb includes—for example, the seventy-two write-ups of the 1959 Paris production of *The Blacks.* Genet and his works are clearly the subject of much critical interest. Both author and works were catapulted to international fame primarily because of the scandal created by his "pornography" and because of Genet's association with Sartre. Yet, rather than debating the "pornographic" aspect of the works, most modern critics argue about their meanings. Any effort to categorize Genet's work may appear arrogant, but it seems appropriate to identify three subjects or characteristics—nihilism, complexity, and antithesis—pertaining to his entire canon.

Perhaps the most easily defined characteristic is negativism. Although the obvious nihilism may be a pose, it is one which serves several purposes. Ultimately one suspects that Genet used the sordid facts of his life as a means to escape it and that he recognized very early on that success is often founded on a loud, provocative, scandalous attack on bourgeois society. Some critics theorize that he created his own scandal based on nihilism and eroticism in order to become rich and famous and to gain a measure of revenge upon society. But whatever the source or motive, Genet's works reflect his unwavering pursuit of his ideals of nothingness and absolute solitude.

The word "complexity" is constantly present in critics' discussions of Genet's works. Whether the complexity was intentional or the result of literary, educational, or philosophic insufficiency depends on what education Genet received while at the Mettray reformatory and on when exactly he began writing. If we accept Pringsheim's statements, Genet was not only experimenting with verse and prose in 1937, he had already written several manuscripts and was in possession of and reading Shakespeare, language textbooks, and other material—all of this many years before he supposedly wrote *Our Lady of the Flowers* in Fresnes prison and long before he had met either Cocteau or Sartre. His first published novel does clearly reveal sophisticated techniques and classical allusions indicating that the legend of the uneducated convict genius was greatly exaggerated by Sartre, Cocteau, and Genet himself. He may have been primarily self-taught, and it is certain that he spent long hours reading and doing research in libraries. But the story that he was miraculously endowed in prison with literary talent and a vast store of classical and literary knowledge is clearly apocryphal.

Finally, antithesis was the foundation of Genet's literary theories and techniques as well as the basis for his view of the world. Whether they treat the eternal couple of the criminal and the saint or the "sophistry of the Nay," his works are best understood through the figure of the mirror, long a symbol of thesis and antithesis, wherein everything is at once itself and its own opposite. Genet, like the dancer in his ballet "Adame Mirror," creates a series of gestures in front of a mirror that reflects a reversed image of reality. Certainly he used the mirror image throughout his works—Stilitano lost in the house of mirrors at the amusement park in *The Thief's Journal,* the vital role of mirrors in *The Balcony.* Perhaps even more pertinent is the symbol of opposing mirrors, mirrors which reflect reality reversed time and time again; indeed, Genet used just such a technique in *The Balcony* when the gas-meter reader plays the role of the bishop in the whore house, the fake bishop is then forced by the chief of police to play the role of the real bishop who has been killed during the revolution, and then after seeking to betray the chief of police in order to assume power in the real world, the would-be bishop rejects function in favor of "sublime appearance." The entire sequence may be interpreted as a series of reversed reflections of reality caught in opposing mirrors. Genet was undoubtedly a part of that literary tradition in France called "le poete maudit" (the accursed or outcast poet) and represented by Villon, the Marquis de Sade, Baudelaire, Rimbaud, Verlaine, and even Gide and Proust. Generally rejected by society, these writers sought justification, vengeance, or something comparable by rejecting or attacking that society. If there is redemption for these authors, it takes place because of a commitment to art. One can not say that Genet and his works are less acceptable than were Baudelaire and his works in the mid-nineteenth century. Baudelaire was even convicted of pornography for *The Flowers of Evil,* now considered a masterpiece and a source for much twentieth-century poetry. Genet should be read and studied for those same reasons we now read and study those other writers in rebellion—as a way to understand ourselves and our times. Genet—the orphan, the professed homosexual, the convicted criminal—forces his readers to face certain facts of human nature and history. His language and his beliefs may be offensive to some, but his work reflects the reality of the world of criminals and prison life. Genet must not, however, be considered a mere writer of social documents, for his genius lay in his ability to create works of great complexity in a style that interests the reader and challenges the critic. Finally, there is no doubt that his subject matter and his innovative techniques and structures made him one of the most significant and controversial French authors of the twentieth century.

Genet's works, letters, selected texts, and interviews continue to be published long after his death. Among these publications are some older works that have never appeared in print. For example, in 1993, Genet's play *Splendid's: Pièce en 2 Actes* was published in France and two years later was translated into English as *Splendid's.* Although written in 1948, Genet had decided not to publish the work as he kept refining it. Sartre, however, had read the play and, according to Bettin L. Knapp writing in *World Literature Today,* "believed it was superior to *The Maids.*" The play takes place in a luxury hotel named Splendid's, where criminals have kidnapped the daughter of an American millionaire and are holding her for ransom. One of the kidnappers accidentally hugs the daughter to death and the leader of the gang makes an appearance on the balcony of the hotel wearing the daughter's gown. Other criminals roam the hotel in a variety of roles, including acting as Napoleon on St. Helena. Throughout the play, role-playing and allusions abound. Knapp commented, "To read *Splendid's,* even after having experienced Genet's great works, is still an enrichment. For within its pages one not only discerns the poetry of his discourse, the harmonies, cacophonies, and rhythms of his voices, but also the many dramatic elements, styles, and techniques he used-travesty, mystery, pantomime, irony, humor, gesture, stage accessories such as mirrors, shrines, and clothes."

In addition to new published works and reprints, literary critics continue to study Genet. Carl Lavery, writing in the *Journal of European Studies,* noted, "The last ten years have witnessed a significant shift in the way Jean Genet's work has been received. Where earlier critics were perplexed by his scathing attack on all forms of political discourse . . . [his plays and novels] are now valued for their acute social and political insights, and their author is celebrated as a visionary thinker."

BIOGRAPHICAL AND CRITICAL SOURCES:

BOOKS

Abel, Lionel, *Metatheatre: A New View of Dramatic Form,* Hill & Wang (New York, NY), 1963.

Bree, Germaine, *Narcissus Absconditus, the Problematic Art of Autobiography in Contemporary France,* Clarendon Press (Oxford, England), 1978.

Brooks, Peter, and Joseph Halpern, editors, *Genet: A Collection of Critical Essays,* Prentice-Hall (Englewood Cliffs, NJ), 1979.

Brophy, Brigid, *Don't Never Forget: Collected Views and Reviews,* Holt (New York, NY), 1966.

Brustein, Robert, *Seasons of Discontent: Dramatic Opinions, 1959-1965,* Simon & Schuster (New York, NY), 1965.

Brustein, Robert, *The Theatre of Revolt: An Approach to Modern Drama,* Little, Brown (Boston, MA), 1964, pp. 361-411.

Burgess, Anthony, *The Novel Now: A Guide to Contemporary Fiction,* Norton (New York, NY), 1967.

Cetta, Lewis T., *Profane Play, Ritual and Jean Genet: A Study of His Drama,* University of Alabama Press (Tuscaloosa, AL), 1974.

Choukri, Mohamed, *Jean Genet in Tangier,* Ecco Press (New York, NY), 1974.

Coe, Richard N., *The Vision of Jean Genet,* Grove (New York, NY), 1968.

Coe, Richard N., editor, *The Theatre of Jean Genet: A Case-book,* Grove (New York, NY), 1970.

Contemporary Literary Criticism, Thomson Gale (Detroit, MI), Volume 1, 1973, Volume 2, 1974, Volume 5, 1976, Volume 10, 1979, Volume 14, 1980, Volume 44, 1987, Volume 46, 1988.

Driver, Tom F., *Jean Genet,* Columbia University Press (New York, NY), 1966.

Esslin, Martin, *The Theatre of the Absurd,* Anchor Books (Garden City, NY), 1961, pp. 140-67.

Genet, Jean, *The Balcony,* (produced in London at London Arts Theatre Club, April 22, 1957; produced on Broadway at Circle in the Square, March 3, 1960), Faber (Boston, MA), 1957.

Genet, Jean, *Miracle of the Rose,* Grove (New York, NY), 1966.

Glicksberg, Charles I., *Modern Literary Perspectives,* Southern Methodist University Press, 1970.

Goldmann, Lucien, *La Creation culturelle dans la societe moderne,* Denoel (Paris, France), 1971.

Grossvogel, D. I., *Four Playwrights and a Postscript,* Cornell University Press (Ithaca, NY), 1962, pp. 133-74.

Guicharnaud, Jacques, *Modern French Theatre: From Giraudoux to Genet,* revised edition, Yale University Press (New Haven, CT), 1967, pp. 259-77.

Hassan, Ihab, *The Dismemberment of Orpheus,* Oxford University Press (New York, NY), 1971.

Hauptman, Robert, *The Pathological Vision,* Peter Lang (New York, NY), 1983, pp. 1-50.

Hayman, Ronald, *Theatre and Anti-theatre: New Movements since Beckett,* Oxford University Press (New York, NY), 1979.

Jacobsen, Josephine, and William R. Mueller, *Ionesco and Genet,* Hill & Wang (New York, NY), 1968.

Knapp, Bettina, *Jean Genet,* Twayne (New York, NY), 1968.

Kostelanetz, Richard, editor, *On Contemporary Literature,* Avon (New York, NY), 1964.

Kunkle, Francis, *Passion and the Passion: Sex and Religion in Modern Literature,* Westminister (Philadelphia, PA), 1975.

Leyland, Winston, editor, *Gay Sunshine Interviews,* Gay Sunshine Press (San Francisco, CA), 1978.

Littlejohn, David, *Interruptions,* Grossman (New York, NY), 1970.

Mandel, Siegfried, editor, *Contemporary European Novelists,* Southern Illinois University Press (Carbondale, IL), 1968.

McMahon, J. H., *The Imagination of Jean Genet,* Yale University Press (New Haven, CT), 1964.

Nadeau, Maurice, *The French Novels since the War,* Methuen, 1967.

Naish, Camille, *A Genetic Approach to Structures in the Work of Jean Genet,* Harvard University Press (Cambridge, MA), 1978.

Pronko, Leonard Cabell, *Avant Garde: The Experimental Theatre in France,* University of California Press (Berkeley, CA), 1962.

Pronko, Leonard Cabell, *Theater East and West: Perspectives toward a Total Theater,* University of California Press (Berkeley, CA), 1967.

Sartre, Jean-Paul, *Saint Genet, comedien et martyr,* Gallimard (Paris, France), 1952, translation by Bernard Frenchtman published as *Saint Genet: Actor and Martyr,* Braziller (New York, NY), 1963.

Savona, Jeanette L., *Jean Genet,* Macmillan (New York, NY), 1983.

Thody, Phillip, *Jean Genet: A Study of His Novels and Plays,* Stein & Day (New York, NY), 1969.

Webb, Richard C., and Suzanne A. Webb, *Jean Genet: An Annotated Bibliography, 1943-1980,* Scarecrow (Metuchen, NJ), 1982.

Weightman, John, *The Concept of the Avant-Garde: Explorations in Modernism,* Alcove (London, England), 1973.

Wellwarth, George, *Theatre of Protest and Paradox: Developments in the Avant-Garde Drama,* New York University Press (New York, NY), 1964.

White, Edmund, *Genet: A Biography,* Knopf (New York, NY), 1993.

Winkler, Josef, *Flowers for Jean Genet,* translated by Michael Roloff, Ariadne (Riverside, CA), 1996.

PERIODICALS

American Cinematographer, May, 1963.

Atlantic, January, 1965.

Black Theatre, Number 5, 1971, E. Bullins, review of *The Blacks.*

Book Week, October 6, 1963.

Commentary, July, 1994.

Contemporary Literature, autumn, 1975.

Dance, December, 1969.

Dance News, September, 1957.

Drama, summer, 1972.

Drama Review, fall, 1969.

Drama Survey, spring-summer, 1967.

French Review, December, 1971; October, 1974; December, 1974, April, 1980, December, 1981; May, 1984.

Harper, January, 1965; September, 1974.

Holiday, June, 1965.

Horizon, November 29, 1964.

Kentucky Romance Quarterly, Number 3, 1985.

Kenyon Review, March, 1967.

Le Figaro Litteraire, March 26, 1949; October 15, 1951.

Modern Drama, September, 1967; September 1969; March, 1974; September, 1976.

Nation, March 20, 1954; November 2, 1963; January 14, 1964; December 27, 1971.

New Leader, October 28, 1974.

New Republic, November 23, 1963.

New Statesman, January 10, 1964.

Newsweek, December 20, 1971; May 9, 1983.

New Yorker, January 16, 1965;, October 21, 1974.

New York Times, January 19, 1986.

New York Times Book Review, September 29, 1963; February 19, 1967; June 15, 1969; September 8, 1974.

Oui, November, 1972, pp. 62-102.

Partisan Review, April, 1949.

Playboy, April, 1964, interview, pp. 45-55.

Plays and Players, May, 1974.

Review of Contemporary Fiction, summer, 1994, Irving Maliln, review of *The Selected Writings of Jean Genet,* p. 222.

Saturday Review, June 18, 1960; November 14, 1964; July 12, 1969; November 15, 1969.

Southern Review, March, 1975; March, 1978.

Times Literary Supplement, October 31, 1958; April 8, 1965.

TriQuarterly 30, spring, 1974.

Village Voice, March 18, 1965.

Vogue, December, 1988.

Washington Post Book World, November 3, 1974.

Wisconsin Studies in Contemporary Literature, summer, 1969.

World Literature Today, fall, 1996, Bettina L. Knapp, review of *Splendid's,* p. 91.

OBITUARIES:

PERIODICALS

New York Times, April 16, 1986.

Time, April 28, 1986.

Washington Post, April 16, 1986.

*   *   *

GIBBONS, Kaye 1960-

PERSONAL: Born 1960, in Wilson, NC; daughter of Charles (a tobacco farmer) and Alice Butts; married Michael Gibbons (divorced); married Frank Ward (an attorney), 1995 (divorced); children: Mary, Leslie, Louise (first marriage). *Education:* Attended North Carolina State University and the University of North Carolina at Chapel Hill.

ADDRESSES: Home—Raleigh, NC. *Agent*—Jane Pasanen, Chelsea Forum, Inc., 377 Rector Place, Suite 12-I, New York, NY 10280.

CAREER: Novelist.

AWARDS, HONORS: Sue Kaufman Prize for First Fiction, American Academy and Institute of Arts and Letters, and citation from Ernest Hemingway Foundation, both for *Ellen Foster*; National Endowment for the Arts fellowship, for *A Virtuous Woman*; Nelson Algren Heartland Award for Fiction, *Chicago Tribune,* 1991, and PEN/Revson Foundation Fellowship, both for *A Cure for Dreams*; Critics Choice Award, *Los Angeles Times,* 1995, for *Sights Unseen*; Chevalier de L'Ordre des Arts et des Lettres (French Knighthood), for contribution to French literature, 1996.

WRITINGS:

NOVELS

Ellen Foster, Algonquin Books (Chapel Hill, NC), 1987.

A Virtuous Woman, Algonquin Books (Chapel Hill, NC), 1989.

A Cure for Dreams, Algonquin Books (Chapel Hill, NC), 1991.

Charms for the Easy Life, Putnam (New York, NY), 1993.

Sights Unseen, Putnam (New York, NY), 1995.

On the Occasion of My Last Afternoon, Putnam (New York, NY), 1998.

Divining Women, Putnam (New York, NY), 2004.

The Life All Around Me By Ellen Foster, Harcourt (Orlando, FL), 2005.

Contributor to the *New York Times Book Review.* Her novels have been translated into French.

ADAPTATIONS: Ellen Foster was adapted for audiocassette by Simon & Schuster (New York, NY), 1996, and for the Hallmark Hall of Fame television movie, 1997; movie rights to *A Virtuous Woman* were bought by the Oprah Winfrey production company. *Charms for the Easy Life* was made into a television movie by Showtime Productions, 2001. *A Virtuous Woman* was recorded as an audiobook by Recorded Books, 1998, and *On the Occasion of My Last Afternoon* was recorded as an audiobook by Recorded Books, 1999. *Sights Unseen* was recorded as an audiobook by Chivers, 2001, and was developed into a movie script by the author.

WORK IN PROGRESS: Completing Jeanne Braselton's posthumous novel *The Other Side of Air;* a biography.

SIDELIGHTS: Kaye Gibbons has won a number of literary awards and much praise for her body of fiction, a group of novels predominantly set in rural Southern communities not unlike Nash County, North Carolina, where Gibbons grew up. From the matriarchal folk healer to the uncompromising eleven-year-old, Gibbons's strong central characters—almost always female—possess a grounding and wisdom that transcends the often-difficult circumstances of lives. Writing in *Publishers Weekly,* critic Bob Summer termed them "Southern women who shoulder the burdens of their ordinary lives with extraordinary courage."

Gibbons was born and raised in North Carolina. The daughter of an alcoholic father and a mother who suffered from bipolar disorder and committed suicide when Kaye was ten years old, Gibbons later drew on some of her experiences in her fiction. While she did not go to live with her grandmother, as Ellen Foster does in *Ellen Foster,* she did live with an older brother, and she did and does value books. "Books are the most important thing in my life," she told *Book* writer Liz Seymour in 2002. "I grew up walking three miles to a Bookmobile—books aren't property, they're a whole separate category." Like her mother, from the age of twenty Gibbons has suffered from bipolar disorder, once known as manic depression, in which a person veers dangerously from periods of depression to periods of mania (intense activity and sleeplessness). She wrote her first novel, *Ellen Foster,* during a six-week manic binge and her 1998 novel *On the Occasion of My Last Afternoon* during three months when she would write from forty to sixty hours at a time. And though this condition has become more treatable, Gibbons is careful, for she does not want to sacrifice the creativity that has allowed her to become an award-winning novelist.

The novel *Ellen Foster* began life as a poem Gibbons started while a student at the University of North Carolina at Chapel Hill, initially in the voice of the protagonist's young African-American friend, Starletta. The author admitted to being influenced by the work of early twentieth-century African-American poet James Weldon Johnson, and his use of common speech patterns and idioms in his prose. "I wanted to see if I could have a child use her voice to talk about life, death, art, eternity—big things from a little person," Gibbons told Summer. Ellen Foster's title character is a mere eleven years of age, and the story follows her travails in the rural southern states as she bounces from relative to relative. Speaking in the first person, Gibbons's heroine refers to herself as "old Ellen," and recounts her difficulties in flashback form. Deanna D'Errico described her in *Belles Lettres* as "the embodiment of tenacity, surviving with the tools of intelligence, sensitivity, a strong will, and a remarkable sense of humor." In the novel, Ellen's mother was the frail scion of a well-to-do family whom she alienated by marrying beneath her, and their offspring has it rough from the start. When her mother commits suicide, Ellen is left with a parent whom she describes as "a monster." His attempt at sexual abuse one drunken night leads Ellen to the jurisdiction of the court system, and a judge sends her to live with her wealthy, but extremely resentful, maternal grandmother.

Ellen's grandmother vents her grief at her daughter's suicide on her granddaughter, forcing her to work the family cotton fields and inflicting verbal and emotional abuse upon her. Over the course of Gibbons's novel, Ellen faces her problems with a good nature and determination: she learns to hoard money in a small box that contains all of her other vital belongings. She also befriends the aforementioned Starletta, who is mute. "Gibbons, unlike so many writers of the New South, doesn't evade the racism of Southern life," wrote Pearl K. Bell in a review of *Ellen Foster* for the *New Republic.* Growing up hearing the racial prejudices of her family, Ellen also feels such biases, and reminds herself that no matter how bad her own situation is, it would be worse to be "colored."

When Ellen's grandmother dies, she is sent to live with an aunt, and the aunt and Ellen's cousin also heap abuse upon her—at one point, ridiculing the picture she has drawn for them for a Christmas present as "cheap-looking." When the aunt sends her away, Ellen spends a night at Starletta's home, which eventually leads to the protagonist's realization that "now I know it is not the germs you cannot see . . . that will hurt you or turn you colored. What you had better worry about though is the people you knew and trusted they would be like you because you were all made in the same batch." In the end, Ellen discovers that her small town contains a "foster" family—a single woman who takes in children. She shows up on their doorstep and offers the $160 contents of her box in exchange for a home.

In the *New Republic* review, Bell praised Gibbons's evocation of Ellen's unique personality through her narrative, as did many other reviewers. "The voice of this resourceful child is mesmerizing because we are right inside her head," she noted. Alice Hoffman reviewed *Ellen Foster* for the *New York Times Book Review* and asserted that the first-time author "is so adept at drawing her characters that we know Ellen, and, yes, trust her from the start." Hoffman further noted that "in many ways this is an old-fashioned novel about traditional values and inherited prejudices. . . . What might have been grim, melodramatic material in the hands of a less talented author is instead filled with lively humor . . . , compassion and intimacy." *Sunday Times* critic Linda Taylor termed Gibbons's debut "fresh, instant and enchanting . . . a first novel that does not put a foot wrong in its sureness of style, tone and characterisation."

In her second novel, *A Virtuous Woman,* Gibbons again sets her characters in the rural South and allows them to speak in the idiomatic, direct language of her own upbringing. The 1989 work opens as Jack Stokes laments the loss of Ruby, his wife of many years, from lung cancer. "She hasn't been dead four months and I've already eaten to the bottom of the deep freeze," the farmer thinks to himself; despite her illness, Ruby had prepared months worth of meals ahead of time for Jack. Such details pointing to the ordinary, yet loving familiarities of the institution of marriage are what Gibbons attempts to call forth in the story. *A Virtuous Woman* is told in alternating first-person flashbacks for most of its course—Jack looking back after she is gone, alternating with Ruby's ruminations on their life together in the months before her death. The reader learns how Ruby's disastrous first marriage ultimately resulted in her inoperable tumors, and why her marriage to Jack was less vivid than her first, but over time, ultimately more satisfying.

As both characters in *A Virtuous Woman* come to grips with their impending tragedy, the interior monologues that Gibbons has Jack and Ruby voice in the novel propel it forward. Toward the end, Gibbons switches to a third-person perspective as the motivations and actions of other characters involved in Jack and Ruby's life come into play. "Too often, lacking a conflict of its own, the story wanders off to peek in at the neighbors," remarked *Los Angeles Times Book Review* critic Susan Heeger of this literary construction. "Pages are spent on the meanness of peripheral folk, whose main raison d'etre is to show up Jack's and Ruby's saintliness and to raise the question of why bad things happen to good people." The critic D'Errico, writing again for *Belles Lettres,* also found this switch disconcerting. "Technique suddenly looms over the tale," she lamented,

"and it is difficult to view the scene without fretting over the strings that are showing."

In 1997 Oprah Winfrey chose *Ellen Foster* and *A Virtuous Woman* for her television book club, exposure that launched the books onto the best-seller lists and thrust their author into the limelight. Gibbons found the publicity both a blessing and a curse: blessing for the sale of books she believes in, but a curse in terms of the distractions of fan mail and telephone calls. *Ellen Foster* has come to be read in many high schools along with such classics as *To Kill a Mockingbird* and *The Adventures of Huckleberry Finn. Ellen Foster* was made into a Hallmark television movie that premiered in December, 1997.

Gibbons's third novel, *A Cure for Dreams,* won the *Chicago Tribune*'s Nelson Algren Heartland award for fiction that same year. In it, Gibbons recounts the multigenerational family saga of a trio of three women: Lottie, her daughter Betty, and granddaughter Marjorie. The novel begins as Marjorie introduces her recently deceased mother Betty to the reader, and relates how much her mother loved to talk. "Talking was my mother's life," she says, and the story is soon overtaken by Betty's own narrative voice. Betty describes her indomitable Irish immigrant grandmother—Lottie's mother—and the harsh life Lottie suffered in rural Kentucky during the early years of the twentieth century. Lottie escapes by marriage, but her workaholic husband isolates her emotionally until Betty arrives as a newborn in 1920.

As some reviewers noted, most of the male characters in *A Cure for Dreams* seem unsympathetic figures, absorbed in their own world of nonverbal communication, while the women ultimately triumph over adversity by virtue of their need to communicate with one another, resulting in strong bonds. In coming together, they manage to overcome both petty and grievous abuses inflicted upon them by the men of their families. Throughout the course of *A Cure for Dreams,* Gibbons lets Betty continue the decades-long tale of her family, recalling how her mother, Lottie, became the de facto community leader of the women around North Carolina's Milk Farm Road in the 1920s. She organized card parties, passed along useful gossip and wisdom, and at one point even protected a friend who may or may not have shot her abusive husband. Betty's own saga of coming of age in the South of the 1930s is also recounted, and the novel ends with the birth of her daughter Marjorie during World War II.

The overwhelming successes of Gibbons's literary career were also accompanied by periods of personal strife during the early 1990s. She went through a divorce, relocated to New York City but returned to North Carolina, and changed publishers. In 1993, her fourth novel, *Charms for the Easy Life,* was published. Like *A Cure for Dreams,* the story follows the exploits of a family of strong women, and develops through the recollections of its youngest member. Set over a forty-year span that ends during World War II, the novel begins with narrator Margaret recounting the courtship of her grandparents in Pasquotank County, North Carolina. Her grandmother, Charlie (Clarissa) Kate, becomes the central figure in the novel through her work as a local midwife and faith healer. Gibbons had originally modeled the character on an African-American midwife who served as the best friend of Lottie in her previous novel, but reconsidered doing a sequel after she began, and instead made Charlie into a completely separate entity.

Like Lottie in *A Cure for Dreams,* Charlie becomes a vital and important force in her rural community. When she saves an African-American man from a lynching, he gives her a rabbit's foot, her "easy-life charm." A folk healer who reads the *New England Journal of Medicine,* Charlie promotes sex education and manages to put a halt to the damaging medical treatment meted out by the charlatan local "trained" doctor. She is also the first person in the community to own a toilet. "She's an implacable force of nature, a pillar of intellect, with insight and powers of intuition so acute as to seem nearly supernatural," remarked Stephen McCauley of Gibbons's creation in the *New York Times Book Review.* As in previous works, the author allowed few compassionate male characters into the story of the three women. "The men in their lives are largely ineffectual," observed McCauley. "They can be relied upon only to disappoint, disappear and die." Charlie's husband simply does not return home one evening, an act which has little impact upon her young daughter, Sophie. Like her mother, Sophie later enters into a marriage with the wrong man, who passes away in the middle of the night; the two then move in with Charlie. Now all three women are free to pursue their ambitions and lend support to one another. They debate literature, Sophie and Margaret act as assistants to Charlie's unofficial doctor/dentist/midwife practice, and Charlie meddles in the affairs of her granddaughter, who in turn finds inspiration from the older woman.

Published in 1995, Gibbons's *Sights Unseen* tells the story, from the perspective of twelve-year-old daughter Hattie, of a mother's struggle with mental illness and its pervasive influence on her family's life. This novel was part of Gibbons's efforts to come to grips with the mental illness that had cost her mother her life and has plagued the author for decades. She struggled in its production, writing five drafts before she was satisfied. Her efforts paid off, for it garnered praised from critics. Comparing *Sights Unseen* to Gibbons's first novel, *Ellen Foster, New Yorker* critic James Wolcott noted that the narrator in each novel portrays "an avid need for normality and acceptance in a world of precarious well-being." A *Publishers Weekly* reviewer cited Gibbons's "restrained prose of unflinching clarity" and praised the novel, declaring it "a haunting story that begs to be read in one sitting." As Donna Seaman noted in *Booklist,* "Gibbons writes seamless and resonant novels, the sort of fiction that wins hearts as well as awards." Indeed, *Sights Unseen* won the *Los Angeles Times* Critics Choice Award for that year.

For her next novel, Gibbons delved into the history of the twentieth-century South that had been the setting of her previous works. *On the Occasion of My Last Afternoon,* so titled because first-person narrator, Emma Lowell, is recalling her life as she prepares to die, follows the narrator's life as the daughter of a Southern slaveowner who follows her own path. In the *Winston-Salem Journal,* Anne Barnhill remarked how well Gibbons's research into the era served her: "It's evident that Gibbons has done a great deal of research for this book. The language has the authentic sound of yesteryear, and interesting details are peppered throughout the novel." *Library Journal*'s Joanna M. Burkhardt likewise praised the novel for its "crystal clarity and brilliant realism." However, while *America* reviewer Jane Fisher found the novel "lively and readable," she questioned Gibbons's characterization of Emma, who, she complained, "seems almost too good to be true." Another reviewer found the novel to be too didactic at times: "Gibbons has wrought a balanced and highly accessible novel which, although well constructed and provocative, descends into cliched and tiresome tirades," wrote *London Times* critic Victoria Fletcher. Because of its fictional memoir structure, the reader knows that the narrator survives any perils, thus eliminating some of the possible suspense. Nevertheless, Dennis Love of the *San Francisco Chronicle* maintained that Gibbons overcomes any difficulties the structure might pose: "We see everything coming from miles away, yet it doesn't matter; this is a master storyteller who, like some arrogant, gifted athlete, telegraphs her every move but still scores at will." Despite any shortcomings, Fisher suggested that Gibbons's "major appeal as a novelist lies in her linking of unrelenting truth with the transformative power of unconditional love" and that she succeeds again in linking the two in *On the Occasion of My Last Afternoon.*

Despite the praise bestowed by critics and the numerous awards she has received, Gibbons admits that the writer's life is a strenuous one. "Nobody ever told me it was going to be easy," she noted in the interview with Bob Summer for *Publishers Weekly*. "If I weren't a writer, I'd probably be a lawyer or an architect. I wouldn't want to do anything easy, and I chose to be a writer." The author reflected that, "as a writer, it's my job to come up with three hundred pages or so every two years. Each time I begin, I know it's going to happen, but I'm scared it won't. It's working with that element of fear that keeps a book going," a process she also likened to "looking over an abyss and knowing I have to jump."

BIOGRAPHICAL AND CRITICAL SOURCES:

BOOKS

Authors and Artists for Young Adults, Volume 34, Thomson Gale (Detroit, MI), 2000.

DeMarr, Mary Jean, *Kaye Gibbons: A Critical Companion,* Greenwood Press (Westport, CT), 2003.

Lewis, Nancy, "Kaye Gibbons: Her Full-Time Women," in *Southern Writers at Century's End,* edited by Jeffrey J. Folks and James A. Perkins, University Press of Kentucky (Lexington, KY), 112-122.

Munafo, Giavanna, "'Colored Biscuits': Reconstructing Whiteness and the Boundaries of 'Home' in Kaye Gibbons's *Ellen Foster,*" pp. 38-61.

Watkins, James, editor, *Southern Selves, from Mark Twain and Eudora Welty to Maya Angelou and Kaye Gibbons: A Collection of Autobiographical Writing,* Vintage (New York, NY), 1998.

PERIODICALS

America, January 2, 1999, Jane Fisher, review of *On the Occasion of My Last Afternoon,* p. 16.

Atlanta Journal-Constitution, June 2, 1998, "In Search of a Novel: Author Kay Gibbons Talks about Her New Civil War Book, the 'Oprah Hoopla' and Why She Tossed out 900 Pages," p. D1.

Belles Lettres, summer, 1987, Deanna D'Errico, review of *Ellen Foster,* p. 9; summer, 1989, Deanna D'Errico, "Two Timers," p. 7; winter 1993-94, Gale Harris, "Beyond the *Scarlett* Image: Women Writing about the South," pp. 16-18.

Book, November-December, 2002, Liz Seymour, "Oh, Kaye!," pp. 24-26.

Booklist, September 1, 1987, Brad Hooper, review of *Ellen Foster,* p. 27; June 1, 1999, reviews of *Ellen Foster* and *A Virtuous Woman,* pp. 1796-1797; August, 1999, review of *Charms for the Easy Life,* p. 2024; February 15, 2000, Donna Seaman, review of *On the Occasion of My Last Afternoon,* p. 1078; September 15, 2001, Karen Harris, review of *Sights Unseen* (audio version), p. 241.

Christian Century, September 23, Ralph C. Wood, "Gumption and Grace in the Novels of Kaye Gibbons," pp. 842-846.

Entertainment Weekly, April 4, 1995, Rebecca Ascher-Walsh, review of *Sights Unseen,* p. 53.

Globe and Mail (Toronto, Ontario, Canada), June 12, 1999, reviews of *A Virtuous Woman* and *Ellen Foster,* p. D4.

Grand Rapids Press (Grand Rapids, MI), April 14, 2002, Ann Byle, "Easter Story Inspires Gibbons' Latest Novel," p. 16.

Journal of American Studies, April, 1999, Sharon Monteith, "Between Girls: Kaye Gibbons's *Ellen Foster* and Friendship As a Monologic Formulation," pp. 45-46.

Kirkus Reviews, March 15, 1987, review of *Ellen Foster,* p. 404; January 15, 2004, review of *Divining Women,* p. 52.

Kliatt Young Adult Paperback Book Guide, September, 1997, p. 4; September, 1998, pp. 4, 61; July, 1999, review of *A Virtuous Woman* (audio version), p. 56.

Library Journal, June 1, 1998, p. 150; September, 1998, pp. 4, 61; February 15, 1999, review of *Ellen Foster* (audio version), p. 126; April 15, 1999, Joanna M. Burkhardt, review of *A Virtuous Woman* (audio version), p. 165; September 15, 1999, Joanna M. Burkhardt, review of *On the Occasion of My Last Afternoon* (audio version), p. 130.

Los Angeles Times Book Review, June 11, 1989, Susan Heeger, review of *A Virtuous Woman,* p. 15; May 19, 1991, Josephine Humphreys, review of *A Cure for Dreams,* p. 13.

New Republic, February 29, 1998, Pearl K. Bell, "Southern Discomfort," pp. 38-41.

New York, April 1, 1991, Rhoda Koenig, "Southern Comfort," p. 63.

New Yorker, June 21, 1993, p. 101; August 21 1995, James Wolcott, "Crazy for You," pp. 115-16.

New York Times Book Review, May 31, 1987, Alice Hoffman, "Shopping for a New Family," review of *Ellen Foster,* p. 13; April 12, 1989, pp. 12-13; April 30, 1989, Padgett Powell, "As Ruby Lay Dying," pp. 12-13; May 12, 1991, James Wilcox, review of *A Cure for Dreams,* pp. 13-14; April 11, 1993, Stephen McCauley, "He's Gone, Go Start the Coffee," pp. 9-10; September 24, 1995, Jacqueline Carey, "Mommy Direst," p. 30.

Observer (London, England), June 2, 1996, Kate Kellaway, review of *Sights Unseen,* p. 16.

People, June 15, 1998, review of *On the Occasion of My Last Afternoon,* p. 49.

Publishers Weekly, March 20, 1987, review of *Ellen Foster,* p. 70; February 8, 1993, Kaye Gibbons, with Bob Summer, "Kaye Gibbons," pp. 60-61; June 5, 1995, p. 48; April 20, 1998, review of *On the Occasion of My Last Afternoon,* p. 43.

San Francisco Chronicle, June 14, 1998, Dennis Love, "Home Is No Refuge for Southern Women in the Civil War," review of *On the Occasion of My Last Afternoon,* p. 3.

San Francisco Review of Books, spring, 1991, Benedict Cosgrove, review of *A Cure for Dreams,* pp. 31-32.

School Library Journal, September, 1993, p. 260; December, 1993, p. 29; September, 1998, Molly Connally, review of *On the Occasion of My Last Afternoon,* p. 229.

Southern Literary Journal, spring, 1994, Tonita Branan, "Women and 'The Gift for Gab': Revisionary Strategies in *A Cure for Dreams,*" pp. 91-101.

Southern Quarterly, winter, 1992, Veronica Makowsky, "'The Only Hard Part Was the Food:' Recipes for Self-Nurture in Kaye Gibbons's Novels," pp. 103-112; summer, 1997, Kathryn McKee, "Simply Talking: Women and Language in Kaye Gibbons's *A Cure for Dreams,*" pp. 97-106.

Southern Studies, summer, 1992, Stephen Souris, "Kaye Gibbons's *A Virtuous Woman,*" 99-115.

Time, April 12, 1993, Amelia Weiss, "Medicine Woman," pp. 77-78.

Times (London, England), May 22, 1999, Victoria Fletcher, "Slave to the Soapbox," review of *On the Occasion of My Last Afternoon,* p. 22.

Times Literary Supplement, November 25, 1988, Andrew Rosenheim, "Voices of the New South," p. 1306; September 15, 1989, Roz Kavaney, "Making Themselves Over," p. 998; July 2, 1999, review of *On the Occasion of My Last Afternoon,* p. 22.

Tribune Books (Chicago, IL), September 15, 1991, p. 7.

Washington Post Book World, July 12, 1998, Susan Dodd, "A Sentimental Education," *On the Occasion of My Last Afternoon,* p. 9.

Winston-Salem Journal (Winston-Salem, NC), July 12, 1998, Anne Barnhill, "Broken Promise: Gibbons' Memoir-Like Tale Lacks Drama," review of *On the Occasion of My Last Afternoon,* p. A22.

Women's Review of Books, July, 1989, Marilyn Chandler, review of *A Virtuous Woman,* p. 21; October, 1993, Judith Beth Cohen, "Daughters of the South," p. 24.

ONLINE

Chelsea Forum, http://www.chelseaforum.com/ (August 17, 2003), "Kaye Gibbons."

Kaye Gibbons Home Page, http://www.kayegibbons.com/ (February 19, 2004).

Syracuse Online, http://syracuse.com/ (August 17, 2003), Laura T. Ryan, "Gibbons Says Manic Depression Fuels Her Art."

Womankind Educational and Resource Center, http://www.womankindflp.org/ (1993), Steve Moore, "Conversation with Kay Gibbons."

*   *   *

GIBSON, William 1914-
(William Mass)

PERSONAL: Born November 13, 1914, in New York, NY; son of George Irving (a bank clerk) and Florence (Dore) Gibson; married Margaret Brenman (a psychoanalyst), September 6, 1940; children: Thomas, Daniel. *Education:* Attended College of City of New York (now City College of the City University of New York), 1930-32. *Politics:* Democrat.

ADDRESSES: Home—General Delivery, Stockbridge, MA 01262-9999. *Agent*—Flora Roberts, 157 West 57th St., New York, NY 10022.

CAREER: Author and playwright. Piano teacher at intervals in early writing days to supplement income. President and cofounder of Berkshire Theatre Festival, Stockbridge, MA, 1966—.

MEMBER: PEN, Authors League of America, Dramatists Guild.

AWARDS, HONORS: Harriet Monroe Memorial Prize, 1945, for group of poems published in *Poetry;* Topeka Civic Theatre Award, 1947, for *A Cry of Players;* Sylvania Award, 1957, for television play *The Miracle Worker;* Antoinette Perry Award Nomination for best play, 1958, for *Two for the Seesaw;* Antoinette Perry Award for best play, 1960, for *The Miracle Worker.*

WRITINGS:

PLAYS

I Lay in Zion (one-act play; produced at Topeka Civic Theatre, 1943), Samuel French (New York, NY), 1947.

(Under pseudonym William Mass) *The Ruby* (one-act lyrical drama), with libretto (based on Lord Dunsany's *A Night at an Inn*) by Norman Dello Joio, Ricordi, 1955.

The Miracle Worker (three-act; originally written as a television drama; produced by Columbia Broadcasting System for *Playhouse 90* in 1957 and by National Broadcasting Company in 1979; rewritten for stage and produced on Broadway at Playhouse Theatre, October 19, 1959; rewritten for screen and produced by United Artists in 1962; also see below), Knopf (New York, NY), 1957.

Dinny and the Witches [and] *The Miracle Worker* (the former produced off-Broadway at Cherry Lane Theatre, December 9, 1959; also see below), Atheneum (New York, NY), 1960.

Two for the Seesaw (three-act comedy; copyrighted in 1956 as *After the Verb to Love*; produced on Broadway at Booth Theatre, January 16, 1958; also see below), Samuel French (New York, NY), 1960.

Dinny and the Witches: A Frolic on Grave Matters, Dramatists Play Service, 1961.

(With Clifford Odets) *Golden Boy* (musical adaptation of Odets's original drama, with lyrics by Lee Adams, and music by Charles Strouse; first produced on Broadway at Majestic Theatre, October 20, 1964), Atheneum (New York, NY), 1965.

A Cry of Players (three-act; produced at Topeka Civic Theatre, February, 1948; produced on Broadway at the Vivian Beaumont Theatre, November 14, 1968), Atheneum (New York, NY), 1969.

John and Abigail (three-act drama; produced at Berkshire Theatre Festival, 1969, later in Washington, DC, at Ford's Theatre, January 9, 1970), published as *American Primitive: The Words of John and Abigail Adams Put into a Sequence for the Theater, with Addenda in Rhyme,* Atheneum (New York, NY), 1972.

The Body and the Wheel (produced in Lenox, MA, at Pierce Chapel, April 5, 1974), Dramatists Play Service, 1975.

The Butterfingers Angel, Mary and Joseph, Herod the Nut, and the Slaughter of 12 Hit Carols in a Pear Tree (produced at Pierce Chapel, December, 1974), Dramatists Play Service, 1975.

Golda (produced on Broadway at the Morosco Theatre, November 14, 1977), Samuel French (New York, NY), 1977.

Goodly Creatures (produced in Washington, DC, at the Round House Theatre, January, 1980), Dramatists Play Service, 1990.

Monday after the Miracle (produced in Charleston, SC, at the Dock Street Theatre, May, 1982, later produced on Broadway at the Eugene O'Neill Theatre, December 14, 1982), Dramatists Play Service, 1990.

Handy Dandy (produced in New York, NY, 1984), Dramatists Play Service, 1986.

Raggedy Ann and Andy (musical; music and lyrics by Joe Raposo), first produced in Albany, NY, 1984, produced in New York City, 1986, as *Raggedy Ann.*

Golda's Balcony (one-act; produced in Lenox, MA, May 18, 2002), Applause Theatre & Cinema Books (New York, NY), 2003.

OTHER

Winter Crook (poems), Oxford University Press (Oxford, England), 1948.

The Cobweb (novel), Knopf (New York, NY), 1954.

The Seesaw Log (a chronicle of the stage production, including the text of *Two for the Seesaw*), Knopf (New York, NY), 1959.

A Mass for the Dead (chronicle and poems), Atheneum (New York, NY), 1968.

A Season in Heaven (chronicle), Atheneum (New York, NY), 1974.

Shakespeare's Game (criticism), Atheneum (New York, NY), 1978.

ADAPTATIONS: The Cobweb was filmed by Metro-Goldwyn-Mayer, 1957; *Two for the Seesaw* was filmed by United Artists, 1962.

SIDELIGHTS: While William Gibson has published poetry, plays, fiction, and criticism, he is best known for his 1957 play *The Miracle Worker.* Originally written and performed as a television drama, and adapted in later years for both stage and screen, *The Miracle Worker* remains Gibson's most widely revived piece. It was filmed again for television in 1979 and also formed the basis for Gibson's 1982 play, *Monday after the Miracle,* which picks up the characters almost twenty years later. Writing in the *Dictionary of Literary Biography,* Stephen C. Coy called the drama "a classic American play—and television play, and film—the full stature of which has yet to be realized."

The story, which is based on real people and actual events, concerns the relationship between Helen Keller, a handicapped child who has been deaf and blind since infancy, and Annie Sullivan, the formerly blind teacher who has been called in to instruct her. When Annie arrives she finds that Helen has been utterly spoiled by well-intentioned parents who, in their sympathy, allow her to terrorize the household. Annie's efforts to civilize Helen and Helen's resistance result in a fierce, and frequently physical, struggle that forms the central conflict of the play. The "miracle" occurs when, after months of frustration, Annie is finally able to reach the child. Coy explained: "Just as the struggle appears to be lost, Helen starts to work the pump in the Keller yard and the miracle—her mind learning to name things—happens before the audience as she feels the water and the wet ground. Annie and others realize what is happening as Helen, possessed, runs about touching things and learning names, finally, to their great joy, 'Mother' and 'Papa.' The frenzy slows as Helen realizes there is something she needs to know, gets Annie to spell it for her, spells it back, and goes to spell it for her mother. It is the one word which more than any other describes the subject of *The Miracle Worker:* 'Teacher.'"

Praising the play's "youthfulness and vigor," *New York Times* reviewer Bosley Crowther described the tremendous concentration of energy apparent in the battle scenes between Helen and Annie: "The physical vitality and passion are absolutely intense as the nurse, played superbly by Anne Bancroft moves in and takes on the job of 'reaching the soul' of the youngster, played by Patty Duke. . . . When the child, who is supposed to be Helen Keller in her absolutely primitive childhood state, kicks and claws with the frenzy of a wild beast at the nurse who is supposed to be Annie Sullivan, the famous instructor of Miss Keller, it is a staggering attack. And when Annie hauls off and swats her or manhandles her into a chair and pushes food into her mouth to teach her habits, it is enough to make the viewer gasp and grunt."

The Broadway production of the play was so well received that a film version with the same stars was made in 1962 and enjoyed similar success. Later revivals have not fared so well. When *The Miracle Worker* was filmed for television in 1979 (with Patty Duke playing Annie Sullivan), Tom Shales commented in the *Washington Post* that the only point in doing *The Miracle Worker* again "was to give Patty Duke Astin a chance on the other side of the food." His objections ranged from what he called "careless casting" to the inappropriateness (almost an insult, he called it) of making a television movie from a screenplay written for live television. For the writing itself, however, Shales had nothing but praise. "William Gibson's play . . . remains, even when not perfectly done, a nearly perfect joy, one of the most assuredly affirmative dramatic works to come out of the optimistic '50s."

Gibson's three-act play, *Two for the Seesaw,* which played on Broadway in 1958, starring Anne Bancroft and Henry Fonda, was a hit, giving momentum to the playwright's career. This "most adroit and refreshing dramatic duet," as Marya Mannes called it in the *Reporter,* revolves around the relationship of Jerry, a lawyer from Nebraska, and Gittel, a girl from the Bronx. Though Lionel Trilling suggested in the *Drama Review* that the play "challenges none of the vested interests, affronts none of the deep-rooted pieties of . . . [the] audience," he remarked that "even a modest comedy about a love affair may be more or less honest, as may any scene in the play, or any speech in a scene." Likening it to a best-selling novel, the *Nation*'s Harold Clurman went on to describe the work as a "conventional tale" lacking concrete characters, but replete with jokes and clichés. When Gibson published the play as *The Seesaw Log,* he prefaced it with a chronicle of the more than two months of work that led up to its Broadway premiere. When the play was revived at the Marin Theatre in Mill Valley, California, in 2002, the director staged it as a period piece. Although *San Francisco Chronicle* critic Robert Hurwitt found the more than two-hour length unjustified for the plot and ill-suited to the modern theatergoer, he praised its undated emotional realism. "As much as its details demonstrate the degree to which things have changed since 1958," he added, "the emotional journeys of its characters haven't dated a bit."

In addition to *The Miracle Worker,* and *Two for the Seesaw,* Gibson wrote several other three-act biographical plays, including *Cry of Players,* about William Shakespeare and Anne Hathaway; *John and Abigail,* about John and Abigail Adams; *Goodly Creatures,* about Anne Hutchinson; and *Golda,* about Israeli prime minister Golda Meir. In 1977 *Golda* appeared on Broadway, starring Anne Bancroft. The play portrays not only Meir's political role, but shows through flashbacks her childhood, life, and work with the Zionist movement. The original had a short and unsuccessful run, yet Gibson felt strongly enough about the work to return to it a quarter-century later. The octogenarian reworked what had been a play with a cast of more than twenty, to a one-act version titled *Golda's Balcony.* With the distance of time between the play and the historical events of the Yom Kippur War, during which the play takes place, *Golda's Balcony* fared much better. While during the original production, the personages and events were often in the news, in the reworked version subtle video projections of personages and events help viewers put the work into historical context. Noting that the play, "imparts a lot of information in its ninety minutes," *Variety*'s Marland Taylor found that "sometimes the transitions from Israel's history to her [Meir's] personal history are too abrupt," and the work seems rather like a lecture. Despite the fact that the play portrays only the Israeli viewpoint about the war, Neil Genzlinger described the play as "enlightening nonetheless" in his *New York Times* review. "Thanks to the vigor of Gibson's writing and actor Annette Miller's strong performance, *Golda's Balcony* is often involving and enlightening," concluded Taylor.

"Despite an age most would consider ripe for retirement, William Gibson (just shy of 90) shows no signs of stopping," wrote Sarah Hart in a sidebar for her 2003 article in *American Theatre*. The Berkshire Theatre Festival opened the 2003 season with Gibson's *American Primitive*, which had premiered at the festival in 1969 as *John and Abigail*. Gibson remained excited about the play that he once thought was not quite right for the theatre. "This production is the first time that this play convinced me it was a theatre piece," Gibson told Hart. "The actors, the direction—It's extraordinary." Festival executive director Kate Maguire noted, "His mind and strength are so intense. I want to be around that, and I want it for the organization. It feels like good karma to open the season with his play, like all the elements have conspired to bring this about."

BIOGRAPHICAL AND CRITICAL SOURCES:

BOOKS

Contemporary Dramatists, 6th edition, St. James Press (Detroit, MI), 1999.
Contemporary Literary Criticism, Volume 23, Thomson Gale (Detroit, MI), 1983.
Dictionary of Literary Biography, Volume 7: *Twentieth-Century American Dramatists,* Thomson Gale (Detroit, MI), 1981.
Gibson, William, *The Seesaw Log,* Knopf (New York, NY), 1959.

PERIODICALS

America, November 10, 1990, p. 350.
American Theatre, November, 2003, Sarah Hart, "An American Revolution: The 75-Year-Old Berkshire Theatre Festival Looks to Its Star-Spangled Past to Inspire a Still-Fermenting Future" (includes sidebar "For William Gibson, Opportunity Knocks Twice"), p. 32.
Back Stage West, January 6, 2000, Terri Roberts, review of *The Miracle Worker,* p. 10.
Cosmopolitan, August, 1958.
Daily Variety, June 5, 2002, Marland Taylor, review of *Golda's Balcony,* p. 9.

Drama Review, May, 1960, Lionel Trilling, review of *Two for the Seesaw,* p. 17.
Los Angeles Times, October 19, 1982; May 13, 1999, Mark Chalon Smith, "Actors Carry *Miracle* in Costa Mesa," p. 6.
Nation, February 1, 1958, Harold Clurman, review of *Two for the Seesaw,* p. 107; December 2, 1968.
New England Theatre, spring, 1970.
New Leader, December 16, 1968.
New Republic, November 9, 1959, Robert Brustein, review of *The Miracle Worker,* p. 28.
Newsweek, March 16, 1959; July 27, 1970.
New York, November 5, 1990, p. 127.
New Yorker, November 23, 1968; November 5, 1990, p. 120.
New York Times, May 24, 1962; May 27, 1962; June 3, 1962; November 16, 1977; December 9, 1980; May 26, 1982; December 15, 1982; March 16, 2003, Shimon Peres, "Always a Lioness, Protecting Her Beloved Israel," p. 7(L); April 1, 2003, Neil Genzlinger, "A 1977 Golda Meir Gets into Shape," review of *Golda's Balcony,* p. E5.
New York Times Book Review, March 15, 1959, Harold Clurman, review of *Two for the Seesaw,* p. 5; April 14, 1968.
Poetry, August, 1948, James Hall, review of *Winter Crook,* pp. 278, 281.
Reporter, March 6, 1958, Marya Mannes, review of *Two for the Seesaw,* p. 36.
San Francisco Chronicle, May 23, 2002, Robert Hurwitt, "*Seesaw*'s Timeless Back-and-Forth; 1958 Broadway Hit Retains Relevance," p. D9.
Saturday Review, March 13, 1954, Charles Lee, review of "The Cobweb," p. 19; March 14, 1959, Henry Hewes, review of *The Seesaw Log,* p. 55; March 23, 1968.
Tulane Drama Review, May, 1960.
Variety, February 21, 1971; June 10, 2002, Marland Taylor, review of *Golda's Balcony,* p. 38; March 31, 2003, Marilyn Stasio, review of *Golda's Balcony,* p. 30.
Washington Post, October 13, 1979; January 20, 1980; January 26, 1980; November 27, 1981; December 3, 1981; October 3, 1982; October 14, 1982.
Writing, Conrad Geller, "A Battle to Free a Human Soul: In *The Miracle Worker,* William Gibson Skillfully Depicts Conflict-The Center of All Successful Drama," p. 14.

*   *   *

GIBSON, William 1948-

PERSONAL: Born March 17, 1948, in Conway, SC; emigrated to Canada; son of William Ford (a contractor) and Otey (a homemaker; maiden name, Williams) Gibson; married Deborah Thompson (a language instructor), June, 1972; children: Graeme, Claire. *Education:* University of British Columbia, B.A., 1977.

ADDRESSES: Home—Vancouver, British Columbia, Canada. *Agent*—Martha Millard Literary Agency, 293 Greenwood Ave., Florham Park, NJ 07932; (for film and television) Martin S. Shapiro, Shapiro-Lichtman Talent, 8827 Beverly Blvd., Los Angeles, CA 90048.

CAREER: Writer.

AWARDS, HONORS: Nebula Award nomination from Science Fiction Writers of America, c. 1983, for short story "Burning Chrome"; Hugo Award for best novel of 1984 from World Science Fiction Society, Philip K. Dick Award for best U.S. original paperback of 1984 from Philadelphia Science Fiction Society, Nebula Award for best novel of 1984 from Science Fiction Writers of America, and Porgie Award for best paperback original novel in science fiction from *West Coast Review of Books,* all 1985, and Ditmar Award from Australian National Science Fiction Convention, all for *Neuromancer; New York Times Book Review* Notable Book for 2003, *Washington Post* Choice Cuts of 2003 pick, and *Los Angeles Times* Best of the Best Book for 2003 selection, all for *Pattern Recognition.*

WRITINGS:

"CYBERSPACE" TRILOGY

Neuromancer Ace (New York, NY), 1984.
Count Zero, Arbor House (New York, NY), 1986.
Mona Lisa Overdrive, Bantam (New York, NY), 1988.

OTHER

(With John Shirley, Bruce Sterling, and Michael Swanwick) *Burning Chrome* (short stories; includes "Burning Chrome," "Johnny Mnemonic," and "New Rose Hotel"), introduction by Bruce Sterling, Arbor House (New York, NY), 1986.
Dream Jumbo (text to accompany performance art by Robert Longo), produced at UCLA Center for the Performing Arts, Los Angeles, CA, 1989.
(With Bruce Sterling) *The Difference Engine* (novel), Gollancz (London, England), 1990, Bantam (New York, NY), 1991.
Virtual Light (novel; first in trilogy), Viking (New York, NY), 1993.

Johnny Mnemonic (screenplay; based on Gibson's short story of the same title), TriStar, 1995.
Idoru (novel; second in trilogy), Putnam (New York, NY), 1996.
All Tomorrow's Parties (novel; third in trilogy), Putnam (New York, NY), 1999.
Pattern Recognition, Putnam (New York, NY), 2003.

Work represented in anthologies, including *Shadows 4,* Doubleday, 1981; *Nebula Award Stories 17,* Holt, 1983; and *Mirrorshades: The Cyberpunk Anthology,* edited with an introduction by Sterling, Arbor House, 1986. Contributor of short stories, articles, and book reviews to periodicals, including *Omni, Rolling Stone, Wired,* and *Science Fiction Review.* Scriptwriter for "Kill Switch," an episode of *The X-Files,* 1999. Contributor to Fox Network series *Harsh Realm,* 2000.

ADAPTATIONS: Neuromancer has been optioned for production as a feature film to be directed by Chris Cunningham.

SIDELIGHTS: Creator of the concept "Cyberspace," science-fiction author William Gibson developed a new fictional landscape for his edgy work—a hallucinatory three-dimensional region built from computer data gathered around the globe. Inventing this fictional setting, he could also leave it behind, which he has in later work. Increasingly, Gibson's creative production has come back from the future to deal with the here and now, forming a distinct arc from his 1984 debut sf novel, *Neuromancer,* set in the gritty futuristic urban world of the Sprawl, to his 2003 mainstream thriller, *Pattern Recognition,* placed in the dystopic present and featuring actual locales from London to Moscow and Tokyo.

Gibson had published only a handful of short stories when he stunned readers with his debut novel, *Neuromancer,* the first work ever to sweep the major honors of science fiction—the Hugo, Nebula, and Philip K. Dick awards. Combining the hip cynicism of the rock music underground and the dizzying powers of high technology, the novel was hailed as the prototype of a new style of writing, promptly dubbed "cyberpunk." Gibson, who was also earning praise as a skillful prose stylist, disliked the trendy label but admitted that he was challenging science fiction traditions. "I'm not even sure what cyberpunk means," he told a contributor for the *Philadelphia Inquirer,* "but I suppose it's useful as a tip-off to people that what they're going to read is a little wilder."

The surface features of Gibson's allegedly cyberpunk style—tough characters facing a tough world, frantic pacing, and bizarre high-tech slang—alienated some reviewers. "Like punk rock . . . Cyberpunk caters to the wish-fulfillment requirements of male teenagers," explained science-fiction novelist Thomas M. Disch in *New York Times Book Review,* "and there is currently no more accomplished caterer than William Gibson." In *Science Fiction Review,* Andrew Andrews criticized the "style and execution" of *Count Zero,* a novel typical of Gibson's work during the 1980s. "It is hodgepodge; spastic; incomprehensible in spots, somehow just *too much,*" the reviewer declared. "I prefer a novel that is concise, with fleshy, human characters." Beneath the flash, however, some admirers detected a serious purpose. Writers like Gibson, suggested J.R. Wytenbroeck in *Canadian Literature,* are really describing the world "in which we live today, with all its problems taken to their logical extreme." In particular, the advance of technology is shown to cause as many problems as it solves. "Technology has *already* changed us, and now we have to figure out a way to stay sane," Gibson observed in *Rolling Stone.* "If you were to put this in terms of mainstream fiction and present readers with a conventional book about modern postindustrial anxiety, many of them would just push it aside. But if you put it in the context of science fiction, maybe you can get them to sit still for what you have to say." Along with "adrenalin verve and random pyrotechnics," wrote Colin Greenland in the *Times Literary Supplement,* Gibson's work is "intellectually substantial." "His style," Greenland wrote, "is deadpan and precise, with the tone of the classic crime thriller: canny, cool and undeceived, yet ultimately the very opposite of the callousness it imitates, because motivated by a desire for justice."

Gibson grew up in a small town in southwest Virginia, Wytheville, on the edge of the Appalachian Mountains, where his widowed mother had grown up and back to which she moved when her husband, Gibson's father, died. "It was a boring, culturally deprived environment," he recalled in the *Sacramento Union.* "The library burned down in 1910, and nobody bothered to rebuild it." In such a place, he told *Interview*'s Victoria Hamburg, "science-fiction books were the only source I had for subversive information." By his late teens Gibson had left behind the conventional authors who filled the genre with shining cities and benevolent scientists. Instead he began to prefer iconoclasts, such as J.G. Ballard and Philip K. Dick, who described a grim and frightening future. Some of his favorites might not qualify with purists as science-fiction writers at all:

both William S. Burroughs and Thomas Pynchon were intricate stylists whose core following was among literary intellectuals. Such writers used the fantastic element of science fiction as a device to explore the ugly potentials of the human heart. Science fiction, Gibson realized, was a way to comment on the reality of the present day.

He escaped Wytheville by attending a private school in Arizona, but before he graduated, his mother died of a stroke. The 1960s youth culture also drew Gibson's attention; a long-term rock fan, he counts the hard-edged music of Lou Reed as a major influence. In 1967 he dropped out of high school and journeyed to Canada, ending up in Toronto, which had a thriving hippie scene. "We had our own version of the Summer of Love there," he said in the *Sacramento Union.* "If I'd gone to New York or San Francisco, I can't imagine what would have happened to me." Reluctant to be drafted into the Vietnam War, he remained in Canada and eventually married Deborah Thompson. The couple settled in Vancouver, where their lives soon centered around the University of British Columbia (UBC). Gibson's wife was a teacher and he was a "permanent pseudo-grad student" who earned his bachelor's degree shortly before he turned thirty. After graduating, "I was clueless," he recalled to an interviewer for the *Chicago Tribune.* "A lot of my friends were becoming lawyers and librarians, things that filled me with horror." So he became a science fiction writer, even though at the time "it seemed like such a goofy, unhip thing to do," as he told a contributor for *Rolling Stone.* Gibson began his career almost in spite of himself, after enrolling in a science fiction course at UBC with the hope of an easy credit. Unwilling to submit a term paper, he accepted the teacher's challenge to compose a short story—an ordeal that lasted three months. As Gibson settled into life as a househusband, however, he realized that writing more stories was the best way he could earn money while watching over his children.

His writing blossomed with amazing speed. He sold his first short story, "Fragments of a Hologram Rose," to *Unearth* magazine for the princely sum of twenty-three dollars in 1977, the year his first child, Graeme, was born. By the early 1980s Gibson was a favorite of fiction editor Ellen Datlow, who helped make *Omni* magazine a showcase of rising science fiction talent. In *Omni* stories such as "Johnny Mnemonic" and "Burning Chrome," Gibson began to sketch his own grim version of the future, peopled with what a *Rolling Stone* contributor called "high-tech lowlifes." The title character of "Johnny Mnemonic," for instance, stashes stolen computer data on a microchip in his brain. He is marked for murder by the Yakuza, a Japanese syndicate that has moved into high-tech crime, but he is saved by Molly Millions, a bionic hitwoman with razors implanted under her fingernails. "I thought I was on this literary kamikaze mission," Gibson told Mikal Gilmore in *Rolling Stone.* "I thought my work was so disturbing it would be dismissed and ignored by all but a few people." Instead, on the basis of a few short stories, he began to gain a powerful reputation: "Burning Chrome" was nominated for a Nebula Award, and Ace Books editor Terry Carr encouraged him to expand his vision into a novel. Meanwhile, "cyberpunk" was becoming a trend throughout the science-fiction world. After writing a third of his novel *Neuromancer,* Gibson went to see the 1982 film *Blade Runner,* director Ridley Scott's stylish, punked-out interpretation of a book by Philip K. Dick. "It looked so much like the inside of my head," reported Gibson in *Saturday Night,* "that I fled the theatre after about thirty minutes and have never seen the rest of it."

Neuromancer, together with its sequels, *Count Zero* and *Mona Lisa Overdrive,* fleshes out the future society of Gibson's short stories. Here technology is the main source of power over others, and the multinational corporations that develop and control technology are more important than governments. The world is a bewildering splatter of cultures and subcultures; Gibson skirts the issue of whether the United States or Canada are still viable countries, but his multinationals are generally based in Europe or Japan. While shadowy figures run the world for their own benefit, a large underclass—the focus of Gibson's interest—endures amid pollution, overcrowding, and pointlessness. People commonly drug themselves with chemicals or with "simstims," a form of electronic drug that allows users to experience vicariously the life of another, more glamorous, human being.

Though the future envisioned by Gibson may seem hopeless, he remains in some sense a romantic, observers note, for he chronicles the efforts of individuals to carve out a life for themselves in spite of hostile surroundings. His misfit heroes often exist on the crime-infested fringes of society, thus lending his works some of the atmosphere of a traditional crime thriller. Along with the expected cast of smugglers, prostitutes, murderers, and thieves, Gibson celebrates a distinctly modern freebooter, the computer hacker. Computers of the future, Gibson posits, will be linked worldwide through "cyberspace"—an electronically generated alternate reality in which all data, and the security programs that protect it, will appear as a palpable three-dimensional universe. Computer operators will access cyberspace by plugging into it with their brains, and hackers—known as "cowboys"—will sneak in to steal data, fill their bank accounts with electronic money, or suffer death when a security program uses feedback to destroy their minds. Gibson wrote in *Rolling Stone,* "The Street finds its own uses for things—uses the manufacturers never imagined."

Gibson's wandering youth did not hinder—and may have helped—his ability to create such a world. "I didn't invent most of what's strange in the [books'] dialogue," Gibson told a contributor for the *Mississippi Review,* as quoted in *Whole Earth Review.* "There are so many cultures and subcultures around today that if you're willing to listen, you start picking up different phrases, inflections, metaphors everywhere you go. A lot of stuff in *Neuromancer* and *Count Zero* that people think is so futuristic is probably just 1969 Toronto dope-dealers' slang, or bikers' slang." Gibson lacked an education in computers, but he knew about computer people. "They have this whole style of language. . . . which attracted me simply for the intensity with which they talked about their machines," he said in *Rolling Stone.* "I immediately heard that in a real echo of the teenagers I grew up with talking about cars." Cyberspace came from watching a new generation of youth in video arcades. "I could see in . . . their postures how *rapt* these kids were," Gibson informed the contributor for *Mississippi Review,* adding: "Everyone who works with computers seems to develop an intuitive faith that there's some kind of actual *space* behind the screen."

The plots of Gibson's works, some reviewers suggest, are less important than the way of life he describes: even admirers find the narratives rather complicated and difficult to summarize. As Gibson told Hamburg, he doesn't "really start with stories" but prefers to assemble images, "like making a ball out of rubber bands." *Neuromancer* centers on Henry Case, a skilled computer "cowboy" who has been punished for his exploits by being given a powerful nerve poison that leaves him unable to plug into cyberspace. As the book opens he is scrounging a living on the seamy side of Japan's Chiba City, when a mysterious patron offers him restorative surgery in exchange for more computer hacking. Case assents, and in the company of Molly Millions (one of Gibson's many recurring characters) he travels from one bizarre setting to the next in pursuit of a goal he cannot even understand. Finally Case arrives on a space station controlled by the wealthy Tessier-Ashpool clan, a family of genetic clones that owns two Artificial Intelligences—powerful computers which, like humans, have self-awareness and free will. Case realizes that one of the computers, named Wintermute, has hired him to help it take control of the other, named Neuromancer; the combined Artificial Intelligence that would result could break free of its human masters.

"*Neuromancer* was a bit hypermanic—simply from my terror at losing the reader's attention," Gibson recalled in *Rolling Stone.* For the sequel, *Count Zero,* "I aimed for a more deliberate pace. I also tried to draw the characters in considerable detail. People have children and dead parents in *Count Zero,* and that makes for different emotional territory." Thus instead of taking one main character on a manic ride throughout human society, *Count Zero* tells the stories of three more fleshed-out individuals whose lives gradually intertwine. The "Count Zero" of the title is really Bobby Newmark, a poor teenage computer "cowboy" with dreams of greatness. On his first illicit run into cyberspace, he finds it much more colorful than Henry Case had found it a few years earlier: the Artificial Intelligences of *Neuromancer* seem to have broken apart into many cyberspace entities, some of which manifest themselves as voodoo gods. The "gods" have human worshippers who take custody of Bobby after he apparently has a religious experience while he is hacking. Meanwhile, art dealer Marly Krushkova tries to find an artist with mysterious powers, only to encounter an old "cowboy" who also believes that God lives in cyberspace. And Turner, a mercenary who rounds up scientists for multinationals, finds himself the protector of a strange young woman named Angie Mitchell. Angie has a unique gift: her scientist father placed microchips in her brain that give her direct access to cyberspace and sometimes make her the mouthpiece for its ghostly inhabitants. "The resolution [of the plot] is figuratively left in the hands of the Haitian Computer Gods," wrote Dorothy Allison in the *Village Voice.* "They are particularly marvelous, considering that the traditional science-fiction model of an intelligent computer has been an emotionless logician."

Gibson's third novel, *Mona Lisa Overdrive,* "brilliantly pyramids the successes of its predecessors," wrote Edward Bryant in *Bloomsbury Review.* The book is set several years after *Count Zero,* using a similar structure of plot-lines that slowly interconnect. When *Mona Lisa Overdrive* opens, Bobby Newmark has grown up into an accomplished cowboy. Now he leaves his body in a coma so that he can explore the electronically generated

universe inside a unique and costly microchip that he stole from the Tessier-Ashpool clan. Angie Mitchell, Bobby's sometime girlfriend, has become a simstim star, struggling against drug abuse and unsure of her future. In *Mona Lisa Overdrive,* wrote Richard Mathews of the *St. Petersburg Times,* "Gibson employs the metaphor of addiction as the central fact of existence. Addictions to drugs, information, and sensuality permeate society and form the basis of all economic transactions." The drug-abusing Angie, for example, is herself a "mere fix . . . piped to millions of simstim addicts to enrich [her producers]." Bobby is also a junkie—"a metaphor for society, increasingly techno-dependent, and hopelessly addicted to the excitement of high-tech power trips and head games."

As *Mona Lisa Overdrive* unfolds amid complex intrigues, the power of technology looms so large as to challenge the meaning of human identity itself. Characters seek friendship and advice from the personalities recorded on microchips; Angie comes face-to-face with "Mona Lisa," a confused teenage junkie who has been surgically altered to resemble Angie herself as part of a bizarre abduction plot. In the violent climax of the novel, during which Angie dies of a brain hemorrhage, the simstim producers stumble upon Mona and gladly recruit her as a new star. Then, in an astonishing burst of fantasy, Gibson shows Angie reunited with Bobby in his microchip universe—a computer-generated heaven. By then, Mathews observed, "Gibson has us re-evaluating our concepts of 'life,' 'death' and 'reality,' all of which have been redefined by the impact of the information matrix. What makes Gibson so exceptional a writer is that you haven't just seen or thought about this future; you've been there."

Increasingly Gibson was hailed as a master of observant, evocative, economical prose. Paul Kincaid of the *Times Literary Supplement* observed, "If the pace [of *Mona Lisa Overdrive*] is rather less frantic than in the earlier books, it is because Gibson's writing has improved, and the space given to more vividly presenting mood, place and character slows the action." Even the skeptical Thomas Disch quoted a passage from *Mona Lisa Overdrive* and, as other reviewers have done, observed how deftly Gibson could suggest a whole society with a handful of words. "Gibson is writing brilliant prose," declared Ellen Datlow in the *Philadelphia Inquirer,* "work that can be compared to anything being written inside or outside the science-fiction field." Some critics have called *Mona* Gibson's most absorbing story, while nevertheless observing that the plot is slowed down by too many characters. According to David Hiltbrand of *People, Mona* "has so many plot lines working that it takes most of the book for him to generate much narrative momentum." *Nation* contributor Erik Davis found the experience of following the numerous plot lines dizzying. "Chapters are short, speedy and high-res[olution], and following the various strands of the plot resembles watching four different TV programs by rapidly changing channels." Similarly, Pat Cadigan of *Quill and Quire* felt that "readers will be left not only wanting more but imagining what it might be. That's called science fiction at the top of its form."

Gibson at first seemed bemused by his new life as a best-selling novelist. At book signings he was greeted by disparate groups of hackers and punks whom he termed "M & M's" (for "modems and Mohawks"). As a soft-spoken, conservatively dressed father of two, Gibson realized that his wilder fans were sometimes disappointed to see him in person. "There was a classic case in San Francisco when two huge motorcyclists came screeching up," he continued in the *Chicago Tribune*. "One of them looked at me, picked up a book and shook his head and said, 'You can sign it anyway.'" To Gibson's surprise he quickly attracted the attention of the Hollywood film industry, and two years after *Neuromancer* was published he sold the film rights for $100,000. Soon he was recruited as screenwriter for the projected third film in the highly profitable *Aliens* series. But after he wrote several drafts, the film studio had a management shuffle and he lost his job. Paradoxically, the very fact that he was involved with such a high-profile effort made it easy for him to find more film work. Though Gibson stresses that *Mona Lisa Overdrive* is not autobiographical, he admits that the simstim subplot was inspired by his introduction to America's film capital. As he told a contributor for the *Philadelphia Inquirer:* "Sitting in the Polo Lounge talking to 20-year-old movie producers with money coming out of their ears—*that's* science fiction, boy."

By the time *Mona Lisa Overdrive* was published in 1988, Gibson and many reviewers were glad to say farewell to the cyberpunk era. "It's becoming fashionable now to write 'cyberpunk is dead' articles," he noted in the *Bloomsbury Review*. The author teamed with fellow novelist Bruce Sterling to write *The Difference Engine,* a sort of retroactive science-fiction novel set in Victorian England. The book is named for one of several mechanical computers that were designed during the nineteenth century by mathematician Charles Babbage. Babbage failed to build his most sophisticated machines, for their manufacture was beyond his budget and he was unable to secure public funding. Gibson and

Sterling, however, imagine what might have happened had he succeeded. With the help of mechanical computers, the Victorians develop airplanes, cybernauts, and a huge steam-powered television. *The Difference Engine,* Gibson warned, "sounds cuter than it is. It's really a very, very chilly semi-dystopia." In this novel, as in most of Gibson's work, technology proves to be corrupting, and society is painfully divided between the haves and have-nots. "One of the reasons we cooked this up was so people wouldn't be able to say it was more cyberpunk writing," Gibson told a contributor for the *Chicago Tribune*. "There won't be one guy with a silver Mohawk in the whole book."

After the short vacation from cyberpunk that *The Difference Engine* afforded him, Gibson returned to a familiar dystopian future with his next novel, *Virtual Light.* Set in the geographic conglomerate known as the Sprawl (most likely a fusion of most of North America), the novel centers on the adventures of an unlikely pair of allies who are thrown together by circumstance. While Gibson's trademarks are still present: biotechnology, evil corporate empires, and ghosts in the machines, *Virtual Light* was perceived by critics as more character-driven than the author's previous cyberpunk work. The technology serves the advancement of the plot rather than existing as the locus of the narrative. As one *Publishers Weekly* critic maintained, Gibson "has his finger on the pulse of popular culture and social trends; he molds a near-future world more frighteningly possible than any other recent writer."

In addition to his return to cyberpunk writing, Gibson also revisited the arena of Hollywood scriptwriting. Although his efforts for *Alien 3* were fruitless, he returned to produce a screenplay in 1995. Adapting his short story "Johnny Mnemonic," Gibson worked closely with director and artist Robert Longo (who had previously collaborated with the author on a performance art piece titled *Dream Jumbo*) to bring his vision of the near future to the screen. With slight alterations to the original story—the remorselessly fierce Molly Millions character was turned into a softer, more accessible female mercenary—the film was released to mixed reviews. While many credited the work with faithfully creating the "look" of the Gibson universe, there were numerous complaints regarding the film's pacing and the acting of Keanu Reeves, who played Johnny.

The world of *Virtual Light* has been elaborated on in two subsequent Gibson novels, *Idoru* and *All Tomorrow's Parties.* Both are tales of "the techno-decadent

21st century" that find "semi-innocents wading hip-deep into trouble," to quote a *Publishers Weekly* reviewer. In *Idoru,* the second novel of the trilogy, "Gibson excels . . . in creating a warped but comprehensible future saturated with logical yet unexpected technologies," according to the same reviewer. One of the central characters, the "idoru" of the title, exists only in virtual reality but is the love object of a flesh-and-blood American rock star. *Booklist* contributor Benjamin Segedin noted of the story: "Gibson remains on the cutting edge, but his vision does not now seem far-fetched. Indeed, often *Idoru* seems not to be set in the future at all. It resonates with startling realism as it presents a future not unlike the present, part hell and part paradise." In *Entertainment Weekly,* Ty Burr observed that *Virtual Light* and *Idoru* "reminded readers of what makes Gibson so damned good: a love of Raymond Chandleresque pulp poetry, a knack for visionary squalor, a bone-dry wit, and an insistence that the technology we create will inevitably evolve beyond us." The final novel of the trilogy, *All Tomorrow's Parties,* picks up the trail of Colin Laney, a freakish interpreter of computer data, who has possession of the projector which holds the idoru. Laney and a host of other characters—some original to this title, others returning from its two predecessors—must try to thwart the ambitions of nano-technology billionaire Cody Harwood. "Gibson's prose, as always, is portentous, crosscutting tough-guy understatement and poetic vagary," wrote Tom LeClair in a *New York Times Book Review* piece on the novel. Nevertheless, the critic added: "Compared to 'Idoru' and 'Virtual Light,' the world of 'All Tomorrow's Parties' is lo/rez, but the author appears to have been highly resolved to compose a trilogy, even if the result is 'Virtual Lite.'" Conversely, *Booklist* correspondent Segedin noted that *All Tomorrow's Parties* "is less a cyberpunk novel about virtual reality than one that realizes an almost recognizable future filled with new and exciting technologies. . . . Gibson's vision is inextricably linked to the advent of the Internet, whose possibilities he envisioned in the book that made him a big sf name, *Neuromancer.*"

Gibson has extended his narrative vision to realms beyond the printed page. His work is often exchanged and discussed on the Internet and he has contributed to television series such as *The X-Files.* Much as he envisioned back in 1984, information and communication has become the fastest growth industry of the new millennium. But despite the prophetic aura one can bestow upon Gibson's ideas, it is his storytelling ability that continues to hold his readers' interests.

Gibson's *Neuromancer* has become one of the most anticipated science-fiction films in the history of the genre.

In 1998, the book—called "the Rosetta stone of modern sci-fi" by *Entertainment Weekly*'s Noah Robischon—seemed to be on its way to the screen when a director, Chris Cunningham, signed on to work with Gibson on the project. Though Cunningham was a special-effects expert in the entertainment industry and had never directed a feature film before, he had drawn storyboards for *Neuromancer* after he read it as a teen, which impressed Gibson. Both writer and director were determined to make "an intelligent, human film rather than just another sci-fi blockbuster," noted Robischon, who predicted that the big-screen *Neuromancer* was likely "years away" from fruition. "Then again, when the book was first published in 1984, cyberspace seemed a long way off too."

Gibson was not holding his breath, waiting for the movie, but rather moving on to new ground in his novel writing with 2003's *Pattern Recognition.* The novel features Cayce Pollard, a highly paid, eerily intuitive market-research consultant or "coolhunter," who can find the next big trend in any neighborhood she walks into. Almost physically allergic to brand names herself, she has the buttons on her Levi 501s sanded to erase name recognition. But she can make a brand famous at the snap of her culturally attuned finger. In London on a job, she is offered a secret assignment by her wealthy employer, Hubertus Bigend of the Blue Ant ad agency: to investigate some intriguing snippets of video, known as "the footage," that have been appearing on the Internet. An entire subculture of people is obsessed with these bits of footage, and anybody who can create that kind of brand loyalty, Bigend figures, would be a gold mine for an advertiser. But when her borrowed apartment is burgled and her computer hacked, she realizes there's more to this project than she had expected.

Still, Cayce is her father's daughter, and the danger makes her stubborn. Her father, Win Pollard, ex-security expert, probably ex-CIA, was last seen headed to the World Trade Center on September 11, 2001, and is presumed dead. Win taught Cayce a bit about the way agents work. She is still devastated by his loss, and, as much for him as for any other reason, she refuses to give up this newly weird job, which will take her to Tokyo and on to Russia. With help and betrayal from equally unlikely quarters, Cayce will follow the trail of the mysterious film to its source, and in the process will learn something about her father's life and death.

Writing in the *New York Times Book Review,* Lisa Zeidner welcomed the new direction taken by this "elegant, entrancing . . . novel." Unlike Gibson's other sf and cyber novels, *Pattern Recognition* "is almost nose-thumbingly conventional in design," according to Zeidner, who further praised Gibson's "corpuscular, crenellated" prose, and his "sentences [that] slide form silk to steel, and take tonal rides from the ironic to the earnest." Similarly, Nancy Pearl, reviewing the novel in *Library Journal,* observed that Gibson "moves into the mainstream with this thriller." Pearl also felt that the book "has a lot of charm and surprising amount of non-cloying sweetness that is positively refreshing in a cool and composed postmodern novel." Not all reviewers were so positive about the new work however. Writing in *Print,* Victor Margolin allowed the many charms of the book, but also complained that it was, in the end, "less resonant" than *Neuromancer.* According to Margolin, "Gibson offers little insight into global advertising and, in fact, plays on the most widely accepted perceptions of it." Additionally, as Margolin observed, "Whereas *Neuromancer* retains an air of mystery and uncertainty at its conclusion, the loose ends in *Pattern Recognition* are tied up too neatly."

On the whole, though, *Pattern Recognition* was a critical success. "Global networking meets terrorism," a reviewer noted of this novel in the *Washington Post Book World.* Noah Robischon commented in his *Entertainment Weekly* review that "far-out ideas and densely worded sentences bear Gibson's unmistakable imprimatur," and that the author of *Neuromancer* demonstrates with this book that he is "just as skilled at seeing the present." *New Scientist*'s Dave Longford likewise wrote that Gibson's tale "glows with SF verve and glitter as future shock overtakes the present." Praise continued in a review from a *Publishers Weekly* contributor, who felt that this was "Gibson's best book since *Mona Lisa Overdrive.*" *Time* magazine's Lev Grossman dubbed the book a "serious thriller set in the dystopian present," while Christine C. Menefee, writing in *School Library Journal,* described the novel as a "headlong race through an unsettling but recognizable world to a surprisingly humane conclusion."

On his author Web site, Gibson addresses the issue of why he set *Pattern Recognition* in the present: "I've been threatening to do it for a while. The last three books feel to me more like 'alternate presents' than imaginary futures. Science fiction is always, really, about the period it's written in, though most people don't seem to understand that. The way that September 11 changed the world is a major theme in this book. How would you describe that change? By writing this book. And I'd leave it at that. I'm more interested in finding questions than answers. Questions are more enduring."

BIOGRAPHICAL AND CRITICAL SOURCES:

BOOKS

Contemporary Literary Criticism, Volume 39, Thomson Gale (Detroit, MI), 1986.

Contemporary Novelists, 6th edition, St. James Press (Detroit, MI), 1996.

Contemporary Popular Writers, St. James Press (Detroit, MI), 1997.

McCaffery, Larry, editor, *Across the Wounded Galaxies: Interviews with Contemporary American Science Fiction Writers,* University of Illinois Press (Champaign, IL), 1990.

St. James Guide to Science Fiction Writers, 4th edition, St. James Press (Detroit, MI), 1996.

St. James Guide to Young Adult Writers, 2nd edition, St. James Press (Detroit, MI), 1999.

Sterling, Bruce, editor, *Mirrorshades: The Cyberpunk Anthology,* Arbor House (New York, NY), 1986.

PERIODICALS

Adweek, April 7, 2003, "William Gibson on the Spot," p. 64.

Analog, November, 1984, p. 167; December, 1986, p. 179; January, 1987, p. 182; April, 1989, p. 178; October, 1989, p. 93; January, 1994, p. 304; September, 1995, p. 160; March, 1997, Tom Easton, review of *Idoru,* p. 147.

Austin American-Statesman, November 27, 1988.

Best Sellers, July, 1986.

Bloomsbury Review, September, 1988, Edward Bryant, review of *Mona Lisa Overdrive.*

Booklist, June 1, 1993, p. 1734; March 15, 1995, p. 1301; August, 1996, Benjamin Segedin, review of *Idoru,* p. 1853; September 1, 1999, Benjamin Segedin, review of *All Tomorrow's Parties,* p. 7.

Canadian Forum, October, 1994, p. 40.

Canadian Literature, summer, 1989, J.R. Wytenbroeck, "Cyberpunk," pp. 162-164.

Chicago Tribune, November 18, 1988; November 23, 1988.

College English, November, 2000, Daniel Punday, "The Narrative Construction of Cyberspace: Reading *Neuromancer,* Reading Cyberspace Debates," p. 194.

Computer Weekly, January 23, 2003, Mark Lewis, review of *Pattern Recognition,* p. 34.

Entertainment Weekly, January 31, 1992, p. 54; August 13, 1993, p. 66; August 26, 1994, p. 106; November 17, 1995, Ty Burr, review of *Johnny Mne-*

monic, p. 86; February 13, 1998, Ken Tucker, review of "Kill Switch" episode of *The X-Files,* p. 48; October 8, 1999, Noah Robischon, "Virtual Celebrity," pp. 10, B16; October 29, 1999, Ty Burr, "Slight of Hand," p. 104; February 7, 2003, Noah Robischon, review of *Pattern Recognition,* p. 86.

EuropeMedia, April 29, 2003, "William Gibson Stops Blogging to Focus on Writing."

Extrapolation, fall, 2003, Dominick M. Grace, "From Videodrome to Virtual Light," pp. 344-356.

Fantasy Review, July, 1984; April, 1986.

Film Comment, January, 1990, p. 60.

Fortune, November 1, 1993.

Guardian, October 7, 1999, Jim McClellan, "Cyperpunk 2000," p. S14; April 26, 2001, Sean Dodson, "The Original Cyperpunk," p. S16.

Impulse, winter, 1989.

Interview, January, 1989, Victoria Hamburg, "The King of Cyberpunk," pp. 85-86.

Isaac Asimov's Science Fiction Magazine, August, 1986.

Library Journal, August, 1993, p. 159; August, 1996, p. 120; October 15, 1999, Jackie Cassada, review of *All Tomorrow's Parties,* p. 110; February 1, 2003, Roger A. Berger, review of *Pattern Recognition,* p. 116; July, 2003, Nancy Pearl, review of *Pattern Recognition,* p. 152.

Listener, October 11, 1990.

Locus, August, 1988.

Los Angeles Times Book Review, January 29, 1989; May 12, 1991, John Sladek, "A Byte Out of Time," p. 9.

Maclean's, April 29, 1991, p. 63; September 6, 1993, p. 52; June 5, 1995, Brian D. Johns, "Mind Games with William Gibson," p. 60.

Magazine of Fantasy and Science Fiction, August, 1985, p. 28; August, 1986, p. 64; October, 1990, p. 31; February, 1997, Charles de Lint, review of *Idoru,* p. 40.

Mississippi Review, Volume 16, numbers 2 and 3, 1988.

Mosaic, March, 1999, Tony Fabijancic, "Space and Power: 19th-Century Urban Practice and Gibson's Cyberworld," p. 105.

Nation, May 8, 1989, Erik Davis, "A Cyberspace Odyssey," pp. 636-639; May 6, 1991, p. 598; November 5, 1993, p. 580.

National Review, June 26, 1995, John Simon, review of *Johnny Mnemonic,* p. 65.

New Scientist, May 31, 2003, Dave Longford, review of *Pattern Recognition,* pp. 50-51.

New Statesman, June 20, 1986; September 26, 1986; September 24, 1993, p. 55; October 11, 1996, Charles Shaar Murray, review of *Idoru,* p. 44.

New Yorker, August 16, 1993, p. 24; June 12, 1995, p. 111.

New York Times Book Review, November 24, 1985, p. 33; October 30, 1988, p. 40; December 11, 1988, p. 23; March 10, Thomas M. Disch, review of *The Difference Engine,* 1991, p. 5; August 29, 1993, p. 12; September 12, 1993, p. 36; September 8, 1996, Laura Miller, review of *Idoru,* p. 6; November 21, 1999, Tom LeClair, review of *All Tomorrow's Parties,* p. 15; January 19, 2003, Lisa Zeidner, review of *Pattern Recognition,* p. 7.

Oregonian (Portland, OR), November 24, 1988.

People, December 12, 1988, David Hiltbrand, review of *Mona Lisa Overdrive,* p. 49; June 10, 1991, Edward Zuckerman, "William Gibson: Teen Geek Makes Good, Redefines Sci-Fi," pp. 103-108; October 25, 1993, p. 45; July 10, 1995, p. 33.

Philadelphia Inquirer, April 15, 1986; October 30, 1988, Ellen Datlow, review of *Mona Lisa Overdrive.*

Pittsburgh Press, October 19, 1986.

Popular Science, October, 2001, "Q&A: William Gibson," p. 63.

Print, November-December, 2003, Victor Margolin, review of *Pattern Recognition,* pp. 54-56.

Publishers Weekly, July 12, 1993, review of *Virtual Light,* p. 72; September 6, 1993, p. 70; August 5, 1996, review of *Idoru,* p. 435; December 2, 1996, review of *Idoru* (audiobook), p. 30; October 11, 1999, review of *All Tomorrow's Parties,* p. 59; January 20, 2003, review of *Pattern Recognition,* pp. 57-58.

Punch, February 6, 1985.

Quill and Quire, December, 1988, Pat Cadigan, "Accessing Gibson's Peculiar Realm of Cyberspace," p. 20.

Reason, November, 1991, p. 61.

Rolling Stone, December 4, 1986, Mikal Gilmore, "The Rise of Cyberpunk," pp. 77-78; June 15, 1989.

Sacramento Union, October 26, 1988.

St. Petersburg Times, December 18, 1988, Richard Mathews, review of *Mona Lisa Overdrive.*

San Francisco Chronicle, January 1, 1987.

Saturday Night, March, 1989, p. 69.

School Library Journal, May, 2003, Christine C. Menefee, review of *Pattern Recognition,* p. 179.

Science Fiction Review, fall, 1985; summer, 1986; winter, 1986.

Science-Fiction Studies, March, 1995, Istvan Sciscery-Ronay, Jr., "Antimancer: Cybernetics and Art in Gibson's 'Count Zero,'" p. 63; November, 1998, Ross Farnell, "Posthuman Topologies: William Gibson's 'Architexture' in *Virtual Light* and *Idoru,*" p. 459.

Seattle Times, October 24, 1988.

Spin, December, 1988.

Time, spring, 1995, p. 4; December 6, 1999, Michael Krantz, review of *All Tomorrow's Parties,* p. 120; February 10, 2003, Lev Grossman, review of *Pattern Recognition,* p. 80.

Times Literary Supplement, December 7, 1984; June 20, 1986; August 12, 1988, Paul Kincaid, review of *Mona Lisa Overdrive;* September 27, 1996, Paul Quinn, review of *Idoru,* p. 25; October 15, 1999, Keith Miller, review of *All Tomorrow's Parties,* p. 25.

Utne Reader, July, 1989, p. 28.

Variety, November 20, 2000, Ken Eisner, review of *No Maps for These Territories,* p. 19.

Village Voice, July 3, 1984; July 16, 1985; May 6, 1986; January 17, 1989.

Washington Post Book World, July 29, 1984, Charles Platt, review of *Neuromancer,* p. 11; March 23, 1986; October 25, 1987; November 27, 1988; February 15, 2004, Jennifer Howard, review of *Pattern Recognition,* p. T14.

West Coast Review of Books, September, 1985.

Whole Earth Review, January, 1985, p. 39; summer, 1989, "Cyberpunk Ezra: Interviews with William Gibson," pp. 78-82.

Writer, January, 2003, review of *Pattern Recognition,* pp. 10-11.

ONLINE

Guardian Online, http://www.guardian.co.uk/ (May 1, 2003), Hamish Mackintosh, "Talk Time: William Gibson."

Science Fiction Weekly Online, http://www.scifi.com/sfw/issue146/interview.html/ (February 24, 2004), Peter Darling, "Sandpapering the Conscious Mind with William Gibson."

William Gibson Official Web Site, http://www.williamgibsonbooks.com/ (February 25, 2004).

OTHER

No Maps for These Territories (documentary film), Mark Neal Productions (London, England), 2000.

*   *   *

GILCHRIST, Ellen 1935-
(Ellen Louise Gilchrist)

PERSONAL: Born February 20, 1935, in Vicksburg, MS; daughter of William Garth (an engineer) and Aurora (Alford) Gilchrist; children: Marshall Peteet Walker, Jr., Garth Gilchrist Walker, Pierre Gautier Walker. *Education:* Millsaps College, B.A., 1967; University of Arkansas, postgraduate study, 1976. *Hobbies and other interests:* Love affairs (mine or anyone else's), all sports, children, inventions, music, rivers, forts and tents, trees.

ADDRESSES: Home and office—Fayetteville, AR. *Agent*—c/o Warner Books, Author Mail, 1271 Avenue of the Americas, New York, NY 10020.

CAREER: Author and journalist. *Vieux Carre Courier,* contributing editor, 1976-79. National Public Radio, Washington, DC, commentator on *Morning Edition* (news program), 1984-85.

MEMBER: Authors Guild, Authors League of America.

AWARDS, HONORS: Poetry award, Mississippi Arts Festival, 1968; poetry award, University of Arkansas, 1976; craft in poetry award, *New York Quarterly,* 1978; National Endowment for the Arts grant in fiction, 1979; Pushcart Prizes, Pushcart Press, 1979-80, for the story "Rich," and 1983, for the story "Summer, An Elegy"; fiction award, *Prairie Schooner,* 1981; Louisiana Library Association Honor book, 1981, for *In the Land of Dreamy Dreams;* fiction awards, Mississippi Academy of Arts and Science, 1982 and 1985; Saxifrage Award, 1983; National Book Award for fiction, Association of American Publishers, 1984, for *Victory over Japan;* J. William Fulbright Award for literature, University of Arkansas, 1985; literature award, Mississippi Institute of Arts and Letters, 1985, 1990, 1991; national script-writing award, National Educational Television Network, for the play *A Season of Dreams;* D. Litt., Millsaps College, 1987; L.H.D., University of Southern Illinois, 1991; O. Henry Short Story Award, 1995.

WRITINGS:

SHORT STORIES

In the Land of Dreamy Dreams, University of Arkansas Press (Fayetteville, AR), 1981.

Victory over Japan: A Book of Stories, Little, Brown (Boston, MA), 1984.

Drunk with Love, Little, Brown (Boston, MA), 1986.

Two Stories: "Some Blue Hills at Sundown" and "The Man Who Kicked Cancer's Ass," Albondocani Press, 1988.

Light Can Be Both Wave and Particle: A Book of Stories, Little, Brown (Boston, MA), 1989.

I Cannot Get You Close Enough, Little, Brown (Boston, MA), 1990.

The Age of Miracles: Stories, Little, Brown (Boston, MA), 1995.

Rhoda: A Life in Stories, Little, Brown (Boston, MA), 1995.

The Courts of Love: A Novella and Stories, Little, Brown (Boston, MA), 1996.

Flights of Angels: Stories, Little, Brown (Boston, MA), 1998.

The Cabal and Other Stories, Little, Brown (Boston, MA), 2000.

Collected Stories, Little, Brown (Boston, MA), 2000.

I, Rhoda Manning, Go Hunting with My Daddy, and Other Stories, Little, Brown (Boston, MA), 2002.

NOVELS

The Annunciation, Little, Brown (Boston, MA), 1983.

The Anna Papers, Little, Brown (Boston, MA), 1988.

Net of Jewels, Little, Brown (Boston, MA), 1992.

Starcarbon: A Meditation of Love, Little, Brown (Boston, MA), 1994.

Anabasis: A Journey to the Interior, University of Mississippi (University, MS), 1994.

Sarah Conley, Little, Brown (Boston, MA), 1997.

OTHER

The Land Surveyor's Daughter (poetry), Lost Roads (Fayetteville, AR), 1979.

Riding out the Tropical Depression (poetry), Faust, 1986.

Falling through Space: The Journals of Ellen Gilchrist, Little, Brown (Boston, MA), 1987.

Also author of *A Season of Dreams* (play; based on short stories by Eudora Welty), produced by the Mississippi Educational Network. Work represented in anthologies, including *The Pushcart Prize: Best of the Small Presses,* Pushcart (Wainscott, NY), 1979-80, 1983. Contributor of poems, short stories, and articles to magazines and journals, including *Atlantic Monthly, California Quarterly, Cincinnati Poetry Review, Cosmopolitan, Iowa Review, Ironwood, Kayak, Mademoiselle, New Laurel Review, New Orleans Review, New York Quarterly, Poetry Northwest, Pontchartrain Review, Prairie Schooner,* and *Southern Living.*

WORK IN PROGRESS: A novel; a play; a screenplay.

SIDELIGHTS: The author of poems, numerous short stories, and several novels, Ellen Gilchrist opens for her readers a side door through which to view the world of the gracious, upscale South. With prose steeped in the traditions of her native Mississippi, Gilchrist's fiction is unique: As Sabine Durrant commented in the London *Times,* Gilchrist's writing "swings between the familiar and the shocking, the everyday and the traumatic." Durrant continued, "She writes about ordinary happenings in out of the way places, of meetings between recognizable characters from her other fiction and strangers, above all of domestic routine disrupted by violence." Surprise endings are characteristic of her work. "It is disorienting stuff," noted Durrant, "but controlled always by Gilchrist's wry tone and gentle insight." A writer in *Contemporary Novelists* praised Gilchrist as "one of America's best contemporary fiction writers."

With the publication of her first short story collection in 1981, Gilchrist gained the attention of literary critics, publishers and, most importantly, the reading public. In its first few months in print, *In the Land of Dreamy Dreams* sold nearly ten thousand copies in the Southwest alone, a particularly impressive phenomenon, since the book was published by a small university press, unaccompanied by major promotional campaigns. The book's popular appeal continued to spread, generating reviews in major newspapers, until it reached the attention of a major publishing company, which offered Gilchrist a cash advance on both a novel and a second collection of short stories. In the meantime, the critical review of *In the Land of Dreamy Dreams* reflected that of the public. As Susan Wood remarked in a review for the *Washington Post Book World,* "Gilchrist may serve as prime evidence for the optimists among us who continue to believe that few truly gifted writers remain unknown forever. And Gilchrist is the real thing alright. In fact," added Wood, "it's difficult to review a first book as good as this without resorting to every known superlative cliché—there are, after all, just so many ways to say 'auspicious debut.'"

In the Land of Dreamy Dreams is a collection of fourteen short stories. Most are set in the city of New Orleans and many focus on the lives and concerns of young people. They are "traditional stories," according to Wood, "full of real people to whom things really happen—set, variously, over the last four decades among the rich of New Orleans, the surviving aristocracy of the Mississippi Delta, and Southerners transplanted . . . to southern Indiana." The main characters in the stories, many of them adolescents, exhibit flaws of character such as envy, lust, and avarice; however, Wood noted that more positive motivations lay underneath the surface: "It is more accurate to say that *In the Land of Dreamy Dreams* is about the stratagems, both admirable and not so, by which we survive our lives." Jim Crace, in a *Times Literary Supplement* review of *In the Land of Dreamy Dreams,* indicated that Gilchrist's text "is obsessively signposted with street names and Louisiana landmarks . . . But *In the Land of Dreamy Dreams* cannot be dismissed as little more than an anecdotal street plan. . . . The self-conscious parading of exact Southern locations is a protective screen beyond which an entirely different territory is explored and mapped. Gilchrist's 'Land of Dreamy Dreams' is Adolescence."

The adolescent struggle to come to terms with the way one's dreams and aspirations are limited by reality figures largely in these fourteen stories. Gilchrist introduces her readers to a variety of characters: an eight-year-old girl who delights in masquerading as an adult and commiserates with a newly widowed wartime bride; a girl who fantasizes about the disasters that could befall the brothers who have excluded her from their Olympic-training plans; a young woman who gains her father's help in obtaining an abortion; another girl who discovers the existence of her father's mistress; and an unruly teenager who disrupts the order of her adoptive father's world, challenges his self-esteem, and so aggravates him that he finally shoots her and then commits suicide. "Domestic life among the bored, purposeless, self-indulgent and self-absorbed rich" is the author's central focus, according to reviewer Jonathan Yardley in the *Washington Post Book World.* But domestic is not to be confused with tame. As Yardley observed, the "brutal realities that Gilchrist thrusts into these lives are chilling, and so too is the merciless candor with which she discloses the emptiness behind their glitter." And John Mellors similarly remarked in *Listener:* " *In the Land of Dreamy Dreams* has many shocks. The author writes in a low, matter-of-fact tone of voice and then changes key in her dramatic, often-bloody endings."

Gilchrist completed her second collection of short stories, *Victory over Japan,* three years later. Winner of the 1984 National Book Award for fiction, *Victory over Japan* was hailed by reviewers as a return to the genre, style, and several of the characters of *In the Land of Dreamy Dreams.* Beverly Lowry, reviewing *Victory over Japan* in the *New York Times Book Review,* commented: "Those who loved *In the Land of Dreamy Dreams* will not be disappointed. Many of the same characters reappear. . . . Often new characters show up with old

names. . . . These crossovers are neither distracting nor accidental. . . . Ellen Gilchrist is only changing costumes, and she can 'do wonderful tricks with her voice.'" *Drunk with Love,* published in 1986, and *Light Can be Both Wave and Particle,* released three years later, expanded the author's exploration of her characters' many facets. While continuing to praise her voice, critics have found Gilchrist's later work to be of a more "uneven" quality than her early writing. Reviewing *Light Can be Both Wave and Particle* for the *Chicago Tribune,* Greg Johnson noted that Gilchrist "seems to get carried away with her breezy style and verbal facility. The stories read quickly and are often enjoyable, but they lack the thought and craft that make for memorable fiction." However, Roy Hoffman praised the book in the *New York Times Book Review* as full of "new energy" and noted of the title story that "it brings together lovers from different cultures more spiritedly than any past Gilchrist story."

The "voice" and characters that Gilchrist employs throughout her fiction are the hallmarks of her work. David Sexton remarked of her voice in a *Times Literary Supplement* review of *Victory over Japan* that it had its roots in the "talk of the Mississippi Delta," adding that "the drawly 'whyyyyy not' world of the modern South which she creates is a great pleasure to visit." Equally important in her prose are the characters who appear time and again throughout her writing. "Without much authorial manicuring or explanation, [Gilchrist] allows her characters to emerge whole, in full possession of their considerable stores of eccentricities and passion," commented reviewer Lowry. The central characters in her works are usually women; whether they are young, as in *The Land of Dreamy Dreams,* or more mature, they are usually spirited, spoiled, and fighting their way out of poverty or out of a bad relationship. "Ms. Gilchrist's women . . . are unconventional, nervy, outspoken," noted Hoffman. "As grown-ups they are passionate to the point of recklessness, romantic in the midst of despair. As youngsters they vex adults."

Eight of the sixteen short stories in *The Age of Miracles,* a collection published in 1995, feature Rhoda Manning, a familiar character who appeared as a child in *Victory over Japan* and as a wife and mother in *Net of Jewels.* In this collection Gilchrist portrays Rhoda as a divorced and matured writer in midlife, with her failed relationships and drinking problems behind her. Julia Glass observed in a *Chicago Tribune* review, "As always, [Rhoda's] adventures are brazen and self-indulgent, seedy yet oddly heroic." In one story, "A Statue of Aphrodite," Gilchrist describes a burgeoning romance between Rhoda and a wealthy doctor who attempts to persuade Rhoda to accompany him to his daughter's wedding dressed in a prim Laura Ashley dress. Though noting that this collection is not Gilchrist's best, Bharat Tandon wrote in a *Times Literary Supplement* review, "there are in this new collection moments of more profound and graceful achievement than she has shown before." While critical of Rhoda's overbearing personae and tendency toward irrelevance, critics praised Gilchrist for several of the pieces that do not include that character. In "Madison at 69th, a Fable," Gilchrist describes how a woman's facelift is averted when her children kidnap her and talk her out of the procedure. Glass commented that the story is "a wholly original comedy that enfolds a dark tangle of fears and betrayed obligations," highlighted by the mother's wish to regain youth while her children revolt against novelty. Diane Cole concluded in the *New York Times Book Review* that "at her best [Gilchrist] blends a sense of poignancy with an often outrageously Gothic humor."

Both new and familiar characters appeared in the collection *Flights of Angels,* rated as "easily her best book in years" by a *Publishers Weekly* reviewer. While the weak-willed men, needy middle-aged women, and their various friends, servants, and relatives are all familiar types in Gilchrist's fiction, the power of her writing remains fresh. "Her dual senses of comedy and poignancy continue in close partnership, the typical laugh-and-cry reaction to a Gilchrist story is both anticipated and realized in every piece," stated Brad Hooper in a *Booklist* review. The *Publishers Weekly* writer found that the best of these stories "convey the old-fashioned idea that charity, compassion and good works can change the world. One reads this collection entertained [Gilchrist's] distinctive prose, beguiled by her vivid characters and buoyed by the insistent touches of humor and hope that she brings to her vision of chaotic lives."

In *The Cabal and Other Stories,* the title novella tells of a psychiatrist who goes mad and begins ranting publicly about his wealthy clients' innermost secrets. Subsequent stories go on to uncover more about the doctor's clientele and the details of their lives. The collection showcases Gilchrist's "fantastic imagination and skill in creating a short story that becomes a world in itself, full of irony and wisdom," according to Patricia Gulian in *Library Journal.* Jim Gladstone, reviewing *The Cabal* in the *New York Times,* commented that "Gilchrist's writing emanates love for the shaggy, uncontainable nature of life; she refuses to contain her characters in stories that offer any artificial sense of closure."

The author personally chose thirty-four of her favorite tales for inclusion in *Collected Stories,* described by

Donna Seaman in *Booklist* as "a potent and pleasingly cohesive volume that showcases her deep sense of place and, the most salient feature of her work, her lusty, unpredictable, and unapologetic heroines." In Seaman's estimation, Gilchrist's "dulcet yet tensile voice has become an integral part of American literature."

In 1983, Gilchrist's first novel, *The Annunciation,* was published. It recounts the life of Amanda McCarney, from her childhood on a Mississippi Delta plantation where she falls in love with and, at the age of fourteen, has a child by her cousin Guy, to her marriage to a wealthy New Orleans man and a life of high society and heavy drinking. Eventually rejecting this lifestyle, Amanda returns to school, where she discovers a gift for languages that has lain dormant during the forty-some years of her life, and where she is offered the chance to translate the rediscovered poetry of an eighteenth-century Frenchwoman. She divorces her husband and moves to a university town in Arkansas to pursue her translating where, in addition to her work, Amanda finds love and friendship among a commune of hippie-type poets and philosophers in the Ozarks. *The Annunciation* received mixed reviews from critics. Yardley, critiquing the book in the *Washington Post Book World,* asserted that for most of its length "*The Annunciation* is a complex, interesting, occasionally startling novel; but as soon as Gilchrist moves Amanda away from the conflicts and discontents of New Orleans, the book falls to pieces." The critic noted that once Amanda moves to the Ozarks, *The Annunciation* "loses its toughness and irony. Amid the potters and the professors and the philosopher-poets of the Ozarks, Amanda McCarney turns into mush." However, Frances Taliaferro, reviewing *The Annunciation* in *Harper's,* deemed Gilchrist's novel "'women's fiction' par excellence," and described the book as "a cheerful hodgepodge of the social and psychological fashions of the past three decades." Taliaferro felt that "Amanda is in some ways a receptacle for current romantic clichés, but she is also a vivid character of dash and humor. . . . Even a skeptical reader pays her the compliment of wondering what she will do next in this surprisingly likable novel." Taliaferro concluded that, despite some tragedy, the "presiding spirit of this novel is self-realization, and Amanda [in the end] has at last made her way to autonomy."

Gilchrist has gone on to write several more books in the novel or novella genre. *The Anna Papers* begins with the short story "Anna, Part I," which concluded *Drunk with Love.* Published in 1988, the novel begins with the suicide of 43-year-old Anna Hand, who decides to conclude her life after being diagnosed with cancer. The work deals with the aftermath of her death, as family and friends are left to the influence of Anna's legacy; the recollection of her full and joyous, yet unconventional, life. Although the critical reception of the novel was mixed, *The Anna Papers* was praised for both the quality of its prose and the complexity of Gilchrist's fictional characters. Ann Vliet in the *Washington Post Book World* ascribed to Gilchrist "a stubborn dedication to the uncovering of human irony, a tendency, despite temptations toward glamour and comfort, to opt for the harder path." *I Cannot Get You Close Enough* is a continuation of *The Anna Papers,* in the form of three novellas, each focusing on one of the characters in the previous book. Ilene Raymond of the *Washington Post Book World* praised the work. "Not since J.D. Salinger's Glass family has a writer lavished so much loving attention on the eccentricities and activities of an extended clan," Raymond commented, adding that the novellas were not "easy tales, but stories rich with acrimony, wisdom, courage and, finally, joy."

In *Starcarbon: A Meditation of Love,* Gilchrist returns to the Hand family of North Carolina, whose various members appeared in *The Anna Papers, I Cannot Get You Close Enough,* and *Net of Jewels.* Prefaced by an extensive genealogical chart that includes some forty-five names, the novel recounts the summer excursions of several family members, including Olivia de Havilland Hand, a half-Cherokee college freshman who visits her maternal grandparents in Oklahoma; Jessie, her half-sister who prepares for the birth of her first child in New Orleans; their Aunt Helen, who leaves her marriage and children to pursue an Irish poet in Boston; and Daniel, brother of Helen, who remains in North Carolina to wallow drunkenly in a midlife crisis. "Ellen Gilchrist's writing tumbles and spills off the page, seemingly without effort, like a voluble cousin breathlessly bringing you up to date on the liaisons and adventures of various members of a sprawling family," wrote *Chicago Tribune* reviewer Victoria Jenkins. Offering tempered praise, Trev Broughton commented in the *Times Literary Supplement,* "The novel's ageing roues and their gold-digging mistresses, the psychiatrists, even the horses are crisply drawn." A writer in *Kirkus Reviews* noted that "*Starcarbon* is soap at its most elegant." Sarah Ferguson concluded in the *New York Times Book Review,* "Ms. Gilchrist has blended these resolutely individual voices to create a richly textured family fugue."

In *Anabasis: A Journey to the Interior,* Gilchrist ventures away from the Deep South to create a novel set in ancient Greece during the Peloponnesian War (431-404 B.C.). Inspired by the storytelling of her mother, Gilchrist first conceived of this book as a child. The main character, an orphaned slave named Auria, receives an early education from renowned healer Philokrates, then escapes her cruel master, adopts his abandoned newborn daughter, and joins a band of runaway slaves who retreat into the mountains to plot rebellion. Among the rebels, Auria finds love and marries Meion, the grandnephew of Pericles, and plies her skills as healer and teacher. A *Publishers Weekly* review described the work as a "richly textured but overly idealized historical novel." Though similarly critical of the novel's improbable plot, Margaret A. Robinson in the *New York Times Book Review* noted, "Such fiction demands suspension of disbelief, and Auria, an appealing heroine, often makes that faith possible."

Gilchrist described to Wendy Smith in an interview for *Publishers Weekly* her evolution from short story writer to novelist: "The thing about the short story form is that in order to do a good job with it you've got to concentrate on no more than two characters; you've got to pretend that nobody has any children or parents." The novel provides her with a larger canvas on which to set forth her fictional world. "I think that in order to serve the vision I currently have of reality, I'm going to have to have at least five or six characters interplaying," she noted. However, Gilchrist has found that the novel format presents its own set of problems. As she told Walker, "You can't go back to the easy fix you learn as a short story writer, where you kill somebody off or get somebody laid to create a climax. What I'm trying to do now is make a study of existence—that's the high ground, but I perceive it as that. I want it to be as true to what I know about human beings as it can be." Commenting on *Net of Jewels,* Gilchrist explained that the more she writes about a character in a short story or a novel, the more she discovers about that character. She decided to "serve that knowledge" in *Net of Jewels,* an account of character Rhoda Manning's emotional growth in college and beyond, as her protagonist becomes involved with a succession of other characters. "This is the difference between writing novels and writing short stories," commented Gilchrist, "there aren't any tricks."

In 1987 Gilchrist published *Falling through Space,* a collection of brief journal excerpts. Originally broadcast as segments of her National Public Radio commentary, the journal reflects the life of a working writer. "I write to learn and to amuse myself and out of joy and because of mystery and in praise of everything that moves, breathes, gives, partakes, is," Gilchrist once told *CA.* "I like the feel of words in my mouth and the sound of them in my ears and the creation of them with my hands. If that sounds like a lot of talk, it is. What are we doing here anyway, all made out of stars and talking about everything and telling everything? The more one writes the clearer it all becomes and the simpler and more divine. A friend once wrote to me and ended the letter by saying: 'Dance in the fullness of time.' I write that in the books I sign. It may be all anyone needs to read."

Critics have repeatedly praised Gilchrist for her subtle perception, unique characters, and sure command of her writer's voice. Yardley remarked of *In the Land of Dreamy Dreams,* "Certainly it is easy to see why reviewers and readers have responded so strongly to Gilchrist; she tells home truths in these stories, and she tells them with style." Crace concluded that her "stories are perceptive, her manner is both stylish and idiomatic—a rare and potent combination." Miranda Seymour, reviewing Gilchrist's first short story collection for the London *Times,* noted that her "stories are elegant little tragedies, memorable and cruel," and compared her writing to that of fellow southerners Carson McCullers and Tennessee Williams, in that all three writers share "the curious gift for presenting characters as objects for pity and affection." And Wood observed: "Even the least attractive characters become known to us, and therefore human, because Gilchrist's voice is so sure, her tone so right, her details so apt."

BIOGRAPHICAL AND CRITICAL SOURCES:

BOOKS

Contemporary Literary Criticism, Thomson Gale (Detroit, MI), Volume 34, 1985, Volume 48, 1988.
Contemporary Novelists, seventh edition, St. James Press (Detroit, MI), 2001.
Contemporary Popular Writers, St. James Press (Detroit, MI), 1997.
Contemporary Southern Writers, St. James Press (Detroit, MI), 1999.
McCay, Mary A., *Ellen Gilchrist,* Twayne, 1997.

PERIODICALS

Book, December, 1998, review of *Flights of Angels,* p. 63; January, 2001, Penelope Mesic, review of *Collected Stories,* p. 69.
Booklist, January 15, 1994; September 1, 1994; August, 1998, Brad Hooper, review of *Flights of Angels,* p. 1922; December 1, 1999, Brad Hooper, review of *The Cabal and Other Stories,* p. 661; September 15, 2000, Donna Seaman, review of *Collected Stories,* p. 188.

Chicago Tribune, October 14, 1986; October 9, 1987; October 2, 1988; October 1, 1989; May 22, 1994; June 11, 1995.
Entertainment Weekly, October 9, 1998, review of *Flights of Angels,* p. 78.
Harper's, June, 1985.
Kirkus Reviews, February 15, 1994, p. 162; July 1, 1994, p. 867; August 15, 1998, review of *Flights of Angels,* p. 1137; October 1, 2000, review of *Collected Stories,* p. 1388.
Kliatt, May, 1998, review of audio version of *The Courts of Love,* p. 44.
Knight-Ridder/Tribune News Service, December 27, 2000, Nancy Pate, review of *Collected Stories,* p. K582; January 10, 2001, Polly Paddock Gossett, review of *Collected Stories,* p. K5769.
Library Journal, March 1, 1994; August, 1994, p. 128; January, 2000, Patricia Gulian, review of *The Cabal and Other Stories,* p. 165; October 15, 2000, Christine DeZelar-Tiedman, review of *Collected Stories,* p. 107.
Listener, January 6, 1983.
Los Angeles Times Book Review, September 14, 1986; November 27, 1988; November 8, 1998, review of *Flights of Angels,* p. 10.
Ms., June, 1985.
New Statesman, March 16, 1984.
Newsweek, January 14, 1985; February 18, 1985.
New Yorker, November 19, 1984.
New York Times, May 7, 2000, Jim Gladstone, review of *The Cabal and Other Stories.*
New York Times Book Review, September 23, 1984; October 5, 1986; January 3, 1988; January 15, 1989; October 22, 1989; November 4, 1990; October 13, 1991; April 12, 1992; June 19, 1994, p. 33; October 30, 1994, p. 48; May 21, 1995, p. 32; October 18, 1998, Erica Sanders, review of *Flights of Angels,* p. 29; December 17, 2000, Katherine Dieckmann, review of *Collected Stories,* p. 8.
Observer, November 24, 1991.
Publishers Weekly, March 2, 1992; January 31, 1994; August 8, 1994, p. 382; September 14, 1998, review of *Flights of Angels,* p. 47; February 14, 2000, review of *The Cabal and Other Stories,* p. 172.
Times (London), November 25, 1982; June 7, 1990; November 21, 1991.
Times Literary Supplement, October 15, 1982; April 6, 1984; May 24, 1985; March 6, 1987; October 27, 1989; November 29, 1991; September 7, 1990; July 1, 1994, p. 21; October 20, 1995, p. 23.
Vogue, May, 1994, p. 184.
Washington Post, September 12, 1984; September 28, 1986; December 31, 1987; October 20, 1988; De-

cember 15, 1989; July 9, 2000, Jane Kollias, review of *The Cabal and Other Stories*, p. X6.

Washington Post Book World, January 24, 1982; March 21, 1982; May 29, 1983; December 31, 1987; December 16, 1990; September 3, 1995, p. 6.

*   *   *

GILCHRIST, Ellen Louise
See GILCHRIST, Ellen

*   *   *

GINSBERG, Allen 1926-1997

PERSONAL: Born June 3, 1926, in Newark, NJ; died of a heart attack while suffering from liver cancer, April 5, 1997, in New York, NY; son of Louis (a poet and teacher) and Naomi (Levy) Ginsberg. *Education:* Columbia University, A.B., 1948. *Politics:* "Space Age Anarchist." *Religion:* "Buddhist-Jewish."

CAREER: Writer. Spot welder, Brooklyn Naval Yard, Brooklyn, NY, 1945; dishwasher, Bickford's Cafeteria, New York, NY, 1945; worked on various cargo ships, 1945-56; literary agent, reporter for New Jersey union newspaper, and copy boy for *New York World Telegram*, 1946; night porter, May Co., Denver, CO, 1946; book reviewer, *Newsweek*, New York, NY, 1950; market research consultant in New York, NY, and San Francisco, CA, 1951-53; instructor, University of British Columbia, Vancouver, Canada, 1963; founder and treasurer, Committee on Poetry Foundation, 1966-97; organizer, Gathering of the Tribes for a Human Be-In, San Francisco, 1967; cofounder, codirector, and teacher, Jack Kerouac School of Disembodied Poetics, Naropa Institute, Boulder, CO, 1974-97. Gave numerous poetry readings in the United States, England, Russia, India, Peru, Chile, Poland, and Czechoslovakia; presenter at conferences. Film appearances included *Pull My Daisy*, 1960; *Guns of the Trees*, 1962; *Couch*, 1964; *Wholly Communion, Chappaqua*, and *Allen for Allen*, all 1965; *Joan of Arc* and *Galaxie*, both 1966; *Herostratus, The Mind Alchemists*, and *Don't Look Back*, all 1967; *Me and My Brother*, 1968; *Dynamite Chicken*, 1971; *Renaldo and Clara*, 1978; *It Doesn't Pay to Be Honest*, 1984; *It Was Twenty Years Ago Today*, 1987; *Heavy Petting*, 1988; *John Bowles: The Complete Outsider* and *Jonas in the Desert*, both 1994; and (narrator) *Kaddish* (TV film), 1977. Performer on recordings, including *San Francisco Poets*, Evergreen Records, 1958; *Howl and Other Poems*, Fantasy, 1959; and *Holy Soul Jelly Roll: Poems and Songs, 1949-1993*, Rhino/Word Beat, 1995.

MEMBER: National Institute of Arts and Letters, PEN, New York Eternal Committee for Conservation of Freedom in the Arts.

AWARDS, HONORS: Woodbury Poetry Prize; Guggenheim fellow, 1963-64; National Endowment for the Arts grant, 1966, and fellowship, 1986; National Institute of Arts and Letters Award, 1969; National Book Award for Poetry, 1974, for *The Fall of America;* National Arts Club Medal of Honor for Literature, 1979; Poetry Society of America gold medal, 1986; Golden Wreath, 1986; Before Columbus Foundation Award, 1990, for lifetime achievement; Harriet Monroe Poetry Award, University of Chicago, 1991; American Academy of Arts and Sciences fellowship, 1992; named chevalier, French Order of Arts and Letters, 1993.

WRITINGS:

POETRY COLLECTIONS

Howl and Other Poems, introduction by William Carlos Williams, City Lights (San Francisco, CA), 1956, revised edition, Grabhorn-Hoyem, 1971, Fortieth anniversary edition, City Lights, 1996.

Siesta in Xbalba and Return to the States, privately printed, 1956.

Kaddish and Other Poems, 1958-1960, City Lights (San Francisco, CA), 1961.

Empty Mirror: Early Poems, Corinth Books (Chevy Chase, MD), 1961, new edition, 1970.

A Strange New Cottage in Berkeley, Grabhorn Press, 1963.

Reality Sandwiches: 1953-1960, City Lights (San Francisco, CA), 1963.

The Change, Writer's Forum, 1963.

Kral Majales (title means "King of May"), Oyez (Kensington, CA), 1965.

Wichita Vortex Sutra, Housmans (London, England), 1966, Coyote Books (Brunswick, ME), 1967.

TV Baby Poems, Cape Golliard Press, 1967, Grossman, 1968.

Airplane Dreams: Compositions from Journals, House of Anansi (Toronto, Ontario, Canada), 1968, City Lights (San Francisco, CA), 1969.

(With Alexandra Lawrence) *Ankor Wat*, Fulcrum Press, 1968.

Scrap Leaves, Tasty Scribbles, Poet's Press, 1968.

Wales—A Visitation, July 29, 1967, Cape Golliard Press, 1968.

The Heart Is a Clock, Gallery Upstairs Press, 1968.

Message II, Gallery Upstairs Press, 1968.

Planet News, City Lights (San Francisco, CA), 1968.

For the Soul of the Planet Is Wakening . . . , Desert Review Press, 1970.

The Moments Return: A Poem, Grabhorn-Hoyem, 1970.

Ginsberg's Improvised Poetics, edited by Mark Robison, Anonym Books, 1971.

New Year Blues, Phoenix Book Shop (New York, NY), 1972.

Open Head, Sun Books (Melbourne, Australia), 1972.

Bixby Canyon Ocean Path Word Breeze, Gotham Book Mart (New York, NY), 1972.

Iron Horse, Coach House Press (Chicago, IL), 1972.

The Fall of America: Poems of These States, 1965-1971, City Lights (San Francisco, CA), 1973.

The Gates of Wrath: Rhymed Poems, 1948-1952, Grey Fox (San Francisco, CA), 1973.

Sad Dust Glories: Poems during Work Summer in Woods, 1974, Workingman's Press (Seattle, WA), 1975.

First Blues: Rags, Ballads, and Harmonium Songs, 1971-1974, Full Court Press (New York, NY), 1975.

Mind Breaths: Poems, 1972-1977, City Lights (San Francisco, CA), 1978.

Poems All over the Place: Mostly Seventies, Cherry Valley (Wheaton, MD), 1978.

Mostly Sitting Haiku, From Here Press (Fanwood, NJ), 1978, revised and expanded edition, 1979.

Careless Love: Two Rhymes, Red Ozier Press, 1978.

(With Peter Orlovsky) *Straight Hearts' Delight: Love Poems and Selected Letters,* Gay Sunshine Press (San Francisco, CA), 1980.

Plutonian Ode: Poems, 1977-1980, City Lights (San Francisco, CA), 1982.

Collected Poems, 1947-1980, Harper (New York, NY), 1984, expanded edition published as *Collected Poems: 1947-85,* Penguin (New York, NY), 1995.

Many Loves, Pequod Press, 1984.

Old Love Story, Lospecchio Press, 1986.

White Shroud, Harper (New York, NY), 1986.

Cosmopolitan Greetings: Poems, 1986-1992, Harper-Collins (New York, NY), 1994.

Illuminated Poems, illustrated by Eric Drooker, Four Walls Eight Windows (New York, NY), 1996.

Selected Poems, 1947-1995, HarperCollins (New York, NY), 1996.

Death and Fame: Poems, 1993-1997, edited by Bob Rosenthal, Peter Hale, and Bill Morgan, foreword by Robert Creeley, HarperFlamingo (New York, NY), 1999.

Also author, with Kenneth Koch, of *Making It Up: Poetry Composed at St. Mark's Church on May 9, 1979.*

OTHER

(Author of introduction) Gregory Corso, *Gasoline* (poems), City Lights (San Francisco, CA), 1958.

(With William Burroughs) *The Yage Letters* (correspondence), City Lights (San Francisco, CA), 1963.

Prose Contribution to Cuban Revolution, Artists Workshop Press, 1966.

(Translator, with others) Nicanor Parra, *Poems and Antipoems,* New Directions (Newton, NJ), 1967.

(Author of introduction) John A. Wood, *Orbs: A Portfolio of Nine Poems,* Apollyon Press, 1968.

(Author of introduction) Louis Ginsberg, *Morning in Spring* (poems), Morrow (New York, NY), 1970.

(Compiler) *Documents on Police Bureaucracy's Conspiracy against Human Rights of Opiate Addicts and Constitutional Rights of Medical Profession Causing Mass Breakdown of Urban Law and Order,* privately printed, 1970.

(Author of commentary) Jean Genet, *May Day Speech,* City Lights (San Francisco, CA), 1970.

Indian Journals: March 1962-May 1963; Notebooks, Diary, Blank Pages, Writings, City Lights (San Francisco, CA), 1970, Grove Press, 1996.

Notes after an Evening with William Carlos Williams, Portents Press, 1970.

Declaration of Independence for Dr. Timothy Leary, Hermes Free Press, 1971.

(Author of introduction) William Burroughs Jr., *Speed* (novel), Sphere Books, 1971.

(Author of foreword) Ann Charters, *Kerouac* (biography), Straight Arrow Books, 1973.

The Fall of America Wins a Prize (speech), Gotham Book Mart (New York, NY), 1974.

Gay Sunshine Interview: Allen Ginsberg with Allen Young, Grey Fox (San Francisco, CA), 1974.

The Visions of the Great Rememberer (correspondence), Mulch Press (San Francisco, CA), 1974.

Allen Verbatim: Lectures on Poetry, Politics, and Consciousness, edited by Gordon Ball, McGraw (New York, NY), 1975.

Chicago Trial Testimony, City Lights (San Francisco, CA), 1975.

The Dream of Tibet, City Moon, 1976.

To Eberhart from Ginsberg (correspondence), Penmaen Press (Great Barrington, MA), 1976.

Journals: Early Fifties, Early Sixties, edited by Gordon Ball, Grove (New York, NY), 1977.

(With Neal Cassady; and author of afterword) *As Ever: Collected Correspondence of Allen Ginsberg and Neal Cassady,* Creative Arts, 1977.

(Author of introduction) Anne Waldman and Marilyn Webb, editors, *Talking Poetics from Naropa Insti-*

tute: *Annals of the Jack Kerouac School of Disembodied Poetics,* Volume I, Shambhala (Boulder, CO), 1978.

Composed on the Tongue (interviews), edited by Donald Allen, Grey Fox (San Francisco, CA), 1980.

Your Reason and Blake's System, Hanuman Books, 1989.

Allen Ginsberg: Photographs, Twelvetrees Press (Pasadena, CA), 1991.

(Author of introduction) Ernesto Cardenal, *Ergo! The Bumbershoot Literary Magazine,* Bumbershoot, 1991.

(Author of foreword) Anne Waldman, editor, *Out of This World: The Poetry Project at the St. Mark's Church in the Bowery, an Anthology, 1966-1991,* Crown (New York, NY), 1991.

(Author of introduction) Andy Clausen, *Without Doubt,* Zeitgeist Press, 1991.

(Author of introduction) Jack Kerouac, *Poems All Sizes,* City Lights (San Francisco, CA), 1992.

(Author of introduction) Sharkmeat Blue, *King Death: And Other Poems,* Underground Forest/Selva Editions, 1992.

(Author of afterword) Louis Ginsberg, *Collected Poems,* edited by Michael Fournier, Northern Lights, 1992.

Snapshot Poetics: Allen Ginsberg's Photographic Memoir of the Beat Era, introduction by Michael Kohler, Chronicle Books (San Francisco, CA), 1993.

(Editor, with Peter Orlovsky) *Francesco Clemente: Evening Raga 1992,* Rizzoli International (New York, NY), 1993.

Honorable Courtship: From the Author's Journals, January 1-15, 1955, edited and illustrated by Dean Bornstein, Coffee House Press (Minneapolis, MN), 1994.

(Author of introduction) Edward Leffingwell, *Earthly Paradise,* Journey Editions, 1994.

Journals Mid-Fifties, 1954-1958, edited by Gordon Ball, HarperCollins (New York, NY), 1995.

(Contributor and author of foreword) *The Beat Book: Poems and Fiction of the Beat Generation,* edited by Anne Waldman, Shambhala (Boston, MA), 1996.

(Author of foreword) Ko Un, *Beyond Self: 108 Korean Zen Poems,* Parallax Press (Berkeley, CA), 1997.

(Editor, with Eliot Katz and Andy Clausen) *Poems for the Nation: A Collection of Contemporary Political Poems,* Seven Stories Press (New York, NY), 1999.

Deliberate Prose: Selected Essays, 1952-1995, edited by Bill Morgan, HarperCollins (New York, NY), 2000.

Spontaneous Minds: Selected Interviews, 1958-1996, edited by David Carter, HarperCollins (New York, NY), 2001.

(With Louis Ginsberg) *Family Business: Selected Letters between a Father and Son,* edited by Michael Schumacher, Bloomsbury (New York, NY), 2001.

Contributor of essays to books, including David Solomon, editor, *The Marijuana Papers,* Bobbs-Merrill (New York, NY), 1966; Charles Hollander, editor, *Background Papers on Student Drug Abuse,* U.S. National Student Association, 1967; Donald M. Allen, editor, *Robert Creeley, Contexts of Poetry: Interviews 1961-1971,* Four Seasons Foundation (San Francisco, CA), 1973; Jonathan Williams, editor, *Madeira and Toasts for Basil Bunting's Seventy-fifth Birthday,* Jargon Society (East Haven, CT), 1977; and *Nuke Chronicles,* Contact Two (Bowling Green, NY), 1980. Work included in anthologies, including *The Beat Generation and the Angry Young Men,* edited by Gene Feldman and Max Gartenberg, Citadel Press, 1958; Bob Booker and George Foster, editors, *Pardon Me, Sir, but Is My Eye Hurting Your Elbow?* (plays), Geis, 1968; and *The New Oxford Book of American Verse,* edited by Richard Ellmann, Oxford University Press, 1976. Contributor of poetry and articles to periodicals, including *Evergreen Review, Journal for the Protection of All Beings, Playboy, Nation, New Age, New Yorker, Atlantic, Partisan Review,* and *Times Literary Supplement.* Correspondent, *Evergreen Review,* 1965; former contributing editor, *Black Mountain Review;* former advisory guru, *Marijuana Review.*

Ginsberg's papers are housed at Stanford University.

ADAPTATIONS: "Kaddish" was adapted as a film, with Ginsberg as narrator, National Educational Television, 1977; author's poems were adapted as a libretto for Elodie Lauten's opera *Waking in New York,* produced in New York, NY, 1999.

SIDELIGHTS: Allen Ginsberg was a controversial poet who gained a prominent place in post-World War II U.S. culture. He was born in 1926 in Newark, New Jersey, and raised in nearby Paterson, where his father worked as a high school English teacher. Ginsberg's mother, a native Russian who supported the Communist Party, suffered from mental instability and experienced repeated nervous breakdowns. Her relationship with her son served as an underlying influence in much of Ginsberg's writing, which includes the long poems "Kaddish" and "Howl" as well as numerous poetry collections.

In 1943, while studying at Columbia University, Ginsberg befriended William Burroughs and Jack Kerouac; the trio eventually became pivotal figures in what became known in the United States as the Beat movement. Ginsberg and his friends regularly experimented with drugs and indulged their enthusiasms for rambunctious behavior. On one occasion, the poet used his college room to store stolen goods acquired by an acquaintance. Faced with prosecution, he decided to plead insanity and subsequently spent several months in a mental institution.

After graduating from Columbia, Ginsberg remained in New York City and worked various jobs. In 1954, however, he abruptly moved to San Francisco, where the Beat movement was developing through the activities of such poets as Kenneth Rexroth and Lawrence Ferlinghetti.

Ginsberg first came to public attention in 1956 with the publication of *Howl and Other Poems.* "Howl," a long-line poem in the tradition of Walt Whitman, is an outcry of rage and despair against a destructive, abusive society. Kevin O'Sullivan, writing in *Newsmakers,* deemed "Howl" "an angry, sexually explicit poem" and added that it is "considered by many to be a revolutionary event in American poetry." The poem's raw, honest language and its "Hebraic-Melvillian bardic breath," as Ginsberg called it, stunned many traditional critics. In his *American Free Verse* critic Walter Sutton dubbed "Howl" "a tirade revealing an animus directed outward against those who do not share the poet's social and sexual orientation." While Sutton reflected the view of many, some critics responded more positively to Ginsberg's work, with Paul Carroll judging "Howl" "one of the milestones of the generation" in his book *The Poem in Its Skin.*

In addition to stunning many critics, "Howl" also stunned the San Francisco Police Department. Because of the graphic sexual language of the poem, they declared the book *Howl and Other Poems* obscene and arrested the publisher, poet Lawrence Ferlinghetti. The ensuing trial attracted national attention, as prominent literary figures such as Mark Schorer, Kenneth Rexroth, and Walter Van Tilberg Clark spoke in defense of "Howl." The testimony eventually persuaded Judge Clayton W. Horn to rule that "Howl" was not obscene.

The qualities cited in its defense helped make "Howl" the manifesto of the Beat literary movement. The Beats—popularly known as Beatniks—included novel-

ists Jack Kerouac and William Burroughs and poets Gregory Corso, Michael McClure, Gary Snyder, and Ginsberg, all of whom wrote in the language of the street about previously forbidden and unliterary topics. The ideas and art of the Beats greatly influenced popular culture during the 1950s and 1960s.

Ginsberg followed "Howl" with *Kaddish and Other Poems, 1958-60* in 1961. "Kaddish," a poem similar in style and form to "Howl," is based on the traditional Hebrew prayer for the dead and tells the life story of Ginsberg's mother, Naomi. The poet's complex feelings for his mother, colored by her struggle with mental illness, are at the heart of this long-line poem, which is considered to be one of Ginsberg's finest.

Ginsberg's early poems were greatly influenced by fellow Paterson, New Jersey, resident William Carlos Williams. Ginsberg recalled being taught at school that Williams was unsophisticated, but upon talking to Williams about his poetry, Ginsberg realized that Williams heard poetry in a different way, and upon this understanding he knew that he needed to make some changes. Ginsberg acted immediately on this sudden understanding. He adapted his prose writings by taking fragments and turning them into lines, broken up in the same way a person would actually talk it out. Williams was very impressed and asked for more just like it.

Another major influence on Ginsberg was his friend Kerouac, who wrote novels in a "spontaneous prose" style Ginsberg admired and adapted in his own work. Both Williams and Kerouac emphasized a writer's emotions and natural mode of expression over traditional literary structures; for his part Kerouac wrote some of his books by putting a roll of white paper into a typewriter and typing continuously in a "stream of consciousness." Ginsberg began writing poetry by remembering or thinking of an idea, writing it down and completing it in one sitting. He cited as historical precedents for this method the works of poet Walt Whitman, novelist Herman Melville, and writers Henry David Thoreau and Ralph Waldo Emerson.

A major theme in Ginsberg's life and poetry was politics. In his *American Poetry in the Twentieth Century,* Kenneth Rexroth called this aspect of Ginsberg's work "an almost perfect fulfillment of the long, Whitman, Populist, social revolutionary tradition in American poetry." In a number of poems, Ginsberg refers to the union struggles of the 1930s, popular radical figures of the day, the McCarthy Era communist scare, and other leftist touchstones. In "Wichita Vortex Sutra" he attempts to end the Vietnam War through a kind of magical, poetic evocation, while in "Plutonian Ode," a similar feat—ending the dangers of nuclear power through the magic of a poet's breath—is attempted. Other poems, such as "Howl," although not expressly political in nature, have been nonetheless considered by many critics to contain strong social criticism.

Ginsberg's political activities were libertarian in nature, echoing his poetic preference for individual expression over traditional structure. In the mid-1960s he was closely associated with the hippie and antiwar movements and advocated "flower power," a strategy in which antiwar demonstrators would promote abstract values like peace and love to dramatize their opposition to the Vietnam War. The use of flowers, bells, smiles, and mantras became common among demonstrators for some time. In 1967 Ginsberg helped organize the "Gathering of the Tribes for a Human Be-In," an event modeled after the Hindu *mela,* a religious festival. This gathering was the first of the hippie festivals and served as an inspiration for hundreds of others. In 1969, when some antiwar activists staged an "exorcism of the Pentagon," Ginsberg composed the mantra they chanted. He also testified for the defense in the Chicago Seven conspiracy trial, in which antiwar activists were charged with "conspiracy to cross state lines to promote a riot."

Ginsberg's politics sometimes prompted reaction from law-enforcement authorities. He was arrested at an antiwar demonstration in New York City in 1967 and tear-gassed at the Democratic National Convention in Chicago in 1968. In 1972 he was jailed for demonstrating against then-President Richard Nixon at the Republican National Convention in Miami. Six years later he and companion Peter Orlovsky were arrested for sitting on train tracks in order to stop a trainload of radioactive waste coming from the Rocky Flats Nuclear Weapons Plant in Colorado.

Ginsberg's political activities caused him problems in other countries as well. In 1965 he visited Cuba as a correspondent for *Evergreen Review.* After he complained about the treatment of homosexuals at the University of Havana, the Cuban government asked Ginsberg to leave the country. In the same year the poet traveled to Czechoslovakia, where he was elected King of May by thousands of Czech citizens. The next day the Czech government requested that he leave, ostensibly because he was unkempt. Ginsberg attributed his expulsion to the Czech secret police department's embarrassment at the acclaim given to him, considering his appearance and sexual-orientation.

Another aspect of Ginsberg's poetry is the focus on the spiritual and visionary. His interest in these matters was inspired by a series of visions he had while reading nineteenth-century British writer William Blake's poetry. Ginsberg recalled hearing a voice that he was certain belonged to Blake.

Such visions prompted an interest in mysticism that led Ginsberg to experiment with various drugs, and he claimed that some of his best poetry was written under the influence of drugs: the second part of "Howl" with peyote, "Kaddish" with amphetamines, and "Wales—A Visitation" with LSD. After a journey to India in 1962, however, during which he was introduced to meditation and yoga, Ginsberg changed his mind about drugs. He became convinced that meditation and yoga were far superior to drugs in raising one's consciousness, while still maintaining that psychedelics could prove helpful in writing poetry.

Ginsberg's study of Eastern religions was spurred on by his discovery of mantras, rhythmic chants used for spiritual effects. The mantra's use of rhythm, breath, and elemental sounds seemed to him a kind of poetry. In a number of poems he incorporated mantras into the body of the text, transforming the work into a kind of poetic prayer. During poetry readings he often began by chanting a mantra in order to set the proper mood.

Ginsberg's interest in Eastern religions eventually led him to the Venerable Chogyam Trungpa, Rinpoche, a Buddhist abbot from Tibet who had a strong influence on Ginsberg's writing. The early 1970s found the poet taking classes at Trungpa's Naropa Institute in Colorado as well as teaching poetry classes there. In 1972 Ginsberg took the Refuge and Boddhisattva vows, formally committing himself to the Buddhist faith.

A primary aspect of Trungpa's teaching is a form of meditation called shamatha in which one concentrates on one's own breathing. Ginsberg's book *Mind Breaths,* dedicated to Trungpa, contains several poems written with the help of shamatha meditation. In 1974 Ginsberg and fellow-poet Anne Waldman co-founded the Jack Kerouac School of Disembodied Poetics as a branch of Trungpa's Naropa Institute.

Ginsberg lived a kind of literary "rags to riches"—from his early days as the feared and criticized poet to his later position as what some critics would call one of the most influential poets of his generation. In the words of James F. Mersmann in his *Out of the Vietnam Vortex,* "a great figure in the history of poetry." According to *Times Literary Supplement* contributor James Campbell, "No one has made his poetry speak for the whole man, without inhibition of any kind, more than Ginsberg." Because of his rise to influence and his staying power as a figure in American art and culture, Ginsberg's work continued to remain the object of much scholarly attention throughout his lifetime. A documentary directed by Jerry Aronson, *The Life and Times of Allen Ginsberg,* was released in 1994. The same year, Stanford University spent a large amount of money to acquire the poet's personal archives. New poems and collections of Ginsberg's previous works continued to be published regularly, while his letters, journals, and even his photographs of fellow Beats provided critics and scholars new insights into his life and work.

Journals Mid-Fifties, 1954-1958, published in 1995, is one example of the continuous supply of new information available on Ginsberg in his later years. Jim Krusoe, writing in the *Los Angeles Times Book Review,* maintained that this book "provides plenty of food for thought about genius in general and about Ginsberg's development in particular." For some reviewers, however, these journals shed less light on the poet than previous works. Alexander Theroux commented in Chicago's *Tribune Books,* "Sadly these pages are often remarkably dull and rarely original and insightful." According to Guy Mannes-Abbott in the *New Statesman,* these journals "have interest but lack the vitality of earlier and later journals, or the generosity of his letters from this time." A reviewer for the *Economist* recognized the shortcomings of Ginsberg's personal writings, but also saw their merits. "Though maddeningly interested in his most banal reactions," the reviewer noted that Ginsberg "is at least open about his self-fascination. . . . In most writers self-preoccupation is usually mortal. But Mr. Ginsberg has the balancing gifts of promiscuous curiosity and an almost sappy, American optimism." For Krusoe, in the end, "the brilliance of these journals is exactly the brilliant persistence of a man who will not quit until his dream life, his love life and his poems are melded into a single whole."

In the spring of 1997, plagued with diabetes and chronic hepatitis, Ginsberg was diagnosed with liver cancer. After learning of this illness, he promptly produced twelve brief poems; the next day he suffered a stroke and lapsed into a coma, and died two days later. In the *New York Times,* Ginsberg was remembered by William Burroughs as "a great person with worldwide influence."

Ginsberg's final poems were collected in *Death and Fame: Poems, 1993-1997.* A *Publishers Weekly* re-viewer, who acknowledged that "there has never been an American poet as public as Ginsberg," described *Death and Fame* as "a perfect capstone to a noble life." Ray Olson and Jack Helberg, writing in *Booklist,* found Ginsberg's poetry "polished if not constrained," while Rochelle Ratner, in a *Library Journal* assessment, observed that "Ginsberg's tenderness and caring is . . . very much in evidence."

Another of Ginsberg's posthumous publications, *Deliberate Prose: Selected Essays, 1952-1995,* presents more than 150 essays on such subjects as nuclear weapons; the Vietnam War; censorship; poets such as Walt Whitman and Beat figure Gregory Corso; and other cultural luminaries, including musician John Lennon and photographer Robert Frank. A *Publishers Weekly* critic appraised *Deliberate Prose* as "sometimes lovely, sometimes slapdash" and added that the book is "sure to appeal" to the late poet's "broad contingent of fans." However, David Adox, in his *New York Times Book Review* assessment, declared that "Ginsberg's pieces on writers read like a series of insipid thank-you notes." *Booklist* reviewer Ray Olson, meanwhile, found Ginsberg's essays "more immediately approachable than much of his verse," and *Library Journal* critic William Gargan affirmed that the book serves as "a good overview of [Ginsberg's] life and art." Still another reviewer, James Gartner, wrote in *National Review* that *Deliberate Prose* constitutes "a window into a slice of American social and literary history, the creative process, and the soul of a beautiful man."

BIOGRAPHICAL AND CRITICAL SOURCES:

BOOKS

Carroll, Paul, *The Poem in Its Skin,* Follett, 1968.

Charters, Ann, *Scenes along the Road,* Gotham Book Mart (New York, NY), 1971.

Charters, Ann, *Kerouac,* Straight Arrow Books, 1973.

Charters, Samuel, *Some Poems/Poets: Studies in American Underground Poetry since 1945,* Oyez, 1971.

Concise Dictionary of American Literary Biography: 1941-1968, Thomson Gale (Detroit, MI), 1987.

Contemporary Literary Criticism, Thomson Gale (Detroit, MI), Volume 1, 1973, Volume 2, 1974, Volume 3, 1975, Volume 4, 1975, Volume 6, 1976, Volume 13, 1980, Volume 36, 1986, Volume 69, 1992.

Contemporary Poets, sixth edition, St. James Press (Detroit, MI), 1996.

Cook, Bruce, *The Beat Generation,* Scribner (New York, NY), 1971.

Dictionary of Literary Biography, Thomson Gale (Detroit, MI), Volume 5: *American Poets since World War II,* 1980, Volume 16: *The Beats: Literary Bohemians in Postwar America,* 1983, Volume 169: *American Poets since World War II, Fifth Series,* 1996.

Erlich, J. W., editor, *Howl of the Censor,* Nourse Publishing, 1961.

Faas, Ekbert, editor, *Toward a New American Poetics: Essays and Interviews,* Black Sparrow Press (Santa Barbara, CA), 1978.

Fielder, Leslie A., *Waiting for the End,* Stein & Day (Briarcliff Manor, NY), 1964.

Gay and Lesbian Biography, St. James Press (New York, NY), 1997.

Gay and Lesbian Literature, St. James Press (New York, NY), 1994.

Gay Sunshine Interview: Allen Ginsberg with Allen Young, Grey Fox Press (San Francisco, CA), 1974.

Gross, Theodore L., editor, *Representative Men,* Free Press (New York, NY), 1970.

Kramer, Jane, *Allen Ginsberg in America,* Random House (New York, NY), 1969, new edition, Fromm International Publishing, 1997.

Kraus, Michelle P., *Allen Ginsberg: An Annotated Bibliography, 1969-1977,* Scarecrow (Metuchen, NJ), 1980.

Lipton, Lawrence, *The Holy Barbarians,* Messner (New York, NY), 1959.

McNally, Dennis, *Desolate Angel: Jack Kerouac, the Beats, and America,* Random House (New York, NY), 1979.

Merrill, Thomas F., *Allen Ginsberg,* Twayne (New York, NY), 1969.

Mersmann, James F., *Out of the Vietnam Vortex: A Study of Poets and Poetry against the War,* University Press of Kansas, 1974.

Miles, Barry, *Two Lectures on the Work of Allen Ginsberg,* Contemporary Research Press (Dallas, TX), 1993.

Morgan, Bill, *The Works of Allen Ginsberg, 1941-1994: A Descriptive Bibliography,* Greenwood Press (Westport, CT), 1995.

Morgan, Bill, *The Response to Allen Ginsberg, 1926-1994: A Bibliography of Secondary Sources,* foreword by Ginsberg, Greenwood Press (Westport, CT), 1996.

Mottram, Eric, *Allen Ginsberg in the Sixties,* Unicorn Bookshop, 1972.

Parkinson, Thomas F., *A Casebook on the Beats,* Crowell (New York, NY), 1961.

Poetry Criticism, Volume 4, Thomson Gale (Detroit, MI), 1992.

Portuges, Paul, *The Visionary Poetics of Allen Ginsberg,* Ross-Erikson (Santa Barbara, CA), 1978.

Rather, Lois, *Bohemians to Hippies: Waves of Rebellion,* Rather Press (Oakland, CA), 1977.

Reference Guide to American Literature, third edition, St. James Press (Detroit, MI), 1994.

Rexroth, Kenneth, *American Poetry in the Twentieth Century,* Herder, 1971.

Rosenthal, Mocha L., *The Modern Poets: A Critical Introduction,* Oxford University Press (Oxford, England), 1960.

Rosenthal, Mocha L., *The New Poets: American and British Poetry since World War II,* Oxford University Press (Oxford, England), 1967.

Roszak, Theodore, *The Making of a Counter Culture,* Doubleday (Garden City, NY), 1969.

Schumacher, Michael, *Dharma Lion,* St. Martin's Press (New York, NY), 1994.

Shaw, Robert B., editor, *American Poetry since 1960: Some Critical Perspectives,* Dufour (Chester Springs, PA), 1974.

Simpson, Louis, *A Revolution in Taste,* Macmillan (New York, NY), 1978.

Stepanchev, Stephen, *American Poetry since 1945,* Harper (New York, NY), 1965.

Sutton, Walter, *American Free Verse: The Modern Revolution in Poetry,* New Directions (New York, NY), 1973.

Tyrell, John, *Naked Angels,* McGraw (New York, NY), 1976.

Widmer, Kingsley, *The Fifties: Fiction, Poetry, Drama,* Everett/Edwards (DeLand, FL), 1970.

PERIODICALS

Advocate, February 22, 1994.

American Poetry Review, September, 1977.

Antioch Review, spring, 1994, p. 374.

Ariel, October, 1993, pp. 21-32.

Art Press, number 188, 1994, pp. E24-E26.

Atlanta Journal and Constitution, November 19, 1994, p. WL23.

Best Sellers, December 15, 1974.

Black Mountain Review, autumn, 1957.

Bloomsbury Review, March, 1993, p. 5.

Booklist, April 15, 1994, p. 1503; April 15, 1995, p. 1468; February 1, 1999, Ray Olson and Jack Heilbig, review of *Death and Fame: Poems, 1993-1997,* p. 959; February 15, 2000, Ray Olson, review of *Deliberate Prose: Selected Essays, 1952-1995.*

Book World, May 25, 1969.

Bulletin of Bibliography, December, 1993, pp. 279-293.

Carolina Quarterly, spring-summer, 1975.

Chicago Review, summer, 1975.

Denver Post, July 20, 1975.

Detroit News, April 18, 1997.

Dionysos, winter, 1993, pp. 30-42.

East West Journal, February, 1978.

Economist, November 11, 1995, p. 8.

Encounter, February, 1970.

Entertainment Weekly, October 11, 1996, p. 92.

Esquire, April, 1973.

Evergreen Review, July-August, 1961.

Globe and Mail (Toronto, Ontario, Canada), February 23, 1985.

Harper's, October, 1966.

Hudson Review, autumn, 1973.

Interview, June, 1994, p. 16.

Journal of American Culture, fall, 1993, pp. 81-88.

Journal of Popular Culture, winter, 1969.

Lambda Book Report, July, 1993, p. 42; July, 1994, p. 47; September, 1994, p. 34.

Library Journal, June 15, 1958; February 1, 1987; May 1, 1994; August, 1995, p. 79; January, 1999, Rochelle Ratner, review of *Death and Fame,* p. 103; March 15, 2000, William Gargan, review of *Deliberate Prose.*

Life, May 27, 1966.

Los Angeles Times, April 18, 1985; February 16, 1994, p. F1; February 17, 1994, p. F3.

Los Angeles Times Book Review, January 2, 1994, p. 12; May 29, 1994, p. 8; September 3, 1995, p. 4.

Michigan Quarterly Review, spring, 1994, pp. 350-359.

Nation, February 25, 1957; November 11, 1961; November 12, 1977; May 20, 1991.

National Observer, December 9, 1968.

National Review, September 12, 1959; May 19, 1997, p. 54; May 22, 2000, James Gartner, "Manic Mensch."

National Screw, June, 1977.

New Age, April, 1976.

New Republic, July 25, 1970; October 12, 1974; October 22, 1977.

New Statesman, May 12, 1995, p. 38; October 27, 1995, p. 47.

New Times, February 20, 1978.

New Yorker, August 17, 1968; August 24, 1968; May 28, 1979.

New York Times, February 6, 1972; May 21, 1994, p. A13; September 20, 1994, p. C15; September 25, 1994, sec. 2, p. 34; October 29, 1994, p. A19; September 29, 1995, p. C18.

New York Times Book Review, September 2, 1956; May 11, 1969; August 31, 1969; April 15, 1973; March 2, 1975; October 23, 1977; March 19, 1978; May

29, 1994, p. 14; March 26, 2000, David Adox, review of *Deliberate Prose.*

New York Times Magazine, July 11, 1965.

Observer (London, England), June 11, 1995, p. 16.

Parnassus, spring-summer, 1974.

Partisan Review, number 2, 1959; number 3, 1967; number 3, 1971; number 2, 1974.

People, July 3, 1978; November 25, 1996, p. 27.

Philadelphia Bulletin, May 19, 1974.

Playboy, April, 1969; January, 1995, p. 24.

Plays and Players, April, 1972.

Poetry, September, 1957; July, 1969; September, 1969.

Progressive, May, 1994, p. 48; August, 1994, pp. 34-39.

Publishers Weekly, January 25, 1999, review of *Death and Fame;* January 31, 2000, review of *Deliberate Prose.*

Salmagundi, spring-summer, 1973.

San Francisco Oracle, February, 1967.

Saturday Review, October 5, 1957.

Small Press Review, July-August, 1977.

Stand, autumn, 1995, p. 77.

Thoth, winter, 1967.

Time, February 9, 1959; November 18, 1974; March 5, 1979.

Times Literary Supplement, July 7, 1978; September 1, 1995, p. 22.

Tribune Books (Chicago, IL), June 11, 1995, p. 5.

Unmuzzled Ox, Volume 3, number 2, 1975.

USA Today, July, 1995, p. 96.

Vanity Fair, March, 1994, p. 186.

Village Voice, April 18, 1974.

Washington Post, March 17, 1985.

Washington Post Book World, March 20, 1994, p. 12.

Western American Literature, spring, 1995, pp. 3-28.

Whole Earth Review, fall, 1995, p. 90.

World Literature Today, winter, 1995, p. 146.

ONLINE

Allen Ginsberg Trust Web Site, http://allenginsberg.org/ (April 20, 2004).

OTHER

The Life and Times of Allen Ginsberg (film), First Run Features, 1994.

OBITUARIES:

BOOKS

Newsmakers, Thomson Gale (Detroit, MI), 1997, pp. 493-495.

PERIODICALS

Detroit News, April 6, 1997.
Economist, April 12, 1997, p. 87.
Entertainment Weekly, April 18, 1997, p. 18.
Los Angeles Times, April 6, 1997, p. A1.
Maclean's, April 14, 1997, p. 11.
Nation, April 28, 1997, p. 8.
National Review, May 5, 1997.
Newsweek, April 14, 1997, p. 60.
New York Times, April 7, 1997, pp. A1, A42; April 8, 1997, p. B10.
Observer, April 6, 1997, p. 4.
People, April 21, 1997, p. 169.
Progressive, May, 1997, p. 10.
Rolling Stone, May 29, 1997, p. 34.
Time, April 14, 1997, p. 31.
Times (London, England), April 7, 1997.
Washington Post, April 6, 1997, p. B8.

* * *

GINZBURG, Natalia 1916-1991
(Alessandra Tornimparte)

PERSONAL: Born July 14 (one source says July 5), 1916, in Palermo, Italy; died October 7 (one source says October 8), 1991; daughter of Carlo (a novelist and professor of biology) and Lidia (Tanzi) Levi; married Leone Ginzburg (an editor and political activist), 1938 (died, 1944); married Gabriele Baldini, 1950.

CAREER: Novelist, short story writer, dramatist, and essayist. Worked for Einaudi (publisher), Turin, Italy. Elected representative of Independent Left Party, Parliament of Italy, 1983.

AWARDS, HONORS: Strega prize, 1964, for *Lessico famigliare;* Marzotto Prize for European drama, 1968, for *The Advertisement;* Milan Club Degli Editori award, 1969; Bagutto award, 1984; Ernest Hemingway Prize, 1985.

WRITINGS:

(Under pseudonym Alessandra Tournimparte) *La strada che va in citta* (two short novels), Einaudi (Turin, Italy), 1942, reprinted under own name, 1975, translation by Frances Frenaye published under own name as *The Road to the City* (contains "The Road to the City" and "The Dry Heart"), Doubleday (New York, NY), 1949.

E stato cosi, Einaudi (Turin, Italy), 1947, reprinted, 1974.

Valentino (novella; also see below), Einaudi (Turin, Italy), 1951.

Tutti i nostri ieri (novel), Einaudi (Turin, Italy), 1952, translation by Angus Davidson published as *A Light for Fools,* Dutton (New York, NY), 1956, translation published as *Dead Yesterdays,* Secker & Warburg^, 1956.

(With Giansiro Ferrata) *Romanzi del 900,* Ediziono Radio Italiana (Turin, Italy), 1957.

Sagittario (novella; also see below), Einaudi (Turin, Italy), 1957, translation published as *Sagittarius,* 1975.

Le voci della sera, Einaudi (Turin, Italy), 1961, new edition edited by Sergio Pacilici, Random House (New York, NY), 1971, translation by D.M. Low published as *Voices in the Evening,* Dutton (New York, NY), 1963.

Le piccole virtu (essays), Einaudi (Turin, Italy), 1962, translation by Dick Davis published as *The Little Virtues,* Seaver Books, 1986.

Lessico famigliare (novel), Einaudi (Turin, Italy), 1963, translation by D.M. Low published as *Family Sayings,* Dutton (New York, NY), 1967, translation by Judith Woolf published as *The Things We Used to Say,* Carcanet (Manchester, England), 1997, Arcade Pub. (New York, NY), 1999.

Cinque romanzi brevi (short novels and short stories), Einaudi (Turin, Italy), 1964.

Ti ho sposato per allegria (plays), Einaudi (Turin, Italy), 1966.

The Advertisement (play; translation by Henry Reed first produced in London at Old Vic Theatre, September 24, 1968), Faber^, 1969.

Teresa (play), [Paris, France], 1970.

Mai devi domandarmi (essays), Garzanti (Milan, Italy) 1970, translation by Isabel Quigly published as *Never Must You Ask Me,* M. Joseph^, 1973.

Caro Michele (novel), Mondadori (Milan, Italy), 1973, translation by Sheila Cudahy published as *No Way,* Harcourt (New York, NY), 1974, published as *Dear Michael,* P. Owen^, 1975.

Paese di mare e altre commedie, Garzanti (Milan, Italy), 1973.

Vita immaginaria (essays), Mondadori (Milan, Italy), 1974.

Famiglia (contains novellas "Borghesia" and "Famiglia"), 1977, translation by Beryl Stockman published as *Family,* Holt (New York, NY), 1988.

La citte e la casa, 1984, translation by Davis published as *The City and the House,* Seaver Books, 1987.

All Our Yesterdays, translation by Angus Davidson, Carcanet, 1985.

The Manzoni Family, translation by Marie Evans, Seaver Books, 1987.

Valentino and Sagittarius, translation by Avril Bardoni, Holt (New York, NY), 1988.

E difficile parlare di se, edited by Cesare Garboli and Lisa Ginzburg, Einaudi (Turin, Italy), 1999, translated by Louise Quirke and published as *It's Hard to Talk about Yourself,* University of Chicago Press (Chicago, IL), 2003.

Non possiamo saperlo: saggi 1973-1990, Einaudi (Turin, Italy), 2001.

Opere, Mondadori (Milan, Italy), 2001.

A Place to Live: And Other Selected Essays, edited and translated by Lynne Sharon Schwartz, Seven Stories Press (New York, NY), 2002.

Also author of *Fragola e panna,* 1966, *La segretaria,* 1967, and "I Married You for the Fun of It," 1972.

SIDELIGHTS: Natalia Ginzburg remains one of the best-known post-war Italian writers. Her cool, controlled, simple style of writing has continued to impress critics, while her intimate explorations of domestic life have been praised for their authenticity and concern for traditional values. Annapaola Concogni, writing in the *New York Times Book Review,* explained that Ginzburg possessed an "ear tuned in to the subtlest frequencies of domestic life, its accents, its gestures, its ups and downs and constant contradictions." In her introduction to Ginzberg's *Never Must You Ask Me,* Isabel Quigly compared Ginzburg to Russian playwright Anton Chekhov, finding that, when reading Ginzburg's fiction, "Inevitably, Chekhov comes to mind: not only because the long summer days, the endless agreeable but unrewarding chat, the whole provincial-intellectual set-up, recall him, but because the Italian charm, and volatility, and loquacity, and unselfconscious egocentricity, and inability to move out of grooves, and so on, that Miss Ginzburg so brilliantly captures, are all Chekhovian qualities."

Other reviewers were critical of Ginzburg's method of characterization. In the *Saturday Review,* Thomas G. Bergin wrote that the characters in *Voices in the Evening* "are, for the most part, like excellent line drawings, quite real but somehow not 'filled in.' Their bone structure is magnificent, but there is no flesh." And although Otis K. Burger found the same novel to be "crisp, brittle, entertaining, and informative" in his review for the *New York Times,* he also remarked that "the very coolness of the style tends to defeat the subtle theme of

the death of a family (and a love) through sheer lack of gumption. The brevity of the book and its semicomic treatment of a muted tragedy come to seem, not a strength but part of the general, fatal weariness. The 'voices in the evening' tend to cancel each other out—succeeding only too well in presenting people who, pallid to begin with, end as mere phantoms."

Although Ginzberg's *Family Sayings* is on the surface a simple family tale, what is beneath and between the lines reveals the weight and worth of the novel. In a review for the *New Leader,* Raymond Rosenthal wrote that "what started as a simple family chronicle takes on the timeless, magnificent aspect of an ancient tale, a Homeric saga. It is magical, exhilarating. In the last pages, after all is accomplished and the deaths, the bereavements, the terrible losses of war and social struggle have been counted up, so to speak, the mere fact that Natalia's mother is still telling the same old stories, and that her father—the counter-muse, the rationalistic ogre—is still there to provide the antiphonic accompaniment of grumbles and complaints, becomes mythical in the truest sense. The surface of this book is also its depths."

In *London Magazine,* Gavin Ewart also praised *Family Sayings.* The book exhibits, Ewart noted, "a simple, distilled style, a reliance on the virtues of repetition, an awareness of the ridiculousness of human beings; a great love (reading between the lines) for both her father and her mother; the shadow of Proust. All these are in it. Dealing with more 'tragic' material, it has the control and the only slightly edited reality that one finds in *My Life and Hard Times* (remember Thurber?). Though this is verbal comedy and not farce, it still seems, like that masterpiece, to imply that life can be terrible, but also terribly funny."

No Way concerns Michael, a young revolutionary living in a basement apartment. Ginzburg develops the relationships between Michael and his friends through letters (most of which are written to Michael, few of which he answers). "While Michael is expending what turn out to be his last days," Martin Levin commented in the *New York Times Book Review,* "his father dies, his girlfriend Mara runs through a half dozen patrons, and his mother is jilted by her lover Philip. All of these relationships are assembled by epistolary connections that have the intricacy and the fragility of an ant city. The wit is mordant and comes directly out of paradox." "What makes this book so wonderful," In a *New Yorker* review L.E. Sissman declared: "magical even—is that we are never bored by the imprisoned pacings and abortive flights of its people. They all become real and individual and fascinating through the technical gifts of the author. . . . *No Way* is a novel of the curdling of aspirations and the enfeebling of powers among those who heretofore held sway. Its quality lies in its reportorial accuracy, in its fine, warm, rueful equanimity, in its balance in the face of toppling worlds. It is a most remarkable book."

Writing in the *Los Angeles Times Book Review,* Peter Brunette praised Ginzberg's body of work, calling her "the undisputed doyenne of contemporary Italian letters. Both a successful playwright and essayist, she has also become, through a steady outpouring of quietly memorable fiction . . . a world-class novelist."

BIOGRAPHICAL AND CRITICAL SOURCES:

BOOKS

Bullock, Alan, *Natalia Ginzburg: Human Relationships in a Changing World,* St. Martin's Press (New York, NY), 1991.
Contemporary Literary Criticism, Thomson Gale, Volume 5, 1976, Volume 11, 1979, Volume 54, 1989.

PERIODICALS

Commonweal, December 4, 1992.
Library Journal, November 1, 2003, Valeda Frances Dent, review of *It's Hard to Talk about Yourself,* p. 82.
London Magazine, May, 1967.
Los Angeles Times Book Review, December 27, 1987.
New Leader, March 13, 1967.
New Republic, September 14, 1974.
New Yorker, October 21, 1974.
New York Review of Books, January 23, 1975.
New York Times, January 5, 1957; October 6, 1963.
New York Times Book Review, September 1, 1974; June 26, 1988.
Saturday Review, September 21, 1963.
Spectator, August 24, 1956.
Times Literary Supplement, February 5, 1971; April 13, 1973; June 15, 1973; February 21, 1975; March 28, 1975; June 2, 1978.
World Literature Today, August, 1991.

OBITUARIES:

PERIODICALS

Chicago Tribune, October 9, 1991, p. 12, sec. 3.
Current Biography, November, 1991, p. 59.

Los Angeles Times, October 12, 1991, p. A34.
New York Times, October 9, 1991, p. D24.
Time, October 21, 1991, p. 79.
Times (London, England), October 9, 1991, p. 20.
Washington Post, October 10, 1991, p. C4.

*   *   *

GIOVANNI, Nikki 1943-
(Yolande Cornelia Giovanni, Jr.)

PERSONAL: Born Yolande Cornelia Giovanni, Jr., June 7, 1943, in Knoxville, TN; daughter of Gus Jones (a probation officer) and Yolande Cornelia (a social worker; maiden name, Watson) Giovanni; children: Thomas Watson. *Ethnicity:* "Black." *Education:* Fisk University, B.A. (with honors), 1967; postgraduate studies at University of Pennsylvania School of Social Work and Columbia University School of Fine Arts, 1968.

ADDRESSES: Office—English Department, Shanks Hall, Virginia Tech, Blacksburg, VA 24061. *E-mail*—ngiovann@vt.edu.

CAREER: Poet, writer, and lecturer. Queens College of the City University of New York, Flushing, assistant professor of black studies, 1968; Rutgers University, Livingston College, New Brunswick, NJ, associate professor of English, 1968-72; Ohio State University, Columbus, visiting professor of English, 1984; College of Mount St. Joseph on the Ohio, Mount St. Joseph, Ohio, professor of creative writing, 1985-87; Virginia Tech, Blacksburg, VA, professor of English, 1987-99, Gloria D. Smith Professor of Black Studies, 1997-99, university distinguished professor, 1999—; Texas Christian University, visiting professor in humanities, 1991. Founder of publishing firm, NikTom Ltd., 1970; participated in "Soul at the Center," Lincoln Center for the Performing Arts, 1972; Duncanson Artist-in-Residence, Taft Museum, Cincinnati, 1986; Cochair, Literary Arts Festival for State of Tennessee Homecoming, 1986; director, Warm Hearth Writer's Workshop, 1988—; appointed to Ohio Humanities Council, 1987; member of board of directors, Virginia Foundation for Humanities and Public Policy, 1990-93; participant in Appalachian Community Fund, 1991-93, and Volunteer Action Center, 1991-94; featured poet, International Poetry Festival, Utrecht, Holland, 1991. Has given numerous poetry readings and lectures worldwide and appeared on numerous television talk shows.

MEMBER: National Council of Negro Women, Society of Magazine Writers, National Black Heroines for PUSH, Winnie Mandela Children's Fund Committee, Delta Sigma Theta (honorary member).

AWARDS, HONORS: Grants from Ford Foundation, 1967, National Endowment for the Arts, 1968, and Harlem Cultural Council, 1969; named one of ten "Most Admired Black Women,"*Amsterdam News,* 1969; outstanding achievement award, *Mademoiselle,* 1971; Omega Psi Phi Fraternity Award, 1971, for outstanding contribution to arts and letters; Meritorious Plaque for Service, Cook County Jail, 1971; Prince Matchabelli Sun Shower Award, 1971; life membership and scroll, National Council of Negro Women, 1972; National Association of Radio and Television Announcers Award, 1972, for recording *Truth Is on Its Way;* Woman of the Year Youth Leadership Award, *Ladies' Home Journal,* 1972; National Book Award nomination, 1973, for *Gemini: An Extended Autobiographical Statement on My First Twenty-five Years of Being a Black Poet;* Best Books for Young Adults citation, American Library Association, 1973, for *My House;*Woman of the Year citation, Cincinnati Chapter of YWCA, 1983; elected to Ohio Women's Hall of Fame, 1985; Outstanding Woman of Tennessee citation, 1985; Post-Corbett Award, 1986; *Spirit to Spirit* received the Silver Apple Award from Oakland Museum Film Festival; Woman of the Year, National Association for the Advancement of Colored People (Lynchburg chapter), 1989. Honorary Doctorate of Humanities, Wilberforce University, 1972, and Fisk University, 1988; Honorary Doctorate of Literature, University of Maryland (Princess Anne Campus), 1974, Ripon University, 1974, and Smith College, 1975; Honorary Doctorate of Humane Letters, College of Mount St. Joseph on the Ohio, 1985, Indiana University, 1991, Otterbein College, 1992, Widener University, 1993, Albright College, 1995, Cabrini College, 1995, and Allegheny College, 1997; Honorary Doctor of Humane Letters, Manhattanville College, 2000; Honorary Doctorate of Humane Letters, Central State University, 2001. Keys to numerous cities, including Dallas, TX, New York, NY, Cincinnati, OH, Miami, FL, New Orleans, LA, and Los Angeles, CA; Ohioana Book Award, 1988; Jeanine Rae Award for the Advancement of Women's Culture, 1995; Langston Hughes Award, 1996; NAACP Image award, 1998; Tennessee Governor's award, 1998; Virginia Governor's Award for the Arts 2000; SHero Award for Lifetime Achievement, 2002; the first Rosa Parks Woman of Courage Award, 2002; Black Caucus Award for nonfiction, American Library Association, and NAACP Image Award for Outstanding Literary Work, both 2003, both for *Quilting the Black-Eyed Pea: Poems and Not Quite Poems.*

WRITINGS:

POETRY

Black Feeling, Black Talk, Broadside Press (Detroit, MI), 1968, 3rd edition, 1970.

Black Judgement, Broadside Press (Detroit, MI), 1968.

Black Feeling, Black Talk/ Black Judgement (contains *Black Feeling, Black Talk,* and *Black Judgement*), Morrow (New York, NY), 1970, selection published as *Knoxville, Tennessee,* illustrated by Larry Johnson, Scholastic (New York, NY), 1994.

Re: Creation, Broadside Press (Detroit, MI), 1970.

Poem of Angela Yvonne Davis, Afro Arts (New York, NY), 1970.

Spin a Soft Black Song: Poems for Children, illustrated by Charles Bible, Hill & Wang (New York, NY), 1971, illustrated by George Martins, Lawrence Hill (Westport, CT), 1985, revised edition, Farrar, Straus (New York, NY), 1987.

My House, foreword by Ida Lewis, Morrow (New York, NY), 1972.

Ego-Tripping and Other Poems for Young People, illustrated by George Ford, Lawrence Hill (Chicago, IL), 1973.

The Women and the Men, Morrow (New York, NY), 1975.

Cotton Candy on a Rainy Day, introduction by Paula Giddings, Morrow (New York, NY), 1978.

Vacation Time: Poems for Children, illustrated by Marisabina Russo, Morrow (New York, NY), 1980.

Those Who Ride the Night Winds, Morrow (New York, NY), 1983.

The Genie in the Jar, illustrated by Chris Raschka, Holt, 1996.

The Selected Poems of Nikki Giovanni, 1968-1995, Morrow (New York, NY), 1996.

The Sun Is So Quiet, illustrated by Ashley Bryant, Holt (New York, NY), 1996.

Love Poems, Morrow (New York, NY), 1997.

Blues: For All the Changes: New Poems, Morrow (New York, NY), 1999.

Quilting the Black-Eyed Pea: Poems and Not Quite Poems, Morrow (New York, NY), 2002.

Prosaic Soul of Nikki Giovanni, HarperCollins (New York, NY), 2003.

The Collected Poetry of Nikki Giovanni: 1968-1998, Morrow (New York, NY), 2003.

Girls in the Circle, illustrated by Cathy Ann Johnson, Scholastic (New York, NY), 2004.

OTHER

(Editor) *Night Comes Softly: An Anthology of Black Female Voices,* Medic Press (Newark, NJ), 1970.

Gemini: An Extended Autobiographical Statement on My First Twenty-five Years of Being a Black Poet, Bobbs-Merrill (Indianapolis, IN), 1971.

Truth Is on Its Way (album), Atlantis, 1971.

(With James Baldwin) *A Dialogue: James Baldwin and Nikki Giovanni,* Lippincott (Philadelphia, PA), 1973.

Like a Ripple on a Pond (album), Collectibles, 1973.

(With Margaret Walker) *A Poetic Equation: Conversations between Nikki Giovanni and Margaret Walker,* Howard University Press (Washington, DC), 1974.

The Way I Feel (album), Atlantic, 1975.

Legacies—The Poetry Of Nikki Giovanni—Read By Nikki Giovanni (album), Folkways, 1976.

The Reason I Like Chocolate (And Other Children's Poems) (album), Folkways, 1976.

Cotton Candy on a Rainy Day (album), Folkways, 1978.

(Author of introduction) *Adele Sebastian: Intro to Fine* (poems), Woman in the Moon, 1985.

Sacred Cows . . . and Other Edibles (essays), Morrow (New York, NY), 1988.

(Editor, with C. Dennison) *Appalachian Elders: A Warm Hearth Sampler,* Pocahontas Press (Blacksburg, VA), 1991.

(Author of foreword) *The Abandoned Baobob: The Autobiography of a Woman,* Chicago Review Press (Chicago, IL), 1991.

Nikki Giovanni and the New York Community Choir (album), Collectibles, 1993.

Racism 101 (essays), Morrow (New York, NY), 1994.

(Editor) *Grand Mothers: Poems, Reminiscences, and Short Stories about the Keepers of Our Traditions,* Holt (New York, NY), 1994.

(Editor) *Shimmy Shimmy Shimmy Like My Sister Kate: Looking at the Harlem Renaissance through Poems,* Holt (New York, NY), 1995.

In Philadelphia (album), Collectibles, 1997.

Stealing Home: For Jack Robinson (album), Sony, 1997.

(Editor) *Grand Fathers: Reminiscences, Poems, Recipes, and Photos of the Keepers of Our Traditions,* Holt (New York, NY), 1999.

Our Souls Have Grown Deep Like the Rivers (compilation), Rhino, 2000.

(Author of foreword) Margaret Ann Reid, *Black Protest Poetry: Polemics from the Harlem Renaissance and the Sixties,* Peter Lang (New York, NY), 2001.

The Nikki Giovanni Poetry Collection (CD), HarperAudio, 2002.

Rosa (children's book), illustrated by Bryan Collier, Henry Holt (New York, NY), 2005.

Contributor to *Voices of Diversity: The Power of Book Publishing,* a videotape produced by the Diversity Committee of the Association of American Publishers and Kaufman Films, 2002. Contributor to numerous anthologies. Contributor of columns to newspapers. Contributor to periodicals, including *Black Creation, Black World, Ebony, Essence, Freedom Ways, Journal of Black Poetry, Negro Digest,* and *Umbra.* Editorial consultant, Encore American and Worldwide News.

A selection of Giovanni's public papers is housed at Mugar Memorial Library, Boston University.

ADAPTATIONS: Spirit to Spirit: The Poetry of Nikki Giovanni (television film), 1986, produced by Corporation for Public Broadcasting and Ohio Council on the Arts.

SIDELIGHTS: One of the best-known African-American poets to reach prominence during the late 1960s and early 1970s, Nikki Giovanni has continued to create poems that encompass a life fully experienced. Her unique and insightful verses testify to her own evolving awareness and experiences as a woman of color: from child to young woman, from naive college freshman to seasoned civil rights activist, and from daughter to mother. Frequently anthologized, Giovanni's poetry expresses strong racial pride and respect for family. Her informal style makes her work accessible to both adults and children. In addition to collections such as *Re: Creation, Spin a Soft Black Song,* and *Those Who Ride the Night Winds,* Giovanni has published several works of nonfiction, including *Racism 101* and the anthology *Grand Mothers: Poems, Reminiscences, and Short Stories about the Keepers of Our Traditions.* A frequent lecturer and reader, Giovanni has also taught at Rutgers University, Ohio State University, and Virginia Tech.

Giovanni was born in Knoxville, Tennessee, in 1943, the younger of two daughters in a close-knit family, and had a reputation for being strong-willed even as a child. She gained an intense appreciation for her African-American heritage from her outspoken grandmother, Louvenia Terrell Watson, Giovanni. "I come from a long line of storytellers," she once explained in an interview, describing how her family influenced her poetry through oral traditions. "My grandfather was a Latin scholar and he loved the myths, and my mother is a big romanticist, so we heard a lot of stories growing up." This early exposure to the power of spoken language would influence Giovanni's career as a poet, particularly her tendency to sprinkle her verses with colloquialisms, including curse words. "I appreciated the quality and the rhythm of the telling of the stories," she once commented, "and I know when I started to write that I wanted to retain that—I didn't want to become the kind of writer that was stilted or that used language in ways that could not be spoken. I use a very natural rhythm; I want my writing to sound like I talk."

When Giovanni was a young child, she moved with her parents from Knoxville to a predominantly black suburb of Cincinnati, Ohio. She remained close to her grandmother, however, spending both her sophomore and junior years of high school at the family home in Knoxville. Encouraged by several schoolteachers, Giovanni enrolled early at Fisk University, a prestigious, all-black college in Nashville, Tennessee. Unaccustomed to Fisk's traditions, the outspoken young woman came into conflict with the school's dean of women and was asked to leave. She returned to Fisk in 1964, however, determined to be an ideal student. She accomplished her goal, becoming a leader in political and literary activities on campus during what would prove to be an important era in black history.

Giovanni had experienced racism firsthand during her childhood in the South. Random violence that erupted in and near Knoxville "was frightening," she later recalled in an autobiographical essay for CA. "You always felt someone was trying to kill you." Yet when Giovanni re-entered the freshman class at Fisk she had not yet found her later radical stance. She was decidedly conservative in political outlook: during high school she had been a supporter of Republican presidential candidate Barry Goldwater, as well as an avid reader of books by Ayn Rand, famous for her philosophy of "objectivism" (based on self-assertion, individualism, and competition). The poet credits a Fisk roommate named Bertha with successfully persuading her to embrace revolutionary ideals. In the wake of the civil rights movement and demonstrations against U.S. involvement in the Vietnam conflict, demands for social and political change were sweeping college campuses around the country. "Bertha kept asking, 'how could Black people be conservative?', " Giovanni wrote in *Gemini: An Extended Autobiographical Statement on My First Twenty-five Years.* "'What have they got to conserve?' And after a while (realizing that I had absolutely nothing, period) I came around."

While Giovanni was at Fisk, a black renaissance was emerging as writers and other artists of color were finding new ways of expressing their distinct culture to an increasingly interested public. As Chauncey Mabe put it in a November, 2002, *Knight Ridder* article, "The Black

Arts Movement [was] a loosely organized aesthetic and political movement that rejected European concepts of art for its own sake, insisting instead that art must benefit and uplift blacks." In addition to serving as editor of the campus literary magazine, *Elan,* and participating in the Fisk Writers Workshop, Giovanni worked to restore the Fisk chapter of the Student Non-Violent Coordinating Committee (SNCC). At that time, the organization was pressing the concept of "black power" to bring about social and economic reform. Giovanni's political activism ultimately led to her planning and directing the first Black Arts Festival in Cincinnati, held in 1967.

Later that year, Giovanni graduated magna cum laude with a degree in history. She decided to continue her studies at the University of Pennsylvania School of Social Work under a grant from the Ford Foundation, and then took classes at Columbia University's School of Fine Arts. This period was darkened, however, when Giovanni's beloved grandmother died. The loss "stirred in her a sense of guilt and shame both for the way in which society had dealt with this strong, sensitive woman, to whom she had been so close and who had deeply influenced her life, as well as for the way she herself had left her alone to die," according to Mozella G. Mitchell in the *Dictionary of Literary Biography.*

Giovanni's first published volumes of poetry grew out of her response to the assassinations of such figures as Martin Luther King, Jr., Malcolm X, Medgar Evers, and Robert Kennedy, and the pressing need she saw to raise awareness of the plight and the rights of black people. *Black Feeling, Black Talk* (which she borrowed money to publish) and *Black Judgement* (with a grant from Harlem Council of the Arts) display a strong, militant African-American perspective as Giovanni explores her growing political and spiritual awareness. "Poem (No Name No. 2)," from the first volume shows the simple forcefulness of her voice: "Bitter Black Bitterness / Black Bitter Bitterness / Bitterness Black Brothers / Bitter Black Get / Blacker Get Bitter / Get Black Bitterness / NOW." "These were the years," as Calvin Reid in a 1999 *Publishers Weekly* article observed, "she published such poems as 'Great Pax Whitie' (1968), with its intermingling of classical history, irony and antiracist outrage, and 'Woman Poem,' which considered the social and sexual limits imposed on black women."

These early books, which were followed by *Re: Creation,* quickly established Giovanni as a prominent new African-American voice. *Black Feeling, Black Talk,* "-sold more than ten thousand copies in its first year alone, making the author an increasingly visible and popular figure on the reading and speaking circuit. Because of Giovanni's overt activism, her fame as a personality almost preceded her critical acclaim as a poet. She gave the first public reading of her work at Birdland, a trendy New York City jazz club, to a standing-room-only audience." Mitchell described the poems Giovanni produced between 1968 and 1970 as "a kind of ritualistic exorcism of former nonblack ways of thinking and an immersion in blackness. Not only are they directed at other black people whom [Giovanni] wanted to awaken to the beauty of blackness, but also at herself as a means of saturating her own consciousness." *Dictionary of Literary Biography*contributor Alex Batman heard in Giovanni's verse the echoes of blues music. "Indeed the rhythms of her verse correspond so directly to the syncopations of black music that her poems begin to show a potential for becoming songs without accompaniment," Batman noted.

Critical reaction to Giovanni's early work focused on her more revolutionary poetry. Some reviewers found her political and social positions to be unsophisticated, while others were threatened by her rebelliousness. "Nikki writes about the familiar: what she knows, sees, experiences," Don L. Lee observed in *Dynamite Voices I: Black Poets of the 1960s.*"It is clear why she conveys such urgency in expressing the need for Black awareness, unity, solidarity . . . . What is perhaps more important is that when the Black poet chooses to serve as political seer, he must display a keen sophistication. Sometimes Nikki oversimplifies and therefore sounds rather naive politically." A contributor to the Web site *Voices from the Gaps: Women Writers of Color* added, however, "In *A Poetic Equation: Conversations between Nikki Giovanni and Margaret Walker,* she again raises the issue of revolution. When Walker says to Giovanni, 'I don't believe individual defiant acts like these will make for the revolution you want,' Giovanni replies, 'No, don't ever misunderstand me and my use of the term "revolution." I could never believe that having an organization was going to cause a revolution'. Throughout *A Poetic Equation,* the two talk about issues from how to raise a child to the Vietnam War to how to save the African-American race that white America is trying to destroy."

Giovanni's first three volumes of poetry were enormously successful, answering as they did a need for inspiration, anger, and solidarity in those who read them. She was among those who publicly expressed the feelings of people who had felt voiceless, vaulting beyond the usual relatively low public demand for modern poetry. *Black Judgement* alone sold six thousand copies in three months, almost six times the sales level expected of a book of its type. As she traveled to speaking engagements at colleges around the country, Giovanni was often hailed as one of the leading black poets of the new black renaissance. The prose poem "Nikki-Rosa," Giovanni's reminiscence of her childhood in a close-knit African-American home, was first published in *Black Judgement.* In becoming her most beloved and most anthologized work, "Nikki-Rosa" also expanded her appeal to an audience well beyond followers of her more activist poetry. During this time, she also made television appearances, out of which the published conversation with Margaret Walker and one with James Baldwin emerged.

In 1969, Giovanni took a teaching position at Rutgers University. That year she also gave birth to her son, Thomas. Her decision to have a child out of wedlock was understandable to anyone who knew her. Even as a young girl she had determined that the institution of marriage was not hospitable to women and would never play a role in her life. "I had a baby at twenty-five because I *wanted* to have a baby and I could *afford* to have a baby," she told an *Ebony* interviewer. "I did not get married because I didn't *want* to get married and I could *afford* not to get married."

Following her success as a poet of the black revolution, Giovanni's work exhibited a shift in focus after the birth of her son. Her priorities had shifted to encompass providing her child with the security of a stable home life. As she remarked to an interviewer for *Harper's Bazaar,* "To protect Tommy there is no question I would give my life. I just cannot imagine living without him. But I can live without the revolution." During this period Giovanni produced a collection of autobiographical essays, two books of poetry for children, and two poetry collections for adults. She also made several recordings of her poetry set against a gospel or jazz backdrop. Martha Cook, in an article in *Southern Women Writers,* explained, "'Truth Is on Its Way' includes a number of poems from Giovanni's Broadside volumes, with music by the New York Community Choir under the direction of Benny Diggs. According to *Harper's Bazaar,* Giovanni introduced the album at a free concert in a church in Harlem. Following her performance, 'the audience shouted its appreciation'." Reviewing these works, Mitchell noticed "evidence of a more developed individualism and greater introspection, and a sharpening of her creative and moral powers, as well as of her social and political focus and understanding."

In addition to writing her own poetry, Giovanni used her boundless energy to offer exposure for other African-American women writers through NikTom,

Ltd., a publishing cooperative she founded in 1970. Gwendolyn Brooks, Margaret Walker, Carolyn Rodgers, and Mari Evans were among those who benefited from Giovanni's work in the cooperative. Travels to other parts of the world, including the Caribbean, also filled much of the poet's time and contributed to the evolution of her work. As she broadened her perspective, Giovanni began to review her own life. Her introspection led to *Gemini: An Extended Autobiographical Statement on My First Twenty-five Years of Being a Black Poet,* which earned a nomination for the National Book Award.

Gemini is a combination of prose, poetry, and other "bits and pieces." In the words of a critic writing in *Kirkus Reviews,* it is a work in which "the contradictions are brought together by sheer force of personality." From sun-soaked childhood memories of a supportive family to an adult acceptance of revolutionary ideology and solo motherhood, the work reflected Giovanni's internal conflict and self-questioning. "I think all autobiography is fiction," Giovanni once observed in an interview, expressing amazement that readers feel they will learn something personal about an author by reading a creative work. "The least factual of anything is autobiography, because half the stuff is forgotten," she added. "Even if you [write] about something terribly painful, you have removed yourself from it. . . . What you have not come to terms with you do not write." While she subtitled *Gemini* an autobiography, Giovanni denied that it offered a key to her inner self. But the essays contained in the volume—particularly one about her grandmother—were personal in subject matter and "as true as I could make it," she commented. But, as Giovanni noted in an interview several decades later, "I also recognize that there are [parts of] the book in which I'm simply trying to deal with ideas. I didn't want it to be considered *the definitive.* It's far from that. It's very selective and how I looked at myself when I was twenty-five."

In addition to writing for adults in *Gemini* and other works during the early 1970s, Giovanni began to compose verse for children. Among her published volumes for young readers are *Spin a Soft Black Song, Ego-Tripping and Other Poems for Young People,* and *Vacation Time.* Written for children of all ages, Giovanni's poems are unrhymed incantations of childhood images and feelings. *Spin a Soft Black Song,* which she dedicated to her son, Tommy, covers a wealth of childhood interests, such as basketball games, close friends, moms, and the coming of spring. "Poem for Rodney" finds a young man contemplating what he wants to be when he grows up. "If" reflects a young man's daydreams about

what it might have been like to participate in a historic event. In a *New York Times Book Review* article on *Spin a Soft Black Song,* Nancy Klein noted, "Nikki Giovanni's poems for children, like her adult works, exhibit a combination of casual energy and sudden wit. No cheek-pinching auntie, she explores the contours of childhood with honest affection, sidestepping both nostalgia and condescension."

Ego-Tripping and Other Poems for Young People contains several poems previously published in *Black Feeling, Black Talk.* Focusing on African-American history, the collection explores issues and concerns specific to black youngsters. In "Poem for Black Boys," for example, Giovanni wonders why young boys of color do not play runaway slave or Mau-Mau, identifying with the brave heroes of their own race rather than the white cowboys of the Wild West. "Revolutionary Dreams" and "Revolutionary Music" speak to the racial strife of the 1960s and 1970s and look toward an end to racial tension. Commenting on *Ego-Tripping,* a *Kirkus Reviews* contributor claimed: "When [Giovanni] grabs hold . . . it's a rare kid, certainly a rare black kid, who could resist being picked right up."

Vacation Time contrasts with Giovanni's two earlier poetry collections for children by being "a much more relaxed and joyous collection which portrays the world of children as full of wonder and delight," according to Kay E. Vandergrift in *Twentieth-Century Children's Writers.* In *Vacation Time* Giovanni uses more traditional rhyme patterns than in *Spin a Soft Black Song.* Reviewing the work for the *Bulletin of the Center for Children's Books,* Zena Sutherland argued that the rhythms often seem forced and that Giovanni uses "an occasional contrivance to achieve scansion." But other critics praised the poet's themes. "In her singing lines, Giovanni shows she hadn't forgotten childhood adventures in . . . exploring the world with a small person's sense of discovery," wrote a *Publishers Weekly* reviewer. Mitchell, too, claimed: "One may be dazzled by the smooth way [Giovanni] drops all political and personal concerns [in *Vacation Time*] and completely enters the world of the child and brings to it all the fanciful beauty, wonder, and lollipopping."

Giovanni's later works for children, include *Knoxville, Tennessee* and *The Sun Is So Quiet.* The first work, a free-verse poem originally published in *Black Feeling, Black Talk, Black Judgement,* celebrates the pleasures of summer. Many of the warm images presented in the picture book came directly from the author's childhood memories. Ellen Fader, writing in *Horn Book,* called

The Sun Is So Quiet "a celebration of African-American family life for all families." Published in 1996, *The Sun Is So Quiet* is a collection of thirteen poems, ranging in topics from snowflakes to bedtime to missing teeth. "The poems," wrote a *Publishers Weekly* reviewer, "hover like butterflies, darting in to make their point and then fluttering off."

Giovanni says she has found writing for children particularly fulfilling because she is a mother who reads to her son. "Mostly I'm aware, as the mother of a reader, that I read to him," she once observed in an interview. "I think all of us know that your first line to the child is going to be his parent, so you want to write something that the parent likes and can share." According to Mitchell, the children's poems have "essentially the same impulse" as Giovanni's adult poetry—namely, "the creation of racial pride and the communication of individual love. These are the goals of all of Giovanni's poetry, here directed toward a younger and more impressionable audience." Love is not excluded by outrage.

Throughout the 1970s and 1980s Giovanni's popularity as a speaker and lecturer increased along with her success as a poet and children's author. She received numerous awards for her work, including honors from the National Council of Negro Women and the National Association of Radio and Television Announcers. She was featured in articles for such magazines as *Ebony, Jet,* and *Harper's Bazaar.* She also continued to travel, making trips to Europe and Africa.

Giovanni's sophistication and maturity continue to grow in *My House.* Her viewpoint, still firmly seated in black revolutionary consciousness, expanded further, balancing a wide range of social concerns. Her rhymes became more pronounced, more lyrical, more gentle. The themes of family love, loneliness, and frustration, which Giovanni had raged over in her earlier works, find softer expression in *My House.* " *My House* is not just poems," commented Kalumu Ya Salaam in *Black World.* "*My House* is how it is, what it is to be a young, single, intelligent Black woman with a son and no man. It is what it is to be a woman who has failed and is now sentimental about some things, bitter about some things, and generally always frustrated, always feeling frustrated on one of various levels or another." In a review for *Contemporary Women Poets,* Jay S. Paul called the book "a poetic tour through . . . a place rich with family remembrance, distinctive personalities, and prevailing love." And in the foreword to *My House,* Ida Lewis observed that Giovanni "has reached a simple

philosophy more or less to the effect that a good family spirit is what produces healthy communities, which is what produces a strong (Black) nation."Noting the continued focus on self-discovery and the connectedness of self to community throughout *My House,* critic John W. Conner suggested in *English Journal* that Giovanni "sees her world as an extension of herself . . . sees problems in the world as an extension of her problems, and . . . sees herself existing amidst tensions, heartache, and marvelous expressions of love." *My House* contained the revelations of a woman coming to terms with her life. *The Women and the Men* continued this trend.

When Giovanni published *Cotton Candy on a Rainy Day,* critics viewed it as one of her most somber works, singing a note of grief. They noted the focus on emotional ups and downs, fear and insecurity, and the weight of everyday responsibilities. Batman also observed the poet's frustration at aims unmet. "What distinguishes *Cotton Candy on a Rainy Day* is its poignancy," the critic maintained. "One feels throughout that here is a child of the 1960s mourning the passing of a decade of conflict, of violence, but most of all, of hope."

During the year *Cotton Candy* was published, Giovanni's father suffered a stroke. She and her son immediately left their apartment in New York City and returned to the family home in Cincinnati to help her mother cope with her father's failing health. After her father's death, Giovanni and her son continued to stay in Cincinnati with her mother. Giovanni thus ensured the same secure, supportive, multigenerational environment for Tommy that she had enjoyed as a child.

The poems in *Vacation Time* turn again to reflect, perhaps, the poet's growing lightness of spirit and inner stability as she enjoys her family. Similarly, *Those Who Ride the Night Winds* reveals "a new and innovative form," according to Mitchell, who added that "the poetry reflects her heightened self-knowledge and imagination." *Those Who Ride the Night Winds* echoes the political activism of Giovanni's early verse as she dedicates various pieces to Phillis Wheatley, Martin Luther King, Jr., and Rosa Parks. In *Sacred Cows . . . and Other Edibles* she presents essays on a wide range of topics: African-American political leaders, national holidays, and termites all come under her insightful and humorous scrutiny. Such essays as "Reflections on My Profession," "Four Introductions," and "An Answer to Some Questions on How I Write" were described by *Washington Post Book World* critic Marita Golden as "quintessential Nikki Giovanni—sometimes funny, nervy and unnerving with flashes of wisdom."

As Giovanni moved through her middle years, her works continued to reflect her changing concerns and perspectives. *The Selected Poems of Nikki Giovanni, 1968-1995,* which spans the first three decades of her career, was heralded by *Booklist* critic Donna Seaman as a "rich synthesis [that] reveals the evolution of Giovanni's voice and charts the course of the social issues that are her muses, issues of gender and race." Twenty of the fifty-three works collected in *Love Poems* find the writer musing on subjects as diverse as friendship, sexual desire, motherhood, and loneliness, while the remainder of the volume includes relevant earlier works. "Funny yet thoughtful, Giovanni celebrates creative energy and the family spirit of African-American communities," Frank Allen wrote of *Love Poems* in a *Library Journal* review.

Giovanni continues to supplement her poetry with occasional volumes of nonfiction. In *Racism 101* she looks back over the past thirty years as one who influenced the civil rights movement and its aftermath. Characterized by a *Publishers Weekly* reviewer as "fluid, often perceptive musings that beg for more substance," this collection of essays touches on diverse topics. Giovanni gives advice to young African-American scholars who are just starting an academic career, and she reflects on her own experiences as a teacher. She also provides a few glimpses into her personal life—for instance, she admits to being a confirmed "Trekkie." The book is a rich source of impressions of other black intellectuals, including writer and activist W.E.B. DuBois, writers Henry Louis Gates, Jr. and Toni Morrison, Supreme Court Justice Clarence Thomas, and filmmaker Spike Lee. "Giovanni is a shrewd observer and an exhilarating essayist," maintained Seaman in *Booklist,* "modulating her tone from chummy to lethal, hilarious to sagacious as smoothly as a race-car driver shifts gears." She does not believe in padding black realities in cotton wool and rainbows, admiring Native American writer Sherman Alexie for his honesty about "warts and all" depictions of Indian life. In addition to publishing original writings, Giovanni has edited poetry collections like the highly praised *Shimmy Shimmy Shimmy Like My Sister Kate.* A compilation of works composed by African-American writers during the Harlem Renaissance of the early twentieth century, *Shimmy* helps students of black writing to gain an understanding of the past.

Giovanni told Mabe that the Black Arts movement wasn't about presenting black culture as "Hallmark" perfect, and she feels that "the hip-hop movement took that from us, as we took it from the Harlem Renaissance before us." She is an avid supporter of hip-hop, "calling it," as she said to Mabe, "the modern equivalent of what spirituals meant to earlier generations of blacks. She admires OutKast, Arrested Development, Queen Latifah, and above all, Tupac Shakur. "We're missing Tupac like my generation missed Malcolm X," she said. "It's been six years and people feel like he was just here. He brought truth and we're still trying to learn what he was trying to teach us." Rather than trying to imitate black culture, white rappers, Giovanni noted, could get at the heart of racialism in America. "It would be great to learn from whites why white supremacy is so prevalent. Most people have rejected it, but they still know something about it they aren't saying. I want them to jump into hip-hop and address it."

Two new volumes, *Blues: For All the Changes* and *Quilting the Black-Eyed Pea: Poems and Not Quite Poems* mark the crossover from the twentieth to the twenty-first century with poetry that is "socially conscious, outspoken, and roguishly funny,"according to Donna Seaman in *Booklist.* "Giovanni makes supple use of the irony inherent in the blues, writing tough, sly, and penetrating monologues that both hammer away at racism and praise the good things in life." *Blues,* published after a battle with lung cancer and her first volume of poetry in five years, "offers thoughts on her battle with illness, on nature, and on the everyday—all laced with doses of harsh reality, a mix of socio- political viewpoints, and personal memories of loss," wrote Denolynn Carroll of *American Visions* who quotes from "The Faith of a Mustard Seed (In the Power of a Poem)": "I like my generation for trying to hold these truths to be self-evident. I like us for using the weapons we had. I like us for holding on and even now we continue to share what we hope and know what we wish." In an interview with *Publishers Weekly* 's Calvin Reid, Giovanni "described *Blues* as 'my environmental piece,' and there are impressions of the land around her home in Virginia, but this collection also salutes the late blues singer Alberta Hunter; it reveals her love of sports as well as her love of Betty Shabazz; jazz riffs mingle with memories of going to the ballpark with her father to see the Cincinnati Reds." *Quilting* includes, as the title already tells, "anecdotes, musings, and praise songs," according to Tara Betts of *Black Issues Book Review.* There is a prose poem honoring Rosa Parks, reflecting the honor recently bestowed on Giovanni when she was recognized with the first Rosa Parks Woman of Courage Award in 2002. Mabe noted that "single motherhood, a bout with lung cancer, showers of literary awards and an academic career have enriched but not blunted her edge," in the volume, though, she adds wryly, "being radical today has sometimes meant being reduced to voting for Ralph Nader." But as Tara Betts pointed out, Giovanni continues to fight against racism with her words wherever it crops up, as "revealed in 'The Self-Evident Poem': 'We just can't keep bomb / -ing the same people over and over again because we don't want / to admit the craziness is home grown.'" In an interview at the time of *Quilt* 's publication, Samiya Bashir of *Black Issues Book Review* felt Giovanni has maintained a "broad fan base, perhaps because she has always put love at the forefront of her life and work," a love that sometimes sparks protective rage, which still comes out in her writing.

In 2003, Giovanni published *The Nikki Giovanni Poetry Collection,* an audio compilation. Spanning her poetry from 1968 to the present and ranging in content from "from racism and Rosa Parks and Emmett Till to love and motherhood to boxes of yummy chicken," according to Sandy Bauers of *Knight Ridder,* the collection brings the poet's voice to life. "On the page, much of Giovanni's writing seems rhetorical," claimed Rochelle Ratner in *Library Journal,* but "hearing her read, dogma is replaced by passion." Bauers praised the production: "The poems are worth the price all by themselves. Giovanni reads with gobs of energy and enthusiasm. Hers is the poetry of plainspeak. None of the metaphorical mumbo jumbo that baffles so many of us. Her hopeful view of the future: 'Maybe one day the whole community will no longer be vested in who sleeps with whom. Maybe one day the Jewish community will be at rest, the Christian community will be content, the Moslem community will be at peace, and all the rest of us will get great meals on holy days and learn new songs and sing in harmony.'"

In 2005 Giovanni published *Rosa,* a children's book version of Rosa Park's famous refusal to give up her seat on the bus and other pivotal events of the Civil Rights movement. Reviewing the book for *School Library Journal,* Margaret Bush called it "striking" and "a handsome and thought-provoking introduction to these watershed acts of civil disobedience" A *Publishers Weekly* reviewer similarly praised the book as a "fresh take on a remarkable historic event and on Mrs. Parks's extraordinary integrity and resolve."

"Most writers spend too much time alone; it is a lonely profession," Giovanni once explained. "I'm not the only poet to point that out. Unless we make ourselves get out and see people, we miss a lot." Teaching, lecturing, sustaining close family ties, and remaining active in her community have allowed the poet to balance the loneliness of writing with a myriad of life experiences. "[Teaching] enriches my life, I mean it keeps reminding

all of us that there are other concerns out there," Giovanni said. "It widens your world . . . . I have certain skills that I am able to impart and that I want to, and it keeps me involved in my community and in a community of writers who are not professional but who are interested. I think that's good."

"Writing is . . . what I do to justify the air I breathe," Giovanni wrote, explaining her choice of a vocation in *CA.* "I have been considered a writer who writes from rage and it confuses me. What else do writers write from? A poem has to say something. It has to make some sort of sense; be lyrical; to the point; and still able to be read by whatever reader is kind enough to pick up the book." Giovanni believes one of her most important qualities is to have experienced life and to have been able to translate those experiences into her work—"apply the lessons learned," as she termed it in *CA.* "Isn't that the purpose of people living and sharing? So that others will at least not make the same mistake, since we seldom are able to recreate the positive things in life." She continues to look back on her contributions to American poetry with pride. "I think that I have grown; I feel that my work has grown a lot," she once told an interviewer. "What I've always wanted to do is something different, and I think each book has made a change. I hope that the next book continues like that. Like all writers, I guess, I keep looking for the heart." She concluded, "human beings fascinate me. You just keep trying to dissect them poetically to see what's there." To Mabe, she added, "People say writers need experience. You don't need experience, you need empathy. It's so limiting to think that you have to go do something in order to write about it. It's important to raise our ability to empathize and listen. I don't need to be enslaved to write about it."

BIOGRAPHICAL AND CRITICAL SOURCES:

BOOKS

Contemporary Literary Criticism, Volume 64, Gale (Detroit, MI), 1991.

Contemporary Poets, St. James Press (Detroit, MI), 1996, pp. 390-391.

Dictionary of Literary Biography, Gale (Detroit, MI), Volume 5: *American Poets since World War II,* 1980, Volume 41: *Afro- American Poets since 1955,* 1985, pp. 135-151.

Evans, Mari, editor, *Black Women Writers, 1950-1980: A Critical Evaluation,* Doubleday (New York, NY), 1984.

Fowler, Virginia, *Nikki Giovanni,* Twayne (Boston, MA), 1992.

Fowler, Virginia, editor, *Conversations with Nikki Giovanni,* University Press of Mississippi (Jackson, MS), 1992.

Georgoudaki, Ekaterini, and Domna Pastourmatzi, editors, *Women: Creators of Culture.* Hellenic Association of American Studies (Thessaloníki, Greece), 1997.

Giovanni, Nikki, *Gemini: An Extended Autobiographical Statement on My First Twenty-five Years of Being a Black Poet,* Bobbs-Merrill (Indianapolis, IN), 1971.

Inge, Tonette Bond, editor, *Southern Women Writers: The New Generation,*University of Alabama Press (Tuscaloosa, AL), 1990.

Josephson, Judith P., *Nikki Giovanni: Poet of the People,* Enslow Publishers, 2003.

Lee, Don L., *Dynamite Voices I: Black Poets of the 1960s,* Broadside Press (Detroit, MI), 1971, pp. 68-73.

Lewis, Ida, introduction to *My House,* Morrow (New York, NY), 1972.

Mitchel, Felicia, editor, *Her Words: Diverse Voices in Contemporary Appalachian Women's Poetry,* University of Tennessee Press (Knoxville, TN), 2002.

Tate, Claudia, editor, *Black Women Writers at Work,* Crossroads Publishing, 1983.

Twentieth-Century Children's Writers, 4th edition, St. James Press (Detroit, MI), 1995, p. 388.

Twentieth-Century Young Adult Writers, St. James Press (Detroit, MI), 1994, pp. 245- 246.

Weixlmann, Joe, and Chester J. Fontenot, editors, *Studies in Black American Literature,* Volume II: *Belief vs. Theory in Black American Literary Criticism,* Penkevill Publishing, 1986.

PERIODICALS

American Visions, February-March, 1998, p. 30; October 1999, p. 34.

Black Issues Book Review, November-December 2002, pp. 1, 32; March-April 2003, p. 31.

Black World, July, 1974.

Booklist, December 1, 1993, p. 658; September 15, 1994, p. 122; December 15, 1995, p. 682; October 15, 1996, p. 426; January 1, 1997, p. 809; August 1998, p. 2029; March 15, 1999, p. 1276; June 1, 1999, p. 1807; February 15, 2001, p. 1102; December 15, 2002, p. 727; December 15, 2003, Donna Seaman, review of *The Collected Poems of Nikki Giovanni: 1968-1998,* p. 721.

Bulletin of the Center for Children's Books, October, 1980, p. 31; June, 1996, p. 334.

Capital Times (Madison, WI), February 7, 1997, p. 13A.

Christian Science Monitor, March 20, 1996, p. 13.

Cimarron Review, April 1988, p. 94.

Cincinnati Enquirer (Cincinnati, OH), June 3, 1999, p. B01.

Ebony, February, 1972, pp. 48-50.

English Journal, April, 1973, p. 650.

Essence, May, 1999, p. 122.

Griot, spring, 1995, p. 18.

Harper's Bazaar, July, 1972, p. 50.

Horn Book, September- October, 1994, p. 575.

Jet, April 4, 1994, p. 29.

Kirkus Reviews, September 15, 1971, p. 1051; January 1, 1974, p. 11; March 15, 1996, p. 447.

Knight Ridder/Tribune News Service, February 16, 1994, p. 0216K0139; July 3, 1996, p. 703K4426; January 24, 2001, p. K3551; November 20, 2002, p. K1262; January 7, 2003, p. K5130.

Library Journal, January, 1996, p. 103; February 1, 1997, p. 84; May 1 1999, p. 84; November 1, 2002, p. 114; November 15, 2002, p. 76; February 1, 2003, p. 136.

New York Times, August 1, 1996, p. C9; May 14, 2000, p. A40.

New York Times Book Review, November 28, 1971, p. 8.

Publishers Weekly, May 23, 1980, p. 77; December 13, 1993, p. 54; December 18, 1995, pp. 51-52; October 21, 1996, p. 83; June 28, 1999, p. 46; July 12, 1999, p. 96; December 19, 1999, p. 51; March 11, 2002, p. 14; August 29, 2005, review of *Rosa,* p. 56.

School Library Journal, April, 1994, p. 119; October, 1994, p. 152; May, 1996, p. 103; January 1997, p. 100; July 1999, p. 107; November 17, 2003, review of *The Collected Poems of Nikki Giovanni,* p. 59; September, 2005, Margaret Bush, review of *Rosa,* p. 192.

Virginian Pilot, March 2, 1997 p. J2.

Voice of Youth Advocates, December, 1994, p. 298; October, 1996, pp. 229- 230.

Washington Post Book Review, February 14, 1988, p. 3.

Washington Post Book World, February 13, 1994, p. 4.

ONLINE

African-American Literature Book Club, http://authors.aalbc.com/ (March 9, 2004), author profile.

BlackEngineer, http://www.blackengineer.com/ (January 14, 2003), discussion with Giovanni.

Nikki Giovanni Home Page, http://nikki-giovanni.com/ (March 9, 2004).

Paula Gordon Show, http://www.paulagordon.com/ (January 22, 2003), interview with Giovanni.

Poets, http://www.poets.org/ (March 9, 2004), "Nikki Giovanni."

Voices from the Gaps: Women Writers of Color, http://voices.cla.umn.edu/ (March 9, 2004).

Writers Write, http://www.writerswrite.com/ (March 2, 2006), interview with Nikki Giovanni.

OTHER

Spirit to Spirit: The Poetry of Nikki Giovanni, a PBS special, 1987.

* * *

GIOVANNI, Yolande Cornelia, Jr.
See GIOVANNI, Nikki

* * *

GLÜCK, Louise 1943-
(Louise Elisabeth Glück)

PERSONAL: Surname is pronounced "Glick"; born April 22, 1943, in New York, NY; daughter of Daniel (an executive) and Beatrice (Grosby) Glück; married Charles Hertz, Jr., 1967 (divorced); married John Dranow (a writer and vice president of the New England Culinary Institute), 1977 (divorced); children: Noah Benjamin. *Education:* Attended Sarah Lawrence College, 1962, and Columbia University, 1963-66, 1967-68.

ADDRESSES: Home—Cambridge, MA. *Office*—Williams College, English Department, Williamstown, MA 01267. *E-mail*—Louise.E.Gluck@williams.edu.

CAREER: Poet. Fine Arts Work Center, Provincetown, MA, visiting teacher, 1970; Goddard College, Plainfield, VT, artist-in-residence, 1971-72, member of faculty, 1973-74; poet-in-residence, University of North Carolina, Greensboro, NC, spring, 1973, and Writer's Community, 1979; visiting professor, University of Iowa, Iowa City, IA, 1976-77, Columbia University, New York, NY, 1979, and University of California—Davis, Davis, CA, 1983; Goddard College, member of faculty and member of board of M.F.A. Writing Program, 1976-80; University of Cincinnati, Cincinnati, OH, Ellison Professor of Poetry, spring, 1978; Warren Wilson College, Swannanoa, NC, member of faculty and member of board of M.F.A. Program for Writers, 1980-84; University of California—Berkeley, Berkeley, CA, Holloway Lecturer, 1982; Williams College, Williamstown, MA, Scott Professor of Poetry, 1983, senior lecturer in English, 1984-2004; Yale University, New Haven, CT, Rosenkranz Writer-in-Residence, 2004—. Regents Professor, University of California—Los Angeles, Los Angeles, CA, 1985-87; Phi Beta Kappa Poet, Harvard University, 1990; Fanny Hurst Professor, Brandeis University, 1996. Special consultant, Library of Congress, Washington, DC, 1999. Poetry panelist or poetry reader at conferences and foundations, including Mrs. Giles Whiting Foundation and PEN Southwest Conference; judge of numerous poetry contests, including Yale Series of Younger Poets, 2003-07.

MEMBER: American Academy of Arts and Letters, Academy of American Poets (chancellor, 1999), PEN (member of board, 1988—).

AWARDS, HONORS: Academy of American Poets Prize, Columbia University, 1966; Rockefeller Foundation fellowship, 1967; National Endowment for the Arts grants, 1969, 1979, fellowship 1988-89; Eunice Tietjens Memorial Prize, *Poetry* magazine, 1971; Guggenheim fellowship, 1975, 1987-88; Vermont Council for the Arts individual artist grant, 1978-79; Award in Literature, American Academy and Institute of Arts and Letters, 1981; National Book Critics Circle Award for poetry, *Boston Globe* Literary Press Award, and Melville Cane Award, Poetry Society of America, 1985, all for *The Triumph of Achilles*; Sara Teasdale Memorial Prize, Wellesley College, 1986; Bobbitt National Prize (with Mark Strand), 1990, for *Ararat*; Pulitzer Prize, and William Carlos Williams Award, Poetry Society of America, 1993, both for *The Wild Iris*; Martha Albrand Award for nonfiction, PEN, 1994, for *Proofs and Theories: Essays on Poetry*; Special Consultant in Poetry, Library of Congress, 1999-2000; M.I.T. Anniversary Medal, 2000; Bingham Poetry Prize, *Boston Book Review,* and best poetry book, *New Yorker* Awards, both 2000, both for *Vita Nova*; Böllingen Prize, Yale University, 2001; National Book Critics Circle Award nomination, 2002, for *The Seven Ages*; U.S. Poet Laureate Consultant in Poetry, Library of Congress, 2003-04; D.Litt. from Williams College, Skidmore College, and Middlebury College.

WRITINGS:

Firstborn, New American Library (New York, NY), 1968.

The House on Marshland, Ecco Press (New York, NY), 1975.

The Garden, Antaeus (New York, NY), 1976.

Descending Figure, Ecco Press (New York, NY), 1980.

The Triumph of Achilles, Ecco Press (New York, NY), 1985.

Ararat, Ecco Press (New York, NY), 1990.

The Wild Iris, Ecco Press (New York, NY), 1992.

(Editor, with David Lehman) *The Best American Poetry 1993,* Collier (New York, NY), 1993.

Proofs and Theories: Essays on Poetry, Ecco Press (New York, NY), 1994.

The First Four Books of Poems, Ecco Press (New York, NY), 1995.

Meadowlands, Ecco Press (New York, NY), 1996.

Vita Nova, Ecco Press (New York, NY), 1999.

The Poet and the Poem from the Library of Congress—Favorite Poets. Louise Glück (sound recording), includes interview by Grace Cabalieri, Library of Congress (Washington, DC), 1999.

The Seven Ages, Ecco Press (New York, NY), 2001.

October (chapbook), Sarabande Books (Louisville, KY), 2004.

Author of introduction to *The Clerk's Tale* by Spencer Reece, Mariner Books (Boston, MA), 2004. Work represented in numerous anthologies, including *The New Yorker Book of Poems,* Viking (New York, NY), 1970; *New Voices in American Poetry,* Winthrop Publishing (Cambridge, MA), 1973; and *The American Poetry Anthology,* Avon (New York, NY), 1975. Contributor to sound recordings from the Library of Congress (Washington, DC), including *Poetry and the American Eagle,* 2000, and *Poetry in America,* 2000. Contributor to various periodicals, including *Antaeus, New Yorker, New Republic, Poetry, Salmagundi,* and *American Poetry Review.*

SIDELIGHTS: Considered by many critics to be one of America's most talented contemporary poets, Louise Glück creates verse that has been described as technically precise, sensitive, insightful, and gripping. In her work, Glück freely shares her most intimate thoughts on such commonly shared human experiences as love, family, relationships, and death. "Glück demands a reader's attention and commands his respect," stated R.D. Spector in the *Saturday Review.* "Glück's poetry is intimate, familial, and what Edwin Muir has called the fable, the archetypal," added *Contemporary Women Poets* contributor James K. Robinson. Within her work can be discerned the influences of poets Stanley Kunitz, with whom Glück studied while attending Columbia University in the mid-1960s, and the early work of

Robert Lowell; shadows cast by the confessional poets Sylvia Plath and Anne Sexton also haunt her earliest poetry.

From her first book of poetry, *Firstborn,* through her more mature work, Glück has become internationally recognized as a skilled yet perceptive author who pulls the reader into her poetry and shares the poetic experience equally with her audience. Helen Hennessey Vendler commented in her *New Republic* review of Glück's second book, *The House on Marshland,* that "Glück's cryptic narratives invite our participation: we must, according to the case, fill out the story, substitute ourselves for the fictive personages, invent a scenario from which the speaker can utter her lines, decode the import, 'solve' the allegory. Or such is our first impulse. Later, I think . . . we read the poem, instead, as a truth complete within its own terms, reflecting some one of the innumerable configurations into which experience falls."

Looking over Glück's early body of work, Dave Smith appraised her ability in a review of *Descending Figure* in the *American Poetry Review:* "There are poets senior to Louise Glück who have done some better work and there are poets of her generation who have done more work. But who is writing consistently better with each book? Who is writing consistently so well at her age? Perhaps it is only my own hunger that wants her to write more, that hopes for the breakthrough poems I do not think she has yet given us. She has the chance as few ever do to become a major poet and no one can talk about contemporary American poetry without speaking of Louise Glück's accomplishment."

For admirers of Glück's work, the poetry in books such as *Firstborn, The House on Marshland, The Garden, Descending Figure, The Triumph of Achilles, Ararat,* and the Pulitzer Prize-winning *The Wild Iris* take readers on an inner journey by exploring their deepest, most intimate feelings. "Glück has a gift for getting the reader to imagine with her, drawing on the power of her audience to be amazed," observed Anna Wooten in the *American Poetry Review,* adding, "She engages a 'spectator' in a way that few other poets can do." Stephen Dobyns maintained in the *New York Times Book Review* that "no American poet writes better than Louise Glück, perhaps none can lead us so deeply into our own nature."

One reason reviewers cite for Glück's seemingly unfailing ability to capture her reader's attention is her expertise at creating poetry that many people can understand, relate to, and experience intensely and completely. Her poetic voice is unique and her language is deceptively straightforward. In a review of Glück's *The Triumph of Achilles*, Wendy Lesser noted in the *Washington Post Book World:* "'Direct' is the operative word here: Glück's language is staunchly straightforward, remarkably close to the diction of ordinary speech. Yet her careful selection for rhythm and repetition, and the specificity of even her idiomatically vague phrases, give her poems a weight that is far from colloquial." Lesser went on to remark that "the strength of that voice derives in large part from its self-centeredness—literally, for the words in Glück's poems seem to come directly from the center of herself."

Because Glück writes so effectively about disappointment, rejection, loss, and isolation, reviewers frequently refer to her poetry as "bleak" or "dark." For example, Deno Trakas observed in the *Dictionary of Literary Biography* that "Glück's poetry has few themes and few moods. Whether she is writing autobiographically or assuming a persona, at the center of every poem is an 'I' who is isolated from family, or bitter from rejected love, or disappointed with what life has to offer. Her world is bleak; however, it is depicted with a lyrical grace, and her poems are attractive if disturbing. . . . Glück's poetry, despite flaws, is remarkable for its consistently high quality." Addressing the subdued character of her verse, *Nation*'s Don Bogen felt that Glück's "basic concerns" were "betrayal, mortality, love and the sense of loss that accompanies it . . . She is at heart the poet of a fallen world. . . . Glück's work to define that mortal part shows dignity and sober compassion." Bogen elaborated further: "Fierce yet coolly intelligent, Glück's poem disturbs not because it is idiosyncratic but because it defines something we feel yet rarely acknowledge; it strips off a veil. Glück has never been content to stop at the surfaces of things. Among the well-mannered forms, nostalgia and blurred resolutions of today's verse, the relentless clarity of her work stands out."

Readers and reviewers have also marveled at Glück's custom of creating poetry with a dreamlike quality that at the same time deals with the realities of passionate and emotional subjects. Holly Prado declared in a *Los Angeles Times Book Review* critique of *The Triumph of Achilles* that Glück's poetry works "because she has an unmistakable voice that resonates and brings into our contemporary world the old notion that poetry and the visionary are intertwined." Prado continued to reflect: "The tone of her work is eerie, philosophical, questioning. Her poems aren't simply mystical ramblings. Far from it. They're sternly well-crafted pieces. But they

carry the voice of a poet who sees, within herself, beyond the ordinary and is able to offer powerful insights, insights not to be quickly interpreted."

"Glück's ear never fails her; she manages to be conversational and lyrical at the same time, a considerable achievement when so much contemporary poetry is lamentably prosaic," asserted Wooten in the *American Poetry Review.* "Her range is personal and mythical, and the particular genius of the volume rests in its fusion of both approaches, rescuing the poems from either narrow self-glorification or pedantic myopia." This mythical voice, echoing the emotional quandaries of the twentieth century, can be quickly identified in *Meadowlands,* through the voices of Odysseus and Penelope. Describing the collection as "a kind of high-low rhetorical experiment in marriage studies," *New York Times Book Review* critic Deborah Garrison added that, through the "suburban banter" between the ancient wanderer and his wife, *Meadowlands* "captures the way that a marriage itself has a tone, a set of shared vocal grooves inseparable from the particular personalities involved and the partial truces they've made along the way." Commenting on the link between Glück's work and the narrative of Homer, Leslie Ullman added in *Poetry* that the dynamic of *Meadowlands* is "played out through poems that speak through or about principle characters in *The Odyssey,* and it is echoed in poems that do not attempt to disguise their origins in Glück's own experience."

Vita Nova earned Glück the prestigious 50,000 dollar Böllingen Prize from Yale University. In an interview with Brian Phillips of the *Harvard Advocate,* Glück stated: "This book was written very, very rapidly. . . . Once it started, I thought, this is a roll, and if it means you're not going to sleep, okay, you're not going to sleep. I wrote poems in airplanes and hotel rooms and elevators, and as a houseguest in California, and it just didn't matter where I was, it didn't matter who was with me." Phillips observed: "Something . . . that struck me about *Vita Nova* as a title was the irony of its historical reference. Obviously, in the late middle ages in Italy the phrase 'vita nuova' was used by Dante and others to indicate a new commitment of a romantic ideal of love. But you [Glück] seem to sort of update that phrase to mean life after the disintegration of the romantic relationship."

Reviewing *Vita Nova* for *Publishers Weekly,* a critic remarked: "Glück's psychic wounds will impress new readers, but it is Glück's austere, demanding craft that makes much of this . . . collection equal the best of her previous work—bitter, stark, careful, guiltily inward. . . . It is astonishing in its self knowledge, and above all, memorable." Offering a similar interpretation from a far more critical perspective was William Logan of *New Criterion* who declared: "Reading Louise Glück's new poems is like eavesdropping on a psychiatrist and a particularly agony-ridden . . . shape shifting analysand. . . . The discomfort in *Vita Nova* is not lessened by the suspicion that the psychiatrist may also be the patient, that all roles may be one role to this quietly hand-wringing playactor. . . . It's hard to convey the oppressive weight of these doomed, sacrificial poems." Although the ostensible subject matter of the collection is the examination of the aftermath of a broken marriage, *Vita Nova* is a book suffused with symbols drawn from both personal dreams and classic mythological archetypes. "The poems in this . . . collection allude repeatedly to Greek and Roman myths of the underworld as well as the Inferno," observed Bill Christophersen of *Poetry,* while James Longenbach, writing in *Southwest Review,* noted: "Vita Nova is built around not one but two mythic backbones—the stories of both Dido and Aeneas and of Orpheus and Eurydice." Tom Clark of the *San Francisco Chronicle* observed that "Glück examines her dream material with unsparing honesty. . . . and inscribes it with a quiet, at times painful, candor, willing to suspend judgment and entertain stubborn unclarities to find the epiphanies she obsessively seeks." Clark characterized *Vita Nova* as "a brave and risky book, daring to explore those obscure places by the flickering light of dreams." Taking a different slant on the collection from that of some other reviewers, Longenbach found the central theme of *Vita Nova* to be the poet's desire for change, and Glück's ultimate resolution to involve an embracing of recurrence rather than transcendence. "Having recognized that real freedom exists within repetition rather than in the postulation of some timeless place beyond it," Longenbach concluded, "Glück now seems content to work within the terms of her art. . . . The result is a book suggesting that Glück's poetry has many more lives to live."

Echoing Longenbach's assertion in a review of Glück's next collection, *The Seven Ages,* for the *New York Times Book Review,* Melanie Rehak stated: "It's a book in which repetition functions as incantation, forming a hazy magic that's alternately frightening and beautiful." *The Seven Ages* contains forty-four poems whose subject matter ranges throughout the author's life, from her earliest memories to the contemplation of death. A writer for *Kirkus Reviews* remarked on how the author uses "common childhood images" as a way "to resurrect intense feelings that accompany awakening to the sensual promises of life, and she desperately explores

these resonant images, searching for a path that might reconcile her to the inevitability of death." While Rehak acclaimed "every poem in *The Seven Ages* [as] a weighty, incandescent marvel," a *Publishers Weekly* reviewer remarked: "Considering age and aging, summer and fall, 'stasis' and constant loss, Glück's new poems often forsake the light touch of her last few books for the grim wisdom she sought in the 1980s."

According to Longenbach: "The works of poet Louise Glück focus on the changeability of self and the definition of identity. She compares the actions of her poem's characters with their feelings, giving them credibility through colloquial diction. Glück uses extreme situations to augment character complexities and heighten the emotions involved in their search."

In 2003 Glück was named the twelfth Poet Laureate Consultant in Poetry by the Library of Congress. On making the appointment, James H. Billington stated, "Louise Glück will bring to the Library of Congress a strong, vivid, deep poetic voice, accomplished in a series of book-length poetic cycles. Her prize-winning poetry and her great interest in young poets will enliven the Poet Laureate's office during the next year." Glück, an intensely private individual, was quoted in *USA Today* as saying that her first undertaking as Poet Laureate will be "to get over being surprised." Then she hopes to promote young poets and poetry contests.

BIOGRAPHICAL AND CRITICAL SOURCES:

BOOKS

American Writers, Supplement 5, Charles Scribner's Sons (New York, NY), 2000.
Contemporary Literary Criticism, Thomson Gale (Detroit, MI), Volume 7, 1977, Volume 22, 1982, Volume 44, 1987.
Contemporary Poets, 7th edition, St. James Press (Detroit, MI), 2000.
Contemporary Women Poets, St. James Press (Detroit, MI), 1997.
Dictionary of Literary Biography, Volume 5: *American Poets since World War II,* Thomson Gale (Detroit, MI), 1980.
Dodd, Elizabeth Caroline, *The Veiled Mirror and the Woman Poet: H. D., Louise Bogan, Elizabeth Bishop, and Louise Glück,* University of Missouri Press (Columbia, MO), 1992.

Poetry Criticism, Volume 16, Thomson Gale (Detroit, MI), 1996.

Poetry for Students, Thomson Gale (Detroit, MI), Volume 5, 1999, Volume 15, 2002.

Trawick, Leonard M., editor, *World, Self, Poem: Essays on Contemporary Poetry from the "Jubilation of Poets,"* Kent State University Press (Kent, OH), 1990.

Upton, Lee, *The Muse of Abandonment: Origin, Identity, Mastery in Five American Poets,* Bucknell University Press (Lewisburg, PA), 1998.

Vendler, Helen, *Part of Nature, Part of Us: Modern American Poets,* Harvard University Press (Cambridge, MA), 1980.

Vendler, Helen, *The Music of What Happens: Poems, Poets, Critics,* Harvard University Press (Cambridge, MA), 1988.

PERIODICALS

America, April 25, 1998, Edward J. Ingebretsen, review of *Meadowlands,* pp. 27-28.

American Poetry Review, July-August, 1975, pp. 5-6; January-February, 1982, pp. 36-46; September-October, 1982, pp. 37-46; November-December, 1986, pp. 33-36; July-August, 1990, Marianne Boruch, review of *Ararat,* pp. 17-19; January-February, 1993, Carol Muske, review of *The Wild Iris,* pp. 52-54; January-February, 1997, Allen Hoey, "Between Truth and Meaning," pp. 37-46; July-August, 2003, Tony Hoagland, "Three Tenors," pp. 37-42.

Antioch Review, spring, 1993, Daniel McGuiness, review of *The Wild Iris,* pp. 311-312; winter, 1997, Daniel McGuiness, review of *Meadowlands,* pp. 118-119.

Belles Lettres, November-December, 1986, pp. 6, 14; spring, 1991, p. 38.

Booklist, February 1, 1999, Donna Seaman and Jack Helbig, review of *Vita Nova,* p. 959; March 15, 2001, Donna Seaman, review of *The Seven Ages,* p. 1346.

Chicago Review, winter, 1997, Maureen McLane, review of *Meadowlands,* pp. 120-122; summer-fall, 1999, Steven Monte, "Louise Gluck," p. 180.

Christianity and Literature, autumn, 2002, William V. Davis, "'Talked to by Silence,'" pp. 47-57.

Classical and Modern Literature, spring, 2002, Sheila Murnaghan and Deborah H. Roberts, "Penelope's Song," pp. 1-32.

Contemporary Literature, spring, 1990, Diane S. Bonds, "Entering Language in Louise Gluck's *The House on the Marshland,*" pp. 58-75; summer, 2001, Ann Keniston, "'The Fluidity of Damaged Form,'" pp. 294-324.

Georgia Review, winter, 1985, pp. 849-863; spring, 1993, Judith Kitchen, review of *The Wild Iris,* pp. 145-159; summer, 2002, Judith Kitchen, "Thinking about Love," pp. 594-608.

Hudson Review, spring, 1993, David Mason, review of *Ararat* and *The Wild Iris,* pp. 223-231; autumn, 2001, Bruce Bawer, "Borne Ceaselessly into the Past," pp. 513-520.

Kenyon Review, winter, 1993, David Baker, review of *The Wild Iris,* pp. 184-192; winter, 2001, Linda Gregerson, "The Sower against Gardens," p. 115, and Brian Henry, review of *Vita Nova,* p. 166; spring, 2003, Willard Spiegelman, "Repetition and Singularity," pp. 149-168.

Kirkus Reviews, April 1, 2001, review of *The Seven Ages,* p. 468.

Landfall, May, 2001, Emma Neale, "Touchpapers," pp. 143-142.

Library Journal, September 15, 1985, p. 84; April 1, 1990; July, 1990, p. 17; May 15, 1992, Fred Muratori, review of *The Wild Iris,* p. 96; September, 1994, Tim Gavin, review of *Proofs and Theories: Essays on Poetry,* p. 71; March 15, 1996, Frank Allen, review of *Meadowlands,* p. 74; March 1, 1999, Ellen Kaufman, review of *Vita Nova,* p. 88; April 15, 2001, Barbara Hoffert, review of *The Seven Ages,* p. 98.

Literary Imagination, fall, 2003, Isaac Cates, "Louise Glück: Interstices and Silences," pp. 462-77.

Literary Review, spring, 1996, Reamy Jansen, review of *Proofs and Theories,* pp. 441-443.

Los Angeles Times Book Review, February 23, 1986, p. 10.

Mid-American Review, Volume 14, number 2, 1994.

Naples Daily News (Naples, FL), October 20, 2003, Justin Pope, "Media-Shy Poet Laureate Won't Follow in Predecessors' Footsteps."

Nation, January 18, 1986, pp. 53-54; April 15, 1991, p. 490; April 29, 1996, p. 28.

New Criterion, June, 1999, William Logan, "Vanity Fair," p. 60; June, 2001, William Logan, "Folk Tales," p. 68.

New England Review, fall, 1991, Bruce Bnod, review of *Ararat,* pp. 216-223; fall, 1993, Henry Hart, review of *The Wild Iris,* pp. 192-206; fall, 2001, Ira Sadoff, "Louise Gluck and the Last Stage of Romanticism," pp. 81-92.

New Letters, spring, 1987, pp. 3-4.

New Republic, June 17, 1978, pp. 34-37; May 24, 1993, Helen Hennessey Vendler, review of *The Wild Iris,* pp. 35-38.

New Yorker, May 13, 1996, Vijay Seshadri, review of *Meadowlands,* pp. 93-94.

New York Review of Books, October 23, 1986, p. 47.

New York Times, August 29, 2003, Elizabeth Olson, "Chronicler of Private Moments Is Named Poet Laureate," p. A14; November 4, 2003, Andrew Johnston, "Poet Laureate: Louise Gluck and the Public Face of a Private Artist," p. A24.

New York Times Book Review, April 6, 1975, pp. 37-38; October 12, 1980, p. 14; December 22, 1985, pp. 22-23; September 2, 1990, p. 5; August 4, 1996; May 13, 2001, Melanie Rehak, "Her Art Imitates Her Life. You Got That?"

North American Review, July-August, 1994, Annie Finch, review of *The Wild Iris,* pp. 40-42.

Parnassus, spring-summer, 1981.

People Weekly, May 5, 1997, review of *Meadowlands,* p. 40.

PN Review, Volume 25, number 3, Steve Burt, "The Dark Garage with the Garbage," pp. 31-35.

Poetry, April, 1986, pp. 42-44; November, 1990, Steven Cramer, "Four True Voices of Feeling," pp. 96-114; May, 1993; March, 1997, p. 339; December, 2000, Bill Christophersen, review of *Vita Nova,* p. 217; December, 2001, David Wojahn, review of *The Seven Ages,* p. 165.

Prairie Schooner, summer, 2000, Richard Jackson, review of *Vita Nova,* p. 190.

Publishers Weekly, February 16, 1990, p. 63; May 11, 1992, p. 58; July 4, 1994, review of *Proofs and Theories,* p. 49; March 18, 1996, review of *Meadowlands,* p. 66; December 21, 1998, review of *Vita Nova,* p. 62; March 12, 2001, review of *The Seven Ages,* p. 84.

Salmagundi, winter, 1977; spring-summer, 1991, Calvin Bedient, review of *Ararat,* pp. 212-230; fall, 1999, Terence Diggory, "Louise Gluck's Lyric Journey," pp. 303-318.

San Francisco Chronicle, April 4, 1999, Tom Clark, "Poet Finds Dreams Leave Traces in the Waking World," p. 3.

Saturday Review, March 15, 1969, p. 33.

Sewanee Review, winter, 1976.

South Carolina Review, fall, 2000, John Perryman, "Washing Homer's Feat," pp. 176-184.

Southwest Review, spring, 1999, James Longenbach, "Nine Lives," p. 184.

Times Literary Supplement, May 16, 1997, Stephen Burt, review of *The Wild Iris,* p. 25; July 30, 1999, Oliver Reynolds, "You Will Suffer," p. 23; May 25, 2001, Josephine Balmer, review of *Vita Nova,* p. 26.

USA Today, August 29, 2003, "Pulitzer Prize-winner Glück Named Poet Laureate."

Village Voice, September 8, 2003, Joshua Clover, "Time on Her Side."

Virginia Quarterly Review, summer, 1998, Brian Henry, "The Odyssey Revisited," pp. 571-577.

Washington Post Book World, February 2, 1986, p. 11.

Women's Review of Books, May, 1993, Elisabeth Frost, review of *The Wild Iris,* pp. 24-25; November, 1996, Elisabeth Frost, review of *Meadowlands,* pp. 24-25.

Women's Studies, Volume 17, number 3, 1990.

World Literature Today, autumn, 1993, Rochelle Owens, review of *The Wild Iris,* p. 827; winter, 1997, Susan Smith Nash, review of *Meadowlands,* pp. 156-157.

Yale Review, October, 1992, Phoebe Pettingell, review of *The Wild Iris,* pp. 114-115; October, 1996, James Longenbach, review of *Meadowlands,* pp. 158-174.

ONLINE

Academy of American Poets Web Site, http://www.poets.org/ (April 20, 2004), "Louise Glück."

Harvard Advocate, http://www.hcs.harvard.edu/~advocate/ (summer, 1999), Brian Phillips, "A Conversation with Louise Glück."

Library of Congress Web Site, http://www.loc.gov/poetry/ (April 22, 2004), "About the New Poet Laureate, Louise Glück."

Louise Glück: Image and Emotion, http://www.artstomp.com/gluck/ (April 22, 2004).

Modern American Poetry Web Site, http://www.english.uiuc.edu/maps/ (April 20, 2004), "Louise Glück."

*   *   *

GLÜCK, Louise Elisabeth
See GLÜCK, Louise

*   *   *

GODWIN, Gail 1937-
(Gail Kathleen Godwin)

PERSONAL: Born June 18, 1937, in Birmingham, AL; daughter of Mose Winston and Kathleen (an educator and writer; maiden name, Krahenbuhl) Godwin; married Douglas Kennedy (a photographer), 1960 (divorced, 1961); married Ian Marshall (a psychiatrist), 1965 (divorced, 1966). *Education:* Attended Peace Junior College, 1955-57; University of North Carolina, B.A., 1959; University of Iowa, M.A., 1968, Ph.D., 1971.

ADDRESSES: Home—P.O. Box 946, Woodstock, NY 12498-0946. *Agent*—John Hawkins, Paul R. Reynolds, Inc., 71 West 23rd St., New York, NY 10010. *E-mail*—gail@gailgodwin.com.

CAREER: Miami Herald, Miami, FL, reporter, 1959-60; U.S. Embassy, London, England, travel consultant in U.S. Travel Service, 1962-65; *Saturday Evening Post,* editorial assistant, 1966; University of Iowa, Iowa City, instructor in English literature, 1967-71, instructor in Writer's Workshop, 1972-73; University of Illinois, Center for Advanced Studies, Urbana-Champaign, fellow, 1971-72; freelance writer. Special lecturer in Brazil for United States Information Service, State Department Cultural Program, spring, 1976; lecturer in English and creative writing at colleges and universities, including Vassar College, 1975, and Columbia University, 1978, 1981.

MEMBER: Authors Guild, Authors League of America, American Society of Composers, Authors, and Publishers (ASCAP).

AWARDS, HONORS: National Endowment for the Arts grant in creative writing, 1974-75; National Book Award nomination, 1974, for *The Odd Woman;* Guggenheim fellowship in creative writing, 1975-76; National Endowment for the Arts grant for librettists, 1977-78; American Book Awards nomination, 1980, for *Violet Clay,* and 1982, for *A Mother and Two Daughters;* Award in Literature, American Institute and Academy of Arts and Letters, 1981; Thomas Wolfe Memorial Award, Lipinsky Endowment of Western North Carolina Historical Association, 1988; Janet Kafka Award, University of Rochester, 1988. Honorary doctorates from University of North Carolina, 1987, University of the South—Sewanee, 1994, and State University of New York, 1996.

WRITINGS:

NOVELS

The Perfectionists, Harper (New York, NY), 1970.
Glass People, Knopf (New York, NY), 1972.
The Odd Woman, Knopf (New York, NY), 1974.
Violet Clay, Knopf (New York, NY), 1978.
A Mother and Two Daughters, Viking (New York, NY), 1982.
The Finishing School, Viking (New York, NY), 1985.
A Southern Family, Morrow (New York, NY), 1987.
Father Melancholy's Daughter, Morrow (New York, NY), 1991.
The Good Husband, Ballantine (New York, NY), 1994.
Evensong, Ballantine (New York, NY), 1999.

Evenings at Five, illustrated by Frances Halsband, Ballantine (New York, NY), 2003.
Queen of the Underworld, Random House (New York, NY), 2006.

OTHER

Dream Children (short stories), Knopf (New York, NY), 1976.
Mr. Bedford and the Muses (a novella and short stories), Viking (New York, NY), 1983.
(Editor, with Shannon Ravenel) *The Best American Short Stories, 1985,* Houghton Mifflin (New York, NY), 1985.
Dream Children: Stories, Ballantine (New York, NY), 1996.
Heart: A Personal Journey through Its Myths and Meanings (nonfiction), Morrow (New York, NY), 2001.
The Making of a Writer: Journals (nonfiction), edited by Rob Neufeld, Random House (New York, NY), 2006.

Author of introduction for *Pushcart Prize VIII: Best of the Small Presses, 1983-84,* edited by Bill Henderson, Pushcart Press, 1983; and *Woodstock Landscapes: Photographs,* by John Kleinhans, Golden Notebook Press (Woodstock, NY)/Precipice Publications (West Hurley, NY), 2000. Contributor to books, including *The Writer on Her Work* (essays), edited by Janet Sternburg, Norton (New York, NY), 1980; and *Real Life* (short stories), Doubleday, 1981. Also contributor of essays and short stories to periodicals, including *Atlantic, Antaeus, Ms., Harper's, Writer, McCall's, Cosmopolitan, North American Review, Paris Review,* and *Esquire.* Reviewer for *North American Review, New York Times Book Review, Chicago Tribune Book World,* and *New Republic.* Member of editorial board, *Writer.*

Librettist of musical works by Robert Starer, *The Last Lover,* produced in Katonah, NY, 1975; *Journals of a Songmaker,* produced in Pittsburgh, PA, with Pittsburgh Symphony Orchestra, 1976; *Apollonia,* produced in Minneapolis, MN, 1979; *Anna Margarita's Will,* recorded by C.R.I., 1980; and *Remembering Felix,* 1987, recorded by Spectrum, 1989.

ADAPTATIONS: Dream Children was made into a sound recording with narration by Godwin, for American Audio Prose Library (Columbia, MO), c. 1986;

Evenings at Five was made into an audio recording, narrated by Godwin for Random House Audio (New York, NY), 2003.

WORK IN PROGRESS: The Making of a Writer: The Journals of Gail Godwin, One (memoir), edited by Rob Neufeld.

SIDELIGHTS: "More than any other contemporary writer, Gail Godwin reminds me of nineteenth century pleasures, civilized, passionate about ideas, ironic about passions," reflected Carol Sternhell in a *Village Voice* review of *The Finishing School.* "Her characters—sensible, intelligent women all—have houses, histories, ghosts; they comfortably inhabit worlds both real and literary, equally at home in North Carolina, Greenwich Village and the England of *Middlemarch.*" Yet Godwin, a best-selling novelist who has been nominated for the American Book Award, creates protagonists who are modern women, often creative and frequently Southern. And like many other writers of her era, she tends to focus "sharply on the relationships of men and women who find their roles no longer clearly delineated by tradition and their freedom yet strange and not entirely comfortable," as Carl Solana Weeks wrote in *Dictionary of Literary Biography.* "Godwin's great topic," noted Lee Smith, reviewing *Father Melancholy's Daughter* in the *Los Angeles Times Book Review,* "is woman's search for identity: A death in the family frequently precipitates this search. The tension between art and real life (many of her women are artists or would-be artists) is another thematic constant in her work. Her literate, smart women characters possess the free will to make choices, to take responsibility for their lives."

Literature has figured in Godwin's life from an early age. She grew up in Asheville, North Carolina, in the shadow of another writer, Thomas Wolfe. During World War II her mother was a reporter, and Godwin recalled in an essay in *The Writer on Her Work* that "whenever Mrs. Wolfe called up the paper to announce, 'I have just remembered something else about Tom,'" her mother "was sent off immediately to the dead novelist's home on Spruce Street." Godwin's parents were divorced, and while Godwin was growing up, her mother taught writing and wrote love stories on the weekend to support her daughter, while Godwin's grandmother ran the house. And although her mother never sold any of her novels, Godwin wrote in the essay, "already, at five, I had allied myself with the typewriter rather than the stove. The person at the stove usually had the thankless task of fueling. Whereas, if you were faithful to your vision at the typewriter, by lunchtime you could make two more characters happy—even if you weren't so happy yourself. What is more, if you retyped your story neatly in the afternoon and sent it off in a manila envelope to New York, you'd get a check back for $100 within two or three weeks (300 words to the page, 16-17 pages, 2 cents a word: in 1942, $100 went a long way)." Godwin once told *CA* that her mother was her first teacher, saying, "She was doing things with her mind, using her imagination and making something out of nothing, really. I remember when she would read to me at night. My favorite book that she read was a little empty address book—it had a picture of some faraway place on the front—and she would read stories out of this blank book. It was just fascinating."

Not that her grandmother was dispensable. Godwin indicated in *The Writer on Her Work* that "in our manless little family, she also played the mother and could be counted on to cook, sew on buttons, polish the piano, and give encouragement to creative endeavors. She was my mother's first reader, while the stories were still in their morning draft; 'It moves a little slowly here,' she'd say, or 'I didn't understand why the girl did this.' And the tempo would be stepped up, the heroine's ambiguous action sharpened in the afternoon draft; for if my grandmother didn't follow tempo and motive, how would all those other women who would buy the magazines?"

Godwin did not meet her father until he showed up many years later at her high school graduation when, as she recalled in her essay, he introduced himself and she flung herself, "weeping," into his arms. He invited her to come and live with him, which she did, briefly, before he shot and killed himself like the lovable ne'er-do-well Uncle Ambrose in *Violet Clay.*

After graduating from the University of North Carolina, Godwin was hired as a reporter for the *Miami Herald* and was reluctantly fired a year later by a bureau chief who felt he had failed to make a good reporter out of her. She married her first husband, newspaper photographer Douglas Kennedy, around that time. After her divorce, she completed her first novel, the unpublished "Gull Key," the story of "a young wife left alone all day on a Florida island while her husband slogs away at his job on the mainland," according to Godwin in *The Writer on Her Work.* (She worked on the book during her slow hours at the U.S. Travel Service in London.) Having submitted the manuscript to several English publishers without good results, she related that she even sent a copy to a fly-by-night agency that advertised in a magazine, "WANTED: UNPUBLISHED NOVELS IN WHICH WOMEN'S PROBLEMS AND LOVE INTERESTS ARE PREDOMINANT. ATTRACTIVE TERMS." She was never able to track down the agency or anyone associated with it.

Not satisfied with her work at the time, Godwin found it helpful to focus on characters and themes outside of herself. She got the idea for one of her most highly regarded short stories, "An Intermediate Stop" (now included in her collection *Dream Children*), in a writing class at the London City Literary Institute after the teacher instructed the students to write a 450-word story beginning with the sentence, "'*Run away*,' he muttered to himself, sitting up and biting his nails." Godwin wrote in *The Writer on Her Work* that "when that must be your first sentence, it sort of excludes a story about a woman in her late twenties, adrift among the options of wifehood, career, vocation, a story that I had begun too many times already—both in fiction and reality—and could not resolve. My teacher wisely understood Gide's maxim for himself as writer: 'The best means of learning to know oneself is seeking to understand others.'"

Godwin described "An Intermediate Stop" as a story "about an English vicar who has seen God, who writes a small book about his experience, and becomes famous. He gets caught up in the international lecture-tour circuit. My story shows him winding up his exhausting American tour at a small Episcopal college for women in the South. He is at his lowest point, having parroted back his own written words until he has lost touch with their meaning." *New York Times* critic Anatole Broyard indicated that, here, "another kind of epiphany—in the form of a [young woman]—restores his faith. The brilliance with which this girl is evoked reminds us that love and religion both partake of the numinous." A draft of the story also got the author accepted into the University of Iowa Writer's Workshop.

Godwin's novel *The Perfectionists*, a draft of which was her Ph.D. thesis at Iowa, was published in 1970. It relates the story of the disintegrating "perfect" marriage of a psychiatrist and his wife while they are vacationing in Majorca with the man's son. Robert Scholes wrote in the *Saturday Review* that "the eerie tension that marks this complex relationship is the great achievement of the novel. It is an extraordinary accomplishment, which is bound to attract and hold many readers." Scholes described the book as "too good, too clever, and too finished a product to be patronized as a 'first novel.'" Joyce Carol Oates, writing in *New York Times Book Review*, called it "a most intelligent and engrossing novel" and "the paranoid tragedy of our contemporary worship of self-consciousness, of constant analysis."

In Godwin's *Glass People*, Francesca Bolt, a pampered and adored wife in a flawless but sterile marital environment, leaves her husband in a brief bid for freedom. This book, too, was praised as "a formally executed, precise, and altogether professional short novel" by Oates in the *Washington Post Book World*. Weeks, however, felt that in *Glass People*, Godwin is exploring "a theme introduced in *The Perfectionists*, that of a resolution of woman's dilemma through complete self-abnegation; but the author, already suspicious of this alternative in her first novel, presents it here as neither fully convincing nor ironic." As a critic asked in the *New York Times Book Review*, "Are we really to root for blank-minded Francesca to break free, when her author has promised us throughout that she's totally incapable of doing so?" Genevieve Stuttaford, though, argued in the *Saturday Review* that "the characters in *Glass People* are meticulously drawn and effectively realized, the facets of their personalities subtly, yet precisely, laid bare. The author is coolly neutral, and she makes no judgments. This is the way it is, Godwin is saying, and you must decide who the villains are."

"Marking a major advance in Godwin's development as a novelist," wrote Weeks in the *Dictionary of Literary Biography*, "her third book, *The Odd Woman*, is twice as long as either of her previous novels, not from extension of plot but from a wealth of incidents told in flashback and in fantasy and a more thorough realization of present action." The odd woman of the book, "odd" in this case meaning not paired with another person, is Jane Clifford, a thirty-two-year-old teacher of Romantic and Victorian literature at a Midwestern college, who is engaged in a sporadic love affair with an art historian who teaches at another school. For Jane, Susan E. Lorsch pointed out in *Critique*, "the worlds of fiction and the 'real' world are one." Not only does Jane experience "literary worlds as real," continued Lorsch, "she treats the actual world as if it were an aesthetic creation." Lorsch further noted that "the entire book moves toward the climax and the completion of Jane's perception that the worlds of life and art are far from identical."

The Odd Woman's major theme, Anne Z. Mickelson suggested in *Reaching Out: Sensitivity and Order in Recent American Fiction by Women*, is "how to achieve freedom while in union with another person, and impose one's own order on life so as to find self-fulfillment." Because literature is explored in the novel as one means of giving shape to life, the book is generally regarded as cerebral and allusive. In the *Times Literary Supplement*, critic Victoria Glendinning said the book is "too closely or specifically tied to its culture" to be considered universal. *New York Times Book Review* writer Lore Dickstein, however, called the novel "a pleasure to read. Godwin's prose is elegant, full of nuance and feeling, and sparkling with ironic humor."

Violet Clay, Weeks commented, confirms Godwin's "mastery of the full, free narrative technique of *The Odd Woman*—the integration of fantasy and flashback into the narrative line—while also recalling the clean, classic structure of her two earlier novels." Weeks continued, "In *Violet Clay* Godwin raises a question that is central to understanding her work as a whole: what is the relationship between the artist and her art? The answer implied in Violet Clay's achievement as a painter reflects directly Godwin's ideals as a writer."

The title character of the novel, Violet Clay, leaves the South for New York at age twenty-four to become an artist, but "nine years later," John Leonard explained in the *New York Times,* "all that she paints are covers on Gothic romances for a paperback publishing house." Violet finally loses her job at Harrow House because the new art director wants to use photographs of terrorized women on the jackets of the romances rather than the idealized paintings Violet creates. When Violet finds out that her only living relative, Uncle Ambrose, a failed writer, has shot himself, she journeys to the Plommet Falls, New York, cabin in which he died to claim his body and bury him. Then, in *Washington Post Book World* critic Susan Shreve's words, "she decides to stay on and face the demons with her paint and brush."

Violet Clay reflects "the old-fashioned assumption that character develops and is good for something besides the daily recital to one's analyst," pointed out a *Harper's* critic. In Leonard's opinion, however, *Violet Clay* is "too intelligent for its own good. It is overgrown with ideas. You can't see the feelings for the ideas." Katha Pollitt commented in the *New York Times Book Review* that *Violet Clay* "has the pep-talk quality of so many recent novels in which the heroine strides off the last page, her own woman at last." As Sternhell argued, though, Godwin's novels "are not about book-ness, not about the *idea* of literature, but about human beings who take ideas seriously. Clever abstracts are not her medium: her 'vital artistic subject,' like Violet Clay's is, will always be the 'living human figure.'"

Godwin's next novel, *A Mother and Two Daughters,* is a comedy of manners that portrays women who "are able to achieve a kind of balance, to find ways of fully becoming themselves that don't necessitate a rejection

of everything in their heritage," as Susan Wood related in the *Washington Post Book World.* Set against a current-events background of the Iranian revolution, Three Mile Island, and Skylab, the novel opens in the changing town of Mountain City, North Carolina (a fictional city), with the death of Leonard Strickland of a heart attack as he is driving home with his wife from a party. The book records "the reactions and relationships of his wife Nell and daughters Cate and Lydia, both in their late thirties, as the bereavement forces each of them to evaluate the achievement and purpose of their own lives," Jennifer Uglow explained in the *Times Literary Supplement.* Josephine Hendin wrote in the *New York Times Book Review,* "As each woman exerts her claims on the others, as each confronts the envy and anger the others can inspire, Gail Godwin orchestrates their entanglements with great skill." And "for the first time," according to John F. Baker in *Publishers Weekly,* "Godwin enters several very different minds and personalities, those of her three protagonists."

Godwin once told Baker that she thinks of *A Mother and Two Daughters* as "a broadening of my canvas," remarking, "It most surprised me that I could get into the head of an elderly woman, but in fact it was easy. Nell's state of calm acceptance, her ability to sense the stillness at the center of things, is what I most aspire to." Nell, Lisa Schwarzbaum commented in the *Detroit News,* "raised to be a gracious gentlewoman—albeit sharper, more direct, less genteel, more 'North-thinking' than the other good ladies of Mountain City, N.C.— faces her future without the philosophical, steadying man on whom she had relied so thoroughly for support and definition." Here, according to Anne Tyler in the *New Republic,* Godwin provides the reader with a "meticulous" documentation of small-town life with its "rituals of Christmas party and book club meeting."

Not content to focus only on the three main characters, though, Godwin portrays "one great enormous pot of people," declared Caroline Moorhead in the *Spectator,* a whole "series of characters in all their intertwined relationships with each other, each other's lovers, children, parents, acquaintances." According to Uglow, the cast of *A Mother and Two Daughters* includes "a Southern *grande dame* with a pregnant teenage protégé; a pesticide baron with two sons, one retarded, the other gay; a hillbilly relative whose nose was bitten off in a brawl; [and] a one-legged Vietnam veteran whose wife runs a local nursery school." Christopher Lehmann-Haupt said in the *New York Times* that these characters are amazingly vivid, citing "the sense one gets that their lives are actually unfolding in the same world as yours." Tyler indicated that "there's an observant, amused, but kindly eye at work here, and not a single cheap shot is taken at these people who might so easily have been caricatures in someone else's hands."

A Mother and Two Daughters is "the richest, and most universal" of Godwin's books, "with a wholeness about its encompassing view of a large Southern family," according to Louise Sweeney in the *Christian Science Monitor,* and it is widely regarded as an unusually artful best-seller, appealing not only to the general public but also to Godwin's longtime followers. *Washington Post Book World* reviewer Jonathan Yardley considered *A Mother and Two Daughters* to be "a work of complete maturity and artistic control, one that I'm fully confident will find a permanent and substantial place in our national literature." He further commented that Godwin "turns out—this was not really evident in her four previous books—to be a stunningly gifted novelist of manners."

In *The Finishing School,* Godwin uses a first-person voice to create "a narrative of humanly impressive energies, as happy-sad in its texture as life itself may be said to be," according to William H. Pritchard in the *New Republic.* Shifting from one age perspective to another, Justin Stokes, a successful forty-year-old actress, tells the story of the summer she turned fourteen and her life changed forever when she underwent what *Time* reviewer Paul Gray called "a brief but harrowing rite of passage toward maturity." After her father and grandparents die in quick succession, the young Justin, her mother, and her brother leave Fredericksburg, Virginia, to live with her aunt in an upstate New York industrial town. There she makes friends with the local bohemian, Ursula DeVane, a forty-four-year-old failed actress who lives with her brother Julian, a talented musician of little consequence, in an old rundown home.

Ursula takes Justin on as her protégé, and they begin to meet in an old stone hut in the woods, the "Finishing School," in which Ursula "enthralls Justin with tales of her past and encourages her artistic aspirations," as Susan Wood put it in a *Washington Post Book World* review. The novel "charts the exhilaration, the enchantment, the transformation, then the inevitable disillusionment and loss inherent in such a friendship and self-discovery," according to Frances Taliaferro in the *New York Times Book Review.* And, as Sternhell related, it is essentially "the tale of a daughter with two mothers." Where *A Mother and Two Daughters* "was symphonic—many movements, many instruments—*The Finishing School* plays a gentle, chilling theme with variations." Sternhell further commented that the book,

despite its realistic form, "often reads like a fable, a contemporary myth; daughters love mothers, and—variations on a theme—daughters betray mothers, repeatedly, inevitably."

The Finishing School may be "old fashioned," according to Lehmann-Haupt, "in its preoccupation with such Aristotelian verities as plot, reversal, discovery, and the tragic flaw. But Miss Godwin's power to isolate and elevate subtle feelings makes her traditional story seem almost innovative." Although it doesn't quite meet the definition of true tragedy, the book is "a finely nuanced, compassionate psychological novel, subtler and more concentrated" than *A Mother and Two Daughters,* Taliaferro maintained. And Lehmann-Haupt pointed out that Godwin's characters serve to lend the novel a variety "as well as to distinguish the two worlds that Justin Stokes inhabits—the two dimensional world of the [industrial] look-alikes and the rich, mysterious kingdom where 'art's redemptive power' is supposed to prevail." The characterization of Justin "is one of the most trustworthy portraits of an adolescent in current literature" said Taliaferro, and the book itself, she concluded, is "a wise contribution to the literature of growing up."

With her seventh novel, 1987's *A Southern Family,* Godwin returns to the setting of Mountain City first found in *A Mother and Two Daughters.* Another novel of manners in the Victorian tradition, this work revolves around the death of a member of the Quick family. Theo, a twenty-eight-year-old divorced father of a young son, is found dead after he apparently killed his girlfriend and committed suicide. The novel focuses on reactions from family members, including novelist Clare, her quirky mother, Lily, and Clare's alcoholic half-brother, Rafe. *A Southern Family,* according to Susan Heeger in the *Los Angeles Times Book Review,* "takes off from Theo's death on a discursive exploration of family history and relationships as the Quicks struggle to measure their blame and—belatedly—to know the brother and son they failed in life." Several reviewers considered *A Southern Family* to be one of Godwin's most accomplished works. "Suffice it to say that *A Southern Family* is an ambitious book that entirely fulfills its ambitions," declared Yardley in the *Washington Post Book World.* "Not merely is it psychologically acute, it is dense with closely observed social and physical detail that in every instance is exactly right." Likewise, Beverly Lowry, writing in the *New York Times Book Review,* proclaimed that Godwin's *A Southern Family* "is the best she's written," concluding that Godwin's works "all give evidence of a supple intelligence working on the page."

Father Melancholy's Daughter is the story of Margaret Gower, whose mother, Ruth, leaves the family when

Margaret is six years old and is killed in a car crash a year later. Margaret and her father, Walter, an Episcopal priest, are thrust into an especially close father-daughter relationship in which much of their time is devoted to puzzling over Ruth's absence. The narrative switches time tracks from twenty-two-year-old Margaret, who is in love with a fortyish counselor named Adrian Bonner, to the younger Margaret of Ruth's disappearance. Calling the novel "a penetrating study of a child's coming to terms with her world," Nancy Wigston wrote in Toronto's *Globe and Mail* that "the real achievement here is Margaret herself: Gail Godwin has created that rarity in fiction, a character who evolves, believably." *New York Times Book Review* contributor Richard Bausch, however, expressed dissatisfaction with Margaret's lack of self-awareness, but he attested that the novel has "a number of real satisfactions, namely the characters that surround Margaret and her father—the parishioners of St. Cuthbert's. . . . Gail Godwin is almost Chaucerian in her delivery of these people, with their small distinguishing characteristics and their vibrant physicality." "Born in the South," Gray wrote in *Time,* "Godwin appears to be one of those writers who inherited a subject for life; then she developed the wisdom and talent to make her birthright seem constantly fresh and enthralling."

In her ninth novel, *The Good Husband,* Godwin portrays four characters undergoing profound change. Magda is a middle-aged English professor who is dying of cancer, while her dutiful husband, Francis, copes gamely with her impending death. Meanwhile, their friends Alice and Hugo Henry are facing the collapse of their marriage. As Alice visits Magda to comfort her during her illness, Alice gradually falls in love with Francis. "It is [Alice's] chaste pursuit of [Francis,] which the dying woman encourages, that holds our attention through much of the novel," remarked Chicago *Tribune Books* reviewer Penelope Mesic. Although critical of the "small defects" in Godwin's prose—"Sentences too often trickle to a vague conclusion"—Mesic praised the author's handling of Magda's feverish, combative decline and "steady, lucid exposition of the action." Writing in the *New York Times Book Review,* Sara Maitland commended many of the novel's elements: "The four main characters are interesting and convincing; their difficulties are real and persuasive; the principal plot is well constructed and involving." However, Maitland faulted Godwin for trying to infuse the plot with more symbolic significance than it can carry. She concluded, "Gail Godwin is a good writer, but *The Good Husband* is not a good novel." While conceding that readers will find the novel "either extremely moving or extremely sentimental," Anita Brookner, writing in the

Spectator, commended Godwin's "calm and unassuming" style and felt that the book is "guileless, dignified, and ultimately persuasive."

With 1999's *Evensong,* Godwin returns to her characters from *Father Melancholy's Daughter.* Margaret is now a fully grown woman and married to Adrian; she has also become an ordained Episcopal pastor at All Saints High Balsam. Much admired in her Smoky Mountain community, she seems like a model of goodness, proving her selflessness to her neighbors in one episode by preventing a mugging without thought to her own safety. She is frequently praised by her parishioners for her inspirational speaking ability and community leadership. But beneath this surface of model citizenry there are many problems and doubts in Margaret's life. Her husband, who is the local school headmaster, is harried in his schedule and plagued by self-doubt, which has led to his becoming distant toward his wife. Also, as the town endures tough economic times with the approach of the millennium, Margaret doubts her own abilities to help her community. This is seen more clearly as several characters enter her life, including a teenager from Adrian's school who has been expelled and has come to live with them, and a poor, elderly man named Tony who also requests aid from the Bonners. Added into this mix is a woman named Grace Munger, who begins preaching in town, saying that she has been divinely inspired to organize a "Millennium Birthday March for Jesus." Grace urges Margaret to help her in her cause, but Margaret resists such outwardly showy expressions of religious faith in favor of quietly performing good deeds. Nevertheless, Grace's presence causes Margaret to question her own character more deeply.

Several critics found much to praise in Godwin's tenth novel. For one thing, *Time* reviewer Gray found the ending refreshing, as it "not only ties up loose ends but also dares to be, in these uncertain times, optimistic." Mary Kaiser, writing in *World Literature Today,* particularly enjoyed Godwin's accurate portrayal of the daily life of a priest. However, she felt that there was too much melodrama and "coincidence of an almost Dickensian implausibility. . . . The high drama conflicts with the otherwise believable presentation of Margaret's routine as the rector of a small parish." On the other hand, a *Publishers Weekly* contributor asserted, "Gracefully written and embracing a worldly but genuine sense of goodness and human possibility, this kind of book is rare these days"; and Karen Anderson concluded in her *Library Journal* assessment that *Evensong* is "a touching portrait of love and loss and the many paths to redemption."

Although the two books to follow *Evensong* are very different in nature, they both deal with matters of the heart. *Heart: A Personal Journey through Its Myths and Meanings* is a nonfiction journey through the history of what the heart has come to symbolize in human civilization, while *Evenings at Five* is a very personal novel that fictionalizes the last years of a very important relationship in Godwin's life. A *Publishers Weekly* writer was impressed by the amount of research that went into *Heart,* which goes back in time to the depiction of the heart on cave walls and notes the symbolism of the heart in the arts, sciences, and lore of humanity up through the more recent times when it has lost ground to the preeminence of the brain and intellectualism. But while the critic said that fans of Godwin "will appreciate her occasional references to her characters and the glimpses of her personal life here, her scholarly approach is unlikely to capture the fancy of most of the readers of her novels." *Library Journal* contributor Richard Burns further considered *Heart* a mere "historical curiosity" whose desultory organization results in a book "without firm definition."

Similarly, reviewers considered Godwin's *Evenings at Five* to be a minor addition to her fiction oeuvre, although it is a work of interest because of its links to the author's own life. Godwin completed this short novel after the death of her longtime companion, composer Robert Starer. Though she and Starer never married, they had a relationship that lasted almost thirty years, and Godwin especially cherished the cocktail hours they shared together, a time when they could reflect on the events in their lives and take the time to enjoy each other's company. In the novel, Godwin fictionalizes this relationship to create the characters Christina and Rudy; she explores their relationship deeply, as well as Christina's grief after Rudy passes away. "For a book that can be read in an hour," observed a *Publishers Weekly* reviewer, "it is remarkably dense." *Book* contributor Beth Kephart described *Evenings at Five* as "heartrending" and composed of "brilliantly webbed scenes." Ann H. Fisher concluded in her *Library Journal* assessment that "fans of Godwin's other fiction will be fascinated by this minor piece."

Godwin told *CA:* "At this point I have four favorite [books], each for its own reason. I love *Father Melancholy's Daughter* because I loved the sheer intensity and preoccupation of writing about a girl growing up with a father, an experience I hadn't had. I am increasingly attracted by *The Good Husband*; it seems to have been written by unfamiliar parts of myself. Though I remember how it disappointed and angered some readers when it first came out ('This isn't like your other

novels!') my admiration for it continues to build, and it seems to be gathering its coterie of devotees. I cherish *Evenings at Five* because it taught me I could write in a different way, almost like creating a musical composition, a sonata in words, with its meshing of themes leading to a resolution that wasn't there before. And I can't wait to get up in the mornings and go back to *Queen of the Underworld,* with its young heroine—she's twenty-two—and her energies and schemes. She drags me willingly into all these places she doesn't know about yet, and I know better to patronize her with my 'adult wisdom' because I want to feel her experiences exactly as she feels them.

"A lifetime of reading and writing fiction has greatly increased my capacity for empathy, that activity of imagining from the inside out what it's like to be someone else. I want my novels to be vehicles for what Ortega y Gasset called 'the transmigration into other souls.'

"I am just now realizing how much I depend on the act of writing—I mean the physical setting down (or crossing out) one word after another, then reading it over, then adding or changing or subtracting more—to clarify my thoughts and orient myself in the world. Now there's a daunting challenge to empathy: imagining and getting inside the self I might have been without the gift of literacy."

BIOGRAPHICAL AND CRITICAL SOURCES:

BOOKS

Anthony, Carolyn, editor, *Family Portraits: Remembrances by Twenty Distinguished Writers,* Doubleday (New York, NY), 1989.

Contemporary Literary Criticism, Thomson Gale (Detroit, MI), Volume 5, 1976, Volume 8, 1978, Volume 31, 1985, Volume 69, 1992.

Contemporary Novelists, 7th edition, St. James Press (Detroit, MI), 2001.

Dictionary of Literary Biography, Volume 6: *American Novelists since World War II,* Thomson Gale (Detroit, MI), 1981.

Halpern, Daniel, editor, *Our Private Lives: Journals, Notebooks, and Diaries,* Ecco Press (New York, NY), 1998.

Hill, Jane, *Gail Godwin,* Twayne (New York, NY), 1992.

Kissel, Susan S., *Moving On: The Heroines of Shirley Ann Grau, Anne Tyler, and Gail Godwin,* Bowling Green State University Popular Press (Bowling Green, OH), 1996.

Mandelbaum, Paul, editor, *First Words: Earliest Writing from Favorite Contemporary Authors,* Algonquin Books (Chapel Hill, NC), 1993.

Mickelson, Anne Z., *Reaching Out: Sensitivity and Order in Recent American Fiction by Women,* Scarecrow (New York, NY), 1979.

Neubauer, Alexander, editor, *Conversations on Writing Fiction: Interviews with 13 Distinguished Teachers of Fiction Writing in America,* Harper Perennial (New York, NY), 1994

Powell, Danny Romine, *Parting the Curtains: Interviews with Southern Writers,* John F. Blair, (Winston Salem, NC), 1994.

Sternburg, Janet, editor, *The Writer on Her Work,* Norton (New York, NY), 1980.

Xie, Lihong, *The Evolving Self in the Novels of Gail Godwin,* Louisiana State University Press (Baton Rouge, LA), 1995.

PERIODICALS

America, December 21, 1974; April 17, 1982.

Atlantic, May, 1976; October, 1979.

Book, May-June, 1995, Beth Kephart, review of *Evenings at Five,* p. 77.

Booklist, June 1, 1994, p. 1724.

Boston Globe, February 21, 1982; March 10, 1991, Gail Caldwell, "A Father and Daughter Making Peace with the Past," p. B17; April 10, 1991, Patti Doten, "A Daughter of Father Melancholy," p. 67; February 28, 1999, Gail Caldwell, "Fire and Ice," p. F1.

Chicago Tribune Book World, January 10, 1982; October 16, 1983; January 27, 1984; October 25, 1987.

Christian Century, November 6, 1991, p. 103; November 16, 1994, p. 1088.

Christian Science Monitor, November 20, 1974; April 1, 1976; June 23, 1978; July 21, 1983; September 2, 1983; March 18, 1999, review of *Evensong,* p. 19; February 22, 2001, review of *Heart: A Personal Journey through Its Myths and Meanings,* p. 18.

Commonweal, June 1, 1984; March 25, 1988, p. 187.

Critique: Studies in Modern Fiction, winter, 1978; number 3, 1980.

Detroit Free Press, March 10, 1985.

Detroit News, April 11, 1982; October 16, 1983; February 10, 1985.

Entertainment Weekly, September 16, 1994, p. 109.

Globe and Mail (Toronto, Ontario, Canada), April 13, 1991, p. C6.

Harper's, July, 1978.

Library Journal, January, 1988, p. 41; February 1, 1991, p. 103; June 1, 1994, p. 158; December, 1998, Karen Anderson, review of *Evensong,* p. 154;

February 15, 2001, Richard Burns, review of *Heart,* p. 176; March 1, 2003, Ann H. Fisher, review of *Evenings at Five,* p. 119.

Listener, June 9, 1977.

Los Angeles Times, November 13, 1981.

Los Angeles Times Book Review, September 11, 1983; February 24, 1985; February 9, 1986; October 4, 1987; March 3, 1991, pp. 2, 11; March 14, 1999, review of *Evensong,* p. 15.

Miami Herald, February 29, 1976.

Mississippi Quarterly, spring, 1993, Lihong Xie, "A Dialogue with Gail Godwin," p. 167.

Ms., January, 1982.

National Review, September 15, 1978.

New Republic, January 25, 1975; July 8, 1978; February 17, 1982; December 19, 1983; February 25, 1985; February 29, 1988, p. 38.

New Statesman, August 15, 1975.

Newsweek, February 23, 1976; January 11, 1982; September 12, 1983; February 25, 1985.

New York, March 11, 1991, p. 86.

New Yorker, November 18, 1974; January 18, 1982.

New York Review of Books, February 20, 1975; April 1, 1976; July 20, 1978.

New York Times, September 21, 1972; September 30, 1974; February 16, 1976; May 18, 1978; December 22, 1981; September 6, 1983; October 4, 1983; January 24, 1985; December 15, 1985; September 21, 1987.

New York Times Book Review, June 7, 1970; October 15, 1972; October 20, 1974; February 22, 1976; May 21, 1978; January 10, 1982; September 18, 1983; January 27, 1985; August 10, 1986; October 11, 1987; March 3, 1991, p. 7; September 4, 1994, p. 5; April 4, 1999, Claire Messud, review of *Evensong,* p. 8; April 8, 2001, review of *Heart,* p. 20; April 6, 2003, John Hartl, review of *Evenings at Five,* p. 24.

New York Times Magazine, December 15, 1985.

Observer (London, England), February 5, 1984.

Pacific Sun, September 23-29, 1983.

Progressive, October, 1978.

Publishers Weekly, January 15, 1982; August 14, 1987, p. 93; August 1, 1994, p. 94; January 4, 1999, review of *Evensong,* p. 69; January 8, 2001, review of *Heart,* p. 61; February 17, 2003, review of *Evenings at Five,* p. 55.

Saturday Review, August 8, 1970; October 28, 1972; February 21, 1976; June 10, 1978; January, 1982.

Southern Literary Journal, spring, 2001, Ron Emerick, "Theo and the Road to Sainthood in Gail Godwin's *A Southern Family,*" p. 134.

Southern Living, May, 1988, p. 118; May, 1991, p. 83.

Spectator, January 15, 1977; September 2, 1978; February 6, 1982; November 5, 1994, p. 51.

Sunday Star-Telegram (Fort Worth, TX), February 14, 1982.

Time, January 25, 1982; February 11, 1985; October 5, 1987, p. 82; March 25, 1991, p. 70; September 26, 1994, p. 82; March 29, 1999, Paul Gray, "Millennium Fevers: In Her Absorbing New Novel, Gail Godwin Tracks Modern Maladies into a Mountain Town," p. 216.

Times (London, England), February 18, 1982; March 28, 1985.

Times Literary Supplement, July 23, 1971; July 4, 1975; September 15, 1978; March 5, 1982; February 17, 1984; November 20, 1987, p. 1274; May 24, 1991, p. 21; November 4, 1994, p. 22.

Tribune Books (Chicago, IL), August 28, 1994, p. 3.

Village Voice, March 30, 1982; February 26, 1985.

Washington Post, February 7, 1983; March 7, 1991, p. D1.

Washington Post Book World, October 1, 1972; May 21, 1978; December 13, 1981; September 11, 1983; February 3, 1985; September 13, 1987; March 17, 1991, p. 4; March 28, 1999, review of *Evensong,* p. 5.

World Literature Today, summer, 2000, Mary Kaiser, review of *Evensong,* p. 606.

Writer, September, 1975; December, 1976.

ONLINE

Gail Godwin's Web site, http://www.gailgodwin.com/ (November 26, 2003).

OTHER

Gail Goodwin Interview with Kay Bonetti (sound recording), American Audio Prose Library (Columbia, MO), c. 1986.

*   *   *

GODWIN, Gail Kathleen
See GODWIN, Gail

*   *   *

GOLDEN, Arthur 1956-

PERSONAL: Born 1956, in Chattanooga, TN; married Trudy Legge, 1982; children: two. *Education:* Harvard College, B.A. (art history); Columbia University, M.A. (Japanese history), 1980; Boston University, M.A. (English), 1988. *Hobbies and other interests:* Classical guitar.

ADDRESSES: Home—P.O. Box 419, Brookline, MA 02446.

CAREER: Writer. Worked for an English-language magazine in Tokyo, 1980-82.

WRITINGS:

Memoirs of a Geisha, Knopf (New York, NY), 1997.

ADAPTATIONS: Memoirs of a Geisha was recorded as an audiobook, Random House (New York, NY), 1997. *Memoirs of a Geisha* has been translated into thirty-three languages, and rights were sold for an American film adaptation in 1997 to Red Wagon Productions. *Memoirs of a Geisha* will be adapted for a film directed by Steven Spielberg. Production begins in September 2004.

WORK IN PROGRESS: A historical novel set in the United States.

SIDELIGHTS: Arthur Golden made a splash when he came on the literary scene in 1997 with the publication of his novel *Memoirs of a Geisha,* the fictional autobiography of a Japanese geisha during the 1920s and 1930s. A phenomenal best seller, this novel sold more than four million copies in English alone in a little over three years and has been translated into thirty-three languages. Many reviewers have praised the work for its portrayal of an obscure and little-understood part of Japanese culture and have marveled that a white American male should write such a work. *Newsweek* reviewer Jeff Giles called it "a faux autobiography ten years and 2,300 pages in the making. . . . A few reservations aside, Golden has written a novel that's full of cliff-hangers great and small, a novel that is never out of one's possession, a novel that refuses to stay shut." Film rights were sold to an American motion picture company, and work proceeded slowly on the project, which was still a work-in-progress in 2004.

Golden was raised in a literary family; his cousin Arthur Ochs Sulzberger is publisher of the *New York Times.* After earning a bachelor's degree in art history from Harvard University, a master's degree in Japanese history from Columbia University, and another master's degree in English from Boston University, Golden worked for an English-language magazine in Tokyo from 1980 to 1982. While in Japan, he met a man whose mother was a geisha and found the topic interesting. When Golden began toying with the idea of writing a novel, he remembered the intrigue he had felt about geishas and believed the topic would adapt well to a fictional treatment. Although an oft-taught tenet of writing is to write about topics the writer knows, Golden decided it was "better to write about what sparks . . . [the] imagination," he told *Maclean's* writer Tanya Davies, "and the geisha district in Kyoto, Japan, sparked mine."

Golden is well-versed in the Japanese language, and even in Mandarin Chinese, so the language posed no barrier to his research. After conducting copious research about geishas in secondary sources, he embarked on the writing of a third-person novel that begins with the son of a geisha as a child. He discarded the novel when he decided that the geisha as the central character would be more interesting. Golden began his "second" novel after meeting Mineko Iwasaki, who had been a geisha during the 1960s and 1970s. From Iwasaki, whom he interviewed for several weeks, Golden learned details of geisha life that helped in the writing of the new version; but the second version, also in third-person, earned the epithet of "dry" from several of Golden's friends, who are professional writers. Not wanting to give up on a project with six years of effort invested, Golden rethought the novel, obsessing over it for a week. Finally he decided to make the leap to writing in first-person, which turned out to be the right move.

Even so, Golden knew that he had several cultural divides to bridge and that the success of his endeavor would be judged by how well he managed these issues: another and non-Western culture, another time period, and another gender. Even after deciding on the first-person voice and relying on his new research, Golden had to find a way to integrate the information needed by non-Japanese readers to understand the culture. The solution turned out to be placing his Japanese heroine in the West and employing the device of a fictional translator, as Golden explained at the Random House Web site: "The content is entirely fiction, although the historic facts of a geisha's life are accurate. The translator is also an invention. . . . I had to find a way to make it believable for Sayuri to annotate the story as she told it. . . . I wanted the reader to know from the beginning of the book that she is living in New York City, telling her story, looking back at her life . . . and talking to a Westerner. Under these circumstances, she would naturally annotate her story as she told it."

As Joanne Wilkinson wrote in *Booklist,* Golden "melds sparkling historical fiction with a compelling coming-of-age story." The work recounts the tale of young Chiyo Sakamoto, born to a poor family in a Japanese fishing village. Following their mother's death during the depression years, their father sells nine-year-old Chiyo and her older sister Satsu. Satsu's fate is to become a prostitute, but the lovely Chiyo is bought by the madam of the Nitta okiya. Chiyo learns music, dance, and the tea ceremony, and wears the heavy costumes and makeup of the geisha. Her beauty soon surpasses that of the scheming Hatsumomo, until then the okiya's head geisha. Chiyo loses her virginity to a man who pays a record price in a bidding war.

Many reviewers discussed the author's ability to adequately portray the thoughts and feelings of a woman. "What is striking about the novel is Mr. Golden's creation of an utterly convincing narrator, a woman who is, at once, a traditional product of Japan's archaic gender relations and a spirited . . . heroine," wrote Michiko Kakutani in the *New York Times Book Review.* "Mr. Golden allows her to relate her story in chatty, colloquial terms that enable the reader to identify with her feelings of surprise, puzzlement and disgust at the rituals she must endure. . . . Mr. Golden gives us not only a richly sympathetic portrait of a woman, but also a finely observed picture of an anomalous and largely vanished world." Chiyo is tutored by Mameha, a renowned geisha, and becomes very successful during the 1930s and 1940s. As a professional, she takes a new name, Sayuri. After many men and years, she becomes mistress of the Chairman of an electrical supply company, whom she first met in the okiya; and he cares for her until his death. Golden has often been asked about the role of geisha in Japan as compared to the Western notion of the prostitute; he likens the geisha, to a mistress maintained by a single lover in Western culture.

Not all reviewers found Golden's characters convincing, however. While *New Leader* critic Gabriel Brownstein praised Golden's use of inanimate details, he found that his characters "fail to convey any emotional, psychological or historical complexities. His narrative is imposed on an exotic world rather than organic to it" and felt Sayuri's desire for the Chairman "is not demonstrated through the logic of the story either. She merely reiterates it in a series of widely spaced asides to the reader." Almost as if answering Brownstein's critique, Golden, commented in an *Amazon.com* interview: "I was not able . . . to really create a fully developed character in the Chairman. . . . Because my father and mother divorced when I was young, my father moved away when I was seven or eight, died when I was thirteen, and for some reason I suppose it's emotionally toxic territory. And I just have a difficult time writing about it. And the Chairman was in many ways based upon my father. . . . When the Chairman was on the page, things were inert. I had so much trouble trying to create a believable person!"

Other reviewers also found fault with Golden's characterizations, including John David Morley, who wrote in *Working Woman* that Golden's "decision to write an autobiographically styled novel rather than a nonfiction portrait is most obviously justified in terms of empathy. . . . Unfortunately, Sayuri's personality seems so familiar it is almost generic. . . . What about the woman inside the sumptuous kimono, underneath the white mask?" Morley said the character Hatsumomo has "the potential one looks for and finds wanting in the heroine . . . with as many bad sides as Sayuri has good ones." Morley felt that if Golden "had been willing to develop this richer, more complex character, he might have been able to rouse the kind of empathy the novel needs—and perhaps one or two other qualities besides. Eroticism, for example." Morley said the book is much more successful with its facts, "filled as it is with colorful nuggets of information."

Much of the novel's verisimilitude results from Golden's use of detail, as Golden himself told Repps Hudson of the *St. Louis Post-Dispatch,* "Absolutely everything's in the details. The book will fail, at least by my standards, if you don't get the details right." Lindsley Cameron wrote of Sayuri in the *Yale Review:* "By the time she is living happily ever after at the Waldorf, the reader has learned quite a lot about geisha culture. . . . Many of these 'facts' are sartorial: not since reading the memoirs of that delightful seventeenth-century transvestite the Abbe de Choisy . . . have I encountered such drooling dwelling on the details of costume. The effect is piquant, something like reading soft-core pornography that keeps turning, as though in a dream, into the catalogue of a textile auction at Christie's." Brownstein also contended that Golden "is masterful at describing teahouses, hairdressers' shops and alleyways of Gion, the Geisha district of Kyoto. He excels, too, at teaching us about the way geisha put on makeup, the stages of their education and how they earn their living." "The meticulous research makes Gion come alive," wrote Hannah Beech in *Time International.* "Hatsumomo slathers on facial cream made of nightingale droppings, and geishas burn one-hour incense sticks to keep track of how much to bill per night. . . . Like a geisha who has mastered the art of illusion, Golden creates a cloistered floating world out of the engines of a modernizing Japan." Among the work's other enthusiasts was *Library Journal*'s Wilda Williams, who asserted that Golden "has brilliantly revealed the culture and traditions of an exotic world, closed to most Westerners," and a *Publishers Weekly* reviewer, who wrote, *Memoirs* is "rendered with stunning clarity. . . . Golden effortlessly spins the tale."

Memoirs of a Geisha sparked controversy in one arena. In 2000, after publication of the Japanese translation, former geisha Mineko Iwasaki brought suit against Golden for supposedly breaching her promised anonymity and for libeling her. "I spent seven to eight hours a day for two weeks talking to him, but he did not get anything right," Iwasaki complained to *U.S. News & World Report*'s Joseph L. Galloway. Because of the fictional memoir format, used in the West in such classic works as *Robinson Crusoe* and *Moll Flanders* and because of the author's acknowledgment of Iwasaki's help at the book's opening, Iwasaki contended that Japanese readers believe she has done everything the main character of the book has done. In 2002 Iwasaki published her own memoir, *Geisha of Gion*. Golden has continually maintained that although Iwasaki influenced his portrayal of Sayuri in *Memoirs of a Geisha,* the "character of Sayuri and her story are completely invented," as he wrote in the preface to *Memoirs of a Geisha.*

After *Memoirs of a Geisha,* Golden began work on another historical novel, this time to be set in the United States. As he told Hudson, "My pep talk to myself now is that I did this by permitting myself to take a risk and giving myself a real challenge and figuring out how to rise to it. My job now is to do exactly the same thing."

BIOGRAPHICAL AND CRITICAL SOURCES:

PERIODICALS

Booklist, September 1, 1997, Joanne Wilkinson, review of *Memoirs of a Geisha,* p. 7.

Commonweal, December 3, 1999, Robin Antepara, review of *Memoirs of a Geisha,* p. 25; April 1, 2000, Brad Hooper, review of *Memoirs of a Geisha,* p. 1442.

Daily Telegraph (London, England), August 4, 2001, Colin Joyce, "The Real Memoirs of a Geisha," p. 18.

Entertainment, January 23, 1998, p. 59; February 19, 1999, review of *Memoirs of a Geisha,* p. 128.

Globe and Mail (Toronto, Canada), April 17, 1999, review of *Memoirs of a Geisha,* p. D17.

Kirkus Reviews, August 15, 1997, review of *Memoirs of a Geisha,* pp. 1240-1241.

Kliatt Young Adult Paperback Book Guide, January, 1999, review of *Memoirs of a Geisha* (audio version), p. 46; March, 1999, review of *Memoirs of a Geisha* (audio version), p. 58.

Library Journal, August, 1997, Wilda Williams, review of *Memoirs of a Geisha,* p. 128; February 15, 1999, R. Kent Rasmussen, review of *Memoirs of a Geisha* (audio version), p. 200.

Los Angeles Times, November 30, 1997, review of *Memoirs of a Geisha,* p. 8; February 15, 1999, Elizabeth Mehren, "*Geisha* a Golden Moment for Author," p. NA; April 26, 2001, Elizabeth Mehren, "Geisha Charges Writer's Fiction Is Her Truth," p. E-1.

Maclean's, March 1, 1999, Tanya Davies, "A Cross-cultural King of the Kimonos," p. 53.

New Leader, November 3, 1997, Gabriel Brownstein, review of *Memoirs of a Geisha,* p. 18.

Newsweek, October 13, 1997, Jeff Giles, review of *Memoirs of a Geisha,* p. 76.

New Yorker, September 29, 1997, review of *Memoirs of a Geisha,* pp. 82-83.

New York Times, January 7, 1999, Sheryl WuDunn, "A Japanese Version of *Geisha*? Well It May Sound Easy," p. E2; June 19, 2001, Calvin Sims, "A Geisha, a Successful Novel and a Lawsuit," p. E1.

New York Times Book Review, October 14, 1997, Michiko Kakutani, review of *Memoirs of a Geisha,* p. 32; February 14, 1999, review of *Memoirs of a Geisha* (audio version), p. 32.

People, December 1, 1997, Lan N. Nguyen, review of *Memoirs of a Geisha,* p. 49.

Publishers Weekly, December 16, 1996, review of *Memoirs of a Geisha,* p. 25; August 11, 1997, p. 255; July 28, 1997, review of *Memoirs of a Geisha,* p. 49; July 1, 2001, "Second Golden Signing at Knopf," p. 14.

Romance Reader, February 9, 1999, review of *Memoirs of a Geisha* p. ONL.

St. Louis Post-Dispatch (St. Louis, MO), February 22, 1999, Repps Hudson, "It's All in the Details," p. E1.

Sunday Times (London, England), April 29, 2001, Cherry Norton, "Betrayal of a Geisha," p. 14.

Time International, March 30, 1998, Hannah Beech, review of *Memoirs of a Geisha,* p. 49.

Times Literary Supplement, December 12, 1997, review of *Memoirs of a Geisha,* p. 21.

U.S. News & World Report, March 13, 2000, Joseph L. Galloway, "Protests of a Geisha," p. 12.

Wall Street Journal, April 25, 2001, "Former Geisha Sues Author, Random House over Book," p. B10.

Washington Post Book World, February 27, 1999, review of *Memoirs of a Geisha,* p. 7.

Working Woman, October 5, 1997, John David Moreley, review of *Memoirs of a Geisha.*

Yale Review, January, 1998, Lindsley Cameron, review of *Memoirs of a Geisha,* pp. 167-178.

ONLINE

Amazon, http://www.amazon.com/ (1998), "Interview with Arthur Golden."

BBC Books, http://www.bbc.co.uk/ (August 6, 2003), Ruth Green, "Arthur Golden."

Behind the Books, http://www.randomhouse.com/vintage/ (May 8, 2003), Arthur Golden, "A Conversation with Arthur Golden."

CNN, http://www.cnn.com/books/ (March 23, 1999), Miles O'Brien, "A Talk with Arthur Golden."

*   *   *

GOLDING, William 1911-1993
(William Gerald Golding)

PERSONAL: Born September 19, 1911, in St. Columb Minor, Cornwall, England; died of a heart attack June 19, 1993, in Perranarworthal, near Falmouth, England; son of Alex A. (a schoolmaster) and Mildred A. Golding; married Ann Brookfield, 1939; children: David, Judith. *Education:* Brasenose College, Oxford, B.A., 1935, M.A., 1960. *Hobbies and other interests:* Sailing, archaeology, and playing the piano, violin, viola, cello, and oboe.

CAREER: Writer. Worked in a settlement house, c. 1935; Bishop Wordsworth's School, Salisbury, Wiltshire, England, teacher of English and philosophy, 1939-40, 1945-61; actor, producer, and writer, 1934-40, 1945-54. Writer-in-residence, Hollins College, 1961-62; honorary fellow, Brasenose College, Oxford, 1966. *Military service:* British Royal Navy, 1940-45; became rocket ship commander.

MEMBER: Royal Society of Literature (fellow), Saville Club.

AWARDS, HONORS: Commander, Order of the British Empire, 1965; D.Litt., University of Sussex, 1970, University of Kent, 1974, University of Warwick, 1981, Oxford University, 1983, and University of Sorbonne,

1983; James Tait Black Memorial Prize, 1980, for *Darkness Visible;* Booker-McConnell Prize, 1981, for *Rites of Passage;* Nobel Prize for literature, 1983, for body of work; LL.D., University of Bristol, 1984; knighted, 1988.

WRITINGS:

FICTION

Lord of the Flies (also see below), Faber & Faber (London, England), 1954, introduction by E.M. Forster, Coward (New York, NY), 1955, reprinted, Berkley (New York, NY), 2003.

The Inheritors, Faber & Faber (London, England), 1955, Harcourt (New York, NY), 1962.

Pincher Martin, Faber & Faber (London, England), 1955, new edition, 1972, published as *The Two Deaths of Christopher Martin,* Harcourt (New York, NY), 1957.

(With John Wyndham and Mervyn Peake) *Sometime, Never: Three Tales of Imagination,* Eyre & Spottiswoode (London, England), 1956, Ballantine (New York, NY), 1957.

Free Fall, Faber & Faber (London, England), 1959, Harcourt (New York, NY), 1960.

The Spire, Harcourt (New York, NY), 1964.

The Pyramid (novellas), Harcourt (New York, NY), 1967.

The Scorpion God: Three Short Novels (includes *Clonk Clonk, Envoy Extraordinary* [also see below], and *The Scorpion God*), Harcourt (New York, NY), 1971.

Darkness Visible, Farrar, Straus (New York, NY), 1979.

Rites of Passage (first novel in trilogy), Farrar, Straus (New York, NY), 1980.

The Paper Men, Farrar, Straus (New York, NY), 1984.

Close Quarters (second novel in trilogy), Farrar, Straus (New York, NY), 1987.

Fire down Below (third novel in trilogy), Farrar, Straus (New York, NY), 1989.

The Double Tongue: A Draft of a Novel, Farrar, Straus (New York, NY), 1995.

OTHER

Poems, Macmillan (New York, NY), 1934.

The Brass Butterfly: A Play in Three Acts (based on *Envoy Extraordinary*; first produced in Oxford, then London, England, 1958; produced in New York, NY, 1965), Faber & Faber (London, England), 1958, new edition with introduction by Golding, 1963.

Break My Heart (radio play), BBC Radio, 1962.

Lord of the Flies (screenplay; adapted from his novel), Two Arts/Continental, 1963.

The Hot Gates, and Other Occasional Pieces (nonfiction), Harcourt (New York, NY), 1965.

A Moving Target (essays and lectures), Farrar, Straus (New York, NY), 1982.

Nobel Lecture, 7 December 1983, Sixth Chamber (Leamington Spa, England), 1984.

An Egyptian Journal (travel), Faber & Faber (London, England), 1985.

Also author of radio plays. Contributor to periodicals, including *Encounter, Holiday, Listener, New Left Review,* and *Spectator.*

ADAPTATIONS: *Pincher Martin* was produced as a radio play by the British Broadcasting Corp., 1958. A new screenplay of the novel *Lord of the Flies* was filmed by Castle Rock Entertainment, 1990, and it was adapted for the stage by Nigel Williams, 1996.

SIDELIGHTS: William Golding has been described as pessimistic, mythical, spiritual: an allegorist who used his novels as a canvas to paint portraits of man's constant struggle between his civilized self and his hidden, darker nature. With the appearance of *Lord of the Flies,* Golding's first published novel, the author began his career as both a campus cult favorite and one of the late twentieth century's distinctive—and much debated—literary talents. Golding's appeal was summarized by the Nobel Prize committee, which while awarding him its literature prize in 1983 stated that Golding's "books are very entertaining and exciting. They can be read with pleasure and profit without the need to make much effort with learning or acumen. But they have also aroused an unusually great interest in professional literary critics [who find] deep strata of ambiguity and complication in Golding's work, . . . in which odd people are tempted to reach beyond their limits, thereby being bared to the very marrow."

The novel that established Golding's reputation, *Lord of the Flies,* was rejected by twenty-one publishers before London-based Faber & Faber accepted the forty-three-year-old schoolmaster's book. While the story has been compared to such works as Daniel Defoe's *Robinson Crusoe* and Richard Hughes's *A High Wind in Jamaica,* Golding's novel is actually the author's "answer" to nineteenth-century writer R.M. Ballantyne's children's classic *The Coral Island: A Tale of the Pacific Ocean.* These two books share the same basic plot line and even some of the same character names; two of the lead characters are named Ralph and Jack in both books. The similarity, however, ends there. Ballantyne's story about a trio of boys stranded on an otherwise uninhabited island shows how, by pluck and resourcefulness, the young castaways survive with their morals strengthened and their wits sharpened. *Lord of the Flies,* on the other hand, is "an allegory on human society [a century later], the novel's primary implication being that what we have come to call civilization is, at best, not more than skin-deep," James Stern explained in the *New York Times Book Review.*

Initially, the tale of a group of schoolboys stranded on an island during their escape from atomic war received mixed reviews and sold only modestly in its hardcover edition. But when the paperback edition was published in 1959, the book was made more accessible to students and began to sell briskly. Teachers, aware of student interest and impressed by the strong theme and stark symbolism of the work, assigned *Lord of the Flies* to literature classes. As the novel's reputation grew, critics reacted by drawing scholarly theses out of what was previously dismissed as just another adventure story.

In his study *The Tragic Past,* David Anderson discerned biblical implications in Golding's novel. "*Lord of the Flies,*" wrote Anderson, "is a complex version of the story of Cain—the man whose smoke-signal failed and who murdered his brother. Above all, it is a refutation of optimistic theologies which believed that God had created a world in which man's moral development had advanced *pari passu* with his biological evolution and would continue so to advance until the all-justifying End was reached." *Lord of the Flies* presents moral regression rather than achievement, Anderson argued. "And there is no all-justifying End," the critic continued, "the rescue-party which takes the boys off their island comes from a world in which regression has occurred on a gigantic scale—the scale of atomic war. The human plight is presented in terms which are unqualified and unrelieved. Cain is not merely our remote ancestor: he is contemporary man, and his murderous impulses are equipped with unlimited destructive power."

The novel has also been interpreted as Golding's response to the popular artistic notion of the 1950s: that youth is a basically innocent collective whose members are victims of adult society. In his 1960 review for *Critical Quarterly,* C.B. Cox deemed *Lord of the Flies* "probably the most important novel to be published" during the 1950s. As the critic continued: "[To] suc-

ceed, a good story needs more than sudden deaths, a terrifying chase and an unexpected conclusion. *Lord of the Flies* includes all these ingredients, but their exceptional force derives from Golding's faith that every detail of human life has a religious significance. This is one reason why he is unique among new writers in the '50s. . . . Golding's intense conviction [is] that every particular of human life has a profound importance. His children are not juvenile delinquents, but human beings realising for themselves the beauty and horror of life."

Golding took his theme of tracing the defects of society back to the defects of human nature a step further with his second novel, *The Inheritors.* This tale is set at the beginning of human existence itself, during the prehistoric age. A tribe of Neanderthals, as seen through the characters of Lok and Fa, live a peaceful, primitive life. Their happy world, however, is doomed: evolution brings in its wake the new race, *Homo sapiens,* who demonstrate their acquired skills with weapons by killing the Neanderthals.

The Inheritors, which Golding called his favorite, was well received by several critics. Inevitably, comparisons were also made between *The Inheritors* and *Lord of the Flies.* To Peter Green, in *Review of English Literature,* for example, "it is clear that there is a close thematic connection between [the two novels]: Mr. Golding has simply set up a different working model to illustrate the eternal human verities from a new angle. Again it is humanity, and humanity alone, that generates evil; and when the new men triumph, Lok, the Neanderthaler, weeps as Ralph wept for the corruption and end of innocence" in *Lord of the Flies.* Reviewer Bernard Oldsey, quoted in the *Dictionary of Literary Biography,* saw the comparison in religious terms, noting that the *Homo sapiens* "represent the Descent of Man, not simply in the Darwinian sense, but in the Biblical sense of the Fall. Peculiarly enough, the boys [in *Lord of the Flies*] slide backward, through their own bedevilment, toward perdition; and Lok's Neanderthal tribe hunches forward, given a push by their *Homo sapiens* antagonists, toward the same perdition. In Golding's view, there is precious little room for evolutionary slippage: progression in *The Inheritors* and retrogression in *Lord of the Flies* have the same results."

Just as *Lord of the Flies* was a revisioning of *The Coral Island,* Golding claimed he wrote *The Inheritors* to refute H.G. Wells's controversial sociological study *Outline of History.* Readers familiar with both works "can see that between the two writers there is a certain filial relation, though strained," commented a *Times Literary*

Supplement critic. "They share the same fascination with past and future, the extraordinary capacity to move imaginatively to remote points in time, the fabulizing impulse, the need to moralize. There are even similarities in style. And surely now, when Wells's reputation as a great writer is beginning to take form, it will be understood as high praise of Golding if one says that he is our Wells, as good in his own individual way as Wells was in his." Taken together, Golding's first two novels are, according to Lawrence R. Ries in *Wolf Masks: Violence in Contemporary Fiction,* "studies in human nature, exposing the kinds of violence that man uses against his fellow man."

Golding's third novel, *Pincher Martin*—published in the United States as *The Two Deaths of Christopher Martin* due to its publishers' concern that U.S. readers would not know that "pincher" is British slang for "petty thief"—found the author moving away from his examination of primitive human nature. Stylistically similar to Ambrose Bierce's famous short story "An Occurrence at Owl Creek Bridge," *Pincher Martin* is about a naval officer who, after his ship is torpedoed in the Atlantic, drifts aimlessly before latching on to a barren rock. Here he clings for days, eating sea anemones and trying his best to retain consciousness. Delirium overtakes him, though, and through his rambling thoughts he relives his past. The discovery of the sailor's corpse at the end of the story in part constitutes what has been called a "gimmick" ending, and gives the book a metaphysical turn—the reader learns that Pincher Martin has been dead from the beginning of the narrative.

The author's use of flashbacks throughout the narrative of *Pincher Martin* was discussed by Avril Henry in *Southern Review:* "On the merely narrative level" Goulding's plot device "is the natural result of Martin's isolation and illness, and is the process by which he is gradually brought to his ghastly self-knowledge." In fact, added Henry, the flashbacks "function in several ways. First the flashbacks relate to each other and to the varied forms in which they themselves are repeated throughout the book; second, they relate also to the details of Martin's 'survival' on [the rock]. . . . Third, they relate to the six-day structure of the whole experience: the structure which is superficially a temporal check for us and Martin in the otherwise timeless and distorted events on the rock and in the mind, and at a deeper level is a horrible parody of the six days of Creation. What we watch is an unmaking process, in which man attempts to create himself his own God, and the process accelerates daily."

While acknowledging the influences present in the themes of *Pincher Martin*—from Homer's *Odysseus* to *Robinson Crusoe* again—Stephen Medcalf in his *William Golding* suggests that the novel is Golding's most autobiographical work to date. The author, said Medcalf, assigned to Martin "more of the external conditions of his own life than to any other of his characters, from [his education at] Oxford . . . through a period of acting and theatre life to a commission in the wartime Navy." Golding also added a dimension from his own past, noted Medcalf, citing the author's "childhood fear of the darkness of the cellar and the coffin ends crushed in the walls from the graveyard outside [his childhood home]. The darkness universalizes him. It becomes increasingly but always properly laden with symbolism: the darkness of the thing that cannot examine itself, the observing ego: the darkness of the unconscious, the darkness of sleep, of death and, beyond death, heaven."

To follow *Pincher Martin,* Golding "next wanted to show the patternlessness of life before we impose our patterns on it," according to Green. However, the resulting book, *Free Fall,* Green noted, "avoids the amoebic paradox suggested by his own prophecy, and falls into a more normal pattern of development: normal, that is, for Golding." Not unlike *Pincher Martin, Free Fall* depicts through flashbacks the life of its protagonist, artist Sammy Mountjoy. Imprisoned in a darkened cell in a Nazi prisoner-of-war camp, Mountjoy, who has been told that his execution is imminent, has only time to reflect on his past.

Despite the similarity in circumstance to *Pincher Martin,* Oldsey found one important difference between that novel and *Free Fall.* In *Free Fall,* a scene showing Sammy Mountjoy's tortured reaction on (symbolically) reliving his own downfall indicates a move toward atonement. "It is at this point in Golding's tangled tale that the reader begins to understand the difference between Sammy Mountjoy and Pincher Martin," Oldsey explained. "Sammy escapes the machinations of the camp psychiatrist, Dr. Halde, by making use of man's last resource, prayer. It is all concentrated in his cry of 'Help me! Help me!'—a cry which Pincher Martin refuses to utter. In this moment of desperate prayer, Sammy spiritually bursts open the door of his own selfishness."

Medcalf saw the story as Dantesque in nature—Mountjoy's romantic interest is even named Beatrice—and remarked that "Dante, like Sammy, came to himself in the middle of his life, in a dark wood [the cell, in Sammy's case], unable to remember how he came there. . . . His only way out is to see the whole world, and himself in its light. Hell, purgatory and heaven are revealed to him directly, himself and this world of sense in glimpses from the standpoint of divine justice and eternity." In *Free Fall* Golding's intent "is to show this world directly, in other hints and guesses. He is involved therefore in showing directly the moment of fall at which Dante only hints. He has a hero without reference points, who lives in the vertigo of free fall, therefore, reproachful of an age in which those who have a morality or a system softly refuse to insist on them: a hero for whom no system he has will do, but who is looking for his own unity in the world—and that, the real world, is 'like nothing, because it is everything.' Golding, however, has the advantage of being able to bring Dante's world in by allusion: and he does so with a Paradise hill on which Beatrice is met."

In Golding's fifth novel, *The Spire,* "the interest is all in the opacity of the man and in a further exploration of man's all-sacrificing will," wrote Medcalf. Fourteenth-century clergyman Dean Jocelin "is obsessed with the belief that it is his divine mission to raise a 400-foot tower and spire above his church," Oldsey related. "His colleagues protest vainly that the project is too expensive and the edifice unsuited for such a shaft. His master builder—obviously named Roger Mason—calculates that the foundation and pillars of the church are inadequate to support the added weight, and fruitlessly suggests compromises to limit the shaft to a lesser height. The townspeople—amoral, skeptical, and often literally pagan—are derisive about 'Jocelin's Folly.'" Dean Jocelin, nonetheless, strives on. The churchman, in fact, "neglects all his spiritual duties to be up in the tower overseeing the workmen himself, all the while choosing not to see within and without himself what might interrupt the spire's dizzying climb," Oldsey continued. The weight of the tower causes the church's foundations to shudder; the townspeople increasingly come to see Jocelin as a man dangerously driven.

The Spire "is a book about vision and its cost," observed *New York Review of Books* critic Frank Kermode. "It has to do with the motives of art and prayer, the phallus turned spire; with the deceit, as painful to man as to God, involved in structures which are human but have to be divine, such as churches and spires. But because the whole work is a dance of figurative language such an account of it can only be misleading." Characteristic of all Golding's work, *The Spire* can be read on two levels, that of an engrossing story and of a biting analysis of human nature. As Nigel Dennis found in the *New York Times Book Review,* Golding "has always written on these two levels. But *The Spire* will be of particular interest to his admirers because it can also

be read as an exact description of his own artistic method. This consists basically of trying to rise to the heights while keeping himself glued to the ground. Mr. Golding's aspirations climb by clinging to solid objects and working up them like a vine. This is particularly pronounced in [*The Spire*], where every piece of building stone, every stage of scaffolding, every joint and ledge, are used by the author to draw himself up into the blue."

By 1965 Golding appeared to be on his way to continuing acclaim and popular acceptance, but then his output dropped dramatically: for the next fifteen years he produced no novels and only a handful of novellas, short stories, and occasional pieces. Published during this period, *The Pyramid* is a collection of three interrelated novellas detailing the episodic story of a man's existence in the suspiciously named English town of Stilbourne. Generally regarded as one of the writer's weaker efforts, *The Pyramid* proved a shock to "even Golding's most faithful adherents [who] wondered if the book contributed anything to the author's reputation. To some," added Oldsey, "it seemed merely three weak stories jammed together to produce a salable book." *The Pyramid,* however, did have its admirers, among them John Wakeman, writing in the *New York Times Book Review,* who called the work Golding's "first sociological novel. It is certainly more humane, exploratory, and life-size than its predecessors, less Old Testament, more New Testament." To a *Times Literary Supplement* critic the book "will astonish by what it is not. It is not a fable, it does not contain evident allegory, it is not set in a simplified or remote world. It belongs to another, more commonplace tradition of English fiction; it is a low-keyed, realistic novel of growing up in a small town—the sort of book H.G. Wells might have written if he had been more attentive to his style."

The Scorpion God: Three Short Novels, another collection of novellas, was somewhat better received. One *Times Literary Supplement* reviewer, while calling the work "not major Golding," nonetheless found the book "a pure example of Golding's gift. . . . The title story is from Golding's Egyptological side and is set in ancient Egypt. . . . By treating the unfamiliar with familiarity, explaining nothing, he teases the reader into the strange world of the story. It is as brilliant a *tour de force* as *The Inheritors,* if on a smaller scale."

Golding's reemergence within the literary world occurred in 1979 with the publication of *Darkness Visible.* Despite some fifteen years' absence from novel writing, the author "returns unchanged," Samuel Hynes observed in a *Washington Post Book World* article. Golding was seen as "still a moralist, still a maker of parables. To be a moralist you must believe in good and evil, and Golding does; indeed, you might say that the nature of good and evil is his only theme. To be a parable-maker you must believe that moral meaning can be expressed in the very fabric of the story itself, and perhaps that some meanings can only be expressed in this way; and this, too, has always been Golding's way."

The title *Darkness Visible* derives from Milton's description of Hell in *Paradise Lost,* and from the first scenes of the book Golding confronts the reader with images of fire, mutilation, and pain—which he presents in biblical terms. For instance, noted *Commonweal* reviewer Bernard McCabe, the novel's opening describes a small child, "horribly burned, horribly disfigured," "out of the flames at the height of the London blitz. . . . The shattered building he emerges from . . . is called 'a burning bush,' the firemen stare into 'two pillars of lighted smoke,' the child walks with a 'ritual gait,' and he appears to have been 'born from the sheer agony of a burning city.'" The rescued youth, dubbed Matty, the left side of whose face has been left permanently mutilated, grows up to be a religious visionary.

"If Matty is a force for light, he is opposed by a pair of beautiful twins, Toni and Sophy Stanhope," continued Susan Fromberg Schaeffer in her *Chicago Tribune Book World* review of *Darkness Visible.* "These girls, once symbols of innocence in their town, discover the seductive attractions of darkness. Once, say the spirits who visit Matty, the girls were called before them, but they refused to come. Instead, obsessed by the darkness loose in the world, they abandon morality, choosing instead a demonic hedonism that allows them to justify anything, even mass murder." "Inevitably, the two girls will . . . [embark on a] spectacular crime, and just as inevitably, Matty, driven by his spirit guides, must oppose them," summarized *Time* reviewer Peter S. Prescott. "The confrontation, as you may imagine, ends happily for no one."

Some of the ideas explored in 1980's *Rites of Passage* trace back to *Lord of the Flies* and to Golding's view "of man as a fallen being capable of a 'vileness beyond words,'" stated *New Statesman* reviewer Blake Morrison. Set in the early nineteenth century, *Rites of Passage* tells of a voyage from England to Australia as recounted through the shipboard diary of young aristocrat Edmund Talbot. Talbot "sets down a vivid record of the ship and its characters," explained Morrison, listing among these characters "the irascible Captain Anderson. . . , the 'wind-machine Mr Brockleband,' the whorish 'painted Magdalene' called Zenobia, and the meek and ridiculous 'parson,' Mr. Colley, who is satirised as mercilessly as the clerics in [Henry] Fielding's *Joseph Andrews.*" This latter character is the one through which much of the dramatic action in *Rites of Passage* takes place. For Colley, this "country curate . . . this hedge priest," as Golding's Talbot describes him, "is the perfect victim—self-deluding, unworldly, sentimentally devout, priggish, and terrified. Above all he is ignorant of the powerful homosexual streak in his nature that impels him toward the crew and especially toward one stalwart sailor, Billy Rogers," noted Robert Towers in the *New York Review of Books.* Driven by his passion yet torn by doubt, ridiculed and shunned by the other passengers on the ship, Colley literally dies of shame during the voyage.

The author faced his harshest criticism to date with the publication of his 1984 novel, *The Paper Men.* A farce-drama about an aging, successful novelist's conflicts with his pushy, overbearing biographer, *The Paper Men* "tells us that biography is the trade of the con man, a fatuous accomplishment, and the height of impertinence in both meanings of the word," according to London *Times* critic Michael Ratcliff. Unfortunately for Golding, many critics found *The Paper Men* to be sorely lacking in the qualities that distinguish the author's best work. In a typical commentary, Michiko Kakutani wrote in the *New York Times:* "Judging from the tired, petulant tone of [the novel], Mr. Golding would seem to have more in common with his creation than mere appearance—a 'scraggy yellow-white beard, yellow-white thatch and broken-toothed grin.' He, too, seems to have allowed his pessimistic vision of man to curdle his view of the world and to sour his enjoyment of craft."

Golding saw the publication of two more novels before his death in 1993. *Close Quarters,* published in 1987, and *Fire down Below,* published in 1989, complete the trilogy begun with *Rites of Passage.* The first volume in the series, according to Bernard F. Dick in *World Literature Today,* "portrayed a voyage to Australia on a ship that symbolized class-conscious Britain (circa 1810) facing the rise of the middle class. . . . *Close Quarters* continues the voyage, but this time the ship, which is again a symbol of Britain, is near collapse." The story is told through the journal entries of Edmund FitzHenry Talbot, "a well-meaning, somewhat uncertain, slightly pompous officer and gentleman enroute to Sydney and a career in His Majesty's service," as a *Publishers Weekly* reviewer observed. When an inexperienced sailor's error destroys the ship's masts, the crew and passengers are left to ponder their mortality. "As with most of Golding's fiction," David Nokes asserted in the *Times Literary Supplement,* "it is impossible to escape a brooding, restless intensity which turns even the most trivial incident or observation into a metaphysical conceit." As the ship founders and its captives become increasingly agitated, it seems to become a living thing itself, with twigs sprouting from its timbers and discernable creeping movements in its deck planks underfoot. Noting that Golding's "touch never falters," Nokes concluded that the novelist's "attention to details of idiom and setting show a reverence for his craft that would do credit to a master-shipwright. It is in the dark undertow of his metaphors and in the literary ostentation of his allusions that a feeling of strain and contrivance appears. As he steers us through the calms and storms, we are never quite sure whether we are in the safe hands of a master-mariner or under the dangerous spell of an Old Man of the Sea."

New York Times Book Review contributor Robert M. Adams had high hopes for the final book of the trilogy based on his reading of *Close Quarters.* He asserted that the second volume "will not stand up by itself as an independent fiction the way *Rites of Passage* did. . . . But this is the wrong time to pass final judgment on a project, the full dimensions of which can at this point only be guessed. In one sense, the very absence from this novel of strong scenes and sharply defined ironies confirms one's sense of a novelist who is still outward bound, firmly in control of his story, and preparing his strongest effects for the resolutions and revolutions to come." *Los Angeles Times Book Review* critic Richard Hough also found *Close Quarters* unable to stand alone: "This reviewer confesses to being totally mystified by Golding's sequel to *Rites of Passage.* It is neither an allegory, nor a fantasy, nor an adventure, nor even a complete novel, as it has a beginning, a middle (of sorts) but an ending only at some unspecified future date when Golding chooses to complete it, if he does."

The final volume of the trilogy, *Fire down Below,* appeared in 1989. The title refers to a plan for repairing the ship's masts that entails creating iron bands to pull together the split wood preventing the masts from bearing the weight of the sails. Implementing the plan also carries the danger of starting a fire in the hold while forging the iron. *Quill and Quire* reviewer Paul Stuewe described *Fire down Below* as an "ambitious and satisfying novel" and "a rousing finale to an entertaining exercise in historical pastiche." While asserting that neither *Fire down Below* nor *Close Quarters* "works as powerfully and coherently as *Rites of Passage* with its

strongly structured story of a parson who literally died of shame," *New Statesman & Society* contributor W.L. Webb observed that "what keeps one attending still, as to the other ancient mariner's tales of ice mast-high, are [Golding's] magic sea pictures: faces on the quarterdeck masked in moonlight, the eerie 'shadow' that falls behind solid bodies in mist and spray, storm-light and a droning wind, and the sailors swarming out like bees as the wounded ship yaws close to the ice cliffs. There's nothing quite like it in our literature."

"As a novelist, William Golding had the gift of terror," Joseph J. Feeney wrote in an obituary for *America* following the author's death in 1993. "It is not the terror of a quick scare—a ghost, a scream, a slash that catches the breath—but a primal, fearsome sense of human evil and human mystery. . . . Golding was, with Graham Greene, the finest British novelist of [the second half of the twentieth century]. . . . His fellow novelist Malcolm Bradbury memorialized him as 'a writer who was both impishly difficult, and wonderfully monumental,' and a teller of 'primal stories—about the birth of speech, the dawn of evil, the strange sources of art.'" Upon Golding's death his novel *The Double Tongue,* remained incomplete. Set in ancient Greece during the age of Caesar, the novel was published in 1996 in its unfinished form.

BIOGRAPHICAL AND CRITICAL SOURCES:

BOOKS

Anderson, David, *The Tragic Past,* John Knox Press, 1969.

Biles, J. I., and Robert O. Evans, editors, *William Golding: Some Critical Considerations,* University Press of Kentucky, 1979.

Bloom, Harold, *William Golding's Lord of the Flies,* Chelsea House (New York, NY), 1996.

Burgess, Anthony, *The Novel Now: A Guide to Contemporary Fiction,* Norton (New York, NY), 1967.

Contemporary Literary Criticism, Thomson Gale (Detroit, MI), Volume 1, 1973, Volume 2, 1974, Volume 3, 1975, Volume 8, 1978, Volume 10, 1979, Volume 18, 1981, Volume 27, 1984, Volume 58, 1990, Volume 81, 1994.

Dictionary of Literary Biography, Volume 15: *British Novelists, 1930-1959,* Thomson Gale (Detroit, MI), 1983.

Dictionary of Literary Biography Yearbook: 1983, Thomson Gale (Detroit, MI), 1984.

Friedman, Lawrence S., *William Golding,* Continuum (New York, NY), 1993.

Johnson, Arnold, *Of Earth and Darkness: The Novels of William Golding,* University of Missouri Press, 1980.

McCarron, Kevin, *The Coincidence of Opposites: William Golding's Later Fiction,* Sheffield Academic Press, 1995.

Medcalf, Stephen, *William Golding,* Longman (London, England), 1975.

Reilly, Patrick, *Lord of the Flies: Fathers and Sons,* Twayne (New York, NY), 1992.

Ries, Lawrence R., *Wolf Masks: Violence in Contemporary Fiction,* Kennikat Press, 1975.

Siegl, Karin, *The Robinsonade Tradition in Robert Michael Ballantyne's The Coral Island and William Golding's Lord of the Flies,* Edwin Mellen Press, 1996.

Swisher, Clarice, editor, *Readings on Lord of the Flies,* Greenhaven Press, 1997.

PERIODICALS

America, July 31, 1993, pp. 6-7.

Antiquity, December, 1996, Paul Graves-Brown, review of *The Inheritors,* p. 978.

Atlantic, May, 1965; April, 1984.

Booklist, November 15, 1999, review of *Lord of the Flies,* p. 601.

Chicago Tribune, October 7, 1983.

Chicago Tribune Book World, December 30, 1979; October 26, 1980; April 8, 1984.

Children's Literature, 1997, p. 205.

Commentary, January, 1968.

Commonweal, October 25, 1968; September 26, 1980.

Contemporary Review, May, 2002, Jonathan W. Doering, "The Fluctuations of William Golding's Critical Reputation," p. 285.

Critical Quarterly, summer, 1960; autumn, 1962; spring, 1967.

Critical Survey, January, 1997, Kevin McCarron, "'A Simple Enormous Grief': Eighteenth-Century Utopianism and 'Fire down Below,'" p. 36.

Critique, Volume 14, number 2, 1972.

Detroit News, December 16, 1979; January 4, 1981; April 29, 1984.

English Review, February, 2003, p. 34.

Explicator, spring, 1999, Arnold Kruger, review of *Lord of the Flies,* p. 167.

Kenyon Review, autumn, 1957.

Library Journal, November 15, 2003, Michael Rogers, review of *Lord of the Flies,* p. 103.

Life, November 17, 1967.

Listener, October 4, 1979; October 23, 1980; January 5, 1984.

London Magazine, February-March, 1981.

London Review of Books, June 17, 1982.

Los Angeles Times Book Review, November 9, 1980; June 20, 1982; June 3, 1984; June 7, 1987, pp. 3, 6.

New Republic, December 8, 1979; September 13, 1982.

New Statesman, August 2, 1958; April 10, 1964; November 5, 1965; October 12, 1979; October 17, 1980; June 11, 1982.

New Statesman & Society, April 14, 1989, p. 34.

Newsweek, November 5, 1979; October 27, 1980; April 30, 1984.

New Yorker, September 21, 1957.

New York Post, December 17, 1963.

New York Review of Books, April 30, 1964; December 7, 1967; February 24, 1972; December 6, 1979; December 18, 1980.

New York Times, September 1, 1957; November 9, 1979; October 15, 1980; October 7, 1983; March 26, 1984; June 22, 1987.

New York Times Book Review, October 23, 1955; April 19, 1964; November 18, 1979; November 2, 1980; July 11, 1982; May 31, 1987, p. 44.

Publishers Weekly, May 15, 1987, p. 267.

Quill and Quire, July, 1989, p. 47.

Review of English Literature, Volume 1, number 2, 1960, Peter Green, "The World of William Golding," pp. 67-72.

Saturday Review, March 19, 1960.

South Atlantic Quarterly, autumn, 1970.

Southern Review, March, 1976.

Spectator, October 13, 1979.

Time, September 9, 1957; October 13, 1967; October 17, 1983; April 9, 1984; June 8, 1987.

Times (London, England), February 9, 1984; June 11, 1987.

Times Literary Supplement, October 21, 1955; October 23, 1959; June 1, 1967; November 5, 1971; November 23, 1979; October 17, 1980; July 23, 1982; March 2, 1984; June 19, 1987, p. 653.

Twentieth Century Literature, summer, 1982; fall, 2001, p. 391.

Village Voice, November 5, 1979.

Washington Post, July 12, 1982; October 7, 1983; January 12, 1986.

Washington Post Book World, November 4, 1979; November 2, 1980; April 15, 1984.

World Literature Today, spring, 1988, p. 81; autumn, 1989, p. 681; summer, 1996, Carter Kaplan, review of *The Double Tongue,* p. 691.

Yale Review, spring, 1960.

GOLDING, William Gerald
See GOLDING, William

*   *   *

GOODKIND, Terry 1948-

PERSONAL: Born 1948, in Omaha, NE; married; wife's name Jeri. *Hobbies and other interests:* Walking in the woods, painting.

ADDRESSES: Agent—Russell Galen, Scovil, Chichak, Galen Literary Agency, Inc., 381 Park Ave. S., Ste. 1020, New York, NY 10016.

CAREER: Writer. Worked previously as a carpenter, violin-maker, hypnotherapist, wildlife artist, and restorer of rare artifacts.

WRITINGS:

NOVELS; "SWORD OF TRUTH" SERIES

Wizard's First Rule, Tor Books (New York, NY), 1994.
Stone of Tears, Tor Books (New York, NY), 1995.
Blood of the Fold, Tor Books (New York, NY), 1996.
Temple of the Winds, Tor Books (New York, NY), 1997.
Soul of the Fire, Tor Books (New York, NY), 1999.
Faith of the Fallen, Tor Books (New York, NY), 2000.
The Pillars of Creation, Tor Books (New York, NY), 2001.
Debt of Bones, Gollancz (London, England), 2001.
Naked Empire, Tor Books (New York, NY), 2003.
Chainfire, Tor Books (New York, NY), 2005.
Phantom, Tor Books (New York, NY), 2006.

Contributor to anthologies.

ADAPTATIONS: Many of the authors novels have been adapted as audio books, including *Blood of the Fold; Soul of the Fire;* and *The Pillars of Creation* Brilliance Audio, 2001.

SIDELIGHTS: Terry Goodkind's first novel, *Wizard's First Rule,* was sold at auction in 1994 for more than six times the record price ever paid for a first fantasy novel at that time, and it went on to become an international bestseller. Goodkind followed with other novels, all part of a series called "Sword of Truth."

Wizard's First Rule introduces the series' protagonists: a naive and reluctant woods guide named Richard Cypher and the beautiful and enigmatic Kahlan Amnell, a woman who tries to conceal her past. Swept up into a war, Richard is called upon to become the "Seeker" and is given the Sword of Truth. He is also the only one who knows the arcane truths contained in the "Book of Counted Shadows." As *Wizard's First Rule* opens, Richard has just learned of the death of his father, who was slain because he refused to reveal the location of the Book of Counted Shadows. After roaming in the forest, Richard sees Kahlan, who is being pursued by assassins who have driven her from her magical Midlands. Richard rescues Kahlan, and the two then join a wizard called Zedd to stop the Midlands' evil tyrant Darken Rahl. Using the wizard's "first rule," Richard tricks Darken Rahl into opening the wrong Box of Orden, which causes Rahl to disappear into another world and thereby saves humanity.

During the novel, readers are introduced to such secondary characters as the old woman who uses bones to traffic in Underworld magic, an abused child who wants evenly trimmed hair, and Mistress Denna, a scarlet-clad dominatrix who tortures Richard. Though most of the violence is not explicit, there are frequent references to unsavory things, even rape, torture, and ritual murder. According to *Library Journal* contributor Jackie Cassada, *Wizard's First Rule* "offers an intriguing variant on the standard fantasy quest"; Cassada suggested that it will "appeal to mature fantasy aficionados."

In the second book of the series, *Stone of Tears,* a reluctant Richard discovers that Darken Rahl, whom he dispatched to another world, was actually his father—and that the good wizard, Zedd, is his grandfather. Worse still, Rahl's opening the wrong box has made it possible for the Keeper of the Underworld to reach into Richard's world and seize control of the living. To prevent this, Richard has to accept his birthright as a wizard. While he struggles with his gift of magic, Kahlan leads her underage troops against the hardened warriors Rahl left behind, "in one of the most vigorous battle sequences written for a heroine in modern fantasy," commented a *Publishers Weekly* contributor. Again, as in Goodkind's first novel, there are graphic scenes of sex and violence.

In *Blood of the Fold,* Kahlan goes into hiding to avoid execution by her former people, while Richard has to accept his ancestry and take on the rule of D'Hara in order to unite the Midlands to stand against the evil Emperor Jagang. He also has to keep the prophecies from falling into Jagang's hands and save his beloved Kahlan, who, as Roland Green wrote in *Booklist,* "emerges here as one of the outstanding female principals in current fantasy." The fourth book in the series, *Temple of the Winds,* has the protagonists seeking a legendary temple that disappeared three thousand years ago and will aid them in finding a cure for a plague released by the fanatical Imperial Order. A *Publishers Weekly* contributor wrote that readers of this series "will delight in a complex epic fantasy that crackles with vigor and magical derring-do."

Soul of the Fire sets Kahlan and Richard against the Chimes—otherworldly beings capable of destroying magic. The Chimes were accidentally set loose in a desperate moment, and Kahlan and Richard must find a way to contain them once again before they drain the world of all its magical properties. A *Publishers Weekly* contributor praised the author for his "ingenious world-building" evidenced in this novel, as well as his "engaging secondary characters" and "flashes of sly wit." *Faith of the Fallen* finds Kahlan gravely wounded and hidden away in a mountain retreat by Richard. But Richard is soon endangered himself when Nicci, the cruel, beautiful mistress of the evil Emperor Jagang, entices him into bondage. She casts a spell that ensures that any harm befalling her also visits Kahlan. A desperate Kahlan leads an army against the emperor's forces, who are protected by black magic. The story gives Goodkind "an ample canvas for . . . disemboweling, spit roasting and miscellaneous mutilating of men, women, and children," reported another *Publishers Weekly* contributor, who predicted that Goodkind's fans would "revel in vicarious berserker battle scenes," which make an "indelible impact." Reviewing the novel in *Booklist,* Roland Green praised Goodkind for his ability to build "marginally plausible plot elements into a credible story," and even manages to say "something serious about the abuse of guilt and selflessness to motivate social behavior."

In *The Pillars of Creation,* Richard must depose his aging father and compete with his illegitimate brothers for the throne. Violence abounds, as do the political commentaries that marked the other books in the series. A *Publishers Weekly* contributor found the author's exposition somewhat "clumsy," marked by "unlikely coincidences and feeble attempts at humor," yet assured that it will certainly "please Goodkind's legions of fans." Goodkind has added to the "Sword of Truth" canon with *Debt of Bones,* published in 2001. This expanded version of a novella originally published in a fantasy anthology illuminates events that took place before the "Sword of Truth" saga. It is, according to Jackie Cassada in *Library Journal,* a "gracefully written story."

Goodkind's eighth book in the "Sword of Truth" series, *Naked Empire,* finds Richard and Kahlan and their group continuing their battle with Emperor Jagang as they are recruited to help the pacifistic Bandakaran Empire, which has been conquered by the Imperial Order. Fortunately, the empire has a weapon in human form that may be just as powerful as Emperor Jagang. Rick Kleffel, writing on the *Agony Column Book Reviews and Commentary* Web site, noted that the author's incorporation of the philosophies of writer Ayn Rand in the story provides the novel with "a kick that this genre certainly requires." Kleffel went on to note: "Goodkind has a nice way of contracting and expanding time with this prose. The result is that pages are easily whisked aside as scenes of action unfold." Noting that the book can be read as a stand-alone novel by people who are not familiar with the series, Kleffel added: "Goodkind writes with enough passion to provide an emotional payoff."

Chainfire, unlike its predecessors, ends as a cliffhanger. When Richard awakes to find Khalan missing, his group thinks he's hallucinating. No one seems to know who Khalan is. In the meantime, Richard is being hunted by an amorphous magical creature created by Jagang. Since the divide between the old and new world has fallen, prophecies indicate that unless Richard is able to lead the final battle against Jagang, the emperor will prevail. The story "is an excellent beginning to a trilogy that may prove to be an exciting conclusion to the 'Sword of Truth' series" wrote Gary Romero in an article posted on the *Fantastic Reviews* Web site. Throughout the review, Romero noted that not only has the story in the series evolved, but so, too, has Goodkind's craft. Goodkind's "ability to bring his world to light has gotten much stronger," he stated. Romero ultimately concluded that "waiting for the next book will not be easy for any Terry Goodkind fan."

BIOGRAPHICAL AND CRITICAL SOURCES:

BOOKS

St. James Guide to Fantasy Writers, St. James Press (Detroit, MI), 1996.

PERIODICALS

Bangor Daily News, November, 1995, Lynn Flewelling, interview with Terry Goodkind.

Booklist, September 1, 1994, Roland Green, review of *Wizard's First Rule,* p. 28; October 1, 1995, Roland Green, review of *Stone of Tears,* p. 254; November 15, 1996, Roland Green, review of *Blood of the Fold,* p. 576; November 1, 1997, Roland Green, review of *Temple of the Winds,* p. 576; May 1, 1999, review of *Soul of the Fire,* p. 1582; February 15, 2000, Whitney Scott, review of *Blood of the Fold,* p. 1128; August, 2000, Roland Green, review of *Faith of the Fallen,* p. 2073.

Half Moon Bay Review, October 23, 1996, Stacy Trevenon, "Top Fantasy Author Terry Goodkind Visits."

Kirkus Reviews, October 1, 1996, review of *Blood of the Fold,* p. 1434; March 1, 1999, review of *Soul of the Fire,* p. 340.

Kliatt, January, 1999, review of *Temple of the Winds,* p. 16; March, 2003, Ginger Armstrong, review of *The Pillars of Creation,* p. 34.

Library Journal, June, 1994, Carolyn Cushman, review of *Wizard's First Rule,* p. 35; September 15, 1994, Jackie Cassada, review of *Wizard's First Rule,* p. 94; October 15, 1995, Jackie Cassada, review of *Stone of Tears,* p. 91; May 15, 1999, Jackie Cassada, review of *Soul of the Fire,* p. 131; September 15, 1999, December, 2001, Jackie Cassada, review of *Debt of Bones,* p. 181; February 15, 2004, Barbara Perkins, review of *Naked Empire,* p. 179.

Publishers Weekly, August 29, 1994, review of *Wizard's First Rule,* p. 65; September 25, 1995, review of *Stone of Tears,* p. 48; October 7, 1996, review of *Blood of the Fold,* p. 66; October 13, 1997, review of *Temple of the Winds,* p. 60; April 19, 1999, review of *Soul of the Fire,* p. 66; July 24, 2000, review of *Faith of the Fallen,* p. 73; November 19, 2001, "December Publications," p. 52; December 3, 2001, review of *The Pillars of Creation,* p. 45; December 3, 2001, review of *The Pillars of Creation,* p. 45; December 17, 2001, John F. Baker, "The Selling of Goodkind," p. 13; August 4, 2003, Daisy Maryles, "Building Momentum," briefly discusses author's book *Naked Empire,* p. 18.

Voice of Youth Advocates, February, 1995, Elaine M. McGuire, review of *Wizard's First Rule,* p. 347; June, 1996, Elaine M. McGuire, review of *Stone of Tears,* p. 107; April, 1997, review of *Stone of Tears,* p. 12; April, 2002, review of *The Voice of Youth Advocates,* p. 51.

ONLINE

Agony Column Book Reviews and Commentary, http://trashotron.com/agony/ (March 8, 2006), Rick Kleffel, review of *Naked Empire.*

Fantastic Reviews, http://www.geocities.com/fantasticreviews/ (March 14, 2006), Gary Romero, review of *Chainfire.*

Terry Goodkind Home Page, http://www.terrygoodkind.com/ (March 8, 2006).

*   *   *

GORDIMER, Nadine 1923-

PERSONAL: Born November 20, 1923, in Springs, Transvaal, South Africa; daughter of Isidore (a jeweler) and Nan (Myers) Gordimer; married Gerald Gavronsky, March 6, 1949 (divorced, 1952); married Reinhold H. Cassirer (owner and director of art gallery; deceased), January 29, 1954; children: (first marriage) Oriane Taramasco; (second marriage) Hugo, one stepdaughter. *Education:* Attended private schools and the University of the Witwatersrand.

ADDRESSES: Home—Johannesburg, South Africa. *Agent*—Farrar, Straus & Giroux, 19 Union Square W., New York, NY 10003.

CAREER: Writer. Ford Foundation visiting professor, under auspices of Institute of Contemporary Arts, Washington, DC, 1961; lecturer, Hopwood Awards, University of Michigan, Ann Arbor, 1970; writer in residence, American Academy in Rome, 1984; has also lectured and taught writing at Harvard, Princeton, Northwestern, Columbia, and Tulane universities; has been goodwill ambassador of the United Nations Development Programme.

MEMBER: International PEN (vice president), Congress of South African Writers, Royal Society of Literature, American Academy of Arts and Sciences (honorary member), American Academy of Literature and Arts (honorary member).

AWARDS, HONORS: W.H. Smith and Son Commonwealth Literary Award, 1961, for short story collection *Friday's Footprint and Other Stories;* Thomas Pringle Award, English Academy of South Africa, 1969; James Tait Black Memorial Prize, 1973, for *A Guest of Honour;* Booker Prize for Fiction, National Book League, 1974, for *The Conservationist;* Grand Aigle d'Or, 1975; CNA awards, 1974, 1979, 1981, and 1991; Neil Gunn fellowship, Scottish Arts Council, 1981; Commonwealth Award for Distinguished Service in Literature, 1981; Modern Language Association of America award,

1982; Nelly Sachs Prize, 1985; Premio Malaparte, 1986; Bennett Award, *Hudson Review,* 1986; Benson Medal, 1990; Commandeur de l'Ordre des Arts et des Lettres (France), 1991; Nobel Prize for literature, Nobel Foundation, 1991; rejected candidacy for Orange Award in 1998 because the award was restricted to women writers; Booker Prize long-list nomination for *The Pickup,* 2001; Commonwealth Writers Prize, Africa Region, best book category for *The Pickup.* Awarded honorary degrees from University of Leuven, 1980, Smith College, City College of the City University of New York, and Mount Holyoke College, all 1985, Harvard University, Columbia University, Yale University, and York University, England, 1987, New School for Social Research, 1988, University of the Witwatersrand, South Africa, University of Cape Town, South Africa, University of Cape Town, South Africa, Cambridge University, 1991, Oxford University, 1994, University of Durban-Westville, and Ben Gurion University, 1996.

WRITINGS:

NOVELS

The Lying Days, Simon & Schuster (New York, NY), 1953, published with new introduction by Paul Bailey, Virago (New York, NY), 1983.

A World of Strangers, Simon & Schuster (New York, NY), 1958.

Occasion for Loving, Viking (New York, NY), 1963, published with new introduction by Paul Bailey, Virago (New York, NY), 1983.

The Late Bourgeois World, Viking (New York, NY), 1966.

A Guest of Honour, Viking (New York, NY), 1970.

The Conservationist, J. Cape (London, England), 1974, Viking (New York, NY), 1975.

Burger's Daughter, Viking (New York, NY), 1979.

July's People, Viking (New York, NY), 1981.

A Sport of Nature (Book-of-the-Month Club dual selection), Knopf (New York, NY), 1987.

My Son's Story, Farrar, Straus & Giroux (New York, NY), 1990.

None to Accompany Me, Farrar, Straus & Giroux (New York, NY), 1994.

Harald, Claudia, and Their Son Duncan, Bloomsbury (New York, NY), 1996.

The House Gun, Farrar, Straus (New York, NY), 1998.

The Pickup, Bloomsbury (New York, NY), 2001.

Get a Life, Farrar, Straus and Giroux (New York, NY), 2005.

SHORT STORIES

Face to Face (also see below), Silver Leaf Books (Johannesburg, South Africa), 1949.

The Soft Voice of the Serpent and Other Stories (contains many stories previously published in *Face to Face*), Simon & Schuster (New York, NY), 1952.

Six Feet of the Country (also see below), Simon & Schuster (New York, NY), 1956.

Friday's Footprint and Other Stories, Viking (New York, NY), 1960.

Not for Publication and Other Stories, Viking (New York, NY), 1965.

Livingstone's Companions, Viking (New York, NY), 1971.

Selected Stories (contains stories from previously published collections), Viking (New York, NY), 1975, also published as *No Place Like: Selected Stories,* Penguin (London, England), 1978.

Some Monday for Sure, Heinemann Educational (London, England), 1976.

A Soldier's Embrace, Viking (New York, NY), 1980.

Town and Country Lovers, Sylvester & Orphanos (Los Angeles, CA), 1980.

Six Feet of the Country (contains stories from previously published collections selected for television series of same title), Penguin (New York, NY), 1982.

Something Out There, Viking (New York, NY), 1984.

Reflections of South Africa: Short Stories, Systime, 1986.

Crimes of Conscience: Selected Short Stories, Heinemann, 1991.

Jump and Other Stories, Farrar, Straus (New York, NY), 1991.

Why Haven't You Written?: Selected Stories, 1950-1972, Viking (New York, NY), 1993.

Loot: And Other Stories, Farrar, Straus (New York, NY), 2003.

OTHER

(Compiler and editor, with Lionel Abrahams) *South African Writing Today,* Penguin (New York, NY), 1967.

African Literature: The Lectures Given on This Theme at the University of Cape Town's Public Summer School, February, 1972, Board of Extra Mural Studies, University of Cape Town (Cape Town, South Africa), 1972.

The Black Interpreters: Notes on African Writing, Spro-Cas/Ravan (Johannesburg, South Africa), 1973.

On the Mines, photographs by David Goldblatt, C. Struik (Cape Town, South Africa), 1973.

(Author of appreciation) *Kurt Jobst: Goldsmith and Silversmith; Art Metal Worker,* G. Bakker (Johannesburg, South Africa), 1979.

(With others) *What Happened to "Burger's Daughter"; or, How South African Censorship Works,* Taurus (Johannesburg, South Africa), 1980.

Lifetimes under Apartheid, photographs by David Goldblatt, Knopf (New York, NY), 1986.

The Essential Gesture: Writing, Politics and Places, edited and introduced by Stephen Clingman, Knopf (New York, NY), 1988.

(With Hugo Cassirer) *Berlin and Johannesburg: The Wall and The Colour Bar,* television documentary film.

Three in a Bed: Fiction, Morals, and Politics, Bennington College (Bennington, VT), 1991.

(With Ruth Weiss) *Zimbabwe and the New Elite,* Tauris (Johannesburg, South Africa), 1993.

Writing and Being: The Charles Eliot Norton Lectures, Harvard University Press (Cambridge, MA), 1995.

Living in Hope and History: Notes from Our Century, Farrar, Straus (New York, NY), 1999.

(Editor) *Telling Tales,* Picador (New York, NY), 2004.

Also author of television plays and documentaries, including *A Terrible Chemistry,* 1981, *Choosing for Justice: Allan Boesak,* with Hugo Cassirer, 1985, *Country Lovers, A Chip of Glass Ruby, Praise,* and *Oral History,* all part of *The Gordimer Stories* series adapted from stories of the same title, 1985. Contributor to periodicals, including *Atlantic, Encounter, Granta, Harper's, Holiday, Kenyon Review, Mother Jones, New Yorker, Paris Review,* and *Playboy. New York Times,* syndicated columnist, January, 2003—. Gordimer's novels, short stories, and essays have been translated into twenty-five languages and are available in audio cassette form.

Indiana University, Lilly Library, houses a collection of Gordimer's papers.

ADAPTATIONS: Screenplays for four of the seven television dramas based on her own short stories, collectively titled *The Gordimer Stories,* 1981-82; *City Lovers,* based on Gordimer's short story of the same title, was filmed by TeleCulture Inc./TelePool in South Africa in 1982.

SIDELIGHTS: "Nadine Gordimer has become, in the whole solid body of her work, the literary voice and conscience of her society," declared Maxwell Geismar in the *Saturday Review.* In numerous novels, short stories, and essays, she has written of her South African homeland and its apartheid government—under which its blacks, coloreds, and whites suffered for nearly half a century. "This writer . . . has made palpable the pernicious, pervasive character of that country's race laws, which not only deny basic rights to most people but poison many relationships," maintained Miriam Berkley in *Publishers Weekly.* Others, like Judith Chettle of the *World and I,* were more critical, noting that Gordimer "has adroitly over the years written books that drew world attention to the political situation in South Africa. Never jailed or exiled (though some books were briefly banned in the 1970s), Gordimer came to be regarded as the preeminent recorder of life under apartheid. Books like *Burger's Daughter* and *The Conservationist* gained her an international audience," but adding the caveat: "In these books, Gordimer astutely described the liberal politics of white and mostly English-speaking South Africa. She was much less incisive in dealing with those Afrikaners supporting the regime and was least successful in describing the blacks."

However, Gordimer's insight, integrity, and compassion inspire critical admiration among many. "She has mapped out the social, political and emotional geography of that troubled land with extraordinary passion and precision," commented Michiko Kakutani of the *New York Times,* observing in a later essay that "taken chronologically, her work not only reflects her own evolving political consciousness and maturation as an artist—an early lyricism has given way to an increased preoccupation with ideas and social issues—but it also charts changes in South Africa's social climate." One of only nine women so recognized, she was honored with the Nobel Prize in literature for her novels in 1991—a sign of the esteem in which the literary world holds her work.

When she began, Gordimer was only one of a number of novelists working in South Africa after World War II. "Some of the writers, like [Alan] Paton, turned to nonfiction or political work; even more, most notably [Peter] Abrahams and Dan Jacobson, expatriated," explained John Cooke in *The Novels of Nadine Gordimer: Private Lives/Public Landscapes.* "By the early sixties Gordimer was almost the only member of the postwar group to continue producing fiction from within the country. That she should be the survivor was not altogether surprising, for she was in essential ways more a product of South Africa than her contemporaries. She attended university at home, not in England as colonial writers so regularly have; she did not travel abroad until she was thirty."

"Gordimer seemed particularly unsuited to prosper as a writer in her arid land," Cooke continued, "because of the disjunction between her temperament and the situation she confronted. More than any of her contemporaries, Gordimer was initially drawn to private themes." Her novels and short stories are, at bottom, about complicated individuals caught in awkward or impossibly complex situations. "Her writing [is] so subtle that it forces readers to find their way back from her works into her mind," remarked Firdaus Kanga in the *Times Literary Supplement;* "her characters are powerful precisely because you cannot sum them up in a line or even a page."

Much of Gordimer's fiction focuses upon white middle-class characters. It frequently depicts what Geismar described as "a terrified white consciousness in the midst of a mysterious and ominous sea of black humanity." But the "enduring subject" of her writing has been "the consequences of apartheid on the daily lives of men and women, the distortions it produces in relationships among both blacks and whites," noted Kakutani. Her first novel, *The Lying Days,* is drawn from her personal experience and tells about a young woman who comes into contact with the effects of apartheid when she has an affair with a social worker. *A World of Strangers* is about the efforts of a British writer to bring together his white intellectual friends and his black African intellectual friends. In *Burger's Daughter,* considered by some to be her best novel, Gordimer examines white ambivalence about apartheid in the person of Rosa, who can no longer sustain the antiapartheid cause of her imprisoned Afrikaner father after his death. This work, like several others before it, was banned in South Africa, but the ban was quickly removed due to the critical attention the novel had attracted in the West. The story of the banning and unbanning of *Burger's Daughter* is related in *What Happened to "Burger's Daughter"; or, How South African Censorship Works,* published in 1980.

Both *The Lying Days* and *A World of Strangers* end with a note of hope for a better future for South Africans. Gordimer's later novels, however, take a more pessimistic tone. *A Guest of Honour,* which won the James Tait Black Memorial Prize in 1973, tells of the return of Colonel James Bray to his African homeland. Bray had been exiled by the previous government for his espousal of black revolutionary ideology. Upon his return, however, Bray discovers that the new revolutionary government is just as corrupt and self-interested as the previous government was. When he speaks out publicly against the new government, it targets him for assassination. *The Conservationist,* awarded the Booker

Prize (England's highest literary honor) the following year, tells about the uneasy relationship between a white landowner and black squatters who have settled on his estate, bringing up the question of "whose land is it anyway?" "Beginning with *A Guest of Honour,*" Cooke concluded, "Gordimer's novels are informed by a tension between . . . two impulses: she at once observes her world from without and envisions it from within. Through this double process, the fruit of her long apprenticeship, Gordimer creates masterful forms and shapes despite the 'low cultural rainfall' of her world."

These forms and shapes also appear in Gordimer's short fiction. *Jump and Other Stories*—published shortly before the author received the Nobel Prize—contains stories that approach her favorite themes in a variety of ways. She tells about a white man out for a jog, who is caught up in a black gang-killing and is saved by a black woman who shelters him. "A single truth is witnessed," wrote John Edgar Wideman in the *New York Times Book Review,* "a truth somehow missing in most fiction by white Americans that purports to examine our national life. No matter how removed one feels oneself from the fray, race and race relations lie at the heart of the intimate, perplexing questions we need to ask of ourselves: Where have I been? Where am I going? Who am I?" "Ms. Gordimer can be a merciless judge and jury," Wideman concluded. "Her portraits obtain a Vermeer-like precision, accurate and remorseless, with no room for hope, for self-delusion, no room even for the small vanities of ego and self-regard that allow us to proceed sometimes as if at least our intentions are honorable."

The Swedish Academy had considered Gordimer as a Nobel Prize nominee for years before she finally received the award in 1991. Several commentators, while congratulating her on her accomplishment, noted that the struggle against apartheid remained unfinished. "On the day of the announcement that Nadine Gordimer would receive the 1991 Nobel Prize for literature, a tribute to the complex and intimate stories she has written about racism's toll on people's lives in her native South Africa," wrote Esther B. Fein in the *New York Times,* "Nelson Mandela still did not have the right to vote." Mandela had been released from his political prison, but the basic tenets of apartheid prevented him from exercising the rights of citizenship. When South African president F.W. De Klerk announced that the policy of separation would end, reviewers wondered where the Nobel laureate would turn her attention. "With apartheid finally ended," Diana Jean Schemo declared in the *New York Times,* "the novelist waxes exultant over a sense of renewal in her homeland; the urgency is gone, but the turn of mind remains."

"For the whole of her literary career, Gordimer has grappled with the intricacies and distortions of life under a certain political system, a specific regime of oppression," noted Diane Simon in the *Nation*. With the ending of apartheid and the enfranchisement of South African blacks, critics scanned Gordimer's fiction for evidence of how this supremely political writer's focus would change. Her novel, *None to Accompany Me*, looks at the fortunes of two families—one black, one white—as they move into the new, postapartheid, era. "The repressions, the curle laws and persecutions, the campaigns of resistance, the exiles, the detentions, the bannings and brutalities—all these horrors of the past are finished," observed Sonya Rudikoff in the book *African Writers*, continuing: "What remains is the damage done to society and to personal relations." "*None to Accompany Me* is a sustaining achievement, proving Gordimer once again a lucid witness to her country's transformation and a formidable interpreter of the inner self," Anne Whitehouse commented in *Tribune Books*. While some viewed this work as a step away from the public themes of her earlier novels and short stories, Simon observed that all of Gordimer's main characters are actively involved in the political life of the new South Africa.

By contrast, Gordimer's second postapartheid novel, *The House Gun*, while it also explores the relationships between blacks and whites in the newly transformed South Africa, is arguably more concerned with the politicization of her characters' personal lives. The Lindegards are an affluent white couple who learn that their only son, Duncan, has committed a murder using a gun intended to protect the house from thieves. They hire a black lawyer to represent him, and begin the painful process of emerging out of the sheltered lives they have created. Through these events, Gordimer explores the question, "Does a violent society provoke violence in nonviolent individuals?" "The story deftly brings home a tricky truth," remarked Walter Kirn in *Time*: "Peace can be as perilous as war, and even more confusing to negotiate," especially when it is a peace that follows bitter internal strife. The novel's other underlying question, which asks if the level of violence in South Africa is higher than in Europe because of its large black population or because of the way blacks have long been treated by racist whites, is the "question that haunts Gordimer's novel," according to Jack Miles in the *New York Times Book Review*. Miles described *House Gun* as an "elegantly conceived, flawlessly executed novel." While Michiko Kakutani in the *New York Times* dubbed the novel "little more than a courtroom thriller, dressed up with some clumsy allusions to apartheid's legacy of violence and the uses and misuses of freedom," *Library*

Journal reviewer Edward B. St. John contended that *House Gun* is "much more ambitious" than the courtroom dramas of Scott Turow or John Grisham, adding that "Gordimer's trademark prose style . . . seems especially well suited to capturing the moral ambiguities of South African life." "Gordimer's great fiction has always personalized the political," observed Hazel Rochman in *Booklist*, but in this novel, the author "moves in the opposite direction, taking the personal intimacy of family, friend, and lover into the glare of the public sphere."

Gordimer's turn of mind reaches out in two directions: politically, she follows the fortunes of other first-class "third-world" writers such as Egyptian Naguib Mahfouz, Nigerian Chinua Achebe, and Israeli Amos Oz. "Her attention is turned on writers whose work seems most engaged in the questions that have absorbed her for much of her life," Schemo wrote, "how justice, wealth, power and freedom are parceled out in a society, and the repercussions for its people." In the essays collected in *Living in Hope and History: Notes from Our Century*, the author addresses politics and morals, writers and culture, and first of all, life as a white liberal in South Africa. Here especially, Gordimer "speaks with the authority of the insider," according to Hazel Rochman in *Booklist*, "bearing witness to what it has been like, as a white citizen and writer, to live in Johannesburg" during the years of apartheid and through the upheavals that accompanied the transition to a postapartheid regime. Critics noted that Gordimer herself has frequently called her fiction more truthful than her nonfiction, and agreed that, as a reviewer for *Publishers Weekly* claimed, the pieces found in *Living in Hope and History* "shouldn't be expected to attain the nuance and depth of Gordimer's best fiction, but some of them are devastating."

Another novel, *The Pickup*, and a volume of short stories, *Loot: and Other Stories*, followed, pursuing further the complexity of individual struggles with racial and cultural differences in racist societies. A *Booklist* reviewer called *The Pickup* "a compelling, unsentimental exploration of the paradox of privilege." Robert Ross in the *World and I* praised the novel, which, he noted, was published on the eve of the fall of the Twin Towers in New York: "underneath what might appear a less gloomy treatment of human experience, there lies a muted but strong concern with the dispossessed: those trapped in economic strife, the victims of racism, those affected by official corruption, and those on the move, facing the obstacles of immigration." The setting is that a young, disaffected woman from a wealthy white family meets an illegal Arab immigrant when her car breaks down. She becomes enthralled with the (to her) simplicity and connectedness of the home he is trying to escape, while he longs for the (to him) glittering cosmopolitan ease of the surroundings she is running from. Their love affair could be seen as a lighter side of Gordimer—a cross-cultural romance or a South African *Romeo and Juliet,* as several critics have observed—or, as Ross suggested, as an exploration of the contradictions that appear when one who has too much material ease and too little meaning in her life intertwines with another yearning towards the life she abhors. Gordon Houser, in the *Christian Century,* pointed out that in this novel Gordimer again shows that she is looking further into the world for her themes following the end of apartheid. He wrote, Gordimer "moves outward to the complexities of the global community, where people seek refuge from poverty and hopelessness by going to more prosperous countries. She juxtaposes Abdul's desperate desire to escape economic chaos with Julie's desire for stability and a loving family." An *Entertainment Weekly* reviewer commented, "Gordimer, deploying the finest kind of irony and attuned to the tiniest gestures, spins an eloquent tale about the ways in which romance ratifies self-image."

Loot, includes both "fragments of crystallized insight" and three longer pieces, one almost a novella, according to Chettle. Gordimer, remarked *Spectator*'s Sebastian Smee, "still displays a natural short-story writer's feeling for the intimate moments and quiet epiphanies that can alter people's lives." He also, however, found her writing style to be "lazily allusive and unkempt" and reading the stories "a pleasureless slog" because of her convoluted prose, but he recommended parts of "Karma," "Mission Statement," and "Generation Gap," a tale about the break-up of a marriage from the point of view of the grown-up children. Carmen Callil in the *New Statesman,* however, argued that "you have to sit up straight to read her, open your mind, extend your understanding, watch every word. It's worth it." She continued, "In 'Mission Statement', a middle-aged Englishwoman, Roberta Blayne, who works for an international aid agency of the Clare Short kind, falls into an affair with the deputy director of land affairs, Gladwell Shadrack Chabruma, in some unnamed African state, the sort of country that has old hospitals 'still known by the name of a deceased English Queen.' Gordimer can capture bodies, black and white, in a word, and sexual attraction in a sentence, as when Roberta sees her lover's torso and its 'gleaming beauty, sweat-painted, of perfectly formed muscle, the double path below pectorals, left and right, of smooth ribbing beneath lithe skin. Black. Simply Black.' The ironic ending of their love affair is perfectly conceived." Callil

noted: "In Gordimer's Africa, too much has happened for easy endings. Her Europeans, her whites, are as soulless as their predecessors. What followed apartheid, after all, was AIDS: today's relics of 'imperial compassion' tend what they have produced—the AIDS children, the 'rags of flesh and bone,' 'the new-born-to-die.'" "The Gordimer of these stories inhabits a stern world."

Chettle was one critic who saw Gordimer struggling to find a new voice since the fall of apartheid. She stated: "While Gordimer's [work] will continue to be read as distilled portraits of a particular society that behaved in a particular way at a particular time, her characters have often been more articulate vehicles for ideas than vivid creations who strut their stuff off the pages and into our hearts." This presents, in Chettle's view, a problem: "Gordimer . . . has valiantly, if with mixed success, been trying to make the necessary adjustments. Her latest book, *Loot,* a collection of ten short stories, exemplifies these adjustments as it describes moments of transition when lives are changed by insight or action. The stories typically reflect both Gordimer's weaknesses and strengths. She has a reporter's eye for the defining detail, but the characters themselves are often disembodied shades, held hostage to the workings out of the authorial intellect rather than following the wayward devices of their own hearts." She especially found the long story, "Karma" a "long mediation (more an intellectual than spiritual examination)." However, Chettle engagingly described stories whose characters "all share moments of abrupt change, signaled often by the acquisition of what is suddenly, or long, desired." Callil, though, found "Karma" to be "as good as anything she has written. Complex and inventive, it depicts worlds within worlds, yet each life recounted is vividly rooted in family and neighbourhood. The history and stories of her country and ours weave in and out of each episode as a wandering soul is born, again and again, sometimes female, sometimes male (it is always better to be male), reaching eventually a view that seems to be Gordimer's own. For our misdeeds, in whatever human form we take, 'we are condemned to live forever.' And so the villainy continues."

In 2004 Gordimer served as sole editor of the *Telling Tales* anthology. The collection contains short stories from 21 well-known international writers, and all profits are donated to help fight HIV/AIDS in South Africa. Gordimer contributed "The Ultimate Safari," which is "a searing, unforgettable account of a desperate refugee child hiding . . . in a famous game park," according to Hazel Rochman in *Booklist.*

The following year, Gordimer once again focused her attention on novels, publishing *Get a Life.* In the story,

Paul Bannerman, an ecologist fighting the development of a dam and nuclear reactor in South Africa, is diagnosed with throat cancer. He stays with his parents until risks associated with radiation therapy subside. As he recovers, he reflects on his troubled marriage to Berenice, or Benni, an advertising executive who works for companies that thwart his land preservation efforts. "Paul's doubts simply trail off in the novel's second half, when Gordimer shifts her focus to escalating troubles between Paul's parents," noted Jennifer Reese in *Entertainment Weekly*. Digby Durrant, reviewing the book for *Spectator,* called it "a difficult read." Durrant continued, "It's as if to write a simple sentence is an error of taste or sloppy thinking. Gordimer strains too hard for an originality a writer of her stature doesn't need" A *Publishers Weekly* reviewer felt Gordimer's effort was "a lacerating novel, one in which conflicted professional and domestic lives are played for all their contradictory possibility."

Gordimer herself once told interviewer Beth Austin in the *Chicago Tribune:* "I began to write, I think, out of the real source of all art, and that is out of a sense of wonderment about life, and a sense of trying to make sense out of the mystery of life. That hasn't changed in all the years that I've been writing. That is the starting point of everything that I write."

BIOGRAPHICAL AND CRITICAL SOURCES:

BOOKS

Bardolph, Jacqueline, editor, *Telling Stories: Postcolonial Short Fiction in English,* Rodopi (Amsterdam, Netherlands), 2001.

Bazin, Nancy Topping, and Marilyn Dallman Seymour, editors, *Conversations with Nadine Gordimer,* University Press of Mississippi (Jackson, MS), 1990.

Brodsky, Joseph, *New Censors: Nadine Gordimer and Others on Publishing Now,* Cassell Academic, 1996.

Brownley, Martine Watson, *Deferrals of Domain: Contemporary Women Novelists and the State,* St. Martin's Press (New York, NY), 2000.

Chapman, Michael, editor, *The Drum Decade: Stories from the 1950s,* University of Natal Press (Pietermaritzburg, South Africa), 1989.

Clingman, Stephen, *The Novels of Nadine Gordimer: History from the Inside,* University of Massachusetts Press (Amherst, MA), 1992.

Cooke, John, *The Novels of Nadine Gordimer: Private Lives/Public Landscapes,* Louisiana State University (Baton Rouge, LA), 1985.

Cox, C. Brian, editor, *African Writers,* Scribner (New York, NY), 1997, pp. 277- 290.

Driver, Dorothy, Ann Dry, Craig MacKenzie, and John Read, *Nadine Gordimer: A Bibliography of Primary and Secondary Sources, 1937-1992,* Hans Zell, 1994.

Dubbeld, Catherine Elizabeth, *Reflecting Apartheid: South African Short Stories in English with Socio-Political Themes, 1960-1987: A Select and Annotated Bibliography,* South African Institute of International Affairs, 1990.

Ettin, Andrew Vogel, *Betrayals of the Body Politic: The Literary Commitments of Nadine Gordimer,* University Press of Virginia (Charlottesville, VA), 1993.

Foster, John Burt, Jr., and Wayne Jeffrey Froman, editors, *Thresholds of Western Culture: Identity, Postcoloniality, Transnationalism.* Continuum (New York, NY), 2002.

Hardwick, Elizabeth, *Sight Readings,* 1998.

Head, Dominic, *Nadine Gordimer,* Cambridge University Press (New York, NY), 1995.

Kamm, Antony, *Biographical Companion to Literature in English,* Scarecrow (Lanham, MD), 1997, pp. 215-216.

King, Bruce, editor, *The Later Fiction of Nadine Gordimer,* St. Martin's Press (New York, NY), 1993.

Lentricchia, Frank, and Andrew DuBois, editors, *Close Reading: The Reader,* Duke University Press (Durham, NC), 2003.

Mwaria, Cheryl B., Silvia Federici, and Joseph McLaren, editors, *African Visions: Literary Images, Political Change, and Social Struggle in Contemporary Africa.* Praeger (Westport, CT), 2000.

Nell, Racilia Jilian, *Nadine Gordimer: Novelist and Short Story Writer: A Bibliography of Her Works and Selected Criticism,* University of the Witwatersrand, 1964.

Newman, Judie, *Nadine Gordimer,* Routledge (New York, NY), 1990.

Newman, Judie, editor, *Nadine Gordimer's "Burger's Daughter": A Casebook,* Oxford University Press (New York, NY), 2003.

Nyman, Jopi, and John A. Stotesbury, editors, *Postcolonialism and Cultural Resistance,* Faculty of Humanities, University of Joensuu (Joensuu, Finland), 1999.

Smith, Rowland, editor, *Critical Essays on Nadine Gordimer,* G.K. Hall (Boston, MA), 1990.

Wagner, Kathrin, *Rereading Nadine Gordimer,* Indiana University Press (Bloomington, IN), 1994.

Yelin, Louise, *From the Margins of Empire: Christina Stead, Doris Lessing, Nadine Gordimer,* Cornell University Press (Ithaca, NY), 1998.

Yousaf, Nahem, editor, *Apartheid Narratives,* Rodopi (Amsterdam, Netherlands), 2001.

PERIODICALS

Africa News Service, July 19, 2001, p. 1008200u3067.

Alternation: Journal of the Centre for the Study of Southern African Literature and Languages, 2000, p. 29.

America, October 31, 1981, p. 264; December 15, 1984, p. 410; November 18, 1989, p. 361; June 6, 1992, p. 518; December 12, 1998, p. 15.

Anglophonia: French Journal of English Studies, 2000, p. 179.

Atlanta Journal- Constitution, November 28, 1999, p. K8; October 7, 2001, p. F5.

Atlantic Monthly, January, 1960; October, 1994, p. 131; February, 1998.

Atlas, January, 1980, p. 30.

AUMLA: Journal of the Australasian Universities Language and Literature Association, November, 2001, p. 135.

Austin American- Statesman, January 25, 1998, p. D6.

B.A.S.: British and American Studies/Revista de Studii Britanice si Americane, 1999, p. 73; 2001, p. 71.

Booklist, October 1, 1958; January 10, 1960; August, 1992, p. 2022; June 1, 1994, p. 1862; September 15, 1995, p. 129; October 15, 1997, p. 362; August, 1999, p. 2025; September 1, 1999, p. 57; July 2001, p. 1949; January 1, 2002, p. 761; January 1, 2003, p. 807; October 1, 2004, Hazel Rochman, review of *Telling Tales,* p. 312.

Boston Herald, May 18, 2003, p. 040.

Bulletin of Bibliography, Volume 36, 1979; Volume 42, number 1, 1985.

Business Week, September 8, 1980, p. 17.

Canadian Forum, February, 1984, p. 17; April, 1989, p. 27.

Cardozo Studies in Law and Literature, fall, 2001, p. 299.

Chicago Sunday Tribune, September 21, 1958.

Chicago Tribune, May 18, 1980; December 7, 1986; November 12, 1987; October 4, 1991.

Chicago Tribune Book World, September 9, 1979; June 7, 1981; July 29, 1984; December 11, 1988, pp. 8-9; September 25, 1994, section 14, pp. 1, 9.

Christian Century, May 26, 1982, p. 642; Nov 21, 2001, p. 33.

Christian Science Monitor, January 10, 1963; November 4, 1971; May 19, 1975; September 10, 1979.

CLA Journal, December 2001, p. 187.

Commentary, February, 1992, p. 51.

Commonweal, October 23, 1953; July 9, 1965; November 4, 1966; December 5, 1980, p. 702; November 30, 1984, pp. 662, 667-668; March 10, 1989, p. 150.

Contemporary Literature, spring, 2000, p. 554.

Cosmopolitan, August, 1981, p. 24.

Courier-Mail (Brisbane, Australia), March 18, 2000, p. W09; December 29, 2001, p. M05.

Critical Survey, 1999, p. 64.

Critique: Studies in Contemporary Fiction, winter, 1998, p. 115; winter, 1999, p. 161.

Current Writing: Text and Reception in Southern Africa, April, 2001, p. 49.

Daily Telegraph (London, England), September 15, 2001; May 31, 2003, p. 02; June 7, 2003, p. 09.

Daily Telegraph (Surry Hills, Australia), March 28, 1998, p. 110.

Denver Post, May 25, 2003, p. EE-02.

Detroit News, September 2, 1979; June 7, 1981; May 31, 1989.

Economist (U.K.), September 15, 2001, p. 94.

Editor and Publisher, December 9, 2002, p. 25.

Encounter, August, 1971; February, 1975.

English in Africa, May, 2002, pp. 27, 55.

English Journal, March, 1990, p. 70.

Entertainment Weekly, January 24, 1992, p. 52; November 4, 1994, p. 69; October 5, 2001, p. 128; December 2, 2005, Jennifer Reese, "A Lioness in Winter: In *Get a Life,* Nadine Gordimer Grapples with Life in Postapartheid South Africa," p. 85.

Estudios de Asia y Africa, September-December, 2000, p. 475.

Evening Standard (London, England), September 10, 2001, p. 50.

Explicator, summer, 1998, p. 213.

Extrapolation, spring, 1992, pp. 73-87.

Financial Times, March 14, 1998, p. 5.

Glamour, November, 1990, p. 174.

Globe and Mail (Toronto, Ontario, Canada), July 28, 1984; June 6, 1987; January 5, 1991; October 5, 1991.

Guardian (London, England), October 27, 2001, p. 6; October 12, 2003, p. 30; January 25, 2003, p. 7; February 28, 2003, p. 23; April 19, 2003, p. 7; May 22, 2003, p. 8; July 5, 2003, p. 27.

Harper's, February, 1963; April, 1976; November, 1990, p. 27.

Houston Chronicle, February 15, 1998, p. 26.

Hudson Review, spring, 1980.

Independent (London, England), November 17, 1999, p. 5.

Independent on Sunday (London, England), February 1, 1998, p. 31; February 21, 1999, p. 13; September 9, 2001, p. 15; June 8, 2003, p. 16.

Insight on the News, January 9, 1995, p. 27.

Interview, December, 1988, p. 140.

Irish Times (Dublin, Ireland), November 2, 2002, p. 62; June 14, 2003, p. 60.

Journal of Southern African Studies, 1999, p. 633.

Journal of Modern Literature, winter, 2001-2002, p. 50.

Kenyon Review, summer- fall, 1998, p. 94.

Kirkus, September 15, 2004, review of *Telling Tales,* p. 883.

Library Journal, September 1, 1958; September 1, 1980, p. 1751; March 15, 1981, p. 680; December, 1985, p. 99; March 1, 1987, p. 70; April 15, 1987, p. 98; January, 1988, p. 41; July, 1988, p. 70; October 15, 1988, p. 91; May 15, 1990, p. 120; November 1, 1990, p. 124; August, 1991, p. 149; March 1, 1993, p. 122; April 1, 1993, p. 148; August, 1994, p. 1989; February 1, 1995, p. 114; September 1, 1995, p. 176; November 1, 1997, p. 115; August 2001, p. 161; March 1, 2003, p. 121.

London Magazine, April-May, 1975.

Los Angeles Times, July 31, 1984; December 7, 1986; May 4, 2003, p. R-12.

Los Angeles Times Book Review, August 10, 1980; April 19, 1987; April 3, 1988; April 2, 1989; October 28, 1990.

Maclean's, August 3, 1981, p. 43; November 2, 1981, p. 21; August 13, 1984, p. 52; June 1, 1987, p. 50; November 14, 1994, p. 104.

Modern Fiction Studies, summer, 1987; spring, 2000, p. 139.

Mother Jones, June, 1984, p. 56; December, 1988, p. 50.

Ms., July, 1975; June, 1981, pp. 41, 90; July, 1984, p. 33; September, 1987, p. 28.

Nation, June 18, 1971; August 18, 1976; January 3, 1981, p. 22; June 6, 1981, p. 226; June 25, 1983, p. 809; May 2, 1987, p. 578; May 30, 1987, p. 731, December 26, 1988, p. 726; December 17, 1990, p. 777; October 16, 1995, p. 431; March 2, 1998, p. 25; December 13, 1999, p. 36.

National Review, December 25, 1981, p. 1561.

New Leader, June 29, 1981, p. 17; June 25, 1984, p. 18; April 20, 1087, p. 18.

New Orleans, December, 1984, p. 87; November, 1985, p. 31.

New Republic, May 18, 1987, p. 33; November 28, 1988, p. 28; October 24, 1994, p. 34.

New Statesman, May 16, 1980, p. 751; September 11, 1981, p. 18; March 23, 1984, p. 27; April 10, 1987, p. 27; December 4, 1987, p. 30; September 10, 2001, p. 55; June 23, 2003, p. 50.

New Statesman and Nation, August 18, 1956.

New Statesman and Society, September 23, 1988, p. 35; December 15, 1989, p. 39; September 21, 1990, p. 40; September 16, 1994, p. 38.

Newsweek, May 10, 1965; July 4, 1966; March 10, 1975; April 19, 1976; September 22, 1980; June 22, 1981, p. 78; July 9, 1984, p. 71; August 4,

1986, p. 29; May 4, 1987, p. 78; October 1, 1990, p. 40; October 14, 1991, p. 40.

New York, August 25, 1980, p. 54; June 22, 1981, p. 64; February 3, 1986, p. 40; October 22, 1990, p. 119.

New Yorker, June 7, 1952; November 21, 1953; November 29, 1958; May 12, 1975; June 22, 1981, p. 114; June 29, 1987, p. 87.

New York Herald Tribune Book Review, May 25, 1952; October 4, 1953; October 21, 1956; September 21, 1958; January 10, 1960; April 7, 1963.

New York Review of Books, June 26, 1975; July 15, 1976; October 23, 1980, p. 46; August 13, 1981, p. 14; July 16, 1987, p. 8; March 30, 1989, p. 12; November 21, 1991, p. 27; December 5, 1991, p. 16; December 1, 1994, p. 12.

New York Times, June 15, 1952; October 4, 1953; October 7, 1956; September 21, 1958; May 23, 1965; October 30, 1970; September 19, 1979; August 20, 1980; November 8, 1990, p. 8; May 27, 1981; December 28, 1981; July 9, 1984; January 14, 1986; April 22, 1987; December 28, 1987; October 5, 1990; January 1, 1991; October 4, 1991, pp. A1, C28; October 10, 1991, p. C25; December 8, 1991, p. 22; September 16, 1994, p. C31; November 28, 1994, pp. C11, C15; January 16, 1998, pp. B43, E49; November 14, 1999, p. WK1; October 9, 2001, p. E7; May 10, 2002, p. A4; May 4, 2003, p. 8; May 8, 2003, p. A11.

New York Times Book Review, January 10, 1960; September 11, 1966; October 31, 1971; April 13, 1975; April 18, 1976; August 19, 1979; August 24, 1980, pp. 7, 31; December 7, 1980, p. 51; June 7, 1981, pp. 26, 226; February 7, 1982, p. 38; August 8, 1982, p. 23; December 5, 1982, p. 75; June 24, 1984, p. 40; July 29, 1984, p. 7; August 16, 1984, p. 3; February 16, 1986, p. 29; August 31, 1986, p. 20; May 3, 1987, pp. 1, 22; July 19, 1987, p. 1; November 27, 1988, p. 8; October 21, 1990, pp. 1, 21; December 2, 1990, p. 81; June 2, 1991, p. 21; September 29, 1991, p. 7; September 25, 1994, p. 7; December 24, 1995, p. 11; October 6, 1996, p. 102; January 16, 1998; February 1, 1998, p. 10; December 16, 2001, p. 10; December 23, 2001, p. 14; January 6, 2002, p. 18; January 13, 2002, p. 22; June 2, 2002, p. 23; October 20, 2002, p. 28; May 4, 2003, p. 8.

Observer (London, England), November 21, 1999, p. 13.

Paris Review, summer, 1983.

People, March 26, 1984, p. 104; August 20, 1984, p. 15; January 5, 1987, p. 18; May 4, 1987, p. 22; October 18, 1991, p. 14; October 21, 1991, p. 52; January 19, 1998, p. 37.

Plain Dealer (Cleveland, OH), September 30, 2001, p. J9.

Playboy, January, 1992, p. 32.

Progressive, January, 1982, p. 53; January, 1992, p. 30.

Publishers Weekly, June 27, 1980, p. 79; April 20, 1984, p. 82; May 23, 1986, p. 99; March 6, 1987; April 10, 1987, p. 80; November 6, 1987, p. 40; September 30, 1988, p. 54; August 17, 1990, p. 53; August 30, 1991, p. 69; October 18, 1991, p. 14; July 11, 1994, p. 61; August 14, 1995, p. 63; November 11, 1996, p. 66; October 20, 1997, p. 52; March 16, 1998, p. 21; August 16, 1999, p. 66; July 16, 2001, p. 155; September 12, 2005, review of *Get a Life,* p. 38.

Record (Bergen County, NJ), December 19, 1997, p. 013.

Research in African Literatures, spring, 2000, p. 95.

Roanoke Times, March 10, 2002, p. 6.

Rocky Mountain News (Denver, CO), December 27, 1998, p. 1E.

St. Louis Post-Dispatch, March 29, 1998, p. E5.

St. Petersburg Times, December 30, 2001, p. 4D.

San Francisco Chronicle, May 26, 1952; November 9, 1953; January 24, 1960; January 11, 1998, p. 3; December 12, 1999, p. 5.

Saturday Review, May 24, 1952; October 3, 1953; September 13, 1958; January 16, 1960; May 8, 1965; August 20, 1966; December 4, 1971; March 8, 1975; September 29, 1979; May, 1981, p. 67.

School Library Journal, May, 2000, p. 194.

Scotland on Sunday (Edinburgh, Scotland), June 1, 2003, p. 4.

Scotsman (Edinburgh, Scotland), September 15, 2001, p. 11; June 14, 2003, p. 8.

Seattle Post- Intelligencer, January 27, 1998, p. D2; August 22, 1998, p. D2.

Seattle Times, February 1, 1998, p. M2; July 24, 1998, p. E1; September 9, 2001, p. J12; April 13, 2003, p. L8.

Sewanee Review, spring, 1977.

Spectator, February 12, 1960; June 7, 2003, p. 45; December 3, 2005, Digby Durrant, "Come, Rap for the Planet," p. 51.

Star-Ledger (Newark, NJ), February 22, 1998, p. 006; January 9, 2000, p. 004; October 14, 2001, p. 004; April 6, 2003, p. 004.

Sunday Telegraph (London, England), Sept 16, 2001; June 1, 2003.

Sunday Times (London, England), September 23, 2001, p. 42; June 15, 2003, p. 44.

Tikkun, January- February, 1990, p. 67; May-June, 1995, pp. 76, 79.

Time, October 15, 1956; September 22, 1958; January 11, 1960; November 16, 1970; July 7, 1975; August 11, 1980, p. 70; June 8, 1981, p. 79; July 23, 1984, p. 95; April 6, 1987, p. 76; October 29, 1990, p. CT12; October 14, 1991, p. 91; January 19, 1998, p. 66.

Times (London, England), December 16, 1982; March 22, 1984; April 2, 1987; September 6, 1990; October 14, 2000, p. 18; September 5, 2001, p. 15; September 22, 2001, p. 20.

Times Literary Supplement, October 30, 1953; July 13, 1956; June 27, 1958; February 12, 1960; March 1, 1963; July 22, 1965; July 7, 1966; May 14, 1971; May 26, 1972; January 9, 1976; July 9, 1976; April 25, 1980; September 4, 1981; March 30, 1984; April 17, 1987; September 23-29, 1988; October 4, 1990; October 11, 1991, p. 14; April 1, 1994, pp. 10-11.

Tribune Books (Chicago, IL), April 26, 1987; December 11, 1988, pp. 8-9; October 14, 1990; September 25, 1994, pp. 1, 9.

U.S. News and World Report, January 27, 1986, p. 65; May 25, 1987, p. 74.

Village Voice, September 17, 1980.

Voice Literary Supplement, September, 1984.

Wall Street Journal, January 20, 1998, p. A16.

Washington Post, December 4, 1979; January 30, 1998, p. D03; February 8, 1998, p. X15; August 5, 2001, p. T08; September 30, 2001, p. T09.

Washington Post Book World, November 28, 1971; April 6, 1975; August 26, 1979; September 7, 1980; May 31, 1981; July 15, 1984; May 3, 1987; November 20, 1988; October 2, 1994.

Washington Times, February 1, 1998, p. 6; May 4, 2003, p. D06.

Weekend Australian (Sydney, Australia), March 28, 1998, p. R29; March 11, 2000, p. R13; November 24, 2001, p. B06.

Wilson Library Journal, February, 1994, p. 94.

World and I, November, 1998, p. 277; March, 2002, p. 245; July, 2003, p. 219.

World Literature Today, autumn, 1984; spring, 1992, pp. 390-391.

World Press Review, October, 1987, p. 61.

World Watch, July- August, 2002, p. 17.

Yale Review, winter, 1982, p. 254; winter, 1988, p. 243.

ONLINE

Atlantic Online, http://www.theatlantic.com/ (February 9, 2000), interview with Gordimer.

BBC Audio Interviews, http://www.bbc.co.uk/bbcfour/ (October 18, 1998).

Gifts of Speech, http://gos.sbc.edu/ (December 7, 1991), Nobel lecture.

University Scholars Programme, National University of Singapore http://www.scholars.nus.edu.sg/ (March 10, 2004), Gordimer page.

South African Review of Books, http://www.uni-ulm.de/ (March 2, 2006), "Nadine Gordimer at 70."

United Nations Development Programme—South Africa, http://www.undp.org.za/ (March 10, 2004), biography of Gordimer.

*   *   *

GORYAN, Sirak
    See SAROYAN, William

*   *   *

GOTTESMAN, S.D.
    See POHL, Frederik

*   *   *

GOULD, Stephen Jay 1941-2002

PERSONAL: Born September 10, 1941, in New York, NY; died of cancer, May 20, 2002, in New York, NY; son of Leonard (a court reporter) and Eleanor (an artist; maiden name, Rosenberg) Gould; married Deborah Lee (an artist and writer), October 3, 1965; children: Jesse, Ethan. *Education:* Antioch College, A.B., 1963; Columbia University, Ph.D., 1967. *Hobbies and other interests:* Baseball.

CAREER: Antioch College, Yellow Springs, OH, instructor in geology, 1966; Harvard University, Cambridge, MA, assistant professor and assistant curator, 1967-71, associate professor and associate curator, 1971-73, professor of geology and curator of invertebrate paleontology at Museum of Comparative Zoology, beginning 1973, Alexander Agassiz Professor of Zoology, beginning 1982. Member of advisory board, Children's Television Workshop, 1978-81, and *Nova* (television program), 1980-92.

MEMBER: American Association for the Advancement of Science, American Academy of Arts and Sciences, American Society of Naturalists (president, 1979-80), National Academy of Sciences, Paleontological Society (president, 1985-86), Society for the Study of Evolution (vice president, 1975; president, 1990), Society of Systematic Zoology, Society of Vertebrate Paleontology, History of Science Society, European Union of Geo-

sciences (honorary foreign fellow), Society for the Study of Sports History, Royal Society of Edinburgh, Linnaean Society of London (foreign member), Sigma Xi.

AWARDS, HONORS: National Science Foundation, Woodrow Wilson, and Columbia University fellowships, 1963-67; Schuchert Award, Paleontological Society, 1975; National Magazine Award, 1980, for "This View of Life"; Notable Book citation, American Library Association, 1980, and National Book Award in science, 1981, both for *The Panda's Thumb: More Reflections in Natural History;* Scientist of the Year citation, *Discover,* 1981; MacArthur Foundation Prize fellowship, 1981-86; National Book Critics Circle Award, and American Book Award nomination in science, both 1982, and Outstanding Book Award, American Educational Research Association, 1983, all for *The Mismeasure of Man;* Medal of Excellence, Columbia University, 1982; F.V. Haydn Medal, Philadelphia Academy of Natural Sciences, 1982; Joseph Priestley Award and Medal, Dickinson College, 1983; Neil Miner Award, National Association of Geology Teachers, 1983; silver medal, Zoological Society of London, 1984; Bradford Washburn Award and gold medal, Boston Museum of Science, 1984; Distinguished Service Award, American Humanists Association, 1984; Tanner Lecturer, Cambridge University, 1984, and Stanford University, 1989; Meritorious Service Award, American Association of Systematics Collections, 1984; Founders Council Award of Merit, Field Museum of Natural History, 1984; John and Samuel Bard Award, Bard College, 1984; Phi Beta Kappa Book Award in science, 1984, for *Hen's Teeth and Horse's Toes: Further Reflections in Natural History;* Sarah Josepha Hale Medal, 1986; Creative Arts Award for nonfiction, Brandeis University, 1986; Terry Lecturer, Yale University, 1986; Distinguished Service Award, American Geological Institute, 1986; Glenn T. Seaborg Award, International Platform Association, 1986; In Praise of Reason Award, Committee for the Scientific Investigation of Claims of the Paranormal, 1986; H.D. Vursell Award, American Academy and Institute of Arts and Letters, 1987; National Book Critics Circle Award nomination, 1987, for *Time's Arrow, Time's Cycle: Myth and Metaphor in the Discovery of Geological Time;* Anthropology in Media Award, American Anthropological Association, 1987; History of Geology Award, Geological Society of America, 1988; T.N. George Medal, University of Glasgow, 1989; Sue T. Friedman Medal, Geological Society of London, 1989; Distinguished Service Award, American Institute of Professional Geologists, 1989; fellow, Museum National d'Historie Naturelle (Paris, France), 1989; fellow, Royal Society of Edinburgh, 1990; City of Edinburgh Medal, 1990; Britannica Award and Gold Medal, 1990, for dissemination of public knowledge; Forkosch Award, Council on Democratic Humanism, and Phi Beta Kappa Book Award in Science, both 1990, and Pulitzer Prize finalist and Rhone-Poulenc Prize, both 1991, all for *Wonderful Life: The Burgess Shale and the Nature of History;* Iglesias Prize, 1991, for Italian translation of *The Mismeasure of Man;* Distinguished Service Award, National Association of Biology Teachers, 1991; Golden Trilobite Award, Paleontological Society, 1992; Homer Smith Medal, New York University School of Medicine, 1992; University of California—Los Angeles medal, 1992; James T. Shea Award, National Association of Geology Teachers, 1992; Commonwealth Award in Interpretive Science, State of Massachusetts, 1993; J.P. McGovern Award and Medal in Science, Cosmos Club, 1993; St. Louis Libraries Literary Award, University of St. Louis, 1994; Gold Medal for Service to Zoology, Linnaean Society of London; Distinguished Service Medal, Teachers College, Columbia University. Recipient of numerous honorary degrees from colleges and universities.

WRITINGS:

NONFICTION

Ontogeny and Phylogeny, Belknap Press/Harvard University (Cambridge, MA), 1977.

Ever since Darwin: Reflections in Natural History (essays), Norton (New York, NY), 1977.

The Panda's Thumb: More Reflections in Natural History (essays), Norton (New York, NY), 1980.

(With Salvador Edward Juria and Sam Singer) *A View of Life,* Benjamin-Cummings (Menlo Park, CA), 1981.

The Mismeasure of Man, Norton (New York, NY), 1981, revised and expanded edition, 1996.

Hen's Teeth and Horse's Toes: Further Reflections in Natural History (essays), Norton (New York, NY), 1983.

The Flamingo's Smile: Reflections in Natural History (essays), Norton (New York, NY), 1985.

(With Rosamund Wolff Purcell) *Illuminations: A Bestiary,* Norton (New York, NY), 1986.

Time's Arrow, Time's Cycle: Myth and Metaphor in the Discovery of Geological Time, Harvard University Press (Cambridge, MA), 1987.

An Urchin in the Storm: Essays about Books and Ideas, Norton (New York, NY), 1987.

(With others) *Frederic Edwin Church,* National Gallery of Art (Washington, DC), 1989.

Wonderful Life: The Burgess Shale and the Nature of History, Norton (New York, NY), 1989.

The Individual in Darwin's World: The Second Edinburgh Medal Address, Edinburgh University Press (Edinburgh, Scotland), 1990.

Bully for Brontosaurus: Reflections in Natural History, Norton (New York, NY), 1991.

(With Rosamund Wolff Purcell) *Finders, Keepers: Eight Collectors,* Norton (New York, NY), 1992.

(Editor) *The Book of Life,* Norton (New York, NY), 1993.

Eight Little Piggies: Reflections in Natural History, Norton (New York, NY), 1993.

Dinosaur in a Haystack: Reflections in Natural History, Harmony Books (New York, NY), 1995.

Full House: The Spread of Excellence from Plato to Darwin, Harmony Books (New York, NY), 1996.

Questioning the Millennium: A Rationalist's Guide to a Precisely Arbitrary Countdown, Random House (New York, NY), 1997.

Leonardo's Mountain of Clams and the Diet of Worms: Essays on Natural History, Harmony (New York, NY), 1998.

Rocks of Ages: Science and Religion in the Fullness of Life, Ballantine (New York, NY), 1999.

(With Rosamond Wolff Purcell) *Crossing Over: Where Art and Science Meet,* Three Rivers Press (New York, NY), 2000.

The Lying Stones of Marrakech: Penultimate Reflections in Natural History, Harmony Books (New York, NY), 2000.

The Structure of Evolutionary Theory, Belknap Press/Harvard University Press (Cambridge, MA), 2002.

I Have Landed: The End of a Beginning in Natural History, Harmony Books (New York, NY), 2002.

The Hedgehog, the Fox, and the Magister's Pox: Mending the Gap between Science and the Humanities, Harmony Books (New York, NY), 2003.

Triumph and Tragedy in Mudville: A Lifelong Passion for Baseball, Norton (New York, NY), 2003.

OTHER

(Editor, with Niles Eldredge) Ernst Mayr, *Systematics and the Origin of Species,* Columbia University Press (New York, NY), 1982.

(Editor, with Niles Eldredge) Theodosius Dobzhansky, *Genetics and the Origin of Species,* Columbia University Press (New York, NY), 1982.

(Author of foreword) Gary Larson, *The Far Side Gallery 3,* Andrews & McMeel (Fairway, KS), 1988.

(Editor) *Best American Essays,* Mariner Books, 2002.

Author of *An Evolutionary Microcosm: Pleistocene and Recent History of the Land Snail P. (Poecilozonites) in Bermuda,* [Cambridge, MA], 1969. Also author, with Eric Lewin Altschuler, of *Bachanalia: The Essential Listener's Guide to Bach's "Well-Tempered Clavier."*

Contributor to books, including *Models in Paleobiology,* edited by T.J.M. Schopf, Freeman, Cooper (San Francisco, CA), 1972; *The Evolutionary Synthesis: Perspectives on the Unification of Biology,* edited by Ernst Mayr, Harvard University Press (Cambridge, MA), 1980; *Darwin's Legacy: Nobel Conference XVIII, Gustavus Adolphus College, St. Peter, Minnesota,* edited by Charles L. Hamrum, Harper (New York, NY), 1983; *Between Home and Heaven: Contemporary American Landscape Photography,* National Museum of American Art (Washington, DC), 1992; and *Understanding Scientific Prose,* edited by Jack Selzer, University of Wisconsin Press (Madison, WI), 1993; Contributor to *Melancholies of Knowledge: Literature in the Age of Science,* State University of New York Press, 1999. Contributor to proceedings of the International Congress of Systematic and Evolutionary Biology Symposium, 1973; contributor to *Bulletin of the Museum of Comparative Zoology,* Harvard University, and contributor of numerous articles to scientific journals. Author of monthly column, "This View of Life," in *Natural History.*

General editor, *The History of Paleontology,* twenty volumes, Ayer, 1980; and *The Book of Life,* Norton (New York, NY), 1993. Associate editor, *Evolution,* 1970-72; member of editorial board, *Systematic Zoology,* 1970-72, *Paleobiology,* 1974-76, and *American Naturalist,* 1977-80; member of board of editors, *Science,* 1986-91.

SIDELIGHTS: Stephen Jay Gould, a Harvard University professor and evolutionary biologist, was renowned for his ability to translate difficult scientific theories into prose understandable to the layman. In his books and essays on natural history, Gould, a paleontologist and geologist by training, popularized his subjects without trivializing them, "simultaneously entertaining and teaching," according to James Gorman in the *New York Times Book Review.* With his dozen essay collections, Gould won critical acclaim for bridging the gap between the advancing frontier of science and the literary world. With coauthor Rosamond Wolff Purcell, he addressed particularly the interface of art and science in the 2000 publication *Crossing Over: Where Art and Science Meet.* "As witty as he is learned, Gould has a born essayist's ability to evoke the general out of fasci-

nating particulars and to discuss important scientific questions for an audience of educated laymen without confusion or condescension," Gene Lyons commented in *Newsweek.* "What made Steve different was that he didn't make a cartoon out of science. He didn't talk down to people," Harvard professor Richard Lewontin told John Nichols of the *Nation.* "He communicated about science in a way that did not try to hide the complexities of the issues and that did not shy away from the political side of these issues. Steve's great talent was his ability to make sense of an issue at precisely the point when people needed that insight." Hallmarks of Gould's style include the use of metaphors and analogies from a variety of disciplines. Gould wrote a single draft on a typewriter, following a detailed outline, and editors soon learned not to touch his prose.

Gould's focus on the unexpected within nature reflects the worldview that permeates his entire body of work: that natural history is significantly altered by events out-of-the-ordinary and is largely revealed by examining its "imperfections." "Catastrophes contain continuities," explained Michael Neve in the *Times Literary Supplement.* "In fact Gould made it his business to see the oddities and small-scale disasters of the natural record as the actual historical evidence for taking evolution seriously, as a real event." Through imperfections, continued Neve, "we can . . . see how things have altered by looking at the way organic life is, as it were, cobbled together out of bits and pieces some of which work, but often only just." The thumb of the panda, highlighted in Gould's American Book Award-winning essay collection *The Panda's Thumb: More Reflections in Natural History,* particularly demonstrates this. Not really a thumb at all, the offshoot on the panda's paw is actually an enlarged wristbone that enables the animal to efficiently strip leaves from bamboo shoots. "If one were to design a panda from scratch, one would not adapt a wrist bone to do the job of a thumb," observed *Times Literary Supplement* reviewer D.M. Knight. An imperfection, the appendage "may have been fashioned by a simple genetic change, perhaps a single mutation affecting the timing and rate of growth."

Gould's writings also emphasize science as a "culturally embedded" discipline. "Science is not a heartless pursuit of objective information," he once told the *New York Times Book Review;* "it is a creative human activity." Raymond A. Sokolov, in the same publication, remarked that Gould's "method is at bottom, a kind of textual criticism of the language of earlier biologists, a historical analysis of their 'metaphors,' their concepts of the world." Gould frequently examines science as the output of individuals working within the confines of specific time periods and cultures. In a *New Yorker* review of *The Flamingo's Smile,* John Updike wrote of "Gould's evangelical sense of science as an advancing light, which gives him a vivid sympathy with thinkers in the dark." Updike continued: "Gould chastens us ungrateful beneficiaries of science with his affectionate and tactile sense of its strenuous progress, its worming forward through fragmentary revelations and obsolete debates, from relative darkness into relative light. Even those who were wrong win his gratitude." Sue M. Halpern noted in the *Nation:* "Gould is both a scientist and a humanist, not merely a scientist whose literary abilities enable him to build a narrow bridge between the two cultures in order to export the intellectual commodities of science to the other side. His writing portrays universal strivings, it expresses creativity and it reveals Gould to be a student of human nature as well as one of human affairs."

In his writing Gould also demonstrates instances where science, by factually "verifying" certain cultural prejudices, has been misused. *The Flamingo's Smile* contains several accounts of individuals victimized as a result of cultural prejudices used as scientific knowledge, such as the "Hottentot Venus," a black southern African woman whose anatomy was put on public display in nineteenth-century Europe, and Carrie Buck, an American woman who was legally sterilized in the 1920s because of a family history of mentally "unfit" individuals. And in his award-winning *Mismeasure of Man,* Gould focuses on the development of intelligence quotient (IQ) testing and debunks the work of scientists purporting to measure human intelligence objectively. "This book," writes Gould in the introduction, "is about the abstraction of intelligence as a single entity, its location within the brain, its quantification as one number for each individual, and the use of these numbers to rank people in a single series of worthiness, invariably to find that oppressed or disadvantaged groups—races, classes or sexes—are innately inferior and deserve their status." Halpern pointed out that, "Implicit in Gould's writing is a binding premise: while the findings of science are themselves value-free, the uses to which they are put are not."

In a *London Review of Books* essay on *Hen's Teeth and Horse's Toes: Further Reflections in Natural History,* John Hedley Brooke summarized some of the major themes that appear in Gould's writings: "The 'fact' of evolution is 'proved' from those imperfections in living organisms which betray a history of descent. The self-styled 'scientific creationists' have no leg to stand on and are simply playing politics. Natural selection must not be construed as a perfecting principle in any strong sense of perfection. Neo-Darwinists who look to adaptive utility as the key to every explanation are as myopic as the natural theologians of the early nineteenth century who saw in the utility of every organ the stamp of its divine origin." Citing yet another recurrent theme, Brooke noted Gould's focus on "the extent to which the course of evolution has been constrained by the simple fact that organisms inherit a body structure and style of embryonic development which impose limits on the scope of transformation." This last principle was enhanced by Gould's field work with the Bahamian land snail genus *Cerion,* a group displaying a wide variety of shapes, in addition to a permanent growth record in its shell. "More orthodox evolutionists would assume that the many changes of form represent adaptations," noted James Gleick in the *New York Times Magazine.* "Gould denies it and finds explanations in the laws of growth. Snails grow the way they do because there are only so many ways a snail *can* grow."

Gould's *Wonderful Life: The Burgess Shale and the Nature of History* focuses on the fossil-rich remains discovered in a small area in the Canadian Rockies in 1909. The organisms preserved there display a much greater diversity than fossil sites from later eras, and their meaning has been hotly debated ever since their discovery. Gould chronicles the early studies of the Burgess Shale, then offers his own speculations on what the fossils reveal. In the process, he discredits the long-held notion that evolution is inevitably a progression toward higher and increasingly perfect life forms. Reviewing *Wonderful Life* in *New Statesman & Society,* Steven Rose related: "Far from being the mechanism of ordered transformation along a great chain of being towards adaptive perfection, evolution is a lottery in which winners and losers are determined by forces over which they have little control. Nearly everything is possible; what survives, including ourselves, confirms the truth that nothing in biology makes sense except in the context of history." High praise for *Wonderful Life* also came from Robin McKie, who wrote in the London *Observer* that Gould's "book is written with such clarity and breathtaking leaps of imagination that it successfully moulds a mass of detail and arcane taxonomy into a lucid and highly entertaining whole." McKie took exception to Gould's contention that biologists have purposely presented evolution in anthropomorphic terms, yet McKie concluded that "*Wonderful Life* remains a masterly scientific explanation" of the Burgess Shale and evolution in general.

In essay collections such as *Eight Little Piggies: Reflections in Natural History, Bully for Brontosaurus: Reflections in Natural History,* and *Dinosaur in a Hay-*

stack: Reflections in Natural History, Gould upheld the standards of accessibility and scientific integrity he set in earlier books. "What makes Gould so good?" Robert Kanigel asked in the Washington Post Book World. The critic went on to answer his own question: His essays transport readers "into a cozy little world where we are left in intimate touch with Gould's heart and mind. Gould is one part Harvard intellectual, nine parts curious little boy; that's one element of his distinctive appeal. For another, he has a commanding knowledge of his discipline, evolutionary biology, and the fields, like geology and paleontology, that flank it. He doesn't have to parade it around; but he has so much to draw upon, and does." Kanigel described Gould's characteristic technique: beginning with some odd fact and proceeding from there to sweeping insights as another special charm, along with his delight in interesting digressions. "This is a feast," declared Bryan C. Clarke in his Nature commentary on Eight Little Piggies, citing the work as "a lovely mixture of bizarre facts, nice arguments, clever insights into the workings of evolution and a quality of writing that can make your skin prickle."

While some reviewers have commented that Gould's writings display a repetition of key principles and themes—in critiquing Hen's Teeth and Horse's Toes, Brooke remarked that "the big implications may begin to sound familiar"—Gould earned consistent praise for the range of subjects through which he illustrates evolutionary principles. "Gould entices us to follow him on a multifaceted Darwinian hunt for answers to age-old questions about ourselves and the rest of the living world," commented John C. McLoughlin in the Washington Post Book World. "Like evolution itself, Gould explores possibilities—any that come to hand—and his range of interest is stupendous. . . . Throughout, he displays with force and elegance the power of evolutionary theory to link the phenomena of the living world as no other theory seems able." Steven Rose wrote in the New York Times Book Review: "Exploring the richness of living forms, Mr. Gould, and we, are constantly struck by the absurd ingenuity by which fundamentally inappropriate parts are pressed into new roles like toes that become hooves, or smell receptors that become the outer layer of the brain. Natural selection is not some grandiose planned event but a continual tinkering. . . . Gould's great strength is to recognize that, by demystifying nature in this way, he increases our wonder and our respect for the richness of life."

In a New York Times Book Review critique of Full House: The Spread of Excellence from Plato to Darwin, David Papineau stated that Gould's "central contention

is that trends, in any area, should never be considered in isolation, but only as aspects of an overall range of variation (the full house of the title)." In terms of evolution, this means that the mechanism of natural selection does not always progress toward greater complexity; in fact, according to Gould, it is just as likely to run toward simplicity. Gould based this argument on "a very clear statistical insight. . . . The first is his own experience as a statistic, when he was a cancer patient. The second is an extended analysis of the disappearance of .400 batters in major league baseball," stated Lucy Horwitz in the Boston Book Review, who concluded that Gould's argument is "convincing" and "elegantly presented."

Questioning the Millennium: A Rationalist's Guide to a Precisely Arbitrary Countdown focuses on three questions posed by Gould: "What does the millennium mean? When does a millennium arrive? Why are we interested in it and other divisions of time?" Gould uses "wit and style" to "launch an inquiry into the human 'fascination with numerical regularity'" and to seek this regularity "as one way of ordering a confusing world," according to New York Times contributor Michiko Kakutani. The critic also stated that the book "is not one of Mr. Gould's more important books, but . . . it beguiles and entertains, even as it teaches us to reconsider our preconceptions about the natural world."

After writing columns regularly over twenty-four years, in 2000 Gould served up a new selection of these short journalistic pieces in The Lying Stones of Marrakech: Penultimate Reflections in Natural History, in which he discusses the misconception of inevitable progress being made in scientific endeavors. Among the work's enthusiasts, Booklist reviewer Gilbert Taylor remarked that the work "evinces no dimming of Gould's humanistic brilliance," and Audubon critic Christopher Camuto dubbed them "elegant, complexly wrought essays." Gould's final essays for Natural Science were compiled into the 2002 work I Have Landed: The End of a Beginning in Natural History, which coincided with the publication of his major scholarly work The Structure of Evolutionary Theory. Included in I Have Landed are pieces of a slightly more personal nature, including a short essay titled "September 11, 2001." As a Publishers Weekly critic acknowledged, "Gould is at the peak of his abilities in this latest menagerie of wonders" for which, according to Gregg Sapp in Library Journal, his "many fans and foes alike should congratulate him."

Between 1999 and 2003, three works by Gould appeared that focus on the interstices of science and religion: Rocks of Ages: Science and Religion in the Full-

ness of Life, Crossing Over, and *The Hedgehog, the Fox, and the Magister's Pox: Mending the Gap between Science and the Humanities.* In the first, Gould explains what he perceives are the differences in subject matter, method, and intention between the disciplines of science and religion. Then he proposes what he terms "non-overlapping magisteria," that is, a "respectful non-interference—accompanied by intense dialogue between the two distinct subjects," which he dubbed NOMA. While *American Scientist*'s Ursula Goodenough viewed this work as vintage Gould, with "graceful language flecked with occasional irreverence [and] wonderful anecdotes," she pointed out contradictions in his arguments. So too, in *Commentary* George Weigel pointed to Gould's failure to adequately deal with the common aspects of science and religions, "both of which aim to understand the truth of the human condition. To treat science and religion as 'utterly different' is convenient for certain kinds of scientists (deeply skeptical about religion but 'tolerant') and certain kinds of religious believers (tepid and/or intellectually insecure). But it does not help us think very seriously about either realm."

Unlike many of his contemporaries, Gould also warred constantly against what he considered "bad science," often ending up in the public spotlight, and he believed that paleontology as a science could add to the discussion of evolution. In his magnum opus, the 1,464-page study *The Structure of Evolutionary Theory,* he discusses how three principal tenets of Darwinism developed throughout modern works on evolutionary theory and, in the process, "presents Gould in all his incarnations: as a digressive historian, original thinker and cunning polemicist," to quote a *Publishers Weekly* reviewer. *Booklist*'s Donna Seaman admitted that "this astonishing feat of scholarship and creativity is intimidating at first glance," yet found that Gould's style makes it readable. On the other hand, Gregg Sapp, writing in *Library Journal,* dubbed *The Structure of Evolutionary Theory* both "indispensable" for collections on the subject and "bloated, redundant, and self-indulgent," the last because Gould wrote 250 pages about his own theory of evolution, known as punctuated equilibrium. Calling the work so full of "asides, digressions, polemics and hobbies that it is positively obese," an *Economist* (U.S.) reviewer found it both difficult to review and "enormously irritating." Yet the critic added, "it is also a book of great power, scope and learning. In the end, its impressive features far outweigh its irritations." Also noting Gould's "remarkably undisciplined prose" was H. Allen Orr, who, writing in the *New Yorker,* suggested that "while Gould's popular essays are perhaps the most widely read texts in the history of biology, his magnum opus risks becoming one of the least." "What

should be incisive analysis is intermittently swamped in highly creative persiflage," complained *Spectator* reviewer John R.G. Turner, who added, "Gould stands here to be judged not on his many literary merits but on the quality of his theory." Despite any perceived stylistic flaws, Orr deemed the first half of the work—the history of evolutionary theory—"particularly impressive."

Gould was a life-long baseball fan—a Yankee fan, in particular—an avidity that is amply evident in his posthumously published essay collection *Triumph and Tragedy in Mudville: A Lifelong Passion for Baseball.* Compiled upon the suggestion of his friend Stephen King, the essays were written over the course of two decades and first appeared in a wide variety of periodicals ranging from the *New York Times* to *Vanity Fair.* While there is, therefore, some repetition of information in the book, in the opinion of *Booklist* reviewer GraceAnne A. DeCandido, the pieces are "uniformly wonderful." *Sports Illustrated* writer Charles Hirshberg pointed to the essay "Why No One Hits .400 Anymore" as the "book's most profound and challenging essay." In it Gould proposed that the lack of .400 hitters "is a sign of improvement, not decline" because modern players are better trained; thus, the difference between the best athletes and average players is slighter than it was in the past. While Gould called this work "baseball scribblings," reviewers had a more respectful view, as in the case of a *Publishers Weekly* writer who dubbed *Triumph and Tragedy in Mudville* a "glorious testament to Gould's remarkable insights and passionate writing." Praising Gould's judgments of teams' and players' abilities, his assessments of books on the game, and his actualities of the game itself as "smart, well-written, and eminently entertaining" was a *Kirkus Reviews* critic.

Gould passed away in May of 2002, after suffering from cancer for several years. In contemplating Gould's contribution to the field of paleontology, Orr suggested that it might not have so much to do with the evolutionary theory of snails or other organisms in the fossil record, but in his effect on his scientific colleagues. "Gould might well . . . represent something new in the historical strata of science: the first self-consciously revolutionary scientist—the first scientist who set out to create a revolution at least in part because he felt that the field just needed one." Orr explained, "Just as old and hopelessly constrained species can do nothing interesting unless they get periodically shaken, so old and hopelessly conservative paradigms can't give way to new science unless they receive a good swift kick now and then."

BIOGRAPHICAL AND CRITICAL SOURCES:

BOOKS

Gould, Stephen Jay, *The Mismeasure of Man*, W.W. Norton and Company (New York, NY), 1996.

Gould, Stephen Jay, *Questioning the Millennium: A Rationalist's Guide to a Precisely Arbitrary Countdown*, Random House (New York, NY), 1997.

Gould, Stephen Jay, *Rocks of Ages: Science and Religion in the Fullness of Life*, Ballantine (New York, NY), 1999.

PERIODICALS

America, May 24, 1986.

American Scientist, May-June, 1999, Ursula Goodenough, review of *Rocks of Ages: Science and Religion in the Fullness of Life*, pp. 264-265; May-June, 2003, Margaret Pizer, "The Steve Wars," p. 213.

Antioch Review, spring, 1978.

Asia Africa Intelligence Wire, January 26, 2003, "Vidal, Ehrenreich Stars of Essay Collection."

Audubon, March, 2000, Christopher Camuto, review of *The Lying Stones of Marrakech: Penultimate Reflections in Natural History*, p. 156.

Book, March-April, 2003, Chris Barsanti, review of *Triumph and Tragedy in Mudville: A Lifelong Passion for Baseball*, p. 81.

Booklist, December 1, 1999, review of *Dinosaur in a Haystack* (audio version), p. 718; January 1, 2000, Gilbert Taylor, review of *The Lying Stones of Marrakech*, p. 832; December 1, 2000, Donna Seaman, review of *The Lying Stones of Marrakech*, p. 686; December 15, 2001, review of *The Structure of Evolutionary Theory*, p. 682; March 1, 2002, review of *I Have Landed: The End of a Beginning in Natural History*, p. 1050; December 15, 2002, Donna Seaman, review of *The Structure of Evolutionary Theory*, p. 682; February 15, 2003, GraceAnne A. DeCandido, review of *Triumph and Tragedy in Mudville*, p. 1031; April 1, 2003, Donna Seaman, review of *The Hedgehog, the Fox, and the Magister's Pox: Mending the Gap between Science and the Humanities*, p. 1354.

Boston Book Review, March 1, 1997.

Bulletin with Newsweek, May 15, 2001, Ashley Hay, review of *Crossing Over: Where Art and Science Meet*, p. 77.

Chicago Tribune, December 2, 1981; January 20, 1988.

Choice, March, 2000, F.M. Szasz, review of *Rocks of Ages*, p. 1312; July-August, 2002, F.S. Szalay, review of *The Structure of Evolutionary Theory*, p. 1985; November, 2002, J. Nabe, review of *I Have Landed*, p. 495.

Christian Century, June 2, 1999, review of *Rocks of Ages*, p. 624.

Christian Science Monitor, July 15, 1987; March 18, 1999, review of *Rocks of Ages*, p. 19.

Commentary, May, 1999, George Weigel, review of *Rocks of Ages*, p. 67.

Commonweal, April 23, 1999, review of *Rocks of Ages*, p. 29.

Detroit News, May 22, 1983.

Economist (U.K.), November 10, 2001, review of *Rocks of Ages*, p. 111.

Economist (U.S.), May 16, 1987; November 10, 2001, review of *Rocks of Ages*, p. 77; December 7, 2002, review of *The Structure of Evolutionary Theory*.

Globe and Mail (Toronto, Ontario, Canada), July 24, 1999, review of *Rocks of Ages*, p. D14; March 23, 2002, review of *The Structure of Evolutionary Theory*, p. D3.

Journal of Chemical Education, June, 2002, Hal Harris, review of *The Lying Stones of Marrakech*, p. 651.

Kirkus Reviews, February 15, 2002, review of *I Have Landed*, p. 236; January 15, 2003, review of *The Hedgehog, the Fox, and the Magister's Pox*, p. 125, and review of *Triumph and Tragedy in Mudville*, p. 125.

Kliatt, July, 1999, review of *Leonardo's Mountain of Clams and the Diet of Worms: Essays on Natural History* (audio version), p. 59; May, 2001, review of *Crossing Over*, p. 40; September, 2001, review of *The Lying Stones of Marrakech*, p. 42.

Library Journal, March 1, 1999, review of *Leonardo's Mountain of Clams and the Diet of Worms*, p. 47; February 15, 2000, Gregg Sapp, review of *The Lying Stones of Marrakech*, p. 193; February 15, 2002, Gregg Sapp, review of *The Structure of Evolutionary Theory*, pp. 174-175; April 15, 2002, Gregg Sapp, review of *I Have Landed*, p. 122; October 1, 2002, Denise J. Stankovics, review of *The Best American Essays 2002*, p. 94; February 1, 2003, Paul Kaplan and Robert C. Cotrrell, review of *Triumph and Tragedy in Mudville*, p. 90; March 1, 2003, Gregg Sapp, review of *The Hedgehog, the Fox, and the Magister's Pox*, p. 113.

Listener, June 11, 1987.

London Review of Books, December 1, 1983.

Los Angeles Times, June 2, 1987.

Los Angeles Times Book Review, July 17, 1983; November 29, 1987.

Magazine of Fantasy and Science Fiction, February, 1999, review of *Questioning the Millennium*, p. 35.

Nation, June 18, 1983; November 16, 1985; June 10, 2002, David Hawkes, review of *The Structure of Evolutionary Theory,* p. 29.

Natural History, January, 1988.

Nature, November 19, 1987; August 26, 1999, review of *Rocks of Ages,* p. 830; May 25, 2000, Henry Gee, review of *The Lying Stones of Marrakech,* p. 397.

New Criterion, October, 2002, Paul R. Gross, "The Apotheosis of Stephen Jay Gould," pp. 77-80.

New Republic, December 3, 1977; November 11, 1981; November 8, 1999, review of *Questioning the Millennium,* p. 76.

New Scientist, September 11, 1999, review of *Leonardo's Mountain of Clams and the Diet of Worms,* p. 53; May 12, 2001, review of *The Lying Stones of Marrakech,* p. 52.

New Statesman, February 19, 2001, review of *Rocks of Ages,* p. 49.

New Statesman and Society, Frebruary 23, 1990, Steven Rose, "Nature's Lottery: Wonderful Life," review of *Wonderful Life: The Burgess Shale and the Nature of History,* p. 36.

Newsweek, November 9, 1981; August 1, 1983.

New Yorker, December 30, 1985; September 30, 2002, H. Allen Orr, "The Descent of Gould."

New York Review of Books, June 1, 1978; February 19, 1981; October 22, 1981; May 28, 1987; October 18, 2001, Frederick Crews, review of *Rocks of Ages,* pp. 51-54; May 23, 2002, Tim Flannery, "A New Darwinism," reviews of *The Structures of Evolutionary Theory* and *I Have Landed,* pp. 52-54.

New York Times, October 17, 1987; November 11, 1997, p. E8.

New York Times Book Review, November 20, 1977; September 14, 1980; November 1, 1981; May 8, 1983; September 22, 1985; December 7, 1986; September 11, 1987; November 15, 1987; January 21, 1996, p. 9; September 22, 1996, p. 9; November 9, 1997, p. 9; March 17, 2002, review of *The Structure of Evolutionary Theory,* p. 11.

New York Times Magazine, November 20, 1983.

Observer (London, England), February 18, 1990, p. 57.

Odyssey, January, 2003, Barbara Krasner-Khait, "A Passion for Writing," pp. 24-25.

People Weekly, June 2, 1986.

Publishers Weekly, January 17, 2000, review of *The Lying Stones of Marrakech,* p. 49; February 11, 2002, review of *The Structure of Evolutionary Theory,* p. 179; April 1, 2002, review of *I Have Landed,* p. 64, "*PW* Talks with Stephen Jay Gould," p. 65; September 2, 2002, review of *The Best American Essays 2002,* pp. 65-66; February 17, 2003, review of *The Hedgehog, the Fox, and the Magister's Pox,* p. 63, and review of *Triumph and Tragedy in Mudville,* p. 65.

Quarterly Review of Biology, June, 2000, Richard A. Watson, review of *Rocks of Ages,* p. 159; September, 2002, Kevin Padian, review of *The Book of Life,* pp. 318-319.

Rolling Stone, January 15, 1987.

Ruminator Review, spring, 2002, review of *The Structure of Evolutionary Theory,* p. 12.

Science, May, 1983; October 29, 1999, Craig B. Anderson, review of *Rocks of Ages,* p. 907; April 26, 2002, Douglas J. Futuyma, review of *The Structure of Evolutionary Theory,* pp. 661-663.

Science Books & Films, November, 1999, review of *Leonardo's Mountain of Clams and the Diet of Worms,* p. 249, and reviews of *Leonardo's Mountain of Claims and the Diet of Worms* and *Wonderful Life* pp. 271-272.

Science News, July 20, 2002, *The Structure of Evolutionary Theory,* p. 47; August 10, 2002, review of *I Have Landed,* p. 95.

Scientist, June 10, 2002, Barry A. Palevitz, "Love Him or Hate Him, Stephen Jay Gould Made a Difference," pp. 12-13.

Spectator, November 24, 2001, review of *Rocks of Ages,* p. 44; June 29, 2002, John R.G. Turner, reviews of *The Structure of Evolutionary Theory* and *I Have Landed,* pp. 36-37.

Sports Illustrated, March 17, 2003, Charles Hirshberg, "Thinking Baseball: Renowned Scientist Stephen Jay Gould Was No Snob When He Focused His Intellect on His Favorite Game," p. R4.

Time, May 30, 1983; September 30, 1985.

Times Higher Education Supplement, April 6, 2001, Nick Petford, review of *The Lying Stones of Marrakech,* p. 26; June 21, 2002, Brian Charlesworth, review of *The Structure of Evolutionary Theory,* p. 36.

Times Literary Supplement, May 22, 1981; February 10, 1984; October 25, 1985; June 6, 1986; September 11-17, 1987; July 2, 1999, review of *Leonardo's Mountain of Clams and the Diet of Worms,* p. 28.

Tribune Books (Chicago, IL), November 30, 1980; June 26, 1983.

Voice Literary Supplement, June, 1987.

Wall Street Journal, March 29, 1999, review of *Rocks of Ages,* p. A24.

Washington Post Book World, November 8, 1981; May 8, 1983; September 29, 1985; April 26, 1987; April 14, 2002, review of *The Structure of Evolutionary Theory,* p. 4.

Whole Earth Review, spring, 2002, Lulu Winslow, review of *Crossing Over,* p. 85.

ONLINE

Salon, http://www.salon.com/ (May 20, 2002).

Unofficial Stephen Jay Gould Archive, http://www.stephenjaygould.org/ (May 8, 2003).

OBITUARIES:

PERIODICALS

Africa News Service, May 24, 2002.
Economist (U.S.), May 25, 2002.
Financial Times, July 6, 2002, p. 5.
Nation, June 17, 2002, p. 6.
Newsweek, June 3, 2002, p. 59.
U.S. News & World Report, June 3, 2002, p. 15.

ONLINE

Popular-Science, http://www.popular-science.net/ (May 8, 2002).

*   *   *

GOYTISOLO, Juan 1931-

PERSONAL: Born January 5, 1931, in Barcelona, Spain; immigrated to France, 1957. *Education:* Attended University of Barcelona and University of Madrid, 1948-52.

ADDRESSES: Home—Marrakesh, Morocco. *Agent*—c/o Author Mail, Serpent's Tail, 4 Blackstock Mews, London N4 2BT, England.

CAREER: Writer. Worked as reporter in Cuba, 1961, Bosnia, 1993, Algeria, 1994, and Chechnya, 1995; associated with Gallimard Publishing Co., Paris, France. Visiting professor at universities in the United States.

AWARDS, HONORS: Premio Europalia, 1985; Nelly Sachs prize, 1993; Premio Octavio Paz, 2002.

WRITINGS:

NOVELS

Juegos de manos, Destino (Barcelona, Spain), 1954, 4th edition, 1969, translation by John Rust published as *The Young Assassins,* Knopf (New York, NY), 1959.

Duelo en el Paraíso, Planeta (Barcelona, Spain), 1955, reprinted, Destino (Barcelona, Spain), 1981, translation by Christine Brooke-Rose published as *Children of Chaos,* Macgibbon & Kee (London, England), 1958.

El circo (first novel in "Mañana efímero" trilogy; title means "The Circus"), Destino (Barcelona, Spain), 1957, recent edition, 1982.

Fiestas (second novel in "Mañana efímero" trilogy), Emece, 1958, Destino (Barcelona, Spain), 1981, translation by Herbert Weinstock published as *Fiestas,* Knopf (New York, NY), 1960.

La resaca (third novel in "Mañana efímero" trilogy; title means "The Undertow"), Club del Libro Español, 1958, J. Mortiz (Mexico), 1977.

La isla, Seix Barral (Barcelona, Spain), 1961, reprinted, 1982, translation by José Yglesias published as *Island of Women,* Knopf (New York, NY), 1962, published as *Sands of Torremolinos,* J. Cape (London, England), 1962.

Señas de identidad (first novel in "Alvaro Mendiola" trilogy), J. Mortiz (Mexico), 1966, translation by Gregory Rabassa published as *Marks of Identity,* Grove (New York, NY), 1969, reprinted, Serpent's Tail (New York, NY), 2003.

Reivindicación del conde don Julián (second novel in "Alvaro Mendiola" trilogy), J. Mortiz (Mexico), 1970, reprinted, Catedra (Madrid, Spain), 1985, translation by Helen R. Lane published as *Count Julian,* Viking (New York, NY), 1974.

Juan sin tierra (third novel in "Alvaro Mendiola" trilogy), Seix Barral (Barcelona, Spain), 1975, translation by Helen R. Lane published as *Juan the Landless,* Viking (New York, NY), 1977.

Makbara, Seix Barral (Barcelona, Spain), 1980, translated by Helen R. Lane, Seaver Books (New York, NY), 1981.

Paisajes despues de la batalla, Montesinos (Barcelona, Spain), 1982, translation by Helen R. Lane published as *Landscapes after the Battle,* Seaver Books (New York, NY), 1987.

Las virtudes del pájaro solitario, Seix Barral (Barcelona, Spain), 1988, translation published as *The Virtues of the Solitary Bird,* 1993.

La cuarentena, Mondadori (Madrid, Spain), 1991, translation by Peter Bush published as *Quarantine,* Dalkey Archive Press (Normal, IL), 1994.

Cuaderno de Sarajevo, Aguilar (Madrid, Spain), 1993.

La saga de los Marx, Aguilar (Madrid, Spain), 1993, translation published as *The Marx Family Saga,* City Lights Books (San Francisco, CA), 1999.

El sitio de los sitios, Alfaguara (Madrid, Spain), 1995, translation by Helen R. Lane published as *State of Siege,* City Light Books (San Francisco, CA), 2002.

Las semanas del jardín; un círculo de lectores, Alfaguara (Madrid, Spain), 1997, translation by Peter Bush published as *The Garden of Secrets: As Written Down,* Serpent's Tail (New York, NY), 2002.

El universo imaginario, Espasa Calpe (Barcelona, Spain), 1997.

Cogitus interruptus, Seix Barral (Barcelona, Spain), 1999.

Carajicomedia: de Fray Bugeo Montesino y otros pajaros devario plumaje y pluma, Seix Barral (Barcelona, Spain), 2000, translated as *A Cock-eyed Comedy,* Serpent's Tail (New York, NY), 2002.

Telón de bois, Aleph (Barcelona, Spain), 2003.

SHORT STORIES

Para vivir aquí (title means "To Live Here"), Sur (Buenos Aires, Argentina), 1960, reprinted, Bruguera (Barcelona, Spain), 1983.

Fin de fiesta: Tentativas de interpretacion de una historia amorosa, Seix Barral (Barcelona, Spain), 1962, translation by José Yglesias published as *The Party's Over: Four Attempts to Define a Love Story,* Weidenfeld & Nicolson (London, England), 1966, Grove (New York, NY), 1967.

Aproximaciones a Gaudí en Capadocia, Mondadori (Madrid, Spain), 1990.

TRAVEL NARRATIVES

Campos de Nijar, Seix Barral (Barcelona, Spain), 1960, Grant & Cutler (London, England), 1984, translation by Luigi Luccarelli published as *The Countryside of Nijar* in *The Countryside of Nijar* [and] *La chanca,* Alembic Press (Plainfield, IN), 1987.

La chanca, Librería Española, 1962, Seix Barral (Barcelona, Spain), 1983, translation by Luigi Luccarelli published as *The Countryside of Nijar* [and] *La chanca,* Alembic Press (Plainfield, IN), 1987.

Pueblo en marcha: instantaneas de un viaje a Cuba (title means "People on the March: Snapshots of a Trip to Cuba"), Librería Española (Paris, France), 1963.

Cronicas sarracinas (title means "Saracen Chronicles"), Iberica (Barcelona, Spain), 1982.

Estambul otomano, Planeta (Barcelona, Spain), 1989, translation published as *Marrakesh Tales,* Serpent's Tail (New York, NY), 2000.

Argelia en el vendaval, Aguilar (Madrid, Spain), 1994.

OTHER

Problemas de la novela (literary criticism; title means "Problems of the Novel"), Seix Barral (Barcelona, Spain), 1959.

Las mismas palabras, Seix Barral (Barcelona, Spain), 1962.

Plume d'hier: espagne d'aujourd'hui, compiled by Mariano José de Larra, Editeurs Français Reunis, 1965.

El furgon de cola (critical essays; title means "The Caboose"), Ruedo Iberico, 1967, reprinted, Seix Barral (Barcelona, Spain), 1982.

Spanien und die Spanien, M. Bucher, 1969.

(Author of prologue) José Maria Blanco White, *Obra inglesa,* Formentor, 1972.

Obras completas (title means "Complete Works"), Aguilar (Madrid, Spain), 1977.

Libertad, libertad, libertad (essays and speeches), Anagrama (Barcelona, Spain), 1978.

(Author of introduction) Mohamed Chukri, *El pan desnudo* (title means "For Bread Alone"), translated from the Arabic by Abdellah Djibilou, Montesinos (Barcelona, Spain), 1982.

Coto vedado (autobiography; also see below), Seix Barral (Barcelona, Spain), 1985, translation by Peter Bush published as *Forbidden Territory: The Memoirs of Juan Goytisolo,* North Point Press (San Francisco, CA), 1989.

(Author of commentary) Omar Khayyam, *Estances,* translated into Catalan by Ramon Vives Pastor, del Mall (Barcelona, Spain), 1985.

Contracorrientes, Montesinos (Barcelona, Spain), 1985.

En los reinos de taifa (autobiography; title means "Realms of Strife"; also see below), Seix Barral (Barcelona, Spain), 1986.

Space in Motion (essays), translation by Helen R. Lane, Lumen Books (New York, NY), 1987.

De la ceca a la meca, Alfaguara (Madrid, Spain), 1997.

Cartas de Americo Castro a Juan Goytisolo, 1968-1972: el epistolario, Pre-Textos (Valencia, Spain), 1997

With Sami Naïr el Paeje del Vida) *Integración o rechazo de la emigracioón en España,* Aguilar (Madrid, Spain), 2000.

Paisajes de guerra con Chechnia al fondo (articles; formerly published in *El País*), Aguilar (Madrid, Spain), 1996, translation published as *Landscapes of War,* City Lights Books (San Francisco, CA), 2001.

Pájaro que ensucia su propio nido, Galaxia Tugenberg (Barcelona, Spain), 2001.

Telón de boca, Aleph (Barcelona, Spain), 2003.

España y sus ejidos, Hijos de Mule-Rubio (Madrid, Spain), 2003.

Forbidden Territory and Realms of Strife: The Memoirs of Juan Goytisolo (translations of *Coto vedado* and *En los reinos de taifa*), edited by Peter Bush, Verso (New York, NY), 2003.

Also author of *Disidencias* (essays), 1977. Work represented in collections and anthologies, including *Juan Goytisolo,* Ministerio de Cultura, Direccion General de Promocion del Libro y la Cinematografia, 1982. Contributor to periodicals, including *Ínsula* and *El País.*

SIDELIGHTS: "Juan Goytisolo is the best living Spanish novelist," wrote John Butt in the *Times Literary Supplement.* The author, as Butt observed, became renowned as a "pitiless satirist" of Spanish society during the dictatorship of Generalissimo Francisco Franco, who imposed his version of conservative religious values on the country from the late 1930s until his death in 1975. Goytisolo, whose youth coincided with the rise of Franco, had a variety of compelling reasons to feel alienated from his own country. He was a small child when his mother was killed in a bombing raid, a casualty of the civil war Franco instigated to seize power from a democratically elected government. The author then grew up as a bisexual in a country dominated, in Butt's words, by "frantic machismo." Eventually, writes Goytisolo in his memoir *Coto vedado—Forbidden Territory*—the author became "that strange species of writer claimed by none and alien and hostile to group s and categories."

In the late 1950s, when his writing career began to flourish, Goytisolo left Spain for Paris and remained in self-imposed exile until after Franco died. The literary world was greatly impressed when Goytisolo's first novel,*Juegos de manos—The Young Assassins*—was published in 1954. Goytisolo was identified as a member of the Spanish "restless generation" but his first novel seemed as much akin to the work of Fedor Dostoevski as it did to American Beat author Jack Kerouac. The plot is similar to Dostoevski's *The Possessed:* a group of students plot the murder of a politician but end up murdering the fellow student chosen to kill the politician. Some reviewers saw the theme as the self-destructiveness and hedonism of the smug and self-righteous.

Duelo en el paraíso—Children of Chaos—is seen as a violent extension of *The Young Assassins.* Like Anthony Burgess's *A Clockwork Orange* and William Golding's *Lord of the Flies, Children of Chaos* focuses on the terror wrought by adolescents. The children have taken over a small town after the end of the Spanish Civil War causes a breakdown of order.

Fiestas begins a trilogy referred to as "Ephemeral Morrow" (after a famous poem by Antonio Machado). Considered the best volume of the trilogy, this novel fol-lows four characters as they try to escape life in Spain by chasing their dreams. Each character meets with disappointment in the novel's end. *El circo,* the second book in the "Ephemeral Morrow" trilogy, was deemed by critics as too blatantly ironic to succeed as a follow-up to *Fiestas.* It is the story of a painter who manages a fraud before being punished for a murder he didn't commit. The third book, *La resaca,* was also a disappointment, the novel's style considered too realistic to function as a fitting conclusion to the trilogy.

After writing two politically oriented travelogues, *Campos de Nijar (The Countryside of Nijar)* and *La chanca,* Goytisolo returned to fiction and the overt realism he had begun in *La resaca.* Unfortunately, critics have implied that both *La isla (Island of Women)* and *Fin de fiesta (The Party's Over)* suffer because they ultimately resembled their subject matter, a small world of intellectuals who operate in a vacuum.

Goytisolo abandoned his realist style after *The Party's Over. Señas de identidad—Marks of Identity*—focuses on an exile who returns to his native Barcelona after the Spanish Civil War. The book is the first in a trilogy that includes *Reivindicación del conde don Julián—Count Julian—*and *Juan sin tierra—Juan the Landless. Count Julian* has been widely considered as Goytisolo's masterpiece to date. In it, the novelist uses techniques borrowed from James Joyce, Celine, Jean Genet, filmmaker Luis Bunuel, and painter Pablo Picasso. *Count Julian* is named for the legendary Spanish nobleman who betrayed his country to Arab invaders in the Middle Ages. In the shocking fantasies of the novel's narrator, a modern Spaniard living as an outcast in Africa, Julian returns to punish Spain for its cruelty and hypocrisy. Over the course of the narration, the Spanish language itself gradually transforms int o Arabic. Writing in the *New York Times Book Review,* Carlos Fuentes called *Count Julian* "an adventure of language, a critical battle against the language appropriated by power in Spain. It is also a search for a new/old language that would offer an alternative for the future." Reviews for *Juan the Landless* were generally less favorable than those for either *Marks of Identity* or *Count Julian,* an *Atlantic* critic suggesting that the uninformed reader begin elsewhere with Goytisolo.

Even after the oppressive Franco regime was dismantled in the late 1970s, Goytisolo continued to write novels that expressed deep alienation by displaying an unconventional, disorienting view of human society. *Makbara,* for example, is named for the cemeteries of North Africa where lovers meet for late-night trysts. "What a poignant central image it is," wrote Paul West in the *Washington Post Book World,* "not only as an emblem of life in death . . . but also as a vantage point from which to review the human antic in general, which includes all those who go about their daily chores with their minds below their belts." The characters Goytisolo "feels at home with," West declared, "are the drop-outs and the ne'er do wells, the outcasts and the misfits." In *Paisajes despues de la batalla—Landscapes after the Battle*—the author moves his vision of alienation to Paris, where he had long remained in exile. This short novel, made up of seventy-eight nonsequential chapters, displays the chaotic mix of people—from French nationalists to Arab immigrants—who uneasily coexist in the city. "The Paris metro map which the protagonist contemplates . . . for all its innumerable permutations of routes," explained Abigail Lee in the *Times Literary Supplement,* "provides an apt image for the text itself." *Landscapes after the Battle* "looked like another repudiation, this time of Paris," Butt wrote, adding: "One wondered what Goytisolo would destroy next."

Accordingly, Butt was surprised to find that the author's memoir of his youth, published in 1985, had a markedly warmer tone than the novels that had preceded it. "Far from being a new repudiation," the critic observed, *Forbidden Territory* "is really an essay in acceptance and understanding. . . . Gone, almost, are the tortuous language, the lurid fantasies, the dreams of violation and abuse. Instead, we are given a moving, confessional account of a difficult childhood and adolescence." Goytisolo's recollections, the reviewer concluded, constitute "a moving and sympathetic story of how one courageous victim of the Franco regime fought his way out of a cultural and intellectual wasteland, educated himself, and went on to inflict a brilliant revenge on the social system which so isolated and insulted him."

In *Las virtudes del pájaro solitario—The Virtues of the Solitary Bird*—Goytisolo explores the Christian, Jewish, and Moorish heritage of Spain and the hybrid mysticism that emerged from the intermingling of the three religions, particularly as expressed in the writings of Saint John of the Cross and Arabian poet Ibn al Farid. Goytisolo juxtaposes the persecution of Saint John with a contemporary narrator who entertains imaginary conversations with the sixteenth-century saint while living in exile and suffering from AIDS. Mirroring the author's own political oppression and departure from Franco's Spain, the book "is also the story of the independent thinker throughout history, flushed out by those fearful of 'contaminating ideas,'" observed a *Publishers Weekly* reviewer. Jack Byrne noted in the *Review of Contemporary Fiction* that Goytisolo's version of the

martyred saint's verse "modernize[s], while not sanitizing, the horror of heresy—theological, political, social, moral—wherever and whenever it appears." Amanda Hopkinson wrote in the *Times Literary Supplement* that "Goytisolo expects to be read as a parable of our time, with all its complexities and obscurities. This is not prose, at least as conventionally punctuated, it is poetry full of rhapsodic psalms and oriental mysticism."

Goytisolo's *Quarantine,* another complex, experimental novel, follows the spiritual wandering of a recently deceased female writer whose soul, according to Islamic tradition, must embark on a forty-day journey to eternal rest. Through an unnamed narrator, Goytisolo likens this spiritual quarantine to the creative writing process, whereby an author remains in isolation for a time to summon memory and the imagination. In effect, the fictional author's meditations on death and writing become the story itself as he imagines his own death, encounters the soul of his dead friend among angels and a Sufi mystic, and considers parallels to Dante's *Divine Comedy.* Jack Shreve noted in a *Library Journal* review that Goytisolo "multiplies levels of interpretation in order to 'destabilize' the reader." Goytisolo also interjects a strong antiwar theme through surreal news reports that describe the carnage of the Persian Gulf War.

In his novel *La saga de los Marx—The Marx Family Saga*—Goytisolo tackles the political theme of the fall of communism in Europe and the West's reaction it. The wry, satirical, and funny story focuses on Albanian refugees in an Italian resort who are searching for a paradise called "Dallas" and who are confronted by locals outraged at their presence. The family is, in essence, a reincarnation of Karl Marx and his family, all living in a type of historical limbo, watching the televised crumbling of the system the father of communism created. Sophia A. McClennen, writing in the *Review of Contemporary Fiction,* said the novel "provides a brutally vivid characterization of the intricacies of social commitment in a world which consumes more television than literature." *New Statesman* contributor Abigail Lee Six commented that "*The Marx Family Saga,* like most of Goytisolo's recent fiction, is very funny as it makes serious literary an d socio-political points."

Goytisolo's *The Garden of Secrets* tells the story of the young poet Eusebio, who is confined by his family in a psychiatric center and diagnosed as schizophrenic. Eusebio ultimately escapes and flees Franco's Spain. A reading group later tries to arrange the various facts of the poet's case, each telling their own respective versions of the story. Writing in the *Review of Contempo-*

rary Fiction, Thomas Hove noted that Eusebio resembles Goytisolo in many biographical aspects and went on to note that "his story develops the author's frequent Joycean theme of exile as both liberation and alienation." Writing in the *Library Journal*, Jack Shreve called *The Garden of Secrets* an "intriguing collective portrait by one of Spain's foremost writers."

Goytisolo tackles the Roman Catholic Church and its secret society Opus Dei in his satirical novel *Carajico-media: de Fray Bugeo Montesino y otros pajaros de-vario plumaje y pluma*, translated as *Cock-eyed Comedy*. The novel includes a wide cast of historical characters, including Roland Barthes, Jean Genet, and a character who keeps popping up throughout the centuries under different guises to expose the hypocrisy of the Spanish priesthood. Writing in the *Library Journal*, Nelly S. Gonzalez noted that in Goytisolo's "parody of our times, humor and cynicism are omnipresent but unexaggerated, and nobody escapes Goytisolo's mordant wit."

The siege of Sarajevo is the setting for Goytisolo's *El sitio de los sitios*, which centers on the mystery surrounding the disappearance of a Spanish visitor's corpse. The missing visitor has left behind various writings signed "J. G." The novel is made up of these and other texts, including stories and poems, police reports, and testimonies by people who saw or knew the vanished man. Writing in *Booklist*, Frank Sennet noted that the novel has "all the earmarks of magic realism" and concluded that the story is "effective in underscoring the tragic absurdity of sieges whose victims can only guess at the rationale of their persecutors." *Review of Contemporary Fiction* contributor Megan A. McDowell noted that in *State of Siege* "Goytisolo exposes the most basic quality of consciousness that both feeds on and creates literature, the part that spawns violence and madness, humor and language."

In 2003, the author's two memoirs were published together in English translation as *Forbidden Territory and Realms of Strife: The Memoirs of Juan Goytisolo*. Describing the work as "literary history up close," a *Publishers Weekly* contributor noted that "style is king here, and it is wonderful, infiltrating Goytisolo's chronological narrative like one of his characters." Nedra Crowe Evers, writing in *Library Journal*, commented that the memoir's lack of an index is the book's only drawback and added, "The writing is powerful but never crude; many passages are, quite simply, beautiful."

BIOGRAPHICAL AND CRITICAL SOURCES:

BOOKS

Amell, Samuel, editor, *Literature, the Arts, and Democracy: Spain in the Eighties*, Fairleigh Dickinson University Press (Madison, NJ), 1990.

Contemporary Literary Criticism, Thomson Gale (Detroit, MI), Volume 5, 1976, Volume 10, 1979, Volume 23, 1983.

Epps, Bradley S., *Significant Violence: Oppression and Resistance in the Later Narrative of Juan Goytisolo*, Clarendon (New York, NY), 1996.

Gazarian Gautier, Marie-Lise, *Interviews with Spanish Writers*, Dalkey Archive Press (Normal, IL), 1991.

Goytisolo, Juan, *Forbidden Territory*, translation by Peter Bush, North Point Press (San Francisco, CA), 1989.

Pope, Randolph D., *Understanding Juan Goytisolo*, University of South Carolina Press (Columbia, SC), 1995.

Schwartz, Kessel, *Juan Goytisolo*, Twayne (New York, NY), 1970.

Schwartz, Ronald, *Spain's New Wave Novelists 1950-1974: Studies in Spanish Realism*, Scarecrow Press (Lanham, MD), 1976.

PERIODICALS

Atlantic, August, 1977.

Best Sellers, June 15, 1974.

Booklist, October 1, 2002, Frank Sennett, review of *State of Siege*, p. 301.

Journal of Spanish Studies, winter, 1979, pp. 353-364.

Kirkus Reviews, March 1, 1994, p. 234.

Lettres Peninsulares, fall-winter, 1990, pp. 259-278.

Library Journal, October 1, 1990, p. 89; March 1, 1994, p. 117; December, 2000, Jack Shreve, review of *The Garden of Secrets*, p. 187; August, 2001, Nelly S. Gonzalez, review of *Cock-eyed Comedy*, p. S34; July, 2003, Nedra Crowe Evers, review of *Forbidden Territory and Realms of Strife: The Memoirs of Juan Goytisolo*, p. 80.

Los Angeles Times Book Review, January 22, 1989.

Nation, March 1, 1975.

New Republic, January 31, 1967.

New Statesman, July 19, 1991, p. 38; December 17, 1993, p. 46; August 9, 1996, Abigail Lee Six, review of *The Marx Family Saga*, p. 47.

New York Times Book Review, January 22, 1967; May 5, 1974; September 18, 1977; June 14, 1987; July 3, 1988; February 12, 1989.

Publishers Weekly, November 30, 1992, p. 48; March 7, 1994, p. 55; May 19, 2003, review of *Forbidden Territory and Realms of Strife: The Memoirs of Juan Goytisolo,* p. 64.

Review of Contemporary Fiction, fall, 1993, p. 213; fall, 1999, Sophia A. McClennen, review of *The Marx Family Saga,* p. 176; January 8, 2001, Maya Jaggi, "Juan Goytisolo" (interview with author), p. 42; fall, 2001, Thomas Hove, "Landscapes of War: From Sarajevo to Chechnya," p. 197; spring, 2003, Megan A. McDowell, review of *State of Siege,* p. 148.

Saturday Review, February 14, 1959; June 11, 1960; June 28, 1969.

Texas Quarterly, spring, 1975.

Times Literary Supplement, May 31, 1985; September 9, 1988; May 19, 1989; November 17, 1989; July 12, 1991, p. 18.

Washington Post Book World, January 17, 1982; June 14, 1987.

World Press Review, April, 1994. p. 51.

ONLINE

Juan Goytisolo Web site, http://www.cnice.mecd.es/tematicas/juangoytisolo/ (April 15, 2004).

* * *

GRAFTON, Sue 1940-

PERSONAL: Born April 24, 1940, in Louisville, KY; daughter of Chip Warren (an attorney and writer) and Vivian Boisseau (a high school chemistry teacher; maiden name, Harnsberger) Grafton; married third husband Steven F. Humphrey (a professor of philosophy), October 1, 1978; children: (first marriage) Leslie Flood; (second marriage) Jay Schmidt, Jamie Schmidt. *Education:* University of Louisville, B.A., 1961. *Hobbies and other interests:* Walking, reading, cooking, bridge.

ADDRESSES: Home—Montecito, CA, and Louisville, KY. *Office*—P.O. Box 41447, Santa Barbara, CA 93140. *Agent*—Molly Friedrich, Aaron Priest Agency, 708 Third Ave., 23rd Fl., New York, NY 10017-4103.

CAREER: Screenwriter and author. Has worked as a hospital admissions clerk, cashier, and clerical/medical secretary. Lecturer, Los Angeles City College, Long Beach, CA, City College, University of Dayton, Dayton, OH, and various writers' conferences, including Los Angeles Valley College, Albuquerque, Smithsonian Campus on the Mall, Antioch Writers Conference, Yellow Springs, OH, and Midwest Writers Conference, Canton, OH.

MEMBER: Writers Guild of America (West), Mystery Writers of America (president, 1994-95), Private Eye Writers of America (president, 1989-90).

AWARDS, HONORS: Christopher Award, 1979, for teleplay *Walking through the Fire;* Mysterious Stranger Award, Cloak and Clue Society, 1982-83, for *A Is for Alibi;* Shamus Award for best hardcover private eye novel, Private Eye Writers of America, and Anthony Award for best hardcover mystery, Mystery Readers of America, both 1985, both for *B Is for Burglar;* Macavity Award for best short story, and Anthony Award, both 1986, both for "The Parker Shotgun"; Edgar Award nomination, Mystery Writers of America, 1986, for teleplay *Love on the Run;* Anthony Award, 1987, for *C Is for Corpse;* Doubleday Mystery Guild Award, 1989, for *E Is for Evidence;* American Mystery Award, best short story, 1990, for "A Poison That Leaves No Trace"; Falcon Award for best mystery novel, Maltese Falcon Society of Japan, and Doubleday Mystery Guild Award, both 1990, both for *F Is for Fugitive;* Doubleday Mystery Guild Award, Shamus Award, and Anthony Award, all 1991, all for *G Is for Gumshoe;* Doubleday Mystery Guild Award, and American Mystery Award, both 1992, both for *H Is for Homicide;* Doubleday Mystery Guild Award, 1993, for *I Is for Innocent,* and 1994, for *J Is for Judgment;* Shamus Award, 1995, and Doubleday Mystery Guild Award, 1995, both for *K Is for Killer.*

WRITINGS:

DETECTIVE NOVELS, EXCEPT AS NOTED

Keziah Dane (novel) Macmillan (New York, NY), 1967.

The Lolly-Madonna War (novel; also see below), P. Owen (New York, NY), 1969.

A Is for Alibi (Mystery Guild main selection; also see below), Holt (New York, NY), 1982.

B Is for Burglar (Mystery Guild main selection; also see below), Holt (New York, NY), 1985.

C Is for Corpse (Mystery Guild main selection; also see below), Holt (New York, NY), 1986.

D Is for Deadbeat, Holt (New York, NY), 1987.

E Is for Evidence, Holt (New York, NY), 1988.

F Is for Fugitive, Holt (New York, NY), 1989.

G Is for Gumshoe, Holt (New York, NY), 1990.

H Is for Homicide, Holt (New York, NY), 1991.

I Is for Innocent, Holt (New York, NY), 1992.

(Editor) *Writing Mysteries: A Handbook,* Writer's Digest (Cincinnati, OH), 1992, 2nd edition, 2002.

Kinsey and Me (short stories), Bench Press (Columbia, SC), 1992.

J Is for Judgment, Holt (New York, NY), 1993.

K Is for Killer, Holt (New York, NY), 1994.

L Is for Lawless (Mystery Guild and Literary Guild main selections), Holt (New York, NY), 1995.

M Is for Malice, Holt (New York, NY), 1996.

N Is for Noose, Holt (New York, NY), 1998.

(Editor, with Otto Penzler) *The Best American Mystery Stories 1998,* Houghton Mifflin (Boston, MA), 1998.

O Is for Outlaw, Holt (New York, NY), 1999.

Three Complete Novels ("A" Is for Alibi, "B" Is for Burglar, and "C" Is for Corpse) Wings Books (New York, NY), 1999.

P Is for Peril, Penguin Putnam (New York, NY), 2001.

Q Is for Quarry, Penguin Putnam (New York, NY), 2002.

R Is for Ricochet, Penguin Putnam (New York, NY), 2004.

S Is for Silence, Penguin Putnam (New York, NY), 2005.

Contributor of "Kinsey Millhone" short stories to anthologies, including *Mean Streets: The Second Private Eye Writers of America Anthology,* edited by Robert J. Randisi, 1986; *Sisters in Crime,* edited by Marilyn Wallace, 1989; and *A Woman's Eye,* edited by Sara Paretsky and Martin H. Greenburg, 1991. Contributor to periodicals, including *California Review* and *Redbook.* The "Kinsey Millhone" novels have been translated into numerous languages, including Dutch, Russian, Polish, Spanish, and French, and have also been released as audiobooks.

SCREENPLAYS AND TELEPLAYS

(With Rodney Carr-Smith) *Lolly-Madonna XXX* (adapted from Sue Grafton's novel *The Lolly-Madonna War),* Metro-Goldwyn-Mayer, 1973.

Walking through the Fire (adapted from the novel by Laurel Lee), Columbia Broadcasting Corp. (CBS-TV), 1979.

Sex and the Single Parent (adapted from the book by Jane Adams), CBS-TV, 1979.

Nurse (adapted from the book by Peggy Anderson), CBS-TV, 1980.

Mark, I Love You (adapted from the book by Hal Painter), CBS-TV, 1980.

(With husband, Steven F. Humphrey) *Seven Brides for Seven Brothers* (pilot), CBS-TV, 1982.

(With Steven F. Humphrey) *A Caribbean Mystery* (adapted from the novel by Agatha Christie), CBS-TV, 1983.

(With Steven F. Humphrey and Robert Aller) *A Killer in the Family,* American Broadcasting Co. (ABC-TV), 1983.

(With Steven F. Humphrey and Robert Malcolm Young) *Sparkling Cyanide* (adapted from the novel by Agatha Christie), CBS-TV, 1983.

(With Steven F. Humphrey) *Love on the Run,* National Broadcasting Co. (NBC-TV), 1985.

(With Steven F. Humphrey) *Tonight's the Night,* ABC-TV, 1987.

Contributor of scripts to television series, including *Rhoda,* 1975. Story editor, Steven F. Humphrey, for television series *Seven Brides for Seven Brothers,* 1982-83.

SIDELIGHTS: Sue Grafton, according to Andrea Chambers in *People,* "is perhaps the best of the new breed of female mystery writers, who are considered the hottest segment of the market." In her mystery stories featuring California private investigator Kinsey Millhone, Grafton has chosen to feature a heroine rather than the traditional male hero. Nonetheless, as Deirdre Donahue observed in *USA Today,* "Grafton draws on elements of the classic private-eye genre." In Millhone, David Lehman of *Newsweek* told prospective readers, "you'll find a thoroughly up-to-date, feminine version of Philip Marlowe, Raymond Chandler's hard-boiled hero."

The hard-boiled detective story traditionally features a male protagonist and a lot of action—gunplay, bloodshed, and general mayhem. Heroes such as Dashiell Hammett's Sam Spade, Raymond Chandler's Marlowe, and Ross MacDonald's Lew Archer defined masculinity for a generation of readers with their "loner" mentalities and their sensitivity to the profound difference between the mean streets and the normal world. Yet Grafton's Millhone is as popular as any of her precursors, male or female. *New York Times Book Review* contributor Vincent Patrick suggested that the reason behind her popularity is that Millhone is, in fact, a traditional hero: "Chandler's concept of a detective hero was that 'he must be the best man in his world, and a good enough man for any world.' Gender aside, Kinsey [Millhone] fills that prescription perfectly."

Along with Sara Paretsky, Grafton is credited with establishing female detectives in the hard-boiled genre. The two authors introduced their characters, V.I. Warshawski and Kinsey Millhone, within a few months of each other in 1982. "There had been female sleuths in crime fiction before, of course," wrote Josh Rubins in the *New York Times Book Review,* "like the eponymous heroine of the 1910 book *Lady Molly of Scotland Yard,* Miss Marple, Nancy Drew and Amanda Cross's Kate Fansler. There had even been a thoroughly believable homicide cop named Christie Opara (in Dorothy Uhnak's landmark police novels of the 1960's and 70's) . . . . However, Kinsey and V. I. were the first women to . . . [bury] the stereotypes about 'lady detectives' and [clear] a path for the dozens of tough-minded, ready- for-anything heroines who have become a major element in the genre."

Other than establishing a heroine in a traditionally male role, Grafton, according to certain critics, has left intact the framework of the hard- boiled detective story. Ed Weiner wrote in the *New York Times Book Review* that neither Grafton nor her peers "have gone so far as to redefine the genre. They play it fairly safe and conventional. But in their work there is thankfully little of the macho posturing and sluggish rogue beefcake found so often in the male versions, no Hemingwayesque mine-is-bigger-than-yours competitive literary swaggering." *Women's Review of Books* contributor Maureen T. Reddy declared that Grafton's books "implicitly question, and undermine, received wisdom about gender-specific character traits, but are not otherwise feminist." Instead, Weiner explained, "she has successfully replaced the raw, masculine-fantasy brutality and gore of the [Robert] Parkers and [Jonathan] Valins and [Elmore] Leonards with heart-pounding, totally mesmerizing suspense." "Millhone . . . got our attention by crashing the private eyes' stag party," Rubins declared. She's "kept it by building, in fits and starts, [her] own rather lonely, increasingly distinctive worlds."

Grafton has also kept readers and attracted new ones by allowing Millhone to develop throughout her novels. "Grafton, always competent, comes roaring out of the '80s with an expanded vision of her heroine and a willingness to take risks," declared *Chicago Tribune* contributor Kevin Moore in a review of *G Is for Gumshoe.* "People buy and read Grafton's books because they believe in Kinsey Millhone, and want to know what's happening in her life," wrote Dick Adler in a *Chicago Tribune* review of *J Is for Judgment* several years later. "In her ten books [Grafton] has managed . . . to create a deeper, softer, more approachable central character."

But some of the elements in the series remain the same. "Like those Saturday afternoon serials of yore," declared *Washington Post Book World* reviewer Maureen Corrigan, writing about *K Is for Killer,* "many a mystery novel has tied its readers up in knots over some subplot complication and abandoned them on the railroad tracks of anticipation, only to delay rescue till the next installment." Corrigan traced some new complications introduced in the previous volume, *J Is for Judgment* (Millhone, introduced as an orphan in the beginning of the series, turns out to have some distant relatives), and noted that "curious Kinsey fans will fling open *K Is for Killer* . . . and race through its pages only to discover . . . that Kinsey is still mulling over what to do about her relatives." In an earlier example taken from *G Is for Gumshoe,* Millhone moves back into her apartment which had been partly destroyed by a bomb in the previous book. "You know you are deep in the land of fiction," wrote *New York Times Book Review* contributor Alex Kozinski, "when you find a landlord in Southern California willing to rent a newly renovated apartment for $200 a month, particularly to a tenant known to be a target for bombers."

This question of resolution is something that regularly troubles Grafton. The writer once stated that her late father C. W. Grafton (who published three mysteries during his lifetime) was "very passionate about mystery novels, which he wrote at the office in the evenings . . . . At this point, I would love to sit down and talk to him about plotting, which to me is the great 'bug-a-boo' of mystery." In order to bring the plots under control, Grafton told Enid Nemy of the *New York Times,* she keeps a comprehensive notebook containing all the information she has researched on a topic. "Every three or four weeks, I go through it and highlight what interests me," she said. "Then the story emerges, and from that, the angle of attack, who hires Kinsey, what she's hired to do. Sometimes I walk down roads that don't go anywhere." When plot complications held up the publication of *K Is for Killer,* for instance, reported *Wall Street Journal* contributor Tom Nolan, hundreds of readers called their bookstores to complain. Grafton told Nolan, "A bookstore owner in Pasadena called me and said, 'You have no idea what rumors are circulating!'"

In the fourteenth installment in the series, *N Is for Noose,* Millhone leaves her home base of Santa Teresa, California, to investigate circumstances surrounding the death of Sheriff Tom Newquist in Nota Lake, Nevada. Although Newquist apparently died of natural causes, his wife, Selma, suspects the stress of a recent case involving a double homicide was what brought it on. As Millhone seeks the dead Sheriff's missing notebook, she confronts hostile townsfolk and endures a serious beating. Writing in *Library Journal,* Wilda Williams observed that *N Is for Noose* serves up less violence and plot action than the average Millhone caper, with "more emphasis on character" and "an almost melancholic mood." While praising "Grafton's easy-reading prose and her heroine's sharp humor," a *Publishers Weekly* reviewer lodged a similar reaction, complaining of "a slew of plot weaknesses." However, Emily Melton of *Booklist* found *N Is for Noose* to be "one of the best to date in Grafton's supremely popular series." Melton also commented: "Grafton has such a strong following . . . that virtually anything she writes shoots to the top of the best-seller lists. Fortunately, the fame is, by and large, well deserved."

In *O Is for Outlaw* Grafton further develops Millhone's history and character as the private investigator is drawn into a case involving her own past. Dubbed "one of the very best entries in a long-lived and much-loved series" by a *Publishers Weekly* reviewer, the mystery begins with an undelivered letter discovered in an abandoned storage locker. The fourteen-year-old letter concerns Millhone's first ex-husband, Mickey Magruder, a former vice officer once accused of beating a man to death. It contains evidence that might exonerate Mickey of the crime, which not only caused his expulsion from the police force but prompted Millhone to divorce him only months into their marriage. The plot thickens and accelerates as Mickey is shot with Millhone's gun and hospitalized in a coma. Millhone must delve back into the sixties and the Vietnam War to discover Mickey's assailant and determine his own guilt or innocence. "Kinsey is sassier than ever," noted Karen Anderson of *Library Journal,* "the supporting characters are amusingly eccentric, and the mysteries, both past and present, are intriguing." According to Melton, in *O Is for Outlaw* Grafton delivers "a novel of depth and substance that is, in every way, the class of the series."

Entering the new millennium with *P Is for Peril,* Millhone finds herself embroiled in a missing persons case involving a rich doctor, a disgruntled and suspicious ex-wife, Medicare fraud at a nursing home, a confused teenager, and an ex-stripper. Meanwhile, the sleuth has become romantically involved with the twin brother of her office landlord, a man accused of murdering his parents ten years earlier. "As always," remarked Connie Fletcher in *Booklist,* "Grafton gives us a truly complex heroine, marvelous depictions of Southern California architecture and interiors, and a writing style that can make a weed path interesting." Williams gave Grafton "an A for maintaining her series's high standard of excellence."

On her Web site, Grafton shares with fans the evolution of *R is for Ricochet.* Referring to the extensive notes she keeps when writing, she explains: "I'd written the first 15 pages of the manuscript, double-spaced. At that same point in time, I had 100 pages, single-spaced, written in my journal . . . . On January 26, 2004, twenty-three months from the time I began, I completed the manuscript, which was 500 pages, double-spaced. The 9 journals I'd written simultaneously totaled 516 single- spaced pages. Yes, I'm nuts."

In 2005 Grafton completed the nineteenth novel in her alphabet series, *S Is for Silence.* Kinsey Millhone returns to investigate a case that remains unsolved after thirty-four years. Violet Sullivan disappeared from a Fourth of July party in 1953; in 1987 her now adult daughter Daisy hires Kinsey to put the mystery to rest. In the novel, Grafton's storytelling alternates between the current investigation and flashbacks from the fifties, creating "the freshest, tautest installment in quite a while," according to Mark Harris in *Entertainment Weekly.* "Grafton has hit upon an ingenious solution, one that enlivens the writing and the reading of the book without compromising the friendship readers have developed with Kinsey and with Grafton," noted Marta Salij in *Detroit Free Press.* Fletcher, again writing in *Booklist,* commented, "this novel also presents strong character portrayals, a mosaic of motives, and a stunning climax."

"When I decided to do mysteries," Grafton explained to Bruce Taylor in an interview in *Armchair Detective,* "I chose the classic private eye genre because I like playing hardball with the boys. I despise gender-segregated events of any kind." Part of Millhone's appeal lies in Grafton's concept of her character, whom she sees as "a stripped-down version of me," she told Taylor. "She's the person I would have been had I not married young and had children. She'll always be thinner and younger and braver, the lucky so-and-so. Her biography is different, but our sensibilities are identical. At the core, we're the same . . . . Because of Kinsey, I get to lead two lives—hers and mine. Sometimes I'm not sure which I prefer." In a question and answer session on the McDougal Littell Web site, Grafton stated: "I do enjoy being a writer. The truth is, there's nothing I'd rather do with my life, but writing is 'fun' in the same way lifting weights is fun. It's hard and it hurts."

BIOGRAPHICAL AND CRITICAL SOURCES:

BOOKS

Kaufman, Natalie Hevener, and Carol McGinnis Kay, *"G" Is for Grafton: The World of Kinsey Millhone,* Henry Holt (New York, NY), 1997.

PERIODICALS

Armchair Detective, spring, 1988; winter, 1989; fall, 1989, p. 368; spring, 1991, p. 229.

Belles Lettres, summer, 1990.

Booklist, February 15, 1998, Emily Melton, review of *N Is for Noose,* p. 948; June 1, 1999, Emily Melton, review of *O Is for Outlaw,* p. 1742; March 15, 2001, Connie Fletcher, review of *P Is for Peril,* p. 1332; September 15, 2005, Connie Fletcher, review of *S Is for Silence,* p. 6.

Chicago Tribune, May 6, 1990, p. 6; May 4, 1992, p. 3; May 4, 1993, p. 3.

Detroit Free Press, Marta Salij, "*S Is for Silence*: Sue Grafton Does a Little Time Traveling for Alphabet Mystery No. 19."

English Journal, February, 1992, p. 95.

Entertainment Weekly, Mark Harris, "Alphabet Snoop: P.I. Kinsey Millhone Returns to Form in Sue Grafton's New Mystery, *S Is for Silence*," p. 91.

Globe and Mail (Toronto, Ontario, Canada), June 20, 1987; May 21, 1988.

Kirkus Reviews, March 1, 2001, review of *P Is for Peril,* p. 296.

Library Journal, March 1, 1998, Wilda Williams, review of *N Is for Noose,* p. 127; August 1999, Karen Anderson, review of *O Is for Outlaw,* p. 146; April 15, 2001, Wilda Williams, review of *P Is for Peril,* p. 131.

Los Angeles Times Book Review, August 4, 1985; May 14, 1989; May 12, 1991; October 8, 1995.

Newsweek, June 7, 1982; June 9, 1986.

New Yorker, June 27, 1994.

New York Times, May 8, 1991, p. C19; August 4, 1994, pp. C1, C10.

New York Times Book Review, May 23, 1982; May 1, 1988, pp. 11-12; May 21, 1989, p. 17; May 27, 1990, p. 13; July 28, 1991, p. 8; May 24, 1992, p. 25; May 2, 1993, p. 22; May 1, 1994, p. 24; October 8, 1995, p. 24.

People, July 10, 1989, Andrea Chambers, "Make No Bones about It, Sue Grafton's Detective Heroine Is a Real Pistol," p. 81; May 9, 1994, Lorenzo Carcaterra, review of *K is for Killer,* p. 29.

Publishers Weekly, February 16, 1998, review of *N Is for Noose,* p. 206; April 5, 1985, p. 66; March 14, 1986, p. 104; August 30, 1999, review of *O Is for Outlaw,* p. 55; May 21, 2001, review of *P Is for Peril,* p. 84.

Reason, December, 1994, p. 52.

Spectator, September 27, 1969.

USA Today, July 27, Deirdre Donahue, 1989.

Wall Street Journal, August 29, 1995, Tom Nolan, p. A12.

Washington Post Book World, May 18, 1986, pp. 8, 13; June 21, 1987; May 19, 1991; May 24, 1992, p. 6; April 17, 1994.

Women's Review of Books, December, 1986, p. 8; July, 1989.

ONLINE

McDougal Littell Web site, http://www.mcdougallittell.com/ (June 6, 2001), "Your Conversation with Sue Grafton."

Sue Grafton Web site, http://www.suegrafton.com/ (August 4, 2004).

*   *   *

GRAHAM, Jorie 1950-

PERSONAL: Born May 9, 1950, in New York, NY; daughter of Curtis Bill (a scholar of religion and theology and head of *Newsweek* Rome bureau) and Beverly (Stoll) Pepper (a noted sculptor); married James Galvin (a poet), 1983; children: Emily. *Education:* Sorbonne (Paris); New York University, B.F.A., 1973; University of Iowa, M.F.A., 1978.

ADDRESSES: Office—Harvard University, Department of English and American Literature, 12 Quincy Street, Cambridge, MA 02138.

CAREER: Writer and teacher of poetry. Murray State University, Murray, KY, assistant professor of English, 1978-79; Humboldt State University, Arcata, CA, assistant professor of English, 1979-81; Columbia University, associate professor and Writer's Community workshop instructor, 1981-83; University of Iowa, professor of English and Writers' Workshop instructor, 1983-99; Harvard University, Boylston Professor of Rhetoric and Oratory, 1999—. Gives poetry readings.

MEMBER: The Academy of American Poets (chancellor, 1997—).

AWARDS, HONORS: Prize from Academy of American Poets, 1977; Young Poet Prize from *Poetry Northwest,* 1980; Pushcart Prize from Pushcart Press, 1980, for "I Was Taught Three," and 1982, for "My Garden, My Daylight;" award from Great Lakes Colleges Association, 1981, for *Hybrids of Plants and of Ghosts;* grant from Ingram-Merrill Foundation, 1981; Bunting fellow at Radcliffe Institute, 1982; prize from *American Poetry Review,* 1982, for *The Age of Reason* and other poems; Guggenheim fellow, 1983; National Endowment for the Arts grant, 1985; Whiting award, 1985; MacArthur Foundation Grant, 1990; Academy of American Poets Lavan Award, 1991; Morton Dauwen Zabel Award, Academy and Institute of Arts and Letters, 1992; Pulitzer Prize for Poetry, 1996, for *The Dream of the Unified Field: Poems, 1974-1994.*

WRITINGS:

POETRY

Hybrids of Plants and of Ghosts, Princeton University Press (Princeton, NJ), 1980.

Erosion, Princeton University Press (Princeton, NJ), 1983.

The End of Beauty, Ecco Press (Hopewell, NJ), 1987.

Region of Unlikeness, Ecco Press (Hopewell, NJ), 1991.

Materialism: Poems, Ecco Press (Hopewell, NJ), 1993.

The Dream of the Unified Field: Poems, 1974-1994, Ecco Press (Hopewell, NJ), 1995.

The Hiding Place (audio recording), Archive of Recorded Poetry and Literature, Library of Congress (Washington, DC), 1995.

Karen Alkalay-Gut and Jorie Graham Reading Their Poems in the Montpelier Room, Library of Congress, October 19, 1995, (sound recording), Library of Congress (Washington, DC), 1995.

The Errancy, Ecco Press (Hopewell, NJ), 1997.

Jorie Graham and James McMichael Reading Their Poems in the Mumford Room, Library of Congress, March 12, 1998 (sound recording), Library of Congress (Washington, DC), 1998.

Swarm, Ecco Press (New York, NY), 2000.

Never: Poems, Ecco Press (New York, NY), 2002.

OTHER

(Editor, with David Lehman) *The Best American Poetry 1990,* Scribners' (New York, NY), 1991.

(Editor) *Earth Took of Earth: 100 Great Poems of the English Language,* Ecco Press (Hopewell, NJ), 1996.

(With Jeannette Montgomery Barron) *Photographs and Poems,* Scalo (New York, NY), 1998.

Work represented in anthologies, including *Golden Gate Harvest,* edited by Philip Dow, 1983; *Vintage Book of Contemporary American Poetry,* J.D. McClatchy, Vintage (New York, NY), 1990; and *New American Poets of the '90's,* edited by Jack Myers and Roger Weingarten, Godine (Boston, MA), 1992. Contributor of articles and poems to magazines, including *American Poetry Review, Antaeus, Georgia Review, Iowa Review, Nation, New England Review, New Yorker, Paris Review, Ploughshares,* and *Poetry Northwest.* Poetry editor of *Crazyhorse,* 1978-81.

SIDELIGHTS: Jorie Graham writes, teaches, and evangelizes poetry. She is perhaps the most celebrated poet of the American post-war generation, for, as Peyton Brien wrote in *Dictionary of Literary Biography,* Graham is a poet who is "at the forefront of the effort to revitalize and redefine American poetry" by writing "deeply searching and skillfully wrought poems that emerge from her firsthand . . . experience of art, literature, history, and religious thought." When Graham replaced Nobel Laureate and poet Seamus Heaney as Boylston professor in Harvard's Department of English and American Literature and Language—a chair whose occupants date back to John Quincy Adams—she became the first woman to be awarded this position.

Born in New York City, Graham was reared and educated in Italy and France. She attended the Sorbonne in Paris, where she studied philosophy, until she was expelled for participating in student riots. Returning to New York, she studied filmmaking at New York University. Graham was drawn to poetry, however, when she passed by a class being taught by poet and literary critic M.L. Rosenthal. Graham overheard him read the lines from T.S. Eliot's "The Love Song of J. Alfred Prufrock": "I have heard the mermaids singing, each to each. / I do not think that they will sing to me." Graham is quoted on the Web site *Connection* as saying, "It was like something being played in the key my soul recognized."

Graham's love of art and philosophy are central to her work. The influences of her artist mother and theological scholar father, her ability to speak three languages, and her early immersion in European culture are all evident in her poetry. Her influences are predominantly modernists—William Butler Yeats, T.S. Eliot, and Wallace Stevens—and help explain the shape and flow of her poetry, what Brien sees as "a diachronic passage of events, one of ever-shifting and weaving patterns."

What emerges from these patterns is a constant exploration of the dualities and polarities of life, of the creative and destructive tensions that exist between spirit and flesh, the real and the mythical, stillness and motion, the interior and exterior existence.

Hybrids of Plants and Ghosts was called "as promising a first book as any recently published" by Dave Smith in *American Poetry Review,* due to Graham's "sustained control and a music not like anyone else's among us." The collection, which began as "a form of journal keeping," according to Brien, was built around her poems that appeared in periodicals; it derives its title from Nietzsche's characterization of human beings. Smith noted the influence of Wallace Stevens "and his verbal sleight of hand," which he found evident in Graham's preoccupation with what is real and what is not. Graham is not a poet who often finds answers, let alone arrives at closure in her poems; instead, she is "a poet of process more than completion," noted William Logan in *Parnassus,* making her what Brien called a "mysterious" poet who calls upon the human imagination to go beyond the limitation of human perceptions.

In *Erosion,* according to Helen Vendler in the *New York Times Book Review,* Graham "brings the presence of poetry into the largest question of life, the relation of body and spirit," and more specifically, "the split between body and mind, flesh and spirit," as Sven Birkerts observed in *Boston Review.* Graham told Ann Snodgrass, in an interview cited by Brien, that "*Erosion* seems to me a book about accountability, and accountability seems to me a very American obsession," especially with what Brien calls her "continuing preoccupation with moral experience." This is evident in the poem "Reading Plato" in which Graham describes a fisherman friend who ties flies in the winter for use in the summer, creating a body, the fly, that is created from the fly's image in the maker's mind, or what Peter Stitt in *Georgia Review* called "a Platonic notion, the ideal form of fly, which he is trying to translate into reality," and evident in the poem.

The End of Beauty presented a new direction for Graham's poetry, making what Sven Birkerts, writing in *Voice Literary Supplement,* saw as "a decisive turn—away from accessibility and resolution and into a realm of difficult ambiguity." Graham's poetry challenges readers on new levels in this volume, as the poems become shaped more by sentence than by stanza, more by collage than by continuation, more by consequence than by closure. Birkerts called this a kind of "flux and transformation" in which Graham "discovers in her narrative the critical or pivotal moment: she then slows the action to expose its perilous eventual consequences," though for Graham, the poem has always been more process than product. Helen Vendler believes that it is because Graham is exploring new territory that she must necessarily explore a new form to fit it, for "When poets shift ground, they shift form too," Vendler noted in the *New Yorker.* Several of the poems are broken into numbered sections, often of seemingly unrelated fragments that are pieces of a larger collage; at times, the poet offers a kind of "close" reading that requires readers both to participate in the poem by filling in the blank and for Graham to present her own inability to express the not-yet-conceivable. Robert Miltner, writing in *No Exit,* saw similarities in many of Graham's poems in this collection to traits of the language poetry movement, especially in her use of the sentence as a measure equivalent to the poetic line, as in "Self-Portrait as Both Parties." It is such poetic experimentation that lead Jessica Greenbaum in *Nation* to note that "Graham's new poems are radically different not only from her previous ones, but from anything else around."

Region of Unlikeness is a sequence of poems which, according to Marjorie Marks in the *Los Angeles Times Book Review,* form "an extended meditation on the idea of history." Helen Vendler, writing in *New York Review of Books,* saw the book as one of tensions, the "grand metaphysical theme" being the tension between "existence and death" and the supplemental tensions of "openness versus shape" and of "continuity and closure, indeterminacy and outline, being and temporality, or experience and art." Where *Region of Unlikeness* moves forward from Graham's earlier works lies in its attempt to connect together these polarities through intersections in time and space, however disparate or oddly juxtaposed. Vendler noted that Graham moves beyond the linear story line and seeks to connect through what in "From the New World" she calls a "coil," so that resemblances spiral and interlace, prompting Vendler to note that "Deciphering the coiled sequencing of memory on different planes is the artist's task—finding (or inventing) likenesses in a region of unlikeness."

In its form and conception, *Materialism: Poems* shows the influence of Czeslaw Milosz's *Unattainable Earth,* in which the poet intersperses texts by other writers. In Graham's case, these include Jonathan Edwards, Ralph

Waldo Emerson, Wittgenstein, and Dante. David Baker, writing in *Kenyon Review,* observes that "In many ways *Materialism* reads like a single, sustained poetic effort, a long poem whose methods strive toward a coherent stability," and which offers readers "an intermixture of songs and stories, of meditation, experiment, and assertion, of Graham's voice amidst the polyphonic chorus of others." This leads the reader, according to Annie Finch in *North American Review,* through interaction with both poet and included texts, to make "implicit connections that urge the reader to wrestle with the philosophical assumptions underlying Western Culture." The duality Graham explores in *Materialism* is the tension that results from the universal difficulty in perceiving and communicating the real, in how art is an attempt to express in some concrete way what humans experience through the senses, as evident in "Notes on the Reality of the Self." William Logan, in *New York Times Book Review,* saw a common pattern in the poems in this book: the poems "commonly begin with a small domestic crisis (taking a leotard to her forgetful daughter, picking up a dead monarch butterfly) and attend with an almost nightmarish intensity to the flux of mental phenomena that follows." *Materialism,* wrote Baker, "is a book about America, its Old World heritage and its perilous New World freedom and responsibility," and added that Jorie Graham is "a challenging and important poet, and *Materialism* shows her working at the height of her powers."

The Dream of a Unified Field, a selection of poems representing five books and spanning twenty years, received the Pulitzer Prize in Poetry in 1996, about which Graham told Timothy Cahill of *Christian Science Monitor,* "It made me very happy that the language of my medium, poetry, is situated among these other languages," that is, the "dramatic, novelistic, journalistic, poetic, biographical," all of which "seem to be searching for versions of what one would call 'the truth.'" Peter Sacks, in the *New York Times Book Review,* praised the book for allowing "followers of her rapid and ever-changing development to review her achievement to date," and, Paja Faudree commented in *Village Voice Literary Supplement,* this collection "verifies her status as one of our best living poets."

The Errancy takes its title from the old idea that erring is a way of learning from mistakes and miscues, as a way of discovery and movement, so that the poems in this collection, according to a reviewer in *Publishers Weekly,* describe "not so much our world but our turns of mind as we proceed without a theory of what we're doing," extending a process-orientation that has characterized Graham's poetry throughout her career, though in this book discovery learning is offered as the only valid method in a postmodern era devoid of a dominant set of cultural values and beliefs upon which one can rely. The polarities which dominate this book are "the very limits of language and meaning," according to Graham Christian in *Library Journal,* though, as James Longenbach noted in *Nation,* if "each of her books has interrogated the one preceding it," then "*Errancy* feels like a culmination," for the poet "is exploring the very notion of what it means for a poet to have a style—an exterior mark of an inner vision." This is a book of angels (the immaterial) and aubades (new beginnings), of "sophisticated meditations on identity, language and culture," notes Longenbach, who called *Errancy* Graham's "most challenging, most rewarding book" because it "provides all the satisfactions we expect from poetry—aural beauty, emotional weight—along with an intellectual rigor we don't expect. No one but Jorie Graham could have written it."

Swarm recalls the mythological past through archetypal women such as Calypso, Clytemnestra, Daphne, Eve, and Eurydice. Donna Seaman for *Booklist* remarked that the idea of the poem cycle "Underneath" is that "we feel the same passions and sorrows and ask the same questions our ancestors felt and asked since the dawn of our being." William Logan viewed the work in a different light, however. In *New Criterion,* he called the work "a pocket Inferno of poetic sins. Most of these poems," he wrote, "haven't been consigned to hell—they've just chosen to live there. The poet of *Erosion* and *The End of Beauty* now puts little of her intelligence into her work (little of her intelligence and less of her logic), the words hurled scrappily onto the page, the poetic line fussed with until it lies tangled like yarn." Josephine Balmer, writing for the *Times Literary Supplement,* was more positive in her assessment. She wrote, "The fractured lines and deconstructed forms of Graham's verse, however, suggest a more ambiguous fragmented relationship with this inherited [archetypal] tradition, which she casts as both blessing and curse . . . In *Swarm,* the past is a constant presence, which, in order to survive, we have both to escape and to understand—a burden we can neither baulk at nor evade, a treat we have long been denied.

Never: Poems, contains twenty-seven poems that originally appeared in publications such as the *New Yorker* and the *Times Literary Supplement.* Of this, her ninth book of collected poems, a reviewer for *Publishers Weekly* wrote, "More than anything else, this book shows Graham to be a most formidable nature poet, finding in her speaker's environment perfect analogues for states of consciousness."

Brien places Graham "among the most important poets in North American literature today," for, by her mid-forties, she had "already seen more of her work in print and achieved more honors than many poets hope to accomplish in a lifetime." The reason for her success is perhaps best expressed by *Kenyon Review*'s Baker, who states that he "can think of no other current American poet who has employed and exposed the actual mechanics of narrative, of form, of strategic inquiry more fully than she has—at least no other readable poet—and no other poet able to deploy so fruitfully and invitingly the diverse systems of philosophy, science, and history. If anyone can unify the disjoined fields of contemporary discourse, I think it might be Jorie Graham."

BIOGRAPHICAL AND CRITICAL SOURCES:

BOOKS

Benbow-Pfalzgraf, Taryn, editor, *American Women Writers: A Critical Reference Guide from Colonial Times to the Present,* 2nd edition, St. James Press (Detroit, MI), 2000.

Blain, Virginia, editor, *Feminist Companion to Literature in English,* Yale University Press (New Haven, CT), 1990.

Contemporary Literary Criticism, Thomson Gale (Detroit, MI), Volume 48, 1988, Volume 118, 1999.

Dictionary of Literary Biography, Volume 120: *American Poets since World War II, Third Series,* Thomson Gale (Detroit, MI), 1992.

Encyclopedia of World Literature in the Twentieth Century, 3rd edition, St. James Press (Detroit, MI), 1999.

Green, Carol Hurd, editor, *American Women Writers: A Critical Reference Guide from Colonial Times to the Present,* Volume 5, Continuum Publishing (New York, NY), 1994.

Hamilton, Ian, editor, *Oxford Companion to Twentieth-Century Poetry in English,* Oxford University Press (New York, NY), 1994.

Perkins, George, editor, *Benet's Reader's Encyclopedia of American Literature,* HarperCollins (New York, NY), 1991.

Riggs, Thomas, editor, *Contemporary Poets,* 6th edition, St. James Press (Detroit, MI), 1996.

Vendler, Helen, *The Breaking of Style: Hopkins, Heaney, Graham,* Harvard University Press (Cambridge, MA), 1995.

Vendler, Helen, *The Given and the Made: Strategies of Poetic Redefinition,* Harvard University Press (Cambridge, MA), 1995.

PERIODICALS

America, October 30, 1993, p. 17.

American Poetry Review, January-February, 1982, pp. 36-46; November-December, 1983, pp. 40-6; March, 1987, p. 22; September, 1987, p. 31.

Antioch Review, summer, 1984, pp. 363-74; fall, 1994, p. 659.

Black Warrior Review, spring, 1988, pp. 136-43.

Bloomsbury Review, January, 1995, p. 19; March-April, 1996, p. 23.

Booklist, October 15, 1995, p. 380; January 1, 1996, p. 735; December 1, 1999, Donna Seaman, review of *Swarm,* p. 128.

Bookwatch, January 19, 1992, p. 8; May 22, 1994, p. 11; January, 1996, p. 4.

Boston Review, August, 1983, Sven Birkerts, review of *Erosion,* p. 38.

Carrell: Journal of the Friends of the University of Miami Library, 1989, pp. 35-9.

Chicago Tribune, January 12, 1992, p. 5.

Choice, November, 1980, p. 395.

Christian Science Monitor, August 12, 1987, p. 17; June 24, 1996, Timothy Cahill, review of *The Dream of the Unified Field,* p. 16.

Commentary, January, 1992, p. 59.

Commonweal, March 9, 1984, p. 155; December 2, 1994, p. 26.

Contemporary Literature, summer, 1992, pp. 373-95.

Denver Quarterly, spring, 1992, pp. 76-104; spring, 1994, pp. 136-41.

Economist, July 13, 1996, p. 91.

Georgia Review, winter, 1983, pp. 894-905; spring, 1984; winter, 1987, p. 800.

Hollins Critic, October, 1987, pp. 1-9.

Hudson Review, winter, 1988, p. 684; winter, 1992, p. 676; spring, 1995, pp. 170-172.

Kenyon Review, fall, 1994, David Baker, review of *Materialism,* pp. 161-165.

Library Journal, May 15, 1980, p. 1170; May 1, 1983, p. 909; March 15, 1987, p. 80; September 15, 1990, p. 80; October 15, 1995, p. 65; June 15, 1997, Graham Christian, review of *The Errancy,* p. 72.

Los Angeles Times Book Review, September 8, 1991, p. 11; March 20, 1994, p. 11.

Multicultural Review, January, 1992, p. 51.

Nation, September 6, 1987, Jessica Greenbaum, review of *The End of Beauty,* pp. 206-8; July 21, 1997, James Longenbach, review of *The Errancy,* pp. 40-2.

New Criterion, June 2000, William Logan, review of *Swarm,* p. 63.

New England Review, summer, 1982, p. 617; summer, 1986, p. 532; fall, 1992, pp. 251-61.

New Republic, January 27, 1992, p. 36; July 11, 1994, pp. 27-30.

New Yorker, July 27, 1987, pp. 74-7; June 28, 1993, p. 103.

New York Review of Books, November 21, 1991, Helen Vendler, review of *Region of Unlikeness,* pp. 50-56.

New York Times, July 26, 1987, p. 9; October 11, 1987, p. 29

New York Times Book Review, July 17, 1983, pp. 10, 15; July 26, 1987, p. 9; November 21, 1991, p. 50; July 31, 1994, p. 18; May 5, 1996, Peter Sacks, review of *The Dream of the Unified Field,* pp. 16-7; May 17, 1998, review of *The End of Beauty,* p. 48.

No Exit, summer, 1995, Robert Miltner, review of *The End of Beauty,* pp. 19-28.

North American Review, May, 1993, p. 40; March, 1988, p. 72; July-August, 1994, Annie Finch, review of *Materialism,* p. 40-2; July 1998, review of *The Errancy,* p. 29.

Parnassus, spring-summer, 1983, pp. 211-30; spring, 1985, p. 588.

Partisan Review, March, 1988, p. 508.

Ploughshares, winter, 2001, Robert N. Casper, "About Jorie Graham," p. 189.

Poetry, April, 1982, pp. 35-7; July 1998, review of *The Errancy,* p. 233.

Prairie Schooner, fall, 1989, p. 117.

Publisher's Weekly, August 31, 1990, p. 59; September 25, 1995, p. 49; June 30, 1997, review of *The Errancy,* p. 72; February 25, 2002, review of *Never: Poems,* p. 56.

Small Press Review, February, 1994, p. 11.

Southwest Review, summer, 1982, pp. 345-9.

Threepenny Review, fall, 1988, p. 12; summer, 1994, p. 18-20.

Times Literary Supplement, May 17, 1996, pp. 26-7; November 20, 1998, review of *The Errancy,* p. 29; May 25, 2001, Josephine Balmer, "Ancient Ladies," review of *Swarm,* p. 26.

Tribune Books (Chicago), January 12, 1992, p. 5.

Village Voice Literary Supplement, June, 1987, Sven Birkerts, review of *The End of Beauty,* p. 5; November, 1995, Paja Faudree, review of *The Dream of the Unified Field,* p. 12, 14.

Virginia Quarterly Review, autumn, 1980, p. 146; autumn, 1983, p. 133.

Washington Post, January 19, 1992, p. 8; May 22, 1994, p. 11.

Wilson Library Bulletin, October, 1987, p. 93.

Women's Review of Books, March, 1994, pp. 11-12.

ONLINE

Academy of American Poets Web site, http://www.poets. org/poets/ (October 15, 2001), biography of Jorie Graham.

Connection Web site, http://www.theconnection.org/ archive/ (December 17, 1999), Christopher Lydon, "The Poetry of Jorie Graham."

Harvard University Gazette Web site, http://www.hno. harvard.edu/gazette/ (October 7, 1999), Lee Simmons, "Jorie Graham, Ambassador for Poetry."

New York Times Web site, http://www.search.nytimes. com/ (January 2, 2000), Richard Eder, "A State of Withdrawal," review of *Swarm.*

*   *   *

GRANT, Skeeter
See SPIEGELMAN, Art

*   *   *

GRASS, Günter 1927-
(Günter Wilhelm Grass)

PERSONAL: Born October 16, 1927, in the Free City of Danzig (Gdansk), (later incorporated into Poland); married Anna Schwarz, 1954 (marriage ended); married Utte Grunert, 1979; children: (first marriage) Franz, Raoul, Laura, Bruno. *Education:* Attended Künstakademie (Düsseldorf, Germany); attended Berlin Academy of Fine Arts, 1953-55. *Politics:* Social Democrat. *Religion:* Roman Catholic.

ADDRESSES: Home—Glockengiesserstrasse 21, Lübeck 23552, Germany. *Office*—Niedstrasse 13, Berlin-Grunewald 41, Germany.

CAREER: Novelist, poet, playwright, graphic artist, and sculptor. Former farm laborer in the Rhineland; worked in potash mine near Hildesheim, Germany; black marketeer; apprentice stonecutter during late 1940s, chiseling tombstones for firms in Düsseldorf, Germany; worked as a drummer and washboard accompanist with a jazz band. Speech writer for Willy Brandt during his candidacy for the election of Bundeskanzler, West Germany. Lecturer at Harvard University, Yale University, Smith College, Kenyon College, and at Goethe House and Poetry Center of YM and YWCA, New York, NY, c. 1960s; writer-in-residence at Columbia University, 1966. *Exhibitions:* Drawings, lithographs, and sculptures have been exhibited in the show "Too Far Afield: Graphics, 1970-2000," Jan van der Donk Gallery, New York, NY, 2001. *Military service:* German Army, drafted during World War II; aide with German Luftwaffe; prisoner of war in Marienbad, Czechoslovakia, 1945-46.

MEMBER: American Academy of Arts and Sciences, Berliner Akademie der Künste (president, 1983-86), Deutscher PEN, Zentrum der Bundesrepublik, Verband Deutscher Schriftsteller, Gruppe 47.

AWARDS, HONORS: Lyrikpreis, Süddeutscher Rundfunk, 1955; prize from Gruppe 47, 1958; Bremen Literary Award, 1959; literary prize from Association of German Critics, 1960; *Die Blechtrommel* (*The Tin Drum*) selected by a French jury as the best foreign-language book of 1962; a plaster bust of Grass was placed in the Regensburger Ruhmestempel Walhalla, 1963; Georg Büchner Prize, 1965; Fontane prize (West Germany), 1968; Theodor Heuss Preis, 1969; *Local Anaesthetic* selected among ten best books of 1970 by *Time;* Carl von Ossiersky Medal, 1977; Premio Internazionale Mondello, Palermo, 1977; International Literature Award, 1978; *The Flounder* selected among best books of fiction by *Time,* 1979; Alexander-Majokowski Medal, 1979; awarded distinguished service medal, Federal Republic of Germany (declined), 1980; Antonio Feltrinelli award, 1982; Leonhard Frank ring, 1988; Karel Capek prize (Czech Republic), 1994; Nobel Prize for literature, Swedish Academy, 1999. Honorary doctorates from Harvard University and Kenyon College.

WRITINGS:

Die Vorzüge der Windhühner (poems, prose, and drawings; title means "The Advantages of Windfowl"; also see below), Luchterhand (Darmstadt, Germany), 1956, 3rd edition, 1967.

(Author of text; with Herman Wilson) *O Susanna: Ein Jazzbilderbuch: Blues, Balladen, Spirituals, Jazz,* illustrated by Horst Geldmacher, Kiepenheuer & Witsch, 1959.

Die Blechtrommel (novel; also see below), Luchterhand (Darmstadt, Germany), 1959, illustrated by Heinrich Richter, 1968, with an afterword by Hans Mayer, 1984, translation by Ralph Manheim published as *The Tin Drum,* Vintage (New York, NY), 1962, reprinted, Knopf (New York, NY), 1993.

Gleisdreieck (poems and drawings; title means "Rail Triangle"), Luchterhand (Darmstadt, Germany), 1960.

Katz und Maus (novella; also see below), Luchterhand (Neuwied am Rhine, Germany), 1961, edited by Edgar Lohner, Blaisdell (Waltham, MA), 1969, with English introduction and notes, edited by H.F. Brookes and C.E. Fraenkel, Heinemann Educational (London, England), 1971, translation by Ralph Manheim published as *Cat and Mouse,* Harcourt (New York, NY), 1963, reprinted, Harcourt (San Diego, CA), 1991.

Hundejahre (novel; also see below), Luchterhand (Neuwied am Rhine, Germany), 1963, translation by Ralph Manheim published as *Dog Years,* Harcourt (New York, NY), 1965, reprinted, Harcourt (San Diego, CA), 1989.

Die Ballerina (essay), Friedenauer Presse (Berlin, Germany), 1963.

Rede über das Selbstverständliche (speech), Luchterhand (Berlin, Germany), 1965.

(Illustrator) Ingeborg Buchmann, *Ein Ort für Zufaelle,* Wagenbach (Berlin, Germany), 1965.

Dich singe ich, Demokratie, Luchterhand (Berlin, Germany), 1965.

Fünf Wahlreden (speeches; contains "Was ist des Deutschen Vaterland?," "Loblied auf Willy," "Es steht zur Wahl," "Ich klage an," and "Des Kaisers neue Kleider"), Nuewied (Berlin, Germany), 1965.

Selected Poems (in German and English; includes poems from *Die Vorzüge der Windhühner* and *Gleisdreieck;* also see below), translated by Michael Hamburger and Christopher Middleton, Harcourt (New York, NY), 1966, published as *Poems of Günter Grass,* Penguin (Harmondsworth, England), 1969.

Ausgefragt (poems and drawings; title means "Questioned") Luchterhand (Darmstadt, Germany), 1967.

Der Fall Axel C. Springer am Beispiel Arnold Zweig: Eine Rede, ihr Anlass, und die Folgen, Voltaire (Berlin, Germany), 1967.

Die Vorzüuge der Windhühner, Luchterhand (Berlin, Germany), 1967.

New Poems (includes poems from *Ausgefragt;* also see below), translation by Michael Hamburger, Harcourt (New York, NY), 1968.

Günter Grass, edited by Theodor Wieser, Luchterhand (Berlin, Germany), 1968.

Über meinen Lehrer Döblin, und andere Vorträge, Literarische Colloquium Berlin (Berlin, Germany), 1968.

Über das Selbstverständliche: Reden, Aufsätze, offene Briefe, Kommentare (title means "On the Self-Evident"; also see below), Luchterhand (Berlin, Germany), 1968, revised and supplemented edition published as *Über das Selbstverständliche: Politische Schriften,* Deutscher Taschenbuch (Munich, Germany), 1969.

(With Pavel Kokout) *Briefe über die Grenze: Versuch eines Ost-West-Dialogs von Günter Grass und Pavel Kohout* (letters), C. Wegner (Hamburg, Germany), 1968.

Über meinen Lehrer Döblin und andere Vorträge (title means "About My Teacher Döblin and Other Lectures"), Literarisches Collequium (Berlin, Germany), 1968.

Günter Grass: Ausgewählte Texte, Abbildungen, Faksimiles, Bio-Bibliographie, edited by Theodor Wieser, Luchterhand (Darmstadt, Germany), 1968, also published as *Porträt und Poesie,* 1968.

(With Kurt Ziesel) *Kunst oder Pornographie?: Der Prozess Grass gegen Ziesel,* J.F. Lehmann (Munich, Germany), 1969.

Speak Out: Speeches, Open Letters, Commentaries (includes selections from *Über das Selbstverständliche: Reden, Aufsätze, offene Briefe, Kommentare*), translation by Ralph Manheim, introduction by Michael Harrington, Harcourt (New York, NY), 1969.

Örtlich betäubt (novel), Luchterhand (Neuwied, Germany), 1969, translation by Ralph Manheim published as *Local Anaesthetic,* Harcourt (New York, NY), 1970, reprinted, Harcourt (San Diego, CA), 1989.

Die Schweinekopfsülze, illustrated by Horst Janssen, Merlin Verlag (Hamburg, Germany), 1969.

Poems of Günter Grass, translated by Michael Hamburger and Christopher Middleton, with an introduction by Hamburger, Penguin (Harmondsworth, England), 1969.

Originalgraphik (poem with illustrations), limited edition, Argelander, 1970.

Gesammelte Gedichte (title means "Collected Poems"; also see below), introduction by Heinrich Vormweg, Luchterhand (Neuwied, Germany), 1971.

Dokumente zur politischen Wirkung, edited by Heinz Ludwig Arnold and Franz Josef Goertz, Richard Boorherg, 1971.

Aus dem Tagebuch einer Schnecke, Luchterhand (Darmstadt, Germany), 1972, translation by Ralph Manheim published as *From the Diary of a Snail,* Harcourt (New York, NY), 1973.

Mariazühren Hommageamarie Inmarypraise, photographs by Maria Rama, Bruckmann (Munich, Germany), 1973, bilingual edition with translation by Christopher Middleton published as *Inmarypraise,* Harcourt (New York, NY), 1973.

Der Schriftstellar als Bürger: Eine Siebenjahresbilanz, Dr. Karl Renner Institute (Vienna, Germany), 1973.

Liebe geprüft (poems), [Bremen], 1974.

Günter Grass: Radierungen 1972-1974, Die Galerie (Berlin, Germany), 1974.

Der Bürger und seine Stimme (speeches, essays, and commentary; title means "The Citizen and His Voice"), Luchterhand (Darmstadt, Germany), 1974.

Günter Grass Materialienbuch, edited by Rolf Geissler, Luchterhand (Darmstadt, Germany), 1976.

Der Butt (novel), Luchterhand (Darmstadt, Germany), 1977, translation by Ralph Manheim published as *Flounder,* Harcourt (New York, NY), 1978.

In the Egg and Other Poems (contains poems from *Selected Poems* and *New Poems*), translated by Michael Hamburger and Christopher Middleton, Harcourt (New York, NY), 1977.

Über meinen Lehrer Alfred Döblin, issued with *Döblin's Die drei Sprünge des Wang-lun,* Walter (Olten, Czech Republic), 1977.

Denkzettel: Politische Reden und Aufsätze (title means "Note for Thought"), Luchterhand (Darmstadt, Germany), 1978.

Das Treffen in Telgte, Luchterhand (Darmstadt, Germany), 1979, with a preface by Stephan Hermlin, Reclam (Leipzig, Germany), 1984, translation by Ralph Manheim published as *The Meeting at Telgte,* with an afterword by Leonard Forster, Harcourt (New York, NY), 1981.

Werkverzeichnis der Radierungen (catalogue), Galerie Andre A. Dreher (Berlin, Germany), 1979.

(With Volker Schlöndorff) *Die Blechtrommel als Film,* Zweitausendeins (Frankfurt am Main, Germany), 1979.

Aufsätze zur Literatur, 1957-1979 (title means "Essays on Literature, 1957-1979"), Luchterhand (Darmstadt, Germany), 1980.

Danziger Trilogie (title means "Danzig Trilogy"; contains *Die Blechtrommel, Katz und Maus,* and *Hundejahre*), Luchterhand (Darmstadt, Germany), 1980, translation by Ralph Manheim published as *The Danzig Trilogy,* Harcourt (San Diego, CA), 1987.

Kopfgeburten; oder Die Deutschen sterben aus, Luchterhand (Darmstadt, Germany), 1980, translation by Ralph Manheim published as *Headbirths; or, The Germans Are Dying Out,* Harcourt (New York, NY), 1982.

Zeichnen und Schreiben: Das bildnerische Werk des Schriftstellers Günter Grass, Luchterhand (Darmstadt, Germany), 1982, translation published as *Graphics and Writing,* edited by Anselm Dreher, Harcourt (San Diego, CA), 1983.

Radierungen und Texte 1972-1982, edited by Anselm Dreher, text selection and afterword by Sigrid Mayer, Luchterhand (Darmstadt, Germany), 1984.

Zeichnungen und Texte 1954-1977, edited by Anselm Dreher, text selection and afterword by Sigrid Mayer, Luchterhand (Darmstadt, Germany), 1982.

Günter Grass: Katalog zur Ausstellung im Winter 82/83 der Galerie Schürer, CH-Regensberg: Ausstellung über das zeichnerische, grafische und plastische Werk, Die Galerie (Regensberg, Germany), 1982.

Kinderlied (poems and etchings; originally published in *Gesammelte Gedichte*), Lord John, 1982.

Zeichnungen und Texte, 1954-1977, Luchterhand (Darmstadt, Germany), 1982, translation by Michael Hamburger and Walter Arndt published as *Drawings and Words, 1954-1977,* edited by Anselm Dreher, text selection and afterword by Sigrid Mayer, Harcourt (San Diego, CA), 1983.

Ach, Butt!: Dein Märchen geht böse aus, Luchterhand (Darmstadt, Germany), 1983.

Radierungen und Texte, 1972-1982, Luchterhand (Darmstadt, Germany), 1984, translation by Michael Hamburger and others published as *Etchings and Words, 1972-1982,* edited by Anselm Dreher, text selection and afterword by Sigrid Mayer, Harcourt (San Diego, CA), 1985.

Widerstand lernen: Politische Gegenreden, 1980-1983 (title means "Learning Resistance: Political Countertalk"), Luchterhand (Darmstadt, Germany), 1984.

On Writing and Politics: 1967-1983 (essays), translated by Ralph Manheim, introduction by Salman Rushdie, Harcourt (San Diego, CA), 1985.

Geschenkt Freiheit: Rede zum 8. Mai 1945, Akademie der Künste (Berlin, Germany), 1985.

Werk und Wirkung, edited by Rudolf Wolff, Bouvier (Bonn, Germany), 1985.

(With Heinrich Vormweg) *Günter Grass: Mit Selbstzeugnissen und Bilddokumenten,* Rowohlt (Reinbek bei Hamburg, Germany), 1986.

In Kupfer, auf Stein: Das grafische Werk, edited by G. Fritze Margull, Steidl (Göttingen, Germany), 1986, new edition, 1994.

Die Rättin, Luchterhand (Darmstadt, Germany), 1986, translation by Ralph Manheim published as *The Rat,* Harcourt (San Diego, CA), 1987.

(With Werner Timm) *Günter Grass: Graphik und Plastik,* Museum Ostdeutsche Galerie (Regensburg, Germany), 1987.

Werkausgabe, ten volumes, edited by Volker Neuhaus, Luchterhand (Darmstadt, Germany), 1987.

Ausstellung anlässlich des 60: Geburtstages von Günter Grass, edited by Jens Christian Jensen, Kunsthalle zu Kiel (Kiel, Germany), 1987.

Günter Grass: Radierungen, Lithographien, Zeichnungen, Plastiken, Gedichte, Kunstamt Berlin-Tempelhof (Berlin, Germany), 1987.

Günter Grass: Mit Sophie in die Pilze gegangen, Steidl (Göttingen, Germany), 1987.

Die Gedichte 1955-1986 (poems), afterword by Volker Neuhaus, Luchterhand (Darmstadt, Germany), 1988.

Calcutta: Zeichnungen, Künsthalle Bremen (Bremen, Germany), 1988.

Zunge Zeigen, Luchterhand (Darmstadt, Germany), 1988, translation by John E. Woods published as *Show Your Tongue,* Harcourt (San Diego, CA), 1989.

Skizzenbuch, Steidl (Göttingen, Germany), 1989.

Meine grüne Wiese: Geschichten und Zeichnungen, Manesse (Zurich, Switzerland), 1989.

Meine grüne Wiese: Kurzprosa, Manesse (Zurich, Switzerland), 1989.

Deutscher Lastenausgleich: Wider das dumpfe Einheitsgebot; Reden und Gespräche, Texte zur Zeit, Luchterhand (Frankfurt am Main, Germany), 1990, translation by Krishna Winston with A.S. Wensinger published as *Two States—One Nation?,* Harcourt (San Diego, CA), 1990.

Günter Grass: Begleitheft zur Ausstellung der Stadt-und Universitätsbibliothek Frankfurt am Main, 13. Februar bis 30. März 1990, Die Bibliothek (Frankfurt am Main, Germany), 1990.

Ein Schnäppchen namens DDR: Letzte Reden vorm Glockengeläut, Luchterhand (Frankfurt am Main, Germany), 1990.

Schreiben nach Auschwitz, Luchterhand (Frankfurt am Main, Germany), 1990.

(And illustrator) *Totes Holz,* Steidl (Göttingen, Germany), 1990.

(With Rudolf Augstein) *Deutschland, einig Vaterland?: ein Streitgespräch,* Steidl (Göttingen, Germany), 1990.

Nachdenken über Deutschland, edited by Dietmar Keller, introductory essays by Christoph Hein and others, Der Nation (Berlin, Germany), 1990–91.

Vier Jahrzehnte: Ein Werkstattbericht, edited by G. Fritze Margull, Steidl (Göttingen, Germany), 1991, updated edition published as *Fünf Jahrzehnte: ein Werkstattbericht,* Ettag, 2001.

Rede vom Verlust: Über den Niedergang der politischen Kultur in geeinten Deutschland (speech), Steidl (Göttingen, Germany), 1992.

Unkenrufe (title means "Toad Croaks"), Steidl (Göttingen, Germany), 1992, translation by Ralph Manheim published as *The Call of the Toad,* Harcourt (New York, NY), 1992.

(With Regine Hildebrandt) *Schaden begrenzen, oder auf die Füsse treten: Ein Gespräch,* edited by Friedrich

Dieckmann and others, Volk & Welt (Berlin, Germany), 1993.

Novemberland: 13 Sonette, Steidl (Göttingen, Germany), 1993, translation by Michael Hamburger published as *Novemberland: Selected Poems, 1956-1993,* Harcourt (New York, NY), 1996.

Cat and Mouse and Other Writings, edited by A. Leslie Willson, foreword by John Irving, Continuum (New York, NY), 1994.

Ein Weites Feld, Steidl (Göttingen, Germany), 1995, translation by Krishna Winston published as *Too Far Afield,* Harcourt (New York, NY), 2000.

(With Kenzaburo Oe) *Gestern, vor 50 Jahren: Ein Deutsch-Japanischer Briefwechsel* (correspondence), Steidl (Göttingen, Germany), 1995, translation by John Barrett published as *Just Yesterday, Fifty Years Ago: A Critical Dialogue on the Anniversary of the End of the Second World War,* Alyscamps Press (Paris, France), 1999.

Die Deutschen und Ihre Dichter, edited by Daniela Hermes, Deutscher Taschenbuch (Munich, Germany), 1995.

Der Schriftsteller als Zeitgenosse, edited by Daniela Hermes, Deustcher Taschesbuch (Munich, Germany), 1996.

Aesthetik Des Engagements, P. Lang (New York, NY), 1996.

Fundsachen für Nichtleser, Steidl (Göttingen, Germany), 1997.

Rede über den Standort (speech), Steidl (Göttingen, Germany), 1997.

Ohne die Feder zu wechseln: Zeichnungen, Druckgraphiken, Aquarelle, Skulpturen, edited by Peter Joch and Annette Lagler, Steidl (Göttingen, Germany), 1997.

Aus einem fotografischen und politischen Tabebuch: Berlin jenseits der Mauer = Da un diario fotografico e politico: Berlino oltre il muro, photographs by Rean Mazzone, ILA Palma (Palermo, Italy), 1997.

(With Reinhard Höppner and Hans-Jochen Tschiche) *Rotgrüne Reder,* Steidl (Göttingen, Germany), 1998.

(With Harro Zimmerman) *Vom Abentauer der Aufklaerung,* Steidl (Göttingen, Germany), 1999.

Für-und Widerworte, Steidl (Göttingen, Germany), 1999.

Auf einem anderen Blatt: Zeichnungen, Steidl (Göttingen, Germany), 1999.

Mein Jahrhundert, Steidl (Göttingen, Germany), 1999, translation by Michael Henry Heim published as *My Century,* Harcourt (New York, NY), 1999.

Wort und Bild: Tübinger Poetik Vorlesung & Materialien, edited by Jürgen Wertheimer, with Ute All-mendinger, Konkursbuchverlag (Tübingen, Germany), 1999.

Fortsetzung folgt—: Literature und Geschichte, Steidl (Göttingen, Germany), 1999.

(With Michael Martens) *Ich werde die Wunde offen halten: ein Gespräch zur Person und über die Ziet,* H. Boldt (Winsen, Germany), 1999.

(With Harro Zimmermann) *Vom Abenteuer der Aufklärung* (interviews) Steidl (Göttingen, Germany), 1999.

(Editor) *Gemischte Klasse: Prosa, Lyrik, Szenen & Essays,* Swiridoff (Kunzelsau, Germany), 2000.

Ohne Stimme: Reder zugunsten des Volkes der Roma und Sinti, Steidl (Göttingen, Germany), 2000.

Günter Grass: Mit Wasserfarben: Aquarelle, Steidl (Göttingen, Germany), 2001.

(With Daniela Dahn) *In einem reichen Land: Zeugnisse alltäglichen Leidens an der Gessellschaft,* edited by Johano Strasser, Steidl (Göttingen, Germany), 2002.

Im Krebsgang, Steidl (Göttingen, Germany), 2002, translation by Krishna Wilson published as *Crabwalk,* Harcourt (Orlando, FL), 2002.

Günter Grass: Gebrannte Erde, photographs by Dirk Reinartz, Steidl (Göttingen, Germany), 2002.

(With Helen Wolff) *Briefe 1959-1994* (correspondence), edited by Daniela Hermes, translated from the English by Eva Maria Hermes, Steidl (Göttingen, Germany), 2003.

Letzte Tänze, Steidl (Göttingen, Germany), 2003.

PLAYS

Die bösen Köche: Ein Drama in fünf Akten (first produced in West Berlin, Germany, 1961; translation by A. Leslie Willson produced as *The Wicked Cooks* on Broadway, 1967), Luchterhand (Darmstadt, Germany), 1982.

Hochwasser: Ein Stück in zwei Akten (two acts; also see below), Suhrkamp (Frankfurt am Main, Germany), 1963, 4th edition, 1968.

Onkel, Onkel (four acts; title means "Mister, Mister"; also see below), Wagenbach (Berlin, Germany), 1965.

Die Plebejer proben den Aufstand: Ein deutsches Trauerspiel (also see below; first produced in West Berlin, Germany, 1966), Luchterhand (Berlin, Germany), 1966, translation by Ralph Manheim published as *The Plebeians Rehearse the Uprising: A German Tragedy* (produced in Cambridge, MA, at the Harvard Dramatic Club, 1967), with an introduction by Grass, Harcourt (New York, NY), 1966.

The World of Günter Grass, adapted by Dennis Rosa, produced off-Broadway at Pocket Theatre, April 26, 1966.

Hochwasser [and] *Noch zehn Minuten bis Buffalo* (title of second play means "Only Ten Minutes to Buffalo"; also see below), edited by A. Leslie Wilson, Appleton (New York, NY), 1967.

Four Plays (includes *The Flood* [produced in New York, NY, 1986], *Onkel, Onkel* [title means "Mister, Mister"], *Only Ten Minutes to Buffalo,* and *The Wicked Cooks*), with an introduction by Martin Esslin, Harcourt (New York, NY), 1967.

Davor: Ein Stuck in dreizehn Szenen (also see below; first produced in West Berlin at Schiller Theatre, February 16, 1969, translation by Wilson and Ralph Manheim produced as *Uptight* in Washington, DC, 1972), edited by Victor Lange and Frances Lange, Harcourt (New York, NY), 1973, translation by A. Leslie Wilson and Ralph Manheim published as *Max: A Play,* Harcourt (New York, NY), 1972.

Theaterspiele (includes *Hochwasser, Onkel, Onkel, Die Plebejer proben den Aufstand,* and *Davor;* first produced in West Berlin, Germany, 1970), Luchterhand (Neuwied, Germany), 1970.

(With Aribert Reimann) *Die Vogelscheuchen* (ballet in three acts), Ars Viva (Mainz, Germany), 1977.

Other plays include *Beritten hin und zurück* (title means "Rocking Back and Forth"), *Goldmaeulchen,* 1964, and *Zweiunddreizig Zaehne.*

OTHER

Also collaborator with Jean-Claude Carriere, Volker Schlondorff, and Franz Seitz on screenplay for film adaptation of *Katz und Maus,* Modern Art Film, 1967. Author of material for catalogues to accompany his artwork. Work represented in anthologies, including *Deutsche Literatur seit 1945 in Einzeldarstellunger,* edited by Dietrich Weber, Kröner, 1968, and *Danzig 1939: Treasures of a Destroyed Community,* edited by Sheila Schwartz, Wayne State University Press (Detroit, MI), 1980. Contributor to *Der Traum der Vernunft: vom Elend der Aufklärung: eine Veranstaltungsreihe der Akademie der Künste, Berlin,* Luchterhand (Darmstadt, Germany), 1985; *Alptraum und Hoffnung: zwei Reden vor dem Club of Rome,* Steidl (Göttingen, Germany), 1989; and *Die Zukunft der Erinnerung,* edited by Martin Wälde, Steidl (Göttingen, Germany), 2001. A recording of selected readings by the author, *Örtlich betaeubt,* has been produced by Deutsche Grammophon Gesellschaft, 1971. Editor, with Heinrich Boell and Carola Stern, of *L-80.* Author of foreword, *Seventeenth*

Century German Prose, Hans J. von Grimmelshausen, Continuum (New York, NY), 1992; Contributor of an "Essay on Loss" to *The Future of German Democracy,* edited by Robert Gerald Livingston and Volkmar Sander, Continuum (New York, NY), 1993.

ADAPTATIONS: Die Blechtrommel (The Tin Drum) was adapted for film, New World Pictures, 1980.

SIDELIGHTS: Through his poems, plays, essays, and especially his novels, Nobel Prize-winning author Günter Grass became the conscience of post-World War II Germany. His first published novel, *Die Blechtrommel*—translated into English as *The Tin Drum*—was one of the first works of recognized merit to come out of Germany after 1945, and it has continued to remain a classic. In this book, and in the rest of his writings, Grass attempts to come to terms with Germany's collective guilt regarding World War II and the Holocaust and to figure out where the country should go in the future.

Grass was born in the Free City of Danzig in the period between the World Wars. The city, with its strategic position at the mouth of the Vistula River, changed hands often in European wars. It was historically German and had a mostly German population, but at the time Grass was born it was a free city, under the protection of the League of Nations and closely tied to Poland. The Nazi Party, growing in strength throughout Grass's childhood, dreamed of restoring the German empire and wanted to return the city to German control. The party was popular among the Germans of Danzig, and Grass himself joined the Hitler Youth as a child.

In 1944, at age fifteen, Grass was drafted into the German military. He was wounded, later found himself in an American prisoner-of-war camp, and at one point was forced to see what remained of Dachau, a notorious concentration camp. He was discharged in 1946, still only eighteen years old. His home was gone—the German population of Danzig had fled or been driven out, and the city became Gdansk, Poland. Grass eventually found his parents and sister, who were trying to scratch out a living as refugees in West Germany. Bitter and unhappy, Grass tried to return to school, dropped out, became a tombstone carver, and finally entered the Düsseldorf Academy of Art to study painting and sculpture. He also started to write.

Grass transferred to the Berlin Academy of Art in 1953 and married in 1954. The next year his wife, Anna, sent some of his poems in to a contest sponsored by a radio station, and he won third prize. This brought him to the attention of Group 47, an informal writing workshop that also counted as members now-famous authors Heinrich Böll, Uwe Johnson, and Martin Walser. Grass first attended a meeting of this group in 1955, at the invitation of its founder, Hans Werner Richter. His verse was well received by the members of Group 47, and the following year Grass published his first volume, a slim book of drawings and poetry titled *Die Vorzüge der Windhühner* (*The Advantages of Windfowl*). While this collection of apparently surrealistic poems and fine-lined drawings of oversized insects was hardly noticed at the time—an English translation of certain of its poems was first published in *Selected Poems* in 1965—it contains the seed of much of his future work. Grass's specific kind of creative imagination has been identified as the graphic and plastic arts combined with lyric inspiration. As Kurt Lothar Tank explained in *Günter Grass:* "One thinks of Paul Klee when one takes . . . lines in this volume of poetry and, instead of actually reading them, visualizes them. One feels with tender fervor the gaiety, light as a dream with which the poet nourishes the windfowl of his own invention that lend wings to his creative act."

In 1958 Grass won the coveted prize of Group 47 for a reading from his manuscript *Die Blechtrommel* (*The Tin Drum*), published the following year. This book, which tells the story of the Nazi rise to power in Danzig from the perspective of a gifted but crazed three year old, transformed the author into a controversial international celebrity. Grass commented on the inspiration for and evolution of the book, which he wrote while living with his wife in a basement apartment in Paris, in a 1973 radio lecture, reprinted in *Günter Grass Materialienbuch.* He said that while he was traveling in France in 1952 and constantly occupied with drawing and writing, he conceived a poem whose protagonist is a "Saint on a Column" and who, from this "elevated perspective," could describe life in the village. But, later, tiny Oskar Matzerath, the tin-drummer, became the exact reverse of a pillar-dweller. By staying closer to the earth than normal, the protagonist of *The Tin Drum* acquires a unique point of view. Presumably it took not merely an adventurer in imagination but also a student of sculpture and drawing to discover this unusual perspective.

The viewpoint of a precocious three year old allowed Grass an honest insider's approach to the problem with which all the writers of Group 47 were struggling: the task of coming to terms with the overwhelming experience of World War II, with what had led up to it and with what had followed in its wake as "economic miracle." In January of 1963, shortly before *The Tin Drum* was published in the United States, a writer for *Time* pronounced Grass's work the "most spectacular example" of recent German literature "trying to probe beneath the surface prosperity to the uneasy past." The reviewer called Grass, whose *Tin Drum* was winning prizes and stirring anger all over Europe, "probably the most inventive talent to be heard from anywhere since the war" and described his central character, Oskar, as "the gaudiest gimmick in his literary bag of tricks. . . . For Oskar is that wildly distorted mirror which, held up to a wildly deformed reality, gives back a recognizable likeness." Two decades later, while reviewing Grass's latest volume, John Irving wrote in *Saturday Review:* "In the more than twenty years since its publication, *Die Blechtrommel* . . . has not been surpassed; it is the greatest novel by a living author."

In Germany, reaction to Grass's bestselling novel ranged from critical endorsement to moral outrage. Characteristic of the honors and scandals surrounding the book was the literature prize of Bremen, voted by the jury but withheld by the city senate on moral grounds. Similar charges against Grass's writings took the form of law suits in 1962, were repeated with political overtones on the occasion of the Büchner Prize in 1965, and continued as confrontations with the Springer Press and others.

The formidable task of coming to grips with his country's past, however, is not something Grass could accomplish in one novel, no matter how incisive. By 1963, when *The Tin Drum* appeared in the United States, he had published a second volume of poetry and drawings, *Gleisdreieck* (*Rail Triangle*); a novella, *Katz und Maus* (translated as *Cat and Mouse*); and another novel of epic dimensions, *Hundejahre* (translated as *Dog Years*). The drawings and poems of *Gleisdreieck,* which are translated in *Selected Poems* and in *In the Egg and Other Poems,* make up a volume of more imposing format than Grass's first poetry collection and clearly show his development from a playful style obsessed with detail to a bolder, more encompassing form of expression.

Together with *The Tin Drum, Cat and Mouse* and *Dog Years* form what is called the "Danzig Trilogy," and deal respectively with the pre-war, inter-war, and post-war periods in that city. In the novella *Cat and Mouse,* the central focus and, with it, a sense of guilt are diverted from the first-person narrator, Pilenz, to Mahlke, his high school friend. Mahlke's protruding adam's apple causes his relentless pursuit of the Iron Cross—never referred to by name—with which he intends to cover up his "mouse." But in the end the narrator, who has set up the cat-and-mouse game, can no longer fathom the depth of his friend's fatal complex nor his own role in it.

The years from the prewar to the postwar era are presented in *Dog Years* through the perspective of three different narrators, a team directed by Amsel—alias Brauxel—who makes scarecrows in man's image. The seemingly solid childhood friendship of Amsel and Matem evolves into the love-hate relationship between Jew and non-Jew under the impact of Nazi ideology. When the former friends from the region of the Vistula finally meet again in the West, the ominous führer dog who followed Matem on his odyssey is left behind in Brauxel's subterranean world of scarecrows. While *Dog Years,* like *The Tin Drum,* again accounts for the past through the eyes of an artist, the artist is no longer a demonic tin-drummer in the guise of a child but the ingenious maker of a world of objects reflecting the break between the creations of nature and those of men. Referring to Amsel's "keen sense of reality in all its innumerable forms," John Reddick wrote in *The Danzig Trilogy of Günter Grass:* "Any serious reader of Grass's work will need little prompting to recognize that Grass is in fact describing his own, as well as his persona's art."

In 1961, well into his *Tin Drum* fame, Grass revealed at a meeting of theater experts in Hamburg that, departing from his early poetry, he had written four long plays and two one-act plays during "the relatively short time, from 1954 to 1957." Not all of the plays to which he referred had been staged or published at that time; some, like *Onkel, Onkel (Mister, Mister),* appeared later in revised editions. Grass's earliest plays, *Beritten hin und zurück (Rocking Back and Forth)* and *Noch zehn Minuten bis Buffalo (Only Ten Minutes to Buffalo),* have a clearly programmatic character. They stage diverse attitudes about approaches to drama or poetry. As presentations of Grass's "poetics," they belong in the same category as his important early essays "Die Ballerina" ("The Ballet Dancer") of 1956 and "Der Inhalt als Widerstand" ("Content as Resistance") of 1957.

Die bösen Köche (The Wicked Cooks), written in 1956 in Paris and initially performed in 1961 in Berlin, was, in 1967, Grass's first play to be staged in the United States. In 1961 Martin Esslin had included discussion of Grass's early dramatic works in *The Theatre of the Absurd.* But in 1966 Peter Spycher argued in a *Germanisch-Romanische Monatsschrift* article that, at least in the case of *The Wicked Cooks,* the criteria of absurdist theater do not apply. In the play a team of five

restaurant cooks find their reputations threatened by the popular "Gray Soup" cooked on occasion by a guest referred to as "the Count." The play revolves around the intrigues of the cooks to obtain the Count's soup recipe. They even try to trade him a nurse, the girlfriend of one of them, in return for the secret. Unfortunately for the cooks, the Count and the nurse fall in love, and when the cooks invade their idyllic existence, the Count shoots both the woman and himself. Spycher justifiably sees the play as an "allegorical parable" or "anti-tale," for the Count assures the cooks that "it is not a recipe, it's an experience, a living knowledge, continuous change."

Grass's initial limited success as a playwright took on the dimensions of a scandal with the 1966 production in West Berlin of *Die Plebejer proben den Aufstand: Ein deutsches Trauerspiel (The Plebeians Rehearse the Uprising),* subtitled *A German Tragedy.* The play is loosely based on the 1953 revolt in East Berlin, in which workers in that sector of the city protested the failure of the Communist authorities to deliver on their promises of better conditions. To many members of the audience, Grass's character "The Boss" was interpreted to be Bertolt Brecht, a Communist East German playwright, and they did not find Grass's perspective on Brecht flattering. As Andrzej Wirth explained in *A Günter Grass Symposium,* "The Boss [of the play] was a Versager [failure], a Hamletic victim of his own theorems. . . . And the Berlin audience interpreted the play as a challenge to Brecht's image, as a case of Günter Grass versus Bertolt Brecht." However, as Wirth continued, "the American premiere of *The Plebeians Rehearse the Uprising* (1967) in the Harvard Dramatic Club presented an interesting alternative." Due to the English translation and certain changes in the staging, "the play succeeded in exposing a more universal theme—the dilemma of the artist: the aesthetic man versus the man of action, ideal versus reality."

Throughout the 1960s Grass become more overtly involved in politics, supporting, campaigning for, and even writing speeches for Willy Brandt, a Social Democrat and the mayor of West Berlin. Grass's third volume of poetry and drawings, *Ausgefragt,* reflects the political controversies of the decade. One cycle of poems in this volume is titled "Indignation, Annoyance, Rage" and is inspired by the protest songs of the early 1960s. Intoning the "powerlessness" of the guitar protesters, Grass points to the futility of their ritualistic peace marches. However, student protests gained momentum after 1966 and became a force to be reckoned with. Thus Grass's hope of engaging the protesters in constructive election activity was crushed by the demands of the new, increasingly radical Left.

Within the literary developments of the 1960s, Grass's *New Poems,* which range in subject matter from the private to the public sphere, and from aesthetics to politics, have been described by Heinrich Vormweg—in the introduction to Grass's *Gesammelte Gedichte (Collected Poems)*—as reality training. The perception of individual and social reality has been exceptional in German literature, and as Vormweg pointed out, Grass, in his poems, ignores the most obvious change in the literature of the late 1950s and 1960s. The current objective of literature, as reflected for example in "concrete poetry," was to expose language itself as an unreliable medium, inadequate for identifying things and situations as they are. Grass, however, evinces a fundamental trust in language and its ability to communicate reality. In *New Poems* he attempts to make perfectly visible the inescapable contradictions and conflicts of everyday life, including his own.

Grass's political essays of this period are collected in the volume *Über das Selbstverständliche* (translated as *On the Self-Evident*). The title comes from his acceptance speech for the prestigious Büchner Prize in 1965; in that year the Social Democrats had lost the elections, and Grass was dubbed a bad loser by critics of his speech. Another collection of his speeches, open letters, and commentaries from the 1960s is translated in the volume *Speak Out!,* which also contains Grass's 1966 address—"On Writers as Court Jesters and on Non-Existent Courts"—at the meeting of Group 47 in Princeton, New Jersey. While Grass's references to some of his literary colleagues and himself were rigorously criticized in Germany, the last statement of his Princeton speech became renowned: "A poem knows no compromise, but men live by compromise. The individual who can stand up under this contradiction and act is a fool and will change the world." Three more volumes of political essays and commentaries—*Der Bürger und seine Stimme (The Citizen and His Voice), Denkzettel (Note for Thought)* and *Widerstand lernen: Politische Gegenreden (Learning Resistance: Political Countertalk)*—demonstrate that Grass has remained politically outspoken through the 1970s and beyond.

In 1969, six years after *Dog Years,* Grass published another novel, *Örtlich betäubt* (translated as *Local Anaesthetic*). For the first time he left the Danzig origins of his earlier prose works, concentrating instead on his new home town, the Berlin of the 1960s, and on the student protests against the Vietnam War. Starusch, a high school teacher, while undergoing extensive dental treatment, is confronted with the plan of his favorite student, Scherbaum, to set fire to his dog on Kurfürstendamm. By this act the seventeen year old hopes to awaken the populace to the realities of the war. Yet in the end the dog is not burned, and the student is about to undergo a dental treatment similar to his teacher's.

The reception of this novel in Germany was predictably negative. War protest reduced to the level of a dachshund was conceived as belittlement of the real problems at hand. In the United States, however, *Local Anaesthetic* earned Grass some enthusiastic reviews and a *Time* cover story. The caption read, "Novelist between the Generations: A Man Who Can Speak to the Young." Perhaps the only problem with this hopeful statement was that "the young" did not listen, nor did they read the book; they preferred Hermann Hesse's *Siddhartha.* However, the *Time* essayist provided a lucid interpretation of *Local Anaesthetic,* while other reviewers of the book found it difficult to make the switch from the generous epic panorama of the "Danzig Trilogy" to the contemporary outrages of the 1960s.

From the Diary of a Snail contains some of Grass's most openly autobiographical statements. It is also a diary recording his experience during Brandt's election campaign of 1969. Most important, however, this book marks a change of emphasis from politics to the more private occupation with the visual arts. Grass writes in the *Diary:* "It's true: I am not a believer; but when I draw, I become devout. . . . But I draw less and less. It doesn't get quiet enough any more. I look out to see what the clamor is; actually it's me that's clamoring and somewhere else." In the context of this self-portrait in the *Diary,* readers also find revealing remarks about Grass's inspiration and technique as graphic artist: "I draw what's left over. . . . A rich, that is, broken line, one that splits, stutters in places, here passes over in silence, there thickly proclaims. Many lines. Also bordered spots. But sometimes niggardly in disbursing outlines."

The image of the snail indicates Grass's withdrawal into an increasingly meditative phase. Although he adopted the snail as his political emblem—"the snail is progress"—his entire field of vision is affected by it. The snail replaces one of the eyeballs in two self-portraits, etchings in copper produced in 1972. Moreover, the English version of the *Diary* contains a reproduction of fifteenth-century artist Albrecht Dürer's engraving "Melancolia I." The "Variations on Albrecht Dürer's Engraving" are summarized in a speech celebrating Dürer's five hundredth birthday in 1971 and appended to the *Diary.* The personifications of both "Melancholy" and her twin sister, "Utopia," are supplemented by a narrative on "Doubt," whose story provides an excursion into the past—a report to the children about the fate of the Jewish community of Danzig during the war. With the exception of this narrative thread, the *Diary* dispenses almost entirely with plot; yet the importance of this book in defining Grass's concerns and motivations has gradually become clear to critics of his work.

Around 1974 Grass again began work on a major novel. At first he referred to it as a "Cookbook." Already in *The Diary of a Snail* he had toyed with plans of writing "a narrative cookbook: about ninety-nine dishes, about guests, about man as an animal who can cook." At a later stage, the working title for the new novel was modified: "The (female) cook in me." At a still later stage the book was said to be a variation on the Grimms' tale of "The Fisherman and His Wife." When after numerous public readings, including one in New York, the work was published in August 1977, it was titled *Der Butt* (translated as *The Flounder*) and comprised 699 pages of prose laced with forty-six poems.

The Flounder is structured around the nine months of a pregnancy and "nine or eleven" female cooks, each representing a major phase in prehistory and history from the neolithic to the present. The talking flounder functions as an archetypal male element, the tempter, who gradually destroys the mythic golden age of the matriarch. He is duly sentenced and punished by a group of feminists but will resume his destructive influence as future advisor and assistant to womankind instead of mankind. Clearly, the novel is purporting to correct some misconceptions about the roles of women in history and in the present. But the strength of this epic account lies not in its feminist argument but rather, as is usual with Grass, in its historical panorama. The setting for the mythical and historical events, all told by an ever-present first-person narrator, is once again the Baltic shore around the mouth of the Vistula. The representation of major cultural phases and personages, through individual female characters who provide life and nourishment, accounts for much of the fascination the work exerts. In the context of historical settings and figures, many of the images Grass had etched in copper—the fishheads, the mushrooms, and the portraits of women—became dynamic agents of the narrative.

A majority of reviewers, including *New Yorker* contributor John Updike, felt that the richness of the "stew" demands too much digestion. They objected to its length, its preoccupation with food and cooking, with sex and scatology. For some readers, Grass's cooks did not come across as real characters. Nigel Dennis in the *New York Review of Books* labeled *The Flounder* "a very bad novel." Morris Dickstein, on the other hand, concluded in the *New York Times* that "Grass's cooks save him for they give body to his politics. . . . The cooks bring together Grass the novelist and Grass the socialist." With regard to the issue of feminism, *The Flounder* was labeled by Richard Howard in his *New Leader* review as both "an antifeminist tract" and "a feminist tract." In a more thorough study of *The Flounder* within the context of Grass's overall work, Michael Hollington speculated in *Günter Grass: The Writer in a Pluralistic Society* "that critical reaction to the book in English-speaking countries was short-sighted" and "that as the novel is digested its distinction will gradually be recognized."

In 1979 Grass published *Das Treffen in Telgte* (translated as *The Meeting at Telgte*). This relatively short narrative is dedicated to Hans Werner Richter, founder of Group 47, in honor of his seventieth birthday. *The Meeting at Telgte,* like *The Flounder,* employs historical material, but because of its compact action, provides more suspenseful reading. Set in 1647, the novel portrays some twenty historical German writers who undertake a fictitious journey to Westphalia because they wish to contribute their share to the peace negotiations that ended the devastating Thirty Years' War. Although the situation parallels that of the writers of Group 47 after World War II, the story is not a *roman à clef*. Still, several of the seventeenth-century writers in Grass's "meeting" have twentieth-century counterparts in Group 47. For example, the mischievous Gelnhausen, who becomes the author of the *Simplicissimus* epic, reflects certain traits of Grass himself, and Simon Dach functions as a seventeenth-century image of Richter. The iconography on the dust jacket, a human hand with a quill rising above a sea of rubble, may represent as wishful a dream for the modern age as it was for the seventeenth century. But its execution in *The Meeting at Telgte* produces a masterpiece, as *German Quarterly* contributor Richard Schade contended, by means of the thistle and writer's hand imagery.

Described alternately as science fiction and fable, Grass's novel *Die Rättin* (*The Rat*) opens with a Christmas scene in which the protagonist—Grass himself—asks for and receives a rat as his present. As the rat observes Grass at work, the author becomes increasingly distracted until, eventually, the rat begins to tell a dream-like, prophetic tale about the extinction of the human race as a result of atomic war, followed by the survival of a race of rats. "This is not a book about what *may* happen; it is a novel, built on our profound need for fable, about what *has* happened to western civilization," Eugene Kennedy declared in Chicago's *Tribune Books*. Also offering praise for the novel, Richard Locke commented in the *Washington Post Book World*: "*The Rat* asks to be read as a kind of modern Book of Revelation, with Grass the St. John of our time, the delirious prophet of Apocalypse, a nuclear Big Bang that will end human life and leave the earth populated with rats feasting on radioactive human garbage."

Unlike *The Rat*, Grass's novel *Unkenrufe* (*The Call of the Toad*) received mixed reviews. *The Call of the Toad* depicts a couple who sell cemetery plots located in the Polish city of Gdansk to Germans who wish to be buried in what was once their homeland. While the business is successful, the couple becomes plagued by escalating greed and tyranny: "[what they] had envisioned as a peace-promoting, free-will enterprise becomes a symbol of German greed and tyranny in the wake of reunification," thought Donna Rikfind of *Washington Post Book World*. Many reviewers faulted the novel for its stylistic flatness, often commenting that Grass's characters lack depth and interest, despite the interesting intellectual premise of the book.

In the heady year of 1990, when the Berlin Wall had fallen and the world was discussing the potential reunification of East and West Germany, Grass published a collection of speeches and essays arguing against this path. Throughout *Deutscher Lastenausgleich: Wider das dumpfe Einheitsgebot; Reden und Gespräche, Texte zur Zeit*—translated as *Two States—One Nation?*—Grass points to the atrocities of the Holocaust as evidence of the potentially destructive force of a powerful Germany motivated by national self-interest and fear: "German unity has so often proved a threat to our neighbors that we cannot expect them to put up with it anymore," he declared. While a reviewer for the *Los Angeles Times Book Review* found the collection "challenging and disturbing," J.P. Stern in the London *Observer* rejected Grass's arguments as "gripes and sour grapes," and without foundation in terms of the contemporary social reality in Germany. Germans also generally rejected his arguments, and German reunification occurred on October 3, 1990.

Grass returned to the subject of reunification in his 1995 novel *Ein Weites Feld* (*Too Far Afield*), which also generated controversy and skeptical reviews. The novel draws upon the historical figure Theodore Fontane, a nineteenth-century writer who was skeptical of Germany's original unification in 1871. "As always, Grass is interested in how the past inundates the lives of ordinary people as they try desperately to swim with

or against history's treacherous tides," noted *New York Times Book Review* critic James J. Sheehan. *Spectator* reviewer Christian Caryl objected to the novel's approach to the satirizing contemporary politics in Germany "in the harsh light of history," noting that "the construction [of *Ein Weites Feld*] takes absolute precedence over the life of the characters. . . . Never before has [Grass] allowed his self-image as the Great German Writer to weigh so heavily on his style."

The subject of German unification is also a focus of the essays and speeches collected in *On Writing and Politics: 1967-1983*. "Grass, as these speeches show, remains stubbornly loyal to his own vision of Europe, to a 'third force' notion of a continent which must liberate itself from Soviet and American hegemony and from the burden of their armaments," observed Neal Ascherson in the *London Review of Books*. Grass also addresses larger political questions concerning the nature of political power on a global scale and the implications for the future of a world characterized by what Jon Cook in *New Statesman* called "a pretense of democracy," in which "everything is done in the name of the popular will, but in reality crucial areas of decision-making are withheld from the difficult, democratic process of negotiating consent."

Originally published in 1993 as *Novemberland: 13 Sonette, Novemberland: Selected Poems 1956-1993*, a bilingual volume of Grass's poems, was published in 1996. The fifty-four poems cover the tumultuous period of German history from World War II to the beginning of German reunification. An *America* critic noted that "Grass's style is allegorical, or perhaps fable-esque; readers familiar and comfortable with a direct access to the poet in a 'confessional' mode may not always know what to do with these poems." Grass's personal connection with the material is not always clear, according to the reviewer, as the style is surrealistic and works against such direct connections. For example, some poems include a lamentation over the ruins of Berlin, two bitten apples that recall Paradise, and a prophetic glove at the beach.

My Century, which came out in 1999, is an historical novel that consists of one hundred brief vignettes—one for each year of the twentieth century—each told in the first person. The narrators are a diverse lot, ranging from former Nazis to ordinary working-class people. "The sheer variety of Grass's inventions is impressive," observed *New York Times Book Review* contributor Peter Gay, who nonetheless felt that the book is "a collection of fragments that fail to cohere." A *Publishers*

Weekly critic had a different view, finding that this "cacaphony . . . is finally resolved into a complex, multipart harmony." Gay did compliment the individual tales: "Not that the episodes are badly told. Grass's old power of engaging the reader is still there. But the selection of witnesses seems arbitrary." Some critics thought that Grass refers too indirectly to the World War II era, including the Nazi Holocaust; the narrators for this period are a group of war correspondents meeting many years later. "Grass, always before able to face horror and disaster, seems at this late date to be losing his nerve," Gay remarked. *Booklist* contributor Frank Caso, however, found the device of the correspondents looking back to be "most effective."

In his 2002 novel *Im Krebsgang* (*Crabwalk*), Grass returns to Danzig to tell the story of a forgotten tragedy. In January of 1945, as Soviet troops were advancing on the eastern borders of Germany, tens of thousands of refugees crammed onto ships headed for safety further west. One such ship, the *Wilhelm Gustloff*, was torpedoed by a Russian submarine and sank on January 30, 1945. Because no one knows exactly how many people were on board, the total death toll remains uncertain, but estimates run as high as 10,000—mostly women and children. In Grass's tale, one such woman was Tulla, a pregnant teenage refugee who gives birth to a son, Paul, the night the ship sinks.

A grown-up, fifty-something Paul narrates the tale. Through three generations of his family, Grass weaves together numerous threads from the past and present of Germany, and "the dexterity with which Grass handles them makes this his most powerful book since *The Tin Drum*," contended *Knight Ridder/Tribune News Service* contributor Michael Upchurch. Speaking about the sufferings of Germans who were ethnically cleansed from the country's former eastern lands was—and for many still is—taboo, because it has been generally accepted that as the instigators of World War II, the German people deserve little sympathy. However Tulla, despite having become a loyal East German communist, still wants the story of the *Wilhelm Gustloff* to be preserved. She pleads with Paul, a journalist, to write about it, but he refuses. Paul, who fled to West Germany and adopted left-wing politics, wants nothing to do with his mother's Nazi past. But Paul's teenage son Konny is another story. He inhabits the fever-swamps of Neo-Nazi Web sites and chat rooms and wants not only the ship *Wilhelm Gustloff* to be recognized, but also the man—a Nazi who was assassinated by a Jewish student named David Frankfurter. Using the handle "Wilhelm," Konny argues with a "David" online. "Their real-life meeting provides the grim climax of a narrative that views fascist hate-mongering, Stalinist lies, capitalist corruption, and the eternal failures of parents with the same angry disdain," wrote a *Kirkus Reviews* contributor. To *Financial Times* reviewer Giles Macdonough, the purpose of the tale is "clearly didactic: too little openness about the past breeds Konnys, who are too often left alone, intentionally uninformed, to fester in their resentment." But Upchurch took a different lesson from the book: "Remembrance, Grass suggests, can end up being repetition."

In 1999 Grass was awarded the Nobel Prize in literature by the Swedish Academy for his body of work, beginning with *The Tin Drum* and continuing through *My Century*. The Swedish Academy commented in its press release that when *The Tin Drum* was published, "it was as if German literature had been granted a new beginning after decades of linguistic and moral destruction." The Academy went on to say that "Grass recreated the lost world from which his creativity sprang, Danzig, his home town, as he remembered it from the years of his infancy before the catastrophe of war. . . . He is a fabulist and a scholarly lecturer, recorder of voices and presumptuous monologist, pasticheur and at the same time creator of an ironic idiom that he alone commands."

BIOGRAPHICAL AND CRITICAL SOURCES:

BOOKS

Brandes, Ute Thoss, *Günter Grass,* Edition Colloquium (Berlin, Germany), 1998.

Contemporary Literary Criticism, Thomson Gale (Detroit, MI), Volume 1, 1973, Volume 2, 1974, Volume 4, 1975, Volume 6, 1976, Volume 11, 1979, Volume 15, 1980, Volume 22, 1982, Volume 32, 1985, Volume 49, 1988, Volume 88, 1995.

Dictionary of Literary Biography, Thomson Gale (Detroit, MI), Volume 75: *Contemporary German Fiction Writers, Second Series,* 1988, Volume 124: *Twentieth-Century German Dramatists, 1919-1992,* 1992.

Diller, Edward, *A Mythic Journey: Günter Grass's "Tin Drum,"* University Press of Kentucky (Lexington, KY), 1974.

Enright, D. J., *Man Is an Onion: Reviews and Essays,* Open Court (LaSalle, IL), 1972.

Esslin, Martin, *Reflections: Essays on Modern Theatre,* Doubleday (New York, NY), 1960.

Esslin, Martin, *The Theatre of the Absurd,* Doubleday (New York, NY), 1961.

Grass, Günter, *Gesammelte Gedichte* (title means "Collected Poems"), introduction by Heinrich Vormweg, Luchterhand (Neuwied, Germany), 1971.

Grass, Günter, *Aus dem Tagebuch einer Schnecke,* Luchterhand (Darmstadt, Germany), 1972, translation by Ralph Manheim published as *From the Diary of a Snail,* Harcourt (New York, NY), 1973.

Hollington, Michael, *Günter Grass: The Writer in a Pluralistic Society,* Marion Boyars (New York, NY), 1980.

International Dictionary of Theatre, Volume 2: *Playwrights,* St. James Press (Detroit, MI), 1993.

Leonard, Irene, *Günter Grass,* Oliver & Boyd, 1974.

Mason, Ann L., *The Skeptical Muse: A Study of Günter Grass' Conception of the Artist,* Herbert Lang, 1974.

Mayer, Hans, *Steppenwolf and Everyman,* translated by Jack D. Zipes, Crowell (New York, NY), 1971.

Mews, Siegfried, editor, *Günter Grass's "The Flounder" in Critical Perspective,* AMS Press (New York, NY), 1983.

Miles, Keith, *Günter Grass,* Barnes & Noble (New York, NY), 1975.

Neuhaus, Volker, *Günter Grass,* Metzler, 1979.

Newsmakers 2000, issue 2, Thomson Gale (Detroit, MI), 2000.

O'Neill, Patrick, *Günter Grass: A Bibliography, 1955-1975,* University of Toronto Press (Toronto, Ontario, Canada), 1976.

O'Neill, Patrick, *Günter Grass Revisited,* Twayne (New York, NY), 1999.

Panichas, George, editor, *The Politics of Twentieth-Century Novelists,* Hawthorn (New York, NY), 1971.

Preece, Julian, *Günter Grass: His Life and Work,* St. Martin's Press (New York, NY), 2000.

Reddick, John, *The Danzig Trilogy of Günter Grass,* Harcourt (San Diego, CA), 1974.

Steiner, George, *Language and Silence,* Atheneum (New York, NY), 1967.

Tank, Kurt Lothar, *Günter Grass,* 5th edition, Colloquium, 1965, translation by John Conway published as *Günter Grass,* Ungar (New York, NY), 1969.

Thomas, Noel, *The Narrative Works of Günter Grass,* John Benjamins (Philadelphia, PA), 1982.

Willson, A. Leslie, editor, *A Günter Grass Symposium,* University of Texas Press (Austin, TX), 1971.

PERIODICALS

America, October 26, 1996, review of *Novemberland: Selected Poems 1956-1993,* p. 26.

Atlantic, June, 1981, Phoebe-Lou Adams, review of *The Meeting at Telgte,* pp. 101-102; April, 1982, Phoebe-Lou Adams, review of *Headbirths; or, The Germans Are Dying Out,* p. 110; June, 1989, Phoebe-Lou Adams, review of *Show Your Tongue,* p. 96; November, 1992, Phoebe-Lou Adams, review of *The Call of the Toad,* p. 162; February, 2000, Phoebe-Lou Adams, review of *My Century,* p. 105.

Book, March-April, 2003, Sean McCann, review of *Crabwalk,* p. 74.

Booklist, September 15, 1992, Stuart Whitwell, review of *The Call of the Toad,* p. 100; November 15, 1999, Frank Caso, review of *My Century,* p. 579; July, 2000, Brian Kenney, review of *Too Far Afield,* p. 1973; February 15, 2003, Frank Caso, review of *Crabwalk,* pp. 1047-1048.

Books Abroad, spring, 1972.

Chicago Review, winter, 1978.

Chicago Tribune, October 29, 1978; June 27, 1980.

Commonweal, May 8, 1970; July 16, 1982, David H. Richter, review of *Headbirths,* pp. 409-410; February 9, 1990, Abigail McCarthy, "'Einig Vaterland!,'" pp. 72-73.

Contemporary European History, May, 2003, Robert G. Moeller, "Sinking Ships, the Lost Heimat and Broken Taboos: Günter Grass and the Politics of Memory in Contemporary Germany."

Contemporary Literature, summer, 1973; winter, 1976; winter, 1993, Reiko Tachibana, "Günter Grass's *The Tin Drum* and Oe Kenzaburo's *My Tears:* A Study in Convergence," pp. 740-766.

Critique, number 3, 1978; spring, 1989, Wayne P. Lindquist, "The Materniads: Grass's Paradoxical Conclusion to the 'Danzig Trilogy,'" pp. 179-192.

Detroit Free Press, October 1, 1999, p. 10A.

Detroit News, May 9, 1982.

Diacritics, number 3, 1973.

Dimension, summer, 1970.

Economist (U.S.), August 2, 1986, review of *Die Rättin,* p. SB13; November 28, 1992, review of *The Call of the Toad,* p. 104; September 2, 1995, "Grass and the Drum of Discord," p. 43; October 18, 1997, review of *Fundsachen für Nichtleser,* pp. S14-S15; October 25, 1997, "Günter Grass, Ever Unmown," p. 57; October 16, 1999, "What the World Is Reading," p. 15; February 16, 2002, review of *Im Krebsgang.*

Encounter, April, 1964; November, 1970.

Entertainment Weekly, October 23, 1992, L.S. Klepp, review of *The Call of the Toad,* pp. 56-57.

Europe, July-August, 1993, Christine Bednarz, "Writer's Corner: Günter Grass," pp. 44-45; March, 2000, Claire Bose, "The Grass Century," p. 25.

Europe Intelligence Wire, May 17, 2003, review of *Crabwalk.*

Financial Times, August 26, 1995, Wolfgang Munchau, "Fiery Reviews Scorch Grass," p. 7; October 1, 1999, Christopher Brown-Humes and Jan Dalley, "Günter Grass Wins Nobel Literature Prize," p. 4; February 16, 2002, Frederick Studemann, review of *Im Krebsgang,* p. 4; April 26, 2003, Frederick Studemann, review of *Crabwalk,* p. 43; November 1, 2003, Giles Macdonough, review of *Crabwalk,* p. 26.

Foreign Policy, March-April, 2003, Robert Gerald Livingston, review of *Im Krebsgang,* pp. 80-82.

Germanic Review, fall, 1993, Lawrence O. Frye, "Günter Grass, *Katz und Maus,* and Gastro-Narratology," pp. 176-184.

Germanisch-Romanische Monatsschrift, number 47, 1966.

German Quarterly, number 54, 1981; number 55, 1982; winter, 1997, Monika Shafi, "Gazing at India: Representations of Alterity in Travelogues by Ingeborg Drewitz, Günter Grass, and Hubert Fichte," pp. 39-56.

Harper's, December, 1978.

Hindu, October 17, 1999, Ravi Vyas, "Reality at Grass Level."

Journal of European Studies, September, 1979; March, 1989, Carl Tighe, "*The Tin Drum* in Poland," pp. 3-20.

Kirkus Reviews, January 1, 2003, review of *Crabwalk,* pp. 11-12.

Kliatt, January, 2002, Bernard D. Cooperman, review of *The Tin Drum* (audiobook), p. 48; November, 2003, Hugh Flick, Jr., review of *Crabwalk* (audiobook), p. 46.

Knight Ridder/Tribune News Service, November 22, 2000, Carlin Romano, review of *Too Far Afield,* p. K3110; January 10, 2001, Jay Goldin, review of *Too Far Afield,* p. K5668; April 30, 2003, Michael Upchurch, review of *Crabwalk,* p. K1370.

Library Journal, March 15, 1981, Gari R. Muller, review of *The Meeting at Telgte,* p. 689; March 15, 1982, review of *Headbirths,* p. 650; July, 1987, Paul E. Hutchison, review of *The Rat,* p. 94; September 15, 1990, Marcia L. Sprules, review of *Two States—One Nation?: Against the Unenlightened Clamor for German Reunification,* p. 90; September 15, 1992, Michael T. O'Pecko, review of *The Call of the Toad,* p. 94; May 15, 1996, Michael T. O'Pecko, review of *Novemberland,* p. 65; January, 2000, Eric Bryant, review of *My Century,* p. 159; September 15, 2000, Mirela Roncevic, review of *Too Far Afield,* p. 112; January, 2003, Edward Cone, review of *Crabwalk,* p. 154.

Literary Review, summer, 1974.

London Magazine, October, 1978.

London Review of Books, February 5-18, 1981; May 6-19, 1982; October 17, 1985, p. 6; October 17, 1996, p. 3.

Los Angeles Times, May 22, 1981; April 18, 1982; May 20, 1983, "Has Our Writing Lost Its Politics?," p. 3; March 4, 1984, Charles Solomon, review of *Günter Grass: Drawings and Words 1954-1977,* p. 6; June 16, 1985, Salman Rushdie, "A Political Author Migrates from Certainty to Doubt," p. 2; July 21, 1985, Art Seidenbaum, review of *On Writing and Politics, 1967-1983,* p. 2; August 13, 1989; November 29, 1992; September 18, 1995, William Pfaff, "Günter Grass's New Novel Unleashes the PC Censors," p. B5; September 22, 1995, Mary Williams, "The Plot Sickens, German Critics Say," p. A5; October 1, 1999, Carol J. Williams, "Germany Hails Grass's 'Overdue' Literature Nobel," p. A1; March 28, 2002, Carol J. Williams, review of *Im Krebsgang,* p. E-1; April 13, 2003, Thomas McGonigle, review of *Crabwalk,* p. R-4.

Los Angeles Times Book Review, November 17, 1991, p. 14.

Michigan Quarterly Review, winter, 1975.

Midwest Quarterly, autumn, 2001, Ronald Charles Epstein, review of *Too Far Afield,* pp. 113-114.

Modern Fiction Studies, spring, 1971; summer, 1986, p. 334.

Modern Language Review, October, 1995, Julian Preece, "Sexual-Textual Politics: The Transparency of the Male Narrative in *Der Butt* by Günter Grass," pp. 955-966; April, 2001, K.F. Hilliard, "Showing, Telling and Believing: Günter Grass's *Katz und Maus* and narratology," p. 420.

Nation, December 23, 1978; April 24, 1982, Richard Gilman, review of *Headbirths,* pp. 502-504; December 24, 1990, John Leonard, review of *Two States—One Nation?* and overview of Grass's work, pp. 810-816; November 16, 1992, Irmgard Elsner Hunt, review of *The Call of the Toad,* pp. 580-584; July 3, 2000, Pierre Bourdieu, interview with Grass, p. 25; March 31, 2003, Hugh Eakin, review of *Crabwalk,* p. 31.

National Interest, summer, 2000, Jacob Heilbrunn, "Germany's Illiberal Fictions," p. 88.

National Review, October 25, 1999, David Pryce-Jones, "The Failure of Günter Grass: Another Nobel Bomb," p. 30; December 6, 1999, James Gardner, review of *My Century,* p. 67.

New Leader, October 29, 1973; December 4, 1978; December 13, 1999, Rosellen Brown, review of *My Century,* p. 29; March-April, 2003, Benjamin Taylor, review of *Crabwalk,* pp. 24-25.

New Republic, June 20, 1970; April 14, 1982, Joel Agee, review of *Headbirths,* pp. 30-32; August 12,

1985, Timothy Garton Ash, review of *On Writing and Politics,* pp. 31-33; July 13, 1987, Jasoslav Anders, review of *The Rat,* pp. 29-32; January 31, 2000, Ian Buruma, review of *My Century,* p. 31; August 11, 2003, Ruth Franklin, review of *Crabwalk,* p. 30.

New Review, May, 1974.

New Statesman, June 7, 1974; June 26, 1981, Salman Rushdie, review of *The Meeting at Telgte,* p. 21; April 23, 1982, Mike Poole, review of *Headbirths,* p. 27; September 20, 1985, p. 27; June 26, 1987, Michelene Wandor, review of *The Rat,* p. 26; March 19, 1999, Lavinia Greenlaw, review of *Selected Poems: 1956-1993,* pp. 48-49; December 4, 2000, William Cook, review of *Too Far Afield,* p. 55; April 7, 2003, Sarah Schaeffer, review of *Crabwalk,* p. 54.

New Statesman & Society, June 22, 1990, Aafke Steenhuis, interview with Grass, pp. 35-38; October 9, 1992, Martin Chalmers, review of *The Call of the Toad,* p. 37.

Newsweek International, March 11, 2002, Andrew Nagorski and Stefan Theil, review of *Crabwalk,* p. 51.

New York, November 16, 1992, Rhoda Koenig, review of *The Call of the Toad,* p. 78.

New Yorker, April 25, 1970; October 15, 1973; November 27, 1978; August 3, 1981, John Updike, review of *The Meeting at Telgte,* pp. 90-93; June 14, 1982, John Updike, review of *Headbirths,* pp. 129-131; February 6, 1984, review of *Günter Grass: Drawings and Words, 1954-1977,* pp. 128-129; October 19, 1992, Ian Buruma, "Günter's Ghosts: Postcard from Berlin," pp. 45-46; April 21, 2003, John Updike, review of *Crabwalk,* p. 185.

New York Review of Books, November 23, 1978; June 11, 1981, Stephen Spender, review of *The Meeting at Telgte,* pp. 35-38; March 18, 1982, D.J. Enright, review of *Headbirths,* p. 46; July 5, 1987; September 24, 1987, D.J. Enright, review of *The Rat,* pp. 45-46; May 21, 1989; September 30, 1990; November 1, 1992; November 19, 1992, Gabriel Annan, review of *The Call of the Toad,* p. 19; November 30, 2000, Gabriele Annan, review of *Too Far Afield,* pp. 39-41.

New York Times, April 15, 1977; November 9, 1978; November 25, 1978; May 31, 1979; January 26, 1980, John Vincour, "In Any Language, Grass Chooses His Words with Care," p. 2; April 6, 1980, John Vincour, review of *The Tin Drum,* p. D1; April 11, 1980, Vincent Canby, review of *The Tin Drum,* p. C6; April 30, 1981, John Leonard, review of *The Meeting at Telgte,* pp. 19, C21; February 26, 1982, Christopher Lehmann-Haupt, review of *Headbirths,* pp. 21, C22; March 6, 1983, John Rus-

sell, "Günter Grass as a Printmaker, Poet, Storyteller, and Fabulist," p. H29; March 8, 1983, Herbert Mitgang, "Author Activism a Topic at German Book Fair," pp. 19, C11; April 18, 1983, "Seven Authors Assail U.S. over Nicaragua Policy," p. 7; June 17, 1985, Christopher Lehmann-Haupt, review of *On Writing and Politics,* pp. 17, C17; January 15, 1986, Edwin McDowell, "Grass Challenges Bellow on U.S. at PEN Meeting," pp. 19, C15; January 19, 1986, "Eavesdropping at a Writers' Conference," p. E6; February 5, 1986, James M. Markham, "The Cold War of Letters Raging in Günter Grass," pp. 19, C21; June 2, 1986, Walter Goodman, review of *Flood,* pp. 21, C14; June 29, 1987, Christopher Lehmann-Haupt, review of *The Rat,* pp. 19, C18; October 3, 1990, Herbert Mitgang, review of *Two States—One Nation?,* pp. B2, C17; February 19, 1991, "Günter Grass Wants Kohl Out," p. A4; November 18, 1992, Herbert Mitgang, review of *The Call of the Toad,* pp. B2, C25; December 29, 1992, Esther B. Fein, "Günter Grass Finds Politics Inescapable," pp. B1, C11; October 1, 1999, Roger Cohen, "Günter Grass Gets Nobel Prize in Literature," p. A13; October 3, 1999, Roger Cohen, "A Nobel for Günter Grass," p. WK2, and James Atlas, "Polemical Prize," p. WK17; January 5, 2000, Richard Bernstein, review of *My Century,* pp. B10, E10; December 14, 2000, Alan Riding, review of *Too Far Afield,* pp. B1, E1; January 26, 2001, Ken Johnson, review of "Too Far Afield: Graphics, 1970-2000," pp. B35, E37; April 8, 2003, Alan Riding, interview with Grass, p. E1; April 24, 2003, Richard Eder, review of *Crabwalk,* p. E8.

New York Times Book Review, August 14, 1966; March 29, 1970; September 30, 1973; November 12, 1978; November 23, 1978; May 17, 1981, Theodore Ziokowski, review of *The Meeting at Telgate,* pp. 7-8; March 14, 1982, review of *Headbirths,* pp. 11-13; May 16, 1982, review of *The Meeting at Telgte,* p. 39; December 5, 1982, review of *Headbirths,* p. 40; February 27, 1983; March 27, 1983; February 19, 1984, Ronald Radosh, review of *Trouble in Our Backyard: Central America and the United States in the Eighties,* pp. 5-6; June 23, 1985, James Markham, review of *On Writing and Politics,* p. 17; July 5, 1987, Janette Turner Hospital, review of *The Rat,* p. 6; May 21, 1989, review of *Show Your Tongue,* p. 12; September 30, 1990, Ralf Dahrendorf, review of *Two States—One Nation?,* p. 9; November 1, 1992, John Bayley, review of *The Call of the Toad,* p. 1; October 22, 1995, Stephen Kinzer, "Günter Grass: Germany's Last Heretic," p. 47; December 19, 1999, Peter Gay, review of *My Century,* p. 9; November 5, 2000,

James J. Sheehan, review of *Too Far Afield,* p. 20; January 6, 2002, Scott Veale, review of *Too Far Afield,* p. 20; April 27, 2003, Jeremy Adler, review of *Crabwalk,* p. 12; May 4, 2003, review of *Crabwalk,* p. 26.

New York Times Magazine, April 29, 1984, John Vincour, "Europe's Intellectuals and American Power," pp. 60-69.

Observer (London, England), July 16, 1989, p. 43; October 14, 1990, p. 64.

Publishers Weekly, January 22, 1982, Barbara A. Bannon, review of *Headbirths,* p. 60; March 27, 1982, review of *The Meeting at Telgte,* pp. 42-43; May 3, 1985, review of *On Writing and Politics,* p. 59; May 22, 1987, Sybil Steinberg, review of *The Rat,* p. 64; April 21, 1989, Penny Kaganoff, review of *Show Your Tongue,* pp. 85-86; June 16, 1989, Sybil Steinberg, interview with Grass, pp. 54-55; September 7, 1990, Genevieve Stuttaford, review of *Two States—One Nation?,* p. 70; August 10, 1992, review of *The Call of the Toad,* p. 50; October 4, 1999, "Germany's Grass Wins 1999 Nobel," p. 10; November 15, 1999, review of *My Century,* p. 57; November 6, 2000, review of *Too Far Afield,* p. 72; March 3, 2003, review of *Crabwalk,* p. 51.

Review of Contemporary Fiction, spring, 2001, Richard J. Murphy, review of *Too Far Afield,* p. 192.

San Francisco Review of Books, July-August, 1981.

Saturday Review, May 20, 1972; November 11, 1978; May, 1981, Donald Newlove, review of *The Meeting at Telgte,* p. 71; March, 1982, John Irving, review of *Headbirths,* pp. 57-60.

Scala, number 6, 1981; number 1, 1982.

Spectator, May 18, 1974; January 27, 1996, Christian Caryl, review of *Ein weites Feld,* p. 28; October 17, 1992, Michael Hulse, review of *The Call of the Toad,* p. 6; October 9, 1999, Stephen Schwartz, "Ignoble Nobel," p. 18; January 1, 2000, Robert Macfarlane, review of *My Century,* pp. 26-27; March 29, 2003, Andrew Gimson, review of *Crabwalk,* pp. 49-50.

Statesman (India), January 28, 2001, review of *Show Your Tongue* and profile of Grass.

Time, January 4, 1963; April 13, 1978; April 28, 1980; May 18, 1981, Paul Gray, review of *The Meeting at Telgte,* p. 87; January 27, 1986; July 20, 1987, Paul Gray, review of *The Rat,* p. 73; October 11, 1999, "Milestones," p. 31; April 28, 2003, Michael Elliott, review of *Crabwalk,* p. 70.

Times (London, England), June 22, 1981; April 22, 1982; September 19, 1985; June 21, 1995, Robert Boyes, "Is the Writer a Traitor?," p. 37.

Times Educational Supplement, December 4, 1992, Brian Morton, review of *The Call of the Toad,* p. S10.

Times Literary Supplement, October 13, 1978; September 26, 1980; June 26, 1981; April 23, 1982; June 15, 1990, Peter Graves, review of *Deutscher Lastenausgleich: Wider das dumpfe Einheitsgebot: Reden und Gespräche, Texte zur Zeit* p. 631; June 19, 1992, "High Priests or Nut-Cases?," p. 14; October 9, 1992, Philip Brady, review of *Call of the Toad* and *Vier Jahrzehnte: Ein Werkstattbericht,* p. 24; October 13, 1995, Anne McElvoy, review of *Ein wFeld,* p. 26; August 20, 1999, Chris Greenhalgh, review of *Selected Poems: 1956-1993,* p. 21; October 8, 1999, Rudiger Gorner, review of *Mein Jahrundert,* p. 10; December 24, 1999, Hugh MacPherson, review of *My Century,* p. 20; December 8, 2000, Hugh MacPherson, review of *Too Far Afield,* p. 22; April 4, 2003, Jonathan Fasman, review of *Crabwalk,* p. 22.

Tribune Books (Chicago, IL), May 10, 1981; March 21, 1982; May 21, 1989; November 15, 1992.

Village Voice, October 25, 1973.

Virginia Quarterly Review, spring, 1975; winter, 1988, review of *The Rat,* p. 20.

Washington Post, March 2, 1972; April 10, 1982; February 15, 1993, David Streitfeld, review of *The Call of the Toad,* p. C1; September 26, 1995, Rick Atkinson, "Roar of the Literary Lion: His Book Mauled, Günter Grass Goes on the Attack," p. E1; October 1, 1999, Marc Fisher and Linton Weeks, "Günter Grass Wins Nobel for Literature," p. A01; December 17, 2000, Dennis Drabelle, review of *Too Far Afield,* p. T14.

Washington Post Book World, September 23, 1973; November 5, 1978; August 9, 1981; August 11, 1985, review of *On Writing and Politics,* p. 9; July 12, 1987, p. 5; November 8, 1992, p. 6.

World Literature Today, spring, 1981; autumn, 1981; winter, 1986, p. 194; summer, 1989, Ulf Zimmermann, review of *Zunge zeigen,* p. 477; spring, 1991, Patricia Pollock Brodsky, review of *Totes Holz,* pp. 299-300; autumn, 1991, Wes Blomster, review of *Ein Schnappchen namens DDR: Letzte Reden vorm Glockengelaut,* pp. 703-704; spring, 1993, Patricia Pollock Brodsky, review of *Unkenrufe,* p. 366; summer, 1994, Irmgard Elsner Hunt, review of *Novemberland: 13 Sonette* and *Rede vom Verlust: Uber den Niedergang der politischen Kultur im geeinten Deutschland,* pp. 559-560; summer, 1995, Irmgard Elsner Hunt, review of *In Kupfer, auf ein Stein: Das Grafische Werk,* pp. 578-579; spring, 1996, Christian Grawe, review of *Ein weites Feld,* pp. 387-388; winter, 2000, Theodore Ziolkowski, "Günter Grass's Century," p. 19; April-June, 2003, Irmgard Hunt, review of *Im Krebsgang,* pp. 128-129.

ONLINE

Nobel Prize Internet Archive, http://nobelprizes.com/ (October 1, 1999).

*   *   *

GRASS, Günter Wilhelm
   See GRASS, Günter

*   *   *

GRAVES, Robert 1895-1985
   (John Doyle, Robert von Ranke Graves, Barbara Rich, a joint pseudonym)

PERSONAL: Born July 24, 1895, in London, England; died after a long illness, December 7, 1985, in Deya, Majorca, Spain; son of Alfred Perceval (an Irish poet and ballad writer) and Amalia (von Ranke) Graves; married Nancy Nicholson, 1918 (divorced, 1929); married Beryl Pritchard, 1950; children: (first marriage) Jenny, David, Catherine, Samuel; (second marriage) William, Lucia, Juan, Tomas. *Education:* Attended King's College School and Rokeby School, Wimbledon, Copthorne School, Sussex, Charterhouse School, Godalming, Surrey, 1907-14; St. John's College, Oxford, B.Litt., 1926.

CAREER: Egyptian University, Cairo, Egypt, professor of English literature, 1926; cofounder with Laura Riding of Seizin Press, 1928, and *Epilogue* semiannual magazine, 1935, coeditor with Riding of *Epilogue,* 1935-37; Clarke Lecturer, Trinity College, Cambridge University, 1954-55; lecturer in United States, 1958; Oxford University, Oxford, England, professor of poetry, 1961-65; lecturer in United States, 1966-67. Arthur Dehon Little Memorial Lecturer at Massachusetts Institute of Technology, 1963. *Military service:* Royal Welch Fusiliers, 1914-18; served in France; became captain.

MEMBER: American Academy of Arts and Sciences (honorary member).

AWARDS, HONORS: Bronze Medal for poetry at Olympic Games in Paris, 1924; James Tait Black Memorial Prize, 1935, for *I, Claudius* and *Claudius, the God and His Wife Messalina;* Hawthornden Prize, 1935, for *I, Claudius;* Femina-Vie Heureuse Prize, and Stock Prize, both 1939, both for *Count Belisarius;* Russell Loines Memorial Fund Award, 1958; Gold Medal of Poetry Society of America, 1959; Foyle Poetry Prize, 1960; M.A., Oxford University, 1961; Arts Council award, 1962; Italia Prize for radio play, 1965; Gold Medal for poetry at Cultural Olympics in Mexico City, 1968; Queen's Gold Medal for Poetry, 1969; honorary fellow of St. John's College, 1971; Sol de Oro Medal, Madrid, 1973.

WRITINGS:

POETRY

Over the Brazier, Poetry Bookshop, 1916.
Goliath and David, Chiswick Press, 1916.
Fairies and Fusiliers, Heinemann (London, England), 1917, Knopf (New York, NY), 1918.
The Treasure Box, Chiswick Press, 1919.
Country Sentiment, Knopf (New York, NY), 1920.
The Pier-Glass, Knopf (New York, NY), 1921.
The Feather Bed, L. and V. Woolf (Oxford, England), 1923.
Whipperginny, Knopf (New York, NY), 1923.
Mock Beggar Hall, Hogarth Press (Oxford, England), 1924.
Welchman's Hose, Fleuron, 1925.
Robert Graves, Benn (London, England), 1925.
(Under pseudonym John Doyle) *The Marmosite's Miscellany,* Hogarth Press (Oxford, England), 1925.
Poems, 1914-1926, Heinemann (London, England), 1927, Doubleday, Doran (New York, NY), 1929.
Poems, 1914-1927, Heinemann (London, England), 1927.
Poems, 1929, Seizin Press, 1929.
Ten Poems More, Hours Press (Paris, France), 1930.
Poems, 1926-1930, Heinemann (Chicago, IL), 1931.
To Whom Else?, Seizin Press, 1931.
Poems, 1930-1933, Barker, 1933.
Collected Poems, Random House (New York, NY), 1938.
No More Ghosts: Selected Poems, Faber (London, England), 1940.
(With Alan Hodge and Norman Cameron) *Work in Hand,* Hogarth Press (Oxford, England), 1942.
Poems, 1938-1945, Creative Age Press, 1946.
Collected Poems, 1914-1947, Cassell (London, England), 1948.
Poems and Satires, Cassell (London, England), 1951.
Poems, 1953, Cassell (London, England), 1953.
Collected Poems, 1955, Doubleday (New York, NY), 1955.

Robert Graves: Poems Selected by Himself, Penguin Books (New York, NY), 1957.

The Poems of Robert Graves Chosen by Himself, Doubleday (New York, NY), 1958.

Collected Poems, 1959, Cassell (London, England), 1959, Doubleday (New York, NY), 1961, 3rd edition, Cassell, 1962.

The Penny Fiddle: Poems for Children, Cassell (London, England), 1960, Doubleday (New York, NY), 1961.

More Poems, Cassell (London, England), 1961.

Selected Poetry and Prose, edited, introduced, and annotated by James Reeves, Hutchinson (London, England), 1961.

Poems, Collected by Himself, Doubleday (New York, NY), 1961.

The More Deserving Cases: Eighteen Old Poems for Reconsideration, Marlborough College Press, 1962.

New Poems, Cassell (London, England), 1962, Doubleday (New York, NY), 1963.

Ann at Highwood Hall: Poems for Children, Cassell (London, England), 1964.

Man Does, Woman Is, Doubleday (New York, NY), 1964.

Love Respelt, Cassell (London, England), 1965, Doubleday (New York, NY), 1966.

Collected Poems, Cassell (London, England), 1965, Doubleday (New York, NY), 1966.

Seventeen Poems Missing from Love Respelt, Stellar Press, 1966.

Colophon to "Love Respelt," Bertram Rota, 1967.

(With D.H. Lawrence) *Poems,* edited by Leonard Clark, Longman (London, England), 1967.

Poems, 1965-1968, Cassell (London, England), 1968.

Beyond Giving, Bertram Rota, 1969.

Love Respelt Again, Doubleday (New York, NY), 1969.

Poems about Love, Cassell (London, England), 1969.

Poems, 1968-1970, Cassell (London, England), 1970, Doubleday (New York, NY), 1971.

Advice from a Mother, Poem-of-the-Month Club, 1970.

Green-Sailed Vessel, Bertram Rota, 1971.

Poems, 1970-1972, Cassell (London, England), 1972.

Timeless Meeting, Bertram Rota, 1973.

At the Gate, Bertram Rota, 1974.

Collected Poems 1975, Cassell (London, England), 1975, published as *New Collected Poems,* Doubleday (New York, NY), 1977.

Poems about War, Moyer Bell, 1992.

Across the Gulf, New Seizin Press, 1994.

Robert Graves: The Centenary Selected Poems, edited by Patrick Quinn, Carcanet (Manchester, England), 1995.

Complete Poems, Volume I, edited by Beryl Graves and Dunstan Ward, Carcanet (Manchester, England), 1995, published as *The Complete Poems in One Volume,* 2000.

Also author of *Deya,* 1973, *Eleven Songs,* 1983, *Selected Poems,* edited by Paul O'Prey, 1986.

FICTION

My Head! My Head! Being the History of Elisha and the Shunamite Woman; With the History of Moses as Elisha Related It, and Her Questions Put to Him, Secker (London, England), 1925.

The Shout, Mathews and Marrot, 1929.

(With Laura Riding, under joint pseudonym Barbara Rich) *No Decency Left,* J. Cape (London, England), 1932.

The Real David Copperfield, Barker, 1933.

I, Claudius, Smith & Haas, 1934, revised edition, Random House (New York, NY), 1977.

Claudius, the God and His Wife Messalina, Barker, 1934, Smith & Haas, 1935.

"Antigua, Penny, Puce," Constable (London, England), 1936, published as *The Antigua Stamp,* Random House (New York, NY), 1937.

Count Belisarius, Random House (New York, NY), 1938.

Sergeant Lamb of the Ninth, Methuen (London, England), 1940, published as *Sergeant Lamb's America,* Random House (New York, NY), 1940.

Proceed, Sergeant Lamb, Random House (New York, NY), 1941.

The Story of Marie Powell, Wife to Mr. Milton, Cassell (London, England), 1943, published as *Wife to Mr. Milton: The Story of Marie Powell,* Creative Age Press, 1944.

The Golden Fleece, Cassell, 1944, published as *Hercules, My Shipmate,* Creative Age Press, 1945.

King Jesus, Creative Age Press, 1946, 6th edition, Cassell (London, England), 1962.

The Islands of Unwisdom, Doubleday (New York, NY), 1949, published as *The Isles of Unwisdom,* Cassell (London, England), 1950.

Watch the North Wind Rise, Creative Age Press, 1949, published as *Seven Days in New Crete,* Cassell (London, England), 1949.

Homer's Daughter, Doubleday (New York, NY), 1955.

Catacrok! Mostly Stories, Mostly Funny, Cassell (London, England), 1956.

They Hanged My Saintly Billy: The Life and Death of Dr. William Palmer, Doubleday (New York, NY), 1957.

Collected Short Stories, Doubleday (New York, NY), 1964, published as *The Shout and Other Stories,* Penguin (New York, NY), 1978.

Complete Short Stories, edited by Lucia Graves, St. Martin's Press (New York, NY), 1996.

NONFICTION

On English Poetry; Being an Irregular Approach to the Psychology of This Art, From Evidence Mainly Subjective, Knopf (New York, NY), 1922.

The Meaning of Dreams, Palmer, 1924.

Poetic Unreason and Other Studies, Palmer, 1925.

Contemporary Techniques of Poetry: A Political Analogy, Hogarth Press (Oxford, England), 1925.

Another Future of Poetry, Hogarth Press (Oxford, England), 1926.

Impenetrability; or, The Proper Habit of English, L. and V. Woolf (Oxford, England), 1926.

(With Laura Riding) *A Survey of Modernist Poetry,* Heinemann (London, England), 1927, Doubleday, Doran (New York, NY), 1928.

Lawrence and the Arabs, J. Cape (London, England), 1927, published as *Lawrence and the Arabian Adventure,* Doubleday, Doran (New York, NY), 1928.

Lars Porsena; or, The Future of Swearing and Improper Language, Dutton (New York, NY), 1927, revised edition published as *The Future of Swearing and Improper Language,* K. Paul, Trench, Trubner, 1936.

Mrs. Fisher; or, The Future of Humour, K. Paul, Trench, Trubner, 1928.

(With Laura Riding) *A Pamphlet against Anthologies,* J. Cape (London, England), 1928.

Goodbye to All That: An Autobiography, J. Cape (London, England), 1929, revised edition, Doubleday (New York, NY), 1957.

T.E. Lawrence to His Biographer, Doubleday (New York, NY), 1938, published with Liddell Hart's work as *T.E. Lawrence to His Biographers,* Doubleday, 1963, 2nd edition, Cassell (London, England), 1963.

(With Alan Hodge) *The Long Week-End: A Social History of Great Britain, 1918-1939,* Faber (London, England), 1940, Macmillan (New York, NY), 1941.

(With Alan Hodge) *The Reader over Your Shoulder: A Handbook for Writers of English Prose,* Macmillan (New York, NY), 1943, revised edition published as *The Use and Abuse of the English Language,* Paragon, 1990.

The White Goddess: A Historical Grammar of Poetic Myth, Creative Age Press, 1948, amended and enlarged edition, Vintage Books (New York, NY), 1958.

The Common Asphodel: Collected Essays on Poetry, 1922-1949, H. Hamilton, 1949.

(With Joshua Podro) *The Nazarene Gospel Restored,* Cassell (London, England), 1953, Doubleday (New York, NY), 1954.

(With Joshua Podro) *Nazarene Gospel,* Cassell (London, England), 1955.

Adam's Rib, and Other Anomalous Elements in the Hebrew Creation Myth: A New View, Trianon Press, 1955, Yoseloff, 1958.

The Greek Myths, two volumes, Penguin Books (New York, NY), 1955, condensed edition, Viking (New York, NY), 1992, published as *The Greek Myths: Complete Edition,* 1993.

The Crowning Privilege: The Clark Lectures, 1954-1955 (includes sixteen new poems), Cassell (London, England), 1955, Doubleday (New York, NY), 1956.

(With Joshua Podro) *Jesus in Rome: A Historical Conjecture,* Cassell (London, England), 1957.

5 Pens in Hand, Doubleday (New York, NY), 1958.

Steps: Stories, Talks, Essays, Poems, Studies in History, Cassell (London, England), 1958.

Food for Centaurs: Stories, Talks, Critical Studies, Poems, Doubleday (New York, NY), 1960.

Greek Gods and Heroes, Doubleday (New York, NY), 1960, published as *Myths of Ancient Greece,* Cassell (London, England), 1961.

Oxford Addresses on Poetry, Doubleday (New York, NY), 1962.

Nine Hundred Iron Chariots, Massachusetts Institute of Technology (Cambridge, MA), 1963.

(With Raphael Patal) *Hebrew Myths: The Book of Genesis,* Doubleday (New York, NY), 1964.

Mammon (lecture; also see below), London School of Economics (London, England), 1964, expanded as *Mammon and the Black Goddess,* Doubleday (New York, NY), 1965.

Majorca Observed, Doubleday (New York, NY), 1965.

Spiritual Quixote, Oxford University Press (New York, NY), 1967.

Poetic Craft and Principle (collection of Oxford lectures), Cassell (London, England), 1967.

(Author of introduction) *Greece, Gods, and Art,* Viking (New York, NY), 1968.

The Crane Bag, Cassell (London, England), 1969.

Difficult Questions, Easy Answers, Cassell (London, England), 1972, Doubleday (New York, NY), 1973.

Selected Letters of Robert Graves, edited by Paul O'Prey, Hutchinson (London, England), Volume I: *In Broken Images: 1914-1946,* 1982, Volume II: *Between Moon and Moon: 1946-1972,* 1984.

Conversations with Robert Graves, edited by Frank L. Kersnowski, University Press of Mississippi (Jackson, MS), 1989.

Dear Robert, Dear Spike: The Graves-Milligan Correspondence, edited by Pauline Scudamore, Sutton, 1991.

Collected Writings on Poetry, edited by Paul O'Prey, Carcanet (Manchester, England), 1995.

FOR CHILDREN

The Big Green Book, illustrated by Maurice Sendak, Crowell (New York, NY), 1962.

The Siege and Fall of Troy, Cassell (London, England), 1962, Doubleday (New York, NY), 1963.

Two Wise Children, Harlin Quist, 1966.

The Poor Boy Who Followed His Star, Cassell (London, England), 1968, Doubleday (New York, NY), 1969.

The Ancient Castle, P. Owen, 1980.

EDITOR

(And author of introduction and critical notes) *The English Ballad: A Short Critical Survey,* Benn (London, England), 1927, revised edition, Heinemann (London, England), 1957, published as *English and Scottish Ballads,* Macmillan (New York, NY), 1957.

John Skelton (Laureate), 1460(?)-1529, Benn (London, England), 1927.

(Compiler) *The Less Familiar Nursery Rhymes,* Benn (London, England), 1927.

(And author of foreword) Algernon Charles Swinburne, *An Old Saying,* J.S. Mayfield, 1947.

(And author of foreword) *The Comedies of Terence,* Doubleday (New York, NY), 1962, published as *Comedies,* Aldine, 1962.

TRANSLATOR

(With Laura Riding) Georg Schwarz, *Almost Forgotten Germany,* Random House (New York, NY), 1937.

Lucius Apuleius, *The Transformations of Lucius, Otherwise Known as "The Golden Ass,"* Farrar, Straus (New York, NY), 1951.

Manuel de Jesus Galvan, *The Cross and the Sword,* Indiana University Press (Bloomington, IN), 1954.

Pedro Antonio de Alarcon, *The Infant with the Globe,* Faber (New York, NY), 1955.

Marcus Annaeus Lucanus, *Pharsalia: Dramatic Episodes of the Civil Wars,* Penguin Books (New York, NY), 1956.

George Sand, *Winter in Majorca,* illustrated by Maurice Sand, Cassell (London, England), 1956.

Suetonius, *The Twelve Caesars,* Cassell (London, England), 1957, reprinted, Penguin (New York, NY), 2003.

The Anger of Achilles: Homer's "Iliad" (produced at Lincoln Center, New York, 1967), Doubleday (New York, NY), 1959.

Hesiodu Stamperia del Santuccio, *Fable of the Hawk and the Nightingale,* 1959.

(With Omar Ali-Shah) *The Rubaiyyat of Omar Khayaam* (based on the twelfth-century manuscript), Cassell (London, England), 1967, published as *The Original Rubaiyyat of Omar Khayaam,* Doubleday (New York, NY), 1968.

Solomon's "Song of Songs," Cassell (London, England), 1968, Doubleday (New York, NY), 1969.

OTHER

John Kemp's Wager: A Ballad Opera, S. French (New York, NY), 1925.

But Still It Goes On: An Accumulation (includes the play "But It Still Goes On"), J. Cape (London, England), 1930.

(Rewriter) Frank Richards, *Old Soldiers Never Die,* Faber & Faber (New York, NY), 1933.

(Rewriter) Richards, *Old-Soldier Sahib,* Smith & Haas, 1936.

Occupation: Writer (includes the play "Horses"), Creative Age Press, 1950.

Nausicaa (opera libretto; adapted from his novel *Homer's Daughter;* music by Peggy Glanville-Hicks), produced in Athens, Greece, 1961.

Some Speculations on Literature, History, and Religion, edited by Patrick Quinn, Carcanet Press (Manchester, England), 2000.

(With Laura Riding), *Essays from "Epilogue,"* Carcanet (Manchester, England), 2001.

Also author of television documentary, *Greece: The Inner World,* 1964.

Recordings by Graves include *Robert Graves Reading His Own Poems,* for Argo and Listen; *Robert Graves Reading His Own Poetry and The White Goddess,* for Caedmon; and *The Rubaiyyat of Omar Khayaam,* for Spoken Arts.

Graves' letters and worksheets, as well as an autograph diary, are in the Graves Manuscript Collection at the University of Victoria, British Columbia, Canada. Other papers are in the collections of Lockwood Memorial Library, State University of New York at Buffalo; Berg Collection, New York City Library; Humanities Research Center, University of Texas, Austin; and University of Southern Illinois, Carbondale.

SIDELIGHTS: Robert Graves often stirred controversy in his endeavors as a poet, novelist, critic, mythographer, translator, and editor. Stephen Spender in the *New York Times Book Review* characterized Graves as a free thinker: "All of his life Graves has been indifferent to fashion, and the great and deserved reputation he has is based on his individuality as a poet who is both intensely idiosyncratic and unlike any other contemporary poet and at the same time classical." A rebel socially, as well as artistically, Graves left his wife and four children in 1929 to live in Majorca with Laura Riding, a Russian Jewish poet. Douglas Day commented on the importance of this move in *Swifter than Reason: The Poetry and Criticism of Robert Graves:* "The influence of Laura Riding is quite possibly the most important single element in his poetic career: she persuaded him to curb his digressiveness and his rambling philosophizing and to concentrate instead on terse, ironic poems written on personal themes. She also imparted to him some of her own dry, cerebral quality, which has remained in much of his poetry. There can be little doubt that some of his best work was done during the years of his literary partnership with Laura Riding."

It has been suggested that one of Graves's debts to Riding was his long-standing fascination with the Muse of poetry. Anne Fremantle noted in *Nation* that T.S. Matthews gave Riding credit for Graves's "mystical and reverent attitude to the mother goddess," that muse to whom he referred by a variety of names, including Calliope and the White Goddess. In his *Third Book of Criticism,* Randall Jarrell noted that Muse symbolism permeates Graves's writing: "All that is finally important to Graves is condensed in the one figure of the Mother-Mistress-Muse, she who creates, nourishes, seduces, destroys; she who saves us—or, as good as saving, destroys us—as long as we love her, write poems to her, submit to her without question, use all our professional, Regimental, masculine qualities in her service. Death is swallowed up in victory, said St. Paul; for Graves Life, Death, everything that exists is swallowed up in the White Goddess."

Critics often described the White Goddess in paradoxical terms. Patrick Callahan, writing in the *Prairie Schooner,* called her a blend of the "cruelty and kindness of woman." He contended: "Cerridwen, the White Goddess, is the apotheosis of woman at her most primitive. Graves finds the women he has loved an embodiment of her. If Cerridwen is to be adored, she is also to be feared, for her passing can rival the passing of very life, and the pendulum of ecstasy and anguish which marks human love reaches its full sweep in her." Martin Seymour-Smith also noted the complex personality of the Muse, describing her in *Robert Graves* as "the Mother who bears man, the Lover who awakens him to manhood, the Old Hag who puts pennies on his dead eyes. She is a threefold process of Birth, Copulation, and Death." Brian Jones, however, found the Goddess one-dimensional. He wrote in *London Magazine:* "It is interesting that it is often impossible to tell whether the feminine pronoun [in *Poems, 1965-1968*] refers to woman or Goddess or both; not that this is necessarily an adverse criticism, but in Graves both the woman and the Goddess [are] sentimental, belittled, simplified male creation[s]. The dignity and 'otherness' of the woman is missing."

Graves explored and reconstructed the White Goddess myth in his book *The White Goddess: A Historical Grammar of Poetic Myth.* J.M. Cohen noted in his *Robert Graves:* "The mythology of The White Goddess, though its elements are drawn from a vast field of ancient story and legends, is in its assemblage Graves's own creation, and conforms to the requirements of his own poetic mind." One of Graves's prerequisites was spontaneity. Muse poetry, wrote Graves in his *Oxford Addresses on Poetry,* "is composed at the back of the mind; an unaccountable product of a trance in which the emotions of love, fear, anger, or grief are profoundly engaged, though at the same time powerfully disciplined." Graves gave an example of such inspiration, explaining that while writing *The Golden Fleece* he experienced powerful feelings of "a sudden enlightenment." According to Cohen, this insight was into a subject Graves knew "almost nothing" about. Cohen wrote that "a night and day of furious cogitation was followed by three weeks of intense work, during which the whole 70,000 words of the original were written." Monroe K. Spears deplored this method of composition in the *Sewanee Review:* "Graves's theory of poetry—if it can be dignified by the name of theory—is essentially a perfectly conventional late Romantic notion of poetry as emotional and magical; it is remarkable only in its crude simplicity and vulnerability." Still, Randall Jarrell asserted that "Graves's richest, most moving, and most consistently beautiful poems—poems that almost deserve the literal *magical*— are his mythic/archaic pieces, all those the reader thinks of as 'White Goddess' poems."

"Unsolicited enlightenment" also figured in Graves's historical method. Peter Quennell wrote in *Casanova in*

London: "The focal point of all of [Graves's] scholarly researches is the bizarre theory of Analeptic Thought, based on his belief that forgotten events may be recovered by the exercise of intuition, which affords sudden glimpses of truth 'that would not have been arrived at by inductive reasoning.' In practice . . . this sometimes means that the historian first decides what he would *like* to believe, then looks around for facts to suit his thesis." Quennell suggested a hazard of that method: "Although [Graves's] facts themselves are usually sound, they do not always support the elaborate conclusions that Graves proceeds to draw from them; two plus two regularly make five and six; and genuine erudition and prophetic imagination conspire to produce some very odd results." Spears also questioned Graves's judgment, claiming that "he has no reverence for the past and he is not interested in learning from it; instead, he re-shapes it in his own image . . . he displays much ingenuity and learning in his interpretations of events and characters, but also a certain coarseness of perception and a tendency to oversimplify."

The story of Graves's translation of *The Rubaiyyat of Omar Khayaam* served to exemplify the stir he was capable of making when he brought his own theories about history to his writing. First, critics and scholars questioned the veracity of his text. Graves had worked from an annotated version of the poem given him by Ali-Shah, a Persian poet; although Ali-Shah alleged that the manuscript had been in his family for 800 years, L.P. Elwell-Sutton, an Orientalist at Edinburgh University, decried it as a "clumsy forgery." Next came the inevitable comparisons with Edward FitzGerald's standard translation, published in 1859. FitzGerald's depiction of romanticized Victorian bliss is epitomized by the much-quoted lines, "A Book of Verse underneath the Bough / A Jug of Wine, a Loaf of Bread, and Thou." Graves's translation, on the other hand, reads: "Should our day's portion be one mancel loaf, / a haunch of mutton and a gourd of wine." A *Time* critic defended FitzGerald's translation by quoting FitzGerald himself: "'A translation must live with a transfusion of one's own worse life if he can't retain the original's better. Better a live sparrow than a stuffed eagle.'" The critic added that "Graves's more dignified *Rubaiyyat* may be an eagle to FitzGerald's sparrow. But FitzGerald's work is still in living flight, while Graves's already sits there on the shelf—stuffed." Similarly, Martin Dodsworth commented in *Listener:* "Graves does not convince here. He has produced a prosy New English Bible sort of Khayaam, whose cloudy mysticism raises more questions than it answers."

Despite his detractors, Graves maintained his characteristically independent stance (he once told his students

that "the poet's chief loyalty is to the Goddess Calliope, not to his publisher or to the booksellers on his publisher's mailing list") in defending his translation against the more commercially directed attempt he felt FitzGerald made. In Graves's opinion, the poet was writing about the ecstasy of Sufi mysticism, not—as he says FitzGerald implies—more earthly pleasures. In an extensive apologia for his translation, Graves wrote in *Observations:* "Any attempt at improving or altering Khayaam's poetic intentions would have seemed shocking to me when I was working on the *Rubaiyyat.* . . . My twin principles were: 'Stick as strictly to the script as you can' and 'Respect the tradition of English verse as first confirmed by the better Tudor poets: which is to be as explicit as possible on every occasion and never play down to ignorance.'"

Some critics have felt that such statements reveal an admirable strength of character. John Wain, for one, felt that Graves demonstrated an unswerving dedication to his ideals in his writing. He commented in the *New York Times Magazine:* "Graves's long, eventful and productive life has certainly been marked by plenty of fighting spirit, whatever name you give to it—combativeness, magnificent independence or just plain cussedness. He has faith in his own vision and his own way of doing things—legitimately, since they are arrived at by effort and sacrifice, by solitude and devotion—and when he has arrived at them, he cares nothing for majority opinion. He has never been in the least daunted by the discovery that everybody else was out of step. Whatever is the issue—the choice of a life style, a knotty point in theological controversy, a big literary reputation that should be made smaller, or a smaller one that should be made bigger—Graves has reached his own conclusions and never worried if no one agreed with him." Considering Graves's output, Wain concluded: "He is not an easy writer. He does not make concessions. He has achieved a large readership and a great fame because of the richness of what he has to offer—its human depth, its range, its compelling imaginative power—rather than by fancy packaging or deep-freeze convenience."

The publication of *The Centenary Selected Poems* and *Collected Writings on Poetry* offered additional insight into Graves's creative preoccupations. *Collected Writings on Poetry* is based on a series of lectures Graves delivered at Cambridge in 1954 and 1955 and Oxford between 1961 and 1965, as well as several addresses made during visits to the United States. "[Graves] believed you had to *live* like a poet, and so he did," wrote Lorna Sage in *Observer,* adding, "He spoke with an Outsider's edgy authority, as you can see in *Collected*

Writings on Poetry." Neil Powell noted in the *Times Literary Supplement,* "[Graves] was certainly not a reliable nor even a wholly competent critic, yet the essays and lectures are worth reading for quite other reasons. One consequence of his curiously innocent egocentricity is that his comments on other poets often reveal much more about himself than about their ostentatious subjects." While praising *Collected Writings on Poetry,* Powell questioned the omission of Graves's love poetry and humorous verse from *The Centenary Selected Poems* which, in his view, "present[s] Graves as a much duller writer than he is."

Together *Dear Robert, Dear Spike,* a volume of correspondence, and Miranda Seymour's biography *Robert Graves: Life on the Edge* expanded public and critical understanding of the poet. *Dear Robert, Dear Spike,* contains selected letters from the decade-long correspondence between Graves and Spike Mulligan, a veteran of war twenty years Graves's junior and the author of *Adolf Hitler, My Part in His Downfall.* Despite the age difference and their widely dissimilar social backgrounds, they apparently shared much in common, particularly the lasting physical and emotional scars of combat experience. "Both had compelling reasons to hate war," remarked Patrick Skene Catling in *Spectator.* "As a result, they both rejected authority and always maintained a defiant sort of artistic integrity." According to Mulligan, quoted by Catling, "The common bonding of our friendship was his mischievous, iconoclastic perorations on all stratas of stupidity and unreasonableness."

An *Observer* review praised the "great insight" provided by the Graves-Mulligan correspondence, which began in 1964. Their letters, as Catling noted, appear "in the easy style of love letters, recounting the small colorful details of their work, opinions, domestic arrangements and moods." Sage similarly commended Seymour's *Robert Graves: Life on the Edge,* described by the critic as a "balanced, convincing, rounded" portrait. Commenting on the biographer's description of Graves's near-death wounding on the Somme in 1916, Sage noted, "as Miranda Seymour says—it would have been hard [for Graves] not to feel a touch mythic, 'as if he had been borne again.'"

Mark Ford summarized Graves's "wholesale rejection of 20th-century civilization and complete submission to the capricious demands of the Goddess" with a quote from *The White Goddess:* "Since the age of 15 poetry has been my ruling passion and I have never intentionally undertaken any task or formed any relationship that seemed inconsistent with poetic principles; which has sometimes won me the reputation of an eccentric."

BIOGRAPHICAL AND CRITICAL SOURCES:

BOOKS

Carter, D.N. G., *Robert Graves: The Lasting Poetic Achievement,* Barnes & Noble (New York, NY), 1989.

Cohen, J. M., *Robert Graves,* Oliver & Boyd, 1960.

Concise Dictionary of British Literary Biography, Volume 6: *Modern Writers, 1914-1945,* Thomson Gale (Detroit, MI), 1991.

Contemporary Literary Criticism, Thomson Gale (Detroit, MI), Volume 1, 1973, Volume 2, 1974, Volume 6, 1976, Volume 11, 1979, Volume 39, 1986, Volume 44, 1987, Volume 45, 1987.

Day, Douglas, *Swifter than Reason: The Poetry and Criticism of Robert Graves,* University of North Carolina Press (Columbia, SC), 1963.

Dictionary of Literary Biography, Thomson Gale (Detroit, MI), Volume 20, *British Poets, 1914-1945,* 1983, Volume 100: *Modern British Essayists, Second Series,* 1991.

Dictionary of Literary Biography Yearbook: 1985, Thomson Gale (Detroit, MI), 1986.

Enright, D. J., *Conspirators and Poets,* Dufour, 1966.

Graves, Richard Perceval, *Robert Graves: The Assault Heroic, 1895-1926,* Viking (New York, NY), 1987.

Graves, Richard Perceval, *Robert Graves: The Years with Laura, 1926-1940,* Viking (New York, NY), 1990.

Graves, Robert, *Goodbye to All That: An Autobiography,* J. Cape (London, England), 1929.

Graves, Robert, *Oxford Addresses on Poetry,* Doubleday (New York, NY), 1962.

Graves, Robert Perceval, *Robert Graves and the White Goddess, 1940-85,* Weidenfeld and Nicolson (London, England), 1995.

Graves, William, *Wild Olives: Life in Majorca with Robert Graves,* Pimlico, 1996.

Higginson, F. H., *A Bibliography of the Works of Robert Graves,* Shoe String, 1966.

Hoffman, D. G., *Barbarous Knowledge,* Oxford University Press (New York, NY), 1967.

Jarrell, Randall, *The Third Book of Criticism,* Farrar, Straus (New York, NY), 1969.

Nemerov, Howard, *Poetry and Fiction,* Rutgers University Press, 1963.

Poetry Criticism, Volume 6, Thomson Gale, 1993.

Quennell, Peter, *Casanova in London,* Stein & Day, 1971.

Seymour, Miranda, *Robert Graves: A Life on the Edge,* Henry Holt (New York, NY), 1995.

Seymour-Smith, Martin, *Robert Graves,* Longman Group (London, England), revised edition, 1965.

Seymour-Smith, Martin, *Robert Graves: His Life and Work,* 1982, revised edition, Bloomsbury (London, England), 1995.

Swinnerton, Frank, *The Georgian Literary Scene,* Dent (London, England), 1951.

PERIODICALS

Atlantic, January, 1966.

Commentary, February, 1967.

Daily Variety, December 10, 1985.

Harper's, August, 1967.

Horizon, January, 1962.

Hudson Review, spring, 1967.

Life, June 24, 1963; October 15, 1965.

Listener, May 4, 1967; November 9, 1967; December 24, 1970.

Literary Times, April, 1965.

London Magazine, February, 1969.

London Review of Books, September 7, 1995, p. 26.

Los Angeles Times Book Review, December 28, 1980; January 23, 1983.

Nation, March 18, 1978.

National Observer, March 17, 1969.

National Review, December 31, 1985.

New Leader, October 27, 1969.

New Statesman, December 3, 1965.

Newsweek, May 20, 1968; July 28, 1969; December 16, 1985.

New York Times, December 1, 1966; October 26, 1967; September 20, 1979; December 25, 1981.

New York Times Book Review, July 20, 1969; October 12, 1969; March 11, 1973; April 29, 1979; May 30, 1982; October 17, 1982; January 18, 1987, p. 34.

New York Times Magazine, October 30, 1966.

Observations, July, 1968.

Observer (London, England), July 2, 1995, p. 15; July 16, 1995, p. 13.

Playboy, December, 1970.

Poetry, January, 1969.

Prairie Schooner, summer, 1970.

Publishers Weekly, August 11, 1975; December 20, 1985.

School Library Journal, February, 1986.

Sewanee Review, fall, 1965.

Shenandoah, spring, 1966.

Spectator, March 16, 1991, p. 40.

Time, November 3, 1967; May 31, 1968; December 16, 1985.

Times (London, England), May 27, 1982; July 26, 1985.

Times Literary Supplement, October 7, 1965; December 7, 1967; June 26, 1969; November 21, 1980; September 27, 1985; November 3, 1995, p. 6.

Variety, July 26, 1972.

Washington Post Book World, November 29, 1981.

Yale Review, autumn, 1968.

OBITUARIES:

PERIODICALS

Chicago Tribune, December 9, 1985.

Los Angeles Times, December 8, 1985.

New York Times, December 8, 1985.

Times (London, England), December 9, 1985.

Washington Post, December 8, 1985; December 9, 1985.

*   *   *

GRAVES, Robert von Ranke
See GRAVES, Robert

*   *   *

GRAVES, Valerie
See BRADLEY, Marion Zimmer

*   *   *

GRAY, Alasdair 1934-
(Alasdair James Gray)

PERSONAL: Born December 28, 1934, in Glasgow, Scotland; son of Alex Gray (a machine operator) and Amy (Fleming) Gray (a homemaker); children: Andrew. *Education:* Glasgow School of Art, diploma (design and printmaking), 1957. *Politics:* "Socialist. Supporter of Scottish Home Rule and Campaign for Nuclear Disarmament." *Religion:* "Rational pantheism."

ADDRESSES: Home—2 Marchmont Terrace, Glasgow G12 9LT, Scotland. *Agent*—Giles Gordon, 6 Ann St., Edinburgh EH 4 1PJ, Scotland.

CAREER: Part-time art teacher in Lanarkshire and Glasgow, Scotland, 1958-62; theatrical scene painter in Glasgow, 1962-63; freelance playwright and painter in Glasgow, 1963-75; People's Palace (local history museum), Glasgow, artist-recorder, 1976-77; University of Glasgow, writer-in-residence, 1977-79, professor of creative writing, 2001—; freelance painter and maker of books in Glasgow, 1979-2001.

MEMBER: Society of Authors, Glasgow Print Workshop, various organizations supporting trade unions and nuclear disarmament.

AWARDS, HONORS: Bellahouston Travelling Scholarship, 1957; Three grants from Scottish Arts Council, between 1968 and 1981; Booker Prize nomination, Book Trust (England), 1981, award from Saltire Society, 1982, and Niven Novel Award, all for *Lanark: A Life in Four Books;* award from Cheltenham Literary Festival, 1983, for *Unlikely Stories, Mostly;* award from Scottish branch of PEN, 1986; Whitbread Prize, and Guardian Fiction Prize, both 1992, both for *Poor Things.*

WRITINGS:

(And illustrator) *Lanark: A Life in Four Books* (novel), Harper (New York, NY), 1981, revised edition, Braziller (New York, NY), 1985.

(And illustrator) *Unlikely Stories, Mostly* (short stories; includes "The Star," "The Spread of Ian Nicol," and "Five Letters from an Eastern Empire"), Canongate Books (Edinburgh, Scotland), 1983, revised edition, Penguin (London, England), 1984.

1982 Janine (novel), J. Cape (London, England), 1984, revised edition, Penguin (New York, NY), 1985.

The Fall of Kelvin Walker: A Fable of the Sixties (novel; adapted from his television play of the same title; also see below), Canongate Books (Edinburgh, Scotland), 1985, Braziller (New York, NY), 1986.

(With James Kelman and Agnes Owens) *Lean Tales* (short-story anthology), J. Cape, (London, England), 1985.

Saltire Self-Portrait 4, Saltire Society Publications (Edinburgh, Scotland), 1988.

(And illustrator) *McGrotty and Ludmilla; or, The Harbinger Report: A Romance of the Eighties,* Dog and Bone Press (Glasgow, Scotland), 1989.

(And illustrator) *Old Negatives: Four Verse Sequences,* J. Cape (London, England), 1989.

Something Leather (novel), Random House (New York, NY), 1990.

Poor Things: Episodes from the Early Life of Archibald McCandless, M.D., Scottish Public Health Officer (novel), Harcourt (New York, NY), 1992.

Why Scots Should Rule Scotland, Canongate Books (Edinburgh, Scotland), 1992.

(And illustrator) *Ten Tales Tall and True: Social Realism, Sexual Comedy, Science Fiction, and Satire,* Harcourt (New York, NY), 1993.

(And illustrator) *A History Maker,* Canongate Books (Edinburgh, Scotland), 1994, Harcourt (New York, NY), 1996.

(And illustrator) *Mavis Belfrage: A Romantic Novel with Five Shorter Tales,* Bloomsbury (London, England), 1996.

The Artist in His World: Prints, 1986-1997 (poetry; prints by Ian McCulloch), Argyll (Gelndaruel, Argyll, Scotland), 1998.

(And illustrator) *The Book of Prefaces,* Bloomsbury (London, England), 2000.

Sixteen Occasional Poems, Morag McAlpine (Glasgow, Scotland), 2000.

A Short Survey of Classical Scottish Writing, Canongate Books (Edinburgh, Scotland), 2001.

The British Book of Popular Political Songs, Bloomsbury (London, England), 2002.

Ends of Our Tethers: 13 Sorry Stories, includes "Big Pockets with Buttoned Flaps, Swan burial," and "No Bluebeard," Canongate Books (Edinburg, Scotland), 2003.

STAGE PLAYS

Dialogue (one-act; first produced in Edinburgh, Scotland, at Gateway Theatre, 1971), Scottish Theatre (Kirknewton, Scotland), 1971.

The Fall of Kelvin Walker (two-act; adapted from his television play of the same title; also see below), first produced in Stirling, Scotland, at McRoberts Centre, University of Stirling, 1972.

The Loss of the Golden Silence (one-act), first produced in Edinburgh, Scotland, at Pool Theatre, 1973.

Homeward Bound (one-act), first produced in Edinburgh, Scotland, at Pool Theatre, 1973.

(With Tom Leonard and Liz Lochhead) *Tickly Mince* (two-act), first produced in Glasgow, Scotland, at Tron Theatre, 1982.

(With Liz Lochhead, Tom Leonard, and James Kelman) *The Pie of Damocles* (two-act; also see below), first produced in Glasgow, Scotland, at Tron Theatre, 1983.

McGrotty and Ludmilla, first produced in Glasgow, Scotland, at Tron Theatre, 1987.

(And illustrator) *Working Legs: A Play for People without Them* (first produced by Birds of Paradise Company, 1998), Dog and Bone Press (Glasgow, Scotland), 1997.

RADIO PLAYS

Quiet People, British Broadcasting Corporation (BBC), 1968.

The Night Off, British Broadcasting Corporation (BBC), 1969.

Thomas Muir of Huntershill, British Broadcasting Corporation (BBC), 1970.

The Loss of the Golden Silence, British Broadcasting Corporation (BBC), 1974.

McGrotty and Ludmilla, British Broadcasting Corporation (BBC), 1976.

The Vital Witness (documentary), British Broadcasting Corporation (BBC), 1979.

Near the Driver, translation into German by Berndt Rullkotter broadcast by Westdeutsche Rundfunk, 1983, original text broadcast by British Broadcasting Corporation (BBC), 1988.

TELEVISION PLAYS

The Fall of Kelvin Walker, British Broadcasting Corporation (BBC), 1968.

Dialogue, British Broadcasting Corporation (BBC), 1972.

Triangles, Granada, 1972.

The Man Who Knew about Electricity, British Broadcasting Corporation (BBC), 1973.

Honesty (educational documentary), British Broadcasting Corporation (BBC), 1974.

Today and Yesterday (series of three twenty-minute educational documentaries), British Broadcasting Corporation (BBC), 1975.

Beloved, Granada, 1976.

The Gadfly, Granada, 1977.

The Story of a Recluse, British Broadcasting Corporation (BBC), 1987.

OTHER

(Designer and illustrator) Wilma Paterson, *Songs of Scotland,* Mainstream, 1995.

Author and reader of *Some Unlikely Stories* (audiocassette), Canongate Audio, 1994, and *Scenes from Lanark, Volume 1* (audiocassette), Canongate Audio, 1995.

WORK IN PROGRESS: A Life in Pictures: Paintings, Murals, and Graphic Work, for Canongate Books.

SIDELIGHTS: After more than twenty years as a painter, and a scriptwriter for radio and television, Alasdair Gray rose to literary prominence with the publication of several of his books in the 1980s. His works have been noted for their mixture of realistic social commentary and vivid fantasy augmented by the author's own evocative illustrations. Jonathan Baumbach wrote in the *New York Times Book Review* that Gray's work "has a verbal energy, an intensity of vision, that has been mostly missing from the English novel since D.H. Lawrence." David Lodge of the *New Republic* said that Gray "is that rather rare bird among contemporary British writers—a genuine experimentalist, transgressing the rules of formal English prose . . . boldly and imaginatively."

In his writing, Gray often draws upon his Scottish background, and he is regarded as a major force in the literature of his homeland. Author Anthony Burgess, for instance, said in the London *Observer* that he considered Gray the best Scottish novelist since Sir Walter Scott became popular in the early nineteenth century. Unlike Scott, who made his country a setting for historical romance, Gray focuses on contemporary Scotland where the industrial economy is deteriorating and many citizens fear that their social and economic destiny has been surrendered to England. Critics praised Gray for putting such themes as Scotland's decline and powerlessness into a larger context that any reader could appreciate. "Using Glasgow as his undeniable starting point," Douglas Gifford wrote in *Studies in Scottish Literature,* "Gray . . . transforms local and hitherto restricting images, which limited [other] novelists of real ability. . . . into symbols of universal prophetic relevance." As noted above, Gray became prominent as a writer only after several years of working as an artist and illustrator. Gray traces his own literary and artistic development to the early years of his life, once explaining that "as soon as I could draw and tell stories, which was around the age of four or five, I spent a lot of time doing these or planning to do them. My parents were friendly to my childish efforts, as were most of my teachers, though they also told me I was unlikely to make a living by either of these jobs. . . . I was delighted to go to art school, because I was a maturer draftsman and painter than writer. My writings while at art school were attempts to prepare something I knew would take long to finish: though I didn't know how long."

Gray went on to say that although his first novel took years to complete, the story line of what would become his now acclaimed first novel, *Lanark: A Life in Four Books,* had essentially been worked out in his mind by the time he was eighteen. A long and complex work that some reviewers considered partly autobiographical, *Lanark* opens in Unthank, an ugly, declining city explained in reviews as a comment on Glasgow and other Western industrial centers. As in George Orwell's *Nineteen Eighty-four*, citizens of Unthank are ruled by a domineering and intrusive bureaucracy. Lanark is a lonely young man unable to remember his past. Along with many of his fellow-citizens, he is plagued with "dragonhide," an insidious, scaly skin infection seen as symbolic of his emotional isolation. Cured of his affliction by doctors at a scientific institute below the surface of the Earth, Lanark realizes to his disgust that the staff is as arrogant and manipulative as the ruling elite on the surface. Before escaping from this underworld, Lanark has a vision in which he sees the life story of a young man who mysteriously resembles him—Duncan Thaw, an aspiring artist who lives in twentieth-century Glasgow.

Thaw's story, which comprises nearly half the book, is virtually a novel within a novel. It echoes the story of Lanark while displaying a markedly different literary technique. As William Boyd explained in the *Times Literary Supplement*, "The narration of Thaw's life turns out to be a brilliant and moving evocation of a talented and imaginative child growing up in working-class Glasgow. The style is limpid and classically elegant, the detail solidly documentary and in marked contrast to the fantastical and surrealistic accoutrements of the first 100 pages." Like Gray, Thaw attends art school in Glasgow, and, as with Lanark, Thaw's loneliness and isolation are expressed outwardly in a skin disease, eczema. With increasing desperation, Thaw seeks fulfillment in love and art, and his disappointment culminates in a violent outburst with tragic consequences. Boyd considered Thaw's story "a minor classic of the literature of adolescence," and Gifford likened it to James Joyce's novel *A Portrait of the Artist As a Young Man.* The last part of Gray's book focuses once more on Lanark, depicting his futile struggle to improve the world around him. Readers have often remarked on the various diseases the characters in *Lanark*'s Unthank suffer from: dragonhide, mouths, twittering rigor, softs. When asked if these diseases had allegorical significance, Gray once commented: "Probably, but I came to that conclusion after, not before, I imagined and described them. And it would limit the reader's enjoyment and understanding of my stories to fix on one 'allegorical significance' and say 'This is it.'" While some critics felt *Lanark* to be hampered by its size and intricacy, it rapidly achieved critical recognition in Britain, and Burgess featured it in his book *Ninety-nine Novels: The Best in English since 1939—A Personal Choice,* declaring, "It was time Scot-

land produced a shattering work of fiction in the modern idiom. This is it."

Although *Lanark* rapidly achieved critical recognition in Britain, it was Gray's second novel, *1982 Janine,* that was the first to be widely known in the United States. When asked why his work had finally attained critical notice in the United States, Gray once commented: "*Lanark* was the first novel I had published in the U.S.A., by Harper & Row in 1981. It was speedily remaindered, because Harper & Row classified it as science fiction, only sent it to sci-fi magazines for review, and the sci-fi reviewers were not amused. . . . . I suppose my books have been published in the United States because they sold well in Britain, and were praised by authors of *A Clockwork Orange* [Anthony Burgess] and *The History Man* [Malcolm Bradbury]."

1982 Janine records the thoughts of Jock McLeish, a disappointed, middle-aged Scottish businessman, during a long night of heavy drinking. In his mind, Jock plays and replays fantasies in which he sexually tortures helpless women, and he gives names and identities to his victims, including Janine of the title. Burgess expressed the opinion of several reviewers when he wrote in the *Observer* that such material was offensive and unneeded. But admirers of the novel, such as Richard Eder of the *Los Angeles Times,* felt that Jock's sexual fantasies were a valid metaphor for the character's own sense of helplessness. Jock, who rose to a managerial post from a working-class background, now hates himself because he is financially dependent on the ruling classes he once hoped to change. Eder observed that Jock's powerlessness is in its turn a metaphor for the subjugation of Scotland. Jock expounds on the sorry state of his homeland in the course of his drunken railings. Scotland's economy, he charges, has been starved in order to strengthen the country's political master, England; what is more, if war with the Soviet Union breaks out, Jock expects the English to use Scotland as a nuclear battlefield. As the novel ends, Jock resolves to quit his job and change his life for the better. Eder commended Gray for conveying a portrait of helplessness and the search for self-realization "in a flamboyantly comic narrator whose verbal blue streak is given depth by a winning impulse to self-discovery, and some alarming insight."

Gray's short-story collection, *Unlikely Stories, Mostly,* is "if anything more idiosyncratic" than *1982 Janine,* according to Jonathan Baumbach of the *New York Times Book Review*. Many reviewers praised the imaginativeness of the stories while acknowledging that the collection, which includes work dating back to Gray's teenage years, is uneven in quality. Gary Marmorstein observed in the *Los Angeles Times Book Review,* some of the stories are "slight but fun," including "The Star," in which a boy catches a star and swallows it, and "The Spread of Ian Nicol," in which a man slowly splits in two like a microbe reproducing itself. By contrast, "Five Letters from an Eastern Empire" is one of several more complex tales that received special praise. Set in the capital of a powerful empire, the story focuses on a talented poet. Gradually readers learn the source of the poet's artistic inspiration: the emperor murdered the boy's parents by razing the city in which they lived, then ordered him to write about the destruction. "The tone of the story remains under perfect control as it darkens and deepens," according to Adam Mar-Jones in the *Times Literary Supplement,* "until an apparently reckless comedy has become a cruel parable about power and meaning." While responding to a question about *Lanark* and the possible allegorical significance of its characters, Gray related an anecdote about the story "Five Letters from an Eastern Empire": "I wrote [the story] when [I was] writer-in-residence at Glasgow University. When I finished, it occurred to me that the Eastern Empire was an allegory of modern Britain viewed from Glasgow University by a writer-in-residence. A year ago I met someone just returned from Tokyo, who said he had heard a Chinese and a Japanese academic having an argument about my Eastern Empire story. The Chinese was quite sure the empire was meant to be China, the Japanese that it was Japan. My only knowledge of these lands is from a few color prints, Arthur Waley's translation of the novel *Monkey* [by Wu Ch'eng-en] and some translated poems."

Gray's third novel, *The Fall of Kelvin Walker: A Fable of the Sixties,* was inspired by personal experience. Still struggling to establish his career several years after his graduation from art school, Gray was tapped as the subject of a documentary by a successful friend at the British Broadcasting Corporation (BBC). Gray, who had been living on welfare, suddenly found himself treated to airline flights and limousine rides at the BBC's expense. In *The Fall of Kelvin Walker* the title character, a young Scotsman with a burning desire for power, has a similar chance to use the communications media to fulfill his wildest fantasies. Though Kelvin arrives in London with little besides self-confidence and a fast-talking manner, his persistence and good luck soon win him a national following as an interviewer on a television show. But in his pride and ambition, Walker forgets that he exercises such influence only at the whims of his corporate bosses, and when he displeases them, his fall from grace is as abrupt as his rise.

The Fall of Kelvin Walker, which Gray adapted from his 1968 teleplay of the same title ("I sent it to a [BBC] director I know. He gave it to a producer who liked it"), is shorter and less surrealistic than his previous novels. The *Observer*'s Hermione Lee, though she stressed that Gray "is always worth attending to," felt that this novel "doesn't allow him the big scope he thrives on." By contrast, Larry McCaffery of the *New York Times Book Review* praised *The Fall of Kelvin Walker* for its "economy of means and exquisite control of detail." Gray "is now fully in command of his virtuoso abilities as a stylist and storyteller," McCaffery said, asserting that Gray's first four books—"each of which impresses in very different ways—indicate that he is emerging as the most vibrant and original new voice in English fiction."

As reviewers became familiar with Gray's work, they noticed several recurring features: illustrations by the author, typographical eccentricities, and an emphasis on the city of Glasgow. When asked about the illustrations, Gray explained a little about the process of creating this kind of manuscript: "The illustrations and cover designs of my books are not essential to them, being thought of after the text is complete. I add them because they make the book more enjoyable. The queer typography, in the three stories which use it, was devised in the act of writing, not added after, like sugar to porridge."

As Gray continued to write, critical reception of his work varied widely. Many reviewers acknowledged his genius in such works as *Lanark,* while books such as *Something Leather* and *McGrotty and Ludmilla; or, The Harbinger Report: A Romance of the Eighties* were criticized for lacking the intensity of his earlier work. Gray himself was remarkably candid about the quality and intent of some of these efforts. For example, he described *McGrotty and Ludmilla; or, The Harbinger Report* as an Aladdin story set in modern Whitehall, "with the hero a junior civil servant, wicked uncle Abanizir a senior one, and the magic lamp a secret government paper which gave whoever held it unlimited powers of blackmail." And works such as *Something Leather,* said Gerald Mangan in the *Times Literary Supplement,* placed Gray in "an unfortunate tradition in Scottish fiction, whereby novelists have tended to exhaust their inspiration in the effort of a single major achievement." That *Lanark* was a major achievement Mangan had no doubt. "*Lanark* is now so monumental a Scottish landmark," he wrote, "that few readers would have reproached him if a decade of silence had followed it." Instead, Gray brought out "a good deal of inferior material that had evidently subsidized or distracted him during the composition of his epic." A *New York Times*

Book Review article by John Kenny Crane further explained the circumstances under which Gray composed *Something Leather.* According to Crane, a publisher had been pushing Gray for years to produce a new novel. Getting nowhere and needing money, Gray shuffled around in his rejected short-story manuscripts and came up with one about a conventional working woman in Glasgow who decides to shave off her hair and begin dressing in leather clothing. The publisher sent Gray a substantial advance, and the tale of the bald, leather-clad Glaswegian woman became his first chapter, "One for the Album." Other unpublished stories, unstaged plays, and early radio and TV scripts were also pressed into service and ultimately published as *Something Leather.* Crane commented in his review: "Gray, who has published some very creditable works of fiction, shamelessly admits to absolutely everything in his epilogue." Yet, the critic added, "Taken on their own, some of the interior chapters have artistry and merit. I particularly liked the reflections on war in one titled 'In the Boiler Room' and the comical friction caused by the divergent life styles of boarders in 'Quiet People.' As short stories, some are quite fine. I would recommend the reader take them as such, even though Mr. Gray insists they are part of a novel." And despite his own criticism of *Something Leather,* Mangan said that in the five stories that comprise the work, Gray's "prose is generally notable for its refusal of second-hand definitions; and it is not surprising to find, among other consolations, a divertingly cynical diatribe on Glasgow's current status as culture-capital."

With the publication of *Poor Things: Episodes from the Early Life of Archibald McCandless, M.D., Scottish Public Health Officer,* purportedly edited by Gray, the author returns to form, suggested Philip Hensher in the *Spectator,* "after a rather sticky patch." The work drew comparisons to such authors as Daniel Defoe and Laurence Sterne, partly because of its eccentric humor and setting and partly because of Gray's skillful use of the traditions of Victorian novels, which, according to Barbara Hardy in the *Times Literary Supplement,* "embodied their liberal notions of providence and progress in realistic narratives which often surge into optimistic or melioristic visions on the last page."

Set in Glasgow during the 1880s, the novel is narrated by Archie McCandless, a young medical student, who befriends the eccentric Godwin Baxter, another medical student. Baxter has been experimenting on the body of a beautiful and pregnant young woman who committed suicide to escape her abusive husband, and has created "Bella" by transplanting the brain of the fetus into its mother's skull. Bella is sexually mature and wholly amoral, and McCandless wants to marry her. She, however, runs off with a wicked playboy whom she soon drives to insanity and death. A clever final twist produces a book that Hensher described as "a great deal more than entertaining only on finishing it. Then your strongest urge is to start reading it again."

Gray uses his visual and writing talents in *Ten Tall Tales and True: Social Realism, Sexual Comedy, Science Fiction, and Satire.* He illustrates the cover with ten animal tails, then showing each animal in its entirety within the covers. A critic for the *Review of Contemporary Fiction* asked: "Is Gray suggesting perhaps the fragmented and nonhuman character of our life when we do not exist in a state of wholeness?" Set in present-day Scotland, the stories explore human relationships with humor and feeling. "[Gray's] stories most often dramatize those symbioses of oppression in which people find just the right partner, family or group to dominate or be dominated by," wrote Ron Loewinsohn in the *New York Times Book Review.* Observed Christopher Bray in the *Spectator,* "Stories and characters like these ought to make you downcast, and they would, were it not for the pithy intensity with which Gray sketches things in."

Gray expresses his concern for modern society in *A History Maker,* a political allegory set in a twenty-third-century Scotland that seems reminiscent of more ancient times. Society has become matriarchal, and men have little to do but kill each other; their war games are televised as entertainment. "Gray's touch is light and wry, and there is enough strangeness in his future to whet conventional SF appetites. But there is no mistaking the relevance of his allegory to the situation of nation-states in today's uneasy post-Cold War peace," maintained a *Village Voice Literary Supplement* reviewer. A *Publishers Weekly* reviewer stated that *A History Maker* succeeds on "all of its many levels" and is a fine work of social satire: "The wit is sharp, the social commentary on target and, most important, the quirky, arch-voiced storytelling is unfailingly entertaining."

The Book of Prefaces is an unusual volume, which took Gray years to compile and edit. It is, as the title suggests, a collection of what he considers the greatest prefaces in works of literature written in English. It begins with the seventh-century author Caedmon and progresses through the twentieth century. Michael Kerrigan in the *Times Literary Supplement* had mixed feelings about *The Book of Prefaces;* while crediting Gray with choosing "prefaces that motivate the reader to seek out in their entirety the works they introduce, and to acknowledge the alternative futures that past achievements have made," he criticized the book for adhering too closely to a "rigid and restrictive" selection of works, and called it "striking in its portentousness." A very different point of view was expressed by Peter Dollard in *Library Journal* who found *The Book of Prefaces* to be "a delightfully original, ironic, and humorous compilation," a genuine "work of literature" in its own right, thanks to the "fascinating and often idiosyncratic commentary" by Gray.

When Sam Phipps reviewed *The Ends of our Tethers: 13 Sorry Stories,* for the *Spectator,* he remarked that Gray's first fiction in seven years "confirms that at the age of sixty-eight he is in rude, wry and irascible health, compellingly inventive and perceptive—and never afraid to send himself up. Indeed an ambivalent mood of defiance and self-ridicule runs through the collection, beginning with the jacket, which as always Gray has designed himself: a naked, athletic, bearded man bearing a close resemblance to the author." The entire collection is dedicated to Agnes Owens, an excellent although little-known Scottish author, and, in it, Gray's characters develop largely as what Irvine Welsh, reviewing the book for the *Guardian,* called "disappointed idealists, saddened by setbacks both political and personal, the latter usually of a romantic nature, and their progress charts more than the customary replacement of youthful idealism with the cynicism of old age." Welsh commented that Gray's "new collection of short stories contains almost everything we have come to associate with its author. The pages glow with keen and incisive wit, are stuffed with quirky and downright weird occurrences, while the philosophical ruminations make us pause for thought, and the sad, flawed, often cowardly, but ultimately humane and decent protagonists are back with a vengeance. Once again, the book is beautifully illustrated by the author's own hand, and in the appendix the critics are playfully baited in advance."

BIOGRAPHICAL AND CRITICAL SOURCES:

BOOKS

Bernstein, Stephen, *Alasdair Gray,* Associated University Presses (Cranbury, NJ), 1999.

Burgess, Anthony, *Ninety-nine Novels: The Best in English since 1939—A Personal Choice,* Allison & Busby (London, England), 1984.

Contemporary Literary Criticism, Volume 41, Thomson Gale (Detroit, MI), 1987.

Crawford, R., and T. Naim, editors, *The Arts of Alasdair Gray,* Edinburgh University Press (Edinburgh, Scotland), 1991.

Dictionary of Literary Biography, Volume 194: *British Novelists since 1960, Second Series,* Thomson Gale (Detroit, MI), 1998.

Moore, Phil, editor, *Alasdair Gray: Critical Appreciations and Bibliography,* British Library (London, England), 2001.

PERIODICALS

Booklist, March 1, 1994, Gilbert Taylor, review of *Ten Tales Tall and True: Social Realism, Sexual Comedy, Science Fiction, and Satire,* p. 1180; October 1, 2000, Mary Ellen Quinn, review of *The Book of Prefaces,* p. 374.

Books, September, 1993, p. 9.

Christian Science Monitor, October 5, 1984.

Daily Telegraph, August 30, 1992, Kate Chisholm, review of *Poor Things: Episodes from the Early Life of Archibald McCandless, M.D., Scottish Public Health Officer;* December 17, 1994, David Profumo, review of *A History Maker;* November 11, 1995, Candida Clark and Jason Thompson, review of *A History Maker;* January 18, 1997, Miranda France, interview with Alasdair Gray.

Guardian, September 2, 1992, Francis Spufford, interview with Alasdair Gray; June 18, 1998, Jonathan Jones, interview with Alasdair Gray; October 11, 2003, Irvine Welsh, review of *The Ends of our Tethers: 13 Sorry Stories,* p. 26.

Kirkus Reviews, February 1, 1994, review of *Ten Tales Tall and True,* p. 87; February 15, 1996, review of *A History Maker,* p. 247.

Library Journal, May 1, 1991, Francis Poole, review of *Library Journal,* p. 108; August, 2000, Peter Dollard, review of *The Book of Prefaces,* p. 102.

Los Angeles Times, November 21, 1984, Richard Eder, review of *1982 Janine.*

Los Angeles Times Book Review, December 9, 1984, Gary Marmorstein, review of *Unlikely Stories, Mostly.*

New Republic, November 12, 1984.

New Statesman, November 25, 1994, p. 48.

New Statesman & Society, September 11, 1992, Christopher Harvie, review of *Poor Things,* p. 38; November 25, 1994, Boyd Tonkin, review of *A History Maker,* p. 48.

Newsweek, March 22, 1993, Malcolm Jones, Jr., review of *Poor Things,* p. 70.

New York, March 8, 1993, Rhoda Koenig, review of *Poor Things,* p. 84.

New Yorker, April 12, 1993, review of *Poor Things,* p. 121.

New York Review of Books, April 25, 1991.

New York Times Book Review, October 28, 1984, Jonathan Baumbach, review of *Unlikely Stories, Mostly,* p. 9; May 5, 1985; December 21, 1986, Larry McCaffery, review of *The Fall of Kelvin Walker: A Fable of the Sixties,* p. 7; August 4, 1991, John Kenny Crane, review of *Something Leather,* p. 15; March 28, 1993, review of *Poor Things,* p. 8; March 6, 1994, Ron Loewinsohn, review of *Ten Tales Tall and True,* p. 11; August 18, 1996, Nicholas Birns, review of *A History Maker,* p. 18.

Observer (London, England), April 15, 1984; March 31, 1985; September 27, 1994, p. 21; December 10, 1995, p. 15.

Publishers Weekly, April 19, 1991, Sybil Steinberg, review of *Something Leather,* p. 58; January 25, 1993, review of *Poor Things,* p. 78; January 31, 1994, review of *Ten Tales Tall and True,* p. 76; March 4, 1996, review of *A History Maker,* p. 61.

Review of Contemporary Fiction, fall, 1994, Lynne Diamond-Nigh, review of *Poor Things* and *Ten Tales Tall and True,* p. 204.

Spectator, February 28, 1981; September 5, 1992; October 30, 1993, p. 35; October 18, 2003, Sam Phipps, review of *The Ends of Our Tethers,* p. 61.

Stage, November 30, 1972.

Studies in Scottish Literature, Volume 18, 1983, article by Douglas Gifford.

Sunday Times (London, Engalnd), December 11, 1994, Andro Linklater, review of *A History Maker.*

Times (London, England), April 1, 1986.

Times Literary Supplement, February 27, 1981; March 18, 1983; April 13, 1984; March 29, 1985; May 10, 1985; July 6-12, 1990, Gerald Mangan, "Lucrative Lines," p. 731; April 3, 1992; August 28, 1992; December 9, 1994, p. 22; August 11, 2000, Michael Kerrigan, review of *A Book of Prefaces,* p. 10.

Village Voice Literary Supplement, December, 1984; April, 1996, p. 8.

Washington Post Book World, December 16, 1984; August 31, 1986; June 16, 1991.

Whole Earth Review, December 22, 1995, James Donnely, review of *Ten Tales Tall and True.*

*   *   *

GRAY, Alasdair James
   See GRAY, Alasdair

GRAY, Francine du Plessix 1930-

PERSONAL: Born September 25, 1930, in Warsaw, Poland (some sources say France); immigrated to U.S., 1941; naturalized U.S. citizen, 1952; daughter of Bertrand Jochaud (a diplomat and pilot for the Resistance) and Tatiana (Iacovleff) du Plessix; married Cleve Gray (a painter), April 23, 1957; children: Thaddeus Ives, Luke Alexander. *Education:* Attended Bryn Mawr College, 1948-50, and Black Mountain College, summers, 1951-52; Barnard College, B.A., 1952. *Politics:* Democrat. *Religion:* Roman Catholic. *Hobbies and other interests:* Growing vegetables, hiking, cooking Provencal food.

ADDRESSES: Home—102 Melius Road, Cornwall Bridge, CT 06754. *Agent*—Georges Borchardt, Inc., 136 East 57th St., New York, NY 10022.

CAREER: United Press International, New York City, reporter at night desk, 1952-54; *Realites* (magazine), Paris, France, editorial assistant for French edition, 1954-55; freelance writer, 1955—; *Art in America,* New York City, book editor, 1964-66; *New Yorker,* New York City, staff writer, 1968—. Distinguished visiting professor at City College of the City University of New York, spring, 1975; visiting lecturer at Saybrook College, Yale University, 1981; adjunct professor, School of Fine Arts, Columbia University, 1983—; Ferris Professor, Princeton University, 1986; Annenberg fellow, Brown University, 1997.

MEMBER: International PEN, Authors Guild, American Academy of Arts and Letters, Institute of Humanities at New York University.

AWARDS, HONORS: Putnam Creative Writing Award from Barnard College, 1952; National Catholic Book Award from Catholic Press Association, 1971, for *Divine Disobedience: Profiles in Catholic Radicalism;* Front Page Award from Newswomen's Club of New York, 1972, for *Hawaii: The Sugar-Coated Fortress;* LL.D. from City University of New York, 1981, Oberlin College, 1985, University of Santa Clara, 1985, St. Mary's College, and University of Hartford; Guggenheim fellow, 1991-92; National Book Critics Circle Award for autobiography, 2006, for *Them: A Memoir of Parents.*

WRITINGS:

Divine Disobedience: Profiles in Catholic Radicalism, Knopf (New York, NY), 1970.

Hawaii: The Sugar-Coated Fortress, Random House (New York City), 1972.

Lovers and Tyrants (novel), Simon & Schuster (New York, NY), 1976.

World without End (novel), Simon & Schuster, 1981.

October Blood (novel), Simon & Schuster, 1985.

Adam and Eve and the City: Selected Nonfiction, Simon & Schuster, 1987.

Soviet Women: Walking the Tightrope, Doubleday (New York, NY), 1990.

Rage & Fire: A Life of Louise Colet—Pioneer Feminist, Literary Star, Flaubert's Muse, Simon & Schuster, 1994.

At Home with the Marquis de Sade: A Life, Simon & Schuster, 1998.

Simone Weil, Viking, 2001.

Them: A Memoir of Parents, Penguin (New York, NY), 2005.

Contributor of articles, stories, and reviews to periodicals, including *New Yorker, New York Review of Books, New York Times Book Review,* and *New Republic.*

WORK IN PROGRESS: A novel.

SIDELIGHTS: In 1976 *New Yorker* columnist Francine du Plessix Gray published *Lovers and Tyrants,* a book Caryl Rivers describes in *Ms.* as being "as rich in its texture as the lace tablecloths women of my grandmother's generation used to crochet." The novel, a startling and often touchingly autobiographical *bildungsroman,* gained the attention of many critics. "Every woman's first novel about her own break-through into adulthood is significant—liberation of any kind is significant—but Francine du Plessix Gray has created, in hers, something memorable," comments Kathleen Cushman in the *National Observer.* "To the cathartic throes of autobiography she has added a good dose each of humor, irony, and skill; *Lovers and Tyrants* transcends its limited possibilities as a book about *Woman Oppressed* and crosses into the realm of art."

The eight parts of this novel of "ascent and liberation," as Joan Peters calls it in the *Nation,* describe various periods in the life of Stephanie, the heroine. It begins with her childhood in Paris as the daughter of a Russian mother and an aristocratic French father who wanted her to be a boy. She is raised by a hypochondriac governess and her childhood, she writes in the opening lines of the book, was "muted, opaque, and drab, the color of gruel and of woolen gaiters, its noises muted and monotonous as a sleeper's pulse. . . . My tempera-ture was taken twice a day, my head was perpetually wrapped in some woolen muffler or gauze veiling. I was scrubbed, spruced, buffed, combed, polished, year round, like a first communicant." After her father's death in the Resistance, Stephanie and her mother move to New York where Stephanie attends a fancy boarding school. Later, a young adult, she returns to France to visit her relatives and has an affair with a French prince who describes himself as "style incarnate." Nearing thirty, she marries an architect, bears two sons, and continues her career as a journalist. She feels confined and dissatisfied in her marriage and leaves to tour the Southwest, writing about bizarre religious cults and taking up with a twenty-five-year-old homosexual who longs to be both a bisexual and a photographer and who continuously begs Stephanie to feed him. The theme of the novel, as Stephanie points out, is the tyranny of love: "Every woman's life is a series of exorcisms from the spells of different oppressors: nurses, lovers, husbands, gurus, parents, children, myths of the good life. The most tyrannical despots can be the ones who love us the most."

That theme, Gray acknowledges, came from experiences in her own life. In an essay for the *New York Times Book Review,* Gray writes that her late start in writing fiction was partially due to fear of disapproval from her father—even though he had died when she was eleven. *Lovers and Tyrants* grew out of her frustration as a young wife and mother. "I was married and had two children," Gray stated in a *New York Times Book Review* "Making of an Author" column, "and since I live deep in the country and in relative solitude, encompassed by domestic duties, the journal [that I kept] became increasingly voluminous, angry, introspective. The nomad, denied flight and forced to turn inward, was beginning to explode. One day when I was 33, after I'd cooked and smiled for a bevy of weekend guests whom I never wished to see again, I felt an immense void, a great powerlessness, the deepest loneliness I'd ever known. I wept for some hours, took out a notebook, started rewriting one of the three stories that had won me my Barnard prize. It was the one about my governess. . . . It was to become, 12 years and two books of nonfiction later, the first chapter for *Lovers and Tyrants.* The process of finishing that book was as complex and lengthy as it was painful."

"There is something very French—Cartesian—in the orderly, rigid pattern that Francine's novel imposes on the random richness of Stephanie's life," remarks Audrey Foote in *Washington Post Book World.* "It is convenient, too; Gray herself has compared it to stringing beads. Once the themes are established, Stephanie-

Francine is absolved of all problems of plot construction, free to proceed methodically yet meaningfully through the heroine's life, devoting every stage, every chapter to the unmasking of another 'jailer.' *Lovers and Tyrants* is an apt and total title; the book is a litany of oppressors, a rosary of named identities." It is that process of naming her oppressors that is central to Stephanie's story, for, to her, that is the way to liberation. "We must name the identities of each jailer before we can crawl on toward the next stage of freedom," Stephanie writes in her journal. "To herself, and to me," says Peters, "Stephanie is simply a person trying to acknowledge and accommodate the forces that have acted on her and which remain a part of her."

The process of naming her oppressors and liberating herself from them (and from the strangling memories of past "jailers") forms the crux of *Lovers and Tyrants*. But it is not only a personal liberation that Stephanie seeks. She views her situation as part of the historical oppression of women. When she leaves her husband and takes to the road, she says that she rebels "for all women, because we are killing each other in our doll's houses." Her ultimate desire, she tells the reader, is "to be free, to be a boy, to be God." Comments Rivers in *Ms.*: "[Stephanie] sees dropping out as the prelude to rebirth. She will be Kerouac, Dean; she will infringe on male territory. . . . *Lovers and Tyrants* may be a classic in a new genre of literature—the woman as wanderer, seeker of truth. . . . To take this journey with her is to confront not only the questions of love and freedom, but those of death and immortality and existence as well." Sara Sanborn considers the novel to be a feminist fable. "The theme of this novel," Sanborn writes in *Saturday Review*, "[is] the perpetual seduction of women by those who will offer tenderness and authority, the feminine materials of feminine transcendence."

The first three-fourths of the novel—the first-person sections describing her childhood, her return to France, and her marriage—is widely praised for its wit, fine writing, and evocative detail. "The author has no trouble persuading the reader that there was once a small girl in Paris named Stephanie," says *Time*'s Timothy Foote, as he notes the similarities between Stephanie's life and that of her creator's (the French and Russian parentage, the immigration to New York, the private schools, the fling in Paris, the career as a journalist, an artistic husband, two sons, even, notes Foote, the same high cheekbones and large eyes). "Stephanie's remembrance of things past flashes with literary style and wit. Remarkable siblings, and sexual suitors are summoned up, often in hilarious detail, though they are mostly kept fro-

zen at the edge of caricature by Stephanie's satiric perceptions." These early sections of the novel, writes Julian Moynahan in the *New York Times Book Review*, "are crammed with unforgettably drawn characters, rich emotion and complex social portraiture. In counterpoint they bring out contrasted aspects of French life that are both immemorial and contemporary, and that perhaps only a cultural 'amphibian' like Mrs. du Plessix Gray would clearly see." Joan Peters in the *Nation* deems "the depiction of Stephanie's relationship with Paul . . . as complex a portrait of love and marriage as I have seen in recent novels."

While critical opinion of the beginning sections of *Lovers and Tyrants* is overwhelmingly favorable, reviews of the last chapters tend to be negative. Michael Wood, for example, in his *New York Review of Books* article, calls the final chapters of *Lovers and Tyrants* "truly lamentable," citing sloppy writing and a final section that "has expanded too far into fantasy" as his reasons for such harsh criticism. "There is a great deal that goes on in the eighth, last, longest, and presumably climactic chapter of *Lovers and Tyrants*," Christopher Lehmann-Haupt comments in the *New York Times*. "There is abundant activity. . . . There is sex. . . . But nowhere in that concluding chapter is it possible to find anything to rouse the reader from his intensifying somnolence. Nowhere is there an interesting unanswered question about the plot or the heroine's development. Nowhere is there activity or thought that one hasn't long since been able to predict. Nowhere is there articulation of Stephanie's problem that we haven't heard uttered before. ('God, I hate puritanism, wasp puritanism, all kinds. Do you realize it's puritanism got us into Vietnam?') Nowhere is there surprise. And that is why *Lovers and Tyrants*, for all the wit and thrust of its prose, is finally so exasperating. The drone of its intelligence ultimately bores."

Village Voice book editor Eliot Fremont-Smith also finds *Lovers and Tyrants* intelligent but at the same time lacking because of that intelligence. "I think something more basic is wrong," he remarks, referring to the abrupt change in the book's tone in the last sections, "and it has to do with intelligence and class. And tone. And tonyness. *Lovers and Tyrants* is nothing if not wonderfully intelligent. For much of the novel, the intelligence is presumed and shared; the reader is in really interesting company, and feels there by right of respectful invitation, and is so honored. But toward the end, the intelligence—not so much of Stephanie or her witty companion, but of the *book*—turns into something else, a sort of shrill IQ-mongering. Intellectual references from the very best places are tossed around like Frisbees; it becomes a contest, and a rather exclusion-ary one, with the reader on the sidelines. This subverts, first, credibility. (Such *constant* smartness, such unflagging articulation of sensibility, such memories! Don't they ever say Stekel when they mean Ferenczi? Don't they ever get tired?) It subverts, second, a sense of caring. A defensive reaction but that's what happens when one feels snubbed, or made the fool. In the end, *Lovers and Tyrants* seems more crass than Class; there is an unpleasant aftertaste of having been unexpectedly and for no deserving reason, insulted. This is inelegant."

Credibility is also seen as a problem by other reviewers of *Lovers and Tyrants.* A major criticism of the novel is that, in the end, the story is not believable. "There is so much in this book to admire that I wish I could believe Stephanie's story. I don't," says Sara Sanborn in *Saturday Review.* "Stephanie seems twice-born, her sensibility as narrator formed more by other writers, from Henry James to Kate Millet, than by the events recounted, which also have their haunting familiarity. I don't believe for one minute that Stephanie really has two children: in twenty years the chief effect they have on her is to supply her with wise-child sayings. Finally, I don't believe in Stephanie's unvarying superiority. Even in her bad moments, she is more thoughtful, sensitive, and self-perceptive, more humorous, open, and finally free than anyone she encounters. The other characters seem to have their existence only to further her self-exploration." *Newsweek* reviewer Peter S. Prescott also agrees: "For three-quarters of its route, *Lovers and Tyrants* is a remarkably convincing, even exhilarating performance. [However,] toward the end, in a long section in the third person, I sensed the author striking poses, lecturing us a bit to emphasize points already amply developed, introducing two characters—a radical Jesuit and a homosexual youth—who are not as engaging as I suspect the author means them to be."

Time's Timothy Foote questions Stephanie's credibility as a character and narrator because, he says, "Stephanie's cries rise to heaven like those of De Sade's Justine, a girl one recollects, with far more justification for complaint." At the point Stephanie leaves her husband (who, Foote mentions, is a "fine husband, a kind man, a devoted father") and goes on the road, "Mrs. Gray abruptly switches from the first-person 'I' narrative form that has preserved whatever degree of credibility the story maintains. Stephanie in the third-person, Stephanie as 'she,' makes fairly ludicrous fiction. . . . This is an age that has learned any grievance must be accepted as both genuine and significant if the public weeping and wailing are long and loud enough. It would therefore be wise to take seriously Mrs. Gray's passionate meditation on the tyranny of love. Not as a novel,

though." In the end, Michael Wood in *New York Review of Books* finds that "this hitherto solid and patient novel has expanded too far into fantasy, and has lost even the truth of seriously entertained wishes."

Concomitant to the lack of credibility that Stephanie suffers is what is perceived by some critics as her inability to reconcile her feminist beliefs with her actions. Writing in the *Nation,* Joan Peters observes that "one of the problems with *Lovers and Tyrants* is that not all the contradictions are accounted for or, it seems, planned for. Among the most perplexing of these is the tension between Stephanie's feminist analysis of her life and her persistent identification with men. On the one hand, she is quite strong in her analysis of how confining it is to be a woman, how discrimination operates, how few models women have, etc. . . . On the other hand, the actual record of Stephanie's life is a Freudian's delight and a feminist's nightmare. Again and again Stephanie realizes that she wants to be a boy." Peters then points out contradictions that belie Stephanie's words: "[her] need to be with men, her desire to be a boy, the absence of female friends, the Henry Milleresque sexual descriptions, her assumption that it is because Mishka couldn't love men that she was so cruel." Moynahan calls Stephanie "the unsatisfactory representation or symbol of modern woman in the throes of an unprecedented process of liberation." Earlier in his article, Moynahan had questioned the value of Stephanie's liberation, noting that despite her access to almost every pleasure desired and freedom from most worries, Stephanie slips "into madness out of a conviction that her freedom is obstructed."

Audrey Foote in *Washington Post Book World* says, "Gray writes with such passion, grace and wit, and her themes are so fashionable, that the reader is swept along in sympathetic credulity until he begins to scrutinize these tyrants." Stephanie's tyrants—governess, family, husband, lovers, friends—Foote points out, are hardly that, loving and indulging Stephanie in any way they can. Continues Foote: "Surely none of these 'lovers' in the wide sense she intends, can seriously be classified as 'tyrants.'. . . *En fin,* there is only one clue that her obsession with tyranny is not pure paranoia: the sex scenes. . . . They are significant in showing that Stephanie, so heroic if quixotic in defiance of imagined oppression, is, alas, a sexual masochist. 'He ordered,' 'she asked permission,' 'he commanded'—she *chooses* these dominating lovers, and her compliance, her collaboration explains her conviction: 'Our enslavers segregate us into zoos, with our full consent.' Speak for yourself, Stephanie! Thus finally the provocative title and grand design of this novel turn out to be based on little more than a retrogressive sexual taste, a dreary and dubious cliche. . . . She is in search of freedom—to do what? What does she want? What do women want? Francine never quite tells us about Stephanie (does *she* know?)."

Despite reservations about *Lovers and Tyrants,* most critics have, in the end, judged it favorably. Peters concludes that in spite of the book's limitations, "what *Lovers and Tyrants* does do, and does beautifully, is exploit the limited strength of the autobiographical genre. Gray presents a fascinating, intelligent woman whose personal contradictions concerning tradition, freedom, sex, culture, and religion shed light on the larger society in a way that is sometimes inadvertent, more often artistically controlled." Michael Wood concedes that *Lovers and Tyrants* "is an absorbing and intelligent book, if a little too icy to be really likeable." Finally, the *Village Voice*'s Fremont-Smith observes: "*Lovers and Tyrants* has all sorts of problems and gets tiresomely narcissistic and irritating; still, it is one of the very truly interesting and stimulating—one wants to argue with it and about it—books I've read all year. . . . If Gray's book burns a bit, and it does, that should suggest fire as well as ice at its core."

World without End, Gray's second novel, is also noted for its sensitivity and intelligence. The story of three lifelong friends who reunite in middle age to tour Russia and, hopefully, to "learn how to live the last third of our lives," *World without End* is "an ambitious novel about love and friendship, faith and doubt, liberty and license," comments Judith Gies in *Saturday Review.* D.M. Thomas, writing in the *Washington Post Book World,* considers *World without End* to be "clearly the work of a richly talented writer. . . . The book is struggling with an important subject: the conflict within each of us between the psychological hungers symbolized by America and Russia—individualism and brotherhood, anarchy and order. It is no small achievement to have explored interestingly one of the most crucial dilemmas of our age."

Doris Grumbach in *Commonweal* calls *World without End* "a prime entry in the novel of intelligence. It is just that: the lives [Gray] tells about ring with authenticity for their times and their place." It is the novel's "intelligence"—its lengthy discourses on a variety of subjects and the articulate growing self-awareness of its characters—that holds the attention of many of its reviewers. The *New York Times*'s John Leonard notes the "lyric excess" of the characters' musings, but believes that Gray "has chosen to satirize the art, the religion

and the politics of the last 35 years" through characters Sophie, Claire, and Edmund. "[Gray] has also chosen to forgive the creatures of her satire," says Leonard. "They are more disappointed in themselves than readers will be in them as characters."

For other critics, the intellectual discussions in *World without End* are a hindrance to an appreciation of the novel. "Anyone not conversant with the intellectual and esthetic upheavals in American art and politics over the last 30 years ought not attempt to read this novel," suggests Henrietta Epstein in the *Detroit News,* "for these concerns, along with those of friendship and love, are at the heart of Francine du Plessix Gray's work." *Newsweek* reviewer Annalyn Swan concurs with Leonard that "some of this is obviously satire" and says that "when Gray is not trying to be wry, or brilliant, she can be wonderful." Swan concludes that Gray, "like many social critics who cross the line into fiction, . . . has not yet mastered the difference between show and tell, between writing fiction that lives and using fiction as a forum for ideas. What she aspires to here is a highbrow critique of art and society in the last twenty years. What she has written is a novel that strives too hard to impress. The prose is full of bad breathiness, the characters suffer from terminal solipsism, and the social criticism is often as cliched as the attitudes it attacks."

Esquire columnist James Wolcott also comments on Gray's satiric designs: "Tripping through *World without End,* I kept telling myself that the book might be a spoofy lark—a Harlequin romance for art majors—but I have a lurking suspicion that Gray is serious. After all, the novel's theme—the pull and persistence of friendship—is buttressed by quotations from Catullus and from Roland Barthes, and floating through the text are the sort of flowery phrases only a tremulously sincere epicurean would use." *Commentary*'s Pearl K. Bell is also highly critical of Gray's second novel. "Francine Gray's sententious dialogue about love and death and self-fulfillment does not blind us to the poverty of thought in what seems to have been conceived as a novel of ideas," the critic contends. "*World without End* is not a novel of ideas, it is an adolescent daydream, an orgy of pseudo-intellectual posturing, a midnight bull session in a college dorm."

Grumbach finds that a distance is placed between the reader and the characters because of the intense intellectualism of the novel. She asserts that "despite the impressive and always accurate documentation of place (Edmund's visit to the Hermitage and the art he looks at there consumes five dense pages) and the character, social movements, parental backgrounds, lovers, husbands, visits with each other, letters and postcards [the three friends] exchange for all those years, do we ever feel close to these people? Curiously, not really. They are so detailed and cerebral, their talk is so elevated and informed, we know so many facts about their milieus that, somehow, passion is smothered." But, other critics disagree. Reynolds Price in the *New York Times Book Review,* for instance, finds that in *World without End,* Gray "displays the one indispensable gift in a novelist—she generates slowly and authoritatively a mixed set of entirely credible human beings who shunt back and forth through credible time and are altered by the trip. Ample, generous and mature, the book is stocked with the goods a novel best provides."

Leonard also finds the book—and the characters in it—touching. "The reader chooses sides," he writes. "In this novel about Renaissance art and Puritanism, about Anglican convents and academic departments of art, about friendship and that televised soap opera *General Hospital*—about lust and literature and missing fathers and saints full of greed and pride and envy—in this popcorn-popper of ideas, in which Edmund is the tourist of art, Claire the tourist of suffering and Sophie the tourist of everything, we are blessed with real people in the middle of an important argument about art and religion and sexuality. We are persuaded. . . . I chose Sophie to root for. It's been a long time in novels since I was a fan. Mrs. Gray tells us that 'Orpheus dismembered will continue to sing, his head floating down our rivers.' A real friend will either scoop up the head or hit it with a stick. Mrs. Gray scoops and sings."

Gray's second father was artist Alexander Liberman, art director of *Vogue* magazine. Her mother once worked at Saks Fifth Avenue, New York City, in the fashion industry. Drawing from this heritage, *October Blood* satirizes "the peculiar world of high fashion" and "sets out to tell a serious, even painful, story about three generations of remarkable women," Judith Viorst remarks in the *New York Times Book Review.* Though *October Blood* received mixed reviews, Joanne Kaufman of the *Washington Post Book World* notes that "Gray is successful at showing that the concerns of the fashion world are as lightweight as a Chanel chemise."

Gray's next bestselling nonfiction book looks at another facet of her heritage, the Russian ancestry of her mother and the other emigres who raised her in Paris. *Soviet Women: Walking the Tightrope* records Gray's observations of contemporary Soviet life and women's concerns she gathered on a visit to her mother's homeland.

"The distinguished American journalist and novelist Francine du Plessix Gray has now brought us a rich and contradictory selection of Soviet women's opinions," Mary F. Zirin comments in the *Los Angeles Times Book Review.* Reading it, says Zirin, "is like turning a kaleidoscope—a new pattern emerges with every chapter. . . . Gray uses her novelistic skills to record talks with some women in which psychological pressure and suppressed rage can be sensed under a facade of stoic cheer." The government encourages women to hold jobs and to raise large families; abortion is the most well-known method of birth control, Gray reports. Each woman expects to have between seven and fourteen abortions before menopause; there are between five and eight abortions for every live birth, and one out of five babies is born with a defect. Women form deep commitments to each other but tend to see men as crude liabilities.

Carroll Bogert of *Newsweek* relates that *Soviet Women* offers some surprises: "Gray turns a predictable tale of oppression upside down. . . . Traditions have ensured a peculiar female dominance in a society where tremendous male chauvinism persists. . . . Ninety-two percent of Soviet women work, and they do nearly all domestic chores. One woman admits many women have 'a need to control that verges on the tyrannical, the sadistic.'" Furthermore, though the reforms of *glasnost* are viewed by outsiders as a move toward greater personal liberty for Soviet citizens, "the Bolshevik ideal of sexual equality is being trampled in the retreat from socialism," Bogert points out. Bogert concludes, "For Westerners who think Gorbachev's reforms will make Them more like Us, this fine writer has a valuable lesson to teach."

Gray's biography *Rage and Fire: A Life of Louise Colet, Pioneer Feminist, Literary Star, Flaubert's Muse,* portrays the life of nineteenth-century novelist Gustave Flaubert's mistress from 1846 to 1855. Reviewers noted that the passionate nature of Colet's life, in addition to her affiliation with several major figures, including Flaubert, constitutes fascinating material for biography. Born in Provence, Colet moved to Paris at a young age and employed what Gray calls "her great gift for self-promotion" to establish her own literary salon. Gray's biography recounts Colet's series of distinguished lovers, her ongoing struggle to assert herself as a successful writer, and her loneliness and decline during her later years. Throughout the biography, Gray refutes Colet's trivialized historical reputation (largely based on negative comments written by Flaubert's friends) as merely a beautiful and volatile woman with whom Flaubert had an affair, emphasizing the fact that some of Flaubert's most important insights concerning the writing process were articulated in letters to Colet, as well as the fact of Colet's literary fame during her lifetime.

While critics acknowledged the often slanderous nature of earlier commentary on Colet, opinions diverged on the subject of Colet's status as a writer and feminist. Most noted that while her life and career were impressive, her writings evidence a modest and uneven level of skill. "The difficult truth is that a rereading of Colet's considerable creative legacy does not prove her testiest critics wrong," observes Barbara Meister in *Belles Lettres*. Gabriele Annan of the *Times Literary Supplement* also expresses skepticism concerning Gray's attempt to rehabilitate Colet as a writer: "Unfortunately, Colet doesn't emerge as a better feminist than she was a writer." *Rage and Fire* is nevertheless regarded as an important and successful biography in its depiction of an outstanding woman's life and for the historical insights Gray provides. "Ms. Gray gives rich background material on the mores of the times and has interesting things to say about the repression of female militancy in the wake of the [French] Revolution," observes Victor Brombert in *New York Times Book Review*.

Gray attempts to expand understanding of the notorious eighteenth-century sexual deviant and pornographer known as the Marquis de Sade by highlighting his married life in her biography *At Home with the Marquis de Sade: A Life*. Sade was married to Renee-Pelagie de Montreuil, a religious-minded young woman of the bourgeois class who remained devoted to her aristocratic husband for nearly three decades, despite his arrests for violent sex crimes, before she finally divorced him.

The response to Gray's biography was somewhat mixed. D. Keith Mano claims in a piece in the *National Review* that Gray's deemphasis of her subject's sexual escapades shows her lack of "courage," and the import she places on his domestic life fails to elicit his interest: "Occasion for this new biographical effort was given by the discovery of further correspondence between Sade and his long-suffering but loyal wife, Renee-Pelagie— hence Gray's folksy title. But this segment of her narrative drags: correspondence with a cranky prisoner seldom scintillates." Others praised Gray's focus on the context that produced Sade: "This biography is not some titillating list of transgressions but rather a complicated, contradictory life portrayed in full cultural, political and psychological context," contended a reviewer for *Publishers Weekly*. That context includes significantly the

high incidence of what is now termed "sado-masochism" in the French culture at large during those times, heavily influenced as it was by the Jesuits, whose favorite educational tool was intricately staged public whippings, Gray notes. Indeed, gaining pleasure from the infliction of pain was common at all levels of French society during this century. Gray recounts that Louis XV received tantalizing daily reports on Sade's sexual escapades for more than a decade. Mano notes the sadomasochism inherent in the public executions that attended the Terror at the turn of the eighteenth century. A reviewer for the *Economist* was less convinced, however, by Gray's attempt to locate the source of Sade's psychological malady in "the marquis's emotionally deprived childhood," adding that "few 18th-century aristocrats could have expected the caring ministrations of a nuclear family."

BIOGRAPHICAL AND CRITICAL SOURCES:

BOOKS

Contemporary Authors Autobiography Series, Volume 2, Thomson Gale (Detroit), 1985.
Contemporary Literary Criticism, Volume 22, Thomson Gale, 1982.
Gray, Francine du Plessix, *Lovers and Tyrants*, Simon & Schuster, 1976.
Gray, *World without End*, Simon & Schuster, 1981.

PERIODICALS

American Spectator, January, 1982; July, 1990.
Belles Lettres, summer, 1994.
Booklist, February 1, 1994, p. 990.
Books and Bookmen, March, 1971.
Book World, October 13, 1985.
Chicago Tribune Book World, May 31, 1981; August 15, 1982; March 25, 1990.
Commentary, August, 1981.
Commonweal, May 22, 1981.
Contemporary Review, January, 1996, p. 53.
Detroit News, December 16, 1981.
Economist, February 13, 1999.
Esquire, June, 1981.
Harpers, November, 1976.
Listener, February 25, 1971; June 2, 1977.
Los Angeles Times Book Review, March 25, 1990.
Maclean's, April 9, 1990.
Ms., November, 1976; July, 1981.

Nation, February 1, 1971; November 20, 1976; June 4, 1990.

National Observer, December 18, 1976.

National Review, November 12, 1976; December 31, 1998, p. 44.

New Republic, June 27, 1970; May 9, 1994, p. 39.

Newsweek, October 11, 1976; June 22, 1981; March 26, 1990.

New Yorker, October 12, 1998, p. 85.

New York Review of Books, November 11, 1976; May 26, 1994, p. 12.

New York Times, October 8, 1976; September 15, 1979; May 19, 1981; August 20, 1981; April 6, 1992.

New York Times Book Review, May 31, 1970; October 17, 1976; May 24, 1981; September 12, 1982; October 6, 1985; March 11, 1990; March 20, 1994.

Progressive, November, 1981.

Publishers Weekly, January 17, 1994, p. 376; October 5, 1998, p. 65.

Quill & Quire, July, 1990.

Saturday Review, June 13, 1970; October 30, 1976; May, 1981.

Time, November 1, 1976.

Times Literary Supplement, May 20, 1977; July 22, 1994.

Village Voice, November 22, 1976.

Wall Street Journal, October 25, 1976; June 1, 1981.

Washington Post Book World, August 29, 1976; October 24, 1976; May 24, 1981; March 11, 1990.

Women's Review of Books, December, 1990.

*   *   *

GRAY, Spalding 1941-2004

PERSONAL: Born June 5, 1941, in Providence, RI; died, January, 2004, in New York, NY; son of Rockwell (a factory employee) and Margeret Elizabeth (a homemaker; maiden name, Horton) Gray; married Renee Shafransky (a writer and stage director), August, 1991 (divorced); married Kathleen Russo; children: three. *Education:* Emerson College, B.A., 1965.

CAREER: Actor and writer. Actor in Cape Cod, MA, and Saratoga, NY, 1965-67; actor with Alley Theater, Houston, TX, 1967; actor with Performance Group (experimental theater company), New York, NY, 1967-79; cofounder of Wooster Group (theater company), New York, NY, 1977; writer, beginning 1979. Actor in summer stock plays, including *The Curious Savage, Long Day's Journey into Night,* and *The Knack;* actor in *The Best Man,* 2000; actor in films, including *The Killing Fields,* 1983, *Swimming to Cambodia,* 1985, *True Sto-*

ries, 1987, *Stars and Bars,* 1988, *Clara's Heart,* 1988, *Beaches,* 1989, *Straight Talk,* 1992, *King of the Hill,* 1993, *The Paper,* 1994, *Diabolique,* 1996, *Drunks,* 1997, and *Kate and Leopold,* 2001. Visiting instructor at University of California, Santa Cruz, summer, 1978, and at Columbia University, 1985; artist-in-residence at Mark Taper Forum, Los Angeles, CA, 1986-87.

AWARDS, HONORS: Grants from National Endowment for the Arts, 1978, Rockefeller Foundation, 1979, and Edward Albee Foundation, 1985; fellowships from National Endowment for the Arts, 1978, and Rockefeller Foundation, 1979; Guggenheim fellowship, 1985; Obie Award, *Village Voice,* 1985, for *Swimming to Cambodia.*

WRITINGS:

DRAMATIC MONOLOGUES

Sex and Death to the Age 14 (also see below), produced off-Broadway, 1979.

Booze, Cars, and College Girls (also see below) produced off-Broadway, 1979.

India (and After), produced off-Broadway, 1979.

A Personal History of the American Theatre, produced off-Broadway, 1980.

(With Randal Levenson) *In Search of the Monkey Girl* (produced off-Broadway, 1981), Aperture Press (New York, NY), 1982.

Swimming to Cambodia (produced off-Broadway, 1985; also see below), Theatre Communications Group (New York, NY), 1985.

Sex and Death to the Age 14 (collection; includes *Booze, Cars, and College Girls*), Random House (New York, NY), 1986.

Travels through New England, produced off-Broadway, 1986.

Terrors of Pleasure, produced in New York, NY, at Lincoln Center, 1986.

Swimming to Cambodia: The Collected Works of Spalding Gray (includes *Sex and Death to the Age 14, Booze, Cars, and College Girls, Forty-seven Beds, Nobody Wanted to Sit behind a Desk, Travels through New England,* and *Terrors of Pleasure*), Picador (New York, NY), 1987.

Monster in a Box (produced in New York, NY, at Lincoln Center, 1990), Vintage (New York, NY), 1992.

Gray's Anatomy (produced in New York, NY, 1993), Vintage (New York, NY), 1994.

It's a Slippery Slope (produced in New York, NY, at Lincoln Center, 1996), Noonday Press (New York, NY), 1997.

Morning, Noon, and Night (produced in Chicago, IL, 1999), Farrar, Straus & Giroux (New York, NY), 1999.

Contributor of *Rivkala's Ring* (based on Anton Chekhov's short story "A Witch"; produced in Chicago, IL, 1986, as part of a production titled *Orchards*), to *Orchards* (anthology), Knopf (New York, NY), 1986.

OTHER

(With Elizabeth LeCompte) *Sakonnet Point* (one-act play), produced off-Broadway, 1975.
(With Elizabeth LeCompte) *Rumstick Road* (one-act play), produced off-Broadway, 1977.
(With Elizabeth LeCompte) *Nyatt School* (one-act play), produced off-Broadway, 1978.
(With Elizabeth LeCompte) *Three Places in Rhode Island* (play trilogy; includes *Sakonnet Point, Rumstick Road,* and *Nyatt School*), produced off-Broadway, 1979.
Point Judith (one-act play; epilogue to *Three Places in Rhode Island*), produced off-Broadway, 1979.
Seven Scenes from a Family Album (short stories), Benzene Press, 1981.
Impossible Vacation (novel), Knopf (New York, NY), 1992.

Also producer of improvisations, including "Interviewing the Audience," 1981, and "Art in the Anchorage," 1985. Contributor of articles to drama journals and periodicals, including *Elle, Rolling Stone, Gentleman's Quarterly, Performing Arts Journal,* and *Drama Review.*

ADAPTATIONS: Several of Gray's performances of *Swimming to Cambodia* were adapted by director Jonathan Demme for the 1987 film of the same title, with music by Laurie Anderson; *Terrors of Pleasure* was filmed as an HBO Comedy Special; *Monster in a Box* was released as a film by Fine Line Features in 1992, with music by Laurie Anderson; *Gray's Anatomy* was directed by Steven Soderberg and filmed in 1997.

SIDELIGHTS: Dubbed "our bard of self-absorption" by *Nation* critic Laurie Stone, actor and performance artist Spalding Gray was known for his critically acclaimed autobiographical dramatic monologues in which he drew upon some of the most intimate areas of his personal history in order to produce observant, humorous, and insightful stories of contemporary life. "Recycling

negative experience is one of the things the monologues are about," Gray once explained to Don Shewey in the *New York Times.* "I go out and digest what could be disturbing situations and convert them into humor in front of an audience." As Stone further noted, Gray learned to see such self-absorption "with detachment, turning it into a subject, a hot tub big enough for a group soak." Many of these monologues, such as *Swimming to Cambodia, Monster in a Box, Gray's Anatomy, It's a Slippery Slope,* and *Morning, Noon, and Night* were adapted for books and some for popular movies. Writing in *Contemporary Literature,* Gay Brewer noted that Gray's "art is the autobiographic monologue, a composite of reality and artifice." According to Brewer, Gray's works "share adventures achieved in the pursuit of artistic expression and colored by an obsession with the unattainable—life as art, encapsulated and preserved." In 2004 Gray was at work on yet another monologue, "Black Spot," about a near-fatal car accident he had in Ireland, when he died in New York, an apparent suicide.

Born in Rhode Island to middle-class parents, Gray became interested in the theater as a teenager. He studied acting at Emerson College, and after his 1965 graduation he performed for two years in summer stock theater in New England and in New York state. In 1967 he traveled to Texas and Mexico, and upon his return several months later he learned his mother had committed suicide. The loss and subsequent family trauma caused him to suffer a prolonged depression that resulted in a nervous breakdown nine years later. Gray eventually used events from his childhood and college life as well as experiences as a struggling actor as material for his dramas and monologues.

In the late 1960s Gray moved to New York City, where he joined the Performance Group, an experimental off-Broadway theater company. There he composed his first autobiographical dramatic works, and in 1977 he founded the Wooster Group with Elizabeth LeCompte. Also with LeCompte, Gray wrote *Sakonnet Point* and *Rumstick Road,* two experimental dramas which explored his mother's mental illness and suicide and their effects on his youth and on his family, and *Nyatt School,* a satire of poet and dramatist T.S. Eliot's play *The Cocktail Party.* The three plays made up a trilogy titled *Three Places in Rhode Island,* which Gray produced collectively in 1979.

Gray became interested in the dramatic monologue's possibilities during his tenure as a summer workshop instructor at the University of California's Santa Cruz campus in 1978. As related by David Guy in the *New York Times Book Review,* Gray lamented what he foresaw as the demise of white middle-class life to a friend who replied, "During the collapse of Rome the last artists were the chroniclers." Gray consequently decided to "chronicle" his own life orally in dramatic monologue form; the performer felt that writing it down implied a faith in the future that he did not possess. In 1979 Gray performed *Sex and Death to the Age 14,* his first monologue, at SoHo's Performing Garage. This confessional account of Gray's boyhood experiences with family turmoil and sexuality was followed by an examination of his life at college titled *Booze, Cars, and College Girls* and then by *India (and After),* the story of his nervous collapse when he returned from a tour of India in 1976. "I'll never run out of material as long as I live," *Newsweek*'s Cathleen McGuigan quoted the actor describing his work's content. "The only disappointment is that I probably won't be able to come back after I die and tell that experience." After the success of these first monologues, Gray began giving performances across the country.

In the early-1980s Gray used the monologue form to produce *Interviewing the Audience* and *In Search of the Monkey Girl.* In the former Gray elicited stories from audience members, while the latter was the product of a trip that Gray, hoping to generate new material for his monologues, took to interview carnival members and sideshow freaks at the 1981 Tennessee State Fair. The resulting monologue was published as the text of a book of photographs by the same name in 1982. During this time Gray also published his first fictional work, *Seven Scenes from a Family Album,* a book of short, interrelated autobiographical sketches depicting, with satire as well as humor, the sexual tensions and complex emotional relationships in a suburban family.

Publicity from Gray's one-man performances resulted in his being cast as an American ambassador's aide in the 1983 feature film *The Killing Fields,* the story of the friendship between an American correspondent and his Asian assistant during the 1970s war in Cambodia. The two months Gray spent filming on location in Thailand became the subject of his next effort, *Swimming to Cambodia,* considered by many critics to be his masterpiece. The monologue premiered in 1985 and evolved improvisationally at New York City's Performing Garage. Gray, who performed the monologue sitting at a desk with only a glass of water, a notebook, and two maps of Southeast Asia as props, narrated anecdotes and observations from several levels of his own experience—as an individual coping with personal problems, as a professional actor in a large-scale movie pro-

duction, as an American facing the aftermath of U.S. policy in Cambodia since the Vietnam War, and as a human being learning of the atrocities committed by the Khmer Rouge, a guerrilla group that terrorized the country in 1975. The monologue takes its title, as quoted by Janet Maslin in the *New York Times,* from Gray's remark in the piece that "explaining the upheaval in that country 'would be a task equal to swimming there from New York.'"

Swimming to Cambodia met with an enthusiastic reception. Critics admired the pace and fluidity of Gray's narrative, the numerous descriptive details in his recollections, and the honesty with which he presented his stories. "What really makes [*Swimming to Cambodia*] work is its shifting frames of reference, as Gray contracts and expands his point of view to move from meticulously described immediate experience to a detached global-historical vision," assessed Dave Kehr in the *Chicago Tribune. New York Times* writer Mel Gussow was similarly impressed, asserting that Gray's "stream of experience has the zestful, first-hand quality of a letter home from the front." And David Richards, writing for the *Washington Post,* called the actor "an original and disciplined artistic temperament at work," concluding that when Gray is "talking about himself—with candor, humor, imagination and the unfailingly bizarre image—he ends up talking about all of us."

Gray's stage success with *Swimming to Cambodia* inspired him to collaborate with future wife Renee Shafransky on a movie version of the monologue. The film version of *Swimming to Cambodia* was produced by Shafransky, directed by Jonathan Demme, and released in 1987 to widespread critical acclaim. Deemed by Kehr a "documentary on the face and voice of Spalding Gray," the movie was filmed in the Performing Garage and later embellished only with music and a few clips from *The Killing Fields.*

Gray published as well as performed his monologues. *Swimming to Cambodia,* issued in 1985, 1993's *Gray's Anatomy,* and a 1986 collection titled *Sex and Death to the Age 14* are among the transcriptions of Gray's many performances through which the printed form of each monologue evolved. "Almost all of my writing has grown out of speaking it in front of an audience," Gray once explained to *CA.* "Then, after a great number of performances, I take the best tape, get it transcribed, and rework it for print." Critical responses to Gray's monologues in book form, however, have been mixed: some readers, while admiring the author's storytelling ability, have questioned the literary merit of his material. Lisa Zeidner, for instance, wrote in the *New York Times Book Review* that *Swimming to Cambodia* "is surprisingly successful on the page—breezy and theatrical," while *New Statesman* reviewer Nick Kimberley complained that in the writing Gray "simply comes across as a cartoon version of the self-dramatising, all-American alternative culturist. . . . He lazily spews up the world in an endless burble of 'me-me-me.'"

Gray followed the popular *Swimming to Cambodia* with two more monologues: *Terrors of Pleasure,* which premiered at the Lincoln Center for the Performing Arts in New York City in 1986, and *Rivkala's Ring.* The story of Gray's purchase of a dilapidated house in New York's Catskill Mountains and his resultant frustration in learning that the structure's rotting foundations were causing it to sink, *Terrors of Pleasure* was praised by Gussow, who remarked that the "narrative has dramatic cohesiveness as well as comic insight." Gray was also commissioned in 1986 by the Juilliard Theater School's Acting Company to write a theatrical adaptation of a short story by Russian author and dramatist Anton Chekhov for a production called *Orchards.* For the project Gray penned *Rivkala's Ring*—a monologue to be performed by an actor other than Gray in which an insomniac, upon receiving a copy of Chekhov's short story "The Witch" in the mail, begins a winding narrative having little overt connection to the story. Some reviewers found Gray's contribution to the program too far removed from Chekhovian themes, but John Beaufort, in the *Christian Science Monitor,* called the monologue "a windy word-scape, effectively recited." Again Gussow admired Gray's work, describing his contribution to *Orchards* as "a stream of fascinating experience," and concluded that "even more clearly than before, one realizes the extent of Mr. Gray's creativity as dramatist as well as performance artist."

In line with his autobiographical bent, Gray also wrote an autobiographical novel. Titled *Impossible Vacation* and published in 1992, the novel had its genesis in the monologue *Monster in a Box,* which was first performed at New York's Lincoln Center in 1990. The monologue featured "a man who can't write a book about a man who can't take a vacation"; the "monster" of the title refers to the stack of handwritten manuscript pages that multiply—but to no conclusive "The End"—during the monologue's performance. In *Impossible Vacation* that man becomes Brewster North—a thinly disguised Gray—who cannot hold down a job because of his belief that something better is just around the corner, whose emotionally troubled mother eventually commits suicide, and whose own emotional and financial instability occasionally topples him into lulls of depression

as well. The continuous frustration of each of North's goals is the lifeblood of the work; while David Montrose commented in the *Times Literary Supplement* that later portions of the novel are "without Gray's usual humour and charm," *Spectator* reviewer Cressida Connolly noted of *Impossible Vacation:* "Its hero spends many years trying to relax, hang out and enjoy life: his failure to do so makes hilarious reading." Meanwhile, *Monster in a Box,* which was a play, book, and movie, continued Gray's rise in the estimation of many critics. For Stanley Kauffmann, writing in the *New Republic,* it showed Gray as "earnestly funny and, above all else, articulate." Others were less impressed. For example, *National Review* critic Joe Queenan failed "to see what all the fuss is about." According to Queenan, Gray seems "not near as funny as the young Woody Allen or even the young Eddie Murphy. He is NPR's idea of what a comic should be: a Bob Newhart who has been to Europe." Lawrence O'Toole, reviewing the same movie for *Entertainment Weekly,* felt that Gray's second film effort lacks the punch of *Swimming to Cambodia.* Stone wrote, "this time self-reference has given way to self-fascination."

Throughout the 1990s Gray continued to mine personal experience and misadventure for his monologues, including *Gray's Anatomy,* which explores his reactions to and treatment for an eye affliction; *It's a Slipper Slope,* detailing his attempts on skis and the breakup of his marriage when his current girlfriend became pregnant with his baby; and *Morning, Noon, and Night,* a very domestic day-in-the-life of the new Spalding family at their Long Island home. Reviewing the book publication of *Gray's Anatomy,* a critic for *Publishers Weekly* found Gray to be "always entertaining, and sometimes hilarious." Reviewing the movie version, Steve Hayes noted in *American Theatre* that the "film is a visual delight, a creative effort of a talented team." Kauffmann, however, writing in the *New Republic,* viewed the film as "padded," and that both "speaker and director are nervous about the material."

Robert Simonson, writing in *Back Stage,* found the stage version of *It's a Slippery Slope* an "engaging production," while Stone, writing in the *Nation,* was less laudatory in her assessment, complaining that the play is a "scrapbook of [Gray's] narcissism." Still Stone praised Gray's monologue as "bravura stand-up unreeled with grand minimalism." Reviewing the book version of the monologue, *Booklist*'s Benjamin Segedin called it the story of a "midlife crisis" and a "welcome addition to the Gray oeuvre." A reviewer for *Publishers Weekly* noted that the monologue looks at more "commonplace human crises" than Gray's previous works. Here the themes are "adultery, separation, fatherhood." The same *Publishers Weekly* critic concluded that *It's a Slippery Slope* is a "portrait of a man in the painful process of being disabused." *People*'s Jim Brown, however, found less to like, noting that in the book version "the vaunted Gray charm is for the most part lacking. He comes off here as a major worrywart."

Similar mixed reactions greeted both the stage and book versions of Gray's next work, *Morning, Noon, and Night.* Jonathan Abarbanel, writing in *Back Stage,* found the stage version a "day in the domestic life of Gray— horny house husband, homeowner, gardener, yoga master, bicyclist, day sailor, stepdad, and proud papa in his fifties, lover of children and small animals." For Abarbanel "something more affirming has taken hold" in this monologue. Abarbanel described this "something else" as "contentment and joy and living in the moment, rather than pondering the unanswerables." *Variety* critic Chris Jones, however, found the "newly cheery Gray" more suited to "the Family Channel than Bravo," and opined that Gray "has gone soft and paternal in middle age." Reviewing the book of the monologue, a critic for *Publishers Weekly* described it as a "portrait of the artist as bemused dad," "by turns funny, meditative and self-absorbed." *Booklist*'s Jack Helbig allowed that Gray "remains a gifted storyteller," but also feared that the author/artist's "longtime fans will miss the hilarity of his earlier work."

Gray's domestic bliss suffered a setback with a car accident in Ireland in 2000 in which he was nearly killed. But true to form, he was in the process of turning this misfortune into his twentieth monologue when depression overcame him. He tried to commit suicide by jumping off a bridge but was talked down by a passerby. In January of 2004, he went missing in New York, and several months later his body was found in the East River, an apparent suicide.

BIOGRAPHICAL AND CRITICAL SOURCES:

BOOKS

Contemporary Dramatists, 6th edition, St. James Press (Detroit, MI), 1999.
Contemporary Literary Criticism, Thomson Gale (Detroit, MI), Volume 49, 1988, Volume 112, 1999.
Contemporary Theatre, Film, and Television, Thomson Gale (Detroit, MI), Volume 7, 1989, Volume 15, 1996, Volume 24, 2000, Volume 49, 2003.

PERIODICALS

American Theatre, November, 1996, Steve Hayes, "Gaze Anatomy," p. 70.
Back Stage, November 29, 1996, Robert Simonson, review of *It's a Slippery Slope,* p. 53; September 17, 1999, Jonathan Abarbanel, review of *Morning, Noon, and Night,* p. 71; March 12, 2004, p. 6.
Booklist, September 1, 1997, Benjamin Segedin, review of *It's a Slippery Slope,* p. 51; August, 1999, Jack Helbig, review of *Morning, Noon, and Night,* p. 1981.
Chicago Tribune, July 9, 1986; April 7, 1987; May 20, 1987.
Christian Science Monitor, April 30, 1986.
Contemporary Literature, summer, 1996, Gay Brewer, "Talking His Way Back to Life: Spalding Gray and the Embodied Voice," p. 23.
Daily Variety, March 9, 2004, p. 1.
Entertainment Weekly, January 29, 1993, Lawrence O'Toole, review of *Monster in a Box,* p. 63; October 1, 1999, Megan Harlan, review of *Morning, Noon, and Night,* p. 70.
Library Journal, July, 1997, Thomas E. Luddy, review of *It's a Slippery Slope,* p. 84; October 1, 1999, Barry X. Miller, review of *Morning, Noon, and Night,* p. 96.
Los Angeles Times, January 15, 1985; January 18, 1985; April 3, 1987; May 20, 1987; January 8, 1988.
Nation, April 18, 1987; December 23, 1996, Laurie Stone, review of *It's a Slippery Slope,* p. 33.
National Review, July 20, 1992, Joe Queenan, review of *Monster in a Box,* p. 43.
New Republic, July 6, 1992, Stanley Kauffmann, review of *Monster in a Box,* p. 26; April 7, 1997, Stanley Kauffmann, review of *Gray's Anatomy,* p. 26.
New Statesman, September 7, 1987.
Newsweek, July 28, 1986.
New York Times, November 16, 1984; March 28, 1986; April 23, 1986; May 11, 1986; May 15, 1986; March 7, 1987; March 13, 1987; March 22, 1987; April 24, 1987; November 11, 1996.
New York Times Book Review, January 12, 1986; May 4, 1986; May 22, 1992; July 12, 1992, pp. 9-10; October 12, 1997.
New York Times Magazine, March 8, 1987.
Observer (London, England), February 15, 1987.
People, October 13, 1997, Jim Brown, review of *It's a Slippery Slope,* p. 36; February 2, 2004, "Without a Trace," p. 86.
Publishers Weekly, January 20, 1992, p. 59; November 22, 1993, review of *Gray's Anatomy,* p. 58; July 7, 1997, review of *It's a Slippery Slope,* p. 56; August

23, 1999, review of *Morning, Noon, and Night,* p. 37; May 13, 2002, John F. Baker, "Spalding Gray and His 'Black Spot,'" p. 24.

Spectator, January 16, 1993, p. 30.

Time, April 27, 1987.

Times (London, England), February 7, 1987.

Times Literary Supplement, January 8, 1993, p. 17.

Variety, September 27, 1999, Chris Jones, review of *Morning, Noon, and Night,* p. 159.

Village Voice, January 27, 1982.

Washington Post, June 2, 1979; April 1, 1985; May 1, 1987.

OBITUARIES:

PERIODICALS

American Theatre, July-August, 2004, Eric Bogosian, "Spalding Gray: 1941-2004; The Perfect Moment," p. 22, Mark Russell, *Spalding Gray: 1941-2004; One True Thing at a Time,* p. 23.

Back Stage West, March 11, 2004, p. 2.

Newsweek, March 22, 2004, p. 10.

Variety, March 14, 2004, Robert Hofler, "Gray Was Pithy Speaker," p. 57.

Village Voice, March 17-23, 2004, Mark Russell, "Spalding Gray 1941-2004."

ONLINE

CNN.com, http://www.cnn.com/ (March 9, 2004).

New York Times Online, http://www.nytimes.com/ (March 9, 2004).

*   *   *

GREELEY, Andrew M. 1928-
(Andrew Moran Greeley)

PERSONAL: Born February 5, 1928, in Oak Park, IL; son of Andrew T. (a corporation executive) and Grace (McNichols) Greeley. *Education:* St. Mary of the Lake Seminary, A.B., 1950, S.T.B., 1952, S.T.L., 1954; University of Chicago, M.A., 1961, Ph.D., 1962. *Politics:* Democrat *Religion:* Roman Catholic

ADDRESSES: Home—1012 E. 47th St., Chicago, IL 60653. *Office*—National Opinion Research Center, University of Chicago, 1155 E. 60th St., Chicago, IL 60637; Department of Sociology, The University of Arizona, Social Sciences Bldg., 400, P.O. Box 210027, Tucson, AZ 85721-0027. *E-mail*—Agreel@aol.com.

CAREER: Ordained Roman Catholic priest, 1954. Church of Christ the King, Chicago, IL, assistant pastor, 1954-64; University of Chicago, National Opinion Research Center, Chicago, IL, senior study director, 1961-68, program director for higher education, 1968-70, director of Center for the Study of American Pluralism, 1971-85, research associate, 1985—; University of Chicago, lecturer in sociology of religion, 1962- 72, professor of social science, 1991—; University of Arizona, Tucson, professor of sociology, beginning 1978, currently adjunct professor. Professor of sociology of education, University of Illinois—Chicago. Member of planning committee, National Conference on Higher Education, 1969; member of board of advisers on student unrest, National Institute of Mental Health; consultant, Hazen Foundation Commission. Has made a number of appearances on radio and television programs.

MEMBER: American Sociological Association, American Catholic Sociological Society (former president), Society for the Scientific Study of Religion, Religious Research Association.

AWARDS, HONORS: Thomas Alva Edison Award, 1962, for *Catholic Hour* radio broadcasts; Catholic Press Association award for best book for young people, 1965; C. Albert Kobb award, National Catholic Education Association, 1977; Popular Culture Award, Center for the Study of Popular Culture (Bowling Green State University), 1986; Mark Twain Award, Society for the Study of Midwestern Literature, 1987; Freedom to Read Award, Friends of the Chicago Public Library, 1989; *U.S. Catholic* Award, 1993, for furthering the cause of women in the Church; Illinois Outstanding Citizen Award, College of Lake County. LL. D., St. Joseph's College (Rensselaer, IN), 1967; Litt.D., St. Mary's College (Winona, MN), 1967; honorary Doctor of Humane Letters, Bowling Green State University (Bowling Green, OH), 1986; honorary Doctorate of Humanities, St. Louis University (St. Louis, MO), 1991; honorary Doctorate, Northern Michigan University.

WRITINGS:

RELIGION

The Church and the Suburbs, Sheed, 1959.

Strangers in the House: Catholic Youth in America, Sheed (London, England), 1961, revised edition, Doubleday (New York, NY), 1967.

(Editor, with Michael E. Schlitz) *Catholics in the Archdiocese of Chicago,* Chicago Archdiocesan Conservation Council, 1962.

Religion and Career: A Study of College Graduates, Sheed (London, England), 1963.

Letters to a Young Man, Sheed (London, England), 1964.

Letters to Nancy, from Andrew M. Greeley, Sheed (London, England), 1964.

Priests for Tomorrow, Ave Maria Press, 1964.

And Young Men Shall See Visions: Letters from Andrew M. Greeley, Sheed (London, England), 1964.

(With Peter H. Rossi) *The Education of Catholic Americans,* Aldine, 1966.

The Hesitant Pilgrim: American Catholicism after the Council, Sheed (London, England), 1966.

The Catholic Experience: An Interpretation of the History of American Catholicism, Doubleday (New York, NY), 1967.

(With William Van Cleve and Grace Ann Carroll) *The Changing Catholic College,* Aldine, 1967.

The Crucible of Change: The Social Dynamics of Pastoral Practice, Sheed (London, England), 1968.

Uncertain Trumpet: The Priest in Modern America, Sheed (London, England), 1968.

Youth Asks, "Does God Talk?," Nelson, 1968, published as *Youth Asks, "Does God Still Speak?,"* 1970.

(With Martin E. Marty and Stuart E. Rosenberg) *What Do We Believe? The Stance of Religion in America,* Meredith, 1968.

From Backwater to Mainstream: A Profile of Catholic Higher Education, McGraw, 1969.

A Future to Hope In: Socio-Religious Speculations, Doubleday (New York, NY), 1969.

Life for a Wanderer: A New Look at Christian Spirituality, Doubleday (New York, NY), 1969.

Religion in the Year 2000, Sheed (London, England), 1969.

New Horizons for the Priesthood, Sheed (London, England), 1970.

The Life of the Spirit (also the Mind, the Heart, the Libido), National Catholic Reporter, 1970.

(With William E. Brown) *Can Catholic Schools Survive?,* Sheed (London, England), 1970.

The Jesus Myth, Doubleday (New York, NY), 1971.

The Touch of the Spirit, Herder & Herder, 1971.

What a Modern Catholic Believes about God, Thomas More Press, 1971.

Priests in the United States: Reflections on a Survey, Doubleday (New York, NY), 1972.

The Sinai Myth, Doubleday (New York, NY), 1972.

The Unsecular Man: The Persistence of Religion, Schocken, 1972.

What a Modern Catholic Believes about the Church, Thomas More Press, 1972.

The Catholic Priest in the United States: Sociological Investigations, United States Catholic Conference, 1972.

(Editor, with Gregory Baum) *The Persistence of Religion,* Seabury, 1973.

The Devil, You Say! Man and His Personal Devils and Angels, Doubleday (New York, NY), 1974.

(With Gregory Baum) *The Church as Institution,* Herder & Herder, 1974.

May the Wind Be at Your Back: The Prayer of St. Patrick, Seabury, 1975.

(With William C. McCready and Kathleen McCourt) *Catholic Schools in a Declining Church,* Sheed (London, England), 1976.

The Communal Catholic: A Personal Manifesto, Seabury, 1976.

Death and Beyond, Thomas More Press, 1976.

The American Catholic: A Social Portrait, Basic Books, 1977.

The Mary Myth: On the Femininity of God, Seabury, 1977.

An Ugly Little Secret: Anti-Catholicism in North America, Sheed (London, England), 1977.

Everything You Wanted to Know about the Catholic Church but Were Too Pious to Ask, Thomas More Press, 1978.

(Editor, with Gregory Baum) *Communication in the Church Concilium,* Seabury, 1978.

Crisis in the Church: A Study of Religion in America, Thomas More Press, 1979.

The Making of the Popes, 1978: The Politics of Intrigue in the Vatican, Sheed (London, England), 1979, revised edition published as *The Making of the Pope, 2005,* Little, Brown, and Company (New York, NY), 2005.

Catholic High Schools and Minority Students, Transaction Publications (New Brunswick, NJ), 1982, reprinted, with a new preface by Greeley, Transaction Publishers, 2002.

The Bottom Line Catechism for Contemporary Catholics, Thomas More Press, 1982.

Religion: A Secular Theory, Free Press, 1982.

The Catholic WHY? Book, Thomas More Press, 1983.

How to Save the Catholic Church, Penguin (New York, NY), 1984.

(With Mary G. Durka) *Angry Catholic Women,* Thomas More Press, 1984.

American Catholics since the Council: An Unauthorized Report, Thomas More Press, 1985.

Patience of a Saint, Warner Books (New York, NY), 1986.

Catholic Contributions: Sociology and Policy, Thomas More Press, 1987.

When Life Hurts: Healing Themes from the Gospels, Thomas More Press, 1988.

Religious Indicators, 1940-1985, Harvard University Press, 1989.

God in Popular Culture, Thomas More Press, 1989.

Myths of Religion, Warner Books (New York, NY), 1989.

Religious Change in America, Harvard University Press, 1989.

Complaints against God, Thomas More Press, 1989.

Year of Grace: A Spiritual Journal, Thomas More Press, 1990.

(With Jacob Neusner) *The Bible and Us: A Priest and a Rabbi Read Scripture Together,* Warner Books, 1990, revised edition published as *Common Ground: A Priest and a Rabbi Read Scripture Together,* Pilgrim Press (Cleveland, OH), 1996.

The Book of Irish American Prayers and Blessings, Thomas More, 1991.

The Catholic Myth: The Behavior and Beliefs of American Catholics, Macmillan (New York, NY), 1991.

(Contributor) *The Seven Deadly Sins: Stories on Human Weakness and Virtue,* Liguori Publications, 1992.

Love Affair: A Prayer Journal, Crossroad (New York, NY), 1992.

Religion as Poetry, Thomas More Press, 1994.

Sociology and the Religion: A Collection of Readings, Harper (New York, NY), 1994.

Sacraments of Love: A Prayer Journal, Crossroad (New York, NY), 1994.

Windows: A Prayer Journal, Crossroad (New York, NY), 1995.

(With Albert Bergesen) *God in the Movies: A Sociological Investigation,* Transaction Publishers (New Brunswick, NJ), 2000.

The Catholic Imagination, University of California Press (Berkeley, CA), 2000.

My Love: A Prayer Journal, Sheed & Ward (London, England), 2001.

Catholic High Schools and Minority Students, (with a new preface by the author), Transaction Publishers, 2002.

The Great Mysteries: Experiencing Catholic Faith from the Inside Out, Sheed & Ward (London, England), 2003.

The Catholic Revolution: New Wine, Old Wineskins, and the Second Vatican Council, University of California Press, 2004.

Priests: A Calling in Crisis, University of Chicago Press, 2004.

Also author of *Teenage World: Its Crises and Anxieties,* Divine Word Publications, and of a number of shorter works. Author of syndicated column "People and Values," appearing in approximately eighty newspapers. Contributor to Catholic magazines.

SOCIOLOGY

Why Can't They Be like Us?: Facts and Fallacies about Ethnic Differences and Group Conflicts in America (also see below), Institute of Human Relations Press, 1969.

A Fresh Look at Vocations, Clarentian, 1969.

(With Joe L. Spaeth) *Recent Alumni and Higher Education,* McGraw, 1970.

Why Can't They Be like Us?: America's White Ethnic Groups (includes portions of *Why Can't They Be like Us?: Facts and Fallacies about Ethnic Differences and Group Conflicts in America*), Dutton (New York, NY), 1971.

The Denominational Society: A Sociological Approach to Religion in America, Scott, Foresman, 1972.

That Most Distressful Nation: The Taming of the American Irish, Quadrangle, 1972.

The New Agenda, Doubleday (New York, NY), 1973.

Building Coalitions: American Politics in the 1970s, New Viewpoints, 1974.

Ethnicity in the United States: A Preliminary Reconnaissance, Wiley, 1974.

MEDIA: Ethnic Media in the United States, Project IMPRESS (Hanover, NH), 1974.

The Sociology of the Paranormal: A Reconnaissance, Sage Publications, 1975.

Ethnicity, Denomination, and Inequality, Sage Publications, 1976.

The Great Mysteries: An Essential Catechism, Seabury, 1976.

(With William C. McCready) *The Ultimate Values of the American Population,* Sage Publications, 1976.

(Also photographer) *Neighborhood,* Seabury, 1977.

No Bigger than Necessary: An Alternative to Socialism, Capitalism, and Anarchism, New American Library, 1977.

(Editor) *The Family in Crisis or in Transition: A Sociological and Theological Perspective,* Seabury, 1979.

The Irish Americans: The Rise to Money and Power, Times Books, 1980.

(With William C. McCready) *Ethnic Drinking Subcultures,* Praeger, 1980.

The Sociology of Andrew M. Greeley, Scholars Press, 1993.

Religion in Europe at the End of the Second Millennium: A Sociological Profile, Transaction Publishers, 2003.

Editor, *Ethnicity.* Contributor to sociology and education journals.

RELATIONSHIPS

The Friendship Game, Doubleday (New York, NY), 1970.
Sexual Intimacy, Thomas More Press, 1973.
Ecstasy: A Way of Knowing, Prentice-Hall (New York, NY), 1974.
Love and Play, Thomas More Press, 1975.
Faithful Attraction: Discovering Intimacy, Love, and Fidelity in American Marriage, Tor, 1991.
The Sense of Love, Ashland Poetry Press, 1992.

NOVELS

Nora Maeve and Sebi, illustrated by Diane Dawson, Paulist/Newman, 1976.
The Magic Cup: An Irish Legend, McGraw (New York, NY), 1979.
Death in April, McGraw (New York, NY), 1980.
The Cardinal Sins, Warner Books (New York, NY), 1981.
Thy Brother's Wife (book 1 of the "Passover Trilogy"), Warner Books (New York, NY), 1982.
Ascent into Hell (book 2 of the "Passover Trilogy"), Warner Books (New York, NY), 1984.
Lord of the Dance (book 3 of the "Passover Trilogy"), Warner Books (New York, NY), 1987.
Love Song, Warner Books (New York, NY), 1988.
All about Women, Tor (New York, NY), 1989.
The Search for Maggie Ward, Warner Books (New York, NY), 1991.
The Cardinal Virtues, Warner Books (New York, NY), 1991.
An Occasion of Sin, Jove (New York, NY), 1992.
Wages of Sin, Putnam (New York, NY), 1992.
Fall from Grace, Putnam (New York, NY), 1993.
Angel Light: An Old-Fashioned Love Story, Forge (New York, NY), 1995.
A Midwinter's Tale, Tom Doherty Associates, 1998.
Younger than Springtime, Forge (New York, NY), 1999.
A Christmas Wedding, Forge (New York, NY), 2000.
September Song, Forge (New York, NY), 2001.
Second Spring: A Love Story, Forge (New York, NY), 2003.

Golden Years, Forge (New York, NY), 2004.
The Priestly Sins, Forge (New York, NY), 2004.
The Senator and the Preist, Forge (New York, NY), 2006.

"FATHER 'BLACKIE' RYAN" MYSTERY NOVELS

Virgin and Martyr, Warner Books (New York, NY), 1985.
Happy Are the Meek, Warner Books (New York, NY), 1985.
Happy Are Those Who Thirst for Justice, Mysterious Press, 1987.
Rite of Spring, Warner Books (New York, NY), 1987.
Happy Are the Clean of Heart, Warner Books (New York, NY), 1988.
St. Valentine's Night, Warner Books (New York, NY), 1989.
Happy Are the Merciful, Jove (New York, NY), 1992.
Happy Are the Peacemakers, Jove (New York, NY), 1993.
Happy Are the Poor in Spirit, Jove (New York, NY), 1994.
Happy Are Those Who Mourn, Jove (New York, NY), 1995.
White Smoke: A Novel about the Next Papal Conclave, Forge (New York, NY), 1996.
The Bishop and the Missing L Train, Forge (New York, NY), 2000.
The Bishop and the Beggar Girl of St. Germain, Forge (New York, NY), 2001.
The Bishop in the West Wing, Forge (New York, NY), 2002.
The Bishop Goes to the University, Forge (New York, NY), 2003.
The Bishop in the Old Neighborhood, Tom Doherty Associates (New York, NY), 2005.

SCIENCE FICTION NOVELS

Angels of September, G.K. Hall, 1986.
God Game, Warner Books (New York, NY), 1986.
The Final Planet, Warner Books (New York, NY), 1987.
Angel Fire, Random House (New York, NY), 1988.

"NUALA MCGRAIL" NOVELS

Irish Gold, Forge (New York, NY), 1994.
Irish Lace, Forge (New York, NY), 1996.

Irish Mist, Tom Doherty Associates (New York, NY), 1999.

Irish Eyes, Forge (New York, NY), 2000.

Irish Love, Forge (New York, NY), 2001.

Irish Stew, Forge (New York, NY), 2002.

Irish Whiskey, Forge (New York, NY), 2005.

Irish Cream, Forge (New York, NY), 2005.

Irish Crystal, Forge (New York, NY), 2006.

OTHER

Come Blow Your Mind with Me (essays), Doubleday (New York, NY), 1971.

(With J.N. Kotre) *The Best of Times, the Worst of Times* (biography), Nelson Hall, 1978.

Women I've Met (poetry), Sheed (London, England), 1979.

A Piece of My Mind . . . on Just about Everything (selection of newspaper columns), Doubleday (New York, NY), 1983.

Confessions of a Parish Priest: An Autobiography, Simon & Schuster (New York, NY), 1986.

An Andrew Greeley Reader (essays), edited by John Sprague, Thomas More Press, 1987.

Andrew Greeley's Chicago, Contemporary Books, 1989.

(Author of introduction) John Appel, *Pat-Riots to Patriots: American Irish in Caricature and Comic Art,* Michigan State University Museum, 1990.

Andrew Greeley (autobiography), Tor (New York, NY), 1990.

"The Crooked Lines of God," in *Authors of Their Own Lives: Intellectual Autobiographies, by Twenty American Sociologists,* edited by Bennett M. Berger, University of California Press, 1990.

(Editor, with Michael Cassutt) *Sacred Visions* (science fiction anthology), Tor (New York, NY), 1991.

An Epidemic of Joy: Stories in the Spirit of Jesus, ACTA Publications (Chicago, IL), 1999.

Furthermore: Memories of a Parish Priest, Tom Doherty Associates (New York, NY), 1999.

(With Jacob Neusner and Mary Greeley Durkin) *Virtues and Vices: Stories of the Moral Life,* Westminster John Knox Press (Louisville, KY), 1999.

(Editor) *Emerald Magic: Great Tales of Irish Fantasy,* Tor Books (New York, NY), 2004.

Also author of *Star Bright, Summer at the Lake, The Bishop and the Three Kings, Contract with an Angel,* and *I Hope You're Listening, God.*

Also author of forwards to Janet Fredericks's *From the Principal's Desk,* P. Lang, 1991; Jason Berry's *Lead Us Not into Temptation: Catholic Priests and the Sexual Abuse of Children,* Doubleday (New York, NY), 1992; George A. Hillery's *The Monastery: A Study in Freedom, Love, and Community,* Praeger, 1992; and Mary E. Andereck's *Ethnic Awareness and the School: An Ethnographic Study,* Sage, 1992.

Author of a weekly column that appears in the *Chicago Sun-Times* and other newspapers. Contributor to *America,* the *National Catholic Reporter,* the *New York Times,* and *Commonweal.* Contributor of "Incidence and Impact of Childhood Sexual Abuse," to *Bad Pastors: Clergy Misconduct in Modern America,* edited by Anson Shupe, William A. Stacey, and Susan E. Darnell, New York University Press, 2000.

SIDELIGHTS: Andrew M. Greeley is, according to a *Time* writer, "a Roman Catholic priest, a sociologist, a theologian, a weekly columnist, the author of [numerous] books, and a celibate sex expert. He is an informational machine gun who can fire off an article on Jesus to the *New York Times Magazine,* on ethnic groups to the *Antioch Review,* and on war to *Dissent.*" *Time* reported that Greeley's friend, psychologist-priest Eugene Kennedy, called him "obsessive, compulsive, a workaholic . . . . He's a natural resource. He should be protected under an ecological act." While dividing his time between the National Opinion Research Center at the University of Chicago, where he has been involved in sociological research since 1961, and the University of Arizona, where he holds a professorship, Greeley has also published scores of books and hundreds of popular and scholarly articles, making him one of the nation's leading authorities on the sociology of religion.

The adjective "controversial" arises often in articles on Greeley and in reviews of his many books. Much of the controversy surrounding Greeley stems from the difficulty critics have experienced in trying to label him. As another *Time* reporter explained: "On practically any topic, Greeley manages to strike some readers as outrageously unfair and others as eminently fair, as left wing and right wing, as wise and wrong-headed." Greeley advocates a great many changes within the Catholic church, including the ordination of women, liberalized policies on birth control and divorce, and a more democratic process for selecting popes, cardinals, and bishops; as a result, he is often at odds with church leaders. On the other hand, he feels that priests are most effective in serving the people when they remain celibate and that the church has taken the correct stand on abortion; he is, therefore, open to criticism from his more liberal colleagues. He maintains, the *Time* writer continued, that "the present leadership of the church is morally, intellectually, and religiously bankrupt" and has referred to the hierarchy as "mitred pinheads." At the same time, he feels no affinity for the more radical element within the church and has said of activist Jesuit Daniel Berrigan, "As a political strategist, he's a great poet."

Greeley has further fueled the fires of controversy by writing more than a dozen bestselling mystery, fantasy, and science fiction novels, often filled with corruption, murder, and lurid sex. Because many of these novels— such as *The Cardinal Sins* and *Thy Brother's Wife* —feature priests and other members of the clergy as principle characters, they are regarded by critics as a forum in which Greeley can air the church's dirty laundry. Other critics have simply dismissed him as a pulp writer. Greeley wrote in *Contemporary Authors Autobiography Series (CAAS)*: "I became in the minds of many the renegade priest who wrote 'steamy' novels to make money." Furthermore, he has been ostracized from the Archdiocese of Chicago, refused a parish, and treated as a "non-person" by the Catholic church. (He related in *CAAS:* "When I tried to pledge a million dollars from my book royalties for the inner-city Catholic schools, [Chicago's] Cardinal Bernardin bluntly turned down the pledge without giving a reason—arguably the first time in history the Catholic Church has turned down money from anyone.")

Despite his marginal status within the church, Greeley still considers himself a man of the cloth first. "I am not a novelist or a sociologist or a writer or any of those things, not primarily, not essentially, not in the core of my being," he told *CAAS*. "I'm a priest who happens to do these other things as a way of being a priest . . . . I will never leave the priesthood. If ecclesiastical authorities try to throw me out—a serious danger in these days of Thermidor against the Vatican Council—I won't go." As to his novels, and their subject matter, he explained in the *New York Times Magazine* that he attempts in his fiction to address those religious issues closest to him: "Stories have always been the best way to talk about religion because stories appeal to the emotions and the whole personality and not just to the mind."

As a young man in Catholic school, Greeley was enthralled by the works of such Catholic poets and novelists as G.K. Chesterton and Evelyn Waugh. "It seemed to me that fiction was a brilliant way of passing on religion," he recalled in *CAAS*. "I thought that it must be challenging and rewarding to write 'Catholic fiction,' even if I never expected to do it myself." Still, within a

few years Greeley was contributing articles and essays to Catholic magazines and conferences; the first of these were written pseudonymously, but later he grew bold enough to use his own name. In 1958 an editor at the Catholic publishers Sheed and Ward offered to expand two of Greeley's articles into a book titled *The Church and the Suburbs*. He wrote in *CAAS:* "This was a big step, much bigger, it would turn out, than I had expected. For a priest to set a word on paper in those days was a dangerous move (it still is). To write a book was to cut oneself off from most of the rest of the priesthood."

Though *The Church and the Suburbs* was, in the author's own words, "not exactly a best-seller," it awakened in Greeley a desire not only to express his controversial viewpoints, but to express them in print. Within twenty-five years he would produce more than sixty works of religious and sociological study. "It would be many years [after the publication of *The Church and the Suburbs*] before I would think of myself as a writer," he told *CAAS*, "but in fact the writer in me was out of the box and would not go back into it ever again."

Greeley's writings have covered myriad topics, many of which deal with the role of religion in modern life. His subjects have included ethnicity, religious education, church politics, secular politics, the family, death and dying, vocations, history, and the future. His opinions in most of these areas have proven controversial to some extent, but when he tackles the subject of sex— particularly as it relates to religion today—he stirs up more than the usual amount of critical commentary. A good example is his book *Sexual Intimacy,* which the *Time* writer called "a priest's enthusiastic endorsement of inventive marital sex play," and which J. W. Gartland of *Library Journal* recommended to Catholics who "seek a 'sexier' sexual relationship with their spouse and need supportive religious sanctions." In a much-quoted chapter titled "How to Be Sexy," Greeley portrays a wife greeting her husband "wearing only panties and a martini pitcher—or maybe only the martini pitcher." According to the *Time* critic, "One right-wing Catholic columnist declared that even discussing the book would be an occasion of sin." But, Greeley explained to Pamela Porvaznik in an interview for the *Detroit News Sunday Magazine,* "a vigorous sexual life is one of the biggest problems confronting married couples. How can people grow in intimacy? How can they consistently reassure themselves and each other of their own worth? These are real issues, and it's time the Church put them into perspective."

In a review of *Sexual Intimacy* for *America,* T.F. Driver wrote: "Whatever scholarship may lie behind the book's judgments has been carefully (or do I mean carelessly) hidden. Though the book contains precious little theological reflection, it is based, I think, on an erroneous theological assumption namely, that the God we have known all along as Yahweh is the same who presides over the modern sexual revolution. It sounds to me like the old game of baptizing everything in sight." However, Charles Dollen of *Best Sellers* called it "by far one of the best books on marriage and sexuality that has been published in many, many years . . . . [Greeley's] style is witty, charming and far above average. But it is the content that sets this book apart. He has some vital insights into what sex and sexuality are all about."

One of Greeley's best-known nonfiction works is *The Making of the Popes, 1978: The Politics of Intrigue in the Vatican*. In this book he details the series of startling events that took place in Rome beginning in the summer of 1978: the death of Pope Paul VI in July; the subsequent election of John Paul I, who died after only thirty-three days in office; and the election of John Paul II, the first non-Italian pope since 1522. The book is particularly noteworthy for its inclusion of little-known "inside information" on the process of electing a new pope, much of it supplied by an informant that Greeley called "Deep Purple." The title of the book and the use of stylistic devices such as a diary format are intentionally reminiscent of Theodore H. White's *Making of the President* books, reinforcing Greeley's thesis that papal elections have all of the mystery, the jockeying for power, and the behind-the-scenes intrigue of an American presidential election. Several reviewers, including R. A. Schroth of the *New York Times Book Review,* noted that Greeley's choice of the name "Deep Purple" for his unnamed source suggests that "he clearly identifies with Woodward and Bernstein." Thus, although the author sees himself as a journalist covering what is, essentially, a political event, he still leaves himself the option of injecting personal comments (as White is known to do) on the various candidates, the election process, and the diverse political powers that subtly influence the voting. "The White model works pretty well," wrote Robert Blair Kaiser of the *New York Times,* "freeing the author to present an account of [the] doings in Rome, which, for all its ambiguous partisanship, tells us more about the election of two popes (and the future of the church) than less knowing reporters ever could."

Greeley's partisanship leads him to offer in *The Making of the Popes* the opinion that the church did not need another leader like Paul VI, "a grim, stern, pessimistic, solemn-faced pope who did not appeal to the world as a man who is really possessed by the 'good news' he claims to be teaching." He would prefer, Kaiser said, "a hopeful holy man who smiles," a man "whose faith makes him happy and whose hope makes him joyful." Greeley was satisfied with the choice of John Paul I and just as happy with his successor, John Paul II, but his approval of the cardinals' choices has not altered his view of papal elections. He told Linda Witt of *People:* "The cardinals are a closed group of men who have spent their whole lives strictly in ecclesiastical activities. Their average age is over sixty, and they are extremely cautious and conservative. In many cases they are totally out of touch with the world. There were between thirty and thirty-five cardinals—about one-third of those voting—who had no notion of what was going on, and who drifted from candidate to candidate depending on who seemed likely to win." Asked what kind of election process he would prefer, Greeley replied: "In the early church, the Pope and all the bishops were elected by the people of their diocese. The cardinals would go into St. Peter's and pick a man and bring him out. If the faithful applauded, he was the Pope. If they booed, the cardinals went back inside and tried again. I'm not suggesting we revert to that, but I would like to see a gradual sharing of power with the rest of the church." J.J. Hughes of *America,* while expressing a few misgivings about Greeley's reportage, concluded that "the book is a remarkable achievement. We are fools, and guilty fools, if we dismiss it as unworthy of serious consideration."

Though the research Greeley conducts at Chicago's National Opinion Research Center is not officially opposed by the Catholic church, each of Greeley's many sociological and religious studies inevitably sparks at least some discussion among church leaders; on more than one occasion, this discussion has turned quickly to open hostility toward the author. "My colleagues and I soon became accustomed to the pattern of reaction to our work," he related in *CAAS.* "First of all it would be distorted, ridiculed, rejected. The attacks would never touch the work itself (with which no competent scholar has ever found serious fault) but would rather concentrate on my character and personality and on distortions of what the research actually reported. Then, sometimes in a year or two, certainly in five years, our findings would be accepted as what everyone knew to be true, rarely with credit to those who originally reported it." Even liberal Catholics, such as the editors of *Commonweal,* have railed against Greeley's research, accusing him of aspiring to bishophood. "I was astonished at the hostility of Catholic 'liberals,'" he continued in *CAAS.* "In their world . . . there was no such thing as objective evidence if it seemed to go against their biases. To disagree with them on the basis of evidence was grounds for character assassination."

The gap between Greeley and the rest of the Catholic Church was further widened in 1981 with the publication of *The Cardinal Sins.* Though not his first work of fiction, *The Cardinal Sins* was attacked by church officials for its unflattering portrayal of Cardinal Patrick Donahue, a fictional character who swiftly ascends to the top of Chicago's religious hierarchy despite his penchant for brutal sex. The church accused Greeley of using this character to slander the late John Cardinal Cody, then Archbishop of Chicago and a longtime rival of Greeley's. These accusations are not unsubstantiated: *The Cardinal Sins*'s Patrick Donahue funnels church funds to his mistress sister-in-law in South America; at the time of the novel's publication, coincidentally, Cardinal Cody was under investigation for allegedly channeling close to one million dollars to a female companion who also happened to be his step-cousin. Greeley denied any connection between the fictional cardinal and Chicago's Archbishop. "Patrick Donahue is a much better bishop than Cody and a much better human being [than Cardinal Cody]," he explained in the *New York Times.*

Greeley produced several additional novels in the 1990s. *Fall from Grace* centers on Irish Catholic clergy and laity in Chicago and their involvement in several scandals, mainly a priest's alleged pedophilia and an aspiring political candidate's secret homosexuality and spousal abuse. Though reflecting actual events in contemporary Chicago, Greeley noted in the introduction that the novel "was drafted before the explosion of the pedophile crisis in the Archdiocese." In *Irish Gold* an American commodities broker embarks for Dublin to investigate mysterious circumstances surrounding his grandparents' emigration to Chicago in 1922. There he falls for a beautiful Trinity College student who translates his grandmother's diaries, leading to the discovery that his grandparents knew who murdered a prominent Free Irish patriot during the period of the "Troubles" in Ireland. Mary Ellen Elsbernd praised Greeley's "piquant characters" and "delightful Irish mystery" in a *Library Journal* review.

In *White Smoke: A Novel about the Next Papal Conclave,* reminiscent of his exposé *The Making of Popes,* Greeley reintroduces the character Father "Blackie" Ryan to address the contentious and often vicious politics behind the selection of a new pontiff. Upon the death of the incumbent pope, Father Blackie leaves Chicago for Rome with Cardinal Cronin to lobby for the election of a more liberal successor. Their cause is aided by a *New York Times* reporter and his ex-wife, a CNN correspondent, who implicate the Vatican in an investment scandal. A *Publishers Weekly* reviewer con-

cluded, "Greeley knows his material *and* his opinions, and sets both into delicious spins here."

Greeley has also written several mystery novels featuring an Irish-American folksinger, Nuala McGrail, and her husband, Dermont Coyne. Gifted with second sight, McGrail is drawn into such mysteries as the 1898 sinking of a passenger ship on Lake Michigan and the 1927 assassination of Irish rebel Michael Collins. Reviewing *Irish Mist* for *Booklist,* Margaret Flanagan called McGrail "a delightfully fey and unconventional sleuth" and rated *Irish Mist* a "supremely entertaining mystery-romance."

Greeley continued his "Nuala McGrail" series with *Irish Cream* and *Irish Crystal. Booklist* reviewer Flanagan called *Irish Cream* "irresistibly predictable" and noted that it contains "an intriguing historical whodunit that adds a little more substance." *Irish Crystal,* which is the ninth novel in the series, is "cute," according to a *Publishers Weekly* reviewer. The same reviewer commented, "the shifts in Irish dialects, Dermot's internal asides and the document extracts can confuse the uninitiated." In addition, a *Kirkus Reviews* critic agreed by stating that the book is "for the faithful only. For the rest, Irish treacle."

Generally speaking, Greeley's novels have not received much critical praise. Christine B. Vogel, writing in the *Washington Post Book World,* described them as "distinctly unscholarly and unpriestly," bearing "dubious literary merit." *America*'s Sean O'Faolain observed that the author is "all too visible" in his novels, "constantly manipulating both character and plot and infusing everybody, most notably the women, with his own often silly romantic notions." The novels' protagonists are, according to Elaine Kendall, writing in the *Los Angeles Times Book Review,* "so tormented by temptations of the flesh that a questioning reader wonders whatever made them take the vow of celibacy in the first place." And *New York Times Book Review* contributor Sheila Paulos proclaimed: "Andrew M. Greeley may be a great priest, a great sociologist, even a great fellow. But . . . a great novelist he is not." However, if not a great novelist, Greeley is undeniably a popular one. His novels consistently reach the bestseller lists and linger there for weeks or months. Even his critics have admitted, at times, to his novels' appeal. "To give credit where it's due," *Washington Post Book World* reviewer Maude McDaniel wrote, "anybody who reads Andrew Greeley's fiction gets involved." Webster Schott supported this claim in the *New York Times Book Review:* "He is never dull, he spins wondrous romances and he has an admirable ideal for what his church should become." Toronto *Globe and Mail* critic John Doyle attributed the author's popularity to the mystique of the clergy: "Greeley's novels have all been bestsellers because they help satisfy a natural need to know about the private lives of powerful, celibate men. Ecclesiastical power is as much an aphrodisiac as any other type." Abigail McCarthy of the *Chicago Tribune* offered a similar opinion, noting Greeley's ability to combine "an apparently inside view of Catholic Church politics" with "a judicious mixture of money and clinically detailed sex."

"In recent years," Greeley told *CAAS,* "critical writers have begun to understand the themes of my fiction and to attribute considerable value to the books." However, this has had little impact on the Catholic church's determination to treat him as a peripheral member; although Greeley has since made peace with Chicago's Cardinal Bernardin, his "celebrity" status keeps him outside the fold. It is this continuing marginality that is hardest for Greeley to endure. He once told a *CA* interviewer: "I have to say in fairness to the Catholic hierarchy that, off the record and privately, many of them are very friendly and encouraging . . . . The thing I find hard in the church . . . is the criticism from other priests who define me as a success because I have published a lot of books, do a lot of traveling, and get my name in the paper. Their resentment is, first of all, a big surprise, and it is also very hard to bear."

In 1994 Greeley published *Sacraments of Love: A Prayer Journal,* containing the author's private meditations recorded between September, 1991, and December, 1992. Greeley reports daily activities and shares his own struggles with mortality, public personae, conflicting demands as priest and novelist, church reform and scandals, friendships, and most importantly his relationship with God, whom he addresses as "My Love." According to *Kirkus Reviews,* the book represents "the journal of an exceptionally active man whose life, or so he prays, is 'possessed by love.'" A *Publishers Weekly* reviewer noted that Greeley's avowed "relationship with Spirit is indeed intimate and accessible."

Greeley has no plans to stop writing novels; rather, he defends both his fiction and nonfiction writing as portraying the church and clergy as real people. "I'm saying here's my church, made up of human beings with all the weaknesses and frailties and yet with the capacity to transcend those limitations and to produce great people, great art, great mysticism and great missionaries," Greeley explained in the *New York Times.* "If it shocks people to hear a priest say we're not perfect,

then it's high time they be disabused of wrong notions about us." As for his reputation as a greedy author of "steamy" novels, he contended in *CAAS:* "The books were not 'steamy' (and research on the readers indicates that they don't think so) and I gave most of the money away . . . . My stories of God's love and the presence of Grace in the universe were vilified and denounced without being understood and often without being read (many of the bishops who complained had only read passages torn out of context) . . . . The objections seemed to be that (1) a priest ought not to know anything about sex and (2) a priest ought not to write novels that millions of people read. But there is nothing wrong with sex. And a priest would not 'know' about sex only if he were not human."

Greeley examined his own sense of aesthetics, and that of millions of others, in his book *The Catholic Imagination.* In it, he put forth the idea that those raised in the Catholic faith—even if they later abandon the practice of that faith—have a unique way of seeing the world, one that is filled with enchantment and an expectation of the miraculous. "As a sociologist of religion, Greeley claims that there is a correspondence between the works of Catholic high art and the sensibilities of ordinary Catholics," explained Leo D. Lefebure in *Christian Century.* "He presents the central arguement of his essay as sociological rather than theological, grounded in studies of the opinions and practices of Catholics and Protestants in ten North Atlantic nations . . . . Greeley repeatedly protests that he is not expressing a preference for being Catholic rather than Protestant (or Hindu or Buddhist). Nonetheless, his own enchantment with the enchanted world of the Catholic imagination comes through clearly." The author asserts that Catholics are more likely to enjoy and patronize the arts, and even that they are likely to have more imaginative, enjoyable sexual relations than non- Catholics. His "central arguement is quite persuasive," decided Lefebure, "and his perspectives are often thought-provoking."

Priests: A Calling in Crisis and *The Priestly Sins,* both published in 2004, examine the sexual abuse crisis of the clergy, one from the viewpoint of sociology, the other fictionally. In the *National Catholic Reporter* Paul Philibert wrote that *Priests: A Calling in Crisis* "is the prophetic outcry of a public intellectual who wants to weigh in on the significance of the scandal with empirically based interpretations of its impact for the future." The protagonist of *The Priestly Sins* is "tall, handsome, blond, broad-shouldered, slow-moving, right thinking, straightly lusty Father Herman Hugo Hoffman, Ph.D., witness to the brutal rape of an altar boy by a priest now dead of AIDS," a *Kirkus Reviews* critic noted. A *Publishers Weekly* reviewer commented that it "makes its valuable point without resorting to unnecessary violence or cheap and easy shock effects."

Greeley once said: "I never courted controversy, but I also never walked away from it." That willingness to create and confront controversy, Jacob Neusner claimed in *America,* makes Greeley exactly what the Catholic Church has needed: a catalyst. "He has defined the issues, set forth the propositions for analysis and argument and brought public discourse to the public at large . . . . He has taught us what it means to be religious in the United States in our time." Neusner concluded: "Had Greeley not lived and done his work, I may fairly claim that we religious people in the United States—Christians and Jews alike—should understand ourselves less perspicaciously than we do."

BIOGRAPHICAL AND CRITICAL SOURCES:

BOOKS

Becker, Allienne R., *The Divine and Human Comedy of Andrew M. Greeley,* foreword by Andrew M. Greeley, Greenwood Press (New York, NY), 2000.

Contemporary Authors Autobiography Series, Volume 7, Gale (Detroit, MI), 1988.

Contemporary Literary Criticism, Volume 28, Gale (Detroit, MI), 1984.

Harrison, Elizabeth, *Andrew M. Greeley: An Annotated Bibliography,* Scarecrow Press (Metuchen, NJ), 1994.

The Incarnate Imagination: Essays in Theology, the Arts, and Social Sciences in Honor of Andrew Greeley: A Festschrift, edited by Ingrid H. Shafer, Bowling Green State University Popular Press, 1988.

Shafer, Ingrid, *The Womanliness of God: Andrew Greeley's Romances of Renewal,* Loyola University Press, 1986.

Shafer, Ingrid, editor, *Andrew Greeley's World: A Collection of Critical Essays, 1986-1988,* Warner Books (New York, NY), 1989.

PERIODICALS

America, February 10, 1968, p. 196; March 2, 1968, p. 297; May 4, 1968, p. 617; September 11, 1971, p. 153; November 20, 1971, p. 438; October 7, 1972, p. 270; December 8, 1973; November 30, 1974, p. 352; April 26, 1975, p. 326; May 15, 1976, p. 425; November 13, 1976, p. 326; April 9, 1977; May 26, 1979; September 15, 1979, p. 117; June 4, 1982, p. 342; October 22, 1983, p. 236; October 4, 1986, p. 170; May 13, 1989, p. 459; May 12, 1990, p. 481; June 16, 1990, p. 611; August 25, 1990, p. 113; June 1, 1991, p. 604; August 14, 1992, p. 18; April 8, 2000, Paul Wilkes, review of *A Sense of the Sacred,* p. 31.

Best Sellers, November 15, 1973.

Booklist, January 1, 1993, p. 771; September 1, 1997, review of *Star Bright,* p. 7; March 15, 1998, review of *Irish Whiskey,* p. 1205; April 1, 1998, review of *Contract with an Angel,* p. 1277; January 1, 1999, Margaret Flanagan, review of *Irish Mist;* August 19, 1999, Mary Ellen Quinn, review of *Younger than Springtime,* p. 1986; October 15, 1999, Ray Olson, review of *Furthermore!: Memories of a Parish Priest,* p. 394; February 15, 2000, Mary Carroll, review of *Irish Eyes;* March 1, 2000, Margaret Flanagan, review of *The Catholic Imagination,* p. 1174; July, 2000, Margaret Flanagan, review of *The Bishop and the Missing L Train,* p. 2012; September 1, 2000, Kathleen Hughes, review of *A Christmas Wedding,* p. 7; May 15, 2001, Kathleen Hughes, review of *The Bishop and the Beggar Girl of St. Germain,* p. 1707; August, 2001, Kathleen Hughes, review of *September Song,* p. 2086; February 15, 2005, Margaret Flanagan, review of *Irish Cream,* p. 1064; December 15, 2005, Margaret Flanagan, review of *The Bishop in the Old Neighborhood,* p. 68.

Chicago Tribune, March 3, 1985; August 22, 1989.

Chicago Tribune Book World, May 24, 1981; May 2, 1982; June 26, 1983; November 25, 1984; August 31, 1986.

Christian Century, February 20, 1985, p. 196; September 30, 1987, p. 836; April 18, 1990, p. 410; March 20, 1991, p. 345; October 18, 2000, Leo D. Lefebure, review of *The Catholic Imagination,* p. 1051.

Christian Literature World, June, 1998, review of *I Hope You're Listening, God,* p. 44.

Commonweal, December 14, 1973; June 18, 1976; August 31, 1979; July 17, 1987, pp. 412-417; January 23, 1988, pp. 63-66; May 18, 1990, p. 323; December 7, 1990, p. 727; August 14, 1992, pp. 18-21; May 5, 2000, James T. Fisher, review of *The Catholic Imagination,* p. 20.

Detroit News, September 7, 1980; May 20, 1984; February 23, 1986.

Detroit News Sunday Magazine, February 2, 1975.

Economist, April 7, 1990, p. 102.

Globe and Mail (Toronto, Ontario, Canada), March 2, 1985; August 20, 1988; July 13, 1991, p. C6.

Kirkus Reviews, December 15, 1992, p. 1524; December 1, 1993, p. 1504; September 15, 1994, p. 1230; April 1, 1996, p. 467; August 1, 1997, review of *Star Bright,* p. 1135; December 15, 1997, review of *Irish Whiskey,* p. 1792; April 15, 1998, review of *Contract with an Angel,* p. 515; September 15, 1998, review of *A Midwinter's Tale,* p. 1310; February 1, 2004, review of *The Priestly Sins,* p. 100; January 1, 2005, review of *Irish Cream,* p. 23; August 15, 2005, review of *The Bishop in the Old Neighborhood,* p. 885; December 15, 2005, review of *Irish Crystal,* p. 1302.

Kliatt, September, 1998, review of audio version of *Star Bright,* p. 64; January, 1999, review of audio version of *Contract with an Angel,* p. 42.

Library Journal, November 15, 1973; January, 1994, p. 126; November 1, 1994, p. 110; May 15, 1996, p. 84; December, 1997, review of *Irish Whiskey,* p. 152; September 15, 1998, review of *A Midwinter's Tale,* p. 112; November 1, 1998, review of *The Bishop and the Three Kings,* p. 127; November 15, 1999, Leroy Hommerding, review of *Furthermore!: Memories of a Parish Priest,* p. 73; February 15, 2000, David I. Fulton, review of *The Catholic Imagination,* p. 170.

Los Angeles Times, May 6, 1982.

Los Angeles Times Book Review, March 28, 1982; September 4, 1983, p. 6; December 9, 1984, p. 16; April 7, 1985, p. 4; March 16, 1986, p. 4; September 14, 1986, p. 3; February 15, 1987, p. 4; April 30, 1989, p. 6; April 15, 1990, p. 8; September 16, 1990, p. 10; April 28, 1991, p. 14; March 14, 1993, p. 7.

National Catholic Reporter, January 15, 1988, p. 7; March 4, 1988, p. 9; March 19, 1999, John L. Allen, Jr., "Still Telling Stories of Sin, Sex and Redemption," p. 14; June 18, 2004, Paul Philibert, "Debunking Stereotypes about Priestly Life," review of *Priests: A Calling in Crisis,* p. 21.

National Review, April 15, 1977; February 22, 1985, p. 42; December 5, 1986, p. 48; April 16, 1990, p. 51; December 5, 1994, p. 77.

New Republic, December 17, 1984, p. 35; September 24, 1990, p. 33.

Newsweek, July 30, 1990, p. 46.

New York Review of Books, March 4, 1976.

New York Times, March 13, 1972; March 6, 1977; September 21, 1979; March 22, 1981; October 31, 1985; March 24, 1993, p. B2.

New York Times Book Review, June 24, 1979; July 26, 1981; April 11, 1982; July 3, 1983, p. 8; January 6, 1985, p. 18; March 10, 1985, p. 13; September 29, 1985, p. 46; March 30, 1986, p. 10; September 14, 1986, p. 14; September 21, 1986, p. 31; February 8, 1987, p. 31; July 31, 1988, p. 32; August 14, 1988, p. 16; January 22, 1989, p. 23; September 17, 1989, p. 24; January 7, 1990, p. 18; April 22, 1990, p. 9; September 2, 1990, p. 9; December 30, 1990, p. 14; June 23, 1991, p. 28; June 30, 1991, p. 20; October 6, 1991, p. 32.

New York Times Magazine, May 6, 1984, p. 34.

People, July 9, 1979; May 3, 1993, p. 36.

Publishers Weekly, April 10, 1987, p. 78; December 14, 1992, p. 38; February 14, 1994, p. 65; October 17, 1994, p. 65; April 29, 1996, p. 50; May 19, 1997, review of *Summer at the Lake,* p. 65; September 1, 1997, review of *Star Bright,* p. 96; October 20, 1997, review of *The Bishop at Sea,* p. 73; December 8, 1997, review of *Irish Whiskey,* p. 57; August 3, 1998, review of *A Midwinter's Tale,* p. 71; February 15, 1999, review of *Irish Mist,* p. 90; August 30, 1999, review *Younger than Springtime,* p. 53; November 29, 1999, review of *Furthermore: Memories of a Parish Priest,* p. 67; March 6, 2000, review of *The Catholic Imagination,* p. 104; March 27, 2000, Heidi Schlumpf, review of *The Catholic Imagination,* p. S22; May 22, 2000, review of *The Bishop and the Missing L Train,* p. 72; October 2, 2000, review of *A Christmas Wedding,* p. 55; January 1, 2001, review of *Irish Love,* p. 71; July 9, 2001, review of *The Bishop and the Beggar Girl of St. Germain,* p. 47; July 30, 2001, review of *September Song,* p. 58; February 2, 2004, review of *The Priestly Sins,* p. 57; December 19, 2005, review of *Irish Crystal,* p. 45.

Time, January 7, 1974; July 16, 1978; August 10, 1981; July 1, 1991, p. 71.

Times Literary Supplement, August 31, 1984.

Tribune Books (Chicago, IL), January 27, 1991, p. 6.

U.S. Catholic, November, 2000, review of *White Smoke: A Novel about the Next Papal Enclave,* p. 42.

Village Voice, January 29, 1985, p. 47.

Virginia Quarterly Review, winter, 1990, p. 27.

Wall Street Journal, March 4, 1986, p. 28.

Washington Post, June 11, 1981; January 24, 1984; April 6, 1984, p. D8; June 27, 1986; July 21, 1986; August 19, 1986; June 13, 1987; November 16, 1987.

Washington Post Book World, July 10, 1983, pp. 3, 18; February 24, 1985, p. 1; March 24, 1985, p. 6; January 27, 1986; March 11, 1990, p. 13.

West Coast Review of Books, May, 1985, p. 32; number 4, 1986, p. 33; number 6, 1988, p. 44; number 2, 1989, p. 26; number 2, 1991, p. 35.

ONLINE

Andrew Greeley's Web Page, http://www.agreeley.com/ (November 28, 2000).

GREELEY, Andrew Moran
    See GREELEY, Andrew M.

*   *   *

GREEN, Brian
    See CARD, Orson Scott

*   *   *

GREENE, Graham 1904-1991
    (Graham Henry Greene)

PERSONAL: Born October 2, 1904, in Berkhamsted, Hertfordshire, England; died of a blood disease April 3, 1991, in Vevey, Switzerland; son of Charles Henry (a headmaster); married Vivien Dayrell Browning, 1927; children: one son, one daughter. *Education:* Balliol College, Oxford, B.A., 1925. *Religion:* Roman Catholic.

CAREER: Writer. *Times,* London, England, sub-editor, 1926-30; film critic for *Night and Day,* c.1930s; *Spectator,* London, film critic, 1935-39, literary editor, 1940-41; with Foreign Office in Africa, 1941-44; Eyre & Spottiswoode Ltd. (publishers), London, director, 1944-48; Indo-China correspondent for *New Republic,* 1954; Bodley Head (publishers), London, director, 1958-68. Member of Panamanian delegation to Washington for signing of Canal Treaty, 1977.

AWARDS, HONORS: Hawthornden Prize, 1940, for *The Power and the Glory;* James Tait Black Memorial Prize, 1949, for *The Heart of the Matter;* Catholic Literary Award, 1952, for *The End of the Affair;* Boys' Clubs of America Junior Book Award, 1955, for *The Little Horse Bus;* Anotinette Perry ("Tony") Award nomination for best play, 1957, for *The Potting Shed;* Pietzak Award (Poland), 1960; D.Litt., Cambridge University, 1962; Balliol College, Oxford, honorary fellow, 1963; Companion of Honour, 1966; D.Litt., University of Edinburgh, 1967; Shakespeare Prize, 1968; named chevalier, Legion d'Honneur (France), 1969; John Dos Passos Prize, 1980; medal of City of Madrid, 1980; Jerusalem Prize, 1981; Grand Cross of the Order of Vasco Nunez de Balboa (Panama), 1983; named commander, Order of Arts and Letters (France), 1984; named to British Order of Merit, 1986; named to Order of Ruben Dario (Nicaragua), 1987; Royal Society of Literature Prize; honorary doctorate, Moscow State University, 1988.

WRITINGS:

FICTION, EXCEPT AS NOTED

Babbling April (poems), Basil Blackwell (London, England), 1925.
The Man Within, Doubleday (New York, NY), 1929.
The Name of Action, Heinemann (London, England), 1930, Doubleday (New York, NY), 1931.
Rumour at Nightfall, Heinemann (London, England), 1931, Doubleday (New York, NY), 1932.
Orient Express, Doubleday (New York, NY), 1932, published as *Stamboul Train,* Heinemann (London, England), 1932.
It's a Battlefield, Doubleday (New York, NY), 1934, with new introduction by author, Heinemann (London, England), 1970.
The Basement Room, and Other Stories, Cresset (London, England), 1935, title story revised as "The Fallen Idol" and published with *The Third Man* (also see below), Heinemann (London, England), 1950.
England Made Me, Doubleday (New York, NY), 1935, published as *The Shipwrecked,* Viking (New York, NY), 1953, reprinted under original title, with new introduction by author, Heinemann (London, England), 1970.
The Bear Fell Free, Grayson & Grayson (London, England), 1935.
Journey without Maps (travelogue; also see below), Doubleday (New York, NY), 1936, 2nd edition, Viking (New York, NY), 1961, reprinted, 1992.
This Gun for Hire (also see below), Doubleday (New York, NY), 1936, published as *A Gun for Sale,* Heinemann (London, England), 1936.
Brighton Rock, Viking (New York, NY), 1938, with new introduction by author, Heinemann (London, England), 1970, reprinted, 1981.
The Confidential Agent (also see below), Viking (New York, NY), 1939, with new introduction by author, Heinemann (London, England), 1971.
Another Mexico, Viking (New York, NY), 1939, reprinted, 1982, published as *The Lawless Roads* (also see below), Longmans, Green (London, England), 1939.
The Labyrinthine Ways, Viking (New York, NY), 1940, published as *The Power and the Glory,* Heinemann (London, England), 1940, Viking, 1946, with new introduction by author, Heinemann, 1971, reprinted, Penguin (New York, NY), 2003.
British Dramatists (nonfiction), Collins (London, England), 1942, reprinted, Folcroft (Folcroft, PA), 1979.

The Ministry of Fear (also see below), Viking (New York, NY), 1943.

Nineteen Stories, Heinemann (London, England), 1947, Viking (New York, NY), 1949, revised and expanded as *Twenty-one Stories,* Heinemann, 1955, Viking (New York, NY), 1962.

The Heart of the Matter, Viking (New York, NY), 1948, with new introduction by author, Heinemann (London, England), 1971, reprinted, Penguin (New York, NY), 1999.

The Third Man (also see below), Viking (New York, NY), 1950, reprinted, 1983.

The Lost Childhood, and Other Essays, Eyre & Spottiswoode (London, England), 1951, Viking (New York, NY), 1952.

The End of the Affair, Viking (New York, NY), 1951, reprinted, Penguin (New York, NY), 1991.

The Quiet American, Heinemann (London, England), 1955, Viking (New York, NY), 1982, reprinted, Penguin (New York, NY), 2002.

Loser Takes All, Heinemann (London, England), 1955, Viking (New York, NY), 1957.

Our Man in Havana (also see below), Viking (New York, NY), 1958, with new introduction by author, Heinemann (London, England), 1970.

A Burnt-out Case, Viking (New York, NY), 1961.

In Search of a Character: Two African Journals, Bodley Head (London, England), 1961, Viking (New York, NY), 1962.

Introductions to Three Novels, Norstedt (Stockholm, Sweden), 1962.

The Destructors, and Other Stories, Eihosha (Tokyo, Japan), 1962.

A Sense of Reality, Viking (New York, NY), 1963.

The Comedians, Viking (New York, NY), 1966.

(With Dorothy Craigie) *Victorian Detective Fiction: A Catalogue of the Collection,* Bodley Head (London, England), 1966.

May We Borrow Your Husband?, and Other Comedies of the Sexual Life, Viking (New York, NY), 1967.

Collected Essays, Viking (New York, NY), 1969.

Travels with My Aunt, Viking (New York, NY), 1969.

(Author of introduction) Al Burt and Bernard Diederich, *Papa Doc,* McGraw (New York, NY), 1969.

A Sort of Life (autobiography), Simon & Schuster (New York, NY), 1971.

Graham Greene on Film: Collected Film Criticism, 1935-1940, Simon & Schuster (New York, NY), 1972, published as *The Pleasure Dome,* Secker & Warburg (London, England), 1972.

The Portable Graham Greene (includes *The Heart of the Matter,* with a new chapter; *The Third Man;* and sections from eight other novels, six short stories, nine critical essays, and ten public statements), Viking (New York, NY), 1972, updated and revised, Penguin (New York, NY), 1994.

The Honorary Consul, Simon & Schuster (New York, NY), 1973, reprinted, 2000.

Collected Stories, Viking (New York, NY), 1973.

Lord Rochester's Monkey, Being the Life of John Wilmot, Second Earl of Rochester, Viking (New York, NY), 1974.

The Human Factor, Simon & Schuster (New York, NY), 1978, reprinted, Knopf (New York, NY), 1992.

Doctor Fischer of Geneva; or, The Bomb Party, Simon & Schuster (New York, NY), 1980.

Ways of Escape, Simon & Schuster (New York, NY), 1981.

Monsignor Quixote, Simon & Schuster (New York, NY), 1982.

J'accuse: The Dark Side of Nice, Bodley Head (London, England), 1982.

Getting to Know the General: The Story of an Involvement, Simon & Schuster (New York, NY), 1984.

The Tenth Man, Bodley Head (London, England), 1985.

(Author of preface) *Night and Day* (journalism), edited by Christopher Hawtree, Chatto & Windus (London, England), 1985.

Collected Short Stories, Penguin (London, England), 1988.

The Captain and the Enemy, Viking (New York, NY), 1988.

Yours, etc.: Letters to the Press, 1945-1989, edited by Hawtree, Reinhardt, 1989.

Reflections (essays), Viking (New York, NY), 1990.

The Graham Greene Film Reader: Reviews, Essays, Interviews, and Film Stories, Applause Theatre Book Publishers (New York, NY), 1994.

A World of My Own: A Dream Diary, Reinhardt (New York, NY), 1994.

The Last Word and Other Stories, Penguin (New York, NY), 1999.

Contributor to books, including *Twenty-four Short Stories,* Cresset (London, England), 1939; *Alfred Hitchcock's Fireside Book of Suspense,* Simon & Schuster, 1947; and *Why Do I Write?,* Percival Marshall, 1948. Contributor to *Esquire, Commonweal, Spectator, Playboy, Saturday Evening Post, New Statesman, Atlantic, London Mercury, New Republic, America, Life,* and other publications.

PLAYS

(With Terrence Rattigan) *Brighton Rock* (screenplay), 1947.

The Fallen Idol (screenplay; based on Greene's short story "The Basement Room"), 1949.

(With Carol Reed) *The Third Man: A Film* (screenplay; based on Greene's novel; produced 1950), Simon & Schuster (New York, NY), 1968.

The Living Room (two-act; produced in London, England, 1953), Heinemann (London, England), 1953, Viking (New York, NY), 1957.

The Potting Shed (three-act; produced in New York, NY, 1957; produced in London, England, 1958), Viking (New York, NY), 1957.

The Complaisant Lover (produced in London, England, 1959), Heinemann (London, England), 1959, Viking (New York, NY), 1961.

Our Man in Havana (screenplay; based on Greene's novel), 1960.

Three Plays, Mercury Books, 1961.

Carving a Statue (two-act; produced in London, England, 1964; produced in New York, NY, 1968), Bodley Head (London, England), 1964.

The Comedians (screenplay; based on Greene's novel), 1967.

The Return of A.J. Raffles (three-act comedy; based on characters from E.W. Hornung's *Amateur Cracksman;* produced in London, England, 1975), Simon & Schuster (New York, NY), 1976.

Yes and No [and] *For Whom the Bell Chimes* (comedies; produced in Leicester, England, 1980), Bodley Head (London, England), 1983.

Collected Plays, Vintage (London, England), 2002.

OMNIBUS VOLUMES

Three: This Gun for Hire; The Confidential Agent; The Ministry of Fear, Viking (New York, NY), 1952.

The Travel Books: Journey without Maps [and] *The Lawless Roads,* Heinemann (London, England), 1963.

Triple Pursuit: A Graham Greene Omnibus (includes *This Gun for Hire, The Third Man,* and *Our Man in Havana*), Viking (New York, NY), 1971.

Works also published in additional collections.

FOR CHILDREN

This Little Fire Engine, Parrish (London, England), 1950, published as *The Little Red Fire Engine,* Lothrop, Lee & Shepard (New York, NY), 1952.

The Little Horse Bus, Parrish (London, England), 1952, Lothrop, Lee & Shepard (New York, NY), 1954.

The Little Steamroller, Lothrop, Lee & Shepard (New York, NY), 1955.

The Little Train, Parrish (London, England), 1957, Lothrop, Lee & Shepard (New York, NY), 1958.

The End of the Party, Creative Education (Mankato, MN), 1993.

EDITOR

The Old School (essays), J. Cape (London, England), 1934.

H.H. Munro, *The Best of Saki,* 2nd edition, Lane (London, England), 1952.

(With brother, Hugh Greene) *The Spy's Bedside Book,* British Book Service (London, England), 1957.

(And author of introduction) Marjorie Bowen, *The Viper of Milan,* Bodley Head (London, England), 1960.

The Bodley Head Ford Madox Ford, 2 volumes, Bodley Head (London, England), 1962.

(And author of epilogue) *An Impossible Woman: The Memories of Dottoressa, Moor of Capri,* Viking (New York, NY), 1976.

(With brother, Hugh Greene) *Victorian Villainies,* Viking (New York, NY), 1984.

ADAPTATIONS: Screenplays based on Greene's books and stories include *Orient Express,* 1934; *This Gun for Hire,* 1942; *The Ministry of Fear,* 1944; *The Confidential Agent,* 1945; *The Smugglers,* 1948; *The Heart of the Matter,* 1954; *The End of the Affair,* 1955, 2000; *Loser Takes All,* 1957; *The Quiet American,* 1958, 2002; *Across the Bridge,* 1958; *The Power and the Glory,* 1962; *The Living Room,* 1969; *The Shipwrecked,* 1970; *May We Borrow Your Husband?,* 1970; *The End of the Affair,* 1971, 2000; *Travels with My Aunt,* 1973; *England Made Me,* 1973; *A Burned-out Case,* 1973; *The Human Factor,* screenplay by Tom Stoppard, directed by Otto Preminger, 1980; *Beyond the Limit,* 1983; and *Strike It Rich* (based on the novella *Loser Takes All*), 1990. Several of Greene's novels have been adapted as audiobooks.

SIDELIGHTS: Graham Greene is among the most widely read of all major English novelists of the twentieth century. Yet Greene's popular success—which David Lodge in *Graham Greene* held partly responsible for a "certain academic hostility" toward the British author—came neither quickly nor easily. Of Greene's initial five novels, the first two were never published, and two others, *The Name of Action* and *Rumour at Nightfall,* sold very poorly. In his first autobiographical volume, *A Sort of Life,* Greene lamented that, in his earliest novels, he did not know "how to convey physical excitement," the ability to write a "simple scene of action . . . was quite beyond my power to render exciting." Even as late as 1944, Greene confessed in his introduction to *The Tenth Man,* he had "no confidence" in sustaining his literary career.

Greene's string of literary failures drove him to write *Stamboul Train,* a thriller he hoped would appeal to film producers. The novel, filmed two years later as *Orient Express,* is recognized by critics as Greene's coming-of-age work. Writing in a taut, realistic manner, Greene sets *Stamboul Train* in contemporary Europe; gathers a train load of plausibly motivated characters; and sends them on their journey. Retaining such stock melodramatic devices as cloak-and-dagger intrigue, flight and pursuit, hair-breadth escapes, and a breakneck narrative pace, Greene shifts the focus away from the conventional hero—the hunter—and onto the villain and/or ostensible villain. What emerges is less a formula than a set of literary hardware that Greene would use throughout the rest of his career, not just to produce further entertainments, but to help give outward excitement to his more morally centered, more philosophical novels.

Stamboul Train is the first of several thrillers Greene referred to as "entertainments"—so named to distinguish them from more serious novels. In his next two such entertainments, *A Gun for Sale*—published in the United States as *This Gun for Hire*—and *The Confidential Agent,* Greene incorporates elements of detective and spy fiction, respectively. He also injects significant doses of melodrama, detection, and espionage into his more serious novels *Brighton Rock, The Power and the Glory*—published in the United States as *The Labyrinthine Ways*—*The Heart of the Matter, The End of the Affair, The Quiet American, A Burnt-out Case, The Comedians, The Honorary Consul,* and *The Human Factor.* Indeed, so greatly did Greene's entertainments influence his other novels that, after 1958, he dropped the entertainments label.

Intrigue and contemporary politics are key elements of Greene's entertainments, and in at least two of his thrillers Greene eulogizes the tranquility of European life prior to World War I. "It was all so peaceful," Dr. Hasselbacher muses about Germany in *Our Man in Havana,* "in those days. . . . Until the war came." And Arthur Rowe, dreaming in *The Ministry of Fear,* notes that his mother, who "had died before the first great war, . . . could [not] have imagined" the blitz on Lon-

don of the second. He tells his mother that the sweet Georgian twilight—"Tea on the lawn, evensong, croquet, the old ladies calling, the gentle unmalicious gossip, the gardener trundling the wheelbarrow full of leaves and grass"—"isn't real life any more." Rowe continues: "I'm hiding underground, and up above the Germans are methodically smashing London to bits all round me. . . . It sounds like a thriller, doesn't it, but the thrillers are like life . . . spies, and murders, and violence . . . that's real life."

Suffering, seediness, and sin are also recurring motifs that typify Greene's work. When, in one of the very early novels Greene later disowned, a character moans, "I suffer, therefore I am," he defines both the plight and the habit of mind of many protagonists who would follow him. In *A Burnt-out Case* Dr. Colin sees suffering as a humanizing force: "Sometimes I think that the search for suffering and the remembrance of suffering are the only means we have to put ourselves in touch with the whole human condition." Colin also adds what none of Greene's other characters would dispute: "suffering is not so hard to find."

Greene's characters inhabit a world in which lasting love, according to the narrator of the story "May We Borrow Your Husband?," means the acceptance of "every disappointment, every failure, every betrayal." By Greene's twenty-second novel, *Doctor Fischer of Geneva; or, The Bomb Party,* suffering has become a sufficient cause for having a soul. When the narrator of *Doctor Fischer of Geneva* tells his wife, "If souls exist you certainly have one," and she asks "Why?," he replies, "You've suffered." This statement may well sound masochistic—"Pain is part of joy," the whiskey priest asserts in *The Power and the Glory,* "pain is a part of pleasure." This ideal is behind the saintly Sarah's striking statement in *The End of the Affair:* "How good You [God] are. You might have killed us with happiness, but You let us be with You in pain."

According to Kenneth Allott and Miriam Farris Allot in their *The Art of Graham Greene,* "seediness . . . seems to Greene the most honest representation of the nature of things." One recurring character embodying this trait in Greene's fiction, for example, appears as early as the opening chapters of *The Man Within.* From the "shambling," bored priest in that novel who sniffles his way through the burial service for Elizabeth's guardian; to the wheezing old priest smelling of eucalyptus at the end of *Brighton Rock;* to the whiskey priest in *The Power and the Glory;* to the broken-down Father Callifer in *The Potting Shed* with his "stubbly worn face," "bloodshot eyes," and "dirty wisp of a Roman collar," Greene anoints a small cathedral of seedy priests. In his critical study *Graham Greene,* Francis Wyndham summarized an objection whose validity each reader must judge for himself: "Some find [Greene's] continual emphasis on squalor and seediness . . . overdone."

Also typical of Greene's characters is their predilection for sin. Greene "seems to have been born with a belief in Original Sin," John Atkins suggested in his *Graham Greene,* and certainly the author's characters have been tainted by it. Raven in *A Gun for Sale* is but one of many Greene protagonists who "had been marked from birth." Another is the whiskey priest's illegitimate daughter in *The Power and the Glory:* "The world was in her heart already, like the small spot of decay in the fruit." Likewise, D. the "confidential agent": "Give me time," he thinks, "and I shall infect anything." Atkins "can almost hear [Greene's] teeth gnashing at those who omitted to sleep with someone else's wife or husband . . . it is difficult to read Greene's fiction without sensing a contempt for sinlessness." Atkins concludes: Greene's "concern with sin has become so intense he finds a life without sin to be devoid of meaning." But George Orwell's witty complaint about Greene in *The Collected Essays, Journalism, and Letters of George Orwell* is the best known. Labeling his subject the leader of the "cult of the sanctified sinner," Orwell declares that Greene shows a Catholic's "snobbishness" about sin: "there is something *distingue* in being damned; Hell is a sort of high-class nightclub, entry to which is reserved for Catholics only."

Although Greene's conversion to Catholicism has generated an intense critical debate, only five or six of his more than twenty novels actually focus on the faith: *Brighton Rock, The Power and the Glory, The Heart of the Matter*—the so-called "Catholic trilogy"—*The End of the Affair, Monsignor Quixote,* and, perhaps, *A Burnt-out Case.* In exploring Catholicism in his fiction, Greene eschewed propaganda. He noted in *Ways of Escape,* his second volume of autobiography, that he was "not a Catholic writer but a writer who happens to be a Catholic." That is, Catholicism does not provide a dogma he wishes to promulgate in his novels but instead supplies a framework within which he can measure the human situation. "I'm not a religious man," Greene once told *Catholic World* interviewer Gene D. Phillips, "though it interests me. Religion is important, as atomic science is."

Despite the attention paid his Catholicism, Greene explained to Phillips that religion occupied only "one period" of his writing career: "My period of Catholic nov-

els was preceded and followed by political novels." Greene's first successful novels were written in the 1930s, a decade G.S. Fraser in *The Modern Writer and His World* maintained "forced the writer's attention back on the intractable public world around him." In *Ways of Escape* Greene defines the mid-1930s as "clouded by the Depression in England . . . and by the rise of Hitler. It was impossible in those days not to be committed, and it is hard to recall details of ones' private life as the enormous battlefield was prepared around us." Greene's earlier political novels are set in Europe, usually in England, but more recent political novels move from one Third-World trouble spot to another even as they explore the author's characteristic themes: commitment, betrayal, corruption, sin, suffering, and the nature of human sexuality, often against a backdrop of Catholicism.

In both religion and politics, Greene opposed the dogmatic and the doctrinaire, sided against those who sacrifice the corrupt but living human spirit for a grand but bloodless thesis. For example, in *Monsignor Quixote,* however much the good-natured priest and the equally good-natured communist politician quibble, both reject the intellectual rigidities of those whose commitment to their respective causes is ideologically absolute. Politics and religion, then, are closely related. *Monsignor Quixote* is at once political and religious in nature; and, while nobody denies that *The Power and the Glory* is one of Greene's Catholic works, it can also be studied as a political novel.

Not only a novelist, Greene wrote in more than a dozen other genres, including novellas, short stories, plays, radio plays, screenplays, essays, memoirs, biographies, autobiographies, travel books, poetry, and children's literature. Although Greene made his mark primarily in the novel form, his stories, plays, and nonfiction prose have all attracted critical consideration.

About the short story genre, Greene wrote in *Ways of Escape:* "I remain in this field a novelist who happens to have written short stories." Unfailingly modest in appraising his own literary efforts, Greene said in a introductory note to his *Nineteen Stories,* "I am only too conscious of the defects of these stories. . . . The short story is an exacting form which I have not properly practised." He dismissed his stories as "merely . . . the by-products of a novelist's career." However true this evaluation might be for *Nineteen Stories,* and however correct Lodge might be in calling the short story a "form in which [Greene] has never excelled," some of Greene's stories do merit reading. Even Atkins, who in

Graham Greene also found that the "short story is not one of Greene's successful forms," conceded that the four newer works in the expanded collection *Twenty-one Stories* "show an improvement" over those in the earlier volume. And in *Ways of Escape* Greene registered contentment with "The Destructors," "A Chance for Mr. Lever," "Under the Garden," and "Cheap in August": "I have never written anything better than" these works, he declared.

Less distinguished than his fiction, Greene's dramas provided him with, if nothing else, diversion. He recorded—indeed, almost bragged about—his lifelong attempt to escape depression and boredom, starting with Russian roulette as a teenager and culminating in a career as a restless, wandering novelist who, when his mainstay got boring, tried to escape by shifting genres. Writing plays, he declared in *Ways of Escape,* "offered me novelty, an escape from the everyday:" "I needed a rest from novels."

As with Greene's short fiction, critics have not been overly enthusiastic about the novelist's plays, although *The Complaisant Lover* attracted some applause. In *Faith and Fiction,* Philip Stratford called it an "outstanding and original achievement," while to Atkins it ranks as "vital as many of the Restoration comedies." Of Greene's plays overall, Smith pointed to a "curious lack . . . of memorable characters," a quality not shared with Greene's novels. On the whole most critics shared Lodge's assessment that "it does not seem likely that Greene will add a significant chapter to the history of British drama." Despite this dismissal, Greene's plays—which include *The Living Room, The Potting Shed,* and *Carving a Statue*—remained in print decades after their first mid-twentieth-century productions.

Greene's nonfiction prose, though not widely analyzed, has been more appreciated. Metaphorical and speculative, his travel books are distinctly literary, and record spiritual no less than physical journeys. Greene's first travel book, *Journey without Maps,* is representative of his work in the genre. Believing Africa to be "not a particular place, but a shape, . . . that of the human heart," Greene imagined his actual trip as, simultaneously, a descent, with Sigmund Freud as guide, into the collective soul of humanity in a quest of "those ancestral threads which still exist in our unconscious minds." Greene finds in Africa "associations with a personal and racial childhood;" and when in the end he returns to civilization, the conclusion he draws about his experience affirms the "lost childhood" theme about which he so frequently wrote: "This journey, if it had done nothing else, had reinforced a sense of disappointment with what man had made out of the primitive, what he had made out of childhood."

The essay collection *Reflections,* which brings together various nonfiction pieces such as film reviews, travel essays, and examinations of communism, Catholicism, and major literary figures, as well as *A World of My Own: A Dream Diary,* which presents dreams Greene recorded throughout his life, provide readers with greater insight onto the novelist. Malcolm Bradbury, writing in the *New York Times Book Review,* concluded of the latter volume: "It's not surprising that the strange tales told here—and they do emerge as tales, not as random notes on disconnected, chaotic events—are as powerful as his fiction, and interweave with it. Greene's *World of My Own*—a carefully organized and edited selection from his dream diaries, which he made and introduced himself, just before his death—is equally the world of his novels, his distinctive, adventurous life as an author, his enigmatic character as a man"

Not surprisingly, commentators have frequently turn to Greene's nonfiction pieces to aid their understanding of his fiction; "Fresh and stimulating," as Wyndham noted, the author's essays throw "much light on [Greene's] own work as a novelist." But the essays are worth reading in their own right. Atkins contended that "When Greene's criticism is gathered together we realize how very good it is," that Greene "has unerring good judgment in all literary matters. He can always be relied upon to see through falsity and to detect the ring of truth in others." Atkins went so far as to maintain that Greene's "criticism is much more free of fault than his fiction."

From 1935 to 1940 Greene wrote film reviews for the *Spectator* and in 1937 performed the same service for *Night and Day.* These reviews have been collected in *The Graham Greene Film Reader,* which also includes reviews of film books, interviews, lectures, letters, scripts he wrote for short documentaries, film stories, and film treatments. "What provides pleasure in these musings on the movies," noted Pat Dowell in the *Washington Post Book World,* "is the glittering nuggets of a prose stylist who writes of the young Bette Davis's 'corrupt and phosphorescent prettiness' or pens a hilariously exasperated description of the unintentionally magnificent surrealism of 'The Garden of Allah.'" Writing in the *New Republic* Stanley Kauffmann commented that, "Overall, this assemblage of Greene's criticism is a boon."

In addition, more than twenty of his own novels and stories have been filmed, some with his own screenplays. Furthermore, Greene wrote original screenplays, including the 1949 classic *The Third Man*. It is, then, understandable that to the *Paris Review* interviewers he called himself a "film man."

Greene's cinematic prose method is evident in his first successful novel, *Stamboul Train*. Creating this work admittedly with one eye on the film camera, Greene intersperses passages of extended narrative with brief cuts from one character or group of characters to another. This device both sustains the novel's full-throttle pace by generating a sense of motion—appropriate to a story whose center is a speeding express train—and, with great economy, evokes the stew of humanity thrown together at a railway station or on a train. The union of film and fiction is even pondered in *Stamboul Train* by the character Q.C. Savory, who seems to describe Greene's own ambition to incorporate aspects of film into his fiction: "One thing the films had taught the eye, Savory thought, the beauty of the landscape in motion, how a church tower moved behind and above the trees, how it dipped and soared with the uneven human stride, the loveliness of a chimney rising towards a cloud and sinking behind the further cowls. That sense of movement must be conveyed in prose."

Although acclaimed for his work in various genres, it is as a novelist that Greene remains most respected. Indeed, some critics have cited him as the leading English novelist of his generation; in Lodge's view, among the British novelists who were Greene's contemporaries, "it is difficult to find his equal." Smith's evaluation—that Greene navigated "one of the more remarkable careers in twentieth-century fiction"—may seem by some to be understated when considered alongside the judgment of a *Times Literary Supplement* reviewer that Greene follows in the tradition of writers as Henry James, Joseph Conrad, and Ford Madox Ford. But it was, perhaps, Wyndham who came closest to explaining Greene's sustained popularity when he stated, simply, that "everything [Greene wrote] is readable."

BIOGRAPHICAL AND CRITICAL SOURCES:

BOOKS

Allain, Marie-Françoise, *The Other Man: Conversations with Graham Greene*, Bodley Head (London, England), 1983.

Allen, Walter, *The Modern Novel*, Dutton (New York, NY), 1965.

Allott, Kenneth, and Miriam Farris Allott, *The Art of Graham Greene*, Hamish Hamilton (London, England), 1951, Russell & Russell, 1965.

Atkins, John, *Graham Greene*, Roy, 1958.

Bestsellers 89, Issue 4, Thomson Gale (Detroit, MI), 1989.

Boardman, Gwenn R., *Graham Greene: The Aesthetics of Exploration*, University of Florida Press, 1971.

Cassis, A. F., *Graham Greene: An Annotated Bibliography of Criticism*, Scarecrow (Metuchen, NJ), 1981.

Contemporary Literary Criticism, Thomson Gale (Detroit, MI), Volume 1, 1973, Volume 3, 1975, Volume 6, 1976, Volume 9, 1978, Volume 14, 1980, Volume 18, 1981, Volume 27, 1984, Volume 37, 1986, Volume 70, 1992, Volume 72, 1992.

DeVitis, L. A., *Graham Greene*, Twayne (New York, NY), 1964.

Dictionary of Literary Biography, Thomson Gale (Detroit, MI), Volume 13: *British Dramatists since World War II*, 1982, Volume 15: *British Novelists, 1930-1959*, 1983, Volume 77: *British Mystery Writers, 1920-1939*, 1989.

Dictionary of Literary Biography Yearbook: 1985, Thomson Gale (Detroit, MI), 1986.

Duraan, Leopoldo, *Graham Greene: An Intimate Portrait by His Closest Friend and Confidant*, Harper (San Francisco, CA), 1994.

Evans, R. O., editor, *Graham Greene: Some Critical Considerations*, University of Kentucky Press (Lexington, KY), 1963.

Falk, Quentin, *Travels in Greeneland: The Cinema of Graham Greene*, Quartet (London, England), 1984.

Fraser, G. S., *The Modern Writer and His World*, Verschoyle (London, England), 1953.

Gordon, Hayim, *Fighting Evil: Unsung Heroes in the Novels of Graham Greene*, Greenwood Press (New York, NY), 1997.

Greene, Graham, *Orient Express*, Doubleday (New York, NY), 1932, published as *Stamboul Train*, Heinemann (London, England), 1932.

Greene, Graham, *Journey without Maps*, Doubleday (New York, NY), 1936, 2nd edition, Viking (New York, NY), 1961, reprinted, 1992.

Greene, Graham, *The Confidential Agent*, Viking (New York, NY), 1939, with new introduction by author, Heinemann (London, England), 1971.

Greene, Graham, *The Labyrinthine Ways*, Viking (New York, NY), 1940, published as *The Power and the Glory*, Heinemann (London, England), 1940, Viking, 1946, with new introduction by author, Heinemann, 1971, reprinted, Penguin (New York, NY), 2003.

Greene, Graham, *The Ministry of Fear*, Viking (New York, NY), 1943.

Greene, Graham, *Nineteen Stories,* Heinemann (London, England), 1947, Viking (New York, NY), 1949, revised and expanded as *Twenty-one Stories,* Heinemann, 1955, Viking (New York, NY), 1962.

Greene, Graham, *The End of the Affair,* Viking (New York, NY), 1951, reprinted, Penguin (New York, NY), 1991.

Greene, Graham, *The Potting Shed* (three-act; produced in New York, NY, 1957; produced in London, England, 1958), Viking (New York, NY), 1957.

Greene, Graham, *Our Man in Havana,* Viking (New York, NY), 1958, with new introduction by author, Heinemann (London, England), 1970.

Greene, Graham, *A Burnt-out Case,* Viking (New York, NY), 1961.

Greene, Graham, *May We Borrow Your Husband?, and Other Comedies of the Sexual Life,* Viking (New York, NY), 1967.

Greene, Graham, *A Sort of Life,* Simon & Schuster (New York, NY), 1971.

Greene, Graham, *Doctor Fischer of Geneva; or, The Bomb Party,* Simon & Schuster (New York, NY), 1980.

Greene, Graham, *Ways of Escape,* Simon & Schuster (New York, NY), 1981.

Greene, Graham, with A.F. Cassis, *Graham Greene: Man of Paradox,* Loyola University Press (Chicago, IL), 1994.

Hill, William Thomas, *The Search for Dwelling and Its Relationship to Journeying and Wandering in the Novels of Graham Greene,* International Scholars Publication, 1998.

Hoskins, Robert, *Graham Greene: An Approach to the Novels,* Garland (New York, NY), 1998.

Hynes, Samuel, editor, *Graham Greene: A Collection of Critical Essays,* Prentice-Hall (New York, NY), 1973.

Kermode, Frank, *Puzzles and Epiphanies,* Chilmark (New York, NY), 1962.

Kunkel, Francis L., *The Labyrinthine Ways of Graham Greene,* Sheed (London, England), 1959.

Living Writers, Sylvan Press, 1947.

Lodge, David, *Graham Greene,* Columbia University Press (New York, NY), 1966.

Malamet, Elliott, *The World Remade: Graham Greene and the Art of Detection,* P. Lang (New York, NY), 1998.

Mauriac, François, *Great Men,* Rockliff, 1952.

Mesnet, Maire-Beatrice, *Graham Greene and the Heart of the Matter,* Cresset (London, England), 1954.

Miller, Robert H., *Graham Greene: A Descriptive Catalog,* University of Kentucky Press (Lexington, KY), 1979.

Mueller, Walter R., *The Prophetic Voice in Modern Fiction,* Association Press, 1959.

Newby, P. H., *The Novel: 1945-1950,* Longmans, Green (London, England), 1951.

O'Faolain, Dean, *The Vanishing Hero,* Atlantic Monthly Press (Boston, MA), 1956.

Orwell, George, *The Collected Essays, Journalism, and Letters of George Orwell,* edited by Sonia Orwell and Ian Angus, Harcourt (New York, NY), 1968.

Parkinson, David, editor,*The Graham Greene Film Reader: Reviews, Essays, Interviews, and Film Stories,* Applause Theatre Book Publishers (New York, NY), 1994.

Pendleton, Robert, *Graham Greene's Conradian Masterplot: The Arabesques of Influence,* St. Martin's Press (New York, NY), 1996.

Prescott, Orville, *In My Opinion,* Bobbs-Merrill (Chicago, IL), 1952.

Reed, Henry, *The Novel since 1939,* Longmans, Green (London, England), 1947.

Rostenne, Paul, *Graham Greene: Temoin des temps tragiques,* Juilliard, 1949.

Shelden, Michael, *Graham Greene: The Enemy Within,* Random House (New York, NY), 1994.

Sherry, Norman, *The Life of Graham Greene,* Viking (New York, NY), Volume 1: *1904-1939,* 1989, Volume 2: *1939-1955,* 1995.

Stratford, Philip, *Faith and Fiction,* University of Notre Dame Press, 1964.

Vann, Jerry Donn, *Graham Greene: A Checklist of Criticism,* University of Kentucky Press (Lexington, KY), 1970.

Watts, Cedric Thomas, *A Preface to Greene,* Longman (London, England), 1997.

West, W. J., *The Quest for Graham Greene,* St. Martin's Press (New York, NY), 1998.

Wobbe, R. A., *Graham Greene: A Bibliography and Guide to Research,* Garland (New York, NY), 1979.

Wyndham, Francis, *Graham Greene,* Longmans, Green (London, England), 1955.

Zabel, Morton Dauwen, *Craft and Character in Modern Fiction,* Viking (New York, NY), 1957.

PERIODICALS

America, January 25, 1941.

Atlantic, July-August, 2002, Peter Godman, "Graham Greene's Vatican Dossier," p. 84.

Booklist, April 15, 1999, Mary McCay, review of *The Third Man,* p. 1542.

British Heritage, February-March, 2002, Barbara Roisman-Cooper, "Graham Greene: The Man behind the Mask," p. 48.

Catholic World, December, 1954, pp. 172-175; August, 1969, pp. 218-221.

College English, October, 1950, pp. 1-9.

Explicator, spring, 2003, David Robertson, "Greene's 'Jubilee,'" p. 168.

First Things, November, 1999, Robert Royal, "The (Mis)Guided Dreams of Graham Greene," p. 16.

Globe and Mail (Toronto, Ontario, Canada), September 29, 1984.

Kliatt, July, 2002, Janet Julian, review of *The Comedians,* p. 49.

Library Journal, February 1, 1999, p. 138; July, 2001, p. 149; January, 2002, Nancy Pearl, review of *The End of the Affair,* p. 188.

Life, February 4, 1966.

London Magazine, June-July, 1977, pp. 35-45.

Los Angeles Times, September 25, 1980; January 2, 1981; March 20, 1985.

Los Angeles Times Book Review, October 23, 1988; October 23, 1994.

Modern Fiction Studies, autumn, 1957, pp. 249-288.

New Republic, December 5, 1994, p. 30.

New Statesman, November 27, 2000, John Gray, "A Touch of Evil," p. 51; December 3, 2001, Maureen Freely, "On Graham Greene's *The Quiet American,*" p. 55.

New Yorker, April 11, 1994, p. 46.

New York Review of Books, March 3, 1966; June 8, 1995; June 22, 1995; February 13, 2003, Pico Iyer, review of *The Quiet American,* p. 19.

New York Times, February 27, 1978; May 19, 1980; January 18, 1981; September 24, 1982; October 25, 1984; March 4, 1985; June 6, 1985; October 17, 1988; January 17, 1995.

New York Times Book Review, January 23, 1966; January 8, 1995.

Playboy, November, 1994, p. 32.

Renascence, winter, 1999, p. 133; fall, 2002 (special Greene issue).

Smithsonian, June, 2002, Bob Cullen, "Heart of the Matter: Graham Greene's Letters to His Paramour, Catherine Walston, Trace the Hazy Line between Life and Fiction," p. 112.

Southwest Review, summer, 1956, pp. 239-250.

Time, September 20, 1982.

Times (London), September 6, 1984; September 7, 1984; March 14, 1985; February 5, 1990.

Times Literary Supplement, January 27, 1966; March 28, 1980; March 15, 1985.

Washington Post, April 3, 1980; September 20, 1988.

Washington Post Book World, May 18, 1980; October 16, 1988; March 12, 1995.

World Press Review, December, 1981, pp. 31-32; April, 1983, p. 62.

OBITUARIES:

PERIODICALS

Detroit Free Press, April 4, 1991.

* * *

GREENE, Graham Henry
See GREENE, Graham

* * *

GREER, Richard
See SILVERBERG, Robert

* * *

GREGOR, Lee
See POHL, Frederik

* * *

GRISHAM, John 1955-
(Al Hayes)

PERSONAL: Born February 8, 1955, in Jonesboro, AR; son of a construction worker and a homemaker; married Renee Jones; children: Ty, Shea (daughter). *Education:* Mississippi State University, B.S., University of Mississippi, J.D. *Religion:* Baptist.

ADDRESSES: Home—Charlottesville, VA. *Agent*—c/o Doubleday Publicity, 1745 Broadway, New York, NY 10019.

CAREER: Writer and lawyer. Admitted to the Bar of the State of Mississippi, 1981; lawyer in private practice in Southaven, MS, 1981-90. Served in Mississippi House of Representatives, 1984-90.

AWARDS, HONORS: Inducted into Academy of Achievement, 1993.

WRITINGS:

NOVELS

A Time to Kill, Wynwood Press (New York, NY), 1989.
The Firm, Doubleday (New York, NY), 1991.

The Pelican Brief, Doubleday (New York, NY), 1992.
The Client, Doubleday (New York, NY), 1993.
John Grisham (collection), Dell (New York, NY), 1993.
The Chamber, Doubleday (New York, NY), 1994.
The Rainmaker, Doubleday (New York, NY), 1995.
The Runaway Jury, Doubleday (New York, NY), 1996.
The Partner, Doubleday (New York, NY), 1997.
The Street Lawyer, Doubleday (New York, NY), 1998.
The Testament, Doubleday (New York, NY), 1999.
The Brethren, Doubleday (New York, NY), 2000.
A Painted House, Doubleday (New York, NY), 2001.
Skipping Christmas, Doubleday (New York, NY), 2001.
The Summons, Doubleday (New York, NY), 2002.
The King of Torts, Doubleday (New York, NY), 2003.
The Bleachers, Doubleday (New York, NY), 2003.
The Last Juror, Doubleday (New York, NY), 2004.
The Broker, Doubleday (New York, NY), 2005.

Also author of screenplays *The Gingerbread Man* (under pseudonym Al Hayes), and *Mickey.*

ADAPTATIONS: The Firm was adapted as a film, directed by Sydney Pollack and starring Tom Cruise, Gene Hackman, and Jeanne Tripplehorn, Paramount, 1993; *The Pelican Brief* was adapted as a film, directed by Alan J. Pakula and starring Julia Roberts and Denzel Washington, 1994; *The Client* was adapted as a film, directed by Joel Schumacher and starring Susan Sarandon and Tommy Lee Jones, 1994; *The Chamber* was adapted as a film, directed by James Foley and starring Chris O'Donnell and Gene Hackman, 1996; *A Time to Kill* was adapted as a film, directed by Schumacher and starring Matthew McConaughey and Sandra Bullock, 1996; *The Rainmaker* was adapted as a film, directed by Francis Ford Coppola and starring Matt Damon and Claire Danes, 1997; *Runaway Jury* was adapted as a film, directed by Gary Fleder and starring Hackman and Dustin Hoffman, 2003; *Skipping Christmas* was adapted as a film, starring Tim Allen and Jamie Lee Curtis, Columbia, 2004.

SIDELIGHTS: The author of seventeen back-to-back bestsellers, many of which have been turned into blockbuster movies, John Grisham can count his revenues and copies sold of his legal thrillers in the hundreds of millions. With his works translated into more than thirty languages, Grisham was one of the major success stories in publishing during the 1990s. As Malcolm Jones noted in *Newsweek,* Grisham was "the best-selling author" of the decade with his formula of "David and Goliath go to court," and the success of his books has helped to make legal thrillers one of the most popular genres among U.S. readers. Jones further com-

mented, "As part of an elite handful of megaselling authors that includes Stephen King, Danielle Steele, Michael Crichton and Tom Clancy, Grisham has literally taken bookselling to places it's never been before—not just to airport kiosks but to price clubs and . . . online bookselling." Grisham's bestsellerdom even extends to countries with a legal system completely different than that in the United States. "He sells to everyone," Jones continued, "from teens to senior citizens, from lawyers in Biloxi to housewives in Hong Kong."

When Grisham began writing his first novel, he never dreamed he would become one of America's best-selling novelists. Yet the appeal of his legal thrillers such as *The Firm, The Pelican Brief, The Client, The Rainmaker,* and *The Summons,* among others, has been so great that initial hardcover print runs number in the hundreds of thousands and the reading public regularly buys millions of copies. The one-time lawyer now enjoys a celebrity status that few writers will ever know. "We think of ourselves as regular people, I swear we do," Grisham was quoted as saying of himself and his family by Keli Pryor in *Entertainment Weekly.* "But then someone will drive 200 miles and show up on my front porch with books for me to sign. Or an old friend will stop by and want to drink coffee for an hour. It drives me crazy." As he told Jones, "I'm a famous writer in a country where nobody reads."

As a youth, Grisham had no dreams of becoming a writer, although he did like to read. Born in Jonesboro, Arkansas, in 1955, he was the son of a construction-worker father and a homemaker mother. His father traveled extensively in his job, and the Grisham family moved many times. Each time the family took up residence in a new town, Grisham would immediately go to the public library to get a library card. "I was never a bookworm," he maintained in an interview for *Bookreporter.com.* "I remember reading Dr. Seuss, the 'Hardy Boys,' *Emil and the Detectives,* Chip Hilton, and lots of Mark Twain and Dickens." Another constant for Grisham was his love of baseball, something he has retained in adulthood. One way he and his brothers gauged the quality of each new hometown was by inspecting its little-league ballpark.

In 1967 the family moved to a permanent home in Southaven, Mississippi, where Grisham enjoyed greater success in high school athletics than he did in English composition, a subject in which he earned a D grade. After graduation, he enrolled at Northwest Junior College in Senatobia, Mississippi, where he remained for a year, playing baseball for the school team. Transferring to Delta State University in Cleveland, Mississippi, he continued with his baseball career until he realized that he was not going to make it to the big leagues. Transferring to Mississippi State University, Grisham studied accounting with the ambition of eventually becoming a tax attorney. By the time he earned his law degree from the University of Mississippi, however, his interest had shifted to criminal law, and he returned to Southaven to establish a practice in that field.

Although his law practice was successful, Grisham grew restless in his new career. He switched to the more lucrative field of civil law and won many cases, but the sense of personal dissatisfaction remained. Hoping to somehow make a difference in the world, he entered politics with the aim of reforming his state's educational system. Running as a Democrat, he won a post in the state legislature; four years later, he was reelected. After a total of seven years in public office, Grisham became convinced that he would never be able to cut through the red tape of government bureaucracy in his effort to improve Mississippi's educational system, and he resigned his post in 1990.

While working in the legislature, Grisham continued to run his law office. His first book, *A Time to Kill,* was inspired by a scene he saw one day in court when a preadolescent girl testified against her rapist. "I felt everything in those moments," Grisham recalled to Pryor. "Revulsion, total love for that child, hate for that defendant. Everyone in that courtroom wanted a gun to shoot him." Unable to get the story out of his mind, be began to wonder what would happen if the girl's father had killed his daughter's assailant. Grisham disclosed to an interviewer with *People,* "I became obsessed wondering what it would be like if the girl's father killed that rapist and was put on trial. I had to write it down." Soon he had the core of a book dealing with a black father who shoots the white man who raped his daughter. "I never felt such emotion and human drama in my life," he said in the interview.

Writing his first novel, let alone publishing it, was no easy task for Grisham. "Because I have this problem of starting projects and not completing them, my goal for this book was simply to finish it," he revealed to *Publishers Weekly* interviewer Michelle Bearden. "Then I started thinking that it would be nice to have a novel sitting on my desk, something I could point to and say, 'Yeah, I wrote that.' But it didn't consume me. I had way too much going on to make it a top priority. If it happened, it happened." Working sixty- to seventy-hour weeks between his law practice and political duties, Grisham rose at five in the morning to write an hour a day on his first novel, thinking of the activity as a hobby rather than a serious effort at publication.

Finishing the manuscript in 1987, Grisham next had to look for an agent. He was turned down by several before finally receiving a positive response from Jay Garon. Agent and author encountered a similarly difficult time trying to find a publisher; 5,000 copies of the book were finally published by Wynwood Press, and Grisham received a check for 15,000 dollars. He purchased 1,000 copies of the book himself, peddling them at garden-club meetings and libraries and giving many of them away to family and friends. Ironically, *A Time to Kill* is now rated by some commentators as the finest of Grisham's novels. Furthermore, according to Pryor, "Those first editions are now worth 3,900 dollars each," and after being republished, "the novel Grisham . . . couldn't give away has 8.6 million copies in print and has spent eighty weeks on the best-seller lists."

Despite the limited initial success of *A Time to Kill,* Grisham was not discouraged from trying his hand at another novel. The second time around, he decided to follow guidelines set forth in a *Writer's Digest* article for plotting a suspense novel. The result was *The Firm,* the story of a corrupt Memphis-based law firm established by organized crime for purposes of shielding and falsifying crime-family earnings. Recruited to the practice is Mitchell McDeere, a promising Harvard law school graduate who is overwhelmed by the company's apparent extravagance. When his criminal bosses discover that McDeere has been indulging his curiosity, he becomes an instant target of both the firm and the authorities monitoring the firm's activities. When he runs afoul of the ostensible good guys, McDeere finds himself in seemingly endless danger.

Grisham was not as motivated when writing *The Firm* as he had been when composing *A Time to Kill,* but with his wife's encouragement he finished the book. Before he even began trying to sell the manuscript, he learned that someone had acquired a bootlegged copy of it and was willing to give him 600,000 dollars to turn it into a movie script. Within two weeks, Doubleday, one of the many publishers that had previously rejected *A Time to Kill,* offered Grisham a contract.

Upon *The Firm*'s publication, several reviewers argued that Grisham had not attained a high art form, although it was generally conceded that he had put together a compelling thriller. *Los Angeles Times Book Review* critic Charles Champlin wrote that the "character penetration is not deep, but the accelerating tempo of paranoia-driven events is wonderful." Chicago *Tribune Books* reviewer Bill Brashler offered similar praise, proclaiming that *The Firm* reads "like a whirlwind." The novel was listed on the *New York Times* bestseller list for nearly a year and sold approximately ten times as many copies as its predecessor. By the time the film version was released, there were more than seven million copies of *The Firm* in print. This amazing success gave Grisham the means he needed to build his dream house, quit his law practice, and devote himself entirely to writing.

In a mere one hundred days, Grisham wrote another legal thriller, *The Pelican Brief,* which introduces readers to brilliant, beautiful female law student Darby Shaw. When two U.S. Supreme Court justices are murdered, Shaw postulates a theory as to why the crimes were committed. Just telling people about her idea makes her gravely vulnerable to the corrupt law firm responsible for the killings.

In reviewing the book, some critics complained that Grisham follows the premise of *The Firm* too closely, with John Skow writing in his review for *Time* that *The Pelican Brief* "is as close to its predecessor as you can get without running *The Firm* through the office copier." However, Grisham also received praise for creating another exciting story. Frank J. Prial, writing in the *New York Times Book Review,* observed that, despite some flaws in *The Pelican Brief,* Grisham "has an ear for dialogue and is a skillful craftsman." The book enjoyed success comparable to *The Firm,* selling millions of copies.

In just six months, Grisham put together yet another bestseller titled *The Client.* This legal thriller focuses on a young boy who, after learning a sinister secret, turns to a motherly lawyer for protection from both the mob and the FBI. Like *The Firm* and *The Pelican Brief,* the book drew lukewarm reviews but became a bestseller and a major motion picture. During the spring of 1993, after *The Client* came out and *A Time to Kill* was republished, Grisham was in the rare and enviable position of having a book at the top of the hardcover bestseller list and books in the first, second, and third spots on the paperback bestseller list as well.

Grisham acknowledged to an *Entertainment Weekly* interviewer that his second, third, and fourth books are formula-driven. He described his recipe for a bestseller

in the following way: "You throw an innocent person in there and get 'em caught up in a conspiracy and you get 'em out." He also admitted to rushing through the writing of *The Pelican Brief* and *The Client,* resulting in "some damage" to the books' quality. Yet he also complained that the critical community treats popular writers harshly. "I've sold too many books to get good reviews anymore," he told Pryor. "There's a lot of jealousy, because [reviewers] think they can write a good novel or a best-seller and get frustrated when they can't. As a group, I've learned to despise them."

With his fifth novel, Grisham departs from his proven formula and proceeds at a more leisurely pace. Not only did he take a full nine months to write *The Chamber,* a book in which the "good guys" and "bad guys" are not as clearly defined as in his previous efforts, but the book itself, at almost 500 pages, takes time to unravel its story line. The novel is a detailed study of a family's history, an examination of the relationship between lawyer and client, and a description of life on death row. *The Chamber* is "a curiously rich milieu for a Grisham novel," according to *Entertainment Weekly* critic Mark Harris, "and it allows the author to do some of his best writing since [*A Time to Kill.*]" Skow credited Grisham with producing a thought-provoking treatise on the death penalty, and noted in *Time* that *The Chamber* "has the pace and characters of a thriller, but little else to suggest that it was written by the glib and cheeky author of Grisham's legal entertainments . . . . Grisham may not change opinions with this sane, civil book, and he may not even be trying to. What he does ask, very plainly, is an important question: Is this what you want?" A reviewer for the London *Sunday Times* stated that "Grisham may do without poetry, wit and style, and offer only the simplest characterisation. The young liberal lawyer may be colourless and the spooky old prisoner one-dimensional; but there is no doubt that this ex-lawyer knows how to tell a story." While *The Chamber* was less obviously commercial than his previous three books, Grisham had little trouble selling the movie rights for a record fee.

The Rainmaker features a young lawyer, Rudy Baylor, recently graduated from law school, who finds himself desperate for a job when the small firm he had planned to work for is bought out by a large, prestigious Memphis firm that has no use for him. After going to work for Bruiser Stone, a shady lawyer with underworld clients, Baylor finds himself averting an FBI raid on Stone's firm while also trying to pursue a lawsuit brought by a terminally ill leukemia patient against an insurance company that has refused to pay for her treatment. While some reviewers again directed harsh criticism at Grisham for his "pedestrian prose" and "ridiculously implausible" plot—in the words of *New York Times* critic Michiko Kakutani—others praised the novel. Garry Abrams, for instance, writing in the *Los Angeles Times Book Review,* commended the author's "complex plotting," noting: "In his loping, plain prose, Grisham handles all his themes with admirable dexterity and clarity."

Grisham also garnered warm critical comments for *The Runaway Jury,* a novel that details the ability of a few individuals to manipulate a jury in the direction that will bring them the greatest financial reward. Writing in the *New York Times,* Christopher Lehmann-Haupt remarked that Grisham's "prose continues to be clunky, the dialogue merely adequate and the characters as unsubtle as pushpins." But the critic also felt that "the plot's eventual outcome is far more entertainingly unpredictable" than Grisham's previous novels, and he declared that Grisham "for once . . . is telling a story of genuine significance."

Grisham continued his streak of phenomenally popular novels with *The Partner,* about a law-firm partner who fakes his own death and absconds with ninety million dollars. Discussing his less-than-virtuous protagonist, Grisham told Mel Gussow of the *New York Times,* "I wanted to show that with money you can really manipulate the system. You can buy your way out of trouble." *Philadelphia Inquirer* reviewer Robert Drake called *The Partner* "a fine book, wholly satisfying, and a superb example of a masterful storyteller's prowess captured at its peak."

With *Street Lawyer* Grisham once again presents a young lawyer on the fast track who has a life-altering experience. The fast pace and moral stance of the novel attracted a chorus of praise. Reviewing the book in *Entertainment Weekly,* Tom De Haven noted that "success hasn't spoiled John Grisham. Instead of churning out rote legal thrillers, his court reporting keeps getting better." De Haven further noted that Grisham, while lacking the "literary genius" of John Steinbeck, "does share with him the conscience of a social critic and the soul of a preacher." *People* reviewer Cynthia Sanz similarly reported that Grisham "has forsaken some of his usual suspense and fireworks in favor of an unabashedly heart-tugging portrait of homelessness." However, Sanz further noted that the author does not sacrifice his "zippy pacing" to do so. Praise not only appeared in the popular press: "In a powerful story," wrote Jacalyn N. Kolk in the *Florida Bar Journal,* "John Grisham tells it like it is on both sides of the street." Kolk felt that this "entertaining" novel "may stir some of us [lawyers] to pay more attention to the world around us."

The Testament provides another departure from the usual Grisham formula. As a reviewer for *Publishers Weekly* noted, "Grisham confounds expectations by sweeping readers into adventure in the Brazilian wetlands and, more urgently, into a man's search for spiritual renewal." Grisham has firsthand experience of Brazil, having traveled there often and once even helping to build houses there for the poor. His novel eschews the legal wrangling and courtroom suspense his readers have come to expect. Instead, in this tale he proves he "can spin an adventure yarn every bit as well as he can craft a legal thriller," according to *Newsweek* reviewer Jones. A reviewer for *Publishers Weekly* felt that while the storytelling is not "subtle," Grisham's use of the suspense novel format to "explore questions of being and faith puts him squarely in the footsteps of Dickens and Graham Greene." The same reviewer concluded that *The Testament* is "sincere, exciting, and tinged with wonder." Speaking with Jones, Grisham remarked, "The point I was trying to make . . . was that if you spend your life pursuing money and power, you're going to have a pretty sad life."

Lawyers and judges of a much different ilk populate Grisham's eleventh novel, *The Brethren.* Noting that Grisham veers away from his usual David-and-Goliath scenario, a reviewer for *Publishers Weekly* still felt that "all will be captivated by this clever thriller that presents as crisp a cast as he's yet devised, and as grippingly sardonic yet bitingly moral a scenario as he's ever imagined." Writing in *Entertainment Weekly,* De Haven also commented on the novel's cast of ne'er do wells, noting that "if you can get past [Grisham's] creepy misanthropy, he's written a terrifically entertaining story."

With *A Painted House,* initially serialized in *The Oxford American*—a small literary magazine Grisham co-owns—the author does the unpredictable: he presents readers with a book with no lawyers. "It's a highly fictionalized childhood memoir of a month in the life of a seven-year-old kid, who is basically me," Grisham explained to *Entertainment Weekly* writer Benjamin Svetkey. *Book* contributor Liz Seymour called the novel "genre-busting," and "the unsentimental story of a single harvest season in the Arkansas Delta as seen through the eyes of the seven-year-old son and grandson of cotton farmers." Though the tale may be without lawyers, it is not without conflict and incident, including trouble between the migrant workers young Luke Chandler's family brings in for the cotton harvest and a tornado that threatens to destroy the Chandler livelihood. A reviewer for *Publishers Weekly* noted that Grisham's "writing has evolved with nearly every book," and though the "mechanics" might still be visible in *A Painted House,* there are "characters that no reader will forget, prose as clean and strong as any Grisham has yet laid down and a drop-dead evocation of a time and place that mark this novel as a classic slice of Americana."

Some critics differed with these opinions, however. Writing in *Booklist,* Stephanie Zvirin called into question the merits of Grisham's coming-of-age novel: "The measured, descriptive prose is readable . . . and there are some truly tender moments, but this is surface without substance, simply an inadequate effort in a genre that has exploded with quality over the last several years." As usual with a Grisham novel, however, there was a divergence among critical voices. What Zvirin found "inadequate," *Entertainment Weekly* contributor Bruce Fretts described as a "gem of an autobiographical novel." Fretts further commented, "Never let it be said this man doesn't know how to spin a good yarn." In *Time,* Jess Cagle criticized the book's slow pace but concluded that Grisham's "compassion for his characters is infectious, and the book is finally rewarding—a Sunday sermon from a Friday-night storyteller."

With *The Summons,* Grisham returns to his lawyer roots, to thrillers, and also to Ford County, Mississippi, which was the setting for *A Time to Kill.* Reviewing the book in *Entertainment Weekly,* Svetkey found *The Summons* "not all that tough to put down," and with "few shocking surprises." Nonetheless, shortly after publication, *The Summons* topped the list of hardcover best sellers, selling well over 100,000 copies in its first week of publication alone.

Grisham's next three books—*The King of Torts, The Bleachers,* and *The Last Juror*—all attained best-seller status despite mixed reviews. Of the first, a reviewer for the *Yale Law Journal* commented that, while Grisham's approach is "badly hobbled . . . by a cliche-driven plot . . . [and] failure to support his argument with substantive, realistic criticisms," the author's talent for powerful storytelling and a simple thesis "may yet move millions of casual readers to support serious reform of American tort law." Jennifer Reese of *Entertainment Weekly* was highly critical of *The Bleachers,* describing the story as "a sloppy gridiron mess, a thin and flimsy meditation on football and the dubious role it can play in the lives of young men." "Never a terrific stylist," Reese continued, "Grisham doesn't show any flair for character here." A *Publishers Weekly* reviewer called *The Bleachers* a "slight but likable novel," stating: "Many readers will come away having enjoyed the time

spent, but wishing there had been a more sympathetic lead character, more originality, more pages, more story and more depth."

The Last Juror became Grisham's seventeenth book and seventeenth best-seller. Despite its popularity among readers, Rosemary Herbert of the *Boston Herald* warned: "If you expect to be on the edge of your seat while reading John Grisham's latest, think again. The experience is bound to be more like sitting in a jury box. Occasionally, the presentation you'll witness will be riveting. Then again, you've got to listen to a good deal of background material." The story is set in Canton, Mississippi, in the 1970s, and follows aftermath of the rape and murder of a widow that is witnessed by her two young children. Herbert called Grisham "the consummate legal eagle who knows how to pull heartstrings even when the suspense is not thrill-a-minute." Praising *The Last Juror* as Grisham's "best book in years," Sean Daly noted in *People* that the novel quickly bounded to best-seller status.

In 2005, Grisham published *The Broker,* a novel about Joel Blackman, a former powerbroker who has been incarcerated for six years for his role in a billon-dollar deal involving software that controls a satellite spies. The CIA sends Joel to Italy as bait to see who tries to kill him, thus making the determination as to which country has the greatest investment in the software. Bob Minzesheimer, writing for *USA Today,* noted that the novel contains "a fresh approach and strong sense of place." Minzesheimer further commented, "it's Grisham living up to his reputation as a great storyteller." A *Publishers Weekly* reviewer stated that "the novel reads like a contented afterthought to a memorable Italian vacation, with little action or tension." However, Alan M. Dershowitz, writing in *New York Times Book Review,* concluded, "the spy-versus-spy intrigue is well constructed and fast-paced."

In little more than a decade, Grisham realized greater success than most writers enjoy in a lifetime. Despite such success, the former lawyer and politician remained realistic about his limitations and maintained that a time might come when he would walk away from writing just as he previously abandoned both law and politics. In his interview with Bearden in *Publishers Weekly,* he compared writers to athletes and concluded: "There's nothing sadder than a sports figure who continues to play past his prime." However, well into his second decade as a novelist, Grisham seemed far from that point. Book ideas "drop in from all directions," he told Svetkey in *Entertainment Weekly.* "Some gestate for years and some happen in a split second. They'll rattle around in my head for a while, and I'll catch myself mentally piecing it together. How do I suck the reader in, how do I maintain the narrative tension, how do I build up to some kind of exciting end? . . . Some of those will work, some won't."

BIOGRAPHICAL AND CRITICAL SOURCES:

BOOKS

Contemporary Literary Criticism, Volume 84, Gale (Detroit, MI), 1995, pp. 189- 201.

PERIODICALS

Asia Africa Intelligence Wire, March 15, 2004, Ruel S. De Vera, review of *The Last Juror.*

Book, January, 2001, Liz Seymour, "Grisham Gets Serious," pp. 34-36.

Booklist, February 1, 1993, p. 954; September 15, 2000, p. 259; February 1, 2001, Stephanie Zvirin, review of *A Painted House,* p. 1020.

Boston Herald, March 2, 2004, Rosemary Herbert, review of *The Last Juror,* p. 40.

Christianity Today, October 3, 1994, p. 14; August 9, 1999, p. 70.

Christian Science Monitor, March 5, 1993, p. 10.

Detroit News, May 25, 1994, p. 3D.

Entertainment Weekly, April 1, 1994, Keli Pryor, interview with Grisham, pp. 15-20; June 3, 1994, Mark Harris, "Southern Discomfort," p. 48; July 15, 1994, p. 54; July 29, 1994, p. 23; February 13, 1998, Tom De Haven, review of *The Street Lawyer,* pp. 64-65; February 4, 2000, Tom De Haven, "Law of Desire," p 63; February 11, 2000, Benjamin Svetkey, "Making His Case" (interview), pp. 63-64; February 9, 2001, Bruce Fretts, "Above the Law," pp. 68-69; February 15, 2002, Benjamin Svetkey, "Trial and Errors," pp. 60-61; September 12, 2003, Jennifer Reese, review of *The Bleachers* p. 155.

Florida Bar Journal, June, 1998, Jacalyn N. Kolk, review of *The Street Lawyer,* p. 115.

Forbes, August 30, 1993, p. 24; January 8, 2001, p. 218.

Globe & Mail (Toronto, Ontario, Canada), March 30, 1991, p. C6.

Kirkus Reviews, February 1, 2001.

Library Journal, August, 2000, p. 179; March 1, 2001, p. 131; September 1, 2001, p. 258; December, 2001, Samantha J. Gust, review of *Skipping Christmas,* pp. 170-171.

Los Angeles Times, December 25, 2001, p. E4; February 26, 2002, p. E3.

Los Angeles Times Book Review, March 10, 1991, Charles Champlin, "Criminal Pursuits," p. 7; April 5, 1992, p. 6; April 4, 1993, p. 6; May 14, 1995, Garry Abrams, review of *The Rainmaker,* p. 8.

National Review, April 6, 1998, pp. 51-52.

New Republic, August 2, 1993, p. 32; March 14, 1994, p. 32; August 22, 1994, p. 35.

Newsday, March 7, 1993.

New Statesman, June 9, 1995, p. 35.

Newsweek, February 25, 1991, p. 63; March 16, 1992, p. 72; March 15, 1993, pp. 79-81; December 20, 1993, p. 121; February 19, 1999, Malcolm Jones, "Grisham's Gospel," p. 65.

New York, August 1, 1994, pp. 52-53.

New Yorker, August 1, 1994, p. 16.

New York Times, March 5, 1993, p. C29; July 29, 1994, p. B10; April 19, 1995, Michiko Kakutani, review of *The Rainmaker,* pp. B1, B9; April 28, 1995, p. C33; May 23, 1996, Christopher Lehmann-Haupt, review of *The Runaway Jury,* p. C20; March 31, 1997, Mel Gussow, review of *The Partner,* p. B1; February 4, 2002, p. B1; February 5, 2002, p. B7.

New York Times Book Review, March 24, 1991, p. 37; March 15, 1992, Frank J. Prial, "Too Liberal to Live," p. 9; October 18, 1992, p. 33; March 7, 1993, p. 18; December 23, 2001, p. 17; February 24, 2002, p. 13; January 9, 2005, Alan M. Dershowitz, "Pardon Me," p. 18.

People, April 8, 1991, pp. 36-37; March 16, 1992, pp. 43-44; March 15, 1993, pp. 27-28; June 27, 1994, p. 24; August 1, 1994, p. 16; March 2, 1998, Cynthia Sanz, review of *The Street Lawyer,* p. 37; February 12, 2001, p. 41; February 18, 2002, p. 41; February 23, 2004, Sean Daly, review of *The Last Juror,* p. 45.

Philadelphia Inquirer, March 23, 1997, Robert Drake, review of *The Partner.*

Publishers Weekly, February 22, 1993, Michelle Bearden, "*PW* Interviews: John Grisham," pp. 70-71; May 30, 1994, p. 37; May 6, 1996, p. 71; February 10, 1997; February 1, 1999, review of *The Testament,* p. 78; January 10, 2000, p. 18; January 31, 2000, review of *The Brethren,* p. 84; January 22, 2001, review of *A Painted House,* p. 302; October 29, 2001, p. 20; November 5, 2001, review of *Skipping Christmas,* p. 43; February 18, 2002, p. 22; August 18, 2003, review of *The Bleachers,* p. 56; January 10, 2005, review of *The Broker,* p. 39.

Southern Living, August, 1991, p. 58.

Sunday Times (London, England), June 12, 1994, review of *The Chamber,* p. 1.

Time, March 9, 1992, John Skow, "Legal Eagle," p. 70; March 8, 1993, p. 73; June 20, 1994, John Skow, review of *The Chamber,* p. 67; August 1, 1994; February 26, 2001, Jess Cagle, review of *A Painted House,* p. 72.

Tribune Books (Chicago, IL), February 24, 1991, Bill Brashler, review of *The Firm,* p. 6; September 8, 1991, p. 10; February 23, 1992, p. 4; February 28, 1993, p. 7.

USA Today, January 13, 2005, Bob Minzesheimer, "Grisham Takes a Detour to Italy," p. 7D.

Voice Literary Supplement, July-August, 1991, p. 7.

Wall Street Journal, March 12, 1993, p. A6.

Washington Post, January 29, 2002, p. C3.

Yale Law Journal, June, 2003, review of *The King of Torts,* p. 2600.

ONLINE

Bookreporter.com, http://www.bookreporter.com/ (April 8, 2004), "Author Profile: John Grisham."

John Grisham Web Site, http://www.jgrisham.com/ (April 8, 2004).

University of Mississippi Web Site, http://www.olemiss. edu/ (April 8, 2004), "John Grisham."

*   *   *

GRUMBACH, Doris 1918-
(Doris Isaac Grumbach)

PERSONAL: Born July 12, 1918, in New York, NY; daughter of Leonard William and Helen Isaac; married Leonard Grumbach (a professor of physiology), October 15, 1941 (divorced, 1972); companion of Sybil Pike; children: Barbara, Jane, Elizabeth, Kathryn. *Education:* Washington Square College, A.B., 1939; Cornell University, M.A., 1940. *Politics:* Liberal *Religion:* Episcopalian

ADDRESSES: Home—Sargentville, ME. *Agent*—c/o Tim Seldes, Russell & Volkening, 50 West 29th St., New York, NY 10001.

CAREER: Writer. Metro-Goldwyn-Mayer, New York, NY, title writer, 1940-41; *Mademoiselle,* New York, NY, proofreader and copyeditor, 1941-42; Time Inc., associate editor of *Architectural Forum,* 1942-43; Albany Academy for Girls, Albany, NY, English teacher, 1952-55; College of Saint Rose, Albany, instructor, 1955-58, assistant professor, 1958-60, associate profes-

sor, 1960-69, professor of English, 1969-73; *New Republic,* Washington, DC, literary editor, 1973-75; American University, Washington, DC, professor of American literature, 1975-85. Visiting University fellow, Empire State College, 1972-73; adjunct professor of English, University of Maryland, 1974-75. Literary critic; *Morning Edition,* National Public Radio, book reviewer, beginning 1982. Board member for National Book Critics Circle and PEN/Faulkner Award; judge for writing contests. *Military service:* U.S. Navy, Women Accepted for Volunteer Emergency Service, 1941-43.

MEMBER: PEN, American Association of University Professors, Phi Beta Kappa.

AWARDS, HONORS: Lambda Literary Award, Lesbian Biography, 1997, for *Life in a Day;* Whitehead Award for Lifetime Achievement, Publishing Triangle, 2000.

WRITINGS:

NOVELS

The Spoil of the Flowers, Doubleday (New York, NY), 1962.

The Short Throat, the Tender Mouth, Doubleday (New York, NY), 1964.

Chamber Music, Dutton (New York, NY), 1979.

The Missing Person, Putnam (New York, NY), 1981.

The Ladies, Dutton (New York, NY), 1984.

The Magician's Girl, Macmillan (New York, NY), 1987.

The Book of Knowledge: A Novel, Norton (New York, NY), 1995.

NONFICTION

The Company She Kept (biography), Coward (New York, NY), 1967.

Coming into the End Zone (memoir), Norton (New York, NY), 1991.

Extra Innings: A Memoir, Norton (New York, NY), 1993.

Fifty Days of Solitude (memoir), Beacon Press (Boston, MA), 1994.

Life in a Day (nonfiction), Beacon Press (Boston, MA), 1996.

The Presence of Absence: On Prayers and an Epiphany, Beacon Press (Boston, MA), 1998.

The Pleasure of Their Company (memoir), Beacon Press (Boston, MA), 2000.

The author's papers and correspondence are housed at the New York Public Library. Also author of introductions and forewords for books. Contributor to books, including *The Postconcilor Parish,* edited by James O'Gara, Kennedy, 1967, and *Book Reviewing,* edited by Silvia E. Kameran, Writer, Inc. (Boston, MA), 1978. Columnist for *Critic,* 1960-64, and *National Catholic Reporter,* 1968—; author of nonfiction column for *New York Times Book Review,* 1976—, column, "Fine Print," for *Saturday Review,* 1977-78, and fiction column, *Chronicle of Higher Education,* 1979—. Contributing editor, *New Republic,* 1971-73; book reviewer for *MacNeil-Lehrer Newshour,* Public Broadcasting Service (PBS). Contributor of reviews and criticism to periodicals, including the *New York Times Book Review, Chicago Tribune, Commonweal, Los Angeles Times, Nation, Washington Post, Washington Star,* and *New Republic.*

SIDELIGHTS: Doris Grumbach, a biographer and respected literary critic, is the author of several novels with historical, biographical, and autobiographical elements. Early in her career, Grumbach worked as a title writer, copy and associate editor, literary editor, and an English teacher; her career as a novelist did not begin until she was in her early forties, but it continued for three decades. After leaving the hustle and bustle of New York City to settle with her long-time companion, Sybil Pike, in rural Sargentville, Maine, where Pike runs Wayward Books, Grumbach wrote two books of reflections on religion and four volumes of memoirs.

In an essay for *Contemporary Authors Autobiography Series (CAAS),* the author recalled the time when she sought to have her first book published: "The manuscript was in a typing-paper box, wrapped in a shopping bag from the A. & P., and taped shut with scotch tape. I left it with the receptionist, remembering too late that I had not put my name and address on the outside of the box. I expected, as one does with an unlabeled suitcase at the airport, never to see it again. Two weeks later I got a phone call from an editor at Doubleday telling me they wished to publish the novel. Two years later they published a second novel." These first two books, *The Spoil of the Flowers,* about student life in a boardinghouse, and *The Short Throat, the Tender Mouth,* about life on a college campus three months before Hitler's march on Poland, "were by a beginner at a time in my life when I no longer should have been a beginner," Grumbach related in *CAAS.* "There are some good things, I believe, in both novels: had I much time ahead of me now, I would rewrite them and resubmit them for publication."

Upon the request of the publisher, Grumbach wrote her third book, *The Company She Kept,* a literary biography of the acerbic novelist Mary McCarthy. This book became the subject of a threatened lawsuit before its publication and of a volatile critical debate after its release. *The Company She Kept* parallels events and characters in McCarthy's novels with those in her life. "The fiction of Mary McCarthy is autobiographical to an extraordinary degree, in the widest sense of autobiography," Grumbach explains in the foreword to the book. "In the case of Mary McCarthy there is only a faint line between what really happened to her, the people she knew and knows, including herself, and the characters in her fictions." To prepare the biography, Grumbach spent a year reading McCarthy's work and criticism of it and interviewed the author extensively at her Paris home. Difficulties with McCarthy arose, Grumbach says, when McCarthy, who suggested she read the galleys of the book to catch any factual errors, protested against some of the information Grumbach had included in the manuscript.

In a *New York Times Book Review* article on her dispute with McCarthy, Grumbach reported that McCarthy voluntarily provided her with intimate biographical details in conversation and in a detailed memorandum. McCarthy's anger over their inclusion therefore came as a surprise, said Grumbach. "I was unprepared for the fury of her response when she saw the galleys . . . and realized that I had used the autobiographical details she had, as she said, given me," commented Grumbach. "She had said, once, that it felt strange to have a book written about one, 'a book that includes you as a person, not just a critical analysis of your writings.' Now she insisted that the *curriculum vitae* had been sent to be 'drawn upon,' not used, although just how this was to be done continues to be a mystery to me. . . . [McCarthy's] feeling was that the tapes and her letters to me had been intended solely for 'your own enlightenment.'"

For all the attendant publicity, however, *The Company She Kept* was not well received by the literary establishment. Stephanie Harrington wrote in *Commonweal:* "To anyone who has read *The Company She Kept* . . . the newspaper stories that followed the book's publication must have seemed too preposterous to be anything but a desperate attempt by the publisher's publicity department to drum up business for a clinker." A *Times Literary Supplement* contributor, who described *The Company She Kept* as "sparkily written and often critically sharp," felt that Grumbach falls short of her stated goal of "weaving one fabric of [the] diverse threads of McCarthy's biography and her fiction." Grumbach, asserted the reviewer, "never fully succeeds in dramatizing the complex interactions that go into such a process; [therefore, *The Company She Kept*] is likely to end up as required reading for gossips." Ellen Moers, writing in the *New York Times Book Review,* did not argue the validity of Grumbach's attempt to find the facts in Mary McCarthy's fiction—the process of "set[ting] out to name names," as Moers called it—but instead claimed that Grumbach misread McCarthy and thus arrived at erroneous conclusions. To Grumbach's statement that "there is only a faint line" between fact and fiction for McCarthy, Moers responded: "This simply cannot be true. The husbands in McCarthy fiction . . . are such dreary mediocrities, her artist colonies and political oases are so bare of talent or distinction, her suites of college girls are so tediously third-rate—only a powerful imagination could have made such nonentities out of the very interesting company that Mary McCarthy actually kept." *Saturday Review* critic Granville Hicks, however, did not find Grumbach's approach in *The Company She Kept* objectionable and approved of her straightforward manner in tackling it. "Although there is nothing novel about finding Miss McCarthy in her books, critics are usually cautious about identifying characters in fiction with real people, and I am grateful for Mrs. Grumbach's refusal to beat around that particular bush."

In the wake of the harsh reviews *The Company She Kept* received, Grumbach tried to deflect some of the criticism from herself by discussing the circumstances leading to her decision to write the McCarthy biography. Explaining in the *New York Times Book Review* that she was asked to write the book on McCarthy, rather than instigating the project herself, Grumbach stated, "An editor asks, somewhere in the inner room of a dim New York restaurant, would you do a book on Her? And because you do not ordinarily eat and drink such sumptuous lunches in the proximate company of so many successful-looking people, and because you need the money, and because after all, She *is* a good writer (you've *always* thought this) and apparently a *fascinating* woman, you say yes, I will." Commented Harrington: "Mrs. Grumbach's apologia in the *Times* . . . [indicates] that it was foolhardy to expect a serious piece of work in the first place when she only decided to take on Mary McCarthy because an editor asked 'somewhere in the inner room of a dim New York restaurant, would you do a book on Her?'" Recognizing the shortcomings of *The Company She Kept,* Grumbach summarized her difficulties with the book in the *New York Times Book Review:* "The value of the whole experience lies, for me," she said, "in the recognition of how difficult, even well-nigh impossible, it is to write a book that deals with a living person. It does not matter in the least that the living person is willing

to assist the writer (beware the Greeks bearing. . .) in conversation or letter; the fact remains, the law being what it is, the subject can give with one hand, take back with the other, and in this process of literary Indian-giving the writer is virtually helpless."

Ten years after publishing *The Company She Kept* and fifteen years after writing her novels, *The Short Throat, the Tender Mouth* and *The Spoil of the Flowers,* Grumbach returned to fiction. Her first novel after the hiatus was *Chamber Music,* written as the memoirs of ninety-year-old Caroline MacLaren, widow of a famous composer and founder of an artists' colony in his memory. Released with a 20,000 copy first printing and a $20,000 promotional campaign, *Chamber Music* won the popular and critical acclaim that eluded Grumbach's earlier books. Writing in the *Atlantic Monthly,* Peter Davison called the book "artful, distinctive, provocative, [and] compassionate." *Chamber Music,* remarked Victoria Glendinning in the *Washington Post Book World,* "is a book of originality and distinction."

Chamber Music is the story of "the chamber of one heart," says narrator Caroline MacLaren in the introduction to her memoirs. The novel's plot revolves around the subjugation of Caroline to her husband Robert and to Robert's music. Their marriage is a cold and barren one and *Chamber Music* charts its course through Robert's incestuous relationship with his mother, his homosexual affair with a student, and, finally, to his agonizing death in the tertiary stage of syphilis. Especially noted for its sensitive handling of its delicate subject matter and for its characterizations, *Chamber Music* was called by the *New York Times*'s John Leonard, "one of those rare novels for adults who listen." The characters in *Chamber Music,* Leonard continued, "are all stringed instruments. The music we hear occurs in the chamber of Caroline's heart. It is quite beautiful." With her third novel, Grumbach "makes us hear the difficult music of grace," wrote Nicholas Delbanco in the *New Republic.*

Although *Chamber Music*'s "revelations of sexuality are meant to shatter," as one *Publishers Weekly* contributor commented, and the passage on Robert's illness gives "a clinical description so simply precise, so elegantly loathsome, that it would do nicely either in a medical text or in a book on style," as Edith Milton observed in the *Yale Review,* it is the contrast between *Chamber Music*'s action and its language that gives the novel its impact. While much of the material in *Chamber Music* is meant to shock, the language is genteel and full of Victorian phrases. "What gives the main part of this book its polish and flavor is the contrast between matter and manner," maintained Glendinning. "Clarity and elegance of style account . . . for the distinction of *Chamber Music,*" wrote Eleanor B. Wymard in *Commonweal,* and other critics offered high praise for Grumbach's writing. For example, a *Washington Post Book World* reviewer claimed the book's language is "as direct and pure as a Hayden quartet," and Abigail McCarthy in *Commonweal* stated that *Chamber Music* has "the classical form, clarity, and brilliance of a composition for strings." Because it is Caroline's story, the novel adopts her voice—a voice that is "slightly stilted, slightly vapid, of the genteel tradition," one *Atlantic* contributor observed. Milton further asserted: "The novel is wonderfully written in [Caroline's] voice to evoke a time gone by, an era vanished. . . . The prose, understated, beautiful in its economies, supports a story of almost uncanny bleakness."

In her short preface to *Chamber Music,* Grumbach states that the novel's characters "are based vaguely upon persons who were once alive" but stresses that the book is fiction. "*Chamber Music* is a thinly, and strangely, fictionalized variation on the life of Marian MacDowell, [composer] Edward MacDowell's widow, who . . . founded an artist's colony in New Hampshire. . . . The names are changed; though not by much considering what else changes with them," wrote Milton. Gail Godwin, writing in the *New York Times Book Review,* suspected that the parallels between the MacDowells and the MacLarens "handicap . . . [Grumbach's] own possibilities for creating a fictional hero who might have come to life more vividly." However, other critics, including Glendinning, found that "the illusion of authenticity is strengthened by the inclusion of real people." "Robert MacLaren himself is given a semihistorical glamour by the parallels between his career and that of . . . Edward MacDowell—the two share teachers, musical styles, even a Boston address, and MacDowell's widow did indeed found an artist's colony in his name," noted Katha Pollitt. "Such details give Caroline's memoirs the piquancy of a historical novel."

Franny Fuller, the protagonist of Grumbach's novel *The Missing Person,* is also patterned after an actual figure. Franny, a 1930s movie star and sex symbol, closely resembles actress Marilyn Monroe. Written as a series of vignettes interweaving the events of Franny's career with an ongoing commentary by a gossip columnist, *The Missing Person* traces the actress's life from her sad beginnings in Utica, New York, through her rise to stardom, and finally to her disappearance from both Hollywood and the public consciousness. "Here, with certain sympathetic changes, is quite visibly another tale about the sad life of Marilyn Monroe," observed the *New York Times*'s Herbert Mitgang. "Missing person," wrote Cynthia Propper Seton in the *Washington Post Book World,* refers to "this sense that one is all facade, that there is no self inside." Franny is supposed to serve as a prototype for all the "missing persons" who are, "above all, missing to themselves," claimed Herbert Gold in the *New York Times Book Review.* "There seems evidence," Abigail McCarthy wrote in *Commonweal,* "that Doris Grumbach may initially have thought of Franny Fuller's story as a feminist statement in that women like Franny whom America 'glorifies and elevates' are sex objects made larger than life. But if so, as often happens in the creative process, she has transcended the aim in the writing. The creatures of the Hollywood process she gives us, men as well as women, are all victims."

Grumbach, in a prefatory note to the novel, comments on the nature of the book. "This novel is a portrait, not of a single life but of many lives melded into one, typical of the women America often glorifies and elevates, and then leaves suspended in their lonely and destructive fame," she says. Still, commented Richard Combs in the *Times Literary Supplement,* "there is no prize for guessing that the novel's heroine is Marilyn Monroe." The close correlation between Marilyn Monroe's life and Franny's life was disturbing to many critics. "The question that poses itself about a book like this is, Why bother? If you must write about Marilyn Monroe then why not do so in fiction or otherwise?," asked James Campbell in the *New Statesman.* "Real names thinly disguised are a bore." Combs believed Grumbach's reliance on the facts of Marilyn Monroe's life hindered her ability to substantiate the point she makes in the preface. "The more the real Hollywood shows through [in the novel], the less satisfying the portrait becomes," Combs maintained. "The author's assumption . . . seems to be that since Hollywood put fantasy on an anonymous, mass-production basis, the results can be freely arranged by the inspired do-it-yourselfer. . . . But in refantasizing the fantasy factory, Mrs. Grumbach allows herself the license of fiction without taking on the responsibility . . . to find revised truth in the revised subject."

"It is hard for [Franny] to have a separate imaginary existence in the mind of the reader," stated McCarthy. "But this flaw, if it is one, is more than compensated for by the writer's evocation of the scene against which Franny moves—tawdry, wonderful Hollywood at its peak." Indeed, Grumbach is praised for her fine writing and for "the adroit structure of the novel," as Gold called it. "There is in this prose a certain leanness, a sparseness that separates most of the characters into a chapter each, surrounded by an implied emptiness. Instead of the usual crowded Hollywood narrative, [*The Missing Person*] has the melancholy air . . . of an underpopulated landscape," stated Combs. Seton commented on Grumbach's ability to capture the tone and feeling of old Hollywood films and newsreels in her writing. "Doris Grumbach's special gift lies in her ability to suit the style and structure of her novels to the world in which she writes," McCarthy said. "*The Missing Person* is itself like a motion picture—a pastiche of scenes centered on the star, complete with flashbacks, close-ups and fade-outs."

About her intentions in writing *The Missing Person,* Grumbach told Wendy Smith of *Publishers Weekly:* "I was interested in seeing what you could do, given a catafalque of fact that I assumed might be known to any literate person who came to the book. I wanted to fantasize about it, to imagine things that probably were not so, and by that process make them true." However, Grumbach was disappointed in her readers, she continued: "I thought you could make that move and people would forget what the catafalque was, but they don't; they superimpose what they know, or think they know, upon what you've written, and they become critical about it."

Grumbach switched her topic from the rise and then demise of a 1930s starlet in *The Missing Person,* to the public ostracism then acceptance of two aristocratic lesbian lovers of the eighteenth century in her novel *The Ladies.* "Grumbach compellingly recreates the lives of two women who so defied convention and so baffled their contemporaries that they became celebrities," lauded Catharine R. Stimpson in the *New York Times Book Review.* The story relates Grumbach's concept of how Eleanor Butler and Sarah Ponsonby, two Irish aristocrats known as "the Ladies of Llangollen," shocked the community with their lesbian relationship but were eventually accepted and visited by such noteworthy individuals as Anna Seward, the Duke of Wellington, and Walter Scott. Stimpson noted that the book "eloquently documents the existence of women who lived as they wished to, instead of as society expected them to."

As Grumbach relates, Lady Eleanor, feeling the lack of love from her parents because she wasn't a boy, becomes the boy in her behavior and dress. Always looking to fulfill her need for acceptance and love, Eleanor falls in love with the orphan, Sarah Ponsonby, who is being sexually harassed by her guardian. Eleanor attempts to rescue Sarah, but the two are caught before

they get far. A second attempt prompts the families to allow the couple to leave together, but under the condition that Lady Eleanor is banned from Ireland forever. After a few years of wandering, Eleanor and Sarah settle with a former servant and create their own haven in Wales. Eleanor and Sarah "seemed to each other to be divine survivors, well beyond the confines of social rules, two inhabitants of an ideal society. . . . They had uncovered a lost continent on which they could live, in harmony, quite alone and together," writes Grumbach in *The Ladies.* Eventually, visited by other aristocrats, they become more secure within the outer community; however, problems arise in their relationship as their greed and fame alters their lives.

The Ladies met with good reviews. Stimpson, while recognizing Grumbach's pattern of blurring biography and fiction, praised the book, noting that "*The Ladies* is boldly imagined, [and] subtly crafted." Comparing Grumbach's work with the likes of Virginia Woolf and Charlotte Perkins Gillman, Sandra Gilbert commented in the *Washington Post Book World* that Grumbach has "recounted their story with grace and wit," and she applauded "the sureness with which Grumbach accumulates small details about the lives of her protagonists and the tough but loving irony with which she portrays their idiosyncrasies." She observed, though, that while the protagonists' "road to reposeful Llangollen is strewn with obstacles for the runaway ladies. . . . All ends well once the weary travelers arrive in friendship's vale." Thus Gilbert maintained that "if there is anything problematic about *The Ladies,* it is that all seems to go almost too well" in the novel and "like Grumbach's earlier *Chamber Music,* seems here and there to flirt with the conventions of an increasingly popular new genre: The Happy Lesbian novel."

The title for Grumbach's next novel, *The Magician's Girl,* is borrowed from Sylvia Plath's poem "The Bee Meeting." In this story Grumbach writes about three women who were college roommates and grew up during the twenties and thirties. In episodic fashion, the stories of Minna, Liz, and Maud are related from their childhood to their sixties, and from their hopes and dreams to their reality. Pretty, shy Minna marries a doctor, has a son, and becomes a history professor. After surviving years in a loveless marriage, at the age of sixty she finally develops a loving relationship with a young man in his twenties. Not long after they meet and she experiences this fulfillment, she is killed in a car accident. Maud, the daughter of a nurse and army sergeant, marries a handsome man whom she eventually rejects, has twins whom she neglects, and spends most of her time writing poetry. Her poetry is good but she destroys it all, except for the copies she sends to Minna in her letters; she commits suicide before realizing the true success of her writings. Liz, the only survivor, lives with her partner in a lesbian relationship, achieving fame as a photographer. Summarizing the book's theme, Anita Brookner in her review for the *Washington Post Book World,* stated that the formulaic stories about these three women demonstrate "the way early beginnings mature into not very much, for despite the achievements that come with age, a sense of disillusion persists." Brookner asserted that Grumbach asks more questions about women's lives than she answers in her story, including the question, "Is that all?," and surmises that this may be more important than the answers. In conclusion, she praised *The Magician's Girl* as "a beautifully easy read, discreet and beguiling, and attractively low-key. It is an honorable addition to the annals of women's reading."

Several critics faulted Grumbach for too closely describing the lives of Sylvia Plath and Diane Arbus as the characters of Maud and Liz, respectively. Other critics found Grumbach's writing weak in definition and description. The *Times Literary Supplement*'s Marianne Wiggins found events "unlocated in time" and places "without a sense of period." She asserted that it is written "as if the text were a rehearsal for a talent contest"; she considered this especially disconcerting since she regards Grumbach as the "master of the quick sketch" and pointed out that generally "when her narrative shifts to describing the specific, it soars." In contrast, Paula Deitz in the *New York Times Book Review* commended Grumbach's attention to detail in *The Magician's Girl.* She deemed that the characters described "are all rich images, informed with the magic conveyed by the small details that reveal the forming of these lives." Deitz further maintained that *The Magician's Girl* is most disturbing, and therefore at its best, in its acute awareness of the pains endured unflinchingly by the young." *Christian Science Monitor*'s Merle Rubin summarized: "What is most poignant about this novel is that its special aura of serenity tinged with sadness comes not from the pains and losses the characters endure, although there are many of these, but from the conviction it conveys that life, for all its sorrows, is so rich with possibilities as to make any one life—however long—much too short."

As she turned seventy, Grumbach found herself looking inward and asking important religious and philosophical questions. Because her seventieth birthday "was an occasion of real despair," as she told Smith, Grumbach decided to put pen to paper with a new view in mind—to alleviate her despair. "I thought, well perhaps it would help if I just take notes on this year," she continued; "whatever happens may throw some light on why I'm still here, make some sense out of living so long." What resulted was the first of what would be four autobiographical and reflective volumes: *Coming into the End Zone: A Memoir.* "What is most delightful about *Coming into the End Zone*—[is] the wry, spry, resilient, candid recording of present happenings and suddenly remembered past happenings which fill almost every page with anecdotes and reflections," exclaimed *Washington Post Book World*'s Anthony Thwaite. Grumbach comments on a wide range of topics, including contemporary annoyances such as phrases like "the computer is down," the death of several friends from the complications of acquired immunodeficiency syndrome (AIDS), her dislike of travel, her move to rural Maine, her memories of being fired from the *New Republic,* and Mary McCarthy's last curt comment to her. "The best moments are the passages in which the author seems least to be writing for posterity, merely trying to capture herself on the page, moments when the need to maintain a public persona gives way to the vulnerability of the private person, sometimes even to the young girl still inside this old woman," declared Carol Anshaw in *Tribune Books.* "The book that Ms. Grumbach intended as a confrontation with death winds up being a celebration of life," commented Noel Perrin in the *New York Times Book Review,* adding that "it is a deeply satisfying book." "Grumbach's reflections record—with honesty, fidelity, much important and unimportant detail, and with much grace and informal wit—her feelings of the time. I know no other book like it," wrote Thwaite, who concluded: "This is a book to grow old with even before one is old. The best is yet to be."

Grumbach continues her reminiscences in *Extra Innings: A Memoir.* Reviewers disagreed about how satisfactorily the author presents her experiences. In the *Washington Post Book World,* Diana O'Hehir defined a memoir as a grab bag and, directing her comments to Grumbach, wrote: "I felt yours wasn't enough of a grab bag. Not enough gossip about people. Not enough detail about you, not enough specific detail about relationships, family." However, Kathleen Norris presented the view in the *New York Times Book Review* that the book is "more of a hodgepodge" than *End Zone.* Norris maintained that "for all its recounting of ordinary events, *Extra Innings,* like *End Zone,* is a document still too rare in literary history, an account of a woman who has lived by words. Ms. Grumbach wittily chronicles the absurdities and ambiguities of the modern American writer's life."

She returned to fiction with her 1995 historical novel *The Book of Knowledge.* In it Grumbach introduces four central characters as adolescents the summer before the great stock market crash of 1929, then touches on each of their lives into adulthood, through the Great Depression and World War II. Two of the characters are a brother and sister who become intimate, sexually and emotionally, that summer. The other two are the vacationing son and daughter of a wealthy stockbroker, with whom the brother and sister become friends. All strive for selfhood in various fashions; and the two young men eventually have a homosexual relationship. According to *Tribune Books*'s Nina Mehta, "Grumbach cuts right to sexuality, condemning her main characters to lives stunted by their inability to deal honestly with their sexual feelings." As Julia Markus of the *Los Angeles Times Book Review* remarked, "The stories of [the four] and their families are told and interwoven with great irony, subtlety and beauty." Markus concluded that "with masterful conciseness and with her own unique haunting force, Doris Grumbach has brilliantly delineated the tragedy of an entire generation."

But other reviewers faulted Grumbach for not delving into the interior lives of the foursome. Grumbach makes "a lot of tendentious commentary about puberty and the chasteness of homosexual inclinations," pointed out Mehta, "but what's most disheartening . . . is the book's lack of insight." Mehta further maintained that "by neglecting to ventilate her characters' lives with even a breeze of introspection, Grumbach gives them less personality, less psychological weight, than they deserve." Likewise, Sara Maitland asserted in the *New York Times Book Review:* "Ms. Grumbach prods at her four central characters with a sharp stick, but when they turn over, she withdraws her authorial attention in disgust." Maitland decried that the reader is "never shown the painful workings through of . . . personal choices that we are *told* the characters have to endure."

During the 1990s Grumbach published two works about her spiritual journey: *Life in a Day,* in which she writes about solitude and thanksgiving as she recounts a day at seventy-seven years old, and *The Presence of Absence: On Prayers and an Epiphany.* In the later, which *Cross Currents* reviewer Kenneth Arnold called a "story of spiritual hunger," Grumbach describes a profound religious event that she experienced while in her twenties and her subsequent search for a renewal of that intense experience. After decades of going to church services that only felt sterile, Grumbach has tried solitude and contemplative prayer. "I had discovered how necessary it was (for me) to discard my stale concepts of God and ritual practices in order to approach the pure core of prayer," she explains in *The Presence of Absence.* "A long life in the church had formed me into a half-hearted, secular worshiper. It was a condition I had to cast off." At the time also suffering from the shingles, a painful inflammation of the nerves, and because the pain was so intense as to prevent prayer, she read works by Simone Weil, Thomas Merton, Kathleen Norris, and Thomas Kelly. "Her experiences are set out in graceful prose and with compelling honesty," wrote Notre Dame theology professor Lawrence S. Cunningham in *Commonweal.* And Kathleen Norris, who is herself a writer on spirituality, wrote about the currency of this "brief and forceful" work: "It is an important book for pastors in that Grumbach . . . conveys something that many older people experience but do not articulate—a profound disappointment with the churches to which they have devoted their lives." "One must thank Grumbach for penning an authentic work," Cunningham added. "Anyone who despairs of the church but still clings to prayer will benefit from this woman's struggles and insights."

Grumbach's memoir *The Pleasure of Their Company* ostensibly deals with the author's upcoming eightieth birthday, yet that is only the framework around which she attaches her musings. These include sketches of deceased friends, as well as her former husband and current companion, and reflections on literature, memory, and prayer. Enthusiasts of the work included *Booklist*'s Donna Seaman, who dubbed it "quietly compelling and always satisfying," *Commonweal*'s Lawrence S. Cunningham, who described it as an "elegantly written and very moving memoir," and *Library Journal*'s Carol A. McAllister, who called the author "vibrant and perceptive," and found her observations "meaningful" and ramblings "wise." *Atlanta Journal-Constitution* reviewer Steve Harvey also praised Grumbach's ability to get to the heart of the matter: "[She] has gotten very good at getting under the skin of her own life. She is able in a few words to reveal the heart of the matter, in this case fear of growing old and dying, and yet she approaches it all with such wit, good feeling and candor that we find ourselves delighted, rather than disconcerted by her words." Finally, in the *Lambda Book Report* Karla Jay compared the work favorably to a memoir by Judith Barrington and to exemplars of the genre as a whole: "Memoirs generally tackle thematic issues that reach beyond the immediate life of the author, and these two works are brilliant examples of the genre."

In 2000 Grumbach was awarded the Whitehead Award for Lifetime Achievement by Publishing Triangle, the publishing association of gay men and lesbians in the publishing industry.

BIOGRAPHICAL AND CRITICAL SOURCES:

BOOKS

Contemporary Authors Autobiography Series, Volume 2, Thomson Gale (Detroit, MI), 1985.

Contemporary Literary Criticism, Thomson Gale (Detroit, MI), Volume 13, 1980, Volume 22, 1982, Volume 64, 1991.

Grumbach, Doris, *Coming into the Endzone,* Norton (New York, NY), 1991.

Grumbach, Doris, *Extra Innings: A Memoir,* Norton (New York, NY), 1993.

Grumbach, Doris, *Fifty Days of Solitude,* Beacon Press (Boston, MA), 1994.

Grumbach, Doris, *Life in a Day,* Beacon Press (Boston, MA), 1996.

Grumbach, Doris, *The Presence of Absence: On Prayers and an Epiphany,* Beacon Press (Boston, MA), 1998.

Grumbach, Doris, *The Pleasure of Their Company,* Beacon Press (Boston, MA), 2000.

PERIODICALS

America, June 2, 1979.

American Spectator, January, 1982.

Atlanta Journal-Constitution, June 4, 2000, Steven Harvey, "The Unexpected 'Pleasure' of Growing Older," review of *The Pleasure of Their Company,* p. L10.

Atlantic Monthly, March, 1979.

Booklist, October 1, 1993; May 1, 2000, Donna Seaman, review of *The Pleasure of Their Company,* p. 1639.

Choice, January, 1999, review of *The Presence of Absence: On Prayers and an Epiphany,* p. 905.

Christian Century, May 19, 1999, Kathleen Norris, review of *The Presence of Absence,* pp. 567-569.

Christian Science Monitor, February 26, 1987, p. 22.

Commonweal, October 6, 1967; June 22, 1979; January 15, 1982; March 26, 1999, Lawrence S. Cunningham, review of *The Presence of Absence,* pp. 25-28; January 12, 2001, Lawrence S. Cunningham, review of *The Pleasure of Their Company,* p. 28.

Cross Currents, spring, 1999, Kenneth Arnold, review of *The Presence of Absence,* 140-143.

Globe and Mail (Toronto, Ontario, Canada), August 4, 2001, review of *The Pleasure of Their Company,* p. D12.

Lambda Book Report, September, 2000, Karla Jay, "Writing beyond the Margins," review of *The Pleasure of Their Company,* p. 18.

Library Journal, March 1, 1979; May 1, 2000, Carol A. McAllister, review of *The Pleasure of Their Company,* p. 112.

Listener, August 9, 1979.

London Review of Books, August 20, 1992.

Los Angeles Times Book Review, July 16, 1995, p. 3.

Ms., April, 1979.

Nation, March 28, 1981, pp. 375-376.

National Review, June 8, 1979.

New Republic, March 10, 1979.

New Statesman, August 17, 1979; August 28, 1981.

Newsweek, March 19, 1979.

New Yorker, April 23, 1979.

New York Times, March 13, 1979; July 20, 1989.

New York Times Book Review, June 11, 1967; March 25, 1979; March 29, 1981, pp. 14-15; September 30, 1984, p. 12; February 1, 1987, p. 22; September 22, 1991, Noel Perrin, "Be Cranky while You Can," review of *Coming into the End Zone;* November 21, 1993, p. 11; October 21, 1993; November 21, 1993, Kathleen Norris, "Not Cranky; Not Grumpy; Not Any of Those Things," review of *Extra Innings: A Memoir;* October 2, 1994, Le Anne Schreiber, "Home Alone," review of *Fifty Days of Solitude;* June 25, 1995, p. 19; August 6, 2000, Leslie Chess Feller, review of *The Pleasure of Their Company,* p. 16.

Observer, August 12, 1979.

Publishers Weekly, January 15, 1979; February 13, 1981; April 24, 2000, review of *The Pleasure of Their Company,* p. 75.

Sewanee Review, January, 1995.

Spectator, August 11, 1979.

Time, April 9, 1979.

Times Literary Supplement, December 7, 1967; November 30, 1979; September 11, 1981; July 12, 1985; June 19, 1987, p. 669.

Tribune Books (Chicago, IL), September 29, 1991; August 13, 1995, p. 6.

Village Voice, August 24, 1987.

Washington Post, June 4, 2000, David Guy, "Look Homeward, Author," review of *The Pleasure of Their Company,* p. X08.

Washington Post Book World, March 18, 1979; February 10, 1980; April 5, 1981, pp. 9, 13; September 30, 1984, p. 7; January 4, 1987, pp. 3, 13; September 8, 1991; October 24, 1993, p. 5; October 10, 1996.

Women's Review of Books, December, 1993; December, 1995.

Yale Review, autumn, 1979.

*   *   *

GRUMBACH, Doris Isaac
See GRUMBACH, Doris

For Reference

Not to be taken from this room